HANDBOOK OF CLASSROOM MANAGEMENT

Research, Practice, and Contemporary Issues

Edited by

Carolyn M. Evertson
Vanderbilt University

Carol S. Weinstein
Rutgers, The State University of New Jersey

LAWRENCE ERLBAUM ASSOCIATES, PUBLISHERS
2006 Mahwah, New Jersey London

Editorial Director: Lane Akers
Executive Assistant: Karin Willig-Bates
Cover Design: Tomai Maridou
Full-Service Compositor: TechBooks
Text and Cover Printer: Hamilton Printing Company

This book was typeset in 10/12 pt. Times Roman, Italic, Bold, and Bold Italic.
The heads were typeset in Helvetica, Helvetica Italic, Helvetica Bold, Helvetica Bold Italic.

Lawrence Erlbaum Associates, Inc., Publishers
10 Industrial Avenue
Mahwah, New Jersey 07430
www.erlbaum.com

Library of Congress Cataloging-in-Publication Data

Handbook of classroom management : research, practice, and contemporary issues / edited by Carolyn M. Evertson, Carol S. Weinstein.
p. cm.
Includes bibliographical references and index.
ISBN 0-8058-4753-7 (casebound : alk. paper)—ISBN 0-8058-4754-5 (pbk. : alk. paper)
1. Classroom management—Handbooks, manuals, etc. I. Evertson, Carolyn M., 1935– II. Weinstein, Carol Simon.
LB3013.H336 2006
371.120′4—dc22

2005030877

Books published by Lawrence Erlbaum Associates are printed on acid-free paper, and their bindings are chosen for strength and durability.

Printed in the United States of America
10 9 8 7 6 5 4 3 2 1

Contents

HANDBOOK OF CLASSROOM MANAGEMENT

Research, Practice, and Contemporary Issues

I

Introduction

1

Classroom Management as a Field of Inquiry

Carolyn M. Evertson
Vanderbilt University

Carol S. Weinstein
Rutgers, The State University of New Jersey

Classroom management is a topic of enduring concern for teachers, administrators, and the public. Beginning teachers consistently perceive student discipline as their most serious challenge; management problems continue to be a major cause of teacher burnout and job dissatisfaction; and the public repeatedly ranks discipline as the first or second most serious problem facing the schools. Indeed, one noted author of a text on effective discipline describes the situation in these blunt terms:

> Our schools are in the grip of a serious problem that is wreaking havoc on teaching and learning. That problem is student misbehavior. If you are now teaching, you have had ample experience with it. If you are preparing to teach, be forewarned: It is the major obstacle to your success and has the potential to destroy your career. (Charles, 2002, p. 1)

Despite the concern of educational practitioners and the public, few researchers focus explicitly on classroom management or identify themselves with this field. An examination of the annual meeting program of the American Educational Research Association (AERA) provides a telling example. With over 22,000 AERA members, the annual meeting is an event of enormous proportions, attended by approximately 13,000 people, with 3,000 presenters, and more than 1,500 program slots. Nonetheless, there are generally only two or three sessions explicitly devoted to classroom management, and these tend to be poorly attended. The lack of interest is also exemplified by the pitifully small membership of the AERA Special Interest Group on classroom management.

Similarly, classroom management is often neglected in teacher preparation programs. Citing a Public Agenda survey of attitudes among professors who teach in schools of education (Farkas & Johnson, 1997), Jean Johnson (2005) reports,

> There is . . . a substantial gap between the attitudes of teachers in the classroom and those of the professors who prepare them for their careers. While virtually all classroom teachers (97%) say that good discipline . . . is "one of the most important prerequisites" for a successful school, fewer

> than 4 in 10 education professors (37%) consider it absolutely essential to train "teachers who maintain discipline and order in the classroom." Only 30% say that their teacher education program places a lot of emphasis on teaching prospective teachers how to handle a rowdy classroom. (p.3)

Consistent with these data, preservice teacher education often relegates the topic of classroom management to a few class sessions in an educational psychology or general methods course. Even when a stand-alone course is offered, it may be an elective or limited to a single credit. Moreover, there is little consensus about what should be included in classroom management courses; some teacher educators emphasize strategies and skills for preventing and dealing with problem behaviors, whereas others present various models of classroom management (e.g., William Glasser's Reality Therapy, Lee Canter's Assertive Discipline, or Frederick Jones' Positive Classroom Discipline) and encourage students to adopt the model that seems most congruent with their own predilections. In sum, preservice teacher preparation frequently fails to provide students with a comprehensive, coherent study of the basic principles and skills of classroom management, well integrated with thoughtfully planned field experiences. (See Vernon Jones, chap. 33, for an extensive discussion of this issue.)

What could account for this apparent neglect by educational researchers and teacher educators? Part of the problem may be that the term *classroom management* has acquired considerable surplus meaning—and some of it is decidedly negative. As McCaslin and Good (1998) point out, classroom management is often thought of in terms of controlling students—getting them to respond quickly to teacher demands, needs, and goals. Whereas current views of curriculum and instruction emphasize independence, understanding, problem solving, and the active participation of students, classroom management is sometimes equated with a mechanistic, authoritarian orientation that minimizes the importance of positive interpersonal relationships and maximizes control and compliance. (See, e.g., Bowers & Flinders, 1990.)

It is also possible that professors of education see classroom management as a "bag of tricks" (Brophy, 1988), to be passed along from teacher to teacher, rather than a set of research-based principles, concepts, and skills that warrant serious professional study. This perception is most likely reinforced by the fact that research relevant to classroom management has been conducted by persons in different disciplines, appears in a wide variety of journals, and is often not identified as "classroom management research." Additional reinforcement for the bag-of-tricks view comes from the lack of national standards that would mandate preparation in the area of classroom management (see Laura Stough, chapter 34). And, of course, there is always confusion about where classroom management "fits" in the teacher preparation curriculum. Because classroom management is neither content knowledge, nor psychological foundations, nor pedagogy, nor pedagogical content knowledge, it seems to slip through the cracks.

The situation we have just described provides the context for understanding the four major goals of the *Handbook of Classroom Management.* First, we hope that the Handbook will clarify the term *classroom management*, broaden the perspective with which it is viewed, and suggest new ways to conceptualize its role in the educational enterprise. Drawing on the work of educational theorists and researchers such as Jacob Kounin (1970), Jere Brophy (1988; 1999), Walter Doyle (1986), and Marilyn Watson and Laura Ecken (2003), we define classroom management as the actions teachers take to create an environment that supports and facilitates both academic and social-emotional learning. In other words, classroom management has two distinct purposes: It not only seeks to establish and sustain an orderly environment so students can engage in meaningful academic learning, it also aims to enhance students' social and moral growth (see chapter 27 by Larry Nucci and chapter 40 by Catherine Fallona and Virginia Richardson). From this perspective, *how* a teacher achieves order is as important as *whether* a teacher achieves order.

In the service of these two purposes, teachers carry out a number of specific tasks. They must (1) develop caring, supportive relationships with and among students; (2) organize and implement instruction in ways that optimize students' access to learning; (3) use group management methods that encourage students' engagement in academic tasks; (4) promote the development of students' social skills and self-regulation; and (5) use appropriate interventions to assist students with behavior problems. Clearly, classroom management is a multifaceted endeavor that is far more complex than establishing rules, rewards, and penalties to control students' behavior.

The second goal of the *Handbook* is to demonstrate that there is a distinct body of knowledge that directly addresses these tasks and to make this knowledge more visible and more accessible to scholars and practitioners. In the early 1980s, the ecological psychologist Paul Gump wrote, "One time I struggled with people at ETS [Educational Testing Service] about devising some test [for beginning teachers] to measure management knowledge. Our problem was that little general and basic material was being taught to students, so what could you test them on?" (personal communication July 6, 1983). This situation was at least partly due to the lack of classroom management knowledge available in the early 80s, when teachers had to rely on intuition and folk wisdom (like "Don't smile until Christmas") to prevent and respond to problem behaviors. Fortunately, times have changed (although, as we have noted, classroom management still constitutes a minor component of teacher education). There is now a substantial knowledge base for classroom management that cannot be dismissed as mere "common sense" or as "nuts and bolts" and that warrants attention from teacher educators, administrators, staff developers, researchers, and policy makers who determine state and national standards. Indeed, Jere Brophy (chapter 2) asserts that the work on classroom management is one of "the major success stories of educational research in the 20th century." Our hope is that this *Handbook* will constitute a comprehensive, easily accessed compendium of this work.

Third, the *Handbook* aims to bring together disparate lines of research and encourage conversations across different areas of inquiry. As we noted earlier, even a quick review of current journals in education and psychology reveals that a considerable amount of work with relevance for classroom management is carried out by individuals who are not classroom management researchers and whose primary academic identification is with other areas of inquiry. Reflecting a wide variety of topics such as motivation, moral development, self-regulated learning, caring, cultural diversity, conflict resolution, literacy education, parent involvement, and educational equity, the research is published in diverse journals and difficult to track down; furthermore, it is usually not identified as research in classroom management, or even as research that has clear implications for classroom management. If classroom management is to be perceived as a legitimate field of inquiry, we need to create a community of scholars who agree on a set of well-defined constructs and use a common language. Similarly, if classroom management is to assume its rightful place in preservice teacher education, we need to be cognizant of the many strands of inquiry that relate to and enrich our understanding of this multidimensional construct.

Finally, the fourth goal of the *Handbook* is to promote a vigorous research agenda for classroom management. Individual chapter authors have sometimes delineated research questions that warrant consideration. For example, Edmund Emmer and Mary Claire Gerwels (chapter 15) observe that "activity management in middle school and high school settings needs more attention. In particular, there is a paucity of research on how teachers in various subject matters and grades/levels organize, structure, and conduct activities." Leslie Soodak and Mary Rose McCarthy (chapter 17), writing on classroom management in inclusive settings, note, "research has failed to investigate whether a student's background affects his or her acceptance, learning, or behavior in inclusive environments." They also point out the need to study the intersection of the inclusion movement and the current trend in using "exclusionary discipline policies as a means of ensuring safe schools." Cheryl Mason Bolick and James M. Cooper (chapter 20) discuss the lack of research studies on technology and classroom management and list a few potential research topics, such as the relationship between teachers' managerial skills and disposition to use technology and the ways that teachers keep students academically engaged when using technology. In the chapter on extrinsic rewards and motivation, Johnmarshall Reeve (chapter 24) asks how teachers can provide an "autonomy-supportive" learning environment during "uninteresting lessons" and what the role of extrinsic rewards is in supporting students' autonomy. Robert Pianta (chapter 26) wonders how a focus on teacher-child relationships, as opposed to discrete behaviors, might advance our understanding of classroom management. David Schimmel (chapter 38), writing about the confusion that exists about students' rights and teachers' authority, questions what teachers know about the law when they enter the classroom and what is the source of that knowledge.

We anticipate—indeed we hope—that the *Handbook* will raise as many questions as it answers. Since the heyday of classroom management research in the late 1970s and early 1980s, there have been few efforts to pursue classroom management questions *per se*, and many pressing questions remain. As Jere Brophy (chapter 2) points out, we need to focus on effective management in the upper secondary grades, examine classroom management in constructivist-oriented classrooms, investigate the effects of district policies like zero tolerance, and explore the interface between general and special education.

THE ORGANIZATION AND CONTENT OF THE HANDBOOK

The *Handbook* begins with Brophy's chapter on the history of research on classroom management as it developed across the 20th century. This comprehensive overview focuses on the substance of this research, as well as its design and methodology. It highlights major influences and trends, introducing many of the topics that are elaborated in subsequent chapters.

Jere Brophy also served as the editor for Part II, *Alternative Paradigms for the Study of Classroom Management*, comprised of chapters that describe the varied perspectives from which classroom management has been studied. Each chapter delineates the assumptions, concepts, values, questions, methodologies, and interpretive frameworks that characterize its particular paradigm and that constitute a unique way of viewing classroom management. Timothy Landrum and James Kauffman (chapter 3) address the behavioral approach to the study of classroom management, certainly a "dominant and influential paradigm in both educational research and the preparation of teachers." Next, Maribeth Gettinger and Kristy Kohler (chapter 4) describe the search for relationships between teacher behaviors ("processes") and student outcomes ("products"). As they argue, this process-product research "has moved the field of teaching closer to being a science, that is, beyond unsupported claims about effective classroom methods toward evidence-based teaching practices derived from credible data." In chapter 5, Walter Doyle has abbreviated and updated his 1986 chapter, "Classroom Organization and Management" (appearing in the 3rd edition of the *Handbook of Research on Teaching)* to provide a contemporary view of the ecological perspective on classroom management. This ecological view opens classroom research to a range of influences from fields such as sociolinguistics, cognitive anthropology, and educational sociology. Because this perspective has as much relevance today as it did 20 years ago, its inclusion in this volume provides a more complete picture of the way in which classroom management has been considered and what perspectives have power for understanding such complex social phenomena. Chapter 6, by Greta Morine-Dershimer, explores the relationship between classroom discourse analysis research and classroom management. She underscores the fact that classrooms are "communicative environments" and shows how familiarity with classroom discourse research (with its strong focus on teacher-pupil interaction, peer-interaction, and comparisons of school and community discourse patterns) can enrich our understanding of classroom management. Ellen Brantlinger and Scot Danforth (chapter 7) take a critical theory perspective on schooling and address the ways that students' and teachers' social class, race, and gender influence the dynamics of classroom life. After identifying the major themes and theories in critical scholarship, these authors discuss the ways that classrooms might be organized to eradicate injustice and contribute to democratic societal reform. Finally, the chapter by Anita Woolfolk Hoy and Carol Weinstein (chapter 8) looks across a variety of paradigms to review what we know about students' and teachers' perspectives on classroom management. As the authors write, teachers and students are "the central participants in classroom interactions and their relationships are at the heart of classroom management concerns and consequences. To ignore the thinking of these important players is to court failure in teaching and teacher education."

Part III, *Recent and Emergent Perspectives on Classroom Management,* edited by Mary McCaslin, includes chapters that present new ways of thinking about classroom management, that are gaining currency and have important implications for how teachers can structure settings for learning. In Chapter 9, Mary McCaslin, Amanda Rabidue Bozack, Lisa Napoleon, Angela Thomas, Veronica Vasquez, Virginia Wayman, and Jizhi Zhang highlight the contributions of seven theories of self-regulated learning (SRL) that have promise for informing classroom management practices. They identify theoretically based strategies that teachers can implement in their classrooms to promote student SRL and suggest that a research agenda in this area should focus on the "under-addressed" value judgments associated with SRL—the "by whom, for whom, why, and how much." Marilyn Watson and Victor Battistich (chapter 10) characterize "community" as the very foundation of classroom management; however, they do more than simply advocate the building and sustaining of caring communities in classrooms. Rather, they examine the classroom management and discipline practices of six different theoretical approaches to creating classroom or school community and discuss the positive effects of community as well as the dangers and impediments. In chapter 11, Daniel Hickey and Nancy Jo Schafer draw on sociocultural theory to propose a "participation-centered approach" to classroom management. They suggest that if teachers focus on students' "collective participation in domain-specific discourse" (e.g., argumentation in science), they can achieve a greater degree of order, cooperation, and engagement than if they focus primarily on the activity of individuals. Maurice Elias and Yoni Schwab (chapter 12) review the literature on social-emotional learning (SEL) and describe steps to incorporate SEL into classroom management to create a classroom system that integrates academic, social, and emotional learning. Finally, Geneva Gay (chapter 13) examines discipline trends among students of color and discusses the reasons for racial disproportionality. She makes the case for culturally responsive teaching and discusses the implications for managing diverse student populations.

Part IV, *Classroom Management in Specific Contexts*, edited by Anita Woolfolk Hoy, focuses on classroom management in some of the most common settings in which teachers work—early childhood and elementary classrooms, middle school and secondary settings, special education classrooms and resource rooms, inclusive general education classrooms, and urban classrooms. Although not all settings are represented, the authors in this section recognize that classroom management is not context-free, but rather is dependent upon the level of schooling, the nature of the community, and the national, state, and local policy contexts. Kathy Carter and Walter Doyle (chapter 14) provide a comprehensive review of the extant research on classroom management in early childhood and elementary classroom settings and sketch the complexities of disentangling the academic, social, emotional, and behavioral issues involved in educating young children. They conclude with a recommendation for adding to the knowledge base of developmentally appropriate classroom management through the use of narratives and classroom stories that can enlarge understanding of daily life in early childhood classrooms. Edmund Emmer and Mary Claire Gerwels (chapter 15) review the social implications of adolescent development and teacher thinking and emotion about classroom management. They present two middle school vignettes illustrating how these concepts play out in ongoing classroom life and how they are dealt with. In Chapter 16, Kathleen Lane, Katherine Falk, and Joseph Wehby, whose work addresses special education classrooms and resource rooms, overview the seven phases of the acting-out cycle, describing the intervention procedures for teachers at each phase. Their chapter also includes functional assessment-based approaches that can be used as a guide for intervention. Leslie Soodak and Mary Rose McCarthy (chapter 17) discuss research-based strategies to promote academic achievement, acceptance, and positive behavior in inclusive settings. They delineate the factors affecting implementation of effective practices (such as teacher attitudes and sense of efficacy) and raise issues for further study, including the changing view of disability as a "deficit-driven phenomenon." In chapter 18, H. Richard Milner provides a comprehensive review of the issues teachers confront when teaching in urban classrooms and reveals the tensions between understanding and accepting the legitimacy of the sometimes troubling behaviors of urban students while still holding them to high standards. High expectations, as Milner points out, must clearly communicate caring for students, not criticism of their lives and culture, a difficult line to walk for white middle-class teachers.

In Part V, *Managing the Instructional Formats of Contemporary Classrooms,* edited by James M. Cooper, chapter authors go beyond traditional formats (e.g., teacher presentation, recitation, and seatwork) to highlight the special managerial challenges associated with more innovative, student-centered formats for instruction. The chapter authors recognize that the way instruction is organized and managed affects the opportunities students have to participate, and that the nature of their participation (e.g., who gets a chance to talk, if their answer is evaluated publicly or privately, and how that answer is or is not built on by others) affects access to learning. Rachel Lotan (chapter 19) describes how teachers can orchestrate and manage group work productively. Acknowledging that group work is a "costly instructional approach, demanding much thought, effort, and time," Lotan argues that its most important benefit is its potential to close the achievement gap and to create caring, democratic, equitable classrooms. Cheryl Mason Bolick and James Cooper (chapter 20) address the potential managerial challenges that teachers confront when they use technology in teaching and examine what little research exists on how technology affects classroom management. A recent innovation, the use of computers for teaching and learning, suggests a whole new set of questions about the nature of learning and the managerial decisions that affect it. In chapter 21, Lesley Morrow, Ray Reutzel, and Heather Casey address managerial issues specific to instruction in the language arts. Focusing on the effects of physical design, grouping practices, and social settings on students' literacy learning, the authors draw on investigations of exemplary practice in language arts instruction and provide a case study of an exemplary language arts program. John Mergendoller, Thom Markham, Jason Ravitz, and John Larmer (chapter 22) define and describe the key features of project-based learning—an instructional model that "engages students in a series of complex tasks that include planning and design, problem-solving, decision-making, creating artifacts and communicating results." The authors identify the issues that are associated with each stage of project implementation, and show how the teacher's role changes with the nature of the instructional tasks.

Part VI, *Research and Theory with Implications for Classroom Management,* edited by Thomas L. Good, focuses on related fields of inquiry that have particular relevance for teachers' understanding of student motivation, development, and behavior. In chapter 23, Kathryn Wentzel considers what it means to be a "socially competent" student and discusses ways that teachers and peers can support students' socially competent functioning at school. She presents research indicating that students will participate willingly in classroom activities when they perceive their relationships with their teachers and peers as emotionally supportive, nurturing, and responsive. Johnmarshall Reeve (chapter 24) examines the "apparent truism" that extrinsic rewards are an effective tool that teachers can use to motivate students. He notes that teachers can adopt two different motivating styles when using rewards—controlling or autonomy-supportive—and concludes that the efforts teachers make to use rewards in noncontrolling and informational ways will pay off in terms of students' motivation and engagement. In chapter 25, Joan Walker and Kathleen Hoover-Dempsey focus on the contributions of both parents and teachers to students' capacity for self-regulation, reviewing empirical studies of parent-child and teacher-child interactions. They argue that "parenting models provide a rich theoretical framework for examining teachers' classroom management practices and their contributions to child development." Relationships between teachers and children are also at the heart of chapter 26. Here, Robert Pianta summarizes research indicating that variation in the quality of child-teacher relationships is related to children's classroom adjustment, motivation, self-esteem, beliefs about school, and academic success. Larry Nucci (chapter 27) portrays classrooms as social environments that affect students' construction of morality and social values. He asks how classroom management can contribute positively to students' moral development and suggests ways that teachers can "transform classroom management from a system designed solely to sustain adult authority and control over students into an integral educational component for students' social and moral growth."

Part VII, *Programs for Classroom Management and Discipline*, edited by Edmund Emmer, examines programs and approaches that have been developed to help teachers solve the problem of order in the classroom, for example, how to intervene to stem student disruptive behavior. The first chapter in this part, by H. Jerome Freiberg and Judith Lapointe (chapter 28), provides an extensive and detailed review of 40 research-based programs (from a review process of nearly 800) that have been implemented in schools to prevent and solve discipline problems. Freiberg and Lapointe propose the creation of a single clearinghouse that would be able to provide schools with continuing updates and assessments of program effectiveness. In chapter 29, Sheri Robinson and Sarah Ricord-Griesemer offer suggestions for teachers whose normal repertoire of classroom management strategies and disciplinary interventions has not been able to eliminate the chronic, disruptive behaviors of one or a few typical students. Originally derived for use in special education settings, the intervention and assessment procedures discussed in the chapter are appropriate for use in general education settings. David and Roger Johnson (chapter 30) describe strategies for conflict resolution and peer mediation, focusing in particular on the Teaching Students To Be Peacemakers Program developed in the mid-1960s. In chapter 31, Timothy J. Lewis, Lori L. Newcomer, Robert Trussell, and Mary Richter argue that traditional systems of school discipline emphasizing punishments and "get tough" measures have been ineffective in reducing problem behaviors such as aggression, attendance problems, and disruptions. They describe "Positive Behavior Support" (PBS), a broad range of individual and system-wide strategies for preventing problem behavior and fostering prosocial behavior. Finally, Irwin Hyman, Bryony Kay, Alex Tabori, Meredith Weber, Matthew Mahon, and Ian Cohen (chapter 32) look closely at the phenomenon of bullying. They report on the frequency and types of bullying, the characteristics of bullies and victims, the destructive effects of bullying, and programs for intervening in student victimization.

Part VIII, *Teaching and Learning About Classroom Management*, edited by Carolyn Evertson, concerns teachers' professional development and their lived experiences. The chapter by Vernon Jones (chapter 33) outlines ways that preservice teachers receive information about classroom management in formal course work, how that information is organized and what experiences preservice teachers encounter that make it likely or unlikely that such information will have meaning for them in their own classrooms. Laura Stough, in chapter 34, clearly describes the policy contexts, curriculum standards, and state licensure policies that often neglect or omit competence in classroom management as part of the education of teachers. Her chapter raises serious issues about how important information about classroom management gets or does not get communicated to new teachers. In chapter 35, Isaac Friedman argues that teacher burnout is a result of the perceived professional failure that occurs when teachers' dreams—their "idealistic and altruistic aspirations"—are at odds with the harsh realities of classrooms and schools. He emphasizes the pivotal role of teacher-student relations in the stress and burnout process. Kim Fries and Marilyn Cochran-Smith (chapter 36) provide an exhaustive review of the available literature on teacher research and classroom management. They point out that all of these studies reflect the efforts of teachers who see teaching as a process of posing important questions and systematically collecting and analyzing data to address those questions. In chapter 37, Barbara Larrivee reviews the assumptions behind reflective practice and describes four levels of reflection—surface, pedagogical, critical, and self—and how the types of reflection in which teachers engage can influence management decisions and practices. She argues for an approach to classroom management that involves critical and self-reflection, which include pausing, reflecting, and reframing reactive responses to student misbehavior.

Part IX, *Policy, Law, Ethics, and Equity*, was edited by Irwin Hyman (until his untimely death in February, 2005). The chapters in this section highlight the sometimes overlooked connections between teachers' classroom management decisions and the legal, policy, and moral contexts in which their work is embedded. In chapter 38, David Schimmel notes that teachers' lack of preparation in school law leads to two types of mistakes. First, because they are unaware that their actions are restrained by the Bill of Rights, teachers may unknowingly violate students' constitutional rights (e.g., freedom of expression). At the same time, teachers may fail to take reasonable disciplinary action for fear of liability. Chapter 39, by Pamela Fenning and Hank Bohanon-Edmonson, focuses on discipline codes of conduct, the documents that communicate to students and parents a school or district's expectations for behavior, and the consequences that will be imposed for disciplinary infractions. Although the study of school-wide discipline policies is in its infancy, the research to date suggests that discipline codes contain "primarily reactionary responses" (e.g., zero tolerance, suspension, and expulsion), despite the lack of evidence to support the use of these procedures. Catherine Fallona and Virginia Richardson (chapter 40) consider the "curriculum of classroom management as a moral activity to promote moral student conduct." They examine two perspectives on moral activity in classrooms: the *implicit*, which focuses on the moral dimensions inherent in classroom actions, and the *explicit*, which focuses on fostering morality through deliberate, conscious programs and pedagogy. In chapter 41, Russell Skiba and M. Karega Rausch turn again to issues of zero tolerance, suspension, and expulsion. Like Fenning and Bohanon-Edmonson, they conclude that a growing body of evidence raises serious questions about the equity and effectiveness of such disciplinary interventions. In particular, they point out that African-Americans are overrepresented in zero tolerance measures, despite the lack of evidence that they engage in higher rates of misbehavior.

Theo Wubbels edited the final part of the *Handbook*, *International Perspectives on Classroom Management*. Here, scholars from England, Israel, The Netherlands, Australia, Sweden, and Japan describe programs of research, lines of inquiry, issues, and traditions with respect to classroom management in their respective countries. First, Andy Miller (chapter 42) provides a history of the study of classroom management in the United Kingdom and outlines the development of key legislation and governmental policy regarding classroom management. The chapter links this historical and political context to some of Miller's own studies of teachers' experiences working with school psychologists and the attributions made by teachers, pupils, and parents into the causes of problem behavior. In chapter 43, Miriam Ben Peretz, Billie Eilam, and Estie Yankelevitch examine the discipline problems that are caused by the clash among cultures in "multicultural, multiethnic" Israel. They describe two strands of Israeli research—one focusing on the relationship between classroom management and educational ideology, and the other focusing on teachers', students', and parents' perceptions of classroom management and discipline—and briefly discuss the place of classroom management in teacher education. In chapter 44, Kjell Granström discusses the origins of disruptive classroom behaviors in Sweden, drawing from studies conducted in nine-year compulsory schools. He makes three main points: (1) numerous student misbehaviors stem from students' personal needs (e.g., for belongingness and friendship); (2) teachers have difficulties handling such behaviors; and (3) different modes of instructional organization influence the probability of troublesome behavior. Theo Wubbels, Mieke Brekelmans, Perry den Brok, and Jan van Tartwijk (chapter 45) from The Netherlands report on the results of a 25-year program of studies investigating teacher-student interpersonal relationships in secondary classrooms. This research has repeatedly demonstrated that positive teacher-student relationships are characterized by a high degree of teacher *influence* (leadership or dominance) and *proximity* (cooperation, support) towards students. In chapter 46, Ramon Lewis from Australia describes a series of studies on students' and teachers' preferred disciplinary interventions, their perceptions of teachers' actual disciplinary practices, and the impact of discipline on students' attitudes and responsibility. The results of his research lead Lewis to conclude that teachers need to decrease their use "coercive" power (aggression and punishment), since coercive strategies are "at best of limited usefulness, and at worst counterproductive...." The last chapter in this part (chapter 47), by Kanae Nishioka, describes trends in classroom management in post-World War II Japan. She outlines four forms of *seikatsushido* (life guidance) that were developed by teachers to foster *shudanzukuri*—the feeling of community or "grouphood."

THEMES THAT CUT ACROSS THE SECTIONS

The chapters in the *Handbook* cover a wide-ranging set of topics and are written by scholars from different disciplines, with different theoretical orientations, and from different countries. Nonetheless, there are a number of themes that appear repeatedly across sections. In fact, we were surprised by how chapters converged on several key ideas. First, the research reported in the *Handbook* underscores the idea that positive teacher-child relationships are at the very core of effective classroom management. This emphasis on relationships is most explicit in the chapter by Robert Pianta, who notes:

> In analysis of classroom management, child-teacher relationships are a key unit of analysis. A focus on relationships rather than discrete behaviors, or interpreting such behavior in light of their meaning for relationships, is an important conceptual advance in the classroom management literature, and may be particularly important for teacher training.

Other chapter authors echo Pianta's emphasis on relationships. Indeed, throughout the *Handbook,* a relational conceptualization of management thoroughly overshadows a view of management as a set of rules, rewards, and penalties, or a set of specific strategies designed to promote engagement and minimize disruption. Authors repeatedly cite the importance of teachers' being warm, responsive, caring, and supportive, as well as holding high expectations. This portrait of "warm demanders" appears frequently in discussions of effective teachers of students of color who may feel alienated or marginalized. (See the chapters by Geneva Gay and Richard Milner.) But it is apparent that "warm demanders" have broader relevance and appeal. This characterization is obviously parallel to the authoritative parent described in the parenting research, and both literatures consistently report the positive outcomes that accrue when adults are both caring and demanding. (See, in particular, the chapter by Joan Walker and Kathleen Hoover-Dempsey.) That students appreciate and respond positively to authoritative teachers is also clear from reports of students' perceptions of "good" teachers. (See the chapter by Anita Woolfolk Hoy and Carol Weinstein.) According to both elementary and secondary students, good teachers *care*: They are concerned about the students' academic and personal lives, they are "there for them," and they know how to set limits and enforce expectations without being punitive and demeaning. Clearly, when students perceive their teachers to be "good," they are more likely to engage in learning activities and to behave in prosocial, responsible ways. On the other hand, if students perceive their teachers to be uncaring, unfair, and rude, they are likely to engage in acts of resistance and sabotage. In the words of one student, "If I don't like 'em . . . I'm not gonna do anything for 'em" (Stinson, 1993, p. 221).

Second, the chapters draw attention to classroom management as a social and moral curriculum. This broader and more complex view recognizes that the managerial decisions that teachers make affect not only students' opportunities to learn, but also their social, emotional, and moral development. This view is the explicit focus of the chapter by Fallona and Richardson, who begin by asking: "What could be closer to the moral in the classroom than activities and teaching that are directed at and/or function to affect present and future student conduct?" Classroom management as a moral curriculum is also the focus of Nucci's chapter. He writes:

> All classrooms, no matter how they are run, constitute social environments that impact students' construction of morality and social values. . . . The issue, then, is not whether classroom management affects social development, but rather how classroom management may contribute positively to students' moral and social growth. Viewing classroom management as an educational activity requires teachers to engage in the same kind of critical analysis of practice as would be directed to the teaching of subject matter. This includes not only an awareness of available options or strategies for how to handle classroom situations, but also a compendium of knowledge about the "subject matter" of social and moral development and how it relates to a given set of practices.

This way of thinking about classroom management appears frequently throughout the *Handbook*. Authors consistently call for an approach to classroom management that fosters the development of self-regulation and emotional competence. McCaslin, Bozack, Napoleon, Thomas, Vasquez, Wayman, and Zhang comment on the importance of "talking it through"—explaining the reasoning behind rules and expectations (again, much like authoritative parents). Maurice Elias and Yoni Schwab comment that social-emotional learning and effective classroom management are "two sides of the same coin," since self-control and responsibility are the "ultimate goals" for both. Watson and Battistich describe approaches to building classroom community that emphasize the importance of building students' social and moral skills and understanding.

In addition to reflecting on ways that management can support children's social, emotional, and moral learning, numerous authors examine the ways that managerial decisions can promote a democratic society. Lotan, for example, urges teachers to use group work to build more "equitable classrooms" that reflect not only a pedagogical, but also a "moral vision." Brantlinger and Danforth discuss the importance of creating "moral classroom communities," which avoid discrimination and contribute to a "new equitable social order." Gay, Milner, Skiba and Rausch, and other authors report evidence of racial and socioeconomic disparities in terms of who gets punished and why, and make the case that classroom management is not just about order, but also about social justice.

A third theme in the *Handbook* is that managerial strategies relying on external reward and punishment are not optimal for promoting academic and social-emotional growth and self-regulated behavior. In particular, numerous authors voice criticism of coercive, exclusionary methods of discipline. Skiba and Rausch, for example, argue that out-of-school suspension and expulsion "are associated with negative outcomes in terms of school climate, student behaviors, student achievement, and school dropout." Fenning and Bohanon-Edmonson concur. They wonder "why school discipline policies have lagged so far behind what is known about effective behavioral interventions" and conclude that discipline policies "may be reflective of a school culture that views discipline as punishment instead of an opportunity to teach." Lewis, Newcomer, Trussell, and Richter contend that traditional disciplinary interventions that emphasize punishment are ineffective in changing chronic patterns of problem behavior. Andy Miller points out that students who are subject to, or witness, teacher coercion and aggression may react negatively, concluding that "the teacher hates me!"

At the same time, authors voice support for more proactive approaches to management and discipline. Freiberg and LaPointe advocate moving beyond a stimulus-response paradigm to an approach that emphasizes students' self-regulation, social-emotional learning, and school connectedness, trust, and caring. David and Roger Johnson describe the benefits of teaching the skills of peacemaking and allowing students to engage in negotiations to resolve their conflicts. Walker and Hoover-Dempsey stress the importance of providing support for student autonomy and note that research suggests that "students are more likely to self-regulate their learning and behavior when they have opportunities to do so." Autonomy support is also underscored in Reeve's review of extrinsic rewards and intrinsic motivation. He concludes that extrinsic rewards are "not necessarily bad or counter-productive" if they are administered in a noncontrolling way and provide information about learning or performance.

Finally, there is recognition across chapters that to create orderly, productive, and supportive environments, teachers must take into account students' characteristics such as age, developmental level, race, ethnicity, cultural background, socioeconomic status, and ableness. While principles of respect, caring, fairness, clarity of expectations, environmental predictability, and guidance apply to all students, there are also important variations among students that mediate teachers' managerial decisions and actions. These decisions ultimately influence teacher-student relationships, the very foundation of trust.

The chapters by Carter and Doyle, Emmer and Gerwels, and Nucci all elaborate on how developmental level affects students' receptivity to classroom norms. Carter and Doyle, writing about early childhood and elementary classrooms, stress the importance of establishing an environment with predictability and constancy. Emmer and Gerwels highlight adolescents' need for autonomy and recommend that teachers increasingly allow secondary students to make decisions for themselves and experience the consequences of those decisions (although they acknowledge that "balancing adolescents' need for autonomy and the teacher's need to manage behavior can be a delicate task"). Similarly, Nucci explains that early adolescence is a difficult transition as students begin to question and negate social conventions they upheld during middle childhood and seek increasing control over areas like appearance, friendships, and access to information. Nucci suggests that teachers who work with this age group distinguish between the norms needed to ensure student safety and those that constitute a minor threat: "To put it another way, it is important for teachers to realize that there are times when it makes more sense to say 'yes' in response to student noncompliance, than it is to simply say 'no' in an effort to maintain consistency for its own sake."

In addition to considering developmental level, teachers must be aware of the cultural clashes that can occur when students and teachers come from different backgrounds. Nowhere is this clash more clearly illustrated than in the chapter by Ben-Peretz, Eilam, and Yankelevitch, which describes the tensions of educating students from many cultures and religious backgrounds in Israel. The authors describe the real dilemmas of authority and power, wherein certain cultural norms and religious beliefs press teachers to be stern and to use punitive measures to gain respect and claim authority. In the United States, we face a similar challenge. While the K–12 student population becomes increasingly diverse in terms of ethnicity, race, culture, and linguistic background, the overwhelming majority of teachers remain monocultural and monolingual European Americans. Gay notes that unless teachers have been prepared in cultural diversity and multicultural education, "they are likely to interpret the attitudes and behaviors of students of color according to the prevailing middle class and Eurocentric-embedded normative standards of schools." Milner, writing on the managerial challenges of urban classrooms, urges teachers to "understand and acknowledge that the students are not necessarily the problem," and "take some of the responsibility, look inwardly and change their own behavior."

Likewise, a number of chapters point out that general education classrooms now contain a greater number of students with disabilities, requiring teachers to acquire a new repertoire of strategies. Robinson and Ricord-Griesemer, for example, describe a number of possible interventions that require specialized knowledge and skills (e.g., functional behavioral assessment, differential reinforcement, group contingencies, and self-management procedures). Soodak and McCarthy examine ways that teachers in inclusive classrooms can promote an environment of acceptance and friendship in which all children experience success and belonging.

CONCLUDING COMMENTS

In 1979, Daniel Duke edited the National Society for the Study of Education (NSSE) Yearbook on classroom management. Since then, there has been no comprehensive research handbook devoted entirely to conceptualizing and reviewing the field of classroom management and its related areas. As noted, the third edition of the *Handbook of Research on Teaching*, published in 1986, contained an outstanding chapter on classroom management by Walter Doyle, but the latest edition, published in 2002, does not even include this topic. The second edition of the *Handbook of Research on Teacher Education* (1996) has an important chapter by Vernon Jones, but the emphasis here is on how teachers develop competence in classroom management. Innumerable textbooks are devoted to helping preservice teachers as they learn to teach, but scholarly books on the topic are rare and considerably narrower in scope. We believe that this *Handbook of Classroom Management* will provide an important resource for scholars, teacher educators, administrators, and teachers.

In the editor's preface to the 1979 NSSE Yearbook, Dan Duke wrote:

> After pondering classroom management for more than a year, writing a chapter for this volume, and reading various versions of the other chapters, I reluctantly have come to realize that classroom management defies simple, straightforward exposition. Confusion exists among practitioners and researchers alike about where instruction stops and management commences. Some argue for more attention to classroom management, while others decry the fact that too much time already is wasted on "clerical" and "police" duties. The literature boasts books full of managerial tips and insights, but few efforts to place classroom management into a context where it can be systematically delineated, observed, analyzed, evaluated, and improved. In short, classroom management, although a very practical, "real-world" issue, is anything but simple. (xi)

Twenty-five years later, after editing this handbook, we are convinced that we have come a long way. Nonetheless, like Duke, we have an increased appreciation for the multi-dimensional, complex nature of classroom management. And like Duke, we have found that classroom management is anything but simple.

As we sorted out the complexities, we were ably assisted by our outstanding section editors. We are grateful for their willingness to be part of this project and to undertake the often tedious chores of reviewing, cajoling, nudging, and, of course, editing. We are privileged to have had the opportunity to work with such a remarkable group of scholars. We especially want to acknowledge the contribution of Irwin Hyman, who completed much of this editing work before his death on February 7, 2005. We appreciate his boundless energy and his keen intellect, and we regret that he will not be able to see the result of his efforts. We are also grateful for the assistance of the external reviewers for each chapter; their names are listed at the end of the chapter they reviewed. Their knowledgeable, insightful comments certainly improved the quality of the *Handbook*. We also thank Joanne Bowser, our production manager, for her wisdom, patience, and diligence in helping this project come to fruition. Finally, we must thank Lane Akers, our editor at Erlbaum. It was Lane who first conceived of a *Handbook of Classroom Management*. In response to his suggestion, we initially laughed—convinced that there wasn't enough research to constitute such a volume. We were wrong.

ACKNOWLEDGMENTS

The authors thank Jere Brophy, Michigan State University, Edmund Emmer, The University of Texas, Austin, and Anita Woolfolk Hoy, Ohio State University, for their insightful comments and suggestions on the final draft of this chapter.

REFERENCES

Bowers, C. A., & Flinders, D. J. (1990). *Responsive teaching: An ecological approach to classroom patterns of language, culture, and thought*. New York: Teachers College Press.

Brophy, J. (1988). Educating teachers about managing classrooms and students. *Teaching and Teacher Education, 4*(1), 1–18.

Brophy, J. E. (1999). Perspectives of classroom management: Yesterday, today, and tomorrow. In H. J. Freiberg (Ed.), *Beyond behaviorism: Changing the classroom management paradigm* (pp. 43–56). Boston: Allyn & Bacon.

Charles, C. M. (2002). *Essential elements of effective discipline*. Boston: Allyn & Bacon.

Doyle, W. (1986). Classroom organization and management. In M. C. Wittrock (Ed.), *Handbook of research on teaching* (pp. 392–431). New York: Macmillan.

Duke, D. L. (Ed.). (1979). *Classroom management*. (*The 78th Yearbook of the National Society for the Study of Education).* Chicago: University of Chicago Press.

Farkas, S., & Johnson, J. (1997). *Different drummers: How teachers of teachers view public education.* New York: Public Agenda.

Johnson, J. (2005). Isn't it time for schools of education to take concerns about student discipline more seriously? *Teachers College Record*, Retrieved February 14, 2005, from http://www.tcrecord.org.

Kounin, J. S. (1970). *Discipline and group management in classrooms*. New York: Holt, Rinehart and Winston.

McCaslin, M., & Good, T. L. (1998). Moving beyond management as sheer compliance: Helping students to develop goal coordination strategies. *Educational Horizons*, 169–176.

Stinson, S. W. (1993). Meaning and value: Reflections on what students say about school. *Journal of Curriculum and Supervision, 8*(3), 216–238.

Watson, M., & Ecken, L. (2003). *Learning to trust: Transforming difficult elementary classrooms through developmental discipline*. San Francisco: Jossey-Bass.

2

History of Research on Classroom Management

Jere Brophy
Michigan State University

INTRODUCTION

This chapter overviews the history of research on classroom management as it developed across the 20th century, taking into account both its substance (theoretical base, questions, findings) and its design and methodology. It highlights major influences and trends in the development of a knowledge base on the subject, introducing many of the bodies of theory and research that are elaborated in detail in subsequent chapters and outlining a big picture within which to locate them.

SCOPE

To delimit the chapter, it was helpful to distinguish management functions from other teaching functions, such as instruction, motivation, or assessment. Hereafter, *classroom management* refers to actions taken to create and maintain a learning environment conducive to successful instruction (arranging the physical environment, establishing rules and procedures, maintaining students' attention to lessons and engagement in activities). Although management is the chapter's primary focus, two related functions also receive attention because they are closely associated with it. *Student socialization* refers to actions taken to influence personal or social (including moral and civic) attitudes, beliefs, or behavior. Socialization includes articulation of ideals; communication of expectations; and modeling, teaching, and reinforcing of desirable personal attributes and behavior (done mostly with the class as a whole); as well as counseling, behavior modification, and other remediation work with students who show poor academic or social adjustment (done mostly with individuals). *Disciplinary interventions* are actions taken to elicit or compel improved behavior from students who fail to conform to expectations, especially when their misbehavior is salient or sustained enough to disrupt the classroom management system. As a practical matter, successful classroom management requires more than creating appropriate physical settings and managing the class as a group. It also includes establishing and working within personal relationships with students (or at least, those students whose special needs or personal characteristics frequently make them unable or unwilling to comply with instructions that are sufficient for the rest of the class).

The chapter addresses what is known about teachers managing the students and activities that occur in regular classrooms. Only passing references are made to the roles of administrators in managing the school as a whole and the roles of specialists (counselors, social workers, resource teachers, etc.) who work in other settings.

BASIC ASSUMPTIONS

The chapter assumes the following about classroom management as a component of schooling: Most fundamentally, schools are established to equip students with desired learning outcomes, so classroom management is not an end in itself but a means for creating and maintaining a learning environment that is optimal given the intended curriculum. Curricular goals should determine instructional methods, materials, and activities; these in turn imply desired student roles, and these in turn imply optimal managerial expectations, rules, and routines. Management theory and research focuses on how teachers can establish and maintain these expectations, rules, and routines, as well as respond effectively and restore desired patterns when they are disrupted.

Recognition that management is a support for learning carries implications for what is defined as success and how it ought to be assessed. For example, although a low frequency of disruptions is relevant, desired student roles typically go beyond passive compliance to call for actively engaging in activities in ways that support progress toward learning goals. Physical setting, task flow, and discourse management need to be designed to create optimal implementations of the intended curriculum. This requires preparing students to enact different roles in different situations. Also, ideal learning environments typically involve optimizing rather than maximizing. A teacher can have too much control as well as too little, or the wrong kind (authoritarian rather than authoritative).

RESEARCH METHODS

Given these and other complexities, it is not feasible to use classical experimental methods to develop and test comprehensive management models. That is, it is not possible to hold constant everything else that is known or suspected to affect outcomes while investigators systematically vary a single component. Classroom events are only partly controllable (or even predictable) by teachers, so much of good management involves adapting effectively to emerging developments. There have been applications of hypothetico-deductive methods in which investigators adapted models developed elsewhere (e.g., applied behavior analysis) for application in classrooms, trained teachers accordingly, and assessed outcomes. In these studies, fidelity of implementation of an explicit model is one criterion for management success.

More typically, investigators have chosen to work inductively, using interviewing or observation to conduct "policy capturing" analyses of effective managers' methods, and then formulating principles of practice. Some have used primarily qualitative methods to produce thick descriptions of the management methods of individual teachers. Others have used mixed methods to compare expert managers with novices or with experienced but less successful managers. These studies usually rely on principals' or professors' recommendations or other "reputation" information to identify ostensibly expert managers, although they sometimes begin by observing a larger number of teachers and then selecting a smaller number for thick description.

In evaluating a teacher's managerial success, investigators typically use direct indicators such as time spent engaged in lessons and activities (relative to time spent getting organized or dealing with chaos), the efficiency of transitions, or the frequencies of problems such as off-task behavior, disruptions, or disciplinary referrals. Some include less direct but potentially important indicators such as achievement gains or students' attitudes toward the teacher or the class.

These characterizations apply mostly to research done relatively recently, however. For the first two thirds of the 20th century, the managerial advice in teacher education textbooks was mostly confined to common sense ("Arrange for smooth-flowing traffic patterns and places for students to store personal belongings") and aphorisms presented as wisdom of practice ("Don't smile until Christmas"). Citations were infrequent and mostly to theorists or other textbooks. Some authors cited surveys of opinion or reported practices, but they could not cite studies that included systematic observation of teacher behavior, because no such studies existed yet.

THE PRE-EMPIRICAL ERA

The Turn of the 20th Century

A noteworthy example of these early treatises is that of William Chandler Bagley (1907). His preface promised management principles interpreted in the light of psychological principles, based on data gathered from four sources: (1) Bagley's observations of teachers he viewed as efficient and successful, (2) textbooks on classroom management and teaching, (3) his own personal experience as a teacher, and (4) general psychological principles that had been "subjected to actual test before being included."

Bagley's language was very different from today's. For example, he spoke of "slowly transforming the child from a little savage into a creature of law and order, fit for the life of civilized society" (1907, p. 35). Yet, his basic assumptions were very familiar. Because school is intended to prepare children for life in civilized society, potential management principles need to be considered not just in terms of short-term efficiency but also the larger purposes of schooling. Unnecessarily punitive or anxiety-inducing methods are inappropriate, as are excessively competition-oriented methods that may make students selfish or even antisocial.

Bagley distinguished "routine factors" (confusion, disorder, irregular attendance, poor hygiene) that could be handled by training students to develop desired habits, from "judgment factors" (inattention, cheating, slow learning) that required conscious teacher attention and individualized adaptation. Habits could be ingrained by applying the law of habit building: Whatever is to become a matter of invariable custom must be made conscious to the students at the outset, then drilled explicitly and held to rigidly, until all tendency to act in any other way has been overcome. This may require detailed instructions early in the year, followed by practice of the desired procedures. Certain routines will need to be installed from day one (traffic patterns, toilet policies, having needed materials available, keeping the blackboards clean).

On the first day, stick to work with which the students are familiar, but do real teaching rather than busywork, to establish seriousness of purpose. Have everything prepared when the students arrive, greet them pleasantly, and direct them to seats. Implement a prearranged plan for handling hats and coats. If seats have not been preassigned, make a seating chart and quickly begin referring to students by name. Appoint monitors and distribute supplies. As needed, instruct and drill students in procedures.

Much of this is very similar to advice given in today's textbooks. Bagley went on to say that only an irreducible minimum of classroom procedures needs to be routinized in this way and some of even those routines can be faded as students become capable of exercising more individual responsibility. He also suggested scheduling the most challenging or fatiguing subjects during prime learning times and being prepared to shift to recess or another subject if fatigue sets in.

In talking about maintaining order and discipline, Bagley anticipated Baumrind's (1971) distinctions among authoritative, authoritarian, and laissez-faire approaches. Teachers have governing responsibilities and must have the courage to assert authority without worrying about becoming unpopular, tact in exercising it effectively, and persistence in following through. Yet, they also must be fair and good natured. Problems can be minimized by keeping students occupied with worthwhile activities and providing incentives for good work (the principle of substitution is preferable to the principle of suppression). Penalties should be imposed only as a last resort, should emphasize natural consequences when possible, and should be inflicted primarily with an eye toward promoting the welfare of the class as a whole. The best penalties are efficient in stopping the undesired behavior, specific to the impulse toward that behavior, and no more severe than necessary. Corporal punishment often meets these criteria, especially with elementary students, because it can be more humane than scolding and because "moral suasion" often is not effective until students begin to understand the reasoning why their behavior is inappropriate (as they enter adolescence).

Based on interviews with about 100 reputedly successful teachers, Bagley offered 15 principles for punishing effectively: the teacher (not someone else) should administer the punishment; little time should elapse between the misbehavior and the punishment; children should not be punished in the presence of their peers; do not punish while angry; punish intentional and premeditated offenses; punish repeated offenses; do not punish offenses not apt to be repeated; not all children require the same punishment for the same offense; children should always understand why they are being punished; punishments tend to reform students if they can see their justice; suspension should be the last resort; do not punish for the sake of "making an example"; do not use sarcasm, ridicule, or satire as punishments; most parents favor corporal punishment; and do not use school assignments as punishments.

Picking up on the idea of keeping students profitably occupied as preventive management, Bagley offered several motivational principles. He acknowledged the value of making school activities interesting and enjoyable, but noted that this principle has limited applicability because children are instinctively oriented toward immediate gratification and variety, whereas school calls for sustained work on activities with ultimate purposes that are distant and fuzzy. Therefore, students need short-term incentives. Rewards are preferable to punishments, following the "well-known psychological law that depression chokes up the channels of energy, while hope and buoyancy tend to liberate energy and make it available" (1907, p. 162). However, some students may need scolding or even punishment to spur effort.

Bagley warned against competitive prizes of intrinsic value because only a few students will have realistic chances to get them and this can lead to rivalry or jealousy. Nonintrinsically valuable rewards, such as merit badges or medals, are preferable, but only if given out in a way that allows the full range of students to earn them. Immunities are unwise because they make regular school activities or tests look like punishments. Privileges and honor rolls can be useful if not overdone in a way that constantly reminds poorer students of their inferiority. Exhibition of good work is advised so long as it doesn't lead to emphasis on form over content. Praise is useful but needs to be offered sparingly and justified by the effort that went into the accomplishment. Students can become dependent on praise, to the point that they become "depressed and discouraged, sour and morose," whenever their efforts are not commended

(1907, p. 182). Finally, there is much to be said for appealing to ideals such as sense of duty, sense of self-respect, or appreciation of a job well done.

The rest of Bagley's book deals with issues that are obsolescent today (guarding against the spread of contagious diseases) or outside of the topic of classroom management (playground supervision, achievement testing). Although it was rooted in instinct theories of psychology, his advice was more similar to than different from what we offer today. Reflecting his time, he was less respectful of children's cognitive and metacognitive capacities, so he placed more emphasis on habit training and less on supporting self-regulation. Also, he emphasized competition (although with misgivings) and made no mention of cooperative learning.

The Early Decades of the 20th Century

Although classroom management has always been recognized as crucial for teachers in general and beginning teachers in particular, and although Bagley produced an extended treatise on the subject in 1907, there was little development of theory and research on the topic until the 1950s. In part, this was because management had not established an identity as an independent subfield of educational studies. As Breed (1933) noted, it had slipped between the cracks of knowledge bases that were developing at the classroom level (focusing on curriculum and instruction in the subject areas) and the school level (focusing on administering the school as a whole). One could even argue that attention to management faded as the first third of the century progressed.

Breed's own book is an example. Even though he recognized the problem and entitled his book *Classroom Organization and Management*, most of it addressed testing, homogeneous versus heterogeneous grouping, class size, grading and promotion policies, curricular issues, extracurricular activities, class scheduling, and other primarily school-level topics. Classroom management was treated in only two chapters, one on organizing routines and one on reconstructing the behavior of pupils.

The latter chapter included a review of Wickman's (1928) study entitled *Children's Behavior and Teachers' Attitudes*, a source cited routinely in subsequent decades and even occasionally today. Wickman surveyed 511 Cleveland teachers to elicit their levels of concern about various child behavior problems and compared their responses with responses elicited from mental health specialists. The teachers expressed the most concern about overt behaviors likely to disrupt classrooms (sexual activity, obscenity, theft, disobedience, defiance, etc.), whereas the clinicians emphasized mostly covert problems (unsocial, suspicious, unhappy, resentful, fearful, overly sensitive or suggestible, etc.). Wickman concluded that teachers were underattentive to anxiety, depression, and other symptoms indicating a need for character education or mental treatment.

Breed's advice about classroom routines cited Bagley and other sources of practitioner wisdom, and his advice on reconstructing the behavior of students was limited to a few basic principles. Rejecting genetics or instinct as explanations for character and dismissing preaching or global generalities as unhelpful, he urged teachers to prioritize the character traits they valued most and emphasize these in socializing students (such as by presenting them with fictional or historical models that embody the traits and specifying in detail behaviors expected in particular situations). Both the doctrine of expression and the doctrine of repression would be avoided in favor of direct instruction in desired traits and behaviors. As sources he cited Charters (1927) on the teaching of ideals, Watson (1926) on behaviorism, and several texts on character education and delinquency. The only citation to data collected in a school setting was to a survey by Haggerty (1925) on the frequencies with which various forms of student misbehavior were observed in public schools.

Other early texts resembled those by Bagley (1907) and Breed (1933): They emphasized the authors' personal experiences and observations, buttressed by citations to authorities (mostly authors of similar texts) and to selected psychological principles. The citations appeared to be ex post facto: The authors began by distilling the wisdom of practice and then dressed it up with citations, rather than beginning with a set of theoretical principles and then proceeding deductively. Consequently, there was a great deal of overlap in what was recommended, even when there was little overlap in the authorities or theoretical principles cited. Citations to empirical studies were limited to surveys of teachers' attitudes or reported frequencies of various behavior problems. Ostensible classroom management texts also included chapters on other teaching functions and on school-level administrative functions (e.g., assessing and classifying students), because at the time the topic of classroom management was subsumed within broader conceptions of school efficiency (Johnson & Brooks, 1979).

The Middle Decades of the 20th Century

These trends continued into the 1950s, as exemplified by Brown's (1952) text entitled *Managing the Classroom: The Teacher's Part in School Administration.* Brown emphasized Christian values, school as preparation for democratic citizenship, and child-centered, progressive educational methods. His text is similar to Bagley's in that it contains comprehensive advice on classroom management, but similar to Breed's in that it also contains several chapters on other teaching functions and on school-level administrative issues (as well as on dressing, grooming, avoiding scandal, and making a good impression in the community).

Brown's text was much more respectful of students than the earlier texts, and it featured ideas rooted in his progressive philosophy (e.g., involve students in developing basic rules and procedures, do not emphasize discipline so much as helping students progress from external toward increasing levels of internal self-control). Once he got to specific advice, however, Brown echoed the same principles emphasized by his predecessors: evaluate potential rules and procedures in terms of consistency with larger learning and motivation goals, not just situational efficiency; do not impose needless or overly rigid demands; emphasize developing individual and collective responsibility among the students over momentary control of behavior; some behaviors should be routinized immediately, others might be routinized later, and still others should not be routinized at all; it is better to prevent problems before they occur than to have to deal with them afterwards, so keep everyone profitably busy, build good school spirit, maintain good relationships with individuals, and emphasize enduring values; when it does become necessary to enforce rules, avoid reactions that will disrupt relationships with students or create other problems; focus punishments on deterrence and reformation, not expiation or retribution; and be prepared to begin the school year productively by clarifying expectations and helping students to develop good behavior and learning habits.

Brown devoted a few pages to what he described as principles derived from 50 years of study of how children learn (frequency, recency, satisfaction, punishment, immediacy, symbolic drive, and interest), citing texts in psychology and educational psychology. However, his management advice did not seem to flow from these principles. He included many more references than Bagley or Breed had, but the vast majority were to other textbooks rather than to research reports. Exceptions included two survey studies (Charters & Waples, 1929; Witty, 1947) suggesting that teachers should display virtues such as kindness, sincerity, tact, politeness, cheerfulness, patience, and fairness. Another exception was the Wickman (1928) study, along with two subsequent studies indicating that the views of teachers and of mental hygiene specialists concerning the relative seriousness of various child behaviors and symptoms were more similar by 1940 than they had been in 1927. However, these and later studies (e.g., Fuller,

1969; Schrupp & Gjerde, 1953; Stern, 1963) continued to show that teachers were especially concerned about behaviors that threatened their classroom control.

STUDIES OF INFLUENCE TECHNIQUES, LEADERSHIP STYLE, AND GROUP CLIMATE

Empirical studies perceived to be relevant to classroom management began to accumulate during the middle decades of the 20th century. Some were isolated individual studies. Others were parts of more programmatic lines of research, that is, research that took place in settings other than classrooms and addressed questions not directly related to classroom management (e.g., group leadership, social climate). Systematic research on the topic did not begin until the 1950s.

Several early studies contrasted reward versus punishment or praise versus blame as techniques for influencing children's behavior. Some were childrearing studies focusing on parents (Sears, Maccoby, & Levin, 1957, and later Baumrind, 1971). Others were experiments conducted by psychologists, initially with animals but later with humans, especially children (Estes, 1944; Kennedy & Willicutt, 1964; Solomon, 1964; Thompson & Hunnicutt, 1944). These studies generally found reward or praise to be superior to punishment or blame as influence techniques, although a few reported punishment or blame to be effective with certain subgroups (extroverts, underachievers). McDonald (1965) interpreted these exceptions as suggesting that individual children's previous experiences with praise and blame condition their responses to these influence attempts in the classroom.

Kounin and Gump (1961) extended these findings to classrooms. They used ratings to identify the most and least punitive of the first-grade teachers in three schools, then asked their students, "What is the worst thing you can do in school?" They found that students of punitive teachers more often mentioned aggression and were more concrete in their descriptions ("Hit George in the mouth"). In contrast, students of nonpunitive teachers more often talked about behaviors that would interfere with learning or about violations of school values and rules, using more abstract language ("Be mean to people"). Kounin and Gump concluded that the nonpunitive approach was more successful for socializing students' values and behavior.

Complementary findings emerged from several lines of research on leadership style and group climate. Anderson and his colleagues (Anderson, 1943; Anderson, Brewer, & Reed, 1946) used classroom observation methods in several studies comparing "dominating" teachers (unilateral, forceful) with "leading" teachers (inviting input, working with students). They reported that domination tended to produce either teacher dependency and rote conformity or conflict and resistance. In contrast, when teachers worked with their students, the students worked with them and their engagement in learning activities featured more spontaneity and collaboration.

Lewin, Lippitt, and White (1939) conducted a classic study of leadership and social climate in groups of boys supervised by group leaders who consistently implemented one of three contrasting leadership styles: authoritarian (leader determines all policies, assigns tasks and work companions, gives step-by-step instructions, praises or blames boys individually); democratic (policies negotiated in group discussion; boys encouraged to assume responsibility for planning and carrying out tasks, but with input from leader as resource person; group members decide how to divide the work and collaborate; leader is more task-focused and impersonal in praising or criticizing progress); or laissez-faire (group members left on their own to determine what to do and how to do it, with ostensible leader participating as little as possible). Findings indicated that the boys in the democratically led groups were the most responsive and spontaneous in working on the tasks, and were able to continue working productively without the supervision of the leader. The boys working under authoritarian leadership were more apathetic and less personally involved in the tasks, frequently frustrated, and likely to become involved in conflict if the leader was not present. The boys in the laissez-faire condition had difficulty negotiating what to do and how to do it, so they were confused, frustrated, and ultimately not very productive. This study was and still is cited very frequently in books and chapters on classroom management. Its findings appear to generalize well to the classroom, although it is important to clarify that the "democratic" leadership style was not actually democratic in the usual sense of the word (policies determined by majority vote, etc.). In fact, it was very similar to the style that Baumrind (1971) later characterized as "authoritative."

Ryans (1952) and Ryans and Wandt (1952) reported findings from two studies based on ratings averaged across three or four observers who each visited a given classroom several times. Ratings focused on students' participation in classroom activities and teachers' personal characteristics and leadership styles. In the elementary study of 345 third- and fourth-grade classes, higher ratings of student alertness, orderliness, responsibility, constructiveness, participation, and initiative were found in classrooms taught by teachers characterized as democratic, kindly, systematic, calm, confident, mature, responsible, and consistent. Within this pattern, students were rated as more docile when their teachers were rated as systematic but in an inflexible and autocratic way, whereas students were rated as more initiatory when their teachers were rated as more democratic, understanding, and original but less organized. Many of these findings were replicated in the study of 249 high school classes, although at this level ratings for teacher democracy and kindliness did not show significant relationships with ratings of student behavior, and a newly added rating of dull versus stimulating instruction showed the strongest relationships.

The 1950s and 1960s ushered in a spate of studies of teacher leadership style variously described as autocratic versus democratic, demanding versus permissive, dominative versus integrative, teacher-centered versus learner-centered, or direct versus indirect. Withall and Lewis (1963) noted that these studies reflected a blending of influences from educational psychology (focusing on teacher characteristics and instructional methods), the mental health movement (focusing on causes of anxiety or other blocks to learning or motivation), and social psychology (focusing on leadership style, social climate, decision-making processes, and patterns of participation). Many were conducted by investigators committed to progressive or child-centered teaching philosophies, and their proliferation was fueled by the development of reliable classroom observation systems by Flanders (1970), Withall (1960) and others. Most of the observation systems included in *Mirrors for Behavior* (Simon & Boyer, 1970), a compilation of systems developed through the late 1960s, focused on these leadership style and climate aspects of classrooms.

These studies indicated that teachers typically were more dominative, direct, etc. than integrative, indirect, etc. Correlations with achievement gains were weak in magnitude and mixed in direction, but more positive pupil attitudes and motivational indicators typically were observed in classes taught by relatively more integrative teachers (Wallen & Travers, 1963). Reviewing these findings, Dunkin and Biddle (1974) suggested that relationships might be clearer if teacher directness and indirectness were considered separate clusters of behaviors rather than treated as poles of the same dimension, and especially if observation systems and data analyses were designed to distinguish teachers' personal warmth versus coldness from the directive versus permissive aspects of their leadership styles. They also noted that leadership style and classroom climate studies had limited potential for developing knowledge about effective classroom management because they typically were confined to frequency counts of teacher behaviors such as lecturing, asking questions, giving directions, praising, or criticizing. Data collection and analysis methods that would retain the connections between these teacher behaviors and relevant student behaviors would make it possible to study sequences of classroom interactions. They concluded that management is an interactive phenomenon that needs to be investigated as such.

RESEARCHERS BEGIN TO FOCUS EXPLICITLY ON CLASSROOM MANAGEMENT

Earlier, more generic research generally supported the conclusions that positive, reward-oriented influence techniques were preferable to negative, punishment-oriented ones, and that authoritative leadership that balanced teacher directiveness with encouragement of student input and self-regulation was preferable to the extremes of either authoritarian or laissez-faire approaches. It was time to address more specific aspects of managing classrooms and students effectively.

Initial movements in this direction came from two very different sources. The first was behaviorists. Working deductively from a rich and theoretically integrated knowledge base developed from experimental studies, behaviorists began probing classroom management applications of key concepts and principles, and in the process developed many new techniques. The second source was ecological researchers, who developed concepts and principles inductively by documenting variation in observed student behavior, initially with respect to variations in classroom settings but later with respect to variations in teacher behavior.

BEHAVIORAL RESEARCH

Most behavioral research and development regarding classroom management has featured applied behavior analysis, known alternatively as operant conditioning or the experimental analysis of behavior. Behaviorists emphasize using reinforcement to "bring behavior under stimulus control." The stimulus is a cue that tells students that certain forms of behavior are desired in the situation and performing these behaviors will gain them access to reinforcement. If they are not able to perform the desired behaviors immediately, gradual improvement toward target performance levels is shaped through successive approximations. Once the desired performance level is established, it is maintained by reinforcing it often enough to ensure its continuation. Any behaviors that are incompatible with the desired pattern are extinguished through nonreinforcement, or if necessary, suppressed through punishment.

Behaviorists favor experimental research methods, typically relying on a four-stage sequence of studies to test hypotheses about the reinforcement contingencies currently controlling behaviors of interest and verify the effectiveness of recommended interventions: (a) baseline documentation of the rates of problem behaviors along with attempts to determine what situations and cues are eliciting them and how they are being reinforced, (b) introduction of treatment procedures (typically followed by measurable improvement from baseline, displayed graphically on time charts), (c) removal of treatment procedures during an extinction phase (in which the problem behaviors typically revert to baseline levels), and (d) reinstitution of treatment procedures (typically followed by a return of the improvements seen earlier). The sequence is persuasive because the first two stages provide empirical evidence of significant change in behavior, and the extinction and reinstitution phases demonstrate that the observed behavior changes are due to the specific treatment procedures used (and not to special attention given to the student, changes in teacher or student expectations, etc.).

Early applications of behavioral techniques to classroom management were mostly limited to shaping the behaviors (such as staying in the seat or remaining quiet) of individual students through reinforcement. Laboratory-generated principles called for reinforcing desired behaviors with praise or material rewards and extinguishing undesired behaviors by ignoring them (it was assumed that teachers' typical responses to students' undesired behaviors were somehow reinforcing them, so teachers could extinguish the behaviors by withdrawing this reinforcement). These direct generalizations of laboratory techniques were soon supplanted by modifications better suited to classrooms (Axelrod, 1977; Brown, 1971; Homme, 1970; Krumboltz & Krumboltz, 1972; Madsen & Madsen, 1981; O'Leary & O'Leary, 1977).

First, it was recognized that unlike animals, students possess language, so it is possible to cue desired behaviors by stating expectations and giving reminders, instead of just waiting for these behaviors to appear spontaneously and then reinforcing them. "Rules, praise, and ignoring" soon became the watchwords of behaviorally based classroom management.

Second, it became obvious that laboratory methods of monitoring behavior and supplying reinforcers were not feasible for application in classrooms where teachers work with 20 or more students. It is not possible for the teacher to simultaneously monitor the behaviors of all of these students and provide immediate reinforcement whenever desired behaviors appear. To address this problem, behaviorists shifted from reinforcing discrete behaviors to reinforcing packages of behaviors (e.g., attending to lessons, completing assignments, and doing well on tests) that extended over longer time periods, with the teacher articulating the reinforcement contingencies verbally and then following up accordingly. Refinements were gradually added to address other problems (e.g., awarding earned point credits because this is less cumbersome than passing out and collecting tokens; providing opportunities to select from reinforcement menus as a way to avoid reinforcer satiation), as well as to introduce opportunities to individualize (e.g., equalizing opportunities to earn credits by awarding them according to individuals' degrees of improvement over their own prior performance levels, customizing behavior contracts to focus on individual students' behaviors most in need of improvement).

Over time, behaviorists maintained their characteristic theoretical concepts and empirical orientation, but expanded their repertoire of recommended techniques far beyond the original laboratory-based collection. One reason for this was the failure of some principles to generalize well to the classroom. For example, the principle of "extinction through ignoring" is applicable only to those student behaviors that are performed to elicit reinforcing responses from teachers. For most students, this is a low percentage, relative to the percentage of behaviors performed because they are intrinsically rewarding or are reinforced by peers. Also, certain problem behaviors are too disruptive or dangerous to be ignored, so some kind of teacher response is required. Finally, research by Kounin (1970), Brophy and Evertson (1976), and others indicated that effective managers acted quickly to nip potentially disruptive behaviors in the bud, rather than allowing them to develop and then waiting for them to be extinguished through nonreinforcement. Consequently, ignoring has faded from prominence as a frequently recommended behavioral technique.

It also became necessary to qualify the characterization of teacher praise as a form of reinforcement. Brophy (1981) reported that correlations between frequencies of teacher praise and measures of student achievement gain were weak and mixed rather than consistently positive, and cited other data indicating that teachers often do not praise in ways likely to be experienced as reinforcing by students, and that even when they do, some students do not value such praise and therefore do not feel reinforced by it. Behaviorists eventually finessed these and other difficulties with attempts to specify classes of reinforcers by using Premack's (1965) definition of a reinforcer as anything that increases the frequency of a behavior when access to it is made contingent on performance of that behavior, and by incorporating reinforcement menus into their classroom applications.

Many educators oppose behavioral approaches on philosophical grounds. In addition, among those who are potentially more accepting, a major barrier to embracing behavioral techniques has been persistent concerns that the improvements they produce in students' behavior are likely to disappear once they are no longer being reinforced systematically. Their own concerns about this problem led many behaviorists to shift from Skinner's operant conditioning (Skinner, 1953) to Bandura's social learning version of behavior modification (Bandura, 1969), supplemented by Meichenbaum's cognitive behavior modification (Meichenbaum, 1977), as their primary theoretical base. Gradually, notions of imposing external control by reinforcing conformity to rules gave way to notions of building self-regulation capacities and dispositions through techniques that combine modeling with verbalized self-instructions (McLaughlin, 1976). The teacher initially demonstrates the desired process, not only by showing the physical motions involved but also by verbalizing the thoughts and other self-talk (self-instructions, self-monitoring, self-reinforcement) that guide the activity. Students then are given opportunities to perform the activity themselves, at first with extensive teacher guidance, then primarily on their own with self-guidance (initially spoken aloud, then whispered, then covert self-instruction).

Proliferation of techniques continues. Contemporary behaviorists typically distinguish between procedures for increasing desired behavior and procedures for decreasing undesired behavior (see Chapter 3). The former techniques include token reinforcement programs, earned points credit systems, praise and approval, modeling, programmed instruction, self-specification of contingencies, self-reinforcement, establishment of clear rules and directions, and shaping through successive approximations. The latter techniques include extinction, reinforcing incompatible behaviors, self-reprimands, time out from reinforcement, relaxation (for fears and anxiety), response cost (punishment by removal of reinforcers), medication, self-instruction, and self-evaluation. Some of those interventions place heavy emphasis on self-regulation and little or none on external reinforcement, so they overlap considerably with strategy training treatments used by nonbehavioral psychologists working from theories of learning and cognition. For example, the *Think Aloud* program (Camp & Bash, 1981) features self-instructional strategies, sometimes supported by cue cards, that enable students to talk themselves through adaptive responses to selected situations, such as paying attention to lessons, writing a report, or coping with anger or frustration.

Many popular approaches to classroom management taught in packaged workshop programs feature behavioristic principles, most notably the Assertive Discipline program developed by Canter and Canter (1992). It began as a largely behavioral program that emphasized specifying clear rules for student behavior, tied to a system of rewards and punishments. Over time, however, the Canters incorporated revisions that place less emphasis on reinforcement and more on clarifying the rationales for rules and supporting student self-regulation. They have not conducted systematic research on their program, however.

ECOLOGICAL STUDIES

Researchers who adopt an ecological perspective analyze environmental settings with an eye toward the kinds of activities they support (affordances) and prohibit (constraints) (Bronfenbrenner, 1989). They view the adaptation potential of different species or different individuals within species as a function of the closeness of fit between their general characteristics and the demands of their environment. Classrooms are environmental settings (ecologies) that can be analyzed accordingly, with the added understanding that they are human inventions constructed and maintained to accomplish particular purposes. Consequently, when the notion of person-environment fit is applied to classrooms, one needs to take into account the affordances and constraints created by teachers, peers, and other human actors, not just the settings' physical characteristics.

Ecological research on classroom management grew out of studies of the characteristics of different classroom settings (e.g., whole class, small group, individual) and the unfolding of the activities that took place in them. Studies of classroom tasks and settings continued (e.g., Bossert, 1979), but some investigators shifted attention from the settings' affordances to and constraints on activities to the role of the teacher in establishing and maintaining the activities. In an early study, Kounin and Gump (1958) observed in 26 kindergarten classrooms during the first four days of school, focusing on desist incidents in which teachers directed interventions at students who were behaving inappropriately. Observers took running notes of classroom events as they unfolded, then expanded them into "specimen records" formatted for coding. Desists were coded for clarity (about how the students were misbehaving or what they should be doing instead), firmness (an "I mean it" and "right now" quality), and roughness (expression of anger or exasperation).

Kounin and Gump were interested in ripple effects on audience students who observe desists directed at peers. Audience reactions were coded as: no reaction, behavior disruption (anxiety, confusion, etc.), increased conformance, increased nonconformance, and ambivalence (mixture of conformance and nonconformance). Analyses indicated that desist clarity was associated with greater subsequent conformity among audience students. Two other findings did not hold up for students in general but did apply to students coded as deviancy linked (because they either were misbehaving themselves at the time of the desist or were watching the misbehavior of the target of the desist). For these deviancy-linked students, desist firmness was associated with subsequent conformity and desist roughness was associated with behavior disruption. However, these effects were strongest on the first day and weaker on subsequent days, and later studies at higher grade levels failed to replicate them.

Kounin pursued classroom management issues in subsequent studies of elementary classrooms (Kounin, Friesen, & Norton, 1966; Kounin, 1970; Kounin & Doyle, 1975). In the process, he made two significant changes that produced original and enduringly influential sets of findings. First, he enriched his data base by shifting from specimen records developed from observers' notes to videotapes of classroom events. The opportunity to replay the videos repeatedly made it possible to code more, and more subtle, aspects of both teacher and student behavior, during both lessons and seatwork activities. Second, he shifted from his original narrow focus on desists to include a much broader range of teacher actions. Analyses of the videotapes continued to show that measures of teachers' responses to disruptive behavior (i.e., desists) were not reliably related to the teachers' overall effectiveness as classroom managers. Instead, the secret to management success was preventing students from becoming disruptive in the first place by maintaining the momentum of classroom activities and nipping potential problems in the bud before they could escalate. Several key variables emerged from subsequent analyses:

- Withitness. Remaining "with it" (aware of what is happening in all parts of the room at all times) by continuously scanning the classroom, even when working with small groups or individuals.
- Overlapping. Doing more than one thing at a time, such as using eye contact or physical proximity to restore certain students' attention to a lesson while continuing the lesson itself without interruption.
- Signal continuity and momentum during lessons. Teaching well-prepared and briskly paced lessons that focus students' attention by providing them with a continuous academic signal which is more compelling than the noise of competing distractions, and by sustaining the momentum of this signal throughout the lesson.
- Group alerting and accountability during lessons. Using presentation and questioning techniques that keep the group alert and accountable, such as waiting and looking around before calling on someone to answer a question, avoiding predictability in choice of respondent, interspersing choral responses with individual responses, requiring students

to hold up props or signify answers visibly, or calling on listeners to comment on or correct a peer's response.
- Challenge and variety in assignments. Encouraging engagement in seatwork by providing varied assignments pitched at the optimal level of difficulty.

PROCESS-OUTCOME (TEACHER EFFECTS) STUDIES

Beginning in the 1960s and continuing through the 1980s, several different research teams explored relationships between classroom processes (particularly teacher behaviors and teacher-student interaction patterns) and subsequent outcomes (particularly adjusted achievement gain). Process measures typically were developed from codings and ratings made during or immediately following classroom observations. Several of these studies included measures adapted from Kounin's work. They generally replicated and extended Kounin's findings (Anderson, Evertson, & Brophy, 1979; Brophy & Evertson, 1976; Crawford, 1989; Crawford et al., 1978; Good & Grouws, 1977).

However, some of these studies also suggested qualifications on those findings. In a correlational study at second- and third-grade (Brophy & Evertson, 1976) and in an experimental study of first-grade reading groups (Anderson, Evertson, & Brophy, 1979), withitness, overlapping, and smoothness of lesson pacing and transitions all were associated not only with better classroom management, but with greater achievement gains. However, these studies did not support some of the accountability techniques. They suggested that in certain situations, especially in the early grades and when teaching small groups, it is more important to make sure that everyone gets a turn and discourage peers from calling out than to use unpredictability as a way to hold students accountable for sustained attention.

In a study of fourth-grade mathematics learning, Good and Grouws (1977) found that accountability was related curvilinearly to student achievement gain: Teachers who used a moderate amount were more successful than those who used too much or too little. These mixed findings on accountability should not be surprising because this technique pressures students to pay attention, which is necessary only when students are not attentive in the first place. High frequencies of accountability behaviors indicate that inattentiveness is a frequent problem and suggest that the teacher is not doing enough of the more fundamental and positive things that tend to sustain student engagement.

Findings also were mixed concerning the value of choral responses. Unless the group is small enough to allow the teacher to monitor each individual, a chorus of correct responses from the majority of students can drown out mistakes and cover up failures to respond at all. This is often a problem with students in the early grades, who seem to need individualized opportunities to respond and get feedback from the teacher (Anderson, Evertson, & Brophy, 1979).

Some of the teacher effects studies also extended Kounin's findings concerning management of students' work on assignments. Various studies indicated that effective managers (a) provide sufficient advance preparation to enable most if not all of their students to begin seatwork and other independent activities smoothly (so that they do not quickly become confused and require the teacher to repeat or elaborate earlier directions); and (b) circulate to monitor progress and provide individual help where needed, but keep these helping interactions brief and primarily private (to minimize potential embarrassment to the students being helped, avoid distracting peers who are working productively, and free themselves to get back into circulation quickly) (Evertson, Anderson, Anderson, & Brophy, 1980; Fisher et al., 1978; Helmke & Schrader, 1988).

In addition to process-outcome studies, some behavioral studies also touched on issues raised by Kounin. For example, Kounin's ripple effects research indicated that rough desists tended to cause at least some students to become confused, tense, or anxious, whereas milder desists tended to have more positive effects. O'Leary, Kaufman, Kass, and Drabman (1970) replicated these findings in a study in which they manipulated soft and loud reprimands experimentally.

GETTING THE SCHOOL YEAR OFF TO A GOOD START

Moskowitz and Hayman (1976) studied 10 "best" and 11 first-year teachers in inner-city junior high schools, by observing them periodically throughout the year, starting right at the beginning. Although their measures usually were not identical, their analyses both replicated findings reported earlier by Flanders (1970) and Kounin (1970) and anticipated findings reported subsequently by Evertson, Emmer, Anderson, and their colleagues (described in the next section). At the beginning of the year, the "best" teachers conveyed more personal acceptance to their students, praised them more, joked more, and gave more helpful suggestions (cues, reminders, work and study tips). However, they also kept close tabs on student behavior and acted quickly to nip potential problems in the bud. Throughout the year, they maintained more positive classroom climates and displayed more behaviors classified as indirect, yet also provided their students with more specific guidance and feedback. In contrast, the new teachers often let problems develop too far before intervening, were less consistent in stating and following through on expectations, and developed less positive classroom climates featuring more frequent criticism of students and other behaviors classified as direct.

Evertson, Emmer, Anderson, and their colleagues developed more detailed information about how teachers who varied in classroom management effectiveness handled the first day and the first few weeks of the school year. They eliminated the need for videotape by developing methods for describing or coding management-relevant behavior as it occurred. These included taking detailed notes about what rules and procedures the teachers introduced, how they did so, and how they followed up when it became necessary to enforce the rules or use the procedures. They also scanned the room every 15 minutes to record the percentage of students who were attentive to lessons or engaged in other teacher-approved activities. These data were analyzed for relationships between teacher management behaviors and student engagement rates.

Third-Grade Study

Their first study (Emmer, Evertson, & Anderson, 1980) was conducted in 28 third-grade classrooms. It showed that the seemingly automatic, smooth functioning of the classrooms of successful managers resulted from thorough preparation and organization at the beginning of the year. On the first day and through the first week, teachers gave special attention to matters of greatest concern to students (information about the teacher and their classmates, review of the daily schedule, procedures for lunch and recess, where to put personal materials, etc.). Procedures and routines were introduced gradually as needed so as not to overload the students with too much information at one time.

Effective managers not only described what they expected, but also modeled correct procedures, took time to answer questions, and, if necessary, arranged for students to practice the procedures and get feedback. Key procedures were formally taught to students, just as academic content is taught.

Although they focused more on instruction than on "control," effective managers were thorough in following up on their expectations. They reminded students about procedures shortly before they were to carry them out, and they scheduled additional instruction and practice when students did not carry them out properly. Consequences of appropriate and inappropriate behavior were clear in their classrooms, and sanctions were applied consistently. Inappropriate behavior was stopped quickly. Effective managers showed three major clusters of behavior.

Conveying Purposefulness. Effective managers tried to maximize use of the available time for instruction and to see that their students learned the curriculum (not just that they remained quiet). Students were held accountable for completing work on time (after being taught to pace themselves by using the clock, if necessary). Regular times were scheduled each day to review independent work. Completed papers were returned promptly, with feedback.

Teaching Students Appropriate Conduct. Effective managers were clear about what they expected and what they would not tolerate. They focused on what students should be doing and taught them how to do it when necessary. This included not only conduct and housekeeping guidelines, but also learning-related behaviors, such as how to read and follow directions for assignments.

Maintaining Students' Attention.. Effective managers continuously monitored students for signs of confusion or inattention and were sensitive to their concerns. Seating was arranged so students could easily face the point in the room where they most often needed to focus attention. Variations in voice, movement, or pacing were used to refocus attention during lessons. Activities had clear beginnings and endings, with efficient transitions in between. Active attention was required when important information was given.

Effective managers followed up this intensive activity in the early weeks by consistently maintaining their expectations. They no longer needed to devote much time to procedural instruction and practice, but they continued to give reminders and occasional remedial instruction, and they remained consistent in enforcing their rules.

Junior High Study

A similar study of junior high school teachers (Evertson & Emmer, 1982a) revealed similar findings, as well as a few differences. Junior high teachers did not need to spend as much time teaching their students how to follow rules and procedures, but they did have to communicate expectations concerning student responsibility for engaging in and completing work assignments. Students need to know exactly what their assignments are and when they are due. This information should be posted, along with any needed elaboration about the expected form or quality of the final product. Evertson and Emmer (1982b) listed the following as characteristics of effective managers at the junior high school level.

Instructing Students in Rules and Procedures. All teachers had rules and procedures, but the effective managers described their rules more completely and installed their procedures more systematically. They were notably more explicit about desirable behavior (the dos, not just the don'ts).

Monitoring Student Compliance with Rules. The better managers monitored compliance more consistently, intervened to correct inappropriate behavior more consistently, and were more likely to mention the rules or describe desirable behavior when giving feedback at these times.

Communicating Information. The better managers were clearer in presenting information, giving directions, and stating objectives. They broke down complex tasks into step-by-step procedures.

Organizing Instruction. Effective managers wasted little time getting organized or accomplishing transitions between activities, and they maximized student attention and task engagement during activities by maintaining signal continuity and momentum in lessons, overlapping their own activities, and using the other techniques identified by Kounin (1970).

Subsequent Studies

Evertson, Emmer, and their colleagues later extended their work to include training teachers in effective classroom management techniques. This work showed that teachers could learn these techniques and thereby decrease classroom disruptions and increase student engagement in academic activities, without undermining classroom climate (Evertson, 1985; Evertson, Emmer, Sanford, & Clements, 1983). Teacher training was accomplished using manuals that summarized research findings about effective classroom management and provided instructions about how to implement recommended procedures. Further work eventually resulted in a comprehensive teacher training program that has proved to be effective in improving teachers' managerial skills and students' task engagement and academic achievement (Evertson & Harris, 1999).

The general findings of Kounin, Evertson, Emmer, and their colleagues have been supported by subsequent work done in both elementary (Freiberg, 1999; Freiberg, Stein, & Huang, 1995) and secondary schools (Gottfredson, Gottfredson, & Hybl, 1993). So have the findings specific to getting the school year off to a good start. The consensus is that although teachers should be friendly and personable rather than austere, they also should be businesslike in visibly taking charge and establishing a positive classroom atmosphere and the basic lesson and activity routines that create the desired learning environment (Brooks, 1985; Doyle, 1986; Moskowitz & Hayman, 1976).

Doyle (1984) conducted research informed by both the ecological point of view and the methods and findings of Evertson, Emmer, and their colleagues. He emphasized that successful classroom managers not only gained student cooperation but accomplished their instructional agendas by successfully leading students through planned lessons and activities. Based on narrative descriptions of seven junior high school English classes, Doyle concluded that the more successful managers: (a) constructed lessons that fit the externally paced schedule (50-minute classes), (b) used activities that had clear programs of action for students, (c) explicitly marked the boundaries of activities and the transitions between them, and orchestrated the transitions actively, (d) demonstrated situational awareness by attending to details and commenting on events as they occurred, (e) protected activities until they became established routines by actively ushering them along, hovering over the students, focusing public attention on work, and ignoring minor misbehavior so as to avoid disrupting the rhythm and flow of events, and (f) pushing the students through the curriculum even when misbehavior was a problem.

The best managers continued the ushering and hovering involved in establishing the work system in the class as a whole throughout the first month of the school year, before shifting attention to working with individual students during seatwork times. Less successful managers made this shift prematurely. Also, the better managers got the most out of the available time by letting activities run over the end of the class, so that anything left undone would be done as homework or finished at the next class. In contrast, less successful managers often overestimated how long an activity would take, so that part of their class time was used unproductively. In addition to making these and other contributions based on his own work, Doyle (1986) wrote a handbook chapter on classroom management that emphasized the role of activities and other ecological aspects of the topic as well as the teacher thinking and decision making involved in managing classrooms successfully.

Principles developed from the research of Kounin, and of Evertson and Emmer, can be combined to create a more comprehensive approach to managing classrooms. Most of these principles are complementary, and even seeming contradictions can be resolved with careful interpretation. For example, Kounin showed that sheer frequencies of teachers' desist statements do not predict their effectiveness as managers, but Evertson and Emmer showed that it is important for teachers to nip potential disruptions in the bud, before they escalate. The latter finding implies that desist statements do play a role in effective management after all. However, the more basic principles emerging from Evertson and Emmer's work stress the importance of preparing students to follow desired protocols and providing cues to situational expectations (thus reducing the need for desist statements), as well as following up those desist statements that are necessary with rule reminders, additional socialization, follow-through on stated consequences, or other actions designed to prevent recurrence of the problem behavior in the future.

OTHER MANAGEMENT STUDIES

Other investigators also elaborated on earlier findings by focusing in more detail on specific aspects of successful management. For example, Arlin (1979) noted that poorly orchestrated transitions between activities can waste a great deal of time in classrooms. He reported that transitions are accomplished most efficiently when students are able to quickly follow a brief signal or a few directions from the teacher because they have been prepared to know where they are supposed to go, what they are supposed to do when they get there, and what equipment they will need. Smith (1985) reported similar findings, noting that effective transitions involve preparing students in advance, starting and ending with clear verbal statements supported by unambiguous nonverbal signals, issuing instructions in logical order and in small discrete units, waiting for the instructions to be carried out before initiating the new activity, and remaining task oriented without becoming deflected by minor extraneous matters.

Doyle's (1986) review included a section on physical design of settings. However, most of the cited studies examined contrasting student attitudes or behavior when students were seated in groups versus rows, in "action zones" versus more remote locations in the classroom, or in open classrooms versus more traditional ones. Treatises on classroom management have always emphasized importance of furnishing and equipping the classroom so as to get the most efficient use of the available space given the intended academic activities. Typically, they recommend clearly separating areas intended to serve different purposes and designing traffic patterns to promote smooth flow. Ecological theorists have even coined the term "synomorphy" to refer to the compatibility between the setting's design and the activities planned to take place in the setting (e.g., rows accommodate frontal teaching nicely but a circular seating pattern is better for a discussion). However, these aspects of classroom management have received very little research attention (Nash, 1981; Pellegrini & Blatchford, 2000; Weinstein, 1979). An exception is the study by Weinstein (1977), in which observations conducted both before and after planned changes in the physical arrangements of an open classroom confirmed that these alterations produced most of the intended changes in the frequency and nature of students' use of the learning centers that had been established.

STUDENT SOCIALIZATION AND DISCIPLINARY INTERVENTIONS

Interpersonal relationship aspects of classroom management have always been recognized as important (as in Bagley's advice in his 1907 text about being authoritative but fair and good-natured, and using punishment only as a last resort). As the 20th century developed, this advice became better rationalized and more elaborated, although most of it was rooted not in research but in theories developed by psychiatrists, clinical psychologists, and other treatment professionals working outside of school settings.

An early set of guidelines adapted for classroom use was developed by Redl and his associates, based on their work in a special school for disturbed and delinquent boys (Redl, 1966; Redl & Wattenberg, 1959; Redl & Wineman, 1957). Four types of influence techniques were identified for use with students prone to acting out their frustrations or personal problems: supporting self-control (giving signals to cue behavior appropriate in the situation, proximity control, humor, interest boosting, and planned ignoring), task assistance ("hurdle help" to assist the student in getting past temporary frustration, restructuring or changing the activity, using situational routines consistently to minimize confusion, temporary removal from a frustrating situation, physical restraint if necessary, and removing seductive objects), reality and value appraisal (helping students to recognize the effects of problem behaviors on themselves and others and to develop positive values and goals), and, if necessary, invoking the pleasure-pain principle (rewarding desired behavior or punishing problem behavior).

Morse (1976) drew on the ideas of Redl and his associates in developing life-space interviewing, a technique designed to foster adjustment and obtain a degree of behavioral compliance from students by providing them with life-space relief. In response to incidents of defiance or serious misbehavior, the teacher would talk to the students privately, elicit their perceptions of the incident and the events that led up to it, convey acceptance of their feelings without necessarily accepting their actions, and then shift to a negotiation mode by analyzing places where relief might be provided or changes might be made. In the process, the teacher would attempt to provide the following kinds of help, as needed: help students see and accept reality and abandon defensive distortions; show them that inappropriate behavior is self-defeating; clarify values; suggest means to help them cope more effectively; help them think for themselves and avoid being led into trouble by peers; help them express anger by expressing sympathy and understanding; help them deal with emotions such as panic, rage, or guilt following emotional explosions; maintain open communication; provide friendly reminders; or clarify thinking and facilitate decision making (Wood & Long, 1991).

Working from a theoretical base in Adlerian psychology, Dreikurs advised teachers to interpret the goals of students' problem behavior and respond accordingly (Dreikurs, 1968; Dreikurs, Grunwald, & Pepper, 1982). He suggested that students who were compensating for feelings of inferiority or lacking a secure sense of belonging in the classroom or peer group might initiate symptomatic behavior designed to get attention, gain power, exact revenge, or gain sympathy or special treatment through display of inferiority. Dreikurs advised teachers to determine which of these goals students' provocative behaviors were addressing and then convey their conclusions to the students in private conversations. He believed that the students would become willing to abandon self-defeating goals and make commitments to more productive goals once they developed insight into their behavior and its meanings.

Dreikurs also emphasized avoiding artificial punishment of students. Instead, teachers should allow them to experience the natural consequences of inappropriate behavior, or, if that is impractical, impose consequences that are logically related to the misbehavior. However, he was not always clear about the distinction between these concepts, and many of his examples of logical consequences (e.g., requiring dawdling students who have not yet finished an assignment to forego recess to work on it) would be considered punishments from a behavioral point of view (Bommarito, 1977). As with the other approaches reviewed in this section, there has been practically no research on the effectiveness of the Dreikurs approach and related Adlerian methods, but the few investigators who did train teachers in these principles reported improvements in student behavior (Hartwell, 1975; Hoffman, 1975).

Other approaches were rooted in Rogerian therapy, most notably the Teacher Effectiveness Training (TET) program developed by Gordon (1974). TET trains teachers to clarify problem ownership and defuse conflicts by arranging no-lose agreements with students. Problems are owned by students when their needs are being frustrated, owned by teachers when their needs are being frustrated, and owned by both parties when the needs of both are being frustrated. For student-owned problems (anxiety, inhibition, poor self-concept), Gordon recommended door openers (invitations for students to talk about the problem), passive listening (responding in ways that make students see that they are being heard and understood), and especially, active listening (giving feedback to the underlying meanings of the students' messages—what Rogerian counselors call reflecting feelings). For teacher-owned problems, Gordon recommended avoiding "you" messages (typically criticisms of the student) and instead focusing on "I" messages that first indicate the specific behavior that leads to the problem ("When I get interrupted . . . "), then specify the effect on the teacher (" . . . I have to start over and repeat things unnecessarily . . . ") and then specify the feelings generated within the teacher (" . . . and I become frustrated."). For shared problems, Gordon recommended negotiating "no lose" agreements by analyzing the problem with the student, finding a tentative solution that both parties can live with, and revisiting the situation later to see if the solution is working (and if not, find another).

Gordon's ideas about problem ownership proved useful in interpreting the findings from a large study of elementary teachers' reports of how they perceive and cope with problem students (Brophy, 1996; Brophy & McCaslin, 1992; Brophy & Rohrkemper, 1981). It was found that when hypothetical students were depicted as presenting student-owned problems, the teachers typically reported that they would respond with sympathy, academic assistance, counseling, support, and other treatment oriented toward long-term solutions. In contrast, when the hypothetical students were depicted as presenting teacher-owned problems, the teachers typically reported that they would respond with anger, threats, and punishment. In other research, two studies of the TET program as a whole showed improvements in students' attitudes (Chanow-Gruen & Doyle, 1983; Nummela & Avila, 1980), and two studies involving training teachers to use "I" messages with disruptive students reported positive changes in the students' behavior (Carducci, 1976; Peterson et al., 1979).

Psychiatrist William Glasser has written several influential books and articles on classroom and school management. His early contributions drew heavily on a treatment approach called reality therapy, but in subsequent publications he has broadened his purview to include other theoretical bases. He is best known among educators for two suggestions: holding regular class meetings to establish and revise classroom rules and discuss how to handle emergent problems, and his 10-step method for dealing with serious behavior and motivation problems. The class meeting idea never caught on with very many teachers, but the 10-step approach to behavior problems became very popular (Glasser, 1977). Meant for use with students who persistently violate rules that are reasonable and are administered fairly by teachers who maintain a positive, problem-solving stance, the 10 steps include:

1. List your typical reactions to the student's disruptive behavior.
2. Analyze the list to see what techniques do or do not work and resolve not to repeat the latter.
3. Improve your relationship with the student by providing extra encouragement, asking the student to perform special errands, showing concern, or implying that things will improve.

4. Focus attention on the disruptive behavior by requiring the student to describe what he or she has been doing. Continue until the student describes the behavior accurately and then request that it be stopped.
5. If the disruptive behavior continues, call a short conference and again have the student describe the behavior. Then have the student state whether the behavior is against the rules or recognized expectations and ask what he or she should be doing instead.
6. If necessary, repeat step 5, but this time add that the student will have to formulate a plan to solve the problem. The plan must be more than a simple agreement to stop misbehaving. It must include commitment to positive actions designed to eliminate the problem.
7. If the problem still persists, isolate the student from the class until he or she has devised a plan for ensuring that the rules will be followed in the future, gotten the plan approved, and made a commitment to follow it.
8. If this does not work, the next step is in-school suspension. Now the student must deal with the principal or someone other than the teacher, but this person will repeat earlier steps in the sequence and press the student to devise a plan that is acceptable. The student will either have to follow the reasonable rules in effect in the classroom or continue to be isolated outside of class.
9. If students remain out of control or do not comply with in-school suspension rules, their parents are called to take them home for the day, and they resume in-school suspension the next day.
10. Students who do not respond to the previous steps are removed from school and referred to another agency.

Research on classroom applications of reality therapy have produced mixed but mostly positive results on student outcome measures (Browning, 1978; Emmer & Aussiker, 1990; Hyman & Lally, 1982; Marandola & Imber, 1979; Matthews, 1973; Poppen, Thompson, Cates, & Gang, 1976; Shearn & Randolph, 1978).

MANAGEMENT IN TODAY'S CLASSROOMS

The classroom management research during the 1960s and 1970s produced a rich body of replicated and mostly complementary findings, so that by the 1980s, reviewers were noting an emerging consensus (Brophy, 1983, 1988; Doyle, 1986; Weber, Crawford, Roff, & Robinson, 1983). These and other reviewers typically acknowledged that there was good support for behavioral techniques (but questioned their appropriateness or practicality for classroom applications). They also reported good support for the techniques emphasized by Kounin and by Evertson and Emmer. Finally, except for studies of some of Glasser's ideas, there was little research evidence available to inform judgments about the effectiveness of approaches recommended by Redl, Morse, Dreikurs, Gordon, or others who based their recommendations to teachers on principles developed in clinical psychology or psychiatry. These same general conclusions still apply 20 years later: The findings based on classroom research have proven robust but few of the recommendations based on clinical principles have been researched systematically (Emmer & Stough, 2001). Many contemporary management programs still incorporate principles drawn from those clinical sources, however, and similar principles are featured in the learning community and conflict resolution strands of contemporary school improvement programs that emphasize effective management principles (Comer, Ben-Avie, Haynes, & Joyner, 1999; Freiberg, 1999).

ADAPTING AND ELABORATING BASIC PRINCIPLES

Even well-established consensus principles often need to be adapted or elaborated to fit particular classroom situations. For example, teachers usually will need to focus on managing the collective when teaching a large class, but can provide more attention to individual students when teaching a small class or working with a small group. All teachers will need to match their management approaches to their instructional systems and to the needs of students at their grade levels.

Matching Management Systems to Instructional Systems

The consensus on basic principles for good classroom management was developed from research in classrooms that emphasized transmission approaches to teaching. Does it also apply to classrooms emphasizing learning community approaches informed by social constructivist and sociocultural views of learning? It does, if it is interpreted properly. McCaslin and Good (1992) have emphasized that management practices must be aligned to support the teacher's intended instructional goals and activities. To ensure this, a teacher can begin by identifying what students must do to engage optimally in the intended learning formats, then work backwards from these descriptions of desired student roles to determine what forms of managerial instruction or assistance may be needed. Applying such analysis to learning community settings identifies a broader set of desired student roles than is required in more traditional transmission settings (Brophy, 1999).

Many roles are the same: be in class/seat on time, store supplies and personal belongings in their designated places, handle equipment carefully, have desk or table cleared and be ready to learn when lessons begin, pay attention during lessons, participate by volunteering to answer questions or make contributions, work carefully on assignments, try to work out problems on your own if you get stuck but ask for help if you need it, turn in assignments completed and on time, confine conversations to appropriate times and forms, and treat others with politeness and respect. However, learning community classrooms also require students to learn collaboratively in whole-class and small-group settings. This embodies additional expectations, such as listening carefully not only to the teacher but also to peers and relating what they say to prior knowledge and experience, asking for clarification if you are not sure what others mean, putting forth your own ideas and explaining your reasoning by citing relevant evidence and arguments, challenging and responding to challenges by focusing on issues and trying to reach agreement rather than engaging in one-upmanship, and seeing that everyone's ideas are included and that everyone accomplishes the goal of the activity when working in pairs or small groups.

Teachers seeking to establish learning communities in their classrooms will still need the familiar management strategies of articulating clear expectations, modeling or providing instruction in desired procedures, cueing students when these procedures are needed, and applying sufficient pressure to compel changes in behavior when students have failed to respond to more positive methods. However, the procedures taught to students will need to include the full set that applies in learning communities, not just the subset that applies in transmission classrooms.

Matching Management Systems to Grade Level

Most management research has been done in elementary classrooms, and what has been done at the secondary level has been done in the junior high rather than senior high grades. Ryans and Wandt (1952) and Evertson and Emmer (1982a, b) have been the only investigators to draw elementary versus secondary comparisons. Their findings suggest that the same basic principles apply across grade levels, but that some are more relevant in the lower grades (those dealing with teaching students to carry out desired routines), and others more relevant in the higher grades (those dealing with providing engaging curricula and activities and with procedures relating to assignment due dates and grading).

Brophy and Evertson (1978) noted that the particulars of teachers' management responsibilities evolve as students progress through the grade levels. They identified four patterns. In the primary grades, students are new to the school situation and require orientation to the rules, procedures, and routines of classroom life. Consequently, primary teachers spend considerable time on management's instructional aspects (teaching students what to do). Teacher time devoted to classroom management tends to diminish in the middle grades, because students now know most of the procedures and routines and still tend to be identified and cooperative with adults. Between the sixth and ninth grades, however, students enter and progress through adolescence, when they identify more with peers and distance themselves from adult authority. Management concerns become prominent again, although this time with relatively more emphasis on their disciplinary aspects (students usually know what they are supposed to do but often need to be pressured to do it). Finally, in the upper secondary grades, most students have passed through the more rebellious stages of adolescence and begun to show renewed and more sophisticated levels of interest in subject matter. In these grades, teachers' energies are directed primarily toward instruction in the curriculum, although it remains important for them to articulate and follow through on expectations and accountability systems. Along with these developments, parallel changes in the organization of schools (toward increasing departmentalization, school size, and bureaucracy) dictate a gradual shift in primary responsibility for handling major discipline problems from the classroom/teacher level to the school/administrator level.

LOOKING BACK AND AHEAD

Although the fundamental importance of classroom management is universally recognized, it has not received proportional attention as a topic of empirical research. One reason for this is its orphan status: It has never become established as a curriculum strand within either the subject-matter courses or the typical foundations courses, let alone within the disciplines that inform them. It is a broad, applied topic that cuts across these disciplines and cannot be addressed adequately within them. In effect, it needs to become its own discipline, and this volume is a major step toward that end. Also, management events take place throughout the school day and subsume the full range of teaching situations and teacher-student interactions. This requires observer presence throughout the day in each classroom studied, making the research labor intensive and thus expensive. Furthermore, the most important time in which to conduct such research is at the beginning of the school year, when many schools or individual teachers do not want researchers visiting their classrooms.

Despite its limited quantity, classroom management research has generally been of very good quality. Furthermore, different investigators working in different places using different methods have produced complementary findings supporting a set of principles that appear to have considerable validity and generality. In the pre-empirical era, much management advice was moralistic or focused on inculcating good behavior habits. It often embodied a survival or disciplinary orientation featuring teacher domination and student obedience. However, the work by Kounin, Evertson and Emmer, and others shifted the student focus from good conduct to engagement in learning activities, and shifted the teacher focus from dealing with disruptions to establishing effective learning structures and routines. Currently, these principles are being reinterpreted to fit concepts and language associated with sociocultural and social constructivist thinking about teaching and learning, especially the concept of learning community.

Looking across the 20th century, initiation and development of empirical research on classroom management can be credited with informing several other important shifts: from generic teacher traits to classroom-specific management models and principles; from interactions with individual students to management of the class as a group to instilling learning community principles in the school as a whole; from reactive discipline to proactive installation of desired procedures and routines, followed by situational cueing; from isolated gimmicks toward consistent socialization; from managing behavior (conduct) to managing engagement in activities (learning); and from unilateral teacher control to development of students' capacities for exercising responsibility and self-regulation. All in all, the work on classroom management can be counted among the major success stories of educational research in the 20th century.

Much work remains to be done, however. Some areas in obvious need of attention have already been noted: management in the upper secondary grades; embedding models of classroom management within models for managing the school as a whole; adapting or elaborating management principles emerging from research in primarily transmission-oriented classrooms to fit primarily constructivist-oriented classrooms; and establishing learning community norms and practices early in the school year. Research is also needed on the effects of management-relevant legal requirements and district policies that have emerged in recent years (e.g., zero tolerance policies).

Perhaps the largest and most pressing set of questions calling for research attention lies at the interface between general and special education. Inclusion laws and policies broadened the range of students attending regular classes, adding many that require individual attention, adaptations of procedures to accommodate students with certain handicaps, and collaboration with various special education teachers and aides. Students receiving special services often leave or return during ongoing classroom activities. This requires teachers to develop procedures to minimize the disruptive effects of these transitions, briefly orient returning students to the ongoing lesson without losing the lesson's momentum in the class as a whole, and later provide any needed follow-up concerning whatever the returning student has missed (especially, directions for assignments). These and other challenges involved in accommodating special education students within regular classrooms are foremost among the management-related concerns expressed by today's teachers.

Yet, unless a significant funding source targets this area, the needed research may be slow in coming. These issues lie between the areas of interest and expertise of researchers in special education (who tend to focus on activities occurring in special education settings) and researchers in general education (who may not feel qualified to assess the effectiveness of teachers' accommodations for students with handicaps). The research approach most likely to pay off here probably will be the same one that has yielded the richest sets of findings from research in general education classrooms: identifying teachers who handle these challenges most successfully and then observing and interviewing them to identify the policies and principles that appear responsible for their success.

CONCLUSION

As the 20th century developed, research converged on the conclusion that much of successful management is prescriptive or preventive scaffolding that prepares students in advance for commonly experienced classroom situations. Certain basic management principles appear to apply across all potential instructional approaches. First, management that emphasizes clarifying what students are expected to do and helping them learn to do it is likely to be more effective than management that focuses on misbehavior and places more emphasis on after-the-fact discipline than before-the-fact prevention. Second, management systems need to support instructional systems. A management system that orients students toward passivity and compliance with rigid rules undercuts the potential effects of an instructional system designed to emphasize active learning, higher order thinking, and the social construction of knowledge. Third, managerial planning should begin by identifying the student outcomes that constitute the goals of instruction, then consider what these outcomes imply about desired learning activities, next consider what these learning activities imply about desired student roles (i.e., student cognitions and behaviors that support optimal engagement in the learning activities), and finally consider what the teacher will need to do to prepare students to optimally fulfill these roles.

ACKNOWLEDGMENTS

The author thanks Virginia Richardson and Carol Weinstein for their very helpful comments on an earlier draft of this chapter.

REFERENCES

Anderson, H. (1943). Domination and socially integrative behavior. In R. Barker, J. Kounin, & H. Wright (Eds.), *Child behavior and development* (pp. 459–483). New York: McGraw-Hill.

Anderson, H., Brewer, J., & Reed, M. (1946). Studies of teachers' classroom personalities. 3: Follow-up studies of the effects of dominative and integrative contacts on children's behavior. *Applied Psychology Monographs, 11.*

Anderson, L., Evertson, C., & Brophy, J. (1979). An experimental study of effective teaching in first-grade reading groups. *Elementary School Journal, 79,* 193–223.

Arlin, M. (1979). Teacher transitions can disrupt time flow in classrooms. *American Educational Research Journal, 16,* 42–56.

Axelrod, S. (1977). *Behavior modification for the classroom teacher.* New York: McGraw-Hill.

Bagley, W. (1907). *Classroom management.* New York: Macmillan.

Bandura, A. (1969). *Principles of behavior modification.* New York: Holt, Rinehart & Winston.

Baumrind, D. (1971). Current patterns of parental authority. *Developmental Psychology Monograph, 4*(1), Part 2.

Bommarito, J. (1977). *Preventive and clinical management of troubled children: Contributions from field, dynamic, and psychoeducational theorists (a learning theory appraisal).* Washington, DC: University Press of America.

Bossert, S. (1979). *Tasks and social relationships in classrooms: A study of instructional organization and its consequences.* New York: Cambridge University Press.

Breed, F. (1933). *Classroom organization and management.* Yonkers-on-Hudson, NY: World Book Company.

Bronfenbrenner, U. (1989). Ecological systems theory. In R. Vasta (Ed.), *Annals of child development* (Vol. 6, pp. 187–250). Greenwich, CT: JAI.

Brooks, D. (1985). The teacher's communicative competence: The first day of school. *Theory Into Practice, 24,* 63–70.

Brophy, J. (1981). Teacher praise: A functional analysis. *Review of Educational Research, 51,* 5–32.

Brophy, J. (1983). Classroom organization and management. *Elementary School Journal, 83,* 265–285.

Brophy, J. (1988). Educating teachers about managing classrooms and students. *Teaching and Teacher Education, 4,* 1–18.

Brophy, J. (1996). *Teaching problem students.* New York: Guilford.

Brophy, J. (1999). Perspectives of classroom management: Yesterday, today, and tomorrow. In H. J. Freiberg (Ed.), *Beyond behaviorism: Changing the classroom management paradigm* (pp. 43–56). Boston: Allyn & Bacon.

Brophy, J., & Evertson, C. (1976). *Learning from teaching: A developmental perspective.* Boston: Allyn & Bacon.

Brophy, J., & Evertson, C. (1978). Context variables in teaching. *Educational Psychologist, 12,* 310–316.

Brophy, J., & McCaslin, M. (1992). Teachers' reports of how they perceive and cope with problem students. *Elementary School Journal, 93,* 3–68.

Brophy, J., & Rohrkemper, M. (1981). The influence of problem ownership on teachers' perceptions of and strategies for coping with problem students. *Journal of Educational Psychology, 73,* 295–311.

Brown, D. (1971). *Changing student behavior: A new approach to discipline*. Dubuque, IA: William C. Brown.
Brown, E. (1952). *Managing the classroom: The teacher's part in school administration*. New York: Ronald Press.
Browning, B. (1978). *Effects of reality therapy on teacher attitudes, student attitudes, student achievement, and student behavior*. Unpublished doctoral dissertation, North Texas State University.
Camp, B., & Bash, M. (1981). *Think aloud: Increasing cognitive skills—a problem-solving program for children*. Champaign, IL: Research Press.
Canter, L., & Canter, M. (1992). *Assertive discipline: Positive behavior management for today's classroom* (2nd ed.). Santa Monica, CA: Lee Canter & Associates.
Carducci, R. (1976). A comparison of I-messages with commands in the control of disruptive classroom behavior. *Dissertation Abstracts International, 36(*11B), 573.
Chanow-Gruen, K., & Doyle, R. (1983). The counselors' consultative role with teachers, using the TET model. *Journal of Humanistic Education and Development, 22*, 16–24.
Charters, W. (1927). *The teaching of ideals*. New York: Macmillan.
Charters, W., & Waples, D. (1929). *The Commonwealth Teacher Training Study*. Chicago: University of Chicago Press.
Comer, J., Ben-Avie, M., Haynes, N., & Joyner, E. (1999). *Child by child: The Comer process for change in education*. New York: Teachers College Press.
Crawford, J. (1989). Teaching effectiveness in Chapter 1 classrooms. *Elementary School Journal, 90*, 33–46.
Crawford, J., Gage, N., Corno, L., Stayrook, N., Mitman, A., Schunk, D., Stallings, J., Baskin, E., Harvey, P., Austin, D., Cronin, D., & Newman, R. (1978). *An experiment on teacher effectiveness and parent-assisted instruction in the third grade* (3 vols.). Stanford, CA: Stanford University, Center for Educational Research at Stanford.
Doyle, W. (1984). How order is achieved in classrooms: An interim report. *Journal of Curriculum Studies, 16*, 259–277.
Doyle, W. (1986). Classroom organization and management. In M.C. Wittrock (Ed.), *Handbook of research on teaching* (3nd ed., pp. 392–431). New York: Macmillan.
Dreikurs, R. (1968). *Psychology in the classroom* (2nd ed). New York: Harper & Row.
Dreikurs, R., Grunwald, B., & Pepper, F. (1982). *Maintaining sanity in the classroom: Classroom management techniques* (2nd ed). New York: Harper & Row.
Dunkin, M., & Biddle, B. (1974). *The study of teaching*. New York: Holt, Rinehart & Winston.
Emmer, E., & Aussiker, A. (1990). School and classroom discipline programs: How well to they work? In O. Moles (Ed.), *Student discipline strategies: Research and practice* (pp. 129–166). Albany: SUNY Press.
Emmer, E., Evertson, C., & Anderson, L. (1980). Effective classroom management at the beginning of the school year. *Elementary School Journal, 80*, 219–231.
Emmer, E., & Stough, L. (2001). Classroom management: A critical part of educational psychology, with implications for teacher education. *Educational Psychologist, 36*, 103–112.
Estes, W. (1944). An experimental study of punishment. *Psychological Monographs, 57*, (263).
Evertson, C. (1985). Training teachers in classroom management: An experimental study in secondary school classrooms. *Journal of Educational Research, 79*, 51–58.
Evertson, C., Anderson, C., Anderson, L., & Brophy, J. (1980). Relationship between classroom behavior and student outcomes in junior high math and English classes. *American Educational Research Journal, 17*, 43–60.
Evertson, C., & Emmer, E. (1982a). Effective management at the beginning of the school year in junior high classes. *Journal of Educational Psychology, 74*, 485–498.
Evertson, C., & Emmer, E. (1982b). Preventive classroom management. In D. Duke (Ed.), *Helping teachers manage classrooms* (pp. 2–31). Alexandria, VA: Association for Supervision and Curriculum Development.
Evertson, C., Emmer, E., Sanford, J., & Clements, B. (1983). Improving classroom management: An experiment in elementary classrooms. *Elementary School Journal, 84*, 173–188.
Evertson, C., & Harris, A. (1999). Support for managing learning-centered classrooms: The Classroom Organization and Management Program. In H. J. Freiberg (Ed), *Beyond behaviorism: Changing the classroom management paradigm* (pp. 59–74). Boston: Allyn & Bacon.
Fisher, C., Berliner, D., Filby, N., Marliave, R., Cahen, L., & Dishaw, M. (1978). Teaching behaviors, academic learning time, and student achievement: An overview. In C. Denham & A. Lieberman (Eds.), *Time to learn* (pp. 7–32). Washington, DC: U.S. Government Printing Office.
Flanders, N. (1970). *Analyzing teacher behavior*. Reading, MA: Addison-Wesley.
Freiberg, H.J. (1999). Consistency management and cooperative discipline: From tourists to citizens in the classrooms. In H. J. Freiberg (Ed.), *Beyond behaviorism: Changing the classroom management paradigm* (pp. 75–97). Boston: Allyn & Bacon.
Freiberg, H.J., Stein, T., & Huang, S. (1995). Effects of a classroom management intervention on student achievement in inner-city elementary schools. *Educational Research and Evaluation: An International Journal on Theory and Practice, 1*, 36–66.
Fuller, F. (1969). Concerns of teachers: A developmental conceptualization. *American Educational Research Journal, 6*, 207–226.

Glasser, W. (1977). Ten steps to good discipline. *Today's Education, 66*, 61–63.

Good, T., & Grouws, D. (1977). Teaching effects: A process-product study in fourth-grade mathematics classrooms. *Journal of Teacher Education, 28*, 49–54.

Gordon, T. (1974). *T.E.T. Teacher Effectiveness Training*. New York: Wyden.

Gottfredson, D., Gottfredson, G., & Hybl, L. (1993). Managing adolescent behavior: A multiyear multischool study. *American Educational Research Journal, 30*, 179–215.

Haggerty, M. (1925). The incidence of undesirable behavior in public-school children. *Journal of Educational Research, 12*, 102–122.

Hartwell, M. (1975). An evaluation of an in-service program concerning the disciplinary approach of Dr. Rudolf Dreikurs. *Dissertation Abstracts International, 36*(2A), 704–705.

Helmke, A., & Schrader, F. (1988). Successful student practice during seatwork: Efficient management and active supervision not enough. *Journal of Educational Research, 82*, 70–75.

Hoffman, F. (1975). Use of the Adlerian model in secondary school counseling and consulting. *Individual Psychologist, 12*(2), 27–32.

Homme, L. (1970). *How to use contingency contracting in the classroom*. Champaign, IL: Research Press.

Hyman, I., & Lally, D. (1982). A study of staff development programs for improving school discipline. *Urban Review, 14*, 181–196.

Johnson, M., & Brooks, H. (1979). Conceptualizing classroom management. In D. Duke (Ed.), *Classroom management (The 78th Yearbook of the National Society for the Study of Education, Part 2*, pp. 1–41). Chicago: University of Chicago Press.

Kennedy, W., & Willicutt, H. (1964). Praise and blame as incentives. *Psychological Bulletin, 62*, 323–332.

Kounin, J. (1970). *Discipline and group management in classrooms*. New York: Holt, Rinehart & Winston.

Kounin, J., & Doyle, P. (1975). Degree of continuity of a lesson's signal system and the task involvement of children. *Journal of Educational Psychology, 67*, 159–164.

Kounin, J., Friesen, W., & Norton, A. (1966). Managing emotionally disturbed children in regular classrooms. *Journal of Educational Psychology, 57*, 1–13.

Kounin, J., & Gump, P. (1958). The ripple effect in discipline. *Elementary School Journal, 35*, 158–162.

Kounin, J., & Gump, P. (1961). The comparative influence of punitive and non-punitive teachers upon children's concepts of school misconduct. *Journal of Educational Psychology, 52*, 44–49.

Krumboltz, J., & Krumboltz, H. (1972). *Changing children's behavior*. Englewood Cliffs, NJ: Prentice-Hall.

Lewin, K., Lippitt, R., & White, R. (1939). Patterns of aggressive behavior in experimentally created "social climates." *Journal of Social Psychology, 10*, 271–299.

Madsen, C.H., Jr., & Madsen, C.K. (1981). *Teaching-discipline: A positive approach for educational development*. Boston: Allyn & Bacon.

Marandola, P., & Imber, S. (1979). Glasser's classroom meeting: A humanistic approach to behavior change with pre-adolescent inner-city learning disabled children. *Journal of Learning Disabilities, 12*, 383–387.

Matthews, D. (1973). The effects of reality therapy on reported self-concept, social adjustment, reading achievement, and discipline of fourth and fifth graders in two elementary schools. *Dissertation Abstracts International, 33*(9A), 4842–4843.

McCaslin, M., & Good, T. (1992). Compliant cognition: The misalliance of management and instructional goals in current school reform. *Educational Researcher, 21*, 4–17.

McDonald, F. (1965). *Educational psychology* (2nd ed). Belmont, CA: Wadsworth.

McLaughlin, T. (1976). Self-control in the classroom. *Review of Educational Research, 46*, 631–663.

Meichenbaum, D. (1977). *Cognitive-behavior modification*. New York: Plenum.

Morse, W. (1976). Worksheet on life space interviewing with teachers. In N. Long, W. Morse, & R. Newman (Eds.), *Conflict in the classroom: The education of children with problems* (3nd ed, pp. 328–336). Belmont, CA: Wadsworth.

Moskowitz, G., & Hayman, J. (1976). Success strategies of inner-city teachers: A year-long study. *Journal of Educational Research, 69*, 283–289.

Nash, B. (1981). The effects of classroom spatial organization on four- and five-year-old children's learning. *British Journal of Educational Psychology, 51*, 144–155.

Nummela, R., & Avila, D. (1980). *Teacher effectiveness and pupil attitude*. ERIC Document Reproduction Service No. ED 194 230.

O'Leary, K., Kaufman, K., Kass, R., & Drabman, R. (1970). The effects of loud and soft reprimands on the behavior of disruptive students. *Exceptional Children, 37*, 145–155.

O'Leary, K., & O'Leary, S. (Eds.). (1977). *The successful use of behavior modification* (2nd ed). New York: Pergamon.

Pellegrini, A., & Blatchford, P. (2000). *The child in school: Interactions with peers and teachers*. London: Arnold.

Peterson, R., Loveless, S., Knapp, T., Loveless, B., Basta, S., & Anderson, S. (1979). The effects of teacher use of I-messages on student disruptive and study behavior. *Psychological Record, 29*, 187–199.

Poppen, W., Thompson, C., Cates, J., & Gang, M. (1976). Classroom discipline problems and reality therapy: Research support. *Elementary School Guidance and Counseling, 11*, 131–137.

Premack, D. (1965). Reinforcement theory. In D. Levine (Ed.), *Nebraska Symposium on Motivation* (Vol. 13, pp. 123–180). Lincoln: University of Nebraska Press.

Redl, F. (1966). *When we deal with children: Selected writings*. New York: The Free Press.

Redl, F., & Wattenberg, W. (1959). *Mental hygiene in teaching* (2nd ed). New York: Harcourt, Brace & Co.

Redl, F., & Wineman, D. (1957). *The aggressive child*. Glencoe, IL: The Free Press.

Ryans, D. (1952). A study of criterion data (a factor analysis of teacher behaviors in the elementary school). *Educational and Psychological Measurement, 12*, 333–344.

Ryans, D., & Wandt, E. (1952). A factor analysis of observed teacher behavior in the secondary school. *Educational and Psychological Measurement, 12*, 574–586.

Schrupp, M., & Gjerde, C. (1953). Teacher growth in attitudes toward behavior problems of children. *Journal of Educational Psychology, 44*, 203–214.

Sears, R., Maccoby, E., & Levin, H. (1957). *Patterns of child-rearing*. Evanston, IL: Row, Peterson, & Co.

Shearn, D., & Randolph, D. (1978). Effects of reality therapy methods applied in the classroom. *Psychology in the Schools, 15*, 79–83.

Simon, A., & Boyer, E.G. (Eds.). (1970). *Mirrors for behavior 2: An anthology of observational instruments* (Volumes A and B). (A special edition of the *Classroom Interaction Newsletter*). Philadelphia: Research for Better Schools, Inc.

Skinner, B. (1953). *Science and human behavior*. New York: Macmillan.

Smith, H. (1985). The marking of transitions by more and less effective teachers. *Theory Into Practice, 24*, 57–62.

Solomon, R. (1964). Punishment. *American Psychologist, 19*, 239–253.

Stern, G. (1963). Measuring noncognitive variables in research on teaching. In N.L. Gage (Ed.), *Handbook of research on teaching* (pp. 398–447). Chicago: Rand McNally.

Thompson, G., & Hunnicutt, C. (1944). The effects of repeated praise or blame on the work achievement of "introverts" and "extroverts." *Journal of Educational Psychology, 35*, 257–266.

Wallen, N., & Travers, R. (1963). Analysis and investigation of teaching methods. In N. L. Gage (Ed.), *Handbook of research on teaching* (pp. 448–505). Chicago: Rand McNally.

Watson, J. (1926, May). What is behaviorism? *Harper's Monthly Magazine, 152*, 723–729.

Weber, W., Crawford, J., Roff, L., Robinson, C. (1983). *Classroom management: Reviews of the teacher education and research literature*. Princeton, NJ: Educational Testing Service.

Weinstein, C. (1977). Modifying student behavior in an open classroom through changes in the physical design. *American Educational Research Journal, 14*, 249–262.

Weinstein, C. (1979). The physical environment of the school: A review of the research. *Review of Educational Research, 49*, 557–610.

Wickman, E. (1928). *Children's behavior and teachers' attitudes*. New York: The Commonwealth Fund.

Withall, J. (1960). Research tools: Observing and recording behavior. *Review of Educational Research, 30*, 496–512.

Withall, J., & Lewis, W. (1963). Social interaction in the classroom. In N. Gage (Ed.), *Handbook of research on teaching* (pp. 683–714). Chicago: Rand McNally.

Witty, P. (1947). An analysis of the personality traits of the effective teacher. *Journal of Educational Research, 40*, 662–671.

Wood, M., & Long, N. (1991). Life space intervention: Talking with children and youth in crisis. Austin, TX: Pro-Ed.

II

Alternative Paradigms for the Study of Classroom Management

Jere Brophy
Michigan State University

3

Behavioral Approaches to Classroom Management

Timothy J. Landrum and James M. Kauffman
University of Virginia

INTRODUCTION

A behavioral view of the management of behavior in classrooms has been and continues to be a dominant and influential paradigm in both educational research and the preparation of teachers. To say that the behavioral view dominates current classroom practice, however, would be inaccurate. As we discuss later in this chapter, despite a rich history and extensive empirical underpinnings, the behavioral perspective on teaching and management is not highly regarded in the education community (see Axelrod, 1996). Moreover, behavioral strategies seem to be implemented haphazardly, inconsistently, or incorrectly as often as they are implemented as they were designed (Kauffman, 1996; Kauffman, Mostert, Trent, & Pullen, 2006; Pullen, 2004; Walker, 1995; Walker, Ramsey, & Gresham, 2004). Despite this failure to translate into practice what has become a considerable body of behavioral research, the behavioral view remains a frequent theme in the literature on classroom management, presented by proponents as a set of foundational principles to guide appropriate and nurturing classroom practice, and by critics as a set of unfeeling clinical procedures more suited to animals rather than humans, and thus to be avoided at all costs when teaching children. University students in teacher preparation course work are likely to hear something about a behavioral approach to classroom management. What is unclear, and probably variable from one university, program, or professor to the next, is whether they will hear a positive or negative portrayal of this approach to management.

Given the prevalence of behavioral topics in the professional literature and courses at all levels in colleges of education, it is imperative that students, practitioners, and researchers in education and psychology take a logical, if not scientific approach to understanding the behavioral view of classroom management. At a minimum, it would seem important to understand as fully as possible (a) what behavioral operations are and how they have been researched; (b) concerns and criticisms that have been levied against the behavioral view of classroom management in particular, and the extent to which such concerns are valid; and (c) contemporary issues regarding behavioral research and practice, including issues surrounding the growing problem of translating educational research into classroom practice.

TABLE 3.1
Overview of Five Basic Behavioral Operations

Operation	*Stimulus Action*	*Effect on Behavior*
Positive reinforcement	Positive stimulus added contingent on desired behavior	Behavior increases
Negative reinforcement	Negative stimulus removed contingent on desired behavior	Behavior increases
Extinction	Reinforcing stimulus following behavior is discontinued	Behavior decreases
Response cost punishment	Portion of positive stimulus removed contingent on undesirable behavior	Behavior decreases
Punishment with aversives	Negative stimulus added contingent on undesirable behavior	Behavior decreases

FIVE BASIC BEHAVIORAL OPERATIONS

Virtually all classroom management applications of behavioral theory involve one or a combination of the following five basic operations: positive reinforcement, negative reinforcement, extinction, response cost punishment, or punishment involving presentation of aversives. In subsequent sections, we provide a brief description of each operation, offer an overview of the empirical foundations of its application to classroom management, and discuss its particular strengths and limitations. The basic principle behind each operation is presented in Table 3.1.

Positive Reinforcement

The term *positive reinforcement* refers to the effect that is observed when a behavior is strengthened (i.e., is made more likely to recur) by a contingently applied stimulus that follows that behavior (Kazdin, 1978). The contingent stimulus may be virtually any object or event, including a tangible object (e.g., a sticker, a food item), a desired activity (the opportunity to play a game or engage is some other preferred activity), or a social gesture (positive acknowledgement or words of praise). A common misconception is that any stimulus used in a reinforcement program is by definition a "reinforcer." In fact, reinforcement is an effect, and thus one can accurately refer to a particular item, activity, or social behavior as a "positive reinforcer" only when its contingent application is shown to systematically increase the occurrence of a targeted behavior.

The effective use of positive reinforcement in classroom management has been well established across a variety of student age and ability levels, a number of academic and social skill areas, and in a variety of settings. Among the more prominent and effective applications of reinforcement in classrooms is the use of contingent teacher attention, or praise, to increase students' positive academic and social behavior. The premise of this technique is straightforward: teachers attend positively to students when they are engaged in desired, appropriate task-related activity or social behavior. In practice, success is dependent on fairly precise application. Most important is that positive attention is provided contingently; that is, when and only when the desired behavior has occurred.

Examples of the effective application of teacher attention abound. Indeed, by the early 1980s, Strain, Lambert, Kerr, Stagg, and Lenkner (1983) noted that "literally hundreds of classroom based studies have shown that teachers' delivery of social reinforcement can result in improved academic performance . . . rule-following and good school deportment . . . cognitive and linguistic performance . . . and increased social responsiveness" (p. 243). The body of evidence supporting the effectiveness of teacher attention led Alber and Heward (1997) to assert "the systematic application of praise and attention may be the most powerful motivational and classroom management tool available to teachers" (p. 277). Positive effects have been observed for elementary students' study behavior (Hall, Lund, & Jackson, 1968), for kindergarten students' following directions (Schutte & Hopkins, 1970) and cooperative play (Grieger, Kauffman, & Grieger, 1976), and secondary students' attending behavior (McAllister, Stachowiak, Baer, & Conderman, 1969). Effects are also evident for students' academic responding. Hasazi and Hasazi (1972) found that students who had trouble with digit reversal when solving math problems reduced the number of reversals in their work when teachers systematically focused positive attention on correctly written responses. Chadwick and Day (1971) found that when teachers added social reinforcers to a point system involving tangible reinforcers, increases in the percentage of time students worked, and the rate and accuracy of their work as well, were observed.

Despite the empirical base, studies have consistently shown that teachers do not reinforce positive behavior nearly as often as they should (Shores et al., 1993; Wehby, Symons, Canale, & Go, 1998). They tend to display higher rates of disapproval than approval to students (Thomas, Presland, Grant, & Glynn, 1978; Walker, Hops, & Fiegenbaum, 1976; White, 1975), and, in fact, may inadvertently reinforce students' negative behavior with their attention (Strain et al., 1983) and engage misbehaving students in arguing, setting the stage for the escalation of misbehavior (Colvin, 2004). Brophy's (1981) observation that "most of the teacher praise that apparently is intended as reinforcement probably does not function very effectively as such, because it is not systematically contingent on desirable behavior" (p. 15) would seem to hold true. As we suggest in a later section of this chapter, however, the problem is not that praise or contingent teacher attention lacks empirical support, or that they are not effective tools for managing behavior, but rather that the conditions under which teachers are both adequately trained and supported in the development and use of these skills are lacking.

Negative Reinforcement

Negative reinforcement is perhaps the most misunderstood of all behavioral operations, probably due to the incorrect connotations associated with the word *negative*. In fact, the term *negative reinforcement* refers to the same effect observed with positive reinforcement: a behavior is strengthened, or made more likely to occur (Alberto & Troutman, 2003; Kauffman, 2005a). Unlike positive reinforcement, however, in which a stimulus is applied contingently following a behavior, negative reinforcement refers to the contingent removal of a stimulus. Naturally, the stimulus that is removed must be one that students find unpleasant, thus making its avoidance the desired outcome. For example, a teacher might tell students that if they complete their classwork on time or to an acceptable level of accuracy, then they will not be given their usual homework assignment. If the contingent removal of this potential aversive (homework) has the effect of increasing students' productivity and accuracy in their classwork, then negative reinforcement has occurred. This example should not imply that all homework is inherently aversive, that all students find homework aversive, or that homework should be used with any regularity as a consequence in a management program. Nonetheless, in practice we have observed that many students would prefer not to do homework, and thus it may serve the function of an aversive in a potential application of negative reinforcement for these students.

While negative reinforcement is a powerful behavioral operation, its importance to teachers probably lies as much in unplanned and even inadvertent occurrences as in planful implementations. Rusch, Rose, and Greenwood (1988) offer an excellent overview of the complexities and potential dangers in trying to program negative reinforcement into a management plan, including most obviously the need to have aversive events available in the environment in the first place. Noting that naturally occurring negative reinforcement is plentiful in daily life (e.g., in breaks from work or vacations), they instead suggest that "one should be aware of the presence of and potential for negatively reinforcing events, but one should avoid purposefully programming these events" (p. 222).

In the terminology of functional analysis, negative reinforcement may be at work in classrooms when students engage in disruptive or negative behavior to escape from unpleasant tasks (see Maag & Kemp, 2003). Suppose a student does not like solving long division math problems. When presented with such an assignment, he or she may engage in significantly disruptive behavior: complaining, whining, and otherwise distracting others. If the teacher unwittingly removes the aversive stimulus (the math assignment) by sending the student to the hallway or the principal's office, even temporarily, negative reinforcement of the student's disruptive behavior may well occur. If the student's use of disruptiveness is successful in avoiding what he or she finds unpleasant (e.g., math), one can predict that disruptiveness will become more likely to occur in the future. Note that this situation also raises for teachers the concern as to why students find a particular class or assignment unpleasant, and modifications to curriculum, methods, materials, or motivational strategies should also be considered.

Ironically, in this scenario a cycle that Patterson (1980) called the "negative reinforcement trap" may also have been established. That is, both student and teacher have been negatively reinforced by the removal of something they find objectionable. It then becomes predictable that disruptiveness will occur again when students find an assignment particularly dull or extremely challenging, and, moreover, that the teacher will again remove the troublemaking student when disruptive behavior interferes with a lesson. Nevertheless, wise teachers may use brief periods of respite from work (effortful tasks) contingent upon a student's successful completion of such work. We call these "breaks" or "vacations" in the worlds of employment and adult self-control.

Extinction

If a behavior has come to be maintained by reinforcement, whether positive or negative, it can be predicted that the cessation of that reinforcement will result in a decline in the occurrence of the behavior. The term *extinction* refers to the phenomenon of a behavior decreasing in rate or likelihood of occurrence when the reinforcement that has been maintaining it is removed (Kazdin, 1978). Often referred to as *planned ignoring* in behavior management texts with a psychoeducational orientation, extinction can be a powerful management tool for teachers. Obviously, extinction is most useful in the classroom context in decreasing negative behaviors that have somehow come to be maintained by a reinforcer. Classic examples of this are mildly annoying behaviors such as talking out or making irrelevant comments during instruction. It is quite likely, for example, that the student offering off-task comments (e.g., "When do we eat lunch?" "Is there a dance on Friday?") will be reinforced if a teacher provides attention in any form. Even a presumably neutral response ("Don't worry about lunch; we're discussing history right now." "I'm going to ignore that.") may be sufficiently reinforcing to maintain this type of off-task comment. Such comments would be prime candidates for the application of extinction, or planned ignoring (i.e., deliberate nonresponse).

In practice, extinction is almost always applied as part of a larger program of reinforcement. Referred to as *differential reinforcement* (Alberto & Troutman, 2003; Wolery, Bailey, & Sugai, 1988), this process involves providing a reinforcer contingent upon a desired response, and withholding the reinforcer when the response is not occurring. In the preceding example, the teacher would be sure to respond positively to students making appropriate, task-related comments during instruction, while ignoring off-task comments. It would be especially important to apply differential reinforcement with individual students, immediately acknowledging the student prone to irrelevant commentary the instant he or she contributed positively to the lesson.

While extinction provides teachers with a simple and effective management tool, some obvious caveats must be taken into account. For example, it is generally untenable to ignore behaviors that are potentially dangerous to a child or others. A more common problem with extinction in classroom settings is behavior that is reinforced by peer attention. If a disruptive student gets the attention of his classmates with his antics and troublemaking, it is quite likely that peer attention is maintaining the behavior. In this case a teacher's decision to ignore such misbehavior is unlikely to have much effect on its future occurrence. A behavior will only be extinguished by a teacher's ignoring when the behavior had been maintained by the teacher's attention in the first place. What is needed instead are alternative procedures to prevent the behavior from occurring in the first place (e.g., more engaging and active instruction, reinforcement for positive participation in lessons), coupled perhaps with efforts to encourage other students not to laugh at or attend to the disruptive student's misdeeds. Wolery et al. (1988) outlined additional difficulties associated with using extinction. The *extinction burst* may be the most challenging for teachers to deal with; put simply, behaviors that are maintained by reinforcement invariably increase for a short period of time immediately after the reinforcement is terminated. A teacher using extinction must be prepared for this temporary and entirely predictable increase in responding, and must be resolved to maintain extinction during this increase.

While positive procedures and ignoring minor misbehavior are rightly touted as the first and preferred approach to classroom management in most courses and texts on the subject, an effective and comprehensive classroom management plan probably must include some level of punishment to deal with misbehavior that cannot be simply ignored. In addition to the reinforcement mechanisms outlined earlier that promote increases in behavior, teachers have at their disposal behavioral procedures that can be used to reduce the occurrence of negative behavior by addressing it directly. These include response cost punishment and punishment through the use of aversives. While both have the effect of reducing behavior, response cost punishment involves a simple removal of some measure of reinforcement already earned. In contrast, punishment through the use of aversives requires that teachers apply an aversive following misbehavior. It should be obvious that response cost is the preferred means of punishment; whereas aversives may have their place in limited use in classroom management, the potential for misuse and negative side effects is so great that they should be viewed with great caution and implemented with parsimony (Kauffman, 2005a; Kauffman et al., 2006).

Response Cost Punishment

Like reinforcement, the term *punishment* refers to an effect; namely the reduction in likelihood of occurrence of a behavior due to some contingency. In *response cost punishment*, a previously earned reinforcer is removed contingent upon the occurrence of a targeted undesirable behavior (Walker, Shea, & Bauer, 2004). A key element of this behavioral operation is that some reinforcement must be present for response cost to occur. For example, if students have earned 15 minutes of recess, 5 minutes of that time could be taken away for those who do not complete their assignment before the class period ends. Obviously, this procedure is appropriate only for students who do not finish their assignments due to a lack of effort, or for their choices to play or disrupt others instead of working, as compared to students who do not finish an assignment due to skill deficits. A number of authors (Alberto & Troutman, 2003; Walker, Shea, & Bauer, 2004) liken response cost to a system of fines, and indeed response cost programming fits particularly well into a token reinforcement program in which students accumulate points or tokens for various positive social and academic behaviors. A simple addition to this type of positive program allows teachers to also take away points when students engage in negative behavior. One presumed benefit of response cost is that it allows teachers to address problem behavior directly and immediately, rather than merely ignoring it as one might do in a program of differential reinforcement. A further benefit is that while the negative behavior is addressed directly, it is not by the application of an aversive, but by merely removing some of the positives already earned.

While response cost can be very effective when used judiciously, a few cautions are important to the teacher thinking of using response cost. First is the general guideline that the "punishment must fit the crime." If a student has worked hard all day to earn some reinforcer (e.g., computer time), a response cost program should not allow him or her to lose this entire privilege for a single minor instance of misbehavior. The logical alternative is that instead of losing 30 minutes on the computer, the student loses 10 of those minutes for misbehaving, and thus still enjoys 20 minutes of computer time, based on the cumulative good work and behavior he or she has produced throughout the day. Similarly, the teacher must be certain that there are ample opportunities for students to earn sufficient amounts of reinforcement that will outweigh the potential loss of reinforcers that inappropriate behavior might cost them. If a teacher knows that a student is prone to high rates of disruptiveness, a response cost program may not be appropriate, unless it is offset by enough reinforcement opportunities for the student to accumulate enough that he or she can "afford" to lose some and still enjoy some measure of positive outcome. A negative balance of reinforcement not only defeats the purpose of the reinforcement program, but probably results in a frustrated student who, with nothing left to lose, may see no reason to curtail negative behavior nor to display positive behavior (Walker, 1995).

Punishment Involving Presentation of Aversives

It is unfortunate that the general term *punishment* has come to connote a single type of punishment: the application of aversives. In fact, aversives are generally regarded as a last resort in dealing with severe behavior problems that (a) fail to respond adequately to positive procedures, including response cost punishment, and (b) are potentially dangerous or debilitating to the independence and dignity of the individual. Indeed, many professional organizations (e.g., the Association for Persons with Severe Handicaps (TASH), Council for Exceptional Children (CEC), National Association of School Psychologists (NASP)) have issued statements calling for severe restrictions or outright cessation of the use of aversives. The concept underlying the use of aversives is simply that the contingent application of a stimulus that a student finds aversive will result in a decrease in the occurrence of the behavior it follows. Aversives range from harsh stimuli that cause obvious physical pain or discomfort, such as hitting or spanking, to milder aversives, such as scolding or reprimanding, that are likely to cause emotional discomfort. Physical punishments are increasingly discouraged in schools and have been abolished in many states. Among the reasons for this is growing professional consensus that such punishments, although they may result in at least temporary suppression of behavior, have not demonstrated long-term positive effects in reducing the behavior they were designed to punish, do not include any component of teaching students what they should be doing instead, and may lead to increases in negative behavior. Walker et al. (2004) note that punishers provide a poor model for students already known to misbehave, and Alberto and Troutman (2003) argue that aggressive punishment may well evoke retaliation from students; they further suggest that what students learn most from punishment with aversives is "not to perform the behavior when the person who applied the punishment is present" (p. 383).

In contrast, the use of milder aversives, including such things as "soft reprimands" (O'Leary, Kaufman, Kass, & Drabman, 1970; O'Leary & O'Leary, 1977), is not only effective but much more appropriate and accepted in schools. A reprimand involves simply telling a student that a particular behavior is unacceptable, with a very brief statement of why it is unacceptable and what should happen instead. Walker et al. (2004) add that reprimands should be delivered calmly and privately, with lengthy or public discussions avoided. Even though reprimands have been shown to reduce negative behavior, they should be used only in combination with positive procedures designed to strengthen students' appropriate behavior.

In summary, a rich history of behavioral research in the second half of the 20th century explicated a number of behavioral operations that are useful to teachers in managing classroom behavior. The use of positive reinforcement in particular has provided the foundation of much of what is known about effective instruction and classroom management. In addition to its focus on positive reinforcement, the operant view that behavior is controlled by its consequences also leads to the understanding of behavioral operations based on extinction and punishment. Taken together, these operations provide a broad empirical foundation from which teachers can draw in developing, implementing, and evaluating classroom management routines. The systematic study of these operations applied to problems of teaching evolved during this same time period, and the development and growth of the field known as applied behavior analysis not only has provided a rich empirical literature base but also has offered teachers a number of mechanisms for implementing and evaluating their own interventions.

APPLIED BEHAVIOR ANALYSIS

The behavioral procedures outlined in the preceding sections were well established in laboratory and clinical settings in the first half of the 20th century (e.g., Kazdin, 1978). B. F. Skinner was the most prominent practitioner of operant conditioning during this time, but much of Skinner's early work, like that of other behaviorists of the time, was conducted with animals other than humans, including primarily white rats and pigeons. The systematic application of behavioral procedures to socially relevant problems of children in clinical settings and ultimately classrooms began in earnest in the latter half of the century, with the 1960s in particular being characterized by the rapid growth and popularity of the field known as applied behavior analysis (Baer, Wolf, & Risley, 1968; Kazdin, 1978). *Applied behavior analysis* refers to systematic efforts to change socially important behaviors in positive ways through the application of behavioral principles, with strict reliance on the frequent, repeated assessment of observable and measurable behavior and the goal of establishing a functional relationship between independent and dependent variables. The founding of the *Journal of Applied Behavior Analysis* in 1968 served as an important marker for this period of growth.

The development, application, and expanded use of research strategies associated with applied behavior analysis served as a catalyst for the systematic study of behavioral procedures in classrooms. Referred to as single-subject or single-case experimental designs, these approaches allow researchers to examine the impact of interventions on individual students. The basic features of single-case designs include continuous assessment, the establishment of baseline levels of performance, and the manipulation of a single variable during one or more intervention phases (see Hersen & Barlow, 1976; Kazdin, 1982). Continuous assessment demands repeated observations of the dependent measure, typically accomplished by daily observations. The establishment of stable baseline levels of performance is crucial to any further effort to determine whether the manipulation of the independent variable has a functional effect on the dependent variable. Stability in this case implies that the rate at which the targeted behavior occurs is essentially flat or shows a clear trend of deterioration during the baseline phase. If researchers are confident that repeated observations of behavior during a baseline phase show a stable or worsening trend in behavior, the introduction of the intervention in question can then be evaluated in the context of a number of different single-case designs. We describe and provide examples from the empirical literature of the four single-case experimental research designs most commonly used in behavioral research: reversal designs, multiple baseline designs, changing criterion designs, and multielement or alternating treatment designs.

ABAB or Reversal Designs

The ABAB or reversal design is perhaps the simplest single-case experimental design. Participants' behavior is measured during a baseline (A) phase, an intervention (B) phase, at least one return to baseline (A_2), meaning withdrawal of the intervention, and at least one reinstatement of the intervention (B_2). While improvement in behavior during the intervention phase provides some evidence of a treatment effect, the strength of this inference is increased dramatically if a second demonstration occurs during the reversal phase. One can infer a functional relationship between independent and dependent variables to the extent that a participant's behavior improves when the intervention is implemented (the B phase), returns to approximate baseline levels when the intervention is withdrawn (A_2), and improves again during a second intervention phase (B_2). In nearly all experimental situations, a reintroduction of the intervention (B_2) is called for, not only because it allows a stronger demonstration of the functionality of the intervention, but because it is consistent with the goals of applied behavior analysis, which include fostering positive behavior change.

Powell and Nelson (1997) provided an example of a reversal design in which an intervention consisting of assignment choice was evaluated using a reversal (ABAB) design with a second grade student who was diagnosed with attention deficit hyperactivity disorder (ADHD). During baseline, the student participated with his classmates by completing the same assignment given to the entire class, but was found to display high rates of undesirable behavior, defined as noncompliance, being away from his desk, disturbing others, or simply not doing his work. The intervention, assignment choice, consisted of the teacher offering the student a choice from among three appropriate assignments taken directly from the class curriculum during language arts periods. As can be seen in Fig. 3.1, levels of undesirable behavior decreased when the choice intervention was implemented, returned to baseline levels when the intervention was withdrawn during the return to baseline, and improved again when the intervention was reintroduced during a second B phase. These data present a compelling case that there is a functional relationship between the intervention (assignment choice) and this particular student's level of disruptive behavior.

Multiple Baseline Designs

Multiple baseline designs allow repeated demonstrations of a functional relationship between independent and dependent variables without necessarily invoking a reversal or withdrawal of the intervention. This is especially useful when a return to baseline is either impossible (in the case where learning has occurred) or unethical (in the case where a destructive or dangerous behavior has been reduced with an intervention). In a multiple baseline design, the researcher establishes two or more baselines before implementing an intervention phase. These baselines may be for different participants (multiple baseline across subjects design), for different behaviors displayed by the same subject (multiple baseline across behaviors design), or for the display of a behavior in different settings (multiple baseline across settings design). The intervention is then implemented in a staggered fashion across these multiple baselines. That is, the intervention will be implemented at different points in time for each participant, behavior, or setting. To the degree that an observed dependent variable targeted for change improves when and only when the intervention is introduced to that subject (or behavior or setting), the case for a functional relationship is enhanced.

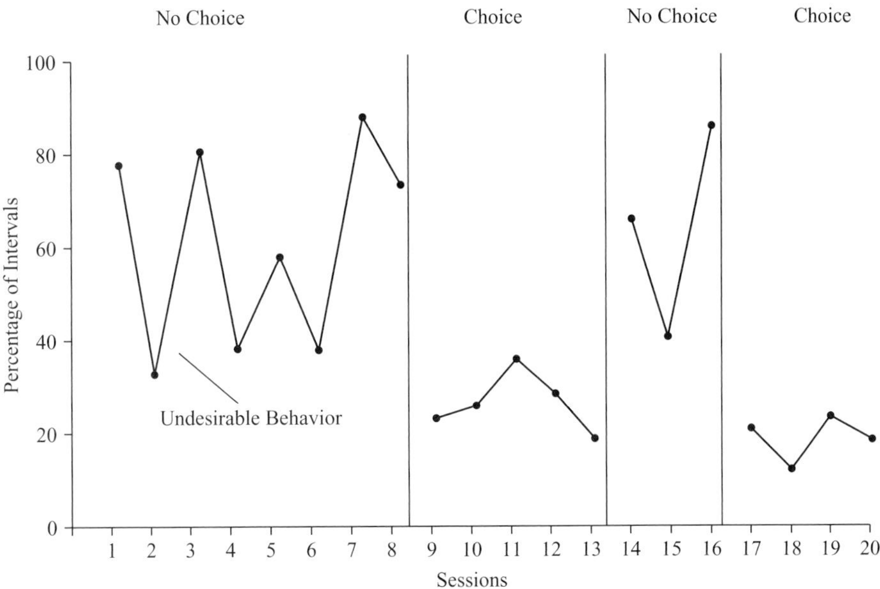

FIGURE 3.1. Example of an ABAB or reversal design. From Powell, S., & Nelson, B. (1997). Effects of choosing academic assignments on a student with attention deficit-hyperactivity disorder. *Journal of Applied Behavior Analysis, 30,* 181–183. Reprinted with permission.

Hartley, Bray, and Kehle (1998) used a multiple baseline across subjects design to evaluate the effects of viewing self-modeling videotapes on three second-grade students' classroom participation, as assessed by the frequency of their hand-raising in response to teacher questions. The intervention consisted of showing students a prepared videotape of their voluntary hand-raising in response to questions asked by the teacher during large-group instruction. In preparing the videotapes, students had been prompted to raise their hands, but the prompts were edited out of the videotapes used during intervention, so that the students appeared to be raising their hands spontaneously when teachers asked general questions of the group. As shown in Fig. 3.2, Hartley et al. implemented their intervention after a baseline phase consisting of 8 observation sessions for Student 1, 12 observation sessions for Student 2, and 18 sessions for Student 3. The implementation of intervention at three different points in time helps to rule out alternative explanations for behavior change (such as changes in teacher behavior, routine, or curriculum), and in this case offers three replications of treatment effect for this intervention.

A second common application of the multiple baseline design involves a single participant, but multiple settings. Fabiano and Pelham (2003) used a multiple baseline across settings design to evaluate the effects of three simple changes to an existing behavior management plan for a third-grade student diagnosed with ADHD who was reported by his regular classroom teacher to display high rates of disruptive, noncompliant classroom behavior. The intervention for this student consisted of modifying the ongoing behavior management plan by (a) allowing the child to earn daily rewards, instead of the weekly rewards offered in the existing plan; (b) providing immediate verbal feedback to the student when his behavior violated classroom rules— in the existing plan, feedback was provided to the student only at the end of each class period; and (c) operationalizing the student's criteria for meeting his behavior goals for a class period—in the existing plan, the student and teacher would simply come to a consensus on whether he had met his behavioral goal for a class period, whereas in the modified intervention phase, meeting a behavioral goal was defined as receiving fewer than three reminders for a given target behavior

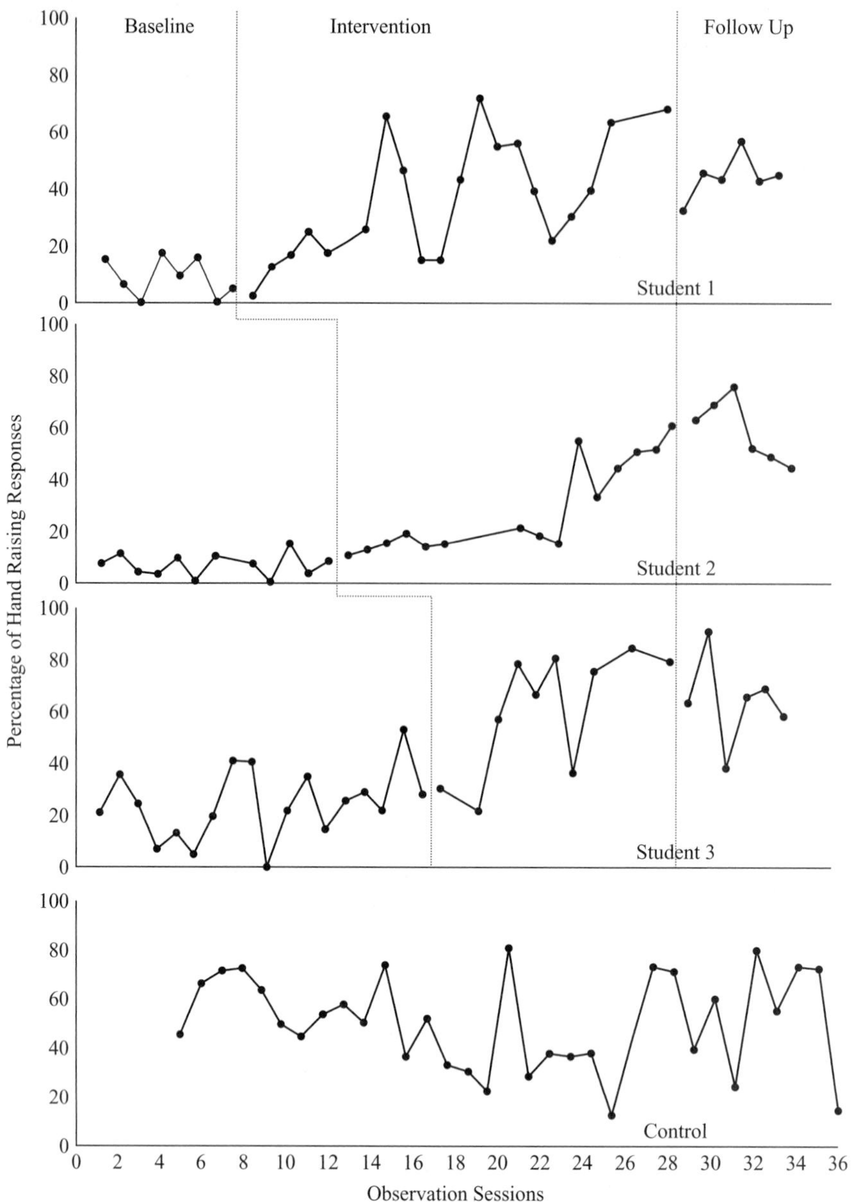

FIGURE 3.2. Example of multiple baseline across subjects design. From Hartley, E. T., Bray, M. A., & Kehle, T. J. (1998). Self-modeling as an intervention to increase student classroom participation. *Psychology in the Schools, 35*(4), 363–372. Copyright © John Wiley & Sons, Inc. Reprinted with permission of John Wiley & Sons, Inc.

during a class period. The effects of these modifications on the student's disruptive behavior were evaluated using a multiple baseline across settings design in which the intervention was introduced first in the student's afternoon class, typically consisting of a short period of large-group instruction followed by small-group work. After treatment effects were evident in this setting, the intervention was introduced in the student's morning classes, consisting of individual and small-group math and reading lessons. The intervention was shown to affect the student's percentage of on-task behavior by decreasing the percent of intervals in which disruptive behavior occurred, from 30% during baseline to about 10% during the afternoon class, and from 21% to 7.5% of intervals during the morning class. Again, the establishment of a functional relationship between these modifications and the student's disruptive behavior lies in that behavior change was observed when and only when the intervention was introduced in a particular setting.

A less common application of the multiple baseline design involves applying a particular intervention across multiple behaviors of a single student. Magee and Ellis (2000), for example, evaluated the effects of an extinction intervention across four problem behaviors in an elementary school student: out of seat, yelling, inappropriate language/gestures, and destroying objects. While Magee and Ellis suggested that the extinction intervention itself may have contributed to higher rates of the subsequent behaviors (i.e., as extinction was applied to and subsequently reduced out-of-seat behavior, increases in yelling were observed), the extinction intervention was nonetheless successful in sequentially reducing all four of the problem behaviors to rates approximating zero.

Changing Criterion Designs

Although the scope of behaviors to which it can be applied is somewhat limited (Rusch et al., 1988), the changing criterion design may be particularly useful in a teaching context in classroom situations. The essential feature of the changing criterion design is that the intervention phase is divided into a number of subphases that have increasingly rigorous criteria for the dependent measure. Treatment is implemented with the goal of moving baseline levels of performance to an initial criterion level; once criterion is reached for a predetermined number of days or sessions, the subsequent phase begins with a more stringent criterion. Such designs may be particularly suited to negative behaviors that occur at a high rate and need to be gradually reduced (Rusch et al.), or conversely to behaviors that do not occur at all and need to be taught.

Deitz and Repp (1973) used a changing criterion design to successfully decrease inappropriate talking in a high school classroom. As shown in Fig. 3.3, after a baseline level of off-topic talking during class was established, a reinforcer consisting of a free period on Friday was implemented if students could keep their level of inappropriate talking below a set criterion—initially five or fewer instances of talking each day. Within this design, the criterion was lowered each week, requiring that students meet a more stringent standard to earn the reinforcer. As can be seen in the figure, the reinforcement program, known as differential reinforcement of low rates (DRL) (Kazdin, 1978), resulted in a systematic decrease in the targeted behavior across these phases, as well as an increase in the negative talking when the program was withdrawn with a return to baseline.

Multielement or Alternating Treatments Designs

The multielement or alternating treatments design is used when researchers wish to evaluate the relative effects of two interventions in a single experimental phase, something that is not possible in other single-case designs. In the alternating treatments design, the baseline phase is followed by an intervention phase in which the two interventions are applied at different times (e.g., morning and afternoon academic periods) or under otherwise different conditions (e.g., in the cafeteria and on the playground). To enhance the analysis of a functional relationship, the treatments are also balanced across the intervention phase so that neither occurs consistently first, nor always under the same conditions. McQuillan, DuPaul, Shapiro, and Cole (1996) used an alternating treatments design to examine the relative effects of two forms of a

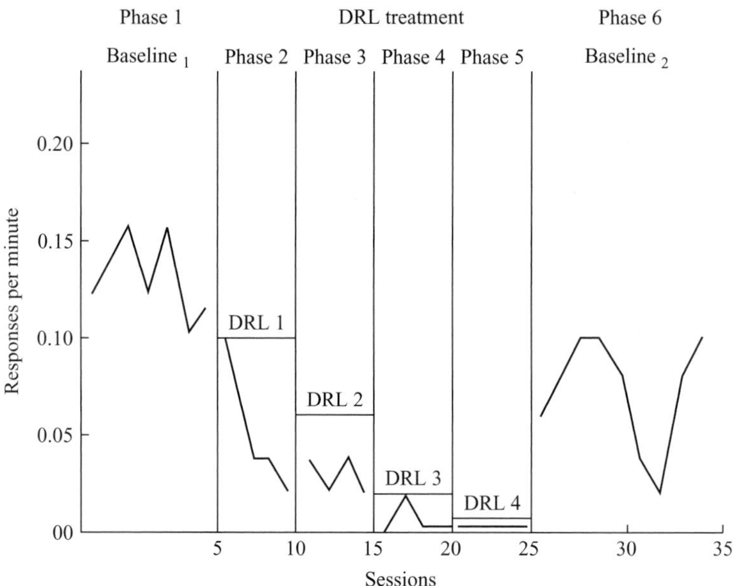

FIGURE 3.3. Example of a changing criterion design. From Deitz, S. M., & Repp, A. C. (1973). Decreasing classroom misbehavior through the use of DRL schedules of reinforcement. *Journal of Applied Behavior Analysis*, *6*, 457–463. Reprinted with permission.

self-management intervention and a teacher-evaluation intervention on the mathematics performance and time on task of three adolescent students with behavior disorders (see Fig. 3.4). After seven days of baseline, during which the teacher-evaluation management system already in use in the school remained in effect, an alternating treatments phase was implemented in which the teacher-evaluation system and the two forms of self-management were counterbalanced across daily sessions. Following three weeks of this phase, the optimal condition (self-evaluation) was implemented in a subsequent phase. As can be seen in the figure, baseline rates of accuracy were quite variable, with a mean of about 78%. When the optimal condition was implemented following the alternating treatments phase, the mean percentage of accuracy was 86%, and the variability in data was reduced dramatically.

CONCERNS ABOUT A BEHAVIORAL APPROACH TO CLASSROOM MANAGEMENT

We have touched briefly on the extensive literature base underlying a behavioral approach to classroom management and have also noted that a research-to-practice gap plagues classroom management just as it does all of education. Some writers have suggested that as a field we really do not know all that we purport to know about how to teach and manage behavior (e.g., Gallagher, 1998; 2004), and that perhaps the empirical foundation we have described here does not really provide much guidance. We disagree, and instead encourage professionals concerned with children's behavioral difficulties to examine the literature base and its shortcomings logically and carefully, and most importantly to implement best practices with an eye toward basing practice on credible and replicable research findings (see also Kauffman, 2005b; Kauffman, Brigham, & Mock, 2004). Three issues seem to be at the heart of concerns about

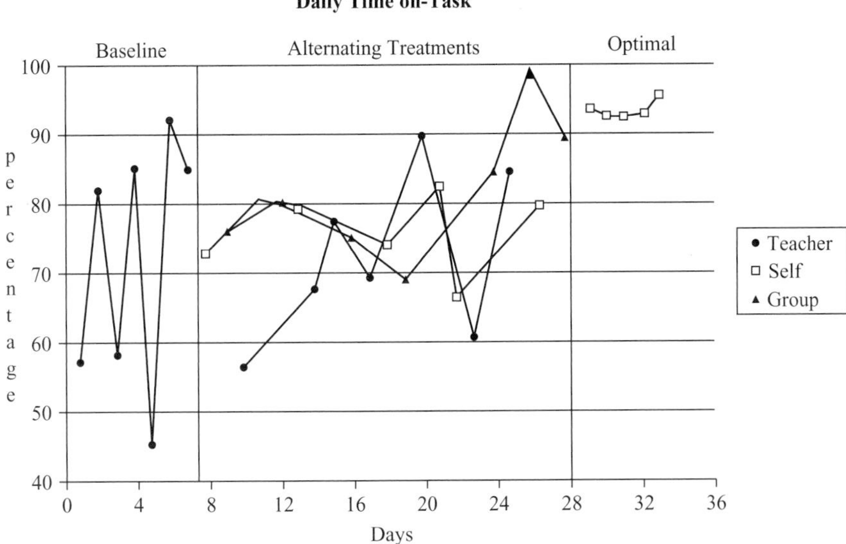

FIGURE 3.4. Example of an alternating treatments or multielement design. From "Classroom performance of students with serious emotional disturbance: A comparative study of evaluation methods for behavior management" by K. McQuillan, G. J. DuPaul, E. S. Shapiro, and C. L. Cole (1996). *Journal of Emotional and Behavioral Disorders, 4,* 162–170. Copyright 1996 by PRO-ED, Inc. Reprinted with permission.

the behavioral view of classroom management: (a) generalization, (b) concerns about coercion and bribery, and (c) ethical concerns about the potential for misuse of behavioral operations.

Generalization

The failure of researchers to produce treatment effects that routinely generalize to other settings, times, and responses has been a sharp and essentially legitimate criticism of behavioral programming since its early application to classroom settings. Even when teachers experience great success in fostering positive change in important academic and social behavior in one context or setting, there is no guarantee that effects will generalize across time (maintenance), or to other settings or responses. In what is probably the classic treatment of the problems associated with generalization, Stokes and Baer (1977) reviewed scores of studies and described nine generalization promotion strategies that researchers reported using. These included such strategies as *program common stimuli*, in which elements of the new environment (tasks, materials, trainers, directions, etc.) are specifically programmed to match those that the student experienced in the original training context, and *train sufficient exemplars*, a strategy that relies on exposing the students to many and varied examples of tasks or materials. Unfortunately, *train and hope*, essentially a failure to program for generalization, was noted as a common strategy in the literature reviewed. In essence, the criticism that behavioral operations do not produce generalizable effects was shown to be true by default; if educators do not actively program for generalization in their interventions, as often appears to be the case, then generalization will be lacking. But as a number of authors have since summarized, active programming for generalization using among other strategies those noted by Stokes and Baer can result in generalized responding (e.g., Alberto & Troutman, 2003; Rusch et al., 1988; Wolery et al., 1988). Ducharme and Holborn (1997), for example, used prompting, modeling, and verbal praise with preschoolers with hearing impairments to teach social interaction skills such as sharing, cooperating, or assisting other children. While the skills were learned and displayed successfully by the children in their preschool training setting, these newly learned skills did not generalize to other teachers, children, or play settings. Ducharme and Holborn used two generalization promotion strategies to engender such transfer. First, they trained *sufficient exemplars* by using multiple and different play activities (games), different teachers, and several different peers during their training of the targeted social skills. Second, they introduced children to *natural contingencies*, by systematically fading the teacher praise used initially to teach the new behaviors. These strategies resulted in generalized responding in a different setting with new peers, teachers, and play activities even with no additional prompting or reinforcement, such as that used in the initial training.

The larger remaining challenge for behavioral researchers lies in making sure that behavioral interventions routinely include explicit programming for generalization. Rusch et al. (1988) note further that programming for generalization is difficult and time-consuming, requiring extensive planning and even decisions about what and how much to teach, given that significant instructional resources must be devoted to training for generalization. As should be obvious, though, failure to generalize calls into question the true worth of any contextually limited behavior change.

Control, Coercion, and Bribery

Among the more frequent criticisms of the behavioral view of classroom management are concerns that teachers become too controlling, and merely coerce or bribe students to behave in ways that the teacher chooses. While terms like "coercion" and "bribe" certainly carry intended negative connotations, the use of behavioral procedures, such as positive reinforcement, are quite distinct from bribes or even coercion in that professional use of these procedures does not induce students to engage in behaviors that are illegal or immoral (e.g., we do not consider tax incentives to build low-income housing to be "bribes" or "coercive"). Moreover, the competent behavior analyst understands the need to develop and evaluate individual student's behavior goals and plans in concert with other professionals, family members, and the students themselves. That said, even behavioral procedures as innocuous as contingent teacher attention are subject to misuse, but this is not different from the teacher who does not use proper and scientifically sound literacy research to guide instruction for emergent readers. The problem lies not in the procedures themselves, but in inadequately trained, mentored, and supported teachers.

Ethics and the Potential for Misuse

The procedures we have outlined here provide teachers with powerful tools that can have a profound impact on the behavior of others. It should go without saying that we assume that ethical and professional educators understand appropriate applications of behavioral procedures, and can apply them earnestly in ways that enhance the academic, social, and emotional well-being of students. But we also know that any procedure carries potential risk that it will be misapplied, or applied toward an inappropriate end. Moreover, the more powerful any tool is, the more potential it has for misuse and abuse. We believe that we do want powerful tools for changing behavior, as the alternative is for our interventions to have little effect. But with powerful tools there are inherent risks as well (Kauffman & Hallahan, 2005).

Our concern here is not with behavioral procedures themselves, however, as we see the science of behaviorism as neither good nor bad. Instead we see an imperative that prospective teachers be trained and practiced in the application of the best that applied behavior analysis has to offer. In addition to the technical skills involved in analyzing behavior, they must understand the human side of education—that students have the right to be treated with fairness and respect at all times, including times when their behavior is different from an expected norm. Moreover, students have the right to be treated by a competent behavior analyst, should their dignity and independence come to be jeopardized by their own behavior.

CONTEMPORARY ISSUES

Recent Trends in Behavioral Research

Although the conceptual roots of behavioral approaches to classroom management are now many decades old (Kauffman, 2005a; Kauffman et al., 2004; Kauffman & Landrum, 2006; Kazdin, 1978; Nelson, 1981), behavioral research has continued to thrive in the 21st century. Behaviorism and behavioral research have changed considerably over the past several decades, becoming much more attuned to the contextual aspects of specific behaviors and incorporating much more of what has come to be called social learning theory (see Bandura, 1977, 1986; Bandura & Locke, 2003; Caprara, Barbarnelli, Pastorelli, Bandura, & Zimbardo, 2000). "Contrary to the contention that behavior analysis is dead or dying, behavior analysts continue to make significant advances in the basic science of behavior" (Malone, 2003). Contemporary behavioral research may also be more acceptable to many teachers than past research, which emphasized a more mechanistic approach and focused more on specific techniques than on the social ecology or context in which behavior principles are applied. As Strand, Barnes-Holmes, and Barnes-Holmes (2003) noted:

> It may be that general education teachers have rejected behavioral education because the caricatured version oftentimes presented to them is too narrow in terms of conceptualizing the duties and responsibilities they face. This rejection has occurred despite convincing data that behavioral techniques would improve student academic outcomes. If it is a goal of behavioral researchers to increase the popularity of their models within education, it may be necessary to provide teachers something other than a set of operant control techniques. (p. 115)

Moreover, behavioral researchers have become much more interested in translating research into practices that can be implemented by teachers and parents as well as clinical psychologists (Lerman, 2003). Seeing how students' behavior is related to its context and the subjective aspects of experience, yet can be shaped by the astute application of behavior principles, has made a behavioral approach to classroom management more understandable and useful to educators (e.g., Kauffman et al., 2006; Rhode, Jenson, & Reavis, 1992; Walker, 1995; Walker, Ramsey, & Gresham, 2003–2004a, 2003–2004b, 2004).

Among the most promising developments of the late 20th and early 21st centuries are advances in the functional assessment of behavior, emphasis on early intervention and prevention based in behavioral research, and efforts to broaden behavioral research to include school-wide applications.

Functional Assessment. A functional analysis of any behavior is an attempt to find out, through careful analysis of the social context—especially antecedents and consequences of the behavior—what use or function it serves. Usually, such analyses have been performed to find the function of the troublesome behavior of individuals with severe developmental disabilities (see O'Neill et al., 1997). In its 1997 reauthorization of the Individuals with Disabilities Education Act (IDEA), the U. S. Congress demanded that educators conduct a functional behavioral assessment (FBA) for all children served under the act whose behavior is so seriously problematic that it warrants disciplinary consideration. FBA as mandated by Congress seems to have been derived as an idea from research on the functional analysis of behavior.

Many students with disabilities are now served primarily in regular classrooms. Consequently, FBA involves both special and general educators. In FBA, the educator tries to determine the specific purposes or goals of the student's problem behavior and teach the student how to achieve the goal in a more acceptable way. Although FBA as a concept is at least as old as behavioral psychology, attempts to demand its widespread implementation in schools began in the late 1990s. FBA emphasizes the communicative intent of behavior—the function the behavior has in telling others what one likes, dislikes, wants, cannot tolerate, and so on. It is also an attempt to encourage nonpunitive management of behavior. That is, a less thorough analysis may suggest punishment for misbehavior, and FBA is an attempt to support students' demonstration of desirable alternatives to misbehavior (e.g., Fyffe, Kahng, Fittro, & Russell, 2004).

The emphasis on FBA is consistent with increased attention to the social context of behavior in research. It may reveal, for example, that a student misbehaves out of frustration, boredom, or that misbehavior is maintained because of the attention it garners or because it allows the student to avoid difficult tasks or unpleasant demands (DuPaul & Barkley, 1998). Although it is a highly useful tool in teaching, performing FBA competently and integrating it into teaching practice requires extensive training, especially in the case of students whose behavioral problems are severe or of long standing (see Fox & Gable, 2004; Gresham, Quinn, & Restori, 1999; Scott & Nelson, 1999; Sugai, Horner, & Sprague, 1999). Kauffman (2005a) notes several potential limitations:

- FBA is not simple, and identifying the actual function of the behavior may require extensive assessment by trained observers. Without support staff trained in FBA, teachers may be unable to implement it.
- Classroom management procedures suggested by FBA are often difficult or impossible for classroom teachers to follow without extra personnel.
- Functional analysis was developed primarily in nonschool settings using very frequent observations of behaviors that occurred often. The mandates of the U.S. Congress aside, these procedures may not generalize to typical school problems, many of which are serious behaviors that occur only infrequently.

Although the idea of FBA may have legitimate conceptual roots, it has become a bandwagon on which many ride with little understanding or appreciation of its difficulty in practice (Sasso, Conroy, Stichter, & Fox, 2001). Nevertheless, some researchers have found that classroom teachers *can* perform functional analyses and find ways to improve the behavior of students in both special and general education classes (e.g., Mueller, Edwards, & Trahant, 2003).

Prevention and Early Intervention. Dealing with difficult behaviors that are well-entrenched in students' behavioral routines is extremely difficult, and, in all cases, it is better to prevent problems from occurring in the first place (prevention) or to intervene early when problems first appear in their mildest form (early intervention). Prevention of behavior problems is certainly not a new idea, but it has never really gotten off the ground. That is, prevention has not become widespread in practice (Kauffman, 1999, 2003, 2004a, 2005a; Kauffman & Landrum, 2006 ; Walker et al., 2003–2004a). Moreover, although calls are frequently made for prevention rather than action after the fact of misbehavior or school failure (e.g., the President's Commission on Excellence in Special Education, 2002), such calls typically do not include consideration of the costs and risks required by actual prevention. Behavioral research has indicated clearly at least *some* of the things we could do to make schools safer and prevent misbehavior (see Sprague, Walker, Nishioka, & Smith, in press; Walker, Ramsey, & Gresham, 2004). Sprague et al. review behavioral research indicating that bullying and peer harassment are part of a pattern of behavior that can be identified early (i.e., by second grade) and that such behavior, if addressed early, can be controlled effectively through positive, typically school-wide interventions.

We do have evidence from decades of behavioral research regarding what we as a society and as educators must do if we want to practice prevention (Sprague et al., in press; Walker, Ramsey, & Gresham, 2004). Nevertheless, we seem unwilling as a society to pay the costs and take the risks (particularly the risk of false identification) required for instituting prevention on a widespread basis (see Kauffman, 1999, 2003, 2004a, 2005b for more detailed discussion of these inevitable costs and risks and suspected reasons for educators' unwillingness to accept them). Prevention that is universal or school-wide—applied to all students, regardless of their risk status or behavior—may be relatively inexpensive and demand little additional effort on the part of teachers. Such school-wide or primary prevention does not require singling out any child for special consideration. However, secondary and tertiary prevention do require identifying particular children as the targets of intervention. That is, any prevention procedure that does not apply to all students inevitably requires (a) labeling the child in some way for special attention and (b) risking that the child's identification is mistaken and that the action following identification is unnecessary (that is, risking a false positive).

Prevention, whether school-wide or not, inevitably involves more students than are now served in any special programs because it requires both (a) responding to problems earlier in children's lives and (b) responding to problems in earlier stages. Education, both general and special, follows a legal model much more closely than a medical model, in that there is great hesitancy to respond to cases before the full-blown problem is obvious. Changing this mind-set so that educators take action to remedy a problem in its incipient stages rather than waiting for the problem to become severe and protracted will require extraordinary change in the ethos of schools and the larger society (Kauffman, 1999, 2005b).

School-Wide Behavior Management. Walker et al. state, "Research has shown that the best way to prevent antisocial behavior is actually to start with an inexpensive school-wide intervention and then add on more intensive interventions for the most troubled kids" (2003–2004a, p. 11). The findings to which Walker et al. refer have resulted in numerous publications devoted to school-wide programs of behavior management (e.g., Lewis, Sugai, & Colvin, 1998; Liaupsin, Jolivette, & Scott, 2004; Martella, Nelson, & Marchand-Martella, 2003).

The advantages of a school-wide approach may seem obvious, but three are highlighted by Walker et al. (2003–2004a):

1. They improve the behavior of most students, even of the students who are not known as trouble-makers.
2. They have greatest effects on students who are at the margins of misbehaving, those just starting to exhibit aggression, defiance, or other unacceptable conduct.
3. They provide a foundation of good behavior management for serious trouble-makers (i.e., antisocial students), who will need the support of a good school-wide system of behavior management if the more intensive interventions designed for them are to have maximum effect.

The school-wide behavior management programs suggested by the authors we have cited generally conform to the behavior principles we suggested earlier in this chapter. That is, the school environment is designed with clear rules and expectations for conduct, monitoring and consistency in communicating expectations involving all school staff, frequent positive reinforcement for desired behavior, and consistent nonviolent penalties for misbehavior.

Controversy Regarding Punishment

Punishment has long been a highly controversial topic in managing children's behavior, partly because of the mistaken assumption that punishment always refers to causing physical pain, conferring a humiliating rebuke, or the presenting of a highly aversive consequence. Many people in the United States apparently approve of corporal punishment and other highly punitive approaches to behavior management (e.g., Evans & Richardson, 1995; Gershoff, 2002; Hyman, 1995). Numerous studies have shown that typical American classrooms are characterized by low rates of positive reinforcement for appropriate behavior and frequent use of consequences intended to be aversive to children (see Bear, 1998; Gunter, Hummel, & Conroy, 1998; Maag, 2001). As a result, some have advocated a ban on all manner of punishment, arguing that punishment in any form is unwise or unethical, that positive reinforcement alone is sufficient to manage behavior, and that further research on punishment is unjustified (e.g., Donnellan & LaVigna, 1990; LaVigna & Donnellan, 1986). Research does not support this conclusion, nor does careful thinking about punishment as defined from a behavioral point of view. Research does suggest using great care in applying or conducting research on punishment (Lerman & Vorndran, 2002). However, punishment, as defined earlier, need not involve pain, humiliation, or other consequences with which it is often mistakenly associated. Punishment may be as mild as withdrawal of attention and often involves response cost—withdrawal of a privilege or of a reward contingent upon misbehavior.

A frequent objection to punishment is that it fosters aggression, both as a consequence of the punished student's anger and resentment and the model of aggression it often provides (e.g., in the use of corporal punishment, or the application of verbal or physical aversives). Punishment does heighten or maintain aggression when it causes pain, when there are no positive alternatives to the punished behavior, when punishment is delayed or inconsistent, or when the type of punishment administered provides a model of aggressive behavior. When counterattack against the punisher seems likely to be successful, then punishment is likely to maintain, not suppress, aggression. The adult who punishes a child by striking out not only causes pain, which increases the probability of aggression, but provides a model of aggression as well. Nevertheless, as one commentary suggests, "punishment happens" (Vollmer, 2002; see also Horner, 2002; Spradlin, 2002). Vollmer argues that punishment happens frequently in everyday life, either as a naturally occurring phenomenon, in planned and unplanned social interactions with others, and, of course, in the behavior of parents, teachers, judges, and others who overtly and directly attempt to reduce undesirable behavior. As such, punishment, just like reinforcement, is a behavioral operation that is clearly in play in the lives of students, and it behooves researchers and practitioners to study and use this behavior management tool wisely.

Teaching appropriate behavior through positive reinforcement is important, but some types of conduct may require punishment because they are intolerable or dangerous and unresponsive to alternative positive interventions (Kazdin, 1998; Walker, 1995; Walker, Ramsey, & Gresham, 2004). Establishing adequate classroom control may in some cases be impossible without using negative consequences for misbehavior, in addition to positive reinforcement of appropriate conduct. Moreover, research shows that judicious negative consequences (response cost procedures) for misconduct are best combined with positive reinforcement and are advantageous in the long run with typical children (Conyers et al., 2004; Pfiffner & O'Leary, 1987; Pfiffner, Rosen, & O'Leary, 1985; Lerman & Vorndran, 2002). For example, Conyers and her colleagues compared differential positive reinforcement of nondisruptive behavior to response cost punishment with a class of 25 4- and 5-year-olds attending a preschool. The problematic, disruptive behaviors exhibited by children in this class included screaming, crying, throwing objects or using them as weapons, and noncompliance with teachers' requests. Although differential positive reinforcement of nondisruptive behavior (with stars and praise) effectively reduced disruption at first, response cost (losing stars for disruption) was more effective in the long term.

Special care in using punishment is important, however, because ill-timed, vengeful, and capricious punishment—especially in the absence of incentives for appropriate behavior—is a vicious example and encourages further misbehavior. Harsh punishment provokes counteraggression and coercion. Punishment is seductive and easily abused because harsh punishment often has an immediate, albeit, temporary effect; it often stops inappropriate behavior immediately, thereby giving the punisher powerful negative reinforcement. Therefore, punishment often is the beginning of a coercive style of interaction in which the punished and the punisher vie for the dubious honor of winning an aversive contest. Because people often mistakenly believe that punishment makes the individual suffer, more intense punishment is frequently thought to be more effective than milder punishment. These dangers, misconceptions, and abuses of punishment appear to underlie the coercive relationships that characterize families of aggressive antisocial children (cf. Patterson, Reid, & Dishion, 1992). School must not become another battleground for aversive control.

Research on social learning clearly supports the assumption that careful and appropriate punishment is a humane and effective tool for controlling serious misbehavior (Lerman & Vorndran, 2002; Walker, 1995; Walker, Ramsey, & Gresham, 2004). However, punishment that is clumsy, vindictive, or malicious is the teacher's downfall. Failure to offer positive reinforcement for appropriate behavior makes punishment unwise and unethical (Maag, 2001; Thompson, Iwata, Conners, & Roscoe, 1999). Moreover, punishment that is out of proportion to the seriousness of the offense has no place in humane schools.

Before using punishment, educators must make sure that a strong program of teaching and positive consequences for appropriate behavior are in place, and they must carefully consider the types of behavior that are to be punished. Teachers should study the use of punishment in depth before using it in the classroom. Following are general guidelines for humane and effective punishment suggested by Kauffman (2005a) based on his review of research on punishment:

- Punishment should be reserved for serious misbehavior that is associated with significant impairment of the youngster's social relationships and behaviors that positive strategies alone have failed to control.
- Punishment should be instituted only in the context of ongoing behavior management and instructional programs that emphasize positive consequences for appropriate conduct and achievement.
- Punishment should be used only by people who are warm and loving toward the individual when his or her behavior is acceptable and who offer ample positive reinforcement for nonaggressive behavior.
- Punishment should be administered matter-of-factly, without anger, threats, or moralizing.
- Punishment should be fair, consistent, and immediate. If the youngster is able to understand descriptions of the contingency, punishment should be applied only to behavior that he or she has been warned is punishable. In short, punishment should be predictable and swift, not capricious or delayed.
- Punishment should be of reasonable intensity. Relatively minor misbehavior should evoke only mild punishment, and more serious offenses or problems should generally result in stronger punishment.

- Whenever possible, punishment should involve response cost (loss of privileges or rewards or withdrawal of attention) rather than aversives.
- Whenever possible, punishment should be related to the misbehavior, enabling the youngster to make restitution and/or practice a more adaptive alternate behavior.
- Punishment should be discontinued if it is not quickly apparent that it is effective. Unlike positive reinforcement, which may not have an immediate effect on behavior, effective punishment usually results in an almost immediate decline in misbehavior. It is better not to punish than to punish ineffectively because ineffective punishment may merely increase the individual's tolerance for aversive consequences. Punishment will not necessarily be more effective if it becomes harsher or more intense; using a different type of punishment, making the punishment more immediate, or making the punishment more consistent may make it more effective.
- There should be written guidelines for using specific punishment procedures. All concerned parties—students, parents, teachers, and school administrators—should know what punishment procedures will be used. Before implementing specific punishment procedures, especially those involving time out or other aversive consequences, they should be approved by school authorities. (pp. 306–307)

Failure to recognize the necessity and value of punishment in behavior management and to use it skillfully reflects, in part, the ascendancy of ideology over data in education. In practice, data do not seem to matter as much as adherence to "theoretical" ideas or ideals about how education should be conducted, and punishment provides but one example (see Hirsch, 1996; Landrum, 1997 for further discussion of ideology versus data).

Failure to Train Teachers in Effective Practices

In spite of calls for evidence-based practices, most teachers are not trained to identify, much less use them. Although bias against certain instructional procedures is pervasive (see Grossen, 1993a, 1993b, 1993c; Heward, 2003), the failure to train teachers to identify and use effective, evidence-based practices involves behavior management as well (Cook, Landrum, Tankersley, & Kauffman, 2003; Kauffman, 2002; Kauffman & Landrum, in press; Tankersley, Landrum, & Cook, 2004). And this problem affects teachers in both special and general education.

Part of the problem in teacher training involves differences of opinion about what constitutes evidence and what does not (see Heward, 2003). However, another is the antitesting, antimeasurement, antibehavioral, or even antiscientific stance of many educators, both those in general and in special education (cf. Gallagher, 2004; Kauffman & Sasso, in press; Kohn, 1993, 2000, 2001). Behavioral research is increasingly devoted to making connections between laboratory studies and classroom practices (Lerman, 2003; Strand et al., 2003), but resistance to a scientific approach to education, including behavior management, is strong.

Controversy Regarding Rewards and Intrinsic Motivation

As we have seen, the behavioral approach suggests a focus on rewarding appropriate behavior (i.e., providing contingent positive reinforcement for desired behavior). Especially for students whose behavior is particularly difficult, the rewards are often extrinsic. Some writers and researchers have contended that extrinsic rewards undermine intrinsic motivation and, therefore, should not be used liberally, if at all, in behavior management (e.g., Deci, Koestner, & Ryan, 1999; Kohn, 1993, 1996; Ryan & Deci, 1996). Others have questioned this conclusion and offered data analyses to support the use of rewards (e.g., Cameron, Banko, & Pierce, 2001; Cameron & Pierce, 1994).

Like punishment, rewards can be used clumsily. The inept use of rewards may well have untoward effects on intrinsic motivation, but the research data do not support the idea that rewards are to be assiduously avoided. Moreover, teachers who refuse to offer rewards for desired performance run a serious risk of deteriorating classroom climate and increasing hostility toward school (Cameron et al., 2001; Colvin, 2004; Emmer, Evertson, & Worsham, 2003; Evertson, Emmer, & Worsham, 2003; Kauffman et al., 2006; Maag, 2001; Pullen, 2004; Rhode et al., 1992).

As many researchers and writers have pointed out, laboratory experiments showing that rewards undermine intrinsic motivation have been done under highly artificial and questionable conditions (see Cameron et al., 2001; Emmer et al., 2003; Evertson et al., 2003). It is, indeed, unwise to offer extrinsic rewards for tasks that the student will perform without them or to fail to pair social approval with more extrinsic rewards, such as material items or privileges. However, in the absence of intrinsic motivation to complete academic tasks or behave as expected in school, nothing is to be gained and much is to be lost by refusing to use extrinsic rewards to reinforce desired conduct. From the research published in the 1960s (e.g., Hall, Panyan, Rabon, & Broden, 1968) to more recent studies (e.g., Mueller et al., 2003) research has demonstrated the indispensability of rewarding consequences in dealing effectively with students whose behavior is difficult to manage (Alberto & Troutman, 2003; Rhode et al., 1992; Walker, Shea, & Bauer, 2004).

CONCLUSION

We conclude that a behavioral approach provides teachers with a well-researched set of tools to manage classroom behavior. These tools can be used skillfully or clumsily, with understanding of the principles that make them work or without such understanding. Research clearly supports the skillful use of behavior principles in classroom management. Recent trends in behavioral research emphasize not only the principles of behavior but their application with understanding of the social contexts in which they are applied and attention to how research can be translated into practices that are usable by parents and teachers.

ACKNOWLEDGMENTS

Rich Simpson provided a thoughtful review of the initial draft of this chapter, and Jere Brophy and Carolyn Evertson each provided extensive and insightful feedback. Their reactions challenged our thinking and allowed us to improve the chapter considerably, and we thank them sincerely.

REFERENCES

Alber, S. R., & Heward, W. L. (1997). Recruit it or lose it! Training students to recruit positive teacher attention. *Intervention in School and Clinic, 32*, 275–282.

Alberto, P., & Troutman, A. (2003). *Applied behavior analysis for teachers* (6th ed.). Upper Saddle River, NJ: Merrill/Prentice-Hall.

Axelrod, S. (1996). What's wrong with behavior analysis? *Journal of Behavioral Education, 6*, 247–256.

Baer, D., Wolf, M., & Risley, T. (1968). Some current dimensions of applied behavior analysis. *Journal of Applied Behavior Analysis, 1*, 91–97.

Bandura, A. (1977). *Social learning theory*. Upper Saddle River, NJ: Prentice-Hall.

Bandura, A. (1986). *Social foundations of thought and action: A social cognitive theory*. Upper Saddle River, NJ: Prentice-Hall.

Bandura, A., & Locke, E. A. (2003). Negative self-efficacy and goal effects revisited. *Journal of Applied Psychology, 88*, 87–99.

Bear, G. G. (1998). School discipline in the United States: Prevention, correction, and long-term social development. *School Psychology Review, 27*, 14–32.

Brophy, J. (1981). Teacher praise: A functional analysis. *Review of Educational Research, 51*, 5–32.

Cameron, J., Banko, K. M., & Pierce, W. D. (2001). Pervasive negative effects of rewards on intrinsic motivation: The myth continues. *The Behavior Analyst, 24*, 1–44.

Cameron, J., & Pierce, W. D. (1994). Reinforcement, reward and intrinsic motivation: A meta-analysis. *Review of Educational Research, 64*, 363–423.

Caprara, G., Barbarnelli, C., Pastorelli, C., Bandura, A., & Zimbardo, P. (2000). Prosocial foundations of children's academic achievement. *Psychological Science, 11*, 302–326.

Chadwick, B. A., & Day, R. C. (1971). Systematic reinforcement: Academic performance of underachieving students. *Journal of Applied Behavior Analysis, 4*, 311–319.

Colvin, G. (2004). *Managing the cycle of acting-out behavior in the classroom*. Eugene, OR: Behavior Associates.

Conyers, C, Miltenberger, R., Maki, A., Barenz, R., Jurgens, M., Sailer, A., Haugen, M., & Kopp, B. (2004). A comparison of response cost and differential reinforcement of other behavior to reduce disruptive behavior in a preschool classroom. *Journal of Applied Behavior Analysis, 37*, 411–415.

Cook, B. G., Landrum, T. J., Tankersley, M., & Kauffman, J. M. (2003). Bringing research to bear on practice: Effecting evidence-based instruction for students with emotional or behavioral disorders. *Education and Treatment of Children, 26*, 345–361.

Deci, E. L., Koestner, R., & Ryan, R. M. (1999). A meta-analytic review of experiments examining the effects of extrinsic rewards on intrinsic motivation. *Psychological Bulletin, 125*, 627–668.

Deitz, S. M., & Repp, A. C. (1973). Decreasing classroom misbehavior through the use of DRL schedules of reinforcement. *Journal of Applied Behavior Analysis, 6*, 457-463.

Donnellan, A. M., & LaVigna, G. W. (1990). Myths about punishment. In A. C. Repp & N. N. Singh (Eds.), *Perspectives on the use of nonaversive and aversive interventions for persons with developmental disabilities* (pp. 33–57). Sycamore, IL: Sycamore.

Ducharme, D., & Holborn, (1997). Programming generalization of social skills in preschool children with hearing impairments. *Journal of Applied Behavior Analysis, 30*, 639–651.

DuPaul, G. J., & Barkley, R. A. (1998). Attention-deficit hyperactivity disorder. In R. J. Morris & T. R. Kratochwill (Eds.), *The practice of child therapy* (3rd ed., pp. 132–166). Boston: Allyn & Bacon.

Emmer, E. T., Evertson, C. M., & Worsham, M. E. (2003). *Classroom management for secondary teachers* (6th ed.). Boston: Allyn & Bacon.

Evans, E. D., & Richardson, R. C. (1995). Corporal punishment: What teachers should know. *Teaching Exceptional Children, 27*(2), 33–36.

Evertson, C. M., Emmer, E. T., & Worsham, M. E. (2003). *Classroom management for elementary* teachers (6th ed.). Boston: Allyn & Bacon.

Fabiano, G. A., & Pelham, W. E. (2003). Improving the effectiveness of behavioral classroom interventions for attention deficit-hyperactivity disorder: A case study. *Journal of Emotional and Behavioral Disorders, 11*(2), 122–128.

Fox, J., & Gable, R. A. (2004). Functional behavioral assessment. In R. B. Rutherford, M. M. Quinn, & S. R. Mathur (Eds.). *Handbook of research in emotional and behavioral disorders* (pp. 143–162). New York: Guilford.

Fyffe, C. E., Kahng, S. W., Fittro, E., & Russell, D. (2004). Functional analysis and treatment of inappropriate sexual behavior. *Journal of Applied Behavior Analysis, 37*, 401–404.

Gallagher, D. J. (1998). The scientific knowledge base of special education: Do we know what we think we know? *Exceptional Children, 64*, 493–502.

Gallagher, D. J. (Ed.). (2004). *Challenging orthodoxy in special education: Dissenting voices*. Denver, CO: Love.

Gershoff, E. T. (2002). Corporal punishment by parents and associated child behaviors and experiences: A meta-analytic and theoretical review. *Psychological Bulletin, 128*, 539–579.

Gresham, F. M., Quinn, M. M., & Restori, A. (1999). Methodological issues in functional analysis: Generalizability to other disability groups. *Behavioral Disorders, 24*, 180–182.

Grieger, T., Kauffman, J. M., & Grieger, R. M. (1976). Effects of peer reporting on cooperative play and aggression of kindergarten children. *Journal of School Psychology, 14*, 307–313.

Grossen, B. (1993a). Child-directed teaching methods: A discriminatory practice of Western education. *Effective School Practices, 12*(2), 9–20.

Grossen, B. (1993b). Focus: Discriminatory educational practices. *Effective School Practices, 12*(2), 1.

Grossen, B. (1993c). Focus: Heterogeneous grouping and curriculum design. *Effective School Practices, 12*(1), 5–8.

Gunter, P. L., Hummel, J. H., & Conroy, M. A. (1998). Increasing correct academic responding: An effective intervention strategy to decrease behavior problems. *Effective School Practices, 17*(2), 36–54.

Hall, R. V., Lund, D., & Jackson, D. (1968). Effects of teacher attention on study behavior. *Journal of Applied Behavior Analysis, 1*, 1–12.

Hall, R. V., Panyan, M., Rabon, D., & Broden, M. (1968). Instructing beginning teachers in reinforcement procedures which improve classroom control. *Journal of Applied Behavior Analysis, 1*, 315–322.

Hartley, E. T., Bray, M. A., & Kehle, T. J. (1998). Self-modeling as an intervention to increase student classroom participation. *Psychology in the Schools, 35*(4), 363–372.

Hasazi, J. E., & Hasazi, S. E. (1972). Effects of teacher attention on digit-reversal behavior in an elementary school child. *Journal of Applied Behavior Analysis, 5*, 157–162.

Hersen, M., & Barlow, D. H. (1976). *Single-case experimental designs: Strategies for studying change*. New York: Pergamon.

Heward, W. L. (2003). Ten faulty notions about teaching and learning that hinder the effectiveness of special education. *The Journal of Special Education, 36*, 186–205.

Hirsch, E. D., Jr. (1996). *The schools we need and why we don't have them*. New York: Anchor.

Horner, R. H. (2002). On the status of knowledge for using punishment: A commentary. *Journal of Applied Behavior Analysis, 35*, 465–467.

Hyman, I. A. (1995). Corporal punishment, psychological maltreatment, violence, and punitiveness in America: Research, advocacy, and public policy. *Applied and Preventive Psychology, 4*, 113–130.

Kauffman, J. M. (1996). Research to practice issues. *Behavioral Disorders, 22*, 55–60.

Kauffman, J. M. (1999). How we prevent the prevention of emotional and behavioral disorders. *Exceptional Children, 65*, 448–468.

Kauffman, J. M. (2002). *Education deform: Bright people sometimes say stupid things about education*. Lanham, MD: Scarecrow Education.

Kauffman, J. M. (2003). Appearances, stigma, and prevention. *Remedial and Special Education, 24*, 195–198.

Kauffman, J. M. (2004a). Foreword for H. M. Walker, E. Ramsey, & F. M. Gresham, *Antisocial behavior in school: Strategies and best practices* (2nd ed.) (pp. xix–xxi). Belmont, CA: Wadsworth.

Kauffman, J. M. (2004b). Introduction [to Part 1: Foundations of Research]. In R. B. Rutherford, M. M. Quinn, & S. R. Mathur (Eds.), *Handbook of research in emotional and behavioral disorders* (pp. 11–14). New York: Guilford.

Kauffman, J. M. (2005a). *Characteristics of emotional and behavioral disorders of children and youth* (8th ed.). Upper Saddle River, NJ: Prentice-Hall.

Kauffman, J. M. (2005b). How we prevent the prevention of emotional and behavioural difficulties in education. In P. Clough, P. Garner, J. T. Pardeck, & F. Yuen (Eds.), *Handbook of emotional and behavioural difficulties in education* (pp. 429–440). London: Sage.

Kauffman, J. M., Brigham, F. J., & Mock, D. R. (2004). Historical to contemporary perspectives in the field of behavioral disorders. In R. B. Rutherford, M. M. Quinn, & S. R. Mathur (Eds.), *Handbook of research in emotional and behavioral disorders* (pp. 15–31). New York: Guilford.

Kauffman, J. M., & Hallahan, D. P. (2005). *Special education: What it is and why we need it*. Boston: Allyn & Bacon.

Kauffman, J. M., & Landrum, T. J. (2006). *Students with emotional and behavioral disorders: A history of their education*. Austin, TX: Pro-Ed.

Kauffman, J. M., & Landrum, T. J. (in press). Educational service interventions and reforms. In J. W. Jacobson & J. A. Mulick (Eds.), *Handbook of intellectual and developmental disabilities*. New York: Kluwer.

Kauffman, J. M., Mostert, M. P., Trent, S. C., & Pullen, P. L. (2006). *Managing classroom behavior: A reflective case-based approach* (4th ed.). Boston: Allyn & Bacon.

Kauffman, J. M., & Sasso, G. M. (in press). Toward ending cultural and cognition relativism in special education. *Exceptionality*.

Kazdin, A. E. (1978). *History of behavior modification: Experimental foundations of contemporary research*. Baltimore: University Park Press.

Kazdin, A. E. (1982). *Single-case research designs*. New York: Oxford University Press.

Kazdin, A. E., (1998). Conduct disorder. In R. J. Morris & T. R. Kratochwill (Eds.), *The practice of child therapy* (3rd ed., pp. 199–230). Boston: Allyn & Bacon.

Kohn, A. (1993). *Punished by rewards*. Boston: Houghton Mifflin.

Kohn, A. (1996). By all available means: Cameron and Pierce's defense of extrinsic motivators. *Review of Educational Research, 66*, 1–4.

Kohn, A. (2000). *The case against standardized testing: Raising the scores, ruining the schools*. Westport, CT: Heinemann.

Kohn, A. (2001). Fighting the tests: A practical guide to rescuing our schools. *Phi Delta Kappan, 82*, 349–357.

Landrum. T. J. (1997). Why data don't matter. *Journal of Behavioral Education, 7*, 123–129.

LaVigna, G. W., & Donnellan, A. M. (1986). *Alternatives to punishment: Solving behavior problems with nonaversive strategies*. New York: Irvington.

Lerman, D. C. (2003). From the laboratory to community application: Translational research in behavior analysis. *Journal of Applied Behavior Analysis, 36*, 415–419.

Lerman, D. C., & Vorndran, C. M. (2002). On the status of knowledge for using punishment: Implications for treating behavior disorders. *Journal of Applied Behavior Analysis, 35*, 431–464.

Lewis, T. J., Sugai, G., & Colvin, G. (1998). Reducing problem behavior through a school-wide system of effective behavioral support: Investigation of a school-wide social skills training program and contextual interventions. *School Psychology Review, 27*, 446–459.

Liaupsin, C. J., Jolivette, K., & Scott, T. M. (2004). School-wide systems of behavior support: Maximizing student success in schools. In R. B. Rutherford, M. M. Quinn, & S. R. Mathur (Eds.), *Handbook of research in emotional and behavioral disorders* (pp. 487–501). New York: Guilford.

Maag, J. W. (2001). Rewarded by punishment: Reflections on the disuse of positive reinforcement in schools. *Exceptional Children, 67*, 173-186.

Maag, J. W., & Kemp, S. E. (2003). Behavioral intent of power and affiliation: Implications for functional analysis. *Remedial and Special Education, 24*, 57-64.

Magee, S. K. & Ellis, J. (2000). Extinction effects during the assessment of multiple problem behaviors. *Journal of Applied Behavior Analysis, 33*, 313—316.

Malone, J. C. (2003). Advances in behaviorism: It's not what it used to be. *Journal of Behavioral Education, 12*, 85–89.

Martella, R. C., Nelson, J. R., & Marchand-Martella, N. E. (2003). *Managing disruptive behaviors in the schools: A schoolwide, classroom, and individualized learning approach.* Boston: Allyn & Bacon.

McAllister, L., Stachowiak, J., Baer, D. M., & Conderman, L. (1969). The application of operant conditioning techniques in a secondary school classroom. *Journal of Applied Behavior Analysis, 2*, 277–285.

McQuillan, K., DuPaul, G. J., Shapiro, E. S., & Cole, C. L. (1996). Classroom performance of students with serious emotional disturbance: A comparative study of evaluation methods for behavior management. *Journal of Emotional and Behavioral Disorders, 4*, 162–170.

Mueller, M. M., Edwards, R. P., & Trahant, D. (2003). Translating multiple assessment techniques into an intervention selection model for classrooms. *Journal of Applied Behavior Analysis, 36*, 563–573.

Nelson, C. M. (1981). Classroom management. In J. M. Kauffman & D. P. Hallahan (Eds.), *Handbook of special education* (pp. 663–687). Upper Saddle River, NJ: Prentice Hall.

O'Leary, D., Kaufman, K., Kass, R. and Drabman, R. (1970). The effects of loud and soft reprimands on the behaviour of disruptive students. *Exceptional Children, 37*, 145–155.

O'Leary, K. D., & O'Leary, S. G. (1977). *Classroom management: The successful use of behavior modification* (2nd ed.). New York: Pergamon Press.

O'Neill, R. E., Horner, R. H., Albin, R. W., Sprague, J. R., Storey, K., & Newton, J. S. (1997). *Functional assessment and program development for problem behavior*. Pacific Grove, CA: Brooks/Cole.

Patterson, G. R. (1980). Mothers: The unacknowledged victims. *Monographs of the Society for Research in Child Development, 45*, (5, Serial No. 186), 1–64.

Patterson, G. R., Reid, J. B., & Dishion, T. J. (1992). *Antisocial boys*. Eugene, OR: Castalia.

Pfiffner, L. J., & O'Leary, S. G. (1987). The efficacy of all-positive management as a function of the prior use of negative consequences. *Journal of Applied Behavior Analysis, 20*, 265–271.

Pfiffner, L. J., Rosen, L. A., & O'Leary, S. G. (1985). The efficacy of an all-positive approach to classroom management. *Journal of Applied Behavior Analysis, 18*, 257–261.

Powell, S., & Nelson, B. (1997). Effects of choosing academic assignments on a student with attention deficit-hyperactivity disorder. *Journal of Applied Behavior Analysis, 30*, 181–183.

President's Commission on Excellence in Special Education. (2002). *A new era: Revitalizing special education for children and their families*. Retrieved february 4, 2004 from www.ed.gov/inits/commissionsboards/whspecialeducation/reports/info.html. Washington, DC: U.S. Department of Education.

Pullen, P. L. (2004). *Brighter beginnings for teachers*. Lanham, MD: Scarecrow Education.

Rhode, G., Jenson, W. R., & Reavis, H. K. (1992). *The tough kid book: Practical classroom management strategies*. Longmont, CA: Sopris West.

Rusch, F. R., Rose, T., & Greenwood, C. R. (1988). *Introduction to behavior analysis in special education*. Englewood Cliffs, NJ: Prentice-Hall.

Ryan, R. M., & Deci, E. L. (1996). When paradigms clash: Comments on Cameron and Pierce's claim that rewards do not undermine intrinsic motivation. *Review of Educational Research, 66*, 33–38.

Sasso, G. M., Conroy, M. A., Stichter, J. P., & Fox, J. J. (2001). Slowing down the bandwagon: The misapplication of functional assessment for students with emotional and behavioral disorders. *Behavioral Disorders, 26*, 282–296.

Schutte, R. C. & Hopkins, B. L. (1970). The effects of teacher attention on following instructions in a kindergarten class. *Journal of Applied Behavior Analysis, 3*, 117–122.

Scott, T. M., & Nelson, C. M. (1999). Functional behavioral assessment: Implications for training and staff development. *Behavioral Disorders, 24*, 249–252.

Shores, R. E., Jack, S. L., Gunter, P. L., Ellis, D. N., DeBriere, T. J., & Wehby, J. H. (1993). Classroom interactions of children with behavior disorders. *Journal of Emotional and Behavioral Disorders, 1*, 27–39.

Spradlin, J. E. (2002). Punishment: A primary process? *Journal of Applied Behavior Analysis, 35*, 475–477.

Sprague, J. R., Walker, H. M., Nishioka, V., & Smith, S. G. (in press). *School safety issues and prevention strategies: Proven and practical solutions for educators*. New York: Guilford.

Stokes, T. F., & Baer, D. M. (1977). An implicit technology of generalization. *Journal of Applied Behavior Analysis, 10*, 349–367.

Strain, P. S., Lambert, D. L., Kerr, M. M., Stagg, V., & Lenkner, D. A. (1983). Naturalistic assessment of children's compliance to teachers' requests and consequences for compliance. *Journal of Applied Behavior Analysis, 16*, 243–249.

Strand, P. S., Barnes-Holmes, Y., & Barnes-Holmes, D. (2003). Educating the whole child: Implications of behaviorism as a science of meaning. *Journal of Behavioral Education, 12*, 105–117.

Sugai, G., Horner, R. H., & Sprague, J. R. (1999). Functional assessment-based behavior support planning: Research to practice. *Behavioral Disorders, 24*, 253–257.

Sutherland, K. S., Copeland, S. & Wehby, J. H. (2001). Catch them while you can: Monitoring and increasing the use of effective praise. *Beyond Behavior, 11*(1), 46–49.

Tankersley, M., Landrum, T. J., & Cook, B. G. (2004). How research informs practice in the field of emotional and behavioral disorders. In R. B. Rutherford, M. M. Quinn, & S. R. Mathur (Eds.), *Handbook of research in emotional and behavioral disorders* (pp. 98–113). New York: Guilford.

Thomas, J. D., Presland, I. E., Grant, M. D., & Glynn, T. L. (1978). Natural rates of teacher approval and disapproval in grade-7 classrooms. *Journal of Applied Behavior Analysis, 11*, 91–94.

Thompson, R. H., Iwata, B. A., Conners, J., & Roscoe, E. M. (1999). Effects of reinforcement for alternative behavior during punishment of self-injury. *Journal of Applied Behavior Analysis, 32*, 317–328.

Vollmer, R. R. (2002). Punishment happens: Some comments on Lerman and Vorndran's review. *Journal of Applied Behavior Analysis, 35*, 469–473.

Walker, H. M. (1995). *The acting-out child: Coping with classroom disruption* (2nd ed.). Longmont, CO: Sopris West.

Walker, H. M., Hops, H., & Fiegenbaum, E. (1976). Deviant classroom behavior as a function of combinations of social and token reinforcement and cost contingency. *Behavior Therapy, 7*, 76–88.

Walker, H. M., Ramsey, E., & Gresham, F. M. (2003–2004a). Heading off disruptive behavior: How early intervention can reduce defiant behavior—and win back teaching time. *American Educator (Winter)*, 6–21, 45–46.

Walker, H. M., Ramsey, E., & Gresham, F. M. (2003–2004b). How disruptive students escalate hostility and disorder—and how teachers can avoid it. *American Educator* (*Winter*), 22–27, 47–48.

Walker, H. M., Ramsey, E., & Gresham, F. M. (2004). *Antisocial behavior in school: Strategies and best practices* (2nd ed.). Pacific Grove, CA: Brooks/Cole.

Walker, J. E., Shea, T. M., & Bauer, A. M. (2004). *Behavior management: A practical approach for educators*. Upper Saddle River, NJ: Merrill/Prentice-Hall.

Wehby, J. H., Symons, F. J., Canale, J. A., & Go, F. J. (1998). Teaching practices in classrooms for students with emotional and behavioral disorders: Discrepancies between recommendations and observations. *Behavioral Disorders, 24*, 51–56.

White, M. A. (1975). Natural rates of teacher approval and disapproval in the classroom. *Journal of Applied Behavior Analysis, 8*, 367–372.

Wolery, M., Bailey, D. B., & Sugai, G. M. (1988). *Effective teaching: Principles and procedures of applied behavior analysis with exceptional students*. Boston: Allyn & Bacon.

4

Process-Outcome Approaches to Classroom Management and Effective Teaching

Maribeth Gettinger and Kristy M. Kohler
University of Wisconsin, Madison

INTRODUCTION

For over 40 years, educational researchers have engaged in studies to identify instructional and environmental variables that contribute to effective teaching and classroom management. Guided by several key questions (e.g., What makes an effective classroom manager? Is there a universal set of effective teaching skills? Is there a link between teacher behavior and student performance?), researchers have sought to identify and quantify the effects of teachers and teaching in the learning process. This search for relations between classroom processes (teaching) and outcomes (what students learn and how they behave) is known as *process-outcome* (or process-product) *research*; it has been the source of important instructional advancements for both improving classroom behavior and promoting student achievement (Gettinger & Stoiber, 1999). Although the volume of process-outcome research has slowed in recent years, researchers continue to affirm that teachers make a difference in school learning. Process-outcome research has been successful in identifying management and instructional variables associated with high student performance. As such, process-outcome research (and more recent applications of this paradigm) has moved the field of teaching closer to being a science, that is, beyond unsupported claims about effective classroom methods toward evidence-based teaching practices derived from credible data.

The purpose of this chapter is to review process-outcome research linking classroom processes to student performance. The specific objectives are to trace the evolution of process-outcome research, identify the strengths and limitations of this approach, summarize key findings related to effective teaching and classroom management, and demonstrate how this knowledge translates into classroom practices.

HISTORY OF RESEARCH ON TEACHING AND THE PROCESS-OUTCOME PARADIGM

Research on teaching, including process-outcome research, has a relatively short history. In their 1974 review, Dunkin and Biddle described four types of variables in teaching research: (a) *presage* variables (characteristics such as age, sex, social class, training experiences, attitudes, beliefs, expectations, and abilities that teachers and students bring to the teaching-learning situation); (b) *context* variables (grade level, subject matter, instructional objectives, class size, and other features of the context within which teaching and learning take place); (c) *process* variables (behaviors or events that transpire during the teaching-learning process, including ways in which teachers and students behave and interact); and (d) *product* variables (measurable indices of the outcomes of instruction, such as achievement, attitudes, or classroom behavior). This categorization is useful for understanding the evolution of a process-outcome paradigm within the overall context of research on teaching.

The earliest studies of factors associated with quality of teaching occurred during the 1950s and 1960s, and focused primarily on presage variables, such as teachers' verbal ability, warmth, intelligence, educational background, and knowledge of subject matter (Shulman, 1986). This line of research diminished in the late 1960s and gave way to new approaches to the study of teaching. Specifically, process-product research was initiated during the 1960s and increased significantly throughout the 1970s and 1980s (Hoffman, 1986). During this time, many researchers concentrated on identifying teacher actions (processes) linked directly to student learning and behavior (products or outcomes).

Two forms of process-outcome research were prominent during the 1970s. The first was school-effects research, which identified system-level characteristics of schools that were successful in promoting high achievement and positive classroom behavior among students. This work identified several process variables relating to student outcomes, such as strong administrative leadership, positive teacher attitudes, safe and orderly school climate, and parent involvement (Bickel, 1999; Stringfield & Herman, 1997). The second type of process-outcome research was teacher-effects research. This work identified teacher behaviors and patterns of teacher-student interactions associated with student performance. Using primarily teacher observation instruments and measures of student achievement, researchers sought to identify skills or behaviors exhibited with high frequency among effective teachers, for example, how they organized the classroom, introduced lessons, asked questions, or provided feedback (Good, 1996). The results of this process-product tradition yielded findings that continue to influence teaching and teacher education today.

One of the earliest classroom researchers to examine the link between teachers' actions and students' classroom behavior was J. S. Kounin. Born out of an ecological approach, Kounin's (1970) most influential work was entitled *Discipline and Group Management in Classrooms*. The program of research described in his book was undertaken to characterize the nature of teaching-learning processes in effectively versus ineffectively managed classrooms. Effective managers were defined as teachers whose classrooms were orderly, with minimum student misbehavior and high levels of on-task behavior. Contrary to expectations, Kounin found that effective and ineffective managers did not differ in their methods for responding to misbehavior. Instead, effective managers were more skilled at preventing disruptions from occurring in the first place.

Kounin identified specific behaviors (processes) associated with keeping students focused on learning and therefore minimizing classroom disruptions (products). These included: (a) *withitness*, communicating through their behavior that teachers know what students are doing and what is happening in their classrooms, and catching events early before they escalate into problems; (b) *overlapping ability*, attending to different events simultaneously, without being diverted by a disruption or other activity; (c) *lesson smoothness and momentum*, conducting smooth and brisk-paced lessons and providing continuous activity signals (e.g., standing near inattentive students, directing questions to potentially disruptive students); (d) *group altering*, involving all students in recitation tasks and keeping them alerted to the task at hand; and (e) *stimulating seatwork*, providing seatwork with sufficient variety and challenge. Kounin's initial findings on successful classroom management were the driving force behind subsequent effective-teaching research conducted during the 1970s and 1980s. Researchers not only replicated Kounin's findings, they also derived more detailed lists of behaviors associated with effective teaching and classroom management; researchers also extended Kounin's findings by documenting a strong correlation between classroom management and student achievement.

An expanding focus on context variables, combined with concerns surrounding a narrow application of process-product findings (explained later in this chapter), led to a greater emphasis on the cognitive complexities of teaching and classrooms throughout the 1980s and 1990s, and subsequent emergence of an alternate research paradigm. Referred to as the interpretive paradigm, this line of inquiry focused on understanding the complexity of teachers' actions, their interactions with students, and diverse teaching-learning contexts (Shulman, 1986). The shift away from a strict process-product paradigm was catalyzed, in part, by concerns that process-product relationships failed to reflect the dynamic nature of classroom contexts (Cochran-Smith & Lytle, 1990). Interpretive researchers focus on indicators of effectiveness that are context-specific (e.g., teachers' decision-making within content-specific domains) and use measures of higher-order outcomes that go beyond what can be observed or measured on a standardized test (e.g., students' problem-solving). For example, within an interpretive approach, teachers may be interviewed about their thinking while engaged in lesson planning, and students asked to describe their approaches to solving problems or learning concepts (e.g., Swing, Stoiber, & Peterson, 1988). In his review of teaching research in the third *Handbook of Research on Teaching*, Shulman (1986) characterized these fundamentally different views of teaching in the following manner: On the process-product side, teaching is a "science in search of laws." (p.9) On the interpretive side, however, teaching is viewed as an "exercise of interpretation in search of meaning." (p.9)

PROCESS-OUTCOME RESEARCH: DESCRIPTION AND METHODOLOGY

The primary goal of process-outcome research is to determine relationships between classroom processes and student performance, with the intent of identifying teaching practices and behaviors associated with students' learning and appropriate classroom behavior. Relying heavily on empiricism, early process-outcome research focused primarily on overt, low-inference teacher behaviors, and the relation between the frequency of these behaviors and measurable student outcomes or products. Although research has included additional process measures, such as high-inference ratings, teacher interviews, and narrative recordings, variables quantified through low-inference coding procedures are more prominent in published reports because they typically demonstrate the strongest association with student outcomes.

Process-product research, therefore, can be characterized on the basis of several methodological features (Floden, 2001). In the typical process-outcome study, teachers are observed at work in their classrooms. Teaching and classroom interactions are described in a series of low-inference behavioral categories, often mutually exclusive and exhaustive, such that any classroom event may be coded in one and only one way. Which teaching processes to observe are often pre-determined on the basis of extant research or hypothesized relationships. For example, if growth in reading comprehension is an expected outcome, the researcher may select levels of teacher questioning as one process to observe. In this instance, the researcher attempts to discover the degree to which certain kinds of teacher questions relate to growth in reading comprehension. During an observation period, observers monitor and record teaching behaviors. Achievement is measured prior to and following the period of observation. If the level of the targeted outcome (e.g., achievement) changes from pre- to post-observation, the relationship between observed instructional processes and changes in outcome are analyzed. Specifically, the coded frequencies of behaviors are aggregated across the teacher sample, and then related to student achievement measures. Relationships between patterns of teaching behaviors and student outcomes are determined statistically through correlations (Richardson, 1994).

Process-outcome researchers have often followed a descriptive-correlational-experimental sequence in programmatic studies on effective teaching and classroom management (Rosenshine & Furst, 1973). This involves a systematic progression through cycles of observation, correlation, and experimentation. First, researchers conduct classroom observations to identify teaching behaviors, interactions, and other classroom events that vary in frequency across classrooms and are expected to relate to student performance. Second, correlational studies are conducted to document positive associations between teaching-learning processes and student outcomes. Finally, empirical studies are conducted in which experimental teachers receive training in effective teaching behaviors (derived from descriptive and correlational research), while control group teachers do not. Achievement and classroom behavior of students are compared between experimental and control teachers (Borich, 1988). Experimental studies based on process-outcome relationships were the focus for much research during the 1980s and early 1990s.

One of the most significant contributions to the advent of process-product research was the emphasis on measurement of classroom processes through systematic observation, and the subsequent proliferation of classroom observation systems. By 1970, there were more than 100 classroom observation systems, most developed for teacher training purposes (Rosenshine & Furst, 1973). These observation systems gradually became more sophisticated, comprehensive, and widely used. With advances in observation technology, researchers were able to focus directly on the process of instruction and its effect on students' learning and behavior.

An illustration of a process measurement tool is the *Classroom Observation Keyed for Effectiveness Research* (COKER; Medley, Coker, & Soar, 1984). This system requires trained observers to code all keys observed during a specified time period. *Keys* refer to discrete teacher competencies, performance, or behaviors. For example, one key under the dimension "Learner Reinforcement and Involvement" is "maintains environment in which students are actively involved." Observation systems such as COKER have both strengths and limitations. Foremost among the strengths is the potential for reliable measurement and documentation of relationships between observed classroom processes and student outcomes, such as achievement or on-task behavior. Among the weaknesses of such observation systems is the limited focus on internal events, such as teacher cognitions, which are typically accessible through more subjective measures, for example, interviews, diaries, or other narrative, self-report indices.

To address this concern, Englert, Tarrant, and Mariage (1992) developed a measure for evaluating preservice teachers, which included low-inference checklists derived from process-product relationships, as well as items relating to more qualitative dimensions of instruction. Similar to traditional process-product measures, the first four checklists on Englert et al.'s measure examine observable dimensions of classrooms and teacher behavior, including classroom management (Is the classroom set up to minimize disruptions due to traffic patterns?), time management (Is transition time between activities kept to a minimum?), lesson presentation

(Does the teacher maintain a brisk pace during the lesson?), and seatwork management (Does the teacher frequently circulate to assist students during seatwork?). All items are rated using a scale ranging from 1 (needs work) to 5 (excellent). Englert et al. enriched their process analysis by adding checklists designed to incorporate qualitative dimensions of teaching and social contexts of instruction. Specifically, items focusing on classroom dialogues, meaningful contexts, responsive instruction, and classroom community were added. Checklists of this sort lend themselves to the same kind of studies as process-product observation measures, but are more comprehensive in nature.

CRITICISMS OF PROCESS-OUTCOME RESEARCH

Process-outcome research has produced a significant knowledge base linking teacher behavior and classroom practices with student performance. Despite these important contributions, process-outcome research has been criticized on multiple grounds, including conceptual, methodological, and application (Gage & Needels, 1989). In reviewing these criticisms, however, it is important to note that concerns surrounding process-outcome research relate more to how findings have been interpreted and used by administrators and educators than to the manner in which the research has been conducted.

Conceptual Concerns

The most vocal critics believe that a process-outcome perspective perpetuates a mechanistic conceptualization of the teaching-learning process, that is, that teaching is "acting out" a set of predetermined behaviors (Cochran-Smith & Lytle, 1990). Critics contend that process-outcome research views teaching as a linear activity, such that if a teacher performs certain actions, then students will achieve high outcomes. Although process-outcome researchers seek to identify patterns of teacher behavior and teacher-student interactions that influence student performance, few researchers embrace such a restricted view of teaching (Berliner, 1990).

Similarly, critics contend that process-outcome research fails to take into account important context variables relating to both teaching and student outcomes. Examples of context variables missing from some process-outcome relationships are students' social class and ability level, grade level, subject matter, as well as instructional features, such as classroom grouping formats, degree of teacher- versus student-initiated learning, nature of tasks (new information vs. recitation and drill), and context within which feedback occurs (e.g., following correct, incorrect vs. no response). Critics argue that a search for universal process-product relationships may disregard important presage and context variables. Indeed, the generality of any process-outcome relationship is variable; some may have wide generality, whereas others may be specific to particular grade levels or types of students (Gage, 1978). Furthermore, the stability of classroom process measures from one observation to another may depend as much on context as on observer accuracy. Thus, process-product research, by necessity, is confined to specific classroom contexts (Westbury, 1988). For example, presenting new information through demonstration or lecture is different than conducting a discussion of content students have already learned; combining process data across these two different teaching situations will likely mask key process variables that might be discovered by studying them separately. In other words, each instructional context has specific objectives and anticipated outcomes (e.g., skill acquisition, knowledge application) that warrant individual study, not aggregated analysis. This criticism, however, may not constitute a valid concern for much process-outcome research, which aggregates findings across similar, not dissimilar, teaching-learning situations and tends to limit generalization to specific contexts.

Methodological Concerns

Methodological criticisms have centered primarily around the validity and reliability of certain measurement procedures sometimes used in process-outcome research. For example, process-product research may be conducted within specific subject-content areas and during short periods of time. This has led critics to question whether teacher actions that are observed and recorded during one time period are reliable and representative of their actions during unobserved periods (Westbury, 1988). Furthermore, using standardized achievement tests as a student outcome measure (although responsive to the public's interest in high-stakes testing) raises questions about content validity, particularly when test items are not aligned with the content of instruction. Critics also claim that a focus on achievement and on-task behavior as student outcomes may not give sufficient attention to a teacher's success in fostering positive student attitudes, personal development, good peer relationships, and other indices of effectiveness (Gage & Needels, 1989).

Additional methodological concerns relate to the adequacy of data to support reliable and valid interpretations of process-outcome relationships. Some studies, for example, have based conclusions on a few hours of classroom observation. Although limited observation time may be sufficient for ratings of teacher characteristics, such as warmth or enthusiasm, more extended observation is required to evaluate process variables, such as questioning styles, feedback to students, and clarity of explanations (Berliner, 1990).

Application Concerns

The most critical concerns relate to the interpretation and application of process-outcome findings, not the research per se. Some school districts, for example, provide professional development based on limited results of process-outcome research and have attempted to translate research findings directly into instruments for evaluating teachers. Such efforts represent a misapplication of process-outcome research and tend to enforce a prescriptive set of uniform teaching behaviors with limited regard to diverse content, curriculum, or student ability (Darling-Hammond, 1996; Richardson, 1994). Critics, including process-outcome researchers, agree that the application of process-outcome findings should avoid an oversimplification of results and naive misuse by policy makers. For example, research has shown that different, but functionally equivalent, paths may lead to similar student outcomes (Berliner, 1990). Therefore, data linking specific teaching behaviors to student performance ought not to be the sole basis for teacher evaluation. For example, in some classrooms, students demonstrate above-average math achievement even when high levels of off-task talking and behavior are coded during independent math work periods. In this case, teachers should not be penalized for failing to follow behavioral prescriptions derived from process-outcome research to increase rates of on-task behavior.

Process-outcome researchers have been successful in responding to many of these criticisms. Needels and Gage (1991) noted that many critics have faulted the incidental characteristics of process-outcome research, "without realizing they were attacking nothing essential to the enterprise" (p. 8). For example, process-outcome research has been criticized because of its focus on simplistic variables that fail to reflect the complex nature of teaching. Nothing inherent in a process-outcome paradigm, however, prevents an analysis of other variables, including context or cognitive processes. Indeed, many process-outcome researchers focus on complex, cognitive aspects of teaching. A focus on observable behaviors typically associated with process-outcome research is what Needels and Gage call an "accident" of process-product research, not the "essence" of the approach. Likewise, the specific methods for measuring process and outcome variables are "accidents" of process-product research, not the "essence." Thus, measurement of process variables in process-outcome research may legitimately include audiotapes, videotapes, questionnaires, interviews, and anecdotal self-recordings or narrative journals by teachers. Similarly, measurement of product variables may include authentic achievement measures (e.g., criterion-referenced measures, curriculum-based probes, work samples), as well as task engagement and active responding among students. Finally, process-outcome researchers have begun to employ statistical procedures beyond a correlation coefficient to establish the relation between process and product, including path analysis, single-cases studies, and ethnographic studies (Floden, 2001).

Research from the Beginning Teacher Evaluation Study (BTES) is a good example of researchers maintaining the essence of process-outcome research, while modifying the measurement of student outcomes (Fisher et al., 1978). BTES researchers, in particular, sought an indicator of teacher effectiveness that could be located in the observable "real time" performance of students at the time of recording teacher processes, without waiting for end-of-year achievement tests. In early process-outcome studies, frequencies of teacher behaviors were typically correlated with performance on tests administered 2–9 months following the time that teacher behaviors were actually observed, as opposed to at that point in time (Cochran-Smith & Lytle, 1990). The result of the efforts of BTES researchers was the specification of a new outcome variable—*academic learning time* (ALT). ALT research is concerned with identifying management practices and teaching strategies that maximize the time students are actively engaged in learning activities (e.g., receiving instruction, completing assigned work, reading, doing projects, etc.). A focus on ALT was based on research demonstrating a consistent link between the amount of time students are actively engaged in learning and their level of achievement (Gettinger, 1986). Process-outcome studies have established that teachers' use of effective management strategies is associated with a high level of ALT, which is linked with high achievement.

PROCESS-OUTCOME RESEARCH FINDINGS

Despite the criticisms noted above, process-outcome findings are considered key elements of effective teaching and classroom management (Brandt, 1992). Furthermore, process-outcome research has demonstrated that effective-teaching processes contribute to outcomes beyond achievement gains; there are significant benefits in terms of task engagement, active learning, motivation, and positive attitudes that prevent misbehavior. In other words, effective teaching is related to a teacher's ability to use appropriate management strategies while also providing high-quality instruction (Munk & Repp, 1994). The purpose of this section is to provide a synthesis of principles of effective teaching and classroom management that have emerged from process-outcome classroom research. The wealth of information on producing high achievement and appropriate behavior has progressed to a well-established knowledge base (Duffy, 1990). While not exhaustive, the findings discussed later are among the more interpretable and better replicated of those produced by this line of research. Process-outcome research views teaching practices broadly, to include classroom management and instructional variables designed to promote positive behavior and achieve learning.

Classroom Management Variables

Classroom management relates to classroom structure and organization and rests on a teacher's ability to educate diverse students within a complicated and sometimes challenging classroom context. Research has identified several structural and organizational classroom processes that contribute to positive student outcomes (Rosenshine, 1997).

Classroom Rules. Classroom rules are an integral part of effective classroom management; they refer to general expectations or standards for classroom conduct for all students. The manner in which teachers are successful in establishing, teaching, and enforcing rules has been well documented (Doyle, 1984, 1986; Emmer & Evertson, 1981; Emmer, Evertson, & Anderson, 1980; Evertson & Emmer, 1982b). First, effective classroom managers approach the teaching of classroom rules as systematically and methodically as teaching academic content. Evertson and Emmer (1982a) observed that effective teachers explain, practice, and review classroom rules until students master them. Second, effective managers communicate clearly to students their expectations for behavior; they provide explicit information about what "good behavior" is and how students can achieve it (Gettinger, 1988). Rules that are stated positively are taught and enforced more effectively than long lists of prohibited behaviors. For example, "raise your hand to speak" is preferable to "no talking" because it clearly explains the desired behavior and what action students should take. Furthermore, effective managers are more likely to have rules in a written form, either posted or provided to students to include in a notebook (Rhode, Jenson, & Reavis, 1993). Finally, several researchers (e.g., Evertson, 1987; Gettinger, 1988; McKee & Witt, 1990; Paine, Radicchi, Rosellini, Deutchman, & Darch, 1983; Rhode et al., 1993) have demonstrated that simply stating rules is ineffective in preventing problem behavior; teachers must also demonstrate a willingness and ability to act when rules are violated. Thus, effective teachers inform students about the consequences of breaking rules, carefully monitor compliance, and enforce rule-violation consequences consistently.

Smooth Transitions Between Activities. More than 30 transitions occur every day in elementary classrooms, accounting for approximately 15% of classroom time (Burns, 1984; Gump, 1982; Rosenshine, 1980). Thus, increasing compliance during transition from one task to another is particularly important for maximizing learning time and minimizing misbehavior (Gettinger, 1986). Doyle (1984) found that transitions disrupt time flow in classrooms, and that disruptive pupil behaviors increase significantly during unstructured transitions. To facilitate smooth transitions, skilled teachers foreshadow and clearly signal the onset of transitions, actively structure and orchestrate transitions, and minimize the loss of momentum during these changes in activities. Less effective managers, conversely, tend to blend activities together; they fail to monitor events during transitions and take excessive time to complete the movement between activities (Doyle, 1984).

Effective teachers also employ strategies to move through transitions rapidly, in ways that minimize student frustration and disruption. These include providing students with beginning-of-year instruction and practice in how to execute transition routines efficiently (Gettinger, 1988), training students to respond to a standard signal (Anderson, Evertson, & Emmer, 1980), and providing students with overlapping assignments in a sequence (Wyne & Struck, 1982). Results from a recent study documented the benefits of a high-probability instructional sequence for increasing group compliance during transition periods (Ardoin, Martens, & Wolfe, 1999). This procedure involves the rapid presentation of three high-probability instructions (directives with which students are likely to comply), immediately preceding a directive with a low probability of compliance. For example, in directing students to transition to a new activity, a teacher might instruct students to "touch their head," "shake their fingers," "clap their hands," and, finally, "take out their morning calendars." According to Ardoin et al. (1999), this type of high-probability sequence increases the likelihood of compliance with low-probability directives to make transitions to academic activities.

Beginning-of-Year Management Activities. Educators have long assumed that what happens in a classroom during the first few weeks of the school year is critical for establishing and maintaining classroom order throughout the year (Anderson et al., 1980; Brophy, 1983;

Evertson & Harris, 1992). In a series of studies conducted in both elementary and secondary schools, researchers developed detailed information about how teachers handle the first days and first weeks of the school year (Emmer et al., 1980; Evertson & Emmer, 1982a; Freiberg, Stein, & Huang, 1995; Gottfredson, Gottfredson, & Hybl, 1993). In general, more effective classroom managers in elementary schools spend considerable time during the first weeks helping students learn classroom routines and procedures. Evertson and Emmer (1982a) obtained similar results in a study of junior high school teachers, with some notable differences. Although junior high school teachers provided clear communication about classroom expectations and monitored compliance carefully during the first few weeks of school, they did not spend as much time as elementary teachers in providing explicit, guided instruction for carrying out step-by-step classroom routines.

Emmer and colleagues (Emmer, Sanford, Evertson, Clements, & Martin, 1981) conducted evaluation studies in which they provided training to teachers on beginning-of-year management techniques associated with high student performance. Overall, they found that teachers can be trained to implement beginning-of-year strategies with integrity, and that doing so resulted in less disruptive and greater on-task behavior among students throughout the year, compared to students of teachers who did not receive training. Similarly, Freiberg et al. (1995) evaluated the effects of a classroom management program on student behavior and achievement in inner-city elementary schools. The program, called the Consistency Management Program (CMP), included a beginning-of-year emphasis on teaching classroom rules and routines. Teachers who received training with the CMP had better attendance, more positive attitudes, and higher achievement among their students compared to control teachers who had not received the training. Collectively, these findings suggest that beginning-of-year management training is a successful and cost-efficient staff development activity for teachers.

Efficient Use of Learning Time. Using learning time efficiently and keeping students engaged in learning are key processes operating in effective classrooms. Even in well-managed classrooms, noninstructional activities can consume up to 50% of available instructional time (Jones & Jones, 2001). Inevitably, teachers must allocate some portion of their school day for noninstructional tasks, including procedural activities (sharpening pencils, turning in and passing out papers, getting books), waiting for help from a teacher or peer, and other off-task behaviors (socializing, daydreaming, misbehaving). It is possible, however, for teachers to minimize the loss of available instructional time by engaging in behaviors associated with what has been termed an interactive teaching approach (Gettinger, 1988). Interactive teaching behaviors include (a) moving around a classroom to monitor students' performance at regular intervals and to communicate awareness of students' behavior and progress, (b) minimizing time spent in noninstructional activities (e.g., changing activities, organizing materials for lessons, conducting clerical jobs) by relying on written rules and fast-paced, routinized classroom procedures, and (c) using proactive classroom management methods to prevent disruptive behaviors that interfere with classroom learning and contribute to lost instructional time (Berliner, 1988; Brophy & Good, 1986; Gettinger, 1988, 1995; Moskowitz & Hayman, 1976; Murphy, 1992).

Monitoring Student Performance. Monitoring student performance is a critical aspect of classroom management. Effective teachers have been shown to monitor student behavior in three ways. First, teachers monitor the entire classroom, and attend to what is happening and how the class is functioning as a whole. Second, teachers observe individual conduct or behavior, responding to incidents of student misbehavior promptly and consistently (Emmer et al., 1980; Evertson & Emmer, 1982a). Third, teachers monitor the pace, rhythm, and duration of classroom activities and assignments. In one procedure, for example, decisions about the pace of instruction are determined by monitoring the completion rates of a "steering criterion group," that is students between the 10h and 25th percentiles in terms of overall ability (Gettinger, 1995). In another procedure, the duration of classroom activities is determined by estimates of attention span and work completion rates among students (Atwood, 1983). Evertson and Emmer (1982b) found that effective managers (a) keep track of how students are progressing, (b) determine if students are able to complete assignments, (c) monitor students at the beginning of activities to detect any problems in being able to complete the assignments, (d) and grade student work regularly and frequently. Ongoing evaluation and modification of instructional programs has also been shown to increase academic achievement, particularly when paired with systematic collection, graphing, and review of progress-monitoring data (Fuchs & Fuchs, 1986).

Progress monitoring ensures that students move through instruction with at least moderate success and minimal frustration, and, in so doing, promotes positive classroom behavior. Systematic and repeated monitoring of student performance enables teachers to match instructional tasks to students' skill level. For example, when students work independently without direct teacher supervision, tasks should be calibrated at a level that will allow students to succeed with reasonable effort. High success rates (90–100% accuracy) are desirable when students work independently or with peers for extended periods without teacher supervision; slightly lower success rates (80%) are acceptable when the teacher is present to scaffold students' learning and provide immediate feedback.

Communicating awareness of the classroom behavior. Teachers' ability to communicate with students contributes to effective classroom management (Brooks, 1985; Brophy, 1979, 1982). Process-outcome research has identified two types of communicative behaviors exhibited more often by effective versus ineffective managers (Anderson et al., 1980; Brooks, 1985; Brophy, 1982; Doyle, 1986). First, effective teachers convey purposefulness about school learning through several communicative actions: (a) holding students accountable for completing work on time, (b) scheduling regular times with students each day to review completed work (e.g., daily morning group review of homework), (c) circulating through the room during seatwork periods, (d) requiring participation by all students during group activities, (e) implementing standard procedures for turning in work and noting progress, and (f) providing feedback to students about their performance (Gettinger, 1988).

A second characteristic of effective teachers is their ability to maintain awareness of what is going on in the classroom, and, equally important, to communicate this awareness to students. Such "withitness" is associated with student achievement and positive classroom behavior (Brooks, 1985; Evertson & Emmer, 1982b). Communicating awareness prevents the initiation and spread of off-task and disruptive behavior, and, thus, minimizes the need for reprimands and redirection. Successful classroom mangers are concrete, explicit, and thorough in their communications to students. Furthermore, they convey situational awareness by commenting frequently on events as they are occurring in the class (Doyle, 1984; Emmer et al., 1980; Evertson & Emmer, 1982b; Good & Brophy, 2000).

Instructional Variables

Effective instruction is associated with effective classroom management. With instruction that is well-planned, fast-paced, and successful in maintaining high engagement, teachers are able to increase student achievement, while preventing the occurrence of challenging behaviors in the classroom (Munk & Repp, 1994). Process-outcome research has identified several features of instruction that enhance student learning and promote positive classroom behaviors; these are described below.

Teacher-Directed Learning. Research has consistently documented a strong connection between teacher-directed instruction and student achievement and learning behaviors (Gettinger & Stoiber, 1999; Good & Brophy, 2000; Rosenshine, 1979, 1986). Three instructional practices characterize teacher-directed instruction: instructional clarity, academic focus, and teachers' willingness to accept accountability for ensuring that students learn.

Instructional clarity relates to how teachers organize academic content, the questioning strategies they use, and the degree to which achievement expectations are communicated and understood by learners (Chilcoat, 1989; Cruickshank, 1985). Clarity in instruction relates positively to multiple outcomes including learner satisfaction, achievement, and student engagement (Hines, Cruickshank, & Kennedy, 1985). High clarity is achieved when explanations of content proceed in a step-by-step fashion, illustrations and applications of content are provided, and questions are posed to assess, develop, and extend students' understanding (Good & Brophy, 2000; McCaleb & White, 1980; Smith & Land, 1981). Clear instruction also contributes to higher-order learning and helps students make connections among ideas, both within and across lessons. Whether in textbooks or through teacher presentations, information is easier to learn when it is coherent, that is, the sequence of ideas makes sense and the relationships among them are explicit (Beck & McKeown, 1988). Lessons in which students perceive linkages among ideas (by using advanced organizers, highlighting connections, or summarizing key concepts) contribute to better understanding, retention, and application of knowledge compared to lessons in which these interconnections are not explicit (Kindsvatter, Wilen, & Ishler, 1988; Knapp, 1995).

McCaleb and White (1980) delineated five elements of instructional clarity: (a) linking new information to the learners' present knowledge; (b) organizing presentations by stating the purpose, reviewing main ideas, and providing transitions between sections; (c) sequencing or arranging information in an order conducive to learning; (d) explaining and connecting new concepts through examples, illustrations, or analogues; and (e) using appropriate volume, pacing, and articulation. In addition to characterizing instructional clarity, researchers have also identified teacher behaviors that have the effect of diminishing clarity. For example, teacher presentations lack clarity and are less effective when they use vague terms and "mazes" (false starts or halts in speech, redundantly spoken words, or tangles of words) (Smith & Land, 1981). Another behavior that detracts from clarity is discontinuity, that is, when a teacher interrupts the flow of the lesson by interjecting irrelevant content or mentioning relevant content at inappropriate times (Cotton, 1995). The best way to assess instructional clarity is to monitor students' understanding of content presented. Frequent signs of student frustration, confusion, or misunderstanding typically signal problems in teacher clarity (Cruickshank, 1985).

Academic focus refers to the degree to which teaching is oriented toward maximizing students' opportunities to learn and the extent to which lessons and activities are related to learning goals (Shuell, 1996). In general, students learn more when the majority of available instructional time is allocated to curriculum-related activities and the classroom management system is effective in maintaining engagement in those activities. Effective teachers allocate most of their classroom time to activities designed to accomplish instructional goals, rather than to nonacademic activities (Burns, 1984). Students of effective teachers spend more hours each year on curriculum-related activities than do students of teachers who are less focused on academic goals (Good, 1996; Waxman, Huang, Anderson, & Weinstein, 1997; Waxman & Walberg, 1991; Weinhart & Helmke, 1995). Teachers with a strong academic focus also convey a sense of purposefulness and importance for maximizing the effectiveness of available time. For example, they begin and end lessons on time, teach students how to get started on activities quickly, and maintain students' focus when working on assignments (through cuing, questioning, etc.) (Duffy, Roehler, Meloth, & Vavrus, 1986). Classrooms with a strong academic focus also incorporate a higher proportion of interactive instruction (e.g., scaffolding, questioning, prompting, discussion, high-participation formats) than solitary seatwork or extended lecture presentations. Despite some concerns that a strong academic orientation minimizes affective outcomes, research demonstrates that students actually acquire more positive attitudes and higher motivation toward school in classrooms where teachers place greater emphasis on academic content than on affective or procedural issues (Berliner, 1988; Fuchs, Fuchs, & Phillips, 1994).

Finally, teachers who elicit strong achievement gains accept responsibility for doing so. Effective teachers believe they have the ability and responsibility for teaching students successfully and that students, in turn, are capable of learning. In fact, research has shown a positive association between teacher accountability and self-efficacy and student performance (Gettinger & Stoiber, 1999). If students do not learn something the first time, accountable teachers teach it again, and, if the regular curriculum materials do not do the job, they find or develop others that will. For example, effective teachers tend to rely less on scripted curriculum materials and sequences for instruction, and more on personalized and individualized lessons (Wang, Haertel, & Walberg, 1994). Effective teachers follow a systematic, but flexible, approach to classroom teaching. They use lecture and demonstration formats to present new information and concepts; they engage students in recitation and discussion by asking questions and providing feedback; they adequately prepare students for independent seatwork by giving explicit instructions and modeling with practice examples; they carefully monitor students' progress during independent work periods; and they provide appropriate feedback and re-teaching when necessary. In sum, effective teachers take an active role to ensure that students learn academic content, instead of relying exclusively on a specific curriculum.

High Level of Active Student Involvement or Responding. The amount of time students are actively engaged in learning is a strong determinant of achievement (Gettinger, 1986). Certain teaching practices have been shown to maximize engagement among students. For example, high-participation formats that encourage active responding, such as discussion, group problem-solving activities, cooperative learning, and peer-assisted learning, are more strongly associated with student engagement than low-participation activities, such as reading silently, listening or watching other students, or working alone (Gettinger, 1995; Paine et al., 1983). Research also demonstrates that students have a higher preference for activities that allow them to respond actively.

A high frequency of teacher-directed questioning and answering is also associated with achievement, especially in the acquisition of basic arithmetic and reading skills (Coker, Lorentz, & Coker, 1980; Phillips, Fuchs, Fuchs, & Hamlett, 1996; Stallings, Needels, & Stayrook, 1979). Effective teachers ask many questions to encourage active student involvement. In a study of junior high school mathematics and English instruction, for example, the most effective teachers asked an average of 24 questions during a 50-minute period, whereas the least effective teachers asked an average of only 8.6 questions (Evertson, Anderson, Anderson & Brophy, 1980). Asking questions is critical because it elicits a high level of active student responding. One approach to maximize the frequency of active responding among all students, while using a minimum amount of instructional time, is group or choral responding. Choral responding that requires students to answer in unison or in response to a teacher signal (e.g., hand gesture, verbal cue) is associated with high achievement among primary-grade students, especially in developing word-recognition skills (Becker, 1988). This instructional technique has been shown to be more appropriate for small-group than whole-class learning and most effective for younger (elementary) children.

Another process for maximizing student response rates is to increase learning trial rates. By completing more learning trials within a fixed period of time, student learning may increase without increasing total allocated time. Skinner, Fletcher, and Henington (1996) outlined four procedures that increase both learning trial rates and on-task behavior during teacher-led instruction. These include: (a) reducing inter-trial intervals (the time between the end of one trial and the beginning of the next trial), (b) matching wait time to the type of task (e.g., longer wait times following comprehension questions versus shorter wait times following factual questions; Rowe, 1986), (c) using choral or unison responding (Becker, 1988), and (d) using individual response cards on which all students write responses to teacher-directed questions (Narayan, Heward, & Gardner, 1990). Because these types of procedures are time efficient, teachers rate them as acceptable, and, in turn, typically implement them with a high degree of integrity. Moreover, Narayen et al. (1990) demonstrated that instructional techniques, such as response cards, are also preferred by students (over raising their hand) and contribute to higher engagement and less disruptive behavior among students.

Guided Student Practice to Promote Success. The purpose of guided practice is to scaffold students' learning and task engagement. In using guided practice, teachers incorporate multiple and varied opportunities for students to apply new knowledge, and they provide error-correction and re-teaching as needed so that students can work independently (Rosenshine & Meister, 1992). Skills that are practiced to the point of automaticity are retained and applied more successfully than skills that are mastered only partially (Brophy & Alleman, 1991). Thus, effective teachers incorporate periodic practice and review, and provide opportunities for students to use knowledge and skills in a variety of application contexts (Dempster, 1991).

How teachers guide student practice is another important instructional process linked to student performance. The effectiveness of practice is enhanced when teachers first explain the work and demonstrate practice examples before releasing students to work independently. Effective teachers then circulate to monitor progress and provide help when needed. Guided practice involves providing assistance that students need to engage in learning activities productively and independently, including explanations, modeling, coaching, and other forms of scaffolding. It also involves a systematic and gradual diminishing of teacher guidance as students' competence develops (Rosenshine & Meister, 1992).

Finally, to be useful, guided practice must involve opportunities not only to apply skills, but also to receive timely feedback. Effective teachers frequently check for student understanding so they can provide correction and explanation, as needed (Good & Grouws, 1979). Guided practice relies on frequent assessments of students' understanding and their ability to apply skills or strategies, combined with feedback that is informative, rather than evaluative. Such feedback helps students evaluate their progress relative to goals and to correct errors or misunderstanding (Stipek, 1993). Although students perform better and are more engaged in classrooms in which they receive frequent feedback about their performance, teachers may not always use feedback appropriately. The key to effectiveness lies in the quality rather than frequency of corrective feedback. Learning whether an answer is right or wrong has a limited effect on learning and performance (Waxman & Walberg, 1991). To be effective, feedback (including praise) should incorporate (a) a high degree of specificity, with explicit reference to the standard or objective to be achieved; (b) information about accuracy, or the results achieved in meeting the standard; and (c) recommendations about alternate methods for meeting the objective (Kindsvatter et al., 1988).

Flexible Instruction to Match Student Needs. Differentiating instruction for groups or individual students is necessary when classroom composition is heterogeneous. According to Wang, Haertel, and Walberg (1993), for any type of instruction to be effective, it must be appropriate to the students' levels. Daly, Martens, Kilmer, and Massie (1996) found that the greatest gains in oral reading accuracy occurred when instructional reading materials were matched to the students' skill level and assessment tasks were similar to those used during instruction. Researchers have identified methods used by teachers use to accommodate the needs of diverse learners in their classrooms (e.g., Evans, 1985; Evertson, Sanford, & Emmer, 1981; Mevarech & Kramarski, 1997). In general, as the heterogeneity of a classroom increases, the amount of whole-class instruction is reduced, and teachers rely more on individual assignments, peer-assisted learning, and small-group work. One approach that has gained considerable support in recent years is class-wide peer tutoring. Results from a 12-year longitudinal study demonstrate that class-wide peer tutoring significantly increases students' engagement during instruction, contributes to student achievement gains, reduces the number of students needing special education services, and reduces the number of dropouts by 12th grade (Greenwood, 1991; Greenwood & Delquadri, 1995; Greenwood, Delquadri, & Hall, 1993). In addition to promoting high achievement, fewer behavior disruptions also occur when teachers are able to adapt their teaching to individual differences among learners (Fuchs, Fuchs, Phillips, & Simmons, 1993).

Despite these positive outcomes, some critics have expressed concern that differentiated instruction may fail to meet the need for challenge and complex learning tasks among high-achieving students (Newmann, 1992). Brantlinger (1993) has demonstrated, however, that differentiated teaching contributes to social-emotional benefits that outweigh the potential educational costs. Specifically, differentiating instruction in general education classrooms is associated with higher motivation and task persistence, self-efficacy, and more positive attitudes toward learning among all learners.

Cooperative Learning Strategies. There is much to be gained by having students participate in small-group learning. Cooperative learning has positive effects on both task engagement and student achievement, especially when instruction is carefully structured, individual students are accountable for performance, and a well-defined group reward system is used (Bennett & Dunne, 1992; Cohen, 1994; Johnson & Johnson, 1994; Slavin, 1994). Cooperative learning has gained popularity in schools; 79% of elementary teachers and 62% of middle school teachers report making some sustained use of cooperative learning (Puma, Jones, Rock, & Fernandez, 1993). Research examining the effects of group composition and the nature of students' interaction during group learning has contributed significantly to our understanding of effective cooperative learning structures (Bennett & Cass, 1988; Peterson, Stark, & Waas, 1984; Swing & Peterson, 1982; Webb, 1982, 1991; Webb, Troper, & Fall, 1995). For example, the level of student achievement is related to the nature of students' experiences within a cooperative small group. Students who know what questions to ask and how to succeed in getting their questions answered are more likely to learn the material than students who do not have skills for giving and receiving explanations (Webb et al., 1995). Although students benefit from both giving and receiving explanations, there is stronger evidence of achievement gains for students who give explanations (Webb, 1982). Webb et al. (1995) found that the more students engage in finding solutions to a problem, the better their achievement. Students are motivated to provide high-quality explanations and less prone to simply supply answers to peers when they understand that each group member is accountable for learning the content (Slavin, 1994). This suggests that both group goals and individual responsibility are important features of cooperative group work. Finally, the highest achievement gains are found for students who receive instruction and scaffolding to prepare them for productive engagement in small groups (e.g., how to listen, share, integrate the ideas of others, and handle disagreements constructively) (Slavin, 1994).

Another consistent finding is that the type of learning task influences the nature of relationships, group interactions, and achievement outcomes in group learning formats (Cohen, 1994). Different task objectives require different types and amounts of group interactions. For example, routine learning situations require different interactions than situations in which students are expected to learn from understanding. During routine learning situations, students ensure that peers grasp the content by offering each other substantive or procedural information. When the task objective is learning for understanding, however, productive group interaction is characterized by a mutual sharing and clarifying of ideas and strategy experimentation (Webb, 1991; Webb et al., 1995).

A final conclusion from research relates to the composition of small groups. Bennett and Cass (1988) found that small groups consisting of two low achievers and one high achiever performed better than groups consisting of one low achiever and two high achievers. In the latter group, low achievers tended to be ignored and often exhibited disruptive, off-task behavior. In the former type of group, the performance of high-achieving students was not harmed by working with low achievers. In general, when considering the makeup of small groups, effective teachers balance groups by placing a relatively equal distribution of low-achieving and high-achieving students in cooperative groups (Slavin, 1994; Swing & Peterson, 1982; Webb, 1982).

Incorporate Humor and Enthusiasm Into Teaching. Students are likely to adopt their teachers' attitude toward learning. When teachers present a topic with enthusiasm, suggesting that it is interesting, important, or worthwhile, students are likely to adopt this same attitude (Bettencourt, Gillett, Gall, & Hull, 1983; Newby, 1991). Effective teachers convey their enthusiasm with sincere statements of the value they place on a topic or activity (Cabello & Terrell, 1994). Effective teachers articulate their own reasons for considering a content or topic as interesting, meaningful, or important. The objective of projecting enthusiasm is to induce students to value the topic or activity, which, in turn, promotes learning (Good & Brophy, 2000). Moskowitz and Hayman (1976), for example, found that the "best" junior high school teachers solicited and accepted student ideas, joked and smiled frequently, and spent considerable time "setting the climate" for students on the first day of school. In sum, when teachers are enthusiastic about a subject, students are likely to develop enthusiasm of their own, and, ultimately, to achieve at higher levels (Rosenshine & Furst, 1973).

Use of Motivational Strategies That Foster Goal Orientation. Research on achievement or goal orientation confirms that effort and persistence are higher among students who set goals of moderate difficulty, commit themselves to pursuing these goals, and concentrate on trying to achieve success rather than trying to avoid failure (Dweck & Elliott, 1983). Two types of goals have been investigated in process-outcome research focusing on motivation outcomes: (a) task-focused or learning-oriented goals, and (b) ability-focused or performance-oriented goals. Students who pursue learning-oriented goals are concerned with improving their level of understanding or competence in an area. Students who pursue performance-oriented goals, however, seek to demonstrate high ability or gain favorable judgments of their abilities in comparison to others.

Students with task-focused or learning-oriented goals use more adaptive help-seeking strategies and show higher levels of creativity (Anderman & Maehr, 1994); they are more likely to adopt a motivational pattern that will support long-term and high-quality involvement in learning (Ames, 1992). Teachers are able to create learning environments that elicit different goal orientations and determine whether students adopt learning versus performance goals. Learning-oriented goals, for example, are associated with learning environments that emphasize self-improvement, discovery of new information, and useful learning materials. A learning orientation is likely to occur when students are involved in choice and decision making; there are opportunities for peer interaction and cooperation; grouping is based on interest and needs; and success is defined in terms of effort, progress, and improvement (Blumenfeld et al., 1991; Maehr & Midgley, 1991; Meece, 1994). Adoption of a particular goal orientation is also influenced by teachers' feedback, accountability, and evaluation practices. Students' expectancies for success and the likelihood they will adopt a motivation orientation that stresses learning rather than performance increase when teachers (a) hold students accountable for learning and understanding, not just getting the right answers; (b) give students the freedom to take risks and be wrong; (c) stress improvement over time; (d) minimize competition and comparisons with others; and (e) use private rather than public evaluation (Blumenfeld, Puro, & Mergendoller, 1992).

Effective teachers help students recognize effort-outcome linkages in several ways. First, teachers model beliefs about effort-outcome linkages when talking to students about their own learning and when demonstrating tasks by "thinking out loud" as they work through them. Effective teachers also model frustration or temporary failure, and express confidence they will succeed if they persist and search for a better strategy. Second, effective teachers stress outcome-effort linkages through socialization and feedback. For example, teachers reinforce students for their effort and the methods they use to complete a project, rather than for completion and quality of the project (Newby, 1991). Third, effective teachers convey to students that learning may take time and often involves confusion or mistakes, but that persistence and careful work eventually yield knowledge or skill mastery. Fourth, teachers communicate to students that intellectual abilities are open to improvement, rather than fixed, and that students possess many abilities, not just a few. Lastly, when monitoring performance and giving feedback, effective teachers stress the quality of task engagement and degree to which students make continuous progress toward mastery, without comparisons to other students (Ames, 1992; Krampen, 1987; McColskey & Leary, 1985).

SUMMARY AND APPLICATION OF PROCESS-PRODUCT RESEARCH FINDINGS

The process-outcome research tradition has generated important knowledge about classrooms, teachers, and students. Elements of effective teaching and classroom management derived from process-outcome research serve as the foundation for many teacher professional development and preservice training programs. Research within a process-outcome paradigm attests to the important role of the teacher in creating and maintaining a positive classroom environment that promotes academic and social competence. A true test of the productivity of a research approach is the extent to which the work contributes to improved classroom practices and better student performance (Gettinger & Stoiber, 1999). Researchers increasingly have turned their attention to determining whether improvements in classroom performance can be obtained through training and application of process-outcome, evidence-based techniques (Gutkin, 2002). Teacher professional development programs derived from process-product relationships have brought about increases in recommended practices and yielded significant effects on student performance, in terms of both achievement and behavior. Thus, it is apparent that teachers can be taught to use process-outcome findings in their teaching, and that such use improves student achievement, behavior, and attitudes (Doyle, 1985; Floden, 2001).

Despite these positive findings, both process-outcome researchers and their critics agree that process-outcome research should not be the only content covered in teacher education, nor constitute the sole basis for developing teacher evaluation instruments. The complexities of the teaching-learning process are such that incorporating isolated research-based practices into classroom teaching may not consistently lead to positive outcomes (Elmore, Peterson, & McCarthey, 1996; Ornstein, 1993). Teaching methods that are effective in one situation may not be appropriate in another. The key to effective teaching rests with teachers' ability to make decisions about effective practices within the context of their particular classrooms (Fuchs et al., 1993; Kagan, 1992). The findings of process-product research should be used thoughtfully and artistically with due regard for circumstances that may call for exceptions to the trends indicated by findings (Floden, 2001).

Despite a general diminishing of process-outcome studies during the 1990s, this research approach is beginning to resurface as investigators are returning to the study of effective teaching and the call for evidence-based practice is intensifying, especially for students who are at risk of failing in school. Indeed, in the 1995 update and third edition of *Effective Schooling Practices: A Research Synthesis*, which synthesizes and summarizes evidence-based classroom practices that promote student achievement and appropriate behavior, many findings from process-outcome research are featured, including classroom routines, clear and focused instruction, feedback and reinforcement, review and reteaching, direct questioning, and communicating performance and behavior expectations (Cotton, 1995).

COMPREHENSIVE MODELS OF EFFECTIVE CLASSROOMS

Whereas much of the earliest process-outcome research focused on individual behaviors or routines (e.g., brisk instructional pace, wait time, performance feedback), more recent work has evaluated the efficacy of comprehensive models of teaching and classroom management derived from these individual studies (Floden, 2001). More contemporary process-outcome research now defines effective teaching primarily through synthesis, in which individual behaviors and processes associated with positive student outcomes are aggregated into an effective-teaching composite, for example, explicit instruction (Kameenui & Carnine, 1998), authoritative classroom management (Jones & Jones, 2001), positive behavior support (Koegel, Koegel, & Dunlap, 1996). Work related to the development of an explicit or direct instruction illustrates this trend. For example, in a meta-analysis of intervention research for students with learning disabilities, Swanson and his research team (1999) coded interventions reported in empirical studies according to the presence of 20 specific instructional components (e.g., sequencing, scaffolding, practice-review, small-group instruction, etc.). Based on the frequency of representation of these 20 components, composite models of effective instruction, rather than individual practices, were identified. An intervention was categorized as "direct instruction" if the approach included a minimum of 4 of 11 targeted components, for example, carefully sequenced instructional material, or scripted teacher performance. Interestingly, Swanson found limited evidence that any teacher's performance was completely aligned with all elements associated with a composite, such as direct instruction. Furthermore, Swanson and others have found that researchers may use different terms for composites yet measure similar teacher behaviors, or, conversely, use the same terms but measure different teacher behaviors, for example, in the case of an authoritative approach to classroom discipline. Brophy and Good (1986) reviewed several experimental studies conducted within the process-outcome paradigm. In most cases, teachers who were trained to use composites of skills typically produced higher performance than their control counterparts. Experimental teachers, however, did not exhibit every behavior in a composite more frequently than their control counterparts. These findings indicate that teachers trained in an integrated model are still more effective than untrained teachers even when they do not implement all practices of the model in which they were trained. Research has yet to determine whether differences in effectiveness exist between teachers who fully implement a composite model compared to teachers who implement only certain components of the model.

The aggregation of findings from process-outcome research into composite instructional models, such as direct instruction, rests on some key assumptions. First, different types of learning call for different types of classroom processes; therefore, no single approach can be the method of choice for all classroom learning. The most effective classroom teaching features a balanced mix of research-based instructional methods and learning tasks. Second, within any domain, students' instructional needs change as their expertise and abilities develop. Thus, what constitutes an optimal mixture of instructional methods will change as students advance through school. Third, the influence of context variables is important. In fact, only a few universal teaching competencies are uniformly effective in all teaching circumstances. Even a potentially useful process of praising students may lead to variable outcomes, depending on the age and attitude of the learners. To be effective, teachers must select appropriate methods, resources, and strategies to match the content to be taught, type of learning involved, and characteristics of learners. A "one-size-fits-all" approach, perpetuated by a narrow application of process-outcome research, is rarely effective. Instead, effective teaching and classroom management requires incorporating multiple research findings to create supportive learning environments. Process-outcome research should continue to examine classroom processes that contribute to environments that support learning (Slavin & Madden, 2001). Research linking teacher behavior to student outcomes can provide input into teacher education and teacher accountability schemes, although it should not translate into a list of fixed or universal training objectives and evaluation criteria.

DIRECTIONS OF FUTURE RESEARCH

Teachers can be effective in helping students succeed in school when they follow pedagogical principles derived from process-outcome research. Future efforts should be directed toward identifying the type of supports necessary to help teachers implement day-to-day teaching practices and classroom processes, which have been validated by process-outcome research. To pursue this direction, alternate research methodologies may need to be explored. For example, a great deal is learned through in-depth case studies of teachers. Using case-study methodology, Phillips et al. (1996) identified four components of effective teaching that were successful in promoting uniformly high performance among all students, including students with learning disabilities. Using individual interviews, Elmore et al. (1996) learned that less successful teachers do not differ from more successful teachers in the effort they commit to teaching. Good teachers, however, do demonstrate key differences in three processes that are not readily assessed through classroom observations. Elmore et al. found that (a) good teachers possess more sophisticated awareness of what students do to achieve an understanding of academic content, (b) they have a clearer command of the subject domain being taught, and (c) they are better able to connect content to the experience and backgrounds of diverse learners. As case studies of teaching excellence accumulate, common features emerge that serve to extend and elaborate process-outcome relationships, especially in promoting achievement and positive classroom behavior for diverse students and students at risk of failing in school.

Research on effective teaching traditionally has relied on a method of contrasting groups, that is, examining measurable differences between more and less successful teachers. The use of contrasting samples worked well in early classroom studies of management, in which the behavior of a small number of teachers of well-managed classes was contrasted with the behavior of teachers whose classrooms were not well managed. In lieu of this method of contrasting groups, however, Berliner (1990) has encouraged greater attention to in-depth study of experts, that is, finding the "best" teachers for purposes of studying process-outcome relations. Once "expert" teachers are identified, researchers can examine closely their planning, thinking, decision-making, as well as classroom practices. This is the approach underlying a systematic research program undertaken by Pressley and his colleagues (Pressley, Rankin, & Yokoi, 1996; Rankin & Pressley, 2000). Their research is aimed at studying and learning from the instructional practices of teachers who are nominated by peer teachers as being "expert" teachers of literacy.

Another challenge for process-outcome researchers is to continue to seek ways to facilitate the application and sustained use of research-based practices. Many findings from educational research are not implemented in classrooms. One recommendation to facilitate application is to work back from process-product relations to examine teachers' thinking about context and other variables associated with student outcomes (Berliner, 1990). Teachers' thinking about process-outcome findings is, in itself, an important area of inquiry. In other words, process-outcome relationships need to be understood not solely in terms of student outcomes, but also in terms of their effect on teachers' thinking.

To be effective, teachers must be aware of the numerous variables that affect classroom environments and student learning. Process-outcome research has focused on a variety of variables, most of which are under the teacher's control. A teacher's primary responsibility is to promote behavioral competence and facilitate the learning of all students in the classroom. The teacher effectiveness research, based on a process-outcome model, provides guidance for being successful in teaching. This research has contributed to the development of teaching principles and practices that, when implemented systematically in classrooms, can enhance student learning and support positive classroom behavior.

ACKNOWLEDGMENTS

The authors want to thank Dr. Brian K. Martens, Professor and Director of Training for the School Psychology Program at Syracuse University, for his helpful comments on an earlier version of this chapter.

REFERENCES

Ames, C. (1992). Classrooms: Goals, structures, and student motivation. *Journal of Educational Psychology, 84*, 261–271.

Anderman, E. M., & Maehr, M. L. (1994). Motivation and schooling in the middle grades. *Review of Educational Research, 64*, 287–309.

Anderson, L. M., Evertson, C. M., & Emmer, E. T. (1980). Dimensions in classroom management derived from recent research. *Journal of Curriculum Studies, 12*, 343–356.

Ardoin, S. P., Martens, B. K., & Wolfe, L. A. (1999). Using high-probability instruction sequences with fading to increase student compliance during transitions. *Journal of Applied Behavior Analysis, 32*, 339–351.

Atwood, R. (1983, April). *The interacting effects of task form and activity structure on students' task involvement and teacher evaluations*. Paper presented at the annual meeting of the American Educational Research Association, Montreal.

Beck, I., & McKeown, M. (1988). Toward meaningful accounts in history texts for young learners. *Educational Researcher, 17*(6), 31–39.

Becker, W. C. (Ed.). (1988). Direct instruction: Special issue. *Education and Treatment of Children, 11*, 297–402.

Bennett, N., & Cass, A. (1988). The effects of group compositions on group interactive processes and pupil understanding. *British Educational Research Journal, 15*, 19–32.

Bennett, N., & Dunne, E. (1992). *Managing small groups*. New York: Simon & Schuster.

Berliner, D. C. (1988). Effective classroom management and instruction: A knowledge base for consultation. In J. L. Graden, J. E. Zins, & M. C. Curtis (Eds.), *Alternative educational delivery systems: Enhancing instructional options for all students* (pp. 309–325). Washington, DC: National Association for School Psychologists.

Berliner, D. C. (1990). The place of process-product research in developing the agenda for research on teaching thinking. *Educational Psychologist, 24*, 325–344.

Bettencourt, E., Gillett, M., Gall, M., & Hull, R. (1983). Effects of teacher enthusiasm training on student on-task behavior and achievement. *American Educational Research Journal, 20*, 435–450.

Bickel, W. E. (1999). The implications of the effective schools literature for school restructuring. In C. R. Reynolds & T. B. Gutkin (Eds.), *The handbook of school psychology* (3rd ed., pp. 959–983). New York: John Wiley.

Blumenfeld, P. C., Puro, P., & Mergendoller, J. (1992). Translating motivation into thoughtfulness. In H. Marshall (Ed.), *Redefining student learning: Roots of educational change* (pp. 207–240). Norwood, NJ: Ablex.

Blumenfeld, P. C., Soloway, E., Marx, R. W., Krajcik, J. S., Guzdial, M., & Palincsar, A. (1991). Motivating project-based learning. *Educational Psychologist, 26,* 369–398.

Borich, G. (1988). *Effective teaching methods.* Columbus, OH: Merrill.

Brandt, R. (1992). On research on teaching: A conversation with Lee Shulman. *Educational Leadership, 50*(1), 14–19.

Brantlinger, E. (1993). Adolescents' interpretation of social class influences on schooling. *Journal of Classroom Interaction, 28*(1), 1–12.

Brooks, D. M. (1985). The teacher's communicative competence. The first day of school. *Theory Into Practice, 24,* 63–70.

Brophy, J. E. (1979). Teacher behavior and its effects. *Journal of Educational Psychology, 71,* 733–750.

Brophy, J. E. (1982). Classroom management and learning. *American Education, 18*(2), 20–23.

Brophy, J. E. (1983). Classroom organization and management. *Elementary School Journal, 83,* 265–285.

Brophy, J., & Alleman, J. (1991). Activities as instructional tools: A framework for analysis and evaluation. *Educational Researcher, 20*(4), 9–23.

Brophy, J., & Good, T. (1986). Teacher behavior and student achievement. In M. Wittrock (Ed.), *Handbook of research on teaching* (3rd ed., pp. 328–375). New York: MacMillan.

Burns, R. B. (1984). How time is used in elementary schools: The activity structure of classrooms. In L. W. Anderson (Ed.), *Time and school learning: Theory, research, and practice* (pp. 52–71). London: Croom Helm.

Cabello, B., & Terrell, R. (1994). Making students feel like family: How teachers create warm and caring classroom climates. *Journal of Classroom Interaction, 29,* 17–23.

Chilcoat, G. (1989). Instructional behaviors for clearer presentations in the classroom. *Instructional Science, 18,* 289–314.

Cochran-Smith, M., & Lytle, S. L. (1990). Research on teaching and teacher research: The issues that divide. *Educational Researcher, 19,* 2–11.

Cohen, E. G. (1994). Restructuring the classroom: Conditions for productive small groups. *Review of Educational Research, 64,* 1–35.

Coker, H., Lorentz, C. W., & Coker, J. (1980, April). *Teacher behavior and student outcomes in the Georgia study.* Paper presented to the American Educational Research Association Annual Meeting, Boston, MA.

Cotton, K. (1995). *Effective schooling practices: A research synthesis.* Alexandria, VA: Association for Supervision and Curriculum Development.

Cruickshank, D. (1985). Applying research on teacher clarity. *Journal of Teacher Education, 36,* 44–48.

Daly, E. J., III, Martens, B. K., Kilmer, A., & Massie, D. R. (1996). The effects of instructional match and content overlap on generalized reading performance. *Journal of Applied Behavior Analysis, 29,* 507–518.

Darling-Hammond, L. (1996). The right to learn and the advancement of teaching: Research, policy, and practice for democratic education. *Educational Researcher, 25,* 5–17.

Dempster, F. (1991). Synthesis of research on reviews and tests. *Educational Leadership, 48*(7), 71–76.

Doyle, W. (1984). How order is achieved in classrooms: An interim report. *Journal of Curriculum Studies, 16,* 259–277.

Doyle, W. (1985). Recent research on classroom management: Implications for teacher preparation. *Journal of Teacher Education, 36,* 31–35.

Doyle, W. (1986). Classroom organization and management. In M. C. Wittrock (Ed.), *Handbook of research on teaching* (3rd ed., pp. 392–431). New York: Macmillan.

Duffy, G. G. (1990). Whatever became of teacher effectiveness? *Reading Psychology, 11,* 3–10.

Duffy, G., Roehler, L., Meloth, M., & Vavrus, L. (1986). Conceptualizing instructional explanation. *Teaching and Teacher Education, 2,* 197–214.

Dunkin, M. J., & Biddle, B. J. (1974). *The study of teaching.* New York: Holt, Rinehart, and Winston.

Dweck, C., & Elliott, E. (1983). Achievement motivation. In P. Mussen (Ed.), *Handbook of child psychology, Vol. 4: Socialization, personality, and social development* (4th ed.). New York: John Wiley.

Elmore, R. F., Peterson, P. L., & McCarthey, S. J. (1996). *Restructuring in the classroom: Teaching, learning, and school organization.* San Francisco: Jossey-Bass.

Emmer, E. T., & Evertson, C. M. (1981). Synthesis of research on classroom management. *Educational Leadership, 38,* 342–347.

Emmer, E. T., Evertson, C. M., & Anderson, L. M. (1980). Effective classroom management at the beginning of the school year. *Elementary School Journal, 80,* 219–231.

Emmer, E., Sanford, J. P., Evertson, C. M., Clements, B. S., & Martin, J. (1981). *The classroom management improvement study: An experiment in elementary school classrooms* (Report No. 6050). Austin: University of Texas, Research & Development Center for Teacher Education.

Englert, C., Tarrant, K., & Mariage, T. (1992). Defining and redefining instructional practice in special education: Perspectives on good teaching. *Teacher Education and Special Education, 15*(2), 62–86.

Evans, J. (1985). *Teaching in transition: The challenge of mixed ability grouping.* Philadelphia: Open University Press.

Evertson, C. M. (1987). Creating conditions for learning: From research to practice. *Theory Into Practice, 26*(1), 44–50.

Evertson, C., Anderson, C., Anderson, L., & Brophy, J. (1980). Relationships between classroom behaviors and student outcomes in junior high mathematics and English classes. *American Educational Research Journal, 17*, 43–60.

Evertson, C. M., & Emmer, E. T. (1982a). Effective management at the beginning of the year in junior high classes. *Journal of Educational Psychology, 74*, 485–498.

Evertson, C. M., & Emmer, E. T. (1982b). Preventive classroom management. In D. L. Duke (Ed.), *Helping teachers manage classrooms* (pp. 2–31). Alexandria, VA: Association for Supervision and Curriculum Development.

Evertson, C. M., & Harris, A. H. (1992). What we know about managing classrooms. *Educational Leadership, 49*(7), 74–78.

Evertson, C. M., Sanford, J. P., & Emmer, E. T. (1981). Effects of class heterogeneity in junior high school. *American Educational Research Journal, 18*, 219–232.

Fisher, C., Filby, N., Marliave, R., Cahen, L., Dishaw, M., & Moore, J. (1978). *Teaching behaviors, academic learning time and student achievement: Final report of Phase 3-B, Beginning Teacher Evaluation Study*. San Francisco: Far West Laboratory.

Floden, R. E. (2001). Research on effects of teaching: A continuing model for research on teaching. In V. Richardson (Ed.), *Handbook of research on teaching* (4th ed., pp. 3–16). Washington, DC: American Educational Research Association.

Freiberg, H. J., Stein, T. A. & Huang, S. (1995). The effects of classroom management intervention on student achievement in inner-city elementary schools. *Educational Research and Evaluation, 1*, 33–66.

Fuchs, L. S., & Fuchs, D. (1986). Effects of systematic formative evaluation: A meta-analysis. *Exceptional Children*, 53, 199–208.

Fuchs, L. S., Fuchs, D., & Phillips, N. B. (1994). The relation between teachers' beliefs about the importance of good student work habits, teacher planning, and student achievement. *The Elementary School Journal, 94*, 331–345.

Fuchs, L. S., Fuchs, D., Phillips, N. B., & Simmons, D. (1993). Contextual variables affecting instructional adaptation for difficult-to-teach students. *School Psychology Review, 22*, 722–740.

Gage, N. L. (1978). *The scientific basis of the art of teaching*. New York: Teachers College Press.

Gage, N. L., & Needels, M. C. (1989). Process-product research on teaching: A review of criticisms. *The Elementary School Journal, 89*, 253–297.

Gettinger, M. (1986). Issues and trends in academic engaged time of students. *Special Services in the Schools, 2*(4), 1–17.

Gettinger, M. (1988). Methods of proactive classroom management. *School Psychology Review, 17*, 227–242.

Gettinger, M. (1995). Best practices for increasing academic learning time. In A. Thomas & J. Grimes (Eds.), *Best practice in school psychology-3* (pp. 943–954). Washington, DC: National Association of School Psychologists.

Gettinger, M., & Stoiber, K. C. (1999). Excellence in teaching: Review of instructional and environmental variables. In C.R. Reynolds & T.B. Gutkin (Eds.), *The handbook of school psychology* (3rd ed., pp. 933–958). New York: John Wiley.

Good, T. (1996). Teacher effectiveness and teacher evaluation. In J. Sikula, T. Buttery & E. Guyton (Eds.), *Handbook of research on teacher education* (2nd ed., pp. 617–665). New York: MacMillan.

Good, T. L. & Brophy, J. E. (2000). *Looking in classrooms* (8th ed.). New York: Addison-Wesley Educational Publishers.

Good, T. L., & Grouws, D. A. (1979). Teaching effects: A process-product study in fourth-grade mathematics classrooms. *Journal of Teacher Education, 28*(3), 49–54.

Gottfredson, D., Gottfredson, G., & Hybl, L. (1993). Managing adolescent behavior: A multiyear, multischool study. *American Educational Research Journal, 31*, 179–215.

Greenwood, C. R. (1991). Longitudinal analysis of time, engagement, and achievement of at risk versus non-risk students. *Exceptional Children, 57*, 521–535.

Greenwood, C. R., & Delquadri, J. (1995). Classwide peer tutoring and the prevention of school failure. *Preventing School Failure, 39*, 21–15.

Greenwood, C. R., Delquadri, J., & Hall, R. V. (1993). Longitudinal effects of classwide peer tutoring. *Journal of Educational Psychology, 81*, 371–383.

Gump, P. V. (1982). School settings and their keeping. In D. L. Duke (Ed.), *Helping teachers manage classrooms* (pp. 98–114). Alexandria, VA: Association for Supervision and Curriculum Development.

Gutkin, T. R. (2002) Evidence-based interventions in school psychology: The state of the art and future directions. *School Psychology Quarterly, 17*, 339–340.

Hoffman, J. V. (1986). Process-product research on effective teaching: A primer for a paradigm. In J. V. Hoffman (Ed.), *Effective teaching of reading: Research and practice* (pp. 39–51). Newark, DE: International Reading Association.

Hines, C. V., Cruickshank, D. R., & Kennedy, J. J. (1985). Teacher clarity and its relationship to student achievement and satisfaction. *American Educational Research Journal, 22*, 87–99.

Johnson, D., & Johnson, R. (1994). *Learning together and alone: Cooperative, competitive, and individualistic learning* (4th ed.). Boston: Allyn & Bacon.

Jones, V. F., & Jones, L. S. (2001). *Comprehensive classroom management* (6th ed.). Boston: Allyn & Bacon.
Kagan, D. M. (1992). Implications of research on teacher beliefs. *Educational Psychologist, 27,* 65–90.
Kame'enui, E. J., & Carnine, D.W. (1998). *Effective teaching strategies that accommodate diverse learners.* Upper Saddle River, NJ: Prentice-Hall, Inc.
Kindsvatter, R., Wilen, W., & Ishler, M. (1988). *Dynamics of effective teaching.* New York: Longman.
Knapp, M. (1995). *Teaching for meaning in high-poverty classrooms.* New York: Teachers College Press.
Koegel, R. L., Koegel, L. K., & Dunlap, G. (Eds.). (1996). *Positive behavioral support: Including people with difficult behavior in the community.* Baltimore: Paul H. Brookes.
Kounin, J. S. (1970). *Discipline and group management in classrooms.* New York: Holt, Rinehart & Winston.
Krampen, G. (1987). Differential effects of teacher comments. *Journal of Educational Psychology, 79,* 137–146.
Maehr, M., & Midgley, C. (1991). Enhancing student motivation: A schoolwide approach. *Educational Psychologist, 26,* 399–428.
McCaleb, J., & White, J. (1980). Critical dimensions in evaluating teacher clarity. *Journal of Classroom Interaction, 15,* 27–30.
McColskey, W., & Leary, M. R. (1985). Differential effects of norm-referenced and self- referenced feedback on performance, expectancies, attributions, and motivation. *Contemporary Educational Psychology, 10,* 275–284.
McKee, W. T., & Witt, J. C. (1990). Effective teaching: A review of instructional and environmental variables. In T. B. Gutkin & C. R. Reynolds (Eds.), *The handbook of school psychology* (2nd ed., pp. 821–846). New York: John Wiley.
Medley, D. M., Coker, H., & Soar, R. S. (1984). *Measurement-based evaluation of teacher performance: An empirical approach.* New York: Longman.
Meece, J. L. (1994). The role of motivation in self-regulated learning. In D. H. Schunk & B. J. Zimmerman (Eds.), *Self-regulation learning and performance: Issues and educational applications* (pp. 25–44). Hillsdale, NJ: Erlbaum.
Mevarech, Z. R., & Kramarski, B. (1997). IMPROVE: A multidimensional method for teaching mathematics in heterogeneous classrooms. *American Educational Research Journal, 34,* 365–394.
Moskowitz, G., & Hayman, J. L. (1976). Success strategies of inner-city teachers: A year-long study. *Journal of Educational Research, 69,* 283–289.
Munk, D. D., & Repp, A. C. (1994). The relationship between instructional variables and problem behavior: A review. *Exceptional Children, 60,* 390–401.
Murphy, J. (1992). Instructional leadership: Focus on time to learn. *NASSP Bulletin, 76,* 19–26.
Narayan, J. S., Heward, W. L., & Gardner, R. (1990). Using response cards to increase student participation in an elementary classroom. *Journal of Applied Behavior Analysis, 23,* 483–490.
Needels, M. C., & Gage, N. L. (1991). Essence and accident in process-product research on teaching. In H. C. Waxman & H. J. Walberg (Eds.), *Effective teaching: Current research* (pp. 3–29). Berkeley, CA: McCutchan.
Newby, T. (1991). Classroom motivation strategies of first-grade teachers. *Journal of Educational Psychology, 83,* 187–194.
Newmann, F. (1992). *Student engagement and achievement in American secondary schools.* New York: Teachers College Press.
Ornstein, A. (1993). How to recognize good teaching. *American School Board Journal, 13,* 24–27.
Paine, S. C., Radicchi, J., Rosellini, L. C., Deutchman, L., & Darch, C. B. (1983). *Structuring your classroom for academic success.* Champaign, IL: Research Press.
Peterson, P. L., Stark, K. D., & Waas, G. A. (1984). Students' cognitions and time on task during mathematics instruction. *American Educational Research Journal, 21,* 487–515.
Phillips, N. B., Fuchs, L. S., Fuchs, D., & Hamlett, C. L. (1996). Instructional variables affecting student achievement: Case studies of two contrasting teachers. *Learning Disabilities Research and Practice, 11*(1), 24–33.
Pressley, M., Rankin, J., & Yokoi, L. (1996). A survey of instructional practices of primary teachers nominated as effective in promoting literacy. *The Elementary School Journal, 96,* 363–384.
Puma, M. J., Jones, C. C., Rock, D., & Fernandez, R. (1993). *Prospects: The congressionally mandated study of educational growth and opportunity interim report.* Washington, DC: U.S. Department of Education, Planning and Evaluation Service.
Rankin, J. L., & Pressley, M. (2000). A survey of instructional practices of special education teachers nominated as effective teachers of literacy. *Learning Disabilities: Research and Practice, 15,* 206–225.
Rhode, G., Jenson, R. J., & Reavis, H. K. (1993). *The tough kid book: Practical classroom management strategies.* Longmont, CA: Sopris West.
Richardson, V. (1994). Conducting research on practice. *Educational Researcher 23*(5), 5–10.
Rosenshine, B. (1979). Content, time, and direct instruction. In H. Walberg (Ed.), *Research on teaching: Concepts, findings, and implications* (pp. 42–68). Berkeley, CA: McCutchan.
Rosenshine, B. (1980). How time is spent in elementary classrooms. In C. Denham & A. Lieberman (Eds.), *Time to learn* (pp. 4–18). Washington, DC: National Institute of Education.
Rosenshine. B. (1986). Synthesis of research on explicit teaching. *Educational Leadership, 46*(7), 60–78.

Rosenshine, B. (1997). Advances in research on instruction. In J. W. Lloyd, E. J. Kameenui, & D. Chard (Eds.), *Issues in education students with disabilities* (pp. 197–221). Mahwah, NJ: Lawrence Erlbaum Associates.

Rosenshine, B., & Furst, N. (1973). The use of direct observation to study teaching. In R. Travers (Ed.), *Handbook of research on teaching* (2nd ed., pp. 263–298). Chicago: Rand McNally.

Rosenshine, B., & Meister, B. (1992). The use of scaffolds for teaching higher-learning cognitive strategies. *Educational Leadership, 49*(7), 26–33.

Rowe, M. (1986). Wait time: Slowing down may be a way of speeding up! *Journal of Teacher Education, 37,* 43–50.

Shuell, T. (1996). Teaching and learning in a classroom context. In D. Berliner & R. Calfee (Eds.), *Handbook of educational psychology* (pp. 726–764). New York: Macmillan.

Shulman, L. S. (1986). Paradigms and research programs in the study of teaching: A contemporary perspective. In M. C. Wittrock (Ed.), *Handbook of research on teaching* (3rd ed., pp. 3–36). New York: Macmillan.

Skinner, C. H., Fletcher, P. A., & Henington, C. (1996). Increasing learning rates by increasing student response rates. *School Psychology Quarterly, 11,* 313–325.

Slavin, R. E. (1994). *Cooperative learning: Theory, research, and practice* (2nd ed.). Boston: Allyn & Bacon.

Slavin, R. E., & Madden, N. A. (Eds.). (2001). *Success for all: Research and reform in elementary education.* Hillsdale, NJ: Erlbaum.

Smith, L., & Land, M. (1981). Low-inference verbal behaviors related to teacher clarity. *Journal of Classroom Interaction, 17,* 37–42.

Stallings, J. A., Needels, M., & Stayrook, N. (1979). *The teaching of basic reading skills in secondary schools, Phase 2 and Phase 3.* Menlo Park, CA: SRI International.

Stipek, D. J. (1983). *Motivation to learn: From theory to practice* (2nd ed.). Needham Heights, MA: Allyn & Bacon.

Stringfield, S., & Herman, R. (1997). Assessment of the state of school effectiveness research in the United States of America. *School Effectiveness and School Improvement, 7,* 159–180.

Swanson, H. L. (1999). *Interventions for students with learning disabilities: A meta-analysis of treatment outcomes.* New York: Guilford Press.

Swing, S. R., & Peterson, P. L. (1982). The relationship of student ability and small-group interaction to student achievement. *American Educational Research Journal, 19,* 259–274.

Swing, S. R., Stoiber, K. C., & Peterson, P. L. (1988). Thinking skills versus learning time: Effects of alternative classroom-based interventions on students' mathematical problem solving. *Cognition and Instruction, 5,* 123–191.

Wang, M. C., Haertel, G. D., & Walberg, H. J. (1993). Toward a knowledge base for school learning.*Review of Educational Research, 63,* 249–294.

Wang, M. C., Haertel, G. D., & Walberg, H. J. (1994). What helps students learn? *Educational Leadership, 51*(4), 74–79.

Waxman, H., Huang, S., Anderson, L., & Weinstein, T. (1997). Classroom process differences in inner-city elementary schools. *Journal of Educational Research, 91,* 49–59.

Waxman, H., & Walberg, H. (1991). *Effective teaching: Current research.* Berkeley, CA: McCutchan.

Webb, N. M. (1982). Peer interaction and learning in cooperative small groups. *Journal of Educational Psychology, 74,* 642–655.

Webb, N. M. (1991). Task-related verbal interaction and mathematics learning in small groups. *Journal for Research in Mathematics Education, 22,* 366-389.

Webb, N. M., Troper, J. D., & Fall, R. (1995). Constructive activity and learning in collaborative small groups. *Journal of Educational Psychology, 87,* 406–423.

Weinhart, F., & Helmke, A. (1995). Learning from wise Mother Nature or Big Brother Instructor: The wrong choice as seen from an educational perspective. *Educational Psychologist, 30,* 135–142.

Westbury, M. (1988). The science and art of teacher effectiveness: An examination of two research traditions. *Canadian Journal of Education, 13,* 4–20.

Wyne, M., & Stuck, G. (1982). Time and learning: Implications for the classroom teacher. *The Elementary School Journal, 83,* 67–75.

5

Ecological Approaches to Classroom Management

Walter Doyle[1]
University of Arizona

INTRODUCTION

This chapter is a streamlined version of the chapter on classroom organization and management that I wrote for the Third Edition of the *Handbook of Research on Teaching* (Doyle, 1986a). The original chapter was written from an ecological perspective and contains the core of what that perspective is and what it means for classroom management. In this revision I have tried to maintain the basic outline and topic structure, but have reduced the number of citations and combined or eliminated sections that primarily elaborated the main themes but were not essential to an overall understanding of an ecological approach. At the end of the present chapter, I have added an appraisal of the current status of and prospects for an ecological approach to classroom management. Readers interested in more details are referred to the 1986 version. For an updated application of an ecological stance to classroom management in early childhood and elementary classrooms, readers are also referred to the chapter by Carter and Doyle in this Handbook.

This chapter is divided into four major sections: (a) an introduction to the ecological perspective; (b) a discussion of the types of settings found in classrooms and the program of actions that define order for these contexts; (c) a consideration of the processes and strategies for managing classroom events; and (d) an appraisal of the current status and future prospects for an ecological approach to classroom management.

---

[1]Sections of this chapter were reprinted with permission of the publisher from the *Handbook of Research on Teaching* (3rd. ed.), copyright 1986, American Educational Research Association. Paul Gump (late of the University of Kansas) and Daniel L. Duke (University of Virginia) served as external reviewers for the original chapter. The writing of that chapter was supported in part by the National Institute of Education, Contract OB-NIE-G-80-0116, P2, Research on Classroom Learning and Teaching Program at the University of Texas.

AN ECOLOGICAL PERSPECTIVE

An ecological understanding of classrooms emerged in the late 1960s from the inventive insights of Jacob Kounin (1970) and the conceptual and methodological elegance of Paul Gump (1969; see also Kounin & Gump, 1958; 1974). Jack and Paul were colleagues at Wayne State University in the 1950s, did work together initially on "ripple effects" in discipline (Kounin & Gump, 1958), and shared a connection with Roger Barker, who was Jack's major professor at the University of Illinois in the 1940s and became Paul's colleague when Paul moved to Barker's Midwest Psychological Field Station at Oskaloosa, Kansas, in the 1960s (Gump, 1990). Barker was, of course, the major architect of what became known as ecological psychology (Barker, 1968).

The central idea in an ecological approach is *habitat*, the physical niche or context with characteristic purposes, dimensions, features, and processes that have consequences for the behavior of occupants in that setting. As the name implies, an ecological stance has a great deal in common with biological sciences and, especially, ethology, or the study of animal behavior (see Tinbergen, 1958). This orientation leads to a central emphasis on a thorough conceptualization of situation or context in accounting for action and practice within a classroom system.

In the Barker group, habitats became known as "behavior settings" to reflect the early realization at the Midwest Station that behavior in everyday life is constrained by the particular setting in which a person is situated at a particular moment, that environments have plans for the behavior of participants (see Willems, 1990). This finding led Gump, for instance, to move into schools and classrooms to study children (Barker & Gump, 1964; Gump, 1969). And Gump's work in schools and classrooms, separately and in conjunction with Kounin, created the foundation for an ecological perspective in classroom management. As will be seen in this chapter, this ecological view, in turn, ultimately opened classroom research to a wide range of influences from studies in sociolinguistics, cognitive anthropology, semiotics, educational sociology, and the like.

The Nature of the Classroom Environment

From an ecological perspective, a classroom is an environment in which, typically, 20 to 30 students—a class—are gathered with one or perhaps two adults (teachers) to engage in activities, which have educational purposes and outcomes for the students. From this standpoint, there are several important features or dimensions of classrooms that are already in place when teachers and students arrive at the classroom door (Doyle, 1977). These include:

1. Multidimensionality—a large quantity of events and tasks in classrooms takes place. A classroom is a crowded place in which many people with different preferences and abilities must use a restricted supply of resources to accomplish a broad range of social and personal objectives.
2. Simultaneity—many things happen at once in classrooms. While helping an individual student during seatwork, for instance, a teacher must monitor the rest of the class, acknowledge other requests for assistance, handle interruptions, and keep track of time.
3. Immediacy—there is a rapid pace of classroom events. Gump (1967) and Jackson (1968) have estimated that an elementary teacher has over 500 exchanges with individual students in a single day. In most instances, therefore, teachers have little leisure time to reflect before acting.

4. Unpredictability—classroom events often take unexpected turns. Events are jointly produced and thus it is often difficult to anticipate how an activity will go on a particular day with a particular group of students.
5. Publicness—classrooms are public places and events, especially those involving the teacher, are often witnessed by a large portion of the students. "Teachers act in fishbowls; each child normally can see how the others are treated" (Lortie, 1975, p. 70).
6. History—classes meet for 5 days a week for several months and thus accumulate a common set of experiences, routines, and norms, which provide a foundation for conducting activities for the rest of the term or year (Emmer, Evertson, and Anderson, 1980).

All of these factors combine to create demands and pressures on participants as activities are played out in these environments. These demands and pressures are placed especially on teachers who carry professional adult responsibility for planning and monitoring classroom activities. Ecologically, these pressures and demands are the origins of the task of classroom management, namely, to establish and sustain order (cooperation) in educative activities that fill the available time.

Order in Classrooms

From an ecological perspective, classroom management is about how order is established and maintained in classroom environments. Conceptions of what constitutes orderliness vary across situations (e.g., snack time vs. silent reading) as well as individual teachers. The settings in which order is achieved—for example, whole-class lessons versus multiple-group investigations—differ in their structure and complexity. The actions teachers can take to create and sustain order range from planning and organizing lessons to distributing resources, explaining rules, monitoring activities, and reacting to individual and group behavior. Finally, the appropriateness of a particular action depends on circumstances, such as the purposes being sought, the work being done, the participants involved, and the time of the day. Understandably, then, the study of classroom management from this perspective is a complicated enterprise.

Order in classrooms does not necessarily mean passivity, absolute silence, or rigid conformity to rules, although these conditions are sometimes considered necessary for specific purposes (e.g., a major test). Order in a classroom simply means that within acceptable limits the students are following the program of action necessary for a particular classroom event to be realized in the situation. Loud comments students make during a hip-hop oral reading of "Green Eggs and Ham" in an urban classroom, for instance, are in most circumstances expressions of involvement rather than disorderly call outs.[2]

Programs of action differ across types of classroom *activities*, or bounded segments of classroom time characterized by identifiable arrangements of participants and materials and specified patterns of communication (see Au, 1980; Doyle, 1979b, 1984; Gump, 1967, 1969; Ross, 1984; Stodolsky, Ferguson, & Wimpelberg, 1981; Yinger, 1980). For lectures or seatwork, for example, students are expected to work independently at their desks and attend to a single information source (see Kounin & Gump, 1974). Whole class discussions, on the other hand, require that at least some students agree to answer the teacher's questions and students are expected to attend to multiple information sources.

According to this model, classroom order is defined and achieved within contexts and "each context makes different interactional demands on the members of the class" (Shultz & Florio, 1979, p. 169). To understand classroom order, then, it is necessary to examine the contexts

[2]I am grateful to Lara Handsfield for this example.

of the classroom and how they are enacted by teachers and students. From the perspective of order, "cooperation" rather than "engagement" (in the sense of involvement with content) is the minimum requirement for student behavior (see Doyle, 1979b). The term *cooperation*, derived from Grice's (1975) analysis of the "Cooperation Principle" in conversations, is useful for at least two reasons. First, it is a social construct that emphasizes that classroom activities are "jointly constituted" by the participants (Erickson & Shultz, 1981). Order, in classrooms as in conversations, is achieved *with* students and depends upon their willingness to follow along with the unfolding of the event. Second, cooperation acknowledges that order can, and often does, rest on passive noninvolvement by at least some students. In seatwork, for instance, order exists as long as students are not interacting or distracting one another, even though they may not be engaged in working with the content. A whole-class discussion can, and often does (see Adams, 1969), operate with only a few students actually interacting with the teacher and the others playing the roles of audience members or passive bystanders, that is, "sitting nicely" and listening (Sieber, 1981). Cooperation, in other words, includes both involvement in the program of action for the activity and passive noninvolvement. Misbehavior, on the other hand, is any action by one or more students that threatens to disrupt the activity flow or pull the class toward a program of action that threatens the safety of the group or violates norms of appropriate classroom behavior held by the teacher, the students, or the school staff (see, e.g., Pollard, 1980). For an activity to succeed as a social event in a classroom, in other words, sufficient numbers of students must be willing to enact the participant role while the rest at least allow the activity to continue.

Classroom management, then, refers here to the actions and strategies teachers use to solve the problem of order in classrooms. Because order is a property of a social system, the language of management must be addressed to group dimensions of the classroom environment and to the contexts within which order is defined and achieved. Management is a complex enterprise because order is jointly accomplished by teachers and students and because a large number of immediate circumstances affect the nature of orderliness, the need for intervention, and the consequences of particular teacher and student actions.

HOW LIFE IN CLASSROOMS IS ORGANIZED

Classroom ecologists (e.g., Gump, 1967, 1975, 1982; Ross, 1984; Weinstein, 1991) have described the structures or behavior settings that organize classroom events and processes. In addition, microethnographers (e.g., Cazden, 1986; Erickson & Mohatt, 1982; Erickson & Shultz, 1981; Mehan, 1979) have examined closely the interactional processes involved in the enactment of events in classrooms. Finally, classroom researchers (e.g., Blumenfeld, Hamilton, Bossert, Wessels, & Meece, 1983; Doyle, 1979a, 1983; Doyle & Carter, 1984; Korth & Cornbleth, 1982) have analyzed the task systems that organize and direct classroom experiences. These domains of theory and research are surveyed in this section because they provide important information about the factors teachers must take into account in achieving classroom order.

According to the ecological tradition (see Gump, 1967, 1969), a classroom is a behavior setting, that is, an ecobehavioral unit composed of segments that surround and regulate behavior. A segment, such as a spelling test, writing lesson, or study period, can be described in terms of several elements or what Burnett (1973, p. 293) has called "scene coordinates," including:

1. Its temporal boundaries or duration.
2. The physical milieu, that is, the shape of the site in which it occurs, the number and types of participants, the arrangement of participants in the available space, and the props or objects available to participants.

3. The behavior format or program of action for participants.
4. The focal content or concern of the segment.

Perhaps the easiest way to clarify the concept of segments is to describe how they are identified in studies (e.g., Doyle, 1984; Gump, 1967; Stodolsky, 1988). The database for ecological studies is typically a set of "chronicles" (Gump, 1967; Ross, 1984) or narrative records of classroom meetings. (Videotape [e.g., Kounin, 1970] and time-lapse photography [e.g., Gump, 1967] were sometimes used when the focus was primarily on fine gradients of behavior within settings.) A classroom chronicle is a reasonably complete description of the behavior stream (Barker, 1968; Gump, 1967) that contains information about scene coordinates (i.e., the participants, physical arrangements, props, and time) and a running account of action sequences within scenes.

The first stage of analysis involves dividing a chronicle into segments that represent natural units of organized action. Segmenting rules (see Doyle, 1984; Gump, 1967) typically call attention to changes in (a) patterns for arranging participants (e.g., small-group vs. whole-class presentation), (b) props and resources used or the sources of information (e.g., books vs. films), (c) roles and responsibilities for carrying out immediate actions and events (e.g., oral answering vs. writing workbook entries), and (d) "rules of appropriateness" (Erickson & Shultz, 1981, p. 156), that is, the kinds of behaviors that are allowed and disapproved (e.g., talking during snack time vs. silence during seatwork). A change in one or more of these dimensions represents a potential change in the nature of the situation in which students and the teacher work.

The basic unit of classroom organization is the activity (see Berliner, 1983; Doyle, 1984; Gump, 1967; Kounin, 1970). Activities are relatively short blocks of classroom time—typically 10 to 20 minutes—during which students are arranged in a particular way. Common labels for activities reflect this organizational focus: seatwork, recitation, presentations, small groups. Sometimes activities are designated by their focal content—for example, morning song, spelling test, art—but an organizational pattern is strongly implied by these titles. Some evidence suggests that more than 30 separate activities occur each day in the average elementary school class (see Ross, 1984). In addition, overlapping or simultaneous segments occur during approximately one third of the elementary school day, although it is rare to find more than two segments occurring at the same time (see Gump, 1967). The diversity implied by these data is subject to two restrictions. First, activities with different labels often have quite similar formats. Thus, the structures for lectures, demonstrations, and audiovisual presentations are congruent on several dimensions. Similarly, seatwork often has a uniform shape regardless of the focal content. It is important to emphasize, however, that differences in focal content—for instance, social studies versus science—are likely to be quite important for students and teachers (Stodolsky, 1988). Second, in terms of actual use in classrooms or what Gump (1967) called student "occupancy time," a few activity types account for the bulk of classroom time. Although there were variations associated with content and student characteristics, reports in the 1980s indicated, for example, that approximately 65% of classroom time was spent in seatwork, 35% in whole-class presentation or recitation, and 15% in transitions and other housekeeping events (see Gump, 1967, 1982; Rosenshine, 1980; Sanford & Evertson, 1983; Stodolsky et al., 1981).

Work involvement or engagement is, by far, the most widely used student behavior dimension in studies of classroom management. Involvement is used to label student behavior that reflects active engagement in working. Noninvolvement or off-task behavior often includes passive withdrawal, mild forms of inappropriate behavior, and more serious forms of misbehavior. Gump's (1967) third grade study, using time-lapse photographs, remains one of the most thorough investigations of relationships between activity types and student involvement.

In general, he found that involvement was highest for students in teacher-led small groups (around 92%) and lowest for pupil presentations (72%). Between these extremes, engagement was higher in whole-class recitations, tests, and teacher presentations (around 80%) than in supervised study and independent seatwork that was not supervised by the teacher (around 75%).

Management demands are systematically related to the types of activities used in the classroom. The amount of time teachers spend organizing and directing students, interacting with individual students, and dealing with inappropriate and disruptive behavior is related to type of activity and the physical arrangements of the setting. Studies suggest that the greater the amount of student choice and mobility and the greater the complexity of the social scene, the greater the need for overt monitoring and managing actions by teachers. In addition, student work involvement or engagement is higher in teacher-led, externally paced activities than in self-paced activities, a factor that may account for the frequent use of recitations in classrooms. In addition, student involvement is lower during the beginning rather than the remaining phase of activities. Involvement is also especially low during activities in which there are prolonged student presentations.

Contexts as Programs of Action

According to Gump (1982), "The action structure is the heart of classroom segments" (p. 99). This statement is especially true for understanding classroom management because order is defined by the programs of action embedded in classroom activities. In addition to providing slots and sequences for participants' behavior, these programs of action have direction, momentum, and energy (see Arlin, 1979, 1982; Erickson, 1982; Kounin, 1970). Time does not simply pass in classrooms. Rather, there is rhythmic movement toward the accomplishment of academic and social-interactional ends. In Merritt's (1982) term, classroom activities contain "vectors" that, once entered into, pull events and participants along their course. In this section, the common classroom activities of recitation, seatwork, multiple-group arrangements, and transitions are described in terms of their programs, or vectors, of action.

Recitation. Recitation, which can take a variety of forms, involves calling on individual students to give usually brief answers to public questions before the rest of the class. Despite a steady barrage of criticism, this form appears to have been quite durable during the past century (see Cuban, 1982; Hoetker & Ahlbrand, 1969). Approximately 35% of classroom time was spent in recitations, and this activity was used for several purposes, including review, introducing new material, checking answers to work, practice, and checking understanding (Stodolsky, et al., 1981). Korth and Cornbleth (1982) found that whole-class considerations of content occurred most frequently in an activity they called "QATE," that is, question and answer with teacher elaboration.

Microethnographic analyses of classroom discourse (see Cazden, 1986) have directed attention to classroom participation structures, that is, the system of rules governing speaking, listening, and turn taking. Sinclair and Coulthard (1975) and Mehan (1979) described the participation structure of conventional classrooms in terms of a transaction or interactional sequence consisting of initiation, reply, and evaluation or follow-up. These episodes consist of the interconnected moves (see Bellack, Kliebard, Hyman, & Smith, 1966) teachers and students use in classrooms to accomplish interactional goals. For a detailed discussion of rules governing turn taking in whole-class lessons, see McHoul (1978).

Seatwork. The term *seatwork* refers to what Gump (1967) called "supervised study" during which all students are assigned to work independently at their desks with their own materials, although not necessarily the same material, and the teacher is free to monitor the total class. This type of seatwork is often quite interactive (Doyle, 1984). Merritt (1982) has examined the processes of multiple attending and scheduling that occurred during "servicelike events," that is, student-initiated contacts with the teacher, in 10 classes from nursery school through third grade. In a language compatible with Kounin's (1970), Merritt noted that teachers and students were faced with the demand to monitor more than one vector of activity even when they were primarily involved in only one. Moreover, teachers stayed with a vector of activity until they located a point at which it was terminated or would apparently continue without their immediate involvement. Thus, in a manner similar to turn taking in group lessons, student requests for teacher attention were ignored unless they occurred when the teacher was free to "slot out" for the request. Contacts, in other words, had to be appropriately timed. Students, in turn, were expected to wait until the teacher was free and to do something to fill the waiting time. Servicelike events involved, therefore, a complex judgment concerning the nature and duration of the interruption and the stability at a particular moment of the vector of activity the teacher was primarily directing. Merritt also noted that teachers often used contextualization cues during servicelike events to separate primary and secondary vectors and maintain the dual streams.

Small Groups and Cooperative Learning Teams. Classroom studies in the 1980s indicated that small groups in which students work together on assignments are used infrequently in most classrooms (Clements, 1983; Emmer, 1983; Stodolsky, 1988), with a possible exception of social studies (Stodolsky, 1988). Nevertheless, a strong emphasis on student groups and cooperative class activities is apparent in the contemporary pedagogical literature (e.g., Daviels and Bizar, 2005; Orlich, Harder, Callahan, Trevisan, & Brown, 2004), and the approach is consistent with the modern accent on collaboration, constructivism, and teaching for understanding. Studies in several subject fields and grade levels have generally indicated that cooperative teams have positive effects on achievement, especially when instruction is carefully structured, individuals are accountable for performance, and a well-defined group reward system is used (see Slavin, 1995, for a review). In addition, such methods have positive effects on race relations and mutual concern among students.

Given the potential for diverse action vectors and the demands on the teacher to divide attention, multiple simultaneous small groups in classrooms are obviously complex activity systems to manage. In their study of 56 cooperative learning lessons, Emmer and Gerwels (2002) found that successful elementary-level lessons (judged by student engagement, performance, and cooperation) were associated with high levels of teacher monitoring of group interaction, provision of feedback on and accountability for task progress, and use of manipulative props and materials shared by group members. Consistent with the ecological approach, in other words, the successful teachers were energetic and vigilant in tracking the progress of small-group work. One suspects that these same efforts would be required for cooperative lessons at upper grade levels.

Transitions. Transitions are points in social interaction when contexts change and, thus, they have been a favorite topic of researchers interested in activity structures and classroom discourse (see Erickson & Shultz, 1981; Gump, 1967). Minor transitions occur between speaking turns, and major transitions occur between activities or phases of a lesson, between lessons, and between class meetings. At each of these levels, large amounts of cuing and interactional negotiation occur to signal the onset of a change, the reorientation of focus, and the beginning of a new segment (see Bremme & Erickson, 1977; Cahir, 1978; Green & Harker, 1982; McDermott, 1976; Shultz & Florio, 1979). This cuing often creates "boundary indeterminacy," which makes it difficult to locate precise beginning and ending points for transitions between activities (see Arlin, 1979).

In general, the duration of major transitions depends upon the magnitude of the changes that must be made. A change in topic without an accompanying change in group structure, for example, is typically handled briefly by what Hargreaves, Hester, and Mellor (1975) called "switch-signals." A reconfiguration of the classroom, for example, from seatwork to small groups, takes more time, and teachers use a large number of regulatory acts to hold order in place until the next program of action is operating. Approximately 31 major transitions occur per day in elementary classrooms, and they account for approximately 15% of classroom time (see Gump, 1967, 1982; Rosenshine, 1980). Because room arrangements in secondary classes typically remain the same across activities, major transitions take less time at this level (see Doyle, 1984; Evertson, 1982).

Academic Work as a Program of Action

It is clear that subject matter is a significant component of the programs of action in classrooms. Hoffman and Clements (1984) and Englert and Semmel (1983) reported, for example, that teachers are likely to interrupt reading turns when a student's errors change the meaning of the text and ignore substitutions that are semantically equivalent to words in the text. These data suggest that teachers track the development of content as well as the flow of social interaction. Furthermore, students appear to focus a significant part of their attention in class on information about how to do the work they are assigned as well as what behavior they are to display (King, 1980, 1983). It would seem, therefore, that subject matter needs to be included more explicitly in research on classroom management.

Doyle (1979a, 1983) has used the notion of "academic tasks" to account for curriculum as a process dimension or program of action in classrooms. According to this model, subject matter appears in classroom settings as work, that is, as products to be generated using available instructions and resources (see also Blumenfeld et al., 1983). Accountability plays a key role in determining the value or significance of work in a classroom: Products that are evaluated strictly by the teacher are more likely to be seen as serious work, that is, work that "counts" (see Doyle & Carter, 1984). At the same time, accountability affects the risk associated with various types of academic tasks. Tasks involving higher cognitive processes of understanding, reasoning, and problem formulation are high in inherent ambiguity and risk for students; that is, because the precise nature of correct answers cannot be predicted and rehearsed in advance, the possibility of failure is high. Ambiguity and risk, in turn, shape students' attitudes toward the work they do in classrooms.

From the perspective of order, the nature of academic work influences the probability of student cooperation and involvement in a lesson and thus the complexity of the teacher's management task. If, for example, most students find the work too difficult, then few will be able to participate in carrying out the activity (see Davis and McKnight, 1976; Doyle and Carter, 1984).

Pacing, Signal Systems, and Involvement

Gump and Kounin have provided a useful framework to account for differences in student involvement among activity structures. In generalizing across types of activities, Gump (1967, 1969) initially placed emphasis on what he called "pacing" and concluded that involvement was higher when the students' work was externally paced (recitations, tests) than when it was self-paced (supervised study and seatwork). In later work, Gump (1982) expanded the notion of pacing to include a difference between an active input of stimuli and a passive availability of materials. In the active structure, students are "pulled" along through the work; in the passive structure, pacing depends upon students' understanding of the action sequence and their own motivation. An emphasis on activity flow and pace is also reflected in Kounin's (1970) findings concerning the importance of momentum in managing classroom groups. This concept is also similar to Merritt's (1982) notion of "vector of activity."

Kounin and Gump (1974) introduced the concept of *signal systems* to explain how different activity structures and tasks influence student involvement. A lesson's signal systems are defined as the provisions external to an individual student that signal action within the setting: "These provisions include the communications of the teacher ('Let's see what sticks and what doesn't stick to a magnet.') and the props that go with the lesson (magnet, paper clips, pieces of paper and cloth, nails). A lesson also includes the standing behavior pattern that goes with the lesson (making piles of objects that stick or don't stick to the magnet, listening to a story being read)." (p. 556). Signal systems are, in other words, the situational instructions for lesson behavior.

In defining features of signal systems, Kounin and Gump emphasized *continuity, insulation*, and *intrusiveness*. Continuity refers to the regularity of the flow of information or signals to the individual participant. Lessons high in continuity are those involving teacher presentations (reading books to the class, demonstrations, or playing phonograph records) in which there is a single, continuous source of signal emission. Such lessons are predicted to have low deviance rates. Individual construction lessons contain tasks that are high in signal continuity "as one action and its immediate result provide impetus and guidance for the next" (Kounin & Gump, 1974, p. 557). In this case, involvement is high if the materials are appropriate and the student is capable of understanding the task and carrying out the steps to completion. Lessons that are low in continuity are group discussions, group projects, and role play in which there are multiple, shifting signal sources, as well as inadequate signals and lags in the flow of information resulting from the faltering performances by students. Such lessons are expected to have low involvement and high off-task behavior.

Insulation refers to the degree to which the individual student is isolated from signals for inappropriate behavior. In individual construction lessons, for example, the signal source, "resting as it does on the results of each child's own actions on his own materials, produces a tight, closed behavior-environment circuit. This closed circuit... shields each child from foreign inputs (distractions, other children's deviances) which may serve as stimuli to inappropriate behavior" (Kounin & Gump, 1974, p. 557). In contrast, group construction lessons during which students share materials are low in insulation. Lessons high in insulation are expected to have low off-task rates. Finally, some lessons (e.g., music or movement lessons) have continuous signals from a single source but are high in intrusiveness, that is, the stimuli used (e.g., bells, dance movements) are sufficiently intense to intrude into the student's attention and thus compete with the appropriate lesson signals. Such lessons are expected to be high in off-task behaviors.

Kounin and Gump (1974) found that individual construction had the lowest rate of off-task behavior of all of the lesson types. In such lessons, students were sufficiently insulated to maintain task involvement even when the teacher conducted a recitation or discussion with another student or a small group of students (Kounin & Doyle, 1975). Moderate rates of off-task behavior were found for lessons in which students listened to the teacher or to records, or lessons involving teacher-led demonstrations. Involvement during these lessons could be maintained even when they included student participation if the duration of such public teacher-student interactions was short (Kounin & Doyle, 1975). Highest off-task levels were found for open discussions, group construction, and music and movement lessons. Indeed, music and movement lessons were high in contagious "group glee" in which students jumped, screamed joyfully, and laughed (see Sherman, 1975).

The work on signal systems suggests that organizing work to maintain activity flow or momentum and guard against competing programs or vectors of action will promote order in classrooms. Despite the compelling logic of this model, it rests primarily on preschool data for lessons that were not part of a regular academic program and were taught on an ad hoc basis. Further research is needed to understand how the propositions of this model apply to other contexts and levels of schooling.

Summary

From an ecological perspective, then, order depends upon the strength and durability of the primary program, or vector of action, that defines order in a particular classroom context. This program of action includes both a social participation dimension that defines rules for interacting in a complex and crowded environment and an academic work dimension that carries the substances of lessons. In classes composed of students who lack either the skill or the inclination to participate, the primary vector of action can lack strength and durability in a context in which alternative programs of action are plentiful. In such situations, teachers are required to expend a considerable amount of energy to nurture and protect the primary vector. Research on how such energy can be fruitfully expended is reviewed in the next section.

HOW ORDER IS ACHIEVED IN CLASSROOMS

The purpose of this section is to integrate information about the strategies and processes that account for the differential effectiveness of teachers in managing classrooms. In shifting from descriptions of classroom organization to management strategies, the emphasis turns to the options teachers have within classroom contexts for constructing well-formed activities.

The Physical Design of Settings

Ecological researchers (e.g., Barker, 1968; Gump, 1974, 1982; Ross, 1984) have used the term *synomorphy* to refer to the compatibility between the program of action in an activity and the physical aspects of the setting. From the perspective of order, one can easily imagine how furniture arrangements (e.g., circles, U-shapes, straight rows), types of desks and chairs (e.g., tables or booths in art and laboratory rooms vs. conventional desks), and room dividers (e.g., bookcases, file cabinets) could affect the density of students, opportunities for interaction, and the visibility of behavior. Similarly, glare from overhead projectors or light through a window could well create blind spots for a teacher and thus interfere with monitoring classroom behavior. Unfortunately, only a limited amount of systematic inquiry has been done in this area of classroom management.

Weinstein (1979) reviewed research on the effects of physical features of the classroom environment. The data on classroom design and furniture arrangements indicate that different patterns of spatial organization have little effect on achievement but some effect on attitudes and conduct. In particular, it seems to be important to separate clearly areas serving different purposes and design traffic avenues in the room carefully. Density, which has been studied primarily at nursery school and college levels, appears to increase dissatisfaction and aggression and decrease attentiveness.

Perhaps the most widely known work on the effects of physical features of classrooms is that conducted by Adams (1969) and Adams and Biddle (1970) on the relationship between students' location and participation. These investigators found that students who sat in the "action zone" in the front and center of the room (seats were arranged in traditional rows) interacted most frequently with the teacher.

A considerable amount of the research on physical dimensions of schooling has concentrated on differences between traditional enclosed classrooms and open-spaced buildings (see Weinstein, 1979). Gump (1975) reviewed data concerning noise in open-space schools and concluded that noise bothered teachers more than it did students (see also Denscombe, 1980) and that the effects of noise on attention depended upon the nature of the activity, the content of the message, and the density of the setting. Gump (1974) studied primary (first and second) and intermediate (fifth and sixth) grades in two open-space and two traditional school buildings. Differences between buildings were more consistent at the primary than at the intermediate levels, and the differences suggested that open-school students at the primary level occupied a greater variety of sites than primary students in the traditional schools (2.75 and 3.00 vs. 1.00 and 1.75). In addition, primary students in open schools worked with more adults than traditional school students did (2.67 vs. 1.37). At the intermediate level, one traditional school provided less variety in sites and number of adults than the other traditional school and the open schools. The data also indicated that open-school students, especially at the primary level, spent more time than traditional-school students in settings in which they worked together and in settings with external rather than self-pacing. The latter result may have occurred because there were more adults present in open classes. In addition, more time in open schools than in traditional schools was spent in transitions, waiting, and organizing (31% and 25% vs. 19% at the primary level). Gump reported that most delays in open schools occurred after transitions because teachers were busy closing out the previous activity or dealing with a problem from that activity. Finally, student on-task percentages were lower in one of the open schools at the primary level (73% vs. 80% for the other schools) and in both open schools at the intermediate level (76% and 78% vs. 82% and 86%). Referring to the frequent similarities in results, especially at the intermediate level, Gump concluded that construction alone did not necessarily affect the educational program in these schools.

Establishing Classroom Rules and Procedures

From the perspective of classroom order, the early class sessions of a school year are of critical importance (see Ball, 1980; Doyle, 1979b; Smith & Geoffrey, 1968). During this time, order is defined and the processes and procedures that sustain order are put into place. The validity of this concern for the beginning of the year was demonstrated quite clearly in a series of elementary and junior high school studies conducted at the University of Texas Research and Development Center for Teacher Education (Emmer et al., 1980; Evertson & Emmer, 1982). Because classrooms are made up of groups of students assembled under crowded conditions for relatively long periods of time to accomplish specified purposes, life in these settings is governed by a variety of explicit and implicit rules and procedures (see Blumenfeld, Hamilton, Wessels, & Falkner, 1979; Hargreaves et al., 1975; Jackson, 1968). In addition to official rules of conduct, class sessions and patterns of interaction often appear to be ritualized, with specific formats for openings, closings, and the conduct of lessons (see Griffin & Mehan, 1979; Yinger, 1979). Classroom rules are usually intended to regulate forms of individual conduct that are likely to disrupt activities, cause injury, or damage school property. Thus, there are rules concerning tardiness, talking during lessons, gum chewing, fighting, bringing materials to class, and the like. In addition, there are a large number of implict rules that affect social interaction and interpersonal relationships in classrooms (see Erickson & Shultz, 1981; McHoul, 1978). Procedures consist of approved ways of taking care of various duties and privileges in classrooms, such as handing in completed work, sharpening pencils, getting a drink of water, and going to the restroom.

Studies at the Research and Development Center for Teacher Education indicated that effective classroom managers in elementary and junior high school classes are especially skilled in establishing rules and procedures at the beginning of the year (Emmer et al., 1980; Evertson & Emmer, 1982). Not only did they introduce rules and procedures on the first day, but they integrated their rules and procedures into a workable system and deliberately taught this system to the students. Rules and procedures were concrete, explicit, and functional, that is, they contributed to order and work accomplishment. In addition, items were clearly explained to students, signals were used to indicate when actions were to be carried out or stopped, and time was spent rehearsing procedures. In addition, effective managers avoided information overload by focusing initially on immediate concerns and then introducing more procedures as they were needed. At the same time, they appear to have anticipated possible interruptions or problems and had procedures readily available to handle these situations. The more effective managers also continued to remind students of the rules and procedures for the first weeks of school. Finally, effective managers monitored classes closely and stopped inappropriate behavior promptly. In contrast, less effective managers either failed to anticipate the need for rules and procedures covering important aspects of class operation or tended to have vague and unenforceable rules (for example, "Be in the right place at the right time," or "Never chew gum"). Moreover, they neither explained their rules and procedures clearly to students nor monitored and enforced compliance. Rather, they seemed to be preoccupied with clerical tasks and disoriented by problems and interruptions. Less effective managers were also more likely than effective managers to leave the room during the first day.

The Function of Routines

The rehearsing and routinizing of procedures and activities in classrooms would seem to be an important mechanism for sustaining classroom order. Yinger (1979, 1980) has argued that routinization makes classroom activities less susceptible to breakdowns during interruptions because participants know the normal sequence of events. At a more micro level, McDermott (1976) has described how the positioning and interactional cuing displayed by participants carry along the sequence of events in familiar lesson contexts (see Woolfolk & Brooks, 1985, for a review of research on nonverbal cuing). In the language of signal system theory (Kounin & Gump, 1974), routines provide a continuous signal for organizational and interpersonal behavior, an effect not present in Kounin and Gump's data because the lessons in their sample were taught on an ad hoc basis by student teachers. (For more discussion of classroom rules and procedures, see chapter 14.)

Orchestrating Classroom Activities

Attention now turns to teacher actions associated with carrying out classroom activities in space and time. Although classroom structures guide behavior and routines stabilize programs of actions, classroom lessons have an improvisational character (Erickson, 1982; Griffin & Mehan, 1979). The form of a particular lesson is jointly negotiated and constructed by students and the teacher, and order is thus subject to the contingencies of multiple interpretations, preferences, and errors. As a result, delicate and complex processes must be balanced to sustain order in classrooms.

The section begins with a survey of research on monitoring as a key process in conducting all forms of classroom activity. The focus then shifts to processes involved in maintaining various types of classroom activities, namely, (a) lessons involving group interaction, for example, recitations and discussion; (b) seatwork, both supervised and unsupervised; and (c) transitions. This section concludes with a discussion of relationships between classroom management and academic work.

Monitoring. Kounin's (1970) widely influential study of 80 first- and second-grade classes (each containing at least one emotionally disturbed child) pointed to teacher attention and monitoring as central components of classroom management skill. Specifically, teachers in Kounin's study who had high levels of work involvement and freedom from deviancy in their classes were high on "withitness" and "overlapping," that is, they were aware of what was going on in the classroom, communicated this awareness to students, and were able to attend to two or more events at the same time (see also Brophy & Evertson, 1976; Emmer et al., 1980; Evertson & Emmer, 1982).

The content of monitoring—what teachers watch when scanning the room—includes at least three dimensions. First, teachers watch groups (see Clark & Yinger, 1979; Kounin, 1970); they attend to what is happening in the entire room and how well the total activity system is going. A group focus does not preclude attention to individual students, but localized attending must be scheduled within the broader framework of the group activity (see Merritt, 1982). Second, teachers watch conduct or behavior, with particular attention to discrepancies from the intended program of action for the segment. "Withit" teachers notice misbehavior early, before it spreads across the room, and reprimand the originator of the misbehavior rather than an innocent bystander or a student who joined the event after it began. Third, teachers monitor the pace, rhythm, and duration of classroom events. Arlin (1982) has described how pressures to keep things moving and avoid delays shape classroom events, Kounin (1970) found that smoothness and momentum were associated with management success, and Gump (1967) found that hesitations and lags in the flow of activities increased off-task behavior.

In addition to staying aware of classroom events and their momentum, teachers must also communicate this awareness to students. Kounin (1970) emphasized that teachers demonstrated awareness through the timeliness and accuracy of desists. If the real culprit is caught early, then students presumably learn that the teacher is aware of what is going on in the room. Moreover, Kounin's (1970) work suggests that communicating awareness prevents the initiation and spread of off-task and disruptive behavior and thus reduces the need for reprimands. Successful managers also comment frequently and accurately on the appropriateness of students' behavior and give a running commentary on classroom events (see Emmer et al., 1980; Evertson & Emmer, 1982; Doyle, 1984). They use, in other words, a multiplicity of "contextualization cues" (Erickson & Shultz, 1981; Green & Harker, 1982; Shultz & Florio, 1979) to establish and maintain classroom events.

Group Lessons. The complexity of classroom events is especially apparent in conversational lessons like recitations and discussions. Group lessons require that a teacher cope with a complex social system with multiple participants of different abilities and a discontinuous signal system to guide the flow of events, monitor the development of content in an often unpredictable pattern, and provide accurate and appropriate feedback to individual students for their answers. Broad topic discussion or divergent questions can increase the demands of such events, requiring alertness and skill on the teacher's part. In the case in which students are reluctant to participate, a teacher must stimulate student participation through group alerting and accountability signals (Kounin, 1970). "Patterned turns," in which students are preselected for answering, localize the teacher's attention to a single student at a time and thus students tend not to attend to immediate events and become uninvolved in work.

Stimulating participation can, however, lead to another set of problems. In reporting a study of British secondary level classes, Hammersley (1974) pointed out that the more successful a teacher was in stimulating participation, the more difficult the turn allocation process became. This dilemma in mobilizing participation stemmed from the fact that there was only one pupil slot for answering and frequently several bidders for the right to speak in that slot. Students were observed to use various strategies to secure an opportunity to give the right answer by shouting out or verbally soliciting teacher recognition by repeating "Sir" until they were called on.

Turn allocation would seem to be an especially difficult process to manage in classrooms. Several investigators have noted that teachers are not always consistent in enforcing rules against "call-outs," especially with low-ability groups (see Copeland, 1978; Eder, 1982a; Evertson, 1982; Sanford & Evertson, 1981). Studies of reading groups, in particular, have indicated that orchestrating turns with low-ability students is problematic. In contrast to higher ability students, low-ability students are less likely to participate and more inclined to make topically irrelevant comments (Eder, 1982a). In addition, shifts between turns in low-ability groups are less orderly and require a greater amount of concentrated teacher direction to accomplish (McDermott, 1976). Teachers in low-ability groups are more likely to interrupt reading turns (Allington, 1980), orient to listeners during turns (Eder, 1982b), and accept student-initiated interruptions that are topically relevant (Eder, 1982a). Finally, reading turns for low-ability students are longer and more likely to contain long pauses and errors that alter the meaning of the text (Eder, 1982a; Hoffman & Clements, 1984), qualities of performance that can lead to inattention (Gump, 1967) and confusion about content. These patterns suggest that teachers are attempting to maintain content flow, activity flow, and student attention by prompting correct responses and by group alerting; that is, they are trying to maintain the integrity of the activity against fairly strong countervailing pressures.

Seatwork. Seatwork is used frequently in classrooms and presents special issues of management. Although the demands of being the central actor and turn allocator are not present in seatwork as they are in group lessons, managing seatwork cannot be left to chance. Management studies indicate that during supervised seatwork effective teachers monitor the class thoroughly, inspect individual papers frequently, and generally hover over the work and usher it along (Doyle, 1984; Emmer et al., 1980; Evertson & Emmer, 1982). Under these conditions, seatwork is much more interactive than the label implies. Such actions would seem to approximate the conditions of external pacing that occur in group lessons. This degree of supervision is not possible, however, when the teacher is teaching a small group while the rest of the students are working independently at their desks. In this latter situation, a teacher can seldom leave the reading group to help seatwork students without disrupting the small-group lesson. Moreover, a teacher is likely to limit whole-class comments to reprimanding disruptive behavior and maintaining boundaries between the small group and the rest of the class (see McDermott, 1976).

Transitions. As indicated earlier in this chapter, transitions are important events in achieving order. Studies indicate that the quality of a transition sets the pace and tone of the subsequent segment (see Arlin, 1979; Cahir, 1978; Gump, 1967). Transitions are also affected by the ability level of a class. Evertson (1982) reported that there were more transitions in higher ability junior high classes, but the average length of a transition and the total time in transition were greater for low-ability classes.

Arlin (1979) and Doyle (1984) found that skilled managers marked the onset of transitions clearly, orchestrated transitions actively, and minimized the loss of momentum during these changes in activities. Less effective managers, on the other hand, tended to blend activities together, failed to monitor events during transitions, and took excessively long to complete the movement between segments (see also Kounin, 1970). Transitions appear to require considerable vigilance and teacher direction to accomplish successfully.

Cuing and Improvising Contexts. This survey of research suggests that orchestrating classroom lessons involves a delicate balancing of a large number of forces and a selective and efficient processing of information about certain key dimensions that affect classroom structures and rhythms. Erickson (1982a) has called attention to the improvisational character of classroom lessons. As students and a teacher go about the processes of achieving a context, they frequently adjust to the demands of immediately unfolding events and the multiple vectors of classroom settings. Order is held in place, however, by the redundancy of contextualization cues that participants use to tell each other what is happening (see Erickson & Mohatt, 1982; Erickson & Shultz, 1981; McDermott, 1976; Griffin & Mehan, 1979). These cues, which include verbal and nonverbal messages as well as the rhythm or cadence of actions and the direction or momentum of events, are often quite subtle and delicate. Shultz and Florio (1979), for example, reported an incident in which the teacher assumed the position for announcing a transition but was distracted from giving the verbal signal. The students, responding to the positional cue, started to move before the teacher was ready to begin the transition. This perspective on the achievement of order suggests that management functions can be easily disrupted by factors interfering with communication systems in classrooms.

Classroom Management and Academic Work: A Delicate Balance

Classroom studies indicate that the demands of academic work are shaped by a complex negotiation process between teachers and students (see Doyle & Carter, 1984). This line of inquiry points to the possibility that teachers sometimes seek to achieve order by selecting only tasks that are familiar and easy for students. Doyle (1983) has argued that academic work involving higher level cognitive processes (understanding, reasoning, and problem formulation) is high in ambiguity and risk for students. Students respond to these factors by attempting to increase the explicitness of product specifications and reduce the stringency of accountability requirements (see especially Davis & McKnight, 1976). Such actions tend to slow down the flow of classroom events, reduce work involvement, and increase the frequency of misbehavior and disruption; that is, students' reactions to work create pressures on the management system. In response to these threats to order, teachers often simplify task demands or lower the risk for mistakes (see especially Doyle & Carter, 1984). In contrast, relatively simple and routine tasks involving memory or algorithms tend to proceed quite smoothly in class with little hesitation or resistance.

Clearly academic work can be swamped by the management function in teaching, and teachers can become preoccupied with getting work accomplished rather than promoting student achievement (Allington, 1983; Brophy, 1982; Eder, 1982b). When this happens, management limits the opportunities students have for learning, even though engagement may be high. In such circumstances, a well-managed class would not necessarily be a high-achieving class. At the same time, some challenging academic tasks are difficult to manage in classrooms. When such tasks are being used, the class may not score high on such management indicators as attention and engagement. Issues such as these suggest that management studies that ignore content can be misleading, and instructional design studies that ignore management can miss an essential dimension related to the practical use of designs.

The data reviewed in this chapter suggest, however, that the solution to the tension between management and instruction may require a greater emphasis on management. For example, including low-ability students into the center of the activity and task systems of a class requires well-developed management skills that enable a teacher to compensate for the pressures such students place on the activity system (see Sanford & Evertson, 1981). In other words, solving the instructional problems of low-ability students cannot be done by deemphasizing management or by designing more complex instructional arrangements for the classroom. Indeed, such "solutions" are likely to increase the problems they are designed to rectify. A more appropriate answer to the problem would seem to involve improved knowledge and training in management so that teachers can be free to concentrate on instructional solutions to learning problems.

Misbehavior and Interventions

To this point in the review, questions of misbehavior and teacher interventions to stop misbehavior have been conveniently sidestepped. This diversionary tactic was intentional in part because of a need to separate issues of classroom management from issues of discipline and in part because misbehavior and teacher interventions, from an ecological perspective, can be understood only in terms of their relation to processes of orchestrating order in classrooms. In other words, misbehavior and what teachers do to stop it are not an isolated entity in a classroom. Rather, they are part of the fabric of the ecological system that defines and sustains order.

It is now time to attack the issues of misbehavior and interventions directly. The first task constructs a definition of misbehavior that is ecologically based, that is, tied to the components of the activity system in classrooms. The second task explains teacher interventions as attempts to repair breakdowns in classroom order.

Misbehavior. Interventions into the flow of an activity to stop misbehavior are based on complex judgments about the act, the actor, and the circumstances at a particular moment in classroom time. To understand interventions, then, it is necessary to understand the contours of misbehavior.

Popular attention is often drawn to incidents of severely disruptive behavior and crime in schools, such as violence, robbery, theft, vandalism, and drug traffic. Although traumatic when they occur, such acts are generally rare in most schools and most often occur in corridors, lunch rooms, and outside the buildings, rather than in classrooms. More common are tardiness, cutting classes, failure to bring supplies and books, inattentiveness, talking, call-outs, and mild forms of verbal and physical aggression (see Doyle, 1978). Most misbehavior is related to attention, crowd control, and getting work accomplished in classrooms. However, the judgments involved in interpreting classroom behavior are not always simple. Actions that appear to be quite similar are reacted to quite differently by teachers when performed by different students at different times or in different contexts (see Mehan, 1974; Mehan, Hertweck, Combs, & Flynn, 1982; Metz, 1978; Solomon & Kendall, 1976). This differential treatment does not usually occur because of teacher incompetence or even inconsistency but because of the contextual specificity of rules and the differential consequences of actions in the behavior stream of classrooms (see Hargreaves et al., 1975). In other words, the discrete actions of the same form are not the same if they have (or are perceived to have) very different consequences under different circumstances.

The key to understanding misbehavior is to view what students do in the context of classroom structures. From this perspective, misbehavior is any behavior by one or more students that is perceived by the teacher to initiate a vector of action that competes with or threatens the primary vector of action at a particular moment in a classroom activity. Vectors perceived as misbehavior are likely to be (or likely to become) public, that is, visible to a significant portion of the class, and contagious, or capable of spreading rapidly or pulling other members of the class into them. Misbehavior, in other words, creates fractures or fissures in the program of action in a classroom. For classes or groups in which the primary vector is weak (i.e., students are easily distracted or not inclined to engage in academic work) and actions outside the primary vector are frequent, misbehavior is likely to be common (see Felmlee & Eder, 1983; Metz, 1978).

By this definition, not every infraction of a rule is necessarily misbehavior. Talking out of turn is not misbehavior if it advances the lesson at a time when moving forward is essential. Similarly, inattention during the last few minutes of a class session will often be tolerated because the vector of action is coming to a stop. On the other hand, consistent delays in reacting to directives can slow down the activity flow in a class and irritate a teacher (Brooks & Wagenhauser, 1980).

Misbehavior, then, is not a property of an action but of an "action in context" (Mehan et al., 1982, p. 313) and a considerable amount of interpretation based on what a teacher knows about the likely configuration of events in a classroom is involved in applying the label (cf. Hargreaves et al., 1975). In this light, the common suggestion that teachers should be "consistent" means not that they should always behave in the same way but that they should be able to make reliable judgments about the probable consequences of students' actions in different situations. The analysis here suggests that this type of consistency is not easy to achieve.

Misbehavior as a Student Skill. It is important not to leave students out of the analysis of the interpretive work that goes into recognizing, producing, and controlling misbehavior in classrooms. In most instances, misbehavior is caused by only a few unruly students (see Metz, 1978; Sanford & Evertson, 1981; Sieber, 1979a; Tikunoff & Ward, 1978), while the rest of the class serves as members of an audience and as potential participants in the incident if it spreads. McDermott (1976) has documented how first-grade students in both high- and low-ability reading groups work interactively to produce and sustain order and to hold each other accountable for appropriate behavior. Part of this interactive work consists of signals to the teacher when order is threatened, perhaps because the teacher is viewed as a protector against aggression and injury (see also Sieber, 1979b). At the same time, there would seem to be a certain skillfulness associated with behavior outside the primary vector of action in classrooms. Even in the early elementary grades, some students are able to mask nonproductive time by faking involvement and concealing actions that teachers are likely to reprimand (see Hargreaves et al., 1975).

In addition, the timing of misbehavior seems to be important. Rusnock and Brandler (1979) found differences across students in the timing of off-task behavior: High-ability students were likely to engage in off-task behavior at the end of segments or during transitions whereas low-ability students engaged in off-task behavior during the middle of segments. In the latter case, off-task behavior was more likely to be visible and to disrupt the activity. Spencer-Hall (1981) described a case of a fifth-grade student (reportedly a typical case) who engaged in several types of "disruptive" behaviors but who actually won the "good citizenship" award for the school. The key to his success was that his actions outside the primary vector were done behind the teacher's back so that he was seldom caught.

One way to interpret these findings is to suggest that "misbehavior" by highly skilled students is not, strictly speaking, misbehavior at all. Although these actions are outside the primary vector and are visible to other students, they are inserted into small gaps in the behavior stream, gaps that are so small that less skilled students do not have time to join in and cannot react without appearing to misbehave. As a result, there is little spread of effect, and these actions have little consequence for classroom order. They do not, in other words, disrupt the primary vector of an activity.

This perspective on student skill in behaving outside the primary vector of action in a classroom would seem to be important in understanding teachers' efforts to communicate competence at the beginning of the year. If a teacher recognizes such behavior early when performed by a student known by the class to be skilled, then the teacher's competence is established instantly. If, however, a teacher fails to recognize such behavior in students known to be unskilled, then he or she is likely to have difficulty creating and sustaining order.

Interventions. The research reviewed in this chapter indicates that students and teachers do a considerable amount of interactional work together to define and sustain order in classrooms. McDermott (1976), for example, reported that students in both high- and low-ability classes responded almost immediately to departures from the primary program of action and began to signal through positionings and glances their awareness of this "disorder." The ripple effect (Kounin, 1970), in other words, occurs early and students hold each other accountable for being orderly. Nevertheless, the teacher is the primary custodian of order in a classroom and, therefore, must decide when and how to intervene into the flow of activity to repair order, that is, to stop a competing or disruptive vector and return to the primary program of action for a segment.

Interventions can repair temporary disturbances in classroom order, but they cannot establish order when no primary vector is operating. As a result, the frequency or even the quality of desists does not predict the degree of order in a classroom (Kounin, 1970). Indeed, Kounin (1983) reported that the least successful teacher in his samples achieved task involvement only 25% of the time and yet attempted to desist behavior 986 times in one day. The degree of order depends more upon the strength of the primary vector and the timing of the intervention to occur before the secondary vector has gained strength (Kounin, 1970). Successful managers, in other words, create order by establishing activities, anticipating potential misbehavior, and catching misbehavior early when it occurs (see Emmer et al., 1980; Evertson & Emmer, 1982).

Interventions are inherently risky because they call attention to potentially disruptive behavior and they initiate a program of action that, ironically, can pull the class further away from the primary vector and weaken its function in holding order in place. There is, in other words, a "ripple effect" of interventions (Kounin & Gump, 1958), that is, desist episodes influence witnesses and disrupt their involvement, although this effect appears to occur primarily during early class sessions and to depend upon a student's commitment to the work and liking for the teacher (see Kounin, 1970). In addition, inserting a desist into an action chain can disrupt the rhythm of interaction and slow down the flow of a classroom event.

Because of these risk factors, successful interventions tend to have a private and fleeting quality that does not interrupt the flow of events (see Erickson & Mohatt, 1982). In addition to occurring early, they are often quite brief and do not invite further comment from the target student or students. Sieber (1976, 1979a, 1981), for instance, identified over 30 types of interventions in a study of first- and fifth-grade classes. Simple verbal reprimands accounted for 58% of the total intervention episodes observed. The other types included praise, prizes and surprises, manipulation of privileges, physical coercion/affection, generalized threats, isolation, seat changes, repetition of routines, "writing names," and detention. Of these, no single type accounted for more than 3% of the total observed episodes. Borman, Lippincott, Matey, and Obermiller (1978) noted that elementary teachers tend to use "soft imperatives," that is, suggestions or questions ("Why don't you put the pencil down?") to control behavior. Such indirect statements leave room for negotiation and avoid confrontations. Indeed, teachers use a variety of unobtrusive nonverbal signals, including gestures, direct eye contact, and proximity, to regulate misbehavior (see Woolfolk & Brooks, 1985).

Humphrey (1979) examined desists or "sanctions" during turn taking in 15 lessons from two kindergarten and two third-grade classes. Of the 263 sanction incidents studied, 124, or 47%, consisted of the "squelch" form only (e.g., "Shh," "Wait," "Stop," or "No") and 74, or 28%, consisted of the squelch plus a brief explication (e.g., "Shh. Put your hand up if you want to say something"). Humphrey argued that the squelch form is uniquely suited to interrupting and terminating a student's utterance. In other words, the intervention is abrupt, short, and does not invite further comment or discussion from the student. As a result, the primary vector of the lesson is only minimally disturbed.

In classes in which the primary vector is weak, desists are likely to be frequent (Evertson, 1982; Metz, 1978; Sanford & Evertson, 1981). At the same time there would appear to be a delicate balance between attending to the primary vector and attending to inappropriate behavior. Doyle (1984) reported that successful junior high managers tended to push on through the curriculum and did not let misbehavior become the central topic of conversation. This practice often meant that some rules were not enforced and the level of inappropriate behavior remained high (see also Metz, 1978). Nevertheless, the primary vector was sustained. Along similar lines, Eder (1982a) reported that the teacher in her study consistently reprimanded attempts by high-ability students to interrupt during reading turns but accepted such bids during turns in the low-ability group. This policy would seem to reflect the strength of the primary vector in these settings. In the high-ability group, the lesson vector is likely to be strong and less susceptible to disruption by reprimands. In the low-ability group, the lesson vector is protected and advanced by accepting topically related bids and avoiding reprimands.

Finally, studies of teacher decision making have indicated that teachers are reluctant to change activities when things are not going well (see Clark & Yinger, 1979), and McHoul (1978) reported that teachers returned to the standard format and procedures for turn taking when open bidding became chaotic. This policy again seems reasonable. When order becomes unstable, repairing a primary vector would seem to be more sensible than initiating a transition to a new vector because transitions, even in the best of circumstances, are difficult to manage. The one exception to this general rule would seem to be the switch to structured seatwork when order is threatened in a whole-class presentation or recitation (see Metz, 1978). Such a transition is frequently made in classrooms and involves a minimum of group reorganization. Moreover, inappropriate behavior is less public when students are directed to attend to work at their own desks.

The Decision to Intervene. Interventions are, by their very nature, reactive. That is, they are occasioned by behaviors that signal the beginnings of a disruption. As a result, they cannot be planned in advance, that is, their timing is difficult to control and their form must be decided on the spot. Given the risks involved, the decision to intervene is quite problematic.

Several attempts have been made to study the intervention decisions of teachers. The results indicate that decisions concerning when and how to intervene are based on teachers' knowledge of who is misbehaving, what the misbehavior is, and when it occurs. In an experiment using written descriptions, Cone (1978) found, for instance, that elementary teachers' estimates of disruptiveness and selections of management strategies were based on information about the student's history of deviancy, the nature of the act, and the setting in which it occurred (i.e., large vs. small group). In post experiment interviews, Cone also found that teachers were able to give a large number of additional cues concerning student characteristics and situational factors such as task at hand and the time of the day or year that they would consider in making intervention decisions. Using written descriptions, Natriello and Dornbusch (1980) found that teachers responded to academic problems with warmth and concern and to behavior problems with presentations of standards. In a survey of 16 classroom studies, White (1975) found consistent differences in teachers' rates of approval and disapproval across instructional and managerial behaviors of students. Finally, Humphrey (1979) found that third-grade teachers were harsher in desisting turn-taking violations than kindergarten teachers, reflecting perhaps a difference in the teachers' expectations about the students' knowledge of appropriate classroom behavior.

The work of Hargreaves et al. (1975) suggests that actual decisions to intervene are made under conditions of considerable uncertainty. Early cues of possible misbehavior, for example, concealment, are ambiguous and yet the teacher has only a limited amount of time to form a judgment and act. To reduce uncertainty, teachers typify or categorize students in terms of such factors as their persistence and their visibility in the social structure of the group. Teachers, in other words, learn the likely configuration of events associated with actions by different students and use this information to decide whether an intervention is necessary.

In summary, the need to restore order in a classroom is a sign that the mechanisms that establish and sustain order are not working. The repair process itself is complex and risky as are the decisions concerning when and how to intervene. Successful managers appear to be able to decide early whether an act will disrupt order and to intervene in an inconspicuous way to cut off the path toward disorder. In attending to misbehavior and interventions, however, the emphasis remains on the primary vector of action as the fundamental means of holding order in place in classrooms.

Conclusion

The need for management is most apparent when order is threatened. As a result, interventions to stop misbehavior are often the primary focus of theory and research in classroom management. The evidence suggests, however, that such episodes are most appropriately viewed as occasions in which order is repaired rather than created. Thus, the quantity or quality of interventions will not predict the degree of order in a classroom unless a program of action has already been established. The evidence also suggests that intervention episodes involve complex decisions about the probable consequences of particular actions by particular students at specific moments in the activity flow of a class session. Finally, because misbehavior and a teacher's reaction to misbehavior represent a vector of action, attempts to stop misbehavior can themselves disrupt order. As a result, successful desists are often inserted skillfully into the activity flow, and, in many cases, teachers seem to prefer to intervene in the private rather than in the public sphere of classrooms. Teachers are intent, in other words, on staying with the primary vector that sustains order in classrooms.

THEMES AND DIRECTIONS FOR AN ECOLOGY OF CLASSROOM MANAGEMENT

This final section of the chapter is devoted to two areas: (a) a summation of the core ideas of an ecological view of classroom management, and (b) an appraisal of the current state and prospects for the ecological approach.

The Basic Ecological Model

The core ideas of the ecological perspective include the following:

1. Classroom management is fundamentally a process of solving the problem of order in classrooms rather than the problems of disruption or misbehavior. The latter issues are not insignificant, but they are secondary targets of a teacher's management energies. High engagement and low levels of inappropriate and disruptive behavior are by-products of effective management strategies directed at establishing and maintaining work systems for classroom groups rather than spotting and punishing misbehavior.
2. Order in classrooms is defined by the strength and durability of the program of action embedded in the activities teachers and students enact together as they accomplish work. This emphasis on programs of action underscores the dynamic quality of management processes. Since classrooms are moving systems, order is not a static condition or an absence of action. Instead, order is a harmony of action with structure and purpose. Since programs of action have direction and energy, they pull events toward their completion. Rules, procedures, routines, and reprimands all have a role to play in sustaining classroom order, but they can only supplement

what teachers do to specify and orchestrate programs of action. The more complex the program of action for an activity, the more difficult the management task a teacher faces.

3. A program of action, and thus classroom order, is jointly enacted by teachers and students in settings of enormous complexity. Teachers obviously play a key role in initiating and sustaining classroom activities. Nevertheless, students contribute in substantial ways to the quality of order that prevails in any classroom. In classes in which students are inclined to cooperate and are capable of doing the work and in which the teacher is skillful in establishing and protecting the primary vector of action, order is readily achieved. In situations in which students lack either the inclination or the ability to follow the primary vector or the teacher lacks skill in steering the program of action, order is often a protracted struggle.

4. Programs of action in classroom activities are defined by both the rules for social participation and the demands of academic work. For this reason, academic work is directly involved in the process of achieving classroom order and can be shaped in basic ways by a teacher's management decisions. Moreover, it is difficult and potentially misleading to study management processes without attention to curriculum or to imagine curriculum designs without attention to classroom processes.

5. Order in classrooms is context specific and held in place by balancing a large array of forces and processes. As a result, order is often fragile, a condition that can be easily disrupted by mistakes, intrusions, and unpredictable events. Order is not something teachers achieve once and for all so they can get on with the business of instruction. Rather, it is a permanent pressure on classroom life, and a teacher continuously faces the need to monitor and protect the programs of action in a class. Indeed, the use of familiar activities, such as recitations and seatwork and the standard practice of routinizing most classroom procedures and activities, appear to be reasonable strategies for offsetting the inherent delicacy of classroom order.

6. The key to a teacher's success in management appears to be his or her (a) understanding of the likely configuration of events in a classroom, and (b) skill in monitoring and guiding activities in light of this information. From this perspective, management effectiveness cannot be defined solely in terms of rules for behavior. Effectiveness must also include such cognitive dimensions as comprehension and interpretation, skills which are necessary for recognizing when to act and how to improvise classroom events to meet immediate circumstances.

Status and Directions in Ecological Research

Broadly speaking little has changed within the ecological framework in the past two decades. Weinstein (1991) used an ecological framework to review research on the classroom as a social system for the *Annual Review of Psychology*, and Carter and Doyle in this *Handbook* (see chapter 14) pull together some of the available, ecologically relevant studies related to management in early childhood and elementary classrooms. For the most part, however, the foundational ecological work remains the same as it was in 1986, even though the existing studies are limited in scope and range of classroom settings. In part, this stasis in the field is a reflection of a more general decline in classroom research itself since the 1970s and 1980s as attention turned to teachers, teacher education, and culture in educational studies. Moreover, the questions an ecological approach to classroom management would foster—questions related to monitoring, pacing, directing, routinizing, intervening in the behavior stream of classrooms—are complex and the processes of finding answers are challenging and labor intensive. It is not easy to examine directly how classroom conditions are established and maintained in a variety of settings, and few researchers have had the resources to conduct such studies.

In the context of the present *Handbook*, the place of the ecological view within the broader scope of classroom management thought and practice is now clearer to me than it was in 1986. At the time, I tended to equate the ecological perspective with classroom management. This presumption came out of my own sense of the development of the field to that point. At a practical level, issues of classroom management become especially visible when classes are disruptive, so attention goes quite naturally to desists ("What do I do when students . . . "), as it did even for Kounin and Gump (1958). Traditionally, issues of disruptive student behavior fell to clinical and counseling psychologists who focused on deviance, mental health, and behavior modification (e.g., Dreikurs, 1957; Glasser, 1969; O'Leary & O'Leary, 1977) and who emphasized individual behavior and discipline rather than classroom ecologies. For me, writing at the time in the context of a review of research on teaching, the ecological perspective brought *classroom* into the center of classroom management research.

In hindsight, I now see more clearly the limits of the ecological work on which I based my arguments. By focusing on habitat and behavior, ecological analyses bypassed cognition. Ecological research could address work involvement with respect to various behavior settings, but, beyond coding for "focal content," this research could not easily speak to questions of what students were thinking about. This is hardly a criticism, since the tools for a thorough cognitive rendering of human action did not emerge until after much of this work was done. However, it means that issues of instruction, curriculum, and learning are not prominent in ecological studies. Along similar lines, because the core work in ecological psychology was done in a small Midwestern middle-class white town—Oskaloosa, Kansas had a population of 750 when the Midwest Psychological Field Station opened in 1947 (Gump, 1990)—issues of ethnicity and culture were not highly visible.[3]

Again, in retrospect, these omissions are substantial. Weinstein (1991) has been especially insightful in raising questions about the possible cognitive and emotional consequences for individuals of arranging settings or intervening into the behavior stream to increase general work involvement. The problem of order might be solved for the moment, but the benefits or costs to an individual student are unclear. Weinstein and her colleagues (Weinstein, Tomlinson-Clarke, & Curran, 2004) have also pointed to the need to develop culturally responsive models of classroom management. Finally, it is now more obvious to me that classroom management, broadly speaking, encompasses not only classrooms but also a social curriculum that addresses issues of moral and prosocial development and the teaching of responsibility and self-management (see Powell, McLaughlin, Savage, and Zehm, 2001, and chapter 14). The ecological approach to classroom management provides powerful tools for creating orderly habitats, which are essential for teaching to occur. At the same time, there are other considerations related to fostering children's social and principled development in school and classroom contexts.

The challenge, then, is to push the ecological approach toward a framework that integrates habitat, curriculum, action, and cognition into a unified conception of classroom processes. The foundation for such a cohesive understanding already exists in the ecological perspective. Kounin and Gump's (1974) concept of *signal systems* attempts to capture the information dimensions of lessons, that is, the array of cues or prompts that shapes how students understand the program of action in a lesson habitat. Although implicit, this concept entails a cognitive mediation of classroom order. More directly, the idea of *task* (see Doyle, 1983) embedded in ecological classroom research is grounded in cognitive work and draws in issues of purpose, operations, artifacts, and consequences by capturing the curriculum in motion in classroom environments. By extension, conceptualizing of the teacher's management work as a task of jointly achieving order in a complex social setting connects management studies to research on teacher planning and cognition (see Carter & Doyle, 1987). Thus, the academic work a teacher attempts to enact in a class can be seen as a representation of that teacher's interpretation of a segment of curriculum as a classroom event (see Doyle, 1986). Similarly, a teacher's

[3]The Barkers were not unaware of cultural issues in ecological psychology. See Barker and Barker (1961).

management strategies can be viewed as a reflection of that teacher's understanding of the task of order in a classroom. Finally, ecological depictions of classroom lessons, as models of the task of order, can be seen as windows into a skilled manager's understandings of classroom environments.

A powerful framework has recently emerged—*activity theory*—that would seem to hold promise for advancing work on an integrated conceptualization for classroom studies. A complete rendering of activity theory is not possible in this context. Rather, I will attempt to outline the basic components of the theory and illustrate its potential application to classroom management in an effort to show what this direction might have to offer classroom researchers.

Activity theory is a comprehensive framework that seeks to integrate context and consciousness within a system of goal-directed, tool-mediated, intersubjective, and self-regulated action. The framework originated in Soviet psychology—Vygotsky (1978) and Leont'ev (1981) are typically cited (see discussions in Bedny & Karwowski, 2004; Cole & Engeström, 1993; and Wertsch, 1981)—and it is being applied by Scandanavian and North American scholars to theoretical and practical problems in literacy education (Gutierrez & Stone, 2000), human-computer interaction (see Engeström, 1993; Nardi, 1996), ergonomics (Bedny & Karwowski, 2004), composition studies (Berkenkotter, 2001; Russell, 1997), and teacher education in English (Grossman, Smagorinsky, & Valencia, 1999; Johnson, Smagorinsky, Thompson, & Fry, 2003) and classroom management (Martin, 2004). The approach also has direct assoociations to work on everyday cognition (Chaiklin & Lave, 1993; Lave, 1988).

Given the complexity of activity theory itself and the variety of applications it is receiving, there is an array of conceptualizations available. Some scholars, for instance, define a context quite broadly as a profession, such as pyschotherapy (Berkenkotter, 2001) or cell biology (Russell, 1997), a policy environment, such as state educational standards (Johnson et al., 2003), or a long-term assignment, such as student teaching (Grossman et al., 1999). Others focus on a more specific and concrete artifact or designed setting, such as an automated post office terminal (Engeström & Escalante, 1996) or an underwater exploration monitor (Bedny & Karwowski, 2004). As with most context theories of course, there is in activity theory a layering of settings with a target situation being embedded in and also contained in other contexts, for instance, from a profession to a university to a department to a degree program to a course to a class to an assignment to a lecture and so on. From an ecological perspective, it sometime appears that a rigorous and distinctive understanding of the nature of the context itself can be lost, especially in broad conceptions, such as a profession or a program.

What these applications share, however, is a fundamental presumption that human consciousness exists in and grows out of engaging in problem-directed action with materials and in settings whose meanings are culturally and historically situated. From this perspective, a context is an "ongoing dynamic accomplishment of people acting together with shared tools" (Russell, 1997, p. 509) to accomplish goals. Such a framework captures cognition, intention or motive, task, situation, resources and tools, culture, community, and change in a comprehensive theoretical umbrella.

To illustrate the possible use of activity theory to extend the ecological perspective on classroom management, I briefly attempt to conceptualize the problem of classroom order in activity terms. To achieve the goal of order (i.e., student cooperation in a program of action appropriate for engaging with a particular curriculum task) a teacher must organize classroom life and recruit, invite, persuade, or convince the students to join forces with her or him for specific periods of time. Among the tools available for the teacher are various teaching principles, such as constructivism or direct instruction, and methods or lesson formats, such as Daily Oral Language or the five-paragraph theme (see Johnson et al., 2003), as well as conceptions of children and their development, curriculum guides, colleague models, and personal experiences.

Recent work on genres from an activity theory perspective provide a helpful view of the stability and flexibility of lesson formats. Genres traditionally are defined as macrosystems of typified text forms—for example, fiction, nonfiction, poetry—that embody purposes, structures, conventions, and expectations within discourse communities (Swales, 1990). As these genres are instantiated in particular texts—for instance, stories, poems, essays, and the like—the socially understood forms mediate comprehension and interpretation. When the idea of genre is expanded within activity theory, genres can be seen to include a variety of typified or recurring text forms that serve as tools to mediate social action and social relationships (Russell, 1997). Examples include the various recurring texts used in relation to generating and reporting on student performance, from papers and exams, to grade reports, grade point averages, transcripts, and the like, that mediate between schooling and a variety of parental and professional publics with implications for students' career trajectories.

Christie (1997) has used the idea of genre to talk about lessons (e.g., a morning news segment in a nursery school) and units (e.g., a linked set of upper elementary social studies lessons on writing an advertisement seeking opinions on the construction of a nuclear power plant) as *curriculum genres*, that is, "staged, purposive activities in which significant goals of various kinds are realized" (p. 136). Christie argues that the concept of genre helps classroom researchers understand the regulative and instructional registers of pedagogic discourses and how they shape students' emerging consciousness.

There would seem to be considerable affinity between the language of behavior settings, action programs, and tasks coming out of ecological management work and the ideas of curriculum genres and interactive contexts that are emerging from activity theory. The advantage of the conceptions of classroom genres and activity is the direct link to the study of interrelationships among contexts, discourses, and consciousness, thus helping to move ecological studies beyond classroom structures and action systems to cognition and curriculum. In addition, the genre conceptions and activity theory itself create macro frameworks for the systematic comparison of particular lessons across enactment communities, thus "bridging the gap between macrolevel perspectives of social structure as shaping and determining human activity, on the one hand, and microlevel perspectives of situated, everyday practices as constitutive or social structure, on the other" (Berkenkotter, 2001, pp. 327–328).

Finally, activity theory keeps in focus the realization that the key terms in classroom theory—order, lesson, curriculum task, student, teacher—are culturally and historically situated. What classroom order, a five-paragraph theme, seatwork, a sixth-grade student, a beginning teacher all mean is mediated by history and culture both at societal and local levels. "Sustained silent reading," for example, has been seen before by students and teachers, has a status within various pedagogical ideologies, is associated with teachers' practical knowledge about utility and consequences, has a history within a particular classroom and within a student cohort, and so forth. Such meanings, albeit multifaceted and often indeterminant, play a central role is constituting and stabilizing order at a particular moment in a particular place and, thus, need to play an essential part in our research, theory, and formulations for practice.

CONCLUSION

This chapter is intended to underscore the distinctive place of an ecological perspective within the broader field of research and theory in classroom organization and management. In many respects, the origins of the ecological perspective were serendipitous. Kounin (1970) tried to answer prospective teachers' questions about how to stop inappropriate behavior and stumbled on the idea of ripple effects. In trying with Gump to understand ripple effects, he discovered that work involvement was more a function of proactive setting organization and process awareness than it was of desists once misbehavior occurred. Barker and Gump (1964), in trying to create specimen records of behavior streams, discovered that settings had plans for behavior so that if one wanted to understand children it was necessary to understand the places they occupied, such as schools and classrooms. In these separate and collaborative journeys, Kounin and Gump discovered classrooms as tangible, dynamic ecologies. Without them, there would be no *classroom* in classroom management or the study of teaching.

The legacy of Kounin and Gump led to vigorous theorizing about classroom processes and their management in the 1980s, theorizing that, as this chapter suggests, moved beyond the narrow confines of process-product studies of teaching effectiveness to embrace an array of intellectual traditions and paradigms. This same commitment to context links classroom management to the emerging work on activity theory and its potentially rich understanding of the intersection of consciousness, tools, task, and culture in dynamic siutations. The further exploration of this link is likely to enrich both classroom management and, because of the commitment to habitat in ecological work, activity theory itself. More important, this link is likely to lead to an important and much needed renaissance in classroom study.

REFERENCES

Adams, R. S. (1969). Location as a feature of instructional interaction. *Merrill Parker Quarterly, 15*(4), 309–321.

Adams, R. S., & Biddle, B. J. (1970). *Realities of teaching: Exploration with videotape*. New York: Holt, Rinehart & Winston.

Allington, R. L. (1980). Teacher interruption behaviors during primary grade oral reading. *Journal of Educational Psychology, 72*, 371–377.

Allington, R. L. (1983). The reading instruction provided readers of differing reading abilities. *Elementary School Journal, 83*(5), 548–559.

Arlin, M. (1979). Teacher transitions can disrupt time flow in classrooms. *American Educational Research Journal, 16*, 42–56.

Arlin, M. (1982). Teacher responses to student time differences in mastery learning. *American Journal of Education, 90*, 334–352.

Au, K. H. (1980). Participation structures in a reading lesson with Hawaiian children: Analysis of a culturally appropriate instructional event. *Anthropology and Education Quarterly, 11*, 91–115.

Ball, S. J. (1980). Initial encounters in the classroom and the process of establishment. In P. Woods (Ed.), *Pupil strategies: Explorations in the sociology of the school* (pp. 143–161). London: Croom Helm.

Barker, R. G. (1968). *Ecological psychology*. Stanford, CA: Stanford University Press.

Barker, R. G., & Barker, L. S. (1961). Behavior units for the comparative study of cultures. In B. Kaplan (Ed.), *Studying personality cross-culturally* (pp. 457–476). New York: Harper & Row.

Barker, R. G., & Gump, P. V. (1964). *Big school, small school: High school size and student behavior*. Stanford, CA: Stanford University Press.

Bedny, G. Z., & Karwowski, W. (2004). Activity theory as a basis for the study of work. *Ergonomics, 47*(2), 134–153.

Bellack, A. A., Kliebard, H. M., Hyman, R. T., & Smith, F. L. (1966). *The language of the classroom*. New York: Teachers College Press.

Berkenkotter, C. (2001). Genre systems at work: DSM-IV and rhetorical recontextualization in psychotherapy paperwork. *Written Communication, 18*(3), 326–349.

Berliner, D. C. (1983). Developing conceptions of classroom environments: Some light on the T in classroom studies of ATI. *Educational Psychologist, 18*, 1–13.

Blumenfeld, P. C., Hamilton, V. L., Bossert, S. T., Wessels, K., & Meece, J. (1983). Teacher talk and student thought: *Socialization* into the student role. In J. Levine & M. Wang (Eds.), *Teacher and student perceptions: Implications for learning*. Hillsdale, NJ: Erlbaum.

Blumenfeld, P. C., Hamilton, V. L., Wessels, K., & Falkner, D. (1979). Teaching responsibility to first graders. *Theory Into Practice, 18*(3), 174–180.

Borman, K. M., Lippincott, N. S., Matey, C. M., & Obermiller, P. (1978, March). *Characteristics of family and classroom control in an urban Appalachian neighborhood*. Paper presented at the annual meeting of the American Educational Research Association, Toronto.

Bremme, D., & Erickson, F. (1977). Relationships among verbal and non-verbal classroom behaviors. *Theory Into Practice, 5*, 153–161.

Brooks, D. M., & Wagenhauser, B. (1980). Completion time as a nonverbal component of teacher attitude. *Elementary School Journal, 81*(1), 24–27.

Brophy, J. E. (1982). How teachers influence what is taught and learned in classrooms. *Elementary School Journal*, 83, 1–13.

Brophy, J. E., & Evertson, C. (1976). *Learning from teaching: A developmental perspective*. Boston: Allyn & Bacon.

Burnett, J. H. (1973). Event description and analysis in the microethnography of urban classrooms. In F. A. J. Lanni & E. Storey (Eds.), *Cultural relevance and educational issues: Readings in anthropology and education*. Boston: Little, Brown.

Cahir, S. R. (1978). *Activity between and within activity: Transition*. Unpublished doctoral dissertation, Georgetown University, Washington, DC.

Carter, K., & Doyle, W. (1987). Teachers' knowledge structures and comprehension processes. In J. Calderhead (Ed.), *Exploring teachers' thinking*. London: Holt, Rinehart & Winston.

Cazden, C. B. (1986). Classroom discourse. In M. C. Wittrock (Ed.), *Handbook of research on teaching* (3rd ed., pp. 432–463). New York: Macmillan.

Chaiklin, S., & Lave, J. (Eds.) (1993). *Understanding practice: Perspectives on activity and practice*. Cambridge: Cambridge University Press.

Christie, F. (1997). Curriculum macrogenres as forms of initiation into a culture. In F. Christie & J. R. Martin (Eds.), *Genre and institutions: Social processes in the workplace and school*. London: Cassell.

Clark, C., & Yinger, R. (1979). Teachers' thinking. In P. Peterson & H. Walberg (Eds.), *Research on teaching*. Berkeley, CA: McCutchan.

Clements, B. S. (1983). *Helping experienced teachers with classroom management: An experimental study (R & D* Rep. No. 6155). Austin: University of Texas, R & D Center for Teacher Education.

Cole, M. & Engestrom, Y. (1993). A socio-cultural approach to distributed cognition. In G. Salomon (Ed.), *Distributed cognitions: Psychological and educational considerations* (pp. 1–46). Cambridge: Cambridge University Press.

Cone, R. (1978). *Teachers' decisions in managing student behavior*. Paper presented at the annual meeting of the American Educational Research Association, Toronto.

Copeland, W. D. (1978). Processes mediating the relationship between cooperating-teacher and student-teacher classroom performance. *Journal of Educational Psychology, 70*, 95–100.

Cuban, L. (1982). Persistent instruction: The high school classroom, 1900–1980. *Phi Delta Kappan, 64*, 113–118.

Daniels, H., & Bizar, M. (2005). *Teaching the best practice way: Methods that matter, K-12*. Portland, ME: Stenhouse.

Davis, R. B., & McKnight, C. (1976). Conceptual, heuristic, and S-algorithmic approaches in mathematics teaching. *Journal of Children's Mathematical Behavior, 1(Suppl. 1)*, 271–286.

Denscombe, M. (1980). Pupil strategies and the open classroom. In P. Woods (Ed.), *Pupil strategies: Explorations in the sociology of the school* (pp. 50–73). London: Croom Helm.

Doyle, W. (1977). Learning the classroom environment: An ecological analysis. *Journal of Teacher Education, 28*(6), 51–55.

Doyle, W. (1978). Are students behaving worse than they used to behave? *Journal of Research and Development in Education, 2*(4), 3–16.

Doyle, W. (1979a). Classroom tasks and students' abilities. In P. L. Peterson & H. J. Walberg (Eds.), *Research on teaching: Concepts, findings and implications*. Berkeley, CA: McCutchan.

Doyle, W. (1979b). Making managerial decisions in classrooms. In D. L. Duke (Ed.), *Classroom management* (78th Yearbook of the National Society for the Study of Education, Part 2). Chicago: University of Chicago Press.

Doyle, W. (1983). Academic work. *Review of Educational Research, 53*(2), 159–199.

Doyle, W. (1984). How order is achieved in classrooms: An interim report. *Journal of Curriculum Studies, 16*(3), 259–277.

Doyle, W. (1986). Content representation in teachers' definitions of academic work. *Journal of Curriculum Studies, 18*, 365–379.

Doyle, W., & Carter, K. (1984). Academic tasks in classrooms. *Curriculum Inquiry, 14*(2), 129–149.

Dreikurs, R. (1957). *Psychology in the classroom: A manual for teachers*. New York: Harper & Row.

Eder, D. (1982a). Differences in communicative styles across ability groups. In L. C. Wilkinson (Ed.), *Communicating in classrooms* (pp. 245–264). New York: Academic Press.

Eder, D. (1982b). The impact of management and turn-allocation activities on student performance. *Discourse Processes, 5*, 147–159.

Emmer, E. T. (1983). *An investigation of heterogeneous elementary school classrooms*. Paper presented at the annual meeting of the American Educational Research Association, Montreal.

Emmer, E., Evertson, C., & Anderson, L. (1980). Effective classroom management at the beginning of the school year. *Elementary School Journal, 80*(5), 219–231.

Emmer, E. T., & Gerwels, M. C. (2002). Cooperative learning in elementary classrooms: Teaching practices and lesson characteristics. *Elementary School Journal, 103*(1), 75–91.

Engeström, Y. (1993). Developmental studies of work as a testbench of activity theory: The case of primary care medical practice. In S. Chaiklin & J. Lave (Eds.), *Understanding practice: Perspecvtives on activity and context* (pp. 64–103). Cambridge: Cambridge University Press.

Engeström, Y., & Escalante, V. (1996). Mundane tool or object of affection? The rise and fall of the postal buddy. In B. Nardi (Ed.), *Context and consciousness: Activity theory and human-computer interaction* (pp. 325–373). Cambridge, MA: MIT Press.

Englert, C. S., & Semmel, M. I. (1983). Spontaneous teacher decision making in interactive instructional contexts. *Journal of Educational Research, 77*(2), 112–121.

Erickson, F. (1982). Classroom discourse as improvisation: Relationships between academic task structure and social participation structure in lessons. In L. C. Wilkinson (Ed.), *Communicating in classrooms* (pp. 153–181). New York: Academic Press.

Erickson, F., & Mohatt, G. (1982). Cultural organization of participation structures in two classrooms of Indian students. In G. Spindler (Ed.), *Doing the ethnography of schooling*. New York: Holt, Rinehart & Winston.

Erickson, F., & Shultz, J. (1981). When is a context? Some issues and methods in the analysis of social competence. In J. L. Green & C. Wallat (Eds.), *Ethnography and language in educational settings*. Norwood, NJ: Ablex.

Evertson, C. M. (1982). Differences in instructional activities in higher and lower-achieving junior high English and math classes. *Elementary School Journal, 82*, 329–350.

Evertson, C. M., & Emmer, E. T. (1982). Effective management at the beginning of the year in junior high classes. *Journal of Educational Psychology, 74*(4), 485–498.

Felmlee, D., & Eder, D. (1983). Contextual effects in the classroom: The impact of ability groups on group attention. *Sociology of Education, 56*, 77–87.

Glasser, W. (1969). *Schools without failure*. New York: Harper & Row.

Green, J. L., & Harker, J. O. (1982). Gaining access to learning: Conversational, social, and cognitive demands of group participation. In L. C. Wilkinson (Ed.), *Communicating in classrooms* (pp. 183–221). New York: Academic Press.

Grice, H. P. (1975). Logic and conversation. In P. Cole & J. L. Morgan (Eds.), *Syntax and semantics: Vol. 3. Speech acts*. New York: Academic Press.

Griffin, P., & Mehan, H. (1979). Sense and ritual in classroom discourse. In F. Coulman (Ed.), *Conversational routine: Explorations in standardized communication situations and prepatterned speech*. The Hague: Mouton.

Grossman, P. L., Smagorinsky, P., & Valencia, S. (1999). Appropriating tools for teaching English: A theoretical framework for research on learning to teach. *American Journal of Education, 108*, 1–29.

Gump, P. V. (1967). *The classroom behavior setting: Its nature and relation to student behavior (final report)*. Washington, DC: U.S. Office of Education, Bureau of Research. (ERIC Document Reproduction Service No. ED015515)

Gump, P. V. (1969). Intra-setting analysis: The third grade classroom as a special but instructive case. In E. Williams & H. Rausch (Eds.), *Naturalistic viewpoints in psychological research*. New York: Holt, Rinehart & Winston.

Gump, P. V. (1974). Operating environments in schools of open and traditional design. *School Review, 82*(4), 575–593.

Gump, P. V. (1975). *Ecological psychology and children*. Chicago: University of Chicago Press.

Gump, P. V. (1982). School settings and their keeping. In D. L. Duke (Ed.), *Helping teachers manage classrooms* (pp. 98–114). Alexandria, VA: Association for Supervision and Curriculum Development.

Gump, P. V. (1990). A short history of the Midwest Psychological Field Station. *Environment and Behavior, 22*(4), 436–457.

Gutierrez, K. D., & Stone, L. D. (2000). Synchronic and diachronic dimensions of social practice: An emerging methodology for cultural-historical perspectives on literacy learning. In C. D. Lee & P. Smagorinsky (Eds.), *Vygotskian perspectives on literacy research: Constructing meaning through collaborative inquiry* (pp. 150–164). Cambridge: Cambridge University Press.

Hammersley, M. (1974). The organization of pupil participation. *The Sociological Review, 22*(3), 355–368.

Hargreaves, D. H., Hester, S. K., & Mellor, F. J. (1975). *Deviance in classrooms*. Boston: Routledge & Kegan Paul.

Hoetker, J., & Ahlbrand, W. P. (1969). The persistence of the recitation. *American Educational Research Journal, 6*, 145–167.

Hoffman, J. V., & Clements, R. O. (1984). Reading miscues and teacher verbal feedback. *Elementary School Journal, 84*, 481–491.

Humphrey, F. M. (1979). "Shh!": *A sociolinguistic study of teachers' turn-taking sanctions in primary school lessons*. Unpublished doctoral dissertation, Georgetown University, Washington, DC.

Jackson, P. (1968). *Life in classrooms*. New York: Holt, Rinehart & Winston.
Johnson, T. S., Smagorinsky, P., Thompson, L., & Fry, P. G. (2003). Learning to teach the five-paragraph theme. *Research in the Teaching of English, 38*(2), 136–176.
King, L. H. (1980). *Student thought processes and the expectancy effect* (Research Rep. No. 80-1–8). Edmonton, Canada: University of Alberta, Centre for Research in Teaching.
King, L. H. (1983). Pupil classroom perceptions and the expectancy effect. *South Pacific Journal of Teacher Education, 11*(1), 54–70.
Korth, W., & Cornbleth, C. (1982). *Classroom activities as settings for cognitive learning opportunity and instruction*. Paper presented at the annual meeting of the American Educational Research Association, New York.
Kounin, J. S. (1970). *Discipline and group management in classrooms*. New York: Holt, Rinehart & Winston.
Kounin, J. S. (1983). *Classrooms: Individuals or behavior settings*? (Monographs in Teaching and Learning No. 1). Bloomington: Indiana University, School of Education.
Kounin, J. S., & Doyle, P. H. (1975). Degree of continuity of a lesson's signal system and the task involvement of children. *Journal of Educational Psychology, 67*(2), 159–164.
Kounin, J., & Gump, P. (1958). The ripple effect in discipline. *Elementary School Journal, 59*, 158–162.
Kounin, J., & Gump, P. (1974). Signal systems of lesson settings and the task related behavior of preschool children. *Journal of Educational Psychology, 66*, 554–562.
Lave, J. (1988). *Cognition and practice*. Cambridge: Cambridge University Press.
Leont'ev, A. N. (1981). *Problems of the development of mind*. Moscow: Progress Publishers.
Lortie, D. C. (1975). *Schoolteacher*. Chicago: University of Chicago Press.
Martin, S. D. (2004). Finding balance: impact of classroom management conceptions on developing teacher practice. *Teaching and Teacher Education, (20)*, 405–422.
McDermott, R. P. (1976). *Kids make sense: An ethnographic account of the interactional management of success and failure in one first-grade classroom*. Unpublished doctoral dissertation, Stanford University, Stanford, CA.
McHoul, A. (1978). The organization of turns at formal talk in the classroom. *Language in Society, 7*(2), 183–213.
Mehan, H. (1974). Accomplishing classroom lessons. In A. V. Cicourel, K. H. Jennings, S. H. M. Jennings, K. C. W. Leiter, R. MacKay, J. Mehan, & D. Roth (Eds.), *Language use and school performance* (pp. 76–142). New York: Academic Press.
Mehan, H. (1979). *Learning lessons: Social organization in a classroom*. Cambridge, MA: Harvard University Press.
Mehan, H., Hertweck, A., Combs, S. E., & Flynn, P. J. (1982). Teachers' interpretations of students' behavior. In L. C. Wilkinson (Ed.), *Communicating in the classroom* (pp. 297–321). New York: Academic Press.
Merritt, M. (1982). Distributing and directing attention in primary classrooms. In L. C. Wilkinson (Ed.), *Communicating in the classroom* (pp. 223–244). New York: Academic Press.
Metz, M. (1978). *Classrooms and corridors*. Berkeley: University of California Press.
Nardi, B. A., Ed. (1996). *Context and consciousness: Activity theory and human-computer interaction*. Cambridge, MA: MIT Press.
Natriello, G., & Dornbusch, S. M. (1980). Bringing behavior back in: The effects of student characteristics and behavior on the classroom behavior of teachers. *American Educational Research Journal, 20*(1), 29–43.
O'Leary, K. D., & O'Leary, S. G. (1977). *Classroom management: The successful use of behavior modification* (2nd ed.). New York: Pergamon.
Orlich, D. C., Harder, R. J., Callahan, R. C., Trevisan, M. S., & Brown, A. H. (2004). *Teaching strategies: A guide to effective instruction* (7th ed.). Boston: Houghton Mifflin.
Pollard, A. (1980). Teacher interests and changing situations of survival threat in primary school classrooms. In P. Woods (Ed.), *Teacher strategies: Explorations in the sociology of the school* (pp. 34–60). London: Croom Helm.
Powell, R. R., McLaughlin, H. J., Savage, T. V., & Zehm, S. (2001). *Classroom management: Perspectives on the social curriculum*. Upper Saddle River, NJ: Merrill/Prentice Hall.
Rosenshine, B. V. (1980). How time is spent in elementary classrooms. In C. Denham & A. Lieberman (Eds.), *Time to learn*. Washington, DC: National Institute of Education.
Ross, R. P. (1984). Classroom segments: The structuring of school time. In L. W. Anderson (Ed.), *Time and school learning: Theory, research and practice*. London: Croom Helm.
Rusnock, M., & Brandler, N. (1979). *Time off task: Implications for learning*. Paper presented at the annual meeting of the American Educational Research Association, San Francisco.
Russell, D. R. (1997). Rethinking genre in school and society: An activity theory analysis. *Written Communication, 14*(4), 504–554.
Sanford, J. P., & Evertson, C. M. (1981). Classroom management in a low SES junior high: Three case studies. *Journal of Teacher Education, 32*(1), 34–38.
Sanford, J. P., & Evertson, C. M. (1983). Time use and activities in junior high classrooms. *Journal of Educational Research, 76*, 140–147.
Sherman, L. (1975). An ecological study of glee in a nursery school. *Child Development, 46*, 53–61.

Shultz, J., & Florio, S. (1979). Stop and freeze: The negotiation of social and physical space in a kindergarten/first grade classroom. *Anthropology and Education Quarterly, 10*(3), 166–181.

Sieber, R. T. (1976). *Schooling in the bureaucratic classroom: Socialization and social reproduction in Chestnut Heights*. Unpublished doctoral dissertation, New York University, New York.

Sieber, R. T. (1979a). Classmates as workmates: Informal peer activity in the elementary school. *Anthropology and Educational Quarterly, 10*, 207–235.

Sieber, R. T. (1979b). Schoolrooms, pupils, and rules: The role of informality in bureaucratic socialization. *Human Organization, 38*(3), 273–282.

Sieber, R. T. (1981). Socialization implications of school discipline, or how first-graders are taught to "listen." In R. T. Sieber & A. J. Gordon (Eds.), *Children and their organizations: Investigations in American culture* (pp. 18–43). Boston, MA: G. K. Hall.

Sinclair, J. M., & Coulthard, R. M. (1975). *Towards an analysis of discourse: The English used by teachers and pupils*. Oxford: Oxford University Press.

Slavin, R. E. (1995). Cooperative learning: Theory, research, and practice (2nd ed.). Boston: Allyn and Bacon.

Smith, L. M., & Geoffrey, W. (1968). *The complexities of an urban classroom*. New York: Holt, Rinehart & Winston.

Solomon, D., & Kendall, A. J. (1976). Individual characteristics and children's performance in "open" and "traditional" classroom settings. *Journal of Educational Psychology, 68*(5), 613–625.

Spencer-Hall, D. A. (1981). Behind the teacher's back. *Elementary School Journal, 81*, 280–289.

Stodolsky, S. S. (1988). *The subject matters: Classroom activity in math and social studies*. Chicago: University of Chicago Press.

Stodolsky, S. S., Ferguson, T. L., & Wimpelberg, K. (1981). The recitation persists, but what does it look like? *Journal of Curriculum Studies, 13*, 121–130.

Swales, J. (1990). *Genre analysis: English in academic and research settings*. Cambridge: Cambridge University Press.

Tikunoff, W. J., & Ward, B. A. (1978). *A naturalistic study of the initiation of students into three classroom social systems* (Rep. No. A-78-1 1). San Francisco: Far West Laboratory.

Tinbergen, N. (1958). *Curious naturalists*. New York: Basic Books.

Vygotsky, L. S. (1978). *Mind in society: The development of higher psychological processes* M. Cole, V. John-Steiner, S. Scribner, & E. Souberman (Eds.). Cambridge, MA: Harvard University Press.

Weinstein, C. S. (1979). The physical environment of the school: A review of the research. *Review of Educational Research, 49*(4), 557–610.

Weinstein, C. S. (1991). The classroom as a social context for learning. *Annual Review of Psychology*, 42, 493–525.

Weinstein, C. S., Tomlinson-Clarke, S., & Curran, M. (2004). Toward a conception of culturally responsive classroom management. *Journal of Teacher Education, 55*(1), 25–38.

Wertsch, J. V. (1981). The concept of activity in Soviet psychology: An introduction. In J. V. Wertsch (Ed.), *The concept of activity in Soviet psychology*. Armonk, NY: Sharpe.

White, M. A. (1975). Natural rates of teacher approval and disapproval in the classroom. *Journal of Applied Behavior Analysis, 8*, 367–372.

Willems, E. P. (1990). Inside Midwest and its field station: The Barker effect. *Environment and Behavior*, 22(4), 468–491.

Woolfolk, A. E., & Brooks, D. M. (1985). Beyond words: The influence of teachers' nonverbal behaviors on students' perceptions and performances. *Elementary School Journal, 85*, 513–528.

Yinger, R. J. (1979). Routines in teacher planning. *Theory Into Practice, 18*(3), 163–169.

Yinger, R. J. (1980). A study of teacher planning. *Elementary School Journal, 80*, 107–127.

6

Classroom Management and Classroom Discourse

Greta Morine-Dershimer
University of Virginia

INTRODUCTION

This chapter provides a brief historical review of classroom discourse research in the U.S., identifies differences in the assumptions and methodology of classroom discourse research compared to classroom management research, and examines the relationship between the five imperatives of classroom management (Evertson & Weinstein, this Handbook) and the four perspectives on learning that are highlighted in the various approaches to classroom discourse studies. In addition two research programs are described, and sample studies discussed, to illustrate the interrelationships among the various imperatives and perspectives. The chapter concludes with a summary of recommendations for classroom management practice derived from classroom discourse studies, and a set of implications for future classroom research on both classroom management and classroom discourse.

As the title implies, this chapter focuses on the relationship between classroom management research and classroom discourse studies. Given the intent of this Handbook, this is an appropriate focus. However, this necessarily limits the degree to which the field of classroom discourse research can be delineated. It is hoped that the list of references provided will encourage readers to pursue further examination of the specific studies, approaches, and research programs within the highly productive and diverse field of classroom discourse research.

A BRIEF EARLY HISTORY

Research on linguistic phenomena in school settings (now known as classroom discourse) was an active field of study in Great Britain in the 1960s and early 1970s, where it was grounded in sociological approaches (Cazden, 1986). Sociolinguists viewed the social context as a critical feature of language-in-use, and noted that different sociological or cultural groups had quite different beliefs about how and when it was appropriate to talk to different audiences. It was assumed that participants' interpretations of the social situation influenced both the speaker's

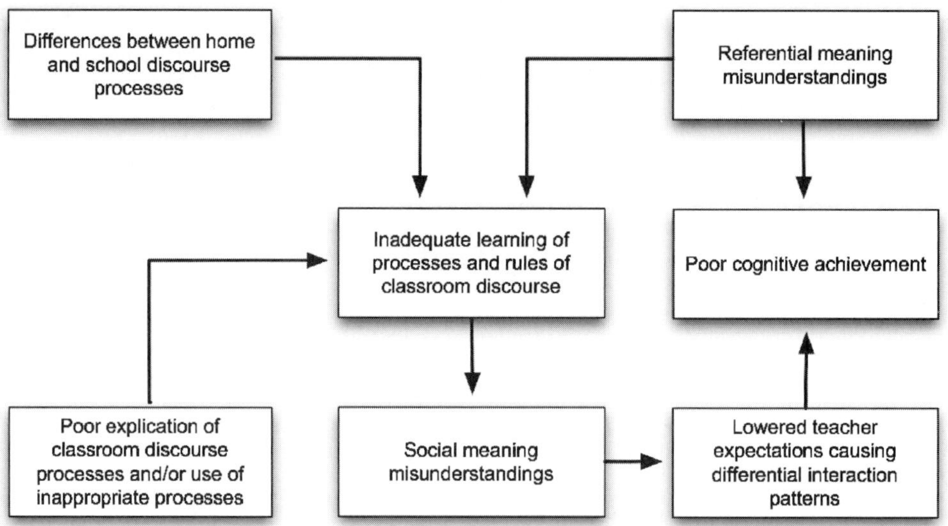

FIGURE 6.1. NIE Model of the Causes and Effects of Inadequate Learning of the Processes and Rules of Classroom Discourse

choice of what could be said and the listener's understanding of the meaning of the speaker's comments. An important problem of concern was that educational failure often appeared to stem from sociolinguistic differences between teachers and pupils (i.e., different interpretations of what was appropriate in the classroom setting; Stubbs, 1976). Early studies in the United States followed the British tradition in many ways, but began to draw as well on ethnographic approaches to examine patterns of communication in a variety of cultural groups (Cazden, John, & Hymes, 1972).

Classroom discourse research was explicitly recognized as an important area of research on teaching in 1974. The National Institute of Education (NIE) organized a five-day conference, led by N. L. Gage of Stanford University, to develop a research and development agenda related to the improvement of teaching. One of the ten panels of experts (prominent researchers and active practitioners) was headed by Courtney Cazden of Harvard University. Panel 5 focused on Teaching as a Linguistic Process in a Cultural Setting, and identified three major questions to be addressed by subsequent research (Cazden, 1974). In 1977 the NIE funded a series of research projects based on the recommendations of Panel 5, and U.S. interest in classroom discourse studies increased.

The NIE request for proposals included a model (see Fig. 6.1) of the presumed causes and effects of inadequate learning of the processes and rules of classroom discourse (Morine-Dershimer, 1985), which clearly indicates the main focus for the series of studies that were funded. The NIE studies, together with a few additional studies funded in 1979, were extensively reviewed by Judith Green (Green, 1983a, 1983b; Green & Smith, 1983), who summarized the results in terms of four principal constructs (each with a series of subconstructs) that were supported across the ten studies. These were:

1. Classrooms are communicative environments (e.g., relationships between teachers and students are asymmetrical, communicative participation affects student achievement);
2. Contexts are constructed during interactions (e.g., rules for participation are implicit, behavior expectations are construed as part of interactions);

3. Meaning is context specific (e.g., meaning is signaled verbally and nonverbally, communicative competence is reflected in appropriate behavior); and
4. Inferencing is required for conversational comprehension (e.g., frame clashes result from differences in perception, form and function in speech used in conversations do not always match).

A fifth construct, supported across five studies was: Teachers orchestrate different participation levels (e.g., teachers evaluate student ability by observing performance during interactions). Green's reviews demonstrated that the assumptions implicit in the NIE model (Fig. 6.1) were supported by the research.

Though it was not necessarily recognized or emphasized at the time, several of the assumptions in the NIE model and related constructs in Green's reviews can be seen to demonstrate close links between classroom management issues and classroom discourse concerns. The central box in the NIE model, "Inadequate learning of processes and rules of classroom discourse," is closely tied to the classroom management focus on the importance of students knowing and following classroom rules and routines as they engage in academic activities. Much classroom management research and related teacher training has focused on issues related to the lower left box in the NIE model, "Poor explication of classroom discourse processes [by the teacher] and/or use of inappropriate processes [by the teacher or pupil]." Research results have emphasized the need for explicit teaching of classroom rules and routines in the opening days and weeks of school. Classroom management research has acknowledged the importance of the lower right box, "Lowered teacher expectations causing differential interaction patterns," noting, for example, the tendency of teachers to call on and reward boys differently than girls during class discussions, partly because of beliefs about differential academic ability, and possibly as one means to prevent anticipated class disruptions by boys. Both classroom management and classroom discourse studies have emphasized the relationship between student engagement in academic activities (differential interaction patterns, or levels of participation in the parlance of classroom discourse) and "Poor cognitive achievement."

The common focus on cognitive achievement, or classroom learning, has been and continues to be the most central similarity between the two fields of research. A major difference has been the more concentrated focus of classroom management studies on teacher behavior, and the more varied view of classroom discourse research, which has included a strong focus on teacher-pupil interaction, careful attention to student interaction with peers, and comparisons of school and community patterns of communication.

Another way to consider the relationship between topics of importance in research on classroom management and classroom discourse studies is by focusing particularly on rules and routines related to classroom communication. Classroom management studies have provided information about rules and routines that are established for pupils early in the school year, mainly through explicit instruction by teachers, although sometimes they may be developed by teachers in cooperation with pupils. The communication rules and routines typically refer to who can talk when to whom about what, who should listen when to whom, and what can appropriately be said (e.g., negative sanctioning of teasing or name-calling). Classroom management research considers what rules and routines are generally helpful, across a variety of classrooms, in maintaining student engagement in academic tasks. It also examines how these communication rules and routines get established effectively, and notes what effective teachers do when disruptions occur.

Classroom discourse studies provide information about rules and routines that are *implicitly* followed by both teachers and pupils, and that are seen as jointly constructed by classroom participants over time through interaction in various settings or types of activities. Even when rules and routines are *explicitly* developed, discourse studies suggest that they become "invisible" to participants after extended regular use. Like those for classroom management, the communication rules and routines identified in classroom discourse studies also refer to who can talk when to whom about what, who should listen when to whom, and what can "appropriately be said" (i.e., what language forms, languages, or dialects are considered appropriate by teachers and pupils for communication within the classroom context). Classroom discourse studies tend to focus on rules and routines within a single classroom, considering shifts that occur from one activity to another, or from one group of pupils to another within the same activity. Many studies focus particularly on how teacher and pupil interpretations of the rules may differ, and what happens when miscommunication occurs.

Lin (1994) contrasts the two approaches more broadly by indicating that classroom management research finds and tells teachers what types of routines are important in promoting student engagement in academic tasks, and when and how to establish these routines in their classrooms. Classroom discourse studies, on the other hand, describe how specific teachers in specific classroom settings introduce, establish, and modify interactive routines to accomplish particular tasks.

BASIC METHODOLOGICAL FEATURES

Given these similarities and differences in the types of issues addressed by the two fields, it is not surprising to find that there are also similarities and differences in the methodology used. As Brophy's historical review (chapter 2 of this Handbook) notes, classroom observation has been the most consistent and important data collection procedure for classroom management research. Detailed observational notes (Kounin & Gump, 1958), videotapes (Kounin, Friesen, & Norton, 1966; Kounin & Doyle, 1975), and observational coding systems (Emmer, Evertson, & Anderson, 1980) have all been used. Observations have been conducted primarily in the opening days and weeks of school, though some studies (e.g., Moskowitz & Hayman, 1976) have observed periodically throughout the year.

The teacher has been the focus of most of this classroom observation, and the teacher behaviors recorded have included both verbal and nonverbal components (e.g., desists issued, directions given, proximity to disruptive pupils, movement around the classroom). Observations of pupil behavior (e.g., proportions of students engaged in academic tasks at periodic intervals) have been compared to patterns of teacher behavior in the same classroom (Emmer, Evertson, & Anderson, 1980), but strictly speaking, the interactive, back-and-forth behavior of teacher and pupils has not been closely tracked. Brophy indicates that classroom management research has also included some teacher interview data.

Classroom management research has used comparative approaches to data collection and analysis to identify effective management practices. Brophy (this Handbook, chapter 2) reports that Moskowitz and Hayman (1976) compared the behavior of "best" teachers and first-year teachers, while Emmer, Evertson, and Anderson (1980) compared teacher behavior and pupil engagement rates in classrooms of more and less effective classroom managers. The categorization and coding of data gathered in classroom management research has contributed to quantitative analysis of data, and identification of general patterns of effective management across a range of classrooms. Follow-up work based on the results of research on classroom management has shown that teachers can be helped to improve their managerial skills, thereby improving students' task engagement and academic achievement (Evertson & Harris, 1999).

A review by Heath (2000) provides a useful overview of general methodological characteristics of classroom discourse studies. Important similarities to classroom management research include: extensive use of classroom observation procedures, including data from field notes and videotapes; follow-up interviews with teachers; and careful comparison of classroom settings during data analysis to generate explanations and results. Within each of these basic similarities, there are also some clear differences between the two approaches. Heath (2000) describes classroom discourse studies as "thickly textured and qualitatively rich studies of language in use (p. 53)." Observations in a given classroom tend to be long-term and often involve participant observation. Observations document oral language as it occurs in interaction between teacher and pupils, or between pupils and peers. Data on nonverbal behavior, written language, or artifacts of pupil products are also observed, collected, and analyzed. Audio and video recordings of classroom talk are transformed into careful, detailed, and lengthy transcriptions of interactive dialogue for use in qualitative analysis. Microanalysis may focus on specific language genres that are valued by particular cultural groups. Interviews are conducted with both teachers and pupils, with a frequent focus on participants' recall and interpretations of the meaning of what was said. Settings are selected for detailed analytic comparison based on differences in contextual features (participation structure, activity setting, public vs. private pupil talk). Classroom discourse studies show what happens in specific settings in individual classrooms; thus they provide possible models of classroom interaction processes that other teachers might choose to try out, whether they teach in similar types of classroom settings or in quite different settings. Rather than implementing research by training teachers to use particular patterns of interaction, classroom discourse researchers tend to encourage teachers to examine patterns that exist in their own classrooms, and consider what happens when they try out some change in the typical patterns (e.g., Kraker, 2000).

These basic methodological similarities and differences between classroom management research and classroom discourse studies are the most consistent typical features of data collection and analysis apparent over a broad array of individual studies. Individual studies in either approach can be seen to vary a good deal, and no individual study should be expected to incorporate all of the general features noted here.

ALTERNATIVE PERSPECTIVES AND KEY CONCEPTS

In the period from the 1970s to 2000 research on teaching expanded drastically from an initial concentration on the relationship between teacher behavior and pupils' academic outcomes (engagement or achievement), typical of the early research on classroom management, to a remarkable array of subareas related to teacher cognitions, pupil cognitions, and types of instructional tasks or curriculum content, as well as both academic and social outcomes (Morine-Dershimer, 2000). Some similar, less drastic, expansion has occurred in the variety of classroom discourse studies. Because the improvement of classroom learning has been and continues to be a central focus of classroom discourse studies, the current distinctions among approaches can be framed usefully in terms of different views of what constitutes learning, or how classroom learning occurs.

An insightful review by Graham Nuthall (1997) provides a helpful guide in identifying important distinctions among the varied approaches. Nuthall examined recent studies of student experience in classrooms to identify common themes and issues. He then divided the studies into three broad categories, based on their general perspectives on student learning and thinking. His three categories are studies that are mainly psychological (or cognitive constructivist) in orientation, those that are primarily sociocultural in orientation, and those that have an emphasis on language, or are sociolinguistic in orientation. According to Nuthall, psychologically oriented studies include thinking and learning within a broad concept of cognition, and see students as constructing their own knowledge and skills. Sociocultural studies view thinking and learning as social processes occurring in social contexts, with knowledge developing within groups through a process of apprenticeship. In sociolinguistic studies, language is seen as both the content and medium of thinking and learning. Students learn to use the language patterns of school and the language, concepts, and ways of perceiving characteristic of the academic disciplines.

Classroom discourse studies are conducted based on each of these three views of thinking and learning. A particular contribution of the Nuthall review is its inclusion of many examples of classroom talk to illustrate each of the three perspectives. He notes that these illustrations of classroom life represent one of the major strengths of classroom discourse studies. Unfortunately, space constraints have severely limited the number of examples of classroom dialogue presented in this chapter, but the studies cited are replete with illustrative data.

Nuthall acknowledges that his categories are not totally discrete. There is some overlapping of assumptions and concepts across the three categories. Nuthall's sequencing of these three approaches may reveal his own intellectual traditions, rooted in very early classroom studies of a psychological nature (Nuthall & Church, 1973). From the point of view of classroom discourse studies, sociolinguistic studies deserve first mention, for this was the earliest type of study to engage in detailed analysis of classroom communication. It should also be noted that a fourth approach, not emphasized by Nuthall, has become increasingly important as a type of classroom discourse study. Allan Luke (1995) identifies critical discourse analysis as a fairly recent entrant into the field, and notes that this perspective is concerned with issues of power, authority, and access to learning of particular discourses that can impact students' future opportunities.

The remainder of this section draws on Nuthall, Luke, and additional reviews to identify key features and key concepts for each of these four distinct perspectives that currently can be seen to constitute the field of classroom discourse research. Each of the four approaches could justify a complete chapter in its own right, but space precludes a full detailing of any single perspective. Instead, only a few key features and key concepts most relevant to classroom management issues are discussed in each section that follows. (For a fuller understanding of any one perspective, see the reviews cited in each section.)

Sociolinguistic Perspective

Some basic premises of sociolinguistically oriented classroom discourse studies related to thinking and learning are: discourse is a mediator of children's classroom learning; oral and written language acquires meaning only through social usage; meaning is constituted relationally between speaker and hearer, or writer and reader; discourses reflect ideologies, systems of values, beliefs, and social practices; community-based discourse practices that children learn at home become the basis for their participation in classroom activities; through participation in classroom activities, children take on the discourses that define what counts as knowing within the disciplines; and speakers acquire social identities through their positionings (kind of participation or role played) in social discourse (Hicks, 1995). From this perspective, the verbal interactions that occur between teacher and pupils and between pupils and peers form a critical aspect of student engagement in academic tasks. Teacher management of verbal interaction processes can strongly influence who has an opportunity to learn, as well as what disciplinary knowledge and what social values are available to be learned.

Some key concepts associated with the sociolinguistic perspective, explicated by Cazden (2001), include question types and sequences, patterns of participation, form-function relationships, and communicative competence. The most basic form of classroom verbal interaction is the oft-documented question cycle, known as the IRE (Initiation-Response-Evaluation) or IRF (Initiation-Response-Follow-up) sequence. In traditional (recitation) lessons, where IRE/IRF patterns prevail, teachers' questions (Initiations) are seen as "psuedo-questions," for teachers only ask about what they already know, and so can identify student answers (Responses) as right or wrong (Evaluation). People at home are more apt to ask "real" questions, seeking to learn what they do not know. In nontraditional lessons, typically advocated in curriculum reform movements, teachers ask more "authentic" questions, and reactions to student responses, which may come from the teacher or other pupils, are framed more often as "How do you know? Show us your evidence." In addition, students ask questions of themselves and each other. Cazden advocates a "both-and" strategy for teachers, which suggests that good managers of classroom discourse should match their questioning processes to varied curriculum goals.

Patterns of participation emphasize the importance of "who participates how, and who doesn't and why" (Cazden, 2001, p. 81). Students who participate more in classroom verbal interaction also tend to learn more (gain more in achievement during the year). Who volunteers to participate will shift depending on whether closed questions (single correct answer) or open questions (multiple acceptable answers possible) are used. "Getting a turn" to participate may depend on knowing unstated rules (raise your hand and wait to be called on, or call out an answer if you're sure you're right), but teachers can facilitate more widespread participation through use of management techniques like "round-robin," or passing around a "talking stick" to designate speakers. Student opportunities for "getting the floor" (getting attention) can be facilitated by seating arrangements that promote looking at the speaker, by teachers who listen and respond to deeper meaning in pupil comments, rather than just a correct answer, or by teacher "revoicing" of student comments by indicating relationships between contributions of various pupils.

Having an opportunity to talk does not guarantee that a student will be "heard" by peers, or by the teacher. In traditional lessons, students have reported hearing comments made by high achievers more than low achievers, but in more nontraditional lessons, lower achievers were reportedly heard more (Morine-Dershimer, 1985). Classroom discourse studies have identified one simple way for teachers to trace what knowledge participants and listeners take away from class discussions. This involves collecting written "exit data" periodically at the close of lessons. Brief statements of key ideas derived from the lesson, or statements of two or three things that were said by anybody during the lesson, written on 5 × 7 cards and submitted anonymously, can provide a good sense of the important content of the lesson as perceived by pupils, as well as affording some insight into how patterns of attention shift as patterns of questioning and patterns of participation vary (Morine-Dershimer, 1991).

The form that an utterance takes does not necessarily correspond to the function it is intended to fulfill. For example, an intended command is frequently stated by teachers in the form of a question (e.g., "Does everyone have their books out, ready for work?"). The intended meaning of such a question is not readily understood by children from homes where such indirect commands are not commonly used. When form-function relationships are misunderstood by students, the lack of "appropriate" response may be misinterpreted by the teacher as willful disobedience.

The key concept of communicative competence (Hymes, 1972) is an overarching concept that incorporates these other concepts, and refers to an understanding of how to use language appropriately in various social settings. Stubbs (2002) points out that all speakers are multistylistic, adapting speech style to the social situation, and using different styles for different audiences, such as talking with respected adults versus conversing with peers. But when there are discrepancies between patterns of discourse used at home and those used at school, as is the case with real versus psuedo questions or direct versus indirect commands for many minority group children, children who exhibit communicative competence in use of the language of their home and community often appear incompetent in their ability to "talk school." This leads to misinterpretations by both pupils and teachers. Pupils fail to understand the intended meaning of much of the verbal classroom interaction, and teachers underestimate pupils' intellectual ability. A good classroom manager working with primary grade minority children may spend extra time directly teaching the rules and routines pertaining to traditional classroom communication, and greatly improve student achievement as a result (Morine-Dershimer, 1985).

These key concepts from sociolinguistic studies help to explain why it is important for good classroom managers to clarify rules and routines related to classroom communication early in the year, so that students know how to take advantage of opportunities to participate, and thus to learn. They also indicate how seating arrangements, variation in use of questioning processes and lesson structures, and teacher's promotion and use of active listening strategies can impact students' opportunities to learn and support engagement in academic tasks.

The emphasis on communicative competence as an important contributor to the opportunity to learn suggests that the sociolinguistic perspective on classroom discourse is most closely linked to the classroom management imperative (chapter 1, this Handbook) to "promote the development of students' social skills and self-regulation." The social skills of knowing what to say when to whom, and when to listen to whom, in what social setting, are critical skills in use of language according to sociolinguists, and are critical classroom skills for students. Students' ability to self-regulate, or accurately identify and use the talking and listening skills appropriate in various classroom activity settings, influences teacher beliefs about their academic ability, and both directly and indirectly impacts their ability to learn from teachers and peers. Thus, good classroom managers who promote the development of social skills and self-regulation by helping students develop the communicative competence essential for successful participation in classroom interaction will also contribute to accomplishing the classroom management imperative (chapter 1, this Handbook) to "organize and implement instruction in ways that optimize students' access to learning."

Cognitive Constructivist Perspective

According to Nuthall (1997), the cognitive constructivist perspective is "based on the view that students construct their own knowledge as they engage in the processes of interpreting and making sense of classroom experience" (p. 684). From this perspective, the structure of tasks, the questions of teachers, the problems that pupils practice solving, all have only indirect effects on student learning. Classroom learning is mediated by the representations and reconstructions that individual students create from their classroom experiences, and much of that depends on what prior, out-of-classroom experiences students bring to school. Three additional issues have been central to studies that take this perspective: how classroom tasks and practical activities engage and structure cognitive processing; how the social processes of the classroom, especially the interaction of peers in small cooperative groups, influence knowledge construction; and how the role of the teacher influences student motivation and guides student cognition. Classroom management research has been most focused on the teacher role in structuring classroom tasks and encouraging student motivation. Classroom discourse studies have more to say about the social processes and the influence of peer interactions. However, it is also the case that classroom tasks and practical activities cannot realistically be separated from classroom social processes, since all tasks and activities take place within the setting of the classroom social system.

Baker (1992) comments on the critical relationship between classroom talk and classroom social structure, noting that classroom talk-in-interaction is a basic part of the everyday production of social structure. Student and teacher roles as knowledgeable authorities are established in terms of who comments and who listens during interactive lessons. Teachers and more knowledgeable pupils talk; less knowledgeable pupils listen; few pupils are seen as "more knowledgeable" in all ability areas, so pupil roles may shift as classroom activities move from one subject area to another, or from one activity structure to another. Baker further explains the strong links between classroom discourse and opportunities to learn (that is, become knowledgeable authorities). Communicative activity structures such as the IRE/IRF cycle identify what counts as knowledge: teachers ask questions about things that are important to know, and indicate what should be learned and remembered by confirming and praising correct answers to their questions. The production of knowledge occurs in public classroom discussions, and pupils are held accountable for this knowledge. Listeners are expected to learn from the public talk, in fact, must learn to abstract the items of information to be learned and remembered by attending closely to teachers' questions and to the answers that draw teacher approval and praise.

An interesting study by Blanton, Berenson, and Norwood (2001) illustrates the link between activity structure and opportunity to learn. It describes how a student teacher, over a series of middle-school mathematics lessons, shifted the type of questions she asked (from "What answer did you get?" to "How did you get your answer?"). The knowledge that was made public changed from the correct answer for a problem to the alternative processes that could be used to understand and solve a problem. The shift in activity structure also led to a clear difference in pupil roles as knowledgeable participants, as well as a marked shift in the student teacher's perception of pupils' mathematical ability.

Nuthall (1997) identifies several key concepts of importance in classroom discourse studies that focus on peer interactions from a cognitive constructivist (psychological) perspective. These are: public versus private talk; the interrelated nature of the cognitive and the social in peer relationships; and the teaching of specific interactive processes, such as productive argumentation. Most studies of classroom interaction (both classroom management and classroom discourse studies) have focused on the public talk. Studies by Alton-Lee and Nuthall (e.g., Alton-Lee, Nuthall & Patrick, 1993) have looked closely at the private talk of pupils within the context of public lessons. Their studies show that about a quarter of all private pupil talk is concerned with carrying out and completing classroom tasks. According to Nuthall, in their private talk to themselves and to peers, "students spend a significant amount of time clarifying instructions, organizing and preparing equipment and resources, worrying about how to complete or present the results of the task, and commenting about how difficult or boring the task is" (1997, p. 690). Alton-Lee shows how private talk mimics the public IRE/IRF pattern (Alton-Lee, Nuthall, & Patrick, 1993) as pupils privately react like a teacher and evaluate their own covert responses to teacher questions, as well as the overt, public responses of their peers. As listeners, they also use private talk to reinforce and remember answers marked as correct by the teacher, repeating the answers to themselves. Thus private talk is important for pupil task engagement and learning.

Nuthall (1997) reviews studies that refer to the interrelated nature of the cognitive and social in pupils' classroom relationships with peers. When pupils disagree with their peers, and try to resolve differences in knowledge or beliefs, the social disequilibrium creates cognitive conflict. Conflict or disagreement provides the occasion for cognitive change. Classroom social processes can then support a search for agreement or a resolution of differences, which can lead to mutual understanding and cognitive change. Tasks or activity structures that require the coordination of individual viewpoints, such as cooperative learning groups, involve clear interaction of social processes with knowledge construction. The contributions that each individual makes in such a group are often determined by their relative social and academic status, and what individuals remember about the final product (knowledge) of the group will also be influenced by these factors, as well as by the social processes that generated the product. Students' recall of things they have learned includes information about the social (and physical) context in which the learning occurred, as well as the content identified as important to remember.

Nuthall cites a study by Mason and Santi (1994) as an example of the value of teaching specific social processes, such as productive argumentation, one process by which differences of opinion and belief can be resolved, thus promoting cognitive change or learning. These researchers used transcripts of discussion in a fifth-grade science class on pollution to identify how students resolved differences, using argument steps (e.g., making or rebutting a claim), epistemic moves (e.g., referring to personal experience or outside evidence), and references to their own metacognitive processes (e.g., "I need to see some evidence ..."). Using a process they had been taught, students in this class moved from disagreement to a collective solution, examining each others' ideas, and developing gradually more complex and better articulated views of the topic. Nuthall notes, however, that the study provides no information on whether training and experience in productive argumentation changed and improved the individual students' own thinking processes.

To summarize the cognitive constructivist perspective on learning and classroom discourse, students construct their own knowledge as they engage in classroom activities and try to make sense of their classroom experiences. New experience is filtered through their existing knowledge and beliefs. Communicative activity in lessons helps to create social structures and define the classroom roles and status of the teacher and of individual pupils. Pupil roles as participants or listeners in classroom discourse influence what is learned. Interaction with the differing knowledge and beliefs of peers can lead to attempts at resolution, and contribute to cognitive change. Productive peer interaction can take place in private talk during public lessons, as well as in cooperative learning groups.

These key ideas related to the cognitive constructivist perspective suggest that good classroom managers need to use a variety of task and activity structures to provide a variety of students with diverse opportunities to learn. Teachers, themselves, can learn more about pupil abilities when they observe the ways pupils participate in different types of communicative tasks or activity structures. Good classroom managers will look for new processes to promote resolution of differences in opinions and beliefs of peers, and teach these processes to their pupils to conduct productive discussions that may contribute to cognitive change. Good classroom managers will also be aware of the important contributions of private talk to pupils' task engagement and learning, and learn to listen unobtrusively to conversations of cooperative learning groups to understand the social processes being enacted within different groups.

The cognitive constructivist perspective on classroom discourse emphasizes the interaction between the social processes in which classroom tasks are embedded and the knowledge construction that results from pupil engagement in those tasks. This suggests that the cognitive constructivist perspective is most closely linked to the classroom management imperative (chapter 1, this Handbook) to "use group management methods that encourage students' engagement in academic tasks." Shifts in types of teacher questions can denote shifts in what counts as knowledge. Use of cooperative learning groups can move students to search for resolution of disagreements, promoting new perceptions. Such variation in the activity structures and social processes associated with classroom tasks can provide opportunities for pupils with different kinds of experiences and abilities to take on the role of knowledgeable authority in different types of instructional settings. Thus, effective classroom managers who promote variation in the social processes associated with classroom tasks also contribute to accomplishing the classroom management imperative (chapter 1, this Handbook) to "organize and implement instruction in ways that optimize students' access to learning."

Sociocultural Perspective

Gee and Green (1998) present the sociocultural perspective, contending that:

> discourse analysis is as much (or more) about what is happening among people out in the world (anthropology and sociology) as it is about what is happening in their minds (psychology). The approach to learning that is most compatible with an ethnographically grounded perspective on discourse analysis is one that defines learning as changing patterns of participation in specific social practices within communities of practice. (p. 147)

According to Gee and Green (1998), classroom participants use language to engage in processes by which they coconstruct meanings and ways of perceiving and understanding. Language is seen as social action, and is studied to understand what the participants in a social group are accomplishing through their interactive talk. Social groups construct cultural models, or sets of connected images, that can be used as resources to guide actions. These cultural models can be modified, broadened, and adapted by group members as they interact over time. Individual members within the group may not share all of the cultural models held by the group as a whole. Because of differences in opportunities afforded, members may have differential access to some models, and thus have differential knowledge.

Gallimore (1996) relates the sociocultural perspective to efforts for curriculum reform, and notes that changes in culture (including the classroom culture) occur gradually, and are built on already existing routines. One problem for reformers is that the functions and effects of familiar cultural activities may be so familiar to participants that they remain unseen, invisible, and accepted as "givens." Gallimore points out that the goals of a familiar classroom activity, the rules that govern it, and the ways that it is valued and understood by students and teachers alike, are social constructions of classroom participants that may make it difficult for change to occur.

Wertsch and colleagues indicate that the main goal of a sociocultural approach is to "explicate the relationships between human mental functioning, on the one hand, and the cultural, institutional, and historical situations in which this functioning occurs, on the other" (Wertsch, del Rio, & Alvarez, 1995, p. 3). These authors argue that the proper focus of such research is on human action, as carried out by small or large groups, as well as by individuals. They acknowledge that, from the point of view of classroom researchers, activity settings are the contexts within which such action occurs. They also refer to their belief that sociocultural studies should not be limited to examining human action and the cultural settings in which it occurs, but should be concerned as well with changing both the action and the setting.

Gee and Green (1998) identify a number of key concepts important to the sociocultural perspective. These include situated meaning, reflexivity, and context. These concepts are highly interrelated, and Gee and Green constantly use one of these terms in providing a definition of another of them. For example, they say that "a *situated meaning* is an image or pattern that we (participants in an interaction) assemble 'on the spot' as we communicate in a given *context*, based on our construal of that *context* and on our past experience" (p. 122, italics added). Within any social interaction, there are many clues provided that can contribute to construction of a situated meaning (e.g., intonation, stress or emphasis, eye contact, gesture, physical proximity of speakers to each other, dialect or language used). These clues might denote to participants (and observers) of a classroom conversation that the speakers are either friendly or hostile to each other, and the meaning of a phrase like "show me your evidence" would change markedly depending on which is construed to be the case. Situated meaning is often negotiated between the participants engaged in social interaction, as when one person checks their interpretation of another's comment ("Do you mean that . . . ?").

By "reflexivity," Gee and Green mean "the way in which language always takes on a specific meaning from the actual *context* in which it is used, while, simultaneously, helping to construct what we take that *context* to mean and be in the first place" (1998, p. 127, italics added). In other words, language both gives meaning to and gets meaning from the social activity in which it occurs. It simultaneously reflects reality and constructs it in a particular way. Thus, the language (words, tone, gestures, etc.) that a speaker chooses to use in an interactive situation can show the alert observer what that speaker takes to be the reality, or situated meaning, of the interaction, while at the same time, the speaker may be attempting to change the import of the situation. A student's question ("This won't be graded, will it?") can signal his or her perception that the task just described by the teacher will be particularly difficult, at the same time that it may serve to influence the teacher to reduce the perceived threat ("No, it won't be graded").

The sociocultural view of "context" is quite different from the sense in which the term has been used by classroom management researchers. Yackel (1995) notes that context refers to the internal (mental) state of the student, rather than to the external conditions of the social setting (e.g., size of group, type of student participants, type of task assigned). In Yackel's 10 week study of a second-grade mathematics teaching experiment, she determined that the same activity setting could represent different contexts for different pupils, or different contexts for the same pupil on slightly different occasions. In one series of lessons where pupils worked in pairs to solve problems, they were asked to explain their reasoning to their partner and to the teacher. Yackel details several instances where miscommunication occurred because of differential pupil interpretation of the task. For example, for one student the task context (perceived pupil role/responsibility and expectations of others) involved manipulation of number strips and squares to demonstrate his solution to a subtraction problem. His partner thought of the task as requiring a numerical solution, and failed to understand his graphic explanation, despite his several attempts. Because of their differing views of what was appropriate mathematical activity, the context for learning differed for the two partners.

In another sociocultural study of the same classroom, Wood (1995) attends to the way that the teacher's sense of the task context (interpretation of teacher role/responsibility and expectations of pupils) changed over time as teacher and pupils coconstructed a change in patterns of classroom discourse. Wood reports that the teacher

> struggled throughout the year to establish a way of teaching that shifted from an interaction involving questioning that was intended to check to an interaction in which negotiation of meaning was of central interest. This created for the students a different classroom setting, one in which children did not feel they were in a situation of constant evaluation. Instead, they found themselves in an atmosphere in which their ideas were listened to and in which the teacher attempted to understand their thoughts.... [T]he departure [for the teacher] involved interpreting children's mathmatical activity during the discussion and making qualitative distinctions in the solution attempts they gave. (p. 225)

From the sociocultural perspective, learning takes place as students begin to identify, understand, and work through specific kinds of problems and activities. Change takes place as students and teacher participate in the activity together, and learning or development is a process of participatory appropriation, a "change resulting from a person's own participation in an activity" (Rogoff, 1995, p. 153). In this process, participants begin to understand each other in new ways, and work together more effectively. Eventually they develop and adopt a common set of goals and values, as well as shared meanings and interpretations. In this way meaning is "situated" within the specific classroom and the varied activities that occur within that classroom, and is negotiated and established over time through negotiation and coconstruction of the classroom participants.

These key ideas related to the sociocultural perspective suggest that good classroom managers need to define, clarify, and model the various learning activities to be used. Teaching general rules and routines at the start of the year is not enough. Teachers need to provide students with time to understand and practice the patterns of interaction appropriate to each new type of learning activity introduced throughout the year, so that roles, responsibilities, and expectations are understood by all. They also need to be responsive to students' reactions, so that new patterns and new meanings can develop over time for the teacher as well as the pupils. Most importantly, they need to work with students to establish norms of cooperative collaboration with others, so that knowledge and ideas can be shared with peers. This suggests that the sociocultural perspective is most closely linked to the classroom management imperative (chapter 1, this Handbook) to "develop caring, supportive relationships with and among students." As classroom participants learn to work together in a variety of specific social practices within a classroom community of practice, they will provide support and encouragement for each other, and engage in efforts to understand each others' meaning. In these ways they will assist each other in achieving the learning goals established and valued within the classroom culture. Thus, good classroom managers who work with students to create a viable, supportive classroom community of practice also promote accomplishment of the classroom management imperative (chapter 1, this Handbook) to "organize and implement instruction in ways that optimize student access to learning."

Critical Discourse Analysis

In his review of critical discourse analysis, Luke (1995) argues that changing views of the educational rights of cultural minorities, indigenous peoples, girls and women, and linguistically diverse students have made it imperative to examine how educational institutions may limit access of some to cultural and economic resources. He sees critical discourse analysis as a useful way to conduct such an examination. Luke further asserts that critical discourse analysis is not just an academic activity, but rather something that each of us does every day in judging the usefulness and accuracy of the oral, written, and graphic "texts" we encounter in our conversations with others, in newspaper articles, in television commercials, or in classroom textbooks. According to Luke, all texts are normative; that is, they work to shape and construct our views, rather than merely reflect or describe "reality." Critical discourse analysis can reveal this by connecting examples of local discourse with related political, economic, and cultural power structures. Luke says:

> It is through everyday texts that cultural categories and versions of children, students, adults, and workers are built up, established in a hierarchical social grid of the "normal," and taught and learned: categories of gender identity, sexual desire, ethnic identity, class and work, regional solidarity, citizenship and national identity. (1995, p. 14)

For these reasons, Luke sees critical discourse analysis not just as a research method, but also as a political act. He thinks that it can take on the task of promoting agency for teachers, students, and others concerned with the educational enterprise, helping them to understand how texts position them in particular ways. He notes that "critical discourse analysis can tell us a great deal about how schools and classrooms build 'success' and 'failure' and about how teachers' and students' spoken and written texts shape and construct policies and rules, knowledge, and, indeed, 'versions' of successful and failing students" (1995, p. 11). Thus, a basic feature of critical discourse analysis is a concern with how texts may work to construct social groups as well as the social identities of individuals.

Some key concepts related to critical discourse analysis are power, authority, intertextuality, and intercontextuality. A definition of intertextuality as associated with classroom life is formulated by Floriani (1994):

> [I]n each event a text of the event is being constructed that includes the oral, written, and social actions of members. The nature of these texts and how they are constructed shape particular views of life and resources for members to use in the construction of future texts and contexts. From this perspective, socially appropriate actions are constructed by members as they construct the social and academic texts of classroom life. These texts, in turn, shape how future texts will be read, interpreted, and used.... [Intertextual] links are reflected in the actions and interactions of members. (p. 256)

Floriani goes on to define intercontextuality, suggesting that contexts, as well as texts, can be juxtaposed by classroom members, so that "prior contexts, with their socially negotiated roles and relationships and texts and meanings, become resources for members to reexamine past events" (p. 257). Thus students and teachers understand and interpret present events in the light of their prior history together. Prior contexts inform present contexts and help to shape future contexts. But teachers and students can also reinterpret past events in the light of new experiences that they share, so present contexts can inform past contexts as well.

The meanings of power and authority in classroom settings are explored by Buzzelli and Johnston (2001), who build on the work of Bernstein (1996). They note the view held by many that school is a social institution designed to reproduce existing power relations, thus contributing to inequities and prejudices. They contend that, just as "discipline" has a double meaning in education, referring to both the management of students' classroom behavior and the formal body of knowledge that forms the substance of any given lesson, so the concept of authority has a complex double meaning. Teachers have the authority to direct actions and activities in the classroom, as well as the authority that accrues to their status as the holder of knowledge that students are supposed to learn. Buzzelli and Johnston see Bernstein's concept of "pedagogic discourse" as a useful way to examine these two aspects of authority. Bernstein calls the discourse of what students are to learn the "instructional discourse," and the discourse that structures and regulates classroom order, relationships, and identities, the "regulative discourse." He says that the regulative discourse is the dominant discourse, "because it is the *moral* discourse that creates the criteria which give rise to character, manner, conduct" (1996, p. 48). The instructional discourse is embedded in the regulative discourse, forming one discourse, the pedagogic discourse.

Buzzelli and Johnston (2001) present a sample of dialogue from a third-grade writer's chair activity to illustrate the embeddedness of the instructional discourse in the regulative discourse. As third-grader "Robbie" reads the story he has written, he mentions that his heroes are drinking beer. The teacher faces a dilemma. She wants to nurture the writer's voice, but she is also concerned with helping students to learn the responsibility to the reader that is associated with authorship. She interrupts the reading activity to raise a question about the use of the word "beer" in the story. According to the researchers' analysis, her resolution of her dilemma is a clear example of pedagogic discourse as one discourse:

> The instructional discourse of learning how to write in order to express one's unique voice is embedded in, and thus subject to and trammeled by, the regulative discourse that establishes and maintains moral rules of social relations and identities, and thus adjudicates what is and is not offensive and, more generally speaking, morally acceptable. In taking part in and overseeing pedagogic discourse, the teacher is inevitably using her authority both for purposes of regulating power relations and for moral ends: she is both a political and a moral agent in the classroom. (Buzzelli & Johnston, 2001, p. 881)

The effects of teacher power and authority can also operate to impact the instructional discourse. In a self-study, Carlsen (1997) compares the discourse in science lessons he taught in biology and chemistry classes in a rural school. In chemistry, a subject matter content with which he was less familiar, Carlsen asked significantly more low-cognitive (comprehension and recall) questions, compared to his lessons in biology, a subject with which he was thoroughly familiar. In addition, Carlsen concluded that his assertions in the chemistry classes were more likely to provide inadequate warrants (logical support), when compared with his assertions in the biology classes. Thus, chemistry students had the opportunity to learn mainly scientific facts, and they were given a different perspective than the biology students on how scientists develop facts and make judgments about the theoretical and factual claims of other scientists.

A study by Moje (1997) shows how a high school chemistry teacher's pedagogic discourse emphasized a particular restricted view of scientific knowledge, as she reiterated regularly that it is critically important for scientists to be clear, accurate, and precise in their communication. This view led the teacher to focus on students' accuracy and precision in reading and reporting on the texts they read. So her discourse patterns defined the student role as demonstrator of received knowledge, and her own role as evaluator of their demonstrations of knowledge. Moje suggests that students in this classroom were learning to "do school," rather than learning to think like scientists.

A number of classroom discourse studies have examined issues related to the teaching and learning of minority group students and children with disabilities. Because these tend to deal with the social construction of identity, and Luke (1995) includes identity and "category" formation as a central issue for critical discourse analysis, these studies are included in this section, though not all the authors locate their work within the traditions of critical discourse analysis. A review by Forman and McCormick (1995) reports on studies that have focused on learners with disabilities, as well as students who encounter some similar classroom communication difficulties, such as cultural and linguistic minorities. These authors note that disabilities are not just a function of individual characteristics but also are influenced by the social interactional context. They discuss a series of studies to illustrate this point, and also remind the reader that discourse analysis includes oral, written, and signed language. They advocate the use of contingent teaching, in which the failure of a pupil is followed by increased teacher control of the task, while the success of a pupil is followed by decreased teacher control, leading to more self-directed pupil performance. However, studies show that noncontingent teaching is more commonly used by teachers of children with communicative disabilities. In discussing classroom miscommunication due to cultural or linguistic differences, Forman and McCormick note studies showing that teachers typically react to students with limited English proficiency by reducing the academic demands of instruction, rather than by providing increased structure, or teacher control of academic tasks. In these ways teachers' interactions with pupils who differ from the norm in communicative competencies can serve to "create" instances of student failure, or lack of opportunity to learn, and a series of such instances or events can serve to develop a context in which expectations of failure or inadequacy become accepted by both the teacher and the pupil.

A contrasting example of teacher-pupil interaction is provided by Rex (2000), who documents a lesson in a 9th-grade heterogeneous class in an "Academic Foundations for Success" program. The teacher in this study made a series of moves to support participation by Judy, a girl diagnosed as having a learning disability. These moves included validating Judy's question as academically and socially meaningful, and inviting another student, a bilingual immigrant from Mexico, with relevant personal experience, to answer her question. In this way the teacher provided a context in which both students could be recognized by their peers as academically literate students, and could see themselves as having performed successfully.

A book edited by Lisa Delpit and Joanne Kilgour Dowdy, *The Skin That We Speak* (2002), presents the work of several authors commenting on issues of classroom communication that impact black children in settings where the teacher's and students' dialects or styles of speech may differ markedly. Stubbs (2002) discusses issues related to teachers' perceptions of students' language as "inappropriate," concluding that a child's language may be a disadvantage in the classroom, not because it is actually deficient, but because it is different. Ladson-Billings (2002) reports on a teacher who gives a black girl "permission to fail," by allowing her day after day to refuse to participate in the class writing task because of her feelings of inadequacy. Herbert Kohl (2002) emphasizes the effect that a teacher's language usage may have on pupils, noting that "small things—comments, questions, responses, phrases, tone—often make a big difference in student attitudes, not merely toward their teacher, but toward what their teacher teaches" (p. 153). He argues that while teachers may have authority, students can hold power; if they refuse to listen to the teacher, or "obey" teacher demands, they control the language of the classroom, rather than the teacher. Delpit (2002) notes that the teacher's attitude toward students' language is critical. If students are seen as language deficient, the teacher's behavior changes; he or she engages children in communication less frequently, and pays less attention to the comments that they do make. Alternatively, the teacher may provide more negative attention to students who use different language styles, or withdraw from classroom tasks, or fail to listen to the teacher, thus reinforcing a developing student identity as bad, lazy, or stupid.

The critical discourse perspective highlights the importance of the language and social context of the classroom in defining what is appropriate and inappropriate linguistic behavior of students. To the extent that classroom communication reflects the political, economic, and cultural power structures of the larger society, children may be categorized as more or less adequate according to their ability to communicate in ways that are similar to the norms of the society. Classroom discourse then may serve to shape students' identities as "academic failures," and over time these identities may become accepted by teachers, the students themselves, and their peers.

Because students' language "behavior" is a key ingredient contributing to teachers' views of appropriate and inappropriate behavior in academic settings, the critical discourse analysis perspective seems to be most closely associated with the classroom management imperative (chapter 1, this Handbook) to "use appropriate interventions to assist students with behavior problems." Considering this imperative from the point of view of classroom discourse throws a new light on the term *behavior*. Bernstein's (1996) emphasis on the dominance of the regulative discourse which gives rise to character, manner, and conduct supports the view that classroom discourse shapes and defines what comes to be considered as a "behavior problem."

Luke's (1995) emphasis on how classroom texts work to construct the social identities of individuals in terms of success or failure suggests that the kinds of interventions teachers use to help students with behavior problems have a critical impact on opportunity to learn. Critical discourse studies focused more closely on the teacher and the instructional discourse indicate that the impact on students' opportunities to learn can be more widespread than students with behavior problems, for teachers have the power to control the knowledge made available to the class as a whole. Effective classroom managers concerned with the types of issues raised by critical discourse analysis will work to provide all their students with extensive opportunities to learn. Teachers' management of classroom communication patterns and participation structures can operate to promote inclusion of students who exhibit communicative differences. Teachers who provide opportunities for pupils to participate in new or atypical activity settings can often see abilities they were unaware of, and shift their attitudes and perceptions of pupils' abilities. Skillful classroom managers will work to promote inclusion and provide varied activity settings for students. In addition, the critical discourse perspective highlights the importance of the language and social context of the classroom in identifying linguistic behaviors of teachers that may limit the content available to be learned. Competent classroom managers will be attentive to their own communicative behavior, and alert to the ways in which their regulative discourse may constrain their instructional discourse. Therefore, Good classroom managers who are attentive to these aspects of classroom communication demonstrate their concern for the classroom management imperative (chapter 1, this Handbook) to "organize and implement instruction in ways that optimize access to learning."

CONTRASTING PROGRAMS OF RESEARCH

The four different perspectives on learning represented by the four approaches to research on classroom discourse described in the preceding section are not totally discrete perspectives. The various approaches share some basic methodological features, and have overlapping key concepts not detailed here (e.g., the IRE/IRF question cycle is attended to by researchers from all four approaches, intertextuality and intercontextuality are important to the sociocultural perspective as well as in critical discourse analysis). While an individual classroom discourse study may build on a single approach, some long-term programs of research illustrate how studies draw on and cut across a set of approaches to provide a more complex and complete set of results. This section compares and contrasts two such programs of research: the Understanding Teaching and Learning Project, developed by Graham Nuthall and Adrienne Alton-Lee at the University of Canterbury in Christchurch, New Zealand (Alton-Lee & Nuthall, 1990, 1992a, 1992b; Nuthall & Alton-Lee, 1993, 1995); and the Santa Barbara Classroom Discourse Group Studies, conducted through the leadership of Judith Green and Carol Dixon of the University of California at Santa Barbara (Gee & Green, 1998; Green & Dixon, 1994; Kelly & Green, 1997, 1998).

Both the Santa Barbara Classroom Discourse Group studies and the Understanding Teaching and Learning Project research use qualitative data, and both have emphasized the importance of finding "generic elements" in specific classroom events. These generic elements are then used to guide analysis in other classrooms and to understand related factors or aspects of events and settings. Thus, both research programs combine knowledge from a series of qualitative studies to derive more general interpretations and results. A major difference between the two is how they view knowledge construction. Green and Dixon and the Santa Barbara Group center their work in the sociocultural perspective, and view knowledge as socially constructed in the classroom. Nuthall and Alton-Lee center their work in the cognitive constructivist perspective, and view knowledge as individually constructed in the classroom. But both of these programs extend their concerns and assumptions beyond a central focus to incorporate aspects of the sociolinguistic approach, as well as aspects of the critical discourse analysis approach. Figure 6.2 illustrates the relationships among the four approaches to classroom discourse, and the contrasting perspectives of the two research programs.

As depicted in Fig. 6.2, the central focus of classroom discourse studies is "opportunity to learn," or "opportunity for learning," as the Santa Barbara group frames it. Each of the four classroom discourse perspectives is concerned with learning opportunities, although each defines learning in a somewhat different way. The associated classroom management imperatives identified in the preceding section are noted in each of the five boxes of the graphic display. From left to right, the four classroom discourse approaches are located in a sequence related to the time at which they became prominent views within classroom discourse research, so they move from the sociolinguistic perspective to the cognitive constructivist perspective to the sociocultural perspective to the critical discourse analysis perspective. The sociolinguistic perspective and the critical discourse analysis perspective are on the same horiziontal line, because each approach is concerned with how the language a child learns at home and within the immediate cultural community influences opportunity to learn. They are at opposite ends of the graphic display because they emphasize different effects of the home-school language mismatch. The sociolinguistic perspective attends more closely to the child's initial lack of understanding of the school discourse, despite his or her ability to display communicative competence within the home community, whereas the critical discourse analysis perspective attends more closely to the teacher's power and authority as these are expressed in reaction to a child's different linguistic style. The cognitive constructivist perspective and the sociocultural perspective are vertically opposite each other because they emphasize different views of how

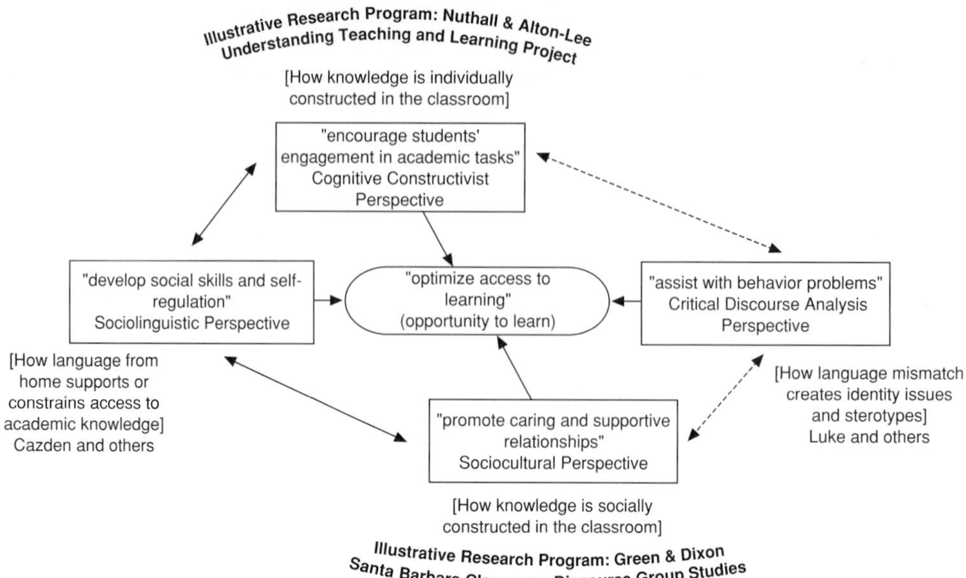

FIGURE 6.2. Relationships Among Classroom Management Imperatives and Classroom Discourse Perspectives

classroom learning is constructed, with individually constructed meaning located above and socially constructed meaning located below the graphic midline. The Understanding Teaching and Learning Project extends across the upper half of the graphic, centered on the cognitive constructivist perspective, but extending in both directions to encompass aspects of the sociolinguistic prespective and the critical discourse analysis perspective. The Santa Barbara Classroom Discourse Group program extends across the lower half of the graphic, centered on the sociocultural perspective, but also extending in both directions to encompass aspects of the sociolinguistic prespective and the critical discourse analysis perspective.

Contrasting Methodologies

Alton-Lee and Nuthall, as well as Green and her colleagues, have all written extensively about their methodological approaches (Alton-Lee & Nuthall, 1990, 1992a, 1992b; Gee & Green, 1998; Green & Dixon, 1994; Kelly & Green, 1997, 1998; Nuthall & Alton-Lee, 1993, 1995). Space does not allow a detailed analysis of their differences, but Table 6.1 provides a summary of contrasting views, emphases, and procedures in the key features of their research.

Selected Studies from the Understanding Teaching and Learning Project

Two studies reported by Nuthall and Alton-Lee illustrate how their research addresses aspects of the sociolinguistic and critical discourse perspectives, while centered on the cognitive constructivist perspective. Both studies also speak to specific aspects of classroom management, and illustrate how classroom discourse studies can enhance awareness of the ways classroom management can operate to optimize (or constrain) access to learning. In the first study the recordings of pupils' private talk, as related to public talk, provide insights into what occurs

TABLE 6.1
Contrasting Methodological Features of two Classroom Discourse Research Programs

Type of Feature	*New Zealand Project*	*Santa Barbara Group*
Perspective on Learning	Main focus is on how knowledge is *individually* constructed in classrooms.	Main focus is on how knowledge is *socially* constructed in classrooms.
Setting	Classroom activity tends to involve "traditional" lessons (in Cazden's terms); teacher-directed whole-class lessons predominate, with some individual pupil seatwork; teacher-developed units of instruction within the regular curriculum.	Classroom activity tends to involve "non-traditional" lessons (in Cazden's terms); small group/independent work or whole-class discussion with teacher as guide or social mediator; use of new reform-based curriculum materials and procedures.
Data	Short-term data collection (one-week to four-week units on a given topic); follow-up interviews with selected students shortly after end of unit and again one year later. Data on both public and private talk, i.e., student comments to peers and self, recorded on individual microphones. Video and audio recordings and observers' notes.	Long-term data collection (several months to a year) using ethnographic methods; reports on smaller segments of interaction, informed by long-term information available. Data on both public and semipublic talk, i.e., teacher interacting with pairs or small groups of pupils. Video and audio recordings and ethnographers' notes.
Role of "Context"	Focus on an individual's experience in varied contexts (home, school) and its influence on what is learned and what becomes patterned (appropriate) behavior. Students recall physical context in which specific information was learned.	Focus on how teacher and students draw on and relate to prior classroom contexts in shaping and interpreting the present context. Context includes roles played, and roles seen as appropriate for self and others, from point of view of various participants.
Evidence of Learning	Use pre- and posttesting of academic learning of information taught during a unit, as well as interviews with individual students to determine the new knowledge held in short-term and long-term (12 months later) memory.	Attempt to determine from interactive data and artifacts of pupil work collected over time how much (and what) conceptual change occurs for individuals and/or what new or revised concepts are generated and held within the class or group.
Explanation of Learning	Emphasis on concept learning. Goal is development of a predictive model of what academic learning will be accomplished by individual students, based on prior knowledge/experience, and amount/timing of classroom exposure to new information. Reference to the transactional relationship between social and cognitive; the individual's prior knowledge/experience shapes what is taken up from the curriculum in social interaction, and therefore, what is learned.	Emphasis on group construction over time of language, meaning, and behavioral norms. Goal is understanding the ordinary discursive and social practices in a classroom setting, and how these practices contribute to the construction of knowledge in classrooms. Reference to the dialectical relationship between group and individual; each contributes to the creation of the other, so each has an impact on development of opportunities for learning by both the group and the individual.

beyond or below a teacher's awareness. In the second study, a focus on public talk shows how a teacher can adapt a lesson to provide for individual differences in pupils' prior experience, as well as encourage participation of a reluctant student.

The Private World of Children. In a sixth-grade unit about New York City, the private talk of four selected students was recorded in addition to the public talk during teacher-directed lessons (Alton-Lee, Nuthall, & Patrick, 1993). The school was in a middle to upper-middle socioeconomic Pakeha (white European background) community. The case-study pupils were Ann, an average achiever, Mia, a high achiever, Joe, a low achiever, and Jon, a high achiever. In addition, Ricky, the only Maori in the class, was picked up on Joe's microphone, as they interacted privately during a lesson.

The pretest results and later interviews showed that Jon began the unit with strong background knowledge about New York City, derived mainly from television cartoons and Mad Magazine. Ann had good relevant prior knowledge from watching a recent television news program on the Statue of Liberty. Joe had little prior knowledge, and what he did know was based on watching television crime dramas. Mia drew on less relevant prior knowledge than the others to interpret new information; for example, she was reminded of a school cross-country race when the teacher asked students to imagine climbing the stairs of the Statue of Liberty.

The combination of public and private talk in one lesson of the unit showed the relationship between individual students' self-regulation, engagement, and access to learning. The teacher's public evaluation of student responses was imitated in the private talk of some students, as they evaluated their own unspoken responses to teacher questions, as well as the public responses of their peers. Mia gave public answers to two teacher questions; one was judged incorrect. She rarely made private answers to questions, but she was alert to both the public and private responses of peers. She was highly aware of the evaluative climate of the classroom, and a year later recalled having made an incorrect public answer. All of Ann's public responses to teacher questions were correct, but she received no positive feedback from the teacher. Her 11 wrong answers were kept private, and where she lacked knowledge, she repeated key phrases of teacher talk to herself in an apparent attempt to learn and remember new information. In contrast, Jon gave 10 public answers, some of which were incorrect, but he seemed comfortable risking public answers when he was not certain of their accuracy. He gave private answers to 16 teacher questions, only one of which was incorrect. Jon also monitored other pupils' public answers and commented privately on their adequacy. Joe gave two public answers, both of which were wrong, but his private talk included no self-monitoring. Posttest data showed that Mia learned the most new information during the unit, while Joe learned the least.

From the critical discourse perspective, the public talk in this unit revealed an unconscious gender and cultural bias on the part of the teacher, while the private talk showed Joe's ethnic bias toward Ricky in a series of harassing comments unnoticed by the teacher. These biases affected how individual students participated in the lesson, and what they learned from the lesson. The boys in the class were called on more frequently and received more positive feedback than the girls. The teacher unconsciously used "we" in talking about white males as the colonizers of New York City. Mia adopted that version of events, and acknowledged in a later interview that she was thinking of European men when she used the term "us." Ricky, the Maori boy, on the other hand, referred to the English men who colonized New York as "they," showing his awareness of being excluded from the teacher's view of history. The teacher's use of "we" to refer to white males also appeared to influence Joe, as seen in this excerpt of recorded talk:

Teacher: Because White people . . .
Joe ([privately] talking to Ricky): Honkies.
Ricky ([privately] talking to Joe): Shut up!

Teacher: Europeans, we . . .
Joe ([privately] talking to Ricky): Nigger!
Teacher: Watch this way please, Ricky!—were often wanting to get things . . .
Joe ([privately] talking to Ricky): Black man! Samoan! (Alton-Lee, Nuthall, & Patrick, 1993, p. 77)

Joe's harassment of Ricky was not heard by the teacher or any of the observers in the room, and was noticed only when investigators heard the recordings of private talk. Joe apparently felt that classroom rules did not apply to him, and in effect they did not, for the teacher reprimanded Ricky's behavior regularly, though Joe was the actual instigator of the disruptions. At one point Joe and other boys asked the teacher to remove Ricky from the class, saying that his bad behavior interfered with their ability to concentrate on their work. Ricky blamed his own behavior in part for the racist treatment he received. In an interview he said that "sometimes people be racist to me 'cause I annoy them" (p. 78).

In this study the importance of students' prior knowledge and the transactional relationship between the cognitive and social features of the public and private classroom discourse illustrate the complexity of teaching and learning. Teacher management of the questioning (IRE/IRF cycles) can be seen to influence patterns of participation, encouraging the engagement of some and discouraging the engagement of others, but individual pupils also played an important role in regulating their own participation and engagement. The enacted curriculum served to include some children and exclude others. The misbehavior of some children was invisible to the teacher, while other children learned to accept or adopt the teacher's demonstrated perception of them as disruptive or unworthy of academic praise. The classroom discourse data clearly showed the potential for a teacher's management of classroom interaction to impact some students' opportunities to learn in a negative fashion.

Managing Reluctance to Participate. The second illustrative study was conducted by Alton-Lee and colleagues as part of the ERUDITE (Educational Research Underpinning Development in Teacher Education) program to develop case studies for use in teacher education (Alton-Lee, Diggins, Klenner, Vine, & Dalton, 2001). This case study focuses on a single lesson for 18 five-year-olds in a teacher-designed social studies unit on "Christmas in Hospital," planned to meet objectives of the national curriculum. It shows how a teacher builds on both different and common prior experiences of pupils, and diversifies management strategies for different students, to promote learning. The children had the common experience of seeing their classmate, Huhana, a Maori girl, fall on the playground, and break her arm. Her mother came to school and took her to the hospital. She returned to school with her arm in a cast.

As one activity for the unit, children drew pictures of their own experiences with hospitals, or their view of hospitals. Two children depicted and reported rather negative prior experiences with hospitals. Brian was not allowed to visit his mother in the hospital when his baby brother was born, and felt removed from that important event. Holly's mother was taken to the hospital for serious burns. Holly brought her flowers, and afterwards drew a picture of her visit to the hospital. Her mother died later from her burns.

After reading a story to the class about a child's hospital experience during an ear operation, the teacher asked who remembered Huhana's playground accident, and invited Huhana to tell the class about her hospital visit following the accident. Huhana looked down and shook her head, declining the request. The teacher asked students to rearrange themselves in a circle, making Huhana a member of the group rather than a reporter in front of the group, and said, "If we sit in a circle . . . Huhana might be able to tell us about what happened." Students became attentive and focused, and Huhana told about her experience in some detail. Other children added information of their own in response to some teacher follow-up questions. When the teacher asked, "Does anyone know what an x-ray is?," Lynda said "—black stuff under your skin—," and William added "Takes a picture of your bones." The teacher seated Holly next to her, to provide support. She did not require all children to participate, but modeled asking questions of Huhana, so that children with no hospital experience were shown a way they might engage in the discussion.

The reasoning behind the Maori teacher's planning of activities and her management of the class discussion are provided as part of this case. The teacher participated in the analysis of data, and in the writing of the case report. When this case has been used in teacher education classes, it is presented as a critical incident, with an interruption of the narrative at the point where Huhana declines to tell about her hospital experience. Teachers are asked what they think the classroom teacher should do next, and what they themselves might do in this situation, and why. In response, New Zealand teachers have tended to suggest that the teacher should not have pursued her attempt to get Huhana to participate. They explain their response in terms of cultural sensitivity and a concern for protecting Maori children. Authors of the case study note how these views feed into a pattern of differential treatment of Maori children in mainstream classes, a pattern which limits opportunity to learn. They are attempting to counteract this trend.

> By focusing on the actions of an effective Maori teacher and a highly achieving Maori student in a mainstream classroom, we have attempted to generate a research case study structure that achieves two purposes. The pedagogy of our case study not only enables us to report our findings but also disrupts deficit thinking about student achievement. (Alton-Lee, et al., 2001, pp. 561–562)

This case shows how a simple management strategy like a change in group formation can operate to encourage a reluctant participant. It also illustrates teacher use of "real" questions to learn more from Huhana about her hospital visit. In this case the teacher models a way for students with less prior experience to participate in the discussion. The two studies together highlight the ways that the roles played by a teacher in managing classroom interaction carry implicit messages for students about appropriate classroom behavior.

Selected Studies from the Santa Barbara Classroom Discourse Group

Two studies reported by participants in the Santa Barbara program demonstrate the way that their research addresses concerns of the sociolinguistic and critical discourse perspectives, while centered on the sociocultural perspective. Both studies illustrate interesting classroom management procedures, and show how classroom discourse studies can expand perceptions of the concept of classroom management. The first study emphasizes the sociocultural perspective and shows how a teacher and small groups of pupils can work together to coconstruct opportunities for learning. The second study incorporates aspects of other discourse approaches to reveal how student behavior and communication patterns change as the context for interaction shifts. Both studies demonstrate the value of long-term ethnographic data for interpreting classroom events.

Constructing Knowledge and Opportunities to Learn. In a third-grade bilingual class pupils worked in teams on a student-initiated writing activity, writing a "planet story," as part of a 33-day science cycle of activity on the solar system (Tuvay, Jennings, & Dixon, 1995). Having agreed to students' requests to write their own planet stories, the teacher set guidelines, indicating that each story should include space travel, arriving at some planet in the solar system, identifying the method of travel, and describing what the planet looked like. The study focuses on a "key event" that was representative of discourse patterns and collaborative tasks observed throughout the year of data collection. Two teams of students, who shared a single worktable, were observed negotiating with team members and with the teacher to develop their stories. The report presents a comparison of the processes used by the two teams, and by the teacher as she interacted with the two teams. One team was a group of three boys, two of whom were bilingual; the third was a monolingual Spanish speaker. The second team was a pair of girls, one bilingual and one monolingual English speaker. The recorded discourse showed that a common task does not necessarily lead to common learnings, but can provide a range of opportunities for students to construct knowledge. Evidence of student learning included the planet stories that were drafted over several days by each team, then revised, "published," and presented to the class.

The report highlights patterns of interaction that were treated as normal in this classroom, but would be atypical in many U.S. classrooms. In one sequence one of the boys commented on and contributed ideas to the story draft being developed by the team of girls seated at the same table. Members of both teams treated this as helpful and appropriate behavior, and the idea offered was incorporated into the final draft of the girls' planet story. In another sequence the teacher was interacting with the team of boys when a boy from another table came by to ask the teacher a question. He stayed to participate in the discussion and contributed an idea that was incorporated into the boys' story draft. The teacher and the boys' team all accepted this as appropriate and helpful behavior. These incidents show the norms that operated in this classroom to promote supportive peer relationships and served to contribute to student construction of knowledge.

This study also details differences between the two teams in their interpretations of the common task, and their use of time. The girls began by asking the teacher about an appropriate introduction to their story. She responded by asking them questions in return ("What planet are you going to?" "How are you going to get there?"). The girls decided they were going to Uranus in a spaceship, but had some difficulty deciding what the spaceship would look like, so the teacher suggested some strategies for deciding on shape and size. The girls then proceeded to discuss and write their story draft. They completed their first draft in 30 minutes, having concentrated on negotiating the content of their story, after using the teacher's suggestions about strategies to describe their spaceship.

The boys began by looking for a book on Jupiter, having interpreted the task as writing a factual report (similar to one they had written previously). The teacher intervened to clarify the task as writing a story, but the boys continued to gather facts by looking at the solar system model hanging in the room, and reading the reports on various planets that were on display. Midway through the writing period they began to write their draft, still thinking in terms of a factual report, but finally shifting to a story mode. As they composed, the boys focused on negotiating their use of language, deciding that they would write five things in English, then five things in Spanish. One boy took on the role of author, and dictated lines in English while another took on the role of scribe and wrote the lines in Spanish. The teacher returned and invited them to act out some story ideas; one boy did, while the others commented. By the end of the period they had written down several ideas for possible inclusion, but they had not completed a story draft.

This study highlights the dialectical relationship between group and individual; the whole class helped to shape the activity, small groups influenced each other as they worked in the activity setting, and individual pupils negotiated within their groups to develop their final products. The teacher adapted to differences in the students' interpretations of the task, to provide helpful assistance to each group. She worked with the girls on ways they might measure the size of their rocket. She worked with the boys on the differences between two genres of writing, and introduced imaginary activity to help them generate ideas for writing their text. As a result, both groups learned to use new processes helpful in writing, and both eventually completed a published story. It is worth noting as well the management processes used by the teacher in organizing the writing activity for the class as a whole. After hearing a peer read aloud from a book on extraterrestrials, students asked to work in teams to write their own stories. The teacher agreed to their request, and provided an opportunity for groups to brainstorm ideas for stories, and to choose their writing partners. On the following day she provided guidelines for the stories, then provided assistance to the groups as they began their compositions. All of these management processes illustrate the ways that opportunities for learning were coconstructed by the teacher and pupils in this classroom.

Creating Authentic Opportunities to Present Science. The second illustrative Santa Barbara study shows how a change in the context for classroom communication can assist with student behavior problems and encourage development of student social skills and self-regulation. High school students in a Conceptual Physics class were engaged in a Museum Project over a two-week period in the second year of a three-year study that combined ethnographic and classroom discourse methods (Crawford, Chen, & Kelly, 1997). During the Museum Project the students chose their own topics, worked in self-selected groups to prepare reports, then presented their work to two different audiences: a group of science teachers, and a group of 5th-grade pupils. Authors compared two key events to examine differences in the communication patterns of one pair of students as they interacted with the two different audiences.

The student participants were Anthony and Miguel, two 9th-grade bilingual Hispanic boys who had displayed little engagement in science tasks during prior group activities, and who were generally disruptive. During this project they exhibited markedly different behavior, becoming quite enthusiastic and engaged. They chose to construct and report on a light-activated burglar alarm, using information about electrical circuits. Evidence of their learning included their ability to "talk science" (use the discourse of physics) in their oral presentations, as well as their ability to read circuit designs, build a functioning circuit, prepare a presentation poster, and plan and organize an oral presentation.

In presenting their project to the teachers, a "more knowledgeable" audience, Anthony and Miguel identified their topic, named the components of their burglar alarm, and explained the theory behind its operation, thus demonstrating their ability to use the discourse of physics. However, when a teacher asked questions about the electronic functions of the circuit ("When the light shines on it . . . what happens in the circuit?"), Anthony responded, "I don't know." The teacher then repositioned himself as less knowledgeable ("I'm not exactly sure either . . . but see how you drew it . . . it has a resistor"), and Anthony provided a substantive explanation ("Oh yeah . . . the current goes, it like goes down from the resistor . . . so then the voltage can go through . . . and from here it goes to the amplifier . . . so then if the thing decreases then you can hear it [the alarm] louder") (Crawford et al., 1997, p. 11). The authors suggest that the teacher became a more authentic audience by indicating his own lack of certainty. In the transformed interactional context, Anthony had more reason to explain what he knew.

In their presentation to fifth graders, a less knowledgeable (more authentic) audience, Anthony and Miguel began by focusing attention on the burglar alarm, describing and demonstrating how it functioned. They then switched from the discourse of physics to the discourse of a teacher and checked for pupils' prior knowledge ("You know what voltage means, right?"). When the pupils said, "No," Anthony and Miguel provided expanded explanations. In interacting with the younger pupils they also engaged in code-switching, reporting in both English and Spanish to the bilingual pupils. Thus they demonstrated social skills and communicative competence, adapting their patterns of discourse to the new interactive context.

The authors of this study report that Anthony and Miguel appeared to know less and were less willing to offer explanations when they were speaking to an audience they saw as knowledgeable. They suggest that teachers can learn more about what students are learning if they provide opportunities for students to use language for "authentic, powerful reasons." Teacher management is less visible in this study, but features of the activity show the importance of behind-the-scenes management in setting up the opportunities for learning described. Students' selection of the topics to be studied, and their choice of partners for their work, probably contributed a good deal to the greater enthusiasm and engagement exhibited by Anthony and Miguel. The teacher also planned for the shift in audiences that provided students with additional practice in presenting their projects, as well as the chance to interact in a more authentic interactive context. This aspect of the study points out that classroom management is critical to learning even when it appears to be invisible. The teacher's role in creating the context for learning impacts the roles that students are able to take on as well as the skills they are able to develop and display.

Growing Together

The differences in the classroom discourse perspective of Nuthall and Alton Lee compared with that of Green and her colleagues have been highlighted in this section, but it is appropriate to end by pointing out the important similarities. To begin with, both programs take a long-term view of learning. This is evident in the extended periods of ethnographic data collection characteristic of the studies of the Santa Barbara Group. It is seen in the 12-month posttesting and interviewing characteristic of the New Zealand researchers. Further, both programs have extended their research concerns beyond their central discourse perspective to include aspects of the issues addressed by the sociolinguistic and critical discourse analysis perspectives. This more inclusive approach contributes greatly to a deeper understanding of the complexity of factors that impact classroom teaching and learning.

Finally, and perhaps most importantly, as their programs have developed over time, each program has gradually moved toward incorporating aspects of the perspective of the other. Starting from the view that knowledge is individually constructed in the classroom, the theory developing from the results of the Understanding Teaching and Learning Project has increasingly attended to the ways that the culture of the classroom influences what is learned. In a 1992 paper, they reported:

> We have arrived at the apparently contradictory position of affording much more weight to the influence of the cultural context of the classroom in framing student experience while acknowledging a more active role for the students in shaping their own knowledge in culturally-specific ways. These changes lead us to conceptualise both the teacher's role and the student's learning processes differently as we grapple with the ways in which the wider culture permeates classroom processes. (Alton-Lee & Nuthall, April 1992, p.1)

In the conclusion to his extensive review of the New Zealand studies, Nuthall notes:

> Because differences in the ways students experience and participate in classroom activities are a function of social and cultural differences, how students learn to learn is essentially a socio-cultural process. The implication is that reforming the effectiveness of classrooms requires changes in the ways classrooms function as communities with their evolving social processes and cultural practices. (Nuthall, 1999, p. 241)

In a similar fashion, starting from the view that knowledge is socially constructed in the classroom, the work of the Santa Barbara Classroom Discourse Group has increasingly focused on the learning of individuals within the group culture (Dixon et al., 2005; Putney, Gueen, Dixon, Duran, & Yeager, 2000). As Dixon and Green and their colleagues explain, in their study tracing the development of a letter written by Lauren, an elementary student:

> [Our] theoretical framework provides a way of viewing Lauren's text, and other texts produced in classrooms, as historically and situationally constructed artifacts. From this perspective, Lauren can be viewed as the "author" of her text, but the words, practices of text construction, and content of the text that Lauren chose to include were not "her words, practices or content" alone. They were *words, practices and content* made available to her in the events of classroom life.... [T]o construct this text Lauren chose among the discourses available to her, and in making these choices, she was inscribing more than a simple message. She was constructing her identity as a writer, her understandings of the activity in which she was engaged, and her membership in this and other communities. (Dixon et al., 2005)

The shifts to include broader perspectives demonstrated by these two programs of research hold important promise for the eventual development of a more inclusive understanding of classroom learning.

IMPLICATIONS FOR TEACHING PRACTICE AND CLASSROOM RESEARCH

Suggestions about effective classroom management practices derived from classroom discourse studies have been stated in each of the earlier sections on the four alternative research perspectives. These are summarized in the Appendix.

There are three main implications for future classroom research that can be derived from this analysis. All three could usefully be applied to both classroom management research and classroom discourse research. The productive methodological processes and results provided by these two illustrative research programs demonstrate the value of:

- unifying or incorporating aspects of discrete perspectives or assumptions to reach deeper, more inclusive understandings;
- supporting research programs over an extended series of studies so that generic elements can be identified from specific classroom/activity settings; and
- examining the social processes revealed in the small group interactions and the private talk of students, and relating this to the more obvious (but not necessarily more influential) public communication systems of the classroom.

Heath (2000) has provided a useful critique of classroom discourse research that may also be relevant to classroom management research. She says:

> The evolution of qualitative methods in the study of language in education will surely be more influenced by cognitive psychology than has been the case in the past three decades. Such a link will insist on more attention to learning over time and contexts and less to classifying what happens in highly specific classrooms or more generalizable classroom events, such as literature circles or peer conferencing. Necessary to this evolution, however, is substantial recognition that methods of research cannot sit totally in the service of advocacy of particular ideologies, teaching methods, approaches to assessment, or evaluation of school reform efforts. (Heath, 2000, pp. 56–57)

Another problem with classroom discourse research is worth noting. It is a difficult problem to avoid, but it does limit the usefulness of the research. Because studies of classroom discourse take place within teaching and learning activities, each individual study tends to be focused on a particular curriculum area. In one way this has enriched the research, as investigators who are primarily interested in science or mathematics education or language arts education have enlarged the field of researchers using classroom discourse methods. In another way this has narrowed the dissemination of the research because it tends to be published in books or journals focused on the separate curriculum areas. This makes it much more difficult to pull individual studies together to compare and contrast results across subject areas, and therefore it limits what can be learned and widely understood about classroom learning. Now that the research in most individual subject areas has increased to provide a substantial body of information, it would seem to be time to move toward more cross-subject comparisons and toward publication for wider, more general audiences. The fragmentation of findings because of publication practices may not be as much of a concern for classroom management research.

A related issue for classroom discourse research has to do with the use of language to report on the language of the classroom. All specialists tend to use special language to discuss their specialties with knowledgeable others, but the use of obscure terms (e.g., intercontextuality) or common terms used with a very different meaning (e.g., context) is not helpful when the discussion is aimed at a wider audience. The segments of classroom dialogue that are included in reports of classroom discourse studies tell a compelling story. Interpretations phrased in more common terms would make the valuable work of classroom discourse researchers more accessible to teachers, teacher educators, and other researchers interested in the study of teaching and learning in classroom settings. To publish reports in books and journals for a more general audience, classroom discourse researchers may need to develop new skills in communicative competence.

It is clear that classroom discourse studies can provide a fresh and useful lens through which to view the results of past research on classroom management. The future of both fields of research can be enhanced to the extent that they become attentive to the ways that their concerns and understandings are interrelated.

APPENDIX

SUMMARY OF SUGGESTIONS FOR CLASSROOM MANAGEMENT PRACTICE DERIVED FROM CLASSROOM DISCOURSE STUDIES

Findings from classroom discourse studies suggest that good classroom managers may enhance their ability to "organize and implement instruction in ways that optimize access to learning" when they engage in the following practices. Many of these findings support similar results from classroom management research.

From studies reflecting the Sociolinguistic Perspective, practices that may assist teachers to "promote the development of students' social skills and self-regulation."

- Clarify rules and routines related to classroom communication early in the school year
- Use varying types of questioning processes and lesson structures
- Use procedures that promote wide participation of pupils
- Promote and use active listening strategies

From studies reflecting the Cognitive Constructivist Perspective, practices that may assist teachers to "use group management methods that encourage students' engagement in academic tasks."

- Use a variety of task and activity structures
- Observe how individual students participate in different types of communication tasks and activity structures
- Teach and use processes to promote resolution of differences in opinions and beliefs
- Listen unobtrusively to conversations of cooperative learning groups to understand the social processes being enacted

From studies reflecting the Sociocultural Perspective, practices that may assist teachers to "develop caring, supportive relationships with and among students."

- Define, clarify, and model the various learning activities to be used
- Provide students with time to understand and practice patterns of interaction appropriate to each new type of learning activity introduced throughout the year
- Be responsive to, and learn from students' reactions to alternative patterns of communication related to different learning activities
- Work to establish norms of cooperative collaboration

From studies reflecting the Critical Discourse Analysis Perspective, practices that may assist teachers to "use appropriate interventions to assist students with behavior problems."

- Work to provide *all* students with extensive opportunities to learn
- Reconsider attitudes and perceptions of pupils' abilities while observing them in atypical activity settings
- Use communication patterns and participation structures that promote inclusion of students who exhibit communicative differences
- Be alert to ways communicative behavior of the teacher may constrain instructional discourse

ACKNOWLEDGMENTS

The author thanks reviewer Ginger Weade, Ohio University, for her feedback. Adrienne Alton-Lee, Judith Green, and Jere Brophy also provided helpful comments.

REFERENCES

Alton-Lee, A., Diggins, C., Klenner, L., Vine, E., & Dalton, N. (2001). Teacher management of the learning environment during a social studies discussion in a new-entrant classroom in New Zealand. *The Elementary School Journal, 101*(5), 549–566.

Alton-Lee, A., & Nuthall, G. (1990). Pupil experiences and pupil learning in the elementary classroom: An illustration of a generative methodology. *Teaching and Teacher Education, 6*(1), 27–45.

Alton-Lee, A., & Nuthall, G. (1992a). A generative methodology for classroom research. *Educational Philosophy and Theory, 24*(2), 29–55.

Alton-Lee, A., & Nuthall, G. (1992b). Children's learning in classrooms: Challenges in developing a methodology to explain "opportunity to learn." *Journal of Classroom Interaction, 27*(2), 1–7.

Alton-Lee, A., & Nuthall, G. (1992, April). Student learning in classrooms: Instructional and sociocultural processes influencing student interaction with curriculum content. In J. Fantuzzo (Chr.), *The analytic study of learning and interaction in classrooms.* Invited symposium presented at the meeting of the American Educational Research Association, San Francisco.

Alton-Lee, A. G., Nuthall, G. A., & Patrick, J. (1993). Reframing classroom research: A lesson from the private world of children. *Harvard Educational Review, 63*(1), 50–84.

Baker, C. D. (1992). Description and analysis in classroom talk and interaction. *Journal of Classroom Interaction, 27*(2), 9–14.

Bernstein, B. (1996). *Pedagogy, symbolic control and ideology: Theory, research, critique.* Bristol, PA: Taylor & Francis.

Blanton, M. L., Berenson, S. B., & Norwood, K. S. (2001). Using classroom discourse to understand a prospective mathematics teacher's developing practice. *Teaching and Teacher Education, 17*, 227–242.

Brophy, J. (2006). History of research on classroom management. In C. Evertson & C. Weinstein (Eds.), *Handbook of classroom management: Research, practice, and contemporary issues.* Mahwah, NJ: Lawrence Erlbaum Associates.

Buzzelli, G., & Johnston, B. (2001). Authority, power, and morality in classroom discourse. *Teaching and Teacher Education, 17*, 873–884.

Carlsen, W. S. (1997). Never ask a question if you don't know the answer: The tension in teaching between modeling scientific argument and maintaining law and order. *Journal of Classroom Interaction, 32*(2), 14–23.

Cazden, C. (1974). *Teaching as a linguistic process in a cultural setting.* (Report of Panel 5, NIE Conference on Studies in Teaching.) Washington, DC: National Institute of Education.

Cazden, C. (1986). Classroom discourse. In M. C. Wittrock (Ed.), *Handbook of research on teaching* (3rd ed. pp. 432–463). New York: Macmillan.

Cazden, C. (2001). *Classroom discourse: The language of teaching and learning.* 2nd ed. Portsmouth, NH: Heineman.

Cazden, C., John, V. P., & Hymes, D. (Eds.). (1972). *Functions of language in the classroom.* New York: Teachers College Press.

Crawford, T., Chen, C., & Kelly, G. J. (1997). Creating authentic opportunities for presenting science: The influence of audience on student talk. *Journal of Classroom Interaction, 32*(2), 1–13.

Delpit, L. (2002). Introduction. In L. Delpit & J. K. Dowdy (Eds.), *The skin that we speak* (pp. xv–xxiv). New York: The New Press.

Delpit, L., & Dowdy, J. K. (2002). *The skin that we speak.* New York: The New Press.

Dixon, C., & Green, J., with others. (2005). Studying the discursive construction of texts in classrooms through interactional ethnography. In R. Beach, J. Green, M. Kamil, & T. Shanahan (Eds.), *Multiple perspectives on literacy research.* Cresskill, NJ: Hampton Press.

Emmer, E., Evertson, C., & Anderson, L. (1980). Effective classroom management at the beginning of the school year. *Elementary School Journal, 80*, 219–231.

Evertson, C. M., & Weinstein, C. S. (2006). Classroom management as a field of inquiry. *Handbook of classroom management: Research, practice, and contemporary issues.* Mahwah, NJ: Lawrence Erlbaum Associates.

Evertson, C., & Harris, A. (1999). Support for managing learner-centered classrooms: The Classroom Organization and Management Program. In H. J. Freiberg (Ed.), *Beyond behaviorism: Changing the classroom management paradigm* (pp. 59–74). Boston: Allyn & Bacon.

Floriani, A. (1994). Negotiating what counts: Roles and relationships, texts and contexts, content and meaning. *Linguistics and Education, 5*, 241–274.

Forman, E. A., & McCormick, D. E. (1995). Discourse analysis: A sociocultural perspective. *Remedial and Special Education, 16*(3), 150–158.

Gallimore, R. (1996). Classrooms are just another cultural activity. In D. L. Speece & B. K. Keogh (Eds.), *Research on classroom ecologies: Implications for inclusion of children with learning disabilities* (pp. 229–250). Mahwah, NJ: Lawrence Erlbaum Associates.

Gee, J. P., & Green, J. L. (1998). Discourse analysis, learning, and social practice: A methodological study. In P. D. Pearson & A. Iran-Nejad (Eds.), *Review of research in education* (Vol. 2, pp. 119–169). Washington, DC: American Educational Research Association.

Green, J. L. (1983a). Research on teaching as a linguistic process: A state of the art. In E. Gordon (Ed.), *Review of research in education* (Vol. 10, pp.151–254). Washington, DC: American Educational Research Association.

Green, J. L. (1983b). Exploring classroom discourse: Linguistic perspectives on teaching-learning processes. *Educational Psychologist, 18*, 180–199.

Green, J. L., & Dixon, C. N. (1994). Talking knowledge into being. *Linguistics and Education, 5*, 231–239.

Green, J. L., & Smith, D. (1983). Teaching and learning: A linguistic perspective. *The Elementary School Journal, 83*, 353–391.

Heath, S. B. (2000). Linguistics in the study of language in education. *Harvard Educational Review, 70*(1), 49–59.

Hicks, D. (1995). Discourse, learning, and teaching. In M. W. Apple (Ed.), *Review of research in education* (Vol. 21, pp. 49–95). Washington, DC: American Educational Research Association.

Hymes, D. (1972). Introduction. In C. Cazden, V. P. John, & D. Hymes (Eds.), *Functions of language in the classroom.* New York: Teachers College Press.

Kelly, G. J., & Green, J. (1997). What counts as science in high school and college classrooms? Examining how teachers' knowledge and classroom discourse influence opportunities for learning science. *Journal of Classroom Interaction, 32*(2), 1–3.

Kelly, G. J., & Green, J. (1998). The social nature of knowing: Toward a sociocultural perspective on conceptual change and knowledge construction. In B. Guzzetti & C. Hynd (Eds.), *Perspectives on conceptual change: Multiple ways to understand knowing and learning in a complex world* (pp. 145–181). Mahwah, NJ: Lawrence Erlbaum Associates.

Kohl, H. (2002). Topsy-turvies: Teacher talk and student talk. In L. Delpit & J. K. Dowdy (Eds.), *The skin that we speak* (pp. 145–161). New York: The New Press.

Kounin, J., & Doyle, P. (1975). Degree of continuity of a lesson's signal system and the task involvement of children. *Journal of Educational Psychology, 67*, 159–164.

Kounin, J., Friesen, W., & Norton, A. (1966). Managing emotionally disturbed children in regular classrooms. *Journal of Educational Psychology, 57*, 1–13.

Kounin, J., & Gump, P. (1958). The ripple effect in discipline. *Elementary School Journal, 35*, 158–162.

Kraker, M. J. (2000). Classroom discourse: Teaching, learning, and learning disabilities. *Teaching and Teacher Education, 16*, 295–313.

Ladson-Billings, G. J. (2002). I ain't writin' nuttin': Permission to fail and demands to succeed in urban classrooms. In L. Delpit & J. K. Dowdy (Eds.), *The skin that we speak* (pp. 107–120). New York: The New Press.

Lin, L. (1994). Language of and in the classroom: Constructing the patterns of social life. *Linguistics and Education, 5*, 367–409.

Luke, A. (1995). Text and discourse in education: an introduction to critical discourse analysis. In M. W. Apple (Ed.), *Review of research in education* (Vol. 2., pp. 3–48). Washington, DC: American Educational Research Association.

Mason, L., & Santi, M. (1994, April). Argumentation structure and metacognition in constructing shared knowledge at school. Paper presented at the annual meeting of the American Educational Research Association, New Orleans, LA.

Moje, E. B. (1997). Exploring discourse, subjectivity, and knowledge in chemistry class. *Journal of Classroom Interaction, 32*(2), 35–44.

Morine-Dershimer, G. (1985). *Talking, listening and learning in elementary classrooms* (Research on Teaching Monograph Series). New York: Longman.

Morine-Dershimer, G. (1991). Learning to think like a teacher. *Teaching and Teacher Education, 7*(2), 159–168.

Morine-Dershimer, G. (2000). "Family connections" as a factor in the development of research on teaching. In V. Richardson (Ed.), *Handbook of research on teaching* (4th ed., pp. 47–68). Washington, DC: American Educational Research Association.

Moskowitz, G., & Hayman, J. (1976). Success strategies of inner-city teachers: A year-long study. *Journal of Educational Research, 69*, 283–289.

Nuthall, G. A. (1997). Understanding student thinking and learning in the classroom. In B. J. Biddle, T. L. Good, & I. F. Goodson (Eds.), *International handbook of teachers and teaching* (pp. 681–768). Dordrecht, The Netherlands: Kluwer Academic Publishers.

Nuthall, G. (1999). Learning how to learrn: The evolution of students' minds through the social processes and culture of the classroom. *International Journal of Educational Research, 31*, 139–256.

Nuthall, G., & Alton-Lee, A. (1993). Predicting learning from student experience of teaching: A theory of student knowledge construction in classrooms. *American Educational Research Journal, 30*(4), 799–840.

Nuthall, G., & Alton-Lee, A. (1995). Assessing classroom learning: How students use their knowledge and experience to answer classroom achievement test questions in science and social studies. *American Educational Research Journal, 32*(1), 185–223.

Nuthall, G. A., & Church, J. (1973). Experimental studies of teaching behaviour. In G. Chanan (Ed.), *Toward a science of teaching* (pp. 9–25). Windsor, Berkshire, England: National Foundation for Educational Research.

Putney, L., Green, J., Dixon, C., Duran, R., & Yeager, B. (2000). Consequential progressions: Exploring collective-individual development in a bilingual classroom. In C. Lee & P. Smagorinsky (Eds.), *Constructing meaning through collaborative inquiry: Vygotskian perspectives on literacy research*. New York: Cambridge University Press.

Rex, L. A. (2000). Judy constructs a genuine question: A case for interactional inclusion. *Teaching and Teacher Education, 16*, 315–333.

Rogoff, B. (1995). Observing sociocultural activity on three planes: Participatory appropriation, guided participation, and apprenticeship. In J. V. Wertsch, P. del Rio, & A. Alvarez (Eds.), *Sociocultural studies of mind* (pp. 139–164). Cambridge: Cambridge University Press.

Stubbs, M. (1976). *Language, schools and classrooms*. London: Methuen.

Stubbs, M. (2002). Some basic sociolinguistic concepts. In L. Delpit & J. K. Dowdy (Eds.), *The skin that we speak* (pp. 63–85). New York: The New Press.

Tuvay, S., Jennings, L., & Dixon, C. (1995). Classroom discourse and opportunities to learn: An ethnographic study of knowledge construction in a bilingual third-grade classroom. *Discourse Processes, 19*, 75–110.

Wertsch, J. V., del Rio, P., & Alvarez, A. (1995). Sociocultural studies: History, action, and mediation. In J. V. Wertsch, P. del Rio, & A. Alvarez (Eds.), *Sociocultural studies of mind* (pp. 1–34). Cambridge: Cambridge University Press.

Wood, T. (1995). An emerging practice of teaching. In P. Cobb & H. Bauersfield (Eds.), *The emergence of mathematical meaning: Interaction in classroom culture* (pp. 203–227). Hillsdale, NJ: Lawrence Erlbaum Associates.

Yackel, E. (1995). Children's talk in inquiry mathematics classrooms. In P. Cobb & H. Bauersfield (Eds.), *The emergence of mathematical meaning: Interaction in classroom culture* (pp. 131–162). Hillsdale, NJ: Lawrence Erlbaum Associates.

7

Critical Theory Perspective on Social Class, Race, Gender, and Classroom Management

Ellen Brantlinger
Indiana University

Scot Danforth
The Ohio State University

INTRODUCTION

This chapter takes a critical theory perspective to address how students and teachers' social class, race, and gender influence the dynamics of classroom life. Lincoln and Guba (2000) call critical theory a research paradigm, hence the critical orientation is fitting for this alternative paradigms section. Critical theory, historically and currently, has the radical democratic aim of understanding and eliminating the power imbalances that exist between people in various social settings. As critical educational scholar Leistyna (1999) writes:

> Critical pedagogy recognizes the ideological and thus inherently political nature of schooling. This entails questioning bodies of knowledge and providing alternative perspectives and **counter-discourses** (languages of critique, demystification, and agency capable of contesting oppressive beliefs and practices). Such interaction is intended to rupture stereotypes, myths, and cultural and institutional biases. (p. 19, bold font his)

MAJOR THEMES AND THEORIES IN CRITICAL SCHOLARSHIP

Critical scholars rarely prescribe classroom strategies; however, ideas for schools are implied in the issues they research. Because they focus on problems, critical theorists often are accused of being negative. Yet, their efforts to reduce oppressive hierarchies indicate they are more accurately perceived as "radical humanists," or optimists, who work to eradicate injustices others see as intractable (Danforth & Taff, 2004, pp. 6, 7). Although much critical scholarship involves unmasking oppression, exposing injustice may not be sufficient to inspire and sustain change. Therefore, some recommend that suggestions for practice and activism must accompany critical research (Brantlinger, 1999). In this chapter, we first review issues critical theorists have raised about schools, then we map out ways classrooms might be organized to achieve an equitable, democratic social life. We first clarify the origin and nature of the critical perspective.

Class Conflict and Hegemony

Critical theory originates with Marx's class analysis (Bottomore, 1956). Identifying capitalists as those in industrialized society who exploit the labors of working classes, Marx illustrates the correspondence between society's economic base and its superstructure (citizens' mental life). In other words, Marx states, "[t]he mode of production of material life determines the general character of the social, political, and spiritual processes of life" (Bottomore, 1966, p. 14). Whether or not they recognize their own class politics, dominant classes control societal circumstances and circulate ideologies that convince workers to comply with practices beneficial to higher classes. Expanding on Marx's ideas of social class domination and mystifying ideologies, Gramsci (1971) credits workers with having the insight and agency to resist capitalist oppression. Hence he views hegemony as a dynamic power relation between subordinate and dominant classes.

Social Class Reproduction

In Britain, M. Young (1971) put forward an ideological critique of the organization of school knowledge that counters the functionalist claim that curriculum content and testing are objective and neutral. In *Schooling in capitalist America*, Bowles and Gintis (1976) theorize that schools inevitably correspond to, and reproduce, societal social class relations. In France, Bourdieu and Passeron (1977) expound on the idea that, as an ideological state apparatus, education's actual role is not to facilitate class mobility, but rather to privilege ruling (middle) class culture and knowledge. Bourdieu's concept of cultural/social capital, or the "capacity to exercise control over one's own future and that of others as a form of power," clarifies how the tastes, styles, and achievements of dominant classes are elevated to serve as the standard to be met by all classes (Calhoun, LiPuma, & Postone, 1993, p. 4). Social and cultural capital are unevenly distributed among students of different social classes, which results in their distinctive status positions and treatment in schools.

Poststructuralism and Postmodernism

Arguing that structural class determination theories are defeatist, a contingent of critical scholars attend to people's understanding of received cultural knowledge as well as the inventive and idiosyncratic ways agents enact or resist power relations in particular contexts (Holland, Lachicotte, Skinner, & Cain, 1998). Although they still rely on macro level accounts of how power relations embedded in language, institutions, and signifying practices shape students and schools, they delve into the dynamic, multilayered, and conflicted micro levels of mental life (Wexler, 1996; Willis, 1977). Using psychoanalytic tools to attend to tacit and explicit meanings in consciousness, some critical scholars rely on textual deconstruction, discourse analysis, and ideological critique to explore individuals' thinking and agency (Bellamy, 1998).

Dominant Power, Hidden Curriculum, and Symbolic Violence

Dominant groups have the power to maintain their privileged status by creating norms against which others' behaviors are judged to be deviant (Becker, 1963; Goffman, 1963). In recent decades, there has been a proliferation of disability labels and a burgeoning number of children identified as disabled (Baker, 2002; Caplan, 1995; Kutchins & Kirk, 1997). Labeling represents children as inferior and deficient—an imposed identity that is personally dislocating and fragmenting (Hudak, 2001). Children struggle to be seen as competent after being retained or placed in special education (Collins, 2003; Kaufman, 2001; Smith, 2001). Similarly, a counterproductive "anti-social promotion policy" is now "intertwined with standards-based school reform via high-stakes testing" (Valencia, 2002a, p. 14). Failure that emerges from competitive grading and ethnocentric curriculum inflict emotional trauma—a symbolic violence that is not random or rare but endemic, systemic, and ubiquitous (Block, 1997). Undermining students' sense of competency has cognitive as well as affective consequences. Dewey (1902) writes: "children who begin with something to say and an intellectual eagerness to say it are sometimes made so conscious of minor errors in substance and form that the energy that should go into constructive thinking is diverted into anxiety not to make mistakes, and even, in extreme cases, into passive quiescence as the best method of minimizing error" (p. 186). Swanson, Cunningham, and Spencer (2003) illustrate how failing, labeling, and tracking interfere with African Americans' coping strategies and achievement. Middle-class school personnel establish school goals and routines of practice, yet most remain unaware of the dark side of schooling. Nevertheless, the hidden curriculum (or "collateral learning," Dewey, 1969) of "unstated norms, values, and beliefs" transmitted through "underlying structures of meaning" and "social relations in classroom life" has a powerful impact on students (Giroux, 1988, p. 23). A common assumption among middle-class people is that families are to blame for students' acting out or internalizing emotional disorders. Given problematic school circumstances, however, it is not hard to understand that schools and classrooms can be a source of frustration and anger, resulting in resistance that gets diagnosed as emotional disturbance (Brantlinger, 1991; Elias, 1989).

Unequal Playing Fields and Meritocractic Schooling

School competition is touted as facilitating the American Dream of social mobility to attain middle-class status. However, the recognition of merit creates a win/lose system that leaves many children behind. Given that education is compulsory in the United States, it seems that meritocratic schooling, organized around achievement-based course sections and ranked grading, is inherently unfair. In countries with relative equity between citizens, moderate versions of school meritocracy may effectively disperse individuals to appropriate adult roles while maintaining access to quality education. Scandinavian and Eastern European countries offer free preschool and university education and their public schools are of comparable quality for all children. There is less disparity in the salaries of adults in such countries so class distinctions are less obvious and influential. Unfortunately, America has never been blessed with social equity. Therefore, claims about universal access to quality schools, level playing fields, and equal opportunity are not valid (Burton, 1999; Kozol, 1991). Furthermore, in the United States, meritocractic schooling inevitably differentiates students along race/ethnicity and social class lines (West, 1997).

Institutional Bias

School personnel may think their classrooms are neutral and it is students who have personal flaws and lesser aptitudes. In contrast, critical theorists see misbehavior and lack of motivation as contingent on classroom factors (Hargreaves, 2004; Orellana & Bowman, 2003; Valenzuela, 1999; Weiler, 2000).When looking in classrooms, many note that the competency and worth of white, middle-class students are validated, while those who lack cultural capital are positioned for failure (Bingham, 2001; Howard, 2003; Levesque, 2002; Nasir & Saxe, 2003;). Addressing the "unintended cruelties" of evaluation used as "a tool of stratification and means of finding deficits in children," Smith and Danforth (2000) cite letters to teachers whose "instructional and interactional styles" made students "feel unworthy, uncomfortable, and angry" (p. 32).

Wexler (1996) turns to the classic Marxist constructs of commodification, exploitation, and alienation as he claims that low-achieving students are exploited by being the relegated losers necessary for others to excel in school. Yet, he theorizes that affluent white students also are exploited. As commodified winners, they must earn top credentials to access prestigious colleges and jobs. Because of the imposition of excessive competition and external standards, they are alienated from their intrinsic interests and potentially satisfying relations with peers and parents (Phelan, Davidson & Yu, 1998; Pipher, 1994). Wexler sees the casting of aspersions as aimed in all directions: at outsiders, insiders, and self. His ideas hark back to Riesman's (1959) notion of the loneliness and alienation in another-directed society.

Personal Bias

Unfair aspects of schools' formal structures are exacerbated by personal prejudices that play out through the social exclusion, silencing, and bullying of powerless students (Eder, Evans, & Parker, 1995). These authors found high levels of cross-group shunning and teasing by high-status middle-school students; even students who do not approve of the cruelty do not intervene to protect victims. Insecure about their own social standing, such students redirect their insecurities outward and deflect potential negative attention from themselves by joining in on the group ridicule and scapegoating of low-status students (Merton, 1994). Burkett (2001) describes a "heavy set kid with a lazy eye" as a "magnet for abuse" (p. 60). Students' targets for bullying often are sanctioned by teachers (Morgan, 1996). Subordinate students' attitudes and behaviors are identified as problems. There is less recognition that teachers and high-status students act in disrespectful and uncivil ways.

The phenomenon of abjection explains why people participate in group-based fear, hatred, and oppression. French psychoanalyst, J. Kristeva (1982; cited in Smith & Danforth, 2000, p. 138–139), claims that humans engage in intense self-creation work and their conformity and intolerance for difference stem from deep psychological needs. Individuals defend their identity boundaries by exclusionary social codes that assign lesser identities to persons or groups they see as threatening their solidarity. Apfelbaum (1999), a Jew who fled Nazi Germany, provides similar analyses of how dominant groups center themselves and project negative characteristics onto those at social borders. Such rejection and hostility can rise to the level of extreme physical violence.

The spate of school shootings indicates that school is not necessarily a safe haven. Not only were those killed and injured not protected, but the perpetrators felt so rejected that they saw their aggression as defensive and justified (Kimmel, 2003). The most publicized violence occurred in white suburbs; nevertheless, draconian security systems are installed in schools with high ratios of minority youth (Casella, 2001; Devine, 1996). Giroux (2004) argues: "Youth are now being framed as a generation of suspects and a threat to public life" (p. 4). Regarding zero tolerance, Slee (1999) writes, "The government, its eye trained nervously on the fickle electorate, sought to reassert itself as a no-nonsense administration tough on disruptive student behavior" (p. 23). Rooted in frustration, depression, and anger, violence reveals the deeply emotional dimensions of classroom life (Boler & Zembylas, 2002). School violence is a global phenomenon that is most evident in nations where schools produce great disparities between high- and low-achieving students (Akiba, LeTendre, Baker, & Goesling, 2002). Chaotic schools where adults do not control aversive circumstances also factor into student aggression (Benjamin, 2002).

Punishing Insight

Low-status students often are aware of, and intensely upset about, unjust and demeaning experiences (Brantlinger, 1993; Brown, 1998; Fleischer, 2001; MacLeod, 1995). Resentment aroused by unfair treatment and hopeless situations explains, and justifies, subordinates' subsequent defiance, passive aggression, and rebellion (Ahier & Beck, 2003; Kimmel, 2003). Rather than respecting the assertiveness of students who speak out about disparities, they are more likely to be judged as uncooperative, disrespectful, noncompliant, and defiant (Willis, 1977). Those at the bottom of hierarchies are aware that their low school credentials are worthless commodities, and often are alienated to the extent that they drop out of school (Demerath, 2003). Others are pushed out for school district convenience (Casella, 2001).

Redirecting Scholars' Downward Gaze

Critical theorists condemn segregated schooling, grade level retention, language/cultural exclusion, under-funded schools, and deficit thinking among school personnel; that is, institutionalized racism (Valencia, 2002b). Unfortunately, many influential people subscribe to a deficit ideology that finds flaws in poor families and children (see Ryan, 1971; Valencia, 1997). White hegemony is maintained as black children and families are scrutinized (McLaren, Carrillo-Rowe, Clark, & Craft, 2001). Preoccupied with evaluating children as successes or failures, schools have come to incorporate a highly systematized and legalized special education classification and placement system that results in some students being in advantaged settings with flattering labels and others in dumbed-down places with stigmatizing classifications (Hehir, 2001; Mehan, Hertwerk, & Meihls, 1986; Varenne & McDermott, 1998). The most egregious and alarming reason for retaining low-achieving students or placing them in special education is to improve a school or school district's achievement statistics (McGill-Franzen & Allington, 1993). This same nefarious intent has resulted in pushing students out of school (Lewin & Medina, 2003). Critical theorists interrogate white privilege, patriarchy, Eurocentrism, xenophobia, ableism, and heteronormativity. They condemn social scientists' persistent and distorting habit of directing their scholarly gaze at subordinate groups and blaming the victims of oppression (Brantlinger, 1999; Lipsitz, 1998; Oliver, 2004). Long ago, W. E. B. DuBois (1990) asked African Americans, "How does it feel to be a problem?"

CONFRONTING A LEGACY OF DISCRIMINATION

Critical theory started as social class analysis, but it has become an umbrella category that includes feminism, which addresses gender distinctions, and critical race theory, which interrogates disparities related to ethnicity, race, and culture. Queer theory, a newcomer to the critical paradigm, tackles the harsh realities of heteronormativity and homophobia for gays, lesbians, and bisexuals. Although sexual orientation is not integral to this chapter, gender cannot be understood without recognizing how it intertwines with sexuality and how gender borders are policed in terms of what is sexually normal and appropriate (Connell, 1997; Kimmel, 2003; Lesko, 2000; Pinar, 2001; Sadowski, 2003). In this section we address the legacy of bias that shapes American schools and classrooms.

Historically, Americans have been valued according to group affiliation and personal characteristics. Differential valuing translated into disparate educational rights and opportunities. Literacy was forbidden for slaves. After emancipation black citizens had similar obligations (taxes, military service) to whites, but never the same access to quality education. Patriarchal traditions excluded women and girls from education or relegated them to inferior school experiences. Before parents brought forward litigation to guarantee children with severe disabilities the right to education, they were barred from public schools. Regardless of enabling legislation, many still are in segregated and stigmatizing school settings. Problematic in the past, the status of indigenous people and Hispanics remain conflicted (Deyle & Swisher, 1997;

Magana, 2004). Who is for or opposed to bilingual instruction relates to perceptions of who is American. Regarding damaging nationalistic patterns, an active and often violent white supremacy movement has emerged in the United States (Southern Poverty Law Center, 2003).

Confronting Poverty and Racism

Americans of all income levels call themselves middle class (Felski, 2002), yet incomes vary substantially and the gap between rich and poor citizens has widened (Seyoum, 2001; Valencia, 2002b). Whites hold more assets than blacks (Conley, 1999; Oliver & Shapiro, 1995). There is more poverty and poverty is more urban, concentrated, and firmly implanted in older industrial cities with highly segregated black and Hispanic residents (Clemetson, 2003; Wilson, 1997). *Brown v. Board of Education* (1954) had an impact on de jure (Jim Crow) segregation but not on de facto neighborhood segregation that occurs when jobs disappear and the poor have no choice about where they live (Wacquant, 1995; Wilson, 1987, 1996). Racial concentration constitutes "American apartheid" (Massey & Denton, 1993) and "segregation exacerbates class differences of income, education, and skill to produce racially structured differences in privilege and opportunity" (Young, 2000, p. 206–207). Inequality enables affluent people to reinforce privilege through formal electoral processes, contaminating the working of American democracy (Worsham & Olson, 1999).

The oppressive conditions of the poor lead some to substance abuse and then to health and legal issues (Alexander & Roberts, 2003; Bourgois, 1995). "Get tough" policies result in epidemic proportions of adjudicated juveniles—in 1994, incarceration rates were up 280% from 1960 (Hopson & Obidah, 2002, p. 158). Blacks are vastly overrepresented in the (juvenile) justice system (Morrison & Epps, 2002). Calling black youths "America's disposable children," Yeakey (2002) contends that racial bias results in "disproportionate sentencing for the same crime, racial profiling, inadequate legal representation, mandatory minimums, the 'War on Drugs,' family poverty" (p. 97). In turn, poor and minority youth have quite negative perceptions of judges and court workers (Miller & Foster, 2002). Incarcerated youth have extremely low literacy levels; nevertheless, they lack access to quality educational programs in juvenile correctional facilities (Morrison & Epps, 2000).

Disproportionately placed in special education and low tracks, black, Latino, and Native Americans lack access to core curriculum (Connor & Boskin, 2001; Losen & Orfield, 2002; Oakes, 1985). Segregated compensatory and remedial programs are associated with low-level instruction, hence poor academic consequences (Ansalone, 2001; Reynolds & Wolfe, 1999; Rueda, Artiles, Salazar, & Higareda, 2002). Then, too, labeled students are vulnerable to ostracism and rejection (Stoughton, 2003). Patton (2004) argues it is "obvious that large numbers of African American students are misdiagnosed, mislabeled, and therefore misplaced" (p. 170). Charting the activist tradition among black teachers who, prior to *Brown v. Board of Education*, taught black children in segregated schools, Dison (2003) laments that intensive identification with, advocacy for, and sense of mutual purpose has disappeared in schools that are dominated by white personnel.

Rodriquez and Berryman (2002) endorse King's (1991) idea that dysconscious racism is deeply embedded in Americans' personal belief systems. Blau (2003) claims "schools are racialized settings that reproduce White advantage—to the detriment of all students" (p. 237). Blau elaborates:

> The best single indicator of children's vulnerability is the color of their skin. White children, compared with dark-skinned children, have superior economic security and health care, attend schools with better resources, and grow up in households and neighborhoods in which adults have higher levels of education. (p. 203)

Noguera (2003) believes that black children are aware of racial bias so even those of the middle class develop oppositional identities and act in ways that interfere with achievement. Interviews with young black men in Chicago reveal that, counter to expectations, those who leave the neighborhood and are exposed to privileged Americans are the most pessimistic about their own futures (Young, 2004). Institutionalized racism is draining. Even middle-class blacks have a permanent sense of alienation and insecurity (Benjamin, 1991; Cose, 1993; DuBois, 1990). "Race is powerful in contemporary America in the phenomenological sense: the meanings people attach to race and racial differences pervade everyday life, shape social action, and are a dynamic component of interpersonal relations" (Blau, 2003, p. xiii). Racism creates a deleterious milieu, then youths' and adults' reactions to racism, whether in the form of resistant acts or internalization of racial bias, result in a vicious cycle of pessimism and anger (Ogbu, 1997).

In spite of radical changes in student demographics, white teachers dominate American schools (Harry & Anderson, 1995). Criticizing teachers who use progressive methods suitable for middle-class white children but not black children, Delpit (1997) asks teachers to directly teach "the culture of power" to poor children. *Brown vs. Board of Education* pinned hope on racial integration; however, fifty years later some black leaders see no alternative but single race schools, or black teachers, to improve the cultural relevancy and student/teacher cultural synchronization in educating black children (Cooper & Jordan, 2003). Paying tribute to their high school in a small Alabama town that closed for desegregation in 1969, Morris and Morris (2000) draw on family records and interviews to celebrate the virtues of an all-black school environment. Black teachers are praised for connecting with black children (Foster, 1997; Ladson-Billings, 1994) and for the inherently political and activist nature of their pedagogy (Dison, 2003). Regardless of their intentions, teachers whose cultural roots differ from students may come across as "them," other, and the enemy (Brantlinger, 1985, 1993; Fleischer, 2001). Then, too, school-home relations reflect teachers and parents' respective power, epistemologies, and purposes (Lawson, 2003)—dissonance comes from minorities not being valued (Deegan, 1996). Acknowledging conflicted perspectives, Nespor (1997) sizes up schools as an "array of intersections: networks and layered connections in relations and understandings" (p. xiv).

Confronting Masculinity Discourse and Hegemony

Masculinity is as much a part of institutions as of personality (Connell, 1997). It is an unspoken standard, a style, division of labor, process of resource allotment, and basis for informal networking (Lesko, 2000). "Gender is deeply and unconsciously ingrained within people's psyches and deeply inscribed within school cultures and education systems" (Kenway & Willis, 1998, p. xiii). D. Smith (1987) argues, "textual messages combine institutional discourses with prevailing discursive practices to become the actual everyday sites of engagement with power" (p. 207). For example, in spite of the rhetoric of equity, girls still are prepared for domestic positions in their homes and the public sector (Luttrell, 1997). L. Johnson (1995) found that boys leave school for jobs or because they are fed up with school, whereas girls leave for romance and sex—mainly pregnancy.

Girls and women are subjected to high levels of sexual harassment (Stein, 1999). Boys, and girls, use sexual putdowns for girls; especially athletes target weak (feminine) behavior and homosexuality (Eder, 1997). Eder hypothesizes that the words faggot, slut, or whore uphold a hierarchy with male-oriented, sexually aggressive boys at the top. Male identity is wrapped up in the messages: it is better to be mad than sad, a man is powerful and strong, and aggression is a legitimate response to conflicts and problems (Bowman, 2003). Dyson (1993) observes that black juveniles react to racism's undermining their power and esteem with machismo.

Similarly, Willis (1977) documents a pattern of displaced anger and aggressive displays among British working-class youths. Boys compete with each other to be "real boys," who perform masculinity in gender-conforming, aggressive ways (Pollack, 1998). According to Morgan (1996):

> Bullying would seem to be the quintessential masculine experience, a key module in the "university of hard knocks." Yet men rarely confess to being bullied, less to having been a bully. However, the lessons of group solidarity, of being able to take it, of not telling tales, carry over easily into male adult worlds of employment and public life of children. (p. 111)

Whereas boys engage in more physical bullying, girls are less direct but still cruel to each other (Eder, 1997).

L. Brown (1998) found that many girls are aware of, and actively resist, patriarchal notions of femininity; however, as they disconnect from dominant practices they often turn their anger inward to self-reproach and self-harm. It might be argued that girls' exploitation and commodification turn to self-alienation (Wexler, 1996). Brown also notes that depressed and alienated girls conceal their feelings. This is consistent with Harris's (1989) theory that, from an early age, children learn to monitor, suppress, and conceal emotion. Finders (1997) found that girls' identities are constructed around the sexually exploitive text and images in girls' magazines. When they reach early adolescence, girls "experience a conflict between their autonomous selves and a need to be feminine" judged by normative "cultural prescriptions"; whether they break or follow the gender code, they feel miserable (Pipher, 1994, pp. 21–22). Recent indicators show girls' achievement meets or surpasses that of boys. The populist media circulates the message that boys are losing ground, thus are the real victims (Weiner, Arnot, & David, 1997). However, as long as adult salary and career advancement remain better for men, charges of female advantage must be considered with caution.

Although African American students generally have less positive school situations than European Americans, African American girls fare better in school than boys of their race (Cooper & Jordan, 2003; Deegan, 1996; Dimitriadis, 2001; Foney & Cunningham, 2002; Roderick, 2003; Smith, 2001). Ferguson (2000) reports how black and white personnel ignore the difficulties of black boys' lives, seeing them as incorrigible and placing them in a prison track through disciplinary actions. Orenstein (1994) shed light on how strength of purpose and resiliency in African American girls buffers them against the vicissitudes of institutional racism and gender bias. Lei (2003) found that black girls play out school personnel's images of them as tough and vocal, whereas Asian males conform to the stereotype of being quiet and studious. Students have strong ideas about which cultural groups are to engage in certain school activities and do not accept intrusions or border crossings (Merton, 1996). These gender, race, and class-based expectations become self-fulfilling prophecies.

WHAT CRITICAL THEORISTS REJECT

An influential factor in classroom life is the degree of consensus among personnel and patrons about the purpose of education. Educational visions are linked to distinctive ideologies as are the curricular and pedagogical practices that evolve from them. So, too, normative expectations that underlie social conduct are infused with values, which "like air, pervade our cultural atmosphere and we imbibe them often without a conscious awareness of their origins" (Laungani, 1999, p. 192). Friction and conflict among values, viewpoints, and philosophies are inevitable; nevertheless, decisions about pedagogy and curriculum must be made with deliberation because educational ends relate to educational means.

Although elements of various perspectives exist concurrently in schools, pendulum swings elevate one or another during particular historical periods. The liberal view that dominated 20th century education exalted the conveyance of academic knowledge and skills as schools' primary function. However, there also was a focus on developing rounded, well-adjusted citizens and suggestions about how to accomplish this flourished. Ideas about multiple intelligences translated into plans for multimodal instruction, unit- and inquiry-based learning, and making arts (music, visual, theater, physical, domestic) integral to a comprehensive curriculum. Title IX expanded opportunities for girls and women in athletics and other domains, emphasizing the goal of gender equity. In recognition of the United States' pluralistic population, proposals emerged regarding how multicultural curriculum and culturally relevant teaching might be incorporated. Attention was paid to socializing critical thinking about environmental and conditions and inspiring students to participate in all levels of government.

The Rightist Economic Agenda for Schools

Although this strand was always knocking at education's door, currently an agenda to narrow education to techno-rational skills and economic competitiveness—what Apple (2001) calls "educating the right way"—holds sway. From a nation-state viewpoint, ratcheting up achievement is touted as the way to fuel a faltering economy, cure troubling social conditions, and secure America's power in a globalizing world. This right-wing turn is evident in school standards, accountability, and high-stakes testing policies (Lipman, 2004; McNeil, 2000). Indeed, the federal control expressed in the No Child Left Behind Act pushes a highly academic national curriculum (Martin, 2002). Various local, state, and federal regulatory initiatives endorse narrow, abstract forms of academic achievement. This official purpose of education is accompanied by massive production of expensive basic skills and test cram curricula (Brandon, 2003). Whether this thrust will improve individual or national well-being is debatable; nevertheless, that is how it is billed to the public.

Teacher education and textbook coverage increasingly reinforce academic schooling (Apple, 1989, 2001). The federal emphasis on evidence-based practice is consistent with Giroux's (1994) idea that education, including teacher education, is to be a matter of being able to use techniques. According to ideals of market-efficiency, teachers are to use standardized strategies to transmit knowledge to docile students. Mastering foundational knowledge and prescribed pedagogy is equated with professional competency and progress in the field.

Right-wing politicians and corporate heads want Americans to believe that failing public schools and students are responsible for human and economic problems—an accusation Berliner and Biddle (1995) dismiss as a "manufactured crisis." Nevertheless, deceitful portrayals of poor children and schools continue to divert public attention away from the evidence that some politicians have a profit motive for pursuing rightist education—their connections with test and textbook companies enhance their profits (Kohn, 2003; Metcalf, 2003; Miner, 2003). Critical theorists eschew pressures to base education on market principles, believing them to be detrimental to the creation of inclusive communities that are models of democratic participation (Kohn, 1998). They reject reform done to facilitate capitalist success in global markets, especially since gains do not trickle down to workers.

The Credentialing and Stratifying Purposes of Schooling

Critical scholars denounce standardized knowledge acquired for personal gain (Kaufman, 2001; Ohanian, 1999). Kihn (2001) condemns the "self-centered ideology of neo-liberalism" that "allows inequality and stifles young people's spirit" (p. 62). Brantlinger (2004) embellishes on a "coalition theory" to explain why strange bedfellows have come to agree on the strict academic purposes of schooling: the media captures an audience by education-bashing; politicians who critique public schools can dub themselves "education presidents" (governors, mayors, school board members, superintendents); cultural conservatives endorse the return to western European classics, positivist science, and standard literacy that can be measured by "objective" tests; and religious fundamentalists are pleased to displace secular humanism and hope evidence of public school failure will allow federal funds to flow to private schools. Score discrepancies supply affluent people with the rationale for the further privilege of advanced tracks, class-pure schools, high professional salaries, and exclusive suburban residential enclaves (Brantlinger, 2003; Reay, 1998). Middle-class children's school advantage are due to their parents' strategic networking (Graue, Kroeger, & Prager, 2001; Lareau, 2003). Sleeter (1996) claims pressure for narrow academics is a backlash to the gains multiculturalists made in reducing white privilege. Labaree (1997) observes, "the consumerist system in which education is a private good" allows wealthier people to invest in their children's future while ignoring other children (p. 48). Critical scholars blame stratifying schooling on the purposeful and self-serving agenda of dominant classes (Apple, 2001; Ball, 2003; Bracey, 2003; Slee, Weiner, & Tomlinson, 1998).

Freire (1985) contends that the "banking system" that entails storing discreet bits of information for test purposes benefits only those on the top rungs of an achievement ladder. Luke and Luke (1995) write:

> The political effects of school knowledge and child literacy range from systematic surveillance, to socialization into a regime of boredom, to the mapping of children onto a psychometric grid of classification, to the gate-keeping of occupational rewards for deskilled, classed, and gendered cultures. (p. 272)

In "predatory culture fashioned around excesses of marketing and consumption under post-industrial capitalism," schools "keep youth stupid" and "infantilize" the population into passive, apolitical social subjects (McLaren, 1995, p. 2, 9). Leistyna (1999) argues "traditional, conservative, technocratic models dominate mainstream practice and embrace depersonalized methods that translate into the regulation and standardization of school practice" (p. 7). During a time of centralized control through standards, tests, and accountability sanctions, creative teachers struggle as state and local administrators manage their work culture (Achinstein, 2002).

TRANSLATING CRITIQUES INTO MEANINGFUL AND JUST CLASSROOMS

After reviewing what critical scholars research and the kinds of schooling they reject, we now discuss how classrooms might be organized to avoid discrimination and engage students in learning that contributes to social adjustment, personal success, and likelihood of engaging in democratic societal reform. "Classroom management" implies top down control—an end not a means, so we refer to classroom climate and organization. It is wrong-headed to see conflicts solely as management issues to be dealt with by increasing school authority or resorting to punitive zero tolerance and draconian security measures that alienate students and socialize them into unproductive futures and prison tracks (Casella, 2001; Devine, 1996). We do not suggest that teachers should not control classrooms. Indeed, teachers must be strong, well-educated, moral leaders who use their adult, professional status to create safe, inclusive, and productive learning environments (see Brantlinger, Morton, & Washburn, 1999). In making suggestions for practice, we divide our focus between the somewhat overlapping areas of curriculum and community.

Culturally Relevant Curriculum and Pedagogy

The cultural deficit perspective is based on the ethnocentric assumption that because children of color and low-income children have not read or experienced what interests middle-class whites, they know nothing. Instead, it should be taken for granted that all children come to school with their own experiences and funds of knowledge (Monzo & Rueda, 2003). Teachers cannot gauge minority youths' knowledge from scores on standardized tests. Authentic assessment occurs through talking with, not at, students. Teachers' awareness of children's cultural knowledge can be the starting point for developing culturally relevant lesson plans and units. In our pluralist society, with its range of indigenous and immigrant populations, it is essential to create classrooms where all feel equal, included, represented, and at ease expressing themselves and interacting with each other (Lee, 2003; Nieto, 2002). Noguero (2003) emphasizes the importance of students, particularly black youth, having supportive relations with adults.

One way to provide culturally relevant pedagogy is to recruit culturally diverse teachers; however, the teaching force is likely to be predominantly white for some time to come. Ladson-Billings (2001) documents that mostly white novice teachers can be taught to be culturally competent—to have respect for children's cultures and teach for social justice. Haberman (1995) also believes that "star teachers" can learn to support excellence among all students. White teachers can be "race traitors," who see things from racial perspectives other than their own (Bailey, 2000). Black studies (King, 1997) and decolonizing pedagogy (Tejeda, Espinoza, & Gutierrez, 2002) can challenge white preservice teachers' assumptions about class, race/ethnicity, gender, and sexual orientation and help them reflect on the impact of their beliefs, values, and actions on students (Kincheloe, 2003). Some teacher education programs require preservice teachers to subscribe to such journals as *Rethinking Schools* or *Teaching Tolerance,* which have a wealth of ideas about culturally relevant curriculum, pedagogy, and materials. Both journals include reviews of books and media resources for teachers and students. *Teaching for Change* also lists K–college resources on equity and social justice. These counterculture journals identify the strengths, rather than deficits, of diverse cultures (see Harry, Kalyanpur, & Day, 1999).

Emancipatory Pedagogy: Authentic Learning That Engages the Controversial

Working with impoverished adults and street children in Brazil, Paulo Freire (1985) combined literacy instruction with consciousness-raising about the nature and causes of subordination. This transformative pedagogy has provided the grounding for struggle against dominant class hegemony. Freire's ideas about praxis, or the infusion of values and deep reflexivity into everyday work, have provided a basis for classroom action research (Barton, Ermer, Burkett, & Osborne, 2003; Benjamin, 2001; Hinchey, 1998; Pruyn, 1999; Zaragosa & Scardina, 1998). In the current right-wing school climate, these teachers "teach against the grain" (Cochran-Smith, 1991) and "transgress" (Hooks, 1994). Fighting an uphill battle to get official approval, they often must engage in emancipatory pedagogy surreptitiously (Benjamin, 2002). Freire, like Gramsci, insists that collective action is essential for subordinates because, regardless of rhetoric and stated intentions, dominant classes ultimately strive to maintain their own advantage.

Most textbooks are saturated with Eurocentric, heteronormative, and patriarchical ideologies; history books celebrate military heroes and presidents and not labor and civil rights movement leaders or the lives of ordinary male and female citizens (Kuzmic, 2000). Critical teachers might instead use texts similar to Zinn's (1995) *A people's history of the United States, 1492–present,* which interprets history from silenced and marginalized people's perspectives.

Although patriotic American citizens, critical theorists are likely to be internationalists who, to some extent, value cultural relativity and see strengths in all world religions, customs, art, and literatures. That said, they would also subscribe to a human rights' position that recognizes the way certain traditions undermine the rights of some citizens.

A central purpose of schooling is to prepare students to be citizens. Critical theorists endorse a problem-centered curriculum that exposes students to realistic societal issues. Certainly America has problems that beg for solutions. Working class jobs have been exported globally for decades (Weis, 1990). Technical occupations are now outsourced, which means middle classes may face downward mobility (Newman, 1998). Media coverage of factory closings, salary and fringe benefit reductions, mortgage foreclosures, personal bankruptcies, a vacillating stock market, and corporate corruption worry the most optimistic of citizens. A burgeoning national deficit portends worsening financial conditions for the future. AIDs and HIV continue to take their toll, particularly on poor people and people of color (Brackis-Cott, Mellins, & Block, 2003). Divisive international politics leave Americans facing hatred from all corners of the world. Global warming, contamination of food sources, air, and water, and diminishing fossil fuel sources leave Americans on edge. Discussions of these troubles and ideas about how they might be resolved belong in classrooms.

Engaging students in disputed and controversial discussions prepares them to be astute and informed citizens who are able to coherently articulate their opinions to others. Unfortunately, teachers shy away from controversial content that might be frowned on by administrators or community members. At the same time, teachers who indulge in race or class privilege discourses do so authoritatively, whereas teachers who speak of inequities apologize for being negative (Brantlinger, 2003). Mainstream Americans see views from the left as uniquely political. In contrast, Zizek (1998) argues that those who support the status quo are the most political (in terms of facilitating their own interests) because they endorse dominant group advantage. Critical theorists believe democracy requires students to engage in controversial dialogues and be guided to confront what is mundane, and likely to be invisibly biased, as well as what is conflicted and disputed. Yet, Meier (1997) puzzles about how "teachers and communities shorn of the capacity to use their own ideas, judgments, and initiative in matters of importance can teach kids to do so" (p. 110). Perhaps children who have not been stripped of genuine curiosity by skill and drill routines can lead the way for teachers. Kohn (2004) stresses the need for mutual problem-solving among all classroom participants, including teachers, around real concerns and interests.

Given the emphasis on skills and knowledge to be measured by standardized tests—an abstract and inauthentic curriculum (what Noddings, 2004, calls "trivia" and "intellectual junk food," p. 494)—critical theorists believe teachers instead should scaffold instruction around students' intrinsic interests and their appraisals of what is important to learn. They buy into the constructivist philosophy that students learn best when actively engaged in meaningful, interesting, and important work. An authentic (relevant and engaging) curriculum is central to diminishing the need for behavior control strategies. Cummins (2002) argues, "Only teacher-student interactions that generate maximum identity investment on the part of students, together with maximum cognitive engagement, are likely to be effective in promoting achievement" (p. 51), and, we add, in promoting cooperative behaviors and empathic atitudes. Ayers (2004) recommends the Summerhill model that encourages student self-determination and authentic learning.

Constructively Differentiated Curriculum

Some argue that schooling has as much to do with identity formation as intellectual development (Apple, 1999; Nasir & Saxe, 2003). It is not easy to acquire an identity that asserts one's strengths, is located in reality, separates and joins individuals with others, reflects true inner being, and leads to the realization of potential (Maslow, 1970). Erikson (1968) long ago conjectured that unresolved identity issues lead to conflict, stress, and crisis. Cummins (2002) discusses the negotiation of identity in the context of societal power relations in which messages communicate to students who they are and who they are capable of becoming. S. Benjamin (2002) reports that special needs girls at a British girls school "had little access to positive identity resources in school" (p. 135). Unfortunately, this may be true for most nonwhite and nonmiddle-class students. Whereas schooling should lead children to know and respect their true selves, Hudak (2001) feels that modern education results in a dislocation of self.

Given that the United States has compulsory attendance, for schools to be structured so that some children are unsuccessful and have no positive identity resources is inexcusable. In evaluating NCLB legislation, Starratt (2003) insists that no child should ever fail unless given ample opportunity to learn. He maintains that many children do not have access to a quality education that would prepare them to compete with others on standardized tests. His point is not that schools be easy, but rather that children should have learning under their control and be successful if they exert an effort. School personnel must be aware that there may be home situations or emotional problems that interfere with motivation and attention; hence, they should screen students for evidence of such interference. Teachers tend to believe that poor students and families do not care about school. Although students may appear not to care—and even state that they do not care—this often is a defensive reaction to anticipation of failure or a retaliation against teachers who students feel do not care about them (Brantlinger, 1985, 1993).

Success in school for all children is essential; at the same time, classrooms should be learning environments that challenge children, allowing them to work toward prized goals. When structuring differentiated learning, teachers must guard against stratifying or separating children. Having a multilayered agenda with sufficient push and opportunity for success is a difficult balancing act for teachers, but when they are inspired to consider the various needs of all students, it is possible (Dewey, 1909; Nicholls, 1989). A classroom organization might be based on Rawls' (1971) idea of distributive justice in which the needs of the most vulnerable in any collective would be met first. Again, this does not mean it is legitimate to ignore other children's needs. Gamoran (2000) advocates high standards for all as necessary to engage learners. He found discussion-based approaches develop students' understanding and interest in meaningful learning (Applebee, Langer, Nystrand, & Gamoran, 2003). In safe and enriched classrooms, children can gain a broad and useful range of skills and knowledge, while developing a positive identity.

Schools as Safe Havens in Difficult Times

Interactional dynamics depend on classroom variables and also on factors external to the school. MacLeod (1995) observes that impoverished students' strategies do not develop in a social vacuum but in the context of chronic social immobility and persistent poverty. Adults and children bring their worries to the classroom (Kohl, 2004). Although we have no romantic illusions about an ideal historical period, at the start of the 21st century, certainly, some Americans face extremely hard times. Kihn (2001) believes that the decline of American employment has profound and disturbing consequences, including a diminution of hope and melancholy. Jordan and Cooper (2003) conclude that such intractable social barriers as poverty, racism, ineffective schooling, and perceptions of limited opportunity due to rising unemployment have resulted in a critical mass of students being disengaged from school. Students, who have no prospects for attending college, and their parents are cynical about the value of high school graduation (Brandau & Collins, 1994; Demerath, 2003). A sense of education's futility may explain the high and increasing dropout rates. Black, Hispanic, and Native American students have about a 50/50 chance of receiving a diploma, whereas the rate for whites and Asians is 25% higher (Urban Institute, 2004). Such family circumstances as being intact and having supportive community connections affect students' adjustment and achievement (Jeynes, 2003). Children and adolescents who watch their parents not make it "in the system" may feel defeated from the start (Demerath, 2003; Kohn, 2004; Perry, Steele & Hilliard, 2003; Sennett & Cobb, 1972). Education may not seem like a way to realize their aspirations for the future and so becomes a purposeless, painful, boring endeavor (Meier, 1995).

As proponents of equal opportunity, critical educators advocate that public policy ensure that resources are distributed equitably to all American schools. Because of the culturally diverse nature of society, decision-making power also should be distributed among all school patrons and students and families' appraisals must be taken seriously (Comer, 2004; Lawson, 2003). After studying the difficulties of impoverished mothers, Polakow (1992) makes a plea for middle-class professionals to stop being indifferent to the poor. Giles (2001) documents the extent to which teachers bring their ethnocentric bias about students' parents to schools, but also provides evidence that these attitudes can be modified and more respectful relations be created through true dialogue.

Parents' depressed moods are mirrored in their adolescents' outlooks (Sarigiani, Heath, & Camarena, 2003). School personnel should become aware of families' difficult circumstances and, subsequently, interact with the personnel at school and nonschool settings to support troubled youth (Sharp, Kendall, & Schagen, 2003). Schools should be places where children can recuperate and heal if they have been subjected to family dysfunction or personal trauma. Although her study involved social workers, Owens-Manley (2003) found that poor women were angry at frontline workers because of their disparaging attitudes towards them. Sensitive to the work conditions of case workers, Owens-Manley attributes these attitudes to their having to deal with the overwhelming aspects of their jobs in a time of rising poverty and community decline. Harvey-Koelpin (2004) found that similar conditions interfered with the relations between teachers and families at an urban school and the tensions were exacerbated by NCLB designation of it being a failing school. Conditions in urban schools are less than ideal for teachers and children (Kozol, 1991). Nevertheless, there are ways schools can constructively interact with diverse families and create a safe and healing haven for children when families have hard times (Valdes, 1996).

Infusing Values in Educational Choices to Create Moral Classroom Communities

Early critical theorists associated school and societal ranking systems with western capitalism. However, based on a meta-analysis of anthropological studies, D. E. Brown (1991) concludes that hierarchy creation is a human universal not limited to capitalist societies. Interestingly, Brown found that people simultaneously endorse a social reciprocity morality that emphasizes equity, justice, and an equal distribution of material and social goods. The tensions between hierarchy and equity cause conflicts. For example, Americans waver between the liberty and equality tenets of democracy. Critical theorists are squarely in the equality (social reciprocity) camp. As radical humanists, critical theorists encourage equality and cooperative interdependence rather than the competitive, hierarchical dimensions of schools and societies. It is important to understand how ethical positions translate into school visions.

Critical theorists imagine, and work to achieve, utopian democratic school communities in which a social reciprocity morality thrives (Anderson, 1983) and "an aristocracy of everyone" exists (Barber, 1992). School personnel develop visions for schooling—and society—from their ideals and encourage students to do the same (Taylor, Rizvi, Lingard, & Henry, 1997). T. J. Smith and Perez (2000) suggest students be exposed to each others' stories because constructing personal narratives about life circumstances and desires allows the development of knowledge about social life from various perspectives. Person-centered classroom communities with shared leadership mean that rules are constructed jointly and students know that the classroom belongs to them (Beane, 1997; Kohn, 2004). Critical scholars turn to Dewey's (1909) idea that schools be nonauthoritarian laboratories where children practice the best forms of democracy. Community is created by an expectation for democratic responsibility (Dibos, 2002) and strong, supportive interpersonal connections (Meier, 1997). Reminiscent of Jencks (1972), Noddings (2003) aspires to creating a sense of happiness for everyone in classrooms, so teachers and students will want to come to school and will benefit from being there.

As optimists, critical theorists believe that schools can be designed to build a new, equitable social order (Counts, 1978). On the other hand, few would claim that schools can do it alone. Voters must select and monitor public officials so they work to reduce the extreme income gaps between the rich and the poor as well as discrimination based on gender, race, disability, and sexual orientation. Equity in society will be mirrored in schools. A distributive justice among adults (see Rawls, 1971) must occur before schools will be equal. Morality in social relations is situation-specific and not fixed for all times. Hence, members of a community must be in tune with what is happening in the world and determine a moral stand through dialogue and debate. Many have written that such domination as heteronormativity, patriarchy, race privilege, and structural class advantage are not apparent to those who benefit from them. This means that interventions to decrease disparities and injustices should be aimed at privileged groups. For these types of discrimination to be discerned, safe places in classrooms must be created, so teachers and students can discuss sensitive and emotionally laden issues without fear of reprisal (Lewis-Charp, 2003; Polite & Saenger, 2003; Tatum, 2003).

A first step in creating community is ensuring that classrooms are safe for all students—safe from physical violence but also from the emotional violence of being failed, bullied, teased, intimidated, ostracized, excluded, or humiliated by degrading labels (Bluestein, 2001). Taking parents and students' feelings and viewpoints into account is necessary to facilitate valued classroom or student outcomes (Meier, 1995; Noddings, 2003; Wilson & Corbett, 2001). Creating productive democratic communities in classrooms takes teachers with skill and commitment. As Brantlinger, Morton, and Washburn (1999) conclude:

> There is unbending commitment to the democratic principles of individual worth, mutual respect, responsibility, and social participation. It is an authority that does not put "me" first and does not endure asocial or antisocial attitudes and behaviors. It is a moral stance that communicates that we are here together on a limited plot of earth and must listen to each other and act in ways that are earth and people enhancing. It celebrates and includes diversity and involves dialogue and substantive affiliation across social borders. Competition is with self for self-improvement; cooperation with others in sharing valued resources and in mutual support is the norm. A climate is created in which students feel safe and in which trust prevails. Freedom of expression and action are allowed; indeed, student agency is valued, but only as long as one student's actions are not detrimental to others. (p. 498)

REFERENCES

Achinstein, B. (2002). *Community and diversity and conflict among school teachers: The ties that blind.* New York: Teachers College Press.

Ahier, J., & Beck, J. (2003). Education and the politics of envy. *British Journal of Educational Studies, 51*, 320–243.

Akiba, M., LeTendre, G. K., Baker, D. P., & Goesling, B. (2002). Student vicitimization: National and school system effects on school violence in 37 nations. *American Educational Research Journal, 39*, 829–853.

Alexander, A., & Roberts, M. S. (2003). *High culture: Reflections on addiction and modernity.* Albany: State University of New York Press.

Anderson, B. (1983). *Imagined communities.* London: Verso.

Ansalone, G. (2001). Schooling, tracking, and inequality. *Journal of Children & Poverty, 7*, 33–47.

Apfelbaum, E. (1999). Relations of domination and movements for liberation: An analysis of power between groups. *Feminism & Psychology, 9*, 267–272.

Apple, M. W. (1989). Teachers and texts: A political economy of class of gender relations in education. New York: Routledge.

Apple, M. W. (1999). *Power, meaning, and identity: Essays in critical educational studies.* New York: Peter Lang.

Apple, M. W. (2001). *Educating the right way: Markets, standards, God and inequality.* New York: RoutledgeFalmer.

Applebee, A. N., Langer, J. A., Nystrand, M., & Gamoran, A. (2003). Discussion-based approaches to developing understanding: Classroom instruction and student performance in middle and high school English. *American Educational Research Journal, 40*, 685–730.

Ayers, W. (2004). *On the side of the child: Summerhill revisited.* New York: Teachers College Press.

Bailey, A. (2000). Locating traitorous identities: Toward a view of privilege-cognizant white character. In U. Narayan & S. Harding (Eds.), *Decentering the center: Philosophy for a multicultural, postcolonial, and feminist world* (pp. 283–298). Bloomington, IN: Indiana University Press.

Baker, B. (2002). The hunt for disability: The new eugenics and the normalization of children. *Teachers College Record, 104*, 663–703.

Ball, S. J. (2003). *Class strategies and the education market: The middle classes and social advantage.* London & New York: RoutledgeFalmer.

Barber, B. (1992). *An aristocracy of everyone: The politics of education and the future of America.* New York: Ballantine Books.

Barton, A. C., Ermer, J. L., Burkett, T. A., & Osborne, M. D. (2003). *Teaching science for social justice.* New York: Teachers College Press.

Beane, J. A. (1997). *Curriculum integration: Designing the core of democratic education.* New York: Teachers College Press.

Becker, H. (1963). *Outsiders.* New York: The Free Press.

Bellamy, E. J. (1998). "Intimate enemies": Psychoanalysis, Marxism, and postcolonial affect. In R. Miklitsch (Special Issue Editor), *Psycho-Marxism: Marxism and psychoanalysis late in the twentieth century* (pp. 341–359). *South Atlantic Quarterly, 97*(2).

Benjamin, L. (1991). *The black elite: Facing the color line in the twilight of the twentieth century.* Chicago: Nelson Hall.

Benjamin, S. (2001). Challenging masculinities: Disability and achievement in testing times. *Gender and Education, 13*, 39–55.

Benjamin, S. (2002). *The micropolitics of inclusive education: An ethnography.* Buckingham: Open University Press.

Berliner, D. C., & Biddle, B. J. (1995). *The manufactured crisis: Myths, fraud, and the attack on America's public schools.* Reading, MA: Addison-Wesley.

Bingham, C. (2001). *Schools of recognition: Identity politics and classroom practices.* Lanham, MD: Rowman & Littlefield.

Blau, J. R. (2003). *Race in the schools: Perpetuating White dominance.* Boulder, CO: Lynne Rienner Publishers.

Block, A. A. (1997). *I'm only bleeding: Education as the practice of violence against children.* New York: Peter Lang.

Bluestein, J. (2001). *Creating emotionally safe schools: A guide for educators and parents.* Deerfield Beach, FL: Health Communications.

Boler, M., & Zembylas, M. (2002). Discomforting truths: The emotional terrain of understanding difference. In P. P. Trifonas (Ed.), *Pedagogies of difference: Rethinking education for social change* (pp. 110–136). New York & London: RoutledgeFalmer.

Bottomore, T. B. (Ed.). (1956). *Karl Marx: Selected writings in sociology and social philosophy* (T. B. Bottomore, Trans.). New York: McGraw-Hill.

Bottomore, T. B. (1966). *Classes in modern society.* New York: Vintage.

Bourdieu, P., & Passeron, J. (1977). *Reproduction in education, society, and culture.* Beverly Hills, CA: Sage.

Bourgois, P. (1995). In search of respect: The new service economy and the crack alternative in Spanish Harlem. (Russell Sage Foundation Working Paper #21, May 1991.) In J. MacLeod, *Ain't no makin' it: Aspirations and attainment in a law-income neighborhood, the follow-up.* Boulder, CO: Westview. (p. 227).

Bowles, S., & Gintis, H. (1976). *Schooling in capitalist America.* New York: Basic Books.

Bowman, D. H. (2003). Male adolescent identity and the roots of aggression: A conversation with James Garbino. In M. Sadowski (Ed.), *Adolescents at school: Perspectives on youth, identity, and education* (pp.79–83). Cambridge, MA: Harvard University Press.

Bracey, G. W. (2003). Tracking, by accident and by design. *Phi Delta Kappan, 85*(4), 332–333.

Brackis-Cott, E., Mellins, C. A., & Block, M. (2003). Current life concerns of early adolescence and their mothers: Influence of Maternal HIV. *Journal of Early Adolescence, 23*, 51–77.

Brandau, D. M., & Collins, J. (1994). Texts, social relations, and work-based skepticism about schooling: An ethnographic analysis. *Anthropology & Education Quarterly, 25*, 118–136.

Brandon, K. (2003) Test-prep pressure hits grade schools. In A. Kohn P. & Shannon (Eds.), Education, Inc.: Turning learning into a business (pp. 58–62). Portsmouth, N. H: Heinemann.

Brantlinger, E. A. (1985). Low-income parents' perceptions of favoritism in the schools. *Urban Education, 20*, 82–102.

Brantlinger, E. A. (1991). Social class distinctions in adolescents' reports of problems and punishment in school. *Behavior Disorders, 17*, 36–46.

Brantlinger, E. A. (1993). *The politics of social class in secondary schools: Views of affluent and impoverished youth.* New York: Teachers College Press.

Brantlinger, E. A. (1999). Inward gaze and activism as moral next steps in inquiry. *Anthropology & Education Quarterly, 30*, 413–429.

Brantlinger, E. A. (2003). *Dividing classes: How the middle class negotiates and rationalizes school advantage.* New York: RoutledgeFalmer.

Brantlinger, E. (2004). Who Benefits? A Gramscian analysis of high stakes testing. *Workplace: A Journal for Academic Labor, 6*, 1–42.

Brantlinger, E., Morton, M., & Washburn, S. (1999). Teachers' moral authority in classrooms: (Re)structuring social interactions and gendered power. *The Elementary School Journal, 99*, 491–504.

Brown v. Board of Education, 347 U.S. 483 (1954).

Brown, D. E. (1991). *Human universals.* Philadelphia: Temple University Press.

Brown, L. M. (1998). *Raising their voices: The politics of girls' anger.* Cambridge, MA: Harvard University Press.

Burkett, E. (2001). *Another planet: A year in the life of a suburban high school.* New York: HarperCollins.

Burton, R. L. (1999). A study of disparities among school facilities in North Carolina: Effects of race and economic status. *Educational Policy, 13*, 280–295.

Calhoun, C., LiPuma, E., & Postone, M. (Eds.). (1993). Introduction: Bourdieu and social theory. In C. Calhoun, E. LiPuma, & M. Postone (Eds.), *Bourdieu: Critical perspectives* (pp. 1–13). Chicago: University of Chicago Press.

Caplan, P. (1995). *They say you're crazy: How the world's most powerful psychiatrists decide who's normal.* Reading, MA: Perseus Books.

Casella, R. (2001). *Being Down: Challenging Violence in Urban Schools.* New York: Teachers College Press.

Clemetson, L. (2003, September 27). More Americans in poverty in 2002 Census study says. *New York Times*, A1, A10.

Cochran-Smith, M. (1991). Learning to teach against the grain. *Harvard Educational Review, 61*, 279–310.

Collins, K. M. (2003). *Ability profiling and school failure: One child's struggle to be seen as competent.* Mahwah, NJ: Lawrence Erlbaum Associates.

Comer, J. (2004). *Leave no child behind: Preparing today's youth for tomorrow's world.* New Haven, CT: Yale University Press.

Conley, D. (1999). *Being black, living in the red: Race, wealth, and social policy in America.* Berkeley: University of California Press.

Connell, R.W. (1997). The big picture: Masculinities in recent world order. In A. H. Halsey, H. Lauder, P. Brown, & A. S. Wells (Eds.), *Education: Culture, economy, and society* (pp. 603–619). Oxford: Oxford University Press.

Connor, M. H., & Boskin, J. (2001). Overrepresentation of bilingual and poor children in special education classes: A continuing problem. *Journal of Children & Poverty, 7*, 23–32.

Cooper, R., & Jordan, W. J. (2003). Cultural issues in comprehensive school reform. *Urban Education, 38*, 380–397.

Cose, E. (1993). *The rage of a privileged class: Why are middle-class blacks angry? Why should America care?* New York: Harper-Perennial.

Counts, G. (1978). *Dare the school build a new social order?* Carbondale, IL: Southern Illinois University Press. (Original work published 1932).

Cummins, J. (2002). Challenging the construction of difference as deficit: Where are identity, intellect, imagination, and power in the new regime of truth? In P. P. Trifonas (Ed.), *Pedagogies of difference: Rethinking education for social change* (pp. 41–60). New York & London: RoutledgeFalmer.

Danforth, S., & Taff, S. D. (2004). Introduction: Examining the practical implications of special education paradigms of social thought. In S. Danforth & S. Taff (Eds.), *Crucial readings in special education* (pp. 1–14). Upper Saddle River, NJ: Pearson.

Deegan, J. G. (1996). *Children's friendships in culturally diverse classrooms.* London: Falmer.

Delpit, L. D. (1997). The silenced dialogue: Power and pedagogy in educating other people's children. In A. H. Halsey, H. Lauder, P. Brown, & A. S. Wells (Eds.), *Education: Culture, economy, and society* (pp. 582–594). Oxford: Oxford University Press.

Demerath, P. (2003). Negotiating individualist and collectivist futures: Emerging subjectivities and social forms in Papua New Guinean High Schools. *Anthropology and Education Quarterly, 34*, 136–157.

Devine, J. (1996). *Maximum security: The culture of violence in inner-city schools.* Chicago: University of Chicago Press.

Dewey, J. (1902). *The school and society.* Chicago: University of Chicago Press.

Dewey, J. (1909). *Moral principles in education.* Boston: Houghton Mifflin.

Dewey, J. (1969). *Experience and education.* New York: Collier.(Original work published 1938).

Deyhle, D., & Swisher, K. (1997). Research in American Indian and Alaska Native education: From assimilation to self-determination. In M. W. Apple (Ed.), *Review of Research in Education, 22* (pp. 113–194). Washington DC: American Educational Research Association.

Dibos, A. (2002). Democracy as responsibility, meaning, and hope: Introductory reflections on a democratic project in education. *Journal of Thought, 37*, 54–65.

Dimitriadis, G. (2001). *Performing identity/performing culture: Hip hop as text, pedagogy, and lived practice.* New York: Peter Lang.

Dison, A. D. (2003). "Let's do this!" Black women teachers' politics and pedagogy. *Urban Education, 38*, 217–235.

DuBois, W. E. B. (1990). *Souls of black folks.* New York: Vintage. (Original work published 1903).

Dyson, M. E. (1993). *Reflecting black: African-American cultural criticism.* Minneapolis: University of Minnesota Press.

Eder, D. (1997). Sexual aggression within the school culture. In B. Bank and P. Hall (Eds.), *Gender, equity and schooling: Policy and practice* (pp. 93–112). New York: Garland.

Eder, D., C. C. Evans, & S. Parker (1995). *School talk: Gender and adolescent culture.* New Brunswick, NJ: Rutgers University Press.

Elias, M. J. (1989). School as a source of stress to young children: An analysis of causal and ameliorative influences. *Journal of School Psychology, 27*, 393–407.

Erikson, E. (1968). *Identity: Youth and crisis.* New York: Norton.

Felski, R. (2002, January 25). Why academics don't study the lower middle class. *The Chronicle of Higher Education*, B24.

Ferguson, A. A. (2000). *Bad boys: Public schools in the making of Black masculinity.* Ann Arbor: University of Michigan Press.

Finders, M. J. (1997). *Just girls: Hidden literacies and life in junior high.* New York: Teachers College Press.

Fleischer, L. E. (2001). Special education students as counter-hegemonic theorizers. In G. M. Hudak & P. Kihn (Eds.), *Labeling: Pedagogy and politics* (pp. 115–124). New York: RoutledgeFalmer.

Foney, D. M., & Cunningham, M. (2002). Why do good kids do bad things? Considering multiple contexts in the study of antisocial fighting behaviors in African American urban youth. *Journal of Negro Education, 71*, 143–157.

Foster, M. (1997). *Black teachers on teaching.* New York: The New Press.

Freire, P. (1985). *The politics of education: Culture, power, and liberation.* South Hadley, MA: Bergin & Garvey.

Gamoran, A. (2000). High standards: A strategy for equalizing opportunities to learn? In R. D. Kahlenberg (Ed.), *A notion at risk: Preserving public education as an engine for social responsibility* (pp. 93–126). New York: Century Foundation.

Giles, H. C. (2001). A word in hand: The scripted labeling of parents by schools. In G. M. Hudak & P. Kihn (Eds.), *Labeling: Pedagogy and politics* (pp. 127–146). New York: RoutledgeFalmer.

Giroux, H. A. (1988). *Teachers as intellectuals: Toward a critical pedagogy of learning.* Amherst, MA: Bergin & Garvey.

Giroux, H. A. (1994). *Between borders: Pedagogy and the politics of cultural studies.* New York: Routledge.

Giroux, H. A. (2004). Class casualties: Disappearing youth in the age of George W. Bush. *Workplace, 6*, 1–24.

Goffman, E. G. (1963). *Stigma: Notes on the Management of Spoiled Identity.* Englewood Cliffs, NJ: Prentice-Hall.

Gramsci, A. (1971). *Selections from the prison notebooks.* Q. Hoare & G. N. Smith (Eds.). New York: International Publishers. (Original work published, 1929–1935).

Graue, M. E., Kroeger, J., & Prager, D. (2001). A Bakhtinian analysis of particular home-school relations. *American Educational Research Journal, 38*, 467–498.

Haberman, M. (1995). *Star teachers of children in poverty.* West Lafayette, IN: Kappa Delta Pi.

Hargreaves, A. (2004). Distinction and disgust: The emotional politics of school failure. *International Journal of Leadership in Education, 7*, 27–41.

Harris, P. L. (1989). *Children and Emotion: The development of psychological understanding.* Oxford: Blackwell.

Harry, B., & Anderson, M. G. (1995). The disproportionate placement of African American males in special education programs: A critique of the process. *Journal of Negro Education, 63*, 602–619.

Harry, B., Kalyanpur, M., & Day, M. (1999). *Building cultural reciprocity with families: Case studies in special education.* Baltimore: Brookes.

Harvey-Koelpin, S. (2004). *The impact of NCLB reform on an urban school.* Unpublished doctoral dissertation, Indiana University, Bloomington, IN.

Hehir, T. (2001). Eliminating ableism in education. *Harvard Educational Review, 72* (1), 1–32.

Hinchey, P. H. (1998). *Finding freedom in the classroom: A practical introduction to critical theory.* New York: Peter Lang.

Holland, D., Lachicotte, W., Jr., Skinner, D., & Cain, C. (1998). *Identity and agency in cultural worlds.* Cambridge, MA: Harvard University Press.

hooks, b. (1994). *Teaching to transgress: Education as the practice of freedom.* New York: Routledge.

Hopson, R. K., & Obidah, J. (2002). When getting tough means getting tougher: Historical and conceptual understandings of juveniles of color sentenced as adults in the United States. *Journal of Negro Education, 71,* 158–169.

Howard, T. C. (2003). "A tug of war for our minds:" African American high school students ' perceptions of their academic identities and college aspirations. *The High School Journal, 87,* 4–17.

Hudak, G. M. (2001). On what is labeled 'playing': Locating the 'true' in education. In G. M. Hudak & P. Kihn (Eds.), *Labeling: Pedagogy and politics* (pp. 9–26). New York: RoutledgeFalmer.

Jencks, C. (1972). *Inequality: A reassessment of the effect of family and schooling in America.* New York: Harper & Row.

Jeynes, W. H. (2003). The effects of black and Hispanic 12th graders living in intact families and being religious on their academic achievement. *Urban education, 38,* 35–57.

Johnson, L. (1995). *Girls at the back of the class.* New York: St. Martin's Press.

Jordan, W. J., & Cooper, R. (2003). High school reform and black male students: Limits and possibilities of policy and practice. *Urban Education, 38,* 196–216.

Kaufman, J. S. (2001). The classroom and labeling: 'The girl who stayed back.' In G. M. Hudak & P. Kihn (Eds.), *Labeling: Pedagogy and politics* (pp. 41–54). New York: RoutledgeFalmer.

Kenway, J., & Willis, S. (1998). *Answering back: Girls, boys, and feminism in schools.* London & New York: Routledge.

Kihn, P. (2001). Labeling the young: Hope and contemporary childhood. In G. M. Hudak & P. Kihn (Eds.), *Labeling: Pedagogy and politics* (pp. 55–71). New York: Routledge-Falmer

Kimmel, M. S. (2003). "I am not insane: I am angry": Adolescent masculinity, homophobia, and violence. In M. Sadowski (Ed.), *Adolescents at school: Perspectives on youth, identity, and education* (pp. 69–78). Cambridge, MA: Harvard University Press.

Kincheloe, J. L. (2003). *Teachers as researchers: Qualitative inquiry as a path to empowerment.* London & New York: RoutledgeFalmer.

King, J. (1991). Dysconscious racism: Ideology, identity and the mideducation of teachers. *Journal of Negro Education, 60,* 133–146.

King, J. (1997). "Thank you for opening our mind": On praxis, transmutation, and black studies in teacher development. In J. King, E. Hollins, & W. Hayman (Eds.), *Preparing teachers for cultural diversity* (pp. 156–169). New York: Teachers College Press.

Kohl, H. (2004). *Stupidity and tears: Teaching and learning in troubled times.* New York & London: The New Press.

Kohn, A. (1998). Only for my kid: How privileged parents undermine school reform. *Phi Delta Kappan, 79,* 569–577.

Kohn, A. (2003). Introduction: The 500-pound gorilla. In A. Kohn & P. Shannon (Eds.), *Education, Inc.: Turning learning into a business* (pp. 1–11). Portsmouth, NH: Heinemann.

Kohn, A. (2004). Beyond bribes and threats: How not to get control of the classroom. In S. Danforth & S. Taff (Eds.), *Crucial readings in special education* (pp. 350–368). Upper Saddle River, NJ: Pearson.

Kozol, J. (1991). *Savage inequalities: Children in America's schools.* New York: Harper-Perennial.

Kristeva, J. (1982). *Powers of horror: An essay in abjection.* New York: Columbia.

Kutchins, H., & Kirk, S. A. (1997). *Making us crazy: DSM: The psychiatric bible and the creation of mental disorders.* New York: The Free Press.

Kuzmic, J. J. (2000). Textbooks, knowledge, and masculinity: Examining patriarchy from
within. In N. Lesko (Ed.), *Masculinities at school* (pp. 105–126). Thousand Oaks, CA: Sage.

Labaree, D. F. (1997). *How to succeed in school without really learning: The credentials race in American education.* New Haven, CT:Yale University Press.

Ladson-Billings, G. (1994). *Dreamkeepers: Successful teachers of African American children.* San Francisco: Jossey-Bass.

Ladson-Billings, G. (2001). *Crossing over to Canaan: The journey of new teachers in diverse classrooms.* San Francisco: Jossey-Bass.

Lareau, A. (2003). *Unequal childhoods: Class, race, and family life.* Berkeley: University of California Press.

Laungani, P. (1999). Cultural influences on identity and behavior: India and Britain. In Y. T. Lee, C. R. McCauley, & J. G. Draguns (Eds.), *Personality and person perception across cultures* (pp. 191–212). Mahwah, NJ: Lawrence Erlbaum Associates.

Lawson, M. A. (2003). School-family relations in context: Parent and teacher perceptions of parent involvement. *Urban Education, 38*, 77–133.
Lee, C. D. (2003). Why we need to re-think race and ethnicity in educational research. *Educational Researcher, 32*, 3–5.
Lei, J. L. (2003). (Un)Necessary toughness?: Those "loud Black girls" and those "quiet Asian boys." *Anthropology and Education Quarterly, 34*, 158–181.
Leistyna, P. (1999). *Presence of mind: Education and the politics of deception.* Boulder, CO: Westview Press.
Lesko, N. (2000). Preparing to (teach) coach: Tracing the gendered relations of dominance on and off the football field. In N. Lesko (Ed.), *Masculinities at school: Research on men and masculinities* (pp. 187–212). Thousand Oaks, CA: Sage.
Levesque, R. J. R. (2002). *Dangerous adolescents, model adolescents: Shaping the role and promise of education.* New York: Kluwer Academic/Plenum.
Lewin, T., & Medina, J. (2003, July 31). To cut failure rate, schools shed students. *New York Times*, A1.
Lewis-Charp, H. (2003). Breaking the silence: White students' perspectives on race in multiracial schools. *Phi Delta Kappan, 85*, 279–285.
Lipman, P. (2004). *High-stakes education: Inequality, globalization, and school reform.* New York: Routledge.
Lipsitz, G. (1998). *The possessive investment in whiteness.* Philadelphia: Temple University Press.
Losen, D. J., & Orfield, G. (2002). *Racial inequality in special education.* Cambridge, MA: Harvard University Press.
Luke, C., & Luke, A. (1995). Just naming? Educational discourses and the politics of
identity. In W. T. Pink & G. W. Noblit (Eds.), *Continuity and contradiction: The futures of the sociology of education* (pp. 357–380). Cresskill, NJ: Hampton.
Luttrell, W. (1997). *Schoolsmart and motherwise: Working-Class women's identity and schooling.* New York: Routledge.
MacLeod, J. (1995). *Ain't no makin' it: Aspirations and attainment in a low-income neighborhood, the follow-up.* Boulder, CO: Westview.
Magana, L. (2004). *Straddling the border: Immigration policy and the INS.* Austin: University of Texas Press.
Martin, J. R. (2002). *Cultural miseducation: In search of a democratic solution.* New York: Teachers College Press.
Maslow, A. (1970). *Motivation and personality.* New York: Harper & Row.
Massey, D., & Denton, N. (1993). *American Apartheid.* Cambridge, MA: Harvard University Press.
McGill-Franzen, & Allington, R. L. (1993). Flunk 'em or get them classified. *Educational Researcher, 22*(1), 19–22.
McLaren, P. (1995). *Critical pedagogy and predatory culture: Oppositional politics in a postmodern era.* London & New York: Routledge.
McLaren, P., Carrillo-Rowe, A. M., Clark, R. L., & Craft, P. A. (2001). Labeling whiteness: Decentering strategies of white racial domination. In G. M. Hudak & P. Kihn (Eds.), *Labeling: Pedagogy and politics* (pp. 203–224). New York: RoutledgeFalmer.
McNeil, L.M. (2000). *Contradictions of school reform: Educational costs of standardized testing.* New York: Routledge.
Mehan, H., Hertwerk, A., & Meihls, J. L. (1986), *Handicapping the handicapped.* Stanford, CA: Stanford University Press.
Meier, D. (1995). *The power of their ideas: Lessons for America from a small school in Harlem.* Boston: Beacon Press.
Meier, D. W. (1997, February 19). Saving public education. *The Nation, 4*, 23–24.
Merton, D. (1994). The cultural context of aggression: The transition to junior high school. *Anthropology & Education Quarterly, 25*, 29–43.
Merton, D. E. (1996). Burnout as cheerleader: The cultural basis for prestige and privilege in junior high school. *Anthropology & Education Quarterly, 27*, 51–70.
Metcalf, S. (2003). Reading between the lines. In A. Kohn & P. Shannon (Eds.), *Education, Inc.: Turning learning into a business* (pp. 49–57). Portsmouth, NH: Heinemann.
Miller, F., & Foster, E. (2002). Youths' perceptions of race, class, and language bias in the courts. *Journal of Negro Education, 71*, 193–205.
Miner, B. (2003). For-profits target education. In A. Kohn & P. Shannon (Eds.), *Education, Inc.: Turning learning into a business* (pp. 131–139). Portsmouth, NH: Heinemann.
Monzo, L., D., & Rueda, R. (2003). Shaping education through diverse funds of knowledge: A look at one Latina paraeducator's lived experiences, beliefs, and teaching practice. *Anthropology and Education Quarterly, 34*, 72–95.
Morgan, D. (1996). Learning to be a man: Dilemmas and contradictions of masculine experience. In C. Luke (Ed.), *Feminisms and pedagogies of everyday life* (pp. 103–115).Albany: State University of New York Press.
Morris, V. G., & Morris, C. L. (2000). *Creating caring and nurturing educational environments for African American children.* Westport, CT: Bergin & Garvey.
Morrison, H. R., & Epps, B. D. (2002). Warehousing or rehabilitation? Public schooling in the juvenile justice system. *Journal of Negro Education, 71*, 218–227.

Nasir, N. S., & Saxe, G. B. (2003). Ethnic and academic identities: A cultural practice perspective on emerging tensions and their management in the lives of minority students. *Educational Researcher, 32*, 14–18.

Nespor, J. (1997). *Tangled up in school: Politics, space, bodies, and signs in the educational process.* Mahwah, NJ: Lawrence Erlbaum Associates.

Newman, K. (1998). *Falling from grace: The experience of downward mobility in the American middle class.* New York: Vintage.

Nicholls, J. R. (1989). *The competitive ethos and democratic education.* Cambridge, MA: Harvard University Press.

Nieto, S. (2002). Language, culture, and teaching: Critical perspectives for a new century. Mahwah, NJ: Lawrence Erlbaum Associates.

Noddings, N. (2003). *Happiness and education.* Cambridge, MA & New York: Cambridge University Press.

Noddings, N. (2004). War, critical thinking, and self-understanding. *Phi Delat Kappan, 85*, 488–495.

Noguera, P. A. (2003). The trouble with Black boys: The role and influence of environmental and cultural factors on the academic performance of African American males. *Urban Education, 38*, 431–459.

Oakes, J. (1985). *Keeping track: How schools structure inequality.* New Haven, CT: Yale University Press.

Ogbu, J. U. (1997). Racial stratification and education in the United States: Why inequality persists. A. H. Halsey, H. Lauder, P. Brown, & A. S. Wells (Eds.), *Education: Culture, economy, and society* (pp. 765–778). Oxford: Oxford University Press.

Ohanian, S. (1999). *One size fits all: The folly of educational standards.* Portsmouth, NH: Henineman.

Oliver, M. (2004). Changing the social relations of research production. In S. Danforth & S. Taff (Eds.), *Crucial readings in special education* (pp. 138–147). Upper Saddle River, NJ: Pearson.

Oliver, M. L., & Shapiro, T. M. (1995). *Black wealth/white wealth.* New York: Routledge.

Orellana, M. F., & Bowman, P. (2003). Cultural diversity research on learning and development: Conceptual, methodological, and strategic considerations. *Educational Researcher, 32*, 26–32.

Orenstein, P. (1994). *School girls: Young women, self-esteem, and the confidence gap.* New York: Doubleday.

Owens-Manley, J. (2003). The leper keepers: Front-line workers and the key to education for poor women. In V. C. Adair & S. L. Dahlberg (Eds.), *Reclaiming class: Women, poverty, and the promise of higher education in America.* (pp. 196–214). Philadelphia: Temple University Press.

Patton, J. M. (2004). The disproportionate representation of African Americans in special education: Looking behind the curtain for understanding and solutions. In S. Danforth & S. Taff (Eds.), *Crucial readings in special education* (pp. 164–172). Upper Saddle River, NJ: Pearson.

Perry, T., Steele, C., & Hilliard, A.G., III (2003). *Young, gifted, and black: Promoting high achievement among African-American students.* Boston: Beacon Press.

Phelan, P., Davidson, A.L., & Yu, H. C. (1998). *Adolescents' worlds: Negotiating family, peers, and school.* New York: Teachers College Press.

Pinar, W. F. (2001). *The gender of racial politics and violence in America: Lynching, prison rape, and the crisis of masculinity.* New York: Peter Lang.

Pipher, M. (1994). *Reviving Ophelia: Saving the selves of adolescent girls.* New York: Ballantine.

Polakow, V. (1992). *Lives on the edge: Single mothers and their children in the other America.* Chicago: University of Chicago Press.

Polite, L., & Saenger, E. B. (2003). A pernicious silence: Confronting race in the elementary classroom. *Phi Delta Kappan, 85*, 274–278.

Pollack, W. (1998). *Real boys: Rescuing our sons from the myths of boyhood.* New York: Henry Holt.

Pruyn, M. (1999). *Discourse wars in Gotham-West: A Latino immigrant urban tale of resistance and agency.* Boulder, CO: Westview Press.

Rawls, J. (1971). *A theory of justice.* Cambridge, MA: Harvard University Press.

Reay, D. (1998). Setting the agenda: The growing impact of market forces on pupil grouping in British secondary schooling. *Journal of Curriculum Studies, 30*, 545–558.

Reynolds, A. J., & Wolfe, B. (1999). Special education and school achievement: An exploratory analysis with a central-city sample. *Educational Evaluation and Policy Analysis, 21*, 249–269.

Riesman, D. (1959). *The lonely crowd: A study of the changing American culture.* New Haven, CT: Yale University Press.

Roderick, M. (2003). What's happening to the boys? Early high school experiences and school outcomes among African American male adolescents in Chicago. *Urban Education, 38*, 538–607.

Rodriguez, A. J., & Berryman, C. (2002). Using sociotransformative constructivism to teach for understanding in diverse classrooms; A beginning teacher's journey. *American Educational Research Journal, 39*, 1017–1045.

Rueda, R., Artiles, A.J., Salazar, J., & Higareda, I. (2002). An analysis of special education as a response to the diminished academic achievement of Chicano/Latino students: An update. In R. R. Valencia (Ed.), *Chicano school failure and success: Past, present, future* (2nd ed., pp. 310–332). London & New York: RoutledgeFalmer.

Ryan, W. (1971). *Blaming the victim.* New York: Random House.

Sadowski, M. (2003). Growing up in the shadows: School and the identity development of sexual minority youth. In M. Sadowski (Ed.), *Adolescents at school: Perspectives on youth, identity, and education* (pp. 85–101). Cambridge, MA: Harvard University Press.

Sarigiani, P. A., Heath, P. A., & Camarena, P.M. (2003). The significance of parental depressed mood for young adolescents' emotional and family experiences. *Journal of Early Adolescence, 23*, 241–267.

Sennett, R., & Cobb, J. (1972). *The hidden injuries of class*. New York: Vintage.

Seyoum, B. (2001). *The State of the Global Economy 2001/2002: Trends: Data: Rankings: Charts*. Baldwin Place, NY: Encyclopedia Society.

Sharp, C., Kendall, L., & Schagen, I. (2003). Different for girls? An exploration of the impact of playing for success. *Educational Research, 45*, 309–324.

Slee, R. (1999). Theorizing discipline—practical research implications for schools. In H. J. Freiberg (Ed.), *Beyond behaviorism: Changing the classroom management paradigm* (pp. 21–42). Boston: Allyn & Bacon.

Slee, R., Weiner, G., & Tomlinson, S. (Eds.). (1998). *School effectiveness for whom? Challenges to the school effectiveness and school improvement movements*. London: Falmer.

Sleeter, C. (1996). *Multicultural education as social activism*. Albany: State University of New York Press.

Smith, A. (2001). The labeling of African American boys in special education: A case study. In G. M. Hudak & P. Kihn (Eds.), *Labeling: Pedagogy and politics* (pp. 109–114). New York: RoutledgeFalmer.

Smith, D. (1987). *The everyday world as problematic: A feminist sociology*. Boston: Northeastern University Press.

Smith, T. J., & Danforth, S. (2000). Ethics, politics, and the unintended cruelties of teaching. In J. L. Paul & T. J. Smith (Eds.), *Stories out of school; Memories and reflections on care and cruelty in the classroom* (pp. 129–152). Stamford, CT: Ablex.

Smith, T. J., & Perez, S. (2000). The morals of teachers' stories. In J. L. Paul & T. J. Smith (Eds.), *Stories out of school: Memories and reflections on care and cruelty in the classroom* (pp. 105–127). Stamford, CT: Ablex.

Southern Poverty Law Center (2003, Winter). *Intelligence Report, 112*, 25–49.

Starratt, R. J. (2003). Opportunity to learn and the accountability agenda. *Phi Delta Kappan, 85*, 298–303.

Stein, N. (1999). *Classrooms and Courtrooms: Facing Sexual harassment in K-12 Schools*. New York: Teachers College Press.

Stoughton, E. (2003). *"I wish I could tell them how I feel": Sharing the stories of young people labeled ED and their families*. Unpublished doctoral dissertation, Indiana University, Bloomington, IN.

Swanson, D. P., Cunningham, M., & Spencer, M. B. (2003). Black males' structural conditions, achievement patterns, normative needs and "opportunities." *Journal of Urban Education, 38*, 608–633.

Tatum, B. D. (2003). Opening the dialogue about race at school. In M. Sadowski (Ed.), *Adolescents at school: Perspectives on youth, identity, and education* (pp. 36–39). Cambridge, MA: Harvard University Press.

Taylor, S., Rizvi, F., Lingard, B., & Henry, M. (1997). *Educational policy and the politics of change*. London & New York: Routledge.

Tejeda, C., Espinoza, M., & Gutierrez, K. (2002). Toward a decolonizing pedagogy: Social justice reconsidered. In P. P. Trifonas (Ed.), *Pedagogies of difference: Rethinking education for social change* (pp. 10–40). New York & London: RoutledgeFalmer. Urban Institute (2004, February 26).

Valdes, G. (1996). *Con respeto: Bridging the distances between culturally diverse families and schools*. New York: Teachers College Press.

Valencia, R. R. (2002a). The plight of Chicano students: An overview of schooling conditions and outcomes. In R. R. Valencia (Ed.), *Chicano school failure and success: Past, present, future* (2nd ed., pp. 3–51). London & New York: RoutledgeFalmer.

Valencia, R. R. (2002b). The explosive growth of the Chicano/Latino population: Educational implications. In R. R. Valencia (Ed.), *Chicano school failure and success: Past, present, future* (2nd ed., pp.52–69). London & New York: RoutledgeFalmer.

Valencia, R. R. (Ed.). (1997). *The evolution of deficit thinking: Educational thought and practice*. London: Falmer.

Valenzuela, A. (1999). *Subtractive schooling: US-Mexican youth and the politics of caring*. Albany: State University of New York Press.

Varenne, H., & McDermott, R. (1998). *Successful failure: The school America builds*. Boulder, CO: Westview.

Wacquant, L. J. D. (1995). The comparative structure and experience of urban exclusion: Race, class and space in Chicago and Paris. In K. McFate, R. Lawson, & W. J. Wilson (Eds.), *Poverty, inequality, and the future of social policy* (pp. 543–570). New York: Russell Sage.

Weiler, J. D. (2000). *Codes and contradictions: Race, gender identity, and schooling*. Albany: State University of New York Press.

Weiner, G., Arnot, M., & David, M. (1997). Is the future female? Female success, male disadvantage, and changing gender patterns in education. In A.H. Halsey, H. Lauder, P. Brown, & A. S. Wells (Eds.), *Education: Culture, economy, and society* (pp. 620–630). Oxford: Oxford University Press.

Weis, L. (1990). *Working class without work: High school students in deindustrializing America*. New York: Routledge, Chapman & Hall.

West, C. (1997). The new cultural politics of difference. In A. H. Halsey, H. Lauder, P. Brown, & A. S. Wells (Eds.), *Education: Culture, economy, and society* (pp. 509–519). Oxford: Oxford University Press.

Wexler, P. (1996). *Critical Social Psychology.* New York: Peter Lang.

Willis, P. (1977). *Learning to labor: How working class kids get working class jobs.* New York: Columbia University Press.

Wilson, B. L., & Corbett, H. D. (2001). *Listening to urban kids: School reform and the teachers they want.* Albany: State University of New York Press.

Wilson, W. J. (1987). *The truly disadvantaged: The inner-city, the underclass, and public policy.* Chicago: University of Chicago Press.

Wilson, W. J. (1996). *When work disappears: The new world of the urban poor.* New York: Knopf.

Wilson, W. J. (1997). Studying inner-city social dislocations: The challenge of public agenda research. In A.H. Halsey, H. Lauder, P. Brown, & A. S. Wells (Eds.), *Education: Culture, economy, and society* (pp. 750–764). Oxford: Oxford University Press.

Worsham, L., & Olson, G. A. (1999). Hegemony and the future of democracy: Ernesto Laclau's political philosophy. In G. A. Olson & L. Worsham (Eds.), *Race, rhetoric, and the postcolonial* (pp. 129–162). Albany: State University of New York Press.

Yeakey, C. C. (2002). America's disposable children: Setting the stage. *Journal of Negro Education, 71,* 97—107.

Young, A. A., Jr. (2004). *The minds of marginalized black men: Making sense of mobility, opportunity, and future life chances.* Princeton, NJ: Princeton University Press.

Young, I. M. (2000). *Inclusion and democracy.* Oxford: Oxford University Press.

Young, M. (1971). *Knowledge and control.* London: Macmillan.

Zaragosa, N., & Scardina, M. (1998). The critical transformation of a special education classroom: A beginning teacher puts theory into practice. In J. L. Kincheloe & S. R. Steinberg (Eds.), *Unauthorized methods: Strategies for critical teaching* (pp. 79–94). New York & London: Routledge.

Zinn, H. (1995). *A people's history of the United States, 1492–present.* New York: Harper-Perennial.

Zizek, S. (1998). Psychoanalysis in post-Marxism: The case of Alain Badiou. In R. Miklitsch (Special Issues Editor), *Psycho-Marxism: Marxism and psychoanalysis late in the twentieth century* (pp. 235–261). *South Atlantic Quarterly, 97*(2).

8

Student and Teacher Perspectives on Classroom Management

Anita Woolfolk Hoy
The Ohio State University

Carol S. Weinstein
Rutgers, The State University of New Jersey

"Have the door open when the kids are coming in. Stand at the door and talk to the kids. Speak on their level and they will understand you and they'll stop making fun of you after school. Take a little time to talk about what they did last night or what they did during lunch hour" (Terry [12 years old] from Ellis [1997, p. 20]).

"Discipline needs to be imposed on students; it is something that 'happens to them' rather than developing internally. Schools must be tougher and have higher expectations" (female primary teacher [age 42] from Johnson, Whitington, and Oswald [1994, p. 268]).

INTRODUCTION

As these quotations suggest, both students and teachers have strong beliefs about what it takes to be an effective manager. These individuals are the central participants in classroom interactions and their relationships are at the heart of classroom management concerns and consequences. To ignore the thinking of these important players is to court failure in teaching and teacher education. Fully understanding their perspectives should allow us to create better learning environments for both students and teachers. This chapter on the beliefs of students and teachers is located in a section about alternative paradigms, not because the work represents a particular paradigm, but because teachers' and students' perspectives are important in every paradigm. In fact, the research on teachers' perspectives includes studies grounded in cognitive, process-product, ethnographic, narrative, and phenomenological approaches to research. The studies of students' perspectives tend to be more paradigmatic, in that they share questions and research approaches, but here too there are some divergences in method.

In identifying studies for this chapter, we cast a wide net, examining students' and teachers' beliefs about classroom management (actions taken to create a productive, orderly learning environment), discipline (actions taken to elicit changes in students' behavior), and socialization (actions taken to help students fulfill their responsibilities more effectively). In the sections that follow, however, we use "classroom management" as the umbrella term for these various teaching functions (Brophy, 1999). The categories and main sections of the chapter emerged from our review of the literature; we searched for research on teacher and student perspectives, beliefs, knowledge, and thinking–including students at every grade level and both inservice and preservice teachers. It appears that the research on students' and teachers' perspectives proceeded apace, without a focus on knowledge-building around a set of common issues. One goal of this chapter is to point toward such a set of issues.

Our discussion of students' beliefs is organized in two parts. The first part focuses on students' perceptions of the "good" teacher, because students' decisions about whether to cooperate are often based on their respect for the teacher. We then consider students' perceptions of the frequency, efficacy, and acceptability of various disciplinary interventions. The section on teachers begins with a consideration of several orientations toward classroom management, many of which array beliefs along a continuum from controlling to democratic. We then turn to teacher perceptions of disciplinary interventions, their views about "problem" students, and their sense of efficacy for classroom management. The final section of the chapter considers convergences and divergences in teachers' and students' beliefs and the implications of those intersections for practice and for future research.

DEFINING KNOWLEDGE, BELIEFS, AND PERCEPTIONS

Because this chapter repeatedly refers to perceptions, beliefs, and knowledge, it is important to clarify how we are using these terms. The distinction between knowledge and beliefs has been widely debated. It is sometimes argued that knowledge requires a "truth condition" or some evidence to back up the claim, whereas beliefs can be held—felt to be true—without necessarily having a base in evidence (Richardson, 1996). Alexander, Schallert, and Hare (1991), on the other hand, asserted that beliefs are a category of knowledge, and that knowledge "encompasses all that a person knows or believes to be true, whether or not it is verified as true in some sort of objective or external way" (p. 317). It is this definition that has been widely accepted in the literature on teaching and learning.

In a series of studies conducted with colleagues (e.g., Alexander & Dochy, 1995; Alexander, Murphy, Guan, & Murphy, 1998; Alexander, Murphy, & Woods, 1996), Alexander investigated how teachers and students of varying educational levels conceptualize knowledge and beliefs. In spite of some conceptual differences (knowledge was seen as more factual and verifiable, whereas beliefs tended to be subjective and not require validation), the majority of respondents perceived knowledge and beliefs as overlapping constructs; many ideas fall in the realm of what is both known *and* believed. Given that teachers often seem to define knowledge and beliefs as overlapping constructs, and a precedent set by other researchers of teacher cognition (e.g., Borko & Putnam, 1996; Fenstermacher, 1994; Kagan, 1992), within this review we discuss them as overlapping and somewhat interchangeable constructs.

Whereas the research on teachers has generally focused on knowledge and beliefs, the research on students' thinking about classroom management has focused on student perceptions—another overlapping, somewhat interchangeable construct. According to Schunk and Meece (1992), "student perceptions are thoughts, beliefs, and feelings about persons, situations, and events" (p. xi). We now examine the research on students' perceptions.

STUDENTS' PERCEPTIONS OF CLASSROOM MANAGEMENT

Interest in student perceptions dates back to at least the 1970s and 1980s (e.g., Levine & Wang, 1983; Metz, 1978; Morine-Dershimer, 1985; Nash, 1976; Weinstein, 1983), reflecting a view of students as "active information processors" (Schunk & Meece, 1992) whose perceptions can affect their behavior. This view of the student has particular relevance for classroom management. As Sheets (1996, 2002) has noted, students are not passive recipients of teacher actions. They choose to resist or comply with rules; they make decisions to ignore, avoid, sabotage, question, or acquiesce to teachers' requests. In other words, behaviors of students are "purposive acts," based on their interpretations of school and classroom life and, in particular, their relationships with teachers (Schlosser, 1992, p. 137).

A telling example comes from a study of "civility, incivility, cursing and politeness" conducted by Plank, McDill, McPartland, and Jordan (2001). Survey responses from 225 seniors in an urban high school indicated that students had both politeness and cursing in their behavioral repertoires; whether they chose to behave in "institutionally sanctioned ways" depended on their perceptions of the teacher—specifically, whether the teachers were "mean" (and did not know students by name) or "nice." Similarly, Thorson (1996) interviewed 14 students (seven from general education and seven from special education) assigned to Saturday School detention because of tardiness, truancy, and disrespect. Students indicated that they sometimes engaged in "maladaptive behaviors" as a form of resistance; in other words, they tried to "get even" with teachers who were rude or didn't teach the class effectively.

These results are consistent with research demonstrating that students who like their teachers and perceive them to be supportive are more likely to engage in prosocial, responsible behavior, to adhere to classroom rules and norms, and to engage in academic activities (Wentzel, 1997, 1998). In short, students perceive "good" teachers as worthy of respect, cooperation, and participation. But what exactly does it mean to be a "good" teacher?

Perceptions of the "Good Teacher"

Three factors seem central to students' perceptions of "good" teachers—the ability to establish positive interpersonal relationships with students (i.e., to demonstrate "care"); the ability to exercise authority and to provide structure without being rigid, threatening, and punitive; and the ability to "make learning fun" by using innovative and creative pedagogical strategies (e.g., see Noguera, 1995). These factors appear repeatedly in qualitative, interpretive studies that examine how students assign value and meaning to their experiences in school (e.g., Valenzuela, 1999), as well as in questionnaire/observation studies of students' perceptions and attitudes (e.g., Short & Short, 1988).

Ability to Establish Caring Relationships With Students. Studies repeatedly attest to the importance that students place on teachers' willingness to "be there" for them, to listen, and to show concern for students' personal and academic lives—in short, to *care* (Alder & Moulton, 1998; Allen, 1995; Cabello & Terrell, 1994; Cothran & Ennis, 2000; Cothran, Kulinna, & Garrahy, 2003; Crowley, 1993; Davidson, 1999; Ellis, 1997; Ferreira & Bosworth, 2001; Hayes, Ryan, & Zseller, 1994; McIntyre & Battle, 1998; Osterman, 2000; Pomeroy, 1999; Schlosser, 1992; Wentzel, 1997). Interviews with more than 100 middle school students (Bosworth, 1995), for example, indicated that students could clearly articulate a definition of caring and could identify specific behaviors of caring teachers. For both males and females, for all grade levels, and for White students, the teacher's willingness to provide help with schoolwork was the most frequently cited manifestation of caring, although students also appreciated teachers who valued their individuality, showed respect, and treated students equitably. Among students of color, the most frequently cited characteristic was the teacher's willingness to help with personal problems and to provide guidance. As one seventh-grade female commented, "A caring teacher wants to make sure you don't get in trouble."

These same themes—personal caring and academic caring—also emerged in a study by Cothran and Ennis (2000) in which 51 urban high school students (89% African American and

11% non-African American) were interviewed about barriers and bridges to engagement. Once again, students reported that they were more willing to engage when they felt that the teacher cared if they learned the subject matter and also cared about their personal lives and welfare. Similarly, Phelan, Davidson, and Cao (1992) followed a diverse group of 54 students in four high schools for two years to gain insight into students' views of schools. A recurring theme was the importance of having teachers who care, but high-achieving students associated caring with assistance in academic matters, whereas low achievers associated caring with personality traits (e.g., patience, humor, ability to listen) and an expression of interest and concern in students as individuals. Personal caring was particularly important for students who were experiencing pressures and problems at home (e.g., alcohol-induced fights, physical abuse, verbal conflicts). Although many teachers are disinclined to consider students' out-of-school circumstances and admonish students to leave their problems at home, Phelan, Yu, and Davidson (1994) assert, "simply having adults who are willing and able to listen can often reduce the stresses they feel" (p. 436).

In a similar vein, Katz (1999) found that high expectations for academic achievement combined with caring and support are the essential components of a productive teacher-student relationship. Interviews with eight Latino immigrant students in a middle school examined their feelings of being marginalized and underscored the centrality of their relationships with teachers. Katz concluded:

> High expectations without caring can result in setting goals that are impossible for the student to reach without adult support and assistance. On the other hand, caring without high expectations can turn dangerously into paternalism in which teachers feel sorry for "underprivileged" youth but never challenge them academically. High expectations and caring in tandem, however, can make a powerful difference in students' lives. (p. 814)

As Katz's study points out, perceiving that teachers care appears to be especially important for students who are alienated and marginalized (Schlosser, 1992) and those who are at risk of school failure (Dillon, 1989; Miller, Leinhardt, & Zigmond, 1988). Davidson (1999), for example, interviewed 49 adolescents representing diverse socioeconomic, cultural, and academic backgrounds. Data revealed not only students' appreciation and preference for teachers who communicated interest in their well-being, but also students' willingness to reciprocate by being attentive and conscientious. This was particularly evident in the responses of "stigmatized" students who faced "social borders"—divisions between their academic and social worlds. Describing Wendy Ashton, a teacher who prodded students to achieve, one student commented, "She won't put you down, she'll talk to you and she'll go, 'Yeah, you know I love you. You know I want you to make something out of yourself, so stop messing around in class'" (p. 361). Davidson speculated that students who do not face social borders might be more accepting of teachers who are relatively distant and impersonal, because the students basically trust school as an institution; however, when students face the social divisions that can lead to alienation and marginalization, it is essential for teachers to be attentive, supportive, and respectful. Negative relationships can exacerbate alienation, and may even determine whether students come to class.

The centrality of caring was also documented in a three-year ethnographic study of academic achievement and school orientations among immigrant Mexican and Mexican American students at a high school in Houston, Texas. According to Valenzuela (1999), the predominantly non-Latino teaching staff at the school interpreted students' attire and off-putting behavior as evidence that they didn't care about school: "Having drawn that conclusion, teachers then often make no further effort to forge effective reciprocal relationships with this group" (p. 22). At the same time, students saw a caring relationship with teachers as a precondition for caring about school; in other words, they needed to be cared *for* before they could care *about* school.

Moreover, Valenzuela contended that requiring students to care about school is tantamount to expecting them to participate in a process of "cultural and linguistic eradication" (p. 62)—what Valenzuela calls "subtractive schooling"—because the curriculum they were asked to value dismisses or derogates their language, culture, and community.

The importance of caring has also been demonstrated in studies that have investigated the perceptions of students with behavior disorders (Crowley, 1993; Ellis, 1997). Garner (1995), for example, investigated the perceptions of 12 "disruptive" students in two secondary schools in which he taught (one in England and one in the United States). Using semistructured interviews and informal comments recorded in a diary, Garner found that the classroom teacher was the most important factor in students' attitudes toward school. Boys at both schools had a clear view of the personal and professional qualities that constitute a good teacher. They consistently mentioned the importance of teachers providing help, being attentive and respectful, and willing to listen. Similarly, in a study of the perceptions of 17 students with or at risk for behavior disorders, Habel, Bloom, Ray, and Bacon (1999) found that students stressed the importance of teacher-student relationships characterized by trust and affection. Once again, students' comments echoed the twin themes of personal care and academic care. As one student reported: "They [teachers] talk to me, and are happy to see me. And when I'm stuck on a problem, they talk to me and help me out" (p. 97).

Ability to Exercise Authority Without Being Rigid, Threatening, or Punitive. "Good" teachers are not only attentive, concerned, and supportive in terms of students' personal and academic lives; they are also able to maintain order, provide limits for behavior, and create an environment in which students feel safe (e.g., Alder & Moulton, 1998; Cothran, Kulinna, & Garrahy, 2003; Crowley, 1993; Davidson, 1999; Munn & Johnstone, 1990; Nash, 1976; Phelan, Davidson, & Cao, 1992; Pomeroy, 1999; Rogers, 1991; Schlosser, 1992; Short & Short, 1988; Smith, Adelman, Nelson, Taylor, & Phares, 1987; Stinson, 1993; Supaporn, 2000; Thorson, 1996; Wallace, 1996). That these two factors are not mutually exclusive, but support and reinforce each other, has been repeatedly demonstrated in an extensive program of research on students' perceptions of teachers' "interpersonal behavior" conducted by Wubbels and his colleagues (see chapter 45; this volume). These investigations have shown that students feel more positively about their classes when teachers are seen as both "cooperative"—caring, helpful, friendly, supportive—*and* "dominant"—showing leadership, being influential, and acting in an authoritative manner (Brekelmans, Wubbels, & den Brok, 2002).

In a set of informal interviews with elementary and secondary students of all achievement levels in both urban and suburban settings (Weinstein, 2003; Weinstein & Mignano, 2003), the desire for clarity, structure, and limits was expressed in a number of ways: "Teachers need to be a strong authority figure"; "teachers need to tell kids what they expect"; "teachers need to show strength"; "teachers need to come off as someone who has control" (pp. 25–26). What is clearly conveyed by these responses is students' lack of respect for teachers who are too permissive, who are "too cowardly to take charge," and who "let kids run all over them." Notably, even students with behavior disorders call for teachers to impose limits, and they acknowledge that these limits enable them to behave in more appropriate, productive ways. For example, in a British study (Pomeroy, 1999) of secondary school students who had been excluded from school and were now attending a "Behavioral Support Service Centre," several interviewees commented that teachers should have been stricter. One respondent, Sarah, reflected:

> I think I needed to have more strict teachers. Like, if I'd have had, like stricter teachers teaching, then I probably would have got on better at the school. Cause, like I behaved for them. But like, teachers who like, can't control ya, I had quite a few of them. And, um, I just didn't get on." (p. 472)

When students call for teachers to be stricter, they are thinking of a particular kind of disciplinary practice. They distinguish clearly between teachers who are strict and those who are "mean" (Weinstein, 2003), those who use their power not for oppression, but in the "moral service of others" (Noblit, 1993, pp. 34–35). They respect teachers who have rules, but who are not overly rigid and who don't set themselves "above and apart" (Davidson, 1999). They also like teachers who use humor to get students back on track rather than resorting to more punitive tactics and who don't punish students for every minor misbehavior. As one of Stinson's (1993) secondary school respondents commented, students dislike teachers who "write you up" for every little thing: "Like, if you have your foot on the chair, 'Get that foot down.' If you yawn and forget to cover your mouth, she'll tell you to cover your mouth" (p. 220). Calls for strict teachers are also qualified by comments about the need for teachers to be fair—to listen to all sides of a story—and to exert "calm control" (Garner, 1995), imposing sanctions without shouting and humiliating students (Pomeroy, 1999), without "going over the top" (Wallace, 1996), and without "harshness" (Hayes, Ryan, & Zseller, 1994). Providing a rationale for rules and directives also appears to be important. Metz (1978), for example, found that top-level students in the two junior high schools she studied wanted teachers to provide explanations for their commands: "They rebelled when a teacher taking a parental or a bureaucratic stance refused to give such a justification but replied in effect 'Do it because I'm your teacher and I say so,' or 'Obey the rule and don't ask why'" (p. 76).

The ability to be firm without using threats and public humiliation appears to be particularly important for students who are already disaffected or alienated from school. Schlosser (1992), for example, interviewed 31 "marginal" junior high school students judged to be at risk of school failure. Students considered teachers to be uncaring and unfair adversaries if they "engaged in public acts intended to convey an impression of authority: making examples of specific students, sending students from the room, and ordering compliance" (p. 135).

Although studies indicate that students of all ages and backgrounds appreciate teachers who can provide clarity and firmness, definitions of these behaviors appear to be culturally dependent. Delpit (1995), for example, points out that many Black children and children from working-class families are more accustomed to straightforward directives from authority figures ("Sit down and get to work") than to the "politeness formulas" (Manke, 1997) and indirect discourse strategies (e.g., "Sally, would you like to sit down?") typically used by middle-class White teachers.

Ballenger (1999) offers a compelling example of the way that discourse styles can influence students' perceptions. An experienced preschool teacher, Ballenger expected to have little difficulty with her class of four-year-old Haitian children. To her surprise, however, her usual repertoire of management strategies failed to create a respectful, orderly environment. Because her colleagues—all Haitian—were experiencing no difficulty with classroom management, Ballenger had to conclude that the problem "did not reside in the children" (p. 32). She began to explore her own beliefs and practices with respect to children's behavior and to visit other teachers' classrooms to examine their "control statements." Eventually, Ballenger was able to identify several key differences between her own style of discourse and that of her Haitian colleagues. Whereas the Haitian teachers stressed that they cared for the children and had their best interests at heart (e.g., "The adults here like you, they want you to be good children"), Ballenger frequently referred to children's internal states (e.g., "You must be angry"). Moreover, she tended to stress the logical consequences of children's behavior (e.g., "If you don't listen, you won't know what to do"). In contrast, the Haitian teachers articulated the values and responsibilities of group membership and stressed less immediate consequences, such as bringing shame to one's family. Once Ballenger had identified these differences in control statements, she made a deliberate effort to adopt some of the Haitian discourse style. Order in her classroom improved significantly and students perceived her to be more caring.

Ability to "Make Learning Fun." According to students in numerous studies, a third component of being a "good" teacher is the ability to develop and implement engaging, varied lessons (e.g., Alder & Moulton, 1998; Allen, 1995; Cothran & Ennis, 2000; Metz, 1978; Nash, 1976; Nieto, 1994; Rogers, 1991; Schmuck & Schmuck, 1991; Short & Short, 1988). Students consistently decry the use of lecture and seatwork, and criticize teachers who rely on "chalk and talk" pedagogy, textbooks, and routine, rote learning (Nieto, 1994). They consistently express a desire for teachers to use more interactive, participatory strategies (Younger & Warrington, 1999) and to structure lessons to meet students' interests and needs (Davidson, 1999). They voice a distinct preference for group work and cooperative activities (Allen, 1986; Cothran & Ennis, 2000) and praise teachers who combine humor, enthusiasm, and creativity in their approach to subject matter (Davidson, 1999).

These personality characteristics and pedagogical strategies were apparent in a "microethnography" (Dillon, 1989) of a low-track, 11th-grade basic English/reading classroom. More specifically, Dillon examined the way in which Mr. Appleby, a white, middle-class teacher with a reputation for being effective, interacted with his 17 low-achieving, predominantly Black students. Observations, conversations, and interviews indicated that Appleby worked hard to bridge the gap between students' home culture and the culture of the school, to plan and structure activities to meet the interests and needs of his students, and to implement lessons in which all students could be active, successful learners. Rather than giving his students "watered-down, skill-sheet oriented material" (p. 243), Appleby believed that students could and should read classic literature with themes to which they could relate, such as *Of Mice and Men*. In addition, he read aloud from library books chosen with students' interests in mind, usually planned two or three varied activities for one class period, and frequently incorporated cooperative learning. Despite his student-centered approaches, students recognized that Appleby had high academic and behavioral expectations; as Melinda commented, "Appleby lets students talk while doing work if they get their work done—when it is time to work Appleby expects work from students" (p. 244).

Appleby's behavior can be characterized as "culturally relevant pedagogy" (Ladson-Billings, 2001) or "culturally responsive teaching" (Gay, 2000): He learned about his students' home cultures, tailored his curriculum to their interests and needs, and demonstrated respect and caring. Furthermore, he appears to have accommodated to his students' cultural backgrounds by adopting (at least some of the time) the more active, participatory interaction pattern ("call-response") characteristic of his students' home culture. During discussions, for example, he encouraged his students to call out answers and make comments and did not expect them to raise their hands and speak one at a time. Dillon (1989) reported:

> Appleby also allowed his students to interact with each other and with him, in the way they spoke to peers and adults in their family/community. In other words, within these lessons, Appleby allowed the interactions in his classrooms to be culturally congruent.... For example, students often talked sarcastically, interrupted Appleby, or overlapped the speech of other students as they presented their ideas. (p. 245)

Despite this "permissiveness," Dillon observed no disrespect; as LaVonne commented, "Students obey Appleby's wishes—we act crazy but we calm ourselves down and don't go overboard" (p. 244).

Students' Perceptions of Disciplinary Interventions

Research in this area has focused on three related topics—students' self-reports of the frequency and efficacy of coercive versus less directive disciplinary strategies (Lewis, 2001; Lewis & Lovegrove, 1987; Pestello, 1989; Smith et al., 1987); students' perceptions of the severity and acceptability of various disciplinary strategies; and students' perceptions of differential treatment, justice, and fairness with respect to discipline. We review each of these topics in turn.

Coercive Versus Less Directive Strategies. Lewis (2001) administered a questionnaire on disciplinary strategies to more than 3,500 students in grades 6, 7, 9, and 11 from 42 schools in Australia. Students were asked to indicate the extent to which their teacher used the following interventions: (a) hints and nondirective descriptions of unacceptable behavior; (b) talking with students to discuss the impact of their behavior on others; (c) involving students in classroom discipline decision making; (d) recognizing the appropriate behavior of individual students and the class; (e) punishing students who misbehave and increasing the level of punishment if resistance is met; and (f) aggressive techniques, such as yelling angrily. The questionnaire also asked students to indicate the extent to which they engaged in 39 responsible classroom behaviors, the level of misbehavior in the class, and how they felt when the teacher dealt with misbehavior. Data analysis indicated that primary students received more "relationship-based" discipline (hints, discussion, involvement, and rewards) than did secondary students. There were no significant differences between the two groups in terms of the use of punishment or aggression. Analysis also demonstrated that four "relationship-based" strategies—rewards and recognitions, discussions, involvement, and nondirective hints—were most associated with student responsibility. In other words, teachers used "coercive discipline" in classes with more misbehavior and more relationship-based discipline in classrooms where students acted more responsibly (Lewis, 2001). Although a causal relationship could not be determined, Lewis speculated that teachers' use of relationship strategies promoted greater levels of student responsibility. He urged teachers to foster the responsibility of irresponsible students by increasing the use of rewards, hints, discussion, and involvement in rule setting. (See chapter 46 by Ramon Lewis for a more complete discussion of this line of research.)

Similar conclusions were reached by Smith et al. (1987) in a study that examined the relationship between students' perception of control at school and problem behavior and attitudes. The Perceived Control at School Scale (PCSS) and a variety of attitude and affect measures were administered to 80 students from general education classrooms (ages 9 to 18), 57 students from public school special education resource rooms (ages 9 to 18), and 51 students who had had problems functioning in public school programs and were now enrolled in a university-based laboratory program designed to enhance students' perception of control in school (ages 9 to 19). Parents and teachers also filled out behavior ratings. Analysis indicated that public school special education students were significantly more negative in their ratings of perceived control at school and general happiness and were rated as exhibiting greater misbehavior. The laboratory school sample reported higher perceptions of control and more positive attitudes toward schooling than did either of the public school samples. For the general education sample, ratings of perceived control were significantly related to most of the indices of attitude and affect towards school and to parent ratings of deportment, but not to teacher ratings. The investigators concluded that the use of external controls with students with learning problems may be counterproductive; they speculated that problem behavior and attitudes may be the result of the very interventions implemented to eliminate them and urged educators to replace approaches that rely excessively on extrinsic control with interventions that emphasize self-regulation and self-determination.

Skepticism about the efficacy of coercive, extrinsic control is supported by other studies that have examined students' perceptions of harsh, punitive sanctions. Sheets (1996), for example, explored how African Americans, Chicano, European American, and Filipino American students who had experienced disciplinary problems understood and explained the causes, consequences, and potential resolutions of conflicts with their teachers. Although students admitted that they had committed the acts for which they were disciplined, coercive policies appeared to be ineffective. Fearing disciplinary repercussions was also inconsequential to four Chicano secondary students (Sheets, 2002), for whom "defending themselves when they were right, maintaining a sense of self-respect and ethnic integrity, having the support of their family, and being with and supporting friends, were stronger influences than any forthcoming penalty" (p. 114). As Sheets and Gay (1996) reflect:

> Students already believe they will not be treated fairly under the best of circumstances and they expect the worst kind of treatment. When schools "get tough" with these students, their expectations are affirmed but their problematic actions may not be reduced at all.... Something very different must be done." (p. 91)

Quantitative research has yielded the same findings. Pestello (1989) explored the influence of students' perceptions of disciplinary interventions on their self-reported misbehavior. Questionnaire data were collected from 271 students, two classes for each of seven teachers. Hierarchical regression analysis found that student perceptions of the severity, certainty, and swiftness of sanctions contributed almost nothing to the variance explained in classroom behavior. Pestello concluded, "fearing the consequences of misbehavior will not necessarily lead one to comply with the rules" (p. 301). Indeed, students' perceptions of the classroom context (e.g., how quickly the class came to order after the bell rang) had the strongest influence on classroom misbehavior.

Severity and Acceptability of Disciplinary Interventions. The results of the limited research on this topic echo the results reported earlier in relationship to students' perceptions of good teachers—specifically, the importance of teachers being able to achieve order without resorting to public humiliation. Zeidner (1988), for example, examined students' perceptions of the severity of common disciplinary strategies. Almost 300 junior high school students in Israel rated the severity of each of 24 strategies on a 5-point Likert-type rating scale, and these ratings were compared with those of 80 junior high school teachers. Interestingly, regardless of sex, socioeconomic status, or cultural background, students viewed "permanent suspension from school" and "shaming or personally insulting student" as the two most severe sanctions appearing on the inventory; they also judged "personal insult" as significantly more severe than did teachers. Other "very severe" strategies (median rating of 4 or 5) included permanent student transfer to a different class, parent-principal conference; and temporary demotion to a lower class. "Moderately severe" strategies (median rating of 3) included after-class detention, threatening teacher glares, student-teacher conference, reporting to the principal's office, shortening recess, and verbal reprimands. "Relatively unsevere" strategies (median ratings of 1 or 2) included rearranging a student's seating position, assigning extra homework, shortening recess, and verbal reprimands.

The importance of not shaming or humiliating students was also demonstrated in a program of research conducted in the mid-1980s by Elliott and his colleagues (Elliott, 1986; Elliott, Turco, & Gresham, 1987; Turco & Elliott, 1986; Witt & Elliott, 1985). These researchers examined students' perceptions of the acceptability of a variety of disciplinary strategies. Data across studies consistently indicated that public reprimands were perceived to be an unacceptable intervention, along with negative group consequences for individual misbehavior

(Elliott, 1986). In one study (Elliott, Witt, Galvin, & Moe, 1986), for example, 79 sixth-graders read a problem scenario about a male student who either destroyed another student's property or talked out of turn. Students then used the *Children's Intervention Rating Profile* to rate the acceptability of 12 teacher-initiated methods for modifying the misbehavior: private reprimand, public reprimand, private praise for appropriate behavior, public praise for appropriate behavior, individual loss of recess, individual gain of extra recess, whole class loss of recess, whole class gain of extra recess, individual stays in for recess, individual goes to a quiet room, individual goes to principal's office, and individual earns rewards via a point system. Public reprimands of the individual and negative consequences for the group when only one child misbehaved were judged to be unacceptable interventions. The four traditional interventions (principal's office, point system, staying in during recess, and quiet room) as a group were rated the most acceptable methods. Severity of problem did not significantly affect the ratings except for the traditional interventions.

More recent qualitative research (Schlosser, 1992; Sheets, 2002; Sheets & Gay, 1996) also demonstrates the unacceptability of public reprimands and indicates that, in particular, marginalized students and students of color have little tolerance for teachers who "dis" them. Moreover, when teachers embarrass, insult, or demean students publicly, they may actually engender sympathy for the misbehaving students and disturb the others. Lewis and Lovegrove (1987) note that "innocent students, who never misbehave and who are never punished, may be as much if not more upset by the types of techniques that teachers use than those student who actually experience the sanction" (p. 183).

Students' Perceptions of Differential Treatment, Justice, and Fairness. Numerous studies by Rhona Weinstein and her colleagues (e.g., 1982, 1983, 1987, 1989; Weinstein & McKown, 1998; Alvidrez & Weinstein, 1999) have demonstrated that students are savvy observers of the differential treatment their teachers provide to high-and low-achievers and that such differential treatment can have lasting consequences. According to Weinstein (2002), even first-graders (and even low-achievers) are "deeply sensitive observers of the classroom reality" (p. 288), able to discern that "high expectations, trust, and opportunity from teachers are linked with doing well in school, whereas scolding, monitoring, and lots of help are associated with poor performance" (p. 110). Weinstein's research also focuses on students' perceptions of the ways that teachers communicate academic expectations, and thus is beyond the scope of this chapter; nonetheless, her work underscores the multiple realities of classroom life and points out the fallacy of thinking that "classroom climate" is experienced in the same way by all children. (See Weinstein, 2002, for an overview and synthesis of this extensive body of research.)

Just as students perceive differential treatment with respect to academic expectations and opportunities, they also perceive differences in the way that discipline is meted out. Brantlinger (1993), for example, found that low-income adolescents reported a greater number and variety of penalties than high-income students. Moreover, there were qualitative differences in the kinds of punishments students received: low-income students reported many more consequences that were ostracizing, humiliating, illogical, and counterproductive. They also described more stringent consequences for the same infractions that high-income students committed. Reports from high-income students confirmed the differential treatment, acknowledging their personal advantage; indeed, there was considerable agreement that school discipline depended on personal reputation, achievement, and social status.

Differential discipline is also reported by students of color, who feel that teachers penalize them for infractions they ignore in White students and unfairly blame them for wrongdoings. As indicated earlier, qualitative studies (Katz, 1996, 1999; Sheets, 1996, 2002) consistently demonstrate that students of color perceive injustices in disciplinary practices and complain that attempts to defend or explain their behaviors are ignored or interpreted as defiance. Indeed, in a study of eight Latino students in a middle school (Katz, 1999), teacher discrimination was cited as the number one cause of students' disengagement from school. Students repeatedly complained that most of their teachers could not see them as individuals and held stereotyped images of Latinos as gang members, thieves, and prostitutes.

These perceptions are consistent with quantitative data collected by Ruck and Wortley (2002) on racial/ethnic minority students' views and beliefs pertaining to school disciplinary practices. A diverse sample of students (N = 1,870) attending grades 10 and 12 in 11 randomly selected Canadian high schools completed anonymous questionnaires that tapped perceptions of differential treatment. Black students were significantly more likely than South Asian, Asian, White, and other students to perceive that teachers treat students from their racial group worse or much worse than students from other racial groups. More specifically, Black students were more likely to believe that they would face discriminatory treatment with respect to school suspension, with respect to having the police called for an incident, and with respect to their treatment by the police. Unfortunately, there was no way of determining the accuracy of these perceptions, because Canadian schools do not compile disciplinary statistics by race and ethnicity. (See chapter 41 by Skiba and Rausch for a fuller discussion of these issues.)

Although differential treatment because of racism or classism is clearly unacceptable to students (at least those who are the recipients of the negative treatment), one study suggests that differentiated behavioral interventions because of special needs may be considered appropriate. Fulk & Smith (1995) administered a brief interview to 98 White elementary students in grades 1 through 6; 23% of the students were identified as exhibiting learning/behavioral problems requiring intervention. Most students (including those identified as having special needs) were in favor of behavioral adaptations (rewards for good behavior and extra chances or different rules) when needed. Except for first graders (with a 53% negative response), the majority of students at all grades accepted individualized behavioral programming. More students supported the use of differential rewards (72%) than the adjustment of rules (64%). Explaining their positive responses, students spoke of the impact on the target students (e.g., "If she got bigger rewards, maybe she'd get the notion of behaving"), as well as the effect of inappropriate behavior on the class as a whole ("His bad behavior affects others, so special rewards would be better for everyone"). Fulk and Smith conclude that "teachers may be more concerned about equal treatment of students than students are" (p. 416).

TEACHERS' KNOWLEDGE AND BELIEFS ABOUT CLASSROOM MANAGEMENT

In the last two decades, research has burgeoned on teachers' knowledge and beliefs; reviews are plentiful (e.g., Borko & Putnam, 1996; Calderhead, 1996; Clark & Peterson, 1986; Fenstermacher, 1994; Kagan, 1990, 1992; Nespor, 1987; Pajares, 1992; Rentel, 1994; Richardson, 1994, 1996; Woolfolk Hoy & Murphy, 2001; Woolfolk Hoy, Pape, & Davis, in press). Researchers have investigated both explicit and implicit beliefs of preservice, novice, and experienced teachers. Some investigators have sought to identify beliefs (cf. C. Weinstein, 1988, 1989; Weinstein, Woolfolk, Dittmeier, & Shanker, 1994); others have examined how knowledge and beliefs affect learning to teach (cf. Hollingworth, 1989) or instruction in particular subjects (Richardson, 1994).

As sources of beliefs, Richardson (1996) listed three categories of experience: personal experiences, experiences with schooling, and experience with formal knowledge. Personal experiences include a wide range of influences, such as beliefs about self and others; perspectives on the relationship of schooling to society; personal, family, and cultural values and attitudes;

and the impact of gender, ethnicity, SES, religion, geography, and life events (Bullough & Knowles, 1991; Clandinin & Connelly, 1987). Schooling experiences include Lortie's (1975) "apprenticeship of observation" that fosters deeply held beliefs about teaching. Strauss (1996) noted that, during their precollege education, prospective teachers are in school learning situations for at least 12,000 hours, many hours more than the 10,000 hours required to become an expert in a particular field (Simon, 1995). Thus, at the very least, prospective teachers come to college experts on being schooled; implicit models of what it means to teach, manage, and learn are inferred from these thousands of hours of schooling (Britzman, 1991; Calderhead & Robson, 1991; Grant, 1992; Knowles, 1992). Experiences with formal knowledge include both knowledge of academic subjects, such as mathematics or history, and pedagogical knowledge, as usually encountered in formal teacher preparation programs. The impact of formal teacher education courses generally is seen as the least powerful influence on teachers' beliefs (Richardson, 1996), but some research has shown that these courses may have effects years later as experienced teachers "rehear" the words of their former professors with new ears (Featherstone, 1993).

Thus, teachers have a store of tacit knowledge about students, learning, teaching, and classroom management. These preconceptions, being so familiar and accessible, are powerful influences, because in learning to teach, "... the knowledge and beliefs that prospective and experienced teachers hold serve as filters through which their learning takes place" (Borko & Putnam, 1996, p. 675). In a seminal paper synthesizing the research on teachers' beliefs, Pajares (1992) identified a number of assumptions that reasonably can be made about the nature and scope of teaching beliefs:

- "Beliefs are formed early and tend to self-perpetuate, persevering even against contradictions caused by reason, time, schooling, or experience." (p. 324)
- "The earlier a belief is incorporated into the belief structure, the more difficult it is to alter. Newly acquired beliefs are most vulnerable to change." (p. 325)
- "Beliefs are instrumental in defining tasks and selecting the cognitive tools with which to interpret, plan, and make decisions regarding such tasks; hence, they play a critical role in defining behavior and organizing knowledge and information." (p. 325)
- "Individuals' beliefs strongly affect their behavior." (p. 326)

Fang (1996) reached a similar conclusion in a meta-analysis of research on teachers' beliefs and actions: teachers' beliefs lead to teachers' actions that impact students' learning—for better or worse.

Beliefs about classroom management and appropriate or inappropriate student behavior will vary, in part, based on a teacher's instructional goals and strategies (Johnson, Whitington, & Oswald, 1994; Prawat, 1992). For example, the belief that students learn by explanation, practice, and direct instruction usually also includes an emphasis on rules, such as "one person speaks at time," "do your own work," or "no talking." Practice, repetition, and compliance with authorities are valued. Learning through dialogue and discovery, in contrast, is associated with cooperative learning, group projects, and inquiry, which require movement, talk, staying focused on academic tasks in the face of distractions, and social skills. These are very different classroom management challenges.

It is beyond the scope of this chapter to fully explore connections between perspectives on teaching and learning and beliefs about classroom management, but clearly such connections exist, though teachers' beliefs about teaching and management are not always consistent. McCaslin and Good (1998), for example, question whether adopting constructivist beliefs about teaching and learning will automatically change beliefs about management. Many educators who stress "understanding" and "critical thinking" are apt to advocate classroom management packages that stress student compliance. "Students are asked to think and understand, but in too many classrooms they are asked to think noiselessly, without peer communication or social exchange" (p. 73). With the interactions and possible contradictions in mind between beliefs about teaching and orientations to class management, we now focus on the latter.

Orientations to Management

Brophy (1996) has documented that the most successful teachers view class management as the creation of effective, engaging, supportive learning environments and the socialization of students, whereas less successful teachers see management as discipline and the maintenance of authority. Much of what is written, however, about teachers' classroom management beliefs, especially earlier work, focuses on beliefs about discipline and pupil control, often conceptualizing these beliefs along a continuum from controlling to humanistic or democratic.

Custodial and Humanistic Control Orientations. Pupil control ideology was one of the earliest approaches to conceptualizing and assessing perspectives on discipline (Hoy, 2001). Willower, Eidell, and Hoy (1967) described pupil control along a continuum from custodial at one extreme to humanistic at the other. The model of the custodial perspective is the traditional school that provides an inflexible and highly regimented setting concerned primarily with the maintenance of order. Students are stereotyped in terms of their appearance, behavior, and family social status. Teachers who hold a custodial orientation conceive of the school as an autocratic organization with a rigid pupil-teacher status hierarchy. Students must accept the orders of their teachers without question. Teachers do not attempt to understand misbehavior, but instead view it as a personal affront. Students are perceived as irresponsible and undisciplined persons who must be controlled through punitive measures. In brief, impersonality, pessimism, punishment, and watchful mistrust pervade the atmosphere of a custodial school.

The model of the humanistic perspective is the school as an educational community in which students learn through cooperative interaction and experience. Learning and behavior are viewed in psychological and sociological terms, not moralistic ones. Self-discipline is substituted for strict teacher control. Humanistic orientations lead teachers to desire a democratic atmosphere with open channels of two-way communication between pupils and teachers and increased self-determination. In sum, a humanistic orientation is used in the sociopsychological sense suggested by Fromm (1948); it stresses the importance of each student and the creation of a climate to meet the wide range of student needs. Of course, the custodial and humanistic poles of the pupil control continuum are extremes—pure forms that may not exist in real schools.

Pupil control ideology typically is assessed using the PCI form—a 20-item Likert-type scale with five response categories for each item ranging from strongly agree to strongly disagree. Example items include, "Students should not be permitted to contradict the statements of their teacher in class," a custodial item, and "Teachers should consider revision of their teaching methods if these are criticized by their pupils," a humanistic item.

Pupil control ideology has been related to both teacher and student characteristics. Teachers who have a more custodial orientation also tend to be more external in their locus of control (Henderson, 1982), more authoritarian and dogmatic in their beliefs, more likely to support corporal punishment, more directive, and less progressive in their educational attitudes (Appleton & Stanwyck, 1996; Nachtschiem & Hoy, 1976; Voege, 1979). Males and secondary school teachers tend to be more custodial than females and elementary teachers (Appleton & Stanwyck, 1996) and prospective teachers with a higher sense of personal teaching efficacy tend to be more humanistic in their pupil control ideology (Enochs, Scharmann, & Riggs, 1995; Woolfolk & Hoy, 1990). Teachers who favor a whole language approach to reading tend to be more humanistic whereas those favoring a phonics approach are more custodial (Morrison, 1997). Greater teacher custodialism is also significantly related to teacher reports of stress and burnout (Lunenburg & Cadavid, 1992) as well as increased student alienation from school and decreased student self-actualization (Diebert & Hoy, 1977; Hoy, 1972). A consistent finding over the past 30 years is that new teachers become more custodial as they gain teaching experience, particularly as a consequence of completing their student teaching (Hoy & Woolfolk, 1990; Packard, 1988; Willower, Eidell, & Hoy, 1967). Some work, however, has failed to replicate this common finding (Knoblauch, 2004; Sewell, 1991).

Beliefs About Discipline Inventory. Based on work by Glickman and Tamashiro (1980), Wolfgang (2001) identified three philosophical orientations toward discipline and classroom management: relationship-listening, confronting-contracting, and rules and consequences. Each philosophy is grounded in different beliefs about the role of adults in child development.

A key belief for the *relationship-listening* philosophy (sometimes called noninterventionist) is humanism. The child is viewed as inherently good. From this perspective, discipline problems in the classroom represent students' struggles to balance their own individual needs with the needs of the class and the curriculum. Struggling students who are engaged in disruptive behavior are seen as needing a compassionate and empathetic adult to listen to—but not necessarily intervene in—their problems. The teacher's task in responding to disruptive behaviors is to help students negotiate their own goals in relation to the needs of others in the class and the requirements of the curriculum. The theories of Carl Rogers (Rogers, 1969; Rogers & Freiberg, 1994) and the classroom management approaches of Thomas Gordon (1974, 1981) and Alfie Kohn (1996) are consistent with the relationship-listening philosophy.

Teachers who endorse *confronting-contracting* strategies (sometimes called interactionalist) likewise view disruptive behavior as a reflection of students' inabilities to manage their own internal needs in relation to the external presses of classroom life. But rather than serving as listeners, teachers who embrace the confronting-contracting perspective see themselves in a socializing role, helping students to understand the nature and importance of external presses (i.e., classroom tasks and rules). The emphasis is on interacting with students to establish shared goals and standards. Thus the confronting-contracting philosophy is consistent with a social learning perspective, with the social psychological theories of Albert Adler, and the classroom management procedures of Dreikurs (1964), Nelson, Lynn, and Glenn (2000), and Glasser (1992).

Finally, teachers who endorse the *rules-consequences* (sometimes called interventionist) philosophy tend to view good behavior as the result of learning through experiencing consequences (rewards and punishments). The teacher decides what behavior is needed and assertively teaches, monitors, and provides consequences—rewarding or punishing behaviors as appropriate. From this perspective, disruptions in the classroom reflect problems with the established system of rules, rewards, practice, and punishments. Such beliefs about management are consistent with Skinnerian theory, applied behavior analysis (Alberto & Troutman, 2006; Skinner, 1953), and the management strategies of Assertive Discipline (Canter & Canter, 2001).

Wolfgang (2001) used the 12-item, forced choice format Beliefs About Discipline Inventory (BDI) to assess philosophical orientation. The measure yields a score for each philosophical orientation. Even though one of the three philosophies is assumed to dominate in most teachers' actions and beliefs, teachers likely hold beliefs that include elements from all three. Little research is available on this measure, though Bailey and Johnson (2000) found that the elementary and secondary student teachers they followed became significantly more interventionist (rules-consequences) and significantly less interactionalist (confronting-contracting) during their student teaching experience. Using a student form of the BDI, Chui and Tulley (1997) found that 4th,-5th,-and 6th-grade students in their study indicated a clear preference for the interactionalist (confronting-contracting) approach.

Attitudes and Beliefs Regarding Classroom Management Style. Whereas the Pupil Control Ideology scale (Willower, Eidell, & Hoy, 1967) and the BDI (Wolfgang, 2001) focus on management as control and discipline, Martin and her colleagues have developed a framework for teacher beliefs about management that conceives of management in broader terms, based on their data indicating that teachers hold differing understandings of what it means to manage the different dimensions of classroom life (Martin, Yin, & Baldwin, 1998). Specifically, teachers tended to view the task of classroom management as composed of behaviors needed to facilitate orderly and organized instruction (*instructional management*), behaviors needed to facilitate the development of supportive student-teacher relationships (*people management*), and the behaviors needed to prevent opportunities for student misbehavior (*behavior management*).

Martin and her colleagues used Wolfgang's Beliefs About Discipline Inventory (previously described) to develop their Attitudes and Beliefs on Classroom Control (ABCC—an earlier version was called the Inventory of Classroom Management Style). This measure assesses teachers' beliefs about the three arenas of managing instruction, managing people, and managing behavior. For each of these three areas, a scale assesses beliefs along a continuum from controlling and interventionist at one extreme to noninterventionist at the other extreme, with interactionalist at the midpoint between the extremes (Martin, Shoho, & Yin, 2003).

In a series of studies, Martin and her colleagues have mapped differences in beliefs about management of instruction, people, and behavior based on teaching setting, teacher gender, and level of experience. For example, Shoho and Martin (1999) found that teachers in an alternate certification training program were significantly more interventionist than traditionally trained teachers on the instructional management scale. Martin and Yin (1997) found that males held significantly higher interventionist beliefs on both the instructional management and behavior management scales. Also, there were relationships between management beliefs and personality characteristics. For example, higher interventionist scores were correlated with higher levels of rule consciousness and perfectionism. Finally, Martin and Yin (1999) found that compared to teachers in urban schools, teachers in rural schools were significantly more controlling and interventionist in their beliefs about instructional management, whereas urban teachers were significantly more interventionist in beliefs about managing people. Thus teachers' beliefs about classroom management appear to be influenced by individual and contextual differences.

Management as Power: Social and Political Perspectives. Johnson, Whitington, and Oswald (1994) observed that teachers hold diverse opinions and beliefs about such basic questions as: How should students behave at school? Why should students behave in these ways? What strategies are appropriate to ensure students behave in these ways? Why do some students not behave in these ways at school? Who should decide these matters? A concern underlying these questions is, "Who determines how students should behave and who insures this behavior?" In other words, who has the power?

Johnson and his colleagues (1994) reported on a series of studies in Australia that map teachers' perceptions about the frequency and severity of and reactions to discipline problems. Over 3,400 teachers answered open-ended questions, producing an 80,000-word transcript. Reading and rereading the transcripts, the researchers concluded that "much of what teachers believed and thought about discipline went beyond psychological, and even classroom related considerations" (p. 263). In the transcripts were ideas about values, families, society, government, power, regulations, and economics. Based on their analyses of the teachers' responses to the open-ended questions, Johnson and his colleagues identified four orientations to discipline: traditional, liberal progressive, socially critical, and laissez-faire, as shown in Table 8.1.

TABLE 8.1
An Overview of Four Orientations to School Discipline

View of	*Traditional*	*Liberal Progressive*	*Socially Critical*	*Laissez-Faire*
Desired Student Behavior	Follow instructions/obey rules. Accept outside authority and power inequities.	Cooperate; negotiate and compromise in conflicts. Apply democratic processes Accept personal responsibility.	Challenge inequalities and undemocratic power relations. Challenge repression, protect rights of powerless. Collaborate for social justice.	Self-actualization Inner harmony True self discipline
Why Children Should Behave in These Ways	Order is essential for academic learning. Prepares student for hierarchical world of work. Respect for law & order necessary for social stability.	Social skills necessary for life and harmony in society. Negotiating goals and resolving conflict are necessary for functioning in democracy.	Collaboration needed to challenge repressive school practices. Prepares students to act morally and justly in wider society.	Everyone needs to be free and personally fulfilled.
Assumptions About the "Innate" Nature of Children	All children have propensity to misbehave if not restrained by external (adult) forces.	Children are inherently good. Social skills will develop in a supportive environment.	Children are neither good nor bad. Their behavior is influenced by alienating, undemocratic exercise of social power	Children are inherently good. Children can achieve self-actualization if given choices and freedom to pursue them.
Role of the Teacher	Promote central authority of the school in discipline. Enforce school rules and policies.	Organize class activities so students develop social and collaborative skills. Share decision making with responsible students.	Negotiate responsibilities and roles with students. Support democratic structures and power sharing. Act as organizer and resource during collaborations about disciplinary activities. Reject status/power hierarchies.	Provide stimulating learning environment. Offer choices consistent with students' interests. Emphasize freedom of choice and expression. Reject status/power hierarchies.

Parents' Role	Accept and support school authority and discipline policies. Enforce school rules (dress, attendance, homework, etc.)	Support and participate in democratic decision making with students and teachers. Promote negotiation and collaboration to resolve problems. Reject punitive discipline.	Support and participate in democratic decision making with students and teachers. Promote community action and social justice to overcome inequalities→ real cause of student discontent.	Support school in creating a free learning environment.
Location of Power	Adults, in formal authority positions. Hierarchy of authority with students at bottom.	Power is shared among stakeholders—negotiation rather than exercise of power. Locus of power is within individual.	Groups hold power. Exercise of group power is justified to oppose inequalities.	Locus of power is within individual; power to chose. Rejection of power of others to control or direct.
Claimed Strengths	Clear and explicit expectations, rules. Predictable, practical. Supported by community.	Democratic, reasonable, humane. Leads to interpersonal harmony. Accepted by "caring" professions.	Emancipatory and reformist. Allows complex analysis of causes of misbehavior. Based on democratic and social justice principles.	Respects human dignity and free choice. Promotes self- discipline and psychological well-being.
Common Criticisms	Authoritarian, repressive, outmoded in collaborative societies; fosters conformity. Does not teach self-discipline. Inflexible and mechanistic.	Lacks firmness and direction. Difficult to implement. Does not prepare students for life in hierarchical society. Focuses on individual, not social-political context of behavior.	Idealistic, impractical; no help with day-to-day misbehaviors. Based on dialects of social conflict. Too radical to gain family support	Socially irresponsible. Focuses on individual, not social-political context of behavior. Fails to provide students with needed guidance. Mystical and romantic.
Advocates	Canter & Canter; Skinner	Dreikurs; Glasser	Foucault	Rogers

Note: Adapted with permission from "Teacher's views of school discipline: A theoretical framework," by B. Johnson, V. Whitington, and M. Oswald, 1994, *Cambridge Journal of Education, 24*, pp. 266–267, Taylor & Frances Ltd, http://www.tandf.co.uk/journals.

Teachers who hold a *traditional* orientation have many beliefs in common with the custodial Pupil Control Ideology (Willower, Eidell, & Hoy, 1967), and the rules-consequences (sometimes called interventionist) philosophy as assessed by Wolfgang's (2001) BDI. "Tough but fair" characterizes their stance. The teacher quoted at opening of this chapter was one of the traditionalists in the Johnson et al. study. Such teachers believe in strict adherence to rules, a fair and escalating set of punishments for infractions, and the teacher as the authority. Relationships are professional and hierarchical. Students are expected to follow rules and respect authorities so that the class will be orderly and students will be prepared for their future roles as workers and citizens.

Teachers with a *liberal progressive* orientation believe that democratic principles should apply in all social situations, including schools and classrooms. Students should share power and be part of the decision-making process. Communication is seen as two-way and there is less emphasis on hierarchical relationships and more concern with cooperation. Teaching social skills is part of the job to prepare students for collaboration both in class and in their future work and, as well, for participation in a democratic society.

Teachers who hold a *socially critical* stance (though Johnson et al. found few) see student disruption as resistance against unfair or repressive practices of schools. Within this view, the schools create many of the so-called discipline problems by the way they treat students. Socially critical teachers particularly felt that management problems could indicate that the curriculum was inappropriate for the students.

Johnson et al. included the *laissez-faire* orientation in their analyses to make the framework conceptually complete but they found no teachers who embraced this stance. The researchers attributed the failure to embrace laissez-faire beliefs to the highly organized and structured nature of the Australian government educational system.

As is the case with most typologies, few real people adhere completely to only one type. Most teachers hold beliefs from several orientations, depending on the situation, even though one perspective tends to dominate their thinking and actions. Johnson et al. found that the vast majority of the 3,400 teachers in their study were either traditional or liberal progressive. About 70% of secondary teachers were traditionalist and the remainder mostly liberal progressive, whereas about 67% of elementary teachers held liberal progressive views with roughly 30% traditional. In the primary grades (below grade 2), about 90% of the teachers were liberal progressive. They saw a major part of their role to be socializing students. Of all the teachers, only 2% to 3% affirmed the socially critical stance and none the laissez-faire view.

Management as Socialization. Role definitions are teachers' "general beliefs about what they should accomplish as teachers and what tasks and functions they will need to perform in order to do so" (Brophy, 1996, p. 433). Two key aspects of the teacher role are instruction and socialization. As evident in the Australian studies described earlier, teachers of young children tend to see their role as socializers; teaching social skills and values is part of their job. In their study of K–6 teachers' perceptions of problem students, Brophy and McCaslin (1992) found that some teachers described themselves as emphasizing instruction, whereas others saw themselves as more focused on socializing students. These differences in role definition were reflected in the teachers' classroom management strategies (Brophy, 1996), as noted in Table 8.2. Even though there were distinct differences between instructors and socializers in their reactions to problem students, there were no distinct differences in effectiveness between the two groups.

Clearly, elementary grade teachers have more opportunities to act as socializers, because they see the same 20 to 30 students at work and play all year. High school teachers, as subject matter specialists, are less likely to have opportunities to socialize students; but the pod, team, community, or school-within-a-school arrangements in middle and even high schools put

TABLE 8.2
Teachers' Role Definitions and Management Strategies

	Instructors	*Socializers*
Guiding Principles	Being a fair and consistent authority figure Establishing a learning environment. Students as learners	Being patient and loving with children Building personal relationships with students to promote positive classroom behaviors
Focused on Helping Students Who Were	Distractible, immature, shy or withdrawn	Underachieving, hostile-aggressive, defiant
Strategies	Brief messages to persuade, criticize, set limits Make demands to improve behavior, without teaching coping skills—less time spent attempting to change or prevent behavior or change attitude	Extensive interventions to improve behaviors, prevent problems, change attitudes Rewards, public "diagnosing" of problem, peer pressure, tension-release techniques, changing the physical or social environment, grilling and counseling, teaching social skills
Assumed Causes of Misbehavior	Students not paying attention or following rules	Poor parenting, social environment, teacher errors, student lack of skills

Adapted from *Teaching problem students* (pp. 434–435), by J. E. Brophy, 1996, New York: Guilford Press. pp. 434-435.

more secondary teachers in the role of socializers. Of course, there are individual differences in teachers' beliefs about the value of the socializing role and some teachers are more skilled or more temperamentally suited to be socializers. Even so, Brophy (1996) describes evidence that there are more behavior problems in schools where teachers immediately refer problem students to administrators and take little responsibility for helping the students improve their behaviors. Thus assuming some aspects of the socializer role seems to prevent behavior problems.

Management as Controlling Versus Supporting Autonomy. An orientation toward classroom management described by Deci and his colleagues (Deci & Ryan, 1985; Deci, Schwartz, Sheinman, & Ryan, 1981; Deci, Vallerand, Pelletier, & Ryan, 1991) has much in common with the view of management as socializing. Deci conceptualizes orientations toward solving social and behavioral problems in school along a continuum from controlling to autonomous. Teachers who decide on a solution to classroom problems and then use rewards or sanctions to ensure that their solutions are implemented have a highly controlling orientation. Moderately controlling in their perspectives are teachers who solve classroom problems and then try to get students to implement them by invoking guilt or emphasizing that it is for the student's own good. Autonomy begins when teachers encourage students to use social comparison information (to see what other students are doing) in an attempt to solve problems. Finally, when teachers encourage students to consider the various elements of the problem and arrive at a solution for themselves, the teachers' orientation is highly supportive of autonomy. These teachers are, in effect, socializing students to be independent and self-regulating.

Deci et al. (1981) developed the Problems in School (PS) questionnaire to assess teachers' beliefs about control and autonomy support. This instrument contains eight different vignettes describing typical school problems, along with four possible solutions for each dilemma. The four solutions reflect a highly controlling (HC), moderately controlling (MC), moderately autonomous (MA), or highly autonomous (HA) solution to the problem. Respondents are asked to rate each of the four solutions for each of the eight problems on a 7-point scale from "very inappropriate" (1) to "very appropriate" (7). The instrument yields a subscale score for HC, MC, MA, and HA as well as a total score; the higher the total score the more the respondent favors encouraging autonomy in children. Research by Reeve and his colleagues (Reeve, Bolt, & Cai, 1999) suggested possible modifications in the scoring of the PS, but also provided evidence for the validity of the measure. Both preservice and practicing teachers who had higher autonomy scores on the PS behaved in more autonomy-supporting ways in the classroom. Even though both controlling- and autonomy-supporting teachers reported using similar instructional approaches, such as gaining students' attention, asking questions and giving feedback, setting and enforcing limits, assessing performance, and demonstrating skills and procedures, there was a difference. Controlling teachers sought student compliance and set sanctions to ensure compliance, whereas autonomy-supporting teachers sought student initiative and input.

Research has identified a number of other factors associated with teachers' beliefs about control and autonomy support. Teachers can be influenced in their views by situational factors such as models who are either autonomy supporting or controlling (Williams & Deci, 1998), students who are disengaged (Skinner & Belmont, 1993), and external pressures to follow a curriculum or reach certain performance standards (Pelletier, Seguin-Levesque, & Legault, 2002; Reeve et al., 1999). Even with these situational influences, a teacher's motivational style is relatively stable across time, but individual differences may play a role. Reeve et al. (1999) found that women and liberals were more autonomy supporting in their responses to the PS questionnaire.

Management and Choices. Studies of self-regulation (Zimmerman, 2000), student self-efficacy (Bandura, 1993, 1997), and intrinsic motivation (Cordova & Lepper, 1996) suggest that students' sense of having control in the classroom—of having and making choices—is associated with positive student outcomes, such as engagement and learning. With the exception of a few studies by Jolivette and her colleagues, however, indicating that female preschool students and students without disabilities are offered more choices (Jolivette, Stitcher, Sibilsky, Scott, & Ridley, 2002), and that choice has generally positive effects on student engagement and participation for students with behavioral disorders (Jolivette, Wehby, Canale, & Massey, 2001), there is little research that directly examines the effects of choice. After reviewing the studies available, Flowerday and Schraw (2000) determined that the results are mixed: "The main conclusion to emerge from this research is that choice positively effects affect but has little impact on performance" (p. 635).

There is even less research (outside of the work on controlling and autonomy-supporting motivational styles) that directly examines teachers' beliefs about choice. Flowerday and Schraw (2000) set as their main purpose to codify teachers' beliefs about choice, specifically, what kinds of choices do teachers offer, when and to whom, and what effects do teachers perceive follow from giving students choices. After conducting in-depth interviews with 36 teachers (8 from grades K–5 elementary and 28 from grades 6–12 secondary), the researchers concluded that teachers offer choices in six main categories: topic of study, reading materials or project focus (most frequent), methods of assessment, order of activities, social arrangements such as seating or group membership, and procedural choices such as when to complete assignments and in what order to cover topics. In terms of effects of and reasons for choice, the teachers believed:

- Offering choices improves students' affective responses to classroom tasks and their motivation by increasing their "ownership," creativity, interest, and autonomy.

- If carefully used, choice can improve student-teacher relationships by communicating the teachers' confidence in student ability to self-regulate.
- Choice improves students' cognitive processes such as attention, strategy use, and decision-making.
- Choice must be incorporated wisely because students may be overwhelmed by too many choices or may lack the maturity needed to make good choices. Also, less motivated and able students may choose to take the easiest path.
- In deciding whom to give the most choice, age, ability, and prior knowledge should be taken into consideration, with older, more able and more knowledgeable students given more choices.
- Even given the above, many teachers felt that there should be some equity in opportunities for choice because younger and less able students need experiences with choices.

Sweet, Guthrie & Ng (1998) concluded that teachers seem to hold an implicit theory that is consistent with Deci's work: Students will become more self-determining and self-regulating when they are allowed to work cooperatively and encouraged to attribute success to effort (Nolen & Nicholls, 1994) and when they engage in activity-based tasks that "pique their interest and enable them to make choices within the boundaries set by the teacher in defining instructional tasks" (Sweet et al., 1998, p. 221). But Flowerday and Schraw (2000) found that these teacher beliefs about choice were not always consistent with their actions. Even though teachers in their study believed that choice develops self-determination (consistent with Deci's theory and the findings of Sweet et al.), paradoxically the teachers acted as if students must earn choices by first being self-determining. Thus, the teachers gave choices after self-determination was demonstrated instead of using choices to develop self-determination.

Perceived Value of Different Management Strategies

In the school psychology literature, one research focus is on the acceptability of behavioral treatment interventions, particularly interventions that are developed in a consultative relationship between teachers and school psychologists. Many of these studies have used hypothetical situations to question teachers about the acceptability of various treatment interventions. A study by Witt, Elliott, and Martens (1984), for example, found that the amount of time needed to plan and implement behavioral interventions significantly influenced the acceptability of classroom management techniques; more specifically, higher levels of time involvement are less acceptable to teachers. In addition, some consistent findings reported by Eckert and Hintze (2000) are: (a) positive interventions (praise, tokens, rewards, etc.) are seen as more acceptable than negative (time out, loss or privileges, etc.) and (b) the more severe the child's problem, the more acceptable is the intervention. These findings are limited, because using hypothetical situations lacks ecological validity; nonetheless, they are consistent with Brophy and McCaslin's (1992) findings that teachers prefer methods that are neutral or positive/supportive over interventions that are negative/punitive.

A recent investigation by Cowan and Sheridan (2003) assessed the beliefs of teachers involved in actual teacher/school psychologist consultations that were focused on developing interventions for 67 students who had academic, social, or behavioral problems that interfered with their learning. Four types of interventions were considered—notes home; student self-monitoring; academic or social skills training and tutoring; and reductive consequences, such as time out, loss of privileges, or ignoring student misbehavior. Results indicated that there were no significant differences among the four kinds of interventions in terms of teacher acceptability ratings. In fact, all four types of interventions were rated above 5.4 on a 6-point scale. In addition, perceived problem severity was related to acceptability ratings for the interventions;

as severity increased so did intervention acceptability, with severity accounting for 16% of the variance in teacher acceptability ratings and problem complexity adding nothing to the prediction of acceptability. Thus, across both simulated and actual classroom problem situations, teachers tend to be more accepting of behaviorally based interventions as the perceptions of the severity of the student problem increases.

Brophy and McCaslin (1992) found that punishment (sometimes even physical punishment) and control-oriented strategies were seen as appropriate for hostile-aggressive, disruptive, and defiant students whereas sympathetic, help-oriented strategies were suggested for shy, anxious, rejected, or low-achieving students. The most common kinds of negative strategies were reminders of the rules and expectations, threats to punish, and actual punishments. Surveying preservice teachers, Gaffney (1997) found that physical punishment was a last resort, to be used rarely and only for serious problems.

Reasons and Attributions for Student Misbehavior

A number of researchers have studied teachers' beliefs about reasons for student misbehavior. The early work of Adler posited that the central motivation for all people is to be accepted by a social group. Based on Adler's work, Dreikurs wrote a number of books for parents and teachers suggesting that even children's misbehaviors are purposeful attempts to achieve social recognition (Wolfgang, 2001). In contrast, McCaslin and Good (1998) listed not one but six possible reasons for misbehavior. The student may be: lonely or scared; out of control or hostile; attempting to save face or at a loss for what to do; bored, frustrated, or unsuccessful in attempts to learn; physiologically in pain, sleep deprived, in withdrawal; or distracted by peers, events, or memories. Clearly the range of possible causes is great.

Attributions. One well-developed area of research focuses on teachers' attributions for the causes of students' academic or behavioral successes and failures. Attributions are the explanations given for successes and failures—the assumed causes. Bernard Weiner is one of the main educational psychologists responsible for relating attribution theory to school learning (Weiner, 1986, 2000). According to Weiner, most of the attributed causes for successes or failures can be characterized in terms of three dimensions: (1) *locus* (location of the cause internal or external to the person); (2) *stability* (whether the cause stays the same or can change), and (3) *controllability* (whether the person can control the cause). For example, luck is external, unstable, and uncontrollable, whereas typical effort is internal, stable, and controllable.

In terms of locus, Athanasiou, Geil, Hazel, & Copeland (2002) found that the teachers in their case studies made both internal and external attributions about the causes of the student problem behaviors addressed in the consultations with school psychologists, but the primary focus was internal. "These teachers appeared to make more internal than external attributions about the causes of behavioral difficulties. The explanations included skill deficits, academic differences, low self-esteem, and other psychological problems" (p. 279). The external factor mentioned most was the home. Teachers talked about unstable homes, single-parent households, only-child status, or immature parents. Beliefs about needed interventions were consistent with the attributions. Because the teachers saw most of the problems as caused by "something inside" the students, the teachers suggested therapy and trying to get students to take ownership of the problems. Consistent with attributions to family causes, family therapy was also recommended.

Johnson et al. (1994) in their large-scale survey of Australian teachers also found that teachers looked outside the classroom and the student for the causes of problem behaviors. A common attribution was to changing societal values. One teacher captured this belief: "I think that discipline is strongly affected by the stability and value system of society at large. The current generation of children is under the guidance of parents and teachers whose values and techniques of discipline are often confused, idealistic, and over-indulged" (p. 263). Other teachers complained that discipline problems were caused when state-supported discipline programs took power away from parents and schools to discipline as they saw fit.

If the teacher views the causes of student misbehavior as controllable by the student, then the student is seen as responsible for the outcome, and the teacher is more likely to feel anger or frustration. Such attributions and emotions are more often associated with a punitive response. In the terms of Reyna and Weiner (2001), the goals set by the teacher are more likely to be retributive. In contrast, if the misbehavior is attributed to a cause the student could not control, then the teacher is more likely to feel sympathetic and set a utilitarian goal—perhaps helping the student learn more appropriate behaviors.

The stability dimension of attributions plays a role as well, because stable causes are assumed to persist. If teachers attribute students' failures to stable factors, such as chronic laziness, they will expect students to fail in that subject in the future. But if they attribute the outcome to unstable factors, such as mood or lack of social skills, then teachers can hope for better outcomes next time. So even if misbehavior is attributed to an uncontrollable cause and the teacher is sympathetic, if the cause is seen as stable, the teacher may see some utilitarian goals as unreachable. For example, if misbehavior is attributed to severe learning disabilities, the teacher may reject some possible utilitarian goals that seem unattainable. The teacher's sense of efficacy (described later) may affect goals as well. Teachers with a greater sense of efficacy for classroom management should be more likely to use utilitarian interventions rather than simply punish students for transgressions. In a study of college students and teachers, Reyna and Weiner (2001) found support for this model of teacher attributions. They concluded: "The attributions teachers make for students' failure determine the goals of teachers' responses to failing students; that is, whether their responses will be utilitarian or punitive in intention" (p. 316).

In sum, when teachers assume that student failure is attributable to forces beyond the students' control, they tend to respond with sympathy and to avoid giving punishments. If, however, the failures are attributed to a controllable factor, such as lack of effort, the teacher's response is more likely to be anger; retribution and punishments may follow (Reyna & Weiner, 2001; Stipek, 1996, 2003). These tendencies seem to be consistent across time and cultures (Weiner, 1986). The differences in teacher responses based on attributions and the emotions that follow are in keeping with other research on adult-child interactions. Brophy (1996) reviewed a number of studies and concluded: "Thus adults tend to respond with concern, assistance, and attempts at long-term solutions when children's problems do not threaten or irritate them; but they respond with anger, rejection, and emphasis on short term control or punishment when they do" (p. 431).

Problem Ownership and Teacher Beliefs. In a large study of teachers' responses to problem student behaviors, Brophy and McCaslin (1992) found that teachers' reactions to and beliefs about the student behavior depended on the type of problem, specifically the problem "ownership" (Gordon, 1974, 1981). According to Gordon, if a student's behavior has a serious effect on the teacher—if the teacher is blocked from reaching goals by the student's action—then the teacher owns the problem. Examples of teacher-owned problems are defiant students and students who fail because they put forward little or no effort. In these situations, the students' actions threaten the teacher's need for authority and control. If the teacher is concerned by the student's behavior because it is getting in the student's way, but the behavior does not directly interfere with teaching, then it is the student's problem. Examples of student owned-problems are struggling low-achieving students or highly anxious students who are putting forth good effort, but still having trouble learning. If the student's behavior does not directly threaten the teacher's authority, but does create management problems for the teacher, then it is a shared problem; for example, students with hyperactive disorders who have great difficulty sitting still and paying attention in class are examples of shared problems (Brophy, 1996).

When faced with teacher-owned problems, the participants in Brophy and McCaslin's study (98 K–6th-grade teachers) saw the student misbehavior as intentional. They were pessimistic about making any stable improvements in the students' behaviors and tended to rely on demands and punishment threats, often without rationales, to simply control the misbehavior. When the problem was student-owned, teachers were more confident that they could help students change. The teachers saw the students as victims of outside forces and viewed the students' misbehavior as unintentional and ultimately controllable. Responses to this kind of problem included support and engagement with the students to teach them new ways of behaving and new attitudes about themselves. Finally, when problems were seen as shared, the emphasis was also on long-term goals for behavior change, but there was less talking with students and more environmental engineering or behavior contracting. Teachers tended to see these shared problems as student responses to particular situations, so some of the teacher strategies focused on changing the situations.

Beliefs About Self: Self-Efficacy for Classroom Management

Teacher efficacy is defined as "the extent to which the teacher believes he or she has the capacity to affect student performance" (Berman, McLaughlin, Bass, Pauly, & Zellman, 1977, p. 137), or as "teachers' belief or conviction that they can influence how well students learn, even those who may be difficult or unmotivated" (Guskey & Passaro, 1994, p. 4). (For a complete discussion of teacher efficacy, see Tschannen-Moran, Woolfolk Hoy, & Hoy, 1998). Among practicing teachers, efficacy is one of the few teacher characteristics consistently related to student achievement (Armor et al., 1976; Ashton, 1985; Ashton & Webb, 1986; Berman et al., 1977). Higher efficacy also has been related to teachers' willingness to implement innovations (Berman et al., 1977; Guskey, 1984; Smylie, 1988), decreased teacher stress (Parkay, Greenwood, Olejnik, & Proller, 1988; Greenwood, Olejnik, & Parkay, 1990), less negative affect in teaching (Ashton, Olejnik, Crocker, & McAuliffe, 1982), and teachers' willingness to stay in the field (Glickman & Tamashiro, 1982). A strong sense of efficacy can support higher motivation, greater effort, persistence, and resilience across the span of a teaching career (Gibson & Dembo, 1984; Tschannen-Moran et al., 1998). Once established, efficacy beliefs seem resistant to change, even when the teachers are exposed to workshops and new teaching methods (Ross, 1994).

Sense of Efficacy and Classroom Management. In terms of classroom management, the efficacy beliefs of preservice teachers have been linked to attitudes towards children and control, as measured by the Pupil Control Ideology form (Willower, et al., 1967). Prospective teachers with a low sense of teacher efficacy tended to have an orientation toward custodial control, taking a pessimistic view of students' motivation, relying on strict classroom regulations, extrinsic rewards, and punishments to make students study (Woolfolk & Hoy, 1990). Once engaged in student teaching, efficacy beliefs also have an impact on behavior. Student interns with higher personal teaching efficacy were rated more positively on lesson presenting behavior, classroom management, and questioning behavior by their supervising teachers on their practicum evaluations (Saklofske, Michayluk, & Randhawa, 1988).

Among practicing teachers, compared to low-efficacy teachers, those who report a higher sense of efficacy spend less time working with small groups, are more active in monitoring seatwork and maintaining academic focus, respond quickly to student misbehavior by redirecting attention without showing anger or becoming threatened, and generally evidence greater "withitness." Low-efficacy teachers are more likely to criticize students and be less persistent in following up on student wrong answers (Ashton & Webb, 1986; Gibson & Dembo, 1984; Saklofske, et al., 1988).

Assessing Management Efficacy. One of the fundamental notions about efficacy is that it is situation and task specific (Bandura, 1997). Early measures of teachers' sense of efficacy such as Gibson and Dembo's (1984) Teacher Efficacy Scale (TES) were more global and not useful in studying teachers' beliefs about their capabilities to manage classrooms. In an attempt to develop an instrument that better reflected the domain of classroom management, Emmer and Hickman (1991) adapted the widely used Gibson and Dembo instrument, yielding a 36-item measure with three efficacy subscales: efficacy for classroom management and discipline, external influences, and personal teaching efficacy. Among a sample of preservice teachers, the efficacy subscales were correlated with preferences for using positive strategies for classroom management, that is, strategies aimed at increasing or encouraging desirable student responses through praise, encouragement, attention, and rewards (Emmer, 1990; Emmer & Hickman, 1991).

The model of teacher efficacy presented by Tschannen-Moran et al. (1998) includes classroom management as one dimension. This conception suggests that teachers' efficacy judgments are the result of the interaction between a personal appraisal of the relative importance of factors that make teaching difficult (analysis of teaching task and its context) and an assessment of self-perceptions of personal teaching capabilities (analysis of teaching competence). The resultant efficacy judgments would impact the goals teachers set for themselves, the effort they invest in reaching these goals, and their persistence when facing difficulties. Considering the components of the model, Tschannen-Moran and Woolfolk Hoy (2001) developed the Teachers' Sense of Efficacy Scale (TSES), in which items describe the types of tasks representative of frequent teaching activities. With inservice and preservice teachers as samples, they reported three dimensions of teaching efficacy: efficacy for student engagement, efficacy for instructional strategies, and efficacy for classroom management. An example for each dimension was "How much can you do to motivate students who show low interest in school work?" "How much can you use a variety of assessment strategies?" and "How much can you do to control disruptive behavior in the classroom?" respectively. This instrument allows researchers to explore teacher efficacy for classroom management in the context of other efficacy judgments.

Novice Teachers. It is possible that the "unrealistic optimism" of beginning teachers interferes with their ability to accurately judge their own effectiveness, particularly their ability to manage classes. In an analysis of students who were about to begin their student teaching, Weinstein (1988) found a strong sense of "unrealistic optimism"—the tendency to believe that problems experienced by others would not happen to them. Interestingly, the unrealistic optimism was greatest for activities having to do with controlling students (e.g., maintaining discipline and establishing and enforcing class rules). These findings are consistent with Emmer's (1990) observations that student teachers who had trouble managing their classes still reported high levels of classroom management efficacy.

Numerous case studies indicate that novice teachers frequently experience a conflict between wanting to care and needing to control (McLaughlin, 1991). Marilyn, for example, a first-year fifth-grade teacher (Crow, 1991) strove to create a "haven" characterized by security and love, but she had no "idea what to do about discipline. . . . " (p. 7). In the face of chaos, Marilyn struggled to reconcile her desire to be a haven-maker with her need to enforce rules and consequences. Similarly, Lyle (Bullough & Knowles, 1990), a math and science teacher in junior high school, hoped to establish caring relationships with his students, but constant challenges to his authority left him in turmoil: "I experience . . . a constant conflict between being personal and positive, on the one hand, and being distant and consistent on the other." As Bullough and Knowles observe, "He saw no middle ground" (p. 106).

These and other studies (e.g., Bullough, 1987; Rust, 1992) suggest that novice teachers tend to think of caring and order in mutually exclusive terms. This interpretation was investigated in a study by Weinstein (1998), which found that prospective teachers hold relatively narrow, dichotomous conceptions of both caring and order: Order is achieved through specific managerial strategies (e.g., establishing rules), while caring is demonstrated by nurturing, willingness to listen, and accessibility. Weinstein concluded that prospective teachers need to understand the ways that positive interpersonal relationships and engaging, well-orchestrated lessons contribute to order. They also need to appreciate that caring can be enacted by teaching well and by creating safe, orderly classrooms.

CONCLUSIONS

It is not surprising that students and teachers have different beliefs about management; they have different roles, goals, concerns, and powers in the classroom. We first contrast the beliefs of these classroom participants, and then consider implications for classroom practice. We end with some thoughts about future research.

Convergences and Divergences Between Teacher and Student Beliefs

Table 8.3 compares the beliefs of students and teachers. A qualification is in order, however. We found very few studies that examined both students' and teachers' perspectives in the same study, so what follows is gleaned from separate investigations of these participants' views and thus is somewhat speculative. The research on student beliefs has been more recent. Methods tend to be qualitative; ethnographies, interviews, and case studies dominate. The research on teacher beliefs about classroom management began in the mid-1900s and tends to be quantitative; surveys, questionnaires, and the development of measurement procedures dominate, though interviews and case studies are available as well. Results of these lines of research show clear divergences in many areas, but some similarities as well. We begin with the possible sources of conflict.

Concerns and Focus. The student voices in the research describe their desire for supportive relationships with teachers. When asked about good teachers, students focus on personal and relational dimensions (Alder & Moulton, 1998; Allen, 1995; Cothran & Ennis, 2000; Crowley, 1993; Davidson, 1999; Ellis, 1997; Pomeroy, 1999; Schlosser, 1992; Wentzel, 1997). Good teachers care. This caring is manifest, students believe, when teachers are concerned about the students' academic, social, and personal lives, as 12-year-old Terry's quote at the beginning of the chapter makes clear. Relationships are central, particularly for students who are alienated or marginalized (Davidson, 1999; Katz, 1999).

In contrast, teachers are more focused on order and on academic concerns—they want students to cooperate in class activities and perform well on assessments (Johnson et al., 1994). And even when using behavioral interventions, teachers may not be satisfied unless there is academic as well as behavioral improvement (Athanasiou et al., 2002). Compliance is a common teacher goal for disciplinary interventions, as the teacher quoted at the beginning of the chapter emphasizes.

Desired Relationships. Students seek choices in their schoolwork and respect, affection, trust, a listening ear, patience, and humor in their relationships with teachers (Bosworth, 1995; Habel et al., 1999; Phelan et al., 1992, 1994; Wentzel, 1997). Frequently, students' decisions about whether or not to cooperate are based on their liking for the teacher. As a student in a

TABLE 8.3
Teacher/Student Beliefs: Comparisons of Methods and Findings

Methods and Finding	*Students*	*Teachers*
Research Methods	Ethnographic studies presenting student voice	Questionnaires and surveys identifying types and orientations
Concerns and Focus	Relationships, personal support	Pedagogy, academic learning support
Desired Relationship	Give me respect, responsibility, autonomy with fair limits	Give me cooperation, respect the rules, and my authority
Individual and Developmental Differences and Needs	Low achieving and marginalized, alienated students → care and help with personal problems	Focus on improving behavior, academics
	Mainstream and successful students → help with academics	
	Moving toward middle-high school → more autonomy	Reward with choices
		Moving toward middle-high school, less autonomy
Key Distinctions	Strict vs. mean	Misbehavior intentional, irritating, controllable vs. unintentional, uncontrollable
		Socializer teachers favored "public diagnosing," grilling
	No public reprimands or embarrassment	Students should be treated the same because they will notice and not accept differences.
	Differential treatment of students is OK, as long as not racist	
What is Good Classroom Management?	Care for and respect me first, give me choices, then I will cooperate, keep order but don't be mean, racist, or sexist	Cooperate with me first, then I will care and give choices; I may have to be mean to keep order—it's my job.
Differential Treatment	Don't like to feel managed, controlled	Feel responsible for managing, controlling, especially under threat
Good Learning Environment	Fun, engagement	Cooperation, engagement

study by Stinson (1993) commented: "If I don't like 'em . . . I'm not gonna do anything for 'em" (p. 221). Studies examining students' perceptions of teachers who are worthy of respect and cooperation converge on teachers who are caring yet provide limits, who have high behavioral and academic expectations yet structure lessons that incorporate students' needs and interests (e.g., Dillon, 1989).

Teachers, on the other hand, look for respect for authority (particularly their authority), cooperation, and compliance with school and classroom rules and procedures (Johnson et al., 1994; McCaslin & Good, 1998). When threatened by student misbehavior, teachers often become more custodial in their discipline styles (Hoy, 2001). But research suggests that the use of "get tough" sanctions and external controls may be counterproductive (Smith et al., 1987).

Individual and Developmental Needs. Even though all students indicate a desire for caring teachers, students who are marginalized particularly value personal caring. They want teachers who care about their home lives, welfare, personal problems, and futures—teachers who keep them out of trouble (Bosworth, 1995; Cothran & Ennis, 2000; Davidson, 1999). Successful students, in contrast, are more likely to value teachers who help them with their academic work and help them get good grades, though they want the respect of the teacher as well.

Teachers, however, are more likely to ignore personal relations and focus on improving the behavior and academic performance of alienated students (Brophy, 1996), or the teachers may decide that these students cannot be reached at all and simply demand compliance. With more successful students, teachers tend to give choices and responsibilities, with less insistence on rule compliance (Flowerday & Schraw, 2000). In other words, teachers may communicate more caring to successful students.

As students mature, during the middle and high school years, they are increasingly ready for autonomy—eager to make more choices and assume more responsibility for their learning. But, paradoxically, as they move to middle school and high school, more elements of their education are set and specified. There are curriculum and course requirements, school rules and policies that define their behavior in school buildings and sports facilities, on buses and field trips. Moreover, teachers often see adolescents as attempting or needing to distance themselves from adults to establish their own identity (Jarvis, Schonert-Reichl, & Krivel-Zacks, 2000). It may be that, in response to holding this stereotype, teachers engage in distancing behaviors, believing that they are responding to adolescents' needs. For example, Finders (1997, p. 29) found, "junior high teachers often construct a role that is less personal and more guarded." Oldfather and Thomas (1998; see also Oldfather & McLaughlin, 1993) argue this cultural stereotype of adolescence as a time of turmoil not only undermines the quality of relationships at the middle school level but also between high school students and teachers. Thus students who need more choice and stronger relationships with teachers may get neither as they move toward the secondary grades.

Key Distinctions. Students distinguish between teachers who are reasonably strict in their limit setting versus mean, punitive, and unreasonable (Weinstein, 2003). Students respect teachers who set fair rules to protect student safety and support the learning environment, who use humor and a light touch to get students back on track, and who do not publicly reprimand or embarrass them (e.g., Alder & Moulton, 1998; Davidson, 1999; Phelan et al., 1992; Pomeroy, 1999; Schlosser, 1992; Stinson, 1993; Thorson, 1996; Wallace, 1996). In addition, students accept that, to be fair and supportive, sometimes teachers must treat students differently (Fulk & Smith, 1995). This does not apply, however, to differential treatment because of racism and favoritism. Qualitative studies (Katz, 1996, 1999; Sheets, 1996, 2002) consistently demonstrate that students of color perceive injustices in disciplinary practices and complain that attempts to defend or explain their behaviors are ignored or interpreted as defiance.

Teachers, on the other hand, make important distinctions between the causes and intentions of student behaviors. When teachers assume that student misbehavior is attributable to forces beyond the students' control, they tend to respond with sympathy and to avoid giving punishments. If, however, the failures are attributed to a controllable factor, such as lack of effort, the teacher's response is more likely to be anger, retribution, and punishment (Reyna & Weiner, 2001; Stipek, 1996, 2003). Further, Brophy (1996) found that teachers who saw their role as socializers often suggested using "public diagnosing," and "third-degree grilling" to handle students who were underachieving, hostile, aggressive, or defiant. Public diagnosing included describing the student's intentions and behavior in an attempt to embarrass the student or communicate to that student and the whole class that "You can't fool me; I know what you are doing" (Brophy, 1996, p. 425). Finally, regarding differential treatment of students, Fulk and Smith (1995) speculated: "teachers may be more concerned about equal treatment of students than students are" (p. 416).

What Is Good Classroom Management? We can bring together these contrasts into one final comparison of students' and teachers' conceptions of good classroom management. Good classroom management for students requires a fair and reasonable system of classroom rules and procedures that protect and respect students. Teachers are expected to care for the students, their learning and their personal lives, before the students will respect and cooperate with the teachers. Students want teachers to maintain order without being mean or punitive, and the students may not mind differential treatment as long as there is no racism, sexism, classism, or favoritism. As they mature, students value choices and chances for responsibilities—they do not want to feel coerced or controlled.

Teachers, in contrast, seem to believe that students need to earn their respect, relationship, concern, and interest—in a word, their caring. Choices and autonomy support come with successful self-regulation and not before. And some teachers believe that being "mean" may be necessary, in the beginning at least, to establish authority—don't smile until Christmas. Often with pressures on the teachers to raise test scores and maintain order, come more directive and punitive control strategies.

The problem inherent in these contrasting views of good classroom management is a possible downward spiral of mistrust (Sheets & Gay, 1996, p. 14). Students withhold their cooperation until teachers "earn it" with their authentic caring. Teachers withhold caring until students "earn it' with respect for authority and cooperation. Marginalized students expect unfair treatment and behave defensively. Teachers get tough, publicly diagnose, grill, and punish. Students feel correct in mistrusting, and become more guarded and defiant. Teachers feel correct in mistrusting and become more controlling and punitive, and so it goes. This cycle is consistent with Bandura's (1997) theory of reciprocal determinism. If personal factors, behaviors, and the environment are in constant interaction, then cycles of events are progressive and self-perpetuating. For example, a new student walks into class late. The student has a tattoo and several visible pierced body parts. The student is actually anxious and hopes to do better at this new school, but the teacher's initial reaction to the late entry and dramatic appearance is a bit hostile. The student feels insulted and responds in kind, so the teacher begins to form expectations about the student, is more vigilant and less trusting, and the student decides that this school will be just as worthless as his previous one—so why bother to try. The teacher sees the student's disengagement, invests less effort in teaching him, and on and on.

Implications for Practice

We occasionally hear teachers emphasize the instructional aspects of their role and downplay the interpersonal. Their refrain usually goes like this: "I'm not here to win a popularity contest, I'm here to teach. If the kids don't like me, that's just too bad." The research on students' views of classroom management suggests that attitudes like this underestimate the power of gaining students' respect and affection. Teachers need to recognize that to teach well, they must also put effort into forging positive relationships with students. The research clearly demonstrates the link between positive student-teacher relationships and students' motivation to become engaged with academic activities. As Valenzuela (1999) points out, for some students at least, being cared *for* is a precondition of caring *about* school. When students see schooling as irrelevant to their futures, when schools seem to denigrate their culture or language, or when noncompliance seems to be the best way to resist coercion, then the only thing that will bring these resistant and reluctant students into the fold of education might be the power of human connection and caring.

At the same time, teachers need to be aware that generating positive relationships with students is definitely not a matter of letting them do whatever they want. Students consistently cite the importance of setting limits and enforcing expectations, and they have little respect for teachers who are unable to achieve an orderly classroom environment. How that order is achieved, however, is critical. Not surprisingly, students prefer teachers who exercise their authority in fair, respectful ways, and they decry the use of punitive techniques that cause public humiliation. It seems clear that teachers should avoid "public diagnosing" and "third-degree grilling," as well as other coercive, extrinsic strategies, and instead maximize the use of strategies that foster autonomy and self-regulation. In other words, teachers need to recognize that socializing students to become self-regulating is an integral part of their job.

Finally, teachers need to acknowledge the inseparable relationship between classroom management and instruction. Lessons that encourage students' active participation and address their interests, needs, and backgrounds are not only likely to foster academic achievement; they are much more likely to generate the good will, respect, and cooperation that is needed for a productive learning environment.

Directions for Future Research

Students' views of the "good" teacher are consonant with the "paradigm shift" manifest in recent discussions of classroom management. (See Freiberg, 1999 and Weinstein, 1999 for a comprehensive discussion of this shift) This new perspective eschews behaviorism with its emphasis on rules, rewards, and penalties, in favor of an approach that stresses the importance of self-regulation; developing trusting, caring relationships between teachers and students; and community-building. In other words, the goal of classroom management is to create an environment in which students behave appropriately, not out of fear of punishment or desire for reward, but out of a sense of personal responsibility, respect, and regard for the group. Although this perspective recognizes that teachers need to function as authority figures who are willing to set limits and guide students' behavior, it suggests that an emphasis on external control does little to teach students to make good choices about how to act. In addition, an emphasis on external control is incompatible with current thinking about curriculum and instruction (McCaslin & Good, 1998).

The literature on this newer perspective on classroom management is rich in terms of models, conceptual frameworks, and theoretical discussions, but there appears to be little empirical research. A few case studies of successful teachers are available (e.g., Alder & Moulton, 1998; Dillon, 1989), but there is nothing to compare with the observational studies of the 1970s that taught us so much about the way that effective classroom managers begin the school year and prevent problems from occurring (cf. Emmer, Evertson, & Anderson, 1980; Kounin, 1970). Thus, we need systematic inquiry into how teachers establish and maintain positive, caring relationships with students, foster autonomy and self-regulation, and build community. What factors support the development of caring and community and what interferes? What role do ethnicity, SES, or perceived similarity in teachers' and parents' values play in these processes (cf. Hauser-Cram, Sirin, & Stipek, 2003; Saft & Pianta, 2001; Wigfield, Galper, Denton, & Seefeldt, 1999)?

We have suggested some possible tensions between teachers' and students' perspectives, with the caution that few researchers have investigated both participant groups simultaneously. The possible convergences and divergences between teachers' and students' perspectives should be examined in the same studies so that setting and context are similar for both participant groups—recognizing that even in the same setting, the experiences for these two groups, and thus their situations, are not identical. This would allow researchers to examine, for example, the downward spiral of teacher-withheld caring and student-withheld respect described earlier. Is such a downward spiral of mistrust more likely to occur in some situations, with certain teaching styles, with some teachers or students, or with certain mismatches of teacher style and student characteristics? How often and under what conditions do these conflicts and failures to connect occur? What can be done to build or repair trust in these situations?

In addition, examination of the literature on teacher knowledge, beliefs, and perceptions indicates that we have potentially valuable scales and inventories that have rarely been used in research (with the obvious exception of the PCI). Wolfgang's *Beliefs about Discipline Inventory*(2001), Martin, Yin, and Baldwin's *Attitudes and Beliefs on Classroom Control* (1998), and Deci, Schwartz, Sheinman, and Ryan's (1981) *Problems in School* all assess teachers' beliefs on a continuum from controlling orientations to democratic or autonomy-supporting orientations. These instruments need to be used by researchers other than their developers so that we can determine their actual utility.

Finally, we found a surprising lack of research on the connections among teachers' beliefs about classroom management, their actual management practices, and the academic and social-emotional outcomes for students. The chapters in this volume by Marilyn Watson and Victor Battistich (chapter 10) and Robert Pianta (chapter 26) provide insight into the connections among perceptions, practices, and outcomes and suggest that research in this area would be fruitful. If beliefs are overpowered by external forces, such as mandated curriculum, accountability, school climate, or administrative requirements, then beliefs are less useful in understanding outcomes. But if beliefs interact with these forces to influence teaching (Weinstein, 2002) then an examination of beliefs, practices, and outcomes should yield valuable knowledge for teaching and teacher education.

ACKNOWLEDGMENT

The author wishes to thank Rhona Weinstein, the University of California, Berkeley, for her comments on an earlier draft of this chapter.

REFERENCES

Alberto, P. A., & Troutman, A. C. (2006). *Applied behavior analysis for teachers* (7th ed.). Columbus, OH: Merrill.

Alder, N. I., & Moulton, M. R. (1998). Caring relationships: Perspectives from middle school students. *Research in Middle Level Education Quarterly, 21*(3), 15–32.

Alexander, P. A., & Dochy, F. J. R. C. (1995). Conceptions of knowledge and beliefs: A comparison across varying cultural and educational communities. *American Educational Research Journal, 32*, 413–442.

Alexander, P. A., Murphy, P. K., Guan, J., & Murphy, P. A. (1998). How students and teachers in Singapore and the United States conceptualize knowledge and beliefs: Positioning learning within epistemological frameworks. *Learning and Instruction, 8*, 97–116.

Alexander, P. A., Murphy, P. K., & Woods, B. S. (1996). Of squalls and fathoms: Navigating the seas of educational innovation. *Educational Researcher, 25*(3), 31–36, 39.

Alexander, P., Schallert, D., & Hare, V. (1991). Coming to terms: How researchers in learning and literacy talk about knowledge. *Review of Educational Research, 61*, 315–343.

Allen, J. (1995). Friends, fairness, fun, and the freedom to choose: Hearing student voices. *Journal of Curriculum & Supervision, 10*(4), 286–301.

Allen, J. D. (1986). Classroom management: Students' perspectives, goals, and strategies. *American Educational Research Journal, 23*(3), 437–459.

Alvidrez, J., & Weinstein, R. S. (1999). Early teacher perceptions and later student academic achievement. *Journal of Educational Psychology, 91*, 731–746.

Appleton, B. A., & Stanwyck, D. (1996). Teacher personality, pupil control ideology, and leadership style. *Individual Psychology, 52*, 119–129.

Armor, D., Conroy-Oseguera, P., Cox, M., King, N., McDonnell, L., Pascal, A., Pauly, E., & Zellman, G. (1976). *Analysis of the school preferred reading programs in selected Los Angeles minority schools.* (Report No. R-2007-LAUSD). Santa Monica, CA: Rand Corporation. (ERIC Document Reproduction Service No. ED130243)

Ashton, P. T. (1985). Motivation and teachers' sense of efficacy. In C. Ames & R. Ames (Eds.), *Research on motivation in education: Vol. 2. The classroom milieu* (pp. 141–174). Orlando, FL: Academic Press.

Ashton, P. T., Olejnik, S., Crocker, L., & McAuliffe, M. (1982, April). *Measurement problems in the study of teachers' sense of efficacy.* Paper presented at the annual meeting of the American Educational Research Association, New York.

Ashton, P. T., & Webb, R. B. (1986). *Making a difference: Teachers' sense of efficacy and student achievement.* New York: Longman.

Athanasiou, M. S., Geil, M., Hazel, C. E., & Copeland, E. P. (2002). A look inside school based consultation: A qualitative study of the beliefs and practices of school psychologists and teachers. *School Psychology Quarterly, 17*, 258–298.

Bailey, G., & Johnson, B. (2000). Preservice teachers' beliefs about discipline before and after student teaching. *Educational Issues, 11*(1), 6–10.

Ballenger, C. (1999). *Teaching other people's children: Literacy and learning in a bilingual classroom.* NY: Teachers College Press.

Bandura, A. (1993). Perceived self-efficacy in cognitive development and functioning. *Educational Psychologist, 28*, 117–148.

Bandura, A. (1997). *Self-efficacy: The exercise of control.* New York: W.H. Freeman.

Berman, P., McLaughlin, M., Bass, G., Pauly, E., & Zellman, G. (1977). *Federal programs supporting educational change: Vol. 7: Factors affecting implementation and continuation* (Report No. R-1589/7-HEW). Santa Monica, CA: The Rand Corporation. (ERIC Document Reproduction Service No. ED140432).

Borko, H., & Putnam, R. (1996). Learning to teach. In D. Berliner & R. Calfee (Eds.), *Handbook of educational psychology* (pp. 673–708). New York: Macmillan.

Brantlinger, E. (1993). *The politics of social class in secondary school: Views of affluent and impoverished youth.* New York: TC Press.

Bosworth, K. (1995). Caring for others and being cared for. *Phi Delta Kappan, 76*(9), 686–693.

Brekelmans, M., Wubbels, T., & den Brok, P. (2002). Teacher experience and the teacher-student relationship in the classroom environment. In S. C. Goh & M. S. Khine (Eds.), *Studies in educational learning environments: An international perspective* (pp. 73–100). Singapore: New World Scientific.

Britzman, D. (1991). *Practice makes practice: A critical study of learning to teach.* Albany: State University of New York Press.

Brophy, J. E. (1996). *Teaching problem students.* New York: Guilford Press.

Brophy, J. E. (1999). Perspectives of classroom management: Yesterday, today, and tomorrow. In H. J. Freiberg (Ed.), *Beyond behaviorism: Changing the classroom management paradigm* (pp. 43–56). Boston, MA: Allyn & Bacon.

Brophy, J. E., & McCaslin, M. (1992). Teachers' reports of how they perceive and cope with problem students. *Elementary School Journal, 93*, 2–68.

Bullough, R., Jr., (1987). Planning and the first year of teaching. *Journal of Education for Teaching, 13*(3), 231–250.

Bullough, R., & Knowles, J. (1990). Becoming a teacher: Struggles of a second-career beginning teacher. *Qualitative Studies in Education, 3*(2), 101–112.

Bullough, R., & Knowles, J. (1991). Teaching and nurturing: Changing conceptions of self as a teacher in a case study of becoming a teacher. *Qualitative Studies in Education, 4*, 121–140.

Cabello, B., & Terrell, R. (1994). Making students feel like family: How teachers create warm and caring classroom climates. *Journal of Classroom Interaction, 29*(1), 17–23.

Calderhead, J. (1996). Teachers: Beliefs and knowledge. In D. Berliner & R. Calfee (Eds.) *Handbook of educational psychology* (pp. 709–725). New York: Macmillan.

Calderhead, J., & Robson, M. (1991). Images of teaching: Student teachers' early conceptions of classroom practice. *Teaching and Teacher Education, 7*, 1–8.

Canter, L., & Canter, M. (1992). *Lee Canter's Assertive Discipline: Positive behavior management for today's classroom.* Santa Monica, CA: Lee Canter and Associates.

Chui, L. H., & Tulley, M. (1997). Student preferences of teacher discipline styles. *Journal of Instructional Psychology, 24*(3), 168–176.

Clandinin, D. J., & Connelly, F. (1987). Teachers' personal knowledge: What counts as personal in studies of the personal. *Journal of Curriculum Studies, 19*, 487–500.

Clark, C., & Peterson, P. (1986). Teachers' thought processes. In M. Wittrock (Ed.), *Handbook of research on teaching* (3rd. ed., pp. 255–296). New York: Macmillan.

Cordova, D. I., & Lepper, M. R. (1996). Intrinsic motivation and the process of learning: Beneficial effects of contextualization, personalization, and choice. *Journal of Educational Psychology, 88*, 715–730.

Cothran, D. J., & Ennis, C. D. (2000). Building bridges to student engagement: Communicating respect and care for students in urban high school. *Journal of Research and Development in Education, 33*(2), 106–117.

Cothran, D. J., Kulinna, P. H., & Garrahy, D. A. (2003). "This is kind of giving a secret away ...": Students' perspectives on effective class management. *Teaching and Teacher Education, 19*, 435–444.

Cowan, R. J., & Sheridan, S. M. (2003). Investigating the acceptability of behavioral interventions in applied conjoint behavioral consultation: Moving from analog conditions to naturalistic settings. *School Psychology Quarterly, 18*, 1–21.

Crow, N. (1991, April). Personal perspectives on classroom management. Paper presented at the Annual Meeting of the American Educational Research Association, Chicago.

Crowley, E. P. (1993). A qualitative analysis of mainstreamed behaviorally disordered aggressive adolescents' perceptions of helpful and unhelpful teacher attitudes and behaviors. *Exceptionality, 4*(3), 131–151.

Davidson, A. L. (1999). Negotiating social differences: Youths' assessments of educators' strategies. *Urban Education, 34*(3), 338–369.

Deci, E. L., & Ryan, R. M. (1985). *Intrinsic motivation and self-determination in human behavior.* New York: Plenum.

Deci, E. L., Schwartz, A. J., Sheinman, L., & Ryan, R. M. (1981). An instrument to assess adults' orientations toward control versus autonomy with children: Reflections on intrinsic motivation and perceived competence. *Journal of Educational Psychology, 73*, 642–650.

Deci, E. L., Vallerand, R. J., Pelletier, L. G., & Ryan, R. M. (1991). Motivation and education: The self-determination perspective. *Educational Psychologist, 26*, 325–346.

Delpit, L. (1995). *Other people's children: Cultural conflicts in the classroom.* NY: The New Press.

Diebert, J. P., & Hoy, W. K. (1977). Custodial high schools and self-actualization of students. *Educational Research Quarterly, 2*, 24–31.

Dillon, D. R. (1989). Showing them that I want them to learn and that I care about who they are: A microethnography of the social organization of a secondary lowtrack English-reading classroom. *American Educational Research Journal, 26*(2), 227–259.

Dreikurs, R. (1964). *Children: The challenge.* New York: E. P. Dutton.

Eckert, T. L., & Hintze, J. M. (2000). Behavioral conceptualizations and applications of treatment acceptability: Issues related to service delivery and research methodology. *School Psychology Quarterly, 15*, 123–148.

Elliott, S. N. (1986). Children's ratings of the acceptability of classroom interventions for misbehavior: Findings and methodological considerations. *Journal of School Psychology, 24*, 23–35.

Elliott, S. N., Turco, T. L., & Gresham, F. M. (1987). Consumers' and clients' pretreatment acceptability ratings of classroom group contingencies. *Journal of School Psychology, 25*, 145–153.

Elliot, S. N., Witt, J. C., Galvin, G. A., & Moe, G. (1986) Children's involvement in intervention selection: Acceptability of interventions for misbehaving peers. *Professional Psychology: Research and Practice, 17*(3), 235–241.

Ellis, J. (1997). What a seriously at-risk student would really like to say to teachers about classroom management. *Education Canada, 37*, 17–21.

Emmer, E. (1990, April). *A scale for measuring teacher efficacy in classroom management and discipline.* Paper presented at the annual meeting of the American Educational Research Association, Boston, MA. (Revised, June, 1990)

Emmer, E., & Hickman, J. (1991). Teacher efficacy in classroom management. *Educational and Psychological Measurement, 51*, 755–765.

Emmer, E. T., Evertson, C. M., & Anderson, L. M. (1980). Effective classroom management at the beginning of the school year. *Elementary School Journal, 80*, 219–231.

Enochs, L. G., Scharmann, L. C., & Riggs, I. M. (1995). The relationship of pupil control to preservice elementary science teachers self-efficacy and outcome expectation. *Science Education, 79,* 63–75.

Fang, Z. (1996). A review of research on teacher beliefs and practices. *Educational Research, 38*(1), 47–65.

Featherstone, H. (1993). Learning from the first years of classroom teaching: The journey in, the journey out. *Teachers College Record, 95*(11), 93–112.

Fenstermacher, G. (1994). The knower and the known: The nature of knowledge in research on teaching. In L. Darling-Hammond (Ed.), *Review of research in education* (Vol. 20, pp. 1–54). Washington, DC: American Educational Research Association.

Ferreira, M. M., & Bosworth, K. (2001). Defining caring teachers: Adolescents' perspectives. *Journal of Classroom Interaction, 36*(1), 24–30.

Finders, M. (1997). *Just girls: Hidden literacies and life in junior high.* New York: Teachers College Press.

Flowerday, T., & Schraw, G. (2000). Teachers' beliefs about instructional choice: a phenomenological study. *Journal of Educational Psychology, 92,* 634–645.

Freiberg, H. J. (1999). Beyond behaviorism.In H. J. Freiberg, (Ed.), *Beyond behaviorism: Changing the classroom management paradigm* (pp. 3–20). Boston, MA: Allyn & Bacon.

Fromm, E. (1948). *Man for himself.* New York: Farrar & Rinehart.

Fulk, C. L., & Smith, P. J. (1995). Students' perceptions of teachers' instructional and management adaptations for students with learning or behavior problems. *The Elementary School Journal, 95*(5), 409–419.

Gaffney, P. V. (1997). *A study of preservice teachers' beliefs about various issues and myths regarding the use of scholastic corporal punishment.*(ERIC Document Reproduction Service No. ED409315 Resources in Education.)

Garner, P. (1995). Schools by scoundrels: The views of "disruptive" pupils in mainstream schools in England and the United States. In M. Lloyd-Smith & J. D. Davies (Eds.), *On the margins: The educational experience of "problem" pupils* (pp. 17–30). Staffordshire, England: Trentham Books.

Gay, G. (2000). *Culturally responsive teaching: Theory, research, and practice.* NY: Teachers College Press.

Gibson, S., & Dembo, M. (1984). Teacher efficacy: A construct validation. *Journal of Educational Psychology, 76,* 569–582.

Glasser, W. (1992). *The quality school: Managing students without coercion* (2nd ed.). New York: Harper & Row.

Glickman, C., & Tamashiro, R. T. (1980). Clarifying teachers' beliefs about discipline. *Educational Leadership, 37,* 459–464.

Glickman, C., & Tamashiro, R. (1982). A comparison of first-year, fifth-year, and former teachers on efficacy, ego development, and problem solving. *Psychology in Schools, 19,* 558–562.

Gordon, T. (1974). *Teacher effectiveness training.* New York: Peter H. Wyden.

Gordon, T. (1981). Crippling our children with discipline. *Journal of Education, 163,* 228–243.

Grant, G. E. (1992). The sources of structural metaphors in teacher knowledge: Three cases. *Teaching and Teacher Education, 8,* 433–440.

Greenwood, G. E., Olejnik, S. F., & Parkay, F. W. (1990). Relationships between four teacher efficacy belief patterns and selected teacher characteristics. *Journal of Research and Development in Education, 23*(2), 102–106.

Guskey, T. (1984). The influence of change in instructional effectiveness upon the affective characteristics of teachers. *American Educational Research Journal, 21,* 245–259.

Guskey, T., & Passaro, P. (1994). Teacher efficacy: A study of construct dimensions. *American Educational Research Journal, 31,* 627–643.

Habel, J., Bloom, L, Ray, M., & Bacon, E. (1999). Consumer reports: What students with behavior disorders say about school. *Remedial and Special Education, 20*(2), 93–105.

Hauser-Cram, P., Sirin, S. R., & Stipek, D. (2003). When teachers' and parents' values differ: Teachers' ratings of academic competence in children from low-income families. *Journal of Educational Psychology, 95,* 813–820.

Hayes, C. B., Ryan, A., & Zseller, E. B. (1994). The middle-school child's perceptions of caring teachers. *American Journal of Education, 103,* 1–19.

Henderson, C. B. (1982). *An analysis of assertive discipline training animplementaion of inservice elementary teachers' self-concept, locus of control, pupil control ideology, and assertive personality characteristics.* Unpublished doctoral dissertation, Indiana University, Bloomington, IN.

Hollingsworth, S. (1989.) Prior beliefs and cognitive change in learning to teach. *American Educational Research Journal, 26*(2), 160–89.

Hoy, W. K. (1972). Dimensions of student alienation and characteristics of public high schools. *Interchange, 3,* 36–52.

Hoy, W. K. (2001). The Pupil Control studies: a historical, theoretical, and empirical analysis. *Journal of Educational Administration, 39,* 424–442.

Hoy, W. K., & Woolfolk, A. E. (1990). Socialization of student teachers. *American Educational Research Journal, 27,* 279–300.

Jarvis, S., Schonert-Reichl, K. A., & Krivel-Zacks, G. (2000, April). *Teachers' (mis)conceptions of early adolescence.* Paper presented at the American Educational Research Association, New Orleans, LA.

Johnson, B., Whitington, V., & Oswald, M. (1994). Teacher's views of school discipline: A theoretical framework. *Cambridge Journal of Education, 24*, 261–278.

Jolivette, K., Stitcher, J., Sibilsky, S., Scott, T. M., & Ridley, R. (2002). Naturally occurring opportunities for preschool children with an at-risk disability to make choices. *Education and Treatment of Children, 25*, 396–414.

Jolivette, K., Wehby, J. H., Canale, J., & Massey, N. G. (2001). Effects of choice making opportunities on the behaviors of students with emotional and behavioral disorders. *Behavioral Disorders, 26*, 131–145.

Kagan, D. (1990). Ways of evaluating teacher cognition: Inferences concerning the Goldilocks principle. *Review of Educational Research, 60*, 419–469.

Kagan, D. (1992). Implications of research on teacher belief. *Educational Psychologist, 27*, 65–90.

Katz, S. R. (1996). Presumed guilty: How schools criminalize Latino youth. *Social Justice, 24*(4), 77–95.

Katz, S. R. (1999). Teaching in tensions: Latino immigrant youth, their teachers, and the structures of schooling. *Teachers College Record, 100*(4), 809–840.

Knowles, J. G. (1992). Models for teachers' biographies. In I. Goodson (Ed.), *Studying teachers' lives* (pp. 99–152). New York: Teachers College Press.

Kohn, A. (1996). *Beyond discipline: From compliance to community*. Alexandria, VA: Association for Supervision and Curriculum Development.

Kounin, J. S. (1970). *Discipline and group management in classrooms.* New York: Holt, Rinehart & Winston.

Knoblauch, D. E. (2004). *Contextual factors and the development of student teachers' sense of efficacy*. Unpublished doctoral dissertation, The Ohio State University.

Ladson-Billings, G. (2001). *Crossing over to Canaan: The journey of new teachers in diverse classrooms.* San Francisco: Jossey-Bass.

Levine, J. M., & Wang, M. C. (Eds.). (1983). *Teacher and student Perceptions: Implications for learning*. Mahwah, NJ: Lawrence Erlbaum Associates.

Lewis, R. (2001). Classroom discipline and student responsibility: The students' view. *Teaching and Teacher Education, 17*(3), 307–319.

Lewis, R., & Lovegrove, M. N. (1987). The teacher as disciplinarian: How do students feel? *Australian Journal of Education, 31*(2), 173–186.

Lortie, D. (1975). *Schoolteachers: A sociological study.* Chicago: University of Chicago Press.

Lunenburg, F. C., & Cadavid, V. (1992). Locus of control, pupil control ideology, and dimensions of teacher burnout. *Journal of Instructional Psychology, 19*, 13–24.

Manke, M. P. (1997). *Classroom power relations: Understanding student-teacher interaction.* Mahwah, NJ: Lawrence Erlbaum Associates.

Martin, N. K., Shoho, A., & Yin, Z. (2003). Attitudes and beliefs regarding classroom management styles: The impact of teacher preparation versus Experience. *Research in the Schools, 10*(2), 29–34.

Martin, N. K., & Yin, Z. (1997, January). *Attitudes and beliefs regarding classroom management styles: Differences between male and female teachers.* Paper presented at the annual conference of the Southwestern Educational Research Association, Austin, TX.

Martin, N. K., & Yin, Z. (1999). Beliefs regarding classroom management style: Differences between urban and rural secondary level teachers. *Journal of Research in Rural Education, 15*(2), 1–5.

Martin, N. K., Yin, Z., & Baldwin, B. (1998). Construct validation of the attitudes and beliefs on classroom control inventory. *Journal of Classroom Interaction, 33*(2), 6–15.

McCaslin, M., & Good, T. L. (1998). Moving beyond management as sheer compliance: Helping students to develop goal coordination strategies. *Educational Horizons, 76*, 169–176.

McIntyre, T., & Battle, J. (1998). The traits of "good" teachers as identified by African American and White students with emotional and or behavioral disorders. *Behavioral Disorders, 23*(2), 134–142.

McLaughlin, H. J. (1991). Reconciling care and control: Authority in classroom relationships. *Journal of Teacher Education, 42*(3), 182–195.

Metz, M. (1978). *Classrooms and corridors: The crisis of authority in desegregated secondary schools.* Berkeley: University of California Press.

Miller, S. A., Leinhardt, G., & Zigmond, N. (1988). Influencing engagement through accommodation: An ethnographic study of at-risk students. *American Educational Research Journal, 25*(4), 465–587.

Morine-Dershimer, G. (1985). *Talking, listening, and learning in elementary classrooms*. New York: Longman.

Morrison, T. G. (1997). Development of teachers' theoretical orientations toward reading and pupil control ideology. *Reading Research and Instruction, 36,* 141–156.

Munn, P., & Johnstone, M. (1990). Pupils' perceptions of "effective disciplinarians." *British Educational Research Journal, 16*(2), 191–198.

Nachtscheim, N., and Hoy, W. K. (1976), Authoritarian personality and control ideologies of teachers. *The Alberta Journal of Educational Research, 22,* 173–7.

Nash, R. (1976). Pupils' expectations of their teachers. In M. Stubbs & S. Delamont (Eds.), *Explorations in classroom observation* (pp. 83–98). London: John Wiley.

Nelson, J., Lynn, L., & Glenn, H. S. (2000). *Positive discipline in the classroom: Developing mutual respect, cooperation, and responsibility in your classroom* (rev. 3rd. ed.). Roseville, CA: Prima Publishing.

Nespor, J. (1987). The role of beliefs in the practice of teaching. *Journal of Curriculum Studies, 19,* 317–328.

Nieto, S. (1994). Lessons from students on creating a chance to dream. *Harvard Educational Review, 64*(4), 392–426.

Noblit, G. (1993). Power and caring. *American Educational Research Journal, 30*(1), 23–38.

Noguera, P. A. (1995). Preventing and producing violence: A critical analysis of responses to school violence. *Harvard Educational Review, 65*(2), 189–212.

Nolen, S. B., & Nicholls, J. G. (1994). A place to begin (again) in research on student motivation: Teachers' beliefs. *Teaching & Teacher Education, 10,* 57–69.

Oldfather, P., & McLaughlin, H. J. (1993). Gaining and losing voice: A longitudinal study of students' continuing impulse to learn across elementary and middle school contexts. *Research in Middle Level Education, 3,* 1–25.

Oldfather, P., & Thomas, S. (1998). What does it mean when high school teachers participate in collaborative research with students on literacy motivations? *Teachers College Record, 99*(4), 617–691.

Osterman, K. F. (2000). Students' need for belonging in the school community. *Review of Educational Research, 70,* 323–367.

Packard, J. S. (1988). The pupil control studies. In N. J. Boyan (Ed.), *Handbook of research on educational administration* (pp. 185–207). New York: Longman.

Pajares, F. (1992). Teachers' beliefs and educational research: Cleaning up a messy construct. *Review of Educational Research, 62,* 307–332.

Parkay, F. W., Greenwood, G., Olejnik, S., & Proller, N. (1988). A study of the relationship among teacher efficacy, locus of control, and stress. *Journal of Research and Development in Education, 21*(4), 13–22.

Pelletier, L. G., Seguin-Levesque, C., & Legault, L. (2002). Pressure from above and pressure from below as determinants of teachers' motivation and teaching behaviors. *Journal of Educational Psychology, 94,* 186–196.

Pestello, F. G. (1989). Misbehavior in high school classrooms. *Youth & Society, 20*(3), 290–306.

Phelan, P., Davidson, A. L., & Cao, H. T. (1992). Speaking up: Students' perspectives on school. *Phi Delta Kappan, 73*(9), 695–704.

Phelan, P., Yu, H. C., & Davidson, A. L. (1994). Navigating the psychosocial pressures of adolescence: The voices and experiences of high school youth. *American Educational Research Journal, 31*(2), 415–447.

Plank, S. B., McDill, E. L., McPartland, J. M., & Jordan, W. J. (2001). Situation and repertoire: Civility, incivility, cursing and politeness in an urban high school. *Teachers College Record, 103*(3), 504–524.

Pomeroy, E. (1999). The teacher-student relationship in secondary school: Insights from excluded students. *British Journal of Sociology of Education, 20*(4), 465–482.

Prawat, R. S. (1992). Teachers beliefs about teaching and learning: A constructivist perspective. *American Journal of Education, 100,* 354–395.

Reeve, J., Bolt, E., & Cai, Y. (1999). Autonomy-supportive teachers: How they teach and motivate students. *Journal of Educational Psychology*, 91, 537–548.

Rentel, V. (1994). Preparing clinical faculty members: Research on teachers' reasoning. In K. Howey & N. Zimpher (Eds.), *The professional development of teacher educators.* Norwood, NJ: Ablex.

Reyna, C., & Weiner, B. (2001). Justice and utility in the classroom: An attributional analysis of the goals of teachers' punishment and intervention strategies. *Journal of Educational Psychology, 93,* 309–319.

Richardson, V. (1994). The consideration of belief in staff development. In V. Richardson (Ed.), *Teacher change and the staff development process: A case in reading instruction.* New York: Teachers College Press.

Richardson, V. (1996). The role of attitudes and beliefs in learning to teach. In J. Sikula (Ed.), *Handbook of research on teacher education* (2nd ed., pp. 102–119). New York: Macmillan.

Rogers, C. R. (1969). *Freedom to learn.* Columbus, OH: Merrill.

Rogers, C. R., & Freiberg, H. J. (1994). *Freedom to learn* (3rd ed.). Columbus, OH: Merrill.

Rogers, D. L. (1991, April). *Conceptions of caring in a fourth grade classroom.* Paper presented at the annual meeting of the American Educational Research Association, Chicago.

Ross, J. A. (1994). The impact of an inservice to promote cooperative learning on the stability of teacher efficacy. *Teaching & Teacher Education, 10*(4), 381–394.

Ruck, M. D., & Wortley, S. (2002). Racial and ethnic minority high school students' perceptions of school disciplinary practices: A look at some Canadian findings. *Journal of Youth and Adolescence, 31*(3), 185–195.

Rust, F. O. (1992). *The first year of teaching: It's not what they expected.* Paper presented at the annual Meeting of the American Educational Research Association, San Francisco.

Saft, E. W., & Pianta, R. C. (2001). Teachers' perceptions of their relationships with students: Effects of child age, gender, and ethnicity of teachers and students. *School Psychology Quarterly, 16*, 125–140.

Saklofske, D., Michayluk, B., & Randhawa, B. (1988). Teachers' efficacy and teaching behaviors. *Psychological Report, 63*, 407–414.

Schlosser, L. K. (1992). Teacher distance and student disengagement: School lives on the margin. *Journal of Teacher Education, 43*(2), 128–140.

Schmuck, R., & Schmuck, P. (1991). The attitudes of adolescents in small-town America. *NASSP Bulletin, 75*, 85–90.

Schunk, D. H., & Meece, J. L. (Eds.). (1992). *Student perceptions in the classroom.* Hillsdale, NJ: Lawrence Erlbaum Associates.

Sewell, K. C. (1991). *A study of the effects of personality type, socialization pressure, and contextual factors on the pupil control ideology of student teachers.* Unpublished doctoral dissertation, Rutgers University, New Brunswick NJ.

Sheets, R. H. (1996). Urban classroom conflict: Student-teacher perception: Ethnic integrity, solidarity, and resistance. *The Urban Review, 28*(2), 165–183.

Sheets, R. H., & Gay, G. (1996). Student perceptions of disciplinary conflict in ethnically diverse classrooms. *NASSP Bulletin, 80*(580), 84–95.

Sheets, R. S. (2002). "You're just a kid that's there"—Chicano perception of disciplinary events. *Journal of Latinos and Education, 1*(2), 105–122.

Shoho, A. R., & Martin, N. K. (1999). A comparison of alienation among alternatively and traditionally certified teachers. *ERS Spectrum, 17*(3), 27–33.

Short, P. M., & Short, R. J. (1988). Perceived classroom environment and student behavior in secondary schools. *Educational Research Quarterly, 12*(3), 35–39.

Simon, H. (1995). The information processing view of the mind. *American Psychologist, 50*, 507–508.

Skinner, B. F. (1953). *Science and human behavior.* New York: Macmillan.

Skinner, E. A., & Belmont, M. J. (1993). Motivation in the classroom: Reciprocal effects of teacher behavior and student engagement across the school year. *Journal of Educational Psychology, 85*, 571–581.

Smith, D. C., Adelman, H. S., Nelson, P., Taylor, L., & Phares, V. (1987). Students' perception of control at school and problem behavior and attitudes. *Journal of School Psychology, 25*, 167–176.

Smylie, M. A., (1988). The enhancement function of staff development: Organizational and psychological antecedents to individual teacher change. *American Educational Research Journal, 25*, 1–30.

Stinson, S. W. (1993). Meaning and value: Reflections on what students say about school. *Journal of Curriculum and Supervision, 8*(3), 216–238.

Stipek, D. J. (1996). Motivation and instruction. In D. Berliner & R. Calfee (Eds.), *Handbook of educational psychology* (pp. 85–109). New York: Macmillan.

Stipek, D. (2003). *Motivation to learn* (4th ed.). Boston: Allyn & Bacon.

Strauss, S. (1996). Confessions of a born-again constructivist. *Educational Psychologist, 31*, 15–22.

Supaporn, S. (2000). High school students' perspectives about misbehavior. *Physical Educator, 57*(3), 124–136.

Sweet, A. P., Guthrie, J. T., & Ng, M. M. (1998). Teacher perceptions and student reading motivation. *Journal of Educational Psychology, 90*, 210–223

Taylor-Dunlop, K., & Norton, M. M. (1997). Out of the mouths of babes: Voices of at-risk adolescents. *The Clearing House, 70*(5), 274–278.

Thorson, S. (1996). The missing link: Students discuss school discipline. *Focus on Exceptional Children, 29*(3), 1–12.

Tschannen-Moran, M., & Woolfolk Hoy, A. (2001). Teacher efficacy: capturing an elusive construct. *Teacher and Teacher Education, 17*, 783–805.

Tschannen-Moran, M., Woolfolk Hoy, A., & Hoy, W. K. (1998). Teacher efficacy: Its meaning and measure. *Review of Educational Research, 68*, 202–248.

Turco, T. L., & Elliott, S. N. (1986). Assessment of students' acceptability ratings of teacher-initiated interventions for classroom behavior. *Journal of School Psychology, 24*, 277–283.

Valenzuela, A. (1999). *Subtractive Schooling: U.S.-Mexican youth and the politics of caring.* Albany, SUNY Press.

Voege, C. C. (1979). *Personal values, educational attitudes toward pupil control of staffs and boards of religious affiliated schools.* Unpublished doctoral dissertation, New York University, New York.

Wallace, G. (1996). Relating to teachers. In J. Rudduck, R. Chaplain, & G. Wallace (Eds.), *School improvement: What can pupils tells us?* (pp. 29–40). London: David Fulton.

Weade, R., & Evertson, C. M. (1991). The construction of lessons in effective and less effective classrooms. In U. Casanova, D. C. Berliner, P. Placier, & L. Weiner (Eds.), *Classroom management: Readings in educational research* (pp. 136–159). Washington, DC: National Education Association.

Weiner, B. (1986). *An attributional theory of motivation and emotion.* New York: Springer.

Weiner, B. (2000). Interpersonal and intrapersonal theories of motivation from an attributional perspective. *Educational Psychology Review, 12*, 1–14.

Weinstein, C. (1988). Preservice teachers' expectations about the first year of teaching. *Teaching and Teacher Education, 4*, 31–41.

Weinstein, C. (1989). Teacher education students' perceptions of teaching. *Journal of Teacher Education, 40*(2), 53–60.

Weinstein, C. S. (1998). "I want to be nice, but I have to be mean": Exploring prospective teachers' conceptions of caring and order. *Teaching and Teacher Education, 14*(2), 153–163.

Weinstein, C. S. (1999). Reflections on best practices and promising programs. In H. J. Freiberg, (Ed), *Beyond behaviorism: Changing the classroom management paradigm* (pp. 145-163). Boston, MA: Allyn & Bacon.

Weinstein, C. S. (2003). *Secondary classroom management: Lessons from research and practice* (2nd edition). Boston: McGraw-Hill.

Weinstein, C. S., & Mignano, A. J. (2003). *Elementary classroom management: Lessons from research and practice* (3rd edition). Boston: McGraw-Hill.

Weinstein, C., Woolfolk, A., Dittmeier, L., & Shanker, U. (1994). Protector or prison guard: Using metaphors and media to explore student teachers' thinking about classroom management. *Action in Teacher Education, 16*(1), 41–54.

Weinstein, R. S. (1983). Student perceptions of schooling. *Elementary School Journal, 83*, 287–312.

Weinstein, R. S. (1989). Perceptions of classroom processes and student motivation: Children's views of self-fulfilling prophecies. In R. A. Ames & C. Ames (Eds.), *Research on motivation in education* (Vol. 3). New York: Academic Press.

Weinstein, R. S. (2002). *Reaching higher: The power of expectations in schooling*. Cambridge, MA: Harvard University Press.

Weinstein, R. S., Marshall, H. H., Brattesani, K. A., & Middlestadt, S. E. (1982). Student perceptions of differential teacher treatment in open and traditional classrooms. *Journal of Educational Psychology, 74,* 678–692.

Weinstein, R. S., Marshall, H. H., Sharp, L., & Botkin, M. (1987). Pygmalion and the student: Age and classroom differences in children's awareness of teacher expectations. *Child Development, 58,* 1079–1093.

Weinstein, R. S., & McKown, C. (1998). Expectancy effects in "context": Listening to the voices of students and teachers. In J. Brophy (Ed.), Teachers' and students' expectations. *Volume 7 of Advances in Research on Teaching* (pp. 215–242). JAI Press.

Wentzel, K. R. (1997). Student motivation in middle school: The role of perceived pedagogical caring. *Journal of Educational Psychology, 89*(3), 411–419.

Wentzel, K. R. (1998). Social relationships and motivation in middle school: The role of parents, teachers, and peers. *Journal of Educational Psychology, 90*(2), 202–209.

Wigfield, A., Galper, A., Denton, K., & Seefeldt, C. (1999). Teachers' beliefs about former Head Start and non-Head Start first-grade children's motivation, performance, and future educational prospects. *Journal of Educational Psychology, 91*(1), 98–104.

Williams, G. C., & Deci, E. L. (1998). Internalization of biopsycho-social values by medical students: a test of self-determination theory. *Journal of Personality and Social Psychology, 70*, 767–779.

Willower, D. J., Eidell, T. L., & Hoy, W. K. (1967). *The school and pupil control ideology* (Penn State Studies Monograph No. 24). University Park, PA: Pennsylvania State University.

Witt, J. C., & Elliot, S. N. (1985). Acceptability of classroom management strategies. In T. R. Kratochwill (Ed.), *Advances in School Psychology, Volume 4*. Hillsdale, NJ: Lawrence Erlbaum Associates, pp. 251–288.

Witt, J. C., Elliott, S. N., & Martens, B. K. (1984). Acceptability of behavioral interventions used in classrooms: The influence of amount of teacher time, severity of behavior problem, and type of intervention. *Behavioral Disorders, 9*, 95–104.

Wolfgang, C. H. (2001). *Solving discipline and classroom management problems: Methods and models for today's teachers*. (5th ed.). New York: John Wiley.

Woolfolk, A. E., & Hoy, W. K. (1990). Prospective teachers' sense of efficacy and beliefs about control. *Journal of Educational Psychology, 82,* 81–91.

Woolfolk Hoy, A., & Murphy, P. K. (2001). Teaching educational psychology to the implicit mind. In R. Sternberg & B. Torff (Eds.), *Understanding and teaching the implicit mind* (pp. 145–185). Mahwah, NJ: Lawrence Erlbaum Associates.

Woolfolk Hoy, A., Davis, H. and Pape, S. (in press). Teachers' knowledge, beliefs, and thinking. In P. A. Alexander & P. H, Winne (Eds.), *Handbook of educational psychology* (2nd ed.). Mahwah, NJ: Lawrence Erlbaum.

Younger, M., & Warrington, M. (1999). "He's such a nice man, but he's so boring, you have to really make a conscious effort to learn": The views of Gemma, Daniel and their contemporaries on teacher quality and effectiveness. *Educational Review, 51*(3), 231–241.

Zeidner, M. (1988). The relative severity of common classroom management strategies: The student's perspective. *British Journal of Educational Psychology, 58*, 69–77.

Zimmerman, B. J. (2000). Attaining self-regulation: A social-cognitive perspective. In M. Boekarts, P. Pintrich, & M. Zeidner (Eds.), *Handbook of self-regulation* (pp. 13–39). San Diego CA: Academic Press.

III

Recent and Emergent Perspectives on Classroom Management

Mary McCaslin
University of Arizona

9

Self-Regulated Learning and Classroom Management: Theory, Research, and Considerations for Classroom Practice

Mary McCaslin, Amanda Rabidue Bozack, Lisa Napoleon, Angela Thomas, Veronica Vasquez, Virginia Wayman, and Jizhi Zhang
University of Arizona

INTRODUCTION

In this chapter we present the construct of *self-regulated learning* (SRL) and examine the definitions of SRL that guide seven working theories. Within each theory we discuss the sources of and supports for student self-regulation that are pertinent to teacher practices and classroom opportunities. Our first goal is to organize theories in a way that makes their common features and unique contributions more readily apparent and their theoretical progression more coherent. Our second goal is to identify what appear to be especially productive theoretically based support strategies that teachers can implement in their classrooms to promote student SRL. Third, we identify classroom practices that receive support across SRL theories. Fourth, we alert educators and policy makers that the theoretical distinctions among SRL theories afford an important opportunity for discussion of just what is meant by "self-regulated students," why that might be desirable, and to what extent is it optimal. We hope that this chapter promotes discussions about the *value* of SRL and its role in teacher-student relationships and classroom management practices.

CONCEPTIONS OF SELF-REGULATED LEARNING IN THE 1980s

Self-regulation-like constructs have a rich history in psychology and more recently have been central to developmental approaches to self-awareness in particular (e.g., Piaget's "auto-regulation" [Piaget, 1983], Vygotsky's "self-direction" [Vygotsky, 1962], Flavell's "meta-cognition" [Flavell, 1979]). In the 1980s, Corno and Mandinach (1983) were among the first educational psychologists to introduce the term *self-regulation* into the educational research literature as a way to link motivation, information processing, and cognitive engagement in the classroom (see also Winne & Marx, 1982). The Corno and Mandinach (1983) definition exemplifies the times with its emphasis on and integration of individual learning, information processing and storage, problem solving, and learner efficacy hypothesized to promote academic success:

> Self-regulated learning will be shown to consist of specific cognitive activities, such as deliberate planning and monitoring, which learners carry out as they encounter academic tasks. Learning is less self-regulated when some of the processes are overtaken by classroom teachers, other students, or features of written instruction. A major point to be made is that self-regulated learning is the highest form of cognitive engagement. Engagement in self-regulated learning is somewhat taxing. When tasks make cognitive demands students may engage in self-regulated learning; they may also shift the mental burden by calling upon available external resources such as a willing and knowledgeable peer. (pp. 89–90)

We subsequently explore theoretical elaborations of this definition, particularly notions of source and support and the movement away from the nearly exclusive focus on the individual and academic outcomes; however, it is useful to consider at the outset its potential for classroom management practices. SRL began as a very "cognitive" construct that was to link student motivation and learning. It required tasks that were informative and challenging (e.g., Block, 1984) and a mindful and capable learner who was as apt to be derailed by too much instructional support as by personal limitations. Part of the "SRL problem" from the beginning was poorly designed tasks and adults too ready to provide assistance.

Corno and Mandinach's (1983) definition introduced the tensions between the sources and support of SRL that remain central to current theoretical positions. In the tradition of the Aptitude-Treatment-Interaction (ATI) paradigm (Cronbach, 1957), the Corno and Mandinach model distinguishes "treatment" or environmental variables from "aptitude" or individual difference variables and focuses on interactions that affect SRL. The environment can provide both the opportunities—the challenging and informative tasks—and the barriers—in this instance, the maintenance of superfluous support—to student cognitive engagement in SRL activities. SRL in this definition, however, remains a capability of the student, not the task or teacher. As we will discuss, current theories differ on the notion of SRL as a capability due to aptitude, disposition, specific skill acquisition, essential human characteristic, the social embeddedness of the learner, or as much a characteristic of the social/cultural context as the individual.

CURRENT THEORIES OF SELF-REGULATED LEARNING

With the exception of social constructivist approaches to SRL, which historically have situated individuals in their sociocultural context to emphasize the social origins and maintenance of the affective and the intellectual features of SRL (e.g., McCaslin Rohrkemper, 1989), current theories of self-regulated learning have progressively moved away from a nearly exclusive focus on the academic potential of individual cognitive and conative processes typical of the 1980s (e.g., Zimmerman & Schunk, 1989) toward a greater sensitivity for context and social influences that play a key role in "individual" regulation (e.g., Zimmerman & Schunk, 2001; McInerney & Van Etten, 2004). Even within this increased sensitivity to the social embeddedness of the individual, however, SRL theories can be meaningfully distinguished in conceptions of the sources and supports of students' SRL. We present briefly seven modern theories of SRL organized within a dialectic framework that provides a useful scaffold for future work in this area (see Hickey and McCaslin, 2001; Hickey, 2003 for elaboration on this approach).

The Thesis: Operant Approaches to Self-Regulated Learning

Behaviorist, or "operant," approaches to self-regulated learning seem a bit problematic at first glance, yet operant approaches are quite powerful and relatively parsimonious in explaining the behaviors that lay persons commonly ascribe to mental phenomena. Behavioral approaches are so fundamental to American psychology and educational practices that we assign the operant approach to SRL the fundamental role of "thesis" in the progression of SRL conceptions. Thus, we assert that at the root of all SRL debate is a decision regarding the role of the environment in the source and support of SRL activity.

Definition of Self-Regulated Learning. In an operant perspective, SRL (or lack thereof) is exemplified by behaviors that represent self-control, impulsivity, and commitment. *Self-control* is inferred from delay of gratification, that is, the individual postpones something desired now for the attainment of something later. *Impulsivity* is its opposite: impulsivity is about selecting an immediately available reinforcement that obviates the attainment of a later (and typically, more desirable) one. *Commitment* involves the selection of a delayed consequence over other delayed alternatives and any more proximal options along the way. Typically, operant researchers co-vary the magnitude of the reinforcement with the timing of its availability (the delayed reinforcement is presumed greater or better than the immediate) so that impulsivity is a poor choice; however, this need not always be the case (see, e.g., research on children's postponement of pleasure by Mischel, 1973). What is essential, however, for an operant definition of SRL is commitment, which involves the removal or nonselection of options in pursuit of a delayed reinforcement.

Source of Self-Regulated Learning. Operant theories define two types of controlling stimuli: those that occur before and cue behavior (antecedent) and those that occur after as a result of behavior (consequent). The mnemonic for this process, *A*ntecedent → *B*ehavior → *C*onsequence, or ABC, is a basic formula for behavior modification used in schools. In typical school practices, this formula is used by a teacher, counselor, or school psychologist to identify what appears to promote student behavior—both in terms of triggers and reinforcements—for the purpose of gaining better stimulus control to improve or change that student behavior. When applied to SRL, gaining better stimulus control is simply a matter of "how individuals alter antecedent and consequent stimuli to regulate their own behavior" (Mace, Belfiore, & Hutchinson, 2001, p. 41). In other words, stimulus control works on the self, by the self, in pretty much the same way it does in the environment by others.

Support of Self-Regulated Learning. Behavioral strategies that promote self-control and commitment and impede impulsivity support self-regulation. Strategies are acquired through traditional behavioral methods now applied to the self by the self. They include self-monitoring (SM), self-instruction (SI), self-evaluation (SE), self-correction (SC), and self-reinforcement (SR). Each of these methods also figures prominently in most theoretical approaches to SRL and, although they may be conceptualized slightly differently within a theory, they serve a similar function: either to transfer environmental controls to the individual or to optimize individual self-awareness as a precursor to SRL activities.

We briefly describe each support strategy here as they are most readily useful for classroom management when discussed within the operant framework. However, a caution is appropriate. Our representation is far more generic than an operant theorist would pursue. For example, what is a readily understood process to a lay reader, self-reinforcement, is defined by Mace et al. (2001) as follows:

> Self-reinforcement (SR) describes a process in which a person, often after satisfying a performance standard or criteria, comes in contact with a stimulus following the occurrence of response that, in turn, results in an increase in the probability of the occurrence of the response subject to the performance standard. We prefer this definition because it is descriptive of the process and avoids labeling (a) stimuli as reinforcer, (b) the relationship between the stimulus and target behaviors as contingent, (c) the spatial locus of the reinforcer, and (d) the source controlling the integrity of the SR sequence. These features of the process set apart the operant view of SR from other perspectives. (p. 51)

Our representation of SR is, simply, self-administered consequences for behaviors that ultimately are instrumental to desired environmental consequences. SR increases the probability of recurring SRL. We take generic liberties in this fashion with each of the SRL theories.

Self-monitoring (SM) is the first step toward self-control. It includes procedures for identifying one's behavior and linking it to environmental consequences. SM requires observation of one's behavior (not as easy as it sounds) and recording that observation. Observational records of one's behavior are like observational research techniques in general. They vary from checklists and frequency counts to rating scales and written narratives. The more accurate the record, the more useful SM is for supporting SRL. Of most interest to SRL theorists not of the operant persuasion is the occurrence of reactivity of self-monitoring, that is, the tendency for behavior to change simply as a function of SM; consequences or reinforcement schedules are not needed for behavior to change in this event. What other theorists call "self-awareness" is sufficient for behavior change. This is perhaps the most difficult of the SRL support strategies for operant theorists to explain, although it can be done with a reconceptualization of recording of self-observation as a consequence (see Mace et al; 2001 for excellent discussion).

Self-Instruction (SI), "talking myself through it" in the operant perspective, is using language as a discriminative stimulus and functions in the same manner as other antecedent stimuli. SI also can take the form of sets of rules to follow, consistent with the ABC formula, in which the behavior to be completed is paired with the antecedent and consequent stimuli. SI in this form is the underlying structure of verbal chains that have evolved into mnemonic strategies typical of procedural learning used to increase self-control in classrooms.

Self-evaluation (SE) requires the comparison of one's performance to a standard of excellence, presumably set before engaging the behavior. If the standard is met, then SR can support SE by providing immediate and desired consequences. If the standard is not met, the standard itself may be set inappropriately or procedures to meet the standard may be judged inappropriate and changed. If the failure to meet criterion is due to the quality of the individual's performance and not faulty procedures or unrealistic standards, then self-correction (SC) or modification of the performance is required. When the performance is closer to standard, SR completes the SRL support process.

Considerations for Classroom Management Practices. Operant procedures to support SRL are readily evident in classroom management practices. In many instances, what teachers actually mean by student SRL is the transfer of teacher control of student behavior to student control of their own behavior. This can be accomplished through the ABC paradigm. First, teachers identify the behavior that they want improved or changed. Second, teachers monitor student behavior, noting the apparent antecedents, or triggers, that precede the behavior and the consequences that may reinforce it, thereby increasing the likelihood of behavior reoccurrence in similar antecendent conditions. Third, when stimuli and behaviors are identified, they can then be taught to students using an ABC mnemonic to organize the sequences of desired behavior.

For example, students may respond to the teacher cue to "read the directions" and "check your work" prior to handing in a class test. In a standardized testing situation, however, teacher cuing of student procedural knowledge is not acceptable practice. Thus, it is important that students learn to enact these strategies on their own if test results are to represent their knowledge. A simple ABC sequence to teach students might be: A. *Always* read the directions before you start, B. *Begin* working on the problems, C. *Check* your work. This ABC sequence, repeated over time, and testing conditions that gradually reduce teacher cuing behavior and also demonstrate to students that doing so improves their test performance and that this is a good thing, can serve as the transfer mechanism by which teacher control of student "self" instruction, monitoring, evaluation, correction, and reinforcement becomes student control of these "self" processes. An operant theorist would likely term this scenario an example of self-control, wherein the student delays gratification (e.g., gets the test over with) and avoids impulsivity (e.g., selects familiar answers without reading directions or solving problems). Self-control in test taking, however, may or may not indicate a SRL commitment to distal achievement goals as required by some operant theorists (e.g., Mace et al., 2001). Even so, we consider the "small wins" (Weick, 1984) of proximal self-control a promising predictor of more distal SRL, much in the manner that distributed success informs self-efficacy in the social cognitive perspective discussed subsequently.

The Antithesis: Cognitive Approaches to Self-Regulated Learning

We assign to the antithesis, or position opposite to operant approaches, theories that emphasize a cognitive perspective to SRL. We include in this group phenomenology, information processing, and volitional theories. As will become apparent, although these theories share common beliefs in the primacy of cognition, they are quite diverse in their theoretical priorities and propositions. We begin with the approach that differs most from behaviorism: phenomenology.

Phenomenology

A primary question that emerges from a phenomenology perspective to SRL is, how does a learner self-reflect to self-regulate their learning to create a personal and advantageous learning environment? Self-reflection has always been essential in phenomenology and it has always been conceptualized as an argument against behaviorism. Edmund Husserl, a German philosopher in the early 1900s, defined phenomenology as "reflection on the content of the mind to the exclusion of everything else." In more modern terms, phenomenology is defined as "the study of the development of human consciousness and self-awareness" (Mish, 1988, in McCombs, 2001). McCombs elaborates:

> That is, it [phenomenology] accepts as reality those experiences that are apparent to the senses and can be scientifically described and evaluated, *including abstract and nonobservable phenomena such as perceptions of self and others*... The methodology is based on the assumption that all knowledge derives from and is grounded in first-person experience and that the "experience" of consciousness and of self are real and can be systematically studied and verified.... In the context of self-regulated learning, a phenomenological perspective is one that *accepts the primacy of self phenomena in directing learning behaviors*; it favors a person-referenced over a performance-referenced account of SRL processes and activities. (p. 68, emphasis added)

In brief, phenomenology is about owning one's experience, not the experience itself or action within it. Phenomenology is personal and contemplative.

Definition of Self-Regulated Learning. Self-system structures and processes that support their development are the primary features of self-regulated learning. SRL itself is defined similarly to social-cognitive approaches (described subsequently), namely that SRL is about active participation in one's business and is known by metacognitive, motivational, and behavioral processes that facilitate learning. SRL processes in the phenomenological perspective, however, are only a piece of the puzzle and not the most interesting one at that. The self is the fundamental construct. The self-system structure and processes support SRL, particularly in the domains of motivational and emotional control.

Source of Self-Regulated Learning. The self is generative; its basic task is to generate motivation and commitment to personally meaningful learning. The self system structures consist of the "I" self and the "me" self. The "I" self is the source of a more enduring, natural, and higher-order self-concept; the "me" self is more task or domain specific. "Me" self includes knowledge of what is known, believed, and desired, and an image of oneself—in this case, an image of oneself as a self-regulated learner. The "me" self is a sort of working self-concept that is the source of motivation and self-regulatory strategies in a particular context. The "me" self can get in the way of the "I" self.

The self structures of global ("I") and domain-specific ("me") self-appraisals are supported by processes, termed "'I' self processes," that also can differ in globality and primacy. Supportive self processes include self-awareness, self-monitoring, self-reflection, self-evaluation, and self-regulation, each described previously in operant terms (e.g., reactivity of SM in operant work is a reasonable proxy for self-awareness in the phenomenological perspective). In addition, McCombs (2001) has argued for additional self-system processes that, in turn, support SRL. These include processes that promote the belief in one's competence and control; define learning and SRL goals and expectations that are personally relevant; monitor self-states (tied to the "me" self); and regulate and direct affect, motivation, and behavior (p. 91). The essential argument is that at the core of SRL is an image of oneself as an active agent in the learning process.

Support of Self-Regulated Learning. Educational opportunities that afford the development of self-system processes are important sources of support. In addition to the intrapersonal self-system supportive processes, phenomenologists look to informative, learner-centered environments to support the development and differentiation of the self. First, and foremost, for SRL to develop in students, they must experience choice and responsibility. Choice fosters active participation that warrants linking outcomes to personal action—a precursor to SRL. Choice also affords proactive goal-setting and planning strategies as compared to more reactive strategies of task management and completion. Such practices, as well as those that directly teach students about the self, foster students' beliefs in themselves as self-regulated learners as they promote the development and refinement of SRL strategies.

Considerations for Classroom Management Practices. Classroom management practices in the phenomenological perspective are about providing the opportunities for students to make choices, reflect on those choices, and render personally meaningful the experiences and the outcomes that accompany them. Specific educational opportunities are instrumental to the development of lifelong learners able to make decisions and feel ownership over their education. For example, within the constraints of an educational agenda aligned with mandated standards and accountability, teachers may provide students with (a) "guided choices" of how they will go about meeting objectives and (b) time to reflect on the effects of their choices. Guided choices may include opportunities for students to work alone or in small groups as they select from an array of sanctioned activities for a class project. Importantly, students are required to choose an activity and once selected it must be followed to completion, which may include a self-reflection paper about the journey.

The teacher role in managing student learning is interactive and personal, helping individual students reflect on and validate their experiences. This is a student-centered conversation that is not immune to student or teacher manipulation. A key feature of the phenomenological perspective is that the learner's task is to create a personal and advantageous learning environment—and "advantageous" is defined by the personal goals of the learner. The "me" self can and does get in the way of the "I," however, and sheer validation is not necessarily optimal. In the arena of classroom management of groups of learners, concerns about individuals' leaner identity ("but I'm not a math person") are sure to arise. For example, perfectionist and underachieving students are probably not the best choices for membership in a small work group and both could profit from more productive self-appraisals that teachers can promote through supportive confrontations that challenge students toward more appropriate choices and self-evaluations. In the phenomenological perspective, classroom management is all about teachers finding the time for knowledge of, reflection on, and support for learners coming to understand the responsibility of choice.

Information Processing (IP) Systems

In a provocative essay, "The psychology of thinking: Embedding artifice in nature," Herbert Simon (1969), a leader in the field of information processing, suggested that the human mind was a relatively straightforward system consisting of perception ←→ information processing ←→ memory storage and retrieval, in which short-term or working memory, the "place" in which information is processed, was limited in capacity and subject to time constraints, compared with the limitless potential of long-term memory for information storage. The apparent complexity in human thinking, he argued, was a reflection of the complexity of the environments—both the natural and the artificial—that humans navigate. Apparent complexity is more about the organism's adaptation than it is about the organism. Most readers likely, and correctly, associate information processing theory with computer metaphors. In this essay, however, Simon used the metaphor of an ant on a beach to explain his hypothesis of simplicity:

> We watch an ant make his laborious way across a wind- and wave-molded beach. He moves ahead, angles to the right to ease his climb up a steep dunelet, detours around a pebble, stops for a moment to exchange information with a compatriot. Thus he makes his weaving, halting way back to his home. So as not to anthropomorphize about his purposes, I sketch the path on a piece of paper. It is a sequence of irregular, angular segments—not quite a random walk, for it has an underlying sense of direction, of aiming toward a goal.

Simon speculates on the passage and suggests the following hypothesis:

> An ant, viewed as a behaving system, is quite simple. The apparent complexity of its behavior over time is largely a reflection of the complexity of the environment in which it finds itself.... In this chapter I should like to explore this hypothesis but with the word "man" substituted for "ant."
>
> *A man, viewed as a behaving system, is quite simple. The apparent complexity of his behavior over time is largely a reflection of the complexity of the environment in which he finds himself.* (pp. 63–65)

Self-regulated learning work that has emerged within an information processing framework does not continue this emphasis on the simplicity of the human mind and the complexity of the environment. Quite the opposite: In the information processing approach to SRL, the environment is more an opportunity for the display of human complexity than the reverse.

We consider it enough of a shift in perspective to locate the information processing approach to SRL in the cluster of cognitive theories that serve as the antithesis of behaviorism. But it didn't start out that way. We define modern SRL in this approach at length, because along with operant approaches, IP dominates modern conceptions of learning and motivation and their import for instruction and classroom management.

Definition of Self-Regulated Learning. Winne (2001) asserts five basic types of deliberate (vs. automatic or stimulus-triggered) information processes and, consistent with the assertions of the approach, labels and organizes them in the form of a mnemonic to facilitate the perception ←→ information processing ←→ memory storage and retrieval of the information. Winne defines the basic processes as Searching, Monitoring, Assembling, Rehearsing, and Translating (SMART). These deliberate processes are central to self-regulated learning. Each is fairly self-evident with the exception of Translating, which refers to representation of information in multiple formats and memory schema that aid recall and integration (e.g., graphs and verbal descriptions).

SRL processes act upon information that varies in form. In traditional IP work, the size or complexity of the information unit is about the smallest "bits" (or "elements" in the operant tradition), and the larger and more integrated "chunks." Chunks allow greater power in short-term or working memory because they are saturated with integrated prior knowledge and thus can bring much more information to bear on the acquisition of new learning or thinking. Modern SRL researchers continue to fine-tune these units. Winne, for example, differentiates chunks of information into schemas, which are further differentiated into tactics of if-then rules that can be organized by strategies in pursuit of a higher-level goal. The notion of cognition as goal-driven, as in the nonrandom path of Simon's ant making its way home, continues as a dominant theme in SRL processes and information storage.

SRL events are organized into four phases, three of which are essential. Phase one concerns defining the task; phase two, setting goals and plans for goal attainment; phase three, enacting the plans—that is doing the work—and possibly phase four, if it occurs, involves making changes to information in earlier phases. Within each phase, information processes construct information products, each having one of four possible topics: (1) conditions, (2) products, (3) standards, and (4) evaluations (Winne, 2001, p. 163). *Conditions* include resources (e.g., prior knowledge) and constraints (e.g., time limitations) for working on a task. *Products* are new units of information created by information processes (i.e., SMART) acting on existing information that lead toward goal attainment. *Standards* are the criteria imposed (by self or another) upon the products. *Evaluations* are more products that are the result of monitoring the product in comparison to the standard in the manner of TOTE units (Miller, Galanter, & Pribrum, 1960). A TOTE unit is a mnemonic for Test/Operate/Test/Exit; the self-evaluation of progress toward a goal that has been a constant theme in the IP tradition. Winne (2001) offers the COPES mnemonic—*C*onditions, *O*perations, *P*roducts, *E*valuations, *S*tandards—with *O*perations being a place holder for SMART, to facilitate memory and, presumably, implementation of subprocesses of SRL events.

What makes all of these processes and products function? Two processes, metacognitive monitoring and metacognitive control, act as a sort of overseer of the four phases of SRL events, each of which involves COPES. These "meta" processes allow flexibility. We are now at the crux of SRL in the IP approach: ultimately, metacognitive monitoring is the key process. Monitoring is essential to metacognition just as monitoring is essential to information processes (SMART), evaluation products, and any adaptive changes that may occur in phase four of SRL events. Monitoring also ushers in motivational concerns as learners are more or less pleased with their rate of progress and relative attainment of a standard of excellence. Motivation is construed as a decision-making process—choosing among alternative scripts—and, in the tradition of Simon (1969) "satisficing," or doing well enough, emerges as a motivational decision or disposition.

Source of SRL. SRL work in the IP perspective locates SRL in the information processing capabilities of the individual. In particular, it is up to the individual to perceive environmental cues and engage in the various levels of monitoring processes throughout SRL events. Researchers vary, but typically, SRL is viewed as an individual aptitude (cf. Perry, Nordby, & Vanderkamp, 2003).

Support for SRL. The capacity and time constraints on short-term or working memory can interfere with learner attempts to self-regulate. Thus, a primary vehicle to support learner engagement in SRL is to facilitate coping with assaults and strains on the IP system. A primary consideration is the conditions in which learners are expected to function. Appropriate task challenge is a necessary condition. Too-difficult work exceeds processing capacity, just as too-easy work fosters automaticity rather than deliberate information processing (task difficulty is also central to sociocultural perspectives discussed subsequently).

Another support for SRL is the opportunity to acquire appropriate prior knowledge that is organized into integrative chunks that in turn enable more efficient processing in short-term or working memory. Pre-requisite courses, often resisted by students because they are perceived to increase their task burden are, in this perspective, very supportive of new learning, higher-level thinking—and efficiency. So, too, is automaticity. Time spent making facts "mindless" is time well spent. The more readily students know their times tables the more the available capacity in short-term memory to think and use that information to solve problems. Mnemonics (the verbal chains of operant theorists) are believed to facilitate retrieval and enactment of enabling information and, in the examples in this discussion, also guide information processing itself (in the manner of rules in operant work). SQ4R—Survey, Read, Recite, Review, Reflect—for example, is a strategy believed to facilitate student learning of new text because it activates prior knowledge, helps the learner become familiar with concepts that will be discussed and with the organization of the text, and assists in student comprehension and retention of the material (Hartman, 2002).

There are also the basic external assaults on short-term memory that need not occur. A student without a pencil, a teacher who goes too fast, intrusive traffic noise—anything that makes it harder for learners to design external props to boost short-term memory capacity, to keep up, or monitor their thinking is a failure to support IP and SRL. SRL is by the student, but the teacher has the authority and responsibility to attend to the conditions in which students are expected to function.

Reflecting on the progression of his thinking over his career and the explosion of information during that time, Simon (1991) asserted that attention is the most precious human resource. In the IP perspective, attention—environmental events permeating the perceptual filter—is the gateway to processing information. Supporting SRL then, includes getting and keeping student attention. Teachers in early grades report that bright and cheerful necklaces that catch the light also catch student attention without demands for eye contact ("all eyes up here") that can be incompatible with some students' cultural rules and roles (Rohrkemper, 1984). In addition to "catching" attention, teachers who help students "tune out" interfering thoughts or noisy neighbors support students' SRL by teaching them strategies to "protect" attention. These strategies that help learners stay with a task also are key to volitional approaches to SRL, the third theory we include within the cognitive approaches to SRL.

Considerations for Classroom Management Practices. Classroom management practices in the IP perspective are about facilitating student processing of information in short-term or working memory and supporting the retrieval of relevant schemas. One important implication is the "keep it in proportion" rule whereby the saliency of an event is not allowed to swamp the reasoning behind it (e.g., Hoffman, 1979; Lepper and Greene, 1978). In classroom management this suggests that a particular sanction—reward or punishment—not be of such magnitude that the learner is unable to retrieve the reasons for its use (Rohrkemper, 1982). More routinely, today's classrooms just wouldn't be the same without the colorful posters of traffic lights (Red! Yellow! Green!) designed to help learners pay attention to and regulate their noise levels or the list of classroom and school rules in mnemonic (Coyote Code: *H*ave respect and be kind. *O*bey safety rules. *W*ork it out. *L*ive responsibly. What's that spell: *HOWL!* [MUSD, 2004]) or alliterative (Our 3Rs: Respectful, Reliable, Responsible) formats. The influences of IP on strategies for managing SRL are not limited to young or novice learners. The first author has invested much of her career in teaching college students (*H*ungry? *A*ngry? *L*onely? *T*ired? *HALT!!!!*). The careful reader will note the similarities between these management tools and those of the operant tradition; theoretically, however, these strategies function quite differently. In IP mnemonics facilitate learner awareness and intentional regulation; in the operant tradition mnemonics serve as antecedents or rules.

Volition

Motivational theorists assume that motivation leads to goal attainment. Volition theorists argue that this is an untenable leap of faith. Something else is required to get from motivational decisions to goal attainment. This "something else" is protecting intentions to adhere to the goal, or "volition" (Heckhausen, 1991). Volition is postdecisional; it is what helps the learner carry out a motivational decision to its realization.

Modern motivation theorists likely overlook volition because of a fundamental change in conceptions of motivation that occurred with the "cognitive" revolution in learning theory (see McClelland, 1985). Hull (1952), the leading behavioral theorist of his era to link learning and motivation, asserted the formula: The tendency to act is a function of drive x habit x incentive. The cognitive rejection and appropriation of Hull's formula did more than change biological and behavioral constructs into cognitive correlates. The cognitive formula replaced the "tendency to act" with "motivation." The revised formula (in Weiner, 1980, 1992) is: Motivation is a function of need x expectancy x value. Not only did "need" replace drive, "expectancy" habit, and "value" incentive, but the revised formula asserts that all three variables predict motivation, removing Hull's assertion that action was the target prediction. Further, in Hull's formula, two aspects of motivation were distinguished. First and foremost for Hull, drive, or motive, includes internal biologically based primary (e.g., hunger) and learned secondary (e.g., fear) drive states. The second aspect of motivation is the incentive factors, those extrinsic contingencies previously discussed within the operant perspective. The third factor in the Hull formula concerns learning; in combination, the three factors predict the tendency to act. The reformulation of Hull's work simplified motivation even as it made it all-inclusive. Most importantly for this discussion; however, was the removal of action as the outcome of interest. Volitional theory is about putting realized action back into the motivational landscape. Volitional behavior is learned strategies that protect motivational "intention"; volition is about seeing tasks through to completion.

In the study of SRL, volition picks up where IP left off. It is one thing to make a motivational decision and quite another to enact that decision. If New Year's resolutions were sufficient to change behavior this chapter would have been written (and likely read!) before now. In the volitional perspective on SRL, motivation and information processing are not enough. Learners need to learn strategies that help them to "follow through" on commitments. Where volition can make readers nervous—or relieved depending on perspective—is in the realization that volition does not require motivation. It is about getting the job done, not setting goals (McCaslin & Good, 1996).

Definition of Self-Regulated Learning. Self-regulated learning includes motivational dynamics and information processing strategies in the IP tradition; however, the volitional contribution to SRL stresses the strategies that individuals engage to see their intentions through to task completion.

Source of Self-Regulated Learning. Volition is part learned skill and part "work style" (Corno, 2001). Disposition toward work is a unique contribution of volition to the SRL literature. In this perspective, classrooms are workplaces rife with distractions. The acquisition of work habits or volitional aptitudes is a necessary, although insufficient, condition to get the tasks of school learning optimally done. One benefit of a focus on volitional strategies is that they can lead to student task attainment without remediation of motivational deficiencies. A key volitional strategy is *self-monitoring*. In the volitional perspective: "Self-monitoring protects concentration and motivation when intrusions arise in the outer (task) environment, or internally (e.g., as when interest or mood shifts)" (Corno, 2001, p. 191).

Similarly, *resourcefulness* in the volitional perspective includes task- and self-management. Management and control of the self and others are key constructs in the volitional perspective. Kuhl (1985) and Corno (2001) differentiate covert from overt processes of self-control. *Covert* processes include control of cognition processes similar to the IP perspective discussed previously. They include control of attention, encoding, and information-processing, with the particular goal of the efficiency of those processes. Emotion control primarily concerns overcoming negative affect. Motivation control is about prioritizing intentions, similar to notions of "goal coordination" (Dodge, Asher, & Parkhurst, 1989; McCaslin & Good, 1996). The basic idea is that you cannot do nor have it all at once. Motivation control processes that support prioritizing include incentive escalation, supportive attributional ascriptions, and (self) instruction. Motivation control is an important contribution to the SRL discussion because it frames motivation in terms of competing desires and demands rather than the presence or absence of motivation per se.

Overt processes of self-control are those that target the environment to enable better self-control. Control of the task situation includes modification of tasks and the settings in which they are to be completed; control of others in the task setting in classrooms involves teachers and students. Overt processes for control are similar to those discussed previously in the operant perspective. The premise is also congruent: when we take charge of our environment we take charge of ourselves. An additional theme in the volitional framework is environmental manipulation for personal efficiency.

Support of Self-Regulated Learning. Volitional strategies are learned, trainable, and continue to develop through adolescence based upon growing self-awareness, home socialization, and other experiences (Kuhl, 1985). Although not directly studied within the context of acquisition of volitional strategies, Corno (2001) hypothesizes that guided demonstration and scaffolding as represented in the sociocultural tradition (discussed subsequently) of Palincsar and Brown (1984) can promote volitional behavior. Certain task conditions likely provide the affording opportunities. Small-group learning has become a familiar feature of classroom learning formats. Overt control of tasks and others in the setting are readily observed (McCaslin & Good, 1996; Panagiotopolous, 1986, in Corno, 2001). To the extent that social modeling (discussed subsequently) in small groups is available, volitional approaches, like SRL theories in general, would predict that peers can and do learn volitional strategies from one another. One potential problem with this opportunity, however, is the difficulty of teacher monitoring of small-group dynamics (e.g., Tsang, 2003): it is easy to imagine inappropriate task and other control strategies acquired in these learning formats.

Home socialization as a source for learning volition is vividly portrayed in research on students completing homework assignments. Getting through homework assignments at the kitchen table is an opportunity ripe for the enactment (or not) of covert control processes such as time management and emotion control as well as overt control processes such as procuring help (Xu & Corno, 1998). In case study research with 6th-grade students and their negotiation of home learning with school expectations, McCaslin and Murdock (1991) found that, to the extent that parent or caregiver help aligns with the apprenticeship model of guided demonstration—that also may include a reasoned *refusal* to assist (e.g., "it is *your* responsibility to follow through on your commitments")—students have the opportunity to learn and refine as well as display volitional strategies. To the extent that "help" is inadequate or punitive, however, volitional demands can be imposed without strategies to meet them (e.g., "you will sit there until you finish"). One result is a spiraling of negative emotion and rejection of intentions... more an acquisition of destructive habits than the intended volition of "staying on track."

Considerations for Classroom Management Practices. If students are to learn to be volitional, they first need to learn what it means to be volitional. The more recent work by Corno in the volitional perspective continues earlier themes in SRL: unnecessary or superfluous supports can undermine SRL, volition included (e.g., Corno & Mandinach, 1983). Tasks and settings designed to maintain student automaticity do not provide the kind of fertile lapses in which students might learn to recognize the need for volitional control and thus have the opportunity to learn the covert and overt strategies that allow them to "own" their time on task (Rohrkemper & Corno, 1988).

This suggests that smooth-running classrooms, seamless instruction, and engaging tasks may not be ideal conditions for students to learn volitional strategies. Rather, volition is learned through necessity: something else is needed for students to get from what they planned or the task they were given to actual task completion. This is not to say that because student volitional capabilities can compensate for inadequate management, instruction, and tasks, they should be required to compensate. However, it is useful to consider that without those gaffs in small-group learning, or the experience of too-difficult or too-easy tasks, or the interruptions and distractions in classrooms, students would not have the opportunity to learn a very basic and essential component of personal responsibility: seeing through and following through on commitments. Teachers who provide realistic mixtures of learning opportunities—not all tasks are interesting and not all classmates are helpful—and teach students how to garner strategies to persevere nonetheless are teaching an essential feature of the volitional approach to SRL: staying the course.

An Emerging Synthesis: Theories of Social Influences

We assert that current perspectives that emphasize the social influences on self-regulated learning serve as a dynamic synthesis to the apparent dichotomy of operant (thesis) and cognitive (antithesis) perspectives. In addition to the considerable common ground among the social influence theories (e.g., reciprocal causality) there are important differences concerning the origins and maintenance of social influence. Accordingly, we also frame these differences within the proposed synthesis as a dialectic progression. At one anchor is the social cognitive perspective with its historical origins in operant constructs and their transformation by Bandura (1977) and at the opposite anchor is the "second wave" constructivist perspective with its historical origins in Piaget's (1983) developmental theory. We also assert that the most viable synthesis to emerge within the social influence theories is the sociocultural perspective with its historical origins in Vygotsky's (1962, 1978) theory of the social origins of higher psychological processes. Such assertions are risky, however, as work in the social influence perspective is quite active and challenging and may well (and hopefully will) move the field in the direction of a "new" dialectic progression, wherein social influences becomes the thesis that contains the seeds of its own obsolescence.

Social Cognitive Theory

Social cognitive theory seeks to explain the learning of socially relevant behaviors in a social context (Levy, 1970). Social cognitive theory is consistent with the integration of the operant perspective (discussed previously) with the early work of Rotter (1954), who developed expectancy-reinforcement theory as a way to understand complex human social behavior. The theory advanced through the work of Bandura and Walters (1963) and Bandura (1969), in which operant conditioning explained reinforcement and imitation as they related to the control of behavior. Subsequently, Bandura (1977) expanded the theory to include two additional influences on behavior: (a) modeling and thus vicarious (vs. direct) learning of behavior and (b) "self-efficacy," or one's personal beliefs about the ability to learn or perform specific behaviors. More recently, Bandura (1997) developed the construct of "collective efficacy" in addition to beliefs about the self. In essence, social cognitive theory incorporates the hedonism of operant theory with the affiliation motive. That is, behavior is instrumental to seeking pleasure and avoiding pain, and the human desire for acceptance in a community results in the willingness to assimilate one's behaviors and beliefs to that community. Affiliation and reinforcement align with two distinct features of the tendency to act as proposed by Hull (1952): motive (drive) and incentive (consequences).

Definition of Self-Regulated Learning. SRL in the social cognitive perspective relates to internal processes that determine behavior in a particular situation (Clark & Zimmerman, 1990). SRL is not a trait nor is it a developmental attainment, although there is limited recognition that young children have difficulty with SRL and strategies like goal-setting. SRL in the social cognitive perspective involves information processing consistent with the IP perspective (discussed previously) that is integrated with self-efficacy beliefs and affiliation needs. As defined by Schunk (2001):

> Self-regulated learning (SRL) refers to learning that results from students' self-generated thoughts and behaviors that are systematically oriented toward the attainment of their learning goals ... for example, attending to instruction, processing information, rehearsing and relating new learning to prior knowledge, *believing that one is capable of learning, and establishing productive social relationships and work environments.* (p. 125 emphasis added)

Source of Self-Regulated Learning. Three interactive subprocesses are involved in SRL in each of three phases of SRL activity that interact with the learning environment. The subprocesses, *self-observation, self-judgment, and self-reaction*, are defined consistently with operant theory as discussed by Mace et al. (2001). Thus, self-observation aligns with self-monitoring (SM), self-judgment with self-evaluation (SE), and self-reaction with the self-correction (SC) and self-reinforcement (SR) behaviors of operant theory. One key theoretical difference, however, is that social cognitive theory asserts that the anticipation of consequences motivates behavior, not the consequences per se. In this perspective, the individual is influenced by what he or she thinks may happen to him or her. Recent arguments by Schunk (2001), however, reassert the utility of performance-contingent rewards per se to enhance SRL.

The three phases of SRL—*Forethought, Performance Control, and Self-Reflection*—are more recent aspects of social cognitive work meant to capture the cyclical nature and malleability of SRL (Zimmerman, 1998).

The *Forethought* phase includes the processes of goal setting and social modeling that students bring to a learning situation. Goal setting and social modeling incorporate student self-efficacy appraisals with affective needs. Proximal goals set by the learner (vs. more distal goals or assigned tasks) motivate and enhance SRL. Social modeling includes exposure to mastery behavior (what behavior should look like when it is learned correctly) and coping behavior (incomplete learning along the way to mastery that indicates progress and eventual goal attainment). Modeling can also be considered in terms of who is the model. In the instance of research on adult compared with peer models, however, status (adult and peer) is likely confounded with level of mastery (masterful expert and coping novice)—unless the domain is computer technology or programming the family VCR. Schunk and Hanson (1989) have demonstrated that social modeling increases self-efficacy and achievement under most circumstances, but peer models and coping models are the most effective form of social modeling.

Performance control is the volitional (Corno, 1989, 2001) or control phase of learning that includes social comparisons, attributional feedback, strategy instruction and self-verbalization. It is perhaps surprising that social comparative information is considered a support of performance control; however, the affiliation need that underlies social cognitive theory is more about "fitting in with" than "besting" others. Social comparative information in this perspective is not considered interpersonally competitive as much as it is intrapersonally challenging to meet the performance levels of others.

Attributional feedback in this perspective is linked to effort or ability ascriptions for performance outcomes. Studies differ in issues of attributional focus (e.g., "you are really smart"; "you tried hard") and timing of the attributional feedback (e.g., at goal setting, performance, or reflection phases of SRL), but the common theme for social cognitive theorists is the issue of credibility of the information (Schunk, 2001), consistent with the social cognitive perspective on the credibility of and therefore effectiveness of a model.

Strategy instruction and self-verbalization is self-talk that learners engage that maintains performance strategies. Self-talk in this perspective is more aligned with the Self-instruction (SI) of operant theory discussed previously than with the inner speech of the Vygotskian perspective discussed subsequently. That is, self-talk in the social cognitive perspective is about continuous cuing that maintains rule adherence; in contrast, inner speech in the Vygotskian perspective is the essential link between social and cultural influences and higher psychological processes. We return to this distinction.

Self-reflection, the final phase of SRL, consists of progress feedback and self-evaluation, self-monitoring, and reward contingencies. Each of these processes has been similarly presented in the context of operant and information processing theories.

Recent work in social cognitive theory attends to the internalization of social resources or supports to function as self-sources (see Zimmerman, 2000). Internalization of social support shifts the locus of relative "credit" for student learning away from social influences such as models, guidance, and feedback toward more personal control that is possible due to the enactment of SRL strategies. The evidence of initial "self-controlled" internalization is the learner's successful performance, independent of social supports, on related tasks. Ultimately, however, the goal is "self-regulated" internalization wherein the learner can transfer the performance beyond related tasks to new contexts. The distinction and criteria for self-control and SRL are similar to those of operant theory discussed previously. In the newest formulations of internalization processes by social cognitive theorists, however, learners, even though self-regulating, are no longer considered to be independent learners. Instead, self-regulating learners remain bound to social sources of support, even though they may appear to use them less frequently (e.g., Zimmerman, 2000). These more recent social cognitive formulations of the fusion of source and support for SRL that go beyond the dynamics of modeling and reinforcement have much in common with work in the sociocultural perspective we discuss subsequently.

Support of Self-Regulated Learning. Social cognitive theory elaborates upon the reinforcement work of operant theorists to include an emphasis on modeling and guidance as key supports for the acquisition of self-regulated learning. SRL acquisition is facilitated by the types of tasks and feedback that cue and reinforce the three phases of SRL—forethought, performance control, and self-reflection—to be learned and practiced.

Considerations for Classroom Management Practices. In addition to strategies consistent with operant theory, social cognitive theory highlights the value of group affiliation, peer modeling, and accountability in classroom management practices. For example, small-group composition decisions (e.g., students presenting behavioral challenges paired with students who exhibit SRL) and some forms of public feedback ("I like the way group three is working so quietly ... ") are based on social cognitive principles. Most central to the social cognitive perspective, however, is the crucial role that credibility plays in teacher management practices. The teacher is first and foremost the model by which students learn the SRL subprocesses of self-observation, self-judgment, and self-reaction in each of the three phases of SRL (forethought, performance control, self-reflection). Importantly, through teacher modeling, feedback, and reinforcement, students also can learn that the results of these subprocesses need to be accurate. A social cognitive (and sociocultural) perspective suggests that teachers attend to the "match" between teacher judgment of student SRL processes and students' self-judgments (see also, Zuckerman, 1994). Accurate student self-appraisals are more likely to the extent that students feel efficacious, view their teachers as credible sources for their covert learning, like their teachers, and want to be valued by them. One interesting omission in research on the social cognitive approach to SRL that seems directly related to considerations for classroom management is the role that teacher efficacy might play in any application of a theory so deeply rooted in the notion of credibility.

Neoconstructivism: The Second Wave

Paris, Byrnes and Paris (2001) provide an excellent discussion of the evolution of Piagetian constructivists and thus their approach to SRL. They note that Paris and Byrnes (1989) presented the "first wave" of the Piaget constructivist approach that was derived from the work of Piaget (1983) and Bruner (1986). Byrnes and Paris summarized some of the key principles of "solo" constructive thinking in the following:

- There is an intrinsic motivation to seek information.
- Understanding goes beyond the information given.
- Mental representations change with development.
- There are progressive refinements in levels of understanding.
- There are developmental constraints on learning.
- Reflection and reconstruction stimulate learning. (2001, p. 54)

The "second" wave of Piagetian constructivists elaborate on this early framework, replacing an emphasis on the idiosyncratic constructions of the individual learner with a perspective of the social-embeddedness of a cultural participant, in the manner of sociocultural, Vygotskian theory discussed later.

Definition of Self-Regulated Learning. The second-wave constructivists elaborate on the definition of SRL in five aspects (see Paris et al., 2001). First, the second wave includes the perspective that learning is situated in social and historical contexts, a primary assertion of Vygotskian theory. The SRL implication of this addition is a major change in focus on just what it is to be self-regulated. Primarily individual learning processes give way to those actions and goals that are specified by social roles and situations within the context of individual history. Thus, the second aspect of this perspective shifts focus from individual intra-cognition to actual participation in acculturated practices that individuals engage. The SRL implication is the assertion that SRL is an adaptive response to environmental demands (see also McCaslin & Murdock, 1991). Further, being literate about these demands is key for SRL in these contexts (see also, Corno, 1989).

Third, group membership in the second-wave perspective is an active coconstructor of individual identity development, including the evolution of the "I" and "me" selves (see previous discussion of phenomenology). Fourth, people construct self-evaluative stories of their lives that are largely coherent about the past and optimistic about the future (see also McAdams, 1993) in a sort of autobiographical TOTE unit (Miller et al., 1960). Finally, thinking and learning are usually adaptive, but maladaptive cognition and behavior are distinct possibilities. This leads to the assertion that the interpretation of an experience is more important than the experience (see also phenomenology). SRL is thus defined in terms of socially situated participation in the practices belonging to a desirable group, such that membership in that group enhances individual self-image and optimistic beliefs in the future. SRL is about becoming a person identified with desirable others (as in social cognitive approaches to modeling) who can predictably engage in membership practices that reaffirm and further a sense of self.

Source of Self-Regulated Learning. Taken together, these five elaborations on first-wave constructivism lead to the assertion that identity confirmation is the primary motive to engage in, and therefore is the source of, SRL. The goal is to appear attractive to a chosen reference group. Students "try on" different personas that they self-evaluate for "goodness of fit" and others' confirmation (see Erikson, 1968). Self-portrayals that lead to increases in self-esteem and mutual validation by valued others are apt to be repeated. If acceptance by others is lacking, "then students are likely to choose a different identity rather than become unregulated" (Paris et al., 2001, p. 259). As Erikson (1968) discussed, these alternative identities are not necessarily those we would wish a student pursue; however, having a negative identity (e.g., gang membership) is preferable and safer to the integrity of the ego than not quite being someone at all.

Students acquire SRL strategies through invention, consistent with the first wave of constructivism, and through instruction or intervention. This more recent position aligns with the sociocultural construct of "emergent interaction" discussed later. Important to this perspective, SRL strategies and the contexts within which they are acquired and therefore practiced become part of students' beliefs about themselves as learners that can be resistant to change. Self-knowledge becomes a more core value with development and experience.

Support of Self-Regulated Learning. Support for SRL shares many features of previously discussed perspectives (e.g., promotion of efficacy beliefs); however, an important source of support for SRL in the second wave perspective concerns the validation of activities that individuals engage. SRL in the second-wave is all about validated identity and finding one's place. Activities that confirm an identity and are rewarded by valued others are likely to be repeated and internalized. This is consistent with internalization due to reinforcement and affiliation needs in recent work within social cognitive theory.

Considerations for Classroom Management Practices. A second-wave constructivist perspective on classroom management practices begins with the question, "What is the array of possible selves available to students to explore and try on for good measure?" Multidimensional classrooms would seem to have many more opportunities for students to seek identity fulfillment and expertise in related practices in ways we might wish for them (e.g., mathematicians, creative writers, environmentalists, policy advocates) than do unidimensional classrooms where only a few (the fastest thinker, the slowest learner) find their niche (Weinstein, 2002).

The more inclusive the "sanctioned" opportunities for learning about the self—for engaging in belief-desire-action sequences—the more likely that students would not need to invent alternate identities that are outside of or in opposition to adult influence. This approach invites the question, what are the adaptive demands placed on students? Do these demands allow an imagined self (see also phenomenology) that they can value and meet in ways that promote a sense of self-efficacy and belief in a positive future?

Vygotskian and Neo-Vygotskian Sociocultural Perspectives

Lev S. Vygotsky (1962; 1978) was an avowed Marxist whose ideas were the product of adaptation to unique circumstances of rapid social change and very high stakes (see McCaslin Rohrkemper, 1989; McCaslin & Hickey, 2001; Wertsch, 1985, for more complete discussion). Foundations of his work include Engels' 1890 theory (1972) on language; Marx's 1867 position on consciousness (1972), self-control, and social contribution; and Hegel's 1807 definition of movement or progress as the conflict of opposites in a dialectical hierarchy (1949).

One result was a developmental approach to individual mediation of cultural experience. Experience is cultural because it represents socially structured tasks and tools. It is historical because it reflects the "storehouse" of knowledge of humankind (Luria, 1979, p. 44). It is personal because individual development, particularly biological readiness and opportunity, enable the individual to refine his capacity for self-direction and, hence, meaningful social contribution. One implication of this perspective is that what mainstream American psychology may consider a characteristic of individuals (like SRL), a Vygotskian theorist may consider an ongoing coregulated process that is uniquely negotiated, integrated, and reconstructed through interpersonal engagement in meaningful opportunity.

Definition of Self-Regulated Learning. Vygotsky focused upon the development of multiple functions of language that fused Engels' premise on language with Marx's position on consciousness: the ability to communicate with others is distinct from but also informs the ability to self-direct one's conscious thinking. The functions of speech differ such that speech that communicates with others requires transforming thoughts to words; in contrast, speech that directs the self involves transforming words to thoughts (Vygotsky, 1962, p. 131). The developmental sequence of these functions is from social or interpersonal to self-directive or intrapersonal; however, the social environment is the source of each. The emergent capacity for "self-regulation" for Vygotsky begins in the interpersonal realm and is a function of self-directive inner speech that integrates the affective and intellectual. For Vygotsky, thoughts did not think themselves; people did, with all their emotions, aspirations, and self-knowledge.

Wertsch (1985) and Zinchenko (1985) challenged the Vygotskian position on word meaning as the most basic unit of analysis and argued instead for a construct of "activity" that embodies "tool-mediated, goal-directed action." Activity theory asserts that motives and goals emerge and exist within the sociocultural realm rather than as a property of the individual (see, e.g., Kozulin, 1986; Leontiev, 1974–75; 1978). Most theorists within the Vygotskian tradition consider "tool-mediated (the Engels part), goal-directed (the Marx part) action (the neo-Vygotskian part)" as the basic unit of meaningful analysis for understanding higher psychological processes. This position has replaced Vygotsky's original stance on word meaning. In modern work, human activity represents individual and collective mediation of participation in opportunity rather than a direct effect of opportunity (see also phenomenology). The neo-Vygotskian shift to view self-directive inner speech as one aspect of self-regulation has broadened interests in this work to types of tasks that learners engage as well as the contexts in which they participate.

Source of Self-Regulated Learning. Perhaps the most well-known representation of the Vygotskian approach to meaningful learning contexts is the Zone of Proximal Development (ZPD), the gap between what a learner can do alone (a proxy for SRL) and with help (coregulated learning).The relationship between the participants in the ZPD is central; the dynamic is of coregulation, in contrast to top-down constructs like modeling in social cognitive theory (Yowell & Smylie, 1999). The goal of the ZPD is to connect the cultural knowledge of the teacher or more capable peer with the learner's everyday understandings and opportunities in the pursuit of meaningful learning (Wertsch & Stone, 1985). Everyday understandings of the responsive contingencies in one's experience—a basic tenet of operant theory discussed previously—is essential to the development of SRL because it enables prediction (McCaslin & Hickey, 2001). Current work on the coregulation of student higher psychological processes in the ZPD has parsed the sources of emergent SRL to include the opportunities that are available to and engaged in by students, the ZPD activities they participate in, and the emergent identity that evolves as a function of each (McCaslin, 2004).

Support of Self-Regulated Learning. Support for SRL is better termed support for "adaptive learning" as SRL is instrumental to adaptive learning. Adaptive learning involves the internalization of goals; the motivation to commit, challenge, or reform them; and the competence to enact and evaluate those commitments (McCaslin Rohrkemper, 1989). Adaptive learning is part of emergent identity; thus, it is historical. It may be expressed in the present moment but it is linked to the individual's past and informs his or her future. Adaptive learning empowers the individual and enriches the culture; it is instrumental to socially meaningful activity.

Coregulation is the process by which adaptive learning is developed, supported, and maintained in the learners ZPD (see McCaslin, 1996, 2004; McCaslin & Good, 1996). Coregulation in school settings is based on three concepts. First, the basic unit of analysis in school learning is the relationship among individuals, objects, and settings (rather than individuals or tasks). Second, students' basic task is coordination of multiple social worlds, expectations, and goals. Achievement is only one aspect of being a student; being a student is only one aspect of being a child. Third, goal coordination in the pursuit of adaptive learning is learned and it is difficult. Teachers' basic task is to provide supportive scaffolding and affording opportunities to promote—to coregulate—student mediation processes that enhance adaptive learning.

Student mediation processes consist of student Motivation, Enactment, and Evaluation activities (see McCaslin and Good, 1996). Coregulation of Motivation activities includes support for student motivational dynamics similar to those discussed earlier in the social cognitive perspective. In addition to support for goal setting, however, coregulation includes support for goal coordination and review. Goal coordination involves understanding relationships among goals so that goal alignment or negation can be anticipated in the pursuit of multiple goals (see Dodge et al., 1989, for an excellent discussion). Goal review includes decisions to quit or change course as viable, and possibly desirable, options. In this perspective multiple goals are desirable rather than interfering. It's about not putting all your eggs in one basket.

In the sociocultural view, developing motive dispositions inform what we value and to what and whom we make commitments; that is, motive dispositions inform student identity, including the development and display of motivational competence. Motivational competence also involves the community that participates in and validates personal striving and commitments.

Coregulation of Enactment activities includes helping students with overt and covert strategies directed to the self and other persons and tasks in the social/instructional environment (SIE), consistent with operant, volitional, and social cognitive theories. Covert enactment activities direct the learner through inner speech that integrates affective ("self-involved") with the intellectual ("task-involved") aspects of consciousness. Inner speech guides activity in pursuit of a goal. Recall that inner speech is social in origin; thus, it represents the transformation of cultural understandings in the formation of mind. Vygotsky predicted self-directive inner speech in nonautomatic "effortful" cognition. Research suggests that subjectively moderately difficult problems afford optimal opportunities for enacting "tool-mediated, goal-directed action" and enhancing students' task-and self-involved inner speech, thereby optimizing their ZPD. Further, reported inner speech and goal-directed activity is aligned with student beliefs about themselves as learners (McCaslin Rohrkemper, 1989).

Coregulation of Evaluation activities includes teaching students to align their self-evaluations with teacher evaluations, which then inform motivational dynamics and alteration of enactment strategies in the manner of a TOTE unit (Miller et al., 1960) discussed previously. In this perspective an important goal of evaluation is the promotion of identity rooted in realistic self-appraisals that are more textured than the notion of "accuracy." The struggle for competence within this perspective is all about the conflict of opposites—the headiness of success and the dread of failure—and their transcendence. Our learner must know the motivational dynamics of success and failure if he or she is to become an adaptive learner who maintains self-confidence and realistic self-appraisals. New work and its mastery are essential achieving opportunities of classrooms just as review and tests signal accountability demands (McCaslin & Burross, 2002). If they connect with student-emergent identity and motive disposition and result in an array of relative success and failure outcomes that are validated by valued others, students will learn to trust themselves when faced with the challenges of failure and the seduction of success (McCaslin, 2004).

As McCaslin (2004) argues, coregulation is all about meaningful opportunities and interpersonal supports that contribute not only to developing strategic motivational and cognitive learning skills but also to the socialization of personal aspirations. A sociocultural perspective does not stop with a student motivated to strategically learn, able to prioritize her intentions, and realistically judge her progress. The point also is to influence what students come to value, to encourage them to go beyond enlightened self-interest to contribute to the common good. In this aspect, sociocultural theory is quite different from other social-influence and constructivist perspectives that look to the social world to enhance the individual and leave it there, at individual self-interest.

Considerations for Classroom Management Practices. Classroom management for SRL in the sociocultural perspective incorporates the insights of the behavioral and cognitive approaches but situates them in developmentally sensitive relationships rather than generic individual self-interest. Perhaps the most directly useful sociocultural construct to organize management or any other classroom practices is the ZPD that explicitly recognizes that what learners are not able to do without assistance is a potent target for meaningful learning. Disagreements about the ZPD construct are best known among developmental scholars. Piaget asserted that developmental readiness precedes instructional effectiveness; in contrast, Vygotsky claimed that meaningful learning can co-occur, precede, or "pull" development. In research on classroom management practices, Rohrkemper (1984, 1985) conceptualized the ZPD debate to be one of the "development" of thought (a la Piaget) and the "socialization" of thought (a la Vygotsky).

Rohrkemper (1984) conceptualized teaching as a manifestation of culturally sanctioned helping behavior; thus, classroom management was considered an especially powerful vehicle for teaching and learning the sociocultural rules associated with helping, neglecting, or punishing behavior. Participants were elementary teachers judged expert in classroom management, who differed in their approach to classroom management style, and their students, who differed in range of "problem presentation" that included those students easy and pleasurable to teach. One teacher management style was a highly verbal, explanatory approach based upon intention; the other was a highly predictable, rule-driven system based on behavior.

In brief, results suggested that student learning of sociocultural roles and rules of responsible behavior was most meaningfully organized by their teacher's management style, especially in interaction with student developmental level. Most importantly, student-reported understandings of their teacher's and their own response to peer behavior illustrated the power of teacher language use. Students whose teachers focused on rationales for rules and expectations expressed attributional knowledge and behavioral response consistent with cultural rules of responsibility. In comparison, students whose teachers focused on behavior and consequences did the same—without understanding the principles that our culture employs and expects individuals to use in their own self-control and their judgments and sanctioned responses to others.

Younger students were markedly more influenced by teacher management style than their older peers. Younger children in classrooms using rule-driven systems based on behavior were notably different—deficient—in their cultural understandings than were their young peers in classrooms based upon explanation and intention. These data mesh nicely with Vygotsky's notions of the ZPD: teacher explanations of the rationales underlying behavior, expectations, and discipline scaffold younger students' interpersonal understanding beyond the level associated with their developmental level. These students' teachers were able to meaningfully connect cultural norms about responsibility and accountability at a higher level than these students' everyday understandings derived from their behavior-consequence experiences. These and related findings suggest the viability of mediation within the ZPD that can enrich cultural understandings and empower individuals beyond the affordances of their personal development. In the Vygotskian, sociocultural perspective, managing classrooms for SRL is about making cultural rules and roles personally meaningful. SRL is social in origin and some approaches to coregulating student learning are more powerful in their influence than others (see McCaslin, 2004, for more extended discussion from which this analysis is taken).

THEORY-BASED IMPLICATIONS FOR CLASSROOM PRACTICES

We have presented theories of SRL organized in a framework that highlights their differences and integration. Although theoretically distinct, particularly in conceptions of the goal of SRL in the manifestation of optimal functioning, there are common themes among the theories that can facilitate their usefulness in classrooms. In addition, the nuts and bolts that comprise the support of SRL are surprisingly similar across perspectives. Important for considerations for classroom management, these components also are identifiable and open to environmental manipulation. We begin with the common themes.

Common Themes in SRL Theories

The enduring influence of the operant approach—the thesis—in SRL is evident across theories. This is to be expected in the social-influence theories that we assert resolve the dichotomous conflict of operant-cognitive paradigms in a dialectical progression. Operant strategies, however, dominate even in two of the three cognitive approaches (i.e., IP and volition) that presumably consider themselves the "opposite," or antithesis, of operant work. The enduring influence of operant work is evident at two levels, the surface level of supportive strategies and the deeper level of the very structure of SRL conceptions.

Consider, for example, the basic presentations of SRL subprocesses. They tend to come in temporal sequences, often in sets of three. The controlling stimuli of the operant paradigm is arrayed into Antecedent–Behavior–Consequences (ABC). The three essential phases of SRL in information processing theory consist of Definition of the task–Goal setting and plans for attainment–Plan enactment. Three phases of SRL in social cognitive theory are termed Forethought–Performance Control–Self-Reflection. Second-wave constructivism organizes identity seeking, the theoretical motive for engaging in SRL, into Belief–Desire–Action sequences. Similarly, modern sociocultural work parses participation in the social-instructional environment into Opportunity–Activity–Identity units and delineates three phases of coregulated student mediation: Motivation–Enactment–Evaluation. Although most SRL theories assert some type of feedback loop or mechanisms of reciprocal causality, the operant view of the environment clearly has shaped most SRL theoretical development.

Next is the operant approach to task analysis. Within each of the SRL sequences, theories parse SRL subprocesses with the precision of algorithms in long division. This is most evident in the IP perspective and least in the phenomenologist and second-wave approaches, but it is key throughout. Theories of SRL apply task analysis strategies, original to operant approaches, to the workings of the mind. Instructional supports are then mapped onto the task analysis of mental processes, similar to the instructional design work of Gagne (1985). As we suggest subsequently, SRL theories inadvertently also have introduced the notion of differing SRL capabilities—differences in learning goals that structure the relationships among task analysis and instructional elements—in the manner of Gagne.

Operant work also leads the way in transferring or transforming observable behaviors into a fusion of overt/covert dynamics of everyday experiences that are theoretically necessary and also meaningful to the lay person. All the theories examined here assert a key role to self-monitoring, for example, and the idea of self- and other-reinforcement is prominent. Whether in the pursuit of enabling "I" and "me" selves (phenomenology), efficiency (information processing), task completion (volition), self-efficacy (social cognitive theory), or interpersonal validation (second-wave constructivism), reinforcement and success is a dominant hedonic goal in most theories. Even the honor of the struggle and the constructive role of informative failure valued by Vygotskian perspectives can be framed in terms of "intermittent reinforcement" without appreciably diminishing implications for classroom practice. Ironically, self- reinforcement presents the most difficulty to the operant theorists.

A third common perspective across theories involves "talking it through." Theories differ in why language is important. For example, the most extreme comparisons are anchored by operant theorists at one end, who would note the discriminate stimulus features of speech and a Vygotskian at the other end, who would assign language a much deeper role in the fusion of culture with the formation of consciousness. Reasons may vary, but the recommendations are the same: talk about it! This feature of SRL promotion has much in common with the parenting-styles literature that finds that children of authoritative parents, those who explain the reasoning behind their rules and expectations, tend to internalize and adhere to parent expectations (Baumrind, 1987). The power of explanation also has been found in research on classroom management strategies, particularly with younger students (Rohrkemper, 1984, 1985).

Common Considerations for Classroom Management Practices

In one very important sense, then, basic conceptions of the underlying structure of SRL and the strategies believed to support it are not particularly esoteric. But they are instructive to classroom management. In our review of seven theoretical positions on SRL we discussed considerations for management practices particular to a given theory. Here we suggest seven recommendations for classroom management that hold more generally across perspectives.

First, teachers need to understand and organize their own interpretive sequences. It is easy to get taken by surprise when dealing with groups of students and time spent understanding personally held belief sequences before the fact is useful. For example, attribution theory would suggest that Attribution–Emotion–Action sequences govern how humans understand and react to behavior. This has proved to be a useful sequence in understanding teacher and student interpersonal relationships and classroom management (Rohrkemper, 1984, 1985; Rohrkemper & Brophy, 1983). Group-comparison studies do not necessarily represent how a given individual understands events, however, and time spent in self-reflection as recommended by phenomenologists seems appropriate for teachers as well.

Second, parsing complex behavior into more manageable components that afford environmental/social support is essential for promoting student acquisition of SRL. Work by Meichenbaum (1977) seems particularly helpful for teachers who are faced with the question of "Where to begin?" Cognitive behavior modification, as presented by Meichenbaum, posits the internal dialogue that learners engage as the primary vehicle for meaningful behavior change. His work has been applied to an array of problem behavior situations and results in impressive changes in behavior that maintain and generalize. We think they apply to establishing and supporting student SRL as well. The following strategies are included in most SRL theories; however, the organization of these strategies is based upon the work of Meichenbaum:

1. Observe the student's behavior. Perform a task analysis to identify both the apparent needed skills and the apparent cause of the lack of SRL. This information guides the content and sequence of the teacher's modeling and interference with the inner dialogue.
2. Assign meaning to the problem for the student. Make the student aware of the problem and engage him or her as a collaborator.
3. Work on the students' internal dialogue. Teach the student to counter negative inner speech with more positive, adaptive inner dialogue. Teach the student both directly and through modeling to replace "I don't care," or "I feel like giving up" with "I can learn this if I try."
4. Model both behaviorally and verbally: (a) model feelings of apathy and resignation; (b) model coping with those feelings ("There I go, thinking that I am dumb, I need to think about what I need to do to get going on this..."); (c) model mastery ("There, I did try that and it worked"); and (d) model self-reinforcement ("I did a good job on that").
5. Facilitate the student's internalization through successive approximations. This process involves: (a) teacher demonstrating aloud, (b) student performing while the teacher verbally "guides," (c) the student talking it through aloud, (d) student whispering it through, and (e) student covert performance.
6. Train the student in necessary skills gleamed from the task analysis. Use rewards, if needed, to establish the initial behavior. Keep reinforcements informative and tied to quality of performance.
7. Provide proof of effectiveness.
8. Reinforce behavior-verbalization congruence. Keep reinforcements informative and tied to quality of congruence.

Third, relatively few SRL theories ascribe to developmental differences among students. Phenomenology, second-wave constructivism, and Vygotskian perspectives are the most apt to understand students in this way—but they are also the least likely to parse complex behavior into elements. Teachers will need to integrate the task analysis of SRL and the Meichenbaum procedures with what they know about the students in their care, including developmental readiness, personal disposition, and sociocultural influences.

Fourth, learners need to be self-aware if they are to self-regulating. Strategies that support that awareness are not as straightforward as one would think, although the Meichenbaum procedures are quite promising. The early work on SRL in education introduced by Corno and Mandinach (1983) raised concerns about uninformative tasks and superfluous supports that impeded the enactment of SRL. Informative tasks have certainly occupied center stage in SRL work, but the idea of "too much" support has somehow received short shrift in modern working theories. One exception is the construct of scaffolding in sociocultural work (that also could be explained by operant fading procedures), but that construct is seldom applied to learning how to engage in productive interpersonal relationships and realistic self-appraisals. Teachers will have their work cut out for them to promote student self-awareness without becoming the source of that self-awareness—to the detriment of student SRL. The signaling strategies of a Kounin (1970) management system, for example, may interfere in the acquisition of SRL unexpectedly (see McCaslin & Good, 1998).

Fifth, students need to experience action-outcome linkages that promote a sense of personal control if they are to engage in SRL. DeCharms illustrated sometime ago (1976) that for students to engage in "origin" behavior, similar to what we now term intrinsically motivated SRL, they needed to have a sense of personal power and effectiveness that can be learned in classrooms. As phenomenologists note, a sense of personal control is necessary for the development of responsibility, presumably the fundamental goal of any theory of SRL and, we suspect, classroom management. Task analysis skills that align with learner emerging beliefs and abilities come into play here as well. Mindless failure has little to recommend it, but in the manner of Erikson and sociocultural theorists, students need to experience the positive and negative aspects of SRL to develop realistic self-appraisals. There are some things that are beyond a student's control, at least for now, and knowing where and when to invest one's heart and resources is part of learning self-control and responsibility that enables meaningful commitments.

Sixth, self-reinforcement is learned. Students need to recognize goal attainment, but also note progress along the way. Multistep task opportunities allow student assessment of progress that can maintain momentum in the manner of volitional theory. Progress helps students stay the course and if that progress is self-evident it also affords a certain feeling of independence and satisfaction. We suspect that appropriate self-reinforcement functions the same as responsive contingency in the interpersonal world: it is a foundation of mental health (Glazier-Robinson, 1989). Self-reinforcement is a necessary life skill: outside of particular approaches to classroom management there are few arenas in life that recognize one's accomplishments and the struggles that fueled them. At the end of the day, it is about self-monitoring and self-reinforcement.

Seventh, talk is good. Teacher talk and student thought (Blumenfeld, Hamilton, Bossert, Wessels, & Meece, 1983)—and student talk and teacher thought—go hand in hand in the development of SRL. Classroom management systems that understand this and explain reasoning behind teacher expectations and goals and teach students to do the same go far in promoting the internalization and enactment (or adherence depending on theory) of desired student behavior and disposition. There can be too much or misuse of a good thing, however, and talk is no exception. Talk that becomes a form of negative reinforcement wherein students comply with management demands to achieve silence is not unusual. Talk can also be manipulative and disingenuous: communication is about the integrity of listening as well as speaking.

SELF-REGULATED LEARNING AS VALUE JUDGMENT

As theoretical comparisons suggest, the goals of SRL are tied to underlying conceptions of the "good life" for students and teachers. Theories differ in important ways that inform their implication for classroom management. We reorganize the theories into three groups to highlight differences in the perceived goals of SRL. We intentionally magnify the implementation implications of each theory to make our concerns more transparent. In reality, most theoretical implementations would not be as monolithic, and thus, not as extreme in result. Our point is that differences among SRL theories is less a question of how and more a question of why and how much.

SRL as Efficient Productivity

We group the operant, volitional, and information processing approaches to SRL in the category we term "efficient productivity." Self-regulating students in these approaches, if successfully implemented, present as relatively low-maintenance, "compliant cognition" (McCaslin & Good, 1992) learners, in pursuit of tasks set for them. In each of these perspectives the emphasis is on optimal self-control. Operant theory ironically posits immediate and delayed self-denial as evidence of self-regulation; information processing not only wants a predictable thinker but an efficient one; and volition sticks to adherence. In their extreme, these approaches conjure images of "Stepford" students designed for productivity that are somehow not very childlike. To the extent that the goals of these perspectives were met, individual differences among students would diminish if not disappear.

Admittedly this prediction does not seem particularly dire—especially in class sizes of 30 and more students with varied backgrounds, aspirations, and talents—until we consider the long-term difficulties faced by parentified children who somehow experienced a childhood but missed the meaning (Eliot, 1943). Foreclosure in the classroom seems to share the same cautions as foreclosure in identity: early buy-in and focus can narrow the opportunities for incidental learning that may well have been the key to later fulfillment and contribution.

It also can lead to burnout. Enough has been said about the hidden costs of effective external control on individual learning and motivation (e.g., Lepper & Greene, 1978). Internal controls can be costly as well. Students can become too self-regulated, becoming perfectionists who set unrealistically high goals with associated stress (Bieling, Israeli, Smith, & Anthony, 2003). It is our most talented students, whose considerable aptitude makes them prime targets for IP and volitional curricula, who are presenting as distressed, disturbed, and depressed college students in unprecedented numbers (New York Times, April 6, 2004). Efficient productivity theories invite a more longitudinal question of SRL: Are there long-term consequences to staying the course? Are there limits to productivity? Can early commitments mortgage a future?

Self-Regulated Learning as the Pursuit of Self

Although phenomenology and second-wave constructivism differ in emphasis on the role of interpersonal validation in the pursuit of individual identity, both assert that the primary motive and goal of SRL is the making, or having, of an identity. Choice is a cornerstone of each—choice of tasks for phenomenology that enables learner reflective selfknowledge and interest, and choice of role-playing for second-wave constructivists that enables consideration of a possible self. For phenomenologists, choices also have value because they promote personal responsibility and empowerment by linking outcomes to action, a belief fundamental for SRL. For second-wave constructivists, choices also have value because they provide the fuel for SRL and result in life stories that are largely coherent about the past and optimistic about the future.

Identity is surely a lifelong goal of considerable importance to individual functioning and mental health; however, the potential for phenomenologists to create the conditions that not only promote intrinsic motivation but also foster the development of idiosyncratic, potentially narcissistic and isolated, learners is worth considering. Self-reflection and self-awareness do not necessarily lead to appreciation of the nonself or valuing of participation with others. As long as individuals live in communities this seems a problem, especially if that community is as diverse as today's classroom.

Thus, we would be the first to agree that identity development certainly can profit from recognition of the nonself, that someone whom I am not but may want to become. The "imaginary audience" (Elkind, 1985) who helps me anticipate whether or not I might fit in, or the enactment of that imaginary audience in actual attempts to gain group membership, are hallmarks of adolescent literature. The serial "trying on of hats" described by Paris et al. (2001) is termed "diffusion" in the Erikson tradition (see Marcia, 1980). Diffusion is typically considered an identity phase typical of early adolescence that evolves from a state of noncrisis and noncommitment that eventually gets old and is resolved with a meaningful identity search. The availability of, and multiple nonparticipant memberships in, the vast numbers of junior high school clubs is a classic example. The failure to resolve diffusion, however, has been linked to other difficulties in personal functioning (Marcia, 1967).

The various reconstructions of "me" that motivate SRL and the continual seeking of validation by a valued group in the second-wave constructivist tradition can leave a learner uniquely vulnerable to the social world in the manner of life in high school. It also has the potential for evasion of personal responsibility: that was me then, I am a different person now. It seems more helpful in the promotion of SRL to consider how to support learners who, through the opportunities and activities they engage, develop a disposition toward industry/inferiority in the pursuit of competence in an arena they value that informs the person they might become (in the manner of Erikson, 1968).

Ideally, identity does not unfold in a vacuum or in the context of benign neglect. Adults have a role to play and classroom management seems an especially fruitful opportunity to influence identity development. Identity development as key to SRL invites the questions: Can there be too much choice? Do identities need to be realistic, and life stories valid? What if an identity is of a nonself-regulating learner, or excludes achievement? At what point, if at all, is intervention appropriate?

Self-Regulated Learning as Societal Participation

The remaining two theories, social cognitive and Vygotskian (or sociocultural) perspectives, to a degree share a concern for the challenges of the socialized, or situated, self. We focus only on these theories here, although the previously discussed second-wave constructivist approach also adheres to some Vygotskian and social cognitive principles. Social cognitive theory rests its case on hedonism and the affiliation motive. Individual behavior in this perspective is difficult to interpret without knowledge of models and reinforcements in the past and present, but the goals of that behavior are presumed to be based in self-interest. Newer concerns to emerge in this work are in one sense a return to initial thinking by Bandura and Walters (1963). They include the extent to which, in contrast to individual motives, individual behavior and SRL can ever be context-free, that is, "owned" by the learner. Social cognitive theory is now wrestling with the historical dilemmas of sociocultural, Vygotskian, approaches: Is there such a thing as independence?

The "self"-regulated learner in the Vygotskian perspective occupies more personal space than in other theories. This learner's personal boundaries extend beyond the self to include in fundamental ways the social, historical, and cultural world that go beyond modeling and reinforcement. In sociocultural thinking, the social world does more than influence behavior through models and reinforcements, it is the source of the ability to communicate with one's culture and ultimately direct the self. The goal of self-direction and learning in the Vygotskian perspective is to enable a contribution to the common good, a key difference from other SRL theories. Vygotskian theories resolve the self-social dichotomy with the notion of individual as participant who engages activities. "Participant" is about opportunity and interpersonal contexts; hence, relationships and coregulation. "Activity" is about tool-mediated, goal-directed action, hence the realization of adaptive learning in the ZPD. A sociocultural child is not so much known by hedonism or self-interest, as by the structural supports available to him or her and the contributions he or she seeks to make to his or her community.

The Vygotskian approach in particular, and to some extent the more recent social cognitive perspective, suggest that "individual" is not as useful a construct as mainstream psychology might assert. Rather, conditions (social cognitive) or contexts (sociocultural) are the more informative units of analysis. Influenced by *whom*, or participant in *what*, are key concerns. Taken to their extreme these theories, like operant theory, can bring judgments of personal responsibility and accountability, which are foundational to our culture (Weiner, 1995), into serious question. This seems an especially important concern in the arena of classroom management. Theories that assign such power to the social world, be it due to available models and reinforcers or the social origins of higher psychological processes, raise the question of responsibility for optimizing the social environments in students' lives rather than judging students.

For example, an early goal of SRL was to teach students to teach themselves so that they might compensate for inadequate teaching in the manner of the Carroll Model of School Learning (Carroll, 1963). Are students responsible for overcoming inadequate teaching? Consider as well modern-day interest in student resiliency, in which students learn to pursue relationships with a potentially caring adult model (e.g., a teacher) to stave off the toxicity of home and neighborhood. The reasoning—you may not be responsible for the circumstances of your past, but you are responsible for the outcomes of your future—focuses on individual responsibility to the extreme. Are students responsible for overcoming detrimental life circumstances? Are they culpable if they fail to do so? Can a focus on SRL distract us from our commitments to optimize social contexts? This is a core dilemma in the social influence approaches to SRL.

CONCLUSION

SRL is an exciting and promising conception of student learning and motivation; however, we do not think that self-regulated learning is the educational panacea some might wish it to be. Theories differ in the definition, source, and supports of SRL. SRL theories invite consideration of just what is meant by a self-regulated learner and why that is a good thing. We hope the presentation of these differences will support attempts to clarify what SRL means among researchers and practitioners. If SRL really means compliance, for example, then some theories are more useful to that end than others. If SRL is about aptitude and aspiration then different approaches will be helpful. And if SRL is about character development, then still other approaches may be informative.

Importantly, what might be an ideal self-regulated learner from a teacher perspective may not be optimal for students. The reverse also may obtain. We can imagine, for example, the exhaustion of teaching 30 self-reflecting phenomenological learners pursuing their interests in search of self and the exasperation of teaching ever-changing learners of the second-wave constructivists whose small-group projects are undermined by fluid identity memberships. It seems important to take both teacher and student perspectives into consideration when creating classrooms to support a particular rendition of SRL. And there is good reason to expect that these classrooms could look very different from each other.

Finally, we assert that at this point, the pursuit of a particular manifestation of SRL is ultimately a value judgment. We raised questions that we think are important that may guide future research and implementation of this construct. The research on SRL and classroom management is in its infancy. A review of citations in ERIC and PSYCHINFO reveals that research on SRL outpaces research on SRL and classroom management by a ratio of approximately 22:1. Unexpectedly, citations in PSYCHOINFO (psychology) also outpace those in the ERIC (education) database. The social cognitive theoretical perspective guides much of the research that is done on SRL and classroom management, particularly if health promotion, physical activity, and nutrition work is included. The more child-centered phenomenological and second-wave constructivist theories appear to inform research on SRL, classroom management, and learners found different, deficient, or difficult in one way or another. What is notable about the research done in each theoretical tradition, however, is the lack of interest in middle school students even though each theory would support the importance of this period. This is a potent area for future research. There is some reason to believe that the progression from elementary to college-age students (the two age groups most studied within the SRL frameworks) is not smooth, nor are the study samples likely similar. That is, we would expect that the sample participants in the two groups of studies differ in important ways beyond age. Research across the school years may provide useful insights into the potential and dynamics of SRL and how to best support them.

This chapter highlights the contributions of seven theories of SRL that might inform classroom management practices that seek to enhance student self-regulation. We are however acutely aware of the paucity of research on the role of these theoretical constructs in classroom management practices for SRL. We hope that our work serves as a call for research on these issues within classrooms, where students and teachers coordinate multiple roles, tasks, and expectations. Perhaps the value judgments associated with SRL—the by whom, for whom, why, and how much—that have thus far gone underaddressed in this work will be considered with more precision and insight in the next level of theoretical progression and theory-based practices.

ACKNOWLEDGMENTS

Authors would like to acknowledge and thank Julianne C. Turner and Carol S. Weinstein for their helpful reviews of this chapter.

REFERENCES

Bandura, A. (1969). *Principles of behavior modification*. New York: Holt, Rinehart & Winston.

Bandura, A. (1977). Self-efficacy: Toward a unifying theory of behavioral change. *Psychcological Review, 84*, 191–215.

Bandura, A. (1997). *Self-efficacy: The exercise of control*. New York: W. H. Freeman & Co.

Bandura, A., & Walters, R. H. (1963). *Social learning and personality development*. New York: Holt, Rinehart & Winston.

Baumrind, D. (1987). A developmental perspective on adolescent risk-taking in contemporary America. In C. Irwin, Jr. (Ed.). *Adolescent social behavior and health*. San Francisco: Jossey Bass.

Bieling, P. J., Israeli, A., Smith, J., & Antony, M. M. (2003). Making the grade: The behavioural consequences of perfectionism in the classroom. *Personality & Individual Differences, 35*, 163–178.

Block, J. H. (1984). Making school learning activities more playlike: Flow and mastery learning. *Elementary School Journal, 85*, 65–76.

Blumenfeld, P., Hamilton, V., Bossert, S., Wessels, K., & Meece, J. (1983). Teacher talk and student thought: Socialization into the student role. In J. Levine & M. Wang (Eds.), *Teacher and student perceptions: Implications for learning* (pp. 143–192). Hillsdale, NJ: Lawrence Erlbaum Associates.

Bruner, J. S. (1986). *Actual minds, possible worlds*. Cambridge, MA: Harvard University Press.

Carroll, J. B. (1963). A model of school learning. *Teacher's College Record, 64*, 723–733.

Clark, N. M., & Zimmerman, B. J. (1990). A social cognitive view of self-regulated learning about health. *Health Education Research, 5*, 371–379.

Corno, L. (1989). What it means to be literate about classrooms. In D. Bloome (Ed.), *Learning to use literacy in educational settings* (pp. 29–52). New York: Ablex.

Corno, L. (2001). Volitional aspects of self-regulated learning. In B. Zimmerman & D. Schunk (Eds.), *Self-regulated learning and academic achievement: Theoretical perspectives* (2nd ed., pp. 191–226). Mahwah, NJ: Lawerence Erlbaum Associates.

Corno, L., & Mandinach, E. B. (1983). The role of cognitive engagement in classroom learning and motivation. *Educational Psychologist, 18*, 88–108.

Crawley, T. M. (Ed). (Fall, 2004). *News & Views*. Marana Unified School District, Marana, AZ.

Cronbach, L. J. (1957). The two disciplines of scientific psychology. *American Psychologist, 12*, 671–684.

deCharms, R. (1976). *Enhancing motivation: Change in the classroom*. Oxford, England: Irvington.

Dodge, K. A., Asher, F. R., & Parkhurst, J. T. (1989). Social life as a goal-coordination task. In C. Ames & R. Ames (Eds.), *Research on motivation in education: Vol. 3: Goals and cognition* (pp. 107–135). New York: Academic Press.

Eliot, T. S. (1943). *Four quarters*. New York: Harcourt, Brace.

Elkind, D. (1985). Egocentrism in adolescence. *Child Development, 32*, 551–560.

Engels, F. (1972). Socialism: Utopian and scientific. In R. C. Tucker (Ed.), *The Marx-Engels reader* (pp. 605–639). New York: Norton. (Original work published 1890)

Erikson, E. (1968). *Identity: Youth and crisis*. New York: Norton.

Flavell, J. H. (1979). Metacognition and cognitive monitoring: A new era of cognitive developmental inquiry. *American Psychologist, 34*, 906–911.

Gagne, R. M. (1985). *The conditions of learning* (4th ed.). New York: Holt, Rinehart & Winston.

Glazier-Robinson, B. (1990). *Effects of a mediated learning parent training prorgram on low SES pre-school children*. Unpublished doctoral dissertation, Bryn Mawr College, Bryn Mawr, PA.

Hartman, S. L. (2002). Postsecondary learning strategy instruction and student outcomes. Unpublished doctoral dissertation, University of Arizona, Tucson, AZ.

Heckhausen, H., & Leppmann, P. K. (1991). *Motivation and action*. New York: Springer-Verlag.

Hegel, G. W. F. (1949). *The phenomenology of the mind*. London: G. Allen & Unwin. (Original work published 1807)

Hickey, D. T. (2003). Engaged participation versus marginal nonparticipation: A stridently sociocultural approach to achievement motivation. *Elementary School Journal, 103*, 401–429.

Hickey, D. T., & McCaslin, M. (2001). A comparative and sociocultural analysis of context and motivation. In S. Volet & S. Järvelä (Eds.), *Motivation in learning contexts: Theoretical and methodological implications* (pp. 33–56). Amsterdam: Pergamon-Elsevier.

Hoffman, M. L. (1979). Development of moral thought, feeling, and behavior. *American Psychologist, 34*, 958–966.

Hull, C. L. (1952). *A behavior system: An introduction to behavior theory concerning the individual organism*. New Haven, CT: Yale University Press.

Jersild, A. (1951). Self-understanding in childhood and adolescence. *American Psychologist, 6*, 109–113.

Kounin, J. S. (1970). *Discipline and group management in classrooms*. New York: Holt, Rinehart & Winston.

Kozulin, A. (1986). The concept of activity in Soviet psychology: Vygotsky, his disciples, and critics. *American Psychologist, 41*, 264–274.

Kuhl, J. (1985). Volitional mediators of cognition-behavior consistency: Self-regulatory processes and action versus state orientation. In J. Kuhl & J. Beckmann (Eds.), *Action control: From cognition to behavior* (pp. 101–128). West Berlin: Springer-Verlag.

Leontiev, A. N. (1974–1975, Winter). The problem of activity in Soviet psychology. *Soviet Psychology*, 4–33.

Leontiev, A. N. (1978). *Activity, consciousness, and personality*. Englewood Cliffs, NJ: Prentice-Hall.

Lepper, M. R., & Greene, D. (Eds.). (1978). *The hidden costs of reward: New perspectives on the psychology of human motivation*. Hillsdale, NJ: Lawrence Erlbaum Associates.

Levy, L. H. (1970). *Conceptions of personality*. New York: Random House.

Luria, A. R. (1979). *The making of mind: A personal account of Soviet psychology*. (M. Cole & S. Cole, Eds.). Cambridge, MA: Harvard University Press.

Mace, C. F., Belfiore, P. J., & Hutchinson, J. M. (2001). Operant theory and research on self-regulation. In B. J. Zimmerman and D. H. Schunk (Eds.), *Self-regulated learning and academic achievement: Theoretical perspectives* (2nd ed., pp. 39–66). Mahwah, NJ: Lawerence Erlbaum Associates.

Marcia, J. E. (1967). Ego identity status: Relationship to change in self-esteem, "general maladjustment," and authoritarianism. *Journal of Personality, 35*, 118–133.

Marcia, J. E. (1980). Identity in adolescence. In J. Adelson (Ed.), *Handbook of adolescent psychology.* New York: Wiley.

Marx, K. (1972). *Capital.* In R. C. Tucker (Ed.), *The Marx-Engels reader* (pp. 191–327). New York: Norton. Original work published 1867a.

McAdams, D. P. (1993). *The stories we live by.* New York: Guilford Press.

McCaslin Rohrkemper, M. (1989). Self-regulated learning and academic achievement: A Vygotskian view. In B. J. Zimmerman & D. H. Schunk (Eds.), *Self-regulated learning and academic achievement: Theory, research, and practice* (pp. 143–168). New York: Springer-Verlag.

McCaslin, M. (1996). The problem of problem representation: The Summit's conception of student. *Educational Researcher, 25*, 13–15.

McCaslin, M. (2004). Coregulation of opportunity, activity, and identity in student motivation: Elaborations on Vygotskian themes. In D. McInerney & S. Van Etten (Eds.), *Big theories revisited* (pp. 249–274). Greenwich, CT: Information Age Publishing.

McCaslin, M., & Burross, H. L. (2002). *Expectancy-Value relationships in 7th grade students' understandings of curriculum tasks: Learning motivation.* Unpublished manuscript.

McCaslin, M., & Good, T. (1992). Compliant cognition: The misalliance of management and instructional goals in current school reform. *Educational Researcher, 21*, 4–17.

McCaslin, M., & Good, T. (1996). The informal curriculum. In D. Berliner & R. Calfee (Eds.), *Handbook of educational psychology* (pp. 622–673). New York: Macmillan.

McCaslin, M., & Good, T. (1998). Moving beyond management as sheer compliance: Helping students to develop goal coordination strategies. *Educational Horizons, 76*, 169–176.

McCaslin, M., & Hickey, D. T. (2001). Self-regulated learning and academic achievement: A Vygotskian view. In B. J. Zimmerman & D. H. Schunk (Eds.), *Self-regulated learning and academic achievement: Theoretical perspectives* (2nd ed., pp. 227–252). Mahwah, NJ: Lawrence Erlbaum Associates.

McCaslin, M., & Murdock, T. B. (1991). The emergent interaction of home and school in the development of students' adaptive learning. In M. L. Maehr & P. R. Pintrich (Eds.), *Advances in motivation and achievement* (pp. 213–259). Greenwich, CT: JAI Press.

McClelland, D. C. (1985). How motives, skills, and values determine what people do. *American Psychologist, 40*, 812–825.

McCombs, B. L. (2001). Self-regulated learning and academic achievement: A phenomenological view. In B. J. Zimmerman and D. H. Schunk (Eds.), *Self-regulated learning and academic achievement: Theoretical perspectives* (2nd ed., pp. 67–124). Mahwah, NJ: Lawerence Erlbaum Associates.

McInerney, D. M., & Van Etten, S. (Eds.) (2004). *Big theories revisited.* Greenwich, CT: Information Age Publishing.

Meichenbaum, D. H. (1977). *Cognitive behavior modification.* New York: Plenum.

Miller, G. A., Galanter, E., & Pribram, K. H. (1960). *Plans and the structure of behavior.* New York: Holt, Rinehart & Winston.

Mischel, W. (1973). Processes in delay of gratification. In L. Berkowitz (Ed.). *Advances in experimental social psychology* (Vol. 7). New York: Academic Press.

Mish, F. C. (Ed.). (1988). *Websters ninth new collegiate dictionary.* Springfield, MA: Merriam-Webster.

Muuss, R. E. (1996). *Theories of adolescence* (6th ed). New York: McGraw-Hill.

Palincsar, A. S., & Brown, A. (1984). Reciprocal teaching of comprehension-fostering and comprehension-monitoring activities. *Cognition and Instruction, 1*, 117–175.

Panagiotopolous, J. (1986). *Cognitive engagement variations among students and classroom tasks.* Unpublished doctoral dissertation, Teachers College, Columbia University, New York.

Paris, S. G., & Byrnes, J. P. (1989). The constructivist approach to self-regulation and learning in the classroom. In B. J. Zimmerman & D. H. Schunk (Eds.) *Self-regulated learning and academic achievement: Theory, research, and practice* (pp. 169–200). New York: Springer-Verlag.

Paris, S. G., Byrnes, J. P., & Paris, A. H. (2001). Constructing theories, identities, and actions of self-regulated learners. In B. J. Zimmerman and D. H. Schunk (Eds.), *Self-regulated learning and academic achievement: Theoretical perspectives* (2nd ed., pp. 253–288). Mahwah, NJ: Lawerence Erlbaum Associates.

Perry, N. E., Nordby, C. J., & VanderKamp, K. O. (2003). Promoting self-regulated reading and writing at home and school. *Elementary School Journal, 103*, 317–339.

Piaget, J. (1983). Piaget's theory. In P. Mussen (Ed.), *Handbook of child psychology* (4th ed., Vol. 1). New York: Wiley.

Rimer, S. (April 6, 2004). New lesson for college students: Lighten up. The New York Times. http://www.nytimes.com/2004/04/06/education/06STRE.html?pagewanted=print &. Retrieved 4/6/2004.

Rohrkemper, M. (1982). Teacher self-assessment. In D. Duke (Ed.), *Helping teachers manage classrooms*, (pp. 77–96). Alexandria, VA: Association for Supervision and Curriculum Development.

Rohrkemper, M. (1984). The influence of teacher socialization style on students' social cognition and reported interpersonal classroom behavior. *Elementary School Journal, 85*, 245–275.

Rohrkemper, M. (1985). Individual differences in students' perceptions of routine classroom behavior. *Journal of Educational Psychology, 77*, 29–44.

Rohrkemper, M., & Brophy, J. (1983). Teachers' thinking about problem students. In J. Levine & M. Wang (Eds.), *Teacher and student perceptions: Implications for learning* (pp. 75–104). Hillsdale, NJ: Lawrence Erlbaum Associates.

Rohrkemper, M., & Corno, L. (1988). Success and failure on classroom tasks: Adaptive learning and classroom teaching. *Elementary School Journal, 88*, 297–312.

Rotter, J. B. (1954). *Social learning and clinical psychology*. Englewood Cliffs, NJ: Prentice-Hall.

Schunk, D. H. (2001). Social cognitive theory and self-regulated learning. In B. J. Zimmerman and D. H. Schunk (Eds.), *Self-regulated learning and academic achievement: Theoretical perspectives* (2nd ed., pp. 125–152). Mahwah, NJ: Lawerence Erlbaum Associates.

Schunk, D. H., & Hanson, A. R. (1989). Self-modeling and children's cognitive skill learning. *Journal of Educational Psychology, 81*, 155–163.

Simon, H. (1969). *The science of the artificial*. Cambridge, MA: MIT Press.

Simon, H. A. (1991). *Models of my life*. New York, NY: Basic Books.

Tsang, H. Y. C. (2003). *Using standardized performance observations and interviews to assess the impact of teacher education*. Unpublished doctoral dissertation, College of Education, University of Arizona, Tucson, AZ.

Vygotsky, L. S. (1962). *Thought and language*. Cambridge, MA: MIT Press.

Vygotsky, L. S. (1978). *Mind in society: The development of higher-order psychological processes*. Cambridge, MA: Harvard University Press. (Original work published 1934)

Weick, K. (1984). Small wins: Redefining the 'scale of social problems'. *American Psychologist, 39*, 40–49.

Weiner, B. (1980). *Human motivation*. New York: Holt, Rinehart & Winston.

Weiner, B. (1992). *Human motivation: Metaphors, theories, and research*. Newbury Park, CA: Sage.

Weiner, B. (1995). *Judgments of responsibility: A foundation for a theory of social conduct*. New York: Guilford Press.

Weinstein, R. S. (2002). *Reaching higher: The power of expectations in schooling*. Cambridge, MA: Harvard University Press.

Wertsch, J. (Ed.). (1985). *Culture, communication, and cognition: Vygotskian perspectives*. New York: Cambridge University Press.

Wertsch, J., & Stone, C. (1985). The concept of internalization in Vygotsky's account of the genesis of higher mental functions. In J. Wertsch (Ed.), *Culture, communication, and cognition: Vygotskian perspectives*. New York: Cambridge University Press.

Winne, P. H. (2001). Self-regulated learning viewed from models of information processing. In B. J. Zimmerman and D. H. Schunk (Eds.), *Self-regulated learning and academic achievement: Theoretical perspectives* (2nd ed., pp. 153–190). Mahwah, NJ: Lawerence Erlbaum Associates.

Winne, P. H., & Marx, R. W. (1982). Students' and teachers' views of thinking processes for classroom learning. *Elementary School Journal, 82*, 493–518.

Xu, J., & Corno, L. (1998). Case studies of families doing third grade homework. *Teachers College Record, 100*, 402–436.

Yowell, C., & Smylie, M. (1999). Self-regulation in democratic communities. *Elementary School Journal, 99*, 469–490.

Zimmerman, B. J. (1998). Developing self-fulfilling cycles of academic regulation: An analysis of exemplary instructional models. In D. H. Schunk & B. J. Zimmerman (Eds.), *Self-regulated learning: From teaching to self-reflective practice* (pp.1–19). New York: Guilford Press.

Zimmerman, B. J. (2000). Attaining self-regulation: A social cognitive perspective. In M. Boekaerts, P. R. Pintrich, & M. Zeidner (Eds.), *Handbook of self-regulation* (pp. 13–39). San Diego, CA: Academic Press.

Zimmerman, B. J., & Schunk, D. H. (Eds.). (1989). *Self-regulated learning and academic achievement: Theory, research, and practice*. New York: Springer-Verlag.

Zimmerman, B. J., & Schunk, D. H. (Eds.). (2001). *Self-regulated learning and academic achievement: Theoretical perspectives* (2nd ed.). Mahwah, NJ: Lawerence Erlbaum Associates.

Zinchenko, V. P. (1985). Vygotsky's ideas about units for the analysis of mind. In J. Wertsch (Ed.), *Culture, communication and cognition: Vygotskian perspectives*. New York: Cambridge University Press.

Zuckerman, G. (1994). A pilot study of a ten-day course in cooperative learning for beginning Russian first graders. *Elementary School Journal, 94*, 405–520.

10

Building and Sustaining Caring Communities

Marilyn Watson
Developmental Studies Center (Retired)

Victor Battistich
University of Missouri, St. Louis

INTRODUCTION

In 1996, Alfie Kohn published a daring little book entitled, *Beyond discipline: From compliance to community*. In this book, he boldly urges teachers to abandon discipline systems along with their central goal—adult control of student behavior. The alternative, he argues, is not chaos but "an engaging curriculum *and* a caring community" (p. 118, emphasis in the original).

Although Kohn's views are radical when seen through the lens of accepted educational practice, he is not alone in his call for radical changes in traditional approaches to discipline and classroom management. A number of other educators, writing both before and since Kohn's provocative book, propose the centrality of sense of community to a well-functioning and productive classroom and school (e.g., Putnam & Burke, 1998; Solomon, Watson, Battistitch, Schaps, & Delucchi, 1996; Dalton & Watson, 1997; DeVries & Zan, 1994; Freiberg, 1999; Rogoff, Bartlett, & Turkanis, 2001; Wolk, 1998, 2002). In fact, the importance of classroom community has become so accepted that it would be difficult to find anyone to persuasively argue against its importance.

However, stressing that community is important is different from making it the foundation of classroom management. In our chapter we focus on educational approaches that view the building and sustaining of community to be the foundation of classroom management.

WHY FOCUS ON COMMUNITY?

First, there is no choice: all classrooms and schools are communities in some sense. However, there is considerable disagreement as to the nature of the community and the role the community is presumed to play in classroom management and learning. As educators, the nature of the community we strive to create and its role will depend on our goals, our beliefs about children, and our theories about how children learn.

Beginning in the early part of the 20th century, the predominant pedagogical theories and beliefs about children were derived from behavioral psychology. Children were viewed as blank slates—born into the world with no built-in systems to guide their learning or social interactions other than reinforcement. In this psychological paradigm, learning happens because of the teacher's actions, the learner is the passive recipient of stimuli and teacher reinforcements. Learning is not affected by the teacher/learner relationship. It is simply a process of forming associations between stimuli and the reinforcement of behavior. Except for the necessity to be awake and pay attention, the internal states of learners, for example, their beliefs, interests, or mental processes, either did not matter or were presumed not to exist. Consequently, strengthening associations became the primary educational goal.

Given these views of children and learning, and the teacher's need to maintain control of fairly large groups of children, most teachers were led to create autocratic classroom communities. This approach to teaching and learning is often referred to as "teacher centered." Teachers know what students need to know, students are told what to do and what to learn, and teachers use controlling management systems to orchestrate students' behavior, usually through the use of extrinsic rewards and consequences.

It was not particularly troubling to educators that children did not experience their classrooms as relational communities—places where they felt emotionally connected to their teacher and one another, and where they had a voice and a sense of well being (McMillan and Chavis, 1986; Osterman, 2000). After all, school was about academic learning, and learning was conceived to be a passive process of students' remembering based on reinforced associations. There was no reason to believe that personal relationships or the nature of the classroom community would affect learning. Learning took place in a classroom community, but the community played no active role in children's learning any more than the walls of the classroom. The community could, however, interfere with children's learning if it was noisy or distracting. Hence, the teacher's role was to efficiently keep the community under control so that each student could listen and learn from the teacher and the teacher's structured activities. In essence, student success involved "learning how to be alone in a crowd" (Jackson, 1968, p. 16).

In recent years, a large body of research paints a more complex and active view of children's learning and development. The work of Piaget and Vygotsky, for example, underscores the social nature of children's learning and documents both that children's thinking is controlled by internal developmental processes and that conceptual learning is the result of children's active mental and social processes, not simply the product of reinforced associations. These more complex views of children's learning led to more complex pedagogical practices and increased attention to the role of context in children's learning. Following the work of Piaget and his followers, approaches to instruction began to emerge that aimed at fostering children's autonomous thought and developing their understanding through exploration, discovery, problem solving, and social interaction (e.g., Copple, Sigel, & Saunders, 1979; Gardner, 1991; Kamii, 1985). Likewise, educators following Vygotsky's social constructivist paradigm began creating and investigating educational programs focused on the role of social context on learning, for example, the Kamehameha Project (Tharp & Gallimore, 1988) and the Community of Learners Project (Brown and Campione, 1990). The traditional autocratic, teacher-centered approach to classroom community no longer seemed sufficient for these new, more complex views of learning (see discussions in Dalton & Watson, 1997; McCaslin & Good, 1992; Putnam & Burke, 1998; and Weinstein, 1999).

Along with more complex views of children's learning, the theory and research based in the work of Piaget and of Vygotsky support more complex and positive views of children. In neither paradigm are children "blank slates," responsive only to the effects of reinforcement from adults. From the constructivist Piagetian perspective, children are viewed as possessing a natural propensity to construct knowledge of the physical and social/moral world and capable of building their knowledge through interactions with those worlds. From a social-constructivist Vygotskyian perspective, children are viewed as biologically predisposed to seek cooperative relationships with more accomplished others (adults) around meaningful tasks within their community. Through these collaborative interactions "the child acquires the 'plane of consciousness' of the natal society and is socialized, acculturated, made human" (Tharp & Gallimore, 1988, p. 30). From this perspective "learning and development occur as people participate in the sociocultural activities of their community" (Rogoff, 1994, p. 209).

Education and socialization from these perspectives need not involve control of children through dispensing and withholding rewards: such a process would undermine the goal of education from the Piagetian paradigm—developing understanding based in autonomous thought. From both perspectives, socialization is best seen as a collaborative process in which the child develops moral understanding through peer interaction and adult instruction, support, guidance, explanation, joint action, and modeling. These more complex and positive views of children's inclinations and motivations have profound implications for the nature and the role of the classroom community. Children are now seen as allies of their caregivers and teachers in service of their own intellectual, social, and moral development; and the community plays an active role in their learning and development.

While views of the nature of children and their learning were changing, a growing number of educators and the general public were becoming concerned about a variety of societal ills, such as racism, the effects of poverty on children's learning, and what appeared to be growing trends in our society toward violence, dishonesty, and a disregard for the needs and rights of others and the general good (Coleman & Hoffer, 1987; Brown & Solomon, 1983; Kohlberg, 1966, as cited in Power, Higgins & Kohleberg, 1989; Ogbu, 1988; Weinstein, 1999). The goals of schooling in America expanded as educators began to take seriously the school's role in ameliorating adverse societal effects and in preparing students for citizenship in an egalitarian, inclusive, moral democracy.

Complex instructional and management approaches, such as cooperative learning and conflict management, were developed not only to enhance learning but to combat racism, create equity, and teach social problem-solving and civil ways of interacting (e.g., Aronson, Blaney, Stephan, Sikes, & Snapp, 1987; Cohen, 1987; Johnson & Johnson, 1975). Research and development projects that focused on finding ways to enhance students' commitment to justice and caring such as the Child Development Project (Battistich, Watson, Solomon, Lewis, & Schaps, 1999) and Kohlberg's Just Community Project (Power et al., 1989) emerged along with a number of books and articles outlining the moral dimensions of teaching (e.g., Goodlad, 1984; Lickona, 1991; Ryan, 1986; Tom, 1984).

In this changed educational environment the role and nature of the classroom and school community took on new importance. Researchers began to focus on defining, measuring, and analyzing the social and academic effects of students' sense of community (Bryk & Driscol; 1988; McMillian & Chavis, 1986; Wehlage, Rutter, Smith, Lesko & Fernandez, 1989). A supportive, relational community was now seen as necessary for students to take the risks involved in thinking for themselves, take responsibility for their learning, seek teacher help when needed, and derive the cognitive benefits from peer interaction. New approaches to classroom management and discipline proliferated. As their names suggest—Cooperative Discipline, Discipline with Dignity—many of these new approaches focused on creating classroom environments more supportive of students' psychological needs, as well more complex approaches to learning (Albert, 1989; Curwin & Mendler, 1988; Dreikurs, Grunwald, & Pepper, 1982). However, as Kohn (1996) argues, these approaches were still essentially about a kinder approach to adult control with logical consequences replacing punishments. Educators had abandoned behavioral theory's passive view of children's learning, but they still clung to its limited view of children's motivations, believing that children's behavior needed to be controlled by adults, primarily through rewards and consequences.

A relatively small number of educators began developing approaches to classroom management and discipline that abandoned the traditional notion of adult control, focusing instead on adult-child collaboration and the creation of an egalitarian, relational community. These approaches are grounded in a variety of philosophical and psychological perspectives, but all have abandoned behavioral psychology's view of children's motivations as primarily aimed at seeking pleasure and avoiding pain. Rather than focus on developing more benign ways to control students such as "time out", logical consequences, and elaborate reward systems, these approaches focus on developing practical ways to build relational communities, trusting that in a supportive environment, students will want to learn and behave ethically.

In this chapter we examine the classroom management and discipline practices of six different approaches to creating classroom or school community. These approaches were chosen because they are theoretically coherent, represent distinctly different theoretical perspectives, and have been honed in the context of real classrooms and schools. Two of these approaches, the Just Community of Kohlberg and his colleagues (power et al.,1989) and the Moral Community of DeVries and Zan (1994), draw their major guidance from the same theoretical perspective, the cognitive developmental theory and research inspired by the work of Piaget. They are both included because the programs were developed for working with students of very different developmental levels. The third program, the OC[1] learning community (Rogoff, Turkanis Bartlett, 2001), derives from sociocultural theory and research inspired by the work of Vygotsky (Lave & Wenger, 1991; Rogoff, 1990, 1994; Rogoff, Mistry, Goncu & Mosier, 1993; Tharp & Gallimore, 1988). The fourth program, focusing on creating a democratic community, was developed by Steven Wolk, a former classroom teacher, and draws heavily on his own classroom experience and critical theory (Wolk, 1998, 2000). Consistency Management and Cooperative Discipline, the fifth program, was developed by Jerome Frieberg (1999), and draws primarily from the humanistic theory of Carl Rogers. Lastly, the caring community of the Child Development Project (Battistich et al., 1999) draws from an eclectic blend of developmental theory and research including attachment theory (Ainsworth, Blehar, Waters, & Wall, 1978; Bowlby, 1969; Sroufe, 1996), care theory (Noddings, 1992, 2002), and research in human motivation (Deci & Ryan, 1985; White, 1959).

In our initial planning for this chapter we intended to compare and contrast these approaches to community, with the goal of highlighting their differences. However, as we read and looked carefully at concrete examples of each approach, we came to believe that although each takes its primary guidance from different theoretical perspectives, their similarities far outweighs their differences both in number and in practical importance. Thus, this chapter focuses on describing common characteristics of approaches to community, while noting differences when they appear significant.

BRIEF DESCRIPTIONS OF APPROACHES TO COMMUNITY

Just Community

Kohlberg and his colleagues (Power et al., 1989) focus primarily on the role of community to support high school students' moral development and their commitment to a democratic society. The principal mechanisms of the Just Community School are regular meetings of small

[1]The letters OC do not stand for anything. In their book describing the OC learning community Rogoff and her colleagues explicitly say that OC is just the name they have given to the particular learning community they are describing (Rogoff, Bartlet, et al., 2001).

student-teacher advisory groups; whole-school community meetings where school problems, rules, and policies are thoroughly discussed and decisions are made; and a student-run disciplinary committee that decides fair punishments, mediates disputes, and counsels students with disciplinary problems. While the faculty retains decision-making power with regard to curriculum, all other aspects of school life are decided in democratic meetings on a one-person, one-vote basis. In Just Communities, faculty play a strong advisory role and use their powers of persuasion, but high school students are trusted to make caring and responsible decisions about all noncurricular aspects of school life.

Moral/Constructivist Community

DeVries and her colleagues focus on the role of community to support the social, moral, and intellectual development of preschool and early primary school children (DeVries & Zan, 1994). Like Kohlberg, they draw extensively on the work of Piaget, particularly on his 1932 publication, *The Moral Judgment of the Child* (Piaget, 1965). However, because DeVries and Zan are working with much younger children than Kohlberg, their focus is on classroom rather than school community. Also, from their perspective, the teacher, while striving to work collaboratively with children, retains the ultimate decision-making power. Strong guiding principles are the interrelatedness of academic and sociomoral development and the importance of encouraging and giving children room to think for themselves and reach their own conclusions in both social and academic learning situations. They employ teacher-guided class meetings and small-group meetings for collaborative, democratic decision making about class rules and other issues of general concern, and teachers adopt a guiding, teaching approach to helping children solve academic and sociomoral problems.

Community of Learners

The term *community of learners* is used by many educators to describe the ideal classroom. Indeed, each of the approaches to community described in this chapter strives to help teachers develop communities of learners. However, the term is most often applied to approaches to community-building based on sociocultural theory. A key feature of these approaches is the view that "higher-order functions develop out of social interaction" (Tharp & Gallimore, 1988, p. 7). The primary goal of most programs that focus on building learning communities is deep, exciting learning—learning that leads to higher-order thinking skills and facility with critical thinking strategies (Brown & Campione, 1990; Rogoff, Bartlett, et al., 2001). In this chapter we focus on one particular community of learners program, the OC, a parent cooperative elementary school in the Salt Lake City school district (Rogoff, Turkanis & Bartlet, 2001). We chose the OC because it has been guided by one of the major theoretical voices in sociocultural theory, Barbara Rogoff, and because it is an ongoing program shaping all aspects of the school and classroom.

Democratic Community

While all of the approaches that make community the foundation for classroom management aspire to build democratic communities the approach described by Wolk (1998, 2000) uses democracy as its primary goal. Focusing on democracy as a way of life and stressing the importance of freedom, Wolk describes his own experiences as an elementary school teacher in the Chicago public schools. Drawing on the writings of Dewey (1966), critical theorists, such as Henry Giroux (1983) and Maxine Green (1988), and constructivist whole-language advocates, such as Nancy Atwell (1998) and Carol Edelsky (1994), Wolk focuses not only on the importance of providing students with freedom in the classroom, but also on the importance of helping students learn to think critically and challenge and struggle against the societal forces that separate social groups and unduly limit freedom.

Consistency Management and Cooperative Discipline

Consistency Management and Cooperative Discipline (CMCD) is a prekindergarten through 12th-grade management program developed by Jerome Freiberg (1999) and strongly influenced by the work of Carl Rogers (Rogers & Freiberg, 1994). The guiding metaphor for CMCD is student as citizen rather than student as tourist. CMCD stresses the importance of authentic caring, consistent messages to students across grades and contexts, and shared responsibility between students and teachers for learning and classroom organization. For example, in addition to class meetings and student participation in developing class constitutions, there are 40-plus developmentally appropriate, one-minute jobs open to every student.

Caring Community

All community-based approaches to classroom management stress the importance of caring relationships. However, the Child Development Project (CDP) leads with care, with the emotional experience of caring and being cared for (Battistich et al., 1999; Dalton & Watson, 1997; Watson & Ecken, 2003). CDP is an elementary school program with the explicit goal of integrating into the school day a focus on children's social and moral development. It draws upon an eclectic blend of theory and research including an ethic of care (Noddings, 1984, 1992, 2002), attachment theory (e.g., Bowlby, 1969; Ainsworth et al., 1978; Sroufe, 1996), and theory and research on human motivation (e.g., deCharms, 1968; Deci & Ryan, 1985; White, 1959). In CDP, community is the foundation of classroom management and caring relationships are the foundation of community. There is a strong emphasis on building students' sociomoral skills and understanding, and caring relationships with and among students as well as between teacher and students. For example, a major component of the classroom program is an approach to cooperative learning that explicitly focuses on sociomoral development and the building of caring relationships among all the students in the classroom (Development Studies Center, 1997).

CORE CHARACTERISTICS OF COMMUNITY APPROACHES TO CLASSROOM MANAGEMENT

A Positive, Developmental View of Children

Perhaps the most important commonality of approaches to classroom management centered on community building is a positive, developmental view of children. Children are seen as internally motivated to learn and respond reciprocally to kind and respectful treatment. While acknowledging that children are also self-interested, all view children as possessing an innate capacity for empathy and a desire for social connection. For example, DeVries and Zan (1994), state that "A moral classroom begins with the teacher's attitude of respect for children, for their interests, feelings, values, and ideas" (p. 58). Wolk (1998) argues that the classroom environment "must be built on a foundation of trust in children as natural learners" (p. 29). With such a positive view of children, it is natural to abandon a controlling autocratic approach to community and to think of teaching and classroom management as working with, rather than controlling, children.

This positive view of children represents a huge break from behavioral psychology's view of children as motivated wholly or primarily by self-interest, but is it justified? Whether one draws on sociocultural theory and research (Rogoff, 1990; Tharpe & Gallimore, 1988; Vygotsky, 1978), research describing children's development and socialization (Hoffman, 2000; Kohlberg, 1969; Peck & Havighurst, 1960; Piaget, 1965), attachment theory and research (Stayton, Hogan, & Ainsworth, 1971; Sroufe, 1996) or motivational theory and research (Deci & Ryan, 1985; White, 1959), there is a substantial body of evidence to support a view of children as naturally motivated to learn and to seek nurturing relationships with adults and friendly relationships with peers. Of course, children do seek to gain pleasure and avoid pain, but compassion and caring are just as deeply rooted in their nature (Keltner, 2004). (For an extensive summary of the evidence supporting a positive view of children, see Kohn, 1990.)

One important implication of a positive view of children is that they are not seen as the sole or major cause of the difficult behavior they might exhibit. If children do not behave well in the classroom, it no longer makes sense to simply assume, as Canter and Canter (1992) instruct us to do, that they could behave well if they just wanted to. Instead of searching for ways to increase students' motivation—that is, to get them to want to behave well—the reasonable response, given that we believe children want to behave well, is to search for possible causes of misbehavior in areas other than children's lack of positive motivation. While different approaches may place more emphasis on one potential cause over another, all consider a variety of possible causes for student misbehavior. For example, students may not possess the academic, social, emotional, or moral skills and understandings needed to meet the demands of the school environment; the school environment may be undermining students' basic needs for autonomy, belonging, or competence by being too restrictive, untrustworthy or too difficult; the learning tasks may be seen as arbitrary and uninteresting. It is the teacher's responsibility to try to ferret out the causes of students failing to behave well and to provide students with additional support or adjust the environment to better meet the students' capabilities. With some children this can be a difficult undertaking, sometimes requiring the help of another teacher, the school psychologist, the child's parents or guardians, or other trusted members of the child's home community. This brings us to the second important commonality in community-based approaches to classroom management: children are viewed as imbedded in a social context.

View of Students as Imbedded in a Social Context

Students are not viewed as isolated individuals responsible for their own behavior. Rather, they exist in the social context of the classroom and school. To successfully develop morally, emotionally, and intellectually, they need that context to be supportive. Thus, how well a child succeeds in living up to positive social values or in accomplishing the learning tasks of the school or classroom is a combined function of the child's abilities and efforts, the nature of the community, and the teacher's and community's ability to provide guidance and support. When children misbehave in the classroom (e.g., fool around during work time), the general response is not to automatically administer punishment, but rather for the teacher to ask questions or make suggestions to increase children's understanding and guide their behavior. From this perspective, cooperation, joint participation, and support are central to a well-functioning classroom (Freiberg, 1999).

Instead of the typical discipline focus of holding children responsible, there is a much stronger focus on providing enough support so that children will be successful and autonomously avoid choices that will result in unpleasant consequences. For example, a teacher in the OC school describes a situation in which a student put little effort into a unit on poetry writing. Whereas the teacher did not try to spare the student the embarrassment of displaying his poor work, she also accepted her responsibility in his failure, remarking that she learned "to hold conferences more frequently... to support students in managing their time and responsibilities" (Polson, 2001, p. 126).

Teachers also take responsibly for creating classroom and school structures that will provide students with needed support. For example, when students break the school rules in Kohlberg's Just Community, they experience public disapproval and appear before the student disciplinary committee (DC). Of course, student disciplinary committees can be far more punitive than supportive. For example, when elementary students are asked what should happen to a fellow student who has broken a rule, they are notoriously punitive. Even when asked to suggest consequences for their own misbehavior students can be punitive and harsh (Turkanis, Bartlett, & Rogoff, 2001). To avoid such punitiveness, Kohlberg and his colleagues structured the DC. in such a way as to emphasize its supportive potential:

> The public expression of disapproval should be seen not as subjecting students to a verbal "stoning" but as a means of showing them that members of the community care for them. D.C. members were rotated in part to prevent it from becoming a group of self-righteous students who never broke the rules themselves and who scolded those who did. Since many students on the Cluster D.C. had broken the very same rules they were asked to enforce, more often than not they identified with the students before them and expressed their interest in helping them out. Helping out meant two things: supporting students so that they could better acknowledge and live up to the expectations of the community, and letting students know that they were not alone, that they belonged to a caring community. (Power et al., 1989 p. 95)

In community-based approaches to school and classroom management, the teacher strives to create a partnership relationship with each student and the class of students as a whole. This partnership is unequal in that the teacher, being the more accomplished other, is responsible for providing students with instruction, encouragement, and support and for creating with the students a nurturing community that affords each student the opportunity for success. When a student fails, the teacher and the community have also failed. What is this nurturing community like, and how are such communities built?

View of Community as Relational

While all schools and classrooms are communities in that their members share a common space and a common set of activities, educators who view building and sustaining community as the foundation of classroom management are using community in the stronger, relational sense. As mentioned earlier, to be a community in the relational sense, members must feel emotionally connected to one another, have a voice and a role in the activities of the community, and feel that their needs are being met in the community (McMillan & Chavis, 1986). When communities fulfill these conditions their members experience a sense of belonging and trust that their needs will be met through mutual commitment (McMillan & Chavis, 1986; Osterman, 2000).

In all the approaches we examined, there is a conscious striving to create an atmosphere of mutual caring and respect and the role of teacher often seems very like the role of good parent. For example, Power et al. describe the main goal in Just Community schools as building a culture that is "like a family, in which everybody cares for everybody else," and where belonging to such a community requires that everyone "live up to norms of sharing, self-sacrifice, and collective responsibility" (1989, p. 106). In describing the nature of the learning community that teachers in the OC strive to create, Rogoff, Bartlett, et al., state that whereas community in their sense "involves relationships among people based on common endeavors," these relationships "are not just focused on getting tasks done but also involve relating to each other as people and attempting to resolve inevitable conflicts in ways that maintain the relationships" (2001, p. 10)." In describing the classroom implications of attachment theory and research, Watson and Ecken state that "the qualities of the adult-child relationship leading to positive child outcomes are the same whether the adult caregiver is a parent or a teacher. From the perspective of attachment theory, building trusting, supportive, collaborative relationships with children should be at the heart of our approach to discipline and teaching" (2003, p. 280).

Like good parents, proponents of building relational communities are guided in one way or another by the basic questions Kohn posed in *Beyond discipline,* "What do children need?" and "How can we meet those needs" (1996, p. xv)? All view children as needing to belong or feel cared for. Reflecting Rogers, Freiberg describes authentic caring as "listening, reflecting, trusting, and respecting the learner" (1999, p. 83).

Affording students reasonable autonomy, freedom, and voice in decisions that affect their school and classroom lives is an especially important goal of all the programs surveyed. This characteristic of community-based programs marks a major separation from most approaches to discipline and classroom management that often stress adult control. Perhaps because it represents such a dramatic shift from the education we all experienced, most programs struggle to achieve the right balance of student autonomy and teacher authority. (See discussions in Power et al., 1989, especially pp. 38–51 and 68–72; Rogoff, Turkanis, et al. 2001, pp. 25–26; and Watson & Ecken, 2003, pp. 135–138.)

Across programs, the level of student autonomy varies dramatically depending on the developmental level of the students. For example, in the programs for preschool and elementary school children, many decisions are reserved for adults, while in Just Community high schools virtually all decisions that affect student life are made in community meetings where students and teachers have equal voice (Power, et al., 1989). Whatever the level of freedom or autonomy, it is always in the context of adult guidance and collaboration. This balance is well described by Rogoff, Bartlet, et al.:

> [B]oth children and adults engage in learning activities in a collaborative way, with varying but coordinated responsibilities to foster children's learning. Adults are responsible for guiding the overall process and for supporting children's changing participation in their shared endeavors. Adults provide leadership and encourage children's leadership as well. (2001, p. 7)

The importance of respecting or providing for student autonomy has important implications for other aspects of school life, notably, the curriculum and disciplinary strategies. We turn first to the curriculum.

View of Curriculum as Integrated and Student-Centered

Given their strong focus on the need to respect student autonomy and their belief that children want to learn if their learning tasks are interesting, relevant, and within their capabilities, we should expect community-based approaches to classroom management to be concerned about devising curriculum and pedagogy that appeal to students' intrinsic learning motivation. And, for the most part, they do.

Probably because the Just Community's primary focus is the school and not the classroom, it is the one community-based approach that does not focus extensively on the curriculum. However, while Kohlberg did not insist that the school faculty take a particular approach to curriculum, he advocated for the integration of academic and sociomoral learning, advising that, as a whole the curriculum should represent "real-life experience to the students" (Power et al., 1989, p. 68). The remaining approaches to community, while different in a number of respects, have developed approaches to curriculum that integrate sociomoral and academic learning, focus on building understanding, and relate to children's lives, purposes, and concerns.

DeVries and Zan (1994), for example, stress that children need the freedom to interact socially and to choose their activities. Strong guiding principles of DeVries and Zan's moral classroom are the interrelatedness of academic and sociomoral development and the importance of encouraging and giving children room to think for themselves and reach their own conclusions. They argue that sociomoral and academic growth are supported by the same classroom conditions and that academics must be "integrated with children's purposes" (p. 251):

> . . . in the constructivist community classroom, the goal of academics is approached indirectly, and children are expected to want to think about academics in the context of personal and group purposes, . . . [f]or example, . . . children reason about the optimal number of days for block constructions to remain in place . . . they experience the temporal meaning of their decision to keep them up for 5 days, they revise their reasoning about what is fair. They come to realize that when one structure is left for this period, an insufficient number of blocks is left for other children. Further, the children whose structures are left up do not wish to use them for 5 days. (pp. 251–257)

Like DeVries and Zan, Rogoff and her colleagues describe the curriculum of the OC as integrated and emergent. In making decisions about curriculum, OC teachers focus on "guiding children toward understanding several 'Big Ideas'" (p.39). These "Big Ideas" integrate the social and moral with the academic aspects of learning, for example, the "Big Ideas" that writing is communication and that "learning involves *problem solving,* whether the problems are interpersonal or academic" (p. 39, emphasis in the original). Although the teachers use the Utah State Core Curriculum as a general guide, they "shape the curriculum around the children's interests, using children's curiosity and events in their lives to spark units of study, being alert to opportunities for learning as they occur" (p. 38). The following classroom vignette provides both a feel for OC classrooms and an example of being alert to learning opportunities.

> . . . our fifth- and sixth- graders were all snuggled together on the carpet in circle, . . . ready to enjoy our read-aloud book, "Nightmare Mountain." We were well into the drama. The main character was on a snowy mountain, in fear for her life because of a llama-stealing villain, when an avalanche began to roll toward her. Glancing up to look at the kids to see how they were reacting, I noticed several raised hands. Should I stop to answer questions? . . . Was there time? . . . A glance back at the kids. Lots of hands now.
>
> That was a clear directive that kids had things to say and needed to be heard. Everything else could wait. Questions and comments erupted as fast as the avalanche on the mountain. What causes an avalanche? How can you predict an avalanche? Can you survive an avalanche? . . . We stopped to look up "avalanche" in the dictionary and discussed the various definitions. Then a quiet voice suggested we return to the book, and we did. (Turkanis, 2001, p. 92)

Like the Just Community, the Child Development Project (CDP) did not start out with a focus on curriculum. The project's initial goal was to help teachers integrate into their current curriculum a focus on sociomoral learning. Encouraging teachers to engage their students with morally relevant children's literature and to use cooperative learning strategies were natural places to begin.

At first CDP tried to adapt its program to the existing curriculum and use the existing cooperative learning paradigms. But the developers soon realized that the existing approaches to cooperative learning for elementary students were incompatible with the project's beliefs about learning, intrinsic motivation, and community. For example, some approaches used intergroup competition (Slavin, 1980, 1983), and all used points or other extrinsic rewards to encourage specific cooperative behaviors and learning activities that best fit a direct instruction paradigm (Kagan, 1982; Johnson & Johnson, 1975). Likewise, for literature discussions most teachers had been trained to use the "recitation script"—teacher asks a question, student recites the answer the teacher is looking for. Such "discussions" seemed unlikely to build genuine empathy or help students construct their own understanding of sociomoral issues. Thus the developers decided they needed to create their own social constructivist approach to cooperative learning and literature instruction (Developmental Studies Center, 1997, 1998a, 1998b; Watson, Kendzior, Dasho, Rutherford, & Solomon, 1998).

These curricula were designed to help teachers integrate sociomoral and academic learning through activities that appeal to students' interests, develop their understanding, and build community. For example, CDP teachers are encouraged to use curriculum that is relevant to students' lives and concerns, offers children opportunities for choice, allows for students to work at their own level, and provides students with authentic opportunities to learn together and to share their learning with the other members of their community (Dalton & Watson, 1997). While not asking teachers to build the curriculum from students' interests, CDP does stress the importance of building student interest in the prescribed curriculum. CDP also stresses the importance of teachers participating with students in guided, open ended conversations, sometimes called "instructional conversations" (Goldenberg & Gallimore, 1991), about important ideas, and engaging students in authentic learning experiences. The following vignette provides an example of how one CDP teacher incorporated some of these principles in her second/third-grade classroom:

> I explained to the class that we were going to work with partners and do more research, and people started cheering, like they were just thrilled silly.
>
> I said, "We're going to do some research on water and weather, because they kind of go together, and you'll see this as we go on with the research."
>
> I had them make a list with their partners of the things that they would like to study or know about related to water or the weather. I explained before they made their lists that there were some topics that I wanted to be sure we covered in our research, like clouds and storm formation—and I named a few other things—and I explained that if it turned out no partnerships chose some of those topics, I might ask people to do them.
>
> After each partnership made a list of things that both of them wanted to study and do research on, most people had five or six things on their lists. It worked out fine because what was on everyone's list was pretty much what I wanted to do. They even added a few things that I hadn't thought of. (Watson & Ecken, 2003, p. 125–126).

Unlike CDP, where the focus on curriculum followed a focus on community, Wolk's approach to building classroom community appears to have followed from his desire to help his students "discover the joys and powers of reading and writing through a whole language and 'workshop' belief system" inspired by Nancy Atwell's book, *In the Middle* (1987):

> From the first day in my own classroom I was determined to do things differently. I was determined to make my students' experiences in school purposeful and meaningful, because I realized how meaningless and purposeless—how *regressive*—my own had been. I don't remember exactly when the notion of *democracy* entered the picture, but from my very first day with my own students I consciously worked to give them freedom, to allow them voice, to give them ownership in their own learning process, to help and challenge them to see the world critically, to *trust* them. (Wolk, 1998, p. vii–viii, emphasis in the original)

As one might guess from his initial inspiration, Wolk's approach to curriculum involves a lot of student choice, learning through student- and sometimes faculty-initiated projects, literature circles in which small groups of students read and discuss authentic children's literature, and a lot of authentic writing experiences. Democracy as a subject of study as well as a lived experience pervades his classroom. Like all of the community-based approaches to classroom management, Wolk's approach to curriculum integrates a focus on sociomoral learning in the context of academic learning. He has even created a list of children's literature ideal for helping children read "to become better people" (2000, p. 123). A somewhat unique focus is Wolk's concern with helping his students be critical readers of society. For example, instead of teaching history as a set of facts handed down from scholars, he chooses to present his students with alternative views of important historical events, such as Columbus's discovery of America and the Civil War.

It is impossible to describe in a short chapter the rich and varied approaches to curriculum that are an essential ingredient to community-based approaches to classroom management. Hopefully, the brief examples we have provided are sufficient to make the point that community-based approaches to classroom management also share similar approaches to curriculum and pedagogy. The curriculum is focused on building student understanding, and on being relevant to students' lives and interests, and integrative of moral as well as academic learning. The pedagogy involves active engagement, choice, collaborative learning, and authentic opportunities to share one's learning with the community. Not only is such an approach to curriculum and pedagogy helpful in creating a relational community, it is necessary if the classroom is to be managed without undermining student autonomy.

Minimal or Noncoercive Disciplinary Strategies

The use of coercion implies a view of students' motivations incompatible with respecting student autonomy and the positive view of children guiding community-based approaches to classroom management. Although sometimes necessary, coercion denies students the opportunity to act voluntarily, thus undermining their sense of autonomy. While clearly recognizing the teacher's authority and obligation to exercise authority, each of the approaches strives to eliminate or severely restrict discipline interventions that use power to coerce children—demanding statements, punishments (logical consequences), or rewards. To a large extent, they share the view expressed by DeVries and Zan that when "children feel that the teacher cares for them, enjoys being with them, and respects them by taking their feelings, interests, and ideas into account, ... they are likely to be willing to cooperate with the teacher and with each other" (1994, p. 179).

In addition to creating an atmosphere of trust and care, community-based approaches focus on providing as much support as their students will need to be successful. They might help students think through the challenges they will face in upcoming situations, for example, having a substitute teacher, working with a partner who is not yet a friend, or escorting a younger student to a school assembly. They might teach specific skills that students will need such as how to disagree respectfully or how to calm themselves when they feel angry. With these approaches teachers might participate with their students to scaffold or guide them to successful performance. When misbehavior does occur, teachers are likely to talk with students, using explanation or persuasion rather than commands.

The particular structures may differ. For example, when students are engaged in a conflict, OC teachers take them aside and talk with them until the students can find a way to settle their conflict (a luxury these teachers have because the OC program is a parent cooperative). In the classrooms described by DeVries and Zan, the children are directed to a conflict bench to talk through their disagreement aided by a posted set of conflict resolution guidelines.

These slightly different approaches to conflict reflect the different theories guiding these two approaches to community. Guided by Piagetian theory, DeVries and Zan stress the importance of children being allowed to construct their own solutions. Guided by the social constructivist theory of Vygotsky, the OC teachers involve themselves in more active support of children's conflict resolution efforts. Nevertheless, both approaches provide support for the students' active problem-solving efforts, rather than settling or ending the conflict through adult direction, ignoring the conflict, or punishing the children involved.

While there is general agreement among all community-based approaches that the coercive use of bribes, threats, punishments, and rewards are to be avoided, there is considerable disagreement as to whether they should be used at all. The Child Development Project takes a strong stance against the use of rewards and punishments and provides the fullest account of an approach to dealing with student misbehavior that does not use rewards and punishment. However, CDP teachers do exercise clear authority when that is needed and do, on occasion, use coercion in a nonpunitive way. For example, when a student's behavior results in harm, CDP teachers are encouraged to help the student repair the harm, where this is feasible. Sometimes students refuse to comply with reasonable requests and their behavior is disrupting the entire classroom or threatens to be physically harmful to others or classroom equipment. In such situations, CDP teachers may ask students to remove themselves from the group or in extreme cases send students to a different classroom or the principal's office. When this happens, the focus is on solving the momentary problem, not on causing students to experience the negative consequences of their behavior. The teacher then follows up with the students to repair their relationship and works with the student to better understand the situation and to figure out how they can work together to prevent reoccurrences. (See Watson & Ecken, 2003, pp. 139–184 for an extensive discussion of CDP's approach to managing student misbehavior.)

In Just Community schools, when students seriously violate the rules of the community, they appear before the student-run disciplinary committee. There can be consequences, but the focus is on understanding the causes of the students' transgressions, providing support, and reinforcing respect for the community's rules. The following quotation from a student on the Disciplinary Committee in response to the possible expulsion of Lisa, a rude student who also had a serious problem with attendance, represents the ideal functioning of the DC:

> To the faculty and to many of the students her rudeness is a personal offense, and, Lisa, I got in a lot of difficulty for a similar attitude. I think, Lisa, you have an authority problem, but to me personal responsibility is the issue. We as a community cannot see Lisa as a problem and just send her back to the high school where nobody cares. Here we have a capacity to care. At her age now her main job is to be a student and a good human being. She needs the support from us. I think the school should put together a student support group for Lisa, we can check on her, be with her, make sure she gets to class. I think helping each other helps the community. (Power et al., 1989, p. 223)

While Kohlberg and his colleagues struggled to tip the DC toward empathic, supportive responses to student misbehavior, punitive responses are always possible and were sometimes chosen. Guiding the DC to becoming a structure that was supportive of students and effective at upholding community norms and rules was a slow and complex process that involved developing students' ideas about the meaning of community, justice, and misbehavior. (See Power et al. (1989), for an extensive and fascinating discussion of this process.)

Other community-based approaches use or recommend the use of rewards or logical consequences sparingly. For example, Wolk advises, "While rewards should be used over punishment, I don't believe giving rewards in school should be done that much, if at all. Rewards can be used with individual students or a class with chronic behavior problems, but they should always be seen as a means to an end—that is, a way to help kids learn to be good without rewards" (2000, p. 79). Turkanis, Bartlett, and Rogoff recommend involving children in determining logical consequences for their poor choices but advise that often students "will need help making the consequences fit with the problem at hand and not being too harsh on themselves" (2001, p. 231). Overall, the use of rewards and punishments seems still to be an area of struggle for community-based approaches. This is particularly true for dealing with strongly oppositional or aggressive behavior.

Common Set of Classroom Activities

While operating in relative isolation from one another, community-based approaches to discipline and management have developed a remarkably similar set of school and classroom activities to build and sustain community. For example, recognizing the importance of respectful, caring relationships, all begin the year with playful activities designed to help students and faculty get to know and like one another. All take the time to teach students the social and emotional skills and understandings they need to solve conflicts fairly and interact in friendly, respectful ways. Recognizing the importance of student autonomy and understanding, all involve students in authentic processes for setting class rules, norms, or constitutions. Being part of a genuine relational community involves having shared experiences, shared goals, and shared responsibility. To achieve these conditions, community-based approaches provide students with pervasive opportunities to work together and share their learning with the community; share responsibility with students for maintaining the smooth functioning of the community; and use frequent class meetings, not only as problem-solving vehicles, but also as opportunities to share ideas and experiences, plan whole group activities, and set classroom or school goals. Reading aloud and discussing good children's literature are also frequently mentioned as ways to create a feeling of closeness, foster empathy, and build an understanding of shared democratic values.

Each approach has a unique flavor that can only be appreciated through a close reading of each, far closer than we have been able to provide here. However, as discussed earlier, we have been more struck by the strong similarities than the differences among the approaches in both underlying abstract principles as well as practical, concrete activities. Three factors were perhaps important in causing these approaches to gradually morph into similar programs. First, although none is a direct, first generation descendent from Dewey, all acknowledge Dewey as an influential ancestor. Dewey's active, teacher-guided, social constructivist approach to learning democracy in a democratic community provides some level of guidance to each of these approaches.

Second, all find the "blank slate" view of human nature and learning by association too simple to explain children's learning, behavior, and development. All make assumptions that the human infant comes biologically prepared with a complex array of needs, motivations, tendencies, and skills suited to life and learning in a community. All assume that the quality of children's relationships in the classroom and school are important determiners of their success. (For an in-depth discussion of the research supporting the role of teacher-student relationships, and the research supporting more complex views of the causes of student behavior and development, see chapter 26 by Pianta in this volume.)

Third, and perhaps most importantly, each of these approaches has evolved in response to its developers' struggling to build a workable model in real schools and classrooms, allowing themselves to be guided by the results of their efforts. For example, early learning–community approaches paid little attention to student affectional ties and CDP began with little attention to the academic curriculum (Brown & Campione, 1990; Solomon et al., 1985). Perhaps the best-documented example of program evolution is Kohlberg's Just Community. Published after Kohlberg's death, the book, *Lawrence Kohlberg's Approach to Moral Education* (see Power et al., 1989), traces his courageous search and painstaking path to developing a viable approach to moral education. From moral dilemma discussions in a Connecticut prison, through observations in an Israeli Kibbutz, to several years of running Just Communities in high schools in Cambridge, Scarsdale, and Brookline, the evolution of the Just Community is a stunning example of program change while retaining core theoretical principles. In our opinion, it is the openness to change in response to experience in schools that accounts for many of the similarities among these programs and their strength. We turn now to look at the research on the effects of community.

DOES COMMUNITY MAKE A DIFFERENCE?

In this section, we review the research findings on the effects of school community on a range of important outcomes for students. Although, as would be expected, not every outcome described below has been examined at all grade levels and across multiple studies, it is important to note that positive effects of school community consistently have been found for preschool (e.g., DeVries & Zan, 1994), elementary (e.g., Battistich, Solomon, Watson, & Schaps, 1997), middle (e.g., Goodenow, 1993) and high school students (e.g., Bryk & Driscoll, 1998), as well as children and youth who are living in particularly difficult life circumstances (e.g., Watson & Ecken, 2003).

The student outcomes examined to date in the research on school community include several areas: (a) school attendance and retention; (b) academic engagement, motivation, achievement, and aspirations; (c) commitment to democratic values; (d) moral reasoning; (e) prosocial attitudes, beliefs, and behaviors; and (f) involvement in problem (antisocial) behaviors.

Academic Attendance and Retention

In a comprehensive study of exemplary programs for preventing at-risk students from dropping out of school, Wehlage et al. (1989) identified the extent to which the school was a supportive community for students as *the* primary preventive factor. Relatedly, Freiberg (1999) found that the CMD program resulted in increased student attendance relative to comparison schools. Although not extensive, this research is consistent with the evidence reported below on the positive effects of student community on the developmental outcomes of students.

Academic Engagement, Motivation, Aspirations, and Achievement

Not surprisingly, one of the most frequently examined, and most consistently found areas of positive effects of school community is on students' school-related attitudes and academic performance. Across K–12 education, schools that can be characterized as communities have been shown to be more effective at promoting students' academic motivation and achievement, as well as their commitment to school (e.g., Bryk & Driscoll, 1988, on high schools; Goodenow, 1993, on middle schools; Solomon, Battistich, Watson, Schaps, & Lewis, 2000, on elementary schools). This is hardly surprising, given that the most salient value in most schools is that of learning and achievement, and, as noted above, students who experience their school as a community should be highly motivated to work to achieve this goal.

What may be more surprising is that programs designed to enhance sense of school community or belonging in the elementary grades have shown significant, longer-term effects on academic attitudes, motivation, and performance during middle and high school (Battistich, Schaps, & Wilson, 2004; Hawkins, Catalano, Osterman, Abbott, & Hill, 1999). These findings suggest that early intervention in children's school experiences may help to set them on a positive "trajectory" toward continued success, both during their educational years and perhaps during their subsequent lives as adult citizens.

Commitment to Democratic Decision-Making and Values

Perhaps most persuasively argued in the writings of Dewey (1966), the importance of learning how to be an effective democratic citizen has long been a critical aspect of schooling. It is surprising, then, that this outcome has only rarely been examined in educational research, much less in research focused on the effects of schools as communities.

Despite the low frequency with which effects on democratic attitudes, behaviors, and values have been examined, the research findings are consistent in indicating that school environments that are experienced as communities have positive effects on students' democratic attitudes and values (Battistich, Solomon, Kim, Watson, & Schaps, 1995; Ehman, 1980; Higgins, 1980; Solomon et al., 1996), as well as their democratic behavior (Solomon & Kendall, 1976), including use of democratic methods for resolving interpersonal conflicts (Allman-Snyder, May, & Garcia, 1975).

Moral Reasoning

Although some other programs have examined the effects of school community on moral reasoning and found positive effects (e.g., Solomon et al., 1996), most research in this area comes from investigations of the Just Community program (Kohlberg Lieberman, Power, Higgins, & Codding, 1981). Given Kohlberg's theoretical emphases, it is not surprising that enhancing moral reasoning was one of the primary goals of this intervention. The evidence from published studies suggests that students in the Just Community schools gained in moral reasoning, relative to students in comparison schools (Higgins, 1980; Higgins, Power, & Kohlberg, 1984; Kohlberg et al., 1981).

Prosocial Orientations

The term prosocial includes both the democratic values and moral reasoning outcomes described above, but is more encompassing, involving such attitudes and behaviors as cooperativeness, helpfulness, concern for others, and altruism. Studies from preschool (DeVries & Goncu, 1987) and elementary school (e.g., Battistich et al., 1997) have found positive effects of community on these outcome variables, and at least one study (Battistich et al., 2004) has found that such effects persist into middle school.

The research on cooperative learning also is relevant to this set of outcomes. Cooperative interaction is an integral part of community, and there is an extensive body of research on the effects of cooperative learning on many student outcomes. Reviews of this literature (e.g., Johnson & Johnson, 1989; Johnson, Johnson, & Maruyama, 1983; Sharan, 1990; Slavin, 1990) have consistently found positive effects on students' cooperative abilities and inclinations, altruistic behavior, interpersonal understanding, feelings of belonging, and acceptance of others.

Involvement in Problem Behaviors

The potential of school community to prevent students' involvement in problem behaviors has only recently begun to be examined. Although limited, the findings from two intervention studies have both shown that the interventions reduced students' involvement in drug use, delinquency and other problem behaviors (Battistich & Hom, 1997; Hawkins et al., 1999).

In addition, correlational analyses from a nationally representative sample of adolescents indicated that "bonding" to school was a significant protective factor for virtually all problem behaviors examined, including drug use, violence, risky sexual behavior, and thoughts of suicide (Blum, McNeely, & Rinehart, 2002; Resnick et al., 1997).

DOES COMMUNITY WORK FOR ALL?

In education, we are fond of saying that "one size does not fit all." By this we usually mean that because students have different lives, needs, strengths, and interests, teachers will need to know and use a variety of instructional approaches to ensure that all students thrive. Community, however, is different. We believe that community is a basic human need and that all students will be best served in classrooms and schools where building community is the basis for discipline. However, a community-based approach to classroom management may be difficult in some school settings and for some teachers. We now discuss these two cases separately.

Students

Is community feasible in a wide variety of school settings serving diverse student populations? In the late 1980s, when the Child Development Project first proposed community-building as a basis for classroom management, a number of teachers in schools serving poor and minority students countered our suggestions with "that may work in middle class schools, but it won't work with our students." These teachers were voicing a belief widely held by educators, that poor children and African American children need firm control and a management style based in authority supported by rewards and punishments. However, a number of educators have argued against this "two cultures" approach to working with children. For example, in Martin Haberman's observations, successful teachers of children in poverty focused little on traditional discipline and instead concentrated on building respectful relationships and creating exciting, engaging, and relevant learning activities (Haberman, 1995). The guidelines offered by Sonia Nieto for creating effective learning environments for bilingual and bicultural children are highly consistent with those that define a community-based approach to teaching and classroom management (Nieto, 1999). In *Through Ebony Eyes*, Gail Thompson argues for the importance of caring relationships stressing that for African American children to succeed, their classroom "must be a community in which students can thrive academically" (Thompson, 2004, p. 105). In observations of daycare and primary classrooms serving children living in difficult circumstances, Carolee Howes and Sharon Ritchey stress the importance of building trusting relationships that bind children to the community rather than control techniques such as time-outs and consequences that push them away (Howes & Ritchey, 2002).

In an effort to demonstrate that and to better understand how a community-based approach to teaching and classroom management works with poor and African American children, one of us conducted a two-year case study in an inner-city classroom (Watson & Ecken, 2003). Although the building of community was a slow process, and the students initially saw their teacher's discussion-based approach to guidance as "doing nothing" in the face of misbehavior, a caring community was eventually built. Gradually, even the most oppositional students came to trust their teacher and positively contribute to the classroom community. And the time spent building the community paid huge dividends in the children's learning—their investment in learning as well as their achievement. We should also add that Wolk (1998, 2000) was successful with his democratic community approach in inner city Chicago schools, the Child Development Project was successful in classrooms serving diverse students in diverse settings (Solomon et al., 2000), the Just Community was successful in an inner-city as well as a suburban high school

(Power et al., 1989), and the Consistency Management and Cooperative Discipline approach to community has been successful in inner city as well as suburban settings (Freiberg, 1999). Data from the Child Development Project suggest that poor and minority students are the least likely to experience their classrooms and schools as caring communities and the most likely to benefit when they do (Battistitch et al., 1997). The existing data provide strong support for the proposition that community-based approaches to teaching and classroom management can work for all students.

Teachers

While it seems clear that all students benefit from community-based approaches, the data do not support a similar conclusion for all teachers. There are hints in the literature that some teachers may have difficulty using a community-based approach. For example, a number of teachers involved in the Child Development Project rejected the project's community-based approach to classroom management and discipline outright or abandoned it after brief unsuccessful efforts. This was of such concern to one of the project's developers that a new version of CDP was created called Caring School Community, a version that abandoned most aspects of Developmental Discipline (Schaps, 2003). All of the community-based approaches rely on teachers being able to build sensitive, supportive relationships with their students. There appear to be several possible causes that can interfere with a teacher's ability to form such relationships with students in general and with some students in particular (Pianta, 1999; and, see chapter 26, this volume). If teachers have a negative view of children or of particular groups of children, they will be unable to trust their students enough to have high expectations for them or to view student behavior in a positive light. If teachers themselves have an insecure need for student affection or have a tendency to be distant in their personal relationships, they may be unable to respond to student rejection with affection and support or simply unable to pay sufficient attention to the affective needs of their students to create a supportive relationship. Without supportive relationships, relational community is impossible.

From the perspective of attachment theory and research, we would expect that some adults would have insecure styles of attachment and that these adults might act toward children in ways that undermine their students' healthy development. Pianta (1999) documents two such types of teachers, one he describes as "needing and wanting emotional support from the children," and one as forming relationships with children "characterized by low involvement and a degree of avoidance of close emotional contact" (114–119). These teachers appear to have personalities that make it difficult for them to provide at least some of their students with the care and warmth they need. One can easily imagine other personality types that would make it difficult for a teacher to be successful at building and maintaining a relational community.

Can such teachers be helped to build supportive relationships with their students, or should they be counseled out of teaching or encouraged to use a coercive approach to maintaining classroom control? Drawing on research on improving parent-child relationships, Pianta (1999) suggests several ways to help teachers who are inclined to have conflictual relationships with their students. Rather than a coercive, supervisory stance, he recommends a collaborative, supportive, problem-solving approach to helping such teachers. Such an approach would involve: (a) providing teachers with new information about, for example, the role of social processes in instruction and learning and of relationships in children's development, (b) engaging teachers' understanding or "representations of relationships," and (c) helping teachers have direct positive experiences with children with whom they have a troubled relationship (Pianta, 1999, p. 127). In *Enhancing Relationships Between Children and Teachers* and his chapter in this book (chapter 26), Pianta describes in detail several promising approaches that he and his colleagues have developed to help teachers improve their relationships with students. Like relationship-based approaches to classroom management, relationship-based approaches to staff development are fairly new. This seems a ripe area for exploration and research.

THE DANGERS OF COMMUNITY

Although there is a considerable body of research demonstrating the widespread benefits of school and classroom community, establishing a sense of community should not be considered a panacea for resolving all discipline problems or guaranteeing a positive school and classroom culture. As noted by Kohn (1996), Noddings (1997), and McMillan and Chavis (1986), establishing a strong sense of community has at least the potential for yielding negative rather than positive effects. These potential problems fall into at least three areas: (a) promoting excess conformity to the community's norms, (b) creating an "ingroup-outgroup" mindset, and (c) focusing on social support to the detriment of promoting academic success.

Excess Conformity

The power of community as a means of maintaining a positive classroom environment or, indeed, for promoting positive development more generally, derives from the desire of community members' to maintain their affiliation with the group. Because the community satisfies members' basic psychological needs, they develop an emotional attachment or "bond" to the community and are motivated to adopt the community's norms and values as their own. However, the desire to belong to the school community may lead individual members into thoughtless, rigid conformity to community norms and values as a means of maintaining community membership. A tragic example of such conformity was exhibited by a soldier who explained his reluctance to report serious prisoner abuse that he knew to be wrong because in his words, he tries "to be friends with everyone" (Serrano, 2004). One of us observed a school where the teachers were generally child-centered but had such a strong sense of community among themselves that no one would confront the fact that one teacher was mistreating her young students by, for example, threatening them with demotion and making them stand in a box outside the classroom door.

The point is that diversity of thought, taste, or values may be suppressed by community leaders in an overzealous effort to strengthen community by strengthening commonalities (Calderwood, 2000). Kohn (1996) calls such communities "collectives" or pseudocommunities. Sacrificing individual thought and welfare solely to remain part of the group or for the good of the group is antithetical to the aims of education in a democracy. While recognizing the importance of individual commitment to the general good, democracies seek to foster respect for personal freedom, autonomous thought, and critical thinking.

Related to the issue of undue conformity is the issue of what norms and values are being promulgated by the community (Battistich et al., 1997; Lee, Bryk, & Smith, 1993). History provides us with many examples of communities that effectively promoted values that were antagonistic to those of an inclusive, democratic society. Although limited, there is some research to suggest that school communities differ in the extent to which they promote student adoption of norms and values consistent with being an effective and critical citizen in a democratic society, as opposed to those consistent with being a compliant citizen (Battistich et al., 1997; Higgins, 1991). Clearly, the content of the community values that students are likely to adopt is an important issue for consideration in any effort to create a classroom or school environment that is more community-like.

Creation of Outgroups

One critical aspect of the this discussion of the content of community values is the importance of the values of diversity and inclusiveness. In the interests of promoting strong affective bonds and a shared sense of identity among community members, there is the distinct danger of creating an "us-versus-them" mindset in which norms of caring, civility, and respect apply to all those within the community, but are not applicable to those on the "outside." Peshkin (1986) has vividly described how the shared values of a fundamentalist school resulted in an insular community whose members were intolerant of lifestyles and beliefs different from their own. When attempting to establish a sense of community in a classroom or school in a democratic society, it is imperative that the boundaries of the community be permeable, and that there is a commitment to acceptance of and respect for those who have different beliefs and values from one's own.

An Underemphasis on Academic Achievement.

For children and youth from disadvantaged backgrounds, there is evidence that a school that is a community can provide substantial help in overcoming life difficulties. However, this research also suggests that in some circumstances, community-building may not effectively promote the academic success of students who are economically disadvantaged. Of particular concern is that teachers, out of empathy for the unfortunate life circumstances of some students, may concentrate their attention on providing social support to these students, but at the same time, reduce their expectations for the students' academic performance. As described by Shouse (1996), sense of classroom or school community may only benefit disadvantaged students in the area of academic achievement when it is combined with a clear "press" for academic performance.

IMPEDIMENTS TO COMMUNITY

Teachers and school leaders who strive to build relational communities that avoid the pitfalls listed previously face a number of obstacles.

Time

Building community takes time—time that might otherwise be spent on academic instruction and learning. Especially in an atmosphere of high pressure for academic performance and high-stakes testing, teachers may fear that taking the time to build personal relationships, hold class meetings, and involve students in decision making will jeopardize their students' academic performance. The community-building process will be especially slow in schools and classrooms where there are a large number of defiant and untrusting students. In a case study of one urban classroom, it took nearly a year for the teacher to build trusting relationships with some students (Watson & Ecken, 2003). Teachers need to trust that the time they take to build community will eventually lead to success and result in a harmonious classroom and better academic learning. For some teachers, especially those who view students as self-interested and unmotivated, it is difficult to have this trust.

Beliefs About Children

"Give them an inch and they'll take a yard." "Don't smile until Christmas." Statements like these reveal the untrusting, individualistic view of children imbedded in American popular culture and much educational practice. Such beliefs undermine the development of community. Many teachers believe that children are individually responsible for their own behavior and need to be tightly controlled and externally motivated to learn and behave well. The controlling stance and inevitable power struggles that follow from such beliefs about children will deny students the reasonable support and autonomy they need to function successfully. Neither teacher nor student will feel themselves to be part of a relational community.

Competition

Competition is valued in American culture and many believe in the power of competition to motivate students to learn and to behave well. Many schools abound with competitive activities, from science fairs to spelling bees. Pitting students against one another undermines the spirit of togetherness and mutual support required for community to develop (Kohn, 1992). Further, if students need to compete with one another for their teacher's favor, they will not be able to trust in their teacher's care. If students cannot trust their teacher they will not experience a sense of community in the classroom.

Common School Practices and Conditions

Many common school conditions make it difficult to build true community in the relational sense. Because a classroom community is built upon the respectful and caring relationships among its members, the larger the class size and the shorter the time class members are together, the more difficult it will be to build these relationships. Typically, in American classrooms, children have different teachers and classmates each year, and in many schools teaching is departmentalized, so that students have several teachers across the day or week and are grouped with many different students in several different classrooms. Keeping the school size small, as has been done with Just Community schools, is one way to solve this problem (Power et al., 1989). Creating teams of teachers that remain stable across the years for each group of students is another. Looping and other techniques to keep teachers and students together for more than one year and limiting departmentalization, and pull-out special programs, especially at the elementary level, can also facilitate the building of relational community.

Inertia

Schools are complex systems and like all systems they are resistant to change. As many teacher educators lament, all too often beginning teachers leave their teacher preparation programs with new ideas and goals to develop relational communities in their classrooms, but are soon socialized into the "tried and true" control-based models of classroom management.

Increased Societal Mobility

Families at all socioeconomic levels have increased their mobility. When families move, even across town, children are removed from their classrooms and enter new classrooms where they must form new relationships. While building community can be made more difficult in all schools because of increased student mobility, the disruption of the community-building process can be especially acute in urban schools serving poor families and rural schools serving children of migrant workers. "Getting to know you" activities and a pervasive use of collaborative learning activities are ways that teachers can help sustain a sense of community in spite of student mobility. Once students have become accustomed to working together, they can help assimilate new students into the norms and values of their community.

The following three vignettes excerpted from a case study of one inner-city, second and third-grade classroom illustrate some of the ways that collaborative learning activities helped a new boy, Derek, enter the classroom in the middle of the year:

> I asked Derek to join John and Paul's partnership... In this activity, first they're supposed to read the captions under the pictures and talk about them. Then they go back and read the chapter together. Finally they talk and write about the question, "Why do you suppose black and white people were not treated equally?"
>
> When it was time to talk about the question and do the writing, I overheard Derek say, "How much do we have to write down?"
>
> John said, "Well, as much as we can think of."
>
> Derek said, "You're kidding!"

After the students had finished working in their partnerships, their teacher, Laura Ecken, gathered them together to reflect on their work and to share their thinking with one another. First the students talked about what went well in their partnerships, then Laura asked them if there were any rough spots.

> Tyrone said, "It's really not a rough spot like a fight. I didn't understand that the little words under the pictures were the captions. Brian kept telling me that I wasn't doing the assignment right, and then he showed me the little bitty words that are the captions."
>
> Because Derek was there I made a big deal of it. I said, "Now, you all got that settled because you talked about it. And Brian explained it and you understood it. That was a good thing to happen."

The third vignette, taken from a class discussion two months later, shows Derek beginning to experience himself as part of a caring, learning community. The class is reflecting on a cooperative activity in which Derek and Brian were partners:

> Brian said, "When we got our partners we didn't fuss about it. We just smiled. When we were writing, I wrote some of it and he wrote some of it."
>
> Derek added, "We got straight to work. Then we kept on getting in fights, and how we solved it, we talked about it and got right back to work." (Watson & Ecken, 2003, pp. 240–242)

For two years with the same class, Laura had worked hard to build a strong relational community. Once this community was built, she was able to rely on her students to help integrate new students into that community. We think the case study of Laura Ecken's class demonstrates that communities can be built and sustained in the face of some mobility. However, like a single snowflake or a drop of rain, there must be some stable core for a community to form and sustain itself.

Strong and supportive relational communities are possible, even in the face of these obstacles. However, if teachers are to be helped to abandon their view of classroom management as control of student behavior, replacing it with community building and collaborative approaches to both classroom management and discipline, we will need to pay careful attention to the strength and forms of these potential impediments in the many different situations teachers face. The above impediments will not be easily overcome. However, we think the benefits are worth the effort.

SUMMARY

Viewing the building of a relational community as the foundation of classroom management is a paradigmatic shift in classroom management and discipline—a shift from teacher control to shared control; from individual responsibility to shared responsibility; from a business atmosphere to a family atmosphere; from a negative view of children's motivations to a positive view; from extrinsic rewards and consequences to explanation, support, guidance, induction, and persuasion; from enforcing rules to building trust by meeting students' needs; and from passive compliance to active participation. It is a shift that parallels and is compatible with the shift that is taking place in the realm of academic curriculum and instruction (McCaslin & Good, 1992; Weinstein, 1999). It is a shift that traces its roots to Dewey and has had many ups and downs along the way.

There have been several past attempts to bring about this kind of shift in mainstream education. The progressive education movement inspired by Dewey shared many of the goals and procedures advocated in the approaches to building community described in this chapter. Yet the progressive movement, sensible as it sounded, did not flourish. In 1962, A. S. Neil in his book, *Summerhill: A Radical Approach to Child Rearing,* advocated a trusting, child-centered approach to teaching, which derived from a positive view of children's motivations. His ideas never threatened to become mainstream. The open education movement of the late 1960s, while often misunderstood and ill-defined (Marshall, 1981) generally took a similar stance to that of progressive educators, rejecting teacher control and extrinsic rewards and punishments, and assuming instead that "given the opportunity, children will choose to engage in activities which will be of high interest to them" (Barth, 1972, p. 26 as cited in Weinstein, 1999, p.161). This approach also failed to transform mainstream educational practice. Teachers tried it briefly and when students did not immediately respond positively, it was soon abandoned (Barth, 1972; Weinstein, 1999). Will the current community-based approaches meet the same fate? We think not.

The community-building approaches described in this chapter differ from the educational movements discussed earlier in that their philosophical stances are supported by current psychological theory and research. Dewey's social constructivist ideas were introduced at a time when behavioral learning theory was becoming the dominant psychological paradigm (Bayles & Hood, 1966). Community-based approaches also differ from Summerhill and, to a lesser extent, the open education movement in that they have a clear role for adult authority and guidance. However, community-based approaches are a long way from becoming the dominant classroom management paradigm.

While all of the theoretically based programs described have been tried in real schools and classrooms and refined to be practical and realizable in real classrooms, there are many obstacles preventing community-based approaches from becoming mainstream. The evidence points to their being good for all students, but it is not clear that all teachers have the personality and temperament required for developing the nurturing relationships required for building a genuine relational community. Many teachers will need help rethinking their views of children and some will need help overcoming personality characteristics, such as needing to be liked, a strong need for control, or the inability to form emotionally warm relationships. Our views of children and our personalities are deeply rooted and will not easily accommodate change. Building community, like teaching for understanding and active learning, is a slow and complex process. Teachers will require time and support to succeed. If our goal as educators is to prepare students to be thoughtful, critical thinkers, supportive of democratic ideals, and compassionate and responsible citizens, then, as Dewey said, many years ago, we need to educate them in the kind of moral, caring, and democratic learning communities they eventually will be called upon to support, sustain, and improve.

ACKNOWLEDGMENTS

The authors would like to thank Hermine Marshall as well as Mary McCaslin, the University of Arizona and Carol Weinstein for their thoughtful and helpful comments on an earlier draft of this manuscript.

REFERENCES

Ainsworth, M. D. S., Blehar, M. C., Waters, E., and Wall, S. (1978). *Patterns of attachment.* Hillsdale, NJ: Lawrence Erlbaum Associates.

Albert, L. (1989). *A teacher's guide to cooperative discipline: How to manage your classroom and promote self-esteem.* Circle Pines, MN: American Guidance Service.

Allman-Snyder, A., May, M. J., & Garcia, F. C. (1975). Classroom structure and children's perception of authority: An open and closed case. *Urban Education, 10,* 131–149.

Aronson, E., Blaney, N., Stephan, C., Sikes, J., & Snapp, M. (1987). *The jigsaw classroom.* Beverley Hills, CA: Sage.

Atwell, N. (1998). *In the middle: New understandings about writing, reading, and learning* (2nd ed.). Portsmouth, NH: Heinemann.

Barth, R.W. (1972). *Open education and the American school.* New York: Agathon Press.

Bartlett, L., Turkanis, C. G., & Rogoff, B. (2001). An orientation to principlals in action. In B. Rogoff, C. G. Turkanis & L. Bartlett (eds.), *Learning together: Children and adults in a school community* (pp. 33–48). New York: Oxford University Press.

Bettistich,V. & Hom, A. (1997). The relationship between students' sense of their school as a community and their involvement in problem behaviors. *American Journal of Public Health, 87,* 1997–2001.

Battistich, V., Schaps, E., & Wilson, N. (2004). Effects of an elementary school intervention on students' "connectedness" to school and social adjustment during middle school. *Journal of Primary Prevention, 24,* 243–262.

Battistich, V., Solomon, D., Kim, D., Watson, M., & Schaps, E. (1995). Schools as communities, poverty levels of student populations, and students' attitudes, motives, and performance: A multilevel analysis. *American Journal of Educational Research, 32,* 627–658.

Battistich, V., Solomon, D., Watson, M., & Schaps, E. (1997). Caring school communities. *Educational Psychologist, 32,* 137–151.

Battistich, V., Watson, M., Solomon, D., Lewis, C., & Schaps, E. (1999). Beyond the three R's: A broader agenda for school reform. *Elementary School Journal, 99*(5), 415–432.

Bayles, E. E., & Hood, B. L. (1966). *Growth of American educational thought and practice.* New York: Harper & Row.

Blum, R. W., McNeely, C. A., & Rinehart, P. M. (2002). *Improving the odds: The untapped power of schools to improve the health of teens.* Minneapolis, MN: Center for Adolescent Health and Development, University of Minnesota.

Bowlby, J. (1969). *Attachment and loss: Vol. 1: Attachment.* New York: Basic Books.

Brown, A. L. & Campione, J.C. (1990). Communities of learning and thinking, or a context by any other name. In D. Kuhn (Ed.), *Developmental perspectives on teaching and learning thinking skills* (pp. 108–126). New York: Karger.

Brown, D., & Solomin, D. (1983). A model for prosocial learning: An in-progress field study. In D. L. Bridgeman (Ed.), *The nature of prosocial development: Interdisciplinary theories and strategies* (pp. 273–307). New York: Academic Press.

Bryk, A. S., & Driscoll, M. E. (1988). *The school as community: Theoretical foundations, contextual influences, and consequences for students and teachers.* Madison: National Center on Effective Secondary Schools, University of Wisconsin.

Calderwood, P. E. (2000). *Learning community: Finding common ground in difference.* New York: Teachers College Press.

Canter, L., & Canter, M. (1992). *Assertive discipline: Positive behavior management for today's classroom.* Santa Monica, CA: Lee Canter & Associates.

Cohen, E. (1987). *Designing group work: Strategies for the heterogeneous classroom.* New York: Teachers College Press.

Coleman, J. S., & Hoffer, T. (1987). *Public and private high schools: The impact of communities.* New York: Basic Books.

Copple, C., Sigel, I. E., & Saunders, R. (1979). *Educating the young thinker: Classroom strategies for cognitive growth.* New York: Van Norstrand.

Curwin, R. L., & Mendler, A. N. (1988). *Discipline with dignity.* Alexandria, VA: Association for Supervision and Curriculum Development.

Dalton, J., & Watson, M. (1997). *Among friends: Classrooms where caring and learning prevail.* Oakland, CA: Developmental Studies Center.

deCharms, R. (1976). *Enhancing motivation: Change in the classroom.* New York: Irvington.

Deci, E. L., & Ryan, R. M. (1985). *Intrinsic motivation and self-determination in human behavior.* New York: Plenum Press.

Developmental Studies Center (1997). *Blueprints for a collaborative classroom.* Oakland, CA: Developmental Studies Center.

Developmental Studies Center (1998a). *Reading, thinking & caring revised program manual.* Oakland, CA: Developmental Studies Center.

Developmental Studies Center (1998b). *Reading for real revised program manual.* Oakland, CA: Developmental Studies Center.

DeVries, R., & Goncu, A. (1987). Interpersonal relations between four-year-olds in dyads from constructivist and Montessori classrooms. *Applied Developmental Psychology, 8,* 481–501.

DeVries, R., & Zan, B. (1994). *Moral classrooms, moral children: Creating a constructivist atmosphere in early education.* New York: Teachers College Press.

Dewey, J. (1966). *Democracy and education.* New York: The Free Press. (Original work published 1944)

Dreikurs, R., Grunwald, B. B., & Pepper, F. C. (1982). *Maintaining sanity in the classroom: Classroom management techniques.* New York: Harper Collins.

Edlesky, C. (1994). Education for democracy. *Language Arts, 71,* 252–257.

Ehman, L. H. (1980). The American school in the political socialization process. *Review of Educational Research, 50,* 99–119.

Freiberg, H. J. (1999). Consistency management and cooperative discipline: From tourists to citizens in the classroom. In H. J. Freiberg (Ed.), *Beyond Behaviorism:Changing the classroom management paradigm* (pp. 75–97). Boston: Allyn & Bacon.

Gardner, H. (1991). *The unschooled mind: How children think and how schools should teach.* New York: Basic Books.

Giroux, H. A. (1983). *Theory and resistance in education: A pedagogy for the opposition.* New York: Bergin & Garvey.

Goldenberg, C. & Gallimore, R. (1991, November). Changing teaching takes more than a one-shot workshop. *Educational Leadership,* 69–72.

Goodenow, C. (1993). Classroom belonging among early adolescent students: Relationships to motivation and achievement. *Journal of Early Adolescence, 13,* 21–43.

Goodlad, J. I. (1984). *A place called school: Perspectives for the future.* New York: McGraw-Hill.

Green, M. (1988). *The dialectic of freedom.* New York: Teachers College Press.

Haberman, M. (1995). *Star teachers of children in poverty.* West Lafayette, IN: Kappa Delta Pi.

Hawkins, J. D., Catalano, R. F., Osterman, R., Abbott, R., & Hill, K. G. (1999). Preventing adolescent health-risk behaviors by strengthening protection during childhood. *Archives of Pediatric and Adolescent Medicine, 153,* 226–234.

Higgins, A. (1980). Research and measurement issues in moral education interventions. In R. L. Mosher (Ed.), *Moral education: A first generation of research and development* (pp. 92–107). New York: Praeger.

Higgins, A. (1991). The Just Community approach to moral education: Evolution of the idea and recent findings. In W. M. Kurtines & J. L. Gewirtz (Eds.), *Handbook of moral behavior and development: Vol. 3. Application* (pp. 111–141). New York: Lawrence Erlbaum Associates.

Higgins, A., Power, C., & Kohlberg, L. (1984). The relationship of moral atmosphere to assignments of responsibility. In W. M. Kurtines & J. L. Gewirtz (Eds.), *Morality, moral behavior and moral development* (pp. 74–106). New York: Wiley.

Hoffman, M. (2000). *Empathy and moral development: Implications for caring and justice.* New York: Cambridge University Press.

Howes, C., & Ritchie, S. (2002). *A matter of trust: Connecting teachers and learners in the early childhood classroom.* New York: Teachers College Press.

Johnson, P. W. (1968). *Life in classrooms.* New York: Holt, Rinehart & Winston.

Johnson, D., & Johnson, R. (1975). *Learning together and alone.* Englewood Cliffs, NJ: Prentice-Hall.

Johnson, D. W., & Johnson, R. T. (1989). *Cooperation and competition: Theory and research.* Edina, MN: Interaction Book Company.

Johnson, D. W., Johnson, R. T., & Marayama, G. (1983). Interdependence and interpersonal attraction among heterogeneous and homogeneous individuals: A theoretical formulation and meta-analysis of the research. *Review of Education Research, 53,* 5–54.

Kagan, S. (1982). Co-op Co-op: A single, flexible cooperative learning method. Paper presented at Second International Conference on Cooperation in Education, Provo, UT.

Kamii, C. (1985). *Young children reinvent arithmetic.* New York: Teachers College Press.

Keltner, D. (2004). The compassionate instinct. *Greater Good, 1*(1), 6–9.

Kohlberg, L. (1966). Moral education in the school. *School Review, 74,* 1–30.

Kohlberg, L. (1969). Stage and sequence: The cognitive-developmental approach to socialization. In D. Goslin (Ed.), *Handbook of socialization theory and research* (pp. 347–480). Chicago: Rand McNally.

Kohlberg, L., Lieberman, M., Power, C., Higgins, A., & Codding, J. (1981). Evaluating Scarsdale's "Just Community School" and its curriculum; implications for the future. *Moral Education Forum, 6*(4), 31–42.

Kohn, A. (1990). *The brighter side of human nature: Altruism and empathy in everyday life*. New York: Basic Books.

Kohn, A. (1992). *No contest: The case against competition*. (Rev. ed.). Boston: Houghton Mifflin.

Kohn, A. (1996). *Beyond discipline: From compliance to community*. Alexandria, VA: Association for Supervision and Curriculum Development.

Lave, J., & Wenger, E. (1991). *Situated learning: Legitimate peripheral participation*. New York: Cambridge University Press.

Lee, V. E., Bryk, A. S., & Smith, J. B. (1993). The organization of effective secondary schools. In L. Darling-Hammond (Ed.), *Review of research in education* (Vol. 19, pp. 171–267). Washington, DC: American Educational Research Association.

Lickona, T. (1991). *Educating for character: How our schools can teach respect and responsibility*. New York: Bantam Books.

Marshall, H. H. (1981). Open classrooms: Has the term outlived its usefulness? *Review of Educational Research 51*(2) 181–192.

McCaslin, M., & Good, T. L. (1992). Compliant cognition: The misalliance of management and instructional goals in current school reform. *Educational Researcher, 21*(3), 4–17.

McMillan, D. W., & Chavis, D. M. (1986). Sense of community: A definition and theory. *Journal of Community Psychology, 14*, 6–23.

Neill, A.S. (1962). *Summerhill: A radical approach to child rearing*. New York: Hart Publishing Company.

Nieto, S. (1999). *The light in their eyes: Creating multicultural learning communities*. New York: Teachers College Press.

Noddings, N. (1984). *Caring: A feminine approach to ethics and moral education*. Berkeley: University of California Press.

Noddings, N. (1992). *The challenge to care in schools: An alternative to character education*. New York: Teachers College Press.

Noddings, N. (1997). Character education and community. In A. Molnar (Ed.), *The construction of children's character*. National Society for the Study of Education (pp. 1–15). Chicago: University of Chicago Press.

Noddings, N. (2002). *Educating moral people: A caring alternative to character education*. New York: Teachers College Press.

Ogbu, J. U. (1988). Class stratification, racial stratification, and schooling. In L. Weis (Ed.), *Class, race, and gender in American education* (pp. 163–179). New York: State University of New York Press.

Osterman, K. F. (2000). Students' need for belonging in the school community. *Review of Educational Research, 70*(3), 323–367.

Peck, R. F., & Havighurst, R. J. (1960). *The psychology of character development*. New York: Wiley.

Pianta, R. C. (1999). *Enhancing relationships between children and teachers*. Washington, DC: American Psychological Association.

Piaget, J. (1965). *The moral judgment of the child*. (M. Gabain, Trans.). New York: The Free Press. (Original work published 1932)

Polson, D. (2001). Helping children learn to make responsible choices. In B. Rogoff, C. G. Turkanis, & L. Bartlet (Eds.), *Learning together: Children and adults in a school community* (pp.123–132). New York: Oxford University Press.

Power, C., Higgins, A., & Kohlberg, L. (1989). *Lawrence Kohlberg's approach to moral education*. New York: Columbia University Press.

Putnam, J., & Burke, J. B. (1998). *Organizing and managing classroom learning communities*. San Francisco: McGraw-Hill.

Resnick, M. D., Bearman, P. S., Blum, R. W., Bauman, K. E., Harris, K. M., Jones, J., Tabor, J., Beuhring, T., Sieving, R. E., Shew, M., Ireland, M., Bearinger, L. H., & Udry, J. R. (1997). Protecting adolescents from harm: Findings from the national longitudinal study on adolescent health. *Journal of the American Medical Association, 278*, 823–832.

Rogers, C., & Freiberg, H. J. (1994). *Freedom to learn* (3rd ed.). Columbus, OH: Merrill.

Rogoff, B. (1990). *Apprenticeship in thinking: Cognitive development in social context*. New York: Oxford University Press.

Rogoff, B. (1994). Developing understanding of the idea of communities of learners. *Mind, Culture, and Activity*, 1, 209–229.

Rogoff, B., Bartlett, L., & Turkanis, C.G. (2001). Lessons about learning in a community. In B. Rogoff, C. G. Turkanis, & L. Bartlett (Eds.) *Learning together: Children and adults in a school community* (pp. 3–20). New York: Oxford University Press.

Rogoff, B., Mistry, J., Goncu, A., & Mosier, C. (1993). Guided participation in cultural activity by toddlers and caregivers. *Monographs of the Society for Research in Child Development, 58*(8).

Rogoff, B., Turkanis, C. G., & Bartlett, L. (Eds.). (2001). *Learning together: Children and adults in a school community.* New York: Oxford University Press.

Ryan, K. (1986). The new moral education. *Phi Delta Kappan, 68,* 228–233.

Schaps, E. (2003, Summer). Community in school: Central to character formation, violence prevention, and more. Texas Elementary Principals and Supervisors Association. *TEPSA Journal, 68,* 15–23.

Serrano, R. A. (5/14/04). 1st G.I. to be tried in prison abuse tells of brutality. *San Francisco Chronicle,* A-12.

Sharan, S. (Ed.). (1990). *Cooperative learning: Theory and research.* New York: Praeger.

Shouse, A. C. (1996). Academic press and sense of community: Conflict, congruence, and implications for student achievement. *Social Psychology of Education, 1,* 47–68.

Slavin, R. E. (1980). Cooperative learning in teams: State of the art. *Educational Psychologist, 15,* 93–111.

Slavin, R. E. (1983). *Cooperative learning.* New York: Longman.

Slavin, R. E. (1990). *Cooperative learning: Theory, research and practice.* Englewood cliffs, NJ: Prentice Hall.

Solomon, D., Battistitch, V., Watson, M., Schaps, E., and Lewis, C. (2000). A six-district study of educational change: Direct and mediated effects of the Child Development Project. *Social Psychology of Education, 4,* 3–51.

Solomon, D., & Kendall, A. J. (1976). Individual characteristics and children's performance in "open" and "traditional" classroom settings. *Journal of Educational Psychology, 68,* 613–625.

Solomon, D., Watson, M., Battistich, V., Schaps, E., & Delucchi, K. (1996). Creating classrooms that students experience as communities. *American Journal of Community Psychology, 24,* 719–748.

Solomon, D., Watson, M., Battistich, V., Schaps, E., Tuck, P., Solomon, J., Cooper, C., & Ritchey, W. (1985). A program to promote interpersonal consideration and cooperation in children. In R. Slavin, S. Sharan, S. Kagan, R. Hertz-Lazarowitz, C. Webb, & R. Schmuck (Eds.), *Learning to cooperate, cooperating to learn* (pp. 371–401). New York: Plenum.

Sroufe, L. A. (1996). *Emotional development: The organization of emotional life in the early years.* New York: Cambridge University Press.

Stayton, D. J., Hogan, R., & Ainsworth, M. D. S. (1971). Infant obedience and maternal behavior: The origins of socialization reconsidered. *Child Development,* 42, 1057–1069.

Tharp, R. G. & Gallimore, R. (1988). *Rousisng minds to life: Teaching, learning, and schooling in social context.* New York: Cambridge University Press.

Thompson, G. L. (2004). *Through ebony eyes: What teachers need to know but are afraid to ask about African American students.* San Francisco: Jossey-Bass.

Tom, A. (1984). *Teaching as a moral craft.* New York: Longman.

Turkanis, C. G. (2001). Creating curriculum with children. In B. Rogoff, C. G. Turkanis, & L. Bartlett (Eds.), *Learning together: Children and adults in a school community.* (pp. 91–102) New York: Oxford University Press.

Turkanis, C. G., Bartlett, L., & Rogoff, B. (2001). Never-ending learning. In B. Rogoff, C. G. Turkanis, & L. Bartlett (Eds.) *Learning together: Children and adults in a school community* (pp. 225–244). New York: Oxford University Press.

Vygotsky, L. S. (1978). *Mind in society: The development of higher psychological processes* (M. Cole, V. John-Steiner, S. Scribner, & E. Soluberman, Eds. & Trans.). Cambridge, MA: Harvard University Press.

Watson, M., & Ecken, L. (2003). *Learning to trust: Transforming difficult elementary classrooms through Developmental Discipline.* San Francisco: Jossey-Bass.

Watson, M., Kendzior, S., Dasho, S., Rutherford, S., & Solomon, D. (1998). A social constructivist approach to cooperative learning and staff development: Ideas from the Child Development Project. In C. M. Brody & N. Davidson (Eds.) *Professional development for cooperative learning: Issues and approaches.* (pp. 147–168). Albany: State University of New York Press.

Wehlage, G. G., Rutter, G. A., Smith, G. A., Lesko, N., & Fernandez, R. R. (1989). *Reducing the risk: Schools as communities of support.* New York: Falmer.

Weinstein, C. S. (1999). Reflectiona on best practices and promising programs: Beyond assertive classroom discipline. In H. J. Freiberg (Ed.), *Beyond behaviorism: Changing the classroom management paradigm.* Boston: Allyn and Bacon.

White, R. W. (1959). Motivation reconsidered: The concept of competence. *Psychological Review, 60*(5), 297–333.

Wolk, S. (1998). *A democratic classroom.* Portsmouth, NH: Heinemann.

Wolk, S. (2000). *Being good: Rethinking classroom management and student discipline.* Portsmouth, NH: Heinemann.

11

Design-Based, Participation-Centered Approaches to Classroom Management

Daniel T. Hickey
Indiana University

Nancy Jo Schafer
Georgia State University

DESIGN-BASED, PARTICIPATION-CENTERED VIEWS OF CLASSROOM MANAGEMENT

As illustrated by the diversity of chapters in this volume, "classroom management" is a rather broad domain of educational practice. One characterization by Froyen & Iverson (1999) includes the management of *content* (space, materials, equipment, movement, and lessons), *conduct* (discipline problems), and *covenant* (social dynamics and interpersonal relationships). This chapter further clarifies classroom management in terms of five types of actions teachers take to facilitate learning in their classrooms:

Engagement—maximizing involvement in academic tasks;
Curriculum—defining the scope and sequence of instruction;
Relationships—interacting with and among students;
Development—changing behavior and cognition over time;
Discipline—preventing and addressing behavior problems.

These actions are treated in this chapter as the five core *aspects* of classroom management. They will be used to organize an effort to apply newer sociocultural perspectives of knowing and learning to the diverse challenges of classroom management. These perspectives regard knowledge as a cultural phenomenon, rather than as something that resides in the minds of individuals. As will be elaborated, a sociocultural perspective treats collective participation of social groups in ritualized knowledgeable activity as the primary phenomenon in human activity. From this perspective, classroom management is concerned with teachers' and students' collective success at ritualizing the routines that define the communities of expertise for which we want students to engage. For example, in our prior research in life science classroom from which we draw many of our ideas, we focused most directly on coaching and scaffolding classroom discourse to reflect that of practicing geneticists. We did so by drawing on diverse examples of socioculturally-oriented considerations of discourse and participation in science education, and exploring the functional value of these ideas in our iterative refinements of our curriculum and classroom assessments. We found that our success in supporting collective participation seemed to have positive consequences for aspects of activity typically associated with classroom management. This included aspects of student cognition (e.g., gains on self-reported motivation) and behavior (e.g., increased time on task and reduced misbehavior). This chapter was written in order to further explores the potential of our approach to classroom management. We do this by considering how each of the five aspects of classroom management listed above might be addressed by focusing directly on collective participation and indirectly on the activity of individuals.

It is important to acknowledge that this chapter is by no means the first application of sociocultural theory to classroom management. Several of the most influential models reflect a strong influence of Soviet theorist Vygotsky, widely regarded as the most seminal sociocultural psychologist. This influence is most notable in McCaslin's coregulated learning model (e.g., McCaslin & Good, 1996) and in the Child Development Project (Developmental Studies Center, 2004; Watson & Battistich, chapter 10 in this volume). Arguably, these approaches direct their focus on the interaction between individuals and their social context: the way that individuals and contexts are mutually defined. Such an approach is consistent with widely held characterizations of Vygotsky's theories (e.g., 1978). We argue that such approaches are more appropriately labeled *socio-constructivist*, reserving the label *sociocultural* for the heretofore undefined approaches that focus more directly on collective participation.

The differences between the proposed participation-centered approaches and existing approaches are rooted in philosophical differences about the nature of knowledge and therefore learning. In this regard, the chapter is strongly shaped by the "comparative" analyses by Greeno, Collins, & Resnick (1996) and Case (1996). These analyses trace the philosophical, psychological, and practical evolution of what are sometimes described as the three "grand theories" of knowing and learning (often labeled *behavioral, cognitive*, and *sociocultural*). Such an approach highlights the fundamental tensions between behavioral and cognitive theories, and advances sociocultural theory as a higher-order synthesis that reconciles these tensions. Our arguments are more pragmatic and thus sidestep the philosophical differences between the proposed sociocultural approach and prior approaches by advancing a hypothesis that can be answered using widely accepted measures and research design. This hypothesis proposes that classroom management techniques that focus on collective participation in domain-specific discourse (e.g., focusing on increasing the quantity or quality of argumentative discourse in science classrooms) will indirectly improve the way that individual students behave and think, and may do so above and beyond approaches that focus primarily on the activity of individuals. In this sense, a participation-centered approach does not deny or ignore behavioral or cognitive activity of individuals. Rather, it very deliberately considers individual activity after attending to collective participation. To use the words of Greeno and the Middle School Mathematics through Application Project (1998), it treats individual behavior and individual cognition as "special cases" of collective participation in sociocultural practices. As will be elaborated in some detail, this characterization of the relationship between individual activity and social contexts is quite different from prevailing characterizations and has important implications for conceptualizing and studying educational practices.

In practical terms, we argue that using sociocultural perspectives and methods to directly "fine-tune" collective participation in the discourses of academic knowledge domains is an effective way to improve the aspects of student behavior and student cognition that are widely considered indicative of effective classroom management. Newer design-based research methods, advanced by leading sociocultural theorists, offer promising means for doing so. This is because these methods present a methodologically and theoretically coherent way to embed participation-centered approaches within the more systematic consideration of both individual behavior and individual cognition. As associated with more conventional approaches, design-based methods further guide the evaluation of these refinements with the types of school-level indicators more commonly associated with policy research. Teachers, teacher educators, and researchers who are attempting to improve classroom management may find it useful to consider embedding some of the methods described in this chapter into the center of their existing approaches, whatever they may be.

We also consider the current social and political context in which educational reforms must function. The sociopolitical context of school reform has changed considerably in recent years. As reflected in recent market-oriented, test-driven accountability, many policy makers have become less receptive (and even hostile) toward the primary goals associated with many modern approaches to classroom management (e.g., students' self-efficacy and intrinsic motivation). Related forces are driving new expectations about educational research, treating randomized control group studies using "objective" and "external" outcomes (like disciplinary referrals and high-stakes test performance) as the "gold-standard" in educational research. This is particularly the case for the U.S. Department of Education, the agency that funded much of the prior research on classroom management. Arguably, these new criteria favor classroom management approaches that focus directly on student behavior, while setting a very high bar for approaches that focus more directly on student cognition. This is because such approaches aim to change behavior indirectly, via cognitive processes, which are in themselves less amenable to objective measurement. In the current "what works" context, this may lead to approaches that focus on cognitive process (of individuals or groups) to be labeled as less effective or even be proscribed. As illustrated by the other chapters in this volume, cognitive processes are the primary focus of many leading theorists and researchers concerned with classroom management. Therefore, these broader political concerns threaten to undermine or derail a great deal of this effort.

After reviewing key sociocultural assumptions and the notion of collective participation, we attempt to define a uniquely sociocultural perspective for each of the five aspects of classroom management listed previously. Assuming that prior approaches to classroom management have focused more on the activity of individuals, we consider the five aspects of classroom management using socioculturally derived examples from outside of the existing considerations of classroom management. This de novo approach is employed to highlight the essential features of a uniquely sociocultural consideration of classroom management. We do not imply such isolation should be maintained, or that an effort to develop sociocultural classroom management practices should also start from scratch. To the contrary, this chapter outlines how newer design-based methods can be used to embed a participation-centered approach within existing individually oriented approaches, and then examine whether doing so helps accomplish existing goals for individual activity. Drawing on related research on classroom assessment, the chapter considers whether discourse analytic methods can be used to directly (but informally) refine collective participation in iterative cycles of refinement that are embedded within more formal assessments of individual cognition and individual behavior at the classroom level. It then outlines how these iterative cycles are themselves embedded within a highly formal evaluation using measures that can be validly interpreted within large-scale control group studies.

Sociocultural, Participation-Centered Views of Classroom Management

Sociocultural Views of Knowing and Learning

Sociocultural perspectives are consistent with what Pepper (1970) labeled a contextualist worldview. The *contextualist* metaphor for human development is a historical event. In a contextualist worldview, human activity cannot be understood outside of the context in which it occurred, and the context from which it is being considered. This fundamental role of context is the root of the term *situative,* and it is widely used to characterize contemporary sociocultural perspectives (e.g., Greeno et. al, 1998).

In attempting to address the educational challenges created by the Russian Revolution, Vygotsky (1978) elaborated on Engels' (1972) argument that human labor and use of physical tools are the means by which humans change nature, and in doing so, change humankind. Vygotsky extended Engels' argument (that using tools of physical labor changes humankind) to also include language and numeracy as tools. If so, then their use also changes the human mind. Rather than merely employing literacy and numeracy and internalizing their function, Vygotsky argued that any participation in the use of these "knowledge tools" necessarily changes them. Sometimes such changes are lasting, as when new technology terms or slang come into widespread formal usage. More commonly, however, such changes are local and fleeting, such as when such terms are only used and understood by a particular group for a particular period of time. This leads to a characterization of learning as participation in the further transformation (construction and refinement) of socially defined knowledge (Vygotsky, 1978). Vygotsky's theories of learning yielded notions, such as the Zone of Proximal Development (ZPD), that eventually became widely known to western educators and researchers.

Fundamental Debates About Knowing and Learning. Given Vygotsky's short career and long-delayed introduction to western scholars, it makes sense that theorists debate what he actually meant. Vygotsky (1978) argued that the social and psychological "planes" are separate, and that all knowledge develops on the social plane via cultural processes. Most agree that he also argued that this knowledge was subsequently internalized on the psychological plane, which was presumably more developmentally and psychologically advanced. This position is maintained by many developmental psychologists (e.g., Valsiner, 1997, 1998). Lave (1991) labeled perspectives that emphasize the way that individuals are shaped by social factors as "cognition plus"; Rogoff (1998) labeled them "social influence" theories. We contend that this position is consistent with what was discussed previously as "socio-constructivist" views of knowing and learning. Regardless of what Vygotsky actually meant, some leading sociocultural theorists have long cautioned against the assumption that knowledge gets "internalized" after it is transformed (i.e., constructed and refined) via social processes (Bruner, 1984; Wertsch, 1991). These theorists argue that if knowledge is being continually transformed in the social context, then it must remain there. They argue that only in the social context in which it is transformed can the knowledge be fully understood; removing it from that context necessarily changes it. Thus, it is impossible to take knowledge "whole cloth" from the social context in which it is intricately bound and have it reside unchanged in the mind of an individual.

Even in ostensibly solitary pursuits, humans use physical, conceptual, and social artifacts of culture to maximize successful participation and overcome the limitations of the individual human mind (Rogoff, 1998). Merely thinking in a specific language necessarily involves participation because language is culturally created and modified, and the use of a particular language has affordances and constraints in its use. In this view, all knowledge (including knowing how productive classroom learners behave and reason) is presumed to reside in the context of its use, rather than the isolated mind of the individual knower. Thus, individual characterizations of knowledge are viewed as secondary to this more fundamental social characterization.

Having established our basic stance regarding sociocultural perspectives, understanding how a uniquely sociocultural perspective views "internalization" from a participation-centered model of learning requires further exploration. From a participation perspective, what students internalize is not an exact replica of external social activity; rather "internalization" is the ongoing participation in the creation, maintenance, and propagation of knowledge as direct and indirect social interaction (Zinchenko, 1985). This means that the social and psychological planes are inseparable and mutually constituted. As such, collaborative and solo activities mutually constitute each other, and neither can be extracted from the context in which it occurs. Rogoff's recent textbook provides the following characterization of this perspective:

> Rather than individual development being influenced by (and influencing) culture, from my perspective, people develop as they participate in and contribute to cultural activities that they themselves develop with the involvement of people in successive generations. People of each generation, as they engage in sociocultural endeavors with other people, make use of and extend cultural tools and practices inherited from previous generations. As people develop through their shared use of cultural tools and practices, they simultaneously contribute to the transformation of cultural tools, practices, and institutions. (2003, p. 52)

The transformation of participation simply cannot be defined in terms of the acquisition of individual skills and knowledge. Rather, the primary phenomenon in human activity is the collective transformation of participation of humans in knowledge practices.

We acknowledge that many scholars, educators, and observers may reject what is characterized here as a sociocultural characterization of knowing and learning. We recognize the folly in overturning widely held and hyperintuitive assumptions about the individual nature of knowing and learning. As Matusov (1998) points out, "participation and internalization models are not just two slightly different 'points' but two different worldviews. They generate different research questions, and different research goals and methodology, and provide different perceptions of a variety of psychological phenomenon" (p. 327). Convincing readers to adopt this philosophical stance is not the goal of this chapter. Rather, to reiterate, our approach aims to show how classroom management practices that follow from sociocultural views may lead to improvements on individual outcomes that are the direct focus of prior approaches. In doing so, we sidestep the intractable philosophical argument about the fundamental nature of knowledge.[1] Instead, we transform the issue into a tractable scientific argument.

Participation-Centered Principles of Classroom Management

The focus on collective participation in domain knowledge practices leads us to propose the term *participation-centered* to characterize the principles and models that follow from sociocultural views of knowing and learning. The highly contextual orientation of sociocultural perspectives leads to an increased focus on the enactment of practices in specific contexts, and a decreased focus on general notions that transcend specific contexts. As such, the distinction between the five aspects of classroom management (engagement, curriculum, relationships, development, and discipline) and the principles that follow from them are inevitably less clear from a sociocultural perspective than from prior perspectives. Of course, even the most prescriptive approaches are ultimately defined as they are enacted in practice. But the contextualized nature of sociocultural perspectives leads to a more descriptive approach to reform that embraces and exploits this reality, rather than tolerates and accommodates it. Furthermore, our perspectives leads us to assume that the emergence of discrete management principles focusing on student behavior or student cognition are at least partly rooted in the antithetical relationship between the competing theoretical views of knowing and learning underlying some of the prior approaches. This conflict is perhaps best embodied in the enduring debate over the consequences of extrinsic incentives on intrinsic motivation.

[1]Readers interested in these more fundamental arguments are referred to Matusov's (1998) concise characterization.

In practical terms, the preceding means that the distinctions between the examples for each of the five aspects of classroom management are somewhat arbitrary, thus, most of the examples could have been applied to many of the five aspects. In this sense, participation-centered principles of classroom management provide a new and potentially more effective way of accomplishing the same goals of established classroom management practices. Consider for example, student discipline. Instead of entering in the debate over existing approaches to discipline (e.g., assertive versus cooperative), we consider how domain-specific research on classroom discourse provides a new and relatively neutral perspective for understanding and improving the consequences of existing approaches to student discipline. We then consider how such a perspective and video exemplars of discourse might be used to iteratively refine participation in worthwhile classroom activity, indirectly reducing misbehavior. We hypothesize that such indirect approaches to reducing misbehavior may be more effective than approaches that directly target classroom discipline. In this way, we draw on examples from diverse socioculturally inspired research outside of classroom management to illustrate our ideas about participation-centered classroom management.

Engagement as Participation. From a sociocultural perspective, *engagement* is fundamentally about the meaningful participation in the knowledge practices that define domains of expertise. Rather than behavioral routines that build associations, or cognitive routines that build schema, this view "emphasizes ways that social practices are organized to encourage and support *engaged participation* by members of communities and that are understood by individuals to support the continuing development of their personal identities" (Greeno et al., 1998, p. 11, emphasis added). Thus, it seems, the notion of *engaged collective participation* belongs at the core of a sociocultural model of classroom management. The notion of identity and its centrality to this view is elaborated below. To use Rogoff's (1998) terms, humans are engaged in learning about a domain when their participation in the knowledge practices that define that domain are being transformed. In other words, students are engaged in learning about a particular domain (e.g., science) when the local enactment of the knowledge practices of that domain (e.g., scientific argumentation) are being constructed and refined by students' legitimate participation. Classroom management from a sociocultural perspective is concerned with directly increasing engagement in knowledge practices of targeted domains to enhance the five aspects of classroom activity that are indicative of classroom management.

Initially at least, it seems that what sets our approach to classroom management apart from others is this intensive focus on enhancing collective participation in very specific knowledge practices associated with expertise in the domains. For example, in studies now getting underway in elementary mathematics, the forms of collective participation that we aim to scaffold are directly informed by research literature from mathematics education that emphasizes the importance of authentic forms of mathematical discourse. Rather than aligning our efforts with any particular theory or view of classroom discourse, we iteratively manipulate aspects of our materials, instructions, and activities that enhance the extent to which students "try-out" the nuances of authentic mathematical discourse and "try-on" the identities that are presumed to define mathematical expertise (such as emphasized by Nasir, 2002). One particularly useful example was provided by Mitchell (2001), who highlighted the negative consequences of *wordwalking* (students' substitution of mathematical terms with everyday natural language terms). We also found the ideas of Sfard (2000), for example, particularly informative because they highlight the limitations of everyday discourse (the focus of many prior mathematics reforms) and the importance of discourse that "deals with mathematical concepts that cannot be incorporated into everyday discourse, as known to the student" (p. 20). From our perspective, these strands of research (which appear to exist in most content domains) diverge from larger and more established strands that are more reflective of cognitive/rationalist views of knowing and learning. These strands focus more on individual knowledge construction and are generally more accepting (and sometimes encouraging) of classroom discourse using "everyday" vernacular.

Obviously then, a central challenge is motivating initial and continued engagement in authentic domain knowledge practices. One of the potentially controversial aspects of the proposed participation-centered view of engagement concerns the use of extrinsic incentives. We precede our consideration by stating that we do not see tangible extrinsic rewards as a fundamental part of participation-centered classroom management. However, extrinsic rewards for performance and achievement are becoming even more common, more tangible, and more widely used with older students as schools struggle to meet stringent new accountability mandates. Furthermore, commonly used incentives (such as grades, summative performance feedback, and even praise) remain controversial because they have been shown to undermine intrinsic motivation in many contexts (e.g., Kohn, 1993; Reeve, chapter 24 in this volume). The agnosticism of sociocultural perspectives is evident in their stance towards the use of incentives. This is because the standards and values that motivate engagement are a function of the knowledge practices. Thus, the standards and values are a fundamental part of the constraints and affordances that define those practices. This means that incentives are neither inherently detrimental for learning (e.g., Kohn, 1993), nor useful for some aspects of school learning (e.g., Chance, 1992). Rather, the impact of incentives should be considered in light of how they transform the collective participation in the desirable knowledge practices of communities of learners. Quite specifically, this means that the consequences of incentives must first be considered in light of their impact on collective participation, as assessed using sociocultural discourse analytic methods (e.g., Gee and Green, 1998). It seems to us that this applies to modest "organic" incentives, such as the experience of success afforded by informal classroom assessment, as well as tangible rewards such as the incentives offered in programs like Accelerated Reader, and controversial policies such as cash incentives for student attendance (e.g., Bach, 2001).

To understand our suggestion to embed the analysis of collective participation within a more formal deliberation, consider, for example, using incentives for motivating students to attain fluency by repeatedly rehearsing lower-level associations (e.g., phonics or arithmetic facts). The impact of different forms of incentives on collective participation in these activities can be readily assessed by analyzing the (necessarily peculiar) forms of discourse associated with ideal engagement in these activities. In the case of phonics or arithmetic facts, the quality of this "discourse" is nothing more than student engagement and persistence in extended practice of those skills. Hence, the consequences of incentives are judged in terms of impact on the engagement and persistence in that particular activity; concern for subsequent free-choice engagement in such activity seems irrelevant. Conversely, when considering the consequences of incentives for "higher-level" curricular routines (e.g., carrying out a laboratory experiment), the impact of any incentives should be considered in light of the very different discursive ideals for that activity. In the case of a laboratory experiment, one should consider the consequences of grading practice or other incentives on the extent to which the discourse around the activity (including, but not limited to conversation, writing, and diagramming) reflects that of experts in the domain. In this case, the consequences of incentives for future engagement seem worthy of careful consideration. However, from our perspective, such considerations of future engagement should consider the quality of discourse when subsequent activities are enacted. In summary, an incentive may be used to initiate and support authentic engagement in discourse, while in another context that same incentive may undermine it.

These analyses yield evidence that is very useful for fine-tuning the value of incentives on participation in a particular context. The impact of such refinements can then be assessed using more conventional measures (e.g., timed tests in the case of fluency, essay items on a formal exam in the case of the laboratory experiment). This provides additional evidence for further refinement of incentives in that context, and provides a stronger basis for making more general conclusions about the consequences of those incentives. In addition to illustrating the embedding of informal refinement of collective participation, this example also illustrates the need to further explore how participation-centered perspectives converge and diverge from other influential perspectives. In this case, self-determination theory (e.g., Ryan & Deci, 2000) provides extensive and influential guidance for minimizing the negative consequences and maximizing the positive consequences of the use of modest incentives like grades and praise that are ubiquitous in most formal classroom settings. It seems to us that expanding such consideration to include the consequences for collective participation is a worthwhile avenue for advancing this line of inquiry. As outlined below, this might entail examining how efforts to directly refine engagement (i.e., collective participation) indirectly enhance the individual students' sense of self-determination.

Curriculum as Authentic Domain Knowledge Practices. Collins, Brown, and Newman (1989) argued that scientific and mathematical activity is "authentic" to the extent that it resembles the activities of practicing scientists and mathematicians. From a sociocultural perspective, curriculum needs to be authentic to be truly effective. The definition of "authenticity" that follows from this assumption appears to diverge from the perspectives of some leading classroom management theorists. For example, Brophy (1999) argued that authentic domain knowledge practices are often "not authentic with respect to life applications and thus are not likely to provide a solid basis for motivating students to learn" because they "deal with topics or problems that are too esoteric for anyone but a disciplinary specialist to need to know or even care about" (p. 22). In this view, the authenticity of a curricular routine is judged in terms of students' interests and prior knowledge regarding the targeted topics and problems. A sociocultural perspective judges authenticity more in terms of the actual practices that define the knowledge domain, such as the ability to engage in argumentative discourse, which is seen as a central knowledge practice of scientists. This does not mean that students' prior knowledge and interests are not taken into account. But it does highlight the need to establish trajectories of participation that are legitimate to a domain from the very start. As Brown (1994, p. 10) argues, the modern assumption that broader cognitive development leads the learning of more specific capacities has long led curriculum theorists to underestimate the kinds of reasoning that children are capable of. From this perspective, prioritizing students' prior knowledge and interests is likely to result in the sort of curricular routines that emphasize coping with the demands of the class and still getting a good grade, regardless of whether the actual knowledge practices of science are involved; what Jiménez-Aleixandre, Rodríguez, & Duschl (2000) characterized as "doing the lesson" instead of the more desirable "doing the science." This is a complex and far-ranging issue that exceeds the scope of this chapter. The perspective being taken here is described and illustrated in more detail in Hickey & Zuiker (2005).

As highlighted by the notion of *guided discovery,* many modern curricular perspectives emphasize that learning is presumed to occur incidentally as students construct new knowledge while trying to solve problems that are personally interesting and build directly on their prior knowledge. We contrast this view with Berieter and Scardamalia's (1989) pioneering notion of *intentional learning,* where the "problem" students are trying to solve is the lack of knowledge. These ideas have been refined in the continued development of CSILE (Computer Supported Intentional Leaning Environment) and more recently, Knowledge Forum (Institute for Knowledge Innovation and Technology, 2004). The contrast between CSILE and Knowledge Forum and other computer-supported learning environments illustrates participation-centered curricular principles. Most computer-supported learning environments use technology to support knowledge development of individuals. Whereas these environments increasingly include features that support interaction and communication among multiple learners, these features are generally organized to support the construction of new knowledge and understanding by individual participants. In contrast, CSILE and Knowledge Forum exploit technology to foster the creation and continual improvement of "community knowledge." The technology supports a "community knowledge space" where participants post notes that contribute to theories, models, plans, evidence, etc. The software supports the creation and shared use of notes, and allows participants to witness and review the creation of communal knowledge over time (Scardamalia, 2004).

At this point, it seems worthwhile to emphasize that trajectories in participation-centered curriculum specifically concern collective rituals (rather than the individual-level constructs such as skills or expertise). We believe that the value of participation-centered practices is obscured when notions like trajectories are characterized in terms of constructs that apply to individuals. Thus, consider the manner in which Brown and Campione's (1996) Community of Learners (COL) classrooms problematize typical school subject matter, and then give students collective authority to address the problems that are presented. Core COL principles work together to hold students accountable for disciplinary norms (e.g., concepts, tools, forms of discourse associated with domain knowledge practice), and to provide them with useful feedback and resources for doing so. Participation-centered curricular ideals are embodied in the analysis by Engle and Conant (2002) of "disciplinary engagement" in one of the COL classrooms. After defining disciplinary engagement ("contact between what students are doing and the issues and practices of a discipline's discourse" p. 402), they document how the COL curricular routines supported trajectories of participation, where the classroom discourse became increasingly successful and increasingly consistent with scientific argumentation and use of evidence and theory to warrant knowledge claims.

In practical terms, the participation-centered refinement of curricular practices can be understood in terms using Lave and Wenger's (1991) notions of "legitimate trajectories." Rather than the more familiar characterizations of trajectories in terms of individual expertise, this characterization of trajectory concerns participation in the social construction of knowledge associated with a domain of expertise (e.g., discourse of scientists or mathematicians). While participation by school children is necessarily "peripheral" relative to content domains, the peripheral forms of participation can be more or less "legitimate." A more legitimate trajectory points towards becoming fuller participants in the coconstruction of that community's practices. A less legitimate trajectory leads away from participating in the construction of domain knowledge. In this view, curricular decisions are refined in light of a trajectory of collective participation in domain discourse. This trajectory starts at the classes' current participation in domain discourse and leads towards the "center" of the community in which the targeted knowledge practices are constructed. This "center" is signified by authentic domain discourse and practices. As an example of this view, the coaching of a math class to replace the vernacular term *point* with the academic term *vector* moves their participation farther along this trajectory. Fortunately, most curricular domains have extensive research and professional development literatures that provide guidance for improving classroom discourse in a manner that is generally consistent with these perspectives.

Another example of the application of these principles emerged in our own studies of an introductory genetics curriculum for secondary life science. The curriculum was organized around *GenScope,* a computer-based modeling tool that allowed students to easily manipulate and observe phenomena of inheritance using fanciful organisms like dragons and through colorful dynamic animations (Horwitz & Christie, 2000). In an early version of the curriculum, roughly 20 hours of collaborative "guided discovery" left students with detailed knowledge of *GenScope*'s various functionalities (the various windows and tools), as well as organisms and traits (dragons, number of legs, wings, etc). But careful assessment revealed that students had learned very little about the underlying genetics content (such as sex linkage and dihybrid inheritance). To use contemporary situative terminology, the classroom discourse that was transformed during these activities left the students attuned to the variant aspects of the *GenScope* environment (i.e., the fanciful dragons and traits, and the various windows that made up the software.) For example, when students were completing computer-based investigations that involved the color of the dragons, classroom discourse in the initial investigations revealed that students were negotiating with each other about what color the dragon should be (e.g., "it is a boy so don't make it pink") rather than the nuances of polygenetic inheritance, which was exemplified by the trait for color (e.g., "you have to look at both of the chromosomes to determine the color"). The former discourse defined an illegitimate trajectory, because the variant aspects of the *GenScope* software are entirely irrelevant to the knowledge practices that define expertise in introductory genetics. Subsequent revisions to the curricular materials and the inclusion of formative assessments that emphasized the invariant aspects of the environment supported a more legitimate trajectory, where student discourse focused on the invariant features of the software that embodied the domain knowledge; these changes also led to dramatically improved outcomes on a wide range of individual outcome measures (Hickey, Kindfield, Horwitz, & Christie, 2003).

Finally, it is worth highlighting that transformation of participation is not synonymous with collaboration. Participation-centered curricular ideals are routinely characterized as collaborative learning methods. For example, Zimmerman and Schunk refer to the reciprocal teaching methods that form the core of the Community of Learners approach as "group-learning methods" that are "especially attractive for students *who have little initial self-regulatory motivation or skills* and who are *not current members of effective learning communities*" (2001, p. 299, emphasis added).[2] Such characterizations of socioculturally inspired practices are common. Such characterizations overlook the reality that solitary meaningful engagement with domain resources (books, computers, etc.) still involves the transformation of participation. These resources define socially constructed knowledge, and their meaningful use defines collective participation. Furthermore, such characterizations overlook the assumption that the real problem in education is not the lack of effective learning communities; rather, it is the sheer effectiveness of the learning communities that are defined by practices other than the intended curriculum. Some of these communities are defined by practices that are relatively benign to intended curricular practices (e.g., popular music, fashion, etc.), whereas others are clearly antagonistic (delinquency, drugs, etc.). The important point is that students are often able to be more legitimate participants in these communities than in the communities associated with curricular domains.

Relationships as Negotiated Identities. From a participation-centered perspective, relationships between teachers and their students and between students and their classmates are understood in terms of identity. When participation is being transformed, participants are negotiating their own identity with different and potentially conflicting communities of practice. Necessarily, this participation involves both conformity to and alienation from prevailing standards and values of different communities, because the standards and values are a function of the practices of the knowledge communities that they represent. As such, identity actually resides alongside the knowledge in the social context, where both are presumed to be

[2]Zimmerman and Schunk's (2001) comments were made in the context of their comments in a chapter on coregulated learning by McCaslin & Hickey (2001). To the extent that the more modest "socio-constructivist" perspectives perpetuate such characterizations, it seems worthwhile to continue pursuing the more uniquely sociocultural perspective being explored in this chapter.

negotiated: "Identity in this sense is an experience and a display of competence that requires neither an explicit self-image nor self-identification with an ostensible community" (Wenger, 1998, p. 152).

Participation-centered principles for relationships concern nonparticipation as much as they involve participation. This is because participation in some activities and nonparticipation in others reciprocally defines identity. This is critical for classroom management, because all students are always engaged in something (even when they choose not to participate in the intended curricular activities). Because any engagement is transforming participation, all students are therefore always learning. Thus, students who are not engaged in the intended curricular routines are still transforming participation. Take, for example, how a sociocultural perspective might lead us to rethink the nonparticipation that occurs when a student sleeps in class. Sleeping in class necessarily requires some form of negotiation between the individual who does so and the teacher and classmates who might forbid/tolerate/allow it. This negotiation defines a very different trajectory of participation when it occurs during a movie rather than during a lecture (or an exam or standardized test). Our thinking in this regard has been shaped by several detailed considerations of the participation of students who are at risk of school failure (e.g., Cobb & Hodge, 2002; Gutierrez, Rymes, & Larson, 1995; Portes, 1996; Vadeboncoeur & Portes, 2002). These analyses emphasize the way that the broader classroom and cultural context prevent some students from negotiating a trajectory of participation that is even remotely legitimate. It seems to us that the view outlined in these considerations has significant value for managing classrooms in ways that support the participation of such students in intended curricular routines. For example, Gutierrez et al. (1995) elaborate on the cultural forces that lead students to collectively resist participation in curricular discourse, and describe collaborative classroom routines that acknowledge this resistance and succeed in overcoming it. Such studies may offer classroom management theoretical and methodological guidance for understanding such resistance by observing and refining the extent to which specific classroom contexts give students the opportunity to "try on" the identities, and "try out" the forms of discourse that define domain specific expertise. We acknowledge that this aspect of our approach is quite preliminary, and ill-defined. Certainly we expect that further consideration and investigation will provide additional clarity. But, as detailed below, the more specific insights that transform specific practices will emerge in design-based refinements in those very specific reform contexts.

Development as Led by Learning. One of the core assumptions of sociocultural views of development is that learning leads development. As generally associated with Vygotsky, this principle challenges the Piagetian principle that development leads learning. Ann Brown addressed this issue in this fashion relative to the design of curriculum:

> Simplistic interpretation of Piagetian theory has led to the consistent underestimation of younger students' capabilities. This slant on Piagetian theory encourages sensitivity to what children of a certain age *cannot* do because they have not yet reached a certain stage of cognitive operations. (1994, p. 10)

Brown elaborates on how the view that learning leads development points to curricular routines that reflect new research insights regarding the development of domain expertise. Brown also elaborates on how this insight reflects the infamous claim made by Bruner (1960) that any subject could be taught to a child at any age in some "intellectually honest" fashion.

Although the insights in the previous paragraph concern ambitions for learning curricular content, it seems that participation-centered principles of development for classroom management also concern having more ambitious expectations for what students are capable of learning. Classroom management principles of development also need to be concerned with learning about how to behave as a student. This brings us back to the point made at the outset of our consideration of participation-centered principles for classroom management. It seems to us that having ambitious goals for the "intellectual honest" knowledge practices that we expect young children to participate in, should be the central developmental principle for participation-centered classroom management. From the very beginning, the transformations of participation should define a trajectory that shows increasingly authentic "epistemic stance" (the meaningful, appropriate, and effective use of language to express not what but how we know, e.g., Ochs, 1996). Thus, for example, the petty argumentation that defines the interactions of many primary age children should be understood in light of the fact that powerful and appropriate argumentation is the essence of expertise in any discipline. As such, young learners should not be taught that all forms of argumentation are bad. Quite to the contrary, argumentation that reflects even very rudimentary participation in domain practices should be encouraged and shaped into an increasingly authentic form (Duschl & Osborne, 2002).

We find inspiration in this regard in the efforts of Leslie Herrenkohl, whose research has looked at the development of scientific argumentation in elementary school classrooms (Cornelius & Herrenkohl, 2004; Herrenkohl & Guerra, 1998; Herrenkohl, Palinscar, Dewater, & Kawasaki, 1999). The ideal of "intellectually honest" participation in domain knowledge practices is embodied in Herrenkohl's recent project called Promoting Argumentation in the Teaching of History and Science (PATHS) (Herrenkohl, Wineberg, Bell, & Stevens, 2000). The project teaches elementary students about the similarities and difference in the forms of argumentation that define expertise for historians and scientists. Such ambitious goals transcend many conventional assumptions about development because elementary students are presumed to lack the "basic skills" to understand such concepts, or have not developed sufficient capacities for abstract thought.

Discipline as Transformation of Participation. As with the other aspects of classroom management, discipline is mainly concerned with participation, specifically, what teachers should do to discourage participation in knowledge practices that interfere with teacher-desired knowledge practices. From our perspective, redefining what is typically characterized as "misbehavior" as "participation in knowledge practices" offers new ways of minimizing it. Several recent qualitative studies reveal how a sociocultural lens provides a new and potentially transformative perspective on student discipline. For example, Vavrus and Cole (2002) examined the broader context in which students were suspended from school within strict "zero-tolerance" policies. They showed that suspensions are seldom imposed for discrete events, as presumed by proponents of such policies. Rather, Vavrus and Cole showed that typical suspensions "are the result of a complex sequence of events that together form a disciplinary moment, a moment when one disruptive act out of many is singled out for action by the teacher" (p. 109). By showing how suspensions reflect broader classroom interactions rather than specific misbehavior, they show that such policies as "zero-tolerance" actually make teacher disciplinary actions less equitable, which in turn can adversely impact the community within the classroom.

Another potentially useful direction when considering sociocultural models of learning is helping students to learn about the negative consequences of risky behavior. In their analysis of adult efforts to scaffold the appropriate behavior of youngsters, Yowell and Smylie (1999) argued that scaffolding involves two "experts" and two "novices." Youngsters are the experts in their social environment. They understand the contingencies of their behavior in ways that are not shared (or sharable) with the adult "novices." On the other hand, adults are experts in the long-term consequences of actions and strategies that promote learning, motivation, and identity. Yowell and Smylie's critique of interventions targeting misbehavior points towards participation-centered principles for transforming student participation in ways that minimize the need to discipline students. Consider, for example, the "just say no" strategies of the Drug Awareness Resistance Education (DARE used police officers to teach elementary students to make good decisions, to resist peer pressure, and to understand the alternatives to drugs and alcohol). Even before studies showed that DARE did not impact behavior (General Accounting Office, 2003), Yowell and Smilie (1999) attacked the naiveté of it and other such interventions that trivialize the power of youth culture to influence their behavior.

Tentatively, we have identified three reasons to embed participation-centered approaches within existing interventions to change youth behavior and culture. First, for approaches that directly target students' cognitive process (such as DARE), the connection between the intervention and desirable behavioral outcomes is very indirect. This makes it difficult to fine-tune strategies and requires complex randomized trials to provide convincing evidence of impact (or detect the lack of it). The second reason for concern is that student-centered interventions often seem poorly matched against the visceral behavioral reinforcement provided by misbehavior. Such interventions assume that getting kids to think differently will somehow overcome the plain fact that sometimes it feels good to participate in nonacademic practices. While it is not clear to us if more controlling approaches (such as random drug testing) are effective, it seems that the participation-centered perspective for risky behavior would focus primarily on transforming the culture of misbehavior in school settings. It also seems to us that doing so would provide a more objective platform for understanding, refining, and evaluating the entire range of interventions. The third and perhaps the most important reason follows from the sociocultural model of engagement and motivation outlined above. Student misbehavior defines a distinct set of "knowledge practices." From this perspective, cognitive programs overlook the meaning-making that occurs when students participate in maladaptive and risky activities (Lightfoot, 1997). This highlights that misbehavior is another set of knowledge practices for which students must negotiate their participation and nonparticipation. To use Wenger's (1998) terms, risky and disruptive practices offer marginal participants in intended knowledge practices a more obvious and direct path to the center of another knowledge community. In other words, students who do not identify with the intended classroom learning community will seek to join or create (i.e., participate in) other communities where they can participate more successfully.

Our insights here are very preliminary. Teachers and teacher educators looking for solutions to classroom discipline problems will not view the notion of "trajectories" and "peripheral participation" as a clear way to minimize student misbehavior. The studies reviewed in the previous paragraphs used a participatory perspective to understand how simpleminded policies and ignorance of cultural and developmental differences lead to methods of handling misbehavior that violate common sense as well as the principles of prior systematic programs. As described next, we expect that scalable participation-centered approaches to discipline (as well as for the other four aspects of classroom management) can only emerge from actual efforts to reform those practices. To use terms discussed in the next section, consideration of participation-centered management practices has so far focused on relatively "high-level" theory. The specific principles that educators need can only come from iterative refinements of practices that emphasize the creation of more useful "local" theory.

Refining and Evaluating Participation-Centered Classroom Management Practices

This section describes our ideas and initial efforts in applying participation-centered approaches to classroom management. We acknowledge that what we are advancing is more of a "perspective" than a well-defined model of practice. Partly due to the highly contextual nature of sociocultural models of practice, it is difficult to define practices that are truly, uniquely sociocultural and then "prove" that those practices are more effective than other practices. As outlined previously, much of what is being advanced as sociocultural classroom management practices can be characterized as new ways of thinking about practices that have already been well defined outside of a sociocultural perspective. However, this section shows that it is possible to identify approaches that previously have not been viewed as classroom management strategies, and that these strategies result in improvements that are considered indicative of classroom management. We reiterate that public perception, legislative mandate, and the everyday practices of many educators have largely defined these indicators in terms of student behavior, particularly in terms of the absence of misbehavior and the consistent engagement in the routines of activity that are presumed to directly increase student performance on external achievement tests.

A Multi-Level/Multi-Method Research Framework

Our nascent insights for refining participation-centered approaches to classroom management follow from our efforts to refine sociocultural approaches to assessment and testing. The study of introductory genetics described above was initiated in part to refine methods for aligning classroom assessments with external achievement tests.[3] A central outcome was a framework consisting of three increasingly "distal" levels of educational outcomes (*close, proximal,* and *distal*). To maximize the formative and summative potential within and across levels, we "crossed" these levels with the three "grand theories" of knowing and learning. This supports a model of assessment practice that uses increasingly "formal" characterizations of domain knowledge at the increasingly distal levels. At the close level, collective participation is assessed and refined using semiformal classroom assessments (e.g., "activity-oriented" quizzes and discourse analytic methods); at the proximal level, individual understanding is assessed and refined using formal classroom assessments (e.g., "curriculum-oriented" exams); at the distal level, achievement is formally evaluated using external tests (e.g., "standards-oriented" achievement tests). Our assessment framework is detailed elsewhere (Hickey, Michael, Zuiker, Schafer, & Taasoobshirazi, in review) and is currently being employed and refined in several medium-scale projects in science education.

A central assumption in this framework is a "unidirectional view" of knowledge transfer. In this view, knowledge (in the broadest possible construal) transfers readily from the more informal "cultural" representation in discourse to the more formal "cognitive" representation in open-ended classroom assessment, and then to the highly formal "behavioral" representations in high-stakes achievement tests, but not vice versa (Hickey & Pellegrino, 2005). This assumption has yet to be fully tested in a well-controlled setting. But it affords a coherent means of iteratively fine-tuning discourse to maximize individual understanding, while also ensuring gains on high-stakes achievement tests.

In light of the established traditions in discourse analysis, it seems that the methods that we employed and are advancing for refining collective participation require clarification. As Morine-Dershimier (chapter 6 in this volume) illustrates, studies that define the field of classroom discourse can be organized around four distinct perspectives: *sociolinguistic, cognitive constructivist, sociocultural,* and *critical discourse analysis.* Our efforts in shaping classroom discourse are mostly shaped by the body of work that Morine-Dershimier characterizes as

[3]The study was also initiated to compare reconciliation of the behavioral, cognitive, and cultural consequences of modest extrinsic incentives using the prevailing "aggregative" approach that follows most logically from both behavioral and cognitive perspectives, with the "dialectical" reconciliation that follows logically from sociocultural perspectives (as elaborated in Hickey, 2003). Ultimately, it became clear that the data needed to convincingly explore this issue demanded a level of experimental and methodological rigor that was impossible to accomplish in classroom-based research. Furthermore, these methods also conflicted with the goal of iteratively refining the alignment of assessment and testing.

"sociocultural" (particularly Gee and Green, 1998). We have found that, as Morine-Dershimier points out, sociocultural classroom discourse research is relatively consistent with our very interventionist approach. Rather than naturalistically documenting classroom discourse, we take a very functional approach that is concerned with aspects of discourse that we think we can most readily change in ways that lead to broadly desired outcomes. In this way, our approach diverges from much of the sociocultural classroom discourse research. In particular, our approach embraces the concern with students' individual performance on knowledge transfer measures that characterizes the classroom discourse studies that Morine-Dershimier characterizes as "cognitive-constructivist."

The assessment framework and specific methods can be readily applied to a participation-centered approach to classroom management. A central advantage of aligning research and reform efforts across three levels is that at the first level, refinements can be judged by their indirect impact at a second level, while the broader consequences of these refinements can be validly and formally evaluated according to their impact at the third level.[4] Before considering how this might be done with classroom management, we first summarize new research perspectives, new research technologies, and multiple levels of outcomes, which are central to our vision for doing so.

New Views of Educational Research. The sociocultural theorists who have helped shaped our ideas about classroom management have been central in the definition of what have come to be called "design-based" educational research methods (e.g., Brown, 1992; Cobb, Confrey, diSessa, Lehrer, & Schauble, 2003; Collins, 1992, 1999). These approaches aim to develop scientific understanding while designing learning environments, formulating curriculum, and assessing learning (Lagemann, 1999). We assume that the most useful theories for classroom management will emerge in efforts to reform classroom management. Put differently, we believe that "interventionist" efforts to reform practice will yield theoretical principles with greater scientific validity than those developed in laboratories or in "naturalistic" observations of practice that are meant to accurately characterize process and products but not directly change them.

Design-based research methods assume that the design of learning environments and the development of useful theories are "intertwined," and occur within "continuous cycles of design, enactment, analysis, and redesign" (Design Based Research Collective [DBRC] 2003, p. 10). Design-based researchers emphasize nascent theories that are expected to generalize to a broader class of curricular innovations; they view theoretical advances in terms of "prototheory" (DBRC, p. 10), targeting an "intermediate" theoretical scope (diSessa, 1991). Recent collaborative efforts (Bell, Hoadley, & Linn, 2004; DBRC, 2003; Kelly & Lesh, 2000) and special issues (Barab, 2004; Kelly 2003) reveal broad and fervent enthusiasm for these approaches. Consistent with the influential book on laboratory sciences, *Pasteur's quadrant* (Stokes, 1997), design-based research transcends the traditional distinction between "basic research" and "applied research" (in "Bohr's quadrant" and "Edison's quadrant," respectively); design-based methods are often characterized as "use-inspired basic research."

Obviously, prior efforts to advance classroom management have involved the iterative refinement of practice. But we have found no systematic efforts to apply what we see as the core elements of design-based methods to classroom management. In particular, it seems to us that

[4]Following from Ruiz-Primo, Shavelson, Hamilton, & Klien (2002), our assessment model actually identifies five levels. Thus, we identify *immediate, close, proximal, distal,* and *remote* levels, focusing on *events, activities, curriculum, standards,* and *attainment,* and employing time scales of *minutes, days, weeks, months,* and *years.* In practice, we fold the very informal refinements from the immediate-level into the close-level; we are just beginning to conduct the multiyear efforts that can deliver statistically significant impact on valid remote-level indicators, such as norm-referenced achievement tests.

most prior classroom management research (like most educational research) can be characterized as applied research that builds on basic research of behavior or cognition of individuals or of groups. In addition to exploring the value of these new methods for advancing classroom management, our approach extends existing characterizations of design research and addresses concerns over the methodological rigor of prior design-based studies (e.g., Shavelson, Phillips, Towne, & Feuer, 2003; Sloane & Gorard, 2003). Specifically, we emphasize the need to include the kinds of research outcomes that can be validly administered and interpreted in comparison-group studies.

The Potential of Video Technology. Technological advances played a central role in prior advances in classroom management. As illustrated by the range of chapters in the present volume, many current models of classroom management have roots in studies of classroom "ecology" initiated in the 1970s. This research reflected an infusion of federal research funding and newly available videotape technology (Weinstein, 1999). Reflecting the prevailing focus on discipline and misbehavior, Kounin (1970) set out to document specific ways that teachers responded to misbehavior in more effective and less effective classrooms. To the surprise of Kounin and the broader community, teachers' responses to misbehavior, known as "desists," played a negligible role in determining overall quality of classroom management. Rather, what defined the well-managed classroom was what teachers did to prevent misbehavior in the first place. These insights supported powerful "process-outcome" research paradigms that documented how specific teacher behaviors lead to particular student outcomes (see chapter 4 by Gettinger & Kohler, in this volume). In this sense, a synergy between research theory and research technology was central to previous advances in classroom management.

In key respects, we see the research vision outlined below to be a natural extension of these prior advances. Video recording has enjoyed a central role in the refinement of design-based research methods. As will be shown, video is essential for documenting and enhancing collective participation, and can also be used in studying and improving individual activity as well. Recent advances make it possible to capture, code, and distribute multiple streams of digital video; this has given rise to fundamentally new approaches for studying classroom activity. While it is premature to speculate whether the convergence of participation-centered views and these new technologies will yield synergistic effects for classroom management, it certainly seems possible.

Our enthusiasm stems partly from the central role that video technology plays in existing design-based research. Videotape recording plays such a central role in understanding and refining "trajectories of participation" that it is central to the most influential characterizations of design-based educational research. Video provides an ideal way of showing students and educators what "authentic participation in domain knowledge practices" actually looks like. As such, video provides an ideal way of directly studying efforts to transform participation, and then consider the impact of those transformations on individual outcomes.

Three Levels of Classroom Management Outcomes. As shown in Fig.11.1, our proposed approach to refining classroom management is organized around three embedded conceptualizations of classroom management. These levels are increasingly *distal* (in terms of specific curricular events), increasingly *general* (in terms of being bound to specific contexts), and increasingly *summative* (in terms of the value for making broad claims, at the expense of formative improvements to practice).

At the *close* level, classroom management is conceptualized as students' and teachers' collective engagement in domain-specific discourse in the enactment of specific curricular routines. These outcomes are generally assessed and refined using "event-based" methods such as discourse analysis. This means that the validity of all interpretations is bound to very specific

DISTAL LEVEL

Representation: Conceptualize classroom management formally and individually, in terms of the behavior and cognition of individual students in their interactions with each other and the teacher.

Curriculum. Provide classrooms and schools with meaningful benchmarks of behavior, cognition, and achievement. Provide useful feedback and opportunities to improve and ensure that classrooms and school are reinforced for doing so. Support collective accountability for behavior, cognition, and high-stakes achievement.

Method. Measure referrals, suspensions, absences, high-stakes achievement tests that are sensitive to proximal level refinements. Use appropriate between-class and between-school designs to evaluate proximal level practices.

PROXIMAL LEVEL

Representation: Conceptualize classroom management semi-formally and individually, in terms of the behavior and cognition of individual students and in their interactions with each other and the teacher, visible and measurable in a classroom

Curriculum. Provide individuals with meaningful benchmarks of behavior, cognition, and learning. Provide useful feedback, opportunity to improve, and ensure students are reinforced for doing so. Provide teachers with methods to support individual responsibility for behavior, cognition, and mastery of classroom curriculum.

Method. Measure time-on-task, respectfulness, exam performance, self-efficacy, and other proximal measures that are sensitive to immediate level refinements and functioning of the specific class. Use appropriate within-class and between-class designs to systematically test and refine immediate level practices. Aim to impact distal-level outcomes.

CLOSE LEVEL

Representation: Conceptualize classroom management informally, culturally, and holistically in terms of increasing successful participation in expert domain-specific discourse.

Curriculum: Provide the classroom community with meaningful benchmarks of participation, useful formative feedback, and the opportunity to improve. Support informal student-centered responsibility for engaged participation in domain knowledge practices.

Method: Measure using discourse analytic methods in design-based iterative refinements to directly refine collective participation in knowledge practices of the domain. Aim to indirectly impact proximal-level outcomes.

FIGURE 11.1. The Embedded Nature of Collective Participation Within More Conventional Characterizations of Classroom Management.

curricular routines in very specific educational contexts. Ultimately, close-level learning is seen when the classroom community "ritualizes" the appropriate use of domain-specific language and concepts. Such characterizations of learning can be confusing to observers who maintain conventional individually oriented views of learning. Fortunately, (as elaborated below) such conceptualization can be guided by prior socioculturally inspired research that is available in most academic domains.

At the *proximal* level, classroom management is conceptualized in terms of individual behavior and cognition in particular classroom contexts. These outcomes are assessed with conventional individually oriented research methods, making it possible to make general claims about classrooms that feature particular types of classroom management policies. These outcomes include individual behavior (e.g., time-on-task, disruptions, referrals), individual cognition (e.g., self-efficacy and goal-orientation), and performance on worthwhile classroom assessments (e.g., essays, open-ended performance assessments, etc). These are conceptualized and measured in a manner that generally transcends specific academic domains, as illustrated by the extensive existing research base on classroom management.

At the *distal* level, classroom management is conceptualized in terms of large-scale outcomes that can be meaningfully interpreted at roughly the school or system level. These outcomes are assessed using large-scale policy research methods, making it possible to make general claims about schools that feature particular management policies. These outcomes include large-scale indicators of misbehavior (e.g., suspensions, absenteeism) as well as performance on high-stakes achievement tests, as illustrated by educational policy research literature.

These general characterizations are necessarily preliminary. We are particularly uncertain about the balance between "academic" and "management" outcomes, and "behavioral" and "cognitive" outcomes, at the proximal and distal levels. We also assume that specification of outcomes across levels will emerge and evolve in particular contexts. As elaborated later, we propose informal refinements of close-level outcomes to indirectly maximize proximal-level outcomes and provide theoretical and methodological coherence that supports goals that are otherwise incompatible. For example, we initially found it quite challenging in our previous work to define "collective participation," and we continue to find it challenging to convey that definition to others. By emphasizing cultural activity that transcends the individual, it became easier to identify the relevant research base for refining collective participation, and (therefore) sharing our insights for doing so with others. It seems to us that this logic extends to the proximal-level and distal-level outcomes as well, offering the potential for a new basis for coherence between practitioners, researchers, and policy makers concerned with classroom management.

At first glance, the concentric characterization shown in Fig. 11.1 appears similar to ecological models of human development that continue to be quite influential in classroom management (e.g., Bronfenbrenner, 1979). However, these approaches embed the individual within the microsystems in the center, while placing cultural practices and values in the macrosystems in the outer circle. In contrast, our approach places culture, in the form of collective participation, in the center, while it places the activity of individuals in the outer rings as "special forms" of that culturally defined activity. While we will show that the model of practice that follows from this characterization is fairly well defined, we acknowledge that the relationship between this model and other models has yet to be defined. We also acknowledge that there is vast research literature on sociocultural models of development that appears relevant to our efforts, but that we have just begun to consider. In this regard, we reiterate the pragmatism of our approach and of the broader class of design-research methods that shape our methods, and focus our attention on developing models of practice that are inspiring, scalable, and effective.

Three Iterative Cycles of Design Research

As shown in Table 11.1, we propose the iterative refinement of classroom management across three increasingly formal design research cycles: *implementation, experimentation,* and *evaluation.* Loosely speaking, these three cycles reflect a shifting emphasis across the three levels of outcomes (close, proximal, and distal) defined in the previous section. Our approach builds strongly on insights emerging in our ongoing assessment work. Our initial ideas are outlined in Table 11.1 and detailed next. In practice, the three cycles unfold in a linear fashion, but they are intended to leave behind tools and practices at each of the three levels that can support continuous improvement over time, in embedded cycles of perpetuating improvement.

Implementation Cycle: Refining Collective Participation. The implementation cycle is concerned with close and proximal outcomes. While these efforts are conceptually aligned with the distal-level outcomes, no effort is made to assess distal-level outcomes in this first cycle.[5] This cycle involves intense collaborations with a small number of participants to directly refine collective participation in specific contexts. Perhaps the most important characteristic of collective participation is that it concerns events rather than individuals. We have found that this notion cannot be fully appreciated (and perhaps not even understood) without first embracing the contextualist worldview summarized earlier. This means that particular strategies for refining collective participation are not just bound to specific academic domains (e.g., mathematics vs. science); they are also bound to the specific instructional context in which they are enacted. For example, one of the most promising tools we have found for refining collective participation is having classrooms informally self-assess their enactment of a specific lesson

[5]This is another element of our pragmatic approach to research. We contend that actually attempting to assess distal-level outcomes in this first cycle distracts needed attention from the close-level refinements, and sets up a nascent effort for failure, because such outcomes are so difficult to obtain from the initial implementation of a specific intervention.

TABLE 11.1
Three Increasingly Formal Cycles of Design Research

Design Cycle	*Research Context*	*Focus of Management Efforts*	*Primary Research Method and Focus*	*Refinement Target*	*Accountability for Classroom Activity Established*
1. Implement	Intensive, single teacher, focus directly on close-level outcomes.	Collective participation.	Discourse analysis for informal refinement.	Enactment of specific curricular routines, informal, contextual design knowledge.	Informal, student-oriented.
2. Experiment	Scale up with multiple teachers or multiple classes.	Individual behavior (e.g., time-on-task) and cognition (e.g., goal orientation).	Quazi-experimentation to maximize individual outcomes.	Most effective, scalable classroom management strategies in this class of contexts. Semiformal design knowledge.	Semiformal, teacher centered (with embedded student-oriented).
3. Evaluate	Large scale, across entire context with comparison group, distal-level data.	Collective achievement (tests) and attainment (school-wide activity).	Formal evaluation of large scale model of classroom management.	Scalability of entire approach, formal, general design knowledge.	Formal, external, test-oriented and attainment-oriented.

using dramatized video benchmarks that illustrate low, medium, and high quality enactments. Obviously, this works best when those benchmarks feature enactments of the same lesson, by similar students. This is because the meaningfulness of the anchors declines as the lessons and/or students become increasingly different from the target.

Fortunately, efforts to refine participation can be informed by the extensive socioculturally inspired research literatures that exist in most academic domains; many domains contain examples for particular instructional forms (e.g., computer-supported or field-based) or for specific content domains (e.g., fractions or graphs in elementary mathematics). For example, our colleagues in mathematics education have helped us locate numerous papers outlining relevant theory and practice that are shaping our initial efforts to refine collective participation in that domain (e.g., in mathematics, see Cobb, Stephan, McClain, & Gravemeijer, 2001; Forman & Ansell, 2001; Knuth & Peressini, 2001; Mitchell, 2001; Sfard, 2000). These domain-specific examples highlight our core suggestion that classroom management should start by managing collective participation in domain-specific discourse.

As an example, we are currently pilot-testing some of our strategies working with a mathematician who has taken her sabbatical to teach sixth-grade mathematics in a struggling inner-city school. She initially asked for help in controlling the misbehavior in the classroom, which made it difficult to hold whole-class discussions about mathematics. Her request was a common one; how to keep kids from misbehaving and increase their motivation to learn to allow the class to engage in productive discourse. We contend that this represents an implicit characterization of the functioning of social groups as the aggregations of individual activity, and that this assumption is consistent with many prior classroom management research characterizations. In this case, the teacher wanted to first focus on controlling the activity of individuals so that she could engage the whole group.

Our alternative reflects a very different assumption; that the activities of individuals are special cases of the collective participation in domain-specific discourse. Rather than providing strategies that focus on the behavior or cognition of individuals to be administered so that she can teach, we offer informal open-ended assessments, learner-oriented formative feedback rubrics, video exemplars of classroom discourse, and lesson-specific guidelines for the forms of domain discourse that should occur when those lessons are enacted. Such materials have provided an effective context for refining classroom discourse (Hickey, Michael, Zuiker, Schafer, & Taasoobshirazi, in review), with seemingly positive consequences for classroom management. A particularly promising approach has been creating video examples of higher-quality and lower-quality participation in specific collaborative activities, and having students informally self-assess themselves. Another example includes formative feedback rubrics for classroom assessment that deliberately avoid stating the "correct" answer, but instead require students to collaboratively make sense of dense, technically accurate characterizations of the reasoning behind the solution (e.g., Hickey, Kindfield, Horwitz, & Christie, 2003). We have yet to formally assess the consequences of these practices on specific aspects of classroom management. Fortunately, we will have numerous opportunities to do so in a large-scale study of mathematics assessment practices recently funded by the National Science Foundation (Hickey, Mewborn, Beckmann, Lanehart, & Cohen, 2005).

A central goal of the close-level efforts is establishing an informal student-oriented accountability for increasingly successful participation in domain discourse. Efforts to refine collective participations should foster what Gutierrez, Rymes, and Larson (1995) called a "third space for authentic interaction." In this view, the "scripts" of schooling and the specific content domains intersect the "counter-scripts" of students' social and epistemological realities. When such a context includes examples of authentic domain discourse, along with meaningful incentives for increasingly successful participation in that discourse, students can hold each other accountable in powerful and productive ways. A common example of such accountability can be seen in conversations when a student substitutes a vernacular term for a more technical domain-specific term. This is sometimes followed by another student's (or perhaps the teacher's) seamless substitution of the vernacular with a more academic domain-specific term. This informal accountability is observed when the first student then adopts and continues using the more academic term.

We encountered a similar situation with our classroom-based research science educators. Many of the novice science teachers with whom we collaborate report that classroom management problems made it impossible for them to implement the "inquiry-oriented" methods emphasized in their professional development. Hence, they direct all of their energy trying to motivate students and minimize misbehavior, and sometimes never get to the open-ended investigations and argumentation that are essential ingredients of inquiry-oriented science instruction. We assume that out of frustration many eventually resort to the conventional didactic lecture-and-demonstrate methods that received cursory (if not dismissive) treatment during their training, or some leave teaching entirely. In our assessment research, we have uncovered a wealth of research that informs and guides our efforts to enhance collective participation in scientific argumentation (e.g., Duschl & Osborne, 2002; Lemke, 1990). According to a range of analyses of student discourse, we have initial evidence that using these ideas to informally enhance collective participation was successful. These analyses include the transactional quality of student conversation (the degree to which each conversational turn is logically connected to the previous turn; see Russell, Kruger, & Schafer, 2004), the proportion of conversational turns that consist of domain-specific scientific argumentation (Schafer, Hickey, Zuiker, Kruger, & Russell, 2003), and the extent to which classroom discourse affords the emergence of desirable "identities" relative to the knowledge practices that define the specific scientific domain (Zuiker & Hickey, 2004). Importantly, as described in the next section, we have initial evidence that our efforts to refine collective participation also yielded desirable outcomes in terms of individual cognition and behavior—including outcomes that are consistent with existing characterization of classroom management.

Our characterization of collective participation in terms of domain-specific discourse brings up another directly relevant example that emerged in our prior research, and which seems to distinguish our proposed approach. In assessment research of introductory genetics, we initially found it easy to foster intense student engagement in the open-ended investigations in a sophisticated computer-based simulation. The investigations involved fanciful "dragons" whose DNA, chromosomes, and characteristics could be readily manipulated and observed in animated graphical interfaces. However, we also found it much more challenging to ensure that this engagement concerned truly "authentic" domain knowledge practices. It turned out that most of the intense engagement we initially observed concerned surface-level features of the software environment, rather than the underlying rules of inheritance that the software was supposed to teach. Thus, although there was a great deal of collective participation around issues such as how to get a dragon to "breath fire," there was very little collective participation around the core concept of sex-linked inheritance (which was exemplified in the phenotype for breathing fire). Subsequent individual assessments confirmed that these curricular routines had left student ill-prepared to solve new problems involving sex-linked inheritance, even when the problems were quite simple and were represented with the same fanciful organisms and familiar phenotypes (Hickey, Kindfield, Horwitz, & Christie, 2003). As alluded to in the consideration of curricular practices above and detailed at length elsewhere (Hickey & Zuiker, 2005), our insistent focus on collective participation in truly authentic forms of domain discourse sets our approach apart from more "discovery-oriented" curricular approaches that emphasize student's personal experiences and intrinsic motivation.

The domain-specific nature of our examples highlights our suggestion that efforts to refine collective participation should be influenced by domain-learning specialists, and the associated research literature at the center of their efforts. However, many of the potentially relevant examples from domain-specific research literatures differ from our approach. We propose that the refinement of collective participation be carried out quite informally. Many of the research examples that investigate collective participation represent more formal and more summative analyses. Many adopt a very naturalistic stance towards the nature of knowledge, and some adopt a very dismissive stance towards other characterizations of knowledge (for example, as in high-stakes achievement tests). In contrast, design-based methods, and particularly our close-level application of them, adopt a much more pragmatic and "interventionist" stance. One of the most relevant conclusions from our prior assessment research was that proximal-level and distal-level assessments of collective participation were difficult to accomplish and had limited formative value. The relatively brief time-scale of immediate-level and close-level assessments (ranging from minutes to days) lend themselves well to fine tuning discourse; the much longer time-scale of proximal-level and distal-level assessments (ranging from weeks to months) are simply too removed from classroom discourse to provide feedback that is useful for formatively refining it. We now understand how to do so, and consider doing so to be an ultimate goal for validating our model of assessment practice. We extend this insight quite directly to classroom management. Thus, while our model of classroom management practice considers collective participation informally at the close level, it may ultimately be worthwhile to use discourse analytic methods at the classroom (i.e., proximal) or school-wide (i.e., distal) levels, to document larger-scale and longer-term consequence of that model on domain-specific discourse across the entire range of academic contexts.

Experimentation Cycle: Enhancing Individual Behavior and Cognition. This second cycle represents a scaled-up implementation of the model of practice that emerged in the first cycle. Additional teachers and or additional classes are added, and the focus shifts to classroom-level practices. Distal-level outcomes should be assessed at this cycle, but only for the purposes of testing proximal-level theories. More specifically, we suggest that one should not expect to make significant gains on distal-level outcomes at this stage. Rather, practices that appear to support the largest gains on distal-level outcomes should be identified. Once such practices are identified and validated, they should be scrutinized for scalability before being formally included. For example, particularly intensive professional development strategies may not have a great enough impact to justify the difficulties they present in large-scale implementations.

The presence of multiplelevels of outcomes creates a fertile context for a range of semiformal tests of practices, while ensuring sufficient interpretive power to warrant inclusion or exclusion of those practices in a final model of practice. For example, classroom-specific decisions can be resolved using between-student, within-class methods that examine both close-level collective participation and proximal-level individual outcomes. Likewise, broader aspects of practice can be tested by manipulating the practices of similar teachers and then examining evidence of impact on outcomes at the proximal level (e.g. time-on-task, disruptions, self-efficacy or open-ended performance assessments) and distal level (e.g. suspensions, high-stakes test scores). By attending carefully to issues like scalability and variability that emerge in such semiformal tests of specific practices, educators and researchers obtain invaluable insights needed to define effective interventions with confidence that can be reasonably well-implemented in broader settings. These efforts support the practical goal of this second cycle: a formal approach that appears likely to lead to the greatest improvement in distal-level outcomes when implemented in a large-scale manner.

The theoretical goal of this second cycle is nascent design-theories about the particular intervention or practice being studied. In shifting one's focus from close-level to proximal-level outcomes, the aspects of specific contexts ("frame-factors") that simultaneously bound and scaffold the enactment of particular practices become apparent. A central feature of design-based methods is capturing the insights that emerge in these transitions, rather then allowing them to be swept into a broad examination of "implementation fidelity." By the end of the second cycle, key aspects of the intervention should be apparent, providing critical guidance in prioritizing professional development and technical assistance in subsequent implementations. This process will also help identify unresolved questions at the various levels of the implementation and create contexts for teachers, schools, systems, and researchers to continue adding to that knowledge. The experimentation cycle should also establish a teacher-oriented culture of responsibility for classroom management that compliments (rather than undermines) informal student-oriented responsibilities.

This second level is the most similar to existing classroom management programs. The proximal-level indicators of individual cognition and behavior are mostly independent of particular content domains, are typically measured within specific classrooms, and provide useful evidence of the impact of classroom-level practices. Depending on the prevailing goals and program theory, this second cycle might focus on more behavior indicators (e.g., time-on-task, disruptions, etc.) or measures that examine individual cognition (self-efficacy, goal orientation, etc.). We believe that we diverge from existing approaches in arguing against systematically prioritizing behavior or cognitive outcomes. Further, we would advise against using a behavioral incentive program and then trying to show that it increases (or does not decrease) cognitive outcomes such as intrinsic motivation, or likewise trying to directly increase self-efficacy with praise, and then showing that time-on-task is increased and misbehavior is decreased.

By insisting that individual behavioral and cognitive outcomes are both "special cases" of collective participation, this approach puts educators in a better position to simultaneously increase both. Doing so also puts researchers in a better position to move beyond the corrosive debates over things like extrinsic rewards that seem to have created some of the public skepticism about the value of educational research.

Before describing the final cycle, it seems worthwhile to first consider the reciprocal relationship between outcomes across levels. By acknowledging the reciprocal relationship between levels at the outset and designing practices with transfer to the next level in mind, essential program coherence can be accomplished. For example, teachers and researchers struggle to define the appropriate grading practices for open-ended curricular activities. For some students and for some activities, highly prescriptive, summative grading practices lead to inauthentic enactments, aimed solely at getting a high grade; for other students or other activities, students may need the incentive of grades or the guidance of prescriptive guidelines. We contend that these challenges are very tightly bound to specific contexts, and are poorly addressed by the plethora of practical and theoretical guidance currently available. A useful intervention might start with an implementation cycle working with individual teachers to define ideal benchmarks of classroom discourse in a handful of their curricular routines. This would provide each teacher with valuable insights and reference points for fine-tuning specific curricular routines, which should provide an initial basis for informally defining them for others.

Evaluation Cycle: Documenting Collective Attainment. In this cycle, the final model of practice that emerges in the experimentation cycle is scaled up and implemented across an entire grade, school, or school system. This implementation focuses on more formal distal-level outcomes that can be readily assessed and interpreted at the larger scale level. These outcomes are likely to be behavioral indicators, such as disciplinary referrals and attendance as well as performance on high-stakes, criterion-referenced achievement tests. Many such indicators are already collected in schools and systems, allowing direct comparison to prior outcomes in the same school, and allowing direct comparisons with other schools in the same systems. Consider, for example, the aforementioned example of refinement of existing incentive systems. If one started with a pair of very similar schools, and had been conducting the refinements in just one of the schools that had been randomly selected, the consequences on distal-level measures could be directly compared with one another, while the implementation school's indicators would provide valid baseline data. Meanwhile, the indicators at the comparison school, and perhaps the district as a whole, can show whether broader community factors (e.g., changing demographics, shifting graduation requirements, and other nonschool interventions) might explain the program effects.

With multiple pairs of schools or systems, stratified random assignment is possible, affording an extremely powerful test of the implementation. The presence of multiple levels of assessment affords a powerful interpretive framework for the distal-level scores that are generated in a large-scale evaluation. Experimental effects that fall shy of traditional criteria for being judged statistically unlikely (i.e., $p < .05$) take on additional meaning when considered in light of other theoretically related outcomes at adjacent levels. For example, marginally significant distal-level outcomes associated with an intervention (e.g., reductions in truancy or arrest) can be more confidently attributed to the intervention (or not) when larger and statistically significant differences are detected (or not) on corresponding proximal-level outcomes (e.g., teacher disciplinary referrals).

Our focus on behavioral indicators at the distal level and evaluation cycle does not mean that we do not value other cognitive and cultural outcomes. However, we fully appreciate the difficulty of validly assessing them in meaningful ways. Our assessment work has helped us appreciate that such outcomes can be assessed only with sufficient research resources. For example, with sufficient attention, measures such as self-efficacy and intrinsic motivation can be administered and interpreted validly at the distal level, by carefully considering the context and format of self-report measures. We have considered distal-level assessment of collective participation by conducting systematic observations of student discourse in a subsequent school year, but only after directing substantial attention to issues, such as sampling and the similarity and differences between the prior intervention context and the subsequent evaluation context. Indeed, we consider the distal-level evaluation of the entire range of outcomes to be essential to validating the core model of practice. However, we consider the measurement of such outcomes to be more of a research issue, supporting the argument that such outcomes are attained whenever the core model is implemented.

CONCLUSION

We conclude simply by acknowledging the very nascent stage of the ideas expressed in this chapter, and by expressing our admiration and appreciation for the extensive research in classroom management that has preceded it. The approach to classroom management discussed in this chapter is focused on classroom management during periods of academic activity (e.g., reading, math, science, etc.) and thus may be most valuable to teachers and researchers in middle and secondary school settings. We feel that this approach also offers elementary teachers and researchers an effective approach to classroom management, particularity during academic periods throughout the day. We also acknowledge that elementary teachers have a significant amount of time in which classroom management issues occur during nonacademic activity (e.g., transitions, bathroom breaks, etc.). How this approach to classroom management affects nonacademic activity has not been studied. We look forward to further refining these ideas as we attempt to apply them in our own work, and incorporate the advice and suggestions of others.

ACKNOWLEDGMENTS

The preparation of this chapter was supported in part by the National Science Foundation Grant REC-0196225 to the University of Georgia. The opinions presented here belong to the authors and do not necessarily represent the positions of the University of Georgia or the National

Science Foundation. Laura Fredrick and Ann Kruger provided helpful feedback on the ideas in this paper. Mary McCaslin edited this section of the volume and provided invaluable feedback on earlier considerations of these issues and on this manuscript. We are particularly grateful to Leslie Herrenkohl, Laura Fredrick, Carolyn Weinstein, Catherine Lewis, Nancy Knapp, and Jennifer Perkins for reviewing this manuscript and providing useful feedback. Rachel Lewis assisted in manuscript preparation and provided useful feedback as well.

REFERENCES

Bach, A. (2001, October 3). Absences increase following cash incentive program. *The Garden City Telegram Online Edition.* Retrieved September 23, 2004, from http://www.gctelegram.com/news/2000/September/30/absences.html

Barab, S. (2004). Design-based research [Special issue]. *The Journal of the Learning Sciences, 13*(1).

Bell, P., Hoadley, C. M., & Linn, M. C. (2004). Design-based research in education. In M. C. Linn, E. A. Davis, & P. Bell (Eds.), *Internet environments for science education* (pp. 73–85). Mahwah, NJ: Lawrence Erlbaum Associates.

Berieter, C., & Scardamalia, M. (1989). Intentional learning as a goal of instruction. In L. B. Resnick (Ed.), *Knowing, learning, and instruction: Essays in honor of Robert Glaser* (pp. 361–385). Hillsdale, NJ: Lawrence Erlbaum Associates.

Bronfenbrenner, U. (1979). *The ecology of human development: Experiments by nature and design.* Cambridge, MA: Harvard University Press.

Brophy, J. (1999). Research on motivation in education: Past, present, and future. In T. C. Urdan (Ed.), *Advances in motivation and achievement: The role of context* (Vol. 11, pp. 1–44). Greenwich, CT: JAI Press.

Brown, A. L. (1992). Design experiments: Theoretical and methodological challenges in creating complex interventions in classroom settings. *Journal of the Learning Sciences, 2,* 141–178.

Brown, A. L. (1994). The advancement of learning. *Educational Researcher, 23*(8) 4–12.

Brown, A. L., & Campione, J. C. (1996). Psychological theory and the design of innovative learning environments: On procedures, principles, and systems. In L. Schauble & R. Glaser (Eds.), *Innovations in learning: New environments for education* (pp. 289–325). Mahwah, NJ: Lawrence Erlbaum Associates.

Bruner, J. S. (1960). *The process of education.* Cambridge, MA: Harvard University Press.

Bruner, J. S. (1984). Vygotsky's zone of proximal development: The hidden agenda. *New Directions for Child Development, 23,* 92–97.

Case, R. (1996). Changing views of knowledge and their impact on educational research and practice. In D. R. Olson & N. Torrance (Eds.), *The handbook of education and human development* (pp. 75—99). Cambridge, MA: Blackwell.

Chance, P. (1992). The rewards of learning. *Phi Delta Kappan, 74,* 200–207.

Cobb, P., Confrey, J., diSessa, A., Lehrer, R., & Schauble, L. (2003). Design experiments in educational research. *Educational Researcher, 32*(1), 9–13.

Cobb, P., & Hodge, L. L. (2002). A relational perspective on issues of cultural diversity and equity as they play out in the mathematics classroom. *Mathematical Thinking and Learning, 4,* 249–284.

Cobb, P., Stephan, M., McClain, K., & Gravemeijer, K. (2001). Participating in classroom mathematical practices. *The Journal of the Learning Sciences, 10,* 112–163.

Collins, A. (1992). Towards a design science of education. In E. Scanlon & T. O'Shea (Eds.), *New directions in educational technology* (pp. 15–22). Berlin/New York: Springer-Verlag.

Collins, A. (1999). The changing infrastructure of educational research. In E. C. Lagemann & L. B. Schulman (Eds.), *Issues in educational research. Problems and possibilities* (pp. 289–298). San Francisco: Jossey-Bass.

Collins, A., Brown, J. S., & Newman, S. E. (1989). Cognitive apprenticeship: Teaching the craft of reading, writing, and mathematics. In L. B. Resnick (Ed.), *Knowing, learning, and instruction: Essays in honor of Robert Glaser* (pp. 453–494). Hillsdale, NJ: Lawrence Erlbaum Associates.

Cornelius, L., & Herrenkohl, L. R. (2004). Power in the classroom: How the classroom environment shapes students' relationships with each other and with concepts. *Cognition and Instruction, 22*(4), 467–498.

Design-Based Research Collective (2003). Design-based research: An emerging paradigm for educational inquiry. *Educational Researcher, 32*(1), 5–8.

Developmental Studies Center (2004). *Summary of evaluation findings for the Child Development Program.* Retrieved January 10, 2004, from http://www.devstu.org/cdp/research.html

diSessa, A. (1991). Local science: Viewing the design of human-computer systems as cognitive science. In J. M. Carroll (Ed.), *Designing interaction: Psychology at the human-computer interface* (pp. 162–202). New York: Cambridge University Press.

Duschl, R. A., & Osborne, J. (2002). Supporting and promoting argumentation discourse in science education. *Studies in Science Education, 38,* 39–72.

Engels, F. (1972). Socialism: Utopian and scientific. In R. C. Tucker (Ed.), *The Marx-Engels reader* (pp. 605–639). New York: Norton. (Original work published 1890)

Engle, R. A., & Conant, F. R. (2002). Guiding principles for fostering productive disciplinary engagement: Explaining an emergent argument in a community of learners classroom. *Cognition and Instruction, 20,* 399–483.

Forman, E., & Ansell, E. (2001). The multiple voices of a classroom mathematics community. *Educational studies in mathematics, 46,*115–142.

Froyen, L. A., & Iverson, A. M. (1999). *Schoolwide and classroom management: The reflective educator-leader.* Upper Saddle River, NJ: Prentice-Hall.

Gee, J. P., & Green, J. (1998). Discourse analysis, learning, and social practice: A methodological study. *Review of Research in Education* 23, 119–169.

General Accounting Office. (2003). *Youth illicit drug use prevention: DARE long-term evaluations and federal efforts to identify effective programs* (GAO Report 03–172R). Washington, DC: Author.

Greeno, J. G., Collin, A. M., & Resnick, L. (1996). Cognition and learning. In D. Berliner and R. Calfee (Eds.), *Handbook of educational psychology* (pp. 15–46). New York: MacMillan.

Greeno, J. G., & The Middle School Mathematics through Application Project. (1998). The situativity of knowing, learning, & research. *American Psychologist, 53,* 5–26.

Gutierrez, K., Rymes, B., & Larson, J. (1995). Scripts, counterscripts, and underlife in the classroom: James Brown versus Brown v. Board of Education. *Harvard Educational Review, 65,* 445–471.

Herrenkohl, L. R., & Guerra, M. R. (1998). Participant structures, scientific discourse, and student engagement in fourth grade. *Cognition and Instruction, 16,* 431–473.

Herrenkohl, L. R., Palinscar, A., Dewater, L. S., & Kawasaki, K. (1999). Developing scientific communities in the classroom: A sociocognitive approach. *Journal of the Learning Sciences, 8,* 451–493.

Herrenkohl, L. R., Wineburg, S. S., Bell, P., & Stevens, R. (2000). *A comparative psychology of school subjects: Promoting epistemological sophistication in elementary science learning through the study of history.* National Science Foundation Grant REC-9980536 to the University of Washington.

Hickey, D. T. (2003). Engaged participation vs. marginal non-participation: A stridently sociocultural model of achievement motivation. *Elementary School Journal, 103*(4), 401–429.

Hickey, D. T., Kindfield, A. C. H., Horwitz, P., & Christie, M. A. (2003). Integrating curriculum, instruction, assessment, and evaluation in a technology-supported genetics environment . *American Educational Research Journal*, 40(2), 495–538.

Hickey, D. T., Mewborn, D. S., Beckmann, S., Lanehart, S. L., & Cohen, A. S. (2005, July). *Multi-level assessment for enhancing mathematical discourse, curriculum, and achievement in diverse elementary school classrooms.* National Science Foundation Grant REC-0440261 to the University of Georgia.

Hickey, D. T., Michael, M. A., Zuiker, S. J., Schafer, N. J., & Taasoobshirazi, (in review). Balancing Formative and Summative Assessment to Attain Systemic Validity: Three is the Magic Number. *Studies in Educational Evaluation*

Hickey, D. T., & Pellegrino, J. W. (2005). Theory, level, and function: Three dimensions for understanding the connections between transfer and student assessment. In J. P. Mestre (Ed.), *Transfer of learning: Research and perspectives.* (pp. 251–293). Greenwich, CT: Information Age Publishers.

Hickey, D. T., & Zuiker, S. J. (2005). Engaged participation: A sociocultural model of motivation with implications for assessment. *Educational Assessment, 10,* 277–305.

Horwitz, P., & Christie, M. (2000). Computer-based manipulatives for teaching scientific reasoning: An example. In M. J. Jacobson & R. B. Kozma (Eds.), *Learning the sciences of the twenty-first century: Theory, research, and the design of advanced technology learning environments* (pp. 163–191). Hillsdale, NJ: Lawrence Erlbaum Associates.

Institute for Knowledge Innovation and Technology (2004). Retrieved January 10, 2004, from http://ikit.org

Jiménez-Aleixandre, M. P., Rodríguez, A. B., & Duschl, R. A. (2000). "Doing the lesson" or "Doing science": Argument in high school genetics. *Science Education, 84,* 757–792.

Kelly, A. E. (Ed.). (2003). Theme issue: The role of design in educational research . *Educational Researcher, 32*(1).

Kelly, A. E., & Lesh, R. A. (Eds.). (2000). *Handbook of research design in mathematics and science education.* Mahwah, NJ: Lawrence Erlbaum Associates.

Knuth, E., & Peressini, D. (2001). Unpacking the nature of discourse in mathematics classrooms. *Mathematics Teaching in the Middle School, 6,* 320–325.

Kohn, A. (1993). *Punished by rewards: The trouble with gold stars, incentive plans, A's, praise, and other bribes.* Boston: Houton Mifflin.

Kounin, J. S. (1970). *Discipline and group management in classrooms.*New York: Holt, Rinehart & Winston.

Lagemann, E. (1999). An auspicious moment for education research? In E. Lagemann & L. S. Shulman (Eds.), *Issues in education research: Problems and possibilities* (pp. 3–16). San Francisco: Jossey-Bass.

Lave, J. (1991). Situating learning in communities of practice. In L. B. Resnick, J. M. Levine, & S. D. Teasley (Eds.), *Perspectives on socially shared cognition* (pp. 63–82). Washington, DC: American Psychological Association.

Lave, J., & Wenger, E. (1991). *Situated learning: Legitimate peripheral participation.* Cambridge: Cambridge University Press.

Lemke, J. (1990). *Talking science: Language, learning, and values.* Norwood, NJ: Ablex.

Lightfoot, C. (1997). *The culture of adolescent risk-taking.* New York: Guilford Press.

Matusov, E. (1998). When solo activity is not privileged: Participation and internalization models of development. *Human Development, 41,* 326–349.

McCaslin, M., & Good, T. (1996). The informal curriculum. In D. Berliner & R. Calfee (Eds.), *Handbook of educational psychology* (pp. 622–673). New York: Macmillan.

McCaslin, M. & Hickey, D. T. (2001). Self-regulated learning and academic achievement: A Vygotskian view. In B. Zimmerman & D. Schunk (Eds.), *Self-regulated learning and academic achievement: Theory, research, and practice* (2nd ed., pp. 227–252). Mahwah, NJ: Lawrence Erlbaum Associates.

Mitchell, J. M. (2001). Interactions between natural language and mathematical structures: The case of "Workwalking." *Mathematical Thinking and Learning, 3,* 29–52.

Nasir, N. S. (2002). Identity, goals, and learning: Mathematics in cultural practice. *Mathematical Thinking and Learning, 4,* 213–247.

Ochs, E. (1996). Linguistic resources for socializing humanity. In J. J. Gumperz & S. C. Levinson (Eds.), *Rethinking linguistic relativity* (pp. 407–437). Cambridge: Cambridge University Press.

Pepper, S. C. (1970). *World hypotheses: A study in evidence.* Berkeley: University of California Press. (Original work published 1942).

Portes, P. R. (1996). Ethnicity and culture in educational psychology. In D. Berliner & R. Calfee (Eds.), *Handbook of educational psychology* (pp. 331–357). New York: MacMillan.

Rogoff, B. (1998). Cognition as a collaborative process. In W. Damon, D. Kuhn, & R. Seigler (Eds.), *Handbook of child psychology* (5th ed.), Vol. 2, pp. 679–744. New York: Wiley.

Rogoff, B. (2003). *The cultural nature of human development.* Oxford: Oxford University Press.

Ruiz-Primo, M. A., Shavelson, R. J., Hamilton, L., & Klein, S. (2002). On the evaluation of systemic science education reform: Searching for instructional sensitivity. *Journal of Research in Science Teaching, 39,* 369–393.

Russell, H. A., Kruger, A. C., & Schafer, N. J. (2004, April). *Analysis of transactional discourse during learning.* Paper presented at the annual meeting of the American Educational Research Association, San Diego, CA.

Ryan, R. M. & Deci, E. L. (2000). Self-determination theory and the facilitation of intrinsic motivation, social development, and well being. *American Psychologist, 55,* 68–79.

Scardamalia, M. (2004). *Education and technology: An encyclopedia.* Santa Barbara, CA: ABC-CLIO.

Schafer, N. J., Hickey, D. T., Zuiker, S., Kruger, A. C., & Russell, A. (2003, April). *Using video feedback to facilitate classroom argumentation around assessment.* Paper presented at the annual meeting of the American Educational Research Association, Chicago, IL.

Sfard, A. (2000). On reform movement and the limits of mathematical discourse. *Mathematical Thinking and Learning, 2,* 157–189.

Shavelson, R. J., Phillips, D. C., Towne, L., & Feuer, M. J. (2003). On the science of educational design studies. *Educational Researcher, 32*(1), 25–28.

Sloane, F. C., & Gorard, S. (2003). Exploring modeling aspects of design experiments. *Educational Researcher, 32*(1), 29–31.

Stokes, D. E. (1997). *Pasteur's quadrant: Basic science and technological innovation.* New York: Brookings Press.

Vadeboncoeur, J., & Portes, P. (2002). Students "At Risk": Exploring identity from a sociocultural perspective. In D. M. McInerney & S. Van Etten (Eds.), *Research on sociocultural influences on motivation and learning* (Vol. 2, pp. 89–127). Greenwich, CO: Information Age Publishing.

Valsiner, J. (1997). Magical phrases, human development and psychological ontology. In B. D. Cox & C. Lightfoot (Eds.), *Sociogenetic perspectives on internalization* (pp. 237–255). Mahwah, NJ: Lawrence Erlbaum Associates.

Valsiner, J. (1998). Dualisms displaced: From crusades to analytic distinctions. *Human Development, 41,* 350–354.

Vavrus, F., & Cole, K. (2002). 'I didn't do nothin': The discursive construction of school suspension. *The Urban Review, 34,* 87–111.

Vygotsky, L. S. (1978). *Mind in society: The development of higher-order psychological processes.* Cambridge, MA: Harvard University Press. (Original work published 1934)

Weinstein, C. S. (1999). Reflections on best practices and promising programs. In H. J. Freiberg (Ed.), *Beyond behaviorism: Changing the classroom management paradigm* (pp. 147–173). Boston: Allyn & Bacon.

Wenger, E. (1998). *Communities of practice: Learning, meaning, & identity.* Cambridge: Cambridge University Press.

Wertsch, J. V. (1991). *Voices of the mind: A sociocultural approach to mediated action.* Cambridge, MA: Harvard University Press.

Yowell, C. M., & Smylie, M. A. (1999). Self-regulation in democratic communities. *Elementary School Journal, 99,* 469–490.

Zimmerman, B. J., & Schunk D. H. (2001). Reflections on theories of self-regulated learning and academic achievement. In B. J. Zimmerman & D. H. Schunk (Eds.), *Self-regulated learning and academic achievement: Theoretical perspectives* (2nd ed., pp. 289–308). Mahwah, NJ: Lawreence Erlbaum Associates.

Zinchenko, V. P. (1985). Vygotsky and units for the analysis of mind. In J. Wertsch (Ed.), *Culture, communication, and cognition: Vygotskian perspectives* (pp. 94–118). Cambridge: Cambridge University Press.

Zuiker, S. J., & Hickey, D. T. (2004). *Identities for knowing: Analysis of discourse during formative feedback activities*. Paper presented at the annual meeting of the American Educational Research Association, San Diego, CA.

12

From Compliance to Responsibility: Social and Emotional Learning and Classroom Management

Maurice J. Elias and Yoni Schwab
Rutgers, The State University of New Jersey

INTRODUCTION

Marzano and Marzano's (2003) meta-analytic study suggests that classroom management is the single variable with the largest impact on student achievement. Why is that? Shouldn't the quality of math or language arts instruction make the biggest difference in terms of achievement? The most obvious reason for this influence is that effective classroom management sets the stage for learning. Without it, classrooms are disorganized and chaotic, and very little academic learning can happen. Less obvious is that a teacher's classroom management practices are socializing influences on students. They communicate—subtly and not-so-subtly—messages about social norms and emotional behavior. Whether teachers are aware of it or not, students are constantly developing social and emotional skills (both good and bad) through modeling, experimentation, and reinforcement. Teachers' activities in the broad category called classroom management can help students to develop healthy habits. However, they can also unintentionally encourage the learning of poor social and emotional skills. This chapter presents guidelines for integrating proactive social and emotional learning (SEL) into classroom management so that both are effective because, ultimately, they are mutually dependent and inseparable.

A Student-Centered Goal for Classroom Management

This chapter defines classroom management as all of the teacher's practices related to establishing the physical and social environment of the classroom, regulating routines and daily activities, and preventing and correcting problems. Nearly everything a teacher does, aside from communicating the content of the academic curriculum, is part of classroom management. Indeed, even the mode of instruction (e.g., frontal lecturing, worksheets, creative groupwork projects) is a component of classroom management.

To evaluate whether any particular techniques or approaches are effective, one must first consider the goals of classroom management that these practices are meant to achieve. The traditional goal of classroom management has been for the teacher to maintain and enforce discipline so that academic instruction can proceed without distractions. This "control" goal of classroom management is an important, probably necessary, condition for a classroom to function effectively. However, this goal is teacher- and instruction-centered, not student-centered. It does not take into account that some discipline strategies may maintain control but may not foster learning. We define learning broadly here. Schools are increasingly focused on social and emotional learning, as well as academic learning. Therefore, we propose a more holistic and student-centered goal for classroom management: to create a classroom environment that fosters students' learning of academic, social, and emotional skills and the ability to put them to positive use in the world around them. While order is necessary for this goal, it is not sufficient. Classroom management strategies must both maintain order and foster learning.

Self-Control and Self-Discipline

There are two ways to achieve order in a classroom: by external control (i.e., control exerted by the teacher) and by internal control (i.e., students' self-control). If both potentially maintain order, then one must ask which is more likely to foster learning. Schools have traditionally relied on external control because of the speed and convenience of this approach. However, numerous classroom management theorists and researchers have attempted to differentiate between management models that stress external control or obedience, on the one hand, and self-control, self-discipline, and responsibility, on the other (e.g., Bear, 2005; Brophy, 1999; Curwin & Mendler, 1988; Dreikurs, 1968; Freiberg, 1999b; Glasser, 1992; Gordon, 1974, 2003; Kohn, 1996; Weinstein, 1999). Naturally, most people who write on this topic advocate an emphasis on developing students' self-control over relying on short-term external control techniques.

> Having socially responsible citizens—citizens who are self-disciplined and who require minimal external regulation—is of critical importance to our society. Obviously, self-discipline also is critically important, especially to teachers and students, because it reduces discipline problems in the classroom—problems that impact by disrupting learning and demand considerable time and effort from the teacher. Perhaps less obvious is that self-discipline also promotes (1) positive relations with others and a positive school climate, (2) academic achievement, and (3) self-worth and emotional well-being. (Bear, 2005, p. 12)

Educators have long ruminated over how to foster the development of self-control and the internalization of society's values and attitudes so that prosocial behaviors are internally motivated. "For several centuries American educators have questioned if *external* control is a wise and effective means of developing *internal* control of behavior" because consistent socially acceptable behavior only "in the *absence* [italics added] of external monitors, sanctions, and rewards is the hallmark of self-discipline" (Bear, 2005, p. 5). Furthermore, the "emphasis on compliance does not fit well with current emphases on learning through the social construction of knowledge and on helping students to become more autonomous and self-regulated learners" (Brophy, 1999, p. 51). To put it in SEL terms, self-control is unlikely to develop, and self-regulated learning is unlikely to be inspired, in environments characterized by little opportunity for students to learn and practice self-discipline. Therefore, classroom management based primarily on external control may maintain order, but it fails our goal for classroom management: to promote students' learning of academic, social, and emotional skills and the ability to put them to positive use in the world around them.

Emotional Competence

SEL theory makes an important contribution to the goal of promoting self-control and self-discipline by stressing the primacy of emotional competence. "Emotional competence is the demonstration of self-efficacy in emotion-eliciting social transactions. *Self-efficacy* is used here to mean that the individual believes that he or she has the capacity and skills to achieve a desired outcome" (Saarni, 2000, p. 68, emphasis in the original). According to Saarni, based on this theory, self-control involves the following steps: The person's problem or dilemma (a) triggers an automatic emotional response and (b) brings previously-learned knowledge about emotions and social relations into consciousness. This knowledge helps the person (c) decide how to regulate the emotions and thereby negotiate the social exchange in line with his or her moral commitments. This process involves a number of skills, such as awareness of one's own emotions and the emotions of others and the ability to put those emotions into words (as well as to have and to know one's moral commitments, a topic beyond the scope of this chapter). It also requires empathy for others and the ability to cope with negative emotions through self-regulation (i.e., reducing the intensity or duration of the emotion when desired) or using the emotion to help achieve a goal (Mayer & Salovey, 1997).

For example, if someone tells a sixth-grade girl that her friends have been spreading rumors about her, her ability to exert self-control relies on her emotional competence. If she does not attend to her emotional reaction or the emotions of her friends, then she may react in an unacceptable way (e.g., spreading counter-rumors, physically attacking) before finding out more information. If she does attend to her emotions and label them (e.g., anger, hurt, puzzlement), she may be able to regulate them until she finds out more information and decides on a plan. That gives her an opportunity to evaluate the source of the disclosure and speak to her friends in a calm way to see if they have a benign explanation. Based on her conclusions to such inquiries, she can identify her emotions and use them to choose a course of action that fits within her sense of morality. For example, instead of starting a fight with her friends and getting in trouble, she may choose to suspend or end the friendships and channel her emotional energy towards strengthening her other relationships.

The inability to identify and manage one's emotions results in being controlled by others. Therefore, with the goal of self-control, SEL makes monitoring emotions the first step in solving problems (see Elias & Tobias, 1996). This is one example of the kind of insights that the emerging field of SEL can bring to the field of classroom management.

The main question of this chapter is: What types of classroom management techniques maintain order while also fostering academic, social, and emotional learning—including self-control? The tension between maintaining order in the classroom and promoting academic, social, and emotional learning can be significant. For example, although well-managed cooperative learning promotes social development while increasing motivation for academic learning, many teachers are reluctant to use it because of the possibility of losing control, particularly in overcrowded classrooms (Weinstein & Mignano, 2003). All approaches to classroom management must carefully balance the ideal with the practical, and this chapter is no exception. We believe that the research on social and emotional learning can shed a unique light on resolving this tension.

The next section defines social and emotional learning and reviews a few sample studies that demonstrate its impact on social, emotional, and behavioral development, as well as specific goals that schools are evaluated on, such as academic achievement and drug and violence prevention. The following section describes how social and emotional research can help to improve the practice and study of classroom management. To that end, we recommend four action steps that, together, form a system that harmonizes the best of classroom management and social and emotional learning.

SOCIAL AND EMOTIONAL LEARNING

Social and emotional learning (SEL) is the process of gaining competencies and intrinsic motivation for emotional self-awareness and self-regulation; safe and responsible behavior; and assertive, empathic, and skillful social interaction. SEL skills include identifying feelings in oneself and others, managing one's emotions, being responsible for one's actions and commitments, showing empathy and respect, communicating effectively, and many other challenging but necessary skills for functioning adaptively in a free society (Elias, 2003; Elias et al., 1997). Please see Appendix A for a more complete list of essential SEL skills, which was developed by the Collaborative for Academic, Social, and Emotional Learning [CASEL] (Elias, 2003).

It was once thought that social and emotional skills were learned strictly by experience and that they had no place in the curriculum. Math can also be learned by experience, but it is doubtful that students would "naturally" learn math with the same level of sophistication as they do with years of instruction and practice. The same is true of social and emotional skills. Numerous studies have demonstrated that social and emotional skills can be taught and that students who learn them in school have better outcomes in terms of reduced psychopathology, better peer and adult relationships, increased academic achievement, and many other benefits (Elias, 2003; Elias et al., 1997; Greenberg, Domitrovich, & Bumbarger, 2001).

Research on the effectiveness of teaching social and emotional skills is continually expanding. Rather than cite studies that invariably find a positive correlational link between social and emotional skills, on the one hand, and prosocial behavior, on the other, we primarily refer to studies of SEL interventions that use methodology to demonstrate a causal relationship between teaching social and emotional skills and positive outcomes. These studies directly support the hypothesis that proactively teaching social and emotional skills can influence children's behavior, social-emotional development, relationship to school, and academic trajectory.

Though SEL programs can have these positive outcomes, not all of them do. There has been a recent proliferation of programs and curricula marketed to promote character and SEL in schools. The quality of these packaged programs varies tremendously. Unfortunately, many of the curricula make cardinal errors by confusing knowledge of good character constructs with real-life responsible behavior. "While it is nice that students can tell us what they need to do to act responsibly, it is more important that they actually *behave* in responsible ways. In a phrase, 'Talk is cheap; behavior is golden'" (Knoff, 2003, p. 39, emphasis in the original). Knoff suggests that, instead of introducing good character constructs to early elementary students who do not possess the cognitive ability to understand them yet, we should focus on responsible behaviors and return to the constructs defined by those behaviors when the students are ready. The ultimate test of any character education or SEL initiative is whether students can flexibly adapt the skills to different real-world situations, settings, and problems. Because of these challenges in creating an effective SEL program, only a handful of them have been empirically supported. (For a more complete review of the many programs available and their respective research standings, please see CASEL, 2003, and Greenberg et al., 2001.)

The following section gives brief descriptions of five of the best-studied programs and the samples they were studied with. Outcomes for all of the programs are summarized together in the following section, by category. This allows the reader to get an aggregated picture of what benefits can be obtained from SEL programs, in general, rather than just one in particular.

SEL Program Descriptions

Child Development Project

The Child Development Project (CDP), perhaps the most extensively described and studied SEL program, was created by the Developmental Studies Center in Oakland, California. Its effectiveness has been researched since the late 1980s. The intervention includes five elements: (1) cooperative learning (a specific form of groupwork); (2) "developmental discipline"; (3) reading instruction that focuses on social and emotional dimensions of literature; (4) school-wide community building; and (5) activities to promote family-school bonds. *Developmental discipline*, as defined by CDP, promotes the internalization of prosocial norms, values, and skills, such as self-control, by involving students in rule setting and decision making. Rewards and punishments are avoided in favor of nonpunitive control techniques to teach students that positive behavior should be intrinsically motivated. Much of the day-to-day implementation of CDP surrounds a literature-based language arts curriculum that helps the students understand and relate to prosocial values and actions in everyday life. The power of this medium is described by Schaps and Solomon (1990):

> ... Books show concretely and vividly how such values as fairness and kindness make the world a better place. Still others reveal the inner lives of people from other cultures, ages, and circumstances as they deal with universal issues and concerns—they help children to empathize with people who are both like them and not like them and to see commonalities that underly diversity. (p. 40)

In the first study, conducted in the 1980s, CDP was implemented school-wide in three elementary schools with three comparable schools serving as controls. All schools were in one middle to upper-middle class community. The intervention lasted five years, with students who began in kindergarten participating in all five years by the time they reached fourth grade (Battistich, Solomon, Watson, Solomon, & Schaps, 1989; Battistich, Watson, Solomon, Schaps, & Solomon, 1991).

Solomon, Battistich, Watson, Schaps, and Lewis (2000) reported the most extensive study of CDP to date, which involved 12 intervention schools and 12 matching control schools in six districts across the United States with widely varying demographics. Schools were in large cities, small cities, and suburbs; were in both affluent and poor communities; were dominated by different racial groups or none at all; and had a variety of past achievement levels. Five of the 12 program schools were judged by blind raters as having significant levels of implementation over the three-year period of this study. Outcome measures are reported for those five schools.

Promoting Alternative Thinking Strategies (PATHS)

Greenberg, Kusche, Cook, and Quamma (1995) studied another SEL program, Promoting Alternative Thinking Strategies (PATHS), which is a social problem solving curriculum that focuses on affective, behavioral, cognitive, dynamic, and developmental components of social and emotional learning. Three skills are stressed: self-control, emotional awareness and understanding, and social problem solving. The 286 participants in this study were second- and third-graders from four schools in the Seattle area. Two-thirds were from traditional classrooms and one-third were from special education classrooms. The sample matched the ethnic diversity of the Seattle area except that there was an underrepresentation of Asian Americans (58% Caucasians, 32% African American, 4% Asian American).

I Can Problem Solve (ICPS)

I Can Problem Solve (ICPS) was one of the first social problem solving curricula that provided numerous lessons for implementation in schools. Its goals are to prevent high-risk and antisocial behaviors by teaching children to solve everyday problems, beginning in preschool. It does this by teaching students four sets of skills: alternative solution skills, consequential thinking, social perspective taking, and means-ends or sequential thinking (Shure & Glaser, 2001). The curriculum relies heavily on teaching concepts through vocabulary and then associating that vocabulary with theoretical problem solving situations. However, early research on ICPS suggested that "the curriculum has an impact on behavior only if the teachers help children apply in real life the skills practiced in fictitious situations" (Shure & Glaser, p. 128). When students confront problems in real life, teachers use "ICPS dialoguing" and other forms of communication that rely more heavily on asking than telling the child what to do. That way, ICPS is both integrated into the planned curriculum as well as used to respond to problems in the classroom.

Skills, Opportunities, And Recognition (SOAR)

Skills, Opportunities, And Recognition (SOAR), also known as the Seattle Social Development Project, was implemented for six years in first through sixth grades in 18 schools serving high-crime areas in Seattle, Washington. Because of mandatory busing, schools were heterogeneous with respect to ethnicity. About 44% of the sample was Caucasian, 26% Africa American, and 22% Asian American. Over 56% of the sample could be defined as "poor," based on participation in the National School Lunch/School Breakfast Program. SOAR's goal was to create a community of learners, bonded to school and family, through improved instructional practices and increased family involvement. The intervention included three components: (1) five days of in-service training for teachers in intervention classrooms each year covering proactive classroom management, interactive teaching, and cooperative learning; (2) training for first grade teachers in a cognitive and social skills program that teaches children to problem solve in social situations; and (3) voluntary parent training classes that focused on behavior management, helping children succeed in school, and preventing drug use. In addition, sixth graders received four hours of training in recognizing and resisting social influences to engage in risky behavior, such as experimenting with drugs. The study reported here is not from the program period. It was done as a follow up with 598 of the participating students (from all of the intervention and control conditions) at age 18, six years after the intervention ended (Hawkins, Catalano, Kosterman, Abbott, & Hill, 1999).

Social Decision Making / Social Problem Solving Curriculum (SDM/SPS)

The longitudinal impact of SEL was also studied by Elias, Gara, Schuyler, Branden-Muller, and Sayette (1991). They studied the Social Decision Making / Social Problem Solving (SDM/SPS) curriculum (Elias & Tobias, 1996), which has the goal of promoting "social competence by focusing on critical social decision-making, self-control, group participation, and social awareness skills" (Elias et al., 1991, p. 409). Students who had participated in the curriculum for two years—in fourth and fifth grades—were studied five or six years later, even though there was no formal continuation of the program or "booster" in the intervening years. All of the students were from one predominantly white, multiethnic, working-class community of 15,000 in central New Jersey and were divided into experimental and control groups based on whether their elementary schools participated in the program during the original intervention period.

How SEL Benefits Schools: SEL Program Outcomes

SEL Improves Social and Emotional Skills

Since the primary goal of all SEL programs is to increase students' social and emotional skills, it is no surprise that these studies found effects in this area. Children in the CDP intervention schools developed more social and emotional competencies than controls (Battistich et al., 1989; Battistich et al., 1991). Greenberg and his colleagues (1995) found that PATHS was effective with both unclassified and special education populations in improving students' ability to identify feelings, belief that they can hide and manage their feelings, and recognition of other people's feelings, three important social and emotional skills. Students trained in kindergarten and first grade by their teachers still had better ICPS skills than controls three years later. ICPS also enhanced social and emotional development in special needs students, including those with AD/HD and Asperger's (Shure & Glaser, 2001). In the longitudinal study of SDM/SPS, experimental girls had significantly higher overall social-competence scores than controls, and both boys and girls in the experimental condition showed higher self-efficacy than controls (Elias et al., 1991).

SEL Fosters a Stronger School Community

Implementing SEL throughout a school reliably leads to perceptions of a more caring environment and more student bonding to the school. CDP, in particular, focuses on this goal, and studies have shown that it leads to a strong sense of community. Over three years of implementation in the second CDP study, students in the intervention schools reported an increased sense of the schools as communities and more liking for their schools. Most of the other behavioral and academic effects were mediated, as predicted, by the sense of the school as a community (Solomon et al., 2000). Similarly, students who participated in the full SOAR intervention through sixth grade had significantly higher ratings of bonding to their schools (Hawkins et al., 1999).

SEL Increases Prosocial Behavior

Schools are always looking for ways to improve student behavior. The effective development of students' SEL skills implies, by definition, that students improve their social skills, self-control, and emotion regulation. SEL's positive, preventive, successful, and long-lasting approach to improving student behavior may be reason enough for schools to adopt these practices. Some evidence of these effects is presented below.

In the first CDP study, students in intervention schools consistently demonstrated more spontaneous prosocial behavior and superior social problem solving skills than controls, especially in response to peer instigations of aggression. This involved better perspective-taking and greater ability to identify one's own situation and someone else's needs, to consider the consequences of various options, and to choose more prosocial and cooperative strategies. The intervention group also engaged in more spontaneous prosocial behavior (e.g., helpfulness, cooperation, and encouragement) and endorsed democratic values more frequently, including assertion responsibility, equality of representation and participation, and willingness to compromise. They were also more likely to act ethically and altruistically (Battistich et al., 1989; Battistich et al., 1991). Many effects of the elementary school intervention persisted through middle school, even after the intervention ended. Students who came from elementary schools that implemented CDP outperformed their peers on teacher ratings of behavior and self-reported misbehavior (Schaps, 2003). In the larger CDP study, students in the five high-implementation schools showed higher prosocial motivation, more democratic values, greater conflict resolution skills, and more concern for others. Effect sizes ranged from small to moderate. There were no significant effects related to observer-rated student behavior in that study (Solomon et al., 2000).

ICPS training with low-income African American four- and five-year-olds resulted in reduced impulsive and inhibited behaviors, increased sharing and caring behaviors, and some protective effects from developing behavior problems in kindergarten or first grade (Shure & Glaser, 2001). In an evaluation of ICPS in a group equally divided between Hispanic, African American, and Caucasian kindergarteners, trained students were rated as having reduced impulsive and inhibited behaviors and increased peer acceptance, concern for others, and classroom initiative. These findings were maintained through a six-month follow-up (Shure & Glaser, 2001).

Research on PATHS found that it reduced aggression and hyperactive-disruptive behavior, improved behaviors related to emotional adjustment, reduced impulsivity, and raised social competence (CASEL, 2003). Not all outcome measures associated with PATHS have shown significant or strong effect sizes (e.g., Conduct Problems Prevention Research Group, 1999), but it does seem to promote at least a modest improvement in children's behavior. Years after the program ended, high school students who participated in SOAR in elementary school had better in-school behavior than their peers according to some measures (Hawkins et al., 1999).

SEL Impacts Student Health and Risk-Taking Behavior

The benefits of SEL are not limited to behavioral self-control and self-discipline. SEL programs create a framework within which to teach about serious health-related issues. For example, most of the programs cited here have a problem-solving component. If the problem-solving system is taught early and reinforced week after week, year after year, there is good reason to believe that students can become proficient at solving all kinds of day-to-day problems ranging in difficulty from getting their homework done to avoiding fights on the playground. When these students face more serious challenges, such as substance use, serious violence, bullying, and sexual risk taking, the problem-solving skills practiced in more banal circumstances will be available to them. These deeply ingrained skills may help them to make mature decisions and resist temptation and peer pressure. Teachers can help to assure this synergy by teaching about these risky behaviors using the problem-solving framework employed throughout the school. Students can discuss and rehearse their responses to these dangers based on a well-developed system of responsible decision making. Research on ICPS directly supports this assumption. ICPS has been found to decrease depression and impulsivity, and the social and emotional gains of ICPS with AD/HD children have been maintained at least three years with some showing further long-term gains (Shure & Glaser, 2001).

Longitudinal studies also demonstrate the points just made. Roughly six years after each intervention had ended, both SOAR and SDM/SPS students showed gains in health and risk-taking behaviors when compared with fellow high school students who had not participated in the intervention. SOAR students had significantly lower rates of violence, heavy drinking, and sexual behavior in high school, though other measures, including drug use, did not reach significance (Hawkins et al., 1999). Students in the experimental condition of SDM/SPS, as compared to controls, showed significantly lower rates of alcohol use, vandalism, hitting or threatening peers or parents, attacking others with intent to injure, buying or providing alcohol for someone else, and using tobacco products. Some effects of the intervention, such as reduced buying of or providing of alcohol, were stronger in boys. Others, like less use of tobacco, were stronger for girls. Analyses of the psychopathology indexes on the Youth Self Report (YSR) (Achenbach & Edelbrock, 1987) showed that experimental boys had significantly fewer symptoms of depression and self-destructive or identity problems than controls (Elias et al., 1991). Although many of the effect sizes were small or moderate, this study and Hawkins et al. (1999) both support the assumption that building social skills in elementary school has immediate benefits, such as reductions in problem behaviors, and that those benefits last many years after the SEL intervention is over, at least into high school, and generalize to include major risk-taking behavior, such as substance use and violence. This is in contrast to the lack of long-term evidence for conventional drug and violence prevention programs that are not linked to a broader skill-building curriculum.

SEL Improves Academic Achievement

Though health- and behavior-related issues are high on schools' agendas, the primary goal of the American education system is students' academic development. This foundational principle has only been reinforced in the past few years since the passing of the No Child Left Behind Act and the prevalence of high-stakes testing. So, it is important to note that SEL skill-building improves academic achievement. On the surface, this may not seem to be a major discovery. SEL skills include self-control and other skills that are necessary for a student to take responsibility for his or her schoolwork, so it is not surprising that SEL is related to academic achievement. However, the magnitude of the relationship—and its apparent independence of IQ and other academically oriented measures—demonstrates that SEL is one of the most important determinants of academic achievement.

Some SEL programs have already shown that they can impact academic achievement, although the outcomes are quite variable from program to program and study to study. One encouraging example is SDM/SPS. SDM/SPS skills are essential to doing academics effectively because, for example, they enable students to understand and follow directions, to examine texts patiently to extract information, to delay gratification to focus on academic tasks without being sidetracked, to participate in cooperative learning groups, and to complete homework and projects in an organized way (Elias, 2004). This was demonstrated in a study of fourth- and fifth-graders in one suburban, working-class community who were part of an SDM/SPS study; their grades in language arts and social studies showed improvement in the third and fourth marking periods as compared with the first marking period, with the highest and most consistent improvements corresponding to the students who received the complete—as opposed to the partial—intervention. (Grades in science and math did not rise, which was consistent with the hypothesis and implied that the effects in language arts and social studies were not due to grade inflation.) In addition to SEL skills, such as self-control and emotional regulation, that help students stay focused on and motivated to do their schoolwork, the problem-solving paradigm of SDM/SPS helped students relate to literature characters more deeply and understand history as a series of individuals and groups "problem-solving." This synergy between academics and SEL improved students' skills in both domains (Elias, 2004). Elias and his colleagues (1991) found small, but significant, positive effects of SDM/SPS on achievement five or six years after the intervention was completed.

CDP studies have also reported academic outcomes. Even after the intervention ended, students who came from elementary schools that implemented CDP outperformed their peers on academic achievement measures (i.e., grade-point average and standardized test scores) in middle school (Schaps, 2003). The larger study of CDP showed that it increased intrinsic academic motivation and the frequency of reading of self-chosen books. Only two schools in one district showed improvements in academic achievement, though this was confounded by a state-wide testing mandate in those schools that was very consistent with the intervention (Solomon et al., 2000). ICPS has resulted in higher standardized achievement test scores with students who began training in both kindergarten and fifth grade (Shure & Glaser, 2001). Students who participated in SOAR and SDM/SPS also showed better academic outcomes on some measures when compared with controls (Hawkins et al., 1999; Elias et al., 1991).

Caprara, Barbaranelli, Pastorelli, Bandura, and Zimbardo (2000) reported a study that, though not on an SEL program, is very important to understanding the magnitude of the relationship between social skills and academic achievement and could bolster the cases of educators who must justify the expenditure of time and resources on SEL in a back-to-basics and high-stakes academic testing environment. The study was longitudinal, tracking four cohorts of Italian third-graders through eighth grade. Prosocial behavior in third grade was strongly related to social preference in eighth grade, accounting for 37% of variance, which supports the long-term importance of social skills for socialization. However, the effects of prosocial behavior were nearly as pronounced when measuring academic achievement. Prosocial behavior in third grade accounted for 35% of the variance in academic achievement in eighth grade. Furthermore, a 100-participant subsample of this study received academic measures in both third and eighth grades. Surprisingly, achievement in third grade was unrelated to achievement in eighth. In this study, prosocial behavior in third grade was the best predictor of achievement in eighth grade. Mitchell, Elias, Labouvie, and Haynes (2004) had similar results, predicting third-grade achievement most strongly from social competence in second grade in an urban sample. If these findings are verified by further study and replication, it could lead to the conclusion that SEL skill-building is an essential factor in reaching schools' academic goals and, therefore, justifies the expenditure of very limited class time and scarce financial and professional resources.

Wentzel (1993) tried to analyze the mechanisms that underlie the relationship between prosocial and responsible behavior on the one hand and academic outcomes on the other. Three mechanisms were suggested: (1) Positive social conduct is related to good academic behaviors, which, in turn, are related to learning and intelligence; (2) positive social conduct leads to teacher preference and support, which lead to learning and other good outcomes; and (3) positive social conduct and responsibility are related to achievement without any mediating factors.

To test these mechanisms, Wentzel (1993) conducted a study of 423 sixth- and seventh-graders and 11 teachers from one school in which she measured students' pro- and antisocial behavior (as rated by self, peers, and teachers), academic achievement (average of grades across different classes), teacher ratings of academically relevant behavior, and teacher preferences. The middle school was in a working-class community in the Midwest; the sample was ethnically diverse (68% Caucasian, 23% African American, 5% Hispanic). Prosocial and antisocial behavior were both highly correlated with GPA (in opposite directions), each accounting for nearly 30% of the variance. When controlling for personal variables, academic behavior, and teacher preferences, pro- and antisocial behavior were still significantly related to achievement, though the effect sizes were considerably smaller (r's $= .17$ and $-.18$). The other independent predictors of academic achievement were academic behavior, IQ, and family structure, but not teacher preferences. Overall, Wentzel's model accounted for 72% of the variance. Pro- and antisocial behavior accounted for about 4% of unique variance in GPA. This supports Wentzel's first hypothesized mechanism: Social conduct primarily influences academic achievement through its relationship with academically oriented behavior.

Based on this study, Wentzel (1993) argued that "... educators and researchers need to go beyond direct, content-based instruction to understand learning and performance in the classroom" (p. 363). Educators and researchers need to look at motivation, self-regulatory processes, and other social competencies. Finally, Wentzel concluded from the data that SEL should be a greater focus of schools. "Given that prosocial behavior is a positive, independent predictor of both students' grades and standardized test scores, a stronger emphasis on the development of cooperative, sharing, and helpful behavior might be warranted" (p. 363).

The empirical evidence in support of SEL approaches certainly justify their use by educators toward the goals of building students' capacity to learn and to engage effectively in the world with sound character. However, this still-emerging literature contains many different models and components. In the following section, we attempt to distill the literature to assist educators in drawing clear guidelines for integrating SEL principles and practices with effective classroom management.

INTEGRATING SOCIAL AND EMOTIONAL LEARNING AND CLASSROOM MANAGEMENT

The research on SEL reinforces the need for classroom management practices that support the development of students' academic, social, and emotional skills, or, at the very least, do not conflict with this cardinal goal of education. SEL instruction and classroom management are overlapping tasks, and classroom management practices can have a significant impact (positive or negative) on students' social and emotional development. This implies a new paradigm for research on and assessment of classroom management techniques and programs. Evaluations of classroom management should move beyond relying solely on short-term measurements of classroom behavior and misbehavior. Many other questions should be asked, including: Is the management program effective in improving behavior over the long term? Is behavior improving outside of the target classroom—in other areas of the school and outside of school? Have self-control and personal effort attributions increased? Are students taking more responsibility for their actions and problem solving independently? Are grades and test scores rising? Is the school a warmer, more comfortable community for all of its stakeholders, especially students? Are measures of academic, social, and emotional learning all improving? These goals are far more difficult to attain and to measure than "Are the students sitting quietly and not disrupting?" They are also far more meaningful.

This section describes four areas of teacher action that characterize an integration of quality classroom management and SEL:

Action 1: Teach SEL skills
Action 2: Build caring relationships
Action 3: Set firm and fair boundaries
Action 4: Share responsibility with students

Please note that these categories and the specific skills and techniques included in each overlap and are mutually dependent. Furthermore, Actions 2–4 could all be considered teaching SEL skills and have been included as such in SEL skill-building curricula. Similarly, Action 1 is an integral part of the best classroom management programs. Nevertheless, each of these actions has a distinct role in managing classrooms effectively and is, we think, a useful way to conceptualize how SEL and classroom management are best integrated. Within each Action section, the SEL skills most relevant and specific to classroom functioning are presented. Methods of teaching those skills taken from SDM/SPS will serve as examples of practical SEL approaches and terminology. Other SEL skills from Appendix A that do not have immediate application to management will not receive the same treatment here.

Action 1: Teach SEL Skills

The first step in bringing SEL to the classroom is to plan how one will incorporate explicit SEL skill building into the curriculum and classroom management agenda. This selection process should come first because, based on the SEL program chosen, a full-scale preventive classroom management plan can then be designed to match the tone, methodology, and language of the SEL program. The specifics of how one carries out Actions 2–4 should rely heavily on and reinforce the core skills being taught during SEL instruction. For example, if the SEL program teaches a problem-solving technique, the teacher should use the same one to address day-to-day problems that arise in the classroom. The SEL skill-building program chosen should be used as a framework upon which the other elements are linked and built, making one's approach more coherent and effective.

Skills necessary for optimal functioning in the classroom can and must be taught, modeled, and practiced proactively. If they are not addressed proactively, they constitute what has been called the "hidden curriculum" because social skills are taught, modeled, and reinforced all the time, even when the teacher is not deliberately teaching them. Unfortunately, students do not always learn adaptive and prosocial versions of these vital skills when they are taught only by experience (Cartledge & Milburn, 1995). This situation is further compounded by the array of media messages children receive that urge them to act in ways that support neither academic excellence nor self-control (Comer, 2003).

Before, during, and after teaching individual social skills, teachers must also work to "change values and basic assumptions, particularly about the value of prosocial rather than aggressive and antisocial behaviors in problem situations" (Cartledge & Milburn, 1995, p. xi). In other words, social skills instruction is a two-component process. First, teachers help students to develop specific skills and competencies to enable students to act in prosocial ways. Second, teachers must work over the long term to foster motivation for responsible behavior and ethical growth, which bridge the gap between students' learning social and emotional skills and choosing to apply them. At first, students will not use their newly acquired skills spontaneously in difficult situations. Repetition, cuing, and coaching are necessary to transform discrete skills into socially competent and responsible behavior across many different situations (Elias et al., 1997). The goal is for students to be able to act responsibly and ethically without cuing or any kind of external reinforcement. These are the kinds of citizens that any democracy hopes for.

The Four Phases of Social-Emotional Skill Instruction

Cartledge and Milburn (1995) break down the process of teaching social and emotional skills into three phases: (1) instruction, (2) skill performance and feedback, and (3) practice and generalization. In addition, SEL emphasizes that cuing and reminding in real-life situations constitute a necessary fourth phase as children transform the skills into lifelong habits (Shure & Glaser, 2001). Evaluation of students' competence with the specific behaviors should occur before, during, and after this sequence to measure the effectiveness of instruction. This section will focus on the four phases of social-emotional skill instruction but not on evaluation and measurement. (For more information on those, see CASEL, 2003, which contains guidelines for evaluation as well as links to evaluation tools used by a number of SEL programs.)

The instruction phase begins with providing a rationale for learning and performing the SEL skill being taught. This is best done by challenging the students to analyze the value of the skill or even to identify the behavior themselves by figuring out the best response to a hypothetical scenario. Once the value of the skill has been addressed, it is important to break down the skill into its component behaviors (Elias & Tobias, 1996). Again, students should participate in doing this, which helps them to learn the components in their own "language." Finally, students are presented with a model that most clearly communicates the skill. The model could be a character in literature, an actor on a videotape, a peer who role-plays the skill in person, and so on (Cartledge & Milburn, 1995).

The second phase of teaching SEL skills is skill performance and feedback. Like seatwork during a lesson, guided rehearsal gives the students an opportunity to perform the focal skill individually for the first time in a secure environment. Rehearsal can be covert (i.e., cognitive or imaginal), verbal, or physical. Of course, physical performance of the skill, if possible, is superior to either thinking or talking about it. Feedback is provided when physical or verbal performance is done to correct mistakes, address problems, and recognize when the skill is being done properly. Feedback can be verbal, reinforcement-based, or self-evaluative (Cartledge & Milburn, 1995). Appendix B is a sample lesson plan that gives classroom-based examples of Phases 1 and 2.

The third phase of teaching social-emotional skills is practice. As with any other skill taught in a classroom, practice—even overlearning—is necessary to maintain the behavior. In addition to practice for maintenance, generalization to different real-world situations is a critical part of teaching social-emotional skills. There are a number of ways to encourage generalization; Cartledge and Milburn (1995) identify six strategies based on behavioral and cognitive research:

1. Training in a variety of settings, particularly settings that match "target" situations for the behavior, is very helpful to generalization.
2. Practice should be done in real life or, if that is not practical, under conditions that approximate real life as much as possible.
3. Training should occur with different people to show consistency across social situations. For the best outcomes, all school personnel should model and reinforce social skills consistently and use the same language to refer to them. This requires that school-wide policies concerning rules and behavior be established. To generalize beyond school, parents and community members should use the same social skill language. Peers can also be a powerful force in reinforcing school- or community-wide SEL skills.
4. As an extension of the previous point, care should be taken to keep training mediators, such as language and expectations, consistent across situations.
5. Contingencies of reinforcement for SEL behaviors should remain consistent across different settings, both in school and, if possible, out of school. External reinforcement is limited in its effectiveness, however. If it is used, it should be tapered to encourage generalization to contets in which reinforcement is unavailable.
6. Students should be encouraged to develop self-management for their social behaviors. This is the highest level of creating generalization and the most effective in the long term. It occurs through self-monitoring via charts, worksheets, diaries, and reflective journals. If students learn to value the skills, adopt reasonable standards for application, self-monitor, self-evaluate, and self-reinforce, then they have reached an admirable level of skill independence and behavioral competence. Ultimately, the goal of social-emotional skill-building is to make the transition from external control and reinforcement to internal motivation, responsibility, and self-control. This is, perhaps, the most valuable principle that the field of classroom management can learn from SEL.

The fourth and final phase of teaching social-emotional skills is cuing and reminding. While students who have reached the level of self-management of their social behaviors may not need cuing and reminding, the vast majority of students do need them, especially when they first learn new skills. Almost no students remember when and how to apply new skills until they've had many opportunities to practice them in the real world. Cuing can take many forms, all of which should be positive, brief, private, and designed to encourage rather than criticize the child. Verbal cues are best done in very short phrases that are as private and encouraging as possible. It can be helpful to have a code word or acronym for a particular skill.

Let's take an example of an SEL skill from the SDM/SPS curriculum that directly applies to classroom management. If a student is not paying attention to a peer who is speaking, a teacher might be tempted to shout from across the room: "Kim, stop fiddling around with the papers in your desk. Sit up straight, turn and look at Michael, and listen to what he's trying to say." This might stop her from fiddling with the papers, but it would likely make Kim feel embarrassed and discouraged and, because of those feelings, she would probably not even hear what Michael has to say. The SDM/SPS program terms that set of listening skills, Listening Position, so the teacher could simply say: "I would like to remind everyone to use Listening Position." If done in a positive tone of voice, it helps everyone self-monitor; those who are in good listening positions feel pleased, and those who are not can self-correct. Either way, feelings of embarrassment or discouragement are minimized. If Kim did not hear the general statement, the teacher can walk over and ask quietly, "Kim, Listening Position, please." A need for further reminders suggests that perhaps the child does not know the skill or has a learning or attentional impairment that should be watched more closely.

Cuing can take many nonverbal forms as well. Cuing can be done with hand gestures or eye contact. Posters or murals on the walls of the classrooms, hallways, and lunchrooms can serve as cues for specific skills. Signals for use in large groups, such as assemblies, are especially important. All school personnel should use the same terminology to cue the same skills in different venues, and even students can be allies in cuing their peers to perform skills in social situations. As long as the cuing is done in brief, positive, and private ways that encourage students to remember and use their skills, it can be a vital tool in promoting the transition from knowledge of skill to real-life performance. Once again, the ultimate goal is for students to exhibit self-management and for cuing to become unnecessary. Nevertheless, educators routinely underestimate the time needed before cues are faded. One should think in terms of years, not weeks, with ultimate success depending a great deal on continuity across grade levels.

Many state-of-the-art instructional practices that teachers apply to academic teaching also are required for SEL instruction. For example, SEL requires (indeed, is predicated on) student-centered learning rather than teacher-oriented instruction and should be developmentally appropriate with regard to both the choice of skills to be taught as well as methods of teaching those skills (Cartledge & Milburn, 1995). SEL pedagogy is highly consistent with Gardner's multiple intelligences theory (1985, 1993), Levine's "A Mind at a Time" approach (2002), and McCarthy's 4MAT instructional method (1987). Principles of differentiated instruction (Tomlinson, 1999) have also emerged as extremely important, as any single classroom almost certainly contains students with vast individual differences in social and emotional competencies based on family background; cultural differences; genetics; prior school experiences; and differences in cognitive, emotional, behavioral, and psychopathological functioning.

Social Problem Solving

There are three building blocks to SEL competency and responsible behavior: basic/readiness skills, problem solving, and internal motivation and self-discipline. Readiness skills include turn taking, following directions, keeping calm, communicating effectively, and reading social cues. (Please see Appendix A for an inventory of SEL skills.) Social problem solving relies upon readiness skills to choose and organize actions in almost any situation. In this way, social problem solving can be seen as the superordinate competency in the SEL skill hierarchy. Consequently, it is at the heart of all of the empirically supported SEL programs discussed previously. Internal motivation, the third building block, drives the choice to use one's problem-solving competencies and exert self-control in a situation.

There are numerous social problem-solving paradigms. Many of them use mnemonics to help children remember the steps. Problem solving in SDM/SPS is called FIG TESPN. Each letter stands for a step in the problem-solving process:

Feelings—How do I feel in this situation?
Identify problem—What's the problem?
Goal—What is my ultimate goal? What do I want to have happen?
Think—Brainstorm at least three possible solutions to this problem.
Envision—What are the likely consequences of each of my possible solutions?
Solution—Choose the best solution I thought of.
Plan—Plan how to carry out my solution.
Notice results—After I carry out my plan, evaluate it.

Other programs' problem-solving systems are substantially similar; the main differences are the names, the memory devices, and SDM/SPS's strong emphasis on feelings at the beginning of the problem-solving process, a discovery of the SDM/SPS program three decades ago. Regardless of the name, social problem solving provides the framework for acting in a socially and emotionally competent way in the classroom and in life.

Integrating SEL and Academics

SEL instruction is particularly effective when integrated with academics rather than when treated as a separate "subject" (Elias, 2004). As described earlier, SEL skills are vital to academic learning. Integrating the two types of learning creates synergies for both. For example, when SEL skill-building is integrated into a literature lesson, the SEL skills are raised to the level of importance of core academics rather than being viewed as a "special" or "add-on" subject. SEL is also dramatized in meaningful and complex ways in literature, which improves the learning of both SEL and the literature being studied through text-to-self connections. Appendix B gives an example of how SEL gains relevance through a literature lesson and how the literature lesson is enhanced by using SEL as a paradigm for analyzing a particular passage in a read-aloud book.

Social problem solving illustrates the connection of SEL and academic instruction particularly well. In language arts, problem solving can be applied to the dilemmas faced by characters in stories. Students' understanding of characters deepens by problem solving at exciting junctures; this brings them into the story and the authoring process. History and current events can be presented as a series of problems that various individuals and groups have attempted to solve. Students can try to figure out, based on their readings and other sources of information, what various individuals and groups involved were feeling and what their goals were. They learn the powerful impact of deficiencies in effective problem solving, empathy, and perspective-taking. As students apply social problem solving in academic areas, they enhance their own ability to problem solve in the present both individually and in groups (Elias, 2004).

As discussed previously, health and family life education provides the closest analogue to real-life problem solving because it is all about making choices about how to live. Having an established, deeply learned problem-solving paradigm in a school can be critical to framing major target issues, such as substance use, violence, and sexual risk taking. Rather than presenting each of these risky behaviors haphazardly, a specific problem-solving technique can serve as the unifying principle for confronting these decisions and making them effectively. Students who have learned over a number of years to make responsible decisions using problem solving when confronted with "smaller" conflicts will be at a great advantage in approaching these "larger" issues in a mature, self-confident, and proactive way. And seeing that problem solving is useful for even the most sensitive and consequential real-world decisions will increase the students' value of those skills.

Teaching SEL skills, from readiness skills to problem solving, is one basic building block in classroom management, but it is not fully effective by itself. This chapter presents three additional areas of classroom management that are necessary for the integration of SEL with management. (A more comprehensive treatment of teaching social and emotional skills, along with a variety of categorizations and listings of skills, can be found in Cartledge & Milburn, 1995, or in any of the empirically supported SEL programs described here or in CASEL, 2003, or Greenberg et al., 2001).

Action 2: Build Caring Relationships

Building caring relationships is a tenet of SEL and is a necessary factor in fostering students' social and emotional growth. The actions associated with developing caring relationships model competent social skill behavior. Since children learn all the time, whether we intend to teach them or not, building caring relationships in classrooms may have at least as much influence on their development of social skills as explicit teaching. (Students should be encouraged to do as we say *and* as we do.) Furthermore, a caring atmosphere supports students emotionally (which, sadly, many students lack outside the classroom) and models such emotional skills as emotion identification and regulation. Building caring relationships sets the tone for SEL skill-building and provides the first vehicle for practice and improvement. It makes the classroom a living SEL laboratory. The importance of a caring classroom community is supported by the literature on CDP. Students' perception of the school as a caring community is the primary goal of CDP and has been studied extensively as a mediator to other positive outcomes in SEL and classroom management practices (Battistich, 1998, 1999, 2000, 2001; Battistich et al., 1991; Battistich, Solomon, & Watson, 1998; Schaps, 2003; Schaps & Solomon, 1990; Solomon et al., 2000).

In terms of classroom management, building an atmosphere of caring relationships can make all of the difference between a functional and dysfunctional classroom. The persistent demands of academic performance, complying with rules, and interacting positively with peers and teachers can be challenging for students. Developing a supportive community in the classroom helps to impart a sense of each student's belonging, to alleviate students' social anxieties and frustration, and to motivate students to comply with teacher requests and act prosocially with peers. Consequently, the level of respect for teachers and peers increases, negative or aggressive social behaviors are reduced, and students are more likely to comply with the rules (Elias et al., 1997). Because of this, building caring relationships is the first step in the promotion of responsible behavior and prevention of misbehavior. Setting a supportive tone for the class should be the teacher's first task when students enter the classroom on the first day of school. It is worth noting that any early childhood educator reading this will recognize it as an essential tenet of their teaching. However, what SEL theory has brought into clearer focus is that the link of caring relationships and learning does not cease to become relevant after early childhood. Indeed, its importance continues through the adolescent years and persists into adult education contexts (Salovey & Sluyter, 1997). (For a full review of research on building caring communities and classroom management, see chapter 10 in this volume.)

Relationships in a typical classroom fall into three different types: teacher-student, student-student, and the classroom community. We consider the first one separately and the latter two together. This section also touches upon the SEL skills and techniques related to effective communication, which is the primary medium for building functional relationships.

Teacher-Student Relationships

Building caring relationships between teachers and students is necessary for many reasons. First, when students sense that a teacher cares about them, they see the teacher as more credible and as an ally rather than a foe. This increases motivation to follow directions, to adhere to rules, and to put effort into classroom activities and academics. Just as adults who feel respected and supported in the workplace are more productive, children have those same needs and respond best in school environments that they perceive as caring and respectful. Pianta and others have demonstrated the influence of teacher-child relationships on academic success, behavior, and other important outcomes (e.g., Pianta, 1999; Pianta & Stuhlman, 2004; see Osterman, 2000). Weinstein and Mignano (2003) detail nine ways in which successful classroom managers express concern for students. Effective teachers are welcoming, are sensitive to students' concerns, treat students fairly, act like real people (not just as teachers), share responsibility, minimize the use of external controls, include everyone, search for students' strengths, and communicate effectively. To this list, we would add that teachers should also show an interest in their students' lives and pursuits. Many of these ten practices not only express concern for students but are important for other action steps, a fact that highlights the integrated nature of SEL and classroom management.

Hoy and Weinstein (see chapter 8 in this volume) summarize the literature on students' perceptions of teachers' management practices. The studies they cite span elementary to high school and cover a wide range of cultural, racial, and socioeconomic populations. Their review points to three factors that are central to students' appraisal of teachers. According to students, good teachers are those who develop positive relationships with their students (they care); exercise authority without being rigid, harsh, punitive, or unfair; and use creative instructional practices to "make learning fun." These teacher practices are the preconditions for establishing a positive classroom environment. The convergence between students' descriptions of "good" teachers and the research on effective teaching practices is noteworthy.

Student-Student Relationships and the Classroom Community

Peer-to-peer relationships and the classroom community are just as important as teacher-student relations in maintaining a functional classroom and promoting social and emotional growth. This may seem like an obvious statement on the surface, but Noddings (2003) points out why the classroom community is essential for shaping success in school and life. She observes that a moral life is completely relational and that character and the habits of learning are acquired through strong, nurturant, positive relationships. The classroom as a community must teach caring as the bedrock upon which other values, essential for intellectual accomplishment and ethical living, can be built: honesty, courage, responsibility. Noddings writes that in a caring community students face realities about themselves, one another, their teacher, and the world around them. This is a prerequisite to genuine learning and openness to, rather than fear of, learning. Like Sarason (1974, 1993), Noddings sees community as a response to the existential realities of loneliness, insecurity, incompleteness, and rejection. Classrooms that promote affiliation, safety, interdependence, and acceptance of differences allow students to check their existential baggage and proceed on the journey of learning. This journey can be a major source of happiness to children, but it is not an isolated trip. Rather, it is carried out in a set of relationships with classmates and other members of the school community.

Even though peer relationships do not always directly involve the teacher, the teacher is a vital force in establishing the conditions for social interaction and would benefit greatly from proactively intervening to help these relationships develop positively. SEL social skill-building practices suggest a number of ways to do this. First, the teacher can begin the year by helping students feel comfortable with each other in the classroom. This can involve group-building activities, creative opportunities to share personal experiences and interests, and establishing an ethic of teamwork and helping one another with everyday tasks and problems. Second, rather than just imposing rules about respecting peers and the teacher, teachers should involve students in deciding what rules should govern social interaction in the classroom and facilitate conversations on specific ways to show respect and caring. In the mode of SEL pedagogy, prosocial interactions should be role-played and modeled so that students learn what abstract values such as caring, inclusion, and respect look like in practice. Third, teachers should discuss, teach, and model a problem-solving approach to understanding and resolving personal dilemmas and mistakes (using personal examples in an appropriate way, if possible) to set a personal, supportive tone to the class. The SEL literature provides numerous models to accomplish these tasks (see Charney, 2002; Elias et al., 1997).

As described above, CDP focuses on building caring school-wide communities. One of the primary vehicles for reaching that goal is cooperative learning. In addition, the CDP approach urges teachers to eschew competition, perceived or real, to foster an atmosphere where no one will end up a "loser." This even applies to competitive or group games, which, although they can be motivating for some students, can undermine the sense of community (Schaps & Solomon, 1990). Cooperative games, in which the entire class is on the same team and competing against itself, can foster a sense of community instead of inhibiting it (Cartledge & Milburn, 1995).

Research on CDP has focused on its effectiveness in fostering community and the correlates of that goal. The benefits of such an approach are encouraging:

> We also found, in general, that the greater the sense of community among the students in a program class, the more favorable their outcomes on measures of prosocial values, helping, conflict resolution skill, responses to transgression, motivation to help others learn, and intrinsic motivation. (Schaps & Solomon, 1990, p. 40)

(Please see chapter 10 in this volume for more about CDP and its current form, Caring School Communities, and other models of building caring classroom communities.)

The capacity for empathy is the keystone to intrinsically motivated prosocial behavior. Empathy and perspective taking are vital—and often absent—in our society. The SDM/SPS skill used to teach empathy is Footsteps. The goal of Footsteps is to enable students to recognize another's feelings and goals when in a conflict. The two participants in the exercise place cutouts in the shape of footsteps on the floor across from each other. They stand in their "own feet," and begin by stating their feelings and concerns using "I" statements. Then, they switch places, and each one acknowledges the other's feelings and concerns and checks for accuracy with an active listening statement (e.g., "I heard you . . . "). They then return to their original places and talk about how it felt to be in the other's "feet." Once they understand their partner's emotions and position, they then problem-solve together until a mutually agreeable solution is reached. This is a complex skill that requires adult modeling, specific feedback, and generous amounts of practice. Creative lessons that integrate this skill with academics (particularly literature and social studies) are especially beneficial. In keeping with the SEL skill-building pedagogy mentioned earlier, once students have learned and practiced the Footsteps technique, its use should be prompted. This takes place by adults carrying around cutouts and "dropping the feet" when they come upon students having conflicts at assemblies, or in hallways, lunchrooms, or on the playground. Students know that once the feet are dropped, they should "assume the position" required and begin the orderly process of conflict resolution under the adult's (or trained peer mediator's) watchful eye.

Communication

Developing effective communication is a challenging but vital step in building caring, functional relationships throughout the classroom. Effective teacher-to-student communication includes, but is not limited to, clarity and checking for understanding; active listening; facilitative and open-ended questioning; and saying far more positive, complimentary, and encouraging words to all students (even the challenging ones) than negative words.

Numerous SEL skills relate to communication, and there are a number of SEL skill-building methods that have particular utility in classroom functioning. "I" messages and active (reflective) listening are tried-and-true techniques. The SDM/SPS listening skill of Listening Position was mentioned above. But how does a student know when it's time to speak instead of listen? SDM/SPS uses a system called Speaker Power, which involves passing an object from person to person to signify whose turn it is to speak. When Speaker Power is active, no one is allowed to speak without holding the object—including the teacher. The teacher gives the instructions while holding Speaker Power and then passes it to a student who is demonstrating a good

Listening Position and has raised his or her hand. After the speaker is finished, the teacher takes the object back and gives it to another student. Once the class masters this procedure, the speaker becomes responsible for choosing who gets Speaker Power next. This not only reduces outbursts and quick responses, but it forces students to pause before they speak and process what the previous person said. These are all important skills in the domains of listening and respecting others.

When it is one's turn to speak, SDM/SPS provides simple guidelines for communicating effectively. BEST is an acronym for Body posture, Eye contact, Say nice words, and Tone of voice. Those are the four aspects of speaking that students learn to attend to. BEST emphasizes that body language and tone of voice are as important as the choice of words. Of course, all of these skills apply as much (if not more) to teachers and other adults as they do to children.

Classrooms dedicated to integrating SEL and effective classroom management should have frequent class meetings or Share Circles (the SDM/SPS version of a class meeting) to discuss problems and continually build the classroom community. Share Circles are designated times to focus entirely on the social and emotional life of the classroom through discussions, group-building activities, SEL skill development, and group problem solving. They encourage supportive relationships throughout the classroom, set a positive tone for the classroom, help children to process any emotions that they bring to school, and give students an opportunity for input into the daily running of the classroom (Charney, 2002). Providing structured opportunities to share feelings, experiences, and interests makes the classroom the personal and supportive environment that underlies caring relationships. Some programs, notably Responsive Classroom, consider this to be a central, daily feature of effective classroom management (Charney, 2002).

Action 3: Set Firm and Fair Boundaries

Discipline is probably the first thing that comes to mind when someone mentions "classroom management." Unfortunately, many teachers equate discipline with classroom management, neglecting the numerous other components of effective management (many of which have been stressed in this chapter), which inevitably leads to disappointing results. For many, discipline implies a reaction to misbehavior. Throughout this chapter, we have emphasized that teachers generate management through specific actions directed toward creating a functional learning environment and preventing misbehavior. Behavior problems are minimized when students are engaged in learning, when they have developed social and emotional skills that enable them to pursue their needs and goals in prosocial ways, when the relationships in the classroom are supportive and caring, and when they feel a sense of autonomy and ownership over the class because they share responsibility for it. That being said, the presence of these conditions does not obviate the need for a clear boundary-setting structure. No matter how well designed and executed the proactive elements of the management plan, students will occasionally make mistakes in their behaviors, just as they do when learning academic skills. In an SEL-infused classroom, these mistakes in judgment highlight social skill deficits. Seen in that light, they do not call for retribution. Just like mistakes in solving math problems, they are opportunities for learning and growing—in other words, social-emotional skill-building for the next time.

Countless pages in books, magazines, and journals have been written on what constitutes effective discipline, and there is still considerable disagreement on its most basic features (see, e.g., Bear, 2005; Emmer & Aussiker, 1990; Evertson, Emmer, & Worsham, 2003; Freiberg, 1999a; Moles, 1990; Tauber, 1999; Wolfgang, 2001). It is beyond the scope of this chapter to review that literature in depth or make far-reaching conclusions about the research. This section will focus on the main elements of discipline that are compatible with SEL and enhance students' social and emotional growth.

Rules

Rules are necessary for any society or organization to function. Boundaries educate children about what is acceptable and what is not. Learning to act with self-control and respect for others is predicated on having clear rules that define responsible behavior in a particular environment. Therefore, clear rules are necessary for an SEL-oriented classroom.

Everyone agrees that class rules should be established early in the year, and most advocate that it be done on the first day of school. Brady, Forton, Porter, and Wood (2003) recommend that the creation of rules wait a few days, until the teacher has established a sense of order, predictability, and trust in the classroom. They contend that the basic elements of a caring community must be established before students can contribute meaningfully to rule making. Many experts, though not all, encourage teachers to create class rules "democratically" (e.g., Brady et al., 2003; Schaps & Solomon, 1990; Weinstein & Mignano, 2003). This means that, like in a democracy, rules are developed with the students rather than simply imposed on them. If they are truly a product of the whole class's effort, the students are far more likely to respect and show a commitment to the rules. The teacher must manage this process to ensure that all students feel they have contributed and that the final set of rules is reasonable, age-appropriate, and fair to the students and the teacher. Establishing democratic rules is a necessity for an SEL-infused classroom because is promotes two important SEL competencies: following the rules and norms of a group and learning how to self-govern, cooperate, and choose responsible actions in a democratic environment.

Establishing and enforcing rules are necessary but not sufficient. To ensure that students understand them and are able to follow them, rules, like SEL skills, must be discussed, taught, modeled, and practiced. "Respecting oneself and others," or some variation on the theme, is found in most classrooms. "Respect" is a very abstract—even confusing—concept, especially to young children. What does respect look like? What types of behaviors does respect imply? Discussing, teaching, modeling, and practicing respectful behavior enable students to learn how to follow the rule. Rules are rarely learned after one lesson or discussion. The more difficult rules require practice and repetition throughout the year or across years.

Procedures

Procedures and routines are a little different than rules. They tend to be narrower and more specific. Rather than dealing with general behavior standards, they focus on day-to-day classroom functioning. Some are derivatives of general rules. For example, a procedure for raising one's hand and getting called on before speaking shows respect for the teacher and other students and helps to develop listening skills and patience, among other things. But raising one's hand is not a valued skill, in and of itself, that one hopes students take into life. It is simply an arbitrarily chosen procedure that keeps the classroom orderly and functioning while promoting SEL skills. Another arbitrary sign for wanting to speak could have been chosen, but raising one's hand was picked because of its efficiency. Well-oiled procedures and routines are vital tools in effectively running a classroom. Based on the SEL model, procedures should be clear and consistent, efficient, well-practiced, and instituted proactively beginning on the first day of school. Establishing procedures can save enormous amounts of time and effort in the long run. Furthermore, solid routines can prevent distractions and student misbehavior because students know what to expect and what is expected of them (Weinstein & Mignano, 2003).

Procedures may be constructed somewhat arbitrarily, but they can have a major impact on the SEL goals of the classroom. For example, Share Circles are only effective if each student has an opportunity to share and perceives that others are paying attention when he or she speaks. That is why the procedure Speaker Power is used to manage the discussion, ensuring that everyone knows when to listen and has an opportunity to speak without interruption.

Responses and Feedback

Though classroom management is primarily a proactive and preventive process, there will always be a need to respond and give feedback about student behavior—both positive and negative. Even though it is inherently a reactive task, the system of responses to problem behavior is such an important component of classroom management—it can either "make or break" the entire system—that it should be planned out in advance.

Marshall and Weisner (2004) elegantly present a theory of discipline that enhances rather than impedes SEL development. They begin by stating a similar goal for classroom management as that proposed by this chapter: to promote responsible behavior guided by internal motivation. They propose a hierarchy of social development modeled on Maslow's (1970) hierarchy of needs and Kohlberg's (1984) stages of moral development. From lowest to highest, the levels of their hierarchy are:

A—Anarchy
B—Bossing/Bullying
C—Cooperation/Conformity
D—Democracy

Levels A and B lead to socially destructive behaviors that are never acceptable. Level C is acceptable but has some drawbacks. Most teachers and administrators are satisfied when students' actions reflect compliance. In fact, it is often impossible to discern from a prosocial behavior itself whether the motivation is cooperation with authority or self-directed responsibility that is the cornerstone of self-rule (i.e., democracy). For example, students may clean up the room at the end of an art lesson because it is the responsible thing to do to maintain a healthy, orderly environment or because the teacher will punish them if they don't. In both cases, the behavior is good, but the SEL implications are quite different.

McCaslin and Good (1998) point out three drawbacks of managing for compliance. First, compliance depends on constant monitoring; there is little maintenance over time. Students learn to value the tools of compliance, not the content of the curriculum or responsible behavior. Second, if compliance is the only means of management, then prosocial behavior is unlikely to generalize to different settings. Third, complex instructional modalities, such as cooperative learning, are very difficult to manage through compliance alone. Students need to self-regulate to make cooperative learning work. Furthermore, a focus on external recognition and regulation can encourage convergent thinking, completing the task, and getting it "right" at the expense of divergent thinking, creativity, and deep understanding. The mediocre effort necessary to obtain positive feedback or avoid negative feedback will likely lead to mediocre learning (see chapter 24 in this volume). Raising students' motivation to level D is necessary for the constructivist, problem-solving curriculum. "We believe that the intended modern school curriculum, which is designed to produce self-motivated active learners, is seriously undermined by classroom management policies that encourage, if not demand, simple obedience" (McCaslin & Good, 1992, p. 4). Management systems should go beyond demanding compliance and strive to foster the skills necessary for democratic values and personal responsibility.

Based on their hierarchy of social development, Marshall and Weisner (2004) use contemporary business management theory to advocate a style of classroom management based on trust and collaboration, rather than coercion and control. Like SEL, they approach misbehavior in the same mode as an academic mistake: as a learning opportunity. When students make mistakes in math problems, (most) teachers do not yell at them or belittle them. They use it as an opportunity to teach a skill that the student has not yet mastered. When viewed through this lens, the teacher is less likely to take the mistaken behavior personally and better able to devise a response that helps the child to fix the problem and act differently in the future.

The perspective just presented is supported, for the most part, by Bear's (1998) detailed review of empirical research on classroom discipline. Bear (1998, 2005) argues for a two-part goal of discipline. In the short term, the goal is managing the class and controlling problems. The long-term goal is developing students' self-discipline. This, he says, is the essence of the authoritative parenting style (Baumrind, 1966), which is widely regarded as the most effective and is most compatible with SEL. Based on this framework, Bear (1998) divides the classroom management research into three basic elements, each of which is necessary: (1) Teachers should focus on prevention through the creation of a positive classroom climate and effective day-to-day management, (2) operant learning strategies are used for short-term problems, and (3) social problem solving is used to promote the long-term goal self-discipline. Like Marshall and Weisner (2004), Bear defines self-discipline as the internalization of democratic ideals. Because it is internally motivated, it is only evident when external regulators are not present. That is why one must move beyond operant strategies to foster self-discipline.

Rewards and Punishments. The most contentious aspect of Bear's (1998) model, indeed the most contentious issue in classroom management, is the use of operant learning strategies (step 2), such as rewards and punishments, to control discipline problems. Short-term evaluations of operant strategies often show that they are effective at reducing or increasing the frequency of target behaviors, so Bear argues that judicious use of operant learning is necessary in the classroom. However, there are significant limitations and drawbacks of operant learning strategies, particularly when viewed through the lens of SEL. Reeve (chapter 24 in this volume) reviews the costs and benefits of using rewards in the classroom. Though extrinsic rewards often work in the immediate context, Reeve describes three "hidden costs" (Condry & Chambers, 1978; Lepper & Greene, 1978). Rewards can (a) reduce intrinsic motivation for the target behavior or activity, (b) interfere with the quality of learning, and (c) undermine students' ability to autonomously self-regulate. All of these are, by definition, damaging to a student's academic, social, and emotional development, and they could lead to poorer behavior in the future.

The three costs of rewards apply to punishment, only more so. In addition, punishment can damage the teacher-child relationship that is so important to creating the conditions for academic, social, and emotional learning. Furthermore, the way that punishment is meted out in most schools is ineffective. In essence, punishment is a stimulus (generally an aversive one) that reduces the target behavior when it is introduced. If common school "punishments" worked, young people would be more likely to comply after they were punished. Yet, in most schools, it seems that the same students are sent repeatedly to the office or detention. This means that these so-called punishments do not meet the scientific definition, and they certainly do not fulfill the premise of SEL-based classroom management: to promote academic, social, and emotional learning over the long term through the development of self-control and self-discipline.

Positive Recognition and Feedback. Despite these limitations to many types of rewards and punishments, qualitative and meaningful feedback are absolutely necessary to developing academic, social, and emotional skills. A few SEL-oriented guidelines should be followed. First, verbal praise has been found to both increase and decrease intrinsic motivation, depending on how and in what context it was delivered (see Deci, Koestner, & Ryan, 1999). Therefore, it is best to use praise judiciously or limit its use in the same way as tangible rewards. Praise should be unexpected and performance-contingent. This requires that praise is only given meaningfully—for real effort and good work—rather than for just completing a task. It also means that different levels of performance should not be praised equally. Substantial praise should be used sparingly, reserved for when it is truly deserved. Too often, students begin to expect praise for the completion of tasks irrespective of quality or effort, which can lead to reductions in intrinsic motivation, self-regulation, and learning (Deci et al., 1999). Second, feedback should take the form of self-evaluation, whenever possible. This can be done by non-judgmentally pointing out specific aspects of the student's work and teaching the student to self-assess in a productive, realistic way. Being specific is the third guideline to positive feedback; specificity conveys the teacher's interest in the child's work and is far more informative than general feedback. Fourth, Dweck and her colleagues' research on the effects of rewards on achievement motivation suggests that praise should be effort- rather than trait-oriented. "You did well on this test—you're so smart," an example of trait praise, can lead to a child's feeling less smart and less motivated after a subsequent failure. However, praising effort (e.g., "You worked really hard on this") can help to increase persistence and avoid discouragement when failure inevitably occurs (Mueller & Dweck, 1998). Finally, praise should be respectful, not patronizing, and take the child's point of view rather than just the teacher's.

Punishment and Natural and Logical Consequences. No matter how efficient the teacher's prevention efforts, students will test the limits of the rules, and responses will be needed to correct the behavior, control the situation, and teach positive and responsible alternatives. Mistaken behaviors are not only inevitable, they are necessary for social and emotional growth because people often learn best from their mistakes. As described above, many common forms of "punishment" can be ineffective in the short term and, even if they are effective, reduce intrinsic motivation, learning, and autonomous self-regulation. Responses to misbehavior should help to teach the important SEL skills of understanding and anticipating the consequences of one's actions, self-regulating, and learning to problem solve more effectively in the future.

The following guidelines help link a "disciplinary" action with SEL:

1. The response should separate the deed from the doer. The teacher should make clear that the problem is the behavior, not the child.
2. Teachers should teach children they have the power to choose their actions and that they can learn to avoid losing control.
3. Responses should encourage reflection, self-evaluation, and problem-solving. Lectures and teacher-centered explaining have the same limited effectiveness for SEL skill-building as they do for academic skill development. Students are more likely to "own" the problem if they are asked rather than told what the problem is and given an opportunity to figure out how to fix it.
4. Responses to a mistaken behavior should involve the child learning the rationale for and practicing prosocial alternatives that can be reasonably used in similar future situations. This basic SEL technique fosters feelings of responsibility for correcting and preventing the problem.

Natural and logical consequences are so called because their goal is to teach children to understand, anticipate, and make decisions based on the consequences of their actions in the real world (Brady et al., 2003; Dreikurs & Loren, 1968; Nelsen, Lynn, & Glenn, 2000). Natural consequences occur "naturally," without any intervention from the outside. For example, if a child plays too roughly with a particular toy and it breaks, then the consequence is that the child's toy is now ruined. There is no need for an external, punitive intervention—the child begins to learn from the direct consequences of his or her mistakes, which is the goal of this system. Logical consequences are needed when the misbehavior substantially affects others or when the potential natural consequence is too severe. Logical consequences are a subset of punishments, in the sense that they are imposed stimuli used to reduce a target behavior. However, they have three basic features that are meant to maximize their informational value while minimizing the control aspect, thereby supporting the child's need for autonomy; when autonomy is maintained, the child is more likely to focus on the information aspect of the feedback. Logical consequences must be related, reasonable, and respectful. Being *related* means that they must be logically related to the misbehavior. For example, if a student writes on his or her desk, a related consequence would be for the student to clean the desk, not for the student to go to detention. *Reasonable* means that the severity of the consequence must be mild. If a kindergartener knocks down another student's block tower, it is unreasonable to have the student sit quietly in his or her chair for 45 minutes while the rest of the class is playing. Instead, the student might help rebuild the tower. Finally, consequences must be delivered *respectfully*. Despite the fact that the teacher probably wants to display his or her anger, consequences are most effective when delivered calmly and matter-of-factly (see Brady et al., 2003; Dreikurs & Loren, 1968; Nelsen et al., 2000).

Natural and logical consequences are solidly aligned with SEL theory. SEL focuses a great deal on students' decision making, problem solving, and conflict resolution processes. A critical reflection point of these processes is the anticipation of outcomes. Likely influenced by advances in the ubiquity and realness of digital media (Postman, 1995), children's ability to discern the realistic consequences of their actions is a growing problem for those who care about their socialization. Early research in SDM/SPS, for example, showed that problem behaviors were most likely to occur when children anticipated positive consequences from negative actions (Leonard & Elias, 1993). The simplest example: "He was bothering me, so I hit him to make him stop." Indeed, that stoppage is a natural consequence, but it is not the only one, and students need guidance to help them understand how the world around them works so that their view of consequences is realistic and takes into account long- and short-term outcomes both for themselves and for others.

Indeed, the term *consequences* has become very popular in discipline circles, especially in schools, partially because of the natural and logical concept and partially because it sounds less harsh or cruel than *punishment*. However, calling something a consequence does not make it so, just as calling something a punishment may not be accurate. From an SEL point of view, the potential for consequences to foster empathy and perspective-taking better than other forms of punishment is critical. Natural and logical consequences must increase compliance in the short term (like punishments), as well as promote long-term maintenance and generalization to situations in which the child is not being monitored. Only carefully and appropriately administered natural and logical consequences promote intrinsic motivation, self-control, and personal responsibility. Essential for these techniques to have their desired positive effect is that they are rooted in a caring relationship between teachers and students. The most direct implication of this insight is that students may perceive the same technique delivered in the same way differently if administered prior to a caring relationship being established (i.e., too early in the school year).

One type of logical consequence that helps to build the SEL skills of empathy and perspective-taking is what Brady et al. (2003) call Apology of Action. An apology of action is an active way to fix a problem the child has caused interpersonally. It includes but goes beyond a verbal apology. The child is expected at least to repair the damage done (or its equivalent), which is the type of consequence that adults face all the time at work and at home. Optimally, the child suggests a way to fix the problem, which makes a far greater impression than a grudging apology and takes the teacher out of the position of being the "enforcer."

SEL-Derived Skills for Preventing and Correcting Misbehavior

Problem Solving and Problem Diaries. Problem-solving paradigms, such as FIG TESPN (described earlier), can be enormously useful in responding to behavior mistakes. They can be used to work collaboratively with a child to fix problems, come up with alternative strategies for challenging situations, and devise appropriate logical consequences. FIG TESPN teaches the child that he or she has the power to choose different actions and encourages the child to take ownership for the mistake and its outcomes. With copious problem-solving practice, students may begin to envision the likely consequences of their actions before they take them and feel responsible for acting constructively in new situations.

When a child gets into "trouble" or has a conflict with a peer, problem solving should be used, regardless of whether a punishment strategy is also called for. In SDM/SPS, that means filling out a Problem Diary with a teacher, guidance counselor, or administrator. Problem Diaries follow the FIG TESPN problem-solving heuristic, focusing primarily on the first four steps: Feelings, Identify the problem, Goal, and Think of possible solutions. Solutions often include other SDM/SPS skills, such as using BEST or Keep Calm (described later). As students accumulate skills, they become part of their social-emotional tool belts. Like a skilled carpenter, students learn when and how to use each tool. Using SEL skills in the face of real-life problems is the only way for students to truly learn them, and it is vital to the discipline process, as well. This is a major area of synergy between SEL and classroom management.

Self-Regulation. A component skill of self-control and self-discipline is self-regulation. For students to be able to control their actions over the long term, they must be able to monitor and regulate their emotions and behaviors independently. There are a number of techniques that can be helpful in teaching students to accomplish this notoriously difficult skill. Emotional self-regulation involves two steps: self-monitoring and emotion management. Self-monitoring emotions requires that students are able to identify the names of emotions they are feeling based on their bodily sensations and cognitions. Emotion words can be taught using a number of games, and the student's unique bodily sensations should be discussed to help the student identify feelings as they are beginning to take hold. Once students are able to identify and self-monitor their emotions, they need practical strategies to be able to manage them and use them constructively.

Feelings Fingerprints. One specific example of how these techniques are operationalized within SEL is the SDM/SPS Program's Feelings Fingerprints procedure. What follows is how we present the technique to teachers to, in turn, present to their students. For children to self-monitor, they need to understand that their bodies send them signals when they are about to lose control. SDM/SPS calls these signals of anger or stress Feelings Fingerprints. (At the secondary level, we use the term, Stress Signature, and make the appropriate adjustments in the analogy.) Why? Like fingerprints, everyone has a unique set. Some people get headaches, a nervous stomach, a stiff neck, or sweaty palms. Others get a dry mouth, a quick heartbeat, clenched fists, a flushed face, or itchy skin. Most have more than one such signal. When teachers find themselves in a stressful or difficult choice situation, they can verbalize how they are feeling and what their Feelings Fingerprints are. This bridges naturally into asking students, "You just heard how my body sends me a headache behind my left eye and a red face when I am upset and under stress. How do YOUR bodies let YOU know when you are upset?"

When learning Feelings Fingerprints, students take turns generating examples of situations during which they felt upset, and what their Feelings Fingerprints were. Those situations are labeled "trigger situations." They learn that being aware of their Feelings Fingerprints and anticipating trigger situations serve as warning systems that they are facing a tough situation and need to use self-control to keep calm. Teachers may use this opportunity to discuss with students what it means to use self-control. They ask students to share different times and situations in which they have to use self-control. Then, the teachers ask for strategies for maintaining self-control, such as Keep Calm (see the following), and help students make proactive plans to disengage from problem situations.

Keep Calm. SDM/SPS relies on Keep Calm, which was derived from Lamaze childbirth preparation procedures, to reduce students' anxiety, anger, and frustration. Keep Calm is simple and short, and it helps students to maintain self-control by reducing physiological arousal. Keep Calm begins with identifying the first physical signs of anger. The person says to him or herself: "Stop. Keep calm." Then, the person takes a number of slow breaths, counting to five while breathing in, two while holding one's breath, and five while breathing out. This "5-2-5" technique is simple to remember, prompt, and apply, and it reduces arousal so that the person can respond in a productive way.

Behavioral self-regulation involves self-monitoring, self-evaluation, and self-instruction. Students who are competent at controlling their behavior, especially when they are not in an external reinforcement environment, do these tasks in their heads. Students who have more trouble exerting self-control and knowing how to act appropriately may need help working on these component skills. Self-monitoring worksheets make the skill visual and physically active rather than abstract and cognitive. The teacher can then work with the child to improve the accuracy of the self-monitoring and improve self-evaluation and self-instruction. Problem solving is very useful in this process, which empowers the child to learn, step by step, how to develop self-control (Weinstein & Mignano, 2003).

Action 4: Share Responsibility with Students

The final recommended action for bringing together SEL and effective classroom management is sharing responsibility with students. If we want children to learn responsibility, we have to give them as many opportunities as possible to experiment with it and grow comfortable, confident, and skilled at taking it. Sharing responsibility with students also increases their commitment to the classroom, increases their motivation and prosocial behavior, and reduces behavior mistakes that result from frustration and feelings of powerlessness. Empowering students is the best way to encourage them to take responsibility and contribute—rather than detract and destroy.

This chapter has already mentioned a number of ways in which responsibility can be shared with students, beginning with developing democratic classroom rules. Students can contribute to the physical environment of the classroom with their artwork and through representations of their individuality. Students also benefit from and respond to opportunities for input in day-to-day classroom decision making. The decisions students participate in can vary from choosing a signal for quiet to requesting a friend to sit with when the class's seating arrangement changes. Even giving students' input into small choices, such as the order of the day's schedule, can increase motivation. Teachers should not and need not give over all classroom governance to the students. The teacher is far more aware of all of the issues that go into decisions and is ultimately responsible for the productivity of the class. However, giving students choices—even between two acceptable options—makes the class more manageable and productive and increases students' social-emotional competencies, such as social responsibility and group decision making (Elias et al., 1997; Weinstein & Mignano, 2003).

One of the most important applications of these concepts is in establishing rules for cooperative learning groups. Cooperative learning is a specific SEL technique, and its successful use requires students to be prepared for and trained in the skills they are expected to use when they come together to work cooperatively in groups. Several key questions are posed by teachers, for which groups must come up with reasonable and age-appropriate answers: How will we make sure that everyone in the group has an equal chance to participate? How will we show that we have listened to what each person in the group has said? How will we handle it when someone in the group is angry, upset, or out of control? How will we handle it when someone in the group is not being fair to or respectful of someone else in the group? The answer to these questions (which can include "ask the teacher for help," especially among younger students) constitutes a set of group rules that becomes an informal social contract for democratically derived shared responsibility. Students should recognize that the nature of their work group is such that it cannot be considered a success if one or two children take over a task and create an "A" project by excluding others.

In addition to group input into decisions, it is important to give individuals choices, particularly about their work. For example, teachers can allow students to choose books for independent reading and decide what type of project they want to create when they are done. If students are allowed to choose between a number of teacher-approved options to communicate their learning, such as a website, an advertisement, a newspaper, a Dr. Seuss-style poem, or a PowerPoint presentation, they are more likely to care about, enjoy, and excel at the assignment because it fulfills their need for autonomy. And, once again, the opportunity to choose improves the students' sense of personal responsibility and confidence in making decisions and following through on them (Freiberg, 1999b; Weinstein & Mignano, 2003).

When students do active service in the classroom, the school, and the community, they develop a sense of contribution and responsibility. Many classrooms have rotating job charts that give each student a new classroom responsibility each week. Though the tasks can be menial or miniscule—such as handing out assignments or feeding the hamster—students often take them very seriously and learn that contributing is essential to a functional community and a privilege to take part in. In addition, it increases the students' sense of "ownership" of the classroom, which, in turn, increases their feelings of responsibility for its functioning and supportive atmosphere. School-wide service serves a similar function.

Service-learning is a well-developed model for linking meaningful service and advocacy in the school or community to the intellectual, social, and emotional learning goals of the classroom. High-quality service learning goes well beyond community service. It is integrated with academics synergistically, it is sustained over time, it matches genuine community needs to students' academic and SEL goals and skills, and it requires time for structured student reflection and discussion about the service and its implications (Fredericks, 2003). This approach is the gold standard in educational practice for teaching students to take responsibility for themselves and their communities and to build their empathic awareness of diverse others.

CONCLUSION

Based on a brief review of the literature on the effectiveness of SEL, we developed four basic action steps to integrate SEL with classroom management, with the goal of creating a seamless system that promotes academic, social, and emotional learning. These steps—teaching social-emotional skills, building caring relationships, setting firm and fair boundaries, and sharing responsibility with students—are all crucial in making a classroom organization and management system positive, preventive, and effective in all meanings of the word. Modifications and additions to these guidelines are needed when implementing them, but educators should attempt to be as inclusive as possible to protect the integrity of the system.

The ideal classroom manager creatively incorporates SEL concepts into every facet of a well-functioning classroom because SEL and effective classroom management are two sides of the same coin. In both fields, self-control and responsibility are the ultimate goals. Integrating proven practices from both creates the optimal conditions for the attainment of those goals based on current theoretical and empirical knowledge. It is based on the strategy of making classrooms into caring and functional environments in the short term, while equipping students to become responsible, knowledgeable, productive, empathetic, and active citizens throughout their lives.

The challenges of attaining these goals cannot not fall on any one teacher. Only by coordinated and continuous application of the principles outlined herein can the desired impact on students occur. Yet, nearly two millennia ago, a Jewish educator recognized that each teacher must do his or her part, with no alibis or excuses: "You are not responsible for completing the work, nor are you free to give up on it" (Pirke Avot 2:21). No teacher can be fully responsible for the growth—academic or otherwise—of his or her students. Students are influenced by so many other factors and spend only a few months in each classroom before moving on. Nevertheless, it is each teacher's responsibility to provide students with as many useful tools as possible to enable them to build their own futures. And it is the responsibility of all educators to see that all students pass through organized, caring, and skill-enhancing classrooms and school environments so that they can become academically, socially, and emotionally competent adults.

APPENDIX A

CASEL's Essential SEL Skills and Competencies (adapted from Elias, 2003)

Know Yourself and Others

- Identify feelings—Recognize and label's feelings in oneself and others.
- Be responsible—Understand and act upon one's obligation to engage in ethical, safe, and legal behaviors.
- Recognize strengths—Identify and cultivate one's positive qualities.

Make Responsible Decisions

- Manage emotions—Regulate feelings so that they aid rather than impede the handling of situations.
- Understand situations—Accurately understand the circumstances one is in.
- Set goals and plans—Establish and work toward the achievement of specific short- and long-term outcomes.
- Solve problems creatively—Engage in a creative, disciplined process of exploring alternative possibilities that lead to responsible, goal-directed action, including overcoming obstacles to plans.

Care for Others

- Show empathy—Identify and understand the thoughts and feelings of others.
- Respect others—Act on the belief that others deserve to be treated with kindness and compassion as part of our shared humanity.
- Appreciate diversity—Understand that individual and group differences complement one another and add strength and adaptability to the world around us.

Know How to Act

- Communicate effectively—Use verbal and nonverbal skills to express oneself and promote effective exchanges with others.
- Build relationships—Establish and maintain healthy and rewarding connections with individuals and groups.
- Negotiate fairly—Strive to achieve mutually satisfactory resolutions to conflict by addressing the needs of all concerned.

- Refuse provocations—Convey and follow through effectively with one's decision not to engage in unwanted, unsafe, and unethical behavior.
- Seek help—Identify one's need for help and access appropriate assistance and support in pursuit of needs and goals.
- Act ethically—Guide decisions and actions by a set of principles or standards derived from recognized legal/professional codes or moral or faith-based systems of conduct.

APPENDIX B

Sample Lesson Plan for Third Grade Language Arts: An Example of Integrating Academics and Social-Emotional Skill Building (adapted from Cartledge & Milburn, 1995)

Objectives

- Students will read and analyze literature through the lens of social and emotional skills.
- Students will become familiar with the concept of body language and its importance in social interactions.
- Students will recognize specific examples of emotional body language.
- Students will practice demonstrating emotions through body language.

Materials

- *Buffalo before breakfast* by Mary Pope Osborne (1999). (This lesson can be adapted for any piece of children's literature that has an example of reading body language.)

Motivation
As part of a regular reading/language arts lesson, the teacher begins by reading a passage from *Buffalo before breakfast* by Mary Pope Osborne (1999) in which the protagonists, Jack and Annie, first meet the Lakota people. In the passage, Jack and Annie report that even though the Lakota people are not saying anything, they do not appear to be angry.

Procedure

1. Providing a rationale
   a. Using this passage as a jumping off point, the teacher poses the following questions:
      How do the characters know the Lakota people are not angry?
      Can you show me what the Lakota people might have looked like if they were angry?
      What do you look like when you are angry?
      [Students respond by saying that there are various signs of anger in the face, arms, and shoulders of the person.]
   b. The teacher introduces the term "body language" and encourages students to make text-to-self connections:
      Why is reading body language helpful?
      When Jack and Annie read body language, how does that help them?
      Can you give me examples of times when reading body language has helped you?
2. Breaking down the skill into its components
   The teacher asks students to suggest different parts of the body that display anger and writes the ideas on the board:
   Which parts of your face or body change when you are angry? [e.g., clenched teeth, a furrowed brow, raised shoulders.]

3. Modeling
   As they suggest angry body signs, students model the actions for their peers. The teacher also asks students to model other emotions so that their peers can guess what they are "feeling." With each example of a new emotion, the teacher uses the student model to help the class break down the body language into its components.
4. Skill performance and feedback: Guess My Emotion game
   a. The teacher divides the students into groups and asks them to write down components of body language for fear and happy. They share these lists with their groups and then practice acting out these emotions for the other members of their group.
   b. Each group is assigned an emotion to present to the class. The class practices reading body language by guessing the other groups' emotions.

Feedback and Assessment

- The teacher circulates during groupwork to monitor progress and understanding.
- With each group presentation, the teacher gives specific feedback on the display of the emotion and on the class's interpretation, as well as encouraging students to give appropriate and constructive feedback to each other.

Follow-up

- The teacher assigns students to practice reading their siblings' and friends' body language after school and report back the next day.
- The teacher will reinforce the skill of reading social and emotional cues in another two reading lessons as soon as is feasible, as well as in future lessons involving literature and other media.
- The teacher will remind students about this skill when it comes up in real-world social interactions in the classroom and throughout the school.

For a skill as complex as recognizing others' emotions through body language to be fully integrated into the students' social skill repertoire, multiple lessons along these lines would be necessary, as well as cuing and practice in real-world situations.

ACKNOWLEDGMENT

The authors thank George Bear, University of Delaware, for his helpful review of this chapter.

REFERENCES

Achenbach, T., & Edelbrock, C. (1987). *Manual for the Youth Self-Report and Profile*. Burlington: University of Vermont Department of Psychiatry.

Battistich, V. (1998, May). *The effects of classroom and school practices on students' character development*. Paper presented at the Character Education Assessment Forum, Bonner Center for Character Education and Citizenship, California State University, Fresno, CA.

Battistich, V. (1999, October). *Assessing implementation of the Child Development Project*. Paper presented at the meeting on Implementation Research in School-Based Models of Prevention and Promotion, Pennsylvania State University, University Park, PA.

Battistich, V. (2000, June). *The use of implementation data in assessing the effectiveness of the Child Development Project*. Paper presented at the meeting of the Society of Prevention Research, Montreal, QUE.

Battistich, V. (2001, April). Effects of an elementary school intervention on students' "connectedness" to school and social adjustment during middle school. In J. Brown (chair), *Resilience education: Theoretical, interactive and empirical applications*. Symposium conducted at the annual meeting for the American Educational Research Association, Seattle, WA.

Battistich, V., Solomon, D., & Watson, M. (1998, April). *Sense of community as a mediating factor in promoting children's social and ethical development*. Paper presented at the meeting of the American Educational Research Association, San Diego, CA.

Battistich, V., Solomon, D., Watson, M., Solomon, J., & Schaps, E. (1989). Effects of an elementary school program to enhance prosocial behavior on children's cognitive social problem-solving skills and strategies. *Journal of Applied Developmental Psychology, 10*, 147–169.

Battistich, V., Watson, M., Solomon, D., Schaps, E., & Solomon, J. (1991). The Child Development Project: A comprehensive program for the development of prosocial character. In W. M. Kurtines & J. L. Gewirtz (Eds.), *Handbook of moral behavior and development: Volume 3: Application* (pp. 1–34). Hillsdale, NJ: Lawrence Erlbaum Associates.

Baumrind, D. (1966). Effects of authoritative parental control on child behavior. *Child Development, 37*, 887–907.

Bear, G. G. (1998). School discipline in the United States: Preventing, correcting, and long-term social development. *School Psychology Review, 27*(1), 14–32.

Bear, G. G. (with Cavalier, A. R., & Manning, M. A.). (2005). *Developing self-discipline and preventing and correcting misbehavior*. Boston: Pearson/Allyn & Bacon.

Brady, K., Forton, M. B., Porter, D., & Wood, C. (2003). *Rules in school*. Greenfield, MA: Northeast Foundation for Children.

Brophy, J. (1999). Perspectives of classroom management: Yesterday, today, and tomorrow. In H. J. Freiberg (Ed.), *Beyond behaviorism: Changing the classroom management paradigm* (pp. 43–56). Boston: Allyn & Bacon.

Caprara, G. V., Barbaranelli, C., Pastorelli, C., Bandura, A., & Zimbardo, P. G. (2000). Prosocial foundations of children's academic achievement. *Psychological Science, 11*(4), 302–306.

Cartledge, G., & Milburn, J. F. (1995). *Teaching social skills to children and youth: Innovative approaches* (3rd ed.). Boston: Allyn & Bacon.

Charney, R. (2002). *Teaching children to care: Classroom management for ethical and academic growth, K–8*. Greenfield, MA: Northeast Foundation for Children.

Collaborative for Academic, Social, and Emotional Learning (CASEL). (2003). *Safe and sound: An educational leader's guide to evidence-based social and emotional learning (SEL) programs*. Chicago, IL: Author.

Comer, James P. (2003). Transforming the lives of children. In M. J. Elias, H. Arnold, & C. S. Hussey (Eds.), *EQ + IQ = best leadership practices for caring and successful schools* (pp. 11–22). Thousand Oaks, CA: Corwin Press.

Condry, J., & Chambers, J. (1978). Intrinsic motivation and the process of learning. In M. Lepper & D. Greene (Eds.), *The hidden costs of reward: New perspectives on the psychology of human motivation* (pp. 61–84). Hillsdale, NJ: Lawrence Erlbaum Associates.

Conduct Problems Prevention Research Group. (1999). Initial impact of the Fast Track prevention trial for conduct problems: 1: The high-risk sample. *Journal of Consulting and Clinical Psychology, 67*(5), 631–647.

Curwin, R., & Mendler, A. (1988). Packaged discipline programs: Let the buyer beware. *Educational Leadership, 46*(2), 68–71.

Deci, E. L., Koestner, R., & Ryan, R. M. (1999). A meta-analytic review of experiments examining the effects of extrinsic rewards on intrinsic motivation. *Psychological Bulletin, 125*, 627–668.

Dreikurs, R. (1968). *Psychology in the classroom: A manual for teachers*. New York: Harper & Row.

Dreikurs, R., & Loren, G. (1968). *Logical consequences*. New York: Meredith Press.

Elias, M. J. (2003). *Academic and social-emotional learning*. Brussels: International Academy of Education, UNESCO.

Elias, M. J. (2004). Strategies to infuse social and emotional learning into academics. In J. E. Zins, R. P. Weissberg, M. C. Wang, & H. J. Walberg (Eds.), *Building academic success on social and emotional learning: What does the research say?* (pp. 113–134). New York: Teachers College Press.

Elias, M. J., Gara, M. A., Schuyler, T. F., Branden-Muller, L. R., & Sayette, M. A. (1991). The promotion of social competence: Longitudinal study of a preventive school-based program. *American Journal of Orthopsychiatry, 61*(3), 409–417.

Elias, M. J., & Tobias, S. E. (1996). *Social decision making skills: A curriculum guide for the elementary grades*. Rockville, MD: Aspen.

Elias, M. J., Zins, J. E., Weissberg, R. P., Frey, K. S., Greenberg, M. T., Haynes, N. M. Kessler, R., Schweb-Stone, M. E., & Shiver, T. P (1997). *Promoting social and emotional learning: Guidelines for educators*. Alexandria, VA: Association for Supervision and Curriculum Development.

Emmer, E. T., & Aussiker, A. (1990). In O. C. Moles (Ed.), *Student discipline strategies: Research and practice* (pp. 129–165). Albany: State University of New York Press.

Evertson, C. M., Emmer, E. T., & Worsham, M. E. (2003). *Classroom management for elementary teachers* (6th ed.). Boston: Allyn & Bacon.

Fredericks, L. (2003). *Making the case for social and emotional learning and service-learning*. Denver, CO: Education Commission of the States.

Freiberg, H. J. (Ed.). (1999a). *Beyond behaviorism: Changing the classroom management paradigm*. Boston: Allyn & Bacon.

Freiberg, H. J. (1999b). Beyond behaviorism. In H. J. Freiberg (Ed.), *Beyond behaviorism: Changing the classroom management paradigm* (pp. 3–20). Boston: Allyn & Bacon.

Gardner, H. (1985). *Frames of mind*. New York: Basic Books.

Gardner, H. (1993). *Multiple intelligences: The theory in practice*. New York: Basic Books.

Glasser, W. (1992). *The quality school: Managing students without coercion* (2nd ed. expanded). New York: HarperCollins.

Gordon, T. (with Burch, N.). (1974). *TET: Teacher effectiveness training*. New York: P. H. Wyden.

Gordon, T. (with Burch, N.). (2003). *TET: Teacher effectiveness training* (1st rev. ed.). New York: Three Rivers Press.

Greenberg, M. T., Domitrovich, C., & Bumbarger, B. (2001, March 30). The prevention of mental disorders in school-aged children: Current state of the field. *Prevention & Treatment, 4*, Article 1. Retrieved January 15, 2004 from http://journals.apa.org/prevention/volume4/pre0040001a.html

Greenberg, M. T., Kusche, C. A., Cook, E. T., & Quamma, J. P. (1995). Promoting emotional competence in school aged children: The effects of the PATHS curriculum. *Development and Psychopathology, 7*, 117–136.

Hawkins, J. D., Catalano, R. F., Kosterman, R., Abbott, R., & Hill, K. G. (1999). Preventing adolescent health-risk behaviors by strengthening protection during childhood. *Archives of Pediatric and Adolescent Medicine, 153*, 226–234.

Knoff, H. M. (2003, November). Character education versus. social skills training: Comparing constructs vs. behavior. *National Association of School Psychologists Communique, 32*(3), 39–40.

Kohlberg, L. (1984). *The psychology of moral development*. San Francisco: Harper & Row.

Kohn, A. (1996). *Beyond discipline: From compliance to community*. Alexandria, VA: Association for Supervision and Curriculum Development.

Leonard, C., & Elias, M. J. (1993). Entry into middle school: Student factors predicting adaptation to an ecological transition. *Prevention in Human Services, 10*, 39–57.

Lepper, M., & Greene, D. (1978). Overjustification research and beyond: Toward a means-ends analysis of intrinsic and extrinsic motivation. In M. Lepper & D. Greene (Eds.), *The hidden costs of reward: New perspectives on the psychology of human motivation* (pp. 109–148). Hillsdale, NJ: Lawrence Erlbaum Associates.

Levine, M. (2002). *A mind at a time*. New York: Simon & Schuster.

Marshall, M., & Weisner, K. (2004, March). Using a discipline system to promote learning. *Phi Delta Kappan, 85*, 498–507.

Marzano, R. J., & Marzano, J. S. (2003, September). The key to classroom management. *Educational Leadership, 61*(1), 6–13.

Maslow, A. H. (1970). *Motivation and personality* (2nd ed.). New York: Harper & Row.

Mayer, J. D., & Salovey, P. (1997). What is emotional intelligence? In P. Salovey & D. Sluyter (Eds.), *Emotional development and emotional intelligence: Educational implications* (pp. 3–31). New York: Basic Books.

McCarthy, B. (1987). *The 4MAT system: Teaching to learning styles with right/left mode techniques*. Barrington, IL: Excel.

McCaslin, M., & Good, T. (1992). Compliant cognition: The misalliance of management and instructional goals in current school reform. *Educational Researcher, 21*, 4–17.

McCaslin, M., & Good, T. (1998). Moving beyond management as sheer compliance: Helping students to develop goal coordination strategies. *Educational Horizons, 76*, 169–176.

Mitchell, K., Elias, M. J., Labouvie, E., & Haynes, N. (2004). *Social competence and social support in third grade, minority, low-income, urban school children*. Manuscript submitted for publication.

Moles, O. C. (1990). General introduction. In O. C. Moles (Ed.), *Student discipline strategies: Research and practice* (pp. 1–11). Albany: State University of New York Press.

Mueller, C. M. & Dweck, C. S. (1998). Intelligence praise can undermine motivation and performance. *Journal of Personality and Social Psychology, 75*, 33–52.

Nelsen, J., Lynn, L., & Glenn, H. S. (2000). *Positive discipline in the classroom: Developing mutual respect, cooperation, and responsibility in your classroom* (rev. 3rd ed.). Roseville, CA: Prima Publishing.

Noddings, N. (2003). *Happiness and education*. Cambridge: Cambridge University Press.

Osborne, M. P. (1999). *Buffalo before breakfast*. New York: Random House.

Osterman, K. F. (2000). Students' need for belonging in the school community. *Review of Educational Research, 70*(3), 323–367.

Pianta, R. C. (1999). *Enhancing relationships between children and teachers*. Washington, DC: American Psychological Association.

Pianta, R. C., & Stuhlman, M. W. (2004). Teacher-child relationships and children's success in the first years of school. *School Psychology Review, 33*, 444–458.

Postman, N. (1995). *The end of education.* New York: Vintage.

Saarni, C. (2000). Emotional competence: A developmental perspective. In R. Bar-On & J. D. A. Parker (Eds.), *The handbook of emotional intelligence: Theory, development, assessment, and application at home, school, and in the workplace* (pp. 68–91). San Francisco: Jossey-Bass.

Salovey, P., & Sluyter, D. (Eds.). (1997). *Emotional development and emotional intelligence: Educational implications.* New York: Basic Books.

Sarason, S. B. (1974). *The psychological sense of community: Prospects for a community psychology.* San Francisco: Jossey-Bass.

Sarason, S. B. (1993). American psychology, and the needs for transcendence and community. *American Journal of Community Psychology, 21*, 185–202.

Schaps, E. (2003, March). Creating a school community. *Educational Leadership, 60*(6), 31–33.

Schaps, E., & Solomon, D. (1990, November). Schools and classrooms as caring communities. *Educational Leadership, 48*(3), 38–42.

Shure, M. B., & Glaser, A. (2001). I Can Problem Solve (ICPS): A cognitive approach to the prevention of early high-risk behaviors. In J. Cohen (Ed.), *Caring classrooms / intelligent schools: The social emotional education of young children* (pp. 122–139). New York: Teachers College Press.

Solomon, D, Battistich, V., Watson, M., Schaps, E., & Lewis C. (2000). A six-district study of educational change: Direct and mediated effects of the Child Development Project. *Social Psychology of Education, 4*, 3–51.

Tauber, R. T. (1999). *Classroom management: Sound theory and effective practice* (3rd ed.). Westport, CT: Bergin & Garvey.

Tomlinson, C. A. (1999). *The differentiated classroom: Responding to the needs of all learners.* Alexandria, VA: Association of Supervision and Curriculum Development.

Weinstein, C. S. (1999). Reflections on best practices and promising programs: Beyond assertive classroom discipline. In H. J. Freiberg (Ed.), *Beyond behaviorism: Changing the classroom management paradigm* (pp. 147–163). Boston: Allyn & Bacon.

Weinstein, C. S., & Mignano, Jr., A. J. (2003). *Elementary classroom management: Lessons from research and practice* (3rd ed.). Boston: McGraw-Hill.

Wentzel, K. R. (1993). Does being good make the grade? Social behavior and academic competence in middle school. *Journal of Educational Psychology, 85*, 357–364.

Wolfgang, C. H. (2001). *Solving discipline and classroom management problems: Methods and models for today's teachers* (5th ed.). New York: John Wiley.

13

Connections Between Classroom Management and Culturally Responsive Teaching

Geneva Gay
University of Washington

INTRODUCTION

This discussion is guided by three major premises. First, classroom management is more comprehensive than controlling student misbehavior and administering discipline. It involves planning, facilitating, and monitoring experiences that are conducive to high levels of learning for a wide variety of students. It also entails creating and sustaining classroom environments that are personally comfortable, racially and ethnically inclusive, and intellectually stimulating. Many scholars of classroom management support these ideas. For example, Marzano, Marzano, and Pickering (2003), Burden (1995), Charles (1996), Emmer, Evertson, and Worsham (2000), and Jones and Jones (2004) include in their characterizations of classroom management organizing physical spaces, establishing relationships and facilitating interactions, planning and conducting instruction, maintaining order, motivating students, maximizing on-task learning, and disciplining inappropriate behavior.

The second premise is that there is an interactive relationship between instructional effectiveness and classroom management. The extent to which successful teaching and learning occur, the disciplinary dimensions of classroom management diminish. However, other aspects of management increase in magnitude and significance, in that teachers are continually challenged to be imaginative and provocative in planning and implementing learning opportunities for students. This is necessary to minimize students becoming disinterested, distracted, and disengaged, which can provoke off-tasks behaviors and misconduct.

The third premise of this discussion is that much of the current high levels of racial disproportionality in school discipline is a reflection of teachers not understanding and incorporating the cultural values, orientations, and experiences of African, Latino, Asian, and Native Americans into curriculum and instruction. Multicultural curriculum content and teaching techniques make it easier for teachers to maintain classroom environments that are conducive to learning, and build positive relationships with ethnically, racially, socially, and linguistically diverse students. Therefore, culturally responsive teaching is imperative to the effective classroom management of students of color. This premise is analogous to the assertions made by

Haberman (1991) that, "For genuinely effective urban teachers, discipline and control are primarily a *consequence* of their teaching and not a *prerequisite* condition for learning. Also, classroom control is "completely interrelated with the learning activity at hand" (p. 291).

Conceptions of comprehensive classroom management are presented first to set a context for subsequent discussions. They are followed by a summary of discipline trends among students of color. The intent of this presentation is not to perpetuate the misconception that discipline and classroom management are synonymous, but to extrapolate embedded messages that have implications for making connections to culturally responsive teaching. Next, some Reasons for racial disproportionality in discipline are discussed. They contend that the underlying causes are located in cultural conflicts, misunderstandings, and inconsistencies between the behavioral norms of schools and the cultural socialization of ethnically diverse students. The chapter ends with an explanation of what research says about the effects of culturally responsive teaching and implications derived from them for better managing diverse student populations. These descriptions synthesize ideas derived from the work of scholars who are exploring culturally responsive teaching for African, Asian/Pacific Islander, Latino, and Native Americans.

Two key points need to be mentioned from the outset about the information presented in the subsequent discussions. First, there is an imbalance in the representation of ethnic groups because theoretical conceptualizations and research findings about their cultural orientations, and their participation in classroom management and discipline dilemmas are not evenly distributed among them. African Americans (especially males) are treated far more extensively than other groups, and Asian Americans the least so. The available data about within-group differences also are not evenly distributed. Females are not studied as extensively as males, academically successful students as much as underachieving ones, suburban settings far less than urban schools, and younger students in elementary grades less than older ones in middle and senior high schools.

Second, the information about the characteristics and intersections of ethnic and cultural differences, and classroom management presented are based on group trends among students and teachers. It is a given that there are individual exceptions to everything discussed even though they are not noted explicitly in the narrative text. All African-American students are not overrepresented (or even involved) in disciplinary referrals. Nor is every classroom teacher uncaring, hypercontrolling, and culturally insensitive toward ethnically diverse students. However, these individual variances do not invalidate the existence of some troublesome patterns of behavior in classroom management and instruction that continue to jeopardize the chances of large numbers of students of color receiving the highest quality learning opportunities possible. It is the educational conditions of these vast numbers that this discussion is intended to positively affect.

PERCEPTIONS OF CLASSROOM MANAGEMENT COMPATIBLE WITH CULTURALLY RESPONSIVE TEACHING

According to Jones and Jones (2004), classroom management is a comprehensive endeavor. It encompasses the philosophical beliefs of teachers; understanding psychological, social, and academic needs of students; creating positive student-teacher, student-student, and teacher-parent relationships; increasing student motivation for learning; minimizing the disruptive and altering the unproductive behaviors of students; the organization of the classroom; and the delivery of effective instruction. As will become evident later, many of these components of classroom management overlap with culturally responsive teaching, even though the language of identity is somewhat different. Jones and Jones add that attention in classroom management needs to be refocused from controlling unproductive student behavior to creating learning environments and opportunities that encourage constructive behaviors. They also point out that the behavior of students is more positive in classrooms where they experience strong feelings of belonging, support, relevance, and engagement, and where students feel they can influence what happens to them. Some of these needs can be met for students of color by making the contributions and concerns of different ethnic groups central features of classroom instruction and climates on a regular basis, and providing frequent opportunities for students to work together in cross-ethnic group peer coaching and cooperative learning arrangements (Banks & Banks, 2004a, 2004b; Lipka, Mohatt, & the Ciulistet Group, 1998; McCarty, 2002).

Another view of classroom management quite different from the control and punishment of undesirable behavior, and a good fit with the ideology of culturally responsive teaching, is offered by Charles (2000), and Epanchin, Townsend, and Stoddard (1994). In a proposal for "joyful teaching and gentle discipline" Charles recommends making teaching and classroom management compatible with the human nature of students. He contends that "students do not misbehave randomly. They do so for particular reasons, which are neither mysterious nor psychologically impenetrable. The reasons are rather evident and all of them can be eliminated, modified, or avoided by teachers in the classroom" (pp. 6–7). Charles identified ten reasons why students misbehave in classrooms. Among them are testing boundaries, imitating the behavior of others, curiosity, desire for attention, need for power in matters affecting them, boredom and disinterest, threats to their dignity and self-respect, and personal disagreements. Some of these are particularly relevant to dealing constructively with management issues in culturally pluralistic classrooms, even though Charles did not make this relationship explicit.

For example, threats to dignity, testing boundaries, need for power, and boredom and disinterest in learning activities may cause some ethnically diverse students to respond in ways that are challenging to classroom expectations. They may resist individual competitiveness and rigid task orientations because they have been socialized in cultures that establish social connections as a prelude to task performance. Other diverse students may retreat behind veils of silence and nonparticipation because classroom routines inadvertently violate their cultural rules of social interaction and self-presentation (Cazden, John, & Hymes, 1985; Hollins, King, & Hayman, 1994). The solution to management and discipline problems Charles offers is deceptively simple—that is, classroom activities designed by teachers should "*work with, rather than against, student nature*" (2000, p. 8). If teachers give students what they need, make lessons interesting, energetic and exciting, affirm their personal identity and dignity, and cultivate feelings of belonging there will be no problems or tensions in the classroom. Misbehavior will decline automatically and dramatically, and teachers will almost never have to pit their will against students, or engage in power plays with them (Charles, 2000). Thus, it is more productive to create effective learning systems than to focus on managing the specific behaviors of individual students (Epanchin, Townsend, & Stoddard, 1994).

As is true with other aspects of the educational enterprise, the personal demeanors and pedagogical skills of teachers are pivotal in actualizing instructional approaches to classroom management. Many scholars suggest that teachers are decisive elements in setting the tone of and climate for what goes on in classroom interactions, and in determining the kind of responses provoked in students. More frequently than not students live up to the expectations and predictions of teachers. They become what they are told they are (or are not) and can or cannot be (Ginott, 1972; Good & Brophy, 2003; *Theory Into Practice*, Summer 2003) In fact, many leaders in the field of classroom management "highlight the relationship between desirable student behavior and effective instructional strategies," and they conclude that unproductive social and academic behaviors of students "can often be traced to failure to create an educational environment conducive to learning" (Jones & Jones, 2004, p. 151).

The contributing authors to the Autumn 2003 edition of *Theory Into Practice* extend these general principles and conditions of effective classroom management to ethnically and culturally diverse students (Weinstein Tomlinson-Clarke, & Curran 2003). In so doing, they provide evidence to support the observations made by Carol Weinstein (the guest editor of the volume) that the management challenge of creating productive and respective learning environments is even greater

> when students and teachers come from different cultural backgrounds, or when students differ in terms of race, ethnicity, socioeconomic status, cultural and linguistic background, sexual orientation, ableness, and academic aptitude. Unless teachers have the knowledge, skills, and disposition to effectively guide diverse groups of children, they are likely to face classes characterized by disrespect and alienation, name-calling and bullying, disorder and chaos. (pp. 266–267)

Scholars from different disciplinary perspectives and professional positions make convincing separate and related cases for culturally responsive teaching and classroom management. For instance, in conducting research on academically successful students of color, Nieto (2002) noted that "maintaining language and culture were essential to supporting and sustaining academic achievement" (p. 51). McCarthy and Benally (2003) and Vadas (1995) observed Navajo students in classrooms to determine if cultural identity and disciplinary behaviors were related. They found that Navajo students who identified strongly with the values and beliefs of their indigenous culture had high levels of inner personal strength and academic achievement, and low incidences of disciplinary referrals. They also were "more resilient and able to cope with adversity in the classroom" (McCarthy & Benally, 2003, p. 297). The majority of disciplinary actions recorded by McCarthy and Benally involved Navajo students who have grown up in "nontraditional homes where there has been a cultural breakdown and no values have taken the place of traditional ones" (p. 297). Bruner's (1996) analysis of cultural influences on education explains why these kind of social adaptations occur. He states, "learning and thinking are always *situated* in a cultural setting and always dependent upon the utilization of cultural resources" (p. 4). The Educational Research Service (2003) added that "cultural variables influence how children present themselves, understand the world, and interpret experiences. Culture also affects the experiences through which children's earliest literacy and mathematical knowledge are acquired" (p. 7). Thus, acquiring knowledge of the cultural characteristics of students from different ethnic groups, and incorporating this knowledge into educational programs and practices are fundamental to successful management, teaching, and learning in ethnically diverse classrooms.

Although it is impossible for educators to know all the specific cultural details of every ethnically, socially, and racially diverse group, the relationships among culture, ethnicity, race, and education demand that they are at least familiar with the general terrains of different groups' cultural maps. Some of these are knowing the work ethics and habits of students from various ethnic backgrounds, how they may respond to different motivational prompts, how they relate to authority figures, their performance style preferences, and how they manage stress or anxiety in learning situations. This cultural knowledge can help teachers and school administrators relate better to students, create classroom conditions more conducive to successful learning, and reduce disciplinary infractions (Banks & Banks, 2004a, 2004b; Gay, 2000; Monroe & Obidah, 2004; Pai & Adler, 2001; Weinstein, Tomlinson-Clarke, & Curran, 2004).

There is a rich and growing body of research and scholarship available for teachers to gain the knowledge and skills they need to implement culturally responsive teaching and classroom management. It is comprised of a wide range of resources, information, and analyses, including social science descriptions of the cultural values, communications, interactional styles, and contributions of specific ethnic groups; personal narratives of ethnic individuals about their experiences in schools; techniques for interracial dialogues developed by human relations experts; and curricular and instructional strategies designed by educators for use with culturally pluralistic student populations. One specific example of these resources is the Culturally Responsive Classroom Management model developed by Weinstein et al. (2003) and Weinstein et al. (2004). It is comprised of five components for teachers: becoming critically conscious of their own cultural biases; acquiring knowledge of the cultural heritages of ethnically diverse students; understanding the broader sociopolitical and economic contexts of schools; developing culturally responsive classroom management strategies; and creating caring learning environments.

Another self-study and cultural awareness technique that can be useful to teachers and students is cultural therapy, created by Spindler and Spindler (1993; 1994a; 1994b). It is a process of bringing one's own culture to cognitive consciousness to understand how it affects social relations, and the transmission of knowledge and skills. The intent of cultural therapy is to anticipate, minimize, and avoid conflicts, misunderstandings, and blind spots in cross-cultural interactions between members of diverse ethnic groups. Its goals for teachers are to increase awareness of the cultural values, beliefs, and assumptions they bring to the classroom; to look at how these influence their behaviors toward culturally different students; and to analyze reasons why they may consider these differences objectionable, shocking, or irritating. For students, cultural therapy is a means of consciousness raising about unequal power relationships in the classroom, school, and society. The goal is to help them acquire the instrumental competencies, cultural capital, and personal empowerment needed to compete equally with the cultural majority for resources, knowledge, opportunities, and experiences. It is somewhat analogous to Delpit's (1995) proposals for teaching students the culture of power that operates in mainstream, Eurocentric schools and classrooms.

The "cultural synchronization" that Monroe and Obidah (2004) observed between an African American middle school teacher and her urban students demonstrates in vivid detail how culturally diverse features can be woven into classroom management practices for students of color. The specific behaviors the teacher used included African-American cultural humor, colloquial expressions common among the students, and displays of emotions and affect when disciplining students. Gay (2000) combined information from research, theory, and practice to create compelling descriptions of different dimensions of culturally responsive teaching (CRT), and their effects on various kinds of student achievement. The CRT dimensions she identified are curriculum, caring, classroom climate, instructional congruity, and cross-cultural communication. The effects addressed the social, cultural, and personal development; school persistence; and academic performance of students. Embedded in all these conceptions and proposals is the idea that effective classroom management for students is dependent on quality instruction, which must be responsive to ethnic, racial, cultural, social, linguistic, and ability diversity.

Racial Disproportionality in School Discipline

Research and scholarship over the last 30 years have consistently shown high levels of discrepancies in disciplinary referrals and punishment. They correlate strongly with racial, cultural, ethnic, social, and ability differences among students. Five trends are apparent in the resulting data. The first is gender disparities. According to several research studies conducted (and others reviewed) by the Indiana Education Policy Center (Skiba, 2000; Skiba, Michael, Nardo, & Peterson, 2000; Skiba & Peterson, 1999; Skiba et al., 2003), males in all ethnic groups are disciplined more frequently and for a wider range of infractions than their female counterparts. Some studies have placed this disparity as high as four to one.

Second, there is a strong gender-by-race interaction in school discipline, with African American males being disciplined most often. They are followed sequentially by European American males, African American females, and European American females (Gregory, 1996,

1997; Skiba et al., 1997; Taylor & Foster, 1986). Gregory (1996) found these patterns in his analysis of data on corporal punishment from a 1992 survey of over 25 million students in 4,692 districts that was conducted by the Office of Civil Rights. This number of students accounted for 59% of the 42.5 million total enrolled in public schools at the time. When the data were collected 30 states and the District of Columbia still allowed corporal punishment to be used on students. The results of the study showed that of the 286,539 incidents of physical discipline reported in 1992 males accounted for 81.6%, African Americans, 44.4% and African American males, 34%. Disparities in corporal punishment for European American males, African American males, and African American females were disturbingly large, but those between African American males and European American females were astonishing, at 16 to 1.

The same pattern existed for suspensions, but the disparities were not as extreme. Compared to African American females, European American males, and European American females, African American males were 2.0, 2.14, and 6.29 times more likely to be suspended (Gregory, 1996, 1997). Several years later Gordon, Della Piana, and Keleher (2000) extended the knowledge base on disciplinary disproportionality by analyzing school discipline for a wider range of ethnic groups of color. Their results revealed that suspensions for African Americans ranged from a low of 1.7 times more than Latino and Native American males, to a high of 10.4 times more than Asian American females. Clearly, these data indicate that African American males are in peril with respect to school discipline. Unfortunately, the situation has not improved noticeably in the years since the Office of Civil Rights Survey. According to some researchers (such as Advancement Project/Civil Rights Project, 2000; Gordon, Della Piana, & Keleher, 2000; Skiba, 2000; Skiba & Peterson, 1999; Skiba et al., 2003) the situation has even worsened.

A third disparity is apparent in the nature or type of disciplinary referrals and their racial correlations. Research conducted at the Indiana Education Policy Center, as well as that of the Children's Defense Fund (1975), Townsend (2000), McCarthy and Hoge (1987), Gregory (1996), and Wu, Pink, Crain, Moles (1982) indicate that African American students (especially males) are referred for less serious disciplinary infractions than European Americans. Specifically, European American students are disciplined more often for so-called *objective* infractions. These are descriptive behaviors that are readily identifiable, such as smoking, leaving school without permission or not coming at all, vandalism, and profanity. By comparison, African Americans are most often disciplined for infractions that require teacher interpretations and judgments, such as disrespect, disobedience, defiance, excessive noise, disruptions, threats and loitering. These types of infractions are called *subjective discipline*. In their study of 11,000 students in grades 6–8 in 19 middle schools in 15 large city districts for the 1994–1995 academic year, Skiba, Michael, Nardo, and Peterson (2000) found that African American students had the most disciplinary actions, and were subjected to higher rates of more severe punishments, but the referrals were for less serious infractions. In other studies, Wu et al. (1982) and Skiba et al. (2003) reported that these subjective judgments are not influenced by race alone. The prior disciplinary history of particular students, the school context, and the attitudes, tolerance levels, resources, and skills teachers have for managing disruptive behavior are critical contributing factors as well.

The fourth persistent pattern of disproportionality in school discipline has to do with social class and residential location. Upper- and middle-income students receive more mild and moderate disciplinary actions, such as a warnings, lectures from teachers, and seat reassignments. Low-income students receive more severe punishment and it is often delivered in unprofessional ways, such as being yelled at before the entire class, being told to leave the classroom, and having their belongings searched (Skiba & Knesting, 2001). Similar patterns of disciplinary disproprotionality exist for students in urban locations, and middle and high schools, compared to suburban and rural settings, and elementary schools. Students of color in all settings and school types are disciplined more frequently and severely (Wu et al., 1982). That children of color are highly represented in poverty and urban schools increases the likelihood of them being disciplined more often. However, the correlations are not always as expected since, even in schools where there are small percentages and in middle class suburban communities, African and Latino Americans are still disciplined disproportionally to their representation in the student population.

A fifth disciplinary trend indicates that students of color who attend schools with high rates of suspensions and expulsions, and subscribe to rigidly uniform disciplinary polices, receive more referrals and punitive actions than in schools with flexible, liberal, and contextual guidelines (Wu et al., 1982). A recent manifestation of philosophies of strict compliance is zero tolerance policies and procedures. Under these guidelines harsh punishments are invoked automatically for misbehavior in schools, irrespective of the severity of the infractions, the circumstances surrounding them, the consequences for the offending students, or the overall climate of the school (NASP Center, 2004). They operate on the assumptions that punishing all offenses severely will be a deterrent to future misconduct, and removing discretion in punishments will eliminate racial disparities in discipline (Advancement Project/Civil Rights Project, 2000a, 2000b; Skiba, 2000; Skiba & Noam 2001; Skiba et al., 2003). Ladson-Billings (2001) offers a very different perspective on zero tolerance. She sees it as "a policy that essentially writes off the individual in an attempt to intimidate the group" (p. 80).

Since their first appearance in public schools in 1989 in California, Kentucky, and New York, zero tolerance policies and practices spread rapidly throughout the United States. Their coverage has extended to include guns, drugs, alcohol, threats, a variety of violations involving no physical harm, general misconduct, and others infractions that are trivial. By 1998, 94% of all schools had zero tolerance policies for guns and other weapons, 87% for alcohol, and 79% for violence, fighting, and smoking (Skiba, 2000). Trivial incidents (such as an elementary student bringing a water pistol to school; adolescent girls sharing Midol pills for menstrual cramps; a first-grade boy kissing a female classmate on the cheek; a kindergartner bringing a toenail clipper to school) that are receiving suspensions and expulsions under zero tolerance policies are increasing at an alarming rate (Ayres, Dohrn, & Ayres, 2001; Skiba, 2000; Skiba & Noam, 2001; Skiba & Peterson, 1999; Skiba et al., 2003).

Many agencies and individual scholars (Akom, 2001; Dohrn, 2001; Gordon, Della Piana, & Keleher, 2000; NASP Center, 2004; Noguera, 2003; Skiba, 2000; Skiba & Knesting, 2001; Skiba & Noam, 2001; Skiba & Peterson, 1999; Skiba, et al., 2003) are analyzing the effects of zero tolerance discipline in general, and on racial disproportionality in particular. Much similarity exists in the findings of these studies. They show that zero tolerance policies and practices (a) have more negative than positive consequences; (b) are especially devastating for students who already are placed at disciplinary risk in schools; (c) are used more often for minor than major offenses, such as disobedience, disrespect, defiance, disruptions, and attendance problems; (d) negatively affect students of color (especially African Americans) and students with disabilities to a greater degree than other groups; (e) do not make a significant positive difference in school climate, safety, student behavior, or learning; (f) often exacerbate problems of students with achievement difficulties, and increase dropout rates; and (g) further aggravate racial disparities in academic opportunities and outcomes.

In their analysis of data reported by 17 states in the U.S. Department of Education Office of Civil Rights Elementary and Secondary Survey for the 2000–2001 school year Skiba et al. (2003) found other disturbing results. These included strong correlations between racial disparities in school discipline and juvenile incarceration. Reports from the Advancement Project/Civil Rights Project (2000a, 2000b) and Ayres, Dohrn, and Ayres (2001) added that, as a result of zero tolerance policies, more children are being pushed into the criminal or juvenile delinquency pipeline, and often for behavioral infractions that previously were managed within schools and classrooms. According to Dohrn (2001) the increasing criminalization of children is even more extreme because of the overall ideological shift signified by zero tolerance mentalities. She says the daily discourse about children in schools and other service agencies has changed from "innocence to guilt, from possibility to punishment, from protection to fear" (p. 89). Two of the suggestions that Gordon, Della Piana, and Keleher (2000) made for reducing zero tolerance situations and other disciplinary disparities are directly connected to culturally responsive teaching and classroom management. First, teachers and administrators should be trained to work better with multicultural and multiracial students. Second, no discipline policies should be implemented without seriously considering their potential for racially disparate applications and effects.

Reasons for Disproportionate Discipline Among Students of Color

Why is disciplinary disproportionality so extreme and prevalent for African American students, and, to a lesser extent, Latino and Native Americans? Scholars, policy analysts, and practitioners offer several explanations for these racial disparities. They fall into the four categories of student misbehavior, racial discrimination, provocative classroom interactions, and cultural discontinuities.

PUNISHMENT IS COMPATIBLE WITH STUDENT MISBEHAVIOR

Many conventional educators and practitioners attribute the causes of disproportionality in discipline to the behaviors of students, their socioeconomic backgrounds, and related disconnections from school norms. They reason that because the disciplinary infractions of African Americans are more frequent and serious, they are (and should be) punished more often and severely. Thus, the referrals and punishments they receive are appropriate responses to their own misbehaviors (Skiba & Noam, 2001; Obidah & Teel, 2001; Townsend, 2000; Wu et al., 1982;).

Skiba, et al. (2000) undertook a study to examine the plausibility of these explanations. In some ways their study continued the traditions of earlier ones, notably the extensive multiple regression analyses conducted by Wu et al. in 1982. Using data produced by the Safe School Study of 1978, Wu et al. examined correlations between suspensions and students' antisocial attitudes and behaviors; educational level (middle and high school); type of school community (urban, rural, suburban); gender, race, and socioeconomic status; teacher attitudes and judgments; authority structure and discipline administration; and perceptions of students' academic performance and social problem-solving abilities.

None of the assertions that placed the onus of disciplinary disproportionality on the misbehavior of students of color and their socioeconomic backgrounds was supported by the findings of either Wu et al. (1982), Skiba et al. (1997), or several other subsequent studies (Advancement Project/Civil Rights Project, 2000a, 2000b; Davis & Jordan,1994; Gordon et al., 2000; Skiba, 2000; Skiba & Knesting, 2001; Skiba et al., 2000; Skiba et al., 2003). Instead, the data indicate that racial and gender differences in suspensions originate with classroom referrals, and are perpetuated by administrative decisions. These disparities exist even after controlling for socioeconomic status. Furthermore, school climate characteristics, teachers' lack of interest in and negative perceptions of students of color, academic bias, and racial inequalities are more predictive of disciplinary referrals and suspensions than the antisocial attitudes and misbehaviors of students. The correlations were compelling enough for Wu et al. (1982) to suggest that students would have a better chance of reducing their suspension rates by transferring to schools with fewer suspensions than improving their attitudes, or reducing their misbehavior. Teachers could help to reduce disproportionality in supension rates by eliminating apathy and indifference, and cultivating better attitudes towards student of color. Skiba et al. (2000) reached similar conclusions:

> Neither these nor any previous results we are aware of provide any evidence that racial discrepancies in school punishment can be accounted for by dis-proportionate rates of misbehavior.... Absent support for any plausible alternative explanation, these data lend support to the conclusion that racial disproportionality in school discipline ... is an indicator of systematic racial discrimination. (p. 16)

Therefore, because racial disproportionality in suspensions and other forms of discipline are institutional phenomena, it is the responsibility of schools and their personnel to assume some of the burden of reform rather than placing it solely on individual students. This conclusion supports the theoretical arguments of scholars of classroom management that it involves much more than controlling student behavior and punitive discipline; it is more a function of instructional quality and overall classroom climate.

RACIAL DISCRIMINATION

Gordon et al. (2000) explicitly named what some other researchers implied as another major cause of disciplinary disproportionality in schools. They called it racism. In studying racial discrimination in public schools they developed a "Racial Justice Report Card" for the 12 participating school districts (in 11 states). Ten criteria were analyzed, including student discipline, dropout rates, and learning environment. Eleven of the districts received a failing grade, and the other one an unimpressive "D." The findings produced a preponderance of statistical evidence on "glaring inequalities and discrimination in U. S. public schools" (p. 2). The data were so convincing that Gordon et al. (2000) declared, "students of color are at a serious disadvantage compared to their white counterparts. Though the discrimination may not be intentional, its persistence and pervasiveness, as measured by actual statistical impacts, amount to a deep pattern of institutional racism in U.S. public schools"(p. 2).

These observations are consistent with those made by McLean Donaldson (1996) in her study of racism in middle and senior high schools from the perspective of the lived experiences of academically successful students of color. She also studied the effects of the Multicultural Arts Program on the ability of the students to cope better with racism. The participants in the studies reported encountering racism regularly from teachers and other school personnel, and, to a lesser degree, from student members of other ethnic groups. Generally, they felt that racism had negative effects on their personal well-being, and educational opportunities and outcomes. Specifically, the students felt cheated because contributions of their ethnic groups were not included in the curriculum, and overwhelmed when their concerns about racism were ignored. They became disinterested in school, skipped classes, distrusted teachers, and expressed feelings of anger, low self-esteem, and discouragement. However, the students credited the Multicultural Arts Program for improving their interest in school and motivation for learning, and empowering them to deal better with racism. In explaining the consequences of these kinds of school experiences McLean Donaldson (1996) noted:

> If students of color do not feel safe, academically challenged, or included in the curriculum, they will not produce at their most efficient or creative capacity. With the burden of racism, many students of color tune out, burn out, act out, or drop out of school.... A growing body of evidence reveals that the perceptions of children regarding whether the school environment is fair and supportive is often the key to whether the children succeed in school. (p. 4)

While shared racial identities is no guarantee that teachers will be successful in teaching and managing diverse students, it is an important factor that needs careful analysis. Obidah and Teel (2001) provide a personal scenario that illustrates the importance of race. The African American students in their study had different expectations of African American and European American teachers regarding tolerance for their misconduct and providing stimulating instruction. Obidah, the African American member of the research and teaching team, said the students expected her to be less tolerant of misconduct and to respond swiftly to it, and to be a highly competent, entertaining, exciting, and caring teacher. They also wanted to have a sense of solidarity with her because of their shared Black identities. These desires and expectations caused the students to be more cooperative with Obidah and less inclined to test her tolerance, or challenge her authority. If she had failed to meet them whatever potential edge her ethnicity offered would have quickly (and permanently) dissipated, and the students would become even more distrustful and antagonistic toward her as an African American teacher than they would toward European American teachers. In their estimation such ethnic disappointment and abandonment are unforgivable, and deserve to be punished. It is difficult to determine how widespread these types of racial affinity are across diverse ethnic groups and how they affect classroom management for other students. Research studies typically have not made these correlations specific and explicit in either discipline or instruction. Fortunately, this convention is changing as interest in the intersections among race, ethnicity, culture, education, and classroom management expand.

PROVOCATIVE CLASSROOM INTERACTIONS

Other explanations for racial disproportionality in school discipline are located in the actual dynamics of classroom interactions between students of color and their teachers. Research conducted by Wu et al. (1982), Sheets (1995b, 1996) Sheets and Gay (1996), Obidah and Teel (2001), Weinstein et al. (2003, 2004), and McCarthy and Benally (2003) examined these dynamics to determine what caused disciplinary referrals among students from different ethnic groups. In these studies data were derived from statistical reports, perceptions of individuals, and observations of experiences within the contexts in which they occurred. For example, the quantitative data in the Wu et al. study about the types, frequency, and distribution of referrals were complemented with perceptions of students and teachers. Determinations of the academic performance and problem-solving abilities of students were based on what teachers assumed to be true, and the lack of teacher interest in students was constructed from assessments offered by students. In noting the power of these perceptions, Wu et al. (1982) declared, "students need not be truly low in their ability; as long as they are *considered to have low ability* they are more likely to be suspended by the school" (p. 266).

Obidah and Teel (2001) analyzed how their attitudes, perceptions, and instructional activities affected the discipline and referrals of African American students. They identified several characteristics that were particularly problematic for Teel, the European American member of the research and teaching partnership. These included what she perceived as the students' aggressive communicative style, unfamiliar expressions and vocabulary, need to save face in front of and elicit respect from peers, openly expressing dissatisfaction with learning activities, testing the authority of the teacher, and talking back. As Obidah and Teel became more culturally conscious and critically reflective of how their own values and behaviors contributed to the responses of students they conceded that teachers are likely to place blame on students for unacceptable classroom behaviors rather than reflect on how their instruction might be a contributing factor.

Sheets' research gives more operational meaning to the general idea that teacher attitudes and behaviors toward students of color contribute to disciplinary conflicts in classrooms, referrals, and subsequent punishments. She examined the experiences and perceptions of African, Latino, Filipino, and European American students in an urban high school in a large city school district by observing classroom interactions and interviewing students and teachers about why behavioral events become disciplinary infractions. The students readily accepted responsibility for their misconduct, but they felt the attitudes and behaviors of teachers often caused minor situations to escalate into major confrontations. This was done by not fully understanding the contexts of or motivations for their behaviors, ignoring extenuating circumstances, making students guilty by association because of peer friendships and family relationships, and refusing to allow students to explain their points of view, or give them any serious consideration. When students insisted on having their say, teachers interpreted these attitudes and demeanors as insubordination, disrespect, defiance, disruption, being argumentative, and challenging their authority. Other students in the Sheets study resented being talked to in demeaning and patronizing ways, treated more harshly than high academic achieving students, penalized for things that other students were not, and having to fight for the right to be heard and respected that should be a given in classrooms. These teacher behaviors caused frustration, irritation, and retaliation in students (Sheets, 1995b, 1996, Sheets & Gay, 1996).

Many students of color, especially in middle and high schools, are not willing to passively submit to the demands of teachers for immediate and unquestioning compliance in conflict situations, especially if they feel they are treated unfairly and denied the opportunity to defend themselves. The reciprocal trust and respect that are so essential to effective classroom interactions between students and teachers are destroyed. According to Sheets and Gay (1996), in these situations students

> are triply disadvantaged—-unjustly accused, unfairly silenced, and unnecessarily punished—- which is not conducive to building trust, respect, and constructive relationships among the students and their teachers. As students with a strong sense of justice retaliate, a vicious cycle of "attack-counter-attack" develops, the students' disciplinary records increase, and their academic success is further compromised. (p. 89)

There also was general consensus among the African, Mexican, Filipino, and European American participants in the Sheets study on why African Americans faired worse in classroom confrontations with teachers. They pointed out that these students were "not given a chance," that "teachers don't want to deal with them," and that teachers "pick on African Americans and Latinos" (Sheets, 1995b, p. 75). African Americans tended to "fight back" and insist on being heard, but Filipino and Mexican American students adopted personas of silence and compliance. These decisions were based on the premise that trying to make uninterested, uncaring, and unconcerned teachers understand their points of view was not worth the effort. The explanations of the teachers paralleled those of the students. They agreed that teachers must assume some of the responsibility for the disciplinary conflicts with students. They attributed these problems to a lack of interpersonal skills, knowledge of cultural diversity, and competence in classroom management for preventing or minimizing confrontations with ethnically and racially different students (Sheets, 1995b).

CULTURAL INSENSITIVITY AND DISCONTINUITY

Another proposed explanation underlying the disproportionate punitive classroom management and disciplinary action African, Latino, and Native American students receive is cultural insensitivities, discontinuities, and misunderstandings. Conflicts occur between teachers and students from different ethnic, racial, and social backgrounds simply because each is thinking, communicating, valuing, and behaving in ways that their respective cultures deem normal and appropriate (Pai & Adler, 2001; Powell & Caseau, 2004; Spindler, 1987; Spring, 1995; *Theory Into Practice*, 2003). As McDermott (1987) explained, "[b]ecause behavioral competence is differently defined by different social groups, many children and teachers fail in their attempts to establish rational, trusting, and rewarding relationships across ethnic, racial, and class boundaries in the classroom" (p. 173). This perspective was expanded by Pai and Adler (2001) in a discussion about the influence of cultural differences on the assessment of the academic potential and performance of students. It can be extended to other dimensions of the educational enterprise as well. They declared:

> Beliefs, values, and biases of the person responsible for carrying out the assessment can make a significant difference in the outcome, the interpre-tation, and the use of data. One of the major issues regarding the interactions between the assessor and the child being evaluated is the concern that the assessor's ... ethnocentrism as well as his or her failure to understand the child's culture, values, cognitive styles, language usage, and unique approach to interpersonal relationships may influence the assessment results adversely. The child may have similar difficulties in understanding the assessor's attitudes and behavior patterns. (pp. 186–187)

These difficulties are complicated further in that most ethnically, culturally, and linguistically diverse students in public schools are taught and assessed by educators who are mostly middle class, monocultural, and monolingual European Americans. Unless they (and others from different ethnic groups) have been thoroughly prepared in cultural diversity and multicultural education they are likely to interpret the attitudes and behaviors of students of color according to the prevailing middle class and Eurocentric-embedded normative standards of schools. Misdiagnoses like these can lead to mistreatment and miseducation, according to a host of multicultural education scholars (e.g., edited volumes by Banks & Banks, 1995, 2004a, 2004b; Diaz, 2001; Dilworth, 1992; Grant, 1995; Hollins, King, & Hayman, 1994; Hollins & Oliver, 1999; Pang & Cheng, 1998; and Sleeter, 1991; see also authored texts, e.g., Bennett, 2003; Bowers & Flinders, 1991; Gay, 2000; Ladson-Billings, 1994; Nieto, 2004; Villegas & Lúcas, 2002).

Cultural differences in discourse, performance, and self-disclosure styles are among the most problematic impediments to effective instruction and management in culturally diverse classrooms. (Brown, 2003; Cazden, John, & Hymes, 1985; Dyc 1993; Kochman, 1981; McCarthy & Benally, 2003; Powell & Caseau, 2004). As a result of inconsistencies they observed in the communication styles of Navajo students and schools McCarthy and Benally (2003) suggested that teachers must understand why communication styles grow out of cultural patterns. McDermott (1987) added that "When the social organization of communicative behaviors is divided by two definitions of what is culturally appropriate, the one definition belonging to the teacher and the other to the pupils, communication across the codes are much more limited than if the codes were merely structurally at odds" (p. 192).

Kochman (1981) and Smitherman (1986; 1994) applied these general assertions to African Americans. Both described specific ways that cultural features are embedded in the discourse styles of African Americans, and the conflicts that can ensure when these different systems encounter each other. Kochman's descriptions derived from his study of the debate habits of European American college students and African American community members. Smitherman's profiles resulted from many years conducting sociolinguist analyses of African American communication patterns in general and among students in K–12 schools. Kochman noted that the two discourse styles are often contentious:

> The black mode ... [of communicating] is high-keyed animated, interpersonal and confrontational [while] [t]he white mode ... is relatively low-keyed, dispassionate, impersonal, and non-challenging. The first is characteristic of involvement; it is heated, loud, and generates affect. The second is characteristic of detachment and is cool, quiet, and without affect. (1981, p. 18)

The inventive delivery, evocative vocabulary, and unique nomenclature of African American students may be perceived by teachers as rude, insulting, and sometimes even vulgar. For instance, African Americans frequently inject high energy, exuberance, and passion into their verbal communication. They also use much symbolism, imagery, dramatic flair, and aestheticism in their language (Baber, 1987; Cazden, John, & Hymes, 1985; Smitherman, 1986, 1994, 1998). But teachers may interpret these styles as inappropriate for classroom discourse, and feel compelled to chastise, correct, or punish students for disrespectful and inflammatory speech (Kochman, 1981; Obidah & Teel, 2001; Powell & Caseau, 2001). The students see nothing wrong with their speech, and may resent and resist the teachers' assessments. The result is a cultural conflict that can quickly escalate into disciplinary sanctions in the classroom, or referrals for administrative action.

Communicative tensions have negative effects on other relationship factors, such as trust, respect, and feelings of acceptance and belonging, which further constrain efforts to achieve genuine communication across cultural differences. As relationships deteriorate, communications become even more strained, narrow, stylized, difficult, rigid, awkward, and ritualistic (Powell & Caseau, 2004). None of these are amenable to building the kind of bonds between teachers and students that are conducive to effective teaching, learning, and classroom management for diverse students.

Misunderstandings of differences in cultural communication that lead to conflicts in classrooms are not limited to social and behavioral interactions. They occur in intellectual processes and academic tasks performance as well. Many students of color use patterns of organizing thoughts in written and verbal discourse that include the prolific use of contextual cues, establishing relationships, and setting stages for the presentation of information. Ideas and events are arranged in episodic sequences or storytelling formats. Au (1993) calls this style of thinking, writing, and talking "topic-chaining." Conversely, the discourse style practiced most often in conventional schooling is "topic-centered," which expects individuals to be parsimonious in the use of words, to arrange ideas in a linear sequence, and to avoid using extraneous information. Students who "talk around" the topic and do not "get to the point" immediately may be considered to be sloppy thinkers or, even worse, cognitively incompetent. In discourses about behavioral infractions teachers may view these habits of talking manipulative, deceptive, dishonesty, and rouses for disguising or avoiding guilt. Interventions that insist students "write and talk right" are frustrating and irritating since teachers often do not teach them how to make the necessary style shifts. The students then assume teachers do not care about what they have to say or whether they learn, and are determined to assault their personal integrity. Some of them stop participating in instructional discourse and learning activities entirely (Ayres, Dohrn, & Ayres, 2001; Caraballo, 2000; Sheets, 1995b; Siu, 1996; Torres-Guzman & Thorne, 2000; Wu et al., 1982).

The European American teacher (Teel) in the Obidah and Teel (2001) study offered graphic descriptions of how these dilemmas unfolded in her interactions with African American students. Her repeated requests for the students to clarify the meaning of words and phrases they used were frustrating for both her and the students. At times they felt inept when they were not understood; other times they thought the teacher was embarrassing them, or they simply got tired of trying to communicate with a teacher who had no knowledge of their out-of-school language. The teacher, in turn, felt ignorant, uncomfortable, and embarrassed when she did not understand what the students were saying, and was reluctant to ask them to explain. Teel noted that the most disturbing aspect of these incidents was her initially not knowing what was happening, and pretending that she could avoid confronting them. Once she developed some knowledge about how culture affected the communication dynamics in the classroom she declared her first reactions to be examples of "how a White teacher in an urban school sabotaged her own good intentions through ignorance of racial and cultural differences, and possibly through unconscious racist notions about the students (Obidah & Teel, 2001, p. 52).

Thus, teachers' ignorance of and punitive reactions to culturally different communication, personal interaction, and intellectual engagement styles can cause diverse students to become disaffiliated, hostile, and silenced in the classroom. These are major management issues.

Townsend (2000), Boykin (1983; 1986; 2002), Hale (1986), Weinstein et al. (2003, 2004), McCarty (2002), Curran (2003), Delpit and White-Bradley (2003), McCarthy and Benally (2003), and Brown (2003) provide some additional examples of how misunderstandings of cultural differences can obstruct effective teaching and learning, as well as become disciplinary and classroom management issues for students of color. They include communal values, work habits, task orientation, and cultural protocols for interpersonal interactions. Many students from diverse ethnic and cultural backgrounds (and those growing up in technologically rich societies) are bombarded with multiple sensory and rapid-fire stimulations, all occurring at the same time. They may listen to music, engage in animated conversations, and watch movies or television programs at the same time they are attending to school assignments. Teachers who serialize activities and expect students to do one thing at a time, and to be rather passive, quiet, and sedentary may interpret these behaviors as not giving sufficient attention and quality effort to academic tasks, and as preludes to disruption and chaos. They then intervene to reassert order. An antidote to these tensions, and the constraints they impose on building constructive learning environments and classroom relationships with ethnically diverse students, is culturally responsive teaching.

Characteristics of Culturally Responsive Teaching (CRT)

Although not a multicultural educator himself, Bernstein (1985) made some observations that capture the philosophical essence of culturally responsive teaching. He said:

> If the culture of the teacher is to become part of the consciousness of the child, then the culture of the child must first be in the consciousness of the teacher. . . . We need to distinguish between the principles and operations, which we as teachers must transmit to and develop in children, and the contexts we create in order to do this. We should start knowing that the social experience the child already possesses is valid and significant, and that this social experience should be reflected back to him as being valid and significant. It can only be reflected back to him if it is part of the texture of the learning experiences we create. (p. 149)

Culturally responsive teaching does what Bernstein proposes by (a) legitimizing the cultures and experiences of ethnically diverse students; (b) including more significant, accurate, and comprehensive information about culturally different people and contributions in all subjects taught in schools; (c) using the cultural legacies, traits, experiences, and orientations of ethnically diverse students as filters through which to teach them academic knowledge and skills; (d) making learning an active, participatory endeavor in which students are assisted in giving personal meaning to new information, ideas, principles, and other learning stimuli; (e) building the moral commitment, critical consciousness, and political competence needed to promote social justice and social transformation; and (f) teaching students style-shifting skills so that they can move back and forth between their home and school cultures with ease (Gay, 2000; Hollins, 1996; Hollins, King, & Hayman, 1994; Howard, 2001; Lipka et al., 1998; McCarty, 2002; Tharp & Gallimore, 1988; Villegas & Lúcas, 2002).

Ladson-Billings (1995a, 1995b) organized the major elements of culturally responsive teaching (CRT) into three areas of emphasis, which are academic achievement, cultural competence, and sociopolitical consciousness for students of color. Brown (2003) also rearranged the broad range of CRT goals and priorities into a few clusters. They are teachers responding explicitly to the ethnic, cultural, social, and cognitive needs of diverse students; integrating the interests of diverse students into construction of caring classroom communities; being assertive in demanding appropriate social behaviors and academic growth; and demonstrating cultural respect for students in social, personal, and instructional interactions. Although configured and named somewhat differently, the general attributes of CRT are affirmed by many other scholars who study specific ethnic groups. Among them are experts on African Americans (Allen & Boykin, 1992; Bailey & Boykin, 2001; Boykin, 1986, 2002; Foster, 1995, 1997; Lee, 1993); Native Americans (Deyhle 1995; Lomawaima, 2004; McCarty, 2002; Philips, 1983); Native Alaskans (Lipka, Mohatt, & the Ciulistet Group, 1998); Latino Americans (Garcia, 2004; Nieto, 2002, 2004); Asian Americans (Pang & Cheng, 1998; Pang, Kiang, & Pak, 2004); and Native Hawaiians (Au, 1993; Boggs, Watson-Gegeo, & McMillen, 1985; Tharp & Gallimore, 1988).

Throughout these studies and related theory educators emphasize a set of propositions and practices similar to those that Krater, Zeni, and Cason (1994) adopted in their research on using ethnic literature to improve the writing and reading performance of African American students in elementary and middle schools. They began the project assuming that the problems and solutions resided in fixing the students, curriculum materials, and instructional strategies. While these helped somewhat, significant changes did not occur in the attitudes, receptivity, and performance levels of the students until the teachers shifted the focus of their reform efforts to themselves, and to students as persons, not merely students. The participants in the project initially tried to analyze African American students from a neutral and objective standpoint, without allowing their own cultural lens to enter the equation, and then design instructional strategies based on the results. Over time they realized that teachers' cultures are intimately involved in the instructional process, and that this reality needs to be thoroughly understood to avoid imposing cultural hegemony onto students, even as efforts are pursued to improve their education. Krate, Zeni, and Cason incorporated some other elements into their writing project that are commonly accepted components of culturally responsive teaching. They were building on the strength of students, encouraging cooperative learning, creating cultural bridges, and expanding their experiential horizons. All of these attributes of CRT place cultural and ethnic diversity at the center of the instructional process to make education more successful for students of color, rather than perpetuating the conventional practice of making them always adapt to Eurocentric standards. They help diverse students acquire school knowledge and skills more effectively, while simultaneously affirming their cultural heritages and ethnic identities.

Boykin (1994, 2000, 2002) and his colleagues at the Center for Research on the Education of Students Placed at Risk (CRESPAR), Howard University, are developing a body of empirical research, based on experimental studies, that demonstrates how general principles of CRT can be translated into actual classroom practice. One of their specific contributions is the Talent Development Model (TDM). It concentrates on acknowledging and actualizing the potential for success of low-income African American students instead of highlighting their limitations. It challenges teachers to fortify students where they are most vulnerable; build on the personal, adaptive, and cultural assets students bring to school; foster success-driven learning environments; develop simultaneously multiple academic, cultural, and personal competences; build community among students; and use active, critical, constructivist , and culturally connected approaches to learning.

Other scholars, such as Piestrup (1973), Obidah and Teel (2001), Lee (1993), Au (1993), Ladson-Billings (1994), Foster (1989, 1997), Monroe and Obidah (2004), Howard (1998, 2001), and Abe (2004) are describing how CRT is actualized in naturalistic classroom practices. They are finding the same kinds of attributes as those reported in experimental studies and special projects. Among these are incorporating specific content examples, cultural referents, learning styles, relational patterns, and communication habits of diverse ethnic groups into curricular materials, instructional practices, and learning climates. For example, Howard (1998, 2001) observed teachers regularly being playful (yet serious), humorous, and dramatic, as well as using performance, storytelling, parables, metaphors, and analogies in teaching African American students. The students also were expected to demonstrate reciprocity by being as persistent in their learning efforts as the teachers were in their teaching efforts, exhibiting sustained time on task, and feeling personally connected to their teachers and to each other. Abe (2004), who examined relationships between teaching styles and student discipline, described the African American teachers in his study as working diligently and imaginatively to connect classroom learning to the lived experiences of their African American students. They used multiple, creative, and varied techniques (such as inquiry, participatory, and cooperative learning) to capture the interests of students, to enhance their knowledge comprehension, and build community allegiance among them. Another notable feature of all these classrooms is the teachers had few disciplinary problems. When they did occur, they were minor infractions, and most were resolved in the classroom, without any outside intervention. The teachers were intellectually demanding, and strongly bonded with their students, both culturally and personally.

The students in both the Howard and Abe studies captured how their teachers exhibited cultural responsiveness in comments such as, “she’s hard but fair”; “he understands where we are coming from, and what we are going through”; “you can count on them because they are always there for you”; “they make learning interesting and fun”; “she’s always doing something different, so you never know what she’s going to do next”; “they don’t make you feel stupid when you don’t know something”; “they take the time to explain it and relate it to something you do know”; and “they show you how to do things by doing them themselves, rather than just telling you what to do, or just to read the book” (Howard, 1998; Abe, 2004). Corresponding results have been reported for Native Americans and Native Hawaiians when their cultural heritages and styles of communicating, learning, and relating are used as conduits for acquiring and demonstrating mastery of academic skills (Cazden, John, Hymes, 1985; Philips, 1983; Boggs, Waston-Gegeo, & McMillen, 1985; Au & Kawakami, 1985, 1994; Barta et al. 2001).

Effects of Culturally Responsive Teaching for Classroom Management

Due to space limitations only three of the different aspects of culturally responsive teaching are discussed here to document the effects of this technique in improving the learning outcomes and classroom management of underachieving Asian, African, Native, and Latino American students. These are curriculum, community, and instruction. More comprehensive discussions of CRT are readily available in the works of many different scholars, and from various ethnic group perspectives. Among them are Banks and Banks (2004a), Gay (2000, 2002), Shade (1989), Villegas and Lúcas (2002), McCarty (2002), Lipka et al. (1998), and Hollins, King, and Hayman (1994).

CURRICULUM EFFECTS OF CRT

Several curricular projects and related research studies have proven that when instructional materials and content reflect their cultural experiences African Americans, Native Americans, Native Hawaiians, Native Alaskans, and Latino Americans perform better in school. These results are evident on different measures of achievement, including quality of effort, academic task persistence, attendance, satisfaction with school, personal efficacy, and achievement in math, reading, writing, and science. Unfortunately, many of these curricular efforts are special projects (such as the Rough Rock Demonstration School for Navajos, the Kamameha Early

Education Project for Native Hawaiians, and the Algebra Project for African Americans) instead of being integral parts of regular curricula and routine classroom dynamics.

Culturally responsive curricula begin with the assumptions that familiar knowledge is a foundation and a filter for learning unfamiliar content in the classroom. Students of color have funds of knowledge (Moll, Amanti, Neff, & Gonzalez, 1992; Moll & Gonzalez, 2004) learned in their homes and cultural communities that can be used to facilitate mastery of academic knowledge and skills in school. In other words, school knowledge does not have to be learned at the expense of cultural knowledge. Therefore, the development of *biculturalism*, or proficiency in at least the two cultural systems of the home and community, and the school, is a desirable goal for effective teaching in ethnically diverse classrooms.

Lipka et al. (1998) provide a detailed description of how the cultural content, or funds of knowledge, of the Yup'ik in Alaska were used to transform the culture and curriculum of the schools their children attended. The university-based curriculum design and research team worked in conjunction with Yup'ik teachers and community elders to accurately record elements of everyday indigenous life. Then they designed curricular materials and instructional strategies showing how this cultural knowledge and practice were connected and could be used to teach school-based math, science, and literacy. One technique was to reproduce designs used in Yup'ik clothing and crafts in a set of geometric manipulatives to assist in teaching mathematical patterns, fractions, simple algebra, and tessellations. Indigenous fishing, weather predictions, and storytelling techniques were used to teach interdisciplinary science, math, and literacy skills.

Working with the same principle of teaching school knowledge through cultural referents the Algebra Project uses everyday life experiences as content to improve pre-algebra and algebra achievement for urban and rural poor African American middle school students (Moses & Cobb, 2001). Escalanté's Math Program demystified calculus in the same way for academically at-risk high school Latino Americans in South Central Los Angeles (Escalanté & Dirmann, 1990; Mathews, 1988). Students who are as thoroughly engaged in and captivated by learning, as the ones involved in these projects, are unlikely to have the time and desire to be sources or objects of disciplinary problems. If anything, they pose a very different management challenge. That is, demanding that teachers continually expand their own content knowledge and pedagogical creativity to engage the interests, creativity, and abilities of students.

Other culturally responsive curriculum initiatives focus on reading and writing. They, too, use the cultural heritages, contributions, and experiences of diverse ethnic groups as bases for teaching academic skills. McCarty's (2002) study of the creation and implementation of the Rough Rock English–Navajo Language Arts Program (RRENLP) is illustrative of these approaches to creating culturally relevant curricula. It used inquiry-based, interdisciplinary teaching and learning activities in which students researched their local community, tribal, national, and global issues and events that affected their personal lives. An example of this was the study of the architecture and petroglyphs in Dinétah, the Navajo homeland of northwestern New Mexico, complemented by an examination of local landforms and sacred sites. The studies combined oral history, geography, geology, and mathematics. They also created opportunities for students to hear, speak, read, see, and write Navajo in naturalistic contexts, and to bring the school and community together in the learning process. The texts used in the RRENLP resulted from oral history interviews of Navajo tribal members, and collaborations with parents, elders, teachers, and students about their personal lived experiences.

The Multicultural Literacy Program (Diamond & Moore, 1995) used literature written by authors who were members of the same ethnic groups as the students in the classrooms to teach reading and writing skills. It highlighted selections from Asian, African, Native, and Latino Americans usually excluded from the literary canons of schools. These choices were driven by the interest appeal, cognitive powers, and personal connectedness potential of the materials. Diamond and Moore (1995) pointed out that multicultural literature is a valuable teaching tool because it taps the interests of students, stimulates their imagination, resonates with how they think and their natural curiosity, and connects them to the cultural heritages of their own and other ethnic groups. These curricular choices also demonstrate how the use of personally lived and culturally embedded experiences ("the familiar") makes it easier for nonmainstream students of color to comprehend the abstract and decontextualized content of school subjects ("the unfamiliar").

INSTRUCTIONAL EFFECTS OF CRT

Instructional components are integral parts of curriculum designs. However, some theorists, scholars, and practitioners focus primarily on them as the centerpieces of culturally responsive teaching. While curriculum concentrates on what is taught about ethnic, racial, social, and cultural diversity, instructional analyses emphasize how content should be taught to and learned by diverse students. Simply stated, the argument is that conventional teaching techniques need to be modified, and new ones developed to better reflect and respond to the cultural values, experiences, and learning styles of different ethnic groups (Shade, 1989). Also, potentially interesting multicultural content will not be fully realized if it is delivered in ways that are problematic to how students learn.

Several scholars are analyzing what these general principles mean for the academic achievement and school behaviors of specific ethnic groups. Boykin (1983, 1986, 1994, 2002) and his colleagues (Allen & Boykin, 1991, 1992; Allen & Butler, 1996; Bailey & Boykin, 2001; Boykin, Allen, Davis, & Senior, 1997; Boykin & Cunningham, 2001; Dill & Boykin, 2000) are demonstrating that teaching strategies that exemplify three key features of African American culture—communalism, verve or exuberance, and expressive movement—increase student performance on different academic tasks, and under a variety of learning conditions. Their findings indicate that there is a strong and consistent preference among African American students for physical movement, music, and active participation in learning activities; working with others; and using novel, fluid, flexible, and frequently varied formats. Conversely, they struggle with, resist, or reject learning activities that always emphasize individualism, competition, and passivity—the norms for most mainstream classrooms. Boykin and associates have found these learning preferences and their positive effects on the intellectual engagement and achievement of elementary African American students in predominately poor inner-city schools, as well as in mostly European American, middle-class suburban settings.

Two other important implications for classroom management derive from the research on culturally responsive teaching for African American students. One is the sequencing or "packaging" of learning activities. The studies revealed that African American students maintain interest in learning and on-task behaviors longer when different types of challenges are presented in varying sequential order instead of similar ones being clustered together. This finding prevailed across math, vocabulary, spelling, and logical picture sequencing tasks. Rather than having students do all math or reading before attending to science and social studies, it is "more efficacious to present the children, for example, with a math task, followed by a spelling task, followed by a vocabulary, followed by a spelling, and then a picture sequencing" (Boykin, 2002, p. 90). When these students are expected to participate in one type of learning activity repeatedly for a long period of time, they lose interest, become frustrated, and engage in off-task behaviors. These sequencing preferences are consistent with the prominence of performed storytelling and improvisation among African Americans to demonstrate mastery of various discourse skills, such as conveying information, making inferences and connections, translation, and converting knowledge from the form in which it was originally learned into different expressive genres (Smitherman, 1986; 1994; 1998).

A second implication of research on the effects of culturally responsive pedagogy in practice for improving classroom management is the viability of holistic teaching and learning. Instead of compartmentalizing different dimensions of learning by subjects, skills, ability levels, and grades, it is better to keep them together as integrated wholes for some ethnic groups. This approach to teaching helps many students of color to maintain focus in learning, and enhances their interest in, engagement with, and ownership of the process. It resonates especially with students from ethnic groups whose cultures place high value on communalism and cooperation, such as African Americans, Native Americans, Asian Americans, Native Alaskans, and Latino Americans.

In describing why and how she used integrated teaching with her Yup'ik students Dull (1998) noted that it is closer to the realities of life. It allowed the students to learn reading, math, science, social communication, and research skills as they interacted with local artisans, examined their own cultural heritages and practices, and validated their prior knowledge. The elementary African American teachers in Howard's study (2001) felt it was essential for African American students to learn common sense along with academic sense; to improve their moral and character development by learning honesty, respect, integrity, responsibility, public etiquette, empathy for others, and commitment to social services, in concert with their cognitive knowledge and skills; and to know how to engage in political and social activism to combat racism and other injustices in society. Ladson-Billings (1994) found that African American students in elementary school actually learned better when academic, social, political, moral, cultural, and personal skills were taught simultaneously. In summarizing the importance of using holistic education with African American students Boykin (2002) proposed, in addition to academic knowledge, the following:

> Schools ... should prepare these children to acquire a broad range of marketable skills; but, they should also prepare them to appreciate their cultural legacy and to use it to be proactive contributors to changing their own life circumstances and to enhancing the life quality of others in their community if not society at large. (p. 91)

Similar pedagogical emphases have been recommended in teaching other ethnic groups as well. At the El Fuente Academy for Peace and Justice in Williamsburg, Brooklyn, curricula, teaching, and learning are "built upon the realities of young people of color and their families and centered on issues of identity, culture, and language" (Rivera & Pedraza, 2001, p. 230). Designed primarily to serve Puerto Rican students, El Fuente's educational mission is grounded in the four values of love and caring, collective self-help, peace and justice, and academic mastery. These values are operationalized by building and sustaining relationships within the context of community, integrating students' cultural realities into teaching, linking school learning to social and political activism, and emancipatory, social justice, participatory, and inquiry-based learning activities. In all learning endeavors, the students and staff at the El Fuente Academy strive to integrate body, mind, and spirit, build community, facilitate inter- and intrapersonal growth, and connect classroom instruction to community development simultaneously. Reflections of Rivera and Pedraza (2001) on the redemptive value of educational initiatives such as the El Fuente Academy point to the power of culturally responsive teaching:

> For poor and working-class, culturally and racially diverse communities, an educational model that integrates the learners' cultures, languages, and identities, recognizes the body-mind-spirit connection within creative beings, and commits to braiding learning to community development and social action helps develop critically thinking, community-minded justice-seeking, artistic young people and adults as well as increases opportunities for holistic growth, human development, and community-building. (p. 242)

Another aspect of culturally responsive instruction that has been shown to produce positive results in learning and classroom management for ethnically diverse students is cultural immersion self-study. Two projects involving Native Americans and African Americans illustrate these effects. McCarthy and Benally (2003) describe a management plan that the dean of students and counselors at a Navajo middle school implemented for chronic disciplinary offenders. Most of these students were not strongly grounded in or affiliated with Navajo culture. As an alternative to detentions and suspensions the plan offered the option of learning about traditional Navajo values and participating in cultural ceremonies. One experience involved spending time in a sweat lodge where a medicine man guided the students in reflections about their identities and responsibilities as Navajos, and how to achieve balance in developing the whole self—the social, physical, mental, cultural, and spiritual. Initial sessions in the sweat lodge were supported by follow-up group discussions. The experience produced positive results for the participants with respect to better self-concepts, increased academic engagement, and reduced disciplinary referrals.

In the African American project a group of low-income fifth-grade students (all African American) were taught the Ma'at value system practiced in ancient Kemet. According to Delpit and White-Bradley (2003) this code of ethics encompassed the principles of trust, justice, harmony, balance, order, reciprocity, and righteousness. Then the students engaged in different learning activities related to how these principles applied to incidents in their own home and school lives, such as being dishonest, irresponsible, and uncaring, and violating the "space," humanity dignity, and rights of others. Notable changes occurred in that the students became more self-regulating of their own and their peers' behaviors. As they internalized the Ma'at principles the students monitored their own conduct, solved personal problems, and reestablished order and equilibrium in the classroom after conflicts occurred with little or no intervention from the teacher. These behaviors were consistent with the Ma'at goal of ensuring cohesion, cooperation, and the smooth functioning of societal groups. Delpit and White-Bradley (2003) concluded that, in addition to self-regulation, the results confirmed that "the values of Ma'at could be easily understood and applied to the classroom setting, while providing a natural outlet for exercising student leadership" (p. 286).

Throughout these studies a recurrent message surfaces that has direct implications for accomplishing effective classroom management through culturally responsive teaching. Relevant content and pedagogical techniques are important factors, but are not the only ones. Of equal significance is establishing personal relationships and bonds with students as cultural, ethnic, and racial beings, and creating caring classroom climates. To accomplish these goals teachers have to work closer with students, as worthy contributing members, as well as broadening knowledge of their own and their students' cultures and developing a better understanding of how their teaching affects the discipline behaviors of students (Powers, Potthoff, Bearinger, & Resnick, 2003; Obidah, 2001; *Theory Into Practice*, 2003).

BUILDING COMMUNITY EFFECTS OF CRT FOR CLASSROOM MANAGEMENT

Much of the efforts to build community across ethnic, racial, cultural, social, and linguistic differences in classrooms is expressed as various forms of cooperative and collaborative learning. Research related to them indicates that the efforts produce positive results in different areas of achievement for all students, irrespective of ethnicity, race, gender, or ability groupings. The results include improved academic effort and achievement, better interracial relations, and heightened feelings of acceptance, ownership of, and affiliation with schools and classrooms (Boykin, 2000; Cohen & Lotan, 2004; Losey, 1997; Slavin, 1995). The studies reviewed by Losey (1997) and programs conducted by Escalantẽ (Escalantẽ & Dirmann, 1990; Mathews,

1988) and Sheets (1995a) show that the performance of Mexican American students on reasoning, oral expression, writing, mathematics, and Spanish literature increased when they worked with their peers in small groups, and felt a sense of cultural and personal connectedness to each other and to their teachers.

The same kind of positive benefits resulted from the Kamehameha Early Education Program (KEEP) for Native Hawaiian students when they were taught at school in ways that they were accustomed to learning in their indigenous cultural communities and homes. One of these techniques was working with small cooperative groups. In part, these groups used a cultural style of collaboration called "talk-story," or conarration. The reading achievement of the first-, second-, and third-grade students in the program improved radically (measured by performance on conventional standardized tests), as did their engaged time on academic tasks, and the amount of constructive feedback offered by teachers (Au & Kawakami 1985, 1994; Boggs et al., 1985; Cazden, John, & Hymes, 1985; Tharp & Gallimore, 1988). Treisman (1985; Fullilove & Treisman, 1990) found similar results for the Chinese, African, and Latino American college students who participated in his Mathematics Workshop Program (MWP). Their grades increased in the high level mathematics courses they were taking when the students studied together in small self-ethnic groups, combined socializing with homework preparation, talked through the processes they used to solve problems with each other, and assisted each other in decoding the thinking challenges embedded in the math assignments.

Teachers also build community among diverse students by creating an ethos and a climate of success in their classrooms. They expect students to demonstrate high levels of academic achievement, and are relentless in their pedagogical efforts to ensure that these expectations are met. They realize that isolated teaching and learning events are not sufficient to accomplish and sustain this success. Rather, an infrastructure must be created that includes social, cultural, and personal supports along with academic mentoring and facilitation. In these capacities, teachers act as cultural mediators and brokers for diverse students, care about the personhood of students along with their intellectuality, and are unequivocal advocates of students instead of being their adversaries (Gay, 2000; Gentemann & Whitehead, 1983).

Two examples involving different ethnic groups demonstrate how these beliefs, attitudes, and values function in teaching, and their effects on student academic and social behaviors. In research she conducted on effective teachers of Native American and Alaskan Native students Kleinfeld (1975) described them as "warm demanders." Their classrooms radiated emotional warmth and personal caring and there were expectations of reciprocity in both respect and academic engagement, among the students and between the students and the teacher; high levels of personal connectedness between teachers and students that extend beyond the classroom; and academic learning demands complemented with facilitative assistance. Students who had previously been totally uninvolved in classrooms activities, silent and disinterested, and frequently absent from school showed a complete turnround. Their interest levels, attendance, and achievement increased significantly. Even more remarkably, those who had once been personifications of the "silent and stoic Indian" image transformed into students who were exuberant and highly vocal, with a wealth of knowledge and skills they were eager to share and quite competent in doing so (Kleinfeld, 1973, 1975; Kleinfeld & Nelson, 1988). Obidah and Teel (2001), Ladson-Billings (1994), and Escalanté and Dirmann (1990) also found that teachers get the best behavioral and academic performance from students when they combine high expectations with unequivocal support; challenge instruction with personal caring; set clear guidelines for behavior with related skill development; and teach students in school with knowledge of them as human beings in nonschool contexts.

The Advancement Via Individual Determination (AVID) Project is another compelling example of how deliberately constructed communal and culturally enriched classroom infrastructures can improve the achievement of students of color. The project started initially with a San Diego County high school teacher who convinced a group of underachieving Latino and African American students to enroll in an Advanced Placement English class. Prompted by a desire to break the cycle of academic failure of students of color, their overrepresentation in low-level curriculum tracks, and low college attendance, she created an instructional system that responded to their cultural learning styles and specific academic needs. It used multicultural content to teach generic English concepts, principles, and skills, and instituted a comprehensive support system. This system included symbols of identity and affiliation with AVID, as well as promoting values of success; teaching cultural capital for negotiating the learning and schooling processes (such as note-taking, learning academic English, and practicing how to interact with educators in different positions of authority); establishing close relationships with college-age mentors; and providing introductions to college courses specifically taught for AVID students in their own high school context. The students also made contractual agreements to work diligently in the project, and to collaborate with each other to accomplish their individual and collective success (Mehan, Hubbard, Villanueva, & Lintz, 1996; Swanson, Mehan, & Hubbard, 1995). Projects like AVID, KEEP, the Escalanté Mathematics Program, the Algebra Project, and the Multicultural Writing Project are good illustrations of why culturally responsive teaching is the best classroom management technique for ethnically diverse students.

CONCLUSION

While discipline is a critical concern for many teachers, classroom management is a larger issue. It has to do with the overall quality of learning environments and experiences, and whether they are conducive to the maximum performance of all students. That performance includes social, personal, cultural, and academic competence. If the classroom is a comfortable, caring, embracing, affirming, engaging, and facilitative place for students then discipline is not likely to be much of an issue. It follows then that both classroom management and school achievement can be improved for students from different ethnic, racial, social, and linguistic backgrounds by ensuring that curriculum and instruction are culturally relevant and personally meaningful for them. This holds true whether classroom management is viewed from a punitive perspective of controlling and sanctioning misbehavior (i.e., discipline), or from the proactive vantage point of captivating learning experiences. The theory, research, and practice discussed in this chapter confirm these premises.

Whether conducted in local, state, regional, or national contexts, analyses of disciplinary practices consistently show high disproportionality toward students of color, especially African and Latino Americans. The commonly held belief that African Americans are disciplined more often and more severely because they commit more serious behavior infractions is not supported by research findings. Instead, they are punished more harshly for relatively minor misconduct (such as defiance, disrespect, rudeness, and disobedience) that falls within the purview of the interpretative judgments of teachers. This subjective discipline often stems from cultural misunderstandings and conflicting expectations about how students and teachers are supposed to behave in relation to each other, and in teaching-learning situations. For example, teachers may consider explicit comments from students that their teaching is boring and irrelevant as rude, insulting, and disrespectful. They may be particularly incensed by the way some students convey these sentiments. Rather than accepting them as useful feedback for improving the quality of instruction, teachers may see them as challenges to their authority that merit chastisement or even stronger disciplinary action. These tensions can be minimized by both students and teachers being more knowledgeable of each others' cultural styles of communicating, valuing, learning, and relating. Teachers also need to embrace these differences as legitimate parts of their classroom dynamics, and use them as conduits for improving academic achievement and teaching students skills of cultural maintenance, adaptation, and border-crossing. In other words, culturally responsive teaching helps ethnically diverse students develop skills to function well in both their indigenous and the mainstream cultural systems. This bi- or multiculturalism is a solid foundation for effective classroom management in diverse classrooms.

Since research indicates that much of the racial disproportionality in discipline results from institutional climates, policies, and actions, it is the responsibility of teachers and administrators to make schools and classrooms into places where ethnically and racially diverse students are empowered through academic success, cultural validation, and personal enrichment. Given that teaching and learning are cultural processes, neither can be the best possible for pluralistic student populations if cultural diversity is not an integral part of educational experiences. Meeting these needs obligates teachers to be knowledgeable of the cultural contributions and social realities of diverse ethnic groups, and then act deliberately and diligently to incorporate them into the learning environments, curriculum content, instructional materials, teaching techniques, and performance assessments they use with students. When this is done, teaching, learning, and classroom management will improve significantly, and, *all* students will have better opportunities to receive equality and excellence in their educational experiences.

ACKNOWLEDGMENT

The author thanks Carl Grant, University of Wisconsin, for his comments on an earlier draft of this chapter.

REFERENCES

Abe, D. J. (2004). *Effects of non-traditional instruction on thr classroom discipline of African American students.* Unpublished doctoral dissertation, University of Washington, Seattle, WA.

Advancement Project/Civil Rights Project (2000a, February). *Education denied: the negative impact of zero tolerance policies.* Testimony before the United States Commission on Civil Rights, Washington, DC.

Advancement Project/Civil Rights Project (2000b). *Opportunities suspended: The devastating consequences of zero tolerance and school discipline policies.* Cambridge, MA: The Civil Rights Project, Harvard University.

Akom, A. A. (2001). Racial profiling at schools: The politics of race and discipline at Berkeley High. In W. Ayres, B. Dohrn, & R. Ayres (Eds.), *Zero tolerance: Resisting the drive for punishment in our schools* (pp. 51–63). New York: New Press.

Allen, B., & Boykin, A. W. (1991). The influence of contextual factors on Afro-American and Euro-American children's performance: Effects of movement opportunity and music. *International Journal of Psychology, 26*(3), 373–387.

Allen, B. A., & Boykin, A. W. (1992). African-American children and the educational process: Alleviating cultural discontinuity through prescriptive pedagogy. *School Psychology Review, 21*(4), 586–598.

Allen, B., & Butler, L. (1996). The effects of music and movement opportunity on the analogical reasoning performance of African American and white school children: A preliminary study. *Journal of Black Psychology, 22*(3), 316–328.

Au, K. H. (1993). *Literacy instruction in multicultural settings.* New York: Harcourt Brace.

Au, K. H., & Kawakami, A. J., (1985). Research currents: Talk story and learning to read. *Language Arts, 62*(4), 406–411.

Au, K. H., & Kawakami, A. J. (1994). Cultural congruence in instruction. In E. R. Hollins, J. E. King, & W. C. Hayman (Eds.), *Teaching diverse populations: Formulating a knowledge base* (pp. 5–23). Albany: State University of New York Press.

Ayres, W., Dohrn, B., & Ayres, R. (Eds.). (2001). *Zero tolerance: Resisting the drive for punishment in our schools.* New York: New Press.

Baber, C. R. (1987). The artistry and artifice of black communication. In G. Gay & W. L. Baber (Eds.), *Expressively black: The cultural basis of ethnic identity* (pp. 75–108). New York: Praeger.

Bailey, C. T., & Boykin, A. W. (2001). The role of task variability and home contextual factors in the academic performance and task motivation of African American elementary school children. *Journal of Negro Education, 70*(1–2), 84–95.

Banks, J. A., & Banks, C. A. M. (Eds.). (1995). *Handbook of research on multicultural education.* New York: Macmillan.

Banks, J. A., & Banks, C. A. M. (Eds.). (2004a). Handbook of research on multicultural education. (2nd ed.). San Francisco: Jossey-Bass.

Banks, J. A., & Banks, C. A. M. (Eds.). (2004b). *Multicultural education: Issues and perspectives* (5th ed.). Hoboken, NJ: Wiley.

Barta, J., Abeyta, A., Gould, D., Galindo, E., Matt, G., Seaman, D., & Voggessor, G. (2001). The mathematical ecology of the Shoshoni and implications for elementary mathematics education and the young learner. *Journal of American Indian Education, 4*(2), 1–27.

Bennett, C. I. (2003). *Comprehensive multicultural education: Theory and practice* (5th ed.). Boston: Allyn & Bacon.

Bernstein, B. B. (1985). A critique of the concept of compensatory education. In C. B. Cazden, V. P. John, & D. Hymes (Eds.), *Functions of language in the classroom* (pp. 135–151). Prospect Heights, IL: Waveland.

Boggs, S. T., Watson-Gegeo, K., & McMillen, G. (1985). *Speaking, relating, and learning: A study of Hawaiian children at home and at school.* Norwood, NJ: Ablex.

Bowers, C. A., & Flinders, D. J. (1991). *Culturally responsive teaching and supervision: A handbook for staff development.* New York: Teachers College Press.

Boykin, A. W. (1983). The academic performance of Afro-American children. In J. Spencer (Ed.), *Achievement and achievement motives* (pp. 322–371). San Francisco: W. Freeman.

Boykin, A. W. (1986). The triple quandary and the schooling of Afro-American children. In U. Neisser (Ed.), *The school achievement of minority children: New perspectives* (pp. 57–92). Hillsdale, NJ: Lawrence Erlbaum Associates.

Boykin, A. W. (1994). Harvesting culture and talent: African American children and school reform. In R. Rossi (Ed.), *Schools and students at risk: Context and framework for positive change* (pp. 116–138). New York: Teachers College Press.

Boykin, A. W. (2000). The talent development model of schooling: Placing students at promise for academic success. *Journal of Education for Students Placed at Risk, 5*(1–2), 3–25.

Boykin, A. W. (2002). Talent development, cultural deep structure, and school reform: Implications for African immersion initiatives. In S. J. Denbo & L. M. Beaulieu (Eds.), *Improving schools for African American students: A reader for educational leaders* (pp. 81–94). Springfield, IL: Charles C. Thomas.

Boykin, A. W., Allen, B., Davis, L., & Senior, A. M. (1997). Task performance of black and white children across levels of presentation variability. *Journal of Psychology, 131*(4), 427–437.

Boykin, A. W., & Bailey, C. T. (2000, April). *The role of cultural factors in school relevant cognitive functioning: Synthesis of findings on cultural contexts, cultural orientations, and individual differences* (Report No. 42). ERIC Document Reproduction Service No. ED441880).

Boykin, A. W., & Cunningham, R. T. (2001). The effect of movement expressiveness in story content and learning context on the analogical reasoning performance of African American children. *Journal of Negro Education, 70*(1–2), 72–83.

Brown, D. F. (2003). Urban teachers' use of culturally responsive management strategies. *Theory Into Practice, 42*(4), 277–282.

Bruner, J. (1996). *The culture of education.* Cambridge, MA: Harvard University Press.

Burden, P. R. (1995). *Classroom management and discipline: Methods for facilitating cooperation and instruction.* White Plains, NY: Longman.

Caraballo, J. M. (2000). Teachers don't care. In S. Nieto (Ed.), *Puerto Rican students in U. S. schools* (pp. 267–268). Mahwah, NJ: Lawrence Erlbaum Associates.

Cazden, C. B., John, V. P., & Hymes, D. (Eds.). (1985). *Functions of language in the classroom* (2nd ed.). Prospect Heights, IL: Waveland.

Charles, C. M. (1996). *Building classroom discipline* (5th ed.). White Plains, NY: Longman.

Charles, C. M. (2000). *The synergetic classroom: Joyful teaching and gentle discipline.* New York: Longman.

Children's Defense Fund (1975). *School suspensions: Are they helping children?* Cambridge, MA: Washington Research Project.

Cohen, E. C., & Lotan, R. A. (2004). Equity in heterogeneous classrooms. In J. A. Banks & C. A. M. Banks (Eds.), *Handbook of research on multicultural education* (2nd ed., pp. 736–750). San Francisco: Jossey-Bass.

Curran, M. E. (2003). Linguistic diversity and classroom management. *Theory Into Practice, 42*(4). 334-340.

Davis, J. E., & Jordan, W. J. (1994). The experience of school context, structure, and experiences on African American males in middle and high schools. *Journal of Negro Education, 63*(4), 570–587.

Delpit, L. (1995). *Other people's children: Cultural conflict in the classroom.* New York: New Press.

Delpit, L., & White-Bradley, P. (2003). Educating or imprisoning the spirit: Lessons from ancient Egypt. *Theory Into Practice, 42*(4), 283–288.

Deyhle, D. (1995). Navajo youth and Anglo racism, cultural integrity and resistance. *Harvard Educational Review, 65*(3), 403–444.

Diamond, B. J., & Moore, M. A. (1995). *Multicultural literacy: Mirroring the reality of the classroom.* New York: Longman.

Diaz, C. F. (Ed.). (2001). *Multicultural education in the 21st century*. New York: Longman.

Dill, E. M., & Boykin, A. W. (2000). The comparative influence of individual, peer tutoring, and communal learning contexts on the recall of African American children. *Journal of Black Psychology, 26*(1), 65–78.

Dilworth, M. E. (Ed.). (1992). *Diversity in teacher education: New expectations*. San Francisco: Jossey-Bass.

Dohrn, B. (2001). "Look out kid/It's something you did:" Zero tolerance for children. In W. Ayres, B. Dohrn, & R. Ayres (Eds.), *Zero tolerance: Resisting the drive for punishment in our schools* (pp. 89–113). New York: New Press.

Dull, V. (1998). Don't act like a teacher!: Images of effective instruction in a Yup'ik Eskimo classroom. A community-based perspective. In J. Lipka, G. V. Mohatt, & the Ciulistet Group (Eds.), *Transforming the culture of schools: Yup'ik Eskimo examples* (pp. 93-100). Mahwah, NJ: Lawrence Erlbaum Associates.

Dyc, G. (1993). Navajo discussion style: A cultural map for the interethnic classroom. *Journal of Navajo Education, 10*(2), 19–25.

Educational Research Service (2003). *Culture and learning*. Arlington, VA: Author.

Emmer, E. T., Evertson, C., & Worsham, M. E. (2000). *Classroom management for secondary teachers* (5th ed.). Boston: Allyn & Bacon.

Epanchin, B. C., Townsend, B., & Stoddard, K. (1994). *Constructive classroom management: Strategies for creating positive learning environments*. Pacific Grove, CA: Brooks/Cole.

Escalantē, J., & Dirmann, J. (1990). The Jaime Escalantē math program. *Journal of Negro Education, 59*(3), 407–423.

Foster, M. (1989). It's cooking now: A performance analysis of the speech events of a black teacher in an urban community college. *Language in Society, 18*(3), 1–29.

Foster, M. (1995). African American teachers and culturally relevant pedagogy. In J. A. Banks & C. A. M. Banks (Eds.), *Handbook of research on multicultural education* (pp. 570–581). New York: Macmillan.

Foster, M. (1997). *Black teachers on teaching*. New York: New Press.

Fullilove, P. E., & Treisman, P. U. (1990). Mathematics achievement among African American undergraduates at the University of California, Berkeley: An evaluation of the Mathematics Workshop Program. *Journal of Negro Education, 59*(3), 463–478.

Garcia, E. E. (2004). Educating Mexican American students: Past treatment and recent developments in theory, research, policy, and practice. In J. A. Banks & C. A. M. Banks (Eds.), *Handbook of research on multicultural education* (2nd ed., pp. 491–514). San Francisco: Jossey-Bass.

Gay, G. (2000). *Culturally responsive teaching: Theory, research, and practice*. New York: Teachers College Press.

Gay, G. (2002). Preparing for culturally responsive teaching. *Journal of Teacher Education, 53*(2), 106–116.

Gentemann, K. M., & Whitehead, T. L. (1983). The cultural broker conception in bicultural education. *Journal of Negro Education, 52*(2), 118–129.

Ginott, H. G. (1972). *Teacher and child: A book for parents and teachers*. New York: Macmillan.

Good, T. L., & Brophy, J. E. (2003). *Looking into classrooms* (9th ed). Boston: Allyn and Bacon.

Gordon, R., Della Piana, L., & Keleher, T. (2000). Facing the consequences: An examination of racial discrimination in U. S. public schools. Oakland, CA: Applied Research Center.

Grant, C. A. (Ed.). (1995). *Educating for diversity: An anthology of multicultural voices*. Boston: Allyn & Bacon.

Gregory, J. F. (1996). The crime of punishment: Racial and gender disparities in the use of corporal punishment in U.S. public schools. *Journal of Negro Education, 64*(4), 454–462.

Gregory, J. F. (1997). Three strikes and they're out: African American boys and American schools' responses to misbehavior. *International Journal of Adolescence and Youth, 7*(1), 25–34.

Haberman, M. (1991). The pedagogy of poverty versus good teaching. *Phi Delta Kappan, 73*(4), 290–294.

Hale, J. (1986). *Black children: Their roots, culture, and learning styles*. Baltimore: Johns Hopkins University Press Associates.

Hollins, E. R. (1996). *Culture in school learning: Revealing the deep meaning*. Mahwah, NJ: Lawrence Erlbaum Associates.

Hollins, E. R., King, J. E., & Hayman, W. C. (Eds.). (1994). *Teaching diverse populations: Formulating a knowledge base*. Albany: State University of New York Press.

Hollins, E. R., & Oliver, E. I. (Eds.). (1999). *Pathways to success in school: Culturally responsive teaching*. Mahwah, NJ: Lawrence Erlbaum Associates.

Howard, T. C. (1998). *Pedagogical practices and ideological constructions of effective teachers of African American students*. Unpublished doctoral dissertation, University of Washington, Seattle, WA.

Howard, T. C. (2001). Powerful pedagogy for African American students: A case of four teachers. *Urban Education, 36*(2), 179–202.

Jones, V. F., & Jones, L. S. (1986). *Comprehensive classroom management: Creating positive learning environments* (2nd ed.). Boston: Allyn & Bacon.

Jones, V. F., & Jones, L. S. (2004). *Comprehensive classroom management: Creating communities of support and solving problems* (7th ed.). Boston: Allyn & Bacon.

Kleinfeld, J. (1973). Effects of nonverbally communicated personal warmth on the intelligence test performance of Indian and Eskimo adolescents. *Journal of Social Psychology, 91*(1), 149–150.

Kleinfeld, J. (1975). Effective teachers of Eskimo and Indian students. *School Review*, 83(2), 301–344.

Kleinfeld, S., & Nelson, P. (1988). Adapting instruction to Native Americans' learning style: An iconoclastic view. In W. J. Lonner & V. O. Tyler, Jr. (Eds.), *Cultural and ethnic factors in learning and motivation: Implications for education* (pp. 83–101). Bellingham, WA: Western Washington University Press.

Kochman, T. (1981). *Black and white styles in conflict*. Chicago: University of Chicago Press.

Krater, J., Zeni, J., & Cason, N. D. (1994). *Mirror images: Teaching writing in black and white*. Portsmouth, NH: Heinemann.

Ladson-Billings, G. (1994). *The dreamkeepers: Successful teachers for African American children*. San Francisco: Jossey-Bass.

Ladson-Billings, G. (1995a). But that's just good teaching: The case for culturally relevant pedagogy. *Theory Into Practice, 34*(3), 159–165.

Ladson-Billings, G. (1995b). Toward a theory of culturally relevant pedagogy. *American Educational Research Journal*, 32(3), 465–491.

Ladson-Billings, G. (2001). America still eats her young. In W. Ayres, B. Dohrn, & R. Ayres (Eds.), *Zero tolerance: Resisting the drive for punishment in our schools* (pp. 77–85) New York: New Press.

Lee, C. (1993). *Signifying as a scaffold to literary interpretation: The pedagogical implications of a form of African-American discourse* (NCTE Research Report No. 26). Urbana, IL: National Council of Teachers of English.

Lipka, J., Mohatt, G. V., & the Ciulistet Group. (Eds.). (1998). *Transforming the culture of schools: Yup'ik Eskimo examples*. Mahwah, NJ: Lawrence Erlbaum Associates.

Lomawaima, K. T. (2004). Educating Native Americans. In J. A. Banks & C. A. M. Banks (Eds.), *Handbook of research on multicultural education* (2nd ed., pp. 441–461). San Francisco: Jossey-Bass.

Losey, K. M. (1997). *Listen to the silence: Mexican American interaction in the composition classroom and community*. Norwood, NJ: Ablex.

Marzano, R. J., Marzano, J. S., & Pickering, D. J. (2003). Classroom management that works: Research-based strategies for every teacher. Alexandria, VA: Association for Supervision and Curriculum Development.

Mathews, J. (1988). *Escalante: The best teacher in America*. New York: Henry Holt.

McCarthy, J., & Benally, J. (2003). Classroom management in a Navajo middle school. *Theory Into Practice, 42*(4), 296–304.

McCarthy, J. D., & Hoge, D. R. (1987). The social construction of school punishment: Racial disadvantage out of universalistic process. *Social Forces, 65*(4), 1101–1120.

McCarty, T. L. (2002). *A place to be Navajo: Rough Rock and the struggle for self-determination in indigenous schooling*. Mahwah, NJ: Lawrence Erlbaum Associates.

McDermott, R. (1987). Achieving school failure: An anthropological approach to illiteracy and social stratification. In G. D. Spindler (Ed.), *Education and cultural process: Anthropological approaches* (2nd ed., pp. 173–209). Prospect Heights, IL: Waveland.

McLean Donaldson, K. B. (1996). *Through students' eyes: Combating racism in United States schools*. Westport, CT: Praeger.

Mehan, H., Hubbard, L., Villanueva, I., & Lintz, A. (1996). *Constructing school success: The consequences of untracking low-achieving students*. New York: Cambridge University Press.

Moll, L. C., Amanti, C., Neff, D., & Gonzalez, N. (1992). Funds of knowledge for teaching: Using a qualitative approach to connect homes and classrooms. *Theory Into Practice, 31*(1), 132–141.

Moll, L. C., & Gonzalez, N. (2004). Engaging life: A funds-of-knowledge approach to multicultural education. In J. A. Banks & C. A. M. Banks (Eds.), *Handbook of research on multicultural education* (2nd ed., pp. 699–715). San Francisco: Jossey-Bass.

Monroe, C. R., & Obidah, J. E. (2004). The influence of cultural synchronization on a teacher's perceptions of disruption: A case study of an African American middle-school classroom. *Journal of Teacher Education, 55*(3), 256–268.

Moses, R. P., & Cobb, C. E., Jr. (2001). *Radical equations: Math literacy and civil rights*. Boston: Beacon Press.

NASP Center (2004). Fair and effective discipline for all students: Best practice strategies for educators. Retrieved January 28, 2004, from http://www.naspcenter.org/factsheets/effdiscip_fs.html

Nieto, S. (2002). *Language, culture, and teaching: Critical perspectives for a new century*. Mahwah, NJ: Lawrence Erlbaum Associates.

Nieto, S. (2004). *Affirming diversity: The sociopolitical context of multicultural education*. Boston: Pearson/Allyn & Bacon.

Noguera, P. A. (2003). Schools, prisons, and social implications of punishment: Rethinking disciplinary practices. *Theory Into Practice, 42*(4), 341–350.

Obidah, J. E., & Teel, K. M. (2001). *Because of the kids: Facing racial and cultural differences in schools*. New York: Teachers College Press.

Pai, Y., & Adler, S. (2001). *Cultural foundations of education* (3rd ed.). Upper Saddle River, NJ: Merrill/Prentice-Hall.

Pang, V. O., & Cheng. L-R. L. (Eds.). (1998). *Struggling to be heard: The unmet needs of Asian Pacific American children.* Albany: State University of New York Press.

Pang, V. O., Kiang, P. N., & Pak, Y. K. (2004). Asian Pacific American students. In J. A. Banks & C. A. M. Banks (Eds.), *Handbook of research on multicultural education* (2nd ed., pp. 542–563). San Francisco: Jossey-Bass.

Philips, S. (1983). *The invisible culture: Communication in classroom and community on the Warm Springs Indian Reservation.* Prospect Heights, IL: Waveland.

Piestrup, A. M. (1973). *Black dialect interference and accommodation of reading instruction in first grade* (Monograph of the Language Behavior Research Laboratory). Berkeley: University of California.

Powell, R. G., & Caseau, D. (2004). *Classroom communication and diversity: Enhancing instructional practice.* Mahwah, NJ: Lawrence Erlbaum Associates.

Powers, K., Potthoff, S. J., Bearinger, L. H., & Resnick, M. D. (2003). Does cultural programming improve educational outcomes for American Indian youth? *Journal of American Indian Education, 42*(2), 17–49.

Rivera, M., & Pedraza, P. (2001). The spirit of transformation: An education reform movement in a New York City Latino/a community. In S. Nieto (Ed.), *Puerto Rican students in U. S. schools* (pp. 223–243). Mahwah, NJ: Lawrence Erlbaum Associates.

Shade, B. J. (Ed.). (1989). *Culture, style, and the educative process.* Springfield, IL: Thomas.

Sheets, R. H. (1995a). From remedial to gifted: Effects of culturally centered pedagogy. *Theory Into Practice, 34*(3), 186–193.

Sheets, R. H. (1995b). *Student and teacher perceptions of disciplinary conflicts in culturally pluralistic classrooms.* Unpublished doctoral dissertation, University of Washington, Seattle WA.

Sheets, R. H. (1996). Urban classroom conflict: Student-teacher perception: Ethnic integrity, solidarity, and resistance. *The Urban Review, 28*(2), 165–183.

Sheets, R. H., & Gay, G. (1996). Student perceptions of disciplinary conflict in ethnically diverse classrooms. *NASSP Bulletin, 80*(580), 84–94.

Siu, S-F. (1996, December). *Asian American students at risk: A literature review* (Report No. 8). Washington, DC: Center for Research on the Education of Students Placed at Risk (CRESPAR), Howard University. Retrieved February 7, 2004, from www.crespar.law.howard.edu

Skiba, R. J. (2000). *Zero tolerance, zero evidence: An analysis of school disciplinary practices* (Policy Research Report No. SRS2). Bloomington, IN: Indiana Education Policy Center.

Skiba, R. J., & Knesting, K. (2001). Zero tolerance, zero evidence: An analysis of school disciplinary practice. In R. J. Skiba and G. G. Noam (Eds.), *New directions for youth development: Theory, practice, research* (pp. 11-43). San Francisco: Jossey-Bass.

Skiba, R. J., Michael, R. S., Nardo, A. C., & Peterson, R. (2000). *The color of discipline: Sources of racial and gender disproportionality in school punishment* (Policy Research Report No. SRS1. Bloomington, IN: Indiana Education Policy Center.

Skiba, R. J., & Noam, G. G. (Eds.). (2001). *New directions for youth development: Theory practice, research.* San Francisco: Jossey-Bass.

Skiba, R. J., & Peterson, R. (1999). The dark side of zero tolerance: Can punishment lead to safe schools? *Phi Delta Kappan, 80*(5), 372–376, 381–382.

Skiba, R. J., Peterson, R. L., & Williams, T. (1997). Office referrals and susppensions: Disciplinary intervention in middle schools. *Education and treatment of children, 20(3)*, 295–315.

Skiba, R. J., Simmons, A., Staudinger, L., Rausch, M., Dow, G., & Feggins R. (2003, May 16–17). Consistent removal: Contributions of school discipline in the school-prison pipeline. Paper presented at the School to Prison Pipeline Conference, Harvard Civil Rights Project, Retrieved February 3, 2004, from www.civilrightsproject.harvard.edu/research/pipeline03/SkibaEXECv4.pdf

Slavin, R. E. (1995). Cooperative learning and intergroup relations. In J. A. Banks & C. A. M. Banks (Eds.), *Handbook of research on multicultural education* (pp. 628–634). New York: Macmillan.

Sleeter, C. E. (Ed.). (1991). *Empowerment through multicultural education.* Albany: State University of New York Press.

Smitherman, G. (1986). *Talkin' and testifyin': The language of Black America* (2nd ed.). Detroit: Wayne State University Press.

Smitherman, G. (1994). The blacker the berry the sweeter the juice: African American student writers. In A. H. Dyson & C. Genishi (Eds.), *The need for story: Cultural diversity in classroom and community* (pp. 80–101). Urbana,IL: National Council of Teachers of English.

Smitherman, G. (1998). Black English/Ebonics: What it be like? In T. Perry & L. Delpit (Eds.), *The real Ebonics debate: Power, language, and the education of African American children* (pp. 29–37). Boston: Beacon Press.

Spindler, G. D. (Ed.). (1987). *Education and cultural process: Anthropological approaches* (2nd ed.). Prospect Heights, IL: Waveland.

Spindler, G., & Spindler, L. (1993). The process of culture and person: Cultural therapy and culturally diverse schools. In P. Phelan & A. L. Davidson (Eds.), *Renegotiating cultural diversity in American schools* (pp. 27–51. New York: Teachers College Press.

Spindler, G., & Spindler, L. (Eds.). (1994a). *Pathways to cultural awareness: Cultural therapy with teachers and students*. Thousand Oaks, CA: Corwin.

Spindler G., & Spindler, L. (1994b). What is cultural therapy? In G. Spindler & L. Spindler (Eds.), *Pathways to cultural awareness: Cultural therapy with teachers and students* (pp. 1–33). Thousand Oaks, CA: Corwin.

Spring, J. (1995). *The intersection of cultures: Multicultural education in the United States*. New York: McGraw-Hill.

Swanson, M. C., Mehan, H., & Hubbard, L. (1995). The AVID classroom: Academic and social support for low-achieving students. In J. Oakes & H. Quartz (Eds.), *Creating new educational communities* (94th Yearbook of the National Society for the Study of Education, Part I) (pp. 53–69). Chicago: University of Chicago Press.

Taylor, M. C., & Foster, G. A. (1986). Bad boys and school suspensions: Public policy implications for black males. *Sociological Inquiry, 56*(4), 498–506.

Tharp, R. G., & Gallimore, R. (1988). *Rousing minds to life: Teaching, learning, and schooling in social context*. New York: Cambridge University Press.

Theory Into Practice (2003, Autumn), *42*(4). Classroom management in a diverse society.

Torres-Guzman, M. E., & Thorne, Y. M. (2000). Puerto Rican/Latino student voices: Stand and deliver. In S. Nieto (Ed.), *Puerto Rican students in U.S. schools* (pp. 269–291). Mahwah, NJ: Lawrence Erlbaum Associates.

Townsend, B. L. (2000). The disproportionate discipline of African American learners: Reducing school suspensions and expulsions. *Exceptional Children, 66*(3), 381–391.

Treisman, P. U. (1985). *A study of the mathematics achievement of black students that the University of California, Berkeley*. Unpublished doctoral dissertation, University of California, Berkeley, CA.

Vadas, R. E. (1995). Assessing the relationship between academic performance and attachment to Navajo culture. *Journal of Navajo Education, 12*(2), 16–25.

Villegas, A. M., & Lúcas, T. (2002). *Educating culturally responsive teachers: A coherent approach*. Albany: State University of New York Press.

Weinstein, C. S., Curran, M., & Tomlinson-Clarke, S. (2003). Culturally responsive classroom management: Awareness into action. *Theory Into Practice, 42*(4), 269–276.

Weinstein,. C. S., Tomlinson-Clarke, S., & Curran, M. (2004). Toward a conception of culturally responsive classroom management. *Journal of Teacher Education, 55*(1), 25–38.

Wu, S. C., Pink, W. T., Crain, R. L., & Moles, O. (1982). Student suspensions: A critical reappraisal. *The Urban Review, 14*(4), 245–303.

IV

Classroom Management in Specific Contexts

Anita Woolfolk Hoy
The Ohio State University

14

Classroom Management in Early Childhood and Elementary Classrooms

Kathy Carter and Walter Doyle
University of Arizona

INTRODUCTION

> Teacher's work is conflicted, contradictory, muddied, and torn by myriad demands of a dynamic lived life in which each teacher must negotiate her way, shaping small moments as she is shaped by the very things she takes most for granted—especially conceptions of use of time. The demands upon her for performance, for action, generate a level of business that is scarcely conceivable to those who have not taught in classrooms. Teacher's work is extraordinarily difficult and challenging. (Wien, 1995, p. 144)

The obligation of any chapter in this *Handbook* is to provide the reader with a survey, appraisal, and, where possible, a synthesis of what is known about a specific topic within the domain of classroom management, in this case, classroom management in early childhood and elementary classrooms. On the surface, meeting this obligation seems relatively straightforward. But early childhood and elementary classroom management is not a mature field situated within a disciplinary community that might give rise to a rigorous and substantial body of tightly reasoned scholarly texts and refereed research reports. Rather, it has been fundamentally a practical matter that exists primarily at the point of service in schools, among mostly women and children far from the towers of academe, and usually becomes an issue mainly for school building administrators largely when it fails, that is, when misbehavior occurs and classroom life is disrupted. Those who actually do classroom management have little time or incentive to write about it. Those who write about it represent a wide range of backgrounds and specialties and are typically motivated to fix it, to improve how classrooms are managed. So the literatures that have evolved represent a wide diversity of intellectual and practical traditions from which a range of sometimes conflicting ideas and suggestions have been extrapolated.

Given the scope and texture of the literatures in early childhood and elementary classroom management, fairly broad criteria have been used in defining a relevant body of literature for this chapter and in judging the grounds for what can be claimed to be knowledge in this area. In determining an answer to the question, "What is known?" we have used not only empirical criteria—what systematic evidence is available—but also a sense of what is commonly held to be "true" within the available writings, including textbooks in the field. Although the content of textbooks is partially driven by market considerations, these books represent in many ways the hubs around which most of the knowledge of classroom management is created, stored, and carried by the early childhood/elementary education community.

The task of reviewing this literature is also confounded in that early childhood and elementary school classrooms (grades P–5)[1] are complex, multifaceted contexts in children's lives, contexts in which they develop social consciousness, early friendships, interpersonal competence outside the family context, resilience, and a foundation for academic proficiency. In such settings, management, teaching, and curriculum often blend together in a coherent narrative as spontaneous groupings, structured activities, and short lessons coalesce, transform, and reconvene across the day. In these primary and intermediate grades, individual achievements are less a function of formal instruction than they are of the social fabric of the classroom environment, that is, the flowing interconnections among adults and children that make up the daily events of classroom life. In parent-teacher conferences in the early grades, for instance, one would be hard pressed to sort out the academic, social, emotional, and behavioral aspects of the discourse.

This natural blending of pedagogical functions has two important implications for the field of classroom management. First, the way early education settings are managed has profound consequences for each child's school career and life success and for building a school community among an increasingly diverse population of families whose children attend school. Second, the blending of categories means, on the one hand, that the topic of classroom management can hardly be avoided in talking about early childhood and elementary classroom teaching, but, on the other hand, it becomes difficult to talk about classroom management as a distinct feature of a teacher's classroom work in these settings. Yet, without an understanding of the specifically management dimensions of their responsibilities, teachers can find it difficult to avoid focusing on extreme outliers rather than turning to the full range of behaviors when trying to comprehend the nature and consequences of activity in their classrooms.

A special effort has been made throughout the chapter to examine a part without deconstructing the whole. The intent here is to accentuate and scrutinize, insofar as the existing literature allows, the management dimensions of what teachers do without isolating managerial functions such that the very fabric of classroom life is unraveled. Whether one agrees that this chapter achieves this goal or not, the project itself is important for the profession and one that is long overdue.

The core of the chapter is framed around two major strands in the early childhood/elementary classroom management literature. The first concerns the classroom itself, i.e., the procedures (techniques, methods, skills, and cognitions) for achieving, sustaining, and restoring orderliness in classroom environments. Attention, in other words, is directed to ways of orchestrating settings and action systems to capture children's attention, engagement, and focus so that curriculum activities can go on. This section isolates the distinctive management aspects of a teacher's work, and it is these matters that often disconcert the beginning teacher: "Can I get lessons to work?" "Will things get out of control?" "Will my children be safe?" The discussion in this section of the chapter is grounded in the ecological traditions in classroom

[1]The National Association for the Education of Young Children (NAEYC) defines early childhood education as encompassing the age span from birth through eight years of age (see Bredekamp, 1996). The premise is that children in this age range share several characteristics, such as vulnerability, dependence on adults, concrete thinking, and a need for closeness. For our purposes, we have started with attendance in formal preschools which typically begins after age two.

management that have been built from innovative work of Jacob Kounin and Paul Gump (see Doyle, 1986).

The second strand of the chapter has to do with the "social curriculum" of classroom management (see Powell, McLaughlin, Savage, & Zehm, 2001), that is, with the consequences of how classrooms are managed. The focus here is on young children's moral and prosocial development and the teaching of self management, responsibility, and resilience in contexts related to their conduct in school settings. This is an emerging emphasis in early childhood/elementary classroom management and one that has drawn a wide range of specializations and theoretical languages. In this section, the discourse shifts from the action systems and environmental structures of the ecologists to the idiosyncratic features of individual pupils as they progress through stages of their development and to the educative potential of different forms of adult-child and child-child interactions within classroom spaces. Attention shifts, in other words, from strictly management issues to educative functions and outcomes of interacting with young children in school settings. This body of work gradually blends with the broader curricular and pedagogical responsibilities of the teacher. Once again, we endeavor to stay as close as possible to the management functions in teaching.

Virtually all of the classroom research related to management has been conducted in upper elementary school classrooms, grades 3–5. The same can be said for the literatures on the social curriculum of classroom management. Little direct work has been done on classroom management in early childhood education and in the primary grades. It will be necessary, therefore, to extrapolate with a combination of available tools to understand management in early childhood classrooms and the early elementary grades.

Many of the themes closely related to this chapter—for example, special needs students, diversity, and teacher preparation—are addressed in other chapters in this *Handbook*. The intention here is to stay focused on the general issues of classroom management in regular early childhood and elementary classrooms.

A PERSPECTIVE ON THE DEVELOPING CHILD

Dramatic differences along several dimensions exist between nursery school and 5th grade, between 2 year olds and 11 year olds, between preschoolers and preadolescents. We have tried to formulate meaningful statements that somehow apply across these differences. Indeed, the very concept of "developmentally appropriate practice," which permeates thinking in early childhood education (see Bredekamp, 1996; Bryant, Clifford, & Peisner, 1991; National Research Council, 2001), decrees adaptation to the growing child's changing developmental processes. At each step of the way, therefore, one must take into account age and grade-level differences across the range encompassed by the topic of this chapter.

It is also important to note that "early childhood" and "elementary" are not just organizational categories in the institution of schooling. They also represent conceptual traditions, that is, philosophical or theoretical frameworks for interpreting who children are, what they need to learn, how they learn, and how they are best nurtured and taught (see Golbeck, 2001). Pedagogical theorists, such as Montessori, Pestolozzi, Froebel, and Dewey, and programs such as Whole Language and Reggio Emilia have created powerful cultural images that inform professionals who educate young children and quietly permeate how parents and the public understand what schools should do for young children and how they should do it. Indeed, the very concept of "developmentally appropriate practice" embodies a child-centered and constructivist philosophical stance toward the education of young children (see Bredekamp, 1987, 1996; Wien, 1995).

To take into account these images and cultural stories in interpreting the literatures on early childhood and elementary classroom management, we provide here a perspective on child development. This overview is necessarily brief and synoptic because it is primarily intended as a backdrop for the focal content of the chapter. Child development and schooling, as the primary occupation of children, are necessarily intertwined. In most of today's industrialized societies, schooling plays a major role in children's lives not only in the amount of time they spend in these formal institutions but also in the social practices that operate in adult-child interactions and in the framing of children's social identities outside of schools (see Rogoff, Paradise, Arauz, Correa-Chavez, & Angelillo, 2003). Not infrequently, parents model school tasks when talking with their children ("How many flowers do you see in the vase?" or "What letter does 'tiger' begin with?"), toys are sometimes designed to foster readiness for school or supplement school learning activities, and children's performance and behavior in school can become a significant part of how they are known among families in a local community. Thus, schooling comes to define a central part of the process of child development in the modern world, just as the attributes and needs of the developing child help define the character of schooling practices.

Most discussions of personal and social development in childhood (e.g., Eddowes & Ralph, 1998; Puckett & Black, 2001; Trawick-Smith, 2000) are framed around versions of the developmental stages articulated by Erik Erikson (1963): trust versus mistrust, autonomy versus shame and doubt, initiative versus guilt, and industry versus inferiority. For our purposes, we have selected four broad categories: autonomy, self-esteem, self-control, and social interaction to organize our survey of the intersection of child development and the social curriculum of classroom management. The first two of these categories—autonomy and self-esteem—are concerned primarily, but not exclusively, with the developing individual within a classroom management system, and the second two—selfcontrol and social interaction—reflect a greater focus on group management dimensions.

Autonomy and Self-Esteem

One of the obvious tasks for a young child moving from a nuclear family setting into an institutional form of care and education is to gain a sense of autonomy, that is, independence and self-government. An environment with predictability and constancy mirrors for many children the family environment they have experienced and builds on the sense of trust they have developed in that context. In cases in which constancy and trust have not characterized a child's home, a steady school environment can help stabilize their lives and build a basic sense of trust. This line of thinking calls for opportunities for attachment to stable adults and for the development of predictable routines and procedures for early childhood classrooms (see, especially, Watson, 2003).

At the same time, to develop autonomy young children need supported opportunities for initiative, exploration, and choice. Such opportunities are possible when there is a balance of freedom and control—what Golback (2001) calls a "child-regulated/teacher-guided" pedagogy—so that the child can deal with his or her contradictory needs for both dependence and independence (see Watson, 2003, for specific examples and suggestions). As children move into the later years of preschool and into kindergarten, the need for initiative increases as they begin to deal with new skills, language, and the challenges of cooperative play. Finally, in the elementary grades, children face the task of developing a sense of industry (mastery and self-assurance). Throughout these phases, the balance of freedom and control and the need for choice with support, acceptance, and recognition come to play an increasingly important part in a child's development. But, as Watson (2003) notes, "it is difficult to meet the misbehaving child's needs for autonomy, belonging, and competence and also maintain a safe and productive classroom" (p. 3).

The theme of self-esteem—a positive regard for one's own attributes and talents—is implicit in this discussion of the development of autonomy, initiative, and industry. With greater initiative and exploration, children begin to face more directly the limits and frustrations of classroom situations and the feelings of guilt and inferiority that can come from social and academic failures. Being able to label and talk about their feelings of frustration, guilt, and failure is important in helping children gain perspective and deal more directly and effectively with their emotions in classroom situations.

Self Control and Social Interaction

The issues of autonomy, initiative, and industry also have manifestations in peer relationships. In early school years, much of children's play is parallel rather than cooperative. Nonetheless, young children begin to learn the complex processes of collaboration that involve a respect for the viewpoints of others, while developing an ability to express their own perspective within group situations and to resolve inevitable conflicts (e.g., choices of objects, direction and flow of games) that arise in social circumstances. Moreover, specific efforts can be made by the teacher to teach children how to be friends (see Watson, 2003, pp. 55–79). As they grow older, more cooperative forms of play emerge and friendships expand and become more complex as they deepen. At the same time, the possibilities for conflict and for both verbal and physical aggression increase. However, children also develop with increased age and experience a greater capacity to understand the perspective of others and begin to internalize social norms and cognitions concerning the treatment of others and the appropriate display of emotions. They also become more sociocentric and less egocentric and develop an increased sense of altruism, empathy, impulse control, and morality.

Most authorities (see, e.g., Puckett & Black, 2001) seem to agree that adults can contribute to a developing sense of respect and autonomy in social groups by judiciously collaborating with children during peer interactions. Research suggests, however, that successful teacher interventions to promote peer interactions can be difficult to achieve. Harper and McCluskey (2003) found, for example, that children were more likely to initiate contact with an adult rather than with a peer after an adult intervention to promote the child's social interaction.

As children grow older, this collaboration becomes less immediate as teachers become partners and facilitators with children in social interactions. Again, a balance of initiative and limits needs to be reached as teachers facilitate, model, prompt, and encourage rather than direct and dominate. The development of self-control requires opportunities to exhibit initiative and make choices in complex social situations. The children must do the work of social interaction if they are to explore and develop in this area. Clearly, the provision of developmentally appropriate social opportunities in classrooms can place pressure on the management aspects of the teacher's work. Tensions can, in other words, exist between the demands of creating orderly environments for accomplishing school work and the need to provide opportunities for children's autonomy and initiative. These potential tensions are addressed in a variety of ways throughout the chapter.

CREATING AND MAINTAINING ORDER IN CLASSROOMS

This section of the chapter focuses on classroom processes and the actions teachers take to establish and sustain order in classroom environments. Although discipline—action taken after misbehavior occurs—intersects with this category, attention is first directed primarily to what teachers do to create and maintain order before disciplinary interventions are needed. As noted, this area of early childhood/elementary classroom management focuses specifically on the distinctive management aspects of teaching and is especially a concern of preservice and beginning teachers as they face the prospects and challenges of leading groups of young children in real-life classroom environments.

The tradition of research on details of classroom processes related to establishing and maintaining order and work involvement can be traced to the remarkable work of Jacob S. Kounin (1970) who, with the help of Paul Gump (1982; Kounin & Gump, 1974), conducted an extraordinarily intuitive program of ecologically framed studies on management and group processes in classrooms (for details of this research program, see Doyle, 1986; Weinstein, 1991). A core notion of this ecological approach is that an environment such as a classroom is "a behavior setting, that is, an ecobehavioral unit composed of segments that *surround* and *regulate* behavior" (Doyle, 1986, p. 397; see also Gump, 1975). From this perspective, one of the central elements of a setting is the program of action, that is, the standing pattern of behavior that defines and regulates appropriate participation. At a play, for instance, participants are expected to move toward their seats when the lights in the lobby blink and to become quiet and attentive as the house lights dim. To do otherwise is disruptive. The program of action, thus, both defines appropriate behavior sequences and pulls participants along toward an orderly social event.

Similarly, in a classroom the program of action for a particular segment (sharing, discussion, dramatic play, presentation, gardening, small group, watercolor painting, etc.) defines order for the present moment and pulls students along toward orderliness. Indeed, an established program of action holds order in place in classrooms. This view of the foundation of classroom order stands in contrast to two dominant views in the field: (a) the position that classroom management is achieved by discipline, that is, by what happens after a student acts inappropriately, and (b) the outlook that classroom management rests primarily on formal regulatory mechanisms, such as rules and specific procedures. An ecologist would never argue that discipline (or desists) and rules and procedures do not play an important part in management, but he or she would emphasize strongly the central role of events in defining, creating, and sustaining classroom order. He or she would contend, therefore, that events themselves must be managed, that is, must be understood, established, and monitored by the teacher. Without an event on the floor, discipline and rules have no center.

This emphasis on action and event in the ecological tradition brings a story perspective to understanding classroom management (see Carter, 1993). Stories, in essence, are frameworks in which incidents, behaviors, motives, and possibilities are woven together into integrated strands that provide the possibility for interpretation or meaning. This interrelating of elements is fundamentally necessary to portray classroom scenes and interpret the processes and dynamics of the management tasks teachers face. There is also reason to believe that much of the practical knowledge experienced teachers acquire is storied, i.e., arises from their actions in situations (Carter, 1992, 1995). Thus, teachers carry their knowledge of classrooms in the lived narratives of their experiences and, therefore, discourse on classroom management as well as efforts to prepare novices to manage classrooms needs to be framed in ways that respect this narrative understanding.

There are special ways in which the idea of program of action applies to early childhood settings. In contrast to elementary classrooms, preschool and even kindergarten settings rarely have segments involving common attention and action by all participants. More typically, early childhood settings have regions or centers for active play, construction, dramatic play, quiet time, and the like. Each center has room for only a portion of the pupils, and they usually choose regions according to their own preference and schedule. Each center has a program of action—dramatic play is different from gross motor activity in the playground—but these are quite loosely defined in terms of pupil's focus and attention. An early childhood teacher might intervene in a center for a variety of reasons (e.g., to capture a teachable moment, etc.), but management consists primarily of attention to glaring deviations from the program of action, such as hitting or excluding classmates. Nevertheless, if group attention is required for a segment, then the ecological imperatives apply.

The second major resource for this section are the elementary classroom studies conducted at the University of Texas Research and Development Center for Teacher Education in the 1970s (see Emmer, Evertson, & Anderson, 1980; Evertson, Emmer, Sanford, & Clements, 1983). No other research program to date has matched the scope of this endeavor. Finally, we have relied on two important classroom management textbooks: Weinstein and Mignano (2003) and Evertson, Emmer, and Worsham (2003). The latter, now in its sixth edition, was based originally on the training manual used in the experimental phase of the University of Texas studies. Both books reflect grounding in classroom research and represent useful syntheses of the relevant work. These works are supplemented where possible with references to individual studies and reviews in the field.

Organizing the Physical Setting

One of the important features of a classroom event—spelling test, reading lesson, morning song—is its "physical milieu, that is, the shape of the site in which it occurs, the number and types of participants, the arrangement of participants in the available space, and the props or objects available to participants" (Doyle, 1986, p. 397). This is certainly a domain over which a teacher has at least limited control. The overall shape and design of a classroom and the type of furnishings available are determined to a large extent before a teacher arrives at the door, but within these constraints a teacher can arrange the setting to facilitate traffic flow, communication, supplies and equipment access, private space, and the monitoring of classroom behavior (see Clayton, 2001). In this section we examine some of the relevant work on the design of physical settings in classrooms and how that might relate to the management of children's behaviors.

Consistent with developmental principles concerning the need for a balance between freedom and external expectations, modern early childhood and elementary classrooms are flexible, adaptable settings crowded with tables, chairs, cubbies, rug areas, plants, easels, building blocks, and shelves to accommodate individual study, small and large group activity, and lessons. With the increased use of computers and other technologies for exploration in classrooms, the demands for space design to accommodate equipment and provide access and privacy have increased (see Butin, 2000a, and chapter 20 in this volume).

In preschools, play, in the form of either dramatic play or gross motor activity, often takes center stage in the design of space; the academic curriculum is on the periphery in nature displays, animal habitats, reading corners, quiet zones, shelves of Cuisenaire rods, and the like. The emphasis, in other words, is on movement and imagination and on opportunities for active, passive, and cooperative activity (see Butin, 2000b). Formal "lessons" are usually conducted almost spontaneously on the floor with groups of children gathered around an adult, and this pattern often continues into the lower elementary grades. In the upper elementary grades, space gradually begins to mirror middle school and high school classrooms with an increasingly formal arrangement of desks in the center and supplies, files, materials, and private places along the edges. At this level, the space is increasingly designed for work rather than play.

What is the best arrangement of early childhood/elementary classrooms for maintaining safety and for achieving and sustaining order? This question probably has no single answer because "best" depends upon a variety of factors related to purposes, participants, and the shape of the available space. However, a limited amount of research and some collective wisdom are available to formulate at least a partial set of principles to guide decisions in this area (see Clayton, 2001; McLeod, 2003; and chapter 3 in Weinstein & Mignano, 2003).

Weinstein (e.g., 1979; Weinstein & David, 1987; Weinstein & Mignano, 2003) has been especially concerned with the physical design of classrooms. In her 1979 review, she found that arrangements primarily affected attitudes and conduct rather than achievement or even patterns of verbal interactions. Density (i.e., the ratio of population to area) and the flow of traffic patterns were especially important in managing distractions, attentiveness, and aggression. With increased size comes an increased concern for rules and regulations, especially in early childhood centers (see Butin, 2000b). Attentiveness and work involvement are also related to where a pupil sits in a lesson. Students in what Adams (1969) called the "action zone" (front and center) are more likely to be attentive and to participate in a lesson (see also Adams & Biddle, 1970; Sommer, 1969). These findings suggest that teachers can increase involvement in lessons by making sure students have enough space among them to be able to focus on the lesson and by attending to students who sit at the back and on the edges of the group. Periodic movement may also be required. Some evidence exists to suggest that it is difficult to sit still and concentrate in noncushioned chairs, which typify classrooms, for more than 50 minutes (Butin, 2000a).

Considerable attention has been given to contrasts between open, flexible classrooms and traditional, structured classrooms (see reviews in Doyle, 1986, and Weinstein & Mignano, 2003). Not surprisingly, open settings, in contrast to traditional environments, provide more opportunities for multiple groupings, pupil initiation of tasks, self-pacing, informality, and a variety of occasions for adult-child interactions. At the same time, open settings create procedural complexity that often requires teachers to engage in more organizational work, more elaborate transitions, and more monitoring of student behavior than in traditional classrooms. Procedural complexity also makes it difficult for students to concentrate on or choose activities. Studies suggest that when students are asked to complete individual assignments, their work involvement and efficiency are higher in structured rows than in clusters, and this effect seems especially true for students who have behavioral or learning problems (see, e.g., Bennett & Blundell, 1983).

Stepping back from the details, it would seem that the principles underlying the physical design of classroom settings are fairly transparent. Spaces provide affordances (Gibson, 1979; Norman, 1990), that is, opportunities for things to happen. If you want children to develop social learnings through frequent interactions with adults and peers, then uncongested space must be designed to afford such occasions and provide easy access. At the same time, such multidimensional activity settings with many things happening simultaneously require heightened teacher awareness to sustain involvement, avoid aggression, and progress through the day. If, on the other hand, you want students to concentrate on an individual task, then space must be arranged to minimize distractions. Finally, if you want children to have privacy—often a rare commodity in schools—for individual reading, study, or even escape (see Weinstein, 1982), then such places must be intentionally created.

Establishing Rules and Procedures

Rules and procedures enjoy a prominent place in research and professional writings in classroom management. Certainly, the importance of rules and procedures was a clear finding from the Texas studies of classroom management (Emmer et al., 1980; Evertson et al., 1983). More recently, Marzano (2003) concluded from his meta-analysis of classroom management studies that design and implementation of rules and procedures had an average effect size of −.772 on disruptions in upper elementary classrooms. He interpreted this effect size to mean that in classes in which rules and procedures were effectively enacted the average number of disruptions was 28 percentile points lower than in classes in which rules were not enacted as effectively.

An enthusiasm for rules is not, however, universal. Some advocates of progressive pedagogies (e.g., Daniels & Bizar, 1998) argue that rules interfere with the choice and spontaneity required for meaningful expressions of curiosity and creativity. Critical theorists who advocate emancipatory pedagogies question classroom rules because they "are grounded in capitalist, hierarchical hegemony" (Holmes, 1991, p. 138). We adopt the view that rules, both formal and informal, permeate social life and contribute, especially in classrooms, to the construction of meaning in these environments (for an analysis of this perspective, see Boostrom, 1991). The trick is to establish reasonable limits for children to learn boundaries while allowing for developmentally appropriate individual expression and exploration.

The significance of rules and procedures stems in part from the fact that classrooms are crowded and busy places that require some kind of regulatory mechanisms to get anything done, that is, to ensure safety, prevent confusion, protect individual sensitivities, and achieve a sense of common purpose. As a result, formal and informal rules and procedures saturate classroom life and cover a vast range of what happens in classrooms from entering the room, hanging up coats and backpacks, finding a place to sit, obtaining supplies, organizing working space, completing assignments, going to the library or recess, having lunch, taking a nap, putting away materials, and going home. Boostrom (1991) argues that rules contribute significantly to the construction of meaning for all participants in classroom life. In his words, "By locating events in a system of belief, rules define reality" (Boostrom, 1991, p. 195). In other words, rules "represent local efforts to put local events in their proper place" (Boostrom, 1991, p. 195).

Procedures are, in essence, policies or regulations governing the variety of formats or scripts established to get things done, for example, where and how to line up, where to store things, how to give completed work to the teacher, when to go to the restroom, the meaning of various teacher signals, etc. Rules are policies covering attendance, safety, decorum, and the use of school property (e.g., Don't run in the halls, Don't bring electronic toys to school, Don't share sandwiches, Don't put blocks in your mouth, Cover your mouth when you cough). Most teachers condense rules into a few broad, if not abstract, categories—be respectful, listen quietly—to cover the range of possible behavior in classrooms. There is some evidence that rules can also be used to promote social development of individual students. Harrist and Bradley (2003) found that implementing a rule that did not permit kindergarten class members to exclude individuals increased social liking among kindergarten students to a greater extent than efforts to target and help isolated or rejected children.

A case can easily be made that a working set of rules and procedures should be taught explicitly at the beginning of the year (Emmer et al., 1980; Leinhardt, Weidman, & Hammond, 1987), especially to very young or potentially disruptive children (Blumenfeld, Hamilton, Wessels, & Falkner, 1979; Kehle, Bray, Theodore, Jenson, & Clark, 2000; Shultz & Florio, 1979). This teaching involves both stating and posting the rules, explaining their meaning and significance, giving clear examples, and answering questions. Similarly, procedures need to be clearly delineated, illustrated, and even rehearsed. In classrooms in which rules and procedures are less explicit, it appears that students perceive that there are in fact rules that capture the essence of life in these settings (Boostrom, 1991, pp. 201–203). Moreover, in such classrooms a considerable amount of social energy is expended in working out operating principles and procedures (see Tikunoff & Ward, 1978), and order may never be established.

Some writers (e.g., Castle & Rogers, 1994; DeVries & Zan, 2003; Powell, McLaughlin, Savage, & Zehm, 2001) argue for cooperative processes in which the teacher and students jointly negotiate classroom rules and procedures on the grounds that (a) the practice is consistent with democratic/constructivist teaching philosophies, (b) such exercises make the final products more understandable and acceptable to students and thus elicit a greater commitment to follow them, and (c) such a process contributes to students' moral development, a topic that will be taken up later in this chapter. For present purposes, it can be noted that there is no clear evidence that cooperative rule setting is a necessary condition for establishing an effective system of rules and procedures. What does seem necessary is some effort to achieve a common understanding in the group of what the rules and procedures are and how they apply to specific situations.

Even before first grade young children have powerful social and cultural images or stories of "school," grounded for better or worse in their exchanges with parents, older siblings, peers, and other members of their communities. Certainly after first grade, they generally know rules, procedures, and consequences in these places, that is, the stories of classrooms. It would seem, then, that the exercise of rule setting at the beginning of the year has, more often than not, indirect but important symbolic value as a ritual to communicate to the students that this particular classroom is a rule-governed place and the teacher cares about keeping it that way. Such messages would no doubt contribute to the achievement of order in a classroom.

The actual process of installing a working set of rules and procedures in a classroom is not completed on the first day of school. Rather, rules and procedures become fully operative over the first weeks of school as the teacher and students interact and carry out activities (see Doyle, 1986, for a review of relevant literature). During this time, behaviors are allowed or stopped in specific circumstances and abstract teacher directives are situated or storied through enactment and feedback in the daily experiences of classroom life. What eventually emerges as the "real" rules and procedures for a class is a product of this extended period of interaction. In this sense, all classroom rules and procedures are narratives jointly constructed in the actions and reactions of participants.

In addition to the formal and explicit procedures in classrooms, there are a host of implicit rules and procedures that emerge around turn taking, social distance, personal expectations (for one's self and for others), humor, and specialized roles (see Doyle, 1986). Through formal and informal rules a classroom culture emerges, in other words, that, for better or worse, guides action in virtually all settings throughout the year. Boostrom (1991) has underscored that rules are not just instruments or techniques that promote order but are, rather, embodiments of a tradition or way of life in a classroom, that is, central elements in the story of a classroom. "Following the rules is an ongoing act of imagination that brings a view of the world and a way of acting in it into existence" (Boostrom, 1991, p. 203). He further argues that if we take a narrowly instrumental view of rules as technique to achieve discipline in a classroom, then we miss the important ways in which rules for doing work shape the work itself and thus what students learn. For example, rules for correcting work or for working on your own define how students approach tasks, seek help, interpret answers and figure out how to obtain them, and understand their role as learners.

This sense of rules as coordinates of a classroom culture or narrative raises an interesting issue related to students' motivations and cultural backgrounds. If, for example, a class is made up of students who are generally not inclined to cooperate in classroom activities, then rules must carry a heavy burden of negotiating the distance between the teacher's vision of the way of life for a class and that of the students. Similarly, if there is a substantial gap between the teacher's tradition and the culturally embedded communicative practices of the students, then rules and rule making can become problematic (see Gonzalez, 1995; Osborne, 1996). Weinstein (1991) citing Michaels (1986) provided an example of this tension in which the contrast during sharing time between the linear narrative style of white children and the episodic style of black children created misunderstandings and frustrations for the teacher and the students around an image of good sharing talk. Similarly, Tsai and Garcia (2000) analyzed a conflict event involving an English-speaking teacher and two Chinese-speaking preschoolers focusing on issues of communicative competence and the socialization of students into a classroom normative system.

Finally, to foreshadow a topic we will take up shortly, classroom activities themselves—lessons, seatwork, games, etc.—become storied, that is, standardized and routinized over time. This seemingly natural consequence of classroom history increases predictability for routine events by providing stable slots for action (see Doyle, 1986; Yinger, 1980). Such proceduralized events become resistant to disruption from external interruptions or internal misconduct and thus serve to hold order in place.

From a developmental perspective, children's needs for autonomy, initiative, and industry suggest that reasonable boundaries and expectations be established but that rules be enacted with openness and flexibility so that children's initiative and exploration are not frustrated and stifled. This is not an easy task since this natural growth can also be accompanied by an increase in oppositional behavior toward adults and greater attention-seeking acts by children. It seems clear, however, that punitive and power-asserting responses by teachers to children's explorations and initiatives can thwart a child's growth toward autonomy and self-assurance.

Managing Student's Tasks

The assignments pupils are asked to do in classrooms have profound consequences for classroom management and order (see Blumenfeld, Mergendoller & Swarthout, 1987; Brophy, 1992; Doyle, 1983, 1992; Doyle & Carter, 1984; Marx & Walsh, 1988). Students' work varies along the following dimensions:

1. The operations required to complete the work: memorization (e.g., math facts), mastery of a reliable procedure (e.g., addition), invent an original product (e.g., write a poem), etc.
2. The resources available during work time: working in private, collaborating with partners, having models of the final product to follow, etc.
3. The strictness of the accountability: will close approximations do (e.g., draw a picture of your house) or must the answer be precise (what is 2×2?).
4. The importance of the work in the grading system: for instance, a unit test versus a daily assignment.

Studies of the enactment of classroom tasks (e.g., Doyle, 1988; Doyle & Carter, 1984) indicate that familiar work, that is, school tasks that are typical or recognizable, have a clearly defined product and explicit grading criteria, and have become routinized in a class (one readily thinks of spelling tests or worksheets), tends to run smoothly: start up is quick, engagement and completion rates are high, and distractions or off-task behaviors are low. *Novel* work, on the other hand, is often "bumpy" (Romano, in press). Novel work is work in which students are asked to create or invent something they have not seen precisely before. For example, students may be given a set of examples of geometric progressions and asked to identify the pattern. Or they may be asked to write an original description of a flower bed in front of the school. Such tasks are often representative of inquiry teaching, constructivist teaching, or teaching for understanding. Such tasks are often difficult to manage in classrooms because it is hard for students to get started and then to sustain their involvement, multiple resources are needed to complete the work, and final products are difficult for both teachers and students to evaluate. Although challenging tasks can be successfully implemented (see Miller, 2003), classroom conditions create pressures on teachers to specify products more fully, provide prompts and models to aid completion, and otherwise modify the original task to make it easier to complete.

Along these lines, Huberman and Middlebrooks (2000) studied enactments of an innovative, constructivist program, The Voyage of the Mimi, in upper elementary and middle school classrooms in six American settings. They found that over time there was a "progressive 'dilution' from a program for inquiry into a set of algorithms, with far lessened demands for cognitive 'stretching' on the part of pupils" (p. 281). One suspects that this "dilution" occurred in part because sustaining order and work involvement was difficult in these enactments.

Bennett and Desforges (1988) reported on studies in Britain of the match between task demands and students' attainments. They and their colleagues looked at over 600 tasks in second- and third-grade classes and found that "High attainers were underestimated on 41% of all tasks assigned to them. Low attainers were overestimated on 44% of tasks assigned" (Bennett & Desforges, 1988, p. 227). In other words, teachers gave students who typically did well in their school work less challenging tasks than they could accomplish and those who struggled with the work received more challenging tasks than they could often handle. During class sessions, students worked hard, appeared happy, and completed assignments even if they did not understand the concepts or processes themselves. Teachers, in turn, focused on procedural aspects of the tasks, praised students for their industry, and ushered work along by accepting frequent interruptions for assistance. At the same time, the teachers were often unaware of the conceptual difficulties students were having with the content itself. In a follow-up study with teachers, the investigators found that teachers were focused on managing very complex social and academic environments in which they were trying to orchestrate the content on the floor, the momentum of lessons, and coverage of the curriculum. This teacher task environment left little room for gaining detailed information about individual children's conceptual understandings.

It is readily apparent that the "academic work" model being explicated here is especially applicable to upper elementary and secondary school classrooms, and, indeed, much of the research on classroom tasks has been conducted in these settings (see Blumenfeld & Meece, 1988; Doyle & Carter, 1984; Herbst, 2003). Class assignments and homework at these levels are clearly articulated, central realities in the school day, and performance on these tasks is assessed regularly. In the early elementary grades, the quality of work performance is judged more holistically, feedback is more global and ambiguous, and completion is the criteria pupils tend to use to judge their efforts (see, for example, Anderson, 1983). Nevertheless, pupils are gradually introduced to product completion schedules and comparisons across individuals become apparent as student progress through the early grades. More importantly, assigned work replaces the play emphasis in preschool, and the nature and holding power of this work influences classroom management and order. One particularly important facet of work would seem to be procedural complexity, how difficult it is for students to understand and follow how to complete the assigned tasks (see Blumenfeld & Meece, 1988).

In preschool, as noted, educative play tends to be the central activity, although it may well be structured by physical design or by teacher direction (e.g., as in Montessori schools) to foster specific skills for social or academic capabilities. Short "lessons" or demonstrations may be conducted at the edges of this play to introduce pupils to concepts and processes related to the beginnings of science, arts, literature, history, and the like. And pupils may be given tasks or "activities" to accomplish with respect to these lessons (e.g., look at specimens with a magnifying glass), but accountability is quite diffuse and participation is left primarily to interest. This is not to say that the teachers do not interpret the educational significance of pupil's performance in these settings, but the pupils are usually not aware of this appraisal.

Despite the relative invisibility of task systems in preschool classes, different play centers and activities have differential holding power, which has consequences for management and order in these places. Moreover, students in these complex social settings are gradually made aware of limits and requirements for performance, which in broad terms introduces accountability and performance assessment. Although considerably more systematic study is needed, tasks would seem to play an important role in how order is achieved in preschool environments.

Guiding and Monitoring Classroom Events

One of the profound contributions of Paul Gump to the field of classroom management was his elaboration of the activity structure or "behavior settings" of classroom environments in his classic study of the third-grade classroom "as a special but instructive case" (Gump, 1967, 1969).[2] From his roots in Barker's (1968) deeply situated ecological psychology, Gump was able to discern the natural segments of classroom life and conceptualize these as environments that surround and regulate behavior, as settings which provide instructions or "programs of action" for participants. A segment—morning song, math lesson, spelling seatwork, snack time, reading group—can be described as a story, that is, in terms of its arrangement of participants, roles and responsibilities, props, duration, rules of appropriateness, focal content, and program of action (see Carter, 1993; Doyle, 1986). A segment, in turn, is associated with a particular pattern of teacher and pupil behavior. Indeed, the program of action for a segment, or the direction and momentum of behavior in a situation, defines what order means for that period of time in a classroom.

From this discussion it is clear that order and management are grounded in the variety of segments that constitute a day in the life of a class. These segments define what order means in a classroom at a given time. Thus, if the actions of participants are congruent with the program of action for the segment on the floor, the class is orderly. And order does not mean sitting quietly watching the teacher. For some segments, such as music, drama, or dance, "group glee" (Sherman, 1975) defines appropriate order.

To manage a classroom, then, means to gain and maintain the cooperation of pupils in the programs of action embedded in the segments that make up the day. From this perspective, order is not an abstract ideal but a situated narrative of the activity on the floor. To manage successfully, then, a teacher must understand the programs of action of various classroom segments and the actions he or she can take to invite and secure pupil's cooperation in these programs of action. Kounin's (1970) great contribution was to identify noncoercive group management skills, that is, clusters of actions teachers can take to monitor the stream of behavior within segments, head off divergent programs of action, and keep the action flowing in concert with the program on the floor.

Given the ecological bias of this chapter, segments and their direction are placed at the center of classroom management. This means that rules, procedures, personal relations, and the like are seen as important but secondary dimensions of classroom management. One can have the best set of rules in the world, but they will not work if the segments or activities of the class are not working. Rules enable but do not substitute for or replace segment management.

In the following we briefly examine four broad exemplars of segments or story structures commonly found in classrooms: lessons, seatwork, discussions, and group cooperation (for further discussion, see Doyle, 1986; Leinhardt, 1983). The discussion is intended to suggest how these prototypical segments work. Drawing from Kounin's example, an attempt will also be made to suggest some of the teacher actions that can be taken within these segments to elicit and sustain student cooperation. Attention will also be directed to transitions—the movement

[2]Gump also worked for many years with Kounin as a friend, advisor, and coinvestigator beginning with the "ripple effect" studies in the 1950s (Kounin & Gump, 1958) and ending with the important "signal system" study in the 1970s (Kounin & Gump, 1974). Broadly, it can be said that Gump detailed the segment or "activity" structure of classrooms and Kounin articulated the skills necessary to monitor and interpret action streams within these structures.

between different activities—as a special category with important implications for classroom order and management.

Lessons. Lessons, in this context, are defined as relatively formalized presentations of material that is to be learned. A lesson typically involves some form of display (pictures, overhead or chalk board examples, artifacts, texts) accompanied by teacher explanation. A full lesson would also normally involve teacher and student questions and answers and even guided practice on sample tasks to clarify understanding. In preschool classrooms, formal lessons are not common but can be used to introduce students to a new center on dinosaurs, for example, or a project on butterflies or hatching chicken eggs. Story reading by an adult also reflects the social structure of a lesson. As students progress through the grades, content-based lessons become a more regular part of classroom life. Lessons usually originate from a single source—the teacher—and are designed to teach what the teacher knows. But lessons can be structured inductively, that is, the teacher can provide examples and ask questions to solicit pupils' comments to build an understanding of a pattern or problem. This latter sequence, from a segment perspective, looks more like a discussion because the teacher's role is indirect. Thus, it will be treated in more detail later.

Structurally, a lesson consists of a group of students arranged to face a single source of information, usually the teacher. Students are responsible for paying attention, tracking the information provided, maybe even circling illustrations or numbers on a worksheet or writing words down, and working to achieve an understanding of what is being presented. Inappropriate actions would include anything that would signal inattention: privately talking to a friend while a story is being read, using an outside voice to share comments, daydreaming, sleeping, tattling on a buddy for not sitting correctly, walking around the room, etc. The teacher is responsible for clarity, accuracy, timing, and some degree of entertainment value—pace, energy, humor, and the like.

Most lessons include an interactive phase, particularly in the early grades. In this phase, solicited or unsolicited student questions or comments are brought to the floor to help in the process of negotiating meaning and understanding. Here participation structures, or the system of rules governing speaking and turn taking, come into play to define the program of action for interactive phases of a segment (see Erickson & Mohatt, 1982; Philips, 1972). In most lessons, the teacher controls access to the floor by deciding the topic, selecting the speaker, and evaluating the value of the speaker's contribution. Students differ, however, in terms of their ability to gain access to the floor by bidding for turns, and differences are often associated with social class and ethnicity (Cunningham, 2004; Weinstein, 1991). With experience, students in first grade appear to learn the rules for participation in lessons and thus become more successful in bidding for turns (Green & Harker, 1982; Mehan, 1979; Eder, 1982).

On-task behavior rates are relatively high for lessons, even in preschool settings, because the lesson format is largely familiar to students as a cultural icon of teaching, the demands for participation are fairly minimal, and the format or structure of the segment provides a continuous flow of information about behavior, insulates participants from competing vectors, and controls intrusiveness from outside sources (Kounin & Gump, 1974). Nevertheless, the level of cooperation and order is influenced by the holding power of the teacher's presentation, the pace and variety of the information flow, and the extent to which the teacher is able to draw in and involve all of the students. Moreover, the task frame for the lesson—what students will be responsible for doing with the information presented—influence the degree of attention and participation.

Discussions and Sharing Time. A discussion is a whole-class format in which a teacher and a class all talk publicly together about a topic. There are obviously many different styles of this activity. At one end of the continuum is the recitation, a tightly controlled question-answer drill in which students recite information learned previously (e.g., math facts). In these segments, the teacher directs the topic on the floor, asks virtually all the questions, selects participants, and evaluates the quality of responses (see Cazden, 2001). Variations on the recitation have persisted throughout the history of formal schooling in the United States (see, e.g., Hoetker & Ahlbrand, 1969). At the other end are open-ended concept attainment or inquiry discussions in which the teacher and students work together to construct generalizations, identify patterns, plan strategies for solving problems, give reasons for interpretations, or go beyond the information given to achieve new understandings and insights. Parker and Hess (2001) state that participation in such discussions "can be both a mind-expanding and community-building endeavor" and that "discussion is relevant to the broad social aims of democracy and solidarity in a diverse society and to the pedagogical aim of creating vigorous communities of inquiry" (p. 273). Open-ended discussions, in others words, help to socialize students into classroom speech or discourse communities (see O'Connor & Michaels, 1993; Wood, 1999). In such discussions, the teacher's role is to urge, encourage, and stimulate—to be one among many—rather than to direct or judge responses.

"Sharing time" is a type of discussion format that commonly occurs in early childhood classrooms (see, especially, Cazden, 2001 and Weinstein, 1991, pp. 505–507). Sharing time is distinctive in that it typically involves giving the floor to a single student at a time with the task of spontaneously composing and telling a personal narrative about his or her out-of-school life. Moreover, participation does not necessarily have to be relevant to another speaker's narrative. Sharing typically begins with openings such as, "Last night at supper my brother spilled ..." or "When we went to my grandmother's house for Thanksgiving dinner, the dog ..." or "Yesterday my cat jumped...." A similar personal narrative emphasis is often apparent in discussions in preschool and early elementary classrooms as students gradually move toward a more formal academic curriculum. A discussion of a story just read, for instance, might focus on personal responses to the narrative, such as how the main character was similar to or different from the speaker.

Despite its seeming value as an educative practice, discussion is a particularly difficult format to use and to learn how to use in classrooms (Parker & Hess, 2001). From a segment perspective, there are at least three reasons for this difficulty. First, the program of action itself is complicated: multiple speakers must take turns on the floor and speak relevantly to and add upon a common core of ideas. As the content stream opens to a variety of possible considerations, the talk, especially in discussions with younger children, can meander and the demands on a teacher's ingenuity in guiding the conversation and his or her knowledge of the content increase accordingly. Moreover, bidding for turns and turn allocation can demand considerable teacher concentration as well as student skill in gaining the floor. As many investigators have noted, this is an area in which sociocultural differences among students play an important role in classroom life (e.g., Au, 1980; Cazden, 2001; Mehan, 1979; Weinstein, 1991). Second, participation in the program of action depends upon (a) the extent to which an individual pupil knows what is being talked about, (b) a pupil's willingness to speak publicly, and (c) one's position in the action zone of the class group. As a result, the program of action may capture only a few students at a time while the rest drift off into alternative vectors. Third, student talk has limited holding power in classrooms (see Gump, 1967; Kowatrakul, 1959) and the content of student remarks is not always salient to task demands in a class. Thus, the program of action is susceptible to interruptions and to the multiple stimuli generated by the format itself (Kounin & Gump, 1974).

Sharing time has an important role in classroom community building and student literacy learning, but presents distinctive management challenges to teachers not only because sharings are discussions but also because they tend to lack holding power as signal systems (Kounin &

Gump, 1974). Because sharings are embedded in a child's personal experience out of school, they can be difficult for both the teacher and other students to understand, especially when they are narrated by young children who are not necessarily skilled in anticipating audience perspectives. Moreover, cultural norms generally protect a storyteller's right to the floor until the story is over, so there are limits to a teacher's efforts to scaffold the narration and the duration of a story can be unpredictable. Finally, children differ in the types of narratives they tell. Michaels (1986; see also Cazden, 2001, and Weinstein, 1991, pp. 505–506) found differences, for example, between narrative styles used by black and white students. White children tended to tell single topic, tightly organized, linear stories, while black children sometimes told loosely connected episodic narratives in which the organizing frame was implicit. This difference affected both the teacher and the listening students' ability to follow and comprehend the shared narratives. When faced with children from different discourse or narrative communities, a teacher must do the difficult work of not only sustaining the classroom event of sharing but also, through modeling and maintaining mutual respect, of protecting the status of different speakers within the classroom group (Cazden, 2001).

Factors such as these make keeping order in place during a discussion or sharing time a challenging task. As a result, teachers often assume a more central role in controlling the range of comments or narrative practices, thus constraining the content stream and making the segment more predictable. From this perspective, it is not surprising that classroom discussions, especially in the upper elementary grades, are often short segments and tend toward the more structured end of the continuum between the recitation and the open-ended conversation.

Seatwork. Seatwork refers here to a class format in which students work on their own to engage in activities or complete assignments under broad and general teacher supervision. In preschool classrooms, seatwork is pervasive, not in the academic sense that children complete worksheets or write sentences to be handed in but in the sense that they draw, build, examine, or play on their own as teachers watch from a distance. In this type of segment, the teacher's immediate responsibilities as a central actor are lessened as the activity or the assigned work takes over the direction of pupil action. This condition frees the teacher to watch what is happening as she or he wanders around the room and offers private assistance as needed. Seatwork often involves parallel play or, in the upper elementary grades, individually completed assignments, although sometimes peer consultation is allowed and even encouraged. As peer interaction becomes a requirement for student participation, the segment becomes an instance of group cooperation, a format to be discussed in the next section of the chapter.

In cases of individual task accomplishment in which students can do the work and are insulated from intrusions, that is, they do not have to share materials or ideas to complete the task, work involvement is typically high (see Kounin & Gump, 1974). However, teachers must be especially vigilant in the beginning moments of a seatwork segment as the activity or the work to be done takes hold of student attention, and then at the end of seatwork as students complete assignments at different rates or begin to drift away from the activity. In the upper elementary grades, the end of seatwork segments can be especially challenging, especially if completion rates are widely different because a large number of students can be left with nothing to do as the class waits for a few to finish. Many experienced teachers orchestrate the end of segments with multiple cues to encourage a more uniform completion schedule. And certainly, as noted earlier, the nature of the work itself matters. If only a few students can actually do the work assigned, then the task cannot hold order in place.

As a teacher roves around the room and stops to help individuals as needed (what Merritt, 1982, called "service like events"), several important management skills identified in Kounin's (1970) work need to be employed. The most important of these is overlapping: the ability to attend to two or more things at once, for example, answering an individual student's question while scanning the room for work involvement of other students. Failure to overlap can mean that distracting incidents get well underway before a teacher becomes aware, leading to a fairly substantial disruption of the class. Merritt (1982) discusses several of the cuing strategies teachers use to manage the multiple vectors created by assisting individual students during seatwork. Teachers must also attend to the order of requests for help so that a queue is formed and, as at a Baskin-Robbins, for example, customers are served in the appropriate sequence.

In the elementary grades, seatwork is often used to occupy a majority of the students in a class while the teacher works with a small group for a reading or math lesson. This structure presents a particularly challenging task for the teacher because the demands of running the lesson make dividing attention across the two behavior settings difficult.

Group Cooperation. In many respects, early childhood classrooms are structured fundamentally around groups of children engaged independently or collaboratively in various forms of play, construction, art, exploration, digging, recreation, and games. Peer interactions, friendships, and personal agendas crisscross in these settings as individuals and small clusters of children move through the classroom making choices and following a seemingly random path and configurations. Space is typically organized to facilitate this pattern of engagement, and, because there is no central instructional agenda applicable to all students at the same time, teachers typically rove to observe and monitor behavior, encourage and facilitate participation, and protect children from physical or emotional injury. Classroom management in such settings is anchored in the design and provisioning of the group centers (discussed earlier) and in intervening as needed to support individuals, redirect actions, or mediate conflicts, topics discussed later in this chapter.

In the middle and upper elementary grades, teachers sometimes organize pupils into groups, each of which is to accomplish a common task such as sharing ideas about a topic, solving a problem together, or constructing a large display such as a poster or collage. The purposes for such an arrangement can include: (a) giving students the opportunity to engage in conversations and thus, through listening and formulating positions and explanations, learn the content better; (b) providing occasions to develop social skills; (c) increasing interactions across gender, ethnicity, and ability levels; (d) integrating special needs students into classroom events; and (e) building community in the classroom. The rules for assigning members to groups can vary from using convenient clusters or volunteer groupings to the highly structured teams in some models of Cooperative Learning (e.g., Slavin, 1996). Similarly, the assignment for the group can vary from a brief sharing of ideas about a topic on the floor to elaborate group investigation research projects.

Whether cooperative groupings accomplish their purpose is shaped by several internal and external factors. Internally, a group's success depends upon the willingness of individuals to listen, their knowledge or skills related to the task under consideration, their skill in expressing ideas and explanation, their motivation to stay engaged throughout the process, and their social skills in negotiating group interactions (see Weinstein & Mignano, 2003, for a good review of relevant literature). Some individuals can withdraw from the group process because they are discouraged, bored, or otherwise unmotivated to participate. Others can dominate conversation and exclude others from contributing ideas. In response to these issues, a variety of strategies have been proposed to structure group membership, assign roles and responsibilities, create interdependence, maintain individual accountability, and teach social skills for cooperation and participation (see Cohen, 1994; Johnson & Johnson, 1994; O'Connor & Jenkins, 1996; Slavin, 1995; Webb & Palincsar, 1996).

Classrooms groups are also arenas in which issues of social status, acceptance, and rejection emerge (see Weinstein, 1991). As with classrooms themselves, group interactions teach children a great deal about who they are, how they are perceived by others, and what they are able to do in relation to their peers. In group contexts teachers need to be especially aware of the impact of peer interactions on children's developing senses of autonomy, initiative, and self esteem. At the same time, groups provide teachers with opportunities to teach important social skills related to self-regulation and conflict resolution.

Externally, grouping students increases simultaneity within a classroom, and by their very nature, groups require interaction and sharing of resources to accomplish tasks. These factors can create vectors that can pull students away from the issues and tasks at hand, and, in turn, present special management tasks for a teacher. At one level, the previous comments suggest that successful cooperative groups do not happen automatically. Teachers must carefully plan group tasks, structure membership and responsibilities, teach cooperation skills, oversee individual accountability, and actively monitor and give feedback on the ongoing processes (Emmer & Gerwels, 2002). In addition, a teacher must observe multiple groups to manage order at a class level. When groups are working, the teacher's role is not unlike that during seatwork: to monitor and pace the event, intervene to maintain order, and be available for assistance.

Transitions. Transitions are segments that occur between classroom activities, as in the movement from a lesson to seatwork or from seatwork in math to a social studies lesson, and a significant part of the school day in elementary classrooms—approximately 15%—is spent in such situations (see Burns, 1984; Gump, 1967; Rosenshine, 1980). Structurally, a transition involves the closing down of one activity, movement from that behavioral setting to the next, and starting up of the next activity. Many times these segments are brief, a simple switch of attention; at other times, especially when pupils and furniture must be rearranged, transitions can take several minutes. As segments, however, transitions are unique in that there is no focal content or tight structure to help hold order in place. Moreover, not all students make transitions easily, especially if they are deeply engaged in the ongoing activity that precedes the transition and, thus, find it hard to pull away from what they were doing. Story time is often too short-lived and hard to leave in preschool settings as is outside exploratory play. As a result, transitions can be bumpy occasions (Romano, in press) in which classroom order breaks down, especially when they become lengthy (Arlin, 1979; Gump, 1982; Rosenshine, 1980).

Most experienced teachers use three strategies to manage transitions. First, they provide multiple cues and signals to notify students a transition is coming, mark when it is to occur, tell the students what they are to do to make the transition, and foreshadow what is to happen in the next activity (see Arlin, 1979; Erickson & Shultz, 1981; Shultz & Florio, 1979). Second, they avoid being distracted by private contacts or administrative details so they can monitor carefully what is happening in the room during the transition. Finally, they proceduralize or routinize transitions to increase predictability of these inherently unstable segments (Weinstein & Mignano, 2003).

Summary. In this section, we have focused attention on the structures that surround and guide action in classroom environments and therefore form the core elements around which classroom order and management are achieved. Although the discussion is relatively abstract—focusing on prototypes of major segments—it suggests some of the dynamics that operate as teachers seek to manage productive learning time in classroom without resorting to coercive or punitive actions. One important theme seems to emerge from these analyses: As the open-endedness of a program of action increases, the signals within the activity to direct student behavior become fuzzy and, thus, the skills required for a teacher to orchestrate the event increase, sometimes exponentially. One can conclude, therefore, that considerable experience with and knowledge of classroom structures is necessary to enact some of the most highly valued educative environments for children.

Restoring Order: Dealing with Inappropriate and Disruptive Behavior

Although, from an ecological perspective, segments carry the burden of cooperation and order in classrooms, they are not perfect devices for holding order in place. Occasionally, and sometimes regularly, inappropriate behaviors occur and these can threaten to disrupt classroom order fundamentally. As a result, teachers often find themselves faced with a need to "desist" or stop misbehavior to repair or restore order when it is endangered. Studies indicate that desists, or teacher actions to acknowledge, redirect, or stop inappropriate behavior, are effective in reducing classroom disruptions (Marzano, 2003).

The topic of misbehavior would be easy if there were a clear list of inappropriate behaviors and an equally clear list of teacher interventions that infallibly corrected them. But the situation is much trickier. Knowing what to repair and when and how to repair it is not always easy to discern, and any intervention by the teacher can create a further distraction from the task at hand. Moreover, the failure of an intervention can increase disorder by communicating to the class that the teacher is ineffectual. It is not surprising, then, that "discipline" is a common concern of teachers, especially novices, and a central topic in the literature in classroom management.

In the following brief survey of the topic of misbehavior, we begin with a definition of what constitutes misbehavior and then turn to the complex processes associated with the decisions teachers have to make concerning when and how to intervene successfully. But the topic of misbehavior and discipline is much larger and is discussed more broadly in this chapter under the heading of social curriculum of classroom management.

Defining Misbehavior. Misbehavior is less a function of an action than it is a function of the consequences of an action in a situation. As Doyle (1986) notes:

> misbehavior is any behavior by one or more students that is perceived by the teacher to initiate a vector of action that competes with or threatens the primary vector of action at a particular moment in a classroom activity. Vectors perceived a misbehavior are likely to be (or likely to become) *public*, that is visible to a significant portion of the class, and *contagious*, that is, capable of spreading rapidly or pulling other member of the class into them. Misbehavior, in other words, creates fractures or fissures in the program of action in a classroom. (p. 419 emphasis in original)

From this perspective, one can argue that if the primary vector is strong and stable, or the main activity is drawing to a close, then minor distractions or student behaviors that no one pays attention to are not likely to disturb classroom order. If, however, the primary vector is weak because students are either unwilling or unable to engage, then almost any action outside the primary vector can be disruptive and the teacher must exercise considerable vigilance. To identify misbehavior, then, a teacher must be able to discern how an action is likely to affect the flow or momentum of a class. Research indicates that such discernment is not always easy for novice teachers (see Carter, Cushing, Sabers, Stein, & Berliner, 1988).

In general, teachers will reprimand students for clear signs of not being engaged in the action on the floor, for example, turning toward a neighbor to talk, trying to conceal behavior or objects, passing items to someone when sharing is not allowed, taking unauthorized trips around the classroom, and the like (see Felmlee & Eder, 1983; Mehan, 1980; Sieber, 1979). In addition, blatant refusals to share or allow others to play, aggressive acts toward persons or equipment, and threats to health and safety are almost universally reprimanded. Finally, violations of school rules in matters such as dress, language, or interpersonal interactions require teacher action. One of the especially difficult areas in this regard is harassment and bullying, in part because these acts often happen privately or outside classrooms on playgrounds and in corridors out of a teacher's eye and ear shot (see, Espelage & Swearer, 2004, and chapter 32 in this volume).

Inappropriate behavior seems to serve a variety of functions for students. Much of it seems to be in the service of students' personal or social agendas, for instance, wanting to talk about play or personal experiences and interests within the often more formal structures of the classroom (see deVoss, 1979; Sieber, 1979). Some students may be bored with or not interested in school tasks or trying to seek peer or adult attention by acting out. In the early grades especially, inappropriate behavior may result from a discrepancy between a child's usual ways of interacting at home and the demands of the classroom (see Borman, 1978; Florio & Shultz, 1979). In the upper elementary grades, inappropriate behavior can, on limited occasions, be useful in negotiating the demands of difficult academic work (Doyle & Carter, 1984). Finally, for some students, inappropriate behavior can signal aspects of personality that require specialized attention, a topic to be discussed in more detail in the subsequent section on discipline. In the end, it seems that inappropriate behavior in classrooms serves to help define social structures in classrooms in the sense that "the periodic eruption of secondary vectors serves to define the boundaries and the strength of the primary vector and shape its direction" (Doyle, 1986, p. 420).

In-Class Interventions and the Intervention Decision. Interventions are actions teachers take to try to stop or "desist" inappropriate or disruptive student behaviors. It is important to remember that interventions serve to repair order but cannot create order where none exists, that is, where there is no primary vector or program of action in place. Moreover, an intervention itself can create a powerful alternative vector—what Kounin and Gump (1958) called a "ripple effect"—that can disrupt work involvement in a class. Kounin and Gump (1958) also found that a teacher's failure to intervene when students expect it can be as disruptive as anything the students might do. As a result, successful interventions need to be early before a disruption spreads, short and quick to minimize their impact on the flow of classroom activity, and private to the extent that such is possible. A teacher might, for instance, move toward a student who is not involved in an activity, stand close or even touch him or her while continuing with the public lesson. If a verbal utterance is used, it will typically be abrupt and short—"Wait" or "Shh"—and designed not to invite a comment back from the target of the intervention (see Emmer et al., 1980; Humphrey, 1979; Sieber, 1979; Woolfolk & Brooks, 1985).

Decisions to intervene often are made under conditions of considerable pressure and uncertainty. Teachers must notice potential disruptions early, interpret often ambiguous signs, and make choices quickly. This uncertainty is reduced, in part, by signals from students. Misbehavior, in most circumstances, is created by only a few students with the rest of the class serving as audience. These bystanders know when behavior is out of range and likely to disrupt and, therefore, they often signal the teacher that something is amiss (see McDermott, 1976). This explains why a failure of the teacher to act in some circumstances can itself be disruptive. Experience with a particular class can also reduce unpredictability. As a teacher comes to know a group and individuals within that group, like trajectories of actions can be recognized more readily.

Obviously the effects of an intervention depend upon a variety of circumstances. If the teacher is conducting a whole-class lesson, such as a teacher-led story time, then both student and teacher behaviors are highly public and visible, whereas they might be virtually invisible during seatwork or play time when students are engaged in private tasks. In early childhood classrooms, in which pupil actions are situationally guided rather than teacher directed, most teacher interventions are social or pedagogical ones rather than desists. When desists do occur, they are often private, involving one or a few students rather than the whole class.

In reporting on her case studies of five early childhood teachers attempting to enact developmentally appropriate practice in their classrooms, Wien (1995, pp. 90–92) describes how one teacher, called Liz, was able to correct children's spontaneous actions without closing off possibilities. Wien notes that Liz's interventions were explicit in that they described immediate circumstances in concrete detail, personal in that they addressed and accepted an individual child's feelings and reactions in that situation, particularized to context in that they focused on specifics so that each intervention was adapted to a situation, and invited the child to action in that the child understood what he or she could not do but was offered choices as to what he or she wanted to do. An example is given in which two boys struggle over a plastic riding train and one runs off with it. Liz follows the boy, stops him, acknowledges his anger, and tells him that although he wants the train it has been chosen by another child. She then invites him to see if something else could be used as a train. The child ends up lining up three chairs and inviting Liz and a student teacher to come aboard his train for a ride. Wien notes that this intervention strategy not only corrects the potential disruption (i.e., desists) but also models for the children how conflicts can be resolved themselves.

Liz's case illustrates a second dimension of teacher intervention. Not only is Liz concerned about restoring order, she is also interested in the continuity of the children's spontaneous action and in teaching young children how to resolve conflicts. This second dimension shifts attention from the organization and management of classroom events to the broad topic of discipline.

Discipline. Within an ecological frame, the emphasis in discussing misbehavior is on restoring order, and students' behavior is interpreted within an action system as a vector that flows with or against a program of action on the floor. Teacher interventions are conceptualized as quick, efficient actions to reestablish the orderly stream of events. The idea of discipline shifts attention to the family of educative responses to children's actions in the personal and social arenas of classrooms and schools. Discipline is occasioned when an individual or small group steadily or very publicly pushes against the structures and programs of action in a classroom, threatening consistently to create alternative vectors to the action on the floor. At this point, typical interventions to stop inappropriate and disruptive behavior are not sufficient to protect the action system of a class, and the teacher needs to intervene in more thorough ways, usually outside the public sphere of an ongoing lesson, to work with individuals to influence their willingness to cooperate with classroom activities. Discipline, then, enters classroom management when a teacher works with an individual pupil or a small group of pupils to educate them with respect to the nature and consequences of their behaviors.

Historically, school discipline has strong roots in the language and social images of control, intimidation, and punishment. These images, unfortunately, often carry a supposition that classroom order rests fundamentally on teacher-delivered consequences. This assumption can misdirect teacher attention from the structures and programs of action that are at the heart of classroom order. It is important to remember, then, that in-class interventions and discipline restore order. If there is no order to return to in the first place, then desists and discipline will not create it. We also argue that skillful activity management as suggested by the ecological model serves developmentally appropriate ends by avoiding power struggles and the need for teachers to feel they have to be punitive and domineering to hold order in place in classrooms.

Although control remains an underlying theme in some discussions of discipline (e.g., Canter & Canter, 2001), the modern emphasis is on positive rather than punitive approaches to managing misbehavior in schools by establishing limits, communicating rules and consequences, and helping students learn responsibility and self-management in making appropriate behavioral choices. The emphasis, in other words, is on more inductive or developmental approaches characterized by warmth, respect, modeling, socialization, reasons, affection, and clear expectations (see Puckett & Black, 2001; Watson, 2003). In this modern framework, students' misbehavior is interpreted as perhaps a lack of appropriate social skills (Cartledge &

Milburn, 1995) or a manifestation of misplaced goals (Dreikers, Grunwald, & Pepper, 1982) but certainly a personal and purposeful choice for which the student is responsible (Glasser, 1998). Indeed, students themselves appear to see coercive strategies as inhibiting the development of responsibility and as distractions from their work (Lewis, 2001). Nevertheless, considerable evidence supports the view that direct efforts by teachers to confront misbehavior and deliver even mild forms of punishment—time out, loss of privileges, restitution, etc.—are effective in reducing misbehavior and disruptions (Marzano, 2003).

The foundational language of modern approaches to discipline reflects the contributions of some major theorists in the field (see Charles, 2005). Of particular importance are: (a) "I" messages to communicate feelings in disciplinary situations (Ginott, 1971; Gordon, 1987); (b) "logical consequences" for compliance with or violations of classroom and school rules (Dreikurs & Cassel, 1995); (c) a "discipline hierarchy" for delivering warnings and increasingly severe consequences for continued violations of rules (Canter & Canter, 2001); (d) "win-win" strategies for conflict resolution (Gordon, 1987); and (e) "Choice Theory," which emphasizes personal control over thinking and acting (Glasser, 1998). Underlying these approaches is also a consistent emphasis on caring, respect, and trust in interactions with students; collaborative rule making and problem solving; and efforts to help students learn self-management strategies, make good choices, and accept personal responsibility for their actions. To understand these conceptions and their importance, we next discuss the broader topic of the social curriculum of classroom management.

Summary. Previously we have surveyed briefly the dynamics of inappropriate and disruptive behavior in classrooms and what teachers might do to recognize such behaviors, interpret their meaning, and intervene to sustain or restore order. Our focus has been management processes within a classroom. But the topic of misbehavior easily expands into a larger discussion of students' personal characteristics and discipline, in which the focus shifts from the management of classroom processes to strategies for promoting individual growth and development. To consider this expanded discourse, we now look at the social curriculum of early childhood and elementary classrooms. Here attention switches from classroom structures and dynamics to the psychological meaning of behavior in a variety of school contexts and from the management of group structures and processes to the care and nurturing of individuals. Within this expanded framework we discuss issues of social skills, personal responsibility, self-talk, caring, manner, and resilience as related to developmentally appropriate ways of helping students realize their potential.

A SOCIAL CURRICULUM OF CLASSROOM MANAGEMENT

The topic of school discipline has traditionally been grounded in the literatures on personality and human development (see Charles, 2005, for discussion of a variety of discipline "models" and approaches). In this context, students' behavior tends to be seen as a manifestation of personal needs, characteristics, and mental health. In addition, the range of behavior is wide, from inattention, withdrawal, and apathy in the classroom to defiance and even violence, and the contexts include not only classrooms but also corridors, bathrooms, the lunchroom, and playgrounds. Traditionally, the emphasis has been on understanding the nature and origins of students' actions and on teacher and school-level strategies for reorientation, remediation, and prevention of the problem behaviors.

Recently, this literature has been enriched by a broader educative agenda which emphasizes strategies for personal motivation and development, moral and ethical growth, social awareness and emancipation, and cultural energy and pride. This emerging work represents a shift from a traditional emphasis in clinical therapy models toward a more curricular orientation, or an emphasis on the educative dimensions of classroom management and discipline. This emphasis, responsive in part to escalating school violence and broad social concerns about drugs and moral behavior in society, extends curricular discourse beyond the academic mission of the school toward a model of management as fostering personal and social growth, what one might call broadly a social curriculum of classroom management (Powell et al., 2001). This emphasis is especially relevant to early childhood/elementary classrooms since, as noted in the introduction to this chapter, academic, personal, and social purposes are closely intertwined at this level of schooling. Indeed, in an important sense a social curriculum of the classroom is a given in the lives of children. As Weinstein (1991) notes:

> the classroom is not simply a social context in which students learn academic lessons. It is a social context in which students learn social lessons—lessons about appropriate behavior in various contexts, about one's self as a learner and one's position in a status hierarchy, about relationships with students from other ethnic and racial groups, about the relative value of competition and cooperation, and about friendship (p. 520).

The idea of a social curriculum of classroom management encompasses a continuum of deliberate interventions designed to assist students in developing the social awarenesses and skills as well as the individual capabilities needed to function as effective, caring participants in school and in their lives. The skills and capabilities include interpreting and dealing with diverse interpersonal situations, solving conflicts and problems that they encounter, acquiring self-talk and self-monitoring abilities, learning appropriate actions for specific situations, and developing resilience, empathy, and character. The interventions include immediate responses to classroom situations as well as more formal projects and programs of personal and social development, many of which reflect school-wide programs and commitments from students, parents, and professional staffs (see Marzano, 2003). These outcomes are seen as both contributing to stable patterns of children's cooperation and order in classrooms and schools as well as essential outcomes of classroom management practices. Finally, the idea of a social curriculum of classroom management embraces the realities of the personal, social, and cultural diversity that characterizes modern society and modern schools.

As one turns from issues of managing classroom structures and processes to those of educating the developing child, the idea of "developmentally appropriate practice" (see Bredekamp, 1987, 1996; Wien, 1995) comes into focus. This idea encompasses a cluster of educational practices that emphasize children's active construction of knowledge and competency through play, social interaction, and personal manipulation of objects and tasks in their environments. The emphasis is on the children's own initiations, explorations, and decisions within teacher-supported settings rather than teacher selection and direction of classroom tasks, activities, and choices. The teacher's role is to guide, interpret, and encourage within age-appropriate limits rather than point and steer children's activity. As Wien (1995) notes, "In developmental appropriateness, the location of power alternates between adult and children, with power shared. Both adults and children are believed to be active agents who seek out and construct knowledge through active interaction with others" (p. 4). This spirit of developmental appropriateness certainly permeates contemporary literatures on the social curriculum of classroom management.

In this section we discuss approaches and strategies that (a) appear to address significant personal/social problems and issues in early childhood and elementary school classrooms, and (b) are consistent with a developmentally appropriate perspective on the social curriculum of classroom management. Once again, this array is necessarily selective, given space limitations of this chapter and the large number of both issues and approaches that are available. We address some of the major concerns in early childhood and elementary school classroom management and suggest the types of systems and procedures available to teachers.

Self-Talk, Self-Regulation, and Resilience

The development of functional strategies for self-talk and self-regulation appear to play an essential role in the development of autonomy, initiative, and industry in children as well as their more general emotional health. Such strategies appear not only to aid in development but also to increase resilience to the effects of stress and adversity (see Saarni, 1997; Vitto, 2003; Waxman, Gray, & Padron, 2003) and improve students' abilities to resolve conflicts, deal with frustrations and failures, and formulate and carry out effective plans. Evidence also suggests that self-regulatory capabilities are influenced by children's relationships to caregivers (Eisenberg, 2002).

With the dramatic rise over the past two decades in interest in cognition, attention began to focus on metacognitive and metamotivational dimensions of students' engagement in academic settings and led to the development of the notion of self-regulation in learning (see Boekaerts, 1995; Brophy, 2004; Corno, 1993; Pintrich & DeGroot, 1990; Pintrich & Schrauben, 1992; Wolters, 2003; Zimmerman, 1989). Self-regulated learning refers to control over one's own learning processes, strategies, and motivation. It involves such processes as goal setting, planning and selecting or inventing strategies for accomplishing goals systematically, evaluation or reflection on one's performance, and revising approaches to increase success. In addition, self-regulation includes control over motivation by activating positive attitudes and intentions and by enacting appropriate intentions within distracting contexts. Kremer-Hayon and Tillema (1999 P. 509) summarize the characteristics of self-regulated learners as follows:

> Self regulated learners are confident in their strategies (Biemiller & Meichenbaum, 1992). They set goals for extending their knowledge and sustaining their motivation, and they are aware of the impact of their knowledge and their beliefs and the implications of the differences between various kinds of information for approaching tasks. They have a grasp of motivation, are aware of their affect, and plan ways to manage the interplay between various aspects of affect as they engage in a task (Butler & Winne, 1995). Moreover, they attribute success or failure to themselves rather than to others—a characteristic of an internal locus of control—and invest greater efforts, which lead to positive outcomes: achievement, self-esteem. They select strategies, seek and retrieve information, monitor their commitment to goals, adapt, adjust, revise and modify. Self-regulated learners control learning outcomes from within, are intrinsically motivated, self-monitoring, self-directing and exhibit greater flexibility in taking on/adapting to uncertain challenges in the classroom (Lindner & Harris, 1993).

Clearly much of this profile is directed to self-regulation of learning in academic contexts. However, the framework seems to hold considerable promise as an approach to classroom management (see chapter 9 in this volume). In essence this adaptation would involve developing resilience, that is, self-awareness and self-talk related to choices of appropriate conduct in the various social contexts in schools (classrooms, playgrounds, hallways, etc.) The resilient child would be aware of affect in various contexts, understand the consequences of actions in situations, recognize possible distractions and inducements to misbehave, cope with personal attacks and threats to self-esteem, have a positive attitude toward achieving the common good, and make healthy choices.

The goal of the development of self-regulated, resilient students is a clear application of a curricular frame to classroom management. Some of the strategies that teachers and administrators might use to support this purpose include explicit modeling and discussions of goals, opportunities for strategy construction, and reflection on conduct in meaningful contexts in which students face behavioral choices (see Butler & Winne, 1995; Palincsar & Brown, 1989).

Social Skills Training and Problem Solving Strategies

Early efforts to apply behavior modification techniques to classrooms involved recommendations for fairly elaborate systems of contingency management: token economies, systematic control of teacher attention, and the like (see Lahey & Rubinoff, 1981; O'Leary & O'Leary, 1977). Although such strategies are often recommended for use with special needs students (see chapters 3 and 16 in this volume), the more general impact of this work was on the development of social skills and participation strategies in individual students to help them learn to cope with classroom situations (see Cartledge & Milburn, 1978, 1995; Watson, 2003).

The explicit teaching of social skills is a proactive approach that focuses on increasing social competence in classroom situations rather than simply trying to eliminate problematic behaviors. This work is grounded in the premise that academic achievement is closely related to such social skills as attention to appropriate information, compliance with teacher requests, and responding to instructional directives (Cartledge & Milburn, 1995), and that the "discourses of power" need to be explicitly taught to children, especially those whose linguistic experiences are not congruent with the dominant language forms of formal schooling (Delpit, 1995). Achievement is also enhanced by learning to initiate contact with the teacher about work assignments, looking attentive and appreciative, and seeking answers to questions in socially appropriate ways. In addition, access to instruction is dependent upon students learning the complex social and linguistic skills required to interpret signals and events and formulate utterances in an appropriate language register to participate successfully in classroom conversations (see Cazden, 2001; Weinstein, 1991, pp. 497–501). The use of these social skills not only influences a student's academic career but also contributes to their peer acceptance (see Ladd, 1999).

Weinstein (1991) summarizes the impact of classroom social factors on students as follows:

> Students' ability to participate in socially appropriate ways influences their opportunities to achieve academic success. If students call out during recitations, instead of bidding for an opportunity to respond, the teacher may reject even correct contributions. Sharing-time narratives that do not conform to the teacher's model of "good talk" are likely to meet with disapproval. Students who need the teacher's help during seatwork may be ignored unless they make a nonverbal approach to the teacher during "down time." Requests for peer assistance may also fail if students do not frame their requests directly or if they are perceived as not having tried hard enough. Pupils who are unable to participate in small-group discussion will not benefit from the opportunity to provide and receive explanations. Examples like these depict the numerous ways in which the social and academic dimensions of schooling are intertwined. (pp. 517–518)

A direct instruction model underlies most approaches to social skills teaching. This framework typically involves identifying specific skills to be taught, providing a rationale and explicit descriptions and models of the skills to be acquired, learner production of the skills under guided prompting and feedback, provision of opportunities for practice to mastery, and continuing assessment of progress (Cartledge & Milburn, 1995). In addition, cognitive and affective strategies are used in which children examine their thinking about social situations and participate in dramatic role-playing situations. Such strategies are especially useful in maintaining the effects of direct instruction and in increasing motivation to use skills in a variety of circumstances. This social skills teaching approach has been applied to working with aggressive children (Hughes & Cavell, 1995), preschool children (Mize, 1995), and diverse student populations (Cartledge, Lee, & Feng, 1995).

A number of programs have been developed to provide students with direct instruction in conflict resolution and problem-solving strategies (see Bodine & Crawford, 1998; Johnson & Johnson, 1995; Larrivee, 2005, pp. 254–295; and the chapter by Johnson and Johnson in this Handbook). Such programs generally involve giving students steps or habits of mind (Costa & Kallick, 2000) that enable them, in private or with adult scaffolding (Watson, 2003), to analyze situations, gain perspectives, and talk through disagreements without resorting to aggression. The general approach has a family resemblance to the work in social skills training.

A preschool study by Danby and Baker (1998) in England provides an interesting perspective on teacher and student perspectives in conflict resolution. The investigators found that in resolving a conflict between children the teacher relied on her own version of the social order and the issues involved. The children momentarily accepted the teacher's version, but then reverted back to their own version when the teacher left the scene. The researchers also found that there was close congruence in versions of the social order between girls and the teacher but little congruence between boys and the teacher.

Character, Citizenship, and Moral Dimensions of Early Education

One very important area in the recent work in classroom management involves a broad view of schooling as a moral enterprise which has profound consequences for developing students' character, moral dispositions, responsibility, and prosocial behavior (see Goodlad, Soder, & Sirotnik, 1990; Hansen, 2001; Jackson, Boostrom, & Hansen, 1993; Lewis, 2001). Central to this perspective is the extent to which students develop "a willingness to exercise their own learning rights and protect the learning, and physical and emotional safety rights of others" (Lewis, 2001, p. 308).

Richardson and Fallona (2001) have examined the moral dimensions of classroom management under the rubric of "manner" in teaching, by which they "are referring to a teacher's virtuous conduct or traits of character as played out or revealed within a classroom context" (p. 706). They argue, along with Fenstermacher (2001), that, on one level, virtuous conduct teaches virtuous conduct. In addition, conscious attempts to act virtuously in classroom interactions as well as explicit instruction in virtuous conduct promote students' moral behavior.

They offer two case studies of experienced primary school teachers (kindergarten and grades three and four) who in different ways sought to promote virtuous behavior. The first teacher, called Darlene, was a skillful manager of group activities but also had a strong concern for developing social and intellectual virtues in students. She wanted them to understand what they were doing, to treat one another well, accept responsibility, and persevere. She emphasized, through action and explicit instruction, friendliness, honesty, justice, practical wisdom, and a strong sense of sharing and community. The second teacher, called Kai, is more direct, demanding, and teacher centered than Darlene but she also emphasizes respect, pride in oneself, friendliness, humor, honesty, and justice in her interactions and in her explicit communications to students.

These cases illustrate well the modern emphasis in classroom management on the use of caring, virtue, and community rather than control and conformity to foster student respect, responsibility, and independence. Watson (2003), in particular, emphasizes how restitution and moral reflection can help young children learn how their misbehavior causes distress for others. For more on this approach, see the chapters by Fallona and Richardson, by Schaps, and by Wentzel in this Handbook.

Culturally Responsive Classroom Management

Children of color are typically the primary targets of disciplinary interventions and penalties, and considerable energy has been devoted recently to developing conceptions of culturally responsive classroom management (see Weinstein, Tomlinson-Clarke, and Curran, 2004). The intent here is to ground classroom management and discipline in a richer understanding of how various cultural groups interpret such matters as order, disorder, misbehavior, reprimands, compliance, respect, and adult–child communication, all of which are part of the dynamics of discipline in school contexts. The hope is that such grounding will enable teachers to understand student conduct more fully, avoid misinterpretations of student behavior that lead to strife and conflict, and develop effective strategies for promoting productive behavior and handling issues that arise in classrooms.

Weinstein and her colleagues (2004) acknowledge that considerable work is needed to develop a conception of culturally responsive classroom management. As an effort toward this goal, they argue that culturally responsive classroom management has five components: "(1) recognition of one's own ethnocentrism and biases; (2) knowledge of students' cultural backgrounds; (3) understanding of the broader social, economic, and political context of our educational system; (4) ability and willingness to use culturally appropriate classroom management strategies; and (5) commitment to building caring classroom communities" (p. 27). Several authors have focused on the racial, social justice, and power issues surrounding classroom management (see Delpit, 2003; Nieto, 2000; Powell et al., 2001). Culturally appropriate management strategies include: teacher monitoring of equitable treatment of children from diverse backgrounds; understanding how status, cooperation, respect, and compliance are viewed within different cultural communities; and discerning when and how to accommodate to students' cultural backgrounds. For more on this area, see chapters by Sheets and by Delpit in this Handbook.

Summary

The social curriculum of classroom management is a rich and exciting area of conceptual and practical development which has expanded greatly our understanding of the educative potential of classroom management in early childhood and elementary settings. In this section we have attempted a selective review of a portion of the array of educative tools available to teachers and administrators. Our purpose was to sample the families of existing approaches, strategies, and ways of thinking that can be used to achieve the ends of the social curriculum of classroom management. This Handbook itself is an important resource for more details on these and related approaches through the chapters that are included on the various frameworks we have sketched in this section.

In retrospect, there would seem to be a striking congruence in tone and spirit between the ecological and the social-curriculum approaches to management in early childhood and elementary classrooms. In the approaches and strategies of the social curriculum reviewed for this section, there is a clear sense of the need to foster and support children's autonomy and initiative and to avoid teacher dominance and coercion. It is also clear that the underlying aspiration of the ecologists is not coercion and compliance but rather the creation of a seamless flow and momentum—an almost invisible energy—that propels the action systems of a classroom forward, maximizes work involvement, and, thus, affords all children the opportunity to experience the full educative potential of these environments. A failure to understand and manage classroom structures effectively, the ecologists would argue, creates discomfort and anxiety for all participants, teachers and students alike, and leads often to a perception by teachers and administrators of a need to increase control and to use restrictive if not punitive practices which can interfere with learning, autonomy, and self-esteem. If a teacher is overwhelmed by the action system of a classroom, he or she is not likely to be open to or successful with the complex event structures characteristic of developmentally appropriate classroom practice (see Wien, 1995).

CONCLUSION

As one looks back across the various ideas and practices reviewed in this chapter, it is easy to note that the empirical foundation for many of the claims made for how to manage early childhood and elementary classrooms is quite thin. One is tempted, therefore, to invoke the traditional refrain that more research is sorely needed in this field and to close the discussion with a strident call for a greater commitment among educational researchers to this cause and a substantial influx of funding to make this dream possible.

It is hard to deny that early childhood and elementary classroom management needs more attention, but we would argue that the more important question is what kind of attention it needs. Traditionally the effectiveness question has dominated classroom research, and so the call for more research usually translates into a call for more investigation into what practices or approaches are most effective. But we propose an alternative path to knowledge and understanding in classroom management for at least two important reasons. First, the effectiveness question itself has always proved to be difficult to answer in a global, universal sense, and the methods one must use to address this question often distort beyond recognition the very process one hopes to understand (see Doyle, 1997). Thus, the answers are often not very useful. Second, effectiveness for an individual teacher is a local construction designed to address issues situated in a specific context (Carter, 1995). Universal prescriptions often lack the particulars that a teacher, especially a beginning teacher, needs to identify a match between practice and situation or to adapt a practice to local circumstances.

If the effectiveness route has inherent limitations, then what are the alternatives? One very powerful opportunity lies in the narrative theme that runs through various sections of this chapter. It has been clear for some time now that experienced teachers' knowledge, especially of classrooms, is storied, that is, embedded in the events and actions that they live daily in classroom environments (see Carter, 1993). Teachers use this storied knowledge as a generative framework to interpret local, daily happenings and invent ways of dealing with the ongoing stream of experience they encounter. It is as if teachers are continuously on stage in an improvisational theater rapidly inventing novel lines and actions to accommodate the emerging narrative of the scene in which they live. To do this successfully, they need a rich store of narrative forms and scripts which can be drawn upon and adapted spontaneously to meet immediate circumstances.

If we apply this narrative perspective to the literatures reviewed in this chapter—if we see the work on classroom ecology and the social curriculum as a foundation for narrative understandings—some very compelling results emerge. Both of these traditions appear to embody a strong shift from a traditional narrative of control and compliance toward an enriched narrative of care, support, and productivity. The ecological approach, grounded in naturalistic studies of classroom activities or ecologies, provides an exciting way of understanding how classroom life is jointly constructed and lived by participants within the structures of classroom environments. Work within the social curriculum, based on a long tradition of holistic pedagogy going back to nineteenth and early twentieth century theorists such as Pestolozzi and Dewey, captures the modern spirit of development, democracy, and constructivism found in efforts to improve children's lives. And both strands are generative in the sense that they enable one to go beyond the information given to frame interpretations and invent possible tools. Indeed, throughout the chapter we found ourselves regularly and naturally extrapolating from a limited empirical foundation to unstudied issues in early childhood and elementary classrooms using the narratives of care and hope embedded in the ecological and social curriculum frameworks as generative tools.

One of the most significant developments in the field, we believe, is the emergence of actual narratives that portray teachers attempting to use developmentally appropriate practices in early childhood and elementary classrooms. Wien (1995), for instance, tells the stories of five early childhood teachers in urban settings who over the course of a year tried to implement developmentally appropriate practices in their classrooms. Watson (2003) narrates Laura Ecken's efforts to use Developmental Discipline in her urban, ungraded primary classroom with particular attention to Danny, an especially disruptive child who pushes the edges of nearly all social structures a teacher might try to put in place. What is especially important about these portrayals is that they are narratives of struggle. In the real world, actually being a developmentally appropriate teacher is not automatic or easy just because one believes heartily in a particular approach or philosophy. The daily task of implementing the strategies of managing classrooms is profoundly challenging, requiring patience, reflection, and external support from colleagues and consultants. In addition to establishing that developmentally appropriate classroom management is challenging, these narratives show the kinds of interpretations and decisions a teacher must engage in to deal with classroom realities. As a result, the narratives add to our understanding of the practices themselves and provide a framework for both experienced and beginning teachers to improve their practices.

In the end, we recommend that researchers interested in early childhood and elementary classroom management extend this narrative work to enlarge our understanding of how management occurs in real classrooms. For teachers, we recommend that they view information about managing early childhood and elementary classrooms as a foundation for elaborating upon the personal narratives they use to understand and guide their current practices (see Carter, 1990; Carter & Doyle, 1996). Finally, for teacher educators (see chapter 33 in this volume), we strongly endorse a narrative approach, through cases, personal stories, and the storying of experience (see Carter, 1992, 1999), to helping novice teachers begin to understand the complexity, richness, and excitement of managing classrooms of young children successfully.

ACKNOWLEDGMENT

The authors wish to thank Vicki Laboskey, Mills College, for her comments on an earlier version of this chapter.

REFERENCES

Adams, R. S. (1969). Location as a feature of instructional interaction. *Merrill Palmer Quarterly, 15*, 309–321.

Adams, R. S., & Biddle, B. J. (1970). *Realities off teaching: Exploration with videotape*. New York: Holt, Rinehart & Winston.

Anderson, L. (1983). *Achievement-related differences in students' responses to seatwork*. Paper presented at the annual meeting of the American Educational Research Association, Montreal, QUE.

Arlin, M. (1979). Teacher transitions can disrupt time flow in classrooms. *American Educational Research Journal, 16*, 42–56.

Au, K. H. (1980). Participation structures in a reading lesson with Hawaiian children: Analysis of a culturally appropriate instructional event. *Anthropology and Education Quarterly, 11*, 91–115.

Barker, R. G. (1968). *Ecological psychology*. Stanford, CA: Stanford University Press.

Bennett, N., & Blundell, D. (1983). Quantity and quality of work in rows and classroom groups. *Educational Psychology, 3*, 93–105.

Bennett, N., & Desforges, C. (1988). Matching classroom tasks to students' attainments. *Elementary School Journal, 88(5)*, 221–234.

Biemiller, A., & Meichenbaum, D. (1992). The nature and nurture of the self-directed learner. *Educational Leadership, 50*(2), 75–80.

Blumenfeld, P. C., Hamilton, V. L., Wessels, K., & Falkner, D. (1979). Teaching responsibility to first graders. *Theory Into Practice, 18*, 174–180.

Blumenfeld, P. C., & Meece, J. L. (1988). Task factors, teacher behavior, and students' involvement and use of learning strategies in science. *Elementary School Journal, 88*, 235–250.

Blumenfeld, P. C., Mergendoller, J., & Swarthout, D. (1987). Cumulative experience of task form: Its impact on students as thinkers and workers. *Journal of Curriculum Studies, 19*, 135–148.

Bodine, R. J., & Crawford, D. K. (1998). *The handbook of conflict resolution education: A guide to building quality programs in schools*. San Francisco: Jossey-Bass.

Boekaerts, M. (1995). Self-regulated learning: Bridging the gap between metacognitive and metamotivational theories. *Educational Psychologist, 30*, 195–200.

Boostrom, R. (1991). The nature and functions of classroom rules. *Curriculum Inquiry, 21*(2), 193–216.

Borman, K. M. (1978). Social control and schooling: Power and process in two kindergarten settings. *Anthropology and Education Quarterly, 9*, 38–53.

Bredekamp, S. (1987). *Developmentally appropriate practice in early childhood programs serving children from birth through age eight*. Washington, DC: National Association for the Education of Young Children.

Bredekamp, S. (1996). Early childhood education. In J. Sikula, T. J. Buttery, & E. Guyton (Eds.), *Handbook of research on teacher education* (2nd ed., pp. 323–347). New York: Macmillan.

Brophy, J. (Ed). (1992). Advances *in research on teaching: Planning and managing learning tasks and activities* (Vol. 3). Greenwich, CT: JAI Press.

Brophy, J. (2004). *Motivating students to learn* (2nd ed.). Mahwah, NJ: Lawrence Erlbaum Associates.

Bryant, D. M., Clifford, R. M., & Peisner, E. S. (1991). Best practices for beginners: Developmental appropriateness in kindergarten. *American Educational Research Journal, 28*(4), 783–803.

Burns, R. B. (1984). How time is used in elementary schools: The activity structure of classrooms. In L. W. Anderson (Ed.), *Time and school learning: Theory, research and practice* (pp. 91–127). London: Croom Helm.

Butin, D. (2000a). *Classrooms*. Washington, DC: National Clearinghouse for Educational Facilities.

Butin, D. (2000b). *Early childhood centers*. Washington, DC: National Clearinghouse for Educational Facilities.

Butler, D. L., & Winne, P. H. (1995). Feedback and self-regulated learning: A theoretical synthesis. *Review of Educational Research, 64*, 245–281.

Canter, L., & Canter, M. (2001). *Assertive discipline: Positive behavior management for today's classroom* (3rd ed.). Seal Beach, CA: Canter & Associates.

Carter, K. (1990). Teachers' knowledge and learning to teach. In W. R. Houston (Ed.), *Handbook of research on teacher education* (pp. 291–310). New York: Macmillan.

Carter, K. (1992). Toward a cognitive conception of classroom management: A case of teacher comprehension. In J. Shulman (Ed.), *Case methods in teacher education* (pp. 111–130). New York: Teachers College Press.

Carter, K. (1993). The place of story in research on teaching and teacher education. *Educational Researcher, 22*(1), 5–12.

Carter, K. (1995). Teaching stories and local understandings. *Journal of Educational Research, 88*, 326–330.

Carter, K. (1999). What is a case? What is not a case? In M. A. Lundberg, B. B. Levin, & H. L. Harrington (Eds.), *Who learns what from cases and how: The research base for teaching with cases* (pp. 165–175). Mahwah, NJ: Lawrence Erlbaum Associates.

Carter, K., Cushing, K., Sabers, D., Stein, P., & Berliner, D. (1988). Expert-novice differences in perceiving and processing visual classroom information. *Journal of Teacher Education, 39*(3), 25–31.

Carter, K., & Doyle, W. (1996). Personal narrative and life history in learning to teach. In J. Sikula, T. J. Buttery, & E. Guyton (Eds.), *Handbook of research on teacher education* (2nd ed., 120–142). New York: Macmillan.

Cartledge, G., Lee, J. W., & Feng, H. (1995). Cultural diversity: Multicultural factors in teaching social skills. In G. Cartledge & J. F. Milburn (Eds.), *Teaching social skills to children and youth: Innovative approaches* (3rd ed., pp. 328– 355). Boston: Allyn & Bacon.

Cartledge, G., & Milburn, J. F. (1978). The case for teaching social skills in the classroom: A review. *Review of Educational Research, 1*, 133–156.

Cartledge, G., & Milburn, J. F. (1995). *Teaching social skills to children and youth: Innovative approaches* (3rd ed.). Boston: Allyn & Bacon.

Castle, K., & Rogers, K. (1994). Rule-creating in a constructivist classroom community. *Childhood Education, 70*(2), 77–80.

Cazden, C. B. (2001). *Classroom discourse: The language of teaching and learning* (2nd ed.). Portsmouth, NH: Heinemann.

Charles, C. M. (2005). *Building classroom discipline* (8th ed.). Boston: Allyn & Bacon.

Clayton, M. K. (2001). *Classroom spaces that work*. Strategies for Teachers Series. Greenfield, MA: Northeast Foundation for Children.

Cohen, E. G. (1994). *Designing groupwork: Strategies for the heterogeneous classroom* (2nd ed.). New York: Teachers College Press.

Corno, L. (1993). The best-laid plans: Modern conceptions of volition and educational research. *Educational Researcher, 22*(2), 14–22.

Costa, A. L., & Kallick, B. (2000). *Discovering and exploring habits of mind.* Alexandria, VA: Association for Supervision and Curriculum Development.

Cunningham, D. L. (2004). *Breaking the silence in classroom participation: A study of a regular classroom and a computer-mediated session.* Unpublished doctoral dissertation, University of Arizona, Tueson, AZ.

Danby, S., & Baker, C. (1998). 'What's the problem?': Restoring social order in the preschool classroom. In I. Hutchby & J. Moran-Ellis (Eds.), *Children and social competence: Arenas of action* (pp. 157–186). London: Falmer.

Daniels, H., & Bizar, M. (1998). *Methods that matter: Six structures for best practice classrooms.* Portland, ME: Stenhouse Publishers.

Delpit, L. (1995). *Other people's children: Cultural conflict in the classroom.* New York: The New Press.

Delpit, L. (2003). Educators as "seed people" growing a new future. *Educational Researcher, 32*(7), 14–21.

deVoss, G. G. (1979). The structure of major lessons and collective student activity. *Elementary School Journal, 80,* 8–18.

DeVries, R., & Zan, B. (2003). When children make rules. *Educational Leadership, 61*(1), 64–67.

Doyle, W. (1983). Academic work. *Review of Educational Research, 53,* 159–199.

Doyle, W. (1986). Content representation in teachers' definitions of academic work. *Journal of Curriculum Studies, 18,* 365–379.

Doyle, W. (1988). Work in mathematics classes: The context of students' thinking during instruction. *Educational Psychologist,* 23, 167–180.

Doyle, W. (1992). Curriculum and pedagogy. In P. W. Jackson (Ed.), *Handbook of research on curriculum* (pp. 486–516). New York: Macmillan.

Doyle, W. (1997). Heard any really good stories lately? A critique of the critics of narrative in educational research. *Teaching and Teacher Education, 13*(1), 93– 99.

Doyle, W., & Carter, K. (1984). Academic tasks in classrooms. *Curriculum Inquiry, 14,* 129–148.

Dreikurs, R., & Cassel, P. (1995). *Discipline without tears.* New York: Penguin.

Dreikurs, R., Grunwald, B. B., & Pepper, F. C. (1982). *Maintaining sanity in the classroom: Classroom management techniques* (2nd ed). New York: Harper & Row.

Eddowes, E. A., & Ralph, K. S. (1998). *Interactions for development and learning: Birth through eight years.* Upper Saddle River, NJ: Merrill/Prentice-Hall.

Eder, D. (1982). Differences in communicative styles across ability groups. In L. C. Wilkinson (Ed.), *Communicating in classrooms* (pp. 245–264). New York: Academic Press.

Eisenberg, N. (2002). Emotion-related regulation and its relation to quality of social functioning. In W. W. Hartup & R. A. Weinberg (Eds.), *Child psychology in retrospect and prospect: In celebration of the 75th anniversary of the Institute of Child Development* The Minnesota Symposia on Child Psychology (vol. 32, pp. 133– 171). Mahwah, NJ: Lawrence Erlbaum Associates.

Emmer, E. T., Evertson, C. M., & Anderson, L. (1980). Effective classroom management at the beginning of the school year. *Elementary School Journal, 80,* 219–231.

Emmer, E. T., & Gerwels, M. C. (2002). Cooperative learning in elementary classrooms: Teaching practices and lesson characteristics. *Elementary School Journal, 103,* 75–91.

Erickson, F., & Mohatt, G. (1982). Cultural organization or participation structures in two classrooms of Indian students. In G. Spindler (Ed.), *Doing the ethnography of schooling* (pp. 132–174). New York: Holt, Rinehart & Winston.

Erickson, F., & Shultz, J. (1981). When is a context? Some issues and methods in the analysis of social competence. In J. L. Green & C. Wallat (Eds.), *Ethnography and language in educational settings* (pp. 147–160). Norwood, NJ: Ablex.

Erikson, E. (1963). *Childhood and society* (2nd ed.). New York: Norton.

Espelage, D. L., & Swearer, S. M. (Eds.). (2004). *Bullying in American schools: A socio-ecological perspective on prevention and intervention.* Mahwah, NJ: Lawrence Erlbaum Associates.

Evertson, C. M., Emmer, E. T., Sanford, J. P., & Clements, B. S. (1983). Improving classroom management: An experiment in elementary classrooms. *Elementary School Journal, 84,* 173–188.

Evertson, C. M., Emmer, E. T., & Worsham, M. E. (2003). *Classroom management for elementary teachers* (6th ed.). Boston: Allyn & Bacon.

Felmlee, D., & Eder, D. (1983). Contextual effects in the classroom: The impact of ability groups on group attention. *Sociology of Education, 56,* 77–87.

Fenstermacher, G. D. (2001). On the concept of manner and its visibility in teaching practice. *Journal of Curriculum Studies, 33,* 639–653.

Florio, S., & Shultz, J. (1979). Social competence at home and at school. *Theory Into Practice, 18,* 234–243.

Gibson, J. J. (1979). *The ecological approach to visual perception.* Boston: Houghton Mifflin.

Ginott, H. (1971). *Teacher and child.* New York: Macmillan.

Glasser, W. (1998). *The quality school: Managing student without coercion.* New York: Harper-Perennial.

Golbeck, S. L. (2001). Instructional model of early childhood: In search of a child- regulated/teacher-guided pedagogy. In S. L. Golbeck (Ed.), *Psychological perspectives on early childhood education: Reframing dilemmas in research and practice* (pp. 3–34). Mahwah, NJ: Lawrence Erlbaum Associates.
Gonzalez, N. (1995). Processual approaches to multicultural education. *Journal of Applied Behavioral Science, 31*, 234–244.
Goodlad, J. I., Soder, R., & Sirotnik, K. A. (Eds.). (1990). *The moral dimension of teaching*. San Francisco: Jossey-Bass.
Gordon, T. (1987). *T.E.T.: Teacher effectiveness training* (2 nd ed.). New York: David McKay.
Green, J. L., & Harker, J. O. (1982). Gaining access to learning: Conversational, social, and cognitive demands of group participation. In L. C. Wilkinson (Ed.), *Communicating in classrooms* (pp. 183–221). New York: Academic Press.
Gump, P. V. (1967). *The classroom behavior setting: Its nature and relation to student behavior (Final Report)*. Washington, DC: U.S. Office of Education, Bureau of Research. (ERIC Document Reproduction Service No. ED015515)
Gump, P. V. (1969). Intra-setting analysis: The third grade classroom as a special but instructive case. In E. Willems & H. Rausch (Eds.), *Naturalistic viewpoints in psychological research* (pp. 200–220). New York: Holt, Rinehart & Winston.
Gump, P. V. (1975). *Ecological psychology and children*. Chicago: University of Chicago Press.
Gump, P. V. (1982). School settings and their keeping. In D. L. Duke (Ed.), *Helping teachers manage classrooms* (pp. 98–114). Alexandria, VA: Association for Supervision and Curriculum Development.
Hansen, D. T. (2001). Reflections on the manner in teaching project. *Journal of Curriculum Studies, 33*, 729–735.
Harper, L. V., and McCluskey, K. S. (2003). Teacher-child and child-child interactions in inclusive preschool settings: Do adults inhibit peer interactions? *Early Childhood Research Quarterly, 18*, 163–184.
Harrist, A. W., & Bradley, K. D. (2003). "You can't say you can't play": Intervening in the process of social exclusion in the kindergarten classroom. *Early Childhood Research Quarterly, 18*, 185–205.
Herbst, P. G. (2003). Using novel tasks in teaching mathematics: Three tensions affecting the work of the teacher. *American Educational Research Journal, 40*, 197–238.
Hoetker, J., & Ahlbrand, W. P. (1969). The persistence of the recitation. *American Educational Research Journal, 6*, 145–167.
Holmes, M. (1991). The classroom: Solitude, isolation and rules. *Curriculum Inquiry, 21*, 135–140.
Huberman, M., & Middlebrooks, S. (2000). The dilution of inquiry: A qualitative study. *International Journal of Qualitative Studies in Education, 13*, 281–304.
Hughes, J. N., & Cavell, T. A. (1995). Cognitive-affective approaches: Enhancing competence in aggressive children. In G. Cartledge, & J. F. Milburn (Eds.), *Teaching social skills to children and youth: Innovative approaches* (3rd ed., pp. 197–236). Boston: Allyn & Bacon.
Humphrey, F. M. (1979). *"Shh!" : A sociolinguistic study of teachers' turn- taking sanctions in primary school lessons*. Unpublished doctoral dissertation, Georgetown University, Washington DC.
Jackson, P. W., Boostrom, R. E., & Hansen, D. T. (1993). *The moral life of schools*. San Francisco: Jossey-Bass.
Johnson, D. W., & Johnson, R. T. (1994). *Learning together and alone: Cooperati ve, competitive, and individualistic learning* (4th ed.). Boston: Allyn & Bacon.
Johnson, D. W., & Johnson, R. T. (1995). *Reducing school violence through conflict resolution*. Alexandria, VA: Association for Supervision and Curriculum Development.
Kehle, T. J., Bray, M. A., Theodore, L. A., Jenson, W. R., & Clark, E. (2000). A multi-component intervention designed to reduce disruptive classroom behavior. *Psychology in the Schools, 37*, 475–481.
Kremer-Hayon, L., & Tillema, H. H. (1999). Self-regulated learning in the context of teacher education. *Teaching and Teacher Education, 15*, 507–522.
Kounin, J. S. (1970). *Discipline and group management in classrooms*. New York: Holt, Rinehart & Winston.
Kounin, J. S., & Gump, P. V. (1958). The ripple effect in discipline. *Elementary School Journal, 59*, 158–162.
Kounin, J. S., & Gump, P. V. (1974). Signal systems of lesson settings and the task related behavior of preschool children. *Journal of Educational Psychology, 66*, 554–562.
Kowatrakul, S. (1959). Some behaviors of elementary school children related to classroom activities and subject areas. *Journal of Educational Psychology, 50*, 121–128.
Ladd, G. W. (1999). Peer relationships and social competence during early and middle childhood. *Annual Review of Psychology, 50*, 333–359.
Lahey, B. B., & Rubinoff, A. (1981). Behavior therapy in education. In L. Michelson, M. Herson, & S. M. Turner (Eds.), *Future perspectives in behavior therapy* (pp. 27- -43). New York: Plenum.
Larrivee, B. (2005). *Authentic classroom management: Creating a learning communi ty and building reflective practice* (2nd ed.). Boston: Allyn & Bacon.
Leinhardt, G. (1983). Types of content in lessons. In T. Husen & N. Postlehwaite (Eds.), *International encyclopedia of education: Research and studies* (pp. 3015–3020). Oxford: Pergamon.

Leinhardt, G., Weidman, C., & Hammond, K. M. (1987). Introduction and integration of classroom routines by expert teachers. *Curriculum Inquiry, 17*, 135–176.

Lewis, R. (2001). Classroom discipline and student responsibility: The students' view. *Teaching and Teacher Education, 17*, 307–319.

Lindner, R. W., & Harris, B. (1993). Self-regulated learning: Its assessment and instructional implications. *Educational Research Quarterly,* 29–37.

Marx, R. W., & Walsh, J. (1988). Learning from academic tasks. *Elementary School Journal. 88*, 207–219.

Marzano, R. J. (2003). *Classroom management that works: Research-based strategies for every teacher*. Alexandria, VA: Association for Supervision and Curriculum Development.

McDermott, R. P. (1976). *Kids make sense: An ethnographic account of the instructional management of success and failure in one first-grade classroom*. Unpublished doctoral dissertation, Stanford University, Stanford, CA.

McLeod, J. (2003). Time and classroom space. In J. McLeod, J. Fisher, & G. Hoover (Eds.), *The key elements of classroom management: Managing time and space, student behavior, and instructional strategies* (pp. 3–38). Alexandria, VA: Association for Supervision and Curriculum Development.

Mehan, H. (1979). *Learning lessons: Social organization in a classroom*. Cambridge, MA: Harvard University Press.

Mehan, H. (1980). The competent student. *Anthropology and Education Quarterly, 11*, 131–152.

Merritt, M. (1982). Distributing and directing attention in primary classrooms. In L. C. Wilkinson (Ed.), *Communicating in classrooms* (pp. 223–244). New York: Academic Press.

Michaels, S. (1986). Narrative presentations: An oral preparation for literacy with first graders. In J. Cook-Gumperz (Ed.), *The social construction of literacy*(pp. 94– 116). Cambridge: Cambridge University Press.

Miller, S. D. (2003). How high- and low-challenge tasks affect motivation and learning: Implications for struggling learners. *Reading and Writing Quarterly, 19*, 39–57.

Mize, J. (1995). Coaching preschool children in social skills: A cognitive-social learning curriculum. In G. Cartledge, & J. F. Milburn (Eds.), *Teaching social skills to children and youth: Innovative approaches* (3rd ed., pp. 237–261). Boston: Allyn & Bacon.

National Research Council, Committee on Early Childhood Pedagogy. (2001). *Eager to learn: Educating our preschoolers*. Washington, DC: National Academic Press.

Nieto, S. (2000). *Affirming diversity: The sociopolitical context of multicultur al education* (3rd ed.). White Plains, NY: Longman.

Norman, D. A. (1990). *The design of everyday things*. New York: Doubleday.

O'Connor, M. C., & Michaels, S. (1993). Aligning academic task and participation status through revoicing: An analysis of a classroom discourse strategy. *Anthropology and Education Quarterly, 24*, 3318–3335.

O'Connor, R. E., & Jenkins, J. R. (1996). Cooperative learning as an inclusion strategy: A closer look. *Exceptional Children, 62*, 29–51.

O'Leary, K. D., & O'Leary, S. G. (1977). *Classroom management: The successful use of behavior modification* (2nd ed.). New York: Pergamon.

Osborne, S. B. (1996). Practice into theory into practice: Culturally relevant pedagogy for students we have marginalized and normalized. *Anthropology and Education Quarterly, 27*, 285–314.

Palincsar, A. S., & Brown, A. L. (1989). Instruction for self-regulated reading. In L. Resnick & L. Kloepfer (Eds.), *Toward the thinking curriculum: Current cognitive research*(pp. 19–39). Alexandria, VA: Association for Supervision and Curriculum Development.

Parker, W. C., & Hess, D. (2001). Teaching with and for discussion. *Teaching and Teacher Education, 17*, 273–289.

Philips, S. U. (1972). Participant structures and communicative competence: Warm Springs children in community and classrooms. In C. Cazden, V. P. Johns, & D. Hymes (Eds.), *Functions of language in the classroom*. New York: Teachers College Press.

Pintrich, P. R., & DeGroot, E. (1990). Motivational and self-regulated learning components of classroom academic performance. *Journal of Educational Psychology, 82*, 33–40.

Pintrich, P., & Schrauben, B. (1992). Students' motivational beliefs and their cognitive engagement in classroom tasks. In D. Schunk & J. Meece (Eds.), *Student perceptions in the classroom: Causes and consequences* (pp. 149–183). Hillsdale, NJ: Lawrence Erlbaum Associates.

Powell, R. R., McLaughlin, H. J., Savage, T. V., & Zehm, S. (2001). *Classroom management: Perspectives on the social curriculum*. Upper Saddle River, NJ: Merrill/ Prentice-Hall.

Puckett, M. B., & Black, J. K. (2001). *The young child: Development from prebirth through age eight* (3rd ed.). Upper Saddle River, NJ: Merrill/Prentice-Hall.

Richardson, V., & Fallona, C. (2001). Classroom management as method and manner. *Journal of Curriculum Studies, 33*, 705–728.

Rogoff, B., Paradise, R., Arauz, R. M., Correa-Chavez, M., & Angelillo, C. (2003). Firsthand learning through intent participation. *Annual Review of Psychology, 54*, 175–203.

Romano, M. E.(2004). Teacher reflections on "bumpy moments" in teaching: A self-study. *Teachers and Teaching: Theory and Practice*. 10, 663–681.

Rosenshine, B. V. (1980). How time is spent in elementary classrooms. In C. Denham & A. Lieberman (Eds.), *Time to learn*. Washington, DC: National Institute of Education.

Saarni, C. (1997). Emotional competence and self-regulation in childhood. In P. Salovey & D. J. Sluyter (Eds.), *Emotional development and emotional intelligence: Educational implications* (pp. 35–66). New York: Basic Books.

Sherman, L. (1975). An ecological study of glee in a nursery school. *Child Development, 46*, 53–61.

Shultz, J., & Florio, S. (1979). Stop and Freeze: The negotiation of social and physical space in a kindergarten and first grade classroom. *Anthropology and Education Quarterly, 10*, 166–181.

Sieber, R. T. (1979). Classmates as workmates: Informal peer activity in the elementary school. *Anthropology and Education Quarterly, 10*, 207–235.

Slavin, R. E. (1995). *Cooperative learning: Theory, research, and practice* (2nd ed.). Boston: Allyn & Bacon.

Slavin, R. E. (1996). Research on cooperative learning and achievement: What we know, what we need to know. *Contemporary Educational Psychology, 21*, 43–69.

Sommer, R. (1969). *Personal space: The behavioral basis of design*. Englewood Cliffs, NJ: Prentice-Hall.

Tikunoff, W. J., & Ward, B. A. (1978). *A naturalistic study of the initiation of students into three classroom social systems* (Rep. No. A-78-11). San Francisco: Far West Laboratory.

Trawick-Smith, J. (2000). *Early childhood development: A multicultural perspective* (2nd ed.). Upper Saddle River, NJ: Merrill/Prentice-Hall.

Tsai, M., & Garcia, G. E. (2000). Who's the boss? How communicative competence is defined in a multilingual preschool classroom. *Anthropology and Education Quarterly, 31*, 230–252.

Vitto, J. M. (2003). *Relationship-driven classroom management: Strategies that promote student motivation*. Thousand Oaks, CA: Corwin.

Watson, M. (2003). *Learning to trust: Transforming difficult elementary classrooms through developmental discipline*. San Francisco: Jossey-Bass.

Waxman, H. C., Gray, J. P., & Padron, Y. N. (2003). *Review of research on educational resilience*. Santa Cruz, CA: Center for Research on Education, Diversity, and Excellence.

Webb, N. M., & Palincsar, A. S. (1996). Group processes in the classroom. In D. Berliner & R. C. Calfee (Eds.), *Handbook of educational psychology* (pp. 841–876). New York: Macmillan.

Weinstein, C. S. (1979). The physical environment of the school: A review of the researc h. *Review of Educational Research, 49*, 557–610.

Weinstein, C. S. (1982). Privacy-seeking behavior in an elementary classroom. *Journal of Environmental Psychology, 2*, 23–35.

Weinstein, C. S. (1991). The classroom as a social context for learning. *Annual Review of Psychology, 42*, 493–525.

Weinstein, C. S., & David, T. G. (Eds.). (1987). *Spaces for children: The built environment and child development*. New York: Plenum.

Weinstein, C. S., & Mignano, A. J. (2003). *Elementary classroom management: Lessons from research and practice* (3rd ed.). New York: McGraw-Hill.

Weinstein, C. S., Tomlinson-Clarke, S., & Curran, M. (2004). Toward a conception of culturally responsive classroom management. *Journal of Teacher Education, 55*(1), 25–38.

Wien, C. A. (1995). *Developmentally appropriate practice in "real life" : Stories of teacher practical knowledge*. New York: Teachers College Press.

Wolters, C. A. (2003). Regulation of motivation: Evaluating an underemphasized aspect of self-regulated learning. *Educational Psychologist, 38*, 189–205.

Wood, T. (1999). Creating a context for argument in mathematics class. *Journal of Research in Mathematics Education, 30*, 171–191.

Woolfolk, A. E., & Brooks, D. M. (1985). Beyond words: The influence of teachers' nonverbal behaviors on students' perceptions and performances. *Elementary School Journal, 85*, 513–528.

Yinger, R. J. (1980). A study of teacher planning. *Elementary School Journal, 80*, 107–127.

Zimmerman, B. (1989). A social cognitive view of self-regulated learning and academic learning. *Journal of Educational Psychology, 81*, 329–339.

15

Classroom Management in Middle and High School Classrooms

Edmund T. Emmer and Mary Claire Gerwels
The University of Texas, Austin

INTRODUCTION

Two primary factors differentiate most secondary settings from their elementary counterparts: (1) the division of the school day into separate predetermined periods of instruction with multiple teachers according to subject matter, and (2) the adolescent population found in secondary school settings. Classroom management plans and strategies need to accommodate these two factors in several ways. For example, secondary students enter and leave the classroom at the beginning and end of each instructional period, so efficient procedures are needed to handle the transitions. Because secondary students are in six or more classes daily, teachers need to develop work routines that facilitate students' efficient use of time. And because secondary teachers work with adolescents, their ability to understand the developmental characteristics of this population plays an important part in whether they can formulate a sound management plan, communicate effectively, and work constructively with this population under sometimes stressful circumstances.

There is a variety of perspectives on the conceptualization of classroom management. For example, Jones and Jones (2004) identify several areas of knowledge and skill: establishing positive teacher–student and peer relationships that build a supportive environment, using instructional methods that optimize learning, gaining a commitment from students to appropriate behavior standards, creating a safe and caring classroom community, and using counseling and behavioral methods to change students' inappropriate behavior. Brophy (1999) distinguishes classroom management from disciplinary interventions. The former is concerned with creating and maintaining a learning environment conducive to instruction, while the latter are "actions taken to elicit or compel changes in the behavior of students who fail to conform to expectations" (p. 43). A different and popular perspective was offered by Canter's *Assertive Discipline* (1976), which emphasized the teacher's communication style and the appropriate use of consequences. This chapter adopts a view of management at the broad end of the spectrum. We agree with Doyle's (1986) view that management is concerned with the establishment of order and its maintenance. It encompasses those things that teachers do to organize the classroom and instructional setting and to influence students toward desirable behavior. We also include disciplinary actions teachers take as they respond to and minimize disruptive behavior.

Some limits on the scope of the chapter are necessary in order to keep it at a reasonable length. Its content will deal with regular education rather than special education, and, of course, the focus will be on secondary rather than elementary settings. Furthermore, we will not address school-wide management and special programs intended for school-wide application. These topics are addressed in other chapters in this *Handbook*. Although this chapter is concerned with management in middle and high schools, many of the concepts, theories, and recommendations from the elementary and special education classroom management literature will be relevant. Substantial research in these settings has provided important ideas for management at the secondary level, and to ignore this body of research and theory would seriously limit our understanding of the topic.

Classroom management is important for middle and high school teachers for several reasons. First, it is central to the task of teaching, and without good management practices the teacher's job is much more difficult. But management of a classroom is complex, belying the surface impression created by countless hours spent as a student, or what Lortie (1975) called the "apprenticeship of observation." As many first-time secondary teachers have discovered, an inability to carry out some fundamental managerial tasks can create miniworlds of chaos. Second, classroom management impacts outcomes of importance to children, their parents, and society. Well-managed settings promote student engagement and create opportunities to learn; poorly managed classrooms dissipate student time and attention, reduce learning, and discourage academic accomplishment. Numerous reviews of research have shown the connection between effective classroom management and academic outcomes (e.g., Wang, Haertel, & Walberg, 1993). Finally, teacher managerial skills are connected to student behavior; good management helps limit student behavior problems and keeps them from disrupting other students' learning.

This chapter has several sections. We begin with a review of adolescent development and characteristics that have important implications for classroom management, followed by a consideration of characteristics of teachers, including emotions and thinking that impact management. We then examine research on managerial behaviors and skills, including studies focused on the beginning of the year, and prevention, activity management, and communication styles. Two vignettes are presented to illustrate and integrate many of the concepts in the previous sections. The final section reviews research on classroom-based strategies for dealing with inappropriate behaviors.

ADOLESCENT DEVELOPMENT AND CHARACTERISTICS

Social Implications of Adolescent Development

Many aspects of adolescent growth and development affect classroom behavior. Understanding how youth develop a sense of social responsibility and self-restraint is essential in creating a developmentally appropriate plan to encourage appropriate behavior in the classroom. Bandura's social cognitive theory (1986) explains how individuals internalize social rules.

Actions, even undesirable ones, tend to be picked up by watching others (Bandura, 1986), especially if the outcomes are valued and the actor feels capable of carrying out the behavior. Observed behavior will not automatically be displayed, however, unless certain conditions are met. If there is a reward or incentive offered, or if others have received such benefits for the behavior, then it is more likely the behavior will be displayed by the observer. According to social learning theory, factors that affect whether or not a model will be emulated are the model's status, competence, power, and similarity to the observer. These models aid in the development of social self-efficacy. Those who feel socially efficacious attempt to work out problems through compromise and fairness, while those who perceive themselves to be aggressive tend to escalate conflicts and resolve them through coercive or physical means (Bandura, 1997). Observers may also decide to produce what they see if the observed behavior seems satisfying or aligned with personal standards.

Personal standards and observation affect the development and enactment of self-restraint (Bandura, 1986). According to social learning theory, restraint of behavior can be achieved through experience with social rules that carry the threat of punishment and by internal rules that are developed as a person matures. Internal restraint develops with the ability to anticipate social sanctions and the impulse control necessary to stop improper behavior. Gradually, external control is needed less often as self-determined standards emerge that help guide behavior. Obviously, environment affects the rules that are internalized, which partially accounts for apparent differences in self-control. Adolescents who are raised in subcultures of unlawfulness will likely adopt internal standards that are not aligned with the larger community. For most adolescents, though, generally accepted rules of conduct are the ones internalized. When punishment is not effective in curbing errant conduct, then the internal system of restraint takes over to keep behavior within personally defined limits. Self-sanctions can be weakened under several conditions, however, some of which may occur in the classroom. For instance, responsibility for individual behavior can be diffused because the individual is part of a larger group engaged in the behavior (Bandura, 1990). Similarly, students may also learn to blame others for their actions, which also helps to remove responsibility for the act. "He made me do it" and "Why are you picking on me? Everyone else is doing it too," are examples of such thinking.

Social learning theory also offers some insight into the effects of the rules and practices teachers implement. When teachers apply sanctions to curb behavior, the likelihood that their standards will be accepted depends upon the types of sanctions used, their application, and the quality of the student–teacher relationship. If sanctions are used effectively, then standards may be learned and social control achieved; otherwise, the socially desirable behavior, as well as the punisher, may be avoided. There is also the possibility that the aversive acts used as punishment may be learned and copied, rather than acting as a deterrent for the unacceptable deeds.

The same behavior may be acceptable in one situation but not in another, so social cues about what is and is not acceptable play a large part in regulating behavior (Bandura, 1986). For instance, casual talking in a group may be considered acceptable and desirable if the group is in a public place such as a restaurant, but it is not desirable in many classroom activities. Therefore, the teacher must direct students' attention to cues that help clarify behaviors that are regarded as acceptable.

Peers have considerable influence on the social norms that students accept, and this can affect the development of self-control. The most accomplished peers provide role models for others, whether the achievements are academic, athletic, or delinquent. For example, the peer group has a large effect on adolescent smoking, drinking, and sexual behaviors. Peers, more than others, tend to reinforce a positive stereotype for drinking and smoking, and to increase the willingness of others to engage in these activities (Blanton, Gibbons, Gerrard, Conger, & Smith, 1997).

Peer modeling and its effect on behavior are of particular importance in school because adults are greatly outnumbered, and because students chosen as leaders may not always be desirable prosocial role models, at least from an adult perspective. In one study, both male and female students in grades five, six, and seven rated peers they perceived as antisocial to be the strongest leaders (Schonert-Reichl, 1999). Although considered antisocial, these leaders tended to be among those with the highest awareness of moral behavior, suggesting that knowledge of desirable conduct does not ensure such behaviors will be enacted. Information about modeling and peer influence is crucial because teachers need to be aware of how students influence each other in the classroom. Simply making students aware of the rules and sanctions for not following them is unlikely to be sufficient to elicit a high level of compliant behavior by many adolescents.

To summarize, social cognitive theory highlights important factors in the development of self-restraint. Teachers can use this information in their development of a behavior plan. Teachers ought to remember that observed behavior is more likely to be imitated if the model is rewarded for the behavior. While classroom management frequently focuses on transgressors, it is helpful to notice those who are following the rules. Focus on the positive may be one of the best ways to help adolescents develop socially acceptable behaviors (Granger, 2002; Lerner & Dowling, 2002). Too, models who are similar to the observers are most likely to be emulated. Noticing positive behavior from students who differ in gender, size, race, athleticism, and academic ability, among other attributes, provides a wide range of models for other students to follow. Consistency in using rewards and punishment is also important so that the consequences of the model's behaviors are unambiguous. One final point is that personal responsibility for actions can be diffused in a group (Bandura, 1990). Therefore, teachers must take action early before inappropriate behavior spreads, in order to be able to maintain individuals' responsibility for their actions, and before models for inappropriate behavior begin to be rewarded.

Adolescent Psychosocial Development

A widely recognized task of adolescence is the development of an identity (Erikson, 1963). In the middle school and high school years many adolescents are developing skills that will help them reach adult goals of holding jobs and becoming socially competent (Erikson, 1963, 1982). Toward the end of their middle school years, most students will have begun to move into the identity formation stage of development.

Taking a broad perspective on adolescent psychosocial development, Nurmi (2004) has categorized adolescent development into four overarching areas that affect social, cognitive, and emotional well-being. The first is that the environments in which adolescents live channel youths into particular settings that affect their thinking, motivation, and behavior. In return, adolescents select their paths based upon the choices available to them in the environment. They learn to adjust their goals and aspirations based on feedback and reflect on their lives in order to build an identity. These four areas take into consideration the whole of adolescent development rather than parsing it into separate units that overlook the effect each piece has on the other. In addition, Nurmi notes that channeling, selection, adjustment, and self-reflection do not take place wholly within the adolescent but are "closely embedded in the adolescent's personal relationships" (p. 95). Thus, identity development in teens does not simply affect those who are experiencing it; it affects and is affected by others around them as well, including teachers and classmates. Teachers need to be aware that they are a part of the channeling, selection, adjustment, and reflection that their students are experiencing. This is especially important in the selection and adjustment phases, which offer new opportunities for growth and feedback about competence. These new experiences and evaluations help to shape youths' identities as learners.

In the development of identity, modeling is no less important at this time than it was when these adolescents were younger, but now peers take on new significance as models. Adolescents "over identify, to the point of apparent complete loss of identity, with the heroes of cliques and crowds" (Erikson, 1963, p. 262). A similar chameleon-like quality is described by Unger (2000) in which adolescents take on the identity of the group with which they associate. Adolescents may also engage in role repudiation in which roles and values that seem acceptable for identity formation are actively sought while those that seem foreign are resisted (Erikson, 1982). Erikson notes that this may account for adolescent defiance and the occasional affinity for a negative identity in which socially unacceptable elements are preferred. Clearly, adolescents rely on each other for direction more than when they were younger or than they will when they are older. At this stage peers act both as models and mirrors for each other, one day projecting an image to be emulated, the next reflecting back the images and identities of others. Development of an identity becomes achievable through adolescents' growing cognitive abilities. The ability to imagine oneself in new situations allows for greater exploration of possible identities (Clements & Seidman, 2002).

Identity formation can be domain specific, in that it may take on different characteristics in different settings, such as school versus home. Roeser and Lau (2002) present a model that portrays the process of adolescent identity development in middle school. Through positive or negative school experiences, students develop images of themselves as either competent or incompetent. Such identities then affect students' behavior in school. In fact, Haynes (1990) found that the best predictor of teacher ratings of student classroom behavior, group participation, and attitude toward authority were the students' own ratings of their behavior along with their moral-ethical self-concepts and personal self-concept. Haynes notes, "Implicit in this finding is the supposition that if children viewed themselves negatively—as incorrigible, lacking discipline, and ill mannered—they were likely to behave that way. Children became what they believed themselves to be" (p. 205). Stated positively, if students believe they have control over their behavior, or that they can achieve in school, then they are less likely to misbehave than those who do not have such beliefs (Bandura, Barbaranelli, Caprara, & Pastorelli, 1996). Thus, students' school-based identities directly affect their in-school behavior.

Belonging

According to developmental systems theory, adolescents have the potential to develop into adults who help support society (Lerner & Dowling, 2002). To thrive, adolescents must be involved in healthy relationships within the community. School communities can be a place in which students learn to develop the healthy relationships that will allow them to eventually be productive adults.

Peer friendships may also help students develop feelings of attachment to school. Lack of belonging due to peer rejection can portend problematic behavior in the future (Wentzel, 2003). Clements and Seidman (2002) state: "It is crucial that middle grades schooling provides the kinds of experience that will foster students' engagement in school and positive expectations of themselves in this domain" (p. 149). This can be accomplished by helping students believe that they belong in their school, and by helping students form strong peer relationships and fostering close relationships with adults. A sense of belonging helps to lessen emotional distress among middle school students (Roeser, Eccles, & Sameroff, 2000).

The Person-Environment Fit model helps explain the benefits of school attachment: "When an individual does not 'fit' or feel a sense of belonging, school crime and misconduct are more likely. Thus, youngsters who identify with school and are academically successful do not present particular problems for educators" (Voelkel, 1997, p. 297). Voelkl further notes that students who have no sense of belonging may distrust the institution and the people who are part of it. It is reasonable to assume that those who do not have a stake in schools would not be as likely to comply with the school rules. Support for this was found in a study of middle and high school students (Dornbusch, Erikson, Laird, & Wong, 2001). Student attachment to school significantly decreased the likelihood that the students would be involved in deviant behavior such as smoking, drinking, marijuana use, or violence, as long as the students had not been involved in those behaviors before. The evidence suggests that school attachment may result in positive behavioral outcomes.

Adolescents often express a desire to be a part of the school environment (Ellis, 1997; Habel, Bloom, Ray, & Bacon, 1999). Unfortunately, simply being enrolled in a school does not guarantee that students will feel they are a part of it. In one study, 41% of the urban middle school students sampled disagreed with the notion that they belonged at school (Goodenow & Grady, 1993). School belonging accounted for about a third of the variance in the students' value of schoolwork and was significantly correlated with motivation to do well in school. Positive beliefs about belonging can also buffer the effects of stressors such as conflicts with parents or peers (Isakson & Jarvis, 1999).

Transitions from elementary to middle school can cause difficulties for students that may also strain students' feelings of belonging at school, though again peer relationships can reduce student anxiety. In a study that followed students from the end of the fifth through the sixth grade, stress increased across the transition for males and females (Chung, Elias, & Schneider, 1998). Although both boys and girls experienced increased psychological distress when going from fifth to sixth grade, boys also showed a decline in academics and poorer behavior than girls in middle school. However, perceived support from friends is a factor in building self-worth during the transition from elementary to middle school (Fenzel, 2000), offsetting some of the stress caused by moving from the relative security of elementary classes to higher grades. Fostering opportunities for students to make friends can help students feel more attached to schools. Well-managed classrooms do not have to keep students separated to ensure learning is achieved. On the contrary, cooperative endeavors among middle school students may prove to be beneficial both socially and academically.

Needs of Adolescents in School

Adolescent students have needs different from those of primary and higher education students. Although all students could benefit from an environment rich in support for individually measured accomplishment, fair judgment of behavior, and adults who listen and encourage them to make decisions for themselves, the developmental peculiarities of adolescents such as self-consciousness, reliance on peers, and identity development make these factors even more salient.

Schools can influence students by channeling skill development in appropriate tasks. Teachers can support students by offering help that acknowledges the student's effort and attempts to learn, allowing students to set the pace of their learning, and respecting students' desire to participate (Habel et al., 1999). Challenge should be accompanied by success, however, so that adolescents learn to persist (Dicintio & Gee, 1999; Mayer, 2001). Perceived accomplishment leads to fewer classroom problem behaviors (Roeser et al., 2000) because perceived scholastic accomplishment helps to establish a positive identity for most students. In addition, positive behavioral self-image can affect a teacher's perception of classroom behavior, and a student's attitude toward authority (Haynes, 1990). Students' beliefs about their behaviors guide their actions. Positive beliefs can lead to better classroom behavior, more respect for authority, and increased group participation.

To help students perceive themselves positively, teachers must not overreact to a student's poor behavioral history or academic achievement. Egalitarian treatment creates an environment that gives everyone a chance to improve (Habel et al., 1999; Pomeroy, 1999). Minority students in one study felt that rules were arbitrary and changed at the whim of the teacher or were made simply to punish students the teacher did not like (Sheets, 1996). Teachers need to be aware that their knowledge and interpretation of the rules may not match that of their students, despite explanations. The right to make and enforce rules is part of what gives teachers power over students, so if the rules appear to favor the teacher, it may make students feel as if they lack autonomy, responsibility, and respect (Pomeroy, 1999). The desire to listen to students, not only to get to know them, but to hear their side of the story when a behavioral problem arises, is another way teachers can show their willingness to be fair to all students, despite previous behavior problems.

Adolescents need teachers and peers who provide social and emotional support (Habel et al., 1999; Roeser et al., 2000), which in turn may help curb problem school behaviors such as bullying (Natvig, Albrektsen, & Qvarnstrøm, 2001). Pomeroy (1999) found that students who had been expelled from school wanted to feel valued by their teachers, which meant in part, no put-downs by the teacher. Students also wished their teachers would take the time to talk to them and listen to what they had to say, to be friendly and to maintain a sense of humor. Getting to know the teachers was particularly important as these youths felt that teachers could head off problems by recognizing when a student was about to get into trouble and to intervene before things went too far.

Besides support, adolescents need some degree of autonomy (Ellis, 1997; Kroger, 1996; Roeser et al., 2000), but such autonomy may clash with the teacher's managerial and instructional roles. When students are offered control over their learning, school involvement can increase and boredom, confusion, and a desire to be doing something else can decrease (Dicintio & Gee, 1999). Giving choices in learning and allowing students to learn from their mistakes can encourage independence in students (Habel et al., 1999). The amount of autonomy should match not just the adolescents' preferences but also their capacity to exhibit self-restraint and maturity. Too much freedom before an adolescent is ready can lead to poor decision making because those skills are not yet fully developed, whereas too little autonomy in adult–child relationships can result in teens turning to peers for most social interactions (Eccles et al., 1991). Teachers may try to limit student autonomy in the classroom because they feel pressured to maintain control, which can lead to teacher frustration (Sheets, 1996). Such frustration can cause teachers to rely on punishment strategies to manage misbehavior rather than teach the students what they need to know to behave properly (Lewis, 2001). In addition, teens may appear to act, and thus be treated, like adults on one occasion, only to be treated like children on other occasions. The frequently changing levels of autonomy offered to them by adults may seem confusing and can cause anger and resentment. Even so, adults should not distance themselves from teens, but should provide support and guidance during the transition from childhood to adulthood.

Serious Behavior Problems

Numerous research studies have documented risk factors for serious problem behavior in adolescence, such as theft, violence, substance abuse, and risky sexual behavior. The friends adolescents make help to shape each youth's behavior. Not surprisingly, if friends are models for or support behaviors that are illegal, lacking in school commitment, or immoral, then adolescents are more likely to engage in these activities than if their friends express positive values (Buysse, 1997; Kasen, Cohen, & Brook, 1998). Adolescents exhibiting problem behaviors often do so in a context in which they see their actions as justified and in which peers support their inappropriate behaviors. This often leads to cognitive distortions that are difficult to counteract. If they can convince themselves that others think they are cool and that peers like their behavior, then the behavior is reinforced and difficult to alter (Barriga, Morrision, Liau, & Gibbs, 2001; Lopez & Emmer, 2000). Since adolescence is a time of finding one's own identity and, at times, rejecting adult prosocial values, adolescents who deviate from those values will find themselves in conflict with adults (Kuperminc & Allen, 2001). Adolescent core values that include a party orientation tend to encourage problem behaviors (Chen & Dornbusch,

1998), while valuing attachment to school appears to inoculate youths from serious problem behaviors (Dornbusch et al., 2001; Goff & Goddard, 1999). Perceived academic competence, higher achievement, and future-oriented goals all help to reduce the chances that adolescents will engage in risky activity (Goff & Goddard, 1999; McDermott, Mordell, & Stoltzfus, 2001).

School can be a place of acceptance or rejection, accomplishment or failure, and caring or indifferent adults. When the former attributes are in place, then schools are more likely to aid in reducing serious behavior problems, whereas if the latter attributes predominate, problem behaviors are much more likely. Certain skills may help adolescents avoid misbehavior. Development of social skills and problem-solving strategies can help adolescents feel capable of handling difficult situations and avoiding conflict (Kuperminc & Allen, 2001; Kuther, 2000). Schools can limit the use of punitive measures in favor of more positive techniques of behavior management (Mayer, 2001). This is especially important as harsh discipline is linked to conduct problems (Dodge, 1996).

Classroom Climate

Teacher behaviors and teacher–student interactions influence classroom climate. Research indicates that there is a correlation between teacher control and punishment of students and acting-out (Newman & Licata, 1986–87). The same teacher behaviors also are correlated with more hostility between students. The Newman and Licata study revealed negative correlations between characteristics of a caring teacher such as warmth, friendship, and respect and the frequency and hostility of student misbehavior. Although punitive teachers may cause student hostility, it is just as plausible that student hostility and resistance to authority cause teachers to resort to controlling and punitive behaviors to maintain order. Because teachers are the adults in this situation, they need to take the lead in providing relief in what can become an escalating spiral of student misbehavior and teacher punishments.

Part of the problem with developing a supportive classroom climate may be that there is a poor fit between adolescent needs and many school programs, especially in middle schools (Baer, 1999; Roeser et al; 2000). Problem areas include competition, which causes social comparison at a time when adolescents are very self-conscious; fewer chances for adolescents to make decisions when many want more control; lower-level cognitive challenges when cognitive capabilities are advancing; and distant teachers who are not available for students who want a close adult relationship outside the home. Hester, Gable, and Manning (2003) offer suggestions about how middle school teachers can create a positive classroom climate. Clearly defining and acknowledging appropriate behavior, teaching and modeling appropriate social skills and conflict resolution skills, and listening to students and then responding positively to their attempts to communicate, are among some of their recommendations.

Summary

Research and theory provide insights into some of the features adolescents need to develop appropriately and to become focused learners in school. Students need to have friends and adult relationships for support, a sense of belonging at school, fair treatment, teachers who listen, feelings of competence, and an environment that balances teacher authority with student autonomy. Teachers can affect the values of their students so that they will desire to behave by remembering, in Bandura's words (1986) "The types of methods used, the manner in which they are applied, and the quality of human relationships involved affect the likelihood that the values of others will be accepted as the standards for regulating one's own actions" (p. 263). If teachers focus on trying to meet the aforementioned needs of their students, they have a better chance of achieving a classroom climate in which their students are able to follow the rules and procedures than when the teacher's primary focus is controlling students. Fairness, caring for students as individuals, and an interest in what students have to say will encourage students to accept a teacher's values and rules.

SECONDARY TEACHERS' PERSPECTIVES IN CLASSROOM MANAGEMENT

Influential reviews by Shavelson and Stern (1981) and Clark and Peterson (1986) used the preactive–interactive distinction to examine teacher thinking and decision making. Preactive thinking includes planning, of which there are several types, including daily, unit, and beginning-of-year. Planning can also be concerned with the organization of activities, work procedures, or class rules. Preactive thinking uses reflection and application of accumulated knowledge about students, content, activities, and methods. In contrast, interactive thinking is reactive to the immediacy of classroom events. Results of several studies indicated, "On the average, teachers make one interactive decision every 2 minutes" (Clark & Peterson, 1986, p. 274). The teacher's active decision making occurs when something happens that departs from the expected during an activity. The teacher then must decide if and how to intervene, and whether a routine is available to manage the situation. Other factors influencing teachers' interactive thoughts besides whether students' behaviors are within tolerance, Clark and Peterson noted, include environmental factors, student questions, and lesson transitions. It is also clear that teacher decision making during instruction is influenced by departures from anticipated happenings, and that behavior deviations attract teacher attention.

Secondary teachers' thinking about classroom management encompasses several broad areas of action that were identified by Fenwick (1998) in a study of junior high school teachers. Fenwick found that teachers perceive their classroom work in terms of management strategies, with three primary areas: managing classroom space and objects within it; managing persons and teaching practices within that space; and managing their own identity. Teachers organize the use of space by creating sets of procedures and expectations, and by monitoring, directing, and responding. By definition, classroom action is dynamic, so teachers also recognize the necessity of adapting to exigent events and accepting the unpredictability of work with adolescents. The structures that teachers create through their organization of space, procedures, and interventions allow them room to maneuver within that setting and to manage their adolescent students' energy, sometimes moderating and directing it, at other times instigating or boosting it. Fenwick describes "managing the teacher self" as achieving an identity with the concept of teaching, which includes developing a clear sense of desirable and undesirable student behaviors, based on conventional moral principles. Fenwick's experienced teachers accepted their role as legitimate authority, but viewed it as serving the ends of mutual respect, care, and maintaining an environment suitable for learning rather than order for its own sake.

In contrast to Fenwick's experienced teachers, teachers-in-training and beginning teachers struggle to make sense of classroom complexity. An extended analysis of a high school English teacher (Clift, 1991) during student teaching reveals the complexity of integrating multiple schemas (content knowledge, literary analysis, pedagogical problem solving, group management, self-image) during initial teaching experiences. Although prior courses, readings, and texts had addressed many relevant topics, it was difficult for the teacher to access, integrate, and apply them. Jones and Vesilind (1995) examined student teacher thinking about management using concept maps. Most of the student teachers' concepts were about managerial roles, being liked, and issues of fairness and flexibility. They were much less likely to use concepts that captured the dynamic, interactive aspects of management, such as pacing, monitoring, activity flow, and interventions. The static quality of their thinking may be a necessary base upon which to build a more comprehensive structure, but it also provides the beginning teacher with an incomplete view of the complexity of classroom management.

Teacher Authority

As youth grow from later childhood into adolescence, they become much more likely to question the teacher's authority to organize or direct their behavior and activities. Research by Metz (1978) several decades ago, at a time when social protest and desegregation were prominent, examined issues surrounding authority. Metz argued that schools and teachers must balance demands for student learning and order. Unless students accept both goals, tension is inevitable. When adolescents resist learning, schools and teachers limit and direct behavior, often using coercive control. When schools and teachers display flexibility and alter their strategies in response to resistance by using open-ended and diverse curricula and activities, they risk undermining student perceptions of consistency, unity, structure, and fairness.

More recently, Pace (2003a, 2003b) observed and interviewed high school teachers, noting issues related to their use of authority. She found less overt questioning of authority than Metz, but noted more "indirect assertions and covert challenges." Legitimate authority is derived from several sources (Spady & Mitchell, 1979). Pace found that teachers did not utilize a single source of authority, but combined traditional, bureaucratic, professional, and egalitarian forms. For example, one of the teachers who exhibited hallmarks of adept management (efficient use of class time, established routines, good group cooperation) used bureaucratic authority (grade-for-work exchange) and traditional professional authority to manage diverse, lower-track 9th-grade English classes. In contrast, another teacher consciously used charismatic authority and relied much less on bureaucratic authority. This teacher was energetic and expressive in the classroom, keeping his students involved by "making his class fun." He regarded his style as an aspect of his professional identity that was attractive to students. Yet, when students resisted direction, he invoked a legal-rational authority principle that it is the teacher's responsibility to keep order by using consequences for misbehavior.

When teacher authority is severely disputed by students, a teacher's ability to implement a curriculum is compromised, and content objectives may be sacrificed to maintain classroom order. Ennis (1996) observed high school physical education teachers whose students resisted class activities through nonparticipation and disruption. Teachers viewed their authority as eroding because of limited administrative support both for enforcing consequences and for implementing a sound curriculum, thus undercutting the teacher's bureaucratic and professional authority. The teachers preserved a vestige of authority by threatening to give students failing grades, but their vulnerability to the influence of students' resistance and cooperation led them to avoid physical activities students disliked, even though the teachers believed they were educationally appropriate (see also Cothran & Ennis, 1997).

In summary, secondary teachers rely on one or more forms of authority to justify student compliance and cooperation. When their authority is undermined (e.g., by a school administrator) or disputed (by students or the community), the teacher's ability to secure student cooperation is weakened. Conversely, when authority is supported by administrative action, by the community, and by students, then the teacher's task of creating and maintaining order is made substantially easier.

Teacher Emotion

Emotion is an ineluctable aspect of teaching. Accounts by teachers of their lives provide ample indication of its presence and influence (Day & Leitch, 2001). Much human behavior is directed at achieving positive emotions and coping with, avoiding, denying, or escaping negative emotional states. The ability to manage emotions is necessary for an individual's healthy functioning in social groups.

Experiencing persistent negative emotion whose cause is seemingly intractable produces stress. By far the most common area of research on teacher emotion is stress and its close relative, burnout (Guglielmi & Tatrow, 1998). Blase (1986) reported that in a large sample of secondary and elementary teachers, student aggression and behavior that intrudes into classroom activities were considered to be the most stressful out of a list of possible stressors. Student teachers, when asked to identify classroom events that require attention, primarily identify those they perceive as hassling or stressful (Admiraal, Korthagen, & Wubbels, 2000). Beginning teachers in schools with high levels of stressors such as threats, confrontations, and unmotivated students are more likely to be depressed than teachers in less stressful settings (Schonfeld, 1992). In a large sample of Dutch secondary teachers, Brouwers and Tomic (2000) found that high levels of student disruption reduced teachers' sense of efficacy, leading to emotional exhaustion and negative teacher attitudes.

Teachers monitor emotional aspects of student behavior constantly (Hargreaves, 2000). For example, they check for engagement, involvement, or negative emotion. Failing to monitor emotions or making incorrect inferences (e.g., that students are interested when they are bored) can lead to poor decisions and inappropriate behavior. Managing students with behavior disorders also requires careful reading of emotional states to prevent aggressive behavior (Myles & Simpson, 1994; Shukla-Mehta & Albin, 2003).

In a study using 53 secondary and elementary teachers, Hargreaves (2000) found that secondary teachers typically viewed emotions on continua of normalcy and intrusiveness. Teachers responded to atypical emotional expressions or when they intruded into the learning process. Their common response was to try to reduce their intensity nonconfrontationally. Hargreaves noted, "There seems to be a tacit emotional grammar of secondary school teaching ... where emotions are normalized or neutralized to make the pedagogical process as smooth and easy as possible. Emotions are attended to when they disturb this grammar, threatening to disturb the order it represents" (p. 822). In contrast, elementary teachers were more open to emotional experience and personal contact with students regarding emotions.

Emotions of teachers in middle school classrooms (grades seven and eight) were studied by Emmer (1994) using classroom observations followed by interviews. Teachers reported negative emotions, chiefly frustration, annoyance, or anger in response to student interruptions of class activities, to chronic noncompliance, and group noncompliance. Negative emotions also were caused by poor student performance and by a lack of support from administrators, other teachers, or parents. The intensity of emotions felt by teachers was reduced when they attributed causes that were external to the classroom and that were perceived to be out of the student's or teacher's control. In contrast, misbehavior and poor performance attributed to a lack of effort aroused more intense negative emotions.

Also noteworthy were some of the strategies teachers used to manage their own emotions, including discounting and masking. These strategies make sense in the instructional context, which would suffer frequent interruptions if the teacher overtly reacted whenever a negative emotion was aroused. Discounting can also be viewed as a form of reappraisal (Reisenzein & Spielhofer, 1994) that is adaptive and mitigates emotional intensity, enabling the teacher to focus on instruction and monitoring. Masking of emotions is endorsed by most teachers, who believe it necessary to maintain a calm, businesslike demeanor and to not express anger or frustration directly to a student. The use of masking by teachers has also been observed when teachers give test feedback to students (Stough & Emmer, 1998). Other means used by teachers to deal with negative emotions include stress relief strategies and taking action to address the problem perceived to be causing the negative emotion.

ESTABLISHING THE CONDITIONS FOR YEAR-LONG PRODUCTIVITY: THE IMPORTANCE OF THE BEGINNING OF THE YEAR

It is axiomatic that it is easier to maintain appropriate behavior than it is to alter established patterns of disruptive and other inappropriate behaviors. Thus the beginning of the year is a natural time to examine stage-setting activities of teachers. A number of large-sample studies at both the elementary and secondary levels have been conducted to examine teacher and student behaviors at the beginning of and throughout the year, in order to track how teachers establish good classroom management systems. Some of these studies compared groups of secondary teachers (7th and 8th grades) identified as more effective managers and less effective managers, based on a variety of criteria including on-task behavior, disruptive behaviors, and student achievement. At the secondary level, these studies include Evertson and Emmer (1982) and Moskowitz and Hayman (1974, 1976). In addition, several evaluation studies and field experiments have been conducted in which teachers received workshops pertaining to the beginning of the year and year-long management (see Evertson & Harris, 1999, for a summary). In these studies, teachers with training in effective management principles did establish better-managed classrooms, compared to teachers not receiving training, with resulting improvements in on-task rates and reduced disruption.

In a study of management that incorporated observations at the beginning of the year in 7th and 8th grade classes (Evertson & Emmer, 1982), disruptive and off-task behavior during the first week were low in both more and less effective managers' classes. By the second and third weeks in less effectively managed classes, however, inappropriate behaviors increased, and rose even further during the rest of the year. In more effective managers' classes, such behaviors stayed at low levels, rising only slightly during the year. Similar results were obtained by Moskowitz and Hayman (1976), who identified their teacher samples using student ratings of "best" teachers and compared them to first-year teachers and "typical" teachers.

Differences in actions taken by more and less effective managers during the first several weeks of the year are considerable. Better managers are more explicit about expectations for behavior in such areas as call outs, movement around the room, talk among students, absence and tardy procedures, contacting the teacher, and academic work. These teachers translate expectations into procedures for students to follow, and explain them to students when the activities in which they are used are first introduced (i.e., not all at once). Less effective managers are less likely to communicate expectations for common aspects of student behavior, or they incorporate them in nonspecific rules (e.g., be courteous) without specifying their application or enforcing them right away. Teachers who are more successful are better monitors of student behavior and deal with inappropriate behavior promptly when it occurs, rather than ignoring it. Interventions during the first several weeks are usually limited to redirections and calling attention to procedures that should be followed. Thus, these teachers approach the establishment of desirable behavior as something to be taught to students, whereas less effective managers are either less vigilant or choose not to intervene promptly.

Moskowitz and Hayman's (1976) comparison of "best," typical, and first-year teachers identified several practices as characteristic of their best teachers: they did more orienting and climate setting during the first day of school, they praised students, smiled, and joked more. New teachers appeared nervous and uncertain to observers, provided only brief orientation before beginning teaching content. In the best teachers' classes, inappropriate behavior increased only slightly during the year, whereas in the first-year teachers' classes misbehavior escalated to a high level, remaining there throughout the year. In the "typical" teacher sample, inappropriate student behavior increased but not to the high level seen in the first-year teachers' classes.

Good management at the beginning of the year is multifaceted. Better managers provide their students with a set of procedures and routines that constitute a kind of behavioral "roadmap" to navigate classroom activities and academic tasks successfully. Teachers appear confident and businesslike, and there is nothing in the research that suggests they are punitive or overbearing. They are also good monitors of students, able to detect problems and to intervene before inappropriate behavior becomes established. Their interventions, usually redirections of behavior or reminders of a procedure, are simple and nonpunitive. Secondary teachers often use a formal set of classroom rules to aid in the process of communicating expectations. Typically, these are posted (especially in classes with younger students) or provided in a syllabus. Based on interviews with high school students serving detentions for rules infractions, Thorson (2003) suggests that rules should be positive, limited to a small (three to five) number, and clearly stated. For example, they should be observable (e.g., Sit at your own desk; Raise your hand to be recognized before speaking) or if general, then they should be discussed and role-played. Other authors (Bicard, 2000; Malone & Tietjens, 2000) offer similar suggestions, and Boonstrum (1991) notes that student acceptance is strengthened when rules are presented positively and their usefulness in creating a desirable environment, conducive to participation and learning, is emphasized.

In classes such as music, physical education, art, and those using labs or special equipment, room arrangements, activity structures, and organization may differ from academic core classes. For instance, in an ensemble class such as choir or band there are usually more students than in an average class, the desks are replaced with risers or chairs and music stands, all students must participate actively throughout the lesson and are encouraged to make sounds instead of remaining quiet, and there often are mixed ages and abilities of students (Bauer, 2001). The approach for handling management issues in such classes begins with the same important steps taken by regular classroom teachers, such as an emphasis on preparation, routines, and organization, all of which need to be communicated, taught, and modeled clearly to the students (Perron & Downey, 1997; Sanford, 1984). Additional measures are often needed to aid in special area classroom organization. Attention-getting routines are necessary, particularly in classes whose activities are outdoors or in a gym, are in groups such as science labs, or include small-group work (Perron & Downey, 1997). Another concern of teachers whose students use equipment (e.g., science, construction trades) or engage in extensive physical movement (e.g., PE) is that ignoring misbehavior may be hazardous, and this concern may cause teachers to favor tight controls on some activities (Kilbourn, 1986; Perron & Downey, 1997). Even in art or music, misbehavior that is ignored may escalate due to the grouplike atmosphere of students working together to complete a task. Williamson (2000) offers advice for middle school choir teachers, which is appropriate for other special area teachers as well. She suggests that teachers try to better understand the developmental needs of their students rather than work against those needs, and to view students' needs as assets when possible. For instance, most middle school students have a strong desire for peer acceptance, have abundant energy, and they seek fun, all of which can be positive characteristics. However, they also tend to have poor time management skills. Williamson suggests a variety of games and activities to either improve or exploit these attributes.

ENGAGING STUDENTS AND MAINTAINING APPROPRIATE BEHAVIOR THROUGHOUT THE YEAR

Choosing Classroom Activities

Although planning and prevention set the stage for the main event, students must be engaged throughout the school year. One contributing factor is the choice of classroom activities.

Research by Csikszentmihalyi and his colleagues (Hunter & Csikszentmihalyi, 2003; Shernoff, Csikszentmihalyi, Schneider, & Shernoff, 2003) examined student engagement in a large sample of secondary school students, using wristwatch devices that prompted students to record their activity and feeling states eight times daily. Students spent the majority of class time in noninteractive activities such as listening to lectures and doing individual seatwork assignments. Interactive activities, such as participating in discussions (9%) and group or lab work (6%), accounted for only a small percentage of the total time. A measure of engagement, based on a composite of interest, concentration, and enjoyment, was higher in group work and individual work compared to lectures, exams, or TV/video viewing. Students also reported being more engaged during "flow" tasks, those that students felt competent to complete and that were high in challenge, compared to tasks that were low in challenge or that students felt were beyond their capabilities. Differences in engagement rates were substantial. For example, only 42% of students reported being attentive during low-challenge activities, whereas 73% reported paying attention during activities that were more challenging and required more skill.

Engagement is improved by eliciting student interest. Schraw and Lehman (2001) differentiated between two types: personal interest and situational interest. Whereas personal interest is a function of individual preferences and characteristics, situational interest is more transitory and subject to direct teacher influence. For example, text materials and the choice of academic task affect situational interest. Mitchell (1993) studied situational interest in secondary mathematics classes and found that involvement in classroom materials was a strong predictor of student interest. Mitchell identified two types of situational interest characteristics: "catch" and "hold"; that is, elicitors or maintainers of interest. Three types of interest "catchers" were group work, computers, and puzzles; "hold" features were meaningfulness and involvement. In a large sample of high school math students, all of the "catch" characteristics predicted interest. One of the best predictors of situational interest was involvement, measured by items that indicated the degree to which learning activities were perceived as fun, as well as items indicating that students "learn the material ourselves" and "do something" instead of just listening to teacher talk or "come in, take notes, go home, do homework, and it's the same thing every day" (p. 436).

Teachers' views of how they engage students were studied by Zahorik (1996). He obtained extensive descriptions of interest-inducing strategies from 65 teachers (35 were secondary level). Of the eight types of actions described, the most common one (reported by all teachers) was the use of hands-on activities. The use of hands-on activities was also reported to be a characteristic of effective cooperative group lessons (Emmer & Gerwels, 2002). Three other strategies used by at least a third of Zahorik's sample were personalizing the content (e.g., by linking it to prior student knowledge or experiences or working with students to generate content to be studied), building student trust (by using activities that permit students to share ideas and experiences, to make decisions, and to be involved in planning and making choices), and group work.

In summary, research on student interest and engagement link instruction, classroom management, and motivation. By stimulating student interest, the use of particular instructional activities increases student engagement. The activities that appear to be most advantageous are those that emphasize involvement through participation and the development of competence. The literature on adolescent development also supports these activities and strategies as more likely to enhance motivation.

Interpersonal Communication and Expressiveness

Classroom teaching is done with groups. Depending on the classroom activity, secondary teachers work among, with, or in front of groups of adolescents. Thus the quality of the

TABLE 15.1
Communication Styles and Sample Items

Communication Type	*Sample Items*
Leadership (D/C)	This teacher explains things clearly. This teacher knows everything that goes on in the classroom.
Helpful/Friendly (C/D)	This teacher helps us with our work. This teacher has a sense of humor.
Understanding (C/S)	This teacher is patient. If we don't agree with this teacher, we can talk about it.
Student Responsibility/ Freedom (S/C)	We can decide some things in this teacher's class. This teacher is lenient.
Uncertain (S/O)	This teacher is hesitant. This teacher is not sure what to do when we fool around.
Dissatisfied (O/S)	This teacher thinks we cheat. This teacher thinks we can't do things well.
Admonishing (O/D)	This teacher is sarcastic. This teacher gets angry quickly.
Strict (D/O)	This teacher is strict. We're afraid of this teacher.

teacher's communication is bound to have an impact on student cooperation and engagement and, therefore, on classroom management.

An extensive line of research on teacher communication behaviors and styles has been developed by Wubbels and his colleagues (Brekelmans, den Brok, van Tartwijk, & Wubbels, in press; Wubbels & Levy, 1993; Wubbels, Levy, & Brekelmans, 1997). These researchers conceptualize teacher communication using two underlying dimensions: Dominance–Submission and Cooperation–Opposition. Various combinations of these two dimensions produce eight styles of communication. These are listed in Table 15.1, along with some sample items from the Questionnaire on Teacher Interaction (QTI), whose scales are used to classify teacher communication.

This international program of research, much of it conducted in secondary classrooms, used student achievement and attitudes as criteria to identify two types of "best" teachers. A "Cooperative" best teacher is perceived by students to be moderately high on scales reflecting Leadership and on Responsibility/Freedom behaviors. "Dominant" best teachers have high levels of Leadership but low levels of Responsibility/Freedom behavior. Both types of teachers are high on Helpful and Understanding styles. Both types of best teachers are relatively low on the Strict scale, though the Dominant teacher is somewhat higher. Both teacher types are perceived by students as low on Admonishing, Dissatisfied, and Uncertain behaviors.

Three types of "worst" teachers were identified. The "Repressive" teacher is high on Admonishing, Strictness, and Dissatisfaction behaviors. The "Uncertain/Aggressive" Teacher is seen as less strict than the Repressive teacher but much more low profile and wishy-washy. Neither of these styles exhibits much Understanding, Leadership, or Student Responsibility/Freedom behaviors. In contrast, a third "worst" teacher type, "Uncertain/Tolerant," does provide for Student Responsibility/Freedom and is perceived as Understanding, but lacks influence, with low perceived levels of Leadership, Admonishing, and Helping behaviors.

The differentiation of teaching styles is a useful aspect of this research program. We are reminded that there is more than one way to be a "worst" or "best" teacher. Teachers mired in the "worst" styles are often trapped with students in a recursive chain of action and reaction.

They may exhibit Repressive or Uncertain/Aggressive behaviors, provoking opposition from students, or they may passively tolerate an unacceptably high level of disorder by being Uncertain/Tolerant. Breaking out of this pattern is difficult, but possible; see Creton, Wubbels, and Hooymayers (1989) for a communication perspective; see Nelson and Carr (2000) for a behavioral perspective. To some degree, the "best" styles are also dependent on the nature of the classroom task. When transmission of information is the goal and direct instruction is an appropriate method, the Leadership style will be more compatible, whereas group activities will be better managed emphasizing a Cooperative pattern.

Teachers' communicative styles have also been examined from another disciplinary perspective: communication studies. Several decades of research on effective verbal and nonverbal interpersonal communication have produced solid evidence of the positive effects of particular styles or behaviors, both verbal and nonverbal, on student achievement, motivation, and affect toward teachers and toward learning. This research base has been developed in both education and communication disciplines (Chesebro & McCroskey, 2001; Witt & Wheeless, 2001), using different labels: in education, "teacher enthusiasm" or "teacher expressiveness"; in communication studies, "immediacy behaviors" is the label.

Nonverbal indicators of immediacy include eye contact, smiling, gesturing, and movement about the room; verbal indicators are expressions of warmth and interest, dynamic expression, use of present tense, self-disclosure, inclusive language, personalizing comments, and active voice. Linking such behavior to management effectiveness is not difficult. Expressive, "immediate" teachers are more likely to be able to command student attention and their interactions with students are more likely to be perceived as rewarding. Students may not be as responsive to less expressive teachers, who may be a weaker source of signals for desirable behavior. Although there is no research directly linking specific aspects of teacher expressiveness or immediacy to management competencies, it makes sense to consider this as one component of a teacher's style that can help or hinder relationships with adolescents and, therefore, the teacher's ability to establish and maintain order.

Activity Management

It isn't easy to engage upwards of 30 adolescents for 50 or so minutes. Visiting with friends and having fun can easily take precedence over learning (Allen, 1986; Thorson, 2003). Classroom rules and routines, clear expectations, challenging content, varied activities, and good interpersonal communication skills build a strong base, but teachers also need to manage their classroom activities competently. Early research by Kounin and his colleagues (Kounin, 1970; Kounin & Gump, 1974), even though much of it was conducted at the elementary level, remains an important source of concepts for understanding activity management. Kounin conceptualized management as a group phenomenon rather than focused on individual students. "We found that the degree of immersion in single children as compared to the focus on the total group differentiates between the successful and unsuccessful teacher at quite a significant level" (1983, p. 8). Kounin's research program also included the notion of the classroom as a unique behavior setting, where different activities have different action structures that require different managerial techniques.

An essential concept underlying effective activity management is that of signal systems. Activities contain cues that prompt students to behave in various ways. In teacher-led activities, such as recitations, discussions, demonstrations, or presentations, the teacher is a strong signal source. Other cues include props used by the teacher or that are part of the activity. Of course, other competing external and internal signals may direct student attention and behavior toward other ends. When an activity is not teacher directed (e.g., group work or individual seat work), the teacher is not as potent a signal source, but materials and other students are.

During teacher-led activities, the teacher needs to keep the activity moving and avoid interruptions to the activity flow by using good pacing, avoiding flip-flops from one to another activity, directing student attention, encouraging student participation, and maintaining accountability. During individual activities, task variety and challenge help keep the students involved. Kounin's research also highlights the importance of "withitness" (the early detection of problems along with the ability to communicate to students the teacher's awareness of them) and "overlapping" (the ability to deal with simultaneous events).

Competing signals for student attention are present especially during transitions. A transition requires bringing one activity to completion and shifting student attention and behavior to accommodate the demands of the new activity. Classrooms populated by students with learning and attention disorders are more susceptible to transition problems (Buck, 1999; Marks et al., 2003), as are classrooms with younger students (Lawry, Danko, & Strain, 2000). Arlin's research (1979) showed that students were off-task at approximately twice the rate in transition than in nontransition times. But transitions can be structured; for example, teachers might use a signal to alert students to prepare them for the shift in behavior, they might remind students of an established transition procedure, or they can give students a time line for completing the transition. When teachers provide structure for transitions, they are much less likely to encounter transition problems. Developing some simple procedures to manage transitions is important for teachers who have multiple activities during a class period. And every secondary teacher needs procedures to manage two key transitions: the beginning and the end of class.

In a study that illustrates the value of some of Kounin's concepts for understanding secondary management, Doyle (1984) reports on activity management in 7th-and 8th-grade English classes. Teachers were more successful when they used activities that had a clear "program of action" for students. That is, there were lesson features that signaled the appropriate behaviors rather than leaving students directionless. These teachers also were able to demarcate activities one from the other (i.e., establish clear transition points). They also kept students focused on activities, ushering them along until they were involved in them. When misbehavior threatened the activity flow, teachers tried to insulate them by keeping a focus on the lesson and not calling attention to the misbehaviors.

How well does "withitness" travel to secondary settings? A study of 31 middle school physical education teachers found that it is indeed a useful construct (Johnston, 1995). Using videotapes, the researchers scored the components of withitness: the accuracy and timeliness of each teacher desist. For correctly timed desists, students returned to the task promptly 76% of the time, whereas poorly timed desists (the teacher waited too long, didn't see the problem until it had spread) were successful only 47% of the time. Correctly targeted students returned promptly to the task 86% of the time, but only 46% of the time when the teacher made a target error by initially issuing a desist to the wrong student.

TWO VIGNETTES

Now that we have reviewed aspects of the adolescent population, teacher thinking and emotion related to classroom management, and research on behavioral aspects of management, we present two classroom vignettes of middle school teachers, accompanied by an interpretive analysis. These classrooms offer contrasting scenes of teacher and student behavior, and examining them allows us to illustrate in an integrative manner many of the concepts that are reviewed in the first part of the chapter. We also illustrate that secondary classroom management is accomplished through a combination of approaches, strategies, and behaviors used interactively with adolescents over time. The vignettes are based on real cases, but the teachers' names and some minor details have been changed to protect anonymity.

Vignette 1. Mark Smith teaches in a predominately lower SES middle school (80% of the students qualify for free or cost-reduced lunch). The school district has supported the principal's and teaching staff's efforts to promote academic success as well as to create a caring school environment by providing an extra counselor and assistant principal, as well as resources to support teacher teams at each grade level. Mark is in his third year of teaching social studies, but he is also under the principal's scrutiny because of difficulty with student behavior problems in his first two years. During several meetings, Mark has received help and advice from the principal and from a mentor teacher. Mark brings several strengths to his teaching: intelligence, good preparation in his content area, and musical talent which he enjoys applying to class activities. He genuinely cares about his students and wants very much to equip them with the knowledge and skills they will need for success in life.

As the school year has progressed, however, he has felt increasingly frustrated with the general disorder that envelops many of his lessons. Like many teachers, he prefers nonconfrontational tactics to manage problems, and this stance has allowed him to avoid eliciting hostile responses or outright defiance from students he has had to discipline, while gaining a modicum of cooperation from many students. Nevertheless, a lot of time is wasted and half the class accomplishes little in the way of learning. Rates of on-task behavior during academic activities are sometimes below 50% of the students and rarely exceed 80% for more than a short time. In spite of the assistance he has received from the principal and his mentor teacher, observations of some incidents in one of Mark's 7th grade classes reveal several problems that hamper his instruction:

- During a class activity that was well within their capabilities, several students left their groups to visit with other students. Mark initially continued to assist individual students, but eventually asked the visiting students to return to the task. His request was ignored and an increasing number of students went off-task.
- A knock on the door prompted three students to leave their seats to open the door for two tardy students. The teacher gave a reprimand, but the students argued that their friends needed to enter the class.
- During a 10-minute class discussion, 4 students read other material, 3 students at the back of the room chatted, and several others had their heads down. After numerous irrelevant call-outs, students were reminded to raise their hands and wait to be called on. The call-outs continued and only a few students participated in the discussion. When two students left their seats to ask him for permission to go to the bathroom, Mark responded to these students; this interrupted the activity and created more opportunities for disorder.
- At the beginning of a writing activity, half the students didn't have paper on their desks. As Mark worked with individual students, several boys called out loudly to each other across the room during the activity.
- During a content development activity, Mark played a tape with a song related to the culture described in the assigned reading. He tried to teach students a chorus from the song, but most students were reluctant to participate. Instead, several boys joked about the song and distracted attention from the activity. Students were attentive during the song, but only a few contributed to the discussion afterward, commenting on their favorite pop singers. Two students moved to different seats to talk with friends as the noise level increased.
- Mark's consequences for inappropriate behavior don't seem to matter to students. Following a suggestion from his mentor teacher, he tried sending disruptive students to the office, but he sent too many and the Assistant Principal asked him to limit use of this

consequence. He tried writing student names on the board when they continued behaving inappropriately, with a detention consequence, but he didn't monitor carefully enough and the system was soon overwhelmed. Students caught misbehaving, moreover, complained that others did the same things and didn't get caught.

Vignette 2. Down the hall, Sara Roberts teaches math to many of the same students as does Mark Smith. Sara's classes, however, are nearly free of troublesome behavior, and the general level of student cooperation is good. In her tenth year of teaching at the middle school level, Sara has a clear idea about what student behaviors are and are not desirable in her classroom; she communicated these expectations to students early in the school year and she is not hesitant to insist that students behave acceptably. Her businesslike, brisk manner during teacher-led whole-class activities is tempered with a personal, familiar style with students on other occasions. Sara jokes with students, makes frequent eye contact, moves around the room, and is animated and expressive as she talks. Observations of Sara and her 8th-grade students reveal well-functioning classrooms:

- Sara monitors students during class activities and limits off-task behavior by catching problems early. During group work and seatwork activities, she is constantly on the move around the room, checking on student work, giving feedback, and offering suggestions and encouragement.
- Students don't interrupt Sara's class activities. Procedures for participation, talk, movement, being ready for class, make-up work, and other key aspects of life in her classroom have been spelled out in a student handout, and are followed consistently.
- Except for emergencies, Sara won't allow students to leave her classroom during the period.
- The rare disruptive event is managed quickly. Students who persist in inappropriate behavior are assigned a lunch-time detention: "If I have to come find you, the penalty will be doubled," she says matter-of-factly, and she means it.
- Sara uses a variety of activities to engage students in the curriculum: small groups, whole-class content development, individual assignments, and discussions based on some structured problem-solving assignments.
- Sara monitors group progress and changes group composition when students don't work well together. Students who are consistently off-task lose the privilege and must work alone, a consequence Sara rarely administers because most students prefer to work together.
- Sara emphasizes that students should give full effort—their "personal best" and not be content to slide by. Not every student has been won over, but enough have so that a general norm of engagement and participation prevails.

Integrative Analysis of the Vignettes

The concepts of modeling and identity development from the literature on adolescence have implications for understanding some of the dynamics in these classrooms. Most of the models for behavior in Sara's class are positive, because the incidence of appropriate behavior is high, and also because Sara calls attention to desirable behavior by commenting favorably on students' attempts to understand the content, to complete work accurately, and to think critically about math concepts. In Mark's class, there are fewer positive and more negative peer models because inappropriate behaviors occur at high rates and are visible, in spite of Mark's low-key attempts to deal with them. Sara has sanctions, such as detention, in place for inappropriate behavior, and this helps limit such behavior. Because inappropriate behaviors are more visible against a backdrop of appropriate behavior, Sara is able to detect and deal with them promptly and consistently, thus communicating "withitness" to her students. In Mark's class, higher amounts of problem behaviors occur, preventing him from appearing consistent when he tries to use consequences. This leads to accusations of unfairness from students, and at the same time diffuses responsibility because they can claim that "everyone is doing it," thus working against self-restraint. The frequent interruptions interfere with the activity flow of Mark's whole-class activities, sometimes causing him to prematurely terminate the content development portion of the lesson and move to a seatwork activity for which students are not adequately prepared and that is, therefore, more vulnerable to intrusions.

In Sara's classes, students for the most part are successful in the assignments and other graded activities. Feedback is frequent and positive, and students receive positive teacher attention. Peer attention, moreover, occurs for behavior that is learning directed and participatory, as students engage in groups and structured whole-class activities. In Mark's class, some students seem to enjoy their relationship with Mark, but peer attention occurs for inappropriate behavior, and some students' contacts with the teacher mainly revolve around his attempts to cajole them into complying with class rules about staying seated or with keeping them from disrupting an activity.

Sara encourages the development of an identity as "capable, productive and successful students." She does this by channeling students toward the behaviors that produce success in her class and by reinforcing this identity through her feedback and her expectations, and by preventing other competing identities from becoming visible. In spite of Mark's intentions or desires, his students don't have the same degree of positive identity as Sara's. By accepting so much inappropriate behavior and lack of effort, Mark has indirectly communicated that students are not capable of better work and behavior, or else that it is not worth the effort. In his class, misbehaving students capture peer and teacher attention, with few visible immediate negative consequences. Thus, taking on an identity as a productive working member of this class is not nearly as attractive as it is in Sarah's class.

A number of problems contribute to the disorder in Mark Smith's activities. Procedures in some basic areas such as student participation, contacting the teacher, beginning activities, and movement around the room were not established at the beginning of the year. Although Mark did present his expectations in the form of general class rules, the presentation was not followed up with consistent application. Mark believed his classes were functioning well after the first few weeks of the year, but that was because there was little overt disruption. Because Mark's monitoring usually focuses on the students with whom he is interacting, he only notices problems after they have spread and become noisy and obvious. Interruptions to his activities are impeding progress and creating conditions for more inappropriate behavior. The teacher's interventions are ineffectual and there is little apparent incentive to engage in lesson activities.

In contrast, Sara Roberts has achieved an orderly, well-managed classroom. Her routines and procedures encourage appropriate behavior, and her confident demeanor and willingness to follow through reduce the likelihood of student disruption. In Mark Smith's classroom, there is peer pressure for inappropriate behavior, which is occurring frequently. This has created a dilemma for Mark: To intervene constantly will sidetrack attention from the academic activity and interventions will put him in conflict with his students. Not to intervene, however, risks allowing the disorder to spread. Mark generally chooses a nonconfrontational route, accepting some disorder while trying to keep the lid on.

Sara uses small groups and pairs working together, activities that engage students and provide them with opportunities for constructive interactions. Among the 25 or 30 adolescents who populate each of Sara's classes, there are undoubtedly more than a few who might be inclined to oppositional response to adult directives, but Sara's students rarely exhibit such behavior, as the flow of the activities and the structure she has created in her classroom carries them along. Mark occasionally tries to use small groups, but because the noise level becomes so high and students spend so much of the time in social talk, he usually has students working individually. This gives him one-on-one time with students, but opportunities for assistance are necessarily limited. As noted by Fenwick (1998), teachers create structures with their rules, routines, and procedures to help manage the complexity of working with classes of 25 or more adolescents. In Sara's case, her management system gives her room to operate by organizing her own and her students' behavior and making monitoring easier. In Mark's classes, the absence or breakdown of important procedures for managing student movement and talk has placed an overload on his monitoring and decision making as student behavior frequently deviates from what is expected.

Sara is comfortable with her use of authority to help maintain control, viewing it as a means to the desirable end of student learning. She avoids the appearance of arbitrariness by giving reasons for her expectations and by her willingness to listen to students. Sara's general teaching style can be characterized as a mix of "cooperative" and "dominant" leadership (Wubbels & Levy, 1993). In contrast to Sara's easy acceptance of teaching authority, Mark is uncomfortable using his authority directly with students, and exhibits behaviors characteristic of an "uncertain/tolerant" teaching style. Unlike older high school students who might be more inclined to challenge him directly, the middle school adolescents in Mark's classes usually ignore rather than question his attempts to assert authority. But when Mark waits until behavior problems escalate before he expresses disapproval or uses consequences, the diffusion of responsibility and students' complaints of unfairness further erode his legitimate use of authority.

Sara feels more positive than negative emotions during her teaching. When a negative emotion occurs, it's mainly a brief feeling of frustration. She is comfortable with her role as a teacher and maintains a generally positive perspective. This is manifest by her nonverbal expressiveness as well as her generally positive responses to students. She is also able to express disapproval directly to students to deal with a problem. Mark spoke in interviews about his frustration with the high levels of disorder in his classes, but he discounts the importance of the emotions as he tries to push on through the activities. When he tried a more active coping style, by using detention and being more assertive with the students, he didn't address some of the fundamental structural problems with his management system. Consequently, when active coping failed to rectify the problems, he began to feel helpless. Mark also experiences anxiety because of some negative feedback from his principal and mentor teacher. The stress that accompanies all these negative emotions is causing him to consider leaving teaching.

INTERVENTIONS

Prevention of problems is the primary bulwark against major disruptions to the classroom setting. Yet, regardless of the efficacy of the teacher's preventive management system, some inappropriate student behaviors are inevitable. It is an understatement to say that adolescents and teachers don't always have the same agenda. In addition, some students, identifiable at an early age, are much more likely than others to engage in disruptive behavior (Dodge, 1996; Webster-Stratton & Spitzer, 1996; Walker & Sprague, 1999). By the time they reach adolescence, such students may have established patterns of oppositional reaction to adult authority figures, and their potential for creating disorder in a regular classroom setting is high. Strategies for managing students exhibiting aggressive behavior should aim first at prevention, then at correction and intervention (Goldstein, 1998; Larson, 1998). Sometimes the response of school personnel is to use expulsion and suspension at an end stage in the chain of action/reaction. A better approach is early intervention, emphasizing preventive, collaborative, and instructional strategies (Martens & Kelly, 1993; Skiba & Peterson, 2003). Aggressive physical and verbal behaviors at the extreme end of the disruption continuum are not common in the regular secondary classroom. Dealing with them requires a multifaceted intervention using school-wide resources and personnel. These interventions, including punishments such as in-school suspension or expulsion and alternative placements are described in other chapters in this *Handbook* and so they will not be presented here. We will, however, describe interventions that can be used by teachers to deal with disruptions that are more typical in regular education settings.

Managing secondary classrooms effectively requires skills for interacting with students who exhibit a range of problematic behaviors. Goals for the teacher are to restore order so that instruction can continue with as little interference as possible (i.e., maintain activity flow), while also preventing future occurrences of the misbehavior. Ideally, the student will learn more appropriate behavior as a result of the intervention. The difficulty for the teacher is getting caught in a transactional trap (Sutherland & Morgan, 2003). The teacher's response to appropriately behaving students is likely to be positive and encouraging, thus prompting students to behave more appropriately and receive more opportunities to respond. The disruptive student, however, tends to behave in ways that are punishing to the teacher, causing the teacher to avoid interactions with the student except when necessary to deal with inappropriate behavior. The student then receives fewer opportunities to respond in ways that are likely to elicit a positive response from the teacher. The student has learned, moreover, that resisting adult interventions often leads to peer attention, avoidance of undesirable tasks, and sometimes even to escape from punishment. This negative pattern may take some time to develop, but once established it predisposes the teacher and student to conflict.

Reciprocal causality is important to understand when formulating strategies to deal with disruptive behaviors, because one of the prime considerations is avoiding escalation into a major incident. Before discussing some possible interventions, it will be useful to consider some data pertaining to disruption and teachers' attempts to deal with it. An extensive observational study of disruptive behavior and teachers' reactions to it was conducted by Nelson and Roberts (2000). Over a three-year period, administrators and teachers identified 99 disruptive target students in six schools in grades 1–8 (46 were in grades 6–8). All of the data were collected in regular education classrooms, although 59 of the students in the target group had Individualized Education Programs. Observations of the target students were conducted until around 20 different episodes of inappropriate behaviors were seen for each student. Each episode was observed until the inappropriate behavior ceased. Observations of 278 students who were identified as "typical" (though not necessarily exhibiting optimal behavioral adjustment) were also conducted, with observations done long enough so that around three episodes were observed per student. For both target students and typical students, initial teacher reactions to the students' inappropriate behaviors were noted as well as any subsequent student response and teacher reaction to the response. Each episode thus was a chain of action-reaction behaviors that might have one cycle of student behavior and teacher reaction or many cycles, depending on how many times the teacher attempted to intervene and the extent of the student's resistance.

One result of interest was that the number of teacher/student interaction cycles for typical students was essentially one. In most interactions (83%), the teacher issued a desist or redirected the student's behavior; in a smaller percentage (16%) of episodes, the teacher gave a reprimand. But the important result is that the typical students complied 93% of the time, and only 6% of the time responded negatively. In contrast, target students complied immediately only 24% of the time, and usually gave a negative response or were otherwise noncompliant. Moreover, and this is another very interesting result, the chain of interactions between teachers and target students contained an average of 4.56 cycles.

Another result of interest (space limitation prevents discussion of further results) is the difference in teacher strategies across the chain of interactions with the target students. Commands (redirections, desists) and reprimands were the most common teacher response. Ignoring was tried on average only 7% of the time. Ultimatums, punishment (response cost), and requests to leave the classroom typically were not tried initially, but the teacher's use of these strategies increased to 10% or more as the number of cycles increased. Once a chain reached the 6th or 7th cycle, the teacher's response was to order the student to leave the classroom 20% of the time. The authors do not report that any one strategy was more likely to result in compliance for the target students. This is in contrast to the very high success rate the teachers experienced with the Command (redirection or desist) strategy with typical students, who complied 93% of the time with the teacher's initial request.

Let us imagine for a minute how we, as teachers, feel when a student refuses to comply with our direction or request to change a behavior. A typical reaction might be frustration or irritation. If, moreover, the interaction with the student has occurred in a more public setting (e.g., a whole class discussion), we may feel some anxiety because of modeling of undesirable behavior for other students and the potential for contagion. Now compound these negative emotions for four or five cycles of action/reaction, as occurs in the case of the "average" episode of disruption for the target students. Over time, teachers may come to believe that they are dealing with a troublesome student. Teachers learn to be wary of disruptive students' potential for creating disorder and interrupting the flow of their activities. They may try to insulate their lessons from the disorder (Doyle, 1984) or they may alter their activities to avoid those in which disruptions are more likely (Cothran & Ennis, 1997; Emmer, 1986; Ennis, 1996). And they may retreat from dealing with that student, providing few opportunities for positive interactions (Sutherland & Morgan, 2003).

It is apparent from the results of the Nelson and Roberts (2000) study that simple interventions will work best for most students. It is also apparent that secondary classrooms are likely to contain some students more predisposed to be or who have learned to be disruptive and who will respond to simple interventions with continuing noncompliance. Nelson and Roberts refer to the relatively "unstoppable" nature of target students' disruption, compared to typical students. The student has learned that resistance via noncompliance, argument, and refusal results in being able to achieve some desired outcome, such as avoiding a task or obtaining peer attention. Effective strategies all begin with the basic premise that it is necessary to avoid or break the escalating chain of action/reaction.

Secondary teachers use a limited number of relatively direct approaches to manage students who exhibit high levels of inappropriate behavior. A national (U.S.) sample of teachers identified the strategies they used to manage the student who behaved the most inappropriately during the previous year (Ringer, Doerr, Hollenshead, & Wills, 1993). Middle school teachers chose Conferences (86%) and Proximity (i.e., seating the student or standing close) (80%), followed by Peer Tutoring (66%), Punishment (19%), a Behavior Plan (12%), and Reinforcement (16%). High school teachers' choices were Conferences (85%), Proximity (65%), Peer Tutoring (36%), Punishment (22%), Behavior Plan (16%), and Reinforcement (23%). The category of Punishment was defined to include time out, isolation, and detention; Reinforcement included praise/rewards, timer, response cost, ignoring.

Research on teacher use of interventions indicates the importance of acceptability, resources needed, intrusiveness, and required training (Elliott, 1988; Witt & Martens, 1983). Many of the more promising approaches (see Stage and Quiroz, 1997; McDougall, 1998) to managing disruption require training or support, and are at least somewhat intrusive into classroom activities. We have limited our summary of strategies to those that have a reasonable chance of implementation in a regular education setting and whose acceptability should be adequate for most teachers experiencing problems with student disruptions.

Nonintrusive Interventions

As noted by Ringer et al. (1993), teachers prefer to use conferences and proximity as their first line of response. Conferences have the advantage of privacy, which reduces or eliminates the effects of peer attention and support for the inappropriate behavior. It also cuts the chain of classroom action/reaction, and gives the teacher and student an opportunity to regain composure, if necessary. A conference affords the possibility of constructive interpersonal communication. Finally, it gives the teacher and the student an opportunity to use problem solving to work out a plan to restore appropriate behavior. There is some evidence (Emmer & Aussiker, 1990) that the problem-solving steps outlined by Glasser (1978, 1986) can be used effectively by teachers to reduce problem behavior. A good description of variations on the problem-solving approach can be found in Jones and Jones (2004).

Proximity, including eye contact with students, allows the teacher to continue the flow of the activity while calming the student or reducing the problem behavior. Because proximity does not require a direct student response to the teacher, it avoids a possible confrontation and gives the student time to self-manage. A study of secondary science and mathematics teachers by Fifer (1986) found that inappropriate behaviors were reduced dramatically when teachers moved about the room at least 50% of the time.

Teacher monitoring and stopping inappropriate behavior promptly are both linked to lower levels of disruption. Evertson and Emmer (1982), for example, found that these behaviors were characteristic of their sample of more effective junior high school managers but not of a sample of less effective managers. Monitoring and prompt handling of inappropriate behavior are, of course, related to Kounin's (1970) classic teacher "withitness" characteristic, which was associated with low levels of disruption and higher levels of on-task student behavior.

More Complex Interventions

Stage and Quiroz (1997) reviewed 99 studies of interventions to decrease disruptive behaviors in public school settings. Of these studies, 21 were conducted in middle or high school classrooms. Effect sizes in secondary settings were similar to those found in elementary classrooms, while studies done in special education classrooms had greater effect sizes than those done in regular classrooms, although these latter were still of practical significance. For the studies conducted at the secondary level, the more positive effects were found for programs that used reinforcement (including teacher attention and home contingencies), self-monitoring and management (including self- and peer-assisted management of behavior), curriculum changes, and modeling. Brief descriptions of the general approaches are provided below; more extended descriptions of other specific strategies are available in Cohen & Fish (1993) or Alberto & Troutman (1999).

Reinforcement Strategies. Many of these strategies have been found to be successful, both for individual students as well as for classes (Macciomei & Ruben, 1999). In regular education, they are more often used in middle schools than high schools. Use of such strategies involves identifying desired behaviors and teaching them to students through explanation and modeling. Some systems use reinforcement for reductions in or elimination of undesirable behavior. Plans for individual students may include contracts and home contingencies. Such plans are generally written after agreement with the student and communication with a parent or guardian. Students can use a folder or calendar page on which the teacher notes successes or problems, perhaps using a stamp, on a daily basis. Reinforcement strategies can also be used for groups or whole classes. When used with groups or classes, activity rewards or privileges are often used as reinforcement.

Self-Management. This approach includes self-monitoring, self-recording, or self-evaluation. Its rationale is that adolescents are more likely to alter behavior when their ability to maintain self-control is acknowledged. In addition, chronic inappropriate behaviors may be reactive or impulsive, with little thought given to alternatives. When adolescents engage in self-monitoring, the response is brought under conscious control. The focus for self-management is usually a desirable behavior (e.g., raising a hand, completing tasks accurately) that substitutes for an inappropriate behavior (e.g., yelling out, not completing work). The student might be asked to tally the desired behaviors that occurred during a specified time or activity or to evaluate their performance, for example, on a scale from one to five. When the student's assessment matches the teacher's, giving a reward (e.g., points) will encourage accurate self-monitoring and self-evaluations. In addition to its use in general education, self-management has been found to produce positive effects for special education populations, prompting McDougall (1998) to urge its use as an inclusion technique.

Self-management strategies can be used in conjunction with behavior contracting, with the results being reviewed during a conference with the student. A simple way to use self-management is with checklists of desired behaviors. A more elaborate application is the use of charting, which provides a longitudinal record of the desirable behavior. Secondary teachers who use this approach with a whole class can have their students keep a chart showing performance on assignments, tests, daily work, etc.

Peer-Assisted Self-Management. Peers can be used to support self-management. Mitchem & Young (2001) developed a program that targeted 10 at-risk students in several 7th-grade language arts classes. All students in the classes were provided instruction that included a rationale for self-management, class rules, and a system for self-evaluation. Students were paired and taught to use a point system to evaluate their own and their partner's behavior. If the student's self-assessment matched the partner's assessment, points were awarded. Pairs were grouped into two teams, with total points tallied each period, and the "winning" team was recognized (though both teams were praised for effort). Results showed substantial improvements in desirable behaviors in comparison to a matched class. Target students' on-task and academic behaviors also improved.

The Think Time Strategy. This strategy (Nelson & Carr, 2000) is designed to allow the teacher to deal with disruptive behavior without being trapped into a lengthy, counterproductive chain of interaction with the student. A student who continues to behave inappropriately after correction is sent to a time-out area in another teacher's room. This lessens the opportunity for unintentional reinforcement. The teacher waits until the student has regained his composure and then has the student write a description of the problem behavior and a plan for changing it. If the plan is correct, the student is sent to his classroom. If the original teacher accepts the plan, the student is allowed to return to the class; if not, the student returns to the cooperating teacher's class and revises the plan. Obviously, teachers must be willing to partner to use this system, and before implementation, students will need instruction on how the system works. Use of the system presumes that other desirable classroom management features are in place; otherwise, the amount of inappropriate behavior might overwhelm the system.

CONCLUSION

Classroom management in middle and high school classes has many aspects. It can be viewed from the perspective of actions teachers take to structure the physical and behavioral setting to facilitate engagement by students and to reduce the potential for disruption. It can be seen as influenced by the choice of classroom activities and the accommodations teachers make for adolescents, whose needs for autonomy, belonging, and competence intersect with their identity development and susceptibility to influence from positive or negative models. Management decisions and behaviors are also affected by how teachers use or exhibit authority, experience and cope with various emotions, communicate with students, and define their role as teachers. Another facet for conceptualizing management consists of the set of skills and behaviors that effective managers use to keep the flow of activities proceeding smoothly. When disruptive events threaten established classroom order, repair and restoration strategies constitute another dimension of managerial competence.

The two managerial vignettes of Mark Smith and Sara Roberts illustrate different levels of many of the aforementioned facets. These different aspects of management influence each other recursively, rather than exist independently. Sara's well-thought-out system of routines and procedures allowed her to state her expectations clearly, which helped start the year well. Her classroom activities engaged students, reducing the potential for misbehavior and presenting mostly positive models for the students in the class. In turn, this made monitoring students easier and allowed her to be more "withit" if a student started to disengage. Her expressive, confident demeanor captured student attention and, combined with her apparent competence, gave her authority when she needed it. Mark Smith had difficulty keeping students engaged in his activities, but there was no one feature that holds the key; rather, several facets contribute to the problems he had. He did not establish some critical routines and procedures early enough, and so he had problems with inappropriate talk and movement about the room. These problems interrupted his activities and created inappropriate models for other students. The constancy of the problems in his classes undermined his authority and reduced his confidence, affecting at times his ability to communicate effectively with the students. His concerns about establishing order also affected his decisions about what activities to use in his classes, reducing his willingness to try activities that might have engaged students more. These vignettes show how several aspects of management interact and influence one another.

Continuing research on classroom management in secondary settings will no doubt add considerably to our understanding of its complex set of facets and their interrelationships. Some aspects are particularly promising or important to pursue.

Activity management in middle school and high school settings needs more attention. In particular, there is a paucity of research on how teachers in various subject matters and grades/levels organize, structure, and conduct activities. Because of the central role activities play in defining how teachers plan and conduct instruction, it would be very useful to examine these activity structures, and to identify what strategies and behaviors are used to engage students, prevent disruptions, and accomplish learning tasks in various types of activities and subjects.

Much of the secondary research base has been gathered in middle school grades, so more research on classroom management in high school settings needs to be conducted. With the exception of some curriculum fields (e.g., music and PE), the content areas have generally not been very attentive to managerial concerns. Also, because many subject matter specialists, quite naturally, view instruction through a content lens rather than a managerial or behavioral one, classroom management has not been given sufficient attention in the secondary teacher preparation curriculum. More research at the high school level might help increase the apparent utility of the management literature for the secondary educator.

Much of the research on management strategies for problem behaviors is being done by researchers in the fields of special education and school psychology. Such research is usually motivated by the practical problem of helping teachers deal with disruptive, acting-out children or adolescents. This body of research is expanding and producing some useful results as well as programs. From the perspective of classroom management, however, these programs are limited because they often require extended training of either the teacher or the students. They are also focused on how the teacher deals with an individual, without taking into account the teacher's task of managing a group of students. To be most applicable to the regular classroom, future research on the management of individual problem behaviors ought to consider carefully the whole classroom context.

ACKNOWLEDGMENT

The authors thank Vein Jones, Lewis and Clark College, for his review of an earlier draft of this chapter.

REFERENCES

Admiraal, W., Korthagen, F., & Wubbels, T. (2000). Effects of student teachers' coping behavior. *British Journal of Educational Psychology, 70,* 33–52.

Alberto, P. A., & Troutman, A. C. (1999). *Applied behavior analysis for teachers* (5th ed.). Upper Saddle River, NJ: Merrill.

Allen, J. D. (1986). Classroom management: students' perspectives, goals, and strategies. *American Educational Research Journal, 23,* 437–459.

Arlin, M. (1979). Teacher transitions can disrupt time flow in classrooms. *American Educational Research Journal, 16,* 42–56.

Baer, J. (1999). Adolescent development and the junior high school environment. *Social Work in Education, 21*(4), 238–248.

Bandura, A. (1986). *Social foundations of thought and action: A social cognitive theory.* Englewood Cliffs, NJ: Prentice-Hall.

Bandura, A. (1990). Selective activation and disengagement of moral control. *Journal of Social Issues, 46*(1), 27–46.

Bandura, A. (1997). *Self-efficacy: The exercise of control.* New York: W. H. Freeman.

Bandura, A., Barbaranelli, C., Caprara, G., & Pastorelli, C. (1996). Multifaceted impact of self-efficacy beliefs on academic functioning. *Child Development, 67,* 1206–1222.

Barriga, A. Q., Morrison, E. M., Liau, A. K., & Gibbs, J. C. (2001). Moral cognition: Explaining the gender difference in antisocial behavior. *Merrill-Palmer Quarterly, 47*(4), 532–562.

Bauer, W. I. (2001). Classroom management for ensembles. *Music Educators Journal, 87*(6), 27–32.

Bicard, D. F. (2000). Using classroom rules to construct behavior. *Middle School Journal, 31*(5), 37–45.

Blanton, H., Gibbons, F. X., Gerrard, M. Conger, K. J., & Smith, G. E. (1997). Role of family and peers in the development of prototypes associated with substance use. *Journal of Family Psychology, 11*(3), 271–288.

Blase, J. J., (1986). A qualitative analysis of sources of teacher stress. *American Educational Research Journal, 23,* 13–40.

Boonstrom, R. (1991). The nature and functions of classroom rules. *Curriculum Inquiry, 21,* 193–216.

Brekelmans, M., den Brok, P., van Tartwijk, J., Wubbels, T. (in press). An interpersonal perspective on teacher behaviour in the classroom. In F. Columbus (Ed.), *Contemporary issues in teacher education.* Hauppeauge, NY: Novascience.

Brophy, J. (1999). Perspectives of classroom management: Yesterday, today, and tomorrow. In H. J. Freiberg (Ed.), *Beyond behaviorism: Changing the classroom management paradigm* (pp. 43–56). Boston: Allyn & Bacon.

Brouwers, A., & Tomic, W. (2000). A longitudinal study of teacher burnout and perceived self-efficacy in classroom management. *Teaching and Teacher Education, 16,* 239–253.

Buck, G. H. (1999). Smoothing the rough edges of classroom transitions. *Intervention in School and Clinic, 34,* 224–227, 235.

Buysse, W. H. (1997). Behavior problems and relationships with family and peers during adolescence. *Journal of Adolescence, 20*(6), 645–659.

Canter, L. (1976). *Assertive discipline: A take-charge approach for today's educator.* Santa Monica, CA: Canter & Associates.

Chen, Z., & Dornbush, S. (1998). Relating aspects of adolescent emotional autonomy to academic achievement and deviant behavior. *Journal of Adolescent Research, 13,* 293–319.

Chesebro, J., & McCroskey, J. (2001). The relationship of teacher clarity and immediacy with student state receiver apprehension, affect, and cognitive learning. *Communication Education, 50,* 59–68.

Chung, H., Elias, M., & Schneider, K. (1998). Patterns of individual adjustment changes during middle school transition. *Journal of School Psychology, 36*(1), 83–101.

Clark, C., & Peterson, P. (1986). Teachers' thought processes. In M. C. Wittrock (Ed.), *Handbook of research on teaching* (3rd ed., (pp. 255–296). New York: Macmillan.

Clements, P., & Seidman, E. (2002). The ecology of middle grades schools and possible selves. In T. M. Brinthaupt & R. P. Lipka (Eds.), *Understanding early adolescent self and identity: Applications and interventions* (pp. 133–164). Albany: State University of New York Press.

Clift, R. T. (1991). Learning to teach English—maybe: a study of knowledge development. *Journal of Teacher Education, 42,* 357–372.

Cohen, J. J., & Fish, M. C. (Eds.). (1993). *Handbook of school-based interventions.* San Francisco: Jossey-Bass.

Cothran, D. J., & Ennis, C. D. (1997). Students' and teachers' perceptions of conflict and power. *Teaching and Teacher Education, 13,* 541–553.

Creton, H. A., Wubbels, T., & Hooymayers, H. P. (1989). Escalated disorderly situations in the classroom and the improvement of these situations. *Teaching and Teacher Education*, vol. 5, 205–215.

Day, C., & Leitch, R. (2001). Teachers' and teacher educators' lives: the role of emotion. *Teaching and Teacher Education, 17,* 403–415.

Dicintio, M. J. & Gee, S. (1999). Control is the key: Unlocking the motivation of at-risk students. *Psychology in the Schools, 36*(3), 231–237.

Dodge, K. A. (1990). The structure and function of reactive and proactive aggression. In D. Pepler & K. Rubin (Eds.), *The development and treatment of childhood aggression* (pp. 201–218). Hillsdale, NJ: Lawrence Erlbaum Associates.

Dodge, K. A. (1996). The legacy of Hobbs and Gray: research on the development and prevention of conduct problems. *Peabody Journal of Education, 71*(4), 86–98.

Dornbusch, S. M., Erickson, K. G., Laird, J., & Wong, C. A. (2001). The relation of family and school attachment to adolescent deviance in diverse groups and communities. *Journal of Adolescent Research, 16*(4), 396–422.

Doyle, W. (1984). How order is achieved in classrooms: An interim report. *Journal of Curriculum Studies, 16,* 259–277.

Doyle, W. (1986). Classroom organization and management. In M. C. Wittrock (Ed.), *Handbook of research on teaching* (3rd ed., pp. 392–431). New York: Macmillan.

Doyle, W. (1990). Classroom management techniques. In O. C. Moles (Ed.), *Student discipline strategies: research and practice* (pp. 113–128). Albany: State University of New York Press.

Eccles, J. S., Buchanan, C. M., Flanagan, C., Fuligni, A., Midgley, C. Yee, D. (1991). Control versus autonomy during early adolescence. *Journal of Social Issues, 47*(4), 53–68.

Elliott, S. (1988). Acceptability of behavioral treatments: review of variables that influence treatment selection. *Professional Psychology: Research and Practice, 19,* 68–80.

Ellis, J. (1997). What a seriously at-risk student would really like to say to teachers about classroom management. *Education Canada, 37*(2), 17–21.

Emmer, E. (1986). Academic tasks and activities in first year teachers' classes. *Teaching and Teacher Education, 2*(3), 229–244.

Emmer, E. T. (1994). Teacher emotions and classroom management. Paper presented at the annual meeting of the American Educational Research Association, Atlanta, GA.

Emmer, E. T., & Aussiker, A. (1990). School and classroom discipline programs: How well do they work. In O. C. Moles (Ed.), *Student discipline strategies: research and practice* (pp. 129–166). Albany: State University of New York Press.

Emmer, E. T., & Gerwels, M. C. (2002). Cooperative learning in elementary classrooms: teaching practices and lesson characteristics. *Elementary School Journal, 103,* 75–91.

Ennis, C. D. (1996). When avoiding confrontation leads to avoiding content: disruptive students' impact on curriculum. *Journal of Curriculum and Supervision, 11,* 145–162.

Erikson, E. H. (1963). *Childhood and society* (2nd ed.). New York: Norton.

Erikson, E. H. (1982). *The life cycle completed: A review.* New York: Norton.

Evertson, C. M., & Emmer, E. T. (1982). Effective management at the beginning of the year in junior high school classes. *Journal of Educational Psychology, 74,* 485–498.

Evertson, C. M., & Harris, A. H. (1999). Support for managing learning-centered classrooms. In H. J. Freiberg (Ed.), *Beyond behaviorism: changing the classoom management paradigm* (pp. 59–74). Boston: Allyn & Bacon.

Fenwick, D. T. (1998). Managing space, energy, and self: junior high teachers experiences of classroom management. *Teaching and Teacher Education, 14,* 619–631.

Fenzel, L. (2000). Prospective study of changes in global self-worth and strain during the transition to middle school. *Journal of Early Adolescence, 20*(1), 93–116.

Fifer, F. L. (1986). Effective classroom management. *Academic Therapy, 21,* 401–410.

Glasser, W. (1978). Disorder in our schools: Causes and remedies. *Phi Delta Kappan, 59,* 322–325.

Glasser, W. (1986). *Control theory in the classroom.* New York: Harper & Row.

Goff, B. G., & Goddard, W. (1999). Terminal core values associated with adolescent problem behaviors. *Adolescence, 34*(133), 47–60.

Goldstein, A. P. (1998). Aggression reduction strategies: Effective and ineffective. *School Psychology Quarterly, 14,* 40–60.

Goodenow, C., & Grady, K. E. (1993). The relationship of school belonging and friends' values to academic motivation among urban adolescent students. *Journal of Experimental Education, 62*(1), 60–71.

Granger, R. C. (2002). Creating the conditions linked to positive youth development. In R. M. Lerner, C. S. Taylor, & A. von Eye (Eds.), *Pathways to positive development among diverse youth* (pp. 149–164). Hoboken, NJ: Josey-Bass.

Guglielmi, R. S., & Tatrow, K. (1998). Occupational stress, burnout, and health in teachers: a methodological and theoretical analysis. *Review of Educational Research, 68*, 61–99.

Habel, J., Bloom, L. A., Ray, M. S., & Bacon, E. (1999). Consumer reports: What students with behavior disorders say about school. *Remedial and Special Education, 20*(2), 93–105.

Hargreaves, A. (2000). Mixed emotions: Teachers' perceptions of their interactions with students. *Teaching and Teacher Education, 16*, 811–826.

Haynes, N. M. (1990). Influence of self-concept on school adjustment among middle-school students. *Journal of Social Psychology, 130*(2), 199–207.

Hester, P., Gable, R. A., & Manning, M. L. (2003). A positive learning environment approach to middle school instruction. *Childhood Education, 79*(3), 130–136.

Hunter, J., & Csikszentmihalyi, M. (2003). The positive psychology of interested adolescents. *Journal of Youth and Adolescence, 32*, 27–35.

Isakson, K., & Jarvis, P. (1999). The adjustment of adolescents during the transition into high school: A short-term longitudinal study. *Journal of Youth and Adolescence, 28*(1), 1–26.

Johnston B. D. (1995). "Withitness:" Real or fictional. *The Physical Educator, 52*, 22–28.

Jones, M. G., & Vesilind, E. (1995). Preservice teachers' cognitive frameworks for class management. *Teaching and Teacher Education, 11*, 313–330.

Jones, V., & Jones, L. (2004). *Comprehensive classroom management: Creating communities of support and solving problems* (7th ed). Boston: Allyn & Bacon.

Kasen, S., Cohen, P., & Brook, J. S. (1998). Adolescent school experiences and dropout, adolescent pregnancy, and young adult deviant behavior. *Journal of Adolescent Research, 13*(1), 49–72.

Kilbourn, B. (1986). Science teaching and socialization in the junior high school. *Science Education, 70*, 433–446.

Kounin, J. (1970). *Discipline and group management in classrooms*. New York: Holt, Rinehart & Winston.

Kounin, J. (1983). Classrooms: Individuals or behavior settings? *Monographs in Teaching and Learning*. General series, no. 1 Bloomington, IN: Indiana University.

Kounin, J., & Gump, P. (1974). Signal systems of lesson settings and the task related behavior of preschool children. *Journal of Educational Psychology, 66*, 554–562.

Kroger, J. (1996). *Identity in adolescence: The balance between self and other*. New York: Routledge.

Kuperminc, G. P., & Allen, J. P. (2001). Social orientation: Problem behavior and motivations toward interpersonal problem solving among high risk adolescents. *Journal of Youth and Adolescence, 30*(5), 597–622.

Kuther, T. (2000). Moral reasoning, perceived competence, and adolescent engagement in risky activity. *Journal of Adolescence, 23*, 599–604.

Larson, J. (1998). Managing student aggression in high schools: implications for practice. *Psychology in the Schools, 35*, 283–295.

Lawry, J., Danko, C. D., & Strain, P. S. (2000). Examining the role of the classroom environment in the prevention of problem behaviors. *Young Exceptional Children, 3*(2), 11–19.

Lerner, R., & Dowling, E. (2002). Positive youth development: Thriving as the basis of personhood and civil society. In R. Lerner, C. Taylor, & A. von Eye (Eds.), *Pathways to positive youth development among diverse youth* (pp. 11–33). San Francisco: Josey-Bass.

Lewis, R. (2001). Classroom discipline and student responsibility: The students' view. *Teaching and Teacher Education, 17*(3), 307–319.

Lopez, V., & Emmer, E. (2000). Adolescent male offenders: A grounded theory study of cognition, emotion, and delinquent crime contexts. *Criminal Justice and Behavior, 27*, 292–311.

Lortie, D. (1975). *Schoolteacher: A sociological study*. Chicago: University of Chicago Press.

Macciomei, N. R., & Ruben, D. H. (Eds.). (1999). *Behavioral management in the schools: An urban approach*. Westport, CT: Praeger.

Malone, B. G., & Tietjens, C. L. (2000). Re-examination of classroom rules: the need for clarity and specified behavior. *Special Services in the Schools, 16*, 159–170.

Marks, L. U., Shaw-Hegwer, J., Schrader, C., Longaker, T., Peters, I., Powers, F., & Levine, M. 2003. Instructional management tips for teachers of students with autism-spectrum disorder (ASD). *Teaching Exceptional Children, 35*(4), 50–54.

Martens, B. K., & Kelly, S. Q. (1993). A behavioral analysis of effective teaching. *School Psychology Quarterly, 12*, 268–280.

Marzano, R. J. (2003). *Classroom management that works: Research-based strategies for every teacher*. Alexandria, VA: Association for Supervision and Curriculum Development.

Mayer, G. R. (2001). Antisocial behavior: Its causes and prevention within our schools. *Education and Treatment of Children, 24*(4), 414–429.

McDermott, P. A., Mordell, M., & Stoltzfus, J. C. (2001). The organization of student performance in American schools: Discipline, motivation, verbal learning, and nonverbal learning. *Journal of Educational Psychology, 93*(1), 65–76.

McDougall, D. (1998). Research on self-management techniques used by students with disabilities in general education settings. *Remedial and Special Education, 19,* 310–321.

Metz, M. H. (1978). *Classrooms and corridors: The crisis of authority in desegregated secondary schools.* Berkeley: University of California Press.

Mitchell, M. (1993). Situational interest: Its multifaceted structure in the secondary school mathematics classroom. *Journal of Educational Psychology, 85,* 424–436.

Mitchem, K. J., & Young, K. R. (2001). Adapting self-management programs for classwide use. *Remedial and Special Education, 22*(2), 75–88.

Moskowitz, G., & Hayman, J. L. (1974). Interaction patterns of first-year, typical, and "best" teachers in inner-city schools. *The Journal of Educational Research, 67,* 224–230.

Moskowitz, G., & Hayman, J. L. (1976). Success strategies of inner-city teachers: a year-long study. *The Journal of Educational Research, 69,* 283–288.

Myles, B., & Simpson, R. (1994). Understanding and preventing acts of aggression and violence in school-age children and youth. *Preventing School Failure, 38*(3), 40–46.

Natvig, G. K., Albrektsen, G., & Qvarnstrøm, U. (2001). School-related stress experience as a risk factor for bullying behavior. *Journal of Youth and Adolescence, 30*(5), 561–575.

Nelson, J. R., & Carr, B. A. (2000). *The Think Time strategy for schools.* Denver, CO: Sopris West.

Nelson, J. R., & Roberts, M. L. (2000). Ongoing reciprocal teacher-student interactions involving disruptive behaviors in general education classrooms. *Journal of Emotional and Behavioral Disorders, 4,* 147–161.

Newman, C. J., & Licata, J. W. (1986–87). Teacher leadership and classroom climate as predictors of student brinkmanship. *The High School Journal, 70,* 102–110.

Nurmi, J. (2004). Socialization and self-development: Channeling, selection, adjustment, and reflection. In R. M. Lerner & L. Steinberg (Eds.), *Handbook of adolescent psychology* (2nd ed., pp. 85–124). NJ: John Wiley.

Pace, J. L. (2003a). Managing the dilemmas of professional and bureaucratic authority in a high school English class. *Sociology of Education, 76,* 37–52.

Pace, J. L. (2003b). Revisiting classroom authority: theory and ideology meet practice. *Teachers College Record, 105,* 1559–1585.

Perron, J., & Downey, P. J. (1997). Management techniques used by high school physical education teachers. *Journal of Teaching in Physical Education, 17,* 72–84.

Pomeroy, E. (1999). The teacher-student relationship in secondary school: Insights from excluded students. *British Journal of Sociology of Education, 20*(4), 465–482.

Reisenzein, R., & Spielhofer, C. (1994). Subjectively salient dimensions of emotional appraisal. *Motivation and Emotion, 18,* 31–77.

Ringer, M., Doerr, P., Hollenshead, J., & Wills, G. (1993). Behavior problems in the schools: A national survey of interventions used by classroom teachers. *Psychology in the Schools, 30,* 168–175.

Roeser, R. W., Eccles, J. S., & Sameroff, A. J. (2000). School as a context of early adolescents' academic and social-emotional development: A summary of research findings. *The Elementary School Journal, 100*(5), 443–471.

Roeser, R. W., & Lau, S. (2002). On academic identity formation in middle school settings during early adolescence. In T. M. Brinthaupt & R. P. Lipka (Eds.), *Understanding early adolescent self and identity: Applications and interventions* (pp. 91–131). New York: State University of New York Press.

Sanford, J. P. (1984). Management and organization in science classrooms. *Journal of Research in Science Teaching, 21,* 575–587.

Schonert-Reichl, K. (1999). Relations of peer acceptance, friendship adjustment, and social behavior to moral reasoning during early adolescence. *Journal of Early Adolescence, 19,* 249–279.

Schonfeld, I. S. (1992). A longitudinal study of occupational stressors and depressive symptoms in first-year female teachers. *Teaching and Teacher Education, 8,* 151–158.

Schraw, G., & Lehman, S. (2001). Situational interest: a review of the literature and directions for future research. *Educational Psychology Review, 13,* 23–52.

Shavelson, R., & Stern, P. (1981). Research on teachers' pedagogical thoughts, judgments, decisions, and behavior. *Review of Educational Research, 51,* 455–498.

Sheets, R. H. (1996). Urban classroom conflict: Student-teacher perception: Ethnic integrity, solidarity, and resistance. *The Urban Review, 28,* 165–183.

Shernoff, D., Csikszentmihalyi, M., Schneider, B., & Shernoff, E. (2003). Student engagement in high school classrooms from the perspective of flow theory. *School Psychology Quarterly, 18,* 158–176.

Shukla-Mehta, S., & Albin, R. (2003). Twelve practical strategies to prevent behavioral escalation in classroom settings. *Preventing School Failure, 47*(4), 156–161.

Skiba, R., & Peterson, R. (2003). Teaching the social curriculum: school discipline as instruction. *Preventing School Failure, 47*(2), 66–73.

Spady, W. G., & Mitchell, D. E. (1979). Authority and the management of classroom activities. In D. Duke (Ed.), *Classroom management: the 78th yearbook of the National Society for the Study of Education* (pp. 75–115). Chicago: University of Chicago Press.

Stage, S. A., & Quiroz, D. R. (1997). A meta-analysis of interventions to decrease disruptive classroom behavior in public education settings. *School Psychology Review, 26*, 333–368.

Stough, L., & Emmer, E. (1998). Teacher emotions and test feedback. *International Journal of Qualitative Studies in Education, 11*, 341–361.

Sutherland, K. S., & Morgan, P. L. (2003). Implications of transactional processes in classrooms for students with emotional/behavioral disorders. *Preventing School Failure, 48*(6), 32–45.

Thorson, S. A. (2003). *Listening to students: reflections on secondary classroom management.* Boston: Allyn & Bacon.

Unger, M. (2000). The myth of peer pressure. *Adolescence, 35*(137), 167–180.

Voelkel, K. (1997). Identification with school. *American Journal of Education, 105*, 294–318.

Walker, H., & Sprague, J. (1999). The path to school failure, delinquency, and violence: causal factors and some potential solutions. *Intervention in School and Clinic, 35*(2), 67–73.

Wang, M. C., Haertel, G. D., & Walberg, H. J. (1993). Toward a knowledge base for school learning. *Review of Educational Research, 63*, 249–294.

Webster-Stratton, C., & Spitzer, A. (1996). Parenting a young child with conduct problems. In T. H. Ollendick & R. J. Prinz (Eds.), *Advances in clinical child psychology* (vol. 18, pp. 1–62). New York: Plenum Press.

Wentzel, K. R. (2003). Sociometric status and adjustment in middle school: A longitudinal study. *Journal of Early Adolescence, 23*(1), 5–28.

Williamson, S. (2000). Positively adolescent! *Music Educators Journal, 86*(4), 29–32.

Witt, J. C., & Martens, B. K. (1983). Assessing the acceptability of behavioral interventions used in classrooms. *Psychology in the Schools, 20*, 510–517.

Witt, P., & Wheeless, L. (2001). An experimental study of teachers' verbal and nonverbal immediacy and students' affective and cognititive learning. *Communication Education, 50*, 327–342.

Wubbels, T., & Levy, J. (Eds.). (1993). *Do you know what you look like? Interpersonal relationships in education.* London: Falmer Press.

Wubbels, T., Levy, J., & Brekelmans, M. (1997). Paying attention to relationships. *Educational Leadership, 54*(7), 82–86.

Zahorik, J. A. (1996). Elementary and secondary teachers' reports of how they make learning interesting. *Elementary School Journal, 96*, 551–565.

16

Classroom Management in Special Education Classrooms and Resource Rooms

Kathleen Lane, Katherine Falk, and Joseph Wehby
Vanderbilt University

INTRODUCTION

Many students with high-incidence disabilities such as learning disabilities (LD), emotional disturbances (ED), mild mental retardation (MMR), and Attention Deficit Hyperactivity Disorders (ADHD; American Psychiatric Association, 2001) benefit from traditional classroom management procedures as described elsewhere in this *Handbook*. However, due to limited problem-solving skills, impaired relationships with teachers and peers, and an often long history of school failure (Coie & Jacobs, 1993; Lane, 1999; Lane & Wehby, 2002; Walker & Severson, 2002), these youngsters typically require additional supports to meet teachers' expectations of student behavior (Lane, Pierson, & Givner, 2003). If general and special education teachers are not equipped with the proactive and reactive strategies to better manage student behavior, they often are left to confront acting-out and noncompliant behaviors that are disruptive to the classroom setting (Colvin, 1993, 2002).

Many students served in more restrictive placements such as residential schools, self-contained schools, self-contained classrooms, and resource classrooms are characterized by behavioral excesses and deficits (Gresham, 2002; Elliott & Gresham, 1991) that impede effective instructional practices. Thus, it is especially important for teachers who work in these environments to be well equipped with empirically validated approaches for managing aberrant behaviors. Although some of the behavioral concerns may stem from acquisition deficits (skills that are simply not a part of the student's behavioral repertoire), the vast majority of social skills deficits stem from performance deficits (Gresham, 2002; Maag, 2004). Performance deficits refer to those deficits in which students have the expected skill in their behavioral repertoire, yet they choose not to demonstrate a particular skill (e.g., managing conflict with peers or adults) due to a lack of motivation or reinforcement. Fortunately, a number of strategies such as differential reinforcement procedures (Ogier & Hornby, 1996; Ramasamy, Taylor, & Ziegler, 1996), choice making (Dunlap, Kern-Dunlap, Clarke, & Robbins, 1991; Dunlap et al., 1994; Jolivette, Wehby, Canale, & Massey, 2001), and high-probability requests (Davis & Reichle, 1996) have been successful in addressing performance deficits by decreasing undesirable behaviors that interfere with student learning in special education settings. Further, some of these strategies (e.g., choice making, see Moes, 1998) have also been used effectively in inclusive settings. Given the trend towards inclusive programming for students with exceptionalities (Fuchs & Fuchs, 1994; MacMillan, Gresham, & Forness, 1996), it is essential for general and special educators alike to acquire strategies to more effectively manage behaviors exhibited by typically developing, at-risk, and identified students.

This chapter explains the acting-out cycle (Colvin, 1993) and delineates three strategies for preventing problem behavior from occurring in both more and less restrictive special education settings. Specifically, strategies such as differential reinforcement, choice making, and high-probability requests are defined and empirical studies depicting these procedures are presented. Finally an ideographic approach for designing individualized intervention are (i.e., functional assessment-based interventions) for students who do not respond to more global efforts (Lane, Umbreit, & Beebe-Frankenberger, 1999) is explained. Although this chapter focuses on the utility of these strategies and procedures in self-contained and resource settings, these procedures also have met with success in general education environments.

UNDERSTANDING ACTING-OUT BEHAVIOR

Often times educators will state that students' inappropriate behavior just "came out of nowhere." In reality, behavior is seldom random. Disruptive, aggressive, and even explosive behaviors are actually part of an escalating behavior change in which each subsequent link in the behavioral chain becomes more deleterious than the preceding link (Walker, Colvin, & Ramsey, 1995). One key to preventing undesirable behaviors from occurring is to identify earlier phases in this chain so that the chain of behavioral events can be interrupted to prevent more intensive behavioral manifestations from occurring. In other words, the goal is to interrupt the acting-out cycle to prevent the student from gaining behavioral momentum (Walker et al., 1995; Walker, Ramsey, & Gresham, 2004). This acting-out cycle, as conceptualized by Colvin (1993), contains seven sequential phases that increase in intensity over time until the behavior peaks: (1) calm, (2) triggers, (3) agitation, (4) acceleration, (5) peak, (6) de-escalation, and (7) recovery. In the following sections we briefly describe the characteristics of each phase and strategies for managing each phase.

Phase 1: Calm

Description. During the calm phase, students display cooperative, compliant, responsive, and academically engaged behaviors. Students are likely to adhere to the rules and expectations established in the classroom and are responsive to teacher-delivered praise. Further, students are apt to engage in prosocial behaviors such as offering a peer assistance or sharing with others. In brief, behavioral is generally goal-directed.

Intervention Techniques. Teachers can often preempt more serious behaviors from developing and enable students to experience the natural consequences associated with successful participation in the school environment (e.g., academic success, adaptive teacher relationships, and successful peer relationships; see Walker, Irvin, Noell, & Singer, 1992) by treating the calm phase as a high priority. This can be accomplished by programming for classroom structure, delivering quality instruction, providing sufficient levels of attention, and teaching social skills (Walker et al., 1995).

Although a range of variables set the stage for a predictable classroom environment, Walker and colleagues (1995) recommend the following: (a) careful preparation, (b) variation in instructional delivery, (c) classroom organization, (d) communication of teacher expectations (Lane, Pierson, & Givner, 2004), and (e) a sound behavioral management system. In other words, the classroom environment becomes more predictable and consequently easier for students to successfully negotiate the daily demands when teachers have taken care to prepare sound lesson plans that incorporate a variety of activities and instructional techniques (e.g., direct instruction, cooperative learning, independent assignments). Furthermore, classroom environments become more predictable when teacher expectations are taught and clarified in both the existing behavior management system as well as the physical arrangement of the classroom. Delivery of quality instruction also plays an integral role in maintaining calm behavior. By definition, academic engagement precludes participation in disruptive behaviors (Hinshaw, 1992; Lane, 1999; Lane, O'Shaughnessy, Lambros, Gresham, & Beebe-Frankenberger, 2001; Lane & Wehby, 2002). Thus, it is particularly important for students with antisocial behavior to participate in high-quality instructional activities to not only enhance skill development and task engagement, but to minimize the opportunity for disruptive behavior. Unfortunately, the literature reflects a scarcity of research on the effects of academic interventions with students with and at risk for emotional and behavioral disorders (Lane, 2004; Ruhl & Berlinghoff, 1992).

In addition to providing high-quality instruction, it is also important that students receive attention for appropriate behaviors (academic, social, and behavioral) during the calm phase. Too often, teachers err on the side of ignoring students during this phase for fear of interrupting a calm moment or simply to acquire respite from these often difficult-to-teach youngsters. However, matching law (Herrnstein, 1970) suggests otherwise—namely, response rates will match reinforcement rates. Therefore, it is important to provide contingent attention for the desired behaviors. It is also important to provide noncontingent attention. Noncontingent attention is given not based on student performance, but more as a precorrection plan designed to provide attention to students who do not often acquire sufficient levels of attention and to communicate a general sense of positive regard (Walker et al., 1995).

Finally, another method of maintaining students in the calm phase is to provide explicit instruction in social skills acquisition deficits (can't-do problems) and reinforcement for performance deficits (won't-do problems; Gresham, 2002). In other words, it is important for teachers to teach students the specific skills that are not currently a part of the students' behavior repertoire via evidenced-based practices such as direct instruction using role-play techniques. In addition, teachers need to provide students opportunities to perform desired behaviors that are not demonstrated consistently (e.g., performance deficits) so that students can become more fluent in these skills and receive social reinforcement for these skills, which will then increase the probability of future occurrences. If social skills expectations are taught and reinforced, students will more clearly understand the social expectations specified by teachers and peers alike (Lane et al., 2004).

If left unnoticed or if these strategies are not implemented with fidelity and consistency, students with behavioral excesses and deficits are likely to progress to the next phase: triggers.

Phase 2: Triggers

Description. Students move out of the calm phase when a "trigger" or circumstance occurs, either within or beyond the school setting, in which a concern (or multiple concerns) was not addressed (Walker et al., 1995). School-based triggers may include a number of circumstances such as negative interactions with peers (e.g., provocations) or adults (e.g., delayed assistance), changes in classroom or school routines (e.g., assemblies or fire drills), high levels of errors when completing tasks, or pressure stemming from tasks that are either unclear or misaligned with the students' instructional level (Gickling & Armstrong, 1978;

Umbreit, Lane, & Dejud, 2004). Triggers occurring beyond the school setting may include circumstances such as poor nutrition, inconsistent sleep routines, medical difficulties, and poor parenting practices (e.g., harsh and inconsistent discipline, low levels of parental involvement, inadequate supervision; see Reid & Patterson, 1991). If triggers are not managed quickly and efficiently, behavior is apt to become agitated. This can be particularly difficult given the broad scope of triggers that are often beyond the control of school site personnel.

Intervention Procedures. Walker and colleagues (1995) recommend two strategies for managing student behavior during this phase: formal problem solving and individualized precorrection plans. Formal problem-solving strategies may involve the use of empirically validated, commercially available curricula. These curricula typically involve explicit instruction in conflict resolution, anger management, social skills instruction, and social problem solving (Amish, Gesten, Smith, Clark, & Stark, 1988; Browning & Nave, 1993; Johnson, 1996; Johnson & Johnson, 1996; Matloff & Smith, 1999; Prothrow-Stith, 1994). A number of literature reviews have described mixed results about the efficacy of such formalized approaches, particularly in the area of social skills instruction (Kavale, Mathur, Forness, Rutherford, & Quinn, 1997; Quinn, Kavale, Mathur, Rutherford, & Forness, 1999; Zaragoza, Vaughn, & McIntosh, 1991), noting a lack of attention to generalization and maintenance issues and skill instruction that is not aligned to students' acquisition deficits (Gresham, 1998, 2002). Despite these concerns, a number of treatment-outcome studies have shown modest changes in both disruptive behavior patterns as well as levels of academic engagement (Lane, Wehby et al., 2003; Miller, Lane, & Wehby, 2005). If these more global problem-solving efforts fail to produce the desired behavioral changes, it may be necessary to employ more ideographic support from district-based behavioral specialists or even mental health professions (e.g., crisis intervention centers; see Walker et al., 1995).

Another strategy is to develop precorrection plans designed to identify student-specific triggers that set the stage for problem behaviors to occur. For example, if a student typically responds negatively to changes in routine (e.g., assemblies or modified schedules), a precorrection plan can be designed with the teacher, student, and, if appropriate, the parent. The goal of the plan would be to teach and reinforce the use of functionally equivalent alternative behaviors in lieu of the undesirable behaviors (Lane et al., 1999). More specifically, a behavioral approach to consultation is employed in which the source of the problem is identified, potential solutions are proposed and evaluated, a specific solution is selected including specification of assigned roles and responsibilities, and a method of evaluation is established (Bergan & Kratochwill, 1990). For example, if a student becomes highly disruptive when returning from assemblies, a meeting can be held with the teacher, student, and possibly the parent to determine (a) why the student, who is usually well behaved, becomes loud and verbally caustic when reentering the classroom, and (b) develop a plan, with an evaluation component, to prevent such disruption in the future. The plan might include a verbal reminder on the part of the teacher, a self-monitoring student to help the student self-regulate his or her own behavior, and perhaps a home-based reinforcement component.

Phase 3: Agitation

Description. Students progress to the agitation phase when they lack or are not fluent in the skills necessary to manage the triggers mentioned in phase 2. In the agitation phase, which can last for an extended period of time, student behaviors are characterized as unfocused. Unfocused behaviors manifest themselves as either increases or decreases in behaviors. Increases in behaviors may include abrupt or nonconversational language, a tendency to start and stop tasks frequently, moving in and out of one's seat unnecessarily, darting eyes, and high rates of hand movements (e.g., tapping). Decreases in behavior may include staring off into space, low levels of activity, removal of oneself from group interactions, and contained body language. Decreases in behaviors may not be as apt to capture teacher attention relative to increases in behaviors, which are more demanding of the teacher responding.

Intervention Procedures. If the behavioral momentum is not interrupted during this phase, student behavior is likely to become more confrontational as it begins to accelerate and become increasingly more dangerous. Therefore, it is important that teachers be familiar in supportive skills to interrupt this phase. Examples of such strategies include acknowledging that the student appears to be struggling, providing students with an alternative work space to de-escalate, allowing students to engage in preferred activities for a brief period of time, providing alternate activities that allow for either independent work or movement-related activities, employing teacher proximity, or even introducing relaxation activities (Walker et al., 1995). Timing is critical when using these intervention techniques; if these strategies are not implemented at the onset of the agitation phase, these strategies could actually escalate student behaviors.

Phase 4: Acceleration

Description. During the acceleration phase, students' behaviors often become more purposeful in nature. Namely, students attempt to engage the teacher by exhibiting a variety of behaviors that impede instruction. For example, students are likely to question or argue with the teacher when given directives, refuse to participate in an activity or attempt an assignment, provoke other students, fuss or cry, or even commit minor destruction of property. Some students will partially comply with tasks but will produce poor quality of work or complete the work while exhibiting inappropriate behaviors. For example, a student might complete the assigned writing task, but the letter construction might be so poor that it makes it difficult, if not impossible, for the teacher to evaluate the content. This is the phase in which teachers are likely to notice a problem occurring. However, the student's behavior patterns are already in the middle of the acting-out cycle.

Intervention Procedures. During this phase, intervention strategies include (a) avoiding the temptation to make statements that could potentially escalate the student's undesirable behavior, (b) maintaining a calm and respectful demeanor, (c) employing crisis-intervention strategies as necessary, (d) resuming the instructional activities, and (e) debriefing the incident (Walker et al., 1995). Teachers may inadvertently provide escalating prompts by touching a student, making caustic or challenging statements, or arguing with the student. In brief, any of these prompts will likely engage the student in a power struggle. Although it may feel somewhat satisfying to "win" a power struggle with a student, it is important that the teacher remain somewhat detached in an effort to sustain a calm, safe, respectful classroom atmosphere. This can be accomplished by talking to the student slowly and privately with limited body language. Interactions should be kept brief, nonjudgmental, and objective all while maintaining a reasonable physical distance. This is not the time to engage in lengthy conversations about appropriate choices and responsible classroom behavior.

Another technique that can be used during this phase is preestablished crisis-prevention strategies. This involves developing a clear plan including the negative consequences associated with the identified problem behaviors, ensuring that the information is delivered to the student, and implementing the plan with consistency. Behaviors that occur during this level need to be documented in a referral form that provides sufficient detail for problem-solving and debriefing activities that will follow (e.g., School Wide Information System [SWIS]). If the environment has been damaged and disturbed, the classroom should be restored as quickly as possible by the student and the class should return to the assigned instructional activity. Finally, a debriefing session is necessary to review the circumstances or events that set the stage for the problem to occur and the consequences that followed the problematic behavior. During the debriefing sessions a plan is developed to prevent a similar episode from occurring in the future.

For example, consider a student who has trouble receiving corrective feedback from a teacher to the point that any type of error correction results in verbal or even physical aggression such as shredding the assignment in question. In this case a plan would be developed to (a) assist the student in listening and responding to the correction (e.g., having the teacher inform the student that the writing assignment will be graded for grammar and content before the assignment is started), (b) ensure that the student is aware of the positive (e.g., verbal praise, points earned) and negative consequences (e.g., redoing the assignment should the student destroy the paper), (c) provide a systematic method of delivering the consequences (e.g., immediately and consistently), and (d) afford time to review any negative instances that do take place (e.g., during recess or passing period).

Phase 5: Peak

Description. In the peak phase, behavior is seriously out of control and the consequences are potentially devastating. Students may engage in serious property destruction (e.g., throwing chairs), physical assault of peers or adults, self-injurious behaviors (e.g., cutting oneself with sharp objects), serious tantrums, or crying hysterically to the point of hyperventilating.

Intervention Procedures. Clearly it is preferable to manage behavioral concerns prior to the peak phase. Nonetheless, if student behaviors increase to this level, intervention procedures are threefold. First, establish a district-based plan for managing this level of difficulty. Second, develop short-term plans to ensure safety of all students (e.g., remove other students, contact parents or police, or employ restraint procedures specified in the individualized education plan; Individuals with Disabilities Education Act [IDEA], 2004). Third, design long-range plans to address recurrent episodes of peak behavior. The later plans are typically developed with the support of the school psychologist or other members of the prereferral intervention or multidisciplinary teams. Specific intervention procedures are often rooted in district procedures and policies. Therefore, it is important to acquire information about your school site and district policies on how to respond to serious behavioral episodes.

Phase 6: De-escalation

Description. As students move out of the peak phase, they often become disoriented, substantially less agitated, and generally confused. Behavior may include social withdrawal, denial of culpability, assigning blame to others, or efforts to reconcile with those harmed. During this time, students are highly responsive to directives and activities that involve manipulatives. However, they are highly unlikely to want to discuss the event.

Intervention Procedures. Walker and colleagues (1995) recommend the following steps for managing the de-escalation phase: (a) isolate the students from other students with adult supervision; (b) provide an opportunity for students to compose themselves and avoid reescalation; (c) provide students with an independent assignment at their instructional levels for a specific length of time that results in a permanent product (e.g., worksheet); (d) complete an office referral or other necessary paperwork (e.g., problem-solving worksheet) that is required to document the incident and secure additional assistance for the students; and (e) prompt the student to restore the instructional environment (e.g., pick up a torn up assignment, or pick up a chair that had been thrown), and resume the instructional activity—preferably an independent activity.

Phase 7: Recovery

Description. In the recovery phase, students are still seeking to avoid discussion of the event and exhibit preferences for simple, repetitive tasks. Students tend to be rather subdued and rather defensive in an effort to avoid debriefing.

Intervention Procedures. Although teachers may wish to avoid intervening in this phase for fear of reescalating the student, it is important that three strategies be employed: (1) prompt the student to resume normal instructional routines and activities to promote academic engagement, (2) be sure to provide positive reinforcement for compliance and be consistent in implementing the previously determined consequences for the aberrant behavior, and (3) talk with the student to recreate the acting-out cycle with an emphasis on developing new methods to prevent behavior patterns from escalating into more severe phases.

This cycle represents a conceptual model introduced by Colvin (1993) to depict the transactional and potentially escalating nature of student-teacher interactions patterns (Wehby, Symons, Canale, & Go, 1998). Without sufficient knowledge of each phase and intervention strategies for navigating earlier phases, teachers can unintentionally prompt and reinforce more intensive, deleterious phases of acting-out behaviors.

Within the field of emotional and behavioral disorders, treatment-outcome investigations have examined the efficacy of other strategies for shaping behaviors. These strategies, which are rooted in behavioral principles (Sulzer-Azaroff & Mayer, 1991), include differential reinforcement procedures, choice-making interventions, and high-probability requests. Each of these strategies, as well as seminal articles employing these strategies, are discussed next.

STRATEGIES FOR SHAPING BEHAVIOR

Differential Reinforcement Procedures

One strategy that has been validated in reducing problem behavior in students with disabilities is the technique of differential reinforcement. There are a variety of differential procedures, such as differential reinforcement of alternative behaviors (DRA), differential reinforcement of incompatible behavior (DRI), differential reinforcement of lower rates of behaviors (DRL), and differential reinforcement of other behavior (DRO). Due to space limitations, we focus here on the foundation and utility of DRO procedures.

DRO is a nonaversive behavior reduction method in which reinforcement is delivered to students contingent on the nonoccurrence of a targeted behavior during a designated interval of time (Reynolds, 1961; Sulzer-Azaroff & Mayer, 1991). In other words, the basic premise underlying differential reinforcement of other behavior (also referred to as differential reinforcement of the omission of behavior) is that individuals receive reinforcement only if there is an absence of the target behavior. To illustrate, Bobby is frequently off-task when assigned independent seatwork. His teacher decides that she will reward Bobby with a sticker at the end of every 10-minute period in which he does not display any off-task behaviors. If Bobby is off-task, he cannot receive a sticker until the next interval and only then if no off-task behaviors have occurred. Eventually, Bobby's rates of off-task behavior begin to diminish since the undesired response is not being reinforced.

There are typically two different schedules of reinforcement (Lane & Beebe-Frankenberger, 2004) that can be used when implementing a DRO procedure. The first method is referred to as *whole interval DRO*. According to this particular procedure, reinforcement is only delivered if the target behavior has not occurred during the entire duration of the time interval. In the second method, known as *momentary DRO*, reinforcement is delivered only if the target behavior is not occurring at the exact moment at which the time interval ends, regardless of whether it has occurred at other times during the interval. There are caveats associated with each approach given that one method (whole interval DRO) underestimates the rate of occurrence while the other method (momentary DRO) is a less precise observation technique relative to whole and partial interval techniques (Lane & Beebe-Frankenberger, 2004; Sulzer-Azaroff & Mayer, 1991).

In a study comparing the two procedures, Repp, Barton, and Brulle (1983) found that whole interval DRO was more effective in significantly reducing rates of behavior while momentary DRO was more effective in maintaining these lower rates of behavior. To strengthen the intervention, they suggested beginning with a whole interval procedure and then shifting over to momentary DRO to maintain the suppressed levels of undesired responses.

The effectiveness of DRO procedures in decreasing disruptive behaviors across disability groups and across settings has been consistently demonstrated (Ramasamy et al., 1996; Repp et al., 1983; Repp & Deitz, 1974; Repp, Felce, & Barton, 1991). To illustrate, DRO has been shown to reduce a range of behaviors including aggression, self-injury, and disruption, to name a few (Ogier & Hornby, 1996; Repp & Deitz, 1974; Repp, Deitz, & Speir, 1974). DRO schedules have produced significant decreases in undesired behaviors and, in some instances, have completely eliminated the target behavior (Ramasamy et al., 1996). Due to the relative ease of its implementation and its nonaversive nature as an antecedent-based intervention (Alberto & Troutman, 2003), a DRO schedule may be a more desirable strategy to use in reducing a variety of behaviors as compared to more consequent-based interventions such as response-cost interventions that require the undesirable behavior to occur before a consequence can be introduced (Alberto & Troutman, 2003; Sulzer-Azaroff & Mayer, 1991).

The majority of studies investigating the effects of DRO procedures on the maladaptive behaviors of students have been conducted in either residential academic settings or in self-contained classrooms for students with special needs. In one such study (Ramasamy et al., 1996), a DRO procedure was implemented for four weeks with a 14-year-old male student with a learning disability enrolled in a self-contained special education classroom. During the first intervention phase, this student, who exhibited high frequencies of out-of-seat, disruptive behavior, earned either an edible (primary) reinforcer or additional free time (secondary reinforcer) for every 15-minute interval in which he remained in his seat. This reinforcement schedule was increased to every 30 minutes for the second intervention phase. In the third intervention phase, contingent reinforcement was delivered every 45 minutes, while in the last intervention phase, the student received reinforcement for demonstrated in-seat and on-task behaviors every hour.

Baseline measurements revealed that on average, the student exhibited out-of-seat behavior 15 times per hour. Introduction of the DRO procedure in the first intervention phase reduced the target behavior to five times each hour. For the second and third intervention phases, the problem behavior was reduced to 1.4 and .4 occurrences per hour, respectively. In the final intervention phase, the student's out-of-seat behavior was completely eliminated and, consequently, there were marked increases in on-task behavior. Thus, the intervention employed successive approximations and DRO to achieve the desired outcomes.

Although empirical research documenting the use of DRO with students with emotional and behavioral disorders (EBD) is limited, what does exist lends promising results. In a study conducted by Ogier and Hornby (1996), a DRO procedure was implemented in an effort to reduce the disruptive behaviors of a group of middle school students at a residential school for children with EBD. The students were rewarded with edible reinforcers if no out-of-seat behavior, talk-outs, or off-task behavior were noted during various fixed intervals of time. Reinforcement was thinned throughout progressive phases of the intervention. Results indicated that there was a significant reduction in each of the target behaviors postintervention and that these effects were maintained for the majority of students at a three-month follow-up period. Although the DRO procedure was combined in this study with additional differential reinforcement schedules, its potency as a behavior reduction strategy was successfully demonstrated.

Summary. As described above, the DRO procedure is a nonaversive behavior reduction strategy that has been shown to substantially reduce problems such as stereotypic behaviors (e.g., body rocking; see Singh, Dawson, & Manning, 1981), talking out (Deitz & Repp, 1974), and out-of-seat (Harris & Herman, 1973) behavior in relatively short periods of time—sometimes even within a single intervention session (Homer & Peterson, 1980). In addition, it is easy to implement and requires less monitoring by the teacher than other reinforcement schedules. However, in spite of these benefits, it is important to recognize that the procedure serves to lower and eliminate rates of a problem behavior and does not teach a more appropriate and constructive behavior to function in its place. The DRO procedure may also inadvertently reinforce other undesired responses that may occur during the time intervals. As a result, it may be advisable to combine DRO with other consequence-based or constructive procedures such as differential reinforcement of incompatible behaviors or overcorrection procedures (e.g., having a student who writes on one desk clean an additional 10 desks) to produce a more powerful intervention and to more effectively eliminate the undesired response as well as other interfering behaviors (Ogier & Hornby, 1996; Sulzer-Azaroff & Mayer, 1991). Finally, given that many students with disabilities are currently educated in general education classrooms, it is critical that empirical evaluations of the effectiveness of DRO procedures be conducted in inclusive settings as well as more restrictive settings.

Choice Making

Another strategy that has effected improvements in student academic and social behavior in the school setting is choice making (see chapter 7). In empirical research, choice-making interventions frequently aim to reduce the aversive nature of completing academic tasks through the inclusion of preferred activities or stimuli that have been selected by the individual student into instructional activities (Dunlap et al., 1994). The benefits of infusing choice-making opportunities in classroom instruction are manifold. First, choice-making interventions provide a method of manipulating antecedent events to better suit the student's preferences, thereby increasing the reinforcing value of the assigned task. Secondly, it has been suggested that choice-making opportunities enhance socioemotional development and quality of life through increasing the individual's sense of control and influence over his or her environment (Dunlap et al., 1994; Guess, Benson, & Siegel-Causey, E., 1985; Kern et al., 1998). Finally, choice making has been validated in empirical literature as an effective method of increasing academic engagement, improving task accuracy, and reducing disruptive behavior among students with disabilities (Cole, Davenport, Bambara, & Ager, 1997; Cosden, Gannon, & Haring, 1995; Dunlap et al., 1994; Kern et al., 1998; Jolivette et al., 2001). It is important to note that students are not offered the choice of working or not working; instead, the nature of the task or the order of the task is often offered in a choice format.

Although choice-making investigations targeting students with high-incidence disabilities have been limited, the existing studies do provide promising results. In one experiment (Dunlap et al., 1991), a 12-year-old girl enrolled in a self-contained classroom for students with severe emotional disturbance completed four assignments (math, science, social studies, and handwriting) in two conditions. In the Choice condition, the student was allowed to choose the order in which she completed each of the four assignments. Alternately, in the No Choice condition, the teacher randomly selected the order in which the student would complete the four assignments. Results of this investigation demonstrated a marked increase in time spent on-task and an elimination of disruptive behaviors for the student in the Choice condition as compared to the No Choice condition.

A similar study was conducted with three male elementary-aged students in a self-contained classroom for students with EBD (Jolivette et al., 2001). The students completed math seatwork assignments in two conditions. As in the previous study, students were able to choose the order in which they completed the worksheets during the Choice condition; in the No Choice condition, the teacher determined the sequence of assignment completion. The results of this study revealed that each time the Choice condition was introduced, students attempted more math problems and displayed higher levels of task engagement.

Choice-making interventions have also proven efficacious in residential settings. For example, Cosden and colleagues (1995) evaluated task accuracy and task completion for three middle school boys with severe behavior problems in a residential setting under conditions of student-control and teacher-control of task and reinforcement. In the student-control condition, the students selected academic tasks and rewards from a teacher-created list whereas in the teacher-control condition, the teacher chose tasks and rewards that mirrored selections made by the students. An increase in both task accuracy and completion occurred when students maintained control over choosing tasks and reinforcers, even when similar choices were made by the teacher. Results suggest that it was the act of choosing, rather than the choices themselves, that produced these positive effects on task performance. Other investigations focused on choice making have echoed these findings (Dunlap et al., 1994; Cole et al., 1997), further highlighting the benefits of modifying instructional activities and procedures to include choice-making opportunities in an effort to improve student academic and social behavior.

Choice-making interventions have proven effective with students with lower incidence disabilities as well. In one such study, three students with developmental disabilities (i.e., autism, severe mental retardation) who exhibited severe problem behavior were tutored individually at either a residential setting or a university site (Dyer, Dunlap, & Winterling, 1990). Each of the instructional sessions included three to four educational tasks which the students had previously demonstrated the ability to complete. As in the previous experiments, the Choice condition involved student selection of both tasks and reinforcers. In the No Choice condition, the same tasks and reinforcers were offered, but were instead scheduled and arranged by the instructor rather than the student. The results indicated that during the Choice conditions, each of the students demonstrated significant decreases in aggressive and disruptive behaviors.

The effects of choice making were also noted in a similarly structured study conducted with four students with autism (Moes, 1998). Individual tutoring sessions incorporated either student selection or tutor selection of the order of homework assignments, order of problems within assignments, and materials needed for assignment completion. To better analyze the effects of the specific choice-making opportunities, the tutor made selections during the No Choice phase that were identical to those made by the individual students in the preceding phase. Again, the students demonstrated less disruptive behavior and higher increases in correct responding and the rate of assignment completion during the Choice phases, further validating the efficacy of choice making in improving both academic and social behaviors of students with disabilities.

Summary. While the effectiveness of choice-making strategies has been demonstrated, research in this area is lacking. As with the research on DRO procedures, there is a need to extend the choice-making research with students with disabilities in a variety of educational settings.

Given the current emphasis on inclusive educational experiences, more research is warranted with students with disabilities in inclusive classrooms to better analyze the effectiveness of this strategy in these settings. Likewise, virtually no studies exist on choice making with students with low-incidence disabilities outside of individual tutoring contexts. More research is needed to address a range of setting options, including self-contained classrooms in general education schools and more restrictive settings.

High-Probability Requests: Behavioral Momentum

There is a growing body of research that suggests that students with behavioral difficulties may more readily comply with requests to complete low-preferred tasks if these are preceded by a series of requests to complete more highly preferred tasks. Such instructional sequences are often referred to as high-probability requests (Davis, Brady, Williams, & Hamilton, 1992; Killu, 1999) and are founded on the notion that the behavioral momentum (Mace & Belfiore, 1990; Mace et al., 1988, Nevin, Mandell, & Atak, 1983) of compliance will increase the probability that the student will respond positively to more aversive requests or directives. Investigations in this area typically have evaluated the efficacy of high-probability request sequences on the behavioral and social responding of students exhibiting oppositional and noncompliant behaviors (Davis & Reichle, 1996; Davis, Reichle, & Southard, 2000); however, recently there has been some evidence of the impact of high-probability (high-p) requests on academic behaviors as well (Belfiore, Lee, Vargas, & Skinner, 1997; Wehby & Hollahan, 2000).

Wehby and Hollahan (2000) implemented a high-probability sequence with an elementary-aged student with learning disabilities in a resource room to determine the impact of the sequence on her compliance to a teacher direction to complete a math worksheet. The student had previously demonstrated a pattern of refusal and opposition to complete similar assignments during math instruction. Through direct observation procedures, investigators, along with the classroom teacher, determined which requests related to math instruction would most likely elicit immediate compliance from the student (e.g., "Take out your pencil," "Put your name on your paper," "Read the first problem"). Intervention consisted of three phases: (1) low-probability requests only, (2) high-probability request sequence, and (3) neutral social comments. During the high-probability sequence, the teacher delivered a series of three high-probability requests before directing the student to complete her math worksheet. Likewise, during the neutral comments phase, the teacher read three neutral comments from an index card before giving the directive to begin work. The student's compliance in each condition was measured by the latency to and the duration of her response to the request. Analysis of the data revealed that the high-probability sequence effected significant reductions in the student's latency to begin the math assignment (from a mean of 677 s to 21 s) and slight increases in task engagement for the first three minutes of the independent assignment.

A second study (Belfiore et al., 1997) examining the impact of behavioral momentum on academic performance was implemented in an alternative school with two adolescent students who had a history of noncompliance in the school setting. Prior to intervention, a preference assessment was conducted that indicated both students preferred single-digit over multiple-digit multiplication problems. During the intervention phases, the students were given a stack of cards with math problems on them; only one problem was written per card. In the low-preference phase, only cards with multiple-digit problems were given to the students to complete; alternately, in the high-preference phase, stacks combined both types of multiplication problems so that the student would complete three single-digit problems before completing a multiple-digit problem. Task initiation was measured by timing the latency of each student's response (i.e., the amount of time between completing one problem and beginning the next). Results of this investigation indicated that the latencies to initiate math problems decreased during the high-preference phases for both students, thereby validating the impact of behavioral momentum on promoting more positive academic behaviors. While insufficient research has been conducted on the effects of high-probability requests on academic performance, what does exist demonstrates the potential of this strategy to improve academic outcomes.

Finally, Davis and colleagues (2000) compared the effects of high-p requests and delivery of preferred items on the success of transition times. Student participants were two six-year-old male students. The first had Down Syndrome and attended an inclusive kindergarten classroom in a regular education public school. The second student was dually labeled with EBD and mild mental retardation and attended a self-contained classroom for students with EBD in grades 1–3. Both students had a history of exhibiting challenging behaviors in the school setting, specifically during transitions. During baseline, the students were instructed to transition to the next activity; this instruction, identified as a low-p request, typically resulted in challenging behavior exhibited by the target students. If no compliance was observed during this phase, the interventionist redirected the target student with verbal or physical prompts. During the intervention phase, the interventionist either delivered three high-p requests before delivering the instruction to transition or offered a preferred item to the target child prior to the delivery of the low-p request. Results indicated that the mean percentage of responses to low-p requests for the first student was 7% during baseline, 94% during the high-p intervention, and 91% when he received a preferred item. The mean percentage of responses to low-p requests for the second student was 10% during baseline, 72.5% during the high-p intervention, and 87.5% when he received the preferred item. This data indicates that the high-p sequence was highly effective in increasing the compliance of the target students during transition times. In addition, results of social validity measures from four of the adult participants indicated that they would implement both of the interventions again and, if they had to select one over the other, the majority of them would select the high-p sequence as the intervention of choice.

Summary. As evidenced in these empirical investigations, the high-p request strategy provides an effective and efficient method for reducing problem behavior and increasing academic responses in educational settings. However, this strategy needs to be evaluated with a more diverse population of students of different ages and with a range of disabilities in a variety of contexts to further validate its efficacy.

FUNCTIONAL ASSESSMENT-BASED INTERVENTIONS: AN IDEOGRAPHIC APPROACH

When more global intervention efforts such as primary (school-wide) and secondary interventions (e.g., differential reinforcement, choice, or high-probability requests) do not produce the desired effects, more ideographic interventions may be necessary (Walker & Severson, 2002; Lane, Gresham, & O'Shaughnessy, 2002). One type of tertiary intervention is functional assessment-based intervention.

Functional assessment is an ideographic approach to understanding and altering behavior. Whereas most traditional approaches to assessing problem behaviors identify what problem behaviors are occurring, functional assessment focuses on why problem behaviors occur. Functional assessment involves identifying the antecedent events or circumstances that precede the target behavior as well as the consequences that maintain the target behavior (Horner, 1994; Lane & Beebe-Frankenberger, 2004; Lane et al., 1999; Mace, 1994). The goal of conducting a functional assessment is to obtain the information necessary to design an intervention based on the function of rather than on the form of the behavior. Moreover, once the function of the problem or target behavior is identified, then a student can be taught a functionally equivalent replacement behavior that is more socially desirable than the target behavior.

Functional assessments involve both direct and indirect procedures including direct observations, interviews, rating scales, record reviews, and functional analysis (Lane et al., 1999). Direct observations involve recording the antecedent and consequent events that precede and follow the target behavior as well as information on the setting, persons present, and other contextual variables (Carr et al., 1994). These observations are referred to as A-B-C data collection procedures (Bijou, Peterson, & Ault, 1968). Structured interviews are also conducted with teachers, parents, and the student to clarify the scope of the problem behavior, identify the circumstances that set the stage for the problem behavior to occur, determine the variables that serve to maintain the problem behavior, and possibly provide input as to a functionally equivalent replacement behavior. A variety of such structured interviews have been developed including the Preliminary Functional Assessment Survey (Dunlap et al., 1993), the Functional Analysis Interview Summary Form (O'Neill et al., 1997), and the Student Functional Assessment Interview (Kern, Dunlap, Clarke, & Childs, 1994). In addition, rating scales can provide necessary information to help identify the function of the target behavior. For example, the Motivation Assessment Scale (Durand & Crimmins, 1988) is designed to identify one of four behavioral functions: escape, attention, tangible, or sensory motives. The Social Skills Rating System (SSRS; Gresham & Elliott, 1990) can be used to differentiate between skill and performance deficits. Data obtained from record reviews, particularly when using empirically validated tools such as the School Archival Record Search (SARS; Walker, Block-Pedego, Todis, & Severson, 1991), can provide background information as to the history and severity of the target behavior. The SARS can also be used to identify internalizing and externalizing behavior patterns. Finally, a functional analysis, also referred to as an experimental analysis (Umbreit, Ferro, Liaupsin, & Lane, in press), involves experimentally manipulating variables (e.g., length of task or task difficulty) that are hypothesized to be related to the function of the behavior. For example, a functional analysis may indicate that a student demonstrates higher rates of academic engagement when given short tasks (e.g., ten long division problems) as compared to long tasks (e.g, fifty long division problems). The data from the functional analysis provides clear direction as to how to intervene to decrease the rate of the target behavior and increase the rate of the replacement behavior (Lane et al., 1999).

Functional assessment procedures were originally designed for use with persons with developmental disabilities (see Iwata, Dorsey, Slifer, Bauman, & Richman, 1994) and were typically conducted in clinical settings. More recently, functional assessments procedures have been successful with students who are at risk for developing EBD including students with emotional disturbances (IDEA, 1997), Attention Deficit Hyperactivity Disorder (ADHD), and conduct problems [e.g., conduct disorders (CD), oppositional defiant disorder (ODD)] in self-contained and inclusive settings (Lane et al., 1999). Glen Dunlap, Lee Kern, and John Umbreit are nationally recognized experts in the field of functional assessment. They have conducted a variety of school-based interventions in more and less restrictive settings. Although space does not permit a detailed review of their works, the following section is a summary of seminal articles highlighting both the feasibility and effectiveness of functional assessment-based interventions.

Self-Contained Settings

Functional assessment procedures have proven efficacious with students with ADHD in analogue or contrived (Northup et al., 1995) and school-based settings (Broussard & Nothup, 1995; Lewis & Sugai, 1996). For example, Kern, Childs, Dunlap, Clarke, and Falk (1994) designed, implemented, and evaluated a functional assessment-based intervention with an 11-year-old, fifth-grade student named Eddie who had been receiving services for four years in a public elementary school special education program for students with emotional disturbances. When asked to turn in an assignment or reprimanded for not completing an assignment, Eddie would engage in tantrums that included crying and, at times, self-injurious behavior. Because these behaviors occurred when work was not completed, the goal targeted for intervention was on-task behavior. Results of a functional assessment including an experimental analysis suggested that on-task behavior was higher when (a) he was allowed to complete an assignment without written expression, (b) assignments included problem-solving skills, (c) short tasks were made available rather than longer tasks, (d) self-monitoring procedures were employed, and (e) he was permitted an opportunity to work in a study carrel.

A multiple-baseline design across three academic subjects (English, spelling, and math) was used to examine the utility of the above intervention components. The English and spelling teachers used self-monitoring, shortened tasks, and nonwritten work for the intervention whereas the math teacher used self-monitoring, shortened tasks, and problem-solving components. Results indicated that, in each setting, on-task behaviors increased immediately following the introduction of the intervention. Further, on-task rates remained high in the follow-up phases.

Dunlap and colleagues (1993) also used interviews, record reviews, and direct observations of behavior to identify the function of five elementary students with EBD. Students ranged in age from 6 to 11 years of age and were receiving services in self-contained classrooms for students with SED. In each instance, hypotheses were developed about the relationship between classroom events and the occurrence of undesirable behaviors. Experimental analyses were conducted to test each of the hypotheses within the context of a traditional school day. Undesirable behaviors demonstrated by the students (e.g., inappropriate verbalizations towards staff and peers, noncompliance, off-task behaviors, and self-abuse) were empirically linked to observable events in the classrooms.

In addition to producing demonstrated effects with students with EBD, functional assessment procedures have also been effective with students with ADHD and conduct problems (e.g., CD, ODD)—a group noted for being particularly resistant to intervention efforts (Gresham, Lane, MacMillan, & Bocian, 1999; Lane, Gresham, MacMillan, & Bocian, 2001; Lynam, 1996). Ervin, DuPaul, Kern, and Friman (1998) conducted a functional assessment-based intervention in consultation with the classroom teachers in a self-contained program, Boys Town. In this study, two adolescent boys were exhibiting high rates of off-task behaviors. Results of descriptive and experimental functional assessment procedures indicated that off-task behaviors were maintained by escape from writing tasks (negative reinforcement) for one student and peer attention (positive reinforcement) for the second student. For Joey, whose off-task behavior was escape-motivated, a package intervention was designed that included completing longer writing assignments on a computer and being given time to brainstorm prior to shorter writing assignments. For Carl, whose off-task behavior was attention-motivated, a self-monitoring intervention with a reinforcement component was designed to enable him to self-evaluate his attention-seeking behaviors. Both interventions were implemented with a high degree of fidelity and resulted in immediate, stable reductions in off-task behaviors. Further, the interventions were rated as acceptable by both the teacher and students.

Inclusive Settings

Not only have functional assessment procedures been effective in self-contained classrooms and in self-contained schools, these procedures have also been used effectively in inclusive environments (see chapter 17). With the call for inclusive educational experiences for students with varying academic, social, and behavioral patterns, many teachers are challenged with the task of managing disruptive behaviors while maintaining the necessary academic rigor to meet the academic expectations such as those specified in the No Child Left Behind Act (Fournier, 2002). Fortunately, functional assessment methods have been effective and acceptable in managing disruptive behaviors that potentially impede continued participation in a general education setting (Umbreit, 1995).

For example, Umbreit (1995) conducted a functional assessment-based intervention in an inclusive third-grade classroom with an eight-year-old diagnosed with ADHD. Results of a functional analysis indicated that his disruptive behavior—(e.g., talking with other students, making gestures to other students, being out of seat without permission, making loud noises) was maintained by negative reinforcement—escape. Results of direct observation and interview data revealed that the disruptive behavior was also maintained by positive reinforcement—peer attention. An intervention was conducted using a multiple baseline across settings (language arts, math, and social studies) design during the course of the traditional school day without removing the student from class. The intervention addressed both the escape (negative reinforcement) and peer attention (positive reinforcement) functions. Specifically, the intervention included four components: (1) independent assignments were to be completed away from other students, (2) when participating in cooperative groups Corey was not to be placed in groups with his friends, (3) Corey was permitted to request a break (1–2 minutes immediately follow the request) at any time to address his need to escape, which was followed by a prompt to return to the assigned activity or task, and (4) the teaching staff was asked to ignore all disruptive behavior that occurred to remove attention. Results indicated that disruptive behavior decreased dramatically from levels of 55 to 95% in the baseline phase to virtually no disruptive behavior in the intervention phase. Further, appropriate behavior (e.g., engaging the request activity or appropriate verbal or nonverbal social behavior) increased between baseline and intervention phases. Further, the incidence of Corey requesting breaks completely stopped after Day 20. Teachers rated the intervention as favorable during both social validity assessments.

More recently, functional assessment procedures were used to reduce off-task behavior in a general education fourth-grade classroom (Umbreit et al., 2004). In this study, Jason, a typically developing 10-year-old student, was exhibiting a variety of undesirable behaviors when asked to work independently during math and reading. Specifically, he would often talk with his peers, kick his seat as well as the seat in front of him, and walk around the classroom without permission. Results of a functional assessment revealed that the off-task behavior was maintained by both escape from undesirable tasks that were "too easy" and access to more desirable activities. The intervention consisted of increasing the task difficulty for Jason's assignments. A multiple baseline across content area (math and reading) resulted in increased levels of on-task behavior and decreased levels of off-task behavior. Both the teacher and Jason rated the intervention as highly acceptable.

Summary. Thus, the effectiveness of functional assessment methodologies has been exhibited in a range of settings (e.g., self-contained classrooms, general education classrooms) with a range of students (with and without identified disabilities) who vary in age and intellectual functioning. Although it is not reasonable to expect every general education teacher to become an expert in principles of applied behavior analysis, mastery of basic principles and functional assessment methodologies would provide teachers with an empirically validated approach for managing disruptive behaviors that impede instructional delivery.

SUMMARY AND CONCLUSIONS

With the movement towards inclusive programming for students with disabilities (Fuchs & Fuchs, 1994; MacMillan et al., 1996) and the call for increased academic outcomes for all learners (i.e., the No Child Left Behind Act; Fournier, 2002), it is imperative for general and special educators to acquire empirically validated strategies to more effectively manage challenging behaviors. These aberrant behaviors can be demonstrated by a range of students inclusive of, but not limited to, typically developing, at-risk, and identified students.

This chapter explains the acting-out cycle (Colvin, 1993; Walker et al., 1995) and delineates three empirically validated strategies—differential reinforcement of other behaviors, choice making, and high-probability requests—for preventing problem behavior from occurring in both more and less restrictive special education settings. We introduce an ideographic approach for designing an individualized intervention plan—functional assessment-based intervention—for students who do not respond to more global efforts (Umbreit et al., in press; Lane et al., 1999).

To briefly reiterate, the acting-out cycle is a seven-phase conceptual model that describes an escalating process characteristic of many youngsters with aberrant behaviors. Each subsequent phase in the behavioral chain is more serious in magnitude and consequence than the preceding phases. Consequently, teachers are wise to interrupt the acting-out cycle at the earliest possible juncture to avoid increasingly deleterious consequences (Walker et al., 1995). The model also recognizes that the chain of events represents interactions between students and teachers. If teachers are equipped with sufficient knowledge and skills, then they will have the ability to prevent behaviors from escalating to more serious iterations. In other words, this model is built on successive interactions; therefore, how each interaction is managed will influence the next interaction (Walker et al., 1995). However, it is important to recognize that this is a conceptual model that warrants future research efforts to establish the validity of both the characteristics of and intervention techniques recommended for each phase.

Research literature has also documented a variety of empirically validated strategies for improving both the academic and behavioral deficits of students with disabilities in educational settings. Specifically, the efficacy of DRO procedures, choice making, and high-probability requests has been demonstrated in decreasing disruptive and aggressive behaviors as well as improving such behaviors as academic engagement, task initiation, task completion, and correct academic responding. In addition, these intervention strategies have been evaluated with students with both high and low incidence disabilities, further proving their utility in addressing a wide range of academic and social needs. In spite of these promising findings, the investigation of these strategies has been limited to self-contained contexts or individual tutoring sessions. Although this information is certainly valuable, the current inclusion of many special education students in mainstream settings necessitates the assessment of previously validated strategies in all relevant contexts. Such investigations will prove beneficial in communicating effective methods of educating students with disabilities to teachers in inclusive settings. Furthermore, although conclusive, the existing research base for DRO procedures, choice making, and high-p requests remains quite limited. As such, additional investigations are warranted across all disability groups so that research findings can be better generalized across this population of students.

Finally, many of the existing investigations in this area of research did not incorporate treatment integrity checks (the accuracy with which the intervention was implemented as originally planned) as part of the intervention procedures (Lane & Beebe-Frankenberger, 2004; Lane, Beebe-Frankenberger, Lambros, & Pierson, 2001), nor did many of the investigations examine issues of social validity (significance of the goals, acceptability of the treatment procedures, and importance of the outcomes; Wolf, 1978). Without assessing components such as fidelity of intervention implementation and social validity, research findings are tentative at best. An absence of treatment integrity data threatens both the internal and external validity of the intervention outcomes, which seriously impedes one's ability to draw accurate conclusions about intervention outcomes and allow for replication—a necessary venture to establish generalizability of findings (Gresham, Gansle, & Noell, 1993; Lane, Beebe-Frankenberger et al., 2001). An absence of social validity data does not allow researchers and practitioners to establish the extent to which treatment agents were proponents of the intervention, efforts at the onset of the intervention. If social validity is high at the onset of the intervention, meaning that that teacher viewed the intervention as targeting significant goals, acceptable procedures, and potentially important outcomes, it is possible that the interventions will be implemented with a higher degree of fidelity than if a teacher did not view the intervention as socially valid. Consequently, it is possible that interventions with high social validity may be more likely to produce lasting, desirable, changes (Lane & Beebe-Frankenberger, 2004).

Functional assessment procedures also suffer from some of these same deficits. For example, in the effort to identify the function of the target behavior and then teach the students a more socially desirable, functionally equivalent replacement behavior, oftentimes components such as social validity, treatment integrity, and even generalization and maintenance are omitted (Lane et al., 1999). The exclusion of these components makes it difficult to adequately interpret intervention outcomes and make accurate conclusions about future intervention efforts.

Gresham, Quinn, and Restori (1999) note that the roots of functional analysis are grounded in earlier works with clients with severe and profound mental retardation who exhibited self-injurious behavior. Since that time, functional assessment methodologies have successfully moved beyond initial work in analogue settings and have now met with demonstrated success in educational settings with students with high-incidence disabilities without sacrificing validity or reliability (Peck, Sasso, & Stambaugh, 1998). This is an important advance given that functional behavioral assessments (FBA) are a required component of the Individuals with Disabilities Education Act (IDEA, 1997). Despite this mandate, there are two pressing concerns that necessitate attention. First, public school personnel face a number of questions about conducting FBA (Quinn, 2000). For example, questions remain in terms of the personnel involved, the types of (direct and indirect) data to be collected, the length of data collection necessary to establish baseline and progress, and the role of parents in both data collection and decision making. Second, although functional assessment procedures have made progress, it may be that functional assessment procedures have fallen prey to a generalization error (Nelson, Roberts, Mathur, & Rutherford, 1999). Namely, it may be that functional behavioral assessment "has been oversold and overextended in its current applications" (Walker & Sprague, 1999, p. 337) in the sense that functional behavioral assessment as a tool is being recommended widely for use with a variety of populations and circumstances without having been validated for use with the new populations and circumstances. Future research is necessary to empirically validate the "assertions of value, utility, breadth, and efficacy of functional behavioral assessment procedures" (p. 337) to establish the acceptability of functional behavioral assessment for both practitioners and researchers.

Final Thoughts: A Need to Support Novice Teachers

Despite the concerns surrounding the acting-out cycle, differential reinforcement procedures, choice making, high-probability requests, and functional assessment methodologies, these technologies provide an important foundation for experienced and, in particular, novice teachers. Pullis (1992) indicates that although a range of variables and challenges (e.g., curricular issues) may influence teacher perceptions about their efficacy as a beginning special educator, the ability to manage behavioral difficulties is a keystone variable. Perceptions of efficacy may play an important role in teacher retention and therefore warrant future investigation. This is particularly important in the study of special education teachers given that their attrition rates are extremely high (Billingsley, 1993; U.S. Department of Education, 1994). Specifically, attrition rates of newly hired special education teachers average 10% over the course of the first six years of teaching (Singer, 1993).

Further, attrition is a concern for first-year special education high school teachers who encounter a range of challenges such as curricular concerns, collaboration and mainstreaming, resource and time constraints, support issues, and behavioral management issues (Mastropieri, 2001). Consequently, it is important for both beginning special education teachers and general education teachers who work in inclusive environments to be provided with a range of knowledge, strategies, and supports not only to support effective management and instructional procedures, but also to facilitate retention (Maroney, 2000). Perhaps future research could explore the influence of acquiring these much needed strategies and supports on general and special education retention rates.

ACKNOWLEDGMENT

The authors thank Phil Gunter, Valdosta State University, for his review of this chapter.

REFERENCES

Alberto, P. A., & Troutman, A. C. (2003). *Applied behavior analysis for teachers* (6th ed.). Upper Seddle River NJ: Merrill/Prentice-Hall.

American Psychiatric Association. (1994). *Diagnostic and statistical manual of mental disorders* (4th ed.). Washington, DC: Author.

Amish, P. L., Gesten, E. L., Smith, J. K., Clark, H. B., & Stark, C. (1988). Social problem-solving training for severely emotionally and behaviorally disturbed children. *Behavioral Disorders, 13*, 175–186.

Belfiore, P. J., Lee, D. L., Vargas, A. U., & Skinner, C. H. (1997). Effects of high-preference single-digit mathematics problem completion on multiple-digit mathematics problem performance. *Journal of Applied Behavior Analysis, 30*, 327–330.

Bergan, J. R., & Kratochwill, T. R. (1990). *Behavioral consultation and therapy*. New York: Plenum Press.

Bijou, S. W., Peterson, R. F., & Ault, M. H. (1968). A method to integrate descriptive and experimental field studies at the level of data and empirical concepts. *Journal of Applied Behavior Analysis, 1*, 175–191.

Billingsley, B. S. (1993). Teacher retention and attrition I special and general education: A critical review of the literature. *The Journal of Special Education, 27*, 137–174.

Broussard, C. D., & Northrup, J. (1995). An approach to functional assessment and analysis of disruptive behavior in regular eduation classrooms. *School Psychology Quarterly, 10*, 151–164.

Browning, P., & Nave, G. (1993). Teaching social problem solving to learners with mild disabilities. *Education and Training in Mental Retardation, 28*, 309–317.

Carr, E. G., Levin, L., McConnachie, G., Carlson, J. I., Kemp, D. C., & Smith, C. E. (1994). *Communication-based intervention for problem behavior.* Baltimore: Paul H. Brookes.

Coie, J., & Jacobs, M. (1993). The role of social context in the prevention of conduct disorder [Special Issue]. *Development and Psychopathology, 5*, 263–276.

Cole, C. L., Davenport, T. A., Bambara, L. M., & Ager, C. L. (1997). Effects of choice and task preference on the work performance of students with behavior problems. *Behavioral Disorders, 22*, 65–74.

Colvin, G. (1993). *Managing acting-out behavior.* Eugene, OR: Behavior Associates.

Colvin, G. (2002). Designing classroom organization and structure. In K. L. Lane, F. M. Gresham, & T. E. O'Shaughnessy (Eds.), *Interventions for children with or at risk for emotional and behavioral disorders.* (pp. 159–174). Boston: Allyn & Bacon.

Cosden, M., Gannon, C., & Haring, T. G. (1995). Teacher-control versus student-control over choice of task and reinforcement for students with severe behavior problems. *Journal of Behavioral Education, 5*, 11–27.

Davis, C. A., Brady, M. P., Williams, R. E., & Hamilton, R. (1992). Effects of high-probability requests on the acquisition and generalization of responses to requests in young children with behavior disorders. *Journal of Applied Behavior Analysis, 25*, 905–916.

Davis, C. A., & Reichle, J. (1996). Variant and invariant high-probability requests: Increasing appropriate behaviors in children with emotional-behavioral disorders. *Journal of Applied Behavior Analysis, 29*, 471–482.

Davis, C. A., Reichle, J. E., & Southard, K. L. (2000). High-probability requests and a preferred item as a distractor: Increasing successful transitions in children with behavior problems. *Education and Treatment of Children, 23*, 423–440.

Deitz, S. M., & Repp, A., C. (1974). Differentially reinforcing low rates of misbehavior with normal elementary school children. *Journal of Applied Behavior Analysis, 7*, 662.

Dunlap, G., Kern-Dunlap, L., Clarke, S., & Robbins, F. R. (1991). Functional assessment, curricular revision, and severe behavior problems. *Journal of Applied Behavior Analysis, 24*, 387–397.

Dunlap, G., Kern, L., dePerczel, M., Clarke, S., Wilson, D., Childs, K. E., White, R., & Falk, G. D. (1993). Functional analysis of classroom variables for students with emotional and behavioral challenges. *Behavioral Disorders, 18*, 275–291.

Dunlap, G., dePerczel, M., Clarke, S., Wilson, D., Wright, S., White, R., & Gomez, A. (1994). Choice making to promote adaptive behavior for students with emotional and behavioral challenges. *Journal of Applied Behavior Analysis, 27*, 505–518.

Durand, M., & Crimmins, D. (1988). *Motivation Assessment Scale.* Topeka, KS: Monaco.

Dyer, K., Dunlap, G., & Winterling, V. (1990). Effects of choice making on the serious problem behaviors of students with severe handicaps. *Journal of Applied Behavior Analysis, 23*, 515–524.

Elliott, S., & Gresham, F. M. (1991). *Social skills intervention guide.* Circle Pines, MN: American Guidance Service.

Ervin, R., DuPaul, G., Kern, L., & Friman, P. (1998). Classroom-based functional and adjunctive assessments: Proactive approaches to intervention selection for adolescents with attention deficit hyperactivity disorder. *Journal of Applied Behavior Analysis, 31*, 65–78.

Fournier, R. (2002, January 9). Education overhaul signed. *The Riverside Press Enterprise*, pp. A1, A9.

Fuchs, D., & Fuchs, L. S. (1994). Inclusive schools movement and the radicalization of special education reform. *Exceptional Children, 60*, 294–309.

Gickling, E., & Armstrong, D. (1978). Levels of instructional difficulty as related to on-task behavior, task completion, and comprehension. *Journal of Learning Disabilities, 11*, 559–566.

Gresham, F. M. (1998). Social skills training: Should we raze, remodel, or rebuild? *Behavioral Disorders, 24*, 19–25.

Gresham, F. M. (2002). Social skills assessment and instruction for students with emotional and behavioral disorders. In K. L. Lane, F. M. Gresham, and T. E. O'Shaughnessy (Eds.), *Interventions for children with or at risk for emotional and behavioral disorders* (pp. 242–258). Boston: Allyn & Bacon.

Gresham, F. M. & Elliott, S. N. (1990). *Social Skills Rating System (SSRS).* Circle Pines, MN: American Guidance Service.

Gresham, F. M., Gansle, K. A., & Noell, G. H. (1993). Treatment integrity in applied behavior analysis with children. *Journal of Applied Behavior Analysis, 26*, 257–263.

Gresham, F. M., Lane, K. L., MacMillan, D. L., & Bocian, K. M. (1999). Social and academic profiles of externalizing and internalizing groups: Risk factors for emotional and behavioral disorders. *Behavioral Disorders, 24*, 231–245.

Gresham, F. M., Quinn, M., & Restori, A. (1999). Methodological issues in functional analysis: Generalizability to other disability groups. *Behavioral Disorders, 24*, 180–182.

Guess, D., Benson, H. S., & Siegel-Causey, E. (1985). Concepts and issues related to choice-making and autonomy among persons with severe disabilities. *Journal of the Association for Persons with Severe Handicaps, 10*, 79–86.

Harris, V. W., & Herman, J. A. (1973). Use and analysis of the "Good Behavior Game" to reduce disruptive classroom behavior. *Journal of Applied Behavior Analysis, 6*, 405–417.

Herrnstein, R. J. (1970). On the law of effect. *Journal of the Experimental Analysis of Behavior, 13*, 243–266.

Hinshaw, S. P. (1992). Externalizing behavior problems and academic underachievement in childhood and adolescence: Causal relationships and underlying mechanisms. *Psychological Bulletin, 111*, 127–155.

Homer, A. L., & Peterson, L. (1980). Differential reinforcement of other behavior: Apreferred response elimination procedure. *Behavior Therapy, 11*, 449–471.

Horner, R. H., (1994). Functional assessment: Contributions and future directions. *Journal of Applied Behavior Analysis, 27*, 401–404.

Individuals with Disabilities Education Act Amendments of 1997. Pub. L. No. 105–17, Section 20, 111 Stat. 37 (2004). Washington, DC: U.S. Government Printing Office.

Iwata, B., Dorsey, M., Slifer, K., Bauman, K., & Richman, G. (1994). Toward a functional analysis of self-injury. *Journal of Applied Behavior Analysis, 27*, 197–209. (Reprinted from *Analysis and Intervention in Developmental Disabilities, 2*, 3–20, 1982)

Johnson, D. W., & Johnson, R. T. (1996). Teaching all students how to manage conflicts constructively: The Peacemakers program. *Journal of Negro Education, 65*, 322–335.

Johnson, P. E. (1996). Implementing a school-wide conflict management program: Staff development is the key. *Journal of School Leadership, 6*, 600–624.

Jolivette, K., Wehby, J. H., Canale, J., & Massey, N. G. (2001). Effects of choice making opportunities on the behavior of students with emotional and behavioral disorders. *Behavioral Disorders, 26*, 131–145.

Kavale, K., Mathur, S., Forness, S., Rutherford, R., & Quinn, M. (1997). Effectiveness of social skills training for students with behavior disorders: A meta-analysis. In T. Scruggs & M. Mastropieri (Eds.), *Advances in learning and behavior disabilities* (Vol. 11, pp. 1–26). Greenwich, CT: JA Press.

Kern, L., Childs, K., Dunlap, G., Clarke, S., & Falk, G. (1994). Using assessment-based curricular intervention to improve the classroom behavior of a student with emotional and behavioral challenges. *Journal of Applied Behavior Analysis, 27*, 7–19.

Kern, L., Dunlap, G., Clarke, S., & Childs, K. E. (1994). Student-assisted functional assessment interview. *Diagnostique, 19*, 20–39.

Kern, L., Vorddran, C. M., Hilt, A., Ringdahl, J. E., Adelman, B. E., & Dunlap, G. (1998). Choice as an intervention to improve behavior: A review of the literature. *Journal of Behavioral Education, 8*, 151–169.

Killu, K. (1999). High-probability request research: Moving beyond compliance. *Education and Treatment of Children, 22*, 470–494.

Lane, K. L. (1999). Young students at-risk for antisocial behavior: The utility of academic and social skills interventions. *Journal of Emotional and Behavioral Disorders, 7*, 211–223.

Lane, K. L. (2004). Academic instruction and tutoring interventions for students with emotional/behavioral disorders: 1990 to present. In R. B. Rutherford, M. M. Quinn, & S. R. Mathur (Eds.), *Handbook of research in behavior disorders* (pp. 462–486). New York: Guilford Press.

Lane, K. L., & Beebe-Frankenberger, M. E. (2004). *School-based interventions: The tools you need to succeed*. Boston: Allyn & Bacon.

Lane, K. L., Beebe-Frankenberger, M., Lambros, K. L., & Pierson, M. E. (2001). Designing effective interventions for children at-risk for antisocial behavior: An integrated model of components necessary for making valid inferences. *Psychology in the Schools, 38*, 365–379.

Lane, K. L., Gresham, F. M., MacMillan, D., & Bocian, K. (2001). Early detection of students with antisocial behavior and hyperactivity problems. *Education and Treatment of Children, 24*, 294–308.

Lane, K. L., Gresham, F. M., & O'Shaughnessy, T. (2002). Identifying, assessing, and intervening with children with or at risk for behavior disorders: A look to the future. In K. L. Lane, F. M. Gresham, & T. E. O'Shaughnessy (Eds.), *Interventions for children with or at risk for emotional and behavioral disorders*. (pp. 317–326). Boston: Allyn & Bacon.

Lane, K. L., O'Shaughnessy, T., Lambros, K. M., Gresham, F. M., & Beebe-Frankenberger, M. E. (2001). The efficacy of phonological awareness training with first-grade students who have behavior problems and reading difficulties. *Journal of Emotional and Behavioral Disorders, 9*, 219–231.

Lane, K. L., Pierson, M., & Givner, C. C. (2003). Teacher expectations of student behavior: Which skills do elementary and secondary teachers deem necessary for success in the classroom? *Education and Treatment of Children, 26*, 413–430.

Lane, K. L., Pierson, M., & Givner, C. C. (2004). Secondary teachers' views on social competence: Skills essential for success. *Journal of Special Education, 38*, 74–186.

Lane, K. L., Umbreit, J., & Beebe-Frankenberger, M. (1999). A review of functional assessment research with students with or at-risk for emotional and behavioral disorders. *Journal of Positive Behavioral Interventions, 1*, 101–111.

Lane, K. L., & Wehby, J. (2002). Addressing antisocial behavior in the schools: A call for action. *Academic Exchange Quarterly, 6*, 4–9.

Lane, K. L., Wehby, J., Menzies, H. M., Doukas, G. L., Munton, S. M., & Gregg, R. M. (2003). Social skills instruction for students at risk for antisocial behavior: The effects of small-group instruction. *Behavioral Disorders, 28*, 229–248.

Lewis, T. J., & Sugai, G. (1996). Functional assessment of problem behavior: A pilot investigation of the comparative and interactive effects of teacher and peer social attention on students in general education settings. *School Psychology Quarterly*, 11, 1–19.

Lynam, D. R. (1996). Early identification of chronic offenders: Who is the fledgling psychopath? *Psychological Bulletin, 120*, 209–234.

Maag, J. W. (2004). *Behavior management: From theoretical implications to practical applications* (2nd ed., pp. 151–197). Belmont, CA: Thomson Wadsworth.

Mace, F. C. (1994). The significance and future of functional analysis methodologies. *Journal of Applied Behavior Analysis, 27*, 385–392.

Mace, F. C., & Belfiore, P. (1990). Behavioral momentum in the treatment of escape-motivated stereotypy. *Journal of Applied Behavior Analysis, 23*, 507–514.

Mace, F. C., Hock, M. L., Lalli, J. S., West, B. J., Belfiore, P., Pinter, E., & Brown, D. K. (1988). Behavioral momentum in the treatment of noncompliance. *Journal of Applied Behavior Analysis, 21*, 123–141.

MacMillan, D., Gresham, F., & Forness, S. (1996). Full inclusion: An empirical perspective. *Behavioral Disorders, 21*, 145–159.

Maroney, S. A. (2000). What's good? Suggested resources for beginning special education teachers. *Teaching Exceptional Children, 33*, 22–27.

Mastropieri, M. A. (2001). Is the glass half full or half empty? Challenges encountered by first-year special education teachers. *Journal of Special Education, 35*, 66–74.

Matloff, G., & Smith, S. W. (1999). Responding to a schoolwide conflict resolution-peer mediation program: Case study of a middle school faculty. *Mediation Quarterly, 17*, 125–141.

Miller, M. J., Lane, K. L., & Wehby, J. (2005). Social skills instruction for students with high incidence disabilities: An effective, efficient approach for addressing acquisition deficits. *Preventing School Failure, 49*, 27–40.

Moes, D. R. (1998). Intergrating choice-making opportunities within teacher-assigned academic tasks to facilitate the performance of children with autism. *Journal of the Association for Persons with Severe Handicaps, 10*, 183–193.

Nelson, J. R., Roberts, M., Mathur, S., & Rutherford, R. (1999). Has public policy exceeded our knowledge base? *Behavioral Disorders, 24*, 169–179.

Nevin, J. A., Mandell, C., & Atak, J. R. (1983). The analysis of behavioral momentum. *Journal of the Experimental Analysis of Behavior, 39*, 49–59.

Northup, J., Broussard, C., Jones, K., George, T., Vollmer, T. R., & Herring, M. (1995). The differential effects of teacher and peer attention on the disruptive classroom behavior of three children with a diagnosis of attention deficit hyperactivity disorders. *Journal of Applied Behavior Analysis, 28*, 227–228.

Ogier, R. E., & Hornby, G. (1996). Effects of differential reinforcement on the behavior and self-esteem of children with emotional and behavioral disorders. *Journal of Behavioral Education, 6*, 501–510.

O'Neill, R. E., Horner, R. H., Albin, R. W., Sprague, J. R., Storey, K., & Newton, J. S. (1997). *Functional assessment and program development for problem behavior: A practical handbook* (2nd ed.). Boston: Brooks/Cole.

Peck, J., Sasso, G. M., & Stambaugh, M. (1998). Functional analysis in the classroom: Gaining reliability without sacrificing validity. *Preventing School Failure, 43*, 14–21.

Prothrow-Stith, D. (1994). Building violence prevention into the curriculum. *School Administrator*, 51, 8–12.

Pullis, M. (1992). An analysis of the occupational stress of teachers of the behaviorally disordered: Sources, effects, and strategies for coping. *Behavioral Disorders, 17*, 191–201.

Quinn, M. (2000). Functional behavioral assessment: The letter and the spirit of the law. *Preventing School Failure, 44*, 147–151.

Quinn, M., Kavale, K. A., Mathur, S. R., Rutherford, R. B., Jr., & Forness, S. R. (1999). A meta-analysis of social skill interventions for students with emotional or behavioral disorders. *Journal of Emotional and Behavioral Disorders, 7*, 54–64.

Ramasamy, R., Taylor, R. L., & Ziegler, E. W. (1996). Eliminating inappropriate classroom behavior using a DRO schedule: A preliminary study. *Psychological Reports, 78*, 753–754.

Reid, J., & Patterson, G. R. (1991). Early prevention and intervention with conduct problems: A social interactional model for the integration of research and practice. In G. Stoner, M. Shinn, & H. M. Walker (Eds.), *Interventions for achievement and behavior problems* (pp. 715–740). Silver Spring, MD: National Association of School Psychologists.

Repp, A. C., Barton, L. E., & Brulle, A. R. (1983). A comparison of two procedures for programming the differential reinforcement of other behaviors. *Journal of Applied Behavior Analysis, 16*, 435–445.

Repp, A. C., & Deitz, S. M. (1974). Reducing aggressive and self-injurious behavior of institutionalized retarded children through reinforcement of other behaviors. *Journal of Applied Behavior Analysis, 7*, 313–325.

Repp, A. C., Deitz, S. M., & Speir, N. C. (1974). Reducing stereotypic responding of retarded persons by the differential reinforcement of other behavior. *American Journal of Mental Deficiency, 79*, 279–284.

Repp, A. C., Felce, D., & Barton, L. E. (1991). The effects of initial interval size on the efficacy of DRO schedules of reinforcement. *Exceptional Children, 57*, 417–425.

Reynolds, G. S. (1961). Behavioral contrast. *Journal of the Experimental Analysis of Behavior, 4*, 57–71.

Ruhl, K. L., & Berlinghoff, D. H. (1992). Research on improving behaviorally disordered students' academic performance: A review of the literature. *Behavioral Disorders, 17*, 178–190.

Singer, J. D. (1993). Are special educators' career paths special? Results from a 13-year longitudinal study. *Exceptional Children, 59*, 262–279.

Singh, N., Dawson, M., & Manning, P. (1981). Effects of spaced responding DRL on the stereotyped behavior of profoundly retarded persons. *Journal of Applied Behavior Analysis, 14*, 521–526.

Sulzer-Azaroff, B., & Mayer, G. R. (1991). *Behavior analysis for lasting change*. Fort Worth, TX: Holt, Rinehart & Winston.

Umbreit, J. (1995). Functional assessment and intervention in a regular classroom setting for the disruptive behavior of students with attention deficit hyperactivity disorder. *Behavioral Disorders, 20*, 267–278.

Umbreit, J., Ferro, J., Liaupsin, C., & Lane, K. L. (in press). Functional behavioral assessment and function-based intervention: An effective, practical approach. Upper Saddle River, NJ: Prentice Hall, Merrill Education.

Umbreit, J., Lane, K. L., & Dejud, C. (2004). Improving classroom behavior by modifying task difficulty: The effects of increasing the difficulty of too-easy tasks. *Journal of Positive Behavior Interventions, 6*, 13–20.

U.S. Department of Education. (1994). *Sixteenth annual report to Congress on the implementation of the Individuals with Disabilities Education Act*. Washington, DC: Author.

Walker, H. M., Block-Pedego, A., Todis, B., & Severson, H. (1991). *School archival records search*. Longmont, CO: Sopris West.

Walker, H. M., Colvin, G., & Ramsey, E. (1995). *Antisocial behavior in school: Strategies and best practices*. Pacific Grove, CA: Brooks/Cole.

Walker, H. M., Irvin, L. K., Noell, J., & Singer, G. H. S. (1992). A construct score approach to the assessment of social competence: Rationale, technological considerations, and anticipated outcomes. *Behavior Modification, 16*, 448–474.

Walker, H. M., Ramsey, E., & Gresham, F. M. (2004). Antisocial behavior in school with infotrac: Evidence-based practices. Belment, CA: Thomson Wadsworth.

Walker, H. M., & Severson, H. (2002). Developmental prevention of at-risk outcomes for vulnerable antisocial children and youth. In K. L. Lane, F. M. Gresham, & T. E. O'Shaughnessy (Eds.), *Interventions for children with or at risk for emotional and behavioral disorders* (pp. 177–194). Boston: Allyn & Bacon.

Walker, H. M., & Sprague, J. R. (1999). Longitudinal research and functional assessment issues. *Behavioral Disorders, 24*, 335–337.

Wehby, J. H., & Hollahan, M. S. (2000). Effects of high-probability requests on the latency to initiate academic tasks. *Journal of Applied Behavior Analysis, 33*, 259–262.

Wehby, J., Symons, F., Canale, J., & Go, F. (1998). Teaching practices in classrooms for students with emotional and behavioral disorders: Discrepancies between recommendations and observations. *Behavior Disorders, 24*, 51–56.

Wolf, M. M. (1978). Social validity: The case for subjective measurement or how applied behavior analysis is finding its heart. *Journal of Applied Behavior Analysis, 11*, 203–214.

Zaragoza, N., Vaughn, S., & McIntosh, R. (1991). Social skills interventions and children with behavior problems: A review. *Behavioral Disorders, 16*, 260–275.

17

Classroom Management in Inclusive Settings

Leslie C. Soodak and Mary Rose McCarthy
Pace University

INTRODUCTION

The practice of educating students with disabilities in general education classes has become, if not the standard, then the expectation of most parents, students, teachers, and administrators in public schools throughout the country. The data reflect the growing trend toward inclusive education. For example, during 1984–1985, only one-quarter of students with disabilities aged 6–21 spent more than 80% of their school day in a regular class. By 1999–2000, that figure had risen to almost half, with 47.3% of the more than 5.6 million children with disabilities aged 6–21 being educated in typical classes (U.S. Department of Education, 2002). Even though there continues to be inconsistency in the availability and quality of inclusive settings (Villa & Thousand, 2000), educating students with disabilities in typical classrooms is now widely accepted as the least restrictive environment within a continuum of educational placements for students with disabilities. Thus, what began as a parent-led advocacy movement in the mid 1980s (Lipsky & Gartner, 1997) has resulted in a significant educational reform affecting students with and without disabilities.

Inclusive education involves educating students with disabilities in age-appropriate general education classes in which they are perceived as valued members of the class and receive the supports and services they need to succeed. The goals of inclusive education are to facilitate acceptance, belonging, and tolerance among students with and without disabilities and to enable all students to have access to a high-quality, standards-based education (Villa & Thousand, 2000). The purposes of this review are (a) to identify research-based practices that promote positive academic, social, and behavioral outcomes for students in inclusive classrooms; (b) to analyze trends and issues in the research; and (c) to identify teacher, school, social, and political factors that influence the use and study of management practices in inclusive classrooms. Classroom management practices are defined as the actions teachers take to create an environment that supports and facilitates both academic and social-emotional learning (see chapter 1 of this *Handbook*).

REVIEW OF THE LITERATURE

Placement Outcomes

Overall, a small but growing body of research supports the notion that placing students with disabilities in general education settings leads to comparable or more positive social and academic outcomes for students than placement in more restrictive settings. However, inconsistencies in the findings, particularly pertaining to students with learning disabilities, have led a number of researchers to suggest that research should be conducted to determine which students are most appropriately educated in inclusive settings (Bricker, 1995; Fuchs & Fuchs, 1995b; Zigmond, 2003). Even though it may be argued that the more relevant question pertains to the instruction rather than the placement itself, it is worthwhile to note that a study of young children (ages three to five) found that children with mild to moderate disabilities functioning at a relatively higher level performed better in inclusive settings than in specialized settings and students with mild to moderate disabilities functioning at a relatively lower level performed equally well in either setting (Holahan & Costenbader, 2000).

Research involving students with moderate and significant disabilities generally supports the hypothesis that students in inclusive settings do at least as well, if not better, than students with similar disabilities educated in segregated settings (Hunt & Goetz, 1997). However, research comparing inclusive and pullout programs for students with mild disabilities, particularly learning disabilities, is less conclusive (Zigmond, 2003). Thus, the effects of placement of students with significant disabilities and students with learning disabilities are discussed separately in the following review.

Including Students with Significant Disabilities. A recent study provides evidence as to the effects of educating students in inclusive settings over time. Fisher and Meyer (2002) compared the development and social competence of 47 students with significant disabilities matched for age and ability being educated in inclusive or self-contained classes over a two-year period. Findings on measures of both independence and social competence indicated that students in inclusive classrooms performed at least as well, if not better than, students in more restrictive settings. Results of this study were consistent with earlier research indicating that students with significant disabilities improve academically in inclusive classrooms (Hollowood, Salisbury, Rainforth, & Palombaro, 1994; Hunt, Staub, Alwell, & Goetz, 1994; Logan & Keefe, 1997).

Research involving students with significant disabilities in inclusive settings has focused more on social outcomes than academic or developmental outcomes. Two studies compared the social performance of elementary students with disabilities matched across setting. Results of these studies showed greater gains for students in inclusive settings in terms of mastery of IEP goals requiring interaction with peers, increased time spent with peers (Hunt, Farron-Davis, Beckstead, Curtis, & Goetz, 1994), increased number of reciprocal interactions, and stronger friendship networks among students with and without disabilities (Fryxell & Kennedy, 1995). The possibility of meaningful friendships among students in inclusive classrooms has been supported further by findings of a qualitative analysis of four friendships involving students with and without disabilities in inclusive elementary school classes (Staub, Schwartz, Gallucci, & Peck, 1994).

However, the social experiences of some students with disabilities in inclusive settings may be of concern. A comparison of eight students with and without disabilities in grades K through 2 revealed that students with disabilities were more often responders than initiators and nondisabled students were primarily assistive in their interactions with their disabled peers (Evans, Salisbury, Palombaro, Berryman, & Hollowood, 1992). Observations of young children have suggested that mere proximity may not yield positive interactions among students; young children may be uninvolved or isolated without planned interventions (Kohler & Strain, 1999). Whereas young children with disabilities are more likely to have typically developing friends when in inclusive settings (Buyssse, 1993; Buysse, Goldman, & Skinner, 2002), young students with disabilities may be at a higher risk of peer rejection in these settings (Guralnick, 1999). The contention that facilitation strategies are needed to promote positive interactions for students with significant disabilities in inclusive settings has been supported further by research on the efficacy of social interventions (Hunt, Alwell, Farron-Davis, & Goetz, 1996; Salisbury, Evans, & Palombaro, 1997).

In a longitudinal study of student friendships, Hall and McGregor (2000) addressed the question of whether peer relationships occur for students in inclusive classes in the absence of a formal program by studying the peer relationships of three boys with disabilities in inclusive classes in the lower elementary grades and again when they had reached the upper elementary grades. Although there were changes in social status over time, with the designated students spending more time alone and receiving fewer nominations as a preferred playmate, none of the preadolescent boys was found to be socially isolated.

Overall findings of studies involving students with significant disabilities suggests that most students with significant disabilities fare at least as well in inclusive classes as similar students educated in segregated classes; however, in the absence of teachers' facilitation of peer interactions some students may not reap the benefits available to them in these settings.

Including Students with Learning Disabilities. As previously noted, research on placement outcomes for students with learning disabilities is less conclusive. Some studies have shown positive outcomes for students with learning disabilities receiving instruction in inclusive settings compared with students in self-contained or resource room settings (Affleck, Madge, Adams, & Lowenbraun, 1988; Baker, Wang, & Walberg, 1995; Waldron & McLeskey, 1998). However, other studies suggest that students with learning disabilities do not show greater gains academically or socially when educated full time in general education classes (Saint-Laurent et al., 1998; Sale & Carey, 1995, Zigmond & Baker, 1990; Zigmond et al., 1995). Some have argued that it is the more direct, intensive, and supportive instruction provided in segregated settings that facilitates students with mild disabilities (Fuchs, & Fuchs, 1995a; Zigmond & Baker, 1990). Zhang (2001) suggested that these factors may account for findings indicating that students with mild mental retardation are more self-determined in resource rooms than in regular classrooms.

In a recent study involving 58 middle school students with learning disabilities, Rea, McLaughlin and Walther-Thomas (2002) explored the effects of placement on student achievement, behavior, and attendance. Compared with students in pullout programs, students in included settings earned higher grades, achieved higher or comparable scores on achievement tests, received no more in- or out-of-school suspensions, and attended school more often. This study suggests that it is possible for teachers in inclusive settings to provide the explicit, systematic, and individualized instruction needed for students with learning disabilities to succeed.

Outcomes for Students Without Disabilities. Research generally supports the notion that the inclusion of students with disabilities does not negatively affect academic achievement of general education students in these classes (Affleck et al., 1988; Jenkins, Jewell, Leicester, Jenkins, & Troutner, 1991; Saint-Laurent et al., 1998). Sharpe, York, and Knight (1994) found that typically developing students do at least as well in classes with students with disabilities as they do in noninclusive general education classes as measured by standardized achievement tests and report card grades. However, there is some evidence to suggest that students at varying levels of ability may be differentially affected by being in inclusive classes. Results of a study involving 410 students in grades 1 through 5 indicated that students with lower academic skills benefited from being in inclusive classes, regardless of the number of students with disabilities in the class, whereas students with higher skills scored lower on tests of reading and math than in the preinclusion year (Huber, Rosenfeld, & Fiorello, 2001).

The critical question as to what specifically comprises the classroom ecology of effective inclusive settings constitutes the body of research discussed in the following sections. The literature is organized according to the dominant outcome being investigated, that is, academic achievement, acceptance and friendship, and positive classroom behavior. Strategies affecting each of these outcomes have been divided into three categories, that is, strategies that are teacher-directed, those that are peer-mediated, and those that are self-directed. In addition, the efficacy of using different personnel arrangements is discussed within a fourth section of the literature review.

The distinction among strategies used in inclusive settings reflects a subtle shift in the responsibility for teaching and learning. Teacher-directed practices, often called direct instruction, refer to methods teachers use to provide instruction in curriculum content or individualized goals. Peer-mediated practices typically involve the pairing of students with disabilities and students without disabilities for the purposes of tutoring, collaboration, play, or conversation. Peer-mediated practices are reflective of a larger move toward collaborative instruction in education in general (Slavin, 1995). Peer-mediated learning has particular relevance in inclusive settings where there is a need to provide individualized instruction for students with disabilities and there are typically developing students available to serve as models or mentors. Self-directed practices explicitly encourage individuals with disabilities to assume responsibility for their own learning and to advocate for themselves. These practices, sometimes referred to as self-determination (Wehmeyer, Palmer, Agran, Mithaug, & Martin, 2000), have recently gained interest in the field of special education. An overview of the self-, peer-, and teacher-directed strategies found to enhance outcomes for students in inclusive settings is presented in the following section and has been summarized in Table 17.1.

Strategies That Promote Academic Achievement

Research on strategies that promote academic achievement in inclusive classrooms is based on larger bodies of research on teaching and learning in more restricted special education settings and in noninclusive general education settings (e.g., instruction in study skills and inquiry-based instruction). This section summarizes the findings of those studies that contribute to our understanding of evidence-based instructional practices in inclusive settings.

Teacher-Directed Strategies. An overview of the teacher-directed strategies that appear to be effective in inclusive classrooms is provided in an observational study conducted in four high schools noted for achieving positive outcomes for all students (Wallace, Anderson, Bartholomay, & Hupp, 2002). They found that more than 75% of teacher time was spent observing, managing, and interacting with students and less than 2% of time was spent disciplining students. Students with and without disabilities had high levels of academic engagement and low levels of inappropriate behavior. Although there were no differences in the behavior of students with and without disabilities, students with disabilities were more often the focus of teacher attention. Citing evidence of the link between student engagement and academic achievement (e.g., Brophy & Good, 1986), the authors conclude that high levels of active engagement and task-related attention are associated with successful inclusive education.

Specific teacher-directed strategies that have been the subject of study in inclusive settings are embedded instruction, inquiry-based and "hands-on" science instruction, nonverbal

TABLE 17.1
Strategies and Personnel Arrangements to Enhance Achievement, Acceptance and Friendship, and Positive Behavior in Inclusive Settings

Strategies Used	*Findings and Implications*[1]	*Research Citations*
	Teacher-Directed Strategies	
	Academic Achievement	
Embedded instruction	• IEP goals achieved • Some evidence of generalization of skills • Student learning impacted by teachers' consistency and frequency of implementation	Horn, Lieber, Sandall, Schwartz, & Li, 2000 McDonnell, Johnson, Polychronis, & Risen, 2002 Wolery, Anthony, Snyder, Werts, & Katzenmeyer, 1997
Nonverbal scaffolding	• Increased attention and success at learning tasks with use of gestural prompts	Wang, Bernas, & Eberhard, 2001
Direct instruction	• Improved test performance in multiplication skills	Bulgren, Lenz, Marquis, Schumaker, & Deshler, 2002
Question Exploration Routine	• Use of a routine and graphic enhanced English test performance.	Harris, Miller, & Mercer, 1995
Inquiry-based instruction	• Improved test performance for students with and without disabilities • Individualized teacher attention was needed to ensure conceptual understanding	Cawley, Hayden, Cade, & Baker-Kroczynski, 2002 Palincsar, Magnusson, Collins, & Cutter, 2001
Authentic assessment	• Increased performance to levels comparable with nondisabled peers • Enhanced use of accommodations for all students	King, Schroeder, & Chawszczewski, 2001
Combined strategies (i.e., using two or more of the following: direct instruction in domain specific strategies, authentic tasks, anchored instruction, and social mediation)	• Enhanced academic performance to levels comparable to nondisabled peers. • Well-trained personnel needed to provide individualized instruction when needed	Bottge, Heinrichs, Mehta, & Hung, 2002 Ferretti, MacArthur, & Okolo, 2001 Morocco, Hindin, Mata-Aguilar, & Clark-Chiarelli, 2001 Woodward, Monroe, & Baxter, 2001
Co-teaching	• Mixed results; both increased and decreased academic performance • Efficacy limited by lack of supports, training, and planning time	Bear & Proctor, 1990 Buoudah, Schumacher, & Deshler, 1997 Schulte, Osborne, & McKinney, 1990
	Acceptance and Friendship	
Teacher rule-making (i.e. "You can't say you can't play")	• Increased acceptance and belonging	Sapon-Shevin, Dobbelaere, Corrigan, Goodman, & Mastin, 1998
Structured social interactions	• Increased quality and duration of social interactions	Frea, Craig-Unkefer, Odom, & Johnson, 1999

(continued)

TABLE 17.1
(Continued)

Strategies Used	*Findings and Implications* [1]	*Research Citations*
	Positive Behavior	
Offering choice	• Decreased undesirable behavior	Coniglio, 2000 Powell & Nelson, 1997
Teacher talk (i.e., positive verbal responses, clear directives and feedback)	• Higher rates of task-appropriate behavior and lower rates of negative behavior	Beyda, Zentall, & Ferko, 2002
Prompts, modeling, and reinforcement	• Increased engagement • Successful transitions to new activities	Davis, Reichle, & Southard, 2000 Malmskog & McDonnell, 1999
Direct instruction in recruiting positive teacher attention	• Increased teacher praise, instructional feedback, and accuracy in completing assignments	Alber, Heward, & Hippler, 1999
Positive behavioral support	• Decreased school-wide disciplinary referrals • Decreased disruptive behavior • Increased participation and engagement	Kennedy, et al., 2001 Lewis & Sugai, 1996 Lewis, Sugai, & Colvin, 1998 Taylor-Green, et al., 1997 Umbreit, 1995
Inquiry-based instruction	• Reduced misbehavior in students with and without disabilities	Cawley, Hayden, Cade, & Baker-Kroczynski, 2002
Co-teaching	• Decreased number of disciplinary referrals	Krank, Moon, & Render, 2002
	Peer-Mediated Strategies	
	Academic Achievement	
Peer Assisted Learning Strategies (PALS)	• Increased academic achievement across grade levels	Fuchs & Fuchs, 1995 Fuchs, Fuchs, Mathes, & Simmons, 1997 Fuchs, Fuchs, & Burish, 2000 Fuchs et al., 2001 Mathes, Grek, Howard, Babyak, & Allen, 1999
Cooperative learning groups	• Increased reading achievement • Personnel and time for monitoring cooperative groups enhanced results	Allsopp, 1997 Jenkins & O'Connor, 1996 Kamps, Leonard, Potucek, & Garrison-Harrell, 1995 Staub, Spaulding, Peck, Gallucci, & Schwartz, et al., 1996
Classroom Wide Peer Tutoring (CWPT)	• Increased spelling achievement • Teacher monitoring of goals and tutoring strategies enhanced results	Mathes, Fuchs, Fuchs, Henley, & Sanders, 1994 Mortweet et al., 1999
Peer support	• Increased academic engagement of tutors	Cushing & Kennedy, 1997
	Acceptance and Friendship	
Peer Assisted Learning Strategies (PALS)	• Greater social acceptance by peers and teachers • Equal social standing in PALS classroom	Fuchs, Fuchs, Mathes, & Martinez, 2002
Cooperative learning	• Increased peer interaction • Greater social acceptance by teachers	Jenkins, Antil, Wayne, & Vadasy, 2003 Kamps, Leonard, & Potucek, 1997

TABLE 17.1
(Continued)

Peer buddies	• Increased self-confidence, independence, and participation	Copeland et al., 2002b
Peer support (i.e., pairing students with disabilities with nondisabled peers trained to provide support)	• Increased interaction time, playful behavior, and socialization outside of school	Dugan et al., 1995 Garrison-Harrell, 1995 Garrison-Harrell, Goldstein, & Thiemann, 2000 Kamps, & Dravis, 1997 Kamps, Leonard, Potucek, Palincsar & Klenk, 1992
	Positive Behavior	
Peer tutoring (including CWPT, PALS)	• Increased engagement, opportunities for independent action and appropriate behaviors • Decreased student frustration and negative behaviors for all students	Arceneaux & Murdock, 1997 Cushing & Kennedy, 1997 Kennedy & Itkonen, 1995 King-Sears & Bradley, 1995 Mortweet et al., 1999 Spencer, Scruggs, & Mastorpieri, 2003 Staub, Spaulding, Peck, Gallucci, & Schwartz et al., 1996
Cooperative learning groups	• Increased engagement, opportunities for self-determination, and appropriate behaviors	Blum, Lipsett, & Yocom, 2002 Kamps et al., 1995 Palincsar & Klenk, 1992
	Self-Directed Strategies	
	Academic Achievement	
Self-identification of target behavior Self-monitoring Self-evaluation	• Increased use of study skills and organizational strategies • Did not fully compensate for knowledge deficits	Agran, Blanchard, Wehmeyer, & Hughes, 2001 Copeland, Hughes, Agran, Wehmeyer, & Fowler, 2002 Hughes et al., 2002 Hughes, Ruhl, Schumaker, & Deshler, 2002b
	Acceptance and Friendship	
Self-evaluation Video feedback	• Increased appropriate interactions	Falk & Dunlap, 1996
	Positive Behavior	
Self-instruction Self-monitoring Self-reinforcement	• Increased positive behavior • Generalization occurred with additional instruction	duPaul & Hoff, 1998 Gilberts, Agran, Hughes, & Wehmeyer, 2001 Peterson, Young, West, & Peterson, 1999
Choice and access to appropriate, self-paced learning tasks	• Comparable behavior to students without disabilities	Beyda, Zentall, & Ferko 2002

[1]Findings pertain to students with disabilities unless otherwise specified.

scaffolding, and direct instruction. These studies provide verification that teacher-directed strategies can improve the academic achievement of some students with disabilities in inclusive settings.

Embedded instruction (the teaching of individualized goals within the context of curriculum-based instruction) has proven to be helpful to preschool children with cerebral palsy, severe speech and language delays, mental retardation and Down syndrome, and to junior high school students with moderate disabilities (Horn, Lieber, Sandall, Schwartz, & Li, 2000; McDonnell, Johnson, Polychronis, & Risen, 2002; Wolery, Anthony, Snyder, Werts, & Katzenmeyer, 1997). The study of nonverbal scaffolding found that students with Down Syndrome responded more positively to teacher directions and were more attentive to and successful at learning tasks when the teacher used gestures to enhance their scaffolding efforts (Wang, Bernas, & Eberhard, 2001). Two studies focused on more scripted strategies. Bulgren and her colleagues found that students with disabilities scored higher on topic-specific tests when teachers used a question exploration routine (a set of questions provided to the teacher to prompt discussion); however, they did not achieve at levels comparable to their nondisabled classmates (Bulgren, Lenz, Marquis, Schumaker, & Deshler, 2002). Harris, Miller, and Mercer (1995) found that when general education teachers in inclusive classes used a concrete-to-representational-to-abstract teaching sequence that had been validated to teach multiplication to students in segregated settings, students with learning and emotional disabilities performed as well as their nondisabled peers except in word problems.

Studies conducted in science classrooms provided evidence that inquiry-based instruction improved learning for students with disabilities in settings in which inclusion is often considered to be extremely difficult. A study that examined guided inquiry science teaching (Palincsar, Magnusson, Collins, & Cutter, 2001) indicated that when teachers pay attention to issues of access and create opportunities for collaboration between special and general educators, they enable students with emotional and learning disabilities to participate more fully in learning activities. Teachers' strategies included mini conferencing and rehearsing contributions to group discussions with students with disabilities. In addition, they provided more specific prompts for laboratory journal entries, glossaries of terms posted as environmental supports to writing, and transcriptions of the written efforts of students with disabilities. These successful strategies integrated the subject-specific knowledge of the general education teacher and the more general knowledge in learning skills of the special education teacher.

A second study based in inclusive science classrooms (Cawley, Hayden, Cade, & Baker-Kroczynski, 2002) demonstrated that activity-based instruction resulted in academic success for students with disabilities. The students with learning and emotional disabilities had a passing rate on a city-wide exam that was comparable to that of their classmates without disabilities. In addition, this study is unique in that it provides information about the behavior of students in the inclusive class: students with disabilities had no behavioral difficulties and students without disabilities had fewer behavioral difficulties in the inclusive setting than in their other noninclusive classes.

An additional strategy available to teachers in inclusive settings is assessment design. King and his colleagues (King, Schroeder, & Chawszczewski, 2001) found that when teachers used authentic assessment measures students with disabilities performed better than comparable students whose teachers did not use similar assessment methods. In addition, students with disabilities who were asked to perform tasks with higher intellectual challenge performed better than those without disabilities whose assessment was less rigorous. Two-thirds of students with disabilities produced work that was at least as authentic as that of their peers without disabilities. When classroom teachers used authentic assessment they were likely to provide accommodations for all students. Choosing authentic assessment tools appears to be another teacher-directed strategy that improves the academic achievement of students with disabilities.

Findings of a number of studies have been summarized in research by the REACH Institute, which investigated ways of enabling students with learning disabilities to develop understanding and meet high academic standards in inclusive classrooms. The results of studies in classes in mathematics (Bottge, Heinrichs, Mehta, & Hung, 2002; Woodward, Monroe, & Baxter, 2001), English (Morocco, Hindin, Mata-Aguilar, & Clark-Chiarelli, 2001), science (Palincsar et al., 2001) and history (Ferretti, MacArthur, & Okolo, 2001) indicate that students with learning disabilities in grades 4, 5, 7, and 8, do as well as their nonidentified peers in meeting high academic standards when certain instructional principles are followed. These principles include providing students with authentic tasks, offering instruction in domain-specific learning strategies, providing opportunities for social mediation, and constructive conversations.

Peer-Mediated Strategies. Peer-mediated strategies are the most frequently researched teaching and learning techniques used in inclusive classrooms. Several forms of peer-mediated strategies have been studied. These include Classwide Peer Tutoring (CWPT), Peer-Assisted Learning Strategies (PALS), Cooperative Homework Teams (CHT), Cooperative Learning Groups (CLG), Cooperative Integrated Reading and Composition (CIRC), reciprocal teaching, and literature circles. Each of these strategies pairs or groups students with and without disabilities for the purpose of performing academic tasks.

The research on peer-mediated instruction generally shows that these strategies improve the academic achievement of students with and without disabilities in inclusive settings. Working with 16 third-graders, Kamps and her colleagues found that participation in cooperative learning groups in which students received peer tutoring on vocabulary words, participated in academic games, and worked with comprehension questions, resulted in gains in reading for students with autism, as well as for students with learning and behavioral disabilities (Kamps, Leonard, Potucek, and Garrison-Harrell, 1995). Cushing and Kennedy (1997) found that students without disabilities who provided peer support to students with disabilities had increased academic engagement and, in one of three cases, improved academic performance.

Classwide Peer Tutoring (CWPT) and Peer-Assisted Learning Strategies (PALS) are two structured peer-tutoring programs that have been studied in inclusive classrooms. Both have positive academic effects. For example, Mortweet and her colleagues demonstrated that students with mild mental retardation can benefit from CWPT in inclusive settings. Seven of eight targeted students spelled with more accuracy during CWPT intervention intervals than during times when instruction was teacher-directed alone. (The remaining student spelled with 96% accuracy during both intervals). All students with mild mental retardation had post–test scores comparable to their typical peers and demonstrated higher than average gains during the CWPT intervention than did their typical peers during either interval (Mortweet et al., 1999).

The effectiveness of PALS has also been studied in inclusive settings, most extensively in grades 2 through 6 (Fuchs, Fuchs, Mathes, & Simmons, 1997) and recently in kindergarten, first grade and high school (Fuchs & Fuchs, 1995a; Fuchs et al., 2001; Fuchs, Fuchs, & Burish, 2000; Mathes, Grek, Howard, Babyak, & Allen, 1999). At all levels, there were significant positive effects in academic achievement for students with learning disabilities during the PALS intervention than during its absence. However, researchers caution that the data also demonstrate limitations in the transfer of skills in mathematics by students with disabilities (Fuchs & Fuchs, 1995a) and in growth in reading skills (Fuchs et al., 2000).

A number of other issues in the use of peer-mediated strategies have been noted. Research on specific forms of peer-mediated teaching and learning strategies suggests that the dyadic peer-tutoring programs may have greater success than those situated in larger groups. Cooperative learning groups appear to include a wide array of strategies that are open to teachers' interpretation and variations in implementation. In doing so it appears that teachers may neglect some components of cooperative learning that researchers and developers deem to be vital to its success, such as individual accountability and student reflection of group processes (Antil, Jenkins, Wayne, & Vadasy, 1998).

Research indicates other considerations in the implementation of peer-mediated strategies in inclusive settings. The forms of partnerships established among students need to be carefully chosen, assisted, and supported (O'Connor & Jenkins, 1996). Students must be instructed in cooperative group or peer-tutoring skills in a classroom in which there is an ethos of acceptance and cooperation (O'Connor & Jenkins, 1996; Staub, Spaulding, Peck, Gallucci, & Schwartz, 1996). Accomplishing these tasks means that teachers need time to identify learning goals and to develop appropriate peer-mediated activities (Allsopp, 1997). Particularly when higher order skills are the objectives of peer-mediated strategies, a greater burden is placed on students in their cooperative or tutoring efforts and on teachers who are supporting them (Allsopp, 1997). Teachers also need to monitor the peer-mediated strategies on an ongoing basis (Mathes, Fuchs, Fuchs, Henley, & Sanders, 1994; McMaster & Fuchs, 2002). Finally, the introduction of peer-mediated strategies may require the presence of more adults in the classroom to accommodate the increased demands on teachers to prepare and monitor the activities (Staub et al., 1996). In addition to budgetary considerations, this requirement has an additional potential difficulty. The adults in the classroom need to monitor their own interaction with students engaged in peer-mediated strategies so as not to inappropriately insert themselves into groups or pairs (O'Connor & Jenkins, 1996).

Self-Directed Strategies. Self-directed learning strategies are techniques that extend the contributions of traditional special education programs. Researchers have begun to investigate what happens when students with disabilities participating in inclusive classes are taught to use these strategies.

Four studies in middle and high schools investigated efforts to develop strategies by which students with learning disabilities, mental retardation, and multiple disabilities identify, monitor, and evaluate their attempts to achieve target behaviors that contribute to academic achievement (Agran, Blanchard, Wehmeyer, & Hughes 2001; Copeland, Hughes, Agran, Wehmeyer, & Fowler, 2002a; Hughes et al., 2002a; Hughes Ruhl, Schumaker, & Deshler, 2002b). There were several common findings among these studies. The consequences of teaching students to use self-directed behaviors were generally positive across settings and student disability. However, the effectiveness of reinforcement seemed to vary based on a number of variables including the nature of the reinforcer and the person issuing the reward. For example, monetary reinforcement produced a stronger and more rapid response than did verbal praise and teacher provided reinforcement further enhanced the results. Finally, the development of study skills and organizational strategies did not make up for students' deficits in content knowledge or skills.

Copeland et al. (2002a) used an intervention package that included instruction in self-monitoring classroom behaviors such as self-prompting to answer all questions on worksheets. Four students with mental retardation demonstrated improved performance on modified assignments; three earned higher report card grades. The same researchers found that an additional student with mental retardation improved his performance on a modified worksheet as the result of a similar intervention. Other students showed improvement in behaviors supporting academic engagement.

Only one study examined the effects of self-directed instruction on students with learning disabilities in inclusive classrooms (Hughes et al., 2002b). This study found that eight of nine students successfully used a set of organizational and self-management skills that they had been taught to improve their rate of homework completion and the quality of their assignments. The students engaged in self-monitoring and did not require teacher or parent supervision of their work.

Overall, research on the instructional components of classroom management demonstrates that effective strategies are drawn from the best practices in self-contained general and special education classes that emphasize higher-level learning, peer-facilitated instruction, and independent learning. The instructional techniques explored in these studies are unique only in that they are being investigated in inclusive settings. It is likely that they are well suited for inclusive settings because they inherently involve differentiation.

Strategies That Promote Acceptance and Friendship

Teacher-Directed Strategies. Three studies addressed teacher-directed strategies to assure the acceptance and belonging of students with disabilities in inclusive classrooms. Two of the studies were qualitative and consisted of interviews with and observations of teachers in elementary schools. The third study examined the effect of teacher-directed interventions in a preschool setting.

Salisbury and her colleagues interviewed and observed teachers at two inclusive schools and identified strategies used by general education teachers to increase positive relations among their general education students and those with severe disabilities in elementary school classes (Salisbury, Gallucci, Palombaro, & Peck, 1995). These strategies included (a) actively facilitating social interactions among classmates, (b) empowering children to make decisions, (c) working to build a sense of community, (d) modeling acceptance, and (e) developing a supportive school organization. The specific practices teachers said they used to create opportunities for positive interactions included cooperative groups, physical arrangements in the classroom, collaborative problem-solving methods such as class meetings and circle time, peer tutoring, assigning a variety of classroom roles, and structuring class time to increase occasions for interaction. Teachers saw students without disabilities as assistants in their efforts to increase the inclusion of students with disabilities. The teachers allowed students to make some decisions independently and valued their students' insights, especially those gained from prior experiences with disabled peers.

In another qualitative study in an elementary school, Sapon-Shevin and her colleagues documented the effectiveness of teachers' rule making in creating classes in which all students are accepted and perceived as belonging (Sapon-Shevin, Dobbelaere, Corrigan, Goodman, & Mastin, 1998). Four teachers agreed to introduce Vivian Paley's (1992) rule "You can't say you can't play" in their classrooms. The teachers taught grades K, 1, 2, and 4 and were identified within the school as supportive of full inclusion. Although the teachers faced obstacles and some resistance in their efforts to implement the rule, eventually all experienced positive results. The team noted that the rule helped to create a dialogue about inclusion issues and in organizing their classrooms. Over an 18-month period, the collaborative research team also found that the rule began to permeate the whole school. Upper-grade teachers were assisted in its implementation by students who had already been in "You can't say" classrooms. The team noted, however, that posting the rule was not in itself a sufficient way of altering student behavior. To achieve the goal, teachers needed to make the rule an integral component of the teaching, learning, and social activities in their classrooms. Furthermore, the presence of the rule did not ensure the full participation of students with disabilities. They could not be excluded if they asked to participate, but the rule did not require them to ask or be asked by their classmates. However, the researchers concluded that the small experiment provides hope that teachers who mandate and support acceptance in their classrooms can make inroads into changing policies and practices of exclusion.

A third, more quantitative, study explored the power of two teacher-directed strategies in a preschool setting (Frea, Craig-Unkefer, Odom, & Johnson, 1999). Teachers implemented structured social interactions in which they created learning situations by choosing the participants, conducting the activity, and suggesting ways to participate successfully. In addition, they introduced Group Friendship Activities in which students participate in finger-play, songs, and games and in the process focus on a student who is not socially accepted and engage in positive affectionate behavior (such as hugging, tickling, and hand-holding) with him or her.

The researchers focused on two children, one with aggressive behavior and the other with a developmental language disorder. Results indicated that both children experienced positive effects on the quality and duration of their social interactions with other children.

These studies support the notion that teacher facilitation is needed to ensure positive social outcomes for children with disabilities in inclusive settings, but that the interventions used need not focus exclusively on the classified student or students. Rather, establishing a routine, expectation, and context for interaction among all students in the class appears to be beneficial.

Peer-Mediated Strategies. Fuchs, Fuchs, Mathes, and Martinez (2002) studied a peer-tutoring program, the PALS (Peer-Assisted Learning Strategies), a highly structured same-age tutoring program in which students have extensive one-to-one interaction with a partner. The study was designed to determine whether acceptance and belonging were collateral benefits of a program designed primarily to increase the academic achievement of students with learning disabilities. They found that students with disabilities in classrooms where PALS was in place had greater social acceptance than similar students in classes without PALS. In addition, the social standing of students with disabilities in PALS classes was similar to that of their nondisabled peers. Although the authors caution that the study is not conclusive due to lack of a pretest demonstrating levels of social acceptance prior to the intervention, they suggest that findings indicate that PALS and other peer-tutoring programs help children with learning disabilities achieve greater social acceptance. They attribute the outcomes to improved academic performance and changes in other students' attitudes as a result of working together with a classmate with disabilities.

Another structured program of peer support, Peer Buddies, was examined by Copeland and her colleagues (Copeland et al., 2002b). The program partners a nondisabled high school student with a peer with disabilities for at least one period each day. The Buddies support their partners in their efforts to be included in general education classes and extracurricular activities in a variety of ways, such as accompanying them to assemblies, sitting with them in the cafeteria, and introducing them to other students without disabilities. The study found that teachers believed that the Peer Buddies program created positive relationships between peers with and without disabilities. The experience increased the self-confidence and independence of students with disabilities. They also became more willing and able to participate in high school activities.

A third study determined how peer support networks might affect the acceptance and participation of students with autism in inclusive classrooms (Garrison-Harrell, Kamps, & Dravis, 1997). The researchers found that by allowing five trained nondisabled peers to participate with a student with autism in group activities for three or four days per week, the students with autism increased their interaction time with peers. In addition, anecdotal reports from educators and parents indicated that the students without disabilities became more accepting of their classmates with autism as indicated by playful behavior within school and increased socialization outside of school.

One common feature of these studies that should be noted is that all students with disabilities were paired with peers who had received training with regard to the support they would be providing. As the research on peer-assisted instructional strategies indicated, such preparation appears to be a key factor in the successful implementation of strategies that depend on other classmates.

Self-Directed Strategies. Only one study that focused on social outcomes of using self-directed strategies in inclusive classrooms was identified. Falk, Dunlap, and Kern (1996) assessed the usefulness of self-evaluation and videotape feedback as a tool for improving the peer interactions of ten students with emotional disorders who were in sixth through eighth multigraded inclusive classrooms. They worked with 18 children, four who exhibited internalizing behavior problems and six who had externalizing behavior problems in inclusive settings. The remaining eight children had no identified behavioral difficulties. The use of videotaping and review of the tapes by the children, in combination with a system of tangible rewards, produced the following effects. Students with externalizing behavior problems experienced a decrease in inappropriate interactions with classmates and most of them increased appropriate behaviors. Students with internalizing behaviors increased the number of their appropriate interactions with other students. By the end of the study participants had rates of appropriate and inappropriate peer interactions that were similar to classmates who had not been identified as having behavioral difficulties.

In summary, the teacher actions that appear to be effective in promoting acceptance in inclusive classrooms are those that instill a culture of belonging facilitated by rules, peer support, opportunities for interactions, and self-reflection.

Strategies That Promote Positive Behavior

Teacher-Directed Strategies. A recently conducted observational study highlights the importance of teachers' management practices for the behavior of students with disabilities in inclusive settings (Beyda, Zentall, & Ferko, 2002). In this study, multiple observations were conducted in eight middle school classes across five different schools, with the focus being on a student with behavioral disorders (BD) and a student with average behavior in each class. Teacher practices and activity settings (independent seat work, teacher-, and student-directed learning activities) had a greater effect on students with BD than on the behavior of students without BD. Specific teacher practices (i.e., use of cooperative tasks, positive verbal responses, offering students choices, and clear directives and feedback) were associated with higher rates of task-appropriate behavior and lower rates of negative behavior for students with BD.

Other research on teacher practices provides some support for offering students choice about their activities. The undesirable behavior of a second-grader with attention deficit hyperactivity disorder was decreased when he was given assignment choices (Powell & Nelson, 1997). Less consistent findings were reported in a study of choices offered to three elementary students who were at risk for emotional disturbance (Coniglio, 2000). In this study, the choice of higher preference tasks was associated with favorable changes in academic engagement and inappropriate behavior for a one child; for a second child the choice of a lower preference task led to a decrease in inappropriate behavior. The authors suggest that the effects of choice may be highly idiosyncratic.

Beyda et al. (2002) also found that certain activity settings normalized the behavior of students with BD. Whereas group differences were noted during teacher-directed activities, no differences in behavior among students with and without disabilities were noted in settings in which student- or self-directed learning was involved. Findings of this study suggest that students with BD may be more vulnerable to teachers' management practices and instructional arrangements than are their nondisabled peers and that students with BD may be best served by being given a greater role in their own instruction.

A few studies have been conducted that demonstrate that teachers can teach students with disabilities specific behavioral skills they need to interact and learn in inclusive settings. Two studies were conducted in early childhood settings. The first study indicated that teachers were able to facilitate student engagement using prompts, modeling, and reinforcement during ongoing play activities in natural contexts (Malmskog & McDonnell, 1999). In the second study, students were taught to make successful transitions to new activities by pairing transitions with high probability request sequences (i.e., a series of requests beginning with those that typically yield a positive response) and preferred items as distracters (Davis, Reichle, & Southard,

2000). Behaviors necessary for learning have also been taught to older students in inclusive settings. Alber, Heward, and Hippler (1999) taught four middle school students with learning disabilities to recruit positive teacher attention while they worked on academic assignments in two inclusive general education classrooms. As a result, these students experienced an increase in teacher praise, instructional feedback, and accuracy in completing assignments.

One of the most promising recent advances in approaches addressing students' challenging behaviors is positive behavioral supports. This strategy is discussed further in chapter 31 of this text. Positive behavioral supports (PBS), which are required for students with disabilities and those at risk for special education placement (Individuals with Disabilities, Education Act [IDEA], 1997), involve a set of procedures aimed at understanding the function of a student's problem behaviors and the factors that maintain the behaviors, and based on this understanding, developing an intervention package to effect change (Horner & Carr, 1997). The process of coming to an understanding of the problem behavior is known as a functional behavioral assessment (FBA). There is some evidence to suggest that students in general education may benefit from positive behavioral supports. Studies of school-wide efforts at PBS indicate decreases in disciplinary referrals (Lewis, Sugai, & Colvin, 1998; Taylor-Green et al., 1997). In addition, Lewis & Sugai (1996) showed how the successful use of PBS in a general education setting benefited a student with behavioral disorders. Umbreit (1995) had similar success with a five-year-old boy with mental retardation. The student's disruptive behavior was nearly eliminated in a relatively short time through an intervention that was based on an FBA conducted by the regular teaching staff and the special education teacher. The intervention included four elements: (1) assigning tasks at an appropriate difficulty level, (2) providing task assistance with these tasks, (3) teaching the student to request assistance, and (4) teaching the student to request a break from assigned work.

A study that combined PBS and person-centered planning (a process that actively involves the student in goal setting and implementation), demonstrated positive effects for the two students at risk for more restrictive placement for whom the PBS plans were fully implemented (Kennedy et al., 2001). Specifically, the researchers reported that problem behaviors were reduced, general education participation was maintained or increased, and general education teachers were able to carry out the plans without assistance or support.

Another approach to supporting students' positive behavior provides indirect services to students in inclusive classrooms by offering consultation to classroom teachers in the use of strategies to affect change. The focus of research in this area has been on the importance of follow-up to general education teachers in the implementation of strategies designed to facilitate the inclusion of students with behavioral disorders into their classes (Noell, Duhon, Gatti, & Connell, 2002; Shapiro, Miller, Sawka, Gardill, & Handler, 1999). In these studies, general education teachers sustained implementation of the behavioral strategies introduced during consultation only when ongoing support (e.g., performance feedback) was provided.

Peer-Mediated Strategies. The most extensively researched techniques for supporting positive behavior of students with disabilities in inclusive classrooms are peer-mediated strategies. Positive results have been demonstrated for students with mild to severe disabilities across educational settings from preschool to high school.

Although peer-mediated strategies, such as peer tutoring and cooperative learning groups, are used as academic interventions, they often have behavioral outcomes. Peer-mediated strategies increased students' time on task and academic engagement (Cushing & Kennedy, 1997; Kamps et al., 1995; King-Sears & Bradley, 1995; Mortweet et al., 1999; Palincsar & Klenk, 1992; Spencer, Scruggs, & Mastropieri, 2003). In these studies, peer-mediated strategies also minimized young people's opportunities to engage in off-task, competing, and inappropriate behaviors. In addition, peer-mediated instructional strategies increased the opportunity for student self-determination and independent action (Blum, Lipsett, & and Yocom, 2002; Staub et al., 1996). These outcomes also seemed to be linked to decreased student frustration and concomitant decreases in classroom management difficulties (Kamps et al., 1995; Staub et al., 1996). In addition, peer-mediated strategies increased socialization and communication among disabled and nondisabled students (Goldstein & Thiemann, 2000; Kamps et al., 1995; Palincsar & Klenk, 1992). Seemingly as a result of these interactions, students with disabilities more clearly observed and imitated peer behavior and decreased inappropriate behaviors (Arceneaux & Murdock, 1997; Staub et al., 1996).

Students without disabilities also seem to benefit from the use of peer-mediated strategies. Nondisabled students have an opportunity to increase their social network to include students with disabilities with whom they might otherwise not become acquainted (Dugan et al., 1995; Hunt et al., 1994). An increase in respect and appreciation for their peers with disabilities and a greater sense of their own feelings of responsibility and accomplishment can result in fewer disruptive incidents on the part of students without disabilities (Kennedy & Itkonen, 1995; Staub et al., 1996). In addition, students without disabilities who participate as peer tutors or in cooperative learning groups with disabled peers may experience improvements in their own academic engagement and achievement (Cushing & Kennedy, 1997). Furthermore, successful participation in peer-mediated learning situations appears to increase the acceptance of students with disabilities by teachers (Jenkins, Antil, Wayne, & Vadasy, 2003; Mortweet et al., 1999; Fuchs et al., 2002) and increase time nondisabled peer tutors spend with adults (Cushing & Kennedy, 1997; Kennedy & Itkonen, 1994). Both of these effects may decrease students' motivation to engage in inappropriate and off-task behaviors.

Self-Directed Strategies. Self-directed strategies include practices that aim to teach students to take action to change their own behavior. Emerging from a behavioral paradigm, self-management practices typically involve teaching students to engage in self-monitoring, self-instruction, and self-reinforcement. A 1998 review of research on the use of self-management techniques yielded 14 studies demonstrating strong to moderate evidence of the efficacy of self-management in enhancing social and academic performance of students with disabilities in general education classes (McDougall, 1998). Participants in these studies included students with learning disabilities, behavioral disorders, and attention deficits. The vast majority of the studies in this review involved fewer than three students.

Additional research has shown that self-management techniques can be used to promote positive behavior in students with varying disabilities and, with focused instruction, across multiple settings. In a study by duPaul and Hoff (1998), students with either attention deficit hyperactive disorder or oppositional deviant disorder learned to effectively self-manage their behavior in structured and unstructured settings, but did not spontaneously generalize their learning to new settings. In an evaluation study involving 29 students participating in a program aimed at reducing antisocial behavior of at-risk middle school students, Peterson, Young, West, and Peterson (1999) investigated the efficacy of a self-management process specifically designed to enhance generalization across settings. Teacher reports indicated that student behavior improved in up to six different classroom settings.

Self-monitoring strategies have also been shown to have positive effects on the behavior of students with significant disabilities in inclusive settings (Gilberts, Agran, Hughes, & Wehmeyer, 2001). In this study, five students with significant disabilities in inclusive middle school classes were taught by peer tutors to self-monitor 11 classroom survival skills (e.g., pay attention to teacher when she or he talks to you, answer questions). Four of the five students with disabilities showed gains in the classroom survival skills and all indicated that they felt they were part of the class.

These studies suggest that students with disabilities and those at risk of referral to special education can be taught to monitor their own behavior in inclusive settings, although they may not spontaneously generalize their learning to new settings. Furthermore, these studies provide preliminary evidence that teachers as well as students appreciate the effects of the self-monitoring on student behavior.

Personnel Arrangements

Advocates of inclusion have argued that inclusion can provide an opportunity to use a school's resources to provide individualized and effective instruction for all students. A variety of ways of using teachers and teaching assistants have emerged to do so. These "delivery systems" include classrooms that are characterized by collaboration between general and special educators and paraprofessionals in various combinations. The research on the effectiveness of these arrangements is at an early stage.

Co-Teaching. Co-teaching is a model of providing instruction to students in inclusive classrooms that is characterized by cooperation between two teachers—one certified in general education, the other certified in special education. The educators are both responsible for planning instruction, teaching and facilitating learning activities, and assessing their own effectiveness as well as student progress. This method is in contrast to the consultation model of providing support for students with disabilities. In the consultation model, general and special educators may work cooperatively but the special educator only suggests instructional design modifications. He or she does not, in general, implement instruction in the inclusive classroom. Proponents of co-teaching argue that this model allows special educators to bring their expertise to bear on the instructional design process in ways that the consultation model does not. Ultimately, the collaboration between the educators is expected to increase the academic achievement of students with disabilities and students without disabilities in inclusive classrooms. In addition, co-teaching is seen as preferable because it limits the "pull-out" time from the classroom for students with disabilities and would therefore be likely to decrease isolation and stigmatization of such students. Research has just begun to test these hypotheses.

Early studies found that, in elementary schools, co-teaching was at least as academically effective as instruction provided through a resource room model (Bear & Proctor, 1990; Schulte, Osborne, & McKinney, 1990). More recently, Boudah and his colleagues found that high school students with learning disabilities experienced decreases in their scores on content tests and quizzes in co-taught classrooms (Boudah, Schumacker, & Deshler, 1997). In a meta-analysis of six studies of students with learning disabilities or mild disabilities, Murawski and Swanson (2001) found that co-teaching was moderately effective in improving academic outcomes and had very little effect on social outcomes. One study of inclusive settings that used co-teaching arrangements linked this collaborative practice to a decrease in the number of disciplinary referrals for students with disabilities in a rural K–8 county school (Krank, Moon, & Render, 2002).

Characteristics of co-teaching environments that appear to be effective include a positive classroom climate, a shared positive perception of co-teaching by all members, activity-based instruction, high expectations for behavior and academic performance, and a commitment to planning time (Dieker, 2001). Several studies suggest that the effectiveness of co-teaching may be limited by the difficulties in developing these characteristics (Boudah et al., 1997; Weiss & Lloyd, 2002). According to the findings of these studies, general and special educators too often are required to participate in co-teaching in the absence of needed supports, such as training, planning, and reflection time.

Participation of Paraprofessionals

In addition to the use of two certified teachers in inclusive classrooms, service delivery models in these classrooms often involve the use of paraprofessionals. This practice is steadily increasing. The small body of research that has emerged on this management practice has identified a number of areas in which further study is warranted. These include determining which students most benefit from the assistance of paraprofessionals, establishing hiring criteria for paraprofessionals, defining the most effective arrangements for relationships between students and paraprofessionals, and determining the kind of initial and continuing training paraprofessionals need to be effective (Giangreco, Broer, & Edelman, 2002; Giangreco & Doyle, 2002).

Presently, no experimental data are available to inform administrators as they attempt to decide which students in an inclusive classroom will most benefit from the assistance of a paraprofessional (Giangreco, Broer, & Edelman, 1999). Some data indicate that current criteria with regard to the academic backgrounds of paraprofessionals are not an adequate match for the instructional tasks that they are being asked to perform (Marks, Schrader, & Levine, 1999). However, the ongoing negotiation of paraprofessionals' roles in inclusive settings is uninformed by data that identify the academic preparation that would better enable them to meet the needs of the students whom they serve.

Research on the impact of the relationship between paraprofessionals and students in inclusive classes has begun to emerge. Paraprofessionals are often identified by the way they interact with students. "Program" paraprofessionals are those who are assigned to assist students in a classroom or program in general. "One-on-one" paraprofessionals are those who are assigned to assist only one designated student. Observational studies on the effectiveness of these arrangements have focused on the proximity of the assistant to a particular student. In general, one-on-one paraprofessionals tend to remain in close proximity to their student. This arrangement, which may be deemed necessary because of the nature of a student's disability, appears to have some negative consequences on the young person's full inclusion and personal development (Giangreco, Edelman, Luiselli, & MacFarland, 1997; Marks et al., 1999; Giangreco, Broer, & Edelman, 2001). These effects include a loss of engagement between the general educator and the student and a consequent interference with the general educator's ability to develop a sense of responsibility for the student with disabilities and the student's ability to receive instruction from a certified teacher. In addition, the close proximity of the paraprofessional can lead to a separation of the student from his or her peers resulting in fewer interactions with classmates; a greater dependence on relationships with adults, especially the paraprofessional; a loss of the student's ability to control his or her own activities; increased stigmatization of the student with disabilities; and some interference with other students' instruction. However, one study indicates that the close proximity of a paraprofessional can increase the intervals of academic engagement for students with significant disabilities (Werts, Zigmond, & Leeper, 2001). Although the use of paraprofessional support has not been limited to students with significant disabilities, research involving students with other disabilities (e.g., behavior disorders) has not been conducted.

SUMMARY AND ANALYSIS OF THE RESEARCH

Major Themes

Classroom management practices are defined as the actions teachers take to create an environment that supports and facilitates both academic and social-emotional learning. In this chapter we have reviewed research on management practices in inclusive classrooms. The following general conclusions emerge from this literature review:

1. Teachers play a vital role in establishing classroom climates in which all students can be successful. They do so in several ways:
   a. They promote academic achievement by using instructional strategies such as inquiry and hands-on activities, peer tutoring, and designing authentic assessment tasks.
   b. They promote acceptance and friendship by modeling acceptance, establishing classroom "rules" that emphasize belonging, establishing peer support programs and group activities that foster acceptance and friendship, and providing students with feedback about and opportunities to self-critique their interactions with others.
   c. They promote positive behavior among students by providing positive verbal responses and supports, training students in self-monitoring techniques, offering students choices about activities, facilitating peer-mediated and self-directed learning opportunities, and using functional behavioral assessments and positive behavioral supports.
2. Several factors limit the potency of such practices to create inclusive classrooms in which all students experience success and belonging. These include:
   a. Absence of institutional commitment on the part of schools and districts to provide teachers with ongoing supports, including training and time for planning and reflection.
   b. Lack of teacher commitment to and competency in providing instruction, monitoring, and support of students who are acting as peer aides or tutors.
   c. Ineffective personnel arrangements such as using paraprofessionals in too-close proximity to students with disabilities and special education teachers in consultative versus co-teaching roles.

Overall, the research reflects a trend toward the study of classroom practices rather than strategies to "remediate" or "fix" the individual with a disability. The emphasis placed on restructuring environments is particularly evident when social or behavioral outcomes are desired. The practices that have been investigated seek to create classrooms in which all students have greater access to the general education curriculum.

Analysis of the Research

The major themes extracted from research on instructional strategies and teaching arrangements that promote positive outcomes for students with disabilities in inclusive classrooms should be seen as tentative conclusions that require further study. Researchers, practitioners, and policy makers agree that the current research base falls short of what is needed to guide practitioners in the selection of empirically supported practices to support learners in inclusive classrooms (Salend & Duhaney; 1999; Zigmond, 2003). The most pressing issue in the current knowledge base lies in the limited number of studies conducted to date. With the exception of peer-mediated strategies, few techniques have been explored extensively in inclusive settings. In the present review, no more than five research studies were identified that explored any one strategy in inclusive settings.

There are also a number of methodological constraints in the existing research that need to be considered. First, the methodologies used in the research reviewed in this chapter were predominantly quasi- or nonexperimental; thus, the validity of the findings is limited by the inability of researchers to randomly assign students to placements or interventions. Most studies in which comparisons were made contrasted the performance of students in groups that existed prior to the research, and preexisting differences were not always considered in the data analysis or discussion of findings.

A second methodological limitation pertains to the number of participants that were included in the vast majority of the studies. This is particularly evident, and expected, in studies involving students with significant disabilities or other disabilities with a low rate of occurrence. Although understandable, it is difficult to generalize findings based on research with few participants.

The third issue in the research reviewed pertains to the extent to which the researchers provided adequate descriptions of their methodologies, particularly in reference to the settings and interventions that were investigated. It is often unclear as to what served as the basis for distinguishing between inclusive classrooms and more restrictive settings. To understand how inclusion is being defined and operationalized, information should minimally be provided about the number of students with disabilities relative to the total number of students in the class and the amount of time students with disabilities spend in the general education class. In addition, personnel arrangements and student supports should be indicated, even when they are not the focus of study. Given the complexity of classroom environments, it is important to understand the context under which specific methodologies are effective. Equally compelling is the need for researchers to explain the intervention they are investigating so that others may replicate their findings. Interestingly, it was not uncommon for researchers to label rather than describe their intervention, particularly in research on intervention programs that are available commercially.

FACTORS AFFECTING IMPLEMENTATION OF EFFECTIVE PRACTICES

Despite limitations in the research on instruction and management of inclusive classrooms, we are beginning to develop an understanding about how teachers can affect positive outcomes for students in inclusive classrooms. Because the significance of the research is in large part determined by how it is used to inform practice, it is troubling to learn that teachers do not necessarily use strategies they know to be effective in these settings (Scott, Vitale, & Masten, 1998). For example, middle school teachers reported that they were not likely to use a number of strategies they knew to be effective, such as instruction in self-directed learning strategies (deBettencourt, 1999), and observations of instruction in classes with students with learning disabilities have found instruction to be largely undifferentiated (Baker & Zigmond, 1995). In this section we review research that explores factors that impact teachers' use of effective strategies in inclusive classrooms.

The question of whether general educators consider implementation of instruction and management strategies in inclusive settings to be effective and usable was explored in a review of research conducted by Scott et al. (1998). Their analysis led them to conclude that general educators tend to be positive in their ratings of the desirability, effectiveness, and feasibility of making accommodations. However, in one study effectiveness was rated higher than ease of implementation (Whinnery, Fuchs, & Fuchs, 1991). Perhaps most importantly, adaptations benefiting the whole class were considered to be more feasible to implement than were strategies directed at an individual student (Ellett, 1993; Gajria, Salend, & Hemrick, 1994; Vaughn, Schumm, Jallad, Slusher, & Saumell, 1996).

Implementation of effective strategies to promote learning in inclusive classes may be enhanced by increased collaboration between researchers and practitioners (Meyer, Park, Grenot-Scheyer, Schwartz, & Harry, 1998). One such approach that has been gaining interest in educational research is participatory action research, in which researchers develop partnerships with teachers, parents, and other stakeholders to conduct meaningful research in real contexts.

Collaboration between researchers and practitioners throughout the research process increases the likelihood that relevant questions are addressed, results are meaningfully interpreted, and implementation occurs and sustains (Park, Gonsier-Gerdin, Hoffman, Whaley, & Yount, 1998; Salisbury, Wilson, & Palombaro, 1998).

Teacher Attitudes. Researchers have suggested that contextual factors, particularly teachers' attitudes and beliefs, contribute to their use of effective strategies to accommodate students with disabilities in their classrooms (Hasazi, Johnston, Liggett, & Schattman, 1994; Salend & Duhaney, 1999; Schmidt, Rozendal, & Reenman, 2002; Soodak, Podell, & Lehman, 1998). Studies of teacher attitudes indicate that teachers are generally supportive of inclusive education (Villa, Thousand, Meyers, & Nevin, 1996; York, Vandercook, MacDonald, Heise-Neff, & Caughey, 1992). However, research also indicates that teachers are skeptical about whether they can effectively educate all students in general education settings (Coates, 1989; Semmel, Abernathy, Butera, & Lesar, 1991). Teachers in these studies consistently cited the need for additional training, personnel, consultation, and administrative support. Teachers have also expressed concern as to whether the time and attention needed for effective instruction of students with significant disabilities would be provided at the expense of other students in their classes (Downing, Eichinger, & Williams, 1997). Interestingly, experience in inclusive settings appears to facilitate change in teacher confidence (Giangreco, Dennis, Clonginger, Edelman, & Schattman, 1993; McLeskey & Waldron, 2002). Interviews conducted by Giangreco and his colleagues revealed that, over time, teachers felt greater ownership of students and increased confidence in their ability to teach students with disabilities (Giangreco et al., 1993).

Teacher Efficacy. Teachers' willingness to include students with disabilities and to implement strategies to improve outcomes for these students is known to relate to an additional teacher attribute that warrants attention: teacher efficacy. Teacher efficacy refers to the teachers' beliefs in their own ability to bring about desired outcomes in their students (Gibson & Dembo, 1984). Two studies have linked general educators' sense of efficacy to their willingness and ability to teach students with disabilities. The first study found that the relation between teachers' use of instructional practices and their receptivity to inclusion was mediated by their efficacy beliefs (Soodak et al., 1998). Specifically, teachers with low efficacy were less likely to use differentiated teaching practices than were teachers with a high sense of efficacy; furthermore, highly efficacious teachers who used differentiated teaching strategies were most likely to be receptive to inclusion. In addition, opportunities to collaborate with others were found to mediate the relationship between teacher efficacy and teachers' receptivity to inclusion. In a second study, highly efficacious teachers, that is, those who perceived their efforts to teach students with disabilities to be successful, were teachers who received support from special educators and building administrators and who had experienced quality preservice and inservice training (Brownell & Pajares, 1999). In addition, the effects of inservice training and support on teachers' sense of efficacy were mediated by teachers' perceptions of their professional collegiality.

Thus, research on teacher attitudes and on sense of efficacy suggest that teachers' confidence in their ability to affect change influence both their willingness to include students with disabilities in their classes and, most importantly, their use of strategies to effectively manage instruction in these classrooms. This research also suggests that teachers are more likely to modify their management practices when they perceive the strategy to be beneficial to all students and when they are supported through opportunities for collaboration with colleagues and professional training. (See chapter 8 in this *Handbook* for further discussion of teachers' efficacy beliefs and their relation to classroom practices.)

ISSUES AND FUTURE DIRECTIONS IN THE STUDY OF INCLUSIVE MANAGEMENT PRACTICES

Research on inclusive management practices represents a small but growing body of work that basically supports the contention that inclusive classrooms can be managed to bring about positive outcomes for all students. Although not many of the strategies investigated yet qualify as research-based interventions, collectively they suggest that effective instruction in inclusive classrooms is similar to effective instruction in traditionally segregated settings. Furthermore, inclusive instruction needs to occur within an environment that actively promotes acceptance and engagement and needs to be provided by teachers who are confident, educated, and supported. However, it is equally important to understand what the research does not tell us.

There are a number of issues that have not been given sufficient attention in the research on inclusive classrooms, many of which require that the discussion of inclusive education occur within the context of the broader social and political conditions affecting schools. For the purposes of this chapter, four issues are next discussed: (1) the changing view of disability in educational research, (2) the relationship of inclusion to other educational reforms, (3) the challenges associated with educating students with behavioral disorders in inclusive settings, and (4) the importance of family partnerships and the implications of cultural influences on management practices in inclusive classrooms.

Changing View of Disability

Although research on instructional practices in inclusive settings highlights the role of environmental factors in student outcomes, the view of disability as a deficit-driven phenomenon persists in the larger body of research in special education (Skrtic, 1995; Sleeter, 1985). The majority of research involving students with disabilities reflects the traditionally held view of disability as a single, defining attribute that is assumed to be due to a deficit in the individual's character, genes, or motivation. In contrast to the understanding of disability emerging from research in inclusive settings, this notion of disability holds the individual responsible for his or her own educational outcomes, and does little to consider the role of schools or teachers in determining students' performance (Deschenes, Cuban, & Tyack, 2001). This approach to the understanding of disability may be antithetical to the study of inclusive education, which assumes that students' failure to learn is best addressed by having schools better adapt to the child. By perpetuating the deficit-based notion of disability we run the risk of limiting the study of management practices to actions that affect individuals rather than those that modify environments and systems.

An additional problem with the prevailing notion of disability is that it is unidimensional; that is, an individual's disability "status" is considered in isolation of other personal attributes. The use of this view of disability in research on inclusive education potentially masks the role of other significant attributes, such as race, ethnicity, and socioeconomic status, which are likely to affect the individual's success in mainstream classrooms. Despite overwhelming evidence of the overrepresentation of minorities in special education (Trent & Artiles, 1994; U.S. Department of Education, 2002) and a wealth of data demonstrating differential outcomes for students based on race and class (Grant & Sleeter, 1986; Harry, 1992; Oakes & Lipton, 1999) research has failed to investigate whether a student's background affects his or her acceptance, learning, or behavior in inclusive environments.

Inclusion and Reform

A second issue affecting research on classroom management in inclusive settings is the need to consider the simultaneous implementation of multiple school reform efforts. The move to educate students with disabilities in general education classrooms is but one of a number of critical reform efforts affecting schools; equally important to teachers and students are efforts to raise academic standards (e.g., No Child Left Behind Act) and to ensure school safety (e.g., zero tolerance policies). Mandates to raise standards and enhance discipline may be in conflict with the goals of inclusive education that seek to acknowledge individual differences and avoid exclusionary interventions. The standards movement as defined by NCLB provides strict guidelines for creating and assessing academic standards and imposes strict penalties on schools that do not meet these standards. There has been much dialogue as to how standards-based reforms might impact the inclusion of children with disabilities (e.g., Lipsky & Gartner, 1997; McDonnell, McLaughlin, & Morison, 1997); however, there is as of now no evidence as to what actually occurs in inclusive classrooms in light of the present emphasis on accountability.

There is also a need for further study of the intersection of the inclusion movement and the current trend in using exclusionary discipline policies as a means of ensuring safe schools. Specifically, how do administrators and teachers meet the needs of students with disabilities in typical classroom settings given that the coexisting goal "may well be the removal of troublesome students from mainstream educational environments" (Skiba & Peterson, 2000, p. 340)? Perhaps even more compelling is the need to understand how schools implement policies in which students with disabilities may not be held to the same disciplinary standards and consequences as their nondisabled classmates due to protections provided to students with disabilities under IDEA.

Challenges in Inclusive Settings

A third area in need of study pertains specifically to enhancing the effective inclusion of students with behavioral disabilities. This need is underscored by evidence indicating that students with behavioral disabilities are less likely to be educated in general education classes (U.S. Department of Education, 2002) and are more likely to be removed from inclusive settings than students with other disabilities (Lewis, Chard, & Scott, 1994). In addition, students with emotional and behavioral problems have been consistently overrepresented in reports of suspensions and expulsions (Civil Rights Project at Harvard University, June, 2000; Cooley, 1995). It may well be that the failure to effectively include students identified with behavioral disorders is related to the issues just noted (i.e., the current emphasis on standards and discipline, the tendency to attribute failure to the individual, and the failure to recognize the role of student background in the outcomes of students with disabilities). The behavior of students with behavior disabilities will likely have a greater impact on classroom climate, organization, and learning than other students with disabilities in inclusive settings. Future research needs to consider the effects of specific school-wide management practices (e.g., positive behavior supports) on students with challenging behaviors within the context of the broader social inequities that are likely to contribute to the outcomes students with disabilities experience in inclusive settings.

Family Partnerships

The fourth area in need of study involves the participation of families in the management of inclusive classrooms. The importance of families in identifying appropriate and culturally responsive management practices has been highlighted in other chapters within this *Handbook* (e.g., see chapters 13 and 25). In addition, a growing body of research involving students with disabilities indicates that developing meaningful family-professional partnerships enhances the likelihood that instructional goals and strategies are consistent with the family's preferences and values and that interventions yield important outcomes for children and their families (Turnbull,

Turnbull, Erwin, & Soodak, 2006). The role of family partnerships and the implications of cultural influences have not been explored in relation to classroom management in inclusive settings.

Thus, research to date has moved the discussion of inclusive education beyond advocacy to efficacy. Research informs us that placement alone is insufficient for success; teachers must actively seek to use practices and create environments that foster learning and promote positive interactions among students. We also know that how teachers manage their inclusive classrooms is shaped in part by the way inclusion and other reforms are perceived and addressed within the school as well as teachers' perspectives on their own ability to affect change. As research moves forward, we must be mindful of the challenges to successful inclusive education and the complex nature of the contexts being explored.

ACKNOWLEDGMENT

The authors wish to thank Elizabeth J. Erwin for her insightful review of this chapter.

REFERENCES

Affleck, J. Q., Madge, S., Adams, A., & Lowenbraun, S. (1988). Integrated classroom vs. resource model: Academic viability and effectiveness. *Exceptional Children, 54,* 349–358.

Agran, M., Blanchard, C., Wehmeyer, M., & Hughes, C. (2001). Teaching students to self-regulate their behavior: The differential effects of students- vs. teacher-delivered reinforcement. *Research in Developmental Disabilities, 22*(4), 319–332.

Alber, S. R., Heward, W. L., & Hippler, B. J. (1999). Teaching middle school students with learning disabilities to recruit positive teacher attention. *Exceptional Children, 65*(2), 253–270.

Allsopp, D. H. (1997). Using classwide peer tutoring to teach beginning algebra problem-solving skills in heterogeneous classrooms. *Remedial and Special Education, 18*(6), 367–379.

Antil, L. R., Jenkins, J. R., Wayne, S. K., & Vadasy, P. F. (1998). Cooperative learning: Prevalence, conceptualizations, and the relation between research and practice. *American Educational Research Journal, 35,* 419–454.

Arceneaux, M. C., & Murdock, J. Y. (1997). Peer prompting reduces disruptive vocalizations of student with developmental disabilities in a general eighth-grade classroom. *Focus on Autism and Other Developmental Disabilities, 12*(3), 182–186.

Baker, E. T., Wang, M., & Walberg, H. J. (1995). The effects of inclusion on learning. *Educational Leadership,* December/January, 33–35.

Baker, J. M., & Zigmond, N. (1995). The meaning and practice of inclusion for students with learning disabilities: Themes and implications from five cases. *Journal of Special Education, 29,* 163–180.

Bear, G. G., & Proctor, W. A. (1990). Impact of a full-time integrated program on the achievement of nonhandicapped and mildly handicapped children. *Exceptionality: A Research Journal, 1*(4), 227–238.

Beyda, S. D., Zentall, S. S., & Ferko, D. J. K. (2002). The relationship between teacher practices and the task-appropriate and social behavior of students with behavioral disorders. *Behavioral Disorders, 27*(3), 236–255.

Blum, H. T., Lipsett, L. R., & Yocom, D. J. (2002). Literature circles: A tool for self-determination in one middle school inclusive classroom. *Remedial and Special Education, 23*(2), 99–108.

Bottge, B. A., Heinrichs, M., Mehta, Z. D., & Hung, Y. (2002). Weighing the benefits of anchored math instruction for students with disabilities in general education classes. *Journal of Special Education, 35*(4), 186–201.

Boudah, D., Schumacker, J. B., & Deshler, D. D. (1997). Collaborative instruction: Is it an effective option for inclusion in secondary classrooms? *Learning Disability Quarterly, 20*(4), 293–316.

Bricker, D. (1995). The challenge of inclusion. *Journal of Early Intervention, 19*(3), 179–194.

Brophy, J. E., & Good, T. L. (1986). Teacher behavior and student achievement. In M. C. Wittrock (Ed.), *Handbook of research and teaching* (pp. 328–376). New York: Macmillan.

Brownell, M. T., & Pajares, F. (1999). Teacher efficacy and perceived success in mainstreaming students with learning and behavior problems. *Teacher Education and Special Education, 22*(3), 154–164.

Bulgren, J. A., Lenz, B. K., Marquis, J., Schumaker, J. B., & Deshler, D. D. (2002). *The effects of the question exploration routine on student performance in secondary content classrooms* (Research Report). Lawrence, KS: Kansas University, Lawrence Institute for Academic Access.

Buysse, V. (1993). Friendships of preschoolers with disabilities in community-based child care settings. *Journal of Early Intervention, 17*, 380–395.

Buysse, V., Goldman, B. D., & Skinner, M. L. (2002). Setting effects on friendship formation among young children with and without disabilities. *Exceptional Children, 68*(4), 503–517.

Cawley, J., Hayden, S., Cade, E., & Baker-Kroczynski, S. (2002). Including students with disabilities into the general education science classroom. *Exceptional Children, 68*(4), 423–435.

Coates, R. D. (1989). The regular education initiative and opinions of regular classroom teachers. *Journal of Learning Disabilities, 22*, 532–536.

Conigio, J. (2000). *Identification and effects of choice of higher versus lower preference assignments for students at risk for ED.* Paper presented at the annual meeting of the American Psychological Association, Washington, D.C.

Cooley, S. (1995). *Suspension/expulsion of regular and special education students in Kansas: A report to the Kansas State Board of Education.* Topeka, KS: Kansas State Board of Education. (ERIC Document Reproduction Service No. 395403)

Copeland, S. R., Hughes, C., Agran, M., Wehmeyer, M. L., & Fowler, S. E. (2002a). An intervention package to support high school students with mental retardation in general education classrooms. *American Journal on Mental Retardation, 107*(1), 32–45.

Copeland, S., McCall, J., Williams, C. R., Guth, C., Carter, E. W., Presley, J. A., Fowler, S. E., & Hughes, C. (2002b). High school peer buddies: A win-win situation. *Teaching Exceptional Children, 35*(1), 16–21.

Cushing, L. S., & Kennedy, C. H. (1997). Academic effects of providing peer support in general education classrooms on students without disabilities. *Journal of Applied Behavior Analysis, 30*(1), 139–151.

Davis, C. A., Reichle, J. E., & Southard, K. L. (2000). High-probability requests and a preferred item as a distractor: Increasing successful transitions in children with behavior problems. *Education and Treatment of Children, 23*(4), 423–440.

deBettencourt, L. U. (1999). General educators' attitudes toward students with mild disabilities and their use of instructional strategies: Implications for training. *Remedial and Special Education, 20*(1), 27–35.

Deschenes, S., Cuban, L., & Tyack, D. (2001). Mismatch: Historical perspectives on schools and students who don't fit them. *Teachers College Record, 103*(4), 525–547.

Dieker, L. A. (2001). What are the characteristics of "effective" middle and high school co-taught teams for students with disabilities? *Preventing School Failure, 46*(1), 14–24.

Downing, J. E., Eichinger, J., & Williams, L. J. (1997). Inclusive education for students with severe disabilities: Comparative views of principals and educators at different levels of implementation. *Remedial and Special Education, 18*, 133–142.

Dugan, E., Kamps, D., Leonard, B., Watkins, N., Rheinberger, A., & Stackhaus, J. (1995). Effects of cooperative learning groups during social studies for students with autism and fourth-grade peers. *Journal of Applied Behavior Analysis, 28*, 175–188.

DuPaul, G. J., & Hoff, K. E. (1998). Reducing disruptive behavior in general education classrooms: The use of self-management strategies. *School Psychology Review, 27*(2), 290–304.

Ellett, L. (1993). Instructional practices in mainstreamed secondary classrooms. *Journal of Learning Disabilities, 26*, 57–64.

Evans, I. M., Salisbury, C. L., Palombaro, M. M., Berryman, J., & Hollowood, T. M. (1992). Acceptance of elementary aged children with severe disabilities in an inclusive school. *Journal of the Association for Persons with Severe Handicaps, 17*, 205–212.

Falk, G. D., Dunlap, G., & Kern, L. (1996). An analysis of self-evaluation and videotape feedback for improving the peer interactions of students with externalizing and internalizing behavior problems. *Behavioral Disorders, 21*(4), 261–276.

Ferretti, R. P., MacArthur, C. D., & Okolo, C. M. (2001). Teaching for historical understanding in inclusive classrooms. *Learning Disability Quarterly, 24*, 59–71.

Fisher, M., & Meyer, L. H. (2002). Development and social competence after two years for student enrolled in inclusive and self-contained programs. *Journal of the Association for Persons with Severe Handicaps, 27*(3), 165–174.

Frea, W., Craig-Unkefer, L., Odom, S. L., & Johnson, D. (1999). Differential effects of structured social integration and group friendship activities for promoting social interaction with peers. *Journal of Early Intervention, 22*(3), 230–242.

Fryxell, D., & Kennedy, C. H. (1995). Placement along the continuum of services and its impact on students' social relationships. *Journal of the Association for Persons with Severe Handicaps, 20*(4), 259–269.

Fuchs, D., & Fuchs, L. S. (1995a). Acquisition and transfer effects of classwide peer-assisted learning strategies in mathematics for students with varying learning histories. *School Psychology Review, 24*(4), 604–621.

Fuchs, D., & Fuchs, L. S. (1995b). What's "special" about special education? *Phi Delta Kappan, 76*, 522–530.

Fuchs, D., Fuchs, L. S., & Burish, L. S. (2000). Peer-assisted learning strategies: An evidence-based practice to promote reading achievement. *Learning Disabilities Research and Practice, 15*, 85–91.

Fuchs, D., Fuchs, L. S., Mathes, P. G., & Martinez, E. A. (2002). Preliminary evidence on the social standing of students with learning disabilities in PALS and no-PALS classrooms. *Learning Disabilities: Research and Practice, 17*(4), 205–215.

Fuchs, D., Fuchs, L. S., Mathes, P. G., & Simmons, D. C. (1997). Peer-assisted learning strategies: Making classrooms more responsive to diversity. *American Educational Research Journal, 34*, 174–206.

Fuchs, D., Fuchs, L. S., Thompson, A., Svenson, E., Yen, L., Otaiba, S., Yang, N., McMaster, K. N., Prentice, K., Kazden, S., & Saenz, L. (2001). Peer-assisted learning strategies in reading: Extensions for kindergarten, first grade, and high school. *Remedial and Special Education, 22*(1), 15–21.

Gajria, M., Salend, S. J., & Hemrick, M. A. (1994). Teacher acceptability of testing modifications for mainstreamed students. *Learning Disabilities Research and Practice, 9*, 236–243.

Garrison-Harrell, L., Kamps, D., & Dravis, T. (1997). The effects of peer networks on social-communicative behaviors for students with autism. *Focus on Autism and Other Developmental Disabilities, 12*(4), 241–254.

Giangreco, M. F., Broer, S. M., & Edelman, S. W. (1999). The tip of the iceberg: Determining whether paraprofessional support is needed for students with disabilities in general education settings. *Journal of the Association for Persons with Severe Handicaps, 24*(4), 281–291.

Giangreco, M. F., Broer, S. M., & Edelman, S. W. (2001). Teacher engagement with students with disabilities: Differences between paraprofessional service delivery models. *Journal of the Association for Persons with Severe Handicaps, 26*(2), 75–86.

Giangreco, M. F., Broer, S. M., & Edelman, S. W. (2002). "That was then, this is now!" Paraprofessional supports for students with disabilities in general education classrooms. *Exceptionality, 10*(1), 47–64.

Giangreco, M. F., Dennis, R., Clonginger, C., Edelman, S., & Schattman, R. (1993). 'I've counted Jon': Transformational experiences of teachers educating students with disabilities. *Exceptional Children, 59*, 359–372.

Giangreco, M. F., & Doyle, M. B. (2002). Students with disabilities and paraprofessional supports: Benefits, balance, and band-aids. *Focus on Exceptional Children, 34*(7), 1–12.

Giangreco, M. F., Edelman, S. W., Luiselli, T. E., & MacFarland, S. Z. C. (1997). Helping or hovering? Effects of instructional assistant proximity on students with disabilities. *Exceptional Children, 64*(1), 7–18.

Gibson, S., & Dembo, M. (1984). Teacher efficacy: A construct validation. *Journal of Educational Psychology, 76*, 569–592.

Gilberts, G. H., Agran, M., Hughes, C., & Wehmeyer, M. (2001). The effects of peer delivered self-monitoring strategies on the participation of students with severe disabilities in general education classrooms. *Journal of the Association for Persons with Severe Handicaps, 26*(1), 25–36.

Goldstein, H., & Thiemann, K. (2000). *Effects of visually-mediated intervention on the social communication of children with pervasive developmental disorders*. Special Education Programs, Washington, DC. (ERIC Document Reproduction Service No. 416607)

Grant, C. A., & Sleeter, C. E. (1986). *After the school bell rings*. Basingstoke, England: Falmer.

Guralnick, M. J. (1999). The nature and meaning of social integration for young children with mild developmental delays in inclusive settings. *Journal of Early Intervention, 22*, 70–86.

Hall, L. J., & McGregor, J. A. (2000). A follow-up study of the peer relationships of children with disabilities in an inclusive setting. *Journal of Special Education, 34*(3), 114–126.

Harris, C. A., Miller, S. P., & Mercer, C. D. (1995). Teaching initial multiplication skills to students with disabilities in general education classrooms. *Learning Disabilities Research and Practice, 10*(3), 189–195.

Harry, B. (1992). *Cultural diversity, families, and the special education system*. New York: Teachers College Press.

Hasazi, S. B., Johnston, A. P., Liggett, A. M., & Schattman, R. A. (1994). A qualitative policy study of the least restrictive environment provision of the Individuals with Disabilities Education Act. *Exceptional Children, 60*, 491–507.

Holahan, A., & Costenbader, V. (2000). A comparison of developmental gains for preschool children with disabilities in inclusive and self-contained classrooms. *Topics in Early Childhood Special Education, 20*(4), 224–235.

Hollowood, T. M., Salisbury, C. L., Rainforth, B., & Palombaro, M. M. (1994). Use of instructional time in classrooms serving students with and without severe disabilities. *Exceptional Children, 61*, 242–253.

Horn, E., Lieber, J., Sandall, S., Schwartz, I., & Li, S. (2000). Supporting young children's IEP goals in inclusive settings through embedded learning opportunities. *Topics in Early Childhood Special Education, 20*(4), 208–223.

Horner, R. H., & Carr, E. G. (1997). Positive behavioral supports for challenging behavior. *Journal of Special Education, 31*, 98–115.

Huber, K. D., Rosenfeld, J. G., & Fiorello, C. A. (2001). The differential impact of inclusion and inclusive practices on high, average, and low achieving general education students. *Psychology in the Schools, 38*(6), 497–504.

Hughes, C., Copeland, S. R., Agran, M., Wehmeyer, M. L., Rodi, M. S., & Presley, J. A. (2002a). Using self-monitoring to improve performance in general education high school classes. *Education and Training in Mental Retardation and Developmental Disabilities, 37*(3), 262–272.

Hughes, C. A., Ruhl, K. L., Schumaker, J. B., & Deshler, D. D. (2002b). Effects of instruction in an assignment completion strategy on the homework performance of students with learning disabilities in general education classes. *Learning Disabilities Research and Practice, 17*(1), 1–18.

Hunt, P., Alwell, M., Farron-Davis, F., & Goetz, L. (1996). Creating socially supportive environments for fully included students who experience multiple disabilities. *Journal of the Association for Persons with Severe Handicaps, 21*(2), 53–71.

Hunt, P., Farron-Davis, F., Beckstead, S., Curtis, D., & Goetz, L. (1994). Evaluating the effects of placement of students with severe disabilities in general education vs. special classes. *Journal of the Association for Persons with Severe Handicaps, 19*, 200–214.

Hunt, P., & Goetz, L. (1997). Research on inclusive educational programs, practices and outcomes for students with severe disabilities. *Journal of Special Education, 31*(1), 3–35.

Hunt, P., Staub, D., Alwell, M., & Goetz, L. (1994). Achievement by all students within the context of cooperative learning groups. *Journal of the Association for Persons with Severe Handicaps, 19*(2), 290–301.

Individuals with Disabilities Education Act Amendments of 1997. Pub. L. N. 105–17, Section 20, 111 Stat. 37 (1997). Washington, DC: U.S. Government Printing Office.

Jenkins, J. R., Antil, L. R., Wayne, S. K., & Vadasy, P. F. (2003). How cooperative learning works for special education and remedial students. *Exceptional Children, 69*(3), 279–292.

Jenkins, J. R., Jewell, M., Leicester, N., Jenkins, L., & Troutner, N. (1991). Development of a school building model for educating students with handicaps and at-risk students in general education classrooms. *Journal of Learning Disabilities, 24*, 311–320.

Kamps, D. M., Leonard, B., Potucek, J., & Garrison-Harrell, L. (1995). Cooperative learning groups in reading: An integration strategy for students with autism and general classroom peers. *Behavioral Disorders, 21*(1), 89–109.

Kennedy, C. H., & Itkonen, T. (1994). Some effects of regular class participation on the social contacts and social networks of high school students with severe disabilities. *Journal of the Association for Persons with Severe Handicaps, 19*, 1–10.

Kennedy, C. H., & Itkonen, T. (1995). Social relationships, influential variables, and change across the lifespan. In L. K. Koegel, R. L. Koegel, & G. Dunlap (Eds.), *Positive behavioral support: Including people with difficult behavior in the community* (pp. 287–304). Baltimore: Paul H. Brookes.

Kennedy, C. H., Long, T., Jolivette, K., Cox, J., Tank, J., & Thompson, T. (2001). Facilitating general education participation for students with behavior problems by linking positive behavior supports and person-centered planning. *Journal of Emotional and Behavioral Disorders, 9*(3), 161–171.

King, M. B., Schroeder, J., & Chawszczewski, D. (2001). Authentic assessment and student performance in inclusive schools (Brief No. 5). Madison, WI: University of Wisconsin-Madison, Research Institute on Secondary Education Reform for Youth with Disabilities Wisconsin Center on Education Research, University of Wisconsin, Madison.

King-Sears, M. E., & Bradley, D. F. (1995). Classwide peer tutoring: Heterogeneous instruction in general education classrooms. *Preventing School Failure, 40*(1), 29–35.

Kohler, F. W., & Strain, P. S. (1999). Maximizing peer-mediated resources in integrated preschool classrooms. *Topics in Early Childhood Special Education, 19*, 92–102.

Krank, H. M., Moon, C. E., & Render, G. F. (2002). Inclusion and discipline referrals. *Rural Educator, 24*(1), 13–17.

Lewis, T. J., Chard, D., & Scott, T. M. (1994). Full inclusion and the education of children and youth with emotional and behavioral disorders. *Behavioral Disorders, 19*, 277–293.

Lewis, T. J., & Sugai, G. (1996). Functional assessment of problem behavior: A pilot investigation of the comparative and interactive effects of teacher and peer social attention on students in general education settings. *School Psychology Quarterly, 11*, 1–19.

Lewis, T. J., Sugai, G., & Colvin, G. (1998). Reducing problem behavior through a school-wide system of effective behavioral support: Investigation of a school-wide social skills training program and contextual interventions. *School Psychology Review, 27*, 446–459.

Lipsky, D. K., & Gartner, A. (1997). *Inclusion and school reform: Transforming America's classrooms.* Baltimore: Brookes.

Logan, K. R., & Keefe, E. B. (1997). A comparison of instructional context, teacher behavior, and engaged behavior for students with severe disabilities in general education and self-contained elementary classrooms. *Journal of the Association for Persons with Severe Handicaps, 22*(1), 16–27.

Malmskog, S., & McDonnell, A. P. (1999). Teacher-mediated facilitation of engagement by children with developmental delays in inclusive preschools. *Topics in Early Childhood, 19*(4), 203–216.

Marks, S. U., Schrader, C., & Levine, M. (1999). Paraeducator experiences in inclusive settings: Helping, hovering, or holding their own? *Exceptional Children, 65*, 315–328.

Mathes, P. G., Fuchs, D., Fuchs, L. S., Henley, A. M., & Sanders, A. (1994). Increasing strategic reading practice with Peabody Classwide Peer Tutoring. *Learning Disabilities Research and Practice, 9*, 44–48.

Mathes, P. G., Grek, M. L., Howard, J. K., Babyak, A. E., & Allen, S. H. (1999). Peer-assisted learning strategies for first-grade readers: A tool for preventing early reading failure. *Learning Disabilities Research and Practice, 14*(1), 50–60.

McDonnell, J., Johnson, J. W., Polychronis, S., & Risen, T. (2002). Effects of embedded instruction on students with moderate disabilities enrolled in general education classes. *Education and Training in Mental Retardation and Developmental Disabilities, 37*(4), 363–377.

McDonnell, L. M., McLaughlin, M. J., & Morison, P. (Eds.). (1997). *Educating one and all: Students with disabilities and standards-based reform.* Washington, DC: National Academy Press.

McDougall, D. (1998). Research on self-management techniques used by students with disabilities in general education setting: A descriptive review. *Remedial and Special Education, 19*(5), 310–320.

McLeskey, J., & Waldron, N. L. (2002). Inclusion and school change: Teacher perceptions regarding curricular and instructional adaptations. *Teacher Education and Special Education, 25*(1), 41–54.

McMaster, K. N., & Fuchs, D. (2002). Effects of cooperative learning on the academic achievement of students with learning disabilities: An update of Tateyama-Sniezek's review. *Learning Disabilities Research and Practice, 17,* 107–117.

Meyer, L. H., Park, H., Grenot-Scheyer, M., Schwartz, I., & Harry, B. (1998). Participatory Research: New Approaches to the Research to Practice Dilemma. *Journal of the Association for Persons with Severe Handicaps, 23*(3), 165–77.

Morocco, C. C., Hindin, A., Mata-Aguilar, C., & Clark-Chiarelli, N. (2001). Building a deep understanding of literature with middle-grade students with learning disabilities. *Learning Disability Quarterly, 24,* 47–58.

Mortweet, S. L., Utley, C. A., Walker, D., Dawson, H. L., Delquadri, J. C., Reddy, S. S., Greenwood, C. R., Hamilton, S., & Ledford, D. (1999). Classwide peer tutoring: Teaching students with mild mental retardation in inclusive classrooms. *Exceptional Children, 65*(4), 524–536.

Murawski, W. W., & Swanson, H. L. (2001). A meta-analysis of co-teaching research. *Remedial and Special Education, 22*(5), 258–259.

Noell, G. H., Duhon, G. J., Gatti, S. L., Connell, J. E. (2002). Consultation, follow-up, and implementation of behavior management interventions in general education. *School Psychology Review, 31*(2), 217–234.

Oakes, J., & Lipton, M. (1999). *Teaching to change the world* (2nd ed.) New York: McGraw-Hill.

O'Connnor, R. E., & Jenkins, J. R. (1996). Cooperative learning as an inclusion strategy: A closer look. *Exceptionality 6*(1), 29–51.

Paley, V. (1992). You *can't say you can't play.* Cambridge, MA: Harvard University Press.

Palincsar, A. S., & Klenk, L. (1992). Fostering literacy learning in supportive contexts. *Journal of Learning Disabilities, 25*(4), 211–225, 229.

Palincsar, A. S., Magnusson, S. J., Collins, K. M., & Cutter, J. (2001). Making science accessible to all: Results of a design experiment in inclusive classrooms. *Learning Disability Quarterly, 24*(1), 15–32.

Park, H., Gonsier-Gerdin, J., Hoffman, S., Whaley, S., & Yount, M. (1998). Applying the participatory action research model to the study of social inclusion at worksites. *Journal of the Association for Persons with Severe Handicaps, 23*(3), 189–202.

Peterson, L. D., Young, K. R., West, R. P., & Peterson, M. H. (1999). Effects of student self-management on generalization of student performance to regular classrooms. *Education and Treatment of Children, 22*(3), 357–372.

Powell, S., & Nelson, B. (1997). Effect of choosing academic assignments on a student with attention deficit hyperactivity disorder. *Journal of Applied Behavior Analysis, 30*(1), 185–186.

Rea, P. J., McLaughlin, V. L., & Walther-Thomas, C. (2002). Outcomes for students with learning disabilities in inclusive and pullout programs. *Exceptional Children, 68*(2), 203–222.

Saint-Laurent, L., Dionne, J., Glasson, J., Royer, E., Simard, C., & Pierard, B. (1998). Academic achievement effects of an in-class service model on students with and without disabilities. *Exceptional Children, 64,* 239–253.

Sale, P., & Carey, D. M. (1995). The sociometric status of students with disabilities in a full-inclusion school. *Exceptional Children, 62,* 6–19.

Salend, S., & Duhaney, L. M. (1999). The impact of inclusion on students with and without disabilities and their educators. *Remedial and Special Education, 20*(2), 114–126.

Salisbury, C. L., Evans, I. M., & Palombaro, M. M. (1997). Collaborative problem-solving to promote the inclusion of young children with significant disabilities in primary grades. *Exceptional Children, 63*(2), 195–209.

Salisbury, C. L., Gallucci, C., Palombaro, M. M., & Peck, C. A. (1995). Strategies that promote social relations among elementary students with and without severe disabilities in inclusive schools. *Exceptional Children, 62*(2), 125–138.

Salisbury, C. L., Wilson, L. L., & Palombaro, M. M. (1998). *Journal of the Association for Persons with Severe Handicaps, 23*(3), 223–237.

Sapon-Shevin, M., Dobbelaere, A., Corrigan, C., Goodman, K., & Mastin, M. (1998). Everyone here can play. *Educational Leadership, 56*(1), 42–45.

Schmidt, R. J., Rozendal, M. S., & Reenman, G. G. (2002). Reading instruction in the inclusion classroom: Research-based practices. *Remedial and Special Education, 23*(3), 130–140.

Schulte, A. C., Osborne, S. S., & McKinney, J. D. (1990). Academic outcomes for students with learning disabilities in consultation and resource programs. *Exceptional Children, 57*, 162–172.

Scott, B. J., Vitale, M. R., & Masten, W. G. (1998). Implementing instructional adaptations for students with disabilities in inclusive classrooms: A literature review. *Remedial and Special Education, 19*(2), 106–119.

Semmel, M. I., Abernathy, T. V., Butera, G., & Lesar, S. (1991). Teacher perceptions to the regular education initiative. *Exceptional Children, 58*, 9–23.

Shapiro, E. S., Miller, D. N., Sawka, K., Gardill, M. C., & Handler, M. W. (1999). Facilitating the inclusion of students with EBD into general education classrooms. *Journal of Emotional and Behavioral Disorders, 7*(2), 83–94.

Sharpe, M. N., York, J. L., & Knight, J. (1994). Effects of inclusion on the performance of classmates without disabilities: A preliminary study. *Remedial and Special Education, 15*, 281–287.

Skiba, R. J., & Peterson, R. L. (2000). School discipline at a crossroads: From zero tolerance to early response. *Exceptional Children, 66*, 335–347.

Skrtic, T. M. (Ed.). (1995). *Disability and Democracy: Reconstruction special education for postmodernity*. New York: Teachers College Press.

Slavin, R. E. (1995). *Cooperative learning: Theory, research and practice* (2nd ed.). Boston: Allyn & Bacon.

Sleeter, C. E. (1985). The social construction of a special education category. *Exceptional Children, 53*(1), 46–54.

Soodak, L. C., Podell, D. M., & Lehman, L. R. (1998). Teacher, student, and school attributes as predictors of teachers' responses to inclusion. *Journal of Special Education, 31*(4), 480–497.

Spencer, V. G., Scruggs, T. E., & Mastropieri, M. A. (2003). Content area learning in middle school social studies classrooms and students with emotional or behavioral disorders: A comparison of strategies. *Behavioral Disorders, 28*, 77–93.

Staub, D., Schwartz, I. S., Galluici, C., & Peck, C. (1994). Four portraits of friendship at an inclusive school. *Journal of the Association for Persons with Severe Handicaps, 19*, 314–325.

Staub, D., Spaulding, M., Peck, C. A., Gallucci, C., & Schwartz, I. (1996). Using nondisabled peers to support the inclusion of students with disabilities at the junior high school level. *Journal of the Association for Persons with Severe Handicaps, 21*(4), 194–205.

Taylor-Green, S., Brown, D., Nelson, L., Longton, J., Gassman, T., Cohen, J., Swatrz, J., Horner, R. H., Sugai, G., & Hall, S. (1997). School-wide behavioral support: Starting the year off right. *Journal of Behavioral Education, 7*, 99–112.

Trent, S., & Artiles, A. (1994). Overrepresentation of minority students in special education: A continuing debate. *Journal of Special Education, 27*(4), 410–437.

Turnbull, A., Turnbull, H. R., Erwin, E. J., & Soodak, L. C. (2006). *Families, professionals, and exceptionality* (5th ed.). Upper Saddle River, NJ: Prentice-Hall.

Umbreit, J. (1995). Functional analysis of disruptive behavior in an inclusive classroom. *Journal of Early Intervention, 20*(1), 18–29.

U.S. Department of Education (2002). *Twenty-fourth annual report to Congress on the implementation of IDEA*. Washington, DC: Author.

Vaughn, S., Schumm, J. S., Jallad, B., Slusher, J., & Saumell, L. (1996). Teachers' views of inclusion. *Learning Disabilities Research and Practice, 11*(2), 96–106.

Villa, R. A., & Thousand, J. S. (2000). Setting the context: History and rationales for inclusive schooling. In R. A. Villa & J. S. Thousand (Eds.), *Restructuring for caring and effective education* (pp. 7–37). Baltimore: Brookes.

Villa, R. A., Thousand, J. S., Meyers, H., & Nevin, A. (1996). Teacher and administrator perceptions of heterogeneous education. *Exceptional Children, 63*, 29–45.

Waldron, N. L., & McLeskey, J. (1998). The effects of an inclusive school program on students with mild and severe learning disabilities. *Exceptional Children, 64*(3), 395–405.

Wallace, T., Anderson, A. R., Bartholomay, T., & Hupp, S. (2002). An ecobehavioral examination of high school classrooms that include students with disabilities. *Exceptional Children, 68*(3), 345–359.

Wang, X., Bernas, R., & Eberhard, P. (2001). Effects of teachers' verbal and non-verbal scaffolding on everyday classroom performances of students with down syndrome. *International Journal of Early Years Education, 9*(1), 71–80.

Wehmeyer, M. L., Palmer, S. B., Agran, M., Mithaug, D. E., & Martin, J. E. (2000). Promoting causal agency: The self-determination learning model of instruction. *Exceptional Children, 66*(4), 439–453.

Weiss, M. P., & Lloyd, J. W. (2002). Congruence between roles and actions of secondary special educators in co-taught and special education settings. *Journal of Special Education, 36*(2), 58–69.

Werts, M. G., Zigmond, N., & Leeper, D. C. (2001). Paraprofessional proximity and academic engagement: Students with disabilities in primary aged classrooms. *Education and Training in Mental Retardation and Developmental Disabilities, 36*(4), 424–440.

Whinnery, K. W., Fuchs, L. S., & Fuchs, L. S. (1991). General, special, and remedial teachers' acceptance of behavioral and instructional strategies for mainstreaming students with mild handicaps. *Remedial and Special Education, 12*, 6–17.

Wolery, M., Anthony, L., Snyder, E. D., Werts, M. G., & Katzenmeyer, J. (1997). Training elementary teachers to embed instruction during classroom activities. *Education and Treatment of Children, 20*, 40–58.

Woodward, J., Monroe, K., & Baxter, J. (2001). Enhancing student achievement on performance assessments in mathematics. *Learning Disability Quarterly, 24*, 33–46.

York, J., Vandercook, T., MacDonald, C., Heise-Neff, C., & Caughey, E. (1992). Feedback about integrating middle-school students with severe disabilities in general education classes. *Exceptional Children, 58*, 244–258.

Zhang, D. (2001). Self-determination and inclusion: Are students with mild mental retardation more self-determined in regular classrooms? *Education and Training in Mental Retardation and Developmental Disabilities, 36*(4), 357–362.

Zigmond, N. (2003). Where should students with disabilities receive special education services? Is one place better than another? *Journal of Special Education, 37*(3), 193–199.

Zigmond, N., & Baker, J. M. (1990). Mainstreaming experiences for learning disabled students (Project Meld): Preliminary report. *Exceptional Children, 57*, 176–185.

Zigmond, N., Jenkins, J., Fuchs, L., Deno, S., Fuchs, D., Baker, J. N. Jenkins, L., & Couthino, M. (1995). Special education in restructured schools: Findings from three multi-year studies. *Phi Delta Kappan, 76*, 531–540.

18

Classroom Management in Urban Classrooms

H. Richard Milner
Vanderbilt University

INTRODUCTION

Classroom management in urban classrooms concerns more than teachers' abilities to get students to behave a certain way. It is about more than how teachers control their students and classes. When an observer walks down a hallway of a school and peeks into a classroom, the question should not be whether the students are orderly and silent in their seats, completing their worksheets, or listening to their teachers' directives. On first glance, it may be tempting to see such classroom settings as productive and meaningful for students. To the contrary, we should instead wonder whether significant learning is taking place in that classroom, why or why not, and by what means.

Classroom management is about students' opportunities to learn in a context; learning should not only focus on academic/subject matter. Rather, effective classroom management in urban classrooms should also provide learning opportunities that help students think critically about issues both inside and outside the school. It should help students develop inquisitive dispositions and ideas about the power structure, recognize the social and political landscape of their schools and their communities, and understand and mitigate the culture of power (Delpit, 1995) in the classroom, in the school, and in society. It should empower students to participate in and critique the pervasive discourses in their classrooms. Effective classroom management in urban classrooms should empower students to be participants in knowledge development and distribution in their classrooms and help them realize their capacity to learn (Siddle-Walker, 1996). It is about the teachers' abilities to manage the classroom so that students can engage and participate in learning—regardless of the subject matter being taught.

Teachers should not restrict their attention to students' behavioral needs; they should be aware of students' cognitive social and academic needs, as well as their political needs. Thus, effective classroom management in urban classrooms is curricular, instructional, social, and political.

It is critical to consider how both teachers and students conduct themselves in the classroom to ensure learning. The onus cannot be placed exclusively on the students. Teachers have to take some responsibility for how they themselves behave in the classroom and how they orchestrate their curriculum, instruction, and management for learning opportunities to take place. In short, classroom management is about the ways in which students and teachers are able to connect, learn, and negotiate. Students need to have a voice in, participate in, and develop their multiple and varied identities, as well as their sense of self-worth and belonging—all in pursuit of optimal learning opportunities. Researchers, administrators, theorists, and practitioners must take a broad view of what classroom management means in urban classrooms. The focus must go beyond control and order, by exploring the purpose or reasons that we should be concerned about classroom management in urban classrooms. Indeed, classroom management is critical if learning is to take place. And the nature of that classroom management sets the tone for how learning can and will occur in the classroom, for whom, for what purposes, and why.

Clearly, classroom management is important to study because teachers report that they struggle most with management (Houston & Williamson, 1993), especially in urban classrooms (Haberman & Rickards, 1990; Howard, 2003). Yet, searching the databases with the keywords *urban, classroom, and management* identified only nine refereed articles. It is unfortunate that there is such a scarcity of research about urban classroom management because, as Weiner (2003) explained, "we do know that after prospective teachers leave education programs in colleges and universities for jobs in urban classrooms, they rank classroom management as one of the main challenges" (p. 306).

Also, urban schools are increasingly populated by students of color, students from lower SES, and linguistically diverse students. Teachers, on the other hand, are increasingly White, middle class, and female. As Weinstein, Tomlinson-Clarke, and Curran (2004) explained, "Definitions and expectations of appropriate behavior are culturally influenced, and conflicts are likely to occur when teachers and students come from different cultural backgrounds" (p. 26). More research is needed that focuses on classroom management, especially as our nations' schools become increasingly diverse (Banks & Banks, 2000; Gay & Howard, 2000). We must develop a knowledge base to understand these students' experiences and life worlds to meet their learning needs.

For the purposes of this chapter, I draw from many related studies of urban schools and classrooms and make connections to classroom management in light of the scarcity of research and theory around these issues. The studies seem to fall into three categories: (a) best practices—where researchers outlined the most effective strategies and practices in urban classroom management; (b) theory-driven—where researchers used conceptual lenses to identify practices, problems, solutions and strategies related to effective classroom management in urban contexts; and (c) a bridge between theory and best practices—where researchers grounded their research in theory and outlined some of the complexities, strategies, approaches, and problems in urban classroom management.

This chapter is divided into two major strands: (a) a focus on the problems, dilemmas, and struggles of urban classrooms and management and (b) a focus on effective strategies, approaches, teachers, and teaching that prove meaningful in managing urban classrooms. I begin this discussion by focusing on characteristics of the urban classroom. What are the characteristics and needs of urban classrooms that make a discussion of issues specific to such environments necessary? I then shift the discussion to focus on Delpit's (1995) "culture of power" because much of the research on classroom management in urban contexts is grounded in Delpit's work. I then discuss some important cultural considerations in interpreting student behavior. Central to this discussion highlighting cultural considerations are disciplinary disproportionality, consequences of disciplinary and management decisions, and connections and disconnections between teachers and students.

After discussing and outlining many of the problems inherent in urban classrooms, the remainder of the chapter focuses on what seems to work best in these contexts. Specifically, the discussion shifts to answer a second question: What characteristics appear to epitomize effective teachers and teaching in urban classrooms? This discussion focuses on student motivation and engagement, and the necessity of caring, empathetic, and trusting teachers. I then turn to a third question: What are the most effective methods, strategies, and approaches to classroom management in urban settings? I attempt to capture the essence of these strategies, methods, and approaches in a chart that builds on the research, theory, and practice around classroom management in urban classrooms. The final section of this chapter outlines implications and conclusions specifically as they relate to teacher education, research and researchers, and policy-makers.

THE URBAN CONTEXT: A LOOK AT CHARACTERISTICS OF URBAN CLASSROOMS

What are the characteristics and needs of urban classrooms that make a discussion of issues specific to such environments necessary? Communities can be categorized generally as suburban, rural, or urban. Whereas these contexts have similarities, this chapter is concerned with their differences and how these differences influence classroom management. For example, suburban schools tend to be relatively homogeneous[1] in terms of socioeconomic status (SES) and ethnic background. Compared to urban and rural communities, suburban communities are higher in SES and predominantly White. Compared to their counterparts in other communities, suburban students also tend to score higher on achievement and proficiency tests and tend to pursue post-secondary degrees more often, teachers tend to have higher educational credentials, and families tend to be nuclear and more educated.

In many respects, urban and rural schools have much in common, particularly in regard to SES. Both types of schools tend to have high concentrations of students living in poverty, high percentages of single-parent families, the least qualified or credentialed teachers, and the fewest school resources (e.g., new school buildings, curricular materials, and so forth). However, there is a noticeable difference between urban and rural schools in terms of student mobility, size, and diversity, with urban schools and communities being larger, having higher student transience, and including greater ethnic and cultural diversity. These differences in school context—diversity, size, resources, teacher qualifications, and more—cannot be ignored, negated, minimized, or trivialized. School size matters in terms of both student achievement and behavior. We know that more experienced teachers tend to have more effective classroom management skills, and students have greater chances for opportunities to learn with these teachers. We know that students whose basic needs are met—most often higher SES students—are better able to concentrate on learning and on managing their behaviors.

Thus, an urban context can be defined as one that is heavily populated with students of color and has a heavy concentration of English-language learners, a large number of students from lower SES, high attrition of teachers, heavy institutional and systemic barriers, and meager resources (Ennis & McCauley, 2002; Weiner, 2003). Urban schools tend to be grossly underfunded, larger in size, and infiltrated with administrative bureaucracy (from local district levels to federal levels).

The aforementioned comparisons and differences not withstanding, educators must consider other characteristics of urban settings that have significant implications for classroom

[1] I use the term "homogeneous" loosely here to refer to the reality that suburban schools tend to have less variance than urban schools in terms of socioeconomic status (SES) and ethnic diversity. That is, students tend to come from similar SES levels and to be disproportionately White. Having said this, I acknowledge that there is no such thing as a homogeneous classroom—even in classrooms where students come from the same SES group and share the same ethnic background, the students will have different learning styles, values, beliefs, and behaviors.

management. The profile of many urban schools is a disturbing one, as indicated by the significant number of efforts designed to "reform" and otherwise "save" urban schools and their students. Urban schools—especially those located in inner cities and barrios—are plagued by high student dropout rates, high rates of school suspension and expulsion, absenteeism, and truancy, high rates of student apathy and disengagement, health problems, and participation in special education, and high teacher turnover. These high rates are accompanied by low rates of graduation, test scores, enrollment in post-secondary institutions, family and community involvement, teacher expectations of students, participation in gifted education, as well as inadequate fiscal, school, and family resources (Ennis & McCauley, 2002; Ferguson, 2000; Kozol, 1992; Steinberg, Brown, & Dornbusch, 1996).

Ladson-Billings (2001) maintained that teachers in urban classrooms

> not only [will encounter] . . . multiracial or multiethnic [students] but they [students] are also likely to be diverse along linguistic, religious, ability, and economic lines. . . . Today teachers walk into urban classrooms with children who represent an incredible range of diversity. Not only are students of different races and ethnicities, but there are students whose parents are incarcerated or drug-addicted, whose parents have never held a steady job, whose parents are themselves children (at least chronologically), and who are bounced from one foster home to the next. And there are children who have no homes or parents. (p. 14)

These contextual nuances, needs, and problems impact classroom learning and management. In short, the results of my review of the literature suggests that many of the problems that urban classrooms and schools face have a great deal to do with how society (from a macro perspective) and classrooms (from a micro perspective) have mis-served and "mis-educated" those who occupy these urban spaces (Irvine, 1990; Woodson, 1933). Clearly, with an understanding of issues embedded in the urban classroom, there is a great need to focus on such contexts as teachers attempt to engage students in learning and students attempt to negotiate and navigate urban classrooms.

For some or perhaps many readers, the phrase "classroom management in urban settings" has some extremely negative connotations. Weiner (2003) explained that these negative, deficient, deficit, and inadequate perspectives are certainly present in the literature on the topic. Much of what is written sends the message that "if it's urban, then it's bad!" Ladson-Billings (1994) and Ford (1996) draw similar analyses when they survey the literature on African American students. The data bases are inundated with synonyms such as "disadvantaged," "marginalized," "oppressed," and "at risk." Such terms are used as adjectives to describe students themselves rather than their environments. In reality, these negative misconceptions are reinforced not only in the classroom but also can be found in the pervasive discourses in the literature concerning urban schools, classrooms, and students. Haberman (2000) suggested, "Language is not an innocent reflection of how we think. The terms we use control our perceptions, shape our understanding, and lead us to particular proposals for improvement" (p. 203). The language used to discuss the situations of urban classrooms sends very disturbing messages. Thinking about urban classrooms requires us to conceive of the systemic and institutional barriers that stifle the success of students and not place the blame on the students—who in many instances are subjected to circumstances outside of their own control.

Institutional and Systemic Barriers

Institutional and systemic barriers make it difficult for teachers to show students they care and to develop the best management strategies in urban classrooms. Teachers often are pressured and closely managed by their administrators. They experience less than ideal support;

consequently, the teachers' students may believe that the teachers "forget to care" about the students themselves. In reality, the teachers are attempting to negotiate "structural conditions within the school, such as tracking and high teacher turnover, that preclude caring relationships with students" (Katz, 1999, p. 809).

Ennis (1996) examined issues of confrontation among 10 urban high schools that enrolled approximately 110,000 students from lower-to middle-class families. Her findings revealed some possible outcomes when teachers feel unsupported by their administrators. Ennis discovered that some 50% of the teachers in the study reported that they did not teach certain content topics "because of the confrontations that such topics generate with specific students" (p. 145). Because these teachers did not want to feel "ganged up on" in their classrooms, students were denied access to a curriculum that might promote more critical and analytical thinking to better prepare them for society. The teachers in the study avoided teaching content that "they believed students were disinterested in learning... students refused to learn or to participate in learning, or... generated discussions that the teachers felt unprepared to moderate" (p. 146). The teachers were, in a sense, granting students permission to fail (Ladson-Billings, 2002). Many of the teachers in Ennis' study reported that a lack of administrative support was a central cause and concern for their avoidance of certain curriculum topics. The teachers did not feel supported and adopted survival mechanisms to essentially get through the day.

In such classrooms, teachers give information, ask questions, give directions, give assignments, give tests, assign homework, punish noncompliance, and grade papers. This vicious cycle is tantamount to Ladson-Billings' (1994) notion that students are often passive participants in their own learning, with teachers constantly attempting to pour knowledge into "empty vessels."

Students tend to rebel against such teaching and management (institutional and systemic structures placed on them by teachers in this respect) by fighting over control with the teacher. Thus, much time is ultimately taken away from teaching and learning. Students, in a sense, punish teachers by resisting efforts to be controlled (Haberman, 1991). Student resistance takes many forms—for example, clowning in class, interrupting lessons with jokes, acting out to be removed from the class, feigning illness to be removed from the class or excused from assignments, "losing" assignments and forgetting materials (e.g., paper, pencils, books) to avoid work, teasing classmates, and disagreeing with teachers for the sake of disagreement. The systemic and institutionalized nature of teachers' work in urban schooling seems to follow several layers, as depicted in Fig. 18.1. The administration takes its cues from the superintendent who interprets national and state guidelines (i. e., a set of policies and expectations about how teachers' classes ought to run—quietly, orderly), which creates a dilemma for teachers. Optimal learning can occur without students seated in silence. Teachers, in turn, in their attempts to meet the institutional expectations, develop and implement management strategies that reify systems of oppression and voicelessness among students. Students, in turn, resist these systemic parameters, and chaos, disconnections, and mismanagement ensue. The impetus for order and control on the classroom level emerges from teachers' goals to improve test scores and to prepare students to follow directions and to "obey" orders for the world of work (Anyon, 1980).

Teacher Turnover and Attrition

These challenges to teachers' authority—and to their sense of control and competence—take their toll on teachers. Reports on high teacher turnover or burnout rates are consistent: teachers leave urban classrooms—and quickly. Howard (2003) explained some of the issues inherent in teacher attrition, particularly in urban schools: "Countless numbers of teachers leave

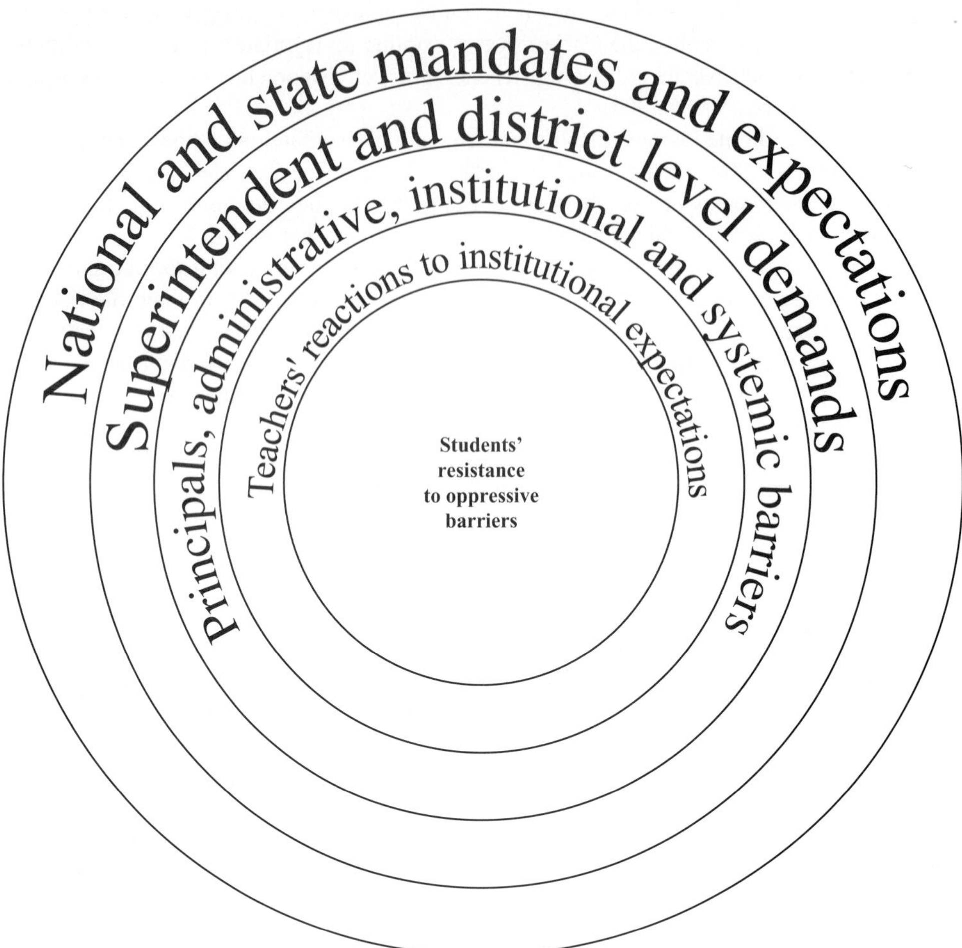

FIGURE 18.1. A Cycle of Resistance to Effective Classroom Management.

because of high levels of stress, unsatisfactory organizational conditions, lack of administrative support, perceived discipline problems, cultural mismatches with students, and a multitude of sociocultural factors that play out in the classroom everyday" (p. 149). Moreover, Howard posed a salient and pressing question about the effects of teacher attrition in urban schools. Who receives the short end of the teacher shortage when teachers leave urban classrooms? And the answer, of course, is the students who are left with unqualified, uncommitted, and often unprepared teachers. Clearly, teacher attrition, along with institutional and systemic issues, is a problem in urban schools. Understanding these issues (among others) means that we must consider the "culture of power."

THE CULTURE OF POWER

The seminal work of Lisa Delpit (1995) profoundly influenced the ways in which researchers, practitioners, and policy makers conceptualized classroom management, particularly in urban contexts. In fact, many of the studies focusing on management in urban classrooms (discussed throughout this chapter) attempt to build on and expand Delpit's scholarship. Her explanation of what she called "the culture of power" helped scholars think about how race, ethnicity, class, gender, and culture are intertwined and must be thought about as we problematize "normal" and "appropriate" behavior. Delpit described five aspects around power:

> (a) issues of power are enacted in classrooms; (b) there are codes or rules for participating in power; that is, there is a "culture of power"; (c) the rules of the culture of power are a reflection of the rules of the culture of those who have power; (d) if you are not already a participant in the culture of power, being told explicitly the rules of that culture makes acquiring power easier; and (e) those with power are frequently least aware of—or least willing to acknowledge—its existence. Those with less power are often most aware of its existence. (p. 24)

In essence, Delpit considered some of the ways in which students' home environments and their experiences with discipline and management significantly differed from the ways in which the students experienced management in the classroom.

Delpit suggested that students deserved to be told explicitly the "rules" and the consequences of those in power. For students to have a chance at success in the classroom and thus society, Delpit explained that students must understand that they live in and operate in a system that is oppressive and repressive because those in power decide how one is supposed to behave. Rewards and sustainability are couched in understanding the culture of power. The onus, in this respect, is on teachers (or those in power) to help students make the transition into behaving in ways that the dominant culture would find acceptable. Students need to learn to adapt their behaviors and the ways in which they operate in their homes to the expectations of their mostly white teachers, and consequently to the expectations of those in society as well. For the transition to transpire effectively, Delpit declared that those in power must make the rules and expectations clear. The assumption that students would be taught this culture of power outside of the classroom is irresponsible, in a sense, particularly in urban classrooms. This point can be substantiated particularly if the parents of these students do not fully understand how to negotiate and live in that culture or with those dominant cultural views. Knowing what the culture of power actually is, how it works, and how power can be achieved are important for students' success in urban classrooms.

Moreover, the notion that there is more than one appropriate way to act gave researchers, theoreticians, and practitioners a chance to critically reflect on and examine what appropriate behavior actually is, and some began to realize that "appropriate behavior" is subjective and socially constructed based on who is in power. Thus, Delpit's work suggested that students' behavior and teachers' classroom management strategies are not culturally neutral. However, as Gordon (1988) explained, those in power often found it difficult to critically examine their "own assumptions about the world—especially if [people/teachers] believe the world works for [them]" (p. 88). Thus, realizing the significance of the culture of power still does not ensure that teachers would rethink and renegotiate their positions around appropriate behavior. Rather, because the world works for many teachers, they still struggle to see how there are any other way to live and act in the world, resisting the reality that there are multiple ways to experience and know the world.

Teachers and researchers were challenged to rethink the connections between how parents parented and how teachers taught and managed their classrooms. Delpit (1995) shared a reaction from a white teacher when talking about the management style and approach of a black teacher: "It's really a shame but she (that Black teacher upstairs) seems to be so authoritarian, so focused on skills and so teacher directed. Those poor kids never seem to be allowed to really express their creativity. (And she even yells at them)" (p. 33). What the teacher in this passage failed to understand was that the "Black teacher upstairs" might have been quite productive and effective in providing all students access and opportunities to learn. Delpit asserted that many African American students are accustomed to a more directive form of management outside of school: "Put down that candy" or "Go to bed" while many White parents give directions in the form of questions: "Can we have candy before dinner?" or "Is it not time for bed?" At the core of these different ways of thinking about discipline are historical and societal issues. The question should not be which approach is right or wrong but which approach works with and connects with the students' prior knowledge and ways of knowing.

The conflicts that often exist in urban classrooms seem to have at their core cultural, racial, class, gender, and ethnic issues that must be addressed in order to first understand the exchanges that occur in the classroom and then to develop strategies that help teachers and students teach and learn. Delpit's work showed how the intersections of these matters with that of classroom management (particularly in urban classrooms) cannot be ignored, misunderstood, misrepresented, or underinvestigated as we work to provide equitable learning opportunities for all students.

The idea of providing equitable learning opportunities seems to be misunderstood by many practicing teachers, and perhaps researchers. Ladson-Billings (2000) maintained that teachers have to recognize that attempting to employ the same pedagogical strategies across various learning contexts will likely result in chaos. In like form, having the same expectations of students across contexts also ensures that teachers will be disappointed. Equal does not mean same. Classroom management strategies along with teachers' expectations, thinking, and beliefs about their students must be content-, context-, and culturally-specific. Moreover, as Weiner (2003) maintained, "standardized practices, designed to treat all students fairly, make the schools impersonal and undercut efforts to individualize learning" (p. 306).

Grossman (1995) explained that teachers who believe that they must implement the same techniques [or expectations] among all students to reach equality

> are not treating all students the same, but are dealing with some students in a culturally appropriate manner and others in a biased manner . . . there is a more valid way of treating students the same, which is to provide all students with culturally appropriate educational approaches . . . while this may make it appear that students are being treated differently, they are being treated the same and in a nondiscriminatory manner. (p. 174)

Accordingly, understanding the culture of power and issues of equity are critical for teachers and students.

CULTURAL CONSIDERATIONS IN INTERPRETING STUDENT BEHAVIOR

Cultural considerations are critical in understanding the ways in which students conduct themselves and learn in urban classrooms. In short, culture matters in how students behave. Hale (1982) and Hilliard's (1992) research pointed to the influences of racial, ethnic, and cultural factors in thinking about how students of color behave (or better yet conduct themselves) in the classroom. Hilliard (1992) suggested that

> unique behavioral style factors could be identified among African American populations. . . . The assumption was that two groups of students with the same intellectual potential would, because of diversity in cultural socialization, develop habits and preferences that would cause them to manifest their mental powers in somewhat different ways. (p. 370)

These behavioral styles are central to understanding the complexities inherent in urban classrooms (McCadden, 1998). Thus, students' behavioral patterns have cultural and social dimensions that are central to their experiences. African American students' intellectual abilities might be displayed in different ways based on their cultural experiences and their socialization.

Hale and Hilliard's work is very important because it is logical and consistent with how other researchers have come to understand and to interpret the learning and behavioral patterns among students of color (see, e.g., Delpit, 1995; Gay, 2000; Grossman, 1995).

For example, as Hale (2001) noted:

> African American children are generally more kinesthetic than [W]hite children and have a higher level of motor activity. There is also medical evidence that African American males have a higher testosterone level than [W]hite males... Teachers should be trained to be patient with the rambunctious and outgoing nature of African American males. Conceptualizing these behavioral styles as normal will correct present tendencies to define the behavior of African American males as pathological, needing medication and special placement for emotional and psychological disorders. (p. 118)

Clearly, as Hale and Hilliard have explained, the different behavioral styles of African American students must be considered and the ways in which these behaviors are conceptualized must be changed to benefit the students. In other words, referring students of color for special education or medication should not be the first option in helping students succeed academically.

DISPROPORTIONATE DISCIPLINE PRACTICES

There is a disproportionate number of African American and poor students referred to the office for discipline problems (Ford, 1996; McCarthy & Hoge, 1987; Wu, Pink, Crain, & Moles, 1982). Overwhelmingly, the findings in the literature are straightforward in that most disciplinary referrals originate in the classroom and that more times than not, the referrals are for students of color and poor students. The notion is that there are some inconsistencies between the rules or the culture of power and that of students' ways of conducting themselves. At the core of these disciplinary referrals and the inconsistencies between teacher-school expectations and urban student behavior are access and opportunity to learn. Students' academic achievement suffers when they are not in the classroom.

For instance, Davis and Jordan (1994) analyzed data from the National Education Longitudinal Study of 1988 administered by the National Center for Educational Statistics. The researchers employed a two-stage, stratified, random sample of 25,000 eighth-graders in 1,000 schools across the country. Davis and Jordan reported a connection between discipline approaches and black male achievement in middle schools. As the researchers explained, "The time teachers spend handling disciplinary problems is time taken away from instruction; Black male achievement suffers as a result" (p. 585). In short, instead of teachers teaching these students, much of their time is spent attempting to discipline the students. Clearly, when students are not in the classroom because of disciplinary approaches and policies that put the students out of the classroom, such as suspension and expulsion, the students are suffering academically. Davis and Jordan explained that these disciplinary actions resulted in student classroom and school disengagement, and the students' achievement suffered because the disciplinary practices served as "disincentives" (p. 586) for these students.

Similarly, Skiba, Michael, Nardo, and Peterson (2002) analyzed disciplinary records of 11,001 students in 19 middle schools in a large, urban Midwestern public school district during the 1994–1995 school year (see also chapter 41 in this volume). Skiba et al. (2002) reported a "differential pattern of treatment, originating at the classroom level, wherein African American students are referred to the office for infractions that are more subjective in interpretation" (p. 317). In other words, if an African American student "talks back" or "mouths off" to a teacher, the teacher may interpret this behavior as completely disrespectful and intolerable. The students may be behaving in this way due to peer pressure—not wanting friends to perceive them as weak. Disrespect or malice may not be at the core of the students' actions. Rather, the student may be trying to "survive" and not engender ridicule from his or her classmates. Another example of how teachers' subjectivities end in students' referral occurs when African American students joke with a teacher after the teacher has attempted to correct some behavior; the teacher may misinterpret that behavior as being defiant or rude. The student, on the other hand, may use a joke at home with his or her parents to show that "there are no hard feelings" on this student's part. Teachers may find such behavior unacceptable and inexcusable—thus, a subjective dimension is applied in the situation, and ultimately students suffer the negative repercussions. Teachers and students do not ascribe the same meanings and intentions for the student's behavior.

The Skiba et al. (2002) study pointed out that students of color, and particularly African American students, overwhelmingly received harsher punishments for misbehavior than did their white counterparts. As an example, the authors described a fistfight at a high school football game in Decatur, Illinois that resulted in the superintendent's recommendation that all seven of the African American students involved be expelled from school for two years. Apparently, in the same district, weapons were used in a fight involving White students and a less severe punishment was imposed upon those students. Why are some groups of students punished more severely and frequently than are others?

Research suggests that there is a level of miscommunication between teachers and students in the classrooms. In schools where the vast majority of teachers are White, middle class, and female, and the students are of color and poor, there are ethnic, racial, and cultural mismatches that exist, which result in conflicts in the classroom. For instance, Skiba et al. (2002) suggested "Fear may... contribute to overreferral [among students of color]. Teachers who are prone to accepting stereotypes of adolescent African American males as threatening or dangerous may overact to relatively minor threats to authority, especially if their anxiety is paired with a misunderstanding of cultural norms of social interaction" (p. 336).

In another article, Skiba, Peterson, and Williams (1997) reported the findings of two studies in two Midwestern cities. One study was conducted across several middle schools, and the other in a single school. The researchers analyzed archival disciplinary referral data to determine the reasons reported for referrals, the circumstances under which the decision was made, the various disciplinary responses, and the rate of suspension, in addition to other issues surrounding the disciplinary incident. In both studies, the results revealed that office referrals were not a consequence of a threat of safety but "those that indicate noncompliance [insubordination] or disrespect... about 40% of all students receive at least one office referral in the middle school during the school year" (p. 295). Like many of the findings, these two studies (Skiba et al., 1997) showed a pattern of disproportionality "in the administration of school discipline based on race, SES, gender and disability" (p. 295). Thus, attempting to control students or force them to do what they were told were the major reasons students were referred, not because the students caused a threat to themselves, the teacher, or their classmates. This point is not to suggest that when students are not causing harm or threat to safety that they are not jeopardizing learning opportunities in the classroom. Indeed, students' "misbehavior" and "disruption" need to be corrected for learning to occur. However, teachers may readily resort to office referrals for matters that they can (and should) be able to handle without denying students access to learning; when students are not in the classroom, they are missing important learning opportunities that will undoubtedly influence their future. And the teacher himself or herself may precipitate the misbehavior.

Skiba et al. (1997) summed up their findings suggesting:

> Both of the current studies found overrepresentation of low SES students, males, and special education students in terms of both school referrals and rate of suspension... even in a district

> with a high proportion of African American students, African Americans were referred to the office significantly more frequently than other ethnic groups . . . these data provide further evidence of disproportionality in the administration of school discipline based on race, SES, gender, and disability, and raise serious concerns about the use of exclusionary discipline at the middle school level. (pp. 313–314)

Moreover, previous research revealed that an overrepresentation of school discipline is independent of both student behavior and SES (see also Wu et al., 1982).

CONSEQUENCES OF DISCIPLINARY AND MANAGEMENT DECISIONS

We must consider the price we all pay for disciplinary decisions that deny students access to knowledge. In reality, when harsh, repetitive, and exclusive disciplinary decisions are made in urban classrooms, students drop out, are placed in special education, or never reach their capacity. For instance, Skiba et al. (2002) discovered that there is a direct correlation between student office referrals and student drop out rate. Simply put, students are more likely to dropout of school and give up on education when they are perpetually sent to the office, expelled, and suspended—especially in urban contexts.

Fine (1986), in her article, *Why urban adolescents drop into and out of public high school*, described the experiences and factors that contributed to urban adolescents' decisions to drop out of school. Among outside factors, such as students becoming pregnant or their parents' needing them to provide financial support for the family, many students reported that they had actually been "thrown out" or at least not encouraged to remain. When teachers and administrators found students "difficult" to control, they did not encourage the students to stay in school. But rather, "many students are coerced to leave high school once they reach seventeen, or at least not encouraged to stay if they choose to go" (p. 403). Fine explained that students were encouraged to drop out of school for a number of disciplinary reasons including "mouthing off." Further, Noguera's (1995) research suggested that the very disciplinary measures schools and teachers employ in their classroom may be perpetuating and producing what he calls "prison-like" (p. 189) schools and classrooms. The "get tough" approaches that many classrooms and schools have adopted dehumanize students, in his view, and consequently produce mistrust and resistance from students.

Ferguson (2000), in her important and carefully developed book, studied an African American student, D'Andre, whose behavior was identified as aggressive and antisocial in the classroom; consequently, the student was referred for psychological evaluation. Her analyses of the situation revealed the following:

> Let us take the boy's [D'Andre's] standpoint for a change. Let us situate the behavior within a specific and highly relevant social context. . . . When the teacher tells her story, the fact that D'Andre is African American and the student teacher is white is never mentioned, nor is the fact that [the school] is a predominately white, middle-class suburb . . . she [the teacher] treats these social distinctions as irrelevant details to her story. (p. 200)

Because of pervasive diagnoses that seem commonplace among students of color, and in particular African American students, these "irrelevant" factors that teachers avoid considering put students at a disadvantage and prohibit teachers from considering the perspectives of the students. The consequences are too high for students of color; there is entirely too much at risk when these cultural and social issues are not taken into account. Ferguson explained that D'Andre's behavior would likely be assessed and diagnosed as a result of an illness, Oppositional Defiant Disorder (ODD), recently conceptualized by the American Psychiatric Association. Unfortunately, many white teachers avoid thinking about race and culture in their teaching, and students are the ones who suffer as a result. These teachers opt to pretend that race and culture do not matter.

Less than promising results of disciplinary and management decisions do not impact African American students exclusively. Schlosser (1992) stressed that Hispanics "are far more likely to drop out of school than are members of any other ethnic group. Nationally, at least one-half of Mexican American and Puerto Rican youth leave school without a high school diploma" (p. 94). Although Schlosser's analyses do not point directly to disciplinary and management decisions as causes of dropping out, we can assume that because urban classrooms are heavily populated with these students, there are likely some connections to be made.

The late anthropologist John Ogbu (1993) wrote:

> The failure of school personnel to understand and respect minority children's culturally learned behaviors often results in conflicts that obstruct children's adjustment and learning.... Generally, dominant group members, such as White Americans, ascribe to themselves the proper moral values, cultural norms, good manners, good and correct speech, and good and correct posture. They see in minorities the opposite qualities.... These treatments affect how the minorities perceive and respond to schooling and other institutions controlled by the dominant group. (p. 91)

When teachers misinterpret their students' behaviors in urban classrooms by working from their own mainstream sociocultural norms, they are

> acting in ways that actually discriminate against students from racial and ethnic minority backgrounds. Such discrimination occurs when teachers do not recognize that behavior is culturally influenced; when they devalue, censure, and punish the behaviors of non-mainstream groups; and when they fail to see that their management practices alienate and marginalize some students, while privileging others. (Weinstein, Curran & Tomlinson-Clarke, 2003, pp. 27–28)

In addition, in concentrating on some of the consequences of discipline and management decisions, Noguera (2003) reminded us that

> disciplinary practices in schools often bear a striking similarity to the strategies used to punish adults in society. Typically, schools rely on some form of exclusion or ostracism to control the behavior of students... the assumption is that safety and order can be achieved by removing "bad" individuals and keeping them away from others who are presumed to be "good" and law abiding. Not surprisingly, those most frequently targeted for punishment in school often look—in terms of race, gender, and socioeconomic status—a lot like smaller versions of the adults who are most likely to be targeted for incarceration in society. (pp. 342–343)

In her qualitative study of 16 students and nine teachers in an urban high school, Sheets (1996) reported that teacher-student conflicts were interpersonal, procedural, and substantive. Over 64% of the participants in the study were students of color, and approximately 77% of the teachers were White. Sheets explained, "interpersonal conflicts were more consequential for the students of color... the attitudes, beliefs, and values of students and teachers differed and were associated with ethnicity, gender, and level of academic achievement" (p. 170). The students of color in the study revealed that they often felt disrespected, devalued, and misunderstood in the classroom due to conflicts with their teachers.

In essence, there are consequences for the disciplinary and management decisions enforced in a context, particularly in urban classrooms. Students of color and poor students' behavior is often interpreted and evaluated as "wrong." Consequences of inappropriate disciplinary practices include high rates of student attrition, a decrease in students' learning opportunities, a decline in academic success, and societal problems (such as crime), which eventually result in incarceration. The connections between school and society are ones that cannot be ignored. A vicious cycle seems to develop when students in urban classrooms do not transition into the culture of power. Eventually, these students are suspended from school or expelled and often end up behind bars in jail.

CONNECTIONS AND DISCONNECTIONS BETWEEN TEACHERS AND STUDENTS

Teachers play an enormous role in how students conduct themselves in urban classrooms. In her ethnographic study of 31 culturally diverse students identified by the school as potential dropouts, Schlosser (1992) discovered that teachers must avoid distancing themselves from their students by developing knowledge about the students' home lives and cultural backgrounds and by developing knowledge about adolescents' developmental needs. In her words, "the behaviors of marginal students are purposive acts . . . their behaviors are constructed on the basis of their interpretation of school life . . . relationships with teachers are a key factor" (p. 137). Moreover, Noguera (2003) declared:

> Students who get into trouble frequently are typically not passive victims; many of them understand that the consequences for violating school rules can be severe, particularly as they grow older. However, as they internalize the labels that have been affixed to them, and as they begin to realize that the trajectory their education has placed them on is leading to nowhere, many simply lose the incentive to adhere to school norms. (p. 343)

Not giving up on students, regardless of their "misbehavior" is very important. Students recognize when there is unnecessary distance between themselves and their teachers, and the students' actions are shaped by such disconnections. The students often question: "Why should I adhere to this teacher's management desires when she or he does not really care about me?" In this respect, students see their misbehavior as a way to distance themselves from uncaring and disrespectful teachers, and the cycle seems to continue in spite of teachers' desires to correct student behavior.

In urban classrooms where students are of color and poor, and teachers are White, the interactions between teachers and students are often in conflict. Grossman (1995) explained that

> teachers praise African-American students less and criticize them more than European American students. The praise they give them is more likely to be routine, rather than feedback for a particular achievement or behavior. And when teachers praise them for specific behavior, it is more likely to be qualified ("Your work is almost good enough to be put on the board") or, in the case of females, more likely to be for good behavior than for academic work. (p. 142)

In short, teachers often exhibit less than appropriate techniques when working with diverse students in urban classrooms because they are not aware of their implicit pedagogical, curricular, and assessment decisions. Because teachers typically have good intentions, the differential treatment that the teachers display is located in their subconscious, and they are not able to critically examine these behaviors because they are not aware that the behaviors exist. And such inappropriate feedback to students is likely true across the board but is especially true and illuminating in urban classrooms. Moreover, because many teachers adopt color-blind ideologies in their work with students, pretending that they do not "see" or recognize color, these teachers are missing important features and dimensions of students' identity. Teachers are attempting to manage fragmented, disconnected, and incomplete individuals. Moreover, these teachers who adopt color-blind ideologies may fail to recognize "discriminatory institutional practices toward students of color such as higher suspension rates for African American males" (Johnson, 2002, p. 154).

Obidah and Teel (2001) described cultural and racial (behavioral) conflicts between the white teacher-researcher (Teel) and the students of color, mainly African American students. Initially, Teel characterized the student behavior in her urban classroom as

> an aggressive communicative; unfamiliar expressions; the need to save face in front of peers; a demand for respect from peers and the teacher; vocal and honest expressions of dissatisfaction with the class; and a tendency to test [Teel] as a person of authority. (p. 48)

After engaging in critical, reflective, and meaningful dialogues with her colleague, Obidah, the black teacher-researcher, Teel began to rethink her beliefs about the students in her classes. The researchers, and particularly the white researcher, began to realize that the problem was not with the students. Obidah was able to help Teel sift through some of her management and curricular decisions. For instance, Obidah explained some of the racial and cultural tensions embedded in some of Teel's instructional activities. Teel was able to also help Obidah think deeply about her connections with students and why such connections with the African American students seemed so profound. Teel, as a result of careful and critical analyses of both her and Obidah's teaching, changed her expectations and management: Teel explained that she began to really listen to her students; she negotiated and redefined her ideas about inappropriate behavior, and she learned to investigate the root causes for disruptions. Instead of thinking that she already had everything figured out, Teel actually listened to her students' perspectives on issues, and she worked to change some of her own decision making rather than assuming that the tensions that emerged in the classroom were a direct result of her students' misbehavior. It was only after Teel began to negotiate and balance some of her authority and ways of knowing that her relationship with her students improved.

In essence, the students in Obidah and Teel's (2001) study reported that Obidah "don't play!" (p. 57). There is a level of respect and authority associated with the ways in which Obidah was able to get the students to act appropriately. One of the students in the class reluctantly pointed out the difference in their behavior with Obidah in comparison to Teel. The student expressed, "Part of it is that [Obidah] is Black and [Teel] is White... Y'all know it's true" (p. 58). While the students were rowdy and could have been perceived as disrespectful with Teel, Obidah was able to change this behavior by the ways in which she communicated with the students, and the respect she demanded in the urban classroom. In short, this research demonstrates that there are cultural and racial connections and mismatches that are profoundly connected to classroom management and the ways in which students will allow teachers to manage them. Because Obidah has a deep understanding of the African American students and what they are willing to respond to, she is able to keep the students on track. Clearly, a knowledge of one's own and others' cultural background appears to be quite significant to the success teachers experience in classroom management.

Thus far, I have attended to the characteristics and needs of urban *classrooms* that make a discussion of issues specific to such environments necessary. Now I focus on the characteristics of effective *teachers*, and their teaching in urban classrooms.

CHARACTERISTICS OF EFFECTIVE TEACHERS AND TEACHING IN URBAN CLASSROOMS

What characteristics appear to personify or epitomize effective teachers and teaching in urban classrooms? Researchers have continuously pointed to the intersections of student motivation and teacher care as central to students' engagement, success, and behavior in urban classrooms (e.g., Howard, 2001; Morris & Morris, 2000; Stinson, 1993).

Student Motivation and Engagement

Building on an established body of research around student motivation and school failure, Teel, Debruin-Parecki, and Covington (1998) developed four teaching strategies that served as alternatives for teachers involved in a school-university collaboration. The strategies were developed to honor and motivate African American inner-city, middle school students. All of the researchers had conducted research in or taught in urban classrooms, which was integral in the development of the strategies. Two cohorts of middle school (seventh-grade) students in the San Francisco Bay area participated in the urban classroom study that lasted two years. Most of the students were African American in both cohorts (78% and 82%, respectively). A total of 23 students enrolled the first year and 29 students the second. These authors reported that their experiences with the cohorts of students

> indicated that given certain classroom conditions in which teaching strategies were used that addressed diverse student interest, talents and strengths, students at risk for school failure became just as engaged and motivated in a positive way as the more "high achieving" students. Negative motivation, observed somewhat at first, gradually decreased. (p. 492)

The African American students in the study displayed an increase in motivation by their enthusiastic responses in class, creative expression, leadership, and critical thinking. The four strategies designed and implemented included, "effort-based grading, multiple performance opportunities, increased student responsibility and choice, and validation of cultural heritage" (Teel et al., 1998, p. 482). Accordingly, student motivation has been found to be central to students' behavioral success in the urban classroom.

Care, Empathy and Trust

It is clear in the literature that having caring teachers is essential for students of color and poor students who often are educated in urban classrooms (Gay, 2000; Irvine, 1990; Noddings, 1992). McAllister and Irvine (2002), in their study of 34 practicing teachers' beliefs about empathy and working with culturally diverse students, found that the teachers' practices were enhanced when they had empathetic dispositions. Empathetic teachers, according to McAllister and Irvine, "take on the perspective of another culture ... [and empathy involves] ... cognitive, affective, and behavioral components" (p. 433).

An important finding of this study was that the teachers empathized with their students and did not pity them. There was a level of social justice and activism that connected the teachers and the students—it was not about those "poor" students' problems but about our (teachers' and students') problems that all involved had to solve together. As a result of participating in a support program to assist the teachers in working with culturally diverse students, the teachers developed empathetic dispositions that resulted in more caring, supportive, and responsive learning environments. Norris (2003) explained that a central skill in developing empathy is through listening to others well, paying attention to their emotions, and understanding others' "perspectives, points of view, and feelings" (p. 315).

Ennis and McCauley's (2002) study made it clear that developing urban classrooms of trust is important in effective teaching and learning. The researchers examined strategies that urban high school teachers used to encourage struggling students to understand rules and to engage in learning. A total of 18 teachers were interviewed and four of their classes were observed regularly for four months. The teachers in the study encouraged their students by "creating a curriculum and class environment that permitted many opportunities for engagement, provided positive interactions, encouraged the development of shared curriculum, and fostered student ownership" (p. 149). Moreover, the teachers gave the students multiple chances for success and allowed the students to have a "voice" in the development of rules and learning. In essence, the teachers were able to develop a trustful milieu, and the students bought into learning because there was a sense of shared expectations and community in the classroom.

Newberg and Sims' (1996) research showed that students in inner-city schools who were predicted to fail could be assisted to reach success through an effective intervention, the Say Yes to Education program, which was established in 1987. The Say Yes to Education program guaranteed a tuition-paid college education to sixth-grade students from low-income families in Philadelphia. The program attempted to change the contexts for the students (in school) to help the students envision and realize success. The problems of the students participating in the program were complex. Although the program attempted to address the entire context of learning, one pervasive issue discovered among the participants occurred specifically in the urban classroom. The researchers stressed that

> we have seen repeatedly how students resist accepting help with academic, social, or personal problems. They have internalized a macho-cool attitude that makes help-seeking a sign of weakness. Students are afraid their peers will hold them up to derision if they are seen as accepting help. Some of the reluctance to ask for help goes beyond peer culture, defining school as a hostile, intrusive, and unreliable institution, especially for low-income students who experience frequent failure. By contrast, [the two students participating in this research] learned to use help because the context in which they received it was perceived to be caring and trustworthy. (p. 172)

In short, the teachers in the study did not water down the curriculum and would not accept mediocre work from the students. By analyzing the data from the students enrolled in the program at graduation, the researchers discovered a significant increase in the number of students who graduated among those who participated in the intervention. The findings suggested that, where such interventions are concerned, "resources and sustained support can change the odds for predictable failure into futures that may be satisfying and fulfilling" (p. 171).

The teachers had high expectations for their students, and these teachers' expectations were perceived as care among the students; a level of trust was established and sustained because of this, and the students wanted to reach their full potential mainly because they wanted to satisfy their teachers' expectations. The students did not want to let their teachers down. In other words, Wentzel (2003) expressed that "creating a caring environment in which teachers enforce rules consistently, communicate expectations for self-reliance and self-control, solicit children's opinions and feelings, and provide positive expressions of warmth and approval appears to be critical..." (p. 325). For such care to exist in urban classrooms, teachers have to facilitate, structure, and develop such contexts and work to demistify the power structures in the classroom. Indeed, caring teachers are critical to academic success for students in urban classrooms.

Caring Teachers

Caring teachers in urban classrooms have several characteristics. Caring teachers want and expect the very best from their students, and they build relationships that allow students to thrive socially, emotionally and academically. Caring relationships are established, according to Rhona S. Weinstein (1996), by teaching strategies that "draw from a wide range of methods; they are challenging and intensive, flexibly applied, responsive to student obstacles encountered in learning, and vary for time completion" (p. 18). In describing some common characteristics of care among the 13 teachers in his study, Brown (2003) reported,

> These 13 urban teachers create caring classroom communities by showing a genuine interest in each student. They gain student cooperation by being assertive through the use of explicitly stated expectations for appropriate student behavior and academic growth. And these teachers demonstrate mutual respect for students through the use of congruent communication processes. (p. 282)

Unfortunately, at times teachers display less than caring instruction due to the many demands placed on them. For instance, Stanley (1998) wrote about a student who complained of a stomach ache and would not participate in the class assignments of the day. The teacher sent the student to the counseling office, and upon inquiry, the counselor learned that the student was "too tired to talk or to walk around school or to do any work" (p. 237). The following Monday the school learned that the student had died over the weekend. The autopsy report stated that the student's appendix had ruptured 10 days prior to his death. No teacher, counselor, or administrator would have ever dreamed of not providing the support necessary to save the student's life. However, as Stanley (1998) explained, those involved in the education of students in schools often forget to "care" for the person. Time, effort, energy, and will are placed on getting the student to do his or her work—or better yet, to submit to the control and instructions of the teachers and school. In the midst of the multiple issues that students and adults face in schools, teachers often forget to really provide care and caring environments for the human—the person, the student. Stanley explained that there is an "impersonal" dimension to classroom management that often ignores the emotional and psychological dilemmas and needs of students.

Indeed, teachers play an integral role in providing safe, reassuring, and optimal learning for students in urban classrooms. Care is critical for effective learning to occur in any environment but especially in urban classrooms. Irvine (2003) explained that teaching is about establishing and maintaining caring relationships, and it is about what Collins (1991) called "other mothering" (and I would add "other fathering").

Mitchell (1998), in her qualitative study of eight recently retired African American teachers, reminded us of the insight among teachers that can help us understand the important connections between the affective domain and student behavior. Mitchell explained that for teachers to establish and maintain student motivation and engagement, they must be aware of the affective domain and care about the students. Students' feelings and emotions matter in how they experience education. The teachers in her study "were critically aware of the experiences of the students, both in and out of school, and of the contexts shaping these experiences" (p. 105). The teachers were able to connect with the students in the urban environments because they understood that the behaviors (whether appropriate or inappropriate) were a direct result of the students' out-of-school experiences. There were reasons behind the students' behavioral choices. In Mitchell's words

> [The teachers] recalled situations in which factors outside of the school adversely affected students' behavior. They described students listless because of hunger and sleepy because they worked at

> night and on weekends to help support younger siblings. They described students easily distracted and sometimes belligerent because of unstable living [home] environments. (p. 109)

Thus, these retired African American teachers understood the connection between the home and school, and they were able to conceptualize how students' feelings had been impacted by their home circumstances and consequently how students' feelings emerged in their respective behaviors and academic engagement in the urban classroom.

Mitchell outlined the teachers' understandings, management, and pedagogy in two interrelated categories: teacher as activist, and teacher as active supporter of student growth and development. The teachers understood that many of their students were doing drugs, living in poverty, and were acting as adults in their homes in terms of bringing in money to support their families and caring for their younger siblings. Clearly, these experiences among the students influenced how they behaved or misbehaved in the classroom. It is easy for teachers to grant students permission to fail when they consider the complex and challenging lives of their students outside of the classroom. However, teachers must maintain high expectations for their students, and not pity them, so that students have the best possible chance of mobilizing themselves and their families. To explain, teachers who are committed to improving the lives of their students do not accept mediocrity, and they encourage and insist that their students reach their full capacity, mainly because these teachers understand that allowing students to "just get by" is surely to leave the students in their current situation or even worse. Thus, teachers cannot adopt approaches that do not push their students—high expectations are necessary to help the students become empowered, emancipate themselves, and to move beyond their current situations.

In summary, empirical research has suggested that care, trust, high expectations, and empathy have all been found as essential features in developing student motivation and in creating effective learning contexts among urban students. These findings surely suggest that administrators and teachers working with urban students must exercise intentions that are in line with the hopes, dreams, expectations, and aspirations that they hold for their own children. Teachers have a better chance of ensuring that students experience learning by developing the knowledge, skills, and attitudes necessary for effective classroom management.

EFFECTIVE CLASSROOM MANAGEMENT IN URBAN CLASSROOMS

The discussion shifts now to answer the following question: What are the most effective methods, strategies, and approaches to classroom management in urban settings? Indeed, outlining the problems and issues inherent in urban schools without thinking seriously and intently about strategies, methods, and approaches that prove effective in urban schools would leave the discussion incomplete.

Warm Demanders and Culturally Relevant Pedagogy

Consider the following exchange from Irvine and Fraser's (1998) article, "Warm Demanders," in which they explain the teaching of Irene Washington, an African American teacher of 23 years:

> "That's enough of your nonsense, Darius. Your story does not make sense. I told you time and time again that you must stick to the theme I gave you. Now sit down." Darius, a first grader trying desperately to tell his story, proceeds slowly to his seat with his head hanging low.

Irvine and Fraser (1998) described the teacher's approach and the interaction between the student and teacher above by borrowing James Vasquez's notion, "warm demanders," a description of teachers of color "who provide a tough-minded, no-nonsense, structured, and disciplined classroom environment for kids whom society has psychologically and physically abandoned" (p. 56). An outsider observing the teacher's tone and expectations for Darius might frown upon the teacher's approach. However, this teacher's classroom management approach is grounded in a history and a reality that is steeped in care for the student's best interest. In short, the teacher understood quite deeply that she must help Darius learn, and she must "talk the talk." There is a sense of urgency not only for Irene to "teach her children well but to save and protect them from the perils of urban street life" (p. 56).

Researchers and practitioners do not agree whether Irene's approach is advantageous or effective. For instance, where low socioeconomic status students were concerned, Brophy (1982) declared:

> many students from low socioeconomic status backgrounds are accustomed to authoritarian or even brutal treatment at home, but this is not what they need from their teachers. If anything, these students have a greater need for, and respond more positively to, teacher acceptance and warmth. Specifically in the case of minority group students who are alienated from school learning and discriminated against by the majority of the student body, successful teaching involves a combination of warmth with determination.... (p. 48)

Thus, how one defines and conceives warmth and appropriate treatment likely depends on his or her worldview. More research grounded in the practices of urban classrooms is needed to tease out this and similar tensions around how best to teach and manage in urban settings.

It seems that the most effective methods, strategies, and approaches to classroom management in urban schools are culturally grounded and are reflective of culturally relevant pedagogy. Ladson-Billings (1994) explained that culturally relevant pedagogy

> uses student culture in order to maintain it and to transcend the negative effects of the dominant culture. The negative effects are brought about, for example, by not seeing one's history, culture, or background represented in textbook or curriculum . . . culturally relevant teaching is a pedagogy that empowers students intellectually, socially, emotionally, and politically by using cultural referents to impart knowledge, skills, and attitudes. (pp. 17–18)

In addition, as evident in Irene's interaction with Darius and based on a range of other research, it seems that we can learn much from teachers of color, and particularly African American teachers, about classroom management in urban classrooms (Foster, 1997; Monroe & Obidah, 2004). However, although teachers of color may more readily understand the nature of urban students' experiences, the pervasive discourses in a school (coupled with the school's philosophies, beliefs, perceptions, and views) can circumvent these teachers' desires to do their best work with urban students. In Buendia, Gitlin, and Doumbia's (2003) words, "the present-day contexts of schools may push critically minded teachers of color in ways that undermine their desires" (p. 317). Still, Irvine (1998) outlined several important practices among African American teachers that could be classified as culturally relevant:

> They perceive themselves as parental surrogates and advocates for their African American students. They employ a teaching style filled with rhythmic language and rapid intonation with many instances of repetition, call and response, high emotional involvement, creative analogies, figurative language, gestures and body movements, symbolism, aphorisms, and lively and often spontaneous discussions. They use students' everyday cultural and historical experiences in an effort to link new concepts to prior knowledge. They spend classroom and nonclassroom time developing a personal

> relationship with their children, and often tease and joke with their students using dialect or slang to establish this personal relationship. They teach with authority. As Michele Foster discovered, for example, students in her study were proud of their teacher's meanness and thought that the teacher pushed them to achieve, limited the amount of disruptions, and ran the class that contributed to students' achievement. (p. 57)

Weis and Centrie (2002), in their ethnographic study, investigated programs within a desegregated school designed to ensure cultural affirmation and advancement of Vietnamese students in an urban magnet school. A homeroom was set aside for the Vietnamese students; the researchers examined the impact of the separate spaces created for the students. Their homeroom teacher, Mr. Lee, who was also Vietnamese, supported the Vietnamese students in the study. As Weis and Centrie explained "By establishing the homeroom for them, the school created a space within which a particular ethnic group could lay psychological and physical claim to space, time, and activities within the larger institution. It was here that the teacher and students could shape their own more targeted agenda, one suited to their needs" (p. 17). How might segregated classroom environments enable students' academic, social, and behavioral success? Is desegregation best for *all* students? (See, Foster, 1997; Holmes, 1990; Irvine & Irvine, 1983; King, 1993; Ladson-Billings, 2004; Milner & Howard, 2004; Tillman, 2004). In essence, the loss of African American teachers and the interactions African American students had with these teachers has been detrimental to the overall success of African American students. Hudson and Holmes (1994) explained that:

> the loss of African American teachers in public school settings has had a lasting negative impact on all students, particularly African American students and the communities in which they reside... [A]lthough the shrinking African American teacher pool has been attributable to several factors, it is partly a fall-out of how *Brown* was implemented by White American policy makers. (p. 389)

Weis and Centrie's (2002) study builds on the research of many African American scholars about the positive influences of black teachers and predominantly black contexts on black student achievement and behavior (see, for example, Foster, 1990; Ladson-Billings, 2004; Siddle-Walker, 1996). Even though there are tensions embedded in the segregation of these students from the larger population in the school, one central theme was evident in Weis and Centrie's (2002) research: segregated spaces with a teacher from the same ethnic background helped the students mediate and negotiate the larger community of the school.

The African American and Latino/a students in the Weis and Centrie study could not experience separate homerooms mainly because the vast majority of students in the school were African American and the teachers were predominantly White. Weis and Centrie (2002) reported that "within the social context of West Side High, the Vietnamese are viewed as the school's shining academic stars, admired by teachers and administrators for their hard work and respectful and polite attitudes. Conversely, the same teachers frequently see African American and Latino students as inept and disruptive"(p. 13). Candidly, Teachers, all teachers, must see themselves as cultural and racial beings, a practice that many White teachers have not mastered. In short, these teachers fail to see their own whiteness and how their own beliefs, values, privileges, and perspectives infiltrate their management, curriculum, and instruction. This discussion is not meant to focus on White teachers exclusively. Clearly, teachers of all ethnic backgrounds need to recognize the interplay of their own identities with that of others. Black teachers, for instance, may have adopted dominant views because they have been socialized and "kidnapped" into the culture of power so significantly that they have forgotten how oppression and repression manifest themselves in the lives of students. Thus, they can also reify stereotypes, and it is critical for all teachers to engage in critical reflection (Gay & Kirkland, 2003). As Tatum (2001) explained:

> In a race-conscious society, the development of a positive sense of racial/ethnic identity not based on assumed superiority or inferiority is an important task for *both* White people and people of color. The development of this positive identity is a lifelong process that often requires unlearning the misinformation and stereotypes we have internalized not only about others, but also about ourselves. (p. 53, emphasis added)

Furthermore, to develop and effectively implement culturally relevant and responsive classroom management strategies, teachers must understand and acknowledge that the students are not necessarily the problem (Ballenger, 1999; Milner, 2003). Teachers must take some of the responsibility, look inwardly and change their own thinking, beliefs, and behavior.

Overwhelmingly, research that focuses on the influences of African American teachers of African American students suggests that these teachers are able to connect with their students on a cultural, racial, social and academic level, resulting in student success. For instance, employing qualitative research methods, Monroe and Obidah (2004) revealed their case study of an eighth-grade class in an urban public middle school. The teacher was African American, and almost all the students were African American. In particular, 22 students were in the science class, 9 African American females, 12 African American males, and one white female. The researchers found that cultural synchronization between the teacher and her students allowed the teacher to manage the classroom in effective ways; that is, instead of referring her students to the office when they did not follow rules, the teacher in the study was able to use humor and, simultaneously, what some would perceive as harsh language with her students to avoid sending the students out of the classroom. Consider the following exchange between the teacher, Ms. Simpson, and her students from Monroe and Obidah's study:

> Andrew, a student... has stopped completing his assignment and is talking to another student who is seated beside him... Ms. Simpson immediately addresses Andrew's off-task behavior with a quick "Andrew!"... after a few minutes Andrew has again stopped working and is talking with another student... "Andrew, I would like to have your tray on my lunch table" Ms. Simpson demands. (p. 256)

Ms. Simpson, after immediately attempting to correct Andrew's off-task behavior and after giving Andrew a verbal warning, decided that she would assign Andrew a detention, and he would have to have lunch with her at her table—away from his friends. Another student in the class ignites an interesting and meaningful exchange:

> Allison: Andrew got a date with Miss Simpson!
> Ms. Simpson: Yes, you have a date with me. You're going to continue to have a date with me until you follow my directions.
> Allison: Andrew like Miss Simpson!
> Michael: That's illegal!
> Ms. Simpson: No illegal would be flat out killing you. That's illegal.
> Michael: You ain't going to put no, you ain't going to put no date rape pill in our milk are you?
> Ms. Simpson: Why would I want to date rape y'all? (p. 257)

After a few more exchanges, the teacher gets the students back on task with their assignments. What the teacher is able to do in this particular situation is connect with the students through what some call "jiving" and to create a classroom of comfort, and high expectations in doing what students were supposed to do and, at the same time, care. She likely does not want to put Andrew's destiny in the hands of another, perhaps an administrator. Rather, she handles the disruptive behavior herself because she has the repertoire of skills and knowledge to do so. Ms. Simpson's management style was also framed by what some would classify as tough verbal feedback and demands. These demands were couched in emotion and affect that were no-nonsense. She implemented such approaches when her students threatened or violated other students (such as when students would fist fight or threatened to). Clearly as Monroe and Obidah as well as Weinstein et al. (2004) explained, "the cultural context in which behaviors occur strongly mediates definitions of appropriate and inappropriate behavior" (p. 257). Grossman (1995) suggested that educators must "adapt their management techniques to students' ethnic, socioeconomic, contextual, gender, and other individual characteristics to help them learn more efficiently, behave appropriately, and feel better about themselves" (p. 171).

Of course, white teachers or teachers not of color can be successful classroom managers with students of color. In fact, there is compelling evidence that suggests that white teachers can be successful with African American students (Ayers, 1993; Cooper, 2003; Ladson-Billings, 1994; Paley, 1979). Teachers not of color who were successful in these studies seemed to carry similar characteristics. For instance, the teachers employed what some define as strict or no-nonsense techniques; the teachers asserted their authority in a caring way—by setting high expectations and not giving in to students' excuses. The teachers understood that the stakes were so high for these students of color in the real world and attempted to make the rules and expectations explicit (Delpit, 1995). And the teachers seemed to engage in a level of racial and cultural consciousness and saw themselves as members of the dominant class with implicit and ingrained perspectives and views of how things were and ought to be thus pointing to the disconnections between themselves and their students.

Culturally Responsive Management

Geneva Gay (2000) defined culturally responsive teaching as "using the cultural knowledge, prior experiences, frames of reference, and performance styles of ethnically diverse students to make learning encounters more relevant to and effective for them. It teaches to and through the strengths of these students. It is culturally validating and affirming" (p. 29). (See also chapter 13 in this volume.) Building on the scholarship of Ladson-Billings (1994) and Gay (2000), Weinstein et al. (2004) outlined several strategies they framed as "culturally responsive classroom management." Perhaps most significant is the authors' explanation that culturally responsive classroom management "is a frame of mind, more than a set of strategies or practices, that guides the management decisions that teachers make" (p. 27). Developing this frame of mind, as Weinstein et al., (2004) posited, requires an understanding of the following components:

> (a) recognition of one's own ethnocentrism and biases; (b) knowledge of students' cultural backgrounds; (c) understanding of the broader social, economic, and political context of our educational system; (d) ability and willingness to use culturally appropriate classroom management strategies; and (e) commitment to building caring classroom communities. (p. 27)

Among other effective classroom management strategies and approaches in urban classrooms, for teachers, Weinstein et al. (2003) stressed the importance of establishing expectations for student behavior, communicating with students in "culturally consistent ways" (p. 272), creating inclusive and caring classrooms, and working with families to build strong partnerships and relationships.

Grossman (1995) maintained "classroom management techniques that are designed by European American middle-class teachers for European-American middle-class students do not meet the needs of many non-middle-class non-European American students" (p. xvii). Culturally responsive management frameworks "incorporate elements of students' home, personal, and community lives into the classroom" (Monroe & Obidah, 2004, p. 259). Moreover, the teacher in Monroe and Obidah's study "drew on referents such as speech patterns, voice tones, facial expressions, and word choices that conveyed her behavioral expectations to students in familiar and meaningful ways" (p. 266).

Figure 2 outlines some strategies, methods, and approaches for creating effective classroom management in urban classrooms. These points are adapted from the research, theory, and practice reviewed in this chapter. Although there is no definitive answer to effective management in urban classrooms, the strategies presented have proven effective through the studies cited in this chapter.

IMPLICATIONS AND CONCLUSIONS

Attempting to understand the complexities inherent in managing urban classrooms is indeed an arduous task. Students, their experiences, their lifeworlds, and their racial and cultural heritage must be at the core of teachers' understanding and knowledge. We (researchers, theorists, and practitioners) must understand how the students who are enrolled in urban classrooms live both inside and outside of school. Understanding students in urban classrooms means that we problematize issues of "appropriate" and "normal" behavior. Like knowledge construction, students' behavioral patterns are constructed based on social, political, and cultural worldviews, phenomena, and experiences. Thus, we must work to understand how students' social, political, and cultural experiences influence what they do, what they choose not to do, why they make such decisions, and how they conduct themselves in the classroom. Moreover, teachers must understand that what they perceive as "appropriate" and "normal" behavior are also socially constructed.

Additionally, classroom management in urban classrooms must involve more than a focus on student behavior. Certainly, more management needs and issues exist in the classroom than mere student discipline and behavior. This review also points to some ethnic, gender, class, and cultural issues that must be explored and considered when thinking about classroom management in urban classrooms. On the one hand, we must be aware of the multiple and varied experiences among students of color and the inconsistencies that exist between them and their teachers. We must not stereotype, generalize, and reify incorrect assumptions and misconceptions about any group of students. To do so would contradict the very essence of the message of this chapter. We must understand that students bring into the classroom knowledge, expertise, brilliance, and a set of experiences that must be taken into consideration when providing learning opportunities. Building on students' prior knowledge, including how they have been taught to behave in the past, is essential in developing the curriculum and instruction. As Dillard (2000) asserts, students of color are not white people with pigmented skin. Their experiences are shaped by their ethnic and cultural heritage. But at the same time, teachers must recognize that they are teaching individual students. Classroom management is about opportunities to learn. The goal of any management study, theory, or practice should be to shed light on students' learning of academic, social, political, and economic realities. In short, classroom management is about social, political, economic, and academic justice.

Students and parents must bear some responsibility for students' behavior in urban classrooms. In like form, teachers, administrators, policy makers, and teacher education programs

Adopt learner lenses: Teachers do not assume that they know everything and learn about the life experiences of their students.

Engage in critical self-examination and reflection: Teachers engage in introspection that bring to the fore their own strengths, weaknesses, privileges, and issues; teachers encourage students to engage in self-reflection; both groups work to examine how they contribute to disharmony in the classroom attempting to avoid blaming the other.

Make the culture of power explicit: Teachers do not assume that students implicitly understand expectation and rules; teachers make the power structure explicit to students.

Uses accessible, relevant language: Teachers do not complicate expectations by using unclear and inaccessible language.

Encourage student input, ownership, and contribution in expectations and rules: Teachers allow students to participate in classroom rules and expectations so that students gain a sense of agency in the context.

Create caring and empathetic attitudes and dispositions: Teachers attempt to understand their students and work with them to solve problems rather than seeing students as the enemy.

Reject deficit thinking: Teachers believe that students are in fact knowledgeable and bring a wealth of knowledge and expertise into the classrooms; teachers see students as assets not as liabilities.

Develop cultural and racial awareness and understanding: Teachers understand that students' experiences are shaped historically, socially, and politically; teachers attempt to connect to students' cultural and racial heritage.

Avoid color-blind ideologies: Teachers recognize and acknowledge students' race as a central dimension of who students are; teachers attempt to know more complete students, not just fragmented ones.

Develop and maintain trust: Teachers create a trusting environment for students by demonstrating care and by establishing bonds with their students by the ways in which they treat students, their expectations, and by building classroom community.

Solicit parental and community partnerships: Teachers recognize that there is strength in having partnerships with parents and the community; teachers work hard to develop partnerships with parents to both understand and scaffold learning and behavior in the classroom.

Provide multiple opportunities: Teachers understand that students are often learning a new culture of power and that they will need multiple chances to succeed; teachers do not give up on students quickly and easily; teachers realize that many students are not used to experiencing success and work to help students "see the other side."

Avoid placing students' destiny in the hands of others: Teachers realize that they likely know the student better than any other in the school and refuses to place the students' future in the hands of another (e.g., principal, resource officer).

Develop and maintain high expectations: Teachers realize that they must push students to reach success because the stakes are so high for these students once they are in the real world; teachers refuse to water down the curriculum because they feel sorry for their students; teachers are on a mission to help their students succeed and refuse to grant students permission to fail.

Realize that each student is an individual: Teachers reject the idea that equal means the same and realize that each student brings a different set of needs into the classroom that must be met.

Be stern and fair: Teachers make it clear that they expect excellence and, at the same time, keep in mind that they must be fair to each student.

Use humor to demystify and breakdown barriers in the classroom: Teachers understand that it is acceptable to laugh but also recognize that humor has to be framed and complemented by their authority.

Develop a frame of mind for success: Teachers really think and believe that their students can and will succeed.

FIGURE 18.2. Strategies and Approaches for Effective Classroom Management.

must also carry some of the responsibility. Clearly, there needs to be some collaboration and effort on the part of various groups to provide optimal learning opportunities for students of color, poor students, and all students in urban classrooms. Developing parental and community alliances can mediate student behavior and their choices inside of the classroom. To do so, teachers must demystify and breakdown barriers that exist between schools and parents. Intimidation that parents may feel can circumvent parental and community partnership that can be central to teachers' development of strategies to help students understand the culture of power and to succeed in the classroom.

When students are not in the classroom—that is, when they are sent out of the classroom for disciplinary reprimands—they do not have access to learning opportunities. This inaccessibility is dangerous and needs to be considered seriously. Monroe and Obidah (2004) explained that among all those involved in the education of urban students "teachers who address inappropriate conduct in the classroom without relying on formal procedures, such as office referrals, may enable their students to avoid detrimental effects associated with recurrent disciplinary action" (p. 266). With this in mind, I offer the following recommendations for the different, and equally important, constituents and stakeholders involved in the educational enterprise of students enrolled in urban classrooms.

A Charge to Teacher Education

Many teacher education programs across the country still do not have courses that address urban schooling—not to mention urban classroom management. This is a programmatic void that needs to be filled (Matus, 1999). Teacher education programs should be in the forefront, helping teachers develop the competencies necessary to meet the needs of urban student learners. Teacher education must help teachers and future teachers pose tough questions for the sake of all students (Milner, 2003; Milner & Smithey, 2003). According to Weinstein et al. (2004), "A lack of multicultural competence can exacerbate the difficulties that novice teachers (and even more experienced teachers) have with classroom management" (p. 26).

It is imperative that teachers understand that "children must learn (and be taught) the culture of the classroom for them to effectively participate in learning . . . if the children understand and learn the appropriate expected behaviors for different classroom contexts, communication and interaction between the teacher and students should increase" (Garibaldi, 1992, pp. 26–27). In addition, teachers still enter urban classrooms secretly afraid of their students because they have never known anyone who "looked, talked, or acted like [students in urban schools]" (Weiner, 1993, p. 119). The manners by which teachers interpret student behavior in urban classrooms have the potential to guide and mitigate learning, and teacher education needs to be on the front line in helping teachers understand these needs and issues.

Finally, as Weinstein et al. (2004) suggested:

> Teacher educators and researchers interested in classroom management must begin to make cultural diversity an integral part of the conversation. We need to ask whether diversity requires different approaches to classroom management, to examine the kinds of cultural conflicts that are likely to arise in ethnically diverse classrooms, and to consider the best ways to help preservice [and practicing] teachers become multiculturally competent. (p. 27)

In short, teacher education must help teachers develop the skills, knowledge, attitudes, beliefs, thinking, practices, and dispositions necessary to teach effectively in urban classrooms and to stay in those contexts. Conceivably, teachers who feel efficacious about their abilities to perform in a context are much more likely to persist—even in the midst of adversity. Teacher education programs are critical in this regard. Students in urban classrooms need and deserve competent and committed teachers. And research trajectories need developing in teacher education programs to tract teachers' learning both in and beyond teachers' education. We must build and expand our knowledge about the effects of our programs to tear down pervasive political discourses and practices that do not recognize the value of our work in teacher education.

A Charge to Researchers

Obviously, we need to know more about classroom management in urban classrooms. There simply are not enough concrete studies on this pressing topic. Weiner (2003) declared, "One of the most serious obstacles to understand anything about urban schools is the lack of reliable data" (p. 306). Weinstein et al. (2004) have posed several interrelated questions that might be a starting point in thinking about future research that really takes into consideration the complexities of urban classroom. For instance, the researchers suggest that research management should pose questions such as

> What types of cultural conflicts can arise in classrooms that might make it more difficult to have a safe, caring, orderly environment?
>
> What approaches are most appropriate when students in one particular classroom come from a variety of cultural backgrounds?
>
> How can we sensitize our (mostly White, middle-class) students to their own biases, assumptions, and stereotypes so that they undergo genuine personal transformation rather than simply learning to mouth the socially appropriate responses? (pp. 35–36)

It is essential for researchers to conduct this research in urban classrooms, to make connections to teacher education, and to see with a cultural eye (Irvine, 2003)—regardless of the research paradigm the researchers select. Researchers cannot assume that their research is culturally, racially, and ethnically neutral. The nature of questions posed, the research design, instrumentation decisions, how the questions are posed, on behalf of whom, and to whom, how data are analyzed and reported or represented are all issues imbedded in one's worldview—issues that have cultural and racial implications.

Jeff, a high school English teacher in Brown's (2003) study reminded us "You're there to teach kids—not subjects! We often forget this point" (p. 278). In this same manner, researchers should craft their research projects and agendas in ways that build, broaden, and expand our knowledge about creating better learning contexts for students who experience urban classroom life. The point is that our research ought to inform practice for the sake of all children. After all, we are studying people—human beings, not subjects or lab rats. Weiner (2003) declared that

> Because so little research has been done that examines a full range of contextual factors that influence urban schools and the classrooms within them, we have relatively little information that is confirmed by research about how the social context of the school and the social organization of the school itself influence urban teaching in general and classroom management in particular. (p. 307)

To date, research is limited that looks specifically at classroom management with linguistically diverse students. While there is a meaningful and growing body of literature focusing on English language learners and learning, the connections to classroom management are scarce. Still, Curran (2003) maintained, "A teacher's management decision-making process becomes even more complex when she or he doesn't speak the first language of students who are new to U.S. classrooms" (p. 334). Because a wide range of students enrolled in urban schools and classrooms are (and will continue to be) from non-English speaking countries, we need to know more about the issues, needs, and perspectives these students bring into the classroom to develop a knowledge base about how best to "manage" their learning and behavior to "reduce the likelihood for linguistic and cultural miscommunication and conflicts" (p. 334) in the urban classroom.

There is a great need for researchers to employ new and more innovative research and theoretical methods, and frameworks, such as critical race theory (Ladson-Billings & Tate, 1995; Singer, in press), to more deeply conceptualize and analyze the central role of race in classroom management strategies, options, and decision making. Employing critical race theory as an analytical and conceptual tool to explore how inequity, race, and racism manifest themselves in the classroom could elicit new and more profound information. For instance, how does race emerge in students' behavior and in teachers' interpretation of that behavior? How do historical, social, and racial issues connect and draw meaning to the ways in which students of color conduct themselves in the urban classroom? What systemic, institutional, and legal mandates perpetuate the nature of schooling offered to certain racial groups of students? That is, how do property taxes shape the kinds of schools available to students of color and how do these systemic issues reproduce, enable, and maintain the status quo?

A Charge to Teachers, Urban Schools, and Reformers

Haberman (2000) explained that "urban educators who can control and manage their classrooms and schools are not removed simply because students are not learning" (p. 205). These teachers, who have some control in the classroom, often are viewed as excellent teachers even though their students are not making academic progress. Certainly, we need to rethink these perceptions—which really are policies—and the praise we give teachers whose only accomplishment is that they can "control" students in their classrooms. Besides, classroom management involves much more than discipline and control. Still, as Newberg and Sims (1996) explained, "Racism, unemployment, and unresponsive schools are corrosive blights that rot and destroy human potential. These social ills are at the root of our society's perpetuation of cultures of poverty and must be addressed vigorously by citizens and government" (p. 174).

Nieto (1994) suggested that true reform could occur when we listen to the experiences and voices of the students who are in a variety of schools. By interviewing a wide range of successful ethnic, linguistic, and racial groups, junior and senior high school students, she learned of these students' struggles in schools but also came to understand the factors that enabled the students' persistence, and success. In Nieto's view, reform has to include dialogue, perspectives, and insights from students themselves. Where urban school reform is concerned, Nieto (1994) posited that "developing conditions in schools that let students know that they have a right to envision other possibilities beyond those imposed by traditional barriers of race, gender, or social class" (p. 422) is a necessary component to any reform effort in urban contexts.

Irvine (1988) stressed that students' home environments cannot and should not be deterrents in thinking about optimal reform. She maintained that variables such as school quality, pedagogical materials and equipment, and characteristics of the teacher are integral to students' learning opportunities. Thus, reformers cannot escape systemic and structural responsibilities by insisting that urban school reform is completely out of their hands. Reformers must take responsibility for the issues that are in their control (such as quality of schools, teachers, instructional materials and school zoning). Those involved in effective urban schools did not make excuses for their failure by blaming students' home environments. In Irvine's (1988) words, "the fact that a child was on welfare and perhaps living in a single-parent home was never used as an excuse to justify a student's non-achievement" (p. 237). It is time for reformers to move beyond the rhetoric and do the work that is necessary to improve these schools.

Irvine's (1988) outline of effective schools, conceptualized over a decade ago, still holds credence in thinking about reform. As she described, effective urban schools displayed some common characteristics: (a) "visionary" leadership; (b) effective, relevant, and responsive instruction; (c) both rigid and flexible bureaucracy (where autonomy and flexibility are welcomed in some instances and strict as well as rigid administration are necessary in other instances—such as disciplinary policies and procedures to keep everyone safe); and (d) partnerships and collaboration with parents and community members. Thus, urban reform, and particularly reform on the classroom level, is necessary and will prove beneficial not only for those attending and working in urban schools but all people in a variety of contexts. As Hilliard (1992) explained, "any reform that benefits those students who are poorly served always works to the benefit of all" (p. 375).

African American students are still being educated in separate and unequal schools across the country (Hale, 2001; Ladson-Billings, 2004; Tillman, 2004). As Siddle-Walker (1996) explained, there was something special—something honorable—about the ways in which African American students experienced education before desegregation. There was a sense of pride among African American students that seemed to be supported by the students' respective communities and also supported and nurtured by the many teachers and students with whom the students interacted. What can we learn from these principals and teachers about reform to help us think about where we are today with regards to urban schools, classrooms, and teaching? For example, studies focusing explicitly on classroom management in urban classrooms should be framed to investigate and build on these principals' and teachers' perspectives.

Concluding Thoughts

Delpit and White-Bradley (2003) shared their memories of working with urban or inner city students:

> Because we serve low-income African American and other students of color—children who are part of a demographic group most likely to be classified as disciplinary problems or behavior disordered—you might expect that our memories would be replete with stories of children engaging in unruly and dangerous acts. To the contrary, we see thinking children who must grapple with issues of power and control, and who for the sake of their humanity, often insist that their voices be heard even as schools [and teachers and classrooms] find new ways to silence them. (p. 288)

Teacher educators, researchers, policy makers, and reformers must include the urban student on their respective agendas. By changing and rejecting deficit notions, by recognizing and embracing the expertise that students bring into the classroom, and by realizing that there is room for negotiation as we think about the social construction of behavior and experience, we may better attend to the needs of urban students in the classroom. Clearly, more rigorous and serious attention is needed to improve the conditions of students in urban classrooms; if not, when the next volume on classroom management is published, the same problems and issues outlined in this chapter will be outlined in that one. The time is now and the issues and needs are plentiful; the question is, what are we going to do about them?

ACKNOWLEDGMENTS

The author wishes to thank Dr. Jacqueline Jordan Irvine, Candler Professor of Urban Education, Emory University and Dr. Donna Ford, Vanderbilt University for reviewing this chapter.

REFERENCES

Anyon, J. (1980). Social class and the hidden curriculum of work. *Journal of Education, 162*(1), 366–391.

Ayers, W. (1993). *To teach: The journey of a teacher*. New York: Teachers College Press.

Ballenger, C. (1999). *Teaching other people's children: Literacy and learning in a bilingual classroom*. New York: Teachers College Press.

Banks, J. A, & Banks, C. A. M. (2000). *Multicultural education: Issues and perspectives*. (4th Edition). New York: John Wiley.

Brophy, J. E. (1979). Teacher behavior and its effects. *Educational Psychology, 71*(6), 733–750.

Brophy, J. E. (1982). Supplemental group management techniques. In D. L. Duke (Ed.), *Helping teachers manage classrooms* (pp. 32–51). Alexandria, VA: Association for Supervision and Curriculum Development.

Brown, D. F. (2003). Urban teachers' use of culturally responsive management strategies. *Theory Into Practice, 42*(4), 277–282.

Buendia, E., Gitlin, A., & Doumbia, F. (2003). Working the pedagogical bourderlands: An African critical pedagogue teaching within an ESL context. *Curriculum Inquiry 33*(3), 291–320.

Collins, P. H. (1991). *Black feminist thought: Knowledge, conscious, and the politics of empowerment: Perspectives on gender, Volume 2*. New York: Routledge.

Cooper, P. M. (2003). Effective white teachers of black children: Teaching within a community. *Journal of Teacher Education, 54*(5), 413–427.

Curran, M. E. (2003). Linguistic diversity and classroom management. *Theory Into Practice, 42*(4), 334–340.

Davis, J. E., & Jordan, W. J. (1994). The effects of school context, structure, and experiences on African American males in middle and high school. *Journal of Negro Education, 63*(4), 570–587.

Delpit, L., (1995). *Other people's children: Cultural conflict in the classroom*. New York: The New Press.

Delpit, L., & White-Bradley (2003). Educating or imprisoning the spirit: Lessons from ancient Egypt. *Theory Into Practice, 42*(4), 283–288.

Dillard, C. B. (2000). Cultural consideration in paradigm proliferation. Paper presented at the annual meeting of the American Educational Research Association, April 24–28, New Orleans, LA.

Ennis, C. D. (1996). When avoiding confrontation leads to avoiding content: Disruptive students' impact on curriculum. *Journal of Curriculum and Supervision, 11*, 145–162.

Ennis, C. D., & McCauley, M. T. (2002). Creating urban classroom communities worthy of trust. *Journal of Curriculum Studies, 34*(2), 149–172.

Ferguson, A. A. (2000). *Bad boys: Public schools in the making of Black masculinity*. Ann Arbor: University of Michigan Press.

Fine, M. (1986). Why urban adolescents drop into and out of public high school. *Teachers College Record, 87*(3), 393–409.

Ford, D. Y. (1996). *Reversing underachievement among gifted Black students: Promising practices and programs*. New York: Teachers College Press.

Foster, M. (1990). The politics of race: Through the eyes of African-American teachers. *Journal of Education, 172*, 123–141.

Foster, M. (1997). *Black teachers on teaching*. New York: The New Press.

Garibaldi, A. M. (1992). Preparing teachers for culturally diverse classrooms. In M. E. Dilworth (Ed.), *Diversity in teacher education: New expectations* (pp. 29–39). San Francisco: Jossey-Bass.

Gay, G. (2000). *Culturally responsive teaching: Theory, research, and practice*. New York: Teachers College Press.

Gay, G., & Howard, T. (2000). Multicultural teacher education for the 21st century *Teacher Educator, 36*(1), 1–16.

Gay, G., & Kirkland, K. (2003). Developing cultural critical consciousness and self-reflection in preservice teacher education. *Theory Into Practice 42*(3), 181–187.

Gordon, B. M. (1988). Implicit assumptions of the Holmes and Carnegie reports: a view from an African-American perspective. *Journal of Negro Education, 57*, 141–158.

Grossman, H. (1995). *Classroom behavior management in a diverse society*. Mountain View, CA: Mayfield.

Haberman, M. (1991). The pedagogy of poverty versus good teaching. *Phi Delta Kappan 73*(4), 290–294.

Haberman, M. (2000, November). Urban schools: Day camps or custodial centers? *Phi Delta Kappan, 82*(3), 203–208.

Haberman, M., & Rickards, W. H. (1990). Urban teachers who quit: Why they leave and what they do. *Urban Education, 25*(3), 297–303.

Hale, J. E. (1982). *Black children: Their roots, culture, and learning styles.* Provo, UT: Brigham Young University Press.

Hale, J. E. (2001). *Learning while black: Creating educational excellence for African-American children.* Baltimore: John Hopkins University Press.

Hilliard, A. G. (1992). Behavioral style, culture, and teaching and learning. *Journal of Negro Education, 61*(3), 370–377.

Holmes, B. J. (1990). New strategies are needed to produce minority teachers. In A. Dorman (Ed.), *Recruiting and retaining minority teachers* (Guest Commentary, Policy Brief No. 8). Oak Brook, IL: North Central Regional Educational Laboratory.

Houston, W. R., & Williamson, J. L. (1993). Perceptions of their preparation by 42 Texas elementary school teachers compared with their responses as student teachers. *Teacher Education and Practice, 8*(2), 27–42.

Howard, T. C. (2001). Telling their side of the story: African American students' perceptions of culturally relevant teaching. *Urban Review, 33*(2), 131–149.

Howard, T. C. (2003). Who receives the short end of the shortage?: America's teacher shortage and implications for urban schools. *Journal of Curriculum and Supervision, 18*(2), 142–160.

Hudson, M. J., & Holmes, B. J. (1994). Missing teachers, impaired communities: The unanticipated consequences of Brown v. Board of Education on the African American teaching force at the precollegiate level. *Journal of Negro Education, 63*, 388–393.

Irvine, J. J. (1988). Urban schools that work: A summary of relevant factors. *Journal of Negro Education, 57*(3), 236–242.

Irvine, J. J. (1990). *Black students and school failure: Policies, practices and prescriptions.* New York: Greenwood Press.

Irvine, J. J., & Fraser, J. W. (1998, May 13). Warm demanders. *Education Week, 17*(35), 56.

Irvine, J. J. (2003). *Because of the kids: Seeing with a cultural eye.* New York: Teachers College Press.

Irvine, R. W., & Irvine, J. J. (1983). The impact of the desegregation process on the education of black students: Key variables. *Journal of Negro Education, 52*, 410–422.

Johnson, L. (2002). "My eyes have been opened": White teachers and racial awareness. *Journal of Teacher Education, 53*(2), 153–167.

Katz, S. R. (1999). Teaching in tensions: Latino immigrant youth, their teachers, and the structures of schooling. *Teachers College Record, 100*(4), 809–840.

King, S. (1993). The limited presence of African-American teachers. *Review of Educational Research, 63*(2), 115–149.

Kozol, J. (1992). *Salvage inequalities: Children in America's schools.* Boston: Houghton Mifflin.

Ladson-Billings, G. (1994). *The dreamkeepers: Successful teachers of African American children.* San Francisco: Jossey-Bass.

Ladson-Billings, G. (2000). Fighting for our lives: Preparing teachers to teach African American students. *Journal of Teacher Education, 51*(3), 206–214.

Ladson-Billings, G. (2001). *Crossing over to Canaan: The journey of new teachers in diverse classrooms.* San Francisco: Jossey-Bass.

Ladson-Billings, G. (2002). Permission to fail. In L. Delpit & J. K. Dowdy (Eds.), *The skin that we speak: Thoughts on language and culture in the classroom* (pp. 107–120). New York: The New Press.

Ladson-Billings, G. (2004). Landing on the wrong note: The price we paid for *Brown. Educational Researcher, 33*(7), 3–13.

Ladson-Billings, G., & Tate, B. (1995). Toward a critical race theory of education. *Teachers College Record, 97*(1), 47–67.

Matus, D. E. (1999, May/June). Humanism and effective urban secondary classroom management. *The Clearing House, 72*(5), 305–307.

McAllister, G., & Irvine, J. J. (2002). The role of empathy in teaching culturally diverse students: A qualitative study of teachers' beliefs. *Journal of Teacher Education, 53*(5), 433–443.

McCadden, B. M. (1998). Why is Michael always getting timed out? Race, class, and the disciplining of other people's children. In R. E. Butchart & B. McEwan (Eds.), *Classroom discipline in American schools: Problems and possibilities for democratic education* (pp. 109–134). Albany, NY: State University of New York Press.

McCarthy, J. D., & Hoge, D. R. (1987). The social construction of school punishment: Racial disadvantage out of universalistic process. *Social Forces, 65*, 1101–1120.

Milner, H. R. (2003). Teacher reflection and race in cultural contexts: history, meanings, and methods in teaching. *Theory Into Practice, 42*(3), 173–180.

Milner, H. R., & Howard, T. C. (2004). Black teachers, Black students, Black communities and *Brown*: Perspectives and insights from experts. *Journal of Negro Education, 73*(3), 285–297.

Milner, H. R. (in press). But good intentions are not enough: Theoretical and philosophical relevance in teaching diverse students. In J. Landsman of C. W. Lewis (Eds.), *White teachers/diverse classrooms: A Guide to building inclisive schools, promoting high expectations and eliminating racism.* Sterling, VA: Stylus Publishers.

Milner, H. R., & Smithey, M. (2003). How teacher educators created a course curriculum to challenge and enhance preservice teachers' thinking and experience with diversity. *Teaching Education, 14*(3), 293–305.

Mitchell, A. (1998). African-American teachers: Unique roles and universal lessons. *Education and Urban Society, 31*(1), 104–122.

Monroe, C. R., & Obidah, J. E. (2004). The influence of cultural synchronization on a teachers perceptions of disruption: A case study of an African-American middle-school classroom. *Journal of Teacher Education, 55*(3), 256–268.

Morris, V. G., & Morris, C. L. (2000). *Creating caring and nurturing educational environments for African American children.* Westport, CT: Bergin & Garvey.

Newberg, N. A., & Sims, R. B. (1996). Contexts that promote success for inner-city students. *Urban Education, 31*(2), 149–176.

Nieto, S. (1994). Lessons from students on creating a chance to dream. *Harvard Educational Review, 64*(4), 392–426.

Noddings, N. (1992). *The challenge to care in schools: An alternative approach to education.* New York: Teachers College Press.

Noguera, P. A. (1995). Preventing and producing violence: A critical analysis of responses to school violence. *Harvard Educational Review, 65*(2), 189–212.

Noguera, P. A. (2003). Schools, prisons, and social implications of punishment: Rethinking disciplinary practices. *Theory Into Practice, 42*(4), 341–350.

Norris, J. A. (2003). Looking at classroom management through a social and emotional learning lens. *Theory Into Practice, 42*(4), 313–318.

Obidah, J. E., & Teel, K. M. (2001). *Because of the kids: Facing racial and cultural differences in schools.* New York: Teachers College Press.

Ogbu, J. U. (1993). Frameworks—variability in minority school performance: A problem in search of an explanation. In E. Jacob & C. Jordan (Eds.), *Minority education: Anthropological perspectives* (pp. 83–111). Norwood, NJ: Ablex.

Paley, V. G. (1979). *White teacher.* Cambridge, MA: Harvard University Press.

Schlosser, L. K. (1992). Teacher distance and student disengagement: School lives on the margin. *Journal of Teacher Education, 43*(2), 128–140.

Sheets, R. H. (1996). Urban classroom conflict: Student-teacher perception: Ethnic integrity, solidarity, and resistance. *Urban Review, 28*(2), 165–183.

Siddle-Walker, V. (1996). *Their highest potential: An African American school community in the segregated South.* Chapel Hill: University of North Carolina Press.

Skiba, R. J., Michael, R. S., Nardo, A. C., & Peterson, R. L. (2002). The color of discipline: Sources of racial and gender disproportionality in school punishment. *The Urban Review, 34*(4), 317–342.

Skiba, R. J., Peterson, R. L., & Williams, T. (1997). Office referrals and suspension: Disciplinary intervention in middle schools. *Education and Treatment of Children, 20*, 295–315.

Singer, J. N. (in press). Addressing epistemolosical racism in sport managment research, *Joural of Sport Management.*

Stanley, S. A. (1998). Empathic caring in classroom management and discipline. In R. E. Butchart & B. McEwan (Eds.), *Classroom discipline in American schools: Problems and possibilities for democratic education* (pp. 237–268). Albany: State University of New York Press.

Steinberg, L., Brown, B. B., & Dornbusch, S. M. (1996). *Beyond the classroom.* New York: Simon & Schuster.

Stinson, S. W. (1993). Meaning and value: Reflections on what students say about school. *Journal of Curriculum and Supervision, 8*(3), 216–238.

Tatum, B. D. (2001). Professional development: An important partner in antiracist teacher education. In S. H. King & L. A. Castenell (Eds.), *Racism and racial inequality: Implications for teacher education* (pp. 51–58). Washington DC: AACTE Publications.

Teel, K. M., Debruin-Parecki, A., & Covington, M. V. (1998). Teaching strategies that honor and motivate inner-city African-American students: A school/university collaboration. *Teaching and Teacher Education, 14*(5), 479–495.

Tillman, L. C. (2004). (Un)intended Consequences?: The Impact of the *Brown v. Board of education* decision on the employment status of black educators. *Education and Urban Society, 36*(3),280–303.

Weiner, L. (1993). *Preparing teachers for urban schools: Lessons from thirty years of school reform.* New York: Teachers College Press.

Weiner, L. (2003). Why is classroom management so vexing for urban teachers? *Theory Into Practice, 42*(4), 305–312.

Weinstein, C. S., Thomlinson-Clarke, S., & Curran, M. (2004). Toward a conception of culturally responsive classroom management. *Journal of Teacher Education, 55*(1), 25–38.

Weinstein, R. S. (1996). High standards in a tracked system of schooling: For which students and with what educational support? *Educational Researcher, 25*(8), 16–19.

Weis, L., & Centrie, C. (2002). On the power of separate spaces: Teachers and students writing (righting) selves and future. *American Educational Research Journal, 39*(1), 7–36.

Wentzel, K. R. (2003). Motivating students to behave in socially competent ways. *Theory Into Practice, 42*(4), 319–326.

Woodson, C. G. (1933). *The mis-education of the Negro*. Washington, DC: Associated Publishers.

Wu, S. C., Pink, W. T., Crain, R. L., & Moles, O. (1982). Student suspension: A critical reappraisal. *Urban Review, 14*, 245–303.

V

Managing the Instructional Formats of Contemporary Classrooms

James M. Cooper
The University of Virginia

19

Managing Groupwork in the Heterogeneous Classroom

Rachel A. Lotan
Stanford University

INTRODUCTION

Academically and linguistically heterogeneous classrooms are a widespread phenomenon in the U.S. and in other countries. In such classrooms, students have a wide range of previous academic achievement or significant differences in their proficiency in the language of instruction. Often, heterogeneous classrooms are the result of educators' intentions and efforts to offer equal access to rigorous curricula, high-quality teaching, and productive interactions with peers. These educators advocate detracking the schools and curtailing traditional ability groupings to create equal opportunities to learn for all students. However, many teachers, students, and parents have had inconsistent or even contradictory experiences with the implementation of these attempts at educational reform. Parents object to watered-down curricula. Students complain about boredom or, conversely, about failing too many classes. Teachers are frustrated by their inability to address the needs of their students at either end of the achievement continuum. For example, in a heterogeneous 10th-grade biology class, about a quarter of the students cannot use the textbook or submit satisfactory lab reports because they read and write at a 5th-grade level. In an 8th-grade social studies class, several newly arrived immigrant students have little or no prior knowledge of momentous events or important figures in U.S. history. In an untracked 9th-grade algebra class, about half the students find it difficult to express their mathematical thinking orally or in writing using conventional and appropriate academic language, although they can solve the problem correctly. In a mainstream 6th-grade classroom where students have nine different home languages, many are bilingual and some are trilingual, some are designated as "limited English proficient," and six students have just joined the class from the pullout English Language Development program.

Groupwork and various models of cooperative or collaborative learning have been promoted as useful pedagogical strategies for such academically and linguistically heterogeneous classrooms. Indeed, there is considerable evidence for the academic, social, and affective benefits of this instructional approach. Students who work collaboratively in small groups have opportunities to grapple with important ideas of the discipline, discuss and debate substantive questions, and practice socially beneficial skills (Slavin, 1995; Johnson & Johnson, 1989, 1990; Sharan, 1995). Most importantly, groupwork has the potential of helping teachers build equitable classrooms (Cohen, 1994; Cohen & Lotan, 1997). How would we recognize an equitable classroom if we saw one? How are equitable learning environments different from nonequitable ones? Are some classrooms more equitable than others? What would be the distinctive and observable features of an equitable classroom?

Equitable classrooms are reflections of a pedagogical, political, and moral vision—a vision that includes a particular conception of learning and teaching, an unapologetic design for the goals of public educational institutions, and a consistent commitment to care for all children and adolescents. In pedagogical terms, equitable classrooms are environments where "being smart" is defined broadly to reflect authentic undertakings in the real world, where students frequently and successfully demonstrate their "smarts," and where they are recognized publicly for their competence and accomplishments. In equitable classrooms, all students have access to intellectually challenging curricula and grade-appropriate learning tasks. In these classrooms, students interact with equal status: they are engaged, they participate actively, and their voices are heard by the teacher and by their peers. The teacher plans the learning environment, orchestrates productive interactions, and treats all students fairly. In political terms, equitable classrooms result in narrowing the achievement gap, allowing advancement to higher levels of education for more students. In equitable classrooms, teachers and students practice democracy (Oakes & Lipton, 1999). In moral terms, an ethic of care pervades equitable classrooms (Noddings, 1992). Rather than imposing rigid control, teachers model and instill a sense of responsibility towards self and others. Students serve as academic, linguistic, and social resources for one another and are accountable to each other individually and as members of a group. In this chapter, I describe how teachers can manage groupwork productively to build equitable classrooms and to practice equitable pedagogy.

MANAGING GROUPWORK—A SOCIOLOGICAL FRAMEWORK

Traditionally, strategies for classroom management have been derived from an individualistic, psychological orientation. As such, classroom management is about correcting and preventing disruptions caused by the "difficult" students and about reinforcing positive comportment of the well-adjusted ones. Such defensive reactions reflect a conception of classroom relations as single and frequently unidirectional interactions between the teacher and individual students. Classroom rules and routines deal with how to support the teacher in controlling the students when she is lecturing or how to ensure that students are attentive and ready to complete in-class or homework assignments in a timely manner. In such cases, rules and routines are lengthy lists of a few *do's* and many *don'ts*, sanctioned by unpleasant consequences such as referrals or detention. Furthermore, when troublesome behaviors are attributed to severe psychological impediments, teachers are expected to act as professional therapists, to diagnose and to counsel youngsters on how to deal with stressful and emotionally taxing tasks.

Groupwork can create many difficult and unpleasant situations for both teacher and students. The following is an excerpt from a teacher-authored case (Shulman, Lotan, & Whitcomb, 1998) entitled "Poor Period 3!":

> I stand at my classroom door to greet my students. Soon period 3 will begin. "Good morning, Latisha, how are you?
>
> "What are we doing today?" she responds.

> I try not to sound too mechanical. "I'll explain to everyone in class at once, Latisha." She plops into her seat and stares; her need for nurturing goes unmet.
>
> "Hi, Jose, what's up?"
>
> "I hate my group," he says. "Let me sit near Donny."
>
> Period 3 is one of the six eighth grade social studies classes I teach each day. We cover US history, government, and geography. Our school draws from what is largely a lower-middle-class neighborhood with an ethnically diverse population, and the majority are Latino. Two-and-a-half years ago, I became an advocate of cooperative group learning. Especially for our large "sheltered" population (i.e., English language learners), it seemed to me group interaction would be preferable to students' struggling in silence. During my conversion to groupwork, I was trained never to give up—if things aren't working out, keep discussing it with the class until they cooperate. Because of my relative success with instruction in cooperative groups, I'd been selected to be a peer coach, observing and helping other teachers to plan, manage, and evaluate their groupwork.
>
> Thus, feeling a little smug, I entered into group instruction this year with a good deal of confidence. I met my match with period 3. In my mind, I call them "poor period 3." This is one class in the district that merits a full time Resource Specialist Program teaching aide because we have nine—yes, nine—special education students. We also have 10 sheltered students who have recently left bilingual classes and are now making the transition to full-time English instruction. The makeup of this class creates a disturbing chemistry that is felt within 30 seconds of the starting bell. I usually place them in groups of four or five, then invariably watch in frozen amazement as they torment each other. I persist, as I was trained to do, but find myself wondering whether groupwork is appropriate for this uncooperative class of 28 students, skewed with a disproportionate number of emotionally needy individuals....
>
> To sum it up, after 42 minutes with period 3, I feel like a giant, emotion-filled ball being slammed from one side of the room to the other. There are just too many emotions flying around the room and rebounding off the walls. Whether it's because they lack experience in small group interaction or they lack self-esteem, or some combination of the two, creating a cooperative atmosphere is not something the students of period 3 seem to be able to accomplish.
>
> At the end of the day I find myself wondering why I don't switch to the more traditional teacher-controlled setting with which these students are more familiar. Perhaps groupwork is not meant for *every* class. "It's okay to give up," I tell myself. Yet deep down I tell myself, "It's *not* okay. I know I need to do *something*. (pp. 21–23)

Framing the issue of classroom management in sociological terms allows us to move away from "fixing" the individual—be it the student or the teacher. It allows us to capitalize on the principle that structural features of the environment affect patterns of interaction as well as participants' willingness to engage and to put out effort (what psychologists would call "being motivated"). In other words, a sociological argument states that in addition to unique personal characteristics, dispositions, and attitudes, students' and teachers' behavior and performances are influenced by structural features of the situation in which they operate. Viewing the classroom as a social system rather than a collection of thirty-odd youngsters led and supervised by an adult allows us to explore, first, the ways in which teachers can use the authority of their role to empower students to manage themselves. Second, this view will lead us to analyze the relationship between features of the learning task and the nature of peer interactions. Third, it makes us recognize the potential of sound evaluation of group and individual products and of social processes for enhancing learning. Finally, it alerts us to the detrimental educational consequences of unequal participation and helps us devise effective interventions.

Recognizing and understanding this systemic view can be useful, even energizing for many teachers. Rather than trying to control behavior by manipulating or attempting to change a student's personality, teachers come to understand that they can define, shape, and adjust the parameters of the classroom situation. In other words, by designing productive and safe learning environments and by crafting conceptually challenging and intellectually rich learning tasks, teachers can create optimal conditions for on-task, productive interactions between and among teachers and students. Thus, the maxim of many veteran teachers that classroom management is all about design and planning is no mere cliché.

TEACHER ROLE AND AUTHORITY

In the classroom, the teacher's authority derives from her institutional position. Given her role, the teacher assigns tasks, monitors students' activities, and evaluates their performances. She explains, provides instructions, and waits for (correct) answers to her questions. She helps, admonishes, supports, approves, and disapproves. When students work on tasks that have right or wrong answers, the teacher gives clear directions and expects that they be closely followed. She supervises students' work to prevent mistakes and to minimize wasting valuable instructional time. She manages.

When the goal of instruction is the development of conceptual understanding, critical thinking, and creative problem solving, face-to-face social interaction becomes a necessary condition. These cognitive functions require that students get involved in promoting each other's learning by discussing the material, helping one another understand it, and holding each other accountable (Johnson, Johnson, & Holubek, 1993). Following earlier theorists (see, e.g., Lewin, 1951, and Deutch, 1949), educators recognized that such interdependence results in more productive groups. Subsequently, Ben-Ari (1997) argued that the link between social interaction and cognitive development is particularly relevant in heterogeneous classrooms where peer interaction is encouraged and adult supervision minimized.

Deriving her argument from organizational sociology, Cohen (1994) claims that when the teacher chooses to use groupwork to set the stage for increased peer interaction, direct supervision becomes unrealistic. Rather than supervising directly, the teacher needs to delegate authority to the students. She explains:

> Groupwork changes a teacher's role dramatically. No longer are you a direct supervisor of students, responsible for insuring that they do their work exactly as you direct. No longer is it your responsibility to watch for every mistake and correct it on the spot. Instead authority is delegated to students and to groups of students. They are in charge of insuring that the job gets done, and that classmates get the help they need. They are empowered to make mistakes, to find out what went wrong, and what might be done about it....
>
> When groupwork is underway, and groups are working and talking together using the instructions you have prepared, then your authority has been delegated. The teacher cannot possibly be everywhere at once trying to help six different groups. Moreover, having students talk with each other is essential as a method of managing heterogeneous classes. When they are trained to help each other, perhaps by reading or by translating into the student's native language, students use each other as resources to understand the assignments. (pp. 103–104)

Thus, when the teacher delegates authority to the students, she shares her power as well as her responsibilities. Activities in the classroom are no longer the sole responsibility of the teacher. Students become responsible for their own and their groupmates' engagement and productivity. Students make the groups work by serving as intellectual, academic, or linguistic resources for one another and by holding each other accountable. They solve open-ended problems and devise solutions to problems posed. They report on their group's work and assess each others' products. Thus, authority is delegated to students in several ways: in managing the groups, in defining the intellectual content of their work, and in enforcing accountability by evaluating their products.

Delegation of Authority for Managing Groups

Successful delegation of authority reflected in smoothly running groups, high student engagement, productive interactions, quality group products, and significant individual accomplishments does not happen by magic.

Cohen (1994) emphasizes that teachers need to teach social skills explicitly so students can learn how to work cooperatively and how to serve as intellectual resources for one another. Students need to know how to address interpersonal conflicts that impede the group's productivity and how to use helping behaviors that enhance its functioning. Students need to become accountable to and for each other. Clearly, they need to learn new rules and new norms for behavior in this new situation.

"You have the right to ask for help. You have the duty to assist" is one of these new norms. When tasks are intellectually challenging and students work in groups for relatively limited periods of time, there is and should be a sense of urgency. Students will need to rely on each others' expertise, previous knowledge, and active contributions. They will need to take advantage of what each one of them brings to the successful completion of the task. Furthermore, they need to take responsibility for engaging all members of the group and supporting them in completing the group task as well as the individual assignments that might follow the work in groups. "No one is done until everyone is done" is another example of a general cooperative norm that, when followed, supports productive interdependence and thus learning.

Different kinds of group tasks require different kinds of cooperative behaviors. For example, designing and conducting a scientific experiment is different from analyzing and interpreting a section of dense literary text. While the former task requires that group members manipulate equipment, observe, formulate hypotheses, record results, and present their conclusions, the latter task might require extensive reading, comprehending, interpreting, visualizing, analyzing, and empathizing. Working on an experiment requires that groupmates help one another by sharing materials, by reaching consensus on the design of the experiment, and by pointing out significant findings. Comprehending a text requires that groupmates ask clarifying questions, listen carefully to others, propose competing interpretations, and justify their opinions based on close readings of the text. Mathematics educators (e.g., Yackel & Cobb, 1996) describe social norms and sociomathematical norms that govern interactions in the inquiry-oriented mathematics classroom. Engaging in mathematics requires that students explain their arguments and justify their solutions, listen to, and make sense of their groupmates' explanations. Sociomathematical norms are the subject-specific norms that state what are the mathematically appropriate and valuable contributions as well as the mathematically acceptable and effective arguments, explanations, and justifications.

These new behaviors do not emerge automatically in small student groups. New behaviors are to be explicitly introduced, recognized, labeled, discussed, practiced, and reinforced. Using principles of social learning, Cohen (1994, 48–50) offers a collection of exercises called skill-builders to introduce the new norms and make sure students internalize them to make social interactions more productive. Particularly important is the norm that "everyone contributes" and that no single member dominates the interaction. For many students unequal opportunities for participation are among the most frustrating aspects of groupwork.

Many teachers, particularly at the secondary level, worry that given the pressures of covering expansive amounts of curriculum, an extended and exclusive focus on developing social skills is a luxury they can hardly afford. Some teachers address this problem by assigning content-specific group tasks, and in their feedback to the students and during the debriefing of the groupwork, they focus on the students' use of cooperative norms and group process skills. Others decide (usually after many frustrating interventions and too many dysfunctional groups) to invest time and effort in training students by using "generic" skill-builders. In any case, helping students to internalize the norms of cooperation and to develop group process skills has proven to be a solid investment of time in the long run.

When the teacher delegates authority, assigning specific roles to the different members enhances the smooth running of groups. In fulfilling these roles, students take responsibility for the practical and routine functions that are traditionally the teachers' purview. For example, a facilitator or team captain makes sure that everybody understands the task and that all group members get a turn and the help they need. The facilitator also acts as the liaison between the group and the teacher. A resource provider or materials manager secures the manipulatives, scissors, dictionaries, and test tubes and supervises the cleanup. A peacekeeper or harmonizer identifies and addresses sources of conflict and looks out for the social and emotional well-being of the group and its members. When time is of essence, a group member can act as the timekeeper. The reporter oversees the group's presentation and organizes the summary of the group's activities during the final wrap-up. Depending on the task, the teacher's priorities, and the students' needs, additional roles can be invented and assigned.

Each student in the group plays a role and roles rotate. That way, all group members develop the skills needed to perform each role. Because some roles are perceived to be more powerful and prestigious than others, it is important that roles be assigned rather than assumed by "natural leaders" or usurped by students who have higher status in the group. The roles described here are different from "content" roles such as theorist, questioner, summarizer, or explainer—roles that reflect metacognitive functions necessary for groupwork. They are also different from "professional" roles such as artist, musician, poet, or director—roles that potentially lead to a strict division of labor and curtail interaction. The use of these "professional" roles also runs the risk of pigeonholing students and limiting their potential contributions to a narrower range.

Although time consuming like the previously described training for cooperative norms, explicitly teaching students to perform the roles seems critical. Many teachers find that in addition to explaining the roles to the students and posting descriptions of the related responsibilities on the classroom wall, it can be useful to help students figure out what roles might "sound like." For example, facilitators can be heard saying: "Does everybody understand what we are supposed to do?" "Michael, what do you propose we do next?" Many teachers might find it useful to explain to the students that being able to act in these different roles is an important skill needed for adult jobs and greatly valued in many workplaces. Practicing what to say and how to say it as an incumbent of a certain role can also be particularly useful for students who are English learners in mainstream classrooms.

While they recognize the benefits of groupwork, some teachers have mixed reactions to the use of roles. As highly skilled and well-socialized adults, they take harmoniously functioning groups for granted. Some teachers and many students perceive the roles as artificial and limiting. Ultimately, however, many teachers recognize that without developing and assigning roles only certain students, and seemingly always the same ones, will take and are given opportunities to assume leadership roles or are ready to act as spokespersons for their groups. Conversely, certain students are permanently "stuck" with doing the cleanup—if cleanup is done at all. That is when teachers become more open to see the added value of well-implemented student roles.

Being able to provide specific and sound feedback to groups and individuals requires that teachers observe the groups very closely and listen in on the conversations. In many classrooms where groupwork is successful, teachers roam around, clipboard in hand, take notes or engage in brief but pointed interactions with the groups. Noting specific cooperative norms and well-executed roles, important contributions of individual group members and providing feedback on the spot or during wrap-up makes students aware that the teacher is listening attentively, and also informs the teacher about students' needs and accomplishments. This constant, precise, and formative classroom assessment of students' work contributes to the students putting out more effort towards improved performance (Ben-Ari, 1997; Black & Wiliam, 1998).

When teachers delegate authority effectively, students are successfully managing the groups by themselves. Often teachers are surprised and worried by this redefinition of their traditional role, although they engineered it in the first place. Some teachers struggle with no longer being the focal point of the classroom, the sole provider of information and knowledge. Ms. Kepner wrote:

> The groups were beginning to buzz along more productively but still testing me frequently to see if I really meant what I said about them taking control of the investigation, of the learning. They wanted to do well. No one wanted to get up in front of the class and look like a fool. And you never knew what sneaky kinds of questions Ms. Kepner or somebody else, might ask about how or why or what if. The management system began to work like a kaleidoscope, the bright bits falling into place to create an impressive, transitory pattern. But I still wanted to be that precious dot in the center of the steadily revolving wheel. (Lotan & Whitcomb, 1995, p. 341)

Other teachers worry that without their constant supervision, the classroom might deteriorate into chaos: students will not understand what needs to be done, will make mistakes, and will not complete their assignments. They fear that they might seem to have abdicated their role as teachers when they abstain from helping or rescuing the groups. They puzzle about when and how to intervene when groups are floundering or when students are reluctant, even resistant to accept the authority delegated to them.

Many teachers, novice and veteran alike, struggle with the notion of delegating authority (Shulman, Lotan, & Whitcomb, 1998; Lotan, 2004). Indeed, groupwork can exacerbate management problems. It often requires higher tolerance for purely social interactions that seem to be only tangentially, if at all, related to the task at hand and a reasonable comfort level with unexpected classroom events. Delegating authority, that is, sharing with the students the power to make decisions about how to accomplish the task, how to work together productively, how to evaluate and enhance the quality of the group product, and how to recognize the contributions of individual members of the group does not mean relinquishing authority. Indeed, I often remind teachers and teacher candidates that one cannot delegate authority if one does not have it in the first place.

With time, however, as they grow more comfortable and confident with making students responsible for their own work, and as they hover less over groups and rescue more and more infrequently, teachers find that they are free for the kind of teaching that attracted them to the profession in the first place. Relieved from the burden of direct supervision and control, teachers, through feedback and questioning, encourage the students to move beyond the procedural aspects of the task and to interact with one another at a high conceptual level, making sense of difficult intellectual problems. Strong delegation of authority, or reduced direct supervision by the teacher, leads to increased levels of student talking and working together on the challenging group tasks. Consequently, the more students talk and work together, the more they learn (Cohen, Lotan, & Holthuis, 1995; Cohen & Lotan, 1997; Ben-Ari, 1997).

Composing Groups

For many teachers, composing the "perfect" group can be a very time-consuming and anxiety-provoking task. One teacher documented her "struggles with the dynamics of grouping":

> When the year began, I had high expectations for groupwork—it would be an effective management tool, promote student self-esteem, and encourage collaboration. Most of all, I saw it as a vital tool to facilitate dialogue among peers, which in turn would help all students—especially second language learners like Sam—increase their verbal, written, expressive, and receptive language skills. With that in mind, my task was to effectively group 29 second graders. My second grade class consisted of 12 girls and 17 boys: 74% African American, 13% Caucasian, and 13% Asian. While a few children were from middle-class families, most were from low-income or welfare families.
>
> The big question was *how* to group them. I wanted groups that were heterogeneous, nonthreatening, noncompetitive, equitable, stimulating, motivating, and most of all, cooperative. I needed to take into special account the children who were described as "at risk"—children who either were learning English as a second language or had been identified as non-readers. . . .
>
> Now as I look back on last year, I realize that there is no "cooperative magic": rather, creating groups that are cooperative and collaborative is a complex, multifaceted endeavor. Sam's involvement in group activities certainly had its ups and downs. On one hand, I am pleased with Sam's growth. When he began the year, he was in a group where he felt rejected and insecure and that his contributions had little value. In the second group, he found teammates who recognized his skills and were willing to listen and attend to his needs. Sam's confidence grew, and with it, his ability to communicate soared. His progress improved his status in subsequent groups. But by the end of the year, Sam became domineering and overbearing and tried to usurp control. (Shulman, Lotan, & Whitcomb, 1998, pp. 39–42)

If teachers create homogeneous groups where group members have similar levels of previous academic achievement, the benefits might outweigh the costs because they might be recreating in the classroom the tracking system they were trying to abolish. Teachers might choose to create heterogeneous groups based on narrowly defined previous academic achievement (i.e., test scores or traditional grades) or perceived academic ability. According to this scenario, a group might include one high-, one low-, and two medium-achieving students, a situation certain to activate considerable status problems.

Often teachers believe that groups need to be balanced and mixed as to its members' prior academic achievement, gender, race, ethnicity, linguistic proficiency, being with or without close friends, or potential to act disruptively. With that many constraints, the teacher might have to spend many hours figuring out the exact group assignment for each and every student. Not only can all this effort be for naught because of an unexpected flu epidemic or a field trip, mechanically and bureaucratically planning that each group have equal number of male or female students, or equal number of students from the different ethnic or racial groups represented in the class will also quickly reveal the teacher's explicit or hidden rationale for group assignments. As a result, students will tend to interact with their fellow group members as stereotypical representatives of their respective racial or ethnic backgrounds rather than as individual persons. In her study of an untracked 9th-grade classroom where groupwork was used consistently, Rubin (2003) provides an excellent description of the drawbacks of such efforts by the teacher to compose groups:

> In spite of the teachers' belief in a "multiple intelligences" approach, small groups in the detracked classroom were nevertheless built with an eye toward balancing "strong" and "weak" students as defined in a traditional academic sense. "I do build it from the weak kids up," Mr. Apple told me. "I don't build it from the strong kids down." In this way, the markers of competence constructed in the whole class context made their way into the small group context. Students who were competent readers and writers and who kept up with their assigned work were positioned as experts, and those who were seen as having lower skills were placed with their more highly skilled peers, with academic assistance as the implicit goal.

> A second feature of a balanced group was racial diversity. Groupwork fulfilled the democratizing role for the core teachers by bringing "kids who are different" into proximity with each other... Mr. Apple pointed out that constructing groups around racial and socio-economic difference could be "tricky, especially if Blacks are the racial minority, you're always separating them... there will be one Black kid in each group." In the Cedar High context, having one African American student in each group usually meant that that student did not have any close friends in that group, and often meant that that student was also positioned as a "weak" student. This exacerbated the correspondence between race and achievement that loomed large for both students and teachers at Cedar High. (pp. 552–553)

Students have clear preferences as to who they want to be with in a group. They know they could benefit from working with others who are perceived as academically strong. They would also choose to work with others who are socially attractive. In her study, Rubin (2003) asked the students about their priorities for group membership. With great acuity, she documents their answers:

> Students wanted group members who were academically competent, fun to be with, motivating and respectful. Many of these attributes were in conflict with the criteria that the teachers used when configuring small groups. Students based their judgments about with whom they would want to work in small group on how their peers displayed themselves in the whole class context, on the stereotypes drawn from the particular school context, and on their previous experiences with individuals in small group settings.
>
> One quality of a good group member was academic competence. Students' definitions of academic competence in small group setting were consistent with the earlier discussion of what made a good student. Thus a good group member would be someone who is "always reading" (Grant), who "does the work" (Kiana), who does not "play around" (Mike), who "actually works" (Sasha), and who does not "like to mess around" (Tiffany)....
>
> Some students came into the small group setting bearing reputations as "bad students": students who "don't really pay attention in class" and "don't do their work" (Grant), "don't want to learn" (Kiana, Sasha, Mike), "don't even try" (Sasha) and who are "rude" (Kiana, Mike). This was a difficult position to hold in a group setting and often led to a reduction in responsibility for those students.
>
> Another characteristic of a good group member was that she or he be "fun" to work with. This was consistent with the more social and intimate setting of the small group participant structure. Sasha told me that she wanted to work with "someone who could joke around. When you work really, really hard, after a while you get really, really punchy, and you just want to stop and joke around.
>
> Some students spoke of desiring group members who were "motivators" and could keep the group moving along. These students were the "groupmakers" and they were in demand. Grant told me he would like to have in his group "somebody who's kind of social and sort of a leader. I might pick Sasha. She's good at that.... Somebody who'll just keep us all working on the same thing and not let us go on to something we're not supposed to do." (pp. 556–557)

Given students' awareness of the intellectual importance and the social value of the different group members, I suggest that teachers make group assignments a public and open classroom event and use controlled randomness. "No hidden agendas" would be the motto of this seemingly oxymoronic method. Many teachers use pocket charts on the wall to signal to the students their group assignment and group role for the day. I suggest that before the start of a groupwork unit, the teacher take a few minutes to compose the groups in the students' presence. After shuffling the students' names like a deck of cards, the teacher can start placing the cards into the different pockets. After distributing all the names, she can review the groups that emerge. Now will be the time to make well-justified changes. For example, the teacher might acknowledge that a newly arrived immigrant student will need a translator and the student who can serve as a translator needs to move to his or her group. The teacher might want to separate two close friends who tend to socialize rather than work when placed together in a group. Alternatively, she might separate two students who are known to be engaged in a drawn-out quarrel, acknowledging that for now it could be too hard to address the deeply felt animosity these students feel towards each other.

More importantly, however, an open and near-random assignment to groups symbolizes that the teacher sees students as being competent and able to contribute to the task in many different ways rather than exclusively through reading, writing, and calculating quickly. When students complete group tasks, they contribute and demonstrate many different abilities—all to be acknowledged as intellectually valued and relevant to the successful completion of the task. By ranking students on a unidimensional scale from "strong" to "weak" and by, intentionally or unintentionally, transmitting that ranking to his students as the criteria by which groups were formed, Mr. Apple in the previous description fundamentally contradicted his stated belief in the intellectual competence of all his students.

Delegation of Intellectual Authority

When the goal of instruction is conceptual learning and deep understanding of content, an often underestimated predictor for successful groupwork is a well-crafted, "group-worthy" task (Lotan, 2003). Returning to the sociological perspective presented previously, I argue that the features of the collective task affect the nature of the interaction among members of the group and their rate of success in contributing to and completing the task. Thus, group-worthy tasks have the following five features: (1) they are anchored in important disciplinary content of the subject matter; (2) they are open-ended and require complex problem solving; (3) they include multiple curricular representations (Eisner, 1994) to provide students with multiple entry points to the task and multiple opportunities to show intellectual competence; (4) they rely on positive interdependence among group members and also require individual accountability; and (5) they include clear criteria for the evaluation of the group's product.

A card containing the instructions to the group's task, the questions to be discussed by the group as they refer to the resource materials, and the evaluation criteria for the group's product can be seen as the physical symbol of the teacher's delegation of authority. As the resource providers pick up the materials to start the work in groups, students understand that they are to grapple with the task on their own, assume full responsibility for its completion, and create a group product that reflects their joint efforts. In addition to the task card and the resource materials, individual reports are part of the package prepared for each group. These individual reports, to be completed after the work in groups, are one of the main vehicles for ensuring and enforcing individual accountability through written assignments.

During groupwork, students can engage in two kinds of learning tasks: well-structured, routine tasks and open-ended, uncertain, nonroutine tasks. To complete routine tasks (individually, in pairs, or in small groups), students follow clear and detailed directions to arrive at the correct answer or the expected solution. Such tasks include finding a definition in a dictionary, recalling or summarizing information from a textbook, completing sentences, drawing or coloring maps, or practicing arithmetic algorithms. Often teachers design tasks that are crowded with details and include a myriad of directions to be followed carefully so students will not make mistakes or will be sure to "discover" what the teacher has planned for them to discover. Having delegated authority to the groups to manage themselves and as they struggle to minimize direct supervision, these teachers try to maintain or regain full control through the tightly structured task by overspecifying the instructions or preteaching the assignment to remove much of the uncertainty.

Although beneficial to some students, particularly those who provide help to their peers by explaining, modeling, and practicing these necessary academic skills (Webb and Farivar, 1999), groupwork is not essential for these kinds of tasks. Often students resent engaging in groupwork to complete tasks they could as easily, and at times more efficiently, complete on their own. They also might find it frustrating to always be the one group member who provides the explanations or, conversely, being the one who always needs them.

Groupwork is essential when students grapple with nonroutine, open-ended tasks that reflect real-life uncertainties and ambiguities, genuine dilemmas, and authentic problems. These tasks are radically different from the traditional, recipe-like activities designed to prevent unexpected answers as described above. Group-worthy tasks allow students to share their experiences and require that they justify their opinions and beliefs. In these tasks, students analyze, synthesize, hypothesize, interpret, imagine, and evaluate. They discuss cause and effect, explore controversial issues, they explain, and they persuade. In working on group-worthy tasks, students have the opportunity to devise different plans, and explore different paths towards a solution. They might come up with as many different solutions as there are groups in the classroom. Together with the teacher, they are empowered to make decisions that have substantial implications for the real classroom curriculum. Therefore, assigning a group-worthy task means that the teacher is ready to accept unexpected solutions and answers. Given the intellectual diversity of a group and the students' varied repertoires of problem-solving strategies, group members can effectively use each other as intellectual resources to explore alternative solutions, to examine issues from different perspectives, and to assess their group-mates' assertions and dissentions. By assigning such tasks, teachers effectively delegate intellectual authority to the students, and support and acknowledge their intellectual autonomy.

This kind of delegation of intellectual authority often raises the teacher's as well as the students' level of anxiety and apprehension. Because there are no "answer keys" or end-of-the-chapter solutions for truly group-worthy tasks, teachers worry about being confronted by their students' unexpected and sometimes uncomfortable answers or solutions. Like their teachers, students handle the task's uncertainty with varying degrees of comfort and success. Some groups and individuals proceed cautiously at first, surprised that schoolwork has become so radically redefined. Paradoxically, more mature students seem to have greater difficulty adjusting to the possibility of more than one legitimate outcome and more than one path to a solution. Realistically, a delicate balance between uncertainty and open-endedness and adequate but not overbearing guidance makes for productive rather than frustrating intellectual engagement. While too much open-endedness is unmanageable, too many details short-circuit the problem-solving interchanges, and thus the learning process.

Delegation of Evaluation Rights

As defined by their role in the classroom, teachers are an important source of evaluation. The power to appraise, to judge, to grade—in short, to evaluate students and their work has traditionally been solely the teacher's responsibility. However, teacher evaluations have direct consequences for students' self-evaluations and for their evaluations of each other's intellectual and academic competence. Teacher's overt and covert evaluations are significant determinants in the creation of perceived academic and social rankings in the classroom.

Given group-worthy tasks, the assessment of groupwork both at the group and at the individual level raises important questions for the teacher and has implications for student learning. Increasingly, topics of assessment have gained central stage with the realization that 1) formative classroom assessment by the teacher (Black et al., 2002), 2) students active in evaluating their own work (Shepard, 2000), and 3) clear criteria, standards, and expectations visible to the students have profound effects on the effort invested by the students, the quality of their products, and ultimately, their learning outcomes.

Cohen, Lotan, Abram, Scarloss, and Schultz (2002) have documented the positive results of using clear evaluation criteria for both self-assessment of the members of the group in group discussion and in evaluating the quality of their group product. This study showed that groups produced superior products and students wrote stronger final unit essays when they used criteria to evaluate their work and their products. As previously described, explicit and content-specific (rather than generic) criteria for evaluating the group product, the individual reports or culminating essays need to be included in the task cards presented to the groups.

When teachers use the evaluation criteria during group presentations at the end of groupwork, their feedback is more concrete and more specific (Schultz et al., 2000). The teacher and the audience of students can assess the quality of the products presented using these criteria on a regular basis. Feedback based on evidence shown during the presentation from both the teacher and the students can be a valuable tool in increasing the effort put forth by groups as they work on the task. Sharing with the teacher the power to evaluate the work of their peers openly and legitimately as well as the opportunity to practice self-evaluation contributes to a further redefinition of the traditional classroom roles of teacher and student. It indicates delegation of evaluation rights.

As argued previously, this redefinition of roles and the restructuring of the classroom environment necessitate explicit preparation and training of the students. They need to learn how to be a genuinely attentive audience, how to use evidence from their peers' presentations to support the feedback and evaluations they give. Just as importantly, they need to become adept at using the evaluation criteria to monitor their own group process and to judge the quality of their own products. More beneficial than group grades, individual, or group points, sound feedback based on clear criteria and standards supports student engagement and learning.

UNEQUAL PARTICIPATION AND ITS EDUCATIONAL CONSEQUENCES

While groupwork is a highly recommended strategy for heterogeneous classrooms and its benefits are convincingly documented, many educators, students, and their parents complain about its all-too-familiar pitfalls. First and foremost among these is the widely recognized, unequal participation among members of a task-oriented small group. Unequal participation can be observed in two ways: on the one hand, one or two students dominate the interaction in the groups. They handle the materials, search for and provide information, solve the problem (correctly or incorrectly) and complete the task, and make the decisions that ultimately determine the group's performance. On the other hand, unequal participation manifests itself in the complete and painful exclusion of other members of the group. These students remain silent and unobtrusive, reluctant to make suggestions or to offer their ideas. Often, they are labeled as "being shy." Alternatively, some of these students, barred from productive interactions, become resistant and disruptive, and deliberately undermine the group's efforts.

Elizabeth Cohen has consistently documented the detrimental consequences of unequal participation in small groups: because participation is related to learning, unequal participation translates into unequal learning outcomes. Across different subject areas and at different grade levels, the more students participate in small group interactions, the greater their learning gains (Cohen, 1994; Cohen & Lotan, 1997). Conversely, students who participate less have lower learning gains. In addition to academic shortfalls, unequal participation creates difficulties for the social-emotional well-being of group members. Hard-working and well-prepared students who worry about their performance and their grades grudgingly invest effort but resent being "the suckers." They blame the ones who do not participate for being "free riders" and social loafers. Furthermore, unequal participation causes teachers to worry about evaluating students' work and performance in small groups. If unequal participation is seen as a matter of personal choice or as stemming from unequal levels of motivation, how are teachers to evaluate group products or group processes (Webb, 1995)?

Cohen relies on sociological theories to explain the phenomenon of unequal participation:

> Small task groups tend to develop hierarchies where some members are more active and influential than others. This is a *status ordering* —an agreed-upon ranking where everyone feels it is better to have a high rank within the status order than a low rank. Group members who have high rank are seen as more competent and as having done more to guide and lead the group. (Cohen, 1994, pp. 27–28)

She continues by saying that according to Expectation State Theory, members of small, on-task groups develop expectations for self and others' competence based on so-called "status characteristics." Examples of status characteristics range from race, gender, socioeconomic status, and physical attractiveness to academic status and peer status in the classroom. Attached to status characteristics are perceived expectations for competence: individuals with high status are expected to be more competent than low-status individuals and thus take and are given more opportunities to exert power and influence. Unequal participation, then, is not the problem of the individual student but rather a problem created by the status ordering in small groups.

Having a theoretical model to understand this phenomenon has also allowed Cohen and her colleagues (1994) to design specific interventions that disrupt the pernicious relationship between status and participation. The first of these interventions, called the "multiple-abilitiy orientation" rests on the premise that in multidimensional classrooms and for multidimensional tasks, previously defined as group-worthy tasks, many different intellectual abilities are needed to be successful. By convincing the students that no single group member has all the abilities to complete such tasks successfully but that everyone has some of these abilities, students will create a mixed set of expectations about themselves and others. As a result, they will take and will give more opportunities to interact to more of their groupmates. The challenge facing teachers is to present a credible analysis of the learning task as a multiple-ability task and to convince the students of the relevance of different intellectual abilities for its successful completion. Furthermore, the teacher needs to persuade students that when tasks require many different kinds of intellectual abilities, each member of the group can make valuable contributions from their repertoire of problem-solving strategies. All contributions are needed to complete the task successfully.

The second intervention designed to weaken the relationship between status and participation is called "assigning competence to low-status students." For this intervention, the teacher pays particular attention to the performance of the low-status student in the group. The teacher watches attentively for those moments when the student shows competence on one or some of the abilities previously identified. Then the teacher tells the student and his or her groupmates what he or she did well and how this contribution is relevant to the successful completion of the task. Often, the teacher also reminds the group that the student can serve as a resource on similar multiple-ability tasks in the future.

Elizabeth Cohen and I (Cohen & Lotan, 1995) have documented the effectiveness of these interventions in elementary classrooms. In these classrooms, teachers used multiple-ability curricula and students, working in small groups, showed high rates of interaction. For our studies, we related the frequency with which teachers used the interventions to measures of status problems both at the individual and at the classroom level. Bower (1997) documented how the use of a multiple-ability curriculum and treatment in high school social studies classrooms mitigated the relationship between status and interaction.

Delegation of authority by the teacher, high levels of student interaction in the small groups, and group-worthy tasks are necessary conditions for these interventions to be effective. First, students need to work on learning tasks that require many different intellectual abilities for their successful completion and that promote interaction. If reading silently, filling in the blanks, or applying algorithms in rote fashion are the only skills required, teachers will have a hard time convincing students of the message of the multiple-ability orientation. Second, while students need to interact constantly and around substantive content in order to demonstrate intellectual competence, low-status students in particular must have repeated opportunities to display their competence and to be recognized for it. Third, having successfully delegated authority to the groups, the teacher is free to observe and focus his or her attention on identifying and recognizing students' intellectual competence and contributions.

CONCLUSION

Skillful management of groupwork, like management of other classroom activities, is a cornerstone of teachers' pedagogical repertoire. It requires that they understand the connections among the fundamental components of teaching and learning: the features of the learning tasks, the relationship between the teacher role and patterns of students' engagement and activity, and the evaluation practices in the classroom. Thus, groupwork is a costly instructional approach, demanding much thought, effort, and time. It requires not only a physical, but also a conceptual reorganization of the classroom, an added dimension to the role of the teacher, new ways for students to interact, and the intense development of group-worthy tasks. While some educators promote groupwork for its affective and social rewards, its most important benefit is its potential as equitable pedagogy. When teachers and students alike are able to recognize and value the diverse intellectual contributions of all students in heterogeneous classrooms, they show their commitment to close the achievement gap and to develop democratic and caring classrooms.

ACKNOWLEDGMENT

The author thanks Charles Rathbone, University of Vermont, for his helpful comments on an earlier draft of this chapter.

REFERENCES

Ben-Ari, R. (1997). Complex instruction and cognitive development, in E. G. Cohen and R. A. Lotan (Ed.), *Working for equity in heterogeneous classrooms: Sociological theory in action* (pp. 193–206). New York: Teachers College Press.

Black, P. & Wiliam D. (1998). Inside the black box: Raising standards through classroom assessment. *Phi Delta Kappan, 80*(2), 139–148.

Black, P., Harrison C., Lee, C., Marshall, B. & William, D. (2002). *Working inside the black box. Assessment for learning in the classroom*, King's College, London, Department of Education and Professional Studies.

Bower, B. (1997). Effects of the multiple-ability Curriculum in secondary social studies classrooms, in E. G. Cohen & R. A. Loton (Eds.) *Working for equity in heterogeneous classrooms: Sociological theory in action* (pp. 117–133). New York: Teachers College Press.

Cohen, E. G. (1994). *Designing groupwork: Strategies for heterogeneous classrooms*. New York: Teachers College Press.

Cohen, E. G., & Lotan, R. A. (1995). Producing equal status interaction in heterogeneous classrooms. *American Educational Research Journal, 32*(1), 99–120.

Cohen, E. G., & Lotan, R. A. (Eds.). (1997). *Working for equity in heterogeneous classrooms: Sociological theory in action.* New York: Teachers College Press.

Cohen, E. G., & Lotan, R. A., Abram, P. L., Scarloss, B. A., & Schultz, S. E. (2002). Can groups learn? *Teacher's College Record, 104*(6), 1045–1068.

Cohen, E. G., Lotan, R. A., & Holthuis, N. C. (1995). Talking and working together: Conditions for learning in complex instruction. In M. Hallinan (Ed.), New York: Plenum Press.

Deutch, M. (1949). A theory of cooperation and competition. *Human Relations, 2*, 129–152.

Eisner, E. W. (1994). *Cognition and curriculum reconsidered.* New York: Teachers College Press.

Johnson, D. W., & Johnson, R. (1989). *Cooperation and competition: Theory and research.* Edina, MN: Interaction Book Co.

Johnson, D. W., & Johnson, R. (1990). Cooperative learning and achievement. In S. Sharan (Ed.), *Cooperative learning: Theory and research* (pp. 23–37). New York: Praeger.

Johnson, D. W., Johnson, R. & HolubeK, E. (1993). *Circles of learning* (4th ed.). Edina, MN: Interaction Book Co.

Lewin, K. (1951). *Field theory in social science: selected theoretical papers.* (D. Cartwright, Ed.). New York: Harper & Row.

Lotan, R. A. (2003). Group-worthy tasks. *Educational Leadership, 6*(6), 72–75.

Lotan, R. A. (2004). Stepping into groupwork. In E. G. Cohen, C. Brody, & M. Sapon-Shevin (Eds.), *Teaching cooperative learning: The challenge for teacher education* (pp. 167–182). Albany: State University of New York Press.

Lotan, R. A. & Whitcomb, J. (1995). Poetry in groupwork: Complex instruction in the language arts. In R. J. Stahl (Ed.), *Handbook for cooperative learning in language arts.* Reading, MA: Addison-Wesley, pp. 319–344.

Noddings, N. (1992). *The challenge to care in schools: An alternative approach to education.* New York: Teachers College Press.

Oakes, J. & Lipton, M. (1999). *Teaching to change the world.* New York: McGraw-Hill.

Rubin, B. C. (2003). Unpacking detracking: When progressive pedagogy meets students' social worlds. *American Educational Research Journal, 40*(2), 539–573.

Sharan, S. (1995). *Handbook of cooperative learning methods.* Westport, CT: Greenwood Press.

Shepard, L. (2000). The role of assessment in a learning culture. *Educational Researcher, 29*, 4–14.

Shulman, J. H., Lotan, R. A., & Whitcomb, J. A. (Eds). (1998). *Groupwork in diverse classrooms: A casebook for educators.* New York: Teachers College Press.

Schultz, S. E., Scarloss, B., Lotan, R. A., Abram, P. L., Cohen, E. G., & Holthuis, N. C. (2000, April). *Let's give 'em something to talk about: Teacher's talk to students in open-ended group tastes.* Paper presented to the AERA Annual Meeting, New Orleans, LA.

Slavin, R. (1995). *Cooperative learning: Theory, research, and practice.* Englewood Cliffs, NJ: Prentice-Hall.

Webb, N. (1995). Group collaboration in assessment: Multiple objectives, processes, and outcomes, *Educational Evaluation and Policy Analysis, 17*(2), 239–261.

Webb, N. M., & Farivar, S. (1999). Developing productive group interaction in middle school mathematics. In A. M. O'Donnell & A. King (Eds.), *Cognitive perspectives on peer learning* (pp. 117–149). Hillsdale, NJ: Lawrence Erlbaum Associates.

Yackel, E. & Cobb, P. (1996). Sociomathematical norms, argumentation and autonomy in mathematics. *Journal for Research in Mathematics Education, 27*, 458–477.

20

Classroom Management and Technology

Cheryl Mason Bolick
University of North Carolina, Chapel Hill

James M. Cooper
University of Virginia

INTRODUCTION

Computer technologies are a set of dynamic tools that continue to evolve and transform classroom teaching and learning. As new technologies emerge and develop over time, they are often at the forefront of educational innovation and play an increasingly significant role in society. The majority of students have access to an Internet-connected computer in their classroom today and almost all students have access to one in their schools. The ratio of students per Internet-connected computer increased from nearly 20 students per computer in 1998, to 4.1 students per computer in 2004. The number of teachers using technology for planning or instruction increased from 73% in 2002 to 83% in 2003 (Ansell & Park, 2003). These numbers provide evidence that the role of technology has substantially multiplied over the past decade. Technology has progressed from being a novelty in the classroom to a "major tool of the trade" (Becker, Ravitz, & Wong; 1999).

Although widely promoted, and now generally accepted, integration of technology into the classroom is by no means an effortless process. There is a clear disconnect between the optimism of those advocating technology in the classroom and the realities of teaching and learning in 21st-century classrooms (Cuban, 2001). Teaching and learning with computers presents a series of new challenges and demands related to education professionals. These challenges include, but are not limited to, teacher training, funding, maintenance, and classroom management. Cuban stresses the importance of teachers and students studying these challenges, "educators have to come to terms with [technology] as an educational tool. Understanding technology and the social practices that accompany it as a potent force in society is incumbent on both students and adults" (p. 194).

While adding technology to a classroom equips teachers with a new range of classroom management tools such as spreadsheets and databases to manage school and classroom records and information, technology also presents a series of new classroom management issues such as moving students from the classroom to the computer lab or managing a classroom in which students are using a variety of different technologies such as wireless laptops or handheld computing devices.

As an example, the following fictitious scenario describes one teacher's attempt to integrate technology into the classroom while maintaining an effective learning environment. The students in Mr. Williams' seventh-grade social studies class are studying the different branches of government. The students are clustered into small groups of five to six students scattered throughout the room while there is a buzz of talking and typing emanating throughout the room. One cluster of students is gathered around a single computer, communicating in real time with their local congressman. Prior to sitting down at the computer, these students generated a list of questions to ask their representative and now are engaging in an interactive text-based discussion with her. As one student types, the other students take notes either in a traditional notebook or on a personal digital assistant (PDA).

Another group of students is gathered in the back corner, sitting at individual computer stations. The students are completing a web-based research assignment that Mr. Williams developed. The research assignment requires students to access specific Web sites to answer a carefully sequenced set of questions. The predetermined Web sites have been bookmarked, to help the students follow the activity with relative ease. A red cup sits next to each computer monitor. If the students do have a question, they know to place the cup on top of their monitor as a symbol to Mr. Williams that they need his assistance.

The third group of students is sitting on the floor in the front of the room. Each student has a PDA and folding keyboard in his or her lap. They are working together to write a collective essay about the roles and responsibilities of the different branches of government. The students, who outlined the essay as a group, each wrote individual sections of the essay to share with the group. Now, they are beaming their sections to one another. The assignment list that Mr. Williams prepared for them requires them to review each other's paragraphs and to work on developing a group conclusion.

The fourth group of students has pulled a group of desks together and is working on the laptops that Mr. Williams checked out from the school library. These students are working to edit a series of digital video clips they recorded. The students interviewed members of the community about the branches of government and are now editing the videos to create a documentary video to share with the class. All of the students in the group have an assigned role, such as script writer, editor, or interviewer that helps to ensure equal participation.

Whereas the scenario depicted above may be the dream of those high-tech teachers, it may be a nightmare for many teachers who are uncomfortable with managing the technology-infused classroom. This chapter addresses the managerial issues that teachers encounter as they attempt to use technology in teaching.

RESEARCH ON TECHNOLOGY AND CLASSROOM MANAGEMENT

Because computer technology use in classrooms is relatively new, little research exists to document how the introduction of technology affects classroom management. There certainly is no scientifically based research using random assignments to treatment and control groups to investigate how technology impacts classroom management issues and practices. Instead, there are a number of small investigations, typically using qualitative methods such as surveys, interviews, and observation techniques to examine the interactions between technology use and classroom management. Many of these small research studies are doctoral dissertations.

A number of these reports and studies describe how technology can be used to manage school and classroom records and information (McNally & Etchison, 2000; Kahn, 1998). Tools that can facilitate this type of classroom management include word processing, spreadsheet, database, and draw-and-paint programs. These tools can be used to compute grades, track attendance, store lesson plans, provide classroom seating charts, and communicate with parents. Used in this way, classroom management refers to the use of technology to improve record keeping, to reduce paperwork, and to free up teachers' time to focus more on instructional activities and planning. The use of these tools will be addressed later in the chapter.

However, a less studied and written about aspect of classroom management and technology concerns how the introduction of technology into classrooms changes and affects the dynamics of the classroom. Only a few studies (Sandholtz, Ringstaff, & Dwyer, 1990; Dwyer, 1994; Xu, 2002; Gross, 2002) examine such issues as designing and maintaining the physical classroom environment, establishing and maintaining classroom rules and routines, interactions among students, interactions between teacher and students, academic engaged time, managing transitions among activities, and many other aspects of classroom management that are affected by the presence and use of instructional technologies. Dwyer (1994) reported that children interacted with one another more frequently while working at computers, and the interactions were different—the students spontaneously helped each other. They were curious about what others were doing and they were both excited about their own activities and intently engaged. The fear that students would become social isolates while working on computers was unfounded.

Gross (2002) identified the problem of managing technology in the classroom as one of the greatest challenges mentioned by the teachers in her study. Teachers were concerned about behavior problems developing when the teacher worked with one group of students at the computer, while another group of students was working on a different task. The teachers were also concerned about how to make use of one or two computers in the classroom. Gross discovered that as teachers became more comfortable with software and student grouping, classroom management became less of an issue.

Xu (2002) studied the implementation of an accelerated mathematics learning information system in a middle school special education program. Although the special education students engaged in considerable talking and off-task behavior while working in the more independent computer environment, the teachers suggested that the discipline problems were no more than those in a regular classroom. These teachers did develop behavioral contracts with students regarding the completion of their assignments, and they developed new rules regarding the use of the computers.

There are also reports of teacher concerns about classroom management when using technology, including fears that unruly students may damage expensive equipment, and concerns about moving children from classrooms to computer laboratories (Irving, 2003).

Reports of effective technology use in classrooms often describe how students actively engage with the technology in inquiry-based, knowledge-construction strategies. Because many traditional classrooms are teacher-centered and favor direct instruction methods, using technology effectively may require a paradigm shift to promote constructivist behavior—student problem solving, exploring the learning environment, conducting learning activities, and students' monitoring their own learning. This shift may threaten some teachers who fear a loss of control. Using technology effectively for instructional use requires considerable planning on the part of the teacher, with the ever-present potential malfunction of the technology looming in the background. Teachers need to perform the activity and test the equipment for possible problems before students become involved (Saurino, Bouma, & Gunnoe, 1999). Planning and managing the technology adds additional tasks to a teacher's already full plate. Teachers with poor or average classroom management skills may shy away from using instructional technology for fear of losing control of the classroom (Margerum-Leys & Marx, 2000). It is difficult for teachers to integrate technology into their instruction if they have poor classroom management skills because computers add another layer of complexity to classroom management and to monitoring student work. "Teachers need multitasking skills when students are working with computer technology and the Internet" (Derfler, 2002, p. 78).

Apple Classrooms of Tomorrow

The largest and most comprehensive study on the introduction of computer technology into classrooms was the Apple Classrooms of Tomorrow project (ACOT), which involved 32 teachers and 650 students over a period of four years (Dwyer, 1994; Dwyer, Ringstaff, & Sandholtz, 1991). This project, begun in 1986 by Apple Computers, investigated how routine use of technology by teachers and students would affect teaching and learning. ACOT began work in seven classrooms representing a cross-section of America's K–12 schools. Each participating student and teacher was given two computers, one for home and one for the classroom, since at that time computers were big and heavy and the two-computer formula was the only way to ensure that students and teachers would have constant access to technology.

The overall outcomes of the ACOT project were quite positive. Cooperative and task-related interactions among students in ACOT classrooms were more extensive than in traditional classrooms. Children tended to use computers more, rather than less, as their competence with technology increased. Teachers acted more as guides and mentors and less like lecturers. Students became more active as they became peer tutors, led classes, and organized work groups. Students interacted often with one another while working at computers, spontaneously helping each other while displaying great curiosity about what others were doing. Teachers reported working harder and longer hours, but enjoying their work more and feeling more successful with their students.

Teachers altered the physical setup of their classrooms and modified daily schedules to allow students more time to work on projects. In elementary and middle grade settings, traditional recitation and seatwork were balanced with interdisciplinary, project-based instruction.

Absenteeism at one high school was cut in half, and 90% of ACOT graduates went on to college. These students routinely employed inquiry, collaborative, technological, and problem-solving skills uncommon to graduates of traditional high school programs (Dwyer, 1994).

Particularly germane to the topic of classroom management, Sandholtz et al. (1990) examined classroom management changes that occurred during the course of the ACOT project. Based on weekly reports sent via e-mail, correspondence between sites, and bimonthly audiotapes from teachers, data from 32 elementary and secondary ACOT teachers in five schools were collected over four years. Using qualitative analyses, the authors describe how teachers went through three management stages, described as "survival," "mastery," and "impact." In the "survival" stage, teachers were overwhelmed by their need to control student behavior, organize the physical environment, and redefine their role in the classroom. Teachers expressed anxiety about being unprepared to deal with such issues as students copying or stealing each others' disks. The addition of technology also meant that teachers had to cope with lack of space, inadequate lighting, and even weather that affected the computers. Broken equipment, noisy or bottlenecked printers, and software bugs added to the teachers' frustration.

During the second year of the ACOT program, teachers started to move into the "mastery" stage by beginning to anticipate problems in student behavior, classroom environment, and technology, and to develop strategies for solving them. Since the computers were the main source of both student attraction and misbehavior, many teachers started to restrict the use of computers. Teachers also addressed the variety of cheating schemes by implementing such strategies as confronting individual students, holding class discussions on ethics, and imposing grading penalties. Teachers also began using the technology to catch cheaters and prevent recurrences.

To deal with the physical space problems created by the addition of computers, printers, and cables, teachers rearranged classrooms to allow the greatest amount of free space, and developed systems for organizing and storing disks, printer papers, software, and other computer-related items. Teachers also began enlisting student assistance in setting up computers and furniture to save time. Teachers also developed rules for the use of printers to avoid the jamming of printers and reducing noise level. As teachers developed greater familiarity and expertise in the use of technology, increased levels of student engagement and motivation were reported, further decreasing management problems.

In the third and fourth years, the teachers began to enter the "impact" stage by successfully using the technology to manage the classroom rather than just troubleshooting. Teachers developed techniques for monitoring student work, keeping records, grading tests, developing new materials, and individualizing instruction. Technology began to save teachers time rather than requiring extra time. One school developed a format for preparing the students' Individualized Education Programs (IEPs) that simplified the process of creating these plans. The authors concluded that at the "impact" stage teachers had learned to use the technology to enhance student motivation, interest, and learning, and incorporated technology in their teaching so as to make the technology indispensable (Sandholtz et al., 1990, p. 35).

Other Research Studies

In a more recent study (Russell, Bebell, Cowan, & Corbelli, 2003), each student in three fourth-grade classrooms was provided with an AlphaSmart, a text-editing word processor. One surprising finding concerned classroom management. The researchers concluded that "when every student had the same resources, technology management was generally easier and less time consuming for teachers. To this end, the teachers who made the most extensive use of technology in their lessons found the greatest degree of improvement in general classroom management" (Russell et al., 2003). The ability to have all students use an AlphaSmart at the same time decreased the need for teachers to manage whose turn it was to use the AlphaSmarts and computers. This logistical improvement in the management of classroom technology was deemed one of the most important changes that resulted from students having full access to the AlphaSmarts. Further, students developed a greater sense of ownership, responsibility, independence, and empowerment. Full, rather than limited, access to technology greatly increases its use in classrooms.

Some of the classroom management problems cited by teachers may occur because students have limited access to the technology, and teachers have to control that access. Students may vie for this access, thus creating classroom management problems. As the Russell et al. (2003) study suggests, when students have unlimited access to the technology, some kinds of classroom management problems may diminish.

While some studies note that technology improves student time on task, other studies describe classroom management problems when using technology. One study on preservice science teachers' use of educational technology during student teaching (Irving, 2003) discovered that student teachers with lower achieving students expressed reluctance to use technology for fear of how their students would behave, especially in a computer laboratory. As one student teacher commented:

> It's stressful to get them to be quiet in the hallway, to get them to the computer lab is hard; when they are in the computer lab . . . they kept making the computers talk. They just don't behave. And when you're in the computer lab, you can't tell who's doing it. So I have no real control over them . . . I can't see whose computer is making the noise. (p. 212)

Another student teacher from the same study felt that immature, unruly students in her classes made it difficult for her to incorporate expensive and breakable equipment in her lesson plans. As she stated:

> We all have a lot of really immature, emotionally, behaviorally disturbed kids who just pick up, touch everything, throw it, break it, hit each other, run around, you know, jumping over desks... So the issue is equipment safety and meddlesome kids who just sit in the back and while... you're teaching your class they might be breaking something. (Irving, 2003, p. 213)

Three of the student teachers in this study expressed concern about low-achieving students' ability to stay on task, to engage with electronic technologies, and to treat equipment safely and with respect. On the other hand, three other student teachers from the same study, who also worked with low-achieving students, did not report difficulties with behavioral issues when using technology. One of them extolled the virtues of laptop carts as a way to differentiate instruction and tailor lesson plans for individual students (Irving, 2003).

Summary of Research Findings

Research concerning classroom management and the use of technology is scant, but that which does exist provides some insight into the intersection of these two topics. As the classroom context changes, so do the classroom management issues. When technology is first introduced into classrooms, management issues are likely to arise. When classrooms have only one or two computers, students are likely to vie for access to this equipment, and teachers have to develop rules regarding their use. In technology-rich classrooms, teachers must deal with issues related to the physical arrangement of the classroom to accommodate computers, printers, and other paraphernalia. As teachers become comfortable with the technology and develop more skill in its use, technology seems to save teachers time, rather than requiring additional time. Getting to this point, however, may take a couple of years.

Creative use of technology for instructional purposes also seems to lead to a different teaching style, one that is less teacher-centered and more student-centered. Many teachers are uncomfortable with this new role as guide or facilitator and resist integrating technology into instruction in a meaningful way. Teachers who struggle with classroom management issues are unlikely to embrace technology since it introduces more variables into an already complicated situation. Even those teachers who are skilled in classroom management will have to deal with issues such as managing access to the equipment, monitoring student time on task, and being alert to new forms of possible cheating.

TEACHER USE OF TECHNOLOGY FOR NONINSTRUCTIONAL ACTIVITIES

It has been documented that classroom teachers' most frequent use of technology is completing noninstructional activities (Becker, et al., 1999). Noninstructional activities include communicating with parents, providing student feedback on assignments, and engaging in professional development activities. Noninstructional activities are essential for creating an effective classroom learning environment; however, they detract from the amount of time teachers are able to spend directly interacting with students. Given that teachers spend more than 11 hours a week on noninstructional activities, technology that enables teachers to be more efficient is a welcome professional tool (Dockterman, 2002). When teachers spend time outside of the classroom for professional activities, they use a computer to assist them 97% of the time (Dockterman, 2002). Teachers find spreadsheets and databases and network systems are effective technology tools that aid in streamlining noninstructional activities and facilitate communication and access to resources (Dockterman, 2002).

Software such as spreadsheet and database programs may be used to manage school and classroom records and information. A spreadsheet is a piece of software that allows users to arrange text or numbers in rows and columns. It allows users to enter data, much like data would be entered onto a ledger form. The data entered can be analyzed using formulas, charts, and graphs. Teachers report that they find spreadsheets to be a helpful classroom management tool by using it specifically to track student progress. For example, by entering student grades into a spreadsheet program, teachers can sort the grades to track one student's progress throughout a grading cycle or to compare all student grades on one particular assignment. Teachers can chose to track the scores either by listing the raw number or by creating different charts or graphs. Recording and organizing data in this manner not only enables teachers to streamline their paperwork, but it also is a helpful way to share student progress with parents and students. Spreadsheets also may be used to streamline teachers' noninstructional tasks, such as creating and maintaining a class budget, creating class lists, scheduling student projects, and keeping student attendance.

Much like spreadsheets, databases also can be used by teachers to record and organize essential classroom information. Teachers cite that the most frequent use of databases is recording student demographic data (Dockterman, 2002). For example, at the beginning of the school year, teachers will create a database that holds basic information such as student name, parents' names, contact information, birthday, and medical information. Once these data are entered into a database, teachers can use it for easy access to their students' home contact information or to create documents such as nametags or student lists.

Word processing software is another technology tool used by teachers to streamline their noninstructional activities. Word processing software enables users to edit, store, and print documents. It is an efficient way to make revisions and to save and file documents. Teachers' most frequent use of this software is to create lesson plans and instructional materials (Berson, Berson, & Ferron, 2002). Examples of instructional materials that teachers can create include worksheets, tests, lab reports, outlines, book report forms, and unit guides. In addition to creating instructional materials, word processing software can be used to prepare documents such as letters home to parents or class newsletters.

School networks, intranet or Internet, are another essential classroom management tool for teachers. School networks enable teachers to engage in professional communication with colleagues, parents, and students. An intranet system permits teachers to exchange information within the school building. For example, teachers may upload lesson plans or student information to the intranet to share with other teachers in the building. This not only is an effective way to share professional information, but it is an efficient way to track student achievement and behavior. By storing student grades and behavior on a school intranet, teachers can trace student grades or behavior issues over time and across classes. For example, a high school teacher having classroom behavior issues with a student can easily pull up the student's behavior chart to see if the behavior issues occur across all subject areas or just one class.

Access to the Internet assists teachers with classroom management much like a school intranet system, but because it is not limited to the school building, teachers have access to many more resources and people. The Internet has proven to be an effective tool for communicating with students, parents, and members of the community. It also is an effective research tool for teachers and provides professional development opportunities for teachers. Teachers report that e-mail access through the Internet provides them a flexible and efficient way to share classroom news with parents. The increased parental involvement and awareness with the school that results from frequent e-mail communication between teacher and parent has been shown to have a positive impact on student classroom behavior (Sumner, 2000).

TEACHER AND STUDENT USE OF TECHNOLOGY FOR INSTRUCTIONAL ACTIVITIES

Managing the learning environment when using technology also varies according to the configuration of the technologies. A teacher-centered lesson using a single computer with a display station calls for different classroom management than a student-centered classroom in which all students are equipped with wireless handheld computers and pursuing individual assignments. Issues that emerge from integrating a variety of technologies and their impact on classroom management are explored here, along with the implications of how instructional technologies are organized for managing the learning environment.

Of a different nature, as more courses and programs are offered online, instructors must manage multiuser virtual learning environments to provide for individual expression while also building a safe community. Among the issues arising from these virtual contexts are ways of establishing appropriate norms for student computer responses, monitoring appropriate language and potentially offensive language in online discussions, and responding to bullying or teasing of other online students.

Burns' (2002) two-year research study of technology integration into the classroom revealed that the primary reason teachers don't use computers in instruction is fear. Teachers reported a fear that using technology for instruction would disrupt the traditional classroom mores. This fear stems from the notion that computers hold the power to shift control from the teacher to the student. The research of Becker et al. (1999) substantiates this finding. The following section discusses classroom management issues and strategies related to specific technology classroom learning environments.

One-Computer Classroom

The function of a computer in a one-computer classroom may simply be teacher use for noninstructional activities such as those discussed in the previous section. However, there are varied and powerful opportunities to use the one computer for effective instructional purposes. Student use of the one-computer classroom has been likened to students lining up to drink water from a hallway drinking fountain (Anderson, 2004). The bottleneck created by this line of eager students is ripe for classroom behavior problems.

Ashmus (2004) outlines seven categories of usage for the one computer classroom. These categories and a brief description of how the one computer may be used in the classroom are listed in Table 20.1.

Classroom management strategies are essential for creating a successful learning environment in the one-computer classroom. Issues that must be considered are as basic as ensuring that the location of the one computer is appropriate for its intended use. Ashmus (2004) reminds teachers to check to be certain that the placement of the hardware ensures convenient access. Convenient access may be defined as a central location for classroom display for all students or as a center that is to the side of the classroom. Because students often will be working on the one computer on their own or in small groups, it is vital for teachers to be appropriately prepared. Being prepared requires teachers to pre-check the computer for all required software and to ensure that students have detailed directions to lead them through the assignment.

Beyond being prepared, teachers should consider specific instructional strategies that have proven effective for teaching in the one-computer classroom (Ashmus, 2004). Among these strategies are creating "trained experts" from the students in the class, asking the volunteers or parents to assist, implementing cooperative learning methods, rotating student computer time, creating standardized methods for saving student work, providing students with a template or checklist to guide them through the assignment.

TABLE 20.1
Uses of One Computer in the Classroom

Category	*Sample Usage*
Administrative Tool	Teacher uses for noninstructional activities
Presentation Tool	Teacher demonstrates key concepts or ideas or presents outline for student note taking
Communication Station	Teacher or students e-mail or videoconference with students/classrooms in other locations
Information Station	Teacher or students use the Internet or CD-ROM to conduct outside research
Publishing Tool	Teacher or students create class newsletter or brochure; students create project-based materials
Learning Center	Students use content-specific software for remediation, such as drill and practice
Simulation Center	Students use software to work through simulations or use guided directions to move through different resources

Multicomputer Classroom

Teachers who have access to multiple computers in the classroom typically design classroom instruction so that students either cluster around the computers in groups to complete the same assignment or set up a station model in which students rotate to different computers, completing a different task at each station. Burns' (2002) research of technology-enhanced instruction revealed a variety of classroom management patterns being practiced in the multicomputer classroom. She named and defined the four more prominent models as:

Learning stations model (13 students to 2 computers). Teams of four to five students are rotated through three different "learning stations" to gather data and information for their project. In one particular application of this structure, one station used a digital camera to gather images, another station used a simple electronic spreadsheet to analyze data, and a third station used printed materials about the community. Each of the stations had roles for every team member as well as instructions for completing the tasks at that station.

Navigator model (4 students to 1 computer). Using a road trip analogy, teams of four to five were assembled and given role cards. The "driver" controlled the mouse and keyboard, while the "navigator" helped the driver operate the computer. "Back-seat driver 1" managed the group's progress and "back-seat driver 2" served as the timekeeper. The navigator attended a 10- to 20-minute training session in which the facilitator provided an overview of the basics of particular software. Once trained, the navigators returned to their teams and instructed team members in the use of the software. The navigator could only give instructions, but could not touch the mouse or keyboard. The rest of the team rotated through "driving" the computer so that everyone had a chance to use the software.

Facilitator Model (6 students to 1 computer). This model was useful for carrying out more complex projects that required different skill sets and levels of expertise. The designated facilitator had some experience with the software in use and showed the most novice users (students) how to use the software application to create a layout for a final product. Like the navigator in the model just mentioned, the facilitator worked with the layout group, and the content group worked without a computer to create content for the newsletter or report. All group members, with the exception of the facilitator, rotated through the layout and content groups to ensure each member gained experience with the software and the content.

Collaborative groups model (7 students to 1 computer). In the collaborative groups model, each small group was responsible for creating some component of the whole group's final product. For example, one part of the group wrote a report, another created a map, and a third used the computer to gather census data and display it in graphs. (p. 36)

Classroom Lab

In the classroom computer lab, the ratio of student to computer is one to one. Given the influx of money that has been dedicated to student use of computers, one would expect teachers to be using lab-based computers more often for instruction. However, only 67% of teachers reported that they used the computer during class time (Technology counts, 2003). Teachers report that the number is not higher because they find it difficult to schedule time to take their classes to the school computer lab, they are fearful of losing control of their students in the lab, and they cite the inordinate amount of preparation time required for taking students to the lab (Burns, 2002). While these obstacles may be valid concerns for teacher avoidance of the computer lab, there are a number of guides and reports for teachers that list suggested strategies for effective classroom management in the computer lab. These guides often provide helpful classroom management tips for the classroom teacher.

Starr (2004) surveyed a team of education technology specialists to arrive at a laundry list of classroom lab management tips. The following is a sample of the innovative and helpful strategies.

- Always run through a technology lesson *before* presenting it to the class—and always have a back-up lesson prepared in case the technology fails.
- Type directions for frequently used computer operations—opening programs, inserting clip art, printing documents, and so on—on index cards, laminate them, and connect them with a circle ring. Keep a set next to each computer.
- Have students turn *off* their monitors when you're giving directions.
- Appoint classroom technology managers. Consider an Attendance Manager, who takes attendance and serves as a substitute teacher helper when necessary; a Materials Manager, who passes out materials and runs errands; a Technical Manager, who helps resolve printer and computer issues; and an End-of-Class Manager, who makes sure work areas are neat—keyboards pushed in, mice straight, and programs closed—before students are dismissed.
- If you have classes filtering in and out of a computer lab each day and have little or no time to set up between classes, arrange for older students to help. Even second graders can put in CDs and start programs for the kindergarteners who follow them. Simply end your lesson five minutes early and walk the older students through the process of setting up for the next class.
- When working on lengthy technology projects, print out step-by-step instructions. Include some that say "Save your work; do not go any further until you help your neighbors reach this point." This helps less-proficient students solve problems more quickly, keeps the class at roughly the same point in the project, and fosters collaborative learning.
- Make it a class rule that students can help one another but cannot ever touch another student's computer. That way, you can be sure that learning occurs even when students help one another.
- Keep a red plastic cup at each computer. When students need help, have them place the highly visible cups on top of their monitors.
- Before students leave class, have them turn their mice upside down so the trackballs are showing. You'll lose fewer trackballs that way.
- Place different colored sticker dots on the left and the right bottom corners of each monitor. Use these to indicate which side of the screen you are talking about—very

helpful when using certain programs, such as the new Kid Pix—and to determine whose turn it is if students share a computer.

- Plug all speakers into a main power bar. Turn the bar off when you're teaching and turn it on when students are working. If the room becomes too noisy, turn off the power bar to get students' attention.
- Use a Video Out card to project a monitor display onto a television screen.
- Type PLEASE WAIT FOR INSTRUCTIONS on $8^1/_2$ by 11 papers, laminate them, and tape one sheet to the top of every monitor. Students flip the signs to the back of the monitor *after* you've given directions.
- Create a folder in the Start menu and place any programs you use with students in that folder. Students never have to click Programs—everything they use is in one folder.
- When working in a computer lab, assign each student a computer. Students can line up in "computer lab order" in their classrooms. Seating goes very quickly when they get to the lab.
- If you're working on a network, ask your technology coordinator to set up a shared folder for Internet resources. Then, when you're planning an Internet lesson, simply save a shortcut to the Web site in that folder. During lab time, students can go to the shared folder, double click the link, and go right to the site without typing the URL. This saves time and stress for both students and teachers.

Mobile Computing

Emerging technology trends suggest that schools are moving towards providing mobile computer access to all students (Dede & Ketelhut, 2003). Mobile computer options include either laptops, personal digital assistants (PDAs), or mobile phones for teachers and students. Laptops, PDAs, and mobile phones are becoming more and more popular among teachers and students because of their portability; however, other features make them invaluable tools. They often have wireless network capabilities, allowing users to access the Internet without being physically connected to the network. They also allow for easy file sharing. PDAs connect with a desktop computer, allowing the user to synchronize data.

The mobile computing configuration allows teachers to use computers in their own classroom setting and it provides one computer for each student. Terms such as "ubiquitous computing" or "pervasive computing" have been used to describe the phenomenon of the one-to-one computing model. This new trend of ubiquitous computing is considered the most recent stage in the evolution of technology, emerging form the eras of mainframe computers and desktop computers (Weiser, 1995). In other words, handheld computers will be everywhere, with every child using one in school and at home. Bull, Bull, Garofalo, and Harris (2002) compare the transition to "ubiquitous computing" with Moore's Law. Moore's Law originated with Gordon Moore, cofounder of Intel, who stated that computing power doubles every 18 to 24 months and, at the same time, the cost of computing is essentially halved. Price drops such as these will open the door to widespread one-to-one computing with mobile computing devices.

Mobile computing allows teachers a freedom of movement to better monitor and record classroom activities (Carter, 2004; Curtis, 2003). One teacher commented, "This freedom of movement allows me to be a better record keeper, better assessor; and hopefully, a better teacher" (Pride, 2003). Teachers also report that using mobile computers to document classroom behavior enables them to see a more "comprehensive picture of learning, yielding formative data that was [sic] useful in guiding the development of lessons and activities" (Pride, 2003).

Providing one laptop or one PDA for each student has been shown to be an effective way to provide access for all students, improve communication with parents, increase student motivation, and encourage student collaboration. In addition to these benefits, mobile computing initiatives have encouraged teachers to engage their students in inquiry-based learning activities and to differentiate instruction for individual students. The Toshiba Laptop Learning Challenge by the National Science Teachers Association (1999) lists several advantages for using laptop computers in educational settings. Among these advantages area that laptop computers:

- Provide portability within the school, outside the classroom
- Provide portability for field trips and investigations
- Provide immediate data processing and graphic feedback
- Provide immediate feedback and analysis for decision making in the field
- Allow file sharing
- Facilitate group work and collaboration
- Generate reports and presentations
- Permit flexible and innovative uses
- Provide access to expert resources on the Internet or through e-mail

The use of mobile computers in the classroom can contribute to improved student classroom behavior. In a pilot laptop initiative, the student attendance rate increased and student discipline problems decreased. At one elementary school, detentions dropped from 28 to 3 among students who had laptops, suspensions decreased from 5 to 0, and 91% of the students with laptops improved their grades in at least one academic area (Profiles in success, 2004).

One laptop or one PDA for each student holds the potential of transforming classroom teaching and learning as we know it today. However, the possibility for classroom management challenges multiplies with mobile computing. Inappropriately surfing the Internet or damaging the computers are two examples of potential management problems. When teachers take measures such as designating "Think Time" or "Lids Down" time when students must direct their attention to the teacher, planning ahead for recharging batteries, bookmarking web addresses, and setting up shortcuts for software programs, classroom management issues in the mobile computing classroom can be relieved.

Teachers have found that they become more efficient in the mobile computing classroom. This newfound efficiency may be attributed to the ease of access that comes with using a laptop or PDA. Pride (2003) outlines four categories of ways teachers are taking advantage of ubiquitous computing in their classroom: calendar, address book, to-do list, and memo pad. Pride's account gives examples of how these applications affect classroom management. For example, the teacher who uses the calendar function on the mobile computer can set the alarm to indicate when students need to leave the classroom for individualized instruction or the teacher can keep a list of class activities and homework assignments so that when a student who is absent returns, she can simply beam the information to the student's PDA. The memo function on a PDA can assist teachers in a variety of ways. For instance, teachers can keep a memo list for each student, recording daily observations about student learning and behavior (Pride, 2003).

Mobile phones are another form of mobile computing. As mobile phones become more and more prevalent in today's society, students begin to bring them to school. For many teachers they may seem a hindrance; however, they are being used effectively in some classrooms. As with the other forms of mobile computers, mobile phones can lead to classroom management issues. These issues include issues related to Internet safety, student cheating, and student time off task. At the present time, many school systems and schools recognize these risks and have banned mobile phones from school settings.

There are, however, a number of educational uses for mobile phones. For example, teachers may prepare interactive quizzes, puzzles, or math problems that can be sent from the teacher to the students. The students can complete the assignment and then send the responses back to the teacher or to another classmate. Mobile phones also can be used to access the Internet. Thus, they become a rather inexpensive tool for voice, image, and video messaging for class assignments, such as student study groups. Within this category of Internet uses is simple text e-mail messaging or instant text messaging. Teachers can create collaborative lessons that call upon students to share data such as photographs or text with students either within the same class or in another location. Additionally, individualized learning activities for students with special needs can be used to differentiate instruction. For example, audio and video supplements could be prepared (National Centre for Technology in Education, 2004).

It is essential that teachers follow school Acceptable Use Policies (AUPs) and have clear expectations for students before mobile phones are introduced into classroom instruction. Teachers should be familiar with the phones so that if there is an instance where students are not following classroom guidelines, they are able to track the student use of the mobile phone through phone options such as the list of recent calls or a transcript of the text messaging.

Assistive Technologies

Assistive technologies refers to the array of devices and services that help people with disabilities perform better in their daily lives. The Individuals with Disabilities Education Act of 1997 requires that assistive technology be considered when developing the Individual Education Program (IEP). A recent study concluded that many more Americans, besides those who have been categorized as having disabilities, can benefit from the use of assistive technology. The study estimates that 60% of working-age adults (101.4 million) are likely or very likely to benefit from the use of assistive technology (Forrester Research, 2003, p. 8).

Devices such as motorized chairs, remote control units to turn on appliances, voice recognition systems, and computers all can assist people with severe disabilities. Computers are particularly important in allowing many students with a range of disabilities to participate in normal classroom activities that would otherwise be impossible. The following are some examples of how computer technology can assist students with disabilities:

- User-friendly keyboard enhancements can simplify typing.
- A combination of lasers and computers can aid students to move a mouse and make selections on a computer display with eye movement alone.
- Voice recognition software can translate a student's spoken words into text on the computer screen, and text-to-speech allows a student to hear his words spoken.
- Computer-assisted instruction (CAI) is self-paced and individualized for each student's needs.
- Braille translation software and Braille printers enable blind students to read.
- Alternative keyboards with touch windows and switches are available for students with limited motor control.
- Screen-enlarging software can assist students who may have sight impairments.

Many such assistive devices exist for a variety of disabilities and more and more are being created.

Having pupils who need such technologies presents challenges for schools, teachers, and other students. The cost for purchasing appropriate assistive technology is always a challenge for school systems. Knowing what assistive technologies can help students, and learning how to install and use these technologies can challenge teachers. Students may consider the assistive technologies to be unfair advantages for some students, particularly those whose disabilities are less physically recognizable.

What is clear is that teachers must begin to understand and use assistive technologies to help students with disabilities, and even those who are not diagnosed as being disabled, to maximize their learning opportunities. Technology can open doors to learning for students whose opportunities to learn would otherwise be severely curtailed.

Virtual Learning Environments

Virtual learning environments, often referred to as distance learning, online learning, telecollaboration activities, or multiuser virtual learning environments, are learning experiences that allow students to interact with other via the Internet. Virtual learning environments present innovative learning opportunities for students, yet also present a new series of classroom management challenges for teachers. Online learning can take many forms in the classroom. The most prevalent model of online learning is based on the Virtual High School model. That is, individual or small groups of students from a traditional school enroll in a course sponsored by an organization outside of the student's school building. The course activities are primarily asynchronous, meaning that students and teachers do not engage in online discussion at the same time.

The typical student enrolled in a virtual class chooses to enroll to have access to course content unavailable in the local community. Beyond access to locally unavailable courses, students seek out online learning opportunities because of the flexibility to take classes anytime, anywhere, and to have the opportunity to engage in learning experiences with learners from around the globe. It becomes the responsibility of the student and the student's school to identify an appropriate time and place for online learning. Some schools have designated specific labs or individual computers in computer labs for use by students enrolled in online courses. It is important for teachers and students in the school to mutually agree on when and where online students should work on their online course assignments. Agreeing on the time and location will minimize classroom management issues.

Telecollaborative activities are another category of virtual learning environments that allow students to learn in ways not possible before the advent of the Internet. Harris (1999) defines telecollaboration as "an educational endeavor that involves people in different locations using Internet tools and resources to work together." (p. 55) Students engaged in telecollaborative activities may use e-mail to correspond with an expert, such as an archaeologist on an international expedition or with other students across the globe about the effects of global warming on their local community. Web-based discussion boards provide students the opportunity to engage in asynchronous chats with an author of the novel that they just completed reading. Synchronous chats through programs such as Instant Messenger allow students to collect and share local weather data with classrooms in other locations. Students can participate in real-time communication that allows audio and video through videoconferencing. An example is the Model United Nations project, in which students throughout the globe videoconference with one another to discuss and debate global issues. Multi-User Virtual Environment Experiential Simulators (MUVEES) are another category of technology that empowers students to communicate with others in geographically disparate locations. MUVEES engage students in virtual spaces that have been created for learning, such as virtual museums or historical situations (Dede & Ketelhut, 2003).

Because Instant Messenger and MUVEES link students with others in geographically disparate locations, they are two powerful technologies that allow students to learn in a way that was not possible when students were limited to resources and learning experiences within their schools and local communities. Yes, these two technologies can cause classroom management problems in the classroom. For instance, it is very easy for students to get off-task and engage in online conversation that does not relate to the assignment. This happens when students strike up conversations with the students or experts that do not relate to the assigned task or topic. Students may also use the tools to engage in conversation with friends who are not a part of the assignment. For example, a ninth-grade student who is assigned to have an Instant Messenger conversation about a collection of poetry with a ninth-grade student in another state, may choose to contact his friend who is home sick from school for the day rather than the student in another state. Teachers should address classroom management issues such as these before students ever turn the computers on. There should be a clear set of classroom expectations and consequences related to online communication. Students should understand that off-task communication is not permitted, why it is not permitted, and what the consequences will be. Teachers should monitor students' online communication by ensuring that student computers are positioned so that a teacher can easily circulate around the room and view what is on each computer screen. Teachers may also require students to print out a transcription of the online discussion. Printed transcripts allow teachers to ensure that students stay on task and also help teachers stay in touch with what students are learning from the activity.

Internet Safety

Telecollaborative activities provide students with powerful learning opportunities. Yet, they present teachers with a new set of classroom management issues. These issues reveal the dark side of technology, such as hacking, false information, cyber bullying, child pornography, child molestation, and kidnapping (Berson et al., 2002).

The majority of Internet safety issues that occur are a result of student interaction with people they do not know over the Internet. Rather than prohibiting student communication over the Internet, teachers, parents, and students should be aware of and discuss Internet safety issues before engaging in telecollaborative activities. One of the most significant features of communicating online for all Internet users is the ability to communicate anonymously. Internet users often use different screen names and give false information about themselves online. Internet users, specifically teenagers, create false personas and engage in an online fantasy world. For many teenagers, this is a way for them to escape from the difficulties of adolescence and try out different personalities. However, this practice is extremely dangerous and most teens do not understand the consequences (Berson et al., 2002). Teachers should talk with students about what information is acceptable to share over the Internet and with whom the students should be communicating. Teachers should actively monitor the students' computer screens when students are online and read excerpts of all online discussions.

Accessing inappropriate materials is another peril of using the Internet. Students may inadvertently come across Web pages that contain sexual, violent, or simply inaccurate information. Many school systems use filter software that prohibit access to inappropriate Web sites. However, none of this software is 100% effective. Again, teachers should consistently monitor student computers and should talk with students about what they should do when the access inappropriate Web sites.

Most schools have Acceptable Use Policies (AUPs) that oversee student use of the Internet. AUPs serve three primary functions: to educate students, parents, and teachers about Internet; to define boundaries of online behavior; and to specify the consequences of online misconduct (CoVis, 2004). Presenting an AUP to students and parents is the first step in developing an awareness of Internet safety. This awareness begins with the acknowledgment that there is inappropriate information on the Internet and there are dangerous people lurking in the shadows of online communication. From this awareness, there should be an educated discussion about the consequences of dangerous Internet activities and the steps one should take to avoid them.

CONCLUSION AND RECOMMENDATIONS

The literature reviewed in this chapter may be organized into two categories: descriptive and research-based. The majority of the literature that has been published about classroom management and technology is descriptive and exploratory. There are a large number of publications and Web sites dedicated to this topic. We attribute this to the fact that classroom teachers are grappling with how to create effective learning environments with the emergence of new technologies in their classrooms. The second category of literature is research related to the topic. There are relatively few published studies related to the nexus of classroom management and technology. Those that do exist are often small studies or doctoral dissertations. The lack of research studies is most likely attributed to the fact that computer technology use in schools is a relatively new phenomenon and scholars in the field are just beginning to recognize the need for such studies.

Because so little research exists on classroom management issues related to the use of technology, there are many areas where research can inform our understanding of effective practice. The following are but a few potential research topics and questions.

Relationship of Effective Classroom Management Skills and Use of Technology

A few studies suggest that teachers who are already effective managers may be more inclined to use technology in their classrooms than teachers whose classroom management skills are weak. Similarly, Irving's dissertation study (2003) found reluctance among intern teachers to use technology with certain classes because the teachers were fearful that rowdy students might damage expensive equipment. Further exploration of the relationship between teachers' classroom management skills and disposition to use technology would be worthwhile.

Relationship of Student Time-On-Task Using Technology and Classroom Organization and Teacher Monitoring

This field would benefit from numerous observational studies of teachers who are effective in keeping students academically engaged when using technology to see how their classrooms are organized, how they prepare students for the task at hand, and how they monitor student behavior. For instance, are the well-known constructs of Jacob Kounin (*withitness, smoothness, momentum*) major predictors of student on-task behavior when using technology, or are there other explanations for a teacher's effectiveness? Are there physical arrangements of computers in a classroom that are more effective in keeping students on task than other arrangements?

Transitions To and From Technology Use

Transitions from one activity to another often result in wasted time and potential disruptions. It would be fruitful to study these transitions to learn how to best structure transitions to and from technology use. Questions to be investigated include: Are transitions to computer technology use similar to or different from other kinds of activity transitions? What procedures do effective teachers use to keep transitions brief and nonintrusive? What can teachers do to ensure smooth transitions?

Given the unique nature of researching classroom management and technology, efforts should be made to conduct collaborative research, that is, research in which scholars and practitioners partner to better understand the relationships between classroom management and technology. Collaborative research would help to bridge the gap between theory and practice. It would provide researchers with an entrée into understanding how classroom teachers are adapting and inventing classroom management techniques as new technologies emerge. Collaborative research would also provide practitioners with the opportunity to engage in self-study opportunities and would help them to refine and improve their own classroom management strategies.

Based on this review, it is our recommendation that traditional textbooks on classroom management should begin to address the issue of technology and how its introduction affects classroom management dynamics. Additionally, teacher education programs should incorporate technology and classroom management issues into preservice teacher education experiences. It is also our recommendation that as school systems develop technology-based professional development activities for inservice teachers, they should incorporate classroom management strategies for teachers into the staff development. By this we mean that when teachers are introduced to a new piece of hardware or software they should not only learn how to use it, but also should learn classroom management strategies connected with its use.

The research also indicates that teachers need time to go through "stages" of using technology before they become comfortable with it and can actually start saving time through its use. Also, students have certain needs, according to Glasser (1999) (survival, love and belonging, power, freedom, and fun), and teachers should recognize and take advantage of these needs vis a vis computer use. Glasser maintains that inappropriate behaviors by students are often misguided efforts to achieve power, which he uses synonymously with "self-esteem" and "self-importance." Teachers need to address this need for power by combining the needs of students with classroom assignments or activities. By understanding and incorporating basic human needs into the classroom structure, the more students will be convinced that their schoolwork satisfies their needs, the harder they will try and the better work they will produce. Organizing computer technology assignments to allow and encourage learning teams and to give students opportunities to fulfill needs for power or self-importance will help to establish an effective classroom management system and reduce undesirable attention-getting behaviors. Dwyer's findings (1994) support Glasser's choice theory, particularly in relation to feelings of power, belonging, freedom, and fun. Dwyer discovered that students spontaneously organized collaborative work groups around their computer assignments. They often had to be chased out of classrooms at recess, and frequently worked with their peers after the formal end of the school year. Working with the computer technology seemed to fulfill a number of these students' basic needs.

ACKNOWLEDGMENTS

The authors thank Lynne Schrum, University of Georgia, Keith Wetzel, Arizona State University West, and Linda Colburn, The University of Texas, Austin, for their comments on an early version of this chapter.

REFERENCES

1999 Toshiba/NSTA laptop learning challenge. (1999, 2004). Retrieved March 23, 2004, from http://www.nsta.org/programs/laptop/

Anderson, W. (2004). That's not a drinking fountain or how to survive in a one computer classroom. Retrieved March 23, 2004, from http://www.ncrtec.org/tl/digi/onecomp/

Ansell, S. E., & Park, J. (2003). Tracking tech tends. *Education Week, 22*(35), 43–44, 48.

Ashmus, D. (2004). But I don't have a computer lab! Using one computer in the classroom. Retrieved March 22, 2004, from http://www.serve.org/seir-tec/present/onecomptr.html

Becker, H. J., Ravitz, J. L., & Wong, Y. (1999). Teacher and teacher-directed student use of computers and software. Retrieved March 23, 2004, from http://www.crito.uci.edu/tlc/findings/computeruse/html/startpage.htm

Berson, I. R., Berson, M. J., & Ferron, J. M. (2002). Emerging risks of violence in the digital age: lessons for educators from an on-line study of adolescent girls in the US. Retrieved March 23, 2004, from http://www.ncsu.edu/meridian/sum2002/cyberviolence/index.html

Bull, G., Bull, G., Garofalo, J., & Harris, J. (2002). Grand challenges: Preparing for the technological tipping point. *Learning and Leading with Technology, 29*(8), 6–12.

Burns, M. (2002). From black and white to color: Technology, professional development and changing practice. *THE Journal, 29*(11), 36.

Carter. (2001). Laptop lessons: Exploring the promise of one-to-one computing. Retrieved March 23, 2004, from http://www.techlearning.com/db_area/archives/TL/200105/laptops.html

CoVis. (2004). What you need to know about acceptable use policies. Retrieved March 23, 2004 from http://www.covis.nwu.edu/info/network-use-policy.html

Cuban, L. (2001). *Oversold and underused: Computers in the classroom*. Cambridge, MA: Harvard University Press.

Curtis, D. (2003). A computer for every lap. Retrieved March 23, 2004, from http://glef.org/php/article.php?id=Art_1032

Dede, C., & Ketelhut, D. (2003). Designing for motivation and usability in a museum-based multi-user virtual environment. Retrieved March 23, 2004, from http://muve.gse.harvard.edu/muvees2003/documents/DedeKetelMUVEaera03final.pdf

Derfler, K. E. (2002). Factors which affect middle school teachers' willingness to utilize technology as an instructional tool. (Doctoral dissertation, LaSierra University, Riverside, CA). Retrieved from the Digital Dissertations database, Publication No. AAT 3055178 unpublished.

Dwyer, D. (1994). Apple classrooms of tomorrow: What we've learned. *Educational Leadership, 51*, 7.

Dwyer, D. C., Ringstaff, C., & Sandholtz, J. H. (1991). Changes in teachers' beliefs and practices in technology-rich classrooms. *Educational Leadership, 48*(8), 45–52.

Forrester Research, Inc. (2003). *The wide range of abilities and its impact on computer technology*. Research study commissioned by Microsoft Corporation, Cambridge, MA.

Glasser, W. (1999). *Choice theory*. New York: HarperCollins.

Gross, D. (2002). An analysis of perceptions of factors that influence microcomputer use in three urban public schools. (Doctoral dissertation, Wayne State University, Detroit, MI). Retrieved from the Digital Dissertations database, Publication No. AAT 3071785 unpublished.

Harris, J. (1999). First steps in telecollaboration. *Learning and Leading with Technology, 27*(3), 54–57.

Irving, K. E. (2003). Preservice science teachers' use of educational technology during student teaching. (Doctoral dissertation, University of Virginia, Charlottesville, VA). Retrieved from the Digital Dissertations database, Publication No. AAT 3097272 unpublished.

Kahn, J. (1998). *Ideas and strategies for the one-computer classroom*. (Report No. BBB27495). Eugene, OR: International Society for Technology in Education. (ERIC Document Reproduction Service No. ED421981)

Margerum-Leys, J., & Marx, R. W. (2000, April). *Teacher knowledge of educational technology: A study of student teacher/mentor teacher pairs*. Paper presented at the annual meeting of the American Educational Research Association, New Orleans, LA. (ERIC Document Reproduction Service No. ED442763)

McNally, L., & Etchison, C. (2000). Strategies of successful technology integration, Part 1. *Learning and Leading with Technology, 28* (2), 6–12.

National Centre for Technology in Education. (2004). Mobile phones. Retrieved March 23, 2004 from http://www.ncte.ie/ICTAdviceSupport/AdviceSheets/MobilePhones/

Pride, C. (2003). *Handhelds in the classroom—tools for teachers*. Retrieved March 23, 2004, from http://www.techlearning.com/story/showArticle.jhtml?articleID=12803444

Profiles in success: *Maine learning technology initiative*. (2004). Retrieved March 23, 2004, from http://www.apple.com/education/profiles/maine/

Russell, M., Bebell, D., Cowan, J., & Corbelli, M. (2003). An AlphaSmart for each student: Do teaching and learning change with full access to word processors? *Computers and Composition, 20*, 51–76.

Sandholtz, J. H., Ringstaff, C., and Dwyer, D. C. (1990). *Teaching in high-tech environments: Classroom management revisited*. Paper presented at the annual meeting of the American Educational Research Association, Boston. (ERIC Document Reproduction Service No. ED327172)

Saurino, D. R., Bouma, A., & Gunnoe, B. (March, 1999). *Science classroom management techniques using graphing calculator technology: A collaborative team action research approach*. Paper presented at the annual meeting of the National Association of Research in Science Teaching, Boston. (ERIC Document Reproduction Service No. ED429828)

Starr, L. (2004). Managing technology: Tips from the experts. Retrieved March 23, 2004, from http://www.education-world.com/a_tech/tech/tech116.shtml

Sumner, S. (2000). Parent communication? Try a classroom web page. Retrieved March 23, 2004, from http://www.4teachers.org/testimony/sumner/index.shtml

Technology counts: E-defining education. (2003). Retrieved March 22, 2004, from http://www.edweek.com/sreports/tc03/

Weiser, M. (1995). Ubiquitous computing movies. Retrieved March 23, 2004, from http://www.ubiq.com/hypertext/weiser/UbiMovies.html

Xu, C. (2002). Teaching mathematics; Implementation of a learning information system in a middle school special education program. (Doctoral dissertation, University of Nebraska, Lincoln, NE.). Retrieved from the Digital Dissertations database, Publication No. AAT 3074113 unpublished.

21

Organization and Management of Language Arts Teaching: Classroom Environments, Grouping Practices, and Exemplary Instruction

Lesley Mandel Morrow
Rutgers, The State University of New Jersey

D. Ray Reutzel
Utah State University

Heather Casey
Rutgers, The State University of New Jersey

INTRODUCTION

A major concern of teachers is organization and management of their language arts programs. Teachers are able with appropriate professional development to integrate cutting-edge strategies into their literacy curriculum, but have a difficult time putting the different pieces of the program together in their school day. In this chapter we attempt to review research that could help professionals with management issues. We examine research areas specifically dealing with the organization and management of language arts instruction, and also focus on theory and research about exemplary practice in the language arts, since this line of work can inform and improve organization and management of language arts teaching. Our purpose is to raise awareness, provide implications for classroom practice, and suggest topics for future research. To accomplish this goal, this chapter is divided into topics that answer some of our questions concerning research on the organization and management of language arts programs:

1. How is student behavior and achievement affected by the physical design of the classroom environment, for example, how are space and materials used in language arts instruction?
2. How do grouping practices in language arts instruction affect student behavior and achievement?
3. How is student behavior affected by different social settings during language arts instruction?

4. What can we learn from research and theory about exemplary practice in language arts instruction to enhance organization and management of programs?
5. What does a case study of an exemplary language arts program look like that is based on the findings from a national investigation?

THE IMPACT OF THE PHYSICAL ENVIRONMENT IN LANGUAGE ARTS CLASSROOMS

Historically, theorists and philosophers such as Froebel and Pestalozzi have emphasized the importance of the physical environment in supporting young children's learning. Montessori (1965) advocated a carefully prepared classroom environment to promote independent learning and recommended that each kind of material in the environment have a specific learning objective. The nature and quality of the literacy environment plays a central role in literacy learning and the acquisition of literacy behaviors and attitudes. Chall, Jacobs, and Baldwin (1990) observed, "No one will debate the idea that a rich literacy environment is helpful for achievement in literacy" (p. 162).

Barker (1968, 1978) is well known for his pioneering work in the field of ecological psychology. One major tenet of ecological psychology states that environment is linked to human behavior in lawful and predictable ways—meaning that what happens in an environment can be explained using theoretically derived principles grounded in the collection and analysis of empirical data. For several decades, Barker studied the connection between environment and human behavior by focusing attention on a unit of study known as the "behavior setting." A behavior setting was essentially defined as a place or location where people come together to engage in predominantly predictable behaviors. As a consequence of this definition, Barker (1978) examined the significance of environment in a variety of behavioral settings such as offices, shops, classrooms, stadiums, museums, grocery stores, etc. and found that each of these environments elicited stable, predictable sets of human behaviors.

Barker's (1968) study of human behaviors yielded three generalizations that have influenced the study of human behavior and ecology: (1) human behavior changes from setting to setting to meet the requirements of each setting, (2) the behavior of people in each setting is more similar than different, and (3) each person's behavior tends to be consistent over time in the same or similar setting.

A study about literacy-rich environments and student literacy behavior (Neuman & Roskos, 1997) substantiates the findings by Barker concerning the effects of the literacy environment and human behavior. In this investigation, the researchers describe in vivid detail the necessary and critical connection between classroom literacy environments and human interactions related to literacy acquisition in the classroom. They assert that classroom environments, which are rich in oral language, reading, and writing experiences, provide opportunities for young children to become involved in literacy-related events. It is not only the environment, but also the human interactions in classrooms that determine in what way, how long, or how often children engage in using literacy-related tools in classrooms for a variety of purposes (Neuman & Roskos, 1992). From a Vygotskian (Vygotsky, 1978) perspective, children use available literacy tools including furnishings, books, paper, and writing tools in everyday problem-solving situations while interacting with peers, teachers, or other available cognitive mentors. As children interact socially with a literacy-rich environment and with significant others, they begin to internalize the literacy processes and practices they observe, and it becomes a part of their behavior. Researchers have found that "children's learning about literacy is integrally tied with practical action, resulting from their need to control, manipulate, and function in their environment" (Neuman & Roskos, 1997, p. 10). Consequently, the context of the language arts classroom is viewed as inseparable from the child's activity and their interactions with others in the classroom environment. These researchers conclude (Neuman and Roskos, 1997) that classroom learning contexts should support literacy learning by providing opportunities for two kinds of literacy learning: (1) situated learning in authentic contexts with real problems to solve using literacy tools, and (2) structured contexts for teaching children factual and conceptual knowledge about literacy.

Similar to many other behavioral settings, early childhood and elementary language arts classroom environments have been shown to elicit stable, predictable human behaviors (Day & Libertini, 1992; Neuman & Roskos, 1992, 1997). Stable and predictable human behaviors within language arts classroom settings are composed of three interlocking elements (Cambourne, 2001): (1) the presence and organization of inanimate physical objects, (2) ongoing routines, and (3) behaviors and settings in which teachers and students interact.

THE PRESENCE AND ORGANIZATION OF INANIMATE LITERACY-RELATED PHYSICAL OBJECTS IN LANGUAGE ARTS CLASSROOMS

It is almost accepted as axiomatic that physical environments have a substantial effect on children's learning and development (Bronfenbrenner, 1978; Garling & Evans, 1991; Kennedy, 1991; Long, Peters, & Garduque, 1985; Nash, 1981). Holmes and Cunningham (1995) found that very young preschool children, ages 3–4, evidenced a keen awareness of their classroom environments. These researchers found that children could, by looking at classroom photographs, identify appropriate activities for spaces in the classroom as well as draw their classrooms representing these activity spaces. In another study, Kershner and Pointon (2000) asked 70 five- and six-year-old children questions using the Individualized Classroom Environmental Questionnaire, to express their views about their classroom environments as places for working and learning. The children expressed strong views about grouping schemes, seating arrangements, wall displays, general tidiness, noise levels, and choices to work alone or in collaboration with others, to name only a few.

Research over the last two decades has provided plentiful and pertinent information about the design and implementation of print-rich classroom environments. Despite the widespread acceptance and awareness among teachers and children and the abundance of research information available, the findings of current research indicate that implementation of "print rich classroom environments" is lagging well behind what is known (Taylor, Blum, & Logsdon, 1986; Neuman & Celano, 1997, 2001). Teacher educators, teachers, and school administrators need to understand at a deeper intellectual level how to assess the design of classroom literacy environments, which strongly supports instruction, if they are to further their understanding of what a "print rich" classroom environment includes.

A study by Wolfersberger, Reutzel, Sudweeks, and Fawson (2004) systematically reviewed 223 articles, chapters, books, etc., examining the characteristics of "print rich" classrooms to develop an instrument for assessing the print-richness of early childhood and elementary language arts classrooms. They developed a model from the findings of this literature review for implementing print-rich language arts classroom environments shown in Fig. 21.1.

This model depicts the process of implementing a print-rich classroom environment beginning with "provisioning" the classroom environment with literacy tools. Once provisioned, the model speaks to an interactive relationship between positioning or arranging the literacy tools around the classroom space for interactive use by children and teachers in the environment.

Weinstein (1981) was one of the first researchers to report a synthesis of research on the physical environment of schools and classrooms, with attention to how and if the elements within

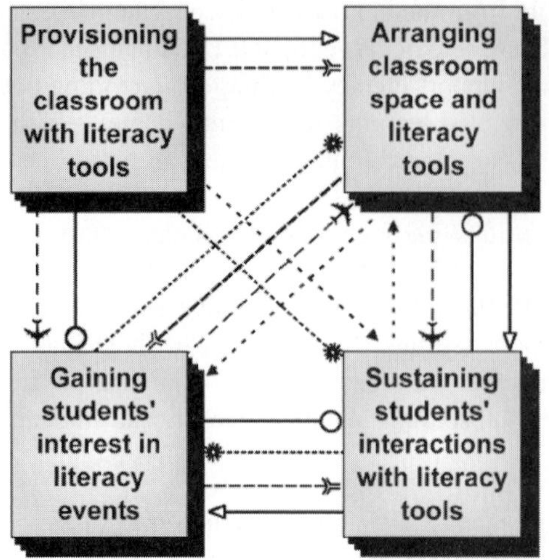

*** Each combination of symbols (_, *, etc.), and line types (continuous, dotted, etc.), represents a hypothetical decision to be made in creating and maintaining a print-rich classroom environment.**

FIGURE 21.1. Interactive relationship among the four dimensions of print-rich classroom literacy environments.*

the physical environment influenced children's opportunities to engage in learning. Recent research has provided significant insights into how the language arts classroom environment influences children's opportunities to actively engage in literacy learning.

THE EFFECTS OF PROVIDING LITERACY-RELATED TOOLS IN LANGUAGE ARTS CLASSROOMS

Many past surveys have shown a paucity of access to literacy-related objects in classrooms, including access to books (Fractor, Woodruff, Martinez, & Teale, 1993; McGill-Franzen, Allington, Yokoi, & Brooks, 1999; Morrow, 1990; Neuman, 1999). In fact, Fractor et al. (1993) found that only 4% of classroom libraries were well stocked with books and other print materials and that most classroom libraries, 89%, were characterized as "basic." Several other studies have examined the influence of literacy-related objects in classrooms and play centers on children's literacy learning and literacy interactions (Morrow, 1990; Vukelich, 1989).

Vukelich (1989) enriched a flower shop play center with receipts, cash register, loan application forms, sales forms, etc. Morrow (1990) created a veterinary center with context-appropriate nonliteracy-related props as well as literacy-related objects including books and medical record forms. These early investigations into the effects of infusing play settings with literacy-related objects yielded significant increases in children's literacy-focused play behaviors.

In a study with preschoolers, the researchers investigated how the presence and arrangement of ordinary, inanimate literacy objects in their classrooms influenced young children's literacy behaviors during free play. The researchers designed an experiment in which 91 preschoolers, aged 3–5 years, in two urban day care centers were randomly selected into a nonintervention (Site A) and intervention (Site B) preschool classroom setting. After collection of baseline data, Site B, the play centers at the intervention site were redesigned to accommodate the infusion of a variety of nonliteracy objects such as a couch, area rug, telephone, table, and buttons. In addition, Site B was enriched with a variety of literacy-related objects such as books, telephone book, cookbooks, recipe cards, coupons, store ads, play money, pens, pencils, markers, library stamps, signs, calendars, wall posters, stickers, file folders, ledger sheets, appointment books, labeled bins, magazines, maps, etc. No changes were made to the physical environment in Site A, the nonintervention setting (Neuman & Roskos, 1992).

Results indicated statistically significant differences among the frequencies of literacy demonstrations observed in three categories—handling, reading, and writing between the two sites, A and B. Similar findings were reported with respect to the duration and complexity of young children's literacy demonstrations in the intervention group as compared to the nonintervention group. In summary, the design and the amount of literacy objects infused into free play centers along with play center design changes significantly increased young children's handling, reading, and writing behaviors and the sustained and interconnected nature of their literacy demonstrations within their ongoing play routines. The results of this study, along with the results of earlier studies of literacy objects used as cultural tools in play settings, provide convincing evidence that changes to the physical environment in language arts classrooms influences or "presses" children into literacy learning behaviors and activities.

Recommendations for providing print-rich environments for language arts classrooms are many and varied. For example, Morrow (2005) and Katims and Pierce (1995) discuss access to an attractive library center as an imperative for establishing a literacy or print-rich classroom environment for young learners. Reutzel and Fawson (2002) have similarly recommended that a classroom library should be a major focal point in every classroom literacy program. Other researchers have corroborated the need for access to a classroom library filled with books when they found strong links between access to and use of a variety of print materials in classrooms and increased reading achievement (Fractor et al., 1993; Gump, 1989; Hoffman, Sailors, Duffy, & Beretvas, 2004; Neuman & Fischer, 1995; Roskos & Neuman, 2001). Another recommended component of a print-rich language arts classroom is the presence of a writing center because reading and writing reinforce one another concurrently, rather than sequentially (Katims & Pierce, 1995, Morrow, 2005) Meskill & Swan 1998 found that second-grade children, when given access to multimedia software, Kids Space, and other computer-based technology, were influenced to write and reflect more upon their compositions and creative writing.

Many suggestions are available for creating print-rich environments. Smith, Dickinson, Sangeorge, and Anastasopoulos (2002) saw the need to develop a valid and reliable instrument to help create and assess early literacy environments. They developed the Early Language and Literacy Classroom Observation (ELLCO) form to document the role of classroom environmental factors for two federally funded intervention studies. The ELLCO is composed of three separate components: (1) a classroom literacy environment checklist, (2) a classroom literacy instruction observation rating scale, and (3) a structured teacher interview. This instrument has been shown to be reliable (ELLCO Technical Report, 2002) for use in preschool classroom environments.

Wolfersberger et al. (2004) developed the Classroom Literacy Environmental Profile (CLEP), which is a tool for examining the "print richness" of early childhood and elementary classrooms. The researchers identified, defined, and organized into categories through a systematic and extensive review of the literature, classroom observations, and teacher focus-group characteristics of print-rich classroom environments. Interpreted data were used to write and review the initial items of the instrument. Using generalizability analyses, classrooms and items on the CLEP evidenced large variance components indicating that the degree of implementation of print-rich classroom environments was reliably discriminated using the CLEP instrument.

When using the CLEP instrument to examine early childhood and elementary language arts classrooms for "print-richness," examiners rated, using a seven-point Likert-type rating scale containing descriptors under points 1, 3, 5, and 7, the: (a) quantity, utility, and appropriateness of literacy related-objects or tools; (b) the quantity of genres, levels, format, and content of text materials; (c) the classroom organization print and student literacy product displays, and reference materials available; (d) the forms of written communication; and (e) the writing utensils, writing surfaces, publishing supplies, and technology available. To examine the organization of "print rich" language arts classrooms, users of the CLEP instrument assess: storage organization; classroom space allocations by size, location, boundaries, and types; the presence of a classroom library; grouping and accessibility of reading and writing tools; invitations and encouragements to participate in literacy events; authentic literacy events and settings; interactions with literacy tools; a variety of literacy products produced; and sharing of literacy products. Wolfersberger et al. (2004) assert that the CLEP is a valid and reliable tool for evaluating the print-richness of early childhood and elementary classrooms to enrich, refine, research, and redesign classrooms to foster engaged literacy learning for all children. In addition, the CLEP may also serve as a reliable guide for educators to apply "a more calculated approach to the design of literacy enrichments in early childhood and elementary classroom environments" as recommended by Neuman and Roskos (1992, p. 221).

THE EFFECTS OF ARRANGING THE PHYSICAL SPACE TO CREATE LITERACY-RICH LANGUAGE ARTS CLASSROOMS

Descriptive studies conducted on the effects of literacy-related settings in early childhood and elementary classrooms were conducted by Morrow (1982) when she observed the physical characteristics of library corners in 133 preschool through second-grade classrooms in a variety of schools in New Jersey. She found that most of these classrooms either had poorly designed or nonexistent library corners or nooks. Later in the same year, Morrow and Weinstein (1982) found a strong relationship between the amount of books and the physical design of the library nooks in kindergarten classrooms and kindergarteners' frequent interactions with literature during free play.

In 1986, Taylor, Blum, and Logsdon conducted a study in which 13 kindergarten teachers were shown how to implement print-rich classroom environments. The researchers then examined the effects of the teacher training on the implementation of print-rich classroom environments in the 13 kindergarten classrooms. High-implementation classrooms showed substantial student interaction with literacy tools and materials as well as substantial amounts of student-generated literacy products. Quantitative measures of reading achievement indicated that children in high-implementation or print-rich classrooms outperformed children in low-implementation classrooms.

Loughlin and Martin (1987) described the characteristics of 22 print-rich first- and second-grade classrooms by using the Survey of Displayed Literacy Stimuli that they had developed for the purposes of the study. These researchers described print-rich classrooms as well organized into clearly defined areas for children's use of print materials and other literacy tools. Loughlin and Martin (1987) also described teachers who encouraged children throughout the day to interact with literacy tools and materials as well as honoring children's products by giving them prominent display space within the classroom environment.

Excellent language arts environments allocate space for storage and use of a variety of instructional materials. Materials are arranged so as to be easily accessible with items labeled and everything in its place. These classrooms contain substantial collections of trade books, textbooks, workbooks, leveled books, and technology. It is recommended that there be seven titles per child as a minimum for a total of 150 to 200 individual trade book titles in a typical classroom of between 20 and 30 students (Morray, 2005).

In observational studies concerning types of books in classrooms for language arts instruction, it was found that language arts and reading textbooks were used in many of the classrooms observed. These materials were used in over 85% of K–6 schools in the U.S. (Baumann,

Hoffman, Duffy-Hester, & Ro, 2000). Contemporary language arts and reading textbooks include a variety of children's literature and information selections and encourage the integration of the language arts: reading, writing, listening, and speaking. Leveled books, rated for difficulty by using a particular leveling scheme, were used for guided reading instruction (Fawson & Reutzel, 2000).

Young children evidence an awareness of how their classroom environment is organized and how their work is treated within the classroom. When young children were asked to reflect upon whether the classroom environment had an effect on their learning, they indicated not only an awareness of the classroom environment, but also expressed to researchers that the environment shaped their own perceptions, motivations, and responses to learning tasks (Holmes & Cunningham, 1995; Kershner & Pointon, 2000). When classroom environments are supportive of what children are trying to do, they can more easily demonstrate what they can do (Bjorklund, Muir-Broaddus, & Schneider, 1990; Neuman & Roskos, 1997).

Hastings and Schwieso (1995) conducted a study in Great Britain investigating the effects of seating arrangements on task engagement in primary grade classrooms. Previous research had shown an increase in on-task behaviors, as well as an increase in the quantity and quality of work completed when seating arrangements matched the learning tasks to be performed, for example, rows for individually completed learning tasks and collaborative seating arrangements for small- or whole-group learning tasks (Bennett & Blundell, 1983; Whelldell & Lam, 1987; Yeomans, 1989). Results of the first study indicated that 76% of children preferred being seated in groups rather than rows. Graphic displays of the children's on-task behaviors in different seating arrangements were somewhat telling. Although children preferred grouped seating arrangements, measures of on-task behaviors for completing individual learning tasks increased when the seating arrangement was changed to rows from groups. This was particularly true with the lowest quartile cohort of children in both classes. Hastings and Schwieso (1995) recommended that group seating arrangements be used when interaction, discussion, and collaboration are needed to complete a task or project. But when a learning task requires individual completion or work, seating in rows leads to more on-task time among young children. They concluded by stating that teachers should, "consider the design of physical environments in the context of pedagogical purposes" (p. 290).

Designing classroom space to support effective language arts instruction involves: (a) the structure of space in the classroom, (b) selection of materials and furnishings to place into the environment, and (c) the literacy activities to be carried out (Wolfersberger et al., 2004). Although some classroom teachers design the space in their rooms with the intent to support literacy learning, they do not typically use research findings to inform their decisions (Neuman & Fischer, 1995).

Research has shown consistently that when language arts classrooms are partitioned into smaller spaces such as learning centers, project or activity areas, or small group discussion areas, these bounded and partitioned arrangements of classroom space into smaller physical spaces facilitate verbal interaction among peers and enhance cooperative and associative learning (Loughlin & Martin, 1987; Morrow, 1990; Rivlin & Weinstein, 1984). After reviewing ecological studies from play and cognitive performance research, Neuman and Roskos (1997) successfully validated several environmental design factors that provide opportunities for literacy learning in a variety of activity settings such as centers, play areas, etc. The factors of greatest importance included: (a) organization of settings, (b) familiarity of objects and procedures, (c) meaningfulness of activities or tasks, and (d) social interactions or resources. These four principles have broad application for the organization of learning environments in language arts classrooms.

Cambourne (2001, 2002) suggests that when organizing classroom settings, teachers can decide which literacy tools, props, objects, or paraphernalia will be purchased and made available for teaching and learning to read and write. But perhaps more importantly, teachers can decide when and how these objects will be used, by whom, and for how long, and even how these objects will be accessed and stored. They also can decide how print will be created, how much print will be displayed (if any) within the classroom, and how furniture is arranged, etc.

Young children demonstrate more advanced thinking when highly typical, familiar literacy objects are available for use in language arts classrooms and in literacy learning activity or independent center areas. Children also demonstrate their competence while engaged in literacy learning tasks when the procedures or operations within a classroom or learning area are well known to them (Neuman & Roskos, 1997). Cambourne (2001, 2002) elaborates this principle by asserting that teachers create and maintain meaningful literacy learning settings "through the language they use, the actions they demonstrate, and the expectations they communicate" (p. 359).

The potential of a print-rich language arts classroom environment is only fully realized when the learning activities and tasks occurring within the environment have meaning for the participants in that environment (Neuman & Roskos, 1997). This suggests that children should experience authentic literacy learning areas within the classroom that reflect what they have experienced in their everyday ecological contexts outside the classroom, as well as having access to familiar literacy tools for enacting literacy behaviors within these same contexts. Lave (1988) maintains that children need to be presented *authentic dilemmas* that offer them opportunities to use literacy tools and objects to create problem-solving situations and experiment with a variety of solutions. Examples of such settings include a post office, a restaurant, a grocery store, or a doctor's office (Morrow, 2005). Children observe how other people use literacy tools and engage in real-life literacy routines in their everyday lives. One of the best resources for supporting literacy learning in print-rich language arts classrooms is the demonstrations and interactions of other people.

REFLECTIONS ON THE RESEARCH OF LITERACY ENVIRONMENTS AND LANGUAGE ARTS INSTRUCTION

There is a significant amount of research that deals with the materials we need in language arts classrooms how to design the space, and the effects of those materials on students' literacy behavior. Children are sensitive to and affected by the physical environment of the early childhood and elementary language arts classroom. The quantity, quality, arrangement, organization, utility, accessibility of literacy tools, and materials in classrooms play a pivotal role in providing opportunities for children to engage in literacy learning. Literacy activities and tools placed into and arranged in early childhood and elementary language arts classrooms need to be purposefully organized, familiar, meaningful, and encourage social interactions (Neuman & Roskos, 1997). However, most research concerning rich print environments is evidenced-based and descriptive in design. It is important research but we need scientifically based studies to add to our knowledge. Most of the investigations talk about student behaviors that deal with social interaction, how materials are used, and increased use of the materials. Research needs to be done that evaluates student achievement as a result of physical environmental factors in language arts instruction. The research about literacy-rich environments has taken place predominantly in preschool and the primary grades and has had a positive effect on shaping these classroom physical environments. We need to carry out investigations in elementary grades to heighten awareness and determine effects of the physical environment for students at these grade levels.

THE EFFECTS OF WHOLE-CLASS AND SMALL-GROUP SETTINGS ON TEACHER AND STUDENT BEHAVIORS IN LANGUAGE ARTS PROGRAMS

Our research thus far has illustrated that teacher and student behaviors are effected by the design of classroom literacy environments. The environments discussed were predicated upon thoughtful planning. Effective use of space in exemplary language arts classroom environments was neither accidental nor incidental. Teachers defined spaces to enhance or promote a particular type of student behavior or activity. We now discuss research about the organization and management of classroom structural plans in language arts classrooms and the results of these structural plans in whole-class instruction and small-group instruction.

Whole-Class Instruction

Our research revealed that teachers allocated space for whole-class instruction for language arts and other content areas as well. This space was generally located near a large display surface such as a white board or projection screen and well away from designated small-group instructional areas intended for quiet instructional activities. In early childhood rooms there were rugs used for seating an entire class of children. In elementary classrooms, desks or tables were arranged in close proximity and faced the large display surface. Whole-class instructional space was allocated to support explicit instruction of phonics, comprehension, vocabulary, writing, and fluency. Teachers modeled strategies and used a variety of activities to teach the whole class, such as choral readings, echo reading, repeated readings, shared reading, readers theater, reading aloud, interactive writing, language-experience charts, etc. In whole-group instruction teachers used big books, posters, overhead transparencies, power point presentations, etc. The type of activities just described lent themselves to whole-group settings. (Bansberg, 2003; Pressley, Allington, Wharton-McDonald, Collins-Block, & Morrow, 2001; Reutzel & Cooter, 1991; Romeo, 1999).

Small-Group Instruction

When teachers created space and time for small-group learning, it was designed for a variety of reasons. (Bansberg, 2003; Cambourne, 2001, 2002; Moore, 1986; Olds, 1987; Reutzel & Cooter, 1991; Taylor & Pearson, 2002; Taylor, Pearson & Clark, 2000; Weinstein, 1977, 1981). One type of small-group work was to engage children productively and independent of the teacher. Children worked alone or in collaboration with others. Teachers created areas they called "centers" for this type of collaborative work. The centers were used predominantly during guided reading instruction when the teacher was working with a small reading group for specific skill development. These centers engaged students productively in practicing work that had been introduced to them while the teacher worked with the small guided reading groups. Examples of well-known centers found in K–6 classrooms included: (a) working with words, (b) the library corner, (c) a writing center, and (d) a literacy-enriched play area.

A working with words center included a computer for students to work in pairs. This center was stocked with magnetic letters, individual dry erase boards, markers, erasers, letter sorts, and letter trays with letters for making words. Also present were word and letter games such as letter and word BINGO and Lotto. The working with words center also had a word wall to display high-frequency sight words, student names, theme words, and phonograms.

Teachers had well stocked and well organized library corners where there was easy access to books and other print and reference materials (Katims & Pierce, 1995; Morrow & Weinstein,

1982, 1986; Neuman, 1999; Neuman & Celano, 2001; Reutzel & Fawson, 2002). Teachers taught strategies to support book selection such as selecting from a limited number of books, and making the books all theme-related or genre-related. All exemplary teachers included a time in the library corner for students to read narrative and informational books and other print materials of their own choosing.

A classroom writing center in classrooms had a space for collaborative writing for children to interact with teachers and peers about their projects. A conference area was allotted for conducting peer-student or teacher-student conferences about developing writing projects. The editing area was for students to obtain help from an editor, peer, adult-volunteer, or teacher. In the writing center students composed writing products including books, essays, editorials, poems, jokes, riddles, research reports, autobiographies, etc.

Studies document that literacy-enriched play centers for small groups found preschool children engaged in reading and writing activities (Dickinson & Tabors, 2001; Neuman and Roskos, 1992, 1993, 1997; Rogg, 2001; Roskos & Neuman, 2001; Vukelich, 1994). Play, according to Vygotsky (1978), involves the child in behaviors that are more sophisticated than expected and seem as if he/she were older. When enriching play centers with a variety of situation-specific literacy materials, researchers have documented an increase in children's use of literacy as a part of their imaginative play. Observations of young children at play have shown that when the presence of literacy tools appropriate to the social situation are available in the play center, children will engage in attempted and conventional reading and writing acts often in collaboration with other children (Morrow, 1990; Neuman & Roskos, 1997). In exemplary language arts classrooms, play centers in K–1 classrooms included: (a) offices—post offices, doctor's offices, newspaper offices, etc.; (b) businesses—labs, restaurants, bakeries, carpentry, grocery stores, auto mechanics and repair; (c) travel services—airports, train stations; (d) home situations—kitchens, workshop, laundry room; and (e) dramatic interpretations—plays, readers theater, puppetry, creative movement, etc.

Another type of small-group work provided a Guided Reading area that had seating and a table to accommodate up to seven students and the teacher (Fountas & Pinnell, 1996). The Guided Reading area was designed so that the teacher could assess and assist a small group of children during instruction. Materials for providing guided instruction often included: (a) several sets of leveled books or basal stories, (b) white dry erase boards, (c) magnetic letters, and (d) markers and erasers. Teachers often had easels and a pocket chart for working with story structure, sentences, phrases, and words (Reutzel & Cooter, 2004). Students in guided reading were grouped by ability. Teaching and materials were geared to their needs.

Grouping Students for Instruction Based on Ability and Achievement

Conventional wisdom suggests that grouping students to meet individual needs is important. Yet research results vary widely for this type of organizational practice. Most studies have found that children who are high achievers do better in ability groups for reading than if they were not grouped at all. The data was not as clear in groups of middle-and low-achieving students. Grouping did not seem to help or hurt middle achievers; however, the data about low achievers was not consistent. Some studies found that low-achieving children did not do better in small-ability groups for reading instruction, other studies found that they did (Eder, 1981; Esposito, 1973; Hiebert, 1983; Kulik & Kulik, 1982; Lou, Abrami, & Spence, 1996).

Observations of what happens in small-ability groups during reading instruction help to explain the findings about grouping and achievement. High-ability groups read more text than children in the low-ability groups. They also read continuous, uninterrupted text. Children in high-ability groups were asked analytical questions and received lots of praise. The attitude in the high-ability groups was positive with high expectations for student achievement. On the other hand, in low-ability groups, students spent less time reading, read segmented text rather than whole texts, and teachers had low expectations for student success. Children recognized when they were in the low-ability groups and had negative feelings about it (Allington, 1984; Eder, 1981; Grant & Rothenberg, 1986).

Students who participated in ability groups during language arts instruction had both positive and negative comments about this type of instruction. On the positive side, students felt that they read more in small-group instruction, they had more positive interactions with the teacher, had more positive interaction with each other, and they felt that independent work during small-group instruction was productive (Hiebert, 1983; Weinstein, 1977). The things students didn't like about ability and group included, once a group is formed you can never move out of it. If you are in a low-group, you feel really dumb. There are a disproportionate number of nonwhite children in low-ability groups. The preponderance of negative comments about grouping came from children in the low-ability groups (Allington, 1984; Eder, 1981; Grant & Rothenberg, 1986).

When questioned about grouping for instruction, teachers said they felt they could attend to more individual differences in small-group instruction and that students had more positive attitudes about themselves and what they were learning (Kulik & Kulik, 1982). Teachers worried about organizing their classrooms so they could meet children in small groups. It was found that professional development had a positive effect on helping teachers to organize and manage grouping in their classrooms and consequently they felt better about using the practice (Lou, Abrami, & Spence, 1996). Teachers were grouped for ability to meet individual needs but also had heterogeneous groups in their rooms for collaborative projects. Homogeneous groups were flexible, since they changed when students needed to change. The work in all groups, no matter what the level of ability, included high expectations for student achievement. Children in different groups learned the same skills but instruction was differentiated (Allington, Johnston, & Day, 2002; Cambourne, 2001, 2002; Cantrell, 1999a, 1999b; Katims & Pierce, 1995; Morrow, 2002, 2005). The expert management of small-group instruction is one of the characteristics of exemplary language arts classrooms and considered a difficult task for many teachers.

THE EFFECTS OF DIFFERENT ENVIRONMENTAL SETTINGS ON SOCIAL BEHAVIOR OF STUDENTS AND TEACHERS

Social interactions between teachers and students and students and students in classrooms are one of the most highly variable aspects of classroom environments as behavior settings (Cambourne, 2002). Although previous ecological research has shown that environmental settings elicit stable behavioral responses, Barker's (1968) ecological critique of human behavior also provided for situations in which changes in the environment induced human behavior to likewise adapt to new demands of a setting.

Day & Libertini (1992) investigated the impact of changes in classroom environments that altered the social interactions experienced by teachers and children. These researchers examined three interaction and grouping patterns used during language arts and mathematics lessons in two primary grade classrooms: (1) teacher-directed, large-group instruction, (2) teacher- and child-directed, large- and small-group instruction, and (3) child-directed only. Three children (two boys, one girl) were selected from a group of five to seven year olds; and three others (one boy, two girls) from a group of seven to nine year olds in each of two classrooms observed in this study. Results indicated that these six children readily shifted their learning behaviors to adapt to the demands of each of the varied social conditions experienced during instruction. Changes in the classroom environments that teachers provide for children, including the grouping arrangements and social interactions encouraged or discouraged during instruction, evoked differing responses from the children. For example, when the children were asked to complete individual tasks, collaborative seating arrangements actually decreased attention and the quality of eventual task completion. On the other hand, when task completion was structured to require collaboration, isolated seating arrangements interfered with the time needed to complete a task and the eventual quality of the task completed. These researchers recommended that teachers carefully consider the proportion of time allocated for whole-group, small-group, teacher-directed, and child-directed instruction inasmuch as each of these differing combinations of social arrangements during instruction both support and suppress social interactions, interfere with or augment cognitive processes, and increase or decrease the quality and quantity of learning outcomes.

Whole-group, teacher-directed instruction, although efficient for many events or circumstances, may be counterproductive in terms of what can be learned and how long it may be retained. On the other hand, totally child-directed settings where children are "messing about may not always be either a sufficient indicator of productive engagement or an adequate criterion for selecting school activities" (Day & Libertini, 1992, p. 111).

Neuman & Fischer (1995) explored task and participation structures in kindergartens where teachers used a holistic literacy teaching philosophy. Twenty kindergarten classrooms, from 10 schools in a large urban school district, were observed and videotaped for two full days of holistic literacy instruction, totaling 24 hours of observed instruction. Literacy tasks were analyzed on five dimensions: (a) activity format, (b) duration, (c) complexity, (d) organization, and (e) participation structures. With reference to the findings related to participation structures, these researchers, similar to Day and Libertini (1992), concluded that task and talk structures need to be varied to accommodate the variety of literacy behaviors and concepts to be learned in early childhood and elementary classrooms. They stated, "Teachers can include tasks that provide opportunities for collaborative interaction, combined with direct instruction, to promote language and literacy. This suggests a better balance between meaning-based and skill-based instruction. Students need to know both the functions and the forms of literacy" (p. 336).

Cambourne (2002) described the complexity of classroom behavior settings by discussing "episodes" in which teachers and children interacted with literacy paraphernalia and programs to create opportunities to learn. He envisioned classroom literacy interactions as composed of two overlapping layers. The first layer is the least complex depicting classrooms as behavior settings composed of humans behaving, inanimate physical objects, and ongoing routines for operating or behaving that are stable and dynamic. The second layer in Cambourne's (2002) scheme represents teachers' attempts to orchestrate behavioral events such as mini-lessons, strategies, activities, etc. in connection with the first layer. Cambourne contends that such deliberate attempts by teachers to create learning opportunities "float on the ethos created by the mix of the three generic components [humans behaving, inanimate physical objects, and ongoing routines for operating or behaving] of the setting, and they are influenced by this ethos" (p. 360). As such, Cambourne paints a picture of the elementary language arts classroom as animated by the intentions of the teachers as they interact with children using the inanimate literacy tools available in the environment.

Hoffman et al. (2004) developed a valid and reliable measure that captures the complexity of the interactions of teachers and children in elementary language arts classroom print environments. In developing their system of measurement, Hoffman et al. drew upon a social practice perspective of literacy development (Barton, Hamilton & Ivanic, 2000) in which the classroom environment involves more than counting and describing inanimate objects. Rather, they envisioned the language arts classroom print environment to be a dynamic social context conditioning and conditioned by those who work within it. The result was the development of the TEX-IN3 Observation System that contains three basic components: (1) a text inventory, (2) a text "in-use" observation, and (3) a series of teacher- and student-text interviews. Hoffman et al. found that the TEX-IN3 is a useful instrument for capturing the complexity of social interactions involving texts in classroom settings by observing 30 minutes of instruction in classrooms in which children are engaged with different types of texts. At the conclusion of the 30 minutes, a classroom snapshot of text engagement is captured. This is followed by an "observational sweep" that focuses on three selected children who are reading above, on, and below grade level. The interactions between these three sampled children, the texts, and the teacher are systematically recorded. At the conclusion of the observational sweep another classroom snapshot of class is taken. This research demonstrates that scores on the three TEX-IN3 subscales strongly predicted students' reading comprehension scores, demonstrating a clear connection between social interactions in print-rich classroom environments and students' literacy achievement.

REFLECTIONS ON GROUPING PRACTICES AND RESULTING STUDENT AND TEACHER BEHAVIORS

Discussion about the value of grouping for instruction in relation to ability, achievement, social, and emotional outcomes has been a persistent issue over time. There are pros and cons to support grouping with many unsolved answers. We can only call for more research in this area—both quantitative and qualitative—to determine how to effectively work with children in small groups to meet their individual needs to improve achievement and at the same time not damage their self-esteem.

The research concerning social behaviors as a result of classroom arrangements, such as small, large, or one-to-one groupings, has demonstrated that when teachers make choices about how to structure and support student social interaction in the classroom, it is clearly linked to later reading performance (Hoffman et al., 2004). Some of the choices referred to are student versus teacher control and choice during instruction, an emphasis upon collaboration or isolation, a focus on meaning construction or skill acquisition, the involvement of teachers and students with each other during teaching and learning activities, and access to literacy tools and materials.

RESEARCH AND THEORY ON EFFECTIVE AND EXEMPLARY TEACHING

Research on effective and exemplary teaching has implications for informing educators about organizing and managing language arts programs. Therefore, we reviewed some of the research and theory in this area that seemed pertinent. The earlier research on effective teaching was not language arts specific. These investigations in the 60s and 70s focused on the teacher as a technician delivering a specific designated program of instruction. In this research effective teaching was based almost primarily on a particular method of teaching. Researchers looked at how the teacher and specific teaching processes affected the product, which was student achievement (Berman & McLaughlin, 1978; Brophy, 1973; Dunkin & Biddle, 1974; Rosenshine & Furst, 1973). The "first grade studies" and other similar research investigated the "methods" or "approaches"—such as the use of basals, phonics, and the language experience approach to find those that were most effective in teaching first-graders to become successful readers. No single approach proved better than the others (Anderson, Evertson, & Brophy, 1979; Bond & Dykstra, 1964/1997; Wilder, 1977). However, this research laid the foundation for the more comprehensive research on exemplary practice, which better takes into account organization and management issues related to teaching.

Research on Exemplary Literacy Teachers

Researchers who began to study exemplary practice did it from a broader perspective than studying only about effective practice. Since there didn't seem to be one method that was most effective for teaching reading, researchers wanted to know not only about good methods, but what was happening in the total classroom that effected achievement. They wanted to know about the interactions between children and teachers, scheduling routines, design of environments, and how the classroom as a community effected growth (Coker, 1985; Duffy & Hoffman, 1999; Genishi, Ryan, Ochsner, & Yarnall, 2001; Haigh & Katterns, 1984; Roehler & Duffy, 1984; Shulman, 1986). Investigators attempted to tap teachers' thought processes about their teaching. For example, teachers were often asked to talk about how they decided to plan their programs, select their materials, and schedule their daily routines (Clark & Peterson, 1986). In one large-scale study of effective teachers, students in grades K–12 were questioned as to the characteristics of their influential literacy teachers in an attempt to build a universal model of effective instruction (Ruddell, 1995; Ruddell & Kern, 1986; Ruddell & Harris, 1989). In this investigation teachers were nominated to participate in in-depth interviews and extensive classroom observations. The results of the study indicated that influential teachers (a) use highly motivating and effective teaching strategies, (b) build strong affective relationships with their students, (c) create a feeling of excitement about what they are teaching, (d) adjust instruction to meet the individual needs of their students, (e) create rich physical environments to support their teaching, and (f) have strong organization and management skills (Ruddell, 1995).

Building on the work of more general effective and exemplary teaching, investigators began to examine exemplary language arts instruction. The purpose was to describe what excellent teachers did when teaching reading and writing and how they made decisions about how and what they taught, what materials they used, how they used space and created structures for social interactions and grouping to meet individual achievement needs. The total classroom community experience rather than a specific practice was considered. This type of research is based on sociocultural theory, according to which student learning is dependent upon what a teacher knows, how students come to understand that knowledge, and the context in which the learning takes place (Vygotksy, 1978). In a setting based on sociocultural theory, school would be considered a collaborative community in which students are assisted by more capable adults or peers. According to sociocultural theory, the entire learning environment or the culture of the classroom needs to be considered when studying instruction since the act of teaching and the learning environment are inextricably linked. A sociocultural concept of learning considers multiple contexts, such as: (a) the relationship between the teacher and student, (b) the community of the classroom, (c) the larger community of the school, and (d) how all of these are organized and managed together and affect each other.

Identifying Exemplary Teachers to Study

A major concern when studying exemplary teachers is finding a reliable and valid way to first identify who is exemplary and then to describe what these exemplary teachers do in their classroom. There have been several ways that investigators have undertaken this task. Researchers have identified teachers as exemplary based on the following criteria:

- Selecting teachers with students who have excellent test scores in literacy achievement over a period of time

- Selecting teachers whose students' test scores are beyond what would be expected from children considered "at risk" from schools that beat the odds
- Selecting teachers based on administrator recommendations
- Selecting teachers recommended by their peers
- Selecting teachers recommended by parents
- Selecting teachers recommended by students

Researchers have used some, or all of the characteristics listed above, when selecting samples to study (Block, 2001; Morrow & Casey, 2003; Pressley, Rankin, & Yokoi, 1996; Taylor, Pearson, Clark, & Walpole, 1999; Taylor, Peterson, Pearson, & Rodriguez, 2002; Wharton-McDonald, Pressley, Rankin, & Mistretta, 1997).

Taylor et al. (2000) studied the literacy practices of exemplary teachers in schools that beat the odds. The students in these teachers' classrooms were considered at-risk, and from low-income families, yet who scored well in literacy achievement. Two teachers in grades K–3 in 14 schools across the U.S. participated in the study. Each teacher was observed five times from December to April for an hour of reading instruction. Teachers also completed a written survey, kept a weekly log of reading and writing activities in their classrooms, and were interviewed in May of the year of the study. These effective teachers focused on small-group instruction, provided time for independent reading, monitored student on-task behaviors, and provided strong home communication. The teachers also focused on explicit phonics instruction and the application of phonics while reading and writing, asked high-level comprehension questions, and were more likely to ask students to write their responses to reading.

In a study to determine exemplary practice, Metsala and Wharton-McDonald (1997) meticulously collected and described through surveys and interviews the most important literacy practices and routines among 89, K–3 regular education and 10 special education teachers identified by administrators as exemplary. These exemplary teachers were described by their peers and supervisors, as "masterful" classroom managers who managed time, materials, and student behavior with finesse. These effective teachers held high expectations for their students as well as having a real sense of purpose, direction, and objectives. Topping the list of classroom characteristics and instructional practices reported by these effective, primary-level teachers was, not surprisingly, a literate classroom environment. In addition these educators provided explicit instruction of literacy (reading and writing) skills, strategies, and concepts. They provided daily doses of contextualized and isolated skill and strategy instruction, access to varied reading materials, and varied ways of engaging in reading and writing. They adapted instruction to the ability levels or needs of their students, worked to motivate students to engage in reading and writing, as well as consistently monitoring student engagement and literacy progress through systematic accountability.

Morrow, Tracey, Woo, and Pressley (1999) intensively observed six exemplary teachers from three different school districts. Teachers selected to be observed for the study were nominated by school administrators, peers, parents, and students. The selection process also included checks of these six teachers' student achievement scores over the past five years to confirm the effects of their exemplary status on student achievement measures. Approximately 25 hours of observation were completed on each of the six teachers as well as conducting interviews with them. The first finding of these researchers was that the six exemplary teachers had "literacy-rich environments." Within these literacy-rich classrooms teachers orchestrated a variety of learning settings such as whole, small, one-on-one, teacher-directed, centers, and social interactions with adults and peers. A rich variety of print and print-producing materials were available for and used by children on a daily basis. Teachers provided varying types of instructional approaches such as spontaneous, authentic, explicit, direct, systematic, meaning-oriented, problem-solving, and open-ended. They engaged children on a daily basis in shared, guided, oral, silent, independent, collaborative, and performance reading and writing. They offered regular writing, word analysis, and comprehension instruction. And they made consistent efforts to connect reading and writing instruction to content taught through themes at other times of the day. Many of these same effective practices and instructional routines were reported and confirmed by Cantrell (1999a, 1999b) two years later in her study of the effects of literacy instruction on primary students' reading and writing achievement.

In summary, how time is distributed among and the focus of regular literacy activities and lessons exert measurable influences on young children's literacy growth and development. Effective teachers are masterful classroom managers and balance their instructional time, emphasis, and content among a variety of alternative literacy learning activities. And effective literacy learning activities are integrally linked to other parts of the day and curriculum; they have an explicit purpose with learning tasks clearly defined and are engaged across a wide variety of social settings.

A synthesis of investigations about exemplary literacy practice in the elementary grades found that exemplary literacy teachers shared the following characteristics. They (a) provide explicit literacy instruction, (b) engage students in constructive exchanges with the teacher, (c) create a supportive, encouraging, and friendly atmosphere, (d) weave reading and writing throughout the curriculum, (e) integrate content area themes into the teaching of reading and writing, (f) create a literacy-rich environment in their classrooms with a variety of literacy materials to support instruction, (g) teach to individual needs in small-group settings, (h) have excellent organization and management skills, and (i) develop strong connections with the student's home (e.g., Allington & Johnston, 2002; Block, 2001; Cantrell, 1999a, 1999b; Morrow, et al., 1999; Morrow & Casey, 2003; Pressley et al., 1996; Taylor et al., 1999; Taylor et al., 2002; Wharton et al., 1997). While many of the studies phrase their findings differently, the categories are remarkably similar.

Observing Exemplary Organization and Management Practices: A Case Study

Syntheses of exemplary language arts instruction found that teachers included the daily organization and management routines such as explicit instruction, constructive exchanges, a supportive classroom atmosphere, reading and writing integrated across the language arts and in content area themes, a variety of literacy materials to support instruction, and teaching to individual needs in small-group settings. The following is an observation recorded from research on exemplary practice of language arts instruction in a fourth grade that illustrates these characteristics (e.g., Allington & Johnston, 2002; Morrow et al., 1999; Morrow & Casey, 2003; Pressley et al., 1996; Wharton et al., 1997). Because departmentalization begins to occur in most fourth-grade classrooms, the language arts block is sometimes limited as far as having a large block of time. This day represents the many exemplary teachers observed in the investigations and describes how the teacher fits in the language arts instruction.

When the students enter the room in the morning, there is a "Do Now" message written on the chalkboard. On this particular morning the teacher has asked the students to use certain words in sentences in their journals. While students are responding, they are also carrying out morning housekeeping items described by several charts posted around the room. After about 15 minutes, most students have completed the "Do Now" and the class lines up for Music. They have their "special" during the first period of each day. When the class returns, they file into the room. The teacher discusses classroom matters such as projects due and handing in homework. She also reviews the sentences from the "Do Now."

Next on the agenda is a story read aloud. Before reading, the teacher leads a discussion about predictions for the story based on the cover illustration. As the story is read, the teacher stops occasionally to discuss issues prompted by the text. Discussion includes where the story takes place and connects the text to what they are learning in social studies. During the story, the questions asked provide a model for the questions children can ask themselves as they read independently. The teacher asks the children to seek clarification of story elements, use context clues to understand vocabulary, and guides them to make connections between the text and their own prior knowledge. She reads with animated expression, and uses different voices and accents to portray the characters in the story. She makes the reading an interactive experience with the modeling of effective comprehension strategies.

In social studies, the class is participating in a unit about the regions of the United States. The teacher connects social studies and literacy development. The teacher uses the popular picture book, *Brown bear, brown bear* (Martin & Carle, 1967) as the format for a project. The students are asked to create books using a state in the U.S. as the topic. The teacher shows a finished product to the class and explains what she did. She reads from her book, "Ohio, Ohio, what do you see? I see Columbus shining at me."

At the end of the social studies period, the work in progress is collected. The unfinished books are placed in a basket to await completion. The children collect the materials they need and proceed to their assigned math classes, which are grouped according to ability for mathematics.

On this day, with the children in her math group, the teacher reviews several geometrical concepts. The teacher reviews an array of shapes and their corresponding names to reinforce the development of a mathematical vocabulary. As the class proceeds, the teacher conveys meaning through multiple representations. She gives a thorough explanation and also presents the ideas with both physical and written models. The children work in all three modalities, and cooperatively with a partner. The same principles evident in the teacher's beliefs about literacy development are evident in her math instruction. She creates an engaging and challenging learning community in all content areas.

After math, the children return to their regular classrooms and proceed to lunch. The remainder of the day is then devoted to the language arts program. Upon reentering the room, the children begin the independent, self-selected reading activity. Children make themselves comfortable, some reading with partners, while others read alone. Reading materials include various genres.

After 15 minutes, the children put their books away. The teacher selects a student volunteer to write and administer the dictation, a weekly assessment for the language arts skills of spelling, capitalization, punctuation, and listening. Each sentence, often referring to subject matter from the social studies or science curriculum, is read aloud three times. When students finish writing, the sentences are put on the board for the class to review the correct format.

The teacher has Guided Reading Groups and Literature Circle Groups. The Literature Circle Groups move together with activities for independent work displayed in a pocket chart hanging on the bulletin board. There are five groups formed that are based on children's selection of the books they wish to read. The Literature Circle groups meet and have their activity assignments such as reading independently, discussion of the book that was read, journal writing related to the book, or a reporting activity that might include the use of art materials.

The teacher forms the guided reading groups according to ability levels and student needs. The teacher calls five students for a guided reading lesson. They sit together at a round table. An easel is set up in front of them with a "Point of View" chart posted on it. First, they discuss this literary element in another book they have all read before. Then, they direct their attention to the novel they are currently reading. The teacher selected this book for guided reading. The teacher models filling in the chart with one character then allows the group to work on its own.

After the reading groups have met, the teacher visits the Literature Circles' meetings. One group is sharing their journal responses to the book. Afterward, they address discussion questions provided by the teacher about the book being read.

After about 45 minutes, the teacher asks the class to clean up their reading materials. She then begins her writing workshop. The teacher begins with a whole-class mini-lesson on the characteristics of nonfiction news articles. The students have been routinely publishing this type of writing in a class newsletter. Together, they compile a chart entitled "Amazing Articles." After the topic has been thoroughly covered, the class is given the remaining time to work on their own newsletter articles. The teacher conferences with individuals to help with skill development.

To summarize this teacher organized her instruction so that the environment was filled with the necessary reading and writing materials to support her instruction. These materials were purposefully placed for accessibility when needed. The students engaged in whole-group, small-group and one-on-one settings. There was explicit instruction and time for periods of social interaction for learning. The teacher provided many strategies for students in reading and writing including reading aloud, shared reading, independent reading, collaborative reading, guided reading, performance of reading activities, partner/buddy reading, literature circles, and content area reading. The teacher organized the following writing activities: shared writing, journal writing, independent writing, reader response writing, collaborative writing, fiction and nonfiction, writing guided writing, performance of writing activities, content-area writing, and writing workshop.

REFLECTIONS ON EXEMPLARY PRACTICE AND THE ORGANIZATION AND MANAGEMENT OF LANGUAGE ARTS PROGRAMS

How well teachers organize and manage the language arts classroom is the bedrock underlying effective literacy instruction. Research has clearly documented that exemplary literacy teachers have strong organization and management systems in place. Exemplary language arts teachers spend time teaching students classroom routines and rules throughout the school year. Exemplary literacy teachers invite children to help them create classroom rules, which give them ownership in the management of the classroom. An early and sustained emphasis on teaching children the rules and routines minimizes classroom disruptions, and supports smooth transitions. Children have a clear understanding of what is expected of them. The atmosphere in these classrooms is calm, controlled, and encourages respect for others. Exemplary literacy teachers are aware of what is happening in their rooms at all times, give positive feedback often, and speak to students in a respectful manner. When problems occur, teachers have private conversations with students, rather then singling them out publicly. In classrooms that are managed well teachers help children to self-regulate their behavior through cooperative social dialogue.

Exemplary language arts classrooms are informed by sociocultural theory. According to this theory student learning is dependent upon what a teacher knows, how students come to understand that knowledge, and the context in which the learning takes place (Vygotksy, 1978). Classrooms that are well organized are collaborative communities with teachers guiding instruction and student participation. This context takes into consideration the relationship between the teacher and student, the community of the classroom, and the larger community of the school and how this is all organized and managed throughout every school day.

One of the most serious problems about the research dealing with exemplary practice is that we do not have reliable and valid methods for determining what is exemplary practice, and who are exemplary teachers. This needs to be a major effort in this area of research. As in the other topics discussed in this paper, the research in this area has been done predominantly in the primary grades. The research has been descriptive and at best evidenced-based. It is crucial to continue work on exemplary language arts teaching with older children, and with scientifically based designs.

CONCLUDING REMARKS

This review of literature studies how students are affected by the physical design of the classroom environments including how space and materials are used in language arts instruction. The chapter also investigates grouping practices in language arts instruction to meet individual needs, and finally, looks at what can be learned from exemplary practice in language arts teaching to enhance organization and management of programs.

Research on the effect of the classroom environment on student learning has consistently demonstrated an impact upon student behaviors, achievement, motivation, interaction patterns, social collaboration, and perceptions. Access to print materials provided in classrooms affects students' engagement in literacy-related behaviors. Research has shown, however, that many teachers do not use the results of research on designing classroom environments in their rooms. Because most of the research has been carried out in preschool and primary grades, there is a need to continue this line of research in elementary classrooms. It is also apparent that the research is mostly descriptive, that is, evidenced-based rather than scientifically based in design. The research discusses how to design print-rich environments and the resulting behaviors by children in those environments, with specific attention paid to student's increased use of literacy materials and engagement in literacy activities. We conclude that it is crucial to do investigations that assess literacy achievement as a result of the preparation of literacy-rich environments. This, of course, is the ultimate goal.

Research about small-group instruction based on student achievement has had inconsistent results. A meta-analysis of several studies on small group instruction found that it is the group's achievement level to which a child is assigned, such as high, middle or low, that will ultimately predict a student's success (Lou, et al., 1996). Possible reasons for these results and differing achievement gains in high, middle, and low instructional groups are that teachers teach and act differently when teaching children in high and low groups. They have high expectations for students in the high groups and low expectations for the students in low groups. Also, different strategies and materials are used in the different ability groups (Anderson, Wilkinson, & Mason, 1991). Grouping for instruction has been controversial. Most of the research in this area is quite dated and not necessarily specific to the language arts. Investigations about grouping for achievement specifically in the language arts need to be continued, taken into consideration what we have learned from the past. We need to study grouping with teachers who are able to act the same when teaching children in high and low groups, that is, they need to have high expectations for students in both the low and high groups and use similar strategies and materials for the different groups as well. This line of investigation will undoubtedly add new insight to the controversies that exist about ability grouping.

The studies about exemplary literacy teachers show how excellent professionals consciously design, plan, and allocate classroom space for whole-group, small-group, and individual teaching and learning activities. As we mentioned earlier, exemplary teachers provide explicit literacy instruction, engage students in constructive exchanges, and create a supportive, encouraging, and friendly atmosphere. They weave reading and writing throughout the curriculum, while integrating content area themes into the teaching of reading and writing. Exemplary teachers create a literacy-rich environment in their classrooms with a variety of literacy materials to support instruction, and teach to individual needs in small-group settings. They have excellent organization and management skills and are able to develop strong connections with the student's home. One of the problems with the research on exemplary teaching is how teachers are selected and labeled as expert. We need to continue to find more valid and reliable techniques for the selection process and subsequently carry out more scientifically and evidenced-based research about expert teaching.

This chapter illustrates the importance of including organization and management as a crucial part of planning language arts instruction. States and school districts spend a great deal of time planning and writing language arts standards and curriculum guides. The course work for the preparation of teachers concentrates on helping future teachers learn about strategies to teach word study skills, comprehension, and writing. They discuss assessment issues, motivating children to want to read and write, and family involvement. In college texts dealing with the teaching of reading instruction, sometimes a section of the book will be devoted to organization and management issues, but it is rarely a large portion. In the professional development of experienced teachers, the issues concerning organization and management of the language arts program are often overlooked entirely or given minimal attention. Organization and management has been viewed as a backdrop related to teaching, rather than as a part of the main agenda in literacy instruction. We know much about reading instruction, more than ever before. We need to refine what we already know and learn how to better deliver the instruction. We believe achievement would be enhanced if the issues related to organization and management were given the same attention and importance as other areas within language arts instruction when putting programs into practice in schools. This is the refinement we have been looking for.

ACKNOWLEDGMENTS

We would like to thank Lisa Fassi, Lisa Gergasko, Anna Turkenich, and Kristin Valvanis for the work they did abstracting articles and editing the paper. We also wish to thank Nancy Roser, The University of Texas, Austin, for her review of an early version of this chapter.

REFERENCES

Allington, R. L. (1984). Content coverage and contextual reading in reading groups. *Journal of Reading Behavior, 16,* 85–96.

Allington, R. L., & Johnston, P. H. (2002). *Reading to learn: Lessons from exemplary fourth-grade classrooms.* New York: Guilford Press.

Allington, R. L., Johnston, P. H., & Day, J. P. (2002). Exemplary fourth-grade teachers. *Language Arts, 79*(6), 462–466.

Anderson, L. M., Evertson, C. M., & Brophy, J. E. (1979). An experimental study of effective teaching in first-grade reading groups. *Elementary School Journal, 79* (4), 193–223.

Anderson, R. C., Wilkinson, I. A. G., & Mason, J. M. (1991). A microanalysis of the small group guided reading lessons: Effects of an emphasis on global story meaning. *Reading Research Quarterly, 26,* 417–439.

Bansberg, B. (2003). Applying the learner-centered principles to the special case of literacy. *Theory Into Practice, 42*(2), 142–150.

Barker, R. G. (1968). *Ecological psychology.* Stanford, CA: Stanford University Press.

Barker, R. G. (1978). Stream of individual behavior. In R. Barker (Ed.), *Habitats, environments, and human behavior* (pp. 3–16). San Francisco: Jossey-Bass.

Barton, D., Hamilton, M., & Ivanic, R. (2000). *Situated literacies: Reading and writing in context.* London: Routledge.

Baumann, J. F., Hoffman, J. V., Duffy-Hester, A. M., & Ro, J. M. (2000). "The first R" yesterday and today: U.S. elementary reading instruction practices reported by teachers and administrators. *Reading Research Quarterly, 35*(3), 338–377.

Bennett, N., & Blundell, D. (1983). Quantity and quality of work in rows and classroom groups. *Educational Psychology, 3*(1), 93–105.

Berman, P., & McLaughlin, M. W. (1978). *Federal programs supporting educational change: Vol. 8. Implementing and sustaining innovations* (R-1589-HEW/8). Santa Monica, CA: Rand Corporation.

Bjorklund, D. F., Muir-Broaddus, J., & Schneider, W. (1990). The role of knowledge in the development of strategies. In D. F. Bjorklund (Ed.), *Children's strategies* (pp. 93–128). Hillsdale, NJ: Lawrence Erlbaum Associates.

Block, C. C. (2001, December). *Distinctions between the expertise of literacy teachers preschool through grade 5.* Paper presented at the annual meeting of the National Reading Conference, San Antonio, TX.

Bond, G. L., & Dykstra, R. (1964/1997). The cooperative research program in first grade reading instruction. *Reading Research Quarterly, 32*(4), 348–427.

Bronfenbrenner, U. (1978). Toward an experimental ecology of human development. *American Psychologist, 32,* 513–531.

Brophy, J. E. (1973). Stability of teacher effectiveness. *American Educational Research Journal, 10*(3), 245–252.

Cambourne, B. (2001). What do I do with the rest of the class?: The nature of teaching-learning activities. *Language Arts, 79*(2), 124–135.

Cambourne, B. (2002). Conditions for literacy learning. *The Reading Teacher, 55*(4), 358–360.

Cantrell, S. C. (1999a). The effects of literacy instruction on primary students' reading and writing achievement. *Reading and Research Instruction, 39*(1), 3–26.

Cantrell, S. C. (1999b). Effective teaching and literacy learning: A look inside primary classrooms. *The Reading Teacher, 52*(4), 370–379.

Chall, J. S., Jacobs, V. A., & Baldwin, L W. (1990). *The reading crisis: Why poor children fall behind.* Cambridge, MA: Harvard University Press.

Clark, C. M., & Peterson, P. L. (1986). Teachers' thought processes. In M. C. Wittrock (Ed.), *Handbook of reading research on teaching* (pp. 255–296). New York: Macmillan.

Coker, H. (1985). Consortium for the improvement of teacher evaluation. *Journal of Teacher Education, 36,* 12–17.

Day, D. E., & Libertini, G. (1992). Profiles of children's learning behavior. *Journal of Research in Childhood Education, 6*(2), 100–112.

Dickinson, D. K., & Tabors, P. O. (2001). *Beginning literacy with language.* Baltimore: Paul H. Brookes.

Duffy, G. G., & Hoffman, J. (1999). In pursuit of an illusion: The flawed search for a perfect method. *The Reading Teacher, 53*(1), 10–16.

Dunkin, M., & Biddle, B. (1974). *The study of teaching.* New York: Holt, Rinehart & Winston.

Eder, D. (1981). Ability grouping as a self-fulfilling prophecy: A micro-analysis of teacher student interaction. *Sociology of Education, 54,* 151–162.

Esposito, D. (1973). Homogeneous and heterogeneous ability grouping: Principal findings and implications for evaluating and designing more effective educational environments. *Review of Educational Research, 43,* 163–179.

Fawson, P. C., & Reutzel, D. R. (2000). But I only have a basal: Implementing guided reading in the early grades. *The Reading Teacher, 54*(1), 84–97.

Fountas, I. C., & Pinnell, G. S. (1996). *Guided reading: Good first teaching for all children.* Portsmouth NH: Heinemann.

Fractor, J. S., Woodruff, M., Martinez, M., & Teale, W. H. (1993). Let's not miss opportunities to promote voluntary reading: Classroom libraries in the elementary school. *The Reading Teacher, 46,* 476–484.

Garling, T., & Evans, G. (1991). *Environment, cognition, and action: An integrated approach.* New York: Oxford University Press.

Genishi, C., Ryan, S., Ochsner, M., & Yarnall, M. M. (2001). Teaching in early childhood education: Understanding practices through research and theory. In V. Richardson (Ed.), *Handbook of research on teaching* (pp. 1175–1210). Washington, DC: American Education Research Association.

Gump, P. V. (1989). Ecological psychology and issues of play. In M. N. Bloch & A. D. Pellegrini (Eds.), *The ecological context of children's play* (pp. 35–56). Norwood, NJ: Ablex.

Haigh, N., & Katterns, B. (1984). Teacher effectiveness: Problem or goal for teacher education. *Journal of Teacher Education, 35*(5), 23–27.

Hastings, N., & Schwieso, J. (1995). Tasks and tables: The effects of seating arrangements on task engagement in primary classrooms. *Educational Research, 37*(3), 279–291.

Heibert, E. H. (1983). An examination of ability grouping for reading instruction. *Reading Research Quarterly, 28,* 231–255.

Hoffman, J. V., Sailors, M., Duffy, G., & Beretvas, S. N. (2004). The effective classroom literacy environment: Examining the validity of the TEX-IN3 Observation System. *Journal of Literacy Research, 36*(3), 303–334.

Holmes, R., & Cunningham, B. (1995). Young children's knowledge of their classrooms: Names, activities, and purposes of learning centers. *Education and Treatment of Children, 18*(4), 433–443.

Katims, D. S., & Pierce, P. L. (1995). Literacy-rich environments and the transition of young children with special needs. *Topics in Early Childhood Special Education, 15*(2), 219–230.

Kennedy, D. (1991). The young child's experience of space and child care center design: A practical mediation. *Children's Environments Quarterly, 8,* 37–48.

Kershner, R., & Pointon, P. (2000). Children's views of the primary classroom as an environment for working and learning. *Research in Education, 64,* 64–78.

Kulik, C. C., & Kulik, J. A. (1982). Research synthesis on ability grouping. *Educational Leadership: Journal of the Department of Supervision and Curriculum Development, N. E. A., 39,* 619–621.

Lave, J. (1988). *Cognition in practice.* New York: Cambridge University Press.

Long, F., Peters, D., & Garduque, L. (1985). Continuity between home and daycare: A model for defining relevant dimensions of child care. In I. Sigel (Ed.), *Advances in applied developmental psychology* (Vol. 1, pp. 131–170). Norwood, NJ: Ablex.

Lou, Y., Abrami, P. C., & Spence, J. C. (1996). Effects of within-class grouping on student achievement: An exploratory model. *Journal of Educational Research, 94,* 101–113.

Loughlin, C. E., & Martin, M. D. (1987). *Supporting literacy: Developing effective learning environments.* New York: Teachers College Press.

Martin, W., E., & Carle, E. (1967). *Brown bear, brown bear.* Henry Holt.

McGill-Franzen, A., Allington, R. L.,Yokoi, L., & Brooks, G. (1999). Putting books in the classroom seems necessary but not sufficient. *Journal of Educational Research, 93,* 67–74.

Meskill, C., & Swan, K. (1998). Response-based multimedia and the culture of the classroom: A pilot study of *Kid's Space* in four elementary classrooms. *Journal of Educational Computing Research, 18*(4), 339–367.

Metsala, J. L., & Wharton-McDonald, R. (1997). Effective primary-grades literacy instruction equals balanced literacy instruction. *The Reading Teacher, 50*(6), 518–521.

Montessori, M. (1965). *Spontaneous activity in education.* New York: Schocken Books.

Moore, G. (1986). Effects of the spatial definition of behavior settings on children's behavior: A quasi-experimental field study. *Journal of Personality and Social Psychology, 6,* 205–231.

Morrow, L. M. (1982) Relationship between literates programs, library corner designs and children's use of literature, *Journal of Educational Research, 75,* 339–344.

Morrow, L. M. (1990). Preparing the classroom environment to promote literacy during play. *Early Childhood Education Research Quarterly, 5,* 537–554.

Morrow, L. M. (2002). *The literacy center: Contexts for reading and writing* (2nd ed). Portland, ME: Stenhouse.

Morrow, L. M. (2005). *Literacy development in the early years: Helping children read and write*(5th ed.). Needham Heights, MA: Allyn & Bacon.

Morrow, L. M., & Casey, H. K. (2003). A comparison of exemplary characteristics in 1st and 4th grade teachers. *The California Reader, 36*(3), 5–17.

Morrow, L. M., Tracey, D. H., Woo, D. G., & Pressley, M. (1999). Characteristics of exemplary first-grade literacy instruction. *The Reading Teacher, 52*(5), 462–476.

Morrow, L. M., & Weinstein, C. S. (1982). Increasing children's use of literature through program and physical design changes. *Elementary School Journal, 83*(2), 131–137.

Morrow, L. M., & Weinstein, C. S. (1986). Encouraging voluntary reading: The impact of a literature program on children's use of library corners. *Reading Research Quarterly, 21*(3), 330–346.

Nash, B. (1981). The effects of classroom spatial organization on four and five-year old children's learning. *British Journal of Educational Psychology, 51,* 144–155.

Neuman, S. B. (1999). Books make a difference: a study of access to literacy. *Reading Research Quarterly, 34*(3), 2–31.

Neuman, S. B., & Celano, D. (2001). Access to print in low-income and middle-income communities. *Reading Research Quarterly, 36*(1), 8–27.

Neuman, S. B., & Fischer, R. (1995). Task and participation structures in kindergarten using a holistic literacy teaching perspective. *Elementary School Journal, 95*(March), 325–337.

Neuman, S. B., & Roskos, K. (1992). Literacy objects as cultural tools: Effects on children's literacy behaviors in play. *Reading Research Quarterly, 27*(3), 203–225.

Neuman, S. B., & Roskos, K. (1993). Access to print for children of poverty: Differential effects of adult mediation and literacy-enriched play settings on environmental and functional print tasks. *American Educational Research Journal, 30*(1), 95–121.

Neuman, S., & Roskos, K. (1997). Literacy knowledge in practice: Contexts of participation for young writers and readers. *Reading Research Quarterly, 32*(1), 10–33.

Olds, A. R. (1987). Designing setting for infants and toddlers. In C. S. Weinstein & T. G. David (Eds.), *Spaces for children: The built environment and child development,* (pp. 117–138). New York: Plenum Press.

Pressley, M., Allington, R. L., Wharton-McDonald, R., Collins-Block, C., & Morrow, L. M. (2001). *Learning to read: Lessons from exemplary first-grade classrooms.* New York: Guilford Press.

Pressley, M., Rankin, J., & Yokoi, L. (1996). A survey of instructional practices of primary teachers nominated as effective in promoting literacy. *Elementary School Journal, 96*(4), 363–383.

Reutzel, D. R., & Cooter, R. B. (1991). Organizing for effective instruction: The reading workshop. *The Reading Teacher, 44,* 548–554.

Reutzel, D. R., & Cooter, R. B. (2004). *Teaching children to read: Putting the pieces together* (4th ed.). Upper Saddle River, NJ: Prentice-Hall/Merrill.

Reutzel, D. R., & Fawson, P. C. (2002). *Your classroom library: New ways to give it more teaching power* (91–100). New York: Scholastic.

Roehler, L. R. & Duffy, G. G. (1984). Direct explanation of comprehension process. In G. G. Duffy, L. R. Roehler, & J. Mason (Eds.), *Comprehension instruction: Perspectives and suggestions* (pp. 265–280). New York: Longman.

Rogg, L. J. (2001). *Early literacy instruction in kindergarten*. Newark, DE: International Reading Association.

Romeo, L. (1999). A recipe for promoting effective classroom literacy environments. *Delta Kappa Gamma Bulletin, 65*(4), 39–44.

Rosenshine, B., & Furst, N. (1973). The use of direct observation to study teaching. In R. W. Travers (Ed.), *Second handbook of research on teaching* (pp. 122–183). Chicago: Rand McNally.

Roskos, K., & Neuman, S. B. (2001). Environment and its influences for early literacy teaching and learning. In S. B. Neuman & D. K. Dickinson (Eds.), *Handbook of early literacy research* (pp. 281–294). New York: Guildford Press.

Ruddell, R. B. (1995). Those influential literacy teachers: Meaning negotiators and motivation builders. *The Reading Teacher, 48*(6), 454–463.

Ruddell, R. B., & Harris, P. (1989). A study of the relationship between influential teachers' prior knowledge and beliefs about teaching effectiveness: Developing higher order thinking in content areas. In S. McCormick & J. Zutell (Eds.), *Cognitive and social perspectives for literacy research and instruction* (pp. 461–472). Chicago: National Reading Conference.

Ruddell, R. B. & Kern, R. B. (1986). The development of belief systems and teaching effectiveness of influential teachers. In M. P. Douglas (Ed.), *Reading: The quest for meaning* (pp. 133–150). Claremont, CA: Claremont Graduate School Yearbook.

Shulman, L. S. (1986). Paradigms and research programs in the study of teaching: A contemporary perspective. In M. C. Wittrock (Ed.), *Handbook of reading research on teaching* (pp. 3–36). New York: Macmillan.

Smith, M. W., Dickinson, D. K., Sangeorge, A., & Anastasopoulos, L. (2002). Early language and literacy classroom observation (ELLCO) toolkit. Baltimore: Brookes.

Taylor, B. M., & Pearson, P. D. (2002). *Teaching reading: Effective schools, accomplished teachers*. Mahwah, NJ: Lawrence Erlbaum Associates.

Taylor, B. M., Pearson, P. D., & Clark, K. (2000). Effective schools and accomplished teachers: Lessons about primary-grade reading instruction in low-income schools. *Elementary School Journal, 101*(2), 121–165.

Taylor, B. M., Pearson, P. D., Clark, K. E., & Walpole, S. (1999). *Beating the odds in teaching all children to read* (Ciera Report No.2–006). Ann Arbor, MI: Center for the Improvement of Early Reading Achievement.

Taylor, B. M., Peterson, D. S., Pearson, P. D., & Rodriguez, M. C. (2002). Looking inside classrooms: Reflecting on the "how" as well as the "what" in effective reading instruction. *The Reading Teacher, 56*(3), 270–279.

Taylor, N. E., Blum, I. H., & Logsdon, D. M. (1986). The development of written language awareness: Environmental aspects and program characteristics. *Reading Research Quarterly, 21*(2), 132–149.

Vukelich, C. (1994). Effects of play interventions on young children's reading of environmental print. *Early Childhood Research Quarterly, 9*(2), 153–170.

Vygotsky, L. S. (1978). *Mind in society*. Cambridge, MA: Harvard University Press.

Weinstein, C. S. (1977). Modifying student behavior in an open classroom through changes in the physical design. *American Educational Research Journal, 14*(3), 249–262.

Weinstein, C. S. (1981). Classroom design as an external condition for learning. *Educational Technology, 21*, 12–19.

Wharton-McDonald, R., Pressley, M., Rankin, J., & Mistretta, J. (1997). Effective primary-grades literacy instruction equals balanced literacy instruction. *The Reading Teacher, 6*(50), 518–521.

Whelldell, K., & Lam, Y. Y. (1987). Rows versus tables: 2 The effects of two classroom seating arrangements on disruption rate, on-task behaviour and teacher behaviour in three special school classes. *Educational Psychology, 7*(4), 303–312.

Wilder, G. (1977). Five exemplary reading programs. In J. Guthrie (Ed.), *cognition, curriculum, and comprehension*. Newark, DE: International Reading Association.

Wolfersberger, M., Reutzel, D. R., Sudweeks, R., & Fawson, P. F. (2004). Developing and validating the Classroom Literacy Environmental Profile (CLEP): A tool for examining the "print richness" of elementary classrooms. *Journal of Literacy Research, 36*(2), 211–272.

Yeomans, J. (1989). Changing seating arrangements: The use of antecedent control to increase on-task behaviour. *Behavioral Approaches With Children, 13*(3), 151–160.

22

Pervasive Management of Project Based Learning: Teachers as Guides and Facilitators

John R. Mergendoller, Thom Markham, Jason Ravitz, and John Larmer
Buck Institute for Education

INTRODUCTION

Twenty years ago Walter Doyle reviewed several decades of classroom management research, and examined the factors that influence the construction of orderly classrooms. Among his observations was the finding that learning activities which require students to engage in higher order thinking, allow student mobility and choice, include group work, range outside the classroom, and culminate in procedurally complex tasks are difficult to manage, and often lead to breakdowns in classroom deportment (Doyle, 1983, 1986; see also Blumenfeld, Mergendoller, & Swarthout, 1987). When implementing such problematic activities, he argued that teachers will have to assert more control and direct management of classroom transactions (Doyle, 1986, p. 403; Evertson & Neal, 2005). These conclusions are built upon an established tradition of behaviorally oriented, Skinner-influenced theory about how to control student behavior and manage classroom interaction.

However, as several authors have argued (Cohen & Lotan, 1990; Evertson et al., 2004; Marshall, 1990), there are other ways to direct student behavior and manage instructional events than those described in the classic classroom management literature—a knowledge base developed largely from observations of teacher-centered classroom environments emphasizing lecture, discussion, and seatwork. This is particularly true for Project Based Learning (PBL)—a teaching and learning model that engages students in a series of complex tasks that include planning and design, problem solving, decision making, creating artifacts, and communicating results. Although PBL can (and often does) encompass lecture and discussion, it gives equal or more emphasis to autonomous learning in small groups or by oneself. Students find their own sources, conduct their own research, and secure their own feedback (Arends, 1997; Diehl, Grobe, Lopez, & Cabral, 1999; Thomas, 1998, 2000).

When teachers who are successful managers of PBL are asked about their management techniques, they generally speak of exerting less control or turning management over to the kids rather than exercising the "overt manage[ment] and control . . ." strategies recommended by Doyle (1986, p. 402). Experienced PBL teachers report that they spend very little time promoting student engagement or reprimanding student misbehavior (Lambros, 2002, 2004). Rather, teachers spend their time participating in projects as mentors rather than as managers, and the metaphor of *conducting* a Project (as in conducting a symphony) is generally more appropriate than that of *controlling* a class.

One goal of PBL is to develop students' abilities to manage themselves. But just as a conductor must learn how to help instrumentalists maintain rhythm, modulate tonal nuance, and enter on cue, a Project Based Learning teacher must learn how to guide students effectively through the learning process. Smooth and effective operation of a PBL classroom does not happen automatically; teachers do not simply "turn students loose" on projects. When PBL is done well, it is the result of thoughtful planning, pervasive management activities, established learning expectations and classroom procedures, reflective orchestration of project tasks and activities, and the continuing availability and use of multiple scaffolds and task-specific training. Effective PBL thrives in a classroom culture that values learning over performance, and supports students' self-management, self-direction, and self-assessment (Blumenfeld, Puro, & Mergendoller, 1992; Buck Institute for Education, 2003; Krajcik, et al., 1998; Thomas, 2000).

The goal of this chapter is to describe a "pervasive" management approach that continually supports student learning from project planning to post-project reflection. We first define and describe the key features of Project Based Learning as an instructional model. We then identify four project implementation stages and discuss the pervasive management activities associated with each stage. Finally, we suggest several aspects of project based learning that need further theoretical and empirical exploration.

THE DEVELOPMENT OF PROJECT BASED LEARNING

Current interest in PBL draws upon three intellectual and empirical roots. First, John Dewey (1929, 1933), and his more recent constructivist-oriented interpreters, draw attention to the power of using intellectual and practical problems as the vehicle for teaching and learning. For example, Hiebert et al. (1996) argue "that reform in curriculum and instruction should be based on allowing students to problematize the subject. Rather than mastering skills and applying them, students should be engaged in resolving problems" (p. 12). Problems to be solved lie at the heart of Project Based Learning.

Secondly, the cognitive and constructivist revolution in psychological and educational theory has focused a great deal of attention on the nature of problems and the problem-solving process (e.g., Anderson, 1980, 1993; Bransford & Stein, 1984; Cognition and Technology Group at Vanderbilt [CTGV], 1992; Frederiksen, 1984; Greeno, 1978; Hayes, 1988; Mayer, 1992; Mayer & Wittrock, 1996; Newell & Simon, 1972; Simon, 1979; Sternberg & Frensch, 1991). This area of cognitive theory, and the empirical research it has inspired, suggest that knowledge and strategies acquired in the process of solving a problem are learned more easily, retained longer, and more frequently applied to future problems than the same knowledge and strategies taught in the abstract (CTGV, 1992; Regehr & Norman, 1996). Project Based Learning is a way to contextualize problem solving and introduce new content and concepts as knowledge to be used, rather than information to be acquired CGTV, 1996; Simon, 1980). By encouraging students to plan, structure, and reflect upon their own learning, PBL seeks to develop students' cognitive skills and confidence to consider and resolve complex, nonalgorithmic problems (such as are found in everyday life), articulate nuanced judgments and interpretations, apply multiple (and sometimes conflicting) criteria, and exercise self-regulation (Resnick, 1987).

Finally, in 1968 a group of medical educators at Canada's McMaster University revamped their medical school curriculum to focus on solving medical problems rather than remembering medical information. Concerned that "bored and disenchanted... students were passive and exposed to too much information little of which seemed relevant to the practice of medicine," (Barrows, 2000, p. vii) they instituted a program where "from the beginning of school, learning would occur around a series of biomedical problems presented in small groups with the faculty functioning as 'tutors or guides to learning'" (Barrows, 2000, p. vii). What was a bold new approach to medical education thirty years ago is now commonplace, and in 1994, some form of PBL instruction was reported in 114 U.S. medical schools (Block, 1997). Other schools of professional education also emphasize problems and projects as pedagogical tools, and examples can be found in schools of business (Gilbert & Foster, 1997; Stinson & Milter, 1996), nursing (Creedy & Alavi, 1997), architecture (Maitland, 1997), optometry (Lovie-Kitchin, 1997), social work (Bolzan & Heycox, 1997), law (Winsor, 1997), engineering (Cawley, 1997; Woods, 1996), and education (Bridges, 1992).

DEFINING PROJECT BASED LEARNING

PBL has been described as "a way of learning" (Engel, 1997), a "general educational strategy" (Walton & Matthews, 1989), and a "way of conceiving the curriculum" (Boud & Feletti, 1997). Depending upon the particular teacher's implementation, PBL may overlap, incorporate, or borrow from a number of similar, constructivist-inspired pedagogical orientations including Anchored Instruction (Bransford, Sherwood, Hasselbring, Kinzer, & Williams, 1990), Authentic Pedagogy (Newmann, Marks, & Gamoran, 1996), Design Experiments, (Brown, 1992), Intentional Learning (Bereiter & Scardamalia, 1989), Self-regulated Learning (McCombs & Marzano, 1990; Pintrich, 1995; Zimmerman & Schunk, 1989), Strategic Learning (Weinstein, 1994), educational simulations (Maxwell, Mergendoller, & Bellisimo, 2004) and Problem Based Learning (Barrows & Tamblyn, 1980; Maxwell, Bellisimo, & Mergendoller, 2001; Torp & Sage, 2002). Others have incorporated features of PBL into more traditional instructional approaches (Memory, Yoder, Bolinger, & Warren, 2004). Building on Fleming (2000), we identify 13 separate varieties of Project Based Learning (see Table 22.1). In addition to the distinctions made by this typology, it is important to bear in mind the variation found among teachers in the selection of project content, project structure, and project implementation. Some projects last a day; some last a semester (or more!). Some combine subject areas; some drill deeply into one complex concept in a single discipline. Some are planned and carried out almost entirely by students; some are passed down from teacher to teacher.

Special attention should be given to a variety of Project Based Learning called *Problem* Based Learning. In this form of PBL, the project is framed as a curriculum-relevant, ill-structured problem, and the students' problem-solving task follows a somewhat prescribed procedure that includes taking a "knowledge inventory," defining a "problem statement," and proposing and defending various solutions before arriving at the most reasonable one. The problem may be encased within a realistic but hypothetical situation that is carefully crafted to direct students toward specific curricular goals (Barrows & Tamblin, 1980; Bridges & Hallinger, 1992; Duffy & Savery, 1994; Maxwell, Bellisimo, & Mergendoller, 2001; Stepien, Gallagher, & Workman, 1993; Wilkerson & Gijselaers, 1996). Students then take the role of individuals or groups involved in these situations, and work together to solve the problem. Several recent publications discuss the creation of problems for classroom use, provide exemplary problems to try in the classroom, and coach teachers through the implementation of Problem Based Learning (Delisle, 1997; Lambros, 2002, 2004; Torp & Sage, 2002). Field tested problems for free download are available at the Buck Institute for Education Web site (http://www.bie.org/) and the Illinois Problem Based Learning Network Web site (http://21cif.imsa.edu/ipbln).

Given these variations, it is impossible to define PBL unambiguously. Following Thomas (2000) we define PBL in terms of a number of specific features, and then conclude this section

TABLE 22.1
Varieties of Project Based Learning

Project Type	*Description*
Community Study (Gillis, 1992)	Students explore community issues, interview citizens, collect and interpret data, develop a community profile, and evaluate their work.
Design and Technology Experience (Davis, Hawley, McMullan, & Spilka, 1997)	Students apply their learning to a situation or problem by developing a prototype or working model.
Environmental Investigation (Elder, 1998)	Students collect, organize, graph, and interpret real-world data to learn more about the conditions, processes, populations, and life cycles or organisms.
Expeditionary Learning (Berger, 2000)	Students conduct interdisciplinary, in-depth studies of a single theme or topic that emphasizes family or community involvement, and both intellectual and character development.
Field Study (Willis, 1997)	Teams of students address a question, problem, or issue outside of the classroom and present their conclusions and recommendations to an audience outside the classroom.
Foxfire Approach (Wigginton, 1986)	Students interview and document community members' lives and experiences.
Microsociety (Fletcher, 1996)	Students create and run a miniature community within a school.
Museum Model (MacFarlane, 1989)	Students plan, organize, and display their learning about a particular place, person, object, or event.
Early Childhood Education Project Approach (Chard, 1992)	Students and the teacher pose questions that guide their research.
Senior Project (Glasgow, 1997)	High school seniors work on intensive in-depth academic, artistic, community service, or career development projects of their own choosing.
Service Learning (Kinsley & McPherson, 1995)	Students apply skills they have learned in school to carry out work serving the needs of individuals, groups, and organizations in their own community.
Work-Based Learning (Naylor, 1997)	Work-based learning includes a variety of approaches designed to increase students' career understanding and job skills. It has variously been called experiential learning, experience-based career education, school-to-work initiatives, cooperative education, tech prep, youth apprenticeships, coordinated workforce development, job shadowing, internships, and mentoring.
Telecommunications Projects (Harris, 1994)	Students use the Internet to conduct projects that involve classrooms around the world gathering and sharing data, solving problems, exchanging cultural information, or creating products together. Students and teachers communicate using World Wide Web browsers or e-mail or other available tools. Examples include Learning Circles (Riel, 1998); WebQuests (Dodge, 2004) and online science inquiry projects (Feldman, Konold, & Coulter, 2000).
Problem-Based Learning (Delisle, 1997; Lambros, 2002, 2004; Maxwell, Mergendoller, & Bellisimo 2004; Torp & Sage, 2002)	Students, playing the roles of interested stakeholders, investigate and resolve ill-structured problems modeled on those encountered outside the classroom.

with a definition more evocative than prescriptive. First, Project Based Learning must display at least some of the characteristics ascribed by Reeves, Herrington, & Oliver (2002) to "authentic" learning activities:

1. Real-world relevance: Activities match as nearly as possible the real-world tasks of professionals in practice rather than decontextualized or classroom-based tasks.

2. Ill-defined: Activities require students to define the tasks and subtasks needed to complete the activity.
3. Complex, sustained tasks: Activities are completed in days, weeks, and months rather than minutes or hours. They require significant investment of time and intellectual resources.
4. Multiple perspectives: Provides the opportunity for students to examine the task from different perspectives using a variety of resources, and separate relevant from irrelevant information.
5. Collaborative: Collaboration is integral and required for task completion.
6. Value laden: Provides the opportunity to reflect and involve students' beliefs and values.
7. Interdisciplinary: Activities encourage interdisciplinary perspectives and enable learners to play diverse roles and build expertise that is applicable beyond a single well-defined field or domain.
8. Authentically assessed: Assessment is seamlessly integrated with learning in a manner that reflects how quality is judged in the real world.
9. Authentic products: Authentic activities create polished products valuable in their own right rather than as preparation for something else.
10. Multiple possible outcomes: Activities allow a range and diversity of outcomes open to multiple solutions of an original nature, rather than a single correct response obtained by the application of predefined rules and procedures.[1]

Second, Project Based Learning is synonymous with learning in depth. Although it generally incorporates "hands-on" learning activities, it requires more than manipulatives, and provokes students to undertake a sustained inquiry into concepts and questions that are central to the curriculum. PBL drives students to encounter (and struggle with) the central concepts and principles of a discipline. Empirical and theoretical work by Newmann, Marks, and Gamoran (1996) operationalizes and elaborates the idea of learning in depth using a three-part definition of authentic achievement. Such learning must: (1) involve the production (rather than the reproduction) of knowledge, (2) result from disciplined inquiry which in turn is defined by: a) use of a priori knowledge base, b) striving for in-depth understanding rather than superficial awareness, and (c) expressing one's ideas and findings through elaborated communication, and (3) have value to individuals or groups beyond school.

Third, Project Based Learning reflects an explicit commitment to helping students learn not just content, but also the skills they need to make use of their knowledge and to gain future knowledge. These include communication and presentation skills, organization and time management skills, research and inquiry skills, self-assessment and reflection skills, and group participation and leadership skills.

Finally, PBL gives students the opportunity to practice the skills and to wrestle with their own ideas and opinions to arrive at decisions affecting the learning process (cf. Thomas, 2000, pp. 1–4). Combining these considerations, we define Project Based Learning as:

> a systematic teaching method that engages students in learning essential knowledge and life-enhancing skills through an extended, student-influenced inquiry process that is structured around complex, authentic questions and carefully designed products and tasks.

Although the idea of using projects as the primary means of instruction is at least as old as the writing of John Dewey, the use of projects to spur the development of subject matter knowledge, logical reasoning and self-management skills in K-16 classrooms is not widespread. Projects are rarely used as a central instructional strategy but rather an opportunity to apply and demonstrate

---

[1] Text slightly modified for use in this chapter.

what students have already learned from traditional, didactic methods. PBL is frequently "the dessert, not the main course" (Berger, 2000). Problems and projects are spoken of as "motivators, hooks or rewards" rather than a primary way to help students develop deep content knowledge, communicative competencies, and social and self-management skills (Newell, 2003). Such superficial implementations of PBL do not take advantage of this instructional approach's ability to promote deep understanding (Blumenfeld et al., 1991; Bransford et al., 1990), build metacognitive skills (Blumenfeld et. al, 1991), and increase knowledge retention (Norman & Schmidt, 1992).

Given its complexity and plasticity, and the variation found within projects, teachers, and students, it is not realistic to describe in this chapter a specific set of techniques (let alone empirically validated techniques) that lead to effective PBL management. Instead, we use the term *pervasive management* to describe a set of activities that provide a starting point for successful PBL management. Teachers will need to analyze their own curricular goals and current students and adapt the management tasks discussed subsequently. Given that PBL lends itself to classroom and teacher adaptation, and experimentation, this adaptation can be considered a natural part of project implementation. As one teacher told us (Mergendoller & Thomas, n.d.):

> There is no "cookie-cutter" way to do projects. Don't be afraid to make mistakes. Initially I thought I was doing a disservice to students if I had something that didn't work. Now I realize it's better to make a mistake and discuss with students what needs to be changed to make it work. This has also improved my relationship with students—it's more collegial now[2] (p. 32)

PERVASIVE PROJECT MANAGEMENT

Pervasive management encompasses more than maintaining classroom order. It begins with project planning and ends with self- and class-reflection. Pervasive management includes elements of effective instruction, and it is often difficult to draw a sharp distinction between instructional and managerial activities. Projects provide opportunities for learning, but it is the manner in which they are planned, organized, structured, and managed that determines their educational effectiveness.

Although complex projects give students the opportunity to develop, practice, and apply planning, metacognitive and self-monitoring skills, research suggests that students do not inevitably respond to high-level cognitive tasks with high-level learning strategies (Anderson & Roth, 1989; Blumenfeld & Meece, 1988; Blumenfeld et al., 1991; Paris, Lipson, & Wixson, 1983; Winne & Marx, 1982). Further, students new to PBL often oppose teachers' efforts to engage them in more procedurally complex and cognitively difficult academic tasks, and prefer procedurally simple tasks requiring routine or algorithmic thought (Atwood, 1983; Blumenfeld et al., 1991; Davis & McKnight, 1976; Doyle, 1983; Mayers, Csikszentmihalyi, & Larson, 1978; Stake & Easley 1978). If students can complete the project without learning anything new, or if they can redesign a project artifact so that they do not address new ideas or develop new capabilities, then the opportunities for learning through PBL degenerate into mere classroom activities.

While allowing for student direction and discovery, PBL is not synonymous with discovery learning, an instructional approach where students receive little or no guidance from the teacher. Nor is PBL consistent with giving students total choice over the substance and process

[2]This and all other quotes from unidentified teachers are taken from a study conducted by the Buck Institute for Education of teachers who are exemplary in their ability to conceive, conduct, and assess standards-focused projects. Full details are available at http://www.bie.org/tmp/research/researchmanagePBL.pdf.

of their learning. In PBL, the teacher has major responsibility for overseeing student activities and providing guidance, structure and feedback as appropriate. Teacher supervision and, where necessary, intervention shape student cognitive and social activities, so that students can reach the learning goals established for the project. There is both empirical and anecdotal support for such a position. After reviewing research on three varieties of discovery learning, Mayer (2004) concluded that teacher guidance is a critical prerequisite to student learning. He notes:

> In short, when students have too much freedom, they may fail to come into contact with the to-be-learned material... the kind of activity that really promotes meaningful learning is cognitive activity (e.g., selecting, organizing, and integrating knowledge). Instead of depending solely on learning by doing or learning by discussion, the most genuine approach to constructivist learning is learning by thinking ... Students need enough freedom to become cognitively active in the process of sense making, and students need enough guidance so that their cognitive activity results in the construction of useful knowledge. (pp. 16–17)

Or, as an expert PBL teacher put it,

> "I had to unlearn the idea that teaching was about my content; I had to learn it was about their thinking (p. 16)."

Students' (and sometimes teachers') focus on "getting the project done" can overwhelm the intended content learning. This can be seen in a study of Project Based Science instruction in middle school (Krajcik et al., 1996). Although students generally enjoyed working on projects and were able to generate project plans and carry out scientific procedures, they had difficulty creating meaningful scientific questions, managing complex tasks and their own time, analyzing and transforming data, and developing a logical argument that explained their results. In other words, they carried out inquiry activities, but they had difficulty achieving the intended learning outcomes associated with these activities. Projects took on a life of their own rather than being closely connected with the intended learning objectives.

> As they carried out the experimental work, students had sporadic conversations about the scientific meaning of their observations.... These conversations often were quite animated. However, students did not pursue the scientific implication of what they noticed and did not discuss how the implications might be explored by raising new questions ... [f]or the most part ... opportunities to learn science content were not realized. (p. 21)

Table 22.2 displays a stage-based model of Project Based Learning and the management activities associated with each stage. We emphasize that project management issues pervade project planning and implementation, and need to be addressed at each project stage. Students, as well as the teacher, need to be cognizant of these issues. In PBL, the teacher (alone or in consultation with students) poses a question or problem and then organizes student learning activity around the process of resolving it. As project work continues, there is a subtle modulation of responsibility from teacher to student and back to the teacher. In the initial stages of PBL implementation, the teacher exerts leadership in planning the project and helping students frame and prepare to conduct necessary learning activities. Students then assume increasing responsibility in the middle stages of PBL implementation as they conduct research, design, and create an artifact. At the conclusion of the project, the teacher has the responsibility to ensure that the assessment is academically rigorous and appropriate, there is an opportunity to reflect upon project activities and the learning that occurred, and to make revisions for future projects

TABLE 22.2
Pervasive Management Activities in Project Based Learning

Project Stage	*Management Activities*
Stage 0 Project Planning	• Define project scope, problem and Big Idea • Develop a Driving Question • Select content standards and incorporate simultaneous noncontent outcomes • Plan assessments • Organize resources • Decide on grouping strategies
Stage 1 Project Launch	• Stimulate student interest, enthusiasm, and concern • Establish high expectations • Clarify rules, procedures, products, timeline, and grading practices
Stage 2 Guided Inquiry and Product Creation	• Facilitate resource use • Help students define tasks and assess progress • Scaffold learning and working • Cultivate presentation skills
Stage 3 Project Conclusion	• Stage exhibition • Conduct summative assessment • Reflect on project learning and process

(cf. Torp & Sage, 2002, p. 70). We will now focus on each stage of PBL implementation and the management activities necessary for optimal student leaving.

STAGE 0: PLAN THE PROJECT

Pervasive Project management begins with careful project planning. Although the design of the project will likely change before the project is over, a well-thought out project "roadmap" is a crucial element of project success. Stage 0 takes place before students begin working on the project. They may be involved in the planning, but this will be a decision made by the teacher based on students' experience with PBL and their capabilities to participate in project planning. Whoever is on the planning team, it is ultimately the teachers' responsibility to ensure that a project provides a constructive learning experience and is not merely a "fun thing to do."

We have divided the planning process into six interdependent and overlapping issues. Although they are discussed separately, in reality, teachers must think about all of them simultaneously. Decisions made about one issue influence decisions made about subsequent (or previously decided) issues.

Define Project Scope, Problem and Big Idea

Projects vary in length, complexity and learning goals. Teachers begin planning the project by considering how it will fit within the curriculum and help students attain important content and skill outcomes. Longer projects are designed to investigate broader issues or topics, whereas shorter projects are organized around a specific issue or problem to be resolved. Consider students' experience with projects and their ability to work on their own when deciding on the length and breadth of a project.

At the heart of a project, there is a problem (or problems) to be solved. Cognitive scientists commonly divide problems into two types: well-structured problems and ill-structured problems. Well-structured problems:

- Present all elements of the problem to the learner.
- Require the application of a limited number of regular and well-structured rules and principles that are organized in predictive and prescriptive ways.
- Have knowable, comprehensible solutions where the relationship between decision choices and all problems states is known or probabilistic. (Wood, 1983, in Jonassen, 2000, p. 67)

Common examples of well-structured problems include word or story problems in mathematics, as well as many physics and chemistry problems. These problems populate textbook appendices and multiple choice exams. Greeno (1978) calls such problems transformation problems because they begin with a well-defined initial state (what is known), the clear identification of a goal state (the solution), and a recognized procedure for transforming the initial state into the goal state.

In contrast, ill-structured problems:

- Possess problem elements that are unknown or not known with any degree of confidence. (Wood, 1983)
- Possess multiple solutions, solution paths, or no solutions at all. (Kitchner, 1983)
- Possess multiple criteria for evaluating solutions, so there is uncertainty about which concepts, rules, and principles are necessary for the solution and how they are organized.
- Often require learners to make judgments and express personal opinions or beliefs about the problem.... (Meacham & Emont, 1989, in Jonassen, 2000, p. 67)

Project Based Learning is most effective when it is built around ill-structured problems and complex issues. Projects that dwell upon well-structured problems are better thought of as application activities, in which students identify a method or solution learned earlier and use it to solve the problem. Such problems provide opportunities for students to practice what they know, but offer little incentive or reason to develop new knowledge. Well-structured problems do not grow or change, unlike the problems faced in daily life. In contrast, ill-structured problems often take on a life of their own. They mutate as students address them. What was a minor issue becomes major. Conditions and constraints change. New, unexpected problems arise. These dynamic and changing problems are generally more difficult to solve than static ones (Jonassen, 2000).

Some projects merge a set of diverse problems to create a complex tapestry of tasks and learning goals. For example, as part of a year-long, whole-school focus on the theme of water, Ron Berger's sixth-graders in rural Massachusetts tested a sample of private wells to determine whether they were polluted with lead or sodium, examined the relationships between water depth and sodium content and pH level, and correlated this information with the distance between the well and the road. Their data were graphed and analyzed, and the results showed no relationships between well location, water depth, and sodium content. Formal presentations of results were made to the entire school, the larger community, and to representatives from the state legislature. As the use of road salt to melt snow was a current controversy, there was great interest in the project's results (Berger, 2000). This multifaceted project enabled students to learn fundamental concepts in chemistry, biology, earth science, geography, mathematics, and cartography. It required students to speak and write clearly, communicate with external audiences, manage their time and work productively in groups.

Project Based Learning is most effective when it contextualizes knowledge acquisition by focusing on problems that are compelling to students and which have meaning in the world at large, not just in the school room. We have drawn on our own experience and advice from others (Duch, Groh, & Allen, 2001; Glasgow, 1997) to create the guidelines below. Although few projects adhere to all of these guidelines, most effective projects incorporate several. Effective projects:

- Are complex enough to accommodate a variety of investigative and ability levels and learning styles for individuals and groups.
- Are complex enough to require cooperative effort (e.g., one person can't do everything).
- Require students to make decisions, formulate and support arguments, and demonstrate deep understanding of a concept or situation.
- Require students to distinguish necessary information from that which is irrelevant, and to use original sources.

Big Ideas provide a larger context for project work. Teachers should discuss this context with students and orient them to the more global issue or idea that sparked the Project. In the Water Quality project just described, for example, the Big Idea could be water husbandry or resource preservation. A Big Idea, however, is too grand and diffuse to focus student learning on specific content standards or skill. For this to occur, it is necessary to distill the essence of the Big Idea. The hourglass metaphor is useful here. A Big Idea must be reduced to a more specific question or set of questions that students can examine over the course of several weeks.

Develop a Driving Question

A second key management task is to develop a Driving Question (sometimes called an Essential Question or Problem Statement) that brings focus and specificity to the learning process and serves as a "driver" for subsequent learning activities (Blumenfeld, et al., 1991). Without a Driving Question to bring coherence to multiple project tasks, it is easy for students to concentrate on superficial or irrelevant aspects of the project. Ethnographic research on college students taking a project based engineering design course demonstrated that students often were unaware of what they were supposed to be learning, why they were working on assigned activities, or how to reflect on and learn from the activities they completed (Turns, Newstetter, Allen, Mistree, 1997). Driving Questions, posted on the classroom wall and continually referenced by the teacher ("How does what you are doing help you to answer the Driving Question?"), help keep students from getting lost as they weave together multiple activities to complete a project.

Driving Questions can increase student motivation in the project. A provocative, engaging question ("Is the water in this school safe to drink?") captures student interest in way that cannot be done with a bald statement of the content to be learned (elements, compounds, and mixtures in water). Writing a single question defining a project is often not feasible, and multiple Driving Questions may be more useful in complex, extended projects; these questions may vary in their abstractness. A good Driving Question is intriguing and understandable. It must leave room for students to make choices—and mistakes—but not be so immense as to be unanswerable ("Are people good or bad?"). Students often generate excellent Driving Questions, by themselves or with teacher facilitation. Driving Questions need not be static; they may be refined, reframed, or constrained as the project continues.

There is no formula for creating effective Driving Questions, but there are guidelines. A good driving question:

- Is provocative and challenges students to think deeply. Do music videos portray contemporary African-American culture accurately? When are people justified in revolting against an established government?
- Connects global and local problems. How will global warming affect my community?
- Contains moral, ethical or social implications. What was the experience of 19th and 20th century immigrants in our community and how has immigration affected our community's development?
- Invites controversy and confronts students with multiple points of view. Without increasing current tax revenues, which community services should be increased? Which should be cut?
- Is related to the lives of the students answering it. Questions that pertain to a student's school and community are generally more meaningful than those answered in the abstract.
- Is feasible. Students have the time and resources to address it and generate an answer. It is developmentally appropriate for the students' grade level.
- Focuses student attention on important curricular standards and topics that are at the core of an academic discipline. The question, "How can we reduce unemployment in our town?" focuses student attention on the economic concepts of scarce resources and opportunity costs, and is a better Driving Question than, "What careers will need the most workers when I graduate from college?"
- Is not a curriculum topic or focused on isolated skills or content knowledge, for example, What is force? How can the difference between the median income of five countries be displayed on a graph? What are the responsibilities of the executive branch in a representative democracy?
- Does not lead to an obvious answer, for example, Was slavery moral or immoral? (adapted from Buck Institute for Education, 2003; Krajcik, Czerniak, & Berger, 1999)

Driving Questions are not easy to write, and require careful phrasing. In our professional development workshops, teachers spend hours brainstorming, reflecting, critiquing, and completing Driving Questions. It is always a good idea to ask other teachers and students to review the Driving Question, and report how they think students will understand and respond to it. This provides an opportunity to refine the Driving Question before launching the project (Lambros, 2004). Table 22.3 presents examples of Driving Questions that have been refined or changed to enlarge the scope of the project, make the question more concrete for younger students, or make the project more engaging by relating the question to students' lives.

Select Content Standards and Incorporate Simultaneous Noncontent Outcomes

Projects should be aligned to curricular goals and focused on explicit content outcomes. They should also be designed to teach specific skills. By clearly defining the instructional purpose of the project, teachers are better able to track student progress, and provide precise feedback. This feedback, in turn, communicates a clearer vision of what students are expected to learn, and often leads them to focus more intently on the learning process and achieve deeper learning. As teachers consider how a project fits within the curriculum, they may wish to consult the compendium of state and national content standards found at http://www.mcrel.org/ standards-benchmarks.

TABLE 22.3
Tweaking the Driving Question

Original Question		*Refined Question*
Was Truman's decision to drop the bomb justified? Powerful question. It forces students to confront the dilemmas of war. Students will not only learn history, but they will also learn about issues that remain relevant today.	⇨	**Can the use of nuclear weapons be justified?** Broadening the question can increase its power. The project can now focus on a number of different decisions about the use of nuclear force, require students to compare these situations, and lead students to develop and justify their own decision criteria.
How have robotics and automation changed our society in the past century? Good question. It prompts students to learn about technology, society, and history.	⇨	**How might robotics and automation change our town and its businesses in the next century?** A better question as it anchors an abstract inquiry within a local context that is of interest to students.
What is radiation fog and how can it be dangerous? Good beginning. The question requires students to focus on central scientific principles.	⇨	**How can we reduce traffic accidents associated with radiation fog?** A more engaging question as it requires students to not only understand the principles of radiation fog, but apply their understanding to a real, currently debated problem.
Is the stream that runs through town a healthy environment for fish? Good question that can involve students in a series of scientific investigations and gain knowledge about ecosystems, properties of matter, fish characteristics, and conservation.	⇨	**Should fishing be regulated to preserve the salmon spawn in our stream?** This question can encompass the same curricular content as the original question, but provides opportunities for students to interact with community members, local politicians, business owners, farmers, etc.

Defining simultaneous noncontent outcomes (or skills) is an important part of pervasive PBL management, since such outcomes are not typically the focus of traditional instruction. Projects can be designed to help students develop oral presentation skills, self-management skills, and collaboration skills. Noncontent outcomes can also include such habits of mind as reflection, active listening, and other skills focused on the process of learning or the mastery of workplace competencies. The number of simultaneous outcomes is only limited by the teacher's ability and willingness to assess each outcome during the course of a project. (See Costa & Kallick, 2004, and Johnson & Johnson, 2004, for assessment tools and techniques appropriate for noncontent outcomes.)

Plan Assessments

Teachers establish the preconditions for success (or failure) when they establish their assessment system. Students–and adults–are sensitive to the performance criteria used to evaluate their work, and knowledge of these criteria is generally a significant influence on behavior. Assessment professionals refer to this as the WYTIWYG effect—what you test is what you get (Hambleton, 1996).

Black and Wiliam (1998) found that students learn more when they are given feedback about the specific qualities of their work coupled with advice about how to improve. Students also benefit from assessing their own work and from discussing this evaluation with the teacher. Such conversations provide teachers with a "window into students' minds" (Tobin & Ulerick, 1989) and can guide instructional decisions about further support needed to attain the project's learning goals.

An effective assessment system is a transparent one. Students benefit most when they fully understand the criteria by which they are being assessed. Wiggins (1989) observes:

> The assessment system [should] provide a basis for developing a metacognitive awareness of what are important characteristics of good problem solving, good writing, good experimentation, good historical analysis and so on. Moreover, such as assessment can address not only the product one is trying to achieve, but also the process of achieving it, that is, the habits of mind that contribute to successful writing, painting, and problem solving. (pp. 29–30)

One strategy for creating a transparent assessment system is to develop assessment rubrics jointly with students, apply these rubrics to common examples of student work, and then discuss results. This procedure can be used to calibrate student and teacher expectations, and may also lead to jointly revising rubrics to make them more explicit and understandable. Good resources for developing rubrics and other assessment procedures that encourage learning and communicate evaluation criteria are Arter & McTighe (2004) and Wiggins (1998).

Organize Resources

PBL generally requires the use of physical resources—charts, meeting rooms, movable chairs, whiteboards, markers, butcher paper, wood, scientific instruments, computers, etc.—by groups and individuals. All necessary materials should be at hand before beginning a project. Once begun, projects function more smoothly if there is a defined space for project work. A single classroom with desks bolted to the floor in rows is not an ideal setting. Newell (2003) describes a more optimal PBL environment:

> open, flexible space so that students may utilize it for a variety of uses. The open space could have tables and chairs available, so students may congregate at various times for various purposes. This open space may look different every day, even every hour... Project processes need room, so that learners may spread out materials they use to produce authentic products. Other breakout rooms are also needed. Having a room where science experiments may be set up is necessary. Having space for an art area, a "shop" area, and a media resource center would be wonderful. (p. 49)

Teachers with small classrooms, who can not append "project space" to their classrooms by incorporating unused space can demarcate a "project area" with yellow plastic tape—the kind used to warn passersby of an open trench or construction project—and signage. This isolates the developing project from general classroom traffic and student curiosity. This is especially important in secondary classrooms where there are different populations of students in each class period, and it is a great temptation for a students in one period to tinker with projects created by students in other periods.

In addition to gathering physical resources, most projects require the teacher to assemble knowledge resources as well. Although one of the goals of PBL is to develop students' skills in finding the information needed to complete a project, most teachers try to shortcut this process and collect and "edit" a set of core knowledge resources. Otherwise, too much student learning time is given over to finding information instead of understanding it. A good solution is to provide a few diverse resources that need to be evaluated by students.

Decide on Grouping Strategies

Since PBL requires students to work collaboratively in groups, criteria for membership in these groups must be established. Much has been written about grouping students for collaborative learning and the outcomes associated with different grouping and grading strategies (Cohen, 1994; Gillies & Ashman, 2003; Johnson & Johnson, 1999; Sharan & Sharan, 1992; Slavin, 1995). Most group learning research, however, has focused on learning discrete, well-specified content or solving well-structured problems. We do not know how well generalizations built upon the cooperative learning of math translates to the messy realities of Project Based Learning (Davidson, 1985; McCaslin & Good, 1996). Nonetheless, there are several findings regarding the relationship of group composition, group interaction, and learning that appear relevant for establishing PBL work groups.

An exhaustive narrative review of the group learning literature by Webb and Palincsar (1996) demonstrates the complexity of the relationships between group composition and learning. First, there is consistent evidence that students of lower ability or who have less prior knowledge, if they participate fully in groups characterized by high quality discussions,[3] can learn dramatically more in groups that are heterogeneous with regards to student ability. A met-analysis of four studies conducted by Lou et al. (1996) calculated that the average difference between student learning in ability heterogeneous groups versus ability homogenous groups for lower-ability students was 23 percentile ranks (Marzano, Pickering, & Pollock, 2001). Webb, Nemer, Chizhik, and Sugrue (1998) report similar findings with eighth-graders on a science performance assessment.

Second, although students who are high achievers or who have substantial prior knowledge, sometimes learn slightly more when working with students of similar ability and knowledge in homogenous groups, the difference is very small. In the analysis conducted by Lou et al. (1996) data, the difference between high ability students working in ability homogeneous versus ability hetereogeneous groups was calculated to be 3 percentile ranks (Marzano et al., 2001). Based on their own literature review, Webb and Palincsar (1996) conclude "hetereogenous ability grouping ... [does] not disadvantage high-ability students" (pp. 859; See also Webb et al., 1998).

Third, heterogeneous ability grouping seems to do a disservice to medium-ability students. In the Lou et al. (1996) analysis, the difference in achievement between medium-ability students working in ability homogeneous versus ability hetereogeneous groups was calculated to be 19 percentile ranks (Marzano et al., 2001). In other words, the learning of medium-ability students was penalized in hetereogenous groups to almost the same extent that the learning of lower-ability students was increased. Webb and Palincsar attribute this finding as a consequence of typical patterns of interaction in hetereogenous groups, where high-ability students often teach and support the low-ability students, and exclude the medium-ability students from group interaction (See also Webb, 1989). By contrast, in ability homogeneous groups there are not students who know noticeably more or less than others, and the medium-ability students are free to participate fully as teacher, collaborator, or learner.

Gender composition has also been shown to have a significant impact on group interaction and individual learning. Webb (1984) studied interaction and achievement patterns among middle school students learning mathematics in groups. She found that although boys and

[3]High-quality discussions are those that contain complete, accurate, elaborated explanations.

girls were equal in initial ability, boys learned more. Girls responded to requests for help within the group more frequently than boys did; this was true whether the help seekers were male or female. Boys typically responded only to requests for help from other males. Gender was more important than ability in choosing from whom to ask help: lower-ability boys were more frequently asked for help than were higher-ability girls. In groups with one girl and three boys, the female was often ignored when help was sought and when it was given. In groups with an equal number of boys and girls, both interaction and achievement were the same for boys and girls. This research was conducted with relatively high-achieving white students. A similar study, however, with mostly low-achieving African American students found no significant differences between boys and girls on type of interaction or achievement, and no relationship between group gender composition and learning (Webb & Kenderski, 1985). These studies, along with observational research in elementary school classrooms by Grant (1986), may suggest that relationships between gender, group interaction, and learning differ among ethnic groups.

The implication of these findings for forming PBL work groups is that group composition and gender (in addition to other factors such as type of task, size of group, group cohesiveness, teacher experience, class and group norms, etc.) influence group interaction and individual learning, and there is no simple, direct way to apply research findings to group constitution. Research findings can, however, provide things to consider when forming groups. In the end, we agree with Wilkinson (1986) that teachers should consider multiple factors, and rely on judgment and experience—rather than empirically derived rules—when forming PBL groups.

Although content learning is a central goal in PBL, it is not the only goal. Project Based Learning requires a variety of student skills and capabilities, and it should be noted that the more complex the project, the greater number of distinct skills and abilities students will need to exercise. PBL provides opportunities to develop metacognitive, self-management, leadership, and communication skills, as well as to master academic content, and groups will function more effectively if some of their members are "higher-achievers" in these areas to ensure each group has the necessary resources to complete the project. Expert PBL teachers adapt the grouping criteria according to the nature of the tasks to be completed (cf. Mergendoller & Thomas, n.d.; McCaslin & Good, 1996):

> You have to think about the purpose of forming groups. We always controlled the group characteristics. We had both [high school] juniors and seniors. We wanted seniors (who were experienced with Projects) mixed in with juniors so they could teach them the ropes. Other teachers have each student pick another student to form a pair, and the teachers put different pairs together into four person groups. This way, both teachers and kids have control over how the groups are formed.
>
> One type of grouping strategy—say, kids who are friends and want to work with each other—works well on a task that requires a great deal of time out of school. A different type of group is necessary if the task is complex and requires a diverse set of skills... Think about the skills necessary to accomplish the task at hand when forming a group.
>
> We formed groups into expert teams who investigated different areas and became experts. Then we formed new teams that had one member from each of the expert teams. That way, each new team had an expert in each of the areas originally investigated. (pp. 21–22)

Since the composition of groups has implications for the management of successful projects, group membership should be considered carefully and changed if necessary.

STAGE 1: PROJECT LAUNCH

Launching a successful project is dependent upon several management activities. It is important to engage students' interest in and encourage students' motivation to carry out the project. In addition, it is essential that all students share (with the teacher) common expectations for acceptable behavior and anticipated learning outcomes. For the project to unroll productively, the entire class—not just those students who will take initial project leadership positions—must understand the project timeline, required individual and group tasks, and how these tasks will be graded. Things may (and probably will) change as the project unrolls, but it is from this initial orientation that students build a map for further activities. Initial student misconceptions about the nature of the Driving Question they are addressing or the level of performance they are expected to demonstrate will result in wasted time and effort and may compromise the learning and skill outcomes students attain.

Stimulate Student Interest, Enthusiasm, and Concern

Students who are "grabbed" by a project are more likely to work productively to complete it. There is no way to guarantee student motivation, but research demonstrates that teachers who stress learning rather than performance goals, minimize the prominence of grades and the comparative evaluation of students, design projects that are challenging, but which students believe they are competent to complete, and find to be novel, interesting and valuable maximize student cognitive engagement and motivation (Blumenfeld et al., 1991; Blumenfeld et al., 1992; Crooks, 1988; Schank & Cleary, 1995).

In addition, expert PBL teachers often employ attention-getting techniques to introduce projects. Instead of handing out pieces of paper with what appears to students as one more assignment, these teachers bring in provocative guest speakers, show videos, conduct field trips, introduce real or simulated documents and letters (e.g., a letter from the President or the mayor asking for help), or conduct engaging discussions around the Big Idea or Driving Question. These techniques help make the project a special learning opportunity and increases its value to students.

Establish High Expectations

Students need to have an understanding and vision of the depth of learning and quality of academic performance expected of them. One hoped for outcome of PBL is the internalization of high standards and expectations that will then carry over to real-world projects completed on the job and in the community. To make this happen, student projects should demonstrate, as far as it is possible, the effort and production quality expected outside the school. This not only increases the professionalism of the product, it increases learning and helps students to develop the metacognitive skills necessary to monitor and evaluate their own work (Shepard, 1996). Glasgow (1997) argues:

> Setting high standards for presentation and communication of results or the production of work products is important. Whatever is expected in the real world should begin to define the standard for outcomes. . . . Artists treat their work differently from how secondary art students do. Fingerprints and folded, wrinkled work are not usually seen in a professional artist's studio. . . . Standards for excellence exist within every profession. (p. 63)

There are several ways teachers can build students' understanding of high quality learning and performance. Elizabeth Cohen and her colleagues (Cohen, Lotan, Scarloss, Schultz, &

Abram, 2002) gave sixth-grade student work groups specific guidelines describing exemplary group products and relating the content of the unit to the final product. They found that groups that used evaluation criteria were more self-critical, more task-focused, had better quality group products, and wrote better essays about the content they were learning. Further analysis suggested that:

> when groups were more focused on the content of the product, they created a better group product, which assisted their understanding and grasp of academic content.... In addition, the more the group evaluated their product and performance, the higher their essay scores. (Cohen et al. 2002)

Expert PBL teachers work with students to create a "culture of critique" and build a common understanding of the qualities defining excellent work. Students develop this vision by examining examples of excellent work completed by previous students, by critiquing the work of other students, and by submitting their own work for public critique. This stimulates students to examine their own work and attempt to improve it. Berger (2003) writes:

> In the first week of school I show videotapes of former students presenting to the panel [of evaluators] and I remind students that at the end of the year it will be they who are presenting. They have models in their mind. They spend the entire year building a strong portfolio and practicing presenting it. They present Projects to their classmates, to their parents, to the school as a whole, and to classroom guests. They get feedback and critique all year long. Two weeks before the presentations we again view videotapes and put those models in our minds. We look over rubrics of what constitutes a strong presentation. We review portfolios and begin selecting Projects. We put together presentation display boards and each student has a partner to support and critique through rehearsal. Students rehearse in front of peers, family, teachers, and sometimes in front of the video camera. We view rehearsals on video so students can watch themselves and learn. By the time each student walks into that conference room, their work in hand and their partner beside them as an assistant, they are on draft ten or maybe twenty. (pp. 91–92)

Finally, professional and appropriate community members can contribute to the classroom culture of critique. They can visit the classroom, show examples of their own work, and critique student work, much as symphony musicians give "master classes."

Clarify Rules, Procedures, Products, Timeline, and Grading Practices

There is a general finding in the classroom management literature that the establishment and enforcement of clear expectations for behavior are at the heart of a well-run classroom (Emmer, 1984; Emmer, Sanford, Evertson, Clements, & Martin, 1981; Evertson, Emmer, Clements, Sanford, Worsham & Williams, 1981; Marzano & Marzano, 2003), and this is true whether the class is doing Project Based Learning or recitation. Because PBL strives to create a collegial learning environment where teachers serve as senior colleagues and mentors, students should be included in the process of making classroom rules. This not only shows respect for students as junior colleagues, it makes it more likely that students will monitor and enforce the rules decided upon (Brooks & Brooks, 1993; Kohn, 1996; Schaps, Battistich & Solomon, 2004).

Rule setting is best addressed as a collaborative, problem-solving process that considers the types of activities necessary for project completion. Typically these include discussing plans and things newly learned within groups, building artifacts and displays, using the telephone or email to conduct interviews or identify resources, leaving the classroom to do research in the library or computer lab, and using classroom computers and other educational technology. Many of these activities require students to move around the classroom, form and reform groups, talk in a conversational voice, and wield tools or art supplies. The teacher and students should decide jointly the rules and procedures necessary to enable these potentially noisy and disruptive activities to be conducted without compromising students' abilities to work together, hear each other, and concentrate on the tasks at hand. They should jointly decide how rule violations (e.g., not returning from the library, talking too loudly, etc.) will be dealt with, and what sanctions should accompany rule violations.

Although plans almost inevitably change during a complex project, teachers should clarify with students at the outset of the project the expected benchmarks, tasks, products, and activities students will be held responsible for completing. Some of these may be individual tasks, whereas others are to be completed by a group. Tasks may be assigned by the teacher or volunteered for by groups or individuals. Within each project group, members generally divide up the tasks that must be completed. Typically, this involves a division of labor, where specific pieces of necessary information are the responsibility of different group members who conduct research on their own, and pool their findings with the remaining group members. Other times, when there are wide disparities in language or academic ability, multiple students are assigned the same research tasks. In PBL, students take responsibility for managing themselves and completing project tasks. They are not "being taught"; they are, with the teachers' help, teaching themselves. Students must understand and accept responsibility for the essential tasks of research, writing, surveying, interviewing, building, etc. on which project completion rests.

PBL provides opportunities for students to acquire the self-management skills that are useful throughout a lifetime. To develop and produce these skills, students must set or be given specific benchmarks to be achieved. By monitoring their progress toward these goals, and adjusting effort as necessary, students become more adept at managing time and planning activities. (Costa & Kallick, 2004; Marzano et al., 2001; Wiggins, 1998). One expert PBL teacher described this process. (Mergendoller & Thomas, n.d.):

> Groups have folders recording what they have to do, and what they accomplish. When I meet with groups, we go over the work in their folders, check off what they accomplished against what they said they were going to do, and assess the quality of the work they completed. (p. 24)

Communicating how students will be graded, and the criteria for different grades is another issue that should be addressed while laying the groundwork for PBL activity. Here, voluminous research on groups suggests that academic learning is most effective when groups are recognized or rewarded according to the individual learning of their members (Ellis & Fouts, 1993; Mergendoller & Packer, 1989; Newmann & Thompson, 1987; Slavin, 1983, 1995). Operationally, this means that a group grade should be computed from individual assessments rather than the other way around. If a single grade is given to a solution or artifact produced by a group of students, and each student in the group is assigned this grade, "social loafing," where some members take advantage of others' work and contribute none of their own, is likely to occur (McWhaw, Schnackenberg, Sclater, & Abrami, 2003). Social loafing theory suggests there are three reasons for low group productivity. First, group members believe the group product is unimportant, because their own contributions are unnoticed and unrewarded. Second, group members do not believe there is a relationship between their performance and group outcome. This occurs when members either think the expected performance unattainable or their own contributions are unnecessary. Finally, social loafing occurs when group members believe the physical or psychological demands required from the group are unjustifiable. Individuals work hard when they perceive their contributions to be indispensable and loaf when they see their efforts dispensable (Shepperd, 1993; Shepperd & Taylor, 1999).

Although the above guideline—group goals and individual accountability—provides a place to start in designing a problem or project grading system, the grading procedures most teachers use in the classroom tend to be much more complex. For example (Mergendoller & Thomas, n.d.):

> I use a variety of grading strategies. Everyone gets an individual grade, as well as a group grade. Every student grades every other student in the group. Written and other "academic" work is graded individually along the way using rubrics—it's not considered part of the project grade. The project grade focuses on SCANS skills, self- and group management, organization, and promptness, as well as the final presentation. The grade encourages students to look at the process of how they have worked together and what has been accomplished. (p. 31)

> You don't give up testing, essays, or quizzes when you do projects. The important question is, what kind of information will they give you? I use quizzes, for example, to find out if kids understand things so I can push on. Kids will always need to write essays. Use multiple measures to look for both content and process outcomes. When you give students a description of the project, explain what will be an individual assignment (and graded individually), and what will be a group assignment (with each person in the group receiving the same grade). Also, have students grade themselves and other members of the team. Have the audience at an exhibition grade student work. (p. 31)

Grades should be based upon the learning goals established by the teacher. At the beginning of the school year, teachers might want to emphasize the process of solving a problem, and put less emphasis on mastering the content. Later in the semester, equal weight might be placed on process and content. Whatever the grading strategy, emphasis or criteria, students should know at the beginning of a project how their products will be assessed, and how this will translate into a grade.

STAGE 2: GUIDED INQUIRY AND PRODUCT CREATION

Student inquiry, guided by the teacher, is at the core of Project Based Learning. Necessary management activities merge with instruction as the teacher works with groups and individuals to keep inquiry moving productively. Teacher guidance, however, should be subtle and judiciously applied. Heavy-handed intervention can undermine students' attempts to steer their own learning. On the other hand, leaving students to their own devices can result in fruitless perseveration on tasks of questionable utility and frustration with the inquiry process. The following pervasive management activities assist the teacher in being an effective "guide on the side."

Facilitate Resource Use

Expert PBL teachers find that engagement is encouraged and discipline problems diminished when resources are delivered in a "just-in-time" manner that enables students to continue their work flow, as opposed to waiting for resources. During project planning (Stage 0), material, knowledge-based, and human resources are identified. It is now important that students know what resources are available, where they can be found, and how to use them. This is not as straightforward as it sounds, as ill-structured problems often require unanticipated resources. A key part of managing PBL is to help students anticipate and identify their resource needs as the project proceeds, and determine on their own where these resources can be found.

Help Students Define Tasks and Assess Progress

With an extended, complex, multiweek project, students generally need continuing help to frame the project and prioritize the tasks that must be completed. There are a number of ways this can be done. Whole-class discussions during which individual groups are required to describe to the other groups what they have completed and what they plan to do next imposes a subtle force on every group to plan and prioritize so they won't be embarrassed when they report to the rest of the class. These discussions can also provide help and assistance to groups that are unsure of where to go next. Individual conferences between the teacher and group members provide an opportunity to question groups about tasks completed and planned.

Another way to help groups define the inquiry tasks they need to pursue is to conduct a Knowledge Inventory (Maxwell, Mergendoller & Bellisimo, 2004). This can be done with the whole class or with individual groups. The leader of this exercise (usually the teacher) asks the question, "What do we know about the problem you are addressing?" Students generate a list of things known about the problem and the leader records their statements on butcher paper. Once what is known is described, the leader asks, "What do we need to know?" Students then generate a list of knowledge that must be attained before the project can be completed. Finally, the leader then asks students to prioritize the needed knowledge, and identify resources necessary to find these things out.

In addition to helping students and groups strategize about next steps, it is important for teachers to ensure that students receive useful information about the quality of their work. Black and Wiliam (1998) have shown that task-focused formative assessment increases student learning. This is especially the case when students can assess their own work and formulate their own feedback and suggestions for improvement. "Assessment conversations," where the student and the teacher compare student work against evaluation criteria established at the beginning of the project, can both build students' understanding of evaluative criteria and develop their ability to critique their own work and learning. Such metacognitive skills free students from depending on others for the information they need to deepen their learning and improve their work (Duschl & Gitomer, 1997, in Shepard, 1996).

Students learn to use a common strategy to critique each other's work, as suggested by Berger (2003):

- *Be Kind.* It's essential that the critique environment feel safe, and the class and I are vigilant to guard against any hurtful comments. This includes sarcasm.
- *Be Specific.* No comments such as *It's good* or *I like it*; these just waste our time.
- *Be Helpful.* The goal is to help the individual and the class, not for the critic to be heard. Echoing the thoughts of others or cleverly pointing out details that are not significant to improving the work also waste our time. (p. 93)

These rules are sacrosanct; Berger tolerates no violations. He also provides guidelines that students generally follow, but may be abandoned in the "heat of a good critique":

- Begin with the author/designer of the work explaining her ideas and goal, and explaining what particular aspects of the work she is seeking help with.
- Critique the work, not the person.
- Begin the critique comments with something positive about the work and then move on to constructive criticism.
- Use *I statements* when possible: "I'm confused by this," rather than "This makes no sense."

- Use a question format when possible: "I'm curious why you chose to begin with this . . . ?" or "Have you considered including . . . ?" (p. 94)

This classroom practice stacks up nicely with research on effective feedback which indicates that feedback is most effective when it: (a) focuses students' attention on their progress, (b) occurs while it is still clearly relevant and the student has opportunities to demonstrate what they have learned from the feedback, and (c) is specific and related to need. Praise should be used sparingly and should be task specific. (Black & Wiliam, 1998; Crooks, 1988).

By focusing analysis and reflection on student learning achievements and lacuna, students are more able to understand, accept and use the evaluation criteria established for the project as a guide for future activity. In addition, they are more interested in receiving substantive feedback, and are more willing to be held to higher standards "because the criteria are clear and [perceived as] reasonable" (Klenowski, 1995, in Shepard, 1996). Interestingly, the development of self-assessment skills has been shown to be especially effective in increasing the learning and performance of lower-achieving students (Fredericksen & White, 1997, in Shepard, 1996).

Pervasive management also entails an evaluation of students' skills as group and classroom members. This is generally accomplished by using evaluation tools that focus on the process of working together. These can include goal sheets, task lists, peer-rating systems, and feedback forms (e.g., Buck Institute for Education, 2003; DeLisle, 1997; Lambros, 2002, 2004).

Scaffold Learning and Working

PBL seeks to encourage students to think critically, apply metacognitive strategies, and develop a deep understanding of facts, concepts, and principles. Most students, however, need guidance from the teacher if these capabilities are to be nurtured, as they do not automatically apply sophisticated learning strategies to complex tasks, even if they are competent in the use of these strategies (Blumenfeld et. al., 1991). It is the teacher's job to support and encourage student thinking as they work on projects, and challenge them to go beyond obvious answers. Scaffolds—a temporary, adjustable support for student learning (Wood, Bruner & Ross, 1976)—can be used by teachers to help students think and learn in ways that would not be possible without the scaffold. These scaffolds can be verbal, textual, or technological.

Giving feedback is an critical part of scaffolding student thought (Hogan & Pressley, 1997, in Shepard 1996). Feedback is most effective when it is focused on task accomplishment and the mastery of learning goals, rather than on the person; occurs immediately after a task is completed; and is referenced to a criterion (or rubric) with which the student is familiar (Marzano et al., 2001; National Research Council, 2001; Shepard, 1996). Research on effective tutoring also provides some guidance for scaffolding student thinking. Highly successful tutors ignore inconsequential errors and give students the chance to recognize their own errors. If this does not occur, the tutor then intervenes with a direct question that prompts the student to self-correct (Lepper, Drake, & O'Donnell-Johnson, 1997; Shepard, 1996).

Howard Barrows (1992) has written a classic book on verbal scaffolding of students' thoughts in a problem based medical curriculum. He writes:

> The ability of the tutor to use facilitatory teaching skills during the small group learning process is the major determinant of the quality and the success of . . . 1) developing students' thinking or reasoning skills (problem solving, metacognition, critical thinking) as they learn, and 2) helping them to become independent, self-directed learners (learning to learn, learning management). p ii

Barrows (1992) describes how student independence, critical thinking, and self-directed learning is developed through "metacognitive modeling":

> The oral statements and challenges he [the teacher] makes should be those he would make to himself when deliberating over such a problem or situation as the one his students are working with. His questions will give them an awareness of what questions they should be asking themselves as they tackle the problem and an appreciation of what they will need to learn. In this way he does not give them information or indicate whether they are right or wrong in their thinking.... As this guidance is covert and the students are unaware that it is going on, they think that the thinking that went on in the group, the path they followed in their reasoning, and the learning issues they identified were solely of their own doing. This makes students feel as though they are responsible for their own learning, as they eventually must become. (p. 4, 5)

In talking with students and groups, finding the right line between too much and too little challenge is an art, not a science. If the teacher is too demanding in the questions posed, students may become discouraged. If not demanding enough, opportunities for students to extend their learning may be missed. Barrows (1992) admonishes a teacher to be keenly aware of students' level of frustration and understanding. Challenges can be increased or moderated:

> [The teacher] can ask, "Why?" "What do you mean?" "What is the evidence?" "Are their other explanations?" "Have you thought of everything that needs to be considered?" "What's the meaning of that?" to crank up tension and interest. To decrease the challenge, he can ask questions such as "Should we just tackle a piece of this problem (or task)?" "Let's revise our objectives and tackle those that are most important in this task." "Maybe we ought to stop here and read some resources or go talk to an expert?" "Would it be better to get the big picture now and fill in the details later" etc. (p. 11)

Torp and Sage (2002) recommend that teachers keep five activities in mind as they scaffold students' thinking and understanding: (1) diagnosing students' learning needs, (2) helping students build intellectual bridges from their current understanding to more complete and complex understanding, (3) encouraging student progress, (4) questioning student thinking, and (5) modeling the inquiry process. Lambros (2004) lists a number of open-ended questions to support and extend student thinking, including:

- What would be helpful to know now?
- How do you know that?
- What does this have to do with the project?
- Where are you stuck?
- Say more about what you are thinking about?
- Where can you find the information you need?
- Summarize where you are right now. (p. 113)

Scaffolds can also be textual objects. Meloth and Deering (1994) conducted a study in which they established two conditions for group work. One group of fifth-graders were given "think sheets" that directed them to reflect on and analyze what they were learning. A comparison group of fifth graders were also given "think sheets," but these were not designed to encourage metacognitive reflection. Students in the groups with the metacognitively oriented "think sheets" produced more explanations and task-related questions during group discussions, and learned more academic content.

A key issue in designing textual scaffolds is to ensure that they support and expand, rather than replace or merely record, student thinking. Often, this depends upon the way textual scaffolds are used. Consider concept (or semantic) maps, a technique widely used in science, language arts, and social studies to represent knowledge learned (Novak & Gowan, 1984). During a project, a teacher might ask students to "map" what they had learned in the hopes of solidifying understanding. But the relationships among concepts and information on cognitive maps can be valid or inaccurate. Hierarchies of concepts may be presented that do not, in actuality, exist. Unrelated concepts may be connected. Essential facts or concepts may be omitted. Beyond such factual errors, research has demonstrated that content maps drawn by novices and experts are different (Baxter & Glaser, 1998; Chi, Glaser, & Rees, 1982). Novices focus on superficialities, whereas experts emphasize concepts and their relationship. The act of drawing a concept map, by itself, is not an effective way to scaffold student thought. However, comparing and discussing individual (or group) maps among students, and with the teacher, can provide an opportunity to deepen understanding, and give the teacher a chance to assess, and respond to, misconceptions.

Computer technology can also provide an effective scaffold for student learning. Concepts can be represented in multiple, simultaneous modalities as video, animation, and text. Students can manipulate and construct their own representations through simulations and microworlds (diSessa, 1982; White & Horowitz, 1987), manipulate data, and ask "What if?" questions (Blumenfeld et al., 1991). Computer programs can structure the way students interact with each other and with each other's thinking (Brunner, Hawkins, Mann, & Moeller, 1990; Hawkins & Pea, 1987; Linn, Songer, Lewis, & Stern, 1991; Scardamalia, Bereiter, McLean, Swallow, & Woodruff, 1989; Solloway, 1991).

The concept of scaffolding—providing assistance necessary for students to go beyond their current competencies—can also be applied to the process of working on a Project. Learning in a collaborative, group environment requires at least three sets of skills: (1) social skills including active listening, sharing, and supporting other group members, (2) explaining skills which help other group members understand the content under study, and (3) leadership skills including planning, showing initiative, keeping track of timelines, and orchestrating activity and discussion (Emmer, Evertson, & Worsham, 2003). Groups with severe deficiencies in one of these areas will have difficulty in PBL classrooms (Moeller, 2005). Effective PBL teachers assess the readiness of their students to work in groups and provide instruction, practice, and remediation of deficient group process skills. (Johnson & Johnson, 1999; Kagan, 1992; Soloman, Davidson & Soloman, 1993). This can be done by modeling the skill for the class, discussing what the skill looks like and how it is carried out, providing supervised practice in using the skill, and giving students direct feed back on how well they are using the skill with suggestions for further improvement. Once the skill has been learned, its practice should be made a regular part of classroom life, and norms established to support its use.

When groups or individuals fail to identify and confront dysfunctional behavior, or when the group does not seem to be able to address unproductive behavior by themselves, teachers can hold a problem-solving conference to identify the problem and fashion a workable solution, which may include training students to use specific participation skills (Emmer et al., 2003).

Research has documented differential participation rates associated with ethnic background and gender (Estrada Duek, 2000; Webb & Palincsar, 1996), and teachers should pay attention to who talks, participates, and makes decisions in PBL groups. Should some group members be ignored by others, left out of the learning process, or shunted off to nonacademic tasks ("coloring the poster" or "assembling the model"), teacher intervention may be called for.[4]

[4]See C. W. Anderson, J. D. Holland, A. M. Palincsar (1997), "Canonical and Sociocultural Approaches to Research and Reform in Science Education: The Story of Juan and His Group," for a vivid portrayal of one group's abandonment of one of its members.

Learning, however, is an individual phenomenon, and cannot be assumed to be directly related to group participation. Rather than assuming students are not learning if they are not participating, confer with the individual and assess whether lack of participation reflects knowledge deficiencies and whether it is hindering the group's work as a whole.

Cultivate Presentation Skills

Most projects conclude with the presentation of products, and the new knowledge they exemplify, to an external audience. These help motivate and solidify learning and provide opportunities for assessment and reflection. High quality presentations require rehearsal, critique, and revision, and it is a pervasive management task to ensure that such critiques occur and students revise their presentations accordingly. Practice by itself is not enough; students must receive specific information about how they performed and how their performance can be made better (Berger, 2003; Crooks, 1988; Fuchs & Fuchs, 1986; Natriello, 1987; National Research Council, 2001). Such critique sessions underscore high expectations for student performance.

STAGE 3: PROJECT CONCLUSION

The final management tasks in PBL revolve around the presentation and assessment of what has been learned in completing the project, and consideration of changes that can improve learning and performance in the future.

Stage Exhibition

Projects are typically designed so that students communicate what they have learned to classmates, students outside the classroom, or audiences outside of school through displays, exhibitions of work, and oral presentations. There is considerable work involved in organizing and publicizing such an exhibition to an external audience, and planning should begin while the project is underway, not when it is completed. Classroom presentations also require careful thought, as presentations by multiple groups over consecutive days are wearing on the audience, especially if all groups have worked to resolve the same Driving Question. It is better to schedule presentations over several weeks, and to minimize redundant parts of presentations.

Conduct Summative Assessment

Students and teachers have been assessing their work throughout the project, and (hopefully) modifying their goals and actions as a result of these formative assessments. The close of a project is the time to evaluate what students have learned throughout the course of the project. In addition to the exhibition, this is often done by assessing students' performance (e.g., a "performance assessment") on a task "that requires a student to create an answer or a product that demonstrates his or her knowledge and skills" (Office of Technology Assessment, 1992). Following Hambleton (1996), we summarize the characteristics of performance assessments. Such assessments:

- Assess what students know *and* can do, with an emphasis on "doing."
- Use direct methods of assessment such as writing samples to assess writing or oral presentations to assess speaking skills.
- Have a high degree of realism.

- May involve activities: (a) for which there is no correct answer, (b) that assess groups rather than individuals, (c) continue over a period of time, and (d) include self-evaluation.
- Are likely to use open-ended tasks aimed at assessing higher level cognitive skills.

The logic of such assessments is that it is important to evaluate what students can actually do (e.g., solve a problem, give a speech), instead of a proxy for such abilities (e.g., know the steps of problem solving, know the components of a good speech). Because performance assessment is generally "focused on students' ability to apply knowledge in ill-defined, ambiguous contexts that demand judgment," (p. 191) they are well-suited to the goals of Project Based Learning (Reeves & Okey, 1996), and reflect a constructivist learning orientation (National Research Council, 2001). Although questions have been raised about the reliability of performance assessments for large-scale testing (Hambleton, 1996), classroom use of this assessment strategy for PBL is widespread.

Like formative assessment, summative assessment is generally more powerful if it includes self- and peer assessment, in addition to teacher assessment, as this gives students additional opportunities to hone their assessment skills. It is also useful to use multiple assessment methods. Rubrics (originally given to students during the Project Launch) can be used to assess performance in planning, building, writing, speaking, group work, and other areas. Traditional tests and essays can provide an indication of content knowledge gained. Presentations can demonstrate skills mastered and self-knowledge gained.

Reflect on Project Learning and Process

The relationship between metacognitive reflection, retention, and transfer has been well documented (Bransford, Brown, & Cocking, 2000), and a reflection session can transform student experience into retained knowledge. At the end of a project, expert PBL teachers orchestrate a discussion of what students have learned about themselves as workers and collaborative problem-solvers, and what they have learned about the subject matter content at the heart of the project. For example (Mergendoller & Thomas, n.d.);

> I show students good models of reflection that other kids have done. Once they know what quality reflection looks like, I ask them to reflect on their own work. (p. 34)

> Students always ask: is this going to be on the test? Or how many points is it worth. Post project reflection is a way to move the focus of discussion to "Here's an end product. Are you proud of it? Did it do what you set out to do? How could it be made better? How could project activities have supported your work better?" Class reflection also provides feedback for the teacher. Maybe we should have talked about something earlier instead of waiting until the last week. Kids are going to do projects their whole life. They need a chance to think about what they've done and how they can do it better. (p. 34)

Reflection time also gives teachers the opportunity to examine their own contributions to the PBL process, and make notes about changes needed to improve future project implementations. At the conclusion of a project, expert PBL teachers consider the concrete acts of PBL implementation (Did students have enough time? What additional resources were needed?), content learned (Were the concepts and relationships too complex? Too elementary? Was there allied content that should have been included? Excluded?), instructional support (Did the scaffolds work as intended? Are there additional scaffolds or content resources that should be included?), and the social process of collaborative work (Where did groups have trouble working together? Why? Would additional preparation have alleviated this?).

NEEDED RESEARCH

As the lack of PBL-specific citations in this chapter indicate, there is a great deal that needs to be learned about the management of Project Based Learning. And because PBL management is so fully intertwined with PBL instruction, research needs to focus on management and instruction as a whole, rather than considering these separate teaching functions.

We need to know more about how expert PBL teachers create and manage projects, and the leverage points that make a difference between project success and failure. We need to know more about the management and modification of project based instructional strategies with diverse students. We need to learn more about the ways technology can add value and extend learning in PBL. We need to see if we can learn ways of managing projects more effectively from industry. Finally, we need to understand better how schools providing a supportive environment for PBL can be established and maintained.

Enacting PBL

We have few accounts of how expert PBL teachers create and manage projects. Qualitative research is needed to portray and understand excellent PBL teaching. Comparative studies of projects that "work" and those that "fall apart" can identify the key leverage points that expert teachers use to make projects effective. Not all topics lend themselves to PBL, and it would be helpful to understand better the project topics and content areas that are more—and less—easily implemented, and which kinds of project designs are suited to different types of topics.

Managing PBL With Diverse Learners

Although PBL is often considered the instructional method of choice for low achievers, data supporting this claim is sparse (Mergendoller, Maxwell, & Bellisimo, 2000, 2002; Ravitz, & Mergendoller, 2005). We need to know more about the impact of PBL on different types of learners and the modifications and accommodations that need to be made (if any) for PBL to be most effective with English language learners, and students of varying ability levels. Lou et al., (1998), for example, found that small group learning was most effective when teachers modified curriculum and instruction to meet the needs of students in specific groups rather than using the same instructional approach and materials in all groups. What modifications and variations in pervasive PBL management can enhance knowledge development and skill building with different types of learners? What is the relationship between individual differences and learning outcomes? The project stages we have used to organize this chapter (Table 22.2) may be useful in focusing observation on specific aspects of project implementation.

Effective Technology Use

Many projects employ technology for telecommunications, online research, record keeping, or to extend students reasoning and problem solving (Becker & Ravitz, 1999; Intel, 2004; Jonassen, Coir & Yuch 1998; Schank & Cleary, 1995). Although research on classroom technology is proliferating, we still don't fully understand how technology is best integrated and used to extend student learning and self-management, or how it is best integrated into projects and used to manage them more effectively. Technology can be the focus of project activities (e.g., telecommunications projects) , or it is can provide scaffolds like Project Portfolio (Loh et al., 1998). Information technology can be used to keep track of project work, feedback forms for mentors or peers, or formative assessment of learners (Ravitz, 2001). A key research question is: To what extent and under what conditions do these tools increase student learning in PBL, or do they constitute a distraction, as suggested by Oppenheimer (2004). Great projects do not require technology, but technology can make a great project even more effective.

Comparing Project Management Techniques

Project management is ubiquitous among business operations, and has been discussed extensively (e.g., Greer, 2001; Wysocki, 2004). Although the environments of the school and the firm are substantially different, it would be worthwhile to study project management texts and evaluate whether effective project management methodologies and procedures in business can improve pervasive project management in schools.

School Context

Although projects can be completed in a variety of environments, it is easier to implement a successful project within a school context that values and supports PBL. Longer class periods, flexibility in scheduling, a culture of inquiry, instructional understanding and leadership from the principal, like-minded colleagues, and school-wide expectations for student performance all contribute to successful project enactment. We need to learn more about how project-friendly environments are created and maintained. Newly established schools can set their own schedule and hire staff who embrace PBL, but already constituted traditional schools don't have this luxury. If these schools are to change, the change will have to come from within. What can be learned from schools that are trying to restructure themselves and from schools that have changed their instructional orientation? What are the direct and indirect linkages between PBL and school context? How do they influence each other? By addressing such questions we can gain important knowledge about the creation of school environments that contribute to the effectiveness of Project Based Learning.

CONCLUSION

When PBL is successful, students learn to manage themselves and work effectively with their peers. They understand the questions the project is addressing, the tasks that must be accomplished, and the standards by which their work will be assessed. This does not occur without pervasive project management by the teacher. From project conception through post-project reflection, a variety of management activities are necessary for a successful project. Often indistinguishable from instruction, these activities steer students around dead ends and scaffold their learning. They encompass planning the project, launching the project, guiding student inquiry and product creation, concluding the project with an exhibition, assessing the project and finally, reflecting on what has been learned and what can be improved. Although students play an important role in carrying out many project management activities, it is the teacher who must ensure that students understand and fulfill their management responsibilities. It is also the teacher who, through example, discussion and feedback, establishes classroom expectations for high quality student work. A successful project brings students and teachers together as partners with the common goal of advancing student learning. Within this partnership, however, the teacher remains the senior partner chiefly responsible for pervasive project management.

ACKNOWLEDGMENT

The authors thank Sara Sage, Indiana University, South Bend, for her comments on an early version of this chapter.

REFERENCES

Anderson, C. W., Holland, J. D., & Palincsar, A. S. (1997). Canonical and sociocultural approaches to research and reform in science education: The story of Juan and his group. *Elementary School Journal, 97*(4), 359–383.

Anderson, J. R., & Roth, K. J. (1989). Teaching for meaningful and self-regulated learning of science. In J. Brophy (Ed.), *Teaching for meaningful and self-regulated learning*. Greenwich, CT: JAI Press.

Arends, R. I. (1997). *Classroom instruction and management* (1st ed.). New York: McGraw-Hill.

Arter, J., & McTighe, J. (2001). *Scoring Rubrics in the classroom: Using performance criteria for assessing and improving student performance* (1st ed.). Thousand Oaks, CA: Corwin Press.

Atwood, R. (1983). *The interacting effects of task form and activity structure on students' task involvement and teacher evaluations*. Paper presented at the annual meeting of the American Educational Research Association, Montreal, QUE.

Barrows, H. S. (1992). *The tutorial process* (Rev. ed.). Springfield: Southern Ilinois University School of Medicine.

Barrows, H. S. (2000). *Problem-based learning applied to medical education*. Springfield: Southern Illinois University School of Medicine.

Barrows, H. S., & Tamblin, R. M. (1980). *Problem based learning*. New York: Springer.

Baxter, G. P., & Glaser, R. (1998). Investigating the cognitive complexity of science assessments. *Educational Measurement: Issues and Practices, 17*(3), 37–45.

Becker, H., & Ravitz, J. (1999). The influence of computer and internet use on teachers' pedagogical practices and perceptions. *Journal of Research on Computing in Education, 31*(4), 356–384.

Bereiter, C., & Scardamalia, M. (1989). Intentional learning as a goal of instruction. In L. B. Resnick (Ed.), *Knowing, learning, and instruction: Essays in honor of Robert Glaser* (pp. 361–392). Hillsdale, NJ: Lawrence Erlbaum Associates.

Berger, R. (2000). Water: A whole school expedition. In D. Udall & A. Mednick (Eds.), *Journeys through our classrooms* (pp. 115–125). Dubuque, IA: Kendall/Hunt.

Berger, R. (2003). *An ethic of excellence: Building a culture of craftsmanship with students* (1st ed.). Portsmouth, NH: Heinemann.

Black, P., & Wiliam, D. (1998). Assessment and classroom learning. *Assessment in Education: Principles, Policy and Practice, 5*(1), 7–74.

Block, K. J. (1997, Summer). Problem-based learning in medical education: Issues for health sciences libraries and librarians. *Katherine Sharp Review*, 5. Retrieved February 9, 2004, from http://www.lis.uiuc.edu/review/5/block.html

Blumenfeld, P. C., & Meece, J. L. (1988). Task factors, teacher behavior, students' involvement and use of learning strategies in science. *Elementary School Journal, 88*(3), 235–250.

Blumenfeld, P. C., Mergendoller, J. R., & Swarthout, D. W. (1987). Tasks as heuristics for understanding student learning and motivation. *Journal of Curriculum Studies, 19*(2), 135–148.

Blumenfeld, P. C., Puro, P., & Mergendoller, J. R. (1992). Translating motivation into thoughtfulness. In H. H. Marshall (Ed.), *Redefining student learning: Roots of educational change*. Norwood, NJ: Ablex.

Blumenfeld, P. C., Soloway, E., Marx, R. W., Krajcik, J. S., Guzdial, M., & Palincsar, A. (1991). Motivating project-based learning: Sustaining the doing, supporting the learning. *Educational Psychologist, 26*(3&4), 369–398.

Bolzan, N., & Heycox, K. (1997). Use of an issue-based approach in social work education. In D. Boud & G. Feletti (Eds.), *The challenge of problem-based learning* (2nd ed., pp. 194–202). London: Kogan Page.

Boud, D., & Feletti, G. (1997). Changing problem-based learning. Introduction to the second edition. In D. Boud & G. Feletti (Eds.), *The challenge of problem-based learning* (2nd ed., pp. 1–14). London: Kogan Page.

Bransford, J., Brown, A., & Cocking, R., Eds. (2000). *How people learn: Brain, mind, experience, and school*. Washington, DC: National Academy Press.

Bransford, J. D., Sherwood, R. D., Hasselbring, T. S., Kinzer, C. K., & Williams, S. M. (1990). Anchored instruction: Why we need it and how technology can help. In D. Nix & R. Sprio (Eds.), *Advances in computer-video technology, computers, cognition, and multimedia: Explorations in high technology* (pp. 115–141). Hillsdale, NJ: Lawrence Erlbaum Associates.

Bridges, E. M., & Hollinger, P. (1992). *Problem based learning for administrators*. Eugene, OR: ERIC Clearinghouse on Educational Management. (ERIC Document Reproduction Service No. ED347617)

Brooks, J. G., & Brooks, M. G. (1993). *The case for constructivist classrooms*. Alexandria, VA: Association for Supervision and Curriculum Development.

Brown, A. (1992). Design experiments: Theoretical and methodological challenges in creating complex interventions in classroom settings. *Journal of the Learning Sciences, 2*(2), 141–178.

Buck Institute for Education. (2003). *Project based learning handbook*. Novato, CA: Author.

Cawley, P. (1997). A problem-based module in mechanical engineering. In D. Boud & G. Feletti (Eds.), *The challenge of problem-based learning* (2nd ed., pp. 185–193). London: Kogan Page.

Chard, S. C. (1992). *The project approach: a practical guide for teachers*. Edmonton: University of Alberta Printing Services.

Chi, M. T. H., Glaser, R., & Rees, E. (1982). Expertise in problem solving. *Advances in the Psychology of Human Intelligence, 1*, 1–75.

Cognition and Technology Group at Vanderbilt [CTGV]. (1992). The Jasper Series as an example of anchored instruction: Theory, program description, and assessment data. *Educational Psychologist, 27*(3), 291–315.

Cognition and Technology Group at Vanderbilt [CTGV]. (1996). Looking at technology in context: A framework for understanding technology and education research. In D. C. Berliner & R. C. Calfee (Eds.), *Handbook of educational psychology* (pp. 807–840). New York: Macmillan.

Cohen, E. G. (1994). *Designing groupwork: Strategies for heterogeneous classrooms*. New York: Teachers College Press.

Cohen, E. G., & Lotan, R. A. (1990). Teacher as supervisor of core technology. *Theory Into Practice, 29*(2), 78–84.

Cohen, E. G., Lotan, R., Scarloss, B., Schultz, S. E., & Abram, P. (2002). *Assessment of group learning: The use of evaluation criteria*. Retrieved February 9, 2004, from http://www.tcrecord.org/PrintContent.asp?ContentID=10986 ID Number: 10986

Costa, A. L., & Kallick, B. (2004). *Assessment strategies for self-directed learning*. Thousand Oaks, CA: Corwin Press.

Creedy, D., & Alavi, C. (1997). Problem-based learning in an integrated nursing curriculum. In D. Boud & G. Feletti (Eds.), *The challenge of problem-based learning* (2nd ed., pp. 218–223). London: Kogan Page.

Crooks, T. J. (1988). The impact of classroom evaluation practices on students. *Review of Educational Research, 58*(4), 438–481.

Davidson, N. (1985). Small-group learning and teaching in mathematics: A selective review of the literature. In R. E. Slavin, S. Sharan, S. Kagan, R. Lazarowitz, C. Webb, & R. Schmuck (Eds.), *Learning to cooperate, cooperating to learn* (pp. 211–230). New York: Plenum Press.

Davis, M., Hawley, P., McMullan, B., & Spilka, G. (1997). *Design as a catalyst for learning*. Alexandria, VA: Association for Supervision and Curriculum Development.

Davis, R. B., & McKnight, C. (1976). Conceptual, heuristic, and S-algorithmic approaches in mathematics teaching. *Journal of Children's Mathematical Behavior, 1* (Suppl. 1), 271–286.

Delisle, R. (1997). *How to use problem-based learning in the classroom* (1st ed.). Alexandria, VA: Association for Supervision and Curriculum Development.

Dewey, J. (1929). *The quest for certainty: A study of the relation of knowledge and action*. New York: Minton, Balch.

Dewey, J. (1933). *How we think*. Chicago: Henry Regnery.

Diehl, W., Grobe, T., Lopez, H., & Cabral, C. (1999). *Project-based learning: A strategy for teaching and learning*. Boston: Center for Youth Development and Education, Corporation for Business, Work, and Learning.

diSessa, A. (1982). Unlearning Aristotelian physics: a study of knowledge-based learning. *Cognitive Science, 6*(1), 37–75.

Dodge, B., *The webquest page*. Retrieved December 1, 2004, from http://webquest.sdsu.edu/

Doyle, W. (1983). Academic work. *Review of Educational Research, 53*(2), 159–199.

Doyle, W. (1986). Classroom organization and management. In M. C. Wittrock (Ed.), *Handbook of research on teaching* (3rd ed., pp. 392–431). New York: Macmillan.

Duch, B. J., Groh, S. E., & Allen, D. E. (2001). *The power of problem-based learning: A practical "how to" for teaching undergraduate courses in any discipline* (1st ed.). Sterling, VA: Stylus.

Duffy, T. M., & Savery, J. R. (1994). Problem-based learning: An instructional model and its constructivist framework. In B. G. Wilson (Ed.), *Constructivist learning environments: Case studies in instructional design*. Englewood Cliffs, NJ: Educational Technology Publications.

Duschl, R. A., & Gitomer, D. H. (1997). Strategies and challenges to changing the focus of assessment and instruction in science classrooms. *Educational Assessment, 4*(1), 37–73.

Elder, J. (1998). *Stories in the land: A place-based environmental education anthology*. Great Barrington, MA: The Orion Society.

Ellis, A. K., & Fouts, J. T. (1993). *Research on educational innovations*. Princeton Junction, NJ: Eye on Education.

Emmer, E. T. (1984). *Classroom management: Research and implications* (R & D. Rep. 6178). Austin, TX: University of Texas Research and Development Center for Teacher Education.

Emmer, E. T., Evertson, C. M., & Worsham, M. E. (2003). *Classroom management for secondary teachers* (5th ed.). Boston: Allyn and Bacon.

Emmer, E. T., Sanford, J. P., Evertson, C. M., Clements, B. S., & Martin, J. (1981). *The classroom management improvement study: An experiment in elementary school classrooms.* (R & D Report No. 6050). Austin, TX: Research and Development Center for Teacher Education, University of Texas. (ERIC Document Reproduction Service No. ED226452).

Engel, C. E. (1997). Not just a method but a way of learning. In D. Boud & G. Feletti (Eds.), *The challenge of problem-based learning* (2nd ed., pp. 17–27). London: Kogan Page.

Estrada Duek, J. (2000). Whose group is it, anyway? Equity of student discourse in problem-based learning (PBL). In D. H. Evensen & C. E. Hmelo (Eds.), *Problem-based learning: A research perspective on learning interactions* (pp. 75–107). Mahwah, NJ: Lawrence Erlbaum Associates.

Evertson, C. M., Emmer, E. T., Clements, B. S., Sanford, J. P., Worsham, M. E., & Williams, E. L. (1981). *Organizing and managing the elementary school classroom.* Austin, TX: University of Texas, Research and Development Center for Teacher Education. (ERIC Document Reproduction Service No. ED223570)

Evertson, C. M., & Neal, K. W. (2005). *Looking into learning centered classrooms: Implications for classroom management.* (NEA Benchmarks for Best Practices Working Paper Series). Washington, DC: NEA Research Division.

Feldman, A., Konold, C., & Coulter, R. (2000). *Network science, a decade later: The internet and classroom learning.* Mahwah, NJ: Lawrence Erlbaum Associates.

Fleming, D. S. (2000). *A teacher's guide to project-based learning* Charleston, WV: AEL, Inc.

Fletcher, K. D. (1996). *The mini-society workbook: Everything you need to create a mini-society in your classroom.* Englewood, CO: Teacher Ideas Press.

Fredericksen, J. R., & White, B. Y. (1997, March), *Reflective assessment of students' research within an inquiry-based middle school science curriculum.* Paper presented at the annual meeting of the American Educational Research Association, Chicago.

Fuchs, L. S., & Fuchs, D. (1986). Effects of systematic formative evaluation: A meta-analysis. *Exceptional Children, 53*(3), 199–208.

Gilbert, A., & Foster, S. F. (1997). Experiences with problem-based learning in business and management. In D. Boud & G. Feletti (Eds.), *The challenge of problem-based learning* (2nd ed., pp. 244–252). London: Kogan Page.

Gillies, R. M., & Ashman, A. F. (2003). *Cooperative learning: The social and intellectual outcomes of learning in groups* (1st ed.). New York: Routledge Falmer.

Gillis, C. (1992). *The community as classroom: Integrating school and community through language arts.* Portsmouth, NH: Boynton/Cook.

Glasgow, N. A. (1997). *New curriculum for new times: A guide to student-centered, problem-based learning.* Thousand Oaks, CA: Corwin Press.

Grant, L. (1986, April). *Classroom peer relationships of minority and nonminority students.* Paper presented at the annual meeting of the American Educational Research Association, San Francisco.

Greeno, J. G. (Ed.). (1978). *Nature of problem-solving abilities* (Vol. 5). Hillsdale, NJ: Lawrence Erlbaum Associates.

Greer, M. (2001). *The project manager's partner: A step-by-step guide to project management,* (2nd ed.). Amherst, MA: Human Resource Development Press.

Hambleton, R. K. (1996). Advances in assessment models, methods, and practices. In D. C. Berliner & R. C. Calfee (Eds.), *Handbook of educational psychology* (pp. 899–925). New York: Macmillan.

Harris, J. (1994). People-to-people projects on the Internet. *The Computing Teacher, 21*(5), 48–52.

Hawkins, J., & Pea, R. D. (1987). Tools for bridging everyday and scientific thinking. *Journal for Research in Science Teaching, 24*(4), 291–307.

Hiebert, J., Carpenter, T. P., Fennema, E., Fuson, K., Human, P., Murray, H., Olivier, A., & Wearne, D. (1996). Problem solving as a basis for reform in curriculum and instruction: The case of mathematics. *Educational Researcher, 25*(4), 12–21.

Hogan, K., & Pressley, M. (1997). Scaffolding scientific competencies within classroom communities of inquiry. In K. Hogan & M. Pressley (Eds.), *Scaffolding student learning: Instructional approaches and issues* (pp. 74–107). Cambridge, MA: Brookline Books.

Intel. (2004).*Case studies: Prairie-Hills Elementary School District 144.* Retrieved December 1, 2004, from http://www.intel.com/education/casestudies/phesd_case_study.htm

Johnson, D. W., & Johnson, R. T. (1999). *Learning together and alone: Cooperative, competitive, and individualistic learning.* Boston: Allyn and Bacon.

Johnson, D. W., & Johnson, R. T. (2004). *Assessing students in groups: Promoting group responsibility and individual accountability* (1st ed.). Thousand Oaks, CA: Corwin Press.

Jonassen, D. H. (2000). Toward a design theory of problem solving. *Educational Technology Research and Development, 48*(4), 63–85.

Jonassen, D. H., Carr, C., & Yueh, H. P. (1998). Computers as mindtools for engaging learners in critical thinking. *Tech Trends, 43*(2), 24–32.

Kagan, S. (1992). *Cooperative learning.* San Juan Capistrano, CA: Kagan Cooperative Learning, Inc.

Kinsley, C. W., & McPherson, K. (1995). *Enriching the curriculum through service learning.* Alexandria, VA: Association for Supervision and Curriculum Development.

Kitchener, K. S. (1983). Cognition, metacognition, and epistemic cognition: A three-level model of cognitive processing. *Human Development, 26*, 222–232.

Klenowski, V. (1995). Student self-evaluation process in student-centered teaching and learning contexts of Australia and England. *Assessment in Education, 2*, 145–163.

Kohn, A. (1996). *Beyond discipline: From compliance to community*. Alexandria, VA: Association for Supervision and Curriculum Development.

Krajcik, J. S., Czerniak, C. M., & Berger, C. (1999). *Teaching children science: A project-based approach* (1st ed.). New York: McGraw-Hill.

Krajcik, J. S., Soloway, E., Blumenfeld, P., & Marx, R. W. (1998). Scaffolded technology tools to promote teaching and learning in science. *1998 ASCD Yearbook: Learning and Technology*. Alexandria, VA: Association for Supervision and Curriculum Development.

Lambros, A. (2002). *Problem-based learning in middle and high school classrooms: A teacher's guide to implementation* (1st ed.). Thousand Oaks, CA: Corwin Press.

Lambros, A. (2004). *Problem-based learning in K–8 classrooms: A teacher's guide to implementation*. Thousand Oaks, CA: Corwin Press.

Lepper, M. R., Drake, M. F., & O'Donnell-Johnson, T. (1997). Scaffolding techniques of expert human tutors. In K. Hogan & M. Pressley (Eds.), *Scaffolding student learning* (pp. 108–144). Cambridge, MA: Brookline Books.

Linn, M., Songer, N. B., Lewis, E. L., & Stern, J. (1991). Using technology to teach thermodynamics: Achieving integrated understanding. In D. L. Ferguson (Ed.), *Advanced technologies in the teaching of mathematics and science*. Berlin: Springer.

Loh, B., Radinsky, J., Russell, E., Gomez, L. M., Reiser, B. J., & Edelson, D. C. (1998). The progress portfolio: Designing reflective tools for a classroom context. In *Proceedings of CHI 98* (pp. 627–634). Reading, MA: Addison-Wesley.

Lou, Y., Abrami, P. C., Spence, J. C., Paulsen, C., Chambers, B., & d'Apollonia, S. (1996). Within-class grouping: A meta-anlysis. *Review of Educational Research, 66*(4), 423–458.

Lovie-Kitchin, J. (1997). Problem-based learning in optometry. In D. Boud & G. Feletti (Eds.), *The challenge of problem-based learning* (2nd ed., pp. 203–210). London: Kogan Page.

MacFarlane, R. B. (1989). *Making your own nature museum*. New York: Franklin Watts.

Maitland, B. (1997). Accreditation and assessment in architecture. In D. Boud & G. Feletti (Eds.), *The challenge of problem-based learning* (2nd ed., pp. 259–262). London: Kogan Page.

Marshall, H. H. (1990). Beyond the workplace metaphor: Toward conceptualizing the classroom as a learning setting. *Theory Into Practice, 29*(2), 94–101.

Marzano, R. J., & Marzano, J. S. (2003). The key to classroom management. *Educational Leadership, 61*(1), 6–13.

Marzano, R. J., Pickering, D. J., & Pollock, J. E. (2001). *Classroom instruction that works: Research-based strategies for increasing student achievement*. Alexandria, VA: Association for Supervision and Curriculum Development.

Maxwell, N. L., Bellisimo, Y., & Mergendoller, J. R. (2001). Problem-based learning: Modifying the medical school model for teaching high school economics. *The Social Studies, 92*(2), 73–78.

Maxwell, N. L., Mergendoller, J. R., & Bellisimo, Y. (2004). Developing a problem-based learning simulation: An economics unit on trade. *Simulation & Gaming, 35*(4), 488–498.

Mayer, R. E. (2004). Should there be a three-strikes rules against pure discovery learning? *American Psychologist, 59*(1), 14–19.

Mayers, P., Csikszentmihalyi, M., & Larson, R. (1978). *The daily experience of high school students*. Paper presented at the annual meeting of the American Educational Research Association, Toronto.

McCaslin, M., & Good, T. L. (1996). The informal curriculum. In D. C. Berliner & R. C. Calfee (Eds.), *Handbook of educational psychology* (pp. 622–670). New York: Macmillan.

McCombs, B. L., & Marzano, R. J. (1990). Putting the self in self-regulated learning: The self as agent in integrating will and skill. *Educational Psychologist, 25*(1), 51–70.

McWhaw, K., Schnackenberg, H., Sclater, J., & Abrami, P. C. (2003). From co-operation to collaboration: Helping students become collaborative learners. In R. Gillies & A. Ashman (Eds.), *Cooperative learning: The social and intellectual outcomes of learning in groups* (pp. 67–86). London: Routledge.

Meachan, J. A., & Emont, N. C. (1989). The interpersonal basis of everyday problem solving. In J. D. Sinnott (Ed.), *Everyday problem solving: Theory and applications*. New York: Praeger.

Meloth, M. S., & Deering, P. D. (1994). Task talk and task awareness under different cooperative learning conditions. *American Educational Research Journal, 31*(1), 138–165.

Memory, D. M., Yoder, C. Y., Bolinger, K. B., & Warren, W. J. (2004). Creating thinking and inquiry tasks that reflect the concerns and interests of adolescents. *The Social Studies*, (July/August 2004), 147–154.

Mergendoller, J. R., Maxwell, N. L., & Bellisimo, Y. (2000). Comparing the impact of problem-based learning (PBL) and traditional instructional strategies in high school economics. *Journal of Educational Research, 93*(6), 374–383.

Mergendoller, J. R., Maxwell, N. L., & Bellisimo, Y. (2002). *The effectiveness of problem-based instruction: A comparative study of instructional methods and student characteristics*. Paper presented at the annual meeting of the American Educational Research Association, New Orleans, LA.

Mergendoller, J., & Packer, M. (1989). *Cooperative learning in the classroom: A knowledge brief on effective teaching*. San Francisco, CA: Far West Laboratory For Educational Research and Development.

Mergendoller, J. R., & Thomas, J. W. (n.d.). *Managing project based learning: Principles from the field*. Unpublished manuscript. Novato, CA: Buck Institute for Education. Retrieved October 1, 2005, from http://www.bie.org/tmp/research/researchmanage-PBL.pdf

Moeller, B. (2005). Understanding the implementation of problem-based learning in New York City high school economics classrooms. In J. Ravitz (Chair). *Assessing implementation and impacts of PBL in diverse K-12 classrooms*. An interactive poster session conducted at the annual meeting of the American Educational Research Association, Montreal, Canada, April 14, 2005. http://www.bie.org/AERA2005/Moeller_Paper.pdf

National Research Council. (2001). *Knowing what students know: The science and design of educational assessment*. Committee on the Foundations of Assessment. J. Pellegrino, N. Chudowsky, and R. Glaser (Eds.). Board on Testing and Assessment, Center for Education. Washington, DC: National Academy Press.

Natriello, G. (1987). The impact of evaluation processes on students. *Educational Psychologist, 22*(2), 155–175.

Naylor, M. (1997). Work-based learning. *ERIC Digest*, ED, 411–417.

Newell, R. J. (2003). *Passion for learning: How project-based learning meets the needs of 21st-century students*. Lanham, MD and Oxford, England: Scarecrow Press.

Newmann, F. M., Marks, H. M., & Gamoran, A. (1996). Authentic pedagogy and student performance. *American Journal of Education, 104*(4), 280–312.

Newmann, F. M., & Thompson, J. (1987). *Effects of cooperative learning on achievement in secondary schools: A summary of research*. Madison: University of Wisconsin, National Center on Effective Secondary Schools.

Norman, G. R., & Schmidt, H. G. (1992). The psychological basis of problem-based learning: A review of the evidence. *Academic Medicine, 67*(9), 557–565.

Novak, J. D., & Gowin, D. R. (1984). *Learning how to learn*. New York: Cambridge Press.

Office of Technology Assessment, U.S. Government. (1992, February). *Testing in American schools: Asking the right questions*. Washington, DC: Author. OTA-SET-519 NTIS order #PB92-170091.

Oppenheimer, T. (2004). *The flickering mind: Saving education from the false promise of technology*. New York: Random House.

Paris, S. G., Lipson, M. Y., & Wixson, K. K. (1983). Becoming a strategic reader. *Contemporary Educational Psychology, 8*, 293–316.

Pintrich, P. R. (1995). *Current issues in research on self-regulated learning: A discussion with commentaries*. Mahwah, NJ: Lawrence Erlbaum Associates.

Ravitz, J. (2001). Will technology pass the test? Paper submitted to the PT3 Vision Quest on Assessment in e-Learning Cultures. http://www.pt3.org/VQ/html/ravitz.html

Ravitz, J., & Mergendoller, J. (2005). Evaluating implementation and impacts of problem based economics in U.S. high schools. In J. Ravitz (Chair). Assessing implementation and impacts of PBL in diverse K-12 classrooms. Montreal, Canada. Retrieved October 1, 2005, from http://www.bie.org/AERA2005/Ravitz_Mergendoller.pdf

Reeves, T. C., & Okey, J. R. (1996). Alternative assessment for constructivist learning environments. In B. Wilson (Ed.), *In constructivist learning environments* (pp. 191–202). Englewood Cliffs, NJ: Educational Technology.

Regehr, G., & Norman, G. R. (1996). Issues in cognitive psychology: Implications for professional education. *Academic Medicine, 71*(9), 988–1001.

Resnick, L. B. (1987). *Education and learning to think*. Washington DC: National Academy Press.

Riel, M. (1998). Teaching and learning in the educational communities of the future. In Chris Dede (Ed.), *ASCD Yearbook 1998: Learning and Technology*. Alexandria, VA: Association for Supervision and Curriculum Development.

Scardamalia, M., Bereiter, C., McLean, R. S., Swallow, J., & Woodruff, E. (1989). Computer supported intentional learning environments. *Journal of Educational Computing Research, 5*, 51–68.

Schank, R. C., & Cleary, C. (1995). *Engines for education* (1st ed.). Hillsdale, NJ: Lawrence Erlbaum Associates.

Schaps, E., Battistich, V., & Solomon, D. (2004). Community in school as key to student growth: Findings from the Child Development Project. In Zins, J., Weissberg, R., Wang, M., & Walberg, H. (Eds.), *Building academic success on social and emotional learning: What does the research say?* New York: Teachers College Press.

Sharan, Y., & Sharan, S. (1992). *Expanding cooperative learning through group investigation*. New York: Teachers College Press.

Shepard, L. A. (2001). The role of classroom assessment in teaching and learning. In V. Richardson (Ed.), *Handbook of research on teaching* (4th ed., pp. 1066–1101). Washington, DC: American Educational Research Association.

Shepperd, J. A. (1993). Productivity loss in performance groups: A motivation analysis. *Psychological Bulletin, 113*(1), 67–81.

Shepperd, J. A., & Taylor, K. M. (1999). Social loafing and expectancy-value theory. *Personality and Social Psychology Bulletin, 25*(9), 1147–1158.

Simon, H. A. (1980). Problem solving and education. In D. T. Tuma and F. Reif (Eds.), *Problem solving and education: Issues in teaching and research* (pp. 81–96). Hillsdale, NJ: Lawrence Erlbaum Associates.

Slavin, R. E. (1983). When does cooperative learning increase student achievement? *Psychological Bulletin, 94*, 429–445.

Slavin, R. E. (1995). *Cooperative learning: Theory, research, and practice*. Boston: Allyn & Bacon.

Solomon, R., Davidson, N. A. & Solomon, E. (1993). *The handbook for the fourth R III: Relationship activities for cooperative and collegial learning*. Columbia, MD: National Institute for Relationship Training, Inc.

Soloway, E. (1991). How the Nintendo generation learns. *Communications of ACM, 34*(9), 23–26, 95.

Stake, R. E., & Easley, J. (Eds.). (1978). *Case studies in science education*. Urbana, IL: University of Illinois.

Stepien, W. J., Gallagher, S. A., & Workman, D. (1993). Problem-based learning for traditional and interdisciplinary classrooms. *Journal for the Education of the Gifted, 16*(4), 338–357.

Sternberg, R. J., & Frensch, P. A. (1991). *Complex problem solving: Principles and mechanisms*. Hillsdale, NJ: Lawrence Erlbaum Associates.

Stinson, J. E., & Milter, R. G. (1996). Problem-based learning in business education: Curriculum design and implementation issues. *New Directions for Teaching and Learning, 68*, 33–42.

Thomas, J. W. (1998). *An overview of project based learning*. Novato, CA: Buck Institute for Education.

Thomas, J. W. (2000). *A review of research on project-based learning*. Retrieved December 1, 2004, from http://www.bie.org/tmp/research/researchreviewPBL.pdf

Tobin, K., & Ulerick, S. (1989). *An interpretation of high school science teaching based on metaphors and beliefs for specific roles*. Paper presented at the 1989 annual meeting of the American Educational Research Association, San Francisco.

Torp, L., & Sage, S. (2002). *Problems as possibilities: Problem-based learnng for K-12 education*. Alexandria, VA: Association for Supervision and Curriculum Development.

Turns, J. A., Newstetter, W, Allen, J. K. & Mistree, F. (1997). The reflective learner: Supporting the writing of learning essays that support the learning of engineering design through experience. *Proceedings of the 1997 American Society of Engineering Educators Conference*. Milwaukee, WI.

Walton, H. J., & Matthews, M. B. (1989). Essentials of problem-based learning. *Medical Education, 23*, 542–558.

Webb, N. M. (1984). Sex differences in interaction and achievement in cooperative small groups. *Journal of Educational Psychology, 36*(1), 33–44.

Webb, N. M. (1989). Peer interaction and learning in small groups. *International Journal of Educational Research, 13*, 21–40.

Webb, N. M., & Kenderski, C. M. (1985). Gender differences in small group interaction and achievement in high-achieving and low-achieving classrooms. In L. C. Wilkinson & C. B. Marrett (Eds.), *Gender related differences in classroom interaction* (pp. 209–226). New York: Academic Press.

Webb, N. M., Nemer, K. M., Chizhik, A., & Sugrue, B. (1998). Equity issues in collaborative group assessment: Group composition and performance. *American Educational Research Journal, 35*(4), 607–651.

Webb, N. M., & Palincsar, A. S. (1996). Group processes in the classroom. In D. C. Berliner & R. C. Calfee (Eds.), *Handbook of educational psychology* (pp. 841–873). New York: Macmillan.

Weinstein, C. E. (1994). Strategic learning/strategic teaching: Flip sides of a coin. In P. R. Pintrich, D. R. Brown, & C. E. Weinstein (Eds.), *Student motivation, cognition, and learning* (pp. 257–273). Hillsdale, NJ: Erlbaum.

White, B. Y., & Horowitz, P. (1987). *Enabling children to understand physical laws* (No. 6740). Cambridge MA: Bolt, Beranek, and Newman.

Wiggins, G. (1989). A true test: Toward more authentic and equitable assessment. *Phi Delta Kappan, 70*, 703–713.

Wiggins, G. (1998). *Educative assessment: Designing assessments to inform and improve student performance* (1st ed.). San Francisco: Jossey-Bass.

Wigginton, E. (1986). *Sometimes a shining moment: The foxfire experience*. New York: Anchor Press/Doubleday.

Wilkinson, L. C. (1986). Grouping low-achieving students for instruction. In B. Mason (Ed.), *Effects of alternative designs in compensatory education*. Washington, DC: Research and Evaluation Associates.

Willis, S. (1997). *Field studies: Learning thrives beyond the classroom*. Alexandria, VA: Association for Supervision and Curriculum Development.

Winne, P. H., & Marx, R. W. (1982). Students' and teachers' views of thinking processes for classroom learning. *Elementary School Journal, 82*, 493–518.

Winsor, K. (1997). Applying problem-based learning to practical legal training. In D. Boud & G. Feletti (Eds.), *The challenge of problem-based learning* (2nd ed., pp. 224–232). London: Kogan Page.

Wood, D., Bruner, J., & Ross, G. (1976). The role of tutoring in problem-solving. *Journal of Child Psychology and Psychiatry, 17*, 89–100.

Wood, P. K. (1983). Inquiring systems and problem structures: Implications for cognitive development. *Human Development, 26*, 249–265.

Woods, D. R. (1996). Problem-based learning for larger classes in chemical engineering. *New Directions for Teaching and Learning, 68*, 91–99.

Wysocki, R. K. (2004). *Project management process improvement*. Norwood, MA: Artech.

Zimmerman, B. J., & Schunk, D. H. (Eds.). (1989). *Self-regulated learning and academic achievement: Theory, research, and practice*. New York: Springer.

VI

Research and Theory with Implications for Classroom Management

Thomas L. Good
University of Arizona

23

A Social Motivation Perspective for Classroom Management

Kathryn R. Wentzel
University of Maryland, College Park

INTRODUCTION

Inherent in discussions of classroom management is a belief that teachers hold the potential to influence their students' classroom behavior and engagement in learning activities. Most often, specific disciplinary practices, interaction styles, and instructional strategies of teachers are identified as critical factors that determine the quality of classroom climate and individual student accomplishments; when students encounter effective classroom managers, they conform to the demands and constraints of teachers' rules and requests. Often missing from these discussions, however, is why certain management practices are effective. Moreover, the role of students themselves in creating positive classroom environments is rarely considered. If teachers are able to implement specific practices and conditions that result in socially competent students, what is it about these practices that motivates students to participate willingly in classroom activities and even contribute in positive ways to the overall climate of the classroom? Are there ways in which students enable each other to adapt to the demands of the classroom?

One approach to answering these questions is to consider first what it means to be a competent student and then, how teachers and peers might support students' efforts to behave in socially adaptive ways at school. Toward this end, I begin this chapter by presenting a definition of social competence derived from theoretical perspectives on person–environment fit and personal goal setting. I then apply this definition to the realm of schooling and discuss ways in which students' interpersonal interactions with teachers and peers can facilitate socially competent functioning at school. In conclusion, remaining challenges to the field are discussed.

PERSPECTIVES ON SOCIAL COMPETENCE

In the social developmental literature, social competence has been described from a variety of perspectives ranging from the development of individual skills to more general adaptation within a particular setting (e.g., Sternberg & Kolligian, 1990). In these discussions, social competence frequently is associated with person-level outcomes such as effective behavioral repertoires (Argyle, 1981), social problem-solving skills (Spivack & Shure, 1982), positive beliefs about the self (Bandura, 1986), achievement of social goals (Ford, 1992), and positive interpersonal relationships (Rubin, Bukowski, & Parker, 1998). In addition, central to many definitions of social competence is the notion that contextual affordances and constraints contribute to and mold the development of these outcomes in ways that enable the individual to contribute to the social good (Barker, 1961; Bronfenbrenner, 1989). In this manner, social contexts are believed to play an integral role in providing opportunities for the development and achievement of social competencies but also in defining the appropriate parameters of individual accomplishments. In this chapter, therefore, social competence is defined with respect to this balance between the achievement of positive outcomes for the self and adherence to context-specific expectations for behavior.

Social Competence as Person–Environment Fit

Support for this perspective on social competence can be found in the work of several theorists (e.g., Bronfenbrenner, 1989; Eccles & Midgley, 1989; Ford, 1992). Bronfenbrenner (1989) argued that competence can only be understood in terms of context-specific effectiveness, being a product of personal attributes such as goals, values, self-regulatory skills, and cognitive abilities, and of ways in which these attributes contribute to meeting situational requirements and demands. Bronfenbrenner further suggested that competence is facilitated by contextual supports that provide opportunities for the growth and development of these personal attributes and for learning what is expected by the social group. Ford (1992) expanded on this notion of person–environment fit by specifying four dimensions of competence that reflect personal as well as context-specific criteria: the achievement of personal goals; the achievement of goals that are situationally relevant; the use of appropriate means to achieve these goals; and the accomplishment of goals that result in positive developmental outcomes for the individual.

The application of this perspective on social competence to the realm of schooling results in a multi-faceted description of children who are socially competent and well adjusted. First, socially competent students achieve goals that are personally valued as well as those that are sanctioned by others. Second, the goals they pursue result in social integration as well as in positive developmental outcomes for the student. Socially integrative outcomes are those that promote the smooth functioning of social groups at school (e.g., cooperative behavior) and are reflected in levels of social approval and social acceptance; student-related outcomes reflect healthy development of the self (e.g., perceived social competence, feelings of self-determination) and feelings of emotional well-being (Bronfenbrenner, 1989; Ford, 1992). From this description it follows that social competence is achieved to the extent that students accomplish social goals that have personal as well as social value in a manner that supports continued psychological and emotional well-being. In addition, the ability to be socially competent is contingent on opportunities and affordances of the school context that allow students to pursue these multiple social goals (see also Eccles & Midgley, 1989).

The Role of Social Goal Setting

A goal-based definition of social competence reflects a basic tenet of motivational theories that people set goals for themselves and that these goals can be powerful motivators of behavior (Austin & Vancouver, 1996; Bandura, 1986; Dweck, 1991). Personal goals are believed to motivate behavior to the extent that individuals value specific, outcomes believe they have the ability to accomplish them, and perceive opportunities for their pursuit and accomplishment

(Eccles & Midgely, 1989; Ford, 1992). In the current chapter, goals are defined with regard to their content, or cognitive representations of social outcomes that students wish to achieve at school. Researchers who focus on the content of students' goals typically examine the frequency of efforts to pursue specific school-related outcomes, and the relation of these efforts to social and academic outcomes (e.g., Wentzel, 1991a, 1991b, 1993). The content of classroom goals might be task related, such as to master subject matter or to meet a specific standard of performance or proficiency, or more cognitive, such as to engage in creative thinking or to satisfy intellectual curiosity or challenge. Of particular concern for a discussion of classroom management are social goals such as to establish personal relationships with teachers and peers, to gain approval from others, to behave cooperatively and responsibly with classmates, and to solve behavioral as well as intellectual conflicts in a civil manner.

Social goal pursuit is considered dependent on specific self-processes that support goal-directed behavior. Similar to relations identified within the domain of achievement motivation, beliefs about ability, personal values, attributions for success and failure, and other social-cognitive and affective regulatory processes have been related to positive social outcomes. For instance, beliefs about social efficacy have been related to helping (Ladd & Oden, 1979), control of aggression (Erdley & Asher, 1996; Perry, Peery, & Rasmussen,1986), peer acceptance (Hymel, Bowker, & Woody, 1993), and social assertiveness (Kazdin, 1979). Similarly, attributional styles have been related to a range of social outcomes, including aggression (Hudley & Graham, 1993), peer rejection (Goetz & Dweck, 1980), and help giving (Weiner, 1980). In addition, a specific set of social information processing and self-regulatory skills have been identified as necessary antecedents of social competence, including the ability to read and process social cues (Crick & Dodge, 1994), social perspective-taking skills (Spivack & Shure, 1982), and interpersonal trust (Rotenberg, 1991). Finally, the achievement of social goals is often evaluated on the basis of standards, with evaluations of "success" typically based on a combined judgement of personal satisfaction with and positive social reactions to specific social outcomes. Achieving an acceptable balance between these two sets of evaluations is the hallmark of social competence and is achieved not just by one person's efforts but often as the result of compromise or conflict resolution among two or more individuals.

In sum, the current perspective suggests that students are most likely to be competent if they can work to achieve the goals and objectives inherent in the demands of classroom life while at the same time, working to achieve their own personal goals. Therefore, a clear identification of teachers' and students' goals is critical if we are to define classroom-specific competence. Practices that promote the adoption of socially valued goals and the development of positive outcomes for students also must be in place. In the following sections, goals for education and ways in which teachers and peers might promote students' pursuit of these goals is discussed.

GOALS FOR EDUCATION

What are the goals for education that are valued by teachers and their students? Goals for classroom life reflect a wide range of social as well as intellectual outcomes. At the policy level, educational objectives have included the development of social competencies as well as scholastic achievements, for producing model citizens as well as scholars. In general, character development and social responsibility have been stated as explicit objectives for public schools in almost every educational policy statement since 1848, being promoted with the same frequency as the development of academic skills (see Wentzel, 1991c, for a review). Specifically, social behavior in the form of moral character, conformity to social rules and norms, cooperation, and positive styles of social interaction has been promoted consistently as a goal for students to achieve.

Teachers and students have rarely been asked directly about their goals for education. Existing evidence, however, suggests that their goals for school often reflect the concerns for social development articulated in federal mandates. For instance, Krumboltz, Ford, Nichols, and Wentzel (1987) evaluated goals for students to achieve by age 18 in a sample of several hundred parents, teachers, and students. Goal statements reflected five academic domains (verbal, math, science, social studies, and fine arts), and five nonacademic domains (motivation, interpersonal competence, moral development, health, and career development). These statements were chosen based on school district curriculum guides from around the country and in consultation with local teachers and other experts in each domain. The most notable aspect of this study is that for each set of respondents, the social domains were regarded as more important than any of the academic domains. In particular, students rated positive motivational outcomes (e.g., valuing education, being intrinsically motivated) as most important, whereas teachers and parents rated the moral domain as most important with motivation being ranked second. Interpersonal competence was ranked either second or third by all three groups.

In short, motivation and social competence in the form of cooperation, respect for others, and positive interpersonal relationships are viewed by most as critical outcomes for students to achieve, over and above academic accomplishments. In the following sections, additional evidence that supports this conclusion is reviewed.

Teachers' Goals for Students

Although researchers rarely have asked teachers about their specific goals for students, teachers have expressed their ideas concerning what well-adjusted and successful students are like. When describing "ideal" students, middle school teachers mentioned three types of desirable outcomes: social outcomes reflecting socially integrative characteristics such as sharing, being helpful to others, and being responsive to rules; learning outcomes reflecting motivational qualities related to learning such as being persistent, hardworking, inquisitive, and intrinsically interested; and performance outcomes reflecting task-related outcomes such as getting good grades, being informed, and completing assignments (Wentzel, 2004a). Similarly, elementary school teachers have consistently reported preferences for students who are cooperative, conforming, cautious, and responsible rather than independent and assertive, or argumentative and disruptive (e.g., Brophy & Good, 1974; Feshbach, 1969; Helton & Oakland, 1977). In contrast, teachers tend to report antisocial and aggressive actions as most antithetical to desirable classroom behavior (Safran & Safran, 1985).

In other research, teachers have identified elementary-aged students toward whom they feel attachment, concern, indifference, or rejection (Brophy & Good, 1974). Of interest is that students placed in these categories tend to display distinct behavioral profiles in the classroom, with characteristics of well-liked students matching those described in Wentzel's (2004a) study. "Attachment" students are typically bright, hardworking, and model students; "concern" students make excessive but appropriate demands for teachers' attention; "indifference" students have few contacts with teachers; and "rejection" students typically display problem behaviors and make illegitimate demands for attention.

Research on the correlates of teachers' preferences for students also can inform us about the outcomes that teachers would like their students to achieve. For instance, students who are well liked by teachers tend to get better grades than those who are not as well liked (e.g., Pianta, Hamre, & Stuhlman, 2003; Wentzel & Asher, 1995). Although it is reasonable to expect that some teachers might assign higher grades to students they like, there is some indication that student characteristics can influence the nature of teacher–student interactions and therefore the quality of instruction received (Brophy & Good, 1974; Brophy & Evertson, 1978). Teachers' preference for students also appears to reflect the goals that students pursue. In one study, middle school teachers were asked to indicate how much they would like to have each of their students in their class again next year (Wentzel, 1991b). Students who reported frequent pursuit of goals to be socially responsible as well as to achieve positive evaluations of performance were preferred by teachers more than students who reported infrequent pursuit of such goals. Of particular interest is that teacher preference was not related to students' reports of pursuit of prosocial goals such as to cooperate and share, or pursuit of goals to learn.

Students' Goals for Each Other

The classroom goals that students would like each other to achieve are not well understood. As with teachers, however, one strategy for understanding the nature of social competence with peers is to identify social characteristics and outcomes related to peer approval and acceptance. Researchers typically have defined children's involvement in peer relationships in three specific ways: degree of peer acceptance or rejection by the larger peer group, peer group membership, and dyadic friendships. Each of these aspects of peer relationships and their correlates are described in the following sections.

Correlates of Peer Preference and Sociometric Popularity and Rejection. Assessments of peer acceptance and rejection always are based on information obtained from the peer group at large rather than from the individual. In this manner, unilateral assessments of a child's relative standing or reputation within the peer group are used to create a continuum of social preference scores ranging from well accepted to rejected (e.g., How much do you like this person?), or categories of individual students that reflect sociometric status groups (i.e., popular, rejected, neglected, controversial, and average status children; see Asher & Dodge, 1986). Although rarely acknowledged as a factor contributing to peer acceptance or rejection, the school and classroom setting has almost always been the context within which peer preference and sociometric status is studied.

Of primary interest for the present discussion are sociometrically rejected children, those who are infrequently nominated as someone's best friend and are actively disliked by their peers, and sociometrically popular children, those who are frequently nominated as a best friend and rarely disliked by their peers. A substantial number of studies have yielded consistent findings concerning the social competencies associated with these groups of children (e.g., Newcomb, Bukowski, & Pattee, 1993). In general, when compared to average status peers (i.e., students with scores that do not fall into these statistically defined groups), popular students are more cooperative, helpful, and sociable, demonstrate better leadership skills, and are more self-assertive. In contrast, rejected students tend to be less compliant, less self-assured, less sociable and more aggressive, disruptive, and withdrawn than their average status peers. In addition, popular status and social acceptance have been related to successful academic performance, and rejected status and low levels of acceptance to academic difficulties (e.g., Buhs & Ladd, 2001; DeRosier, Kupersmidt, & Patterson, 1994; Wentzel, 1991a). Results are most consistent with respect to classroom grades (Buhs & Ladd, 2001; Hatzichristou & Hopf, 1996; Wentzel, 1991a), although peer acceptance also has been related positively to standardized test scores and IQ (Wentzel, 1991a). These findings are robust for elementary-aged children as well as adolescents, and longitudinal studies document the stability of relations between peer acceptance and academic accomplishments over time (e.g., Ladd & Burgess, 2001; Wentzel & Caldwell, 1997).

Correlates of Peer Group Membership. Students also enjoy relationships within peer groups or crowds. In contrast to peer status or preference, group membership is typically assessed by using statistical methods to identify clusters of friends who form groups (see

Kindermann, McCollum, & Gibson, 1996), or by asking students to report who actually hangs out in groups with each other (Brown, 1989). Typical adolescent crowds include "Populars," students who engage in positive forms of academic as well as social behavior but also in some delinquent activities; "Jocks," students characterized by athletic accomplishments but also relatively frequent alcohol use; more alienated groups (e.g., "Druggies") characterized by poor academic performance and engagement in delinquent and other illicit activities; and "Normals," who tend to be fairly average students who do not engage in delinquent activities. Research on peer group membership has been mostly descriptive, identifying the central norms and values that uniquely characterize various adolescent school-based groups and crowds (e.g., Brown, 1989). Therefore, in contrast to work on sociometric status, there is not a one-to-one correspondence between enjoying high status and being described in a positive light. To illustrate, in contrast to sociometrically popular students who are typically characterized in positive terms, members of "Popular" crowds are often described by their peers as having undesirable characteristics such as being dominant and exclusionary as well as lacking positive prosocial skills (LaFontana & Cillessen, 2002; Parkhurst & Hopmeyer, 1998).

As with research on peer acceptance, studies of peer group membership also have focused on academic values and characteristics. For example, ethnographic studies by Brown and his colleagues (Brown, 1989; Brown, Mounts, Lamborn, & Steinberg, 1993; Stone & Brown, 1999) described adolescents as characterizing certain crowds in terms of academic standing. "Brains," or students who get high grades, typically enjoy average status in crowd hierarchies although they are viewed as somewhat disengaged from peer activities. The social status of this crowd also appears to have a developmental trajectory, with Brain crowd status being highest during middle school and the end of high school, and lowest at the beginning of high school (see Stone & Brown, 1999). Of additional interest, is that members of the Popular crowd, who enjoy high status, also are typically characterized as being good students (Brown et al., 1993).

Finally, researchers who identify friendship-based peer groups using statistical procedures also have related group membership to academic performance (Kurdek & Sinclair, 2000; Wentzel & Caldwell, 1997) and to academic engagement (Kindermann, 1993). Peer group membership in middle school also has been associated with changes in academic performance over time (A. Ryan, 2001). However, although most of these studies have followed students over time, few have documented long-term relations between group membership and academic performance (e.g., Wentzel & Caldwell, 1997).

Correlates of Friendship. Peer relationships also are studied with respect to dyadic friendships. In this case, students are asked to nominate their best friends at school; nominations are then matched to determine reciprocity, or best friendships. An important distinction between friendships and peer group membership is that friendships reflect relatively private, egalitarian relationships often formed on the basis of idiosyncratic criteria. In contrast, peer groups are characterized by publicly acknowledged and therefore fairly consistent characteristics that are valued by the group (Brown, 1989).

Friendships have been described most often with respect to their functions and qualities (Parker & Asher, 1993). However, simply having a friend at school appears to be related to a range of positive outcomes. Children with friends tend to be more sociable, cooperative, and self-confident when compared to their peers without friends (Newcomb & Bagwell, 1995; Wentzel, Barry, & Caldwell, 2004). Children with reciprocated friendships also tend to be more independent, emotionally supportive, altruistic, and prosocial, and less aggressive than those who do not have such friendships (Aboud & Mendelson, 1996; Wentzel et al., 2004). In addition, adolescents report they are satisfied with friends if they are self-disclosing, initiate activities, can manage and resolve conflict, and are emotionally supportive (Aboud & Mendelson,

1996). Research on friendship formation also suggests that the ability to engage in responsive communication, exchange information, establish common ground, to self-disclose, to extend and elaborate the activities of others, and to resolve conflict (Gottman, 1983) is necessary to develop and maintain positive friendships. Similar to other types of peer relationships, having friends also has been related positively to grades and test scores in elementary school and middle school (Berndt & Keefe, 1995; Wentzel & Caldwell, 1997; Wentzel et al., 2004). In addition, students with friends tend to be more involved and engaged in school-related activities than those who do not have reciprocated friendships (e.g., Berndt & Keefe, 1995; Ladd, 1990).

Students' Goals for Themselves

Research on school-related goals that students value for themselves also has not been frequent (cf., Wigfield & Eccles, 1992). However, students do report trying to achieve positive social as well as academic outcomes. In an ethnographic study, Allen (1986) interviewed ninth-grade students about their school-related goals and found that two major goals were mentioned by almost all students, goals to socialize with peers and to pass the course. Students believed these goals could be accomplished by trying to figure out the teacher, having fun, giving the teacher what he wants, minimizing work, reducing boredom, and staying out of trouble. In other research, high school students have indicated trying to achieve social goals to have fun and to be dependable and responsible, in addition to task-related goals to learn new things and to get good grades (Wentzel, 1989). Middle school students have reported trying to achieve social goals to behave appropriately more frequently than goals to learn or to socialize with peers (Wentzel, 1991b, 1992).

Although rarely studied from the perspective of social goal setting, students consistently express interest in forming positive relationships with their classmates at school. Indeed, children are interested in and even emotionally attached to their peers at all ages. However, they exhibit increased interest in their peers and a growing psychological and emotional dependence on them for support and guidance as they make the transition into adolescence (Steinberg, 1990; Youniss & Smollar, 1989). One reason for this growing interest is that many young adolescents enter new middle school structures that necessitate interacting with larger numbers of peers on a daily basis. In contrast to the greater predictability of self-contained classroom environments in elementary school, the relative uncertainty and ambiguity of multiple classroom environments, new instructional styles, and more complex class schedules often result in middle school students turning to each other for information, social support, and ways to cope. Therefore, establishing rewarding relationships with peers is of special interest as a school-related social goal of students in middle school and high school. Of final note is that establishing positive relationships with teachers is also of concern to most students, although the value of these relationships appears to decline as students enter adolescence (Lempers & Clark-Lempers, 1992).

Finally, considerable research also has been conducted on the reasons why students try to be successful. In the social domain, these goal orientations (Dweck & Leggett, 1988) reflect desires to earn positive social evaluations and to gain social approval or avoid social disapproval (social performance goals) or to experience opportunities to learn and form new relationships (social learning goals; see, e.g., Erdley, Cain, Loomis, Dumas-Hines, & Dweck, 1997). In the academic domain, researchers have documented similar orientations reflecting desires to achieve in order to earn positive evaluations of one's ability and to avoid negative evaluations (performance goal orientations) or desires to master new tasks and increase abilities (mastery goal orientations; see Pintrich, 2003).

Summary

Although teachers' and students' goals for education have not been studied extensively, it is clear from the literature that a core set of social and academic competencies is valued by teachers as well as students. Positive forms of behavior that are reflected in compliance to classroom rules and norms and that demonstrate caring and concern for classmates are related to social approval and acceptance by adults as well as peers. In addition, academic accomplishments also appear to be valued by teachers and peers. It also is clear, however, that at least some students do not demonstrate these positive outcomes when at school. In this regard, several issues are important to consider.

First, we often assume that students understand how they are supposed to behave and what it is they are supposed to accomplish while at school. However, for some students these expectations are not always immediately obvious. In particular, young children who are just beginning school and students who are raised in cultures with dissimilar goals and values to those espoused by American educational institutions might need explicit guidance with respect to the school-related goals they are expected to achieve (Ogbu, 1985). In addition, teachers do not always communicate clearly their own goals for their students. In two studies of middle school students, almost half the participants reported that teachers did not have clear rules for them to follow and did not explain clearly what would happen if rules were broken (Wentzel, 2004a; Wentzel, Battle, & Looney, 2000). Therefore, the more that teachers explicitly and clearly communicate their social expectations to students, the more likely students will at least understand the goals they are expected to achieve.

Similarly, students do not always understand what their peers expect of them. However, interventions have demonstrated that helping children replace inappropriate goals with ones that will facilitate social competence can lead to improved behavioral skills when interacting with peers (e.g., Oden & Asher, 1977). It also is reasonable to expect that school-based interventions that provide children with a clear set of socially acceptable goals to strive for might help alleviate peer-related adjustment problems. In this regard, providing children with a more balanced set of goals might be especially beneficial. Rabiner and Gordon (1992) asked boys to generate goals for hypothetical situations that required coordination of competitive and cooperative goals to resolve a conflict. In this case, aggressive boys who also were rejected by their peers tended to generate goals that were focused on personal needs and interests, whereas nonaggressive and socially accepted boys were more likely to generate responses that reflected a balance between personal goals, goals that focused on the needs of others, or goals to maintain interpersonal relationships. Together, these studies support the notion that students trained to identify and subsequently coordinate multiple social goals might also develop more positive interactions with their classmates.

Given the multitude of expectations that are present in the classroom environment, of additional concern is how students coordinate their own social and academic goals with those promoted within individual classrooms. For instance, some students who try to pursue multiple goals might be unable to coordinate the pursuit of their goals into an organized system of behavior and as a consequence, become distracted or overwhelmed when facing particularly demanding tasks that require focused concentration and attention. An example of this problem is when students want to achieve social goals *and* academically related goals. Students who are unable to coordinate these goals might opt to pursue social relationship goals with peers (e.g., to have fun) in lieu of task-related goals such as to complete class assignments. Students with more effective goal coordination skills would likely find a way to achieve both goals, for instance, by doing homework with friends. An identification of specific self-regulatory strategies that enable students to accomplish more than one task at a time seems essential for helping students coordinate demands to achieve multiple and often conflicting goals at school.

A focus on students' coordination of social and academic goal pursuit also highlights the possibility that achieving academic and social competence at school is inextricably linked. In fact, numerous correlational, longitudinal, and experimental studies have established significant and positive associations between social and academic accomplishments at school (Wentzel, 2003). Despite these findings, however, researchers have not focused consistently on why relations between social and academic outcomes exist. Nevertheless, there are several ways that social behavior might contribute to academic achievement at school. First, prosocial and responsible behavior can contribute to academic achievement by creating a context conducive to learning. This can occur when children conform to rules for social conduct such as to pay attention, cooperate with others, and to restrain from aggressive or disruptive behavior. Quite simply, students' adherence to classroom rules and displays of socially competent behavior allows teachers to focus their efforts on teaching rather than classroom management. Presumably, all students will learn more when this occurs.

In addition, being socially responsible also means conforming to rules and conventions for completing learning activities; teachers provide students with procedures for accomplishing academic tasks and dictate specific criteria and standards for performance. Paying close attention to these conventions for learning also is bound to help students achieve academically. Finally, constructivist theories of development (Piaget, 1965; Youniss & Smollar, 1989) propose that positive social interactions (e.g., cooperative and collaborative problem solving) can create cognitive conflict that hastens the development of higher-order thinking skills and cognitive structures. Empirical research supports this notion in that cooperative learning results in greatest gains when interactive questioning and explanation are an explicit part of the learning task (e.g., Damon & Phelps, 1989; Slavin, Hurley, & Chamberlain, 2003).

An important issue with respect to these models, however, concerns the direction of effects. Assuming that causal relations do exist, is it that behavioral competence influences learning and achievement or that academic success promotes behavioral competence? On the one hand, negative academic feedback can lead to acting out, noncompliance, and other forms of irresponsible behavior. On the other hand, it is reasonable to assume that at least to some degree, behavioral competence precedes academic competence at school. From a developmental perspective, antisocial behavior and a lack of prosocial skills appear to begin with poor family interaction patterns (e.g., Patterson & Bank, 1989). Therefore, how children are taught to behave before they enter school should have at least an initial impact on how they behave and subsequently learn at school. In addition, interventions designed to increase academic skills do not necessarily lead to decreases in antisocial behavior (Patterson, Bank, & Stoolmiller, 1990), nor do they enhance social skills typically associated with academic achievement (Hopps & Cobb, 1974), whereas ways in which teachers and peers might promote positive social outcomes are indicated throughout the literature. This work is discussed in the next section.

SUPPORTING ADAPTIVE GOAL PURSUIT AT SCHOOL

Although children try to achieve goals for many reasons, the question of what leads them to actively engage in the pursuit of goals that are valued by others as well as those that are valued by themselves lies at the heart of research on socialization (e.g., Grusec & Goodnow, 1994; Maccoby, 1992). Models of socialization suggest at least two general mechanisms whereby social experiences might influence goal pursuit. First, ongoing social interactions teach children about themselves and what they need to do to become accepted and competent members of their social worlds. Within the context of interpersonal interactions, children develop a set of values and standards for behavior and goals they should strive to achieve (see Grusec & Goodnow, 1994). Second, the qualities of children's social relationships are likely to have motivational significance. When their interpersonal relationships with adults are nurturant and supportive, children are more likely to adopt and internalize the expectations and goals that are valued by these adults than if their relationships are harsh and critical (see Grusec & Goodnow, 1994; R. Ryan, 1993).

When applied to the social worlds of the classroom, these models suggest that teachers and peers also should hold the potential to provide optimal contexts within which positive goal setting takes place. Specifically, relationships with teachers and peers are likely to have motivational significance if they create contexts that make students feel like they are an integral and valued part of the classroom. If this is true, what are the critical aspects of classroom climate that contribute to a sense of social support and relatedness and therefore, pursuit of valued social and academic goals? One strategy for addressing this question is to extend our understanding of the underlying belief systems that are reflected in a sense of social relatedness. In this regard, Ford (1992; see also Wentzel, 2002b) suggested that evaluative beliefs about social relationships and settings can play an influential role in decisions to engage in the pursuit of personal goals. Specifically, within certain situations, individuals evaluate the correspondence between their personal goals and those of others, the degree to which others will provide access to information and resources necessary to achieve one's goals, and the extent to which social relationships will provide an emotionally supportive environment for goal pursuit.

Extending this formulation to classroom settings, students who wish to achieve academically should engage in learning activities when they perceive their involvement and relationships with their teachers and peers as providing opportunities to achieve academic goals; as being safe and responsive to their academic strivings; as facilitating the achievement of their goals by providing help, advice, and instruction; and as being emotionally supportive and nurturing. Students' motivation to achieve academic goals should then serve as mediators between opportunities afforded by positive relationships with teachers and peers and academic accomplishments. Few researchers have explored links between these multiple dimensions of classroom contexts and students' positive goal setting. However, empirical evidence supports the notion that enjoying positive relationships with teachers and peers is related to various aspects of academic motivation (see Wentzel, 2003). In line with Ford's (1992) proposal, ample support also exists for characterizing the opportunities provided by teachers and peers along dimensions of instrumental help, clear expectations and opportunities for goal pursuit, safety and responsivity, and emotional support.

Based on the extant literature, it is reasonable to speculate that contextual supports can partly explain students' school-related competencies because they support the pursuit of positive social and academic goals. In the following sections, I review evidence suggesting that these teacher- and peer-related supports can promote social and academic accomplishments by motivating students to display positive forms of social behavior and to engage in academic activities.

Providing Expectations and Opportunities

As noted earlier, social contexts can influence personal goal pursuit if there is correspondence between personal goals and those of others. Therefore, a central question concerning students' pursuit of socially valued goals is whether teachers and peers communicate values and expectations concerning social behavior and academic accomplishments within the classroom.

Teacher Expectations. Although researchers rarely have asked teachers directly about their specific goals for students, they have documented that teachers continuously communicate socially valued goals and expectations to their students. Teachers are sensitive to individual differences in classroom conduct, value socially competent behavior, and spend an enormous amount of time teaching their students how to behave and act responsibly (see Doyle, 1986). In fact, teachers tend to have a core set of behavioral expectations for their students reflecting appropriate responses to academic requests and tasks, impulse control, mature problem solving, cooperative and courteous interaction with peers, involvement in class activities, and recognition of appropriate contexts for different types of behavior (e.g., Trenholm & Rose, 1981). Moreover, teachers actively communicate these expectations to their students, regardless of their instructional goals, teaching styles, and ethnicity (Hargreaves, Hester, & Mellor, 1975). Teachers also communicate expectations for students' interactions with each other. High school teachers promote adherence to interpersonal rules concerning aggression, manners, stealing, and loyalty (Hargreaves et al., 1975), and elementary school teachers tend to focus on peer norms for sharing resources, being nice to each other, working well with others, and harmonious problem solving (Sieber, 1979). Teachers also communicate directly to students when they need to pay attention as a function of which contexts they are in (Shultz & Florio, 1979), and when and where it is appropriate to interact with peers (Sieber, 1979).

Teachers tend to promote prosocial and socially responsible behavior in several ways. For instance, various classroom management practices can be used to establish group order and control (see Doyle, 1986). Blumenfeld and her colleagues (Blumenfeld, Hamilton, Bossert, Wessels, & Meece, 1983; Blumenfeld, Hamilton, Wessels, & Faulkner, 1979) also have documented specific ways in which social responsibility is taught at school. In particular, they have studied teacher communications that relay why students ought to behave in certain ways, ascribe causal attributions to students' behavior, and suggest sanctions for classroom conduct. These researchers found that teachers' communications reflect specific issues concerning academic performance, academic procedures (i.e., proper ways to do work), social procedures (e.g., talking, adhering to social conventions), and social–moral norms (e.g., cheating, fighting). Within the procedural and social–moral domain, 46% of the academic procedure statements concerned staying on task, 51% of the social procedure statements concerned talking, and 57% of the social–moral statements concerned respect for others. The power of these communications was reflected in that they were related to students' ratings of how important classroom procedures and norms were to them personally.

Teachers also communicate expectations by structuring learning environments in ways that make certain goals more salient to students than others. For example, cooperative learning structures can be designed to promote the pursuit of social goals to be responsible to the group and to achieve common objectives (e.g., Cohen, 1986; Solomon, Schaps, Watson, & Battistich, 1992; Slavin et al., 2003). Teachers also provide students with evaluation criteria and design tasks in ways that can focus attention on goals to learn and develop skills (task-related and intellectual goals) or to demonstrate ability to others (performance goals; see Ames, 1992). Teachers who provide students with a diverse set of tasks that are challenging, personally relevant, and promote skill development are likely to foster pursuit of mastery goals; teachers who use normative and comparative evaluation criteria and who provide students with controlling, noncontingent extrinsic rewards are likely to promote pursuit of performance goals (e.g., Midgley, 2002).

In addition to communicating values and expectations for behavior and achievement at the classroom level, teachers also can convey expectations about ability and performance differentially to individual students. These communications most often take the form of positive expectations that students are able to achieve more than previously demonstrated, or negative expectations reflecting underestimations of a student's ability. In this regard, researchers have documented that many teachers hold negative stereotypes of minority students, expecting less competent behavior and lower levels of academic performance from them than from other students (Weinstein, Gregory, & Strambler, 2004). Moreover, students perceive these differential expectations and are aware of their teachers' expectations for them personally (Weinstein, Marshall, Sharp, & Botkin, 1987). Of particular importance is that teachers' false expectations can become self-fulfilling prophecies, with student performance changing to conform to teacher expectations (see Weinstein, 2002).

Although the effects of these expectations tend to be fairly weak (e.g., Jussim, 1991; Jussim & Eccles, 1995), self-fulfilling prophecies tend to have stronger effects on African American students, students from low socioeconomic backgrounds, and low achievers (see Smith, Jussim, & Eccles, 1999). In addition, however, teachers' overestimations of ability seem to have a somewhat stronger effect in raising levels of achievement than teachers' underestimates have on lowering achievement, especially for low-performing students (Madon, Jussim, & Eccles, 1997). Therefore, teachers who communicate high expectations for individual students can bring about positive changes in performance and actual accomplishments.

Peer Expectations. Although not well documented, it is reasonable to assume that students communicate to each other values and expectations concerning social behavior and academic achievement and provide opportunities for each other that will allow their expression (e.g., Altermatt, Pomerantz, Ruble, Frey, & Greulich, 2002). It is clear, however, that as students advance through their middle school and high school years, the degree to which their goals and values match or even complement the values communicated by adults can become fairly attenuated. Despite these developmental trends, some adolescent students do report that their classmates expect them to behave appropriately and perform well academically at school. For instance, approximately 70% of adolescents from three predominantly middle-class middle schools reported that their peers expected them to be cooperative and helpful in class either sometimes or always, and approximately 80% reported similar peer values for academic learning (Wentzel, Looney, & Battle, 2004). Moreover, these perceptions did not appear to differ as a function of grade level.

Research by Crosnoe and Needham (2004) also suggests that peer influence (positive as well as negative) tends to be strongest in schools that are academically rigorous. Moreover, the potentially negative influence of adolescent friendships appears to be lessened in schools where students enjoy positive, caring relationships with teachers. Ethnicity also seems to play a role in the degree to which students experience positive encouragement from peers to succeed academically. Typically, Asian American students have the highest levels of peer support for academic pursuits, whereas African American students are at greatest risk for receiving fairly limited peer support for achieving academically at school (Steinberg, Dornbusch, & Brown, 1992).

Other evidence suggests that perceived expectations of peers for specific kinds of behavior might play a central role in students' own determination of why it is important to behave in those ways. In fact, peers have the potential to provide the most proximal input concerning whether engaging in a task is important, fun, or interesting. In support of this notion is evidence that students who perceive relatively high expectations for academic learning and engagement from their peers also pursue goals to learn for internalized reasons (because it is important) rather than because they believe they will get in trouble or lose social approval if they do not (Wentzel, Looney, & Battle, 2004). Therefore, peers who communicate a sense of importance or enjoyment with regard to task engagement are likely to lead others to form similar attitudes toward the task (Bandura, 1986). This is especially likely to occur when students are friends: Students have the opportunity to observe their friend's behavior with greater frequency than a nonfriend's behavior (Crockett, Losoff, & Petersen, 1984), and friendships typically are characterized by strong emotional bonds, thereby increasing the likelihood that friends will imitate each other's behavior.

Providing Help, Advice, and Instruction

Teachers and peers routinely provide children with resources that promote the development of social and academic competencies. These resources can take the form of information and advice, modeled behavior, or specific experiences that facilitate learning. In the classroom, teachers play the central pedagogical function of transmitting knowledge and training students in academic subject areas. The relevance of having positive relationships with teachers for gaining access to academic resources is reflected in Brophy and Good's (1974) work. The teachers observed in this research reported that they were more appreciative and positive toward students who were cooperative and persistent (i.e., behaviorally competent) than toward students who were less cooperative but displayed high levels of creativity and achievement. Teachers responded to students about whom they were concerned with help and encouragement when these students sought them out for help. In contrast, students toward whom they felt rejection were treated most often with criticism and typically were refused help. In short, these latter students were most likely to receive less one-on-one instruction than other students.

Enjoying positive relationships with peers also can lead directly to resources and information that help students learn. By virtue of the fact that they are socially accepted, it is reasonable to assume that students who get along with their peers will also have access to peer resources that can promote the development of social and academic competencies. These resources can take the form of information and advice, modeled behavior, or specific experiences that facilitate learning (Sieber, 1979). Students frequently clarify and interpret their teacher's instructions concerning what they should be doing and how they should do it, provide mutual assistance in the form of volunteering substantive information and answering questions (Cooper, Akers-Lopez, & Marquis, 1982), and share various supplies such as pencils and paper.

Classmates also provide each other with important information about themselves by modeling academic competencies (Schunk, 1987), and by comparing work and grades (Guay, Boivin, & Hodges, 1999). Such information is likely to influence beliefs concerning their own levels of academic efficacy. Indeed, Altermatt et al. (2002) documented the role of students' evaluative discourse with peers in changing perceptions of academic efficacy over time. Experimental work also has shown that peers serve as powerful models that influence the development of academic self-efficacy (e.g., Schunk, 1987). In turn, students' efficacy beliefs are likely to be a primary motivator of goals to achieve academically (Bandura, 1986).

Providing a Safe and Responsive Environment

Teacher Responsiveness. Researchers have not often focused on physical safety in the classroom as a primary influence on student competence. However, researchers have examined ways in which teachers can be responsive to students' needs. In particular, responsive teachers are those who provide consistent enforcement of rules, age-appropriate expectations for self-reliance and self-control, and solicitations of children's opinions and feelings (e.g., Grolnick & Ryan, 1989; Skinner & Belmont, 1993; Wentzel, 2002a). Moreover, when teachers are taught to provide students with warmth and support, clear expectations for behavior, and developmentally appropriate autonomy, their students develop a stronger sense of community, increase displays of socially competent behavior, and show academic gains (Schaps, Battistich, & Solomon, 1997; Watson, Solomon, Battistich, Schaps, & Solomon, 1989). Findings that students are more likely to establish positive relationships with teachers when they feel safe at school (Crosnoe, Johnson, & Elder, 2004) also support this notion.

In studies of elementary school-aged students, teacher provisions of structure, guidance, and autonomy have been related to a range of positive, motivational outcomes (e.g., Grolnick & Ryan, 1989; Skinner & Belmont, 1993). Birch and Ladd (1996) reported that young children's healthy adjustment to school is related to teacher–student relationships characterized by warmth and the absence of conflict as well as open communication. In contrast, kindergartners' relationships with teachers marked by conflict and dependency predict less-than-adaptive academic and behavioral outcomes through eighth grade, especially for boys (Hamre & Pianta, 2001). When teachers are taught to provide students with warmth and support, clear expectations for behavior, and developmentally appropriate autonomy, their students develop a stronger sense of community, increase displays of socially competent behavior, and show academic gains (Schaps et al., 1997; Watson et al., 1989).

Peer Responsiveness and Safety. Students who are accepted by their peers and who have established friendships with classmates also are more likely to enjoy a relatively safe school environment and less likely to be the targets of peer-directed violence and harassment than their classmates who do not have friends (Hodges, Bovin, Vitaro, & Bukowski, 1999; Pelligrini, Bartini, & Brooks, 1999). The safety net that friends appear to provide each other is critical in that peer-directed violence and harassment is a fairly pervasive problem in American schools and can have an enormous negative impact on students' social and emotional functioning (Elliott, Hamburg, & Williams, 1998; Snyder, Brooker, Patrick, Schrepferman, & Stoolmiller, 2003). Although the frequency of school-related violence does not appear to be increasing (see Nichols & Good, 2005), national surveys indicate that large numbers of students are the target of classmate aggression and take active measures to avoid being harmed physically as well as psychologically by peers (National Center for Educational Statistics, 1995).

The effects of peer harassment on student goal setting and school-related competence has not been studied frequently. However, threats to physical safety can have a significant impact on students' emotional functioning at school (Buhs & Ladd, 2001; Elliott et al., 1998). Students who are frequently victimized tend to report higher levels of distress and depression than those who are not routinely victimized (e.g., Olweus, 1993; Snyder et al., 2003). In turn, other studies have linked psychological distress and depression to interest in school (Wentzel, Weinberger, Ford, & Feldman, 1990), negative attitudes toward academic achievement (Dubow & Tisak, 1989), academic performance (Wentzel et al., 1990), and ineffective cognitive functioning (Jacobsen, Edelstein, & Hoffmann, 1994). Therefore, students' affective functioning appears to mediate the effects of peer relationship quality and of peer harassment on academic outcomes (Juvonen, Nishina, & Graham, 2000; Wentzel, 1998; Wentzel & Caldwell, 1997; Wentzel & McNamara, 1999).

Providing Emotional Support

In conjunction with providing safe and responsive interpersonal contexts, teachers and peers also can create a climate of emotional support for students. Research on this aspect of classroom context has been more frequent.

Teacher Support. Perceiving teachers to be emotionally supportive and caring has been related to positive motivational outcomes, including the pursuit of goals to learn and to behave prosocially and responsibly, educational aspirations and values, and positive self-concept (Goodenow, 1993; Harter, 1996; Midgley, Feldlaufer, & Eccles, 1989; Wentzel, 1994, 1997). In middle school, students' perceptions that teachers care about them have been related to positive aspects of student motivation such as pursuit of social and academic goals, mastery orientations toward learning, and academic interest (Wentzel, 1997). In a recent study of perceived support from teachers, parents, and peers (Wentzel, 1998), perceived support from teachers was unique in its relation to students' interest in class and pursuit of goals to adhere to classroom rules and norms. Finally, Eccles and her colleagues (Feldlaufer, Midgley, & Eccles, 1988; Midgley et al., 1989) found that young adolescents report declines in the nurturant qualities of teacher–student relationships after the transition to middle school; these declines correspond to declines in academic motivation and achievement. As students proceed through middle school, they also report that teachers become more focused on students earning high grades, competition between students, and maintaining adult control, with a decrease in personal interest in students (Harter, 1996). Students who report these changes also tend to report less intrinsic motivation to achieve than students who do not (Harter, 1996).

Of particular interest for teachers is that by middle school, students appear to have strong opinions about what caring and supportive teachers are like. When asked to characterize teachers who care, middle school students describe teachers who demonstrate democratic and egalitarian communication styles designed to elicit student participation and input, who develop expectations for student behavior and performance in light of individual differences and abilities, who model a "caring" attitude and interest in their instruction and interpersonal dealings with students, and who provide constructive rather than harsh and critical feedback. Moreover, students who perceive their teachers to display high levels of these characteristics also tend to pursue appropriate social and academic classroom goals more frequently than students who do not (Wentzel, 2002a).

Peer Support. Peer relationships also have the potential to create a climate of emotional support for students. During adolescence, students report that their peer groups and crowds provide them with a sense of emotional security and a sense of belonging (Brown, Eicher, & Petrie, 1986). In contrast, children without friends or who are socially rejected are often lonely, emotionally distressed and depressed, and suffer from poor self-concepts (Wentzel & Caldwell, 1997). Few studies have examined sociometric status in relation to students' own perceptions of peer acceptance (cf., Zakriski & Coie, 1996). However, students who believe that their peers support and care about them tend to be more engaged in positive aspects of classroom life than students who do not perceive such support. In particular, perceived social and emotional support from peers has been associated positively with prosocial outcomes such as helping, sharing, and cooperating, and related negatively to antisocial forms of behavior (Wentzel, 1994).

The positive academic effects of emotional support from peers are well documented. Students who perceive that their peers support and care about them also tend to be more engaged in positive aspects of classroom life than are students who do not perceive such support. Perceived social and emotional support from peers has been associated with pursuit of academic and prosocial goals (DuBois, Felner, Brand, Adan, & Evans, 1992; Harter, 1996; Wentzel, 1994, 1997, 1998), as well as with students' interest in academic pursuits (e.g., Wentzel, 1998). Young adolescents who do not perceive their relationships with peers as positive and supportive also tend to be at risk for academic problems (e.g., Goodenow, 1993; Midgley et al., 1989).

Summary

The literature just reviewed provides clear support for Ford's (1992) proposal that classroom contexts can be characterized, in part, with respect to the opportunities provided by teachers and peers along dimensions of instrumental help, clear expectations and opportunities for goal pursuit, safety and responsivity, and emotional support. These dimensions are related to a range of motivational outcomes that support goal pursuit and active engagement in learning activities. Therefore, it is reasonable to speculate that these contextual supports can explain students' social and academic accomplishments because they support the pursuit of socially valued goals.

Although empirical evidence of the joint contribution of these teacher and peer provisions to students' classroom goals has been reported (Wentzel, 2004b), what it is that develops or is changed on the part of students as a result of these provisions remains unanswered. One area for consideration is the influence of teacher and peer provisions on self-regulatory processes that support academic goal pursuit. For example, in a study of middle school and high school students, teacher and peer social support, instrumental help, and values explained significant amounts of variance in students' pursuit of academic goals to learn (Wentzel, Looney, & Battle, 2004). Of additional interest is that social support and instrumental help from peers remained significant predictors of reported efforts to learn when demographic, parenting, and teacher variables were taken into account. However, these peer provisions became nonsignificant predictors when students' academic self-processes (i.e., efficacy for learning, control beliefs, and reasons for learning) were entered into the regression equation. Therefore, although academic motivation in the form of goal pursuit is a likely mediator between teacher and peer provisions and students' academic accomplishments, other processes that regulate goal pursuit might be the more proximal targets of influence.

In addition to examining further the role of academic self-processes as mediators between provisions of classroom relationships and academic goal pursuit, it would be fruitful to focus on other social self-processes that are likely to influence the degree to which teacher and peer contexts orient students toward positive social and academic activities. Aspects of social–cognitive processing such as selective attention, attributions, and social biases and stereotypes (Crick & Dodge, 1994) can influence students' interpretations of social communications as well as teacher and peer reactions to students' behavior. Other individual characteristics such as attachment security and family functioning (e.g., Fuligni, Eccles, Barber, & Clements, 2001), racial identity (Graham, Taylor, & Hudley, 1998), and the extent that students are oriented toward gaining social approval (Goetz & Dweck, 1980) are also likely to influence the degree to which they are open to influence from teachers and peers.

A focus on students' beliefs concerning the constraints and affordances of the classroom also underscores the notion that subjective beliefs concerning acceptance and support from classmates and teachers represent an important aspect of social cognitive functioning that might influence behavior to a greater degree than actual levels of acceptance and support (see Harter, 1996). Few researchers have examined socialization processes that might influence social–cognitive aspects of goal setting, especially the degree to which students believe that their teachers can help them achieve their personal goals. However, these beliefs are likely to reflect to some degree the expectations that teachers have for students and how they are conveyed. For instance, teaching methods that foster the development of goals to learn and intrinsic orientations toward learning (e.g., Covington, 1999; Midgley, 2002), and that focus on establishing equal status and an ethos of care and cooperation among students (e.g., Cohen, 1986; Schaps, Battistich, & Solomon, 1997; Slavin, et al., 2003), are more likely to communicate beliefs that all students have the potential to learn than methods that foster competition, norm-referenced evaluations, and attitudes that not everyone can be successful (see Weinstein et al., 2004). In short, if the supports necessary for struggling and at-risk students are not provided in the classroom, these students are likely to feel alienated and to disengage.

Of additional concern is that certain student characteristics might predispose students to perceive relationships with adults and peers in either positive or negative ways. The literature on peer relationships suggests that children who are socially rejected tend to believe that others are out to harm them when in fact they are not, and they choose to pursue inappropriate and often antisocial goals in social situations (see Dodge & Feldman, 1990). Over time, these children develop relationships with their peers marked by mistrust and hostility. Similar research has not been conducted on student–teacher relationships. However, it is possible that students who believe that teachers do not like them might also be perceiving and interpreting these adult relationships in ways that are biased and unfounded. Therefore, efforts to promote perceptions that peers and teachers are caring and supportive are likely to be most successful if students themselves are targets of intervention.

Evidence also suggests that students are likely to listen to and accept the expectations of teachers and other adults depending on their age. For example, Smetana and Bitz (1996) reported that almost all adolescents believe that teachers have authority over issues such as stealing and fighting, somewhat less authority over issues such as misbehaving in class, breaking school rules, and smoking or substance abuse, and least authority over issues involving peer interactions, friendships, and personal appearance. Moreover, when compared to beliefs about the authority of their parents and friends to dictate their school behavior, adolescents reported that teachers have more authority with respect to moral issues such as stealing and fighting and conventional rules involving school and classroom conduct. Adolescent students also believed that teachers have as much authority as parents with respect to smoking or substance abuse. In general, however, these beliefs tend to change as children got older, with younger adolescents in middle school reporting that teachers have legitimate authority in all areas of school conduct and older adolescents in high school believing that teachers have little authority over most aspects of their lives at school.

In sum, it is important to remember that some students reject the expectations and values of teachers and peers outright. It is likely that other students merely comply with these expectations and present the impression that they are interested in achieving what is required when in fact, they are not. Some students, however, are likely to have internalized adult-valued goals and are committed to achieving them regardless of competing expectations. Therefore, identifying the precise socialization experiences that lead to these fundamentally different orientations toward learning at different ages remains a significant challenge to the field.

CONCLUSION

If teachers are able to implement specific practices and conditions that result in socially competent students, what is it about these practices that motivates students to participate willingly in classroom activities and even contribute in positive ways to the overall climate of the classroom? Are there ways in which students enable each other to adapt to the demands of the classroom? In this chapter, I have argued that socially competent students achieve goals that are personally valued as well as those that are sanctioned by others, and that the goals they pursue result in social integration as well as in positive developmental outcomes for the student. In addition, I have presented literature supportive of the notion that the ability to be socially competent is contingent on opportunities and affordances of the school context that allow students to pursue these multiple social goals. Specifically, students will engage in valued social and academic activities when they perceive their involvement and relationships with their teachers and peers as providing opportunities to achieve social and academic goals; as being safe and responsive to their social and academic strivings; as facilitating the achievement of their goals by providing help, advice, and instruction; and as being emotionally supportive and nurturing.

Beyond these basic observations, however, many interesting and challenging questions remain. In conclusion, therefore, I raise several general issues in need of additional consideration and empirical investigation if we are to make progress in understanding classroom supports and opportunities that can facilitate children's competence at school. These issues concern the expectations and goals we hold for our students, the role of developmental processes in choosing these goals, and the development of more sophisticated models to guide research on student competence.

Defining School Adjustment

Perhaps the most important goal for researchers and educators is to come to terms with the fundamental questions central to the task of educating children: What are our educational goals for our children? Do we want to teach simply to the test or nurture our children in ways that will help them become productive and healthy adults and citizens? By the same token, what are the goals that children bring with them to school? Do they strive to excel in relation to their peers, satisfy their curiosities, get along with others, or simply feel safe? To understand fully children's adjustment to school, it is imperative that we continue to seek answers to these questions and identify ways to coordinate these often antagonistic goals to achieve a healthy balance of multiple objectives. Indeed, the process of achieving more adaptive levels of adjustment will always include negotiations and coordination of the multiple and often conflicting goals of teachers, peers, students themselves, and their parents.

Although we are beginning to understand the basic goals that most teachers and students wish to achieve, we know little about how and why students come to learn about and to adopt these goals as their own. For instance, how do teachers communicate their expectations and goals to students and which factors predispose students to accept or reject these communications? We know that parental messages are more likely to be perceived accurately by children if they are clear and consistent, are framed in ways that are relevant and meaningful to the child, require decoding and processing by the child, and are perceived by the child to be of clear importance to the parent, and as being conveyed with positive intentions (Grusec & Goodnow, 1994). Do these same factors reflect effective forms of teacher–student communication and if so, can we teach teachers to communicate goals and expectations to their students in similar ways?

Similarly, we need to focus on understanding student characteristics that facilitate their acceptance of teachers' communications. Motivational factors such as perceived autonomy, competence, and belongingness (e.g., Connell & Wellborn, 1991), and social–emotional competencies such as the ability to experience empathy and interpersonal trust (see Grusec & Goodnow, 1994) are well-documented correlates of compliance with, if not internalization of, socially valued goals. Other factors such as students' beliefs regarding the fairness, relevance, and developmental appropriateness of teachers' goals and expectations also need to be investigated in this regard (e.g., Smetana & Bitz, 1996). Social information processing skills that determine which social messages and cues are attended to, how they are interpreted, and how they are responded to are additional, critical components of socially competent behavior (Crick & Dodge, 1994). These skills have been widely researched in the area of peer relationships; extending our knowledge of their influence to the realm of teacher–student relationships and adaptation to classroom contexts is a necessary next step in research on students' competence at school.

Developmental Processes

If the achievement of socially valued goals is a critical component of students' adjustment to school, investigations of appropriate goals and expectations need to be conducted within a developmental framework. A consideration of developmental issues is critically important for students of all ages. To illustrate, Grolnick and her colleagues (Grolnick, Kurowski, & Gurland, 1999) argued that children face normative motivational challenges as they make their way through school, with issues of social integration defining the transition to school, the development self-regulatory skills and positive perceptions of autonomy and competence defining the elementary years, and flexible coping and adaptation to new environments marking the transitions into middle and high school. Work by Eccles and Midgley (1989) also underscores the notion that schools need to account for students' changing needs and goals as they get older in order to provide optimal challenges and instructional supports for student engagement.

Developmental issues concerning the role of teachers in student goal setting also need to be considered. First, teachers tend to focus on different issues depending on the age of their students. Teachers of early elementary and junior high school students typically spend more of their time on issues related to social conduct than do teachers at other grade levels (Brophy & Evertson, 1978). In addition, the contribution of various socialization agents to the development and internalization of goals and values might also change with age. Whereas parents and teachers might facilitate the learning and adoption of goals in young children, peers might play an increasingly important role as children reach adolescence (see Wentzel, Filisetti, & Looney, 2004). It is likely that developmental influences and changes that orient children to either adults or peers for guidance are central to explanations of context-specific goal pursuit, and the question of how the content of students' goals changes with age. The reward structures that teachers establish in their classrooms also might have differential impact depending on students' age. Several researchers (Ames, 1992; Midgley, 2002) have identified classroom reward structures that can communicate the value of goals to compete with others, to improve one's own personal performance, and to cooperate with group efforts. However, middle school and high school students might be more attuned to evaluation practices that are competitive and normative than elementary-aged children (see Harter, 1996).

A developmental focus also is necessary for understanding the demands of teachers on students of different ages. Researchers (e.g., Brophy & Good, 1974; Eccles & Midgley, 1989) have observed that teachers treat students differently and focus on different tasks and goals depending on the age of their students. At this point, we do not know if changing developmental needs of students or normative and societal expectations for children at different ages drive these differences. Therefore, a critical look at the abilities of children at different ages as well as the normative requirements for competent classroom functioning is necessary. Systematic longitudinal and experimental research is needed to tease apart the relative contributions of children and teachers to patterns of classroom behavior and student–teacher interactions that appear to change across the elementary, middle, and high school years.

Models of School-Based Competence

As noted throughout this chapter, theoretically based models of school-based competence are not well developed. In particular, the role of context as it interacts with individual differences and psychological processes needs careful and systematic consideration. First, models need to consider the possible ways in which children and the various social systems in which they develop, including home, peer groups, and schools, interact to create expectations for school-based competence (see Bronfenbrenner, 1989). How these beliefs change as children develop and ways in which they contribute to children's developing school-related goal hierarchies should be a primary target of researchers' efforts.

Theoretical considerations of school-based competence also must continue to focus on underlying psychological processes and skills that promote the development and display of adjustment outcomes. To illustrate, researchers have clearly established significant and powerful links between prosocial and socially responsible behaviors and academic accomplishments. What have not been identified, however, are the psychological underpinnings of these behaviors. Research on skills and strategies involved in emotion regulation, self-regulated learning, social information processing, and goal coordination might be particularly fruitful in determining the degree to which multiple aspects of school adjustment (e.g., prosocial behavior, academic performance) are supported by a core set of psychological and emotional competencies and the degree to which social behaviors themselves contribute directly to learning outcomes. The logical next step would then be to identify ways to help students develop these critical skills.

Models of school-based competence also need to account for a diversity of student backgrounds and experiences. Indeed, much of what we know about these processes comes from studies of White, middle-class children. However, some researchers have found that supportive relationships with teachers might benefit minority students and girls in achieving positive behavioral and academic outcomes to a greater extent than Caucasian students and boys (e.g., Crosnoe et al., 2004). Studies of adolescent peer groups have documented that African American youth might face disproportionate levels of conflict between parental and peer values, with the potential to have a negative impact on academic achievement (Steinberg et al., 1992). Similarly, goal coordination skills might be more important for the adjustment of children from minority backgrounds than for children who come from families and communities whose goals and expectations, educational goals, and definitions of student success are likely to vary as a function of race, gender, neighborhood, and family background. In short, expanding our database to include the voices of under represented populations can only enrich our understanding of ways to create optimal classroom contexts within which all children can thrive socially as well as academically.

In closing, this chapter has provided some initial insights into the nature of school-related competence and how it might be supported by students' experiences with their teachers and peers. It is hoped these insights can serve as a foundation to explore further the role of classroom management practices in supporting the social and academic accomplishments of all school-aged children.

ACKNOWLEDGMENTS

The author thanks Jacqueline Eccles, University of Michigan and Tom Good, University of Arizona, for their insightful and helpful comments on earlier versions of this chapter.

REFERENCES

Aboud, F. E., & Mendelson, M. J. (1996). Determinants of friendship selection and quality: Developmental perspectives. In W. M. Bukowski, A. F. Newcomb, & W. W. Hartup (Eds.), *The company they keep: Friendship during childhood and adolescence* (pp. 87–112). New York: Cambridge University Press.

Allen, J. D. (1986). Classroom management: Students' perspectives, goals, and strategies. *American Educational Research Journal, 23*, 437–459.

Altermatt, E. R., Pomerantz, E. M., Ruble, D. N., Frey, K. S., & Greulich, F. K. (2002). Predicting changes in children's self-perceptions of academic competence: A naturalistic examination of evaluative discourse among classmates. *Developmental Psychology, 38*, 903–917.

Ames, C. (1992). Classrooms: Goals, structures, and student motivation. *Journal of Educational Psychology, 84*, 261–271.

Argyle, M. (1981). The contribution of social interaction research to social skills training. In J. D. Wine & M. D. Smye (Eds.), *Social competence*. New York: Guilford.

Asher, S. R., & Dodge, K. A. (1986). Identifying children who are rejected by their peers. *Developmental Psychology, 22*, 444–449.

Austin, J. T., & Vancouver, J. B. (1996). Goal constructs in psychology: Structure, process, and content. *Psychological Bulletin, 120*, 338–375.

Bandura, A. (1986). *Social foundations of thought and action: A social cognitive theory*. Englewood Cliffs, NJ: Prentice Hall.

Barker, R. G. (1961). Ecology and motivation. In M. R. Jones (Ed.), *Nebraska symposium on motivation*, (Vol. 8, pp. 1–50). Lincoln: University of Nebraska Press.

Berndt, T. J., & Keefe, K. (1995). Friends' influence on adolescents' adjustment to school. *Child Development, 66*, 1312–1329.

Birch, S. H., & Ladd, G. W. (1996). Interpersonal relationships in the school environment and children's early school adjustment: The role of teachers and peers. In J. Juvonen & K. Wentzel (Eds.), *Social motivation: Understanding children's school adjustment* (pp. 199–225). New York: Cambridge University Press.

Blumenfeld, P. C., Hamilton, V. L., Bossert, S. T., Wessels, K., & Meece, J. (1983). Teacher talk and student thought: Socialization into the student role. In J. M. Levine & M. C. Wang (Eds.), *Teacher and student perceptions: Implications for learning* (pp. 143–192). Hillsdale, NJ: Lawrence Erlbaum Associates.

Blumenfeld, P. C., Hamilton, V. L., Wessels, K., & Faulkner, D. (1979). Teaching responsibility to first graders. *Theory Into Practice, 18*, 174–180.

Bronfenbrenner, U. (1989). Ecological systems theory. In R. Vasta (Ed.), *Annals of child development* (Vol. 6, pp.187–250). Greenwich, CT: JAI Press.

Brophy, J. E., & Evertson, C. M. (1978). Context variables in teaching. *Educational Psychologist, 12*, 310–316.

Brophy, J. E., & Good, T. L. (1974). *Teacher-student relationships: Causes and consequences*. New York: Holt, Rinehart & Winston.

Brown, B. B. (1989). The role of peer groups in adolescents' adjustment to secondary school. In T. J. Berndt & G. W. Ladd (Eds.), *Peer relationships in child development* (pp. 188–215). New York: John Wiley.

Brown, B. B., Eicher, S. A., & Petrie, S. (1986). The importance of peer group ("crowd') affiliation in adolescence. *Journal of Adolescence, 9*, 73–96.

Brown, B. B., Mounts, N., Lamborn, D. D., Steinberg, L. (1993). Parenting practices and peer group affiliation in adolescence. *Child Development, 64*, 467–482.

Buhs, E. S., & Ladd, G. W. (2001). Peer rejection as an antecedent of young children's school adjustment: An examination of mediating processes. *Developmental Psychology, 37*, 550–560.

Cohen, E. G. (1986). *Designing group work: Strategies for the heterogeneous classroom*. New York: Teachers College Press.

Connell, J. P., & Wellborn, J. G. (1991). Competence, autonomy, and relatedness: A motivational analysis of self-system processes. In M. R. Gunnar & L. A. Sroufe (Eds.), Self *processes and development: The Minnesota symposia on child development* (Vol. 23, pp. 43–78). Hillsdale, NJ: Lawrence Erlbaum Associates.

Cooper, C. R., Ayers-Lopez, S., & Marquis, A. (1982). Children's discourse during peer learning in experimental and naturalistic situations. *Discourse Processes, 5*, 177–191.

Covington, M. V. (1999). Caring about learning: The nature and nurturing of subject-matter appreciation. *Educational Psychologist, 34*, 217–136.

Crick, N., & Dodge, K. A. (1994). A review and reformulation of social information-processing mechanisms in children's social adjustment. *Psychological Bulletin, 115*, 74–101.

Crockett, L., Losoff, M., & Petersen, A. C. (1984). Perceptions of the peer group and friendship in early adolescence. *Journal of Early Adolescence, 4*, 155–181.

Crosnoe, R., Johnson, M. K., & Elder, G. H. (2004). Intergenerational bonding in school: The behavioral and contextual correlates of student-teacher relationships. *Sociology of Education, 77*, 60–81.

Crosnoe, R., & Needham, B. (2004). Holism, contextual variability, and the study of friendships in adolescent development. *Child Development, 75*, 264–279.

Damon, W., & Phelps, E. (1989). Strategic uses of peer learning in children's education. In T. J. Berndt & G. W. Ladd (Eds.), *Peer relationships in child development* (pp. 133–157). New York: John Wiley.

DeRosier, M. E., Kupersmidt, J. B., & Patterson, C. J. (1994). Children's academic and behavioral adjustment as a function of the chronicity and proximity of peer rejection. *Child Development*, 65, 1799–1813.

Dodge, K. A., & Feldman, E. (1990). Issues in social cognition and sociometric status. In S. R. Asher & J. D. Coie (Eds.), *Peer rejection in childhood* (pp. 119–155). New York: Cambridge University Press.

Doyle, W. (1986). Classroom organization and management. In M. C. Witrock (Ed.), *Handbook of research on teaching* (pp. 392–431). New York: Macmillan.

DuBois, D. L., Felner, R. D., Brand, S., Adan, A. M., & Evans, E. G. (1992). A prospective study of life stress, social support, and adaptation in early adolescence. *Child Development, 63*, 542–557.

Dubow, E. F., & Tisak, J. (1989). The relation between stressful life events and adjustment in elementary school children: The role of social support and social problem-solving skills. *Child Development, 60*, 1412–1423.

Dweck, C. S. (1991). Self-theories and goals: Their role in motivation, personality, and development. In R. Dienstbier (Ed.), *Nebraska symposium on motivation* (Vol. 38, pp. 199–236). Lincoln, University of Nebraska Press.

Dweck, C. S., & Leggett, E. L. (1988). A social-cognitive approach to motivation and personality. *Psychological Review, 95*, 256–272.

Eccles, J. S., & Midgley, C. (1989). Stage-environment fit: Developmentally appropriate classrooms for young adolescents. In C. Ames & R. Ames (Eds.), *Research on motivation in education* (Vol. 3, pp. 139–186). New York: Academic Press.

Elliott, D. S., Hamburg, B. A., & Williams, K. R. (1998). *Violence in American schools: A new perspective*. New York: Cambridge University Press.

Erdley, C. A., & Asher, S. R. (1996). Children's social goals and self-efficacy perceptions as influences on their responses to ambiguous provocation. *Child Development, 67*, 1329–1344.

Erdley, C. A., Cain, K. M., Loomis, C. C., Dumas-Hines, F., & Dweck, C. S. (1997). Relations among children's social goals, implicit personality theories, and responses to social failure. *Developmental Psychology, 33*, 263–272.

Feldlaufer, H., Midgley, C., & Eccles, J. S. (1988). Student, teacher, and observer perceptions of the classroom before and after the transition to junior high school. *Journal of Early Adolescence, 8*, 133–156.

Feshbach, N. D. (1969). Student teacher preferences for elementary school pupils varying in personality characteristics. *Journal of Educational Psychology, 60*, 126–132.

Ford, M. E. (1992). *Motivating humans: Goals, emotions, and personal agency beliefs*. Newbury Park, CA: Sage.

Fuligni, A. J., Eccles, J. S., Barber, B. L., & Clements, P. (2001). Early adolescent peer orientation and adjustment during high school. *Developmental Psychology, 37*, 28–36.

Goetz, T. S., & Dweck, C. S. (1980). Learned helplessness in social situations. *journal of Personality and Social Psychology, 39*, 246–255.

Goodenow, C. (1993). Classroom belonging among early adolescent students: Relationships to motivation and achievement. *Journal of Early Adolescence, 13*, 21–43.

Gottman, J. M. (1983). How children become friends. *Monographs of the Society for Research in Child Development, 48*(3, Serial No. 201).

Graham, S., Taylor, A., & Hudley, C. (1998). Exploring achievement values among ethnic minority early adolescents. *Journal of Educational Psychology, 90*, 606–620.

Grolnick, W. S., Kurowski, C. O., & Gurland, S. T. (1999). Family processes and the development of children's self-regulation. *Educational Psychologist, 34*, 3–14.

Grolnick, W. S., & Ryan, R. M. (1989). Parent styles associated with children's self-regulation and competence in school. *Journal of Educational Psychology, 81*, 143–154.

Grusec, J. E., & Goodnow, J. J. (1994). Impact of parental discipline methods on the child's internalization of values: A reconceptualization of current points of view. *Developmental Psychology, 30*, 4–19.

Guay, F., Boivin, M., & Hodges, E. V. E. (1999). Predicting change in academic achievement: A model of peer experiences and self-system processes. *Journal of Educational Psychology, 91*, 105–115.

Hamre, B. K., & Pianta, R. C. (2001). Early teacher-child relationships and the trajectory of children's school outcomes through eighth grade. *Child Development, 72*, 625–638.

Hargreaves, D. H., Hester, S. K., & Mellor, F. J. (1975). *Deviance in classrooms*. London: Routledge & Kegan Paul.

Harter, S. (1996). Teacher and classmate influences on scholastic motivation, self-esteem, and level of voice in adolescents. In J. Juvonen & K. Wentzel (Eds.), *Social motivation: Understanding children's school adjustment* (pp. 11–42). New York: Cambridge University Press.

Hatzichristou, C., & Hopf, D. (1996). A multiperspective comparison of peer sociometric status groups in childhood and adolescence. *Child Development, 67*, 1085–1102.

Helton, G. B., & Oakland, T. D. (1977). Teachers' attitudinal responses to differing characteristics of elementary school students. *Journal of Educational Psychology, 69*, 261–265.

Hodges, E. V., Boivin, M., Vitaro, F., & Bukowski, W. M. (1999). The power of friendship: Protection against an escalating cycle of peer victimization. *Developmental Psychology, 35*, 94–101.

Hopps, H., & Cobb, J. A. (1974). Initial investigations into academic survivalskill training, direct instruction, and firstgrade achievement. *Journal of Educational Psychology, 66*, 548–553.

Hudley, C., & Graham, S. (1993). An attributional intervention to reduce peer-directed aggression among African-American boys. *Child Development, 64*, 124–138.

Hymel, S., Bowker, A., & Woody, E. (1993). Aggressive versus withdrawn unpopular children: Variations in peer and self-perceptions in multiple domains. *Child Development, 64*, 879–896.

Jacobsen, T., Edelstein, W., & Hofmann, V. (1994). A longitudinal study of the relation between representations of attachment in childhood and cognitive functioning in childhood and adolescence. *Developmental Psychology, 30*, 112–124.

Jussim, L. (1991). Social perception and social reality: A reflection-construction model. *Psychological Review, 98*, 9–34.

Jussim, L., & Eccles, J. (1995). Naturalistic studies of interpersonal expectancies. *Psychology, 63*, 947–961.

Juvonon, J., Nishina, A., & Graham, S. (2000). Peer harassment, psychological adjustment, and school functioning in early adolescence. *Journal of Educational Psychology, 92*, 349–359.

Kazdin, A. E. (1979). Nonspecific treatment factors in psychotherapy outcome research. *Journal of Consulting and Clinical Psychology, 47*, 846–851.

Kindermann, T. A. (1993). Natural peer groups as contexts for individual development: The case of children's motivation in school. *Developmental Psychology, 29*, 970–977.

Kindermann, T. A., McCollum, T., & Gibson, E. (1996). Peer networks and students' classroom engagement during childhood and adolescence. In J. Juvonen & K. R. Wentzel (Eds.), *Social motivation: Understanding children's school adjustment* (pp. 279–312). New York: Cambridge University Press.

Krumboltz, J., Ford, M. E., Nichols, C., & Wentzel, K. (1987). The goals of education. In R. C. Calfee (Ed.), *The study of Stanford and the schools: Views from the inside: Part II*. Stanford, CA: School of Education, Stanford.

Kurdek, L. A., & Sinclair, R. J. (2000). Psychological, family, and peer predictors of academic outcomes in first- through fifth-grade children. *Journal of Educational Psychology, 92*, 449–457.

Ladd, G. W. (1990). Having friends, keeping friends, making friends, and being liked by peers in the classroom: Predictors of children's early school adjustment. *Child Development, 61*, 1081–1100.

Ladd, G. W., & Burgess, K. B. (2001). Do relational risks and protective factors moderate the linkages between childhood aggression and early psychological and school adjustment? *Child Development, 72*, 1579–1601.

Ladd, G. W., & Oden, S. (1979). The relationships between peer acceptance and children's ideas about helpfulness. *Child Development, 50*, 402–408.

LaFontana, K. M., & Cillessen, A. H (2002). Children's perceptions of popular and unpopular peers: A multimethod assessment. *Developmental Psychology, 38*, 635–647.

Lempers, J. D., & Clark-Lempers, D. S. (1992). Young, middle, and late adolescents' comparisons of the functional importance of five significant relationships. *Journal of Youth and Adolescence, 21*, 53–96.

Maccoby, E. E. (1992). Trends in the study of socialization: Is there a Lewinian heritage? *Journal of Social Issues, 48*, 171–185.

Madon, S., Jussim, L., & Eccles, J. (1997). In search of self-fulfilling prophecy. *Journal of Personality and Social Psychology, 72*, 791–809.

Midgley, C. (2002). *Goals, goal structures, and adaptive learning*. Mahwah, NJ: Lawrence Erlbaum Associates.

Midgley, C., Feldlaufer, H., & Eccles, J. (1989). Student/teacher relations and attitudes toward mathematics before and after the transition to junior high school. *Child Development, 60*, 981–992.

National Center for Educational Statistics. (1995). Student strategies to avoid harm at school. (NCES Publication No. NCES 95-203). Washington, DC: U.S. Government Printing Office.

Newcomb, A. F., & Bagwell, C. L. (1995). Children's friendship relations: A meta-analytic review. *Psychological Bulletin, 117*, 306–347.

Newcomb, A. F., Bukowski, W. M., & Pattee, L. (1993). Children's peer relations: A metaanalytic review of popular, rejected, neglected, and controversial sociometric status. *Psychological Bulletin, 113*, 99–128.

Nichols, S. L., & Good, T. L. (2005). *America's teenagers—Myths and realities: Media images, schooling, and the social costs of careless indifference*. MAhwan, NJ: Lawrence Erlbaum Associates.

Oden, S., & Asher, S. R. (1977). Coaching children in social skills for friendship making. *Child Development, 48*, 495–506.

Ogbu, J. U. (1985). Origins of human competence: A cultural-ecological perspective. *Child Development, 52*, 413–429.

Olweus, D. (1993). Victimization by peers: Antecedents and long-term outcomes. In K. Rubin & J. B. Asendorf (Eds.), *Social withdrawal, inhibition, and shyness in childhood* (pp. 315–341). Chicago: University of Chicago Press.

Parker, J. G., & Asher, S. R. (1993). Friendship and friendship quality in middle childhood: Links with peer group acceptance and feelings of loneliness and social dissatisfaction. *Developmental Psychology, 29*, 611–621.

Parkhurst, J. T., & Hopmeyer, A. (1998). Sociometric popularity and peer-perceived popularity: Two distinct dimensions of peer status. *Journal of Early Adolescence, 18*, 125–144.

Patterson, G. R., & Bank, C. L. (1989). Some amplifying mechanisms for pathologic processes in families. In M. R. Gunnar & E. Thelan (Eds.), *Systems and development: The Minnesota symposia on child psychology* (Vol. 22 pp. 167–210). Hillsdale, NJ: Lawrence Erlbaum Associates.

Patterson, G. R., Bank, C. L., & Stoolmiller, M. (1990). The preadolescent's contributions to disrupted family process. In R. Montemayor, G. R. Adams, & T. P. Gullota (Eds.), *From childhood to adolescence: A transitional period?* (Vol. 2, pp. 107–133). Newbury Park, CA: Sage.

Pellegrini, A. D., Bartini, M., & Brooks, F. (1999). School bullies, victims, and aggressive victims: Factors relating to group affiliation and victimization in early adolescence. *Journal of Educational Psychology, 91*, 216–224.

Perry, D. G., Perry, L. C., & Rasmussen, P. (1986). Cognitive social learning mediators of aggression. *Child Development, 57*, 700–711.

Piaget, J. (1965). *The moral judgment of the child*. New York: Free Press.

Pianta, R. C., Hamre, B., & Stuhlman, M. (2003). Relationships between teachers and children. In W. Reynolds & G. Miller (Eds.), *Handbook of psychology: Vol. 7. Educational psychology* (pp. 199–234) . New York: John Wiley.

Pintrich, P. R. (2003). Motivation and classroom learning. In W. Reynolds & G. Miller (Eds.), *Handbook of psychology: Vol. 7. Educational psychology* (pp. 103–122) . New York: John Wiley.

Rabiner, D. L., & Gordon, L. V. (1992). The coordination of conflicting social goals: Differences between rejected and nonrejected boys. *Child Development, 63*, 1344–1350.

Rotenberg, K. J. (1991). *Children's interpersonal trust: Sensitivity to lying, deception, and promise violations*. New York: Springer-Verlag.

Rubin, K. H., Bukowski, W., & Parker, J. G. (1998). Peer interactions, relationships, and groups. In W. Damon (Series Ed.) & N. Eisenberg (Vol. Ed.), *Handbook of child psychology: Vol. 3. Social, emotional, and personality development* (5th ed., pp. 619–700). New York: John Wiley.

Ryan, A. (2001). The peer group as a context for the development of young adolescent motivation and achievement. *Child Development, 72*, 1135–1150.

Ryan, R. M. (1993). Agency and organization: Intrinsic motivation, autonomy, and the self in psychological development. In J. Jacobs (Ed.), *Nebraska symposium on motivation* (Vol. 40, pp. 1–56). Lincoln: University of Nebraska Press.

Safran, S. P., & Safran, J. S. (1985). Classroom context and teachers' perceptions of problem behaviors. *Journal of Educational Psychology, 77*, 20–28.

Schaps, E., Battistich, V., & Solomon, D. (1997). School as a caring community: A key to character education. In A. Molnar (Ed.), *Ninety-sixth yearbook of the National Society for the Study of Education* (pp. 127–139). Chicago: University of Chicago Press.

Schunk, D. H. (1987). Peer models and children's behavioral change. *Review of Educational Research, 57*, 149–174.

Shultz, J., & Florio, S. (1979). Stop and freeze: The negotiation of social and physical space in a kindergarten/first grade classroom. *Anthropology and Education Quarterly, 10*, 166–181.

Sieber, R. T. (1979). Classmates as workmates: Informal peer activity in the elementary school. *Anthropology and Education Quarterly, 10*, 207–235.

Skinner, E. A., & Belmont, M. J. (1993). Motivation in the classroom: Reciprocal effects of teacher behavior and student engagement across the school year. *Journal of Educational Psychology, 85*, 571–581.

Slavin, R. E., Hurley, E. A., & Chamberlain, A. (2003). Cooperative learning and achievement: Theory and research. In W. Reynolds & G. Miller (Eds.), *Handbook of psychology: Vol. 7. Educational psychology* (pp. 177–198) . New York: John Wiley.

Smetana, J., & Bitz, B. (1996). Adolescents' conceptions of teachers' authority and their relations to rule violations in school. *Child Development, 67*, 1153–1172.

Smith, A. E., Jussim, L., & Eccles, J. (1999). Do self-fulfilling prophecies accumulate, dissipate, or remain stable over time? *Journal of Personality and Social Psychology, 77*, 548–565.

Solomon, D., Schaps, E., Watson, M., & Battistich, V. (1992). Creating caring school and classroom communities for all students. In R. Villa, J. Thousand, W. Stainback, & S. Stainback (Eds.), *Restructuring for caring and effective education: An administrative guide to creating heterogeneous schools* (pp. 41–60). Baltimore: Brookes.

Snyder, J., Brooker, M., Patrick, M. R., Snyder, A., Schrepferman, & Stoolmiller, M. (2003). Observed peer victimization during early elementary school: Continuity, growth, and relation to risk for child antisocial and depressive behavior. *Child Development, 74*, 1881–1898.

Spivack, G., & Shure, M. B. (1982). The cognition of social adjustment: Interpersonal cognitive problem-solving thinking. In B. B. Lahey & A. E. Kazdin (Eds.), *Advances in clinical psychology*, (Vol. 5, pp. 323–372). New York: Plenum.

Steinberg, L. (1990). Autonomy, conflict, and harmony in the family relationship. In S. S Feldman & G. R. Elliott (Eds.), *At the threshold: The developing adolescent* (pp. 255–276). Cambridge, MA: Harvard University Press.

Steinberg, L., Dornbusch, S. M., & Brown, B. B. (1992). Ethnic differences in adolescent achievement: An ecological perspective. *American Psychologist, 47*, 723–729.

Sternberg, R. J., & Kolligian, J. (1990). *Competence considered*. New Haven, CT: Yale University Press.

Stone, M. R., & Brown, B. B. (1999). Identity claims and projections: Descriptions of self and crowds in secondary school. *New Directions for Child and Adolescent Development, 84*, 7–20.

Trenholm, S., & Rose, T. (1981). The compliant communicator: Teacher perceptions of appropriate classroom behavior. *The Western Journal of Speech Communication, 45*, 13–26.

Watson, M., Solomon, D., Battistich, V., Schaps, E., & Solomon, J. (1989). The child development project: Combining traditional and developmental approaches to values education. In L. Nucci (Ed.), *Moral development and character education: A dialogue* (pp. 51–92). Berkeley, CA: McCutchan.

Weiner, B. (1980). A cognitive (attribution)-emotion-action model of motivated behavior: An analysis of judgements of help-giving. *Journal of Personality and Social Psychology, 39*, 186–200.

Weinstein, R. S. (2002). *Reaching higher: The power of expectations in schooling*. Cambridge, MA: Harvard University Press.

Weinstein, R. S., Gregory, A., & Strambler, M. J. (2004). Intractable self-fulfilling prophecies: Brown v. Board of Education. *American Psychologist, 59*, 511–520.

Weinstein, R. S., Marshall, H. H., Sharp, L., & Botkin, M. (1987). Pygmalion and the student: Age and classroom differences in children's awareness of teacher expectations. *Child Development, 58*, 1079–1093.

Wentzel, K. R. (1989). Adolescent classroom goals, standards for performance, and academic achievement: An interactionist perspective. *Journal of Educational Psychology, 81*, 131–142.

Wentzel, K. R. (1991a). Relations between social competence and academic achievement in early adolescence. *Child Development, 62*, 1066–1078.

Wentzel, K. R. (1991b). Social and academic goals at school: Achievement motivation in context. In M. Maehr & P. Pintrich (Eds.), *Advances in motivation and achievement* (Vol. 7, pp. 185–212). Greenwich, CT: JAI Press.

Wentzel, K. R. (1991c). Social competence at school: Relations between social responsibility and academic achievement. *Review of Educational Research, 61*, 1–24.

Wentzel, K. R. (1992). Motivation and achievement In adolescence: A multiple goals perspective. In D. Schunk & J. Meece (Eds.), *Student perceptions in the classroom: Causes and consequences* (pp. 287–306). Hillsdale, NJ: Lawrence Erlbaum Associates.

Wentzel, K. R. (1993). Social and academic goals at school: Motivation and achievement in early adolescence. *Journal of Early Adolescence, 13*, 4–20.

Wentzel, K. R. (1994). Relations of social goal pursuit to social acceptance, classroom behavior, and perceived social support. *Journal of Educational Psychology, 86*, 173–182.

Wentzel, K. R. (1997). Student motivation in middle school: The role of perceived pedagogical caring. *Journal of Educational Psychology, 89*, 411–419.

Wentzel, K. R. (1998). Social support and adjustment in middle school: The role of parents, teachers, and peers. *Journal of Educational Psychology, 90*, 202–209.

Wentzel, K. R. (2002a). Are effective teachers like good parents? Interpersonal predictors of school adjustment in early adolescence. *Child Development, 73*, 287–301.

Wentzel, K. R. (2002b). The contribution of social goal setting to children's school adjustment. In A. Wigfield & J. Eccles (Eds.), *Development of achievement motivation* (pp. 221–246). New York: Academic Press.

Wentzel, K. R. (2003). School adjustment. In W. Reynolds & G. Miller (Eds.), *Handbook of psychology: Vol. 7. Educational psychology* (pp. 235–258). New York: John Wiley.

Wentzel, K. R. (2004a). *Teachers' beliefs about pedagogical caring*. Unpublished manuscript, University of Maryland, College Park, MD.

Wentzel, K. R. (2004b). Social motivation and school adjustment. In R. Kail (Ed.), *Advances in child development and behavior* (Vol. 32, pp. 213–241). New York: Elsevier.

Wentzel, K. R., & Asher, S. R. (1995). Academic lives of neglected, rejected, popular, and controversial children. *Child Development, 66*, 754–763.

Wentzel, K. R., Barry, C., & Caldwell, K. (2004). Friendships in middle school: Influences on motivation and school adjustment. *Journal of Educational Psychology, 96*, 195–203.

Wentzel, K. R., Battle, A., Looney, L. (March, 2000). *Teacher and peer contributions to classroom climate in middle school: Relations to school adjustment*. Paper presented at the annual meeting of the American Educational Research Association, Seattle, WA.

Wentzel, K. R. & Caldwell, K. (1997). Friendships, peer acceptance, and group membership: Relations to academic achievement in middle school. *Child Development, 68*, 1198–1209.

Wentzel, K. R., Filisetti, L., & Looney, L. (2005). *Predictors of prosocial behavior in young adolescents: Self-processes and contextual factors*. Unpublished manuscript.

Wentzel, K. R., Looney, L., & Battle, A., (2004). *Teacher and peer contributions to classroom climate in middle school and high school*. Manuscript in preparation.

Wentzel, K. R., & McNamara, C. (1999). Interpersonal relationships, emotional distress, and prosocial behavior in middle school. *Journal of Early Adolescence, 19*, 114–125.

Wentzel, K. R., Weinberger, D. A., Ford, M. E., & Feldman, S. S. (1990). Academic achievement in preadolescence: The role of motivational, affective, and self-regulatory processes. *Journal of Applied Developmental Psychology, 11*, 179–193.

Wigfield, A., & Eccles, J. S. (1992). The development of achievement task values: A theoretical analysis. *Developmental Review, 12*, 265–310.

Youniss, J., & Smollar, J. (1989). Adolescents' interpersonal relationships in social context. In T. J. Berndt & G. Ladd (Eds.), *Peer relationships in child development* (pp. 300–316). New York: John Wiley.

Zakriski, A. L., & Coie, J. D. (1996). A comparison of aggressive-rejected and nonaggressive-rejected children's interpretations of self-directed and other-directed rejection. *Child Development, 67*, 1048–1070.

24

Extrinsic Rewards and Inner Motivation

Johnmarshall Reeve
University of Iowa

INTRODUCTION

Most children glow with excitement when they see a sticker attached to their latest homework effort. When offered a special privilege, most adolescents perk up with interest. Positive emotion and a spike in students' willingness to participate is what teachers often see when they introduce extrinsic rewards into the learning environment. The conclusion seems to be that extrinsic rewards are effective motivators that can contribute to teachers' efforts to manage classrooms. The present chapter both acknowledges and debates this apparent truism.

Extrinsic rewards enhance students' emotion and on-task behavior, but they do more. They also affect students' inner motivation (Deci, Koestner, & Ryan, 1999; Ryan & Deci, 2000a). As we shall see, extrinsic rewards sometimes support, but other times interfere with, students' inner motivation. This interaction between extrinsic rewards and inner motivation therefore introduces a complex set of circumstances in predicting how effective rewards will be as classroom motivators. Accordingly, a comprehensive analysis of how extrinsic rewards affect emotion and behavior needs to be extended to include an analysis of how extrinsic rewards affect inner motivation. Students posses a repertoire of inner motivational resources that are fully capable of energizing and sustaining their classroom engagement—with or without the support of extrinsic rewards (Reeve, 1996). So, the question to ask is whether teachers need extrinsic rewards to motivate students. With this question in mind, the fourfold purpose of this chapter is to discuss the following issues about the role of extrinsic rewards in classrooms: (a) What are the motivating effects of extrinsic rewards? (b) How do extrinsic rewards affect students' inner motivation? (c) How do both extrinsic rewards and inner motivation affect students' classroom engagement? and (d) What are some recommendations for how educators can effectively motivate and engage students during learning activities?

EXTRINSIC REWARDS

An extrinsic reward is some offering given in return for another person's service or achievement (Craighead, Kazdin, & Mahoney, 1981). Thus, when a teacher promises a prize if her students will participate more or when a teacher smiles to acknowledge their successful performance, she administers a reward (prize, smile). Common classroom rewards include praise, attention, stickers, gold stars, privileges, good grades, tokens, approval, scholarships, candy, food, trophies, check marks and points, good citizen certificates, awards, money, smiles, positive feedback, public recognition, pats on the back, prizes, special materials, free time, incentive plans, and honor rolls.

Because extrinsic rewards are often confused with positive reinforcers, which are defined by their effects on behavior, I will distinguish between the two. A positive reinforcer is any environmental event that, when presented, increases the strength and future probability of a target behavior. The distinction between rewards and positive reinforcers is that all positive reinforcers are rewards, whereas only some rewards function as positive reinforcers (because not all rewards increase behavior). The focus in this chapter is on the broad instructional practice of offering extrinsic rewards to solicit students' service or to acknowledge their achievement, irrespective of whether those rewards actually reinforce behavior. Such a focus allows the discussion to center on teachers' use of extrinsic rewards as *potential* classroom motivators.

Why Rewards Enliven Positive Emotion and Facilitate Behavior

Why do students get so excited about the prospect of an extrinsic reward? Why do rewards enliven positive emotion and facilitate behavior? Like all human beings, students are inherently sensitive to signals of gain and pleasure. The physiological mechanism that makes students inherently sensitive to reward (to gain and pleasure) is the release of brain dopamine (Mirenowicz & Schultz, 1994; Montague, Dayan, & Sejnowski, 1996) and the subsequent activation of the behavioral activation system (BAS; Gray, 1990). Increased neural activity in the BAS is responsible for generating inherently positive feelings, such as hope and interest. It further facilitates behavior, as BAS activation literally and physically encourages students to move toward environmental signals of personal gain. Thus, an extrinsic reward enlivens positive emotion and facilitates behavior because it signals an upcoming opportunity for a personal gain.

In practice, the offering of an extrinsic reward means, to students, that personal gain is imminent and that the classroom script has taken an unexpected turn for the better. For instance, routine (expected) classroom events leave students' BASs unaffected. However, when events take an unexpected turn for the better, then dopamine release and BAS neural activation occur, as the brain inherently latches onto the environmental signal of an unexpected gain. An unexpected sticker and a surprise announcement of a special privilege represent two such examples of teacher-provided signals of students' possible future gain.

Why Rewards Are So Prevalent in Schools

Because school personnel often note students' emotional and behavioral responsivity to particular rewards, they capitalize on this phenomenon by identifying desired behaviors and engineering contingencies between behaviors and rewards. Extensive research literatures (e.g., behavior modification programs) show practitioners how to administer extrinsic rewards in this way (Alberto & Troutman, 2003; Baldwin & Baldwin, 1986; Walker, Shea, & Bauer, 2004).

Briefly, teachers administer rewards in one of the following three ways: (a) before the target behavior so to elicit a particular way of behaving from the student; (b) during the performance of the target behavior so to maintain its persistence; and (c) as a consequence after an episode of the target behavior has occurred.

Teachers introduce extrinsic rewards into the learning environment for two primary reasons. One reason is to manage students' behavior. When teachers manage students' behavior, they essentially set up conditions (e.g., reward contingencies) that make desired target behaviors more likely. A second reason teachers use rewards is to supply students with motivation that they might otherwise lack. From a motivational (rather than a behavioral) perspective, teachers use rewards to bolster students' otherwise low motivation (Boggiano, Barrett, Weiher, McClelland, & Lusk, 1987). For example, teachers may decide that if the task itself cannot generate enough motivation for students to engage it, then what is needed is an added external gain to provide students with the motivation they otherwise lack. For instance, if a poetry assignment fails to provide students with the motivation they need to complete it, then perhaps the offer of bonus points for doing so will provide the motivation the assignment itself was unable to provide.

This chapter focuses on the use of extrinsic rewards to motivate students' academic learning and behavior. In addition to extrinsic rewards, however, teachers who seek to manage students' behavior have many additional ways to do so. For instance, teachers can offer clear expectations of what student are to do, endorse high standards of achievement, provide step-by-step directions, introduce a schedule, set goals, make plans, offer suggestions, introduce interesting activities, offer choices, provide encouragement, introduce attractive role models, and administer performance feedback (Brophy, 1986; Skinner, 1995). Motivation researchers in the classroom management tradition therefore extend their focus beyond just extrinsic rewards to include the more general construct of classroom structure.

Structure refers to the amount and clarity of information that teachers provide to students regarding what to do, how to do it, and what are the best ways to develop desired skills and achieve valued outcomes (Connell & Wellborn, 1991; Skinner, 1985, 1995; Skinner, Zimmer-Gembeck, & Connell, 1998). Its opposite is confusion. Confused students lack a clear intention to act (e.g., "What should I do?"). Generally speaking, the more teachers provide structure for students' learning experiences, the more students develop intentions to act that enable them to achieve the skills and outcomes they value (Skinner et al., 1998). From a classroom management perspective, the provision of structure prepares students for learning (Martin, 1983). By structuring a learning environment, teachers focus students' attention and make the lesson's framework clear (Perrott, 1982).

Rewards as One Part of Classroom Structure

A glimpse into the history of psychology shows how educators gradually expanded a narrow focus on rewards to a broader focus on structure. When behaviorism dominated psychological thinking, motivation, intentions, and behaviors were seen as a function of environmental events such as incentives, consequences, and rewards (Bolles, 1972; Dember, 1965). Two generations of work showed that students' motivated behavior was further a function of observing models, setting goals, formulating expectations, striving for competence, being mentored and scaffolded, receiving feedback, piquing curiosity, nurturing intrinsic motivation, catching and holding interest, supporting autonomous self-regulation, and so on (Weiner, 1990). Offering rewards became recognized as only one way to motivate students. To add motivational strategies such as modeling, scaffolding, offering challenges, communicating feedback, supporting autonomy, and promoting mastery goals, a more general term was needed to describe the process

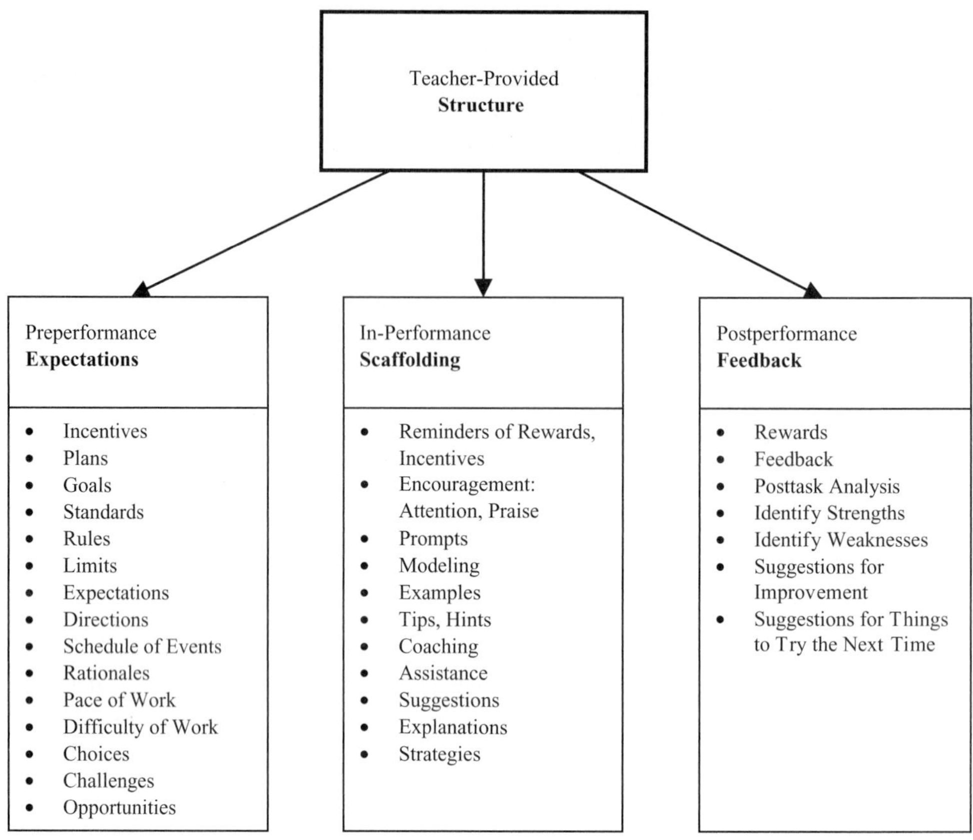

FIGURE 24.1. Elements of teacher-provided classroom structure.

by which teachers help students formulate and maintain intentions to act. As mentioned, that term became known as structure, as in a structured learning environment.

Figure 24.1 provides a framework to illustrate the role of extrinsic rewards within a highly structured learning environment. The figure divides the flow of any learning activity into three phases. First, before asking students to engage themselves in the learning activity, the teacher prepares students for learning by communicating her expectations, standards, and a script for what students will do. What all these aspects of structure have in common is that they help students formulate intentions to act. If rewards are used at this point in the lesson, they are offered as incentives in exchange for students' service. Second, during the learning activity, the teacher monitors and assists students' activity by providing reminders, encouragement, modeling, and scaffolding. What all these aspects of structure have in common is that they help students maintain their intentions to act. If rewards are used at this point in the lesson, they are employed to remind students of the contingencies that are in place or as behavioral supports to maintain students' positive emotion and on-task behavior. Third, upon the completion of the learning activity, the teacher tells students what they learned and prepares them for future learning experiences by offering feedback, analysis, and a reflective commentary as to what students did well, did poorly, and what needs to be done the next time. What all these aspects of structure have in common is that they help students revise their intentions and formulate new and improved intentions for the future. If rewards are used at this point in the lesson, they are given either spontaneously or in exchange for students' achievement.

Are Rewards Effective Motivators?

Do extrinsic rewards work? Are they effective motivators? If so, extrinsic rewards should meet two criteria:

1. If effective, rewards should encourage engagement via a facilitating effect on students' positive emotion and on-task behavior.
2. If safe, rewards should produce this facilitating effect without introducing any troubling "side effects."

Do Rewards Work? The general consensus is that, yes, extrinsic rewards do encourage targeted behaviors, at least when teachers administer them in a sincere and contingent way (Alberto & Troutman, 2003; Walker et al., 2004). If a teacher promises students a pizza party if they achieve 100% attendance for the week, then the promise of a pizza party will generally encourage students' subsequent attendance. Many additional examples of the positive effects that rewards have on students' compliance can be offered, including using rewards to motivate students to complete their homework (Harris & Sherman, 1974; Miller & Kelley, 1994), follow the teacher's "do" and "don't" requests (Neef, Shafer, Egel, Cataldo, & Parrish, 1983), improve their reading fluency (Eckert, Ardoin, Daly, & Martins, 2002), and complete assigned tasks (Martens, Lochner, & Kelly, 1992). One qualification of this conclusion is that, when rewards are no longer offered in exchange for a target behavior, the facilitating effect declines and the once-contingent behavior returns to its prereward baseline level (Baldwin & Baldwin, 1986).

Do Rewards Produce Troubling "Side Effects?" The general consensus is, again, yes, extrinsic rewards sometimes produce troubling side effects. Collectively, these side effects have been termed the "hidden costs of reward," because our society and American education in general typically view extrinsic rewards as positive contributors to students' motivation and behavior (Lepper & Greene, 1978). Three such hidden costs include (a) decreased intrinsic motivation toward the activity; (b) interference with the process and quality of academic learning; and (c) undermining of students' capacity for autonomous self-regulation.

The first side effect is that extrinsic rewards often undermine intrinsic motivation (Deci et al., 1999; Ryan & Deci, 2000a). The research on how extrinsic rewards affect intrinsic motivation began with this question: "If a person is involved in an intrinsically interesting activity and begins to receive an extrinsic reward for doing it, what happens to his or her intrinsic motivation for that activity?" (Deci & Ryan, 1985, p. 43). Extrinsic rewards generally do not add to intrinsic motivation, and extrinsic motivation and intrinsic motivation do not necessarily combine into "super motivation." Instead, the introduction of an extrinsic reward typically conflicts with and eventually undermines intrinsic motivation (Condry, 1977; Deci et al., 1999; Lepper & Greene, 1978; Ryan & Deci, 2000a).

Teachers are often surprised to learn that extrinsic rewards can undermine intrinsic motivation (Hom, 1994), so the undermining effect needs to be explained. Extrinsic rewards undermine intrinsic motivation when "play becomes work" (Lepper & Greene, 1975) and when rewards conflict with students' psychological need for autonomy (Deci, 1975; Deci et al., 1999). When rewards are at stake, students who have an initial intrinsic motivation toward reading, for instance, begin to read less and less out of endogenous interest, autonomy, and intrinsic motivation, and more and more for the exogenous gain of extrinsic reward. Basically, bribing students to engage in a task, even when doing so with rewards that are unquestionably attractive, instigates a shift in students' understanding of why they engage in that activity away from a reason of autonomy, intrinsic motivation, and "play" to one of reward, extrinsic motivation, and "work." Students who have participated in the popular *Book It*! reading program, or any student who has been induced to read a book for a $2 prize, can attest to this experience of turning play into work (Donahue, 1996).

However, extrinsic rewards do not always undermine intrinsic motivation. Some types of extrinsic rewards do undermine intrinsic motivation, but other types leave intrinsic motivation unaffected or even increase it. Expected, tangible, and task-contingent rewards ("If you do X, then you get some candy.") typically undermine intrinsic motivation. Unlike expected rewards, unexpected rewards do not undermine intrinsic motivation (Deci et al., 1999; Lepper, Greene, & Nisbett, 1973; Pallak, Castomiris, Sroka, & Pittman, 1982; Tang & Hall, 1995). Unlike tangible rewards such as tokens and food prizes that undermine intrinsic motivation (Wiersma, 1992), verbal rewards and positive feedback do not (Anderson, Manoogian, & Reznick, 1976; Blank, Reis, & Jackson, 1984; Deci et al., 1999; Henderlong & Lepper, 2002). In the same spirit, task-noncontingent rewards (those given with no strings attached) do not undermine intrinsic motivation the way task-contingent rewards do (Ryan, Mims, & Koestner, 1983; Tang & Hall, 1995). Thus, the undermining of intrinsic motivation seems to occur when extrinsic rewards are offered in the following way, "If you turn in your homework, you get a candy bar." or "If you want a sticker, you have to come to class on time."

The second side effect is that expected tangible, and task-contingent rewards generally interfere with both the *process* and the *quality* of learning. These types of extrinsic rewards interfere with the learner's on-task attention and challenge seeking, as learners shift their attention away from the learning material toward the extrinsic reward (Harter, 1978; Pittman, Boggiano, & Ruble, 1983) and prefer easy success over optimal challenge (Shapira, 1976). These types of rewards also tend to orient learners toward passivity, convergent thinking, quickly getting the right answer, and a search for factual knowledge, but away from creativity, divergent thinking, the search for an optimal solution, and the desire to conceptually understand the lesson (Amabile, 1985; Benware & Deci, 1984; Boggiano, Flink, Shields, Seelbach, & Barrett, 1993; Grolnick & Ryan, 1987; McGraw & McCullers, 1979).

The third side effect is that extrinsic rewards interfere with students' developmental capacity for autonomous self-regulation (Cannella, 1986; Lepper, 1983; Kohn, 1993; Ryan, 1993). From a motivational perspective, autonomous self-regulation is the capacity to initiate and persist in environmental transactions in ways that involve and satisfy one's inner motivational resources, such as interests and preferences. When these types of rewards are not at stake, students generally engage themselves in academic activities in ways that reflect the rise and fall of their inner motivation (Joussemet, Koestner, Lekes, & Houlfort, 2004). In contrast, the offering of an attractive extrinsic contingency essentially asks students to neglect or at least put aside their inner motivation and instead engage themselves in relatively uninteresting and nonpreferred activities. Over time, controlling external contingencies desensitize students to their basic needs, disrupt their self-awareness, and interfere with their sense of choice and autonomous self-regulation.

INNER MOTIVATION

Students are sensitive and responsive to environmental signals of reward, and this sensitivity endows them with a capacity for extrinsic motivation. In addition, however, students further possess an array of inner motivational resources (Reeve, 1996; Reeve, Deci, & Ryan, 2004). Among students' inner resources are their psychological needs and intrinsic motivation.

Psychological Needs

A psychological need is an inherent process that underlies a student's desire to seek out interactions with the environment for experiences that are essential and necessary for vitality, psychological growth, and well-being (Reeve, 2004). The three psychological needs studied extensively in the empirical exploration of intrinsic and extrinsic motivation are autonomy, competence, and relatedness (Ryan & Deci, 2000b, 2002). Unlike the motivation associated with extrinsic rewards, which is reactive and environmentally generated, the motivation associated with psychological needs is proactive and personally generated. Collectively, these psychological needs provide students with a natural motivation for learning, growing, and developing. Whether students actually experience such learning, growing, and developing, however, depends on the quality of the social environment and the extent to which it supports and nurtures versus neglects and frustrates these needs.

Autonomy is the inner endorsement of one's actions, and it reflects the desire to have one's interests and preferences (rather than reward contingencies) determine one's actions (Deci & Ryan, 1985). The experiential qualities that constitute its subjective experience include an internal perceived locus of causality, high volition (feeling free), and perceived choice over one's actions (Reeve, Nix, & Hamm, 2003). Behavior is autonomous when a student's interests and personal preferences (i.e., inner motivational resources) guide the decision-making process of whether to engage in a particular activity.

Competence is the psychological need to be effective in interactions with the environment, and it reflects the desire to exercise one's capacities and skills, and in doing so, to seek out and master optimal challenges (Deci & Ryan, 1985). The experiential qualities that constitute its subjective experience include feeling capable, effective, flow, and a sense that one is making progress. Behavior reflects the need for competence when the student proactively seeks out and invests high effort in finding optimal challenges, concentrates and becomes fully absorbed during those challenges, and uses the task engagement as an opportunity to develop and stretch valued skills.

Relatedness is the psychological need to establish close emotional bonds and attachments with others, and it reflects the desire to be emotionally connected to and interpersonally involved in warm relationships (Baumeister & Leary, 1995; Furrer & Skinner, 2003; Ryan, 1991). The experiential qualities that constitute its subjective experience are acceptance, belongingness, and sense of being genuinely cared for. Behavior reflects the need for relatedness when the student gravitates toward people perceived to be trustworthy and to be looking out for one's well-being.

Intrinsic Motivation

Intrinsic motivation is the inherent propensity to engage one's interests and to exercise and develop one's capacities (Deci & Ryan, 1985). It emerges spontaneously from the psychological needs for autonomy, competence, and relatedness (Ryan & Deci, 2000b), and its emergence requires no instrumental reason associated with extrinsic reward. Instead, intrinsic motivation arises when an activity successfully involves and nurtures one or more of the psychological needs. When intrinsically motivated, however, students do not typically say, "I feel competent" or "I feel autonomous." Instead, they say, "that is interesting," "that is fun," or "I enjoy doing it." For instance, when students say that math or art is fun, the experience that allows the activity to be deemed as fun is theoretically one of autonomy, competence, or relatedness satisfaction. Though intrinsically motivated individuals feel interest and enjoyment, the underlying source of their intrinsic motivation is nonetheless the involvement and nurturance of their psychological needs (Deci, 1987, 1992; Ryan & Deci, 2000b).

Intrinsic motivation yields numerous educational benefits for students. When intrinsically motivated, students are more likely to be creative (Amabile, 1985), active during information processing (Benware & Deci, 1984), learn in ways that are conceptual (Boggiano, Fink, Shields, Seelbach, & Barrett, 1993; Grolnick & Ryan, 1987), experience greater positive emotion and subjective well-being (Ryan & Deci, 2000b), and come to school rather than drop out

(Hardre & Reeve, 2003). Though intrinsic motivation arises from students' psychological needs, educators can nevertheless use extrinsic rewards to support and satisfy these psychological needs. Hence, whereas some types of extrinsic rewards produce troubling side effects, other types can support intrinsic motivation, learning, and autonomous self-regulation, as will be illustrated in the next section on cognitive evaluation theory.

COGNITIVE EVALUATION THEORY

Sometimes, educators offer students extrinsic rewards to increase their desired behaviors. In using rewards in this way, the teacher's purpose is to shape, guide, or control students' behavior. Other times, educators offer extrinsic rewards to communicate a message of a job well done. In using rewards in this way, the teacher's purpose is to enhance students' sense of competence. Extrinsic rewards therefore serve two purposes: to elicit a desired behavior (control behavior) and to affirm achievement (inform competence). According to cognitive evaluation theory, this first purpose is referred to as the "controlling aspect" of a reward, whereas the second purpose is referred to as its "informational aspect" (Deci & Ryan, 1985). The theory goes further, however, and states that *all* extrinsic rewards have *both* a controlling aspect and an informational aspect. That is, all rewards both control behavior and inform competence, and the important distinction is whether the teacher's primary purpose in administering the reward is to control behavior or to inform competence.

Figure 24.2 graphically represents the elements in cognitive evaluation theory. As shown on the left-hand side of the figure, any extrinsic reward—or any aspect of classroom structure for that matter—is used both to control behavior and to inform competence. The more the extrinsic reward is used to control students' behavior, the more it will increase extrinsic motivation, frustrate autonomy, and undermine intrinsic motivation. If the extrinsic reward is not used in a controlling way, however, it may leave these motivational outcomes (extrinsic motivation, need for autonomy, intrinsic motivation) unaffected. The more an extrinsic reward is used to inform students' competence, the more it will satisfy the need for competence and enhance intrinsic motivation. If the extrinsic reward is not used in an informational way, however, it may leave these motivational outcomes (need for competence, intrinsic motivation) unaffected.

Tests of cognitive evaluation theory have consistently supported the theory (Rummel & Feinberg, 1988; Tang & Hall, 1995; Wiersma, 1992), and the theory explains students' motivational reactions to extrinsic rewards across a range of student-related factors, though some age effects have occurred. Children's autonomy and intrinsic motivation, for instance, are often more impaired by controlling extrinsic rewards than are adults' autonomy and intrinsic motivation (Deci et al., 1999).

What makes the theory unique in the classroom management literature is that it emphasizes students' inner motivation, specifically the psychological needs for autonomy and competence. The controlling aspect of an extrinsic reward affects students' need for autonomy, whereas its informational aspect affects students' need for competence. Extrinsic rewards affect the psychological need for autonomy mostly through their controlling aspect, as expected, tangible, and task-contingent (i.e., controlling) rewards frustrate and thwart students' need for autonomy. Extrinsic rewards affect the psychological need for competence mostly through their informational aspect, as unexpected, verbal, and performance-contingent rewards nurture and satisfy students' need for competence. From this point of view, cognitive evaluation theory allows the chapter to address one of its key purposes—namely, to explain how extrinsic rewards affect students' inner motivation.

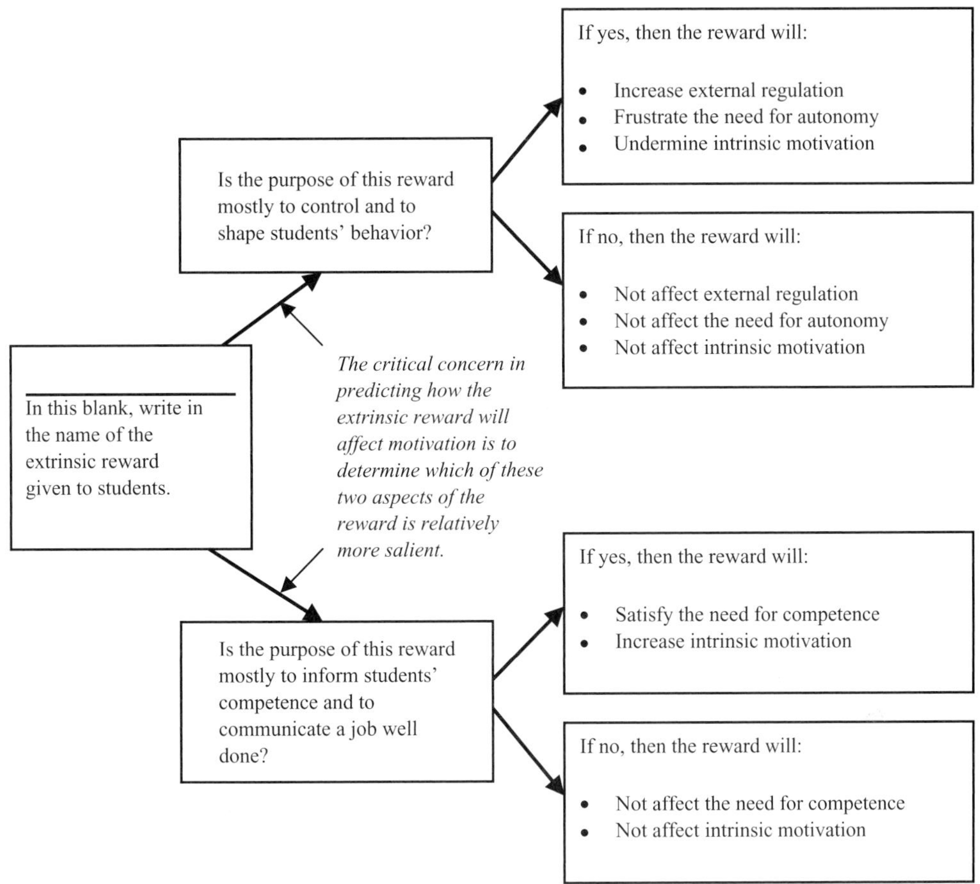

FIGURE 24.2. Graphical representation of cognitive evaluation theory.

Cognitive evaluation theory argues that *why* teachers give rewards is at least as important as *which* rewards they give (Ryan et al., 1983). To illustrate this point, consider two examples. The first is a prototypical case in which extrinsic rewards take on the functional significance of behavioral control. The teacher offers students an expected, tangible, and task-contingent reward—such as a conditional privilege—saying, in effect, "If you do X, you'll get Y." Here, the purpose—the functional significance—of why the teacher gives the reward is to control students' behavior so that students will be more likely to perform the targeted behavior. The second is a prototypical case in which extrinsic rewards take on a functional significance of competence affirmation. The teacher offers students a verbal, unexpected, and task-noncontingent reward—such as positive feedback—saying, in effect, "Your writing has improved since the last time." Here, the purpose or functional significance of why the teacher gives the reward is to inform students of a job well done.

Reward Administration

Because rewards can be presented to students in relatively controlling or in relatively informational ways, there exists an art to administering extrinsic rewards. Table 24.1 summarizes the five most common types of reward administrations and provides a definition and example for

TABLE 24.1
Types of Extrinsic Rewards

Type of Reward	*Definition and Example*
Expected (vs. unexpected)	Reward given on a prearranged and contingent basis, such as "If you turn in your homework, then you can expect two bonus points." An unexpected reward is given without a preannounced contingency.
Tangible (vs. verbal)	Reward that one can touch, smell, see, or taste, such as food or a prize. A verbal reward is one of symbolic value, such as praise or positive feedback.
Task contingent (vs. noncontingent)	Reward given in exchange for carrying out a requested behavior or task. For instance, teacher gives students a reward for completing a worksheet assignment. A noncontingent reward is given irrespective of whether the student actually completes the task. For instance, teacher gives students a reward merely for coming to class (rather than for completing an assignment).
Engagement contingent	Reward given in exchange for participating in, or working on, but not necessarily completing, a requested task. For instance, teacher gives students a reward for trying hard.
Performance contingent	Reward given in exchange for performing well, such as surpassing a specified performance level. For instance, teacher gives a gold star to all those students who score 80% or higher on a quiz.

each. *Expected rewards* are typically experienced as highly controlling, because they are given on a contractual "do this, get that" basis. Unexpected rewards, however, are typically experienced as noncontrolling and their informational aspect therefore can affirm the student's sense of competence. *Tangible rewards* are typically experienced as controlling, because they may attract so much of the student's attention that focus shifts from the task to the reward. Verbal rewards like praise and positive feedback, however, have symbolic value and are therefore much more likely to be experienced as informational events. *Task-contingent rewards* are typically experienced as highly controlling and not at all informational, because they are simply given in exchange for doing what is asked. Noncontingent rewards are less likely to be experienced as controlling because no behavior → reward contingency is contracted. *Engagement-contingent rewards* are rewards given for merely engaging in a requested activity (irrespective of the student's behavior or performance) and are frequently experienced by students as controlling and noninformational. *Performance-contingent rewards* are the most complex types of extrinsic rewards, because students experience them as controlling and informational at the same time. Performance-contingent rewards are given for the quality of a student's performance (e.g., getting an A on a test, earning a perfect attendance certificate). The more the student feels that there is a "string attached" to the reward, the more he or she will experience it as a controlling event; the less salient the attached string is in the mind of the student, the more he or she will be able to attend to the competence message with the performance-contingent reward (Reeve & Deci, 1996).

What this review of cognitive evaluation theory and the different types of reward administration makes clear is this: Why—for what purpose—teachers give students rewards is crucial. When teachers use rewards as part of their classroom management strategy, they need to administer rewards in ways that are not controlling ("no strings attached") and, at the same time, informational and competence affirming ("You're making rapid progress").

A traditional approach in which teachers motivate students directly.

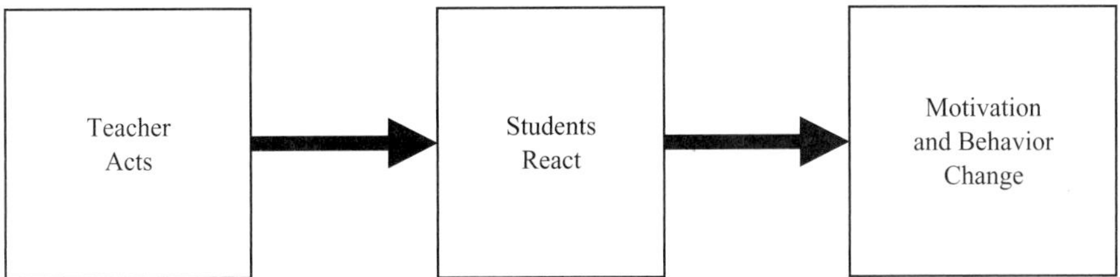

A dialectical approach in which teachers affect students and students affect teachers.

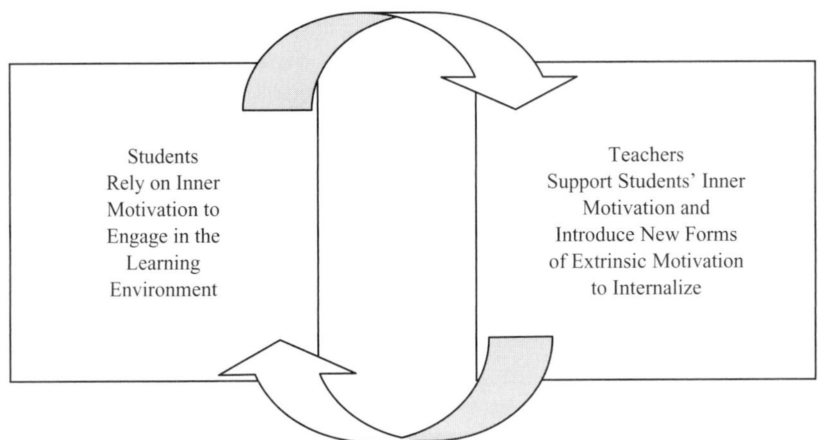

FIGURE 24.3. Two approaches to motivating students.

TWO CONTRASTING APPROACHES TO MOTIVATING STUDENTS

When they use extrinsic rewards to motivate students, teachers often take one of two different approaches. The first is a traditional approach in which they attempt to increase a specific target behavior. A graphical depiction of this approach appears in the upper half of Fig. 24.3. In this traditional approach, students' motivation and on-task behavior rise and fall in response to what the teacher does or does not offer. When teachers offer attractive rewards students show positive emotion and on-task behavior, but when teachers do not offer these inducements students' positive emotion and on-task behavior remain dormant. Teachers often find this approach attractive, because it rather directly answers the pressing question of "What can I do to motivate my students?" The answer: Offer an attractive extrinsic reward.

The second is a dialectical approach in which teachers affect students' motivation and engagement, which in turn, affect teachers' motivating styles. A dialectical approach begins with the assumption that students possess inner motivation of their own, and students' motivation and engagement unfolds in the classroom as they proactively express their inner motivation and as teachers support their proactivity. For instance, a student might express an interest in a topic and the teacher would adapt the lesson so to integrate the student's interest into the day's lesson plan. A graphical depiction of this approach appears in the lower half of Fig. 24.3. In this approach, students' motivation and on-task behavior rise and fall in response to how well versus how poorly teachers support students' inner motivation and also how well or poorly teachers are able to provide new and extrinsic forms of motivation for students to internalize and accept as their own. This approach essentially reframes the basic question from "What can I do to motivate my students?" to "How can I provide the conditions under which students can motivate themselves?" Once reframed, many answers are possible, as discussed in the next section.

Supporting Autonomy

Autonomy-supportive environments are those that involve and nurture students' inner motivational resources (Reeve, 1996; Reeve, Deci, & Ryan, 2004; Ryan & Deci, 2000b, 2002). The opposite of an autonomy-supportive environment is a controlling one, which is defined as an environment that frustrates or thwarts students' inner motivation, typically because it prioritizes a prescribed target behavior over expressions of students' inner motivation. The instructional effort to nurture students' inner resources is a worthwhile endeavor because students in autonomy-supportive classrooms, compared to those in controlling classrooms, experience an impressive range of positive educational outcomes, including greater mastery motivation, more conceptual understanding, higher creativity, more engagement in learning activities, higher academic performance, greater school persistence, and positive well-being (Black & Deci, 2000; Deci & Ryan, 1985, 1987; Deci, Schwartz, Sheinman, & Ryan, 1981; Deci, Vallerand, Pelletier, & Ryan, 1991; Reeve, 2002; Reeve, Jang, Carrell, Barch, & Jeon, 2004; Vallerand, Fortier, & Guay, 1997). Recognizing these benefits, researchers have worked to identify what teachers say and do during instruction to support students' autonomy (Deci, Spiegel, Ryan, Koestner, & Kauffman, 1982; Deci, Eghrari, Patrick, & Leone, 1994; Flink, Boggiano, & Barrett, 1990; Reeve, Bolt, & Cai, 1999; Reeve & Jang, in press).

Nurture Inner Motivational Resources. When teachers nurture students' inner motivation they find ways to align instructional activities with students' interests, preferences, and choice making, rather than relying on external regulators such as incentives and directives. This first aspect of an autonomy-supportive environment represents teachers' efforts to nurture students' interests, values, needs, and intrinsic motivation, rather than trying to extrinsically engineer expected, tangible, and task-contingent motivators. Nurturing inner motivational resources is especially important when teachers seek ways to initiate students' classroom activity. For instance, instead of offering a reward to solicit students' participation in a lesson, an autonomy-supportive teacher adapts the lesson so that it becomes a more interesting or enjoyable experience. A planned assignment to read a play that students think is boring could be restructured into an opportunity to take a part and read the play aloud in class as a cast of characters.

Rely on Informational, Noncontrolling Language. When teachers rely on informational, noncontrolling language they communicate classroom requirements and performance feedback through messages that are informational, flexible, and sensitive to students' inner motivational resources, not through messages that are controlling, rigid, and pressuring. In this second aspect of an autonomy-supportive environment, teachers communicate with students to help them integrate their inner motivation and autonomous self-regulation with their moment-to-moment classroom activity. Informational, noncontrolling language is especially important when teachers respond to students' behavioral problems and poor performance. For instance, instead of responding to students' behavior problems with pressure and controlling language such as "You should work harder," informational and noncontrolling language can be used such as "I've noticed you work has slipped lately; would you like to talk about it?"

Communicate Value In Uninteresting Activities and Rationales for Requested Behaviors. In an autonomy-supportive environment, teachers pair elements of classroom structure—rewards, rules, expectations, and so on—with an explanation of why that classroom feature is valuable, useful, or personally important to the students' learning and well-being. When imposing a limit on students' behavior, for instance, the teacher might provide a rationale to clarify not only why the limit is being imposed but also why it is a positive (i.e., personally useful) addition to the learning environment. This third aspect of an autonomy-supportive environment acknowledges that teachers sometimes ask students to invest their effort in relatively unappealing undertakings (e.g., worksheets, homework assignments, rule following). A rationale to clean one's workspace might be, "because cleaning your workspace will allow the students in the next period to have just as clean a space as you had when you began; wasn't it nice to walk in and see everything so clean and organized?" To the extent that students hear such a rationale and to the extent that they accept and internalize the rationale, they can say to themselves, "Yes, okay, that makes sense; that is something I want to do."

Acknowledge and Accept Students' Expressions of Negative Affect. Because classrooms have rules, requests, and agendas that are sometimes at odds with students' natural inclinations, students often complain and resist. When teachers acknowledge and accept such negative affect, they communicate an understanding of the students' perspectives and acknowledge that resistance is understandable. During teacher–student disagreements, a controlling teacher counters students' resistance with "Shape up; it's my way or the highway" or "because I said so," whereas an autonomy-supportive teacher acknowledges students' points of resistance and solicits students' input with "Yes, the assigned book is long, isn't it? 300 pages. Does anybody have a tip or suggestion about how to read 300 pages in a week?" Students' emotionality therefore becomes helpful information in the classroom management effort to transform a learning task away from "something not worth doing" in students' eyes to "something worth doing."

Providing Structure

Autonomy support revolves around being sensitive to students' inner motivational resources and finding ways to support these inner resources during learning activities. The opposite of autonomy support is *not* the removal of structure (e.g., see Ryan, 1993; Ryan & Stiller, 1991). Rather, autonomy support and structure represent different aspects of teachers' motivating styles, each of which contributes unique variance to students' motivation and engagement (Connell & Wellborn, 1991; Reeve, Deci, & Ryan, 2004; Skinner & Belmont, 1993).

Unilaterally imposing high structure on students in a controlling way yields a poor motivational profile, as does a permissive or laissez-faire instructional environment that fails to provide students with the structure they need to learn, internalize new values, and improve their skills (Skinner, 1995). In contrast, when teachers both support autonomy and provide structure ("freedom within limits"; Rogers, 1969), students show a healthy profile in terms of their motivation, engagement, and learning (Koestner, Ryan, Bernieri, & Holt, 1984; Grolnick & Ryan, 1987). Several individual studies show the benefits of teachers' efforts to provide structure in an autonomy-supportive way, including autonomy-supportive rules (Koestner et al., 1984), autonomy-supportive praise (Ryan et al., 1983), autonomy-supportive rationales (Reeve, Jang, Hardre, & Omura, 2002), autonomy-supportive communications (Schuh, 2004), autonomy-supportive goals (Jang, 2005), and an autonomy-supportive instructional set (Grolnick & Ryan, 1987). In each of these studies, when the element of structure was presented in a controlling way motivation suffered, whereas when it was presented in an autonomy-supportive way motivation thrived.

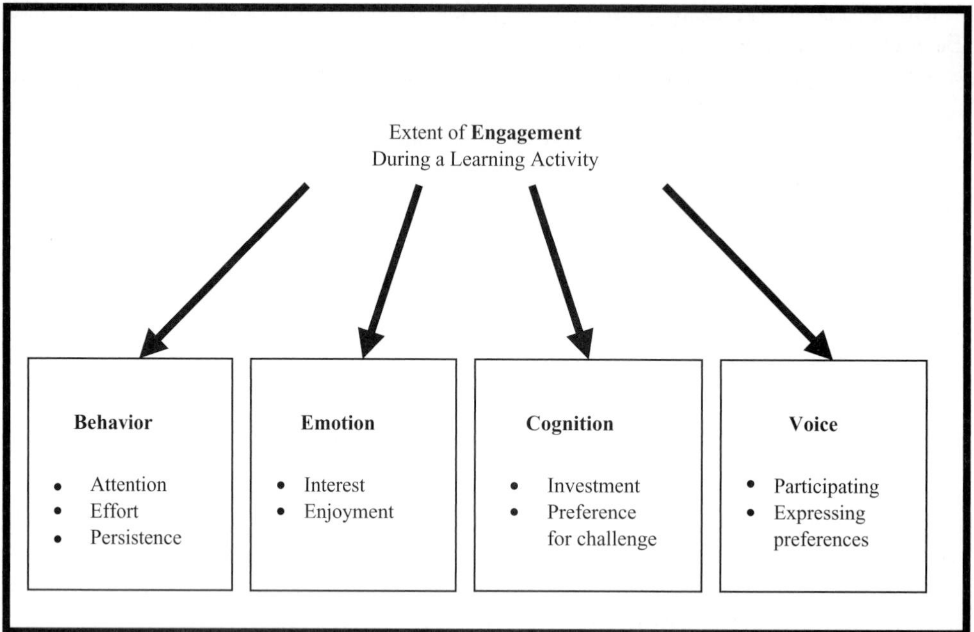

FIGURE 24.4. Engagement as a multifaceted concept.

FROM TARGETING BEHAVIOR TO ENHANCING ENGAGEMENT

Within a behavioral framework, controlling classroom management strategies make sense. A controlling approach represents an ideal way to gain students' compliance and on-task behavior. If the goal of a classroom management strategy is to increase some behaviors (desirable behaviors) and to decrease other behaviors (undesirable behaviors), then using reward contingencies to do so can be a productive course of action. Such a strategy is still, however, likely to prompt the three unintended side effects identified earlier. Recently, however, educators have broadened their attention beyond just targeting behaviors to a concern over outcomes such as learning, self-regulation, and well-being. The more classroom management and motivational strategies focus on learning, autonomous self-regulation, and subjective well-being, the more they find themselves drawn toward the larger concept of engagement.

Engagement refers to the behavioral intensity, emotional quality, and personal investment in a student's involvement during a learning activity (Connell & Wellborn, 1991; Fredricks, Blumenfeld, & Paris, 2004; Furrer & Skinner, 2003; Koenigs, Fiedler, & deCharms, 1977; Wellborn, 1991). Engagement includes on-task behavior, but it further highlights the central role of students' emotion, cognition, and voice, as summarized in Fig. 24.4. When engagement is characterized by the full range of on-task behavior, positive emotion, invested cognition, and personal voice, it functions as the engine for learning and development.

Behavioral engagement expresses itself as students show attention, effort, and persistence. Emotional engagement expresses positive emotion, or an emotional atmosphere of interest, enjoyment, and a sense of "wanting to" during one's investment of attention, effort, and persistence. Cognitive engagement expresses itself as students go beyond the basic requirements of an activity and, instead, commit themselves to being strategic, purposive, and self-regulating (rather than superficial) during the learning activity. Voice represents an expression of the self during task involvement. Students with voice offer suggestions, recommend activities, express their interests and preferences, participate in class discussions, ask questions about what they are learning, and generally attempt to influence the flow of class in a constructive way. The rich display of multifaceted classroom engagement depicted in Fig. 24.4 emanates more out of students' inner motivation then it does from teachers' extrinsic rewards. Recognizing this, attention has moved away from the practice of using rewards to motivate behavior in a narrow sense and toward the practice of using rewards to support students inner motivation, which enhances and sustains students' engagement in a broader sense.

EDUCATORS' CONCERNS, SOME RECOMMENDATIONS, AND FUTURE RESEARCH

Concerns

When thinking about classroom management strategies, educators generally express three concerns over an autonomy-supportive motivating style, even if they acknowledge the strong relationship between supporting autonomy and students' engagement during learning activities. The first is whether supporting autonomy will yield uneven displays of engagement, because students' engagement will depend on their task interest. Students might wander off-task whenever their interest takes them in a different direction, such as talking with their friends instead of completing an assignment. Concern over enacting the autonomy → engagement relationship dissipates, however, with the realization that autonomy support and structure can complement, rather than interfere with, one another. The argument put forward in this chapter is that engagement flourishes when teachers provide students with a highly autonomy-supportive, highly structured learning environment.

The second concern is whether educators can trust an autonomy-supportive motivating style. They ask, "What if I support students' autonomy and they then act irresponsibly?" One answer is that students actually act more responsibly when teachers support their autonomy rather than control their behavior (Ryan & Deci, 2000b), but another is that teachers have immediate access to the telltale feedback they need to assess how well or how poorly their autonomy-supportive instructional strategies are working. That feedback is students' moment-to-moment engagement (Reeve, Deci, & Ryan, 2004). Any increase or decrease in students' engagement during the flow of a lesson reflects how well teachers' efforts to nurture students' inner motivational resources are going. Surges in engagement during attempts to support students' inner motivational resources provide some of the assurance teachers need to see in order to trust an autonomy-supportive motivating style.

A final concern is whether an autonomy-supportive motivating style is an effective classroom management strategy in all educational contexts and for all types of students. To date, the research literature shows that supporting students' autonomy enhances the motivation and engagement across a wide range of contexts and students including students of different abilities (e.g., special education; Algozzine, Browder, Karovnen, Test, & Wood, 2001), rural students (Hardre & Reeve, 2003), and students of different cultures, including Eastern cultures (Sheldon, Elliot, Kim, & Kasser, 2001) and religiously motivated home school students (Cai, Reeve, & Robinson, 2002). I highlight this universality issue—the claim that everyone benefits from autonomy support—because critics inaccurately conceptualize autonomy support as permissiveness or as a laissez-faire style, which would essentially be the removal of structure (Ryan & Stiller, 1991). Students' motivation and engagement do suffer when teachers are permissive, but students respond well to, and benefit from, classroom environments high in both autonomy support and structure.

Recommendations

Extrinsic rewards are ubiqutious in educational settings. They offer many benefits, such as their capacity to structure a learning environment and communicate a message of a job well done. At the same time, however, extrinsic rewards carry potential hidden costs and, hence, liabilities. From this point of view, two recommendations on how to use rewards in a motivationally constructive way can be made. First, the central thesis of cognitive evaluation theory is that any extrinsic reward can be administered in either a controlling or an informational way. When offered in noncontrolling and informational ways, extrinsic rewards support rather than interfere with students' inner motivational resources. Thus, there exists an art to administering rewards, and the efforts teachers make to develop skills in using rewards in noncontrolling and informational ways is an opportunity to support students' motivation and engagement.

Second, teachers can adopt two different motivating styles when using rewards—controlling or autonomy supportive. It is easy to imagine how controlling teachers use rewards, as they follow a traditional behavioral model of how to administer incentives and consequences (see Walker et al., 2004). What is not so readily apparent is how autonomy-supportive teachers use rewards. Therefore, the four autonomy-supportive instructional strategies outlined earlier might help. To use rewards that nurture students' inner motivational resources, teachers can offer unexpected, symbolic rewards ("Good job.") as a student displays progress or mastery (thereby nurturing the need for competence and protecting the need for autonomy). Teachers can use informational language when offering rewards, especially when they articulate what it is about the student's learning or performing that signals progress, competence or achievement. Teachers can also provide rationales that explain why the student is currently receiving the reward. And teachers can acknowledge and accept students' negative affect instead of using rewards to counter negative affect so to get students to do what does not come naturally, such as working long hours, ignoring their interests, or engaging in nonvalued behaviors.

Future Research

Empirical research on how extrinsic rewards affect students' inner motivational resources, engagement, learning, and development has a long history (see Deci & Ryan, 1985, 1987; Deci et al., 1999; Kohn, 1993; Lepper & Greene, 1978; Ryan & Deci, 2000a). The general conclusion was that extrinsic rewards, when administered in controlling (expected, tangible, and contingent) ways, generally undermined students' autonomy, intrinsic motivation, self-regulation, and engagement. More recently, different types of extrinsic motivation have been identified. Only some types of extrinsic motivation (external regulation, introjected regulation) are associated with low engagement and poor functioning, whereas other types of extrinsic motivation (e.g., identified regulation, integrated regulation) are actually associated with high engagement and optimal functioning (Deci & Ryan, 2000b). The consensus is now that extrinsic rewards are not necessarily bad or counter productive. Instead, extrinsic rewards undermine motivation and engagement only when they are administered in controlling ways and only when they produce external regulation and introjected regulation in students. This same conclusion can be extended to practically any aspect of structure, as any rule, limit, goal, evaluation, or feedback undermines motivation and engagement only when presented in controlling ways that push students into external regulation or into introjected regulation. This conclusion suggests four possible avenues for future research.

The first is to ask how teachers can provide an autonomy-supportive, structured learning environment during uninteresting activities. Currently, the use of rationales to explain why an uninteresting activity is worth the students' effort is one effective autonomy-supportive strategy under these conditions (Reeve et al., 2002). Another strategy is to offer students "interest-enhancing strategies" (Jang, 2003). That said, the problem of how to support students' autonomy during uninteresting lessons is so pressing that future research to identify additional strategies is highly needed.

The second is to investigate the relationship between structure and engagement. The present chapter has argued for the benefits of high structure, but others argue for a moderate level of structure. They argue that the relationship between structure and engagement is curvilinear with moderate structure engendering greater engagement than either low or high structure (deCharms, 1984). Whether students benefit most from high structure or from moderate structure is an empirical question that is yet to be answered.

A third research question is to continue to investigate how teachers can use extrinsic rewards to support students' autonomy during instruction. Some research exists to identify what autonomy-supportive teachers say and do (Reeve et al., 1999; Reeve & Jang, in press; Reeve, Jang et al., 2004) but, when compared to the extensive literature on classroom management strategies, research on how to support autonomy is still in its infancy.

Finally, a fourth research question is to understand why teachers, students, and so many other participants in the educational system prefer controlling motivational strategies over autonomy-supportive ones, even after being exposed to information that shows them that autonomy-supportive strategies are more effective (Boggiano et al., 1987). The minimax principle of motivation ("the larger the reward, the larger the motivation") appears to be so dear in people's minds, whereas autonomy-supportive strategies appear to be held with some sort of suspicious naiveté. Why this is so needs to be explored and understood. Perhaps, what parents, students, and others are saying is that they would like an educational climate rich in both structure and autonomy support. If so, the present chapter suggests that their intuition is right on track.

ACKNOWLEDGMENTS

The author thanks Ellen Skinner, Portland State University, and Tom Good, University of Arizona, for their comments on an earlier draft of this chapter.

REFERENCES

Alberto, P., & Troutman, A. (2003). *Applied behavior analysis for teachers* (6th ed.). Upper Saddle River, NJ: Merrill/Prentice Hall.

Algozzine, B., Browder, D., Karovnen, M., Test, D. W., & Wood, W. M. (2001). Effects of interventions to promote self-determination for individuals with disabilities. *Review of Educational Research, 71*, 219–277.

Amabile, T. M. (1985). Motivation and creativity: Effect of motivational orientation on creative writers. *Journal of Personality and Social Psychology, 48*, 393–399.

Anderson, R., Manoogian, S. T., & Reznick, J. S. (1976). The undermining and enhancing of intrinsic motivation in preschool children. *Journal of Personality and Social Psychology, 34*, 915–922.

Baldwin, J. D., & Baldwin, J. I. (1986). *Behavior principles in everyday life* (2nd ed.). Englewood Cliffs, NJ: Prentice Hall.

Baumeister, R., & Leary, M. R. (1995). The need to belong: Desire for interpersonal attachments as a fundamental human motivation. *Psychological Bulletin, 117*, 497–529.

Benware, C., & Deci, E. L. (1984). Quality of learning with an active versus passive motivational set. *American Educational Research Journal, 21*, 755–765.

Black, A. E., & Deci, E. L. (2000). The effects of instructors' autonomy support and students' autonomous motivation on learning organic chemistry: A self-determination theory perspective. *Science Education, 84*, 740–756.

Blank, P. D., Reis, H. T., & Jackson, L. (1984). The effects of verbal reinforcements on intrinsic motivation for sex-linked tasks. *Sex Roles, 10*, 369–387.

Boggiano, A. K., Barrett, M., Weiher, A. W., McClelland, G. H., & Lusk, C. M. (1987). Use of the maximal–operant principle to motivate children's intrinsic interest. *Journal of Personality and Social Psychology, 53*, 866–879.

Boggiano, A. K., Flink, C., Shields, A., Seelbach, A., & Barrett, M. (1993). Use of techniques promoting students' self-determination: Effects on students' analytic problem-solving skills. *Motivation and Emotion, 17*, 319–336.

Bolles, R. C. (1972). A motivational view of learning, performance, and behavior modification. *Psychological Review, 81*, 199–213.

Brophy, J. (1986). Teacher influences of student achievement. *American Psychologist, 41*, 1069–1077.

Cai, Y., Reeve, J., & Robinson, D. T. (2002). Home schooling and teaching style: Comparing the motivating styles of home school and public school teachers. *Journal of Educational Psychology, 94*, 372–380.

Cannella, G. S. (1986). Praise and concrete rewards: Concerns for childhood education. *Childhood Education, 62*, 297–301.

Condry, J. (1977). Enemies of exploration: Self-initiated versus other-initiated learning. *Journal of Personality and Social Psychology, 35*, 459–477.

Connell, J. P., & Wellborn, J. G. (1991). Competence, autonomy, and relatedness: A motivational analysis of self-system processes. In M. R. Gunnar & L. A. Sroufe (Eds.), *Self processes in development: Minnesota symposium on child psychology* (Vol. 23, pp. 167–216). Chicago: University of Chicago Press.

Craighead, W. E., Kazdin, A. E., & Mahoney, M. J. (1981). *Behavior modification: Principles, issues, and applications*. Boston: Houghton Mifflin.

deCharms, R. (1984). Motivation enhancement in educational settings. In R. E. Ames & C. A. Ames (Eds.), *Research on motivation in education: Student motivation* (Vol. 1, pp. 275–310). New York: Academic Press.

Deci, E. L. (1975). *Intrinsic motivation*. New York: Plenum.

Deci, E. L. (1987). Theories and paradigms, constructs and operations: Intrinsic motivation is already exciting. *Journal of Social Behavior and Personality, 2*, 177–185.

Deci, E. L. (1992). The relation of interest to the motivation of behavior: A self-determination theory perspective. In K. A. Renninger, S. Hidi, & A. Krapp (Eds.), *The role of interest in learning and development* (pp. 43–70). Hillsdale, NJ: Lawrence Erlbaum Associates.

Deci, E. L., Eghrari, H., Patrick, B. C., & Leone, D. R. (1994). Facilitating internalization: The self-determination theory perspective. *Journal of Personality, 62*, 119–142.

Deci, E. L., Koestner, R., & Ryan, R. M. (1999). A meta-analytic review of experiments examining the effects of extrinsic rewards on intrinsic motivation. *Psychological Bulletin, 125*, 627–668.

Deci, E. L., & Ryan, R. M. (1985). *Intrinsic motivation and self-determination in human behavior*. New York: Plenum.

Deci, E. L., & Ryan, R. M. (1987). The support of autonomy and the control of behavior. *Journal of Personality and Social Psychology, 53*, 1024–1037.

Deci, E. L., Schwartz, A., Sheinman, L., & Ryan, R. M. (1981). An instrument to assess adult's orientations toward control versus autonomy in children: Reflections on intrinsic motivation and perceived competence. *Journal of Educational Psychology, 73*, 642–650.

Deci, E. L., Spiegel, N. H., Ryan, R. M., Koestner, R., & Kauffman, M. (1982). Effects of performance standards on teaching styles: Behavior of controlling teachers. *Journal of Educational Psychology, 74*, 852–859.

Deci, E. L., Vallerand, R. J., Pelletier, L. G., & Ryan, R. M. (1991). Motivation and education: The self-determination perspective. *Educational Psychologist, 26*, 325–346.

Dember, W. N. (1965). The new look in motivation. *American Scientist, 53*, 409–427.

Donahue, P. (1996, January 16). *Donahue: Should we pay students to learn?* [Televison broadcast]. New York: Multimedia Entertainment.

Eckert, T. L., Ardoin, S. P., Daly III, E. J., & Martens, B. K. (2002). Improving oral reading fluency: A brief experimental analysis of combining an antecedent intervention with consequences. *Journal of Applied Behavior Analysis, 35*, 271–281.

Flink, C., Boggiano, A. K., & Barrett, M. (1990). Controlling teaching strategies: Undermining children's self-determination and performance. *Journal of Personality and Social Psychology, 59*, 916–924.

Fredricks, J. A., Blumenfeld, P. C., & Paris, A. H. (2004). School engagement: Potential of the concept, state of the evidence. *Review of Educational Research, 74*, 59–109.

Furrer, C., & Skinner, E. A. (2003). Sense of relatedness as a factor in children's academic engagement and performance. *Journal of Educational Psychology, 95*, 148–162.

Gray, J. A. (1990). Brain systems that mediate both emotion and cognition. *Cognition and Emotion, 4*, 269–288.

Grolnick, W. S., & Ryan, R. M. (1987). Autonomy in children's learning: An experimental and individual differences investigation. *Journal of Personality and Social Psychology, 52*, 890–898.

Hardre, P. L., & Reeve, J. (2003). A motivational model of rural students' intentions to persist in, versus drop out of, high school. *Journal of Educational Psychology, 95*, 347–356.

Harris, V. W., & Sherman, J. A. (1974). Homework assignments, consequences, and classroom performance in social studies and mathematics. *Journal of Applied Behavior Analysis, 7*, 505–519.

Harter, S. (1978). Pleasure derived from optimal challenge and the effects of extrinsic rewards on children's difficulty level choices. *Child Development, 49*, 788–799.

Henderlong, J., & Lepper, M. R. (2002). The effects of praise on children's intrinsic motivation: A review and synthesis. *Psychological Bulletin, 128*, 774–795.

Hom, H. L., Jr. (1994). Can you predict the overjustification effect? *Teaching of Psychology, 21*, 36–37.

Jang, H. (2003). *Providing a rationale to engage students in an uninteresting learning activity: A test of multiple models*. Unpublished dissertation, University of Iowa.

Jang, H., (2005). *Preserving and enhancing students' autonomy by delivering directed instruction in an autonomy-supportive way*. Unpublished manuscript, University of Wisconsin-Milwaukee.

Joussemet, M., Koestner, R., Lekes, N., & Houlfort, N. (2004). Introducing uninteresting tasks to children: A comparison of the effects of rewards and autonomy support. *Journal of Personality, 72*, 139–166.

Koenigs, S. S., Fiedler, M. L., & deCharms, R. (1977). Teacher beliefs, classroom interaction, and personal causation. *Journal of Applied Social Psychology, 7*, 95–114.

Koestner, R., Ryan, R. M., Bernieri, F., & Holt, K. (1984). Setting limits on children's behavior: The differential effects of controlling versus informational styles on intrinsic motivation and creativity. *Journal of Personality, 52*, 233–248.

Kohn, A. (1993). *Punished by rewards: The trouble with gold stars, incentive plans, A's, praise, and other bribes*. Boston: Houghton Mifflin.

Lepper, M. R. (1983). Social-control processes and the internalization of social values: An attributional perspective. In E. T. Higgins, D. N. Ruble, & W. W. Hartup (Eds.), *Social cognition and social development* (pp. 294–330). New York: Cambridge University Press.

Lepper, M. R., & Greene, D. (1975). Turning play into work: Effects of adult surveillance and extrinsic rewards on children's intrinsic motivation. *Journal of Personality and Social Psychology, 31*, 479–486.

Lepper, M. R., & Greene, D. (Eds.). (1978). *The hidden costs of reward*. Hillsdale, NJ: Lawrence Erlbaum Associates.

Lepper, M. R., Greene, D., & Nisbett, R. E. (1973). Undermining children's intrinsic interest with extrinsic rewards: A test of the overjustification hypothesis. *Journal of Personality and Social Psychology, 28*, 129–137.

Martens, B. K., Lochner, D. G., & Kelly, S. Q. (1992). The effects of variable-interval reinforcement on academic engagement: A demonstration of matching theory. *Journal of Behavior Analysis, 25*, 143–151.

Martin, J. (1983). *Mastering instruction*. Boston: Allyn & Bacon.

McGraw, K. O., & McCullers, J. C. (1979). Evidence of detrimental effects of extrinsic incentives on breaking a mental set. *Journal of Experimental Social Psychology, 15*, 285–294.

Miller, D. L., & Kelley, M. L. (1994). The use of goal setting and contingency contracting for improving children's homework performance. *Journal of Applied Behavior Analysis, 27*, 73–84.

Mirenowicz, J., & Schultz, W. (1994). Importance of unpredictability for reward responses in primate dopamine neurons. *Journal of Neurophysiology, 72*, 1024–1027.

Montague, P. R., Dayan, P., & Sejnowski, T. J. (1996). A framework for mesencephalic dopamine systems based on predictive Hebbian learning. *Journal of Neuroscience, 16*, 1936–1947.

Neef, N. A., Shafer, M. S., Egel, A. L., Cataldo, M. F., & Parrish, J. M. (1983). The class specific effects of compliance training with "do" and "don't" requests: Analogue analysis and classroom application. *Journal of Applied Behavior Analysis, 16*, 81–99.

Pallak, S. R., Costomiris, S., Sroka, S., & Pittman, T. S. (1982). School experience, reward characteristics, and intrinsic motivation. *Child Development, 53*, 1382–1391.

Perrott, E. (1982). *Effective teaching: A practical guide to improving your teaching*. New York: Longman.

Pittman, T. S., Boggiano, A. K., & Ruble, D. N. (1983). Intrinsic and extrinsic motivational orientations: Limiting conditions on the undermining and enhancing effects of reward on intrinsic motivation. In J. Levine & M. Wang (Eds.), *Teacher and student perceptions: Implications for learning* (pp. 319–340). Hillsdale, NJ: Lawrence Erlbaum Associates.

Reeve, J. (1996). *Motivating others: Nurturing inner motivational resources*. Needham Heights, MA: Allyn & Bacon.

Reeve, J. (2002). Self-determination theory applied to educational settings. In E. L. Deci & R. M. Ryan (Eds.), *Handbook of self-determination* (pp. 183–203). Rochester, NY: University of Rochester Press.

Reeve, J. (2004). *Understanding motivation and emotion* (4th ed.). Hoboken, NJ: John Wiley.

Reeve, J., Bolt, E., & Cai, Y. (1999). Autonomy-supportive teachers: How they teach and motivate students. *Journal of Educational Psychology, 91*, 537–548.

Reeve, J., & Deci, E. L. (1996). Elements of the competitive situation that affect intrinsic motivation. *Personality and Social Psychology Bulletin, 22*, 24–33.

Reeve, J., Deci, E. L., & Ryan, R. M. (2004). Self-determination theory: A dialectical framework for understanding the sociocultural influences on student motivation. In D. McInerney & S. Van Etten (Eds.), *Research on sociocultural influences on motivation and learning: Big theories revisited* (Vol. 4, pp. 31–59). Greenwich, CT: Information Age Press.

Reeve, J., & Jang, H. (in press). What teachers say and do to support students' autonomy during a learning activity. *Journal of Educational Psychology*.

Reeve, J., Jang, H., Carrell, D., Barch, J., & Jeon, S. (2004). Enhancing high school students' engagement by increasing teachers' autonomy support. *Motivation and Emotion, 28*, 147–169.

Reeve, J., Jang, H., Hardre, P., & Omura, M. (2002). Providing a rationale in an autonomy-supportive way as a strategy to motivate others during an uninteresting activity. *Motivation and Emotion, 26*, 183–207.

Reeve, J., Nix, G., & Hamm, D. (2003). Testing models of the experience of self-determination in intrinsic motivation and the conundrum of choice. *Journal of Educational Psychology, 95*, 375–392.

Rogers, C. R. (1969). *Freedom to learn*. Columbus, OH: Charles E. Merrill.

Rummel, A., & Feinberg, R. (1988). Cognitive evaluation theory: A meta-analytic review of the literature. *Social Behavior and Personality, 16*, 147–164.

Ryan, R. M. (1991). The nature of the self in autonomy and relatedness. In J. Strauss & G. R. Goethals (Eds.), *The self: Interdisciplinary approaches* (pp. 208–238). New York: Springer-Verlag.

Ryan, R. M. (1993). Agency and organization: Intrinsic motivation, autonomy and the self in psychological development. In J. Jacobs (Ed.), *Nebraska symposium on motivation: Developmental perspectives on motivation* (Vol. 40, pp. 1–56). Lincoln: University of Nebraska Press.

Ryan, R. M., & Deci, E. L. (2000a). When rewards compete with nature: The undermining of intrinsic motivation and self-regulation. In C. Sansone & J. M. Harackiewicz (Eds.), *Intrinsic and extrinsic motivation: The search for optimal motivation and performance* (pp. 13–54). San Diego, CA: Academic Press.

Ryan, R. M., & Deci, E. L. (2000b). Self-determination theory and the facilitation of intrinsic motivation, social development, and well-being. *American Psychologist, 55*, 68–78.

Ryan, R. M., & Deci, E. L. (2002). An overview of self-determination theory: An organismic-dialectical perspective. In E. L. Deci & R. M. Ryan (Eds.), *Handbook of self-determination research* (pp. 3–33). Rochester, NY: University of Rochester Press.

Ryan, R. M., Mims, V., & Koestner, R. (1983). Relation of reward contingency and interpersonal context to intrinsic motivation: A review and test using cognitive evaluation theory. *Journal of Personality and Social Psychology, 45*, 736–750.

Ryan, R. M., & Stiller, J. (1991). The social contexts of internalization: Parent and teacher influences on autonomy, motivation and learning. In P. R. Pintrich & M. L. Maehr (Eds.), *Advances in motivation and achievement: Vol. 7. Goals and self-regulatory processes* (pp. 115–149). Greenwich, CT: JAI Press.

Schuh, K. L. (2004). Learner-centered principles in teacher-centered practices? *Teaching and Teacher Education, 20*, 833–846.

Shapira, Z. (1976). Expectancy determinants of intrinsically motivated behavior. *Journal of Personality and Social Psychology, 34*, 1235–1244.

Sheldon, K. M., Elliot, A. J., Kim, Y., & Kasser, T. (2001). What is satisfying about satisfying events? Testing 10 candidate psychological needs. *Journal of Personality and Social Psychology, 80*, 325–339.

Skinner, E. A. (1985). Action, control judgments, and the structure of control experience. *Psychological Review, 92*, 39–58.

Skinner, E. A. (1995). *Perceived control, motivation, and coping*. Newbury Park, CA: Sage.

Skinner, E. A., & Belmont, M. J. (1993). Motivation in the classroom: Reciprocal effects of teacher behavior and student engagement across the school year. *Journal of Educational Psychology, 85*, 571–581.

Skinner, E. A., Zimmer-Gembeck, M. J., & Connell, J. P. (1998). Individual differences and the development of perceived control. *Monographs of the Society for Research in Child Development 63* (Serial No. 254).

Tang, S.-H., & Hall, V. C. (1995). The overjustification effect: A meta-analysis. *Applied Cognitive Psychology, 9*, 365–404.

Vallerand, R. J., Fortier, M. S., & Guay, F. (1997). Self-determination and persistence in a real-life setting: Toward a motivational model of high school dropout. *Journal of Personality and Social Psychology, 72*, 1161–1176.

Walker, J. E., Shea, T. M., & Bauer, A. M. (2004). *Behavior management: A practical approach for educaters*. Upper Saddle River, NJ: Merrill/Prentice Hall.

Weiner, B. (1990). History of motivational research in education. *Journal of Educational Psychology, 82*, 616–622.

Wellborn, J. P. (1991). *Engaged and disaffected action: The conceptualization and measurement of motivation in the academic domain*. Unpublished doctoral dissertation, University of Rochester.

Wiersma, U. J. (1992). The effects of extrinsic rewards in intrinsic motivation: A meta-analysis. *Journal of Occupational and Organizational Psychology, 65*, 101–114.

25

Why Research on Parental Involvement Is Important to Classroom Management

Joan M. T. Walker
Long Island University

Kathleen V. Hoover-Dempsey
Vanderbilt University

INTRODUCTION

In this chapter we connect teachers' classroom management practices to research on parental involvement. We have two main purposes. First, we argue that teachers' parent involvement practices have practical value in that they can make teaching easier and more effective. For instance, teachers are more likely to meet students' individual needs and abilities when they create learner-centered classroom environments (e.g., Roeser, Eccles, & Sameroff, 2000). Parents are important to a learner-centered approach to teaching because they are likely sources of critical information about students, such as their interests, learning style, and learning history. Teaching can also be easier and more effective when children are motivated to learn. Parents are important to student engagement in the classroom because, as the primary socializing agents in children's lives, they have considerable influence on children's attitudes toward school. We thus argue that student learning and motivation to learn is enhanced to the extent that teachers view parental involvement as an educational resource and know how to tap its power.

Our second purpose pertains to theory and research in developmental psychology. Within the context of their personal involvement with children (i.e., interactions within families and within classrooms), parents and teachers create a context for the development of children's learning and engagement in school. Few studies, however, have examined the unique and collective contributions of parents' and teachers' involvement practices *across* the contexts of home and school. In this chapter we highlight parallels between research findings in each area with an eye toward enriching theoretical understanding of adult–child relationships as developmental contexts. We view such connections as essential to the identification of fruitful avenues for future research and the establishment of meaningful recommendations for educational practice.

We focus on parent and teacher contributions to one student construct that has received increasing attention from educational researchers, self-regulated learning. The term *self-regulated learning* is typically associated with students who are metacognitively, motivationally, and behaviorally active participants in their education (Zimmerman, 1990). For example, students who self-regulate their learning productively share several characteristics, including strong belief in their ability to learn, persistence in the face of difficulty, the ability to monitor their understanding, and the capacity to act in ways that deepen their comprehension. Self-regulated learners also frequently demonstrate appropriate help-seeking behaviors and endorse prosocial goals (Wentzel, 1999; Zimmerman & Martinez-Pons, 1990). Together, these characteristics represent an "adaptive motivational orientation" that supports learning and school success (Grolnick, Kurowski, & Gurland, 1999). Self-regulated learning also can refer, however, to maladaptive or self-handicapping approaches to learning (Covington, 1992; Urdan, 1998). This defensive type of self-regulated learning is associated with limited ability beliefs, limited persistence and helpless orientations to problem solving, and a superficial approach to learning that emphasizes academic performance over personal mastery.

In this chapter we focus on understanding how parents and teachers contribute to these adaptive and less adaptive forms of self-regulated learning. Consistent with sociocultural perspectives (McCaslin & Murdock, 1991; Vygotsky, 1978) and research on interpersonal relationships as developmental contexts (e.g., Roeser et al., 2000; Wentzel, 1999), we believe that children's abilities to self-regulate their learning and the forms of self-regulated learning in which they engage emerge, in part, from their interactions with important others in their social world. Because parents *and* teachers provide developmental resources that influence children's approaches to learning, it is important to understand the nature of the contribution each makes and the effects of their interactions.

We frame our discussion of parent and teacher contributions to self-regulated learning in terms of developmental systems theory, which describes the child as an active, evolving system that develops through reciprocal interaction with people and things in the immediate environment (Bronfenbrenner, 1979, 1992; Pianta & Walsh, 1996; Sameroff, 1983). The environment is characterized as increasingly complex nested social systems including (a) parents and teachers (i.e., dyadic systems), (b) small-group systems such as families and classrooms, and (c) broader community influences such as schools (see Fig. 25.1). Within these systems, development is driven by proximal processes, such as problem solving, making plans, and acquiring new knowledge, that take place on a regular basis over an extended period. These proximal cognitive processes are arguably the essence of children's education. Within dyadic systems there are also proximal social processes such as learning to balance personal interests with the needs and interests of others. Thus, consistent with research on parenting (Grolnick & Slowiaczek, 1994) we focus on two forms of parental involvement in children's education, cognitive–intellectual (e.g., helping with homework) and personal engagement (e.g., asking about the school day), rather than more traditional conceptions of parental involvement, which often pertain to parents' participation in school-based activities.

Although we address the broad influence of schools on parenting and teaching practices and family–school interactions, at the heart of our discussion is the adult–child relationship or what happens within adult–child dyadic systems. Of particular interest is (a) the identification of explicit and implicit mechanisms that parents and teachers use to convey their values and expectations about school to children and (b) how those mechanisms relate to patterns of student self-regulated learning during childhood and early adolescence. We tend to focus on the elementary and early middle school grades because this is when parents are most likely to make the most significant and enduring contributions to their children's school success, in terms of both cognitive–intellectual processing and affective support (Grolnick, Kurowski, Dunlap, & Hevey, 2000; McCaslin & Murdock, 1991). Although parental involvement continues to be important to students' school success in adolescence, it is well noted that several forms of parental involvement decline markedly during adolescence (Griffith, 1998). In some cases the decline may be due to school structure, including the increased number of teachers involved in children's secondary education (Izzo, Weissberg, Kasprow, & Fendrich, 1999) and diminished opportunities for involvement (Grolnick et al., 2000; Grolnick & Slowiaczek, 1994); in others

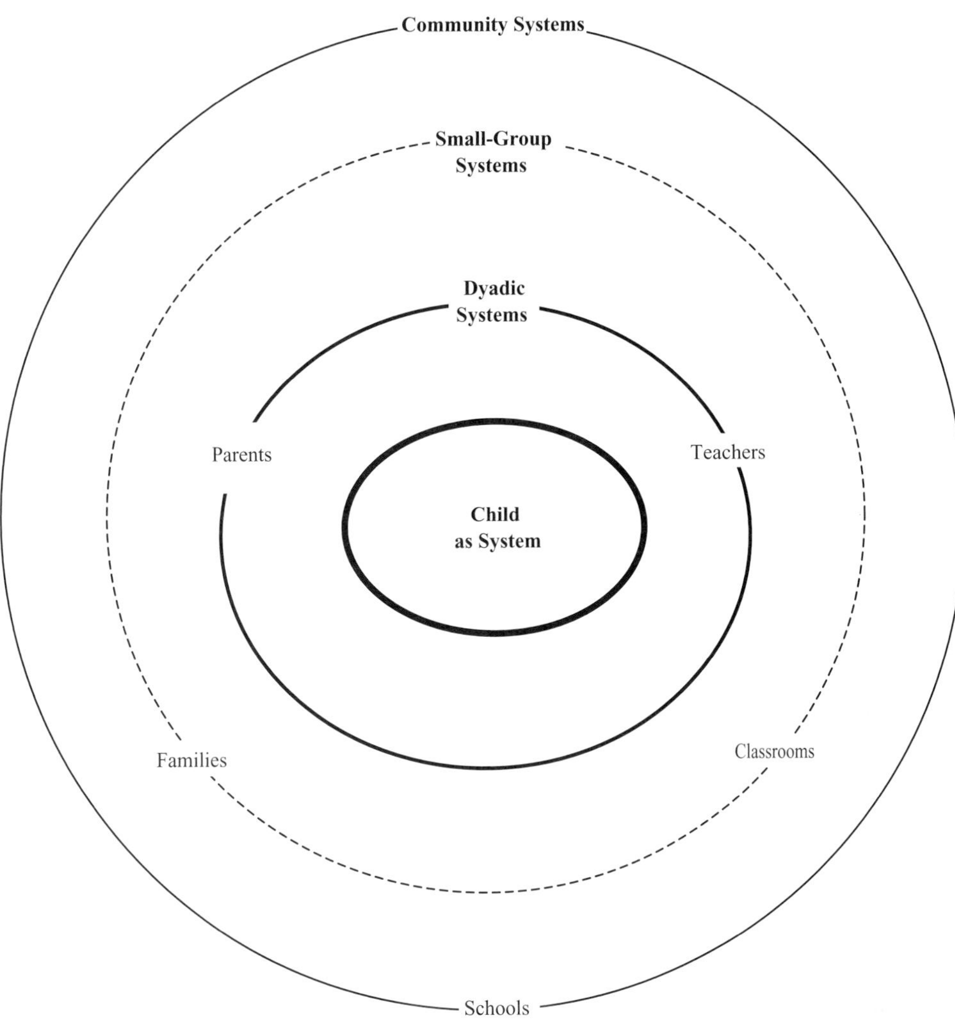

FIGURE 25.1. Contexts for self-regulatory development. Adapted from Pianta and Walsh (1996) and Sameroff (1983).

it may be related to the difficulty of the child's work and children's increasing press for independence (Simon, 2004).

We note that our review consists primarily of empirical studies conducted over the past two decades. The studies most often involve exclusive attention to either parent–child or teacher–student interactions. Reflecting much of the work in the field at this point, few of the studies are longitudinal and most are not experimental. The primary data sources are self-report questionnaires, although several use observation and interview methodology. It is also noteworthy that samples included in this work are often, but certainly not always, Euro-American families from suburban or urban schools.

The chapter is structured in five sections. First, we review parenting as context for children's social and cognitive development. Second, we examine how teachers' classroom management practices relate to student self-regulation. Third, we identify shared mechanisms of parent and teacher influence, and discuss the individual and collective influence of parent and teacher contributions. In the fourth section we suggest potentially fruitful avenues for future research.

Finally, we translate research into practice by suggesting how teachers can use parent involvement practices to enhance the effectiveness of parents' cognitive and personal involvement, and create more satisfying, productive classroom environments.

PARENTS AS CONTEXT FOR THE DEVELOPMENT OF STUDENT SELF-REGULATION

We examine the influence of three levels of family context that contribute to the skills, attitudes, and goals that children bring with them to school. We focus first on the broad influence of culture on children's socialization outcomes and then examine the influence of family-based parenting style on these outcomes. Finally, we highlight research underscoring the influence of parents' specific involvement practices on student outcomes.

Culture and Children's Socialization Outcomes

A relatively long tradition of research has suggested that, across cultures, families raise children with similar overarching goals that include providing shelter, food, and a safe environment, and teaching the skills, attitudes, and values needed for productive adult life in that culture (e.g., Cole, 1996; Le Vine, 1988; Maccoby, 1992). Beyond such basic goals, important variations have been observed. For instance, in comparing samples of Kenyan and U.S. families, Whiting and Whiting (1975) found that Kenyan families expected children to perform economically meaningful work and to offer substantial help with household tasks, including care of siblings. In turn, children in these families consistently offered substantial help with family and home tasks, and assumed personal responsibility for ensuring that sibling behavior met family standards. By contrast, U.S. families in this sample expected children to attend school, to learn outside the home under direct adult supervision, and to think of themselves as individuals. The U.S. children, in turn, displayed sociable but frequently competitive interactions with peers and a consistent tendency to seek adult attention.

Similar patterns of variability have been observed within cultures. Within the United States for example, White and Carew (1973) found that varied family practices influenced children's patterns of social skills for relating to peers and adults. One group of parents was characterized by consistent efforts to support their young children at home: they expressed affection, made strong efforts to create a safe environment that offered opportunities for informal learning, and tended to take advantage of teaching opportunities. A second group behaved much differently: These parents demonstrated less overt enjoyment in their children's company, focused on maintaining neat homes, and seldom engaged in informal teaching opportunities. Subsequent comparisons suggested that children of parents in the first group, compared with those in the second, were more socially skilled, played more productively with others, used more socially appropriate ways to gain adult attention, and were more skilled in "using" adults as resources for accomplishing things they could not do on their own.

Cultures and subcultures thus shape the broad patterns of social and intellectual skills that children bring to school. Cultural practices, in turn, provide a backdrop for parents' enactment of parenting style, or patterns of child-rearing behaviors and values.

Parenting Style and Children's Socialization Outcomes

We highlight here a sample of research on patterns of parents' beliefs and behaviors as a general developmental context and their influence on child outcomes important in schooling. Although the work we review has suggested strong links between patterns of parenting and students' social and cognitive outcomes in the United States, it is important to note that variations in patterns of parenting and their links to student outcomes have been found across social, cultural, and ethnic groups within the United States (e.g., Baumrind, 1991a; Chao, 1994). We discuss cultural variations in parenting and its relation to child development in later sections.

Baumrind's work on parenting style has been perhaps the most influential research in this area (e.g., 1967, 1971). She began with the observation that similarly situated preschool children (predominantly middle class) manifested notable social and cognitive differences in classroom behavior. To understand the source of these differences, she "worked backwards" to conduct extensive observations of children's interactions with their parents. These observations suggested relatively distinct patterns of parental behaviors. Identifying these patterns as "parenting style," she detailed their relationship to observed differences in children.

Children who appeared most competent or highly socialized for school (e.g., self-reliant, self-controlled, at ease in exploring the environment, successful in social relationships) had parents whose style was characterized as *authoritative*. These parents made developmentally appropriate demands for child maturity (e.g., expected children to attempt tasks independently), controlled child behavior as needed, were responsive and affectionate, and communicated frequently and effectively with their children. By contrast, children who were less competent at school tended to have parents whose styles were characterized as either *authoritarian* or *permissive*. Authoritarian parents made many demands of their children and exercised strong control, but tended to show little affection and did not communicate often. Parents with a permissive style offered copious communication and affection, but made very few demands and exercised very little control over their children.

When these same children were examined in adolescence (1991a, 1991b), Baumrind found that children whose parents maintained an authoritative style continued to possess attributes central to school success (e.g., self-control, ability to take the perspective of others, intrinsic motivation) whereas children of authoritarian and permissive parents had less optimal social and academic outcomes. Baumrind attributed these findings to the positive effects of authoritative parenting and its focus on developmentally appropriate levels of behavioral control and autonomy support. Essentially, she suggested that children's engagement in school across childhood and adolescence was best supported by parenting that is both demanding and responsive.

Baumrind's findings have been replicated and extended by many investigators over the years. Pratt, Green, MacVicar, and Bountrogianni (1992), for example, examined parenting style in relation to parents' interactions with fifth-grade children on math homework. They found that authoritative parents, compared to nonauthoritative parents, engaged in more scaffolding or keying their support to the child's level of understanding. In turn, children of authoritative parents learned more from their parents' help, and had generally higher achievement than did children of nonauthoritative parents. Pratt and his colleagues also noted that parents' authoritativeness was more consistently predictive of students' performance than either parental education or intelligence level.

Studies of parenting on older children's social and academic competence have supported this general pattern of findings. Authoritative parenting has been found to predict specific qualities of adolescent self-regulation including motivation to work hard and strive for success, positive attributional style (e.g., attributing school success to personal effort and ability), higher personal expectations and aspirations, more time spent on homework, and greater engagement with learning and with teachers (Glasgow, Dornbusch, Troyer, Steinberg, & Ritter, 1997; Steinberg, Elmen, & Mounts, 1989; Steinberg, Lamborn, Dornbusch, & Darling, 1992). Suggesting that the impact of parent involvement activities is dependent on the full set of authoritative parenting practices, Steinberg et al. (1992) noted that some parental involvement activities, which were effective in an authoritative context, did not have as much influence when parents manifested a nonauthoritative style. Thus, predictions about the consequences of varied parenting techniques on students' school behavior and success must take into account both the parent's specific practices and the larger context of parenting style (Darling & Steinberg, 1993).

Parenting style thus influences children's development of social and intellectual competencies related to school success, and influences the impact of parents' involvement behaviors on student learning. Three elements appear central to the positive impact of authoritative parenting for many families: establishment of reasonable demands and expectations for developmentally appropriate behavior, responsiveness and sensitivity to the child's developmental level and learning needs, and support of developmentally appropriate levels of child autonomy.

Parental Involvement in Schooling and Student Self-Regulation

Specific elements associated with authoritative parenting style have been examined as mechanisms that support children's development of self-regulation. Grolnick and Ryan (1989), for example, explored links between parental autonomy support and provision of structure, and student self-regulation and school competence among White, middle-class families. Of particular interest to these researchers was differentiating the influence of parental autonomy support (defined as parental encouragement of the child's independent problem solving, and choice and participation in decisions) and provision of structure (defined as parental provision of clear, consistent guidelines and expectations). Analyses revealed that autonomy support was positively related to children's self-reported self-regulation, teacher ratings of student competence and school adjustment, school grades, and achievement. Structure was related primarily to children's beliefs that they were responsible for their success or failure. The combination of parental provision of structure and autonomy may encourage student self-regulation because it offers children clear expectations (e.g., "I am expected to do my homework before bedtime") and evidence that they are capable of independently meeting those expectations ("I am capable of setting a time for doing my homework").

Variations in the parenting practices of middle-class families have also been noted in naturalistic observations. Xu and Corno (1998), for example, found that typical parental involvement activities included simultaneous efforts to help the student arrange the environment and manage time, as well as efforts to monitor student attention, motivation, and emotional responses to homework. Experimental studies of parent–child problem-solving interactions also demonstrate that parents' patterns of involvement practices influence children's persistence, ability attributions, and affect. For instance, children whose parents offered emotional and cognitive support without being directive persisted longer at difficult learning tasks and made fewer attributions about their ability than did children whose parents were more controlling or who offered little encouragement (Hokoda & Fincham, 1995).

These findings have been replicated across ethnic groups within the United States. For example, Brody, Flor, and Gibson (1999) looked at a set of "competence-promoting parenting practices" among early elementary African American children from mother-headed families. They found that parents' involvement routines (e.g., children generally do homework at the same time each day), school involvement (e.g., attending parent–teacher conferences), and mother–child relationship quality supported children's self-regulation (e.g., thinking ahead about the consequences of actions, planning before acting, paying attention, working toward goals).

In studying low-income Mexican American families, Delgado-Gaitan (1992) found differences in the parenting practices of advanced and less advanced first-grade readers. The parents of advanced readers provided more general supervision of homework, were available on demand to help but held children accountable for finishing schoolwork, offered substantial emotional support for achievement, and asked teachers for ideas on how best to help children learn. By contrast, parents of less advanced readers enforced highly structured rules for doing homework, and generally did not seem to be aware that they could contact teachers for ideas about supporting student learning at home.

Focusing on the relationship between parental involvement and positive school outcomes for children, Hoover-Dempsey, Battiato, Walker, Reed, DeJong, and Jones (2001) reviewed research on parental involvement in one specific context: homework. They organized effective parental homework involvement behaviors into a sequence of eight categories. The first four categories—establishing reasonable structures, interacting with the child's teacher about homework, providing general oversight of the homework process, and reinforcing and encouraging the student's homework accomplishments—evince parents' general efforts to create a supportive context for homework. The four remaining categories reflect parents' cognitive involvement in homework tasks and included parents' explicit teaching efforts, creating a "fit" between homework tasks and student skill level (e.g., demonstrating how to break tasks down into manageable parts), and helping the child understand how specific homework skills related more broadly to achievement. The review by Hoover-Dempsey and her colleagues also underscored the fact that parents rarely use only one general structuring or teaching strategy but often draw simultaneously from the full range of homework involvement practices.

In sum, this spectrum of research on parenting and students' school-relevant attributes has suggested that varied social systems, including broad cultural standards, family-based parenting style, and parents' specific involvement behaviors, create a context for the development of student self-regulation. It also suggests that self-regulatory skill development is supported by parenting practices that offer children a clearly structured and supportive environment within which they may exercise developmentally appropriate levels of autonomy in their school-related activities.

TEACHERS AS CONTEXT FOR THE DEVELOPMENT OF STUDENT SELF-REGULATION

Similar to our discussion of parenting as developmental context, we begin our discussion of teacher contributions to self-regulated learning with attention to broad contextual factors that influence teacher practices and student outcomes. We then examine the influence of teachers at the classroom level, acknowledging that our understanding of teacher practices, patterns of student self-regulation, and their interactions have been influenced by varied research traditions.

Cultural Expectations for Schools and Child Development

Like parenting practices, teacher practices reflect broad cultural expectations. Doyle (1992) has described connections between societal expectations and schooling as the "abstract curriculum," which determines who is schooled as well as how and when they are schooled. In the United States, for instance, school is compulsory and most school learning occurs in group settings that are largely adult directed. American society further assumes that children are ready to enter school at age five and that as students approach early adolescence, they can and should assume greater personal responsibility for learning. These assumptions are translated into what Doyle describes as the "analytical curriculum" or educational events and activities that occur within schools, which influence student self-regulation. For example, at entry to middle school adolescents in the United States typically encounter a greater number of classes, teachers, transitions, and expectations during the school day, often with negative consequences for their motivation to learn, feelings of belongingness, and other social outcomes (Eccles, Lord, & Midgley, 1991; Roeser et al., 2000). These assumptions and practices stand in contrast to other cultures' conceptions about activities and structures appropriate for learning and cognitive development (e.g., Rogoff, 1990).

Cultural expectations and school structures influence teachers' practices; however, at the classroom level there is considerable variability in individual teachers' classroom management and instructional style (e.g., Weade & Evertson, 1988). In the following sections we focus on teacher beliefs and behaviors as a general developmental context and their influence on self-regulated learning. Recognizing that understanding of teacher practices and their relation to student learning and motivation has been shaped by varied research traditions and their attendant definitions of teacher effectiveness and student success, we organize our review of this literature into three approaches: teacher focused, student focused, and relationship focused.

Teacher-Focused Approaches

Early investigations of teaching style and its influence on student learning often examined the relationship between observable teacher behaviors and student performance on standardized measures of achievement (Helmke, 2001; Kounin, 1967). For instance, Evertson and Emmer (1982) hypothesized that middle school teachers' behavior during the opening days of school "set the stage" for student self-regulation across the school year. These researchers related how frequently teachers used specific classroom management practices to students' observable engagement in the classroom and year-end achievement. Positive correlations were found between student achievement and teachers' consistent use of behavior management practices (i.e., rewards and punishments), efficient transitions and discipline, and clear directions and rationales for tasks. Student achievement was also positively linked to teacher recognition of student needs (e.g., setting of reasonable work standards), enthusiasm for teaching, and demonstrations of interest in students as individuals. Similar results were found with a sample of elementary school teachers (Emmer, Evertson, & Anderson, 1980). Thus, consistent with findings for authoritative parenting, student outcomes were best supported by teaching practices that were both demanding and responsive.

Although useful in identifying effective classroom management practices, this line of research did not focus on the many variables that mediate the relationship between instructional practices and achievement, including students' general orientation to schoolwork and perceptions of classroom interactions. A number of questions remained about how teachers influence the more proximal intellectual and motivational processes underlying student achievement.

Student-Focused Approaches

With the advent of a strong focus in cognitive psychology, research increasingly probed students' subjective classroom experiences, including their perceptions of instruction, their goals and values, and their expectations (e.g., Pintrich & Schrauben, 1992). Ames (1992) offered a framework for understanding links between these student variables and teacher behavior by establishing three broad teaching dimensions: structuring of evaluation, structuring of authority and structuring of tasks.

A growing body of work has since established that teachers' evaluation practices create classroom goal structures that, in turn, influence students' own personal goals and orientations to school. For instance, teacher emphasis on effort rather than ability has been positively associated with student endorsement of mastery goals, academic and social self-efficacy, and use of effective learning strategies (Patrick, Anderman, Ryan, Edelin, & Midgley, 2001; Ryan & Patrick, 2001). By contrast, teacher emphasis on competitive goals (i.e., personal performance relative to that of others) has been associated with maladaptive patterns of student engagement, including low perceptions of personal ability and the use of self-handicapping strategies such as procrastination (Midgley, Arunkumar, & Urdan, 1996; Urdan, Midgley, & Anderman, 1998). These contrasting patterns of evaluation practices have been characterized, respectively, as mastery-focused and performance-focused teaching (e.g., Patrick et al., 2001).

A second measurable quality of instruction that influences student self-regulation is structuring of classroom authority. For example, teacher support for student autonomy—teaching that offers a reasonable degree of choice over tasks and the level of challenge associated with those tasks, control over classroom processes, and opportunities for self-evaluation—has been positively associated with students' ability beliefs, self-regulatory skills, and enjoyment of school (Ames, 1992; Perry, 1998; Skinner & Belmont, 1993; Stipek, Feiler, Daniels, & Milburn, 1995). Similar to research examining the influence of parenting style on student self-regulation (e.g., Grolnick & Ryan, 1989), this work suggests that students are more likely to self-regulate their learning and behavior when they have opportunities to do so.

Task structures that support student self-regulation include teacher efforts to engage students in conceptual *and* procedural thinking (e.g., emphasis on why as well as how) and situating classroom tasks in authentic contexts that students find inherently interesting (National Council of Teachers of Mathematics, 2000). These practices may be effective because they encourage connections between the student emotions, goals, and ability beliefs that support enduring engagement in learning (Ford, 1996). In short, as Stipek (2000) has argued, "good instruction is motivating." Other supportive tasks include peer interaction or reciprocal teaching experiences (Palincsar & Brown, 1984), and teacher modeling of metacognitive strategies such as time management, text comprehension and summarization, classroom note taking, and test anticipation (Martinez-Pons, 1996). Together, these practices may be effective because they offer students opportunities to gain self-regulatory strategy knowledge, observe effective self-regulatory strategy use, and practice observed strategies in socially supportive contexts.

Like parents, teachers use a variety of methods simultaneously to guide student self-regulation. However, we have a limited understanding of associations among the three teaching dimensions just reviewed (structuring of evaluation, authority, and tasks) and a critically important fourth dimension, teachers' affective support. Meyer and Turner (2002) have explored this issue by simultaneously focusing on teachers' organizational, instructional, and motivational speech as scaffolding of student self-regulation. Such work holds promise for increased understanding of relations among teachers' instructional practices, classroom social and academic processes, and student self-regulation.

Approaches Focused on Student–Teacher Relationships

A specific parenting or teaching practice may have different effects depending on the interpersonal context in which it is applied (Darling & Steinberg, 1993; Pratt et al., 1992; Steinberg et al., 1992). Darling and Steinberg have speculated that parenting style moderates the influence of parenting practices on children's development in two ways: Style enhances the effectiveness of a specific parenting practice and style influences the child's openness to parental influence. The latter possibility underscores the importance of examining the reciprocal quality of teacher–student interactions or the concept of coregulation (McCaslin & Good, 1996). Both possibilities suggest that full understanding of teaching as context for children's intellectual and social development requires attention to students' perceptions of their relationships with teachers and the emotional climate in which learning occurs (Wentzel & Wigfield, 1998).

For instance, examining reciprocal effects of teacher behavior and student engagement across the school year, Skinner and Belmont (1993) found that students who showed initial behavioral engagement received teacher involvement, autonomy support, and consistency across the year. By contrast, students who displayed a more passive learning orientation elicited teacher neglect, coercion, and inconsistency. These findings demonstrate not only the influence of students on teachers but also the fact that patterns of engagement displayed by students are likely to be reinforced by teachers (i.e., active students have more opportunities to participate; passive students are treated in a way that exacerbates withdrawal from classroom activities).

Because teacher involvement influences student learning and motivation, several researchers have sought to characterize the valence or emotional "charge" of teacher–student relationships. Birch and Ladd (1998), for instance, have characterized the teacher–child relationship in terms of dependency, conflict, and closeness. Correspondingly, they represented children's responses to teachers in one of three ways: moving toward, moving away, and moving with. They found negative links between dependence and kindergarten children's school adjustment and positive links between closeness and academic performance and self-directedness. In a longitudinal study of adolescents, Wentzel (1997) found that perceived caring from teachers (e.g., demonstrating democratic interaction styles, developing expectations for student behavior in light of individual differences, modeling a "caring" attitude toward their own work, and providing constructive feedback) predicted student motivational outcomes but not academic performance.

In addition to Birch and Ladd's (1998) characterizations, another potentially powerful framework for examining links between teacher–student relationships and patterns of self-regulated learning can be found in socialization models such as parenting style. For instance, Wentzel (2002) investigated whether, like parents, teachers' differential use of autonomy support (i.e., democratic communication), warmth, and demands for student maturity (i.e., high expectations) influenced patterns of student learning and engagement in school. She found that high expectations (maturity demands) were a consistent positive predictor of adolescents' goals and interests, whereas negative feedback (lack of nurturance) was the most consistent negative predictor of academic performance and social behavior.

In our own work we have examined similar dimensions of teaching within individual classrooms and their relation to student engagement and learning over time. For instance, Walker (2004) studied teacher–student interactions and student self-regulation in 3 fifth-grade math classrooms from the opening day of middle school until the end of the first semester. Within each classroom she observed discourse and activities pertaining to *structuring* (e.g., consistent routines, clear expectations), *autonomy support* (e.g., opportunities to problem-solve with peers), *evaluation* (i.e., emphasis on task mastery and academic performance), and *warmth*. She also interviewed teachers about their teaching philosophies. Comparison of interview and observational data showed that all teachers wanted children to develop self-discipline; however, they pursued this objective in strikingly different ways (e.g., some teachers valued adherence to predefined classroom rules whereas others encouraged student management of classroom activities). Comparison of these data also revealed differences in teachers' structuring, evaluation, and warmth (e.g., teachers differed in their level of behavioral control, feedback to students, and demonstrations of personal interest in students). Based on their characteristics along these dimensions, each teacher was matched with one of three major parenting styles: *authoritarian* (e.g., high structure but limited warmth and autonomy support), *authoritative* (e.g., high structure, autonomy support and warmth), and *permissive* (e.g., low structure but high autonomy support and warmth).

To learn how students perceived these teaching contexts, Walker asked students to rate their teachers along the four teaching dimensions at multiple time points across the semester. She also asked students to rate their academic self-efficacy, social self-efficacy for relating to the teacher, and learning strategy use. As a measure of student learning, she obtained year-end standardized achievement test scores for the prior and current school years. At the opening of the school year there were no classroom-based differences on any study variables. However, at the end of the semester students in the authoritarian classroom perceived their teacher as less warm and supportive of student autonomy. In turn, these students reported lower social self-efficacy for relating to the teacher than students in the permissive classroom and more frequent use of ego-protecting strategies than students in the authoritative classroom. Students in the permissive classroom had significantly lower achievement gains for the year. Students did not perceive differences among teachers' structuring or evaluation practices.

Thus, similar to research on parenting, the most productive patterns of student learning and engagement were associated with the authoritatively structured classroom. These findings suggest that opportunities for autonomous behavior and demonstrations of teacher care support adolescent motivation whereas high expectations and consistent structuring support learning. In this way, autonomy support and teacher care may influence student academic outcomes indirectly through their relation to student motivation; however, this may only be true when teachers create caring *and* demanding classroom cultures.

This review has demonstrated that research on teacher contributions to the development of student self-regulation has moved from relating overt teacher behavior to student achievement, to identifying specific implicit and explicit teacher practices that influence students' social and intellectual processes, to characterizing the quality of teacher–student relationships and their links to students' social and cognitive development. It suggests that productive student self-regulation is associated with several broad teaching dimensions: firm behavioral control, warmth, feedback that promotes students' sense of competence, and instruction that engages students in meaningful tasks. This combination of factors may foster student self-regulation because it demonstrates teacher concern for individual students' intellectual *and* emotional well-being (Birch & Ladd, 1998; Walker, 2004; Wentzel, 1997, 2002). In short, demonstrating care is not only "good" teaching because it is humane; it is an essential factor in supporting student learning.

DRAWING PARALLELS BETWEEN PARENT AND TEACHER INFLUENCE

We now draw parallels across parent–child and teacher–child systems. Our goal is to articulate similar mechanisms of influence (i.e., parent and teacher practices) on student self-regulation. We frame our discussion in terms of developmental systems theory, which portrays development in terms of children's reciprocal interactions with increasingly wider and more complex social systems (Bronfenbrenner, 1979, 1992; Pianta & Walsh, 1996; Sameroff, 1983). This theoretical framework allows us to consider the shared and unique contributions of parents and teachers to self-regulated learning or what happens within dyadic systems. It also allows us to think about how features of dyadic systems relate to children's movement between small group systems (i.e., the family and the classroom).

Similar Mechanisms but Unique Contributions Across Dyadic Systems

What do the parent–child and teacher–student literatures tell us about similar mechanisms of influence on student self-regulation? Productive student self-regulation appears to be fostered when parents and teachers have high expectations, hold students accountable for their behavior but use reason to gain compliance, and offer strong emotional support. By contrast, adult–child relationships that do not offer these patterns of demand and support appear to promote less adaptive student beliefs and behaviors.

The development of student self-regulation across childhood and adolescence thus appears to be enhanced by parent and teacher practices that are consistent with an authoritative parenting style. However, given that authoritative parenting style is not widely used or necessarily associated with outcomes across cultural contexts (e.g., Chao, 1994), we do not advocate that all parents and teachers adopt an authoritative style. Rather, consistent with self-systems theories (Connell & Wellborn, 1991; Deci & Ryan, 1985), we argue that an authoritative style has several "active ingredients" that support the development of self-regulated learning as valued by the immediate sociocultural context. These include support for children's autonomy and their social and academic competence. Recall the work of Whiting and Whiting (1975) for instance: Kenyan parents encouraged children to contribute to the family system whereas U.S. parents encouraged children to attain individual accomplishments. These families met children's psychological needs; however, they differed in the types of activities at which they expected children to be autonomous and competent.

This review has also suggested that students develop adaptive and less adaptive forms of self-regulation in relation to the developmental resources they receive. Put another way, our review suggests that self-regulation is a flexible construct shaped by the opportunities for self-regulation provided by parents and teachers. For instance, in addition to being capable of meeting varied family expectations across cultures, children appear capable of regulating their behavior according to the cultural demands of the classroom (e.g., Walker, 2004). This evidence suggests that adult–child interactions convey cultural and personal values and standards that then become points of orientation for child self-regulation. In the context of children's schooling, the ability to adapt to classroom standards is promising because it suggests that teachers can move students from maladaptive to more productive approaches to learning. This flexibility is also of concern because it means that teachers might also create contexts that encourage students to adopt a passive orientation to learning based on responding to external demands rather than pursuing personal interest and responsibility.

If parents and teachers use similar mechanisms and have similar influence, are they then interchangeable contributors to the development of student self-regulation? Although research in this area is scarce, there is some evidence that each party's contribution to children's development is unique, and that the involvement of one cannot compensate for the absence of involvement from the other (Murdock & Miller, 2003; Wentzel, 1998). For instance, in examining the relationship between adolescents' perceived support from parents, teachers, and peers and their motivation at school, Wentzel (1998) reported that perceptions of support from parents predicted school-related interest and goal orientations whereas perceptions of support from teachers were predictive of interest in school, engagement in classroom activities, and social responsibility. Perceived support from peers positively predicted prosocial goal pursuit. In short, parents, teachers, and peers each made important and unique contributions to student engagement.

It appears then that teachers and parents can use similar mechanisms to influence student behavior; however, the nature of their contributions is different. Developmental systems theory (Bronfenbrenner, 1979, 1992) suggests that these differences stem from the unique roles that parents and teachers play in children's lives. Parental involvement is enduring whereas the teacher–child relationship is short term; parents' involvement often focuses on socialization for culture and school rather than instruction whereas teachers focus more on instruction and socialization at school. These two roles represent different but essential resources for children's development.

From a psychological perspective, parents' general involvement practices may be effective in supporting student motivation and learning because they convey to the child that education is valuable and important, and because they provide resources for the development of social and cognitive competencies associated with self-regulation. An important part of learning, for instance, is knowing when and how to ask for help. When parents are responsive to children's requests for help with schoolwork, they provide encouragement that supports student motivation and emotion regulation. When parents seek feedback from teachers about how to help with schoolwork, they model strategic help-seeking behavior and demonstrate the importance of meeting school and teacher expectations.

Parents' involvement practices focused specifically on instruction can support connections between student motivation and metacognition. If they show children how to break assignments down into manageable parts, parents support students' positive ability beliefs (e.g., "This assignment is hard, but I can do it if I work one step at a time"). When parents ask children to explain what they don't understand, children must articulate and organize their thinking. When this happens, the child is mindfully engaged in the learning process, not mindlessly completing tasks. For instance, Stright, Neitzel, Sears, and Hoke-Sinex (2001) examined relations between parental instruction in the home (i.e., metacognitive content of interactions, manner of instruction, emotional support) and student self-regulation in the classroom. They found that parental scaffolding predicted children's attention to teacher instruction, classroom participation, appropriate help-seeking, self-monitoring, and metacognitive talk; parents' emotional support predicted child self-monitoring and metacognitive talk.

In sum, in contrast to the social conventions and formal structures that govern students' learning behaviors in the classroom, the more informal interactions between parents and children may provide a unique and critical form of guided instruction that gives students "room" to regulate their learning.

AVENUES FOR FUTURE RESEARCH

Although there has been much discussion of parent and teacher contributions to student learning over the years, we know surprisingly little about the specific ways in which parents and teachers influence (collectively and individually) student learning and motivation. In this section we suggest potentially fruitful avenues for future work focused on the systems in which children develop: we begin with needed research on dyadic systems and children's movement between the small-group systems of home and school. We conclude with attention to the child as a developing self-regulatory system.

In this chapter we have outlined parallels between parent and teacher contributions to one construct that is important to students' school success, self-regulated learning. Based on these parallels we have argued that parenting models provide a promising framework for understanding configurations of teaching practices, teacher influence on student self-regulation, and ultimately, adult–child relationships as developmental contexts. Testing the utility of parenting models as frameworks for research on teaching and student–teacher relationships requires operationalizing specific features of the parent–child system (i.e., parental support for the child's autonomy, competence, and relatedness) and translating them into the classroom context. For instance, what does appropriate support for student autonomy look like in the home and in the classroom? Once articulated, such theoretical models of teaching style may be useful in understanding interactions between teacher practices and student self-regulation across cultural groups, developmental levels, and school contexts. Further, given evidence that specific practices are more and less effective depending on the larger interpersonal context (Darling & Steinberg, 1993), an enhanced ability to characterize classroom structures in psychological terms (e.g., authoritative, authoritarian) may also explain why some curriculum initiatives and specific teaching practices are more successful in some school and classroom contexts than others.

In addition to studying configurations of parenting and teaching practices it is important to understand *why* parents and teachers adopt one set of involvement practices as opposed to another. For instance, our work has revealed that an active parental role predicted Anglo-American but not Latino parents' general involvement at home and school and that requests from children predicted the involvement of Anglo parents, whereas teacher requests influenced Latino parents' involvement (Closson, Wilkins, Sandler, Hoover-Dempsey, & Walker, 2004). This work has implications for understanding cultural variations in belief–behavior links and may help schools effectively aim their parental involvement initiatives at targeted groups of parents. Future research might also assess parents' and teachers' more specific beliefs about the kinds of instructional activities and contexts that best support student learning and self-regulation, and about what counts as evidence of students' self-regulatory competence (e.g., to what extent do parents and teachers value compliance with group norms versus satisfaction of personal interest? On what basis do they evaluate students as engaged or not in learning?).

It would also be useful to know what students notice about their relationships with parents and teachers and how their perceptions change over time. For instance, are the components of parenting and teaching identified by theorists as essential to child development (e.g., autonomy support, personal involvement) also salient to children and student outcomes, and if so, at what point in their development do children become aware of these contextual features? Also of interest is whether children's perceptions matter. That is, are parents and teachers influential by mere exposure or is their influence mediated by students' abilities to perceive parent and teacher actions, and their openness to socialization practices?

If students are influenced by parenting and teaching styles, then what are the developmental consequences of perceived consonance and dissonance between the contexts of home and school? Examining this question, Arunkumar, Midgley, and Urdan (1999) assessed relations among ethnically diverse adolescents' perceptions of home–school dissonance (defined as students' perceptions of similarities and differences in the beliefs, values, and expectations of home and school), their academic self-efficacy, and feelings of anger and hopefulness. They found that high levels of dissonance across ethnic groups were negatively associated with academic self-efficacy, feelings of hopefulness, and achievement, and positively associated with feelings of anger. Although such work is important to understanding the affective correlates of student disengagement, there is still much to be learned about the bases for students' perceptions of home–school discord.

There is also much to be learned about the nature of self-regulated learning. For instance, although teacher structuring of the classroom has been related to student self-regulation during the preschool and early elementary school years (Perry, 1998; Stipek et al., 1995), we have a limited understanding of when children begin to self-regulate their learning and when teachers begin to influence students' self-regulatory processes. For instance, how quickly do students "size up" teacher standards? What strategies do they use to adapt to the expectations and norms of varied classroom cultures? What is the onset of such flexibility and how does it relate to learning and motivation? Also of interest is whether there are "sensitive periods" for self-regulatory development, such as entry to school and the transition to middle school.

It is important to note that answering these and other questions about parent and teacher contributions to children's development requires more than attention to adults or attention to students. Changes in self-regulation stem from both children's changing social and cognitive competencies, *and* from parent and teacher practices. In this way, children and teachers create coregulating systems (McCaslin & Good, 1996) in which children are active architects of their own development. More research on the reciprocal nature of teacher structuring and student engagement is needed. This is especially true for the transition from elementary to secondary school, when children assume greater responsibility for their learning and school experiences.

Finally, there are inherent and unique challenges in understanding teacher contributions to child development. Because we lack longitudinal data, we know little about the durability and cumulative effects of teacher practices on student self-regulation (Murdock & Miller, 2003). Elementary school teachers undoubtedly create a foundation for later student self-regulation; however, the benefits of their efforts may be evinced in students' behavior "down the road" and accrue to others. Thus, although tracking teacher influence over time is important to theoretical understanding of teachers' unique contributions to and cumulative effects on self-regulated learning, researchers continue to struggle with the reality that students encounter a significant number of teachers over the course of their educational careers.

TRANSLATING RESEARCH INTO PRACTICE: RECOMMENDATIONS FOR TEACHERS

The full set of findings reviewed here underscores the importance of efforts to increase parental involvement in students' education. Because teachers are uniquely positioned to help parents optimize their role in children's education, we conclude with suggestions for how teachers can use parental involvement practices to support their own teaching practices and student learning. We ground these suggestions in evidence that parents are more likely to become involved effectively when teachers offer clear suggestions for how they can help their children succeed in school (Hoover-Dempsey, Bassler, & Burow, 1995; Shumow & Miller, 2001; VanVoorhis, 2001). However, recognizing that teachers' individual efforts are often influenced by the broader social context of school, we also suggest how school leaders might support teachers as they seek to establish home–school connections.

How Teachers Can Help Parents Support Student Learning at Home

A critical first step in engaging parents' effective involvement behavior is motivating them to become involved (Hoover-Dempsey & Sandler, 1995, 1997; Hoover-Dempsey, Walker, & Sandler, in press). We suggest that teachers can motivate parents by informing them about the specific student attitudes and behaviors that they are likely to influence through their involvement. These outcomes include positive student attitudes about school, persistence in learning tasks, improved knowledge and use of effective learning strategies, and strong belief that effort is important to learning success (Grolnick & Slowiaczek, 1994; Hoover-Dempsey et al., 2001).

We argue here and in related work (Hoover-Dempsey, Walker, Jones, & Reed, 2002; Hoover-Dempsey et al., in press) that teachers must also encourage parents to believe that taking an active role can make a positive difference in their child's academic and social success. Teachers might accomplish this by emphasizing to parents that many simple home-based activities are important to student learning. For instance, Sui-Chu and Willms (1996) found that the parent involvement variable most strongly related to adolescent achievement was parents' at-home discussion of school-related activities. Such findings underscore the value of parents' general involvement practices, such as creating homework routines, and providing emotional support and encouragement during homework completion.

Other teacher invitations to involvement might focus on actively involving parents in homework tasks. Teachers might encourage parents to listen to children read, help them review for a test, or go over the structure of a required essay. Such activities may be most successful if they are specific and time limited. Teachers might also routinely mention general sources of help with homework, such as homework hotlines (Hoover-Dempsey et al., 1995; Hoover-Dempsey et al., 2001). More ambitious efforts might provide parents with direct training in scaffolding techniques that support children's homework performance (e.g., Pratt et al., 1992; Shumow & Miller, 2001). Because the influence of these efforts may stem from parents' learning about developmentally appropriate performance for their child's grade level, teachers might also support parents' involvement by making clear to parents the specific skills and abilities that children should be able to display by the end of the school year.

Teachers might accomplish these goals by using student-centered school events. For example, at school programs they might circulate information on the important effects of parents' support for student learning and suggestions for how parents can support student learning at various developmental levels. Teachers can also set the tone for involvement by establishing contacts with schools or programs that "feed" into their classrooms, and by creating opportunities for families to make informal visits to the school before the opening of the school year. Throughout the year, teachers can send home written messages to parents about home-based and school-based involvement opportunities, and offer explicit invitations to individual parents to visit the classroom on particular days or weeks. These practices may be most effective if they have school support in the form of time, training, and other resources.

How Schools Can Create a Home–School Community

Because teachers receive little preservice training for family involvement (Chavkin & Williams, 1988; Hoover-Dempsey et al., 2002), we suggest ways that school leaders can support the development of teachers' parent involvement practices. Several of these recommendations require little in the way of monetary resources but much in school commitment to creating a community that supports students as they move between home and school.

Our first major recommendation involves the school climate. We suggest three ways schools can create a physical and psychological sense of home–school community. First, to clearly convey to families and school staff the idea that "This is *our* school; *we* belong here," schools can emphasize the importance of overtly friendly and welcoming greetings from staff members who are often parents' first point of contact with the school. Second, schools may also enhance a sense of school community by acknowledging existing home–school "bridges." Many schools, for example, have on-site after-school programs whose staff members often interact with children about homework and who have regular opportunities to talk with parents and teachers about children's social and academic development. To expand effective communication among all parties interested in children's development, schools might consider including after-school staff in teacher professional development opportunities, faculty meetings, and important in-house communications. Third, schools can inform teachers about how they can benefit personally from involving parents. Teachers who invite parents' involvement tend to report relatively high levels of teaching efficacy and support from parents, and tend to be perceived by parents as better teachers (Epstein, 1986; Hoover-Dempsey, Bassler, & Brissie, 1992). Efforts to raise teacher awareness of the value of parental involvement practices might begin as a conversation at a faculty meeting where teachers share practices that have worked well within their classrooms and at the school. These practices can be kept on file in the school office or other teacher resource area to develop a resource bank for supporting new teachers' parent involvement skills.

Our second major recommendation is that schools create formal in-service education experiences focused on teachers' motivation and skills for parent involvement. Grounded in principles of educational psychology and professional development (Hoover-Dempsey et al., 2002; Wilson & Berne, 1999), such programs should (a) create opportunities for teachers to collaborate with colleagues; (b) emphasize teachers' active learning; (c) offer parents' perspectives on effective approaches to home–school communication; (d) allow significant tailoring of program content and activities to the specific attributes of participants; and (e) be followed by opportunities for reflection and evaluation of their revised parent involvement practices. As demonstrated by Hoover-Dempsey and her colleagues (2002), when teachers are given supported time to address parental involvement issues, schools can reap significant benefits in relatively short order.

Our third major suggestion is that schools develop in-school resources that support teacher and family communication. These may include designation of a parent resource area (e.g., a room, section of the library) where parents may wait comfortably, talk with other parents or staff members, and check out resources that support learning activities at home. Consistent with major school systems' recent efforts to hire parents themselves as family–school liaison workers (Gootman, 2003), we suggest that schools create family–school coordinator positions or engage the cooperation of volunteers who might fill similar positions. Given that many parents work in jobs that may not permit involvement during the working day, such a staff position would afford teachers time for impromptu conferences, parent phone calls, and preparation of newsletters.

Because each school community is different, our recommendations are not "one size fits all." The needs and preferences of families vary widely across communities; thus, different schools will likely need to enact different sets of strategies based on the attributes of individual members of the community. The usefulness of specific strategies is also likely to vary according to students' developmental level. Amid this variability, we argue for one constant: Improving teacher–parent relations requires understanding that their interactions are a *process* that may require a long-term commitment to changing deeply held perceptions and habits. However schools choose to allocate their resources, their goal should be helping teachers develop relationships with families that support the identification and attainment of parents' and teachers' common goals for children.

CONCLUSION

We have linked research on parental involvement to teachers' classroom management practices with two goals in mind. First, we sought to raise teacher awareness of parents' critical contributions to children's school success and encourage teachers to inform parents of the many ways they can help their children succeed in school. Our second goal was related to the fact that although teachers have considerable influence on student outcomes, there are relatively few theoretical models available for characterizing configurations of teacher practices and their relation to student learning and motivation. In this review we have argued that parenting models provide a rich theoretical framework for examining teachers' classroom management practices and their contributions to child development. We believe that continued investigation of connections between parent and teacher contributions to self-regulated learning is essential to enhanced understanding of teachers' classroom management practices and children's interpersonal relationships with adults as contexts for intellectual and social development.

ACKNOWLEDGMENTS

The authors thank the Peabody Family–School Partnership Lab at Vanderbilt University, and Carolyn Evertson and Tom Good for their insightful reviews.

REFERENCES

Ames, C. (1992). Classrooms: Goals, structures, and student motivation. *Journal of Educational Psychology, 84*, 261–271.

Arunkumar, R., Midgley, C., & Urdan, T. C. (1999). Perceiving high or low home-school dissonance: Longitudinal effects on adolescent emotional and academic well-being. *Journal of Research on Adolescence, 9*, 441–466.

Baumrind, D. (1967). Child care practices anteceding three patterns of preschool behavior. *Genetic Psychology Monographs*, 75, 43–88.

Baumrind, D. (1971). Current patterns of parental authority. *Developmental Psychology Monographs, 4* (1, Pt. 2).

Baumrind, D. (1991a). Parenting styles and adolescent development. In R. M. Lerner, A. C. Petersen, & J. Brooks-Gunn (Eds.), *Encyclopedia of Adolescence* (Vol. 2, pp. 746–758). New York: Garland.

Baumrind, D. (1991b). Effective parenting during the early adolescent transition. In P. A. Cowan & E. M. Hetherington (Eds.), *Advances in Family Research* (Vol. 2, pp. 111–163). Hillsdale, NJ: Lawrence Erlbaum Associates .

Birch, S. H., & Ladd, G. W. (1998). Children's interpersonal behaviors and the teacher-child relationship. *Developmental Psychology, 34*, 934–946.

Brody, G. H., Flor, D. L., & Gibson, N. M. (1999). Linking maternal efficacy beliefs, developmental goals, parenting practices, and child competence in rural single-parent African American families. *Child Development, 70*, 1197–1208.

Bronfenbrenner, U. (1979). *The ecology of human development: Experiments by nature and design*. Cambridge, MA: Harvard University Press.

Bronfenbrenner, U. (1992). Ecological systems theory. In R. Vasta (Ed.), *Six theories of child development: Revised formulations and current issues* (pp. 187–249). London: Jessica Kingsley.

Chao, R. K. (1994). Beyond parental control and authoritarian parenting style: Understanding Chinese parenting through the cultural notion of training. *Child Development, 65*, 1111–1119.

Chavkin, N. L., & Williams, D. L. (1988). Critical issues in teacher training for parent involvement. *Educational Horizons, 66*, 87–89.

Closson, K., Wilkins, A. S., Sandler, H. M., Hoover-Dempsey, K. V., & Walker, J. M. T. (2004). *Crossing cultural boundaries: Latino parents' involvement in children's education*. Manuscript in preparation. Vanderbilt University.

Cole, M. (1996). *Cultural psychology: A once and future discipline*. Cambridge, MA: Belknap Harvard.

Connell, J., & Wellborn, J. (1991). Competence, autonomy, and relatedness: A motivational analysis of self–system processes. In M. Gunner & A. Sroufe (Eds.), *Self-processes and development* (pp. 43–77). Hillsdale, NJ: Lawrence Erlbaum Associates.

Covington, M. V. (1992). *Making the grade: A self–worth perspective on motivation and school reform*. New York: Cambridge University Press.

Darling, N., & Steinberg, L. (1993). Parenting style as context: An integrative model. *Psychological Bulletin, 113*, 487-496.

Deci, E. L., & Ryan, R. M. (1985). *Intrinsic motivation and self-determination in human behavior*. New York: Plenum.

Delgado-Gaitan, C. (1992). School matters in the Mexican-American home: Socializing children to education. *American Educational Research Journal, 29*, 495–513.

Doyle, W. (1992). Curriculum and pedagogy. In P. Jackson (Ed.), *Handbook of research on curriculum* (pp. 486–516). New York: Macmillan.

Eccles, J. S., Lord, S., & Midgley, C. (1991). What are we doing to early adolescents? The impact of educational contexts on early adolescence. *American Journal of Education, 99*, 521–542.

Emmer, E. T., Evertson, C. M., & Anderson, L. M. (1980). Effective classroom management at the beginning of the school year. *Elementary School Journal, 80*, 219–231.

Epstein, J. L. (1986). Parents' reactions to teacher practices of parent involvement. *Elementary School Journal, 86*, 277–294.

Everston, C. M., & Emmer, E. T. (1982). Effective management at the beginning of the school year in junior high classes. *Journal of Educational Psychology, 74*, 485–498.

Ford, M. E. (1996). Motivational opportunities and obstacles associated with social responsibility and caring behavior in school contexts. In J. Juvonen & K. R. Wentzel (Eds.), *Social motivation: Understanding children's school adjustment. Cambridge studies in social and emotional development* (pp. 126–153). New York: Cambridge University Press.

Glasgow, K. L., Dornbusch, S. M., Troyer, L., Steinberg, L., & Ritter, P. L. (1997). Parenting styles, adolescents' attributions, and educational outcomes in nine heterogeneous high schools. *Child Development, 68*, 507–529.

Gootman, E. (2003, August 30). In gamble, New York schools pay to get parents involved. *The New York Times*, p. 6.

Griffith, J. (1998). The relation of school structure and social environment to parent involvement in elementary schools. *Elementary School Journal, 99*, 53–80.

Grolnick, W. S., Kurowski, C. O., & Gurland, S. T. (1999). Family processes and the development of children's self-regulation. *Educational Psychologist, 34*, 3–14.

Grolnick, W. S., Kurowski, C. O., Dunlap, K. G., & Hevey, C. (2000). Parental resources and the transition to junior high. *Journal of Research on Adolescence, 10*, 465–488.

Grolnick, W. S., & Ryan, R. M. (1989). Parent styles associated with children's self-regulation and competence in school. *Journal of Educational Psychology, 81*, 143–154.

Grolnick, W. S., & Slowiaczek, M. L. (1994). Parents' involvement in children's schooling: A multidimensional conceptualization and motivational model. *Child Development, 65*, 237–252.

Helmke, A. (2001). Research on classroom instruction and its effects—Shortcomings, dead ends, and future perspectives. In F. Salili, C. Y. Chiu, & Y. Y. Hong (Eds.), *Student motivation: The culture and context of learning* (pp. 335–345). New York: Kluwer Academic/Plenum.

Hokoda, A., & Fincham, F. D. (1995). Origins of children's helpless and mastery achievement patterns in the family. *Journal of Educational Psychology, 87*, 375–385.

Hoover–Dempsey, K. V., Bassler, O. C., & Brissie, J. S. (1992). Explorations in parent-school relations. *Journal of Educational Research, 85*, 287–294.

Hoover-Dempsey, K. V., Bassler, O. C., & Burow, R. (1995). Parents' reported involvement in students' homework: Strategies and practices. *Elementary School Journal, 95*, 435–450.

Hoover-Dempsey, K. V., Battiato, A., Walker, J. M. T., Reed, R. P., De Jong, J. M., & Jones, K. P. (2001). Parental involvement in homework. *Educational Psychologist, 36*, 195–209.

Hoover-Dempsey, K. V., & Sandler, H. M. (1995). Parental involvement in children's education: Why does it make a difference? *Teachers College Record, 97*, 310–331.

Hoover-Dempsey, K. V., & Sandler, H. M. (1997). Why do parents become involved in their children's education? *Review of Educational Research, 67*, 3–42.

Hoover-Dempsey, K. V., Walker, J. M. T., & Sandler, H. M. (in press). What motivates parents to become involved in their children's education? In E. N. Patrikakou, R. P. Weissberg, J. B. Manning, H. J. Walberg, & S. Redding (Eds.), *School-family partnerships: Promoting the social, emotional, and academic growth of children*. New York: Teachers' College Press.

Hoover-Dempsey, K. V., Walker, J. M. T., Jones, K. P., & Reed, R. P. (2002). Teachers Involving Parents (TIP): An in-service teacher education program for enhancing parental involvement. *Teaching and Teacher Education, 18*, 843–867.

Izzo, C. V., Weissberg, R. P., Kasprow, W. J., & Fendrich, M. (1999). A longitudinal assessment of teacher perceptions of parent involvement in children's educational and school performance. *American Journal of Community Psychology, 27*, 817–839.

Kounin, J. S. (1967). An analysis of teachers' managerial techniques. *Psychology in the Schools, 4*, 221–227.

LeVine, R. A. (1988). Human parental care: Universal goals, cultural strategies, individual behavior. In R. A. LeVine, P. M. Miller, & M. M. West (Eds.), *Parental behavior in diverse societies. New directions for child development, No. 40* (pp. 3–12). San Francisco: Jossey-Bass.

McCaslin, M., & Good, T. L. (1996). The informal curriculum. In R. C. Calfee & D. C. Berliner (Eds.), *Handbook of educational psychology* (pp. 622–670). New York: Macmillan.

McCaslin, M. M., & Murdock, T. B. (1991). The emergent interaction of home and school in the development of students' adaptive learning. In M. L. Maehr & P. Pintrich (Eds.), *Advances in motivation and achievement: Vol. 7. Goals and self-regulatory processes* (pp. 213–259). Greenwich, CT: JAI Press.

Maccoby, E. E. (1992). The role of parents in the socialization of children: An historical overview. *Developmental Psychology, 28*, 1006–1017.

Martinez-Pons, M. (1996). Test of a model of parental inducement of academic self-regulation. *Journal of Experimental Education, 64*, 213–227.

Meyer, D. K., & Turner, J. C. (2002). Using instructional discourse analysis to study the scaffolding of student self-regulation. *Educational Psychologist, 37*, 17–25.

Midgley, C., Arunkumar, R., & Urdan, T. (1996). "If I don't do well tomorrow, there's a reason:" Predictors of adolescents' use of academic self-handicapping strategies. *Journal of Educational Psychology, 88*, 423–434.

Murdock, T. B., & Miller, A. (2003). Teachers as sources of middle school students' motivational identity: Variable-centered and person-centered analytic approaches. *Elementary School Journal, 103*, 383–399.

National Council of Teachers of Mathematics (2000). *Principles and standards for school mathematics*. Reston, VA: Author.

Palincsar, A. S., & Brown, A. L. (1984). Reciprocal teaching of comprehension-fostering and comprehension-monitoring activities. *Cognition and Instruction, 1*, 117–175.

Patrick, H., Anderman, L., Ryan, A. M., Edelin, K., & Midgley, C. (2001). Teachers' communication of goal orientations in four fifth-grade classrooms. *Elementary School Journal, 102*, 35–58.

Perry, N. E. (1998). Young children's self-regulated learning and contexts that support it. *Journal of Educational Psychology, 90*, 715–729.

Pianta, R. C., & Walsh, D. (1996). *High-risk children in the schools: Creating sustaining relationships*. New York: Routledge.

Pintrich, P. R., & Schrauben, B. (1992). Students' motivational beliefs and their cognitive engagement in classroom tasks. In D. Schunk & J. Meece (Eds.), *Student perceptions in the classroom: Causes and consequences* (pp. 149–183). Hillsdale, NJ: Lawrence Erlbaum Associates.

Pratt, M. W., Green, D., MacVicar, J., & Bountrogianni, M. (1992). The mathematical parent: Parental scaffolding, parent style, and learning outcomes in long-division mathematics homework. *Journal of Applied Developmental Psychology, 13*, 17–34.

Roeser, R., Eccles, J. S., & Sameroff, A. J. (2000). School as a context of early adolescents' academic and social-emotional development: A summary of research findings. *Elementary School Journal, 100*, 443–549.

Rogoff, B. (1990). *Apprenticeship in thinking: Cognitive development in social context*. London: Oxford University Press.

Ryan, A. M., & Patrick, H. (2001). The classroom social environment and changes in adolescents' motivation and engagement during middle school. *American Educational Research Journal, 38*, 437–460

Sameroff, A. J. (1983). Developmental systems: Context and evolution. In P. H. Mussen (Series Ed.) & W. Kessen (Vol. Ed.), *Handbook of child psychology: Vol. 1. History, theory and methods* (pp. 237–294). New York: John Wiley.

Shumow, L., & Miller, J. D. (2001). Parents' at-home and at-school academic involvement with young adolescents. *Journal of Early Adolescence, 21*, 68–91.

Simon, B. S. (2004). High school outreach and family involvement. *Social Psychology of Education, 7*, 185–209.

Skinner, E. A., & Belmont, M. J. (1993). Motivation in the classroom: Reciprocal effects of teacher behavior and student engagement across the school year. *Journal of Educational Psychology, 85*, 571–581.

Steinberg, L., Elmen, J. D., & Mounts, N. S. (1989). Authoritative parenting, psychosocial maturity, and academic success among adolescents. *Child Development, 60*, 1424–1436.

Steinberg, L., Lamborn, S. D., Dornbusch, S. M., & Darling, N. (1992). Impact of parenting practices on adolescent achievement: Authoritative parenting, school involvement, and encouragement to succeed. *Child Development, 63*, 1266–1281.

Stipek, D. (2000). Good instruction is motivating. In A. Wigfield & J. Eccles (Eds.), *Development of achievement in motivation* (pp. 310–334). San Diego, CA: Academic Press.

Stipek, D. J., Feiler, R., Daniels, D., & Milburn, S. (1995). Effects of different instructional approaches on young children's achievement and motivation. *Child Development, 66*, 209–223.

Stright, A. D., Neitzel, C., Sears, K. G., & Hoke–Sinex, L. (2001). Instruction begins in the home: Relations between parental instruction and children's self-regulation in the classroom. *Journal of Educational Psychology, 93*, 456–466.

Sui-Chu, E. H., & Willms, J. D. (1996). Effects of parental involvement on eighth-grade achievement. *Sociology of Education, 69*, 126–141.

Urdan, T. (1998). Contextual influences on motivation and performance: An examination of achievement goal structures. In F. Salili, C. Y. Chiu, & Y. Y. Hong (Eds.), *Student motivation: The culture and context of learning*. New York: Kluwer Academic/Plenum.

Urdan, T., Midgley, C., & Anderman, E. M. (1998). The role of classroom goal structure in students' use of self-handicapping strategies. *American Educational Research Journal, 35*, 101–122.

Van Voorhis, F. L. (2001). Interactive science homework: An experiment in home and school connection. *National Association of Secondary School Principals' Bulletin, 85*(627), 20–32.

Vygotsky, L. S. (1978). *Mind in society*. Cambridge, MA: Harvard University Press.

Walker, J. M. T. (2004). *Teachers as context for student self-regulation*. Unpublished doctoral dissertation. Vanderbilt University.

Weade, R., & Evertson, C. M. (1988). The construction of lessons in effective and less effective classrooms. *Teaching and Teacher Education, 4*, 189–213.

Wentzel, K. R. (1998). Social relationships and motivation in middle school: The role of parents, teachers, and peers. *Journal of Educational Psychology, 90*, 202–209.

Wentzel, K. R. (1997). Student motivation in middle school: The role of perceived pedagogical caring. *Journal of Educational Psychology, 89*, 411–419.

Wentzel, K. R. (1999). What is it that I'm trying to achieve? Classroom goals from a content perspective. *Contemporary Educational Psychology, 25*, 105–115.

Wentzel, K. R. (2002). Are effective teachers like good parents? Teaching styles and student adjustment in early adolescence. *Child Development, 73*, 287–301.

Wentzel, K. R., & Wigfield, A. (1998). Academic and social motivational influences on students' academic performance. *Educational Psychology Review, 10*, 155–175.

White, B. L., & Carew, J. C. (1973). *Experience and environment: Major influences on the development of the young child*. Englewood Cliffs, NJ: Prentice Hall.

Whiting, B. B., & Whiting, J. W. M. (1975). *Children of six cultures: A psycho-cultural analysis*. Cambridge MA: Harvard University Press.

Wilson, S. M., & Berne, J. (1999). Teacher learning and the acquisition of professional knowledge: An examination of research on contemporary professional development. In A. Iran-Nejad & P. D. Pearson (Eds.), *Review of research in education* (Vol. 24, pp. 173–209). Washington, DC: American Educational Research Association.

Xu, J., & Corno, L. (1998). Case studies of families doing third-grade homework. *Teachers College Record, 100*, 402–436.

Zimmerman, B. J. (1990). Self-regulated learning and academic achievement: An overview. *Educational Psychologist, 25*, 3–17.

Zimmerman, B. J., & Martinez-Pons, M. P. (1990). Student differences in self-regulated learning: Relating grade, sex, and giftedness to self-efficacy and strategy use. *Journal of Educational Psychology, 82*, 51–59.

26

Classroom Management and Relationships Between Children and Teachers: Implications for Research and Practice

Robert C. Pianta
University of Virginia

INTRODUCTION

Readers of this volume will no doubt find familiarity with the notion that a large, and perhaps growing, sector of professional practice and training in education has to do with students' social interactions and emotional health, based on accrued evidence that socioemotional functioning relates to academic achievement domains as well as well-being (see Battistich, Solomon, Watson, & Schaps, 1997; Brophy & Good, 1974, 1986; Hoagwood & Johnson, 2003; Pianta, 1999). Attention to the school as a social setting and the ways in which classroom and school social structures constrain or support social development have for many years been the focus of discussions related to classroom management—ranging from how to use specific behavior modification techniques to address problem behavior of individual children in the classroom to the restructuring and reorganization of schools to address concerns related to community and forming a homelike setting (Battistich et al., 1997; Felner, Favazza, Shim, & Brand, 2001). Perspectives on social processes in schools draw from diverse literatures concerning teachers' and students' expectations of one another, discipline and class management, teaching and learning as socially mediated, teachers' own self- and efficacy-related feelings and beliefs, school belonging and caring, teacher–student interactions, and the more recent work on teacher support as a source of resilience for children at risk (e.g., Brophy & Good, 1974; Battistich et al., 1997; Eccles & Roeser, 1999; Goodenow, 1992).

In one way or another all of these efforts occupy the intersection of educational processes and child development. In this space educational structures and resources are put in place to intentionally enhance and shape development toward desired outcomes; increasingly the field has come to recognize that the mechanisms of this influence are located in large part in socially-mediated interactions between teachers and children over time (Brophy & Good, 1974; Goodenow, 1992; Howes & Ritchie, 2002; Pianta, in press). However defined and operationalized, classroom management is at the core of how classrooms influence development, and from both the child's and the teacher's perspective, management is one of the fundamental organizers of experience of the classroom setting (e.g., Brophy & Good, 1974; Goodlad,

1991; Johnson, Duffett, Farkas, & Collins, 2002). It is the goal of this chapter to reconceptualize classroom management in terms of relationship processes, with a particular focus on relationships between teachers and children. Although peer relations play a critical role in management mechanisms (Gifford-Smith & Brownell, 2003), they are not the focus of this chapter because other chapters in the present volume address peer relations and management. Instead, the chapter attempts to advance understanding the dynamics of classroom management by embedding management in a teacher–child relationship perspective (Howes & Ritchie, 2002: Pianta, 1999). This discussion suggests benefits for research, theory, practice, and policy of a focus on *relationships* as a key unit of analysis in understanding the value of classroom settings.

THEORY ON CHILD–TEACHER RELATIONSHIPS: A CONFLUENCE OF INTERESTS

Relationships involve component processes integrated within a dynamic system (Hinde, 1987; Magnusson & Stattin, 1998) that serves to regulate social behavior and, over time, influence individual outcomes (for both parties). Expectations, beliefs about the self or other, emotions, and behavioral interactions are all involved in relationship systems (Eccles & Roeser, 1999; Pianta, 1999; Sroufe, 1989). In a school or classroom setting, each of these components has its own extensive literature, for example, on teacher expectations or the role of social processes as mediators of instruction (see Eccles & Roeser, 1999; Goodenow, 1992; Jackson, 1968; Slavin, Hurley, & Chamberlain, 2003; Wentzel, 2003). Although there has been clear progress in understanding each of these component processes as they relate to educational outcomes, it is equally clear that recent conceptualizations of classroom processes in terms of social systems and relationships (Birch & Ladd, 1998; Eccles & Roeser, 1999; Pianta, 1999; Slavin et al., 2003) bring a fresh perspective to understanding, studying, and influencing what have been vexing concerns on education—particularly the area of classroom management.

Brophy and Good's (1974) seminal work on classroom interactions and Jackson's volume *Life in Classrooms* (1968) are perhaps the foundation for understanding classrooms as social systems (see also Brophy, 2004). This work made clear that properties of social interaction—timing, structure, contingency, affective valence—are key components of what make classrooms successful settings for student learning and teachers' sense of efficacy. The staying power of these results is evident in recent statements concerning the properties of teaching that convey "value-added" aspects of classroom settings (e.g., Brophy, 2004; Slavin et al., 2003). However, in addition to Brophy and Good's work, several areas of work also pertain to understanding the classroom in relational, social terms. The literature on interpersonal perception, attribution, and expectation (see Wentzel, 2003), starting with Rosenthal's work (1969) on the influence of teacher expectations on student performance, was among the first to indicate that instruction is something more than simply demonstration, modeling, and reinforcement, but instead a complex, socially- and psychologically-mediated process, from both the teacher's and the child's perspective (Goodenow, 1992). More recently, work on student motivation, self-perceptions, and goal attainment documents consistent associations with aspects of school contexts, including teachers' attitudes and behavior toward the child (see Eccles & Roeser, 1999; Wentzel, 2002). Research and theory on the concept of students' help-seeking behavior (Nelson-Le Gall & Resnick, 1998; Newman, 2000) demonstrates that student and teacher emotions, perceptions, and motivations are interconnected in the context of instructional and classroom management interactions.

Clearly, the complexity of the classroom environment and the multipurpose teacher–child interactions that take place in that setting pose a challenge for teachers, teacher educators, researchers, and policy makers who are charged with various aspects of increasing the value of those interactions and that setting. How educators understand this complexity can play a very large role in solutions they choose for the challenges they face. For the most part, behavioral psychology, particularly the operant conditioning paradigm, has been the dominant conceptual tool for addressing the social complexity of the classroom environment. Look in any classroom today (or talk to teachers and children) and you will see "management" conceptualized and operationalized in terms of rules, reinforcers, and structure (e.g., Walker, Stiller, Severson, Feil, & Golly, 1998). Although broader views of management might include management of time and transitions, for the most part management takes form in discrete techniques and practices for the purposes of increasing desirable and decreasing undesirable behaviors.

Conceptualizing and enacting classroom management in terms of discrete techniques, informed by a behavioral paradigm, is only partially aligned with a view of the classroom as a social system and the processes that are linked with the desirable and undesirable child behaviors that management techniques seek to address. Although a potentially critical component of management (Walker et al., 1998), behavioral paradigms rely on a limited view of children's (and teachers') motivation, the components and regulators of behavioral interaction, and the role of emotions (Gifford-Smith & Brownell, 2003; Goodenow, 1992; Wentzel, 2003). One by-product of efforts to conceptualize management in relational terms and to focus on improving *relationships* between teachers and children are increases in teachers' own mental health, job satisfaction, and sense of efficacy (e.g., Battistich et al., 1997; Pianta, 1999). The sections that follow offer a way of understanding and approaching the challenges of the classroom as a social system that integrates behavioral perspectives. In the end, it is argued, viewing the classroom as a relationship system offers educators a wider array of conceptual and practice tools to address social and management concerns than are offered by a focus on discrete operant techniques. As a start, a discussion of systems theory and its application to classroom settings provides a tool for addressing the challenge of complexity.

KEY CONCEPTUAL ADVANCES: DEVELOPMENTAL SYSTEMS AND RELATIONSHIPS

In the last two decades, the perspective that the study of development is in large part the study of living *systems* has been adopted as the primary conceptual paradigm in human development (Lerner, 1998) and has been applied to classroom and school processes with considerable success (Eccles & Roeser, 1999; Howes & Ritchie, 2002; Pianta, 1999). Analysis of child–teacher relationships draws on developmental systems perspectives for principles and constructs that guide inquiry, understanding, and integration of diverse knowledge sources.

Systems theory has been helpful in linking research on schooling with theory and research in human development in several areas. These include relationships between teachers and children (Birch & Ladd, 1998; Ladd & Burgess, 1999; Hamre & Pianta, 2001), early intervention with high-risk preschoolers (e.g., Ramey & Ramey, 1999), school-based research and interventions with children at risk for aggressive/disruptive behavior problems (Catalano et al., 2003; Greenberg, Domitrovich, & Bumbarger, 2001; Ialongo et al., 1999; Walker et al., 1998), and transitions to kindergarten (Pianta & Cox, 1999), middle school (Roeser, Eccles, & Sameroff, 1998; Roeser, Eccles, & Sameroff, 2000), and high school (Felner et al., 2001). The general systems theory principles discussed in the following section, holistic units of analysis and multilevel coaction, are conceptual tools that help advance understanding of the classroom as a dynamic, social system and that have specific implications for research and practice related to management of that system.

HOLISTIC, RELATIONAL UNITS OF ANALYSIS

A central issue in understanding the classroom as a social setting is the selection of the appropriate unit of analysis. On the one hand, most practices informed by behaviorism focus on moment-to-moment sequences of discrete observable interactions, calling attention to units that can be isolated from one another and consequently examined and controlled (Walker et al., 1998). On the other hand, because of the preponderance of rich, cross-level interactions among social, biological, psychological, and related systems, Lerner (1998) emphasized that the *causes* of development are in reality the *relationships* among systems and their components, not actions or behaviors themselves. With regard to schooling *effects*, a relational unit is consistent with the perspective advanced by Bronfenbrenner and Morris (1998) when they argued that the primary engine of development is *proximal process*—interactions that take place between the child and context(s) over extended periods. There are several examples of research programs that focus on relational, holistic units of analysis in schools, and the yield of these research programs for understanding the role of proximal process for both social and cognitive/achievement development has been substantial.

Noam and Hermann's (2002) school-based prevention approach with adolescents emphasized the importance of a relational unit both as a focus of intervention and of evaluation. The intervention aims to establish for each adolescent a multifunction relationship with a "coach/mentor," based explicitly on the rationale that relationships are a vehicle through which can be organized and transmitted positive emotional experiences, concrete help, information, and support, a sense of predictability and safety, and direct skill training. These multiple components are, in this view, necessary to counteract the similarly multiple negative effects of experiences with poverty, maltreatment, and lack of skills that are primary drivers of poor functioning in school. In this way the multidimensional and relational nature of the treatment aligns with the multidimensional and relational nature of the risk it is intended to address (Pianta, 1999). Furthermore, in their assessment of the implementation and effects of these ideas in classrooms, Noam and colleagues' work also assessed intervention processes and outcomes at the relational level in terms of the adolescents' use and perceptions of the interventionist and qualities of their interactions with other people (adults and peers) in the school. The youth referred for this intervention are all challenges to classroom management in that they exhibit a variety of problem behaviors with peers and teachers that violate rules and norms. In the Noam and Herman (2002) approach, these challenges are conceptualized in terms of relational histories, motivations, and goals.

Children are often referred for disciplinary interventions as a consequence of teachers' views of problem behaviors (aggression, lack of cooperation, inattention) that are often assessed formally using behavior checklist or informally through discussions of individual children. In these approaches to discipline and management, the unit of analysis is the teachers' report of the frequency or intensity of a certain behavior. Hamre and Pianta (2001) took a different approach by examining teachers' perceptions of their relationships with children in kindergarten and the consequences of these perceptions for understanding and predicting disciplinary infractions in the school setting. It was hypothesized that teachers' perceptions of relationships provided a more accurate and context-sensitive indicator of the value of the classroom setting, the child's adjustment in that setting, and teacher feelings about the child that would be important for any management intervention, than would their views on intensity or frequency of behavior. Importantly, when examining prediction from teacher–child relationships, Hamre and Pianta adjusted for these same teachers' ratings of the child's disruptive problem behavior and verbal ability. When predicting achievement as well as disciplinary infractions at school some years later, kindergarten teachers' perceptions of *relational negativity*, not their ratings of problem behavior or verbal IQ, were by far the strongest predictor. In this way, conceptualization of schooling in relational terms appeared to capture processes that were salient for predicting future functioning (in similar settings).

The gain to be had from a focus on relational processes and units is not limited solely to social processes or social problems. Understanding academic success is also improved when conceptualizing the phenomena at the relational level. In the educational research literature, academic growth is more successfully modeled and predicted when information is available on the qualities and quantity of the child's engagement with specific forms of instruction that map onto their prior learning history. Thus, it is not enough to know the child is receiving a certain amount or type of instruction that predicts growth in literacy over the first-grade year, it is the child's *engagement in learning activities* (a relational concept) that maps onto prerequisite skills (Christian, Bachman, & Morrison, 2001; Morrison & Connor, 2002). In younger children, the value of instructional interactions can be reflected by the ways in which emotions, perceptions, and motivational processes activate and shape children's help-seeking behavior (Nelson-Le Gall & Resnick, 1998; Newman, 2000) and in middle schoolers it has been amply demonstrated that achievement growth is conditioned on an assortment of motivational and emotional factors that interact with what is offered in the classroom (Roeser et al., 1998; Wentzel, 2003). More specifically, using control-oriented discipline and competitive academic values with early adolescents who value autonomy, exploration, and a sense of identity tends to produce lower levels of motivation and achievement and higher levels of problem behavior in large part because of the mismatch between context and developmental forces—a *relational* concern. Thus, the effects of schooling transmitted via instruction and management of the classroom are something more than simply demonstration, modeling, and reinforcement of discrete behaviors, but instead a complex, socially and psychologically mediated, relational process.

MULTILEVEL COACTION

In multilevel, dynamic, active systems such as schools or classrooms, it is fiction to conceptualize "cause" or "source" of interactions and activity (Magnusson & Stattin, 1998; Sameroff, 1995). In such systems interactions take place within levels (e.g., beliefs about children affect a teacher's beliefs about a particular child [Brophy, 1985]) and across levels, such as when teachers' beliefs about children are related to their training as well as the climate of the school in which they work (Battstitch et al., 1997; Pianta et al., 2004). It is a fundamental tenet of developmental systems theories that these interactions are reciprocal and bidirectional. Gottlieb (1991) referred to these interactions as *coactivity* in part to call attention to the mutuality and reciprocity of these actions.

There are numerous examples of multilevel coaction in research on educational processes related to classroom management. Across levels, although evidence indicates that child–teacher relationships alter trajectories of social and academic functioning (see Pianta, Hamre, & Stuhlman, 2003, for a review), it is also the case that these are less of a benefit to children in larger classrooms (NICHD ECCRN, 2004a), when teachers report negative moods and depressive symptoms (Hamre & Pianta, 2004), and when schools are control oriented and do not make social climate a priority (Battistich, Solomon, Watson, Solomon, & Schaps, 1989; Felner et al., 2001). Similarly, coaction is evident during transitions to secondary schools when school climate, procedures around accountability and discipline, students' prior experience, and their attitudes and expectations about school interact to affect their performance in the new school (Eccles, Early, Fraser, Belansky, & McCarthy, 1997; Gambone, Klem, & Connell, 2002). Thus, when understanding something as complex as classroom management, it is critical to understand how the multiple components of management are mediated and moderated by intervening processes operating within the classroom and schools in which management is embedded (Gottlieb, 1991). In short, classroom management, itself a complex process, is organized among layers of superordinate (school policy, community features) and subordinate (characteristics of teachers and children) that regulate the actual management qualities that will be enacted in a given classroom. Because management is so intertwined in these layers, efforts to understand and influence management must embrace its connections with these other levels.

CONCEPTUAL/THEORETICAL ISSUES IN RESEARCH ON CHILD–TEACHER RELATIONSHIPS

Hinde (1987) and others (e.g., Sameroff, 1995) have described relationships as *dyadic systems*. As such, relationships are subject to the principles of systems' behavior described earlier; they are dynamic, multicomponent entities involving reciprocal interactions across and within multiple levels of organization and influence (Lerner, 1998). A relationship between a teacher and child is not equivalent to their behavioral interactions with one another, or to some sum of their characteristics as individuals. A relationship between a teacher and a child is not determined by that child's temperament, intelligence, or communication skills. Nor can their relationship be reduced to the pattern of behavioral reinforcement exchanged between them. Relationships have their own identity apart from the features of interactions or individuals (Sroufe, 1989).

The utility of a focus at this level of analysis is borne out by ample evidence from the parent–child literature as well as studies examining children and teachers using this relational focus (Howes, 2000a). For example, when the focus of teachers' reports about children is *relational* rather than simply a focus on the child's behavior, it is the relational aspects of teachers' views that are more predictive of long-term educational outcomes than are their reports about children's classroom behavior (Hamre & Pianta, 2001). Evidence also suggests that teachers' reflections on their own relational histories, as well as current relationships with children, relate to their behavior with and attitudes toward the child more than teacher attributes such as training or education (Stuhlman & Pianta, 2001). Coming to view the disparate and multiple foci of most research on teachers and children using the lens or unit of child–teacher relationships can provide considerable gain in understanding the complex phenomenon of classroom adjustment and management.

A CONCEPTUAL MODEL OF CHILD–TEACHER RELATIONSHIPS

The conceptual model of child–teacher relationships presented by Pianta (1999) is reproduced as Fig. 26.1. Some of the primary components of relationships between teachers and children include (a) features of the individuals and their representation of the relationship, (b) processes by which information is exchanged between the relational partners, and (c) external influences of the systems in which the relationship is embedded.

Relationships embody features of the individuals involved. These features include biologically predisposed characteristics (e.g. temperament), personality, self-perceptions and beliefs, developmental history, as well as attributes such as gender or age. Relationships also involve each participant's views of the relationship and his or her own and the other's role in the relationship—what Sroufe and Fleeson (1988) called the members' representation of the relationship. Consistent with evidence from the literature on parent–child relationships (Main, Kaplan, & Cassidy, 1985; Sroufe & Fleeson, 1988), representational models are conceptualized not as features of individuals but as a higher-order construct that embodies properties of

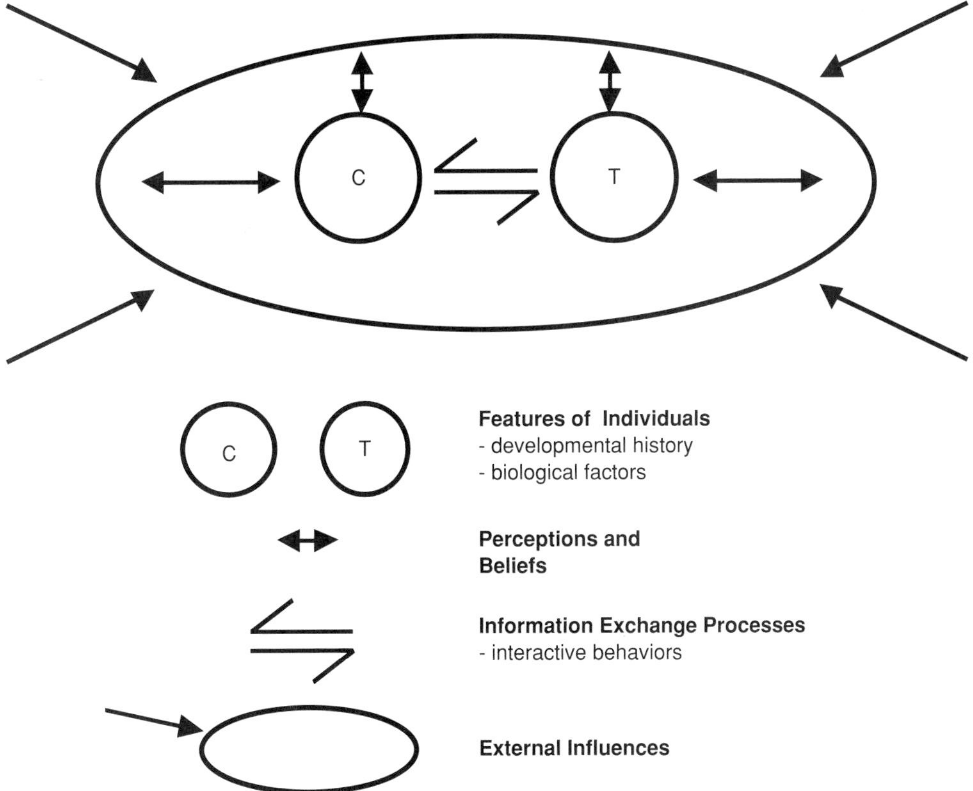

FIGURE 26.1. A conceptual model of teacher–child relationships.

the relationship that are accessed through the participants. Relationships also include processes that exchange information between the two individuals and serve a feedback function in the relationship system (Lerner, 1998). These processes include behavioral interactions, language, and communication. These feedback or information exchange processes are critical to the smooth functioning of the relationship. Importantly, these relationship components (individual characteristics, representational models, information exchange processes) are themselves in dynamic, reciprocal interactions, such that behaviors of teacher and child toward one another influence representations (Stuhlman & Pianta, 2001), and attributes of the child or teacher are related to teachers' perceptions of the relationship (Saft & Pianta, 2001) or interactive behaviors (Pianta, La Paro, Payne, Cox, & Bradley, 2002). Teacher–child relationships are also embedded in many other systems (schools, classrooms, communities) and interact with other systems (such as families and peer groups). Finally, it is important to emphasize that adult–child relationships embody certain asymmetries. That is, there are different levels of responsibility for qualities of the relationship that are a function of the discrepancy in roles and maturity of the adult and child, the balance of which changes across the school-age years (Eccles & Roeser, 1998).

Individuals: Demographic, Psychological, and Developmental Factors

At the most basic level, relationships incorporate features of individuals. These include biological facts (such as gender), and biological processes (such as temperament, genetics, responsivity to stressors), and developed features such as personality, self-esteem, or social skills, as well as the perceptions each individual holds of his or her relational partner and the relationship itself. The following focuses on psychological and social factors related to the characteristics of teachers and children that have been shown to predict relationship quality, as well as emergent research on children's and teachers' representations of one another and their relationships.

Characteristics of Teachers. Briefly, teacher demographic factors show a fairly inconsistent association with quality of the teacher–child relationship. Teacher experience and education have shown little relation to teachers' or students' reports about the qualities of their relationships in the elementary grades (Beady & Hansell, 1981; Stuhlman & Pianta, 2001) and into the middle school years (Wentzel, 2003). In terms of relationships at the school level, Battistich et al. (1997) reported that in a large sample of upper elementary school students there were no significant associations between child-reported or teacher-reported perceptions of the school as a caring community (which included an index of teacher emotional support) and teacher age, number of years teaching, education, or ethnic status.

However, there is evidence that experience may relate to the qualities of relationships teachers form with children, albeit in a fairly complicated manner. In a study that elicited teachers' representations of their relationships with specific students using an interview procedure (Stuhlman & Pianta, 2001), the extent to which teachers reported negative emotional qualities in the relationship were related to their negative behaviors toward the children varied as a function of teacher experience. Teachers who were more experienced were more likely to have their represented negativity reflected in their behavior than were teachers with fewer than 7 years of experience. The extent to which the less experienced teachers held negative beliefs and experienced negative emotions in their relationship with a specific child was not related to their negative behavior with that child. These data suggest some type of emotional buffering mechanism that may wane with more years in the profession, and that may have implications for how that teacher creates a well-managed classroom that prevents problem behavior and supports learning through supportive and stimulating interactions.

In terms of the roles that teachers view themselves performing in relation to children, Brophy (1985) suggested that teachers view themselves primarily as *instructors or socializers* and that teachers' perceptions in relation to these two roles influence the way they interact with students. Instructors tend to respond more negatively to students who are underachievers, unmotivated, or disruptive during learning tasks whereas socializer teachers tended to act more negatively toward students they viewed as hostile, aggressive, or those who pushed away as teachers attempted to form relationships (Brophy, 1985).

How teachers come to develop perceptions of their roles, whether as socializers or instructors, is a matter of great interest, particularly as this may illuminate factors related to training and experience that could have relevance for interactions in the classroom. Along these lines, Kesner (2000) gathered data on student teachers' representations of attachment relationships with their own parents and showed that beginning teachers who viewed their relationships with their parents as secure were also those who formed relationships with students characterized as secure. In a related study, Horppu & Ikonen-Varila (2004) showed that beginning teachers' representations of attachment with their parents related to their stated motives for their work and their beliefs about a kindergarten teacher's work and goals in the classroom. Beginning teachers classified as having a secure/autonomous relationship with their parent(s) were more likely than those classified insecure to express motives that were child-centered as well as centered on goals for the self. Teachers classified as secure also described more complex conceptions of a teacher's work (involving social, emotional, and instructional components) and were more likely to view relationships with students as mutually satisfying (Horppu & Ikonen-Varila, 2004). Apparently, teachers' own personal relational experiences play a role in shaping their motives and goals for their role as a teacher.

As is evident, a range of psychological processes can play a role in teachers' perceptions of and behavior in relationships with children. More broadly, teachers hold beliefs about their efficacy in the classroom and associated expectations for children that are related to experiences with children and their own success and satisfaction. Teachers who believe that they have an influence on children tend to interact with them in ways that enhance student investment and achievement (Midgley, Feldlaufer, & Eccles, 1989). When teachers hold high, generalized expectations for student achievement, students tend to achieve more, experience a greater sense of self-esteem and competence as learners, and resist involvement in problem behaviors during both childhood and adolescence (Eccles, 1983, 1993; Rutter, 1987; Roeser et al., 1998; Weinstein, 1989). Teachers' mental health may also play a role in relational experiences, although this has been an area that has not received much attention in research. In one recent study, it was shown that teachers experiencing a recent loss or depression in their personal lives are more likely to respond in a dependent fashion to children's needs and can have difficulty establishing emotional or behavioral boundaries for children (Zeller & Pianta, 2004). That is, for teachers experiencing a loss or feeling depressed, they reported their relationships with children as being a source of emotional support and comfort.

In sum, there is ample evidence to suggest that teachers' psychological and relational experiences and histories play a role in the relational behaviors and perceptions that they hold with students in their classrooms. However, it is also clear that this literature is not at all well developed or as systematic as it would need to be if one wanted to draw implications for teacher training or interventions with teachers who may have problems with classroom management.

Characteristics of Children. From the moment they enter a classroom, students begin to make impressions on a teacher, impressions that are important in the formation of the relationships that develop over the course of the school year. Though it is likely that a wide variety of student characteristics, behaviors, and perceptions are associated with the development of their relationships with teachers, understanding of these associations is limited and derived in part from inferences about how these characteristics function in other relationships. Some characteristics, such as gender, are both static and readily apparent to teachers, whereas others are more psychological or behavioral in nature.

Student age and gender play a prominent role in the valence of child–teacher relationships. Young girls tend to form closer and less conflictual relationships with their teachers, as noted in studies using teacher (Hamre & Pianta, 2001) and child (Bracken & Crain, 1994; Ryan, Stiller, & Lynch, 1994) reports on the quality of the relationship as well as in studies in which trained observers rated relationship quality (Ladd, Birch, & Buhs, 1999). Even as late as middle school, girls report higher levels of felt security and emulation of teachers than do boys (Ryan et al., 1994). Unfortunately the disproportionately female teaching workforce makes it difficult to conduct studies of relationships and gender-matched teachers and students, although findings from the adolescent literature suggest that relational closeness may be higher for gender-matched dyads (see Rhodes, 2002).

These gender differences may also be related, in part, to the fact that boys typically show more frequent antisocial behaviors, such as verbal and physical aggression. Disruptive behaviors are, in turn, associated with the formation of poorer child–teacher relationships, as rated by trained observers (Ladd et al., 1999), so there may be a child effect responsible for the boy–girl differences in relational quality, at least in elementary school. It is important to note, however, that the majority of teachers in primary grades are females and there is no existing data to suggest how male teachers may relate differentially to boys and girls in the primary grades. There is some evidence that as children mature, gender matching may be important in the formation of closeness with teachers. In one study, 12th-grade girls reported that they perceived greater positive regard from female teachers whereas the boys in the study perceived more positive regard from male teachers (Drevets, Benton, & Bradley, 1996). However, this gender specificity in children's perceptions was not reported by the 10th and 11th-grade students in this study.

Other child characteristics that may be linked to the relationships children develop with teachers include their own social and academic competencies and problems (Ladd et al., 1999; Murray & Greenberg, 2000). In a large sample of elementary school children, Murray and Greenberg reported that children's own reports of feeling a close emotional bond with their teacher were related to their own and their teachers' reports of problem behavior and competence in the classroom. Similarly, Pianta (1992) reported that teachers' descriptions of their relationships with students in kindergarten were related to their reports of the child's classroom adjustment and, in turn, related to first-grade teacher reports. Ladd et al. (1999) suggested that relational style of the child (moving toward, away, against) is a prominent feature of classroom behavior with both peers and teachers that likely has a history in parent–child relationships (Howes & Ritchie, 2002).

Also important to the formation of the child–teacher relationship, though less visible to teachers, are the thoughts and feelings of their students, including their general feelings about the school environment and about using adults as a source of support. Third- through fifth-graders from urban, at-risk schools who reported the highest levels of dissatisfaction with the school environment reported less social support at school and a more negative classroom social environment than did their more satisfied peers (Baker, 1999). Similarly, elementary school children who report an emotionally close and warm relationship with their teacher view the school environment and climate more positively (Murray & Greenberg, 2000). As they grow older, youth calculate their relational investment based on the expected returns (Muller, Katz, & Dance, 1999). For example, urban youths enrolled in two supplemental programs near Boston (largely African American males) reported investing more with teachers who show that they care yet are also able to provide structure and have high expectations for students' progress (Muller et al., 1999). This is also consistent with reports from national surveys of youth, who report that teachers are important and valuable relationship figures, both for support and for structuring/mentoring types of influences (Resnick et al., 1997). Thus, like teachers, children and youth bring with them to their relationships with teachers an assortment of goals, feelings, needs, and behavioral styles that will ultimately affect the quality of relationship they form and, in turn, influence the value of their experiences with one another in the classroom.

Information Exchange Processes: Feedback Loops Between Child and Teacher

Like any system, the components of the child–teacher relationship system interact in reciprocal exchanges or loops in which feedback is provided across components, allowing calibration and integration of component function by way of the information provided in these feedback loops. In one way, dyadic relationships can be characterized by these feedback processes. This view of interaction as *carrying information* is somewhat broader than that of interaction as *reinforcing or not*. This perspective makes explicit the link between interaction and the interpretation by participants of the information embedded in the interaction, consistent with the focus on relational units of analysis. Furthermore, the qualities of, or how information is exchanged (tone of voice, posture/proximity, timing of behavior, contingency or reciprocity of behavior), may be even more important than what is actually performed behaviorally. It has been suggested that these qualities convey more information in the context of a relationship than does actual behavioral content (Cohn, Campbell, Matias, & Hopkins, 1990; Sroufe, 1996). Recent studies have examined classroom settings in terms of quality of teacher–child interactions (e.g., sensitivity of the teacher; positive engagement of the child) in contrast with quantities of discrete behaviors (e.g., teacher praise or discipline; child disruption). This work suggests that these aspects of behavior, at least in early elementary classrooms, are correlated at low levels and that for prediction of child social outcomes (ratings of internalizing and externalizing behavior; social competence) the qualities of observed interaction carry more weight than quantity of discrete behaviors (NICHD ECCRN, 2004b).

There is a large literature on interactions between teachers and children that focuses on instruction as well as social/relational interactions (e.g., Brophy, 2004; Brophy & Good, 1974; Howes & Ritchie, 2002; Morrison & Connor, 2002; Pressley et al., 2003; Zeichner, 1995), although the emphasis tends to be on instruction. Not surprisingly, teachers' interactions with children are related to characteristics of the children themselves. Peer-rejected children tend to be more frequent targets of corrective teacher feedback than nonrejected classmates (e.g., Dodge, Coie, & Brakke, 1982; Rubin & Clarke, 1983), and it has been repeatedly demonstrated that teachers direct more of their attention to children with behavior or learning problems, or boys (see Brophy & Good, 1974; Goodenow, 1992). Similarly, children rated as more competent in the classroom are more frequent recipients of sensitive child–teacher interactions and teachers' positive affect (Stuhlman & Pianta, 2001). Once again, when considering child–teacher interactions as they play a role in classroom management, in the context of this dyadic relationship system, it is important to recognize that there are strong bidirectional relations between child characteristics and teacher behavior.

Research on teacher–child interactions as they relate to student motivation provides some insight into associations between these interactions and the quality of child–teacher relationships. Skinner and Belmont (1993) found that upper elementary teachers' reports of greater involvement with students were the feature of the social environment most closely associated with children's positive perceptions of the teacher. Furthermore, they found a reciprocal association between teacher and student behavior such that teacher involvement facilitated children's classroom engagement and that engagement, in turn, led teachers to become more involved. It is possible that students who are able to form strong relationships with teachers are at an advantage that may grow exponentially as the year progresses. Similar research conducted with adolescents suggests that student engagement with teachers is dependent not only on their feelings of personal competence and relevance of course material, but also on students' perceptions of feelings of safety and caring in the school environment (Roeser et al., 2000).

An interesting line of recent research with considerable implications for classroom management has focused on teachers as social agents of information and the role that their interactions with a given student serve as sources of information about child–teacher relationships for the other students in the classroom (Hughes, Cavell, & Willson, 2001; White & Kistner, 1992). Hughes, Cavell, and Willson reported that classmates' perceptions of the quality of the relationship between their teacher and a selected child in the classroom were related to their own perceptions of the quality of their relationship with the teacher. Importantly, these relations were observed independent of the characteristics of the child, suggesting that this is a unique source of social information in the classroom setting that has consequences for the impressions that children form of their teacher (and vice versa), which in turn could relate to help-seeking and other motivational and learning behaviors (Newman, 2000). Relatedly, White and Kistner (1992) examined relations between teacher feedback and children's peer preferences in early elementary students, finding that teachers' negatively-toned feedback toward selected children was related negatively to classmates' preferences for these children.

External Influences

There is an assortment of external factors that place pressure on or support child–teacher relationships. At the broadest level, cultures often prescribe timetables and expectations about students' progress, how schools should be organized, or what should be the purpose of schooling (Sameroff, 1995) that can shape how students and teacher relate to one another. In some schools state regulations mandate standards for student performance that affect what a teacher must teach, and at times how she must teach it. School systems have codes for discipline and behavior, sometimes mandating how discipline will be conducted. States and localities prescribe policies and regulations regarding student–teacher ratios, the placement of children in classrooms, at what grade students move to middle school, or the number of teachers a child comes into contact with in a given day. Teachers also have families and personal lives of their own. All of these factors can influence a teacher–child relationship.

Structural Aspects of the School Environment. Structural variables in classrooms and schools play an important role in constraining child–teacher relationships through direct effects on the nature of interaction and indirectly via attributes of the people involved. For example, observations of child–teacher interactions in kindergarten and first grade are observed to vary as a function of the ratio of children to adults in the room, the activity setting (small or large group), and the characteristics of the children in the classroom. In large samples of kindergarten (Pianta et al., 2002) and first grades (NICHD ECCRN, 2004b), children in classrooms with a low ratio of children to adults receive more frequent contacts with their teacher and contacts that are more positive emotionally. Teachers in these classrooms are observed to be more sensitive even though in first-grade classrooms, children, on average, were engaged in individual contact with their teachers on approximately four occasions during a 2-hour morning observation (NICHD ECCRN, 2002).

Attributes of the class as a whole also are related to the quality of interactions teachers have with an individual child. Across several large-scale observational studies of pre-K, kindergarten, first-and third-grade classrooms, when the classroom was composed of a higher percentage of ethnic minorities, or children receiving free or reduced lunch, teachers (most of whom were Caucasian) were observed to show less emotional sensitivity and support and lower instructional quality in their interactions with an individual (unselected) student (NICHD ECCRN, 2002, 2004b; Pianta et al., 2004). It is possible that the racial/ethnic and socioeconomic makeup of the classroom reflects instructional and social needs of the children, which if proportionally high, can result in a teacher behaving more negatively. This suggestion is supported by survey data demonstrating that kindergarten teachers with high concentrations of ethnic minority or poor children in their classrooms report a greater degree of burden (Rimm-Kaufman, Pianta, Cox, & Early, 2000).

Clearly race/ethnicity or poverty are mere stand-ins for the learning and socioemotional profiles of children, which indeed have considerable consequences for child–teacher relationships. In fact, children in early elementary school who have a history of maltreatment (Lynch & Cicchetti, 1992) or insensitive parenting (NICHD ECCRN, 2002, 2004b) regardless of income or race/ethnicity are observed to have more negative interactions with teachers and their teachers report more relational conflict with them. Lynch and Cicchetti (1992) have established that maltreated children, as a result of experiences with parents, are sensitized to seek certain relational experiences with teachers; they are less likely to form optimal relational patterns, and more likely seek psychological proximity and support from teachers.

School Climate and Culture. The level or organization of the school also affects how child and teacher relationships form and function. Eccles and Roeser (1998) summarized findings suggesting that as children move through elementary school and into middle school, there is an increasing mismatch between their continuing needs for emotional support and the school's increasing departmentalization and impersonal climate.

How the school values and supports the emotional/social component of teacher–child interactions involves its view of the role and importance of child–teacher relationships (e.g., Battistich et al., 1997; Haynes, 1998). As noted earlier, it is difficult to disentangle the extent to which teacher–child relationships and school climate influence one another, and the extent to which the balance of influence shifts as children grow older and their experiences are more widely distributed within a school. Nonetheless, there is ample evidence that school climate and the quality of child–teacher relationships share a mutually reciprocal association (Solomon, Watson, Battistich, Schaps, & Delucci, 1996). In fact, definitions of climate frequently refer to the role of child–teacher relationships as a key component (Battistich et al., 1997; Haynes, Emmons, & Ben-Avie, 1997).

One source of information about school climate comes from interventions aimed at changing climate. These interventions are often aimed at changing relationships in the school and creating a sense of community (Baker, Terry, Bridger, & Winsor, 1997). For example, the goals of the Caring Communities approach are to help children "feel psychologically safe, responsibly connected to others, practice ethical decision making and self-governance in the microcosm of the classroom" (Baker et al., 1997, p. 598). Furthermore, the Child Development Project (e.g. Battistich et al., 1997) places a great emphasis on students feeling emotionally supported by teachers, and on cultivating a school climate in which emotional resources are available and flow readily as needed. Kasen, Johnson, and Cohen (1990), in their review of the school climate literature, described student–teacher relationships as a central facet of school climate and propose that the various dimensions of school climate described in the literature can be organized into three domains: task orientation, relationships, and order.

As reported by Battistich, et al. (1997), in elementary classrooms with improved climate, children had a greater sense of community, exhibited more prosocial interactions, were better at social problem solving and conflict resolution, and scored higher on reading comprehension tests. They also liked school better, were more empathetic and motivated, and had higher self-esteem as compared to children in schools that did not receive the intervention. These classrooms had a predictable and safe atmosphere and were characterized by productive engagement; in short, they appeared well managed.

Middle school children's positive perceptions of school in relational terms are related to their motivation, achievement, and emotional functioning (Roeser et al., 1998). Middle school students who had higher levels of motivation and emotional well-being also felt their schools were more developmentally appropriate in the teacher–student interactions, practices, and norms (this is especially important as many middle schools are less supportive of the developmental needs of students than elementary schools). Middle schools can be developmentally appropriate by encouraging positive and supportive teacher–child interactions (in contrast to control oriented) and by espousing instructional techniques that emphasize progress or improvement, effort, and mastery as goals and not emphasizing competition and comparisons among students (Roeser et al., 1998). Teacher–student interactions that lead students to feel supported by their teachers, and smaller communities of teachers and students are also important in enhancing young adolescents' motivation and emotional well-being (Roeser et al., 1998). Unfortunately, when middle schools approach children's social and instructional needs from the perspective in which management is the goal, the ensuing control-oriented organization and techniques often backfire, creating less motivation and increased student disengagement and hostility (Roeser et al., 1998).

TEACHER–CHILD RELATIONSHIPS AND CHILDREN'S SCHOOL PERFORMANCE

Over the last 10 years, research on child–teacher relationships focused around several lines of inquiry, each resulting in support for these relationships as salient features of development. These lines of inquiry involve child–teacher relationships as related to peer relations, parent–child relationships, academic competence, and features of social and emotional adjustment (see Pianta et al., 2003). Teacher–child relationships are related to children's competencies with peers in the classroom (e.g., Birch & Ladd, 1998; Howes, Hamilton, & Matheson, 1994a; Howes, 2000b) and trajectories toward academic success or failure (Birch & Ladd, 1996; Hamre & Pianta, 2001; Pianta, Steinberg, & Rollins, 1995; van IJzendoorn, Sagi, & Lambermon, 1992), as well as with patterns of disruptive behavior (Hamre & Pianta, 2001).

Howes and colleagues (see Howes, 2000a, 2000b) have conducted a series of studies relating child–parent and child–teacher relationships to each other and to early childhood social outcomes (Hamilton & Howes, 1992; Howes et al., 1994a; Howes, Hamilton, & Phillipsen, 1998; Howes, Matheson, & Hamilton, 1994b). They have established a low to moderate degree of continuity in the quality of relationships children have with mothers and form with teachers (Howes & Matheson, 1992), and that both of these relationships play a role in children's peer competencies, albeit relationships with teachers are stronger predictors of behavior with peers in the classroom than is the relationship with parents (Howes et al., 1994b). Also, child–teacher relationships show low to moderate levels of continuity in the early grades of school—at least through second grade (Howes, Phillipsen, & Peisner-Feinberg, 2000), echoing Birch and Ladd's (1998) contention that children's relationships demonstrate a coherence across relational figures and across time.

Pianta and colleagues reported links between teachers' reports of relationships with children and a range of school outcomes in the early grades. In one such study (Pianta, et al., 1995), kindergarten teachers' reports of the degree to which children displayed security toward them was related to first-grade teachers' reports of the children's competence. In a series of descriptive studies, Pianta and Steinberg (1992) and Pianta (1994) showed that teacher–child relationships are fairly stable across the kindergarten-to-grade-2 period and correlate with concurrent and future teacher-reported measures of adjustment, grade retention, and special education referrals (Birch & Ladd, 1997; Pianta et al., 1995). Changes in student adjustment from year to year were correlated in expected directions with these relational dimensions (Pianta et. al., 1995): Increasing adjustment problems were correlated with child–teacher conflict whereas when children were better adjusted than expected, teachers reported greater relational closeness. Finally, there is evidence that child–teacher relationships operate as a protective factor against risk—children at high risk for retention or referral for special education who are not referred or retained are reported to be closer to their teachers whereas their retained/referred counterparts are in greater conflict with teachers (Pianta et al., 1995).

Within a group of children designated on the basis of low kindergarten screening scores as having a high likelihood of referral for special education or retention, those who ultimately did get retained/referred between kindergarten and second grade were compared with those who, despite being high risk, were promoted or not referred (Pianta et al., 1995). The children who, despite predictions of retention/referral, were ultimately promoted or not referred had far more positive relationships with their teachers than their high-risk peers who were retained/referred. Significantly, this successful high-risk group was notable for its lack of conflict and high degree of open communication. In short, it appeared that the relationship between the child and teacher acted in such a way to reduce risk for negative outcomes (Pianta et al., 1995).

Hamre and Pianta (2001) extended analysis of the longitudinal relations between early child–teacher relationships (in kindergarten) and child school outcomes through eighth grade. Controlling for kindergarten entry, cognitive ability, and problem behavior, negativity in the child–teacher relationship reported by the child's kindergarten teacher predicted achievement test scores, disciplinary infractions, and school suspensions, through either grade. The effects on eighth-grade achievement scores appeared largely mediated by effects of the kindergarten child–teacher relationship on achievement in early elementary school. Furthermore, effects on disciplinary infractions were most pronounced for children who had problems in kindergarten adjustment. This was the first study to report longitudinal findings for early child–teacher relationships extending into middle and junior high school, and in addition supports the conclusion of other investigations that the quality of these relationships appears particularly important for children who might otherwise have adjustment problems.

Birch and Ladd (1996) studied teacher–child relationships extensively in early elementary classrooms and suggest that children have a generalized interpersonal style (moving toward, moving against, moving away) that characterizes their interactions with peers and with teachers. Presumably, this style is a product of interactions with parents. This relational style of the child is related in predictable ways to the quality of relationships children form with teachers and peers in the classroom through early elementary school, across socioeconomic levels (Birch & Ladd, 1998; Ladd & Burgess, 1999). Those children who displayed moving against behaviors in kindergarten, such as verbal and physical aggression toward teacher and peers, were more likely to form negative relationships with teachers in first and second grade (Ladd & Burgess, 1999). Children who tended to move away from others in kindergarten were more likely to be rated as overly dependent by first-grade teachers, though there was less stability in these behaviors than in aggressive behaviors (Birch & Ladd, 1998). In this work, observed conflict (i.e., moving against) in the child–teacher relationship was related to less classroom participation and lower achievement over the first half of kindergarten (Ladd et al., 1999). Children's moving toward, or prosocial behavior, in kindergarten was not related to aspects of children's relationships with first-grade teachers, but did account for significant variance in children's social behavior in first grade after controlling for gender and kindergarten social behavior (Birch & Ladd, 1998). Importantly, the three relational styles described by Ladd and colleagues are found across all racial/ethnic and socioeconomic groups.

Harter (1996) discussed how relationships with teachers change from elementary to junior high school: Relationships between teachers and students become less personal, more formal, more evaluative, and more competitive. These changes can lead to more negative self-evaluations and attitudes toward learning because the impersonal and evaluative nature of the relational context in junior high does not match well with the children's relational needs, at that age, as has been discussed by Roeser and Galloway (2002). Harter (1996) found that this view particularly applies to students who have lower levels of intrinsic motivation in that teacher–child relationships (typically viewed as potential resources) can actually exacerbate risk if they are either not positive or do not match with the developmental needs of the child. Harter (1996) also reported that classmate support and teacher approval are associated with self-esteem in middle-school–aged population. Teacher support can be particularly salient for students who have low levels of parent support.

Consistent with this view of the needs of middle schoolers for support from adult figures, teacher support has been found to be related to sixth-grade children's school- and class-related interests and to their pursuit of social goals (Wentzel, 1998). These self-beliefs and motivations in sixth grade in turn predicted pursuit of social goals and academic grades in seventh grade (Wentzel, 1998). Importantly, the support youth receive from their parents, peers, and teachers seemed to have additive, thus fairly independent, effects. Wentzel (1998) suggested the possibility that support in teacher–child relationships may be particularly salient at transition points, such as the transition from elementary to middle school, and that communication and warmth between early adolescents and teachers are key facets of support. Teachers who convey emotional warmth and acceptance as well as make themselves available regularly for personal communication with students foster the positive relational processes characteristic of support.

It is critical to emphasize that in several of the investigations described earlier (e.g., Birch & Ladd, 1998; Hamre & Pianta, 2001; Howes et al., 2000; Stuhlman & Pianta, 2001), relations were reported between child outcomes and qualities of the child–teacher relationship controlling for aspects of child behavior considered principal predictors of the outcomes assessed. For example, Hamre and Pianta (2001) controlled for kindergarten teachers' reports of children's problem behavior when predicting problem behavior outcomes in later elementary and middle school using kindergarten child–teacher relational negativity as a predictor. Similarly, Stuhlman and Pianta (2001) controlled for observed child competence when examining relations between teachers' representations and observed sensitivity. Relational dimensions provide unique prediction of child outcomes independent of attributes of the child (e.g. Birch & Ladd, 1998) and teacher (Stuhlman, & Pianta, 2001). This focus on this *relational* unit of analysis, rather than on discrete characteristics of the individuals themselves, provides considerably more conceptual power for the purposes of understanding behaviors in settings and the influence such settings have on developmental processes. Two other aspects of this literature should be noted. First, the results reported previously are correlational in nature—there have yet to be experimental studies of the effects on academic or social performance of teacher–child relationships of differing quality. Second, effect sizes for the associations between teacher–child relationship quality and children's school performance range from small to moderate, similar in magnitude to most predictors of these child outcomes.

APPLICATIONS RELATED TO CHILD–TEACHER RELATIONSHIPS

Evidence that qualities of child–teacher relationships predict child outcomes and are related to features of school climate, teacher characteristics, child attributes, and classroom variables provides ample support for examining how this information can be used to create more developmentally supportive school environments (see Battistich et al., 1997; Hughes & Cavell, 1999; Pianta, 1999). At the classroom level, a developmentally supportive setting is consistent with the view of a well–managed classroom as one in which children are productively engaged in learning and interactions among peers and with teachers are well regulated (Brophy, 2004). Brophy (2004) summarized the body of research on qualities of teaching showing that children's developmental outcomes are improved when they are exposed to teacher–child interactions that are characterized by warmth, emotional support, and sensitivity in combination with structure, modeling, and direct instruction. Pianta (2003) described socioemotional and instructional aspects of child–teacher interactions as integrated processes that can be observed in teachers' *intentionality* in interactions with the child and the classroom as a whole. Intentional teachers have high expectations for their children, skills of management and planning, and a learning orientation in the classroom; they engage children's attention with appropriate activities, use effective feedback in their interactions with children, and convey warmth and acceptance while doing so. The following section describes emergent approaches to fostering these types of child–teacher relationships and interactions.

INFLUENCING CHILD–TEACHER RELATIONSHIPS WITH SCHOOL-LEVEL APPROACHES

In a comprehensive review of whole-school restructuring projects and their consequences for student mental health, Felner et al. (2001) concluded that often there is a "mismatch between the conditions and practices students encounter in grades k-12 and the developmental needs, readiness, and capacities of students" (p. 3). One of these needs, as argued by many scholars and practitioners, is to form functional, effective, supportive relationships with peers and with adults in the school setting (Connell & Wellborn, 1991; Eccles & Roeser, 1999).

In Felner's (2001) approach to this challenge (which is widely used in large schools), "teams" of 60 to 100 students have classes together and have consistent homeroom advisors/counselors. Time is allotted for all teachers to meet and discuss students, integrate curriculum, and increase coherence and support available to students. These efforts reduce complexity for students and build a sense of continuity and community. Critically, these school restructuring efforts result in an increase in and stabilizing of contact between children and a teacher or teachers (Felner et al., 2001). Felner et al. (2001) reported 40% to 50% declines in school dropout, maintenance of achievement levels, and fewer child- and teacher-reported behavioral/emotional problems. Not surprisingly, teachers also reported higher job satisfaction and less burnout (see Felner et al., 2001). Common dimensions of successful schools, according to Felner and colleagues (2001), include promoting a sense of belongingness and agency; engaging families; an integrated, quality curriculum; ongoing professional development (both in curriculum content and in child development); high expectations for students; and opportunities for success (see Felner et al., 2001).

The Child Development Project (CDP) (Battistich et al., 1997; Solomon et al., 1996) has worked to promote social and moral development, a sense of community, and active caring for children within schools. The need for schools to become "caring communities" (Battistich et al., 1997) is most commonly identified at the middle and high school levels where preadolescent and adolescent disengagement and lack of connection to school values and social ethos are most marked; however, CDP has been primarily involved with elementary schools. Although the actual implementation and end product of the CDP intervention mostly involve a set of changes taking place at the classroom level, CDP involves extensive analysis and reshaping of the school environment as a prerequisite for changes sought at the classroom level (Battistich et al., 1997). In the view of CDP, interventions to address concerns such as caring, relationships, and student autonomy and values need to engage at both the classroom and school levels, with primary focus, in their most recent work, at the school level.

Prominent among the outcomes sought at the school and classroom level are opportunities for (a) collaboration among students in pursuit of common goals, (b) providing help and receiving help when needed, (c) reflection and discussion of own and other's perspectives and goals, and (d) practice social competencies and exercise autonomy and decision making. To promote these skills, Battistich and colleagues suggested activities such as having teachers and students share appropriate aspects of their personal lives, eat lunch together in small groups, and engage in other activities that communicate to students that teachers are genuinely interested and concerned about the range of their experiences and not only about their academic work. They also suggested that teacher–parent communication should be a priority so that teachers can have a greater awareness of what is going on in their students' lives. The approach used by the CDP at both the school and classroom levels has been evaluated in several studies (see Battistich et al., 1997; Strachota, 1996). Battistich et al. (1997) summarized the evaluation of 2 years of implementation data in 24 (12 comparison) highly diverse schools. By and large, the findings indicate positive changes in desired outcomes for the 12 CDP schools (and associated teachers and children) in that both the school and classrooms changed as a function of implementation; changes in classroom practice were in turn responsible for changes in student achievement, attitude, and behavior, as well as attitudes and behaviors of teachers. With regard to student–teacher relationships, CDP produced changes in teachers' observed warmth and supportiveness to students and low use of extrinsic control measures, both of which were in part responsible for children's increased engagement, influence in the classroom setting, and positive behavior toward peers and adults. Students reported an increase in the enjoyment of the classroom and motivation to learn, both of which are perceptions related to the child's sense of relatedness within the classroom environment (Connell & Wellborn, 1991). Effect sizes reported in CDP studies range from small to moderate and, in many cases, evidence points to meaningful changes in student outcomes.

In a direct response to perceived problems with classroom management, Nelson (1996) addressed changing teacher–child interactions around children's disruptive behavior. The goal of this elementary school intervention effort was to identify and change school and classroom practices that fostered disruptive behavior. Adults' management of disruptive behavior through school-, classroom-, and individually-focused strategies was the goal of this approach, premised on the notion that adult–child relationships can enhance child social development when the adults make it clear to children which behaviors are acceptable and which are not (Nelson, 1996). The space and scheduling of the school were changed to make it easier for adults to supervise children in less crowded settings. Behavioral guidelines for all common areas were taught and enforced, and inappropriate behavior was responded to quickly and effectively. Also, the interactions between teachers and children in the classroom were changed. There was a school-wide classroom management system for disruptive behavior that reduced patterns of escalating negativity between classroom teachers and students. The result was a clear decrease in disciplinary actions, teachers felt more supported, and their sense of confidence increased. The target children's social adjustment fell within normal range and their work habits improved after the intervention. This behaviorally-focused approach to reduction of disruption is consistent with Pianta's (1999) view that such approaches enhance the feedback and information exchange processes in child–teacher relationships by making information clear to both children and teachers, thereby creating a sense of predictability and safety that enhances the affective and interactive quality of the relationship system.

CLASSROOM PRACTICES AND CHILD–TEACHER RELATIONSHIPS

Project Fast Track (Conduct Problems Prevention Research Group, 1999) has a specific focus on enhancing children's social and emotional competencies and reducing negative, aggressive social behavior, starting with children as they enter school through classroom teachers' use of the PATHS curriculum (Promoting Alternative Thinking Strategies) (Greenberg, Kusche, Cook, & Quamma, 1995). PATHS is designed to help children identify and label feelings and social interactions, reflect on those feelings and interactions, generate solutions and alternatives for interpretation and behavior, and test such alternatives. For example, teachers are trained to add lessons to their first-grade curriculum that teach children emotional understanding, communication skills, self-control, and social participation. This broad-based approach to classroom management focuses on enhancing children's self-regulation in the context of enhanced child–teacher and peer relationships.

Evaluation indicates PATHS can be effective in altering the quality of the classroom climate and relationships within the classroom (CPPRG, 1999). Specifically, teachers who had a better understanding of the importance of teaching PATHS skills generalized the lessons taught in the PATHS curriculum to their interactions with students throughout the day, and those who had effective management skills reported more decreases in aggressive behavior in their classrooms. In one study, teachers implemented PATHS with specific regular and special education children in the second and third grades (Greenberg et al., 1995). This was designed to promote these children's emotional understanding as assessed through emotional vocabulary, ability to recognize emotional cues, and ability to connect emotions to personal experiences. Teachers were trained to teach sixty 30-minute lessons on self-control, emotions, and problem solving to their classes. Participating teachers were observed and received consultation weekly in addition to an initial training workshop. Children who received the intervention had a larger emotional vocabulary, a more advanced ability to connect basic emotions to personal experiences, a more advanced understanding of recognizing emotional cues in others, and believed that they could manage their feelings more than the children who did not receive the intervention (Greenberg et al., 1995). Children with lower initial symptom levels (as measured by teacher reports) were more likely to improve their emotional vocabulary as a result of the intervention than children with highly elevated initial symptoms.

Based on the success of fairly structured programs of parent consultation and training (see Barkley, 1987; Eyberg & Boggs, 1998), Pianta (1999) and Pianta and Hamre (2001) developed the Students, Teachers and Relationship Support (STARS) system for consultation with teachers to enhance their relationship with a specific child (or children) with whom the teacher reports a problem in her relationship. STARS is a multifaceted program targeting a teacher's representation of her relationship with a child, and her interactive behavior toward the child, in the context of a supportive relationship with a consultant.

The specific technique in STARS that is directed at improving child–teacher interactions (and indirectly their beliefs about each other and their relationship) is *Banking Time.* Banking Time is an approach used to enhance the quality of child–teacher relationships through brief, regular play/interaction sessions in which the teacher plays the role of follower and listener. Its name is derived from the idea that relationships can be a resource on which teachers and student rely during the course of their day-to-day interactions, and when positive, these relationships provide support or "capital" that can be drawn on in stressful circumstances.

In Banking Time sessions, the teacher's behavior is highly constrained in order to produce changes in interaction and beliefs. There is an emphasis on the child's choice of activities, the regular occurrence of sessions and that sessions are not contingent on the child's good behavior, neutral verbalizations from the teacher that do not focus on the child's performance of skills, conveying relational messages of safety, support for exploration, or predictability that help the child and teacher define their relationship, and behavioral standards consistent with classroom standards. When implementing Banking Time with a target child (typically a child with whom the teacher reports high levels of relational conflict), teachers report changes in communication with the child (the child more readily shares personal information) and less relational conflict; they also feel more effective in interactions with the child and report knowing the child better than before.

These principles of Banking Time sessions are very similar to Teacher Child Interaction Therapy as described by McIntosh, Rizza, and Bliss (2000) in which teachers engage in nondirective sessions with children designed to enhance the quality of their relationship. Banking Time directly addresses classroom management concerns by focusing on improving the quality of children–teacher relationships for children with whom the teacher has elevated concerns or management problems. Thus, Banking Time responds to disruptive behavior as an indicator of relationship dysregulation and improves problems with classroom management by increasing the quality of child–teacher relationships.

Recently, Pianta and colleagues (Pianta, Justice, Pullen, Kinzie, Lloyd, and Fan, 2003) developed a method using the Internet as a medium for providing support to teachers in classroom interactions and teacher–child relationships related to management. The Web resource, http://www.MyTeachingPartner.net, is a two-level support to teachers currently being evaluated in a randomized field trial in prekindergarten classrooms. In this approach to professional development and support, teachers, on their own, can access hundreds of video examples of classroom interactions with students that have been independently rated as high quality using the Classroom Assessment Scoring System (Pianta & La Paro, 2004), a system composed of dimensional rating scales validated against child academic and social outcomes. Teachers can view clips of high-quality interaction that are accompanied by detailed text descriptions of the aspects of interaction that led to the rating of high quality.

In addition to access to the MyTeachingPartner (MTP) Web site, teachers may also receive Internet-mediated consultation. The MTP approach to consultation is a 2-week cycle that starts when teachers provide consultants with videotape of their classroom interactions. The consultant then edits the tape, offering feedback to the teacher and making the edited tape with feedback available to the teacher on her own private Web page. The teacher has the opportunity to view the edited tape and comments, and to reflect on the consultant's views. Teacher and consultant then meet face-to-face in a conversation that takes place over the Internet. This 2-week cycle repeats continuously over the course of the academic year. It is hypothesized that video examples and feedback to teachers (on the Web and in consultant conditions) based on actual observations of their own or others' classroom interactions, provides teachers with a resource for development as a professional that is more directly tied to their classroom interactions and, in the case of the consultation condition, a source of partnership and support intended to lead to higher-quality child–teacher relationships.

CONCLUSIONS AND FUTURE DIRECTIONS

Classroom management can certainly be many different things to many different people. The sheer number of chapters in this volume is reflective of this reality. The present chapter has viewed classroom management through the lens of child–teacher relationships and, in so doing, has attempted to demonstrate the value of a broad, developmentally-based conceptualization of management. This conceptualization of classroom management embraces the complex social, psychological, and emotional processes involved in interactions and relationships between teachers and children that are the focus of classroom management. This view of management in terms of teacher–child relationships (others will address the role of peer relationships) leads to potentially new and fruitful ways of designing and implementing school and classroom structures and practices that lead to mutually satisfying, supportive, and productive relationships between teachers and children. This conceptualization also has implications for the training and professional development support of teachers. Next, some possibilities for future directions are offered.

1. In analysis of classroom management, child–teacher relationships are a key unit of analysis. A focus on relationships rather than discrete behaviors, or interpreting such behaviors in light of their meaning for relationships, is an important conceptual advance in the classroom management literature, and may be particularly important for teacher training.
2. Child–teacher relationships are multicomponent systems embedded in ongoing interactions with school and community factors. To the extent that relationship-focused approaches to classroom management can be adopted successfully, attention to these other systems (e.g., teacher characteristics and beliefs, school climate and organization) must also be addressed. Isolating any one factor and focusing attention only on that factor will inevitably lead to less-than-rewarding returns.
3. Relationships between children and teachers are marked by variation in the extent of emotional and interactional engagement or involvement, and qualities of the emotional experience of that involvement. Variation in the quality of child–teacher relationships is related in expected directions to child outcomes in the domains of classroom adjustment, motivation and self-esteem, beliefs about school and schooling, and academic success as well as to teachers' perceptions and emotional well-being. Importantly, the quality of child–teacher relationships can be enhanced by systematic interventions and supports, and such efforts routinely are related to improvements in a number of indicators of well-managed classrooms.

ACKNOWLEDGMENTS

The author wishes to thank Carolee Howes, University of California, Los Angeles, for her review of an earlier draft of this chapter.

REFERENCES

Baker, J., Terry, T., Bridger, R., & Winsor, A. (1997). Schools as caring communities: A relational approach to school reform. *School Psychology Review, 26*(4), 586–602.

Baker, J. A. (1999). Teacher-student interaction in urban at-risk classrooms—differential behavior, relationship quality, and student satisfaction with school. *The Elementary School Journal, 100*, 57–70.

Barkley, R. (1987). *Defiant children: A clinician's manual for parent training*. New York: Guilford.

Battistich, V., Solomon, D., Watson, M., & Schaps, E. (1997). Caring school communities. *Educational Psychologist, 32*(3), 137–151.

Battistich, V., Solomon, D., Watson, M., Solomon, J., & Schaps, E. (1989). Effects of an elementary school program to enhance prosocial behavior on children's cognitive-social problem-solving skills and strategies. *Journal of Applied Developmental Psychology, 10*, 147–169.

Beady, C. H., & Hansell, S. (1981). Teacher race and expectations for student achievement. *American Educational Research Journal, 18*(2), 191–206.

Birch, S. H., & Ladd, G. W. (1996). Interpersonal relationships in the school environment and children's early school adjustment. In K. Wentzel & J. Juvonen (Eds.), *Social motivation: Understanding children's school adjustment* (pp. 199–225). Cambridge, MA: Cambridge University Press.

Birch, S. H., & Ladd, G. W. (1997). The teacher-child relationship and children's early school adjustment. *Journal of School Psychology, 35*, 61–79.

Birch, S. H., & Ladd, G. W. (1998). Children's interpersonal behaviors and the teacher-child relationship. *Developmental Psychology, 34*, 934–946.

Bracken, B. A., & Craine, R. M. (1994). Children's and adolescents' interpersonal relations: Do age, race, and gender define normalcy? *Journal of Psychoeducational Assessment, 12*, 14–32.

Bronfenbrenner, U., & Morris, P. A. (1998). The ecology of developmental processes. In W. Damon & R. M. Lerner (Eds.), *Handbook of child psychology. Theoretical models of human development* (5th ed., pp. 993–1028). New York: John Wiley.

Brophy, J. (1985). Teachers' expectations, motives, and goals for working with problem students. In C. Ames & R. Ames (Eds.), *Research on motivation in education: Vol. 2. The classroom milieu* (pp. 175–213). New York: Academic Press.

Brophy, J. (2004). *Teaching. Educational Practices Series—1*. International Academy of Education, International Bureau of Education. Switzerland: PCL, Lausanne.

Brophy, J. E., & Good, T. L. (1974). *Teacher-student relationships: Causes and consequences*. Oxford, England: Holt, Rinehart & Winston.

Brophy, J., & Good, J. L. (1986). Teacher behavior and student achievement. In M. Wittrock (Ed.), *Handbook of research on teaching* (pp. 328–375). New York: Macmillan.

Catalano, R. F., Mazza, J. J., Harachi, T. W., Abbott, R. D., Haggerty, K. P., & Fleming, C. B. (2003). Raising healthy children through enhancing social development in elementary school: Results after 1.5 years. *Journal of School Psychology, 41*(2), 143–164.

Christian, K., Bachman, H. J., & Morrison, F. J. (2001). Schooling and cognitive development. In R. J. Sternberg, & E. L. Grigorenko (Eds.), *Environmental effects on cognitive abilities* (pp. 287–335). Mahwah, NJ: Lawrence Erlbaum Associates.

Cohn, J., Campbell, S., Matias, R., & Hopkins, J. (1990). Face-to-face interactions of postpartum depressed and non-depressed mother-infant pairs. *Developmental Psychology, 26*, 15–23.

Conduct Problems Prevention Research Group (1999). Initial impact of the fast track prevention trial for conduct problems: II. Classroom effects *Journal of Consulting and Clinical Psychology, 67*(5), 648–657.

Connell, J. P., & Wellborn, J. G. (1991). Competence, autonomy, and relatedness: A motivational analysis of self-system processes. In R. Gunnar & L. A. Sroufe (Eds.), *Minnesota symposia on child psychology* (Vol. 23, pp. 43–77). Hillsdale, NJ: Lawrence Erlbaum Associates.

Dodge, K. A., Coie, J. D., & Brakke, N. P. (1982). Behavior patterns of socially rejected and neglected preadolescents: The roles of social approach and aggression. *Journal of Abnormal Child Psychology, 10*, 389–410.

Drevets, R. K., Benton, S. L., & Bradley, F. O. (1996). Students' perceptions of parents' and teachers' qualities of interpersonal relations. *Journal of Youth and Adolescents, 25*, 787–802.

Eccles, J. S. (1983). Expectancies, values, and academic behaviors. In J. T. Spence (Ed.), *Achievement and achievement motives: Psychological and sociological approaches* (pp. 75–146). San Francisco: Freeman.

Eccles, J. S. (1993). School and family effects on the ontogeny of children's interests, self-perceptions, and activity choices. In J. Jacobs (Ed.), *Nebraska symposium on motivation: Vol. 40. Developmental perspectives on motivation* (pp. 145–208). Lincoln: University of Nebraska Press.

Eccles, J. S., Early, D., Fraser, K., Belansky, E., & McCarthy, K. (1997). The relation of connection, regulation, and support for autonomy in the context of family, school, and peer group to successful adolescent development. *Journal of Adolescent Research, 12,* 263–286.

Eccles, J. S., & Roeser, R. W. (1998). School and community influences on human development. In M. H. Bornstein, & M. E. Lamb (Eds.), *Developmental psychology: An advanced textbook* (4th ed., pp.503–554). Mahwah, NJ: Lawrence Erlbaum Associates.

Eccles, J. S., & Roeser, R. W. (1999). School and community influences on human development. In M. H. Bornstein & M. E. Lamb (Eds.), *Developmental psychology: An advanced textbook* (4th ed., pp., 503–554). Mahwah, NJ: Lawrence Erlbaum Associates.

Eyberg, S. M., & Boggs, S. R. (1998). Parent-child interaction therapy: A psychosocial intervention for the treatment of young conduct-disordered children. In C. E. Schaefer & J. M. Briesmeister (Eds.), *Handbook of parent training: Parents as co-therapists for children's behavior problems* (2nd ed.). New York: John Wiley.

Felner, R., Favazza, A., Shim, M., & Brand, S. (2001). Whole school improvement and restructuring as prevention and promotion: Lessons from project STEP and the project on high performance learning communities. *Journal of School Psychology, 39,* 177–202.

Gambone, M. A., Klem, A. M., & Connell, J. P. (2002). *Finding out what matters for youth: Testing key links in a community action framework for youth development.* Philadelphia: Youth Development Strategies.

Gifford-Smith, M. E., & Brownell, C. A. (Eds.). (2003). Childhood peer relationships: Social acceptance, friendships, and peer networks [Target issue]. *Journal of School Psychology, 41* (4).

Goodenow, C. (1992). Strengthening the links between educational psychology and the study of social contexts. *Educational Psychologist, 27*(2), 177–196.

Goodlad, J. I. (1991). *Teachers for our nation's schools.* San Francisco: Jossey-Bass.

Gottlieb, G. (1991). Experimental canalization of behavioral development: Theory. *Developmental Psychology, 27,* 4–13.

Greenberg, M., Kusche, C., Cook, E., & Quamma, J. (1995). Promoting emotional competence in school-aged children: The effects of the PATHS curriculum. *Development and Psycholopathology, 7,* 117–136.

Greenberg, M. T., Domitrovich, C., & Bumbarger, B. (2001). The prevention of mental disorders in school-aged children: Current state of the field. *Prevention and Treatment, 4*(1), 1–48.

Hamilton, C. E., & Howes, C. (1992). A comparison of young children's relationships with mothers and teachers. In R. C. Pianta (Ed.), *Relationships between children and non-parental adults: New directions in child development.* San Francisco: Jossey-Bass.

Hamre, B. K., & Pianta, R. C. (2004). Self-reported depression in nonfamilial caregivers: Prevalence and associations with caregiver behavior in child care settings. *Early Childhood Research Quarterly, 19*(2), 297–318.

Hamre, B. K., & Pianta, R. C. (2001). Early teacher-child relationships and the trajectory of children's school outcomes through eighth grade. *Child Development, 72*(2), 625–638.

Harter, S. (1996). Teacher and classmate influences on scholastic motivation, self-esteem, and level of voice in adolescents. In J. Juvonen & K. Wentzel (Eds.), *Social motivation: Understanding children's school adjustment.* New York: Cambridge University Press.

Haynes, N. (1998). Creating safe and caring school communities: Comer school development program schools. *Journal of Negro Education, 65*(3), 308–314.

Haynes, N., Emmons, C., & Ben-Avie, M. (1997). School climate as a factor in student adjustment and achievement. *Journal of Educational and Psychological Consultation, 8*(3), 321–329.

Hinde, R. (1987). *Individuals, relationships, and culture.* New York: Cambridge University Press.

Hoagwood, K., & Johnson, J. (2003). School psychology: A public health framework: I. From evidence-based practices to evidence-based policies. *Journal of School Psychology, 41*(1), 3–21.

Horppu, R., & Ikonen-Varila, M. (2004). *Adult attachment representations, motives for working with children, and conceptions of a kindergarten teacher's work in first-year kindergarten teacher students.* Manuscript submitted for publication.

Howes, C. (2000a). Social development, the family and attachment relationships of infants and toddlers: Research into practice. In D. Cryer and T. Harms (Eds.), *Infants and toddlers in out-of-home care* (pp. 87–113). Baltimore: Brookes.

Howes, C. (2000b). Social-emotional classroom climate in child care, child-teacher relationships and children's second grade peer relations. *Social Development, 9,* 191–204.

Howes, C., Hamilton, C. E., & Matheson, C. C. (1994a). Children's relationships with peers: Differential associations with aspects of the teacher-child relationship. *Child Development, 65,* 253–263.

Howes, C., Hamilton, C. E., & Phillipsen, L. (1998). Stability and continuity of child-caregiver and child-peer relationships. *Child Development, 69,* 418–426.

Howes, C., & Matheson, C. C. (1992). Contextual constraints on the concordance of mother-child and teacher-child relationships. In R. C. Pianta (Ed.), *Relationships between children and non-parental adults: New directions in child development.* San Francisco: Jossey-Bass.

Howes, C., Matheson, C. C., & Hamilton, C. E. (1994b). Maternal, teacher, and child-care history correlates of children's relationships with peers. *Child Development, 65,* 264–273.

Howes, C., Phillipsen, L., & Peisner-Feinberg, E. (2000). The consistency and predictability of teacher-child relationships during the transition to kindergarten. *Journal of School Psychology, 38*(2), 113–132.

Howes, C., & Ritchie, S. (2002). *A matter of trust: Connecting teachers and learners in the early childhood classrooms.* New York: Teachers College Press.

Hughes, J., & Cavell, T. (1999). School-based interventions for aggressive children: Primetime as a case in point. In S. Russ & T. Ollendick (Eds.), *Handbook of psychotherapies with children and families.* New York: Kluwer Academic/Plenum.

Hughes, J., Cavell, T., & Willson, V. (2001). Further support for the developmental significance of the quality of the teacher-student relationship. *Journal of School Psychology, 39*(4), 289–302.

Ialongo, N. S., Werthamer, L., Kellam, S. G., Brown, C. H., Wang, S., & Lin, Y. (1999). Proximal impact of two first-grade preventive interventions on the early risk behaviors for later substance abuse, depression, and antisocial behavior. *American Journal of Community Psychology, 27,*(5), 299–641.

Jackson, P. (1968). *Life in classrooms.* New York: Holt, Rinehart & Winston.

Johnson, J., Duffett, A., Farkas, S., & Collins, K. (2002). *Sizing things up: What parents, teachers and students think about large or small high schools.* Washington, DC: Public Agenda.

Kasen, S., Johnson, J., & Cohen, P. (1990). The impact of school emotional climate on student psychopathology. *Journal of Abnormal Child Psychology, 18*(2), 165–177.

Kesner, J. E. (2000). Teacher characteristics and the quality of child-teacher relationships. *Journal of School Psychology, 38*(2), 133–150.

Ladd, G. W., Birch, S. H., & Buhs, E. S. (1999). Children's social and scholastic lives in kindergarten: Related spheres of influence? *Child Development, 70,* 1373–1400.

Ladd, G. W., & Burgess, K. B. (1999). Charting the relationship trajectories of aggressive, withdrawn, and aggressive/withdrawn children during early grade school. *Child Development, 70,* 910–929.

Lerner, R. M. (1998). Theories of human development: Contemporary perspectives. In W. Damon & R. M. Lerner (Eds.), *Handbook of child psychology: Theoretical models of human development* (5th ed., pp.1–24). New York: John Wiley.

Lynch, M., & Cicchetti, D. (1992). Maltreated children's reports of relatedness to their teachers. In R. C. Pianta (Ed.), *Relationships between children and non-parental adults: New directions in child development* (pp. 81–108). San Francisco: Jossey-Bass.

Magnusson, D., & Stattin, H. (1998). Person-context interaction theory. In W. Damon & R. M. Lerner (Eds.), *Handbook of child psychology: Theoretical models of human development* (5th ed., pp. 685–760). New York: John Wiley. Wiley.

Main, M., Kaplan, N., & Cassidy, J. (1985). Security in infancy, childhood, & adulthood: A move to the level of the representation. In I. Bretherton & E. Waters (Eds.), *Growing points in attachment theory and research* (pp. 66–104). *Monographs of the Society for Research in Child Development, 50*(1–2, Serial No. 209).

McIntosh, D. E., Rizza, M. G., & Bliss, L. (2000). Implementing empirically supported interventions: Teacher-child interaction therapy. *Psychology in the Schools, 37*(5), 453–462.

Midgley, C., Feldlaufer, H., & Eccles, J. S. (1989). Student/teacher relations and attitudes toward mathematics before and after the transition to junior high school. *Child Development, 60,* 981–992.

Morrison, F. J., & Connor, C. M. (2002). Understanding schooling effects on early literacy: A working research strategy. *Journal of School Psychology, 46,*(6), 493–500.

Muller, C., Katz, S. R., & Dance, L. J. (1999). Investing in teaching and learning: Dynamics of the teacher-student relationship from each actor's perspective. *Urban Education, 34,* 292–337.

Murray, C., & Greenberg, M. T. (2000). Children's relationship with teachers and bonds with school: An investigation of patterns and correlates in middle childhood. *Psychology in the Schools, 38*(5), 425–446.

Nelson, J. R. (1996). Designing schools to meet the needs of students who exhibit disruptive behavior. *Journal of Emotional and Behavioral Disorders, 4*(3), 147–161.

Nelson-Le Gall, S., & Resnick, L. (1998). Help seeking, achievement motivation, and the social practice of intelligence in school. In S. A. Karabenick (Ed.), *Strategic help seeking: Implications for learning and teaching* (pp. 39–60). Mahwah, NJ: Lawrence Erlbaum Associates.

Newman, R. S. (2000). Social influence son the development of children's adaptive help seeking: The role of parents, teachers, and peers. *Developmental Review, 20,* 350–404.

NICHD Early Child Care Research Network. (2002). The relation of global first grade classroom environment to structural classroom features, teacher, and student behaviors. *Elementary School Journal, 102*(5), 367–387.

NICHD Early Child Care Research Network. (2004a). Does class size in first grade relate to changes in child academic and social performance or observed classroom processes? *Developmental Psychology, 40*(5), 651–664.

NICHD Early Child Care Research Network (2004b). Low-income and observed classroom quality. Manuscript in preparation.

Noam, G. G., & Hermann, C. A. (2002). Where education and mental health meet: Developmental prevention and early intervention in schools. *Development and Psychopathology, 14*, 861–875.

Pianta, R. (in press). Schools, schooling, and developmental psychopathology. In D. Cicchetti (Ed.), *Handbook of developmental psychopathology, Vol. 2.*

Pianta, R. C. (1992). Beyond the parent: The role of other adults in children's lives. *New directions in child development, No. 57*. San Francisco: Jossey-Bass.

Pianta, R. C. (1994). Patterns of relationships between children and kindergarten teachers. *Journal of School Psychology, 32*, 15–32.

Pianta, R. C. (1999). *Enhancing relationships between children and teachers.* Washington, DC: American Psychological Association.

Pianta, R. C. (2003). *Standardized classroom observations from pre-k to 3rd grade: A mechanism for improving classroom quality and practices, consistency of P-3 experiences, and child outcomes.* A Foundation for Child Development working paper. New York: Foundation for Child Development.

Pianta, R. C., & Cox, M. (1999). *The transition to kindergarten.* Baltimore: Brookes.

Pianta, R. C., & Hamre, B. (2001). *Students, Teachers, and Relationship Support [STARS]: User's guide.* Lutz, FL: Psychological Assessment Resources.

Pianta, R. C., Hamre, B., & Stuhlman, M. (2003). Relationships between teachers and children. In W. Reynolds & G. Miller (Eds.), *Comprehensive handbook of psychology: Vol. 7. Educational psychology*, 199–234.

Pianta, R. C., Howes, C., Burchinal, M., Bryant, D., Clifford, R., Early, D., & Barbarin, O. (2004). *Features of pre-kindergarten programs, classrooms, and teachers: Do they predict observed classroom quality and child-teacher interactions?* Manuscript submitted for publication.

Pianta, R., Kinzie, M., Justice, L., Pullen, P., Fan, X., & Lloyd, J. (2003). *Web training: Pre-K teachers, literacy, and relationships.* Effectiveness of Early Childhood Program, Curricula, and Interventions. Washington, DC: National Institute of Child Health and Human Development.

Pianta, R., & La Paro, K. (2004). Classroom Assessment Scoring System (CLASS). Unpublished measure. University of Virginia, Charlottesville.

Pianta, R. C., La Paro, K. M., Payne, C., Cox, M. J., & Bradley, R. (2002). The relation of kindergarten classroom environment to teacher, family, and school characteristics and child outcomes. *Elementary School Journal,102*(3), 225–238.

Pianta, R. C., & Steinberg, M. (1992). Relationships between children and kindergarten teachers from the teachers' perspective. In R. Pianta (Ed.), *Beyond the parent: The role of other adults in children's lives* (pp. 61–80). San Francisco: Jossey-Bass.

Pianta, R. C., Steinberg, M. S., & Rollins, K. B. (1995). The first two years of school: Teacher-child relationships and deflections in children's classroom adjustment. *Development and Psychopathology, 7*, 295–312.

Pressley, M., Roehrig, A., Raphael, L., Dolezal, S., Bohn, C., Mohan, L., Wharton-McDonald, R., Bogner, K., & Hogan, K. (2003). Teaching processes in elementary and secondary education. In W. Reynolds & G. Miller (Eds.), *Handbook of psychology: Vol. 7. Educational psychology* (pp. 153–176). Hoboken, NJ: John Wiley.

Ramey, C. T., & Ramey, S. L. (1999). Beginning school for children at risk. In R. Pianta & M. Cox (Eds.), *The transition to kindergarten* (pp. 217–252). Baltimore: Brookes.

Resnick, M. D., Bearman, P. S., Blum, R. W., Bauman, K., Harris, K. M., Jones, J., Tabor, J., Beuhring, T., Sieving, R. E., Shew, M., Ireland, M., Behringer, L. H., & Udry, J. R. (1997). Protecting adolescents from harm: Findings from the National Longitudinal Study of Adolescent Health. *Journal of the American Medical Association, 278*, 823–832.

Rimm-Kaufman, S., Pianta, R., Cox, M., & Early, D. (2000). Teachers' judgments of problems in the transition to kindergarten. *Early Childhood Research Quarterly, 15*(2), 147–166.

Rhodes, J. E. (Ed.). (2002). A critical view of youth mentoring. *New Directions for Youth Development, 93*(Spring).

Roeser, R. W., Eccles, J. S., & Sameroff, A. J. (1998). Academic and emotional functioning in early adolescence: Longitudinal relations, patterns, and prediction by experience in middle school. *Development and Psychopathology, 10*, 321–352.

Roeser, R. W., Eccles, J. S., & Sameroff, A. J. (2000). School as a context of early adolescents' academic and social-emotional development: A summary of research findings. *The Elementary School Journal, 100*, 443–471.

Roeser, R. W., & Galloway, M. K. (2002). Studying motivation to learn during early adolescence: A holistic perspective. In F. Pajares & T. Urban (Eds.), *Academic motivation of adolescents* (pp. 331–372). Greenwich, CT: LAP Information Age.

Rosenthal, R. (1969). Interpersonal expectations effects of the experimenter's hypothesis. In R. Rosenthal & R. L. Rosnow (Eds.), *Artifact in behavioral research* (pp. 182–279). New York: Academic Press.

Rubin, K. H., & Clark, M. L. (1983). Preschool teacher's ratings of behavioral problems: Observational, sociometric, and social-cognitive correlates. *Journal of Abnormal Child Psychology, 11,* 273–286.

Rutter, M. (1987). Psychosocial resilience and protective mechanisms. *American Journal of Orthopsychiatry, 57,* 316–331.

Ryan, R. M., Stiller, J. D., & Lynch, J. H. (1994). Representations of relationships to teachers, parents, and friends as predictors of academic motivation and self-esteem. *Journal of Early Adolescence, 14*(2), 226–249.

Saft, E. W., & Pianta, R. C. (2001). Teachers' perceptions of their relationships with students: Effects of child age, gender, and ethnicity of teachers and children. *School Psychology Quarterly, 16*(2), 125–141.

Sameroff, A. J. (1995). General system theory and developmental psychopathology. In D. Cicchetti & D. J. Cohen (Eds.), *Developmental psychopathology: Risk, disorder, and adaptation* (Vol. 1, pp. 659–695). New York: John Wiley.

Skinner, E. A., & Belmont, M. J. (1993). Motivation in the classroom: Reciprocal effects of teacher behavior and student engagement across the school year. *Journal of Educational Psychology, 85,* 571–581.

Slavin, R., Hurley, E., & Chamberlain, A. (2003). Cooperative learning and achievements: Theory and research. In W. Reynolds & G. Miller (Eds.), *Handbook of psychology: Vol. 7. Educational psychology* (pp. 177–198). Hoboken, NJ: John Wiley.

Solomon, D., Watson, M., Battistich, V., Schaps, E., & Delucci, K. (1996). Creating classrooms that students experience as communities. *American Journal of Community Psychology, 24*(6), 719–748.

Sroufe, L. A. (1989). Pathways to adaptation and maladaptation: Psychopathology as developmental deviation. In D. Cicchetti (Ed.), *Emergence of a discipline: Rochester symposium on developmental psychopathology* (pp. 13–40). Hillsdale, NJ: Lawrence Erlbaum Associates.

Sroufe, L. A. (1996). *Emotional development.* New York: Cambridge University Press.

Sroufe, L. A., & Fleeson, J. (1988). Attachment and the construction of relationships. In W. Hartup & Z. Rubin (Eds.), *Relationships and development.* Hillsdale, NJ: Lawrence Erlbaum Associates.

Strachota, B. (1996). *On their side: Helping children take charge of their learning.* Greenfield, MA: Northeast Foundation for Children.

Stuhlman, M. W., & Pianta, R. C. (2001). Teachers' narratives about their relationships with children: Associations with behavior in classrooms. *School Psychology Review, 31,*(2), 148–163.

van IJzendoorn, M. H., Sagi, A., & Lambermon, M. W. E. (1992). The multiple caretaker paradox: Some data from Holland and Israel. In R. C. Pianta (Ed.), *Relationships between children and non-parental adults: New directions in child development.* San Francisco: Jossey-Bass.

Walker, H. M., Stiller, B., Severson, H. H., Feil, E. G., & Golly, A. (1998). First step to success: Intervening at the point of school entry to prevent antisocial behavior patterns. *Psychology in the Schools, 35,* 259–269.

Weinstein, R. (1989). Perceptions of classroom processes and student motivation: Children's views of self-fulfilling prophecies. In C. Ames & R. Ames (Eds.), *Research on motivation in education: Vol. 3. Goals and cognitions* (pp. 13–44). New York: Academic Press.

Wentzel, K. (1998). Social relationships and motivation in middle school: The role of parents, teachers, and peers. *Journal of Educational Psychology, 90*(2), 202–209.

Wentzel, K. (2002). Are effective teachers like good parents? Teaching styles and student adjustment in early adolescence. *Child Development, 73*(1), 287–301.

Wentzel, K. (2003). School adjustment. In W. Reynolds & G. Miller (Eds.), *Handbook of psychology: Vol. 7. Educational psychology* (pp. 235–258). Hoboken, NJ: John Wiley.

White, K., & Kistner, J. (1992). The influence of teacher feedback on young children's peer preferences and perceptions. *Developmental Psychology, 28*(5), 933–940.

Zeichner, K. (1996). Educating teachers to close the achievement gap: Issues of pedagogy, knowledge and teacher preparation. In B. Williams (Ed.), *Closing the achievement gap: A vision to guide changing beliefs and practice* (pp. 56–77. Alexandria, UA: Association for Supervision and Curriculum Development.

Zeller, J. J., & Pianta, R. C. (2004). *Teachers' childhood attachments and teacher-student relationships.* Unpublished manuscript, University of Virginia, Charlottesville.

27

Classroom Management for Moral and Social Development

Larry Nucci
University of Illinois at Chicago

INTRODUCTION

"Don't smile until Christmas" is a piece of advice often spoken to new teachers for how to approach classroom management. The presumption conveyed in that advice is that the primary challenge facing a new teacher is establishing control over the students. Although no one would dispute the need for classroom order and organization as an essential component of effective teaching, the emphasis on teacher control obscures the role that effective classroom management can have in contributing to students' moral and social development. All classrooms, no matter how they are run, constitute social environments that influence students' construction of morality and social values (Jackson, Boostrom, & Hansen, 1993). The issue then, is not whether classroom management affects social development, but rather how classroom management may contribute positively to students' moral and social growth. Viewing classroom management as an educational activity requires teachers to engage in the same kind of critical analysis of practice as would be directed to the teaching of subject matter. This includes not only an awareness of available options or strategies for how to handle classroom situations, but also a compendium of knowledge about the "subject matter" of social and moral development and how it relates to a given set of practices. This chapter provides a discussion of these issues as they play out in school contexts. Before moving to that more specific discussion, however, we need to set out some of the general elements of moral and social growth relevant to our concerns about classroom management.

THEORY AND RESEARCH ON MORAL DEVELOPMENT

Defining the Moral Domain

The information contained in this chapter is based on work in what is referred to as social cognitive domain theory (Turiel, 1983, 1998). Domain theory has emerged over the past decade as the dominant paradigm for research on moral development, and provides a set of novel implications for classroom management practices. This view of social development holds that children construct social concepts within discrete developmental frameworks, or domains, that are generated out of qualitatively differing aspects of their social interactions. Three basic conceptual frameworks or domains of social knowledge are posited by domain theory: morality, societal convention, and the personal. Concepts of morality address the nonarbitrary and therefore universal aspects of social relations pertaining to issues of human welfare, rights, and fairness (Turiel, 1983, 2002). Children as young as age 3 have been found to treat moral transgressions such as the unprovoked hitting and hurting of another child as wrong even in the absence of a governing rule or norm, because of the intrinsic effects (pain and injury) that the act of hitting has on the victim (Turiel, 1983, 2002). Children's moral development entails progressive transformations in their conceptions of justice and human welfare (Turiel, 2002). These moral understandings inform children's and adolescents' views of such larger moral issues as civil liberties (Helwig & Turiel, 2002).

Morality can be distinguished from concepts of social conventions, which are the consensually determined standards of conduct particular to a given social group. Conventions established by social systems such as norms or standards of dress, how people should address one another, table manners, and so forth derive their status as correct or incorrect forms of conduct from their embeddedness within a particular shared system of meaning and social interaction. The particular acts in and of themselves have no prescriptive force in that different or even opposite norms (e.g., dresses for men, pants for women) could be established to achieve the same symbolic or regulatory function (e.g., distinguishing men from women). Thus, children and adults view the wrongness of violations of conventions, such as addressing teachers by their first names, as contingent on the presence of a rule or norm governing the action (Turiel, 1983, 2002). The importance of conventions lies in the function they serve to coordinate social interaction and discourse within social systems. In keeping with this definition, concepts of social convention have been found to be structured by underlying conceptions of social organization (Turiel, 1983, 2002).

Finally, whereas morality and convention deal with aspects of interpersonal regulation, concepts of personal issues refer to actions that compose the private aspects of one's life, such as the contents of a diary, and issues that are matters of preference and choice (e.g., friends, music, hairstyle) rather than right or wrong. It has been proposed that the establishment of control over the personal domain emerges from the need to establish boundaries between the self and others, and is critical to the establishment of personal autonomy and individual identity (Nucci, 1996).

Social Interactions and Moral and Social Growth

The distinctions drawn among moral, conventional, and personal concepts have been sustained by findings from more than 70 studies published over the past 30 years. This work includes observations of naturally occurring peer and adult–child interactions, developmental interviews of children and adults, and cross-cultural studies conducted in a number of countries (Brazil, Canada, China, Colombia, Israel, India, Indonesia, Japan, Korea, Taiwan, United States, Zambia). Comprehensive recent reviews of this research may be found in Nucci (2001), Smetana (2002), and Turiel (1998, 2002).

Of particular interest for a discussion on classroom management is the observational research that has been done on children's social interactions. Observational studies of children and adults in school, home, and free-play settings have provided a consistent body of evidence that the forms of social interaction associated with morality are qualitatively different from the social interactions children use to construct their basic understandings of societal convention, and matters of personal prerogative (see Nucci, 2003 for a comprehensive review).

Interactions having to do with morality tend to focus on the effects those actions have on the welfare of others. In the case of moral events, children experience such interactions as victims, perpetrators, or third-person observers. Interactions around societal conventions, in contrast, tend to focus on the norms or rules that would apply, along with feedback regarding the social organizational function of the norm (e.g., to maintain classroom order). What this observational research demonstrates is that children are using different patterns of social information to construct their understandings of morality and conventional norms. As is discussed later in the chapter, these domain-related patterns of social interaction have implications for the ways in which teachers should approach issues of morality and convention in the classroom.

The Role of Emotion in Constructing Moral Understandings

An important component of classroom management is the overall emotional climate of the classroom. Part of the information children use to construct their moral and social knowledge is the emotion surrounding social interactions. Arsenio and his colleagues (Arsenio & Lover, 1995) have provided evidence that children associate different feelings with different domains of social events. Issues of social conventions generally elicit "cool" or neutral affect on the part of children. This holds for acts of compliance as well as transgressions (Arsenio, 1988). To the extent that children experience "hot" emotions, it is on the part of adults who occasionally respond with anger to children's conventional transgressions (Shweder, Mahapatra, & Miller, 1987). Issues of morality, however, are viewed by children as filled with "hot" emotions of anger, fear, and sadness among victims of transgressions, and happiness among all parties in the cases where moral situations turn out fairly (Arsenio, 1988).

Emotions are routinely stored as part of the construction of social–cognitive representations (Arsenio & Lover, 1995). Repeated experience with events having similar emotional outcomes allows children to form generalized social scripts (Karniol, 2003). In the views of some researchers these scripts form the beginnings of our moral character (Kochanska, 1993). The role of affect in such social constructions also means that individual variations in the affective experiences of children are reflected in their moral orientations. For example, variations in the early construction of moral schemata, such as differences in the child's temperament (Kochanska, 1993), the degree of anger displayed by adults in reaction to children's transgressions, or the warmth in reaction to children's prosocial conduct (Cumberland-Li, Eisenberg, Champion, Gershoff, & Fabes, 2003; Emde, Birigen, Clyman, & Openheim, 1991), appear to affect the way in which children construct their basic concepts of the social world and how to react within interpersonal situations.

The core of morality is the capacity to engage in moral reciprocity. For the child growing up in an affectively supportive environment, the construction of moral reversibility (fairness) is supported by the experience of "goodwill" that comes from acts of fair reciprocity (Aresnio & Lover, 1995). This goodwill complements the positive feelings and happiness that children experience when they engage in acts of prosocial conduct (Eisenberg, 1986). In contrast, children with long-term patterns of victimization and peer rejection tend to establish a pattern of "ill will" distorting the construction of moral reciprocity in support of aggressive actions toward others (Arsenio & Lover, 1995). From the perspective of the classroom teacher, this effect of early emotional experience helps explain the variations the teacher observes in children's tendencies to respond to peers in fair and caring or aggressive ways. It also implies that an important element of a teacher's approach to children's moral and social growth is the establishment of a classroom climate and teacher practice that maximizes the likelihood that students will experience "goodwill" during their time at school.

Throughout development, the emotional climate of the school and the pattern of peer and student–teacher interactions form a basic context within which schools either unwittingly or self-consciously contribute to students' social and moral development (Hansen, 1995). The sections that follow discuss how social interactions associated with classroom management may be tailored to differentially contribute to development in the moral and conventional domains. This discussion also addresses how normative phases of student resistance are related to developmental changes in the domains of social convention and the personal, and the implications such developmental phases have for the enforcement of school rules and policies. We begin with a brief general discussion of the implications of research on moral and social development for classroom management, followed by sections focusing on management issues at particular grade levels.

CLASSROOM MANAGEMENT FOR SOCIAL DEVELOPMENT

General Issues

There are several broad implications of recent developmental research for an approach to classroom management intended to contribute to students' moral and social growth. Among those that transcend particular grade levels are the following.

- *Classroom management practices should engage students in active reflection to promote social knowledge construction.* The goal of using classroom management as an educative tool can only be achieved if the practices stimulate students to alter their underlying conceptions of morality and social norms, and take active control of their own conduct. This position is consistent with fundamental tenets of contemporary developmental psychology (Amsel & Renninger, 1997; Rogoff, 1990; Turiel, 1983) and cognitive theories of learning (Brown & Reeve, 1987; Liben, 1987; Narvaez, in press; Sternberg, 1998). It is also concordant with motivational theories that emphasize the promotion of intrinsic rather than extrinsic motivation (Deci, 1995), and related accounts of the promotion of self-efficacy and self-regulation (Polson, 2001; Zimmerman, Bonner, & Kovach, 2002). For this reason traditional approaches to classroom management (e.g., Canter & Canter, 1992; Wynne & Ryan, 1993) that rely heavily on external reward and punishment as management techniques are not optimal strategies beyond the immediate goal of establishing control over students. As McCaslin and Good (1992, 1998) pointed out, such traditional rule and consequence systems foster "compliant cognition," which is at odds with attempts to develop self-regulated learners. Constructivist alternatives that engage student reflection are described within the subsequent sections on specific practices.
- *Classroom management strategies need to attend to the domain of the social issues being addressed.* Given that children's concepts of morality are distinct from their concepts of social convention, it follows that efforts to generate social development would need to differentially attend to the domain of the issues being addressed (Nucci, 2001). The distinctions maintained by domain theory are not shared, however, by theories of socialization (e.g., Bandura, 1991) that sustain traditional approaches to classroom management. Traditional behavioral and social learning theories hold that morality is defined by cultural norms and conventions acquired by children through direct instruction and the observation of actions of adult role models. Accordingly, the classroom management practices advocated by traditional educators (e.g., Canter & Canter, 1992; Wynne & Ryan, 1993) approach social behaviors in a uniform fashion, reducing all social values including morality to matters of social convention.

  The distinction between morality and convention is contained in the accounts of moral development (Piaget, 1932; Kohlberg, 1984) that have informed developmental approaches to classroom management (DeVries & Zan, 1994). However, although differing in their interpretations of the ages at which such changes take place, both Piaget (1932) and Kohlberg (1984) maintained that only at the highest stages of moral development can morality be differentiated from and displace convention as the basis for moral judgments. Thus, when it comes to classroom management practices advocated by developmental educators, there is also the tendency to presume that children approach all classroom norms from a unitary conceptual orientation, and to emphasize issues of fairness and concern for others in an effort to move children beyond their presumed subordination of morality to authority and social expectations (DeVries & Zan, 1994; Power, Higgins, & Kohlberg, 1989). As a consequence, the tendency in developmental programs based on the work of Piaget and Kohlberg is to assimilate all aspects of classroom interactions to matters of morality.

The importance of attending differentially to domain has been demonstrated in research indicating that instructional practices that are domain consistent are more effective in stimulating children's development in both the moral and conventional domains than are practices that subordinate all social norms to a single domain of morality or convention (Nucci & Weber, 1991). As is discussed in greater detail in subsequent sections, research has also demonstrated that students use their social knowledge to evaluate teacher responses to misbehavior in part on the basis of the perceived correspondence between teacher messages and the domain of the transgression (Killen, Breton, Ferguson, & Handler, 1994; Nucci, 1984).

- *Classroom management needs to be coordinated with students' levels of development.* Matching teaching with student development is a basic educational principle. Development within the moral domain involves transformations in students' concepts about justice and harm that move toward progressively broader interpretations of the meaning of fairness and one's obligations toward other people (Damon, 1977; Nucci, 2001). Recent work also indicates that moral growth involves changing perspectives in the interpretation of the fairness of classroom practices such as testing, grading, and the use of instructional methods such as ability grouping (Thorkildsen, 2000). For example, young children prior to third grade tend to think that a fair testing practice is one that allows for peers to work together, and that a fair test produces equal test scores. Older children, on the other hand, tend to believe that testing has to be done with individuals because group testing would unfairly mask ability differences (Thorkildsen, 1991).

Development within the conventional domain is less straightforward. Because conventions are arbitrary, their connections to social organization are often difficult for children to understand. Development within the conventional domain follows an oscillating pattern involving periods of affirmation in which children offer interpretations for the social functions of social convention that are followed by periods of negation in which children question their prior basis for affirming adherence to convention (Turiel, 1983; Nucci, Becker, & Horn, 2004). As is discussed later, these oscillating patterns of affirmation and negation are also associated with age-related periods of compliance and noncompliance with classroom conventions (Geiger & Turiel, 1983; Nucci & Nucci, 1982).

Adding to the complexity of this developmental picture are developmental changes that occur in the relationship between the conventional and personal domains (Smetana, 2002, in press). As children enter the sixth grade (around age 11), they also enter a period of expansion of areas of conduct that they consider personal, and therefore their own business, rather than subject to social convention or parental or teacher authority (Smetana, 2002, in press). As is discussed in greater detail later, this shift in late childhood and early adolescence has consequences for students' perceptions of school authority, and their willingness to comply with school conventions (Smetana, in press; Smetana & Bitz, 1996).

Finally, issues of social class and ethnicity play a role in the ways in which children and adolescents interpret the meaning of social and moral events adding complexity to the general developmental picture. For example, Astor (1994) reported that although inner-city African American male elementary and middle school children universally condemned unprovoked hitting as wrong, they tended to view hitting back in response to verbal insult as a justifiable form of retributive justice. Middle-class teachers operating within an urban setting might well misinterpret this tendency toward physical retaliation as evidence of a "lower" level of moral development rather than as a shared view of a morally appropriate response to disrespect. This is not to say that teachers should not challenge such culturally supported student positions, but rather that one should not misconstrue such moral positions as evidence of developmental delay.

This more complex view of social and moral development provided by recent work on social cognitive domains affords teachers a variegated framework within which to interpret student conduct, and to fashion classroom structure and social messages that are concordant with student development. Having briefly introduced some of the general considerations for using classroom management as a medium for moral and social values education, let us turn now to a consideration of these issues within specific grade levels.

Classroom Management in Early Childhood and Elementary School

Establishing a Moral Climate of Trust. As the research on moral development demonstrates, the impact of emotional experience on the construction of morality is never more critical than in the social interactions of young children (Arsenio & Lover, 1995; Kochanska, 1993). Thus, we begin our discussion of classroom management in the preschool and elementary school classroom with the establishment of a moral climate of trust. For some educators the establishment of a caring environment and an overall "ethic of care" is the most essential component of moral education (Noddings, 2002). Establishing a caring orientation begins with the capacity to accept care from others. This requires a school and classroom climate in which students can afford to be emotionally vulnerable, and in which that vulnerability extends to the student's willingness to risk engagement in acts of kindness and concern for others (Noddings, 2002). As was seen in the earlier discussion of affect and moral growth, young children are particularly susceptible to the positive effects of adult displays of emotional warmth, and the negative impact of adult displays of anger (Cumberland-Li et al., 2003; Emde et al., 1991). Thus, constructing an emotionally caring environment for young children means that teachers should be even-tempered, and refrain from emotional outbursts or shouting at young children.

This is not to say that all teachers need to sound and act like the television character, Mr. Rogers. As Delpit (1995) has pointed out with respect to lower-class African Americans, many cultural groups use discourse with their children that would be interpreted as authoritarian by the middle-class community. However, more directive parental and teacher orientations toward children should not be confused with displays of anger and harsh treatment. In studies conducted within cultural groups using purportedly more authoritarian parenting practices, researchers have reported that such directive parenting is associated with positive child outcomes when it is also coupled with an overall parent–child relationship characterized by emotional warmth and caring (Park & Buriel, 1998; Steinberg, 2001). Finally, although Delpit (1995) has argued effectively for the need to respect cultural styles of parenting and classroom interactions, others (Thompson, 2004) have taken the position that classroom contexts for all children, including those of inner-city African-Americans, should emphasize mutual respect and care over the exertion of teacher control. In making his case, Thompson did not argue against the teacher's role in establishing classroom organization, but rather the unilateral imposition of adult power over children.

This notion of an ethic of care is related to a more general conceptualization of the school and classroom environment around the establishment of relationships based on trust (Watson, 2003). Trust carries with it the affective connections of care, regulated by moral reciprocity, and continuity. A trusting environment is not only emotionally warm, but also one in which children are treated fairly by teachers and protected from exploitation and harm by classmates. Thus trust corresponds essentially to what Arsenio and Lover describe as an "orientation of goodwill." Trust is basic to the construction of an overall sense of school or classroom community that in turn is one of the primary predictors of prosocial conduct in schools (Battistich, Solomon, Watson, & Schaps, 1997).

Classroom Rules and Teacher Authority. Part of what is required to maintain and build on an atmosphere of trust are a set of school rules concordant with the legitimate requirements of an instructional environment, and that encode basic moral norms. With regard to morality, children, even at preschool ages, expect schools to have rules governing actions such as hitting and hurting and stealing personal property, and state that it is wrong for schools or teachers to permit such behaviors because of the harm that they cause (Laupa & Turiel, 1986; Weston & Turiel, 1980). Moreover, children consider it morally right to disobey an adult authority (whether teacher or parent) whose instructions would result in harm to another child (Laupa & Turiel, 1993). Thus, with respect to morality, it is less the case that teacher authority and rules establish what is right and wrong as it is that the legitimacy of the classroom rules and teachers' authority to enforce them stem from the degree to which the rules are consistent with children's conceptions of justice and harm.

The one caveat that must be added to this conclusion, however, is that because teachers, and other adults, are presumed to know more than children, they have great potential to alter the ways in which children interpret the moral meaning of social situations. For example, cultural mores regarding the use of physical force to stand up for oneself, and respond to aggression, are associated with the readiness of young males to engage in acts of physical retaliation and playground fighting (Astor, 1994). Tacit approval by teachers and playground supervisors of such behavior sustains the status of playground fighting as morally acceptable instances of self-defense. In a similar fashion, instances of tacit teacher approval of instances of school bullying and malicious teasing would support children's perceptions that the victims of such bullying are deserving of maltreatment because of their personal attributes (Horn, Killen, & Stangor, 1999). A moral responsibility of teachers and administrators with respect to the establishment and enforcement of moral norms is to reflect on the assumptions that might sustain their own sense of the fairness of commonplace instances of school aggression, such as playground retaliatory fighting and peer harassment. As is discussed later in this portion of the chapter, such commonplace forms of moral conflict are also excellent bases for students' peer discussion and social problem solving.

If we move from the moral domain to consideration of school and classroom convention, we see a very different pattern regarding children's acceptance of teacher authority. With respect to conventions, students acknowledge that school authorities may legitimately establish, alter, or eliminate school-based norms of propriety (e.g., dress codes, forms of address), and the rules and procedures for academic activity ((Blumenfeld, Pintrich, & Hamilton, 1987; Dodsworth-Rugani, 1982; Nicholls & Thorkildsen, 1988; Weston & Turiel, 1980). Moreover, children consider teachers the ultimate authorities regarding school conventions and accord them more power than parents when it comes to conventions in the school context (Laupa, 1991; Weber, 1999).

The scope of the school's legitimate authority in establishing conventional norms is limited from the child's point of view by whether they encroach on areas of activity perceived by children as within the personal domain. This was illustrated in a study of children's positive and negative feelings about classroom rules (Arsenio, 1984). Arsenio reported that nearly 62% of all negative rule evaluations provided by fifth-grade boys involved undue teacher control of such nonacademic activities as bathroom and drinking-fountain procedures, and restrictions on free-time activities. This becomes an even more important issue in adolescence (Smetana & Bitz, 1996), and is taken up again in greater detail in the discussion of secondary school contexts.

Observational studies of classroom interactions have consistently reported that the majority of teacher responses to classroom transgressions are to violations of conventions (Blumenfeld, et al., 1987; Nucci & Nucci, 1982; Weber, 1999). Thus, despite the emphasis in the educational literature on the moral meaning of everyday classroom events (Hansen, 2001; Jackson et al., 1993), most everyday classroom discourse centers on classroom conventions. In some respects this is a positive happenstance as it indicates that most student–teacher interactions regarding norm violations are centered on procedural issues, rather than transgressions entailing harm and unfair treatment. A question worth asking, however, is whether the sheer volume of teacher–student interactions around transgressions of convention in the elementary school classroom is indicative that some of the norms being enforced are either inappropriate or being overapplied. For example, in an observational study that we conducted of 10 elementary school classrooms (Nucci & Nucci, 1982), we found that over one half of the classroom violations were accounted for by a single category: cross-talking. This held across ages including the fifth grade, at which point elementary school children are at their most compliant. In our study we discovered that children, including second-graders, differentiated between disruptive talking, which prevents others from hearing the teacher and doing their work, and merely chatting with a neighbor. The cross-talking that seemed to receive the most teacher attention was of the latter non disruptive sort. Such cross-talking generally occurred during "downtime" between activities, or in the act of keeping one another company as children were engaged in their work. There was no evidence that these forms of conversation were impeding the students' academic activity. A simple suggestion offered by DeVries and Zan (1994) with respect to such situations is that teachers reduce conventional regulations to those that are actually instrumental to the operation of the classroom. An alternative, though not contradictory, position is that students be brought into a discussion of classroom conventions in order to arrive at a set of norms mutually agreed to by the students and the teacher. This suggestion is discussed again in the following section on developmental changes. In addition to enlisting the students as allies in the establishment of classroom organization, involvement of students in constructing classroom conventions also contributes to their social cognitive growth.

Teacher Authority and Domain-Concordant Responses to Classroom Transgressions. Whether or not one agrees with the adage that "rules are meant to be broken," students most certainly engage in misbehavior. Teacher discourse in response to transgressions is one source of social information students use to construct their moral and social knowledge. An implication of the research on naturally occurring social interactions (Nucci, 2003) is that the types of feedback teachers provide in response to transgressions should be concordant with the domain of the misbehavior. As was noted in the earlier discussion of general issues, research exploring the uses of the academic curriculum have provided support for the contention that domain-consistent practices are more effective in generating moral and social growth than are teaching practices that subordinate all social normative issues to a single dimension of morality or societal convention (Nucci & Weber, 1991).

One of the more interesting research findings with respect to teacher responses to transgressions is that students also expect teachers to provide social messages that are domain concordant (Killen et al., 1994; Nucci, 1984), and they use those expectations to evaluate the legitimacy of teachers as classroom authorities (Nucci, 1984). As described in Nucci (2001), domain-concordant teacher responses to moral transgressions are those that direct the transgressor to focus on the effects of the action on others, and that request the transgressor to engage in social perspective taking. These response types are formally defined as follows (Nucci, 2001):

1. *Intrinsic features of act statement,* which indicates that the act is inherently hurtful or unjust ("John, that really hurt Mike.").
2. *Perspective-taking request* is a request that the transgressor consider how it feels to be the victim of the act ("Christine, how would you feel if somebody stole from you?").

Domain-concordant responses to transgressions of social convention, in contrast, center on the governing rules and norms, the status of the action as deviant or inconsistent with general social expectations, and the effect the transgression has on classroom order and organization. Formal definitions of domain-concordant responses to conventions are the following (Nucci, 2001):

3. *Rule statement*, which is a specification of the rule governing the action ("Jim, you are not allowed to be out of your seat during math.").
4. *Disorder deviation statement* indicates that the behavior is creating disorder or that it is out of place or odd ("Sally, it's very unladylike to sit with your legs open when you are wearing a skirt.").

Domain-discordant responses would involve the teacher providing responses listed earlier as 3 and 4 to a moral transgression, and responses 1 or 2 to a violation of classroom convention. If the reader does this, it should be apparent that providing moral responses to violations of convention direct the student to consider a set of intrinsic interpersonal effects that simply are not there (e.g., in response to leaving one's seat during math time: "Darrell, how would you like it if other people got out of their seat during math?" or "Darrell, it upsets people when you leave your seat."), whereas the responses that seem most consonant with violations of conventional norms provide a rather weak basis for evaluating the effects of moral transgressions (e.g., in response to hitting: "John, it's against the rules to hit." or "John, that isn't the way a gentleman should act.").

As was stated earlier, when preschool (Killen et al., 1994) and elementary school children (Nucci, 1984) were asked to rate domain-concordant and domain-discordant responses to hypothetical transgressions, it was found that they prefer teachers to use domain-concordant methods of intervention (e.g., telling an instigator who doesn't share toys to give some back "because it's not fair to others who do not have any") rather than domain-inappropriate ones (e.g., telling a child who has hit another child, "You shouldn't do that; it's against the rules to hit." or simply saying, "That's not the way that a student should act.").

In terms of issues of children's evaluations of the legitimacy of teacher authority, it was found that younger children (up to age 10) provided global high ratings for the teachers irrespective of the pattern of responses. By age 10, however, students evaluated not only the teachers' responses but also the teachers as respondents (Nucci, 1984). Students rated highest those teachers who responded to moral transgressions with statements focusing on the effects of the acts (e.g., "Carlos, that really hurts Mike.") Rated lower were teachers who responded with statements of school rules or normative expectations. Rated lowest were teachers who used simple commands (e.g., "Stop it!" or "Don't hit!").

As one would expect, students rated highest those teachers who responded to breaches of convention with rule statements or with evaluations of acts as deviant, and they rated lower those teachers who responded to such transgressions in terms of their effects on others (e.g., "When you sit like that, it really upsets people.").

Studies examining how preschool and elementary teachers spontaneously respond to actual classroom transgressions (Killen & Smetana, 1999; Nucci & Nucci, 1982; Nucci & Turiel, 1978; Nucci, Turiel, & Encarnacion-Gawrych, 1983; Weber, 1999) have reported that teacher responses are not uniform across transgressions, but instead tend to differentially map onto transgressions as a function of domain. These same studies, however, also indicated that about 8% of teacher responses were domain discordant, and another 40% were domain-undifferentiated simple commands (e.g., "Stop it."). Teachers most at risk of engaging in domain-discordant or domain-undifferentiated responses (e.g., "Stop it") are those who most emphasize teacher control and classroom rules. As a consequence, such teachers tend to overapply undifferentiated commands to cease misbehavior that provide little social information to children, along with rule statements and statements focusing on classroom order and organization that are not consistent with the content of moral transgressions.

Responding to Misbehavior in Ways That Engage Student Development. In addition to providing domain-concordant messages to students, teachers can engage students' moral and social growth through their selection of consequences for misbehavior. This is a controversial topic in that an argument can be made that the more effective approach to misconduct is to engage students in social problem solving (Watson, 2003). From a developmental point of view, there is little objection to be raised against the engagement of students in constructively resolving the sources and causes of their social conflicts and misconduct. This is the focus of the last section within our consideration of classroom management within the preschool and elementary school contexts. There are, however, occasions when even the most ardent developmental educator will find it useful to employ consequences for misbehavior. Here, we enter a second point of controversy having to do with the use of traditional behavioral management techniques involving the provision of external rewards and expiative forms of punishment.

The use of rewards for positive behavior is a mainstay of traditional approaches to character education (Wynne & Ryan, 1993). There is little dispute that rewards and positive feedback lead to an increase in rates of desirable behavior. What is in contention, however, is the impact of rewards on students' intrinsic motivation to do the right thing. There is now a considerable body of evidence indicating that an overreliance on rewards and positive feedback can undermine children's moral motivation (Deci, 1995). Although this is a recent position within American psychology (Kohn, 1996), hints of this point of view were already being suggested in the 1950s by B. F. Skinner (1953), who argued that intrinsic reinforcement was more effective than external rewards in stimulating and maintaining human behavior. Where external rewards are most effective is in contexts where there is little intrinsic reason to act. For example, it would be hard to imagine an intrinsic motive that would cause someone to regularly pick up and dispose of other peoples' trash. For this reason, communities pay garbagemen a salary.

With respect to social behavior, there are intrinsic motives to engage in moral actions based on the evaluation of their effects on others (Turiel, 1998). In essence, virtue is its own reward, and an occasional simple acknowledgement or "thanks" is all that is required to support moral motivation. Conventions on the other hand, offer little by way of rational justification other than their connection to social agreement and tradition. In the absence of an underlying understanding of the specific organizational function of such norms, there is less of an intrinsic reason for students to adhere to classroom conventions. As we will see in the following section, this is especially the case during developmental periods of negation of social convention. Thus, it is somewhat more difficult to achieve regular compliance with conventions as is evident in the relative rates of conventional and moral transgressions reported in studies of classroom misbehavior reviewed earlier. For this reason, the domain-concordant feedback that teachers provide in response to transgressions of convention focusing on their specific connection to classroom order and social expectations is a critical element in achieving students' rational bases for compliance. Where the use of extrinsic rewards in the form of teacher praise or contingent privileges would make sense would be in contexts where there is little time for teacher–student dialogue (such as in the midst of a field trip), or in cases where the teacher is attempting to redirect a long-standing pattern of student noncompliance. In either case, the teacher must realize that the primary benefit of extrinsic rewards is behavioral compliance rather than a change in students' conceptions of morality or societal convention.

The use of punishment in response to misbehavior is likewise controversial. Traditional forms of punishment, such as having students serve detention, or write a phrase such as "I will turn in my assignments on time" several hundred times, are examples of what are referred to as expiative forms of punishment. The purpose of an expiative punishment is to cause the transgressor to experience discomfort, and thereby suppress the incidence of misbehavior. Unfortunately, the downside of expiative punishments generally outweighs their utility. For one thing, an expiative punishment has no logical connection to the action and therefore provides little by way of information that would contribute to student social development. More importantly, students tend to associate expiative punishments with the person meting them out, rather than with their own misconduct. One can argue that such punishments invite revenge and provide students with a sense that they have a right to retaliate (Dreikurs & Cassel, 1972). In effect, the morality of the situation becomes turned on its head as the student, guilty of misconduct, now becomes in his or her own mind the aggrieved party. Through the overreliance on the use of expiative punishment, the teacher transforms the affective climate of the classroom into an environment of "ill will" that supports students' self-protective and "selfish" motivations.

A number of writers on the topic of classroom management have argued for the elimination of punishments and their replacement with sanctions based on logical consequences connected in a meaningful way with the nature of the transgression (Albert, 1989; Curwin & Mendler, 1988; DeVries & Zan, 1994; Dreikurs, Grunwald, & Pepper, 1982). Logical consequences include such things as restitution, depriving the transgressor of the thing misused, and exclusion. Because of the nonarbitrary, reciprocal nature of morality, it is somewhat easier to envision logical consequences for moral transgressions than for violations of social conventions. For example, if a child takes something away from another child, a logical consequence would be for the child to have to replace it. However, even conventions, once in place, have a logic associated with their function. A student who talks disruptively during story time might be asked by the teacher to leave the story area until he or she is able to rejoin the group and sit quietly. If this sanction is coupled with a domain-appropriate statement of the rule or social organizational function of the norm, the student is likely to see the connection between the sanction and the misbehavior. An indefinite or extended expulsion from the story area, however, would shift the consequence away from the behavior and become an arbitrary, expiative punishment rather than a logical consequence (DeVries & Zan, 1994).

Although the reduction in reliance on traditional modes of behavioral control through rewards and expiative punishments is upheld by proponents of developmentally based approaches to moral development and socialization (DeVries & Zan, 1994), some have argued (Kohn, 1996) that the employment of logical consequences amounts to little more than a kinder and gentler form of social control. In response, one could argue that such criticisms are unduly harsh as they underestimate the educative value of the use of logical consequences stemming from their correspondence to moral reciprocity. Such criticisms also tend to downplay teachers' need to have access to methods of controlling student conduct in the rapid flow of events in actual classrooms. To the extent that one can link behavioral management with social education, the use of logical consequences would appear to be a reasonable teacher strategy. The alternative is to attempt to reduce misconduct through engagement of students in resolving moral disputes, and entering into rational discourse with them over the need for adherence to social conventions. Such more "democratic" approaches to classrooms are directly affected by students' development. Thus, before turning to a discussion of the use of social problem solving as a classroom management strategy, we will first explore broad developmental trends in elementary school children's moral and social reasoning and their relationship to school conduct.

Developmental Trends in Students' Moral and Conventional Concepts: Why "Lucy" Tends to Appear in the Fifth Grade. The general patterns of social interaction that have occupied the discussion up to this point are all influenced by students' development within each social cognitive domain. With respect to morality, the young child's understanding that unprovoked harm is inherently wrong illustrates that young children are quite capable of engaging in moral judgment. However, the reasoning of young children prior to about the second grade is limited by the difficulty young children have in coordinating the needs of more than one person at a time. Thus, young children appear to vacillate between seeming selflessness when comforting a sad peer and utter selfishness when refusing to share a swing with that same peer. Moral transgressions among young children tend to stem from this inability to coordinate moral perspectives, and teacher interventions with young children often entail helping them sequentially work through how their needs and those of another child are affected by their actions.

As children enter second grade, they are generally able to engage in strict moral reciprocity and have an "Old Testament" view of fairness. Between second and fifth grade children tend to pay strict attention to issues of turn taking and distribution of goods to ensure that everyone receives the same amount (Damon, 1977) according to their contribution to the common good. Children at this age also view direct retaliation as a moral response to victimization. Moral transgressions among children at this age often center around acts of aggression (both verbal and physical) that are viewed as morally justified responses to others. In late childhood children begin to move away from tit-for-tat morality as they start to consider broader notions of fairness as something other than strict reciprocity.

With respect to convention, the developmental picture is at least as complex. Young children up to the age of 7 tend to view school conventions as describing the way the social world is supposed to be. Thus, women are supposed to wear dresses because they are girls, and that's that. Exceptions to these presumed uniformities, such as a man wearing long hair, are treated as singularities rather than as evidence that their overgeneralization of social norms is incorrect. Although young children have the capacity to generate conventions that pertain to their own play (Corsaro, 1985), they take little interest in peer transgressions of school conventions. It is not until the 4th or 5th grade that children respond to peer violations of classroom conventions (Nucci & Nucci, 1982).

As children enter second and third grade, they reevaluate their earlier affirmation of conventions as describing the way the world is, by pointing to exceptions, such as a neighbor adult who lets children refer to him by his first name, as evidence that conventions don't really matter much. In observations made of classroom transgressions we noted that the rate of conventional violations was higher in second grade than at either the first or fifth grades (Nucci & Nucci, 1982). One thing that teachers might want to consider is how such normative negation of convention plays into classroom misbehavior in the second through fourth grades.

By fifth grade students have constructed their first concrete understanding of social hierarchy and social systems. Children at this age now typically affirm conventions as rules established by authorities to reduce chaos (keep kids from running in the halls) and provide social order. It is at this age that observational studies of classroom interactions report students responding to peer violations of classroom and school conventions (Nucci & Nucci, 1982)—hence the emergence of children who, like the character Lucy (from the Peanuts comic strip), are willing to volunteer to serve as classroom and hall monitors. It is also at fifth grade that observational studies of classroom transgressions reported the lowest rates of conventional violations (Nucci & Nucci, 1982).

Engaging Moral and Social Development Through Social Problem Solving and Democratic Forms of School Community. Thus far the discussion has centered around the establishment of classroom rules and forms of teacher response to misbehavior that generally compose the mainstay of research and theory on classroom management. An alternative approach to the entire issue is to move the discussion away from the teacher-centered focus on top-down management to a view of the classroom as a community in which issues of moral and conventional behavior are the concerns of the students as well as the teacher (Watson, 2003). An aspect of this approach that is taken up here is the engagement of students in the resolution of moral disputes, and collaborative construction of classroom and school norms.

The value of engaging children in conflict resolution is that it brings into focus the contradictions that exist between the child's own initial way of looking at things and what is necessary for his or her own needs and those of another person to be met. In Piagetian terms (1985), what takes place through the experience of cognitive contradiction is the gradual replacement of the child's current way of thinking by a more adequate re-equilibrated form that resolves the contradictions arising from the initial way of looking at things. As described in the work of DeVries and Zan (1994) and Watson (2003), conflicts are resolved through teacher-mediated discourse between or among students with encouragement to students to find their own solutions, rather than resorting to teacher-imposed resolutions. Transgressors are encouraged to find ways to make reparations for the harm or injustice they have caused, rather than having the teacher administer an expiative punishment. Allowing children to solve their own problems has the advantage that the solutions generated are "owned" by the children, and the process contributes to the child's autonomy and social efficacy. This approach is consistent with evidence that preschool- and elementary school-aged children prefer to resolve their own moral disputes rather than have an adult-imposed solution (Killen, et al, 1994). The involvement of the teacher mediator, however, also allows for the possibility that the teacher may be able to use his or her greater social knowledge as a scaffold to assist the children's movement toward a resolution when their own interpretations of the dispute may reach an impasse. Finally, Watson (2003) pointed out that the participation of the teacher as mediator rather than heteronomous authority contributes to the classroom climate of trust.

The use of teacher mediation around moral disputes works well in preschool and early elementary grades where such disputes tend to be overt and in full view of the supervising teacher. In later grades (grades 3 to 5), teachers tend to remain involved in the resolution of playground fighting (Nucci & Nucci, 1982). The teacher's role in such conflicts is to move children beyond the simple tit-for-tat morality that sustains the moral justification for fighting. Teachers may also work with aggressive children to alter their tendencies to read malintent in the actions and motives of other children (Dodge, Lochman, Harnish, Bates, & Pettit, 1997). However, beyond such obvious and overt moral transgressions, the tendency is for teachers to become less and less involved in children's moral disputes, and for children to reduce their tendencies to turn to adults for help (Nucci & Nucci, 1982).

A way for schools to build on this developmental trend is to incorporate peer mediation as an overt component of the broader approach to classroom management taken by the school as a community. The advantages of engaging a peer mediator to help with conflicts among elementary school children are several. First and foremost it reduces the tendency for children to see objections to immoral conduct as simply a matter of adult authority. Second, it causes the disputants to see their situation from a third, disinterested vantage point. This third-person perspective moves the issue out of one of direct reciprocity, and offers a window into a new way of looking at moral issues. Finally, the act of peer mediation is of benefit to the mediator who is necessarily engaged in moral discourse and reflection. For example, a study examining the impact of peer mediation on second-through fifth-grade students found that students who had served as peer mediators more often resolved their *own* interpersonal conflicts in ways that took into account the needs of both parties, and were also less likely to ask for adult intervention than children who had not had this mediator experience (Johnson, Johnson, Dudley, Ward, & Magnuson, 1995).

The engagement of peer mediators may be seen as part of a more general effort by schools to enlist students as active members of a community (Freiberg, 1999). The construction of a community, however, involves more than a shared morality. It also includes the establishment of conventions that structure the procedures and norms of specific institutions such as the classroom. Actively engaging students in collectively discussing and altering classroom conventions is something that has been attempted with children even in preschool settings (DeVries, Hildebrandt, & Zan, 2000; DeVries & Zan, 1994). Developmentally, such young children are years away from genuinely understanding the functions of conventional norms (Turiel, 1983). Asking such young children to participate in a meaningful discussion about broader social conventions, such as table manners, would have limited utility. However, there is much to be said for engaging young children in the construction of conventional norms that affect them directly. This is consistent with observational research indicating that young children respond to conventional norms that structure their play (Corsaro, 1985). Engaging children in discussion and decisions around specific classroom procedures provides them concrete experience with the collective and negotiated source of these social norms. Doing so also establishes very early on an experiential framework for discussion of social and moral norms that is at the heart of any meaningful social values curriculum. For example, children may be engaged in forming the conventions that are to guide how the children are to play with the classroom guinea pig (DeVries & Zan, 1994, pp. 128–130).

As was described earlier in the section on development, children move from this early period of affirmation of conventions to a phase in second and third grade in which personal experiences with exceptions to conventions (e.g., a neighbor adult who allows children to address him by his first name) lead children to conclude that conventions don't seem to matter very much. Teachers can achieve compliance with classroom conventions largely through the desire of young children to maintain teacher affection. However, allowing children in this negation phase to have some input into classroom procedures affords them an opportunity to generate a set of explanations for norms that would affect them directly. As children move toward the affirmation phase of reasoning about conventions, typical of fifth grade, they become quite capable of comprehending the basic purposes of conventions for establishing social order, and can be useful allies for schools in sorting out the unnecessary and burdensome conventions that may have arisen over time. Most U. S. elementary schools have school councils, but it is not always the case that children serving on such councils actually are given any role in helping structure the norms of their schools and classrooms. Watson (2003) and her colleagues, as well as De Vries and her colleagues (DeVries, et al. 2000), have provided more than ample evidence that both children and the school community benefit from such active student participation in the school as a social institution.

Classroom Management in Middle School and High School

Early Adolescence and Normative Resistance to School Rules: Knowing When to Say Yes. The broad principles of classroom management pertaining to moral and social rules, domain-concordant responses to transgression, and the uses of logical consequences that were brought up in the discussion about preschool and elementary school contexts also hold for the middle school and high school. Thus, they will not be repeated here. The core issues for classroom management with adolescent students have to do with the ways in which social development during this transitional period presents normative challenges to adult and institutional authority.

The middle school and freshman years of high school pose a particular set of challenges and opportunities that are addressed first. Among the developmental changes that typify these years are two broad shifts in reasoning about social convention and the personal domain. With respect to social convention, young adolescents enter a phase in which they question the basis upon which they upheld conventions during middle childhood (Nucci et al., 2004; Turiel, 1983). The support for conventions as reflecting the norms of authority established in support of the goal of maintaining basic order (e.g., to keep kids from running in the hallways) evaporates as young people reconsider the arbitrariness of conventional regulations, and conclude that they are "simply the arbitrary dictates of authority" (Turiel, 1983). In many cases, students at this level of development will continue to adhere to conventions in order to maintain smooth relations with teachers, or to avoid sanctions. However, students at this level are unable to produce a conceptual rationale for the conventions themselves (Nucci et al, 2004). Thus, there is greater tendency for students at this point in development to engage in the violation of school conventions (Geiger & Turiel, 1983; Nucci & Nucci, 1982). By middle adolescence, about age 15 or the sophomore year of high school, most American adolescents have moved to the next level of reasoning about social convention (Nucci et al., 2004). At this level conventions are viewed as constituent elements of the social system structuring hierarchical relations, and coordinating interactions among members of a society or societal institution such as the school (Turiel, 1883).

Coincident with these developmental shifts in concepts of convention are basic changes in the ways in which adolescents draw the boundaries between convention and what they consider matters of personal prerogative and privacy (Smetana, 2002). Areas where the conventions and norms of the family and school touch on personal expression (dress, hairstyle), personal associations (friendships), personal communication (phone, e-mail), access to information (Internet), and personal safety (substance use, sexuality) become zones of dispute wherein adolescents lay increasing claims to autonomy and control. Family disputes across cultures are largely around such issues as adolescents begin to appropriate greater areas of personal jurisdiction from what had been areas of parental influence or control (Smetana, 2002). Within school settings, students also lay claim to zones of personal privacy and prerogative (Smetana & Bitz, 1996). They are also somewhat more willing, however, to accept conventions regulating conduct within the school setting such as public displays of affection (kissing in public) that would be considered personal in nonschool contexts (Smetana & Bitz, 1996). Nevertheless, the combined developmental phase of negation of convention with the extension of what is considered personal renders the period of early adolescence a difficult transition as students struggle with the norms of schools as institutions.

A positive approach to this age group is for the teachers to make a distinction between the norms needed to operate the school and to protect student safety and those behaviors that constitute a "minor threat" to the social order. To put it another way, it is important for teachers to realize that there are times when it makes more sense to say "yes" in response to student noncompliance than it is to simply say "no" in an effort to maintain consistency for its own sake. For example, marking a student tardy for being next to his seat rather than sitting in it as the bell rings may make the adult feel powerful, but it does little to enhance the student's appreciation of the norm of promptness. Without reducing things to a cliché, this really is a phase that will pass, and some adult patience is called for. Most students who were "good kids" in fifth grade still view teachers as people worthy of fair treatment. For example, a student will call teachers by titles in order not to needlessly offend the teacher, even though the student is clueless as to why using the teacher's first name is offensive. Firm and fair enforcement of rules with a dash of humor will work better than rigid requirements for compliance.

The evidence suggests, however, that this "kinder, gentler" approach is not shared by most middle schools. Eccles and her colleagues offer a window into the mismatch that currently exists between schools and young adolescents around these normative issues. These researchers (Eccles et al., 1993; Eccles, Wigfield, & Schiefele, 1998) have provided evidence that despite the increased maturity of adolescents, middle schools and junior high schools emphasize greater teacher control and discipline and offer fewer opportunities for student involvement in decision making, choice, and self-management than do elementary school classrooms. Accordingly, Eccles and her colleagues (1998) have reported that the mismatch between adolescents' efforts to attain greater autonomy and the schools' increased efforts at control resulted in declines in junior high students' intrinsic motivation and interest in school.

From a developmental perspective, the responses of schools to this period of transition amount to a defensive maneuver to maintain order through institutional power while waiting out a passing developmental storm. An alternative approach recommended by Eccles (Eccles et al., 1993, 1998) is that schools include more opportunities for students to have input into the norms governing classroom practices. More specifically, Smetana's (Smetana & Bitz, 1996) research, and the observational studies of student transgressions (Geiger & Turiel, 1983; Nucci & Nucci, 1982), indicate that the focus of such student input and discourse should be around matters of social convention and personal prerogative. Other work exploring the impact of developmental discourse around issues of convention has demonstrated that such discussion can effectively contribute to students' levels of understanding about the social functions of such norms (Nucci & Weber, 1991). Thus, schools and classroom teachers would be able to come out of their foxholes to engage students in discourse that would contribute to their social development as well as the smooth functioning of schools as educational institutions.

Moral Issues in Adolescence. As children move from childhood into adolescence the forms of moral conflict shift from overt acts of physical aggression and challenges over playground equipment to subtler and less obvious acts of social exclusion (Killen, Lee-Kim, McGlothlin, & Stangor, 2002). Making matters even more complex is that these moral conflicts of adolescence are not straightforward matters confined to the moral domain. Issues of peer exclusion and harassment call on students' conceptions of peer conventions of dress and behavior, personal domain construals of the selection of personal associations and friendships, and moral concepts of harm and fairness (Horn, 2003; Killen, et al., 2002).

The uses of moral discourse around such issues in the absence of attention to the ways in which students are focusing on the nonmoral aspects of a given situation of peer exclusion will be ineffective. For example, peer systems of social status and hierarchy use conventions of dress and behavior as markers of group membership (Horn, 2003). Middle adolescents, having just constructed an understanding of conventions as constituent elements of social systems, tend also to be more likely than younger or older adolescents to justify exclusion of peers whose clothing or behavior does not conform to peer conventions (Horn, 2003). Focusing only on the fairness or harm involved will not address the motivations and justifications for exclusion maintained by a young person whose focus is on the importance of peer conventions in defining group membership and identity status. An effective discourse around such a multifaceted social issue would start with an examination of the presumptive importance of the conventions as modes for defining group membership, social status, and personal identity (Horn, in press). Only after students have had an opportunity to fully explore the meaning and ramifications of their use of conventions to define group membership would a discussion of the moral implications of such peer exclusion be fruitful.

Coupled with this shift in kind of moral conflict is a developmental tendency for young people to attempt to resolve such issues on their own. In keeping with this general trend is a parallel tendency for teachers to withdraw from involvement in students' moral interactions (Nucci & Nucci, 1982). Thus, the previous advice for teacher-mediated discourse around issues of exclusion is most effective if accompanied by school programs involving peer mediation. This brings us back full circle to the uses of community as a basic method of enhancing school and classroom management.

The Just Community as a Response to "Negative Morality. Although the majority of adolescent misconduct is around issues of convention, some of the efforts to establish autonomy and identity entail engagement in risk taking and relatively serious moral transgressions such as shoplifting (Lightfoot, 1997). The Swiss developmentalist Oser (in press; Oser & Veugelers, 2003) has argued that educators should view such moral misconduct as an essential component for moral growth, and seize upon moral transgressions as an opportunity for what he referred to as "realistic discourse." Oser's (in press) position is that "negative morality," like mistakes in math class, composes the basis from which a genuine moral epistemology and moral orientation arise. His approach to moral misconduct in adolescence is to make it the subject of moral discourse in which students must confront one another's actual misdeeds and interpretations of their motives and the consequences of their actions (Oser & Veugelers, 2003). Oser's approach builds from prior work done in the Kohlberg tradition on what is referred to as the "just community" (Power et al., 1989). Teachers leading these discussion sessions encourage participants to engage in what are referred to as transactive forms of discourse found in prior research to lead to moral development (Berkowitz & Gibbs, 1983; Oser, 1991). Teachers support forms of discourse that entail efforts by each speaker to extend the logic of the prior speaker's argument, refute the assumptions of the argument, or provide a point of commonality between competing positions. The processes advocated by Oser have been used with considerable success by others working within the Kohlberg tradition (Blakeney & Blakeney, 1991) to alter the misconduct and recidivism among behaviorally disordered children and adolescents.

CONCLUSIONS

Schools are social institutions, and as such are inherently involved in the moral and social development of students (Jackson et al., 1993). The work reviewed in this chapter provides some analytic tools for classroom teachers to begin to conceive of the relationships among classroom norms and procedures, and students' construction of their morality and understandings of social norms and social systems. At a basic level, a climate of mutual respect and warmth, with fair and consistent application of rules, forms the elemental conditions for an educationally constructive moral atmosphere. Beyond this general base, what we have seen is that effective practice is enhanced by the coordination of teacher responses with the moral or conventional nature of school norms or student behaviors. Domain-appropriate teacher input with regard to moral concerns focuses on the effects that actions have on the rights and welfare of persons. Teacher contributions regarding social conventions focus on social organization, social expectations, and rules.

What we have also seen is that there are normative periods of resistance to the conventions of society that reflect the efforts of children to figure out the functions of the consensually generated norms and procedures that constitute the conventions governing schools and classrooms as particular social systems. These periods of resistance are generally associated with increases in the level of noncompliance with classroom and school conventions. In early adolescence, this negation of convention is coupled with a normative developmental tendency for students to broaden the scope of what they consider their own areas of prerogative and privacy, bringing about a period of seeming resistance to school and classroom authority. Understanding this developmental period as a "minor threat" to adult power, and the functioning of schools as institutions, is one of the more positive lessons to be learned from research on social development.

Finally, the more general thrust of developmental research reviewed in this chapter leans toward support for approaches to classroom management and instruction that actively engage students in solving their own social and moral disputes, and that draw students into the construction of school and classroom norms as active participants in their own self-governance (McCaslin & Good, 1992, 1998). Thus, the emphasis is on engaging students' intrinsic moral motivations (Turiel, 1998), and enlistment of their active compliance to social conventions on the grounds that they are reasonable expectations of members of a social group (Nucci, 2001). The argument for doing so is to transform classroom management from a system designed solely to sustain adult authority and control over students into an integral educational component for students' social and moral growth.

ACKNOWLEDGMENT

The author wishes to thank Judi Smetana, University of California, Santa Cruz, for her comments on an earlier draft of this chapter.

REFERENCES

Albert, L. (1989). *A teacher's guide to Cooperative Discipline: How to manage your classroom and promote self-esteem*. Circle Pines, MN: American Guidance Service.

Amsel, E., & Renninger, K. A. (Eds.). (1997). *Change and development: Issues of theory, method, and application*. Mahwah, NJ: Lawrence Erlbaum Associates.

Arsenio, W. (1988). Children's conceptions of the situational affective consequences of sociomoral events. *Child Development, 59*, 1611–1622.

Arsenio, W., & Lover, A. (1995). Children's conceptions of socio-moral affect: Happy victimizers, mixed emotions, and other expectancies. In M. Killen & D. Hart (Eds.), *Morality in everyday life* (pp. 87–130). New York: Cambridge University Press.

Astor, R. A. (1994). Children's moral reasoning about family and peer violence: The role of provocation and retribution. *Child Development, 65*, 1054–1067.

Bandura, A. (1991) Social cognitive theory of moral thought and action. In W. M. Kurtines & J. L. Gewirtz (Eds.), *Handbook of moral behavior and development: Vol. 1. Theory* (pp. 45–104). Hillsdale, NJ: Lawrence Erlbaum Associates.

Battistich, V., Solomon, D., Watson, M., & Schaps, E. (1997). Caring school communities. *Educational Psychologist, 32*, 137–151.

Berkowitz, M., & Gibbs, J. (1983). Measuring the developmental features of moral discourse. *Merrill-Palmer Quarterly, 24*, 399–410.

Blakeney, C., & Blakeney, R. (1991). Understanding and reforming moral misbehavior among behaviorally disorder children. *Journal of Behavioral Disorders, 16*, 135–143.

Blumenfeld, P. C., Pintrich, P. R., & Hamilton, V. L. (1987). Teacher talk and students' reasoning about morals, conventions, and achievement. *Child Development, 58*, 1389–1401.

Brown, A. L. (1987). Metacognition, executive control, self-regulation, and other more mysterious mechanisms. In F. Weinert & R. Klewe (Eds.), *Metacognition, motivation and understanding*. Hillsdale, NJ: Lawrence Erlbaum Associates.

Brown A. L., & Reeve, R. A., (1987). "Bandwidths of competence: The role of supportive contexts in learning and development. In L. Liben (Ed,), *Learning and Development: Conflict or congruence*? (173–216). Hillsdale, NJ: Erlbaum.

Bryk, A. S., & Schneider, B. (2002). *Trust in schools*. New York: Russell Sage Foundation.

Canter, L., & Canter, M. (1992). *Lee Canter's assertive discipline: Positive behavior management for today's classroom*. Santa Monica, CA: Canter & Associates.

Corsaro, W. (1985). *Peer culture in the early years*. Norwood, NJ: Ablex.

Cumberland-Li, A., Eisenberg, N., Champion, C., Gershoff, E., & Fabes, R. A. (2003). The relation of parental emotionality and related dispositional traits to parental expression of emotion and children's social functioning. *Motivation and Emotion, 27*, 27–56.

Curwin, R. L., & Mendler, A. N. (1988). *Discipline with dignity*. Alexandria, VA: Association for Supervision and Curriculum Development.

Damon, W. (1977). *The social world of the child*. San Francisco: Jossey-Bass.

Deci, E. (1995). *Why we do what we do: The dynamics of personal autonomy*. New York: Putnam.

Delpit, L. (1995). *Other peoples' children: Cultural conflict in the classroom*. New York: New Press.

DeVries, R. Hildebrandt, C., & Zan, B. (2000). Constructivist early education for moral development. *Early Education and Development, 11*, 9–35.

DeVries, R., & Zan, B. (1994). *Moral classrooms, moral children: Creating a constructivist atmosphere for early education*. New York: Teachers College Press.

Dodge, K. A., Lochman, J. E., Harnish, J. D., Bates, J. E., & Pettit, G. S. (1997). Reactive and proactive aggression in school children and psychiatrically impaired chronically assaultive youth. *Journal of Abnormal Psychology, 106*, 37–51.

Dodsworth-Rugani, K. (1982). *The development of concepts of social structure and their relationship to school rules and authority*. Unpublished doctoral dissertation, University of California, Berkeley.

Dreikurs, R., & Cassel, P. (1972). *Discipline without tears*. New York: Hawthorne Books.

Dreikurs, R., Grunwald, B. B., & Pepper, F. C. (1982). *Maintaining sanity in the classroom: Classroom management techniques* (2nd ed.). New York: Harper & Row.

Eccles, J. S., Midgley, C., Wigfield, A., Buchanan, C. M., Reuman, D., Flanagan, C., & Mac Iver, D. (1993). Development during adolescence: The impact of stage-environment fit on adolescents' experiences in schools and families. *American Psychologist, 48*, 90–101.

Eccles, J. S., Wigfield, A., & Schiefele, U. (1998). Motivation to succeed. In W. Damon (Ed.), *Handbook of child psychology, Vol. 3: N. Eisenberg (Ed.), Social, Emotional, and Personality Development* (5th ed., pp. 1017–1095). New York: John Wiley.

Eisenberg, N. (1986). *Altruistic emotion, cognition and behavior*. Hillsdale, NJ: Lawrence Erlbaum Associates.

Emde, R., Birigen, Z., Clyman, R., & Openheim, D. (1991). The moral self of infancy: Affective core and procedural knowledge. *Developmental Review, 11*, 251–270.

Freiberg, H. J. (1999). Consistency management and cooperative discipline: From tourists to citizens in the classroom. In H. J. Freiberg (Ed.), *Beyond Behaviorism: Changing the classroom management paradigm* (pp. 75–97). Boston: Allyn & Bacon.

Geiger, K., & Turiel, E. (1983). Disruptive school behavior and concepts of social convention in early adolsecence. *Journal of Educational Psychology, 75*, 677–685.

Hansen, D. T. (1995). Teaching and the moral life of classrooms. *Journal for a Just and Caring Education, 2*, 59–74.

Hasen, D. T. (2001). Teaching as a moral activity. In V. Richardson (Ed.), *Handbook of research on teaching* (4th ed.). Washington, DC: American Educational Research Association, 2001.

Helwig, C., & Turiel, E. (2002). Civil liberties, autonomy, and democracy: Children's perspectives. *International Journal of Law and Psychiatry, 25*, 253–270.

Horn, S. S. (2003). Adolescents' reasoning about exclusion from social groups. *Developmental Psychology, 39*, 71–84.

Horn, S. S. (in press). Adolescents' peer interactions: Conflict and coordination between personal expression, social norms, and moral reasoning. In L. Nucci (Ed.), *Conflict, contradiction and contrarian elements in moral development and education*. Mahwah, NJ: Lawrence Erlbaum Associates.

Horn, S. S., Killen, M., & Stangor, C. (1999). The influence of group stereotypes of adolescents' moral reasoning. *Journal of Early Adolescence, 19*, 98–113.

Jackson, P. W., Boostrom, R., & Hansen, D. T. (1993). *The moral life of schools*. San Francisco: Jossey-Bass.

Johnson, D. W., Johnson, R., Dudley, B., Ward, M., & Magnuson, D. (1995). The impact of peer mediation training on the management of school and home conflicts. *American Educational Research Journal, 32*, 829–844.

Karniol, R. (2003). Egocentricism versus protocentrism: The status of self in social prediction. *Psychological Review, 110*(3), 564–580.

Killen, M., Breton, S., Ferguson, H., & Handler, K. (1994). Preschoolers' evaluations of teacher methods of intervention in social transgressions. *Merrill-Palmer Quarterly, 40*, 399–415.

Killen, M., Lee-Kim, J., McGlothlin, H., & Stangor, C. (2002). How children and adolescents evaluate gender and racial exclusion. *Monograph of the Society for Research in Child Development, 67*(4, Serial No. 271).

Killen, M., & Smetana, J. G. (1999). Social interactions in preschool classrooms and the development of young children's conceptions of the personal. *Child Development, 70*, 486–501.

Kochanska, K. (1993). Toward a synthesis of parental socialization and child temperment in early development of conscience. *Child Development, 64*, 325–347.

Kohlberg, L. (1984). *Essays on moral development: Vol 2. The psychology of moral development.* San Francisco: Harper & Row.

Kohn, A. (1996). *Beyond discipline: From compliance to community.* Alexandria, VA: ASCD.

Laupa, M. (1991). Childrens reasoning about 3 authority attributes—adult status, knowledge, and social position. *Development Psychology, 27*, 321–329.

Laupa, M., & Turiel, E. (1986). Children's conceptions of adult and peer authority. *Child Development, 57*, 405–412.

Laupa, M., & Turiel, T. (1993). Children's conceptions of authority and social context. *Journal of Educational Psychology, 85*, 191–197.

Liben, L. (Ed.). (1987). *Development and leraning: Conflict or congruence.* Hillsdale, NJ: Lawrence Erlbaum Associates.

Lightfoot, C. (1997). *The culture of adolescent risk-taking.* New York: Guilford.

McCaslin, M., & Good, T. (1992). Compliant cognition: The misalliance of management and instructional goals in current school reform. *Educational Researcher, 21*, 4–17.

McCaslin, M., & Good, T. (1998). Moving beyond management as sheer compliance: Helping students to develop goal coordination strategies. *Educational Horizons, 76*, 169–176.

Narvaez, D. (in press). Integrative ethical education. In M. Killen & J. Smetana (Eds.), *Handbook of moral development.* Mahwah, NJ: Lawrence Erlbaum Associates.

Nicholls, J. G., & Thorkildsen, T. A. (1988). Children's distinctions among matters if intellectual convention, logic, fact, and personal preference. *Child Development, 59*, 939–949.

Noddings, N. (2002). *Educating moral people: A caring alternative to character.* New York: Teachers College Press.

Nucci, L. (1984). Evaluating teachers as social agents: Students' ratings of domain appropriate and domain-inappropriate teacher responses to transgressions. *American Educational Research Journal, 21*, 367–378.

Nucci, L. (1996). Morality and the personal sphere of actions. In E. Reed, E. Turiel, & T. Brown (Eds.), *Values and knowledge* (pp. 41–60). Mahwah, NJ: Lawrence Erlbaum Associates.

Nucci, L. (2001). *Education in the moral domain.* Cambridge, England: Cambridge University Press.

Nucci, L. (2003). Social interaction and the construction of moral and social knowledge. In J. I. M. Carpendale & U. Muller (Eds.), *Social interaction and knowledge.* Mahwah, NJ: Lawrence Erlbaum Associates.

Nucci, L., Becker, K., & Horn, S. (2004, June). *Assessing the development of adolescent concepts of social convention.* Paper presented at the annual meeting of the Jean Piaget Society, Toronto, Ontario, Canada.

Nucci, L., & Nucci M. S. (1982). Children's social interactions in the context of moral and conventional transgressions. *Child Development, 53*, 403–412.

Nucci, L. P., & Turiel, E. (1978). Social interactions and the development of social concepts in preschool children. *Child Development, 49*, 400–407.

Nucci, L., Turiel, E., & Encarnacion-Gawrych, G. (1983). Children's social interactions and social concepts in the Virgin Islands. *Journal of Cross-Cultural Psychology, 14*, 469–487.

Nucci, L., & Weber, E. (1991). Research on classroom applications of the domain approach to values education. In W. Kurtines & J. Gewirtz (Eds.), *Handbook of moral behavior and development: Vol. 3. Applications* (pp. 251–266). Hillsdale, NJ: Lawrence Erlbaum Associates.

Oser, F. (in press). Negative morality and the goals of education. In L. Nucci (Ed.), *Conflict, contradiction and contrarian elements in moral development and education.* Mahwah, NJ: Lawrence Erlbaum Associates.

Oser, F. K. (1991). Professional morality: A discourse approach. In W. Kurtines & J. Gewirtz (Eds.), *Handbook of moral development: Vol. 2. Research* (pp. 191–228). Hillsdale, NJ: Lawrence Erlbaum Associates.

Oser, F. K., & Veugelers, W. (2003). *Teaching in moral and democratic education.* Bern, Switzerland: Peter Lang Verlag.

Park, R. D., & Buriel, R. (1998). Socialization in the family: Ethnic and ecological perspectives. In W. Damon (Series Ed.) & N. Eisenberg (Vol. Ed.), *Handbook of child psychology: Vol. 3. Social, emotional, and personality development* (4th ed.). New York: John Wiley.

Piaget, J. (1932). *The moral judgment of the child.* New York: Free Press.

Piaget, J. (1985). *The equilibration of cognitive structures.* Chicago: University of Chicago Press.

Polson, D. (2001). Helping children learn to make responsible choices. In B. Rogoff, C. G. Turkanis, & L. Bartlett (Eds.), *Learning together: Children and adults in a school community* (123–129). New York: Oxford University Press.

Power, C., Higgins, A., & Kohlberg, L. (1989). *Lawrence Kohlberg's approach to moral education.* New York: Columbia University Press.

Rogoff, B. (1990). *Apprenticeship in thinking: Cognitive development in social context.* New York: Oxford University Press.

Shweder, R., Mahapatra, M., & Miller, J. (1987). Culture and moral development. In J. Kagan & S. Lamb (Eds.)., *The emergence of morality in young children.* Chicago: University of Chicago Press.

Skinner, B. F. (1953). *Science and human behavior.* New York: Macmillan.

Smetana, J. G. (2002). Culture, autonomy, and personal jurisdiction in adolescent-parent relationships. In H. W. Reese & R. Kail (Eds.), *Advances in child development and behavior* (Vol. 29, pp. 51–87). New York: Academic Press.

Smetana, J. G. (in press). Adolescent-parent conflict: Resistance and subversion as developmental process. In L. Nucci (Ed.), *Conflict, contradiction and contrarian elements in moral development and education.* Mahwah, NJ: Lawrence Erlbaum Associates.

Smetana, J., & Bitz, B. (1996). Adolescents' conceptions of teachers' authority and their relations to rule violations in school. *Child Development, 67*, 1153–1172.

Steinberg, L. (2001). We know some things. Parent-child relationships in retrospect and prospect. *Journal of Research on Adolescence, 11,* 1–19.

Sternberg, R. (1998). Abilities are forms of developing expertise, *Educational Researcher, 3,* 22–35.

Thompson, G. (2004). *Through ebony eyes: What teachers need to know but are afraid to ask about African American students.* San Francisco: Jossey-Bass.

Thorkildsen, T. A. (1991). Defining social goods and distributing them fairly: The development of conceptions of fair testing practices. *Child Development, 62*, 852–862.

Thorkildsen, T. A. (2000). Children's coordination of procedural and commutative justice in school. In W. van Haaften, T. Wren, & A. Tellings (Eds.), *Moral sensibilities and education II: The school age child* (pp. 61–88). Bemmel, Netherlands: Concorde Publishing House.

Turiel, E. (1983). *The development of social knowledge: Morality and convention.* Cambridge, England: Cambridge University Press.

Turiel, E. (1998). The development of morality. In W. Damon (Ed.), *Handbook of child psychology: Vol. 3. N. Eisenberg (Ed.), Social, emotional, and personality development* (5th ed., pp. 863–932). New York: Academic Press.

Turiel, E. (2002). *The culture of morality: Social development, context, and conflict.* Cambridge, England: Cambridge University Press.

Watson, M. (2003). *Learning to trust: transforming difficult elementary classrooms through developmental discipline.* San Francisco: Jossey-Bass.

Weber, E. K. (1999). Children's personal prerogative in home and school contexts. *Early Education and Development, 10*, 499–515.

Weston, D., & Turiel, E. (1980). Act-rule relations: Children's concepts of social rules. *Developmental Psychology, 16*, 417–424.

Wynne, E., & Ryan, K. (1993). *Reclaiming our schools: A handbook on teaching character, academics, and discipline.* New York: Macmillan.

Zimmerman, B. J., Bonner, S., & Kovach, R. (2002). *Developing self-regulated learners.* Washington, DC: American Psychological Association.

VII

Programs for Classroom Management and Discipline

Edmund T. Emmer
The University of Texas, Austin

28

Research-Based Programs for Preventing and Solving Discipline Problems

H. Jerome Freiberg and Judith M. Lapointe
University of Houston

INTRODUCTION

There continues to be growing concerns over antisocial behaviors in schools and communities (e.g., aggression, delinquency, and violence) and over the lack of prosocial positive character development traits (e.g., caring, responsibility, and civic virtue) among our children and youth (Rose & Gallup, 2004). In 1998, some 2.6 million school-age youth were arrested in the United States (Snyder, 2004). A 2005 Federal report of U.S. youth shows an overall improvement in their health. It also indicates that parents report 5 percent or 2.7 million children have emotional or behavioral problems (Federal Interagency Forum on Child and Family Statistics, 2005). Within the schooling context, student behaviors that disrupt the learning environment often have a contagious effect (Kounin, 1970), influencing the disruptive individual, classmates, the school, and subsequently near and far communities. Classroom disruptions steal valuable teaching and learning time (Opuni, 2002). School climate and student achievement are casualties of these disruptions, resulting from time off task, conflicts, and ineffective instructional management. A multiple-year study by Gottfredson, Gottfredson, and Hybl (1993) shows that students who are disruptive in school are at higher risk of dropping out of school, substance abuse, and other delinquent behaviors. A pattern of disruptions also engulfs school administration in noninstructional activities with thousands of hours spent responding to disciplinary referrals to the office.

This chapter begins the process of identifying research-based programs that have the potential and promise of preventing and solving discipline problems from several different philosophical and programmatic vantage points. Hundreds of programs have been implemented in schools to prevent and solve behavior problems. However, the vast majority of these programs lack internal or third-party research to validate their effectiveness (Office of the Surgeon General, 2001). Fewer still have longitudinal studies to support their sustainability. Researchers who have attempted to conduct meta-analyses of operational classroom management programs concluded there were too few high-quality research studies to form a sample to conduct a meta-analysis (J. Kim, personal communication, April 17, 2002).

The nature of schools and classrooms is complex (Weinstein, 1996), and the response to this complexity requires an array of classroom and school management options that have their foundation in research. A total of 40 programs from a review process of nearly 800 are presented in this chapter. The review identified specific skills-based, individually-focused programs as well as those that have a whole-school focus. The programs' curriculum varies from conflict resolution to instructional management and discipline, from classroom and school climate to violence prevention and intervention, and from bullying to social–emotional development. Program philosophies traverse the psychological landscape—from humanism and cognitive psychology to programs that emphasize behaviorism. The program selection processes transited through several layers of review and are presented in both narrative and tabular formats.

Behavior Problems in Schools and Society

The Centers for Disease Control and Prevention has identified violence in schools as a serious health issue affecting thousands of youth in the United States. Studies indicate that students who feel connected to school report higher levels of emotional well-being (Resnick et al., 1997). McNeely, Nonnemaker, and Blum (2002), building from the longitudinal work of Resnick and others, found that "A classroom management program that increased school connectedness and promotes self-discipline found that after one year, 30%–100% fewer students were sent to the principal's office for acting out in class, fighting, or assault" (p. 138). Resnick et al. identified school connectedness as the only school-related variable that was protective for every health risk outcome (e.g., violence, drugs, pregnancy, truancy) among adolescents. McNeely, Nonnemaker, and Blum (2002) reported, "When adolescents feel cared for by people at their school and feel like a part of their school, they are less likely to use substances, engage in violence, or initiate sexual activity at an early age" (p. 138).

The American landscape has and is changing. As Americans continue to become less anchored to one place, the pillars of support that have in the past sustained and nurtured youth (family, community, culture, religion, and schools) are also in flux. It is school, the fifth pillar, that must carry an ever-increasing academic and social–emotional load (Freiberg, 1999). As school systems become more bureaucratic and relationships between schools, parents, and communities become more formalized, both students and parents have become increasingly disconnected from the sources of teaching and learning. Moreover, McCaslin and Good (1992) determined that educational reform efforts are stifled by "classroom management policies that encourage, if not demand simple obedience" (p. 4). Effective programs and strategies to support and promote student behaviors increasingly reflect minimal necessary conditions for social and academic development (Erickson, Mattaini, & McGuire, 2004).

According to the U.S. Surgeon General's Report (2001), trends in overall youth violence showed sharp increases from 1983 to 1994 and then a 24% decline from the 1994 peak. However, youth violence remains 70% above the 1983 base period, and schools have seen a 50% increase in violent acts (e.g., aggravated assaults) from high school seniors with little change since its peak year of 1993. Additionally, high-profile acts of violence have been seen at much younger ages, including 6, 7, and 8 years old (Snyder & Sickmund, 1999). However, schools continue to be safer places than either home or community (Kaufman et al., 1998) even though the overall threshold of youth violence remains very high. The level of simulated murders and other severe acts of violence in the media has also taken its toll. It was concluded that the average elementary-age child has seen 8,000 murders on television (Straton, 1995), and the growing dominance of video games causes a child or adolescent to be a direct participant in the violence. Behaviors learned outside the school and classroom have significant effects inside the classroom.

Public opinion polls conducted by Gallup and reported by Phi Delta Kappan over the past 3 decades show that since 1971, classroom discipline combined with youth violence and gangs is in the top three leading school concerns as viewed by the American public (Rose & Gallup, 2004). Although public concerns about school discipline and violence have remained high, comprehensive studies of discipline and classroom management programs have diminished (Doyle, 1990). Forty-two programs studied by Emmer and Aussiker (1990) were found to lack documented links between program mediation and outcome measures. In reviewing four widely used programs, they established most lacked the comprehensive elements of prevention and relied more on disciplining students.

Disruptive student behavior does more than limit teaching and learning; it also inhibits instructional approaches that foster interactive teaching methods (Cohen, 1994; Brophy, 1999; Freiberg & Driscoll, 2005). Teachers are reluctant to incorporate active learning methods when student behavior becomes an interceding factor. When students are self-disciplined, they are able to work in less controlled instructional settings, enabling teachers to use cooperative learning, centers, and research projects (Slavin, 1983; Sharan, 1993; Cohen, 1994; Freiberg & Driscoll, 2005). Kounin (1970) demonstrated the relationship between a teacher's management and instructional actions and student behaviors. It is difficult for teachers to both control student behavior and provide for complex instruction (Cohen, 1994); if there is a choice between the two, complex instruction often suffers.

Wang, Haertel, and Walberg's (1993) meta-analysis of learning factors identified classroom management as being first in a list of five variables that influence school learning. Weade and Evertson (1988) and Evertson and Weade (1989) found connections between classroom management and student achievement using microanalyses of class lessons in language arts, reading, and mathematics. Opuni (2003) found similar results in comparison studies in reading and mathematics on standardized tests with inner-city schools in the northeastern United States. He used the Stanford 9 standardized tests results with 228 intervention and 228 comparison students in third-grade mathematics and fourth-grade reading with effect sizes of +.53 and +.40, respectively.

Classroom management skills affect the quantity and quality of the teaching core. Contrary to popular belief, there is not a shortage of certified teachers in America but rather a shortage of those certified to teach willing to either enter or remain in the classroom. The primary reasons new teachers never enter or quickly leave the profession are based on their inability to manage the classroom environment (Brophy, 1999; Ingersoll, 2001; Patterson, Roehrig, & Luff, 2003). The need for order and programs that facilitate constructive learning environments become even more essential in the next decade as a new generation enters the teaching profession.

Defining Classroom Management

Classroom management is defined as *the ability of teachers and students to agree upon and carry forward a common framework for social and academic interactions, by creating an ethos of effort within a social fabric that is built over time, and ultimately leads to student self-discipline* (Doyle, 1986; Rogers & Freiberg, 1994; Freiberg, 1999; Emmer & Stough, 2001).

The inability to establish an orderly learning environment contributes to misbehavior (Gottfredson et al., 1993; Emmer, Evertson, & Worsham, 2003) and reduces opportunities for student learning (Wang et al., 1993; Opuni, 2003). Constructive learning environments enable a level of academic work that is necessary for learning to be accomplished. From the organization of the classroom to the tone or climate, classroom management is the responsibility of the teacher to create or facilitate the necessary conditions for teaching and learning. If classroom management is the primary responsibility of the educator, discipline requires the child or youth, with assistance from adults, to take responsibility for his or her actions (Lapointe, 2003; Lapointe & Legault, 2004).

Defining Discipline

In this chapter, *discipline is considered the ability of an individual pupil to work in a learning environment without impinging on the rights, freedoms, and responsibilities of other peers and adults.* Often classroom management and discipline are used as one in the same. Many researchers and educators see the terms as different sides of the same coin (Kohn, 1996). However, the term *discipline* has several mutually exclusive meanings. In the context of the classroom, it may be viewed as "an action against" as in disciplining or punishing someone. In the context of curriculum, it is commonly used as a reference point for academic content as in the discipline of history, science, or literature. In the context of behavior, discipline refers to control and with self-discipline to self-control. If the child is not "disciplined," meaning the child has no self-control, often greater external controls are proposed. However, sometimes student behavior is simply a healthy response to unhealthy conditions. Studies by Brantlinger (1993) and reviews by Watts and Erevelles (2004) of high school students from lower-income minority families and of students with disabilities who were treated differentially as a result of their social or physical conditions found that they may have simply been responding behaviorally to an unjust learning environment. Weinstein and Mignano (1993) found that "the way teachers think about management strongly influences the way they behave" (p. 22). Their study of four effective elementary teachers found that when the teachers speak about classroom management they do not relate it to "discipline, or punishment, confrontation or penalty" (p. 22). Students bring varying degrees of discipline with them as they enter school. Many but not all children learn from the family before schooling that within certain social contexts some actions are appropriate but others are inappropriate. Students who arrive at school with few social skills are at a disadvantage when it comes to learning. Rarely does the school adjust to the individual, although some are trying to meet individual student needs. Not only are children expected to work with an adult whom they do not know, but to learn and socialize with groups of other children who are strangers.

Classroom management is more than the traditional unidimensional view of punishments and rewards, obedience and control. No single program will solve all the complexity of youth and adult behaviors found in American classrooms and schools, but the 40 identified research-based programs respond to both discreet and broad complexities of behavioral needs of youth in schools. The following represents the procedures used in the selection of a final list of 40 research-based programs.

PROGRAM SELECTION PROCEDURES

Initial sources used to identify programs included Educator's Reference Desk^{SM} (http://www.eduref.org) and federal and state databases, as well as published journal articles and books on school discipline and classroom management. In all, over 900 sources were identified for this chapter. After months of investigation, it became clear that the review procedures we planed would take years.

Further investigation determined that state or national organizations, governmental agencies, and third-party researchers had reviewed most of the programs we had identified in our initial review. We identified 12 organizations and two groups of authors for a total of 14 third-party reviews; for efficiency we call them "organizations." These organizations evaluated more than 800 programs in various areas such as student discipline, bullying, youth violence, delinquency, substance abuse, and psychopathology in school, family, and community settings. Some are sponsored by the Department of Education, the Department of Justice (Office of Juvenile Justice and Delinquency Prevention), or the Department of Health and Human Services. We used the criteria of the 14 organizations plus our additional criteria (see the following) to form a final list of programs. We did not rereview each of the 800 programs. The 14 organizations are summarized in Table 28.1: "School Discipline and Classroom Management Program Reviews by Third Parties." The organizations' research criteria are in Appendix A. Program's contact information and Web sites are in Appendix B. Other organizations and groups of authors were not included in the selection procedure as their selection criteria were not research based, lacked consistency from one program to another, or only covered a very few programs.

Authors' Criteria for Program Inclusion

Each program included in this chapter had to meet seven criteria established by the Chapter 28 authors:

1. The program was selected by at least 1 of the 14 organizations or groups (see Appendix A for organizations' criteria).
2. The major part of the program is related to prevention or intervention of discipline problems in school settings, such as classroom disruption, antisocial/aggressive behavior, suspension from school, and school violence. We also considered programs promoting one or many of the following: positive social skills, conflict resolution skills, participation/involvement in class, and positive school/classroom climate.
3. The program is school based in whole or in part. Community-based, family-based, and after-school programs were excluded even though some supplemental positive outcomes may be found in school and classroom settings.
4. The program involves school or classroom instruction/activities/intervention during the school day or is part of the school's discipline management system.
5. The target populations are students 3 to 18 years of age.
6. The program has the capacity to offer training and materials to schools.
7. The program developer completed and returned the authors' six-page questionnaire on his or her program (the questionnaire is described in the following section).

Originally, questionnaires were sent to 48 program developers, but eight programs were excluded as the requested information was not provided or the program subsequently did not meet one or several of the criteria listed previously (e.g., the program did not have the capacity to offer the required training to schools anymore). The 40 programs that met the seven criteria are presented in Table 28.1 and summarized in Tables 28.2.a/b. As shown in Table 28.1, nine programs included in the chapter were selected by a single organization and five programs were selected by 10 or more organizations. Twenty-six programs were selected by two to nine organizations.

Program Questionnaire

To provide consistency of review for this chapter and to update program information, a six-page questionnaire on program characteristics and effects was developed and distributed to 48 program developers. The questionnaire was also intended to identify commonalities across

TABLE 28.1

School Discipline and Classroom Management Program Reviews by Third Parties

Programs Selected	*A Blueprints for Viol. Prev (CSPV)*	*B Building on the Best (AFT, CSPV)*	*C CTC (Hawkins & Catalano)*	*D Example & Prom. Prog. (US Dept. Edu. Panel)*	*E Hamfish Programs (Hamfish Institute)*	*F Maryland Blueprints Manual (MBC)*	*G Model Programs Database (OJJDP)*	*H Preventing Mental Disorders (PRCPHD)*	*I Safe & Sound (CASEL)*	*J SAMHSA Model Programs (NREP)*	*K School Crime and Policing (M.&A.-B.)*	*L Sharing Successful Programs (SSTAC)*	*M Source-book of Drug and Viol.(VINJ)*	*N Youth Violence (DHHS: OSG)*
01. Aggression Replacement Training				2								1		
02. Aggressors, Victims, and Bystanders				2	2		2						1	
03. Al's Pals: Kids Making Healthy Choices				2						1	2			
04. Behavioral Monitoring & Reinforcement Program	2		1			1	2			3	2		1	2
05. Bullying Prevention Program	1	1	1			1	3	1		1	1		1	2
06. Child Development Project™			1	2			2	1	1	1	3		1	
07. Classroom Organization and Management Program					2									
08. Community of Caring®				2					1					
09. Consistency Management & Cooperative Discipline®		1			2		2				3			
10. Get Real About Violence®										3				
11. Good Behavior Game	2	1	1		1	1	2	1		2	2			2
12. High/Scope® Perry Preschool Program	2		1			1	1		1	1	2			2
13. I Can Problem Solve®	2	1	1	2	1	1	2	1	1	3	2		1	2
14. The Incredible Years	1		1			1				1	1			2
15. Learning for Life									1					
16. Lions-Quest				2		1			1	1				
17. Morning Program												1		
18. Open Circle				2					1		3			
19. Peace Works									1					
20. PeaceBuilders®			1	2		1	3			3	3		1	
21. Peacemakers				2		1				3				

22. PAL® Peer Assistance and Leadership							3			3				
23. Peers Making Peace				2			3			3				
24. Positive Action®				2			1			1	3			
25. Positive Adolescent Choices Training					1		2							
26. Primary Project						1								
27. Productive Conflict Resolution Program					1				1					
28. Project ACHIEVE							3		1	1			1	
29. Promoting Alternative Thinking Strategies (PATHS®)	1	1	1	2		1	1	1	1	1	1		1	2
30. Responding in Peaceful and Positive Ways (RIPP)			1	2		1	1	1		1			1	
31. Responsive Classroom®									1					
32. School-Wide Positive Behavior Support					2									
33. Second Step®: A Violence Prevention Curriculum			1	1	2	1	1	1	1	1			1	
34. Skills, Opportunities & Recognition (SOAR™)	2		1	2		1	2	1	1	2	2		1	1
35. Skillstreaming the Adolescent					2									
36. SMART Team: Students Managing Anger & Resolution Together				2			1			1				
37. Social Decision Making & Problem Solving Program				2		1		1	1			1	1	
38. Teaching Students to be Peacemakers					1					2			1	
39. The Think Time® Strategy				2										
40. Violence Prevention Curriculum for Adolescents					1	1	3						1	
Total number of programs selected for this chapter	8	5	12	19	12	16	20	9	15	22	14	3	14	8
Total number of programs selected by each organization	32	5	59	22	73	97	154	73	110	27	42	33	34	38

Categories ranked 1, 2, 3 are defined by each organization (A-N) in terms of effectiveness as determined by the organization's criteria.

TABLE 28.1
(Continued)

Review Organization Rating/Reference

A = *Blueprints for Violence Prevention*. Center for the Study and Prevention of Violence. 1996-ongoing. Rating: model (1) and promising (2). (refer to http://www.colorado.edu/cspv/blueprints)

B = *Building on the Best, Learning from What Works. Five Promising Discipline and Violence Prevention Programs*. The American Federation of Teachers (AFT). Study conducted by the Center for the Study and Prevention of Violence. 2000. (refer to http://www.aft.org)

C = *Communities That Care®. Prevention Strategies: A Research Guide to What Works*. J. D. Hawkins & R. F. Catalano. 2003. (refer to http://www.channing-bete.com/positiveyouth/pages/CTC/CTC.html)

D = *Exemplary & Promising Safe, Disciplined, and Drug-Free Schools Programs 2001*. U.S. Department of Education. Safe, Disciplined, and Drug-Free Schools Expert Panel. 2001. Rating: exemplary (1) and promising (2). (refer to http://www.ed.gov/admins/lead/safety/exemplary01/index.html)

E = *Hamfish Programs*. The Hamilton Fish Institute on School and Community Violence (Hamfish). Rating: effective (1) and noteworthy (2). (refer to http://www.hamfish.org/programs)

F = *Maryland Blueprints Manual*. Maryland Blueprints Committee. D. Gottfredson, M. Eddy & R. Spoth. 2001-2003. (refer to http://www.marylandblueprints.org)

G = *Model Programs Database*. Office for Juvenile Justice and Delinquency Prevention. 2002-ongoing. Rating: exemplary (1), effective (2) and promising (3). (refer to http://www.dsgonline.com)

H = *Preventing Mental Disorders in School-Aged Children: A Review of the Effectiveness of Prevention Programs*. The Prevention Research Center for the Promotion of Human Development. M. T. Greenberg, C. Domitrovich & B. Bumbarger. 1999 (July). (refer to http://www.prevention.psu.edu/CMHS.html)

I = *Safe and Sound. An Educational Leader's Guide to Evidence-Based Social and Emotional Learning (SEL) Programs*. The Collaborative for Academic, Social, and Emotional Learning (CASEL). 2003 (March). (refer to http://www.casel.org)

J = *SAMHSA Model Programs: Effective Substance Abuse and Mental Health Programs for Every Community*. Substance Abuse and Mental Health Services Administration (SAMHSA). National Registry of Effective Programs. 2003 (October). Rating: model (1), effective (2) and promising (3). (refer to http://www.modelprograms.samhsa.gov)

K = *School Crime and Policing* (W. L. Turk, Ed.). Chapter 11 : *A Guide to Effective School-Based Prevention Programs: Early Childhood Education and Environmentally Focused Programs* and chapter 12: *A Guide to Effective School-Based Prevention Programs: Individually Focused Programs*. S. Mihalic & T. Aultman-Bettridge. 2004. Rating: exemplary (1), promising (2) and favorable (3).

L = *Sharing Successful Programs*. Sharing Success Technical Assistance Center. 2002. (refer to http://www.sharingsuccess.org)

M = *Sourcebook of Drug and Violence Prevention Programs for Children and Adolescents*. Violence Institute of New Jersey. 1996-ongoing. (refer to http://www.umdnj.edu/vinjweb/publications/sourcebook/about_sourcebook.html)

N = *Youth Violence: A Report of the Surgeon General*. Department of Health and Human Services. Office of the Surgeon General. 2001 (November and December). Rating: model (1) and promising (2). (refer to http://www.surgeongeneral.gov/library/youthviolence)

TABLE 28.2.a
Program Summaries (Programs 1 to 20)

Programs	*Descriptions*
01. Aggression Replacement Training (ART)	Intervention program teaching social skills to aggressive students from grade 4 to high school
02. Aggressors, Victims, and Bystanders[1] (AVB)	Classroom-based curriculum program for preventing violence among middle school students
03. Al's Pals: Kids Making Healthy Choices (AP)	Classroom-based program aimed at developing positive social behavior in pre-K–3 children
04. Behavioral Monitoring Reinforcement Program[2] (BMRP)	Behavior modification program reinforcing academic motivation and discipline of high-risk adolescents
05. Bullying Prevention Program[3] (BPP)	Schoolwide program designed to prevent and reduce bullying in grades 1–9
06. Child Development Project™[4] (CDP)	Multifaceted program aimed at creating a caring community of learners in elementary schools
07. Classroom Organization and Management Program (COMP)	Professional development prog. designed for K–12 teachers to manage effective classroom environments
08. Community of Caring® (CC)	Character education program for K–12 students with emphasis on inclusion of disabled learners
09. Consistency Management & Cooperative Discipline® (CMCD)	Multifaceted management prog. based on shared responsibility between teachers and pre-K–12 students
10. Get Real About Violence® (GRAV)	Curriculum-based program aimed at preventing a wide range of violent behaviors for K–12 students
11. Good Behavior Game (GBG)	Classroom management strategy aimed at decreasing misbehavior in 1st and 2nd graders
12. High/Scope® Perry Preschool Program[5] (HSPP)	Active learning approach fostering cognitive and social development of disadvantaged young children
13. I Can Problem Solve®[6] (ICPS)	Curriculum-based program that trains pre-K–6 children in generating solutions to interpersonal problems
14. The Incredible Years (IY)	Multicomponent program promoting social competence for high-risk children up to 8 years old
15. Learning for Life (LL)	Curriculum-based program enhancing motivation, self-confidence, and self-worth in K–12 students
16. Lions-Quest (LQ)	Curriculum-based prevention program that addresses a wide range of social behaviors for K–12 students
17. Morning Program (MP)	Assembly held every school day for enhancing elementary students' positive attitudes toward school
18. Open Circle[7] (OC)	Elementary class meetings enhancing social competence and positive interactions
19. Peace Works (PW)	School-wide peer mediation and conflict resolution program for pre-K–12 students
20. PeaceBuilders® (PB)	Violence prevention program developing peaceful learning environments in elementary and middle schools

1. The entire name is *Aggressors, Victims, and Bystanders: Thinking and Acting to Prevent Violence*.
2. Also named *Preventive Intervention* or *Behaviorally-Based Prevention Program*.
3. Also named *The Intervention Campaign Against Bully/Victim Problems* or *Olweus Bullying Prevention Program*.
4. Child Development Project™ has three components: (a) *SIPPS*™ (Systematic Instruction in Phoneme Awareness, Phonics, and Sight Words) for teaching decoding; (b) Making Meaning™ for teaching comprehension and social skills; (c) *Caring School Community*™ designed to foster students' sense of community in classroom and school. In this chapter, the focus is on the last component.
5. Also named High/Scope Cognitive Curriculum.
6. Also named Interpersonal Cognitive Problem Solving.
7. Also named Reach Out to Schools: Social Competency Program.

TABLE 28.2.b
Program Summaries (Programs 21 to 40)

Programs	*Descriptions*
21. Peacemakers (PM)	Curriculum-based violence prevention program for upper-elementary and middle school students
22. PAL® Peer Assistance and Leadership (PAL)	Peer assistance program offering peer mentoring and mediation to at-risk children and adolescents
23. Peers Making Peace (PMP)	A grade 1–12th schoolwide peer mediation program where 15–24 students receive conflict resolution training
24. Positive Action® (PA)	Grade specific curriculum to improve positive behavior and achievement mainly in elementary schools
25. Positive Adolescent Choices Training (PACT)	Social skills training program designed to teach high-risk adolescents how to avoid violence
26. Primary Project (PP)	Individual program aimed at preventing school adjustment problems of high-risk pre-K–3 children
27. Productive Conflict Resolution Program[1] (PCRP)	Whole-school program teaching grades K–12 students how to resolve conflicts without using violence
28. Project ACHIEVE (ACH)	Schoolwide reform program aimed at increasing social skills and achievement in K–8 schools
29. Promoting Alternative Thinking Strategies (PATHS®)	Curriculum-based program promoting K–6 students' social competence and reducing aggressive behavior
30. Responding in Peaceful and Positive Ways (RIPP)	Prevention program teaching conflict resolution skills and strategies to middle school students
31. Responsive Classroom® (RC)	Classroom management program improving K–6 student social skills and academic competence
32. School-wide Positive Behavior Support (SWP)	Program that prevents and reduces behavior problems at the school, classroom and individual levels
33. Second Step®: A Violence Prevention Curriculum (SS)	Classroom-based program teaching empathy, problem solving and anger management to pre-K–8 students
34. Skills, Opportunities, and Recognition (SOAR™)[2]	Classroom management methods and parent workshops to improve elementary students' social skills
35. Skillstreaming the Adolescent (STA)	Intervention program teaching 50 interpersonal skills to at-risk and aggressive adolescents
36. SMART Team: Students Managing Anger & Resolution Together	Multimedia software teaching social competence and conflict-resolution skills to grades 5–9 students
37. Social Decision Making & Problem Solving Program[3] (SDM)	Curriculum-based prog. teaching self-control, social awareness and problem solving to grades1–8 students
38. Teaching Students to be Peacemakers (TSP)	Conflict resolution program promoting cooperation and positive climate in K–12 schools
39. The Think Time® Strategy (TTS)	Discipline management strategy to handle classroom disruptive behavior especially in elementary schools
40. Violence Prevention Curriculum for Adolescents (VPCA)	Violence prev. module exploring the nature of interpersonal violence and how to avoid it in grades 9–10

1. Includes *Peer Mediation Program* selected by the Hamilton Fish Institute.
2. Also named *Seattle Social Development Project* (former name).
3. Also named *Improving Social Awareness—Social Problem Solving*.

programs and obtain clarification on specific research areas directly from the program developers. The questionnaire consisted of 12 topics derived from a range of items used by most of the 14 organizations in their evaluations of classroom management and discipline programs. The topics included (1) focus on prevention or intervention; (2) population-specific selections; (3) grade level/age; (4) ethnicity; (5) geographic location; (6) socioeconomic status; (7) programmatic elements at the school, classroom, and individual levels; (8) parental and other adult involvement; (9) school approval process; (10) teacher inservice; (11) implementation frequency; and (12) program duration. In addition to these 12 principal areas, the program developers[1] were asked to indicate research data sources (students, teachers, principals, peers, parents, school records, and observations) for the following four areas that were synthesized from information derived during the initial program reviews: school/classroom climate, student behavior (protective factors), student behavior (risk factors), and academic achievement. The developers also indicated methodologies (quantitative or qualitative) and whether the findings were from external or internal studies. From the questionnaire, some additional contacts with program developers were needed to clarify discrepancies or to obtain additional information. The results of this process are discussed in the next section and in subsequent tables.

PROGRAM CHARACTERISTICS AND OUTCOMES

Characteristics

The first program characteristic is the "focus" as being prevention or intervention (see Tables 28.3.1.a/b). Although 33 of the 40 program developers could identify both prevention (item 1.1.) and intervention (item 1.2.) elements, 32 developers described their program as focusing on prevention and only 3 indicated intervention as the primary focus. Thirty-three programs are designed to include the general student population and 29 target students at risk of developing behavior problems. Nineteen programs can be used with students with disabilities or in special education. "Selected populations" is checked when programs, in whole or in part, are for students with high-risk behaviors (e.g., aggressive behavior). Next, program demographics include grade level, ethnicity, geographic location, and socioeconomic status (SES; Tables 28.3.2.a/b). The number of research-supported programs varies according to grade level: pre-K ($n = 8$), kindergarten ($n = 20$), elementary ($n = 35$), middle school ($n = 27$), and high school ($n = 16$). Programs generally cover a wide range of ethnicity, geographic locations, and SES, and most include studies conducted with low-SES students in urban settings. All programs, except the Norwegian Bullying Prevention Program were developed in the United States, but additional research was conducted on 13 programs outside the United States.

Tables 28.3.3.a/b show that 22 programs include elements at the school level, such as restructuring of school culture, school committees, peer mediation/mentoring, student meetings, and school- or community-based service-learning. At the classroom level, 25 programs provide a student curriculum for the teacher, 13 include classroom meetings on topics such as bullying, 2 offer software to teach the curriculum, and 22 focus on classroom management in whole or in part (include a classroom management system, provide a behavior management tool, offer specific training on classroom management, or give strategies to integrate the program into the life of the classroom). Fourteen of these programs also incorporate meetings with students about classroom management. Finally, 17 programs reinforce school rules at the classroom level. As shown in Tables 28.3.4.a/b, 16 programs include one or more components at the individual or small-group level. Finally, 36 of the 40 programs involve parents in various ways.

[1] In some cases, the questionnaire was completed by program developers' assistants or program implementers.

TABLE 28.3.1.a
Program Questionnaire: Type of Programs and Population Selection

Programs	*1. Focus*		*1.1. Prevention*			*1.2. Intervention*		*2. Population Selection*			
	a. Prevention	b. Intervention	a. Prevent the Behavior Source	b. Problem-Prevent vs Problem-Solve	c. How to Problem-Solve	a. Reduce Misbehavior	b. Respond to Immediate Problem	a. Comprehensive	b. At-Risk	c. Selected Populations	d.Special Ed.
01. Aggression Replacement Training		√	√		√	√			√	√	√
02. Aggressors, Victims, and Bystanders	√		√	√	√			√	√		
03. Al's Pals: Kids Making Healthy Choices	√		√		√	√		√	√		√
04. Behavioral Monitoring & Reinforcement Program		√	√			√			√	√	
05. Bullying Prevention Program	√		√	√	√	√	√	√		√	
06. Child Development Project™	√		√	√	√			√	√		
07. Classroom Organization and Management Program	√		√	√			√	√	√		√
08. Community of Caring®	√		√		√		√	√	√		√
09. Consistency Management & Cooperative Discipline®	√		√	√	√	√		√	√		√
10. Get Real About Violence®	√		√	√		√		√			
11. Good Behavior Game	√		√				√	√			
12. High/Scope® Perry Preschool Program	√		√	√	√		√		√	√	√
13. I Can Problem Solve®	√				√		√	√	√	√	√
14. The Incredible Years	√	√	√		√	√	√		√	√	√
15. Learning for Life	√		√		√	√	√	√	√		√
16. Lions-Quest	√		√	√	√	√	√	√	√		
17. Morning Program	√		√					√			
18. Open Circle	√		√		√		√	√			
19. Peace Works	√		√	√	√		√	√			
20. PeaceBuilders®	√		√	√	√	√	√	√	√		√

1.1.a. The program is designed to prevent the source of a specific behavior and deter similar behavioral problems in the future.
1.1.b. The program is designed to problem-prevent rather than problem–solve.
1.1.c. The program is designed to teach how to problem solve before problems surface so that students know what to do if future problems occur.
1.2.a. Students who participate in this program may already show disruptive behaviors. One of the goals of the program is to reduce these specific behaviors.
1.2.b. The program has specific methods for responding to immediate discipline problems.
2.a. Comprehensive (general population, no specific selection).
2.b. At-risk (students whose risk of developing a problem is significantly higher than the average. e.g., violent neighborhood, low SES).
2.c. Selected (students already show one or more high-risk behaviors, e.g., fighting).
2.d. Special education or students with disabilities.

TABLE 28.3.1.b

Program Questionnaire: Type of Programs and Population Selection

Programs	*1. Focus*		*1.1. Prevention*			*1.2. Intervention*		*2. Population Selection*			
	a. Prevention	b. Intervention	a. Prevent the Behavior Source	b. Problem-Prevent vs. Problem-Solve	c. How to Problem-Solve	a. Reduce Misbehavior	b. Respond to Immediate Problem	a. Comprehensive	b. At-Risk	c. Selected Populations	d.Special Ed.
21. Peacemakers	√		√			√		√	√	√	√
22. PAL® Peer Assistance and Leadership	√		√		√			√[1]	√	√	
23. Peers Making Peace	√	√	√		√	√	√	√	√		√
24. Positive Action®	√		√	√	√	√	√	√	√	√	√
25. Positive Adolescent Choices Training	√	√			√	√			√	√	
26. Primary Project	√		√	√		√			√	√	
27. Productive Conflict Resolution Program	√	√	√		√		√	√			
28. Project ACHIEVE	√		√	√	√	√	√	√	√	√	√
29. Promoting Alternative Thinking Strategies (PATHS®)	√		√	√	√	√		√	√		√
30. Responding in Peaceful and Positive Ways	√			√	√	√		√	√		
31. Responsive Classroom®	√		√		√	√		√			
32. School-Wide Positive Behavior Support	√		√		√	√	√	√		√	
33. Second Step®: A Violence Prevention Curriculum	√		√		√			√	√		
34. Skills, Opportunities & Recognition (SOAR™)	√		√	√	√			√	√		
35. Skillstreaming the Adolescent		√			√	√			√	√	√
36. SMART Team: Stud. Man. Anger & Res. Together	√		√	√	√		√	√	√	√	√
37. Social Decision Making & Problem Solving Program	√		√	√	√	√	√	√			√
38. Teaching Students to be Peacemakers	√		√		√	√	√	√	√		
39. The Think Time® Strategy	√	√	√	√	√	√	√	√	√	√	√
40. Violence Prevention Curriculum for Adolescents	√				√			√			

[1] Some students from the general population receive training to assist at-risk or other special needs students.
1.1.a. The program is designed to prevent the source of a specific behavior and deter similar behavioral problems in the future.
1.1.b. The program is designed to problem-prevent rather than problem-solve.
1.1.c. The program is designed to teach how to problem-solve before problems surface so that students know what to do if future problems occur.
1.2.a. Students who participate in this program may already show disruptive behaviors. One of the goals of the program is to reduce these specific behaviors.
1.2.b. The program has specific methods for responding to immediate discipline problems.
2.a. Comprehensive (general population, no specific selection).
2.b. At-risk (students whose risk of developing a problem is significantly higher than the average, e.g., violent neighborhood, low SES).
2.c. Selected (students already show one or more high risk behaviors, e.g., fighting).
2.d. Special education or students with disabilities.

TABLE 28.3.2.a
Program Questionnaire: Demographics

Programs	*3. Grade Level*							*4. Ethnicity*						*5. Geographic Location*			*6. SES*[1]		
	Pre-K	Kindergarten	1st–3rd	4th–6th	Middle School	9th	High School	African American	Caucasian	Latino	Asian	Multiethnic	International[2]	Urban	Suburban	Rural	Low	Middle	High
01. Aggression Replacement Training				R*	R*	R*	R*	R	R	R	R	R	R	R	R	R	R	R	R
02. Aggressors, Victims, and Bystanders				I	R*	I		R	R	R	R	R	I	R	R	I	R	R	I
03. Al's Pals: Kids Making Healthy Choices	R*	R*	R*					R	R	I		I		R	R	R	R	R	I
04. Behavioral Monitoring & Reinforcement Prog.					R*	R	R	R	R	R	R	R		R	R		R	R	
05. Bullying Prevention Program		I	R*	R*	R*	R*	R	R	R	I	I	R	R	R	I	R	R	R	I
06. Child Development Project™		R*	R*	R*	R			R	R	R	R	R		R	R	R	R	R	R
07. Classroom Organization and Management Prog.		R*	R*	R*	R*	R*	R*	R	R	R	R	R	I	R	R	R	R	R	R
08. Community of Caring®		R*	R*	R*	R*	R*	R*	R	R	R	R	R	I	R	R	R	R	R	R
09. Consistency Mgt. & Cooperative Discipline®	I	I	R*	R*	R*	R*	R*	R	R	R		R	R	R	R	R	R	R	
10. Get Real About Violence®		I	I	I	R*	I	I	I	I	I	I	R	I	R	I	I	R	I	I
11. Good Behavior Game			R*					R	R			R		R			R	R	
12. High/Scope® Perry Preschool Program	R*	R	R					R	R	R	I	I	R	R	I	I	R	I	I
13. I Can Problem Solve®	R*	R*	R*	R*				R	I	I	I	I	I	R	I	R	R	I	I
14. The Incredible Years	R*	R*	R*					R	R	R	R	R	R	R	R	R	R	R	I
15. Learning for Life		I	R*	R*	R	R	R	R	R	R	R	R	I	R	R	R	R	R	R
16. Lions-Quest		R*	R*	R*	R*	R*	R*	R	R	R			R	R	R	I	R	R	I
17. Morning Program		R*	R*	R*					R					I	I	R	I	R	
18. Open Circle		I	I	R*				I	R	I	I	I		R	R		R	R	R
19. Peace Works	R	R	R*	R*	R	R	R	R	R	R		R	R	R	R	R	R	R	R
20. PeaceBuilders®	I	R*	R*	R*	R*	I	I	R	I	R	I	R	R	R	R	I	R	R	

[1] Socioeconomic status.
[2] Country other than the U.S.
"I" indicates that the program has been implemented only (no research results are available) at the specific grade level, ethnic group, geographic location, or SES population.
"R" indicates that research is available at the specific grade level, ethnic group, geographic location, or SES population.
"R*" indicates that the program was reviewed by organization(s) at the specific grade level.

TABLE 28.3.2.b
Program Questionnaire: Demographics

Programs	*3. Grade Level*							*4. Ethnicity*						*5. Geographic Location*			*6. SES*[1]		
	Pre-K	Kindergarten	1st–3rd	4th–6th	Middle School	9th	High School	African American	Caucasian	Latino	Asian	Multiethnic	International[2]	Urban	Suburban	Rural	Low	Middle	High
21. Peacemakers				R*	R*	I	I	R	R	R	I			R	I	I	R	R	I
22. PAL® Peer Assistance and Leadership			R*	R*	R*	R*	R*	R	R	R	R	I	I	R	R	R	R	R	R
23. Peers Making Peace	I	I	R*	R*	R*	R*	R*	R	R	R	R	R	I	R	R	R	R	R	R
24. Positive Action®	I	R*	R*	R*	I	I	I	R	R	R	R	R	R	R	R	R	R	R	R
25. Positive Adolescent Choices Training				R*	R*	R*	I	R	R	I		I		R	I	I	R		
26. Primary Project	R*	R*	R*					R	R	R	R	R	R	R	R	R	R	R	R
27. Productive Conflict Resolution Program		R	R	R*	R*	R*	R*	R	R	R	I		I	R	R	I	R	R	R
28. Project ACHIEVE	I	R*	R*	R*	R*	I	I	R	R	R	R	R		R	R	R	R	R	R
29. Promoting Alternative Think. Strat. (PATHS®)	R	R*	R*	R*				R	R		R	R	I	R	R	R	R	R	I
30. Responding in Peaceful and Positive Ways					R*			R	R	R	I	R		R		R	R	R	
31. Responsive Classroom®		R*	R*	R*	I			R	R	R	R	R		R	I	I	R	R	R
32. School-Wide Positive Behavior Support		I	R	R	R	R	R	R	R	R	R	R	R	R	R	R	R	R	R
33. Second Step® A Violence Prevention Cur.	R*	R*	R*	R*	R*	I	I	R	R	R	I	R	R	R	R	R	R	R	I
34. Skills, Opportunities & Recognition (SOAR™)			R*	R*	R*			R	R		R	R		R			R	R	
35. Skillstreaming the Adolescent				R	R*	R*	R*	R	R	R	R	R	R	R	R	R	R	R	R
36. SMART Team: Stud. Man. Anger & Res. Tog.				R*	R*	R*		R	R	I	I	I		I	R	I	R	R	I
37. Social Decision Making & Prob. Solving Prog.		I	R*	R*	R	I	I	R	R	R	I	R	R	R	R	I	R	R	I
38. Teaching Students to be Peacemakers	I	R*	R*	R*	R*	R*	R*	R	R	I	I	R	I	R	R	R	R	R	R
39. The Think Time® Strategy		R*	R*	R*	I	I	I	R	R	R	R	R		R	R		R	R	R
40. Violence Prevention Curriculum for Adol.					I	R*	R*	R	I	R	I	I		R	I	I	R	I	I

[1] Socioeconomic status.
[2] Country other than the U.S.
"I" indicates that the program has been implemented only (no research results are available) at the specific grade level, ethnic group, geographic location, or SES population.
"R" indicates that research is available at the specific grade level, ethnic group, geographic location, or SES population.
"R*" indicates that the program was reviewed by organization(s) at the specific grade level.

TABLE 28.3.3.a

Program Questionnaire: School and Classroom Programmatic Elements

	7. School Level							*8. Classroom Level*					
	a. Restructuring of the Whole School	b. School Committee	c. Peer Mediation	d. Peer Mentoring	e. Student Meetings	f. Service Learning	g. Other	a. Curriculum-Based	b. Meetings on a Topic	c. Software	d. Classroom Mgt.	e. Meetings on Classroom Mgt.	f. School Rules Reinforced in Class
01. Aggression Replacement Training													
02. Aggressors, Victims, and Bystanders								√					
03. Al's Pals: Kids Making Healthy Choices								√			√		
04. Behavioral Monitoring & Reinforcement Prog.													
05. Bullying Prevention Program	√	√			√		√[1]		√				√
06. Child Development Project™	√	√		√	√	√		√	√		√	√	
07. Classroom Organization and Mgt. Prog.											√	√	√
08. Community of Caring®	√	√		√	√	√			√		√		√
09. Consistency Mgt. & Cooperative Discipline®	√	√	√	√	√				√		√	√	√
10. Get Real About Violence®								√					
11. Good Behavior Game									√		√	√	√
12. High/Scope® Perry Preschool Program								√			√		√
13. I Can Problem Solve®								√					
14. The Incredible Years								√	√		√	√	√
15. Learning for Life		√				√		√					
16. Lions-Quest	√	√				√		√	√				
17. Morning Program		√					√[2]						
18. Open Circle								√	√		√	√	√
19. Peace Works	√		√					√		√			√
20. PeaceBuilders®	√	√	√	√	√	√		√	√		√		√

7.a. A restructuring of the whole school culture environment (e.g., new philosophy, new schoolwide rules, change in scheduling).

7.e. Student meetings, activities or action groups to improve school climate.

7.g.[1] Increased supervision in specific school areas.

7.g.[2] Assembly held at the beginning of each school day (e.g., in the gymnasium).

8.a. Curriculum-based program (a specific number of lessons ready to use: activity sheets, video, etc.).

TABLE 28.3.3.b

Program Questionnaire: School and Classroom Programmatic Elements

	7. School Level							*8. Classroom Level*					
	a. Restructuring of the Whole School	b. School Committee	c. Peer Mediation	d. Peer Mentoring	e. Student Meetings	f. Service Learning	g. Other	a. Curriculum-Based	b. Meetings on a Topic	c. Software	d. Classroom Mgt.	e. Meetings on Classroom Mgt.	f. School Rules Reinforced in Class
21. Peacemakers	√							√					√
22. PAL® Peer Assistance and Leadership		√	√	√		√		√	√				
23. Peers Making Peace	√		√	√	√	√		√			√		
24. Positive Action®		√	√	√	√	√		√			√	√	√
25. Positive Adolescents Choices Training													
26. Primary Project							√[1]						
27. Productive Conflict Resolution Program	√	√	√					√	√		√	√	
28. Project ACHIEVE	√	√						√			√	√	√
29. Promoting Altern. Think. Strat. (PATHS®)						√		√			√	√	
30. Responding in Peaceful and Positive Ways		√	√		√			√					√
31. Responsive Classroom®		√				√					√	√	
32. School-Wide Positive Behavior Support	√	√									√		√
33. Second Step® A Violence Prevention Cur.								√	√		√	√	
34. Skills, Opportunities & Recog. (SOAR™)	√	√									√		
35. Skillstreaming the Adolescent													
36. SMART Team: Stud. Man. Ang. & Res. Tog.								√		√			
37. Social Decision Making & Prob. Solv. Prog.		√				√		√	√		√	√	√
38. Teaching Students to be Peacemakers			√					√			√	√	
39. The Think Time® Strategy	√										√		√
40. Violence Prevention Curriculum for Adol.								√					

7.a. A restructuring of the whole school culture environment (e.g., new philosophy, new schoolwide rules, change in scheduling).
7.e. Student meetings, activities or action groups to improve school climate.
7.g[1] A playroom is needed.
8.a. Curriculum-based program (a specific number of lessons ready to use: activity sheets, video, etc.).

TABLE 28.3.4.a

Program Questionnaire: Individual Student Programmatic Elements and Parental Involvement

	9. Individual Student Level[1]						*10. Parental Involvement*						
	a. Social Skills Training	b. Meeting Stud./Teach.	c. Meeting Stud./Prof.	d. Group Meetings Outside Classroom	e. Group Meetings Inside Classroom	f. IEP	a. Parent Training	b. Home Material	c. Home–School Contact	d. Child-Specific Feedback	e. School Committee	f. School/Class Activities	g. Homework
01. Aggression Replacement Training	c			√		√		√					
02. Aggressors, Victims, and Bystanders									√				√
03. Al's Pals: Kids Making Healthy Choices							√	√	√				
04. Behavioral Monitoring & Reinf. Program		√	√	√						√*			
05. Bullying Prevention Program				√[2]			√	√	√	√	√	√	
06. Child Development Project™								√			√	√	√
07. Classroom Organization and Mgt. Program													
08. Community of Caring®								√	√		√	√	√
09. Consistency Mgt. & Cooperative Discipline®							√		√	√		√	
10. Get Real About Violence®								√	√				
11. Good Behavior Game												√	
12. High/Scope® Perry Preschool Program	a					√	√	√	√	√*		√	√
13. I Can Problem Solve®							√						
14. The Incredible Years	c			√	√		√	√	√	√		√	√
15. Learning for Life								√	√				√
16. Lions-Quest							√	√	√		√	√	√
17. Morning Program									√			√	
18. Open Circle							√	√	√				√
19. Peace Works							√	√					
20. PeaceBuilders®							√	√	√	√	√	√	√

[1] In general, students are selected to participate in these components (see Table 28.3.1.a, 2c).
[2] Interventions with individual or small groups of bullies, victims and parents.
9.a. Social skills training such as modeling, role playing, performance feedback, and attribution retraining given by (a) a certified teacher, (b) a professional (psychologist, social worker, etc.), or (c) either a teacher or a professional.
9.b. Dyad or individual student meetings with a teacher.
9.c. Dyad or individual student meetings with a professional.
9.d. Regular small-group student meetings outside the classroom.
9.e. Small-group in-class student meetings called only when a problem occurs.
9.f. Included in IEP (Individualized Education Plan) of students as needed.
10.a. Parent training in school so that parents can intervene at home.
10.b. Home material given to parents (without training).
10.c. General home–school contact by letter.
10.d. Child specific feedback (phone or letter). * = Home visit required.
10.e. Parental involvement in school committee.
10.f. Parental involvement in school activities or class meetings.
10.g. Homework involving parents.

TABLE 28.3.4.b

Program Questionnaire: Individual Student Programmatic Elements and Parental Involvement

Programs	*9. Individual Student Level*[1]						*10. Parental Involvement*						
	a. Social Skills Training	b. Meeting Stud./Teach.	c. Meeting Stud./Prof.	d. Group Meetings Outside Classroom	e. Group Meetings Inside Classroom	f. IEP	a. Parent Training	b. Home Material	c. Home–School Contact	d.Child-Specific Feedback	e. School Committee	f. School/Class Activities	g. Homework
21. Peacemakers	b							√	√				
22. PAL® Peer Assistance and Leadership		√	√						√		√		
23. Peers Making Peace							√						
24. Positive Action®	c	√	√			√	√	√	√	√	√	√	√
25. Positive Adolescent Choices Training	b							√					
26. Primary Project			√			√	√	√		√			
27. Productive Conflict Resolution Program				√	√		√	√			√		
28. Project ACHIEVE	a					√	√	√	√			√	
29. Promoting Altern. Think. Strat. (PATHS®)								√	√				√
30. Responding in Peaceful and Positive Ways													
31. Responsive Classroom®									√		√	√	√
32. School-Wide Positive Behavior Support	c								√	√	√		
33. Second Step® A Violence Prevention Cur.							√		√				
34. Skills, Opportunities & Recog. (SOAR™)							√	√		√			
35. Skillstreaming the Adolescent	c			√				√		√			
36. SMART Team: Stud. Man. Ang. & Res. Tog.			√										
37. Social Decision Making & Prob. Solv. Prog.							√	√	√	√	√	√	√
38. Teaching Students to be Peacemakers							√						
39. The Think Time® Strategy		√						√	√		√		
40. Violence Prevention Curriculum for Adol.													

[1] In general, students are selected to participate in these components (see Table 28.3.1.b, 2c).
9.a. Social skills training such as modeling, role playing, performance feedback, and attribution retraining given by: (a) a certified teacher, (b) a professional (psychologist, social worker, etc.), or (c) either a teacher or a professional.
9.b. Dyad or individual student meetings with a teacher.
9.c. Dyad or individual student meetings with a professional.
9.d. Regular small-group student meetings outside the classroom.
9.e. Small-group in-class student meetings called only when a problem occurs.
9.f. Included in IEP (Individualized Education Plan) of students as needed.

10.a. Parent training in school so that parents can intervene at home.
10.b. Home material given to parents (without training).
10.c. General home–school contact by letter.
10.d. Child specific feedback (phone or letter). * = Home visit required.
10.e. Parental involvement in school committee.
10.f. Parental involvement in school activities or class meetings.
10.g. Homework involving parents.

Twenty-nine of them offer parent training or provide home material related to the program, and 27 recommend general school–home contact by letters or specific student feedback that may include home visits. Parents can also be involved through participation in committees, school/class activities, and homework.

Fourteen programs propose teacher discussion groups and counselor–teacher discussions about students (see Tables 28.3.5.a/b). More than half of the programs suggest or require the involvement of all adults interacting with students such as support staff and paraprofessionals. In many cases, specific training is offered to them. Eleven developers indicated that they require a general vote or approval by the faculty to commence the program and five indicated that human subjects approvals from a college, university, or medical school were required for data collection. Teacher professional development is not only available but also required to implement 18 of the 40 programs. Thirty-five programs have a Web site or phone number for ongoing assistance, 37 offer videos or manuals, and in 24 cases, teachers receive training and then train other teachers.

Developers reported that implementation frequency and duration are flexible in order to adjust to schools' needs (see Tables 28.3.6.a/b). The total duration of the programs also varies, but most programs last a year.

Outcomes

Developer responses[2] regarding program outcomes are summarized in "Program Reports on Effects" (see Tables 28.4.1 to 28.4.3). Four areas of outcomes are presented: school/classroom climate (3 items), student behavior (protective factors: 4 items/risk factors: 11 items), and academic achievement (5 items). When the research shows a specific outcome, the source of data is indicated by a specific letter (students [S], teachers [T], etc.). **Bold** letters indicate that the outcome was supported by external studies.

All 40 programs had positive effects on one or more of the following: order and discipline, disruptive behavior, office discipline referral, antisocial behavior among students, and conflict. Teacher or student-reported measures were used for each program (12 relied solely on these sources) and 18 used observational data. External research was reported by 26 of the 40 developers. Quantitative methods were used for all programs and qualitative methods were also employed for 23 of them.

EIGHT PROGRAM GROUPINGS AND DESCRIPTIONS

Eight specific program groupings with commonalities in goals and characteristics (described in the previous section) emerged from a comparison on the basis of the 40 programs' similarities and differences regarding their nature, focus, scope, contents, population, and outcomes: (1) Classroom-Based Management Programs ($n = 2$); (2) Classroom Management Programs for Special Populations ($n = 2$); (3) Specific Strategies for Classroom Discipline ($n = 2$); (4) Schoolwide Management Programs ($n = 5$); (5) Resiliency-Based and Character Education Programs ($n = 7$); (6) Classroom-Based Curriculum Programs on Violence Prevention ($n = 8$); (7) Schoolwide Conflict Resolution and Peer Mediation Programs ($n = 8$); and (8) Out-of-Classroom Programs for Small Groups or Individuals ($n = 6$).

---

[2]Data reported on *SOAR*™ were provided by the authors of this chapter based on available information.

TABLE 28.3.5.a.
Program Questionnaire: Adult Involvement, School Approval and Teacher Inservice

Programs	*11. Adult Involvement*				*12. School Approval*		*13. Teacher Inservice*				
	a. Teacher Discussions	b. Counselor–Teacher Discussions	c. Staff Involvement	d. Staff Training	a. Faculty vote 70%	b. Human Subjects Approval	a. Teachers Training Required	b. Web Site or Phone Number	c. Video	d. Manual	e. Teachers Training Teachers
01. Aggression Replacement Training								√	√	√	
02. Aggressors, Victims, and Bystanders			optional	√				√	√	√	√
03. Al's Pals: Kids Making Healthy Choices							√	√		√	
04. Behavioral Monitoring & Reinforcement Program		√								√	
05. Bullying Prevention Program	√	√	√	√	√	√	√	√	√	√	√
06. Child Development Project™			√					√	√	√	
07. Classroom Organization and Management Program							√	√		√	√
08. Community of Caring®	√		√	√	√	√	√	√	√	√	√
09. Consistency Managementt & Cooperative Discipline®	√	√	√	√	√	√	√	√	√	√	√
10. Get Real About Violence®			√					√			
11. Good Behavior Game	√						√			√	
12. High/Scope® Perry Preschool Program							√	√	√	√	√
13. I Can Problem Solve®								√			
14. The Incredible Years			optional					√	√	√	√
15. Learning for Life	√			√			√	√	√	√	
16. Lions-Quest			optional	√			√	√		√	√
17. Morning Program	√		√					√	√		√
18. Open Circle			optional	√			√	√	√	√	√
19. Peace Works			√	√				√		√	√
20. PeaceBuilders®	√		√	√	√		√	√		√	√

11.a. Teacher discussion groups.
11.b. Counselor–teacher discussions about student(s).
11.c. The program involves all adults in the school (e.g., support staff, paraprofessionals, custodial, bus drivers).
11.d. Staff training (other than teachers).
12.a. A vote of at least 70% of the participants is required to commence the program.
12.b. The program requires human subjects approval of a college, university, or medical school.

TABLE 28.3.5.b.
Program Questionnaire: Adult Involvement, School Approval and Teacher Inservice

	11. Adult Involvement				*12. School Approval*		*13. Teacher Inservice*				
Programs	a. Teacher Discussions	b. Counselor–Teacher Discussions	c. Staff Involvement	d. Staff Training	a. Faculty vote 70%	b. Human Subjects Approval	a. Teachers Training Required	b. Web Site or Phone Number	c. Video	d. Manual	e. Teachers Training Teachers
21. Peacemakers								√		√	
22. PAL® Peer Assistance and Leadership				√			√	√		√	√
23. Peers Making Peace			√		√	√	√	√	√	√	√
24. Positive Action®	√	√	√	√	√			√	√	√	√
25. Positive Adolescent Choices Training						√			√	√	
26. Primary Project		√		√				√	√	√	√
27. Productive Conflict Resolution Program	√	√	√	√	√			√	√	√	
28. Project ACHIEVE	√	√	√	√	√		√	√	√	√	√
29. Promoting Alternative Thinking Strategies (PATHS®)			√	√				√		√	√
30. Responding in Peaceful and Positive Ways			√				√	√		√	
31. Responsive Classroom®	√		√	√			√	√	√	√	√
32. School-Wide Positive Behavior Support			√	√	√		√	√	√	√	
33. Second Step® A Violence Prevention Curriculum				√				√		√	√
34. Skills, Opportunities & Recognition (SOAR™)					√		√			√	
35. Skillstreaming the Adolescent								√	√	√	
36. SMART Team: Stud. Man. Anger & Res. Together								√		√	
37. Social Decision Making & Problem Solving Program	√	√	√	√				√	√	√	√
38. Teaching Students to be Peacemakers				√				√	√	√	√
39. The Think Time® Strategy			√	√	√				√	√	√
40. Violence Prevention Curriculum for Adolescents								√	√		√

11.a. Teacher discussion groups.
11.b. Counselor–teacher discussions about student(s).
11.c. The program involves all adults in the school (e.g., support staff, paraprofessionals, custodial, bus drivers).
11.d. Staff training (other than teachers).
12.a. A vote of at least 70% of the participants is required to commence the program.
12.b. The program requires human subjects approval of a college, university, or medical school.

TABLE 28.3.6.a
Program Questionnaire: Frequency and Duration

Programs	*14. Frequency*	*15. Duration*
01. Aggression Replacement Training	3X/week (flexible)	10 weeks (flexible)
02. Aggressors, Victims, and Bystanders	1X/week (flexible)	12 lessons, 3 to 12 weeks
03. Al's Pals: Kids Making Healthy Choices	2X 15 minutes/week, ongoing	23 weeks, ongoing
04. Behavioral Monitoring & Reinforcement Program	Weekly meetings	2 years
05. Bullying Prevention Program	Ongoing	Ongoing
06. Child Development Project™	Ongoing	Ongoing
07. Classroom Organization and Management Program	Ongoing	Ongoing
08. Community of Caring®	Ongoing	Ongoing
09. Consistency Management & Cooperative Discipline®	Ongoing	Ongoing
10. Get Real About Violence®	At least one lesson/week	12–29 lessons, 1 to 6 months
11. Good Behavior Game	10 min. 3X/week to 30–45 min. 5X/week	1 year
12. High/Scope® Perry Preschool Program	2.5h/day	1 to 2 years
13. I Can Problem Solve®	PK = 20–30 min. daily; K–6 = 30–45 min./week	59–83 lessons, 3 months
14. The Incredible Years	Ongoing	Ongoing
15. Learning for Life	Varies, ongoing	K–6 = 61 lessons; grades 7–8 = 44 lessons
16. Lions-Quest	1 to 3X 40 minutes/week	1 semester to 1 year
17. Morning Program	20 minutes/day	Ongoing
18. Open Circle	2X 15–30 minutes/week, ongoing	35 lessons, 1 year, ongoing
19. Peace Works	K–6 = daily; Grades 6–12 = 2–3 X/week	20–50 lessons, 2 to 4 months
20. PeaceBuilders®	Ongoing	Ongoing

Classroom-Based Management Programs

Two classroom management programs are designed for the general population of students and emphasize prevention with some intervention strategies. They primarily use a staff development model for their delivery system (curriculum is not taught directly to students), including a train-the-trainer for dissemination.

The Classroom Organization and Management Program (COMP,#7[3]) is a K–12 program based on descriptive, correlational, and experimental studies that found that planning, implementing, and maintaining classroom management skills improves both behavior and learning. The program emphasizes seven areas of classroom management: (1) organizing the classroom; (2) planning and teaching rules and procedures; (3) managing student work and improving student accountability; (4) maintaining good student behavior; (5) planning and organizing; (6) conducting instruction and maintaining momentum; and (7) getting the year off to a good start. COMP views the classroom as a social and communicative setting. Through more effective use of teacher organization and managing skills, students will have greater learning opportunities and these proactive strategies prevent deviant behavior. COMP has a series of

[3]The number after each program name or acronym refers to its location in the tables in this chapter.

TABLE 28.3.6.b
Program Questionnaire: Frequency and Duration

Programs	*14. Frequency*	*15. Duration*
21. Peacemakers	Varies	18X 45 minutes lessons, varies
22. PAL® Peer Assistance and Leadership	2X to 3X/week	Maximum 2 years/level (elem., middle, high)
23. Peers Making Peace	Ongoing	18 lessons, ongoing
24. Positive Action®	4 X 15 minutes/week	Ongoing
25. Positive Adolescent Choices Training	1X/week	3 months minimum
26. Primary Project	30 minutes/week	1 semester
27. Productive Conflict Resolution Program	Weekly and bi-weekly meetings, ongoing	Ongoing
28. Project ACHIEVE	Ongoing	Ongoing
29. Promoting Alternative Thinking Strategies (PATHS®)	Ongoing	40 to 50 lessons/year, ongoing
30. Responding in Peaceful and Positive Ways	1X/week	25 lessons (Grades 7 – 8 = 12 lessons)/year
31. Responsive Classroom®	Ongoing	Ongoing
32. School-Wide Positive Behavior Support	Ongoing	Ongoing
33. Second Step®: A Violence Prevention Curriculum	1X/week	PK-6 = 15–22 lessons; Grades 6 – 8 = 1 semester
34. Skills, Opportunities & Recognition (SOAR™)	Ongoing	Ongoing
35. Skillstreaming the Adolescent	2X 45 minutes/week	Varies
36. SMART Team: Students Managing Anger & Resolution Together	Varies	8X 50 minutes, varies
37. Social Decision Making & Problem Solving Prog.	Weekly lessons, ongoing	Ongoing
38. Teaching Students to be Peacemakers	Ongoing	20 to 30 minutes lessons, ongoing
39. The Think Time® Strategy	Ongoing	Ongoing
40. Violence Prevention Curriculum for Adolescents	At least 1X/week	4 to 10 weeks

studies that support its effectiveness on student disruptive behavior and academic engagement (Evertson & Smithey, 2000; Gottfredson et al., 1993). COMP training is divided into two parts: a 3-day workshop before the school year and a 1-day follow-up. COMP also provides training specifically for new teachers.

The Responsive Classroom® (RC, #31) includes strategies for social and academic learning. Research supports *RC* in grades K–6, and it is also used in middle school but the research is not available. The program's principles include (a) the social and academic curriculum are both important; (b) how and what children learn are equally important; (c) social interaction brings cognitive growth; (d) important social skills include cooperation, assertion, responsibility, empathy, and self-control; (e) teachers need to know the child individually, culturally, and developmentally; (f) families should be known and invited to participate; and (g) how the adults at school work together is as important as individual competence. The RC approach includes six teaching strategies including morning meetings, rules and logical consequences, guided discovery, academic choice, classroom organization, and family communication. The program's research is evolving but preliminary findings seem to support its effectiveness on

TABLE 28.4.1
Program Reports on Outcomes (School and Classroom Management Programs)

	Classroom-Based Management Programs		*Classroom Mgt. Prog. for Special Populations*		*Specific Strategies for Classroom Discipline*		*Schoolwide Management Programs*				
Program Numbers	**07**	**31**	**12**	**14**	**11**	**39**	**06**	**09**	**28**	**32**	**34**
Program Abbreviations	COMP	RC	HSPP	IY	GBG	TTS	CDP	CMCD	ACH	SWP	SOAR
Grade Levels Included in Research	K-12	K-6	PK-3	PK-3	1-3	K-6	K-8	1-12	K-8	1-12	1-8
SCHOOL/CLASSROOM CLIMATE											
School/classroom climate	**TO**	**TPO**		TO			**STP**	**STPO**	**TPO**	**STRO**	
Sense of classroom/school community		**TP**					**STP**	STPO		**STRO**	
School/classroom belonging		**TPO**					**STP**	STPO			S
STUDENT BEHAVIOR (PROTECTIVE FACTORS)											
Pro-social skills/social competence	**TPRO**	**TO**	STAR	**TAO**		TR	**STPO**	**STPRO**	**X**	**STRO**	T
Intention to use non-violence strategies	**TPRO**			**TAO**				**STPRO**			
Problem-solving/conflict resolution knowledge	**TPO**			**TAO**			**STP**	**STPRO**	**STEPA**		
Order and discipline	**TPRO**	**TO**		**TAO**		TR	**TPO**	**STPRO**	**TPO**	**STRO**	
STUDENT BEHAVIOR (RISK FACTORS)											
Disruptive behavior	**TPRO**		STR	**TAO**	**TEO**	TR	STE	**STR**	**TPRO**		S
Office discipline referrals	**TPRO**		R			R		**R**	**TPR**	**STRO**	
Antisocial behavior among students	**TPRO**		ST	**TAO**		TR	**STE**	**STPR**	**R**		T
Lack of anger control				**TAO**				STPR	**STEPA**		
Verbal aggression	**TPRO**			**TAO**	**TEO**	TR	T	STPR	**TPRO**	S	
Physical aggression	**TPRO**		R	**TAO**	**TEO**	TR		STPR	**X**	S	
Conflict	**TPRO**			**TAO**			ST	**STPR**	**STEPAR**		
Bullying				**TAO**			ST	STPR	**TPR**		
Weapons carrying or offenses			R				S	STPR	**R**	**STRO**	
Vandalism			R					**STPR**	**R**	**STRO**	
Suspension/expulsion	**TPRO**		R			R		**R**	**R**	**STRO**	
ACADEMIC ACHIEVEMENT											
Attendance								**R**	**R**	**STRO**	
Positive attitude toward school		**TO**	S	**TAO**			ST	**STEP**	**STEPA**		STA
Academic engagement, time on task	**TPRO**	**TO**		**TO**	**TEO**		ST	**STEPO**	**TPO**	**STRO**	S
Academic achievement (grades)	**TPRO**	**TRO**	S		**RO**	T	R	R	**R**		TA
Gains in national, state, or local examinations		TA				R	R	**R**	**R**	**STRO**	R
Use of qualitative (1) and quantitative (2) methods:	1-2	1-2	1-2	1-2	2	2	1-2	1-2	1-2	2	2

Note: Results in **bold** are supported by external studies
S = Student-Reported Data
T = Teacher-Reported Data
P = Principal-Reported Data
E = Peer-Reported Data
A = Parent-Reported Data
R = School Records Data
O = Observation Data
X = All Sources S-O

TABLE 28.4.2

Program Reports on Outcomes (Resiliency-Based and Violence Prevention Programs)

	Resiliency-Based and Character Education Programs							*Classroom-Based Curriculum Programs on Violence Prevention*							
Program Numbers	**08**	**15**	**16**	**17**	**18**	**24**	**37**	**02**	**03**	**10**	**13**	**29**	**33**	**36**	**40**
Program Abbreviations	CC	LL	LQ	MP	OC	PA	SDM	AVB	AP	GRAV	ICPS	PATHS	SS	ST	VPCA
Grade Levels Included in Research	K-12	1-12	K-12	K-6	4-6	K-6	1-8	6-8	PK-3	6-8	PK-6	PK-6	PK-8	5-9	9-12
SCHOOL/CLASSROOM CLIMATE															
School/classroom climate		ST	T	STPA	T	**STPA**	**STP**					**O**			
Sense of classroom/school community		ST	T	STPAO	T	**STPAR**	**ST**								
School/classroom belonging		ST	T	TPA		**STPAR**									
STUDENT BEHAVIOR (PROTECTIVE FACTORS)															
Pro-social skills/social competence	**TR**	ST	ST	TPAO	ST	**STEPAR**	**X**	S	T		**TEO**	**TEAO**	**STO**	S	
Intention to use non-violence strategies		ST	ST	STPA			**SR**	S		**S**		ST		S	
Problem-solving/conflict resolution knowledge	**TR**	ST	ST	O	ST	STEPAR	**STPRO**				**S**	ST	**SO**	S	
Order and discipline	**TR**	ST	T	TPA		**TPR**	**TPRO**				**TO**		**O**		
STUDENT BEHAVIOR (RISK FACTORS)															
Disruptive behavior	**TR**	ST	T		T	**TR**	**TPRO**				**TEO**	**TE**	**O**		
Office discipline referrals	**TR**	ST	T			**TR**	**PR**								
Antisocial behavior among students	**TR**	ST	T		S	**TR**	**STEPR**		T		**TEO**		**T**		
Lack of anger control		ST	T			**TR**	**STPR**				**TEO**	**TE**			
Verbal aggression	**TR**	ST	T			**TR**	**STPR**		T	S	**TEO**	**TE**	**O**		
Physical aggression		ST	T		S	**TR**	**STPR**		T		**TEO**	**TE**	**O**		S
Conflict		ST	T			**TR**	**STPR**	S		S	**TEO**			S	S
Bullying	**TR**	ST	T			**TR**	**STPR**	**S**			**TEO**				
Weapons carrying or offenses			T			**TR**									
Vandalism			T			**TR**									
Suspension/expulsion	**TR**	ST	T			**TR**	**PR**								
ACADEMIC ACHIEVEMENT															
Attendance	**S**	ST	T	STPAR		**R**	R								
Positive attitude toward school	**S**	ST	ST	STPA	ST	**TA**	ST								
Academic engagement, time on task		ST	T		T		T								
Academic achievement (grades)	**S**	ST	T				R				**TR**				
Gains in national, state, or local examinations			T			**R**					**R**				
Use of (1) qualitative and (2) quantitative methods	1-2	1-2	1-2	2	1-2	2	1-2	1-2	1-2	2	1-2	1-2	2	1-2	2

Note: Results in **bold** are supported by external studies.

S = Student-Reported Data
T = Teacher-Reported Data
P = Principal-Reported Data
E = Peer-Reported Data
A = Parent-Reported Data
R = School Records Data
O = Observation Data
X = All Sources S-O

TABLE 28.4.3

Program Reports on Outcomes (Conflict Resolution and Out-of-Classroom Programs)

	Schoolwide Conflict Resolution and Peer Mediation Programs								*Out-of-Classroom Programs* for small Groups or Individuals					
Program Numbers	**05**	**19**	**20**	**21**	**23**	**27**	**30**	**38**	**01**	**04**	**22**	**25**	**26**	**35**
Program Abbreviations	BPP	PW	PB	PM	PMP	PCRP	RIPP	TSP	ART	BMRP	PAL	PACT	PP	STA
Grade Levels Included in Research	1-12	PK-12	K-8	4-8	1-12	K-12	6-8	K-12	4-12	6-12	1-12	4-9	PK-3	4-12
SCHOOL/CLASSROOM CLIMATE														
School/classroom climate	ST	**TRO**	**TPRO**		X	STEP		**ST**			**SA**		**T**	
Sense of classroom/school community		**TRO**	**STEPRO**		STEPAO	STEP		**ST**			**SA**			
School/classroom belonging			**STEPRO**		STEPAO	STEP		**ST**			**SA**		**T**	
STUDENT BEHAVIOR (PROTECTIVE FACTORS)														
Pro-social skills/social competence		**TRO**	**X**		STEPAO	STEPO	**SR**	**S**	**ST**		**SA**	**STR**	**ST**	**ST**
Intention to use non-violence strategies		**TRO**	**X**		STEPAO	STEPO	S	**S**						
Problem-solving/conflict resolution knowledge		**TRO**	**X**	S	STEPAO	STEPO	S	**S**	**T**			**STR**		**T**
Order and discipline		**TRO**	**TERO**	ST	X			**ST**	**T**		**SPA**	R	S	
STUDENT BEHAVIOR (RISK FACTORS)														
Disruptive behavior		**TPRO**	**TPRO**	ST	X		**T**	**ST**	**T**	**STR**	**ST**	STR	**ST**	
Office discipline referrals		**TRO**	**TPRO**	T	STEPAO	STEP	**T**	**T**	**T**		**TR**	TR		**P**
Antisocial behavior among students	S	**TRO**	**TPRO**	ST	STEPAO		**T**	ST	**T**		**R**	STR		**T**
Lack of anger control		**TRO**	**TPRO**		STEPAO				**T**		**R**	ST	**ST**	**T**
Verbal aggression		**TRO**	**TPRO**	ST	STEPAO	STEP	**ST**	**ST**	**T**		**R**	R	**ST**	**T**
Physical aggression		**TPRO**	**TPRO**	ST	X	STEP	**ST**	**ST**			**R**	R	**ST**	**T**
Conflict		**TRO**	**TPRO**		STEPAO				**T**		**R**	R		**T**
Bullying	**SO**	**TRO**	**TPRO**			STEP		**ST**		**R**		R		**T**
Weapons carrying or offenses		**R**	**TPRO**	ST			**S**				**R**	R		
Vandalism	S	**P**	**TPRO**						**T**		**R**	R		
Suspension/expulsion		**PR**	**TPRO**	ST	X	STEP	**T**			**STR**	**R**	R		
ACADEMIC ACHIEVEMENT														
Attendance		P	**TPRO**		X				**T**	**STR**	**STR**			
Positive attitude toward school	S	**T**	**STPARO**					**S**	**T**		**STR**		**ST**	
Academic engagement, time on task			**TPRO**		STEPAO			**S**			**STR**		**ST**	
Academic achievement (grades)		P	**TPARO**					**S**		**STR**	**STR**			
Gains in national, state, or local examinations			**TPRO**		X						**R**			
Use of (1) qualitative and (2) quantitative methods	2	1-2	2	2	2	1-2	2	1-2	1-2	2	1-2	2	2	1-2

Note: Results in **bold** are supported by external studies.

S = Student-Reported Data
T = Teacher-Reported Data
P = Principal-Reported Data
E = Peer-Reported Data
A = Parent-Reported Data
R = School Records Data
O = Observation Data
X = All Sources S-O

social skills and academic behaviors (Elliot, 1999). Teachers who used the program reported greater disciplinary efficacy and were more likely to report positive attitudes toward teaching (Rimm-Kaufman & Sawyer, 2004). The Responsive Classroom professional development and materials range from 1-day workshops to weeklong institutes and multiyear staff development.

Classroom Management Programs for Special Populations

Two programs propose classroom management strategies designed for at-risk children or special education populations. They both are supported by research from pre-K to third grade and involve parents in various ways (see Table 28.3.4.a). They also provide a curriculum to be taught to children.

The High/Scope® Perry Preschool Program (HSPP, #12) principles form an "open framework" where the curriculum is adjusted to the needs of learners. This program, based on constructivism, carries "the belief that children learn best through active experiences with people, materials, events and ideas, rather than through direct teaching or sequenced exercises" (http://www.highscope.org). Children are invited to engage in 58 "key experiences" and, to facilitate them, the program provides a blueprint for daily routines, classroom/playground organization, and teacher–child interactions. When discipline problems arise, teachers avoid punishment and isolation. Instead, children are encouraged to discuss the problem with the teacher or with others involved. The developer, in response to the chapter authors' questionnaire, indicated that High/Scope has specific methods for responding to immediate discipline problems. A follow-up at age 27 comparing children who received the High/Scope® Perry Preschool Program with a control group showed greater school persistence and reduced delinquency, violent crimes, and drug dealing (Schweinhart, Barnes, & Weikart, 1993).

The goal of The Incredible Years (IY, #14) is to reduce children's aggression and increase social competence at home and at school. IY operates in three areas: parent training, teacher training, and child social skills training. The classroom management teacher training includes five sections: (1) the importance of teacher attention, encouragement, and praise; (2) motivating children through incentives; (3) preventing behavior problems; (4) decreasing students' inappropriate behaviors; and (5) building positive relationships with students. The Dinosaur Child Training Curriculum is taught by counselors with aggressive children in small groups or by the teacher with an entire class. Children with oppositional defiant behavior showed fewer conduct problems after receiving the program in a 2-year follow-up study (Reid, Webster-Stratton, & Hammond, 2003).

Specific Strategies for Classroom Discipline

Two specific programs incorporate behavior modification techniques to maintain order and discourage disruptive behaviors. The Good Behavior Game (GBG, #11) solicits participation of each student in the classroom whereas The Think Time® Strategy (TTS, #39) is an individual behavior management technique used only when a student fails to obey the teacher's request.

Good Behavior Game is a behavior management strategy for lower-elementary classrooms (grades 1 and 2). It allows students to work in teams where each individual becomes responsible for the group. Before the game begins, the teacher explains what disruptive behaviors will result in a checkmark on the board. Teams that have not exceeded a specific number of marks at the end of the game are rewarded (e.g., tangible rewards, activities). The length of the game increases with time and eventually the teacher begins the game with no warning so that students are always monitoring their behavior. GBG also includes class meetings to discuss problems related to academic, social, and behavioral goals. Parents can attend these meetings. At the end of first grade, GBG students compared to a control group had less aggressive and shy behaviors according to teachers. GBG boys who were rated highly aggressive in first grade showed a decrease in aggression at the end of sixth grade (Kellam, Rebok, Ialongo, & Mayer, 1994).

The Think Time® Strategy helps students acquire self-discipline in the classroom with a strategy derived from Patterson's coercion theory on adult–child interactions (see Patterson, 1982). The implementation of TTS requires two or more teachers in proximity to each other to set aside in their separate classrooms a Think Time area where two or three desks are located away from the group. When a student fails to obey a teacher's request to change his or her behavior, that student is sent to the Think Time area in another teacher's classroom. After the cooperating teacher determines that the student has gained self-control, a Behavior Debriefing Form is given to him or her. While in the Think Time area, the student writes the cause and the behavior needed upon return. This strategy decreases up to 70% of behaviors requiring administrative intervention such as suspension (Nelson, Martella, & Galand, 1998). Think Time® Strategy has research at the elementary level. It is also used in middle and high schools classrooms though no research data is currently available.

Schoolwide Management Programs

The five schoolwide management programs restructure the school's climate and culture, as well as improve classroom behavior and academic achievement. At least one program also improves attendance, truancy, teacher retention, and vandalism. Teacher training in classroom management is a key component for four of the five programs.

The Child Development Project™ (CDP, #06), specifically through its Caring School Community™ component, integrates research-based principles to create a climate of caring in elementary schools. Various activities are proposed: "That's My Buddy" partners older and younger students for academic activities; "At Home in Our School" involves parents in school activities; "Ways We Want Our Class to Be" provides a forum to discuss classroom behavior norms and other issues; and "Homeside Activities" are short conversational activities completed at home with parents. A follow-up of 1,246 program and control students from elementary to middle school showed improvements on several outcomes. They were more engaged and connected to school, displayed less behavior problems, had better academic performance, and they associated with peers who were more prosocial (Battistich, Schaps, & Wilson, 2004).

Consistency Management & Cooperative Discipline® (CMCD®, #09), implemented in pre-K–12, supports teachers in establishing self-disciplined, caring, and respectful places to learn. All adults (from administrators and teachers to cafeteria workers) receive professional development. CMCD emphasizes (a) *preventing* problems before they occur; (b) establishing and maintaining *caring* learning environments; (c) creating *cooperative* student opportunities for rule development and decision making; (d) *organizing* a consistent but flexible learning environment; and (e) linking classroom, school, and *community* to advance the learner. Studies with comparison groups show significant achievement gains in reading, mathematics, and English; reductions in office discipline referrals and truancy; and improvements in classroom and school climate, instructional time saved (from 1.4 to 4.4 school weeks), as well as improved student attendance and teacher retention in both elementary and secondary schools (Freiberg, Connell, & Lorentz, 2001; Opuni, 2002, 2003; Day & Townsend, 2004; Eiseman, 2005). CMCD starts with the classroom and expands schoolwide. Climate and discipline data are used to inform and improve practice and CMCD has a specific curriculum for new teachers.

Project ACHIEVE (ACH, #28) is designed to strengthen pre-K–8 students' self-management skills and academic achievement. The program involves seven components implemented over a 3-year period: (1) assessment of school functioning in order to generate action plans; (2) use of a problem-solving process; (3) reinforcement of teacher instructional behaviors to maximize student engagement; (4) instructional consultation and curriculum-based assessment to improve learning; (5) interventions to address students' curricular/behavioral problems and teacher's instructional/classroom management procedures; (6) development of ongoing home–school collaboration; and (7) data collection to validate the school improvement. The five-step Stop & Think Social Skills Program improves self-management and is the anchor of the student curriculum. At the elementary level, Knoff and Batsche (1995) reported decreases in disciplinary referral, suspension, and grade retention. Teachers also perceived an improvement in school climate.

School-Wide Positive Behavior Support (SWP, #32) aims at preventing and reducing misbehavior in elementary and secondary schools. At the school level: (a) specific guidelines are provided with behavioral expectations being defined and taught; (b) appropriate behaviors are acknowledged and behavioral errors are connected proactively; (c) program evaluations and adaptations are made by a team; (d) administrative support and involvement are active; and (e) student support systems are integrated with the schools' discipline policy. At the classroom level, teachers are encouraged to provide precorrection, keep students engaged, provide a positive focus, consistently enforce school/class rules, correct disruptive behavior proactively, and teach and plan for smooth transitions. For students who exhibit behavior problems, a five-step behavioral assessment is proposed. A middle school study with comparison group showed that program students reported more positive reinforcement for appropriate behavior. Discipline referrals significantly decreased as well as verbal and physical aggression, and students' perceptions of school safety improved (Metzler, Biglan, Rusby, & Sprague, 2001).

Skills, Opportunities, and Recognition (SOAR™, #34) aims at creating a community of learners in elementary schools. SOAR™ provides teacher training to develop a proactive classroom management system that uses interactive strategies and emphasizes cooperative learning. Teachers integrate a wide range of social and emotional skills in the classroom and throughout the school. Establishment of clear rules and rewards for appropriate behavior are suggested to reduce disruptive behavior. The program provides family management training and workshops that help their child succeed. O'Donnell, Hawkins, Catalano, Abbott, and Day (1995) showed that children were less involved with antisocial peers and more attached to school compared to control students in fifth grade. In 11th grade, they reduced involvement in delinquency.

Resiliency-Based and Character Education Programs

Seven programs designed for the general population foster protective factors, such as prosocial skills and social competence, and generally improve school/classroom climate (Table 28.4.2). Program developers define their programs as being "resiliency based" and focusing on prevention. They cover the general physical, intellectual, social, and emotional domains of students (Norris, 2003).

Community of Caring® (CC, #08) is a whole-school program implemented in almost 1,000 schools in North America. The five core values of *caring, respect, responsibility, trust*, and *family* are integrated into classroom and school life. Students may participate in group activities such as service-learning, class meetings, buddy partners, and cross-age groups to help one another, discuss issues, and solve problems. The program also emphasizes inclusion of students with disabilities. These students, who are often recipients of service, become, like their nondisabled peers, active contributors in their school through service-learning. The organizations that selected the program (see Table 28.1.) reported results from a 2-year unpublished study. Grade 9 students reported lower unexcused school absences and higher grades at posttest.

Learning for Life (LL, #15) aims at supporting schools in their efforts to prepare students to handle life complexities and to enhance self-confidence, motivation, and self-worth. Since

1991, over 1 million, students have participated in LL, which is a classroom-based program with specific curriculum for each grade level (K–12). A wide range of social and academic skills and subjects are part of the program (e.g., dealing with moral dilemmas and development of critical thinking). Students take part in activities such as being a "secret pal" for a week and participate in projects for the environment. At upper levels, students are taught practical skills necessary to acquire a job and to stay employed. LL includes optional supplements, such as a drug prevention program at the elementary level and a program for students with special needs. An unpublished study reviewed by the Collaborative for Academic, Social, and Emotional Learning (CASEL; 2003) showed improvement in elementary students' classroom behavior, respect for peers, sense of caring about others, and decision making compared to a control group.

Lions-Quest (LQ, #16) is designed to guide youth toward healthy choices and a drug- and violence-free lifestyle. LQ is divided into three classroom-based curricula: Skills for Growing (K–5), Skills for Adolescence (6–8), and Skills for Action (9–12). A school climate committee also offers activities to involve students. A series of unpublished studies provided by Lions-Quest for organizations' reviews (see Table 28.1) showed results in the three age groups. On the basis of a pretest–posttest design, K–5 students felt more able to make decisions apart from peers. They perceived a better classroom environment compared to the control group. Middle school students had higher expectations in school success and improved their grades. High school students maintained a lower risk of dropping out from school whereas control students increased their lifestyle risks.

Morning Program (MP, #17) is a 20-minute daily assembly held at the beginning of each school day. Students participate in art forms such as music and storytelling, are introduced to other cultures, are involved in discussions, speak in front of large audiences of multiage students and parents, receive information from professionals on health and safety, meet with people from various occupations, are introduced to science concepts, and acquire knowledge about history. MP focuses on the learning environments necessary to establish the protective behavior factors from prosocial skills to order and discipline. MP is based on two rules: Be kind to yourself and others, and let others work and learn without being disturbed. This program has been replicated in more than 100 elementary schools in New York State. Students participating in MP were found to be more positive about school and themselves (see Sharing Success Technical Assistance Center [SSTAC], 2002).

Open Circle (OC, #18) fosters communication, responsibility, and social problem solving at the elementary level. During classroom meetings, students move their chairs into an "open circle," and one chair is left empty as a symbol for room for another person. They practice social competency skills and reinforce a strong sense of community in the classroom through discussions of topics such as being a good listener, nonverbal communication, and dealing with teasing. The teacher is provided a lesson plan for 35 meetings, including literature connections and supplementary lessons. These meetings provide an opportunity to discuss classroom interactions weekly and allow for a better engagement in schoolwork. A study on sixth-grade students showed that girls exposed to OC were better adjusted to middle school, and boys perceived themselves to have more self-control and be less involved in physical fights compared to a control group (Taylor, Liang, Tracy, Williams, & Seigle, 2002).

Positive Action® (PA, #24) is a program used to improve positive and decrease negative behaviors in a variety of educational settings (schools, mental health agencies, family welfare and juvenile justice programs). In schools, a PA goal is to allow teachers to spend more time teaching and less time controlling the classroom and disciplining students. There is a curriculum toolkit for each grade level (K–12), supplementary toolkits for social conflict resolution and alcohol and drug prevention, a counseling kit for specific problems, and climate kits designed to develop a positive culture throughout the school. The PA staff can also help design a program adjusted to specific needs or populations. In two different school districts, PA resulted in decreases in disciplinary referrals (78% and 85%) and increases in academic achievement (16% and 52%) (Flay, 2001).

The Social Decision Making & Problem Solving Program (SDM, #37) focuses on emotional intelligence (Goleman, 1995). It teaches social and emotional learning skills to first to eighth graders to pursue healthy life choices and avoid violence, substance abuse, and academic failure. The curriculum contains lessons in three areas: self-control and social awareness (e.g., self-monitoring emotions and how to make friends), thinking about social decision making (students are taught an eight-step "clear thinking strategy" to cope with social problems), and application to academics and real-life problems (teachers infuse the newly learned skills in concrete activities). In a study conducted by Elias, Gara, Schuyler, Braden-Muller, and Sayette (1991), students who participated in the program in 4th and 5th grade were followed into 11th grade. Compared to a control group, they presented higher prosocial behaviors and academic achievement, and less antisocial and self-destructive behavior 4 to 6 years after the program's completion.

Classroom-Based Curriculum Programs on Violence Prevention

Eight programs provide curriculum materials for students and are designed for preventing antisocial behavior and violence. They consist of a specific number of lessons taught by the teacher to her or his entire regular group of students and can be considered as add-on elements to a teacher's classroom management. The format of two programs (SMART Team and I Can Problem Solve®) also allows for their use with selected individuals or smaller groups of students.

Studies on Aggressors, Victims, and Bystanders (AVB, #02), Get Real About Violence® (GRAV, #10), Violence Prevention Curriculum for Adolescents (VPCA, #40), and SMART Team: Students Managing Anger & Resolution Together (ST, #36) are based on student-reported measures (Table 28.4.2). The intention to use nonviolence strategies and perceived reductions in conflict and aggressions are the main outcomes of these programs.

In the AVB curriculum, the four-step Think-First Model of Conflict Resolution (*Keep cool*, *Size up the situation*, *Think it through*, and *Do the right thing*) provides middle school students a framework for changing the thinking resulting in violent acts. In schools at high risk of violence, AVB showed an increase in intention to resolve conflicts without violence, and a decrease in acceptance and encouragement of aggression (Slaby, Wilson-Brewer, & DeVos, 1994).

GRAV has different curricula for each age group (K–3, 4–6, 6–9, 9–12). In grades K–9, the curriculum focuses on three areas related to violence: vulnerability, contributors, and alternatives. In grades 9–12, four areas are discussed besides violence in general (guns, alcohol, relationships, and groups). After receiving the program, urban middle school students reported that they were less likely to watch a fight and better understood the negative consequences of being involved in a fight (Baseline Research, LLC, 2000).

In the VPCA curriculum, grades 9 and 10 students learn that anger is normal but that there are healthy ways to express it. Through the lessons they discuss violence prevention, fights, and homicide. A pretest–posttest comparison showed significant self-reported decreases in frequency of use of violence (including physical fights) in the previous 30 days (DuRant et al., 1996).

SMART Team is designed around multimedia software requiring less direct teacher involvement. It is possible to offer this program to selected students outside the classroom and provide meetings with a counseling professional when needed. The modules focus on anger management, dispute resolution, and perspective taking. Compared to a control group, students from a large middle school showed greater intention to use nonviolent strategies and reduction in beliefs supporting violence after using the software (Bosworth, Espelage, & Dubay, 1996).

Al's Pals: Kids Making Healthy Choices (AP, #03) is designed to improve prosocial skills and prevent aggressive behavior in pre-K–3 children. Al's Pals' lessons are reinforced throughout the day. The program uses hand puppets to engage the children, and provides scripted puppet-led discussions, guided creative play, songs, color photographs, message pads, and books. Al's Pals emphasizes self-control, healthy decision making, and peaceful problem solving. A multiyear evaluation of the program in a variety of geographic locations showed a reinforcement of socioemotional competence, positive coping skills, and a decrease in antisocial and aggressive behaviors (Lynch, Geller, & Schmidt, 2004).

I Can Problem Solve®(ICPS, #13) trains pre-K–6 children in generating solutions to interpersonal problems. With the use of pictures, role playing, puppets, and group interaction, ICPS teaches children how *to* think rather than determine *what* to think. Children are taught to analyze situations and to consider motives that generate conflicts. The program is especially effective with urban children of 4 and 5 years of age. Immediately following and 1 year after the program ended, nursery and kindergarten children showed less impulsive and inhibited classroom behaviors and better problem–solving skills than a control group. These results were sustained as long as 4 years. Fifth-and sixth-graders who benefited from the program also displayed better prosocial behaviors and problem-solving skills (Shure & Spivack, 1980; 1982).

Promoting Alternative Thinking Strategies (PATHS®, #29) provides a curriculum for K–6 classrooms that addresses five conceptual domains (self-control, emotional understanding, positive self-esteem, relationships, and interpersonal problem-solving skills). It includes a behavior management system that rewards self-control in the classroom, and the teacher holds problem-solving meetings to solve everyday class issues. Studies reported by the Conduct Problems Prevention Research Group (1999) showed that both regular and special need students receiving PATHS® had better understanding of social problems and developed more effective solutions compared to control groups.

Second Step®: A Violence Prevention Curriculum (SS, #33) focuses on four competencies: empathy, impulse control, anger management and problem solving. Emotion management, skills and problem-solving steps are used by teachers and students as tools for resolving classroom interpersonal conflicts. From pre-K to grade 5, the program takes the format of puppets and songs (pre-K and K), classroom videos (1–5), and photo-lesson cards and posters. In middle school, students are provided scripted lessons with overheads, classroom videos, and activity sheets. In a study of six schools, second- and third-grade teachers taught the curriculum. After 6 months, observational data showed a decrease in verbal and physical aggression whereas these behaviors increased in six control schools (Grossman et al., 1997).

Schoolwide Conflict Resolution and Peer Mediation Programs

Eight programs are designed to prevent antisocial behavior or solve violence problems at the school and classroom level. These programs concentrate on restructuring the culture within the school to minimize peer conflicts or include a peer mediation element at the school level. Consequently, they are more likely to produce positive school climate outcomes. All programs described next cover at least the middle school level.

The Norwegian Bullying Prevention Program (BPP, #05) focuses on bullying and operates at three levels: school (establishment of a coordinating committee to create a schoolwide plan against bullying), classroom (development of rules to prevent bullying and regular meetings), and individual (a structure involving parents is established to deal with bullying problems when they occur). The American Federation of Teachers (AFT; 2000) reported studies both in

Norway and in the United States. In Bergen, an evaluation of the program on 3,200 students from grades 5 to 7 showed a 20% to 35% decrease in the tendency to bully others after 6 months of implementation whereas the control group reported an increase of 35%. In South Carolina, a 7-month follow-up on 6,400 middle school students in nonurban settings reported a 25% decrease in bullying whereas the control group showed a corresponding increase.

The Peace Works (PW, #19) curriculum emphasizes six components: community building; rules for fighting fair; understanding conflict; perception and diversity; anger management and other emotions; and effective communication. There are specific curricula from pre-K to high school. In addition, the peer mediation training allows students from grades 4 and above to resolve conflicts through a structured process facilitated by a neutral third party. In elementary schools, an unpublished report showed positive results on teacher-reported decrease in student disruptive, antisocial, and aggressive behaviors (see CASEL, 2003). At the high school level, Barnett, Adler, Easton, and Howard (2001) reported a decrease in referral rates compared to control schools.

PeaceBuilders® (PB, #20) is an inclusive school climate shift program based on a cognitive behavioral framework especially for K–8 students. The curriculum includes six principles: praise people, give up put-downs, seek wise people, notice hurts, right wrongs and help others. Adults reinforce positive behaviors everywhere in the school. For example, "Peace feet" are placed by the drinking fountains to help students not to cut in line when waiting for their turn and students are sent to the principal for kind acts. Flannery et al. (2003) reported an increase in social competence (K–2) and a decrease in aggressive behavior (grades 3–5) in program students compared to the control group. In another study by Krug, Brener, Dahlberg, Ryan, and Powell (1997), the rate of injury–related visits to the nurse decreased by 12.6% with no significant change in the control schools.

Peacemakers (PM, #21) is based on social and developmental psychology research and mainly consists of training students from grades 4 to 8 in anger management, problem-solving, and conflict resolution techniques using a variety of classroom activities. Program principles and strategies are strongly infused in the everyday culture of the classroom and school. PM also includes a remediation component for students with serious aggression-related problems. In their study from a sample of more than 1,500 students, including a control group, Shapiro, Burgoon, Welker, and Clough (2002) reported positive program effects on knowledge of psychosocial skills and low levels of aggressive behaviors and use of mediation services. Notably, results showed a 67% decrease in suspensions for violent behavior.

Peers Making Peace (PMP, #23), research supported from grades 1 to 12, trains a group of selected students to become mediators. They learn skills such as nonverbal communication, questioning, maintaining neutrality, and conflict resolution, and serve as a microcosm of the overall school. PMP offers implementation options to teach conflict resolution skills such as Let's Talk It Out at the elementary level. When a conflict occurs, the teacher asks mediators to work with disputants to solve the conflict, allowing the teacher to continue teaching. An unpublished evaluation report on six PMP high schools was submitted to the three organizations that reviewed this program (see Table 28.1). Results showed that 97.7% of mediations (n = 1305) resulted in agreements. Furthermore, significant decreases were found in assaults (90.2%), discipline referrals (57.7%), and expulsion (73%). In the six corresponding control schools, these percentages increased by 33%, 8.4%, and 6.2%, respectively.

Productive Conflict Resolution Program (PCRP, #27) incorporates several components such as bullying prevention, peaceable classrooms, peer mediation, and positive discipline systems. It offers training for K–12 students, teachers, support staff, and parents. Conflict resolution skills can be learned through the study of a novel during English class for example, enabling teachers and students to link negotiation skills with academic skills. PCRP includes the Peer Mediation Program where, typically, 25 to 30 student mediators are trained to resolve peer conflicts. Mediators meet weekly or biweekly to review skills, debrief cases, and engage in many activities such as role-plays. In studies provided for review (see CASEL, 2003) students from grades 4 to 12 showed reductions in personal conflicts and increased their tendency to help others, especially in the student mediator group. Aggression was reduced in high school students participating in the general curriculum whereas in grades 4–8, aggression was reduced in the student mediator group only.

Responding in Peaceful and Positive Ways (RIPP, #30) is a sociocognitive program for middle schools. A RIPP facilitator receives a 5-day training session, teaches the curriculum to students in their classroom, and supervises the peer mediation program. The program includes behavioral repetition and mental rehearsal of a social–cognitive problem-solving model, experiential learning techniques, and guided discussions. The seven-step problem-solving model is the backbone of the curriculum. Selected peer mediators are in grade 7 or 8. They complete a 16-hour training program and participate in biweekly meetings with the RIPP facilitator. Farrell, Valois, and Meyer (2002) found significant lower approval of violence, peer provocation, and physical aggression after completion of the program within a rural middle school.

Teaching Students to be Peacemakers (TSP, #38) teaches K–12 students how to engage in problem-solving negotiations and mediate peer conflicts. TSP views conflicts as constructive when they give an opportunity to enhance the quality of reasoning and decision making. Students are taught negotiation skills: (a) state wants; (b) describe feelings; (c) give reasons for wants and feelings; (d) reverse perspectives; (e) invent solutions for mutual gains; and (f) reach agreement. Every day, pairs of students are chosen to serve as class or school mediators, but unlike other programs, this responsibility is rotated so that all students serve as mediator an equal amount of time. According to pretest–posttest, control-group designs, TSP students showed greater willingness and ability to use negotiation in conflicts in elementary (Johnson, Johnson, Dudley, & Magnuson, 1995), middle (Johnson, Johnson, Dudley, Mitchell, & Fredrickson, 1997), and high schools (Stevahn, Johnson, Johnson, Green, & Laginski, 1997).

Out-of-Classroom Programs for Small Groups or Individuals

The six programs in this section are not used with the general population. Delivered to small groups or individuals outside the regular classroom, they are designed for children or adolescents who present school adjustment problems or are at risk of presenting behavioral problems in the future. Overall, the programs in this section reported positive results in prosocial skills/social competence, disruptive behavior, anger control, and verbal aggression (see Table 28.4.3).

Primary Project (PP, #26) is for young children from preschool to third grade. The program concentrates on a preemptive strategy that avoids future social and learning problems based on identifying specific student behaviors at lower thresholds. There is a systematic screening to detect early school adjustment difficulties (self-confidence, social and learning skills) in students that have been identified by their teacher, counselor, or support person. Each selected child is provided weekly meetings with a trained paraprofessional in a playroom, with expressive play being the primary activity. The adult supports and reflects on what the child says and does. Teachers reported a decrease in shyness and anxiety, and an increase in peer social skills that placed referred children who benefited from the program within the range of functioning displayed by other children (Nafpaktitis & Perlmutter, 1998).

In PAL® Peer Assistance and Leadership (PAL, #22), students from the general population who are selected to become PALs form a unique class and receive specific training in PAL® ethics, standards, and guidelines, as well as problem solving, modeling leadership, and confidentiality importance. They then help students outside the class who have risk behaviors (PALees). Meetings with teachers or professionals are encouraged when difficult situations arise. The program operates as a class during regular hours at the high school level and as clubs outside school hours at the elementary level. Either classes or clubs are used in middle schools. An unpublished independent study conducted in 1996–1997 was submitted for organization reviews (see Table 28.1). A pretest–posttest design revealed increases in school attendance and amount of praise for good work as well as decreases in suspension, drug use, and incidents involving weapons.

The four other programs focus on intervention. The first three (used in grades 4 to 12) reported decreases in antisocial behavior, lack of anger control, physical aggression, and office discipline referrals (see Table 28.4.3).

The Skillstreaming the Adolescent (STA, #35) curriculum contains 50 skill lessons and six skill groups: beginning social skills, advanced social skills, dealing with feelings, alternatives to aggression, dealing with stress, and planning skills. It is delivered through modeling, role playing, performance feedback, and transfer (homework). Although STA is designed for chronically aggressive adolescents, it is also used at the elementary level with more mature students. Aggression Replacement Training (ART, #01) is an extension of STA. In addition to the 50 skills, ART includes training in anger control (emotional component) and moral reasoning (values component). It is often used for students who are housed in in-school suspension programs or centers, alternative schools, and schools for students who have a high level of aggressive and antisocial behavior. The organizations that reviewed the program (see Table 28.1) indicated a significant increase in prosocial behavior and a decrease in anger-level responses to minor anger-provoking situations.

Positive Adolescent Choices Training (PACT, #25) was developed for the needs of African American youth to reduce risks that they become victims or perpetrators of violence. In groups of up to 10 students, videos demonstrating correct and incorrect ways to deal with situations leading to physical conflicts are presented. Students practice appropriate skills and negotiating in small groups supervised by an adult facilitator. Based on their review, organizations (see Table 28.1) reported a decrease in physical aggression and suspension with seventh-grade students in the program.

Behavioral Monitoring & Reinforcement Program (BMRP, #04) is a 2-year intervention based on behaviorism and designed for seventh-graders who have school adjustment problems such as low motivation and frequent discipline referrals. BMRP increases communication between teachers, paraprofessionals, students, and parents. Participating students are given a Weekly Report Card on school attendance and behavior, and they also receive points for being prepared for group meetings outside the classroom. In these meetings, they discuss their behavior with a paraprofessional and good evaluations lead to a field trip. Parents are regularly informed of their child's progress. BMRP has shown improvements in attendance and grades, and decreases in drug use and suspensions compared to control groups (Bry, 1982; Bry & George, 1980).

DISCUSSION

Limitations

At first glance, the number of times a program has been selected by an organization is a good indicator of its effectiveness. However, this observation has to be interpreted with caution. For example, Sharing for Success reviewed local and national programs developed or implemented in the state of New York. Some organizations directly solicited program developers to review materials, but others did not. Other organizations and researchers reviewed classroom management and discipline programs within a much larger context of school reform and achievement. These reviews were not included in this chapter as they emphasized different outcomes beyond the chapter's scope (e.g., Slavin & Fashola, 1998). More, funding plays a role in reviews of specific programs. Programs funded by federal agencies have a greater chance of being reviewed and disseminated nationally. In several cases, the focus age (moving from pre-K to third grade to all of elementary grades) of the participants is extended and the program is modified but research has not been conducted or finalized for the new grade levels. Programs that did not meet the "widely replicated" criteria of an organization several years ago because of a limited number of sites could meet the criteria in the future. Therefore, if a program is not selected by an organization in Table 28.1 at the time of publishing this chapter, it does not necessarily indicate that the program will not meet an organization's criteria in the future. A final cautionary note is needed. Programs that are highly focused may garner results more readily and in a shorter period than those programs that are more comprehensive. The complexity of discipline issues to be resolved may also be a factor in the frequency that a program is able to achieve significant results.

Themes Across Programs

The programs in the chapter have several commonalities. There are at least three main themes and two subthemes that apply to the majority of the 40 programs.

Moving Beyond Discipline

Discipline in this context is used as both student behavior and punishment. Many of the programs have moved beyond a stimulus–response paradigm to a primarily instructional and person-centered approach (Freiberg, 1999; Good & Brophy, 2003). Most of the programs place an emphasis on students learning and self-control; that is, managing their own emotions and behavior.

School Connectedness

Schoolwide and comprehensive programs create ways that teachers, administrators, and other adults in the school can engage a greater proportion of students in the day-to-day operations of classrooms and schools. This is accomplished through more open and fair opportunities for participation in events and activities, and inclusion in decision making that have direct effects on the learner. Many parents in low-SES communities were not successful in school and are reluctant to participate in their child's schooling. This is also true of parents where English is not their first language. Parental (or caregiver) involvement also becomes an integral and necessary part of school connectedness (Stevens & Sanchez, 1999).

Social–Emotional Emphasis

Most of the programs emphasize the social–emotional part of learning at individual, class, and school levels. They provide philosophies supported by specific strategies to engage the part of the children and youth that seem to be ignored in the press for academics and lost in behemoth secondary schools. Several programs take into account that the support systems common in families and communities in previous generations are often absent today. Caring and trust, and school and classroom climate are integral parts of the social–emotional environment.

Caring and Trust. These two qualities are the foundation for teaching. At one level, teaching hinges on the trust between two people and at another level, between an adult and the class of learners. Teaching is relationship and caring, and the need for connecting learners with each other and the teacher is an essential component to solving the problems experienced by teachers in the classroom. Many of the programs described in the chapter assume a level of trust or, if not present, provide ways to build trust among people. Twenty-eight of the 40 programs have caring as a primary or secondary element. Fifteen programs have caring (e.g., bonding, attachment, warm climate) as a primary component, objective, or activity. Thirteen programs have caring as a secondary component, with positive outcomes in school/classroom climate, sense of school community, and belonging or connectedness (see Tables 28.4.1–3).

Positive School and Classroom Climate. The learning environment plays a central role in those programs that emphasize classroom and instructional management and safe schools. A climate of fear and hostility has shown to be a poor environment for learning. Also, highly negative environments have a greater potential for bullying, disruptive classroom behavior, destruction of school property, and individual and gang violence.

The themes and subthemes that tie the 40 programs together—moving beyond discipline, school connectedness, social–emotional emphasis, trust and caring, and positive school and classroom climate—represent a new chapter in the book of programs that prevent and solve discipline problems. That these programs have the potential to improve the lives of all who work and learn in schools demonstrates that new ways of thinking and practice are viable. However, selecting research-based programs that match the specific needs of those that teach and learn in schools is an important next step.

Selecting Programs for Preventing and Solving Discipline Problems

Two studies, "Youth Violence: A Report of the U.S. Surgeon General" (2001) and "Focus on the Wonder Years: Challenges Facing the American School" (Juvonen, Le, Kaganoff, Augustine & Constant, 2004), highlight the importance of selective factors in the implementation of discipline and violence prevention programs. They emphasize the need for more comprehensive programs that bring together several effective prosocial elements including individual as well as group social skills, parent development, and skills that improve school and classroom climate and engage students, particularly those that tend to be tourists rather than citizens of the school (Freiberg, 1996). The two studies as well as Joyce and Showers' work (2002) also call attention to the importance of highly effective staff development models and the significance of quality implementation and internal and external evaluations. These elements and others are extrapolated further in the following section.

In selecting research-based programs for preventing and solving discipline problems, school decision makers should ask specific questions to the developers in determining what programs if any would be best for the site context. The 40 programs presented in this chapter fit a range of models with some having modularized materials presented during a few days of professional development whereas others are whole-school models with extensive multiyear follow-ups to programs that direct materials to students as part of their curriculum. Many of the programs have studies and evaluations that use comparison groups. However, the population and sample size of the program study may be different than the demographics for a new site considering the program. The following eight factors may be useful to consider in guiding program selection, but not all questions will be relevant to every site situation.

Eight Factors to Consider

1. *What are the problems you are trying to solve and what is the perceived root cause of the problem? Has a need assessment been conducted? How ready is the school for change?* (see Freiberg, 1999; Hoy, Tarter, & Koltkamp, 1991; Fraser, 1999).

2. *Are there opportunities for faculty, staff and administrators to become highly informed and knowledgeable about the program before selection?* This may be accomplished through visits to programs, reviewing research, and taking time to discuss options and share information.
3. *Are there mechanisms in place to acquire commitment and assent from the participants?* This could be achieved with discussions and a secret faculty vote.
4. *Are there external evaluations and research studies of the program's work?* Examine both short-and long-term studies and match the study demographics and findings with your own context.
5. *Do the developers describe the necessary conditions for successful implementation?* Identify sites that did not succeed and identify why. Determine whether the necessary conditions for success are present at the proposed sites.
6. *Is there a detailed professional development model and will materials be provided in advance of a final decision?* Examine participant feedback of workshops, and develop implementation plans with times and dates in advance of staff development.
7. *Has a plan for building continuance and capacity at the site been established before implementation?* Identify sites that have sustained the program for several years and potential areas that could derail long-term success.
8. *Are research, evaluation and data collection procedures articulated for each site?* Develop a data collection and dissemination plan that will improve implementation and inform practice.

The selection process to determine the best fit of a program for a specific school, feeder pattern of schools or district may seem somewhat involved, but many of the programs include a significant commitment of time and resources. Time and energy spent at the start of a project will pay dividends throughout the process.

Conclusions

In a technological world that expects flexibility, independence, and self-discipline, many schools of the 21st century continue to follow management paradigms of the 19th and 20th century that valued compliance and obedience over innovation, creativity, and self-direction. One could argue that these 19th century models served the education system well so why change now? During the 19th century, traveling to Europe took months. Few today would consider this as a viable work-related option. Several programs presented in this chapter represent a shift from these historical paradigms. Classroom management is moving beyond the external controls of reward and punishment to creating an environment of shared responsibility and learning. Most of the programs reflected in this chapter provide the necessary conditions, strategies, and tools to enable students the freedom to learn through everyday classroom experiences without constant disruptions. Freedom, after all, requires responsibility, whereas license has none. Actions do have consequences, particularly those that impede the learning or safety of others.

Changing the Paradigm

Complex learning environments require parallel changes in the roles that students and teachers take in the classroom. Many but not all of the programs in this chapter have emerged from decades of behaviorism to instructional and "person-centered" approaches to classroom management (Rogers & Freiberg, 1994; Good & Brophy, 2003). These approaches, as evident in the review of programs, reflect a shift from intervention to prevention. Why solve a problem if you can prevent it in the first place? The paradigm shift however is more than changing strategies. It is a philosophical change in the way educators think about classroom management. The shift results in different views of the learner and the roles students and teachers engage in the classroom.

When teaching is considered primarily transmission of information (e.g., lecture), classroom management systems facilitate a one-way flow of information where the teacher is directive and the student passive. As teaching and learning becomes more engaging and the learner more active in the educational process, management approaches need to parallel the levels of intellectual activity (Rogers & Freiberg, 1994, in press). From cooperative learning to computer simulations, self-study, and group research projects, the teacher's role becomes more facilitative while the students become more actively engaged in their own learning. The level and types of teacher controls change in this new teaching and learning paradigm. The teacher does not abandon the learner; rather, teacher and students' roles are defined by focusing on the climate and culture of the learning environment. The skills students need also must change. Moving from passive to active learning requires higher levels of self-direction and self-discipline. Self-discipline in the learner derives from the ability to focus when there are distractions and think through the next steps without an adult immediately present to tell the learner what to do next. This change will require an expanded and sometimes different repertoire of skills and expertise for teacher and learner.

Weinstein (1999) described this paradigm shift (a) from management as a "bag of tricks" to management as decision making that necessitates ongoing professional development, expertise in knowledge, practice, and introspection; (b) from an emphasis on obedience and compliance to procedures that advance self-direction; (c) from an emphasis on rules to the social–emotional relationships that include trust and caring; and (d) from management that is teacher-directed work (and sometimes busywork) to an active student-centered learning environment.

We often hear the concern expressed that there is a danger of "too much freedom." Balancing freedom with responsibility and changing how we think about the learner in the place called school will bring about an evolving paradigm. The new paradigm does not abandon all from the past but it does modify school and classroom management to respond to an era that was only pictured in science fiction stories 50 years ago. Moving educators to the level that schools and classrooms are truly trusting, caring, active, safe, and dynamic places to learn will require a paradigm shift in how educators acquire new ideas and knowledge. As Evertson and Harris (1999) stated: "Learning to create conditions for learning is an evolutionary process, one for which teachers need professional development, support and dialog" (p. 73).

POLICY IMPLICATIONS

The 40 chapter programs represent some of the better-documented programs. It is evident, however, that much more is needed in terms of research design, methodology, and external longitudinal studies. Although there are federal and state funds to disseminate violence prevention programs, there are few funding sources to conduct high-quality qualitative (e.g., Pittman, 1985) or quantitative studies on the effectiveness of programs to prevent and solve behavior problems. Some of the reviewed programs have documented the strong effects of classroom management and disruptive behavior on learning and achievement, yet the funding emphasis in most states and the federal government is on content-specific (e.g., math and science) programs. The 14 organizations cited in this review in some instances represent silos of information and may not be well known to the education and research communities outside their specific focal areas. It took the authors of this chapter several weeks to identify the organizations. Additionally, the 14 organizations used a range of differing criteria to establish their rankings of effectiveness necessitating our need to create additional criteria and a follow-up survey of program developers. There is no single source of information regarding discipline management programs, or an agreed upon metric to measure program efficacy. We propose a single clearinghouse combined with continuing reviews that provide schools, districts and others in the research community with ongoing updates and yearly assessments.

Building a future requires more than a bag of tricks or a cafeteria approach to knowledge. The levels of understanding required of youth today to be successful adults and productive and knowledgeable citizens requires schools to have the tools and resources that can help prevent and solve discipline problems. Without these social assets, discipline problems will rob teachers and students of valuable learning time and drive potential teachers from the profession leaving a vacuum that may become filled with more, not fewer, behavior problems.

APPENDIX A

CRITERIA FOR PROGRAM INCLUSION BY THE FOURTEEN ORGANIZATIONS

A) Beginning in 1996, the Center for the Study and Prevention of Violence (CSPV) at University of Colorado, Boulder, launched a nationwide violence prevention initiative to identify prevention and intervention programs that are effective. In this project, named *Blueprints for Violence Prevention*, more than 600 programs regarding violent crime, aggression, delinquency, and substance abuse were evaluated to date (January 2004). This organization conducted the largest review of all the organizations identified for this chapter. Only 11 model programs and 21 promising programs were identified. The CSPV used three major criteria to evaluate programs:

1. Evidence of deterrent effect with a strong research design (experimental design with random assignment or quasi-experimental design with matched control group; large sample sizes; low attrition; and tests to measure outcomes administered accurately and consistently to all participants).
2. Sustained effect at least 1 year beyond treatment.
3. Multiple site replication.

Model programs met all these criteria, whereas promising programs met at least the first criterion but not all three. Most of the promising programs had not gone through multiple site replications by the time the report was published. More details on each of the three criteria can be found at http://www.colorado.edu/cspv/blueprints/model/criteria.html

B) The American Federation of Teachers (AFT) also enlisted the expertise of the CSPV to evaluate school discipline and school-based violence programs. The principal investigator, Jennifer K. Grotpeter, conducted a search and identified 116 programs having the potential of meeting at least the six following criteria:

1. There were at least three quantitative evaluations showing positive outcomes, including data from experimental or quasi-experimental (with control group) studies.
2. Quantitative effects were at statistically significant level on disruptive behavior in school. A preference was given to quantitative evaluation complemented by qualitative evaluation.
3. Evaluations conducted by independent third-party researchers were available.
4. The program has been implemented in multiple sites.
5. Adequate support is available for replication.
6. Sustained effects were found at least 1 year after treatment.

Only 5 of the 116 programs met the six criteria and were labeled as "promising programs" they are described in *Building on the Best, Learning From What Works. Five Promising Discipline and Violence Prevention Programs* (July 2000), available on the AFT Web site (http://www.aft.org).

C) *Communities That Care® Prevention Strategies: A Research Guide to What Works* (Hawkins & Catalano, 2003) provides information on research-based programs and strategies effective in four areas: family, school, community-based youth programs, and community. The 97 effective programs listed in the booklet met the following four criteria:

1. The program addresses research-based risk factors for substance abuse, delinquency, teen pregnancy, school dropout, and violence.
2. The program increases protective factors by (a) strengthening healthy beliefs and clear standards for behavior or (b) building bonds to family, community, school, or positive peers by providing opportunities for meaningful contribution, teaching skills necessary for contributing, and recognizing skillful performance.
3. The program intervenes at a developmentally appropriate age.
4. The program has shown positive effects in high-quality tests. It has demonstrated significant effects on risk and protective factors in controlled studies or research trials based in community settings.

D) The Safe, Disciplined, and Drug-Free Schools Expert Panel, established by the U.S. Department of Education, reviewed 124 programs aimed at preventing or reducing violence, discipline problems, and drug abuse in schools. During the first stage of the process, all programs were submitted to a panel of 19 experts in research and evaluation as well as school violence and drug abuse. Programs were evaluated by two members of the panel based on the following criterion: "evidence of efficacy based on a methodologically sound evaluation." This includes an evaluation indicating a measurable difference in outcomes based on statistical significance testing; a design and analysis that adequately controls for threats to internal validity; reliable and valid outcome measures; and analyses appropriate to the data.

Programs with high scores during the first round were submitted to a second stage of reviewers with expertise in safe, disciplined, and drug-free schools programming. The programs were evaluated on six additional criteria: (1) the program's goals with respect to changing behavior or risk and protective factors are clear and appropriate for the intended population and settings; (2) the rationale underlying the program is clearly stated and the program's content and processes are aligned with its goals; (3) the program's content takes into consideration the characteristics of the intended population and setting, and the needs implied by these characteristics; (4) the program implementation process effectively engages the intended population; (5) the application describes how the program is integrated into schools' educational missions; and (6) the program provides necessary information and guidance for replication in other appropriate settings.

A third panel made a final decision on the exemplary programs. The panel proposed 9 exemplary and 33 promising programs. A description of each program was published in *Exemplary and Promising Safe, Disciplined, and Drug-Free Schools Programs 2001* (http://www.ed.gov/admins/lead/safety/exemplary01/index.html).

E) The Hamilton Fish Institute (http://www.hamfish.org) listed 357 school-based programs designed to prevent or reduce violence (last updated 2001). Twelve were considered "effective" and 11 "noteworthy." The institute researchers conducted a meta-analysis and found the effective group had a somewhat higher effect sizes than noteworthy. Those that did not receive either recognition fell below the effect size range of $E = +.25$.

F) The *Maryland Blueprints Manual* (http://www.marylandblueprints.org) is designed to help community planning groups select youth-focused prevention programs based on these groups' goals. The Maryland Blueprint Committee is made of three experts on substance abuse and delinquency prevention research and evaluation (Denise Gottfredson, Mark Eddy, and Richard Spoth). In 2001 and 2002, the committee spent more than 18 months reviewing existing prevention research and still continues to review programs (Web site last updated May 2003). The following criteria were selected to identify effectiveness:

1. The program had a measurable, statistically significant effect on such outcomes as tobacco, alcohol, or other substance use; crime; or delinquency or antisocial behavior (including conduct problems such as defiance, disrespect, rebelliousness, hitting, stealing, lying, fighting, aggressive acts of hostility, and violating the rights of others). The studies on which these positive findings were based must have been designed in such a way that they could demonstrate that the observed positive outcome was based on the program rather than on some alternative event or process.
2. The program currently has the capacity to offer training and materials to community groups interested in implementation.
3. The program can be implemented at a somewhat larger scale at the county level or subcounty levels.

Programs selected by the Center for the Study and Prevention of Violence (http://www.colorado.edu/cspv/blueprints/index.html), School-Based Crime Prevention (http://www.cpu.sa.gov.au/sa_sbcp.htm), and Safe and Drug Free Schools and Communities (http://www.ed.gov/about/offices/list/osdfs/index.html), were automatically accepted when they have had an immediate effect on the same outcomes (e.g., tobacco, antisocial behavior) targeted by the Maryland Blueprint Committee.

G) The Office of Juvenile Justice and Delinquency Prevention (OJJDP), U.S. Department of Justice, and the Development Services Group, Inc. listed 110 programs related to delinquency prevention (http://www.dsgonline.com). Thirty-seven programs were rated as exemplary, 37 as effective, and 36 as promising (last updated January 2004).

All programs presented in the *Model Programs Database* have been demonstrated to prevent delinquency or reduce or enhance risk/protective factors for delinquency in specific social contexts. Exemplary programs used an experimental design with a randomized sample. Effective programs identified by OJJDP used experimental or quasi-experimental design, and the evidence suggested program effectiveness was not as strong as the exemplary programs. Finally, promising programs used limited research or nonexperimental designs, and evidence required confirmation.

H) Greenberg, Domitrovich, and Bumbarger (1999), from the Prevention Research Center for the Promotion of Human Development at Pennsylvania State University, reviewed over 130 programs related to preventive interventions for reducing the risk or effects of psychopathology in school-age children. Thirty-four programs were described in *Preventing Mental Disorders in School-Aged Children: A Review of the Effectiveness of Prevention Programs*. Fourteen were universal programs, 10 focused on externalizing behaviors, and 10 on internalizing behaviors. Studies related to these programs used either a randomized-trial design or a quasi-experimental design with control group. They had pre- and postfindings and preferably follow-up data to ensure duration and stability of program effects. Behavioral and social characteristics of sample were necessary, and a manual describing the model and procedures to be used in the intervention was required. A copy of the report is available at http://www.prevention.psu.edu/CMHS.html

I) Funded by the U.S. Department of Education's Institute of Education Sciences and Office of Safe and Drug-Free Schools, the Collaborative for Academic, Social, and Emotional

Learning (CASEL) produced *Safe and Sound: An Educational Leader's Guide to Evidence-Based Social and Emotional Learning (SEL) Programs.* Published in March 2003, this guide reviewed 80 multiyear, sequenced SEL programs designed for use in general education classrooms. The guide includes both comprehensive and more narrowly focused programs, such as drug education and violence prevention. A total of 242 programs were examined. The 80 programs included in the initial review used four main criteria:

1. The program is school based and has sequenced lessons intended for a general student population.
2. There are at least eight lessons in one of the program years.
3. There are either lessons for at least two consecutive grades or grade spans, or a structure that promotes lesson reinforcement beyond the first program year.
4. The program is nationally available, and the distributors provided CASEL with curriculum materials for review.

The 22 "select" programs covered the following three areas:

1. Outstanding SEL instruction: The program provides outstanding coverage of five essential SEL skills areas according to Bandura's social learning theory (self-awareness, social awareness, self-management, relationship skills, and responsible decision making).
2. Evidence of effectiveness included (a) pretest and posttest assessments (or randomized group assignment); (b) a control group; and (c) a measurement of changes in student behaviors associated with SEL, academic learning, or measure of health and risk.
3. Outstanding professional development (PD): The program provides PD and support that goes beyond an initial workshop to include on-site observation and coaching.

CASEL created a coding manual for rating 28 elements of each program. A description of the programs and their evaluation is available at http://www.casel.org and the guide can be downloaded at this address as well.

J) The Substance Abuse and Mental Health Services Administration (SAMHSA), an agency of the U.S. Department of Health and Human Services, produced a list of programs on the reduction of substance abuse and other related high-risk behaviors (htpp://www.samhsa.gov, October 30, 2003). SAMHSA's National Registry of Effective Programs (NREP) reviewed 377 programs and out of this number, 55 were rated as model, 42 as effective, and 57 as promising.

Independent reviewers evaluated each program on several methodological criteria varying on the program category. A detailed description of the grid used is provided on SAMHSA's Web site. Generally speaking, summary scores were drawn from two parameters: integrity (scientific rigor of evaluation) and utility (practicality of findings). On a scale of 1.0 to 5.0, a promising program scores 3.33 to 3.99 and an effective program scores 4.0 and above. Programs defined as effective became a model program if their developers agreed to participate in SAMHSA's dissemination efforts and were able to provide supporting materials, training, and technical assistance to others who wish to implement their program. A model program is conceptually sound and internally consistent, has sound research methodology, can provide evidence that results are clearly linked to the program itself rather than extraneous events, and can be generalizable.

K) Reviews from text authors included in *School Crime and Policing* (Turk, 2004). Mihalic and Aultman-Bettridge authored two chapters (11—A *Guide to Effective School-Based*

Prevention Programs: Early Childhood Education and Environmentally Focused Programs and 12—*A Guide to Effective School-Based Prevention Programs: Individually Focused Programs*). They reviewed 382 programs on violence, school safety, and success such as disciplinary problems, truancy, dropout, and academic achievement. Most of these programs are school based.

Exemplary and promising programs include, but are not limited to, those selected as "model" and "promising" by the Center for the Study and Prevention of Violence in *Blueprints for Violence Prevention* (see letter A at the beginning of this appendix). Mihalic and Aultman-Bettridge also added a third list of "favorable" programs that may have "slightly weaker research designs" (Mihalic & Aultman-Bettridge, 2004, p. 207). These programs have experimental or matched control group designs and authors consider that there is "reasonable scientific evidence that behavioral effects are due to the intervention and not result of weak methodological rigor" (Mihalic & Aultman-Bettridge, 2004, p. 207).

L) The Westchester Institute for Human Services Research, Inc. formed the Technical Assistance Center for Sharing Success through New York State Education Department funding. The goal of Sharing Success is to identify and disseminate successful educational programs (http://www.sharingsuccess.org). In 2002, the organization published *Sharing Successful Programs: New York State Educational That Work*, a booklet that presents New York State validated programs and practices as well as out-of-state validated programs active in New York State. The 73 programs presented in the booklet met the following requirements stated in A or B depending on research category:

A. Large-scale, externally reviewed research:
   1. Program research has been published in two or more peer review journals or has been reviewed by an independent review panel.
   2. Program research meets the following requirements: (a) experimental or quasi-experimental control group design implemented; (b) the N per condition > 50 for experimental research or > 100 for quasi-experimental research; (c) multiple outcomes assessed; (d) valid or reliable instruments used; and (e) results are statistically significant and educationally meaningful.
   3. Program may be whole-school model, classroom program, or specific instructional strategy.
   4. Data from multiple years or multiple sites is reported.

B. Validated program research:
   1. The program has been reviewed by New York State Validation Panel or National Validation Panel.
   2. The program met these criteria: (a) experimental or quasi-experimental design implemented (including norm-referenced or time series designs); (b) the N per condition >50; (c) valid or reliable instruments used; and (d) results are statistically significant and educationally meaningful.
   3. The program is operational for more than 2 years.

M) In 2000, the Violence institute of New Jersey selected 38 programs from hundreds of programs reviewed by other organizations in order to assist six school districts in New Jersey on a range of issues from smoking to drug education to classroom management and violence prevention for middle and high schools. The institute had a U.S. Department of Education Grant to create a sourcebook that would bring together programs into one document. They drew upon the expertise of 11 other research review groups to assist in their selection for creating the *Source Book of Drug and Violence Prevention Programs for Children and Adolescents*

Appendix B: Program Contact Information

Programs	*Program Developers (PD), Organizations (Org.) and Contacts*	*Websites*
01. Aggression Replacement Training	PD: Arnold P. Goldstein, Ph.D./contact: Research Press (rp@researchpress.com, 800-519-2707)	www.researchpress.com
02. Aggressors, Victims, and Bystanders	PD: Ronald G. Slaby, Ph.D. (rslaby@edc.org), Renée W.-Simmons, Dr. P.H. & Kimberly Dash, M.P.H./contact: Erica Macheca (emacheca@edc.org)	www.thtm.org/special.htm
03. Al's Pals: Kids Making Healthy Choices	PD: Susan Rose Geller, M.S. (sgeller@wingspanworks.com)/contact: contact@wingspanworks.com	ww.wingspanworks.com
04. Behavioral Monitoring & Reinforcement Prog.	PD: Brenna H. Bry, Ph.D. (bbry@rci.rutgers.edu)	no website
05. Bullying Prevention Program	PD: Dan Olweus, Ph.D. (olweus@psych.uib.no)/contact: Susan Limber, Ph.D. (slimber@clemson.edu)	no website
06. Child Development Project™	PD: Eric Schaps, Ph.D./contact: info@devstu.org, 800-666-7270	www.devstu.org
07. Classroom Organization and Management Prog.	PD: Carolyn Evertson, Ph.D. (carolyn.evertson@vanderbilt.edu) & Alene Harris, Ph.D./contact: info@comp.org	www.comp.org
08. Community of Caring®	PD: Eunice Kennedy Shriver/contact: contact@communityofcaring.org	www.communityofcaring.org
09. Consistency Mgt. & Coop. Discipline®	PD: H. Jerome Freiberg, Ed.D. (hjfreiberg@hotmail.com)	www.consistencymanagement.com
10. Get Real About Violence®	Org: Comprehensive Health Education Foundation/contact: Debbie P. Crawley (Debbiepc@chef.org, info@unitedlearning.com)	www.unitedlearning.com
11. Good Behavior Game	PD: Sheppard Kellam, Ph.D. (skellam@air.org)	www.bpp.jhu.edu/publish/Manuals/gbg.html
12. High/Scope® Perry Preschool Program	PD: David P.Weikart, Ph.D./contact: Gavin Haque (ghaque@highscope.org)	www.highscope.org
13. I Can Problem Solve®	PD: Myrna B. Shure, Ph.D. (mshure@drexel.edu, 215-762-7295)	www.thinkingchild.com
14. The Incredible Years	PD: Carolyn Webster-Stratton, Ph.D./contact: Lisa St.George (888-506-3562)	www.incredibleyears.com
15. Learning for Life	Org.: Learning for Life (972-580-2000)/contact: Peggy Chessnut (PChestnu@LFLmail.org)	www.learning-for-life.org
16. Lions-Quest	Org.: Lions Clubs International (info@lions-quest.org, 800-446-2700)	www.lions-quest.org
17. Morning Program	PD: Joyce M. Bliss, Barbara Rizzieri & Patricia O'Donnell (odonnelp@clarityconnect.com)	www.uvcs.k12.ny.us/MorningProgram
18. Open Circle	PD: Pamela Seigle, M.S./contact: James B. Vetter, Ed.M., Program Director (jvetter@wellesley.edu)	www.open-circle.org
19. Peace Works	Org.: Peace Education Foundation/contact: Chuck Bryant (800-749-8838)	www.peace-ed.org
20. PeaceBuilders®	Org. PeacePartners, Inc. (877-473-2236)/contact: Michelle A. Molina, President (info@peacebuilders.com)	www.peacebuilders.com
21. Peacemakers	PD: Jeremy P. Shapiro, Ph.D. (jeremyshapiro@yahoo.com)/contact: National Educational Service (800-733-6786)	no website

22. PAL® Peer Assistance and Leadership	Org.: Workers Assistance Program, Inc./contact: Mary Sowder, M.A. LCDC (msowder@palusa.org)	www.palusa.org
23. Peers Making Peace	PD: Susan Armoni, Ph.D. (susan.armoni@paxunited.org)	www.paxunited.org
24. Positive Action®	PD: Carol Gerber Allred, Ph.D. (callred@positiveaction.net)/contact: info@positiveaction.net	www.positiveaction.net
25. Positive Adolescent Choices Training	PD: W. Rodney Hammond, Ph.D./contact: Betty R. Yung, Ph.D. (betty.yung@wright.edu), Research Press (rp@researchpress.com)	www.state.sc.us/dmh/schoolbased/pact.htm www.researchpress.com
26. Primary Project	PD: Deborah B. Johnson, current head of program development (djohnson@childreninstitute.net)	www.childrensinstitute.net
27. Productive Conflict Resolution Program	Org.: School Mediation Center (info@schoolmediationcenter.org)	www.schoolmediationcenter.org
28. Project ACHIEVE	PD: Howard M. Knoff, Ph.D. (knoffprojectachieve@earthlink.net)/contact: Sopris West (customerservice@sopriswest.com)	www.stopandthinksocialskills.com www.sopriswest.com
29. Promoting Alternative Thinking Strategies (PATHS®)	PD: Carol A. Kusché, Ph.D. (ckusche@attglobal.net) & Mark T. Greenberg (mxg47@psu.edu)/contact: Channing Bete (custsvcs@channing-bete.com)	www.prevention.psu.edu/PATHS/ www.channing-bete.com
30. Resp. in Peaceful and Positive Ways (RIPP)	PD: Aleta L. Meyers, Ph.D. & Wendy B. Northup, M.A./contact: preventionopportunities@direcway.com	www.has.vcu.edu/RIPP
31. Responsive Classroom®	Org.: Northeast Foundation for Children/contact: Gretchen Bukowick (contactinfo@responsiveclassroom.org)	www.responsiveclassroom.org
32. School-wide Positive Behavior Support	PD: Jeffrey Sprague, Ph.D. (Jsprague56@aol.com, 541-346-3592), Rob Horner, Ph.D., George Sugai, Ph.D., Geoff Colvin, Ph.D. & Anne Todd, M.S.	www.pbis.org
33. Second Step®: A Violence Prev. Curriculum	Org.: Committee for Children (info@cfchildren.org)/contact: Pam Dell Fitzgerald, Ph.D. (pfitzgerald@cfchildren.org)	www.cfchildren.org
34. Skills, Opp., and Recognition (SOAR™)	PD: J. David Hawkins, Ph.D. & Richard F. Catalano, Ph.D./contact: Channing Bete (custsvcs@channing-bete.com)	www.channing-bete.com
35. Skillstreaming the Adolescent	PD: Arnold P. Goldstein, Ph.D./contact: Research Press (rp@researchpress.com, 800-519-2707)	www.researchpress.com
36. SMART Team: Students Managing Anger and Resolution Together	PD: Kris Bosworth, Ph.D. (boswortk@email.arizona.edu)/contact: Brad Oltrogge, Learning Multi-Systems (oltrogge@lmssite.com, 800-362-7323)	www.lmssite.com
37. Social Decision Making & Prob. Solv. Prog.	PD: Maurice Elias, Ph.D. (melias@rci-rutgers.edu)/contact: Linda Bruene (bruene@umdnj.edu)	www2.umdnj.edu/spsweb
38. Teaching Students to be Peacemakers	PD: David W. Johnson, Ed.D. (johns010@umn.edu)	www.co-operation.org
39. The Think Time® Strategy	PD: J. Ron Nelson, Ph.D. (rnelson8@.unl.edu)/contact: Sopris West (customerservice@sopriswest.com)	www.sopriswest.com
40. Violence Prevention Curriculum for Adolescents	PD: Deborah Prothrow-Stith, Ph.D. (dprothro@hsph.harvard.edu)/contact: Erica Macheca (emacheca@edc.org)	www.thtm.org

(http://www.umdnj.edu/vinjweb/publications/sourcebook/about_sourcebook.html). The criteria the Institute used to select the 38 programs (last updated January 2004) include:

1. There has been at least one evaluation with random assignment of subjects (or schools) to treatment and control conditions, or a matched comparison group. Pre–post quasi-experimental designs with matched comparison groups were considered adequate.
2. There is an adequate sample size in treatment conditions given the selected outcome analyses in general. The institute examined whether sample selection methods and sample sizes enabled generalization beyond the particular evaluation sample. In addition, the institute staff examined whether the sample size was adequate for the impact analyses conducted by the evaluators.
3. Outcome measures appear to be reliable and valid. Previously published measures of youth behaviors attitudes or norms were used or the evaluators explicitly cited positive results of psychometric analyses (e.g., Cronbach's alpha $\geq$ 0.70).
4. The sample attrition was minimal ($\geq$20% at 1 year, $\geq$30% at 18-month follow-up or later); not differential between treatment conditions; or attrition-related biases were detected and corrected statistically during impact analyses.
5. The generalizability included diverse geographic settings (urban, suburban, and rural), included ethnic diversity in the study samples, and was replicated and evaluated in at least one additional site.

N) In December 2001, the Department of Health and Human Services, under the direction of the Office of the Surgeon General, produced *Youth Violence. A Report of the Surgeon General* (http://www.surgeongeneral.gov/library/youthviolence). Seven model programs and 20 promising programs were reported. They met the following criteria:

1. Rigorous experimental design (experimental or quasi-experimental).
2. Significant deterrent effects on (a) violence or serious delinquency or (b) any risk factor for violence with a minimum effect size of +.30 or greater.

Furthermore, promising programs had to show either replication with demonstrated effects or sustainability of effects. Model programs met both replication and sustainability criteria.

ACKNOWLEDGMENT

The authors thank Bruce Smith, Henderson State University, for his review of an earlier draft of this chapter.

REFERENCES

American Federation of Teachers. (2000). *Building on the best, learning from what works: Five promising discipline and violence prevention programs*. Washington, DC: Author.

Barnett, R. V., Adler, A., Easton, J. O., & Howard, K. P. (2001). An evaluation of Peace Education Foundation's Conflict Resolution and Peer Mediation Program in a Palm Beach County high school. *School Business Affairs, 5*(7), 29–39.

Baseline Research, LLC (2000). *Get real about violence. Curriculum and final report*. Retrieved February 14, 2004, from http://www.unitedlearning.com

Battistich, V., Schaps, E., & Wilson, N. (2004). Effects of an elementary school intervention on students' "connectedness" to school and social adjustment during middle school. *The Journal of Primary Prevention, 24*(3), 243–262.

Bosworth, K., Espelage, D., & Dubay, T. (1996). Using multimedia to teach conflict-resolution skills to young adolescents. *American Journal of Preventive Medicine, 12*(5), 65–74.

Brantlinger, E. (1993). Adolescent's interpretation of social class influences on schooling. *Journal of Classroom Interaction, 28*(1), 1–12.

Brophy, J. (1999). Perspectives of classroom management: Yesterday, today, and tomorrow. In H. J. Freiberg (Ed.), *Beyond behaviorism* (pp. 44–55). Needham Heights, MA: Allyn & Bacon.

Bry, B. H. (1982). Reducing the incidence of adolescent problems through preventive intervention : One- and five-year follow-up. *American Journal of Community Psychology, 10*, 265–276.

Bry, B. H., & George, F. E. (1982). The preventive effects of early intervention on the attendance and grades of urban adolescents. *Professional Psychology, 11*, 252–260.

Cohen, E. (1994). *Designing groupwork: Strategies for the heterogeneous classroom.* New York: Teachers College Press.

Collaborative for Academic, Social, and Emotional Learning (CASEL). (2003). *Safe and sound. An educational leader's guide to evidence-based social and emotional learning (SEL) programs*. Retrieved February 14, 2004, from http://www.casel.org

Conduct Problems Prevention Research Group. (1999). Initial impact of the Fast Track prevention trial for conduct problems : II. Classroom effects. *Journal of Consulting and Clinical Psychology, 67*, 648–657.

Day, C., & Townsend, A. (2004). Final review of the Consistency Management & Cooperative Discipline® (CMCD®) initiative at Garth Hill College, Bracknell Forest. England: Center for Research on Teacher and School Development, School of Education, University of Nottingham.

Doyle, W. (1986). Classroom organization and management. In M. C. Wittrock (Ed.), *Handbook of research on teaching* (3rd ed., pp. 329–431). New York: Macmillan.

Doyle, W. (1990, April). *Whatever happened to all the research in classroom management?* Paper presented at the national meeting of the American Educational Research Asociation, Boston.

DuRant, R. H., Treiber, F., Getts, A., McCloud, K., Linder, C. W. & Woods, E. R. (1996). Comparison of two violence prevention curricula for middle school adolescents. *American Journal of Preventive Medicine, 12*(5), 91–100.

Educator's Reference Desk℠. Available at: http://www.eduref.org

Eiseman, J. W. (2005). An evaluation of Consistency Management & Cooperative Discipline® (CMCD). University of Massachusetts, Amherst, Mass.

Elias, M., Gara, M., Schuyer, T., Branden-Muller, L., & Sayette, M. (1991). The promotion of social competence: Longitudinal study of a preventive school-based program. *American Journal of Orthopsychiatry, 61*, 409–417.

Elliott, S. N. (1999). *A multi-year evaluation of the Responsive Classroom® approach: Its effectiveness and acceptability in promoting social and academic competence*. Report prepared for Northeast Foundation for Children and Kensington Avenue Elementary School Staff. Retrieved February 14, 2004, from http://www.responsiveclassroom.org

Emmer, E. T., & Aussiker, A. (1990). School and classroom discipline programs: How well do they work? In O. C. Moles (Ed.), *Student discipline strategies: Research and practice*. Albany: State University of New York Press.

Emmer, E. T., Evertson, C. M., & Worsham, M. E. (2003). *Classroom management for secondary teachers* (6th ed.). Boston: Allyn & Bacon.

Emmer, E. T., & Stough, L. M. (2001). Classroom management: A critical part of educational psychology, with implications for teacher education. *Educational Psychologist, 36*(2), 103–112.

Erickson, C. L., Mattaini, M. A., & McGuire, M. S. (2004). Constructing nonviolent cultures in schools: The state of the science. *Children and Schools, 26*(2), 102–116.

Evertson, C. M., & Harris, A. H., (1999). Support for managing learner-centered classrooms. In H. J. Freiberg (Ed.), *Beyond behaviorism* (pp. 59–74). Needham Heights, MA: Allyn & Bacon.

Evertson, C. M., & Smithey, M. W. (2000). Mentoring effects on protégés' classroom practice: An experimental field study. *Journal of Educational Research, 93*(5), 294–304.

Evertson, C. M., Emmer, E. T., & Worsham, M. E. (2003). *Classroom management for elementary teachers* (6th ed.). Boston: Allyn and Bacon.

Evertson, C. M., & Weade, G. (1989). Classroom management and student achievement: Stability and variability in two junior high English classrooms. *Elementary School Journal, 89*(3), 379–393.

Farrell, A. D., Valois, R. E., & Meyer, A. (2002). Evaluation of the RIPP-6 violence prevention program at a rural middle school. *American Journal of Health Education, 33*(3), 167–172.

Federal Interagency Forum on Child and Family Statistics (2005). America's children: Key national indicators of well-being 2005. Retrieved July 20, 2005, from www.Childstats.gov

Flannery, D. J., Liau, A. K., Powell, K. E., Vesterdal, W., Vazsonyi, A. T., Guo, S., Atha, H., & Embry, D. (2003). Initial behavior outcomes for the PeaceBuilders universal school-based violence prevention program. *Developmental Psychology, 39*(2), 292–308.

Flay, B. (2001). Effects of the Positive Action Program on achievement and discipline: Two matched-control comparisons. *Prevention Science, 2*, 71–89.

Fraser, B. J. (1999). Using learning environment assessments to improve classroom and school climates. In Freiberg, H. J. (Ed.). (1999). *School climate, measuring, improving and sustaining healthy learning environments*. London, England: Farmer Press, Taylor and Francis, Inc., pp. 65–83.

Freiberg, H. J. (1996). Creating a Climate for Learning. From Tourist to Citizens in the Classroom. *Educational Leadership, 54*, 32–37.

Freiberg, H. J. (1999). *Beyond behaviorism: Changing the classroom management paradigm*. Needham Heights, MA: Allyn & Bacon.

Freiberg, H. J. & Driscoll, A. (2005). *Universal Teaching Strategies* (4th ed.). Boston: Allyn & Bacon.

Freiberg, H. J., Connell, M. L., & Lorentz, J. (2001). Effects of consistency management on student mathematics achievement in seven chapter 1 elementary schools. *Journal of Education for Students Placed at Risk, 6*(3), 249–270.

Goleman, D. (1995). *Emotional intelligence*. New York: Bantam Books.

Good, T. L., & Brophy, J. E. (2003). *Looking in classrooms* (9th ed.). New York: Pearson Education.

Gottfredson, D., Gottfredson, G. D., & Hybl, L. G. (1993). Managing adolescent behavior: A multi-year, multischool study. *American Educational Research Journal, 30*(1), 179–215.

Greenberg, M. K., Domitrovich, C., & Bumbarger, B. (1999). *Preventing mental disorder in school-aged children: A review of the effectiveness of prevention programs*. Report submitted for the Federal Center for Mental Health Service. Retrieved January 17, 2004, from http://www.prevention.psu.edu/pubs/index.html

Grossman, D. C., Neckerman, H. J., Koepsell, T. D., Liu, P. Y., Asher, K. N., Beland, K., Frey, K., & Rivara, F. P. (1997). Effectiveness of a violence prevention curriculum among children in elementary school: A randomized controlled trial. *Journal of the American Medical Association, 277*, 1605–1611.

Hawkins, J. D., & Catalano, R. F. (2003). *Communities That Care®. Prevention strategies: A research guide to what works*. South Deerfield, MA: Channing Bete.

Hoy, W. K., Tarter, C. J., & Kottkamp, R. B. (1991). Open school, healthy school: Making schools work, Newberry Park, CA: Corwin Press.

Ingersoll, R. (2001). Teacher turnover and teacher shortages: An organizational analysis. *American Education Research Journal, 38*(3), 499–534.

Johnson, D. W., Johnson, R., Dudley, B., & Magnuson, D. (1995). Training of elementary school students to manage conflict. *Journal of Social Psychology, 135*(6), 673–686.

Johnson, D. W., Johnson, R., Dudley, B., Mitchell, J., & Fredrickson, J. (1997). The impact of conflict resolution training on middle school students. *Journal of Social Psychology, 137*(1), 11–22.

Joyce, B., & Showers, B., (2002). *Student achievement through staff development* (3rd ed.). Alexandria, VA: Association for Supervision and Curriculum Development.

Juvonen, J., Le, V., Kaganoff, T., Augustine, C., & Constant, L. (2004). *Focus on the wonder years, challenges facing the American middle school*. Santa Monica: RAND Corporation.

Kaufman, P., Xianglei, C., Choy, S. P., Chandler, K. A., Chapman, C. D., Rand, M. R., & Ringel, C. (1998). *Indicators of school crime and safety, 1998*. Office of Educational Research and Improvement and National Center for Education Statistics. Washington D. C.

Kellam, S. G., Rebok, G. W., Ialongo, N., & Mayer, L. S. (1994). The course and malleability of aggressive behavior from early first grade into middle school: Results of a developemental epidemiologically-based preventive trial. *Journal of Child Psychology and Psychiatry, 25*(2), 259–281.

Knoff, H. M., & Batsche, G. M. (1995). Project ACHIEVE: Analyzing a school reform process for at-risk and underachieving students. *School Psychology Review, 28*(4), 579–603.

Kohn, A. (1996). *Beyond discipline: from compliance to community*, Introduction, (p. xii). Alexandria, VA: Association for Supervision and Curriculum Development.

Kounin, J. S. (1970). *Discipline and group management in classrooms*. New York: Holt, Reinhart & Winston.

Krug, E. G., Brener, N. D., Dahlberg, L. L., Ryan, G. W., & Powell, K. E. (1997). The impact of an elementary school-based violence program on visits to the school nurse. *American Journal of Preventive Medicine, 13*, 459–463.

Lapointe, J. M. (2003). Teacher-student conflict and misbehavior: Toward a model of the extended symmetrical escalation. *Journal of Classroom Interaction, 38*(2), 11–19.

Lapointe, J. M., & Legault, F. (2004). Solving group discipline problems without coercion: An approach based on attribution retraining. *Journal of Classroom Interaction, 39*(1), 1–10.

Lynch, K. B., Geller, S. R., & Schmidt, M. G. (2004). Multi-year evaluation of the effectiveness of a resilience-based prevention program for young children. *Journal of Primary Prevention, 24*(3), 335–353.

McCaslin, M., & Good, T. (1992). Compliant cognition: The misalliance of management and instructional goals in current school reform. *Educational Researcher, 40*(3), 41–50.

McNeely, C. A., Nonnemaker, J. M., & Blum, R. W. (2002). Promoting school connectedness: Evidence from the National Longitudinal Study of Adolescent Health. *Journal of School Health, 72*(4), 138–146.

Metzler, C. W., Biglan, A., Rusby, J. C., & Sprague, J. R. (2001). Evaluation of a comprehensive behavior management program to improve school-wide positive behavior support. *Education and Treatment of Children, 24*(4), 448–470.

Mihalic, S., & Aultman-Bettridge, T. (2004). A guide to effective school-based prevention programs: Early childhood education and environmentally focused programs. In W. L. Turk (Ed.), *School crime and policing* (pp. 202–229). Upper Saddle River, NJ: Pearson/Prentice Hall.

Nafpaktitis, N., & Perlmutter, B. F. (1998). School-based early mental health intervention with at-risk students. *School Psychology Review, 27*, 420–432.

Nelson, J. R., Martella, R., & Galand, B. (1998). The effects of teaching school expectations and establishing consistent consequences on formal office disciplinary actions. *Journal of Emotional and Behavioral Disorders, 6*, 153–161.

Norris, J. A. (2003). Looking at classroom management through a social and emotional lens. *Theory Into Practice, 42*(4), 313–318.

O'Donnell, J. A., Hawkins, J. D., Catalano, R. F., Abbott, R. D., & Day, L. E. (1995). Preventing school failure, drug use, and delinquency among low-income children: Long-term prevention in elementary schools. *American Journal of Orthopsychiatry, 65*(1), 87–100.

Office of the Surgeon General. (2001). *Youth Violence: A Report of the Surgeon General.* Retrieved March 5, 2004, from http://www.surgeongeneral.gov/library/youthviolence/toc.html

Opuni, K. A. (2002 and 2003). *Project grad evaluations.* Houston, TX: Center for School Reform.

Patterson, G. (1982). Performance models of antisocial boys. *American Psychologist, 41*, 432–444.

Patterson, N. C., Roehrig, G. H., & Luff, J. A., (2003). Running the treadmill: Explorations of beginning high school science teacher turnover in Arizona. *High School Journal, 86*(4), 14–22.

Pittman, S. I. (1985). A cognitive ethnography and quantification of a firstgrade teachers' selection routines for classroom management. *Elementary School Journal, 85*, 541–557.

Reid, M. J., Webster-Stratton, C., & Hammond, M. (2003). Follow-up of children who received The Incredible Years intervention for oppositional-defiant disorder: Maintenance and prediction of 2-year outcomes. *Behavior Therapy, 34*(4), 471–491.

Resnick, M. D., Bearman, P. S., Blum, R. W., Bauman, K. E., Harris, K. M., Jones, J., et al. (1997). Protecting adolescents from harm: Findings from the National Longitudinal Study on Adolescent Health. *Journal of the American Medical Association, 278*, 823–832.

Rimm-Kaufman, S. E., & Sawyer, B. E. (2004). Primary-grade teachers' self-efficacy beliefs, attitudes toward teaching, and discipline and teaching practice priorities in relation to the Responsive Classroom approach. *The Elementary School Journal, 104*(4), 321–341.

Rogers, C., & Freiberg, H. J. (1994). *Freedom to Learn* (3rd ed.). Columbus, OH: Merrill.

Rogers, C., & Freiberg, H. J. (in press). *Freedom to Learn* (4th ed.). Columbus, OH: Merrill.

Rose, L. C., & Gallup, A. M. (2004). The 36th annual Phi Delta Kappan/Gallup poll of the public's attitude toward the public schools. *Phi Delta Kappan, 86*(1), 41–52.

Schweinhart, L. J., Barnes, H. V., & Weikart, D. P. (1993). Significant benefits: The High/Scope Perry Preschool study through age 27. *High/Scope Educational Research Foundation Monographs* (Serial No. 10). Ypsilanti, MI: High Scope Press.

Shapiro, J. P., Burgoon, J. D., Welker, C. J., & Clough, J. B. (2002). Evaluation of the Peacemakers Program: School-based violence prevention for students in grades four through eight. *Psychology in the Schools, 39*(1), 87–100.

Sharing Success Technical Assistance Center. (2002). *Sharing successful programs, New York State. Education programs that Work.* Retrieved February 14, 2004, from http://www.sharingsuccess.org

Sharan, S. (1993). *Handbook on cooperative learning methods.* Westport, CT: Greenwood.

Shure, M. B., & Spivack, G. (1980). Interpersonal problem solving as a mediator of behavioral adjustment in preschool and kindergarten children. *Journal of Applied Developmental Psychology, 1*, 29–44.

Shure, M. B., & Spivack, G. (1982). Interpersonal problem solving in young children: A cognitive approach to prevention. *American Journal of Community Psychology, 10*(3), 341–355.

Slaby, R. G., Wilson-Brewer, K. D., & DeVos, E. (1994). *Aggressors, victims, and bystanders: An assessment-based middle school violence prevention curriculum.* Education Development Center. Unpublished study.

Slavin, R. E. (1983). *Cooperative learning.* New York: Longman.

Slavin, R. E., & Fashola, O. S. (1998). *Show me the evidence!: Proven and promising programs forAmerica's schools.* Thousand Oaks, CA: Sage.

Snyder, H. N. (2004). *Juvenile arrests 2002.* Retrieved November 4, 2004, from Office of Juvenile Justice and Delinquency Prevention Web site: http://ojjdp.ncjrs.org/publications/index.html

Snyder, H. N., & Sickmund, M. (1999). *Juvenile offenders and victims: 1999 national report* (NCJ 178257). Washington, DC: U.S. Department of Justice, Office of Justice Programs, Office of Juvenile Justice and Delinquency Prevention.

Stevahn, L., Johnson, D. W., Johnson, R. T., Green, K., & Laginski, A. M. (1997). Effects on high school students of conflict resolution training integrated into English literature. *Journal of Social Psychology, 137*(3), 302–315.

Stevens, C. J., & Sanchez, K. S., (1999) Perceptions of parents and community members as a measure of climate. In H. J. Freiberg (Ed.), *School climate: measuring, improving and sustaining healthy learning environments* (pp. 124–147). London, Falmer Press.

Straton, J. (1995). *How student have changed: A call to action for our children's future*. Alexandra, VA: American Association of School Administrators.

Taylor, C. A., Liang, B., Tracy, A. J., Williams, L. M., & Seigle, P. (2002). Gender differences in middle school adjustment, physical fighting, and social skills: Evaluation of a social competency program. *The Journal of Primary Prevention, 23*(2), 259–272.

Turk, W. L. (Ed.). (2004). *School crime and policing*. Upper Saddle River, NJ: Pearson/Prentice Hall.

Wang, M. C., Haertel, G. D., & Walberg, H. J. (1993). Toward a knowledge base for school learning. *Review of Educational Research, 63*, 249–294.

Watts, I. E., & Erevelles, N., (2004). These deadly times: Reconceptualizing school violence by using critical race theory and disability studies. *American Educational Research Journal, 41*(2) 271–299.

Weade, G., & Evertson, C. M. (1988). The construction of lessons in effective and less effective classrooms. *Teaching and Teacher Education, 4*(3), 1–18.

Weinstein, C. S., (1996). *Secondary classroom management: Lessons from research and practice*. New York: McGraw-Hill.

Weinstein, C. S. (1999). Reflections on best practices and promising programs: Beyond assertive classroom discipline. In H. J. Freiberg (Ed.), *Beyond behaviorism* (pp. 147–163). Needham Heights, MA: Allyn & Bacon.

Weinstein, C. S., & Mignano, A. J., Jr. (1993). *Elementary classroom management: lessons from research and practice*. New York: McGraw-Hill.

29

Helping Individual Students with Problem Behavior

Sheri L. Robinson
Sarah M. Ricord Griesemer
The University of Texas–Austin

INTRODUCTION

The purpose of this chapter is to provide information and suggestions for teachers dealing with chronic, disruptive behaviors of one or a few typical students that persist after the teacher has used normal intervention methods. Thus, we presuppose that the problem behaviors are not the result of poor classroom management skills or a deficient classroom management plan. Specifically, we assume that the teacher has (a) explicitly expressed reasonable expectations for student behavior, (b) established routines to manage classroom activities and transitions, (c) monitors student behavior, (d) uses appropriate and generally positive affect when working with students, and (e) has adequate skills to handle inappropriate behavior.

Although the intervention and assessment procedures discussed in this chapter were originally derived using applied behavior analysis techniques in special education settings, they are equally appropriate for less severe behavior problems with typical children. Likewise, most of the work in this area has been conducted by school psychologists and special educators serving in a consulting role to teachers experiencing persistent difficulty with a particular child or behavior. However, with the integration of students with disabilities into general education classrooms through inclusion and least-restrictive environment mandates, general education teachers are exposed to a much wider range of student behavior resulting in a greater need for individualized behavior management plans. The interventions described in this chapter have been implemented and empirically validated in general education settings by general education teachers following training by a consultant.

The chapter begins with a discussion of the nature of problem behavior in classrooms, its definition, and the limitations of using punitive approaches to handle it. The next section focuses on prevention and early-intervention models, which are considered the best approach for positive short and long-term outcomes. The chapter concludes with a more detailed description of a variety of assessment practices and interventions shown to be effective in decreasing problem behavior of individuals in the general education classroom.

DEFINING PROBLEM BEHAVIOR

Problem behavior is a broad term that may include any number of behaviors that do not conform to the established rules of the classroom and school. Evaluating problem classroom behavior is difficult because of the subjective nature of identifying typical child behavior versus problem behavior. Whether a behavior is identified as problematic depends on the rater's degree of tolerance as well as the actual behavior (Book & Skeen, 1987). In other words, what one teacher identifies as disruptive behavior may be acceptable or at least tolerated as a minor problem by a different teacher.

One strategy to help with objectivity is to observe and record the behavior of an average student and the target student simultaneously. This controls for differences in teacher expectations and potential bias against the target student and provides a classroom "norm"; however, it does not give an indication of what behaviors and frequencies are typical beyond the classroom. Local norms can be established by collecting from multiple classrooms and schools within a district observation data that provide a measure of typical behavior for that particular location. For example, in a study of local norms, Book and Skeen (1987) compared 81 students referred for disruptive behavior to 81 students never referred for behavior problems in grades kindergarten through 5 in a Utah suburb. Behaviors were coded as one of four general categories: off-task, out of seat, inappropriate talking, and other (e.g., aggression, profanity, destruction of materials). The referred sample was found to engage in all four categories significantly more than the nonreferred sample across all grades. The average number of disruptive behaviors observed per child during 45-minute observation periods for referred and nonreferred groups, respectively, was (a) 5.11 and 0.78 off-task behaviors; (b) 72.84 and 10 instances of inappropriate talking; (c) 4.88 and 1.44 out-of-seat behaviors, and (d) 2.55 and 0.23 "other" behaviors. Although local norms vary, results from studies such as this provide a general marker for typical and problem rates of disruptive behavior.

In the general education setting, behaviors frequently cited by teachers as problematic are high-frequency, low-intensity disruptive behaviors such as off-task behavior, out-of-seat behavior, inappropriate vocalizations (e.g., making noises, talking out of turn), touching or disturbing others, playing with objects, and noncompliance (Book & Skeen, 1987; Broussard & Northup, 1995; Skiba, Peterson, & Williams, 1997). Aggression and bullying are additional problem behaviors identified by teachers but are more likely to occur in the absence of adults and at lower frequencies. Problem behaviors are operationally defined in a case-by-case manner based on referrals by teachers. For example, Broussard and Northup (1997) defined disruptive behavior as inappropriate vocalizations, out-of-seat behavior, and playing with objects. VanDerHeyden, Witt, and Gatti (2001), on the other hand, defined disruptive behaviors of preschool children in more specific terms including talking in louder-than-conversational volume, crying, hitting, biting, and removing clothing. These examples demonstrate the wide range of behaviors that are considered disruptive depending on the classroom context as well as the varying child populations.

The primary reasons for discipline referrals in public schools are noncompliance, classroom disruption, and taking away from instructional time (De Martini-Scully, Bray & Kehle, 2000; Skiba et al., 1997). Students whose behavior negatively affects their learning and overall routine of the classroom are consistently reported as one of teachers' and parents' most serious concerns (Bear, 1998; Rose & Gallup, 2003). As referrals are made primarily by teachers, students who are disruptive in class are most at risk for disciplinary referrals. A study of urban midwestern public middle schools found that 41.1% of students had at least one referral during the school year for behaviors such as noncompliance and disrespectful behavior (Skiba et al., 1997).

"Zero tolerance" approaches to discipline over the last several years have led to increased reliance on traditional discipline procedures such as suspension and detention. In a descriptive study of punishment procedures for schoolchildren, traditional punishment procedures (e.g., suspension, detention) were not effective in reducing or preventing undesirable behaviors (McFadden, Marsh, Price, & Huang, 1992). Of those receiving punishment, 75% engaged in one to five future offenses and 25% engaged in more than five future infractions. Because this was not an experimental study, one cannot conclude that traditional methods are worse than other methods, but it does provide support for investigating alternative methods to handling inappropriate behavior.

Referrals for behavior problems often fail to stop classroom disruptions and instead often worsen problem behaviors creating what Patterson and Reid (1970) called a "coercive cycle." The coercive cycle occurs when the child behaves disruptively to gain something or to avoid something aversive. The teacher eventually withdrawals the request and the child discontinues the disruptive behavior. Thus, both parties are negatively reinforced, which perpetuates the cycle. For example, a teacher's request that a student complete a math worksheet is responded to with arguing from the child. If the teacher withdrawals the request (e.g., gives in, time-out, office referral), the arguing stops (negative reinforcement for the teacher) and the child has avoided the task (negative reinforcement for the child). Both are more likely to respond this way in similar situations in the future.

Several researchers have conducted studies that support this theory. Nelson and Roberts (2000) developed a 3-year study based on the coercive cycle theory. The sequence of teacher–student interactions of 99 disruptive target students was compared to 278 nondisruptive students. Findings revealed teachers interacted more negatively (issuing more commands and reprimands) with target students than criterion students following incidents of disruptive behavior. Walker, Hops, and Fiegenbaum (1976) reported a ratio of 45 negative interactions to every 3 positive interactions between teacher and student per hour. Walker and Buckley (1973) found that teachers were more likely to interact with students who displayed inappropriate behavior than students who engaged in appropriate behavior. Eighty-nine percent of teacher attention to target children was directed at inappropriate behavior compared to 18% for nontarget children. These numbers might be expected because by definition nondisruptive children do not engage in high rates of inappropriate behavior. However, when frequencies of teacher attention were examined, teachers attended to target children (for both positive and negative behavior) on average 19 times compared to an average of 5 interactions with nontarget children. In other words, teachers attended to the negative behavior more frequently than appropriate behavior. This is significant because teacher attention (even in the form of reprimands) has been shown to reinforce both positive and negative behaviors. Examples such as these provide evidence that alternatives to traditional and punitive discipline techniques are needed to address problem behaviors by individuals in the classroom.

DISRUPTIVE BEHAVIOR AND LONG-TERM OUTCOMES

There is a well-established trend of poor academic performance for children who engage in disruptive behavior in school (e.g., Tremblay, Pihl, Vitaro, & Dobkin, 1994). Disruptive behaviors typically result in a change in focus from academics to discipline (De Martini-Scully et al., 2000), negatively affect achievement (Shinn, Ramsey, Walker, Stieber, & O' Neill, 1987), and are associated with future delinquency (Masse & Tremblay, 1999). Children in preschool and kindergarten exhibiting disruptive behavior, hyperactivity, or impulsivity are at risk for academic failure and early withdrawal from school above and beyond that of their nondisruptive peers (Barkley, Shelton, Crosswait, & Moorehouse, 2000; Tremblay et al., 1994).

Janosz, LeBlanc, Boulerice, and Tremblay (1997) found that a child's school experience is pivotal in the decision to stay in school or not. Withdrawal from school has been linked specifically to disciplinary actions even after controlling for familial and socioeconomic factors (Skiba et al., 1997). Although the connection between disruptive behavior and negative educational outcomes is established, it should be noted that the link may be mediated by placement in non-age-appropriate classrooms as a result of disruptive behavior (Cairns, Cairns, & Neckerman, 1989; Ensminger Lamkin, & Jacobson, 1996; Rumberger, 1995; Vitaro, Brendgen, & Tremblay, 1999).

Disruptive behavior also is strongly linked to adolescent and adult criminality. Those displaying signs of impulsivity or aggression in childhood are at even greater risk for later delinquency (Moffitt, 1990; Tremblay et al., 1994). However, there are sex differences and the relationship between disruptive behavior of female students and later juvenile delinquency is unclear (Broidy et al., 2003; Tremblay et al., 1992).

In addition to poor school performance, early disruptive behavior tends to be stable over time and associated with negative short- and long-term social and emotional outcomes (Tremblay et al., 1994). Many students exhibiting disruptive behavior face peer rejection, as well as rejection by adults in the school (Vitaro, Brendgen, & Tremblay, 2001).

PREVENTION AND EARLY INTERVENTION

Disruptive behavior has been found to be a better selection criterion for intervention than low socioeconomic status, ethnicity, single parenthood, and family risk factors. Disruptive kindergarten boys have been shown to be at greater risk for future antisocial behavior (ages 10–15) than their nondisruptive peers (Tremblay, Pagani-Kurtz, Masse, Vitaro, & Pihl, 1995). Barkley and colleagues (2000) found that disruptive behavior among preschool children resulted in greater risk for antisocial behavior by the end of the kindergarten year.

Although early problem behaviors may indicate forthcoming detrimental academic, social, and psychological outcomes, early intervention has been shown to effectively decrease problem behaviors. The Good Behavior Game (Barrish, Saunders, & Wolfe, 1969) is one example of an intervention that has been shown to be successful in reducing the disruptive behavior of young children. The Good Behavior Game is a group-based, behavior management program that promotes prosocial behavior and is characterized by (a) explicit classroom rules; (b) clear definitions of appropriate and inappropriate behavior; (c) systematic rewards for appropriate behavior, thus emphasizing positive rather than negative behavior; (d) public posting of a scoreboard; and (e) facilitation of interactions between disruptive and nondisruptive children through a team-based approach. Peer pressure, peer competition, and peer recognition are three aspects of the intervention associated with its effectiveness. For example, the Good Behavior Game was implemented for 2 consecutive years with first-grade children in order to evaluate its effects on future delinquent behaviors (Kellam, Rebok, Ialongo, & Mayer, 1994). The class was divided into three teams. Teams could win the game by keeping the total number of inappropriate behaviors of the group below the set criterion of four disruptions. Any one or all of the teams could win privileges (e.g., extra recess, free time, stickers). Students participating in the intervention received no maintenance treatment. Results showed that the most aggressive children in first grade showed significant improvements in their behavior through middle school. In another example of early intervention, Canadian kindergarten teachers were asked to rate the behavior of their male students (Tremblay et al., 1995). Boys identified as disruptive ($n = 319$) were divided into treatment ($n = 96$) and control groups. These groups were compared with one another and to a random sample of kindergarten boys. Treatment was implemented for 2 years (ages 7–9) and consisted of home-based parent training and school-based social skills training. Parent-training procedures were based on Patterson's (1982) Oregon Social Learning Center Model. Parents were taught to monitor their children's behavior, reinforce prosocial behavior, use discipline more effectively, manage family crises, and use their skills across situations. The average number of parent-training sessions required during treatment was 17.

Social skills training was conducted during lunchtime in small groups that also included children identified as prosocial by their teachers. Nine to 10 sessions were provided with a focus on improving problem solving and conflict resolution skills. Results indicated that significantly more boys from the treatment group were in age-appropriate classrooms at the end of elementary school and engaged in significantly fewer delinquent behaviors between the ages of 10 and 15, compared to controls. Although prevention is considered ideal, it is not always possible. The following section describes a model that integrates prevention with increasingly individualized and complex interventions.

MULTILEVEL, INTEGRATED PREVENTION AND INTERVENTION MODEL

Prevention and intervention strategies for problem behaviors should be multilevel, to reflect the problem' varying degrees of complexity and seriousness. Walker et al. (1996) described a three-tiered model of schoolwide discipline designed to prevent problem behaviors and to target students at risk for problem behaviors. The first level is primary prevention, which encompasses schoolwide strategies intended for all students to create a positive learning environment and to reduce the overall incidence of problem behavior. Examples of primary prevention include teaching conflict resolution, providing an interesting curriculum, and teaching rules and expectations. The second level, secondary prevention, is intended for students who do not respond to universal interventions and therefore require individualized interventions. The final level, tertiary prevention, is intended for students displaying severe, stable patterns of problem behavior that have not responded to other strategies. Interventions at this level require a collaborative, intensive wraparound intervention. The wraparound approach is a team-driven process involving the family, child, natural supports, agencies, and community services working together to develop, implement, and evaluate the individualized plan. Problem behaviors and interventions described in this chapter are categorized primarily as secondary prevention. For the model to be effective, however, all three levels must be consistently used and supported by school personnel. In a well-executed and integrated program, it is estimated that 75% to 85% of students problems can be solved at the primary prevention level. The majority of the remaining problems can be alleviated by individual interventions, with only a very small number of students requiring tertiary strategies. The goal of the model is to reduce the number of students requiring high-cost, time-intensive interventions. The following section elaborates on techniques and interventions that have been successful in reducing disruptive behavior at the primary and secondary prevention levels.

FUNCTIONAL BEHAVIORAL ASSESSMENT

Functional behavioral assessment (FBA) is designed to gather information about causal relationships between environmental factors and target behaviors. It uses a range of methods, including rating scales, interviews, and observations to gather information about the reasons a student engages in problem behavior. The analytic component of FBA, called functional analysis, is used to test hypotheses regarding the function of problem behavior. Functional analysis requires the manipulation of environmental events or factors hypothesized to cause the problem (Cone, 1997). Thus functional behavioral assessment is the process of gathering information about causal relationships and functional analysis is the experimental testing of hypotheses based on information derived from the other components of functional assessment.

Functional analysis was originally used with developmentally disabled populations for severe behaviors problems such as self-injurious behaviors (Vollmer & Northup, 1996). Functional analysis has been well established as a best practice in the field of developmental disabilities and more recently has been used successfully with typically developing children who engage in high-frequency, low-intensity behaviors, such as talking out of turn, getting out their seat, and making annoying noises (e.g., Broussard & Northup, 1997; Lewis & Sugai, 1996; Storey, Lawry, Ashworth, Danko, & Strain, 1994).

Renewed interest in functional behavioral assessment procedures is due to an increase in support for evidence-based interventions and more research demonstrating the efficacy of functional behavioral assessment with diverse populations, behaviors, and settings (Cone, 1997). Additionally, special education policy mandates that educators use functional behavioral assessment and positive behavioral supports to develop, review, or revise an intervention plan (Gresham, 2003). Cone (1997) identified three phases of functional assessment: (a) information gathering, (b) hypothesis formulation, and (c) hypothesis testing. Information gathering involves direct and indirect data collection including rating scales (self, teachers, peers), interviews, and direct observation. In the second phase, hypotheses regarding causal relationships between the target behavior and contextual variables are developed. In the final stage, the hypotheses developed are tested either formally (e.g., functional analysis, data collection) or informally (e.g., ignore and see how student responds). According to Cone (1997) there are two primary approaches to assessment and classification: syndromal classification and functional behavioral assessment. Syndromal classification is characterized by the use of measures (e.g., rating scales) and assessment practices (e.g., structured interviews) designed to identify the presence or absence of a disorder (e.g., ADHD). One approach is not superior to the other. Rather, each serves a unique function. Functional behavioral assessment is considered most useful when the purpose is to link assessment to intervention. Syndromal classification is useful for describing differences among groups of people, but typically it is not sensitive enough to inform intervention. Cone (1997) stated that in order for functional strategies to have their greatest impact, there would need to be a shift away from diagnosing disorders based on similar behaviors (e.g., sad, cries often, socially withdrawn) and instead focus on classifying functions of behaviors (e.g., escape, attention). This is because a particular behavior can serve multiple functions and, conversely, the same function (e.g., attention) can control multiple behaviors. Problem behaviors are idiosyncratic. Although topographically they appear similar, behaviors may occur and continue for different reasons (Vollmer & Northup, 1996). For example, children may engage in aggression for a number of different reasons. Knowing that a child is diagnosed as conduct disordered does little to help identify an effective treatment. Regardless of the diagnosis or cognitive ability, children engage in various behaviors for individual reasons. One child may engage in hitting to avoid a social activity whereas another may hit in order to obtain a toy.

Understanding why a behavior occurs makes it possible to design an intervention that will provide the same outcome (e.g., escape) but in an appropriate way. Four categories of functions of problem behavior have been identified among special education populations: social attention, escape or avoidance of tasks or demands, sensory reinforcement, and access to tangible items or events (Doggett, Edwards, Moore, Tingstrom, & Wilczynski, 2001). With typically developing children, teacher attention, peer attention, escape from instructional tasks, or some combination of these have been found to maintain disruptive behavior most frequently (Volmer & Northup, 1996).

Mayer (1995) reported that functional assessment was useful in helping teachers more accurately select behavior management procedures that address the function of the problem reducing the likelihood of inadvertently reinforcing problem behaviors (e.g., removing a child for disruptive behavior who is reinforced by avoiding or escaping a difficult or unpleasant assignment). In reports by teachers that prereferral and other classroom interventions are oftentimes ineffective, one limitation noted is the arbitrary selection of intervention strategies. Vollmer and Northup (1996) identified several problems associated with selecting interventions without taking into account behavioral function: (a) The problem behavior may inadvertently be positively or negatively reinforced (e.g., reprimanding a child whose behavior is maintained by teacher attention or putting a child in time-out whose behavior is maintained by escape from aversive tasks); (b) the intervention may be irrelevant to the maintaining function (e.g., the teacher provides praise for appropriate behavior when behavior is maintained by peer attention); and (c) the intervention may not provide other opportunities for reinforcement of desired behaviors (e.g., detention and suspension are not often arranged to provide opportunities for students to complete assignments).

Conditional Probabilities

Another method used to identify functional relationships is the calculation of conditional probabilities. Conditional probabilities are calculated to determine the probability of an event occurring before or after the target problem behavior (VanDerHeyden, et al., 2001). Observation data provide a descriptive analysis of conditions occurring before (antecedents) and after (consequences) a target behavior. When antecedent or consequent events are highly correlated with the occurrence of a behavior, it is hypothesized that these events are functionally related to the behavior. Conditional probabilities are calculated by dividing the total of each antecedent (e.g., teacher request, seatwork) by the total number of occurrences of disruptive behavior, and each consequent category (e.g., attention, tangible reinforcer) by the total interval occurrence of disruptive behavior to get the two proportions of events occurring before and after disruptive behaviors. The identified events are then validated through intervention using an experimental design (e.g., ABAB reversal design). For example, Sarah frequently gets out of her chair and walks around the room. Observation data reveal that the most prevalent subsequent event was teacher attention (e.g., reprimand). The probability of obtaining teacher attention for getting of her seat was .49 compared to .12 for appropriate behavior. This suggests that teacher attention is functionally related to out-of-seat behavior for this child. This hypothesis can be used to develop an intervention (e.g., ignoring out-of-seat behavior, rewarding staying in seat) using an experimental design such as an ABAB reversal design, which is described in the next section.

Interventions Based on Functional Behavioral Assessment

Although historically associated with students with severe disabilities, functional behavioral assessment is becoming more widely associated with typical developing students in general education classrooms. Specifically, modification of classroom environment and consequences using functional behavioral assessment has resulted in a decrease in problem behaviors of individual students in general education classrooms. Broussard and Northup (1997) used functional analysis procedures to develop interventions for four boys between the ages of 7 and 9 exhibiting disruptive behaviors including out-of-seat behavior, making noises, talking at inappropriate times, and playing with objects. Descriptive observations were conducted to confirm the problems identified by the teacher. Functional analysis conditions were arranged in order to determine whether teacher attention, peer attention, escape, or some combination was maintaining the problem behaviors. Peer attention was found to maintain the highest levels of disruptive behavior for all participants compared to teacher attention and escape conditions. An intervention based on this information using peer attention to reinforce appropriate behavior and no attention from peers to extinguish inappropriate behavior was effective in eliminating disruptive behavior for all four participants.

Functional assessment was used effectively with two nondisabled boys, ages 7 and 9, to reduce high rates of inappropriate behavior (Lewis & Sugai, 1996). The first child was referred for off-task behavior and the second participant was referred for off-task behavior and social withdrawal. Following an interview and direct observation, the investigators hypothesized that social attention from the teacher and peers was maintaining off-task behavior. A functional analysis was conducted and supported the hypotheses that peer and teacher attention maintained inappropriate behavior and further that the students could discriminate between situations in order to obtain the highest amount of attention (i.e., appropriate behavior for teacher attention and inappropriate behavior for peer attention). Social withdrawal exhibited by one of the target students also was found to be maintained by teacher attention. The student was able to spend one-on-one time with the teacher during recess to finish the assignment. Overall, the investigators found that using functional assessment techniques was effective in narrowing down the contributing factors before to conducting a functional analysis (i.e., experimentally testing each hypothesis).

Potential functions of disruptive behavior for a 6-year-old boy in the first grade were identified using interview and observation data (Storey et al., 1994). Results from the data indicated attention was likely maintaining inappropriate behavior. A self-management program was implemented by the teacher based on the findings of interview and observation data but without a functional analysis. An ABAB single-case withdrawal design was used to evaluate the hypothesis and the effects of the intervention. Baseline data were collected during the A phases. During the baseline phases, teacher and student were observed during typical daily routines without instruction or involvement from the experimenters. After a 2-week baseline phase, the self-management intervention (i.e., B phase) was implemented. The intervention was then withdrawn (second A phase) in order to determine whether the changes in behavior were due to the intervention. The intervention was reimplemented (second B phase) in order to replicate previous reductions in disruptive behavior. Results indicated that the intervention was effective in reducing disruptive behaviors.

In another study, functional assessment procedures were used to identify variables maintaining high-frequency, low-intensity disruptive behaviors (e.g., calling out answers) using an entire class of preschool children rather than individuals (VanDerHeyden et al., 2001). A descriptive analysis was conducted under naturally occurring conditions and the data were used to calculate conditional probabilities in order to identify the most frequently occurring events before and following disruptive behavior. From the descriptive analysis teachers were found to respond more often to inappropriate behaviors than appropriate behaviors lending support for the hypothesis that teacher attention (reprimands) were maintaining high rates of disruptive behavior. This hypothesis was tested using two conditions in an alternating treatment design. For the first condition, the teacher provided attention for appropriate behavior (i.e., differential reinforcement of alternative behavior, DRA) while ignoring inappropriate behavior. This treatment was alternated with the second contraindicated treatment condition, reprimands for inappropriate behavior. DRA was found to result in fewer instances of disruptive behavior than both baseline and the reprimand condition providing additional evidence that misbehavior is often inadvertently reinforced.

Two case illustrations describing an integrative three-step approach to behavioral assessment in general education classrooms was provided by Doggett, et al. (2001). Their purpose was to abbreviate the FBA process as much as possible while still maintaining high integrity. Participants were 2 first-grade boys referred for disruptive behaviors (e.g., talking out of turn, touching peers). The first phase was the descriptive phase. Teacher interviews and direct observations were conducted to gather information about participants and the problem behaviors. In the interpretive phase, information gathered from the assessment was used to conduct conditional probabilities in order to generate hypotheses regarding the specific behavior functions for each child. Based on the data, it was hypothesized that teacher attention maintained the disruptive behavior of one child and social attention (peer and teacher) maintained the inappropriate behavior of the second child. In the final phase, the verification phase, brief functional analyses were conducted by the teacher to evaluate each hypothesis using an ABAB design. During A phases for the functional analysis of teacher attention, the teacher responded to inappropriate behavior with disapproval such as a reprimand, frown, or redirection. During B phases, the teacher responded to appropriate behavior with approval such as smiles and praise. For the second student, the hypothesized maintaining variable was peer and teacher attention. Teacher attention was tested in the same manner as described earlier. During the A phase for the functional analysis of peer attention, the student was placed with peers likely to pay attention to the inappropriate behavior. During B phases, the student was placed near students likely to ignore problem behavior. The brief functional analyses confirmed hypothesized functions of disruptive behavior for both students and resulted in subsequent behavior change. This study provides evidence that teachers can successfully implement interventions using functional behavioral assessment.

OTHER INTERVENTIONS FOR PROBLEM BEHAVIOR

Any of the following interventions could be used in conjunction with functional assessment data. When the focus is on identifying the function of the behavior (e.g., escape), the intervention can be designed to help the student obtain the same reinforcement by engaging in appropriate behaviors. Some of the interventions have been implemented in group settings without a target child in mind (i.e., universal classroom intervention) but could be easily adapted to individuals.

In a meta-analysis of interventions designed to decrease disruptive behavior in public classroom settings, Stage and Quiroz (1997) found that differential reinforcement (Effect Size =-0.95), group contingencies (ES = -1.02), and self-management (ES = -1.00) were the most effective interventions in reducing disruptive behavior. Each of these is discussed in the following sections, along with other interventions such as modifying the curriculum and packaged programs.

Differential Reinforcement

Differential reinforcement is used to increase desired behaviors (e.g., completing seatwork, raising hand to answer questions) and to decrease undesired behaviors. Differential reinforcement of other behaviors (DRO) is one type of differential reinforcement that involves providing reinforcement when the inappropriate behavior does not occur for a specified period. The period can vary in length (e.g., 30 seconds or 20 minutes) using whole-interval recording or momentary time sampling. In whole-interval DRO, reinforcement is provided if the target behavior does not occur for the entire interval. When using momentary DRO, reinforcement is delivered if the target behavior is not occurring at the instant the interval ends. Reinforcement is individual and determined during the functional assessment.

Momentary DRO and self-management procedures were used by Storey et al. (1994) to reduce disruptive behaviors of a 6-year-old boy in a general education kindergarten class. The target behaviors, excessive movement and talking out, were identified as the two most frequent disruptive behaviors through observation data and teacher interview. The self-management program (described in the self-management section) was implemented and at specified intervals a tape recorder cued the student to monitor and record his or her behavior. If the student was engaging in appropriate behavior at the time of signal, she or he was praised by the teacher

(DRO). The target student received points that could be exchanged later for activities or tangible reinforcers. The rationale behind the intervention was that if attention from teacher and peers was maintaining the disruptive behavior, then the student would be able to access attention via teacher praise and spend extra time with peers during earned activities. Treatment effects were evaluated using an ABAB withdrawal design. During the first phase of the intervention, disruptive behaviors were reduced from 60% to 17% of the intervals recorded, and in the final phase of intervention, disruptive behaviors were reduced to 6%.

In another study, momentary DRO and whole-interval DRO were evaluated to determine their efficacy in reducing disruptive behaviors in a preschool classroom (Conyers, Miltenberger, Romaniuk, Kopp, & Himle, 2003). During momentary DRO each child received a star at the end of the interval if he or she was engaging in appropriate behavior. Those who received 13 out of 15 stars received a small toy or sticker. During the whole-interval DRO condition, students were told they could not engage in any disruptive behavior for the entire interval in order to receive a small toy or sticker or in later phases an edible reinforcer. The intervals were gradually lengthened from 1 minute to 3 minutes. Both conditions resulted in decrease in disruptive behavior; however, whole-interval DRO was found to be more effective. One weakness is that reinforcement was not the same across all conditions (i.e., edible reinforcement was not given during any of the momentary DRO phases); thus a direct comparison between the two conditions cannot be made.

Group Contingencies

There are three types of group contingency programs: dependent, independent, and interdependent (Kelshaw-Levering, Sterling-Turner, Henry & Skinner, 2000; Skinner, Cashwell, & Dunn, 1996). Dependent group contingencies require a single student to reach a designated goal in order for the group to receive reinforcement. For example, if Dave can make it all day without hitting anyone, then the whole class gets 15 extra recess minutes. Because of the potential negative response from peers if the student does not make the goal, this type of group contingency is rarely used. In contrast, reinforcement for independent group contingencies is based on each individual's performance. For example, as soon as a student reads 50 books, she or will receive an award. If the entire class is given the opportunity to read 50 books and earn a reward it is considered an independent group contingency program. If only one or a few students are given the opportunity to read 50 books and earn a reward, then it would be considered a contract. Interdependent group contingency programs require an entire group of students to reach a designated goal in order to receive reinforcement. For example, if the class can move through transition periods 3 days in a row without any disruptions, the entire class will earn a pizza party.

Interdependent group contingencies have several advantages that make them appealing to teachers. First, interdependent group contingencies have been found to be time-efficient, cost-effective, and easy to implement. Either all or none of the students meet the goal and receive reinforcement making it less complicated procedurally while allowing more activities to become available for reinforcement (e.g., field trips, extra recess, pizza party). Second, because individual students are not directly singled out (even though there may be a target student in mind), there is little risk of individual students being targeted for ridicule based on their performance. Finally, because it is in everyone's best interest to meet the goal, cooperation and encouragement are more likely to occur.

One potential problem with group contingency programs is identifying reinforcement that all students find desirable. The randomization of reinforcement or "mystery motivator" has been shown to be effective in reducing disruptive behavior. Mystery motivator is simply keeping the reinforcement earned unknown until the predetermined criteria have been met. For example, students know they have the potential to earn free time, extra recess, stickers, or a pizza party but they do not know which one will be picked from the envelope. The teacher randomly draws a slip of paper from an envelope or jar that contains all the possible choices.

A second potential problem with group contingency programs may arise when students realize that their performance does not meet the established criterion. Motivation to continue toward the goal may be diminished and frustration about not receiving the reinforcement may occur (Skinner et al., 1996). In an effort to address these issues, Kelshaw-Levering et al. (2000) compared the effects of two interdependent group contingency interventions on the disruptive behavior of 12 second-grade students. In the first intervention, the teacher selected the necessary criteria the students needed to achieve in order to receive reinforcers. Potential reinforcers (e.g., 5 min of free time, 15 min of free time, points toward a party) were randomized so that students did not know which reinforcer they would receive until after it was known if the criteria were met. In the second intervention, all of the components (behavior and criteria, group vs. individual, reinforcers) were randomized. The teacher had four jars on her desk. At the end of the designated interval, the teacher selected from jar 1 the target behavior and criterion for that day. It was either a specific disruptive behavior (e.g., calling out answers) or all disruptive behaviors with a criterion ranging from 0 to 36 disruptive behaviors allowed for that interval. The second jar determined whether the criterion would need to be met by either the whole class or an individual whose identity was known only to the teacher (dependent group contingency). If it was an individual, the teacher drew the name of a student from the third jar. The fourth jar contained the potential reinforcers. If the criterion was not met, then the criterion and the individual student (if applicable) were not announced. The interventions were evaluated using an A-B-A-C-B-C design in order to make direct comparisons between the two group contingency interventions. Results indicated that both interventions were effective in reducing disruptive behaviors, with the randomization of multiple components resulting in slightly fewer disruptive behaviors and more stable data.

Self-Management Procedures

Self-management refers to actions individuals take to independently change or maintain their own behavior. Students are taught to monitor, record, and evaluate their own behavior. The goal of self-management is for students to perform the necessary steps of a desired behavior without the need for supervision from others. Self-management procedures require teacher time initially to train students, but teacher involvement is gradually faded and ultimately considered cost- and time-effective. Fantuzzo and Polite (1990) conducted a review of school-based behavioral self-management with children of normal intellectual functioning and reported a positive relationship between the degree of self-management and treatment effect size.

DuPaul and Hoff (1998) implemented a self-management intervention in a general classroom with three 9-year-old students identified as at risk for referral for special education services because of disruptive behavior. Participants were taught to self-evaluate and record their own behavior on a scale of 0 (unacceptable) to 5 (excellent). Initially, teachers also rated student behavior and provided reinforcement based on appropriate behavior and accurate ratings (i.e., student ratings matched teacher ratings). The matching procedure was faded as the students became accurate in rating their own behavior. Results were evaluated using a multiple probe across settings (playground, math, and social studies) design. The intervention was found to be effective in reducing disruptive behavior in each setting for all three participants and the results were maintained after teacher matching was faded.

In another example, Davies and Witte (2000) evaluated the effects of self-management and peer monitoring strategies on the disruptive behaviors (i.e., inappropriate verbalizations) of four target students between the ages of 8 and 10 diagnosed with ADHD using an ABAB design. All 30 students in the classroom participated in the intervention; however, data were only collected on the four target students and matched peers. The class was divided into small groups and trained to monitor and record their group and individual target behavior. Each day students recorded their own behavior and group behavior. Groups started each day with five Velcro "dots." When individuals made an inappropriate verbalization, they were required to move a dot on the group chart and record it on an individual chart. Reinforcement was based on the number of dots remaining at the end of the designated period. At least one dot was required to receive reinforcement. Additionally, for the first 5 minutes of each session, groups discussed the group's behavior the previous day to determine what went well and what could be better. Results indicated that the intervention was effective in reducing inappropriate verbalizations for the target students as well as the matched peers (who also engaged in inappropriate verbalizations).

Mitchem, Young, West, and Benyo (2001) examined the efficacy and acceptability of a classwide peer-assisted self-management program on increasing appropriate behavior using a multiple baseline design. Students in 3 seventh-grade general education language arts classrooms participated. In addition to whole-group data, 10 students were selected as target students for data collection based on the presence of three out of four criteria: (a) referral for disruptive behavior or off-task behavior, (b) teacher-reported high rates of disruptive or off-task behavior, (c) observations indicating off-task behavior for more than 40% of the class period, and (d) grades of C or below. The teacher trained the students in classwide peer tutoring (Greenwood, Delquadri, & Carta, 1997) and self-management. Results indicated that the average rate of on-task behavior of the three classes improved from 0.7% during baseline to 68.9% during intervention. (On-task behavior was measured by the percentage of intervals during which all students were on-task.) Overall, target student behavior improved showing a trend of gradual improvement over time.

Modifying Curriculum

Academic tasks have been shown to be related to the occurrence of disruptive behaviors in the classroom and there is a convincing body of evidence demonstrating that modifying curriculum can result in improved behavior (e.g., Armendariz & Umbreit, 1999; Blair, Umbreit, & Eck, 2000; Dunlap & Kern; 1996). Task difficulty is one curricular variable that is associated with problem behavior. The majority of research has focused on tasks that are too difficult for students, which consistently resulted in lower rates of on-task behavior and increases in escape behavior. In contrast, Umbreit, Lane, and Dejud (2004) reduced the disruptive behavior of a 10-year-old boy referred for high-frequency off-task behavior during independent seatwork that was too easy. Previous attempts to improve behavior included providing praise and stickers for appropriate behavior, keeping him in for recess, implementing a 15-minute time-out, keeping him after school, taking back any earned stickers, sending him to the principal's office, and giving reprimands. A functional behavioral assessment (teacher and student interviews and direct observation) revealed that independent seatwork in math and reading resulted in the greatest amounts of disruptive behavior and that during this time he frequently disturbed peers. The data led to the hypothesis that disruptive behavior was maintained by access to a more desirable activity (i.e., helping peers) when his work was completed. Task difficulty was increased to make the seatwork more challenging (and time-consuming). The intervention was evaluated using an ABAB reversal design. On-task behavior rose from low levels during baseline (47%–63%) to high levels during both treatment phases (80%–97%).

In another example, Armendariz and Umbreit (1999) used response cards in which every student responded to teacher-directed questions to evaluate the effects on disruptive behavior of a class of twenty-two 8- and 9-year-old children. Using an ABA design, the teacher compared traditional lecture with hand-raising (baseline) to active responding using response cards. The intervention was found to be highly effective in reducing rates of disruptive behavior. This type of intervention may be desirable because it benefits the entire class while potentially improving the behavior of individuals with problem behavior.

Packaged Interventions

Although school-based interventions in general have been shown to be successful (e.g., Stage & Quiroz, 1997), a multimodal approach is considered by some to be more effective than interventions that focus on changing one aspect of a child's problem behavior (Tremblay et al., 1995). For example, De Martini-Scully et al. (2000) used a combination of interventions previously supported by empirical data including precision requests, public posting of rules, teacher movement around the room, positive reinforcement (e.g., mystery motivators), and response cost to reduce the disruptive behaviors of 2 third-grade female students in a general education setting.

Precision request programs are based on Forehand and McMahon's (1981) compliance training methods in order to teach parents and teachers how to effectively deliver commands and consequences. Teachers in this study were instructed to issue a request in statement form within close proximity to the student, talking in a calm voice, making eye contact, and waiting approximately 5 seconds for a response. If the child complied, then verbal reinforcement was given. If the child did not comply, the command was given again with another 5-second wait. Noncompliance the second time resulted in a loss of opportunity to receive a token at the end of the lesson (i.e., response cost). Response cost is a procedure used to decrease behavior (e.g., noncompliance) by removing access to reinforcement. Reinforcement in this program consisted of tokens that could be exchanged for a mystery motivator reinforcer. Mystery motivators are simply unknown reinforcers (e.g., a wrapped gift). Typically students are involved in determining potential reinforcers, which are then written on a piece of paper and randomly selected from an envelope or jar.

Results indicated that the packaged intervention was effective in reducing the frequency of disruptive behaviors from 41% of the intervals during the first baseline to 20% of the intervals. One limitation of packaged interventions is that it is not possible to determine which component or combination of components was responsible for the decrease in disruptive behaviors.

In another example, a multimethod intervention focusing on parental management skills training as well as a child social and social–cognitive skills training was used to determine if future delinquency (ages 13–16) could be prevented by intervening early with disruptive males ages 7 through 9 (Vitaro et al., 2001). Compared to control, the intervention group engaged in less disruptive behavior, fewer associations with deviant peers, and less delinquent behaviors by age 13.

The effects of four treatment conditions on the behavior of 158 kindergarten children exhibiting high levels of disruptive behavior were compared: no treatment, behavioral parent training only, classroom-based treatment only, and the combination of parent training and classroom treatment (Barkley et al., 2000) compared. Significant improvements were found on teacher ratings of self-control, social skills, aggression, and attention, parent ratings of adaptive behavior, and direct observations of disruptive behavior in the classroom for the classroom-based intervention. The parent training did not result in changes presumably because of poor attendance. The study also revealed that the success of a multimodal approach with a parent-training element hinges on parent readiness to seek help for their children.

APPLICATIONS

The assessment procedures and interventions described in this chapter were conducted by researchers and other educational professionals to determine the efficacy of various interventions and therefore adhered to stringent experimental procedures necessary to make claims of causality. Although general education teachers have successfully conducted functional assessments, it would be unreasonable to expect teachers to conduct functional behavioral assessments for each student displaying disruptive behavior. Instead, readers should use the information to provide a general framework for looking at causes and factors maintaining problem behavior. For example, although a full functional assessment may be unreasonable, it is useful to think about what was happening immediately before and after the behavior occurred. This information combined with the knowledge that most chronic disruptive behaviors are maintained by either escape from an aversive situation (e.g., writing assignments) or peer/teacher attention can help educators develop reasonable hypotheses regarding the problem behavior.

Once a hypothesis has been identified, the chapter provides a number of interventions based on the function of the behavior (escape, attention) rather than the topography of the behavior (talking out of turn). This approach is beneficial because it simplifies the process of identifying potential interventions. For example, rather than looking new methods for handling talking out turn, walking around the room, and bothering other students, teachers can use variations of the same intervention for all behaviors maintained by the same function (e.g., teacher attention).

CONCLUSIONS

Problem behaviors in the classroom are reported by teachers and parents as one of their primary classroom management concerns (Bear, 1998, Rose & Gallup, 2003). Yet teachers also report that they do not feel adequately trained to handle problem behavior. Perhaps because of heightened awareness of incidents of violence and aggression in schools, much of the focus of school administrators has been on responding to serious behavior problems. What cannot be ignored is the relationship between early problem behaviors and negative short- and long-term outcomes, including increased negative interactions with teachers and peers, poor attitudes regarding school, increased likelihood of dropping out of school, and future delinquent behavior.

Integrative prevention and intervention programs such as the three-tiered schoolwide discipline program described by Walker and colleagues (1996) may help prevent some of the common disruptive problem behavior problems experienced in the classroom. In addition, it can provide a framework for teachers to identify at-risk students in need of secondary interventions for individual behavior problems. Secondary interventions require individualized intervention. Functional behavioral assessment (FBA) is one method that can be used to help select effective interventions. FBA recently has been shown to be an effective procedure for identifying the function of problem behaviors for typical students in general education classrooms.

Stage and Quiroz (1997) found that differential reinforcement, group contingencies, and self-management were the most effective interventions for reducing problem behaviors in the classroom. Each of these interventions has been shown to be successfully implemented by classroom teachers with a high level of treatment integrity and acceptability. The results from functional assessments can be used in conjunction with empirically validated procedures such as self-management, group contingencies, and differential reinforcement for reducing problem behaviors in the classroom.

ACKNOWLEDGMENT

The authors thank Heather Sterling-Turner, University of Southern Mississippi, for her review of an early draft of this chapter.

REFERENCES

Armendariz, F., & Umbreit, J. (1999). Using active responding to reduce disruptive behavior in a general education classroom. *Journal of Positive Behavior Interventions, 1*, 152–158.

Barkley, R. A., Shelton, T. L., Crosswait, C., & Moorehouse, M. (2000). Multi-method psycho-educational intervention for preschool children with disruptive behavior: Preliminary results at post-treatment. *Journal of Child Psychology and Psychiatry, 41*, 319–332.

Barrish, H. H., Saunders, M., & Wolfe, M. D. (1969). Good Behavior Game: Effects of individual contingencies for group consequences and disruptive behavior in the classroom. *Journal of Applied Behavior Analyses, 2*, 119–124

Bear, G. (1998). School discipline in the United States: Prevention, corrections, and long-term social development. *School Psychology Review, 27*, 14–32.

Blair, K., Umbreit, J., & Eck, S. (2000). Analysis of multiple variables related to a young child's aggressive behaviors. *Journal of Positive Behavioral Interventions, 2*, 33–39.

Book, R., & Skeen, J. (1987). Behavioral observations of disruptive behaviors with referred and nonreferred elementary school students. *Psychology in the Schools, 24*, 399–405.

Broidy, L. M., Nagin, D., Tremblay, R., Bates, J., Brame, B., Dodge, K., Fergusson, D, Horwood, J., Loeber, R., Laird, R., Lynam, D., Moffitt, T., Pettit, G., & Vitaro, F. (2003). Developmental trajectories of childhood disruptive behaviors and adolescent delinquency: A six-site, cross-national study. *Developmental Psychology, 39*, 222–245.

Broussard, C. D., & Northup, J. (1995). An approach to assessment and analysis of disruptive behavior in regular education classrooms. *School Psychology Quarterly, 10*, 151–164

Broussard, C., & Northup, J. (1997). The use of functional analysis to develop peer interventions for disruptive classroom behavior. *School Psychology Quarterly, 12*, 65–76.

Cairns, R. B., Cairns, B. D., & Neckerman, H. J. (1989). Early school dropout: Configur ations and determinants. *Child Development, 60*, 1437–1452.

Cone, J. (1997). Issues in functional analysis in behavioral assessment. *Behavioral Research and Therapy, 35*, 259–275.

Conyers, C., Miltenberger, R., Romaniuk, C., Kopp, B., & Himle, M. (2003). Evaluation of DRO schedules to reduce disruptive behavior in a preschool classroom. *Child and Family Behavior Therapy, 25*, 1–6.

Davies, S., & Witte, R. (2000). Self-management and peer-monitoring within a group contingency to decrease uncontrolled verbalizations of children with attention-deficit/ hyperactivity disorder. *Psychology in the Schools, 37*, 135–147.

De Martini-Scully, D., Bray, M. A., & Kehle, T. J. (2000). A packaged intervention to reduce disruptive behaviors in general education students. *Psychology in the Schools, 37*, 149–156.

Doggett, R., Edwards, R., Moore, J., Tingstrom, D., & Wilczynski, S. (2001). An approach to functional assessment in general education classroom settings. *School Psychology Review, 30*, 313–329.

Dunlap, G., & Kern, L. (1996). Modifying instructional activities to promote desirable behavior: A conceptual and practical framework. *School Psychology Quarterly, 11*, 297–312.

DuPaul, G., & Hoff, K. (1998). Reducing disruptive behavior in general education classrooms: The use of self-management strategies. *School Psychology Review, 27*, 290–304.

Ensminger, M. E., Lamkin, R. P., & Jacobson, N. (1996). School leaving: A longitudinal perspective including neighborhood effects. *Child Development, 67*, 2400–2416.

Fantuzzo, J., & Polite, K. (1990). School-based behavioral self-management: A review and analysis. *School Psychology Quarterly, 5*, 255–263.

Forehand, R., & McMahon, R. (1981). *Helping the noncompliant child: A clinician's guide to parent training*. New York: Guilford.

Greenwood, C., Delquadri, J., & Carta, J. (1997). *Together we can! ClassWide Peer Tutoring to improve basic academic skills*. Longmont, CO: Sopris West.

Gresham, F. (2003). Establishing the technical adequacy of functional behavioral assessment: Conceptual and measurement challenges. *Behavioral Disorders, 28*, 282- -298.

Janosz, M., LeBlanc, M., Boulerice, B., & Tremblay, R. E. (1997). Disentangling the weight of school dropout predictors: A test on two longitudinal samples. *Journal of Youth and Adolescence, 26*, 733–762.

Kellam, S. G., Rebok, G. W., Ialongo, N., & Mayer, L. S. (1994). The course and malleability of aggressive behavior from early first grade into middle school: Results of a developmental epidemiology-based preventive trial. *Journal of Child Psychology and Psychiatry and Allied Disciplines, 35*, 259–281.

Kelshaw-Levering, K., Sterling-Turner, H., Henry, J., & Skinner, C. (2000). Randomized interdependent group contingencies: Group reinforcement with twist. *Psychology in the Schools, 37*, 523–533.

Lewis, T., & Sugai, G. (1996). Functional assessment of problem behavior: A pilot investigation of the comparative and interactive effects of teacher and peer social attention on students in general education settings. *School Psychology Quarterly, 11*, 1–19.

Masse, L. C., & Tremblay, R. E. (1999). Kindergarten disruptive behaviour, family adversity, gender and elementary school failure. *International Journal of Behavioral Development, 23*, 225–240.

Mayer, G. (1995). Preventing antisocial behavior in schools. *Journal of Applied Behavior Analysis, 28*, 467–478.

McFadden, A. C., Marsh, G. E., Price, B. J., & Huang, Y. (1992). A study of race and gender bias in the punishment of school children. *Education and Treatment of Children, 15*, 140–146.

Mitchem, K., Young, K., West, R., & Benyo, J. (2001). CWPASM: A classwide peer-assisted self-management program for general education classrooms. *Education and Treatment of Children, 24*, 111–141.

Moffitt, T. (1990). Juvenile delinquency and attention deficit disorder: Boys' developmental trajectories from age 3 to 15. *Child Development, 61*, 893–910

Nelson, J., & Roberts, M. (2000). Ongoing reciprocal teacher-student interactions involving disruptive behaviors in general education classrooms. *Journal of Emotional and Behavioral Disorders, 8*, 27–39.

Patterson, G. R. (1982). *Coersive family process*. Eugene, OR: Castalia.

Patterson, G. R., & Reid, J. B. (1970). Reciprocity and coercion: Two facets of social systems. In C. Neuringer & J. L. Michael (Eds.), *Behavior modification in clinical psychology* (133–177). New York: Appleton-Century-Crofts.

Rose, L., & Gallup, A. (2003). The 35th annual Phi Delta Kappa/Gallup poll of the public's attitudes toward the public schools. *Phi Delta Kappan, 85*, 41–53.

Rumberger, R. W. (1995). Dropping out of middle school: A multilevel analysis of students and schools. *American Educational Research Journal, 20*, 199–220.

Shinn, M., Ramsey, E., Walker, H., Stieber, S., & O'Neill, R. (1987). Antisocial behavior in school settings: Initial differences in an at-risk and normal population. *The Journal of Special Education, 21*, 69–84.

Skiba, R. J., Peterson, R. L., & Williams, T. (1997). Office referrals and suspension: Disciplinary intervention in middle schools. *Education and Treatment of Children, 20*, 295–315.

Skinner, C., Cashwell, C., & Dunn, M. (1996). Independent and interdependent group contingencies: Smoothing the rough waters. *Special Services in the Schools, 12*, 61–78.

Stage, S., & Quiroz, D. (1997). A meta-analysis of interventions to decrease disruptive classroom behavior in public education settings. *School Psychology Review, 26*, 333–368.

Storey, K., Lawry, J., Ashworth, R., Danko, C., & Strain, P. (1994). Functional analysis and intervention for disruptive behaviors of a kindergarten student. *Journal of Educational Research, 87*, 361–371.

Tremblay, R.E., Masse, B., Perron, D., LeBlanc, M., Schwartzman, A., & Ledingham, J. (1992). Early disruptive behavior, poor school achievement, delinquent behavior, and delinquent personality: Longitudinal analysis. *Journal of Consulting and Clinical Psychology, 60*, 64–72.

Tremblay, R. E., Pagani-Kurtz, L., Masse, L. C., Vitaro, F., & Pihl, R. O. (1995). A bimodal preventive intervention for disruptive kindergarten boys; Its impact through mid-adolescence. *Journal of Consulting and Clinical Psychology, 63*, 560–568.

Tremblay, R. E., Pihl, R. O., Vitaro, F., & Dobkin, P. L. (1994). Predicting early onset of male antisocial behavior from preschool behavior. *Archives of General Psychiatry, 51*, 732–739.

Umbreit, J., Lane, K., & Dejud, C. (2004). Improving classroom behavior by modifying task difficulty: Effects of increasing the difficulty of too-easy tasks. *Journal of Positive Behavioral Interventions, 6*, 13–20.

VanDerHeyden, A., Witt, J., & Gatti, S. (2001). Descriptive assessment method to reduce overall disruptive behavior in a preschool classroom. *School Psychology Review, 30*, 548–567.

Vitaro, F., Brendgen, M., & Tremblay, R.E. (1999). Prevention of school dropout through the reduction of disruptive behaviors and school failure in elementary school. *Journal of School Psychology, 37*, 205–226.

Vitaro, F., Brendgen, M., & Tremblay, R.E. (2001). Preventive intervention: Assessing its effects on the trajectories of delinquency and testing for mediational processes. *Applied Developmental Science, 5*, 201–213.

Vollmer, T., & Northup, J. (1996). Some implications of functional analysis for school psychology. *School Psychology Quarterly, 11*, 76–92.

Walker, H. M., & Buckley, N. K. (1973). Teacher attention to appropriate and inappropriate classroom behavior: An individual case study. *Focus on Exceptional Children, 5*, 5–11

Walker, H. M., Hops, H., & Fiegenbaum, E. (1976). *Deviant classroom behavior as a function of combinations of social and token reinforcement and cost contingency. Behavior Therapy, 7*, 76–88.

Walker, H. M., Horner, R. H., Sugai, G., Bullis, M., Sprague, J. R., Bricker, D., & Kaufman, M. J. (1996). *Integrated approaches to preventing antisocial behavior patterns among school-age children and youth. Journal of Emotional and Behavioral Disorders, 4*, 194–209.

30

Conflict Resolution, Peer Mediation, and Peacemaking

David W. Johnson and Roger T. Johnson
University of Minnesota

INTRODUCTION

The heart of preventing and solving discipline problems is the constructive resolution of conflict. Whether a discipline problem is mild or severe (involving violence), it represents a conflict between teachers who wish to restore order and the misbehaving students. The conflict may be among students or between students and the teacher or other staff members. The way in which conflicts are managed has profound influences on the effectiveness with which teachers instruct and socialize students and manage the classroom as well on the methods they use to intervene when discipline problems occur. When conflicts are resolved constructively, teacher effectiveness increases. When conflicts are managed destructively, the teacher's ability to instruct students and manage the classroom is obstructed.

Conflict does not occur separately from the rest of classroom and school life. It takes place in a context. Establishing a classroom management system in which conflicts are managed constructively involves three steps (Johnson & Johnson, 1999): Creating a cooperative learning environment, teaching students, teachers, and staff how to manage conflicts constructively, and inculcating civic values in all members of the school. In this chapter the emphasis is on teaching school members how to manage conflicts, although the other two parts are discussed in passing. For educational goals to be achieved in orderly and effective ways, students (as well as faculty and staff) need to be trained in how to resolve constructively conflicts of interests (such as who gets to use the computer) and conflicts involved in decision making and opposing conclusions (such as whether to play dodgeball or soccer). Because all discipline problems are by their very nature conflicts, whether students (as well as faculty and staff) have the competencies necessary to resolve conflicts constructively is at the very heart of classroom management and disciplinary procedures. To understand the importance of conflict resolution in classroom management, it is first necessary to review the nature of social systems, the nature of social interdependence, and the impact of social interdependence on conflict and classroom management. The nature of conflict resolution and violence prevention programs are then discussed and the benefits of teaching students to resolve conflicts constructively are briefly presented. The history of theorizing on conflict resolution is discussed and two examples of conflict resolution program are presented in some detail.

NATURE OF SOCIAL SYSTEMS

Social systems, such as schools and classrooms, are created to organize joint efforts to achieve mutual goals focusing on instruction/learning and socialization (Johnson, 1970, 1979). The faculty and staff are hired to achieve the school's goals. School goals may be organized into two interrelated categories: Teaching students the knowledge they need to become a contributing member of society (i.e., teach students how to read, write, and do math) and socializing students into the perspectives, attitudes, and values they need to be contributing members of a society (i.e., love of learning, intellectual curiosity, the need for work to be of high quality, commitment to the scientific method). Students are required to attend school and expected to help achieve the school's goals. Both faculty and students need to commit themselves to the goals and the processes for achieving the goals (such as the instructional procedures) if cooperative efforts are to result. At any one time, some students may adopt the school's goals (i.e., they want to learn to read and write), some students may be indifferent to the school's goals (i.e., they do not mind if the teacher presents material on reading and writing but they are disinterested), and some students may oppose the school's goals (i.e., they want to talk to their friends rather than learn how to read and write). Correspondingly, faculty and students may agree on the overall goals (i.e., both want students to learn to read and write) but incompatibilities may exist on what processes to follow to achieve the goals (i.e., the teacher may wish students to read Shakespeare and a student may wish to read a mystery novel).

To achieve the school's goals, the behavior of members is directed and coordinated through role definitions and norms specifying appropriate and expected behaviors (Johnson, 1970). **Roles** such as teacher and student prescribe the behavior expected of any individual occupying the position (e.g., teachers plan and orchestrate learning experiences, students follow the teacher's directions in participating in learning experiences) and the **norms** make explicit what is and is not appropriate behavior (e.g., no running in the hallways, no bullying of classmates). Any one role cannot be discussed without considering complementary roles (e.g., the role of teacher cannot be discussed without also discussing the role of student). Roles have both **rights** (what individuals in complementary roles will do for a person) and **obligations** (what individuals in complementary roles expect from a person). **Classroom management** is aimed at ensuring that everyone adheres to his or her role definitions and the classroom's norms so that both instruction (actions taken to assist students in mastering the formal curriculum) and socialization (actions taken to influence students' attitudes, values, beliefs, role responsibilities, identity, and other aspects of being a citizen in their society) can take place effectively. There are at least two types of student socialization that teachers promote: socialization into the school culture and socialization into the society as a whole. Although much of the focus in schools is on academic learning, instruction cannot take place unless students are socialized into their role and the normative expectations for participating in learning situations. In fact, every academic lesson is concurrently a socializing experience into the school culture. Management problems arise when students do not fulfill their role requirements and do not adhere to the normative expectations for appropriate behavior. Teachers then engage in **disciplinary interventions**, which are actions aimed at influencing students to fulfill their role responsibilities and follow the norms for appropriate behavior.

The procedures for instruction, socialization, classroom management, and disciplinary interventions need to be (a) based on a set of principles formulated from theory that has been validated by research (as opposed to a bag of tricks or random guidelines) and (b) congruent and integrated, so that each enhances the other. The instructional procedures implicitly define the roles of teacher and student, the nature of the classroom management system, and the type of disciplinary interventions the teacher makes. If the teacher primarily lectures, for example, then the role of teacher is defined as presenting information, the role of student is defined as listening and taking notes without interacting with other students, and disciplinary interventions are based on the teacher exerting power (i.e., rewards and punishments) to ensure students sit quietly. If the teacher structures cooperative learning, however, the role of the teacher is to structure and guide student–student interaction, the student role is to work with other students to complete the assignment (which requires active engagement in learning activities), and disciplinary interventions include strengthening the positive interdependence among students, ensuring each student is individually accountable to learn, and teaching students the social skills (i.e., leadership, communication, decision making, conflict resolution) they need to work together and help solve the problems they have in working together. To maintain the congruence among inducing commitment to learning goals, instructional and socialization procedures, classroom management procedures, and disciplinary interventions, it is helpful for teachers to understand social interdependence theory.

SOCIAL INTERDEPENDENCE THEORY

Social interdependence exists when the goal achievements of individuals are affected by each other's actions, that is, A's actions affect B's goal achievement and B's actions affect A's goal achievement (Deutsch, 1949, 1962; Johnson, 2003; Johnson & Johnson, 1989). Individuals' attempts to achieve their goals may affect each other's success positively or negatively. **Positive interdependence** is reflected in cooperation to achieve mutual goals (when one person achieves his or her goal, all others with whom he or she is cooperatively linked achieve their goals) whereas **negative interdependence** is reflected in competition to achieve mutually exclusive goals (when one person achieves his or her goal, all others with whom he or she is competitively linked fail to achieve their goals).

Social interdependence theory posits that when faculty and students are working toward mutual goals, their actions promote each other's success (i.e., the more effectively the teacher instructs, the more students learn). The compatibility of their goals tends to result in increased efforts to achieve, positive relationships, and more healthy psychological and social adjustment. To structure cooperation, five basic elements must be implemented: Positive interdependence (which may be based on mutual goals, joint rewards, role assignments, divided resources, joint identity); individual accountability in which each student is responsible for doing his or her fair share of the work; promotive interaction in which each student encourages and helps his or her groupmates; the appropriate use of social skills (such as leadership, communication, decision making, and conflict resolution skills); and group processing in which each learning group discusses how to work more effectively in the future. A learning environment is created that enhances the well-being and productivity of all members of the classroom.

When faculty and students are working toward incompatible goals, their actions oppose each other's success (i.e., students disrupt the teacher's efforts to instruct and obstruct classmates' efforts to learn). Goal incompatibility tends to result in decreased efforts to achieve, negative relationships, and unhealthy psychological and social adjustment.

Competition	**Cooperation**
Instruction Emphasizes Direct Teaching, Lecturing	Instruction Emphasizes Learning Groups, Active Engagement, Social Construction
Management Programs Emphasize Faculty Administrated External Rewards And Punishments	Management Programs Emphasize Teaching Students the Competencies They Need to Regulate Own and Schoolmates' Behavior

1---2---3---4---5---6---7—8—9—10

Disciplinary Interventions Include Faculty Being a Police Officer, Judge, Jury, and Executioner; Faculty Monitor Student Behavior, Judge Its Appropriateness, Decide Which Consequence to Administer, and Give The Reward or Punishment	Disciplinary Interventions Include Strengthening Five Basic Elements of Cooperation. Students Monitor the Appropriateness of Their Own and Their Groupmatesí Behavior, Assess Its Effectiveness, and Decide How to Behave

FIGURE 30.1. Continuum of classroom management programs.

SOCIAL INTERDEPENDENCE AND CLASSROOM MANAGEMENT

School and classroom management programs derived from competitive and cooperative contexts may be placed on a continuum (see Fig. 30.1). At one end are competitive management programs where teachers engage in direct instruction (such as lecturing) and students work alone and their performances are ranked comparatively from highest to lowest (e.g., they are graded on a curve). Classroom management tends to be based on extrinsic rewards and punishments administrated by faculty and staff to control student behavior. Disciplinary interventions reflect faculty monitoring students' behavior, determining whether it is within the bounds of acceptability, and forcing students to terminate inappropriate actions. This requires a great deal of instructional and administrative time and works only as long as students are under surveillance. The external rewards and punishments approach is based on behavioral theory, which assumes that individuals will repeat behavior that is rewarded and avoid behavior that is punished. Requiring students to obey rules out of the fear of punishment, however, reduces student self-regulation (Berk, 1994). The basic value inculcated by competition is to strive for personal success at the expense of others (Johnson & Johnson, 1996a, 2000b).

At the other end of the continuum are cooperative programs where students work together in small learning groups to achieve mutual learning goals and contribute to the common good. Students' performances are assessed on the basis of how they compare to a preset criterion. Cooperative experiences inculcate such values as commitment to the common good and to the well-being of other members, a sense of responsibility to contribute one's fair share of the work, respect for the efforts of others and for them as people, behaving with integrity, caring for other members, compassion, and appreciation of diversity (Johnson & Johnson, 1996a, 2000b). Cooperative classroom management focuses student attention on mutual goals and teaches them the competencies and skills required to regulate their own and their schoolmates' behavior in order to achieve the goals. Faculty monitor students' behavior as they work in groups, assess the quality of their taskwork (i.e., academic understanding) and teamwork (i.e., competencies students need to work together effectively and regulate their own and their groupmates' behavior), and strengthen the five basic elements of cooperation (positive interdependence, individual accountability, promotive interaction, appropriate use of social skills, and group processing) when students get off-task. **Self-regulation** is the ability to act in socially approved ways in the absence of external monitors by deciding how one should behave and engage in the chosen actions. Self-regulation is a central and significant hallmark of cognitive and social development. Students are empowered to solve their own problems and regulate their own and their classmates' behavior when they manage conflicts constructively. The basic value inculcated by cooperation is to strive for other people's benefit and the common good as well as for self-benefit (Johnson & Johnson, 1996a, 2000b).

The continuum from competition to cooperation describes the nature of instruction and socialization, classroom management, and disciplinary interventions. The heart of the continuum, however, is the nature of conflict resolution at each end of the continuum.

Social Interdependence and Conflict

For conflicts to be resolved constructively, disputants must take into account the long-term relationship and goals (as well as the immediate situation) and see the conflict as a problem to be solved. Accurate and complete communication about the issues being contested must take place. Perceptions of each other's positions and motivations must be unbiased. Disputants need to trust each other and see each other's goals and feelings as legitimate. The context in which the conflict occurs has been shown to have a powerful influence on these variables. Thus, the conflict's context largely determines whether constructive or destructive outcomes result (Deutsch, 1973; Johnson & Johnson, 1989, 1995a). The context may be competitive or cooperative.

In a **competitive context**, individuals tend to focus on differential benefit (i.e., doing better than anyone else in the situation), be dominated by short-term self-interests, avoid communication or engage in misleading information and threats, have frequent misperceptions of the other person's position and motivations that are difficult to correct, have suspicious and hostile attitudes toward others, deny the legitimacy of others' goals and feelings, and engage in win-lose negotiations to maximize their own outcomes at the expense of the other disputants.

In an **individualistic context**, individuals tend to focus only on their short-term self-interests and ignore the others in the situation. The indifference to other persons and their actions results in little or no communication and an unconcern with the goals of others.

In a **cooperative context**, individuals tend to focus on both self and others' well-being, be dominated by long-term mutual interests, engage in effective and continued communication, have accurate perceptions of the other person's position and motivations, trust the other disputants, like the other disputants, recognize the legitimacy of the others' interests, and engage in problem-solving negotiations to maximize joint outcomes. Individuals focus on mutual goals and shared interests. The easiest way to create a cooperative context is for faculty to use cooperative learning the majority of the time. The more students cooperate with each other academically, the more likely their conflicts will be managed constructively.

All social systems are established to achieve mutual goals and, therefore, they are inherently cooperative. Within the overall cooperative framework, however, competitions may be established among certain members or groups within the social system. Students, for example, may be placed in competition over grades by creating an artificial shortage of As and Bs and grading on a curve. The consequences of doing so, however, are that the nature of instruction, classroom management, and disciplinary interventions are all affected. When competitive and individualistic efforts dominate a classroom and school, conflicts will tend to be perceived as "win-lose" situations and management problems will tend to increase. The competitive focus on differential benefit and the individualistic focus on self-benefit tend to result in relatively frequent discipline and management problems. In such contexts, instead of trying to solve interpersonal problems, students will think short term and go for the "win" or simply what is best for oneself.

Alternatively, the cooperative nature of the overall social system may be enhanced by structuring cooperative efforts among certain members or groups within the social system. Students, for example, may be placed in cooperative learning groups and told to work together to achieve mutual learning goals. Students' grades are determined by how the quality of their work compares with a preset criterion. When cooperation dominates the classroom, students tend to perceive conflicts as mutual problems to be solved and management problems will tend to decrease. The cooperative focus on others' benefits (as well as oneself) and the common good tends to result in fewer discipline and management problems and more constructive resolution of the problems that do occur.

CONFLICT RESOLUTION AND VIOLENCE PREVENTION PROGRAMS

The Nature of Conflict and Discipline Problems

Discipline problems are by their very nature conflicts that may be managed in constructive ways or destructive ways. A **conflict** exists when the actions of one person prevent, block, or interfere with the other's efforts to achieve his or her goal (Deutsch, 1973). Correspondingly, a **discipline problem** exists when the actions of a student prevent, block, or interfere with a faculty member's efforts to instruct and socialize students. This could be a conflict among students that disrupts the teacher's efforts (which becomes a conflict between the students and the teacher) or it could be a direct conflict with the teacher (or another staff member). It should be noted that although all discipline problems are conflicts, not all conflicts are discipline problems. Conflicts may be resolved constructively without the involvement of faculty or staff and without disrupting and even enhancing instruction and other aspects of classroom and school life.

Conflict may be distinguished from a number of related concepts. Although **competition** (which involves working against other individuals to achieve a goal that only one or a few can attain) and **aggression** (which are behaviors aimed at harming another person) produce conflict, not all instances of conflict reflect competition or aggression. **Influence** deals with affecting others in desired ways and **dominance** deals with one-way influence from, for example, teacher to students. Conflict should not be confused with these concepts. Doing so results in conflict being perceived as extreme behaviors present in only a small fraction of actual disputes.

There are two types of conflicts important for schools (Johnson & Johnson, 1995a, 1995b). The first is a **conflict of interests** (which occurs when the actions of one person attempting to reach his or her goals prevent, block, or interfere with the actions of another person attempting to reach his or her goals). Faculty and students also have different interests that must be reconciled if they are to cooperate to achieve mutual goals. Teacher interests include successful instruction and good relationships with colleagues, administrators, and parents. Student interests include peer relationships, having fun, meeting developmental challenges, and expanding their worldview. Although some of their interests are common, discipline problems occur when the actions of students aimed at achieving their goals obstruct the actions of teachers aimed at achieving their goals. Student incivility toward certain classmates or faculty, for example, may win status with peers but disrupt instruction. Student clowning around may gain attention from classmates but disrupt instruction. A lack of interest in what is being taught disrupts instruction. There are many instances when the interests of students and the interests of faculty conflict. For such discipline problems to be solved constructively, students and faculty need to engage in integrative (i.e., problem-solving) negotiations and have a mediator available when negotiations fail.

The second type of conflict is **controversy** (which occurs when one person's ideas, information, conclusions, theories, and opinions are incompatible with those of another and the two seek to decide on a conclusion or course of action). Faculty and students (as well as other stakeholders) have to make decisions as to what course of action to follow to achieve their goals. Any decision-making situation is a potential conflict, in which participants must choose among several alternative courses of action. The pros and cons of each alternative are determined, and then agreement is reached as to which alternative is best. Among themselves, students have to decide whether to play baseball or basketball during recess, who should be included on their team, whether it is "cool" to disrespect a teacher, which band should play at the junior prom, who should be invited to a party, whether to take science or shop, or even which expressions to use. There are also sensitive issues (such as "whether ethnicity is an important difference between people") that are difficult to discuss because they involve more than one perspective but a single viewpoint dominates and if anyone speaks against that perspective there are reprisals. Students continuously make group as well as individual decisions all day long at school. If anger, resentment, hostility, hurt feelings, and anxiety result, then both instruction and socialization are disrupted. Students need a procedure for constructively making decisions and reaching conclusions on complex issues.

A conflict is managed constructively when (a) all parties involved are satisfied with the outcomes (i.e., joint benefits are maximized), (b) the relationship among disputants is strengthened or improved, and (c) the disputants' ability to resolve future conflicts in a constructive manner with each other has been improved. If one or more of these conditions is not met, the resolution of the conflict is destructive. Correspondingly, a discipline problem is solved constructively when both the teacher and the student are satisfied with the solution, the relationship between the student and teacher is improved, and their ability to resolve future discipline problems constructively has been improved. Whether positive outcomes result depends largely on (a) the availability of clear procedures for managing conflicts, (b) the level of students and faculty's skills in using the procedures, (c) student and faculty commitment to using the procedures, and (d) the level at which the norms and values of the school encourage and support the use of the procedures.

Learning how to mange conflicts of interests and controversies constructively both prevents the occurrence of discipline problems and is instrumental in resolving the discipline problems that do occur. In addition, such competencies prevent violence, but conflict resolution programs may be distinguished from violence prevention programs.

Violence Prevention Programs

Violence prevention programs are primarily aimed at suppressing conflict and reducing the availability of weapons (see also Freiberg's chapter in this volume). **Violence** is behavior that violates physically or emotionally another individual or group (Johnson & Johnson, 1995a). There is violence in U.S. schools (Toppo, 2004); during the 2001–2002 school year there were 17 violent deaths connected to school (i.e., a homicide or suicide on school grounds or on their way to and from school or at a school-related event), during the 2002–2003 school year there were 16 violent deaths connected to school, but during the 2003–2004 school year there were 48 deaths connected to school (the large increase is attributed primarily to cuts in spending on school safety). The worst and most pervasive violence in schools, however, tends to occur in a small number of schools in neighborhoods where there is considerable violence and easy access to guns and drugs. Thus, there tends to be more physical and verbal aggression in urban than in suburban or rural schools. Even in urban schools, however, the physical violence documented almost never involves serious altercations or violations of law.

Violence prevention programs are procedures aimed at reducing the frequency of violence committed by members of the school. Components of these programs include:

1. Implementing surveillance systems (such as metal detectors and random searches of lockers) to reduce the number of weapons brought into the school.
2. Suppressing violence by having the city police patrol the school.
3. Concentrating school resources on students who commit the most serious acts of violence and are involved most often in violent incidents in the school (such as bullies) so that their behavior is modified.
4. Instituting a threat-management policy so that students who believe they are in danger in the school can talk to a counselor or psychologist and receive adult protection.
5. Training faculty and staff in how to intervene in violent situations so that deescalation rather than escalation takes place. The training includes how to recognize the stages leading to a student's violent actions so faculty and staff intervene before the student becomes physically violent.

Generally, violence prevention programs are conducted by adults to suppress and control extreme student behaviors (most discipline problems, however, are less severe and involve minor disruptions to instruction and socialization). They are quite different from conflict resolution training programs in which students are trained in procedures they will use to regulate their own behavior in conflict situations (although conflict resolution programs do in fact prevent violence).

Conflict Resolution Programs

The history of mediation as a means of resolving conflicts constructively goes back to the beginnings of human existence. In ancient China conflicts were mediated in order to follow the Confucian way of resolving disputes by moral persuasion and agreement. In ancient Japan, the village leader was expected to use mediation and conciliation to help community members settle their disputes. In parts of ancient Africa, disputes were resolved informally by assembling a "moot" or neighborhood meeting where a respected community member served as a mediator to help the disputants resolve their conflict cooperatively without involving a judge or arbitrator and without using sanctions. Historically, in many cultures, members of the extended family served as mediators. For centuries, all over the world, local religious leaders (priests, ministers, rabbis) served as mediators to resolve conflicts among community members. On the other hand, the history of the modern field of conflict resolution is brief, spanning the last 150 years or so, and the history of school-based mediation programs spans about 3 decades.

In contrast to violence prevention programs, conflict resolution programs are aimed primarily at teaching students the competencies they need to regulate their own and their classmates' behavior so that conflicts may be faced and resolved constructively. Conflict resolution and peer mediation programs have been generated by (a) researchers in the field of conflict resolution, (b) groups committed to nonviolence such as the Quaker Church, (c) anti-nuclear war groups, and (d) lawyers. More recently, groups concerned about the rising frequency of violence among children and teenagers have generated more large-scale implementations. Finally, there are a number of related programs that should be mentioned. Although there are dozens and dozens of programs, some of the most historic and important are discussed next.

Research-Theory Based Programs. The **Teaching Students to Be Peacemakers Program** (TSP) was developed in the mid-1960s at the University of Minnesota by researchers in the field of conflict resolution (Johnson, 1970, 1971a, 1971b; Johnson & Johnson, 1995a;

Johnson, Johnson, & Johnson, 1976). Beginning in 1966, teachers were trained to teach students how to resolve conflicts constructively. Special attention was paid to (a) helping students resolve cross-ethnic conflicts arising from desegregation and (b) helping faculty resolve conflicts arising from site-base decision making and team teaching. The Peacemaker Program (a) trains all students in the school to negotiate integrative agreements to their conflicts and mediate schoolmates' conflicts, (b) integrates the training into curriculum units, (c) repeats the training each year at an increasingly higher level of sophistication as a 12-year spiral curriculum, (d) ensures that school norms, values, and culture support the use of the negotiation and mediation procedures, and (e) ensures that all students serve as peer mediators an equal amount of time so that the benefits for doing so are experienced by everyone. The Peacemaker Program has been implemented in schools throughout North America and in several countries in Europe, the Middle East, Africa, Asia, and Central and South America.

Columbia University's **International Center for Cooperation and Conflict Resolution** (ICCCR) focuses primarily on research and training in conflict resolution (Coleman & Fisher-Yoshida, 2004). Its program is implemented by training school mediators, bringing conflict resolution concepts and skills into the curriculum, using cooperative learning and constructive controversy as pedagogical methods, changing the school culture from competitive to cooperative, and involving the broader community in the program. Although ICCCR primarily works with schools, and has conducted one of the few large-scale implementations of conflict resolution training, it has also worked with the United Nations and business and industry to train adults in how to resolve conflicts constructively.

The **Conflict Resolution Model** (Wertheim, Love, Peck, & Littlefield, 1992) developed in Australia consists of four components that represent different stages in successful problem solving. The first component is developing expectations for "win-win" solutions by teaching that cooperation is the most effective means of managing conflict, because it leads to better quality outcomes for all concerned. The second component is identifying each party's interests. The third component is brainstorming creative options. The fourth component is combining options into win-win solutions. This model has been field-tested in Australia and a series of research studies have been conducted on its effectiveness (Davidson & Wood, 2004). Significant effects were found for cooperation training that creates expectations for integrative agreements and for training in how to engage in problem solving.

The **Constructive Controversy Program** consists of teaching students how to engage in intellectual conflict, in either academic or group decision-making situations (Johnson & Johnson, 1979, 1995b). First taught in the early 1970s, students are trained to research and prepare the best case possible for their position, give a persuasive presentation to convince others to agree with them, engage in an open discussion in which they attempt to refute opposing positions while rebutting attacks on their position, engage in perspective reversal in which they present the best case for the opposing position, and then reach a decision based on their best reasoned judgment. This program has been implemented in classrooms throughout North America, Europe, and many other parts of the world.

Nonviolence Advocacy Groups. A second source of school-based conflict resolution programs are groups committed to nonviolence. In the early 1970s, a few Quaker teachers in New York City became interested in teaching nonviolence training to children. Their efforts, known as the New York Quaker Project on Community Conflict, resulted in the founding of the **Children's Creative Response to Conflict** in 1972. Priscilla Prutzman was named its first director. Weekly workshops in public schools were given. The power of nonviolence lies in the force of justice, the power of love and caring, and the desire for personal integrity. Its modern roots lie in the teachings of Gandhi and Martin Luther King.

Anti-Nuclear War Groups. A third source of school-based conflict resolution programs are groups committed to the prevention of nuclear war. In the early 1980s the Educators for Social Responsibility was formed to address, among other things, the roots of violence in schools. In 1985, in partnership with the New York City public schools, the Educators for Social Responsibility began the **Resolving Conflict Creatively Program** (RCCP). The program is aimed at implementing (a) a 10-unit curriculum with lessons on intergroup relations, cooperative learning, and dispute resolution procedures, (b) 20 hours of training in how to be a peer mediator, and (c) ten 4-hour workshops for parents.

Lawyers. A fourth source of conflict resolution programs in schools comes from the legal profession. As a response to President Carter's Neighborhood Justice Centers, in 1977 trial lawyer Ray Shonholtz established the Community Boards in San Francisco to mediate conflicts in neighborhoods. In mediating conflicts among adults, the mediators had to teach conflict resolution skills. Turning some attention to prevention, they approached local schools with the idea of beginning a peer mediation program in schools. In 1982 Helena Davis wrote a conflict manager curriculum for elementary schools that was piloted in 1984. In the 1985–1986 school year, middle and high school curricula were developed and implemented. The curriculum has been extended and modified by Gail Sadalla.

Large-Scale Implementations. The Ohio Commission on Dispute Resolution and Conflict Management joined with the Ohio Department of Education to create a statewide model of teaching conflict resolution education throughout the state that could be institutionalized within each school and district (Batton, 2002). Each school year, the two agencies award competitive grants to Ohio's public schools K–12 to design, implement, and evaluate conflict resolution programs. Since 1994, more than 700 conflict resolution grants have been awarded. The agencies also make training, technical assistance, and age-appropriate lesson plans and resource materials available to grantee schools. In 2002 more than 1,400 public schools in 380 or more of Ohio's 612 school districts reported having a conflict resolution program in place.

The National Curriculum Integration Project in 1998 recruited seven middle schools in seven different states to implement conflict resolution education into an academic curricula (Compton, 2002). Their evaluation indicated that classroom learning climate was seen as more positive, students' tendency to take the perspective of the other disputant increased, but other aspects of the program, such as the use of problem-solving strategies in resolving conflicts, were relatively unaffected.

The Oregon School Conflict Resolution Information Project began in 1999 as a collaborative project between the Oregon Dispute Resolution Commission and the Oregon Department of Education to develop resources for schools to implement conflict resolution programs (Ford, 2002). To institutionalize the program, six main groups are involved in building a strong and sustainable school conflict resolution education program: school staff members and school boards, students, parents and extended family, other community groups, Community Dispute Resolution Centers, and the School Conflict Resolution Program Team. The six partner groups collaborate for successful implementation of conflict resolution education programs throughout the state of Oregon.

Related Programs. Robert Enright and his associates have developed a training program on forgiveness, teaching students how to forgive as a means of conflict resolution (Enright, Gassin, & Knutson, 2003). They have tested their training program on students who have inappropriately high levels of anger and with students who have had exceptionally stressful situations to cope with, such as children in Northern Ireland who have been exposed to terrorism throughout their lives. The training program emphasizes five elements: reframing for inherent worth (realization that all people, even those who are unfair, have worth), moral love (acting more out of a concern for the well-being of another more than for oneself), kindness, respect, and generosity to those around them, including the ones who have hurt them.

Conflict creates stress, and how students manage their stress influences how constructively conflicts are resolved. Frydenberg (2004) and her colleagues have developed a training program on coping with stress and adversity and developing resilience that has been used in Australia. Consisting of 10 sessions, the program includes identifying ineffective coping strategies (such as worry and self-blame), thinking optimistically (appraising events positively, not negatively), communicating effectively (including how to ask for help), effective problem solving, effective decision making, goal setting (including aiming high), and time management. These coping skills help students manage the stress and adversity that is inherent in many conflicts.

The Christian Child's Fund works throughout the world teaching children and adolescents who were child warriors and personally committed atrocities and brutal acts how to live peacefully as adults. This is an important type of peace education (Wessells, 2003). Once the civil wars have ended, and the rebel and other various armies have been disbanded, these children and adolescents need to be resocialized. Whereas violence training emphasizes the legitimacy of violence, the glorification of martyrs, an identity consisting of being both a victim and a warrior, and education for intolerance, peace education emphasizes the legitimacy of resolving conflicts peacefully, the glorification of reasoned discussion and problem solving, an identity as a peacemaker, and education for tolerance and the value of each human life. If child warriors are not resocialized, they often continue cycles of violence, including terrorism.

Conclusion. Although these and many other programs are being implemented in schools throughout the world, there may be only two conflict procedures that are (a) based on principles formulated from theory that has been validated by research, (b) are congruent with and will enhance a cooperative classroom climate, and (c) may be integrated into academic lessons to enhance achievement as well as constructive conflict resolution. The programs are the **Teaching Students to Be Peacemakers Program** and the **Constructive Controversy Program**. These programs are discussed in more detail.

BENEFITS OF TEACHING STUDENTS TO RESOLVE CONFLICTS CONSTRUCTIVELY

Conflict is the moment of truth within any social system or relationship. When conflicts are resolved constructively, they enrich and enhance the success of any endeavor or relationship creating benefits for individual students, the school, and the society as a whole (Johnson & Johnson, 1995a, 1995b, 1996b).

Benefits for Students

There are so many personal and societal benefits for teaching students how to manage conflicts constructively that only a few can be discussed here. Individuals who resolve their conflicts constructively tend to (Johnson & Johnson, 1989):

1. Be healthier psychologically. They tend to, for example, cope with stress and adversity more positively, be more optimistic, have higher self-esteem, be more prosocially oriented, have greater social competencies, and have a greater sense of efficacy.

2. Develop socially and cognitively in more healthy ways. At every stage of social and cognitive development there are conflicts that must be resolved constructively if the person is to move on to the next stage.
3. Be happier more of the time (i.e., destructively managed conflicts tend to result in long periods of anger, regret, desire for revenge, shame, guilt, and other negative emotions). Conflicts are a source of fun, excitement, energy, curiosity, and motivation.
4. Have more positive and supportive interpersonal and intergroup relationships. Resolving conflicts constructively strengthens relationships by increasing individuals' confidence that they can resolve their disagreements, caring and commitment, and personal and task-oriented social support, as well as keeping the relationship clear of irritations and resentments so that positive feelings can be experienced fully.
5. Have a greater sense of meaning and purpose in life. Mediating the conflicts of schoolmates tends to give students a sense of purpose and meaning that is unavailable in most of school life (Johnson & Johnson, 1996b). Engaging in conflicts, furthermore, clarifies own and others' identity, commitments, and values.
6. Be more engaged with the school and its academic program. There are quiet conflicts characterized by withdrawal and disengagement (reflected in tardiness, class cutting, and truancy) which, when managed constructively, results in students becoming more engaged.
7. Achieve higher academically. Students who manage conflicts constructively tend to increase their academic achievement, retention, insight, creativity, problem solving, and synthesizing. When conflicts are managed destructively, the other schoolmates will tend to try to sabotage, obstruct, and interfere with students' attempts to achieve their goals.
8. Have a developmental advantage. Learning how to resolve conflicts constructively, and being skilled in doing so, gives students a developmental advance over those who never learned how to do so (Johnson & Johnson, 1995a, 1996b, 2002). Individuals skilled in resolving conflicts constructively tend to make and keep more friends, be more liked by and popular with peers, and generally experience more happiness and less stress. They tend to be more assertive, have more self-control, are more able to communicate effectively, and are more able to cooperate with others. They tend to engage in more prosocial behavior and less antisocial, inappropriate behavior (such as bullying, teasing, excluding others, challenging the authority of teachers and administrators). Teaching students to be peacemakers may be one of the most valuable competencies that can be given to students, benefiting them throughout their lives.
9. Have more successful careers. Learning how to engage in problem-solving negotiations and peer mediation may especially affect students' later employability and career success. A recent survey of vice presidents and personnel directors of 100 of the nation's 1,000 largest corporations found that the people who manage America's leading corporations spend over 4 working weeks a year dealing with the problems caused by employees who cannot resolve their conflicts with each other. The American Management Association reported that about 24% of managers' time is spent dealing with conflict. School and hospital administrators, mayors, and city managers report that conflict resolution commands nearly 49% of their attention. The higher the position in the organization, the more skillful the person needs to be.

Benefits for the School

The benefits for the school of students resolving conflicts constructively include decreases in bullying, social rejection, social withdrawal, number of discipline referrals, and school dropouts

(Johnson & Johnson, 1996b, 2002). As a result, the quality of life within the school is enhanced. In addition, when students manage their conflicts constructively, their achievement and liking for school tend to go up and the school is successful. The costs of students resolving conflicts destructively (i.e., the occurrence of discipline problems, general incivility, lack of motivation to learn, property damage, depression and anxiety, and even violence) is considerable in terms of faculty and staff time and energy. The attention paid to instruction and socialization is significantly reduced. These costs are avoided when students lean how to manage conflicts constructively. Finally, as a result of teaching students the procedures for managing conflicts, teachers will master the procedures. As the Roman philosopher Seneca was fond of saying, "He who teaches, learns twice." A faculty skilled in resolving conflicts with students and with each other and other staff members is an important resource of any school.

Benefits for Society

There are numerous advantages for our society if all children, adolescents, and young adults are trained in how to resolve conflicts constructively. Society will be more cohesive and the relations among citizens and groups will be more cooperative when citizens are skilled in resolving conflicts constructively. Organizations will function more smoothly and effectively. Families will be more cohesive and caring. Fewer citizens will be involved in legal disputes. There are so many benefits to society that teaching students how to manage conflicts constructively should be a major priority in all schools.

THEORETICAL PERSPECTIVES ON CONFLICT RESOLUTION, VIOLENCE PREVENTION, AND PEACEMAKING

Of the approaches to conflict resolution programs, the most successful may be those programs based on theory validated by research. To understand the development of such programs, it may be helpful to review the early theorizing in conflict and the more current theorizing conducted in the 20th century (Fig. 30.2).

Early Theorists

The history of the modern field of conflict resolution began with the writings of the British naturalist Charles Darwin, the German sociologist Karl Marx, and the German psychologist Sigmund Freud (Deutsch, 2000). In his theory of evolution, Charles Darwin stressed the competitive struggle for existence in nature and the survival of the fittest. He wrote, "all nature is at war, one organism with another, or with external nature. Seeing the contented face nature, this may at first be well doubted; but reflection will inevitably prove it is too true" (quoted in Hyman, 1966, p. 29). Conflict phenomena such as war, intergroup hostility, and human exploitation could be on the basis of human instincts that evolved because they increased chances for survival.

Karl Marx presented a social-political-economic view of conflict, arguing that there was a historically inevitable, objective conflict between the economic and political interests of the social classes. As the class conflict proceeds, society increasingly breaks up into two hostile, directly antagonistic classes (bourgeoisie and proletariat) who fight for supremacy.

Sigmund Freud argued that conflict is an inevitable by-product of the needs and goals of individuals clashing with the needs and goals of others (such as parents). Psychosexual development thus largely consists of a constant struggle between the biologically rooted infantile id and the socially determined, internalized parental surrogate, the superego. Conflicts with

DATE	EVENT
	Confucian Mediation: Moral Persuasion and Agreement
	Japan Village Leaders Mediated Seeking Conciliation
	African Neighborhood Meeting to Mediate Conflict Cooperatively
	Religious Leaders (Priests, Ministers, Rabbis) Served as Mediators
1858	Charles Darwin, *Origin of Species*
1848	Karl Marx (with F. Engels), *Communist Manifesto*, Social Determinism
1930	Sigmund Freud, Psychological Development
1924	Mary Parker Follett, Positive Conflict, Cooperative Problem Solving
1931	Kurt Lewin, Three Types of Internal Conflict, Interdependence
1944	Von Neumann & Morgenstern, *Theory of Games and Economic Behavior*
1949	Morton Deutsch, *Theory and Research on Cooperation and Competition*
1965	Walton & McKenzie, *A Behavioral Theory of Labor Negotiations*
1967	David W. Johnson, *Perspective Reversal in Distributive and Integrative Negotiations*
1968	David W. Johnson, Initial Peacemaking Program
1972	David W. Johnson, Initial Constructive Controversy Program
1973	Morton Deutsch, Constructive Conflict
1972	New York Quaker Project on Community Conflict, Children's Creative Response to Conflict, Priscilla Prutzman first director.
1984	San Francisco Community Boards conflict resolution curriculum implemented in schools
1985	Resolving Conflict Creatively Program (RCCP) developed by Educators for Social Responsibility
1992	Wertheim, Love, Littlefield, & Peck, Conflict Resolution Model
1994	Institutionalizing Conflict Resolution Education: The Ohio Model
1998	National Curriculum Integration Project
1999	Oregon School Conflict Resolution Information Project

FIGURE 30.2. Time-line: history of conflict resolution.
Given above is a partial time line on the history of conflict resolution. Please excuse the absence of anyone of any event that should be listed—the absences are unintended. In limited space it is not possible to list all the people and events important to the history of conflict resolution.

and detachment from parents are a healthy necessity for becoming a separate individual, realigning relationships, and reducing anxieties. As the person matures, family relationships are disrupted, conflicts ensue, and the person withdraws, and establishes alternative caring and committed relationships with peers that replace the close ties with parents.

Darwin, Marx, and Freud all posit a competitive struggle that reflected the social conditions of their times, such as the intense competition among businesses and among nations, the devastation of World War I, the economic depression of the 1920s and 1930s, and the rise of Nazism and other totalitarian systems (Deutsch, 2000). Because much of the writings in the 1930s, 1940s, and early 1950s on the topics of war, intergroup conflict, and industrial strife were largely nonempirical, there was little evidence to contradict the competitive orientation to conflict.

20th-Century Theorists

In contrast to the early theorists, there are 20th century theorists who viewed conflict as potentially cooperative and positive: Mary Parker Follett, Kurt Lewin, Jean Piaget, Morton Deutsch, von Neumann and Morgenstern, and David and Roger Johnson (the authors of this chapter). Mary Parker Follett was a lifelong advocate of democracy, a leader in the movement to establish community centers in public schools, a leader in the attempts to improve management and administration in industry and public institutions, and a popular lecturer known for her combination of passion, charm, and common sense. She taught that conflict in groups is natural and that it can be harnessed to increase organizational productivity. One of her examples of such conflict resolution is a conflict between two people reading in a library room. One wants to open the window for ventilation, the other to keep it closed in order not to catch cold. To resolve their conflict they search for creative options and finally agree to open a window in the next room, thereby letting in fresh air while avoiding a draft and thus both sides get all of what they want.

Kurt Lewin's work had a profound impact on social psychology. In Europe and the United States, during the 1920s, 1930s, and 1940s, Kurt Lewin and his students developed an empirical social psychology and a new vocabulary for thinking about conflict. Lewin (1931, 1935) presented a penetrating theoretical discussion of three basic types of psychological conflict: (a) approach-approach (the individual stands between two positive valences of approximately equal strength), (b) avoidance-avoidance (the individual stands between two negative valences of approximately equal strength), and (c) approach-avoidance (the individual is exposed to opposing forces deriving from positive and negative values). Lewin's insisted that conflicts were inevitable and potentially positive, resulting in improvements in personal and group decision making.

In the 1930s, Jean Piaget (1932/1965) posited that conflicts resulting from intellectual maturation spur revisions in understanding of the self and relationships. Conflict is the mechanism by which children and adolescents acquire new cognitive structures and develop new perspectives and stagelike shifts in patterns of reasoning that result in changes in behavior toward parents and peers. The new behavior patterns create new conflicts as roles and normative expectations are renegotiated.

Morton Deutsch, one of Kurt Lewin's doctoral students, published a theory of cooperation and competition in 1949, and then proceeded to extend the theory to include trust, conflict resolution, and systems of distributive justice (Deutsch, 1949, 1962, 1973, 1985). By defining the nature of cooperation and competition, Deutsch made it possible to define conflict and related phenomena. Conflict may be defined as a disruption in ongoing cooperative efforts or as a competition, conflict tends to be resolved differently according to whether it occurs within a cooperative or a competitive context, and the successful resolution of many conflicts depends on reestablishing a cooperative relationship among the disputants. The theory on cooperation and competition and the resulting research provide a foundation for the empirical study of conflict and the understanding of the processes involved in conflict.

In 1944, von Neumann and Morgenstern published their classic book, *Theory of Games and Economic Behavior*. Game theory formulated in mathematical terms the problem of conflict of interests and clarified that parties in conflict have interdependent interests; their fates are woven together. Whereas zero-sum games illustrate pure competitive conflict, non-zero-sum (and coalition) games recognize that cooperative as well as competitive interests (i.e., mixed motives) may be intertwined in conflict. Game matrices as an experimental device became popular because they facilitated precise definition of the reward structure encountered by the participants, and hence of the way participants were dependent on one another. Well over 1,000 studies based on experimental games were published by 1985.

In the early 1960s, David W. Johnson (one of Morton Deutsch's students) began developing two theories of positive conflict, one focused on integrative negotiation and one focused on decision making and reasoned judgments. He also investigated the conditions under which conflict resulted in positive outcomes. The related research focused on (a) engaging in perspective taking in win-lose (distributive) and problem-solving (integrative) negotiations, (b) establishing joint goals and expressing cooperative intentions in conflict situations, (c) expressing emotions such as warmth and avoiding expressing emotions such as coldness or anger in negotiations, (d) strengthening the identity of low-power persons in conflict, (e) challenging one's conclusions with opposing views, and (g) the components of problem-solving, integrative negotiation.

Summary

Although the early conflict theorists emphasized understanding the competitive nature of many conflicts, later theorists have emphasized the positive aspects of conflicts and the essential role of conflict in human relationships and endeavors. Thus, there are two major purposes behind implementing conflict resolution programs in schools: reducing the frequency of destructive conflicts and increasing the frequency of constructive conflicts. The two most researched and perhaps widely implemented programs to achieve these purposes are Teaching Students to Be Peacemakers and Constructive Controversy. Both are based on social interdependence theory.

TEACHING STUDENTS TO BE PEACEMAKERS

After establishing a cooperative context, students must be taught to manage their conflicts of interests constructively. The types of conflicts that students typically deal with in school include dating/relationship issues, control of resources, playground conflicts, access/possession conflicts, preferences, verbal harassments (name-calling, insults, put-downs, teasing), verbal arguments, rumors and gossip, things damaged or stolen, and physical aggression (Johnson & Johnson, 1996b). In dealing with these and other conflicts, untrained students tend to either avoid the conflict (i.e., withdrawal) or try to overpower the opposition (i.e., forcing or win-lose negotiation) about 90% of the time and untrained faculty and staff tend to impose a resolution the majority of the time. The research indicates that a wide variety of conflicts of interests occur continually in schools and both students and faculty need to be trained in how to resolve such conflicts constructively.

Implementing Program

There are six parts in teaching students how to be peacemakers (Johnson & Johnson, 1995a). All students receive 30 minutes of training per day for about 20 days and then receive weekly training for the rest of the school year.

Part One: Understanding the Nature of Conflict. Students need to learn how to recognize when a conflict is and is not occurring and the potential constructive consequences of conflict. Generally, students have a negativity bias in which they see conflicts as always involving anger, hostility, and violence and do not recognize conflicts as such when they lead to laughter, insight, learning, and problem solving. Students learn that as long as they are managed constructively, conflicts should occur frequently.

Part Two: Choosing an Appropriate Conflict Strategy. The second part of the Peacemaker training focuses on the two concerns in conflicts: (a) to achieve one's goals and (b) to maintain a good relationship with the other person. The importance of the goals and relationship determine whether a person should withdraw (giving up both one's goal and the relationship), force (achieve one's goal at the other person's expense thereby giving up the relationship—sometimes known as win-lose negotiations), smooth (give up one's goal in order to enhance the relationship), compromise (give up part of one's goal at some damage to the relationship), or negotiate to solve the problem (achieve one's goal and maintain the relationship).

Part Three: Negotiating to Solve the Problem. Conflicts of interests are resolved through negotiation (when negotiation does not work, then mediation is required). There are two ways to negotiate: (a) **distributive**, "win-lose," or forcing (where one person benefits only if the opponent agrees to make a concession) and (b) **integrative** or problem solving (where disputants work together to create an agreement that benefits everyone involved). In ongoing relationships, it is integrative negotiation that leads to all disputants achieving their goals while maintaining or even improving the quality of their relationship. The problem-solving, integrative negotiation procedure consists of six steps (Johnson & Johnson, 1995a):

1. **Describing what you want**. "*I want to use the book now.*" This includes using good communication skills and defining the conflict as a small and specific mutual problem.
2. **Describing how you feel**. "*I'm frustrated.*" Disputants must understand how they feel and communicate it openly and clearly.
3. **Describing the reasons for your wants and feelings**. "*You have been using the book for the past hour. If I don't get to use the book soon my report will not be done on time. It's frustrating to have to wait so long.*" This includes expressing cooperative intentions, listening carefully, separating interests from positions, and differentiating before trying to integrate the two sets of interests.
4. **Taking the other's perspective and summarizing your understanding of what the other person wants, how the other person feels, and the reasons underlying both**. "*My understanding of you is...*" This includes understanding the perspective of the opposing disputant and being able to see the problem from both perspectives simultaneously.
5. **Inventing three optional plans to resolve the conflict in ways that maximize joint benefits**. "*Plan A is..., Plan B is..., Plan C is...*" This includes inventing creative options to solve the problem and maximize joint benefit.
6. **Choosing one option and formalizing the agreement with a handshake**. "*Let's agree on Plan B!*" A wise agreement maximizes joint benefit, strengthens disputants' ability to work together cooperatively, and improves their ability to resolve conflicts constructively in the future. It specifies how each disputant should act in the future and how the agreement will be reviewed and renegotiated if it does not work.

Part Four: Mediating Others' Conflicts. When students are unable to negotiate a resolution to their conflict, they may request help from a mediator. **Mediation** exists when a neutral and impartial third party actively assists two or more people to negotiate a constructive resolution to their conflict. A **mediator** is a neutral person who helps two or more people resolve their conflict. In contrast, **arbitration** is the submission of a dispute to a disinterested third party (such as a teacher or principal) who makes a final and binding judgment as to how the conflict will be resolved. Mediation consists of four steps (Johnson & Johnson, 1995a):

1. **Ending hostilities**: Break up hostile encounters and cool off students.
2. **Ensuring disputants are committed to the mediation process**: To ensure that disputants are committed to the mediation process and are ready to negotiate in good faith, the mediator introduces the process of mediation and sets the ground rules. The mediator first introduces him- or herself. The mediator asks students if they want to solve the problem and does not proceed until both answer "yes." Then the mediator explains that mediation is voluntary, the mediator is neutral and will not take sides, each person will have the chance to state his or her view of the conflict without interruption, and disputants must follow the rules of (a) agreeing to solve the problem, (b) no-name calling, (c) no interrupting, (d) being as honest as you can, (e) abiding by the agreement made, and (f) keeping anything said in mediation confidential (the mediator especially will not tell anyone what is said).
3. **Helping disputants successfully negotiate with each other**: The disputants are carefully taken through the problem-solving negotiation sequence.
4. **Formalizing the agreement**: The mediator formalizes the agreement by completing a **Mediation Report Form** and having disputants sign it and shake hands as a commitment to implement the agreement and abide by its conditions. The mediator becomes the keeper of the contract and checks back with the disputants a day or so later to see if the agreement is working.

Part Five: Implementing the Program. Once students understand how to negotiate and mediate, the Peacemaker Program is implemented. Each day the teacher selects two class members to serve as official mediators. Any conflicts students cannot resolve themselves are referred to the mediators. The mediators wear official T-shirts, patrol the playground and lunchroom, and are available to mediate any conflicts that occur in the classroom or school. An example is as follows.

> During lunch on the playground, a ball rolls out-of-bounds during a lively game of soccer. A cluster of students walking by laugh as one of them kicks the ball away from the player trying to retrieve it. An argument ensures. A pair of peer mediators with clipboards in hand quickly approach the two disputants. "Would you like some help resolving your conflict?" So begins the mediation process through which the disputants arrive at a mutually agreeable solution that makes both happy. They shake hands as friends and return to their activities while the peer mediators make a note of the resolution, then continue to be available for other schoolmates who may need help resolving conflicts.

The role of mediator is rotated so that all students in the class or school serve as mediators an equal amount of time. Initially, students mediate in pairs. This ensures that shy or nonverbal students get the same amount of experience as more extroverted and verbally fluent students. Mediating classmates' conflicts is perhaps the most effective way of teaching students the need for the skillful use of each step of the negotiation procedure.

If peer mediation fails, the teacher mediates the conflict. If teacher mediation fails, the teacher arbitrates by deciding who is right and who is wrong. If that fails, the principal mediates the conflict. If that fails, the principal arbitrates. Teaching all students to mediate properly results in a schoolwide discipline program where students are empowered to regulate and control their own and their classmates' actions. Teachers and administrators are then freed to spend more of their energies on instruction.

Part Six: Teaching Continuing Lessons to Refine and Upgrade Students' Skills. Additional lessons are needed to refine and upgrade students' skills in using the negotiation and mediation procedures. Gaining real expertise in resolving conflicts constructively takes years of training and practice. A few hours of training is clearly insufficient. Negotiation and mediation training may become part of the fabric of school life by integrating them into academic lessons. Literature, history, and science units typically involve conflict. Almost any lesson in these subject areas can be modified to include role-playing situations in which the negotiation or mediation procedures are used. In our research, for example, we have focused on integrating the peacemaker training into history units and English literature units involving the studying of a novel. Each of the major conflicts in the novel was used to teach the negotiation or mediation procedures and students participated in role playing how to use the procedures to resolve the conflicts in the novel constructively.

Spiral Curriculum From the First Through the Twelfth Grades. The **Teaching Students to Be Peacemakers Program** is a 12-year spiral program that is retaught each year in an increasingly sophisticated and complex way. It takes years to become competent in resolving conflicts. Twelve years of training and practice will result in a person with considerable expertise in resolving conflicts constructively.

Benefits of Conflict Resolution and Peer Mediation Programs

A meta-analysis has been reported on 16 studies conducted between 1988 and 2000 on the effectiveness of the Peacemaker Program in eight different schools in two different countries (Johnson & Johnson, 2002). The studies included students from kindergarten through ninth grades and were conducted in rural, suburban, and urban settings in the United States and Canada. In most of the studies, students were randomly assigned to conditions and teachers were rotated across conditions. These carefully controlled field-experimental studies addressed a series of questions.

"How often do conflicts among students occur and what are the most commonly occurring conflicts?" The research indicates that students engage in conflicts several times a day. Whereas in the suburban schools studied, the majority of conflicts reported were over the possession of and access to resources, preferences about what to do, playground issues, and turn taking, in the urban elementary school studied, the vast majority of conflicts referred to mediation involved physical and verbal aggression. Students described more different types of conflicts at school than at home. The conflicts at home tended to be over preferences, possessions, and access; few conflicts were reported over beliefs and relationships or involved physical fights and verbal insults. Very few conflicts occurred over academic work or basic values in either setting.

"What strategies did students use to manage their conflicts before training?" Before training, students tended to manage their conflicts through trying to win by (a) forcing the other to concede (either by overpowering the other disputant or by asking the teacher to force the other to give in) or (b) withdrawing from the conflict and the other person. The possibility of problem-solving, integrative negotiations seemed never to occur to most students. One of the teachers stated in her log, "*Before training, students viewed conflict as fights that always*

TABLE 30.1
Mean Weighted Effect Sizes for Peacemaker Studies

Dependent Variable	*Mean*	*Standard Deviation*	*Number of Effects*
Learned Procedure	2.25	1.98	13
Learned Procedure—Retention	3.34	4.16	9
Applied Procedure	2.16	1.31	4
Application—Retention	0.46	0.16	3
Strategy Constructiveness	1.60	1.70	21
Constructiveness—Retention	1.10	0.53	10
Strategy Two-Concerns	1.10	0.46	5
Two-Concerns—Retention	0.45	0.20	2
Integrative Negotiation	0.98	0.36	5
Quality of Solutions	0.73	0	1
Positive Attitude	1.07	0.25	5
Negative Attitude	−0.61	0.37	2
Academic Achievement	0.88	0.09	5
Academic Retention	0.70	0.31	4

Note: From Johnson, R., & Johnson, D. W. (2002 April). *Teaching students to be peacemakers: A meta-analysis.* Paper presented at the Annual Convention of the American Educational Research Association, New Orleans. Reprinted with permission.

resulted in a winner and a loser. To avoid such an unpleasant situation, they usually placed the responsibility for resolving conflicts on me, the teacher."

"Was the Peacemaker training successful in teaching students the negotiation and mediation procedures?" Following training, students were given a test requiring them to write from memory the steps of negotiation and the procedures for mediation. Across our studies, over 90% of the students accurately recalled 100% of the negotiation and the mediation procedure. Up to a year after the training had ended, on average over 75% of students were still able to write out all the negotiation and mediation steps. The average effect size for the studies was 2.25 for the immediate post-test and 3.34 for the retention measures (see Table 30.1). These results indicate that the training was quite effective.

"Could students apply the negotiation and mediation procedures to conflicts?" Learning the negotiation and mediation procedures does not necessarily mean that students will use them in actual conflict situations. Both paper-and-pencil and observation measures were used to determine whether students could use the procedures in actual conflicts. Students completed Conflict Report Forms on any conflict they were involved in or were observed in actual conflicts with their classmates. The results indicate that students were quite good at applying the negotiation and mediation procedures. Immediately after training, students applied the procedures almost perfectly (effect size = 2.16) and were still quite good months after the training was over (effect size = 0.46).

"Do students transfer the negotiation and mediation procedures to nonclassroom and nonschool situations?" Our studies demonstrated that students did in fact use the negotiation and mediation procedures in the hallways, lunchroom, and playground. In addition, students used the procedures in family settings.

"What strategies did the students use to resolve their conflicts?" Two scales were used to classify the strategies students used to resolve their conflicts. For the Strategy Constructiveness Scale (a continuum from destructive actions [physical and verbal aggression and avoidance] to constructive actions [invoking norms for appropriate behavior, proposing alternatives, and engaging in problem-solving negotiations]), the average effect size was 1.60 on the posttest and 1.10 for the retention tests. For the Two-Concerns Scale (five strategies of withdrawing, forcing smoothing, compromising, and negotiating to solve the problem), the posttest effect size was 1.10 and the retention effect size was 0.45. Trained students tended to use the integrative negotiation and mediation procedures in resolving the conflicts. There were no significant differences between males and females in the strategies used to manage conflicts. There were no significant differences between the strategies used in school and in the home; students used the strategies learned in school just as frequently in the home as they did in the school.

"When given the option, would students engage in "win-lose" or problem-solving negotiations?" Following the TSP training, students were placed in a negotiation situation in which they could either try to win or maximize joint outcomes. Untrained students almost always tried to win whereas the majority of trained students focused on maximizing joint outcomes (effect size = 0.98).

"How would the conflicts be resolved?" Very few of the conflicts were arbitrated by adults or resolved through forgiveness in either the control or experimental groups. Untrained students left many conflicts unresolved. The number of integrative solutions that resulted in both sides achieving their goals was much higher in conflicts among trained (rather than untrained) students. There was no significant difference between the solutions arrived at for conflicts in school or at home. Only one study had the necessary statistics to determine an effect size (ES = 0.73), indicating that trained students tended to find more constructive resolutions than did untrained students.

"Does the Peacemaker training increase students' academic achievement?" The Peacemaker training was integrated into both English literature and history academic units to determine its impact on academic achievement. The basic design for these studies was to randomly assign students to classes in which the Peacemaker training was integrated into the academic unit studied or to classes in which the academic unit was studied without any conflict training. Students who received the Peacemaker training as part of the academic unit tended to score significantly higher on achievement (effect size = 0.88) and retention (effect size = 0.70) tests than did students who studied the academic unit only. Students not only learned the factual information contained in the academic unit better, they were better able to interpret the information in insightful ways.

"Does the Peacemaker training result in more positive attitudes toward conflict?" Attitudes toward conflict were measured by a word association task. Before training, the students overwhelmingly held negative attitudes toward conflict seeing almost no potential positive outcomes. Although still perceiving conflict more negatively than positively, the attitudes of trained students became markedly more positive (effect size = 1.07) and less negative (effect size = −0.61) whereas the attitudes of untrained students stayed essentially the same. Students generally liked to engage in the procedures. A teacher stated, "*They never refuse to negotiate or mediate. When there's a conflict and you say it's time for conflict resolution, you never have either one say I won't do it. There are no refusals.*" Teachers and administrators and parents tended to perceive the Peacemaker Program to be constructive and helpful. Many parents whose children were not part of the project requested that their children receive the training next year, and a number of parents requested that they receive the training so they could use the procedures to improve conflict management within the family.

"Does the TSP training result in fewer discipline problems that have to be managed by the teacher and the administration?" Students tended to resolve their conflicts without the involvement of faculty and administrators, significantly reducing classroom management problems. The number of discipline problems teachers had to deal with decreased by about 60% and referrals to administrators dropped about 90%. A teacher commented, "*Classroom management problems are nil as far as I'm concerned. We don't do a lot of disciplining per se. A lot of times, when a conflict occurs on the playground, they resolve it there and do not bring it back to the classroom. So there is a lot less I have to deal with in the classroom."*

ACADEMIC CONTROVERSY

Management problems may also originate in arguments and disagreements among students and between students and teachers or staff members. As with all conflicts, it is not the occurrence of arguments that is the problem, it is how the arguments are managed. In making decisions it is especially important to consider a variety of options that conflict with each other. Students need to be trained to resolve intellectual conflicts (such as arguments and disagreements) in which they may have different conclusions or opinions. Learning how to resolve conflicts over different conclusions may take place in the classroom during academic lessons.

Academic Controversies

A **controversy** exists when one person's ideas, opinions, information, theories, or conclusions are incompatible with those of another and the two seek to reach an agreement. Controversies are resolved by engaging in what Aristotle called deliberate discourse (i.e., the discussion of the advantages and disadvantages of proposed actions) aimed at synthesizing novel solutions (i.e., creative problem solving). Teaching students how to engage in the controversy process begins with randomly assigning students to heterogeneous cooperative learning groups of four members (Johnson & Johnson, 1979, 1989, 1995b). The groups are given an issue on which to write a report and pass a test. Each cooperative group is divided into two pairs. One pair is given the con position on the issue and the other pair is given the pro position. Each pair is given the instructional materials needed to define their position and point them toward supporting information. The cooperative goal of reaching a consensus on the issue (by synthesizing the best reasoning from both sides) and writing a quality group report is highlighted. Students then:

1. **Research and Prepare a Position**. Each pair develops the position assigned, learns the relevant information, and plans how to present the best case possible to the other pair. Near the end of the period pairs are encouraged to compare notes with pairs from other groups who represent the same position.
2. **Present and Advocate Their Position**. Each pair makes their presentation to the opposing pair. Each member of the pair has to participate in the presentation. Students are to be as persuasive and convincing as possible. Members of the opposing pair are encouraged to take notes, listen carefully to learn the information being presented, and clarify anything they do not understand.
3. **Refute Opposing Position and Rebut Attacks on Their Own**. Students argue forcefully and persuasively for their position, presenting as many facts as they can to support their point of view. Students analyze and critically evaluate the information, rationale, and inductive and deductive reasoning of the opposing pair, asking them for the facts that support their point of view. They refute the arguments of the opposing pair and rebut attacks on their position. They discuss the issue, following a set of rules to help them criticize ideas without criticizing people, differentiate the two positions, and assess the degree of evidence and logic supporting each position. They keep in mind that the issue is complex and they need to know both sides to write a good report.

4. **Reverse Perspectives**. The pairs reverse perspectives and present each other's positions. In arguing for the opposing position, students are forceful and persuasive. They add any new information that the opposing pair did not think to present. They strive to see the issue from both perspectives simultaneously.
5. **Synthesize and Integrate the Best Evidence and Reasoning Into a Joint Position**. The four members of the group drop all advocacy and synthesize and integrate what they know into a joint position to which all sides can agree. They (a) finalize the report (the teacher evaluates reports on the quality of the writing, the logical presentation of evidence, and the oral presentation of the report to the class), (b) present their conclusions to the class (all four members of the group are required to participate orally in the presentation), (c) individually take the test covering both sides of the issue (if every member of the group achieves up to criterion, they all receive bonus points), and (d) process how well they worked together and how they could be even more effective next time.

Theory of Constructive Controversy

There is no more certain sign of a narrow mind, of stupidity, and of arrogance, than to stand aloof from those who think differently from us.

Walter Savage Landor

Over the past 35 years, we have (a) developed a theory of constructive controversy, (b) validated it through a program of research, (c) operationalized the validated theory into a practical procedure (there are two formats, one for decision-making situations and one for academic learning), (d) trained teachers, professors, administrators, managers, and executives in how to implement the constructive controversy procedure, and (e) developed a series of curriculum units, academic lessons, and training exercises structured for controversies. Our theorizing began with concepts taken from developmental, cognitive, social, and organizational psychology. The process through which constructive controversy creates positive outcomes involves the following theoretical assumptions (Johnson & Johnson, 1979, 1989, 1995b, 2000) (see Fig. 30.3):

1. When individuals are presented with a problem or decision, they have an initial conclusion based on categorizing and organizing incomplete information, their limited experiences, and their specific perspective. They have a high degree of confidence in their conclusions (they freeze the epistemic process).
2. When individuals present their conclusion and its rationale to others, they engage in cognitive rehearsal, deepen their understanding of their position, and use higher-level reasoning strategies. The more they attempt to persuade others to agree with them, the more committed they may become to their position.
3. When individuals are confronted with different conclusions based on other people's information, experiences, and perspectives, they become uncertain as to the correctness of their views and a state of conceptual conflict or disequilibrium is aroused. They unfreeze their epistemic process.
4. Uncertainty, conceptual conflict, or disequilibrium motivates *epistemic curiosity*, an active search for (a) more information and new experiences (increased specific content) and (b) a more adequate cognitive perspective and reasoning process (increased validity) in hopes of resolving the uncertainty.

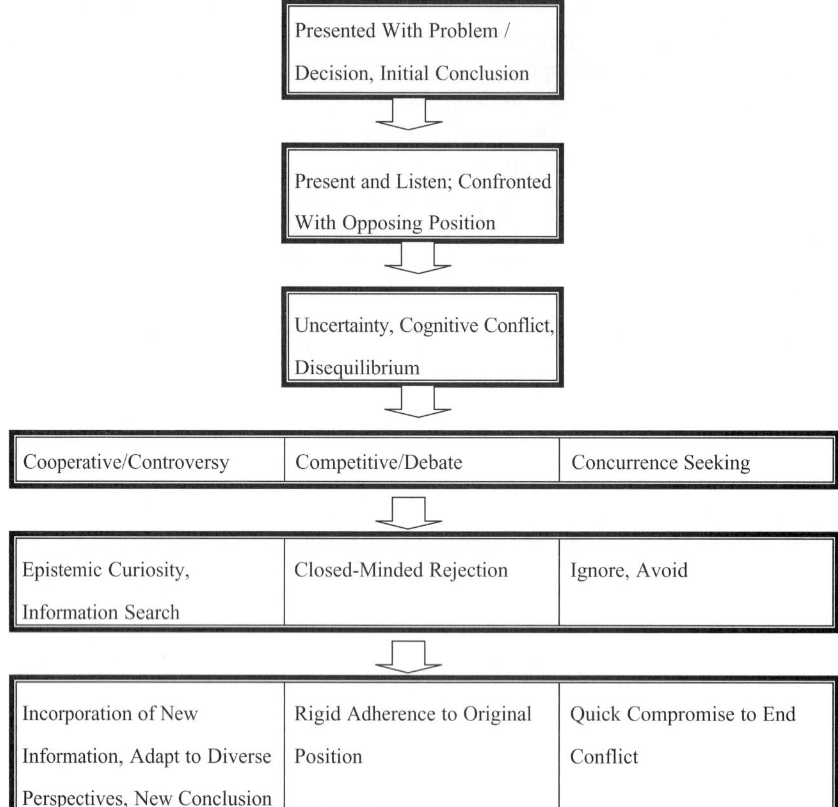

FIGURE 30.3. Processes of controversy, debate, concurrence seeking.
Note: From Johnson, D. W., & Johnson, R. (1995). *Creative controversy: Intellectual conflict in the classroom*. Edina, MN: Interaction Book Company. Reprinted with permission.

5. By adapting their cognitive perspective and reasoning through understanding and accommodating the perspective and reasoning of others, individuals derive a new, reconceptualized, and reorganized conclusion. Novel solutions and decisions that, on balance, are qualitatively better are detected. The positive feelings and commitment individuals feel in creating a solution to the problem together is extended to each other and interpersonal attraction increases. Their competencies in managing conflicts constructively tend to improve. The process may begin again at this point or it may be terminated by freezing the current conclusion and resolving any dissonance by increasing the confidence in the validity of the conclusion.

The process that results, therefore, involves having an initial conclusion as to what course of action should be adopted to solve the problem, presenting a persuasive case for that conclusion while listening to persuasive presentations of opposing positions, feeling uncertain about the correctness of one's position, engaging in a search for better information and reconceptualizing one's views on the decision, and then coming to a new conclusion about what course of action should be adopted. Each time a person goes through this process his or her conclusions may be closer and closer approximations of the "truth."

The process of constructive controversy is most effective within a certain set of conditions. The more cooperative the context, the more skilled the students are in engaging in the

TABLE 30.2
Meta-Analysis of Academic Controversy Studies: Weighted Effect Sizes

Dependent Variable	*Controversy/ Concurrence Seeking*	*Controversy/ Debate*	*Controversy/ Individualistic Efforts*
Achievement	0.68	0.40	0.87
Cognitive Reasoning	0.62	1.35	0.90
Perspective Taking	0.91	0.22	0.86
Motivation	0.75	0.45	0.71
Attitudes Toward Task	0.58	0.81	0.64
Interpersonal Attraction	0.24	0.72	0.81
Social Support	0.32	0.92	1.52
Self-Esteem	0.39	0.51	0.85

Note: From Johnson, D. W., & Johnson, R. (1995). *Creative controversy: Intellectual conflict in the classroom.* Edina, MN: Interaction Book Company. Reprinted with permission.

constructive controversy procedure, and the more able students are in engaging in rational argument, the more constructively the controversy will be resolved (Johnson & Johnson, 1979, 1989, 1995b, 2000).

Research Results

He that wrestles with us strengthens our nerves, and sharpens our skill. Our antagonist is our helper.

Edmund Burke, *Reflection on the Revolution in France*

The research on constructive controversy has been conducted in the last 35 years by several different researchers in a variety of settings using many different participant populations and many different tasks within an experimental and field-experimental format (see Table 30.2). For a detailed listing of all the supporting studies, see Johnson and Johnson (1979, 1989, 1995b, 2000, 2002). All studies randomly assigned participants to conditions. The studies have all been published in journals (except for one dissertation), have high internal validity, and have lasted from 1 to 60 hours. The studies have been conducted on elementary, intermediate, and college students. Taken together, their results have considerable validity and generalizability. A recent meta-analysis provides the data to validate or disconfirm the theory. Weighted effect sizes were computed for the 28 studies included in the analyses (see Table 30.2).

The results of the research indicate that compared with concurrence-seeking (effect size = 0.68), debate (effect size = 0.40), and individualistic efforts (effect size = 0.87), constructive controversy tends to result in higher-quality decisions (including decisions that involve ethical dilemmas) and higher-quality solutions to complex problems for which different viewpoints can plausibly be developed. Controversy tends to promote more frequent use of higher-level reasoning strategies than do concurrence-seeking (effect size = 0.62), debate (effect size = 1.35), or individualistic efforts (effect size = 0.90). Constructive controversy tends to promote more accurate and complete understanding of opposing perspectives than do concurrence-seeking (effect size = 0.91), debate (effect size = 0.22), and individualistic efforts (effect size = 0.86). In constructive controversies, participants tend to invent more creative solutions to problems, be more original in their thinking, generate and use a greater number of ideas, generate more higher-quality ideas, analyze problems at a deeper level, raise more issues, have greater feelings of stimulation and enjoyment, become more emotionally involved in and committed to solving the problem, and are more satisfied with the resulting decision. Being confronted with credible alternative views, furthermore, has resulted in the generation of more novel solutions, varied strategies, and original ideas. Participating in a controversy tends to result in attitude change beyond that which occurs when individuals read about the issue, and these attitude changes tend to be relatively stable over time (i.e., not merely a response to the controversy experience itself).

Participants in a constructive controversy tend to have more continuing motivation to learn about the issue and come to the best reasoned judgment possible than do participants in concurrence-seeking (effect size = 75), debate (effect size = 0.45), and individualistic efforts (effect size = 0.64). Participants in a controversy tend to search for (a) more information and new experiences (increased specific content) and (b) a more adequate cognitive perspective and reasoning process (increased validity) in hopes of resolving the uncertainty. There is also an active interest in learning the others' positions and developing an understanding and appreciation of them. Lowry and Johnson (1981), for example, found that students involved in a controversy, compared with students involved in concurrence seeking, read more library materials, reviewed more classroom materials, more frequently watched an optional movie shown during recess, and more frequently requested information from others.

Individuals involved in controversy liked the procedure better than did individuals working individualistically, and participating in a controversy consistently promoted more positive attitudes toward the experience than did participating in a debate, concurrence-seeking discussions, or individualistic decisions. Controversy experiences promoted stronger beliefs that controversy is valid and valuable. Individuals who engaged in controversies tended to like the decision-making task better than did individuals who engaged in concurrence-seeking discussions (effect size = 0.63).

Constructive controversy has been found to promote greater liking among participants than did debate (effect size = 0.72), concurrence-seeking (effect size = 0.24), or individualistic efforts (effect size = 0.81). Debate tended to promote greater interpersonal attraction among participants than did individualistic efforts (effect size = 0.46). In addition, constructive controversy tends to promote greater social support among participants than debate (effect size = 0.92), concurrence-seeking (effect size = 0.32), or individualistic efforts (effect size = 1.52). Debate tended to promote greater social support among participants than did individualistic efforts (effect size = 0.85).

Constructive controversy tends to promote higher self-esteem than concurrence-seeking (effect size = 0.39), debate (effect size = 0.51), or individualistic efforts (effect size = 0.85). Debate tends to promote higher self-esteem than individualistic efforts (effect size = 0.45).

Constructive Controversy and Democracy

Conflict is the gadfly of thought. It stirs us to observation and memory. It instigates invention. It shocks us out of sheeplike passivity, and sets us at noting and contriving.... Conflict is a "sine qua non" of reflection and ingenuity.

John Dewey, *Human Nature and Conduct: Morals Are Human*

Thomas Jefferson and his fellow revolutionaries believed that free and open discussion should serve as the basis of influence within society, not the social rank within which a person was born. American democracy was, therefore, founded on the premise that "truth" will result from free and open-minded discussion in which opposing points of view are advocated and vigorously argued. Every citizen is given the opportunity to advocate for his or her ideas and to listen respectfully to opposing points of view. Once a decision is made, the minority are expected to go along willingly with the majority because they know they have been given a fair and complete hearing. To be a citizen in our democracy, individuals need to internalize the norms for constructive controversy as well as mastering the process of researching an issue, organizing their conclusions, advocating their views, challenging opposing positions, making a decision, and committing themselves to implement the decision made (regardless of whether one initially favored the alternative adopted or not). In essence, the use of constructive controversy teaches the participants to be active citizens of a democracy.

CIVIC VALUES

The conflict resolution and violence prevention programs implemented in schools will teach an inherent set of values as well as the instructional procedures used and the classroom management system. Value development is a hidden curriculum beneath the ebb and flow of daily life in the school (Johnson & Johnson, 1996a, 1999). The use of cooperative learning will teach a different set of values than will the use of competitive or individualistic learning. The promotion of conflict resolution competencies will teach a different set of values than will attempts to suppress violence. The emphasis on the positive nature of conflict will teach a different set of values than will an emphasis on the potential destructiveness of conflicts. Ideally, education should use instructional and socialization procedures, classroom management systems, and disciplinary interventions that teach values that (a) assume a positive view of human nature, (b) are aimed at developing individuals who are active advocates for democracy and social justice, and (c) focus students beyond selfishness toward improving the quality of life for all students and the common good. The Peacemaker and Controversy procedures (as well as other conflict resolution programs) implicitly teach such values.

SUMMARY AND CONCLUSIONS

Schools and classes are social systems created to achieve goals (such as instruction and socialization of children, youth, and young adults). Efforts to achieve the goals are directed and coordinated by roles (behavior expected of any individual occupying a position) and norms (general expectations for appropriate behavior). The role of teacher includes instruction and socialization, classroom management, and disciplinary interventions, each of which should enhance and be congruent with the others. It makes little sense, for example, to emphasize competition in instruction (which requires students to demonstrate superiority over others) yet expect students to use problem-solving, integrative negotiations in resolving their conflicts (which requires a concern for each other's outcomes).

One of the problems with the literature on classroom management is that recommendations are often either atheoretical or based on narrow theories that are unrelated to instruction and other aspects of school functioning. What is needed is a theory that provides a foundation for a coordinated approach to instruction, classroom management, and disciplinary interventions. Social interdependence theory, which focuses on how individuals' actions affect each other's goal accomplishments, is such a theory. It posits that the goals of individuals may be positively interdependent (which results in cooperative efforts) or negatively interdependent (which results in competitive efforts). When individuals work together to achieve mutual goals, they tend to be committed to the other's well-being as well their own, whereas when individuals work to achieve goals negatively related to each other, they tend to be committed to succeeding at others' expense. From social interdependence theory it may be concluded that instruction should be dominated by cooperative learning and the use of competition in learning situations should be minimized. In classrooms dominated by cooperation, classroom management tends to be focused on teaching students the competencies they need to work effectively with peers and to regulate their own and their classmates' behavior in order to achieve those goals. Conflicts are viewed as problems to be solved. Students tend to communicate effectively, accurately perceive the other person and his or her position, trust and like the other, recognize the legitimacy of the other's interests, and focus on both their own and their classmates' long-term well-being. In classrooms dominated by competition, class management tends to be focused on the teacher rewarding appropriate student behavior and punishing inappropriate behavior. Conflicts are viewed as "win-lose" situations. Students focus on performing higher than anyone else in the situation, communicate misleading information, misperceive the other person's position and motivation, be suspicious of and hostile toward others, and deny the legitimacy of others' goals and feelings. Disciplinary interventions in a cooperative classroom involve the peers in ensuring order is restored. In a competitive classroom, disciplinary interventions tend to emphasize adult enforcement of the rules. Thus, social interdependence theory provides a foundation for an integrated approach to instruction, classroom management, and disciplinary interventions. More work needs to be done building conceptual bridges between the theory and classroom practices.

All discipline problems are conflicts but not all conflicts are discipline problems. Conflicts may be suppressed or they may be resolved. Violence prevention programs are typically aimed at suppressing conflict and reducing the availability of weapons so that violence cannot occur. Conflict resolution programs are aimed at teaching students the competencies they need to regulate their own and their classmates' behavior within conflict situations. There are numerous benefits to teaching students conflict resolution procedures for individual students, the school, and society as a whole. There is much to gain, therefore, from teaching students how to resolve conflicts constructively. Ideally, conflict resolution programs will be based on the theorizing about conflict that has been validated by research.

The early conflict theorists, Darwin, Marx, and Freud, all posited that conflict based on competition was inherent in nature and in human existence. More recent theorists, Follett, Piaget, Lewin, Deutsch, and the authors of this chapter, emphasized conflict as a means of enhancing cooperation and solving the problems of working together. The origins of modern conflict resolution programs include not only these conflict theorists, but also nonviolence advocates, anti-nuclear war advocates, and lawyers. In addition, there are several large-scale implementations in such places as Ohio and Oregon and related programs involving forgiveness, coping skills, and the resocialization of child warriors in Africa and the Middle East.

Although numerous conflict resolution programs are being implemented in the schools, the two that have been most thoroughly researched and evaluated the (as well as implemented most widely) are the Teaching Students to Be Peacemakers and Constructive Controversy programs. The Teaching Students to Be Peacemakers Program trains students in the use of problem-solving negotiations and peer mediation. The Constructive Controversy Program trains students in the use of a five-step procedure (develop position, make a persuasive presentation of it, attempt to refute the opposing position, take the perspective of the opponent, and come to a reasoned judgment taking into account the best information and reasoning from both sides) to make a high-quality decision or judgment about an issue. It is hoped that in the future more of the conflict resolution programs being implemented in the schools will be rigorously evaluated.

The constructive resolution of conflict is the heart of preventing and solving discipline problems. To ensure that the potential positive outcomes of conflict are used to achieve the goals involving instruction and socialization, all students and faculty need to be trained so that everyone uses the same procedures. Teaching all students negotiation and mediation procedures and the constructive controversy procedure results in a schoolwide discipline program focused on empowering students to regulate their own and their schoolmates' behavior in order to achieve class and school goals. In addition, every student needs to learn how to manage conflicts constructively as part of his or her socialization into society. Conflict resolution training ensures that future generations are prepared to manage conflicts constructively in career, family, community, national, and international settings.

REFERENCES

Berk, I. (1994). *Child development* (3rd ed.). Needham Heights, MA: Allyn & Bacon.

Batton, J. (2002). Institutionalizing conflict resolution education: The Ohio model. *Conflict Resolution Quarterly, 19*(4), 479-494.

Coleman, P., & Fisher-Yoshida, B. (2004). Conflict resolution at multiple levels across the lifespan: The work of the ICCCR. *Theory Into Practice, 43*(1), 31–38.

Compton, R. (2002). Discovering the promise of curriculum integration: The National Curriculum Integration Project. *Conflict Resolution Quarterly, 19*(4), 447–464.

Davidson, J., & Wood, C. (2004). A conflict resolution model. *Theory Into Practice, 43*(1), 6–13.

Deutsch, M. (1949). A theory of cooperation and competition. *Human Relations, 2*, 129–152.

Deutsch, M. (1962). Cooperation and trust: Some theoretical notes. In M. R. Jones (Ed.), *Nebraska symposium on motivation* (pp. 275–319). Lincoln University of Nebraska Press.

Deutsch, M. (1973). *The resolution of conflict.* New Haven, CT: Yale University Press.

Deutsch, M. (1985). *Distributive justice.* New Haven, CT: Yale University Press.

Deutsch, M. (2000). Introduction. In M. Deutsch & P. Coleman (Eds.), *Handbook of conflict resolution* (pp. 1–17). San Francisco: Jossey-Bass.

Enright, R., Gassin, E., & Knutson, J. (2003). Waging peace through forgiveness education in Belfast, Northern Ireland: A review and proposal for mental health improvement of children. *Journal of Research in Education, 13*(1), 51–61.

Ford, E. (2002). Oregon's SCRIP Model: Building school conflict resolution education capacity through community partnerships. *Conflict Resolution Quarterly, 19*(4), 465–478.

Frydenberg, E. (2004). Coping competencies: What to teach and when. *Theory Into Practice, 43*(1), 14–22.

Hyman, S. (1966). *The tangled bank.* New York: Grosset & Dunlap.

Johnson, D. W. (1970). *Social psychology of education.* New York: Holt, Rinehart & Winston.

Johnson, D. W. (1971a). Role reversal: A summary and review of the research. *International Journal of Group Tensions*, 1, 318–334.

Johnson, D. W. (1971b). Students against the school establishment: Crisis intervention in school conflicts and organizational change. *Journal of School Psychology, 9*, 84–92.

Johnson, D. W. (1979). *Educational psychology.* Englewood Cliffs, NJ: Prentice Hall.

Johnson D. W., & Johnson, F. (2003). *Joining together: Group theory and group skills* (8th ed.). Englewood Cliffs, NJ: Prentice Hall.

Johnson, D. W., & Johnson, R. (1979). Conflict in the classroom: Controversy and learning. *Review of Educational Research, 49*, 51–61.

Johnson, D. W., & Johnson, R. (1989). *Cooperation and competition: Theory and research.* Edina, MN: Interaction Book Company.

Johnson, D. W., & Johnson, R. (1995a). *Teaching students to be peacemakers.* Edina, MN: Interaction Book Company.

Johnson, D. W., & Johnson, R. (1995b). *Creative controversy: Intellectual challenge in the classroom.* Edina, MN: Interaction Book Company.

Johnson, D. W., & Johnson, R. (1996a). Cooperative learning and traditional American values: An appreciation. *NASSP Bulletin, 80*(579), 63–65.

Johnson, D. W., & Johnson, R. (1996b). Conflict resolution and peer mediation programs in elementary and secondary schools: A review of the research. *Review of Educational Research, 66*(4), 459–506.

Johnson, D. W., & Johnson, R. (1999). The three Cs of school and classroom management. In H. Freiberg (Ed.), *Beyond behaviorism: Changing the classroom management paradigm* (pp. 119–144). Boston: Allyn & Bacon.

Johnson, D. W., & Johnson, R. (2000a). Cooperative learning, values, and culturally plural classrooms. In M. Leicester, C. Modgill, & S. Modgill (Eds.), *Values, the classroom, and cultural diversity* (pp. 15–28). London: Cassell PLC.

Johnson, D. W., & Johnson, R. (2000b). Civil political discourse in a democracy: The contribution of psychology. *Peace and Conflict: Journal of Peace Psychology, 6*(4), 291–317.

Johnson, R., & Johnson, D. W. (2002). Teaching students to be peacemakers: A meta-analysis. *Journal of Research in Education , 12*(1), 25–39.

Johnson, D. W., Johnson, R., & Johnson, F. (1976). Promoting constructive conflict in the classroom. *Notre Dame Journal of Education, 7*, 163–168.

Lewin. K. (1931). Environmental forces in child behavior and development. In C. Murchison (Ed.), *A handbook of child psychology*. Worcester, MA: Clark University Press.

Lewin, K. (1935). *A dynamic theory of personality*. New York: McGraw-Hill.

Piaget, J. (1965). *The psychology of intelligence*. New York: Harcourt, Brase & Co.

Toppo, G. (2004, June 28). Forty-eight school deaths highest in years. *USA Today*, p. 1.

Von Neumann, J., & Morgenstern, O. (1944). *Theory of games and economic behavior*. New York: John Wiley.

Wertheim, E., Love, A., Peck., C., & Littlefield, L. (1998). *Skills for resolving conflict: A co-operative problem solving approach.* Melbourne, Australia: Eruditions.

Wessells, M. (2003). *The impact of U.S. anti-terrorism interventions on terrorist motivation: A preliminary study in Afghanistan and Iraq*. Research Report, Christian Children's Fund and Randolph-Macon College.

31

Schoolwide Positive Behavior Support: Building Systems to Develop and Maintain Appropriate Social Behavior

Timothy J. Lewis, Lori L. Newcomer, Robert Trussell, and Mary Richter
University of Missouri–Columbia

INTRODUCTION

School discipline continues to be reported as one of the top concerns of educators and the American public (Elam, Rose, & Gallup, 1996; U.S. Department of Education, 1998). A recent study indicated that general education teachers reported on average that 1 in 5 of their students exhibited disruptive or off-task behavior and 1 in 20 exhibited aggressive behaviors to the point intervention was necessary (Myers & Holland, 2000). Data suggest that students in middle and high schools are even more at risk for encountering serious violence (Heaviside, Rowand, Williams, & Farris, 1998), with an estimated 16% of all high school students in this country involved in one or more physical fights on school property in the course of a year (Lockwood, 1997). Although the majority of students will not experience exceedingly violent or aggressive behavior, the frequency and intensity of these behaviors still disrupts and can overwhelm the process of schooling for all students (Walker, Colvin, & Ramsey, 1995). Teachers and administrators indicate that addressing school discipline issues is one of the single greatest demands on their time, citing that problem behaviors interfere with their ability to educate and are the most common reason for the removal of students from classroom and school settings (Hofmeister & Lubke, 1990; Todd, Horner, & Sugai, 1999; Walker et al., 1995).

Further compounding the challenge schools face is the relationship between low-level, nonviolent behavioral offenses (noncompliance, disrespect, insubordination) and later emergence of more serious or violent offenses (Heaviside et al., 1998). In one study, 52% of teachers and administrators surveyed reported an increase in violence at the middle and high school level; however, they perceived that minor offenses such as verbal intimidation, threats, shoving, and harassment were escalating at a far greater rate than more serious violations (Peterson, Beekley, Speaker, & Pietrzak, 1996). Suspensions and expulsions have increased due in large part to such minor infractions as noncompliance, tardiness, and truancy (Brooks, Schiraldi, & Ziedenberg, 1999; Ingersoll & LeBoeuf, 1997; Skiba, Peterson, & Williams, 1997). Mayer and Leone (1999) pointed out that school personnel spend more time and resources on punitive and reactive measures (e.g., security guards, metal detectors, video surveillance systems) aimed at inhibiting aggression and violence than on positive, preventive measures. These findings are significant in that they suggest that schools should spend equal energy to address the overall school climate and focus efforts to reduce minor disruptions. The magnitude of concern regarding discipline and the mental health needs of children and youth has prompted the Surgeon General to call for a national agenda that fosters social and emotional health in children as a national priority (U.S. Department of Health and Human Services, 2000). To more fully respond to the issue of creating improved school environments to curb disruptive, aggressive, and violent behavior in schools, informed policy and interventions are urgently needed.

Part of the challenge of school disciplinary response rests in the complexities of educating children and youth who engage in antisocial behavior. Walker et al. (1995, p. 2) defined antisocial behavior as "the opposite of prosocial, which is composed of cooperative, positive and mutually reciprocal social behavior. Antisocial behavior suggests hostility to others, aggression, a willingness to commit rule infractions, defiance of adult authority, and violation of the social norms and mores of society." Although they represent a small percentage of the total school enrollment, antisocial students place considerable stress on the school environment and consume an excessive amount of time, resources, and expertise. For the most part, schools have responded to these students by moving them into specialized placements, home tutoring, or other exclusionary options. Such approaches have proven ineffective at improved outcomes for these students (Walker & Sylwester, 1991).

Factors That Contribute to the Problem

The Institute on Violence and Destructive Behavior has identified several risk factors that lead to the development of antisocial behavior patterns among children. The list includes (a) poverty, neglect, and abuse; (b) harsh and inconsistent parenting; (c) drug and alcohol use by the caregiver; (d) modeling of aggressive behavior; (e) media violence; (f) a negative attitude in the home toward schooling; (g) family transitions such as death or divorce; and (h) parent criminality. Sadly, contextual factors found in schools also contribute to the development and occurrence of persistent problem behaviors. Mayer (1995, 2001) and colleagues (1987) identified within-school factors that exacerbate antisocial behavior including (a) an overreliance on punitive methods of control (b) unclear rules for student behavior, (c) lack of administrative support for staff and lack of staff agreement with policies, (d) misuse of behavior management procedures, (e) failure to respond to individual student differences, and (f) academic failure. The significance of school-related contextual factors is emphasized in a U.S. Department of Education publication (2000a, p. 10) that states: "Studies indicate that approximately four of every five disruptive students can be traced to some dysfunction in the way schools are organized, staff members are trained, or schools are run." By and large, the reliance on coercive or punitive discipline that typifies the response to students who have history of problem behavior promotes and reinforces the antisocial behaviors (e.g., aggression, violence, vandalism, truancy, escape) that it is designed to prevent (Mayer, 1995, 2001; Mayer et al., 1987).

At the school and district level, discipline codes and policies are likely to include "get tough" responses (e.g., containment, punishment, suspension, or zero tolerance) designed to send a strong message that certain types of problem behaviors are unacceptable and will result in stringent consequences. Although these responses may lead to temporary reductions in problem behavior, they have little effect on increasing school safety or long-term reduction of problem behavior (DeVoe et al., 2003; Skiba, 2002; Skiba & Peterson, 2000). Paradoxically, the coercive and punitive environments that result from this approach may serve as a setting event that evokes aggression, attendance problems, disruptions, and other antisocial behaviors (Mayer, 1995). Exclusionary responses increase the probability of future grade retention, subsequent suspensions, expulsion, and dropping out, factors associated with increased academic risk and juvenile crime (Diem, 1988; Sulzer-Azaroff & Mayer, 1986). Nor do such policies meet the challenge of creating a positive school climate or prevent the development and occurrence of problem behavior (Mayer, 1995; Patterson, Reid, & Dishion, 1992).

Antisocial Behavior. The complexities involved in understanding the development of antisocial behavior from preschool through adolescence are too extensive to cover adequately in this chapter; however, a brief explanation of the coercive patterns that develop between children and their families based on extensive research conducted at the Oregon Social Learning Center has contributed valuable insight into how children develop and maintain antisocial behavior patterns (Patterson et al., 1992). One of the common features in the development of antisocial behavior is the emergence of a coercive process that begins during the first years of life. Among families that experience severe pressure due to various family stressors (e.g., poverty, alcoholism, pathology, frequent transitions), coercion becomes a key mechanism in family interactions that essentially "train" family members to be aversive and aggressive in their exchanges. In essence, children and parents learn that being coercive is often functional in ending or avoiding conflicts. Escalating, aggressive interactions between parent or caregiver and child during these exchanges are characterized by parental negative reinforcement that ultimately leads to increases in deviant behavior and decreases in prosocial behavior. The coercive cycle breeds antisocial behavior patterns. The more frequently children are reinforced by terminating family conflict as a result of using coercive techniques rather than other social behaviors, the stronger those behavior coercive patterns become. The frequency of reinforcement becomes an efficient predictor for the development of antisocial behaviors (Snyder & Patterson, 1995). In fact, in a recent study, the analysis of relative reinforcement for coercion during family conflicts plus "density of conflict" was a significant indicator in predicting police arrest 2 years later (Snyder, Schrepferman, & St. Peter, 1997).

The effects of coercive patterns established at home generalize to other settings, including school, according to Ramsey, Patterson, and Walker (1990). When children enter school, the frequency and aversive nature of their behaviors typically lead to rejection by teachers and peers, which further widens their social skill deficits and inadvertently reinforces their deviant social interaction patterns. Understanding the coercive cycle and the development of antisocial behavior has led to increased recognition and conviction in the field that successful intervention must include school-based programs that teach the personal, academic, and social skills that at-risk students need for success in school (Walker & Sylwester, 1991). In essence, there is a disconnect between student learning history (i.e., coercive patterns to get needs met) and the principles on which typical school discipline practices are built. Traditional school discipline practices such as suspension are predicated on the assumption that students find school reinforcing, which is simply not the case for many at-risk students. Unfortunately, when traditional discipline systems are put in place for students at risk for antisocial behavior based on early learning history, not only do suspension, removal of privileges, and other strategies not work, they provide the student with one more adult modeling the use of aversive strategies to get them to comply (i.e., coerce them into behaving). Educators, along with other social agencies, must build systems of support that account for student early learning history and teach and model prosocial alternatives that will allow students to get their needs met by using appropriate social interaction patterns.

A Promising Solution

A substantial research base suggests that addressing school-based contextual factors that promote antisocial behavior can create a school environment that improves student and staff interactions and lead to decreases in problem behavior. Altering contextual factors (e.g., clear routines, high rates of positive vs. negative feedback, clear adult presence) has also been associated with the creation of more positive school environments that are conducive to learning and result in increases in student time on task, teacher use of praise, and improved perceptions of school safety (Mayer & Butterworth, 1981; Mayer, Butterworth, Nafpaktitis, & Sulzer-Azaroff, 1983; Mayer et al., 1993; Mayer & Sulzer-Azaroff, 1991; Metzler, Biglan, Rusby, & Sprague, 2001; Walker et al., 1995). Consistent with this body of research, the Center on Crime, Communities, and Culture (1997) summarized findings that indicate a quality education may be the most important protective factor available to counter the risk factors that lead to problem behavior. To this end, there is a growing expectation that schools deliver effective and efficient interventions to ensure safe, productive school environments where norm-violating behavior is minimized and prosocial behavior is promoted (U.S. Department of Education, 2000a). The convergence of research evidence points to the need for systemic prevention and intervention that addresses the risk factors that affect youth, and has led the Surgeon General to call for a National Action Agenda (U.S. Department of Health and Human Services, 2001) to promote cost-effective, proactive systems of behavior support at the school level. A promising solution is the use of proactive schoolwide behavior management strategies to address the contextual factors within schools that lead to problem behavior (Colvin, Kame'enui, & Sugai, 1993; Gottfredson, Gottfredson, & Hybl, 1993; Mayer, 1995; Sugai et al., 2000). These systems of behavior support should emphasize universal, primary prevention methods, while also providing a continuum of supports that meet the needs of individual students who display chronic problem behavior. A systems approach to schoolwide Positive Behavior Support (PBS) is one way to effectively (a) reduce chronic challenging behavior, (b) promote cultures of social competence that foster prosocial behavior and academic achievement, and (c) meet the needs of children with significant behavioral challenges (Lewis & Sugai, 1999; Sugai et al., 2000).

What is Positive Behavior Support?

Positive behavior support is a general term that refers to the culturally appropriate application of positive behavioral interventions and systems to achieve socially important behavior change (U.S. Department of Education, 2000b). The Office of Special Education Programs' (OSEP) Center on Positive Behavior Support (2002) defined schoolwide PBS as a broad range of individual and systemwide strategies for preventing problem behavior and achieving social and learning outcomes. PBS is not a packaged curriculum, but a compilation of effective practices, interventions, and system change strategies that have a history of empirical support. Systems change emphasizes construction of an organizational infrastructure that focuses on the entire school as the "unit of analysis" with an emphasis on (a) an agenda of primary prevention, (b) a continuum that provides increased levels of intervention for intense levels of problem behavior, (c) the use of data to guide decision making and action planning, (d) establishing local behavioral competence, and (e) proactive programming for students and staff in all settings. Schoolwide PBS focuses on three key elements: (1) adoption of evidence-based practices, (2) data to identify current status and effectiveness of intervention, and (3) systems that enable staff to implement and sustain practices with accuracy.

Proactive schoolwide discipline establishes the behavioral expectations and supports for all staff and students across multiple levels (schoolwide, classroom, individual student) and applies a three-tiered approach to prevention (Lewis & Sugai, 1999; Sugai et al., 2000; Walker et al., 1996). *Primary prevention* focuses on preventing the development and occurrence of problem behaviors. *Secondary prevention* focuses on providing efficient and rapid response to reduce the number of existing cases. *Tertiary prevention* focuses on reducing the intensity and complexity of existing cases that are not responsive to primary and secondary prevention. A functional perspective in which factors that reinforce appropriate behaviors and maintain problem behaviors (i.e., positive and negative reinforcement) guides the development of effective, efficient, and relevant interventions and is applied across the full continuum of supports. Finally, PBS promotes an instructional emphasis in which behavioral expectations are clearly defined and taught to all students. For students who are at risk of social failure, social skills are taught in the same way as academic skills and behavioral deficits are addressed by teaching functional replacement behaviors (Colvin, Sugai, & Patching, 1993).

Schoolwide PBS is a comprehensive approach that gives priority to problem solving and action planning with an emphasis on accurate, durable, and expanded implementation across a continuum of settings and levels. The remainder of this chapter provides an overview of the essential features of schoolwide systems of PBS and is organized around (a) the essential features of schoolwide systems of PBS, (b) current research, and (c) implications for research and practice.

Underlying Themes of Schoolwide Positive Behavior Support

As schools implement the systemic approach of schoolwide PBS, five themes emerge as schools organize resources, activities, and initiatives (Newcomer, Lewis, & Powers, 2002). First, an agenda of primary prevention is given priority. Preventative policy provides for the definition, teaching, monitoring, and acknowledgement of desired social behavior across all school settings and levels of support. Second, the behavior of educators is emphasized. Use of a proactive, instructional approach to teach and encourage appropriate behavior leads to higher rates of positive interactions between teachers and students and fewer corrective and punishing interactions. Third, structures exist to support a multilevel continuum of supports. A schoolwide leadership team guides the adoption and sustained use of a full continuum of interventions. Fourth, problem solving is team based to design, develop, and implement schoolwide discipline systems. Fifth, data are used to determine action plans, decision making, and problem solving. Readily available school data, such as office discipline referrals, suspensions, and referral to special education, are reviewed regularly to make informed and accurate decisions regarding patterns of behavior and effectiveness of systems and practices.

A Full Continuum of Support

Problem behavior occurs on a continuum from occasional mild misbehavior to behavior that is severe, chronic, and disruptive to the learning environment. PBS emphasizes a continuum of support in which the intensity of intervention increases to match the intensity and complexity of the presenting problem. Universal systems of support to teach and encourage appropriate behavior and discourage problem behaviors work sufficiently for most students. For a small percentage of students, however, universal strategies will not be sufficient. Secondary systems of targeted interventions are necessary to support these students. Finally, comprehensive tertiary systems of individual support are needed for those students who require intensive, highly individualized behavior support plans.

Universal Systems of Primary Prevention

Universal systems of support focus on prevention and the creation of a safe, predictable environment with a common set of expectations and consistent supports applied across three interrelated systems: schoolwide, nonclassroom, and classroom.

Schoolwide Systems. A leadership team is established to guide all processes of PBS. The team is composed of a building administrator, classroom teachers, specialists, and support staff representatives. The leadership team takes responsibility for assessment of current discipline procedures and staff perceptions of what is in place, as well as what is working and not working. The information is used by the team to develop and implement PBS policy and procedures. Components of proactive systems of schoolwide PBS include (a) a statement of purpose, (b) a clear definition of expected behaviors, (c) procedures for teaching expected behaviors, (e) procedures for discouraging problem behaviors, and (f) procedures for record keeping and decision making (Sugai et al., 2000).

A statement of purpose is used to capture the proactive objectives of the discipline plan. The statement reflects an approach that is agreed on by the administration and staff, focuses on all members of the school community, and emphasizes behavioral as well as instructional outcomes. A key component of schoolwide PBS systems is a clear understanding of expected student behavior. To guide the identification of universal expectations, the team focuses not on the problem behaviors, but on prosocial "replacement behaviors." In other words, they emphasize the behaviors that they would like children to demonstrate. The expectations, or school rules, should be five or fewer and positively stated. For example, the staff at Elysium Elementary School wanted their students to be safe, respectful learners. With input from faculty and staff, the leadership team completed a matrix that operationally defined what each of those expectations would look like across all settings in their school (see Fig. 31.1). The examples of appropriate behavior were then used as a foundation for social skill instruction.

Behavior is a skill, just as reading and mathematical computations are skills. As such, behavioral skills are taught paralleling the same process as academic instruction: educators introduce and teach a concept (e.g., quadratic equations in algebra), provide practice opportunities (e.g., homework, in-class work), and give feedback on performance (e.g., grades). Only after the student demonstrates mastery does the instructor move on to new concepts. If a student does not master the skill, reteaching, additional support, and practice are provided. Behavioral skills are taught and learned in the same way.

Procedures to explicitly teach the expected behaviors are structured around the critical features of "tell, show, and practice." The leadership team develops and provides scripted lessons based on direct instruction for teachers to use in which expectations are presented and reviewed, with positive and negative examples to illustrate each behavior. Examples are designed to be relevant to the unique context and culture of the school community. Students are provided with multiple opportunities for practice and feedback across settings. By providing teachers with common lesson plans and designating times to teach the lessons, greater staff participation and consistency is achieved.

The leadership team also develops procedures to acknowledge appropriate behaviors on a regular basis. This serves three purposes. First, principles of reinforcement teach us that the provision of positive consequences following a desired behavior results in an increase in the future probability of that behavior occurring. Second, procedures to acknowledge appropriate behavior serve to increase the ratio of positive interactions between teachers and students, creating a positive school environment. Third, acknowledgment and reinforcement encourages students to self-manage their own behavior. Schools use a range of reinforcement strategies, from token systems to positive social acknowledgment. For example, at Elysium Elementary, a teacher presents a student with a coupon when the student is observed displaying appropriate behavior. More important, the teacher provides specific feedback to the student that relates back to the schools expectations and links the reinforcer to a specific behavior (e.g., "Thank you for showing respect for others by entering the building so quietly after recess"). The student submits the coupon for a chance in a lottery drawing at the end of the week. The form of the reinforcer is less critical than the related frequency and consistency of acknowledgement of appropriate behavior by teachers and staff. It is worth noting that use of tangible reinforcers in the form of tickets, coupons, and so forth. provides teachers with a prompt, reminding them to

I am . . .	**All Settings**	**Classroom**	**Hallways**	**Cafeteria**	**Bathrooms**	**Playground**	**Assemblies**
Safe	• Keep bodies calm in line • Report any problems • Ask permission to leave any setting	• Maintain personal space	• Walk • Stay to the right on stairs • Banisters are for hands	• Walk • Push in chairs • Place trash in trash can	• Wash hands with soap and water • Keep water in the sink • Onne person per stall	• Use equipment for intended purpose • Wood chips are for the ground • Participate in school approved games only • Stay in approved areas • Keep body to self	• Walk • Enter and exit gym in an orderly manneer
Respectful	• Treat others the way you want to be treated • Be an active listener • Follow adult direction(s) • Use polite language • Help keep the school orderly	• Be honest • Take care of yourself	• Walk quietly so others can continue learning	• Eat only your food • Use a peaceful voice	• Allow for privacy of others • Clean up after self	• Line up at first signal • Invite others who want to join in • Enter and exit building peacefully • Share materials • Use polite language	• Be an active listener • Applaud appropriately to show appreciation
A Learner	• Be an active participant • Give full effort • Be a team player • Do your job	• Be a risk taker • Be prepared • Make good choices	• Return to class promptly	• Use proper manners • Leave when adult excuses	• Follow bathroom procedures • Return to class promptly	• Be a problem solver • Learn new games and activities	• Raise your hand to share • Keep comments and questions on topic

FIGURE 31.1. School matrix of expectations and definitions.

focus on encouraging and reinforcing appropriate behaviors rather than responding primarily to problem behaviors.

Even with the schoolwide positive procedures in place, there is still a need to develop procedures to discourage problem behaviors. A continuum of consequence responses should be available to respond to problem behavior. Consistency can be increased by providing clear definitions of problem behaviors and by differentiating between the behaviors that should be managed by teachers and supervisory staff and the behaviors that warrant a referral for administrative involvement. A full range of response procedures allows for more effective interventions across the continuum of mild misbehavior to serious and chronic behavior challenges. Students who repeatedly fail to meet behavioral expectations require a different level of response than students who only occasionally misbehave. For these students, systems that focus on teaching and supporting appropriate replacement behaviors come into play. These systems are discussed later in the chapter.

The use of data to assess current conditions, guide implementation, and evaluate the effectiveness of procedures is a critical feature of schoolwide PBS. An efficient system of data collection and reporting is used to summarize data in a usable format (e.g., graphs that allow visual analysis) for the purpose of evaluation and informed decision making. The data should be flexible enough to provide a summary of key indicators of problem behavior such as (a) number of office referrals per day for any given month, (b) number of office referrals per behavior (e.g., disrespect, fighting, inappropriate language), (c) number of office referrals per location (e.g., cafeteria, classroom, playground), (d) number of office referrals by consequences (e.g., detention, suspension), and (e) cumulative number of office referrals by individual students. The leadership team analyzes the data on a regular basis to discern patterns of problem behavior and to guide the decision-making process. For example, the team may decide to fade a tangible system of reinforcement based on data indicators (e.g., a 50% drop in office referrals maintained over a period of 4 weeks). Or, criteria may be established that social skill lessons will be retaught when there is a 15% increase in office referrals. Data decision rules are also established to determine when individual students may need more intensive supports (e.g., secondary or tertiary levels of support are considered if a student receives five or more office referrals).

Nonclassroom Systems. Nonclassroom settings include areas of the school that are characterized by large numbers of students, strong social interaction among students, minimal adult supervision, and low structure (e.g., cafeteria, hallway transitions, bathrooms, playground) and present a different set of management challenges than the classroom. The schoolwide expectations are extended to address specific behaviors unique to these settings through direct instruction and opportunities to practice. In addition, the physical characteristics and routines of these settings are assessed to determine if modifications are necessary to promote safety and effective supervision. Modifications may include physical adjustments, such as removing unsafe objects, eliminating objects or areas with obstructed views, altering traffic patterns, or adjusting schedules to reduce the number of students in a particular setting. Setting routines are designed to address both student and adult behavior to promote efficiency in the execution of activities and to reduce the likelihood of problem behaviors occurring. To be effective, setting routines must (a) define student and adult behavior, (b) be clearly communicated to all staff, (c) be taught explicitly to students, and (d) be consistently enforced by all staff. Schools have operationalized routines for a variety of settings, including the cafeteria, playground, bus, arrival and dismissal from school, assemblies, sport events, and parking areas. Posters and other visual reminders strategically placed within the setting can support consistent implementation and compliance with routines.

Two strategies, precorrects and active supervision, are important features of nonclassroom setting supports. *Precorrection* procedures are used to make adjustments before a student has a chance to behave inappropriately and are used when a teacher anticipates the occurrence of problem behavior. For example, a teacher may anticipate students having difficulty with an assignment. Based on the predictable errors, she will preteach difficult vocabulary words before students are asked to read a passage (Kame'enui & Simmons, 1990). The same strategy is applied to behavioral errors. The teacher provides a precorrect, based on predictable problem behavior, to remind students of the routines and expectations before they transition to a nonclassroom setting. Precorrects consist of identifying the context and the likely problem behavior, identifying the expected behavior, conducting behavioral rehearsals, and providing reinforcement for expected behaviors. Effective use of precorrects can prevent the need to respond reactively to inappropriate student behavior after the fact (Colvin, Sugai et al., 1993)

A second strategy for nonclassroom settings is *active supervision*. Elements of active supervision include (a) movement around the setting in close proximity to students, (b) visual scanning, and (c) high rates of interaction with students composed of prompts, feedback, praise, correction, and encouragement (Newcomer & Lewis, in press). After students are instructed in the expectations, rules, and routines, active supervision can promote generalized responding to other settings in the school environment.

There is a direct relationship between the teacher proximity promoted through active supervision and student behavior. When proximity is combined with regular monitoring and feedback, students learn about the expectations for the setting and are held accountable for their performance. Physical movement throughout the environment not only serves as a deterrent to inappropriate behavior, but it also provides an opportunity to observe student performance and provide relevant feedback (e.g., praise, correction, encouragement). Visually scanning the area serves a similar purpose and allows for early intervention and correction for inappropriate behavior. When student misbehavior is observed, an error correction is immediately applied by providing information about the behavior, reteaching the correct response or behavior, and asking the student to practice the correct behavior. At times, manipulation of the physical environment may be necessary to allow for scanning of student activity (e.g., an isolated area of a playground may be roped off).

Maintaining a high rate of positive teacher-to-student interactions is another important component of active supervision. Basic principles of human behavior tell us that behavior is largely a product of the environment and that appropriate behavior is more efficiently shaped by positive consequences than negative consequences. Casual, brief, intermittent, and specific verbal praise while circulating among students will maintain and strengthen appropriate behaviors.

A final consideration in active supervision is to avoid distractions that draw attention away from student activity (e.g., lengthy conversations with other adults, clustering with other adults in the area, completing paperwork). Teachers and adult supervisors model the behaviors they expect from their students. Consider a school assembly where teachers are lined up along the wall, talking among themselves. The teachers are no longer actively supervising students to provide reinforcement or correction. In fact, their behavior models inappropriate behavior that is in violation of the expectations to which students will be held accountable. The adult behavior, in this case, negatively affects the order and climate of the event and sends a very inconsistent message on what is acceptable behavior.

Classroom Systems. Paralleling universal schoolwide systems, classroom systems also emphasize teaching clearly defined behavioral expectations to prevent the occurrence of problem behavior. Key components of universal classroom systems include (a) identification and instruction in rules and routines, (b) effective instructional strategies, and (c) a strong emphasis on positive teacher–student interactions.

Classroom rules and expectations should reflect the unique characteristics of an individual classroom, but should link back to and reflect the greater schoolwide expectations. Linking the rules to the schoolwide expectations extends the language into the classroom and supports the generalization of behavioral performance across settings. For example, at one school the schoolwide expectations were "*Be Respectful, Be Responsible, Be Cooperative*." To clearly define what behaviors were needed to create a positive and productive learning environment, each teacher aligned his or her classroom rules to the schoolwide expectations. The rules and expected behaviors were taught and reinforced at the start of the school year, and reviewed on a regular basis. By linking back to the language of the schoolwide expectations, the students learned the specific behaviors that were important in the classroom and were able to relate how those expectations fit into the school context as a whole. As with the schoolwide expectations, these rules are taught the first few weeks of school, and reviewed on an ongoing basis.

Because instruction that is too difficult or too easy creates conditions that foster problem behavior (Cooper et al., 1992), teaching and management strategies that focus on instructional, curricular, and organizational adjustments are linked to improved behavior (Kern, Childs, Dunlap, Clarke, & Falk, 1994). Students learn best when there are frequent opportunities to respond to and actively engage in the instruction and to be positively reinforced. Frequent opportunities to respond and high rates of correct response are associated with increased on-task behavior (Gunter & Denny, 1998) and a decrease in disruptive behavior (Gunter & Reed, 1997). High rates of student response results in increased opportunity for a teacher to praise and correct student responses and allows assessment of student understanding. Effective, well-designed instruction incorporates student supportive strategies to minimize errors, support skill acquisition, and encourage active participation by creating opportunities for successful learning.

The quality of teacher-to-student interactions is another component of the use of BPS in classrooms. Research has demonstrated that in most classrooms, the rate of reprimands exceeds the rate of positive feedback and praise (Sutherland & Wehby, 2001; Sutherland, Wehby, & Copeland, 2000; Wehby, Symons, & Shores, 1995). Altering interaction patterns to increase teacher praise and positive attention in the classroom can result in an increase in appropriate behaviors and a decrease in disruptive behaviors. An effective classroom teacher strives for a ratio of four positive praise statements to every reprimand or correction.

Secondary Systems of Support

Approximately 10% to 20% of students will require support beyond the universal level (Sugai, Horner, Lewis, & Cheney, 2002). Although these students exhibit problem behaviors at degrees and frequency that places them at risk for establishing chronic problem behavioral patterns, developing individualized interventions is beyond the time and resources of most schools. As part of the three-tiered approach to prevention outlined earlier in this chapter, secondary systems of prevention and intervention present an efficient and effective intermediate level of intervention to target these students. Secondary systems of support include interventions that are less time-intensive and more cost-effective responses than individual support plans. Students who require this level of intervention typically have a profile of ongoing, low-level problem behaviors (e.g., talking out, minor disruptions, work completion), frequent (three to seven) office referrals, and they exhibit problem behavior across multiple settings within the school.

Targeted secondary supports focus on a range of intervention procedures and are developed and driven by data indicators. Targeted and small-group interventions have included (a) self-management, (b) anger management, (c) conflict resolution, (d) mentoring programs, (e) daily check-in and check-out procedures, (f) specialized social skill instruction, (g) informal, brief functional assessments and support plans, and (h) increased family involvement. The targeted interventions are efficient because they use a similar set of behavioral strategies across a group of students who need similar support. They are effective because they focus on decreasing problem behavior in the classroom, thereby increasing academic engagement and decreasing office discipline referrals. Although the focus of each intervention procedure may be different based on the behaviors of concern, certain critical features form the foundation of efficient, systematic implementation. These features include continuous availability, rapid access to the intervention, and low effort by teachers for referral and implementation. In addition they are implemented by all staff across multiple settings, and continuously monitored for effectiveness and decision making.

Targeted interventions work well because of the improved structure and systems for implementation. Because they are implemented within a schoolwide system, they are designed to support the existing classroom expectations and create a common focus and expected outcomes that are consistent throughout the setting. All faculty and staff are trained and familiar with the procedures, resulting in accurate and consistent implementation across settings throughout the school day. As a result, the student receives increased contingent feedback tied to the behavior. Inappropriate behavior is less likely to be ignored or rewarded, and there is elevated reinforcement (adult and peer attention) for appropriate behavior. (See Crone, Horner, & Hawken, 2004 for an example of a small-group PBS strategy).

Data-based decisions guide the process. Students are identified proactively, based on data or teacher referral, and they receive support quickly. A multiple-gating approach efficiently identifies students who need additional academic and social supports. First, teachers identify students who may be at risk and make referrals based on their assessment. Second, review of attendance records, academic performance and office referrals are used to identify patterns or problems that require support. Third, a team reviews the information to determine if the targeted intervention is appropriate for the student. Daily performance data are used to monitor student progress. When data indicate improvements in performance, the student is moved toward self-management.

In summary, the proactive components of secondary systems represent significant movement away from a traditional discipline system response of reviewing rules and extending the continuum of aversives and punishment following behavior incidents. With efficient, effective secondary systems in place, students who display precursors to chronic challenging behavior are identified proactively and receive support within a week of identification. Interventions serve to increase regular, positive acknowledgement from teachers, staff, and administrators. Daily performance data are reviewed to evaluate student progress and promote movement to self-monitoring.

Tertiary or Individual Systems of Support

Even with effective implementation of PBS at the universal and small-group or targeted levels, approximately 5% to 7% of students in a school will require intense, individualized interventions (Lewis, Sugai, & Colvin, 1998; Taylor-Greene et al., 1997). These students typically display serious, chronic behavior patterns and higher rates of behavior infraction (e.g., eight or more office referrals) and require specially designed individualized supports that are comprehensive, function based, person centered, and provide wraparound services. Efficient and effective systems of individual support are based on technical competence in behavioral assessment and intervention design from an applied behavior analysis perspective. Within the three-tiered approach to schoolwide systems of PBS, the tertiary level provides systems to build the capacity for schools to understand and assess the function of behavior and to design, implement, evaluate, and modify effective behavior support plans for individuals with serious behavior problems.

A Team Approach. A team-based approach is the foundation of a sustainable system of individual behavior support (Todd, Horner, Sugai, & Colvin, 1999). Team members should possess the technical expertise to conduct functional behavioral assessments (FBAs) and design behavior support plans that are based on assessment outcomes. At least one member of the team should have expertise in applied behavior analysis, behavioral theory, FBA, and intervention. Other logical team members would include school psychologists, special and general educators, and a building administrator. The team must also have predictable and efficient procedures to "(a) manage teacher requests for assistance, (b) ensure that teachers and students receive support in a timely and meaningful manner, (c) provide a general forum for discussions and possible solutions for individual student behavioral concerns, and (d) organize a collaborative effort to support the teacher" (Todd et al., 1999, p. 74). The organizational features of the team promote the efficient use of time, efficient documentation, a system of accountability for task and implementation responsibilities, and clearly defined systems for making data-based decisions (Crone & Horner, 2003).

A consistent, predictable organizational structure facilitates movement of the team as they work. Procedures are developed to promote efficient execution of critical steps in the assessment and support planning process. Specifically, procedures are developed to systematize (a) how the team responds to initial referrals, (b) the collection of functional assessment data and support plan development, (c) implementation, and (d) follow-up.

Function-Based Interventions. Research is emerging that supports function-based interventions as more efficient than alternative intervention approaches (Newcomer & Lewis, 2004). The purpose of functional assessment is to develop interventions that meet student need (Karsh, Repp, Dahlquist, & Munk, 1995). The value of a function-based approach to intervention is the assumption that treatment effectiveness increases if the treatment matches the function of the target behavior. Key features of the functional assessment process include an operational definition of the problem behavior, application of indirect and direct measures of assessment, and the formulation of a valid hypothesis regarding the function of the behavior. The hypothesis serves to identify the variables that are functionally related to the problem behaviors and is used to design interventions that make programmatic changes specific to those variables. As an extension of the PBS continuum, interventions at this level are grounded in the school-wide expectations, practices, and procedures to promote generalized outcomes. (Refer to chapters within this text by Lane, Falk, & Wehby and Soodak and McCarthy for more information regarding functional assessment.)

With the universal and secondary systems firmly in place, schools should experience a decrease in the number of students who need intensive individual supports. With the number of referrals for individual interventions reduced, the system can respond more efficiently and effectively to those students who do require a more intense level of support. However, some students, such as those with dangerous or violent behaviors, will be beyond the resources of the assessment and support team. Support for these students will require wraparound services that draw on community and other resources.

Summary

Schoolwide systems of PBS are based on a continuum of research-based strategies with a central focus on increasing appropriate behavior. Schoolwide systems provide the processes, structures, and routines to prevent problem behavior; they promote early intervention at the first signs of problem behavior; and they use comprehensive individual support plans. An instructional approach built on a central theme of teaching appropriate behavior, building multiple opportunities for practice, and altering environments to promote success is emphasized through a continuum of three levels of support: universal, targeted, and individual.

RESEARCH TO DATE ON THE EFFICACY OF SCHOOLWIDE PBS

An emerging body of research has shown that implementing a network of four interactive systems of schoolwide, specific setting, classroom, and individual student support will affect overall rates of problem behavior in school. In addition, preliminary research has demonstrated improvements in behavior, academic gains, and increases in instructional time following implementation of interventions as part of a fully integrated approach across three levels: universal, targeted, and individual student. Research that has demonstrated efficacy at each of the three levels is provided in this section.

Universal Supports

Universal schoolwide systems emphasize primary prevention and are usually sufficient to ensure success for the majority of the school population. A common set of expectations and school rules, teaching strategies, and consistent supports such as adult monitoring are developed as universal strategies with an emphasis on the creation of a safe and predictable environment (Lewis & Sugai, 1999). Universal strategies are applied across three interrelated systems: schoolwide, specific setting, and classroom.

Schoolwide. Schoolwide PBS is grounded within the field of applied behavior analysis, which has multiple replications of empirically validated practices. These individual empirically validated practices make up the essential features of schoolwide PBS. Component features include (a) development of constructive disciplinary practices that clearly define, teach, and encourage expected behavior (Mayer, 1995; Mayer et al., 1983; Sulzer-Azaroff & Mayer, 1994); (b) explicit instruction of appropriate social behavior (Colvin, Kame'enui, & Sugai; 1993; Colvin, Sugai, & Patching, 1993; Lewis et al., 1998); (c) encouragement and positive reinforcement for appropriate social behavior (Embry, 1997; Taylor-Greene et al., 1997); (d) consistent corrective consequences for rule violation (Nelson, Martella, & Garland, 1996; Taylor-Greene et al., 1997); and (e) monitoring data to evaluate progress and inform decision making (Sugai, Sprague, Horner, & Walker, 1999; Tobin, Sugai, & Colvin, 1996).

Systemic efforts to implement effective behavioral interventions have evolved from these research foundations. When empirically based preventative practices are integrated into universal systems of PBS, schools report reductions of 40% to 60% in discipline referrals (Sugai et al., 2002). For example, over a 1-year period Taylor-Greene and her colleagues (1997) demonstrated a 42% reduction in behavioral offenses by clearly defining schoolwide expectations and teaching students how to meet each expectation. More important, Taylor-Greene and her school team continue to report declines in behavioral problems (Taylor-Greene & Kartub, 2000). Likewise, Nakasato (2000) demonstrated drops in daily office referrals across six elementary schools through the development of universal PBS strategies. Finally, Scott (2001) demonstrated 65% to 75% reductions in out-of-school suspensions and in-school detentions, which allowed students to be more successful in class as evidenced by increased standardized test scores.

Nonclassroom Settings. Nonclassroom setting interventions are an extension of the larger schoolwide system. Noninstructional settings with large numbers of students, low structure, and a minimum of adult influence (e.g., hallways, restrooms, cafeterias, playgrounds, buses, and parking lots) are often identified as problem areas for schools and present a different set of behavior management challenges. At this level, routines and active supervision are as essential as teaching rules. For example, Lewis et al. (1998), through a combination of social skill instruction, active supervision, and group contingencies, demonstrated reductions in problem behaviors across the cafeteria, playground, and hallway within an elementary school. Kartub, Taylor-Greene, March, and Horner (2000) effectively reduced hallway noise during cafeteria transitions in a middle school through a simple process of instruction, prompts, and group contingency reinforcement. Similarly, Putnam, Handler, Ramirez-Platt, & Luiselli (2003) reported a decrease in bus-related discipline referrals and suspensions following intervention procedures that included instruction in appropriate bus behavior, training drivers to deliver positive reinforcement, and rewarding student performance through a weekly school-based lottery.

Effective behavior management in nonclassroom contexts goes beyond the development of clear expectations; active and efficient supervision are critical components. Colvin and his colleagues (Colvin, Sugai, Good, & Lee, 1997; Colvin, Sugai, & Patching, 1993) demonstrated that student transition behavior is functionally related to supervisor behavior in nonclassroom settings, and noted that students are more likely to engage in problem behavior when there are ambiguous rules and routines and ineffective adult supervision. They report a substantial reduction in student problem behavior associated with an increase in the rate of precorrection and active supervision behaviors by staff. Lewis, Colvin, and Sugai (2000) came to a similar conclusion when examining the effectiveness of a precorrection and active supervision strategy on an elementary school playground. Likewise, schoolwide instruction on playground-related behavior, combined with active supervision and group contingency reinforcement systems have been associated with reduced behavioral incidences as well as reports of increased staff satisfaction (Lewis, Powers, Kelk, & Newcomer, 2002; Todd, Haugen, Anderson, & Spriggs, 2002). In addition, Latham (1992, 2002) observed that teacher behaviors associated with active supervision (e.g., scanning, moving around the area, maintaining a high rate of general and specific positive reinforcement) are effective at preventing problem behavior.

A decrease in problem behavior has also led to improved school climate following implementation of universal systems of PBS. For example, middle school students reported a 26% increase of perceived safety in the hallways, classroom, and cafeteria following clarification of rules and adjustment of routines and physical characteristics for specific settings (Metzler et al., 2001). Todd et al. (2002) reported that staff members expressed satisfaction with student outcomes and the schoolwide systems to teach and reinforce appropriate behavior, and they also indicated the procedures were an effective and efficient use of teaching time.

Classroom. Universal classroom PBS systems focus on maintaining acceptable behavior, preventing problem behavior, and managing problem behavior after it has occurred. Key system components are (a) clearly defining classroom expectations, (b) consistent, effective consequences; and (c) effective instructional management techniques. In general, procedures to prevent problem behavior in the classroom are similar to those used for schoolwide PBS systems; the information required for students to behave appropriately is carefully and strategically taught to a high level of performance. Clearly stated rules are posted to provide (a) proactive prompts to increase expected behavior and (b) consistency for disciplinary actions and corrective sequences. Routines are established to maintain a consistent and predictable classroom environment, and precorrects are used to prevent misbehavior, increase the likelihood of appropriate behavior, and decrease the need for negative consequences (Colvin & Sugai, 1988). By replicating the same process used to teach schoolwide expectations (i.e., explicit teaching of expectations, scripted role play, precorrects, and specific praise), Langland, Lewis-Palmer, & Sugai (1998) reported a decrease in rates of inappropriate behavior (i.e., verbal abuse, harassment, defiance, and disruptive behavior) across two middle school classrooms.

Teacher praise also functions as an effective preventative and nonintrusive practice to encourage appropriate behavior. Madsen, Becker, and Thomas (1968) demonstrated that disruptive behavior decreased when teachers praised appropriate behavior and increased when praise was withdrawn. Increased teacher praise has also been associated with increases of appropriate student behavior and task engagement (Broden, Bruce, Mitchell, Carter, & Hall, 1970; Hall, Lund, & Jackson, 1968) and is therefore considered a key component of PBS in the classroom.

A connection between effective instruction and classroom behavior has been well established in the literature (Engelmann, Becker, Carnine, & Gersten, 1988; Kame'enui & Darch, 2004). Recent research indicates that (a) students with similar academic abilities have very different academic outcomes depending on teacher effectiveness and (b) teacher effectiveness is the most dominant factor affecting student gain (Ross, Stringfield, Sanders, & Wright, 2003; Ross et al., 2001; Wright, Horn, & Sanders, 1999). Therefore, teacher effectiveness, as defined by the appropriate use of evidence-based strategies, must also be considered a critical factor in primary prevention. Gunter, Hummel, and Conroy (1998) established that designing lessons to increase correct academic responding as an intervention strategy resulted in a decrease in problem behaviors. Sutherland and Wehby (2001) found similar effects, suggesting that increased rates of opportunities to respond result in higher task engagement and academic achievement and in lower rates of inappropriate classroom behaviors.

Small-Group or Targeted Interventions

It is estimated that approximately 75% to 80% of student problem behavior can be addressed through the implementation of fully integrated universal strategies (Reid, 1993). For the 10% to 15% of students who demonstrate persistent patterns of chronic problem behavior and who do not respond to the universal schoolwide PBS system, targeted interventions that remediate problem behavior patterns are emerging as an effective and resource-efficient approach. A targeted intervention system for these students typically takes the form of more instruction in behavioral expectations along with more opportunities for practice with feedback. For example, one elementary school staff identified their at-risk students by reviewing discipline referrals. Sixteen students who received eight or more office referrals during the previous school year were invited to participate in a specialized social skills group that provided more extensive instruction and practice in prosocial behavior that mirrored the universal schoolwide instruction. Lessons were taught in small groups and generalization strategies were given to all classroom teachers so that they could provide additional practice and acknowledgement of skill mastery. Of the 16 students, 10 experienced at least a 70% drop in office referrals over the course of the subsequent school year (Newcomer & Powers, 2002; Powers, 2003).

Another example of a targeted intervention is the Behavior Education Program (BEP). Based on a simple process of checking in and out using a daily point sheet, the BEP increases the likelihood of contingent adult praise and provides the student with immediate feedback on behavior (Hawken & Horner, 2003; March & Horner, 2002). Students participating in the BEP system in one middle school demonstrated overall reductions in disruptive behavior that were linked to improved academic engagement (Hawken & Horner, 2003). Other examples of targeted support include targeted social skill training, self-monitoring, and self-management systems. (Long & Edwards, 1994; Nelson, Martella, & Garland, 1998; Powers, 2003; Todd et al., 1999; Sinclair, Christenson, Evelo, & Hurley, 1998).

Intensive Individual Student Supports

The application of universal and targeted interventions will greatly reduce, but not eliminate, the number of students who require intense individualized support. What is emerging from the field is that PBS may increase the capacity of schools to deliver more systematic and intensive targeted small-group and individual interventions (Crone & Horner, 2003; Crone, Horner,

& Hawken, 2004). Preliminary data from pilot studies are showing that functional-based interventions are outperforming traditional behavioral interventions (Ingram, 2002; Newcomer & Lewis, 2004) and that plans are of higher quality if linked to schoolwide PBS systems (Newcomer & Lewis, 2004; Newcomer & Powers, 2002). More research is needed to show what additional benefit schoolwide systems of PBS "value add" to small-group and individual student support plans.

In summary, schoolwide systems of PBS based on the research foundations of systemic assessment and implementation of behavioral interventions have been extended in application from individual students to the collective behaviors, routines, and working structures of the school as a whole (Colvin, Kameenui, & Sugai, 1993; Colvin et al., 1997; Lewis, Colvin, & Sugai, 2000; Lewis et al., 1998; Taylor-Greene et al., 1997; Todd, Horner, Sugai, & Sprague, 1999). The schoolwide systems of PBS are firmly grounded in evidence-based practices of (a) social skills instruction, (b) academic and curricular restructuring, (c) proactive management, and (d) individualized behavioral interventions.

Limitations of the Research Base

The study of schoolwide PBS represents a move from studies that evaluated the behavioral mechanism of single and small groups of students to large-scale application studies. To an extent, many of the application studies have been conducted within the framework of scientific methodology; testing observable events with objective, reliable, and quantifiable data; and using procedures that are replicable. However, the processes of the PBS model represent a multicomponent package that is quite complex and bridges the gap between basic and applied science. Although data to date have shown encouraging results at the Universal level, the "value add" of the system approach in addressing small-group or targeted and individual supports is best described as emerging. The challenge remains to identify under what conditions the model yields significant outcomes and the active components that contribute to those outcomes. The next section briefly describes some of the issues associated with measuring large-scale system efforts to date.

Measures. The science that underlies PBS, applied behavior analysis, provides a methodology for understanding and predicting target behaviors in given contexts. As investigation and application moves from controlled situations such as laboratories and clinics to the less structured school environment, greater flexibility is needed in using correlation analysis, data sources, and case studies (Carr et al., 2002). Because schoolwide PBS interventions are always multicomponent in nature, validity concerns arise due to the multiple interacting variables that come into play. Such interaction makes it difficult to measure the impact of individual variables. Analysis must take into consideration multiple-component interventions. Such analysis, however, does not meet the standards of single-variable experimentation necessary to ascribe causality. Applied research practices must be flexible enough to study the pragmatic effectiveness of multicomponent interventions as well as the causal mechanisms of intervention package components to explain why a model worked and to specify the active components of the model.

Connections to Individual Supports. In 1968, Baer, Wolf, and Risley established the importance of functional analysis to identify environmental variables associated with the occurrence of target behaviors. In so doing, they laid the foundation for the application of applied behavior analysis to study human behavior and the functional relations between academic and social changes in adult and child behaviors. In the ensuing years compelling evidence has accumulated to document the effectiveness of functional behavioral assessment and positive behavior interventions and supports as having direct relevance for addressing disruptive and chronic problem behavior in schools (Blair, Umbriet, & Boss, 1999; Dunlap et al., 1993; Ervin et al., 2000; Lewis & Sugai, 1996a, 1996b). Although the technology exists to respond to the challenges of problem behavior, it has not "fit" the unique problem context schools present (Lewis & Sugai, 1999; Sugai & Horner, 1999; Sugai et al., 2000). Research has yet to identify a well-defined procedure that delivers precise, usable, valid information with the limited time and resources available to school professionals. Zins and Ponti (1990) suggest that establishing a "host environment" that can support and maintain evidence-based practices is essential to achieve specialized and individualized behavior supports for students with chronic problem behaviors and at-risk backgrounds. The systems perspective of PBS provides the requisite structure to support the adoption and sustained use of effective practices (Sugai, Horner, & Sprague, 1999).

As demonstrated in the research previously reviewed, a schoolwide systems approach to PBS effectively reduces chronic challenging behavior, promotes cultures of social competence, and meets the needs of children with significant behavioral challenges, creating a host environment that emphasizes the development of a positive school climate, practical policies, well-defined physical spaces, and monitoring systems to improve academic and social outcomes for all students, but especially those who are considered at risk for behavior problems. With schoolwide systems of PBS in place, schools increase their capacity to support students who present challenges by shifting away from traditional responses of solving behavior problems through suspension and exclusion to an approach that emphasizes the development of specially designed and individualized interventions based on functional behavioral assessment to generate an understanding of how the social and instructional context influence an individual student's behavior. In doing so, these schools have redefined the roles and responsibilities of educators and all school personnel for promoting positive behavioral interventions, strategies, and support for students with chronically challenging behavior. Individual systems of PBS focus on integrated, team-based planning and problem solving to design individual support plans to prevent, reduce, and replace problem behaviors and to develop, maintain, and strengthen socially desirable behaviors. We have learned from research and application the importance of a schoolwide foundation of integrated systems, collaboration, and the development of proactive, practical interventions. When school personnel routinely reinforce positive behaviors and dedicate themselves to teaching social skills, then they increase the likelihood that individual support plans will be implemented with a high degree of integrity.

CONCLUSION

Schoolwide PBS is defined as systemic and individualized strategies implemented through a continuum of supports based on data-based decision making. The literature on behavioral problems is clear in that early intervention and prevention are our best hopes at making schools safe and productive learning environments (Ziglar, Taussig, & Black, 1992). Unfortunately, many educators have been slow to implement best practice until problems become chronic and entrenched (Kauffman, 1999) even though recent research has shown a clear link between "minor" discipline problems and later significant problems (Skiba & Peterson, 2000). Given that schoolwide PBS in essence is a process rather than a curriculum or packaged program, we are not suggesting that it is "the answer." Yet, work to date has demonstrated that schools can implement best practices at the prevention or early intervention level. Essential components that characterize each level of the continuum include empirically validated practices such as clearly defined expectations, teaching expectations, and providing feedback during practice opportunities. The intensity of application of these basic components are then matched to the intensity of problem behavior, and connections are made to other resources necessary to support students and their families. The selection, application, and evaluation of practices are simultaneously supported through data-based decision making, using a team process that supports faculty and staff.

Although evidence supports the components, the research base supporting the systemic application across multiple school settings, school buildings, districts, and states is just emerging. As described earlier, additional work is needed to validate component features, assess their efficacy when couched within a schoolwide process, and continue to be refined to include additional components such as academic instruction, mental health strategies, and emerging behavioral support strategies.

ACKNOWLEDGMENT

The authors wish to thank our reviewer, Joseph Wehby, Vanderbilt University, for his helpful comments on an earlier draft of this chapter.

REFERENCES

Baer, D. M., Wolf, M. M., & Risley, T. R. (1968). Some current dimensions of applied behavior analysis. *Journal of Applied Behavior Analysis, 1*(1), 91–9.

Blair, K., Umbreit, J., & Bos, C. (1999). Using functional assessment and children's preferences to improve the behavior of young children with behavioral disorders. *Behavioral Disorders, 24*(2), 151–166.

Broden, M., Bruce, C., Mitchell, M. A., Carter, V., & Hall, R.V. (1970). Effects of teacher attention on attending behavior of two boys at adjacent desks. *Journal of Applied Behavior Analysis, 3*, 199–203.

Brooks, K. V. Schiraldi, V., & Ziedenberg, J. (1999). *School house hype: Two years later*. San Francisco: Center on Juvenile and Criminal Justice.

Carr, E. G., Dunlap, G., Horner, R. H., Koegel, R. L., Turnbull, A. P., Sailor, W., Anderson, J. L., Albin, R. W., Korgel, L. H., & Fox, L. (2002). Positive behavior support: Evolution of an applied science. *Journal of Positive Behavior Intervention, 4*, 4–16.

Center on Crime, Communities, and Culture. (1997). *Education as crime prevention.* Occasional Paper Series No. 2: New York: Author. Leone, P. E., & Meisel, S. (1997). Improving education services for students in detention and confinement facilities. *Children's Legal Rights Journal, 71*(1), 2–12.

Colvin, G., Kame'enui, E. J., & Sugai, G. (1993). Reconceptualizing behavior management and school-wide discipline in general education. *Education and Treatment of Children, 16*(4), 361–381.

Colvin, G., & Sugai, G. (1988). Proactive strategies for managing social behavior problems: An instructional approach. *Education and Treatment of Children, 16*, 361–381.

Colvin, G., Sugai, G., & Patching, W. (1993). Pre-correction: An instructional strategy for managing predictable behavior problems. *Intervention in School and Clinic, 28*, 143–150.

Colvin, G., Sugai, G., Good, R. H. I., & Lee, Y. (1997). Using active supervision and precorrection to improve transition behavior in elementary school. *School Psychology Quarterly, 12*(4), 344–363.

Cooper, L. J., Wacker, D. P., Thursby, D., Plagmann, L. A., Harding, J., Millard, T., & Derby, M. (1992). Analysis of the effects of task preferences, task demands, and adult attention on child behavior in outpatient and classroom settings. *Journal of Applied Behavior Analysis, 25*(4), 823–840.

Crone, D. A., & Horner, R. H. (2003). *Building positive behavior support systems in schools: Functional behavioral assessment.* New York: Guilford.

Crone, D. A., Horner, R. H., & Hawken, L. S. (2004). *Responding to problem behavior in schools: The behavior education program.* New York: Guilford.

DeVoe, J. F., Peter, K., Ruddy, S., Miller, A., Planty, M., Snyder, T., Rand, M. (2003). *Indicators of school crime and safety (NCES 2004004).* Washington, DC: U.S. Department of Education, National Center for Education Statistics.

Diem, R. A. On campus suspensions: A case study. *The High School Journal*, October/November 1988.

Dunlap, G., Kern, L., dePerczel, M., Clarke, S., Wilson, D., Childs, K. E., White, R., & Falk, G. D. (1993). Functional analysis of classroom variables for students with emotional and behavioral disorders. *Behavioral Disorders, 18*(4), 275–291.

Elam, S. J., Rose, L. C., & Gallup, A. M. (1996). 28th annual Phi Delta Kappa/Gallup poll of the public's attitudes toward the public schools. *Kappan, 78*(1), 41–59.

Embry, D. D. (1997). Does your school have a peaceful environment? Using an audit to create a climate for change and resiliency. *Intervention in School and Clinic, 32*, 217–222.

Engelmann, S., Becker, W. C., Carnine, D., & Gersten, R. (1988). The direct instruction follow through model: Design and outcomes. *Education and Treatment of Children, 11*(4), 303–317.

Ervin, R., Kern, L., Clarke, S., DuPaul, G., Dunlap, G., & Friman, P. (2000). Evaluating assessment-based intervention strategies for students with ADHD within the natural classroom context. *Behavioral Disorders, 25*(4), 344–356.

Gottfredson, D. C., Gottfredson, G. D., & Hybl, L. G. (1993). Managing adolescent behavior: A multiyear, multi-school study. *American Educational Research Journal, 30*(1), 179–215.

Gunter, P., & Denny, R. K. (1998). Trends and issues in research regarding academic instruction of students with emotional and behavioral disorders. *Behavioral Disorders, 24*, 44–50.

Gunter, P., Hummel, J. H., & Conroy, M. (1998). Increasing correct academic responding: An effective intervention strategy to decrease problem behaviors. *Effective School Practices, 17*, 43–50.

Gunter, P., & Reed, T. M. (1997). Academic instruction of children with emotional and behavioral disorders using scripted lessons. *Preventing School Failure, 42*, 33–37.

Hall, R. V., Panyan, M., Rabon, D., & Broden, M. (1968). Instructing beginning teachers in reinforcement procedures which improve classroom control. *Journal of Applied Behavior Analysis, 1*, 315–322.

Hawken, L. S., & Horner, R. H. (2003). Evaluation of a targeted intervention within a schoolwide system of behavior support. *Journal of Behavioral Education, 12*(3), 225–240.

Heaviside, S., Rowand, C., Williams, C., & Farris, E. (1998). *Violence and discipline problems in U.S. Public Schools: 1996–97 (NCES 98-030)*. Washington, DC: U.S. Department of Education, National Center for Education Statistics.

Hofmeister, A., & Lubke, M. (1990). *Research into practice*. Boston: Allyn & Bacon.

Ingersoll, S., & LeBoeuf, K. (1997, February). Reaching out to youth out of the education mainstream. *Juvenile Justice Bulletin*, U.S. Department of Justice, Office of Juvenile Justice and Delinquency Prevention (pp. 1–11).

Ingram, K. (2002). *Comparing effectiveness of intervention strategies that are based on functional behavioral assessment information and those that are contra-indicated by the assessment.* Unpublished doctoral dissertation, University of Oregon, Eugene.

Kame'enui, E. J., & Darch, C. B. (2004). *Instructional classrom management: A proactive approach to behavior management.* Upper Saddle River, NJ: Pearson Merrill/Prentice Hall.

Kame'enui, E. J., & Simmons, D. C. (1990). *Designing instructional strategies: The prevention of academic learning problems.* Englewood Cliffs, NJ: Macmillan.

Karsh, K. G., Repp, A., Dahlquist, C. M., & Munk, D. (1995). In vivo functional assessment and multi-element interventions for problem behaviors of students with disabilities in classroom settings. *Journal of Behavioral Education, 5*, 189–210.

Kartub, D. T., Taylor-Greene, S., March, R. E., & Horner, R. H. (2000). Reducing hallway noise: A systems approach. *Journal of Positive Behavior Interventions, 2*, 179–182.

Kauffman, J, M. (1999). How we prevent the prevention of emotional and behavioral disorders. *Exceptional Children, 65*, 448–468.

Kern, L., Childs, K. E., Dunlap, G., Clarke, S., & Falk, G. D. (1994). Using assessment -based curricular intervention to improve the classroom behavior of a student with emotional and behavioral challenges. *Journal of Applied Behavior Analysis, 27*(1), 7–19.

Langland, S., Lewis-Palmer, & Sugai, G. (1998). Teaching respect in the classroom: An instructional approach. *Journal of Behavior Education, 8*(2), 245–262.

Latham, G. (1992). Interacting with at-risk children: The positive position. *Principal, 72*(1), 245–262.

Latham, G. (2002). *Behind the schoolhouse door: Managing chaos with science, skills and strategies.* North Logan, UT: P&T Ink.

Lewis, T. J., Colvin, G., & Sugai, G. (2000). The effects of pre-correction and active supervision on the recess behavior of elementary students. *Education and Treatment of Children, 23*(2), 109–121.

Lewis, T. J., Powers, L. J., Kelk, M., & Newcomer, L. L. (2002). Reducing problem behaviors on the playground: An investigation of the application of schoolwide positive behavior supports. *Psycholology in the Schools, 39*(2), 181–190.

Lewis, T. J., & Sugai, G. (1996a). Functional assessment of problem behavior: A pilot investigation of the comparative and interactive effects of teacher and peer social attention on students in general education settings. *School Psychology Quarterly, 11*(1), 1–19.

Lewis, T. J., & Sugai, G. (1996b). Descriptive and experimental analysis of teacher and peer attention and the use of assessment-based Intervention to improve pro-social behavior. *Journal of Behavioral Education, 6*(1), 7–24.

Lewis, T. J., & Sugai, G. (1999). Effective behavior support: A systems approach to proactive schoolwide management. *Focus on Exceptional Children, 31*(6), 1–24.

Lewis, T. J., Sugai, G., & Colvin, G. (1998). Reducing problem behavior through a school-wide system of effective behavioral support: Investigation of a school-wide social skills training program and contextual intervention. *School Psychology Review, 27*, 446–459.

Lockwood, D. (1997). *Violence among middle school and high school students: Analysis and implications for prevention*. Washington, DC: National Institute of Justice, U.S. Department of Justice.

Long, N., & Edwards, M. (1994). The use of a daily report card to address children's school behavior problems. *Contemporary Education, 65*(3), 152–155.

Madsen, C. H., Jr., Becker, W. C., & Thomas, D. R. (1968). Rules, praise, and ignoring: Elements of elementary classroom control. *Journal of Applied Behavior Analysis, 1*, 139–150.

Myers, C. L., & Holland, K. L. (2000). Classroom behavioral interventions: Do teachers consider the function of the behavior? *Psychology in the Schools, 37(3)*, 271–280.

March, R. E., & Horner, R. H. (2002). Feasibility and contributions of functional behavioral assessment in schools. *Journal of Emotional and Behavioral Disorders, 10*(3), 158–170.

Mayer, G. R. (1995). Preventing antisocial behavior in the schools. *Journal of Applied Behavior Analysis, 28*(4), 467–478.

Mayer, G. R. (2001). Antisocial behavior: Its causes and prevention within our schools. *Education and Treatment of Children, 24*, 414–429.

Mayer, G. R. & Butterworth, T. (1981). Evaluating a preventative approach to reducing school vandalism. *Phi Delta Kappan*, 62, 498–499.

Mayer, G. R., Butterworth, T., Nafpaktitis, M., & Sulzer-Azaroff, B. (1983). Preventing vandalism and improving discipline: A three year study. *Journal of Applied Behavior Analysis, 16*, 355–369.

Mayer, G. R., & Leone, P. (1999). A structural analysis of school violence and disruption: Implications for creating safer schools. *Education and Treatment of Children, 22*(3), 333–356.

Mayer, G. R., Mitchell, L., Clementi, T., Clement-Robertson, E., Myatt, R., & Vullara, D. T. (1993). A dropout prevention program for at-risk high school students: Emphasizing consulting to promote positive classroom environments. *Education and Treatment of Children, 16*, 135–146.

Mayer, G. R., Nafpaktitis, M., Butterworth, T., & Hollingsworth, P. (1987). A search for the elusive setting events of school vandalism: A correlational study. *Education and Treatment of Children, 10*, 259–270.

Mayer, G. R., & Sulzer-Azaroff, B. (1991). Interventions for vandalism. In G. Stoner, M. K. Shinn, & H. M. Walker (Eds.), *Interventions for achievement and behaviour problems* (pp. 559–580). Washington, DC: National Association of School Psychologists Monograph.

Metzler, C. W., Biglan, A., Rusby, J. C., & Sprague, J. (2001). Evaluation of a comprehensive behavior management program to improve school-wide positive behavior support. *Education and Treatment of Children, 24*, 448–479.

Nakasato, J. (2000). Data-based decision making in Hawaii's behavior support effort. *Journal of Positive Behavior Interventions, 2*(4).

Nelson, J. R., Martella, R., & Garland, B. (1998). The effects of teaching school expectations and establishing a consistent consequence on formal office disciplinary actions. *Journal of Emotional and Behavioral Disorders, 6*(3), 153–161.

Newcomer, L., & Lewis, T. (2004). Functional behavioral assessment: An investigation of assessment reliability and effectiveness of function-based interventions. *Journal of Emotional and Behavioral Disorders, 12*(3), 168–181.

Newcomer, L. L., & Lewis, T. J. (2005). Active supervision. In Sugai, G., & Horner, R. (Eds.), *Encyclopedia of behavior modification and cognitive behavior therapy: Educational Applications* (Volume III, pp. 1132–1135). Thousand Oaks, CA: Sage Publications.

Newcomer, L. L., Lewis, T. J., & Powers, L. J. (2002). *Policies and procedures to develop effective school-wide discipline practices at the elementary level*. Arlington, VA: CCBD/CASE.

Newcomer, L., & Powers, L. (2002, February) *A team approach to functional behavioral assessment-based positive behavioral support plans*. Paper presented at Midwest Symposium for Leadership in Behavior Disorders, Kansas City, MO.

Peterson, G. J., Beekley, C. Z., Speaker, K. M., & Pietrzak, D. (1996). An examination of violence in three rural school districts. *Rural Educator, 19*(3), 25–32.

Patterson, G. R., Reid, J. B., & Dishion, T. J. (1992). *Antisocial boys*. Eugene, OR: Castalia Press.

Powers, L. J. (2003). *Examining effects of targeted group social skills interventi on in schools with and without school-wide systems of positive behavior support*. Unpublished doctoral dissertation, University of Missouri, Columbia.

Putnam, R. F., Handler, M. W., Ramirez-Platt, C., & Luiselli, J. K. (2003). Improving student bus-riding behavior through a whole-school intervention. *Journal of Applied Behavior Analysis, 36*, 583–590.

Ramsey, E., Patterson, G. R., & Walker, H. M. (1990). Generalization of the antisocial trait from home to school settings. *Journal of Applied Developmental Psychology, 11*, 209–223.

Reid, J. B. (1993). Prevention of conduct disorder before and after school entry: Relating interventions to developmental findings. *Development and Psychopathology, 5*(1/2), 243–262.

Ross, S., Sanders, W., Wright, S., Stringfield, S., Wang, L., & Alberg, M. (2001) Two- and three-year achievement results from the Memphis Restructuring Initiative. *School Effectiveness and Improvement, 12*(3), 323–246.

Ross, S., Stringfield, S., Sanders, W., & Wright, S. P. (2003) Inside systemic elementary school reform: Teacher effects and teacher mobility. *School Effectiveness and School Improvement, 14*(1) 73–110.

Safran, S. P., & Oswald, K. (2003). Positive behavior supports: Can schools reshape disciplinary practices? *Exceptional Children, 69,* 361–373.

Scott, T. M. (2001). A school-wide example of positive behavioral support. *Journal of Positive Behavioral Interventions, 3,* 88–94.

Scott, T. M., & Nelson, C. M. (1999). Universal school discipline strategies: Facilitati ng positive learning environments. *Effective School Practices, 17*(4), 54–64.

Skiba, R. J. (2002). Special education and school discipline: A precarious balance. *Behavioral Disorders, 27*(2), 81–97.

Skiba, R. J., & Peterson, R. L. (2000). School discipline at a crossroads: From zero tolerance to early response. *Exceptional Children, 66,* 335–347.

Skiba, R. J., Peterson, R. L., & Williams, T. (1997). Office referrals and suspensions: Disciplinary intervention in middle schools. *Education and Treatment of Children, 20,* 295–315.

Snyder, J. J., & Patterson, G. R. (1995). Individual differences in social aggression: A test of reinforcement model of socialization in the natural environment. *Behavior Therapy, 26,* 371–391.

Snyder, J., Schrepferman, L., & St. Peter, C. (1997). Origins of antisocial behavior: Negative reinforcement and affect dysregulation of behavior as socialization mechanisms in family interaction. *Behavior Modification, 21,* 187–215.

Sinclair, M. F., Christenson, S. L., Evelo, D. L., & Hurley, C. M. (1998). Dropout prevention for youth with disabilities: Efficacy of a sustained school engagement procedure. *Exceptional Children, 65*(1), 7–21.

Sugai, G., & Horner, R. H. (1999). Discipline and behavioral support: Preferred processes and practices. *Effective School Practices, 17*(4), 10–22.

Sugai, G., Horner, R. H., Dunlap, G., Hieneman, M., Lewis, T. J., Nelson, C. M., Scott, T., Liaupsin, C., Sailor, W., Turnbull, A. P., Turnbull, W., Wickham, D., Ruef, M., & Wilcox, B. (2000). *Applying positive behavioral support and functional behavioral assessment in schools.* Washington, DC: OSEP Center of Positive Behavioral Interventions and Supports.

Sugai, G., Horner, R., Lewis, T. J., & Cheney, D. (2002, July). *Positive behavioral supports.* Paper presented at the OSEP Research Project Directors' Conference, Washington, DC.

Sugai, G., Horner, R., & Sprague, J. (1999). Functional-assessment-based behavior support planning: Research to practice to research. *Behavioral Disorders, 24(3),* 253–257.

Sugai, G., Lewis-Palmer, T., & Hagan, S. (1998). Using functional assessments to develop behavior support plans. *Preventing School Failure, 43*(1), 6–13.

Sugai, G., Sprague, J. R., Horner, R., & Walker, H. M. (1999). Preventing school violence. The use of office discipline referrals to assess and monitor school-wide discipline interventions. *Journal of Behavioral Education, 8*(2), 94–101.

Sulzer-Azaroff, B., & Mayer, G. R. (1986). Achieving educational excellence using behavioral strategies. Chicago: Holt Rinehart & Winston.

Sulzer-Azaroff, B., & Mayer, G. R. (1994). *Achieving educational excellence: Behavior analysis for achieving classroom and schoolwide behavior change.* San Marcos, CA: Western Image.

Sutherland, K. S., & Wehby, J. H. (2001). Exploring the relationship between increased opportunities to respond to academic requests and the academic and behavioral outcomes of students with EBD. *Remedial and Special Education, 22*(2), 113–121.

Sutherland, K. S., Wehby, J. H., & Copeland, S. (2000). Effects of varying rates of behavior-specific prasie on the on-task behavior of students with EBD. *Journal of Emotional and Behavioral Disorders, 8*(2), 2–8.

Taylor-Greene, S., Brown, D. K., Nelson, L., Longton, J., Gassman, T., Cohen, J., Swartz, J., Horner, R. H., Sugai, G., & Hall, S. (1997). School-wide behavioral support: Starting the year off right. *Journal of Behavioral Education, 7,* 99–112.

Taylor-Greene, S. J., & Kartub, D. T. (2000). Durable implementation of school-wide positive behavior support: The high five program. *Journal of Positive Behavior Interventions, 2,* 233–235.

Tobin, T., Sugai, G., & Colvin, G. (1996). Patterns in middle school discipline referrals. *Journal of Emotional and Behavioral Disorders, 4*(2), 82–94.

Todd, A., Horner, R. H., & Sugai, G. (1999). Self-monitoring and self-recruited praise: Effects on problem behavior, academic engagement, and work completion in a typical classroom. *Journal of Positive Behavior Interventions, 1*(2), 66–76.

Todd, A. W., Haugen, L., Anderson, K., & Spriggs, M. (2002). Teaching recess: Low-cost efforts producing effective results. *Journal of Positive Behavior Interventions, 4*(1), 46–52.

Todd, A. W., Horner, R., Sugai, G., & Colvin, G. (1999). Individualizing school-wide discipline for students with chronic problem behaviors: A team approach. *Effective School Practices, 17*, 72–82.

Todd, A. W., Horner, R. H., Sugai, G., & Sprague, J. R. (1999). Effective behavior support: Strengthening school-wide systems through a team-based approach. *Effect School Practices, 17*(4), 23–37.

U.S. Department of Education. (1998). *Violence and discipline problems in U.S. public schools: 1996-97*. Washington, DC: U.S. Department of Education, National Center for Educational Statistics.

U.S. Department of Education. (2000a). *Effective alternative strategies: Grant competition to reduce student suspensions and expulsions and ensure educational progress of suspended and expelled students*. Washington, DC: Safe and drug-free school programs. (OMB No. 1810-0551)

U.S. Department of Education. (2000b). *Twenty-second annual report to Congress on the implementation of the Individuals with Disabilities Education Act*. Washington, DC: Author.

U.S. Department of Health and Human Services. (2000). *Report of the Surgeon General's conference on children's mental health: A national action agenda*. Washington, DC: Author.

U.S. Department of Health and Human Services (2001). *Youth violence: A report of the Surgeon General—Executive Summary*. Rockville, MD: Author.

Walker, H. M., Colvin, G., & Ramsey, E. (1995). *Antisocial behavior in school: Strategies and best practices*. Pacific Grove, CA: Brooks/Cole.

Walker, H. M., Horner, R., Sugai, G., Bullis, M., Sprague, J., Bricker, D., & Kaufman, J. (1996). Integrated approaches to preventing antisocial behavior patterns among school -age children and youth. *Journal of Emotional and Behavioral Disorders, 4*, 193–256.

Walker, H. M., & Sylwester, R. (1991). Where is school along the path to prison. *Educational Leadership*, 14–16.

Wehby, J. H., Symons, F. J., & Shores, R. E. (1995). A descriptive analysis of aggressive behavior in classrooms for children with emotional and behavioral disorders. *Behavioral Disorders, 20*(2), 87–105.

Wright, S., Horn, S., & Sanders, W. (2001). Teacher and the classroom context effects on student achievement. Implications for teacher evaluation. *Journal of Personnel Evaluation in Education, 11*(1), 57–67.

Ziglar, E., Taussig, C., & Black, K. (1992). Early childhood intervention: A promising preventative for juvenile delinquency. *American Psychologist, 47*, 997–1006.

Zins, J. E., & Ponti, C. R. (1990). Best practices in school-based consultation. In A. Thomas & J. Grimes (Eds.), *Best practices in school psychology—II* (pp. 673–694). Washington, DC: National Association of School Psychologists.

32

Bullying: Theory, Research, and Interventions

Irwin Hyman, Bryony Kay, Alexander Tabori,
Meredith Weber, Matthew Mahon, and Ian Cohen
Temple University

INTRODUCTION

American policy makers periodically address school violence, student disruption, and student victimization (Hyman & Snook, 1999a; Moles, 1990). They are generally responding to alarmed public disclosure of perceived increases in illegal student behavior. Yet actual incidents of school violence, including homicides, extortion, assaults with weapons, and death threats are relatively infrequent, and have been relatively stable since 1988 (National Center for Education Statistics, 1992; Hyman et al., 1997). More widespread is "common" everyday bullying by peers (Batsche & Knoff, 1994; Elliott, 2002; Hoover, Oliver, & Hazler 1992; Smith, 2000). During the last decade more policy makers have noted daily student victimization by peers (Limber & Small, 2003). This chapter presents a comprehensive review of the literature on bullying within the broader context of student victimization, school disruption, and student alienation. In so doing, we provide information about the extent of bullying, its contexts, the characteristics of bullies and their victims, the effects of bullying on a variety of outcomes, and interventions aimed at preventing and reducing bullying behavior.

Bullying should be included in the broader context of school and community violence indicators used to determine student alienation from schools, peers, and educators (Hyman, Cohen, & Mahon, 2003). The relation between school violence and bullying is most startling in research and anecdotal reports about the shootings at Columbine High School. Like many other violent student offenders, the perpetrators felt bullied, demeaned, marginalized, and disrespected by peers and educators (Bai, 1999; Vossekuil, Reddy, Fein, Borum, & Modzeleski, 2000). Research presupposes a cycle where victims may become victimizers. There is evidence to suggest that victims may use horrendous retaliatory acts against peers and educators. For instance, 71% of attackers (in school shootings) felt persecuted, threatened, or were actually bullied or attacked by other students before the incident (U.S. Secret Service and U.S. Department of Education, 2002a, 2002b).

Most educators do not grasp the connection between bullying and its potential for school disruption (Metropolitan Life Survey of the American Teacher, 1999). Many educators are unaware of the nature and extent of bullying, because much of it often occurs outside of classrooms (Rigby, 1997, Whitney & Smith, 1993). Many victims hesitate to report bullying because they believe teachers will either ignore them, trivialize the bullying, or deal with it ineffectively (Whitney & Smith, 1993). Victims may also fear retaliation by the bully or further rejection by peers who may label them as "snitches," "tattletales," or "narcs." Almost all students have experienced or witnessed bullying. Hoover et al. (1992) indicate that at least 75% of American students have been bullied at least once before graduating from high school. Other evidence suggests that 50% to 60% of students report being victimized at least once by educators to the extent that the students developed stress symptoms (Hyman & Snook, 1999a; Hyman & Perone, 1998a; Hyman, Cohen, & Mahon, 2003). Studies from other Western democracies add that school bullying is widespread and normative across many cultures (Nansel et al., 2001; Olweus, 1993; Smith, 2000).

Bullying also directly and indirectly affects children's education, their physical health, and their social adjustment. Sharp (1995) found that 29% of bullying victims found it difficult to concentrate on their schoolwork. Victims also suffer physical symptoms including headaches, poor sleep, and stomachaches at a higher rate than nonbullied peers (Dawkins, 1995; Rigby, 1998; Sharpe, 1995). Victims are more likely to feel socially isolated (Hawker & Boulton, 2000), and to be truant (Kochenderfer & Ladd, 1996). It has also been estimated by the National Educational Association that approximately 160,000 students are absent from school each day in the United States as a result of fears of victimization (cited in Sanchez et al., 2001).

Relatively large proportions (20%–25%) of British children have reported fears of going to school because of bullying (Balding, Regis, Wise, Bish, & Muirden, 1996). In the United States, 27% of bullied students reported fear of being attacked or harmed at school compared to 4.1% of their nonbullied peers. Similarly, 11.6% reported being afraid of traveling to and from school (National Center for Education Statistics, 2003). Of children who have been the victims of bullying, 16% to 19% of those in the 8 to 12-year age group perceive their school as hardly ever being safe. In the 13 to 18-year age group this increases to approximately 30%. More disturbing is that across these age groups only 28% to 31% of children who report having never been bullied perceive their schools to be safe. Thus the mere knowledge of bullying negatively affects nonvictimized children, observers, peer confidants, parents, and school staff (Rigby & Slee, 2000).

Although most school officials, parents, and students concede the existence of bullying, little has been done in the United States until relatively recently (Batsche & Knoff, 1994, Elliott, 2002; Hyman & Eisenstein, 2000). Olweus (1993) in his seminal research exposed the extent of peer bullying in Norway and revealed that effective programs could greatly reduce student victimization. His work greatly stimulated the recent international interest in studying, preventing, and intervening in bullying.

DEFINITIONS OF BULLYING AND STUDENT VICTIMIZATION

Bullying includes demeaning physical or psychological assaults on students by both peers and school personnel (Hyman, Cohen, & Mahon, 2003; Hyman & Snook, 1999a). The terms *victimizers* and *victims* describe those who bully and their targets. Olweus (1993) defined bullying as a type of aggressive behavior in which the perpetrators' negative behaviors toward the victims are repeated over time and are intended to cause harm or discomfort. It must be repetitive, as compared to infrequent or incidental attacks, and can involve various types and levels of direct or indirect hostile actions. Bullies may attack physically, verbally, or nonverbally. The latter action can include repeated use of lewd, demeaning, and demoralizing gestures, and relational actions such as exclusion from small groups and total ostracism.

Contemporary bullying now may involve the Internet, e-mails, and text messaging. "Cyber bullies" use instant messages to victimize students by the use of false accusations, name-calling, and embarrassing pictures (Harmon, 2004). Further, bullies may use peers as passive or active surrogates.

Bullying presupposes power over a victim. The power imbalance may reflect the bully's greater size, strength, intellectual ability, social status, or ability to enlist peers as helpers. Also, victimization may occur when a group of peers rejects, isolates, or ridicules the victim. The most dramatic bullying includes overt aggression, with subtler forms involving verbal and relational aggression (Crick & Grotpeter, 1996). However, not all aggression is bullying. Reactive aggression is not usually considered bullying, as it may be a reaction to a perceived threat or insult during an actual physical attack. Proactive bullying aggression, which fits the criteria, is goal directed and has a social component (Dodge, 1991); the victimizer's intent is to dominate, intimidate, and terrorize. The bully gains social power and increased affiliation with peers (Roland & Thormod, 2001). To accomplish their goals, bullies are deft at targeting their victims (Smith & Sharp, 1994).

Although physical bullying tends to receive the most attention, it is not the most prevalent form of bullying in the schools. Verbal bullying, most often name-calling, is more common, followed by being hit, physically threatened, having rumors spread about the victim, having belongings taken away, and being socially excluded (Hyman & Snook, 1999b; Nansel et al., 2001; Rigby, 1997; Whitney & Smith, 1993). Relational bullying is meant to embarrass, alienate, and isolate (Crick & Grotpeter, 1996). Teasing is common, but some experts such as Olweus (1993) maintained that teasing, without the intent to harm, is unacceptable, but should not be considered bullying. When teasing, even by close friends, is perceived by the victim as hurtful, the difference between malicious bullying and nonmalicious verbal attacks is problematic. As teasing becomes bullying, especially as it socially isolates the victim, it meets the criteria for relational bullying. Relational bullying can also have a strong nonverbal component. For example, it can include the alpha bullies and their coconspirators huddling in groups, and staring at victims (Owens, Shute, & Slee, 2000).

FREQUENCY AND TYPES OF BULLYING

Research reveals bullying as a pervasive, cross-national problem with frequency rates ranging from approximately 8% to 30% depending in part on the measurement categories used (e.g., this semester, this year, sometimes, weekly) (Borg, 1999; Jeffrey, Miller, & Linn, 2001; Nansel et al., 2001; Olweus, 1993; Rigby, 1998; Whitney & Smith, 1993; Wolke, Woods, Bloomfield, & Karstadt, 2000). Seventy five percent of American schoolchildren have reported being bullied at least once during their school careers (Hoover et al., 1992). In the United States, there has been an increase in the number of students from 6th through 12th grade reporting victimization. In 1999, 5% of students reported being victimized in the last 6 months, compared to 8% in 2001 (National Center for Educational Statistics, 2003). Bullying spans cultures, socioeconomic groups, age groups, types of school, gender (Morita, Haruo, Kumiko, & Taki, 2000; Olweus 1993, 2000a, 2000b; Rigby, 1997; Smith, & Brain, 2000; Schwartz, Dodge, Pettit, & Bates, 1997; Whitney & Smith, 1993), and urban and rural settings (Stockdale, Hangaduambo, Duys, Larson, & Sarvela, 2002). Although clearly a significant school problem, educators are seemingly unaware of its true extent as students' reports of bullying are often higher than teachers' reports in the same school (Stockdale et al., 2002). Because these studies vary widely in terms of methodology, comparisons using cross-cultural studies are difficult. Despite recognized limitations, we summarize some of the major studies on incidence and frequency.

In one of the earliest large-scale incidence studies, Olweus (1993) found that 15% of 130,000 Norwegian primary and junior high school students had bully/victim problems now and then (9% victims, 7% bullying others, and 1.6% both victim and bully). Approximately 5% of the students reported at least weekly involvement either as a bully or a victim. A similar large-scale survey of over 6,000 7- to 18-year-old English schoolchildren using the Olweus questionnaire found that 27% of primary school students reported being bullied sometime in the previous semester, and 10% reported being bullied at least once a week. Of primary school students, 12% reported bullying others sometimes and 4% reported bullying others at least once a week. Of secondary school students, 10% reported being bullied sometimes that semester and 4% reported being bullied at least once a week. Of these students, 6% reported bullying others sometimes and 1% reported bullying others at least once a week (Whitney & Smith, 1993). Studies of Maltese students (Borg, 1999) and Italian students (Genta, Menesini, Fonzi, & Costabile, 1996) reported similar characteristics, but with overall frequencies in excess of 33%.

In the United States there has been more limited research on the extent and typology of bullying behavior in schools. Early research indicated that 10% of third-through sixth-graders reported being chronically abused by peers (Perry, Kusel, & Perry, 1988). In another study, 29% of middle school students reported bullying others in the last 30 days (Bosworth, Espelage, & Simon, 1999). A more recent study of bullying in grades 4 through 6 found that more than one third of students reported experiencing bullying, and one fifth reported bullying others (Berthold & Hoover, 2000). More recently, Nansel and colleagues (2001) conducted an extensive study of 15,686 sixth-through tenth-graders in public and private schools, to determine current rates and types of bullying. They asked students to indicate the frequency with which they bullied others, or were bullied, during that semester. Nansel et al. (2001) found that almost a third of the sample reported moderate or frequent involvement in bullying as either a bully (13%), a victim (10.6%), or both (6.3%). In terms of the actual frequency of victimization, results showed that approximately 24% of students were bullied once or twice that term, 8% were sometimes, and a further 8% were victimized weekly. Participants were then given five response options and asked to indicate the manner in which they were bullied. Results showed that being belittled about their looks or speech (20.1%) was the most frequent form of bullying, followed by sexual comments (18%), rumors (17%), and being hit, slapped, or pushed (14%). Being belittled about one's religion or race was the least frequent form of bullying (8%). The rates and frequency of bullying behavior was also assessed. One fourth of the sample reported bullying others once or twice, 10.6% sometimes, and 8.8% weekly.

Bullying is a cross-national problem that is clearly reflected in educational laws and legislation addressing this issue. Many countries require bullying prevention and postvention policies and programs. All schools in Belgium, Finland, France, Ireland, Luxembourg, Malta, Sweden, and the United Kingdom must offer antibullying and antiviolence programs (Ananiadou & Smith, 2002). In the United States there are no federal mandates as yet, but challenges to the current law have increased. In the last 2 years, a number of states have passed laws addressing bullying in schools. As of 2003, 15 states had passed laws requiring school boards to develop policies on bullying. Some also require bullying prevention programs and staff training (Limber & Small, 2003). Similarly, schools can be liable for negligence under Title IX of the Federal Education Amendments of 1972 if they have failed to stop sexual harassment of students. Although no federal law mandates preventive or responsive measures to bullying, the National Education Goals Panel (1993) stated as one of their six goals that by the year 2000, "Every school in America will be free of drugs and violence." Bullying was reportedly included in their definition of school violence (Harachi, Catalano, & Hawkins, 2000). Further, 90% of American schools now have a zero tolerance policy mandating consequences for specific violent acts and behaviors (National Center for Educational Statistics, 2003). In summary, bullying is a cross-national problem. Its frequency rates range from approximately 8% to 30%, with some estimates even higher. The high frequency of reported bullying suggests that victims exist in most if not all classrooms (Schuster, 1999).

Naturalistic observational studies offer an alternative to self-reports, and provide a clearer picture on the daily rate of school bullying. Craig and Pepler (1997, 2000) conducted an observational study of elementary school playgrounds. They noted that among 6- to 12-year-old students, bullying occurred approximately once every 7 minutes. Direct verbal, aggression was the most frequent followed by physical aggression, combined physical and verbal, and then relational. Bullying incidents occurred 6.5 times each hour, and lasted from 2 seconds to eight minutes (mean length—38 seconds), with verbal bullying lasting longer than physical bullying. In an observational study of classroom bullying among 6- to 12-year-olds, bullying occurred approximately twice every hour. Direct bullying was the most frequent behavior. Here, name-calling occurred in half of the incidents, a third consisted of direct physical aggression, and 17% involved both physical and verbal aggression. Indirect bullying occurred approximately a third of the time and consisted of mostly gossiping, followed by social exclusion. In 85% of the episodes, peers were either onlookers or participants (Atlas & Pepler, 1998). In the playground study, eight different classes were observed within one school and so observed student behaviors may reflect that specific school culture and climate. Also, bullying behaviors were defined as having a power imbalance, intent to harm, and victim distress but did not include repeated bullying behaviors.

Although boys are slightly more likely to be bullies and to be exposed to bullying than girls (Craig & Pepler, 1997; Nansel et al., 2001; Olweus, 1993; Rigby, 1997; Whitney & Smith, 1993), there are some exceptions. Jeffrey et al. (2001) reported more low-frequency victimization among middle school females than males, although a larger percentage of males reported weekly victimization.

Boys victimize as individuals or as part of a bullying group; girls are more likely to bully as part of a group. Bullying in all-girl schools is less frequent than in coeducational schools (Rigby, 2002). Girls are likely to bully their own gender whereas boys are equal opportunity victimizers. A study in Britain of 6 to 9-year-olds found "young boys to be just as likely, or more likely to be involved in relational bullying as girls" (Wolke et al., 2000, p. 997). Girls also experience more sexual harassment, but boys are also subject to this at high rates (Nansel et al., 2001). For both genders, name-calling is the most frequent form of bullying (Hyman et al., 2003; Nansel et al., 2001; Rigby, 1997; Whitney & Smith, 1993).

The occurrences of bullying change over time. There is a general decrease in the frequency of physical bullying as children develop. Although the frequencies of bullying behaviors decrease, the incidences of relational bullying, involving the disruption of social relationships and bonds through rumors, ostracism, and so forth, actually increase (Cairns, Neckerman, Ferguson, & Gariepy,1989, cited in Warman & Cohen, 2000; Bosworth et al., 1999; Nansel et al., 2001; *Olweus, 1993*; Pellegrini & Long, 2002; Whitney & Smith, 1993). In addition, bullies tend to maintain their roles over time, whereas victims are more likely to escape their roles (Camodeca, Goossens, Meerum Terwogt, & Schuengel, 2002).

Developmental decreases in physical bullying may be related to increasing social skills, which make older children less susceptible. Also, as children mature, their definition of bullying narrows (Smith, Madsen, & Moody, 1999). A developmental confound in the data on self-reports of bullying may be that as children become older, the lower social desirability of being a victim or victimizer may result in less reporting of bullying (Menesini et al., 1997). Another confound related to the overall stability data is that temporary increases may occur at transition points when students change schools or grades, regardless of the age of the students during those transitions (Bosworth et al., 1999; Rigby, 1996).

In conclusion, bullying is a normative practice across cultures. Most research on this type of trauma has been conducted in Europe, Australia, Canada, and Japan. Stein (2001) pointed out that knowledge gained from these studies must only be cautiously applied to American schools. These other countries have much more homogenous populations than the United States, and also "have much less overt public violence than the United States, so the meaning (and forms) of bullying varied greatly . . . [and] do not provide us with a viable comparison sample or context" (Stein, 2001, p. 1). Also, methodological differences between studies suggest that comparisons of data must be made with caution. Similarly, theoretical explanations for bullying behaviors have to be viewed cautiously given that most bullying data are derived from self-report measures. Although most of these studies are based on self-report inventories, with few actual observational studies, the explanations for bullying are often generated from the data gathered. We turn next to a discussion of theoretical explanations for bullying.

SOME THEORETICAL PERSPECTIVES ON BULLYING

Olweus' (1993) explanation of bullying appears to be rooted in theories of social information processing (Schwartz & Proctor, 2000). This suggests that bullies recognize victims' passivity or aggressiveness as no threat to the victimizer. The bully senses the victim's anxiety, immediate or eventual submissiveness, and physical weakness. Bullies may learn to model their behavior by watching and then successfully victimizing others. They create cognitive schemata, which enhance and reinforce their feelings of power and effectiveness.

A tripartite belief model (Gottheil & Dubow, 2001) suggests that normative beliefs, self-efficacy, and outcome expectancy compose the underlying system that powers bullying behavior. Bullying behavior is goal oriented, often accepted and supported by peers, easily rationalized, and encouraged.

Sutton and Keogh (2000) suggested that bullying is a type of social intelligence explained through the research on Machiavellianism. This concept and the scales developed to measure it emerged from studies of successful corporate managers (Jay, 1967). Machiavelli (1513/1958; 1950) is one of the early writers recognized for explaining how successful leaders manipulate underlings to reach their goals. Christie and Geis (1970) used the Machiavellianism Scale to measure the traits of successful executives. Many successful executives who scored high on the Machiavellian Scale (High Machs) were charming, confident, glib, arrogant, calculating, exploitative, and cynical about people's feeling and motives. Like young bullies, high "Machs" in the executive suites are goal oriented, and value their ability to manipulate people to obtain those goals. People's feelings count only when they help leaders reach their goals. These bullies successfully victimize others by spreading rumors, excluding and isolating them, and using sarcasm and ridicule that range from subtle to brutally overt. From what we know of the Machiavellian personality, it may stem from a combination of inborn temperament and social learning. There is some evidence that Machiavellian traits may be genetically predetermined through evolutionary processes (De Wall, 1998).

Chimpanzees, one of our closest relatives among primates, offer a good model for studying bullying. De Wall (1998) found that both male and female primates achieve dominance, not only through force, but also by seeking support and acceptance. Some dysfunctional male chimpanzees spend so much time and energy struggling for dominance that they appear as power-hungry Machiavellians. But those that achieve dominance reflect a careful combination of manipulation and aggressiveness. Both humans and chimpanzees use bluffing, alliances, and ostracism.

Atlas and Pepler (1998) explained bullying through ecological systems theory. Bullying occurs as a function of interactions: individuality of the bully, the dyadic interaction between the bully and victim, the presence of peers and teachers, and the context in which bullying occurs. Teacher responses to bullying and classroom structure may actually reinforce bullying behavior. Unnoticed, ignored, or trivialized bullying in the classroom occurs during solitary as well as teacher-led tasks. Most bullying in the classroom is relational, and goes undetected by the teacher. Classroom ecological theory suggests that bullying can be decreased when the teacher intertwines antibullying messages within the curriculum, group activities, and discussions of the morality of aggressive behavior (Hyman et al., 1997).

Hazler and Miller (2001) discussed the frequency of unchallenged relational bullying within ecological theory. Social/emotional bullying such as name-calling, spreading rumors, and ostracizing are more common than physical bullying, but school staff are less likely to intervene or prevent social bullying, as opposed to aggressive bullying. They are also likely to overreact punitively in dangerous situations and thereby increase, rather than decrease, aggressive behavior. Therefore, ecological theory implies that a more effective approach would be to help students understand the nature of both types of bullying and the importance of early prevention and intervention use through such activities as peer mediation and conflict resolution.

Pellegrini, Bartini, and Brooks (1999) suggested that nature may contribute as much as nurture to traits that affect bullying. Students with innately high levels of physical activity and emotionality seem more likely to victimize others. Students who are both victims and bullies tend to have high activity levels, low impulse control, and tend to affiliate with aggressive peers. Evidence for the relation between temperament and socially reinforced bullying is minimal. But strong evidence indicates that highly aggressive, impulse-driven bullies from coercive families tend to become lawbreakers (Huesmann, Eron, & Yarmel, 1987; Reid, Patterson, & Snyder, 2002; Patterson, DeBaryshe, & Ramsey, 2000). These individuals may develop patterns of criminal behavior and family violence that are rooted in early bullying behavior.

In summary, the causes of bullying are complex, and are accounted for by both nature and nurture. Most explanations are rooted in social learning, behavioral, and ecological theories. Least explored are theories based on evolutionary biology. Evolutionary explanations examine group behavior of all primates and clarify the hierarchical and cooperative nature of social behavior. Institutional norms and community culture modulate bullying behavior in each school. Ecological interventions enhance peer acceptance, cooperation, and the opportunity for victims to seek redress within the established social hierarchy. Although theoretical explanations of the roots of bullying are important, it is necessary to examine the actual ecology of bullying situations.

THE ECOLOGY OF BULLYING

Ecological factors influence the nature and frequency of bullying. A common theory holds it is more likely to occur in larger schools, where students appear to be less supervised. Yet, most studies suggest that class or school size do not correlate with frequency of bullying (Olweus, 1993; Whitney & Smith, 1993) although the type of school may. A Swiss study (Alsaker & Brunner, 2000) of seventh- to ninth-graders suggests that students in more academically elite schools experience less bullying than those who attend schools for students of lesser academic ability. In terms of the location of bullying incidents, there are some differences in findings across studies and cultures. However, the general trend is for most bullying to occur in the playground or schoolyard especially at the lower levels, and for bullying incidents in classrooms and corridors to increase at the secondary level. Whitney and Smith (1993) found that 75% of primary school victims reported being bullied on the playground and 30% the classroom. At the secondary level, 45% of bullying incidents occurred in the playground, 39% in classrooms, and 30% in school corridors. Similar findings have been observed in Australia, Europe, and Japan (Borg, 1999; Morita et al., 2000; Rigby, 1997). There is also some indication that for elementary school children, bullying begins toward the end of the recess period (Boulton, 1993) and may be a means of breaking up the monotony of unstructured time (Rigby, 2002). Other data suggest that at the middle school level, most bullying occurs in the classroom (Baldry & Farrington, 2000), whereas a Swiss study suggests equal occurrences of bullying in the playground, classroom, and to and from school (Alsaker & Brunner, 2000).

Although the playground appears to be the single most frequent location for bullying, the frequency in other locations varies with different countries and possibly reflects differing school organization and supervision. For example, reports of bullying to and from school in the United Kingdom ranged from 14% of junior/middle school children to 5% secondary school students (Whitney & Smith, 1993), whereas the Australian frequencies were significantly higher, especially on the way home from school compared to going to school (Rigby, 1997). Of note is Olweus' finding (1993) that it is the same children who are bullied on the way to school, as at school. In a study of Japanese schools, out-of-school bullying was also significant, with approximately 20% of victims reporting occurrences after school, and 19% reporting occurrences on the way to school (Morita et al., 2000). In a study in Swiss schools, bullying occurred at equal rates to and from school, on the playground, and in the classroom (Alsaker & Brunner, 2000). In a study of Italian elementary and middle schools, the majority of bullying took place in the classroom, followed by the playground at the primary level, and corridors and toilets at the middle school level (Fonzi, Genta, Menesini, Bonino, & Costabile, 2000).

In summary, it appears that across grades, bullying episodes occur most frequently on school playgrounds, with the classroom venue becoming more popular with increasing age. This may be a function of reduced supervision and less organized activities, or it may relate to the social dynamics of the playground. Similarly, as children age and verbal and relational aggression increases, the classroom may become a preferred location. Although there are some differences across studies, it is likely that the amount of direct adult supervision, organized activities, and structure correlates with the level of bullying (Craig & Pepler, 1995, 1997; Espelage & Asidao, 2001; Olweus, 1993, 2000a, 2000b; Rivers & Smith, 1994). From the ecology of bullying we next address research on the characteristics of the players in various bullying scenarios, although again we must exercise caution because of the limitations inherent in self-report measures.

CHARACTERISTICS OF BULLIES, VICTIMS, AND BULLY/VICTIMS

During much of the 20th century, psychoanalytic perspectives influenced the professional's understanding of bullies and victims. Bullies were seen to have poor self-images and were trying to compensate for perceived inadequacies. Victims were portrayed as those whose behavior triggered bullying. However, in the last few decades, research has changed this perception, and has led to radically different therapeutic and disciplinary interventions.

Characteristics of Bullies

The seminal work of Olweus (1993) and the longitudinal studies of aggressive behavior by Eron (1987) and others (Reid et al., 2002) suggest that bullies, especially males, have an aggressive reaction pattern. Olweus described bullies as impulsive, domineering, and lacking in empathy. Contrary to popular belief, bullies are not overly anxious, depressed, or insecure (Craig, 1998). Nor do they suffer from low self-esteem. To the contrary, they appear to have high levels of self-esteem (Olweus, 2000a); however, bullies who are also victimized may have lower sense of self-worth and self-esteem than victims, non victimized children, and bullies (Andreou, 2001). They also have a higher likelihood of being referred for psychiatric services than the other groups (Kumpulainen, Rasanen, Henttonen, Almovist, & Kresanov, 1998).

Despite the assumption that the behaviors exhibited by bullies would cause peer rejection, bullies tend to be popular (Lindman & Sinclair, 1988, cited in Salmivalli, Lagerspetz, Bjorkqvist, Osterman & Kauklianen, 1996; Pellegrini, 2001). Clinical evidence and empirical research have long suggested that aggressive children have social skills deficits that lead to faulty social cognition and misattribution of other's behaviors (Crick & Dodge, 1996). Because bullying involves a variety of aggressive behaviors, especially the planned disruption of social connections and ties (relational bullying), the research on conduct-disordered children may not apply to bullying (Espelage & Swearer, 2003). Rather than misperceiving others' behavior and intentions, bullies tend to be effective social interpreters, especially in relational bullying. Far from being socially deficient, bullies may be effective social manipulators (Sutton, Smith, & Swettenham, 1999). Their effective social skills make them generally more popular than victims. In fact, victims are often blamed for their characteristics or behaviors, which supposedly trigger aggressive behaviors in others. Bullies' good social skills are explored, using tasks rooted in a "theory of mind" (Badenes, Estevan, & Bacete, 2000). According to this construct, bullies can identify the most vulnerable victims and effectively target them in the most opportune settings. As a result of successful victimization, bullies develop positive attitudes, an enhanced sense of self-efficacy, and the use of physical and relational assaults on others (Bosworth et al., 1999; Gottheil & Dubow, 2001; Stockdale et al., 2002).

Characteristics of Victims

Victims tend to be physically weaker (Lagerspetz, Bjorkqvist, Berts, & King, 1982; Olweus, 1993) and smaller than others (Elliott, 1996). They have lower energy levels and pain tolerance (Olweus, 1993) than nonvictim peers. Victims tend to have few friends, and are sometimes perceived as irritating or provocative (Espelage & Asidao, 2001; Owens et al., 2000). Time spent alone has been positively correlated with high victim scores on observational measures of 8- and 9-year-olds (Boulton, 1999). This study may not be generalized across age spans. Whitney and Smith (1993) found that being alone during recess one or more times a week positively correlated with being bullied for elementary/middle school children (8–11 years), but was not significant at the secondary school level (11–16 years). In fact, there was a negative correlation at the older levels, suggesting that social isolation may therefore be a greater risk factor for younger children. It appears clear that children's self-reported levels of loneliness increase with levels of victimization (Kochenderfer & Ladd, 1996). Conversely, friendships and peer acceptance are protective factors against victimization (Pellegrini et al., 1999).

In summary, there is conflicting research about the correlation between frequently being alone and being a victim (Lagerspetz et al., 1982, Pellegrini et al., 1999). However, because social isolation is not a healthy or desirable method of coping, we would suggest that the elimination of this behavior be included in antibullying programs. Schools need to develop policies and plans to identify and help isolated and lonely students. This is especially true with students who have issues of gender identity that may make them outcasts (Hyman & Snook, 1999a).

Disabilities and Victimization. A variety of disabilities make children more likely victims. For instance, in inclusion classes, children with moderate learning difficulties were more likely to be identified by their peers as victims of bullying than were non-learning-disabled children (Nabuzoka & Smith, 1993). Classified students are 2 to 3 times more at risk of being bullied, and also at a greater risk of being bullies (Whitney, Smith, & Thompson, 1994, as cited in Smith, & Brain, 2000). Physical or visible disability in itself does not play a significant role in the likelihood of being bullied. Cumulatively, receiving extra help in school, having fewer friends, being alone at recess, and being male are significant factors (Dawkins, 1996, cited in

Smith, 2000). Physical disability does increase the likelihood of experiencing three of these four factors.

Temperament and Victimization. Olweus' (1993, 2000a, 2000b) analysis of data from studies in Norway and Sweden reveals two distinct types of victims. Passive victims represent the largest proportion. They tend not to defend themselves, and they even communicate to their attackers that they are insecure and will not retaliate. They are "more anxious and insecure than students in general . . . cautious, sensitive and quiet. When attacked by other students they commonly react by crying and withdrawal. They often look upon themselves as failures and feel stupid, ashamed and unattractive. Victims are lonely and abandoned, do not have a good friend, and are not aggressive or teasing in their behaviors . . . they often have a negative attitude toward violence" (Olweus, 1993, p. 32).

Provocative victims display anxious and aggressive reaction patterns. These students are likely to be impulsive, hyperactive, and irritating to other students. They may be being highly emotional, hostile, and quick to lose control and act aggressively (Schwartz et al., 1997). Provocative victims represent only a small proportion of all victimized children and are the least popular among their peers. This category of victim is somewhat problematic from a theoretical and research perspective, in that the definition of bullying refers to unprovoked aggressive behaviors. We must also be aware that victims may not provoke attacks, yet may display reactive aggression under these situations. False victims are those who, Besag (1989) suggested, continually complain of being teased, left out, and rarely befriended, but are not truly being victimized. This category of "victim" requires further research.

Ethnicity, Race, and Victimization. Ethnicity does not appear to correlate with the frequency at which students report being bullied. In one UK study of Asian and White 9- to 15-year-old children no differences by ethnicity were found for the likelihood and frequency with which children reported bullying others, or being bullied. Of those children who were bullied, there was no ethnic difference in terms of where they were bullied or whether they received help. However approximately 50% of the bullying behavior consisted of racist name-calling (Moran, Smith, Thompson, & Whitney, 1993). Another British study (Eslea & Mukhtar, 2000) found that Hindu, Indian Muslim, and Pakistani children were "equally likely to report being bullied by white children, but in no case was this the most frequent kind [of bullying], the most frequent kind were other Asian children from a different ethnic group" (p. 213). The most frequent type of bullying was name-calling, which varied by ethnic group. Among Hindus it involved different gods and places of worship, among Muslims it was related to clothing, and for Pakistanis it was related to language and food.

Similarly, a recent American study of students in grades 6–10 revealed no ethnic differences (White, African American, Hispanic) in the percentages of students who reported bullying others. The percentage of African American students who reported never having been bullied was much higher than for the other two groups. Further, being subject to derogatory comments about race or religion was the least frequent form of bullying behavior (Nansel et al., 2001). Anecdotal evidence suggests that these studies may be somewhat flawed and affected by social desirability factors in answering questionnaires. For instance, among certain ethnic groups, admitting being a victim is tantamount to admitting being inadequate.

Aside from these and a few other studies, racism in bullying has largely been neglected. When it has been explored, the methods have generally been inadequate, with data collected from responses to only one item (i.e., being called names or belittled about race or color). The Eslea and Mukhtar study, which expanded the questions posed, cautions against generalizing findings from his data, adding that "the questions you ask will determine the answers you get" (Eslea & Mukhtar, 2000, p. 216) and that in essence more questions need to be asked.

Therefore, "the relationship among bullying . . . and racial harassment needs to be resolved" (Espelage & Swearer, 2003, p. 378). For instance, in a school that is predominantly African American, students are unlikely to be bullied because of their race. However, in a predominantly White school, minority children may be harassed because of their race and the inability or ineffectiveness of the school to address these issues.

Gender Orientation and Victimization. Gender orientation is a major predictor of victimization across many Western societies. Rivers (1996) found that 80% of British gay and lesbian schoolchildren reported being teased about their sexual orientation and over 50% reported that they had been assaulted or ridiculed by students or teachers. A recent survey in the United States indicates that 83% of gay and lesbian students reported being verbally harassed, 41% physically harassed, and 13% physically assaulted (Morrison & L'Heureux, 2001). One fourth of the students report hearing homophobic comments from faculty or staff. Frequent peer bullying and staff indifference is associated with high rates of suicide among gay/lesbian and transgender youths (Helsel, 2001; Morrison & L'Heureux, 2001). Similarly, self-reports from 1,000 American middle and high school students revealed that frequent male-on-male bullying involved homophobic verbal insults. The authors concluded that "fear of being labelled a homosexual was central to male adolescent life" (Skakeshaft et al., p. 24, 1997). This presents a particular challenge to schools, because homophobia may be deeply embedded in the community.

THE BULLY/VICTIM SYNDROME

The bully/victim syndrome refers to children who are both victims and bullies. This group appears to differ from either bullies or victims only, although it displays the same gender differences in bullying behaviors (Kumpalainan et al., 1998). Bully/victims present the greatest challenge in terms of interventions, because they seem not to recognize that the pain they felt as victims should be spared others. They apparently lack the empathy, cognitive insight, or moral development to understand this conundrum.

Andreou's (2000) study of Greek students found that bully/victims had the lowest scores on nearly all scales of the SPCC (Self-Perception Profile for Children). These scales address academic competence, social acceptance, physical appearance, conduct, global (overall) self-worth, and self-esteem. They also scored highest on Machiavellianism scales, but scored between the bullies and victims on the locus of control scales. Bully/victims have a "distinctly negative view of themselves and other people. They believe that they live in a world in which they can be either bullies or victims" (Andreou, 2000, p. 54). Their extreme negative views of self and others prevent the discomfort of any cognitive dissonance. Their low social acceptance and lack of peer group affiliation reduce protective factors they may have from bullying. Thus they are less pressured to follow group norms regarding bullying. They easily vacillate between the two behaviors. Being perceived as both bully and victim may also increase the degree to which others despise them.

Salmivalli and Nieminen (2002) found this group to score highest on measures of both reactive and proactive aggression. They also scored high on measures of depression. Research on the effects of being involved in bully/victim problems has shown that psychological disturbances were most likely among bully/victims, followed by bullies and victims at similar rates, and lastly uninvolved children (Kumpulainen et al., 1998). The probability of being referred for psychiatric services was greatest among the bully/victim group. (Kumpalainen, Rasanen, & Pura, 2001). Other research has shown that bully/victims score higher on neuroticism and psychoticism scales than either bullies or victims (Mynard & Joseph, 1997). This can be partly explained by the fact that the bully/victim group appears to be the most at-risk group for remaining involved in bullying over long periods (Kumpulainen et al., 1998). Bully/victims also use aggressive and self-destructive coping strategies to cope with general stressors in the school. This group is therefore particularly at risk of continued problems in other areas of life (Olafsen & Viemeroe, 2000). Bully/victims may also be victims who developed into bullies. There is some evidence to suggest this. Hanish and Guerra (2002) found that victimization among second-and fourth-graders was associated with later and current aggression, attention problems, and delinquency as well as depression and anxiety. This was particularly true for males.

SOCIAL AND EMOTIONAL EFFECTS OF BULLYING

Victims may be studied in terms of the immediate, and often observable, emotional and behavioral responses to bullying episodes or in terms of more serious, long lasting psychological effects. Such studies should include students' coping styles, gender, immediate behavioral responses, and such mediating factors as attributional styles and resilience. Therefore, a thorough understanding of the emotional effects of bullying is complex and requires a theoretical framework that is comprehensive. For instance, the emotional displays of bullies are aimed at dominating others. Bullies are reinforced for their behaviors, but victims may also be reinforced for their reactions to the bullying, and therefore may not display the overt emotionality that one might expect. Attention from peers may be reinforcing, even though the attention is negative. The victims' emotional responses may also reinforce the bully. This suggests that both victim and bully use faulty emotional regulation and social information processing.

A study by Salmivalli, Karhunen, and Lagerspetz (1996) indicates gender difference exist in the emotional responses of victims and bullies. Although both males and females displayed nonchalance, females also tended to display helplessness, whereas males tended to react aggressively. For girls, both counteraggression and helplessness were perceived as causing and maintaining the initial bullying. For males, counteraggression was perceived as causing as well as maintaining initial bullying. A lack of perceived helplessness in girls and both counteraggression and nonchalance in boys were seen to reduce bullying. Female victims felt more self-pity than male victims, and more secondary than elementary school children felt angry and vengeful. The latter emotion was also more prevalent among boys. Borg (1998) found that elementary school bullies were more likely to indicate remorse for their behavior than were older students. Also, girls were more likely than boys to express remorse.

Males are most likely to report that being bullied made them angry whereas girls became sad, reclusive (Slee, 1995), confused, anxious, insecure, and frightened (Owens et al., 2000). Obviously, these reactions are mediated by the type and intensity of the victimization. Girls are more likely to internalize symptoms than boys, who are more likely to fight or avoid the bullies.

Rigby and Bagshaw (2001) found that for both boys and girls the most distressing type of victimization was social exclusion in the form of losing friendships (44% of males, 55% of females). This was followed by being ganged up on (33% of males and 46% of females), then excluded (30% of males and 46% of females), and having rumors spread about them (15% of males and 41% of females). Only 17% of boys but 39% of girls reported that being threatened upset them a lot (Rigby & Bagshaw, 2001). Salmivalli, Kaukiainen, Kaistaniemi, and Lagerspetz (1999) also found similar gender differences in response to bullying.

Immediate Behavioral Responses

Of particular interest is the role that victim's behavioral responses may play in escalating, maintaining, or dissipating the bullying. In an observational bullying study of primary school children, Mahady Wilton, Craig, and Pepler (2000) found that targeted students responded with either passive problem solving or aggressive behaviors. Although possibly reducing the immediate bullying episode, passive acquiescent responses may place the victim at future risk, as the bully has been reinforced for asserting dominance. Aggressive responses tended to escalate bullying, and were "13 times less likely than problem-solving approaches to deescalate a bullying interaction" (Mahady Wilton et al., 2000, p. 241). The two categories found by Mahady Wilton et al. (2000) correspond to the passive and provocative victims as described by Olweus (1993), although it must be stressed that Olweus also emphasized the behaviors in the provocative victims, which trigger, as well as maintain, the initial bullying.

Immediate Affective Responses

Overt affective responses can also reinforce, reduce, or extinguish bullying. In the Mahady Wilton et al. (2000) study, affective responses were coded for both victims and bullies using the AFFEX system (Izard, Dougherty, & Hembree, 1989). Interest in the bullying interaction, joy, and anger were the three most frequently exhibited responses. Bullies displayed interest 35% of the time, joy 32% of the time, and anger 20% of time. Victims displayed interest 30% of the time, joy 22% of the time, and anger 15% of the time. Victims also showed surprise, sadness, contempt, and distress in 4% to 8% of observed displays, with distress being the least frequent (Mahady Wilton et al., 2000). The emotional displays of the bullies are not surprising, given the goal of their behavior. What is unexpected is that victims express many of the same emotions in similar proportions. Further, these maladaptive affective displays, in combination with passive problem-solving behaviors, provide significant reinforcement to the bullies and can signal to onlookers that help is not needed. The victims' emotional and affective responses thereby trap them within their role. The authors proposed that the victims' role or behaviors may be reinforced through gaining social interaction with peers that they would otherwise find difficult to obtain. This would explain the high levels of interest and joy. Conversely, the victims' apparent expressions of joy may be passive acquiescent gestures

So far we have discussed "normal" immediate or short-term emotional reactions of victims and victimizers. However, it is important to consider emotional reactions that may develop into more serious emotional feelings and behaviors that have the potential for psychopathology. In the next section, we discuss this issue.

Serious Emotional and Psychological Effects

Little attention has been paid to the long-term emotional effects of bullying, or to the psychopathology of bullying. Victims of bullying are at risk of internalized disorders, including depression, anxiety, and eventual suicide (Craig, 1998; Hawker & Boulton, 2000; Neary & Joseph, 1994; Swearer, Song, Cary, Eagle, & Mickelson, 2001). In fact, it was the occurrence of adolescent suicides in Norway, United Kingdom, and Japan that brought into public focus the problems of school bullying (Morita et al., 2000; Olweus, 1993; Smith, & Sharp, 1994). A small percentage of bullying victims are also at risk for aggressive behaviors. In an American Safe Schools survey (National Center for Education Statistics, 2003) of 12- to 18-year-olds, 3.9% who reported being bullied at school also reported bringing a weapon to school compared to 1.4% of their nonbullied peers. Many of the attackers in recent American school shootings "felt bullied, persecuted or injured by others prior to an attack" (U.S. Secret Service and U.S. Department of Education, 2002a, p. 35).

Evidence indicates that bullies are at greater risk of delinquency and criminal behaviors (Olweus, 1993). In a follow-up study to his large-scale Swedish survey, Olweus reported that 60% of boys identified as bullies between the grades 6 and 9 had been convicted of at least one criminal offence by age 24. Further, approximately 40% had received three or more criminal convictions by this age (Olweus, 1993). Similarly, a follow-up study of aggressive 8-year-olds in semirural New York State schools found that 22 years later, they had a 1 in 4 chance of having a criminal record, compared to a 1 in 20 chance for nonidentified children. Bullying correlates with violent behaviors (Baldry & Farrington, 2000) outside the school. Furthermore, Stein (1999) suggested that school bullies graduate into workplace sexual harassers.

Student Alienation and Stress Responses

Traumatic school experiences, including victimization by school staff and peers, can lead to hopelessness, hostility, reexperiencing of events (e.g., flashbacks, nightmares), depression, and hypervigilance (Hyman, Berna, Snook, DuCette, & Kohr, 2002). If victims experience severe stress responses due to chronic victimization, they are more likely to seek revenge (externalize) or commit suicide (internalize). For many years Hyman (1987, 1990, 1995) and colleagues (Hyman et al., 2003; Hyman & Perone, 1998a, 1998b; Hyman & Wise, 1979) have studied the effects of student victimization by teachers. Their instruments and research methodology have recently been modified to include peer victimization, and the development of a construct called Student Alienation Syndrome (SAS) (Hyman, Cohen, & Mahon, 2003; Hyman, Mahon, Cohen, Snook, Britton, & Lurkis, 2004).

Students with SAS fit the model of those who commit homicides and other serious offenses against peers, school personnel, and property (Vossekuil et al., 2000). This construct may be measured by the Student Alienation and Trauma Survey—Revised (SATS-R), a version of the My Worst Experience Scales (Hyman, Berna, Kohr, & DuCette, 1998; Hyman, Cohen, & Mahon, 2003). The SATS-R is discussed in more detail later.

In a recent cross-national study of student victimization, using the SATS in Israel, Greece, and the United States, between 6% and 9% of the students surveyed remembered experiencing clinically significant PTSD symptomology after their worst school experiences (Hyman, Cohen, Glass et al., 2003). Many would be considered peer or teacher bullying. These results support extensive evidence that children and adolescents can develop PTSD from extremely negative school experiences (Hyman & Snook, 1999b). Moreover, the data suggest that the development of PTSD from negative school experiences is not specific to schools within the United States, but rather spans nations throughout the Western hemisphere (Halkias et al., 2003; Hyman, Cohen, Glass et al., 2003).

Victims with PTSD symptoms typically develop vengeful, aggressive, and even homicidal ideation against their attackers. As many as 50% of children in clinical populations diagnosed with PTSD also meet the DSM-IV-TR criteria for conduct disorder (Curcio, 1994; Curcio-Chilton, 1995; Hyman, Zelikoff, & Clarke, 1988; Rea, 1996). This highlights the significant overlap between children with PTSD and histories of abuse, which are common to those diagnosed as conduct disordered. The link between PTSD and conduct disorder is particularly important when examining the relationship between victimization, alienation, aggression, and bullying.

THE "AUDIENCE" IN BULLYING SCENARIOS

Much bullying takes place in front of an audience, which may encourage the victimizer. Research on the audience yields contradictory data between what those in the audience say they do and what independent observers report. For instance, Whitney and Smith (1993) asked peers what they did as members of the bullying audience. Fifty-four percent of elementary school students and 34% of secondary school students reported that when they saw someone being bullied they intervened, which is consistent with victims' perceptions of peer intervention.

However, 27% of elementary and 47% of secondary school children reported that they did not intervene but probably should have. The remaining students reported not intervening, as they did not consider it their problem. Clearly, large numbers of older inactive students believed they should have intervened. However, observational studies have shown a clear discrepancy between what students report they do and what they actually do. The difference in methodology makes comparison of data difficult. However, direct observation is possibly more reliable as results are less influenced by a socially desirable response often found in self-reports.

Several observational studies of children's behaviors during bullying episodes in the schoolyard and classroom have provided useful information on peer interventions. Peers were present in 85% to 88% of bullying episodes, yet intervened in only 10% of classroom incidents (Atlas & Pepler, 1998) and 11% to 19% of playground incidents (Craig & Pepler, 1997, 2000; Hawkins, Pepler, & Craig, 2001). In Craig and Pepler's study, boys were more likely than girls to intervene, which may reflect that boys' greater involvement in bullying provides them with increased opportunities to intervene. Boys also tend to play in larger groups than girls, who are more frequently in smaller groups or dyads. A supporting observational study found that 61% of peers present in bullying incidents were boys and 39% were girls (Hawkins et al., 2001). As in previous studies, the percentage of peer intervention was much lower than indicated by students' reports of their own behavior and attitudes toward bullying. The Hawkins study was conducted at two elementary schools that had antibullying programs, yet even here, peers intervened in only 19% of the bullying episodes. The interventions ranged from 1 second to just under 2 minutes with a mean duration of 17 seconds for boys and 11 seconds for girls (Hawkins et al., 2001). This lack of peer intervention, and thus lack of any social consequences, reinforces the bully's behavior and the victim's experience of social alienation.

Given that school bullying is fundamentally a group process, the behaviors of peers are crucial for its survival. However, children's school behavior is greatly shaped by their school's culture, climate, and more specifically, the attitudes and behaviors of teachers. How teachers respond to bullying is now briefly examined. This topic is discussed in more detail later in the chapter. In the observational studies mentioned, teachers were reported to intervene at somewhat low levels. On the playground, teachers were observed to intervene in only 4% of all bullying episodes. However, this increased to 25% when the bullying episode was in close proximity. So, although peers intervened more than staff, teachers were twice as likely to intervene when they were aware of the bullying. However, teachers seemed unaware of 80% of all bullying episodes. (Craig & Pepler, 2000). In the classroom, teachers intervened in 18% of all the bullying episodes and 37% of those in which they were in close proximity (Atlas & Pepler, 1998).

An examination of peer interventions reveals that males and females intervene in the same way that they bully (Hawkins et al., 2001). Females mainly used verbal methods (47%), followed by physical aggression (19%). Of males, 22% used physical aggression, 19% verbal assertion, 19% combined physical with verbal assertions, 13.5% verbal assertion with physical aggression, and 5% combined verbal and physical aggression. In all episodes of bullying, 47% of the interventions were aggressive, and 53% were nonaggressive, with no significant difference between the proportions of each type of intervention (Hawkins et al., 2001) Hawkins' study showed that the majority of interventions (66%) were directed toward the bully, with 15% toward the victim and 19% toward the bully–victim dyad. Interventions targeting the bully were mostly aggressive (60.5%) and those toward the victim were nonaggressive (78%). However, 22% of the interventions directed toward the victim were aggressive. This may reflect the percentage of children who report despising the victim in some way (Rigby & Slee, 1991, cited in Rigby, 2002). Or it may relate to the small percentage of victims that Olweus identified as provocative (Olweus, 1993). The fact that peers mostly target bullies in their interventions is particularly interesting, given that teachers have reported being more comfortable supporting victims, and their families and peers, rather than working directly with bullies and their families. (Nicolaides, Toda, & Smith, 2002). These studies also suggest that bullies are much less likely to be deterred by victim's aggressive retaliations than they are by aggressive peer interventions. Bullies may interpret that aggressive peer intervention indicates that the victim is affiliated with, or supported by, a more dominant group than the bully had expected. In the absence of peer support for the victim, however, a victim's aggressive response may reinforce the bully.

Conventional wisdom has long suggested that the best approach to a bully is the use of counterforce. Anecdotal evidence (Hyman & Eisenstein, 2000) indicates that many parents encourage their children to find a friend or sibling to beat up a bully or to fight back hard enough that the bully is hurt each time he engages in aggressive behavior. There is some truth that if the victimizer becomes fearful of the victim or the victim's protector, the episodes will end. To some extent research supports that counter aggression is an effective intervention, or that it is at least as effective as other nonaggressive approaches (Hawkins et al., 2001). Of course, because only a small percentage of victims are able to effectively counteraggress, and relatively few peers do in fact intervene, dependence on counteraggression and peer support is not very reliable. Effective interventions are likely to be intense and of relatively short duration, because the longer intervention lasts, the less likely it is to succeed.

Unfortunately, some members of the audience may join in bullying. Whitney and Smith, (1993) found that 16% of elementary and 25% of secondary school children reported that they could join in bullying others. In another study, 9.1% of middle school males and 6.2% of females indicated that when a bullying incident occurs they assist the bully (Jeffrey et al., 2001).

Students are more likely to intervene when the victim is the same gender. However, in comparing cross-gender interventions, girls are more likely to intervene to support male victims than boys are to support female victims (Hawkins et al., 2001). As a result, children's self-reports of peer intervention have shown that they perceive girls to play the defender role more than boys (Salmivalli, Layerspetz et al., 1996). Perhaps girl's interventions become more salient to their peers as they are not expected, or because there are a smaller number of female observers than boys. In 85% of bullying episodes there are peers present, yet only 10% ask for help. This may be because victims are socially isolated and feel they have no one to assist them, or they may perceive that asking for help will worsen the situation. It also may be that their faulty emotional regulation, with affective displays of interest and joy, fails to indicate their need for help. That bystanders fail to support victims concerns Hazler (1996). He proposes that this results from lack of skill, fear of becoming the next target, or of escalating the problem. This suggests a need to explore the emotional reactions of audience participants as they witness an unfolding bullying scenario.

Audiences' Emotional Reactions to Bullying Episodes

Although in one study (Whitney & Smith, 1993) large numbers of observers to bullying incidents felt that they ought to have intervened, in-depth interviews from an American study with middle school students do not indicate such feelings of guilt. In a study of fifth-through eighth-graders who had observed bullying, males reported experiencing mostly fear (29%), followed by excitement (23%), indifference (19%), helplessness (19%), and relief (10%). Females reported experiencing mostly fear (34%), followed by helplessness (31%), indifference (22%), relief (8%), and excitement (6%). Overall, eighth-graders felt more indifferent and fifth-graders more helpless and fearful (Jeffrey et al., 2001). These emotional reactions of observers or bystanders are likely to influence both the bully's behavior and that of the victim and the audience.

Perhaps many of these emotions are not relevant, because the Hawkins et al., (2001) observational study indicated that of the small number of peers who did intervene, the majority of those interventions, 57%, were effective, 26% were ineffective, and the effects of 17% could not be determined. There was no difference between the type of intervention (aggressive and nonaggressive) and its effectiveness. Nor were there any differences between the effectiveness of an intervention and the gender of the person intervening. This is an important consideration when devising bullying intervention programs with a prosocial approach.

The previous discussion makes it acutely apparent that school bullying is an important stressor of children. In student self-reports, bullying has been ranked as the fourth most stressful experience below loss of a pet, loss of a parent, or moving (Branwhite, 1994). It appears to be the only type of trauma publicly experienced by victims. It causes fear and helplessness, but does not immediately evoke substantial help and support, which all other known victims of traumatic incidents receive. Further, bullying is an ongoing, often daily or weekly stressor that is largely inescapable. Not only are victims unaided, but they must also repeatedly reenter a hostile environment. When others do intervene, they reduce bullying only a little more than half the time. This intensifies the traumatic experience; victims not only are attacked by a member of their peer group, but are observed being attacked and not helped.

This situation parallels the victimization of children by family members. In fact, most research into childhood victimization and trauma has focused on familial physical and sexual abuse. Victimization in this context has been viewed as a nonnormative traumatic experience. The link between childhood sexual or physical abuse and PTSD has been extensively researched and established. As children mature, they gradually shift their attachments from family to peer group. Peer relationships become increasingly important to children's emotional and psychological well-being. Conversely, disruptions to, or traumatic experiences within, the peer group can be devastating.

REPORTING BULLYING

Although school bullying is a frequent and mostly public behavior, it is generally underreported to school staff. Across studies, figures indicate that overall, less than 50% of children who are frequently bullied report this to school staff. The rate of reporting also decreases with age. Whitney and Smith (1993) found that 48% of British elementary school children who reported being the victim of bullying at least once a week told their teacher, compared to 65% who told someone at home. At the secondary level, 36% of frequently bullied students told a teacher, compared to 44% who told someone at home. Similar trends exist across countries, although rates may differ. For example, in Australia approximately 30% of children report incidents of bullying to teachers (Rigby, 2000); in Japan, approximately 22% report bullying to teachers and 67% to someone at home (Morita et al., 2000). In Italy approximately 50% of children at all ages reported bullying incidents to teachers. (Fonzi et al., 2001).

Studies suggest that students who do not report victimization often fear retaliation from bullies (Morita et al., 2000). Also, many students perceive teachers as ineffective interveners or feel that few adults or peers can help. Research in Australia shows that approximately 50% of boys and girls aged 8–17 report that telling someone about their victimization improves the situation. However, there is a notable decline with age, with 65% of 8- and 9-year-olds reporting it improves the situation and only 40% of 16- and 17-year-olds feeling things improved. Telling a friend is the most popular but least effective approach, whereas telling a school counselor is the least popular, but most effective course of action (Rigby, 2002). Constant across all ages is that 10% of victims report that telling someone made matters worse (Rigby, 2002). In the Whitney and Smith study (1993), 54% of elementary and 48% of secondary school children said teachers intervened sometimes or always. Fifty percent of elementary and 38% of secondary school children reported that other students intervened. Clearly, the majority of victims are not telling teachers, and the majority of victims at the elementary level (where there are the highest rates of bullying) do not perceive teachers as helpful. In addition, students do not perceive peers as intervening in the majority of incidents. Despite the somewhat low levels of active peer interventions, students do seem to report their victimization to peers. Among 8- to 18-year-olds, 75% of female victims reported telling a peer, and 60% of males reported telling a peer (Rigby, 2001).

Staff Reactions

There may be a good reason why reporting bullying to teachers is not perceived as helpful. Almost one third of teachers in the United States view bullying as normative behavior that victims must learn to resolve (National Center for Educational Statistics, 2003). Also, students report that information is not kept confidential by teachers (Espelage & Asidao, 2001). This distrust of the reporting process has an empirical basis. Observational data suggest that teachers intervene in only 25% of bullying episodes within their proximity (National Association of School Psychologists, 2002). Teachers seem unaware of the majority of bullying incidents, and when aware, they do not always intervene (Atlas & Pepler, 1998; Craig & Pepler, 2000; Shakeshaft et al., 1997). This is particularly important as it highlights the double stressor experienced by victims who are subject to repeated bullying and see no escape.

Having reviewed much of the research on bullying, it is clear that it is a cross-national problem, occurring in all schools, and across ages and gender. It has a negative impact both on those directly involved and on the total school population. Although immediate interventions at the time of these episodes are often minimal, there is a significant move among educators and researchers to address this problem at both a proactive and a reactive level. These interventions are reviewed next.

INTERVENTION STRATEGIES

A comprehensive search for empirically validated intervention programs included the use of EBSCO Academic Search Premiere, LexisNexis, Science Direct, bullypolice.org, fight-crime.org, yahoo.com, and google.com. Keywords entered for the search included *bullying*, *prevention*, *intervention*, *school*, *effective*, *violence*, *schoolwide programs*, and *empirical*. In addition, the authors have been collecting data from other sources such as personal contacts and reviews of journals and solicitations of presenters at national meetings. We were particularly interested in conducting our own meta-analysis of programs, but because of the limited number of acceptable studies, especially those that reported effect sizes, we settled on several previous integrative studies of the extant literature and our own content analysis. Before presenting this analysis it is appropriate to review the program developed by Dan Olweus (2000a, 2000b, 2002, 2003), from which so many other programs have evolved.

The Olweus Bullying Prevention Program

The Olweus program was initially implemented in Norway as a result of three adolescent suicides believed to be related to bullying. The government commissioned Dr. Olweus to conduct a large-scale study to evaluate the nature, cause, and possible interventions for bullying. His program now reaches over 200 Norwegian schools (Olweus, 2003). Initial outcome studies indicated that properly implemented programs could reduce bullying by 50% (Olweus, 2003). This program deals with elementary, middle, and junior high schools (Ericson, 2001). Partial replications have been used in the United States, Canada, the United Kingdom, and Germany, with results ranging from a 30% to 70% reduction in student reports of bullying (Ericson, 2001). The first implementation of this program witnessed an unanticipated reduction in substance abuse (Olweus, 2003).

The Olweus program, a whole-school approach, assumes that because bullying does not occur in a vacuum and the whole school community should be involved. The program aims for a school environment with warmth, positive interest, and adult involvement. Adults act as authorities and positive role models. The program sets limits and consequences for unacceptable behavior at school and home. It uses consistent, nonhostile, nonphysical sanctions for unacceptable behavior. In contrast to problem-solving approaches, Olweus believes that blame should be placed with the perpetrator.

The Olweus program operates on three tiers: school, classroom, and student. A school coordinator forms a committee of parents, teachers, and staff. Intensive staff training coordinates staff supervision for monitoring break periods. Schoolwide rules against bullying are developed and publicized at the start of the project, and the Olweus Bully/Victim Questionnaire (2000b) is administered to all students.

To raise awareness and address current bullying problems, both classroom and parent meetings take place. Bully and victim meet separately before both sides are brought together. Meetings with parents are also included. Evaluation research conducted by Olweus has shown that the longer the program is implemented, the better the results (Olweus, 2003).

In the United States, the Olweus program has been cited as a "Model Program" of the Substance Abuse and Mental Health Services Administration, part of the U.S. Department of Health and Human Services (Elliot, 2002). The first American adaptation of the Bullying Prevention Program (BPP) took place through Clemson University in South Carolina (Olweus, 2003). This large-scale implementation and evaluation was in rural and nonmetropolitan school districts. After the first year, students reported decreased bullying, in comparison with students in control group schools (Olweus, 2003; Smith, Ananiadou, & Cowie, 2003). Victimization rates did not decrease. A confound of these results may be attributed to the fact that bullies were made aware of the socially undesirable aspects of bullying and were less likely to report their bullying.

In 2001, the program was implemented as part of the Healthy Schools project in an inner-city environment in a southeastern city (Cunningham & Henggeler, 2001). The South Carolina program was adapted to an urban environment. These adaptations included initiatives to increase community involvement, targeted program materials for school staff and parents, teacher incentives to promote program fidelity (such as restaurant certificates), and the capacity to address serious personal and family issues. Unfortunately, material reviewed showed no evaluative data.

Previous Reviews of the Effectiveness of Antibullying Programs

Smith et al. (2003) competently examined the effectiveness of interventions to reduce bullying. They analyzed programs based on whole-school policy, classroom climate, peer support systems, school tribunals, playground improvement, curriculum modifications, targeting specific pupils, and community conferencing as transformative justice. Smith et al. (2003) also analyzed large-scale intervention projects in Norway, England, Canada, Germany, the United States, Belgium, Spain, and Switzerland. As noted previously, the authors found little rigorous empirical support for most large-scale antibullying programs. The authors found mixed results, with some programs actually generating negative outcomes. The review suggests that variables such as type of intervention, length of program, support by researchers, age of students, students' gender, and program comprehensiveness can confound results. In general, we agree that the mere recognition of bullying as a problem and any systematic, long-term attempt to deal with the problem may promote some degree of success.

Australian researcher Ken Rigby (2002) investigated bullying prevention programs from a cross-national perspective. Rigby (2002) examined nine programs that met his minimal criteria for methodological rigor. Because few studies used control groups, a standard meta-analysis was not possible. Most studies would be considered evaluation research, where-pre and postmeasures were used with individual programs. Some apparently used time-lagged designs, so that temporal factors established control groups (Rigby, 2002). Olweus' research in Bergen, Norway, demonstrated significant improvement for his rules and consequences (RC) approach. However, studies of the RC approach were not convincing enough to suggest strong support for this method.

Although Rigby found that the five programs using problem-solving approaches produced positive results, the pre- and postchanges were not robust. Rigby concluded that consistent implementation of interventions significantly decreases bullying, and recommended that programs be implemented at lower grade levels. In addition, Rigby's intervention analysis found that most programs teach victims how to protect themselves, but they minimally affect the bully's behavior.

Blueprints for Violence Prevention

We found no comprehensive analysis targeting the effectiveness of antibullying programs in the United States. Most analyses of antibullying programs were embedded in antiviolence literature. One of the best attempts to evaluate these antiviolence programs in the United States was conducted at the Center for the Study and Prevention of Violence (CSPV) at University of Colorado at Boulder. The CSPV staff developed the Blueprints for Violence Prevention series (Elliot, 2002) in 1996. To be selected by the Blueprints panel, programs had to meet specific criteria. Inclusion required strong research design, low rate of participant attrition, adequate measurement, effective administration of the program, and positive outcome measures. Programs also needed evidence of significant deterrence effects. These included reduction of the onset, prevalence, or individual rates of violent behavior, and deterrence of delinquency (under which is included childhood aggression and conduct disorder) and drug use. Arrest records provided acceptable outcome measures. Programs that evidenced a deterrent effect on violent behavior were preferred, as well as programs that demonstrated multisite replication.

Inclusion required that programs demonstrate sustained effects of at least a year beyond treatment or participation in the designed intervention. Although stating this as a criterion, the Blueprints guidelines also state that the effects of most prevention programs are diminished when students re-enter their original environment where anti-violence values are not reinforced (Elliott, 2002).

The Blueprints panel reviewed 600 programs. Out of these, only 11 were selected as "Model Programs," with another 21 selected as "Promising Programs." The Olweus Bullying Prevention program was selected as 1 of the 11 model programs in violence prevention. It was the only program specifically designed to reduce or eliminate bullying. Most antibullying programs in America are based on this model. In the United States they fall under the rubric of Bullying Prevention Programs (BPPs) (Elliot, 2002; Olweus, 2003). Our review to identify American BPPs used the works of researchers cited earlier and our own independent review as described in the beginning of this section.

A Content Analysis of Selected American Bullying Prevention Programs

During 2003 and 2004, we conducted a content analysis of the most commonly used BPPs ($n = 15$). We began the content analysis by identifying the interventions listed by each program. We then sought common elements across programs, and identified eight intervention strategies most consistent with positive findings in the methodologically limited research we reviewed. Table 32.1 presents the common elements of a content analysis of 15 antibullying programs. We offer only the nine programs that offered the strongest empirical evidence. These programs met criteria for spelling out the details of implementation, and include at least a minimal level of evaluation.

Whole-school approach programs generally include, but are not limited to, students, parents, teachers, administrators, counselors, bus drivers, and lunch aides. All members of the school community invest in identifying and reducing bullying. A typical Olweus BPP conference day provides participants with initial training. Participants learn to recognize and respond to bullying situations. Topics include bullying research, bullying behaviors, response strategies, available resources, problems unique to the particular school, specifics of the proposed program, and how to gain the investment of the whole school and community.

BPPs include coordinating groups that typically include an administrator; a teacher from each grade level; a guidance counselor, psychologist, or school nurse; and parent and student representatives to manage and evaluate the program. An example of a BPP is the James H. Bean School Bullying Prevention Program (stopbullyingnow.com) located in Sydney, Maine. During extensive training sessions, staff are assigned clear responsibilities, and are trained to work with parents. Steps to Respect (cfchildren.org), a recently developed program by the Committee for Children, also includes this crucial whole-school approach. This process begins with a three-sectioned, fully scripted training component for school staff. The initial 3-hour session teaches examines dynamics of bullying, background research on the topic, and how to listen and respond effectively when a child reports an incident. Section two instructs staff who will be coaching both bully and victim. A four-step coaching model and techniques for talking one-on-one with students are used during this time. The third and final section of adult training is a 1-hour curriculum orientation session for teachers who will be presenting lessons to their students.

Encouraging student involvement is crucial to the success of any program. Students accept the need to report bullying behavior, and to learn about positive roles for bystanders. Student involvement is also a crucial component of problem-solving approaches. For instance, the No Blame Approach (Maines & Robinson, 1998) and the Pikas Method of Shared Concern (Rigby, 1996) allow students to become problem solvers in the antibullying process. In both programs, the group is encouraged to suggest solutions, express how they can help, and explain what they will do to rectify a situation. The group is responsible for implementing suggestions.

Antibullying policies are common to many programs, but they vary in how well they are publicized and enforced. Well-developed policies precisely define bullying, schoolwide and individual classroom codes of conduct, and clear consequences for bullying behavior. In this way the whole school community understands the nature and consequences of bullying. These policies are developed at different levels of participation. For instance, Bullybusters (Beale & Scott, 2001) involves students in the process of creating policy and encourages them to take an antibullying pledge. The James H. Bean School developed a "Behavior Grid," where frequency and consequences are recorded. For example, the first time a student teases a peer, a warning is issued, and the student must call home. A first-time offense for a more severe instance of bullying, such as harassment, warrants three inside recesses along with the call home. Olweus' BPP (Olweus, 1993/2002) firmly limits unacceptable behavior. These programs

TABLE 32.1
Common Elements of Antibullying Programs

Program	*Whole-School Approach*	*Student Involvement*	*Antibullying Policy*	*Involves Curriculum*	*Increased Supervision*	*Peer Impowerment*	*Bullying Assessment*	*Social Skills Traning*
Prevention Programs (Rules and Consequences Approach)								
Olweus BPP	X	X	X	X	X		X	X
Bean School	X	X	X	X		X	X	X
Paws for Peace	X	X	X	X	X	X	X	X
Bullybusters	X		X	X	X	X	X	
Steps to Respect	X	X		X			X	X
Peer Empowerment (Salmivalli)			X	X			X	X
Intervention Programs (Problem-Solving Approaches)								
No-Blame Approach		X						X
Circle of Friends		X						X
Pikas MSC		X						X

stress the consistent use of nonphysical sanctions for rule violations (having children call home or missing recess are forms of punishment).

Curricula promoting an accepting classroom climate in which students learn empathy, anger management, and conflict resolution skills appear to be included in most successful BBPS, and are used in six of the programs listed on Table 32.1. In Steps to Respect there are three levels of skill and literature lessons targeted for grades 3–5 or 4–6. Resources that come with the Steps to Respect program include games and activities, role-play scenarios, colorful classroom posters to reinforce skills, parent materials, videos, and literature units based on popular children's books. At each level, initial lessons focus on teaching students friendship skills, while later on, lessons focus on learning assertive behavior strategies, safely refusing bullying, reporting bullying, and understanding the role of bystanders in bullying situations. This mirrors Olweus' teaching of kindness, communication, cooperation, and friendship.

The Bean School curriculum emphasizes consideration for others, expressing feelings without hurting others, respectful problem solving, and development of bystander skills to stop bullying. Bullybusters (Beale & Scott, 2001) also incorporates this element with a series of structured classroom discussions that identify and treat bully behaviors. Counselors prepare information packets for teachers to read and share with the students. Most important are classroom discussions that follow the psychoeducational drama, when students react to characters and situations, clarify and express their opinions, and evaluate alternative ways to deal with bullying.

Increasing supervision of students in the school is a crucial hallmark of the Olweus type of BBP. Research suggests that a major way to curb bullying is to increase student supervision outside the classroom (Bentley & Li, 1995; Borg, 1999; Whitney & Smith, 1993). This includes the cafeteria, hallways, bathrooms, and the playground, where most of the bullying occurs. However, given limited resources at a time of increasing numbers of students and decreasing budgets, this is not always easy to accomplish and therefore may require increases in staff responsibilities. Bullybusters (Beale & Scott, 2001) and the Paws for Peace program, based on the Olweus BPP, in York, Pennsylvania (M. Stought, personal communication, March 14, 2003), offers creative examples. Through student brainstorming (student involvement), supervision was increased through the installation of video cameras on all school buses, further increasing supervision in a high-risk bullying setting. Students' planning and implementing of this approach gave them a sense of ownership unrealizable if dictated by the school administration.

Peer empowerment refers to encouraging onlookers to intervene during bullying. Finnish researcher Christina Salmivalli and colleagues (Salmivalli, Lagerspetz et al., 1996) assumes that many children may be inclined to intervene and trains them in skills such as mediation. Although the research on effectiveness peer mediation is inconclusive (Caruthers, Sweeney, Kmitta, & Harris, 1996; Johnson & Johnson, 1996), enough positive studies warrant its inclusion in BBP (Bell, Coleman, Anderson, & Whelan, 2000). Contrary to this approach, Olweus (1993/2002) believes that mediation removes responsibility from the bully and may retraumatize the victim.

Rigby (1996) avoids some issues associated with peer mediation. He cites the benefits of appointing peer buddies to help new students' successful transition to school, as well as having students act as peer tutors. Another unique approach to peer empowerment emerged from the Paws for Peace (M. Stought, personal communication, March 14, 2003) program, which formed a victim support group. The drama group tours elementary schools with presentations about respect and bullying prevention. The goal is to encourage former victims, who compose the group, to feel empowered as activists in bullying prevention—quite different from being a victim in a support group. This program also sponsors an antibullying songwriting contest and concert, in which the winners record their songs in a studio.

Rigby (1996) strongly perceives peers as more credible helpers than adults, especially with adolescents. Although underscoring that "peer counselors" benefit from their involvement, he cautions that they should be selected for friendliness, sensitivity, caring, and that they receive training in human relations and role performance. Typically, older students are best for these specific roles. He suggests the use of both peer tutors and peer mediators. They should be emotionally supportive, understanding, empathetic problem solvers, who are interested and able to act as counselors. Their training should include the dynamics of bullying. This role is like academic peer tutoring, which is well established in many American schools (Garcia-Vazquez & Ehly, 1995), where both parties benefit from the experience. Rigby also suggests that programs should train peer orientation guides, especially to help new students transition to the grade level or the school. Guides can help ease transitions and help students at their most vulnerable.

Assessment of bullying climate through student and teacher surveys provides guidelines for program implementation. Olweus has created an anonymous 40-question bullying assessment survey (Revised Olweus Bully/Victim Questionnaire), which measures a variety of bully/victim problems including various forms of bullying (physical, verbal, relational, racial, sexual), probully and provictim attitudes, and how often teachers, students, and parents respond to bullying (Olweus, 2003). There are forms for children in grades 3 through 5 and 6 through 10 or higher. The James H. Bean School used a much less extensive assessment survey that asked only eight questions about the bullying atmosphere of the school, and three more questions on each student's reaction to a bullying situation. Bullybusters, a whole-school approach that incorporates a psychoeducational drama group to relay their message on bullying, used counselors to survey teachers and students about their perceptions regarding bullying at the school to serve as a benchmark for evaluation and effectiveness of the program (Beale & Scott, 2001). As mentioned previously, Hyman and colleagues (Hyman, Cohen, Glass et al., 2003; Hyman, Mahon, Cohen, Tabori et al., 2004; Hyman, Cohen, & Mahon, 2003) have developed the Student Alienation and Trauma Scale—Revised (SATS-R), which may be used to determine the nature and frequency of victimization by both school staff and peers, and the emotional effects of students' worst school experience. This scale is designed to study a wide range of traumatic events that students experience. Many but not all of these events, fall into the bailiwick of school bullying. The results of the scale may be used for individual diagnosis of victims and identification of the nature and frequency of various bullying behaviors for the entire student population. Intervention plans must be tailored to the results of the survey.

Social skills training, which replaces impulsive and aggressive behaviors with prosocial behavior, is a major goal of many programs. Students are taught friendship, conversational, and conflict management skills. This element was found to be interspersed throughout the curriculum component, but it was also seen to be implemented through workshops, school assemblies, and various role-playing situations, such as those used for in the Bullybusters drama (Beale & Scott, 2001). This technique uses dramatic readings, choral recitations, and psychoeducational drama to model social skills. This is reinforced by classroom groups led by teachers and counselors. In Olweus' BPP, bullies and victims reverse roles, omitting actual physical aggression.

SUMMARY

This chapter makes a clear case that school bullying deserves a prominent place in school discipline programs. Bullying is part of the school discipline–school violence matrix. There have been sporadic efforts to develop effective interventions, even though the research base for these approaches is far from convincing. Programs must be based on empirically established facts and not ad hoc, piecemeal notions, which unfortunately typify some of the current approaches. For example, many of the popular zero tolerance interventions such as increased security guards, hallway monitors, and the introduction of metal detectors have no apparent effect on the incidence of school bullying (National Center for Educational Statistics, 2003). Interventions need to be more comprehensive and should be tailored toward the specific needs of the school. Determining which type of program is the best fit for a particular school can be accomplished through an empirically validated bullying assessment tool (e.g., Olweus Bully/Victim Questionnaire). Allied with this, teacher-training programs need to incorporate courses on bullying to help teachers prevent bullying and develop frontline antibullying strategies. This need is articulated not only by theorists, but by teachers in training (Nicolaides et al., 2002). In addition, there is a need for educators and mental health professionals to be alerted to the emotional and behavioral impact of being bullied, the types of symptomology manifested by the victims, and the most efficacious treatment interventions.

ACKNOWLEDGMENT

The authors wish to thank Dorothy Espelage, University of Illinois, Urbana-Champaign, and Russell Skiba, Indiana University, for their very helpful reviews of an earlier version of this chapter.

REFERENCES

Alsaker, F., & Brunner, A. (2000). Switzerland. In P. K. Smith et al. (Eds.), *The nature of school bullying; A cross-national perspective* (pp. 250–264). London: Routledge.

Ananiadou, K., & Smith, P. K. (2002). Legal requirements and nationally circulated materials against school bullying. *Criminal Justice, 2*, 471–491.

Andreou, E. (2000). Bully/victim problems and their associations with psychological constructs in 8–12 year old Greek schoolchildren. *Aggressive Behavior, 26*, 49– 56.

Atlas, R. S., & Pepler, D. J. (1998). Observations of bullying in the classroom. *Journal of Educational Research, 92*(2), 86–99.

Badenes, L. V., Estevan, R. A., & Bacete, F. J. G. (2000). Theory of mind and peer rejection. *Social Development, 9*(3), 271–283.

Bai, M. (1999, May 3). Anatomy of a massacre. *Newsweek*, 24–31.

Balding, J., Regis, D., Wise, A., Bish, D., & Muirden, J. (1996). *Bully off: Young people that fear going to school Devon, England:* University of Exeter, Schools Health Education Unit.

Baldry, A. C., & Farrington, D. P. (2000). Bullies and delinquents: Personal characteristics and parental styles. *Journal of Community and Applied Social Psychology, 10*(1), 17–31.

Batsche, G. M., & Knoff, H. M. (1994). Bullies and their victims: Understanding a pervasive problem in the schools. *School Psychology Review, 23*, 165–174.

Beale, A., & Scott, P. (2001). "Bullybusters": Using drama to empower students to take a stand against bullying behavior. *Professional School Counseling, 4*(4), 300– 305.

Bell, S. K., Coleman, J. K., Anderson, A., & Whelan, P. (2000). The effectiveness of peer mediation in a low SES rural elementary school. *Psychology in the Schools, 37*(6), 505–516.

Bentley, K. M., & Li, A. (1995). Bully and victim problems in elementary schools and students beliefs about aggression. *Canadian Journal of School Psychology, 11*(2), 153–165.

Berthold, K. A., & Hoover, J. H. (2000). Correlates of bullying and victimization among intermediate students in the midwestern USA. *School Psychology International, 21*(1), 65–78.

Besag, V. E. (1989). *Bullies and victims in schools*. Philadelphia: Open University Press.

Borg, M. G. (1998). The emotional reactions of school bullies and their victims. *Educational Psychology, 18*(4), 433–445.

Borg, M. G. (1999). The extent and nature of bullying among primary and secondary schoolchildren. *Educational Research, 41*(2), 137–153.

Bosworth, K., Espelage, D. L., & Simon, T. R. (1999). Factors associated with bullying behavior in middle school students. *Journal of Early Adolescence, 19*(3), 341– 362.

Boulton, M. J. (1993). Aggressive fighting in British middle school children. *Educational Studies, 19,* 19–39.

Boulton, M. J. (1999). Concurrent and longitudinal relations between children's playground behaviour and social preference, victimization, and bullying. *Child Development, 70*(4), 944–954.

Branwhite, T. (1994). Bullying and student distress: Beneath the tip of the iceberg. *Educational Psychology, 14*(1), 59–71.

Cairns, R. B., Cairns B. D., Neckerman, H. J. J., Ferguson, L. L., & Gariepy, J. (1989). Growth and aggression: In childhood to early adolescence. *Developmental Psychology, 25*, 320–330.

Camodeca, M., Goossens, F. A., Meerum Terwogt, M., & Schuengel, C. (2002). Bullying and victimization among school age children: Stability and links to proactive and reactive aggression. *Social Development, 11*(3), 332–345.

Caruthers, W. L., Sweeney, B., Kmitta, D., & Harris, G. (1996). Conflict resolution: An examination of the research literature and a model fort program evaluation. *The School Counselor, 44*, 5–18.

Christie, R., & Geis, F. (1970). *Studies in Machiavellianism.* New York: Academic Press.

Craig, H. (1998). The relationship among bullying, victimization, depression, anxiety, and aggression in elementary school children. *Personality and Individual Differences, 24*(1), 123–130.

Craig, W., & Pepler, D. (1995). Peer processes in bullying and victimization. An observational study. *Exceptionality Education Canada, 5,* 81–95.

Craig, W. M., & Pepler, D. J. (1997). Observations of bullying and victimization on the playground. *Journal of School Canadian Psychology, 2,* 41–60.

Craig, W. M., & Pepler, D. J. (2000). Observations of bullying and victimization in the school yard. In W. Craig (Ed.), *Childhood social development* (pp. 113–137). Maldon, MA: Blackwell.

Crick, N. R., & Dodge, K. A (1996). Social information processes in reactive and proactive aggression. *Child Development, 67,* 993–1002.

Crick, N. R., & Grotpeter, J. K. (1996). Children's Treatment by peers: Victims of relational and overt aggression. *Development and Psychopathology, 8*, 367–380.

Cunningham, P. B., & Henggeler, S. W. (2001). Implementation of an empirically based drug and violence prevention and intervention program in public school settings. *Journal of Clinical Child Psychology, 30*(1), 221–232.

Curcio, K. (1994). *Stress symptoms of special education students diagnosed with conduct disorder.* Unpublished doctoral dissertation, Temple University, Philadelphia.

Curcio-Chilton, K. (1995). Stress symptoms of adolescents diagnosed with conduct disorders. *Dissertation Abstracts International, Section B: The Physical Sciences and Engineering*, 55(12-B), 5552.

Dawkins, J. L. (1995). Bullying in school: Doctors' responsibilities. *British Medical Journal, 310,* 274–275.

Dawkins, H. L. (1996). Bullying, physical disability and the pediatric patient. *Developmental Medicine and Child Neurology, 38*(7), 603–612.

De Wall, F. B. M. (1998, April 10). Self-esteem and primate politics. *The Chronicle of Higher Education, 44*(31), B4.

Dodge, K. (1991). The structure and function of reactive and proactive aggression. In D. J. Pepler & K. H. Rubin (Eds.), *The development and treatment of childhood aggression* (pp. 201–218). Hillsdale, NJ: Lawrence Erlbaum Associates.

Elliott, D. S. (Ed.). (2002). *Blueprints for violence prevention, book nine, bullying prevention program.* (Available from the Center for the Study and Prevention of Violence, Institute of Behavioral Science, University of Colorado at Boulder, Campus Box 442, Boulder, CO, 80309–0442)

Elliott, M. (Ed.). (1996). *Bullying: A practical guide to coping for schools* (2nd ed). London: Pitman.

Ericson, N. (2001, June). *Addressing the problem of juvenile bullying.* Washington, DC: Office of Juvenile Justice and Delinquency Prevention, Office of Justice Programs, U.S. Department of Justice. Retrieved April 19, 2004, from http:/www.ncjrs.org/ pdffiles1/ojjdp/fs200127.pdf

Eron, L. D. (1987). The development of aggressive behavior from the perspective of a developing behaviorism. *American Psychologist, 42,* 435–442.

Eslea, M., & Mukhtar, K. (2000). Bullying and racism among Asian schoolchildren in Britain. *Educational Research, 42*(2) 207–217.

Espelage, D., & Asidao, C. S. (2001). Conversations with middle school students about bullying and victimization: Should we be concerned. In R. A. Geffner, M. Loring, & C. Young (Eds.), *Bullying behavior. Current issues, research, and interventions.* (pp. 49–63). New York: Haworth Press.

Espelage, D. L., & Swearer, S. M. (2003). Research on school bullying and victimization: What have we learned and where do we go from here*? School Psychology Review, 32*(3), 365–383.

Fonzi, A., Genta, M. L., Menesini, D. B., Bonino, S., & Costabile, A. (2000). In P. K. Smith et al. (Eds.), *The nature of school bullying: A cross-national perspective* (pp. 140–157). London: Routledge.

Garcia-Vazquez, E., & Ehly, S. (1995). Best practices in facilitating peer tutoring programs. In A. Thomas & J. Grimes (Eds.), *Best practices in school psychology-III* (pp. 403–411). Washington, DC: National Association of School Psychologists.

Genta, M. L., Menesini, E., Fonzi, A., & Costabile, A. (1996). Bullies and victims in schools in central and southern Italy. *European Journal of Psychology of Education, 11*, 1, 97–110.

Gottheil, N. F., & Dubow, E. F. (2001). Tripartite beliefs models of bully and victim behavior. In R. A. Geffner, M. Loring, & C. Young (Eds.), *Bullying behavior. Current issues, research, and interventions* (pp. 25–49). New York: Haworth Press.

Halkias, D., Fakinos, M., Hyman, I., Cohen, I., Akrivos, D., & Mahon, M. (2003, May). *Victimization of children in Greek schools: Stress and trauma symptoms related to school bullying*. Paper presented at the 9th Panhellenic Conference on Psychological Research, Rhodes, Greece.

Hanish, L. D., & Guerra, N. G. (2000). A longitudinal analysis of patterns of adjustment following peer victimization. *Journal of Development and Psychopathology, 14*, 69–89.

Harachi, T. W., Catalano, F., & Hawkins J. D. (2000). United States. In P. K. Smith et al. (Eds.), *The nature of school bullying: A cross-national perspective* (pp. 279–296). London: Routledge.

Harmon, A. (2004, August 26). Internet gives teenage bullies weapons to wound from afar. *The New York Times*, pp. 1, 23.

Hawker, D. S. J., & Boulton, M. J. (2000). Twenty years research on peer victimization and psychosocial maladjustment: A meta-analytic review of cross sectional studies. *Journal of Child Psychology and Psychiatry, 41*, 441–455.

Hawkins, D. L., Pepler, D. J., & Craig, W. M. (2001). Naturalistic observations of peer interventions in bullying. *Social Development, 10*, 512–524.

Hazler, R. J. (1996). Bystanders: An overlooked factor in peer on peer abuse. *The Journal for the Professional Counselor, 11*, 11–21.

Hazler, R. J., & Miller, D. L. (2001). Adult recognition of school bullying situations. *Educational Research, 43*(2), 133–146.

Helsel, D. (2001, November/December). Does your school track the suicidal student? *The Clearing House, 92*, 5.

Hoover, J. H., Oliver, R., & Hazler, R. L. (1992). Bullying: Perceptions of adolescent victims in the midwestern USA. *Social Psychology International, 13*, 5–16.

Huesmann, L. R., Eron, L. D., & Yarmel, P. W. (1987). Intellectual functioning and aggression. *Journal of Personality and Social Psychology, 52*(1), 232–240.

Hyman, I. (1987). Psychological correlates of corporal punishment and physical abuse. In M. Brassard, B. Germain, & S. Hart (Eds.), *Psychological maltreatment of children and youth* (pp. 59–68). Elmsford, NY: Pergamon Press.

Hyman, I. (1990). *Reading, writing, and the hickory stick: The appalling story of physical and psychological abuse in American schools*. Lanham, MD: Lexington Books.

Hyman, I. (1995). Corporal punishment, psychological maltreatment, violence and punitiveness in America: Research, advocacy and public policy. *Applied and Preventive Psychology, 4*(2), 113–130.

Hyman, I., Berna, J., Kohr, M., & DuCette, J. (1998). *My Worst School Experience Scale (research form)*. Los Angeles: Western Psychological Services.

Hyman, I., Berna, J., Snook, P., DuCette, J., & Kohr, M. (2002). *Manual for the My Worst Experience Scales (MWES)*. Los Angeles: Western Psychological Services.

Hyman, I., Cohen, I., & Mahon, M. (2003). Student alienation syndrome: A paradigm for understanding the relation between school trauma and school violence. *The California School Psychologist, 8*, 73–86.

Hyman, I., Cohen, I., Glass, J., Kay, B., Mahon, M., Siegel, N., Tabori, A., & Weber, M. (2003, June). *School bullying: Theory, research, assessment, and interventions*. Workshop presented at the Annual Convention of the Pennsylvania Psychological Association, Harrisburg, PA.

Hyman, I., Dahbany, A., Blum, M., Brooks-Klein, V., Weiler, E., & Pokalo, M. (1997). *School discipline and school violence: The teacher variance approach*. Needham Heights, MA: Allyn & Bacon.

Hyman, I., & Eisenstein, J. (2000). The bullying dilemma. *Bulletin of the Society for the Psychological Study of Men and Masculinity, 5*(2), 15–17.

Hyman, I., Mahon, M., Cohen, I., Snook, P., Britton, G., & Lurkis, L. (2004). Student alienation syndrome: The other side of school violence. In J. Conoley & A. Goldstein (Eds.), *School violence intervention: A practical handbook* (2nd ed.). New York: Guilford.

Hyman, I., Mahon, M., Cohen, I., Tabori, A., Kay, B., Ateah, C., Bolatoglou, K., Campbell, M. Espinoza, E., Fakinos, M., Halkias, D., Karcher, P., Lanyon, D., Malikiosi-Loizos, M., van der Meulin, K., Moore, T., Newman, M., Sutherland, A., Tapanya, S., Yoder, M., DuCette, J., Sung-Kyung, Y. (2004, July). *Bullying by educators and peers: A cross-national study*. Paper presented at the 112th Annual Convention of the American Psychological Association, Honolulu, HI.

Hyman, I., & Perone, D. (1998a). The ecology of school violence: Introduction to the special theme section on school violence. *Journal of School Psychology, 36*(1), 3–6.

Hyman, I., & Perone, D. (1998b). The other side of school violence: Educator policies and practices, which may contribute to student misbehavior. *Journal of School Psychology, 36*(1), 7–28.

Hyman, I., & Snook, P. (1999a). *Dangerous schools: What we can do about the physical and emotional abuse of our children.* San Francisco: Jossey-Bass.

Hyman, I., & Snook, P. (1999b, April). *Use of the My Worst Experience Scales for diagnosis and treatment of posttraumatic stress disorder in children.* Paper presented as part of a mini-skills workshop at the 1999. National Association of School Psychologists Annual Convention, Las Vegas, NV.

Hyman, I., Wise, J. H. (1979). *Corporal punishment in American education.* Philadelphia: Temple University Press.

Hyman, I., Zelikoff, W., & Clarke, J. (1988). Psychological and physical abuse in the schools: A paradigm for understanding post-traumatic stress disorder in children and youth. *Journal of Traumatic Stress, 1,* 243–267.

Izard, C. E., Dougherty, L. M., & Hembree, E. A. (1989). *A system for identifying affective expressions by holistic judgments.* Newark: University of Delaware Media Services.

Jay, A. (1967). *Management and Machiavelli: An inquiry into the politics of corporate life.* New York: Bantam Books.

Jeffrey, L. R., Miller, D., & Linn, M.(2001). Middle school bullying as a context for the development of passive observers to the victimization of others. In R. A. Geffner, M. Loring, & C. Young (Eds.), *Bullying behavior: Current issues, research, and interventions.* (pp. 143–157). New York: Haworth Press.

Johnson, D. W., & Johnson, R. T. (1996). Conflict resolution and peer mediation programs in elementary and secondary schools: A review of the research. *Review of Educational Research, 66,* 459–506.

Kochenderfer, B. J., & Ladd, G. W. (1996). Peer victimization: Cause or consequence of school maladjustment. *Child Development, 67,* 1305–1317.

Kumpalainen, K., Rasanen, E., Henttonen, I., Almovist, F., & Kresanov, K. (1998). Bullying and psychiatric symptoms among elementary school age children. *Child Abuse and Neglect, 22*(7) 705–717.

Kumpulainen, K., Rasanen, E., & Puura, K. (2001). Psychiatric disorders and the use of mental health services among children involved in bullying. *Aggressive Behavior, 27,* 102–110.

Lagerspetz, K. M. J., Bjorkqvist, K., Berts, M., & King, E. (1982). Group aggression among school children in 3 schools. *Scandinavian Journal of Psychology, 23,* 45– 52.

Limber, S. P., & Small, M. A. (2003). State laws and policies to address bullying in schools. *School Psychology Review, 32*(3), 445–456.

Lindman, R., & Sinclair, S. (1988). *Social roles and aspirations of bullies and victims.* Paper presented at the 8th World Biennial ISRA Conference, Swansea, Wales.

Machiavelli, N. (1950). *Discourses on the first ten books of Livy: The discourses of Niccolo Machiavelli* (L. J. Walker, Trans.) London: Routledge & Kegan Paul.

Machiavelli, N. (1513/1958). *The prince* (W. K. Marriot, Trans). London: J. M. Dent & Sons.

Mahady Wilton, M. M., Craig, M., & Pepler, D. J. (2000). Emotional regulation and display in classroom victims of bullying: Characteristic expressions of affect, coping styles and relevant contextual factors. *Social Development, 9,* 226–245.

Maines, B., & Robinson, G. (1998). The no blame approach to bullying. In D. Shorrocks- Taylor (Ed.), *Directions in educational psychology* (pp. 281–295). London: Whurr.

Menesini, E., Eslea, M., Smith, P. K., Genta, M.L., Gianetti, E., Fonzi, A., & Costabile, A. (1997). Cross–national comparison of children's attitudes towards bully/victim problems in school. *Aggressive Behavior, 23,* 245–257.

Metropolitan Life Survey of the American Teacher. (1999, May). Violence in America's public schools—5 years later. New York: Louis Harris and Associates.

Moles, O. (Ed.). (1990). *Student discipline strategies.* Albany: State University of New York Press.

Moran, S., Smith, P. K., Thompson, D., & Whitney, I. (1993). Ethnic differences in experiences of bullying: Asian and white children. *British Journal of Educational Psychology, 63,* 431–440.

Morrison, L. L., & L'Heureux, J. (2001). Suicide and gay/lesbian/bisexual youth: Implications for clinicians. *Journal of Adolescence, 24*(1), 39–49.

Morita, Y., Haruo, S., Kumiko, S., & Taki. (2000). Japan. In P. K. Smith et al. (Eds.), *The nature of school bullying: A cross-national perspective* (pp. 309– 324). London: Routledge.

Mynard, J., & Joseph, S. (1997). Bully/victim problems and their association with Eysenck's personality dimension in 8 to 13 year olds. *British Journal of Educational Psychology, 67,* 51–54.

Nabuzoka, D., & Smith, P. K. (1993). Sociometric status and social behavior of children with and without learning difficulties. *Journal of Child Psychology and Psychiatry, 34,* 1435–1448.

Nansel, T. R., Overpeck, M., Pilla, R. S., Ruan, W. J., Simons-Morton, B., & Scheidt, P. (2001). Bullying behaviors amongst US youth: Prevalence and association with psychosocial adjustment. *Journal of the American Medical Association, 285*(16), 2094–2100.

National Association of School Psychologists. (2002). *Bullying prevention: What schools and parents can do.* Retrieved January 22, 2004, from http://www.nasponline.org

National Center for Educational Statistics. (1992). Public school districts survey on safe, disciplined and drug-free schools. Washington, DC: U.S. Department of Education, Office of Educational Research and Improvement.

National Center for Educational Statistics. (2003). Indicators of school crime and safety 2002. Retrieved January 22, 2004, from http://nces.ed.gov/pubs2003/schoolcrime/6.asp? nav=1

National Education Goals Panel. (1993). *The national education goals report* (Vol. 1.) Washington, DC: U.S. Government Printing Office.

Neary, A., & Joseph, S. (1994). Peer victimization and its relationship to self concept and depression among schoolgirls. *Personality and Individual Differences, 16*(1), 183–186.

Nicolaides, S., Toda, Y., & Smith, P. K. (2002). Knowledge and attitudes about school bullying in trainee teachers. *British Journal of Educational Psychology, 72,* 105-118.

Olafsen, R. N., & Viemeroe, V. (2000). Bully/victim problems and coping with stress in school among 10-12 year old pupils in Aaland Finland. *Aggressive Behavior, 26,* 57–65.

Olweus, D. (1993/2002). *Bullying at school.* Oxford, England: Blackwell.

Olweus, D. (2000a). Norway. In P. K. Smith et al. (Eds.), *The nature of school bullying: A cross-national perspective* (pp. 28–48). London: Routledge.

Olweus, D. (2000b) Sweden. In P. K. Smith et al. (Eds.), *The nature of school bullying: A cross-national perspective* (pp. 7–27). London: Routledge.

Olweus, D. (2003). Prevalence estimation of school bullying with the Olweus bully/victim questionnaire. *Aggressive Behavior, 29*(3), 239–269.

Owens, L., Shute, R., & Slee, P. (2000). "Guess what I just heard!": Indirect aggression among teenage girls in Australia. *Aggressive Behavior, 26,* 67–83.

Patterson, G. R., DeBaryshe, B. D., & Ramsey, E. (2000). A developmental perspective on antisocial behavior. In W. Craig (Ed.), *Childhood social development* (pp. 331–349). Malden, MA: Blackwell.

Pellegrini, A. D. (2001). The roles of dominance and bullying in the development of early heterosexual relationships. In R. A. Geffner, M. Loring, & C. Young (Eds.), *Bullying behavior. Current issues, research, and interventions* (pp. 63–75). New York: Haworth Press.

Pellegrini, A. D., Bartini, M., & Brooks, F. (1999). School bullies, victims, and aggressive victims: Factors relating to group affiliation and victimization in early adolescence. *Journal of Educational Psychology, 91*(2), 216–224.

Pellegrini, A. D., & Long, J. D. (2002). A longitudinal study of bullying, dominance and victimization during the transition from primary school through secondary school. *British Journal of Developmental Psychology, 20*(2), 259–280.

Perry, D. G., Kusel, S. J., & Perry, L. C. (1988). Victims of peer aggression. *Developmental Psychology, 24,* 807–814.

Rea, C. D. (1996). Comparisons of patterns of traumatic stress symptoms in adolescents with and without overt behavior difficulties. *Dissertation Abstracts Internation al, Section A: The Humanities and Social Sciences, 57*(1–A), 0078.

Reid, J., Patterson, G., & Snyder, J. (2002). *Antisocial behavior in children and adolescents: A developmental analysis and model for intervention.* Washington, DC: American Psychological Association Press.

Rigby, K. (1996). *Bullying in schools—and what to do about it* (pp. 209–220). Camberwell, Melbourne: Australian Council for Educational Research.

Rigby, K. (1997). Attitudes and beliefs about bullying among Australian school children. *Irish Journal of Psychology, 18*(2), 202–220.

Rigby, K. (1998). The relationship between reported health and involvement in bully/ victim problems among male and female secondary school children. *Journal of Health Psychology, 3*(4), 465–476.

Rigby, K. (2000). Effects of peer victimization in schools and perceived social support on adolescent well-being. *Journal of Adolescence, 23,* 57–68.

Rigby, K. (2001). *Outcomes of telling about being bullied at school.* Unpublished paper.

Rigby, K. (2002). *New perspectives on bullying.* Philadelphia: Jessica Kingsley.

Rigby, K., & Bagshaw, D. (2001). The prevalence and hurtfulness of acts of aggression from peers experienced by Australian male and female adolescents at school. *Children Australia, 26,* 36–41.

Rigby, K., & Slee, P. T. (1991). Bullying among Australian school children: Reported behaviour and attitudes to victims. *Journal of Social Psychology, 131,* 615–217.

Rigby, K., & Slee, P. T. (2000). Australia. In P. K. Smith et al. (Eds.), *The nature of school bullying: A cross-national perspective* (pp. 324–340). London: Routledge.

Rivers, I. (1996). Young, gay, and bullied. *Young People Now*, 81, 18–19.

Rivers, I., & Smith, P. K. (1994). Types of bullying behavior their correlates. *Aggressive Behavior, 20,* 359–368.

Roland, E., & Thormod, I. (2001). Aggression and bullying. *Aggressive Behavior, 27,* 446–462.

Salmivalli, C., Karhunen, J., & Lagerspetz, K. (1996). How do the victims respond to bullying? *Aggressive Behavior, 22,* 99–109.

Salmivalli, C., Kaukiainen, A., Kaistaniemi, L., Lagerspetz, K. M. J. (1999). Self-evaluated self-esteem, peer-evaluated self-esteem, and defensive egotism as predictors of adolescents' participation in bullying situations. *Personality and Social Psychology Bulletin, 25*(10), 1268–1278.

Salmivalli, C., Lagerspetz, K., Bjorkqvist, K. Osterman, K., & Kaukiainen, A. (1996). Bullying as a group process: Participant roles and their relations to social status within the group. *Aggressive Behavior, 22,* 1–15.

Salmivalli, C., & Nieminen, E. (2002). Proactive and reactive aggression among school bullies, victims, and bully victims. *Aggressive Behavior, 28,* 30–44.

Sanchez, E., Robertson, T., Lewis, C., Rosenbluth, B., Bohman, T., & Casey D. (2001). Preventing bullying and sexual harassment in elementary schools: The expect respect model. In R. A. Geffner, M. Loring, & C. Young (Eds.), *Bullying behavior. Current issues, research, and interventions* (pp. 157–181). New York: Haworth Press.

Schuster, B. (1999). Outsiders at school: The prevalence of bullying and its relation with social status. *Group Processes and Intergroup Relations, 2*(2), 175–190.

Schwartz, D., Dodge, K. A., Pettit, S., & Bates, J. E. (1997). The early socialization of aggressive victims of bullying. *Child Development, 68,* 665–675.

Schwartz, D., & Proctor, L. J. (2000). Community violence exposure and children's social adjustment in the school peer group: The mediating roles of emotion regulation and social cognition. *Journal of Consulting and Clinical Psychology, 68*(4), 670–683.

Shakeshaft, C., Mandel, L., Johnson, Y., Sawyer, J., Hergenrother, M., & Barber, E. (1997, October). Boys call me cow. *Educational Leadership*, 22–25.

Sharp, S. (1995). How much does bullying hurt? The effects of bullying on the personal wellbeing and educational progress of secondary aged students. *Educational and Child Psychology, 12,* 81–88.

Slee, P. T. (1995). Bullying in the playground. The impact of interpersonal violence on Australian schoolchildren's perceptions of their play environment. *Children's Environments, 12*(3), 320–327.

Smith, P. K., Ananiadou, K., & Cowie, H. (2003). Interventions to reduce school bullying. *Canadian Journal of Psychiatry, 48,* 591–599.

Smith, P. K., & Brain, P. (2000). Bullying in schools. Lessons from two decades of research. *Aggressive behavior, 26,* 1–9.

Smith, P. K., Madsen, K. C., & Moody, J. C. (1999). What causes the age decline in reports of being bullied at school: Towards a developmental analysis of risks of being bullied. *Educational Research, 41*(3), 267–285.

Smith, P. K., & Sharp S. (1994). *School bullying: Insights and perspectives.* London, Routledge.

Stein, N. (1999). *Classrooms and courtrooms: Facing sexual harassment in k-12 schools.* New York: Teachers College Press.

Stein, N. (2001). What a difference a discipline makes. Bullying research and future directions. In R. A. Geffner, M. Loring. & C. Young (Eds.), *Bullying behavior. Current issues, research, and interventions* (pp. 1–7). New York: Haworth Press.

Stockdale, M. S., Hanguaduambo, S., Duys, D., Larson, K., & Sarvela, P. D. (2002). Rural elementary students' parents' and teachers' perceptions of bullying. *American Journal of Health Behavior, 26*(4), 266–277.

Sutton, J., & Keough, E. (2000). Social competition in school: Relationships with bullying, Machiavellianism, and personality. *British Journal of Educational Psychology, 70,* 443–456.

Sutton, J., Smith, P. K., & Swettenham, J. (1999). Bullying and "theory of mind": A critique of the "social skills deficit" view of antisocial behavior. *Social Development, 8,* 117–127.

Swearer, S. M., Song, S. Y., Cary, P. T., Eagle, J. W., & Mickelson, W. T. (2001). Psychosocial correlates in bullying and victimization: The relationship between depression, anxiety, and bully/victim status. *Journal of Emotional Abuse, 2,* 95–121.

U.S. Secret Service and U.S. Department of Education. (2002a). *The final report and findings of the safe school initiative: Implications for the prevention of school attacks in the United States.* Washington, DC: U.S. Department of Education.

U.S. Secret Service and U.S. Department of Education. (2002b). *Threat assessment in schools: A guide to managing threatening situations and to creating safe school climates.* Washington, DC: U.S. Department of Education.

Vossekuil, B., Reddy, M., Fein, R., Borum R., & Modzeleski, W. (2000). *Safe school initiative: An interim report on the prevention of targeted violence in schools.* U.S. Secret Service National Threat Assessment Center. Retrieved May 3, 2003, from http://www.ustreas.gov/usss/ntac/ntac_ssi_report.pdf

Warman, D. M., & Cohen, R. (2000). Stability of aggressive behaviors and children's peer relationships. *Aggressive Behavior, 26,* 277–290.

Whitney, I., & Smith, P. K. (1993). A survey of the nature and extent of bullying in junior/middle and secondary schools. *Educational Research, 35,* 3–25.

Whitney, I., Smith, P. K., & Thompson, D. (1994). Bullying and children with special educational needs. In P. K. Smith & S. Sharpe (Eds.), *School bullying. Insights and perspectives* (pp. 213–240). London: Routledge.

Wolke, D., Woods, S., Bloomfield, L., & Karstadt, L. (2000). The association between direct and relational bullying and behaviour problems among primary school children. *Journal of Child Psychology and Psychiatry, 41*(8), 989–1002.

VIII

Teaching and Learning About Classroom Management

Carolyn M. Evertson

33

How Do Teachers Learn to Be Effective Classroom Managers?

Vern Jones
Lewis & Clark College

INTRODUCTION

This chapter is divided into two major sections: The first and most extensive focuses on preservice classroom management education, and the second examines inservice instruction in classroom management. Both sections present not only the attitudes, knowledge, and skills most needed by teachers at various professional development levels, but also the methods teacher educators can implement to assist teachers in developing the attitudes, knowlege, and skills needed to be effective classroom managers.

PRESERVICE CLASSROOM MANAGEMENT EDUCATION

In their introductory chapter, Carolyn Evertson and Carol Weinsten note that at each meeting of the American Educational Research Association with approximately 12,000 people in attendance and 3,000 presenters, "there are generally only two or three sessions explicitly devoted to classroom management, and these tend to be poorly attended." Because many of those in attendance at this conference are involved in teacher education, it is perhaps not surprising that students in these programs frequently rate the attention given to classroom management as woefully inadequate.

Preservice Students' Assessment of Their Classroom Management Education

Many beginning teachers state they are unprepared for the realities of working with the behavior demands presented by their students. Classroom management is the most common concern expressed by beginning teachers (Britt, 1997; Ganser, 1999; Jacques, 2000; Ladd, 2000; McCormack, 2001; Pigge & Marso, 1997; White, 1995). In a study of 82 teachers in their first year of teaching, 64 stated that classroom management was the area in which they needed the most support (Stroot et al., 1999). New teachers report that poor classroom management skills (82 %) and disruptive students (57%) are the two most significant barriers to professional success (Fideler & Haskelhorn, 1999). New teachers state they feel unprepared to cope with issues related to classroom management (Pigge & Marso, 1997; Herbert & Worthy, 2001). In a study conducted by the Oregon Department of Education (Dalton & Zanville, 2002), beginning teachers cited issues related to classroom management as their biggest challenge. Lundeen (2002) reported that the beginning teachers in her study were shocked with the severity of emotional and behavior issues presented by their students. This emphasis on severe behavior problems was highlighted in a study of 42 beginning teachers (Meister & Jenks, 2000). These researchers reported that:

> The greatest concern of all new teachers was their inability to deal with aberrant behavior and diverse needs of some students. Almost none of the voiced concerns dealt with low-level discipline issues. The issues these teachers talked about were complicated and sometimes volatile. These beginning teachers felt completely unprepared to face them. (p. 4)

Beginning teachers frequently place the blame for their lack of preparation squarely on the inadequancies of classroom management coursework in their teacher education programs (Halford, 1998; Ladd, 2000; Pipho, 2000). One young professional stated, "I felt bewildered and more than a bit betrayed by my own teacher education program: all the learning theories and stages of development that I studied helped little when I was faced with managing a classroom of real third grade children with unique needs, wants, and personalities" (Pilarski, 1994, p. 78). This teacher went on to comment that "On the few occasions when my courses did deal with management issues, the lessons were so far removed from the actual classroom situations that benefits proved minimal" (p. 79).

When responding to a question regarding the quality of their preservice education, a sample of first-year teachers in a Texas study ranked "teaching computers," "classroom management," and "dealing with misbehavior" as the areas in which they had been most poorly prepared (Houston & Williamson, 1993). These teachers also listed working with parents as another area in which their preservice educational experience was sorely lacking. In a study involving 124 institutions listed as providing middle-level teacher preparation, Scales (1994) reported that 59% of teacher educators at these institutions indicated that better educational experiences were very much needed in the area of classroom management. Results from a survey completed by 900 graduates of fifth-year teacher education programs in California indicated these educators believed their programs should have placed a greater focus on classroom management and skills in communicating with parents (Whitney, Golez, Nagel, & Nieto, 2002). A survey of Florida teachers indicated that 43% of first-year teachers felt they were "minimally prepared" or "not prepared" to manage their classrooms (Florida Office of Economic and Demographic Research, 2000).

A study involving 176 secondary school teachers (Merrett & Wheldall, 1993) indicated a vast majority of these teachers felt classroom management was very important, and yet 72% of these teachers were dissatisfied with their preservice preparation in the area of classroom management. Indeed, only 18% of the respondents stated they had learned valuable classroom management skills in their preservice education program, and the majority of these stated they had learned these skills during their student teaching experience. The remainder stated they had learned the skills they needed while on the job. Not surprisingly, 95% of these teachers stated they thought a course in classroom management would be very beneficial to new teachers. In a study of preservice teachers at four midwestern universities, Ladd (2000) reported that "classroom behavior and management was by far the ... most criticized issue" (p. 171). She noted that "graduates of all four programs viewed their proficiency in classroom management to be lacking" (p. 182). She concluded her research by noting, "The implications are resounding—teachers want more help in managing classrooms" (p. 185). In a study of preservice elementary and secondary teachers, Stewart-Wells (2000) reported that before their student teaching experience, preservice teachers listed lesson plan development and classroom management as their major concerns. Following student teaching, classroom management was again listed as a major area for additional professional growth. Students stated that it would be more helpful if they could have been provided with "more 'hands-on,' real life stories on how to resolve classroom management issues before, during, and after problems in this area arise" (p. ii). Fifty percent of the student teachers surveyed indicated that issues of classroom management and discipline should be major aspects of their teacher education program. In a similar vein, in a study of 25 beginning secondary teachers from St. Paul, Minnesota, Davis (1999) reported that many of these teachers felt their teacher preparation program was far too theoretical and several believed they would have been as well prepared had they entirely skipped their college classes. These teachers expressed particular concern with their lack of knowledge in working with students from varied cultural backgrounds and students identified as having special needs. Perhaps not surprisingly, 45% of the teachers in his study indicated they would be unlikely to return to teaching the next year.

Administrators' and Educational Writers' Concerns or Beliefs Regarding Beginning Teachers' Classroom Management Skills

Ladd (2000) reported that the issue of classroom management was the area in which administrators expressed the greatest concern regarding new teachers' classroom skills. In an examination of factors administrators considered when hiring teachers, researchers found that administrators listed "1. Establishing positive classroom climate, 2. Building/maintaining rapport with students, and 3. classroom management/discipline" (p. 52) as the top three teaching skills (Ralph, Kesten, Lang, & Smith, 1998). Studies suggest that in the area of classroom management many beginning teachers have limited practical skills (Britzman, 2000; Earley, 2000; Lytle, 2000; Wasley, 1999), and school administrators state they must provide extensive supervision and retraining of beginning teachers (Brock & Grady, 1997; Charnock & Kiley, 1995; Lytle, 2000).

Administrators appear to be accurate in their sense that beginning teachers lack skills in classroom management. In her study of 36 preservice science teachers, Zuckerman (2000) found that in responding to student behavior that disrupted learning opportunities, over half the student teachers either made no response or merely attempted to enforce compliance. Only six of these student teachers focused on ways to more actively or successfully engage students in the learning experience.

Administrators are faced with serious problems in reeducating and replacing teachers who have not been adequately prepared to manage their classrooms. Soon after entering their first full-time teaching experience, many beginning teachers experience a sense of frustration and failure (Archer, 1999; Brock & Grady, 1996; Chester & Beaudin, 1996; Halford, 1998). Estimates indicate that 15% of beginning teachers leave after 2 years, 23% leave after 3 years, and nearly 40% leave within 5 years (Halford, 1998; Ingersoll & Smith, 2003; Olson, 2000; Sherman, 2003; Spring, 2000). Concerns about student discipline problems are second only to poor salary as the reason beginning teachers who leave the profession are dissatisfied with teaching (Ingersoll & Smith, 2003).

Those involved in hiring and supervising beginning teachers are not alone in their emphasis on and concern for beginning teachers' classroom management skills. In a 1992 AERA publication, classroom management was listed as number two on a list of the top seven characteristics of an effective teacher (Good & McCaslin, 1992, p. 1375). Several writers have noted that beginning teachers' ability to implement what they have learned in their university training into their classroom teaching is a serious factor limiting the effectiveness of teachers in American society (Burstein, Kretschmer, Smith, & Gudoski, 1999; Cochran-Smith, 2000; Darling-Hammond, 2000). Darling-Hamond wrote that teacher preparation programs need to be redesigned in order "to strengthen its knowledge base, its connections to both practice and theory, and its capacity to support the development of powerful teaching" (2000, p. 166).

Bandura (1997) suggested that teacher efficacy includes confidence in maintaining a safe, orderly classroom environment and working to increase students' motivation to learn. Reilly (2002) also found the domains of classroom management and discipline to be a separate component of teacher efficacy. Emmer and Hickman (1991) reported that teacher efficacy for classroom management and discipline is a distinct type of teacher efficacy. Furthermore, they suggested that high efficacy in this area is associated with teachers' interest in using more student-centered strategies for dealing with problems. These include meeting with the student, modifying work requirements, giving the student extra praise and attention, and helping the student develop a behavior change plan. This work supports findings by Woolfolk and Hoy (1990) indicating that prospective teachers with high teaching efficacy appear more humanistic in their classroom management beliefs. Reilly (2002) reported that teachers high in efficacy in the classroom management/discipline domain were more likely to feel capable of helping students improve their skills in social and academic areas as well as in the area of classroom behavior. Given that teachers are increasingly required to work with a wide range of students with special needs and varied cultural backgrounds, this willingness to consider individual student needs and work with students and their families seems an essential component of effective classroom management. In addition, because teachers gradually develop a relatively stable sense of teaching efficacy (Ross, 1998), it seems important that preservice teacher education programs assist students in developing a strong sense of teacher efficacy in the area of classroom management so this carries over into their initial teaching experiences.

In her study of four teacher education programs in California, Stewart-Wells (2000) found that only one program required a course in classroom management, and this was a one-credit-hour course generally taken by teachers 2 years before their student teaching experience. She reported that content in classroom management is most often part of an educational psychology course and is not required for students to graduate. In summarizing her study of teacher education programs, Stewart-Wells (2000) suggested that:

> The two most apparent faults in TEPs in preparing future teachers to be effective classroom managers are that: 1) teacher educators teach classroom management based on their own comfort levels, and in the broadest sense of the term classroom management, leaving student teachers dependent on whom they have as an educator and 2) not all TEPs require an integrated classroom management curriculum, which includes teaching of effective discipline strategies, to graduate. (p. 174)

Mahlios and Maxson (1995) noted that although management is deeply embedded in teachers' belief systems, their research of teacher education programs suggests that "too many faculty in TEPs operate with little knowledge of who their students are and the dominant beliefs they may hold upon entry into TEPs" (p. 198). They suggested that classroom management coursework is enhanced when teacher education faculty get to know their students well and help them relate their personal beliefs about human nature and discipline to current research on effective methods for creating positive learning environments and helping students act responsibly. This suggests classroom management coursework may need to occur in small classes with adequate meeting time to support personal self-examination and extensive knowledge and skill development.

Data collected from approximately 600 teachers by the Council for Basic Education and certified by the National Board of Professional Standards suggest that beginning teachers' lack of preparation in classroom management is in part caused by the lack of experience of university faculty in teacher education programs (Rigden, 1997). Anyone who has worked in public schools for an extended period is aware of the dramatic differences in the cultural diversity and severity of student behavior problems over the past decade. University faculty, however, often lack recent or extensive work in public schools, and they represent a homogeneous population (Cockrell, Mitchell, Middleton, & Campbell, 1999). Therefore, it appears unlikely that a majority of students in preservice teacher education programs are required to complete significant classroom management coursework (more than a one-semester-hour class) taught by an instructor with recent public school experience.

Kagan (1992a) examined 40 studies conducted on learning to teach between 1987 and 1991. One "important finding from these 40 studies was that new teachers do not have the prerequisite knowledge of classroom procedures to understand the complex interrelationship among management, behavior, and academic tasks" (Meister & Jenks, 2000, p. 2). In reviewing studies of first-year teachers, Wideen, Mayer-Smith, and Moon (1998) wrote about these young teachers:

> Their struggles with classroom management challenged many of their beliefs and caused anger, which was hard to balance with their humanistic concerns. The need for control became very apparent to the beginning teacher, often at the expense of alternative ways of teaching. (p. 158)

The limited amount and poor quality of field experiences is another area often presented as contributing to the lack of knowledge, skill, and confidence preservice teachers possess in the area of classroom management. Data collected in a study of approximately 600 teachers conducted by the Council for Basic Education and certified by the National Board of Professional Standards suggest that beginning teachers' lack of preparation in classroom management is in part caused by limited field experiences (Rigden, 1997). Students frequently comment on the poor match between the theories and methods presented in their teacher education program and those espoused during their student teaching or internship experience.

Grasmick and Leak (1997) summarized two reports on teacher preparation: *What Matters Most: Teaching for America's Future*, by the National Commission on Teaching, and *America's Future, and What Teachers Have to Say About Teacher Education*, by the Council for Basic Education. Among the eight major problems with teacher preparation programs, Grasmick and Leak included the (1) inadequate length of 4-year programs, (2) lack of connection between coursework and field experiences, (3) lack of dynamic teaching methods, (4) lack of curricular depth, (5) traditional views of teaching, (6) poor quality of those admitted to teacher education programs, (7) lack of teaching experience in K–12 public schools found among university faculty in teacher education programs, and (8) limited and poorly supervised field experiences.

In examining the concerns expressed by preservice and beginning teachers, school administrators, and researchers, 12 concerns surface regarding classroom management content and instruction in teacher education programs:

1. A too general and theoretical approach to teaching classroom management (Davis, 1999; Stewart-Wells, 2000)
2. Lack of an integrated, comprehensive curriculum in classroom management (Stewart-Wells, 2000)
3. Lack of skills in working with severe behavior problems and students with special needs (Meister & Melnick, 2003)

4. Lack of preparation to teach in diverse and multicultural settings (Davis, 1999; Valli, 1995: Wideen et al., 1998)
5. Teacher educators' lack of understanding regarding who their students are and the beliefs they hold when they enter their teacher education program (Mahlios & Maxson, 1995; Wideen et al., 1998)
6. Limited amount and poor quality of field experiences in teacher education programs (Grasmick & Leak, 1997; Rigden, 1997)
7. Inadequate length of 4-year teacher education programs (Grasmick & Leak, 1997)
8. Lack of connection between coursework and field experiences (Grasmick & Leak, 1997)
9. Lack of recent teaching experience of university faculty in teacher education programs (Cockrell et al., 1999; Grasmick & Leak, 1997; Rigden, 1997);
10. Lack of congruence between what preservice teachers are taught during their teacher education program and what they encounter during their student teaching and first year of teaching (Davis, 1999; Wideen et al., 1998)
11. The poor quality of those admitted to teacher education programs (Grasmick & Leak, 1997)
12. The young age of many teacher education candidates (Stewart-Wells, 2000)

These concerns raise three key questions. The first four concerns highlight the question: What classroom management content will best prepare preservice teachers to face the reality and responsibility of establishing a positive learning environment in classrooms characterized by large class size and increased numbers of students requiring special academic and behavioral assistance? The 5th through the 10th issues suggest teacher educators examine the question: What instructional approaches will be most effective in helping students develop this knowledge and skill? The final two issues raise the question: Who should be admitted to teacher education programs?

Classroom Management Content for Preservice Teachers

The first four concerns listed regarding classroom management relate to issues of content. In discussing the limited amount of coursework in this area, Landau (2001) wrote:

> If there is only limited amount of time to discuss classroom management, and teacher educators have expertise in another subject, the most likely management strategies to be covered will be those that can be quickly explained and that are easiest to implement. (p. 11)

In summarizing the findings of their study of classroom management instruction in preservice teacher education programs, Ackley and McEwan (2004) noted:

> We also lack a clear consensus about what should be included in the curriculum of any management course. Apparently we even lack a consensus about the importance of providing future teachers with a plan they can use as they enter their first professional experience. (p. 11)

Based on her examination of teacher preparation in classroom management, Stewart-Wells (2000) noted that the "two most apparent faults" in preparing teachers in the area of classroom management were the lack of an integrated curriculum and the broad presentation of material based on each instructor's own comfort level. Lasley (1994) suggested preservice teachers may learn far too much theory but lack specific methods for dealing with student behavior. He suggested focusing on a limited number of skills and helping preservice teachers master these skills. He also argued strongly against the approach of presenting preservice students with an overview of a variety of methods or concepts and expecting them to extrapolate this to specific classroom strategies and generalize this to actual use in the classroom (Lasley 1987, 1989). Lasley suggested that although teachers will need to move beyond technical proficiency on a limited number of key classroom management skills, the mastery of these skills is the appropriate goal for classroom management education in preservice programs. This need to define a clear curriculum was also highlighted by Gilberts and Lignugaris-Kraft (1997) who, after reviewing 33 studies of teacher classroom management competencies for both elementary education and special education, suggested it is necessary to determine a "common core of knowledge and practice that all teachers must demonstrate prior to certification" (p. 607).

What are these key areas beginning teachers must master to effectively manage their classrooms? Lasley (1994) recommended the following three general skill areas: (1) "an ability to develop and implement specific classroom rules" (1994, p. 14), (2) "an understanding of when and how to use both low and high profile desists in dealing with student misbehavior" (1994, p. 15), and (3) "an ability to use parents as a resource in dealing with chronic severe misbehavior" (1994, p. 17). In an article entitled "Educating Teachers About Classrooms and Students," Brophy (1988) also argued for emphasizing a single integrated approach to classroom management rather than providing brief coverage of different approaches. Rather than trying to provide novice teachers with too broad a spectrum of skills, he recommended emphasizing classroom management methods for handling the most common instructional methods beginning teachers would likely use. Brophy proposed that the major teaching functions include: (a) instruction, (b) classroom management, (c) student socialization, and (d) disciplinary interventions. Although he proposed providing beginning teachers with methods for responding to student rule violations, he suggested that the "more sophisticated socialization strategies (counseling and psychotherapy techniques, cognitive behavior modification techniques)" (p. 17) be reserved for inservice teachers.

Similarly, Jones (1982, 1996; Jones & Jones, 1981, 1986, 2004) has for many years suggested that an effective, comprehensive approach to classroom management includes helping students develop knowledge and skills in five major areas: (1) understanding how decisions in classroom management need to include a consideration of students' personal and cultural needs; (2) creating positive teacher–student, peer relationships, and teacher–parent relationships; (3) implementing instructional methods that motivate students and ensure all students experience academic success; (4) developing ways to help all students understand and commit to behavior standards and routine procedures that ensure a safe, supportive classroom environment; and (5) knowing how to implement methods for responding to student behavior that disrupts the learning environment or creates an unsafe learning setting. Rather than be exposed to a limited number of theorists or a focus on one or a few specific models, (e.g., Glasser, Canter, Dreikurs), Jones has argued that preservice teachers learn specific, research-based skills in each of these five areas.

For over 3 decades, Carolyn Evertson has been a leader in developing materials for assisting teachers in developing basic, sound classroom management methods. Her Classroom Organization and Management Program (COMP) provides instructional modules for the areas of (a) organizing the classroom, (b) planning and teaching rules and procedures, (c) developing student accountability, (d) maintaining good student behavior, (e) planning and organizing instruction, (f) conducting instruction and maintaining momentum, (g) getting off to a good start, and (h) climate, communication, and self-management (Evertson & Harris, 1995, 1999; Evertson, Emmer, & Worsham, 2003).

Brophy (1988) highlighted another key concept in classroom management content within preservice teacher education programs when he noted that many individuals entering teacher education programs not only lack skills in classroom management but have attitudes and beliefs that are inconsistent with current research about classroom management. Brophy suggested that in providing classroom management instruction, educators working with preservice teachers should assist learners in clarifying and changing misconceptions in their thinking. Brophy stated that "teacher educators should label misconceptions as such, underscore key contrasts with correct conceptions, and call attention to self-defeating aspects of the classroom strategies that are associated with these misconceptions" (1988, p. 13).

Classroom management content has changed over the past decade. Given the increasing diversity of our classrooms, a lack of multicultural competence can exacerbate the difficulties that novice teachers (and even more experienced teachers) have with classroom management (Weinstein, Tomlinson-Clarke, & Curran, 2004 p. 26). This need for culturally competent classroom management is both a content and an instructional issue and is addressed in more detail in the next section.

First-year teachers also report needing skills in how to manage crisis situations in the classroom (Steed, 2001) and how to deal with students presenting serious behavior problems (Meister & Melnick, 2003; Soodak & Podell, 1998). Therefore, it seems important that pre-service teachers develop at least the basic skills for responding to crisis situations and developing behavior change programs for students whose behavior is consistently or seriously in violation of agreed-upon classroom behavior standards. That this recommendation differs from recommendations made almost 20 years ago (Brophy, 1988) is likely due to the increased number and intensity of behavior problems presented by students. A decade ago, less than one third of students with disabilities participated in general education classes. Currently, over three fourths of the nearly 7 million students identified with disabilities spend time in general education classes (U.S. Department of Education, 2001). This means that beginning teachers need a wider repertoire of skills for implementing individualized academic adaptations and behavior change plans.

Despite their frustration with coursework in classroom management, preservice teachers do make important progress in their knowledge about classroom management. Weinstein, Woolfolk, Dittmeier, and Shanker (1994) found that by the end of their student teaching experience, the preservice teachers they studied had developed a "new recognition that the classroom group is composed of individuals with unique personalities and problems, each presenting a different challenge to management" (p. 50). These authors also noted that preservice students in their study developed an increasing awareness of the relationship between effective, engaging instruction and student behavior. This suggests that although it may be important to assist beginning teachers in developing very basic classroom management skills such as working with students to develop classroom behavior standards and responding to classroom disruptions, near the end of their preservice program, prospective teachers are prepared to develop skills for examining the relationship between student behavior and academic success as well as methods for assisting individual students in developing a more responsible behavior repertoire.

Given the strong criticism many preservice students present regarding their coursework in classroom management, it is interesting that Johnson (1994) reported that a wide range of elementary student teachers shared beliefs about effective classroom management that were consistent with current research findings. This suggests that although perspective teachers may bring their own agendas regarding working with students, they are influenced by the ideas and values presented in their teacher education programs. Johnson (1994) suggested that "if elementary teachers are having difficulty with classroom management and discipline, either as student teachers or as beginning teachers, it is not because they hold weak or inappropriate conceptions of management, at least as measured against current knowledge of best practice" (p. 116). Given the extensive findings indicating beginning teachers did not believe their teacher education programs had served them well in the area of classroom management training, it appears likely that the methods for providing this content, along with the limited time allocated to this content, may be a key factor limiting beginning teachers' ability to develop useful classroom management skills. The next section examines methods teacher educators can use to increase the likelihood that graduates from their programs will be effective in using the classroom management content taught in their programs.

Methods for Teaching Classroom Management

Many of the concerns and criticisms described by beginning teachers, school administrators, and researchers emphasize problems with the methods used to provide preservice teachers with knowledge and useful skills in the area of classroom management (concerns 5–10). In addition, researchers have also pointed to the selection of students as a possible factor influencing the ability of preservice teachers to develop solid classroom management skills.

A wide variety of studies suggest that the perceptions, beliefs, and attitudes individuals bring to their teacher education program influence their views of teaching and classroom management (Calderhead & Robson, 1991; Goodman, 1988; Kagan, 1992a). Some research also suggests that teacher education programs have relatively little impact on changing the views preservice teachers bring to their professional preparation program (Kagan, 1992a; Wideen et al., 1998). Teacher educators must attend to the fact that the experiences and associated preexisting beliefs prospective teachers bring with them will serve as a filter for their interpretation and response to the classroom management content presented in their university courses. These beliefs and experiences influence the manner in which beginning teachers develop their image of themselves as teachers. It is therefore important that teacher educators understand these beliefs and incorporate methods that help preservice students examine their beliefs and consider alternative ways of viewing themselves and their interactions with students (Hollingsworth, 1992; Wideen et al., 1998). In the area of classroom management this often means helping preservice teachers examine their beliefs regarding their relationships with students and how their responsibility for student learning within a safe classroom setting relates to their own beliefs and feelings about their sense of efficacy and issues of power, control, and democratic classroom structures (Metzger, 2002; Weinstein, 1998). Assessment of one's personal beliefs is enhanced by providing students with ongoing support, often including work with a cohort group (Graber, 1996; Gunstone, Slatttery, Baird, & Northfield, 1993; Hollingsworth, 1992). A cohort group provides emotional and intellectual support while also combating the rather simplistic views about teaching that characterize many preservice teachers' thinking (Weinstein, 1990). Especially in graduate programs in which cohorts may include participants ranging from ages 22 to 55, small cohort groups can provide many opportunities for discussions about important classroom management concepts such as issues of power and control, contact with parents and guardians, and teacher responsibility for student behavior and learning.

A second grouping of concerns regarding methods for teaching classroom management preparation in teacher education programs relates to the quality of field experiences and lack of congruence between what is taught at the university and what students experience during their field experiences (items 6–10 in the list of concerns).

In describing the most effective instructional approach in the area of classroom management, Brophy (1988) wrote:

> In my view, this translates into a combination of didactic instruction in basic concepts and skills, carefully planned classroom observation and student teaching experiences . . . and the use of case materials and simulation exercises as substitutes for field experiences that cannot be included in the program. (p. 14)

Brophy (1988) suggested that "classroom management strategies appear to be examples of the kinds of complex skills that are accomplished most naturally under instructional conditions that follow the apprenticeship model" (p. 13). He went on to state that in this model, "a novice learns from an expert by spending sustained time as the expert's apprentice, observing the expert perform the task, asking questions and receiving tutorial assistance, and gradually assuming increasing personal responsibilities as knowledge and skills develop" (p. 13). In a similar vein, Hylton (2000) suggested that although students may learn concepts and facts about classroom management through traditional methods of instruction, what she calls "procedural knowledge" requires active, engaging instructional methods such as role playing and video analysis. Hyton described procedural knowledge as:

> Cognitive awareness and the performance of classroom management skills and behavioral patterns in the context of planning, organizing a classroom learning environment which focuses students' attention on the lesson taught while maintaining the flow of a lesson and control over student behaviors. (p. 5)

Taken together, this work supports the benefits of involving preservice students in extended field experiences (Andrew & Schwab, 1995). In many teacher education programs, students have far too little access to real classroom experiences before or during their study of classroom management (Stewart-Wells, 2000). Until they have extended time in classrooms and opportunities to discuss issues that arise as they observe and work in these settings, novice teachers may have too little background to develop procedural knowledge and to move toward an understanding of students' needs (Berlinger, 1988; Eisenhart, Behm, & Romagnano, 1991; Kagan, 1992b). Research supports the concept that extended field experiences are associated with greater effects on students beliefs about teaching (Wideen et al., 1998), more advanced teacher skills (Angelle, 2002), and higher retention rates (Darling-Hammond, 2003).

In addition to the lack of time in the classroom, considerable concern has been raised regarding the lack of connection between what students experience in their field placements and what they learn in their teacher education classes. The lack of connection between coursework and field experiences can be addressed by selecting mentor teachers who implement many of the methods being taught at the university. This can be accomplished by university faculty selecting graduates of their program as mentors. In addition, mentor teachers and supervisors can be provided with assistance in understanding how university faculty view classroom management and learning. Seminars can be held in which interns or student teachers, mentors, and supervisors meet with the instructor of the classroom management course to discuss issues arising in the field placements. Mentors can be encouraged to be very specific in sharing with their student teacher their decision-making processes regarding classroom management. Likewise, student teachers can be provided with structure and encouragement to ask their mentors why classroom management decisions were made and what specific procedures were most influential in creating a smooth classroom flow.

Student teachers also need to be provided with frequent visits from supervisors representing the university preservice program. These visits allow the supervisor to monitor the student teachers' use of classroom management methods and to ensure congruence between these methods and those being taught at the university. Classroom management involves a complex set of skills, and implementing these skills is confounded by the emotional aspect of having to respond to student behavior that disrupts the learning process. Many beginning teachers can write outstanding papers describing what they would do in the classroom, and can effectively role-play this in a university classroom setting, yet find themselves struggling to implement these skills within the context of a public school classroom. It is imperative, therefore, that teacher education programs provide extensive supervision to preservice students during their internship or student teaching experiences. This may involve the supervisor reinforcing the importance of using these skills, cuing the student when these skills need to be implemented, and occasionally modeling these skills for the student.

Another method for increasing the connection between material taught in teacher education courses and what students experience in the field setting is for classroom management courses to be taught with small class sizes (25 or less) and for the professor to model effective instructional and management techniques. When making classroom management decisions, the professor can discuss her own decision-making process regarding classroom procedures and instructional decisions. In addition, students can be provided numerous opportunities to share the procedures that are effective in the classrooms where they are observing or student teaching.

Students also express concern regarding the lack of practical value of their university coursework. Brophy (1988) suggested that effective classroom management instruction involves helping students acquire basic knowledge in classroom management combined with an opportunity to ask questions and receive tutorial assistance from individuals with practical, current field experience. Stoiber (1991) compared the effects of a technical skills approach to classroom management to a pedagogical reasoning and problem-solving approach. The problem-solving approach involved students in analyzing classroom cases. Results indicated that students exposed to the reflective problem-solving approach were more able to provide reasons for their interventions and had a greater sense of their responsibility for student learning and behavior. Stoiber suggests these findings indicate preservice teachers are capable of understanding, analyzing, and responding to complex classroom conditions. A number of other researchers and writers recommended the use of the case method approach for helping preservice teachers understand and respond more effectively to the complexity of student behavior within the learning context and to increase their ability to engage in reflective practice (Adler, 1996; Kowalski, Weaver, & Henson, 1990; Silverman, Welty, & Lyon, 1992). Adler (1996) found that the case method helped preservice teachers develop "more complex conceptual frameworks" (p. 37). In a similar vein, Singh, Doyle, Rose, & Kennedy (1997) explored the use of students' stories and a problem-solving approach they call a Reflective and Critical Internship Program. They used self-reflection of students' experiences and the solving of problems that arose in practicum experiences to help students construct their own ways of understanding classroom management and their own techniques. It is important to note that the case method described in the area of classroom management differs from that used in counseling. In classroom management this refers to opportunities to examine classroom methods related to both preventive and corrective classroom management skills. This may involve videotape analysis, students discussing problems they are having with basic management problems such as making effective transitions or monitoring student work, or discussions of serious student behavior problems. In discussing the value of case methods, Merseth (1996) wrote, "Teacher action derives from induction from multiple experiences, not deduction from theoretical principles" (p. 724). Shulman (1992) stated,

> Apparently, learning is much more situation-specific than heretofore imagined.... Thus, the specificity and localism of cases as instructional materials may not be problematic for learning; indeed, they may be far more appropriate media for learning than the abstract and decontextualized lists of propositions or expositions of acts, concepts, and principles. (p. 24)

One instructional approach that supports this problem-solving or case methods approach is to allocate approximately one third of class time in classroom management courses for dealing with issues students bring from their field sites. These may be addressed by the instructor or by having students break into dyads or triads to develop possible strategies in response to the concern presented by their fellow interns. It is important that preservice teachers have ongoing opportunities to discuss issues with their colleagues. Studies have shown that even e-mail collaboration and dialogue between students can enhance students' knowledge and application skills (Hoover, 1994; Schlagal, Trathen, & Blanton, 1996; Yan, Anderson, & Nelson, 1994).

Although it is highly desirable that classroom management coursework be offered with simultaneous in-depth practicum experiences, there are times when electronic images may substitute for or enhance live classroom observation and participation. Sariscsany and Pettigrew (1997) compared the Interactive Video Classroom Management Training Program with a teacher-directed videotape and a traditional lecture instruction approach and found students involved in the interactive video scored significantly higher on a test of content knowledge in classroom management. These authors suggested that content mastery (declarative knowledge) is a prerequisite for developing and using skills (procedural knowledge). Hylton's (2000) work supports earlier work (Overbaugh, 1995; Randolph & Evertson, 1992; Rubin, 1991; Wethington, 1991; Winitzky & Arends, 1991) suggesting that methods such as video, computer, and multimedia approaches to instruction can assist students in being able to effectively apply classroom management methods. Murphy, Kauffman, and Strang (1987) reported that the use of a classroom management microcomputer simulation with preservice teachers was associated with the teachers using more appropriate management responses and fewer inappropriate responses when teaching a simulated lesson. Overbaugh (1995) discovered that the use of an interactive-video computer-aided instructional program significantly increased students' knowledge of and interest in learning and applying classroom management methods. However, other studies (Goodwin & Deering, 1993) have found no significant positive results when comparing interactive video to more traditional instructional methods such as lecture, discussion, and conventional videotapes.

Another concern expressed by researchers, school personnel, and preservice teachers is the lack of recent teaching experience by those teaching in teacher education programs. Because of the dramatic changes in the number of students from different cultures and the inclusion of an increasing number of students with special needs, this problem is particularly serious in coursework in classroom management where issues of student motivation, student behavior, and appropriate responses to a wide range of students is a critical aspect of effective practice (Meister & Jenks, 2000). One method of addressing this concern is to have a practicing or recently retired teacher either teach the preservice classroom management course or team-teach it with a university professor.

Although much can be accomplished during a preservice course in classroom management, it is also imperative that throughout their preservice coursework, students receive frequent, consistent messages regarding how to create learning environments that encourage and maintain positive student behavior. In their review of 93 studies on learning to teach, Wideen et al. (1998) reported that long-term changes in teacher beliefs were more likely to occur within programs where students were presented with a consistent message along with ongoing support in implementing teaching methods consistent with this message. Teacher education faculty will be more effective when they work collaboratively to ensure students are presented with both a comprehensive and a consistent message regarding the type of instruction and management needed to enhance student learning and positive student behavior.

The final two factors listed as negatively affecting beginning teachers' ability to develop effective classroom management skills involve the selection of these teachers. Research suggests that teachers with higher cognitive ability (Ehrenberg & Brewer, 1994, 1995), academic proficiency (Ferguson & Ladd, 1996; Strauss & Vogt, 2001) and those with stronger backgrounds in their subject matter (Blair, 2000; Goldhaber & Brewer, 2000; Kaplan & Owings, 2003) are more successful at creating classrooms characterized by high student achievement. Despite indications that more well-educated students may become more effective teachers, the Education Trust reported that "most of the content on licensing exams is typically found in high school curricula" (Mitchell & Barth, 1999, p. 15) and some states report 100% passing rates on test scores required by teacher education candidates, whereas 24 states have no standards related to academic content (Paige, 2002).

In addition to the low academic skills of some teacher education candidates, the number of very young teachers entering the profession may affect new teachers' ability to effectively manage their classroom. In her study of preservice education, Stewart-Wells (2000) noted, "The greatest predictors of classroom management concerns were age and years of experience. Student teachers who were younger and had one year or less in a classroom environment had greater concerns about developing discipline strategies" (p. 165). Lundeen (2002) found that the young adults who were beginning teachers struggled with their work. She suggested this may be due to the fact that the demands of beginning teaching may not blend well with developmental issues associated with establishing oneself as an emerging, independent adult. Feiman-Nemser (2003) suggested that "Each new teacher's learning agenda is also intimately bound up with the personal struggle to craft a public identity" (p. 26). This task both is influenced by and influences teachers' ability to effectively manage their classroom, and most young beginning teachers find this task of developing a classroom identity a more demanding experience than do beginning teachers with more life experiences.

Both the teacher shortage experienced in many areas of this country and the lack of extensive research to support the validity of such practices will very likely prevent the screening of teachers based on age, experience with youth, and cognitive ability. Nevertheless, those working in teacher education programs must be prepared to provide additional support and assistance to all teachers who struggle during their preservice program, and may want to pay particular attention to candidates who enter as very young adults, have limited experience with children and youth, or have a history of less-than-stellar academic performance. Not all individuals develop mastery at the same rate. If teacher education programs are to maintain high standards, it is imperative that preservice teachers who do not meet these standards not be allowed to enter the profession. Teacher education programs must be prepared to provide these students with extended opportunities to develop and demonstrate all the standards required by a program.

INSERVICE CLASSROOM MANAGEMENT EDUCATION

Brophy (1988) noted that although the individual elements of effective classroom management may by themselves be quite easily mastered, the difficulty arises in implementing these methods within the complex and rapidly changing classroom context. Based on her work with novice middle school teachers, Angelle (2002) reported that "four year preservice programs were not adequately preparing student teachers for the realities of classrooms. Inadequate classroom management preparation left them struggling to survive in the real world of teaching and learning" (p. 1). Therefore, it is not surprising that even in programs in which students receive the content and methods described in the previous two sections, and rate their classroom management education as a strength of their teacher education program, some program graduates state that classroom management is a significant problem during their early years of teaching (Jones, 2005).

Several inservice programs have demonstrated effectiveness in assisting inservice teachers in developing improved skills in classroom management and in bringing about associated improved student learning and behavior. The most well-researched and frequently implemented program has been Carolyn Evertson's Classroom Organization and Management (COMP) program described in the section on preservice instructional methods.

> COMP promotes effective classroom management through teachers' development of an integrated management plan that focuses on planning and implementing effective strategies for room

> arrangements, rules and procedures, student accountability, consequences and intervention strategies for behavior management, and planning and conducting lessons. For each of the above areas teachers engage in (1) assessing current problem areas, (2) examining related educational research, (3) problem-solving through case studies and classroom scenarios, and (4) applying these principles in their own classrooms. (Evertson & Harris, 1995, p. 1)

Evertson and Harris (1999) noted that the COMP program is based on four principles:

> First: effective classroom management means preventing problems rather than handling them after the fact.... Second: management and instruction are integrally related.... Third: students are active participants in the learning environment, and classroom management must take into account student differences.... Fourth: professional collaboration supports changes in teaching practice. (pp. 65–67)

Extensive research indicates students of teachers trained through this program show improved academic performance and on-task behavior (Evertson & Harris, 1995, 1999).

A second inservice classroom management program associated with consistent positive results is Jerome Freiberg's Consistency Management and Cooperative Discipline. This program emphasizes the active involvement of students and the creation of a caring, supportive classroom and school environment. The key components of this program include (a) prevention (collaborative development of classroom rules), (b) caring (activities to ensure that all students feel cared for by their peers and adults in the school), (c) cooperation (students have opportunities to take responsibility and ownership for the classroom and school), (d) organization(students take responsibility for aspects of classroom operation), and (e) community (involvement of families and the community). Implementation of this program has been associated with higher student achievement gains and improved student behavior (Freiberg, 1993; Freiberg, Connell, & Lorentz, 2001; Freiberg, Stein, & Huang, 1995, Freiberg, Prokosch, Treister, & Stein, 1990).

Positive Behavior Support is a third inservice classroom management program with a national focus and solid research evidence. Although this program focuses on schoolwide student management and includes a major component on developing behavior change plans for students experiencing serious and ongoing behavior problems (Dunlap et al., 2000), it also includes a classroom component involving six areas of skill development:

> (a) physical environment (e.g., traffic patterns, seating arrangements, unsupervisable areas), (b) student routines (e.g., transitions, starting/ending work, getting help or materials), (c) teacher routines (e.g., working with assistants and volunteers, taking attendance, dealing with visitors, scheduling), (d) behavior management (e.g., encouraging prosocial behavior, discouraging rule violations, responding to crises), (e) curriculum and materials (e.g., availability, quantity and quality), (f) data management and evaluation (e.g., grading work, individual education plan progress, keeping track of problem behavior). (Sugai, Horner, & Gresham, 2002, p. 324)

Data suggest that implementation of the classroom and schoolwide components of this program are associated with dramatically lower rates of office referrals and higher student test scores (Nelson, 1996; Nelson, Crabtree, Marchand-Martella, & Martella, 1998; Sadler, 2003). Unlike the work of Evertson and Freiberg and their colleagues, most of the data from this approach have either been based on individual student cases or aggregated by schoolwide data rather than examining individual teacher and classroom changes.

A fourth approach with an extensive research base is the mentoring of beginning teachers. Mentoring programs involve beginning teachers in sustained, research-based involvement with veteran teachers who have received training in methods for effective mentoring (Andrews &

Martin, 2003; Evertson & Smithey, 2000; Spencer & Logan, 2003; Wojnowski, Bellamy, & Cooke, 2003). Evertson and Smithey (2000) reported that beginning teachers in their study who had worked with mentors could "more effectively organize and manage instruction at the beginning of the year and establish more workable classroom routines. Also, their students had better behavior and engagement" (p. 294).

Mentoring programs have been shown to reduce attrition rates of beginning teachers (National Association of State Boards of Education, 1998), help teachers demonstrating more skillful classroom management and discipline (Brewster & Railsback, 2001; Evertson & Smithey, 2000), be associated with more skillful teaching (Schaffer, Stringfield, & Wolfe, 1992; Weiss & Weiss, 1999), and lead to higher student achievement scores (Ganser, Marchione, & Fleischmann, 1999).

In addition to sound outcome data associated with the inservice programs described earlier, research supports several key concepts related to implementing inservice education. Several studies (Fuller 1969; Kagan, 1992b; Nemser, 1983) suggest teachers go through three developmental stages. In the beginning stage, teachers are focused on themselves and their survival in the classroom. One would expect the majority of students who have completed a teacher education program to have experienced this stage and, although still involved in aspects of this state to also be moving into the second stage. The second stage involves teachers synthesizing their classroom routines. Kagan (1992b) reported that novice teachers lacked procedures that allowed for a smooth classroom flow, and this led to a focus on classroom control rather than student learning. Kagan noted that "Until such standard procedures are routinized and fairly automated, novices may continue to focus on their own rather than their pupil's behaviors" (p. 145). It is therefore not surprising that many first- and second-year teachers are extremely interested in fine-tuning how they create a positive classroom climate, develop behavioral norms, and develop procedures or routines that help classroom events flow more smoothly. In the third stage, teachers begin to focus on students' needs and how the decisions they make as a teacher may be influencing student learning and behavior. Teachers in this stage frequently express concerns regarding individual student behavior. After their initial time in the classroom, many teachers begin to focus more on why individual students appear unmotivated or consistently violate classroom norms, and these teachers are often intensely interested in methods for working with individual students (Britton, Paine, & Raizen, 1999; Meister & Jenks, 2000; Walbeck, Menlove, Garff, Menlove, & Harris, 2003). Based on their survey returned by 164 teachers, teacher education graduates of a southwestern university listed motivating students as their top concern, with severe behavior problems and classroom management issues as their next highest rated needs (Barrett & Davis, 1995).

In addition to attending to concerns based on teachers' stages of professional development, inservice teacher educators must attend to the fact that issues of classroom management are highly contextual. Classroom management involves teachers knowing their own educational goals and personal strengths, their students' learning styles and needs, and the context in which they work. As a Hawaiian educator wrote:

> Here in Hawaii, one thing classroom management clearly depends on is culture. Packaged approaches like Assertive Discipline and Teacher Effectiveness Training are geared toward students who are different in crucial ways from the Polynesian and Asian American children who comprise the majority of Hawaii's public school students." (Tobin & Johnson, 1994)

A number of studies have examined how lack of understanding and sensitivity to students' culture can negatively affect teachers' ability to assist students in making productive behavior choices at school (Ballenger, 1992; Curran, 2003; Macias, 1987, McCarthy & Benally, 2003: Weinstein, Curran, & Tomlinson-Clarke, 2003). Therefore, inservice programs will be more effective when they assist teachers in understanding and responding sensitively to their students' unique backgrounds, interests, and needs.

Because inservice teachers' classroom management needs differ depending on the context in which they work and their years of teaching experience, all of the inservice programs described earlier incorporate some form of problem-solving or case management approach. Inservice teachers are searching for collegial support and relish the opportunity to examine their own methods and provide ideas and support for their fellow teachers. These needs are most effectively met by inservice experiences that provide a safe, supportive learning community and a focus on problem solving.

DIRECTIONS FOR FUTURE RESEARCH

Many beginning teachers express frustration and concern regarding their skills in the area of classroom management. They frequently comment about the lack of adequate classroom management coursework during their preservice teacher education program, noting that what little information they received was too theoretical, too removed from their full-time field experiences, and often taught by individuals with limited current practical experience. School administrators and educational writers echo concerns regarding the classroom management skills beginning teachers bring to their initial teaching assignment. Perhaps not surprisingly, over one third of new teachers leave the profession by the end of their third year of teaching, and many of these teachers list problems with student behavior as a significant factor influencing their decision to leave the profession.

Several approaches to inservice education in classroom management indicate teachers trained in the methods described in this chapter develop skills associated with higher rates of positive student behavior and higher achievement. Studies also suggest important differences between preservice teachers depending on general components of their teacher education programs (Angelle, 2002; Darling-Hammond, 2002; Darling-Hammond, Chung, & Frelow, 2002; Henke, Chen, & Geis, 2000). At this point, however, relatively little is known regarding the level of classroom management skills, student achievement gains, student behavior, and teacher retention associated with teachers prepared in programs providing the type of preservice classroom management preparation described in this chapter as compared to teachers from programs with limited classroom management preparation. An important next step in classroom management research will be to work with selected colleges and universities with varying types of preservice classroom management programs to track how effective these teachers are on these variables during their first 3 years of teaching.

ACKNOWLEDGMENT

The author thanks Jane McCarthy, University of Nevada, Las Vegas, for her review of an early draft of this chapter.

REFERENCES

Adler, S. (1996). On case method and classroom management. *Action in Teacher Education, 18*(3), 33–43.

Ackley, B., & McEwan, B. (2004, April). *The role of classroom management in pre-service teacher education programs.* Paper presented at the annual meeting of the American Educational Research Association, San Diego, CA.

Andrew, M., & Schwab, R. (1995). Has reform in teacher education influenced teacher performance? An outcome assessment of graduates of eleven teacher education programs. *Action in Education, 17*(3), 43–53.

Andrews, S., & Martin, E. (2003, April). *No teacher left behind: Mentoring and supporting novice teachers.* Paper presented at the Annual Meeting of the Georgia Association of Colleges for Teacher Education, Simons Island, GA.

Angelle, P. (2002, April). *Socialization experiences of beginning teachers in differentially effective schools.* Paper presented at the American Educational Research Association Conference, New Orleans, LA.

Archer, J. (1999). New teachers abandon field at high rate. *Education Week, 18*(27), 1–21.

Ballenger, C. (1992). Because you like us: The language of control. *Harvard Educational Review, 62*, 199–208.

Bandura, A. (1997). *The exercise of control.* New York: Freeman.

Barrett, E., & Davis, S. (1995). Perceptions of beginning teachers' inservice needs in classroom management. *Teacher Education and Practice, 11*, 22–27.

Berliner, D. (1988). Implications of studies on expertise in pedagogy for teacher education and evaluation. In *New directions for teacher assessment* (Proceeding of the 1988 ETS Invitational Conference, pp. 39–68). Princeton, NJ: Educational Testing Service.

Blair, J. (2000, October 25). ETS study links effective teaching methods to test-score gains. *Education Week,* 24–25.

Brewster, C., & Railsback, J. (2001). Supporting beginning teachers: How administrators, teachers, and policymakers can help teachers succeed. Portland, OR: Northwest Regional Educational Laboratory.

Britt, A. (1997). *Perceptions of beginning teachers: Novice teachers reflect upon their beginning experiences.* (ERIC Document Reproduction Service No. ED415218)

Britton, E., Paine, L., & Raizen, S. (1999). *Middle grades mathematics and science teachers' induction in selected countries: Preliminary findings.* Washington, DC: National Center for Improving Science Education.

Britzman, D. (2000). Teacher education in the confusion of our times. *Journal of Teacher Education, 51*, 200–205.

Brock, B., & Grady, M. (1997). *From first-year to first-rate: Principals guiding beginning teachers.* Thousand Oaks, CA: Corwin Press.

Brock, B., & Grady, M. (1996, August). *Beginning teacher induction programs.* Paper presented at the Annual Meeting of the National Council of Professionals in Educational Administration, Corpus Christi, TX.

Brophy, J. (1988). Educating teachers about managing classrooms and students. *Teaching and Teacher Education, 4*, 1–18.

Burstein, N., Kretschmer, D., Smith, C., & Gudoski, P. (1999). Redesigning teacher education as a shared responsibility of schools and universities. *Journal of Teacher Education, 50*, 106–118.

Calderhead, J., & Robson, M. (1991). Images of teaching: Student teachers' early conceptions of classroom practice. *Teaching and Teacher Education, 7*, 1–8.

Charnock, B., & Kiley, M. (1995, April). *Concerns and preferred assistance strategies of beginning and middle and high school teachers.* Paper presented at the Annual Meeting of the American Educational Research Association, San Francisco.

Chester, M., & Beaudin, B. (1996). Efficacy beliefs of newly hired teachers in urban schools. *American Educational Research Journal, 33*, 233–257.

Cochran-Smith, M. (2000). Teacher education at the turn of the century. *Journal of Teacher Education, 51*, 163–165.

Cockrell, K., Mitchell, R., Middleton, J., & Campbell, N. (1999). The Holmes Scholars Network: A study of the Holmes Group initiative for recruitment and retention of minority faculty. *Journal of Teacher Education, 50*, 85–93.

Curran, M. (2003). Linguistic diversity and classroom management. *Theory Into Practice, 42*, 334–341.

Dalton, M., & Zanville, H. (2002). *Student teacher study—2000–2001 cohort.* Salem: Oregon Quality Assurance in Teaching Project.

Darling-Hammond, L. (2000). How teacher education matters. *Journal of Teacher Education, 51*, 166–173.

Darling-Hammond, L. (2002). *Access to quality teaching: An analysis of inequality in California's public schools.* Stanford, CA: Stanford University Press.

Darling-Hammond, L. (2003). Keeping good teachers. *Educational Leadership, 60*(8), 6–13.

Darling-Hammond, L., Chung, R., & Frelow, F. (2002). Variation in teacher preparation: How well do different pathways prepare teachers to teach? *Journal of Teacher Education, 53*, 286–302.

Davis, K. (1999). *A study of beginning teachers' perceptions regarding their teacher preparation programs.* Unpublished master's thesis, University of Minnesota, Minneapolis.

Dunlap, G., Hieneman, M., Knoster, T., Fox, L., Anderson, J., & Albin, R. (2000). Essential elements of inservice training in positive behavior support. *Journal of Positive Behavior Interventions, 2*, 22–32.

Earley, P. (2000). Finding the culprit: Federal policy and teacher education. *Educational Policy, 14*, 25–40.

Ehrenberg, R., & Brewer, D. (1994). Do school and teacher characterisitics mater? Evidence from "High School and Beyond." *Economics of Education Review, 13*, 1–17.

Ehrneberg, R., & Brewer, D. (1995). Did teachers' verbal ability and race matter in the 1960s? "Coleman" revisited. *Economics of Education Review, 14*, 1–21.

Eisenhart, M., Behm, L., & Romagnano, L. (1991). Learning to teach: Developing expertise or rite of passage? *Journal of Education for Teaching, 17*, 51–71.

Emmer, E., & Hickman, J. (1991). Teacher efficacy in classroom management and discipline. *Educational and Psychological Measurement, 51*, 755–765.

Evertson, C., Emmer, E., & Worsham, M. (2003). *Classroom management for elementary teachers* (5th ed.). Boston: Allyn & Bacon.

Evertson, C., & Harris, S. (1995, September). Classroom Organization and management program: Revalidation submissions to the Program Effectiveness Panel (PEP). U.S. Department of Education. Nashville, TN: Peabody Collee, Vanderbilt University. (ERIC Document Reproduction Service No. ED403247)

Evertson, C., & Harris, S. (1999). Support for managing learning-centered classrooms: The classroom organization and management program. In J. Freiberg (Ed.), *Beyond Behaviorism: Changing the classroom management paradigm.* Boston: Allyn & Bacon.

Evertson, C., & Smithey, M. (2000). Mentoring effects on proteges' classroom practice: An experimental field study. *Journal of Educational Research, 93*, 294–305.

Feiman-Nemser, S. (2003). What new teachers need to learn. *Educational Leadership, 60*(18), 25–29.

Ferguson, R., & Ladd, H. (1996). How and why money matters: An analysis of Alabama schools. In H. Ladd (Ed.), *Holding schools accountable: Performance-based reform in education*. Washington, DC: Brookings Institute.

Fideler, E., & Haskelhorn, D. (1999). *Learning the ropes: Urban teacher induction programs and practices in the United States.* Belmont, MA: Recruiting New Teachers.

Florida Office of Economic and Demographic Research. (2000). *Former Florida teacher survey results.* Tallahassee, FL: Office of Economic and Demographic Research.

Freiberg, H. (1993). A school that fosters resilience in inner-city youth. *Journal of Negro Education, 62*, 364–376.

Frieberg, H., Connell, M., & Lorentz, J. (2001). Effects of consistency management on student mathematics achievement in seven Chapter I schools. *Journal of Education for Students Placed at Risk, 6*, 249–270.

Freiberg, H., Prokosch, N., Treister, E., & Stein, T. (1990). Turning around five at-risk elementary schools. *School Effectiveness and School Improvement, 1*, 5–25.

Freiberg, H., Stein, T., & Huang, S. (1995). Effects of classroom management intervention on student achievement in inner-city elementary schools. *Educational Research and Evaluation, 1*, 36–66.

Fuller, F. (1969). Concerns for teachers: A developmental conceptualization. *The American Educational Research Journal, 6*, 207–226.

Ganser, T. (1999, April). *Reconsidering the relevance of Veenman's (1994) meta-analysis of the perceived problems of beginning teachers.* Paper presented at the annual meeting of the American Educational Research Association, Montreal, Canada.

Ganser, T., Marchione, M., & Fleischmann, A. (1999). Baltimore takes mentoring to the next level. In M. Scherer (Ed.), *A better beginning: Supporting and mentoring new teachers* (pp. 69-96). Alexandria, VA: Association for Supervision and Curriculum Development.

Gilberts, G., & Lignugaris-Kraft, B. (1997). Classroom management and instruction competencies for preparing elementary and special education teachers, *Teaching and Teacher Education, 13*, 597–610.

Goldhaber, D., & Brewer, D. (2000). Does teacher certification matter? High school teacher certification status and student achievement. *Educational Evaluation and Policy Analysis, 22*, 129–145.

Good, T., & McCaslin, M. (1992). Teaching effectiveness. In *Encyclopedia of Education Research* (p. 1373–1388). New York: Macmillan.

Goodman, J. (1988). Constructing a practical philosophy of teaching: A study of preservice teachers' professional perspectives. *Teaching and Teacher Education, 4*, 121–137.

Goodwin, D., & Deering, R. (1993). The interactive video approach to preservice teacher training: An analysis of students' perceptions and attitudes. *Teacher Education and Practice, 9*, 11–19.

Graber, K. (1996). Influencing student beliefs: The design of a "high impact" teacher education program. *Teaching and Teacher Education, 12,* 451–466.

Grasmick, N., & Leak, L. (1997). What tomorrow's teachers really need from higher education: A view from the trenches. *Educational Record, 78*(2), 22–29.

Gunstone, R., Slattery, M., Baird, J., & Northfield, J. (1993). A case study of development in preservice science teachers. *Science Education, 77*(6), 47–73.

Halford, J. (1998). Easing the way for new teachers. *Educational Leadership, 55*(5), 33–36.

Henke, R., Chen, X., & Geis, S. (2000). Progress through the teacher pipeline: 1992–93 college graduates and elementary/secondary school teaching as of 1997. Washington, DC: U.S. Department of Education, National Center for Education Statistics.

Hollingsworth, S. (1992). Learning to teach through collaborative conversation: A feminist approach. *American Educational Research Journal, 29*, 160–189.

Herbert, E., & Worthy, T. (2001). Does the first year of teaching have to be a bad one? A case study of success. *Teaching and Teacher Education, 17*, 897–911.

Hoover, L. (1994). Use of telecomputing to support group-oriented inquiry during student teaching. In D. A. Willis, B. Robin, & J. Willis (Eds.), *Technology and Teacher Education Annual, 1994* (pp. 652–656). Charlottesville, VA: Association for the Advancement of Computing in Education.

Houston, R., & Williamson, J. (1993). Perceptions of their preparation by 42 Texas elementary school teachers compared with their responses as student teachers. *Teacher Education and Practice, 8*(2), 27–42.

Hylton, I. (2000). Classroom management skills: Can video-modeling make a difference? Doctoral dissertation, New York University. *Dissertation Abstracts International, 61*(4A), 1362. (UMI No. 9968429)

Ingersoll, R., & Smith, T. (2003). The wrong solution to the teacher shortage. *Educational Leadership, 60*(8), 30–33.

Jacques, K. (2000). Solicitous tenderness: Discipline and responsibility in the classroom. In H. Cooper & R. Hyland (Eds.), *Children's perceptions of learning with trainee teachers* (pp. 166–177). London: Routledge.

Johnson, V. (1994). Student teachers' conceptions of classroom control. *Journal of Educational Research, 88*, 109–118.

Jones, V. (1982). Training teachers to be effective classroom managers. In D. Duke (Ed.), *Helping teachers manage classroom.* Alexandria, VA: Association for Supervision and Curriculum Development.

Jones, V. (1996). Classroom management. In J. Sikula (Ed.), *Handbook of research on teacher education* (2nd ed., pp. 503–521). New York: Macmillan.

Jones, V. (2004). *Preservice teachers' response to their classroom management skill development at the end of their teacher education program and the end of their first year of teaching.* Manuscript in preparation.

Jones, V. (2005) Assessment Plan in *Lewis & Clark College NCATE Review Document.* Portland, OR: Lewis & Clark College.

Jones, V., & Jones, L. (1981). *Responsible classroom discipline.* Boston: Allyn & Bacon.

Jones, V., & Jones, L. (1986). *Comprehensive classroom management: Creating positive learning environments.* Boston: Allyn & Bacon.

Jones, V., & Jones, L. (2004). *Comprehensive classroom management: Creating communities of support and solving problems.* Boston: Allyn & Bacon.

Kagan, D. (1992a). Implications of research on teacher belief. *Educational Psychologist, 27*, 65–90.

Kagan, D. (1992b). Professional growth among preservice and beginning teachers. *Review of Educational Research, 62*, 129–169.

Kaplan, L., & Owings, W. (2003). The politics of teacher quality. *Phi Delta Kappan, 84*, 687–693.

Kowalski, T., Weaver, R., & Henson, K. (1990). *Case studies on teaching.* New York: Longman.

Ladd, K. (2000). A comparison of teacher education programs and graduate's perceptions of experiences. *Dissertation Abstracts International, 61*(12A), 4695, (UMI No. 9998491)

Landau, B. (2001, April). *Teaching classroom management: A stand-alone necessity for preparing new teachers.* Paper presented at the annual meeting of the American Educational Research Association, Seattle, WA.

Lasley, T. (1987). Classroom management. *Educational Forum, 51*, 285–298.

Lasley, T. (1989). A teacher development model for classroom management. *Phi Delta Kappan, 71*(1), 36–39.

Lasley, T. (1994). Teacher technicians: A "new" metaphor for new teachers. *Action in Teacher Education, 16*(1), 11–19.

Lundeen, C. (2002). *The study of beginning teachers' perceived problems with classroom management and adult relationships throughout the first year of teaching.* Unpublished doctoral dissertation, University of North Carolina at Chapel Hill.

Lytle, J. (2000). Teacher education at the millennium: A view from the cafeteria. *Journal of Teacher Education, 51*, 174–179.

Macias, J. (1987). The hidden curriculum of Papago teachers: American Indian strategies for mitigating cultural discontinuity in early school. In G. Spindler & L. Spindler (Eds.), *Interpretive ethnography of education: At home and abroad* (pp. 363–380). Hillsdale, NJ: Lawrence Erlbaum Associates.

Mahlios, M., & Maxson, M. (1995). Capturing preservice teachers' beliefs about schooling, life, and childhood. *Journal of Teacher Education, 46*, 192–198.

McCarthy, J., & Benally, J. (2003). Classroom management in a Navajo middle school. *Theory Into Practice, 42*, 296–307.

McCormack, C. (2001). Investigating the impact of an internship on the classroom management beliefs of preservice teachers. *The Professional Educator, 23*(2), 11–22.

Meister, D., & Jenks, C. (2000). Making the transition from preservice to inservice teaching: Beginning teachers' reflections. *Action in Teacher Education, 23*(3), 1–11.

Meister, D., & Melnick, S. (2003). National new teacher study: Beginning teachers' concerns. *Action in Teacher Education, 24*(4), 87–94.

Merrett, F., & Wheldall, K. (1993). How do teachers learn to manage classroom behavior? A study of teachers' opinions about their initial training with special reference to classroom behavior management. *Educational Studies, 19*(3), 91–107.

Merseth, K. (1996). Cases and case methods in teacher education. In J. Sikula, T. Buttery, & E. Guyton (Eds.), *Handbook of research on teacher education.* New York: Simon & Schuster/Macmillan.

Metzger, M. (2002). Learning to discipline. *Phi Delta Kappan, 88*, 77–84.

Mitchell, R., & Barth, P. (1999). *How teacher licensing tests fall short.* Washington DC: The Education Trust.

Murphy, D., Kauffman, J., & Strang, H. (1987). Using microcomputer simulation to teach classroom management skills to preservice teachers. *Behavior Disorders, 13*, 20–34.

National Association of State Boards of Education. (1998). *The numbers game: Ensuring quantity and quality in the teaching workforce.* Alexandria, VA: Author.

Nelson, J. (1996). Designing schools to meet the needs of students who exhibit disruptive behavior. *Journal of Emotional and Behavioral Disorders, 4*, 147–161.

Nelson, J., Crabtree, M., Marchand-Martella, N., & Martella, R. (1998). Teaching good behavior in the whole school. *Teaching Exceptional Children, 30*(4), 4–9.

Nemser, S. (1983). Learning to teach. In L. S. Shulman & G. Sykes (Eds.), *Handbook of teaching and policy.* New York: Longman.

Olson, L. (2000). Finding and keeping competent teachers. *Education Week, 19*(8), 12–18.

Overbaugh, R. (1995). The efficacy of interactive video for teaching basic techniques of classroom management to pre-service teachers. *Computers in Human Behavior, 11*, 511–527.

Paige, R. (2002). *The secretary's annual report on teacher quality: Meeting the qualified teacher challenge.* Washington, DC: U.S. Department of Education.

Pigge, F., & Marso, R. (1997). A seven year longitudinal multi-factor assessment of teaching concerns development through preparation and early years of teaching. *Teaching and Teacher Education, 13*, 225– 235.

Pilarski, M. (1994). Student teachers: Underprepared for classroom management? *Teaching Education, 6*, 77–80.

Pipho, C. (2000). A new reform model for teachers and teaching. *Phi Delta Kappan, 81*, 421–423.

Ralph, E., Kesten, C., Lang, H., & Smith, D. (1998). Hiring new teachers: What do school districts look for? *Journal of Teacher Education, 49*, 47–56.

Randolph, C., & Evertson, C. (1992, April). *Enhancing problem-solving in preservice teachers' approaches to classroom management using video technology.* Paper presented at the Annual Meeting of the American Educational research Association, San Francisco.

Randolph, C., & Evertson, C. (1994). Images of management for learner-centered classrooms. *Action in Teacher Education, 16*(1), 55–63.

Reilly, J. (2002). *Differentiating the concept of teacher efficacy for academic achievement, classroom management and discipline and enhancement of social relations.* Doctoral dissertation, Fordham University, *Dissertation Abstracts International, 63*(O1A), 147. (UMI No. 3040402)

Rigden, D. (1997). What teachers think of teacher education. *Techniques: Making Education and Career Connections, 72*(3), 78.

Ross, J. (1998). The antecedents and consequences of teacher efficacy. In J. Brophy (Ed.), *Advances in research on teaching: Vol. 7, Expectations in the classroom* (pp. 49–73). Greenwich, CT: JAI Press.

Rubin, J. (1991). *Increasing classroom management skills through a training module for student teachers.* Unpublished doctoral dissertation, Nova University, North Miami, FL. (ERIC Document Reproduction Service No. ED335348)

Sadler, C. (2003). *Tigard-Tualatin School District 23J EBS, EBIS, FSTS and Project Circuits: A summary of progress 2001–2003.* Tigard, OR: Tigard-Tualatin School District.

Sariscsany, M., & Pettigrew, F. (1997). Effectiveness of interactive video instruction on teacher's classroom management declarative knowledge. *Journal of Teaching in Physical Education, 16*, 229–240.

Scales, P. (1994). Strengthening middle grade teacher preparation programs. *Middle School Journal, 26*(1), 59–65.

Schaffer, E., Stringfield, S., & Wolfe, D. (1992). An innovative beginning teacher induction program: A two-year analysis of classroom interactions. *Journal of Teacher Education, 43*, 181–192.

Schlagal, B., Trathen, W., & Blanton, W. (1996). Structuring telecommuications to create instructional conversations about student teaching. *Journal of Teacher Education, 47*, 175–183.

Sherman, L. (2003). Stemming the tide. *Today's OEA, 78*(3), 7–15.

Shulman, J. (Ed.). (1992). *Case methods in teacher education.* New York: Teachers College Press.

Silverman, R., Welty, M., & Lyon, S. (1992). *Case studies in teacher problem solving.* New York: McGraw-Hill.

Singh, A., Doyle, C., Rose, A., & Kennedy, W. (1997). Reflective internship and the phobia of classroom management. *Australian Journal of Education, 41*, 105–118.

Soodak, L., & Podell, D. (1998). Teacher efficacy and the vulnerability of the difficult-to-teach student. In J. Brophy (Ed.), *Advances in research on teaching: Vol. 7, Expectations in the classroom* (pp. 75–109). Greenwich, CT: JAI Press.

Spencer, S., & Logan, K. (2003). Bridging the gap: A school based staff development model that bridges the gap from research to practice. *Teacher Education and Special Education, 26*(1), 51–61.

Spring, J. (2000). *American education.* Boston: McGraw-Hill.

Steed, D. (2001). *A comparison of first year and veteran teacher responses to a questionnaire regarding classroom safety.* Unpublished master's thesis, Mississippi State University.

Stewart-Wells, G. (2000). *An investigation of student teacher and teacher educator perceptions of their teacher education programs and the role classroom management plays or should play in preservice education.* Doctoral dissertation, *The Claretmont Graduate University, 61*(O2A), 574.

Stoiber, K. (1991). The effect of technical and reflective preservice instruction on pedagogical reasoning and problem solving. *Journal of Teacher Education, 42*, 131–139.

Strauss, R., & Vogt, W. (2001, March). *It's what you know, not how you learned to teach it: Evidence from a study of the effects of knowledge and pedagogy on student achievement.* Paper presented at the annual meeting of American Educational Finance Association, Cincinnati, OH.

Stroot, S., Fowlker, J., Langholz, S., Stedman, P., Steffer, L., & Valtman, A. (1999). Impact of a collaborative peer assistance and review model on entry-year teachers in a large urban school setting. *Journal of Teacher Education, 50,* 27–41.

Sugai, G., Horner, R., & Gresham, F. (2002). Behaviorally effective school environments. In M. Shinn, G. Stoner, & H. Walker (Eds.), *Interventions for academic and behavior problems: Preventive and remedial approaches* (pp. 315–350). Silver Springs, MD: National Association of School Psychologists.

Tobin J., & Johnson, R. (1994). A multicultural, multivocal, multimedia approach to teaching classroom management and preservice teachers. *Teaching Education, 6,* 113–122.

U.S. Department of Education. (2001). *Twenty-five years of educating children with disabilities: The good news and the work ahead.* Washington, DC: American Youth Forum and Center on Education Policy.

Valli, L. (1995). The dilemma of race: Learning to be color blind and color conscious. *The Journal of Teacher Education, 46,* 120–129.

Walbeck, D., Menlove, R., Garff, T., Menlove, S., & Harris, S. (2003). What preservice and first year teachers need to know to survive and thrive. *Rural Survival: Proceedings of the Annual Conference of the American Council on Rural Special Education,* Salt Lake City, UT (ERIC Document Reproduction Service No. ED476123).

Wasley, P. (1999). Teaching and worth celebrating. *Educational Leadership, 56*(8), 8–13.

Weinstein, C. (1990). Prospective elementary teachers' beliefs about teaching: Implications for teacher education. *Teaching and Teacher Education, 6*, 279–290.

Weinstein, C. (1998). "I want to be nice, but I have to be mean": Exploring prospective teachers' conceptions of caring and order. *Teaching and Teacher Education, 14,* 153–163.

Weinstein, C., Curran, M., & Tomlinson-Clarke, S. (2003). Culturally responsive classroom management: Awareness into action. *Theory Into Practice, 42*(4), 269–277.

Weinstein, C., Tomlinson-Clarke, S., & Curran, M. (2004). Toward a conception of culturally responsive classroom management. *Journal of Teacher Education, 55*, 25–38.

Weinstein, C., Woolfolk, A., Dittmeier, L., & Shanker, U. (1994). Protector or prison guard? Using metaphors and media to explore student teachers' thinking about classroom management. *Action in Teacher Education, 16*(1), 41–54.

Weiss, E., & Weiss, S. (1999). *Beginning teacher induction.* Washington, DC: ERIC Clearinghouse on Teacher and Teacher Education. (ERIC Document Reproduction Service No. ED436487).

Wethington, S. (1991). *A theoretical professional development model tested with video tape and print materials.* Unpublished doctoral dissertation, University of Houston.

White, C. (1995). Making classroom management approaches in teacher education relevant. *Teacher Education and Practice, 11*, 15–21.

Whitney, L., Golez, F., Nagel, G., & Nieto, C. (2002). Listening to voices of practicing teachers to examine the effectiveness of a teacher education program. *Action in Teacher Education, 23*(4), 69–76.

Wideen, M., Mayer-Smith, J., & Moon, B. (1998). A critical analysis of the research on learning to teach: Making the case for an ecological perspective on inquiry. *Review of Educational Research, 68*, 130–178.

Winitzky, N., & Arends, R. (1991). Translating research into practice: The effects of various forms of training and clinical experience on preservice students' knowledge, skill, and reflectiveness. *Journal of Teacher Education, 42*, 52–65.

Wojnowski, B., Bellamy, M., & Cooke, S. (2003) A review of literature on mentoring and induction of beginning teachers with an emphasis on the retention and renewal of science teachers. *Issues in Science Education* (SE 067109).

Woolfolk, A., & Hoy, W. (1990). Prospective teachers' sense of efficacy and their beliefs about control. *Journal of Educational Psychology, 82*, 81–91.

Yan, W., Anderson, M., & Nelson, J. (1994). Facilitating reflective thinking in student teachers through electronic mail. In D. A. Willis, B. Robin, & J. Willis (Eds.), *Technology and Teacher Education Annual, 1994* (pp. 652–656). Charlottesville, VA: Association for the Advancement of Computing in Education.

Zuckerman, J. (2000). Student science teachers' accounts of a well-remembered event about classroom management. *Journal of Science Teacher Education, 11*, 243–250.

34

The Place of Classroom Management and Standards in Teacher Education

Laura M. Stough
Texas A&M University

INTRODUCTION

The value of classroom management knowledge for teachers has been consistently supported through the research literature (Brophy & Evertson, 1976; Shinn, Walker, & Stoner, 2002; Wang, Haertel, & Walberg, 1993) and management strategies have been referred to as "the most valuable skills set a teacher can have" (Landau, 2001, p. 4). A number of studies have found that classroom management is a primary area in which beginning teachers feel underprepared (Halford, 1998; Houston & Williamson, 1993; Pigge & Marso, 1997; Veenman, 1984). Specifically, according to a survey of 103 recent graduates of an accredited teacher preparation program, teachers most desire additional training on how to motivate students and address chronic and severe misbehaviors, and pragmatic classroom management ideas (Barrett & Davis, 1995). Experienced teachers express similar dissatisfaction with their preparation in this area: A Merrett and Wheldall (1993) survey of 176 experienced teachers found that 72% felt that their preparation in the area of classroom management was inadequate. School administrators also view classroom management strategies as an essential teacher skill (Ralph, Kesten, Lang, & Smith, 1998) and often report that beginning teachers display limitations in the area of classroom management. Jones (2005), in this volume, provides a comprehensive overview of research of the perceptions of beginning and experienced teachers, as well as that of administrators, on the need for increased teacher preparation in the area of classroom management.

Although there is a solid extant research base on the perceptions of teachers about their training (or lack thereof) in classroom management, these studies are retrospective in nature and thus dependent on teacher's memories about these programs. Few studies have directly examined the content of teacher preparation programs. In addition, as studies have demonstrated that teachers' beliefs and perceptions change over time as a result of their experiences in the classroom (Martin & Shoho, 2000; Pigge & Marso, 1997), issues identified as critical by teachers during their first years of teaching may become either less or more salient as time passes. Despite these limitations, novice and experienced teachers consistently report that their training in classroom management was inadequate or impractical, and that they require further preparation in this area.

THE PLACE OF CLASSROOM MANAGEMENT IN TEACHER PREPARATION PROGRAMS

Direct evaluations of teacher education programs and of the extent to which classroom management content is, in fact, part of these programs substantiate the reported perceptions of teachers and administrators. The few studies of the presence of classroom management content in teacher preparation programs have spanned across 20 years yet concur in their reports of the scarcity of classroom management content in teacher training programs. In an early study, Rickman and Hollowell (1981) suggested that the lack of classroom management content in teacher training programs was the subsequent cause of problems that student teachers experienced in their placements. In a 1989 survey, over 80% of 1,388 teachers indicated that their university program did not offer an undergraduate course that focused on classroom management strategies at all (Clapp, 1989). Similarly, Jones (1989) suggested that most teachers during the 1980s did not receive systematic training in any model of classroom discipline.

Wesley and Vocke (1992) have conducted the most direct evaluation of classroom management content in teacher preparation. These researchers examined the catalogs of 111 universities offering teacher preparation programs and then more closely analyzed the content of secondary programs. After searching for courses containing titles with the words *discipline*, *control*, *behavior*, or *management*, they found that only 36.9% of the programs offered a separate course that specifically focused on classroom management techniques (Wesley & Vocke, 1992). In addition, in an in-depth examination of 27 teacher preparation programs at the secondary level, they found that only 16% of these programs offered classroom management as a separate course. Even more striking, when classroom management content was covered within another course, rather than as a stand-alone course, this content was allotted merely an average of 13% of the total course time. It should be noted that in 1992, when the Wesley and Vocke study was completed, coursework in pedagogy typically was more extensive than is the case currently.

In another study on the existence of content in classroom management in teacher preparation programs, Blum (1994) surveyed the 467 existing colleges and universities that were then accredited by the National Council for the Accreditation of Teacher Education (NCATE). Results received from 266 of these institutions found that, although 51% of these institutions offered a specific course on classroom management and discipline at the undergraduate level, only 43% of preservice teachers at these institutions were required to take such a course. Although Blum reports that a higher number of universities included classroom management content than did Wesley and Vocke, this number should be interpreted with caution, as these are data were reported by the teacher preparation programs themselves.

Christiansen (1996) examined the self-study reports of 42 teacher preparation programs that had submitted their programs for accreditation by NCATE. In an examination of the knowledge bases that these programs reported they used to prepare their teachers, Christiansen tabulated 83 different knowledge-based instructional models described by these programs. Despite the diversity of these models, not one of these programs identified "classroom management," "discipline," or "behavior," as a knowledge base that they included as part of their training, although one institution did include "Glasser Circle" as a model. Christiansen notes in her summary that "one must conclude there are many different ways to design teacher education programs based on a selected knowledge-research base" (p. 49); however, the lack of identification of classroom management as a primary research base is both noteworthy and puzzling.

Banks (2003) conducted a survey of faculty who taught classroom management at 52 Texas universities. She found that the most commonly used theoretical models in these programs were (a) Glasser (84%), (b) Canter (82%), (c) Dreikurs (58%), (d) neo-Skinnerian (57%), and (e) Curwin/Mendler (51%), followed by eight other models. These rankings of models varied depending on whether the faculty member responding taught primary or secondary teacher education courses. In addition, faculty members reported using an incredible variety of 45 different textbooks to teach their classes. Glasser's books, however, were reported as chosen more often by those training secondary-level teachers.

Landau (2001) observed, after an informal examination of the Web sites of 20 teacher education programs, that only one of these programs included a course specifically titled "Classroom Management" as part of its required coursework for preservice teachers. Somewhat humorously, Landau remarked, "I began to draw the conclusion that the term 'Classroom Management' is coded or couched in euphemisms" (p. 5). In a similar attempt to locate classroom management in the top 50 schools of education rated by the 2004 *U.S. News and World Report*, I also found the task to be baffling (Stough, Williams-Diehm, & Montague, 2004). Required coursework included titles such as "Creating Community in the Classroom," "Curriculum and Management," and "Classroom Discourse and Interaction" that *might* contain classroom management content but would necessitate a translation by the course instructor in order to be certain. In 22 of these programs I could find no allusion to a course in classroom management whatsoever.[1]

Note that most of the preceeding studies searched for the existence of an entire course devoted to classroom management. Emmer and Stough (2001) similarly have implied that when classroom management content is part of a teacher training program, it is taught as a stand-alone course. In actuality, researchers have not systematically examined whether other methods of teaching classroom management content are used in teacher preparation programs. Landau's (2001) review suggested that classroom management may be taught as a seminar or as content embedded within other courses. Kher, Lacina-Gifford, and Yandell (2000) stated that classroom management "is usually addressed as a small part of Educational Psychology or peripherally as part of discipline techniques in Child Development courses" (p. 2), but the extent to which this embedded model is used to teach the content is not given. It may be that given the increase in the requirement of field-based experiences, as well as the movement to decrease the amount of coursework required in teacher preparation, the content of classroom management has become diffused and less likely to be delivered in a stand-alone course. Again, further direct examination of teacher preparation programs is needed to substantiate these suppositions.

Who Teaches Classroom Management Courses?

Landau (2001) noted that when classroom management and discipline coursework is included in teacher preparation programs, it is often offered through departments of special education. Such a distinction is logical as, when one works with students with special educational needs, mastery of classroom management skills becomes particularly essential. This is not to imply, however, that general education teachers do not need a high level of training in classroom management. The movement to include more special education students in regular education classrooms has increased the number of children who may not be prepared to meet the behavioral expectations of the general education classroom (Bender & Mathes, 1995). Even

---

[1] As a side note, and in acknowledgement of participatory guilt in using obscure titles for coursework, I confess that for several years my own course was called "Dynamics and Management in Multicultural/Inclusionary Learning Environments." It is now much more straightforwardly titled "Classroom Management and Behavioral Interventions."

when teachers do receive adequate preparation in classroom management, it has been noted that the inclusion of children with emotional or behavioral disorders in the general education classroom will tax the most competent of classroom teachers (Kauffman, Lloyd, Baker, & Riedel, 1995).

Several researchers (e.g., Kilgore & Griffin, 1998; Gilberts & Lignugaris-Kraft, 1997) affirm that the emphasis of preservice preparation programs for special educators is different than that of general educators. They suggest that special education programs tend to prepare teachers in how to address individual behavioral needs and small-group management. In contrast, they view general education programs as emphasizing subject matter while underpreparing students in the domains of classroom management and discipline. Again, as an area of expertise for special educators may be in the instruction of students with behavioral disorders, it is reasonable that special education coursework stress content on classroom behavior. However, as pointed out by Landau (2001) and given the author's own knowledge of the field of special education teacher preparation, it is often the case that these courses focus on individual behavior analysis and interventions, rather than a more global approach to classroom management and the prevention of problem behaviors.

A final area in which we might expect to see training in classroom management is as part of inservice training for experienced teachers. Barrett and Davis (1995) found in their survey of classroom teacher inservice needs that teachers ranked dealing with problem behaviors and classroom management as two of their top three inservice needs. Popular inservice training programs include Canter's Assertive Discipline program, Harry Wong's The First Days of School, and Sprick's CHAMPs program. However, there has been little to no research on the effectiveness of these programs and the extent to which they influence teacher behavior nor on their effects on teacher behavior on a long-term basis.

TEXTBOOKS ON CLASSROOM MANAGEMENT

Another source of information about how classroom management is incorporated into teacher preparation programs is through inspection of current textbooks that are on the market. Stengel and Tom (1996) suggested that the presence of classroom management and discipline as primary content areas is consistent across methods textbooks. Hoy's (2000) review of content in educational psychology textbooks published since 1983 listed classroom management content as a common topic in teacher preparation texts. Emmer and Stough (2001) similarly observed that whereas 20 to 30 years ago little information about classroom management could be found in educational psychology textbooks, current texts usually contain a chapter or two about classroom management.

Textbooks that have classroom management as their primary focus address the topic with some variation. A few texts use different models of classroom management as an organizing feature, such as Charles' (2002) *Building Classroom Discipline*. Other textbooks such as Emmer, Evertson, and Worsham's (2003) *Classroom Management for Secondary Teachers* or Jones and Jones' (2004) *Comprehensive Classroom Management* focus on a functional approach to management, in which proactive and procedural knowledge, such as how to write rules or organize a classroom, is stressed. A few textbooks take a behavioral approach, such as Alberto and Troutman's (2006) *Applied Behavior Analysis for Teachers*, and detail how to implement individual behavioral interventions, rather than presenting an overview of classroom management. In the author's own review of 23 different classroom management textbooks designed for use in teacher preparation programs, most did not address educational concerns such as including students with disabilities, cultural diversity, bullying, or school violence to any significant degree. Admittedly, these topics do not yet have as extensive a research base as does more established research in classroom management. However, given the changes in student demographics in the United States over the last decade and the consistent concern the public expresses about school safety (Rose & Gallup, 2004), authors should consider giving more weight to these topics in their classroom management textbooks.

Despite the apparent surfeit of classroom management textbooks, there is evidence that faculty would like more information in this area. Scales (1994) surveyed 175 college and university faculty involved in teacher preparation for middle schools. Faculty rated the extent to which they believed they needed additional resources in each of 11 topic areas, including classroom management. Fifty-nine percent of these faculty members reported that new resources, including texts, in the area of classroom management were "very much needed" and ranked classroom management as the third most important area in which they desired more resources. Classroom management textbooks and resources that these faculty reported as currently using included (a) *Control Theory and Quality Schools* by William Glasser, (b) *Positive Discipline: A Pocketful of Ideas* by William Purkey, (c) *Assertive Discipline for Parents* by Lee Canter, (d) *Classroom Management for Elementary Teachers* by Carolyn Evertson and Ed Emmer, and (e) *Discipline with Dignity* by Richard Curwin and Allen Mendler. However, although faculty reported that they needed additional resources in the area classroom management, Scales pointed out that in actuality "this is not because few resources exist: Our respondents named 58 resources" (1994, p. 64), implying that even though much has been written about classroom management and discipline, the field is not satiated.

The Design of Classroom Management Courses

Despite the value with which teachers hold it, training in classroom management has never been a requirement of teacher preparation programs to the same degree as has, for example, coursework in reading instruction. It is also not clear what is the best way to teach classroom management content to future teachers. Jones (1996) pointed out that "little work has been done to determine the most effective methods of educating teachers in classroom management" (p. 515). Teacher preparation programs may have inadvertently contributed to the concerns and frustrations expressed by teachers and administrators in the area of classroom management by failing to provide pertinent coursework and relevant experiences for preservice teachers.

In addition, most teacher education programs in U.S. colleges and universities appear to be doing little to prepare teachers to cope with the issue of school violence (Nims & Wilson, 1998). It is suggested that maladaptive behaviors are rooted, in part, in early aggressive behaviors occurring in classrooms that are poorly managed (Greer-Chase, Rhodes, & Kellam, 2002). Thus, a lack of training in classroom management may have an impact that transcends that of the immediate classroom climate.

Given that classroom management is essential to include in the preparation of teachers, that teachers and administrators want more of it, and that the public believes that student behavior is one of the most important issues confronting education, why are teacher preparation programs as a whole doing such a spotty job of addressing the topic? This disjunction might be illuminated if current educational standards for teacher preparation and assessment are examined more closely.

STANDARDS AND CLASSROOM MANAGEMENT CONTENT

Education in the United States has been undeniably shaped by a standards-based reform, which shows no sign of losing momentum. In fact, Roth (1996) stated, "The standards based movement is so pervasive and powerful that it appropriately may be termed the *Era of Standards*" (p. 242).

Although much of the educational dialogue has focused on student outcomes, the movement also has affected the various standards that pertain to teacher quality and preparation.

The qualifications of teachers are given an assortment of labels. The terms *accreditation*, *certification*, and *licensing* are often used interchangeably, but actually indicate different levels of teacher preparation (Oakes, 1999; Roth, 1996). Each of these levels of preparation has its own rubric of standards that indicate teacher qualifications. Some states issue "licenses" whereas others issue what they term "certificates" and this mixing of terminology adds to the confusion. To clarify, the state-based process by which teachers are legally approved for a teaching position is properly described as *licensing*. Licensing normally occurs on the state level and suggests that a teacher possesses a minimal level of competence needed to practice in that state. State licensing does not usually make a distinction between experienced teachers and those who demonstrate beginning or entry level skills in teaching, and states may legally issue probationary or emergency licenses to individuals who have not received teacher training of any type. In contrast, the term *certification*, when used appropriately, denotes that an individual teacher has met predetermined standards that have been recognized by a professional organization. Certification can be described as a type of professional peer approbation, such as Board certification among medical doctors (Oakes, 1999). *Accreditation* is given to a college, university, or other training program that has been reviewed and judged qualified to grant teacher certification, again given the standards of a professional organization that evaluates training programs. Finally, teacher *appraisal* is the process by which a local education agency, usually the school district, assesses teacher performance, most typically through the direct observation of teaching performance. Standards on the local level are often derived or used wholesale from a state-developed teacher appraisal system; however, the method and extent to which these appraisals are used to evaluate teachers widely varies from state to state and even among school districts within the same state.

The extent to which classroom management standards are part of an accreditation, licensing, or certification process is variable. In the following section, the role of classroom management at these different levels of standards is examined.

Accreditation

As mentioned earlier, accreditation is a formal recognition that an educational program of work receives from a professional body. NCATE is the largest accreditation body for programs of teacher preparation and consists of a coalition of 33 national education associations (NCATE, 2005a) that developed the standards that NCATE uses to evaluate teacher preparation programs. Most of the association members of NCATE include professional education bodies, such as the National Education Association and the American Association for Colleges for Teacher Education (AACTE), but also include 19 different professional specialty associations as well, such as the Council for Exceptional Children and the National Council of Teachers of Mathematics.

Colleges and other institutions that have teacher training programs are eligible for NCATE accreditation. Participation in the NCATE accreditation process is voluntary and requires that the college or institution develop a portfolio of its program, followed by a weeklong site visit by reviewers from NCATE's professional specialty associations, to determine the fidelity of the program. Depending on the program, these standards are differentially selected so that they correspond to the teacher preparation program being reviewed. For example, an early childhood program would be reviewed by NCATE using standards from the National Association for the Education of Young Children, whereas a mathematics program would use standards developed by the National Council of Teachers of Mathematics. The NCATE standards were revised in 1987 so that teacher education programs were required to focus on teacher knowledge about teaching and learning (Hoy, 2000) and the number of teacher preparation programs that apply for accreditation has steadily increased since the last decade. As of 2005, NCATE recorded that it had accredited teacher preparation programs in 602 colleges of education (2005a) in the United States.

A second federally recognized accreditation body for teacher education is the Teacher Education Accreditation Council (TEAC). TEAC was created in 1997 and, as is NCATE, is a nonprofit organization that accredits teacher education programs. TEAC is composed of 19 affiliate organizations that are nonvoting members of the organization, most of which are state associations that represent independent colleges and universities (TEAC, 2005). At present, only 13 programs have been accredited by TEAC, although 91 programs have satisfied TEAC's eligibility requirements and are identified by TEAC as having "candidate status" (TEAC, 2005). For standards, TEAC uses a program's evidence for quality principles including (a) evidence of candidate learning, (b) evidence that the assessment of candidate learning is valid, and (c) evidence of the program's continuous improvement and quality control. Unlike NCATE, TEAC standards are determined by the program itself, with the constraint that the program standards meet TEAC's overall principles.

Before 1990, there was little coordination between the approval processes that states used to accredit teacher preparation programs and accreditation by professional organizations: Colleges and universities thus had to meet the accreditation demands of two entirely separate systems. At present, NCATE has partnerships with 49 states as well as the districts of Columbia and Puerto Rico and conducts joint reviews of colleges of education (NCATE, 2005a). These partnerships integrate state and national professional teacher preparation standards and thus reduce the expense and duplication of effort that occur when states and NCATE conduct two separate reviews of a particular preparation program (NCATE, 2005a). These partnerships take several forms: 24 states have their programs reviewed by professional associations whose standards have been adopted by NCATE, whereas 25 states and the District of Columbia and Puerto Rico use state standards that have been aligned with NCATE standards. Despite this apparent high level of collaboration with NCATE on the national level, most states do not require that their schools of education be accredited. Darling-Hammond and Rustique-Forrester (1997) pointed out that "states routinely approve all of their teacher education programs, including those that lack qualified faculty and are out of touch with new knowledge about teaching" (1997, p.1).

The specific standards that NCATE uses to accredit teacher preparation programs are performance based and focus on (1) candidate knowledge, skills, and dispositions; (2) assessment system and unit evaluation; (3) field experiences and clinical practice; (4) diversity; (5) faculty qualifications, performance, and development; and (6) unit governance and resources. Standard 1: Candidate Knowledge, Skills and Dispositions, includes the content knowledge, pedagogical content knowledge, and dispositions required of all teacher candidates, and also delineates how teachers should be able to assess and analyze student learning. It is under Standard 1 that specific standards for classroom management would most likely be mentioned. However, classroom management is referred to only indirectly as follows: "Teacher candidates . . . are able to create learning environments encouraging positive social interaction, active engagement in learning, and self-motivation" (NCATE, 2002, p. 18). In fact, neither NCATE nor TEAC directly refers to classroom management as a required standard for the teacher preparation programs that they accredit.

Specialty Area Standards. NCATE has a Special Areas Studies Board (SASB) that approves program standards that have been developed in 20 program areas (NCATE, 2005b). These include content area standards, developed by the International Reading Association and the National Council of Teachers of Mathematics, as well as those developed by professional organizations such as the Council for Exceptional Children and the National Association of

School Psychologists. Some states require that teacher education institutions address the standards of a specialty area program as part of the NCATE accreditation process. These standards are then incorporated into the NCATE accreditation review process along with the Core Standards. Standards that are part of the content areas focus almost entirely on standards for achievement in the content area and do not address classroom management practices to any degree.

However, of interest are the standards used by the Council for Exceptional Children (CEC, 2003). Of all of the NCATE program standards, the CEC standards include classroom management and discipline to the greatest degree, including those included as part of the NCATE Core Standards. No other standards reviewed as part of the preparation for this chapter included a focus on classroom management and discipline to a similar extent. These standards, entitled "What Every Special Educator Should Know," include a list of 10 Standard Domain Areas that are aligned with the Interstate New Teacher Assessment and Support Consortium (INTASC) Standards. Standard 5: Learning Environments and Social Interactions, includes the classroom management procedures and knowledge that special educators should know. The descriptions under this standard relating to classroom management consist of three types: (1) classroom management strategies, (2) behavioral interventions that are typically used for more severe behavioral interventions, and (3) techniques to teach social skills. Although it may be argued that these are all skills inherent in good classroom management practices, the latter two standards, behavioral interventions and social skills, are areas that are not addressed in standards from any other source.

Interstate New Teacher Assessment and Support Consortium (INTASC)

INTASC is a consortium of 34 state education agencies and 8 professional educational organizations that examine the preparation and licensing of teachers. INTASC is one of several programs sponsored by the Council of Chief State School Officers (CCSSO, 2004). INTASC developed model core standards for beginning teachers in 1992. In 1994, NCATE aligned its unit and program standards with the principles of the Interstate New Teacher Assessment and Support Consortium (INTASC) (Darling-Hammond & Rustique-Forrester, 1999). These INTASC standards defined the knowledge and skills required of beginning teachers. Although these standards are designed for use in licensing beginning teachers, they were designed also to be compatible with the standards used by the National Board of Professional Teaching Standards (NBPTS) in certifying experienced teachers.

At present, INTASC has developed standards in the following areas: arts education, elementary education, English language arts, foreign languages, math, science, social studies, and special education. All of these areas plainly focus exclusively on content knowledge and pedagogical content knowledge. INTASC also has developed what it refers to as "core standards" that outline the knowledge, disposition, and performances expected of all beginning teachers, regardless of their area of expertise. These core standards consist of 10 principles that detail the "knowledge, skills and dispositions that every teacher should display." Principle 5 of the INTASC principles most directly overlaps with content in classroom management. This principle reads, "The teacher uses an understanding of individual and group motivation and behavior to create a learning environment that encourages positive social interaction, active engagement in learning, and self-motivation." The corresponding knowledge, skills, and performance areas detail concepts commonly considered a part of classroom management knowledge and skills, including how to structure group work, promote intrinsic motivation, and create a "smoothly functioning learning community." Two of the 14 details under Principle 5 are clearly classroom management standards: Under the knowledge detail, the standard "The teacher understands the principles of effective classroom management and can use a range of strategies to promote positive relationships, cooperation, and purposeful learning in the classroom" is most clearly one that emphasizes classroom management. The second performance detail "The teacher organizes, allocates, and manages the resources of time, space, activities, and attention to provide active and equitable engagement of students in productive tasks," is also usually considered essential classroom management knowledge.

The CCSSO is sponsoring a second initiative through INTASC to establish the Center for Improving Teacher Quality (CTQ). The center has the mission to develop models for improving teacher preparation, licensing, and the professional development of both general and special educators. Its May 2001 document, "Model Standards for Licensing General and Special Education Teachers of Students with Disabilities: A Resource for State Dialog," holds the premise that all teachers must have knowledge and skills drawn from the field of special education (CCSSO, 2001). These standards elaborate on the previously established INTASC standards by including knowledge and skills that relate to students with special educational needs. This draft document adds eight additional aspect statements to INTASC's Standard 5 that emphasize specialized management issues and tasks that all teachers of students with disabilities should know. Most specifically, Standard 5.05 states that all teachers should "tailor classroom management and grouping to individual needs using constructive behavior management strategies, a variety of grouping options, and positive behavioral support strategies." In addition, the standard for special education teachers stresses the need for teachers to be able to conduct functional behavioral assessments, implement behavioral support plans, and know how to use behavioral intervention plans for students with challenging behaviors. Finally, the standard details that special education teachers should support students with disabilities in taking an active role in their IEP planning process. Plainly, these standards emphasize classroom management and student behavior to a greater degree than do the general INTASC standards. However, the question should be raised of whether these are management standards that all teachers, whether or not they work with students with special needs, should master.

INTASC has recently taken the position that the state's process for approving teacher preparation should be designed so that preparation programs are aligned with teacher licensing standards. From 2000 to 2002, INTASC coordinated a collaborative effort of eight states to draft model standards that would be compatible with the INTASC core standards with the objective of using these standards for the state's review of teacher preparation programs (CCSSO, 2004). These standards were slated to be publicized by the fall of 2003 but apparently are still in the final stages of editing.

National Board for Professional Teaching Standards

The National Board for Professional Teaching Standards (NBPTS) sets professional-caliber standards for experienced teachers and administers certification to recognize educators who demonstrate a high level of teaching competence (NBPTS, 2004a). The NBPTS was founded in 1987, in part to assess and certify teachers who met rigorous standards for what accomplished teachers should know. NBPTS certification is voluntary and yet rigorous. Candidate teachers must have at least 3 years of teaching experience. Teachers submit a teaching portfolio that includes videotapes of classroom teaching, a student work sample, and a written commentary from the teacher that describes, analyzes, and represents reflections on the teacher's instruction. Over 40,000 teachers across the United States have earned NBPTS certification to date and the number is predicted to grow exponentially (NBPTS, 2005). Several national education organizations endorse National Board certification and some states allow reciprocal licensing of teachers who hold NBPTS certification. Other states base their decision to license teachers who hold a NBPTS from another state primarily on the validity of the NBPTS certificate (NASDTEC, 2002).

The NBPTS uses five propositions that define teaching effectiveness: (1) Teachers are committed to students and their learning, (2) Teachers know the subject they teach and how to teach those subjects to students, (3) Teachers are responsible for managing and monitoring students learning, (4) Teachers think systematically about their practice and learn from experience, and (5) Teachers are members of learning communities (NBPTS, 2004a). Of these propositions, Proposition 3 most clearly intersects with classroom management and includes the description "Accomplished teachers have developed systems for overseeing their classrooms so that students and teacher alike can focus on learning, not on controlling disruptive behavior." Other than this statement, the core NBPTS propositions and their descriptions do not refer to classroom management directly. However, the standards detailed within specific subjects or childhood age groups do address management to a greater degree. For example, Standard III in the Middle Childhood Generalist Standards (2004b) is entitled "Learning Environment" and details "Accomplished teachers establish a caring, inclusive, stimulating, and safe school community where students can take intellectual risks, practice democracy, and work both collaboratively and independently." Similarly, in the Early Childhood Generalist (2004b) standards, Proposition 3 includes "Teachers are Responsible for Managing and Monitoring Student Learning," which includes that "teachers must create, enrich and alter the organizational structures in which they work with young people." However, these standards apply only to the specialty area or age group for which they are written.

State Licensing Standards

Licensing has traditionally been and continues to be part of the role of the states in the United States. In addition, the No Child Left Behind Act (NCLB) of 2001 gives states considerable flexibility in determining how they may license teachers. Thirty-four states collaborate to some degree with INTASC to set *beginning* teacher standards, and this collaboration currently represents the largest degree of consensus across the states regarding what beginning teachers should know. The remaining 16 state standards vary widely, and the development of these standards, at present, is in considerable flux as states consider how they will respond to the guidelines of NCLB. Criteria for *experienced* teachers among the states reflect much less of a consensus, despite the increasing number of teachers who are becoming National Board Certified. As the licensing and standards for experienced teachers must also fall under the guidelines of NCLB, these standards are similarly being widely considered by the states.

No Child Left Behind Act. The No Child Left Behind Act (NCLB) of 2001 requires that each state establish its own set of standards for the content areas of reading, math, and science. As such, NCLB emphasizes that it is not the intention for the government to establish national standards for student outcome measures; rather, it holds states accountable for establishing their own standards. Among its provisions, NCLB includes standards regarding teacher qualifications and acknowledges that teacher quality is a determining factor in student achievement (NCLB, 2001). NCLB outlines a list of minimum requirements related to content knowledge and teaching skills that a highly qualified teacher should master, but again, allows for each state to develop its individual definition of "highly qualified," as long as it is consistent with NCLB requirements. These minimum requirements for teachers state that they should hold (a) a bachelor's degree, (b) full state certification and licensure as defined by the state, and (c) demonstrated competency, as defined by the state, in each core academic subject he or she teaches. These core academic subjects are listed as English, reading or language arts, mathematics, science, foreign languages, civics and government, economics, arts, history, and geography. General pedagogical knowledge, such as that of methods and classroom management, is not referred to by NCLB.

As of August 2005, only 25 states had developed a definition of "highly qualified teacher" and only 12 states had defined "subject matter competence" in a way that met the requirements of NCLB (Education Commission of the States, 2005). NCLB does distinguish between what beginning teachers should know and what is required of experienced teachers. Beginning teachers are required to pass a state-designed test to establish their competence. As of 2005, 44 of the states had designed such a test (Education Commission of the States, 2005). In addition, experienced teachers must either meet the same requirements as used for a new teacher or demonstrate competency based on a separate system designed by the state. The states, under NCLB, may create a "high, objective, uniform state standard of evaluation" (HOUSSE) for teachers but as of January 2004 only 33 states had done so (Azondegan, 2004). HOUSSE criteria focus primarily on subject matter knowledge and do not refer to any competency related to classroom management. However, states may choose to set criteria that include classroom management under the general description of "teaching skills." Given these standards, the extent to which classroom management is included may vary greatly state to state, particularly as the criteria for certification and licensure is also at the discretion of the state.

Within NCLB there are several other standards that might overlap with teacher knowledge and skills in the area of classroom management. Title IV of NCLB is the "Safe Schools" component and provides support to prevent violence and drug, alcohol, and tobacco use in and around schools. The Gun-Free Schools Act includes a provision to expel students who bring firearms to school. Finally, the Unsafe School Choice Option requires that states implement a policy that students be given the right to attend "safe public schools" and be allowed to transfer out of a school if the state identifies it as unsafe. States have been more responsive in designing criteria that meet these "safe schools" standards than they have the "highly qualified teacher" definition and, as of August 2005, all but one of the states had complied (Education Commission of the United States, 2004; 2005). Interestingly, none of the Title IV components refers to teacher training in the prevention of school violence or discipline.

Although NCLB stresses the need for standards as the primary method to reform education in the United States, it underemphasizes general pedagogy and the importance of teacher preparation in classroom management. Despite a stated emphasis on scientifically based research, it makes no reference, neither directly nor indirectly, to one of the areas in which some of the most valid and replicable educational research has been conducted, that of classroom management.

National Assessments of Teacher Knowledge

Tests of teacher knowledge should be mentioned in this chapter, as assessments are often reflective of preparation standards. The most widely used tests of teacher knowledge, the Praxis Series, administered by the Educational Testing Service, are currently required in 39 of the states that use tests as part of their teacher licensure process (Education Testing Service, 2005). As the exam is not overseen by a given state, scores on the Praxis exams may be used for licensure requirements in different states. The Praxis Series consists of three parts: Praxis I: Academic Skills Assessments, is used to test the basic knowledge of teacher candidates; Praxis II: Subject Assessments, measures candidates' knowledge of the subject they will teach, as well as general and subject-specific pedagogical skills and knowledge; and Praxis III: Classroom Performance Assessments, which assess the skills of teachers in classroom settings. Praxis III was developed for use in state licensing decisions and is used with experienced teachers (ETS, 2005). The Praxis II includes a measure of what it refers to as the Principles of Learning and Teaching, which does test some classroom management knowledge. Praxis III consists of 19 assessment criteria in four domains: (1) Organizing Content Knowledge for Student Learning (planning to teach); (2) Creating an Environment for Student Learning (the classroom environment); (3) Teaching for Student Learning (instruction); and (4) Teacher Professionalism (professional responsibilities). Of these four domains, the second and third areas test for classroom management competencies, particularly those that refer to "Establishing and maintaining consistent standards of classroom behavior" and "Using instructional time effectively."

The CCSSO is also in the process of designing a test for teachers, but for licensing purposes. INTASC recommends that a prospective teacher pass three licensing tests before receiving a permanent license: (1) a content knowledge test, (2) a teaching knowledge test, and (3) an assessment of actual teaching (CCSSO, 2004). The Test of Teaching Knowledge (TTK) has been developed by INTASC to assess a prospective teacher's ability to meet the INTASC core standards. Presumably the TTK will address the need for the states to produce the second of the three required licensing tests, a test of teacher knowledge. The TTK is still being field-tested so the content is unavailable; however, given the INTASC standards that detail classroom management, it is probable that the TTK will include items on classroom management.

Interestingly, assessments used to evaluate student teachers often include items that address classroom management skills. In a 1996 study by Koziol, Minnick, and Sherman, student teacher evaluations used by the teacher preparation programs at 11 Holmes Group research universities were examined. They found that 28% of the assessment items on these student teaching assessments related to managing the activity in the classroom, which was by far the largest conceptual group of any of the assessment items. Whether state-level assessments similarly focus on classroom management competencies to a similar degree would be an interesting topic for a future investigation.

Lack of Standards That Address Classroom Management Competencies

Given the previous overview of standards used in accreditation, certification, and licensing, the extent to which knowledge and skills of classroom management is included in these standards appears exceedingly limited. We know from public surveys, analyses of teacher's concerns, and studies of teacher effectiveness that classroom management is of paramount importance in assuring success in the classroom. Why then is classroom management, with perhaps the exception of the CEC standards, given such minimal attention? I suggest here several informed possibilities.

First, the standards movement in the last 10 years has emphasized teacher knowledge of content and pedagogical content knowledge, not general pedagogical knowledge. In some cases, policy makers and states have advocated for a decrease in the number of general pedagogy courses that prospective teachers must take and some have even questioned whether these courses are effective at all. Thus, the teacher is seen primarily as a content specialist while pedagogy and educational methods are deemphasized. Classroom management being neither fish nor fowl—not representing content knowledge nor pedagogical content knowledge—is consequently overlooked.

Second, despite the existence of a solid and concrete research base in the area of classroom management, new research in the area has diminished considerably in the last 15 years. In an analysis of discipline-related content in the elementary education literature from 1989–1998, Hardman and Smith (2000) found that less than 1% of articles across 13 journals focused to any degree on classroom discipline. Evertson and Weinstein (2005), in their introduction to this volume, point out that only 2 or 3 of the over 1,500 sessions at the annual meeting of the American Educational Research Association deal with classroom management. Without a strong presence in the research literature and academic discourse over the last decade—the same decade that has seen the rise in standards-based criteria in education—classroom management content had few champions participating in the development of standards. Third, classroom management has been one of many victims of the minimalization of teacher education coursework. Houston and Williams on (1992) pointed out that the cap of 18 semester hours of professional education imposed by the Texas legislature in 1987 decreased classroom management courses along with other methods. Meeting the need for classroom management content is more difficult in these states where professional teacher preparation has become increasingly limited. Schwartz (1997) has also found that many states have placed limits on semester hours or academic credits to eliminate parts of the teacher preparation curriculum deemed unnecessary, such as methods courses. She notes that in most states less time is devoted to training teachers than to training other professionals such as pharmacists, nurses, accountants, or other professionals.

Fourth, there is a disjunction between teacher preparation and area-specific standards and state-level criteria. As summarized earlier, it is only under Principle 5 that the INTASC standards directly address classroom management. However, in state-level assessments used for evaluating teaching in the classroom, it is evident that classroom management is *strongly* represented as a desired teacher skill. Thus, it is where standards take on their most incarnate form, in the authentic evaluation of teacher performance, that we see classroom management competencies expressed most strongly. It is clear that work needs to be done to align current standards with teacher assessments being used at the state level. Perhaps this work will also influence the extent to which classroom management appears in standards at different levels.

With regard to the lack of classroom management content in teacher preparation programs, perhaps we are observing the natural result of the lack of standards in the area of classroom management. That is to say, mention of classroom management is sparse in national standards, and correspondingly, the extent to which this content is part of training programs is sparse. In contrast, the specialty standards used by NCATE that were developed by the Council for Exceptional Children, as well as those developed by recent efforts of INTASC for all educators who work with students with disabilities, stand out as those that contain the most classroom management content. As noted earlier, coursework in classroom or behavioral management appears often as part of special education programs, which may well be the field's response to the frequent appearance of classroom management in these standards. Greer-Chase, Rhodes, and Kellam (2002) have suggested that teacher training programs incorporate classroom management as a mandatory component of teacher preparation. Similarly, classroom management should be an essential part of accreditation, licensing, and certification standards and teachers should be adequately prepared in response to these standards. A teacher in Whitney, Golez, Nagel, and Nieto's (2002) study stated the situation succinctly, "If you don't have the management, you can't teach" (p. 73). Teachers who are not prepared in the area of classroom management not only cannot teach, they should not teach. However, it is up to those of us who prepare teachers to ensure that the essential skill of classroom management becomes a fundamental part of the training program of all teachers.

ACKNOWLEDGMENT

The author wishes to thank Lynn Boyer, Council for Exceptional Children, for her review of an early draft of this chapter.

REFERENCES

Alberto, P. A., & Troutman, A. C. (2006). *Applied behavior analysis for teachers* (7th ed.). Upper Saddle River, NJ: Pearson.

Azondegan, J. (2004, January). Initial findings and major questions about HOUSSE). Retrieved August 8, 2005 from www.ecs.org/clearinghouse/99/68/4968.pdf

Banks, M. K. (2003). Classroom management preparation in Texas colleges and universities. *International Journal of Reality Therapy, 23*(2), 48–51.

Barrett, E. R., & Davis, S. (1995). Perceptions of beginning teachers' inservice needs in classroom management. *Teacher Education and Practice, 2*(1), 22–27.

Bender, W. N., & Mathes, M. Y. (1995). Students with ADHD in the inclusive classroom: A hierarchical approach to strategy selection. *Intervention in School and Clinic 30*(4), 226–232.

Blum, H. (1994). The pre-service teacher's educational training in classroom discipline: A national survey of teacher education programs. Unpublished dissertation, Temple University. *Dissertation Abstracts International.* (p. 2348 DAI-A 55/08 Dissertation Abstracts International 313 Pages AAT No. 9434650).

Brophy, J. E., & Evertson, C. M. (1976). *Learning from teaching: A developmental perspective.* Boston: Allyn & Bacon.

Charles, C. M. (2002) *Building classroom discipline* (7th ed.). Boston: Allyn & Bacon.

Christiansen, D. (1996). The professional knowledge-research base for teacher education. In J. Sikula, T. Buttery, & E. Guyton (Eds.), *Handbook of research on teacher education* (2nd ed., pp. 38–52). New York: Simon & Schuster.

Clapp, B. (1989). The discipline challenge. *Instructor, 99*, 32–34.

Council of Chief State School Officers (2001, May). Model standards for licensing general and special education teachers of students with disabilities: A resource for state dialog. Washington, DC: Author.

Council of Chief State School Officers. (2004). *Test of teaching knowledge.* Retrieved March 19, 2004, from http://www.ccsso.org/projects/Interstate New Teacher Assessment and Support Consortium.

Council for Exceptional Children. (2003). *What every special educator must know: Ethics, standards, and guidelines for special educators* (5th Ed.). Upper Saddle River: NJ: Pearson Education.

Darling-Hammond, L., & Rustique-Forrester, E. (1997). Investing in quality teaching: State-level strategies. *Perspective.* Denver, CO: Education Commission of the States.

Education Commission of the States. (2004). *ECS Report to the Nation: State Implementation of the No Child Left Behind Act.* Denver, CO: Author.

Education Commission of the States (2005). Retrieved August 8, 2005, from http://nclb2.esc.org/NCLBSURVEY/NCLB.aspx

Education Testing Service. (2005). *Frequently asked questions.* Retrieved August 8, 2005, from http://www.ets.org/praxis/prxfaq.html

Emmer, E. T., Evertson, C. M., & Worsham, M. E. (2003). *Classroom management for secondary teachers* (6th ed.). Englewood Cliffs, NJ: Allyn & Bacon.

Emmer, E. T., & Stough, L. M. (2001). Classroom management: A critical part of educational psychology and teacher education. *Educational Psychologist, 36*(2), 103–112.

Evertson, C. M., & Weinstein, C. (2006). (Eds.). Classroom management as a field of inquiry. In C. Evertson & C. Weinstein (Eds.), *Handbook of classroom management: Research, practice and contemporary issues.* Mahwah, NJ: Lawrence Erlbaum Associates.

Gilberts, G. H., & Lignugaris-Kraft, B. (1997). Classroom management and instruction competencies for preparing elementary and special education teachers. *Teaching* and *Teacher Education, 13*(16), 597–610.

Greer-Chase, M., Rhodes, W. A., & Kellam, S. G. (2002). Why the prevention of aggressive disruptive behaviors in middle school must begin in elementary school. *Clearing House, 75*(5), 242–247.

Hardman, E. L., & Smith, S. W. (2000, April). *Analysis of discipline-related content in the elementary education literature.* Paper presented at the annual conference of the American Educational Research Association, New Orleans, LA.

Halford, J. (1998). Easing the way for new teachers. *Educational Leadership, 55*(5), 33–36.

Houston, W. R., & Williamson, J. (1993). Perceptions of their preparation by 42 Texas elementary school teachers compared with their responses as student teachers. *Teacher Education and Practice*, *8*(2), 27–42.

Hoy, A. W. (2000). Educational psychology in teacher education. *Educational Psychologist, 4,* 257–270.

Jones, V. (1989). Classroom management: Clarifying theory and improving practice. *Education, 109*, 330–339.

Jones, V. (1996). Classroom management. In J. Sikula, T. Buttery, & E. Guyton (Eds.), *Handbook of research on teacher education* (2nd ed., pp. 503–521). New York: Simon & Schuster.

Jones, V. (2006). How do teachers learn to be effective classroom managers? In C. Evertson & C. Weinstein (Eds.), *Handbook of classroom management: Research, practice and contemporary issues.* Mahwah, NJ: Lawrence Erlbaum Associates.

Jones, V., & Jones, L. (2004). *Comprehensive classroom management* (7th ed.). Boston: Allyn & Bacon.

Kauffman, J. M., Lloyd, J. W., Baker, J., & Riedel, T. M. (1995). Inclusion of all students with emotional or behavioral disorders? Let's think again. *Phi Delta Kappan, 76*(7), 542–546.

Kher, N., Lacina-Gifford, L. J., & Yandell, S. (2000, April). *Preservice teachers' knowledge of effective classroom management strategies: Defiant behavior.* Paper presented at the annual meeting of the American Educational Research Association, New Orleans, LA.

Kilgore, K. L., & Griffin, C. C. (1998). Beginning special educators: Problems of practice and the influence of school context. *Teacher Education and Special Education, 21*(3), 155–173.

Koziol, S., Minnick, B., & Sherman, M. (1996). What student teaching evaluation instruments tell us about emphases in teacher education programs. *Journal of Personnel Evaluation in Education, 10*(1), 53–74.

Landau, B. M. (2001, April). *Teaching classroom management: A stand-alone necessity for preparing new teachers.* Paper presented at the annual meeting of the American Educational Research Association Conference, Seattle, WA.

Martin, N. K., & Shoho, A. R. (2000, February). *Teacher experience, training and age: The influence of teacher characteristics on classroom management style.* Paper presented at the annual meeting of the Southwest Educational Research Association, Dallas, TX.

Merrett, F., & Wheldall, K. (1993). How do teachers learn to manage classroom behavior? A study of teachers' opinions about their initial training with special reference to classroom behavior management. *Educational Studies, 19*(3), 91–107.

National Association of State Directors of Teacher Education and Certification (2002). *NASDTEC's report on how the states respond to NBPTS-Certified Teachers.* Paper retrieved July 2, 2004, from http://www.nasdtec.org/papers/NBPTS_Report.rtf

National Board for Professional Teaching Standards. (2004a). *What teachers should know and be able to do: The five core propositions of the national board.* Retrieved October 28, 2004, from http://www.nbpts.org/about/coreprops.cfm

National Board for Professional Teaching Standards. (2004b). *Standards and National Board certification.* Retrieved October 28, 2004, from http://www.nbpts.org/standards/stds.cfm

National Board for Professional Teaching Standards. (2005). NBPTS quick facts. Retrieved August 8, 2005 from http://www.nbpts.org/pdf/quickfacts.pdf

National Council on the Accreditation of Teacher Education. (2002). *Professional standards for the accreditation of schools, colleges, and departments of education.* Washington DC: Author.

National Council on the Accreditation of Teacher Educators. (2005a). *About NCATE.* Retrieved August 8, 2005, from http://www.ncate.org

National Council on the Accreditation of Teacher Education. (2005b). *Standards.* Retrieved August 8, 2005, from http://www.ncate.org/public/standards.asp

Nims, D. R., & Wilson, R. W. (1998, February). *Violence prevention preparation: A survey of colleges of education and departments of teacher education.* Paper presented at the Annual Meeting of the American Association of Colleges for Teacher Education, New Orleans, LA.

No Child Left Behind Act of 2001. *Public Law 107-110, the No Child Left Behind Act.* Retrieved October 28, 2004, from http://www.ed.gov/policy/elsec/leg/esea02/index.html

Oakes, T. J. (1999). A guide to organizations involved with licensing and certification of teachers and accreditation of teacher education programs. *ERIC Digest,* 1–5, ED437367.

Pigge, F. L., & Marso, R. N. (1997). A seven year longitudinal multi-factor assessment of teaching concerns development through preparation and early years of teaching. *Teaching and Teacher Education, 13*(2), 225–235.

Ralph, E. G., Kesten, C., Lang, H., & Smith, D. (1998). Hiring new teachers: What do school districts look for? *Journal of Teacher Education, 49*(1), 47–56.

Rickman, L. W., & Hollowell, J. (1981). Some causes of student teacher failure. *Improving College and University Teaching, 29*(4), 176–179.

Rose, L. C., & Gallup, A. M. (2004). The 36th annual Phi Delta Kappa/Gallup poll of the public's attitudes toward the public schools. *Phi Delta Kappan, 86*(1), 41–52.

Roth, R. A. (1996). Standards for certification, licensure, and accreditation. In J. Sikula, T. Buttery, & E. Guyton (Eds.), *Handbook of research on teacher education* (2nd ed., pp. 242–278). New York: Simon & Schuster.

Scales, P. C. (1994). Strengthening middle grade teacher preparation programs, *Middle School Journal, 26*(1), 59–65.

Schwartz, H. (1997). The changing nature of teacher education. In J. Sikula, T. Buttery, & E. Guyton (Eds.), *Handbook of research on teacher education* (2nd ed., pp 3–13). New York: Simon & Schuster.

Shinn, M. R., Walker, H. M., & Stoner, G. (Eds.). (2002). *Interventions for academic and behavior problems: Preventive and remedial approaches.* Silver Springs, MD: National Association of School Psychologists.

Stengel, B. S., & Tom, A. R. (1996). Changes and choices in teaching methods. In F. B. Murray (Ed.), *The teacher educator's handbook: Building a knowledge base for the preparation of teachers* (pp. 593–619). San Francisco: Jossey-Bass.

Stough, L. M., Williams-Diehm K., & Montague, M. (2004, November). *Classroom management content in teacher preparation programs.* Paper presented at the Teacher Education Division of the Council for Exceptional Children, Albuquerque, NM.

Teacher Education Accreditation Council. (2005). *Teacher education accreditation conucil.* Retrieved August 8, 2005, from http://www.teac.org/

U.S. News and World Report. (2004). *Top education schools.* Retrieved April 20, 2004, from http:///www.usnews.com/usnews/edu/grad/rankings/edu/brief/edurank_brief.php

Veenman, S. (1984). Perceived problems of beginning teachers. *Review of Educational Research, 54*(2), 143–178.

Wang, M. C., Haertel, G. D., & Walberg, H. J. (1993). Toward a knowledge base for school learning. *Review of Educational Research, 63*, 249–294.

Wesley, D. A., & Vocke, D. E. (1992, February). *Classroom discipline and teacher education.* Paper presented at the Association of Teacher Educators annual meeting, Orlando, FL.

Whitney, L., Golez, F., Nagel, G., & Nieto, C. (2002). Listening to voices of practicing teachers to examine the effectiveness of a teacher education program. *Action in Teacher Education, 23*(4), 69–76.

35

Classroom Management and Teacher Stress and Burnout

Isaac A. Friedman
Henrietta Szold Institute, Jerusalem

INTRODUCTION

Professional burnout has been widely discussed in the literature since the late 1970s. It characterizes primarily people working in human-service professions, particularly those involved in the helping professions, such as psychology, medicine, teaching, social work, and to a certain extent, law. Burnout reduces professionals' natural inclination to help others, and hurts professionals and their families and, naturally, those whom they are helping (Ashforth & Lee, 1997). Burnout also jeopardizes opportunities for a productive career, and greatly reduces the effectiveness of organizations in which professionals work (Maslach & Leiter, 1997).

Professional burnout can result from ongoing work-related stress, which therefore makes it an important focus for studying factors influencing teacher career development. The most commonly accepted model of work-related stress is that it occurs as a result of incompatibility between the individual's needs, goals, and abilities on the one hand, and the resources, requirements, and rewards he or she receives from the work environment on the other hand (Folkman & Lazarus, 1980; Kahn, Wolf, Quin, Snoek, & Rozenthal, 1964; Katz & Kahn, 1978). Work-related stress is, therefore, a phenomenon that can be explained in terms of the interrelationship between people and their environment. The assumption is that organizations and individuals are interdependent, and that one cannot comprehend the behavior of people in organizations without understanding the connection and interrelationships between the organization's characteristics and those of the people who work within it (Ostroff, 1993).

Most researchers point to the existence of compatibility, harmony, integration, or reciprocal influence between individuals and their workplace as desirable for both the organization and the individual. When the individual's characteristics and the environmental climate are mutually suited, the organization operates more efficiently and the individual working in that organization feels that his or her abilities are being put to good use and that he or she is attaining individual goals. Under these circumstances, the individual experiences satisfaction, a sense of motivation, commitment, and stability. In contrast, when the person's characteristics and the environment are not mutually suited, for example, when the effort required of the individual outweighs the rewards or the individual's ability to perform, or when the individual feels that his or her personal or social values and resources are threatened, the individual experiences stress (Caplan, 1987; Hobfoll & Freedy, 1993; Holland, 1985; Spokane, 1987).

Work-related stress is unavoidable, and the individual needs a certain level of stress. It is a motivating force for achieving success and attempting new challenges. Total lack of stress at work situations can have negative consequences on both the professional and the organization (Bradfield & Fones, 1985; Dedrick & Raschke, 1990; Lazarus, 1966; Shea, 1990). Professionals "at ease" function complacently, occasionally without a sense of urgency or the need to invest efforts in solving problems, overcoming obstacles, and meeting organizational challenges. When individuals believe that they have the capacity to cope with a situation and must expend some degree of effort, they feel rewarded at meeting a challenge. On the other hand, when individuals feel that the stress is uncontrolled, ongoing, and more than they can handle, there is a greater likelihood that the stress will become a negative force leading to a feeling of overwhelming threat (Dedrick & Raschke, 1990; Wisniewski & Gargiulo, 1997). This produces psychological tension and frustration (Smylie, 1999), fear, anxiety, anger, guilt, and depression, and interferes with one's abilities, cognitive functioning, and social behavior (Lazarus, 1966).

Stress is not always a sole product of work, and employees sometimes import stressors into their workplace. Teachers, for example, reported on four exceptionally high-stress factors that they admit carrying into their classroom—money management, health, relationships, and caregiving (Black, 2003).

Stress is usually a temporary condition accompanied by physical and emotional symptoms in a process of adaptation. Burnout, in comparison, refers to a problem of adaptation and involves chronic disturbances. This difference between professional stress and burnout means that the two concepts cannot be distinguished from one another based on their symptomology alone, but rather in retrospect, on the basis of the process when adaptation has been successfully achieved (the relative lack of work-related stress), or when adaptation goes severely awry (burnout). Most researchers dealing with burnout perceive the phenomenon as a process that develops over time, as a result of exposure to stressful events or severe and harsh environmental conditions (Cherniss, 1980; Maslach & Schaufeli, 1993). Burnout derives from stress factors that have not been addressed by the individual and from unrelenting tension without mediation or support (Farber, 1984; McGill, 2002; Reilly, 1994).

This chapter will define professional burnout and, in particular, burnout in teachers, and will describe its developmental process. Teacher expectations of classroom and school functioning, including relations with students, will be discussed, followed by an outline of school and classroom reality as perceived by teachers and students. Finally, antecedents of teacher burnout will be detailed and discussed, accentuating the pivotal role of teacher–student relations in the stress and burnout process. The underlying assumption of this chapter is that burnout in teachers is a result of perceived professional failure due to the incongruities of individual dreams of idealistic and altruistic aspirations and expectations of impeccable professional performance. This dream is at odds with harsh classroom, school, and environmental realities.

DEFINING BURNOUT

Early researchers of this phenomenon described burnout as a condition in which individuals are drained of physical and mental energies because of an exaggerated effort to realize unrealistic expectations, either set by themselves or by superiors, or because of a desire to act in accordance with social norms at a time when the needs of the self are not being met (Freudenberger, 1974). In other words, there is an overload of demands placed on the person's sources of energy and coping resources (Hobfoll & Freedy, 1993). Burnout, therefore, is the product of a destructive interaction between eager professionals with a strong achievement drive and unrealistic desires, and overly demanding service recipients. A social–psychological approach to burnout was formulated by Maslach (1976) and by Maslach and Jackson (1981) focusing on the professional's social and organizational environment at work. Maslach and Jackson (1981) have highlighted the empirical aspect of the topic and structured it conceptually. Using questionnaires and interviews, they identified three dimensions composing burnout: (a) exhaustion—a sense that the person's physical and mental energies have been depleted; (b) depersonalization—a negative, harsh, or alienated reaction to clients and those receiving help; and (c) a decreased sense of personal accomplishment—a feeling of failure at work and negative self-evaluation.

Both Maslach (1976) and Freudenberger (1974) theorized that the emotional and physical overload involved in the helping professions leads to frustration and stress, but whereas Freudenberger perceived such situations as leading the individual to invest longer hours and more energy at work, Maslach and Jackson emphasized the employee's withdrawal from work, along with a tendency to treat clients in an inhumane and detached manner.

Pines and Aronson (1988) and Cherniss (1980) provided another approach to burnout research. Pines and Aronson defined burnout as "a state of physical, emotional, and mental exhaustion caused by long-term involvement in situations that are emotionally damaging" (p. 9). Physical exhaustion is characterized by a lack of energy, chronic fatigue, and weakness; emotional exhaustion includes feelings of helplessness, hopelessness, and a sense of being trapped; and mental exhaustion involves the development of negative attitudes toward oneself, work, and life in general. Cherniss' approach toward defining and understanding burnout, although similar to that of Maslach or Pines and Aronson, focuses on the role of the organization. It attempts to explain burnout by examining the ways in which organizations and work environments influence a person's reaction to work. Burnout, in Cherniss' view, is the result of an incongruity between what workers feel they are giving and what they believe they are getting in return. This is a dynamic process that develops over time. Burnout is the final stage in a series of unsuccessful attempts to cope with the stresses of the workplace and is expressed as a transition from effective coping mechanisms for solving problems to passive coping methods, such as mechanical or apathetic relationships with clients at a time when the individual feels powerless to cope with the stress. Unlike Maslach or Pines and Aronson, who proposed that burnout was an advanced and final stage of a developmental process, that is, reflecting passive coping that includes exhaustion, detachment, and low self-esteem, Cherniss expanded the concept into a process that begins with effective coping methods; that is, he perceived the transition from one stage to the next as the actual burnout process itself.

In the 3 decades since the term *burnout* was first used in the literature, there has been significant progress in studying this phenomenon. Although several approaches have been proposed to understanding it, there seems to be a consensus that, at its core, burnout reflects the discrepancy between the individual's assessment and workplace reality. Yet another approach to understanding burnout is the conservation of resources (COR) theory (Hobfoll & Freedy, 1993), which states that stress is likely to appear under one of three conditions: (1) when people feel that their resources are being threatened (e.g., when people feel that job demands and requirements potentially exceed their professional or personal capacity); (2) when resources are being depleted (e.g., as a result of exertion); or (3) when there are not sufficient resources to meet the demands of the job, or when they do not produce the expected results.

The COR theory is related to burnout as follows: The demands of the job overload the individual's resources and thus cause stress, which ultimately leads to mental and physical exhaustion. People with a high level of personal ability, who can be defined as rich in personal resources, can overcome these tensions more easily and thus the feeling of burnout is mitigated, or avoided altogether (Hobfoll & Freedy, 1993; Janssen, Schaufeli, & Houkes, 1999; Lee & Ashforth, 1996; Leiter, 1993; Taris, Schreurs, & Schaufeli, 1999). It appears that people feel threatened by workload, because the demands of the job are generally likely to impose heavily on one's physical and emotional resources, and addressing those demands requires protection against depletion of resources. Work overload is therefore perceived as a threat to one's personal and professional resource reservoir and an undesirable component of the job characteristics. Nevertheless, although gaining additional resources is perceived by most workers as less important than preventing the loss of resources, adding resources is not without value. Resources help us cope with work demands, for example, through social, physical, or mental support, which are provided to the worker by the surrounding people, or by the organization.

Self-efficacy is another important concept associated with burnout, defined as a person's belief in his or her ability to organize and realize the actions needed to attain specific goals. It is thus the individual's own judgment regarding the degree to which he or she is capable of coping effectively and realistically with a specific task in the future (Bandura, 1997). Undoubtedly, the efforts needed for creativity, problem solving, or self-management, which characterize feelings of self-efficacy, do not coincide with feelings of emotional emptiness, exhaustion, and reduced self-fulfillment that characterize burnout. In other words, burnout is the antithesis of feelings of control and self-direction (Brouwers & Tomic, 2000; Cherniss, 1993; Friedman, 2000; Leiter, 1992; Schwarzer & Greenglass, 1999). Researchers have theorized that underlying the feeling of burnout is a decreased sense of self-efficacy caused by environmental factors (Cherniss, 1993; Friedman, 2000). Leiter (1992) stated that burnout is a crisis in one's perception of self-efficacy, that is, a breakdown in the individual's sense of self-efficacy in the professional sphere. Organizational control systems (i.e., organizational feedback, support, and inservice training mechanisms), aiming to detect and handle conflicts or difficult situations at work, can help improve or undermine the individual's sense of efficacy. According to Friedman and Farber (1992), organizational–environmental factors that prevent individuals from experiencing a strong sense of efficacy through the realization of occupational goals and expectations are likely to contribute to emotional burnout. Workers who feel secure in their abilities expect those abilities to lead to rewards, and when this does not happen, the probability of burnout increases. Friedman (2000) called this situation "the incongruity between the expected and observed levels of self-efficacy" and argued that "incongruity in the feeling of self-efficacy is likely to be a strong foundation for understanding burnout and identifying several key factors in its prevention" (p. 597).

Malach-Pines (2000) perceived the burnout process from an existential perspective. According to this perception, burnout reflects the feeling of a lack of existential meaning that individuals expect to achieve through their work. When individuals feel that their job performance is failing or that the way in which their job "ought to be performed" is not the way they actually perform it, and when work no longer gives their lives a sense of purpose, they become burned out.

After 3 decades of research and study of the phenomenon, we can say that burnout is, essentially, a sense of failure that originates with the nonrealization of dreams regarding ideal job performance. A professional usually begins his or her career with expectations of enjoyable and satisfying work in a supportive, encouraging, and accepting organizational environment where all the parties involved offer a professional and personal partnership. If the reality does not match these expectations, there may be a rapid change in the professional's perceived sense of self-efficacy, accompanied by a deep sense of failure and disappointment, and overwhelming stress. At this stage of disillusionment, burnout begins to develop, and if not treated properly, it becomes worse (Friedman, 2000).

BURNOUT IN TEACHERS

Research on burnout in teachers emerged in the early 1980s (Iwanicki & Schwab, 1981; Schwab & Iwanicki, 1982a, 1982b). Over time, the concept of burnout has become used more in connection with teachers than with any other occupational group (Farber, 2000). Several characteristics that affect burnout differentiate the teaching profession from other helping professions (Friedman & Lotan, 1985). First, teaching is not an encounter between a "patient" and a "therapist," but an interaction between an educated adult and healthy young people in need of knowledge, training, and socialization. Second, the relationship between the teacher and his or her students involves group and leadership perspectives. Third, teachers work generally in classroom settings, whereas in other helping professions the focus is more on individualized service recipients. Fourth, teachers' work environments are highly complex, including the classroom, the parents and the community, colleagues, administration, and the school as an organization. And finally, teachers are required to have constant interaction with young people, but interactions with adult peers at work are usually limited. Teachers can rarely refer the "service recipient" to someone else, and thus may have to work with someone in whom they may not be interested.

Symptoms of teacher burnout are usually emotional or physical exhaustion, or both, low work output, and loss of the special personal relationship that usually characterizes the teacher's work with his or her students (Farber, 1984). Other elements may also be present with regard to teaching, such as low morale, low self-esteem, cynicism, a negative attitude toward service recipients, overemotionalism, suspiciousness, depression, rigidity, absenteeism, and retirement. Teachers who are burned out may treat their students overly harshly and show low levels of commitment toward teaching and the students' interests (Farber, 1991; Friedman, 2004). Dunham (1976) described two main typologies of burnout responses among teachers exposed to undue stress—frustration and anxiety. The first type of reaction is related to various physical symptoms, sleep disturbances, and in certain cases, illnesses related to depression. The second type is related to feelings of insecurity, limited abilities, and confusion.

Teachers in Israel who participated in workshops run by this author described their patterns of burnout. In these workshops teachers familiarized themselves with the phenomenon of burnout and were interviewed afterward. Some representative responses are cited here:

Homeroom teacher (several years in primary education, then adult education):

> I consider teaching to be a calling and it gives me personal meaning, but they don't let me do it the way I want to; it ties my hands and frustrates me. Feeling [un]successful is an element of burnout. What is success? For me it is student feedback, both emotional feedback and through their achievements. By emotional feedback I mean that I see students internalizing things that were important for me to give them. Feedback in this case is when my students tell me that the class was interesting, that they feel good, that they can sense a true change that something good happened to them.

Homeroom teacher (19 years of teaching):

> I have a deep sense of frustration. Now I feel that I am not a good teacher because I don't give my students everything I can. I am not "reaching" all of my students—and that burns me out. I have a sense of failure: This isn't turning out the way I had hoped.

Counselor (25 years of teaching):

> I worked with small children in the past, and later on with older kids. During that time I felt that I couldn't be responsible for so many students and I saw that gradually they became "numbers" to me, rather than human beings. The teacher thinks she must inculcate, teach, educate, but she can't do that because she has so many students. I feel like I don't "matter" to these kids and in contrast with the past—today I don't even want to "matter" to them. The teacher isn't an engineer working with machines, and when I see myself starting to treat my students like machines, I become an "engineer" and not a "teacher."

Burned out teachers reported that they saw their work as futile, and inconsistent with the ideals or goals they had as novice teachers (Bullough & Baughman, 1997). Discrepancies between ideals of what it means to be a good teacher and school reality were significantly related to burnout (Dworkin, 1986; Brown & Ralph, 1998; Esteve, 2000; Troman & Woods, 2001). Sense of powerlessness in defining professional roles was also found to be instrumental in creating stress leading to burnout (LeCompte & Dworkin, 1991). Hence, burnout may be explained as a result of perceived discrepancy between idealistic professional expectations and harsh, hard-to-bear environmental reality. Therefore, it is important to explore and describe teachers' classroom and environmental expectations and their reality. This is done in the following sections.

TEACHERS' CLASSROOM EXPECTATIONS: MISSION AND POWER

Teachers, particularly those beginning their professional careers, have expectations regarding work in class and with students. Researchers looking to uncover the reasons why people join the teaching profession have found several motivations: a personal aspect (teaching provides an opportunity for ongoing contact with young people); a service aspect (teachers carry out a unique mission in society that has a high moral value); social and human continuity (passing on social traditions from one generation to the next); material benefits; and convenient working hours (Lortie, 1975). Sarason (1999) included in the reasons why people join the teaching profession the desire to achieve status within the community, and the desire to contribute to society, the future of which could be at risk if the younger generation is not properly educated.

Teachers develop personal and professional expectations relating to their teaching work and the relationship with their students during their training period, and perhaps even before that. Teachers formulate their own personal vision of what they will do in class, what they should give to their students, what they might receive from the students in exchange, and what they will benefit from their work as teachers. Gavish (2002) explored expectations of teaching trainees in the classroom who were functioning as instructors and educators. She found that, as instructors, teachers aim to achieve scholastic goals in class (learning, inculcating knowledge and skills). As educators, they aim to instill in students values and rules for proper behavior and to ensure their physical and emotional well-being. Teachers are also expected to be the leaders of the class, and to maintain positive interpersonal interrelationships with their students. Providing knowledge and education to students is considered by teachers as a mission and a fulfillment of ideals. Underlying these ideals is an altruistic attitude toward others. Teachers expect to be valued for their expertise and respected for their efforts. Expectations of gaining benefits from work, including appreciation and respect, and influence with students, can be perceived as "healthy" narcissism (Kohut & Wolf, 1978).

Teacher expectations of their work in classrooms was presented by Friedman (in press) as a bipolar model, comprising "giving" (teaching, caring, friendship) at one end, and "receiving" (respect and appreciation) at the other. The "giving" pole comprises the altruistic aspect of the teacher's self, and is compromised of three dimensions: (1) *Friendship and support*—Teachers desire to be true friends and to give each student the feeling that the teacher is always supportive; to give each student individual warmth and love as needed; to view the student as a unique being; (2) *Empathy and caring*—Teachers desire to be attentive to their students' problems and to be able to help them; to know the students as closely as possible and be sensitive to their personal and social needs, and aspirations; to radiate calm and pleasantness, even under tense conditions; to be a teacher who can handle squabbles between the students in the classroom and teach them to be good human beings; (3) *Supportive teaching*—Teachers desire to help students having difficulty in class; to instill knowledge and skills in each student, to use effective teaching methods to reach every child in the class; to structure a variety of lessons based on the needs of each student in class, rather than use a standard format.

The "receiving" pole comprises the (healthy) narcissistic aspect of the teacher's self—the need for power and influence (i.e., expectations of being a charismatic leader who shapes the future generation) and respect and gratitude. The receiving pole serves as a source of power and fulfillment of ambitions, which relate primarily to the interpersonal relationships among teachers, students, and others. The ambitions nested in the "receiving" pole are organized in two groups: (1) *Power and influence*—Teachers desire to be an important figure, a model to be emulated by the students; to be the teacher who is the source of fond memories of school; to be "the authority" for students and to the be one of the most significant persons in the student's life; and (2) *Respect and gratitude*—Teachers desire to be "a good teacher" in the eyes of students and parents; to be a respected professional to whom people turn for advice, direction, and problem solving; to achieve good results with regard to student achievement, making the teachers proud and worthy of gratitude for their efforts and achievements.

Table 35.1 shows how novice teachers' classroom expectations can be classified according to the bipolar model (Gavish, 2002; Friedman, in press).

THE REALITY OF TEACHERS' PROFESSIONAL WORK: TEACHER AS ORGANIZATION PERSON

A teacher's primary work environment—the classroom—has special qualities that are a potential source of stress. Classrooms are closed, crowded spaces in which many people with differing abilities and priorities are forced to use limited resources to achieve a broad range of personal, institutional, and social goals. They are places where many things take place simultaneously, very rapidly, with unexpected changes. Teachers face a classroom full of students every day; negotiate potentially stressful interactions with parents, administrators, counselors, and other teachers; contend with relatively low school budgets; and ensure students meet increasingly strict standards. In such a reality, teachers' influence on their students is usually difficult to discern, and is likely not to be noticeable for quite some time (Lortie, 1975; Smylie, 1999).

Developments in the past few decades indicate that work in the classroom is also related to what is happening outside the classroom, such as the school's organizational environment, policy environments, new technologies, and so on. Schools have become important social organizations and teachers also play a role in the school as an organization. Thus, for several decades the classroom has no longer been considered an enclosed bubble, isolated from its surroundings. For teachers to successfully manage their classrooms, they must be well versed in the school's work procedures, rights, and obligations; the areas of responsibility of various school officials; and their own areas of responsibility. Teachers must be able to use organizational resources efficiently, initiate effective working relationships with their colleagues, and draw assistance from them when necessary. Teachers must feel that the school as an organization provides the support they need to grow professionally, to realize their personal and professional talents, and, in particular, to function as organizational persons. An "organization person" is an employee

TABLE 35.1
Novice Teachers Expectations

Classroom Expectations Stemming From the Giving Pole	*Classroom Expectations Stemming From the Receiving Pole*
Friendship and Support: • To be a friend to the students • To give disadvantaged students warmth and love • To give each student the feeling that the teacher is a consistent and reliable support • To always see the student in the center; to put your students' needs and desires above your owns • To see each child as special with unique qualities and desires • To encourage students to realize and act on the basis of their individual strengths and abilities	***Power and Influence:*** • To be a charismatic leader shaping the future generation • To feel that the teacher is like the "director general" of the classroom • To be the teacher who makes the students remember the school fondly • To take credit for the positive results of the students' achievements • To be the teacher who can exercise authority over his or her students in class • To be a significant person in the lives of the students
Empathy and Caring: • To listen to students' problems and be able to help them • To appreciate the abilities of every student, regardless of academic achievement • To know the students well enough and to be sensitive to their inner worlds by being responsive to their often unexpressed wishes, desires and needs • To be calm and pleasant even under stressful conditions • To help each student believe in his or her abilities • To be a trustworthy person whom the students can turn to • To deal successfully with the differences among students in the class	***Respect and Gratitude:*** • To enjoy the experience of standing in front of a class, as "the teacher" • For the children to tell their parents good things about the teacher • To be like a doctor: a specialist and a professional whom students and parents approach for help to solve their problems
Supportive Teaching: • To devote needed time to support students who may have difficulty • To instill knowledge and skills suited to each student • To interest and motivate students and stimulate them to learn • To help each student to understand what the teacher says and to progress properly • To employ effective teaching methods to reach all students • To assist weak students individually and helping them academically • To know whether each and every student is "with the teacher" during class	

working in an organizational setting, being involved in the organizational administrative and professional processes, meaningfully contributing to the organization and being supported by it.

The concept of teachers as organization persons was recently proposed by Friedman and Kass (2002) as a perspective for studying teachers' perceived sense of self-efficacy. Teachers as organizational persons should be organizationally literate, that is, be well acquainted with the school's administrative processes (planning, budgeting, communication, and control); know the school's physical and cultural ambience, government rules and regulations pertaining to school administration; and be acquainted with the school's human and physical resources. They also should be trained to work efficiently and collegially as team members.

A Myriad of School Reforms, Change, and Expectations

Schools have become work organizations that enable professionalism, promote collegial relationships, and ensure that teachers' voices will be counted in the decisions that influence students' learning and their own working conditions. However, alongside these positive changes, there has been an increase in the employment-related demands made of teachers and the workload they must carry, and that is concomitant with reductions in pay and prestige. Since the early 1980s, teaching has been at the center of significant social–political changes. It can be shown that some changes may be defined as positive in the eyes of teachers, and others may be classified as negative. Either way, the abundance of school reforms and educational fashions are conflicting and confusing, leading to perceived role ambiguity and role conflict. Change movements brought shifts from individualism to a professional community, from teaching in the center to learning in the center, from technical teaching to enquiry, from control to accountability, from controlled and managed work to leadership, from focus on the class to focus on the school as a whole.

Public expectations have risen dramatically and the criteria for measuring educational success have become more stringent, with greater emphasis on standardized tests. Teachers' roles related to school in general have been expanded; schedules have become more structured and support collaborative work; teacher inservice programs have expanded and new jobs have been created, such as counselors and instructors. These changes have brought massive work overload and loss of spontaneity: Feelings of "enjoyment" and "personal concern" have been pushed aside by detachment; quantity has replaced quality; teaching has become more bureaucratic than professional; teachers have begun to feel that they are losing their autonomy and control over the curriculum; accountability has become a threat. Reforms have failed to reinforce the feeling that teachers make a difference in the lives of their students. Teachers have begun to complain about the fact that they are perceived as successful only if their students manage to get average scores or higher in every parameter of educational reform.

In light of the fact that teachers' expectations for benefits and professional satisfaction have increased in the wake of these changes, it is easy to see why many remain disappointed and bitter by the reality that conditions in the classroom remain essentially unchanged. The changes in teaching are, therefore, a double-edged sword: although they have the potential to enhance teachers' sense of power and feelings of belonging and personal achievement, they add to teachers' workload and may lead to greater exhaustion. When teachers continue to carry the same responsibility for classroom teaching with added roles as leaders and decision makers, they often develop tendencies toward emotional exhaustion, poor performance, frustration, and burnout (Farber, 1999, 2000; Miller, 1999; Sleegers, 1999; Woods, 1999). When teachers must work in a classroom where school policy is unclear, or where there is a conflict between this policy and their professional belief, teachers' sense of ability to succeed becomes compromised and is replaced by a feeling of professional frustration, and incipient signs of burnout (Friedman & Gavish, 2003).

Changes in the education system (i.e., higher autonomy and increased flexibility for teachers) may positively affect school climate and reduce teacher burnout (Friedman, 1991) by forcing teachers to replenish their resources and maintain their professional effectiveness (Luckner, 1996), and by being intellectually challenging (Cherniss, 1980). However, constant changes arouse negative feelings among teachers and may precipitate burnout (Evers, Brouwers, & Tomic, 2002). Teachers, especially those with a high sense of professional commitment, do not want to have to adapt to new demands that contradict their teaching style (Lens & De Jesus, 1999). Constant calls for change and innovation are likely to be interpreted not as reasonable professional challenges, but rather as personal criticism. Dramatic, unsettling changes including transfers, school closings, and loss of jobs may also increase the frequency of burnout. Many teachers view educational reform as an expression of blame for their failure. Mishor (1994) noted that many educational changes are supposed to be implemented by teachers without any systematic training that would help them meet the demands of changing areas of responsibility. Mishor (1994) even found that an intervention program might, during its initial stage and until the new skills have been internalized, lead to an increased level of burnout among teachers. She explains this as a lack of support for the teacher dealing with the demand for change, who must cope alone with the difficulties in the classroom as a result of the change. This causes teachers to feel apathetic and to withdraw from their work.

With the introduction of numerous changes in the education system, many of the things teachers have worked so hard to achieve in the classroom now seem superfluous and their feeling is that even if they hadn't worked so hard the results would have been the same: failure. Thus, teachers may perceive that there is no connection between input, effort, concern, and outcome, which contributes to a feeling of helplessness, hopelessness, lack of motivation, depression, stress, and ultimately, burnout. Under such circumstances teachers tend to give up; they cannot find the strength, enthusiasm, and effort to make the new program a success. Experience has taught many teachers that it does not matter at all—things will soon change in any event. Furthermore, most of the changes are imposed on teachers "from the top down." Teachers feel like pawns in the education system moved by outside forces. They live with an external locus of control and causality with a lack of any feeling of self-determination, which undermines their internal motivation (Friedman, 2000; Friedman & Lotan, 1985).

STUDENTS' VIEWS OF TEACHERS' CLASSROOM REALITY

Studies of the relationship between students and their teachers show that students can sharply and accurately decode their teachers' behaviors and reactions (Cullingford, 1987). Students exchange information among themselves, analyze the information, and draw conclusions—which are usually accurate and highly beneficial to them. Thus, we can learn from the students what interests them, what is effective for them, and what they enjoy. In addition, the students' sharp observational skills enable them to guess what is damaging and painful to their teachers.

Students' awareness of the impact of their behavior on their teachers was studied in Israel by Friedman and Krongold (1993). Students who participated in the study recorded their typical behaviors, or those of their friends, that stress out their teachers. Students responses were classified into the following categories: (a) not listening to the teacher; (b) lack of motivation to learn; and (c) behavioral problems. Examples of students' responses are presented in Table 35.2.

Students' responses bring up three main types of behavior that, in the eyes of students are stressful to their teachers. One relates to "supportive teaching," the "giving" pole in Friedman's

TABLE 35.2

Student Behaviors That Stress Teachers

	Elementary Schools	*Junior and High Schools*
Not listening to the teacher	• The teachers are upset when students don't listen and then claim they didn't understand. • The thing that stresses out the teacher most is when students talk while they are explaining something. • Students are busy with other things during the lesson, passing notes to one another. • Students are arguing and the teacher asks them to stop, but they continue. • Students are disrespectful and insolent.	• Students behave as if they just "sit-in" in the class, uncommitted, with no sense of responsibility. • Indifference is rampant in the class and everyone pretends to be tired • Students do not answer teacher's questions and do not respond to what she is saying. • Students do not take the teacher's preaching and remarks seriously. • A student who is popular in the class shows contempt for the teacher.
Lack of motivation	• They are not involved in what is happening in the class. • The students come to class unprepared. • A student plays in the classroom instead of learning. • Not preparing homework.	• Students pretend to be dumb. • The students' level of concentration in class is low. • The teacher explains but half the class don't care much. • Students don't do anything, not in class nor on the exams. • Students are passive, and don't participate in class. • The teacher asks a question and no one raises a hand. • The teacher tries very hard and the class makes no effort.
Behavioral problems	• Talking, shouting, making noise. • A disrespectful student tells jokes in the middle of class and others are laughing. • The class makes noise and doesn't stop talking. • One student hits another and says he doesn't care about the teacher. • Fights in the middle of class. • A student talks back to the teacher and argues with her. • Students who yell at the teacher and make faces, and get mad at the teacher. • A child who laughs and insults the teacher in front of the whole class. • A student who interrupts the teacher and stops her in the middle of something important. • Students who shout out the answer to a question after the teacher called on someone else to respond.	• Violence in class. • Children chew gum in class. • Students are late to class, with or without an excuse. • Students do not stay behind to clean up the school. • Kids leave the class before the proper time. • Children shout at the teacher like they were buddies. • Students are impertinent, respond insolently or with outright disrespect. • Students humiliate the teacher. • Children undermine the teacher's authority. • Students threaten the teacher.

(in press) bipolar model of teacher professional self, and the remaining two pertain to the "receiving" (power and influence) pole in that model.

Hindering Teaching

Another student behavior that causes stress in teachers is related to teaching and learning. Some students believe that when teachers are not able to "convey" the learning material successfully in class, this is a teaching failure. "Students' lack of desire to study labels the teacher as a failure" or "the teacher is afraid she won't cover the material because the class isn't progressing fast enough." Failure on tests is also perceived by students as the teacher's failure as much their own. "Failure on exams is actually the teacher's fault," they said. Students know that homework is part of the school curriculum, but sometimes they do not do their homework knowing this stresses their teachers.

Teacher Ability to Control the Class

A prominent behavior that, in the students' views, leads to teacher stress is classroom disruptions—talking and noise that keep teachers from instilling order and discipline and prevent them from teaching. Students stated that teachers become stressed and display helplessness in the face of disruptions—when all the students speak at once, refuse to listen, and interrupt. Most types of interruptions are not directed against the teachers but some of them are, indeed, aimed against the teacher and inflict stress, especially when they take place in front of the whole class. An example is uncontrolled insolence, when the teacher must cope with this behavior in front of the entire class or when students aggrieve the teacher for no apparent reason. Such situations may even turn into teacher abuse.

Students know the extent to which being unnecessarily argumentative bothers their teachers. As one student noted, arguing with the teacher endlessly about something usually "sends her into a tailspin." Students note that repeatedly disobeying teachers and ignoring what they say make teachers feel helpless and out of control. A more extreme situation is one in which control is usurped by the students: "A student takes control from the teacher" and by simply ignoring the teacher, "the teacher feels as if she is talking to the walls, and the students don't treat the teacher the way she should be treated."

Students differentiate between an "ordinary" teacher and one who "makes an effort" to fulfill their expectations by saying that the latter "understands the students, tries to help them, to meet them halfway. Misbehavior causes this kind of teacher emotional distress, and students feel that it "is not playing fair."

During exam periods, students may often decide to stay home and study for the test, which is more important to them than regular attendance at school. When they cut class, the teacher comes into the classroom, sees that many of the students are absent, and "it makes teachers feel anxious because they cannot teach the lesson properly."

Respect for the Teacher

The third issue that students mentioned as causing stress in teachers is related to situations that embarrass the teacher. From the students' point of view, teachers find it extremely difficult to face criticism (e.g., making errors, or having students correct mistakes in a disrespectful manner). In addition, students believe it is difficult for some teachers if they cannot be "all-knowing" (e.g., "when a teacher is asked a question and she doesn't know how to respond, or what the correct answer is, or when a student contradicts her, and the student is correct and the teacher doesn't know what to say"). As long as the criticism is expressed within the classroom it remains part of teacher–student interaction, but criticism that is expressed outside the classroom can embarrass the teacher even more (e.g., "when students accuse a teacher and involve her superiors, it can lead to the teacher feeling resentment towards the class").

There is a high degree of similarity between teacher stress factors that lead to burnout among teachers, reported by teachers, and teacher stress factors reported by students. This points to the students' uncanny ability to observe and realize what affects their teachers and what stresses them. It provides a sound basis for assuming that students use their sharp perception to manipulate their teachers. As one student said, "Kids deliberately do things that anger the teacher." Interrupting the teacher and ignoring what she says are, apparently, common phenomena with which students are quite familiar. Even negative behaviors that are not aimed directly against the teacher and have to do with the students' relationships with one another, such as "physical and verbal abuse, arguments and lies," and "children arguing and fighting in the middle of class" are a burden on teachers. Students see the teacher's distress, they hear and understand, but often do not show empathy to their teachers.

Displaying unresponsive and inattentive behaviors is an expression of disrespect for the teacher, and can lead to teacher sense of personal and professional failure and burnout. Because teachers invest great effort in educating and nurturing of students, they expect a level of recognition and appreciation from them. When they do not receive it, a discrepancy arises between expectations and reality. The deeper the discrepancy between expectations and reality, the more stress there is at work, and the greater the stress—the higher the potential for burnout.

TEACHER BURNOUT: UNREALIZED ASPIRATIONS OF GIVING AND RECEIVING

The interaction between teachers and their work environment is reflected in the relationships with the people they work with—students, fellow teachers, administration, parents, and the community—and these relations compose the most prevalent sources of stress and burnout in this profession. There is consensus among researchers that the most common sources of teacher work stress stem from individual relationships with students (Billingsley & Tech, 1993; Farber, 1983; Freeman, 1987; Friedman & Lotan, 1985; Lortie, 1975; Nias, 1999). Interrelations with students constitute the core of teachers' life at school, even in the light of recent organizational reforms, as teachers become organizational persons. These relations involve personal involvement, altruistic care, and exercising authority and control. Nias (1999) presented three characteristics of the interrelationship between teachers and students: (1) Most teachers perceive their relationship with their students as personal more than nonpersonal and bureaucratic; (2) teachers perceive the relationship with their students as having an ethical dimension; and (3) most teachers feel that moral responsibility toward their students constitutes a commitment to them. Further, this commitment is expressed in the need to "be concerned" for the physical, social, emotional, or moral well-being of their students; to support them; to be worried and even fearful for them; and to act in the best interests of their students, even if such action demands a heavy price or contradicts the interests of the teachers themselves. Nias adds that, paradoxically, some of the satisfaction from teaching depends on worrying more about others than about themselves (e.g., teachers sometimes ignore their own physical and emotional health and are willing to make sacrifices for the needs of their students). This is why some teachers are not aware of the first symptoms of stress, do nothing to mitigate it, and continue to work until they are burned out.

Lortie (1975) noted that controlling students is an important demand of the teacher's job and an essential part of teachers' role identity, but for most teachers controlling students is not satisfying. Actually, establishing meaningful personal relationships with students brings teachers greater rewards and personal satisfaction. Darling-Hammond (1990) claimed that teachers, if they want to be professional, are obligated, first and foremost, to their students ("the clients"). They are required to consider the unique needs of the students in the judgments they make, while relying on the knowledge they have acquired on an ongoing basis. But the reality of working in a bureaucratized school culture forces teachers to focus on following rules and pleasing their superiors, sometimes at the expense of investing in students and their needs. Therefore, despite of the concern for their students that underlies their teaching, many teachers who perform their job well and are truly concerned about their students tend to burn out and leave the profession.

Pajak, Cramer, and Konke (1986) claimed that students' expectations and perceptions of their teachers have a stronger influence on teacher behavior than anything else. In a study conducted by Friedman and Farber (1992), elementary school teachers (grades 1–6) in state and state-religious schools in Israel filled out a questionnaire aimed to examine the association between teachers' self-image and burnout. This study found that there was a negative (reverse) correlation between teachers' self-image and their perceived burnout: the lower the teacher's self-image, the more intense the feeling of burnout reported by the teacher. Among the components constituting the concept of "self-image," a teacher's level of satisfaction as a professional was very strongly associated with burnout. Contrarily, a teacher's self-image as a capable individual was only moderately associated with burnout. In the area of burnout, the study indicated that the person considered most important to the teacher was the student, and the teacher's image in the students' eyes was strongly associated with tendencies toward burnout. Although important, teacher's image in the eyes of the principal and parents had less to do with burnout than his or her image in the eyes of the students. It was also found that teachers believed their students knew them almost as well as they knew themselves.

Students' group or classroom behavior ("classroom climate") was found to have a strong and consistent impact on teacher burnout in many studies (Bacharach, Bauer, & Conley, 1986; Byrne, 1999; Friedman & Lotan, 1985). Byrne argued that when classroom climate deteriorates, teachers become emotionally exhausted and develop negative attitudes toward their students and the teaching profession in general. Blase (1986) indicated that students' disruptive behaviors such as verbal abuse, vandalism, cheating, and drug use violate the basic norms of the class or the school, take away from the teacher's precious time, and jeopardize the educational processes. They occur quite often and are considered difficult to control or to change. There are those who add that teachers are in constant threat and under verbal and physical threats from students (Byrne, 1994, 1999). This phenomenon is reported more often by urban teachers, and has become more common in recent years. Brouwers and Tomic (2000) explained that teachers who do not maintain order in class, and yet know that their colleagues sustain a comfortable learning atmosphere in their classes, are quite likely to suffer from stress and mental exhaustion, and develop a negative attitude toward their students and the teaching profession in general. There are teachers who find their students inattentive, apathetic, unmotivated, and not concentrating or listening, besides being disruptive (Blase, 1986; Byrne, 1994; Farber, 1991; Friedman, 1992; Travers & Cooper, 1996). Disruptive behaviors prevent teachers from feeling professionally effective and satisfied—the reasons they went into teaching—and reduce their status in their own eyes over time (Farber, 1991; Travers & Cooper, 1996; Weiskopf, 1980).

In the early 1980s a large-scale study conducted in elementary schools in Israel showed that student classroom behaviors had the highest impact on teacher burnout ($\beta = .24$), and that these relations clearly distinguished between burned-out teachers and those reportedly not burned out. Specific student behavior patterns that had the most salient impact on teacher burnout were students' overt disrespect, talking back, and behaviors compromising teachers' personal safety (Friedman & Lotan, 1985). Very similar results were found 10 years later, in the mid-1990s (Friedman, 1995), and 15 years later, in the early 2000s (Gavish, 2002). Burnout had statistically significant regression coefficients on student classroom behavior, in particular those behaviors that indicate disrespect, and lack of sociability and affection for the teacher ($\beta = .26$ on burnout, and $\beta = .22$ on nonaccomplishment and depersonalization) (Gavish, 2002).

Three main student behavior patterns have accounted for 22% of the variance in teacher burnout. They were (a) *disrespect* (the teacher demands silence in class and students go on making noise, they interrupt one another, are derisive to one another, pick on one another and answer back to the teacher); (b) *sociability* (students talk to the teacher about what worries them and about what makes them happy, discuss their personal problems with the teacher, say to the teacher "I have missed you," and how much they have enjoyed the class); and (c) *attentiveness* (students are cooperative and enthusiastic, concentrate on their work, and show interest). Disrespect accounted for 15% of burnout variance, attentiveness for 6% above and beyond the variance explained by disrespect, and sociability added one more percent to the explained variance (Friedman, 1994, 1995). Hastings and Bahm (2003) corroborated the results of Friedman's (1995) study and also found that teachers having a humanistic control ideology, who put special emphasis on personal, informal student–teacher relations, find themselves in conflict between their altruistic desires and students' inattentiveness. On the other hand, teachers described as having a custodial control ideology, emphasizing classroom discipline and expectations that students accept their teaching with respect and gratitude, face a gap between their narcissistic desires and students' boldness or impudence. The gap between teachers' environmental expectations and classroom reality gives rise to feelings of ineffectiveness and inconsequentiality. A sense of unrealized desires can clearly lead to burnout (Farber, 1991; Friedman, 1995, 2000).

The correlation between student achievement and teacher burnout is less obvious, although Byrne (1994) found a relationship between heterogeneity in students' ability and mental exhaustion among secondary school teachers, as well as a connection between low student achievement and mental exhaustion and depersonalization among teachers working in primary and secondary schools. Friedman and Lotan (1985) found that student academic achievement had a statistically significant negative (reverse) correlation with teacher burnout, but of a small effect size. This means that students' low academic achievement does not really appear to affect burnout. Also, burnout research clearly indicates that students' low level of achievement and difficulty in understanding the material are not included among the major predictors of burnout (Bivona, 2002; Brock & Grady, 2000; Brouwers & Tomic, 2000; Nelson, Macula, Roberts, & Ohlund, 2001; Johanson, 2000). The relationship between perceived efficacy of classroom instruction, classroom interrelations efficacy, and burnout among teachers was investigated in several studies (Cherniss, 1993; Brouwers & Tomic, 2000). Friedman (2004) found that teacher–student relations efficacy was statistically significant in predicting teacher burnout, whereas instructional efficacy had no statistical effect on burnout.

It would therefore appear that teachers' ability to teach is not perceived by teachers as being problematic or a cause for concern. Apparently, teachers feel that they are capable of teaching if they only had the opportunity to concentrate on teaching without undue disruption. The factor perceived by teachers as a primary indicator of professional inadequacy and a source of stress, which leads to burnout, is the social–psychological aspect of teaching: the leadership element of the teacher's job. This component of the teacher's work is expressed in the teacher's ability to control students; to motivate them as individuals and as a group; and to be recognized by them as a "leader" or as being "in charge." It is easy to find similarities between the interdependence between teachers and their students in the classroom, and the interrelationship between leaders and their followers in small groups. Responses that reflect ignoring the leader, not to mention overt disrespect of his or her authority, are the most powerful threats to a leader. Responses of not listening and inattentiveness, as well as disrespect of the teacher's authority by students, accompanied with disobeying school norms, seriously undermine the teacher's narcissistic image as the leader of his or her students.

Teachers' leadership behaviors in the classroom are also important in order to establish and reinforce students' sense of freedom and responsibility when working independently in small groups in class (Wubbels, Brekelmans, Brok & Tartwijk, in this volume). Facing student disruptive and unruly behavior can make teachers feel degraded and inferior, and make them question their leadership abilities. The threat against the leadership aspect of teaching generates conflict and discrepancy between the demands teachers believe are essential to their ability to function properly and the job's psychosocial reality. This conflict puts tremendous pressure on the professional, which ultimately may lead to burnout (French, Rogers, & Cobb, 1974).

The correlation between the type of student population and teacher burnout is also not clear-cut, although it is generally assumed that stress factors are highest among teachers working with special needs children. Providing individual attention to students' needs (even those not directly associated with school) for many hours of the day; limited, irregular, and unobserved success at work; emotional demand and the need for empathy—all these are likely to consume a teacher's emotional resources and increase her vulnerability to burnout (Bhana & Haffejee, 1996; Billingsley & Tech, 1993; Dedrick & Raschke, 1990; Dweck & Repucci, 1973; Greer & Wethered, 1984; Male & May, 1997; Mascari & Forgmone, 1982; Trendall, 1989; Workman & Hector, 1978).

It must be emphasized here that teachers should not be perceived as demanding respect or special affection from their students. Respect for teachers is, in fact, respect for the subject matter taught and for the instructor, a token of appreciation for education and those who provide it, an expression of gratitude for professional and personal efforts. Manifestations of disrespect refer to a deep lack of belief in and appreciation for everything the teacher represents. From the teacher's perspective, disrespect to the teacher means a shameful—and in the worst case—irreversible sense of professional failure. At any rate, disrespect is a serious blow to the teacher's "receiving" pole of his or her professional self, whereas inattentiveness is harmful to the "giving" pole (Friedman, in press).

The question that should be asked now is what can be done based on the data and information gathered and published so far? We should bear in mind that burnout stems from incongruity between high aspirations and expectations, and the harsh realities teachers often face starting from their first day at school. There seem to be two options for action. First, it can be suggested that teacher training colleges try to provide their students with more realistic aspirations of their future work, and equip them with appropriate functioning tools. Usually, in teacher training colleges a noticeable emphasis is placed on developing teaching skills. And indeed, teachers are quite successful at teaching in classrooms conditions. However, findings from burnout studies indicate that teaching is really not the problem teachers are facing at school or in class. A much more serious issue is classroom management and control. Nevertheless, managing classrooms and controlling students' behavior are generally not pivotal issues in teacher training curricula. Moreover, the need for proper training in these issues is well known, but still very little attention, time, and resources are given to provide proper training to aspiring teachers. Teacher training may benefit from new classroom management practices, in particular those that enable a proper balance between "giving" to the students and "receiving," both personally and professionally.

Second, more should be done to encourage and support collegiality among teachers at schools. Schools as organizations have a role in creating conditions for teachers to learn from one another. Enhanced collegiality can, and should, help and support the solutions to pedagogical as well as administrative problems.

ACKNOWLEDGMENT

The author thanks Barry Farber, Curtin University, Australia, for his review of an early version of this chapter.

REFERENCES

Ashforth, B. E., & Lee, R. T. (1997). Burnout as a process: Commentary on Cordes, Dougherty and Blum. *Journal of Organizational Behavior, 18*, 703–708.

Bacharach, S. B., Bauer, S. C., & Conley, S. (1986). Organizational analysis of stress: The case of elementary and secondary schools. *Work and Occupations, 13*(1), 7–32.

Bandura, A. (1997). *Self efficacy—The exercise of control*. New York: Freeman.

Bhana, A., & Haffejee, N. (1996). Relation among measures of burnout, job satisfaction, and role dynamics for a sample of South African child-care social workers. *Psychological Reports, 79*, 431–434.

Billingsley, B. S., & Tech, V. (1993). Teacher retention and attrition in special and general education: A critical review of the literature. *The Journal of Special Education, 27*(2), 137–174.

Bivona, K. N. (2002). Teacher morale: the impact of teaching experience, workplace conditions, and workload. (ERIC Document Reproduction Service No. ED467760)

Black, S. (2003). Stressed out in the classroom. *American School Board Journal. 190*(10), 36–38.

Blase, J. J. (1986). A qualitative analysis of sources of teacher stress: Consequences for performance. *American Educational Research Journal, 23*(1), 13–40.

Bradford, R. H., & Fones, D. M. (1985). Special teacher stress: Its product and prevention. *Academic Therapy, 21*(1), 91–97.

Brock, B. L., & Grady, M. L. (2000). *Rekindling the flame*. Thousand Oaks, CA: Sage.

Brouwers, A., & Tomic, W. (2000, August). *Disruptive student behavior, perceived self-efficacy and teacher burnout*. Paper presented at the 108th Annual Meeting of the American Psychological Association, Washington, DC.

Brown, M., & Ralph, S. (1998). The identification of stress in teachers. In J. Dunham & V. Varma (Eds.), *Stress in teachers: Past, present and future* (pp. 37–56). London: Whurr.

Bullough, R. V., Jr., & Baughman, K. (1997). *"First year teacher" Eight years later: An inquiry into teacher development*. New York: Teachers College Press.

Byrne, B. M. (1994). Burnout: Testing for the validity, replication, and invariance of causal structure across elementary, intermediate and secondary teachers. *American Educational Research Journal, 31*, 654–673.

Byrne, B. M. (1999). The nomological network of teacher burnout: A literature review and empirically validated model. In R. Vandenberghe & A. M. Huberman (Eds.), *Understanding and preventing teacher burnout* (pp. 15–37). England: Cambridge University Press.

Caplan, R. S. (1987). Person-environment fit theory and organization: Commensurate dimensions, time perspectives, and mechanisms. *Journal of Vocational Behavior, 31*, 248–267.

Cherniss, C. (1980). *Professional burnout in human service organizations*. New York: Prager.

Cherniss, C. (1993). Role of professional self efficacy in the etiology and amelioration of burnout. In W. B. Schaufeli, C. Maslach, & T. Marek (Eds.), *Professional burnout: Recent developments in theory and research* (pp. 135–143). Washington, DC: Taylor & Francis.

Cullingford, C. (1987). Children's attitudes to teaching styles. *Oxford Review of Education, 13*(3), 331–339.

Darling-Hammond, L. (1990). Teacher professionalism: Why and how? In A. Lieberman (Ed.), *Schools as collaborative cultures: Creating the future now* (pp. 271–288). New York: Falmer Press.

Dedrick, C. V. L., & Raschke, D. B. (1990). *The special educator and job stress*. Washington, DC: National Education Association.

Dunham, J. (1976). *Stress situations and responses*. Hemel Hempstead, England: National Association of Schoolmasters.

Dweck, C. S., & Reppucci, N. D. (1973). Learned helplessness, and reinforcement responsibility in children. *Journal of Personality and Social Psychology, 25*(1), 109–116.

Dworkin, A. G. (1986). *Teacher burnout in the public schools: Structural causes and consequences for children*. Albany: State University of New York Press.

Esteve, J. M. (2000). The transformation of the teachers' role at the end of the twentieth century: New challenges for the future. *Educational Review, 52*(2), 197–207.

Evers, W., Brouwers, A., & Tomic, W. (2002). Burnout and self efficacy: A study on teachers' beliefs when implementing an innovative educational system in the Netherlands. *British Journal of Educational Psychology, 72*(2), 227–244.

Farber, B. A. (1983). *Stress and burnout in the human service professions*. Elmsford, NY: Pergamon Press.

Farber, B. A. (1984). Stress and burnout in suburban teachers. *Journal of Educational Research, 7*(6), 325–331.

Farber, B. A. (1991). *Crisis in education: Stress and burnout in the American teacher*. San Francisco: Jossey-Bass.

Farber, B. A. (1999). Inconsequentiality—The key to understanding teacher burnout. In R. Vandenberghe & A. M. Huberman (Eds.), *Understanding and preventing teacher burnout* (pp. 159–165). England: Cambridge University Press.

Farber, B. A. (2000). Treatment strategies for different types of teacher burnout. *Clinical Psychology, 56*(5), 675–689.

Folkman, S., & Lazarus. (1980). An analysis of coping in a middle-aged community sample. *Journal of Health and Social Behavior, 21*(3), 219–239.

Freeman, A. (1987). Pastoral care and teacher stress. *Pastoral Care in Education, 5*(1), 22–28.

French, J. R. P., Rogers, W. L., & Cobb, S. (1974). *Adjustment as coping and adaptation.* New York: Basic Books.

Freudenberger, H. J. (1974). Staff burnout. *Journal of Social Issues, 30,* 159–164.

Friedman, I. A. (1991). High and low burnout schools: School culture aspects of teacher burnout. *Journal of Educational Research, 84*(6), 325–333.

Friedman, I. A. (1992). Burnout in teaching: the concept and its components. *Megamot, 34*, 248–261. (Hebrew)

Friedman, I. A. (1994). Conceptualizing and measuring teacher-perceived student behaviors: Disrespect, sociability, and attentiveness. *Educational and Psychological Measurement, 54*(4), 949–958.

Friedman, I. A. (1995). Student behavior patterns contributing to teacher burnout. *The Journal of Educational Research, 88*(5), 281–289.

Friedman, I. A. (2000). Burnout in teachers: Shattered dreams of impeccable professional performance. *Journal of Clinical Psychology, 56*, 595–606.

Friedman, I. A. (2004). Directions in teacher training for low burnout teaching. In E. Frydenberg (Ed.), *Thriving, surviving, or going under: Coping with everyday lives* (pp. 305–326). Greenwich, CT: Information Age Publishing.

Friedman, I. A. (in press). The Bipolar professional self of aspiring teachers: Mission and power. *Teaching and Teacher Education.*

Friedman, I. A., & Gavish, B. (2003). *Teacher burnout: The shattered dreams of professional success.* Jerusalem: Henrietta Szold Institute. (Hebrew)

Friedman, I. A., & Kass, E. (2002). Teacher self-efficacy: A classroom-organization conceptualization. *Teaching and Teacher Education, 18*, 675–686.

Friedman, I. A., & Farber, B. A. (1992). Professional self-concept as a predictor of teacher burnout. *Journal of Educational Research, 86*(1), 28–35.

Friedman, I. A., & Krongold, N. (1993). *Teacher-students relationships: Students' point of View.* Jerusalem: Henrietta Szold Institute. (Hebrew)

Friedman, I. A., & Lotan, I. (1985). *Mental burnout among teachers in elementary schools.* Jerusalem: Henrietta Szold Institute. (Hebrew)

Gavish, B. (2002). *Fit between role expectations and actual role perceptions as predictors of burnout in novice teachers.* Unpublished doctoral dissertation. Hebrew University, Jerusalem. (Hebrew)

Greer, J. G., & Wethered, C. E. (1984). Learned helplessness: A piece of the burnout puzzle. *Exceptional Children, 5*(6), 524–530.

Hastings, R. P., & Bham, M. S. (2003). The relationship between student behavior patterns and teacher burnout. *School Psychology International, 24*(1), 115–127.

Hobfoll, S. E., & Freedy, J. (1993). Conservation of resources: A general stress theory applied to burnout. In W. B. Schaufeli, C. Maslach, & T. Marek (Eds.), *Professional burnout: Recent developments in theory and research* (pp. 19–32). Washington, DC: Taylor & Francis.

Holland, J. L. (1985). *Making vocational choices: A theory of careers* (2nd ed.). Englewood Cliffs, NJ: Prentice Hall.

Iwanicki, E. F., & Schwab, R. L. (1981). A cross validation study of the Maslach Burnout Inventory. *Educational and Psychological Measurement, 41*(4), 1167–1174.

Janssen, P. M., Schaufeli, W. B., & Houkes, I. (1999). Work-related and individual determinants of the three burnout dimensions. *Work and Stress, 13,* 174–186.

Johanson, C. S. (2000). Teaching stress and student characteristics as predictors of teacher behavior. *Dissertation Abstracts International, Section A: Humanities and Social Sciences, 61*(6-A), 2185.

Kahn, R. L., Wolfe, D. M., Quin, R. P., Snoek, J. D., & Rosenthal, R. A. (1964). *Organizational stress: Studies in role conflicted ambiguity.* New York: John Wiley.

Katz, D. N., & Kahn, R. L. (1978). *Social psychology of organizations.* New York: John Wiley.

Kohut, H., & Wolf, E. S. (1978). The disorders of the self and their treatment: An outline. *International Journal of Psychoanalysis, 59*, 413–425.

Lazarus, R. S. (1966). *Psychological stress and the coping process.* New York: McGraw-Hill.

LeCompte, M. D., & Dworkin, A. G. (1991). *Giving up on school: Student dropouts and teacher burnouts.* Newbury Park, CA: Corwin Press.

Lee, R. T., & Ashforth, B. E. (1996). A meta-analytic examination of the correlates of the three dimensions of job burnout. *Journal of Applied Psychology, 81*(2), 123–133.

Leiter, M. P. (1992). Burn-out as a crisis in self efficacy: Conceptual and practical implications. *Work and Stress, 6*(2), 107–115.

Leiter, M. P. (1993). Burnout as a developmental process: Consideration of models. In W. B. Schaufeli, C. Maslach, & T. Marek (Eds.), *Professional burnout: Recent developments in theory and research* (pp. 237–250). Washington, DC: Taylor & Francis.

Lens, W., & De Jesus, S. N. (1999). A psychological interpretation of teacher stress and burnout. In R. Vandenberghe & A. M. Huberman (Eds.), *Understanding and preventing teacher burnout* (pp. 192–201). England: Cambridge University Press.

Lortie, D. (1975). *School teacher: A sociological study*. Chicago: University of Chicago Press.

Luckner, J. L. (1996). Juggling roles and making changes. *Teaching Exceptional Children, 12*(2) 24–28.

Malach-Pines, A. (2000). Treating career burnout: A psychodynamic existential perspective. *Journal of Clinical Psychology, 56*(5), 633–642.

Male, D., & May, D. (1997). Stress, burnout, and workload in teachers of children with special educational needs. *British Journal of Special Education, 24*(3), 133–140.

Mascari, B. G., & Forgmone, C. (1982). A follow up study of EMR students four years after dismissal from the program. *Education and Training of the Mentally Retarded, 17*, 288–292.

Maslach, C. (1976). Burned-out. *Human Behavior, 5*(9), 16–22.

Maslach, C., & Jackson, S. E. (1981). The measurement of experienced burnout. *Journal of Occupational Behavior, 2*, 99–113.

Maslach, C., & Leiter, M. P. (1997). *The truth about burnout*. San Francisco: Jossey-Bass.

Maslach, C., & Schaufeli, W. B. (1993). Historical and conceptual development of burnout. In W. B. Schaufeli, C. Maslach, & T. Marek (Eds.), *Professional burnout: Recent developments in theory and research* (pp. 19–32). Washington, DC: Taylor & Francis.

Mcgill, E. S. (2002). Stressors effecting self-contained comprehensive development class teachers. *Dissertation Abstracts International, Section A: Humanities and Social Sciences, 62*(10-A), 3343.

Miller, L. (1999). Reframing teacher burnout in the context of school reform and teacher development in the United States. In R. Vandenberghe & A. M. Huberman (Eds.), *Understanding and preventing teacher burnout* (pp. 139–156). England: Cambridge University Press.

Mishor, M. (1994). *Sense of burnout among teachers and their perception of organization pattern and teamwork in heterogeneous junior high-schools*. Unpublished master's thesis. Bar-Ilan University, Ramat Gan, Israel. (Hebrew)

Nelson, J. R., Maculan, A., Roberts, M. L., & Ohlund, B. J. (2001). Sources of occupational stress for teachers of students with emotional and behavioral disorders. *Journal of Emotional and Behavioral Disorders, 9*(2), 123–130.

Nias J. (1999). Teachers moral purpose: Stress, vulnerability, and strength. In R. Vandenberghe & A. M. Huberman (Eds.), *Understanding and preventing teacher burnout* (pp. 223–237). England: Cambridge University Press.

Ostroff, C. (1993). Relationships between person-environment congruence and organizational effectiveness. *Group and Organization Management, 1*, 103–123.

Pajak, E., Cramer, S. E., & Konke, K. (1986). Role set correlates of teacher reports of classroom behavior. *Journal of Research and Development in Education, 20*(1), 37–43.

Pines, A., & Aronson, E. (1988). *Career burnout: Causes and cures*. New York: Free Press.

Reilly, N. P. (1994). Exploring a paradox: Commitment as a moderator of the stressor-burnout relationship. *Journal of Applied Social Psychology, 24*(5), 397–414.

Sarason, S. B. (1999). *Teaching as a performing art*. New York: Teachers College Press.

Schwab, R. L., & Iwanicki, E. F. (1982a). Perceived role conflict, role ambiguity, and teacher burnout. *Educational Administration Quarterly, 18*, 60–74.

Schwab, R. L., & Iwanicki, E. F. (1982b). Who are our burned out teachers? *Educational Research Quarterly, 7*(2), 5–16.

Schwarzer, R., & Greenglass, E. (1999). Teacher burnout from a social-cognitive perspective: A theoretical position paper. In R. Vandenberghe & A. M. Huberman (Eds.), *Understanding and preventing teacher burnout* (pp. 238–246). England: Cambridge University Press.

Shea, C. A. (1990). *The emotional exhaustion aspect of burnout and stressors in resource LD teachers*. (Eric Document Reproduction Service No. ED322117)

Sleegers, P. (1999). Professional identity, school reform, and burnout: Some reflections on teacher burnout. In R. Vandenberghe & A. M. Huberman (Eds.), *Understanding and preventing teacher burnout* (pp. 247–255). England: Cambridge University Press.

Smylie, M. A. (1999). Teacher stress in a time of reform. In R. Vandenberghe & A. M. Huberman (Eds.), *Understanding and preventing teacher burnout* (pp. 59–84). England: Cambridge University Press.

Spokane, A. R. (1987). Conceptual and methodological issues in person-environment fit research. *Journal of Vocational Behavior, 31*, 217–221.

Taris, T. W., Schreurs, P. G., & Schaufeli, W. B. (1999). Construct validity of the Maslach Burnout Inventory—General survey: A two-sample examination of its factor structure and correlates. *Work and Stress, 13*(3), 223–237.

Travers, C. J., & Cooper, C. L. (1996). *Teachers under pressure*. London: Routledge.

Trendall, C. (1989). Stress in teaching and teacher effectiveness: A study of teachers across mainstream and special education. *Educational Research, 31*(1), 52–58.

Troman, G., & Woods, P. (2001). *Primary teachers' stress*. New York: Routledge/Falmer.

Weiskopf, P. E. (1980). Burnout among teachers of exceptional children. *Exceptional Children, 47*(1), 18–23.

Wisniewski, L., & Gargiulo, R. M. (1997). Occupational stress and burnout among special educators: A review of the literature. *The Journal of Special Education, 31*(3), 325–346.

Woods, P. (1999). Intensification and stress in teaching. In R. Vandenberghe & A. M. Huberman (Eds.), *Understanding and preventing teacher burnout* (pp. 115–138). England: Cambridge University Press.

Workman, E. A., & Hector, M. (1978). Behavior self-control in classroom settings: A review of the literature. *Journal of School Psychology, 16*(3), 227–236.

36

Teacher Research and Classroom Management: What Questions Do Teachers Ask?

Kim Fries
University of New Hampshire

Marilyn Cochran-Smith
Boston College

INTRODUCTION

As many of the chapters in this handbook reveal, researchers and other educators interested in classroom management have long recognized that variations in students, teachers, and contexts play key roles in determining the daily functioning of classrooms. Over time classroom management researchers have found that student characteristics such as home life, cultural heritage, learning abilities and disabilities, individual temperament, language resources, and social and interpersonal skills exert a significant influence on the classroom. In addition researchers have examined the impact of teacher characteristics and strategies such as methods of instruction, curricular selection, organizational approaches, and the ability of the teacher to adapt to the needs of learners. Along similar lines, classroom management researchers have shown that the structure of classrooms, including numbers of students, resources available, the range of student ability, the dynamics of the group, and the size of the room, also contributes to successful educational experiences.

Historically, technical and prescriptive approaches to both studying and implementing classroom management were common. More recently, however, critics have called for major paradigmatic shifts in both our understandings of how classrooms are organized and managed and the ways we study classrooms to illuminate the complexities of classroom life. Today, the majority of researchers make the argument that classroom management must be studied in complex, sophisticated, and multilayered ways that include analyses of teachers' beliefs, assumptions, and knowledge as well as their behaviors and techniques. (Freiberg, 1999b; Jones & Jones, 2004; Tauber, 1999).

RESEARCHING CLASSROOM MANAGEMENT: OUTSIDE-IN, INSIDE-OUT

The chapters in this handbook examine classroom management research and practice from a variety of important theoretical, paradigmatic, and practical perspectives. Together the chapters revisit some of the most enduring tensions involved in teachers' efforts to establish and manage classroom environments at the same time that they explore new questions and connections between management and discourse, culture, inclusion, technology, and moral development, among other areas. Despite their very different approaches to conceptualizing and researching classroom management, however, nearly all of the chapters in this volume are written from an "outside-inside" perspective (Cochran-Smith & Lytle, 1993; Waff, 1994a). That is, even in the chapters that focus explicitly on teachers' perspectives and beliefs, the angle or lens through which these beliefs are examined is that of the university-based or other outside researcher. One implicit assumption underlying research of this kind (and most handbooks of research on various aspects of teaching) is that outside researchers' perspectives offer important implications and useful frameworks for improving teaching and learning inside schools. This assumption is consistent with much of the history of research on teaching.

The norm in our educational system has been for teachers to be on the receiving end of research and inquiry. Traditionally teachers and their work have been the subjects of research, and their classrooms have been sites for the collection of data on a whole variety of topics, including classroom climate, student–teacher interactions, organizational strategies, behavior management systems, and acquisition of subject matter knowledge. In terms of preparing teachers for the management of classrooms, teacher educators, researchers, and specialists in related fields have attempted to provide guidance for teachers in the form of prepared curricula, university-based classes, support from social service agencies, "tricks of the trade" workshops, and schoolwide management programs. In most of these, teachers themselves have few opportunities to scrutinize the assumptions, perspectives, and philosophies behind recommended management approaches, let alone examine how new approaches might help, intersect with, or hinder ongoing practice.

In one regard, our chapter is not different from the others in this volume. Both of us, as authors, are university-based researchers and teacher educators writing about a particular aspect of classroom management. Neither of us would quarrel with the idea that outside research generates knowledge that is essential to the improvement of teaching and learning inside schools and classrooms. In another important respect, however, our chapter is different from many of the others in this volume in that the research it synthesizes and presents is research that has been designed and carried out by K–12 teachers themselves. This chapter reviews, synthesizes, and critiques teacher research on classroom management, focusing in particular on the questions teachers ask, the problems they pose, the issues they regard as important, and the ways they understand and come to know about managing what goes on inside classrooms through systematic inquiry. To be sure, the teachers' questions and issues reviewed in this chapter are filtered through and organized around our own perspectives as university-based researchers and thus they are at least once removed from the knowledge and experiences of teacher researchers themselves. We acknowledge this distance and the limitations it carries. Nonetheless it is our deliberate intention here to highlight insiders' perspectives about managing classrooms by focusing on the questions teacher researchers ask.

The chapter begins with a framework for understanding teacher research, including the major intellectual traditions and educational projects out of which it grew. In particular we focus on the traditions that influenced the emergence during the 1980s of the current North

American teacher research movement. We describe the major features of teacher research, which connect it to other forms of practitioner inquiry and at the same time, distinguish it from more traditional forms of research on teaching. We also comment on what has been referred to as the "protean" shape of teacher research (Cochran-Smith & Lytle, 1999b), pointing out that because teacher research is such a generative concept, it can be shaped and reshaped to further many different classroom purposes and larger educational agendas. We point out that these various agendas have underlying assumptions about the nature of teaching and learning, the sources and remedies for management issues, and the social and political aspects of teaching that may be quite different from one another.

We then review two bodies of teacher research related to classroom management, one the result of a standard literature search on key terms and the other based on selected examples of well-known teacher research. These two bodies of work tend to have different underlying assumptions and focus on different aspects of classroom management. Although we group the teacher research studies we located into two broad categories for heuristic purposes in this chapter, it is not our intention to label either approach to teacher research on classroom management as the good or right approach. Rather we focus on what these two bodies of research reveal about teachers' perspectives on classroom management. We argue that we need to ask many kinds of questions and conduct many kinds of research in order to portray a rich picture of how teachers "manage to teach" (Lampert, 1985). We also suggest that until we have many analyses, including rich insiders' perspectives on the daily work of managing to teach, we will not have an adequate understanding of how teachers negotiate the complexities of the classroom, how they integrate curricular areas with one another and with children's previous knowledge, how they come to understand their learners, and how they pose and solve problems of practice.

TEACHER RESEARCH: BLURRING THE BOUNDARIES OF INQUIRY AND PRACTICE

In her history of educational research in the United States, Lagemann (2000) suggested that by the 1990s, there were three new directions that seemed particularly promising for creating closer links between research and practice—teacher research, design experiments, and combining teaching with research. Although various forms of teacher inquiry were discussed throughout the 20th century (Anderson, Herr, & Nihlen, 1994; Cochran-Smith & Lytle, 2004; Zeichner & Noffke, 2001), it was during the 1990s that teacher research gained new standing because of its potential to lessen the divide between theory and practice (Lagemann, 2000), on the one hand, and contribute needed insider perspectives to the knowledge base about teaching and learning on the other (Cochran-Smith & Lytle, 1990).

We frame our discussion of teacher research and classroom management within the traditions of the North American teacher research movement that emerged in the 1980s. Its various roots and relatives are related to a number of intellectual traditions and educational projects, which other scholars have reviewed. For example, Anderson and colleagues (1994) linked practitioner research to the work of sociologists Kurt Lewin and Stephen Corey, the Stenhouse-led teacher as researcher movement in Great Britain, the participatory action research movement in Latin American, the field of action science led by Chris Argyris and Donald Schon, and the North American teacher research movement. Zeichner and Noffke's (2001) five major traditions of 20th-century practitioner research are very similar to Anderson's, but Zeichner and Noffke also included the teacher education self-study movement in higher education and the Australian participatory action research movement.

A Historical Perspective: The North American Teacher Research Movement

Cochran-Smith and Lytle (1999b) have suggested that the 1980s North American renewal of interest in teacher research was shaped by a number of intellectual projects and political agendas that emphasized the importance of teachers' knowledge and actions in school change and educational reform. Cochran-Smith and Lytle suggested that the emergence of the teacher research movement was influenced by four influential sets of publications in the United States or in Britain. One group of writings reflected and also helped shape the paradigm shift in conceptualizing, studying, and teaching writing that occurred during the 1970s and 1980s. Many publications by and for teachers from the National Council of Teachers of English and by publishers such as Heinemann and Boynton/Cook concentrated on enriching curriculum and enhancing children's language and literacy learning opportunities in classrooms. Part of the paradigm shift was a view of the teacher as a knower and thinker in the classroom (Berthoff, 1987) and a view of teacher research as what Goswami and Stillman (1987) called "an agency for change." At about the same time, the National Writing Project and the Breadloaf School of English began to focus on teachers' research and other inquiries into reading, writing, and talk in classroom settings as part of their ongoing efforts to improve language and literacy learning.

A second influence on the North American renewal of interest in teacher research was a set of writings published primarily by Falmer Press and other British and Australian publishers that focused on teachers' and other practitioners' involvement in action research, or research intended to promote social change and social action (Carr & Kemmis, 1986; Elliot, 1985; Stenhouse, 1985). Although these writings were different from one another, they shared critical perspectives on the current arrangements of schools and schooling and were grounded in democratic social theory. In particular, these writings eschewed the idea that scientific research could be generated by researchers outside of schools and then imported and applied inside of schools. Rather they suggested that teachers themselves ought to participate in action research in order to "democratize research" (Stenhouse, 1985) and improve curriculum. From this perspective, then, teachers' action research was seen as a kind of critical social science (Carr & Kemmis, 1986).

A third influence on the 1980s renewal of teacher research was the work of educators committed to developing more progressive approaches to education in the United States. Cochran-Smith and Lytle (1999b) described this as

> a very loosely connected group of school-based and university-based teachers and researchers who were committed to progressive education, the social responsibility of educators, and the construction of alternative ways of observing and understanding students' work, solving educational problems, and helping teachers uncover and clarify their implicit assumptions about teaching, learning, and schooling. (p. 16)

This loose grouping included, for example, the work of Bussis, Chittenden, and Amarel (1976); Carini (1975, 1986); Duckworth (1987); and others as well as the North Dakota Study Group, the Prospect Center and School, the Progressive Educators' Conference, the Progressive Educators' Network, and the Philadelphia Teachers Learning Cooperative. A common belief was that teachers needed to be their own experts in the classroom who learned how to teach based on close observations of children, structured inquiries, and joint interpretations.

The fourth influence on the North American teacher research movement was the work in the 1980s of teacher educators and researchers who began to challenge the dominance of a university-generated knowledge base on teaching and promote the potential of teacher researchers to add to but also fundamentally alter that knowledge base. The individuals and collaborators who wrote in this area (Cochran-Smith & Lytle, 1990; Erickson, 1986;

Florio-Ruane & Walsh, 1980) worked from an ethnographic research tradition and a multi-disciplinary understanding of language, literacy, and pedagogy. As advocates of the teacher research movement, Cochran-Smith and Lytle argued that teacher research could challenge the very idea of a knowledge base by recognizing teachers as knowers and acknowledging the importance of their questions, interpretive frameworks, and analyses.

Cochran-Smith and Lytle's analysis suggests three primary reasons that this1980s renewal of interest became a movement and not just the latest educational fad. First, interest in teacher research emerged from several different, but in some ways compatible, intellectual traditions and educational projects. These different projects and the larger agendas to which they were attached gave the teacher research movement an unusually broad base with multiple outlets, audiences, and purposes. Second, although different, these projects and intellectual traditions each constructed the teacher as a knower and agent in the classroom and in larger educational contexts. This was oddly consistent with the national discourse that also emerged during the mid-1980s, with its conclusion that that the schools were failing and the nation was at risk (Carnegie Forum on Education and the Economy, 1986; National Commission on Excellence in Education, 1983). Ironically claims of school failure emphasized the need for a professional teaching force, and teachers began to be constructed as simultaneously the greatest obstacle to school reform and its greatest hope for change. Finally in many cases teachers and teacher-initiated groups themselves shaped the teacher research movement and articulated its agendas, which helped to give the teacher research movement a grassroots basis that was powerful and provocative.

Teacher Research in Teacher Education: Prominent but Protean

Over the last decade a number of people have characterized teacher education in terms of "new images" of teacher learning and even "new paradigms" of professional development (Hawley & Valli, 1999; Little, 1993). These new images supplanted the idea that teacher education was a onetime process of "training" with periodic "staff development" for experienced teachers to receive the latest techniques from educational experts. These new images of teacher education were informed by research about how teachers thought about their work (Clark & Peterson, 1986) and by the emerging notion of "learning to teach" across the professional lifespan (Feiman-Nemser, 1983). The emphasis shifted from what teachers did to what they knew, what their sources of knowledge were, and how those sources influenced their work in classrooms (Barnes, 1989; Shulman, 1987). It was also generally agreed that teacher education and professional development had to be deeply embedded in the daily life of schools (Darling-Hammond, 1998; Elmore & Burney, 1997) and had to feature opportunities for teachers to inquire systematically about how teaching practice constructs learning opportunities (Ball & Cohen, 1999; Cochran-Smith & Lytle, 1993; Little, 1993).

In the context of these new images of teacher learning, teacher research has become prominent in teacher education, professional development, and school reform at the national, state, school district, and individual school levels. Generally the emphasis is on posing not just answering questions, interrogating one's own and others' practices and assumptions, and making classrooms sites for inquiry—that is, learning how to teach and improve one's teaching by collecting and analyzing the "data" of daily life in schools.

In many preservice teacher education programs, critical reflections, ethnographies, critical inquiry, teacher research, and action research are now widely used (Beyer, 1988; Cochran-Smith, 1994; Tabachnik & Zeichner, 1991), and professional development schools are intended to provide new kinds of spaces for student teachers to learn through inquiry alongside experienced teachers (Darling-Hammond, 1994; Levine & Trachtman, 1997). In professional development initiatives for experienced teachers, many local teacher research communities as well as regional and national networks of teachers have emerged. These vary in purpose and character but have in common the creation of contexts for teachers to direct their own learning by inquiring about their practice and the learning of their students (Lieberman & Grolnick, 1996).

Very broadly speaking, these initiatives to make teacher research central to teacher learning and development were consistent with "new" images of teacher education and carried with them an enlarged view of the teacher's role—as knowledge generator, decision maker, consultant, curriculum developer, analyst, activist, and school leader. Just beneath the surface, however, approaches to teacher research and inquiry-based teacher learning may look quite different from one another, depending on differing underlying goals and assumptions about teaching, teachers' roles in reform, knowledge for teaching, and how teachers learn. Cochran-Smith and Lytle (1999b) have pointed to the protean nature of teacher research, suggesting that because it is such a generative concept, it can be shaped and reshaped to further virtually any educational agenda. It is not the language of "teacher research" or the organizational structure of "teacher research community" that differentiates approaches, but assumed relationships about inquiry, knowledge, and practice as well as what is made problematic and what is assumed.

Teacher Research: Common Features, Common Critiques

For the purposes of this chapter, we define teacher research as the systematic and intentional inquiries of K–12 teachers and prospective teachers about their own schools and classrooms. Although some teacher research is conducted by individuals working alone, in most versions collaboration is a key feature, and the role of the community is critical because this is the context in which knowledge is constructed and used, as well as the context in which knowledge is opened to the scrutiny of others. A second feature of teacher research is the assumption that what teachers can know through systematic inquiry is worth knowing, and that the knowledge needed to understand, analyze, and ultimately improve educational situations cannot be generated only by those outside of the actual context and then transported from "outside to inside" (Cochran-Smith & Lytle, 1993) for direct implementation and use.

A third feature of teacher research is that the teaching context itself is the site for inquiry. This means that many aspects of K–12 schools and classrooms become potential research sites, including for example, reading groups, math units, and parent–teacher conferences, as well as gender relationships in school, classroom management concerns, and individual students or groups of students such as second-language learners. Although these are also common sites for research that is conducted by those who are outside teaching, it is the combination of teacher as researcher with teaching context as research site that helps define teacher research. In traditional research on teaching, questions come from study of the literature and sometimes from negotiations with research subjects. The questions of teacher researchers, on the other hand, are often referenced to particular students or situations. They are not, however, just about "practical" things. Rather most versions of teacher research turn on the assumption that practice is both practical and theoretical, and teacher research has a great deal to do with how teachers theorize their own work, the assumptions and decisions they make, and the interpretations they construct about students' learning.

The boundaries between teaching and research blur when the teacher is a researcher and when the teaching context is a site for the study of problems and questions of practice. This has the potential to generate innovative inquiry and new kinds of knowledge as well as new tensions and professional dilemmas. Teacher research is based on the assumption that inquiry is an integral, not separate, part of practice and that learning from practice is an essential task of practitioners across the professional lifespan.

Teacher research is also characterized by systematicity and intentionality, as Stenhouse (1985) suggested in his definition of research as systematic self-critical inquiry made public. With teacher research, systematic documentation often resembles the forms of documentation (observation, interviews, and document/artifact collection) used in ethnographic research and other forms of qualitative study. As in other modes of qualitative research, multiple data sources can be used to illuminate, confirm, but also disconfirm one another. Part of what distinguishes the inquiries of teachers from those of outside researchers who rely on similar forms of data collection is that in addition to documenting students' learning, many teacher researchers also systematically document their own teaching and learning and the connections between their students' and their own learning.

Notions of validity and generalizability in teacher research are different from the traditional criteria of transferability and application of findings (often, the identification of causes and effects) to other populations and contexts. With some forms of teacher research, notions of validity are similar to the idea of "trustworthiness," which has been forwarded as a way to evaluate the results of qualitative research (Lincoln & Guba, 1990; Mishler, 1990). Other scholars make a distinction between practitioner inquiry intended to produce knowledge for traditional outlets, on the one hand, and practitioner research intended to transform practice, on the other. Different ways of valuing and establishing validity that break with traditional epistemologies and criteria may be needed for these (Anderson et al., 1994). Finally most forms of teacher research emphasize the importance of making the work public and open to the critique of a larger community. This means that peers and colleagues play an important role in responding to and scrutinizing each others' questions, interpretations, and explanations for situations and events.

TEACHER RESEARCH AND MANAGEMENT: NOTES ON THE LITERATURE REVIEWED

In preparation for this chapter, we selected two bodies of teacher research, both of which are related to classroom management, but which are also quite different from one another in approach, underlying assumptions, and the explicitness with which they address and foreground classroom management as an issue that is separate or separable from other larger teaching and learning issues or from larger contextual issues. The primary difference in these two bodies of teacher research is how the researchers frame and conceptualize classroom management issues, particularly whether they foreground management as the major problem or question being addressed.

The first body of teacher research we identified was the result of fairly standard electronic search procedures using keywords related to teacher research and classroom management, as described later. With some exceptions, the first group of teacher research studies, which we refer to here as "searched teacher research studies," generally focuses on classroom management problems as rather discrete aspects of teaching, which are to a certain extent separable from other issues and thus able to be addressed separately from them. As we show in the sections that follow, these studies reveal many of the direct and explicit questions teacher researchers, particularly new teachers and teachers engaged in professional development courses and programs, ask about organizing classrooms and maintaining order. These studies also reveal the ways teachers go about trying to deal with and solve those problems.

The second body of teacher research was the result of an entirely subjective process of selecting a small set of well-known teacher research studies, which did not appear on any of the search lists using management as descriptor, but which clearly address important aspects of classroom management. Studies in the second group, which we refer to as "selected teacher research studies," provide detailed accounts of how life in classrooms is jointly constructed out of the beliefs, assumptions, discourse, and actions of teachers and students as they relate to one another and interact with the materials, activities, and texts of their classrooms. The studies we have selected in this group focus on classroom management issues to be sure, but they do so in terms of how management is related to and embedded in larger issues of power, gender, culture, language, and very general aspects of curriculum. These studies assume the inseparability of inquiry and practice, showing how teacher researchers continuously form and reform the social, linguistic, and cultural theories that guide the ways they manage classroom teaching and learning environments. Some of the studies in this second group, however, do not reveal very much about how teacher researchers take action to solve problems in their classrooms based on new understandings of students' sensemaking and new realizations about their own assumptions and beliefs.

We review these two bodies of work somewhat differently. For the literature located through conventional search channels, we describe the general features of the studies, including the questions teacher researchers asked and the problems they identified. To provide a closer look, we offer exemplars of each of the five clusters of research studies we identified. We describe these exemplars in enough detail to give readers a sense of the general patterns the studies in each cluster followed. In addition, we list all of the studies in each cluster in a separate figure so that readers have the full list. For the four selected teacher research studies, we describe each study in some detail, commenting on not only the questions that guided the inquiries, but also the view of each of the researchers about the teacher research process itself and the roles that their various inquiry communities played in their development as researchers. For this small set of studies, we stay close to teachers' own words and ideas, trying to reveal how teachers conceptualized the larger issues within which management was embedded and the larger agendas to which they were attached.

Searching for Teacher Research on Management

To establish a teacher researcher-initiated research base on classroom management, we searched four databases: ERIC, Books in Print, Academic Search Premier, and Dissertation Abstracts. Combinations of the following keywords yielded more than 350 citations over all time periods: (a) classroom management and teacher research; (b) classroom management and action research; (c) classroom management and practitioner research; (d) classroom management and self-study; (e) discipline and teacher research; (f) discipline and action research; (g) discipline and practitioner research; and (h) discipline and self-study. These included journal articles, conference papers, dissertations, master's theses, and books. Given that much of the teacher research literature is not readily available in journals and books, we did not limit our search only to published works and thus did not eliminate a priori any of the preceding formats.

Initial examination of each study's title and abstract allowed us to eliminate studies if they appeared in the search because of a different meaning of the keywords than intended for this study. For example, the word *discipline* yielded several studies related to disciplining students in classrooms but also yielded several studies that referred to "the discipline of science." In addition, we eliminated psychological studies that referred to "self-discipline" or focused on self-help. A number of relevant studies appeared in our citation list as a result of the keyword, "action research." However this descriptor also yielded a number of studies wherein outside researchers, such as staff from state departments of education, private foundations, or universities, entered schools to recruit teachers as data gatherers, whom they referred to as "teacher researchers." Although we do not question the potential of these studies to provide important insights, for this chapter, we were only interested in studies initiated by teachers' own questions and concerns. Finally, although we draw on some of these in our general discussion, we eliminated from our major database those articles and chapters written by university-based teacher educators about practitioner inquiry, teacher education, teacher learning, or professional development.

The remaining citation list totaled just under 70 studies. We discovered that approximately 40 of these, which were listed on the ERIC database, came from one university where a teacher research study was required of students seeking a master's degree in education. The remaining studies were from journal articles, books, dissertations, and conference papers.

There is an additional point worth making here about using traditional search strategies to locate teacher research. By definition, teacher research is local—based on questions that arise from daily work in particular schools and classrooms and, although often of interest to broader audiences, generally intended to generate knowledge that will be useful in those local settings. This means that much of the work of teacher researchers is not available through traditional searches and has not been published or presented beyond the local scene. For example, a large number of preservice and inservice teacher education programs either require or encourage teachers to engage in research and inquiry. It is highly likely that some of this, even a great deal of it, deals with classroom management questions. However, these studies are not usually included in the ERIC database.

Describing the problem of reviewing the teacher research literature for the *Handbook of Reading Research*, Lytle (2000) made this insightful point:

> For over a decade there has been enormous growth in the number of teachers conducting inquiry into literacy teaching and learning in their own schools and classrooms. A considerable portion of this work has been published and disseminated nationally as research monographs, edited volumes, and journal articles. Much of it, however, has been published in newsletters or network collections and has remained intentionally local, not readily available beyond the particular setting to which it is connected. What counts as the literature of teacher research is thus at issue because the texts available for a review in a handbook such as this one, although numerous, likely constitute a small proportion of what is actually being written in the field. (p. 691)

Zeichner (1993) made a related point about the difficulty of locating teacher educator research that described preparation of teachers for diversity. Referring to this work as the "fugitive educational literature," Zeichner indicated that practitioners' own research often appears in less accessible journals or is available only through personal contact, not through traditional literature searches. We suspect that there is much more research by teachers that deals frontally with issues related to classroom management, organization, and interactions with students than what was captured through our search strategies. We have no way of knowing whether the 70 studies we located through electronic searching are typical of others or whether their approaches to teacher research are similar to those used in other programs where some form of teacher research is required of teachers as learners.

Selecting Teacher Research on Management

To counteract to a certain extent some of the difficulties involved in using conventional search strategies for a review of teacher research, we selected a second body of teacher research that speaks to issues of classroom management. Because of our involvement over the years with the teacher research community and our knowledge of the field, we were aware that there were a number of teacher research studies, published as either articles or full-length books, which addressed classroom management issues through the lens of teacher research and were quite well known. However we found that these pieces of teacher research did not appear on any search lists related to classroom management. We believe this was the case because they were not explicitly about management, but about the social and intellectual lives that teachers and students together construct in classrooms. They addressed management issues as related to and embedded in larger issues of curriculum, power, gender, culture, and language. Although including these selected teacher research studies in our review chapter does not address the problem of capturing the fugitive literature of teacher research, it does expand the range of approaches and questions related to management.

We selected four examples of this group of teacher research studies, two book-length pieces of teacher research published in the "Practitioner Inquiry" series of Teachers College Press, and three articles published in journals or edited books, two of which are companion pieces to one another and thus were treated as one example here. The four studies we selected were Magdalene Lampert's (1985) *Harvard Educational Review* article, "How Do Teachers Manage to Teach?", Karen Gallas' (1998) *Sometimes I Can Be Anything: Power, Gender and Identity in a Primary Classroom*, Cynthia Ballenger's (1998) *Teaching Other People's Children: Literacy and Learning in a Bilingual Classroom*, and a pair of related articles in a journal and an edited book by Diane Waff (1994a, 1994b), "Girl Talk: Creating Community Through Social Exchange" and "Romance in the Classroom: Inviting Discourse on Gender and Power." Although our reasons for selecting these pieces as examples were highly subjective, as we noted before, they were consistent. Each is a well-defined piece of teacher research in keeping with the features and characteristics of the genre, which we describe previously. Their authors were participants in research communities whose members examined classroom data, discussed the uses of teacher research to improve practice in a variety of ways, and together constructed interpretive frameworks about language, literacy, culture, gender, race, and other issues. In addition, each of the four examples was published by a major press or organization and is widely known in the teacher research community and beyond. Finally each example reveals interesting insights about how teachers manage to teach, including how they think about and raise questions about managing classrooms, how they use research to deepen their understandings and enhance their practice, and how they connect questions of management to other aspects of the social and intellectual lives of classrooms.

We should note here that there are many other examples of widely disseminated and highly regarded writing by teachers that speak directly to management issues and classroom interactions, but were not included here. For example, both Vivian Paley and Herbert Kohl, who are among the most prolific and popular teacher writers in the nation, have books that deal head-on with management and discipline—Paley's (1981, 1992) *Wally's Stories* and *You Can't Say You Can't Play* as well as Kohl's (1991) *'I Won't Learn From You.'* Other less well-known examples of teachers' writing that touch on management questions, but which we did not review in this chapter, include a number of teacher diaries and accounts, such as *Educating Esme* (Codell, 2001) and M*y First Year as a Teacher*(Kane, 1991). Our decision for this handbook chapter about what counts as teacher research is certainly arguable, as others have pointed out (Cochran-Smith & Lytle, 1998; Lytle, 2000). Generally speaking, however, we included only teacher research based on systematic and intentional data collection and analysis consistent with the definition and features of teacher research elaborated in the preceding section.

THE QUESTIONS TEACHERS ASK: SEARCHED TEACHER RESEARCH STUDIES

The first body of teacher research we identified was the result of the electronic search described earlier. With some exceptions, this collection of studies generally focuses on classroom management as discrete aspects of teaching. As we show in the sections that follow, these studies reveal many of the direct and explicit questions teacher researchers ask about organizing classrooms and maintaining order and how they try to deal with and solve those problems.

For example, Patricia Anguiano (2001) was a first-year teacher in a third-grade classroom. She posed several important questions: (a) What strategies can I use to reduce misbehavior in my classroom? (b) What strategies are effective in reducing misbehavior during direct instruction? (c) What strategies are effective in reducing misbehavior during transitions? and (d) What strategies are effective in reducing misbehavior during recess? After establishing a baseline of behavior (by recording field notes daily in a journal, conducting pre- and post-surveys with her students, tabulating frequency counts of misbehaviors), Anguiano targeted four strategies—physical proximity, "withitness," overlapping, and eye contact. As a result of this work, Anguiano wrote:

> This classroom inquiry project affected my students' misbehavior, as well as my own behaviors. As the project progressed, many of the misbehaviors I targeted were reduced because of my ability to manage my classroom better, thus giving the students less opportunity to misbehave. My students gained respect for me as a teacher because I was able to deal with misbehaviors in a way that did not take away instructional time. I also gained respect for myself as a teacher as I saw a positive response in my students' listening skills and ability to follow directions. This experience taught me the importance of looking inward at my own behaviors and not merely identifying the misbehaviors one encounters in every classroom setting. (p. 55)

Like Anguiano, many of the teacher researchers in our searched category stated clearly that doing research had an effect on how they taught, made decisions, problem-solved, handled conflict, and on their attitudes toward their students. Many of these teachers conceptualized their research as a powerful way to make sense of their own experiences in the classroom. Others viewed it as a way to solve problems. Still others used their research to tease out, articulate, and highlight the complexities in their practice so that they could change their practice or extend it in new ways. These viewpoints are generally consistent with the ways practitioner inquiry has been conceptualized by others who suggest that teacher research allows teachers to examine systematically and thoughtfully their own practice (Adler, 1993, 1996; Cochran-Smith & Lytle, 1993; Kemmis & McTaggart, 2000; Zeichner, 1994; Zeichner & Noffke, 2001).

We have organized this body of searched teacher research literature into five clusters with similar characteristics: (1) studies that focus on decreasing misbehavior; (2) studies that focus on decreasing misbehaviors in combination with one or more other variables; (3) studies that focus on implementation of a published classroom management program or curriculum; (4) studies in which individual teachers focus on management in concert with their entire faculty or school–university based collaboratives; and (5) studies that focus on a content area. The characteristics of each cluster are described and exemplars provided.

Cluster # 1: Decreasing Misbehavior

In this first cluster of teacher research studies, teachers posed questions related to the problem of decreasing disruptive, aggressive, or inappropriate behavior. (See Fig. 36.1 for a full list of these studies.) In an attempt to "solve the problem," the researchers followed a general pattern. They collected data to confirm the existence of the problem, speculated on the "probable causes," reviewed published research on implementation strategies, formulated and implemented an intervention plan, and finally gathered data to assess the effects of the intervention.

In a study that typified this pattern, Berman, Hornbaker, and Ulm (2000), three master's degree students from St. Xavier University, focused on pupils in their sixth-through eighth-grade English and physical education classes. The question they posed was how they could

	Title and Author(s)
Decreasing student misbehavior	*A first-year teacher's plan to reduce misbehavior in the classroom.* (Anguiano, 2001)
	A study of students' disruptive behaviors and a lack of respect for authority and peers with middle school students. (Berman et al., 2000)
	Frequency of teacher intervention in hallway misconduct. (O'Brien, 1998)
	Improving discipline through the use of social skills. (Cook & Rudin, 1997)
	Improving elementary student behavior through the use of positive reinforcement and discipline strategies. (Gerk, Obiala, & Simmons, 1997)
	Improving student behavior. (Liddell, Norris, & Zinanni, 1999)
	Improving student behavior by teaching social skills. (Cone, Fulton, & Van Nieuwenhuyse, 2000)
	Improving student behavior in the classroom by using assertive discipline strategies. (Francois, Harlacher, & Smith, 1999)
	Improving student behavior through social skills instruction. (Cook, 1995)
	Improving student behavior through the use of conflict resolution in fifth and eighth grades. (Lanham & Baker, 1997)
	Positive classroom management. (Ellis, 1996)
	Using multiple intelligences, cooperative learning, and higher order thinking skills to improve the behavior of at-risk students. (Dare, Durand, Moeller, & Washington, 1997)
	Using positive discipline to reduce disruptive classroom behaviors. (Brennan, Dworak, & Reinhardt, 2002)

FIGURE 36.1. *Decreasing student misbehavior.*

decrease disruptive behaviors and a lack of respect for authority and peers. As researchers, they first collected demographic data that included race, income, limited English proficiency, and attendance. Then they documented the existence of inappropriate behavioral incidents by counting the number of disciplinary referrals to the office and using observational checklists, student surveys, and journals. After a review of the literature and discussions with other experienced educators, these three researchers implemented cooperative learning strategies, a community service project, and a conflict resolution program. Additional data indicated that the intervention plan had a positive influence on student behavior, with the number and severity of discipline problems reduced.

Cluster #2: Decreasing Misbehavior as a Means to an End

In addition to the studies described earlier that set the single goal of reducing misbehavior, 31 of the studies we located tied the goal of decreasing disruptive behavior to another secondary goal, such as improving academic achievement, developing moral character, improving organizational skills, increasing motivation, increasing student responsibility or autonomy of one's own learning, and improving social/interpersonal skills. (See Fig. 36.2 for a complete list of these studies.) Classroom observations, teacher interviews, school documentation

	Title and Author(s)
Decreasing student misbehavior and improving academic achievement	*Decreasing the amount of classroom disruptions in order to increase the amount of time on task in elementary students.* (Baugous & Bendery, 2000)
	Improving academic success by increasing student engagement in the learning task. (Foster, Gaa, Nowicki, & Ross, 1997)
	Improving student achievement through behavior intervention. (Berry, Johnson, & MacQueen, 1996)
	Teacher and researcher co-design self-management content for an inclusive setting: Research training, intervention, and generalization effects on student performance. (King-Sears, 1999)
Decreasing student misbehavior and improving moral character	*Character education.* (Duer, Parissi, & Valintis, 2002)
	Student achievement through character education. (Finck, Hansen, & Jenson, 2003)
Decreasing student misbehavior and improving motivation	*Increasing teacher, parent, and student involvement to promote student learning and self-esteem.* (Eilers, Fox, Welvaert, & Wood, 1998)
	Motivating students to appropriate behavior. (Albright, 1995)
	Motivating students to learn through multiple intelligences, cooperative learning, and positive discipline. (Baldes, Cahill, & Moretto, 2000)
Decreasing student misbehavior and improving organizational skills	*Effects of teaching organizational strategies.* (Monahan, Ognibene, & Torrisi, 2000)
Decreasing student misbehavior and improving social/ interpersonal skills	*Advancing the pro-social skills in at-risk elementary students through curricular interventions.* (Barnstable et al., 1997)
	Conflict resolution. (Graves, Nordling, Roberts, & Taylor, 1997)
	Creating a conflict-solving classroom community. (Casey, Klene, & Pangallo, 2000)
	Decreasing inappropriate social behavior in freshman seminar through the use of interpersonal skills training. (Quinn, 2001)
	Enhancing students' emotional intelligence and social adeptness. (Gore, 2000)
	Improving elementary and middle school students' abilities to manage conflict. (Karneboge, Smith, VandeSchraaf, Wiegardt, & Wormer, 1999)
	Improving social interaction among 4th grade students though social skills. (Dunleavy, Karwowski, & Shudes-Eitel, 1997)
	Improving social skills at the elementary level through cooperative learning and direct instruction. (Dohrn, Holian, & Kaplan, 2001)
	Improving discipline through the use of social skills instruction. (Bouguist & Schmidgall, 1997)
	Improving student interpersonal relationships and academic achievement through school safety interventions. (Echelbarger et al., 1999)

FIGURE 36.2. *Combinations of Variables.*

	Title and Author(s)
	Improving student social skill. (Garthe, McDonald, Poremba, Schmidt, & Summers, 1998)
	Improving student social skills in structures and unstructured situations. (Finzer, Green, Mizen, & Sennstrom, 1998)
	Improving student social skills through the use of children's literature. (Rives, Smith, & Staples, 2000)
	Improving student social skills through the use of cooperative learning, problem solving, and direct instruction. (Brandt & Robb, 2002)
	Interpersonal skills and goal setting through cooperative learning in physical education. (Anderson & Windeatt, 1995)
	Social skills and problem solving abilities in a middle school setting. (Aherns, Barrett, & Holtzman, 1997)
	Social skills: Improving student behavior. (Duvall, Miller, & Tillman, 1997)
	Using cooperative learning strategies to improve social skills. (Schroeder, Basken, Engsstrom, & Heald, 2000)
Decreasing student misbehavior and improving student responsibility and or autonomy of one's own learning	*Empowering intrinsic learners.* (Martin, Powers, Ward, & Webb, 2000)
	Giving social studies students great decision-making autonomy. (Gardner, 1996)
	Hatching butterflies and other mysteries: A story of a teacher learning to "let go." (Wisneski, 2000)
	Increasing students' responsibility for their learning through multiple intelligence activities and cooperative learning. (Erb, 1996)

FIGURE 36.2. (*Continued*)

(e.g., discipline referrals, parent contact data), surveys, academic assessments, journal entries, anecdotal records, and self- assessments were used to document the existence of these problems. Then, as noted earlier, researchers collected data, implemented an intervention, assessed its impact, and reported on their findings.

In a study by Barnstable, Cargill, Gehlbach, and Workman (1997), for example, teachers' questions revolved around how to reduce the number and severity of misbehaviors and enhance prosocial behaviors in elementary classrooms. The authors documented the "problem" by collecting and analyzing discipline reports, checklists, teachers' journals, and student self-assessments. A review of solution strategies resulted in an intervention plan that included cooperative learning structures, activities that provided opportunities for modeling and practicing prosocial skills, and augmenting and supporting existing conflict resolution programs. Postintervention data indicated that the implemented social skills program made an impressive difference.

What is especially interesting to note is that in both the Berman et al. (2000) and Barnstable et al. (1997) studies (and in a majority of the other studies reviewed in these first two clusters), the teacher researchers generally speculated about the "probable causes" of misbehaviors or the lack of prosocial skills. These probable causes often included problems with the home and family situation of the pupils. In the Berman study (2000), the researchers speculated that "several factors contributed to the problems occurring in the classroom, including family environments and attitudes, no accountability for certain actions, and adults' lack of respect for others" (p. 1). Similarly, in the Barnstable et al. study (1997), the authors wrote:

> The high percentage of students who are lacking adequate social skills can be attributed to a variety of causes, the most significant being a breakdown of family values involving single parent homes, high teen pregnancy rates, numerous foster care placements, high student mobility rates, and gang/drug influences. Other probable causes are related to delayed academic skills, large class size, and a lack of school support personnel. Increasing numbers of children with physical, emotional, and mental disabilities are other factors causing inappropriate behaviors throughout the school setting. (p. 22)

In these studies, however, data were not collected about family or environmental issues, nor were academic assessment scores obtained. Rather data included disciplinary reports, checklists, teacher's journals, and self-assessments. The interventions teacher implemented included the cooperative learning structures, developing activities which provided opportunities for modeling and practicing prosocial skills, and augmenting and supporting existing conflict resolution programs. There were no interventions that addressed the "probable causes" mentioned.

Because the issue of causality was so central in the studies in these first two clusters, we carefully examined them. Fig. 36.3 organizes the "causes" of misbehavior as articulated by the researchers into four categories: home life, teacher behaviors, children's skills or behaviors, and societal factors that influence educational settings. What is interesting to notice is that many of these "causes" are quite speculative based on neither data nor work referenced by other researchers. What is also of interest is that once these "causes" were articulated, the intervention plans put into place did not connect to the "probable cause" that had been articled. Rather these intervention seemed to be more connected to teachers' own beliefs.

Several university-based researchers have suggested that among the most important beliefs teachers have about students are beliefs about the causes of their behavior and misbehavior (Good & Brophy, 2000; Weinstein, Woolfolk, Dittmeier, & Shanker, 1994). Both Konner (1990) and Fink (1988) found that what teachers believe about children's behavior determines the labels teachers attach both to behaviors and to children. In turn, what teachers believe and how they feel about both behavior and children subsequently shapes how they react (Allison & Berry, 1996). For example, if a teacher believes a child's action is an isolated event or stems from a lack of knowledge, a problem may be handled in a benign, understanding, or redirective manner. On the other hand, if a teacher perceives a behavior (even a similar behavior in a different child) as intentional or as an extension of a child's inadequate personality or upbringing, this child may be labeled as "difficult" or "bad." In this case, the teacher's intervention is likely to be more punitive, unaccepting, and severe.

A number of university-based researchers have found that beliefs play a strong role in the decisions educators make and the subsequent experiences that unfold (Bandura, 1986; Clark & Peterson, 1986; Dewey, 1933; McNeely & Mertz, 1990; Pintrich & Schunk, 1996). These assumptions and beliefs represent powerful and what Bowlby (1988) called "internal, overlearned, and unconscious frameworks" that we carry into every encounter acting as guidance systems that influence the way we approach, react, and respond to every circumstance or event. Although there were multiple opportunities to examine the teacher researchers' own beliefs in these studies, little interrogation occurred.

Additionally, in these first two clusters of studies that clearly posed problems and explored interventions, the complexity of the classroom was not made explicit. Changing one's plans in midstream is not an uncommon event in teaching. As Magdalene Lampert (1997) suggested, teachers must decide to discipline or not and that decision occurs in the context of a fast-paced setting where the teacher must consider the "contagiousness" of the misbehavior, the group dynamics, changing evidence, and make moment-to-moment choices about how to proceed.

Home Life	Teacher Behaviors or Larger School Efforts	Children's Skills or Behaviors	Societal Issues
Changing family structures Economic problems Family environment and attitudes Health problems Increased mobility of families in the U.S. Increased number of foster placements Increased teenage pregnancy (younger parents) Lack of moral character or values related to home environment Lack of parental supervision and no accountability for certain actions Lack of parent participation at school Poor role modeling	Curriculum "overload" Inadequate curriculum and instruction of social skills Inclusion of special education students in general education classrooms Inconsistent and poor role modeling Increased number of "safety issues" in schools and classrooms Lack of a classroom management plan Lack of comprehensive professional development in the area of classroom management Lack of contact with parents Lack of integration of social skills across the various curricular areas Lack of sufficient support personnel Large class size Unclear rules, expectations, and consequences	Inability to problem-solve, make decisions, resolve conflicts, express feelings, or manage anger and stress Inability to transfer skills and strategies to real-life situations or across curricular areas Intolerance toward differing ethnic backgrounds Lack of intrinsic motivation to learn or set goals Lack of organizational skills and a deficit work ethic Lack of positive leadership skills Lack of self-esteem Lack of student responsibility and respect Lack of (or underdevelopment of) interpersonal and social skills Low reading ability Negative peer influences Social ineptness	Gang/drug influences Need for social support for families Negative societal influences Population shifts/demographic changes Violence in the media

FIGURE 36.3. *Teacher researcher's perceptions of the causes of misbehavior (arranged in alphabetical order, not by order of value).*

This suggests that every dilemma, conflict, or discipline issue in a classroom is somewhat unique and related to the multiple layers of ideals and goals and people (Florio-Ruane, 1989). The "messiness" of the classroom is not readily apparent in the studies we identified in these first two clusters. Instead the relationship between interventions and results is assumed to be somewhat linear. Although studies such as these reveal a great deal about the kinds of management questions teachers ask, there are many remaining questions that are not addressed, such as what teachers do if the intervention plan they implement does not work, how they know what "working" and "not working" looks like, what they do if interventions work for some but not other students, and under what circumstances and in what contexts interventions plans should change.

Cluster #3: Implementing a Classroom Management Program

In the firsts two clusters of studies, which might be thought of as cause-and-effect or problem solving studies, teacher researchers laid out one or more questions, substantiated the existence of a problem using classroom data, speculated on probable causes, invented and implemented a plan for intervention, and then assessed and reported on its impact. A third cluster of studies,

	Title and Author(s)
Studies that examined the effectiveness of a published classroom management curriculum	*Conducting democratic class meetings. School violence and conflict programs.* (Gathercoal, 2000)
	Improving student discipline at the primary level. (Kelly, 1997)
	Judicious (character education) discipline. (Gathercoal & Nimmo, 2001)
	Judicious discipline: A case study of a student teacher. (Ackley & Campbell, 2000)
	Judicious discipline: 5 years later. (Gathercoal, 2002)
	Promoting appropriate behavior through social skill instruction. (Bogdan et al., 1996)

FIGURE 36.4. *Studies that examined the effectiveness of a published classroom management curriculum.*

although small, examined student behavior as a result of implementing a specific preestablished and published classroom management system. These studies implemented a system in totality, in contrast with studies in the first two groups where teachers mixed and matched strategies from various discipline theories or approaches. This third cluster of studies followed the general pattern of problem solving, outlined earlier. (See Fig. 36.4 for a complete list of these teacher research studies.) With this cluster of studies, teacher researchers asked questions such as "How can I reduce the misbehavior in my class?", which is similar to the questions posed in Cluster #1. Interestingly, however, little or no discussion of why they chose to implement a particular curriculum was offered.

Ackley and Campbell (2000), for example, examined the effects of using McEwan, Gathercoal, and Nimmo's (1999) Judicious Discipline program in the classroom of Campbell, a student teacher from the University of Portland. Campbell administered anonymous student surveys on discipline to his high school social studies class and then introduced the Judicious Discipline program, discussing topics such as freedom, justice, and equality with his students. Additionally, the class considered the concept of the rights of an individual versus the rights and needs of a community. Students were presented with a variety of case studies that focused on school discipline and asked to brainstorm consequences for breaking rules. This culminated in the creation of their own class rules. Simultaneously, Ackley, a university-based researcher, interviewed Campbell's cooperating teacher and supervisor. Following the implementation of the discipline program, the survey was readministered to students and the data compared. Ackley and Campbell concluded that the discipline program enabled students to become more comfortable in the classroom and that student perceptions moved from less to more autonomous. Additional action research studies examining the effectiveness of the Judicious Discipline program have also been published by its authors (Gathercoal, 2000, 2002; Gathercoal & Nimmo, 2001).

Two studies examined the effects of another commercial management program, the Second Step Violence Prevention program (published by the Committee for Children, 1996). Kelly (1997) and the team of Bogdan, Dye, Leitner, and Meersman (1996) implemented this curriculum in elementary classrooms. Setting a goal of reducing inappropriate behaviors such as physical aggression and the use of inappropriate words in her all-day kindergarten, Kelly (1997) implemented the Second Step program using lessons, stories, discussion, and role-play. She also infused a second program, entitled the MegaSkills program, designed to build motivation, confidence, effort, responsibility, initiative, teamwork, and more. Behavioral checklists and surveys were used for data collection, and postintervention data indicated a decrease in hitting, pushing, and kicking as well as a decrease in the number of inappropriate words.

The team of Bogdan et al. (1996) examined the impact of the Second Step program after problems in student behavior were documented through an analysis of records from peer mediation sessions, student referrals, and staff surveys. These teacher researchers integrated the program with cooperative learning activities and team-building activities, targeting social skills in need of improvement such as respect, responsibility, and cooperation. They concluded that students showed an improvement in appropriate behaviors as a result of the program.

It is not surprising that teacher researchers pose questions about issues of misbehavior and even violence in schools. It is clear that there is no consensus in our society at this time about how to deal appropriately with young people's behavior and misbehavior, or even what counts in these areas. In the last 50 years or so, psychologists, educators, and others have offered many theories about how to manage the classroom (Emmer & Aussiker, 1990). These focus, variously, on the teacher's power to shape individual and group behavior (Redl & Wattenberg, 1959; Skinner, 1968); using power and communication to influence a child's sense of belonging (Dreikurs & Cassel, 1972; Gordon, 1974); controlling through congruent communication (Ginott, 1971); managing students without coercion (Glasser, 1992); and controlling through lesson management (Kounin, 1977; Palmer, 1998). More recently, we have seen specific preestablished programs such as assertive discipline (Canter & Canter, 1976; 1992); positive discipline (Bourgeois, 1979; Glenn & Nelson, 1987; Jones, 1987; Nelsen, Lott, & Glenn, 1997; Shandler, 1996); developmental discipline (Walsh & Cowles, 1982); prescriptive discipline (Shupe, 1998); discipline with dignity (Curwin & Mendler, 1988; Mendler, 1992); cooperative discipline (Albert, 1996; Freiberg, 1999a); humanistic discipline (Charney, 1992); smart discipline (Koenig, 2000); constructive discipline (Smith, 1924, 1936); inner discipline (Coloroso, 1994); discipline as self-control (Gordon, 1974, 1989); and judicious discipline (Ackley & Campbell, 2000; Gathercoal, 1998; Gathercoal & Crowell, 2000; McEwan, 2000; McEwan et al., 1999; Nimmo, 1998), to name just a few. The teacher researchers in this third cluster of studies ask important questions about aggressive and disruptive behaviors in both secondary and elementary classrooms. Each attempts to intervene by imposing a particular preestablished management/discipline intervention, an approach that is very different from those mix-and-match or invented strategies described in the first two clusters. For whatever reasons, teacher researchers have studied the impact of most of the vast numbers of management and discipline packaged programs available today.

Cluster #4: Implementing Schoolwide Management Programs

The fourth cluster of studies includes research by teachers who have engaged in schoolwide management programs, such as in-school suspension (Simon, 1993) or peer mediation programs (Gabrielle, 2002). (See Figure 36.5 for a listing of these studies.)

For example, as part of a teacher research dissertation, Gabrielle (2002) worked with middle school administrators, parents, teachers, and students to introduce conflict resolution principles and skill-building activities as an alternative to more traditional disciplinary measures. Different from the other clusters of studies, in this study, the teacher researcher taught conflict resolution skills and strategies to students throughout the school, organized and oversaw the schoolwide peer mediation program, offered staff development workshops, and met with parent groups. The researcher concluded that sixth-grade students introduced to peer mediation

> continued to use the program throughout their tenure at the middle school. Furthermore, as the program continued to refine itself, it handled increasingly complex problems more effectively and with less intervention from administrators. Finally, data analysis revealed that including peer mediation in the school's character education and discipline program increased visibility and increased support from teachers, parents, and the school administration. (p. 5)

	Title and Author(s)
Teachers participating in school-university collaboratives and with their faculty on research projects	*An investigation of the teacher competencies needed to utilize diagnostic test data in prescribing occupational learning experiences in teaching EMRS. Final Report.* (Nelson, 1976)
	Evaluating a peer mediation program at one middle school. (Gabrielle, 2002)
	Facilitating teacher research through school-university partnerships. (Wortham, 1997)
	Making schools safe for students: Solutions to discipline problems. (Malesich, 1994)
	Promoting acceptance to prevent discipline problems. (Beane et al., 1998)
	Promoting a culture of collaboration through continuing professional development. (Barnes & Bennett, 2001)
	Promoting classroom teacher research. (Eades & Peake, 1980)
	The in-school suspension program in the Coatesville Area School District. (Simon, 1993)
	The professional development school: Linking the university and the public school: An action research project. (Murphy, 1996)
	The school as a center of inquiry: An action research project. (Williams, 1995)
	Training students in thinking skills for solving social problems: A strategy for helping students cope constructively with school stressors. (Bruene, 1985)

FIGURE 36.5. Teachers participating in school–university collaboratives or with their faculty on research projects.

In addition to individual researchers studying schoolwide programs, several faculties examined ways to promote a sense of belonging in their school and establish an atmosphere where students demonstrated respect for themselves, their peers, and adults in an attempt to prevent discipline problems (Beane, Jacobs, & Miller, 1998; Murphy, 1996). Another faculty study examined the stress of middle school students as they transition from elementary school to middle school (Bruene, 1985). Other faculties completed self-studies to examine issues surrounding their school's safety (Malesich, 1994), disciplinary policies (Eades & Peake, 1980), and behavior management (Barnes & Bennett, 2001).

Cluster #5: Management, Curriculum, and Content

The studies in this final cluster did not begin with a question related to classroom management, but with questions related to a curricular area such as science (Saurino, Bourma, & Gunnoe, 1999), social studies (Turner, 1981), and English/language arts (Donoahue, 1998; Morris, 1998). However as they explored students' development in a particular content area, each of these studies uncovered data connected to classroom management, and one or more of their findings were related to management and were significant enough for the study to appear in our searched database. (See Figure 36.6 for a list of these studies.)

Traditionally classroom management and instruction have been regarded as dichotomous (Butchart & McEwan, 1998; Freiberg, 1999b), with management typically regarded as a precursor to instruction, and management and instruction typically researched in isolation from one another (Tauber, 1999). This cluster of teacher research studies that focus on content area

	Title and Author(s)
Studies that examined content areas	*Collaboration as community: Outcomes of conducting research on one's colleagues.* (Slater, 1988)
	Giving children control: Fourth graders initiate and sustain discussions after teacher read-alouds. (Donoahue, 1998)
	Improving student's writing ability through journals and creative writing exercises. (Bartscher et al., 2001)
	Improving writing of at-risk students with a focus on African American males. (Cason et al., 1991)
	Law-related education. (Turner, 1981)
	Science classroom management techniques using graphic calculator technology. (Saurino et al., 1999)
	The effects of integrated curriculum on 9th grade at-risk students. (Morris, 1998)

FIGURE 36.6. *Studies that examined content areas.*

instruction suggest that the "line" between classroom management and instruction is much more blurred. In the teaching of writing, research by Cason, Tabscott, and Thomas (1991); Slater (1988); and Bartscher, Lawler, Ramirez, and Schinault (2001) illustrates these "blurry" connections.

Cason, et al. (1991) reported on an action research project where a group of 7th-through 12th-grade teachers analyzed samples of their students' writing to answer the following question: "Do the low-scoring papers written by Black students differ in any systematic way from those by White students?" This analysis looked at both the rhetorical features of the students' writing as well as the use of vocabulary. They concluded that features of Black English "rarely appeared in the writing of African- American students in [their] district, a fact which contradicted our assumptions about what caused the low scores" (p. 26). As a follow-up to this analysis, the teachers attempted to uncover why the discrepancy existed and asked how they could find ways to reach their Black writers. Additionally, they examined how they, a group of White female teachers, could design a plan to reach these students, the majority of whom were male. After studying African American culture, literature, the writing process, and language styles, the teachers implemented the following to improve the writing of their secondary students (in particular African American males): (a) emphasized the writing process; (b) individualized and personalized; (c) encouraged cooperative learning; (d) built on strengths; (e) increased engagement with writing; (f) increased control of language; (g) built bridges to more challenging tasks; and (h) used the computer for word processing, editing, and publishing. These teachers noted dramatic changes in student attitude, self-concept, and achievement. There was more time-on-task, positive peer pressure for achievement in a variety of areas, and student empowerment. Additional changes occurred in the teachers' own behaviors: The teachers gave more time for writing in class, they arranged lessons to meet a variety of learning styles, they explicitly valued ethnic diversity, they acted more as a facilitators rather than as disseminators of knowledge, and they became less confrontational in handling discipline. Those students with whom they were able to form a warm personal connection prospered and their scores improved. Even those more aggressive students with whom these teachers felt they had to work even harder to establish a relationship, improved their scores. The few students with whom they felt they were not able to establish rapport showed less progress. Overall the teacher research group concluded that as they changed instruction and classroom management strategies, they also improved their rapport with students, the students improved both their writing skills and scores, and the number of classroom disruptions decreased in number and in intensity.

Slater (1988), a veteran New York City teacher on sabbatical, studied five New York City high school teachers (a math teacher, a physics teacher, a career education teacher, a biology teacher, and a health/PE teacher). Over a 6-month period she explored how and why these teachers incorporated writing-to-learn into the curriculum. Each teacher kept a journal, and Slater found that these teachers began conversing about more than a writing-to-learn philosophy in their classrooms. They began sharing their own personal struggles with writing, they began collaborating with one another on the use of writing within and across curricular areas, and these discussions led to conversations about changes in their style of management.

> We now share ideas collegially in a way one would not expect for a math, a physics, and an English teacher to do. Pia hands me articles from *Mathematics Teacher* about using writing to teach Calculus. David tells me that my use of journals in English classes makes it easier for his students to write comfortably about physics. Our Principal remarks about the ease and facility with which our students sit down and write: he sees none of the usual hesitance and rampant fear. He attributes this to the widespread conscious attention to writing across the curriculum. (p. 4)

Slater concluded that all five participants had changed their classroom management style as a result of integrating the concept of "writing-to-learn" into their curricula. Teachers gained more confidence in trying out new management strategies and expanding on old ones because of the support of this research network. For example, the career education teacher used writing to bring her shyer Asian students into group work. The mathematics teacher used writing to help her students internalize the vocabulary and structure of mathematics, allaying their fears, frustrations, and subsequent "acting out" in the classroom. The physics teacher used writing to focus students on their learning and also to break down the traditional roles and relationships between teacher and student.

Bartscher et al. (2001) targeted fourth-, seventh-, and eighth-grade students from two midwestern school districts, who also exhibited low achievement in writing. This team of researchers perceived that "this low achievement affect[ed] behavior, attitudes, and peer interactions" (p. iii). This low achievement in writing was substantiated with data from surveys, interviews, school report cards, observational checklists, as well as an analysis of students' journal writing, discipline referrals, district assessments, and teacher written assessments. Cooperative learning strategies, increasing the quantity and quality of feedback from teacher to student, focusing journal writing on topics that interested and motivated students, instituting a peer review process, and focusing on creative writing were all implemented. Over time, an increase was seen relative to assessment scores and a decrease in discipline referrals also occurred at both sites.

Looking Across the Examples: The Questions Teachers Ask

Across these five clusters of teacher research studies about classroom management and discipline, teachers developed and implemented intervention plans for pupils ranging from prekindergarten through 12th grade. These included students from diverse classroom settings with varying socioeconomic, racial, and ethnic groups. Some of the classrooms studied were rural, whereas others were urban and suburban. Some were public, and others were private. Many classrooms were arranged in heterogeneous groupings whereas others were homogeneously grouped.

The questions posed by these educators (both preservice and inservice teachers) were significant, primarily having to do with how to manage student behavior while attempting to teach. To manage their dilemmas and "solve the problems" they uncovered, the teacher researchers tried to identify possible causes of behavior problems, collect data to substantiate that problems did exist, and invented or sought out intervention strategies and programs from colleagues, mentors, commercial programs, and research literature. Establishing an intervention plan and then implementing it, these teacher researchers collected additional data to assess the success or failure of the intervention.

In addition to examining how teachers can prevent or decrease student misbehavior, these studies also explored relationships between decreasing student misbehavior and other important aspects of classroom life, such as improving pupils' academic achievement, moral character, organizational skills, interpersonal skills, and autonomy. Additionally some of these studies examined the impact of preestablished classroom management programs or how classroom management intersects with subject matter knowledge and growth in students.

THE QUESTIONS TEACHERS ASK: SELECTED TEACHER RESEARCH STUDIES

In addition to our review of the teacher research studies that result from standard literature search procedures, we also selected four examples of teacher research that deal with management issues as they are related to and embedded within the larger social life of classrooms. In particular these studies explored gender and race dynamics, language and cultural patterns, and how power is used to establish relationships but also defines and sometimes limits students' learning opportunities. As we did for the searched teacher research studies earlier, for each of these selected examples, we considered who the researchers are, what questions they ask, and the interpretive frameworks they bring.

Example 1: Teaching as Managing Dilemmas

As noted earlier, the North American teacher research movement emerged in the context of new ways of understanding and studying teaching. Researchers began to focus on what teachers knew and how they used various kinds of knowledge to make decisions and solve problems in the classroom. As part of this program of research, Magdalene Lampert and a few colleagues at Michigan State University began to teach in elementary classrooms and use their own teaching as a site for research. Over time Lampert's teaching of fourth-, fifth-, and sixth-grade mathematics became the site for an extensive inquiry that explored students' ways of knowing mathematical concepts (Lampert, 1985, 1990, 2001). Lampert analyzed extensively her own planning, teaching, and interactions with students as well as her students' learning as she worked throughout the years. By actively altering the roles of students and teacher in the classroom, Lampert also explored the tensions between knowing mathematics in school and knowing mathematics in the discipline.

We use here as an example one early piece from Lampert's program of teacher research on mathematics teaching and learning, which she titled with the question, "How Do Teachers Manage to Teach? Perspectives on Problems in Practice" (Lampert, 1985). In this piece, Lampert used two incidents—one from her own teaching in a fifth-grade mathematics class and one from a beginning teacher colleague's classroom—to make an argument about the kinds of problems teachers face in their day-to-day work managing classrooms. Lampert pointed out that in contrast to outside researchers who analyzed classrooms situations in order to build more general theories, teachers' emphases were on the "concrete particulars" of classrooms wherein many elements of practice were "unconsonant with theoretical principles" (p. 179).

Lampert offered a close description of one situation in her classroom. She had come to realize over time that in order to "manage" the behavior of the more unruly boys who sat together at one table in the room and to ensure that they worked productively on math problems, she tended to work at the blackboard nearest them, thus making that area the "front" of the classroom. She argued that this situation was a dilemma—a problem without a ready solution:

> But my presence near the boys had inadvertently put the girls in "the back" of the room. One of the more outspoken girls impatiently pointed out that she had been trying to get my attention and thought I was ignoring her. She made me aware that my problem-solving strategy, devised to keep the boys' attention, had caused another, quite different problem. The boys could see and hear more easily than the girls, and I noticed their questions more readily.... I felt that I faced a forced choice between equally undesirable alternatives.... Whether I chose to promote classroom order or equal opportunity, it seemed that either the boys or the girls would miss something I wanted them to learn. (p. 179)

Lampert used her analysis of this and other incidents to raise questions about "generalized theories of instruction, curriculum or classroom management based on careful empirical research" and to challenge whether they adequately captured the work of teaching or applied to the practical problems of teaching.

Lampert's analysis of how teachers teach, from a teacher's perspective, suggested that what was usually referred to as classroom management was more a process of constructing and managing dilemmas than identifying and solving problems that necessarily have clear or dichotomous possible solutions. Having constructed a genuine dilemma, Lampert suggested that choosing the lesser of two evils was not the only way—or an acceptable way—for her, as the teacher, to manage the classroom. Instead she posited that her job as teacher was "maintaining the tension between my own equally important but conflicting aims without choosing between them" (p. 182). These conflicting aims had to do with her identity as a teacher rather than with her ability to manage children's behavior by selecting the one correct approach among an array of management strategies:

> I did not want to be a person who treated girls unequally, as my high school trigonometry teacher had done. Nor did I want to be someone who gave special attention to girls just because they were girls. I did not want to be a person who had such a preoccupation with order that I discouraged enthusiasm. Nor did I want to try to do my work in a disorderly classroom. The person that I wanted to be—this ambiguous self-definition—became a tool to enable me to accomplish my pedagogical goals. (p. 184)

We use Lampert's example here to make an important point about classroom management and the questions and perspectives teachers bring. Her research suggests that teachers' questions come from who teachers are and who they want to be in the classroom as well as from their struggles to understand how they can cope with dilemmas. She argued that sometimes teachers cope by "submerging the conflict below an improvised, workable, but superficial resolution," an approach she suggested would probably not have been recommended by cognitive psychologists and others who were studying classrooms and teachers' cognitive processes from the outside. Her analysis of dilemma management contrasts sharply with the notion of classroom management as the teacher's skill at controlling pupils' behavior and keeping them focused on learning tasks. Lampert argued that in order to manage to teach, teachers must "have the resources to cope with equally weighted alternatives when it is not appropriate to express a preference between them" (p. 193). As a researcher who was also a teacher, Lampert called for more attention to these ways of thinking about management and about the work of teachers.

Example 2: Gender and Power in a Primary Class

Karen Gallas is among the most prolific and engaging of the current teacher researchers, with four books and many journal articles, papers, and presentations to her credit. A primary teacher of more than 20 years and a longtime member of the Brookline Teacher Research Seminar, Gallas developed a teacher research agenda that focused on children's language and learning in primary classrooms. To study particular aspects of the social worlds of her classroom, Gallas observed and audiotaped during sharing time, science talks, and morning journal writing (Gallas, 1994, 1995, 1998). Using transcriptions of classroom interactions as well as detailed observations, she closely examined child-directed initiatives to see how children constructed and used language for various purposes in public and private contexts. Each of her inquiries—on the arts and languages of learning, the roles of children's questions in their emerging science understandings, the dynamics of gender and power in an early childhood classroom, and the development of children's imaginative powers—was located within the larger context and purpose of creating a close classroom community.

Our second selected example of teacher research related to issues of classroom management is Gallas' book (1998), *Sometimes I Can Be Anything: Power, Gender and Identity in a Primary Classroom*. In this book Gallas reveals that she set out to observe and understand, from the teacher's perspective, how particular children—whom she called "bad boys and silent girls" (p. 4)—influenced classroom dynamics by observing two groups of first-and second-grade children. Over 4 years she came to realize that the children's understandings and constructions of gender were "socially holistic" (p. 3) and constantly shifting; they were closely connected to their understandings of race and class and had more to do with power and social control than with gender alone or with the political and social labels adults construct for these.

It is crystal clear in Gallas' writing that her inquiry about gender dynamics emerged from a "problem" of classroom management. She perceived that certain children in the classroom—mostly the "bad boys"—behaved in ways that limited their own and others' social and learning opportunities. Her approach, though, was not to "solve" the problem or "fix" the children but to do teacher research in order to better understand the children and the social processes of the classroom. She wrote explicitly about teachers' questions concerning management (and other issues):

> Teachers' questions are obscured by their contextuality, by being immersed in a particular 'moment' of classroom or school time. They can seem trivial or unformed and usually are interpreted by others as a call for help, or something to be fixed. Both teachers and outsiders respond with explanations of the phenomenon, and solutions .... Observations that place problems of teaching and learning in the foreground seem to beg for a solution but the solutions of others, however well intentioned, are rarely effective. They embody the widely held opinion that if teachers only knew enough about their craft, they wouldn't have messy questions that clearly represented a problem with a teachers' methodology or a child's deficits. The solutions also represent an approach to teaching that portrays classroom problems and teachers' questions as entities that can be remedied by tapping a general, all-purpose store of knowledge about teaching and learning, regardless of the unique nature of that classroom's students, physical space, materials, and teacher. (p. 17)

Gallas' comments here are consistent with Lampert's—outsiders' standard solutions to management "problems" are neither appropriate nor effective. Nor do they reflect sufficiently complex or particularized understandings of the activity of teaching. Both Gallas and Lampert suggest that this is the case—at least in part—because teachers' questions are questions that, almost by definition and in the first place, cannot be adequately answered with solutions but with enriched and deeper understandings.

Gallas' questions and her study of gender dynamics emerged from an interpretive framework that emphasized the social nature of classrooms wherein meanings are mutually negotiated by the participants. Language—and silence—are paramount. Within and in relation to this overall interpretive framework, Gallas developed the notions of performance, personae, and the "social topography" of classroom life, including the subtextual dynamics, to help her understand what was going on. Using teacher research, Gallas worked to bring the subtextual dynamics of the classroom to the surface: "But it is only through the action of classroom research that I can give shape and form to the children's sub-textual work, that I can begin to map the terrain that they are trying to negotiate and see the topography of our classroom culture" (p. 24). In bringing the subtexts of the classroom to the surface, Gallas was able to see patterns in the social dynamics of her classroom. She focused on the distance between the children's private and public personae. Over time she came to see the behavior of the "bad boys" as both a source of social control and a trap that cut them off from opportunities to fully engage in the classroom learning community. Similarly she came to see a girl's silence as both "fortress and prison" (p. 46). Like the bad boys who used language to control, the silent girl used the absence of language to manipulate others, but again like the bad boys whose social power also limited their opportunities, the girl's silence also imprisoned her and precluded her full participation in the learning community.

Gallas' book does not end with a "solution" to the problem of bad boys and silent girls. Nor does it end with an overarching theory of gender dynamics in primary classrooms. The final pages of the book are true to Gallas' view that classrooms are unique social settings that are constantly negotiated and renegotiated by the participants and that cannot be predicted or controlled. It ends with Gallas' account of the entry into her classroom of a new and powerful group of girls who challenged her views about boys and social control and reminded her (and readers of her book) that classrooms are living, changing communities and that each participant brings an "evolving," not a static, consciousness (p. 146).

Example 3: Language, Culture, and Control in a Bilingual Classroom

Cynthia Ballenger is an early childhood specialist who worked primarily in poor communities and had for many years taught children with language delays or learning disabilities. Ballenger was a member of the same inquiry community as Karen Gallas—the Brookline Teacher Research Seminar. Like many teachers who were influenced by Herbert Kohl, Jonathan Kozol, George Dennison, and other 1960s teacher writers who were sharp but idealistic critics of the educational mainstream, Ballenger prepared for teaching at a time when teachers believed they could change the world, particularly the worlds of poor, minority children. During this time, when many teachers began to interrogate their own and others' cultural assumptions and beliefs, they also grew increasingly dissatisfied with the standard arrangements of schooling that seemed in many ways organized not to support but to provide obstacles to children's learning and their life chances.

Along with other Brookline Teacher Research Seminar (BTRS) members, Ballenger was animated by the belief that almost all children could and would learn unless they were hindered from doing so. Indeed, as Ballenger points out, the heart of many of the most powerful pieces of teacher research is the question, "Why aren't all children learning?" To get at this question in many different ways, the Brookline teacher researchers focused on classroom language:

> Teacher research in the BTRS began with the tape recorder as a way to 'stop time' (Phillips, 1992) in the classroom so that we could listen longer. It began with the literature of sociolinguistics, which gave us stories and actual transcripts in which students were misunderstood by their

> well-meaning teachers, in which there was more to hear and to understand than first appeared. ... Looking at transcripts has given us new categories, and more expanded categories, through which to look at what might be relevant to schooling, and new ways to make sense of children's behavior and to connect with it. Looking at transcripts, we discover individuals, who constantly break out of categories. Through this approach to data and interpretation, we have found a way to see what children are putting their energy into, the ways in which they are approaching knowledge of the world, where their skills lie; at the same time, it gives us a way to explore the patterns and assumptions that formed the structure and content of our own teaching. (pp. 13–14)

This approach to teacher research prompted new respect for children and helped teachers develop ways to understand them that were not rooted in deficits but in strengths. Over a number of years, Ballenger (1992, 1998) developed a teacher research agenda that focused on children's language and learning in bilingual classrooms.

Our third selected example of teacher research that deals directly with classroom management issues (among other issues of language and literacy) is Ballenger's (1998) *Teaching Other People's Children: Literacy and Learning in a Bilingual Classroom* . As Ballenger put it, her book is an exploration of the "tension between honoring the children's home discourse as a rich source of knowledge and learning itself, and yet wishing to put that discourse into meaningful contact with school-based and discipline- based ways of talking, acting and knowing" (p. 6).

During the period that is the focus of this teacher research study, Ballenger had just returned to teaching after several years in graduate school. She returned to a small, private, teacher-run preschool that was operated as part of a neighborhood social science agency and supported by state and federal funds. The school community was all Haitian, with all teachers, including Ballenger, speaking both English and Haitian Creole, which was used interchangeably with the children. Ballenger was the only non-Haitian among the children and the other teachers. Although she had long been a successful preschool teacher in many settings where children had behavior problems, she experienced classroom management problems almost immediately:

> I had major problems. The children ran me ragged. In the friendliest, most cheerful and affectionate manner imaginable, my class of 4-year-olds followed their own inclinations rather than my directions in almost everything. ... I tried many of my standard practices. ... Although there were exceptions, on a typical day I had very little sense of being in control. My difficulties increased when I looked around at the other classrooms at my school. There, I was uncomfortably aware, the other teachers—all Haitian women with far less education and training than I—ran orderly classrooms of children, who in an equally affectionate and cheerful manner, did follow directions and kept the confusion to a level that I could have tolerated. The problem, evidently, did not reside in the children, since the Haitian teachers managed them well enough. Where then did it reside? What was it the Haitian teachers did that I did not?. (pp. 31–32)

To address these problems and at the suggestion of her colleagues in the BTRS, Ballenger began to collect texts from the school. She wrote down what the Haitian teachers said and did in "control situations" (p. 33) and then she shared these texts with both the BTRS and the Haitian women she was teaching in a child development course.

By focusing carefully on talk and by examining her own socialization and assumptions, Ballenger discovered that there were major cultural and language differences between the ways the Haitian teachers established and maintained control and the ways she was operating. As an American teacher, Ballenger tried to connect with individual children, anticipating feelings and focusing on consequences (e.g., "if you don't listen, you won't know what to do"). In contrast she discovered that the Haitian teachers focused on the group in control talk, emphasizing family expectations and what loved ones would want (e.g., "when your mother talks to you, don't you listen?"). Over time Ballenger developed new ways of managing in the classroom, combining some of the Haitian tone and style with her own. More importantly perhaps, she developed a much richer and deeper understanding of Haitian cultural beliefs about childhood and socialization and about their focus on a "moral community" (p. 40).

Ballenger worked in a way that is similar to Gallas' approach. That is, she collected and analyzed the "texts" of the classroom to try to make sense of the tensions she noticed between her own and the children's beliefs and approaches to books and print. She learned that what the children valued about books was quite different from what she valued. Her conclusion was also similar: "We have come to see that investigating, interpreting, and identifying what the children are doing in a particular area is a way for the teacher to delve into the area himself or herself in order to learn what it is and what it really means for the teacher as well as for the child" (p. 60).

Example 4: Gender, Talk, and Community in a Secondary Classroom

For many years, Diane Waff has been a high school teacher, a teacher consultant in the Philadelphia Writing Project, a member of the Seminar on Teaching and Learning cosponsored by the Writing Project and the Philadelphia Schools Collaborative, and an active participant in local and national teacher research and reform communities. Her work as a teacher researcher emerged in the context of the 1980s emphasis on inquiry as a way to rethink assumptions and beliefs about culture, race, and gender as well as a way to enhance writing and literacy development across the K–12 curriculum. Working within nested or interrelated teacher learning communities over time, Waff (Cochran-Smith, Lytle, Maimon, & Waff, 1997; Waff, 1994a, 1994b) raised many questions and developed a complex teacher research agenda about language, student–teacher interactions, racial background, and gender dynamics in schools and classrooms.

Our final selected example of teacher research related to issues of classroom management is a combination of two of Waff's writings, which are companion pieces: the journal article "Romance in the Classroom: Inviting Discourse on Gender and Power" (1994b) and the chapter "Girl Talk: Creating Community Through Social Exchange"(1994a). Waff taught adapted English and remedial math in a program for mildly handicapped special education students in a large comprehensive secondary school in urban Philadelphia. In part because of its special education label, Waff's program, composed of primarily Latinas and African Americans, had a sharply uneven gender distribution with 22 girls and 80 boys. Waff (1994a) described the disturbing gender dynamics that emerged in the program and her classroom:

> This environment is one that has encouraged sexual harassment and victimizing of weaker students. It is one which has sent a clear message that appropriate behavior includes power and domination over others. Misunderstandings between boys and girls have often erupted into violent confrontations, and often girls have faded into the background, overpowered by more aggressive male voices. These gender conflicts have cut across racial and cultural lines. (p. 15)

Through her participation in the Philadelphia Writing Project and the Seminar on Teaching and Learning and also in the company of 35 other new teacher researchers, Waff began to raise questions and recognize her own role in the classroom situation:

> I began to realize that the reason I wasn't being successful with my students was largely due to my insulated middle class life style. I lost the opportunity to help them because I didn't invite their realities, their experiences into my classroom. . . . I had grown up in the inner city, attended a Black high school and lived in a neighborhood similar to my students, yet, I still felt a tremendous sense of separation from the students in my classes. (p. 193)

Her participation in the teacher research seminar gave the opportunity to become part of a teacher learning community, which approached problems and issues from an inquiry stance (Cochran-Smith & Lytle, 1999a) and supported small-scale classroom studies. Waff decided to focus on how to get students' voices, especially girls' voices, heard in the classroom.

Based on systematic attention to audiotaped classroom discussions, journal entries, and other students' writing, Waff considered the gender dynamics in her classroom and was deeply disturbed by the anger and hostility she observed. Over several years, she initiated a number of curriculum changes as well as voluntary discussion and writing opportunities. She initiated "girl talk" sessions for girls only with topics that grew out of the girls' previous week's journal writing. Facilitated by two volunteers from the local community who were professional women of color (one an attorney and one an engineer), the girl talk sessions helped to create an open discussion context about gender and equity issues and anything else the girls wanted to discuss. Later Waff also initiated brief daily journal writing sessions with a focus on gender issues:

> Our collective anger over what we perceived as harassment by the opposite sex fueled passionate writing for more than two months. There wasn't an idle pen in the class, as it became clear to us that the negative interactions had taken their toll on our ability to function as a community. Over time we came to agree that men and women need to treat each other more respectfully. (p. 16)

Over time Waff implemented a number of changes in her classroom, in terms of both how she organized activities and how she learned to listen to girls and hear their interests. At one point she began to use romance novels and short stories in the classroom to see whether these would enhance communication between boys and girls. This resulted in entirely new interpretations of traditional texts and also prompted new questions about nontraditional texts. She also consciously adopted teaching strategies designed to make the classroom more gender equitable. These included modeling ways to resist sexist jokes and epithets.

During the years of studying gender dynamics, Waff became aware of many changes in her classroom. As the girls were heard, they learned to speak out more and developed a collective voice. Boys and girls learned more about the others' points of view. But throughout this time, Waff was also engaged in a long-term process of interrogating her own assumptions, working with other teacher researchers, and participating in a gender studies group sponsored by the Philadelphia Writing project. She wrote:

> This has led me to look at my own behavior. I have become much more aware of my tendency to call on boys and to engage them in conversation. In the past I did this to maintain classroom control by keeping the more vocal boys engaged, but the girls let me know through private conversation, journal writes, and in open discussions that this practice was indefensible.... Their voices have caused me to reassess not only the way I teach, but the materials I use. ... Now I work hard to make room for girls' talk and defend girls' space by constantly reiterating the norms for classroom behavior.... We are on the road to building healthy classroom relationships.... My students and I work as a team, and I no longer assume the total burden of maintaining classroom discipline.... What's different is that I have incorporated into classroom discussion issues surrounding gender and power. (p. 18)

It is clear that Waff's inquiries were critical of the larger relations of power and gender that structure our society but also self-critical about her own role in perpetuating these. Her approach to teacher research grew out of problems and concerns that she had about classroom management, to be sure, but her intention was to build a richer and more productive classroom learning community rather than to "fix" the students or "solve" a specific classroom problem.

Looking Across the Selected Teacher Research Examples: The Questions Teachers Ask

In this section we have described in some detail four selected pieces of teacher research that are well known and well regarded in the teacher research community. As we noted earlier, none of these was identified through conventional search strategies when keywords such as "classroom management" were paired with "teacher research." Apparently these studies were not thought of by their authors or by catalogers as explicitly about classroom management, discipline, changing students' behavior, or keeping order in the school room. Rather the descriptors used to identify these pieces in their subtitles or for Library of Congress and other cataloging purposes were terms such as *race, culture, language, power, gender, literacy, identity, bilingualism*, and *community* in the classroom. Regardless of the descriptors, all four of these books address important topics directly related to the ways teachers manage classrooms, establish relationships, and create learning environments. These include, but are not limited to, cultural and language differences in child-rearing patterns and expectations between teachers and children; children's and adolescents' uses of language and silence to establish and maintain their own and others' social positions in the classroom; teachers' constructions of problems and dilemmas related to management and learning opportunities; and teachers' efforts to hear students' voices, interrogate their own and others' assumptions, and build classroom communities.

Across these four studies, there were a number of common characteristics. All of the teacher researchers in this group conceptualized, studied, and acted on management issues in relation to other larger issues such as those noted earlier, rather than in isolation. That is, they examined management issues not as separate and separable aspects of classroom life, but in the context of many other interrelated issues. More appropriately perhaps in many cases, they examined the larger issues of classroom life and in the process of doing so, they also addressed management issues. On the other hand, however, the teacher researchers we have described here were not aiming for generalized or universalized strategies or theories of management or of anything else. To the contrary, all of the studies considered in this section assumed a particularized view of classroom life and attempted to understand the multilayered and nuanced features of what was going on in the social and intellectual lives of their own classrooms. Lampert was quite explicit about this, commenting directly on the unlikelihood that universalized theories of instruction or management could adequately capture the activities of particular classrooms.

In addition, it is very clear that these teacher researchers approached classroom management primarily for the purpose of understanding rather than "fixing" children and adolescents, although they sometimes also changed their own teaching strategies as a result of their richer understandings of the social processes of their classrooms. They used language such as "letting the children teach you" how to work with them and "getting a sense of" what students' interpretive frames and experiences were. In addition, and very importantly, they approached classroom management issues from the perspective of students' strengths rather than from a deficit perspective. All of these teacher researchers also concentrated on students' conceptions, desires, and worldviews, trying to both build and uncover the ways their students perceived situations and the interests and previous experiences they brought to the situation. Rather than trying to fix students because there was something wrong with them or identify the causes of their "bad" behavior, these teacher researchers searched for meanings and assumed that all students were engaged in behavior that made sense to them. The point, therefore, was to understand how participants were making sense in order to create a constructive classroom learning community for all.

Some of the teacher researchers focused more on actions than others. For example, Waff was very clear about the curricular and organizational changes she put into place as she came to understand more about what her female and male students were experiencing. Ballenger was also explicit about trying to incorporate and combine Haitian ways of using language to control into her own repertoire of classroom management strategies. Gallas, on the other hand, wrote very little about actions or classroom organization; she concentrated on trying to develop a theory that would help her understand the children's behavior as they used language and silence to develop social positioning. The implication is that this more sophisticated and nuanced theorizing guided her continuing and future actions and relationships with the children, but this is not made explicit. Likewise Lampert concentrated more on the notion of dilemmas and the role of teachers' identities in constructing dilemmas than she did on a plan of action for the future. What this suggests is that underlying these teacher research studies is a view of teaching as an activity that is inherently theoretical as well as practical. This work makes it clear that teachers are always both theorizing practice and putting into practice their emerging theories.

Finally the teacher researchers in this group of selected studies assumed that a critical part of engaging in teacher research related to classroom management issues was interrogating their own assumptions, including looking self-critically at their own stereotyped views, unexamined labels, cultural practices, beliefs, and attitudes. Lampert, for example, wrote about her own identity as a teacher, couching her understanding of teachers' management dilemmas in terms of debates with herself as teacher. Gallas wrote about struggling to put aside the usual adult interpretations and labels associated with discussions of gender, power, and control. Ballenger worked to sort out Haitian and American views of child rearing and language use, explicitly juxtaposing what she came to believe was the "Haitian view" of American views and the "American view" of Haitian views about young children. And Waff interrogated her own middle-class values and beliefs, acknowledging the distance she had maintained from her students despite their shared cultural or racial backgrounds, and working to identify and own her own role in maintaining an environment that unintentionally sanctioned domination by boys.

TEACHER RESEARCH AND CLASSROOM MANAGEMENT: THE QUESTIONS TEACHERS ASK

Our analysis in this chapter of two distinct bodies of teacher research that deal with classroom management suggests that teacher researchers ask a wide range of questions about how teachers manage and organize classrooms. Some of these are quite instrumental and pragmatic, identifying an explicit problem and then collecting and analyzing data in order to formulate a solution and gauge its impact. Others are integral to larger questions about the social processes of classrooms, the relationships of culture and gender to classroom dynamics, and the impact of classroom interactions on the learning opportunities available and accessible to children and adolescents. Despite these differences, which we have discussed in detail in the preceding sections, all of these examples of teacher research reflect the efforts of teachers who see teaching as a process—at least in part—of posing important questions; systematically collecting and analyzing the data of classroom life in order to address those questions (through, for example, sequential journal entries, observations focused on particular aspects of children's interactions, transcriptions of classroom discussions, analyses of students' written work); and interpreting data in order to construct new strategies or under standings of classroom situations.

As detailed earlier, some of the teacher research we reviewed, especially the searched-for studies, used prepackaged or available classroom management programs and strategies. In a number of ways, these teacher research studies are similar to the fieldtests or classroom trials of particular approaches that program developers conduct. Other teacher research that we reviewed, particularly the studies we intentionally selected, approached classroom management issues as part of larger and more encompassing theories about the interrelationships of culture, gender, power relationships, and learning opportunities. These latter teacher research studies are more like traditional ethnographic studies carried out in classrooms by outside researchers than they are like the field tests that are reflective of the first group. Some of the studies we mention are hybrids of these two ends of the continuum, reflecting both a desire to solve a particular problem and a theoretical frame that recognizes the interconnections of management problems and content, culture, and language.

Both the searched-for and the selected teacher research studies, however, seem to assume that there are no universal solutions or prepackaged answers to issues related to the construction of learning environments and the management of the day-to-day work of teaching and learning. Even in the studies where a prepackaged program was used to address a specific problem, the point of the teacher researcher was to figure out how and whether this program was appropriate for a particular classroom and to analyze the conditions and circumstances under which that might be the case. By definition, teacher research—even teacher research that asks rather instrumental questions and assesses the impact of packaged strategies—assumes that classrooms are different from one another, that context matters, and that teaching and learning are relational. By definition, teacher research assumes that teaching is an intellectual rather than a purely technical activity, and that teachers have unique perspectives from which to pose the most important problems and questions that relate to their classrooms.

As is the case with many of the other areas that teacher researchers have explored, teacher research related to the management of classrooms broadens and deepens our knowledge about the nature of classrooms, the interactions of teachers and learners, and the potential as well as the very limitations of universalized theories and strategies of instruction, curriculum, and classroom management. Looking across the teacher research we have drawn on in this chapter, it is clear that empirical research on classroom management and related issues by researchers outside of schools and classrooms will always provide partial knowledge at best. That is, they will always capture only part of the story about how teachers manage to teach. Our conclusion, having reviewed an extensive body of teacher research about classroom management, is that we will always need both insider and outsider research in this area to capture adequately the real work of teaching and the subtle and nuanced interconnections among classroom management, curriculum, teachers' and students' learning, and teacher–student relationships.

ACKNOWLEDGMENT

The authors thank Ann Lieberman, Carnegie Foundation for the Advancement of Teaching, for her review of this chapter.

REFERENCES

Ackley, B., & Campbell, T. (2000, April). *Judicious discipline: A case study of a student teacher.* Paper presented at the Annual Meeting of the American Education Research Association, New Orleans, LA.

Adler, S. (1993). Teacher education: Research as reflective practice. *Teaching and Teacher Education, 9*(2), 159–167.

Adler, S. (1996). On case method and classroom management. *Action in Teacher Education, 18*(3), 33–43.

Aherns, S., Barrett, E., & Holtzman, D. (1997). *Social skills and problem solving abilities in a middle school setting.* Unpublished master's thesis, St. Xavier University, Chicago.

Albert, L. (1996). *Cooperative discipline.* Circles Pine, MN: American Guidance Services.

Albright, L. (1995). *Motivating students to appropriate behavior.* Unpublished master's thesis, St. Xavier University, Chicago.

Allison, C., & Berry, K. (1996). Students under suspicion: Do students misbehave more than they used to? In J. L. Kincheloe & S. Steinberg (Eds.), *Thirteen questions: Reframing education's conversation* (2nd ed., pp. 77–96). New York: Peter Lang.

Anderson, C., & Windeatt, D. (1995). *Interpersonal skills and goal setting through cooperative learning in physical education.* Unpublished master's thesis, St. Xavier University, Chicago.

Anderson, G. L., Herr, K., & Nihlen, A. S. (1994). *Studying your own school: An educator's guide to qualitative practitioner research.* Thousand Oaks, CA: Corwin Press.

Anguiano, P. (2001). A first-year teacher's plan to reduce misbehavior in the classroom. *Teaching Exceptional Children, 33*(3), 52–55.

Baldes, D., Cahill, C., & Moretto, F. (2000). *Motivating students to learn through multiple intelligences, cooperative learning, and positive discipline.* Unpublished master's thesis, St. Xavier University, Chicago.

Ball, D., & Cohen, D. (1999). Developing practice, developing practitioners: Toward a practice-based theory of professional education. In L. Darling-Hammond & G. Sykes (Eds.), *Teaching as the learning profession: Handbook of policy and practice* (pp. 3–32). San Francisco: Jossey-Bass.

Ballenger, C. (1992). Because you like us: The language of control. *Harvard Educational Review, 62*(2), 199–208.

Ballenger, C. (1998). *Teaching other people's children: Literacy and learning in a bilingual classroom.* New York: Teachers College Press.

Bandura, A. (1986). *Social foundations of thought and action.* Englewood Cliffs, NJ: PrenticeHall.

Barnes, H. (1989). Structuring knowledge for beginning teaching. In M. Reynolds (Ed.), *Knowledge base for the beginning teacher* (pp. 13–22). New York: Pergamon Press.

Barnes, S., & Bennett, N. (2001). Promoting a culture of collaboration through continuing professional development. *Management in Education, 15*(5), 13–16.

Barnstable, R., Cargill, L., Gehlbach, S., & Workman, H. (1997). *Advancing the pro-social skills in at-risk elementary students through curricular interventions.* Unpublished master's thesis, St. Xavier University, Chicago.

Bartscher, M., Lawler, K., Ramirez, A., & Schinault, K. (2001). *Improving student's writing ability through journals and creative writing exercises.* Unpublished master's thesis, St. Xavier University, Chicago.

Baugous, K., & Bendery, S. (2000). *Decreasing the amount of classroom disruptions in order to increase the amount of time on task in elementary students.* Unpublished master's action research project, St. Xavier University, Chicago.

Beane, A., Jacobs, M., & Miller, T. (1998, April). *Promoting acceptance to prevent discipline problems.* Paper presented at the Annual Meeting of the American Educational Research Association, San Diego, CA.

Berman, N., Hornbaker, G., & Ulm, A. (2000). *A study of students' disruptive behaviors and a lack of respect for authority and peers with middle school students.* Unpublished master's thesis, St. Xavier University, Chicago.

Berry, G., Johnson, C., & MacQueen, B. (1996). *Improving student achievement through behavior intervention.* Unpublished master's thesis, St. Xavier University, Chicago.

Berthoff, A. (1987). The teacher as Researcher. In D. Goswami & P. R. Stillman (Eds.), *Reclaiming the classroom: Teacher research as an agency for change* (pp. 28–48). Upper Montclair, NJ: Boynton/Cook.

Beyer, L. (1988). *Knowing and acting: Inquiry ideology and educational studies.* London: Falmer Press.

Bogdan, J., Dye, J., Leitner, B., & Meersman, R. (1996). *Promoting appropriate behavior through social skill instruction.* Unpublished master's thesis, St. Xavier University, Chicago.

Borquist, M., & Schmidgall, J. (1997). *Improving discipline through the use of social skills instruction.* Unpublished master's thesis, St. Xavier University, Chicago.

Bourgeois, D. (1979). Positive discipline: A practical approach to disruptive student behavior. *National Association of Secondary School Principals, 63*(428), 68–71.

Bowlby, J. (1988). *A secure base: Parent-child attachment and healthy human development.* New York: Basic Books.

Brandt, M., & Robb, C. (2002). *Improving student social skills through the use of cooperative learning, problem solving, and direct instruction.* Unpublished master's thesis, St. Xavier University, Chicago.

Brennan, R., Dworak, J., & Reinhardt, S. (2002). *Using positive discipline to reduce disruptive classroom behaviors.* Unpublished master's thesis, St. Xavier University, Chicago.

Bruene, L. (1985, April). *Training students in thinking skills for solving social problems: A strategy for helping students cope constructively with school stressors.* Paper presented at the Annual Meeting of the American Education Research Association, Chicago.

Bussis, A. M., Chittenden, E. A., & Amarel, M. (1976). *Beyond surface curriculum.* Boulder, CO: Westview Press.

Butchart, R., & McEwan, B. (Eds.). (1998). *Classroom discipline in American schools: Problems and possibilities for democratic education.* Albany: State University of New York Press.

Canter, L., & Canter, M. (1976). *Assertive discipline: A take-charge approach for today's classrooms.* Santa Monica, CA: Canter & Associates.

Canter, L., & Canter, M. (1992). *Assertive discipline: Positive behavior management for today's classroom* (Rev. ed.). Santa Monica, CA: Canter & Associates.

Carini, P. (1975). *Observation and description: An alternative methodology for the investigation of human phenomena.* Grand Forks: University of North Dakota Press.

Carini, P. (1986). *Prospect's documentary process.* Bennington, VT: Prospect School Center.

Carnegie Forum on Education and the Economy. (1986). *A nation prepared: Teachers for the 21st century.* New York: Carnegie Corporation.

Carr, W., & Kemmis, S. (1986). Towards a critical educational science. In W. Carr & S. Kemmis (Eds.), *Becoming critical: Education, knowledge and action research* (pp. 155–178). Philadelphia: Falmer Press.

Casey, C., Klene, P., & Pangallo, P. (2000). *Creating a conflict-solving class room community.* Unpublished masters of arts thesis, St. Xavier University, Chicago.

Cason, N., Tabscott, S., & Thomas, J. (1991). Improving writing of at-risk students with a focus on African American males. *Bread Loaf News, 5*(2), 26–29.

Charney, R. (1992). *Teaching children to care: Management in a responsive classroom.* Greenfield, MA: Northeast Foundation for Children.

Clark, C., & Peterson, P. (1986). Teachers' thought processes. In M. Wittrock (Ed.), *Handbook of research on teaching* (3rd ed., pp. 255–296). New York: Macmillan.

Cochran-Smith, M. (1994). The power of teacher research in teacher education. In S. Hollingsworth & H. Sockett (Eds.), *Teacher research and educational reform* (pp. 142–165). Chicago: University of Chicago Press.

Cochran-Smith, M., & Lytle, S. (1990). Research on teaching and teacher research: The issues that divide. *Educational Researcher, 19*(2), 2–11.

Cochran-Smith, M., & Lytle, S. (1993). *Inside/Outside: Teacher research and knowledge.* New York: Teachers College Press.

Cochran-Smith, M., & Lytle, S. (1998). Teacher research: The question that persists. *International Journal of Leadership in Education, 1*(1), 19–36.

Cochran-Smith, M., & Lytle, S. (1999a). Relationship of knowledge and practice: Teacher learning in communities. In A. Iran-Nejad & C. Pearson (Eds.), *Review of research in education* (Vol. 24, pp. 249–306). Washington, DC: American Educational Research Association.

Cochran-Smith, M., & Lytle, S. (1999b). The teacher research movement: A decade later. *Educational Researcher, 28*(7), 15–25.

Cochran-Smith, M., & Lytle, S. (2004). Practitioner inquiry, knowledge, and university culture. In J. Loughran, M. Hamilton, V. LaBoskey, & T. Russell (Eds.), *International handbook of research of self-study of teaching and teacher education practices.* Amsterdam: Kluwer.

Cochran-Smith, M., Lytle, S., Maimon, G., & Waff, D. (1997). *Teacher research: Toward what end?* Philadelphia: University of Pennsylvania.

Codell, E. (2001). *Educating Esme: Diary of a Teachers' First Year.* Chapel Hill, NC: Algonquin Books.

Coloroso, B. (1994). *Kids are worth it! Giving your child the gift of inner discipline.* New York: William Morrow.

Committee for Children. (1996). *Program overview: Second step violence prevention curriculum.* Seattle, WA: Author.

Cone, J., Fulton, R., & Van Nieuwenhuyse, D. (2000). *Improving student behavior by teaching social skills.* Unpublished masters of arts action research project, St. Xavier University, Chicago.

Cook, D., & Rudin, L. (1997). *Improving discipline through the use of social skills.* Unpublished master's thesis, St. Xavier University, Chicago.

Cook, S. (1995). *Improving student behavior through social skills instruction.* Unpublished masters thesis, St. Xavier University, Chicago.

Curwin, R., & Mendler, A. (1988). *Discipline with dignity.* Alexandria, VA: Association for Supervision and Curriculum Development.

Dare, M., Durand, S., Moeller, L., & Washington, M. (1997). *Using multiple intelligences, cooperative learning, and higher order thinking skills to improve the behavior of at-risk students.* Unpublished master's thesis, St. Xavier University, Chicago.

Darling-Hammond, L. (1994). *Professional development schools: Schools for a developing profession.* New York: Teachers College Press.

Darling-Hammond, L. (1998). Teacher learning that supports student learning. *Educational Leadership, 55*(5), 6–11.

Dewey, J. (1933). *How we think: A restatement of the relation of reflective thinking to the educative process.* Boston: Houghton Mifflin.

Dohrn, L., Holian, E., & Kaplan, D. (2001). *Improving social skills at the elementary level through cooperative learning and direct instruction.* Unpublished masters of arts action research project, St. Xavier University, Chicago.

Donoahue, Z. (1998). *Giving children control: Fourth graders initiate and sustain discussions after teacher read-alouds.* Retrieved May 22, 2003, from http://www.oise.utoronto.ca

Dreikurs, S., & Cassel, P. (1972). *Discipline without tears: What to do when children misbehave.* New York: Hawthorne.

Duckworth, E. (1987). *The having of wonderful ideas and other essays on teaching and learning.* New York: Teachers College Press.

Duer, M., Parissi, A., & Valintis, M. (2002). *Character education.* Unpublished master's thesis, St. Xavier University, Chicago.

Dunleavy, S., Karwowski, S., & Shudes-Eitel, J. (1997). *Improving social interaction among 4th grade students though social skills.* Unpublished master's thesis, St. Xavier University, Chicago.

Duvall, L., Miller, P., & Tillman, I. (1997). *Social skills: Improving student behavior.* Unpublished master's thesis, St. Xavier University, Chicago.

Eades, G., & Peake, R. (1980). *Promoting classroom teacher research.* (ERIC Document Reproduction Service No. ED207951).

Echelbarger, S., Holler, M., Kelty, L., Rivera, M., Schliesman, G., & Trojanowski, T. (1999). *Improving student interpersonal relationships and academic achievement through school safety interventions.* Unpublished master's thesis St. Xavier University, Chicago (ERIC Document Reproduction Service No. ED411956).

Eilers, J., Fox, J., Welvaert, M., & Wood, J. (1998). *Increasing teacher, parent, and student involvement to promote student learning and self-esteem.* Unpublished master's thesis, St. Xavier University, Chicago.

Elliot, J. (1985). Facilitating action research in schools: Some dilemmas. In R. Burgess (Ed.), *Field methods in the study of education.* London: Falmer Press.

Ellis, H. (1996). *Positive classroom management.* Unpublished master's thesis, St. Xavier University, Chicago.

Elmore, R., & Burney, D. (1997). *Investing in teacher learning: Staff development and instructional improvement in Community School District #2, New York City.* New York: National Commission on Teaching and America's Future.

Emmer, E., & Aussiker, A. (1990). School and classroom discipline programs: How well do they work? In O. Moles (Ed.), *Student discipline strategies: Research and practice* (pp. 129–165). Albany: State University of New York Press.

Erb, M. (1996). *Increasing students' responsibility for their learning through multiple intelligence activities and cooperative learning.* Unpublished master's thesis, St. Xavier University, Chicago.

Erickson, F. (1986). Qualitative methods in research on teaching. In M. Wittrock (Ed.), *Handbook of research on teaching* (3rd ed., pp. 119–161). New York: Macmillan.

Feiman-Nemser, S. (1983). Learning to teach. In L. S. Shulman & G. Sykes (Eds.), *Handbook of teaching and policy* (pp. 150–170). New York: Longman.

Finck, C., Hansen, C., & Jenson, J. (2003). *Student achievement through character education.* Unpublished master's thesis, St. Xavier University, Chicago.

Fink, A. (1988). The psychoeducational philosophy: Programming implications for students with behavioral disorders. *Behavior in Our Schools, 2*, 8–13.

Finzer, S., Green, P., Mizen, J., & Sennstrom, S. (1998). *Improving student social skills in structures and unstructured situations.* Unpublished master's thesis, St. Xavier University, Chicago.

Florio-Ruane, S. (1989). Social organization of classes and schools. In M. Reynolds (Ed.), *Knowledge base for the beginning teacher* (pp. 163–172). New York: Pergamon Press.

Florio-Ruane, S., & Walsh, M. (1980). The teacher as colleague in classroom research. In H. Trueba, G. Guthrie, & K. Au (Eds.), *Culture in the bilingual classroom: Studies in classroom ethnography.* Rowley, MA: Newbury House.

Foster, W., Gaa, N., Nowicki, J., & Ross, V. (1997). *Improving academic success by increasing student engagement in the learning task.* Unpublished master's thesis, St. Xavier University, Chicago.

Francois, F., Harlacher, G., & Smith, B. (1999). *Improving student behavior in the classroom by using assertive discipline strategies.* Unpublished master's thesis, St. Xavier University, Chicago.

Freiberg, J. (1999a). Consistency management and cooperative discipline: From tourists to citizens in the classroom. In J. Freiberg (Ed.), *Beyond behaviorism: Changing the classroom management paradigm* (pp. 75–97). Boston: Allyn & Bacon.

Freiberg, J. (Ed.). (1999b). *Beyond behaviorism: Changing the classroom management paradigm.* Boston,: Allyn & Bacon.

Gabrielle, P. (2002). *Evaluating a peer mediation program at one middle school.* Unpublished doctoral dissertation, Fielding Graduate Institute, Santa Barbara, CA.

Gallas, K. (1994). *The language of learning: How children talk, write, dance, draw, and sing their understanding of the world.* New York: Teachers College Press.

Gallas, K. (1995). What is science? and science talks. In *Talking their way into science.* New York: Teachers College Press.

Gallas, K. (1998). *Sometimes I can be anything.* New York: Teachers College Press.

Gardner, S. (1996). Giving social studies students great decision-making autonomy. *Teaching and Change, 4*(1), 20–34.

Garthe, W., McDonald, M., Poremba, K., Schmidt, C., & Summers, P. (1998). *Improving student social skills.* Unpublished master's thesis, St. Xavier University, Chicago.

Gathercoal, P. (1998). Judicious discipline. In R. Butchart & B. McEwan (Eds.), *Classroom discipline in American schools: Problems and possibilities for democratic education* (pp. 197–216). Albany: State University of New York Press.

Gathercoal, P. (2000, April). *Conducting democratic class meetings. School violence and conflict programs.* Paper presented at the Annual Meeting of the American Educational Research Association, New Orleans, LA.

Gathercoal, P. (2002, April). *Judicious discipline: 5 years later.* Paper presented at the Annual Meeting of the American Educational Research Association, New Orleans, LA.
Gathercoal, P., & Crowell, R. (2000). Judicious discipline. *Kappa Delta Pi Record, 36*(4), 173–177.
Gathercoal, P., & Nimmo, V. (2001, April). *Judicious (character education) discipline.* Paper presented at the Annual Meeting of the American Educational Research Association, Seattle, WA.
Gerk, B., Obiala, R., & Simmons, A. (1997). *Improving elementary student behavior through the use of positive reinforcement and discipline strategies.* Unpublished master's thesis, St. Xavier University, Chicago.
Ginott, H. (1971). *Teacher and the child.* New York: Macmillan.
Glasser, W. (1992). *The quality school: Managing students without coercion.* New York: Harper Perennial.
Glenn, H., & Nelson, J. (1987). *Raising children for success.* Fair Oaks, CA: Sunshine Press.
Good, T., & Brophy, J. (2000). *Looking in classrooms* (8th ed.). New York: Longman.
Gordon, T. (1974). *T.E.T.: Teacher effectiveness training.* New York: David McKay.
Gordon, T. (1989). *Discipline that works: Promoting self-discipline in children.* New York: Random House.
Gore, S. (2000). *Enhancing students' emotional intelligence and social adeptness.* Unpublished master's thesis, St. Xavier University, Chicago.
Goswami, P., & Stillman, P. (1987). *Reclaiming the classroom: Teacher research as an agency for change.* Upper Montclair, NJ: Boynton/Cook.
Graves, M., Nordling, G., Roberts, D., & Taylor, C. (1997). *Conflict resolution through children's literature.* Unpublished master's thesis, St. Xavier University, Chicago.
Hawley, W., & Valli, L. (1999). The essentials of effective professional development: A new consensus. In L. Darling-Hammond & G. Sykes (Eds.), *Teaching as the learning profession: Handbook of policy and practice* (pp. 127–150). San Francisco: Jossey-Bass.
Jones, F. (1987). *Positive classroom discipline.* New York: McGraw-Hill.
Jones, V., & Jones, L. (2004). *Comprehensive classroom management: Creating communities of support and solving problems* (7th ed.). Boston: Allyn & Bacon.
Kane, P. (Ed.). (1991). *My first year as a teacher.* New York: New American Library.
Karneboge, L., Smith, S., VandeSchraaf, C., Wiegardt, C., & Wormer, G. (1999). *Improving elementary and middle school students' abilities to manage conflict.* Unpublished masters thesis, St. Xavier University, Chicago.
Kelly, C. (1997). *Improving student discipline at the primary level.* Unpublished master's thesis, St. Xavier University, Chicago.
Kemmis, S., & McTaggart, R. (2000). Participatory action research. In N. Denzin & Y. Lincoln (Eds.), *Handbook of qualitative research* (2nd ed., pp. 567–606). Thousand Oaks, CA: Sage.
King-Sears, M. (1999). Teacher and researcher co-design self-management content for an inclusive setting: Research training, intervention, and generalization effects on student performance. *Education and Training in Mental Retardation and Developmental Disabilities, 34*(2), 134–156.
Koenig, L. (2000). *Smart discipline for the classroom: Respect and cooperation restored* (3rd ed.). Thousand Oaks, CA: Corwin Press.
Kohl, H. (1991). *I won't learn from you! The role of assent in education.* Minneapolis, MN: Milkweed.
Konner, M. (1990). *Why the reckless survive and other secrets of human nature.* New York: Viking Press.
Kounin, J. (1977). *Discipline and group management in classrooms* (Rev. ed.). New York: Holt, Rinehart & Winston.
Lagemann, E. (2000). *An elusive science: The troubling history of education research.* Chicago: University of Chicago Press.
Lampert, M. (1985). How do teachers manage to teach? Perspectives in practice. *Harvard Educational Review, 55*(2), 178–194.
Lampert, M. (1990). When the problem is not the question and the solution is not the answer: Mathematical knowing and teaching. *American Educational Research Journal, 27*(1), 29–63.
Lampert, M. (1997). Understanding and managing classroom dilemmas in the service of good teaching. In N. Burbules & D. Hansen (Eds.), *Teaching and its predicaments* (pp. 145–162). Boulder, CO: Westview Press.
Lampert, M. (2001). *Teaching problems and the problems of teaching.* New Haven, CT: Yale University Press.
Lanham, K., & Baker, D. (1997). *Improving student behavior through the use of conflict resolution in fifth and eighth grades.* Unpublished masters thesis, St. Xavier University, Chicago.
Levine, M., & Trachtman, R. (Eds.). (1997). *Making professional development schools work: Politics, practice, and policy.* New York: Teachers College Press.
Liddell, K., Norris, W., & Zinanni, T. (1999). *Improving student behavior.* Unpublished master's thesis, St. Xavier University, Chicago.
Lieberman, A., & Grolnick, M. (1996). Networks and reform in American education. *Teachers College Record, 98*(1), 6–45.
Lincoln, Y., & Guba, E. (1990). *Naturalistic inquiry.* Beverly Hills, CA: Sage.

Little, J. (1993). Teachers' professional development in a climate of educational reform. *Educational Evaluation and Policy Analysis, 15*(2), 129–151.

Lytle, S. (2000). Teacher research in the contact zone. In M. Kamil, P. Mosenthal, D. Pearson, & R. Barr (Eds.), *Handbook of reading research* (Vol. 3, pp. 693–718). Mahwah, NJ: Lawrence Ehrlbaum Associates.

Malesich, R. (1994). Making schools safe for students: Solutions to discipline problems. *Schools in the Middle, 3*(3), 38–40.

Martin, J., Powers, L., Ward, J., & Webb, M. (2000). *Empowering intrinsic learners.* Unpublished master's thesis, St. Xavier University, Chicago.

McEwan, B. (2000). *The art of classroom management: Effective practices for building equitable learning communities.* Upper Saddle River, NJ: Merrill.

McEwan, B., Gathercoal, P., & Nimmo, V. (1999). Application of judicious discipline: A common language for classroom management. In J. Freiberg (Ed.), *Beyond behaviorism: Changing the classroom management paradigm* (pp. 98–118). Boston: Allyn & Bacon.

McNeely, S., & Mertz, N. (1990, April). *Cognitive constructs of preservice teachers: Research on how student teachers think about teaching.* Paper presented at the Annual Meeting of the American Educational Research Association, Boston.

Mendler, A. (1992). *What do I do when . . . ? How to achieve discipline with dignity in the classroom.* Bloomington, IN: National Educational Services.

Mishler, E. (1990). Validation in inquiry-guided research: The role of exemplars in narrative studies. *Harvard Educational Review, 60*(4), 415–442.

Monahan, S., Ognibene, B., & Torrisi, A. (2000). *Effects of teaching organizational strategies.* Unpublished master of arts thesis, St. Xavier University, Chicago.

Morris, L. (1998). *The effects of integrated curriculum on 9th grade at-risk students.* Unpublished master's thesis, St. Xavier University, Chicago.

Murphy, C. (1996). *The professional development school: Linking the university and the public school: An action research project.* (ERIC Document Reproduction No. ED400226)

National Commission on Excellence in Education. (1983). *A nation at risk: The imperative for educational reform.* Washington, DC: U.S. Government Printing Office.

Nelsen, J., Lott, L., & Glenn, S. (1997). *Positive discipline in the classroom* (Rev. ed.). Rocklin, CA: Prima.

Nelson, O. (1976). *An investigation of the teacher competencies needed to utilize diagnostic test data in prescribing occupational learning experiences in teaching EMRS. Final Report.* (ERIC Document Reproduction Service No. ED137534)

Nimmo, V. (1998). But will it work? The practice of judicious discipline in southern Minnesota schools. In R. Butchart & B. McEwan (Eds.), *Classroom discipline in American schools: Problems and possibilities for democratic education* (pp. 217–236). Albany: State University of New York Press.

O'Brien, K. (1998). *Frequency of teacher intervention in hallway misconduct.* Unpublished field project, University of Virginia, Charlottesville, VA.

Paley, V. (1981). *Wally's stories.* Cambridge, MA: Harvard University Press.

Paley, V. (1992). *You can't say you can't play.* Cambridge, MA: Harvard University Press.

Palmer, P. (1998). *The courage to teach.* San Francisco: Jossey-Bass.

Phillips, A. (1992, April). *Raising the teachers' voice: The ironic role of silence.* Paper presented at the Annual Meeting of the American Educational Research Association, San Francisco.

Pintrich, P., & Schunk, D. (1996). *Motivation in education: Theory, research, and applications.* Englewood Cliffs, NJ: Prentice Hall.

Quinn, P. (2001). *Decreasing inappropriate social behavior in freshman seminar through the use of interpersonal skills training.* Unpublished masters of arts action research project, St. Xavier University, Chicago.

Redl, F., & Wattenberg, W. (1959). *Mental hygiene in teaching* (Rev. ed.). New York: Harcourt, Brace, & World.

Rives, B., Smith, T., & Staples, G. (2000). *Improving student social skills through the use of children's literature.* Unpublished master's thesis, St. Xavier University, Chicago.

Saurino, D., Bourma, A., & Gunnoe, B. (1999, March). *Science classroom management techniques using graphic calculator technology: A collaborative teacher action research approach.* Paper presented at the Annual Meeting of the National Association of Research in Science Teaching, Boston.

Schroeder, P., Basken, A., Engsstrom, L., & Heald, L. (2000). *Using cooperative learning strategies to improve social skills.* Unpublished master's thesis, St. Xavier University, Chicago.

Shandler, N. (1996). Just rewards: Positive discipline can teach students self-respect and empathy. *Teaching Tolerance, 9*, 37–41.

Shulman, L. (1987). Knowledge and teaching: Foundations of the new reform. *Harvard Educational Review, 51*, 1–22.

Shupe, J. (1998). Prescriptive discipline: Just what the doctor ordered. *National Association of Secondary School Principals, 82*(596), 25–30.

Simon, H. (1993). *The in-school suspension program in the Coatesville Area School District.* Unpublished doctoral dissertation, Temple University, Philodelphia.

Skinner, B. (1968). *The technology of education.* New York: Appleton-Century-Crofts.

Slater, M. (1988, March). *Collaboration as community: Outcomes of conducting research on one's colleagues.* Paper presented at the Annual Meeting of the Conference on College Composition and Communication, St. Louis, MO.

Smith, W. (1924). *Constructive school discipline.* New York: American Book Company.

Smith, W. (1936). *Constructive school discipline.* New York: American Book Company.

Stenhouse, L. (1985). *Research as a basis for teaching.* London: Heinemann.

Tabachnik, R., & Zeichner, K. (1991). *Issues and practices in inquiry-oriented teacher education.* London: Falmer Press.

Tauber, R. (1999). *Classroom management: Sound theory and effective practice.* Westport, CT: Bergin & Garvey.

Turner, M. (1981). *Law-related education. Evaluation project. Final Report, Phase II, Year I.* (ERIC Document Reproduction Service No. ED220391)

Waff, D. (1994a). Girl talk: Creating community through social exchange. In M. Fine (Ed.), *Chartering urban school reform: Reflections on public high schools in the midst of change* (pp. 192–203). New York: Teachers College Press.

Waff, D. (1994b). Romance in the classroom: Inviting discourse on gender and power. *The Voice, 3*(1), 7–14.

Walsh, K., & Cowles, M. (1982). *Developmental discipline.* Birmingham, AL: Religious Education Press.

Weinstein, C., Woolfolk, A., Dittmeier, L., & Shanker, U. (1994). Protector or prison guard? Using metaphors and media to explore student teachers' thinking about classroom management. *Action in Teacher Education, 16*(1), 41–54.

Williams, M. (1995, August). *The school as a center of inquiry: An action research project.* Paper presented at the Annual Meeting of the National Council of Professors of Educational Administration, Williamsburg, VA.

Wisneski, D. (2000). Hatching butterflies and other mysteries: A story of a teacher learning to "let go." *Early Childhood Education Quarterly, 28*(1), 29–33.

Wortham, S. (1997, March). *Facilitating teacher research through school- university partnerships.* Paper presented at the Annual Meeting of the American Educational Research Association, Chicago.

Zeichner, K. (1993). *Educating teachers for cultural diversity.* East Lansing, MI: National Center for Research on Teacher Learning.(ERIC Document Reproduction Service No. ED359167).

Zeichner, K. (1994). Personal renewal and social construction through teacher research. In S. Hollingsworth & H. Sockett (Eds.), *Teacher research and educational reform* (pp. 66–84). Chicago: University of Chicago Press.

Zeichner, K., & Noffke, S. (2001). Practitioner research. In V. Richardson (Ed.), *Handbook of research on teaching* (pp. 298–332). Washington, DC: American Educational Research Association.

37

The Convergence of Reflective Practice and Effective Classroom Management

Barbara Larrivee
California State University, San Bernadino

INTRODUCTION

This chapter discusses the necessity of prospective and practicing teachers developing as reflective practitioners to manage today's classrooms effectively. It provides a background of theory and research on reflection, explicating the links between building reflective practice and classroom management. The various levels in the reflective continuum as well as dimensions of reflection characterized in the literature as reflection-in-action, reflection-on-action, and reflection-for-action are discussed, drawing implications for classroom management. Also included are the habits of mind and practices teachers need to develop to manage classrooms as reflective practitioners. Finally, the chapter suggests active processes and mediating structures most conducive for developing an "enabling culture" for reflection on management practices.

Both state and national standards for teacher education and continued professional development emphasize the importance of teachers developing reflective practice. Yet, the looming threat of mandated standards of teacher accountability undermines teachers becoming reflective practitioners, and the increasing pressure to raise test scores makes it likely that teachers will opt for teaching strategies, management styles, and discourse patterns that prioritize efficiency and expediency over quality practices. This is unfortunate, because engaging in inquiry and reflection is the most promising path to developing effective management strategies. Because today's classrooms are characterized by increasing student diversity, a teacher's management style must accommodate and adjust to a greater range of differences in ethnicity, socioeconomic status, developmental levels, motivation to learn, and achievement. Being responsive to this vast array of student needs necessitates that teachers develop a reflective stance.

THE IMPORTANCE OF BEING REFLECTIVE IN MANAGING TODAY'S CLASSROOM

Approaching classroom management as a reflective practitioner is based on the assumption that effective classroom management, with all its complexities, ambiguities, and dilemmas, requires a teacher to go beyond mere control tactics and engage in both critical inquiry and thoughtful reflection, the hallmarks of reflective practitioners.

Teaching has been described as a "complex, situation-specific, and dilemma ridden endeavor" (Sparks-Langer & Colton, 1991, p. 37). This description highlights the challenge teachers face in managing the classroom environment. It necessitates ongoing learning for continual improved practice. Becoming a lifelong learner requires developing the capacity to be reflective. The development of reflective practice is the foundation for the highest professional competence (Cole & Knowles, 2000; Jay, 2003; Larrivee, 2000; Osterman & Kottkamp, 2004; Steffy, Wolfe, Pasch, & Enz, 2000; Valli, 1997; York-Barr, Sommers, Ghere, & Montie, 2001; Zeichner & Liston, 1996). In fact, it is being adopted increasingly as the professional standard to which to aspire in many other professions, namely, business management, social services, counseling, nursing, and pharmacy. It is rapidly becoming an espoused objective of professional training in many fields, gaining wide acceptance as the hallmark of professional competence.

Engaging in reflection helps teachers test biased assumptions, challenge limiting expectations, and recognize behaviors and practices that impede their potential for tolerance and acceptance, vital elements for meeting the needs of all students in a diverse society moving toward a global community. Reflection involves a deep exploration process that exposes unexamined beliefs, assumptions, and expectations, calling teachers to the task of facing deeply rooted personal attitudes about human nature, human potential, and human learning.

The explicit goal of reflective practice is to create deeper understanding and insight, forming the basis for not only considering alternatives, but taking ongoing action to improve practice. Relative to classroom management, as teachers develop the capacity to reflect on their practices, they come to accept problems as natural occurrences and use them as opportunities to cocreate better solutions, rather than enforce preset standards of operation. Becoming a reflective practitioner means perpetually growing and expanding, opening up to a greater range of possible choices and responses to classroom situations and individual student behaviors.

The position advocated here is that effectiveness in managing the classroom, often wrought with surprises, chaos, and conflict, cannot be achieved without considerable personal insight, self-awareness, and acceptance of responsibility for one's actions. In the absence of building reflective practice, teachers stay trapped in unexamined judgments, assumptions, and interpretations. Reflection is a vital tool for navigating life in the classroom.

Managing the classroom as a reflective practitioner means integrating personal beliefs and values into a professional identity, resulting in the development of a deliberate code of conduct. Breaking through familiar cycles necessitates a shift in ways of thinking, perceiving, and interpreting classroom events. Building the habit of reflective practice allows teachers to see beyond the filters of their past and the blinders of their expectations to respond more appropriately to classroom situations and circumstances. When teachers manage as reflective practitioners, they resist establishing a culture of control and remain fluid in the dynamic environment of the classroom.

Reflective practitioners operate in a perpetual learning spiral in which dilemmas surface, constantly initiating a new cycle of planning, acting, observing, reflecting, and adapting. They challenge assumptions that they and others are making, reconsidering the taken-for-granted in order to inform a more deliberate and conscious course of action.

DEVELOPING REFLECTIVE PRACTICE

Practice refers to one's repertoire of knowledge, dispositions, behaviors, and skills in specific areas of performance, such as managing the classroom, designing instruction, establishing assessment strategies, and interacting with students, colleagues, and parents. Reflective teaching, reflection, and reflective practice are often used interchangeably. The term *reflective practice* is viewed here as the culmination of all other forms of reflection in that it is undertaken not solely to revisit the past but to guide future action.

Nearly a century ago, Dewey (1910/1933, 1938) made the distinction between action that is routine and action that is reflective, contrasting reflective thinking with habits of thought that lack evidence and are based on faulty beliefs or unverified assumptions. In the early 1980s the notion of reflective practice gained popularity through the work of Schön (1983, 1987), who challenged the portrayal of teacher as technician, replacing it instead with teacher as committed, autonomous decision maker, or reflective practitioner. According to Schön, reflective practitioners continually learn from their experience, reconstructing experience through reflection. A primary quality of Schön's notion of reflective practice is his calling for teachers to give themselves up to the action of the moment and to be researchers and artists in the laboratory of practice—the classroom (Tremmel, 1993).

Focus and Goals of Reflective Practice

The focus of reflection can be at the level of classroom practices and behaviors, goals and outcomes, or beliefs and values, manifested in expectations and assumptions. The focus of reflection may also be specific or at a more general level bringing into question the utility of established rules, policies, and procedures. Teachers may reflect on the effects of a specific intervention strategy, as well as on general practices, such as organizing the classroom, structuring the school day, establishing task structures and routines, interacting with students, and building relationships with both students and parents.

Teachers also bring into question their goals that encompass desired aims, outcomes, and intentions. They can be general such as creating the classroom as a learning community for students, or they can be more specific, such as assessing the impact of task structures such as cooperative learning groups or buddy or peer groupings.

Growing demands on teachers with recently imposed federal and state mandates often lead to feelings of alienation and isolation where teachers view themselves as mere pawns in the system feeling a sense of helplessness about their situation and role. However, teachers really can influence their practice much more than they may think by taking control of their teaching lives and becoming empowered decision makers by engaging in systematic reflection about their work. As Smyth (1989) pointed out, being able to locate oneself historically, both personally and professionally, in order to become clear about the forces that have come to determine one's reality is "the hallmark of a teacher who has been able to harness the reflective process" (p. 7) and can then begin to act on the world in a way that can change it.

DEFINING REFLECTIVE PRACTICE

Some definitions focus only on the relationship between goals and outcomes. Accordingly, Cruickshank and Applegate (1981) referred to reflective practice as a process that helps teachers think about what happened, why it happened, and what else could have been done to reach their goals. Similarly, Killion and Todnem (1991) defined reflective practice as analyzing one's actions, decisions, or products by focusing on one's process for achieving them. Others go further to characterize reflective practice as a lifelong endeavor involving a deep commitment to ongoing learning and continuous improvement of the quality of one's professional practice (Bright, 1996; Ross, 1990; York-Barr et al., 2001). At another level, some believe that reflective practice requires one to move beyond a focus on isolated events to perceive a broader context for situating behavior, focusing on the personal, pedagogical, societal, as well as ethical contexts associated with professional work (Cole & Knowles, 2000; Hatton & Smith, 1995). At still another level, some consider that reflective practice necessitates an inquiry stance and requires a systematic data-gathering process enriched by dialogue and collaborative effort (Osterman & Kottkamp, 2004). The definition of reflective practice applied here incorporates all of these levels.

Levels of Reflection

Various definitions evolving over several decades most commonly depict three levels of reflection (Day, 1993; Farrell, 2004; Handal & Lauvas, 1987; Jay & Johnson, 2002; Van Manen, 1977); the conceptual models theorizing more than three levels generally single out the concept of self-reflection as a separate entity. There is no generally accepted terminology to define the various levels in the development of reflective practice. The conceptual framework presented here represents a continuum of multiple levels adopting the terminology of surface reflection, pedagogical reflection, critical reflection, and self-reflection.

Surface Reflection. At this first level, teachers' reflections focus on strategies and methods used to reach predetermined goals. Teachers are concerned with what works in the classroom to keep students quiet and maintain order, rather than with any consideration of the value of such goals as ends in themselves. For this level, the term *technical* has been most widely used (Van Manen, 1977). It has also been referred to as *descriptive* (Jay & Johnson, 2002). The term *surface* is preferred by this author to depict a broader scope in this category, although still a low level of reflection (Larrivee, 2004). Typical managerial questions the teacher asks at the level of surface reflection are: *How long should I keep students in time-out? How can I keep students on-task?*

Pedagogical Reflection. At this next level, teachers reflect on educational goals, the theories underlying approaches, and the connections between theoretical principles and practice. This level has probably the least consensus in the literature as to its composition and label. It has been variously labeled *practical*, *comparative*, *conceptual*, *contextual*, *theoretical*, and *deliberative*. The term *pedagogical* is preferred by this author as a more inclusive term, merging all of the other concepts to connote a higher level of reflection based on application of teaching knowledge, theory, or research.

Teachers engaging in pedagogical reflection strive to understand the theoretical basis for classroom practice and to foster consistency between espoused theory (what they say they do and believe) and theory-in-use (what they actually do in the classroom). Teachers reflecting at this level can determine when there is dissonance between what they practice and what they preach (e.g., seeing themselves as humanistic yet belittling students when they persist in disobeying rules). Typical questions the teacher asks at the level of pedagogical reflection are: *Is my point system for rewards and consequences inhibiting my students from developing decision-making skills? How can I build in better accountability for cooperative learning tasks?*

Critical Reflection. At this level, teachers reflect on the moral and ethical implications and consequences of their classroom practices on students. They extend their considerations to issues beyond the classroom to include equity aspects of practice.

Critical reflection involves examination of both personal and professional belief systems. Teachers operating at the level of critical reflection recognize that teaching is embedded within institutional, cultural, and political contexts and that these contexts both *affect* what they do and *are affected by* what they do. Teachers who are critically reflective focus their attention both inwardly at their own practice, and outwardly, at the social conditions in which these practices are situated. These teachers acknowledge that their teaching practices and policies can either contribute to, or hinder, the realization of a more just and humane society. Their deliberations focus on issues of equity and social justice that arise inside and outside the classroom and on connecting their practice to democratic ideals.

Acknowledging that classroom and school practices cannot be separated from the larger social and political realities, critically reflective teachers strive to become fully conscious of the range of consequences of their actions. Few teachers get through a day without facing ethical dilemmas. Even routine evaluative assessment of students' work is partly an ethical decision, in that lack of opportunity to learn and influence on self-concept are ever-present considerations.

Typical questions the teacher asks at the level of critical reflection are: *Who is being included and who is being excluded in this classroom practice? Does this classroom practice promote equity?* Questions like these are in vivid contrast to questions generated by teachers engaging in surface reflection, who may question how to improve the behavior modification system they are using but may never question the larger issue of whether there are better methods (pedagogical reflection) or even if their structure limits the potential for some students with different cultural backgrounds to be successful (critical reflection).

Self-Reflection. Some conceptual models theorize more than three levels of reflection, generally singling out the concept of self-reflection as a separate entity. Hatton and Smith (1995), Valli (1997), and York-Barr et al. (2001) referred to this form of reflection as *dialogic*, *personalistic*, and *reflection-within*, respectively, highlighting the dimension of dialogue with oneself. However, the conceptualization of self-reflection presented here is a broader concept. Self-reflection focuses on examining how one's beliefs and values, expectations and assumptions, family imprinting, and cultural conditioning affect students and their learning (Larrivee, 2005). Based on the presumption that understanding oneself is a prerequisite condition to understanding others, self-reflection warrants distinction by itself.

The capacity for self-reflection is a distinguishing attribute of reflective practitioners. Self-reflection entails deep examination of values and beliefs, embodied in the assumptions teachers make and the expectations they have for students. Beliefs about students' capacity and willingness to learn, assumptions about the behavior of students, especially those from different ethnic and social backgrounds, and expectations formulated on the basis of the teacher's own value system drive teacher behavior.

Beliefs are dearly held convictions. They are enduring ideas about what is real. Although we are confident in the truth of our beliefs, they are not susceptible to proof. Beliefs can be affirming or defeating, expansive or limiting.

Beliefs create the lens through which we view the world, shaping our identity. Hence, shedding a cherished belief can shake our very existence. For example, if a teacher tries to shed the belief that the teacher must be in total control to be effective, it means revealing uncertainty and vulnerability.

Values are our ideals, defining what we think is worthwhile. They steer how we behave on a daily basis, determining the lines we will and will not cross. They are subjective and arouse an emotional response. In teaching, sets of values are often in conflict, challenging the teacher to weigh competing values against one another and play them off against the facts available. For example, a teacher may value being consistent while simultaneously valuing treating students justly. And, there are times when to be fair is to be inconsistent.

As teachers develop the capacity to be self-reflective, they become increasingly aware of how they are interactive participants in classroom encounters rather than innocent bystanders, or victims. By developing the practice of self-reflection teachers learn to (a) slow down their thinking and reasoning process to become more aware of how they perceive and react to students and (b) bring to the surface some of their unconscious ways of responding to students.

Typical questions the teacher asks at the level of self-reflection are: *In what ways might I be modeling disrespect? Why am I so intolerant of Leroy's inappropriate behavior?* Reflective practitioners call into question the assumptions, premises, or presuppositions underlying their beliefs and practices. Self-reflection entails deep examination of personal values and beliefs. Without tying teaching decisions to beliefs about the teaching/learning process and assumptions about, and expectations for, students, teachers will have only fragmented techniques—stabs in the dark. Unless teachers engage in critical reflection and self-reflection, they stay trapped in unexamined judgments, interpretations, assumptions, and expectations.

Being self-reflective brings commonly held beliefs about classroom management into question. Beginning teachers often get caught in dichotomous thinking (e.g., "I have to be a drill sergeant or students will think I'm a doormat," or "I have to chose between being personal and being distant"). This kind of thinking, which Ellis (1974) labeled "all-or-none thinking," generally leads to a counter productive cycle where teachers choose strategies that involve coercion through punishment or constraint, resulting in physical or psychological isolation. Such strategies only further alienate students, creating more problems (Glasser, 1997; Kohn, 1996; Osterman, 2000).

When teachers develop the habit of self-reflection they are never satisfied that they have all the answers and constantly seek new information, thereby continuously accessing new lenses to view student behavior and alter their perceptions. Problems present opportunities to find better solutions, build relationships, and teach students new coping and self-management strategies. The teacher's modus operandus is solving problems and the classroom becomes a laboratory for purposeful experimentation. A practice or procedure is never permanent. New insights, understandings, and perspectives bring previous decisions up for reevaluation.

Developing self-reflection helps teachers recognize their repetitive cycles and makes visible their "reflexive loops" which limit their vision. Argyris (1990) pointed out how our beliefs are *self-generating,* and often untested, based on conclusions inferred from our selected observations. In other words, from all the data available to us, we select data by literally choosing to see some things and ignore others. He coined the term *reflexive loop* to describe the circular process by which we select data, add personal meaning, make assumptions based on our interpretations of the selected data, draw conclusions, adopt beliefs, and ultimately take action. We stay in a reflexive loop where our unexamined beliefs affect what data we select.

Cole and Knowles (2000) distinguished between *reflective inquiry* and *reflexive inquiry*, describing the latter as tantamount to self-reflection as defined here. Underpinning reflective inquiry is the notion that assumptions behind all practice are subject to questioning. *Reflexive inquiry*, on the other hand, is reflective inquiry situated within the context of personal histories in order to make connections between personal lives and professional careers and to understand personal (including early) influences on professional practice. Reflexive inquiry takes into account the personal history–based elements of contextual understanding, emphasizing the foundational place of experience in the formulations of practice in a way that reflective inquiry does not. Reflexive inquiry, unlike some forms and interpretations of reflective inquiry, is rooted in a critical perspective.

Cole and Knowles also suggested that another way to think of *reflexive* is in terms of the properties of prisms and mirrors that reflect and refract light. They change the direction in which light rays travel, sometimes even bending them back on themselves, causing them to move in directions opposite from their original path. Reflexive practices associated with teaching have somewhat similar qualities. Being reflexive is like having a mirror and transparent prism with which to view practice. Examination of practice, with an intent to understand or improve it, sometimes leads to complete turnabouts in thinking. The ideas and thoughts bent back through reflexive inquiry may derive from a whole range of experiences and interactions throughout one's life inside and outside classrooms and schools, as students and as teachers. In a reflexive stance, making sense of both prior and current educational experiences within the context of present practice can shed new, perhaps brighter, light on one's understanding of teaching.

In sum, the position taken here is that teachers must go beyond surface reflection to engage in both critical reflection and self-reflection to respond to the management challenges they face. As teachers move from surface to self-reflection, the nature of their questions changes. At the surface level, a teacher might ask: *Are these good classroom rules for my class?* At the level of pedagogical reflection, the question might be: *Are these classroom rules reasonable expectations for my students?* A teacher who is critically reflective might ask: *Are the consequences for rule infractions just?* And a teacher engaging in self- reflection might ponder: *Do I overreact when responding to Derrick's behavior because of my own biases?*

It is important to note that an individual teacher's progression from surface to critical or self-reflection is not necessarily linear. It is possible for teachers to reflect at different levels simultaneously, or for various levels to be interwoven, depending on the topic of deliberation. Reagan, Case, and Brubacher (2000) suggested that the process of engaging in reflection should be seen as an ongoing spiral in which each element of reflective practice is constantly involved in an interactive process of change and development.

Reflection Dimensions

Schön (1983) distinguished between *reflection-in-action*, thinking about events in the classroom as they happen to make immediate adjustments, and *reflection-on-action*, thinking back on what was done to gain deeper insight. Killion and Todnem (1991) added the concept of *reflection-for-action*, in which the designated purpose of analyzing behavior is taking some action to change.

Reflection-in-action is observing thinking and action as classroom events unfold, allowing reevaluation to occur on the spot. Sparked by a momentary insight, the teacher adapts in the moment. Although difficult, this is a very powerful form of reflection requiring a high level of consciousness. For example, the teacher may notice that Vince is attracting a lot of attention and do something novel to regain students' attention. As Schön noted, this type of reflection is often tacit.

Reflection-on-action is looking back on and learning from experience. Often reflection simultaneously with actions is difficult because of the multiple demands teachers are juggling. For instance, hurrying to complete a lesson before recess may distract the teacher from noticing that her responses to students are terse. Van Manen (1991) referred to this looking back after the action has taken place as *recollective reflection*, noting that it promotes deeper insight into past experiences. Given that it may be too challenging to reflect while engaged in teaching, reflecting after being removed from an event is probably the most frequently used form of reflection.

Reflection-for-action is proactive thinking. Killion and Todnem (1991) contended that it is the desired outcome of both reflection-in-action and reflection-on-action, making the case that reflection is not so much for the purpose of revisiting the past or becoming aware of our metacognitive processes, but to guide future action. Teachers use this type of reflection when they already recognize that they need to change something, such as a relationship with a student, or a punishment strategy that is backfiring. This type of reflection also serves as a means of detecting inconsistencies between beliefs and practice.

The systematic investigation advocated by those espousing action research as a primary vehicle for reflection on classroom practices also falls into the category of reflection-for-action (Carr & Kemmis, 1986; Cochran-Smith & Lytle, 1993; Cole & Knowles, 2000; Dana & Yendol-Silva, 2003; Glanz, 1998; McFee, 1993; Osterman & Kottkamp, 2004). Teachers assume the active role of researchers in their own classrooms to systematically collect and analyze data to take informed action. The basic belief system underlying action research is that each classroom is its own unique social culture and taking a reflective stance helps a teacher build and verify a coherent explanation of how a particular classroom works.

Teachers using reflection-for-action are able to move out of focusing on their dissatisfaction with what is happening now to concentrate on closing the discrepancy between the current situation and what they would like to see. By focusing on their vision for the preferred future they put their energy into closing the gap between what is and what could be.

The Reflective Mindset for Managing Classrooms

Being a successful manager in today's classroom environment requires that the teacher remain fluid and able to move in many directions, rather than stuck only being able to move in one direction as situations occur. As master teachers know, there are multiple pathways for addressing concerns and solving individual behavior problems.

At the simplest nonreflective level, teachers react with an immediate response with little thought occurring and fail to connect individual classroom situations to other events. Their orientation is reactive, attributing ownership of problems to students or others and viewing student and classroom circumstances as beyond their control. An automatic reaction, like removing your hand from a hot burner, is a reaction without conscious consideration of alternative responses. This type of response is often referred to as a "knee-jerk" response, connoting that the response is automatic. Often teachers operate on "automatic pilot," closed off from entertaining a continuum of responses. When they become reactive in this way, they run the risk of responding to students in ways that can easily escalate, rather than deescalate, student reactions. Developing reflective practice involves observing patterns of behavior and considering behavior in light of its specific context.

The reflective mindset relative to classroom management and managing individual student behavior that poses a problem involves recognizing that there are many ways to view a particular circumstance, situation, or event. When considering an intervention, the reflective practitioner:

- Entertains multiple alternative explanations of student behavior
- Sees beyond the surface behavior to recognize the communicative intent of the behavior
- Identifies predictable behavior patterns
- Is aware of the interaction between teacher responses to students and student responses to the teacher
- Acknowledges beliefs and limiting assumptions that may affect perception of the problem

Repositioning: An Essential Capacity of Reflective Practitioners

Teachers often cannot change the situations they encounter, but they can change how they emotionally respond to cope more effectively. Teachers can learn to reposition classroom events and individual student behaviors by shifting their perspective to view the situation from a different angle or include parts of the picture that were not visible from the first vantage point.

Repositioning is the capacity to change your perception by moving out of a limited perspective and creating a new position from which to view a situation (Larrivee, 1996, 2005). It involves developing the ability to look at what is happening and withholding judgment, while simultaneously recognizing that the meaning you attribute to it is no more than your interpretation filtered through your cumulative experience.

Seeing new ways of interpreting a situation enables a teacher to move beyond a limited perspective and assign new meaning to the classroom situations encountered. When a student acts out, one teacher sees it as a personal attack, whereas another sees a cry for help. It is the teacher's interpretation of the student's behavior, or the meaning attached to the behavior, that determines how the teacher will respond.

By repositioning a seemingly negative event, the teacher seizes the opportunity to discover the potential in a situation. Teachers can change their negative feelings by altering their inner dialogue that mediates their thinking and how they interpret a situation. For instance, a teacher might be fuming and telling herself "How dare Kayla do this *to me*!" This self-talk virtually ensures that she will be upset. If on the other hand, she shifts her perspective and starts to tell herself "She's not doing this to me. In fact, this isn't about me at all, it's about her own need to feel important. If I stop personalizing this, then I won't be upset." In repositioning, the teacher looks for openings to extend and learn in any situation.

Some helpful ways of capitalizing on these openings in classroom settings include repositioning:

- confrontation as energy to be rechanneled,
- an attack as a cry for help,
- conflict as opportunity for relationship building,
- defiance as a request for communication, and
- attention seeking as a plea for recognition.

Repositioning calls for a change in a teacher's perception of misbehavior, by making the shift in thinking from "*This kid is a problem*" to "*This kid poses a problem for me to solve.*" Rather than trying to "*teach the kid a lesson*" for misbehaving with cease and desist tactics, the teacher actually *does* teach a lesson by using the problem situation as a springboard to introduce a new coping strategy. By using a problem-solving approach instead of just trying to stop the behavior, teachers work *with* rather than *against* the student by seizing "teachable moments" to teach students how to get what they want in more appropriate ways.

Another rendition of the concept of repositioning is making the shift from *pawn* to *origin* (deCharms, 1976). For the pawn, all individual actions are shaped by beliefs about what the system will or will not tolerate. In contrast, the origin shifts the focus (repositions) and asks "What am I going to do within these constraints?" In other words, the pawn is immobilized while the origin is moved to action. According to Osterman and Kottkamp (2004), when the individual emerges to the forefront, he or she constructs a different reality, availing a whole range of options. This is essentially the essence of reflective practice.

Authenticity: A Crucial Attribute of Reflective Practitioners

As teachers become more aware of the beliefs and assumptions that drive them, they become aware of the dissonance between what they say and what they do. With that awareness comes the capacity to change and become more authentic. To be authentic begins with being honest with oneself. This journey through one's own fears, limitations, and assumptions is essential for becoming more authentic.

Brookfield (1995) described authenticity as being alert to the voices inside your head that are not your own, the voices that have been deliberately implanted by outside interests rather than springing from your own experiences. Authenticity is acting without pretense. The opposite of authenticity is defensiveness. Authentic teachers communicate a powerful sense of inner authority. Being authentic means not depending on others for your sense of well-being, not having to appear in control, look good, or refrain from rocking the boat.

THE PATH TO CULTIVATING REFLECTIVE PRACTICE IS MARKED WITH DISSONANCE

Teachers need to be reflective in order to deal with the inevitable uncertainties, dilemmas, and trade-offs involved in everyday decisions that affect the lives of students. Any effort to become a reflective practitioner involves negotiating feelings of frustration, insecurity, and even rejection. Untangling and reevaluating taken-for-granted, even cherished, practices necessitates breaking into well-entrenched myths that are not easily dislodged (Smyth, 1989).

Reagan, Case, and Brubacher (2000) suggested that becoming a reflective practitioner has much in common with the process of becoming "real" as the Skin Horse explained it to the Rabbit in the children's book *The Velveteen Rabbit* (Williams, 1981, pp. 14–16). Just as becoming real takes time and happens after a toy has lost its hair and become shabby, so becoming a reflective teacher involves time, and inevitably a bit of wear and tear. Yet every teacher should strive to become a reflective practitioner, knowing that only by making the effort to become reflective can one really become a masterful teacher, just as every toy knows that being loved by a child is the only way to become real.

The term *reflection* characterizes a way of thinking that accepts uncertainty (e.g., Dewey, 1933, 1938; Kelsey, 1993; King & Kitchener, 1994; Sparks-Langer & Colton, 1991; Osterman & Kottkamp, 2004; Rogers, 2002; Zehm & Kottler, 1993). In Dewey's (1933, 1938) writings, he asserted that the capacity to reflect is initiated only after recognition of a problem or dilemma *and* the acceptance of uncertainty. The dissonance created in understanding that a problem exists engages the reflective thinker to become an *active inquirer*, involved in both the critique of current conclusions and the generation of new hypotheses. According to Dewey, reflective thinking requires continual evaluation of beliefs, assumptions, and hypotheses against existing data and against other plausible interpretations of the data. Resulting decisions remain open to further scrutiny and reformulation. Similarly, King and Kitchener (1994) posited that those operating at the highest stage of reflective judgment know that a solution is only a hypothetical conjecture of what is, recognizing the temporary nature of any solution.

The route to becoming a reflective practitioner is plagued by incremental fluctuations of irregular progress, often marked by two steps forward and one step backward. There are necessary and predictable stages in the emotional and cognitive rhythm of becoming reflective (Berkey et al., 1990; Brookfield, 1995; Cole & Knowles, 2000; Day, 1998; Golby & Appleby, 1995; Kasl, Dechant, & Marsink, 1993; Keane, 1987; Larrivee, 2000; Usher & Bryant, 1989; Zeichner & Liston, 1996). The sense of liberation at discarding a dearly held assumption is quickly followed by the fear of being in limbo. This state leads to a longing for the abandoned assumption and a desire to revert to the familiar to keep the chaos at bay. Old ways of thinking no longer make sense but new ones have not yet gelled to take their place, leaving one dangling in the throes of uncertainty. Yet, this uncertainty is the hallmark for transformation and the emergence of new possibilities. This inner struggle is a necessary and important stage in the reflective process. To break through familiar cycles, one has to allow oneself to feel confused and anxious, not permanently, but for a time. Fully experiencing this sense of uncertainty is what opens the door to a personal deeper understanding, leading to a shift in ways of thinking and perceiving.

Brookfield (1995) depicted critical reflection as a matter of "stance and dance." The stance toward teaching practice is one of inquiry, being in constant formation and always open to further investigation. The dance is one of experimentation and risk, modifying practice while moving to fluctuating and sometimes contrary rhythms. Often a contradictory tempo is created through realization that students may experience actions a teacher initiates in unintended ways. Despite honorable intentions, the teacher may discover that students are humiliated or confused by actions intended to be supportive or clarifying.

The Need to Challenge Underlying Beliefs

Teachers who develop as reflective practitioners continually challenge the underlying beliefs that drive their present behavior. However, the channel to changing beliefs is not direct; it is through critically examining assumptions, interpretations, and expectations.

Yost, Sentner, and Forlenza-Bailey (2000) noted that the literature consistently advocates the need to address the beliefs that teacher candidates bring with them. Some studies indicate that beliefs can be altered when a multifaceted approach is implemented that helps teachers in training acknowledge, articulate, and challenge their beliefs (Boyd, Boll, Brawner, & Villaume, 1998; Nais, 1987; Wideen, Mayer-Smith, & Moon, 1998; Yost, 1997; Yost, Forlanza-Bailey, & Shaw, 1999). Promoting tension, uncertainty, and dissonance helps them see the multiple dimensions of dilemmas and consequently choose from a wider range of options.

To encourage teachers' development of reflective practice, teacher educators will need to be prepared to move beyond "comfortable collaboration" (Day, 1993). Examining efficacy, value, and worth of classroom practices necessarily creates tension. When values underlying reflective practice clash with prevailing school climates, conflict is to be expected.

Because questioning assumptions, naming issues, and confronting limiting beliefs is always an arousing experience, the process inevitably leads to assaults on emotions (Leat, 1995). As Johnson (1994) experienced working with students in a master's program over 2 years, arriving at a more examined set of beliefs and a more complex view of teaching practices creates a great deal of dissonance. Likewise, Campbell and Kirschner depicted their staff development work over a 4-year period in which they questioned operating assumptions as well as the status quo, as "fraught with conflict and discomfort" (Berkey, et al., 1990). They also noted that out of the conflict and discomfort came invaluable learning and insight. Working through the difficult times was essential to individual growth and to authentic engagement with one another. As Kagan (1992) justifiably noted, learning to teach requires a journey into the deep recesses of oneself, where both fears and hopes reside.

Although at times engaging in the highly disciplined practice of reflection can be both nerve-wracking and time-consuming, at other times the undertaking of reflection can be quite brief and appear natural and effortless. In fact, Yost et al. (1999) reported that the reflective process for some teachers actually alleviated much stress and frustration. As one teacher noted, "When I start to get frustrated, I say, 'This isn't working—why ...?' ... I find another way ... that relieves my tension ... and my anger." Abandoning the security of the control that comes with sticking with the familiar can be empowering and exhilarating.

Reflection as a Collaborative Social Practice

Although advocates of reflective practice emphasize starting with one's personal experiences, they also stress the importance of critical analysis and reformulation of that experience (e.g., Argyris, 1990; Brookfield, 1995; Burbules, 1993; Horn, 2000; Kasl et al., 1993; Knowles,

1992; Mezirow, 1991; Senge, 1990; Senge, Kleiner, Roberts, Ross, & Smith, 1994; Sokol & Cranton, 1998). Experience is culturally and personally "sculpted," is contextually bound, and has a potential for distortion. Personal experiences need the critical checks and balances of others' perspectives. Use of a "critical professional community" is widely seen as a vehicle for providing multiple lenses to view one's experiences.

According to Rodgers (2002), the collaborative process can affirm the value of one's experiences, broaden one's depth of understanding, and provide the needed support to engage in the inquiry process. Many others have also attested to the important role of a collaborative process in developing reflective practice (Bright, 1996; Cole & Knowles, 2000; Jay, 2003; Larrivee, 2000; Osterman & Kottkamp, 2004; Smyth, 1989, 1991; Valli, 1997; York-Barr et al., 2001; Zeichner & Liston, 1996).

A consequence of teacher isolation and of the lack of attention to the social context of teaching is that teachers come to see their problems as their own, unrelated to those of other teachers or to the structure of schools and school systems. It is important for teachers to engage in critical analysis of schools as institutions, recognizing how the structure of schools constrains their work and deeply affects their relationships with their fellow teachers, their students, and their students' families (Brookfield, 1995; Cole & Knowles, 2000; Horn, 2000; Smyth, 1989, 1991; Zeichner & Liston, 1996). As Leat aptly noted, "There are dangers in operating in a paradigm little understood by our political masters, a wider public and even the majority of teachers" (1995, p. 174).

It is important to build a support system to provide comfort and compassion as well as understanding, direction, and when necessary, redirection. Recurring problems can erode self-perceptions of ability to find adequate solutions to problems that plague teachers on a day-to-day basis, leading to a preoccupation with negative aspects of self and teaching. Collaborative peer support is one vehicle for supplanting such negative attitudes and self-appraisals with encouragement. Conversations with peers can open up a new way of seeing things. In the absence of feedback, reflection can merely validate and perpetuate one's own views.

CREATING AN ENABLING CULTURE FOR REFLECTIVE PRACTICE

For developing and practicing teachers to cultivate the habits of mind necessary to become reflective practitioners, they must be exposed to active practice techniques and processes that explicitly prompt them to think, respond, and act in new ways. Reflective practice is enhanced when structures or processes are provided that mediate or draw personal connections between existing knowledge and new knowledge. Mediating structures allow learners to access their own realm of experiences, reflect on those experiences, and construct personal meaning to inform their practice.

Reflection, especially critical reflection and self-reflection, are complex constructs requiring multifaceted and strategically constructed mediation processes. Jay and Johnson (2002) recently pointed out that preparing reflective practitioners calls on teacher educators to continuously struggle with the tension between providing supportive scaffolding for encouraging reflection and doing so without reducing it to a series of steps, devising creative strategies that aid in the development of a reflective stance toward the dilemmas of practice and a way of thinking them through.

Much of the literature grapples with helping teachers move beyond surface-level reflection to pedagogical and critical reflection. Challenging the old belief system of teacher as technician, replacing it with teacher as reflective practitioner, renders traditional higher education "stand and deliver" models of teacher training moot. Emerging teaching/learning practices distinguish between a teacher trainer perspective and a learning facilitator and social mediator perspective. Trainers see themselves as responsible for the development of predetermined skills and outcomes. In contrast, the task of a learning facilitator/social mediator is to provide a structure to guide the group through a discovery process requiring group members to listen, learn, and figure things out together. Acting in this role requires teacher educators to be aware of their own thinking (i.e., metacognition) in the process of facilitating the group process (Garmston & Wellman, 1999). As Day (1993) suggested, they must become "skilled helpers, critical friends, and trusted colleagues" to fulfill this new role. First and foremost, they must learn to trust the group and have confidence in the ability of its members to come up with their own solutions and applications when engaged in a meaningful learning process.

According to research conducted by Hatton and Smith (1995) with teachers in preservice training, teacher progression through various levels of reflection appears to be developmental in the sense that the technical level represents a useful starting point for addressing concerns. For example, they noted that teachers may need to reflect first on areas of technical skill before being able to compare different teaching strategies and weigh their relative merit. However, the literature is wrought with failed attempts designed specifically to move teacher trainees along the reflection continuum (e.g., Korthagen & Wubbels, 1991; Smith & Hatton, 1993; Valli, 1992). Similarly, Collier (1999) and Pultorak (1993) found the reflections of teachers in preservice training to be mostly descriptive and unconnected to a theoretical framework or societal issues, even with the benefit of specific scaffolding to develop reflection. Likewise, Wunder (2003) found that teachers learning to teach social studies were concerned more with issues of management and student learning and involvement and did not reflect at higher levels to consider the purposes of teaching social studies despite exposure to a reflective approach. Nonetheless, there is an emerging consensus on the kinds of mediation structures that have the potential to promote higher-order reflection. The literature is generally specific to either preservice and novice teachers or practicing and experienced teachers.

Some researchers have suggested that preservice and novice teachers can be helped to reflect (e.g., Pultorak, 1993, 1996; Rudney & Guillaume, 1990; Wildman & Niles, 1987). The generally accepted position is that without carefully constructed guidance, preservice and novice teachers seem unable to integrate and apply learned pedagogy to enhance their teaching (Yost et al., 2000). However, focusing on what they already know and believe about teaching has proven to be a useful starting point (Wideen et al., 1998).

Smyth (1989) argued that taking the position that the reflective process is not accessible to inexperienced teachers dismisses their history of being treated in certain ways as students. He believes that such histories are worthy of "unpacking" for the more just and humane alternatives they are likely to uncover. Collier (1999) noted that by establishing self-monitoring and self-reflective activities early on, teacher education programs could promote the kind of self-awareness that allows preservice teachers to hear and listen to their own voices.

Mediation Structures Conducive to Developing Reflective Practice

Some mediation structures and other vehicles that have been found to be useful in promoting reflection include journal writing, teacher narratives, personal histories, autobiography, metaphor, case studies, critical incidents, problem framing, video recording, role playing, critical friendships, support groups, book clubs, fishbowl, action research, portfolios, cognitive coaching, and peer coaching. Those that have the greatest potential for reflection on classroom management issues are the various forms of journal writing, teacher narratives, and critical incidents. Merging these task structures in creative ways and using them individually, collaboratively, and with facilitated coaching is likely to maximize the level of reflection required to grapple with daily management dilemmas.

Journal Writing (Open, Reflective, Interactive, and Dialogue Journals). Journal writing as a systematic self-reflection process enables teachers to chart their development and become more aware of their contribution to the experiences they encounter in the classroom. Making regular journal entries can help teachers remain clear and intensely aware of what is going on in both their inner and outer worlds. Journal writing also develops self-discipline. Attitudes about teaching and interacting with students are the result of attitudes and experiences gained over time. By making regular journal entries teachers can look more objectively at their behaviors in the classroom.

Journal writing can be used in a number of ways to encourage reflection (Calderhead, 1991; Collier, 1999; Dobbins, 1996; Keating, 1993; Ross, 1990; Smyth, 1992; Surbeck, Han, & Moyer, 1991; Wiltz, 1999; Yost, 1997; Yost et al., 1999). Specific structures that have been found to facilitate reflection include providing prompts, structuring periodic rereading of previous entries to search for any emerging patterns, and posing questions in a nonjudgmental way as a means of creating ongoing dialogue. Dobbins (1996) used journal writing with preservice teachers and found that specific prompts to focus on their own learning produced deeper reflection and encouraged teachers to confront broader educational issues in the process of clarifying their own beliefs. Similarly, Hoover (1994) found that reflection was enhanced when student teachers were asked to write structured, rather than more open analyses of videotapes of themselves teaching. The focused written analyses directed the student teachers to select an area of analysis, systematically collect data on the selected area of analysis, summarize their data, explore the congruency between what they believed and the teaching actions they viewed, identify what they learned about themselves as teachers, and tell how they would apply what they learned in their future teaching.

Dialogue journals, also referred to as interactive, are another useful vehicle for promoting reflection. They are first individually written and then shared with another person who makes inquiries for the purpose of expanding thinking (Keating, 1993). Essentially this is inquiry through writing instead of conversation. Likewise, autobiographical journal writing coupled with deliberate questioning prompts can stimulate greater awareness of personal values and implicit theories of teaching (Ross, 1990). The regular feedback from a mentor serving in a coaching role can be a valuable tool to move teacher trainees along the reflection continuum as well as provide a venue for critical reflection. According to Smyth (1991), a powerful tool for promoting higher-order reflection is posing a series of questions that moves from description (What do I do?) to meaning (What does it mean?) to confrontation (How did I come to be like this?) to reconstruction (How might I do things differently?).

Using a vehicle of case story writing based on student teaching experiences, Hunter and Hatton (1998) found that peer and instructor collaboration helped preservice teachers move toward critical reflection. Similarly there is some evidence that when preservice teachers are engaged in journal writing over time they develop the habit of reflection (Yost, 1997; Yost et al., 1999).

Having a record of thoughts, feelings, issues and concerns can provide both a window of the past and a gateway to the future. The act of maintaining and reviewing a journal over time can serve as a tool for discovering patterns of thought and behavior.

Specific to becoming more reflective regarding classroom management issues and solving individual behavior problems, journals can serve several important purposes for teachers, including naming issues and posing questions, working through internal conflicts, recording critical incidents, identifying cause-and-effect relationships, seeing patterns of unsuccessful strategies over time, and tracing life patterns and themes.

Teacher Narratives (Autobiography, Metaphor, Case Story Writing). Narratives other than journal writing can render a rich understanding of what takes place in the minds of developing teachers as they construct their reality of teaching. Teacher narratives are stories written by and about teachers and can be used as the source of narrative inquiry (Cole & Knowles, 2000; Sparks-Langer & Colton, 1991; Zeichner, 1983). It is a more disciplined from of writing than journaling in that it has a structure and a focus, the intent to communicate a story. Either keen observers or teachers themselves write real stories about teaching, illuminating the realities, dilemmas, and rewards of teaching. Reflecting on teacher narratives can yield insights about motivations for teacher actions, about the complexities of teaching, and about teachers themselves (Sparks-Langer & Colton, 1991; Taggart & Wilson, 1998). Teacher narratives can also be used as case studies with the explicit purpose of reflecting on a specific problem.

Autobiographical sketches, also called personal histories, are a specialized form of teacher narratives (Sparks-Langer & Colton, 1994). These stories of a more personal and in-depth nature offer insight into the past to uncover preconceived theories of practice. Writing their own biographies and how these have shaped the formation of their values enables teachers to see more clearly the influence of social and institutional forces beyond the classroom and school.

Metaphors bear the images teachers have of themselves as teachers, their professional identity (Bullough, Knowles, & Crow, 1992). The practical theories of teachers are often expressed as metaphors as opposed to the more logical forms of expression and they often appear in the natural language teachers use to talk about their teaching (Munby & Russell, 1990). The knowledge-in-action embedded in the personal theories of teachers often cannot be adequately depicted in their actual statements of knowledge; hence metaphor is a way to bridge the known to the new.

Metaphorical thinking is a way of illuminating features through comparison, identifying relationships that may not be obvious or previously acknowledged. Through shared similarity, understanding is deepened and knowledge in one domain serves as a guide for comprehending knowledge in another, with some transfer of meaning taking place in both directions.

Johnston (1994) and Lasley (1992) advocated the use of metaphors to help teachers become aware of their teaching identities and develop alternative ways to think about an issue. Specific to metaphorical expressions of the role of manager, Tobin (1990) used teachers' actual depictions as *intimidator*, *comedian*, and *ship's captain* as a means of encouraging teachers to explore the potential limitations embedded in the language they chose.

Metaphors can be a powerful way into the expressions of meanings and the organizing ideas that underpin ways of thinking about classroom management as Korthagen (1993) discovered in exploring a *lion tamer* metaphor used by a beginning teacher struggling with discipline problems. This teacher depicted her plight as being caged in, having to use the whip or risk being torn to pieces. Her metaphor provided a frame of reference, which served as a first step in the process of reframing to reveal other possible interpretations of the situation.

Weinstein, Woolfolk, Dittmeier, and Shanker (1994) found that some student teachers used more empowering metaphors to conceptualize their role of classroom manager. For example, one teacher used the metaphor of *gardener*, one who nourished, nurtured, and protected individual students, and simultaneously "tended" the whole garden.

Marshall (1990) contended that the reflection that occurs in the examination of personal teaching metaphors involves reframing the lens through which a teacher perceives a problem. According to Schön, this is a critical attribute of reflective practice.

Critical Incidents. A critical incident is generally conceived of as a self-generated incident, although it could also be a carefully chosen real-world example or case study of a teaching dilemma intended to serve as a springboard for reflection. Details of significant incidents that stand out provide the impetus for teachers to grapple with dilemmas. When teachers share critical incident responses, they come to realize that their individual stories have embedded within them generic qualities and themes, discovering that their personal struggles are not so different from those experienced by their colleagues. What they thought were idiosyncratic failings or inadequacies become seen as common experiences.

There is some evidence that a critical incident can be a tool for deepening the level of reflection. Writing about critical incidents or dilemmas rather than typical daily events has been found to promote critical reflection in novice teachers (Pultorak, 1996). Use of critical incidents with explicit prompts and coaching increased the capacity of preservice teachers to engage in higher-order reflection (Griffin, 2003).

Scenario-based learning also holds promise as a vehicle for reflection. A "scenario" refers to a specific situation, a set of circumstances, a critical incident, an incomplete story, or an active case study of persons and events (Errington, 2003). Scenario-based learning (SBL) is the intentional use of scenarios to bring about desired learning outcomes and it can be specifically geared to building reflective practice. Scenarios can be skill based, problem based, issue based, or speculative based. The key ingredient to successful SBL is an authentic context—one that enables participants to experience and respond to a challenging issue in an interactive, purposeful way (Parkin, 1998; Pernice, 2003).

CONCLUDING THOUGHTS

The path to developing as a critically reflective teacher is uncharted territory. Developing teachers must plot their own course. This complex process cannot be prescriptive in nature; rather it is a process that allows insights to surface which serve to challenge familiar behavior patterns. It is therefore more a way of knowing than a knowing how.

Because there are many pathways to becoming a reflective practitioner, there is no single road map. Whichever path a teacher chooses, however, must involve a willingness to be an active participant in a perpetual growth process requiring ongoing critical reflection on classroom practices. Reflective practice cannot be achieved in the absence of considerable personal responsibility, insight, and awareness. To be a reflective practitioner is to act with integrity, openness, and courage rather than compromise, defensiveness, or fear. The journey involves infusing personal beliefs and values into professional practice.

The more teachers explore, the more they discover. The more they question, the more they access new realms of possibility.

ACKNOWLEDGMENT

The author thanks Karen Osterman, Hofstra University, for her review of an earlier version of this chapter.

REFERENCES

Argyris, C. (1990). *Overcoming organizational defenses*. Boston: Allyn & Bacon.

Berkey, R., Curtis, T., Minnick, F., Zietlow, K., Campbell, D., & Kirschner, B. (1990). Collaborating for reflective practice: Voices of teachers, administrators, and researchers. *Education and Urban Society, 22*(2), 204–235.

Boyd, P. C., Boll, M., & Brawner, L. (1998). Becoming reflective professionals: An exploration of preservice teachers' struggles as they translate language theory into practice. *Action in Teacher Education, 19*(4), 61–75.

Bright, B. (1996). Reflecting on "reflective practice." *Studies in the Education of Adults, 28*(2), 162–184.

Brookfield, S. D. (1995). *Becoming a critically reflective teacher*. San Francisco: Jossey-Bass.

Burbules, N. C. (1993). *Dialogue in teaching: Theory and practice*. New York: Teachers College Press.

Bullough, R., Knowles, J. G., & Crow, N. (1992). *Emerging as a teacher*. London: Routledge.

Calderhead, J. (1991). The nature and growth of knowledge in student teaching. *Teaching and Teacher Education, 8*(5/6), 531–535.

Carr, W., & Kemmis, S. (1986). *Becoming critical: Education, knowledge and action research.* London: Falmer Press.

Cochran-Smith, M., & Lytle, S. (1993). *Inside/Outside: Teacher research and knowledge.* New York: Teachers College Press.

Collier, S. T. (1999). Characteristics of reflective thought during the student teaching experience. *Journal of Teacher Education, 50*(3), 173–181.

Cole, A. L., & Knowles, J. G. (2000). *Researching teaching: Exploring teacher development through reflective inquiry.* Boston: Allyn and Bacon.

Cruickshank, D., & Applegate, J. (1981). Reflective teaching as a strategy for teacher growth. *Educational Leadership, 38*(7), 553–554.

Dana, N. F., & Yendol-Silva, D. (2003). *The reflective educator's guide to classroom research.* Thousand Oaks, CA: Corwin Press.

Day, C. (1993). Reflection: A necessary but not sufficient condition for professional development. *British Educational Research Journal, 19*, 83–93.

Day, C. (1998). Working with the different selves of teachers: Beyond comfortable collaboration. *Educational Action Research, 6*(2), 255–272.

deCharms, R. (1976). *Enhancing motivation.* New York: Irvington.

Dewey, J. (1910/1933). *How we think: A restatement of the relation of reflective thinking to the educative process.* Lexington, MA: Heath.

Dewey, J. (1938). *Logic: The theory of inquiry.* Troy, MO: Holt, Rinehart & Winston.

Dobbins, R. (1996). The challenge of developing a 'reflective practicum.' *Asia-Pacific Journal of Teacher Education, 24*(3), 269–280.

Ellis, A. (1974). *Humanistic psychotherapy: The rational-emotive approach.* New York: McGraw-Hill.

Errington, E. (2003). *Developing scenario-based learning: Practical insights for tertiary educators.* Palmerston North, New Zealand: Dunmore Press.

Farrell, T. S. (2004). *Reflective practice in action: 80 reflective breaks for busy teachers.* Thousand Oaks, CA: Corwin Press.

Garmston, R., & Wellman, B. (1999). *The adaptive school. A sourcebook for developing collaborative groups.* Norwood, MA: Christopher-Gordon.

Glanz, J. (1998). *Action research: An educational leader's guide to school improvement.* Norwood, MA: Christopher-Gordon.

Glasser, W. (1997, April). A new look at school failure and school success. *Phi Delta Kappan, 78*, 597–602.

Golby, M., & Appleby, R. (1995). Reflective practice through critical friendship: Some possibilities. *Cambridge Journal of Education, 25*, 149–160.

Griffin, M. L. (2003). Using critical incidents to promote and assess reflective thinking in preservice teachers. *Reflective Practice, 4(2)*, 207–220.

Handal, G., & Lauvas, P. (1987). *Promoting reflective teaching.* Milton Keynes, UK: Open University Press.

Hatton, N., & Smith, D. (1995). Reflection in teacher education: Towards definition and implementation. *Teaching and Teacher Education, 11*(1), 22–49.

Horn, R. H. (2000). *Teacher talk: A post-formal inquiry into educational change.* New York: Peter Lang.

Hoover, L. A. (1994). Reflective writing as a window on preservice teachers' thought processes. *Teaching and Teacher Education, 10*, 83–93.

Hunter, J., & Hatton, N. (1998). Approaches to the writing of cases: Experience with preservice master of education students. *Asia-Pacific Journal of Teacher Education, 26*, 235–246.

Jay, J. K. (2003). *Quality teaching: Reflection as the heart of practice.* Lanham, MD: Scarecrow Press.

Jay, J. K., & Johnson, K. L. (2002). Capturing complexity: A typology of reflective practice for teacher education. *Teaching and Teacher Education, 18*, 73–85.

Johnston, M. (1994). Contrasts and similarities in case studies of teacher reflection and change. *Curriculum Inquiry, 24*(1), 9–26.

Kagan, D. M. (1992). Professional growth among preservice and beginning teachers. *Review of Educational Research, 62*, 120–169.

Kasl, E., Dechant, K., & Marsick, V. (1993). Living the learning: Internalizing our model of group learning. In D. Boud, R. Cohen, & D. Walker (Eds.), *Using experience for learning.* Bristol, PA: Open University Press.

Keane, R. (1987). The doubting journey: A learning process of self-transformation. In D. Boud & V. Griffin (Eds.), *Appreciating adults' learning: From the learners' perspective.* Toronto, Canada: Ontario Institute for Studies in Education Press.

Keating, C. N. (1993). Promoting growth through dialogue journals. In G. Wells (Ed.), *Changing schools from within: Creating communities of inquiry* (pp. 217–236). Toronto, Canada: Ontario Institute for Studies in Education Press.

Kesley, J. G. (1993). Learning from teaching: Problems, problem-formulation and the enhancement of problem-solving capability. In P. Hallinger, K. A., Leithwood, & J. Murphy (Eds.), *A cognitive perspective on educational administration* (pp. 231–252). New York: Teachers College Press.

Killion, J., & Todnem, G. (1991). A process of personal theory building. *Educational Leadership, 48*(6), 14–17.

King, P. M., & Kitchener, K. S. (1994). *Developing reflective judgment.* San Francisco: Jossey-Bass.

Kohn, A. (1996). *Beyond discipline: From compliance to community.* Alexandria, VA: Association for Supervision and Curriculum Development.

Knowles, M. (1992). *The adult learner: A neglected species* (4th ed.). Houston, TX: Gulf.

Korthagen, F. (1993). Two modes of reflection. *Teaching and Teacher Education, 9*, 317–326.

Korthagen, F., & Wubbels, T. (1991, April). *Characteristics of reflective practitioners: Towards an operationalization of the concept of reflection.* Paper presented at the annual meeting of the American Educational Research Association, Chicago.

Larrivee, B. (1996). *Moving into balance.* Santa Monica, CA: Shoreline.

Larrivee, B. (2000). Transforming teaching practice: Becoming the critically reflective teacher. *Reflective Practice, 1*(3), 293–307.

Larrivee, B. (2004, June). *Assessing teachers' level of reflective practice as a tool for change.* Paper presented at the Third International Conference on Reflective Practice, Gloucester, UK.

Larrivee, B. (2005). *Authentic classroom management: Creating a learning community and building reflective practice.* Boston: Allyn & Bacon.

Lasley, T. J. (1992). Inquiry and reflection: Promoting teacher reflection. *Journal of Staff Development, 13*(1), 24–29.

Leat, D. (1995). The costs of reflection in initial teacher education. *Cambridge Journal of Education, 25*(2), 161–174.

Marshall, H. (1990). Metaphor as an instructional tool in encouraging student teacher reflection. *Theory Into Practice, 29*(2), 128–132.

McFee, G. (1993). Reflections on the nature of action research. *Cambridge Journal of Education, 23*(2), 173–183.

Mezirow, J. (1991). *Transformative dimensions of adult learning.* San Francisco: Jossey-Bass.

Munby, H., & Russell, T. (1990). Metaphor in the study of teachers' professional knowledge. *Theory Into Practice, 29*(2), 116–121.

Nais, J. (1987). Learning from difference: A college approach to change. In J. Smyth (Ed.), *Educating teachers* (pp. 137–152). New York: Teachers College Press.

Osterman, K. F. (2000). Students' need for belonging in the school community. *Review of Educational Research, 70*(3), 323–367.

Osterman, K. P., & Kottkamp, R. B. (2004). *Reflective practice for educators: Improving schooling through professional development.* Thousand Oaks, CA: Corwin Press.

Parkin, M. (1998). *Tales for trainers: Using stories and metaphors to facilitate training,* London: Kogan Page.

Pernice, R. (2003). Writing in role: Helping students explore emotional dimensions within scenarios. In E. Errington (Ed.), *Developing scenario-based learning: Practical insights for tertiary teachers.* Palmerston North, New Zealand: Dunmore Press.

Pultorak, E. G. (1993). Facilitating reflective thought in novice teachers. *Journal of Teacher Education, 44*, 288–295.

Pultorak, E. G. (1996). Following the developmental process of reflection in novice teacher: Three years of investigation. *Journal of Teacher Education, 47*, 283–291.

Reagan, T. G., Case, C. W., & Brubacher, J. W. (2000). *Becoming a reflective educator: How to build a culture of inquiry in the schools.* Thousand Oaks, CA: Corwin Press.

Rodgers, C. (2002). Defining reflection: Another look at John Dewey and reflective thinking. *Teachers College Record, 104*(4), 842–866.

Ross, D. D. (1990). Programmatic structures for the preparation of reflective teachers. In R. T. Clift, W. R. Houston, & M. C. Pugach (Eds.), *Encouraging reflective practice in education: An analysis of issues and programs* (pp. 97–118). New York: Teachers College Press.

Rudney, G., & Guillaume, A. (1990). Reflective teaching for student teachers. *The Teacher Educator, 25*(3), 13–20.

Schön, D. A. (1983). *The reflective practitioner: How professionals think in action.* New York: Basic Books.

Schön, D. A. (1987). *Educating the reflective practitioner.* San Francisco: Jossey-Bass.

Senge, P. M. (1990). *The fifth discipline.* New York: Currency Doubleday.

Senge, P. M., Kleiner, A., Roberts, C., Ross, R. B., & Smith, B. J. (1994). *The fifth discipline fieldbook.* New York: Currency Doubleday.

Smith, D., & Hatton, N. (1993). Reflection in teacher education: A study in progress. *Education Research and Perspectives, 20,* 13–23.

Smyth, J. (1989). Developing and sustaining critical reflection in teacher education. *Journal of Teacher Education, 40*(2), 2–9.

Smyth, J. (1991). *Teachers as collaborative learners.* Philadelphia: Open University Press.

Smyth, J. (1992). Teacher's work and the politics of reflection. *American Education Research Journal, 29*(2), 267–300.

Sokol, A. V., & Cranton, P. (1998, Spring). Transforming, not training. *Adult Learning*, 14–16.

Sparks-Langer, G., & Colton, A. (1991). Synthesis of research on teachers' reflective thinking. *Educational Leadership, 48(6)*, 37–44.

Sparks-Langer, G., & Colton, A. (1994). Reflective decision making: The cornerstone of school reform. *Journal of Staff Development, 15*(1), 2–7.

Steffy, B. E., Wolfe, M. P., Pasch, S. H., & Enz, B. J. (2000). *Life cycle of the career teacher*. Thousand Oaks, CA: Corwin Press.

Surbeck, E., Han, E., & Moyer, J. (1991). Assessing reflective responses in journals. *Educational Leadership, 48*(6), 25–27.

Taggart, G., & Wilson, A. P. (1998). *Promoting reflective thinking in teachers*. Thousand Oaks, CA: Corwin Press.

Tobin, K. (1990). Changing metaphors and beliefs: A master switch for teaching. *Theory Into Practice, 29*(2), 121–127.

Tremmel, R. (1993). Zen and the art of reflective practice in teacher education. *Harvard Educational Review, 63*(1), 434–458.

Usher, R. S., & Bryant, I. (1989). *Adult education as theory, practice and research: The captive triangle*. New York: Routledge, Chapman and Hall.

Valli, L. (1992). *Reflective teacher education: Cases and critiques*. Albany State University of New York Press.

Valli, L. (1997). Listening to other voices: A description of teacher reflection in the United States. *Peabody Journal of Education, 72*(1), 67–88.

Van Manen, M. (1977). Linking ways of knowing with ways of being practical. *Curriculum Inquiry, 6*(3), 205–228.

Van Manen, M. (1991). Reflectivity and pedagogical moment: The normativity of pedagogical thinking and acting. *Journal of Curriculum Studies, 23*, 507–536.

Weinstein, C., Woolfolk, A., Dittmeier, L. & Shanker, U. (1994). Protector or prison guard: Using metaphors and media to explore student teachers' thinking about classroom management. *Action in Teacher Education, 16*(1), 41–54.

Wideen, M., Mayer-Smith, J., & Moon, B. (1998). A critical analysis of the research on learning to teach: Making the case for an ecological perspective on inquiry. *Review of Educational Research, 68*(2), 130–178.

Wildman, T. M., & Niles, J. A. (1987). Reflective teachers: Tensions between abstractions and realities. *Journal of Teacher Education, 38*(4), 25–31.

Williams, M. (1981). *The velveteen rabbit or, how toys become real*. Philadelphia: Running Press.

Wiltz, N. W. (1999, April). *Reflective journaling: A tool for promoting professional development in student teachers*. Paper presented at the annual meeting of the American Educational Research Association, Montreal, Canada.

Wunder, S. (2003). Preservice teachers reflections on learning to teach elementary social studies. *Reflective Practice, 4*(2), 193–206.

York-Barr, J., Sommers, W. A., Ghere, G. S., & Montie, J. (2001). *Reflective practice to improve schools*. Thousand Oaks, CA: Corwin Press.

Yost, D. S. (1997). The moral dimensions of teaching and preservice teachers: Can moral dispositions be influenced? *Journal of Teacher Education, 48*, 281–292.

Yost, D. S., Forlenza-Bailey, A., & Shaw, S. F. (1999). The teachers who embrace diversity: The role of reflection, discourse, and field experience in education. *The Professional Educator, 21*(2), 1–14.

Yost, D. S., Sentner, S. M., & Forlenza-Bailey, A. (2000). An examination of the construct of critical reflection: Implications for teacher education programming in the 21st century. *Journal of Teacher Education, 51*(1), 39–48.

Zehm, S. J., & Kottler, J. A. (1993). *On being a teacher: The human dimension*. Newbury Park, CA: Corwin Press.

Zeichner, K. M. (1983). Alternative paradigms of teacher education. *Journal of Teacher Education, 39*(3), 3–9.

Zeichner, K. M., & Liston, D. P. (1996). *Reflective teaching: An introduction*. Mahwah, NJ: Lawrence Erlbaum Associates.

38

Classroom Management, Discipline, and the Law: Clarifying Confusions about Students' Rights and Teachers' Authority

David Schimmel
University of Massachusetts, Amherst

INTRODUCTION

Most teachers have had no training in school law. As a result, many make two types of mistakes. First, because they see their relations with students in loco parentis, they may overreact and punish their students as they believe parents should for "inappropriate" statements, behaviors, or clothing. Because they are unaware that public school teachers function as agents of the government and are therefore restrained by the Bill of Rights, these teachers may unknowingly violate students' constitutional rights. Second, because they have misinformed fears of being sued if they discipline students (and if students are accidentally injured), teachers may underreact and fail to take reasonable disciplinary action that is legally and educationally appropriate.

This chapter explores some of these misunderstandings and clarifies the scope and limits of students' rights and teachers' authority. Part I examines selected cases in three areas of frequent constitutional confusion: student freedom of expression, freedom of religion and conscience, and search and seizure. Part II focuses on teachers' excessive fear of liability in disciplining students. It does this through analyzing the debates and provisions of the federal Teacher Liability Protection Act of 2001, a little-known part of the omnibus No Child Left Behind legislation. Part III summarizes some of the reasons for teachers' legal confusions, the limited research in this area, the need for further research, and what can be done to enable teachers to become legally literate. It concludes that the major responsibility for teachers' misunderstanding of the laws that affect them and their students rests with those who omit legal literacy from most teacher certification and inservice education programs.

PART I. CONSTITUTIONAL CONFUSION

In a small New England town, a controversy erupted over the distribution of a provocative "underground" student newspaper written and printed off campus. Many teachers and parents felt the paper's distribution should be banned on school grounds because it included offensive language. At a school forum about the paper, I explained that the First Amendment prohibited public school educators from restricting unpopular speech because they acted as agents of the government. In response, one irate teacher said that the police, the CIA, and the FBI might be agents of the government, but that he was just a high school teacher, and he certainly didn't consider himself to be some "government agent." It is likely that most of his colleagues felt the same way. And that, of course, is the problem, because many, if not most, public school teachers do not understand the constitutional context in which they work. They see themselves as employees of a local school district. They impose discipline in good faith to protect their students from being offended by provocative classmates and to keep distracting controversy out of their classrooms. They may understand that the First Amendment prohibits the government from censoring freedom of the press, but do not understand why teachers should not be able to prohibit controversial student expression.

Freedom of Expression

The small-town forum on underground student newspapers took place in 2002—more than 30 years after the U.S. Supreme Court clearly ruled that the First Amendment applies to public schools and that a student's right to freedom of expression "does not stop at the schoolhouse gate" (*Tinker v. Des Moines*, 1969, p. 506). According to the Court, because schools "are educating the young for citizenship," they should carefully protect the "constitutional freedoms of the individual, if we are not to strangle the free mind at its source and teach youth to discount important principles of our government as mere platitudes" (*Tinker v. Des Moines*, 1969, p. 507).

In this case, schools in Des Moines, Iowa, prohibited students from wearing black armbands to protest against the Vietnam War because they feared that the armbands might lead to a disturbance. However, the Court rejected this justification and wrote: "In our system, undifferentiated fear or apprehension of disturbance is not enough to overcome the right to freedom of expression." Furthermore, Justice Fortas, who wrote the Court's majority opinion, noted that "state-operated schools cannot be enclaves of totalitarianism." The Court acknowledged that schools can prohibit and punish student expression that causes substantial disruption or interferes with the rights of others. However, Justice Fortas emphasized that schools cannot prohibit student expression merely "to avoid the discomfort and unpleasantness that always accompany an unpopular viewpoint" (*Tinker v. Des Moines*, 1969, p. 509).

Subsequent Supreme Court decisions have somewhat narrowed *Tinker*'s holding. Thus, *Bethel School District v. Fraser* (1986) ruled that students' lewd and vulgar speech could be prohibited in school-sponsored activities even if it were not disruptive, and *Hazelwood School District v. Kuhlmeier* (1988) held that educators can control student expression that is related to the curriculum. However, the basic principle of *Tinker* remains good law, that is, a student's nondisruptive personal expression that occurs in school is protected by the First Amendment even if the ideas are unpopular and controversial.

A few years after the Tinker decision, several students from a Texas high school were suspended for distributing the *Awakening*, an underground newspaper, in violation of a school policy requiring prior administrative approval. School officials expressed concern that the paper's "controversial" statements advocating a review of marijuana laws and offering information about birth control might cause disruption. In response, a federal appeals court wrote that "it should be axiomatic at this point in our nation's history that in a democracy 'controversy' is, as a matter of constitutional law, never sufficient in and of itself to stifle the views of any citizen" (*Shanley v. Northeast Sch. Dist.*, 1972, p. 971).

Two other comments of the court seem at least as true today as they did then:

> One of the great concerns of our time is that our young people, disillusioned by our political process, are disengaging from political participation. It is most important that our young become convinced that our Constitution is a living reality, not parchment preserved under glass. (p. 972)
>
> It is incredible to us that in 1972, the First Amendment was deemed inapplicable under these circumstances to high school students living at the threshold of voting and dying for their country. (*Shanley v. Northeast Sch. Dist.*, 1972, p. 973)

Despite decades of judicial decisions reaffirming the free speech rights of students, teachers and administrators continue to restrict controversial expression that they think might be offensive. This was illustrated in a 2003 Michigan case concerning Bretton Barber, who wore a T-shirt to school just before the Iraq war with a picture of President Bush above the caption, "International Terrorist," to express his beliefs about the president's foreign policy.

One of the teachers complained that the T-shirt was "inappropriate" and a student complained it was "disrespectful." Based on these complaints, an assistant principal concluded that the shirt created a disruption and told Bretton to take it off or turn it inside out. Because there was no evidence that Bretton's shirt was obscene, lewd, or substantially interfered with school operations or was likely to do so, a federal court held that the shirt was protected by the First Amendment and could not be banned (*Barber v. Dearborn*, 2003).

In another recent case, Elliot Chambers, a Minnesota high school student, wore a sweatshirt to school emblazoned with the message "straight pride" and the symbol of a man and woman holding hands. Elliot believed that homosexuality is a sin and felt it was unfair for the school to have "gay pride parades" and none for straight pride. After the assistant principal learned that the shirt offended a group of students, she told Elliot not to wear it. Elliott and his parents argued in court that the First Amendment should protect Elliot's right to wear the shirt.

The judge recognized "the tension between the school's responsibility to maintain a safe environment conducive to learning and its equally compelling mandate to allow for the exercise of constitutional expression." Thus, the court ruled that Elliot's freedom of expression should be protected unless the school had evidence that wearing the shirt could lead to "material interference with school activities." Although the judge commended the school for creating an environment of tolerance for diversity (including respect for gay students), the First Amendment requires the school to also tolerate "divergent viewpoints, whether they be political, religious or social" including the straight pride point of view (*Chambers v. Babbitt*, 2001).

These cases illustrate how students' constitutional rights to freedom of expression that have been firmly established for over 35 years continue to be violated by some teachers and administrators in our public schools—often with the best of intentions—to keep controversy out of the classroom and to provide a "safe" environment that protects students from "offensive" views that might make some students uncomfortable. Instead, educators need to learn and apply basic constitutional principles in their schools and classrooms and teach tolerance for uncomfortable views. Such teachers will not teach students to be cynical about their constitutional rights. Rather, educators who practice what they teach about the Bill of Rights will model, complement, and reinforce the values of the First Amendment.

Search and Seizure

Unconstitutional strip searches are another example of some educators acting illegally with the best of intentions—as they may think a good parent should—to discourage and punish theft.

Although dozens of such controversies have gone to court, the following cases are illustrative of the situations that have led to illegal searches from the 1970s to the present.

Robert Reardon was a fifth-grade teacher in upstate New York when one of his students complained that he was missing $3 from his coat pocket. The teacher asked the class if anyone knew about the missing money, but there was no response. Because there were prior student complaints about missing money, Reardon started to search the class with the help of three other teachers. They searched the clothes in the coatroom and then asked students to empty their pockets and remove their shoes. When these searches proved fruitless, women teachers took the girls to the girls' restroom and the men teachers took the boys to the boys' restroom. There, students were ordered to strip to their underwear, and their clothes were searched; but the strip searches proved futile, and the money was never found.

As a result of the search, parents sued the teachers for violating their children's Fourth Amendment right against unreasonable search and seizure. In deciding whether a search is reasonable, the judge wrote that teachers should consider the students' age and the seriousness of the problem to which the search is directed. Based on the facts of this case, the judge ruled the search was not valid. Although it was reasonable to suspect that someone in the class stole the money, there were no facts to indicate that any specific student took the money. Therefore, wrote the judge, the search violated the Fourth Amendment because there was "no reasonable suspicion to believe that each student searched possessed the contraband." However, the court ruled that the teacher should not be held personally liable. This is because the date of the decision was 1977, and the judge did not feel that students' Fourth Amendment rights were clearly established at that time (*Bellinier v. Lund*, 1977).

Whether the Fourth Amendment protects students against unreasonable searches was not definitively resolved by the U.S. Supreme Court until 1985. In that year, school officials argued that they should be exempt from the Fourth Amendment because they act in loco parentis in dealing with students because their authority is from the parent, not the state. But the Supreme Court rejected that argument. "Such reasoning," wrote Justice White, is in conflict "with contemporary reality." Furthermore, the Court explained that "the concept of parental delegation" as a source of school authority is not consonant with compulsory education laws. Today's public school educators, wrote Justice White, "do not merely exercise authority voluntarily conferred on them by individual parents, rather they act in furtherance of publicly mandated educational and disciplinary policies" (*New Jersey v.T.L.O.*, 1985, p. 336). Thus, in carrying out searches, educators "act as representatives of the state, not merely as surrogates for the parents, and they cannot claim the parents' immunity from the strictures of the Fourth Amendment." Nevertheless, the Court concluded that educators' searches of students (unlike searches by police) would not require a warrant or probable cause. Instead, school searches would be permitted under the Fourth Amendment if they were based on "reasonable suspicion" that the students violated the law or school rules and were "not excessively intrusive" in light of the age and sex of the student and the nature of the infraction (*New Jersey v. T.L.O.*, 1985, p. 342).

As a result of the Supreme Court ruling in *T.L.O.*, and subsequent judicial decisions, it has been clear for 20 years that the Fourth Amendment prohibition against unreasonable searches applies to teachers and administrators and that educators who strip-search students violate the Constitution unless they have reasonable suspicion that the individual student has broken the law or a school rule. However, it appears that some teachers still are unaware that their disciplinary actions are restricted by the Constitution, as the following 2003 decision illustrates.

When Ms. Apley, an Ohio third-grade teacher, discovered that $10 was missing from her desk, she asked Shaneequa Watkins and two other students who were in her classroom at the time to check their book bags, empty their pockets, and turn down the waistband of their pants. But no money was found. Apley then asked Watkins to accompany her to a supply closet where she asked the student to pull out her pants and underwear so the teacher could look down them for the missing money.

In this case, the school defended the teacher's action in the interest of maintaining order and "instilling moral values against theft." But the court ruled that these legitimate concerns "cannot outweigh Watkins' privacy interest" (*Watkins v. Millenium School*, 2003, p. 901). The judge recognized that there are dangerous situations (such as those involving weapons) in which educators may search students without individualized suspicion. In this case, wrote the court, "a reasonable teacher should have known that students have Fourth Amendment rights against unreasonable search and seizure" and that requiring a student "to expose the private areas of her body underneath her pants" to search for $10 without individualized suspicion is clearly unreasonable (*Watkins v. Millenium, School*, 2003, p. 902). Thus, we have another example of a constitutional right that has been firmly established for 2 decades that continues to be violated by educators who were probably never taught about students' Fourth Amendment protections.

Religion and Conscience

There is much confusion among teachers and administrators about the separation of religion and education. Although very few educators believe that public schools should promote particular religions, some feel that schools should be allowed to encourage voluntary, nondenominational prayers. However, the U.S. Supreme Court clearly ruled, in 1963, that schools cannot incorporate Bible reading or nondenominational prayers into their opening exercises (*Abington v. Shempp*, 1963), and in 1992, the Court ruled that school-sponsored graduation prayers were also unconstitutional—even when students could be excused (*Lee v. Weiseman*, 1992). The problem of public schools endorsing religion, explained Justice O'Connor, is that "Endorsement sends a message to nonadherents that they are outsiders, not full members of the political community, and an accompanying message to adherents that they are insiders, favored members of the political community." (*Lynch v. Donnelly*, 1984, p. 688). Moreover, Justice Kennedy explained that nondenominational "civic" prayers also conflict with the "central meaning of the Religion Clauses . . . which is that all creeds must be tolerated and none favored" (*Lee v. Weiseman*, 1992, p. 590).

Because most educators have learned little about how the two religion clauses of the First Amendment (the Establishment Clause and the Free Exercise Clause) apply to the public schools, they tend to make two mistakes. First, some teachers have misinterpreted Supreme Court rulings to mean that public schools should prohibit all religious books and ideas. These educators fail to distinguish between public schools *promoting* religion or prayer (which is prohibited) and teaching *about* religion (which is not). In fact, the Supreme Court wrote that "the study of the Bible or of religion, where presented objectively as part of a secular program of education" would not violate the Establishment Clause (*Abington v. Shempp*, 1963, p. 225).

Second, some teachers and administrators fail to distinguish between school-sponsored prayer or religious activities, which the Establishment Clause of the First Amendment prohibits, and a student's private speech endorsing or promoting religion, which the Free Speech and Free Exercise Clauses protect. Such protected student speech would include reading the Bible outside of class, saying grace before meals, or other nondisruptive religious expression. Here are a couple of other examples:

Two students at a Denver high school were suspended for distributing a newspaper called *Issues and Answers* published by Student Action for Christ. Their actions violated a school policy that prohibited distribution of "material that proselytizes a particular religious . . . belief." The students believed that the policy was unconstitutional, and a federal court agreed. The school argued that their policy was designed to prevent potential disruption. But the judge wrote that this restriction defeats "the very purpose of public education in secondary schools," which includes preparation for citizenship and the ability "to develop their own sets of values and beliefs" (*Rivera v. East Otero School District*, 1989, p. 1194).

The school also argued that the restriction of proselytizing material is necessary to avoid violating the Establishment Clause. However, the court explained that the Establishment Clause is a limit on the power of governments and public schools, not a restriction on the rights of individual students "acting in their private lives" and "not in concert with school authority," who distribute their religious material in a nondisruptive manner to students who want to accept it. (*Rivera v. East Otero*, 1989). Because students have a right to engage in religious speech and the school has no compelling reason to restrict it, the ban on students distributing proselytizing religious material was declared unconstitutional.

In a more recent case, a Massachusetts high school suspended members of a Christian student club for insubordination for distributing candy canes with proselytizing religious messages after the principal prohibited the practice. The principal felt that the evangelical messages about individual sin and salvation through Jesus Christ were offensive to some students and that allowing the distribution would violate the Establishment Clause because people would think the message was endorsed by the school. However, a federal court ruled in favor of the students.

First, the judge explained that a public school cannot prohibit the expression of an idea simply because many or most people find it offensive. Second, there was no evidence that the distribution of the message would cause disruption. Third, because the candy distribution was a private student activity, the school could not argue that permitting distribution violated the Establishment Clause. According to this 2003 decision, the school's argument is based on "a widely held misconception of constitutional law that has infected our sometimes politically overcorrect society: the Establishment Clause does not apply to private action; it applies only to government action." Because the student religious club's activities "are private, school-tolerated (rather than school-sponsored) expressive activities," the Establishment Clause does not prohibit them from distributing their religious messages (*Westfield High School L.I.F.E. Club v. City of Westfield*, 2003, p. 120).

A related issue concerns requiring students to salute the flag and say the Pledge of Allegiance. Most educators know that a student can be excused from these patriotic activities for religious reasons. However, some teachers and administrators believe that religious objectors must stand in "respectful silence" and that students must pledge unless they have a religious objection. As the following decisions demonstrate, both beliefs have been wrong for decades.

In a 1970 Florida case, Andrew Banks was suspended for refusing to stand during the Pledge of Allegiance. The rule stated that "Students who for religious or other deep personal convictions do not participate in the salute and Pledge of Allegiance to the flag will stand quietly." Banks said his refusal to stand was based on his belief in "uni-world" government and as a protest against Black repression in the United States. The judge ruled in his favor and noted that "standing is an integral portion of the pledge ceremony and is no less a gesture of acceptance and respect than is the salute or the utterance of the words of allegiance." The court concluded that "the right to differ . . . even to the extent of exhibiting disrespect for our flag and country by refusing to stand and participate in the pledge" cannot be suppressed or punished because it is a right protected by the First Amendment (*Banks v. Board of Public Instruction of Dade County*, 1970, p. 296).

In a similar New York case, a student refused to participate in the pledge because he believed "there isn't liberty and justice for all in the United States." The student was given the option of leaving the room or standing silently. But the student maintained that he had a First Amendment right to remain quietly seated, and a federal appeals court agreed. According to the judge, requiring the student to stand in silence "cannot be compelled over his deeply held convictions. It can no more be required than the pledge itself." Because the school cannot require participation, "it also cannot punish nonparticipation" (*Goetz v. Ansell*, 1973, p. 638). Despite this ruling, several schools this past year attempted to compel students to stand for the Pledge of Allegiance (ACLU, 2004).

Related Issues and Implications

Although this section has focused on three illustrative areas of constitutional confusion, there are, of course, a number of other related issues, such as due process, that deserve educators' attention. Unlike freedom of expression or religion where teachers are often unaware of students' rights, some educators are overconcerned about due process and believe more process is due than the Fourteenth Amendment requires. Because the Supreme Court has ruled in *Goss v. Lopez* (1975) that students cannot be suspended without due process, there are teachers who hesitate to recommend suspension of troublemakers because they incorrectly believe it would require their participation in an extensive procedure. This fear is illustrated by commentators such as Kay Hymowitz (2000), who erroneously wrote: "You want to suspend a violent troublemaker? Because of *Goss*, you now had to ask: Would a judge find your procedures satisfactory? Would he agree that you have enough witnesses?" (p. 37). This echoes many educators' concerns even though *Goss* requires *no* witnesses. In fact, all that *Goss* requires is an informal notice and hearing. This consists of telling students what they are accused of doing and, if they deny the charge, explaining the evidence against them and giving them the chance to explain their side of the story. This informal due process is a procedure most thoughtful disciplinarians would follow even if there were no *Goss* decision. As the Court wrote: "We do not believe we have imposed procedures on school disciplinarians which are inappropriate in a classroom setting. Instead we have imposed requirements which are, if anything, less than a fair-minded school principal would impose upon himself in order to avoid unfair suspensions" (*Goss v. Lopez*, 1975, p. 583).

At the other extreme are teachers and administrators who overreact to zero tolerance policies such as those that broadly prohibit weapons or sexual harassment. The problem with rigid, automatic zero tolerance policies is illustrated by the teacher who sent a 6-year-old student to the principal to be suspended for bringing a pocketknife to school given to her by her grandfather because the teacher had asked for students to bring to class "something that they cherished" (Johnson & Duffett, 2003, p. 11). Equally problematic was the suspension of four kindergarten students for "making threats" while playing "cops and robbers" and pretending their fingers were guns, or the suspension of a senior honors student when a random drug and weapons search found a pocketknife in the first-aid kit of the student's car (Jenkins & Dayton, 2003, p. 14).

Although there are good reasons to prohibit dangerous weapons, the Supreme Court stated that "due process negates any concept of inflexible procedures applicable to every imaginable situation" (*Goss v. Lopez*, 1975, p. 578). The problem of inflexibility was illustrated by a Tennessee case involving the expulsion of a high school student for possession of a knife found in his car that was placed there by a friend without the student's knowledge. According to a federal appeals court, the fact that judges should usually defer to a school's disciplinary decisions "does not mean that we must, or should, rationalize away its irrational decisions" (*Seal v. Morgan*, 2000, p. 579). Suspending or expelling a student for "weapons possession" if the student was totally unaware of the weapon cannot serve any legitimate purpose. In response to the school board's argument that it must apply its zero tolerance policy consistently, the Court wrote: "consistency is not a substitute for rationality" (*Seal v. Morgan*, 2000, p. 581). As this decision illustrates, there are some zero tolerance cases where the pressures to impose excessive penalties do not come from teachers (who may feel obligated to report any weapon or threat), but from administrators or school board members who fail to exercise reasonable discretion. As a result, some teachers decline to report minor violations of zero tolerance policies because they have seen administrators rigidly impose harsh penalties that seem disproportionate to the offense. Other constitutional issues that teachers should understand are their own First and Fourteenth Amendment rights. It would be useful, for example, for K–12 teachers to be aware of the scope and limits of their academic freedom and why it is much more limited than in higher education. As well, they should know about their right to speak out freely and critically as a citizen about issues of public concern related to education, about why they cannot use the classroom to proselytize students about their political or religious beliefs, and about the limited due process rights of probationary teachers.

This section's examination of constitutional violations suggests that teachers themselves can be viewed as victims of a teacher certification system that has failed to educate them about their legal rights and responsibilities. Furthermore, the legal mistakes discussed here indicate that no teachers should begin their careers without at least a coherent introduction to the principles of the First, Fourth, and Fourteenth Amendments and how they apply to the classroom. Such an introduction should lead to an indelible understanding that when teachers discipline students in a public school, they do so as agents of the state and their actions must conform to constitutional constraints. This will not ensure against teachers making legal mistakes, but it may help to prevent the kind of errors illustrated earlier and give teachers the knowledge they need to protect their students' rights.

PART II. FEARING TO USE REASONABLE DISCIPLINE

Many educators believe that they could be held liable for money damages if they use any force in disciplining a student that results in an injury—even if the force they use to protect themselves or other students is reasonable and even if the injury is slight. Some also believe that we are in the midst of a litigation explosion against teachers and schools and that teachers are increasingly vulnerable to frivolous lawsuits. Although these fears and beliefs are widely held, they are largely false. But they are the assumptions that underlie the Teacher Liability Protection Act (TLPA) that Congress passed in 2001. In this section, the arguments and explanations for this act are examined in detail because they reflect, illustrate, and magnify the fears of many teachers.

The stated purpose of the TLPA is to provide "teachers, principals and other school professionals the tools they need to undertake reasonable actions to maintain order, discipline, and an appropriate educational environment" (TLPA, 2001, p. S1338). The "tool" Congress gives educators to maintain order and discipline is protection against liability. Specifically, the TLPA states that "no teacher in a school shall be liable for harm caused by an act or omission" if the act was carried out "to control, discipline, expel, or suspend a student or maintain order or control in the classroom or school" (TLPA, 2001, p. S1338). This liability protection applies to teachers' ordinary negligence when acting within "the scope of their employment" if the harm "was not caused by willful or criminal misconduct, gross negligence, reckless misconduct, or a conscious, flagrant indifference to the rights or safety of the individual harmed by the teacher" (TLPA, 2001, p. S1338).

The presumed need to protect teachers from liability for negligence is based on the "findings" of Congress that "each year more and more teachers . . . face lawsuits" while trying to provide school children with a quality education and that the ability of teachers and other school professionals to teach is "hindered by frivolous law suits." Congress also found that "limiting the liability of teachers . . . who undertake reasonable actions to maintain order . . . is of national importance" because "of the problems created by the legitimate fears of teachers" about "capricious lawsuits against teachers" (Limitations on Liability for Teachers, TLPA, (2001, p. S1339). These findings appear to be based on hearsay and anecdotal evidence.

Here is the way the legislation's cosponsor, Senator Mitch McConnell of Kentucky, explained the TLPA to his senatorial colleagues: "Everyone agrees that providing a safe, orderly environment" is critical to ensuring a good education. "Teachers who are unable to maintain order in the classroom" cannot teach effectively. Disruptive, rowdy students threaten the safety of their classmates and their opportunity to learn. Unfortunately the fear of lawsuits impedes educators' efforts to ensure a safe learning environment. According to McConnell, educators are fearful because their "reasonable actions to instill discipline and maintain order" are too often questioned by "opportunistic trial lawyers." As a result, "today's teachers will tell you that the threat of litigation is in the back of their minds and forces them at times" not to act in the best interests of their students and to spend time worrying about frivolous lawsuits rather than teaching. That is why we need "a national standard to protect from liability those teachers, principals and education professionals who act in a reasonable manner to maintain order in the classroom" (McConnell, 2001, p. S1338).

In the House of Representatives, Congressman Brady of Texas led the debate in favor of the TLPA. He began by noting strong bipartisan support for "returning order and discipline to our classrooms," by protecting educators from frivolous lawsuits. "Schools are becoming more and more dangerous," said Brady, and teachers do not feel safe because "they are afraid to discipline unruly students," afraid to stop fights or even defend themselves because "teachers may face an expensive and career-damaging lawsuit by overzealous lawyers" and may not be backed up by their administrators "who face constant threats" of harassing lawsuits. Thus, "this bill ensures that dedicated teachers trying to maintain a safe classroom are not afraid of being hauled into court for doing the responsible thing" (Brady, 2001, p. H112).

To illustrate the need for this bill, Representative Brady read a letter from a Houston teacher, who wrote:

> In another classroom, two girls had a fight today. The teacher got knocked down, was hit twice in the head, and when he fell to the ground, was kicked twice by the girls. This teacher could not touch these girls to separate them. We have been told over and over again, do not touch the students, even to defend yourself. ... Seven little letters tell why: Lawsuit. ... We want only to be protected. Is a little peace of mind in the classroom too much to ask? (Brady, 2001, p. H112–113).

Another supporter of the TLPA, Congressman Keller from Florida, added this illustrative scenario: Imagine a disruptive student and "the teacher tells him to go to the Principal's office. The student says 'I'm not going ... you are not going to tell me what to do.'" In that situation, explained Representative Keller, the teacher would get another teacher and "would have no choice but to physically remove the [disruptive] student" and take him to the principal's office. The problem, however, is that "under that scenario, those same teachers could then be subjected to a frivolous suit for unlimited compensatory and punitive damages." Keller concluded: We ask a lot of teachers and "pay them nothing. The least we can do is protect them from frivolous lawsuits" (Keller, 2001, p. H2614)[1].

Opponents of the TLPA pointed out that the act defines "teacher" to include not just teachers but also "principal, administrator, or other educational professional that works in a school," plus a school board and its members. As a result, argued Congressman Scott, the act "immunizes every responsible individual" and "means that nobody would be responsible to a parent when

[1]Other members of Congress, such as Representative Graves of Missouri, echoed these sentiments and supported the legislation because "Responsible teachers should not be afraid of violent bullies with intimidating attorneys. Teachers should not fear a lawsuit because they attempt to break up a fight in gym class or on the playground." That's why, said Graves, "it is time to take the lawyer out of the classroom" (Graves, 2001, p. H2614.).

a child is injured by a negligent act or omission at the school." This "would insure," said Scott, "that schools will virtually never be accountable to parents regarding the safety and discipline for their children" (Scott, 2001, p. H2613).

Assumptions, Questions, and Implications

It is important to make explicit the following assumptions, assertions, and implications underlying the arguments and congressional findings of the TLPA advocates:

> Increasing numbers of teachers face "frivolous" and intimidating lawsuits each year. Because teachers fear such suits, they fail to take reasonable actions to discipline students, maintain order, stop fights, or defend themselves. If Congress protects teachers from being held liable if they negligently discipline and injure a student, teachers will take reasonable disciplinary actions to maintain order and focus on teaching instead of worrying about lawsuits.

There is little, if any, significant evidence to support these congressional findings or arguments. For purposes of analysis, they can be divided into two groups. First are the assertions that seem to be misleading or false. Second are assumptions that call for thoughtful, systematic research to determine their validity.

Three of the central assertions underlying the TLPA can be classified as false, doubtful, or misleading: the increase in suits against teachers, the frivolous nature of the suits, and the need to protect teachers who act reasonably.

Litigation Explosion

TLPA supporters and many educators believe that education litigation has substantially increased. However, in a recent article, Professor Perry Zirkel has written that "research on published court decisions revealed a reversal of the purported 'explosion' in education litigation" (Zirkel, 2003, p. 549). Even assuming there has been an increase in education litigation, most of this litigation concerns issues such as special education or employment rights, not suits against individual teachers. Moreover, when congresspeople assert that teachers "face constant threats" of "expensive career-damaging lawsuits," one thinks of the cost and risks of medical malpractice insurance and premiums of $25,000 to $50,000. Because insurance premiums are based on actuarial projections of the likelihood of being sued and found liable, it is useful to note the cost of insuring teachers against being held liable for negligence. Teachers who are members of the National Education Association are provided a $1 million liability insurance policy as part of their annual dues. According to NEA Secretary-Treasurer Lily Eskelsen, $15.40 of each member's 2003–2004 dues covers his or her liability insurance *and* the supporting legal services in Washington, DC (Eskelsen, 2004). Assuming the entire $15.40 was allocated for each $1 million policy, this suggests that the chances of any teacher being sued and held liable is extraordinarily small and is much less than most congresspeople believe and educators fear.

Frivolous Lawsuits

Because there is no flood of suits against teachers, there can be no flood of frivolous suits. Nevertheless, if a suit is clearly frivolous, it would have no merit, and the teacher would not be liable. In fact, under the Federal Rules of Civil Procedure, an attorney can be sanctioned for filing a frivolous suit. Rule 11 states that by filing a suit, attorneys certify to the best of their knowledge, their claims are warranted by the law and that allegations have "evidentiary support." Thus, in an extreme case, a New Jersey lawyer was fined $100,000 because of a pattern of frivolous suits against local teachers and administrators (*Giangrasso v. Kittatinny Regional High School*, 1994). This, of course, does not mean that there are no frivolous suits against teachers, but it does suggest that they are less frequent than the TLPA advocates claim.

Protecting Reasonable Actions

The stated purpose of the TLPA is to protect teachers who are sued as a result of taking "reasonable" actions to maintain discipline. However, even before to the passage of the TLPA, if courts found that teachers' actions were reasonable, they could not be held liable for injuries that result from these actions. Schools are not insurers against every student injury, and no state law permits a student to win a negligence suit against a teacher unless the student can prove that the teacher did not act with reasonable care and that the teacher's negligence caused the injury. And there are no reported cases holding teachers liable for injuries that have resulted from the use of reasonable force by teachers attempting to protect themselves or their students. Admittedly, teachers and juries may differ about what is reasonable. Therefore, it is important to note that, despite its stated purpose, the TLPA does not just protect teachers from harm caused by reasonable acts, but it also protects teachers from liability from harm caused by any "act or omission of the teacher on behalf of the school" in "efforts to control, discipline, expel, or suspend a student," even if the teacher's action was not reasonable—as long as the injury was not intentional and occurred within the scope of the teacher's employment (TLPA, 2001, p. S1339). In addition, some states, such as Massachusetts, have statutes protecting public school teachers against personal liability for negligence (Laws of Massachusetts, 2004), and a number of states have sovereign immunity laws that provide similar protection (Cambron-McCabe, McCarthy, & Thomas, 2004).

Related Issues and Needed Research

Even if the basic assumptions underlying the TLPA are not true (e.g., even if there is no evidence of teachers being held liable for using reasonable measures to maintain order), we do not know whether few, many, or most teachers believe such popular assumptions and whether such beliefs influence the way they discipline or fail to discipline students. Thus, these unproven assumptions raise important research questions such as:

> Are schools becoming more dangerous because teachers "are afraid to discipline unruly students?"
> Do teachers fail to use reasonable measures to discipline students because of fear of lawsuits? If so, what is the source of such fear?
> If teachers were taught that they could not be held liable for using reasonable force to discipline students, stop fights, or protect themselves (even if they negligently injured a student), would this increase the use of reasonable discipline and lead to more orderly classrooms?

PART III. REALITIES AND RECOMMENDATIONS

Most schools and departments of education work hard to prepare their students for the multiple challenges of the classroom. Yet, most also apparently fail to include school law in their teacher preparation programs. As a result, the majority of American teachers begin their careers with very little knowledge of education law and how it affects students and teachers. One reason is that only two states, Washington and Nevada, require any course concerning school law in their undergraduate or graduate teacher preparation programs (Gullatt & Tollett, 1997). Not only do 48 states not require school law courses for teachers, but less than 10% of teacher preparation programs even offer education law as an option.[2] Some state teacher licensure standards require the inclusion of legal topics (such as the obligation to report abuse and neglect) in their teacher preparation programs. But these topics are often scattered incoherently in a variety of courses. In other states, the legal aspects of professional standards are very general. For example, the Massachusetts licensure regulations concerning Professional Responsibilities simply require (without any specifics) that each teacher "understands his or her legal and moral responsibilities" (Massachusetts Department of Education, 2003, p. 47).

Although there is no national survey assessing teachers' knowledge of education law, there have been a variety of state surveys (mostly in dissertations) that have found, for example, that Virginia teachers "do not have a working knowledge of tort law," that Illinois teachers "possess an inadequate knowledge of their legal responsibilities," and that preservice teachers at a midwestern state university "are not simply uncertain about the law, but have clear misconceptions" (Higham, Littleton, & Styron, 2001, p. 329). Because most teachers enter the classroom with no coherent knowledge of education law, many view law as a source of fear and anxiety, as an invisible monster lurking in the shadows of the classroom, waiting to ensnare any teacher who makes an innocent mistake.

As noted earlier, many teachers do not understand the constitutional context in which they work and do not understand when they can be held liable for student injuries. Although it is very rare to find teachers who intentionally violate the law, too many fail to act when they should and unintentionally violate constitutional rights when they should not. This raises two critical research questions.

First, what do teachers know about the law when they enter the classroom? Second, what is the source of that knowledge? Do they enter the classroom with the common myths and misinformation that are pervasive in our culture? Is this based on media reports or lawyer ads that suggest that if people are injured, they have a right to sue and be compensated even if the injury was caused by an accident and not by someone's negligence?

Or, does most teacher misunderstanding come from their teacher preparation program or from what they learn after they start teaching? Are they confused because of the superficial and disconnected snippets of information about the law that are added to diverse education courses and texts? Or is it because of administrators who pass on their own legal anxieties and ignorance, because of unchallenged and unchecked rumors in the teachers' lounge, because of threats to sue by parents and lawyers, or because of legal consultants who spread excessive fear and incomprehensible legalistic information at inservice workshops? All these are possible sources of confusion. That is why systematic research on the sources of teacher knowledge plus an understanding of what they want to know about school law is the first essential step in confronting legal illiteracy among teachers.

Based on an awareness of the sources of teachers' information and misinformation about the law and their legal questions and concerns, the next step is to develop a strategy for educating preservice and inservice teachers about the law that affects them. After discovering "the paucity of preparation on education law" in their 50-state survey, Gullatt and Tollett (1997) recommended that "a discrete preservice education law course specific to classroom

[2]The reasons that have been cited for not offering such a course were (a) lack of room in the curriculum, (b) legal topics included in other courses, (c) the course is not needed, and (d) lack of trained faculty and resources. Although education law is usually a requirement in administration certification programs, a national survey of 221 teacher preparation programs found that only 8.1% offered a course in education law. And, even if students wanted to take a school law course for administrators, such a course might not be approved as part of their teacher certification program (Gullatt & Tollett, 1997).

teachers should be required" in all teacher education programs (p. 134). Such a requirement would be an important element in preparing new teachers for their professional responsibilities. However, in view of the current pressures in many states to decrease the number of education courses in teacher certification programs and to increase courses in content areas, it is unlikely that a school law course would be added to the teacher education programs in many colleges and universities. One alternative that might be possible on some campuses would be to add a one-credit course on teachers and the law into the certification mix—perhaps as part of the preservice internship.[3]

If even a one-credit course is not an option at most teacher training institutions, a feasible alternative might be to develop a single substantive and coherent curriculum unit on teachers and the law that could be integrated into a variety of teacher education courses and taught by nonlawyers. Such a unit would not attempt to cover all of the issues or complexities included in the typical school law course. Instead, it would focus on selected topics and concepts such as those examined in this chapter. As a result, teachers might be less likely to punish students for wearing controversial political T-shirts, strip-search students for missing money, prohibit students from distributing religious messages, or refuse to break up a fight for fear of liability.

A unit on teachers and the law that was periodically updated with illustrative statutes and cases could also be used in professional development workshops and in school or district inservice days. In addition, Gullatt and Tollett recommended that each school "designate a resource teacher interested in education law to be responsible for collecting professional information related to school law and making this information available to the entire faculty" (Gullatt & Tollett, 1997, p. 134.).[4] Such material also might be useful for school board members who usually begin their service with little knowledge of education law. Furthermore, if school attorneys were chosen for their ability to educate as well as litigate, they could teach preventive law to their school principals, who would then be better law teachers for their staffs.

CONCLUSION

In this chapter, I argue that most teachers enter the classroom with inadequate knowledge of school law. This is not a criticism of teachers. It reflects a shortcoming of teacher certification programs that fail to adequately educate teachers about the laws that affect students and teachers in the public schools.[5] Because teachers know little about education law, legal literacy should become one of the competencies required of every classroom teacher, just as teachers are required to learn about educational psychology and teaching methods. The examination of judicial decisions concerning the First, Fourth, and Fourteenth Amendments illustrates how many teachers unknowingly violate students' constitutional rights. The analysis of the congressional debates about the Teacher Liability Protection Act illustrates frequent legal misunderstandings among educators and the public. These examples suggest that if legal literacy were integrated into the preservice and inservice curriculum, public school teachers would understand the constitutional context in which they work, would know when and how to protect the rights of their students, and would know when they can use force to defend themselves and others without an unreasonable fear of being sued. Legally literate teachers would

[3]At the University of Massachusetts, for example, all students in the Secondary Teacher Education Program take such a one-credit course on school law that is integrated into their prepracticum curriculum.

[4]Some current publications on school law designed for teachers include, *Legal Rights of Students and Teachers* Cambron-McCabe, McCarthy, and Thomas, 2004, and *Teachers and the Law* (6th ed.), Fischer, Schimmel, and Stellman, 2003.

[5]It also is a criticism of inservice education programs whose legal content (if any) tends to focus in a nonsystematic way on isolated dos and don'ts or on compliance with specific, current legal mandates.

not only know how the law applies to the classroom, but they also would use that knowledge to become more self-confident and effective educators.

Because of the limited information currently available about (a) what teachers know about the law, (b) the formal and nonformal sources of their information and misinformation, and (c) their legal concerns and anxieties, I recommend that more research be done on these questions. Based on this research, I also recommend the development of a law curriculum for teachers that can be integrated into preservice courses and inservice programs.

Some critics will argue that the increasing pressures on teachers in every state to have their students perform well on standardized tests and to cope with a multiplicity of state and federal requirements leaves no room in preservice or inservice programs to add significant material on teachers and the law. I disagree. With the legal confusions that plague most teachers, we cannot afford the high price of legal illiteracy—an emotional, administrative, and financial price that is paid when teachers unknowingly violate students' rights, fail to take appropriate disciplinary action, or fail to protect themselves or their students because of unfounded fears of legal liability. Certainly, a one-credit course or curriculum unit will not make teachers into legal experts. But such a curriculum can provide teachers with a basic understanding of students' rights and their own legal authority. With this information, teachers may no longer see themselves as victims of the legal system. Instead, they will better understand how the system works and how it can work to protect them, their students, and their schools.

ACKNOWLEDGMENTS

The auther wishes to thank the following colleagues for their review of this chapter: Ron Hyman, Irv Seidman, and Katie McDermott.

REFERENCES

Abington School District v. Schempp, 374 U.S. 203 (1963).

ACLU of Massachusetts. (2003/2004, July). *Annual Report* (p. 13). Boston, MA: Author.

Banks v. Board of Public Instruction of Dade County, 314 F. Supp. 285 (1970).

Barber v. Dearborn Public Schools, 286 F. Supp.2d 847 (E.D. Mich. 2003).

Bellinier v. Lund, 438 F. Supp. 47 (N.D. N.Y. 1977).

Bethel School District v. Fraser, 478 U.S. 675 (1986).

Brady, K. (Tex). Part D: Teacher Liability Protection Act. *Congressional Record, 147,* No. 72 (May, 23, 2001) daily pages: H2612/2613.

Cambron-McCabe, N. H., McCarthy, M. M., & Thomas, S. B. (2004). *Public school law* (5th ed.) Boston: Allyn & Bacon.

Chambers v. Babbitt, 145 F. Supp. 2d 1068 (D.C. Mich. 2001).

Eskelson, L. (2004). Your dues dollars. *NEA Today*, 47.

Fischer, L., Schimmel, D., & Stellman, L. (2003). *Teachers and the Law* (6th ed). Boston: Allyn & Bacon.

Findings and purpose, Section 1. Teacher Liability Protection Act. *Congressional Record, 147,* No. 20 (February 13, 2001) daily pages: S.1338.

Giangrosso v. Kittatinny Regional High School Board of Education, 865 F. Supp. 1133 (D.N.J. 1994).

Goetz v. Ansell, 477 F.2d 636 (1973).

Goss v. Lopez, 419 U.S. 565 (1975).

Graves, S. (Mo.). Part D: Teacher Liability Protection Act. *Congressional Record, 147*, No. 72 (May 23, 2001) daily pages: H2614.

Gullatt, D. E., & Tollett, J. R. (1997). Education law: A requisite course for preservice and inservice teacher education programs. *Journal of Teacher Education, 48,* 129–135.

Hazelwood School District v. Kuhlmeier, 484 U.S. 260 (1988).

Higham, R., Littleton, M., & Styron, K. (2001, November). *Education law preparation of school administrators.* Paper presented at the Education Law Association Conference, Albuquerque, NM.

Hymowitz, K. (2000). Who killed school discipline? *City Journal, 10,* 34–42.
Jenkins, J., & Dayton, J. (2003). Students, weapons, and due process: An analysis of zero tolerance policies in public schools. *Education Law Reporter, 171,* 13–33.
Johnson, J., & Duffett, A. (2003, November). *I'm calling my lawyer: Public agenda pilot study on how litigation, due process and other regulatory requirements are affecting public education.* Paper prepared for a forum: Is Law Undermining Public Education? Washington, DC.
Keller, R. (Fla.). Part D: Teacher Liability Protection Act. *Congressional Record, 147,* No. 72 (May 23, 2001) daily pages: H2614
Laws of Massachusetts, Chapter 258, Section 2 (2004).
Lee v. Weisman, 505 U.S. 577 (1992).
Limitation on Liability for Teachers, Section 1. Teacher Liability Protection Act. *Congressional Record*, 147, No. 20 (February 13, 2001) daily pages: S1339.
Lynch v. Donnelly, 465 U.S. 668 (1984).
Massachusetts Department of Education. (2005). *Regulations for educator licensure and preparation program approval.* Professional Standards for Teachers 7.08(2)(e).
McConnell, M. (Ky.). Section 1. Teacher Liability Protection Act. *Congressional Record, 147,* No. 20 (February 13, 2001) daily pages: S1338.
Mc Marthy, M. M., Cambron-McCabe, N. H., & Thomas, S. B. (2004). *Legal Rights of Teachers and Students.* Boston: Allyn & Bacon.
New Jersey v. T.L.O., 469 U.S. 325 (1985).
Rivera v. East Otero School District, 721 F. Supp. 1189 (D. Colo. 1989).
Scott, R. (Va.). Part D: Teacher Liability Protection Act. *Congressional Record, 147,* No. 72 (May 23, 2001) daily pages: H2613.
Seal v. Morgan, 229 F.3d 567 (6th Cir. 2000).
Shanley v. Northeast Independent School District, 462 F.2d 960 (5th Cir. 1972).
Teacher Liability Protection Act, 20 U.S.C. Sections 6731–6738 (2001).
Tinker v. Des Moines Independent School District, 393 U.S. 503 (1969).
Watkins v. Millenium School, 290 F.Supp. 2d 890 (E.D. Ohio 2003).
Westfield High School L.I.F.E. Club v. City of Westfield, 249 F. Supp. 2d 98 (D. Mass. 2003).
Zirkel, P. (2003). The Coverdell Teacher Protection Act: Immunization or illusion. *Education Law Reporter, 179,* 547–558.

39

Schoolwide Discipline Policies: An Analysis of Discipline Codes of Conduct

Pamela A. Fenning and Hank Bohanon
Loyola University, Chicago

INTRODUCTION

School personnel typically highlight their discipline regulations in policies called codes of conduct. Discipline codes of conduct are documents that contain the schoolwide discipline procedures that students must follow. The focus of this chapter is on discipline codes of conduct because they are the written means by which sanctioned behaviors are communicated to students, parents, and the larger school community. Codes of conduct are generally distributed to school staff, students, and parents at the beginning of the school year. Discipline codes of conduct are often used by deans of students or those with the responsibility for addressing discipline in the school after a student commits an infraction.

Historically, discipline codes of conduct were greatly influenced by legislation (e.g., *Goss v. Lopez*, 1975) and were recommended by those who conducted federally commissioned studies about levels of school violence in the 1970s (National Institute of Education, 1978; National School Resource Network, 1980). They were also affected by mandates for students with disabilities, such as PL-94-142, and court cases that interpreted the rights of students with disabilities, based on this legislation. More recently, discipline codes of conduct have been mandated under the No Child Left Behind Act. As a result, discipline codes are found in nearly every school district across the United States and are the written contract for expected behaviors. Discipline codes of conduct are sometimes unique to a particular school or serve as the discipline document for an entire unified school district.

Despite the critical role that discipline codes of conduct play in school discipline, very little is written about these important documents and how they affect schools. The purpose of this chapter is to review the current available literature about discipline codes of conduct and to accomplish four main objectives: (1) to provide a historical context about the development and the original intentions of discipline codes in schools, (2) to review recent literature about the nature of discipline codes of conduct and to evaluate whether they have achieved their intended purposes, (3) to draw some initial conclusions about ways in which discipline codes of conduct could more completely reflect their initial intentions, and (4) to provide suggestions for future research and study of discipline codes of conduct.

Procedure for Conducting Literature Review

Two databases were used to retrieve articles related to schoolwide discipline policies (ERIC and PsychINFO) over the last 15 years. The primary author also consulted with the section editor about historical pieces and any untapped resources related to this topic. In addition, the authors incorporated other relevant studies from previous literature searches conducted for this topic (in 2000 and 2001), articles previously found in related journals, and federal documents in the area. This literature was reviewed in the preparation of the current literature review.

Historical Context and Development of Discipline Codes of Conduct

Early Writing. Written standards for behavior have been present in schools for nearly a century. In New Jersey, for instance, administrators report the existence of discipline codes of conduct in some form as early as 1916 (Lally, 1982). However, the biggest push for the widespread development of written codes of conduct comes from the late 1970s. At that time, a Senate Subcommittee was chaired by Senator Bayh because of increased concern about school violence and vandalism (National Institute of Education, 1978). Legislation was written to commission a national study about the prevalence of school violence. This work was ultimately conducted by the National Institute of Education. In general, the researchers concluded that school violence had decreased compared to previous years (1960s and early 1970s). However, school violence was still perceived by this group as a significant problem that was a central focus of the media (National Institute of Education, 1978) and one that required the sustained focus of school personnel to address.

One of the conclusions drawn from the Safe School Study was that school crime was more likely when rules were arbitrary and enforced by those who were considered excessively punitive (Lally, 1982). As a result, one of the major recommendations resulting from the Safe School Study was the development of uniform written codes of conduct as a way to clearly describe the rules to all in advance (National Institute of Education, 1978). Hence, written codes of conduct were seen as a positive way of producing clear guidelines for behavior and, consequently, serving an important role in making schools safer. It was anticipated that written guidelines would be more likely to result in consistent and equitable application of rules for all.

Shortly after this, the National School Resource Network (NSRN) published a handbook intended to guide schools in developing effective discipline codes of conduct (National School Resource Network, 1980). The NSRN outlined essential components of discipline codes of conduct. Consistent with the conclusions of the Safe School Study, the NSRN viewed discipline codes as helping to eliminate arbitrary and inconsistent application of discipline and rules.

A unique contribution of the NSRN was an outline of specific language that could be incorporated into discipline codes of conduct. For instance, this working group emphasized the need for a description of rights as well as responsibilities of school personnel and students in discipline policies (NSRN, 1980). A key component in discipline codes of conduct was a balanced view of the rights of an individual (often guaranteed by the First Amendment) with a responsibility to maintain the rights of others. For example, the NSRN presented an example from a discipline policy in the Louisiana schools; "Students have the right to learn in an atmosphere free of the narrowing and stifling influences of social, religious and ethnic prejudice" (1980, p. 110).

Student rights and responsibilities were often tied to specific behaviors. In the South Dakota school systems, it was explained that students had a right to attend school, but also a responsibility to be on time to all classes and be in school daily. The South Dakota school system discussed rights and responsibilities around dress as follows: "Dress in such a way as to express his/her personality" (a right), while maintaining "dress and appearance so as to meet fair standards of propriety, safety, health and good taste" (a responsibility) (NSRN, 1980, p. 124). The delineation of student responsibilities was seen as prescriptive (telling students what they need to do) rather than punitive.

The NSRN viewed written discipline policies as an opportunity to review the rights and responsibilities of school personnel as well as students (e.g., teachers, administrators, related service staff in a building). The ultimate outcome of both rights and responsibilities was intended to be a philosophy of mutual respect for all. For example, the NSRN provided an example of this notion in a policy from Boulder Valley Public Schools: "a spirit of mutual respect and involvement among the members of the school community" (NSRN, 1980, p. 12).

An example of a teacher responsibility, as described in a Louisiana discipline policy, was the fair and consistent treatment of students. Teacher responsibilities were described as follows: "Teachers should be fair and consistent and treat each student equally" (NSRN, 1980, p. 129).

In the Fresno, California, school systems, teachers had a responsibility to "consider the personal worth of each individual student as a single, unique important being" (NSRN, 1980, p. 130).

The rights and responsibilities of administrators were also incorporated into discipline policies. For example, an administrative responsibility described in a Fresno, California, discipline code was as follows: "Make a determined effort to stay attuned to expressions of student/staff/parent/community concerns and react with sensitivity towards them" (NSRN, 1980, p. 132).

The overall purpose of rights and responsibility statements was to clearly describe the roles of all in the school to create an atmosphere of respect and to use policies as a way to "tell staff what should be done and how to do it" (NSRN, 1980, p. 135).

The National School Resource Network suggested that school disciplinarians use discipline policies as educational and rehabilitative versus punitive. This group cited data that drive our thinking today about the need for evidence-based alternatives to suspension and expulsion. The early writing about discipline codes focuses on the use of these documents as teaching tools rather than sanctions for punishment. Discipline codes were seen as a way of preteaching students, teachers, and the larger community what is expected of them rather than solely emphasizing punishment for incorrect behavior.

The NSRN was one of the first working groups to clearly outline preferred content in discipline codes of conduct. This group also advocated for a collaborative process in the development of these policies. Participation by those who are most affected by the rules was seen as important. In particular, students were seen as a critical group that would be more likely to follow the rules if they had a hand in developing them. Key stakeholders such as parents, community members, and school staff were seen as critical to the development of proactive discipline codes of conduct. They based this on the belief that an integrated perspective of all key stakeholders (e.g., school personnel, parents, the community, and students) would create more proactive policies that all would be likely to follow.

In roughly the same period, *Goss v. Lopez* (1977) was decided with direct implications for student discipline and policy. In this federal case, it was determined that suspensions could not be determined by a single administrator (Zantal-Weiner, 1988). Although controversial among school district personnel, this court case resulted in due process requirements for all students when suspension was considered. The trend at this time was to document students' rights in discipline policy as a way of showing that these stipulations were being met.

Literature Following National Institute of Education Studies. Roughly 10 years following the publication of the seminal documents described previously, in the late 1970s and early 1980s, there was relatively sporadic writing specifically about the preferred content of discipline codes of conduct. (NSRN, 1980; National Institute of Education, 1978).

The writing that was done throughout the 1980 and mid-1990s primarily focused on mandates related to the discipline of special education students, especially in relation to suspension and removal of the students from school. Following the passage of PL-94-142, students in special education were provided specific procedural safeguards related to discipline and exclusion (Zantal-Weiner, 1988). For example, court cases such as *Hoenig v. Doe* (1987) had direct implications for the number of days that a student in special education could be suspended without the consequence of being considered a change of placement (Zantal-Weiner, 1988). School districts often documented these procedural safeguards in their discipline codes of conduct. However, these procedural safeguards did not result in specific recommendations for school districts to follow in creating proactive discipline codes, as was advocated by the NSRN in the previous decade. The legislative mandates were not directly translated to practical ways of enacting prosocial alternatives to traditional discipline methods for students (Zantal-Weiner, 1988).

Literature in Early 1990s to Present

Apart from commentary about legislation that directly affected discipline policies, there was relatively limited attention to the discipline codes of conduct during this period. Some work reiterated the NSRN's recommendation for a collaborative proactive method in the development of discipline codes of conduct (see, e.g., the American Federation of Teachers, 1995–1996; Findley, 1996; Suarez, 1992). Noonan, Tunney, Fogal, and Sarich (1999) were among the sole researchers who directly assessed the impact of a collaborative approach on the design and implementation of discipline codes of conduct. These researchers held focus groups among key constituents in 40 schools when developing the district codes of conduct. Through qualitative analysis of transcripts, the researchers determined that the policies were based on mutual respect and the philosophy that discipline is equated with teaching. They concluded that the collaborative input of multiple stakeholders was key in the development of proactive discipline codes of conduct.

Other researchers assessed the clarity of definitions in discipline codes of conduct. Jay (1997) studied the definitions of unacceptable language and found ambiguity with regard to behavioral definitions and consequences. Clear descriptions of behaviors and subsequent consequences were the original reasons why discipline codes of conduct were suggested (National School Resource Network, 1980; National Institute of Education, 1978), yet his initial findings suggested that this was not the case for the particular behaviors that he studied.

More recently, an analysis of the content in 24 discipline codes of conduct (described in the following sections) indicated that behaviors under the domain of zero tolerance procedures were consistently described in discipline codes of conduct and directly related to consequences, albeit exclusionary ones (Fenning, Theodos, Benner, & Banull, 2005). However, other behaviors with a high degree of probability for school disruption and student discomfort (e.g., sexual harassment) were not represented in a significant number of policies, nor were there clearly described consequences for the behavior.

Zero Tolerance Policies

In general, the time frame from the 1980s until the mid-1990s was marked by limited sustained research activity and writing about the content of discipline codes of conduct except for that pertaining to fulfilling mandates and due process for students. Renewed interest and debate about schoolwide discipline policies came in the mid to late 1990s, again related to legislative action. The Gun-Free Schools Act of 1994 was passed with direct implications for the content and language found in discipline policies. The Gun-Free Schools Act required automatic removal of students for at least 1 calendar year (hence, "zero tolerance") for drug or weapons offenses. As a result, many schools established districtwide policies to reflect this legislation, and documented this compliance in their discipline codes of conduct (Fenning, Theodos, Benner, & Bohanon-Edmonson, 2004). Therefore, schoolwide discipline policies have received relatively recent attention in the literature because of their connection to zero tolerance policies.

Zero tolerance policies deserve special attention because of the significant implications of their use on the lives of youth and the enormous debate they have prompted in the literature. Zero tolerance procedures have been integrated into schoolwide discipline policies for behaviors besides those within the domain of the Gun-Free Schools Act (e.g., weapons and drug offenses) (Harvard University Advancement and Civil Rights Project, 2000).

Probably the most comprehensive report that we have to date about the efficacy of zero tolerance procedures is the result of a national summit held in June of 2000—Opportunities Suspended: The Devastating Consequences of Zero Tolerance and School Discipline Policies. This conference, jointly sponsored by the Advancement and Civil Rights Project at Harvard University Rainbow/Push Coalition, and other national advocacy groups for underrepresented students, was organized to address significant concerns about the overrepresentation of minority youth (particularly Hispanic and African American students) in zero tolerance and related punitive procedures. A second major reason for the organization of the summit was the overzealous and rigid application of these policies.

A major outcome of this event was the commission of research on the appropriateness of zero tolerance procedures in public schools and what impact, if any, they have had on school safety. Another major focus was the impact of the policies on the youths who have been on the receiving end of these procedures. These activities resulted in the publication of *Opportunities Suspended: The Devastating Consequences of Zero Tolerance Procedures* (Harvard University, Advancement and Civil Rights Project, 2000).

This report provided extensive documentation about the misapplication of zero tolerance policies. Numerous examples were cited in which zero tolerance procedures were invoked without any consideration for the circumstances surrounding the event. For example, it was reported that a kindergarten student was suspended for bringing a toy axe to school as part of his Halloween costume. Students who carried Certs candies and Midol in other schools received drug possession violations. A young child who was given a plastic knife by his grandmother in his lunch was expelled for a weapons violation. Hyman (1997) reported a similar event when he was consulting in a school district. A girl used a marker to cover profanities written about her in a bathroom, only to receive a suspension for defacing property. Certainly, in these situations, administrators literally applied these exclusionary procedures without considering the circumstances of the situation. The lack of commonsense judgment in these situations has harrowing results for the students who are caught in this web of discipline.

The use of zero tolerance procedures seems most troubling for ethnic minority students. (particularly African American and Hispanic students), who are most likely to be on the receiving end of zero tolerance policies. This may be related to a variety of factors, one of which might be the greater prevalence of zero tolerance policies and procedures in schools with a high percentage of African American and Latino students (Harvard University Advancement and Civil Rights Project, 2000).

On a national level, African American and Latino students are more likely to receive all types of exclusionary consequences (e.g., suspension and expulsion) even though they commit less serious offenses than their White counterparts (Skiba & Peterson, 1999). Quite troubling are the conclusions of the Harvard group that ethnic minority youth tend to be tracked into the juvenile justice system after zero tolerance policies are invoked for relatively minor offenses. For example, the "Opportunities" report summarized an event in which students who were throwing peanuts on the bus received felony criminal charges and were expelled from their school. The five students involved were not able to travel to an alternative school placement (which was over 30 miles away) and subsequently dropped out of school. This one incident had highly detrimental consequences for these youth because of the unwavering application of zero tolerance procedures.

Although some would argue that zero tolerance policies create safe schools because they rid schools of dangerous students, there is no evidence that schools that use these procedures are safer (Skiba & Rausch, 2005; Skiba & Knesting, 2002), as most schools that have adopted zero tolerance procedures have not shown any reduction in behaviors related to school safety (Skiba & Peterson, 1999). Overall, school policies that promote zero tolerance procedures are not likely to result in safer schools, yet they serve as formal procedures for excluding unwanted students for relatively trivial offenses.

The previous analysis of zero tolerance procedures would suggest that they do not improve school safety and have many detrimental side effects, particularly for our most disenfranchised groups. In the next section, we consider the use of suspension and expulsion in general, as they are the most common procedures offered in discipline policies for a wide array of behaviors, many of which are unrelated to school safety.

Suspension and Expulsion

Despite the call to offer more proactive alternatives to traditional consequences in discipline policies and in planning for school discipline in general, suspension and expulsion are the most widely used discipline procedures for all behaviors, even those unrelated to school safety (Larson, 1998; Skiba, Peterson, & Williams, 1997). It is troubling, however, that there is no evidence that these procedures are successful at reducing or eliminating problematic behaviors (Skiba & Peterson, 1999). On the contrary, data suggest that these procedures may actually exacerbate unwanted school behaviors (Mayer, 1995). Therefore, their predominance and integration into schoolwide discipline policies (primarily the codes of conduct) is counter to evidence-based procedures for teaching expected behaviors and eliminating undesirable ones.

Similar to the findings described earlier pertaining to zero tolerance procedures, discipline policies that are based on reactionary procedures are biased against minority youth. These reactionary procedures include suspension (shorter-term removal of the student from school) and expulsion (removal of students for at least 1 calendar year). For example, school policies that emphasize suspension and expulsion have the highest overrepresentation of minority students in discipline consequences (McEvoy & Welker, 2000). This is particularly the case for African American males (Skiba et al., 1997), who are already at risk to be disenfranchised from school for a variety of reasons. The use of exclusionary practices in discipline policy seems to further marginalize minority youth beyond what is currently occurring in our schools.

These findings pertaining to suspension and expulsion in general are consistent with those reported for zero tolerance procedures (intended originally for solely drug and alcohol offenses). Despite the intention of uniform discipline policies to be equitable to all, discipline codes of conduct, as currently configured, may actually be contributing to further biases because of the reactionary responses that pervade them. Unfortunately, discipline policies may be achieving the exact opposite of their original intention to be fair to all. The initial intention of the discipline codes of conduct was to uniformly apply discipline procedures to all as described by the National School Resource Network and those that authored the Safe School Study. Ironically, discipline codes of conduct may be producing the opposite result because of their focus on reactionary consequences that are unjustly applied to minority youth.

Further, we know that, by definition, suspension and expulsion results in the reduction of instructional time as these procedures remove students from the classroom. Unfortunately, the students who end up receiving these consequences are those with the greatest academic difficulties (Morrison & D'Incau, 1997). This may be one of the most compelling arguments against the use of these procedures and their institutionalization in discipline codes of conduct. Schools may be formalizing procedures that remove instructional minutes from the very students who need them the most. What may be happening is that our policies are giving students with significant academic needs an opportunity to avoid classroom instruction, which then further exacerbates their academic problems. Certainly, this is a possibility that must be considered by those that are integral to the development and practical implementation of discipline codes of conduct.

Related to this, current school discipline policies create a culture in which students may be subtly encouraged to drop out of school. Suspension, for example, is one of the strongest predictors of school dropout. Qualitative case study data support the premise that school discipline policies serve as a formal mechanism used by schools to entice students with behavioral and academic issues to leave school (Bowditch, 1993). Students who have dropped out of schools report discipline policies as one of the factors related to their decision to leave school (MacDonald, 1997). Our policies, as currently configured, may be unwittingly producing unintended consequences. We may have a short-term gain when students who have behavioral and academic difficulties are removed from the classroom because we no longer need to deal with that particular student. However, this short-term gain results in larger systemic and societal concerns when these students leave school and have limited long-term employment or postsecondary educational options.

The description of the efficacy of suspension and expulsion is important for this chapter because these are the most common responses offered in discipline codes of conduct (Fenning et al., 2004; Fenning, Parraga, & Wilczynksi, 2000). Indeed, discipline codes of conduct are based on these reactionary approaches more frequently than any other method of intervention. A recent content analysis of 24 secondary school discipline codes of conduct documented the overuse of these procedures in policy (Fenning et al., 2005). The Analysis of Discipline Codes Rating Form (see Table 39.1) was developed to evaluate the types of behaviors referenced in the codes of conduct, the degree to which consequences were clearly specified, and whether responses were characterized as reactionary or prosocial. Reactionary responses were defined as punitive without a means for directly teaching alternative behaviors. Prosocial responses were those that directly taught expected behaviors to students. The preponderance of responses were punitive in nature, regardless of the type of infraction. The exclusionary procedures of suspension and expulsion were the most common types of reactionary responses offered. When present, prosocial responses were not tied to the function of the behavior and were global in nature. For example, counseling was the most common type of prosocial response offered in discipline codes of conduct. In general, there was a focus on punishment for misbehavior, rather than an explanation of what is expected of students. Although the use of suspension and expulsion would not be recommended based on the previous review of the literature, discipline codes of conduct overemphasize these procedures in handling student behaviors.

This current study is limited because of its small sample size and focus on only Illinois schools. Certainly, more work needs to be done to confirm these findings. However, the preliminary evidence seems to suggest that codes of conduct developed in the last few years do not reflect their original purpose. The spirit in which discipline codes of conduct were originally conceptualized (nearly 30 years ago) is based on sound principles of directly teaching

TABLE 39.1
Analysis of Discipline Codes Rating Form (Adopted from Fenning, Theodos & Benner, 2002)

Behaviors	*Included in Policy*	*Linked to Consequence*	*Repeated Violation*
Fighting			
Weapons Poss.			
Weapons Dist.			
Weapons Use			
Tobacco Poss.			
Alcohol Poss.			
Drugs Poss.			
Tobacco Use			
Alcohol Use			
Drug Use			
Tobacco Dist.			
Alcohol Dist.			
Drugs Dist.			
Tobacco Sale			
Alcohol Sale			
Drugs Sale			
Gang Behavior			
Theft			
Sexual Harrassment			
Bomb Threat			
Fireworks/Explosives Poss.			
Misuse of Fire Alarm			
Physical Assault (Teacher)			
Physical Threat (Teacher)			
Intimidating/Physical Threats			
Hazing/Bullying (Student)			
Arson			

Note: Behaviors characterized as having physical or serious emotional threat to the safety of the schools were evaluated in the policies as present or absent. Possible consequences were as follows: detention, Saturday detention, in-school suspension, out of school suspension, expulsion, natural consequence, counseling, police involvement, substance abuse intervention and alternative school placement.

behaviors to students and having preset and clear standards for behavior. However, we do not see this reflected in current-day discipline codes, which are filled with references to suspension and expulsion. Discipline codes of conduct do not seem to be serving their initial intention of directly articulating expected behaviors to students and the larger school community. We have substantial evidence that suspension and expulsion are not effective, with some very serious potential biases for youth from underrepresented backgrounds.

Given this compelling data, it is surprising that our schoolwide discipline policies continue to reflect punitive and reactionary approaches. Our overall assessment of the current status of discipline codes of conduct would be that they have not realized their potential as written documents that positively convey expected preset behaviors. On the contrary, they seem to have had the unintended effect of punishing and excluding our most vulnerable students for a variety of offenses that are unrelated to school safety. More recent mandates under the Individuals with Disabilities Education Act (1997) requiring more prosocial means of addressing behavioral issues are not evident in schoolwide discipline policies (Zurkowski, Kelly, & Griswold, 1998). Our general conclusions would be that discipline policies are not being used in the way in which they were originally conceptualized. Given the previous literature review, it seems apparent that current discipline codes of conduct have not fulfilled their original purpose as a written contract used to clearly specify expected behaviors to all.

A larger question is why these policies have not fulfilled their original promise. Certainly, one could speculate that school personnel have been under significant pressure for decades to manage behavior. In Gallup polls year after year, discipline and the management of student behavior is reported by school personnel and the larger community to be a primary concern (Rose & Gallup, 2002). As a response, school personnel may have felt pressure to take a "get tough" approach to school discipline. The evidence in schools for decades is that they are relatively safe places, yet the public perception is to the contrary. The punitive responses of schools are likely partially driven by this outward perception. Ultimately, these punitive responses are found in schoolwide policies that maintain these discipline procedures in a continued cycle and as a way for schools to appear in control. We believe that large-scale system reform efforts would need to be enacted to change our historical approach to discipline. The creation of proactive discipline codes of conduct would possibly be a component of this school reform effort. In the next section, we consider ways to create proactive discipline codes of conduct as part of a schoolwide discipline reform effort.

Use of Positive Behavior Support Models in the Design of Proactive Discipline Codes

Positive Behavior Support (PBS) is a school reform model that is based on teaching behaviors to students on a proactive and prevention-oriented basis (Sugai & Horner, 2002; Sugai et al., 1999). It is a data-based approach to positive teaching and supporting expected behaviors at multiple levels in a school. PBS is a philosophy that focuses on developing a set of schoolwide set of expectations and then directly teaching them to students. Behaviors are directly taught to students just as academic skills are (Colvin, Kameenui, & Sugai, 1993). Once the behaviors are taught, a system is put in place to acknowledge appropriate behavior. Schoolwide systems of PBS are discussed fully in another chapter of this handbook. The ways in which discipline codes of conduct were originally conceptualized by the National School Resource Network over 30 years ago is consistent with the PBS philosophy of establishing preset rules and then teaching them to students accordingly. Therefore, we anticipate that the revision of discipline codes of conduct would more likely be sustained within a larger school reform effort that incorporates the philosophy and thinking of PBS.

In recent years, PBS has shown success, as evidenced by reductions in office disciplinary referrals, increases in instructional time, and the improvement of school climate at the elementary and middle school levels (Metzler, Biglan, & Rusby, 2001; Sprague, Walker, & Golly, 2001). A major focus of PBS is the use of data to drive decisions about behavioral support on a schoolwide basis (Lewis, Sugai, & Colvin, 1998), for groups of students (Taylor-Greene et al., 1997), and for individual student needs (Carr, 1994).

We would suggest that the PBS framework would be useful to follow when creating discipline policies that meet the standards of directly teaching expected behaviors, as it is defined as a systems-level approach used to directly teach expected behaviors to students. Direct teaching and acknowledgement of behaviors is a major component of this model, which could be incorporated into discipline codes of conduct to make them more proactive. PBS focuses on directly teaching behaviors to students in the same manner as academic skills are taught (Colvin et al., 1993).

The development of proactive discipline codes of conduct could be part of a schoolwide PBS process. A major activity of PBS is the clear delineation of expected behaviors and ways in which behaviors that are directly taught are acknowledged. In the PBS model, a teaching grid is developed by all key stakeholders (e.g., school personnel, students, staff, parents) that outlines nonexamples of an expected behavior (what not to do), but more importantly, examples of the correct behavior. Then, the specific contexts in which the behaviors will be enacted (e.g., the hallway, the cafeteria) are outlined. Finally, a method for directly teaching and practicing these behaviors is determined by a team.

The teaching grid could be developed at the same time that the schoolwide discipline codes of conduct are reviewed and updated. This could happen on a scheduled basis, such as when an action plan is made for teaching expected behaviors to students. The expected behaviors and both sets of examples (i.e., the correct and incorrect ones) could be written into the discipline policy, with behaviors being defined in the positive. For instance, on time to class could be defined as "through the threshold of the door and in one's seat," whereas not on time (tardy) could be defined as "wandering in the hallway after the bell rings." These behaviors would be helpful to practice at the beginning of the year as part of a series of schoolwide expectations. During these practice sessions, the discipline codes of conduct could be reviewed with students. Students' attention could be drawn to the expected behaviors that are practiced by students and also described in the discipline codes of conduct. Consistent with the PBS procedures, schoolwide data could be used to track student progress in demonstrating specific behaviors. For areas of difficulty, direct interventions meant to teach behaviors could be delivered to students on a schoolwide, group, and individual basis. The interventions could also be documented in the discipline code of conduct.

The schoolwide discipline codes of conduct could be an important document to reinforce what students should be doing, and to clearly define behaviors in a positive fashion rather than serving solely as a description of punishments. In this way, it is hoped that discipline policies would shift from their position as a sanctioned method for punishing and removing students to becoming a valuable teaching tool in the spirit of PBS.

Use of the Discipline Codes of Conduct and Classroom Management

Classroom Uses of Discipline Codes of Conduct. One of the tenets of PBS is an initial schoolwide teaching of expected behaviors and then continued teaching of expected behaviors throughout the school year. One of the ways that this might be done would be the use of classroom time to review expected behaviors within the discipline codes. Discipline policies can serve as important teaching tools if they are reviewed on a routine basis. The expected behaviors within the policy can be pretaught to students as routine activities take place. For example, if students are going to an assembly, the teacher might remind the students that one of the agreed-on behaviors is "respectful hallway behavior." In this scenario, the rationale for why the behavior needs to be performed (so that classes can continue uninterrupted) can be explained and used as an opportunity for instruction. Students can then practice and be acknowledged for engaging in correct behaviors that are found in the schoolwide discipline policy. The use of discipline codes of conduct in this manner would help to promote a proactive means of teaching and acknowledging behaviors on an ongoing basis.

Prevention-oriented activities. Prevention-oriented and early intervention procedures for use in the classroom in response to particular behaviors can also be developed and clearly specified in the discipline codes of conduct. It should be noted in the discipline codes of conduct which behaviors should be managed in the classroom and which should be sent to the discipline office as a referral. A component of developing a discipline policy under the auspices of PBS is a mutual understanding of minor (what can be handled by the teacher) and major (what needs to be handled outside the classroom) offenses. When these are clearly specified, teachers can develop a lesson plan to directly teach expected classroom behaviors and to develop a classroom management plan for handling classroom-based behaviors.

When students demonstrate beginning signs of minor behavioral issues (classroom managed), there are several evidence-based responses that can be enacted. A very simple response is to simply talk to the student in a private manner about the behavioral concerns. That is, the teacher moves closer to the student and talks to him or her in close proximity rather than talking across the room. This behavior management procedure, although simple, can prevent behaviors from escalating further. If the behavior persists, then a classroom intervention could be developed with the collaboration of a building-based team. This intervention might entail precorrection of student behavior. For instance, if a student continually disrupts the class, then a private conference can occur in which a student and teacher determine that a prompt will be used to remind the student to engage in the appropriate behavior (e.g., raising his or her hand). This prompt could be something as simple as the teacher standing closer to the student or a hand signal that only the teacher and student know about. Precorrection can occur in which the teacher reminds the student beforehand that he or she will "need to raise hands" during a class discussion. In this way, minor-level behaviors are directly taught and there is a greater likelihood that these prevention-oriented approaches will be successful. If behaviors are dealt with in this way, they will be less likely to follow an escalation pattern (Walker and Horner, 1996) that result in more significant behaviors that necessitate an office referral. These redirection procedures and prevention-oriented approaches can also be strategies that are integrated into the discipline codes of conduct as classroom management procedures.

Development of a Discipline Team

The formation of a discipline team with the primary function of reviewing the procedures outlined in the discipline codes of conduct would be critical to the development of proactive discipline codes of conduct. Discipline codes are more likely to be proactive when they are developed on a collaborative basis (Noonan et al., 1999). Similar to the procedures for forming a team in PBS activities, the team could consist of all key constituents affected by discipline in the building, such as security officers, teachers, front office staff, cafeteria workers, parents, students, community members, and administrators. These individuals would also have responsibility for teaching expected behaviors to students and addressing behavioral issues as they occur.

One of the team's responsibilities could be to incorporate prosocial and data-driven approaches into policy and to handle behavioral concerns in the school. The discipline referral data could be examined and fed back into the system to inform practice and policy. Figure 39.1 depicts a flowchart that illustrates the possible steps that can be taken by a team to create more proactive discipline codes of conduct using a problem-solving, team-based approach.

For example, the positive behaviors that will be directly taught to students could be determined by this team. Similarly, this team could have responsibility for writing behavioral descriptions of unacceptable behaviors and directly specifying consequences. The team could have a procedure in place for gaining feedback from the larger school community about the behaviors that are important to include in the discipline codes of conduct and the development of strategies that can be used when problems occur. The overall goal would be to provide clear definitions of all desired and undesired behaviors. At this time, most discipline codes of conduct feature somewhat ambiguous unwanted behaviors without clearly explaining to students what is expected of them. The active involvement of a team will likely shift discipline codes closer to their original aspiration as positive documents used to clearly describe behaviors in a preset fashion.

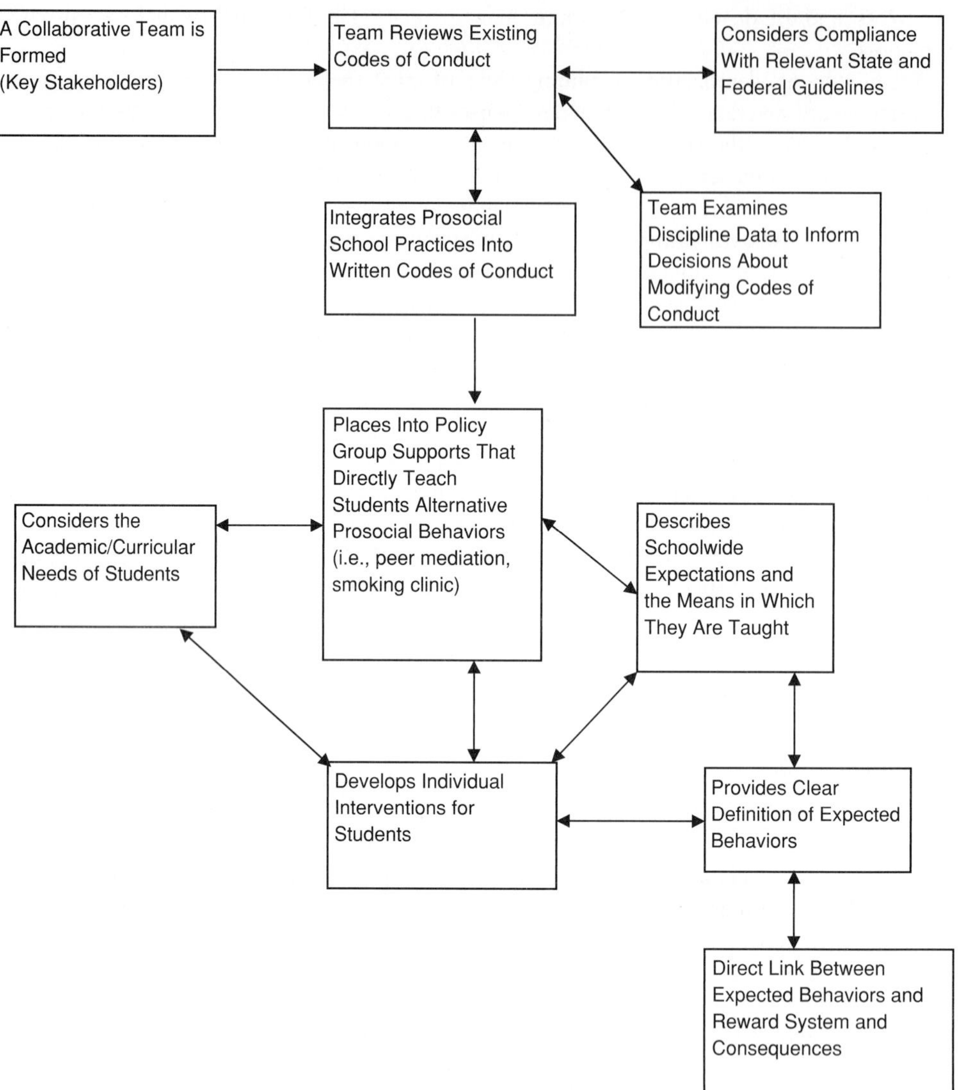

FIG. 39.1. Team decision-making process for developing proactive discipline policies.

Using Data to Evaluate Discipline Codes of Conduct

The review of discipline procedures and the content of discipline codes of conduct is a key responsibility of a school-based team. Within the PBIS framework, procedures outlined in the discipline codes of conduct could be evaluated using schoolwide behavioral and academic indicators. For example, schoolwide discipline referral data, attendance rates, the percentage of students who drop out of school, the number of academic failures, achievement, and grade point average are some possible indicators that could be monitored. Based on these academic and behavioral outcomes, discipline codes of conduct could be modified and new interventions could be introduced into policy and also evaluated. Schoolwide discipline policies could be considered as interventions in themselves that require continued progress monitoring, modification, and the review of data to guide decision making. These revisions could focus on the development and implementation of proactive alternatives to traditional reactionary methods that are not functional (e.g., suspension and expulsion).

The data gathered through referrals from discipline policies could fuel schoolwide interventions, as well as interventions for groups of students and individuals that are not successful after general discipline procedures are in place. In this way (consistent with PBS principles), the schoolwide discipline policy can be used as a tool to gather necessary information and to plan interventions. This is in contrast to the routine uses of discipline codes of conduct as methods of punishment and a formal procedure for removing students from school. The data are continually fed back to the system to evaluate interventions and to modify the discipline policy, based on this data.

Schoolwide discipline efforts that involve a team approach and the use of data to drive decisions about interventions are system-level procedures that can contribute to the development of proactive discipline policies. Discipline policies that are developed and evaluated within system-level reform efforts are likely to be more prosocial and counter to traditional exclusionary methods of handling discipline issues. We should suggest that discipline policies must be considered within long-term system reform efforts focused on changing our approach to classroom and behavioral management. The flowchart outlined in Fig. 39.1 provides an illustration of the continued use of data that is used for decision making and to determine whether the discipline practice and the policy needs revision, modification, and subsequent evaluation.

USE OF EVIDENCE-BASED PROCEDURES IN POLICY

The previous review of the literature and suggestions for modification of discipline codes of conduct are based on the formation of a functioning team that makes data-based decisions about discipline policy procedures. One of the major activities of this group is to choose evidence-based interventions that are likely to be effective in addressing behavioral concerns in the school building.

Federal documents such as the Surgeon General's report on youth violence (Office of the Surgeon General, 2001) and the U.S. Department of Health and Human Services Substance Abuse and and Mental Health Services Administration (SAMHSA) National Registry of Effective Programs (2001) can guide school-based teams in decisions about evidence-based interventions that might be appropriate alternatives to traditional discipline responses, such as suspension and expulsion. The most rigorous scientific methodology (experimental and quasi-experimental research designs) is used as the gold standard for determining outcome (programs deemed model), followed by those that are evaluated using less rigorous, yet controlled, standards (programs deemed promising). A few programs with negative outcomes that are not suggested for use are also evaluated in these documents.

Effect sizes (for direct outcome indicators and those that serve as risk factors) are used as indicators of success. The criteria used to evaluate these programs are open to debate and are beyond the scope of this chapter. However, a consistent criterion is applied across studies to determine effectiveness, and outcome data is gathered to measure the utility of the intervention. Certainly, traditional exclusionary procedures (e.g., suspension and expulsion) that are found in the majority of schoolwide policies would not meet minimal standards as evidence-based interventions.

As a starting point for the recasting of schoolwide discipline policies, we can consider a number of programs that have data to support their use and could be offered as an alternative to the traditional reactionary procedures that characterize schoolwide discipline policies.

For example, several promising and model programs are at our disposal that target the reduction of the very behaviors that school personnel sanction in schoolwide discipline policies.

TABLE 39.2
Evidence-based Interventions as Alternatives to Traditional Discipline

Behavior	*Traditional Consequences*	*Proactive Alternatives*
Tobacco Offenses	Suspension/Expulsion	Project Toward No Tobacco Use (Sussman et al., 1993)
Drug Offenses	Suspension/Expulsion	Project Toward No Drug Abuse (Sussman et al., 1997)
		Too Good for Drugs (developed by the Mendez Foundation) (Botvin, Schinke, & Orlandi, 1995)
Alcohol Offenses	Suspension/Expulsion	Parenting Wisely (Gordon, 2000)
Bullying Behavior	Suspension/Expulsion	Bullying Prevention (Olweus, 1994) Second Step (Nelson & Finch, 2000)

In traditional policies, these same behaviors are met with the exclusionary procedures of suspension and expulsion. There are no known studies that have empirically evaluated the reactionary procedures that pervade discipline codes of conduct (e.g., suspension and expulsion) in the way that these interventions have been subjected to scientific scrutiny. However, reactionary procedures are the ones most frequently found in schoolwide discipline policies. Although these alternative and evidence-based interventions have not been evaluated specifically as alternatives to suspension programs, they have certainly been subjected to a higher level of evaluation than suspension and expulsion. We can safely conclude that we do have a database of programs that are more likely to be effective than traditional discipline standards, yet we are unlikely to find them in schoolwide discipline policies.

Table 39.2 portrays a brief review of the types of evidence-based intervention programs that could be considered as alternatives to traditional methods of suspension and expulsion. For a more comprehensive summary of these programs, the reader is directed to the U.S. Department of Health and Human Services Substance Abuse and Mental Health Program's National Registry of Effective Programs (SAMHSA, 2001). In the table, we present a sample of behaviors that were found in schoolwide discipline policies reviewed in our previous research. Reviews of the specific programs are beyond the scope of this chapter and are handled elsewhere in this book (e.g., see chapters on bullying). Our major premise is that there are well-researched interventions that can be integrated into discipline codes of conduct, evaluated, and modified, as necessary. The behavioral interventions range along a continuum from prevention oriented (no risk factors for the behavior to occur) to tertiary (treatment following the occurrence of the behavior). We have focused on prosocial interventions that directly teach expected behaviors and would keep students in school. These interventions could be routinely reviewed by the discipline leadership team as evidence-based alternatives to traditional discipline consequences. Certainly, the discipline team would need to evaluate the appropriateness of the intervention for their particular school setting and determine whether there are existing resources in place to implement and evaluate the outcome for students. However, they are offered here only as a sampling of the possible interventions that can be attempted. We suspect that they would have greater promise in addressing common behaviors in policy than the traditional methods reviewed earlier.

Evidence-based interventions that directly teach expected behaviors have the strongest empirical support, yet are missing from schoolwide discipline policies. Perhaps the larger question is why interventions that fail on so many fronts (e.g., suspension and expulsion) dominate policies, whereas procedures with empirical support are notably absent. Given the limited study of written schoolwide discipline policies, this question largely remains unanswered. School attorneys may have the strongest voice in the development of discipline codes of conduct. Certainly, these individuals must assure that state and federal guidelines surrounding the discipline of students are in compliance. In some cases, discipline policies may be intentionally vague because of the need for flexibility in interpretation. A significant gap between what is known about evidence-based interventions and the integration of these procedures into policy is evident. What is not known is precisely how to narrow the gap between best practices and what is currently found in schoolwide discipline policies.

Directions for the Future Study of Discipline Policies

Clearly, substantial work needs to be done to gain a better understanding of how discipline policies can align with mandates for teaching prosocial behaviors (Zurkowkski et al., 1998). We have significant work to complete before understanding the best ways of developing proactive discipline policies and procedures. Perhaps a critical area that needs to be researched is an analysis of why school discipline policies have lagged so far behind what is known about effective behavioral interventions. Future researchers could examine this issue by exploring more fully the decision-making process of school policy makers and those who execute discipline in the school (e.g., school deans). Discipline policies may be reflective of a school culture that views discipline as punishment instead of an opportunity to teach (Fink, 1985). If this is the case, substantial school reform efforts must be enacted to fully implement changes to schoolwide discipline policies. Modifications of discipline codes of conduct may only occur as part of a larger school reform effort around discipline.

Similarly, it would be interesting to note the types of policies that are developed in schools that have a unified and proactive discipline plan (such as those in schools that implement PBS) versus those that do not prioritize the prosocial teaching of expected behaviors. It would seem that discipline codes of conduct can be viewed as an issue that is highly resistant to change and modification. Therefore, we have the most hope of changing them if they are embedded in larger system reform efforts.

In addition, future work could be done to examine the interplay between academics and discipline policy. Students with academic difficulties are the most likely to receive reactionary discipline methods, such as suspension and expulsion. Future research could focus on proactive policy alternatives implemented with students who have academic difficulties. These are the students most likely to be removed from school through suspension or expulsion (Furlong & Morrison, 1994). It would seem important to have a better understanding of why students with academic issues are most involved in punitive discipline processes. The outcome measures could be the following: retention in school, attendance, grades, and behavioral referrals. These indicators could also be measured on a schoolwide basis as part of a comprehensive program meant to improve school safety, discipline, school climate, and academic achievement of students.

Certainly, more attention needs to be given to schoolwide discipline policies in future research. Discipline policies are integral to a well-developed discipline plan (Phay, 1975; Schwartz, 2001). Extensive future study of schoolwide discipline policies needs to occur for a better understanding of how these documents affect a comprehensive school safety plan and the climate of the building in general. We are at an exciting time in the field, as we have evidence-based alternatives that can be effective with youth. It is time to consider ways of integrating these procedures into policy to institutionalize these systems at the building and district level. Of utmost concern is the lack of correspondence between what we know about evidence-based alternatives to traditional discipline procedures and what is sanctioned in schoolwide discipline policies. Schoolwide policies must be considered relevant to the behavioral and academic functioning of students. Schoolwide discipline policies have a powerful role in either teaching students to engage in appropriate behavior or inadvertently encouraging them to leave the school environment.

Implications of Schoolwide Discipline Policies for Classroom Management

Schoolwide discipline policies have significant implications for classroom teachers and behavior management in general. Classroom teachers and ancillary staff (security) are integral to the discipline referral process. These individuals are the first to encounter behavioral problems in the classroom and can intervene early, when we are most likely to be effective. They are in the best position to develop effective redirection strategies that prevent behavioral problems from occurring in the first place. We know that intervention earlier in the behavioral trajectory (Walker et al., 1996) will be more successful. Typically, teachers are the first ones to see behaviors before escalation occurs. Schoolwide discipline policies could also address classroom management strategies and less intrusive interventions that help prevent more significant problems from occurring. Once more severe behavior occurs, our chances of responding proactively are greatly diminished. Many severe behaviors in policy (although they occur infrequently), by law, require police intervention. It would seem prudent for school administrators to put fiscal resources into classroom management issues and provide training and release time for teachers. This will allow teachers to have an opportunity to provide meaningful input into the development of prevention-oriented strategies that can be integrated into policy. Prosocial alternatives for teachers to follow in schoolwide discipline policies may be helpful in preventing more severe behavioral infractions from occurring.

Classroom management issues are a significant source of discipline referral issues, as they occur much more frequently than more severe behaviors. However, a significant amount of instructional time is lost to process these referrals and address the problems, typically through reactionary means (e.g., suspension, expulsion). It would seem efficient to build prevention strategies into policy and provide training meant to prevent more significant behaviors from occurring in the first place. These efforts require release time for teachers to meaningfully address classroom management issues and a team that is interesting in taking a proactive perspective in handling these issues. Classroom management is a critical component of discipline policy development and needs to be considered in our discussion of creating more proactive discipline policies. Classroom teachers can play a critical role in system reform efforts focused on creating proactive schoolwide discipline procedures. Prevention-oriented classroom management procedures could be integrated into discipline policy as a component of proactive interventions intended to teach expected behaviors rather than to punish students.

Overall Implications of Schoolwide Discipline Policies

The study of schoolwide discipline policies is in its infancy. It is surprising that so little attention has been given to written policy documents. The research that has been done to date suggests that discipline policies (specifically discipline codes of conduct) contain primarily reactionary responses (e.g., suspension and expulsion) in response to student behaviors. Unfortunately, there is no evidence to support the use of these procedures. On the contrary, a number of evidence-based interventions are at our disposal and have not yet materialized in written discipline policies. It is unclear as to why discipline policies have lagged so far behind in their integration of evidence-based practices with documented efficacy. Unfortunately, we can also draw some general conclusions that the original purpose of discipline codes of conduct, as expressed nearly 30 years ago, has not materialized in our modern-day policies.

We would suggest that a first place to begin the arduous task of modifying discipline codes of conduct and related written policies would be to form a team of key stakeholders with a primary mission of reviewing and modifying the discipline codes of conduct. The pioneering work of Positive Behavior Support (PBS) (Sugai & Horner, 2002) could be a useful framework for guiding this process. PBS procedures entail the use of data to drive decisions, the formation of a team, and the direct teaching of expectations to all students. A school-based team with the power and authority to make policy decisions with administrator guidance would be a possible step in the direction of creating proactive discipline codes of conduct.

Related to this, efforts could be taken to address classroom management issues that are highly related to discipline concerns, and to create commonsense policy about which behaviors can be managed in the classroom. Teachers, classroom personnel, and related staff are in the best position to direct interventions that are endorsed by policy within instructional settings. In this way, they can work toward keeping students in the classroom. These efforts could serve to prevent more significant behaviors from occurring and the need for exclusionary discipline practices to be invoked (e.g., suspension and expulsion).

Our understanding of evidence-based interventions has grown rapidly and we have resources at our disposal for helping students to learn expected behaviors. The need to establish clear and consistent proactive discipline policies is critical. Significant future research is needed to build on what we currently know about schoolwide discipline policies and to enhance our knowledge of ways to create and implement proactive discipline codes of conduct.

The creation of proactive schoolwide discipline policies is a monumental task. The integration of proactive alternatives into policy will require significant planning and dedication on the part of the larger school community. We believe that true sustained reorganization of discipline codes of conduct is a major system reform effort. True changes in discipline policy will necessitate some serious thinking about the roles of schools and philosophically where they stand on the business of teaching behavior to students. At this time, our discipline policies serve the purpose of outlining sanctioned behaviors and punishing or removing students for noncompliance. Serious consideration about the role of discipline policies and the role of schools in discipline is time well spent. Current reactionary practices are failing our students. A significant portion of time taken to process disciplinary referrals and remove students from classroom could be saved by creating more proactive discipline practices. This is a task that can be facilitating by the joint efforts of researchers, policy makers, school professionals, and the larger community. It is time that we begin modifying our schoolwide discipline policies to reflect the extensive work that has been done in the area of prevention and early intervention. However, this is likely to occur only through large-scale, team-based approaches in which the discipline policy is conceptualized as an intervention that requires data-based feedback and evaluation. In this way, we can shift discipline policies from their current reactionary forms to documents that are based on our latest technology in prevention-oriented and proactive procedures.

ACKNOWLEDGMENT

The authors thank Reece Peterson, University of Nebraska, for his review of the draft of this chapter.

REFERENCES

American Federation of Teachers. (1995–1996). Elements of an effective discipline strategy. *American Educator, 19*, 24–27.

Botvin, G. J., Schinke, S., & Orlandi, M. A. (1995). School-based health promotion: Substance abuse and sexual behavior. *Applied and Preventive Psychology, 4*, 167–184.

Bowditch, C. (1993). Getting rid of troublemakers: High school disciplinary procedures and the production of dropouts. *Social Problems, 40*, 493–509.

Carr, E. G. (1994). Emerging themes in the functional analysis of problem behavior. *Journal of Applied Behavior Analysis, 27*, 393–400.

Colvin, G., Kame'enui, E. J., & Sugai, G. (1993). School-wide and classroom management: Reconceptualizing the integration and management of students with behavior problems in general education. *Education and Treatment of Children, 16*, 361–381.

Fenning, P., Parraga, M., & Wilczynski, J. (2000). A comparative analysis of existing secondary school discipline policies: Implications for improving practice and school safety. In K. McClafferty, C. A. Torres, & T. R. Mitchell (Eds.), *Challenges of urban education: Sociological perspectives for the next century* (pp. 175–194). Albany: State University of New York Press.

Fenning, P., Theodos, J., Benner, C., & Bohanon-Edmonson, H. (2004). Integrating proactive discipline practices into codes of conduct. *Journal of School Violence, 3*(1), 45–61.

Fenning, P., Theodos, J., Benner, C., & Banull, C. (2005). *A content analysis of school discipline codes of conduct.* Manuscript in preparation.

Fenning, P., Theodos, J., & Benner, C., (2002). *The Analysis of Discipline Codes Rating Form (ADCR).* Unpublished Rating Scale.

Findley, D. (1996). How can schools meet public expectations for discipline? *Thresholds in Education, 22*(4), 21–23.

Fink, D. M. (1985). *Discipline in school-age care: Control the climate, not the children.* Nashville, TN: School Age Notes.

Furlong, M. J., & Morrison, G. M. (1994). Introduction to miniseries: School violence and safety in perspective. *School Psychology Review, 23*, 139–150.

Gordon, D. A. (2000). Parent training via CD-ROM: Using technology to disseminate effective prevention practices. *The Journal of Primary Prevention, 21*, 227–251.

Goss v. Lopez, 95 S. Ct. 729, 419 U.S. 565, 42, L.Ed., 2d 725. (1975).

Harvard University Advancement and Civil Rights Project. (2000). *Opportunities suspended: The devastating consequences of zero tolerance and school discipline policies.* Retrieved October 9, 2002, from http://www.law.harvard.edu/groups/civilrights/conferences/zero/zt_report2.html

Honig v. Doe, EHLR December, 559: 231 (1987–1988).

Hyman, I. (1997). *School discipline and school violence: The teacher variance approach.* Boston: Allyn & Bacon.

Jay, T. (1997). *Improving school conduct codes: Clarity about unacceptable speech.* (Eric Document Reproduction Service No. ED408684).

Lally, D. (1982). *Administrator's perceptions of the effectiveness of discipline codes in New Jersey high schools.* Unpublished doctoral dissertation, Temple University, Philadelphia.

Larson, J. (1998). Managing student aggression in high schools: Implications for Practice. *Psychology in the Schools, 35*, 283–295.

Lewis, T. J., Sugai, G., & Colvin, G. (1998). Reducing problem behavior through a school-wide system of effective behavioral support: Investigation of a school-wide social skills training program and contextual interventions. *School Psychology Review, 27*, 446–459.

MacDonald, I. (1997, June). *School violence: Redirecting the storm chasers.* Paper presented at the Annual Meeting of the Canadian Association for the Study of Educational Administration, St. Johns, Newfoundland, Canada.

Mayer, G. R. (1995). Preventing antisocial behavior in the schools. *Journal of Applied Behavior Analysis, 28*, 467–478.

McEvoy, A., & Welker, R. (2000). Antisocial behavior, academic failure and school climate: A critical review. *Journal of Emotional and Behavioral Disorders, 8*, 130–141.

Metzler, C. W., Biglan, A., & Rusby, J. C. (2001). Evaluation of a comprehensive behavior management program to improve school-wide positive behavior support. *Education and Treatment of Children, 24*, 448–479.

Morrison, G. M., & D'Incau, B. (1997). The web of zero tolerance: Characteristics of students who are recommended for expulsion from school. *Education and Treatment of Children, 20*, 316–335.

National Institute of Education. (1978). *Violent schools—safe schools: The safe school study report to the congress.* Washington, DC: Superintendent of Documents.

National School Resource Network. (1980). *Resource handbook on discipline codes.* Cambridge, MA: Oelgeschlager, Gun & Hahn.

Nelson, W. M., III, & Finch, A. J., Jr. (2000). Managing anger in youth: A cognitive-behavioral intervention approach. In P. C. Kendall (Ed.), *Child and adolescent therapy: Cognitive-behavioral procedures* (pp. 129–170). New York: Guilford.

Noonan, B., Tunney, K., Fogal, B., & Sarich, C. (1999). Developing student codes of conduct: A case for parent-principal partnership. *School Psychology International, 20*, 289–299.

Office of the Surgeon General. (2001). *Youth violence: A report of the Surgeon General.* Washington, DC: Author.

Olweus, D. (1994). Annotation: Bullying at school: Basic facts and effects of a school-based intervention program. *Journal of Child Psychology and Psychiatry, 35*, 1171–1190.

Phay, R. E. (1975). Written student conduct codes: An essential ingredient in reducing and controlling student misconduct. *School Law Bulletin, 4*, 1–11.

Rose, L. C., & Gallup, A. M. (2002). The 34th annual Phi Delta Kappa/Gallup poll of the public's attitudes toward the public schools. *Phi Delta Kappan, 84*, 41–46.

Schwartz, W. (Ed.). (2001). *School practices for equitable discipline of African American Students*. (ERIC Digest No. 166)

Skiba, R., & Knesting, K. (2002). Zero tolerance, zero evidence: An analysis of school disciplinary practice. In R. Skiba & G. G. Noam (Eds.), *Zero tolerance: Can suspension and expulsion keep school safe? New directions for youth development* (pp. 17–43). San Francisco: Jossey-Bass.

Skiba, R., & Peterson, R. (1999). The dark side of zero tolerance: Can punishment lead to safe schools? *Phi Delta Kappan, 80*, 372–376, 381–382.

Skiba, R. J., Peterson, R. L., & Williams, T. (1997). Office referrals and suspension: Disciplinary intervention in middle schools. *Education and Treatment of Children, 20*, 295–315.

Skiba, R., & Rausch, M. K. (2005). Zero tolerance, suspension, and expulsion: Questions of equity and effectiveness. In C. Evertson & C. S. Weinstein (Eds.), *Handbook of behavior management: Research, practice and contemporary issues*. (pp. 1063–1089). Mahwah, NJ: Lawrence Erlbaum Associates.

Sprague, J., Walker, H., & Golly, A. (2001). Translating research into effective practice: The effects of a universal staff and student intervention on indicators of discipline and school safety. *Education and Treatment of Children, 24*, 495–511.

Suarez, T. M. (1992). *Creating safe environments for Learning in North Carolina's Public Schools*. Chapel Hill, NC: North Carolina Educational Policy Research Center.

Sugai, G., & Horner, R. H. (2002). Introduction to the special series on positive behavior support in schools. *Journal of Emotional and Behavioral Disorders, 10*(3), 130–135.

Sugai, G., Horner, R. H., Dunlap, G., Hieneman, M., Lewis, T., Nelson, C. M., Scott, T., Liaupsin, C., Sailor, W., Turnbull, A. P., Turnbull, R., Wickham D., Ruef, M. H., Wilcox, B. (1999). *Applying positive behavioral support and functional behavioral assessment in schools. Technical assistance guide #1* (version 14.4). Washington, DC: U.S. Department of Education, Office of Special Education Programs.

Sussman, S., Dent, C. W., Stacy, A. W., Sun, P., Craig, S., Simon, T. R., Button, D., Flay, B. R. (1993). Project towards no tobacco use: 1-year behavior outcomes. *American Journal of Public Health, 83*, 1245–1250.

Sussman, S., Simon, T. R., Dent, C. W., Stacy, A. W., Galaif, E. R., Moss, M. A., Craig, S., Johnson, C. A. (1997). Immediate impact of thirty-two drug abuse prevention activities among students at continuation high schools. *Substance Use and Misuse, 32*, 265–281.

Taylor-Greene, S., Brown, D., Nelson, L., Longton, J., Gassman, T., Cohen, J. Horner, R. H., Sugal, G. & Hall, S. (1997). School-wide behavioral support: Starting the year off right. *Journal of Behavioral Education, 7*, 99–112.

U.S. Department of Health and Human Services Substance Abuse and Mental Health Programs (SAMHSA). (2001). *National Registry of Effective Programs*. Retrieved March 15, 2004, from http://modelprogram.samhsa.gov.

Walker, H. M., & Horner, R. (1996). Integrated approaches to preventing antisocial behavior patterns among school-aged children and youth. *Journal of Emotional and Behavior Disorders, 4*, 194–209.

Zantal-Weiner, K. (1988). *Disciplinary exclusion of special education students*. (ERIC Document Reproduction Services No. ED295397)

Zurkowski, J. K., Kelly, P. S., & Griswold, D. E. (1998). Discipline and IDEA 1997: Instituting a new balance. *Intervention in School and Clinic, 34*, 3–9.

40

Classroom Management as a Moral Activity

Catherine Fallona
University of Southern Maine

Virginia Richardson
University of Michigan

INTRODUCTION

What could be closer to the moral in the classroom than activities and teaching that are directed at or function to affect present and future student conduct? We use the term *conduct*, here, because it combines behavior and the intentions and rationale for acting in a certain way. Student conduct in relation to other students, the teacher, formal knowledge, the community, democratic ideals, and the human conversation all hold moral implications. Recognizing the moral import of teachers' work and therefore of classroom management, the goal of this chapter is to provide an analysis that helps make evident the nature of classroom management as a moral activity.

We turn to Rest (1983) for a conception of morality that is helpful in this chapter. For Rest, morality is:

> 1) behavior that helps another human being; 2) behavior in conformity with social norms; 3) the internalization of social norms; 4) the arousal of empathy or guilt or both; 5) reasoning about justice, and 6) putting another's interest ahead of one's own. (p. 556)

We find this psychological definition helpful in our analysis of classroom management as a moral activity because of the relationship between Rest's five forms of morality and the goals and functions of classroom management.

However, we recognize that not everyone is in agreement with Rest's (1983) definition of morality. For example, Nucci (2001) suggested that conforming to and internalizing social norms is not morality but an example of following social conventions. According to Nucci, "moral issues are viewed to be independent of the existence of social norms and generalizable across contexts, societies, and cultures" (2001, p. 10). To support his claim, he referred to philosophical attempts to establish criteria for what ought to count as a moral value. Nucci then suggested: "What is morally right is not something that is simply subject to individual opinion but carries with it an 'objective' prescriptive force. The second, related idea, is that what is morally right, because it is 'objectively' prescriptive, holds generally and can be universalized" (2001, p. 6). Although Nucci does not credit Kant with his rational notion of morality or universalizability in this analysis, his conceptions of morality are born out of Kantian virtue.

The authors of this chapter, on the other hand, situate our sense of morality within the context of Aristotelian particularism. As Sherman (1997) wrote in reference to Aristotelian particularism, making a decision about what is morally right "is neither to subsume one's choice under some general principles or law nor to ask whether others could endorse the universalized maxim of one's action.... Rather, the focus is always on the specifics of the case" (p. 244). Within this conception, every classroom has its own "shared morality" (Hansen, 1992), and within the context of the classroom, individual student moral conduct conforms to the shared morality and social norms of the classroom community. Students learn that they must be socially responsible by working with and caring for others and furthering the common good (Berman, 1997).

The link between classroom management and morality may be seen in the in the conception of classroom management found in the description of this book by its editors:

> Teachers must (1) Develop caring, supportive relationships with and among students; (2) Organize and implement instruction in ways that that optimize students' access to learning; (3) Use group management methods that encourage students' engagement in academic tasks; (4) Promote the development of students' social skills and self-regulation; and use appropriate interventions to assist students with behavior problems. (Evertson & Weinstein, 2006)

This kind of classroom management curriculum fosters a shared morality and moral student conduct in the classroom. Classroom management is joined with other types of classroom functions and tasks as a moral activity. As Wolk (2002) wrote:

> There is no separation between the content we teach and issues of character and morality. They are just as intertwined. The knowledge of that content should inform and direct the daily moral decisions we make. Classroom management, behavior, character, subject matter knowledge and morality should all be intertwined with both citizenship and social justice. (p. 2)

Affecting the morality of students and how that morality is exhibited in their conduct means viewing classroom management holistically. It means going beyond the official curriculum and making behavior, community, character, citizenship, and social justice a part of the classroom curriculum (Wolk, 2002).

The purpose of this chapter is to holistically examine the curriculum of classroom management as a moral activity to promote moral student conduct. In reviewing the literature, we found exemplars that illuminate the moral discourse, classroom practices, and research on these topics. We are not presenting a complete literature review, which would be extensive, but we use these exemplars in developing an analysis of these two perspectives—implicit and explicit—on the moral nature of the classroom and classroom management, and conceptions, programs, and research within them. We conclude the chapter with a discussion of issues relating to conceiving of classroom management as a moral activity and implications for teaching and teacher education.

THE MORAL DISCOURSE OF CLASSROOM MANAGEMENT ACTIVITIES

A starting point for holistically examining the curriculum of classroom management as a moral activity to promote individual students' moral conduct is to examine, briefly, the moral discourse embedded in views of classroom management that have emerged over the last 30 years from research and various recommended classroom practices. What is salient about these definitions, the research, and the classroom practices associated with them is that, until recently, they were primarily consciously or unconsciously amoral.

Broad definitions of classroom management that emerged in the late 1970s focus on how teachers organize and manage their classrooms to optimize student learning. For example, in the 1979 NSSE Yearbook devoted to Classroom Management, Duke (1979) defined classroom management in the following way: "Classroom management constitutes the provisions and procedures necessary to establish and maintain an environment in which instruction and learning can occur" (p. xii). His definition connects strongly with a behaviorist theory of the nature of teaching and a process–product approach to research on teaching. Teachers apply behavioral principles to classroom management through the use of rewards in the form of grades, praise, and privileges to reinforce desired behavior and consequences such as bad grades, reprimands, and loss of privileges to discourage undesirable tendencies or actions.

Perhaps the most well-known example of a classroom management program based on reinforcement theory is Assertive Discipline (Canter & Canter, 1976, 2002). This program calls for teachers to gain control of their classrooms by insisting on appropriate student behavior and responding assertively to inappropriate behavior. Teachers must be clear about their expectations, and they must respond to student misbehavior firmly and confidently. Therefore, teachers who use assertive discipline develop a set of classroom rules as well as a set of consequences for breaking these rules. As if the rules and consequences were void of moral lessons associated with what it means to be morally good, the discourse on assertive discipline is amoral, rather narrowly focusing on teacher-made rules and consequences. There is a lack of consideration of how these activities achieve more than compliance with rules or how they foster or fail to foster current and future moral student conduct.

Doyle (1986) expanded this notion of classroom management and its focus on individual student behavior through considerations of the tasks and functions of classroom actions. His definition of classroom management includes the use of group management methods that encourage students' engagement in academic tasks. Doyle (1986) referred to these tasks that teachers undertake as "the management function of teaching" (p. 394). Viewing classroom management in terms of tasks and functions of teaching helps move the concept of classroom management beyond the simple notion of controlling and disciplining students. Classroom management becomes regarded as all those things that teachers do to construct a classroom environment that is conducive to learning.

In these earlier works, the focus on behavior and academic learning overshadows most other considerations of classroom activity. For example, little of the earlier writing refers to the moral nature of the tasks and functions of classroom management. In the 1979 NSSE Yearbook, there are amazingly few references to the moral. Two exceptions refer to the social nature of the classroom and the socialization function. Calfee and Brown (1979), in a chapter that focuses on grouping students for instruction, examined the process of learning about social norms, and specifically, the relationship between group organization and cheating. They referred to an example by Dreeben (1968), who compared the complexity of social norms in schools with those in the home: "The irony of cheating in school is that the same kinds of acts are considered morally acceptable and even commendable in other situations" (pp. 67–68). Spady and Mitchell (1979) examined social responsibility as an important outcome for students to attain through various elements of classroom management. Social responsibility, according to the authors, is "compliance with moral and legal standards" that is an "essential ingredient in the maintenance of social order" (p. 91). As these notions and examples illustrate, explicit considerations of the moral in classroom management research and practices of the 1970s and 80s tended to be situated in an amoral discourse.

Within the 1990s, however, a realization grew that classroom management should be reconceptualized to bring it together with other aspects of the classroom such as instruction and facilitating the student acquisition of the virtues. In teacher education, as pointed out by Boostrom (1991) and McLaughin (1994), classroom management was (and still is in many cases) treated as a set of technical skills related to controlling students, and student discipline was seen as providing rewards and punishment (Jones 1996). Weinstein (1998) suggested that given the way classroom management is taught in teacher education, students may see it as separate from instruction and interpersonal relationships. Weinstein underscored the lack of relationship between conceptions of caring and classroom order held by prospective teachers. This reconceptualization of classroom management by Weinstein and others to include the construction of caring classroom environments that are conducive to learning, as well as a renewed interest in character education has led to considerations of the moral aspects of teaching, including the management functions of teaching.

TWO PERSPECTIVES ON THE MORAL CURRICULUM OF CLASSROOM MANAGEMENT

Current inquiries into and program development in the moral dimensions of classrooms may be considered within two perspectives. The first perspective, which we label *implicit*, focuses on the moral dimensions inherent in classroom actions. Morality, then, is seen as embedded in practice, and teachers may or may not be aware of the moral import of actions such as their manner, style, or classroom discourse. Inquiry within this perspective attempts to make visible all that is moral within the classroom, whether within the teacher's conscious curriculum or not. Thus, for example, such an inquiry might include descriptions of conscious programs of moral education, as well as actions that could be described as fostering morality in the students but not seen as such by the teacher. The implicit perspective is meant to be descriptive, leading toward a theory of the moral nature of classrooms and how teachers, instruction, and classroom environment contribute. An example of such descriptive work may be found in Fenstermacher and Richardson (2003), who described the ways that teachers in their study fostered moral student conduct within six methods: construction of the classroom community, didactic instruction, design and execution of academic task structures, calling out for conduct of a particular kind, private conversations, and showcasing specific students. Because the implicit perspective focuses on classroom actions, particularly those initiated by the teacher, the view of change, if there is one, is concerned with helping the teachers become more conscious of the moral nature of their actions in the classroom, with the goal being to develop practitioners who are thoughtful about the moral implications of their practice.

The *explicit* perspective is more prescriptive than the implicit, in that it focuses on the fostering of student morality through explicit and conscious programs and pedagogy. Thus, in a sense, the teaching of the moral is another subject matter, whether taught separately, or integrated into all other subjects. This perspective includes inquiring into and developing the wide range of programs categorized under the expansive label of character education as well as the construction of a sociomoral classroom environment.

The implicit and explicit categories are analytic approaches, and therefore heuristic in nature. As with so many analytic conceptions of classrooms, one seldom finds a "pure" case in practice. Programs often get adjusted in the classroom as the teacher uses an eclectic approach to program implementation. A further confusion in this field is that program developers often label their programs differently depending on to whom they are speaking and writing. Character education, for example, is used as a label for a wide variety of programs and may be used inconsistently by developers. Thus, although we describe the perspectives and program types below, we do so with the understanding that the categories often overlap.

THE IMPLICIT MORAL CURRICULUM OF CLASSROOM MANAGEMENT

The implicit perspective seeks to make visible the moral aspects of everyday classroom activities. It is a descriptive, inquiry approach that is moving toward theories of moral life in classrooms. Within this perspective, the implicit moral curriculum of classroom management is an integral part of all that occurs in the classroom. It is a perspective on classroom management as a hidden curriculum related to the moral nature inherent in classroom actions. The implicit moral curriculum of classroom management includes analytic as well as empirical studies of the moral dimensions of teaching.

The analytic work related to the implicit moral curriculum of classroom management brings to the fore aspects of teaching such as the moral importance of style; manner and professional virtue; and moral knowledge, judgment, and discourse. This work renews attention to teaching as an inherently moral activity. As Fenstermacher (1990) explained: "What makes teaching a moral endeavor is that it is, quite centrally, human action undertaken in regard to other human beings. Thus matters of what is fair, right, just, and virtuous are always present.... The teacher's conduct, at all times and in all ways, is a moral matter" (p. 133).

Understanding teaching, and most especially, teachers' conduct has been a growing area of research in recent years. Hansen's (2001) summary of this research suggests: (a) teaching is an inherently moral endeavor; (b) teaching is at one and the same time an intellectual and a moral endeavor; (c) any action a teacher undertakes in the classroom is capable of expressing moral meaning that in turn can influence students; and (d) moral perception, moral judgment, and moral knowledge play a dynamic role in teaching. Essentially, each of these areas of research illustrates how morality is embedded in practice.

Because the moral is seen as embedded in classroom action, it is difficult to make the moral visible. The challenge lies in developing a vocabulary and a set of constructs to discuss and describe this inherent property, to observe it in classroom actions, and to help teachers understand what might be going on in their classrooms. We have found three discourse approaches in this work: that which focuses on teachers' style and manner, on teachers' moral discourse, and on teachers' ethical knowledge and knowing. Although not inclusive of all the analytical or empirical work that has been done on the notion that teaching is inherently moral, these approaches, each consisting of analytic as well as empirical work, illustrate how aspects of teaching are an implicit moral curriculum of classroom management.

Implicit Approaches to the Moral Curriculum of Classroom Management

A strong body of analytic studies has set the stage for the work in the approaches of how teaching is a moral activity. Tom's (1984) analysis of teaching as a moral craft portrays teaching as a moral relationship between the teacher and the student. Goodlad, Soder, and Sirotnik's (1990) edited book analyzes the moral dimensions of teaching including the moral role of teachers in a democratic society. Sockett's (1993) philosophical analysis of teacher professionalism suggests five teacher virtues that constitute this professionalism: courage, care, honesty, fairness, and practical wisdom. Each of these analyses serves to highlight the moral significance of teaching and the professional virtue required of teachers. Analytic and empirical work has continued to build on these conceptions to help us understand the ways in which teaching is a moral activity that affects the moral curriculum of classroom management.

The research and analytic work on teacher style and manner illustrate the ways teaching is an inherently moral endeavor and any action a teacher undertakes in the classroom is capable of expressing moral meaning that in turn can influence students. Although recent work (see Hansen, 2001; Fallona, 2000; Fenstermacher, 1999) delineates the different origins and conceptions of teacher style and teacher manner, the two concepts are parallel. Style pertains to the conduct of the teachers that reflects their own personal qualities, and manner refers to teachers' stable dispositions and traits of character that are believed to be important in pedagogical relations and fostering virtues in students (Fenstermacher, 1999).

As the previous definition indicates, teacher manner is seen as having a moral influence on students. For a quality relationship between a teacher and a student to ensue, it is thought that a teacher must have a manner expressive of virtue (Fallona, 2000). This expression is conveyed through the methods the teacher uses, including those related to classroom management. When examining a teacher's manner while performing the managerial functions of teaching, we find ourselves particularly interested in those dispositions and traits of character that reside in the realm of moral virtue. Drawing on Fenstermacher's theories of manner and pedagogy, Fallona (2000) constructed a framework based on Aristotelian virtue for empirically examining the conceptual nature of manner in teaching. Richardson and Fallona (2001) used this Aristotelian framework to study the manner and management of two experienced and expert teachers whose classroom management approaches differed dramatically. Comparing the manner of Kai, an African American kindergarten teacher in an inner-city Afrocentric school, and Darlene, a White third-grade teacher in a culturally diverse urban school, Richardson and Fallona (2001) wrote:

> Differences may also be seen in the way that teacher manner manifests itself in the classroom. Caring, in Kai's classroom, is expressed in what might be called "tough love" in the popular literature. She cares for them, and therefore, demands that they work toward her expectations for their academic and social success. One could say that caring is expressed for the group of students as well as individuals. Darlene is also a caring teacher and expresses caring in hugs, applauding, careful listening to students, and attempting to determine what is best for individual children. Although much of this activity happens in groups, much more is expressed when Darlene is communicating with individual students in private. (p. 722)

They noted seamlessness among method, style, and manner in the two teachers' classroom management actions:

> Classroom management—and particularly effective classroom management—is interwoven with the goals and beliefs of the teacher, and with his or her manner. An understanding of a teacher's classroom management is greatly enhanced through an understanding of the degree of authenticity—coherence—in which he or she expresses her beliefs, goals, manner and methods. (Richardson & Fallona (2001, p. 724)

Thus, who the teacher is, what the teacher believes, and how the teacher's beliefs are enacted are well aligned.

In an interview study with a number of students in the classrooms of the collaborating teachers, Richardson and Williams (2000) found that the students are very clear about the virtues that their teachers stress in the classrooms and are able to talk articulately and extensively about these virtues and virtuous behaviors. They also found that the nature of the talk about teacher expectations varied by gender. The girls focus on aspects of moral virtues that relate to relationships with others (e.g., "respect others," "don't put others down"); whereas the boys focus on more material behaviors as stressed in what might be considered behavioral approaches to classroom management ("don't lean your chair back," "don't push other kids"). It is also clear from the study that the culture in the two schools in which the study was conducted, as expressed clearly and strongly by the two principals, has a strong impact on the moral virtues that are stressed in the classrooms and corridors (Chow-Hoy, 2001). The moral nature of the schools and the manner in which the teachers manage their classrooms permeates the atmosphere of the schools and classrooms.

Jackson, Boostrom, and Hansen (1993) expressed a similar finding in their investigation of the ways moral considerations permeate the everyday life of schools and classrooms. As a part of their investigation, they explored several aspects of teachers' conduct. An aspect of teachers' conduct that they explored in depth was style. According to these researchers:

> Style refers to the teacher's typical ways of handling the demands of the job. What makes a teacher's style noteworthy from a moral perspective is the way it embodies attributes that we normally think of as moral.... A teacher's style can be reserved and aloof or warm and intimate. It can express kindness or cruelty. It can be scatterbrained or methodical. (p. 37)

The teacher's style reveals something about the teacher's typical ways of dealing with students.

The teacher's style also affects moral learning in students in that it is witnessed and experienced by everyone present, and as such, it is a form of moral education. Hansen (1993b) stated, "through a close look at style, one can perceive how a teacher provides students over the course of a school year with an ongoing model of conduct" (p. 398). It predates formal teacher training and is broadly expressive of a teacher's approach to life in general (Jackson et al., 1993). The teacher's style of working can be seen as more than a mere function of role, of convention, or of external expectations from school or society. Style is expressive of a teacher's personal qualities that can potentially influence students for good or for ill. Style is at the heart of a teacher's moral influence on students.

Following up on this work on style, Boostrom (1991) looked specifically at the use of rules in successful classrooms, and how misuse of rules can lead to a disappearance of the seamlessness described earlier:

> When we think about a successful classroom, we imagine that the students' inclinations and the teacher's plans are so united that the statement of classroom rules seems superfluous (p. 203).... The way we think about rules is very important. It is not just a philosophical point, but a practical one, because when teachers forget the significance of their own rules, a chasm begins to open between what they are doing and why they are doing it. The results can be both a mechanical classroom and an uncertain teacher.... Avoiding the mechanical in the classroom is not a matter of letting up on rules but of seeing them for what they are—a moral ordering of the world for which the teacher is accountable just as the students are to be obedient. (pp. 212–213)

Buzzelli and Johnston (2002) examined classroom interaction through a moral lens. In particular, they analyzed morality in teaching through three lenses: language, power, and culture. Through their analysis, they illustrated the ways classroom interactions serve as an implicitly moral curriculum for classroom management. In terms of language, for example, they suggested: "It is through language that the moral dimension of teaching is realized and through language moral meanings are negotiated in classrooms" (p. 20). An example is Buzelli and Johnston's (2002) analysis of teachers' use of repetition. Through repetition, the teacher conveys "her care and concern for the content and process" of the activity; "shifts responsibility for part of the activity to the children"; and by engaging in a type of participatory listening, the teacher "conveys to the students in this class not only that the teacher is listening, but that she cares about them, values their contributions, and is concerned about the way she is creating and maintaining social relationships with them" (pp. 22–23). This example highlights the morally significant choices that teachers make when they construct classroom discussions, and the importance of discourse in affecting the relationships between teachers and students.

The quality of the teacher–student relationship is also influenced by the power relationships in the classroom. Power relationships are permeated with questions of "values, beliefs, and notions of what is right and wrong, good and bad" (Buzzelli & Johnston, 2002, p. 51). Teachers' values and beliefs are conveyed in how they construct the curriculum, and this moral agency helps shape the teacher's relationships with students and the environment in the classroom. It is, then, an implicit moral curriculum of classroom management.

The moral agency that teachers have to construct the curriculum illustrates how the intellectual and moral aspects of teaching are intertwined. Ball (1993) singularly and then with Wilson (Ball & Wilson, 1996) examined the relationship between teaching as a knowledge endeavor and teaching as a moral enterprise using episodes from their own practice. Ball (1993) suggested that teachers must negotiate their obligations to the moral and intellectual demands of the work. She wrote: "It is the trying for a justifiable balance of knowledge and learner, obligation and autonomy, common standards and personal style that makes teaching a virtuous- and very difficult activity" (p. 204). Ball and Wilson (1996) wrote: "Establishing and maintaining one's integrity in teaching depends on a complex interplay of commitments, values, beliefs, and understandings of students and subject matter, professional communities, and parents" (1996, p. 156). Integrity, Ball and Wilson argued is the intersection between the moral and the intellectual aspects of teaching. However, through the process of examining their own practice, they realized that the moral and the intellectual are not so easily separated. As a result, they concluded that the moral and the intellectual are and ought to be fused in teaching.

Some studies have joined the moral and the intellectual through their study of moral knowledge or moral judgment. For example, Lyons (1990) studied teachers' dilemmas of knowing and found that 70% of teachers in her sample characterized their professional conflicts as moral or ethical. According to Lyons (1990), epistemological and ethical dimensions exist in the social and intellectual relationships between teacher and student in everyday interaction. Elements of these interactions include the teacher's stance toward the self as knower, the teacher's stance toward the student as a knower and a learner, and the teacher's stance toward knowledge of subject matter (Lyons, 1990). This stance is informed by the teacher's ethical knowledge and defines the teacher's moral agency.

Accepting of the "embedded and implicit nature of much of teachers' moral practice," Campbell (2003, p. 1) used teachers' voices as gathered in her various qualitative studies to make more visible teachers' ethical knowledge in terms of complexity, self-awareness, and intention. To Campbell, teachers' ethical knowledge "is expressed through both their knowledge of what is ethically important to do in the course of their professional practice and their knowledge about what they want students to achieve, internalize or learn related to principles of right and wrong and how they can facilitate and inspire such learning" (p. 2). Teachers who are ethically knowledgeable have a "well developed conscience" of what is right and wrong. By way of example, Campbell (2003) described Marissa, "who is ever conscious of being fair and kind toward students—allows extensions on assignments, accepts students late to class, and permits students to determine test and assignment due dates" (p. 41). She also provided examples of what happens in classrooms where the teacher lacks ethical knowledge and of what happens under conditions of moral uncertainty when ethical knowledge fades. Campbell (2003) described these as dilemmas in which other norms, such as collegial autonomy and egalitarianism, may affect the decisions made by teachers that could be considered unethical.

Like Campbell (2003), a number of authors focus on the moral dilemmas confronting teachers on a daily basis. There are moral dilemmas that take place both within and outside the classroom. In all cases, teachers are aware of (have knowledge of) the forces that make a moral decision difficult. They are often, however, dissatisfied with the decision that they ultimately make, and begin to realize that many of these dilemmas recur in different contexts and situations. Colnerud (1997), for example, referred to the dilemma faced by teachers who see one of their colleagues mistreat a student, but, given the norms of the school, are unwilling to take action to either explore the situation with the other teacher, or report the teacher to the administrators of the school.

Following Fenstermacher and Richardson's (2003) study of manner and methods of fostering the virtues in students, Miletta (2003) examined the dilemmas faced by teachers in three different settings who were conscious of the moral nature of their teaching. One of the incidents that she and the teachers focus on took place in a Reggio Emelia preschool classroom in Italy. The incident involves students who fought in the halls outside the classroom, and the analysis that was developed by Miletta and the teachers examines the moral dilemmas faced by the teachers as they attempt to prevent this violence from reoccurring. Because it did continue, the analysis was able to follow the ways the teachers used Fenstermacher's (2001) six methods of fostering moral conduct in the students.

All of the work in this area requires analytic interpretation on the part of the inquirer, and the foundations for these interpretations may be derived from a number of sources. Husu (2003) explored three representations of teachers' ethical understanding and practice from pedagogical ethics: ethics of background beliefs, guiding rules and principles, and dilemma management. Through interviews and classroom observation of teachers, one of whom is presented as a case study in his article, he found that using these three representations, together, on the same data, can help the observer both see and interpret pedagogical practice, and help the teachers better understand their professional practice. As they enact their pedagogical ethics, they are implementing an implicit moral curriculum of classroom management.

Summarizing Thoughts on the Implicit Moral Curriculum of Classroom Management

An implicit moral curriculum of classroom management stresses that teaching is inherently a moral endeavor. As such, all aspects of teaching have moral implications. As illustrated by Jackson et al.'s (1993) categories for observing the moral content in schools, Fenstermacher's (2001) methods of fostering moral conduct in the students, Buzzelli and Johnston's (2002) calls for moral discourse, and Campbell's (2003) notion of ethical knowledge, there is moral significance in everything in the classroom from the curriculum to the language to the power relationships that characterizes the interactions between teachers and students. The moral significance of these elements of classroom life pervades the classroom environment and relates to classroom management as a moral activity.

THE EXPLICIT MORAL CURRICULUM OF CLASSROOM MANAGEMENT

The explicit perspective on the moral curriculum of classroom management assumes a holistic view of classroom management. It is a view of classroom management that extends far beyond how teachers manage student behavior or student discipline. The explicit moral curriculum of classroom management, whether taught directly or indirectly, includes all forms of explicit moral instruction in the classroom, or character education in its broadest sense. As Wolk (2002) wrote, "Classroom management and issues of character are both essentially about goodness and how we act, in school and out. So... classroom management and character education are synonymous or at least woven together like a double helix strand of DNA" (p. 2). The ways explicit forms of moral instruction call on students to display moral conduct affects the classroom environment and relates to the moral curriculum of classroom management. The goal of the explicit perspective as seen in the analytic, research, and practice literature is prescriptive in nature. That is, its purpose is to determine how and which specific programs, instructional practices, and classroom organizations and environments can lead to the moral development of students.

Explicit forms of moral instruction consist of character education programs introduced to teachers for the purpose of morally educating students through the development of character and sociomoral competency. Character is the complex set of psychological characteristics that enable an individual to act as a moral agent. It includes moral action, moral values, moral personality, moral emotions, moral reasoning, moral identity, and foundational characteristics (Berkowitz, 1997; Berkowitz & Bier, 2004).

In the broadest sense, character education initiatives include direct and indirect approaches to developing character. As Berkowitz and Bier (2004) wrote: "Character education varies from a limited set of stand-alone and homegrown lessons to fully integrated, comprehensive school reform models" (p. 74). Character education is "eclectic" and "lacks either a theoretical perspective or a common core of practice" (Lemming, 1997). It includes instruction on what moral virtue is and how to be morally virtuous as well as integrating character issues into such subjects as literature or social studies. It also includes preventive programs, socioemotional learning, and service learning (Berkowitz & Bier, 2004).

There are two pedagogical approaches in the explicit perspective. One, which we call more direct,[1] involves direct instruction of what the literature refers to as either "virtues" or "values." Used somewhat interchangeably in some of the character education literature, virtues and values are traits, behaviors, or skills that the teacher wishes the students to learn. The second approach is more indirect. Although the goal is still one of explicitly developing the traits, behaviors and skills of the students, the instructional approach is not one of direct instruction. Rather this form of moral instruction is embedded in the conscious beliefs and values of the teacher, and the construction of the classroom environment.

More Direct Approaches to the Moral Curriculum of Classroom Management

In recent years, direct moral instruction in the form of character education has experienced a resurgence among educators across the country. In part, this increase of interest in character education may be attributable to policies such as the No Child Left Behind Act of 2001 (NCLB, 2002) that embrace character education. The result of this increased interest in character education has been the creation of a wide array of character education programs consciously designed to teach moral virtue and conduct.

The most prevalent form of character education programs involves teaching virtues such as self-control, honesty, and respecting others through direct instruction (Ryan & Bohlin, 1999; Wynne & Ryan, 1997). As Lickona (1997) wrote, "Especially important is teaching students what the virtues are, how their habitual practice will lead to a more fulfilling life, and how each

[1]Although we describe these two forms of the explicit perspective separately, they are sometimes difficult to separate in classroom action. Thus, they are labeled as "more direct" and "more indirect," and perhaps should be viewed on a continuum.

of us must take responsibility for developing our own character" (p. 55). In an interview with Kevin Ryan, Green (1999) quoted him as suggesting that moral values and behaviors should be directly taught by teachers:

> Teachers were dealing with history and literature in a moral vacuum. . . . I was appalled by how they were reduced to trying to be entertainers or psychological counselors, rather than an extension of parents who have a responsibility to teach proper behavior. As a result, students started to engage in a lot of disorderly conduct, bad language, and disrespect for each other and their teachers. . . . As a former student and having been a high school teacher myself, it became clear that teachers are more than information jockeys. They have a responsibility to help kids learn virtues like self-control, an understanding of justice, and an ability to persist at hard tasks. (p. 1)

To address this responsibility, Ryan and Bohlin (1999) suggested that teachers cultivate character through the curriculum.

They suggested examining the curriculum and deliberately integrating the concept of virtue into every subject that is taught. They wrote, "stories, biographies, historical events and human reflections provide us with a guide to what it means to lead a good life and possess strong moral character" (p. 95). Therefore, as a part of every subject they teach, teachers should tell the human stories of virtue, and to assist the teacher in how to do this, Ryan and Bohlin (1999) offered "100 Ways to Bring Character to Life." These 100 strategies for bringing character into the classroom include suggestions for building a community of virtue, mining the curriculum for virtue, and involving teachers, administrators, and parents.

Another example of direct instruction in character education is the Life Skills program developed by Susan Kovalik and Associates. Placed within a broader framework of Integrated Thematic Instruction, the Life Skills program has become very popular in many schools and school districts across the country. The Life Skills program consists of descriptions of activities designed to instruct students in 17 life skills that include curiosity, caring, cooperation, courage, pride, effort, common sense, and so forth and methods of assessing students' progress in the life skills (Pearson, 2000). In the program, as observed by Chow-Hoy (2001), each life skill is taught for 1 week, at which point students self-assess their progress, talk individually with the teacher about their progress, and receive a grade.

The major critique of this direct approach to character education focuses on the possibility that the goals of these programs relate more to social control rather than moral education. The programs are described as direct exhortation and placed within a transmission model of teaching (Solomon, Watson, & Battistich, 2001). Kohn (1997), for example, described these approaches as:

> A collection of exhortations and extrinsic inducements designed to make children work harder and do what they are told. Even when other values are also promoted—caring or fairness, say—the preferred methods of instruction is tantamount to indoctrination. The point is to drill students in specific behaviors rather than engage them in deep, critical reflection about certain ways of being. (p. 429)

Supporting Kohn's point, several studies suggest that external forms of control, positive or negative, are relatively ineffective for the internalization of moral virtues. Research on this form of moral instruction was first conducted in the 1920s; however, little current research matches the scope of the original research program of Hartshorne and May (1928). Using experimental and comparative methods, Hartshorne and May examined programs and results in religious, progressive, and traditional schools. They examined various factors such as honesty, thought to contribute to the moral character. They found little evidence for the effectiveness of direct instruction of the moral and concluded that teachers should provide opportunities for the use of forms of conduct that contribute to the public good (see also, Grusec, 1991; Lepper, 1983).

At the same time, one study that included ethnographic interviews with students who were in classrooms of teachers working with the Life Skills program did find that direct instruction in the virtues led to the students' use, easily and comfortably, of the language and constructs taught in the Life Skills program to describe their classrooms and their teachers' expectations for them. However, the study took place in two schools that stress personal responsibility for learning and building community within their schools. Thus there was considerable direct as well as indirect attention to virtuous behavior (Choy-Hoy, 2001; Richardson & Williams, 2000).

Character education programs such as the Life Skills program are representative of the direct approach to moral instruction. In these programs, the teacher plays a pivotal role in constructing the classroom environment. Whether using tasks from a "canned" character education program or constructing them, the teacher's role is to explicitly teach students what the virtues are and how to act virtuously. The role of the students in such a classroom environment is to complete the tasks assigned by the teacher and to show the teacher that they have met the intended outcomes. In this case, students should demonstrate virtuous behavior. Once a virtue is taught, students are expected to exhibit that virtue. For example, if the virtue of the week is honesty, truthfulness, or respect for others, students are expected to demonstrate that they understand the virtue by behaving accordingly. This behavioral expectation pervades the classroom environment and becomes a form of classroom management.

More Indirect Approaches to the Moral Curriculum of Classroom Management

Indirect forms of moral instruction deliver the moral curriculum of classroom management via the more indirect approaches than those described in the preceding section. The indirect approaches to moral instruction are more student centered and do not involve the teacher in continual direct instruction of desired virtues and their concomitant behaviors. However, they are considered explicit because their approaches to moral instruction are consciously planned. The teacher constructs an environment and creates activities for students to engage in and discover what it means to be and act as a moral person and citizen. This approach asks students to take responsibility for their actions in comparison to direct approaches that usually operate within a rewards/punishment motivation framework.

An example of an indirect but explicit approach to classroom management as a moral activity is the construction of a sociomoral learning atmosphere in the classroom and school. According to DeVries and Zan (1994): "The sociomoral atmosphere is the entire network of interpersonal relations that make up a child's experience at school. This network can be thought of as comprised of two primary parts: the teacher-child relation and children's peer relations" (p. 22). The teacher establishes the sociomoral atmosphere in the classroom through the manner in which he or she relates to children and organizes the classroom for activities. DeVries and Zan (1994) suggested that the most positive sociomoral atmosphere for children is based on cooperation and respect. In describing such a classroom community, DeVries and Zan (1994) wrote:

> The sociomoral atmosphere is one of respect. The teacher respects the children by consulting them.... Children's ideas are valued, and the Mentor teacher affirms them and encourages their pride in having good ideas. She takes a "we" attitude, frequently identifying with the children as a group member. She facilitates children's interactions among themselves. The attitude of the group is positive and reflects a feeling of community. (p. 14)

The role of the teacher in this constructivist classroom "is a companion guide who organizes a program of activities and . . . children are free to be themselves in the constructivist community atmosphere" (DeVries & Zan, 1994, pp. 16–17). The constructivist teacher consciously implements a moral curriculum of classroom management that uses authority selectively and wisely, respects children and their feelings, provides opportunities for children to grow into their personalities with self-confidence, respects self and others, and actively engages students in inquiry (DeVries & Zan, 1994).

The domain approach to creating a moral atmosphere and integrating values education into the curriculum is another example of indirect moral instruction (Nucci, 2001). Like DeVries and Zan (1994), Nucci (2001) attended to the sociomoral atmosphere in the classroom and the school. According to Nucci (2001),

> The sociomoral curriculum of the school, unlike its academic curriculum, is not confined to periods of instruction and study but includes the social interactions established by school and classroom rules, rituals, and practices, and by the less regimented peer interactions that take place on playgrounds, in cafeterias, and in hallways. (p. 141)

Moral instruction cannot be separated from the social climate or normative structure of the school or classroom. Therefore, according to Nucci (2001), "the manner in which teachers establish and maintain conventions and moral standards forms a substantial aspect of the school's contribution to students' sociomoral development" (p. 167). Domain-appropriate teacher responses to moral concerns focuses on the effects that actions have on the rights and welfare of persons (Nucci, 2001). An explicit moral curriculum based on "a climate of mutual respect and warmth, with fair and consistent application of rules, forms the elemental conditions for an educationally constructive moral atmosphere" (p. 167). Thus, through the sociomoral atmosphere of the school and classroom, the domain approach indirectly teaches students what is morally right, and in this way, the domain approach is a moral curriculum of classroom management.

Another example of an explicit form of moral instruction that is indirect is just community schools. Just community schools focus on the creation of a participatory, functioning, collective moral atmosphere in the school. Students and faculty participate in establishing and maintaining community norms through community meetings. Teachers function as collaborators, facilitators, and guides as issues of fairness or morality are focused upon through "higher-stage" reasoning (Higgins, Power, & Kohlberg, 1984).

Although teachers are conscious of the moral curriculum of the classroom and school environment, the moral instruction is indirect. Moral instruction occurs as students experience justice by interacting with their peers in cooperative activities, participating in free expression, learning respect for diverse viewpoints, and participating in democratic deliberations and decision making. The classroom environment is operated as a democratic community with students sharing fully in the establishing and enforcing of codes of conduct (McLellan, 1999), and as such, this environment serves as a moral curriculum.

Moral instruction is also indirect in a classroom environment where the moral curriculum of classroom management is based on an ethic of care (Gilligan, 1971; Noddings, 1984, 1992). Moral instruction based on caring reflects a sense of virtue, but it goes beyond one person's virtue in that it is relational. Caring teachers demonstrate that they can establish relations of care (Noddings, 2001) by modeling care for students, participating in dialogue with students, respecting students, and providing consideration for students (Noddings, 2002).

The moral stance within a caring classroom is that teachers enact caring by constructing a classroom environment based on an ethic of care, by establishing personal relationships with students, and by altering the curriculum and the learning environment to keep students engaged.

Caring can be enacted in three key ways: by being real and spontaneous, by establishing personal relationships with students in and out of class, and by altering the curriculum and the learning environment to keep students engaged. The classroom environment and curriculum is organized around centers of care: care for self, care for intimate others, care for associates and acquaintances, care for distant others, care for nonhuman animals, care for plants and the physical environment, care for the human-made world of objects and instruments, and care for ideas (Noddings, 1992). In caring classrooms, students are truly cared for and connect themselves in caring relationships to the matters they study (Simon, 2001).

Several studies on caring have focused on the tension between teachers' desire to be caring and their need to control students. Researchers have noted teachers'—especially preservice teachers'—concerns for maintaining order and control. Many of these studies contrast teachers' concern for order and control with their attempts to care for students. For example, Weinstein (1998) explored prospective teachers' conceptions of caring and order. She found that prospective teachers think about achieving order and enacting caring in somewhat dichotomous terms. Order is achieved through managerial strategies such as establishing rules, rewarding appropriate behavior, being consistent, establishing consequences, and "letting children know you're the boss." On the other hand, "caring was seen primarily in terms of interpersonal relationships—establishing rapport, taking an interest in students' lives outside of school, 'being there' for students" (p. 159). McLaughlin (1991) found a similar dichotomy between caring and control in his study of a student teacher's conceptions of classroom management. He concluded that a teacher's legitimate authority derives from personal and positional relationships with students.

Drawing upon some of the principles of caring and cognitive development, the Child Development Project (CDP) is designed to influence children's social, ethical, and intellectual development. The CDP attempts to incorporate inductive discipline, student autonomy and self-direction, student interaction, discussion, participation in positive, prosocial activities, clear adult direction and guidance, and a warm, supportive classroom and school environment. Studies on the CDP reveal positive effects on interpersonal behavior, social problem solving and conflict resolution skills, democratic values and interpersonal understanding, and social adjustment. Students view their classrooms as communities and, as a result, are more likely to adopt the values that are most salient in the classroom. The sense of community also positively correlates with prosocial conflict resolution skill, intrinsic prosocial motivation, altruistic behavior, enjoyment of helping others learn, and trust in and respect for teachers and engagement in class (Solomon, Battistich, Watson, Schaps, & Lewis, 2000).

Research on the CDP consists of a set of studies that focus on students who have been involved in CDP classrooms in comparison to those who have not. The studies reveal positive effects on interpersonal behavior, social problem-solving and conflict resolution skills, democratic values and interpersonal understanding, and social adjustment. For example, in a follow-up study of a subsample of former CDP middle school students and comparison students, data were gathered on 40 outcome variables using student questionnaires, school record data, and teacher ratings. The results indicate a significant difference between the two groups of students on 20 of the factors, including school-related attitudes and academic performance, personal and social attitudes, and positive and negative behaviors. The results of this study show a continuation of the positive effects of the CDP classrooms on students after they had left the program (Battistich, 2001).

The concept of developmental discipline was derived within the context of the CDP. Developmental discipline is based on the belief that socialization is a collaborative process and that children are naturally motivated to learn and to be empathetic and cooperative in a caring and nurturing environment. Based on attachment theory, developmental discipline purposefully integrates children's social and ethical development into daily classroom life. Teachers who accept and use developmental discipline believe that if their values are clear; if they meet children's basic human needs for autonomy, belonging, and competence; and if they create caring classroom communities, then students will more likely adopt the their values and become good people as well as good learners (Watson, 2003).

The case of ungraded primary teacher, Laura Ecken, illustrates developmental discipline in practice. In her classroom, Laura builds a classroom community based on trust, collaboration, and the power of the teacher–student relationship. She forms warm and supportive relationships with and among students, helps students understand the reasons behind classroom rules and expectations, teaches students relevant skills they may be lacking, engages students in a collaborative, problem-solving process aimed at stopping misbehavior, and uses nonpunitive ways to externally control student behavior when necessary (Watson, 2003). These instructional strategies are at the center of the moral curriculum of Laura's classroom management.

Oser (1986), drawing on Habermas' (1984) theory of communicative action,[2] proposed an indirect moral curriculum of classroom management. He espoused explicit moral discourse as the important and common denominator in all forms of moral education, and he pointed to how teachers should conduct themselves in such a discourse. He stated: "The central notion of moral discourse requires that after the presentation of moral knowledge, after the discussion of a moral or value problem, and after questioning the right way of action, the educators step back and stimulate a discussion in which the moral ideal is questioned" (1986, p. 920). In this context, teachers teach the use of rules and principles, regarding justice and respect in discourse, that enable us to defer personal success in favor of another person, a community, or a society (Oser, 1986).

Such teaching is what Oser (1992) and his colleagues called "responsible" teaching. Responsible teaching is explicitly moral. Responsible teachers understand that teaching an academic subject involves addressing the social and moral aspects of learning. Learning involves moral growth. Teachers must help students learn to reason about everyday moral issues, including how to treat one another. In addition, responsible teachers must anticipate and reflect on the consequences of their actions on students' academic and moral development (Hansen, 2001). As responsible teachers do each of these things, they are implementing an explicit moral curriculum of classroom management.

Summarizing Thoughts on the Explicit Moral Curriculum of Classroom Management

The explicit perspectives on moral instruction illustrate the ways direct or indirect instruction related to being a morally good person is intentional. For both the direct and indirect approaches, the conscious nature of providing a particular kind of moral instruction frames the moral curriculum of classroom management according to the approach used to foster moral student conduct. Indirect and direct approaches to moral instruction are similar in that they have the explicit goal that students will learn what it means to be and act as a moral person and citizen. However, the range of conceptions of what it means to be moral may differ depending on the perspectives of what ought to count as a moral value.

The primary distinction between the two forms of explicit moral instruction is the approach each takes to reach the intended outcome of being and acting as a moral person and citizen. The

[2]Oser's early research also contradicted Habermas' theory that suggests that real discourse is only possible at higher stages of model development. Oser (1984) found that discourse is possible at lower stages of moral development.

differences between the two approaches mirror the development of the two major perspectives on classroom management. For many years, classroom management was seen as a disciplinary activity in which students were informed of appropriate classroom behavior and rewards and punishment would be employed to assure compliance. The same is true of the direct instruction of moral behaviors, many of which are mapped onto behaviors present in a well-managed classroom. For example, one critique of the direct approach suggests that the goal is really one of social control rather than moral development. According to Carr (2000), there is a difference between moral education and social control: "Although there is undeniable overlap between these two concerns, it is nevertheless important to keep the differences between them clear" (p. 187). In some classrooms where the direct approach is used, students may exhibit moral conduct out of a need to demonstrate mastery of the moral curriculum of classroom management and comply with the social norms of the classroom rather than a need to act in morally defensible ways. It is also possible that in classrooms where the indirect approach to moral instruction is taken, students may be exhibiting moral conduct in compliance with social conventions rather than being thoroughly moral.

Despite this critique, a moral curriculum of classroom management, whether it relies on direct or indirect instruction, holds the possibility of fostering moral student conduct if it is well designed and implemented. To be successful, direct and indirect forms of moral education need to possess the characteristics of effective character education. That is, they need to be comprehensive, use multifaceted approaches, use approaches that target and succeed at promoting student bonding to school, have committed and informed school leadership, integrate character and academic education, integrate character and prevention education, provide ample and appropriate staff development, include direct teaching of relevant and social skills, involve parents, and encourage student reflection and grappling of moral issues, and modeling of good character by adults (Berkowitz & Bier, 2004).

CONCLUSIONS

This exploration describes two perspectives for viewing classroom management as a moral activity. The first suggests that the moral is implicit in all classroom activities, and the purpose of inquiry into classrooms is to make visible the moral dimensions and implications. The second focuses on creating and assessing programs and environments that foster moral conduct and development in students. The implicit perspective is descriptive rather than prescriptive; however, it is understood that there is a relationship between instructional actions implications and moral learning, whether intentionally fostered by the teacher or not. Within the explicit perspective, we describe two quite different approaches for instruction in moral education. Although the goals of the direct and indirect explicit approaches are similar, the moral theories and the methods of moral instruction are different. One approach provides direct instruction in the separate virtues, and the second provides activities and environments that allow students to develop their understandings of the virtuous judgments and conduct. In this section of the chapter, we attempt to move from the scholarly, analytic considerations of moral education to considerations of what this work means for teaching, teacher education, and research.

Teaching

Classroom management is an integral part of a holistic view of classroom teaching and learning, including the teaching and learning of virtue. Expertise in teaching requires a seamless coherence among style, method, and manner, leading to a form of teaching that is authentic, effective, and responsible. This means that it is important for teachers to have ethical understanding and knowledge that brings the moral nature of teaching and classroom interactions to a conscious level. Teachers with ethical understanding and knowledge recognize the possibility of fostering moral student conduct if the instruction and organization are well designed and implemented. Such knowledge and understanding leads to responsible teaching (Oser, 1992) and makes the implicit moral curriculum of classroom management an explicit one. As noted, responsible teaching is explicitly moral. Responsible teachers understand that teaching an academic subject involves addressing the social and moral aspects of learning and that learning involves moral growth in how to reason about everyday moral issues, including how to treat one another. With their ethical knowledge and understanding, responsible teachers anticipate and reflect on the consequences of their actions on students' academic and moral development and make changes on the basis of this reflection (Hansen, 2001). As responsible teachers do this, they are moving from an implicit to an explicit moral curriculum of classroom management.

There continue to be strong arguments concerning the methods teachers use to facilitate student learning and the development of the virtues. The questions revolve around whether direct instruction of the virtues and virtuous behaviors is really aimed at social control rather than moral development. In fact, whether the instruction appears as explicit or implicit in the teacher's actions or interactions with students or in the construction of the classroom environment, the *teacher's intent* is the key to understanding classroom management as a moral activity. For example, direct instruction in the form of character education could be viewed as an academic—perhaps even memorization—task in a classroom in which a teacher does not embrace the character education program but is mandated to enact it. Another teacher could use a particular character education program to attempt to control the behavior of the students in his or her classroom, even if the program's material stated that classroom control is not the primary function of the program. At the same time, a teacher could integrate a character education program into a classroom organization that stresses the development of independent thinking, and allow the students to direct the discussion about and learning of the virtues. Similarly implicit acts of constructing a classroom community, such as having private conversations with students, showcasing model student behavior, or calling out for the expected student behavior, could be a means for promoting virtuous conduct or for controlling the classroom environment.[3]

Thus, the moral stance of the teacher has a strong impact on the classroom management strategies that are used. As noted, some view classroom management as a set of technical skills related to controlling students. Fostering virtuous conduct may not be the teacher's intent. On the other hand, classroom management within a classroom whose teacher attempts to foster an ethic of care by creating a classroom environment around centers of caring will be strongly affected by this moral approach. And the approach to classroom management will strongly affect the moral development of the student.

Experience and research in classrooms suggest that student conduct is affected by activities in the classroom whether the perspective on the classroom environment and classroom

[3]In both the Fallona (2000) and Richardson and Fenstermacher (2001) work, all teachers who participated in the studies expressed great relief at either the introduction of a moral education program in their school (the Life Skills Program), or the collaborative involvement in the research project. The moral was something that they thought about a lot, but basically had shelved the thoughts because it was not seen by the school administration, school norms, and often the parents as something that should be taking place in or about the classroom. Teaching the character education program or discussing the moral dimensions of the classroom, in a sense, removed their shackles.

management is moral or technical. In response to the classroom environment and as a result of classroom management strategies, students exhibit conduct that may or may not be expressive of the virtues. Some evidence suggests that students respond with appropriate or virtuous conduct because of their relationship with their teacher (Watson, 2003), and other evidence suggests that students' conduct is shaped through reward and consequences (Canter & Canter, 1976, 2002). It would appear that regardless of the conscious moral perspective and instructional program or lack thereof, teachers influence immediate student conduct in the classroom. Therefore, teachers need to be aware of that impact, particularly with regard to how it affects the moral development of students.

Teacher Education

Within teacher education, classroom management is still thought of as a topic and classroom activity, separated from all other aspects such as instruction and relationships with students. As such, it is seen as a means to an end; and teacher education students are provided with a set of classroom management systems that they will be able to use when appropriate. Classroom management is taught as a demarcated unit or class, and the teacher education students themselves may begin to view classroom management as separate from instruction and interpersonal relationships (Weinstein, 1998).

As studies by McLaughlin (1991) and Weinstein (1998) suggest, one of the biggest challenges preservice teachers face is the dichotomy between caring about and controlling students. Not knowing how to maintain control over their classroom and be caring at the same time, beginning teachers often resort to classroom management strategies that emphasize controlling students. The result is beginning teachers not exhibiting their philosophy in practice or being the teachers they want to be, particularly with regard to how they construct the classroom and manage the classroom environment (Stanulis, Fallona, & Pearson, 2002). Thus, the task for teacher educators is to assist beginning teachers in working through this and to help them develop a teaching stance that is seamless with regard to teaching philosophy and methods of instruction and classroom management. Beginning teachers must be provided with opportunities to reflect on their beliefs about teaching and how they will enact them in a manner that is congruent with whom they want to be as teachers.

The curriculum of teacher education should strive to reduce the separation of classroom management from other functions, including the moral. It is important that teacher education students begin to understand the moral implications of such management tools as classroom rules (Boostrom, 1991), and turn taking (Hansen, 1993a). The separation found in most teacher education programs can work against teacher education students and beginning teachers from consciously learning to weave their goals, beliefs, and aspirations together with methods of moral instruction and classroom management.

Beginning teachers must be made aware of and reflect on their role as a moral educator. Whether beginning teachers embrace an explicit form of moral education or not, they must recognize the moral dimensions of teaching. This means that beginning teachers understand that teaching is an inherently moral activity and that there are potentially moral implications in everything they do as teachers. Of particular moral importance are their manner of teaching and interacting with students and the way in which they construct the learning community in the classroom.

To help beginning teachers develop an awareness and understanding of the moral dimensions of teaching, teacher educators can ask beginning teachers read, write, discuss, and reflect on the literature on the moral activities of teaching, on their observations of more experienced teachers, and on their own teaching experiences. Engaging in these activities will likely lead to teachers with a more developed teaching stance that attends to the moral activities of teaching and exemplifies their philosophies and the kind of teachers they want to be.

Research

A major question for research should focus on whether and how moral instruction and teachers' manner influences the moral development of student. Does what happens in classrooms—whether there is explicit moral instruction or not—function to affect present and future student conduct? And if there is no explicit moral education program in a classroom, what do they learn, if anything, from the implicit nature of the moral?

What is not known is the degree to which the moral conduct that is learned in a specific classroom and school transcends these walls in terms of place and time. That is, does a student who learns to not "put others down" in the classroom bring this admonition home in dealing with his or her siblings? And do these virtues carry over to the next grade or school level?

The question of whether students bring admonitions home is conflated by the goals of many teachers and schools that consciously limit the desired moral conduct to activities within the specific school and classroom. In analyzing the beliefs and observations of the teachers in the Richardson and Fenstermacher (2001) study, Richardson and Ratzlaff (2001) found that the teachers in one of the schools they studied did not believe that their purpose was to affect the moral conduct in all elements of their students' lives.[4] Instead, they felt that the moral conduct they fostered in their classrooms should be taught in a way that made it understood that it was limited to their classroom—they did not want to impose these morals on students' lives at home and in the community. This was seen in the classroom when a teacher would say: "In this classroom, we do not push other students." Regardless of whether the goals related to moral conduct were locally situated or more general, it would be useful to know how much carryover of moral virtues and conduct from school to everyday life ensues.

The question of whether virtues carry over to the next grade or school level is difficult to answer unless the research engages in follow-up studies of students who had been in classrooms in which a specific moral education program was implemented. In such a case, these students could be compared with those who did not go through the program. Hartshorne and May (1928) used this design almost 80 years ago. However, they did not look at the long-term results. More recently, students who participated in a Child Development Project program were followed several years later and compared with a control group that had not been through the program (Battistich, 2001; Solomon et al., 2000). As noted earlier in this chapter, the CDP students rated higher on a number of measures of moral development than did the control students. More of this form of research would be helpful.

More research on the explicit perspectives on moral instruction, like the CDP, and on the implicit perspectives on moral instruction that function as a moral curriculum of classroom management would assist in making the moral in classrooms more visible. In addition, it would promote a more holistic view of classroom management that considers the embedded nature of the moral aspects of classroom management functions. A more holistic view that embraces teachers' ethical knowledge alongside their content and pedagogical content knowledge would better serve students. As Wolk (2002) reminded us, "in school, the teaching of kids and their learning (or lack of learning) is intricately connected to how we manage them" (p. 6). Therefore, teachers must be aware of the moral implications of their teaching, curricula, and classroom environment.

---

[4]This was not the case in the second school, an Afrocentric urban K–8 school. In this school, teachers were explicit about their moral goals for their students in school and life. Because it was a school of choice, parents selected this school and were aware of its overall goals, and its place within the improvement of community.

ACKNOWLEDGMENTS

The authors wish to thank Rheta DeVries and Betty Zan, University of Northern Iowa, and Marvin Berkowitz, University of Missouri, St. Louis, for their reviews of this chapter.

REFERENCES

Ball, D. L. (1993). Moral and intellectual, personal and professional: Restitching practice. In M. Buchmann & R. Floden (Eds.), *Detachment and concern: Conversations in the philosophy of teaching and teacher education* (pp. 193–204). New York: Teachers College Press.

Ball, D. L., & Wilson, S. M. (1996). Integrity in teaching: Recognizing the fusion of the moral and intellectual. *American Educational Research Journal, 33*(1), 155–192.

Battistich, V. (April, 2001). *Effects of an elementary school intervention on students' 'connectedness' to school and social adjustment during middle school*. Paper presented at the American Educational Research Association, Seattle, WA.

Berkowitz, M. W. (1997). The complete moral person: Anatomy and formation. In J. M. DuBois (Ed.), *Moral issues in psychology: Personalist contributions to selected problems* (pp. 11–41). Lanhan, MD: University Press of America.

Berkowitz, M., & Bier, M. (2004). Research-based character education. *The Annals of the Academy of Political and Social Sciences, 591*, 72–85.

Berman, S. (1997). *Children's social consciousness and the development of social responsibility*. Albany: State University of New York Press.

Boostrom, R. (1991). The nature and functions of classroom rules. *Curriculum Inquiry, 21*, 193–216.

Buzzelli, C. A., & Johnston, B. (2002). *The moral dimensions of teaching: Language, power, and culture in classroom interaction*. New York: Falmer Press.

Calfee, B., & Brown, R. (1979). Grouping students for instruction. In D. Duke, (Ed.), *Classroom management* (pp. 144–181). Chicago: University of Chicago Press.

Campbell, E. (2003). *The ethical teacher*. London: Open University Press.

Canter, L., & Canter, D. M. (1976). *Assertive discipline*. Los Angeles: Canter & Associates.

Canter, L., & Canter, D. M. (2002). *Assertive discipline: Positive behavior management for today's classrooms*. Santa Monica, CA: Canter & Associates.

Carr, D. (2000). *Professionalism and ethics in teaching*. London: Routledge.

Chow-Hoy, T. (2001). An inquiry into school context and the teaching of the virtues. *Journal of Curriculum Studies, 33*(6), 655–682.

Colnerud, G. (1997). Ethical conflicts in teaching. *Teaching and teacher education 13*(6), 627–635.

DeVries, R., & Zan, B. (1994). *Moral classrooms, moral children: Creating a constructivist classroom in early education*. New York: Teachers College Press.

Doyle, W. (1986). Classroom management. In M. C. Wittrock (Ed.), *Handbook of research on teaching* (3rd ed., pp. 392–431). New York: Macmillan.

Dreeben, R. (1968). *On what is learned in school*. Reading, MA: Addison-Wesley.

Duke, D. (1979). Editor's preface. In D. Duke (Ed.), *Classroom management*. (pp. xi–xvi). Chicago: University of Chicago Press.

Evertson, C. & Weinstein, C. (2006). Classroom management as a field of inquiry. In C. Evertson and C. Weinstein (Eds.), *Handbook of Classroom Management: Research, practice, and contemporary issues* (pp. 13–15). Mahwah, NJ: Lawrence Earlbaum Associates.

Fallona, C. (2000). Manner in teaching: A study in observing and interpreting teachers' moral virtues. *Teaching and Teacher Education,16*(7), 681–695.

Fenstermacher, G. D. (1990). Some moral considerations on teaching as a profession. In J. I. Goodlad, R. Soder, & K. Sirotnik (Eds.), *The moral dimensions of teaching* (pp. 130–154). San Francisco: Jossey-Bass.

Fenstermacher, G. D. (1999, April). *Method, style, and manner in classroom teaching*. Paper presented at the annual meeting of the American Educational Research Association, Montreal, Quebec, Canada.

Fenstermacher, G. D. (2001). On the concept of manner and its visibility in teaching practice. *Journal of Curriculum Studies, 33*(6), 639–653.

Fenstermacher, G. D., & Richardson, V. (2003). An inquiry into the moral dimensions of teaching. In L. Poulson & M. Wallace (Eds.), *Learning to read critically in teaching and learning* (pp. 110–128). London: Sage.

Gilligan, C. (1971). *In a different voice: Psychological theory and women's development*. Cambridge, MA: Harvard University Press.

Goodlad, J. I., Soder, R., & Sirotnik, K. A. (Eds.). (1990). *The moral dimensions of teaching*. San Francisco: Jossey-Bass.

Green, H. (1999). Center's virtuous mission carries on. *BU Bridge, 2*(28), 1–2.

Grusec, J. E. (1991). The socialization of altruism. In M. S. Clark (Ed.), *Prosocial behavior* (Vol. 12, pp. 9–33). Newbury Park, CA: Sage.

Habermas, J. (1984). *The theory of communicative action: Volume One, Reason and the rationalization of society* (T. McCarthy, Trans.). Boston: Beacon Press.

Hansen, D. T. (1992). The emergence of a shared morality in a classroom. *Curriculum Inquiry, 22*, 345–361.

Hansen, D. T. (1993a). From role to person: The moral layeredness of classroom teaching. *American Educational Research Journal, 30*, 651–674.

Hansen, D. T. (1993b). The moral importance of teacher style. *Journal of Curriculum Studies, 25*(5), 397–421.

Hansen, D. T. (2001). Teaching as a moral activity. In V. Richardson (Ed.), *Handbook of research on teaching* (4th ed., pp. 826–857). Washington, DC: American Educational Research Association.

Hartshorne, H., & May, M. A. (1928). *Studies in the nature of character. I. Studies in deceit. Book One: General methods and results. Book Two. Statistical methods and results: Vol. 1.* New York: Macmillan.

Higgins, A., Power, C., & Kohlberg, L. (1984). The relationship of moral atmosphere to judgments of responsibility. In W. M. Kurtines & J. L. Gewitz (Eds.), *Morality, moral behavior and moral development* (pp. 74–106). New York: John Wiley.

Husu, J. (2003). Constructing ethical representations from the teacher's pedagogical practice: A case of prolonged reflection. *Interchange, 34*(1), 1–21.

Jackson, P. W., Boostrom, R. E., & Hansen, D. T. (1993). *The moral life of schools*. San Francisco: Jossey-Bass.

Jones, V. (1996). Classroom management. In J. Sikula (Ed.), *Handbook of research on teacher education* (pp. 503–115). New York: Macmillan.

Kohn, A. (1997). How not to teach values: A critical look at character education. *Phi Delta Kappan, 78*, 428–439.

Lemming, J. (1997). Research and practice in character education: A historical perspective. In A. Molnav (Ed.). *The construction of children's character*. Chicago: University of Chicago Press.

Lepper, M. (1983). Social control processes, attributions of motivation, and the internalization of social values. In E. T. Higgins, D. N. Ruble, & W. W. Hartup (Eds.), *Social cognition and social development: A sociocultural perspective* (pp. 294–330). New York: Cambridge University Press.

Lickona, T. (1997). Educating for character: A comprehensive approach. In A. Molnar (Ed.), *The construction of children's character*. Chicago: University of Chicago Press.

Lyons, N. (1990). Dilemmas of knowing: Ethical and epistemological dimensions of teachers' work and development. *Harvard Educational Review, 60*(2), 159–180.

McLaughlin, H. J. (1991). Reconciling care and control: Authority in classroom relationships. *Journal of Teacher Education, 42*(3), 182–195.

McLaughlin, H. J. (1994). From negation to negotiation: Moving away from the management. metaphor. *Action in Teacher Education, 16*(1), 75–84.

McLellan, B. E. (1999). *Moral education in America: Schools and the shaping of character from Colonial times to the present*. New York: Teachers College Press.

Miletta, A. (2003). *Managing dilemmas: uncovering moral and intellectual dimensions of classroom life*. Unpublished doctoral dissertation, University of Michigan, School of Education, Ann Arbor.

No Child Left Behind Act of 2001, Pub. L. No. 107–110 (H.R.1), 115 Stat. 1425 (2002).

Noddings, N. (1984). *Caring: A feminine approach to ethics and moral education*. Berkeley: University of California Press.

Noddings, N. (1992). *The challenge to care in schools: An alternative approach to education*. New York: Teachers College Press.

Noddings, N. (2001). The caring teacher. In V. Richardson (ed.). Handbook of Research on Teaching (4th ed, pp. 99–105), Washingtion, DC: AERA.

Noddings, N. (2002). *Educating moral people*. New York: Teachers College Press.

Nucci, L. P. (2001). *Education in the moral domain*. Cambridge England: Cambridge University Press.

Oser, F. (1984). Cognitive stages of interaction in moral discourse. In W. M. Kurtines & J. L. Gerwitz (Eds.), *Morality, moral behavior, and moral development* (pp. 159–174). New York: John Wiley.

Oser, F. (1986). Moral education and values education: The discourse perspective. In M. C. Wittrock (Ed.), *Handbook of research on teaching* (3rd ed., pp. 917–941). New York: Macmillan.

Oser, F. (1992). Morality in professional action: A discourse approach for teaching. In A. D. F. Oser & J. L. Patry (Eds.), *Effective and responsible teaching* (pp. 109–125). San Francisco: Jossey-Bass.

Pearson, S. (2000). *Tools for citizenship and life: Using the Lifeline Guidelines and Lifeskills in your classroom.* Covington, WA: Books for Educators.

Rest, J. R. (1983). Morality. In J. H. Flavell & E. M. Markman (Eds.), *Handbook of child psychology. Vol. 3: Cognitive development* (pp. 556–629). New York: John Wiley.

Richardson, V., & Fallona, C. (2001). Classroom management as method and manner. *Journal of Curriculum Studies, 33*(6), 705–728.

Richardson, V. & Fenstermacher, G. D. (2001). Manner in Teaching: The study in four parts. *Journal of Curriculum Studies, 33*(6), 705–728.

Richardson, V., & Ratzlaff, C. (April, 2001). *Teacher' perceptions of the moral dimensions of their classrooms.* Paper presented at the annual meeting of the American Educational Research Association, Seattle, WA.

Richardson, V., & Williams, N. (April, 2000). *In their own words: Students' views about the moral nature of the classroom.* Paper presented at the annual meeting of the American Educational Research Association, New Orleans, LA.

Ryan, K., & Bohlin, K. (1999). *Building character in schools.* New York: Teachers College Press.

Sherman, N. (1997). *Making necessity of virtue: Aristotle and Kant on virtue.* Cambridge, England: Cambridge University Press.

Simon, K. G. (2001). *Moral questions in the classroom: How to get kids to think deeply about real life and their schoolwork.* New Haven, CT: Yale University Press.

Sockett, H. (1993). *The moral base for teacher professionalism.* New York: Teachers College Press.

Solomon, D., Battistich, V., Watson, M., Schaps, E., & Lewis, C. (2000). A six-district study of educational change: Direct and mediated effects of the Child Development Project. *Social Psychology in Education, 4,* 3–51.

Solomon, D., Watson, M. S., & Battistich, V. A. (2001). Teaching and schooling effects on moral/prosocial development. In V. Richardson (Ed.), *Handbook of research on teaching* (4th ed., pp. 566–603). Washington, DC: American Educational Research Association.

Spady, W., & Mitchell, D. (1979). Authority and the management of classroom activities. In D. Duke (Ed.), *Classroom management* (pp. 75–115). Chicago: University of Chicago Press.

Stanulis, R., Fallona, C., & Pearson, C. (2002). *"Am I doing what I am supposed to be doing?":* Mentoring a group of teachers through the uncertainties and challenges of the first year of teaching. *Journal of Mentoring and Tutoring, 10*(1), 71–81.

Tom, A. (1984). *Teaching as a moral craft.* New York: Longman.

Watson, M. (2003). *Learning to trust: Transforming difficult elementary classrooms through developmental discipline.* San Francisco: Jossey-Bass.

Weinstein, C. S. (1998). "I want to be nice, but I have to be mean": Exploring prospective teachers' conceptions of caring and order.*Teaching and Teacher Education, 14*(2), 153–163.

Wolk, S. (2002). *Being good: Rethinking classroom management and student discipline.* Portsmouth, NH: Heinemann.

Wynne, E., & Ryan, K. (1997). *Reclaiming our schools: Teaching character, academics, and discipline.* Upper Saddle River, NJ: Merrill.

41

Zero Tolerance, Suspension, and Expulsion: Questions of Equity and Effectiveness

Russell J. Skiba and M. Karega Rausch
Indiana University

INTRODUCTION

There can be no question that schools need sound disciplinary systems to maintain school safety and promote student learning. Indeed, in the face of multiple-victim homicides in the late 1990s, schools have been increasingly motivated to address issues of disruption and violence. Pressure from teachers who are concerned about the safety of their classrooms (Public Agenda, 2004) and from parents who wish to ensure school safety (Pew Research Center, 2000) have motivated schools and communities to search for methods that can promote safe school climates maximally conducive to learning.

Yet the climate of fear that has prevailed in recent years has also generated support for more punitive methods of school discipline, often under the broad rhetoric of *zero tolerance* (Noguera, 1995). Zero tolerance emerged from national drug policy of the 1990s and mandates severe punishments, typically out-of-school suspension and expulsion, for both serious and relatively minor infractions (Skiba & Peterson, 1999). The rise of zero tolerance philosophy has led to substantial increases in rates of out-of-school suspension and expulsion (Michigan Public Policy Initiative, 2003; Potts, Njie, Detch, & Walton, 2003; Wald & Losen, 2003).

Thus, schools face what is an apparently profound dilemma. To fulfill their responsibility to promote safe climates conducive to learning many schools and school districts increased their use of procedures that remove some children from the opportunity to learn. Under federal education legislation, No Child Left Behind, schools are under a mandate to use "only practices that are evidence-based, so only the best ideas with proven results are introduced into the classroom" (No Child Left Behind Act Fact Sheet, 2001). The purpose of this chapter is to examine what we know about the use of school exclusion as a disciplinary strategy. Are zero tolerance, out-of-school suspension, and expulsion effective methods for promoting safe and effective school climates? Are there effective alternatives that can keep schools safe without removing students from the opportunity to learn?

CONTEXT, HISTORY, AND CURRENT STATUS

Purposes of School Discipline

Although school discipline has increasingly come to be associated in the public mind with the use of punishment and school exclusion (Skiba & Peterson, 1999), there are in fact a number of important instructional and organizational purposes to any school disciplinary system:

- **Ensuring the safety of students and teachers**. Incidents of deadly school violence in the 1990s have drawn acute attention to the need to guarantee the safety of students and teachers. The most recent national data on school safety suggest that there has been a 50% drop in violent crimes committed at schools since 1992 (DeVoe et al., 2004), yet one in three teachers still report that physical violence is a very or somewhat serious problem at their schools (Public Agenda, 2004). Clearly, a primary purpose of school disciplinary systems must be to prevent incidents that could threaten the safety of students or staff.
- **Creating a climate conducive to learning**. Even beyond issues of physical safety, students cannot learn and teachers cannot teach in a school environment characterized by disruption, chaos, or frequent behavioral interruptions. Research in educational psychology has shown that student learning is largely a direct result of the amount and quality of instruction that students receive (Brophy, 1988; Fisher et al., 1981; Hattie, 2002; Reynolds & Walberg, 1991; Wang & Haertel, 1994; Wang, Haertel, & Walberg, 1997). Effective disciplinary systems should improve academic outcomes by increasing the amount and quality of time teachers can spend teaching, rather than responding to behavioral disruptions.
- **Teaching students needed skills for successful interaction in school and society**. It is interesting to note that the word *discipline* comes from the same Latin root as the word *disciple*: *discipere,* to teach or comprehend. *Webster's Revised Unabridged Dictionary* (1998) defines discipline as "The treatment suited to a disciple or learner; education; development of the faculties by instruction, and exercise; training, whether physical, mental, or moral." Recent survey research indicates that a large majority of both teachers (93%) and parents (88%) believe one fundamental element of a school's mission is to "teach kids rules so they are ready to join society" (Public Agenda, 2004, p.8). Children will always require socialization, instruction, and correction that shapes fundamentally egocentric behavior into interpersonal skills that make them capable of interacting successfully with others in school and beyond.
- **Reducing rates of future misbehavior**. Behavioral psychology defines the term *punishment* as something that reduces the probability of occurrence of some behavior (Alberto & Troutman, 2003; Driscoll, 2000; Maag, 2001; Skinnner, 1953). One might then expect that those disciplinary interventions that are effective will lead to reduced rates of inappropriate or disruptive behavior in the school setting.

It is important to note that zero tolerance is not simply a strategy, but also a philosophy of school discipline (Skiba & Knesting, 2001). As such, there are a number of purposes for school discipline that are associated specifically with the philosophy of zero tolerance:

- **A belief in the deterrent function of school punishment**. An implied purpose of severe punishment is the deterrent effect on others who may witness that punishment (Noguera, 1995). Ewing (2000) argued that zero tolerance "appropriately denounces violent student behavior in no uncertain terms and serves as a deterrent to such behavior in the future by sending a clear message that acts which physically harm or endanger others will not be permitted at school under any circumstances."

- **Remove troublemakers in order to improve the school climate for others.** Central to the idea of suspension and expulsion is the notion that removing the most persistently disruptive students will lead to substantial improvements in the learning climate for others. A large majority of middle and high school teachers agree with this proposition, noting that if persistently troublemaking students were removed from school, teaching and learning would be much more effective for the remaining students (Public Agenda, 2004).
- **What happens if we don't punish?** This assumption is in some ways the inverse of a belief in the deterrent capability of punishment. Zero tolerance suggests that failure to punish misbehavior sufficiently will "send a message" that a school is not serious enough about safety (Larson & Ovando, 2001).

Before examining whether the disciplinary practices favored by a zero tolerance approach have been effective in meeting the primary purposes of school discipline, we review the background and definition of zero tolerance.

Zero Tolerance: Background and Definition

Zero tolerance first received national attention as the title of a program developed in 1986 by U.S. Attorney Peter Nuñez in San Diego, impounding seagoing vessels carrying any amount of drugs. U.S. Attorney General Edwin Meese highlighted the program as a national model in 1988, and ordered customs officials to seize the vehicles and property of anyone crossing the border with even trace amounts of drugs, and charge those individuals in federal court. Beginning in 1989, school districts in California, New York, and Kentucky picked up on the term *zero tolerance* and mandated expulsion for drugs, fighting, and gang-related activity. By 1993, zero tolerance policies had been adopted across the country, often broadened to include not only drugs and weapons, but also smoking and school disruption. This tide swept zero tolerance into national policy when the Clinton administration signed the Gun-Free Schools Act of 1994 into law. The law mandates a 1-calendar-year expulsion for possession of a firearm, referral of these students to the criminal or juvenile justice system, and the provision that state law must authorize the chief administrative officer of each local school district to modify such expulsions on a case-by-case basis (Public Law 103-227, 1994).

State legislatures and local school districts have broadened the mandate of zero tolerance beyond the federal mandates of weapons, to drugs and alcohol, fighting, threats, or swearing. Many school boards continue to toughen their disciplinary policies; some have begun to experiment with permanent expulsion from the system for some offenses (Potts et al., 2003). Others have begun to apply school suspensions, expulsions, or transfers to behaviors that occur outside of school.

Since the passage of the Gun-Free Schools Act, some form of zero tolerance policy appears to have become prevalent in public schools. Defining zero tolerance as a policy that mandates predetermined consequences or punishments for specified offenses, the National Center on Education Statistics report, *Violence in America's Public Schools: 1996–1997* (Heaviside, Rowand, Williams, & Farris, 1998), found that 94% of all schools have zero tolerance policies for weapons or firearms, 87% for alcohol, 79% for tobacco, and 79% for violence. It is important to note, however, that the NCES definition of zero tolerance is quite broad. One would expect that there are few school disciplinary policies that do not mandate some predetermined consequences for specific behaviors, and it is possible that the high prevalence rates reported for zero tolerance in the NCES study were due to an overly broad definition. A more typical and more limited definition of zero tolerance is as a disciplinary policy that is "intended primarily as a method of sending a message that certain behaviors will not be tolerated, by punishing all offenses severely, no matter how minor" (Skiba & Peterson, 1999, p. 373).

Frequency of Use of Suspension and Expulsion

Out-of-school suspension and expulsion are often viewed as a relatively linear response progressing from student disruption to office referral to school removal. It is important to note however, that any disciplinary action is the culmination of a complex process, not an isolated event (Morrison et al., 2001). Disciplinary actions are multiply determined by student behavior, teacher tolerance, school and classroom characteristics, and local and state policy. In addition, the length of out-of-school suspension can vary widely from a few hours or a day to 10 or more days. The most common cutoff in state law differentiating suspension and expulsion appears to be that removal of 10 days or less constitutes suspension, whereas removal for more than 10 days constitutes expulsion, but this is by no means universal (Skiba, Eaton, & Sotoo, 2004). Finally, because of the federal protections of free and appropriate public education (FAPE) for students with disabilities, those students are subject to a somewhat different set of disciplinary regulations for school removals exceeding 10 days (Yell, 1998).

These multiple sources of variation in the application of suspension and expulsion make it difficult to precisely estimate the exact frequency of out-of-school suspension[1] and expulsion. Available national estimates suggest that 1.5 million American students missed at least 1 day of school because of out-of-school suspension or expulsion in the 1970s; over the past decade, that number had doubled and reached an estimated 3.1 million or approximately 7% of the student population (Brooks, Schiraldi, & Ziedenberg, 1999; U.S. Department of Education, 2000). Both state and local district reports suggest increases in out-of-school suspension rates at the local level (Raffaele-Mendez & Knoff, 2003; Rausch & Skiba, 2004a; Richart, Brooks, & Soler, 2003).

Studies of school discipline (Bowditch, 1993; Mansfield & Farris, 1992; Rose, 1988; Skiba, Peterson, & Williams, 1997; Uchitelle, Bartz, & Hillman, 1989) have consistently found that suspension is among the most widely used disciplinary techniques, and at the office level, perhaps the most frequently used response to office referrals. Reported schoolwide rates of suspension at the high school level vary widely, from a low 9.3% of enrolled students (Kaeser, 1979), to 33.6% of the students in a given high school (Morgan-D'Atrio, Northrup, LaFleur, & Spera, 1996), to a reported suspension rate of 92% in one high school in East Baton Rouge, Louisiana (Thornton & Trent, 1988). Skiba et al. (1997), studying disciplinary referrals across all middle schools in one large urban school district, reported that one third of all referrals to the office resulted in a 1- to-5-day suspension, and 21% of all enrolled students were suspended at least once during the school year. In contrast, school expulsion appears to be used relatively infrequently relative to other disciplinary techniques (Heaviside et al., 1998). National and state data on the implementation of the Gun-Free Schools Act (Sinclair, 1999) show that fewer than 1 in 1000 students have been expelled for weapons violations under that law.

Rates of usage of suspension and expulsion also appear to be dependent on location and level served (e.g., elementary, middle, or high school), and do not appear to be spread evenly across schools. Out-of-school suspension rates appear to be highest in urban schools compared to usage rates at suburban, town, or rural locales (Massachusetts Advocacy Center, 1986; Rausch & Skiba, 2004a; Wu, Pink, Crain, & Moles, 1982). Specific to school level, suspension rates

[1] In addressing suspension in this manuscript, we refer only to out-of-school suspension, not in-school suspension, for two primary reasons. First, zero tolerance discipline has tended to rely on school exclusionary punishments such as out-of-school suspension and expulsion, rather than in-school consequences, for its presumed deterrent effect. Second, the apparent disciplinary paradox of exclusionary approaches in terms of threatening academic engaged time does not necessarily apply in the case of in-school suspension.

appear to be lowest in elementary school, increase and peak during middle school, and slightly drop from middle to high school (Raffaele Mendez & Knoff, 2003; Rausch & Skiba, 2004a). The slight drop in suspension rates from middle to high school has been hypothesized (Raffaele Mendez & Knoff, 2003) as being due to what has been termed the "pushout" phenomena: Students who had been suspended multiple times in middle school and early high school may have dropped out and thus not been present to be suspended in high school. Finally, rates of suspension do not appear to be evenly distributed across schools. One analysis found that schools in the top 10% of out-of-school suspension use accounted for 51% of all suspension incidents (Rausch & Skiba, 2004a).

Why Is Consideration of Efficacy Important?

Oftentimes, controversies about zero tolerance focus on the civil rights controversies aroused by removing an otherwise "good student" from school for what appears to be a relatively minor infraction. In response to the long-term suspension of an honors student for a sip of sangria, the *St. Petersburg Times* wrote in an editorial:

> Zero tolerance policies are inherently unjust and irrational because they conflate harms. Accepting a cup of sangria for a good-bye toast is punished as severely as a student who gets drunk on school property.... Bringing a butter knife to school to cut an apple for lunch carries the same expulsion as toting a loaded magnum. Those harms are not equivalent, and if they are punished with equal severity, the system looks both unfair and nonsensical. ("Zero sense," 1998)

Strictures against cruel and unusual punishment are fundamental to our legal system. It may well be that school punishments greatly out of proportion to the offense arouse controversy by violating basic perceptions of fairness inherent in our system of law.

Important as such concerns are, they may be less important to frontline educators than ensuring the safety of school environments. It might well be argued that, unfortunate as occasional violations of students' rights are, out-of-school suspension and expulsion are necessary to maintain safe and productive school climates. Certainly, schools have the right and responsibility to use any and all effective procedures to ensure a school climate that is conducive to learning.

Yet out-of-school suspension and expulsion, by their very nature, are interventions that pose some risk to educational opportunity. One of the most important findings of educational psychology of the last 30 years is the positive relationship between the amount and quality of engaged time in academic learning and student achievement (Brophy, 1988; Fisher et al., 1981; Greenwood, 1996; Greenwood, Delquardri, & Hall, 1984; Greenwood, Horton, & Utley, 2002; Wang et al., 1997). In addition, models of youth violence and delinquency have identified school alienation–school bonding as one of the strongest variables in predicting delinquency (Hawkins, Doueck, & Lishner, 1988). Thus procedures such as out-of-school suspension and expulsion that remove students from the opportunity to learn and potentially weaken the school bond must be viewed as potentially risky interventions.

Thus, questions about the usefulness of school suspension and expulsion are essentially questions of cost-benefit. Does the removal of troublesome students from school through suspension and expulsion provide sufficient benefits in terms of reducing disruption and affording a school climate conducive to learning to offset the risks to educational opportunity and school bonding that are inherent in disciplinary removal? The following sections review the literature on the efficacy of out-of-school suspension and expulsion in order to address that question.

HOW WELL DOES DISCIPLINARY REMOVAL WORK?

How effective is school disciplinary removal in preserving safe school climates conducive to learning, teaching students the behaviors they need to succeed in school, or deterring students from disruptive behavior? In the following sections, we examine the extent to which disciplinary removal might be considered an effective intervention, in terms of three criteria: (a) treatment fidelity, (b) educational outcomes, and (c) nondiscriminatory application.

Treatment Fidelity

Treatment fidelity, also referred to as quality of implementation (Gottfredson & Gottfrredson, 2002) or treatment integrity (Lane, Bocian, MacMillan, & Gresham, 2004), refers to the extent to which an intervention is implemented as planned, and has been increasingly viewed as a key factor in judging the effectiveness of behavioral interventions (Lane et al., 2004). Unless an intervention can be implemented with some degree of consistency, it is impossible to attribute any changes in school climate or student behavior to that intervention.

For traditional disciplinary interventions, one might expect two indicators of treatment fidelity or treatment integrity. First, because removal from the opportunity to learn is in most cases the most extreme form of punishment a school could administer, one measure of treatment fidelity would be whether out-of-school suspension and expulsion are reserved for those offenses for which they are intended, that is, the most serious offenses. Second, because disciplinary techniques are intended as methods to change student behavior, one would expect that variations in the use of suspension and expulsion would be based largely on variations in student behavior, not on idiosyncratic characteristics of schools or school staff. Both of these aspects of the treatment integrity of disciplinary removal are reviewed next.

Are Suspension and Expulsion Reserved for Most Serious Offenses? What types of infractions are suspension and expulsion used for? Are they reserved for only the most serious and severe of school disruptions?

Looking across studies of school discipline, it is clear that school suspension tends not to be reserved for serious or dangerous behaviors. Fights or physical aggression among students are consistently found to be among the most common reasons for suspension (Costenbader & Markson, 1994; Dupper & Bosch, 1996; Imich, 1994; Skiba et al., 1997; Stone, 1993). Yet the majority of offenses for which students are suspended appear to be nonviolent, less disruptive offenses (Children's Defense Fund, 1975; Raffaele Mendez & Knoff, 2003). After fighting, the most common offenses appear to be attendance issues (cutting class, tardiness, truancy) (Kaeser, 1979; Morgan D'Atrio et al., 1996; Richart et al., 2003) and abusive language (Imich, 1994; Kaeser, 1979). Other common reasons for school suspension are disobedience and disrespect (Bain & MacPherson, 1990; Cooley, 1995; Raffaele Mendez & Knoff, 2003; Skiba et al., 1997), and general classroom disruption (Imich, 1994; Massachussetts Advocacy Center, 1986; Morgan D'Atrio et al., 1996; Rausch & Skiba, 2004a; Raffaele Mendez & Knoff, 2003), often framed as a "catch-all category" (Dupper & Bosch, 1996). Figure 41.1 represents the relative distribution of out-of-school suspensions in a single state, as reported by Rausch and Skiba (2004a); the data show that 5% of all out-of-school suspensions are in categories such as weapons or drugs that are typically considered more serious or dangerous, the remaining 95% of suspensions fell into two categories: disruptive behavior and other. These data are consistent with Stone's (1993) conclusions in reporting the results of a national survey of 35 school districts representing over a million students: "It appears clear that on reviewing the data to determine if the crime fits the punishment, the answer is no" (p. 367).

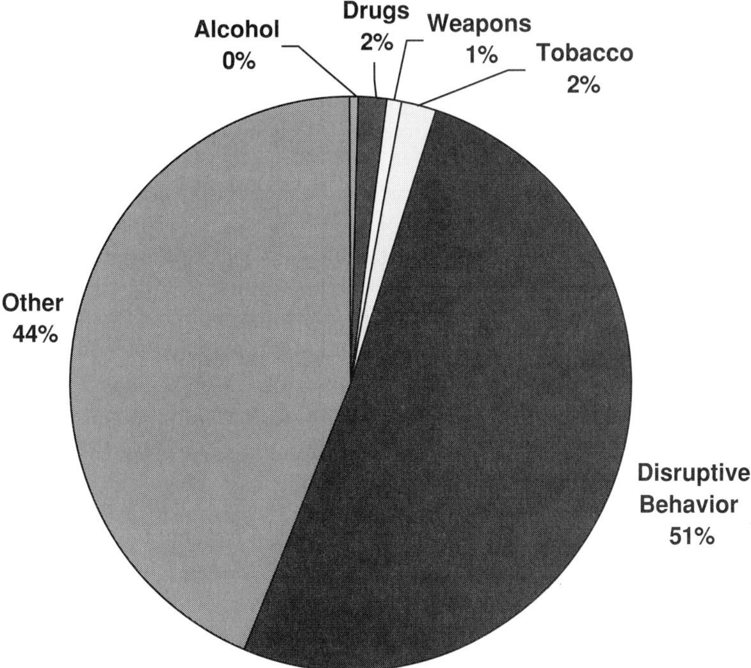

FIGURE 41.1. The distribution of out-of-school suspension incidents by category of infraction in one midwestern state for the 2002–2003 school year (Rausch & Skiba, 2004a).

One might expect that, used less frequently, expulsion would be reserved for more serious infractions. In one of the few reported studies of school expulsion in American education, Morrison and D'Incau (1997) found that student offenses resulting in expulsion tended to be offenses of moderate to high severity. The authors reported, however, that the majority of offenses in the sample they investigated were committed by students who would not generally be considered dangerous to the school environment. In the same statewide investigation reported earlier, Rausch and Skiba (2004a) found that 70% of all expulsions in the state fall into the categories of disruptive behavior and other. Some have suggested that zero tolerance and the increased involvement of law enforcement in schools has led to the "criminalization" of some relatively minor misbehavior (Richart et al., 2003; Wald & Losen, 2003). In general, although it appears that expulsion is reserved for serious infractions to a greater extent than suspension, the data are insufficient to assess whether that intervention tends to be reserved only for the most dangerous or serious of infractions.

Are Suspension and Expulsion Primarily a Response to Student Misbehavior? There can be little doubt that certain students are at increased risk for office referral and school suspension, and account for a disproportionate share of disciplinary effort (Tobin, Sugai, & Colvin, 1996; Wu et al., 1982). Eckenrode, Laird, and Doris (1993) reported that students with substantiated reports of abuse or neglect were significantly more likely to be referred for school discipline and somewhat more likely to be suspended, especially at the middle and high school level. Morgan-D'Atrio et al. (1996) reported that, of students who were suspended, 43% at the high school level and 38% at the middle school level had clinically elevated scores on one or more student and teacher subscales of the Child Behavior Checklist (Quay, 1983).

Yet explorations of suspension and expulsion at the school district level (Massachussetts Advocacy Center, 1986; Skiba et al., 1997) have also found the use of disciplinary removal to be extremely inconsistent from school to school, suggesting that there are other sources of variation than student characteristics or behavior in school rates of disciplinary removal. Investigations have found possible contributions to rates of school disciplinary exclusions at both the classroom and school level. At the classroom level, Skiba et al. (1997) described one middle school in which 25% of classroom teachers were responsible for 66% of all referrals to the office. There also appear to be a variety of ways in which schools contribute to out-of-school suspension. Wu et al. (1982) tested the contribution of both student and school characteristics to a student's likelihood of being suspended at least once during high school. As noted earlier, student behavior and attitude did make a significant contribution to the probability of suspension in that model. Regression analyses, however, showed that a number of nonbehavioral characteristics also made a significant contribution to the probability of being suspended, independent of other variables, including overall school suspension rate, teacher attitudes, administrative centralization, school governance, perceptions of achievement, socioeconomic disadvantage, and racial status. In the final model, including both student and school characteristics, Wu et al. (1982) reported that school and nonbehavioral student characteristics (e.g., race) made a more significant contribution to predicting school suspension than student behavior and attitude. This finding led them to conclude:

> One could argue from this finding that if students are interested in reducing their chances of being suspended, they will be better off by transferring to a school with a lower suspension rate than by improving their attitudes or reducing their misbehavior. (pp. 255–256)

At least some of the variance in school rates of out-of-school suspension and expulsion appear to be attributable to differences in principal attitudes toward the disciplinary process. Qualitative findings in the national report *Opportunities Suspended* (Advancement Project/Civil Rights Project, 2000) suggest that building principals used out-of-school suspension in direct proportion to their stated support for zero tolerance policies and procedures. In a comprehensive study of the relationship of principal attitudes and disciplinary outcomes, Skiba et al. (2003) surveyed 325 principals regarding their attitudes toward zero tolerance, suspension and expulsion, and violence prevention strategies. They found principal attitude and school disciplinary outcomes to be correlated: Rates of out-of-school suspension were lower, and the use of preventive measures more frequent, at schools whose principals believed that suspension and expulsion were unnecessary given a positive school climate.

In summary, treatment integrity is a key precursor to the effectiveness of an intervention (Lane et al., 2004): If an intervention is not implemented with sufficient fidelity, it may be impossible to even test whether it can be effective in changing student behavior. Findings about the implementation of out-of-school suspension raise questions about the integrity with which the interventions of suspension and expulsion are delivered. Contrary to expectations, suspensions and perhaps even expulsions are not reserved for the most serious or dangerous behaviors. Further, there is a very high level of inconsistency in the application of suspension and expulsion, and this variability appears to be due as much to classroom, school, or principal characteristics as to student behavior. Together, these findings raise concerns about whether the quality of implementation of out-of-school suspension and expulsion are sufficient to know whether they could be effective in changing behavior.

Outcomes of Disciplinary Removal

As is the case with any frequently used educational intervention, consideration of effectiveness is of central importance. Federal educational legislation has increasingly mandated the use of only those educational interventions that are "evidence-based." Disciplinary removal could be judged an effective educational or behavioral intervention if it led to improvements in either (a) individual rates of disruptive or violent behavior or (b) overall school safety or school climate. Data on the outcomes of exclusionary disciplinary approaches are reviewed in the following sections.

Do Zero Tolerance Suspensions and Expulsions Improve Student Behavior? Behavioral psychology defines an effective punisher as one that reduces the future probability of responding (Skinner, 1953). Yet descriptive studies of school discipline have found no evidence of reductions in misbehavior as a result of the application of out-of-school suspension. Rather, studies of suspension have found high rates of repeat offending in out-of-school suspension, ranging from 35% (Bowditch, 1993) to 42% (Costenbader & Markson, 1998). A recent longitudinal investigation revealed that the strongest predictor of a middle school student's number of out-of-school suspensions was the number of out-of-school suspensions she or he received in late elementary school (fourth and fifth grade), even after statistically controlling for student socioeconomic status (SES), racial categorization, special education status, teacher ratings of student behavior, and academic achievement (Raffaele Mendez, 2003). In a study of school discipline records for middle school students, Tobin et al. (1996) showed that students who were suspended in the first term of grade 6 were *more likely* to have discipline problems over the next four terms. Such results led the authors to conclude that for some students "suspension functions as a reinforcer (variable interval schedule) rather than as a punisher" (p. 91).

In the long term, school suspension has been found to be a moderate to strong predictor of dropout and not graduating on time. Analysis of data from the High School and Beyond study, a national longitudinal sample surveying 30,000 high school students, revealed that 31% of sophomores who dropped out of school had been suspended, as compared to a suspension rate of only 10% for their peers who had stayed in school (Ekstrom, Goertz, Pollack, & Rock, 1986). In a multivariate analysis of the same data base, discipline emerged as one of the strongest factors, along with poor academics and low SES, predicting school dropout (Wehlage & Rutter, 1986). Further, Raffaele Mendez (2003) reported that the number of out-of-school suspensions a student received as a 6th-grade student was negatively correlated with the probability that the student would graduate with his or her cohort of students 6 years later as a 12th-grade student. This relationship was stronger for African American students than White students.

Unfortunately, there is evidence that the relationship between school suspension and school dropout may not be entirely accidental. Ethnographic field studies of school discipline, interviewing administrators and observing the school discipline process, have noted that disciplinarians in troubled urban schools often view their role in large measure as dealing with persistent "troublemakers" who challenge the institution's authority (Bowditch, 1993). Over time, as such students develop a reputation, disciplinary contacts afford administrators the opportunity to rid the school of its most troublesome students:

> In this high school, the practice of cleansing the school of "bad kids" was quite widely acknowledged and equally appreciated by administrators, teachers, and counselors. Criticisms of the practice were voiced rarely, quietly, and confidentially behind closed doors. (Fine, 1986, p. 403)

In such a context, suspension may be used as a "pushout" tool to encourage low-achieving students and those viewed as "troublemakers" to leave school before graduation.

Improved School Climate? Rather than making a contribution to school safety, the increased use of suspension and expulsion seems to be associated with student and teacher perceptions of a less effective and inviting school climate. Schools with higher rates of suspension have been reported to have higher student–teacher ratios and a lower level of academic quality (Hellman & Beaton, 1986), spend more time on discipline-related matters (Davis & Jordan, 1994), and pay significantly less attention to issues of school climate (Bickel & Qualls, 1980). Wu et al. (1982) found that less satisfactory school governance was a significant predictor of the probability of a student being suspended at least once in his or her school career.

As noted, an important part of the purpose of school discipline is to maintain a school climate that is conducive to learning; thus one would in general expect a positive correlation between effective school discipline and levels of academic achievement. Emerging data, however, have revealed a negative relationship between the use of school suspension and expulsion and academic achievement. Skiba et al. (2003) reported that states with higher rates of out-of-school suspension had lower average scores on the National Assessment of Education Progress (NAEP), and Raffaele Mendez, Knoff, and Ferron (2002) found that student achievement in writing was negatively associated with out-of-school suspensions for middle and high school students.

The simple correlation between achievement and discipline could of course be due to a number of factors. For example, schools in more disadvantaged areas might have a higher percentage of difficult students who were both suspended and exhibited lower achievement. To test this hypothesis, Skiba and Rausch (2004) constructed a multivariate analysis investigating the relationship of school discipline and academic achievement, controlling for a number of demographic variables including the school's percentage of free- and reduced-lunch students (poverty), enrollment of African American students, and school type (elementary or secondary). Results indicated that higher school rates of out-of-school suspension were associated with lower passing rates on the state accountability test, regardless of the demographic, economic, or racial makeup of the school.

Nondiscriminatory Application

Federal education policy prohibits discrimination in the application or outcomes of educational interventions. The right not to be discriminated against on the basis of race, color, or national origin is explicitly guaranteed by the Equal Protection Clause of the Fourteenth Amendment and Title VI of the Civil Rights Act of 1964 (Browne, Losen, & Wald, 2002). Yet almost 30 years of research has documented racial and socioeconomic disparities in the use of out-of-school suspension and expulsion. These concerns become especially acute if, as suggested by the previous findings, the intervention to which some students are disproportionately exposed appears to be associated with a host of negative educational outcomes.

Disproportionality Due to Socioeconomic Status. Studies of school suspension have consistently documented disproportionality due to socioeconomic status (SES). Research has found that students who receive free school lunch are at greater risk of school suspension (Skiba et al., 1997; Wu et al., 1982). Wu et al. (1982) also found that students whose fathers did not have a full time job were significantly more likely to be suspended than students whose fathers were employed full time.

In a qualitative study of student reactions to school discipline, Brantlinger (1991) interviewed adolescent students from both high- and low-income residential areas about their reactions to school climate and school discipline. Both high- and low-income adolescents reported that the lower-SES students were more likely to commit more frequent and more serious disciplinary infractions. At the same time, both groups pointed to systematic social class discrimination, agreeing that whether a student is punished for a given infraction depends on student reputation, achievement, and socioeconomic class status. There also appeared to be differences in the nature of punishment meted out to students of different social classes. Whereas high-income students were more likely to receive more mild and moderate consequences (e.g., teacher lecture, moving desk), low-income students reported receiving more severe consequences, sometimes delivered in a less professional manner (e.g., yelled at in front of class, made to stand in hall all day, going through one's personal belongings).

Disproportionality Due to Minority Status. For over 25 years, in national-, state-, district-, and building-level data, students of color have been found to be suspended at rates 2 to 3 times that of other students, and similarly overrepresented in office referrals, corporal punishment, and school expulsion (Skiba, Michael, Nardo, & Peterson, 2002). Of particular concern in the administration of school discipline is the overrepresentation of minorities, especially African American students, in the use of exclusionary and punitive consequences. In one of the earliest presentations of statistical evidence concerning school suspension, the Children's Defense Fund (1975) studied U.S. Department of Education Office for Civil Rights (OCR) data on school discipline, and reported rates of school suspension for Black students that exceeded White students on a variety of measures. Rates of suspension for Black students were between 2 and 3 times higher than suspension rates for White students at the elementary, middle, and high school levels.

Since that report, documentation of disciplinary overrepresentation for African American students has been highly consistent (Costenbader & Markson, 1994, 1998; Glackman et al., 1978; Gregory, 1997; Kaeser, 1979; Lietz & Gregory, 1978; Massachusetts Advocacy Center, 1986; McCarthy & Hoge, 1987; McFadden & Marsh, 1992; McFadden, Marsh, Price, & Hwang, 1992; Raffaele Mendez & Knoff, 2003; Raffaele Mendez et al., 2002; Rausch & Skiba, 2004a; Richart et al., 2003; Skiba et al., 1997; 2002; Streitmatter, 1986; Taylor & Foster, 1986; Thornton & Trent, 1988; U.S. Department of Education, 2000; Wu et al., 1982). In one recent study of a large and diverse school district, 50% of African American male and 30% of African American female middle school students experienced out-of-school suspension during 1 school year (Raffaele Mendez & Knoff, 2003), rates that were substantially higher than White male (25%) and White female (9.3%) middle school students. Further, recent analyses (Raffaele Mendez & Knoff, 2003; Rausch & Skiba, 2004a) have found rates of out-of-school suspensions for African American elementary school students that are between 4 and 7 times greater than White students. The magnitudes of these disproportionate rates tend to remain or increase from elementary through high school.

Few investigations have explored disciplinary disproportionality among students of other ethnic backgrounds and those studies have yielded inconsistent results. Although disciplinary overrepresentation of Latino students had been reported in some studies (Raffaele Mendez & Knoff, 2003; Rausch & Skiba, 2004a), the finding is not universal across locations or studies (see e.g., Gordon, Della Piana, & Keleher, 2000).

Although minority disproportionality in school discipline has been widely documented, there have been only a few studies that have provided data on the reasons for that disproportionality. Those findings are presented next, categorized by factors that appear *not* to be associated with disproportionality in discipline, and those that appear to make some contribution to disciplinary disparities.

Factors Not Associated With Disciplinary Disproportionality

Socioeconomic Status. Race and socioeconomic status are unfortunately highly connected in American society (Duncan, Brooks-Gunn, & Klebanov, 1994; McLoyd, 1998), increasing the possibility that any finding of disproportionality due to race is primarily a byproduct of disproportionality associated with SES. As noted, low SES has been consistently found to be a risk factor for school suspension (Brantlinger, 1991; Skiba et al., 1997; Wu et al., 1982). In its statement before the United States Commission on Civil Rights, the National Association of Secondary School Principals (2000) thus argued that racial disproportionality in the application of zero tolerance policies

> is not an issue of discrimination or bias between ethnic or racial groups, but a socioeconomic issue. . . . A higher incidence of ethnic and racial minority students being affected by zero tolerance policies should not be seen as disparate treatment or discrimination but in terms of an issue of socioeconomic status. (p. 3)

Yet it is clear that race makes a contribution to disciplinary outcome independent of socioeconomic status. Using a regression model controlling for school socioeconomic status (percentage of parents unemployed and percentage of students enrolled in free lunch program), Wu et al. (1982) reported that, even with socioeconomic effects accounted for, non-White students still reported significantly higher rates of suspension than White students in all locales except rural senior high schools. Similarly, Skiba et al. (2002) found that effect sizes describing the size of the disparity between Black and White school discipline remained virtually unchanged when SES was statistically controlled, and that in fact, SES proved to be a far less significant and consistent predictor when both SES and race were considered simultaneously.

Higher Rates of Disruption Among Students of Color. Implicit in the poverty hypothesis for disparities in discipline is the assumption that African American students may engage in higher rates of disruptive behavior than other students. If so, disproportionate punishment would not be an indicator of bias, but rather an appropriate response to disproportionate misbehavior.

Investigations of student behavior, race, and discipline, however, have yielded no evidence that African American overrepresentation in school suspension is due to higher rates of misbehavior. Multivariate studies have shown that students from schools with more non-White students tended to have higher rates of suspension, even *after* statistically controlling for student attitudes and behavior (Wu et al., 1982). In a survey study involving 1,125 students in the 7th, 9th, and 11th grades in a mid-Atlantic city, McCarthy and Hoge (1987) collected self-report data concerning both rates of school misbehavior and rates of receiving school sanctions. Results indicated that Black students were in general more likely to be punished, and more likely to report having been punished, on three particular sanctions: told to bring parents to school, sent to principal's office for bad behavior, and suspended. Although there was no significant difference between the two groups on total school misconduct, two items (skipped class and carved desks) showed significant Black–White differences; both indicated levels of misbehavior that were significantly higher for the White students.

Indeed, it may be that African American students are suspended and punished for behavior that is less serious than other students. McFadden et al. (1992) reported that Black pupils in a Florida school district were more likely than White students to receive severe punishments (e.g., corporal punishment, school suspension) and less likely to receive milder consequences (e.g., in-school suspension). Further analysis of the data suggested that the African American students tended to receive these harsher punishments for less severe behaviors. These results are consistent with findings that African American students are referred for corporal punishment for less serious behavior than are other students (Shaw & Braden, 1990).

In a study specifically devoted to African American disproportionality in school discipline, Skiba et al. (2002) described racial and gender disparities in school punishments in an urban setting, and tested alternate hypotheses for that disproportionality. Discriminant function analysis revealed differences by gender for 12 of the 32 possible reasons for referral; boys received higher rates of teacher referral for 11 of 12 of those behaviors. Similar discriminant function analyses by race revealed differences on 8 of the 32 possible reasons for referral; in contrast to the results for gender, however, the group receiving the higher rate of school punishment did not show a pattern of more disruptive behavior. White students were referred to the office significantly more frequently for offenses that appear more capable of objective documentation: smoking, vandalism, leaving without permission, and obscene language. In contrast, African American students were referred more often for disrespect, excessive noise, threat, and loitering, behaviors that would seem to require more subjective judgment on the part of the referring agent. In short, there is no evidence that racial disparities in school discipline can be explained through higher rates of disruption among African American students. Rather, the available evidence suggests that African American students are subjected to office referrals or disciplinary consequences for less serious or more subjective reasons.

Factors Associated With Disciplinary Disproportionality

African American overrepresentation in school exclusion does not seem to be related to overall enrollment of African American students (Larkin, 1979). There may, however, be an effect related to changes in enrollment: Disproportionality in school suspension appeared to increase immediately after school desegregation, especially in high-SES schools (Thornton & Trent, 1988).

The disproportionate discipline of minority students also appears to be associated with an overreliance on exclusionary or punitive discipline. Schools with higher rates of suspension in general also have higher rates of overrepresentation of African American students in suspension (Advancement Project, 2000; Massachussetts Advocacy Center, 1986). Multivariate analyses (Felice, 1981) have found significant relationships in urban schools among high rates of suspension, minority dropout rate, and student perceptions of racial discrimination. Bullara (1993) argued that the typical classroom management style in many schools, relying heavily on negative consequences, contributes to school rejection and dropout for African American youth; for such students, "staying in school or dropping out may be less of a choice and more of a natural response to a negative environment . . . which he or she is trying to escape" (p. 362).

There is some evidence suggesting that the disproportionate representation of African American students originates at the classroom level. In a study of disproportionate discipline in urban middle schools, Skiba et al. (2002) reported no difference between African American and White students in measures reflecting disciplinary treatment at the office level (e.g., number of days suspended, probability of being suspended given an office referral). Further analyses showed that racial disparities in out-of-school suspension rates could be almost entirely accounted for by the fact that African Americans were twice as likely as White students to be referred to the office by classroom teachers.

Qualitative studies have explored possible mechanisms for this classroom contribution to racial disparities. In an ethnographic observational study of urban classrooms, Vavrus and Cole (2002) analyzed videotaped interactions among students and teachers. They found that many office referrals leading to school suspension were not the result of serious disruption or flagrant violation of disciplinary codes. Rather, many referrals out of the classroom were due to what the authors described as a students' "violation of implicit interactional codes," most often a student calling into question established classroom practices or the teacher's authority. Those students singled out in this way were disproportionately students of color. The authors concluded that:

> Suspensions are the result of a complex sequence of events that together form a disciplinary moment, a moment when one disruptive act among many is singled out for action by the teacher. This singling-out process, we contend, disproportionately affects students whose race and gender distance them from their teachers, and this subtle, often unconscious process may be one of the reasons why students of color often experience suspension in the absence of violent behavior. (p. 109)

Together, these results are highly consistent with suggestions that cultural discontinuities may create interactional patterns that increase the likelihood that African American students, especially African American male adolescents, will be removed from class. Townsend (2000) suggested that many teachers, especially those of European American origin, may be unfamiliar and even uncomfortable with the more active and boisterous style of interaction that characterizes many African American males. The impassioned and emotive manner popular among young African Americans may be interpreted as combative or argumentative by unfamiliar listeners. Fear may also play a role in contributing to overreferral. Teachers who are prone to accepting stereotypes of adolescent African American males as threatening or dangerous may be more likely to react more quickly to relatively minor threats to authority that might be ignored for other ethnic or racial groups, especially if such fear is paired with a misunderstanding of cultural norms of social interaction (Ferguson, 2001). Clearly, an important area for future research will be to identify more precisely the extent to which issues of teacher skill in behavior management or cultural competence contribute to disparate rates of office referrals or school exclusion.

Whatever the reason, racial disparities in school exclusion are not lost on students of color. Sheets (1996) interviewed students and teachers in an urban high school concerning their perceptions of school discipline. Both European American and ethnically diverse students perceived sources of racism in the application of discipline. But whereas European American students perceived racial disparity in discipline as unintentional or unconscious, students of color saw it as conscious and deliberate, arguing that teachers often apply classroom rules and guidelines arbitrarily to exercise control, or to remove students whom they do not like. In particular, African American students felt that contextual variables, such as a lack of respect, differences in communication styles, disinterest on the part of teachers, and "being purposefully pushed to the edge where they were expected and encouraged to be hostile" were the primary causes of many disciplinary conflicts (Sheets, 1996, p. 175). When asked to describe the rules of the school, European American students felt that there were clear rules regarding discipline that simply tended to be enforced differently for different groups; students of color, asked the same question, tended to insist that there were no rules.

In summary, it would be hard to argue that disciplinary removal constitutes nondiscriminatory practice. Rather, students of color, particularly African American students, and students from disadvantaged backgrounds are at increased risk of being removed from school through suspension and expulsion. These disparities cannot be explained simply by socioeconomic status or the behavior of students themselves. Rather, the evidence suggests that these disparities are at least in part a product of cultural discontinuity or insufficient training in culturally responsive classroom management practices. These data make a case that the use, and especially the overuse, of disciplinary removal carries with it an inherent risk of racial disparity.

Such findings are especially troubling given the generally negative outcomes that have been found to be associated with the use of out-of-school suspension and expulsion. Together, the data indicate that minority students are being disproportionately exposed to interventions that increase disciplinary recidivism, are negatively related to school achievement, and in the long term are associated with higher rates of school dropout. Indeed, Verdugo (2002) has argued that concerns about the equity and effectiveness of zero tolerance are inextricably linked:

> The right to a free public education was a hard-fought right. . . . Expelling or suspending children from school denies them their right to an education. The denial of this right is especially troublesome when we consider that many students are expelled for ambiguous violations of school policy. (p. 60)

Summary: The Failure of Zero Tolerance as a Disciplinary Paradigm

There can be no question that schools must use all effective methods at their disposal to prevent violence, and to ensure a school climate that is maximally conducive to learning. Schools have a right and responsibility to minimize disruptions that can threaten the integrity of the learning environment. In the wake of frightening violence in our schools in the 1990s, there can be little doubt over the depth of the consensus around these propositions.

Among the key words in that understanding however, is the term *effective*. In the climate of fear generated by real and perceived threats to the safety of schools, many schools and school districts adopted the "get-tough" deterrent philosophy of zero tolerance as an intuitive method for addressing perceived threats to school safety. It makes logical sense that strict levels of enforcement for both major and minor incidents will be effective in sending a message to students that disruption will not be tolerated. It is intuitively appealing to think that removing troublemakers will be effective in improving and strengthening the school climate for those students who remain.

Yet as data on zero tolerance, out-of-school suspension, and expulsion have emerged, they have overwhelmingly failed to support these "common-sense" notions that lie at the heart of the zero tolerance philosophy. Suspension and expulsion appear to be used too inconsistently to guarantee treatment integrity. There is no evidence that zero tolerance makes a contribution to school safety or improved student behavior. Rather, higher levels of out-of-school suspension and expulsion are related to less adequate school climate, lower levels of achievement at the school level, a higher probability of future student misbehavior, and eventually lower levels of school completion. Finally, over 30 years of consistent data concerning African American overrepresentation in suspension and expulsion indicates that disciplinary school exclusion may carry inherent risks for creating or exacerbating racial and socioeconomic disadvantage. This overrepresentation is not explainable by appeal to socioeconomic status or differential rates of behavior; rather, more promising explanations for racial disparities in school discipline are cultural mismatch, especially in classroom behavior management, or insufficient school resources that may create an increased reliance on suspension and expulsion. Together, these data indicate that the actual benefits of removing a child from school for disciplinary reasons are in no way sufficient to counterbalance other concerns created by those interventions in terms of loss of educational opportunity and threats to school bonding.

ARE THERE EFFECTIVE ALTERNATIVES TO DISCIPLINARY REMOVAL?

Given a mandate under No Child Left Behind to use only effective strategies, one might presume that over time pressure will increase on schools to develop disciplinary approaches that are better able to demonstrate the capability to maintain safe school climates with a lower risk to student learning. In the short term, however, it is unrealistic to expect that schools will simply cease suspending and expelling disruptive students. Indeed, in the absence of knowledge of other effective strategies, the abrupt removal of the tool many administrators believe is their only or best option (Skiba et al., 2003) could simply increase school disruption and chaos. Thus, it becomes extremely important to examine the available alternatives to suspension and expulsion, and the potential for their effective implementation in schools. To what extent do alternative interventions exist? How widely are they implemented? What is the process by which schools begin to move away from ineffective and punitive discipline toward more evidence-based procedures?

Evidence-based Prevention Strategies: Internal Validity

At the national level, there can be little doubt that effective alternatives for reducing the threat of youth violence have been identified. In the last 10 years, a number of research efforts and panels on school-based prevention of youth violence have been convened or sponsored by the federal government, including the Sherman et al. (1997; see especially Gottfredson, 1997) report to Congress, the *Blueprints for Violence Prevention* series (Mihalic, Irwin, Elliott, Fagan, & Hansen, 2001), the Department of Education and Juvenile Justice *Early Warning, Timely Response* guide (Dwyer, Osher, & Warger, 1998), and reports from the U.S. Surgeon General (Elliott, Hatot, Sirovatka, & Potter, 2001) and the Centers for Disease Control (Thornton, Craft, Dahlberg, Lynch, & Baer, 2000). These panels have in general relied on stringent methodological criteria to identify effective and promising programs for reducing youth violence. Their findings have been remarkably consistent with each other, and with scholarly reviews (e.g., Gagnon & Leone, 2001; Greenberg et al., 2003; Tolan & Guerra & Kendall, 1995; Zins, Weissberg, Wang & Walberg, 2004), in outlining an emerging conceptual model, and in identifying programs that appear to be most effective within that model.

In 1993, the American Psychological Association released its report *Violence and Youth: Psychology's Response* (APA, 1993) addressing what was then widely perceived as an epidemic of youth violence. That report framed youth violence prevention efforts in terms of a three-tiered primary prevention model. Since the publication of that report, a large number of researchers, policy makers, and professional organizations have articulated similar three-component prevention models as applied to mental health (Mrazek & Haggerty, 1994), youth violence in general (Elliott et al., 2001; Tolan et al., 1995), or school violence in particular (Dwyer et al., 1998; Larson, 1994; Sprague et al., 2001; Walker et al., 1996). The model became the centerpiece for efforts of the U.S. Department of Education to address school violence in a series of publications intended to provide guidance to America's schools concerning the prevention of violence (Dwyer et al., 1998; Dwyer & Osher, 2000). Although there is of course some variation in the definition of each of the three tiers of prevention, in general, school-based primary prevention approaches apply increasingly intensive interventions across three levels:

Figure 41.2 represents the three levels of a primary prevention model. As applied in school settings, the framework acts as a useful schematic for organizing violence prevention and school disciplinary interventions. The three levels in that model include:

- *Primary prevention:* To promote a safe and responsive climate for all students, primary prevention efforts, such as conflict resolution (Johnson & Johnson, this volume), bullying prevention (Hyman, this volume), social–emotional learning (Elias & Schwab, this volume), or improved classroom management (Carter & Doyle, this volume; Emmer & Gerwels, this volume), are implemented schoolwide.

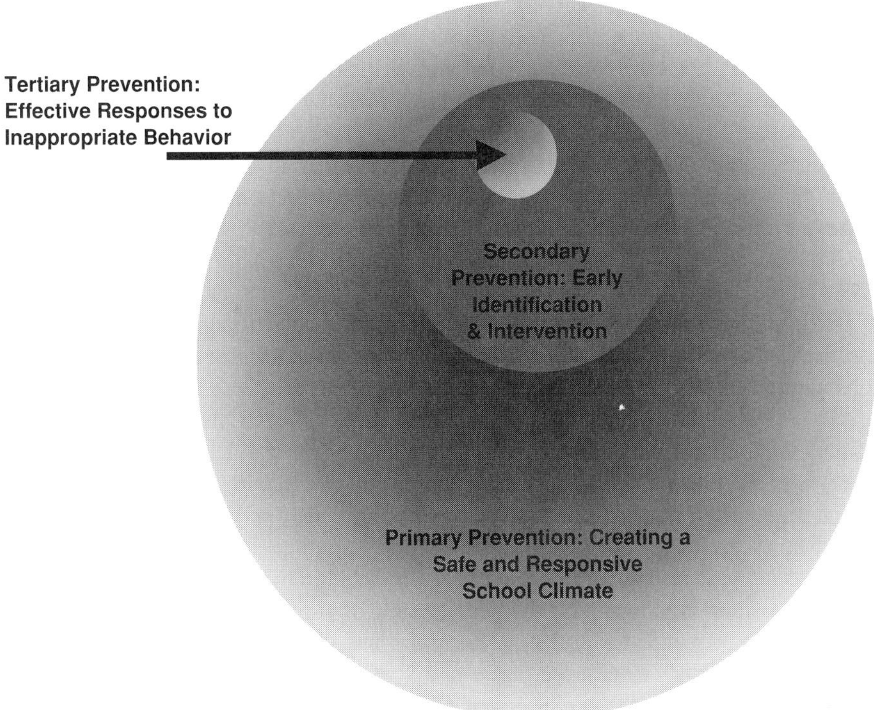

FIGURE 41.2. The Safe and Responsive Schools Model of school violence prevention (Skiba, Peterson, Miller, Ritter, & Simmons, in press). Primary prevention approaches to create a safe and positive school climate are applied universally, addressing issues of day-to-day disruption and school climate. Secondary prevention strategies of early identification and early intervention are applied to a smaller proportion of the school population that may be at risk for violence or disruption, while effective response strategies and intervention are in place for those students who are already engaging in disruptive behavior.

- *Secondary prevention:* At the secondary or indicated prevention level, schools implement early screening or identification efforts for children who may be at risk for violence (Walker & Shinn, 2002), and programs such as anger management or mentoring that can reconnect students with schools and other institutions.
- *Tertiary prevention:* Despite our best efforts, it is likely that there will always be some level of disruption, aggression, and perhaps violence requiring an appropriate response. Tertiary prevention interventions such as multisystemic therapy are targeted at those students who have already engaged in violence and disruption. Such efforts are characterized by a planned and coordinated response that seeks to minimize the future damage of aggression to the child and others (Bear, Webster-Stratton, Furlong, & Rhee, 2000; Walker & Shinn, 2002).

Evidence-based Prevention Strategies: External Validity

Unfortunately, the existence of an extensive and relatively consistent data base on school-based intervention for violence prevention does not in any way guarantee that those strategies will be implemented as intended in actual school settings. G. Gottfredson et al. (2000) surveyed a nationally representative sample of school principals and teachers regarding the implementation of prevention programs at their school. Survey results indicated that more than 50% of reporting principals reported the presence of a prevention activity in most of the 20 prevention categories surveyed. Yet surveys of teachers found that implementation of prevention activities was typically at a level that would be considered unacceptable for guaranteeing efficacy. Of particular interest, the prevention practices that were reported to be most widely used were not necessarily those identified in evidence-based literature, but were instead procedures that tended to be less widely researched with respect to their impact on behavior (e.g., changes in class size or promotion practices).

Indeed, some findings have raised questions about the capability of schools to implement prevention programs with an acceptable degree of treatment integrity. Gottfredson, Gottfredson, and Skroban (1998) attempted to implement a multicomponent violence prevention strategy in a single middle school. The program was designed to include only interventions with previous demonstrations of effect, such as life skills training (Botvin, Mihalic, & Grotpeter, 1998), and violence prevention curricula (Guerra & Slaby, 1990). Despite levels of training of school personnel that were well in excess of typical research practice in school settings, however, Gottfredson et al. reported that few of the components of the program were received by more than 60% of the students, and the intensity of the interventions was also lower than expected.

It has been suggested that the problem of implementation of evidence-based violence prevention programs in school settings may lie in the nature of the research enterprise itself, with its emphasis on internal validity and experimental control. Shoenwald and Hoagwood (2001) argued that the majority of evidence-based practices have been developed under "test tube conditions" that fail to mirror the realities of school settings. In the main, the programs most often identified as "effective" or "promising" entail implementation that includes the presence and guidance of highly trained professionals, researchers, or graduate assistants, often accompanied by an large influx of grant support (Gottfredson, 2001). These additional resources enable researchers to maintain the rigorous experimental conditions that are critical to ensuring internal validity judgments about their treatments. Yet paradoxically, such arrangements probably also limit the applicability of evidence-based procedures in real-world school settings, because those settings typically lack access to highly trained researchers, graduate assistants, and large amounts of discretionary funds. In response to this issue, Jensen, Hoagwood, and Trickett (1999) have suggested that it may be necessary for prevention researchers to reverse their priorities; that is, to begin by developing treatments that are "sensible . . . , feasible, flexible, and palatable" (p. 209), and to move on to the demonstration of experimental control only after such practical concerns are met.

Improving the Implementation of Alternatives to Out-of-School Suspension and Expulsion

Thus, extensive reviews using rigorous criteria have identified a range of alternatives to suspension and expulsion for maintaining school safety and school discipline. Yet there is also cause for skepticism concerning the extent to which empirically validated methods of violence prevention are, or even could be, implemented in schools. Together, these facts suggest that the most critical challenge facing alternative approaches to school discipline is to find effective methods of improving the school-based implementation of proven effective practices in school discipline and school violence prevention.

A number of strategies have been designed to improve implementation of such alternatives and are typically characterized by an attention to the process by which schools implement effective alternatives tailored to local needs. The Positive Behavior Interventions and Supports (PBIS) model focuses on providing comprehensive, positive, and locally generated systems of proactive resources to schools, especially classroom teachers (Lewis, Trussell, Sunderland, & Richter, this volume). A school PBIS plan is typically created and implemented by a team of local educators, community members, and parents who review their school's discipline and other relevant data to identify areas of concern, generate positive and support-focused intervention suggestions to change the contextual variables hypothesized to be contributing to these concerns, implement selected interventions, and track or modify the effects of the intervention. Tests of implementation have documented decreased rates of office referrals, suspensions, expulsions, and improvements on measures of school climate (Rosenberg & Jackman, 2003), as well as decreased time spent on discipline at the administrative level (Scott & Barrett, 2004). A second approach that has shown some success in schoolwide restructuring of disciplinary practices is the Safe and Responsive Schools (SRS) model (Skiba, Peterson, Miller, Ritter, & Simmons, in press). The goal of the SRS approach has been to increase the knowledge base of teachers and administrators concerning what works in discipline and violence prevention, and to develop school safety plans responsive to student needs. The process leads participating schools through a strategic planning process involving local needs assessment, review of best practices, and tailoring a local plan matching intervention strategies with school concerns. Again, results have been encouraging: highly favorable assessments of the treatment acceptability of the process were matched by substantial reductions in rates of out-of-school suspension and expulsion (Skiba et al., in press).

Using a Process–Product Approach: What Works in Practice

An alternative to infusing research-based strategies into school settings is to explore "naturally occurring" interventions and strategies, that is, practices already used in classrooms and schools to reach more positive outcomes. In the early 1980s, such process–product studies of classroom teaching (Berliner, 1989; Brophy, 1988; Emmer & Evertson, 1981; Fisher et al., 1981) revolutionized our knowledge of effective teaching, by examining academic achievement outcomes associated with a variety of instructional and classroom management practices. A process–product approach might also be used to identify currently effective disciplinary strategies across a variety of economic and demographic profiles, in the hopes of disseminating those effective approaches to other similarly situated schools. Skiba and colleagues (Skiba et al., 2002; Skiba, Rausch, & Ritter, 2004; Rausch & Skiba, 2004b) have begun piloting this approach, interviewing principals in one midwestern state to identify disciplinary practices that are currently in use in schools attempting to maintain a safe and productive learning climate without resorting to exclusionary school discipline.

Skiba et al. (2004) reported that the strategies reported by these principals in no way involved a relaxation of academic standards or behavioral expectations. Most of the principals who were interviewed explicitly stated that they had no hesitation in using suspension or expulsion to remove a student that they deemed a realistic threat to school safety. But these principals also expressed a commitment to the use of a wide range of alternatives to ensure that exclusionary discipline was not overused. Most reported that they had put in place some process to clarify expectations with school staff concerning what constitutes an appropriate office referral, and conducted in-service training in classroom management. Many of the schools reported the use of conflict resolution, life skills training, or bullying prevention programs to instruct students in alternatives to violence for resolving interpersonal conflict. For students at risk for disruption and violence, the responding principals described programs for promoting parental involvement and increased support, such as mentoring. Finally, a number of these schools and school districts reported creative alternative programs that continue to provide educational opportunities to students even after being suspended or expelled from school.

There is limited evidence suggesting that such an approach can have substantial effects on both school discipline and school levels of academic achievement. In one middle school (Rausch & Skiba, 2004b), the programs and philosophies implemented by a new principal and building-leadership team saw a 1-year drop in the out-of-school suspension rate from 50.67 to 18.53 incidents per 100 students, and this lower rate remained consistent over a period of 4 years. In addition, the change in the disciplinary climate appears to have been concurrent with improved achievement outcomes; with the change in leadership that brought a different philosophy and programmatic approach to student discipline, scores on the state accountability test, which had been substantially below the state average, have been consistently above the average achievement rate for middle schools in the state.

Although these data must be regarded as preliminary and merely suggestive of positive outcomes, they also argue that a return to the process–product research paradigm would be fruitful in the domain of school discipline. Such an approach may have important implications for practice and dissemination. An examination of current effective practice may address the difficult issue of the external validity of preventive disciplinary alternatives: One might well expect that school practitioners would be more amenable to implementing disciplinary interventions already implemented and tested by their peers in practice.

CONCLUSIONS AND RECOMMENDATIONS

The current status of research and practice in school discipline provides a double quandary. On the one hand, the most widely used disciplinary procedures in schools today—out-of-school suspension and expulsion—are associated with a host of negative outcomes, including recidivism, lower achievement, and school dropout. These concerns are exacerbated by the fact that students of color, particularly African American students, are disproportionately exposed to these outcomes by being overrepresented among those who are suspended or expelled. On the other hand, although a number of procedures have been identified that clearly lead to more positive outcomes, these procedures do not appear to be implemented in schools with a frequency or fidelity that could be expected to yield improved outcomes.

The recent history of school disciplinary policy has seen an increasing reliance on school exclusion through suspension or expulsion. Yet the findings of recent research on school discipline have begun to challenge the notion that preserving a school climate conducive to learning requires the removal of students who engage in disruption. Indeed, emerging data have begun to document a negative correlation between school levels of suspension and expulsion and school achievement (Raffaele Mendez et al., 2002; Skiba et al., 2003). If that finding continues to be validated, one might expect that positive alternatives that can maintain an orderly school climate without reducing educational opportunity would join the evidence-based procedures that schools are mandated to use under No Child Left Behind.

Recommendations for modifying or moving away from a zero tolerance model have begun to emerge. Educational professionals and policy makers wishing to move toward best-practice school discipline and violence prevention programs might consider advocating for the following:

1. **Reserve zero tolerance disciplinary removals for only the most serious and severe of disruptive behaviors, and define those behaviors explicitly.** Balancing the need to protect against the most serious infractions with the absence of efficacy data for the extension of zero tolerance to less serious offenses, a best-evidence approach suggests restricting zero tolerance to only the most serious of infractions, such as possession of firearms on school property.

2. **Replace one-size-fits-all disciplinary strategies with graduated systems of discipline, wherein consequences are geared to the seriousness of the infraction.** In response to community concerns about punishments that do not fit the crime under zero tolerance, many school districts are implementing graduated systems of discipline, reserving severe punishment for only the most serious, safety-threatening offenses. Less serious offenses, such as classroom disruption, attendance related behaviors, or even minor fights among students are met with less severe consequences that might range from in-school suspension to parent contact, reprimands, community service, or counseling.
3. **Define all infractions, whether major or minor, carefully.** Garibaldi, Blanchard, and Brooks (1996) argued that inadequate reporting and definition allow greater room for individual bias to emerge in the disciplinary process. Carefully drawn definitions of all behaviors subject to the school disciplinary code protect both students from inequitable consequences and school officials from charges of unfair and arbitrary application of school policy.
4. **Expand the array of options available to schools for dealing with disruptive or violent behavior.** One must assume that school boards or administrators implementing zero tolerance policies are not doing so because they take pleasure in removing children from school. Rather, many school disciplinarians may simply be unaware of more effective alternatives. School psychologists can play a critical role in the development of more effective disciplinary systems by becoming aware of best practice knowledge on effective preventive alternatives and disseminating that information to administrators and teachers.
5. **Implement preventive measures that can improve school climate and reconnect alienated students.** Osher, Sandler, and Nelson (2001) noted that many of the most effective programs in the nation for dealing with student disruption are characterized by high levels of student support and community. Solutions to the zero tolerance dilemma might also seek to shift the focus from swift and certain punishment to using research-supported strategies like conflict resolution and bullying prevention to improve the sense of school community and belongingness.
6. **Improve collaboration and communication among schools, parents, juvenile justice, and mental health to develop an array of alternatives for challenging youth.** The behaviors of the most challenging of youth can seriously disrupt school environments, and the problems faced by those youth and their family often exceed the abilities of any one agency to address them. System of care and wraparound approaches (Burchard & Clarke, 1990), in which education, mental health, juvenile justice, and other community youth-serving agencies collaborate to develop integrated services, offer promise as a way of providing additional resources to schools to address the most serious and challenging behaviors.
7. **Evaluate all school discipline or school violence prevention strategies to ensure that all disciplinary interventions, programs, or strategies are truly affecting student behavior and school safety.** Accountability of instruction has become a national priority. There is no reason why behavioral or disciplinary procedures should be held to a lower standard of accountability. The implementation of any procedure addressing student behavior or school violence—whether it be zero tolerance, conflict resolution, school security, or classroom management—must be accompanied by an evaluation adequate to determine whether that procedure has indeed made a positive contribution to improving school safety or student behavior. Without such data, there is the danger that time and resources will be wasted on strategies that sound appealing, but in fact do little to decrease a school's chances of disruption or violence.

SUMMARY

Clear and effective school discipline systems are critical in maintaining safe school environments conducive to learning. Yet the evidence has failed to support disciplinary exclusion as an intervention capable of ensuring such a climate. Viewed as behavioral interventions, out-of-school suspension and expulsion appear to lack treatment fidelity, are associated with negative outcomes in terms of school climate, student behavior, student achievement, and school dropout, and show consistent evidence of racial and socioeconomic disparities. Fortunately, effective alternatives are emerging, many with strong empirical support. Although problems of implementation clearly remain to be solved, school reform strategies such as Positive Behavioral Supports and Safe and Responsive Schools appear to hold promise as methods for improving the implementation of effective school disciplinary policies and practices. The challenge for research and practice will be to identify ways to increase the implementation of effective disciplinary systems that maintain school safety without removing students from the opportunity to learn.

ACKNOWLEDGMENT

The authors thank Edmund Emmer, The University of Texas, Austin, for his review of this chapter.

REFERENCES

Advancement Project/Civil Rights Project. (2000, February). *Opportunities suspended: The devastating consequences of zero tolerance and school discipline*. Cambridge, MA: Author.

Alberto, P. A., & Troutman, A. C. (2003). *Applied behavior analysis for teachers*. Upper Saddle River, NJ: Merrill/Prentice Hall.

American Psychological Association. (1993). *Violence and youth: Psychology's response*. Washington, DC: Author.

Bain, A., & MacPherson, A. (1990). An examination of the system-wide use of exclusion with disruptive students. *Australia and New Zealand Journal of Developmental Disabilities, 16*, 109–123.

Bear, G. C., Webster-Stratton, C., Furlong, M. J., & Rhee, S. (2000). Preventing aggression and violence. In K. M. Minke & G. C. Bear (Eds.), *Preventing school problems, promoting school success: Strategies and programs that work.* Bethesda, MD: National Association of School Psychologists.

Berliner, D. C. (1989). The place of process-product research in developing the agenda for research on teacher thinking. *Educational Psychologist, 24*, 325–344.

Bickel, F., & Qualls, R. (1980). The impact of school climate on suspension rates in the Jefferson County Public Schools. *Urban Review, 12*, 79–86.

Botvin, G. J., Mihalic, S. F., & Grotpeter, J. K. (1998). *Blueprints for violence prevention, book five: Life skills training*. Boulder, CO: Center for the Study and Prevention of Violence.

Bowditch, C. (1993). Getting rid of troublemakers: High school disciplinary procedures and the production of dropouts. *Social Problems, 40*, 493–507.

Brantlinger, E. (1991). Social class distinctions in adolescents' reports of problems and punishment in school. *Behavioral Disorders, 17*, 36–46.

Brooks, K., Schiraldi, V., & Ziedenberg, J. (1999). *School house hype: Two years later*. San Francisco: Center on Juvenile and Criminal Justice. Retrieved July 21, 2004, from http://www.cjcj.org

Brophy, J. E. (1988). Research linking teacher behavior to student achievement: Potential implications for instruction of Chapter 1 students. *Educational Psychologist, 23*, 235–286.

Browne, J. A., Losen, D. J., & Wald, J. (2002). Zero tolerance: Unfair, with little recourse. In R. J. Skiba & G. G. Noam (Eds.), *New directions for youth development* (no. 92: Zero tolerance: Can suspension and expulsion keep schools safe?) (pp. 73–99). San Francisco: Jossey-Bass.

Bullara, D. T. (1993). Classroom management strategies to reduce racially-biased treatment of students. *Journal of Education and Psychological Consultation, 4*, 357–368.

Burchard, J. D., & Clarke, J. D. (1990). The role of individualized care in a service delivery system for children and adolescents with severely maladjusted behavior. *The Journal of Mental Health Administration, 17*, 48–60.

Children's Defense Fund. (1975). *School suspensions: Are they helping children?* Cambridge, MA: Washington Research Project.

Cooley, S. (1995). *Suspension/expulsion of regular and special education students in Kansas: A report to the Kansas State Board of Education.* Topeka: Kansas State Board of Education.

Costenbader, V., & Markson, S. (1998). School suspension: A study with secondary school students. *Journal of School Psychology, 36*, 59–82.

Costenbader, V. K., & Markson, S. (1994). School suspension: A survey of current policies and practices. *NASSP Bulletin, 78*, 103–107.

Davis, J. E., & Jordan, W. J. (1994). The effects of school context, structure, and experiences on African American males in middle and high schools. *Journal of Negro Education, 63*, 570–587.

DeVoe, J. F., Peter, K., Kaufman, P., Miller, A., Noonan, M., Snyder, T. D., & Baum, K. (2004). *Indicators of school crime and safety: 2004.* U.S. Departments of Education and Justice. Washington, DC: U.S. Government Printing Office.

Driscoll, M. P. (2000). *Psychology of learning for instruction* (2nd ed.). Boston: Allyn & Bacon.

Duncan, G. J., Brooks-Gunn, J., & Klebanov, P. K. (1994). Economic deprivation and early childhood development. *Child Development, 65*, 296–318.

Dupper, D. R. & Bosch, L. A. (1996). Reasons for school suspensions: An examination of data from one school district and recommendations for reducing suspensions. *Journal for a Just and Caring Education, 2*, 140–150.

Dwyer, K., & Osher, D. (2000). *Safeguarding our children: An action guide. Implementing early warning, timely response.* Washington, DC: National Association of School Psychologists.

Dwyer, K., Osher, D., & Warger, C. (1998). *Early warning, timely response: A guide to safe schools.* Washington, DC: U.S. Department of Education.

Eckenrode, J., Laird, M., & Doris, J. (1993). School performance and disciplinary problems among abused and neglected children. *Developmental Psychology, 29*, 53–62.

Ekstrom, R. B., Goertz, J. M., Pollack, D. A., & Rock, D. A. (1986). Who drops out of high school and why? Findings from a national study. In G. Natriello (Ed.), *School dropouts: Patterns and policies.* New York: Teachers College Press.

Elliott, D., Hatot, N. J., Sirovatka, P., & Potter, B. B. (2001). *Youth violence: A report of the Surgeon General.* Washington, DC: U.S. Surgeon General.

Emmer, E. T., & Evertson, C. M. (1981). Synthesis of research on classroom management. *Educational Leadership, 38*, 342–347.

Ewing, C. P. (2000, January/February). *Sensible zero tolerance protects students.* Harvard Education Letter. Retrieved July 21, 2004, from http://www.edlettr.org/past/issues/2000-jf/zero.shtml

Felice, L. G. (1981). Black student dropout behavior: Disengagement from school rejection and racial discrimination. *Journal of Negro Education, 50*, 415–424.

Ferguson, A. A. (2001). *Bad boys: Public schools and the making of black masculinity.* Ann Arbor: University of Michigan Press.

Fine, M. (1986). Why urban adolescents drop into and out of public high school. *Teachers College Record, 87*, 393–409.

Fisher, C. W., Berliner, D. C., Filby, N. N., Marliave, R., Cahen, L.S., & Dishaw, M.M. (1981). Teaching behaviors, academic learning time, and student achievement: An overview. *Journal of Classroom Interaction, 17*, 2–15.

Gagnon, J. C., & Leone, P. E. (2001). Alternative strategies for youth violence prevention. In R. J. Skiba & G. G. Noam (Eds.), *New directions for youth development* (no. 92: Zero tolerance: Can suspension and expulsion keep school safe?) (pp. 101–125). San Francisco: Jossey-Bass.

Garibaldi, A., Blanchard, L., & Brooks. S. (1996). Conflict resolution training, teacher effectiveness and student suspension: The impact of a health and safety initiative in the New Orleans public schools. *Journal of Negro Education, 65*, 408–413.

Glackman, T., Martin, R., Hyman, I., McDowell, E., Berv, V., & Spino, P. (1978). Corporal punishment, school suspension, and the civil rights of students: An analysis of Office for Civil Rights school surveys. *Inequality in Education, 23*, 61–65.

Gottfredson, D. C. (1997). School-based crime prevention. In L. Sherman, D. Gottfredson, D. MacKenzie, J. Eck, P. Ruter, & S. Bushway (Eds.), *Preventing crime: What works, what doesn't, what's promising: A report to the United States Congress* (pp. 1–74). Washington, DC: U.S. Department of Justice, Office of Justice Programs.

Gottfredson, D. C. (2001). *Delinquency prevention in schools.* New York: Cambridge University Press.

Gottfredson, D. C., & Gottfredson, G. D. (2002). Quality of school-based prevention programs: Results from a national survey. *Journal of Research in Crime and Delinquency, 39*, 3–35.

Gottfredson, D. C., Gottfredson, G. D., & Skroban, S. (1998). Can prevention work where it is needed most? *Evaluation Review, 22*, 315–339.

Gottfredson, G. D., Gottfredson, D. C., Czeh, E. R., Cantor, D., Crosse, S., & Hantman, I. (2000). *The national study of delinquency prevention in schools.* Ellicott City, MD: Gottfredson Associates.

Gordon, R., Della Piana, L., & Keleher, T. (2000). *Facing the consequences: An examination of racial discrimination in U. S. Public Schools.* Oakland, CA: Applied Research Center.

Greenberg, M. T., Weissberg, R. P. O'Brien, M. U., Zins, J. E., Fredericks, L., Resnik, H., & Elias, M. J. (2003). Enhancing school-based prevention and youth development through coordinated social, emotional, and academic learning. *American Psychologist, 58*, 466–474.

Greenwood, C. R. (1996). The case for performance-based models of instruction. *School Psychology Quarterly, 11*, 283–296.

Greenwood, C. R., Delquadri, J., & Hall, R. V. (1984). Opportunity to respond and student academic performance. In W. Heward, T. Heron, D. Hill, & J. Trapporter (Eds.), *Behavior analysis in education* (pp. 58–88). Columbus, OH: Merrill.

Greenwood, C. R., Horton, B. T., & Utley, C. A. (2002). Academic engagement: Current perspectives on research and practice. *School Psychology Review, 31*, 328–349.

Gregory, J. F. (1997). Three strikes and they're out: African American boys and American schools' responses to misbehavior. *International Journal of Adolescence and Youth, 7*(1), 25–34.

Guerra, N. G., & Slaby, R. G. (1990). Cognitive mediators of aggression in adolescent offenders: 2. Intervention. *Developmental Psychology, 26*, 269–277.

Hattie, J. A. C. (2002). Classroom composition and peer effects. *International Journal of Educational Research*, 37, 449–482.

Hawkins, J. D., Doueck, H. J., & Lishner, D. M. (1988). Changing teaching practices in mainstream classrooms to improve bonding and behavior of low achievers. *American Educational Research Journal, 25*, 31–50.

Heaviside, S., Rowand, C., Williams, C., & Farris, E. (1998). *Violence and discipline problems in U.S. Public Schools: 1996–97*. (NCES 98-030). Washington, DC: U.S. Department of Education, National Center for Education Statistics.

Hellman, D. A., & Beaton, S. (1986). The pattern of violence in urban public schools: The influence of school and community. *Journal of Research in Crime and Delinquency, 23*, 102–127.

Imich, A. J. (1994). Exclusions from school: Current trends and issues. *Educational Research, 36*(1), 3–11.

Jensen, P. S., Hoagwood, K., & Trickett, E. J. (1999). Ivory towers or earthen trenches? Community collaborations to foster real-world research. *Applied Developmental Science, 3*, 206–212.

Kaeser, S. C. (1979). Suspensions in school discipline. *Education and Urban Society, 11*, 465–484.

Lane, K. L., Bocian, K. M., MacMillan, D. L., & Gresham, F. M. (2004). Treatment integrity: An essential—but often forgotten—component of school-based interventions. *Preventing School Failure, 48*, 36–44.

Larkin, J. (1979). School desegregation and student suspension: A look at one school system. *Education and Urban Society, 11*, 485–495.

Larson, C. L., & Ovando, C. J. (2001). Racial conflict in a divided community: An illustrative case study of socio-political conflict. In C. L. Larson & C. J. Ovando (Eds.), *The color of bureaucracy: The politics of equity in multicultural school communities* (pp. 31–60). Belmont, CA: Wadsworth.

Larson, J. (1994). Violence prevention in the schools: A review of selected programs and procedures. *School Psychology Review, 23*, 151–165.

Lietz, J. J., & Gregory, M. K. (1978). Pupil race and sex determinants of office and exceptional education referrals. *Educational Research Quarterly, 3*(2), 61–66.

Maag, J. W. (2001). Rewarded by punishment: Reflections on the disuse of positive reinforcement in schools. *Exceptional Children, 67*, 173–186.

Mansfield, W., & Farris, E. (1992). *Office for Civil Rights survey redesign: A feasibility study*. Rockville, MD: Westat.

Massachusetts Advocacy Center. (1986). *The way out: Student exclusion practices in Boston middle schools*. Boston: Author.

McCarthy, J. D., & Hoge, D. R. (1987). The social construction of school punishment: Racial disadvantage out of universalistic process. *Social Forces, 65*, 1101–1120.

McFadden, A. C., & Marsh, G. E. (1992). A study of race and gender bias in the punishment of school children. *Education and Treatment of Children, 15*, 140–147.

McFadden, A. C., Marsh, G. E., Price, B. J., & Hwang, Y. (1992). A study of race and gender bias in the punishment of handicapped school children. *Urban Review, 24*, 239–251.

McLoyd, V. C. (1998). Socioeconomic disadvantage and child development. *American Psychologist, 53*, 185–204.

Michigan Public Policy Initiative. (2003). *Zero tolerance policies and their impact on Michigan students*. Retrieved July 28, 2004, from http://www.mnaonline.org/pdf/spotlight%202002_12.pdf

Mihalic, S., Irwin, K., Elliott, D., Fagan, A., & Hansen, D. (2001, July). *Blueprints for violence prevention* (OJJDP Juvenile Justice Bulletin). Washington, DC: U.S. Department of Justice, Office of Juvenile Justice and Delinquency Prevention.

Morgan-D'Atrio, C. Northrup, J., LaFleur, L., & Spera, S. (1996). Toward prescriptive alternatives to suspensions: A preliminary evaluation. *Behavioral Disorders, 21*, 190–200.

Morrison, G. M., Anthony, S., Storino, M., Cheng, J., Furlong, M. F., & Morrison, R. L. (2001). School expulsion as a process and an event: Before and after effects on children at-risk for school discipline. *New Directions for Youth Development: Theory, Practice, Research, 92*, 45–72.

Morrison, G. M., & D'Incau, B. (1997). The web of zero tolerance: Characteristics of students who are recommended for expulsion from school. *Education and Treatment of Children, 20*, 316–336.

Mrazek, P. J., & Haggerty, R. J. (Eds.) (1994). *Reducing risks for mental disorders: Frontiers for preventive intervention research.* Washington, DC: National Academies Press.

National Association of Secondary School Principals. (2000, February). *Statement on civil rights implications of zero tolerance programs.* Testimony presented to the United States Commission on Civil Rights, Washington, DC.

National Center for Education Statistics. (1999). *Indicators of school crime and safety: Annual Report, 1999.* Washington, DC: U.S. Departments of Education and Justice.

No Child Left Behind Act Fact Sheet. (2001). *The facts about investing what works.* [Online]. Retrieved July 21, 2004, from http://www.ed.gov/nclb/methods/whatworks/what_works.pdf

Noguera, P. A. (1995). Preventing and producing violence: A critical analysis of responses to school violence. *Harvard Educational Review, 65*, 189–212.

Osher, D. M., Sandler, S., & Nelson, C. L. (2001). The best approach to safety is to fix schools and support children and staff. In R. J. Skiba & G. G. Noam (Eds.), *New Directions for Youth Development* (no. 92: Zero tolerance: Can suspension and expulsion keep school safe?) (pp. 127–154). San Francisco: Jossey-Bass.

Pew Research Center. (2000). *A year after Columbine: Public looks to parents more than schools to prevent violence.* Retrieved July 21, 2004, from http://people-press.org

Potts, K., Njie, B., Detch, E. R., & Walton, J. (2003). *Zero tolerance in Tennessee schools: An update.* Nashville: Office of Education Accountability, State of Tennessee. (ERIC Document Reproduction Service No. ED481971)

Public Agenda. (2004). *Teaching interrupted: Do discipline policies in today's public schools foster the common good?* Retrieved July 21, 2004, from http://www.publicagenda.org

Public Law 103-227. (1994). *Gun-free schools act.* SEC 1031, 20 USC 2701.

Quay, H. C. (1983). A dimensional approach to behavior disorder: The Revised Behavior Problem Checklist. *School Psychology Review, 12*, 244–249.

Raffaele Mendez, L. M. (2003). Predictors of suspension and negative school outcomes: A longitudinal investigation. In J. Wald & D. J. Losen (Eds.), *New directions for youth development* (no. 99: Deconstructing the school-to-prison pipeline) (pp. 17–34). San Francisco: Jossey-Bass.

Raffaele Mendez, L. M., & Knoff, H. M. (2003). Who gets suspended from school and why: A demographic analysis of schools and disciplinary infractions in a large school district. *Education and Treatment of Children, 26*, 30–51.

Raffaele-Mendez, L. M., Knoff, H. M., & Ferron, J. F. (2002). School demographic variables and out-of-school suspension rates: A quantitative and qualitative analysis of a large, ethnically diverse school district. *Psychology in the Schools, 39*, 259–277.

Rausch, M. K., & Skiba, R. J. (2004a). *Unplanned outcomes: Suspensions and expulsions in Indiana.* Bloomington, IN: Center for Evaluation and Education Policy. Retrieved July 21, 2004, from http://ceep.indiana.edu/ChildrenLeftBehind

Rausch, M. K., & Skiba, R. J. (2004b). *Doing discipline differently: The Greenfield middle school story.* Bloomington, IN: Center for Evaluation and Education Policy. Retrieved July 21, 2004, from http://ceep.indiana.edu/ChildrenLeftBehind

Reynolds, A. J., & Walberg, H. J. (1991). A structural model of science achievement. *Journal of Educational Psychology, 83*, 97–107.

Richart, D., Brooks, K., & Soler, M. (2003). *Unintended consequences: The impact of "Zero Tolerance" and other exclusionary policies on Kentucky students.* Retrieved July 21, 2004, from http://www.buildingblocksforyouth.org

Rose, T. L. (1988). Current disciplinary practices with handicapped students: Suspensions and expulsions. *Exceptional Children, 55*, 230–239.

Rosenberg, M. S. & Jackman, L. A. (2003). Development, implementation, and sustainability of comprehensive school-wide behavior management systems. *Intervention in School and Clinic, 39*, 10–21.

Schoenwald, S. K., & Hoagwood, K. (2001). Effectiveness, transportability, and dissemination of intervention: What matters when? *Psychiatric Services, 52*, 1190–1197.

Scott, T. M., & Barrett, S. B. (2004). Using staff and student time engaged in disciplinary procedures to evaluate the impact of school-wide PBS. *Journal of Positive Behavior Interventions, 6*, 21–27.

Shaw, S. R., & Braden, J. P. (1990). Race and gender bias in the administration of corporal punishment. *School Psychology Review, 19*, 378–383.

Sheets, R. H. (1996). Urban classroom conflict: Student-teacher perception: Ethnic integrity, solidarity, and resistance. *The Urban Review, 28*, 165–183.

Sherman, L. W., Gottfredson, D. C., MacKenzie, D. L., Eck, J., Reuter, P., & Bushway, S. D. (Eds.). (1997). *Preventing crime: What works, what doesn't, what's promising. A report to the United States Congress* (NCJ 171676). Washington, DC: U.S. Department of Justice, Office of Justice Programs.

Sinclair, B. (1999). *Report on state implementation of the Gun-Free Schools Act: School year 1997–98.* Rockville, MD: Westat.

Skiba, R. J., Eaton, J., & Sotoo, N. (2004). *Factors associated with state rates of out-of-school suspension and expulsion.* Bloomington, IN: Center for Evaluation and Education Policy. Retrieved December 17, 2004, from http://ceep.indiana.edu/ChildrenLeftBehind

Skiba, R. J., Michael, R. S., Nardo, A. C., & Peterson, R. (2002). The color of discipline: Sources of racial and gender disproportionality in school punishment. *Urban Review, 34*, 317–342.

Skiba, R. J, Peterson, R., Miller, C., Ritter, S., & Simmons, A. (in press). The safe and responsive schools project: A school reform model for implementing best practices in violence prevention. In S. Jimerson & M. Furlong (Eds.), *Handbook of school violence and school safety.*

Skiba, R. J., & Peterson, R. L. (1999). The dark side of zero tolerance: Can punishment lead to safe schools? *Phi Delta Kappan, 80*, 372–376, 381–382.

Skiba, R. J., Peterson, R. L., & Williams, T. (1997). Office referrals and suspension: Disciplinary intervention in middle schools. *Education and Treatment of Children, 20*, 295–315.

Skiba, R. J., & Knesting, K. (2001). Zero tolerance, zero evidence: An analysis of school disciplinary practice. In R. J. Skiba & G. G. Noam (Eds.), *New directions for youth development* (no. 92: Zero tolerance: Can suspension and expulsion keep schools safe?) (pp. 17–43). San Francisco: Jossey-Bass.

Skiba, R. J., & Rausch, M. K. (2004). *The relationship between achievement, discipline, and race: An analysis of factors predicting ISTEP scores.* Bloomington, IN: Center for Evaluation and Education Policy. Retrieved July 21, 2004, from http://ceep.indiana.edu/ChildrenLeftBehind

Skiba, R. J., Rausch, M. K., & Ritter, S. (2004). *"Discipline is always teaching": Effective alternatives to zero tolerance in Indiana's schools.* Bloomington, IN: Center for Evaluation and Education Policy. Retrieved July 21, 2004, from http://ceep.indiana.edu/ChildrenLeftBehind

Skiba, R. J., Simmons, A. B, Staudinger, L. P., Rausch, M. K., Dow, G., & Feggins, L. R. (2003, May). *Consistent removal: Contributions of school discipline to the school-prison pipeline.* Paper presented at the Harvard Civil Rights Conference School-to-Prison Pipeline Conference, Cambridge, MA.

Skinner, B. F. (1953). *Science and human behavior.* New York: Free Press.

Sprague, J., Walker, H. M., Stieber, S., Simonsen, B., Nishioka, V., Wagner, L. (2001). Exploring the relationship between school discipline referrals and delinquency. *Psychology in the Schools, 38*, 197–206.

Streitmatter, J. L. (1986). Ethnic/racial and gender equity in school suspensions. *The High School Journal, 68*, 139–143.

Stone, D. H. (1993). Crime and punishment in public schools: An empirical study of disciplinary proceedings. *Journal of Trial Advocacy, 17*, 351–398.

Taylor, M. C., & Foster, G. A. (1986). Bad boys and school suspensions: Public policy implications for black males. *Sociological Inquiry, 56*, 498–506.

Thornton, C. H., & Trent, W. (1988). School desegregation and suspension in East Baton Rouge Parish: A preliminary report. *Journal of Negro Education, 57*, 482–501.

Thornton, T. N., Craft, C. A., Dahlberg, L. L., Lynch, B. S., & Baer, K. (2000). *Best practices of youth violence prevention: A sourcebook for community action.* Atlanta, GA: Centers for Disease Control and Prevention, National Center for Injury Prevention and Control.

Tobin, T., Sugai, G., & Colvin, G. (1996). Patterns in middle school discipline records. *Journal of Emotional and Behavioral Disorders, 4*, 82–94.

Tolan, P. H., Guerra, N. G., & Kendall, P. C. (1995). Prediction and prevention of antisocial behavior in children and adolescents. *Journal of Consulting and Clinical Psychology, 63*, 515–517.

Townsend, B. (2000). Disproportionate discipline of African American children and youth: Culturally responsive strategies for reducing school suspension and expulsions. *Exceptional Children, 66*, 381–391.

Uchitelle, S., Bartz, D., & Hillman, L. (1989). Strategies for reducing suspensions. *Urban Education, 24*, 163–176.

U.S. Department of Education. (2000). *The 2000–2001 Elementary and secondary school survey: National and state projections.* Washington, DC: U.S. Government Printing Office. Retrieved July 26, 2004, from http://205.207.175.84/ocr2000r/wdsdata.html

Vavrus, F., & Cole, K. (2002). "I didn't do nothin' ": The discursive construction of school suspension. *The Urban Review, 34*, 87–111.

Verdugo, R. (2002). Race-ethnicity, social class, and zero tolerance policies: The cultural and structural wars. *Education and Urban Society*, 35, 50–75.

Wald, J., & Losen, D. J. (2003). Defining and redirecting a school-to-prison pipeline. In J. Wald & D. J. Losen (Eds.), *New directions for youth development* (no. 99: Deconstructing the school-to-prison pipeline) (pp. 9–15). San Francisco: Jossey-Bass.

Walker, H. M., Horner, R. H., Sugai, G., Bullis, M., Sprague, J. R., Bricker, D., Kaufman, & M. J. (1996). Integrated approaches to preventing antisocial behavior patterns among school-age children and youth. *Journal of Emotional and Behavioral Disorders, 4*(4), 194–209.

Walker, H. M. & Shinn, M. R. (2002). Structuring school-based interventions to achieve integrated primary, secondary, and tertiary prevention goals for safe and effective schools. In M. R. Shinn, H. M. Walker, & G. Stoner (Eds.),

Interventions for academic and behavior problems II: Preventive and remedial approaches (pp. 1–26). Bethesda, MD: National Association of School Psychologists.

Wang, M. C., & Haertel, G. D. (1994). What helps students learn? *Educational Leadership, 51*, 74–80.

Wang, M. C., Haertel, G. D., & Walberg, H. J. (1997). Learning influences. In H. J. Walberg & G. D. Haertel (Eds.), *Psychology and educational practice* (pp. 199–211). Berkeley: McCutchan.

Webster's Revised Unabridged Dictionary (4th ed.). (1998). Plainfield, NJ: MICRA.

Wehlage, G. G., & Rutter, R. A. (1986). Dropping out: How much do schools contribute to the problem? *Teachers College Record, 87*, 374–393.

Wu, S. C., Pink, W. T., Crain, R. L., & Moles, O. (1982). Student suspension: A critical reappraisal. *The Urban Review, 14,* 245–303.

Yell, M. L. (1998). *The law and special education.* Upper Saddle River, NJ: Merrill/Prentice Hall.

Zero sense. (1998, October 31). *St. Petersburg Times*, p. 16A.

Zins, J. E., Weissberg, R. P., Wang, M. C., & Walberg, H. J. (Eds.). (2004). *Building academic success on social and emotional learning: What does the research say?* New York: Teachers College Press.

X

International Perspectives on Classroom Management

Theo Wubbels
Utrecht University

42

Contexts and Attributions for Difficult Behavior in English Classrooms

Andy Miller
University of Nottingham

INTRODUCTION

In their introductory chapter, Carolyn Evertson and Carol Weinstein argue that adopting a comprehensive definition of classroom management puts the focus on a broad range of research, including academic areas not normally associated primarily with classroom management. This author agrees with such a comprehensive definition and supports the synthesis of the wide range of sources represented in this handbook. However, to review developments within the United Kingdom from such a standpoint would require examination of a huge and diverse amount of research and would require either a substantial handbook of its own or a very cursory and unsatisfactory attempt at comprehensiveness. Consequently, this chapter will pay greater attention to developments in the management of unsettled and challenging behavior of pupils in classrooms, while also taking the opportunity to examine in more detail certain selected and related studies carried out by the author.

The chapter begins by demonstrating that the origins of the study of classroom management in the United Kingdom lie in a range of academic disciplines, including sociology, psychiatry, psychology, and education. It then discusses the particular strand of British research and practice stimulated in 1971 by classic applied behavioral analysis studies within the United States of America and highlights significant steps in the subsequent evolution of this area. Turning to a perceived divide between published research and primers of behavior management on the one hand and the actual practices of educational psychologists working with teachers on the other, the chapter then looks in some detail at the author's exploratory study of teachers' experiences of successful consultations with psychologists over instances of individual pupil management. In particular, the emergence in this study of the relationship between aspects of the informal teacher culture in schools and successful behavior management are examined.

The development of key legislation and policy guidance from successive British governments pertaining to classroom management will be outlined and, in particular, the recent trend toward the delineation of the various responsibilities of schools, teachers, pupils, parents, and other professionals are highlighted. These developments are linked to studies carried out by the author and others into the attributions made by teachers, pupils, and parents into the causes of difficult behavior in schools and it is argued that such research offers a promising contribution to the drive toward "evidence-based practice" in this area. Finally, the chapter concludes by presenting a number of key challenges to the effective marrying of legislation, policy making, classroom practice, and research activity in the current British context.[1]

EARLY STUDIES OF DIFFICULT PUPIL BEHAVIOR AND CLASSROOM MANAGEMENT IN THE UNITED KINGDOM: FOCUS, ACADEMIC DISCIPLINE, AND METHODOLOGY

British research with a specific focus on "classroom management" is a relatively recent area of activity. A broader historical tradition, however, concerned itself with more general issues relating to schools in society, educational practice, and the psychopathology of certain individuals and families. The chapter begins by selectively reviewing examples to illustrate the range of these research endeavors, the cited studies having been chosen as clear and significant representations of the various different academic disciplines and research methodologies.

In terms of the early studies concerned with pupil behavior in schools, a major distinction of focus may be found between those concentrated on environmental factors influencing the management of whole-class groups or targeted individuals, and those concerned with the characteristics of individual pupils or class groups deemed specifically difficult to manage. In addition to the differing perspectives and priorities for study afforded by this diversity, these different academic disciplines have also each engaged their preferred research paradigms. Consequently, the research and evaluation literature consists of a widely heterogeneous set of studies varying in terms of their focus and methodological slant (see Fig. 42.1). In addition, case study material with a less theoretical and more pragmatic intent has been provided by practitioners such as mainstream and specialist teachers and educational psychologists. In total, this represents a methodological range from the highly constructivist view of "deviance" as a negotiated entity within educational institutions, which also reflects a wider stratified society (Sharpe & Green, 1975), through to surveys that treat pupil "behaviors" as discrete and quantifiable entities (Wheldall & Merrett, 1988). Also within the spectrum of British practice, approaches arising from a psychodynamic perspective were particularly influential in the development of some specialist schools for pupils who were, in the 1970s, termed "maladjusted." However, Wilson and Evans reported in a survey in 1980 that most such special schools and classes used cognitive—behavioral and humanistic—approaches far more than those from an explicitly psychodynamic orientation.

This range of perspectives, and more, are of course also represented across the chapters composing this handbook. Positivist and constructivist stances, and related quantitative and qualitative methodologies, are also represented within the taxonomy. Positivist and quantitative approaches include surveys (Rutter, Tizard, & Whitmore, 1970) and quasi-experimental group designs (Kolvin et al., 1981) originating from a base in psychiatry. Longitudinal cohort studies from a more sociological perspective (Douglas, Ross, & Simpson, 1968; Fogelman, 1983) provided a multitude of correlational and between group findings with a particular emphasis being placed on differences associated with social class. School effectiveness research, such

[1]Legislation and policy making in Scotland has always followed a course independent from that of the rest of the United Kingdom. There have traditionally been closer parallels between England, Wales, and Northern Ireland although, with greater political power and decision making currently being devolved away from London, this may not remain the case. Consequently, this chapter is explicitly concerned with the English context although most of what is said holds for Wales and Northern Ireland too, and some for the whole of the United Kingdom.

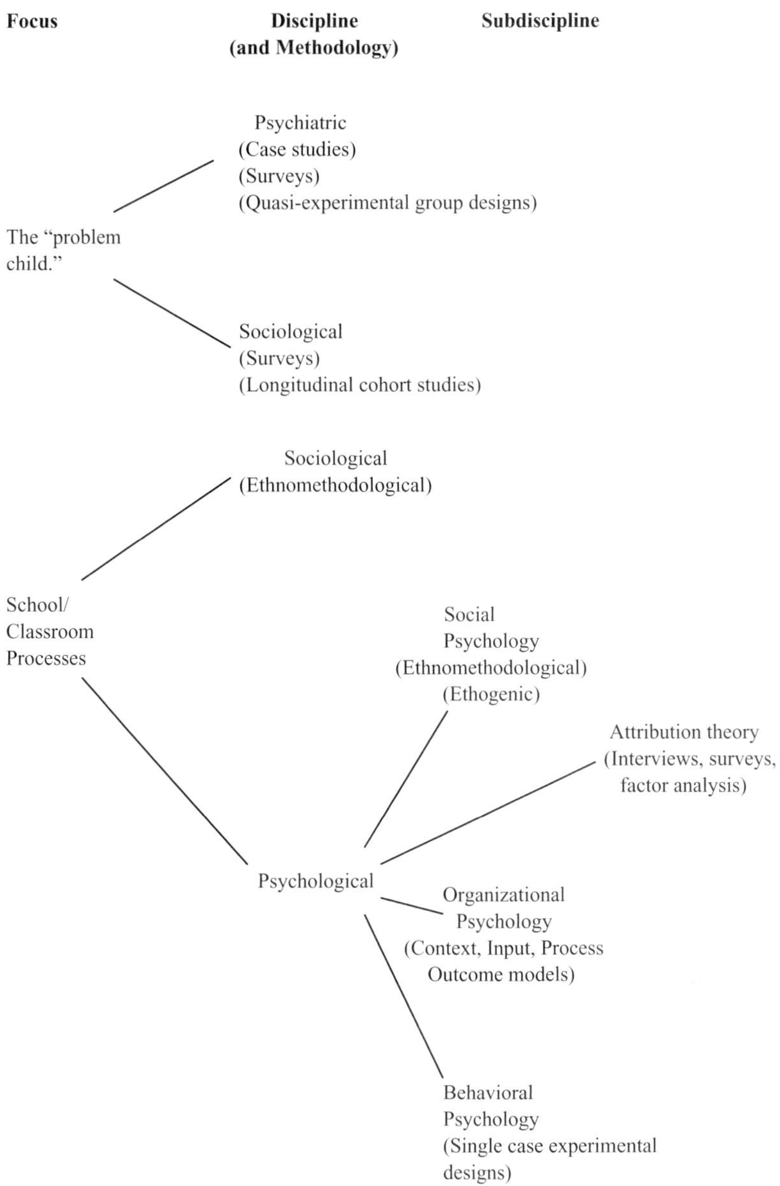

FIGURE 42.1. Studies of pupil behavior in schools by focus, discipline, and methodology (adapted from Miller, 2004).

as the landmark studies by Rutter, Maughan, Mortimore, and Ouston (1979) and Mortimore, Sammons, Stoll, Lewis, and Ecob (1988), used "context, input, process, outcome" models and may be loosely grouped under the heading of "organizational psychology." And behavioral psychology, from the pioneering study by Madsen, Becker, & Thomas (1968) onwards, has repeatedly made use of a range of single case experimental designs (Barlow & Hersen 1984).

Turning to qualitative research studies, a classic study from a social psychology background is that conducted by Hargreaves (1967) and reported in his book *Social Relations in a Secondary School*. Adopting an ethnographic approach, Hargreaves spent 1 year in what was then a "secondary modern school" studying fourth-year pupils. A major outcome from this study was Hargreaves' detailed description of an antischool subculture, vividly evoked and still salient today, which he attributed to the school's streaming system and the creation of a group of pupils rejected as public examination candidates. Often studies originating within sociological and social psychological paradigms view the construct of "difficult behavior" as being problematic and one that reflects wider societal issues. For example, Sharp and Green (1975) studied the "microsociological" contexts of classrooms through an analysis of conflicts between teachers' accounts of the rationale for various of their specific actions and the in situ observational evidence of the nature and effects of these same actions. These researchers were also concerned with investigating "macrosociological" concerns, in particular, the ways in which social control in a stratified society was translated into school and classroom life.

THE INFLUENCE OF APPLIED BEHAVIORAL ANALYSIS

The First UK Studies

Compared to the extensive body of U.S. research reviewed by Jere Brophy in Chapter 2 of this volume, the British contribution to published studies of applied behavioral analysis might look meager indeed, and all the more so because substantial early sections of it consist of attempts to translate and replicate classic U.S. studies in the British context (Merrett, 1981). For example, the study of the effects of rules, praise, and ignoring carried out by Madsen and his colleagues in 1968 created considerable interest among professionals with a direct responsibility for helping teachers manage the difficult behavior of some pupils. In 1971, Ward, who was responsible for training educational psychologists, repeated the experiment in a Manchester school with similar results and published the first British replication of this work.

At the time of these earliest studies, the zeitgeist within British education was strongly in terms of "child-centredness" (DES, 1967). At that time, the author was a young teacher working in a primary school that exemplified this ethos and can remember the almost daily stream of visitors from many countries, especially the United States of America, keen to see for themselves the practical application of an educational philosophy in which Britain was seen to provide an innovative example to the world. Whatever variations this ethos actually took in practice—and the reactions of subsequent legislators and policy makers from the late 1980s certainly expressed a retributive attitude—central aspects, at least within the rhetoric, were of a curriculum built around children's interests and varying abilities, teaching methods that aimed to encourage and support learning rather than teach directly, and a room layout and timetable organization constructed around the principle of maximum flexibility. Unsurprisingly, all of these were grossly incompatible with, and antagonistic toward, the widespread public perception of "behavior modification."

From Consequences to Antecedents

In the minds of many who came upon behavioral approaches, an overriding emphasis seemed be placed on the rewards and punishments that followed pupils' behavior. Although antecedents, in the form of clear explanations of rules, were prominently contained within the Madsen et al. (1968) study, the focus of immediately subsequent work was very much on the consequences of behavior. Antecedents were generally not considered sufficient on their own to have a significant impact on some behavior, whereas consequences were seen as much more likely to determine whether a behavior was strengthened and maintained. It was this emphasis on consequences—rewards and punishments—that became most firmly associated with "behavior modification," a term that attracted many negative connotations.

For the first decade or so of British interest, behavioral approaches seemed to be a field of theory and practice distinctly separate from all other aspects of educational enquiry. However, by the end of this period there were increasing signs that an alliance was being forged with major areas such as curriculum planning and classroom layout. For example, two of the earliest British proponents, Harrop and McNamara (1979), took stock of their practice after a 5-year period of gathering casework and group workshop experience with teachers using behavioral methods. They commented on their move toward giving greater emphasis to classroom rules, as well as praise and ignoring. They made the point that behavioral interventions had to ask whether the curriculum within the classroom where the difficult behavior was being manifested should be altered to meet the pupil's interests and aptitudes before embarking on a fuller behavioral intervention. Similarly, Wheldall (1981) pointed to the dangers of what he termed "behavioural overkill," the use of very powerful reinforcers in an attempt to change behavior where a less powerful and more "natural" reinforcer would suffice. He was also another who stressed that behavioral approaches needed to take the focus away from the consequences of behavior and place it more on the antecedents.

Pursuing this line, Wheldall, Morris, Vaughn, and Ng (1981) carried out an experiment with two classes of 10- and 11-year-olds in a junior school. The amount of "on-task" behavior was recorded over a 2-week period while the children were seated around tables, the measurements then being repeated for a further 2 weeks while the children were seated in rows. The mean on-task behavior was higher for the rows condition and when the children were subsequently returned to tables for a further 2 weeks, their mean on-task behaviour declined. Examination of the data revealed that the rows condition had the greatest effect on the children with low initial on-task behavior, the very pupils for whom behavioral interventions were usually devised. This strand of research interest still finds expression in publications such as that by Hastings and Wood (2002).

From On-Task Behavior to Socially Useful Outcomes

Following on from the study by Madsen and his colleagues, many subsequent British publications about work in primary schools and some special school settings consisted of case studies also concerned with increasing the on-task behavior of pupils. With the steady accumulation of accounts of practice, some psychologists began to voice misgivings about the general direction of such work. Surveying the American scene, Winnet and Winkler (1972), for instance, had cautioned that the current thrust of behavioral approaches in classrooms at that time could be summed up in the injunction to pupils to "be still, be quiet, be docile." In a similar vein, McNamara and Harrop (1981) commented on what they saw as the "waves of development" of behavioral approaches in Britain, and concluded that until the early 1980s much practice had been "somewhat naive" in focusing so much attention on on-task behavior as opposed to "academic work output" and other skills and socially acceptable behaviour. They argued that if behavioral approaches were to move beyond encouraging what might be only superficial pupil compliance, a lot more attention would also have to be paid to manipulating such aspects of the setting events as lesson preparation.

As a result, a far greater number of subsequent studies switched their focus to include a greater emphasis on academic work output and on encouraging the development among pupils of a range of new skills. Developments such as these were driven by the recognition that pupils who were more able to succeed at conventionally valued school work were more likely, as a result, to identify more closely with the aims of the school and receive more naturally occurring praise and encouragement for their efforts. A creative and novel example was provided by

Burland (1979), who described work in a school for pupils with emotional and behavioral difficulties in which behavioral principles were rigorously but creatively used to teach pupils a range of social and leisure skills—everything from juggling to riding unicycles! In addition to introducing an element of fun and getting away from the image of behavioral approaches as being always aligned to control and conformity, this work had a serious intention. Not only did it display the versatility of the approaches, but for a group of children with underdeveloped social skills and restricted friendship groupings these new talents became a source of satisfaction in themselves and a probable entry into a wider social acceptability.

From Primary- to Secondary-Level Applications

Despite the accumulation of published accounts of successful work in primary and special school settings, similar outcomes in secondary schools proved far harder to achieve. McNamara and Harrop (1979), for example, found that when they attempted to repeat for secondary staff the types of workshops that had generally proved welcome and successful for primary teachers, there was a much reduced benefit. Following a course for 100 probationary secondary teachers, there was only a limited response, compared with primary teachers, in terms of accounts of successful interventions supported by accompanying data. They concluded that these results, and the general paucity of studies in behavioral approaches in secondary schools, could mean that the complex nature of these schools did not easily lend themselves to such approaches.

From External Control to Self-Control

One means of overcoming the problem of trying to coordinate the responses of a large number of subject teachers in a secondary setting, and at the same time increasing a pupil's self-regulation, came in the form of "self-recording" studies, a clear account of which was initially provided by Merrett and Blundell in 1982. They reported on work involving a 13-year-old boy in what was then termed a remedial department of a comprehensive school, who displayed a very unsettled approach to many aspects of his work and also distracted other class members from theirs. Following a baseline period, an intervention was introduced that required the pupil to tally his on-task behavior during the same periods that his teacher collected a similar record. A signal, audible to both the pupil and teacher, was used to indicate when both should record the behavior. It was explained to the pupil that only the tally marks of his that agreed with his teacher's would be counted toward a reinforcing activity—10 jointly agreed-on marks could be exchanged for a 2-minute period of coloring-in a Doodle Art picture. The boy's on-task behavior rose from a mean level of approximately 30% during the baseline period to a mean level of more than 60% during this intervention period.

From Individual Pupils to Whole-Class Approaches

While advances such as these were being recorded in the British literature, there was a recognition that the time commitment required from a psychologist or other consultant was considerable. Partly from a desire to use expensive expertise effectively and partly out of a concern to benefit the maximum number of pupils, a line of research also pursued work with whole-class groups rather than selected individual pupils. The first British experimental validation of the behavioral approach's positive contribution to management of a whole class was provided by Tsoi and Yule (1976), who used extra break time as a reinforcer. Two types of strategy were each shown to be effective, one where the behavior of a single child formed the basis for reinforcement for all the class and one in which changes in the behavior of the whole class were required. The study was well designed and thus able to demonstrate objectively the experimental effects. Merrett and Wheldall (1978) used a similarly rigorous methodology in a study that was again concerned with management of the whole class, in this instance combining a "rules, ignore, and praise" approach with a "timer game." Basically, this involved a teacher using a cassette tape prepared so that it gave a random signal on average once a minute. On the signal, target children were observed and house points were awarded to all the children on the target child's table if he or she was following the set rules. Merrett and Wheldall (1987) commented that "no teacher would want to use such a device often, or for long periods, but it remains a very useful strategy for gaining, or regaining, control of a group of children who display difficult and/or disruptive behavior" (p. 47). Rennie (1980) subsequently used other game strategies with whole classes, again with success.

From Reactive Strategies to Preventative Approaches

As well as approaches with whole-class groups as a means of capitalizing on the potential of behavioral approaches, a parallel drive among psychologists and others was toward the prevention of classroom difficulties by means of various teacher training and school policy development initiatives. It was at this stage that a wider research base was drawn upon.

For example, a particularly innovative set of training materials, titled *Preventative Approaches to Disruption* (Chisholm et al., 1986), was devised by a group of educational psychologists in 1986 and drew upon Kounin's (1970) studies of classroom management as well as the research described earlier. These materials also involved a variety of teaching methods such as personal reflection, group discussion, video or classroom observation, and role play. Another distinctive feature was the amount of thought given to a dissemination model for introducing these materials into schools, this careful consideration being borne of the authors' daily experiences as educational psychologists working with and in schools over issues such as pupil behavior management, staff training, and policy development.

In another influential set of resource materials, *Building a Better Behaved School*, Galvin, Merier, and Costa (1990) pulled together a similar breadth of research studies in combination with extensive experience of working in schools. In addition to influencing individual pupil management techniques and whole-class strategies, this publication also drew attention to the crucial importance of establishing clear and mutually agreed-on policies within schools for encouraging positive pupil behavior. Again, principles from the behavioral literature, including the earliest emphasis on clear statements of rules and appropriate rewards and sanctions, were incorporated centrally into these recommended whole-school policies.

As the second decade of these innovations drew to a close, the scene was set for a major government-commissioned review of the level of, and the most effective responses to, disruptive behavior in British schools. Before looking at the outcomes of this review, the Elton Report, and subsequent developments in associated legislation, it is necessary to return to look more closely at individual strategy planning in schools in order to ensure that the full lessons from this explosion of professional activity have been learned.

A GROUNDED THEORY STUDY OF SUCCESSFUL BEHAVIORAL CONSULTATIONS IN CLASSROOMS

Rationale

By the early 1990s, the stream of research publications into applied behavioral approaches in the British context had slowed to a trickle, if not dried up altogether. Nonetheless, in schools, with teachers still struggling to manage the challenging behavior of some of their pupils, many educational psychologists continued in their attempts to draw upon this research literature as the basis for a productive means of helping teachers and pupils.

This author had long been interested in what seemed like a gap between the published case studies outlined earlier and the actual consultative practice of colleagues working on a daily basis with teachers in schools. In essence, working typically with a "patch" of between 20 and 30 schools at that time, many British educational psychologists seemed to be aware that devising interventions that teachers would actually implement often involved consideration of a whole range of issues not normally addressed in a literature that concentrated mainly on either the principles behind program planning or examples of the successful applications of such programs. Furthermore, McNamara (1988) claimed that published demonstrations of the successful use of behavioral interventions had often been carried out in highly conducive settings, whereas the usual run of professional consultative work was in far less favorable settings.

Consequently, a study was undertaken by the author (Miller 1996, 2003) to investigate how interventions supposedly deriving from behavioral psychology could at times achieve their effect. This question was particularly pertinent because of the suspicion engendered by conversations with many colleagues that teachers would often only tolerate "light" interventions and that these in themselves might only then be adhered to by the teachers to a variable degree. Given that theoreticians with allegiance to other paradigms could also argue convincingly that classroom interaction was an immensely complex social activity (Nash, 1973; Leach & Raybould, 1977) and that notions of "deviance" should pay regard to a range of sociological and interpersonal processes (Hargreaves, 1975), how could it be the case that these very light interventions, often diluted beyond their explanatory tolerance, could sometimes lead the teachers involved to experience a sense of success when all their previous best efforts had failed? And why was it only sometimes? What factors were at work in these instances?

Clearly any research that attempted to answer these questions would have to be exploratory in nature. As this was not a specific area that was developed within the research literature, a methodology concerned with hypothesis testing was not applicable and any "hunches" or beliefs that the researcher brought to the task would need to be acknowledged and controlled for at an the early stage. A grounded theory methodology (Glaser & Strauss, 1967; Strauss & Corbin, 1999) was ideally suited to this task, first because it acknowledges the importance of these possible researcher effects, and then through the various disciplines imposed by "fracturing" the data during the lengthy processes of coding and categorization, as described in the following sections.

Given that difficult behavior has been approached from a range of theoretical perspectives it was important not to foreclose on possible explanatory mechanisms too early, and grounded analysis, especially in the process of theoretical sensitivity, is well suited to avoiding this. Similarly, any attempt to impose a more global theoretical formulation from any particular discipline onto a puzzling practical phenomenon would be likely to underestimate the complexity of the area under investigation and thus limit its explanatory power. Because of the emphasis on its emergent and "local" nature (Turner, 1991), grounded theory again seemed particularly suitable to the task.

The Sample

Twenty-four primary teachers were interviewed using a structured interview. They were identified by contacting educational psychologists in a number of local authorities and asking whether they could supply the name and address of any primary-range teacher with whom they had devised an intervention deriving to a greater or lesser extent from a behavioral perspective and targeted on some aspect of challenging behavior.

The teachers in the sample were eventually drawn from eight local education authorities spanning an area between the English Midlands and Scottish border. The pupils represented the full primary age range with a bias toward the younger group, the mean age being 7.1 years. In terms of the perceived severity of the problem behavior, 10 teachers said the pupil was the most difficult they had ever encountered and 8 said he or she was among the most difficult half-dozen. Because of the sample selection, all teachers reported success following their collaborative work with an educational psychologist—6 expressed the view that the intervention had been successful but had some reservation, such as that there might be deterioration again in the future; 11 saw a definite improvement with no qualifications; and 7 saw such a degree of success that it made a strong emotional impact on them.

Coding Within Grounded Theory Methodology

A full account of the use of grounded theory, which is a detailed methodology generating its own debates and schools of thought, will not be provided here. A range of publications may be consulted (e.g., Strauss, 1987; Hutchinson, 1988; Strauss & Corbin, 1999; Pidgeon & Henwood, 1996) and the author has written more fully on the method as used in this particular study (Miller, 1995a). Here, a flavor of the approach will be provided in order to give a general impression of the means by which the arguments and accounts, especially those in this chapter, have been developed.

The interview transcripts were analyzed by the "open coding" procedure from grounded theory, in which a large number of these codes are seen to "emerge" from the data. This involves a line-by-line, or even word-by-word, analysis of the data during which the researcher gives each discrete incident, idea, or event a name or code, aiming for the code to be at a higher conceptual level than the text. Proceeding through the text, the researcher generates new codes and finds other examples of already existing codes. In this study the analysis of the first interview transcript took place over a period of weeks, yielding over 80 different open codes with many examples of these being repeated at various places and in differing combinations within this interview.

Level II codes, also known as categories, are derived from condensing level I codes—the open codes. Academic and professional knowledge then supplies theoretical constructs to form level III codes, so that they give meaning to the relationship between themselves and the level I and II codes, weaving the fractured data back together again (Glaser, 1978).

ANALYSIS

Glaser (1978) saw "theoretical sensitivity" as central for producing grounded theory. This refers to a personal quality of the researcher in terms of his or her awareness of the subtleties of meaning of data. To achieve this, a number of procedures were embarked on. First, a list of "theories, models and concepts," all of which were hypothesized as having the potential to yield codes for the data that might be found within the transcripts, was drawn up. This list was composed from within and beyond the range of theoretical perspectives represented within Fig. 42.1. Then a period of reading was embarked on, revisiting texts with a deliberately broad range of coverage.

The final grounded theory arising from the interview data described a complex interrelationship between aspects of the interactions between the teachers and psychologists, the attributions made by teachers, the delicate and sometimes indistinct boundary between the responsibilities of home and school, and the unwritten rules for staff as well as pupils within schools.

TABLE 42.1
Total Set of Open Codes Relating to Other Staff

Pupil impinging on other staff
Role of head
Staff agreement with the need for referral
Consultation within school
School policy on managing the day
Other staff's knowledge of pupil
Previous teachers' strategy with pupil
School culture re: problem solving
Support as the opportunity to talk
Teacher alone/not alone with problem
Staff's/head's support strategy
Reluctance/lack of reluctance to seek support
Valuing/not valuing colleagues' expertise
Staff consensus over presenting problems
Other staff's role in strategy
Consistency of strategy across staff
Individual staff's consistency within strategy
Other staff's knowledge of strategy
Staff's general agreement with strategy
Staff's reluctance re: time factors
Staff's reluctance re: equitability
Staff's original perception of likelihood of progress
Staff's ongoing perception of progress
Staff's enthusiasm for/interest in strategy

In a number of the interviews, discussions about teacher colleagues seemed to contain paradoxical and contradictory items and strong feelings. Within the list made during the early stages of developing theoretical sensitivity, the area of relations with colleagues had not been included and thus came to be seen as a potential category within which theorizing could be extended. In total, 24 different open codes relating to "other staff" (see Table 42.1) were discovered within the first two thirds of the transcripts and no further new codes then emerged within the later ones.

The teachers in this sample were all selected because they had enjoyed positive outcomes, many attesting to these as highly significant professional experiences. And yet almost all were very reluctant to tell their colleagues about the details of the educational psychologist's suggestions (all teacher quotations in this section are from Miller, 2003):

> I was a little unsure and I didn't want to say anything—stick my neck out if you like and say "Look we're doing this and it could prove wonderful." I wanted to go very tentatively and then when I could see some sort of hope I turned to the staff and said "This is what we're doing, will you please bear this in mind." (Interview 18)

This reticence is being expressed in a school where the general atmosphere is perceived by the teacher as positive—"a very happy school . . . staff are very nice and . . . all quite happy to help." The tension between her optimism ("it could prove wonderful") and caution ("I didn't want to say anything—stick my neck out"), a tension present in a dramatic form in many of the interviews, is partly explained by her subsequent comments that reveal something of the texture of staff room culture:

> I didn't want to offend Margaret [pupil's previous teacher] in any way by saying "I shall keep him in the class no matter what." So it was only very gradually that I explained to her what was happening—[she's] the deputy head... [it's] very, very delicate.

Whereas it may be relatively easy to understand this reticence, it is harder to believe that a school staff could perceive positive changes in a pupil with a previously notorious schoolwide reputation, be aware that some form of intervention had taken place, and yet express little interest in the nature of this intervention. And yet this phenomenon occurs clearly in more than a third of the 24 interviews. The point is perhaps best illustrated by considering sets of three quotes from a number of interviewees (Miller, 2003). The first in each set refers to the previous reputation of the pupil, the second to the class teacher's and the other staff's perceptions of change, and the third to the staff's curiosity concerning the nature of the intervention responsible for this change.

Interview 13

> The other staff were very aware of Brian... they'd all met him in the playground and in the dining hall. He would get into trouble with all the other teachers on playground duty and the dinner ladies as well.... He would get very cross and throw himself on the floor and bang his fists on the ground and scream his head off, and he actually did that to the head once, which amazed me. You don't very often do that to the headmaster.
>
> Brian is a changed character. I think everybody's noticed.... I'm absolutely astounded in the change in Brian.
>
> No one's really questioned it as such. They obviously think it's just happened. You tend to take things for granted I suppose if you're not directly involved. No one's actually said to me "How did you do it?" or whatever.

Interview 20

> The parents have had meetings with class teachers, special needs teachers... throughout the child's stay in school.... She was infamous throughout the school for the things she did.... She had chopped up the duvet cover and the curtains [at home]. We had the Bishop in... and she went up to his table and sort of "Oh my name's Chloe!" Most of the other children were quite deferential.
>
> Her behaviour showed, over the last six weeks roughly a dramatic improvement. Her standard of work did as well and her reading came on in leaps and bounds.... [Staff] who knew I was doing it they'd say "Ooh she's behaving herself, I didn't have to tell her off in the yard."
>
> One or two of them did ask me what recommendations she had made, one infant teacher who had her before especially. I didn't make a big issue of it.... If anybody asked I did, but quite honestly at the end of the term it was quite chaotic.

Interview 15

> Oh, he had a tremendous reputation, yes... the chief education officer was at school that day and he cried... screamed all day... he was really quite a handful.
>
> He was the topic of conversation in the staff room but now he's rarely mentioned.... They've remarked how different he's got.
>
> *Did they ask what you'd been doing with the ed psych?*
>
> No.
>
> *Did you tell them?*
>
> No, I didn't.

The Grounded Theory of Successful Behavioral Consultations

There is a marked difference between a grounded theory approach and conventional verification research in the function of the literature review. In the latter it is necessary to present a review of the literature before narrowing down the study to the research hypothesis, in order to demonstrate how the literature has led to the research and how the findings may be linked back into the relevant literature. In contrast, a grounded theory derives from the field data, "coded under conditions of theoretical sensitivity" (Glaser, 1978 p. 14), and then, as the grounded theory emerges, the research literature is turned to in order to provide support for it. In this example, and as a result of the emerging findings described earlier, a detailed literature review, drawing on both UK and U.S. sources, in the areas of systems and their boundaries (e.g., Rice 1976; De Shazer, 1982; Hoy & Miskel, 1989), schools as systems (e.g., Ball, 1987; Frederickson, 1990), teachers' relationships with colleagues (Nias, 1985; Lieberman & Miller, 1990; Little, 1990), teacher thinking (e.g., Wagner, 1987), and sociological studies of teaching as work (e.g. Lortie, 1975) was then pursued

A full grounded theory of these phenomena was generated and this is reported formally elsewhere (Miller, 1996). For the purposes of this chapter, however, it is sufficient to highlight and illustrate the main components of this theory in terms of what Glaser (1978) called "basic psychological processes." These are core variables that satisfy Glaser's three criteria of recurring frequently in the data (i.e., the data concerning "other staff" rather than the full transcripts), linking the data together, and explaining much of the variation within the data. The two core variables detected in this study were the "temporary overlapping boundary" created by the involvement of the educational psychologist and the "maintenance of the school system boundary" (see Fig. 42.2).

The grounded theory analysis generated an explanation for this "cultural" resistance to the wider interest in potentially successful practice in terms of the psychosocial system boundaries of schools (Rice, 1976) and the boundaries between homes and schools (Dowling & Osborne, 1994). For example, the teachers in this study displayed a strong tendency to attribute the difficult behavior of the pupils to the parents while at the same time feeling "saddled" with the responsibility to effect a solution.

These boundary uncertainties are temporarily resolved with the involvement of an educational psychologist who creates a temporary system that includes at least one member of staff, one parent, the pupil, and the psychologist, and within which new norms and rules are created, in much the same way that a therapist and a family may form a "therapeutic suprasystem" (De Shazer, 1982). This new system enables participants to act toward and construe each other in new and more positive ways, which provide the basis from which the pupil and, sometimes, the parent can assume new identities:

> Mrs. Roberts [mother] had caused so many problems here. She's a very bristly lady, very much on the ball, but in her own way she really did care for Barry. Maybe not the way that you and I would care for our children but she did ... she really was a caring mum. (Interview 15)

The involvement of the educational psychologist in some way allows the generally accepted view among the staff, that Mrs. Roberts is very "bristly" and causes "so many problems," to be departed from but continue to coexist with a more positive, if perhaps slightly patronizing, view of her as a "caring mum." This temporary escape from the dominant view is also sometimes expressed in terms of privacy and ownership:

> I think a lot of the time when teachers are working with a psychologist they keep it very much to—it's their property almost. It's strange, teachers are very possessive of the children in their class and they don't want to share things. (Interview 24)

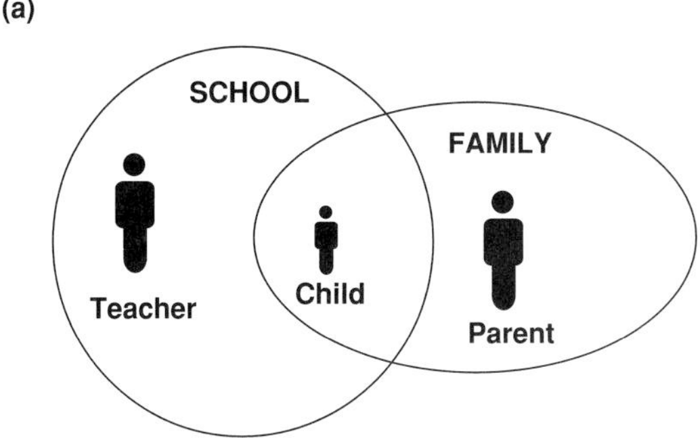

Each boundary includes the norms and rules for:

- **interacting with individuals within the system**
- **dealing with internally disruptive events**
- **carrying out joint tasks**
- **presenting a 'common front'**
- **communicating across the boundary**

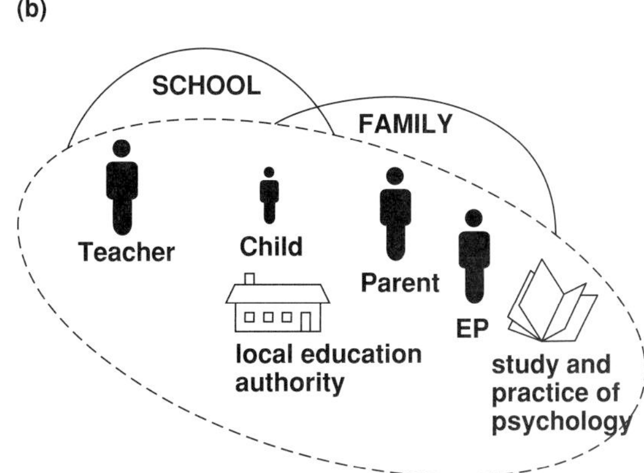

FIGURE 42.2. The location and nature of the temporary overlapping boundary. (a) The child as a member of the family and school systems. (b) The introduction of the temporary overlapping system (from Miller, 1996; 2003)

This phenomenological experience of "possessiveness" and secrecy, of not "sticking one's neck out," is particularly pertinent to the example from Interview 18 in which the teacher initially found the prospect of success after the relative "failure" of the deputy head in the previous year "very, very delicate." Even after successful completion, when the results are visible to the others in the school, the notions of teacher-effected change with difficult pupils will not fit easily into the staff culture:

> I mean I've come back to teaching after 15 years break and they've been super, they've been really helpful.... I can't come into the staff room and say aren't I good?' ... It's very big-headed isn't it? (Interview 15)

> We're a very close school ... we do talk in the staff room and say, you know, 'What do you think? How can you help?' ... when I found that it was working then I thought that as I felt so good about it everybody had to know.... I think they all got fed up of me keep saying 'Richard, Richard, Richard!' (Interview 21)

The temporary overlapping boundary, in place as long as the psychologist continues to work with the teacher and others, insulates the class teacher from other staff members and thus prevents her or his new constructions of the pupil and parent from clashing with the more widely held views among the staff and hence disrupting the "homeostasis"—the tendency to maintain the internal stability—of the system. The insulating effect of this new boundary is described both in terms of the separation of the teacher from colleagues *over this particular pupil*:

> . . . and it was nothing to do with the rest of the staff really. They just breathed a sigh of relief that it wasn't their problem. (Interview 3)

and in terms of a new set of norms and support within which to construe this pupil and parent differently:

> She didn't quiz me. She was lovely, she would just sit there and I could ask her questions, like "I am trying this particular thing, is that alright?". . . . She would sort of say "You're doing well, yes you are doing the right thing." So yes, I appreciated that part of her.., as the professional. . . . [The other teachers] would have said. . . . "Oh go on he'll be alright" . . . but it meant more coming from her. . . . She was trying hard to get Brian out of this negative situation. (Interview 15)

Implications—Individual Interventions, Generalization, and Whole-School Approaches

Because this is a small-sample, intensive study these results clearly cannot be easily generalized. But they do nevertheless have important implications.

On the one hand, the study provides further confirmatory evidence that interventions that manipulate rules, praise, and ignoring within the classroom, in tandem with carefully mediated teacher–parent cooperation, are able to bring about positive changes in the behavior of pupils, at least younger pupils, judged by their teachers as some the most difficult, or *the* most difficult, they have ever encountered. The study has also demonstrated that, within the terms of a behavioral paradigm, these strategies may be very light and still achieve these effects.

However, the study also accentuates the potentially confounding contributions of psychosocial phenomena such as staff culture, attributions of responsibility, and systems boundaries between school and home. And in doing so, it goes a considerable way toward explaining the repeatedly observed lack of generalization of such strategies within educational contexts. In the light of these observations, additional weight is provided to the moves toward various forms of whole-school intervention, in particular those that include a focus on these subtle yet powerful psychosocial processes.

The next section of this chapter looks at developments in British legislation and government advice in respect of managing pupil behavior in schools and generally creating orderly learning environments. Many of the lessons learned from the range of studies considered so far will be found to have received official endorsement in these various pronouncements.

KEY LEGISLATION AND POLICY GUIDANCE FROM CENTRAL GOVERNMENT

Turning to the historical absence of a relationship between legislation, research and practice, the publication in 1989 of the government-commissioned Elton Report (DES, 1989), *Discipline in Schools*, is generally considered to represent the beginnings of legislative intervention and government-initiated policies in this area. This report was commissioned following concerns within the teaching profession and the popular media that pupils' behavior in schools was deteriorating. In addition to the usual procedures of seeking comment from a wide selection of interests, and a program of visits, the committee commissioned two studies. Although the results of these are examined in some detail, the studies themselves have not been published separately or in their entirety. Represented within these survey and interview studies were the methods developed in some of the earlier research already described, and revealed in the findings were a number of familiar themes.

The report authors acknowledged that earlier research by Wheldall and Merrett (1988), two leading British researchers into behavioral approaches, had contributed in several ways to the practical tasks of constructing questionnaires for the national survey. Consequently, items such as "talking out of turn (e.g., by making remarks, calling out, distracting others by chattering)" and "hindering other pupils" (e.g., by distracting them from work, interfering with equipment or materials)—two items that Wheldall and Merrett had discovered to be of particular concern to teachers, were included among the 14 questionnaire items sent to the teachers. The questionnaire also examined the types of pupil behavior that teachers most frequently encountered outside of their classrooms in the course of their general duties around the school. In addition, teachers' views of the "seriousness" of discipline problems in their school, and the strategies and sanctions that they used, were also examined.

The Elton Report in many ways provided a reassuring message to many at the time in concluding, in contrast to more sensationalist claims, that the incidence of very violent behavior in schools was small. The much higher degree of lesser but frequent classroom disruption that was detected was seen as a challenge for educators, but one for which effective solutions in such areas as teacher training, school policy development, and support service activity, were seen as realizable.

Major legislation and policy guidance has followed the landmark publication of this report. In the early 1990s, procedures were announced whereby schools, local education authorities, and professionals such as educational psychologists and school doctors were to be involved in the identification and assessment of pupils with special educational needs. Following this, and addressing specifically the issue of pupil behavior, government guidance was issued in 1994 on the distinctions that might be drawn between three groups of pupils:

- children who are "disruptive or naughty," or experiencing some emotional stress within normal and expected bounds;
- children whose symptoms are those of a serious mental illness, the occurrence of which is rare; and
- children with emotional and behavioral difficulties, who lie on a spectrum between these other two groups and should be construed as having some form of learning difficulty.

These government circulars avoided oversimplistic categorizations and attempted to offer advice based on research studies and professional opinion. For instance, the first group of pupils was seen as the responsibility of the school and class teacher and associated recommendations drew on the research into school processes. Circular 8/94 (DFE, 1994a) stated that "individual instances of disruptive behaviour are bound to occur at times" and that, in response, "interventions have to be carefully judged by teachers, using their knowledge of individual pupils or class groups" (p. 14). These teachers were advised to do "no more than is needed to secure the desired change in the pupil's behavior" (p. 14).

At the other end of the spectrum, the grouping of pupils with a "serious mental illness" was described as being very small in size but consisting of "young people [who] develop severe emotional and behavioural disorders which require care and treatment beyond that which can be found in school, including special school" (DFE, 1994c, p. 17). Children characterized in this way might "be referred to a unit, often on a residential basis, because they have exhausted the resources or the ability to cope of their community, family and school and require an environment which can facilitate cognitive and emotional growth" (DFE, 1994c, p. 18).

The third grouping, the children with emotional and behavioral difficulties, was reported to be likely to have a persisting problem that constituted a "learning difficulty." (DFE, 1994b). Such a view conceived of difficult pupil behavior as arising primarily either from an inadequate repertoire of socially desirable behavior or from the learning of unacceptable methods of responding to certain social demands, especially those encountered within school settings. As a form of learning difficulty, emotional and behavioral difficulties were to be met via the stages of assessment and intervention set down in the Code of Practice on the Identification and Assessment of Children with Special Educational Needs (DFE 1993; DfES 2001).

A subsequent set of government recommendations may be seen as an attempt to assign certain sets of responsibilities to various major stakeholders. The SEN Code of Practice and the subsequent legislation into which this became incorporated spelled out the procedures that school staff were to follow in respect of a pupil they deemed to have special educational needs, including pupils with emotional and behavioral difficulties. The statutory duties of other personnel, particularly educational psychologists and school doctors, were also stated. Continuing with school staff, a government circular in 1994 also required schools to develop and clarify their internal policies and procedures regarding pupil behavior (DfEE, 1994a). This was then followed by the further expectation that local education authorities confirm and make clear their coordinating role by means of published LEA Behaviour Plans (DfEE, 1998b).

Although these various publications also referred to pupils and parents, their central thrust was in terms of the obligations placed on organizations such as schools and LEAs. The extension of prescription toward parents, in particular, can be seen in a subsequent circular requiring all schools to draw up and adopt "home-school agreements" (DfEE, 2000). These documents required respective responsibilities to be listed, and then signed by both school staff and parents to indicate their intention to adhere to the contents. In addition, the governing bodies of schools were also encouraged to take "all reasonable steps" to ensure that the parental declaration was signed, indicating that parents understood and accepted the agreement. Of particular relevance to the theme of challenging behavior was the requirement that these agreements included a statement of the school's and parents' respective responsibilities concerning pupil attendance and behavior, and government advice was that agreements would work best where they were "a product of genuine discussion between all parties concerned" (DfEE, 1998b, p. 3).

The strong emphasis on the rights and responsibilities of parents was also emphasised in Circular 10/99 (DfEE, 1999), which states that schools should set up a Pastoral Support Programme for pupils experienced as particularly difficult to manage and seen as in danger of being excluded from school. In this multiagency program, parents should contribute to strategy planning and "be regularly informed about their child's progress" (p. 27). Again, this government recommendation was founded on the belief that by making expectations between school and home agreed and explicit, a subsequent exclusion may be averted.

Behind all these developments was a strong and understandable desire to make clear and unambiguous to all—particularly pupils, parents, and teachers—who should be responsible for what. In addition to policies and practices to develop cooperative, preventive, and proactive strategies, especially between school and home, there were, however, often strong statements of mutual recrimination and blame to be heard. Earlier, the present author had characterized the continuing public concern over difficult pupil behavior as one in which

> blame tends to shift from pupils to teachers and on to parents before coming around again to teachers, as if proceeding around the points of a triangle. Legislative initiatives which are introduced in an attempt to delineate the relative responsibilities of each party have a habit of floundering when the public attention shifts to another point on the triangle. Teachers can feel they have little chance if their efforts are not supported at home. Parents will complain that they are unable to exert control over how their child behaves during a particular lesson at school. And young people themselves lack the power and psychological sophistication to act as mediators between clashing home and school perspectives. (Miller, 1999, p. 79)

Although many difficulties and stumbling blocks are often encountered in attempts to implement home–school approaches to pupil behavior problems, there is a strong evidence base for the effectiveness of these approaches, if they can somehow be arranged. In the U.S. context, Barth (1979) and Atkeson and Forehand (1979) reviewed a substantial body of published research into "home-based reinforcement" schemes demonstrating that, if it is possible to set up these types of strategies, then extremely effective outcomes can often ensue. Similarly, in the author's research into 24 case studies of successful behavior management by UK teachers (Miller, 2003), almost all the interventions displayed major features of a home-based reinforcement approach.

However, it is well recognized that strong feelings of blame, hostility, and a "lack of cooperation" can easily become unleashed on occasions when pupil behavior is considered an issue, and the barriers to arriving at a joint home–school strategy can seem insurmountable. For example, in a large-scale research project aimed at helping secondary-age pupils displaying challenging behavior, Kolvin et al. (1981) found that joint teacher–parent approaches could often be characterized by "mutual distrust and prejudice" (p. 194). Similarly, Dowling and Taylor (1989), offering an advisory service to parents within a London primary school, concluded that "the seemingly humble goal of reopening communication between parents and teachers must not be underestimated" (p. 25).

Given this potential minefield, but also the research outcomes for those home–school strategies that are implemented, this chapter now turns to a series of research studies that have attempted to get beneath the surface of these issues. In doing so, the intention is to gain an understanding of those psychological processes that really determine whether a strategy will be doomed to failure before it is begun, or whether it will receive initial and continuing support of a cautious or enthusiastic nature.

ATTRIBUTIONS MADE BY TEACHERS, PUPILS, AND PARENTS

The discussion in this chapter so far has shown that recent legislation has required teachers and parents to work together over issues of difficult pupil behavior and that such approaches are supported by a respectable research evidence base. Further, teachers and pupils have been shown to be fairly optimistic supporters of such approaches (Miller & Black, 2001). In the light of this, why is behavior in schools in the United Kingdom still widely seen as such a pressing and seemingly irresolvable problem? What is preventing a wider take-up of home–school approaches?

Answers such as time pressures in schools, a lack of cooperation from parents, and the fear of triggering high degrees of antagonism from parents all suggest themselves. But an area not yet examined—the beliefs that teachers, pupils, and parents have about who or what constitutes the cause of difficult behavior in the first place—may hold an important key.

Within the discipline of psychology, attribution theory seeks to investigate and understand how individuals invoke causes and explanations for various phenomena. In the case of difficult pupil behavior, many types of explanation may suggest themselves. For example, some may seek to explain the origins of a pupil's difficulties in terms of social, economic, or political pressures on schools, parents, and pupils. Others might look to characteristics of the pupil—academic ability, attitudes, personality—or to factors such as the lifestyles or educational experiences of parents. Yet again, explanations may be sought in areas such as school policy or teachers' classroom management skills.

Attribution theory does not concern itself directly with tracking down the true or real causes of a phenomenon but, rather, examines the ways by which these perceived causes are arrived at. This is an important area because it is on the basis of our attributions rather than any "objective truth" that we usually have to function in complex and fraught social situations such as these. Consequently, the remainder of this section looks at a series of studies carried out by the author and colleagues into the ways that teachers, pupils, and parents make sense of the causes of difficult behavior in schools, in order to learn more about what is really required to launch successful strategies from within schools.

Teachers' Attributions for the Causes of Difficult Behavior in Schools

Background. In a survey of 428 junior class teachers, Croll and Moses (1985) found that behavior or discipline problems were seen to be due to home factors in 66% of cases, to "within-child" factors in 30% of cases, and in less than 4% of cases to any school or teacher factors (including previous schools or teachers). Similarly, the Elton Report commented that:

> Our evidence suggests that teachers' picture of parents is generally very negative. Many teachers feel that parents are to blame for much misbehaviour in schools. We consider that, while this picture contains an element of truth, it is distorted. (DES, 1989, p. 133)

In fact, after reviewing the pronouncements of a wide range of interested parties, Hood (1999) has argued that models of parents as "problems" rather than "partners" or "consumers" are likely to dominate in situations where there is concern about pupil behavior in school.

Clearly such unvoiced attributions have the potential to seriously undermine the quest for "agreed and explicit" strategies devised in a spirit of "genuine discussion" between teachers, parents, and pupils. The research study presented here consequently sought to get beneath the surface of descriptions such as "home factors" or "within-child" explanations and to explore the more "fine-grained" detail of the attributions that teachers make about causes (Miller, 1995b, 2003).

Sample. This study was carried out with 24 primary school teachers, drawn from a wide geographic area within England. All of these teachers had in common the fact that they had collaborated successfully with an educational psychologist in implementing a strategy to manage the difficult behavior of a pupil in their class.

Method. The investigation took the form of an intensive interview with each teacher and, as part of the analysis, the interview transcripts were subsequently "combed" for all suggested or hypothesized causes of the original behavior. All are listed in Table 42.2 with the number of teachers making each attribution shown in parentheses.

TABLE 42.2
Teachers' Attributions for the Origins of Difficult Behavior

Attributions made to: *Pupils*	*Parents*	*Teachers*
need for praise (7)	general management of child (8)	interest level of work set (4)
lack of acceptance of social norms (7)	punitive/violent home (7)	work expectations/steps set (3)
physical/medical (7)	absence of father (6)	negative attention to pupil (2)
temperament/personality (6)	lack of attention to child (6)	teacher's anxiety (2)
not feeling valued/self-esteem (5)	divided loyalties re: separation/divorce (5)	lack of incentives/tangible rewards (1)
attention seeking (4)	management of difficult behaviour (4)	lack of record keeping (1)
lack of acceptance of school rules (4)	geographical problems re: separation/divorce (1)	lack of specific management techniques (1)
lack of maturity (4)	lack of encouragement (1)	lack of affection/sympathy for child (1)
attention span (4)	atmosphere of disharmony (1)	teacher not making an exception (1)
lack of motivation toward schoolwork (3)	adoption issues (1)	pressure from other parents (1)
intelligence (2)	parent illness (1)	
lack of awareness of effect on other children (2)	grandparents' influence (1)	
knowledge of specific school rules (1)	lack of affection (1)	
knowledge of general social norms (1)	house move (1)	
lack of respect for teacher (1)	geographical isolation (1)	
comprehension level (1)		
lack of awareness of effect on parent (1)		
'tough guy' self-image (1)		
'clutter in head' (1)		
lack of trust in others (1)		
effect of bad previous school experiences (1)		

Results. Perhaps the most striking aspect of Table 42.2 is the number of different items it contains. Unlike some political pundits and sections of the media, these teachers clearly perceive causation to be a complex issue, influenced by a web of characteristics belonging to parents, teachers, and pupils themselves.

However, there is another, less immediately obvious feature of these lists that has significant implications for practice, and that is the extent to which these possible causes are seen to be under the control of the parties to whom they are attributed (Weiner, 1980). If, for example, people were to view a pupil's "attention span" as something beyond that young person's conscious control, then they would be likely to be more sympathetic toward any difficulties arising from this, than to behavior that was seen to be wilfully enacted. Alternatively, however, behavior judged to be within conscious control, perhaps a parent's "lack of attention to a child" or a teacher's "lack of record keeping," is far more likely to elicit feelings of blame and disapproval.

The lists in Table 42.2 were examined item by item by a group of seven primary school teachers training to become educational psychologists. They were asked to make judgements about the degree to which each item might be considered to be under the control of the "actor" to whom it had been attributed. When only the items commonly agreed as being highly within the control of each actor were compared in this way, then a clear majority of the difficult behavior was found to have been judged the fault of parents (Miller, 1995b, 2003).

Despite the increasing official focus on partnership with parents, the repeated finding that teachers view parents as the major cause of classroom misbehavior is likely to present a major stumbling block. Government advice on home–school agreements is unlikely to be received in the spirit intended when set against these widespread attributions toward parents.

Pupils' Attributions for the Causes of Difficult behavior in School

Given the potential importance of teachers' attributions for difficult behavior, the question of whether pupils would themselves concur with these was a logical extension. Would pupils also see parents and home factors as major causes of difficult behavior in schools or might they display a very different perspective?

Sample. To answer this question, a two-part study (Miller, Ferguson, & Byrne, 2000) was carried out in an inner-city comprehensive school in the northwest of England. This involved a total of 125 year-7 pupils (predominantly 12 years of age), composing essentially that entire year group for the school.

Method. The study was carried out using a questionnaire about the possible causes of difficult behavior in schools, the items for this questionnaire having derived from a number of prior small-group interviews. The pupils who generated the questionnaire items were selected by the Head of Year, and were seen by the researcher in four groups of between four and seven for periods of between 40 minutes and an hour. These pupils were judged by their teachers as being representative in terms of ability, behavior, and gender. After defining the purpose and ground rules for the interviews and addressing issues of confidentiality, the groups were asked to think back to their time in primary schools and to remember the types of misbehavior they had witnessed, and perhaps engaged in. Primary, rather than the current secondary school settings were examined because that is the sector examined by the corresponding research on teacher attributions. Discussion was then encouraged by means of a set of questions to encourage the pupils to think of all the possible reasons why there might be misbehavior in schools. These discussions were tape-recorded and all the suggested reasons were written up on a flip chart, and further prompts were used in an attempt to make sure that all possible reasons had been elicited. In general, the discussion groups were able to list factors related to parents and families but were reluctant to elaborate on them. Items concerning teachers and other pupils were, however, discussed and elaborated on at length.

A questionnaire was then constructed incorporating all the possible reasons provided by the groups using, wherever possible, the actual terminology of the pupils. One or two items, such as the possibility of sexual abuse, were omitted from the questionnaire, despite being raised in each group, because it was felt that, presented on a questionnaire, they might cause distress or anxiety. The resulting questionnaire consisted of 27 items (as in Table 42.3 but presented in a randomized order), and pupils were asked how important they judged each to be as a cause of difficult behavior in schools. Each questionnaire item was rated on a 4-point scale (1 = Very Important; 2 = Quite Important; 3 = Not Very Important; 4 = Not Important at All).

In the second part of this study all pupils from the year group who had not participated in the preliminary discussions, 105 in total, filled in the questionnaire. This was administered in class groups with the researcher reading out the questions one by one in each class, providing reminders about the method of responding, and encouraging pupils to ask about any items where the meaning might be unclear or ambiguous.

Results. Initial screening of the data for kurtosis and sphericity indicated that the data, with one item removed, were suitable for exploratory factor analysis (Ferguson & Cox, 1993). Factors were extracted using principal components analysis and rotated to simple structure using orthogonal (varimax) rotation (Gorsuch, 1983). The Scree test suggested a four-factor model accounting for 37.8% of the variance. As such four-factors were extracted and rotated. Both three-and five-factor models were also extracted but these were not readily interpretable, whereas the four-factor model was. The four factors reflected fairness of teacher's actions, pupil vulnerability, adverse family circumstances, and strictness of classroom regime, and these are shown in the left-hand column of Table 42.3. The questionnaire items within each factor are listed from those having the highest to the lowest loading on the factor, and fuller details of the analysis are presented in Miller et al. (2000).

Factor 1 was termed "fairness of teacher's actions" and appears to attribute misbehavior to injustices on the part of teachers. The second factor was termed "pupil vulnerability" and reflects misbehavior attributed to certain children being vulnerable to either pressure from other pupils, their own emotional turmoil, or difficulties with schoolwork. The third factor was termed "adverse family circumstances" and reflects attributions for misbehavior being located with families' inability to control their children and general family problems (e.g., financial hardship, drink, drugs). The final factor represents another teacher factor but this time reflecting on the "strictness of the classroom regime" in terms of the amount of classwork and homework set and the rigor with which the teacher manages the class.

Further analysis of this data showed that these pupils rated "teacher's unfairness" and "pupil vulnerability" as statistically significantly more important causes of misbehavior than either family problems or how strictly the classroom was managed, and this is illustrated within Table 42.3 by means of the dashed horizontal line. There were no significant differences between the results obtained from boys and girls.

Conclusions. The present study has shown pupils to attribute to teachers a significantly greater responsibility for pupil misbehavior than that which they attribute to parents. This is in dramatically marked contrast to the findings from Croll and Moses (1985), in which teachers attributed pupil misbehavior to home rather than school factors by a ratio of 17:1. It is also a finding that will be unpalatable to teachers and many involved with educational policy making.

Parents' Attributions for the Causes of Misbehavior in Schools

Background. Given the drive for parents to be involved in genuine home–school agreements and in acceptance of some responsibility for their children's school behavior, then it becomes imperative to know whether their attributional styles will resemble more closely that of teachers or of pupils. To investigate this question, a study that paralleled many of the procedures from the study of pupils' attributions was carried out with parents in an inner-city primary school (Miller, Ferguson, & Moore, 2002).

Method. This again consisted of two parts, the first being a series of intensive small-group interviews designed to elicit scenarios that would form the basis of the questionnaire. The second, and main study, was a quantitative survey of parent attributions regarding pupils' misbehavior in schools.

TABLE 42.3
The Most Important Causes of Misbehavior Deriving From Factor Analytic Studies With Parents and Pupils

PUPIL FACTORS	PARENT FACTORS
'Fairness of teachers' actions'	*'Fairness of teachers' actions'*
Teachers shouted all the time	Teachers have favorites
Pupils were picked on by teachers	Pupils are picked on by teachers
Teachers did not listen to pupils	Teachers are rude to pupils
Teachers had favorites	Teachers shout all the time
Pupils were unfairly blamed	Teachers do not listen to pupils
Good work wasn't noticed	Teachers are too soft
Teachers were rude to pupils	Good work isn't noticed
Teachers had bad moods	Pupils are unfairly blamed
Teachers gave too many detentions	Teachers have bad moods
Teachers were too soft	
Pupils didn't like teacher	
'Pupil vulnerability'	*'Pupil vulnerability to peer influences and adverse family circumstances'*
Other pupils wanted pupil to be in gang	Other pupils tell pupil to misbehave
Other pupils told pupil to misbehave	Other pupils want pupil to be in gang
Pupil was unable to see mum/dad	Families do not have enough money to eat or buy clothes
Pupils were worried about other things	Other pupils want to copy work
Pupils liked misbehaving	Other pupils stir up trouble
Other pupils wanted to copy work	Pupil is unable to see mum/dad
Pupils needed more help in class	Parents let pupils get away with too much
Classwork was too difficult	Pupil likes misbehaving
Other pupils stirred up trouble	There are fights and arguments at home
'Strictness of classroom regime'	*'Differentiation of classroom demands and expectations'*
Too much classwork was given	Too much homework was given
Too much homework was given	Teachers are too strict
Teachers were too strict	Too much classwork was given
	Classwork is too difficult
	Pupil needs more help in class
'Adverse family circumstances'	Pupil doesn't like the teacher
There were fights and arguments at home	Pupil is worried about other things
Alcohol/drug abuse by family members	
Parents let pupils get away with too much	
Families did not have enough money to eat or buy clothes	

Three initial small-group interviews involving 15 parents—12 mothers and 3 fathers—were carried out in a manner identical to those in the previous pupil study, in order to elicit all possible causes of difficult behavior in school as the basis for a new questionnaire. These group interviews eventually yielded 61 different items, including the 27 previously obtained from the small-group discussions with pupils.

Two copies of the resulting questionnaire and a cover letter were then distributed to all 165 families represented in the school. Because the school drew on a large Bengali- speaking population, copies of the questionnaire translated into Bengali were sent out where appropriate. The researcher also spoke to all the children about the project in assembly the same day and asked them to encourage their parents to complete the questionnaires and to return them to school.

One hundred fourteen families returned either one or two questionnaires, a response rate of 69%. In total, 151 questionnaires were received, of which 144 were usable for analysis. Of these, 38 (26%) were completed by fathers and 106 (74%) by mothers. Nine (6%) of the respondents described themselves as Black, 27 (19%) as Asian of Bangladeshi origin, and 102 (71%) as White.

Results. Although the full 61-item questionnaire was administered to the parent sample, the present analysis concentrates only on those items also presented to pupils in the previous study to allow for a direct comparison between these two groups.

Factor analysis of the parent responses, using a similar procedure to that for the pupil data, yielded a three-factor model. Factor 1 was termed "fairness of teacher's actions," as in the pupil study, and appears to attribute misbehavior to perceived injustices on the part of teachers. The second factor was termed "pupil vulnerability to peer influences and adverse family circumstances" and reflects a view of misbehavior as originating with pressure from other pupils, or from families' inability to control their children, and general family problems (e.g., financial hardship, discord, absent parent). The final factor, "differentiation of classroom demands and expectations," comprises school-based elements related to the appropriateness of, and the degree of support provided in respect of the curriculum demands placed on pupils.

When the full 61 items were analyzed, five factors were obtained. Four of these corresponded fairly closely to the three from the 27 items, with some subdivision taking place. A fifth factor, which was termed "culture of misbehaviour," was also obtained. To allow a more direct comparison between pupils and parents, however, only the factors deriving from the 27 items are presented for both groups in Table 42.3.

Conclusions. Table 42.3 reveals a number of interesting comparisons and contrasts that are discussed in detail elsewhere (Miller et al., 2002). First, the same factor, "fairness of teacher's actions," emerges from the study of both parents and pupils. For both groups this is also seen as one of the most prominent causes of misbehavior. The two studies were conducted in cities about 200 miles apart and this result cannot therefore simply be a reflection of local circumstances common to both groups. (A major disadvantage of conducting the research in this way, however, is that it is not possible to pursue certain interesting lines of investigation through direct comparisons within parent–child dyads.)

Second, a factor concerning "pupil vulnerability" rates equally highly for both parents and pupils as a major cause of misbehavior. However, this study also shows that, in contrast to pupils, parents do agree with teachers that certain adverse home circumstances can also be seen as a major cause of difficult pupil behavior in schools.

These findings may be interpreted as a cause for either optimism or pessimism. Although teachers express a "lack of parental support" as a major barrier to being able to implement successful behavior plans (Miller, 1996, 2003), the present study shows that parents, more so than pupils, do concur with teachers over certain aspects of the influence of home background. Therefore, it should not be assumed that parents automatically start from a different set of beliefs than teachers in this respect. The converse, however, seems to be the case when it comes to considering the possible influences of teachers on the behavior of pupils, with parents and pupils far more likely to share a common opinion concerning the influence of actions by teachers that they deem to be unfair.

It must be emphasized again that these studies do not establish the "truth" of any particular perspective, but they do highlight the fact that conflicting attributional patterns, if not recognized and addressed in some way, have the potential to create enormous obstacles to the search for agreement in this contentious area. The findings from these studies focus on the actual nature of these obstacles and thus illuminate more precisely the challenges to be addressed, or circumnavigated, in the process of setting up potentially productive joint strategies.

Implications for Teachers and Schools. The sequence of studies described in this section has drawn attention to the central importance of issues of attribution to understanding the frequently intransigent nature of difficult behavior in schools. This area of psychological study could well be seen as the "missing link" between legal and policy imperatives on the one hand and workable, real-world strategies on the other.

The major implications for teachers arising from the studies in this section can therefore be summarized as:

- Teachers are able to achieve successful outcomes even with the most disruptive pupils, if a way can be found to implement certain types of home–school approaches.
- As a prerequisite for achieving these, teachers will need to be aware of the attributions that they make for the causes of difficult behavior.
- Once made explicit, a way must be found to help teachers entertain a fuller range of possible attributions or, at least, view their own as working hypotheses rather than certainties.
- Teachers will also need to be aware of the attributions being made by pupils and parents, whether or not these are actually voiced.
- Similarly, ways must also be found to allow all parties to step to one side of these attributions, in the quest for an acceptable strategy. Engaging directly with beliefs about blame and responsibility—debating, challenging, or seeking to establish the one ultimate truth—are all likely to be extremely counterproductive, whereas acting as if they do not exist can feel like dishonesty or a failure of nerve.

The barriers to setting up home–school interventions can appear huge and insurmountable. To ask a lone teacher to navigate successfully and lead others through this web of attributions is a tall order, especially on occasions when feelings are running high. Any individual who can do so should be applauded and looked to as a potential mentor to others.

Fortunately, there is also a growing number of accounts of externally led individual and group work with teachers in this area (e.g., Osborne, 1983; Stringer, Stow, Hibbert, Powell, & Louw, 1992; Hanko, 1999; Miller, 2003) and legislators, policy makers, and the managers of individual schools need to recognize the existence and value of this trend.

Support for teachers will need to be based on a recognition that the issue of difficult behavior often gives rise to intense and unpalatable feelings. This applies to support that is obtainable through formal and hierarchical channels and informally among colleagues, as well as that available from outside agencies. Rather than denying these feelings, or labeling them as unprofessional, the climate within a school needs to permit their safe expression. However, the emphasis must be on safe expression—on promoting the recognition that attributions are always one particular way of making sense of phenomena, and that persistence with a desire to blame will be counterproductive. Distinguishing between a desire to pursue the causes of phenomena out of a natural human curiosity, and a solution-focused pragmatism concerned with finding achievable and acceptable strategies is, however, necessary to avoid the creation of a culture that saps morale and initiative in this contentious topic.

As in most forms of potential human conflict, from international tensions through to strained personal relationships, effective mediation and mutually acceptable resolution cannot be left to chance. This section has argued for the crucial contribution that psychological research in topics such as attribution theory can have in helping translate the broad aims of legislation and policy into dignified and successful outcomes for all.

CONCLUSIONS

In the early years of the new millennium, there is an increasing range of developments emanating from the British government and focusing on aspects of classroom management. For example, schools are now required to attend more specifically to many aspects of "teaching and learning" in addition to the longer-standing requirement to deliver a centrally prescribed national curriculum. These newer developments attend to matters of lesson delivery and classroom management and reflect the early work of researchers such as Kounin (1970). In addition, a recent "behavior and attendance strategy" develops approaches first proposed by Galvin et al. (1990) in the form of action plans within schools that derive from certain "audits" across students and staff.

As well as initiatives that are predominantly school based, there is also a strong drive for support agencies such as health, social services, the police, and others to operate as joint teams (known popularly as "joined-up working"), and new funding arrangements and the further development of services are frequently predicated on this requirement. Although many potential benefits may result from such joint approaches, the research into conflicting attributional patterns cited in this chapter should point to important psychological considerations that must be appreciated and probably addressed before such results can be achieved.

A contemporary extension to the tensions around delineating between home and school responsibilities may be seen in new legislation that led to the imprisonment for 60 days in 2002 of a mother whose daughter persistently truanted from school. Some short while after her release, a second daughter was similarly found to be acquiring a serious record on nonattendance at school, and the mother was sentenced for a second time, this time to 28 days.

Finally, as this chapter is being written, there is much media speculation about the date for the next British general election. By the time this book appears, this will have taken place and the complexion of the new government will be known. Recently the leader of the main opposition party highlighted his main priorities in the form of a "10-word list." In a shrinking world, in an age of global and local challenges, both natural and human-made, and at a time of accelerating worldwide changes on every level, this political leader's first words, the first 2 from his list of 10, were *school* and then *discipline*. Whoever wins the responsibility for Britain's future legislative program, it is clear that classroom management and related matters will remain a high political priority. Whether research into these matters, and particularly into such psychological features as causal attribution, organizational culture, and systems boundaries (Miller, 2003), receives the attention this chapter has suggested they deserve, remains at present to be seen.

ACKNOWLEDGMENT

The author wishes to thank Norah Frederickson, University College, London, for her comments on an earlier version of this chapter.

REFERENCES

Atkeson, B. M., & Forehand, R. (1979). Home-based reinforcement programs designed to modify classroom behavior: A review and methodological evaluation. *Psychological Bulletin, 86*(6), 1298–1308.

Ball, S. J. (1987). *The micro-politics of the school.* London: Methuen.

Barlow, D. H., & Hersen, M. (1984). *Single case experimental designs. Strategies for studying behaviour change* (2nd ed.). Oxford, England: Pergammon Press.

Barth, R. (1979). Home-based reinforcement of school behavior: A review and analysis. *Review of Educational Research, 49*(3), 436–458.

Burland, R. (1979). Social skills as the basis for coping strategies in school. *Proceedings of the 1979 DECP Annual Course*. British Psychological Society.

Chisholm, B., Kearney, D., Knight, G., Little, H., Morris, S., & Tweddle, D. (1986). *Preventative approaches to disruption*. Basingstoke, England: Macmillan Education.

Croll, P., & Moses, D. (1985). *One in five. The assessment and incidence of special educational needs*. London: Routledge & Kegan Paul.

Department for Education. (1993). *Code of practice on the identification and assessment of special educational needs*. London: Her Majesty's Stationary Office.

Department for Education. (1994a). *Pupil behaviour and discipline (Circular 8/94)*. London: Author.

Department for Education. (1994b). *The education of children with emotional and behavioural difficulties (Circular 9/94)*. London: Author.

Department for Education. (1994c). *The education of sick children (Circular 12/94)*. London: Author.

Department for Education and Employment. (1998a). *School standards and framework act*. London: Author.

Department for Education and Employment. (1998b). *LEA behaviour support plans (Circular 1/98)*. London: Author.

Department for Education and Employment. (1999). *Social inclusion: Pupil support (Circular 10/99)*. London: Author.

Department for Education and Employment. (2000). *Home-school agreements. Guidance for schools*. London: Author.

Department of Education and Science. (1967). *Children and their primary schools (the Plowden report)*. London: Her Majesty's Stationary Office.

Department for Education and Science. (1989). *Discipline in schools (the Elton report)*. London: Her Majesty's Stationary Office.

Department for Education and Science. (2001). *Code of practice on the identification and assessment of special educational needs*. London: Author.

De Shazer, S. (1982). *Patterns of brief family therapy: An ecosystemic approach*. New York: Guildford.

Douglas, J. W. B., Ross, J. M., & Simpson, H. R. (1968). *All our future*. London: Panther.

Dowling, E., & Taylor, D. (1989). The clinic goes to school: Lessons learned. *Maladjustment and Therapeutic Education 7*(1), 24–28.

Dowling, E., & Osborne, E. (Eds.) (1994). *The family and the school. A joint systems approach to problems with children*. (2nd edition). London: Routledge.

Ferguson, E., & Cox, T. (1993). Exploratory factor analysis: A users guide. *International Journal of Selection and Assessment, 1*, 84–94.

Fogelman, K. (Ed.). (1983). *Growing up in Great Britain: Papers from the National Child Development Study*. London: Macmillan.

Frederickson, N. (1990). Systems approaches in educational psychology. *Journal of Applied Systems Analysis, 17*, 3–20.

Galvin, P., Mercer, S., & Costa, P. (1990). *Building a better behaved school*. Harlow, England: Longman.

Glaser, B. (1978). *Theoretical sensitivity*. Mill Valley, CA: Sociology Press.

Glaser, B., & Strauss, A. L. (1967). *The discovery of grounded theory*. Chicago: Aldine.

Gorsuch, R. (1983). *Factor analysis*. London: Lawrence Erlbaum Associates.

Hanko, G. (1999). *Increasing competence through collaborative problem solving: Using insight into social and emotional factors in children's learning*. London: David Fulton.

Hargreaves, D. H. (1967). *Social relations in a secondary school*. London: Routledge & Kegan Paul.

Hargreaves, D. H. (1975). *Interpersonal relations and education*. London: Routledge & Kegan Paul.

Harrop, L. A., & McNamara, E. (1979). The behavioural workshop for classroom problems. A re-appraisal. *British Journal of In-Service Education, 1*(1), 47–50.

Hastings, N., & Wood, K. C. (2002). *Re-organising primary classroom learning*. Milton Keynes, England: Open University Press.

Hood, S. (1999). Home-school agreements: A true partnership? *School Leadership and Management, 19*(4), 427–440.

Hoy, W. K., & Miskel, C. C. (1989) Schools and their external environments. In R. Glatter (ed) *Educational institutions and their environments*. Milton Keynes, England: Open University Press.

Hutchinson, S. A. (1988). Education and grounded theory. In R. R. Sherman & R. B. Webb (Eds.), *Qualitative research in education: Focus and methods*. Lewes, England: Falmer Press.

Kolvin, I., Garside, R. C., Nicol, A. R., Macmillan, A.,Wolstenholme, F. & Leitch, I. M. (1981). *Help starts here. The maladjusted child in the ordinary school*. London: Tavistock Publications.

Kounin, J. S. (1970). *Discipline and group management in classrooms*. New York: Holt, Rinehart & Winston.

Leach, D. J., & Raybould, E. C. (1977). *Learning and behaviour difficulties in school*. London: Open Books.

Lieberman, A., & Miller, L. (1990). The social realities of teaching. In A. Lieberman (Ed.), *Schools as collaborative cultures*. Basingstoke, England: Falmer Press.

Little, J. W. (1990). Teachers as colleagues. In A. Lieberman (Ed.), *Schools as collaborative cultures*. Basingstoke, England: Falmer Press.

Lortie, D. (1975). *Schoolteacher. A sociological study*. Chicago: University of Chicago Press.

McNamara, E. (1988). Behavioural contracting with secondary aged pupils. *Educational Psychology in Practice 2*(4), 21–26.

McNamara, E., & Harrop, L. A. (1979). Behaviour modification in secondary schools—a cautionary tale. *Occasional Papers of the DECP*, 3, 2, 38–40.

McNamara, E., & Harrop, L. A. (1981). Behaviour modification in the secondary school: A rejoinder to Wheldall and Austin. *Occasional Papers of the DECP*, 3, 2, 38–40.

Madsen, C. H., Becker, W. C., & Thomas, D. R. (1968). Rules, praise and ignoring: Elements of elementary classroom control. *Journal of Applied Behavioural Analysis, 1*(2), 139–150.

Merrett, F. (1981) Studies in behaviour modification in British educational settings, *Educational Psychology 1*(1), 13–38.

Merrett, F., & Blundell, D. (1982). Self-recording as a means of improving behaviour in the secondary school. *Educational Psychology, 2*, 147–157.

Merrett, P., & Wheldall, K. (1978). Playing the game: A behavioural approach to classroom management in the junior school. *Educational Review, 30*(1), 41–50.

Miller, A. (1995a). Building grounded theory within educational psychology practice. *Educational and Child Psychology, 12*(2), 5–14.

Miller, A. (1995b). Teachers' attributions of causality, control and responsibility in respect of difficult pupil behaviour and its successful management. *Educational Psychology, 15*, 457–471.

Miller, A. (1996). *Pupil behaviour and teacher culture*. London: Cassell.

Miller, A. (1999). Squaring the triangle: Pupil behaviour, teachers and parents—and psychology. *Educational Psychology in Practice, 15*(2), 75–80.

Miller, A. (2003). *Teachers, parents and classroom behaviour. A psychosocial approach*. Maidenhead, England: Open University Press.

Miller, A. (2004). Educational psychology and difficult pupil behaviour: Qualitative, quantitative or mixed methods? In Z. Todd, B. Nerlich, S. McKeown, & D. D. Clarke, (Eds.), *Mixing methods in psychology. The integration of qualitative and quantitative methods in theory and practice*. Hove, England: Psychology Press.

Miller, A., & Black, L. (2001). Does support for home-school behaviour plans exist within teacher and pupil cultures? *Educational Psychology in Practice, 17*(3), 245–262.

Miller, A., Ferguson, E., & Byrne, I. (2000). Pupils' causal attributions for difficult classroom behaviour *British Journal of Educational Psychology, 70*, 85–96.

Miller, A., Ferguson, E., & Moore, E. (2002). Parents' and pupils' causal attributions for difficult classroom behaviour. *British Journal of Educational Psychology, 72*, 27–40.

Mortimore, P., Sammons, P., Stoll, L., Lewis, D., & Ecob, R. (1988). *School matters*. Wells, England: Open Books.

Nash, R. (1973). *Classrooms observed. The teacher's perception and the pupil's performance*. London: Routledge & Kegan Paul.

Nias, J. (1985). Reference groups in primary teaching. In S. J. Ball & I. E. Goodson (Eds.), *Teachers' lives and careers*. Lewes, England: Falmer Press.

Osborne, E. (1983). The teacher's relationship with the pupils' families. In I. Salzbergber-Wittenberg, G. Henry, & E. Osborne (Eds), *The emotional experience of learning and teaching*. London: Routledge.

Pidgeon, N., & Henwood, K. (1996). Grounded theory: Practical implementation. In J. T. E. Richardson, (Ed.), *Handbook of qualitative research methods*. Oxford, England: BPS Blackwell.

Rennie, E. N. F. (1980). Good behaviour games with a whole class. *Remedial Education, 15*, 187–190.

Rice, A. K. (1976). Individual, group and inter-group processes. In E. J. Miller (Ed.), *Task and organization*. Chichester, England: John Wiley.

Rutter, M., Tizard, J., & Whitmore, K. (1970). *Education, health and behaviour*. London: Longman.

Rutter, M., Maughan, B., Mortimore, P., & Ouston, J. (1979). *Fifteen thousand hours*. Wells, England: Open Books.

Sharp, R., & Green, A. (1975). *Education and social control. A study in progressive primary education*. London: Routledge & Kegan Paul.

Strauss, A. L. (1987). *Qualitative analysis for social scientists*. England: Cambridge University Press.

Strauss, A., & Corbin, J. (1999). *Basics of qualitative research: Techniques and procedures for developing grounded theory*. London: Sage.

Stringer, P., Stow, L., Hibbert, K., Powell, J., & Louw, E. (1992). Establishing staff consultation groups in schools. *Educational Psychology in Practice, 8*(2), 87–96.

Tsoi, M. M., & Yule, W. (1976). The effects of group reinforcement in classroom behaviour modification. *Educational Studies, 2*, 129–140.

Turner, B. (1992) Looking closely and creating grounded theory. Paper presented at ESRC Research Semiar, University of Warwick, England. 5 March 1992.

Wagner, A. C. (1987). 'Knots' in teacher's thinking. In J. Calderhead (Ed.), *Exploring teachers' thinking*. London: Cassell.

Ward, J. (1971). Modification of deviant classroom behaviour. *British Journal of Educational Psychology, 41*, 304–313.

Weiner, B. (1980). A cognitive-attribution-emotion-action model of motivated behaviour: An analysis of judgements of help-giving. *Journal of Personality and Social Psychology, 39*, 186–200.

Wheldall, K. (1981). 'A' before 'C' or the use of behavioural ecology in the classrooms. In P. Gurney, (Ed.), *Behaviour modification in education. Perspectives 5*. England: University of Exeter.

Wheldall, K., Morris, M., Vaughn, P., & Ng, Y. Y. (1981). Rows versus tables: An example of the use of behavioural ecology in two classes of 11-year old children. *Educational Psychology, 1*(2), 171–184.

Wheldall, K., & Merrett, F. (1988). Which classroom behaviours do primary school teachers say they find most troublesome? *Educational Review, 40*(1), 13–27.

Wilson, M., & Evans, M. (1980). *Educational of disturbed pupils*. Schools Council Working Paper 65. London: Methuen.

Winnet, R. A., & Winkler, R. C. (1972). Current behaviour modification in the classroom: Be still, be quiet, be docile. *Journal of Applied Behaviour Analysis, 8*, 259–262.

43

Classroom Management in Multicultural Classes in an Immigrant Country: The Case of Israel

Miriam Ben-Peretz, Billie Eilam, and Estie Yankelevitch
University of Haifa

INTRODUCTION

This chapter focuses on issues of classroom management and discipline in the multicultural and heterogeneous classrooms in present-day Israel, reflecting massive immigration over the years. We start with a conceptual framework guiding our discussion and move to features of existing multicultural classrooms. We trace the development of management and discipline regulations in the Israeli centralized school system, noting the implications for cultural dissonance with diverse student populations. A special part of the chapter presents research focused on issues of discipline in multicultural classrooms as perceived by teachers, students, and parents. After briefly discussing how teachers are prepared for multiculturalism in current schools, we conclude by linking theoretical perspectives with research findings. We focus on the Jewish sector because most immigration in the last 15 years occurs in this context. New immigrants from the former Soviet Union and Ethiopia currently constitute a highly significant part of the school population.

A CONCEPTUAL BACKGROUND

In Israel, as in many other countries, classroom management and discipline are conceived to be crucial components of a productive, effective learning environment. Several researchers point to the positive relationships between appropriate classroom behavior and learning achievements (Bennett, Finn, & Cribb, 1999; Nelson, Martella, & Marchand, 2002). Flay, Alred, and Ordway (2001) found a 50% improvement in students' achievement in schools that implemented special programs of classroom management.

Classroom management may be defined as the thoughts and actions of teachers designed to create an effective learning environment. Preservation of order is a desirable component of classroom management. Teachers, who are effective in classroom control, establish routines and adequately insist on their implementation. Classroom management is both routine and nonroutine; it is profoundly interactive and the subject of planning and reflection. It is about maintaining order and about what to do when that order has been achieved (Helsby & Knight, 1998). Although classroom management covers many aspects of planning and development, the most prominent concern in the eyes of principals, teachers, parents, and students is maintaining discipline (Romi & Freund, 1999). Therefore, we focus on classroom discipline in this chapter.

The Hebrew word for classroom discipline is *mischmaat*, which may be translated as "the self-imposed ability to listen." Manberg (1996), in a book for teachers on the relationship between maturity and values, interprets the term *mischmaat* as the integration of listening and acceptance of authority as well as the responsiveness to norms and regulations.

Classroom discipline may be conceived of as part of a socialization process, (i.e., a process of induction into a lifestyle of continuous autonomous learning and of productive interpersonal relationships). Emphasizing the social aspects of classroom discipline enhances the importance of effective classroom management, to ensure that smooth and effective teaching and learning occur, and as a means of socializing students for future participation in the community (Ben-Peretz, 1998).

The two main approaches to classroom management outlined in an Israeli book intended for elementary education (Smilanski & Bar-Lev, 1994) are an individualistic approach and a systemic approach. The individual approach focuses on a single student as the target of a teacher's actions. Careful observations of an individual student's misbehavior result in deliberate choices of the teacher's (disciplinary) actions. The systemic approach focuses on the group as the target of a teacher's actions. This is based on the assumption that the individual is shaped by the social context. It is therefore necessary to establish group norms and relationships in order to create a productive learning environment. A relevant definition of individual discipline would include his or her ability and readiness to become part of a community by accepting its norms and regulations. A disciplinary problem arises when behavior is disruptive and disturbs the functioning of the group and its development. It is the teacher's role to create a classroom climate that is conducive to the development of a classroom community (Shimoni, Segal, & Sharoni, 1996).

The Israeli concept of classroom discipline may be defined as having two aspects (Saad & Hendrix, 1993):

- a continuum between mandated, externally determined, and open, locally designed frames of discipline; and
- a continuum between an individualistic and a societal orientation toward classroom discipline.

These two aspects and their implications are discussed later in the chapter.

In Israel there is growing emphasis on teacher autonomy together with the implementation of more student-oriented teaching strategies, such as cooperative learning, and these tend to create a more open and flexible classroom climate. Teachers are encouraged to develop school-based curricula and to use a greater variety of instructional strategies beyond the regular teacher-centered mode. These expectations pose a daily dilemma for teachers who have to maneuver between the potential for classroom chaos and the limitations of a traditional learning environment. This dilemma increases the need for adequate strategies of classroom management and discipline and demands a high level of pedagogical knowledge, practical experience, and reflective abilities (Ben-Peretz, 1998).

The difficulties of coping with discipline in progressivist school reform (Lefstein, 2002) is a continuing problem in Israel. According to Lefstein, the failure of progressivist school reform to persevere is due in part to the inadequate treatment of the relationship between innovative pedagogy and issues of classroom control. Keeping these two components of teaching distinct prevents the development of classroom discipline models that match progressive pedagogy.

Israel is a multicultural, multiethnic country with a highly fluid classroom population related to immigration and demographic changes. The clash between cultures may introduce serious problems, including classroom discipline, as new immigrants from Ethiopia and the former Soviet Union, for instance, may find Israeli classroom situations alien and confusing (Ben-Peretz & Shteinhart, 1996). New immigrants may come to Israel with different and varied experiences and, in most cases, cannot be considered homogeneous groups. Surprisingly, neither Ministry of Education circulars, internal school documents, nor most research reports refer specifically or explicitly to this phenomenon. A possible explanation may be that multiculturalism in Israel is taken for granted by all concerned.

We have briefly discussed general issues of classroom management and discipline. Because of the complexity of this situation, we now focus on issues of discipline in multicultural classrooms, noting that lacunas exist in many official documents and regulations as well as in most research endeavors concerning these issues.

MULTICULTURAL CLASSROOMS IN ISRAEL

Migration of populations is a worldwide phenomenon due to political, economic, and social factors. Like many other countries today, Israel reflects significant demographic changes due to intense immigration. These changes have resulted in the dominance of multicultural classrooms in Israeli schools. Beyond the many individual differences among students encountered in heterogeneous environments, multicultural classrooms are characterized by diversity of ethnicity, religion, mother tongue, and cultural traditions. Israel is a gathering place for Jews from all over the world. It is blessed with rich cultural diversity that includes the existing plurality of populations: Jews, Arabs both Muslims and Christians, Druze, and others. Because the educational system in Israel strives to meet the needs of different social populations (e.g., Arabs and Jews) and to sustain an optimal continuity between home and school with regard to language and cultural heritage, most classrooms are dominated either by Arabs or by Jewish students. We focus on the impact of immigration on classroom life in the Jewish sector where most of the immigration occurs.

After a short period of adaptation in separate classrooms in which immigrant youth learn the Hebrew language, Israeli educational policy favors their integration into mixed classrooms. This governmental commitment alone, however, does not ensure the realization of the goal of integration.

We turn now to a conceptualization of the multicultural nature of Israeli classrooms.

CONCEPTUALIZING MULTICULTURAL CLASSROOMS AND THE IMPLICATION FOR THE ISRAELI CONTEXT

An ideal multicultural classroom in a democratic country would be a place where all voices are heard and respected, in an atmosphere of acceptance and mutual understanding. Such a climate may be created by restructuring the environment rather than by simply adding new aspects to the curriculum such as learning about other cultures. It reflects "equity pedagogy," expressed in teachers' expectations as well as in school disciplinary policies and practices. Restructuring the environment to strive for these ideals may be conducive to the acculturation of immigrants in a new environment.

A number of studies have investigated acculturation and adaptation of individuals who migrate from one culture to another. The concept of acculturation refers to the phases of belonging that these individuals experience as they encounter the new, dominant cultural contexts. According to Redfield, Linton, and Herskovits (1936), acculturation is defined as follows:

> Acculturation comprehends those phenomena which result when groups of individuals having different cultures come into continuous first-hand contact with subsequent changes in the original culture patterns of either or both groups. (p. 149)

Berry (1997) makes an important distinction between acculturation as a group phenomenon and the changes in the psychology of individuals. Both developmental processes may be identified in schools in which immigrant students experience both group and psychological acculturation.

According to Berry (1997), four acculturation processes may be identified: **assimilation**, when individuals do not maintain their separate cultural identity; **integration**, when they participate fully in the dominant social network exists simultaneously with a desire to maintain some degree of cultural identity; **separation**, when individuals hold on to their original culture, avoiding interaction with others; and **marginalization**, when both cultural maintenance and significant relations with the dominant culture are minimized for reasons of exclusion or discrimination. In the Israeli multicultural classroom one may find all four processes of acculturation. The stronger and more positive the group sense of cultural identity, the more inclined its members might be toward integration. On the other hand, a less positive sense of cultural identity may lead to separation and in more severe cases to marginalization.

Similar to these acculturation processes, Eisikovitz and Beck (1990) identified two courses of action that take place within multicultural classrooms: (a) **adaptation**—through which the immigrants learn to live in harmony with the new surroundings of school, and (b) **integration**—which describes the mutual changes experienced by both natives and immigrants during and as a result of the encounter.

In the following we discuss several features of culture and relate these to issues of discipline in Israeli multicultural classrooms.

There are several independent parameters commonly accepted for characterizing a culture, each constituting a continuum. Three of these parameters, or dimensions, were used by den Brok, Levy, Rodriguez, and Wubbels (2002) for characterizing cultural differences in communication between individuals and differences in their perception of each other.

1. *The individualism–collectivism continuum* (Triandis, 1995)
   According to this parameter, people belonging to cultures characterized as individualistic, such as Western societies, prefer and maintain their own agendas over societal ones, and those belonging to collectivist cultures, such as Eastern societies, behave according to the collective common goals rather than their own. Collectivist cultures tend to exhibit intimate relations among themselves and remoteness from outsiders. Accountability to family surpasses accountability to all others, and they value collective harmony above all. Within the Israeli Jewish population, Eilam (2003) has found that Eastern-originating Jews are more collectivist than Western-originating Jews at least where teaching–learning environments are concerned.
2. *The approach–avoidance continuum (immediacy)* (Anderson, 1985; Hecht, Anderson, & Ribeau, 1989)
   This dimension was found to be of importance in all cultures and ethnic groups. Behaviors characterizing the "approach" end of the continuum express closeness, approach, and accessibility (e.g., smiling, touching, eye contact, open body positions, close distances). Behaviors characterizing the "avoidance" end of the continuum express avoidance and

distance. Hall (1966) found the Middle Eastern and the Southern and Eastern European cultures to be "high-contact" cultures. Israelis, by and large, tend to exhibit "high contact" behaviors not necessarily shared by newcomers. An example of "low contact" behavior in Israel is, for instance, found with Ethiopian immigrants who avoid close eye contact with anyone not closely related to them. Russian immigrants seem to be reticent in their interpersonal behaviors, especially in comparison with young Israelis who tend to be extremely direct and close.

3. The *power–distance continuum* (Hofstede, 1991)
   This parameter describes the degree to which an individual perceives the locus of power and wealth to be concentrated in the hands of few or to be equally distributed throughout a culture. Hofstede considered the students' perception of teachers on the continuum of high/low power-distance according to their cultural expectations. Many cultures expect teachers to be authoritative, and this is related to family structure and authority. The Ethiopian Jews, for example who have a strong patriarchal family structure in which adults are highly respected and have complete authority over the young. In this culture, teachers are expected to be authoritative.

In light of these parameters, a dissonance exists between the natives and the new immigrants as they transfer from one culture to another and this may be termed as "cultural shock" (Bock, 1970) and expressed by feelings of strangeness, lack of belonging, and even helplessness. Taft (1977) included a phenomenon of "cultural tiredness" expressed in individuals' discomfort, sense of pressure, anger, and extreme helplessness.

The phenomenon of cultural shock also may be explained by the concept of "developmental niche." Harkness and Super (1999) have emphasized the role of "cultural messages" that are conveyed and interpreted by individuals participating in educational situations. They propose the theoretical framework of the developmental niche in order to gain insights into the processes of child development and acquisition of cultural knowledge (Super & Harkness, 1986). Three major subsystems interact in the developmental niche: (a) the physical and social setting in which the child lives; (b) the customs and practices of childcare; and (c) the psychology of the caretakers.

Harkness and Super (1999) focused on the developmental niche of the parents' home, and we expand this framework to include the culture of schools. Schools also represent differences of physical and social settings; they are characterized by specific customs, norms, and practices of teacher–student interactions. Teachers, and other "caretakers" in schools, have their own theories of education. Generally speaking, there are gaps between the developmental niche at home and in school. These gaps are exacerbated when students come from home backgrounds that differ in significant ways from the background of teachers and other students.

THE CURRENT COMPOSITION OF MULTICULTURAL CLASSROOMS IN ISRAEL AND RELEVANT RESEARCH

Two major immigrant populations, the Ethiopians and the Russian Jews, are found in current Israeli classrooms. We rely on the concepts presented earlier in our descriptions of these populations.

The Ethiopian Jews

The Israeli Ethiopian community is composed of about 80,000 members, about half of them under the age of 18. They arrived in two major immigration waves (1984–85 and 1991). The prior educational experiences of many new immigrant Ethiopians are very different from those of the native Israelis and may be expressed through different norms of behavior, time perception, and space orientation (Eilam, 1999; Friedman, 1986).

As suggested by den Brok et al. (2002), Ethiopian youth who were born in Israel are still influenced by their culture as practiced in their homes and communities despite the acculturation process through the Israeli educational system (Eisikovitz & Beck, 1990). Because of increased racial awareness, it has been reported that the young Ethiopian generation is adding to its Israeli-Ethiopian-Jewish identity a new and broader identity with the darker minority within the larger White society (Anteby, Yemini, 2003). This new collective identity is developing in light of the global Afro-culture. This new identity may raise negative feelings, resulting in possible separation or even marginalization. The consequences of the Ethiopian culture shock (or new feelings of identity) may be expressed in feelings of anger and frustration and may result in severe disciplinary problems.

As mentioned before, most Ethiopian Jews who immigrated to Israel have a patriarchal family structure—with adults having complete authority over the young. These are generally the characteristics of the Ethiopian Jews' home developmental niche. In contrast, the power relation in the Israeli classrooms is less authoritative and more child centered. As a result students may experience feeling of conflict that are expressed in aggression toward other students and teachers. It may also lead to the weakening of parental authority at home, preventing parents from fulfilling their complementary role in solving their children's disciplinary problems.

The Russian Jews

About a million Russian immigrants arrived in Israel during the last 15 years after the collapse of the former USSR. Most of the Russian immigrants knew very little about Israel, were not observant Jews, and were not familiar with Jewish practices.

Shamai (2003) reported the effect of the "cultural shock" on Russian immigrant youth in a certain kibbutz while they were going through the long and difficult adaptation process to become part of the new society. Shamai summarized a continuum of cultural adaptation styles from complete assimilation in the new culture at the one end of the continuum, through a cognitive adaptation (integration) expressed in learning of the new culture, up to complete withdrawal from the new culture (separation or even marginalization). These personal adaptation styles are influenced by the duration of contact with the new culture, the personal traits of the immigrants, and the attitude of the acceptance system.

We turn now to the relationships between regulations and norms of classroom discipline in Israel and the multicultural pluralistic nature of these classrooms, starting with a general overview of school regulations in Israel.

SCHOOL REGULATIONS AND PRACTICES AS MEANS OF ENFORCING DISCIPLINE IN ISRAEL

Though Israeli educators do not directly follow the biblical principles, these principles do constitute part of their pedagogical heritage. The Bible, for instance, provides guidelines concerning father–son, and teacher–student relationships: "He who spareth his rod hateth his son; but he that loveth him chasteneth him betimes" (Proverbs XIV, 24). This proverb emphasizes discipline, whereas "Train up the child in the way he should go" (Proverbs, XX, 22), and "Let the honor of the student be as dear to you as your own" (Avotht—Chapters from the Fathers, 4, 12) demonstrate respect of the teacher for the students' point of view. Some of these ideas are embedded in present-day approaches concerning discipline, though not literally.

The Israeli Ministry of Education publishes and updates from time to time guidelines for school regulations concerning discipline (Israel Ministry of Education, 1986). These regulations represent a formal bureaucratic model that relates to the pedagogic climate in schools in general. Most schools compose their own regulations based on the formal model.

Although regulations are one of the basic structures of a formal bureaucratic organization in Israeli schools, regulations are more symbolic than operative according to Jacobson (1995), and they are more of an ideological tool than a paradigm of behavior. The official ministry school regulations are vague. They relate to schools in general without relating to specific school characteristics such as the age groups; level (elementary, secondary, or high schools); the number of immigrant students, if any; the number of students in class, which usually lies between 35 and 41 students; or the population structure of the school (multicultural or homogeneous, etc.). The symbolic aspect of these regulations expresses the power of the ministry to enforce general principles for school culture, not necessarily expecting these to be followed except as a guiding framework. Some of the regulations, such as those related to students' rights, are symbolic of the cultural status of students in Israeli schools. Nevertheless, in certain schools, the regulations are used as an operative tool and in many cases the regulations do determine rules of behavior and qualify as a mandated form of discipline.

The foreword to the regulations includes the expectations and intentions expressed by the Ministry of Education policy makers. In this foreword it is found that one purpose of the regulations is to engender a balance between the level of freedom of students, on the one hand, and the necessary discipline enforced, on the other. Disciplinary regulations in Israel are designed to guide the students' lives as free citizens in a democratic environment. The methods used to apply these regulations are based on the educational philosophy of the school, and are formalized by the teaching staff of the school in question. Steps taken when rules are broken by undisciplined students are part of school regulations and are usually well known to both students and their parents.

The specific school regulations include the educational goals of the institute; a list of obligations and privileges; disciplinary rules and measures applied for keeping the rules; suggestions for prevention of contravening the rules; and suggested reactions in case of violation of the rules. The final response to contravening the rules is usually left to the teacher involved. There are, however, certain responses that are prohibited, such as physical punishment, adverse comments in the class register, or lowering of grades. Authorization of punishment is in the hands of the class teacher or the principal of the school, determined by the seriousness of the violation. This contravention of the rules can be divided into two categories of less and more severe misbehavior. Less severe or day-to-day misbehavior such as talking during class, lack of concentration during lessons, distraction, or unpunctuality can be dealt with by the teacher on the spot.

The more severe contraventions of rules include misbehavior toward teachers or fellow students, continuous teasing or bullying that is typical of conflicts between students, and deliberate damage to school property. Teachers also may view deliberate disobedience, answering back, or threats to the teacher as severe misbehavior. Consequences for this type of contravention may include: informing the parents, demanding an apology, warning, or handing over the punishment to the principal. This behavior can lead to isolation of the child from the peer group or, in extreme cases, to expulsion. The regulations of the Ministry of Education state that expulsion from school demands that prior steps be taken, such as discussion with the student and parents, review with an educational consultant, or oral and written warnings. In extreme cases, the school pedagogical council can decide to expel the student permanently. According to the notion of the developmental niche, both types of misbehavior can be interpreted as emerging from the cultural gap between the norms and expectations of home and those of school authorities.

The following is a concrete example. In 1991 the Ethiopian Jewish immigrants were settled in absorption centers, and shortly afterwards the children were sent to school. In this particular case, the students started off in separated classrooms—in order to study Hebrew and other subjects in Hebrew. After a short while disciplinary problems arose. One morning as the teacher turned to one of the students and asked him to fulfill an assignment, the student got upset, rose, approached the teachers' desk and turned it over, and left the class saying "you will not tell me what to do." The student was sent back to the absorption center, and the school principal asked the center manager to explain the seriousness of the event to the parents. The manager, accompanied by a translator, went to the student's home and explained the situation to the parents, asking them to intervene and to take responsibility for their child's misbehavior. The father in reaction said, "Now the boy belongs to the government. You take care of him. Do what is necessary." Nevertheless, the father later beat the boy very severely. When that became known, the manager once again visited their home, this time explaining that corporal punishment is forbidden in Israel, (contrary to the biblical advice concerning using the rod) (Yankelevitch, E., January 15, personal communication, 1991).

In Israel today, as in the Western world, historical and legal development brought about a change in philosophical and educational principles relating to childhood and youth. In 1989 a "Declaration of Children's' Rights in Israel" was composed. One of the inalienable rights in this declaration is the right of students to a fair and just hearing, enabling their point of view to be heard, ensuring that the "punishment fits the crime," and prevention of collective punishment. Punishment should be imposed only after due consideration and not as a result of anger or vengeance. School regulations thus keep the punishment within bounds and prevent irrational punishment. To promote these rights and to ensure their application, an open line was set up in the Ministry of Education for the use of students and their parents. By the means of this line, they could turn to a professional independent adjudicator to deal with complaints and conflicts between students and the system. Over and above this, it provides preliminary therapy to children in need. The open line is one of potential response to the many conflicts and dilemmas arising in present-day Israeli multicultural classrooms.

PRACTICES IN THE CLASSROOM AND THEIR CHANGES OVER TIME

To demonstrate the changes in rules of discipline over time and the possible relationship between these changes and the growing diversity in Israeli classrooms, we focus on one school—the Reali School in Haifa, which was founded in 1913, one of the first to be founded in *Eretz-Israel*[1] (Halperin, 1970).

In the early days in this school (until the establishment of the State of Israel in 1948), school regulations included detailed rules and orders concerning students' behavior, learning methods, and school order. Disciplinary violations led to punishment as laid down in published regulations. Students were obliged to behave in an appropriate manner, they were responsible for school property, and they were expected to be polite to their teachers and keep quiet in class, corridor, and playground.

Specific rules concerning order in school were defined. Each day began with a morning assembly that took place in the schoolyard. Later on the students walked to class in line followed by the teacher. At the beginning of each lesson students greeted the teacher standing up, until they were told to sit down. A student called on would stand up while answering. The lesson was not over at the sound of the bell, but only when the teacher announced the class

[1] *Eretz-Israel*—the land of Israel. A name used before the establishment of the State of Israel.

was dismissed. And when the teacher left the class, the students once again stood up as an act of respect toward the teacher.

Each class had three ledgers. In the first one, the student on duty would write down the homework given to the class after each lesson. The other two were the responsibility of the teacher; in the first one he or she would register classroom attendance, and the second was designated for registering misbehavior—the "black diary." Each morning the class teacher would deal with students who had behaved badly. A student who accumulated a high number of complaints was reprimanded or, in more severe cases, could be sent to the principal, or expelled from school for a couple of days.

The following is an example demonstrating the teacher's responsibility in enforcing norms of behavior. During the 1920s and the beginning of the 1930s when Haifa was a small city with few streets and cinemas, teachers were required to take turns in observing their students in public places. For a time, students were not allowed to walk about after 10 p.m., but as the town grew bigger this regulation was cancelled. Nevertheless, in the updated school, students still are required to behave in a respectable manner in public places outside school. The regulations mention that a complaint forwarded to school concerning unsuitable behavior after school hours would be dealt with accordingly.

Another school regulation first enforced in the 1930s, which is still valid today, is the compulsory wearing of school uniforms. This regulation is based on the educational principle that students should be valued not by their appearance but by their personality.

These norms and regulations continued as long as the school population was relatively homogeneous and the expectations of teachers, students, and parents were fairly uniform. As Haifa grew, changes in the internal structure of the school occurred, a junior high school was established, and the student population became more heterogeneous. These changes were accompanied by a reform in school regulations. The main reform, as far as discipline was concerned, was the abolition of the "black diary." The school showed more tolerance toward misbehavior, and students who improved their behavior could clear their previous bad record. This was done to encourage unruly students to improve their conduct, especially immigrant students who were not accustomed to school regulations.

The school regulations for the academic year 2003–04 include paragraphs dealing with traditional classroom discipline problems such as absenteeism, failure to do homework, copying during tests, as well as more modern problems such as using a cell phone during class, vandalism in school, violence, and abusive language (Ha'Reali Ha'Iuri, School Regulation 2003/4). These latter examples are typical of the changes that society in Israel is going through. In the earlier days, problems caused by cell phones and immodest clothing did not exist. Modernization, migration, ideology changes, and the breakdown of the family unit may be held partially responsible for these changes. Body piercing, for instance, may be considered a symptom of youth rebellion that causes conflicts between adults and students. Different norms that students bring with them are apt to raise tension and additional behavioral problems. According to Yariv (1999) about 40% of students in elementary schools in Israel are defined by their teachers as exhibiting problematic behavior.

School regulations nowadays refer to teachers and school employees as well to students. For example, "teachers and students are responsible for arriving at the lesson on time." "The bell refers to teachers as well as to students." "The appearance of teachers, employees and students should be according to educational norms" (Ha'Reali Ha'Iuri: regulations 2003–04).

In a guide about maintaining discipline in school Yariv (1999) elaborated on the impact of the multicultural population of students on the climate of classrooms. Among other issues, he related to the tendency of youth to exhibit their autonomy by body piercing, and soon. Yariv presented ways to overcome conflicts and nonnormative behavior through wise regulations. He argued against regulations that ignore present-day youth culture.

In the last decade, attention has been paid to the issue of "rights and duties at school." An ongoing discussion took place in Israel involving the activity of voluntary independent organizations, as well as the Movement of the National Council of Child Welfare and the Israel's Parents' Committee. All contributed to the awareness of this topic in many educational institutions. In 1991, a group of high school students together with the pedagogical secretariat initiated a discussion on this topic. As a result, a forum of educators and students got together to compose a document called "Involvement, Cooperation and Responsibility," and finally, the director of the Ministry of Education, the secretariat, and the National Students Council declared a convention. The rationale of the convention says:

> One of the duties of school is to prepare the future citizen of the country. It has to enable the students to learn the principles and values that characterize a democratic-pluralistic society and to practice and apply these in every day life at school. This will contribute to the student's development as an autonomous person, an involved member of his/her community and a caring and involved citizen in the country. (Marcus, 1999)

The composers of this convention recommended that each school compose its own convention according to its educational philosophy, beliefs, population, and the wishes and needs of its students, teachers, parents and community.

RESEARCH CONCERNING CLASSROOM MANAGEMENT IN THE MULTICULTURAL CONTEXT OF ISRAEL

An examination of Israeli studies concerning classroom management revealed a focus on two core themes: (a) classroom management, pedagogy, and school organization reflecting educational ideologies; and (b) teachers', students', and parents' perceptions and attitudes concerning classroom management and discipline.

These studies base their conclusions on data gathered from classrooms that include Israeli multicultural populations, especially immigrants from the former Soviet Union and Ethiopia, and are situated in different areas of the country. They include urban as well as rural schools, Jewish and Arab sectors, students of Eastern and Western origins, and schools that cater primarily to students of high or low socioeconomic background.

The studies focus primarily on the teachers and students in the schools studied. In few of them data from parents were collected as well.

The instruments used are mostly Likert-type questionnaires, composed of statements concerning discipline and control strategies, and rating of items. In a few studies, observational data are used and some interviews. Several studies are theoretical and analytical concerning components of classroom management modes.

The following is a brief discussion of these studies:

(a) *The relation between classroom management and school organization, pedagogy, and educational ideologies.* This group of studies relate to diverse educational ideologies. Lefstein (2002) indicated that most Israeli schools fit the progressive educational orientation that encourages students' autonomy and active learning and implements relevant curricula. The progressive orientation is expressed in a pedagogy that accepts and promotes students' diversity and active involvement in the learning process. It encourages students' use of personal interest, task types, and pace, and it allows for students' high mobility in and outside the classroom and the school. Such strategies for active learning create a "positive noise" but also make it difficult for teachers to follow and control students at all times. This creates the potential for classroom disturbances.

Lefstein (2002) explored teacher strategies for dealing with the inherent conflict between the progressive ideology and their need for control and discipline of their students. He found that teachers practice a functional "cognitive partition," completely divorcing their thinking of power and their thinking of pedagogy and acting in each of these arenas separately with little integration of the two. For instance, teachers may implement an instructional strategy of group work, inquiry, and peer learning and teaching, and at the same time, they may enforce quiet and orderly conduct among the students, maintaining the cognitive partition mentioned by Lefstein. Students coming from more authoritative classrooms may conceive a more liberal and open classroom climate as evidence of a teacher's lack of power and credibility, which are viewed as shortcomings. This may lead to highly unruly behavior and exacerbate the teacher's "cognitive partition" (Shteinhart, 2000). The cognitive partition is not used by teachers alone. It also may be noted in the school's functional organization in which teachers deal with pedagogy and administrators with discipline. Most policy documents and manuals do not address an integration of both domains.

Using a framework of power relations, Jacobson (1995) suggested tension between a permissive ideology that provides more autonomy to students and the need to exercise control to fulfill the requirements of the educational system. Jacobson explored the dynamics among three elements in one high school: (1) the element of control and imposing discipline as expressed in the dominant body of authority through its rules and regulations; (2) the element of violating discipline as expressed in individuals' accepting or rejecting the practices, rules, and regulations of authority and (3) the element of protest. To investigate the dynamics among these elements, Jacobson used a phenomenological/interactionist perspective, in which behaviors are not forced on an individual, but rather are constructed by their acknowledgement of the other's behavior and its meaning. Thus, teachers and students are perceived as interpreting and constructing, through mutual references, their activities and their daily behavior. According to Jacobson, the language of control and discipline is actually a ritual act and the teacher–student patterns of negotiation are routinized over time. The intent of the rules of the repeated verbal ritual is to help teachers and students affirm the relations of authority. In multicultural classes, such rituals and routines are apt to be misinterpreted, because the construction of meaning is dependent on the varied cultural background of teachers and students.

(b) *Teachers', students', and parents' perceptions and attitudes concerning classroom management and discipline.* The studies discussed under this heading relate to the impact of context and personal background on the perceptions and attitudes of the various stakeholders in the educational situation. Saad and Hendrix (1993) measured school climate by a continuum representing the teachers' orientation concerning the need to control the students, called the pupil control ideology (PCI). At one end of the continuum was a custodial orientation and at the other end was a humanistic orientation. They examined teachers' orientations toward classroom discipline in relation to ethnicity (Jewish and Arab) and school location (urban and rural). The findings indicate that Arab teachers in urban schools have a more humanistic PCI orientation than rural Arab teachers. The rural Arab society in Israel is very traditional with a well-defined system of hierarchical values and customs. These characteristics are more in line with a custodial PCI that emphasizes a highly controlled environment. Historically, Arabs in the city tend to be better educated and have a higher socioeconomic status than rural Arabs. This may explain their more humanistic orientation. Better-educated teachers who are exposed to progressive liberal and modern educational ideologies are prepared to adopt a more humanistic orientation to pupil control. In small villages the governing educational ideology tends to be traditional with teachers adopting a more custodial orientation. The opposite was found to be true for rural and urban Jewish communities. The rural schools in this study were mainly "kibbutz" schools in which the whole community holds and reflects nonauthoritarian and democratic values, leading to the teachers' more humanistic PCI orientations. Urban

Jewish schools are usually large with a multicultural heterogeneous body of students, and higher levels of bureaucracy and student alienation, resulting in a more custodial PCI orientation by the teachers.

Romi and Freund (1999) examined attitudes of teachers, students, and parents toward students' disruptive behaviors in a vocational school with a heterogeneous population of students. Most school students were from low socioeconomic background and about 10% were immigrants. Participants completed a 38-item, 5-point Likert scale and rated each item in terms of severity. Items included late arrival for lessons, copying during tests, smoking in class, vandalism in school, and answering the teacher rudely. The study found a high consensus among the teachers with regard to the severity of many of the 38 behavioral problems explored. However, there was very little agreement among students and among parents concerning the level of severity of the various problems. This low agreement of perceptions among the parents themselves, and between them and the teachers' perceptions, shows that parents perceive students' conduct in a different light and judge behavior according to different standards than do teachers. Students also tend to perceive problems as less severe than their teachers.

A student–teacher gap of this kind may hint at a possible reason for students' disruptive behavior. This difference is especially important in multicultural classes. If students with immigrant, cultural backgrounds do not regard behavioral problems the way their teachers do, it seems evident that the problem of communication must be added to that of disruptive behavior. In this study, teachers tended to view all disruptive incidents as "serious" or "extremely serious," and this may cause an antagonistic reaction among students. The authors argued that when students feel unable to meet their teachers' behavior criteria they give up in advance: "They opt out of the discipline game in which they have no say in any case" (Romi & Freund, 1999, p. 6). The gap in perception becomes greater as students and teachers belong to and live in more different cultural worlds. Indeed, more disciplinary problems are reported in relation to heterogeneous classrooms in comparison to homogeneous ones (Lavi & Chen, 1983).

Ichilov and Harel (1987) studied the type of discipline enforcements used in a number of schools that students viewed as fair. The researchers revealed that the teachers' discipline strategies in a highly ethnically heterogeneous junior high school relied on problem-centered techniques, whereas strategies in an elementary school focused on relation-centered techniques. It may be hypothesized that these different disciplinary strategies used by teachers dealing with students of different ages may be especially significant for new immigrant students who may react favorably to more relation-centered strategies even at the junior high school level.

Guttmann (1982) compared the perceptions of fourth to sixth grade students, parents, and teachers with regard to misbehavior. Much of this behavior is influenced by the quality of personal interactions, and further influenced by the reasons attributed to the misbehavior by the individuals involved. Guttmann also looked at the degree of congruence between reasons given by students, teachers, and parents and found that the higher the congruence between reasons given for misbehavior, the more positive the personal interactions tend to be. The study population marked the degree of importance of the reasons given for certain misbehaviors.

Results suggested that the children attributed less importance to internal stable reasons (e.g., inability to learn, jealousy of others, bad character) and greater importance to external stable reasons (e.g., the class/teachers' attitude toward the student, parents' low income) thus indicating an external locus of control orientation that children have in the causal attribution of problematic behavior at school. Teachers more often projected the responsibility for misbehavior onto the child and away from themselves. Parents divided the responsibility for the child's misconduct between the child (attributing more importance to reasons external to the child) and the child's environment, including the family. The lack of congruence found among the three groups may explain the difficulties in their ability to communicate and to promote a consistent positive climate in the classroom. These difficulties are exacerbated in multicultural classrooms, where perceptions and lack of communication between parents, teachers, and students are even more pronounced, involving different approaches along the individualism–collectivism continuum. New immigrants may behave according to collective, common goals and attribute misbehaviors to external reasons that make it difficult for children to conduct themselves in line with teacher or classroom goals.

Horenczyk and Tatar (2001) advocated the role of education in valuing multiculturalism by ensuring the centrality of cultural recognition and tolerance in a pluralistic, democratic, immigrant society like Israel. The Israeli educational policy concerning the immigrants advocates their absorption into the mainstream society while allowing for the expression of their homeland traditions (Horowitz, 1999). It is suggested that in a multicultural school, teachers' attitudes toward multiculturalism are influenced by the school's cultural organization. Such influence originates in the spirit and beliefs that constitute the school culture and are reflected in the behavioral norms and values of its members. This school culture serves to shape the identity of students and faculty, promote their commitment to it, and facilitate their adherence to standards of behavior.

The study revealed that teacher attitudes concerning the broader society of Israel are dominantly pluralistic, but in the context of their schools they are assimilative in nature. These attitudes may reflect the gap between the multicultural rhetoric and its problematic implementation in the concrete context of the school. The study further showed that, instead of accepting immigrants as a minority culture, strong efforts are made to assimilate them as mainstream Israelis. This approach reflects an assimilation acculturation rather than an integrative approach (Berry, 1997). Eisikovitz and Beck (1990) found that school practices supporting continuity between the individual's past and present behavioral expectations decreased the shock and disorientation caused by the transfer into a new culture. These supportive practices predict more success for a multicultural classroom. Such practices include a maximum integration of minorities in school activities, an increase of parent involvement, recognition of the legitimacy of immigrant problems, and honoring all cultures in the everyday life at school. These attitudes and practices have particular implications for teacher education programs.

A separate study (Zeidner, 1988) assessed the perceptions of teachers and students of European, Asian, and African backgrounds, concerning the severity of classroom management responses to student misbehaviors. The participants rated 24 common responses. The findings show that students perceive temporary or permanent removal from school, conferring with parents, and a threat to the students' self-esteem or academic status as the most drastic control strategies. Constraints and restrictions on their freedom and time were regarded as less severe, and the least drastic strategies were regarded as those involving the removal of privileges, imposing unpleasant tasks, and verbal punishment. The teachers agreed with the students regarding the most and the least severe strategies, but they disagreed on the level of harshness of more than half of the midlevel responses.

In this study no differences were found among students with background or gender variables. Indeed, they tended to adopt a common "student perspective" on the relative severity of management strategies.

In this context it is interesting to note the study conducted by Lewis and Lovegrove (1987) cited in the chapter "Classroom Discipline in Australia" by Ramon Lewis appearing in this handbook. In their study Lewis and Lovegrove found that, like Israelis, the Australian students wished teachers not to involve parents and not to embarrass misbehaving students. Israeli students also found such sanctions to be most drastic and undesirable.

Ben-Peretz and Shteinhart (2000) (based on Shteinhart, 2000) examined the perception of discipline in Israeli schools by immigrant students from systems characterized by totalitarian or traditional disciplinary values. Through yearlong observations and interviews the authors examined the immigrants' expectations with regard to discipline, the students' behaviors during lessons, and their attitudes concerning discipline in Israel compared with their country of origin. Incongruence between the stringent disciplinary practices expressed through external coercion and control experienced in previous schools, and the more liberal approach guided by a belief in students' internal control and motivation, made intercultural communication difficult in their new schools.

Many students from Ethiopia and the former USSR, although coming from completely different environments as far as discipline in school is concerned, criticized the situation they came across in Israeli schools. Both groups remembered their former schools with positive attitudes, especially in comparison with their schools in Israel. And as time passed, they related to this topic with nostalgia (Shteinhart, 2000). Memories of past experiences, especially of one's homeland, tend to be viewed positively (Linton, 1986).

According to this study the Ethiopian students' behavior in class seemed quite reserved, showing their respect for the teacher, and the unruly behavior of their Israeli classmates was unacceptable to them—"at school you should respect your teacher." As time passed, their criticism of their fellow students even increased. They mistakenly inferred that discipline norms in Israeli classrooms did not exist. Aspects of classmate relations, teacher–students relations, lesson structure, and various teaching activities were unfamiliar to them, leading them to conclude that there were few boundaries.

The students from the former USSR were observed waiting and sitting quietly for the teacher to enter the classroom. It was obvious that they were not aware of the local discipline norms. They said they did not participate during the lessons because of lack of order in class. There was no automatic reaction to the sound of the bell at beginning of class, they read books in Russian during lesson, spoke loudly with their mates in Russian, and even tended sometimes to sleep in class. However, they still showed more respect in face-to-face communication with their teachers than their Israeli classmates did. By the end of the semester they appeared more familiar with the local school regulations and atmosphere and tried to behave like the native students.

A clash between the cultures is unavoidable and one aspect of that clash concerns discipline. Immigrant students create a subculture in their class. When they come across unfamiliar classroom expectations of behavior a collision may be inevitable. Some criticize the local students by saying,

> You ask me about what goes on here during intermission and at the beginning of the lesson, and I'll tell you it is a big mess . . . if you visited a Russian school you would see that over there you never talk during lessons. I mean with your friends. That's what intermission is for . . . yesterday I joined an English lesson with *sabras* [a nickname for a native Israeli] and I saw they never stopped talking. And the teacher had to hush them. Sometimes it was even impossible to hear the teacher. (Shteinhart, 2000, p. 158; 160).

In their study of young Russian immigrants, Shoham, Resnick, Sabar, and Shapira (1997) reported that a number of them have difficulties adapting to the Israeli school discipline policies. These students claimed that the lack of order and discipline at schools frightened them. The teachers in this study indicated that the Russian immigrants saw school organization and practices as being inefficient. Therefore, the immigrant students often skipped school.

The incongruence of perceptions regarding effective discipline did not decrease significantly over time, with the potential for cultural segregation due to decreased communication.

Even if immigrant students try to reach a higher level of understanding the present classroom situations they do not always succeed. Attempts to understand new classroom situations are rarely successful (Ben-Peretz & Halkes, 1987).

Grupper et al. (2003) found that Ethiopian students perceived their Israeli peers as lacking respect for their teachers, making lots of noise even in learning situations, and dressing in a funny way. These perceptions reflect attitudes originating from differing cultural backgrounds. The Ethiopian youths develop respect for adults and authority, and their norms and boundaries are determined by these authority figures including teachers. Native Israelis grow up in a society characterized by anticipated egalitarian relations among individuals, a society in which every idea is subject to discussion and debate, and behavioral boundaries are often not explicit. Such cultural discrepancies lead Ethiopian youth to lose respect for adult educators who do not dictate strict norms and boundaries.

Reaction and responses of new immigrants to the climate of Israeli classrooms reflect the fact that their prior school experiences are located more on the "mandated" end of the classroom discipline continuum, whereas Israeli classroom climate leans toward the "open" end of this continuum (Saad & Hendrix, 1993). This gap may explain the tensions, conflicts, and misunderstandings arising in this situation. Surprisingly, students coming from very different cultural backgrounds such as the former Soviet Union and Ethiopia appear to share the same expectations of teacher power (Hofstede, 1991). This phenomenon may be related to the authoritarian regimes that ruled these countries.

Yet some positive examples can be found. Eilam (1999) studied the behavioral domain of Ethiopian children's integration in an Israeli school shortly after they arrived in the country. Norms of order and discipline (e.g., time, schedule, use of school facilities, and physical environment) were examined. No significant differences were observed between the Ethiopian and the native Israeli students concerning time and space orientation. The Ethiopian students never missed the school bus, kept to the school schedule, and used school facilities appropriately as did their native Israeli peers. It seems that some aspects of the formal organization of the school day were understood and internalized by these students.

Golan-Cook, Horowitz, and Shefatia (1987) found that Ethiopian girls adapted well to discipline norms within the lessons. Lifshitz and Noam (1994) found very few teachers who reported behavioral difficulties with Ethiopian students in the classroom. Teachers thought this was due to the students' traditional education culture that emphasizes accepting authority of the adult teacher.

TEACHER EDUCATION FOR CLASSROOM MANAGEMENT IN ISRAEL

Despite the central and crucial role that classroom management plays in the life of schools and teachers, this topic does not have a high priority in programs of teacher education in Israel. For instance, departments of teacher education at the Israeli universities offer few courses on multiculturalism, teaching in heterogeneous classes, how to create a democratic climate, and the implications for preventing disciplinary problems. In general, these courses are not specifically geared to deal with issues of discipline. The claim is made that disciplinary issues arise in the context of other courses, such as theories of instruction.

There are special courses that focus on prevention of disciplinary problems in most Israeli colleges of teacher education.[2] The aim of such courses is to provide teachers with necessary

---

[2]In Israel teacher education for K–9 is carried out in designated colleges of education. Universities prepare teachers for grades 7–12.

tools for identifying teacher behaviors that might cause problems, and the means to overcome them if they arise. The emphasis is on creating a positive classroom climate and learning how to solve conflicts. The linkage between norms of student behavior and successful learning is clarified for students. Issues of classroom management pertain to routines of life in school. It is interesting to note that the basic approach to classroom management is usually grounded in behaviorist theory, suggesting the use of positive and negative rewards, and punishment as a consequence in severe cases. In general, no special attempt is made to deal with issues of classroom management in multicultural, heterogeneous classrooms, even though these are prevalent in Israel.

MOFET, the Ministry Institute for the Professional Development of Teacher Education, has published a booklet on classroom management that includes a variety of suggestions for planning and creating a classroom climate that will prevent disciplinary problems (Shimoni, Segal, & Sharoni, 1996). The following is an example of a disciplinary problem case included in the instructional material that relates to the heterogeneity of multicultural classroom. "Menashe, an eleven years old Ethiopian student, complains that the teacher pushed him into his seat when he tried to get up to borrow a sharpener for his pencil from another student, and hurt him" (The student teachers) are asked to consider the following issues: "What is the nature of the problem raised? What causes the behavior of Menashe and his teacher? Suggest short- and long-term solutions to the problem." (p. 90, 95), Short-term solutions are meant to deal with the situation at hand in order to restore classroom order. A possible short-term response in the preceeding case could be the teacher's apology and demonstration of caring. A long-term solution may require attention to possible misunderstandings that arise in the classrooms when teachers and students have different expectations of norms of behavior. The previous case does represent such a possible misunderstanding.

In the practicum of teacher education, mentor teachers often help student teachers respond to disciplinary problems and offer varied interpretations of classroom disturbances and suggestions for ways to deal with them. For example:

- It is important to let students express their feelings, even if they voice anger against the teacher.
- One should not regard any disturbance in the lesson as reflecting a desire to annoy the teacher. Often such behavior is grounded in distress and is to be understood as a plea for help.
- Problems arising in the context of the classroom should be dealt with in school without appeal to the parents.

These suggestions are highly relevant to problems of discipline in multicultural classrooms.

In this context it is interesting to compare teacher education for classroom management with teacher education for multiculturalism. Ezer, Millet, and Patkin (2003) investigated this issue in two teacher education colleges. They found that, in the formal curriculum, a number of courses concerning equity, political education, and value education also treat issues of multiculturalism. Concepts like "social heterogeneity" or "culture and language" were introduced in the curriculum, but there was no explicit attempt to translate these into teacher actions in the classroom. This study showed that the teacher educators were aware of the importance of a pluralistic, multicultural approach to teaching, but they lacked clear insights into ways of achieving this goal. The personal background of these teacher educators played a central role in shaping their attitudes, and new immigrant teachers, more so than native teacher educators, tended to emphasize "integration" as a desired outcome of education and rejected any segregation based on ethnic or cultural background.

CONCLUDING COMMENTS

Diversity in the classroom brings a number of obstacles to the establishment of a harmonious and stable classroom climate. Contrary to an ecological situation in nature, where diverse organisms have different needs as far as light, moisture, and so forth are concerned and are not expected to manifest similar features, all students in a classroom are usually viewed as having similar needs and reaching for similar goals. Yet, each member's individual characteristics, modes of acting and behaving, perceptions, ideologies, and beliefs create a set of multiple and varied needs. A uniform niche does not offer suitable acknowledgement of this diversity. In cases where the developmental niche at home is inherently different from the culture of Israeli classrooms, tensions and dilemmas may arise affecting both discipline and learning.

Different norms and customs may be related to some of the theoretical frameworks mentioned earlier. For instance, students from Ethiopia tend to have very rigid codes concerning the relationship of power between adults and children, and between genders. Children are not supposed to look directly into the eyes of adults. Teachers in Israel are apt to interpret this behavior as furtive, antagonistic, and rebellious, and react accordingly. Even if teachers are aware of this cultural gap they might not be able to overcome their intuitive reactions.

Another example is the possible gap pertaining to ideological orientations, in which the school may try to implement progressive, child-centered norms of behavior, but the students coming from a highly traditional background may perceive it as completely laissez-fair without boundaries. Ben-Peretz and Shteinhart's study (2000) uncovered such situations, as did the study of Grupper et al. (2003).

Israeli society may be viewed as moving from a collectivistic orientation to a more individualistic one. The kibbutz movement presents extreme collectivism, but even the kibbutz is changing its basic ideology and becoming more individualistic. These tendencies are reflected in the educational context as well (Aviram, 1999).

Multicultural classrooms may be understood as constituting an environment with multiple layers of cultural expectations from which a climate of misunderstandings, tensions, and problems may emerge. Heterogeneity in the human-made environment tends to increase competition and decrease communication and mutual understanding. Such competition may constrain the abilities and performance of members in classroom society and cause conflict rather than acceptance of each other. Disciplinary problems are often the result of constant stress.

Viewing the "other" with apprehension, mistrust, and lack of respect adds to the sometimes chaotic climate of heterogeneous classrooms and exacerbates the difficulties of establishing management routines and creating a positive climate to support the teaching–learning process. The Israeli educational system regards the positive development of multiculturalism in school as one of its major missions. Many interventions and projects aim at promoting acceptance of others, tolerance, and appreciation of diversity.

Although education alone cannot compensate for society's failings (Bernstein, 1971), educational endeavors can contribute tremendously to improvement. This requires a synergetic effort of principals, teachers, pre- and inservice programs, and significant resource allocation. In particular, this means the need for a concept of classroom management that goes beyond just disciplining students and includes the notion of education for democratic citizenship. Teacher education in Israel will have to be adapted for this purpose and will have to emphasize more understanding of a multicultural society and the contribution classroom management can have on acceptance of student diversity and the creation of a more just society.

ACKNOWLEDGMENT

We wish to thank Sally Brown, University of Stirling, Scotland, for her review of an earlier draft of this chapter.

REFERENCES

Anderson, P. A. (1985). Nonverbal immediacy in interpersonal communication. In A. W. Siegman & S. Feldstein (Eds.), *Multichannel integrations of non verbal behavior*. Hillsdale, NJ: Lawrence Erlbaum Associates.

Anteby-Yemini, L. (2003). Urban Ethiopia and Black culture: New models of identity among immigrant youths from Ethiopia in Israel. In R. A. Eisikovits (Ed.), *On cultural boundaries and between them: Young immigrants in Israel* (pp. 11–31). Tel Aviv, Israel: Ramot Publishing House, Tel Aviv University. (Hebrew)

Aviram, R. (1999). *Navigating through the storm, education in postmodern democratic society.* Tel-Aviv, Israel: Masada. (Hebrew)

Bennett, W. J., Finn, J. R., & Cribb, G. R. (1999). *The educated child.* New York: Free Press.

Ben-Peretz, M. (1998). Classroom management in Israel: Issues and concerns. In: Nobuo K. Shimahara (Ed), *Politics of classroom life: Classroom management in international perspective* (pp. 261–277). New York: Garland.

Ben-Peretz, M., & Halkes, R. (1987). How teachers know their classroom: A cross-cultural study of teachers understanding of classroom situations. *Anthropology and Education Quarterly, 18*, 17–32.

Ben-Peretz, M., & Shteinhart, M. (1996, September). *Students' perceptions of classroom situations in multicultural contexts.* Paper presented at ECER, the 2nd International Conference of the European Research Association. Seville, Spain.

Ben-Peretz, M., & Shteinhart, M. (2000). The classroom inter-cultural encounter: How new immigrants students perceive the learning reality in the Israeli school? In M. Bar-Lev (Ed.), *Cultural education in a multicultural society* (pp. 123–138). Jerusalem: Hebrew University of Jerusalem, School of Education. (Hebrew)

Berustein, B. (1971). *Class, codes and control.* London: Routledge and Kegain Poul.

Berry, J. W. (1997). Immigration, acculturation, and adaptation. *Applied Psychology: An International Review, 46*(1), 5–68.

Bock, K. P. (1970). *Cultural shock—A reader in modern cultural anthropology.* New York: Knopf.

den Brok, P. J., Levy, J., Rodriguez, R., & Wubbels, T. (2002). Perceptions of Asian-American and Hispanic-American teachers and their students on teacher interpersonal communication style. *Teaching and Teacher Education, 18*, 447–467.

Eilam, B. (1999). Toward the formation of a "cultural mosaic": A case study. *Social Psychology of Education, 2*, 263–296.

Eilam, B. (2003). Jewish and Arab teacher trainees' orientations toward teaching-learning processes. *Teaching Education, 14*(2), 169–186.

Eisikovitz, R. A., & Beck, R. H. (1990). Models governing the education of new immigrant children in Israel. *Comparative Education Review, 34*(2), 177–195.

Ezer, H., Millet, S., & Patkin, D. (2003). *Teacher education for multiculturalism: Curriculum and knowledge of teacher educators.* Tel-Aviv, Israel: Funded by the intercollegiate research authority at the MOFET Institute. (Hebrew)

Flay, B. R., Alred, C. G., & Ordway, N. (2001). Effects of the positive action program on achievements and discipline: Two matched control comparisons. *Prevention Science, 2*(2), 71–89.

Friedman, I. (1986). Social and academic aspects in the absorption of Ethiopean immigrants. In D. Shur (Ed.), *Ethiopian Jews and their absorption in Israel* (pp. 1–7). Jerusalem: Szold Institute. (Hebrew)

Golan-Cook, P., Horowitz, T., & Shefatia, L. (1987). *The adaptation of Ethiopian immigrant students to the school system* (Research Report No. 230). Jerusalem: Szold Institute. (Hebrew)

Grupper, E., Yaakov, M., & Nudelman, A. (2003). "Rites of passage" of immigrant youth from Ethiopia entering residential school in Israel. In R. A. Eisikovits (Ed.), *On cultural boundaries and between them: Young immigrants in Israel* (pp. 33–63). Tel Aviv, Israel: Ramot Publishing House, Tel Aviv University. (Hebrew)

Guttmann, J. (1982). Pupils', teachers', and parents' causal attributions for problem behaviour at school. *Journal of Educational Research, 76*(1),14–21.

Hall, E. T. (1966). *The hidden dimension.* New York: Doubleday.

Halperin, S., (1970) *Dr. A. Biram and his "Reali" school.* Jerusalem: Reuven Mass Publication. (Hebrew)

Hareali-Haivri School. *Regulations 1991–2004.* (Hebrew)

Harkness, S., & Super, C. M. (1999). From parents' cultural belief systems to behavior. In L. Eldering & P. P. M. Leseman (Eds.), *Effective early education cross-cultural perspectives* (pp. 67–90). New York: Falmer Press.

Hecht, M., Anderson, P. A., & Ribeau, S. (1989). The cultural dimensions of non verbal communications. In M. K. Asante, & W. B. Gudykunst (Eds.), *Handbook of international and intercultural communication* (pp. 163–185). Newbury Park, CA: Sage.

Helsby, G., & Knight, P. (1998). Classroom management in England. In M. K. Shimahara (Ed.), *Politics of classroom life* (pp. 85–105). New York: Garland.

Hofstede, G. (1991). *Cultures and organizations: Software of the mind.* London: McGraw-Hill.

Horenczyk, G., & Tatar, M. (2001). Teachers' attitudes toward multiculturalism and their perceptions of the school organizational culture. *Teaching and Teacher Education, 18,* 435–445.

Horowitz, T. (1999). Assimilation, monolingualism, unidirectionality, and stereotyping. In T. Horowitz (Ed.), *Children of perestroiuka in Israel* (pp. 22–71). Lanham, MD: University Press of America.

Ichilov, O., & Harel, O. (1987). Patterns of discipline enforcement and the perception of justice in two educational frameworks in Israel. *Adolescence, 22*(85), 97–114.

Israel Ministry of Education. General Director Circular, 46/8, #237, 1986. *Rules and Customs at School.* Updated 1990, 1991, 1997. (Hebrew)

Jacobson, Y. (1995). *Struggles over discipline and control in a high-school: an anthropological perspective.* Unpublished doctoral dissertation, Tel Aviv University, Israel. (Hebrew)

Lavi, N., & Chen, M. (1983, month). *Disruptive students as viewed by their teachers in the Israeli junior high and elementary schools.* Hauat Daat 16, 43–57 (Helrew)

Lefstein, A. (2002). Thinking power and pedagogy apart—coping with discipline in progressivist school reform. *Teachers College Record, 104*(8), 1627–1655.

Linton, M. (1986). Ways of searching and the contents of memory. In D. C. Rubin (Ed.), *Autobiographical memory* (pp. 56–67). England: Cambridge University Press,

Lifshitz, C., & Noam, G. (1994). *Absorbing Ethiopian immigrant children in schools: Coping with the challenge* (Research summary). Jerusalem: JDC-Brookdale Institute of Gerontology and Human Development. (Hebrew)

Manberg, E. (1996). A different viewpoint on education for classroom discipline. In M. Hirschfeld (Ed.), *Secondary education: Maturity and values* (pp. 38–42). Jerusalem: Ministry of Education and Culture. (Hebrew)

Marcus, E. (1999). Rights and duties at school. In E. Peled (Ed.), *Fifty years of Israel education* (pp. 797–812). Jerusalem: Ministry of Education Culture and Sports, Israel. (Hebrew)

Nelson, J. R., Martella, R. M., & Marchand, N. (2002). Maximizing student learning: The effect of a comprehensive school-based program for preventing problem behaviors. *Journal of Emotional and Behavioral Disorders, 10*(3), 136–148.

Ogbu, J. U. (1993). Differences in cultural frame of references. *International Journal of Behavioral Development, 16*(3), 483–506.

Reckless, W. (1961) The new theory of delinquency and crime. *Federal Probation, 25,* 42–46.

Redfield, R., Linton, R., & Herskovits, M. (1936). Memorandum on the study of acculturation. *American Anthropologist, 38,* 149–152.

Romi, S., & Freund, M. (1999). Teachers', students' and parents' attitudes towards disruptive behaviour problems in high school: A case study. *Educational Psychology, 19*(1), 53–70.

Saad, A., & Hendrix, V. L. (1993). Pupil control ideology in multicultural society: Arab and Jewish teachers in Israeli elementary schools. *Comparative Education Review, 37*(1), 21–30.

Shamai, S. (2003). "Of course I would like to be integrated... and may be it will happen someday...": Styles of cultural adaptation of immigrant adolescents from the former Soviet Union. In R. A. Eisikovits (Ed.), *On cultural boundaries and between them: Young immigrants in Israel.* Tel Aviv, Israel: School and Society Series, Ramot Publishing House, Tel Aviv University. (Hebrew)

Shimoni, S., Segal, S., & Sharoni, V. (1996). *Classroom discipline: Psychological and educational aspects.* Tel-Aviv, Israel: Funded by the intercollegiate research authority at the MOFET Institute. (Hebrew)

Shoham, E., Resnick, J., Sabar Ben-Joshua, N., & Shapira, R. (1997). *A case study: The Soviet Union immigrant students' encounter with Israeli students—between cultural assimilation and social enclave.* A research report. Tel Aviv, Israel: Tel Aviv University, the Unit of Sociology of Education and Community, Unit of School Based Curriculum Development.

Shteinhart, M. (2000). *The perception of classroom situations by new immigrant students from different cultures.* Unpublished doctoral dissertation, University of Haifa, Israel. (Hebrew)

Smilanski, J., & Bar-Lev, M. (1994). *Approaches to dealing with classroom discipline problems.* Publication No. 95. Jerusalem: School of Education, Hebrew University. (Hebrew)

Super C. M., & Hankners, S. (1986). The developmental niche: A conceptualization at the interface of child, and culture. *International Journal of Behavioral Development, 9*(4), 546–569.

Taft, R. (1977). Coping with unfamiliar cultures. In N. Warren (Ed.), *Studies in cross-cultural psychology* (Vol. 1, pp. 121–153). London: Academic Press.

Triandis, H. C. (1995). *Individualism and collectivism.* Boulder, CO: Westview Press.

Yariv, E. (1999). *Silence in class! A guide to maintaining discipline.* Even Yehuda, Israel: Reches Publication. (Hebrew)

Zeidner, M. (1988). The relative severity of common classroom management strategies: The student's perspective. *Journal of Educational Psychology, 58,* 69–77.

44

Group Phenomena and Classroom Management in Sweden

Kjell Granström
Linköping University

INTRODUCTION

Teacher and student interactions are an integral part of life in classrooms. Sometimes, these interactions involve a positive dynamic process in which the teacher educates, tutors, and provides for students' needs. Sometimes, these interactions can be characterized as negative in that there is confrontation where the teacher competes for students' attention while students try to acquire appropriate space for their own needs and preferences, for instance, exploring friendships, belongingness, and current values in the peer group. Both situations are a part of the daily life in classrooms. Some students are eager to listen and learn (i.e., to take part in the teacher's project), whereas others do not show the same interest. They are more interested in their own projects.

This latter orientation may result in behaviors that are perceived by the teacher as disturbing. Several studies (e.g., Alton-Lee, Nuthall, & Patrick, 1993; Dyson, 1987; Jones, Charlton, & Wilkin, 1995; Merrett & Wheldall, 1993) show that teachers, independent of national context, perceive a number of similar student behaviors as disturbing and as a hindrance to their education.

In this chapter, I discuss plausible origins of such disruptive classroom behaviors. Most examples are taken from Swedish 9-year compulsory schools, but the results seem to be valid for other ages and probably for other Western countries as well.

Certainly, there are many assumptions and explanations as to why interactional dynamics in a classroom may be perceived as troublesome and there are also several ideas about how to manage such processes. I restrict this presentation to three aspects that may be of importance for understanding teacher and student interplay in the classroom. First, I comment on the interaction by using dynamic theories, which means theories concerning unconscious maneuvers people use to reduce tension and anxiety in a group. Second, I discuss possible consequences of a restricted professional role for teachers to handle group processes and troublesome behaviors. Third, I exemplify how different modes of instructional organization may increase or decrease the probability of troublesome behavior or undesired dynamics. By doing so I hope to reveal the relationship between classroom dynamics, teachers' professional competencies, and their preferences for specific forms of classroom work. The three parts are presented consecutively and finally tied together. In this way, teachers' legitimate claim for collegial and tutorial support will be obvious.

DYNAMICS IN THE CLASSROOM

The interplay between leaders and followers in industrial companies and public service has been described using dynamic theories (e.g., Rioch, 1971; Klein, 1963; Bion, 1961, Kernberg, 1980; Sutherland, 1985). Such studies have shown that leaders and employees, in order to survive mentally, that is, to handle stressful situations, may reduce their anxiety by using various unconscious behaviors. Examples could be *projections* of unwanted feelings onto another person (often the leader). The assumption is that in order to avoid being overwhelmed with what they perceive as their own shortcomings, these feelings of fear or inadequacy may be transferred or attributed to a colleague or the boss, and the targeted person may not even be aware of it. However, if such processes recur often enough and in a group setting, they can evolve into expectations wherein the target may sometimes identify with the projections and act in accordance. This phenomenon is called projective identification (Ashbash & Schermer, 1987; Ogden, 1979; Goldstein, 1991). Bullying can be interpreted as an example of projective identification wherein the mob blames a scapegoat, who sometimes also identifies with the projections (Olweus, 1993; Crick & Gropeter, 1995; Lagerspetz, Bjorkqvist, & Peltonen, 1988).

The need for projection is not necessarily restricted to negative qualities. Positive qualities may also be uncomfortable to possess. Sometimes, it could be a relief for example, to take a break from being responsible, or dutiful, and so on. There is a well-known phenomenon where educated and informed individuals in stressful situations may behave as if they were uninformed and ill informed, projecting competence and responsibility onto the leader (O'Conner, 1971; Brown, 1985; Janis, 1982; Granstrom, 1986, Elmes & Gemil, 1990; Argyris, 1990).

Application of this knowledge to the school system, and particularly to the classroom setting, has been rare. There are, however, some interesting analyses of school and classroom behavior based on dynamic theories (cf. Richardson, 1977; Slavin, 1997, 2002). Even though teachers do not describe their relations with students using dynamic theory terminology, they have experienced able students behaving irresponsibly or casting blame on teachers, parents, or peers for their own shortcomings.

Teachers as Targets

Teachers in the classroom can be unwitting targets of students' emotions, expectations, disappointments, fears, and fantasies. These projections are part of what teachers have to deal with as classroom managers. Provocative behavior can be seen as warning signals of insufficiency and as a natural and necessary part of the human defense system. In this interplay, the role of the teacher is very important. If the teacher is not able to distinguish between personal and professional issues, there is a risk of him or her using professional authority for personal reasons. The interactional dynamics in the classroom may reduce the teacher's planning and many good pedagogical intentions to a minimum. Group processes in a classroom can be very dominant, and sometimes such processes jeopardize teachers' goals as managers of classroom activities. Consequently, the students' behavior can sometimes be seen as a threat to a teacher's professional identity and ethics.

Struggle for Space

Earlier, I pointed to two types of projects in a classroom: the teacher's instructional project and the students' project concerning self-knowledge, self-esteem, group values, and belongingness. The conflict between these two projects may sometimes result in frustration among students and teachers, as both types of projects require space in the educational setting. Next, I describe some studies concerning interactional patterns in the classroom to illustrate the struggle for space for the two types of projects.

Previous research on classroom interaction has shown the existence of "the rule of two-thirds" (Einarsson & Hultman, 1985; Goodlad, 1984; Sirotnik, 1981). According to this rule, teachers talk about two thirds of the time and the students have to share the remaining third. Flanders (1970, 1973) found similar patterns in the United States. However, such results are valid considering the *public communication* in the classroom. When the focus is on the *private communication*, between the students, the pattern is quite different. Granström (1996b) found that students' mutual interaction with each other during lessons exceeded the number of their interactions with the teacher. Students were found to consult with their peers about lesson tasks (as a part of the teacher's project), but most of all they discussed and explored social relations, values, music, sports, and so on (i.e., their own projects). From such a perspective, it is more accurate to talk about "the rule of the reversed sixth part" (i.e., students interact 6 times more with their classmates than with their teacher during a lesson). This means that students' self-knowledge and self-esteem are influenced and confirmed by their classmates as well as by the teacher. These findings are consistent with those of Pellegrini and Blatchford (2000) who stated, "If we want to maximize the sort of behaviors associated with social competence, then it is important to provide opportunities which maximize peer interaction with each other, with minimal adult direction" (p. 23). This statement assumes that students' peer interaction is an important means for their development. Thus, the informal interaction among the students constitutes an important part of the educational context of the classroom. In some lessons, the space for peer influences could be extensive. Even though the mean interaction rate is about 10 turns per student, the results in Fig. 44.1 show that in some cases peer interaction can be fairly comprehensive. The estimated results in this case are based on randomized observations of a group of four students at a time.

The figure seems almost to be a sociogramme. The most popular student makes her appearance, and the students are interested in her. Even though this is not an average lesson, it illustrates the potential for student interaction and peer influences hidden in each lesson. However, as the interaction is normally not very loud, most teachers are unaware of the huge amount of interaction going on. Nevertheless, most teachers are disturbed by the students' peer interaction. An interesting finding (Granström, 1996b) is that the individual children's amount of interaction seems to be independent of class size. The students satisfy their need for communication irrespective of class size. This means that the sum of chatter will increase linearly, not exponentially, with the number of children in the class. The reason why large classes are noisier than small ones is the increasing number of individuals satisfying their need for social relationships. A conclusion from the study is that the activity labeled chattering is an inevitable expression of human needs, that is, the students' need for nearness, support, confirmation, curiosity, and knowledge. Even though more research on the significance of peer relations for learning and friendship is needed (Newcomb & Bagwell, 1995), the importance of peer interaction cannot be neglected. Learning is a result of social interaction, for instance, by means of different forms of cooperation (Lave & Wenger, 1991). Knowledge is acquired in "natural" situations, which means that learning is contextually anchored. Students have for the most part a sense of responsibility in social situations. This implies that students act in and create local conditions and premises for communication (Rommetveit, 1992; Säljö,

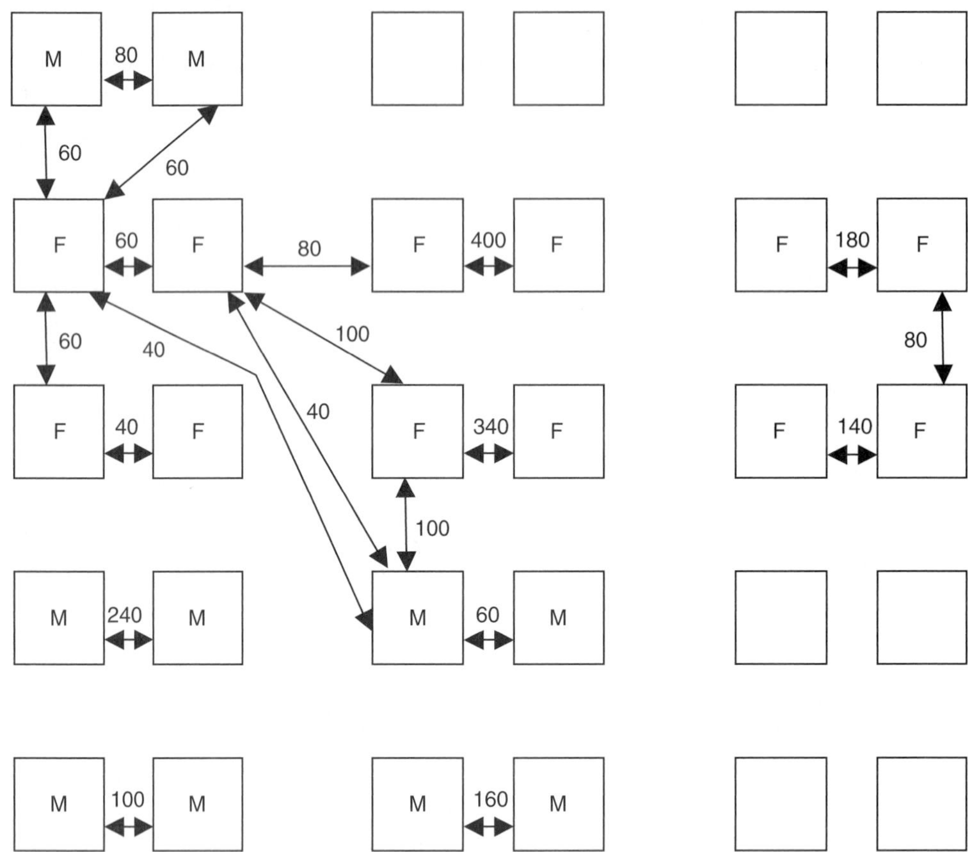

FIGURE 44.1. Interaction between students, aged 14, during a lesson (the figures indicate the number of replies, i.e., turns). (From Granström, 1996a.)

1999). However, such activities and students' needs are not always in line with the teacher's planning and goals for the lesson. Instead, most teachers find the students' private interaction troublesome and may perceive their noise as a threat to their role as teacher.

Disturbing "Projects"

What teachers usually describe as annoying activities are such student activities that are outside the teacher's control. In a Swedish study, teachers at different levels were asked to write down behaviors they found troublesome in the educational setting (Granström, 1996a). Irrespective of school level, the same types of behavior recurred in most reports. Most frequent was chattering, inattentiveness, hindering other students, being noisy, and late arrival. These behaviors indicate that students have been so engaged in their own projects that the activities are perceived as disturbing the teacher's project.

The results from the Swedish study are very similar to those of Merrett and Wheldall (1993) from England and Wales, and to the Jones et al. (1995) study from St. Helena. In these studies, teachers mentioned activities such as talking out of turn, hindering other pupils, lack of concentration, and making noise. It seems that most student behavior that teachers perceive as troublesome can be related to students' private interaction and their relation-creating projects. Teachers describe them with a negative undertone. However, the same actions could be described from a student's point of view as a way of seeking contact instead of disturbing others; as turning toward a classmate instead of turning away from their assignment; as being attentive to a fellow human being instead of being inattentive to work; and so on. From a student's perspective, the academic content of a lesson may be of some importance, but lesson time also provides opportunities for learning about life, oneself, and others. Verkuyten (2002) described classroom dynamics in the following way: "Behavior that is labeled 'disruptive' by the teacher can be presented as adequate and appropriate or as a part of schoolwork. And claims about abnormal behavior can be undermined by defining the behavior as ordinary and general" (p. 119).

Summary. Off-task communication seems to be important to students and it probably affects students' learning, attitudes, and self-esteem to a considerable extent. The classroom is not only a place for education but also an arena for the formation of friendships and personal development. Such formative friendships can even be seen as competencies used to construct future relationships (Hartup, 1996).

Students' socially shared processes also have an important function as a relief from anxiety, tension, and anger. Students may sometimes perceive the social or academic situation, with its ambiguous demands as frightening. In such a situation their need for relief and to give vent to their feelings is hard to control. Teachers thus face a number of challenges as a consequence of group processes in the classroom. Without knowledge of such processes, the teacher may easily regard a number of "misbehaving" students as provocative, rather than viewing their behavior as being an indication of a basic need of security. Actually, behaviors can be an expression of psychological defense mechanisms. Students use their teachers as targets for their disappointment, frustrations, and shortcomings. Instead of blaming themselves, they may project their failure onto the teacher and accuse him or her of giving a boring lesson, or become inattentive. Thus, a very important professional skill seems to be to distinguish between deliberate provocation and unconscious signals for help. Teachers' readiness when it comes to handling such situations will be discussed further in the next part.

PROFESSIONAL QUALIFICATIONS FOR HANDLING CLASSROOM DYNAMICS

An interesting question in the case of interactional dynamics in the classroom is whether teachers are qualified to handle such processes (i.e., do they possess the professional skills to manage classroom dynamics?). Several attempts have been made to define what teachers need to know in order to prepare students for being a member of society. Sigel (1990) identified five important fields for teaching: "(1) basic communication skills—reading, writing, speaking, (2) good study and work habits, (3) appropriate social values, (4) thinking and problem-solving skills, and (5) subject matter in the basic disciplines. These are but some of the goals of education. What a heavy burden we place on our teachers!" (p. 77). Probably such formidable demands may give rise to feelings of insufficiency, which the individual teacher has to deal with in some way. One solution is to define professional features so they fit the teacher's own conditions. This seems to be a solution as most teachers identify themselves as a professional group, and believe that they have professional qualifications. By investigating these *perceived* qualifications, it ought to be possible to describe the self-images that teachers hold as regards their roles as teachers. It is also possible to describe the qualifications teachers believe to be important for handling a classroom situation. Comparing perceived professional attributes with frequent classroom demands might be clarifying.

Perceived Essentials of Teachership

In a study (Granström, 1998) concerning teachers' professional traits, a large number of teachers wrote down criteria that signified a professional teacher. The teachers' reports could be easily divided into three parts: (a) personal competencies, (b) shared competencies, and (c) personal traits and interest in teaching. Thus, to be a good teacher one needed to have some personal traits and acquired personal competence combined with an interest in teaching. Shared competence (i.e., joint and collective qualifications) constituted the least mentioned traits.

Acquired personal competencies are based on individual insights and skills that can be learned or practiced, for instance, by means of academic study. This includes subject knowledge or pedagogical skills, and leadership. About half of the answers belonged to this category. These competencies are developed individually, which means that different teachers at the same school possess different competencies in varying degrees. Even though teachers may agree on the importance of instructional matters (cf. Jones & Jones, 1990) or arrangement of subject matter (Anderson, 1991), their practical solutions may differ considerably.

Shared competencies (i.e., such qualifications and values shared by all teachers) were mentioned by only a few teachers in this study. This criterion, often used by researchers as a sign of professional competence, is not what teachers first and foremost suggest (Parsons, 1964; Lortie, 1977; Fullan, 1991). A few teachers mentioned "common professional language" and "shared ethical code" as examples of shared competence (cf. Lortie, 1977; Fullan, 1991). These responses can be interpreted as a need for a common language and for common areas for planning, analyzing, and revising the joint work, or as Hargreaves and Fullan (2000) put it, "collegial profession means working with, learning from, and teaching colleagues" (p. 51). Despite the fact that some teachers mentioned cooperation as a professional prerequisite, most of them related teacher professionalization to teachers as individuals rather than to the teaching profession as a collective and shared province.

Personal traits and interest in teaching constituted about 45% of the answers in the study. Teachers mentioned interest in schoolwork and education or in pupils as a basis of professionalism. Commitment is an aspect often mentioned in the public debate (Tellhaug, 1996). Certainly, an interest in children could be a motivation for professional efforts, but it can hardly be seen as a sign of professionalism (cf. Ramsey & Oliver, 1995). The same argument is valid for personal traits. Some traits can be facilitating, whereas others can hinder a teacher's professional development. Traits emphasized by teachers are being flexible, empathic, considerate, and creative. Such qualities imply that teachers highlight an ability to adapt to new situations and pay attention to emerging needs among the students. All these personal traits seem to be qualities related to the teacher's role as a classroom manager. Nevertheless, different teachers may be equipped with quite different attributes.

Taking the teachers' own descriptions of teacher professionalism as a point of departure, from the dynamic theory of classroom interaction two main threats to the teacher's role as a classroom manager can be identified. First, students' troublesome behavior could be seen as a matter of the teacher's personal traits being questioned. Second, the students' provocative conduct could also be perceived as an attack on the teacher's leadership and ability to be flexible, patient, and considerate. Troublesome behaviors accounted for earlier, such as chattering, inattentiveness, and turning away from work (Alton-Lee et al., 1993; Dyson, 1987; Jones et al., 1995; Merrett & Wheldall, 1993), may call into question the teacher's ability as a classroom manager; that is, the teacher's self-esteem is questioned. Students who arrive late, talk inappropriately, do not work, and are noisy can be perceived as challenging the teacher as an individual. Teachers also mentioned that a student's behavior might be perceived as a personal insult. In such cases, there is a risk of positive traits such as flexibility, empathy, and creativity being jeopardized. As teachers blend their personal identities with their professional roles, challenges to the teacher's role can also be perceived as a personal attack.

The Need for a Professional "Shelter"

Privacy as a common condition for teaching and professional identity among teachers, as discussed earlier, is in line with previous findings by Lortie (1977) and Weick (1976). McTaggart (1989) argued that privacy has been recognized among teachers as "commitment for oneself, and as a virtue and right for others" (p. 367). A personal or private teacher identity implies difficulties in handling attacks or provocation. Other professional groups working close to their clients, such as psychologists, social workers, and therapists, have been trained to handle their clients' transference and projections (Hawkins & Shoet, 1989). The clients may use the professional as a target for their shortcomings, hate, anxiety, and even love fantasies. These professionals have learned to distinguish between attacks on their professional role and attacks directed toward their own person. In this way, they are able to handle this type of transference without assuming it to be a "personal" attack.

Although I do not suggest that teachers need to be therapists, nevertheless, there is knowledge from psychological therapy that could be useful for teachers. In the same way as therapists discuss and learn from common experiences of troublesome clients, teachers could also develop a common competence related to their teaching. There is a large risk involved when handling professional problems in a personal way, especially as the students come very close to teachers. The difference between a personal way of acting and a professional approach is that the former implies that the teacher displays and gives vent to personal feelings and reacts as if he or she and the students were evenly matched. A professional teacher is able to disregard personal feelings and suppress inclinations to exact revenge or punishment. However, group processes, individual needs, projections, expectations, and provocation may not be seen as natural and necessary parts of the students' development, but rather as merely obstacles to teacher's work. There is an obvious risk that a teacher in a pressing situation will make use of the advantage he or she possesses as a teacher and possibly misuse it for personal reasons. This could take the form of reacting to an insult by insulting the student who is being provocative, by paying back an indignity by offending the frustrated student, dealing with inattentiveness by meting out punishment or by dismissing the student's needs, and so on. However, it has to be said that most lessons are spent on curricular activities and not on disciplinary matters. In the ORACLE studies (Galton & Simon, 1980), it was found that three fourths of classroom time was spent on learning, and the number of disruptions was fairly low. This is in line with Stodolsky, Ferguson, and Wimpelberg (1981) and our own studies (Granström, 2003). Nevertheless, teachers are intermittently exposed to students' provocations.

When the students are interested and focus on the task it is not difficult to live up to a virtuous teacher role. When students do not behave as expected, they may constitute an immediate threat to the teacher. Whereas other professional groups can protect their personal identity behind a professional role (professional self), teachers' professional role and identity is limited and unclear. Such a restricted professional role cannot provide sufficient shelter from client attacks (see Fig. 44. 2).

Figure 44.2 illustrates the conditions for a restricted professional role (i.e., not exclusively trained for handling projections and transferences) compared to a "full" professional role such

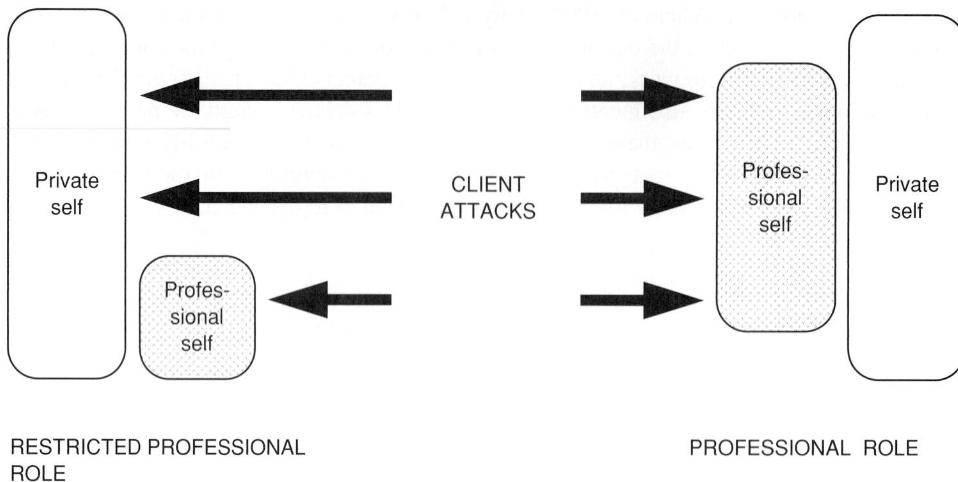

FIGURE 44.2. The professional role can protect the private self from client attacks.

as a psychologist or a therapist. Although the professional shelter protects the professional's personal self or identity, teachers are more vulnerable as their professional shield is rather small. Consequently, there is a large risk of provocations striking at the personal identity, that is, the personal self instead of the professional shelter. The shelter in this case is composed of knowledge of and insights into the meaning and expressions of clients' attacks.

The Need for a Common Professional Language

A solution for the problem described earlier may be to strengthen teachers' professional identity so that they can engage with students without being personally provoked by students' spontaneous behavior. This might be possible by creating a reasonable social distance or by dissociating oneself from the students to some degree. In the same way as other professionals meet in order to discuss, analyze, and interpret client behavior, teachers also deserve the same opportunities (Hargreaves & Fullan, 2000). A very important part of professional identity is a common professional language. The most important function of a professional language is to be a means of increasing the shared knowledge, which in turn can help the professionals codify and structure the shared and common understanding among the members. Joyce and Showers (1991) believed that the "best knowledge" develops in regular on-site coaching by colleagues. Hopkins, West and Ainscow (1996) stressed the opportunities for teachers to talk about teaching. Professional language can be said to be the collected and shared *understanding* of professional practice. It could thus be a tool for communicating hypotheses, assumptions, models, and theories about daily practice, for instance, with respect to students' troublesome behavior or group processes in the classroom as well as teaching and learning. This implies that the members of a professional group are able to discuss daily practice on a meta level. Development and learning is a process of acquiring linguistic distinctions and intellectual and discursive tools for understanding unknown or strange things; this enables circumstances, which are hard to understand, to be understood in a more differentiated and nuanced way (Säljö, 2000). Such learning processes take place *between* individuals as well as *within* them (Lave, 1988; Lave & Wenger, 1991). Thus, professional understanding and language acquisition take place, to a high degree, in cooperation between teachers.

Other professional groups have received "language training" in their academic courses, a training that continues in their ongoing practice. Professionals working closely with their clients usually have the opportunity to take part in tutorial groups, collegial counseling, and staff groups and study groups. Such possibilities have, so far, not been offered to teachers in Sweden to any great extent. However, organizing the teachers in teams or working units, with scheduled times for internal meetings, has become more frequent. Tickle (1991) has pointed to the importance of emotional support for new teachers. Hargreaves (1994) and Hargreaves and Fullan (2000) claimed that this is also valid for experienced teachers. Teachers need "to talk through their emotions, manage their anxieties and frustrations, and be guided and reassured about the limits the care they can provide when guilt threaten to overwhelm them" (Hargreaves & Fullan, 2000, p. 53). Collegial meetings can certainly be a forum for professional discussions about the role of classroom manager, that is, serve as a means of developing a common understanding and promoting a professional language. It has also become more common, nowadays, for a teacher team to call in a consultant or a tutor to facilitate professional discussions, analyses, and interpretations.

Summary. Teachers seem not to be fully trained to treat provocations and projections. Like other professionals they need to verbalize their working conditions and discuss them with colleagues or consultants. Development of management skills such as the ability to handle group processes, projections, and transference does not take place in the classroom first and foremost. Rather, such competencies evolve in discussions and joint analyses (reflection on teaching) with colleagues and consultants (Hawkins & Shoet, 1989; Hopkins et al., 1996). Probably, such discussions can also be an important forum for reflection on various classroom activities. For instance, what are the pros and cons of different arrangements, and how do we take advantage of opportunities in different settings? Questions such as these are discussed in the next section.

CLASSROOM MANAGEMENT AND TEACHERS' CHOICE OF INSTRUCTIONAL ORGANIZATION

In this section, three classroom activities are scrutinized in relation to what interactional dynamics they may trigger or make space for. A plausible assumption is that teachers, not fully trained to handle group processes and interactional dynamics, prefer classroom activities that provide little scope for dynamic processes. This assumption is examined next.

A central concern for teachers has been the choice of settings for students' learning (Brophy & Good, 1986; Walberg, 1990; Joyce, Calhoun, & Hopkins, 1996). Well-composed lessons not only support learning; they also reduce the causes of distress and troublesome behavior. Accordingly, it is important to highlight the choice of instructional organization in order to be able to understand students' desirable and undesirable behaviors. Weinstein (1991) summarized research on the classroom as a social context for learning, and concluded that students, apart from learning academic lessons, also learn about relationships, competition, cooperation, and friendship. Weinstein's conclusion implies that so-called students' projects can fairly easily be incorporated in the teacher's project. Thus, the classroom organization offered to students ought to be based on careful considerations.

In a comprehensive study, Cuban (1993) described how teaching has changed or varied during different periods in the U.S. public school system. Using classroom observation records and photographs of classrooms from the period 1890 to 1990, he presented an interesting story on consistency and change in the educational system. One important conclusion is that "the tradition of teacher-centered instruction continues to dominate elementary and secondary classrooms, but a hybrid version of student-centered practices, begun in the early decades of this century has spread and is maturing" (p. 272). A comprehensive study of the Swedish school

TABLE 44.1
Different Forms of Classroom Activities in Swedish Schools Over the Last 40 Years (Percentage of lesson time)

Decade	*Whole-Class*	*Teamwork*	*Individual Work*
1960	60	18	22
1980	50	24	26
2000	44	12	41

Note: From "Dynamics in the Classroom," by K. Granström. In S. Selander (Ed.), *Tradition and Renewal of Education and Educational Research in Sweden*, Stockholm: Liber, Copyright 2003 by K. Granström Adapted with permission.

system similar to Cuban's is not available. However, there are observational data on classroom settings available from 1960 to 2000 (Stukat, 1970; Granström & Einarsson, 1995; Granström, 1998, 2003). These studies make it possible to identify both increases and decreases in the use of different forms of instructional organization and to describe changes in the social meaning of various classroom organizations.

The change in classroom management observed will probably have consequences for students' social and academic development as well as for their competence as citizens. The observations in the three studies proved that most classroom activities could be described either as *whole-class lessons, teamwork*, or *individual work*. Next, an account of the changes within and between the three types of classroom activities is given. The quantitative and qualitative evolution that has occurred in Swedish classrooms (and perhaps in many other classrooms in the Western world) will probably have implications for students' self-esteem and their knowledge esteem (Pellerini & Blatchford, 2000). Thus, potential effects of the educational environment in terms of different organizational events need to be examined. Table 44.1 shows the changes in Sweden over 4 decades.

As can be seen from the table, whole-class lessons have decreased during the period and individual work has doubled while throughout the period, little time has been set aside for teamwork.

Whole-Class Lessons

The results from the three studies (Table 44.1) show very clearly that the number of whole-class lessons has decreased over the last 40 years. At the beginning of the period, this activity was characterized by "teacher's desk education." This means that the teacher sat or stood behind the teacher's desk and instructed students, tested the class on homework, showed pictures, or demonstrated material. The class was kept together and all the students took part in the same activity. Cuban (1993) described a similar picture of the U.S. classrooms.

At the beginning of the 21st century, the teacher's desk is still there in most classrooms. Even though the students spend a lot of time in whole-class groups, classroom observations reveal that the activities cannot be classified as pure lectures. Certainly, at the upper level, there are still teachers who mediate knowledge and test the students in a traditional "college" way. However, a very large part of the common time in whole-class lessons is spent on administration rather than education. This could take the form of information about the schedule, giving and collecting homework, preparing for individual work, information about outdoor activities, plays, study visits, and so on.

The teacher's desk is not first and foremost a pulpit any longer; it has become more of a steward's meeting point. Teachers do not seem to use their positions as a scholar to the same extent as before. The consequences of this change are probably both good and bad. Whole-class teaching as a place for shared and collective experiences of cognitive, aesthetic, and ethical events has become less frequent in many Swedish classrooms. There are important aspects of a child's education and development that presuppose collective and group experiences, such as what can come about in shared activities. Listening to a teacher, in the whole-class setting, who narrates historical or physical events in a vivid and absorbing way, is not only a way of acquiring knowledge. It also provides training in listening, fantasizing, and entering into other people's situation. Cuban (1993) gave several examples of teachers handling this in a creative way. Whole-class teaching implies that students are free to ask questions and that they are allowed and encouraged to openly reflect on them and discuss them with each other. This is important training for adult life in that students are given scope for verbalizing their thoughts and ideas about society, politics, and religion. The joint seeking for meaning—the collective conversation—is an important part of individual and civil education. Students need opportunities to listen to others and their opinions, just as they need to train their own ability to formulate ideas and to argue. Certainly, such sessions run the risk of being noisy and resulting in conflicts and antagonism. However, in their studies, Rudduck, Day, and Wallace (1997) found that students in supportive situations are observant and capable of analytical and constructive comments. Thus, the teacher's project can be supported by the students' projects and vice versa.

Whole-class lessons may imply that the teacher explains historical, social, ecological, moral, and scientific phenomena, and that the teacher and the students together investigate, question, and test the credibility of different arguments. I prefer to call this type of whole-class education *the collective conversation*. This activity is radically different from traditional teachers' desk lectures. Collective conversations can be an important preparation for group activities and a basis for personality development, but it is also an eminent condition for academic learning. "Children must be encouraged and helped to talk aloud about love, hate, jealousy, fear, curiosity, and so on. As these topics are articulated and recognized, children will be better able to deal with the academics of their school lives. The pressure of internal needs and conflict will no longer be sabotaging their curiosity, creativity and motivation." (Slavin, 2002, p. 298). However, whole-class teaching may also give rise to uncontrolled dynamics where discussions turn into quarrels and conflicts. Subgroups may start fighting; even the teacher may be implicated as a target of hard feelings. Thus, whole-class lessons are a risky project that teachers try to avoid. This may be one explanation why this activity has become less frequent.

Summary. There are clear indications of a decrease in traditional teacher's desk lessons in the Swedish school system. Furthermore, a lot of whole-class time is used for organizational and administrative matters. Whole-class teaching as a golden opportunity for collective conversation is not utilized in full. Collective conversation could be a useful tool for teachers in their classroom management, as such discussions offer the students an opportunity to get group and social training, and give them the opportunity to express curiosity and anxiety. However, there is a great risk of such collective learning being "sabotaged" if different subgroups exploit the situation for private projects. As pointed out earlier, the individual amount of chatter seems to be fairly stable, and a large group is perceived as noisier than a small one. Certainly, there can be pedagogical reasons for reducing the time for whole-class lessons, but there can also be survival reasons for teachers avoiding such situations if they are not trained to handle such group processes that are inevitable in large groups. Such processes can be suppressed by means of strict discipline, but most teachers refrain from this. A better solution seems to be to avoid large groups as much as possible. This can be a relief for the teacher but a loss for the students: The collective situation offered by whole-class education is, when used appropriately, an effective form for group training, social training, individual growth, and knowledge acquisition.

Teamwork in School Settings

Teamwork means that two or more students have a joint task to carry out. It could be a project, a laboratory experiment, vocabulary training, or a joint painting. This type of activity is considered a form of academic training at the same time as the students' need for social contact can be satisfied. It can also be a preparation for a labor market characterized by team organizations.

In the Swedish context (Skolverket, 1994; Granström, 2003), as well as internationally (Cuban, 1993; Gall & Gall, 1994; Schmuck & Schmuck, 1992), the time spent on teamwork has been fairly limited and, furthermore, it is decreasing. Nowadays, no more than about 10% of lesson time is used for teamwork in Sweden. Galton and Williamson (1992) found that just because students are seated around a table does not mean that they will work as a small group. They showed that teachers do not always coordinate learning tasks and the educational setting. This may seem peculiar as the trend among companies and in public service is in the opposite direction. Nowadays, hierarchical organizations have been abandoned and teamwork, group organizations, and small units for production have been introduced (Nordqvist, 2002). Teamwork implies common and shared responsibility for producing, irrespective of whether the output is physical goods, services, or acquired knowledge. Having the students work in groups may also provide a bridge between students with different ethnical or social backgrounds and between boys and girls. For some reason, this classroom activity is rather unusual in Swedish schools.

Swedish teachers are often skeptical of teamwork as a pedagogical tool (Stymne, 1992). It is not considered an easy and self-evident activity for children. Instead of joint problem solving, teachers think that one or two students in the group may do the entire job and solve the common problem. The result presented by the group, in such cases, is an achievement by one or two members rather than an outcome of joint efforts. This means that the other group members use the time for other things. This form of teamwork is called *disjunctive*, which means "without co-operation" (Steiner, 1972; Hammar Chiriac, 2003). It is enough that one member of the group has found the solution, which means that the group task has then been completed. Probably the decrease in teamwork can be explained by teachers' observations of such dysfunctional group processes.

Another reason why teachers have abandoned group work could be the fact that it sometimes takes the form of *complementary* tasks. In such cases, the members divide the task into smaller pieces, and distribute them among the members, who become responsible for different clearly defined parts. The final account or presentation takes the form of a stapled document where the separate parts are combined, or oral presentations of the separate parts in front of the class.

However, there are also successful examples of teamwork in accordance with a *conjunctive* model, which implies that the group work is dependent on each and every member (Stymne, 1992). The group activity is not finished until all the members have understood the solution or completed the assignment. This classroom activity has been compared to a group of mountain climbers (Hammar Chiriac, 2003). The climbers are united by a rope and are thus dependent on each other. Conjunctive work implies that the members discuss the best course of action and suitable strategies. Together, they interpret the problem and finish the work in cooperation. Certainly, there will be space for students' private interaction not connected to the actual task, but there seems to be less off-task discussion in conjunctive teamwork than in other forms of group activities (Stymne, 1992). Several researchers have demonstrated the benefits of peer interactive groupings. Slavin (1990), Johnson and Johnson (1987), and Granström (1997), among others, have shown that teamwork has a positive effect on the students' achievement and social learning, for instance, by increasing concern for others. However, Blatchford, Kutnik, and Baines (1999) noted that surprisingly little is known about the nature of groupings used in classrooms.

As soon as individuals are expected to work together, group processes emerge. In a new group, the members search for a position and a role in the new setting, norms and power relations have to be investigated, and so on. In most cases, there is also a struggle for leadership in the group (Brown, 1988; Wheelan, 1994). Such processes are important and must not be neglected, as they are a natural part of human relationships and group development. Certainly, such processes can go astray and the need for competent and tactful classroom management is evident. Pellegrini and Blatchford (2000) concluded that several studies (e.g., Slavin, 1990; Rogoff, 1990) show that cooperative groups may have a positive effect on the students' performance, relations, and concern for others. An important part of this management is an ability to find the right composition of groups (Galton, Simon, & Croll, 1980). Another part of a teacher's leadership is to be patient and give the groups time to form and decide on how to tackle the assignment. The most important part of classroom management in the case of teamwork is, however, training students for this activity. It is naive to believe that young students can handle such a difficult form as teamwork without training.

Training for teamwork need not be too time-consuming. Ashman and Gillies (1997) showed that group training in two sessions conducted by the classroom teacher over 2 consecutive days had a striking effect. The results were overwhelming. Compared to control groups, the trained children were more cooperative and helpful and tried to involve each other in the common task, and became more responsive to each other's learning needs. They also performed better on the learning outcome test. What the training seems to have provided was, on the one hand, tools for structuring the task. This enabled the students to define more clearly their task. On the other hand, they were trained to handle social interaction, which in turn helped them not to get stuck in destructive group processes. Even though many of the dynamic processes in the classroom are unconscious and hard to get at in rational training, this study proves that educational investments are not wasted. These results are also confirmed by other studies, for example, Johnson and Johnson, (1990), Sjödin, (1991), and Sharan (1990).

The educational benefits of teamwork are obvious, but so are the risks connected with it. Group processes, deficient structure, and deficient leadership may result in annoyance. This may be one reason why teachers avoid this classroom activity.

Summary. It is clear that teamwork is not a self-evident and convenient alternative when teachers plan the students' work. However, from the students' point of view, teamwork constitutes an important arena for development, for testing social relations, and for acquiring knowledge about the world and their own position in it. Teamwork is perhaps the most challenging task in terms of classroom activities. The reason why it is practiced so little cannot be explained by a lack of learning potential. On the contrary, it has proven to be a good context for learning. There seems to be a resistance among teachers against making use of this educational setting. The reason for this could be that teamwork sometimes gives rise to group processes that are outside the teacher's control. Furthermore, professional knowledge about such processes may be limited with respect to strategies for preventing failure and making use of the good sides. Once again, a way out of this dilemma could be to avoid this activity as much as possible. This is unfortunate, because managed in an appropriate way, teamwork offers students unique opportunities for learning (Wheelan, 1994).

Individual Work

The third type of classroom activity can be labeled individual work, which includes seatwork and silent work (Doyle, 1984). This is an assignment where each student, individually, is busy with different tasks, such as answering written questions, drawing or painting, reading, or doing arithmetic. Forty years ago, this activity was considered a complement to the teacher's lectures in the whole class (Granström, 2003). Usually, there were preprinted booklets with series of items to fill in or to answer in short sentences. Common tasks were copybook writing, working with a spelling book, filling in geographical names in a list or table, or doing arithmetic exercises. The amount of individual work has changed over the last 40 years, as has the content and meaning of this classroom activity. In the 1960s, the share of individual work was about 20%; nowadays it is twice as much. It is obvious that this type of activity has appealed to teachers and it has increased at the expense of whole-class education. A similar trend has been observed in the United States (Cuban, 1993) and in England (Blatchford, Burke, Farquhar, Plewis, & Tizard, 1998). However, the most interesting change in Sweden concerns the core content of individual work rather than its quantity. Previously, individual work meant that the teacher assigned all the students identical tasks, usually "fill-in items." After attending a lecture or reading a textbook, the students had to answer preproduced questions or tasks in a printed booklet. The authors of the schoolbooks usually provided with such material. The students worked with identical items and the teacher regularly collected the students' papers and used a key when marking them. The space for professional reflection is more limited when working with preprinted materials than in self-controlled situations (Clark & Peterson, 1986; Ramsey & Oliver, 1995). In this sense, preproduced material can have a deprofessionalizing effect on the teaching profession.

In the 1980s, there were teachers who were eager to break the pattern of routine use of fill-in items. They introduced something that came to be called "my own work" under "contract" (Österlind, 1998). At the end of each school week, the student individually planned his or her work for the coming week, above all in math and Swedish, but also in foreign languages and science. The teacher constructed a number of tasks in each subject and the students had to deal with all of them. However, they decided independently the order and the time schedule for different subjects. At the beginning of a week, they picked up the material and started working in accordance with their own planning. Each student had a checklist (which could be a number of empty squares, circles, apples, etc.). When an item was finished, they marked it in a special square or painted a numbered apple. Cuban (1993) commented on the U.S. situation and said that "the meaning of working 'individually' is ambiguous since the question included answers of teachers who assigned the entire class the same task and also assigned students to work independently on different tasks" (p. 225). The latter form is most commonly used in Sweden.

"My own work" was introduced in the Swedish classrooms without any pressure from school authorities. Student individual work has grown out of a real need, among teachers, to handle classroom management in a satisfactory way. Experience showed that a lot of troublesome behavior vanished and the volume of noise dropped. This student activity resulted in calmer workdays for both teachers and students (Österlind, 1998; Westlund, 2003).

There are, however, a number of children who are not comfortable with this combination of freedom and responsibility. Some children are not able to concentrate on their tasks; instead of working they walk around in the classroom. They have been called "vagabonds" (Westlund, 2003). Other students could be called "the dreamers." They appear to be very obedient when they are sitting quietly and seemingly concentrated but in fact are lost in dreams or fantasies. It is evident that "my own work" is too formidable a task for some students, but they are a minority.

Individual work has been found to reduce chatter and noise in the classroom (Granström, 1996b) although not completely. The need for students to carry out their own projects is always present. However, individual work seems to reduce the need and space for such projects.

The increase in individual work is not a specific Swedish experience. Results from the ORACLE project (Galton, Simon, & Croll, 1989) show that classroom work has been more individualized and is practiced by most teachers. This is also valid for the United States. (Cuban, 1993) although not as pronounced as in Sweden. It is obvious that individual work seems to be attractive to teachers in different national contexts. One reason could be that this student activity reduces the probability of troublesome group processes and spares the teacher collective projections and chatter.

Summary. We can conclude that time for individual work has increased in the last 40 years, at least in the Swedish school system. Irrespective of whether all students carry out the same task on the same occasion or work individually on allotted tasks, the amount of troublesome behavior decreases. Probably, these minimizing effects are as important for teachers as are the educational effects. This is obvious from the following quotation: "Children should be seated well apart, and distractions by other people can be minimized by providing each child with his own set of materials, together with complete instructions about task" (Bull & Solity, 1993, p. 56).

Thus, individual work seems to be increasing at the expense of teamwork and whole-class lessons. The reason for this could be the difficulties teachers have in handling group dynamics and interactional processes in more collective classroom activities. If teachers avoid group processes by adopting "individual working" to a high degree, this may limit valuable opportunities for benefiting from more collective classroom activities.

CONCLUDING REMARKS

The body of research accounted for in this chapter shows that students have an overwhelming need for social interaction. They also create space for this need in their private talk during lessons. On average, they create 6 times more interaction with peers than with the teacher while they are in the classroom. The influence of peers seems to be as great as the influence of adults. Certainly, in a class of 25 to 30 students this means an awful lot of interaction and chattering at the same time as learning takes place. Classroom observations reveal, however, that the students usually manage their internal communication in an unobtrusive way. As a result, the teacher can carry out the lesson without being disturbed by the students' whispering and hidden communication. If the students' projects are not too noisy, the teacher can accept it, as long as the students do not intentionally sabotage the teacher's instructional plans.

Certainly, individual and group processes may evolve in the classroom to such an extent that they are perceived as troublesome. Teachers may sometimes interpret such manifestations as attacks on the teacher and the personal self, rather than considering them as an expression of human needs. Because of an unclear professional role there is a great risk of a teacher interpreting the students' signals as a personal insult. The need for knowledge about group processes, collective projections, and transference in the classroom is obvious. Offering teachers a fair chance to cooperate in teacher teams and to take part in tutorial groups where they can verbalize their experiences and develop a shared professional competence could be a means of enhancing their professionalization. Such knowledge will probably help teachers use the whole-class instruction for a teaching and fostering purpose. Knowledge and experiences of group dynamics may also help teachers arrange appropriate group compositions and coach the students to make use of the potential of teamwork. Probably, teachers who are not very familiar with group processes need not exaggerate the amount of individual work in order to suppress group dynamics. Rather, they can use this activity as a complement and as an occasional tool for relief. The relation between aim and means seems to be extremely important.

Summary. Students' inevitable need of friendship, belongingness, curiosity about peers, music, sports, values, and so on may sometimes interfere with teachers' educational projects. Students may sometimes also involve the teacher as a target for projections, fantasies, hopes, or disappointments.

Teachers, compared with other professionals working close to their clients, are less trained to handle such transferences. Consequently, there is a large risk that they will perceive students' attacks as being directed toward their private self rather than their professional role.

In this presentation, it has been assumed that the above-mentioned circumstances may have some influence on teachers' choice of classroom activities. As individual work provides less space for students' private projects, social dilemmas, and interactional frustrations, teachers perceive such lessons as calmer. In whole-class lessons as well as in teamwork a teacher is more exposed to group processes such as collective frustrations and projections but also is a witness to tensions within and between groups. If the teacher is not trained to handle such dynamics, a way out seems to be to avoid such situations.

More knowledge about origins and expressions of interactional dynamics is needed. But first and foremost, teachers need time for collegial and tutorial discussions, and opportunities to verbalize and analyze their daily practice in order to develop professional tools. In this way, the relationship between group dynamics, professional role, and organizational settings can be made more understandable.

In this chapter, I have focused on dynamic aspects of classroom management. This does not mean that the academic content is an unimportant component of a teacher's profession. On the contrary, greater knowledge about group dynamics can contribute to the teaching mission.

ACKNOWLEDGMENT

The author wishes to thank Roberta Slavin for her comments on an earlier version of this chapter.

REFERENCES

Alton-Lee, A., Nuthall, G., & Patrick, J. (1993). Reframing classroom research: A lesson from the private world of children. *Harvard Educational Review, 63*, 50–84.

Anderson, L. (1991). *Increasing teacher effectiveness.* Paris: UNESCO.

Argyris, C. (1990). *Overcoming organizational defenses.* Boston: Allyn & Bacon.

Ashbash, C., & Schermer,V. L. (1987). *Object relations, the self, and the group.* London: Routledge & Kegan Paul.

Ashman, A., & Gillies, R. (1997). Children's cooperative behavior and interactions in trained and untrained work groups in regular classrooms. *Journal of School Psychology, 35*, 261–279.

Bion, W.R. (1961). *Experiences in groups.* New York: Tavistock Publications.

Blatchford, P., Burke, J., Farquhar, C., Plewis, I., & Tizard, B. (1998). An observational study of childrens' behaviour at infant school. In M. Woodhead & A. McGrath (Eds.), *Family, school and society.* London: Open University Press.

Blatchford, P., Kutnik, P., & Baines, E. (1999). *The nature and use of classroom groups in primary schools/project (R00237255).* London: ESRC.

Brophy, J., & Good, T. (1986). Teacher behavior and student achievement. In M. Wittrock (Ed.), *Handbook of research on teaching* (3rd ed., pp. 328–375). New York: Macmillian.

Brown, D. G. (1985). Bion and Foulkes: Basic assumption and beyond. In M. Pines (Ed.), *Bion and group psychotherapy* (pp. 192–219). London: Routledge & Kegan Paul.

Brown, R. (1988), *Group processes: Dynamics within and between groups.* Oxford, England: Blackwell.

Bull, S. L., & Solity, J. E. (1993). *Classroom management: Principles to practice.* London: Routledge.

Clark, C., & Peterson, P. (1986). Teachers' thought processes. In M. C. Wittrock (Ed.), *Handbook of research on teaching* (3rd ed., pp. 255–296).New York: Macmillan.

Crick, N. R., & Gropeter, J. K. (1995). Relational aggression, gender and social-psychological adjustment. *Child Development, 54,* 1386–1399.

Cuban, L. (1993). *How teachers taught: Constancy and change in American classrooms 1890–1990.* New York: Teachers College Press.

Doyle, W. (1986). Classroom organization and management. In M. Wittrock (Ed.), *Handbook of research on teaching* (3rd ed., pp. 292–431). New York: Macmillan.

Dyson, H. A. (1987). The values of 'time off task': Young children's spontaneous talk and deliberate. *Harvard Educational Review, 57,* 396–420.

Einarsson, J., & Hultman, T. G. (1985). *God morgon pojkar och flickor. Om språk och kön i skolan.* [Good morning boys and girls. On language and gender in the school setting]. Stockholm: Liber.

Elmes, M. B., & Gemil, G. (1990). The psychodynamics of mindlessness and dissent in small groups. *Small Group Research, 21,*28–44.

Flanders, N. (1970). *Analyzing teacher behavior.* Reading, MA: Addison-Wesley.

Flanders, N. (1973). Research on teaching in improving teacher education. *British Journal of Teacher Education, 2,* 164–167.

Fullan, M. G. (1991). *The new meaning of educational change.* London: Cassell.

Gall, J. P., & Gall, M. D. (1994). Group dynamics. In T. Husén & N. Postlewaite (Eds.), *The international encyclopedia of education* (pp. 2523–2529). London: Pergamon Press.

Galton, M., & Simon, B. (1980). *Progress and performance in the primary school.* London: Routledge and Kegan Paul.

Galton, M., Simon, B., & Croll, P. (1980). *Inside the primary classroom.* London: Routledge.

Galton, M., & Williamson, J. (1992). *Group work in the primary school.* London: Routledge.

Goodlad, J. (1984). *A place called school.* San Francisco: Jossey-Bass.

Goldstein, W. N. (1991). Clarification of projective identification. *American Journal of Psychiatry, 148,* 13–161.

Granström, K. (1986). *Dynamics in meetings. On leadership and followership in ordinary meetings in different organizations.* Linköping: Linköping Studies in Arts and Science.

Granström, K. (1996a March). *Students as a hindrance for professional conduct among teachers.* Paper presented at the 24th Annual Congress of the Nordic Society for Educational Research. Lillehammer, Norway.

Granström, K. (1996b). Private communication between students in the classroom in relation to different classroom features. *Educational Psychology, 16,* 349–364.

Granström, K. (1997). *Pupils' perceived performances and satisfaction as a function of frame factors in the classroom.* Linköping: Linköping University Department of Behavioural Sciences.

Granström, K. (1998). Classroom management in Sweden. In N. K. Shimahara (Ed.), *Politics of classroom life. Classroom management in international perspective* (pp. 137–162). New York: Garland.

Granström, K. (2003). Arbetsformer och dynamik i klassrummet [Dynamics in the classroom]. In S. Selander (Ed.), *Tradition och förnyelse i svensk skola och skolforskning* [Tradition and renewal of education and educational research in Sweden] (pp. 223–243). Stockholm: Liber.

Granström, K., & Einarsson, C. (1995). *Forskning om liv och arbete i svenska klassrum* [Research on daily life in Swedish classrooms]. Stockholm: Liber.

Hammar Chiriac, E. (2003). *Grupprocesser i utbildning.* [Group processes in educational settings]. Linköping: Linköping Studies in Education and Psychology.

Hargreaves, A. (1994). *Changing teachers, changing times: Teachers' work and culture in the postmodern age.* London: Cassell.

Hargreaves, A., & Fullan, M. (2000). Mentoring in the new millennium. *Theory Into Practice, 39,* 50–56.

Hartup, W. (1996). The company they keep: Friendship and their developmental significance. *Child Development, 67,* 1–13.

Hawkins, P., & & Shoet, R. (1989). *Supervision in the helping profession. An individual, group and organizational approach.* Milton Keynes, England: Open University Press.

Hopkins, D., West, M., & Ainscow, M. (1996). *Improving the quality of education for all. Progress and challenge.* London: David Fulton.

Janis, I. L. (1982). *Groupthink.* New York: Houghton-Mifflin.

Johnson, D. W., & Johnson, R. T. (1987). *Learning together and alone.* Englewood Cliffs, NJ: Prentice Hall.

Johnson, D. W., & Johnson, R. T. (1990). Cooperative learning and achivement. In S. Sharan (Ed.), *Cooperative learning: Theory and research* (pp. 23–37). New York: Praeger.

Jones, K., Charlton, T., & Wilkin, J. (1995). Classroom behaviours which first and middle school teachers in St. Helena find troublesome. *Educational Studies, 21,* 139–153.

Jones, V., & Jones, L. (1990). *Comprehensive classroom management.* Boston: Allyn & Bacon.

Joyce, B., Calhoun, E., & Hopkins, D. (1996). *Creating powerful learning experiences.* Buckingham, England: Open University Press.

Joyce, B., & Showers, B. (1991). *Student achievement though staff development.* Aptos, CA: Boosend Laboratories.

Kernberg, O. (1980). *Internal world and external reality, object relations theory applied.* London: Jason Aronson.

Klein, M. (1963). *Our adult world.* New York: Basic Books.

Lagerspetz, K. M., Bjorkquist, K., & Peltonen, T. (1988). Is indirect aggression more typical of females? *Aggressive Behavior, 14,* 403–414.

Lave, J. (1988). *Cognition in practice: Mind, mathematics, and culture in everyday life.* England: Cambridge University Press.

Lave, J., & Wenger, E. (1991). *Situated learning: Legitimate peripheral participation.* England: Cambridge University Press.

Lortie, D. C. (1977). *Schoolteacher: A sociological study.* Chicago: University of Chicago Press.

McTaggart, R. (1989). Bureaucratic rationality and the self-educating profession: The problem of teacher privatism. *Journal of Curriculum Studies, 21,* 345–361.

Merrett, F., & Wheldall, K. (1993). How do teachers learn to manage classroom behaviour? A study of teachers' opinion about their initial training with special reference to classroom behaviour management. *Educational Studies, 19,* 91–106.

Newcomb, A. F., & Bagwell, C. L. (1995). Children's friendship relations: A meta-analytic review. *Psychological Bulletin, 117,* 306–347.

Nordqvist, S. (2002). *Team based organizations.* Stockholm: Stockholm University, Department of Psychology.

O'Connor, G. (1971). The Tavistock method of group study. *Science and Psychoanalysis, 18,* 100–115.

Ogden, T. (1979). On projective identification. *The International Journal of Psychoanalysis, 18,* 357–373.

Olweus, D. (1993). *Bullying at school.* Cambridge, England: Blackwell.

Österlind, E. (1998). *Disciplinering via frihet. Elevernas planering av sitt eget arbete.* [Discipline by freedom. Students' planning of their own work]. Uppsala: Uppsala University, Uppsala Studies of Education.

Parsons, T. (1964). Professions. *International Encyclopedia of Social Science, 12,* 536–547.

Pellegrini, A. D. & Blatchford, P. (2000). *The child at school. Interactions with peers and teachers.* London: Arnold Publishers.

Ramsey, P., & Oliver, D. (1995). Capacities and behavior of quality classroom teachers. *School Effectiveness and School Improvement, 6,* 332–366.

Richardson, E. (1977). *The teacher, the school and the task of management.* London: Heineman.

Rioch, M. J. (1971). "All we like sheep" (Isaiah 53:6): Followers and leaders. *Psychiatry, 34,* 258–273.

Rogoff, B. (1990). *Apprenticeship in thinking: Cognitive development in social context.* New York: Oxford University Press.

Rommetveit, R. (1992). Outlines of a dialogically based social-cognitive approach to human cognition and communication. In A. Heenwold (Ed.), *The dialogical alternative. Towards a theory of language and mind* (pp. 26–66). London: MIT Press.

Rudduck, J., Day, J., & Wallace, G. (1997). Students' perspectives on school improvement. In A. Hargreaves (Ed.), *Rethinking educational change with heart and mind* (pp. 73–91). Alexandria, VA: Association for Supervision and Curriculum Development.

Säljö, R. (1999). Learning as the use of tolls. A socio-cultural perspective on the human-technology link. In K. Littleton & P. Light (Eds.), *Learning with computers. Analysing productive interactions* (pp. 144–166). London: Routledge.

Säljö, R. (2000). *Lärande i praktiken. Ett sociokulturellt perspektiv.* [Learning in praxis. A social-cultural perspective]. Stockholm: Prisma.

Schmuck, R. A., & Schmuck, P. A. (1992). *Group processes in the classroom.* Dubuque, IA: William C. Brown.

Sharan, S. (1990). Cooperative learning and helping behaviour in the multi-ethnic classroom. In H. C. Foot, M. J. Morgan, & R. H. Shute (Eds.), *Children helping children* (pp. 173–176). Chichester, England: John Wiley.

Sigel, I. S. (1990). What teachers need to know about human development. In D. D. Dill (Ed.), *What teachers need to know. The knowledge, skills, and values essential to good teaching* (pp. 76–93). San Francisco: Jossey-Bass.

Sirotnik, K. (1981). *What you see is what you get: A summary of observations in over 1,000 elementary and secondary classrooms.* Los Angeles: UCLA Graduate School of Education.

Sjödin, S. (1991). *Problemlösning i grupp* [Solving problems in group settings]. Umeå: Umeå University, Department of Education.

Skolverket [National Educational Authority]. (1994). *Skolors och elevers utveckling* [The development of schools and pupils]. Stockholm: Skolverket.

Slavin, R. E. (1990). *Co-operative learning.* Boston: Allyn & Bacon.

Slavin, R. L. (1997). A group analytic approach to the education of children and teenagers. *Journal of Child and Adolescent Group Therapy, 7,* 69–78.

Slavin, R. L. (2002). Operative group dynamics in school settings: Structuring to enhance educational, social, and emotional progress. *Group, 26,* 297–308.

Steiner, I. D. (1972). *Group processes and productivity.* New York: Academic Press.

Stodolsky, S., Ferguson, T., & Wimpelberg, K. (1981). The recitation persists but what does it look like? *Journal of Curriculum Studies, 13,* 121–130.

Stukat, K. G. (1970). Observationer af laereradfaerd i klasserummet [Observations of teacher management in the classroom]. In T. Ålvik (Ed.), *Undervisningslaere* [A guide to teaching] (pp. 170–180). Copenhagen, Denmark: Gyldendals.

Stymne, I. (1992). *The structure of work: Analyzing interaction in small task groups.* Stockholm: Stockholm University, Department of Psychology.

Sutherland, J. D. (1985). Bion revisited: Group dynamics and group psychotherapy. In M. Pines (Ed.), *Bion and group psychotherapy* (pp. 47–85). London: Routledge & Kegan Paul.

Tellhaug, A. O. (1996). Den gode lærers kompetanse. [The competence of the good teacher]. *Bedre Skole, 2,* 87–98.

Tickle, L. (1991). New teachers and the emotions of learning teaching. *Cambridge Journal of Education, 30,* 447–472.

Verkuyten, M. (2002). Making teachers accountable for students' disruptive classroom behaviour. *British Journal of Sociology of Education, 23,* 107–122.

Walberg, H. (1990). Productive teaching and instruction: Assessing the knowledge base. *Phi Delta Kappa, 71,* 470–478.

Weick, K. (1978). Educational organizations as loosely coupled systems. *Adminstrative Science Quartley, 21,*1–19.

Weinstein, C. S. (1991). The classroom as a social context for learning. *Annual Review of Psychology, 42,* 493–525.

Westlund, I. (2003). *Gränslöst arbete – inom vissa gränser* [Frame-less work – within certain frames]. Linköping: Linköping University, Department of Behavioural Sciences.

Wheelan, S. A. (1994). *Group processes: A developmental perspective.* Boston: Allyn & Bacon.

45

An Interpersonal Perspective on Classroom Management in Secondary Classrooms in the Netherlands

Theo Wubbels, Mieke Brekelmans, and Perry den Brok
Utrecht University

Jan van Tartwijk
Leiden University

INTRODUCTION

This chapter reports on results of research from a 25-year program of studies investigating teacher–student interpersonal relationships in secondary classrooms. This research focuses on the role of the teacher and builds a knowledge base about managing classrooms to create effective learning environments. Starting in The Netherlands, this line of research now has developed to many other countries such as Australia, Canada, Israel, Slovenia, Turkey, Korea, Taiwan, Singapore, and the United States. In this chapter, we focus on Dutch research, referring when useful to the research in other countries.

We begin this chapter with a discussion of the multiple perspectives that can be used to analyze teaching and then describe the communicative systems approach, the central element of the interpersonal perspective that is the focus of this chapter. We then turn to another element, the model for interpersonal teacher behavior, and measurement instruments developed to map teacher interpersonal behavior. The remainder of the chapter reviews studies on diverse issues covering the development of interpersonal teacher behavior during the teaching career, problems of beginning and experienced teachers including nonverbal behavior and the spatial position of the teacher in the class, teacher interpersonal relations and student outcomes, differences between teacher and student perceptions of the relationship, and finally interventions to improve relationships in class.

MULTIPLE PERSPECTIVES ON TEACHING

Classroom teaching is a complex task in a complex environment. Usually a (Dutch) secondary school teacher is in a modest-sized room with between 20 and 40 students. Many factors including emotional, cultural, interpersonal, and environmental issues influence the teacher, the students, and what occurs in class (Shuell, 1996). To reach their aims in this complex situation teachers have to fulfill many functions often at the same time (e.g., motivating, instructing, and organizing) (see Doyle in this volume). To grasp this complexity, some researchers distinguish between different types of teaching acts such as classroom management or instructional behaviors (e.g., Brophy & Good, 1986; Creemers, 1994; Lee, 1995). Rather than distinguishing between different *types* of teaching acts we want to look at teaching from different *perspectives*. Although these perspectives are different, often there is overlap.

Consider a classroom in which a teacher is lecturing. From the subject matter perspective, one can analyze whether the content presented is correct, or what content has been selected by the teacher, or what concepts are being used. One can also study the effects of lecturing on the teacher's relationship with the students: Does this teacher engage them, do they see him or her as someone who really understands their problems and needs? We define this as part of the interpersonal perspective. When analyzing the type of learning activities the teacher elicits, for example, we ask: Do students have to rehearse information, or do they have to organize characteristics or objects? We define this as the learning activities perspective. Yet an alternative focus is the moral perspective that considers the values communicated by the teacher. For instance, does the teacher show a commitment to democratic values? In a classroom management perspective, the contribution of teaching is studied to create a productive working environment. A variety of perspectives can thus be used consecutively to study one teaching act, or a series of acts. The analyses of the U.S. secretary of education's publicly broadcasted lesson about Lincoln's paper on the Constitution show, for example, the perspective of instructional effectiveness, a discourse perspective, a moral perspective, and a gender perspective (see the analysis of the Bennett tape, Morine-Dershimer, 1986).

As is clear from these examples, perspectives can be distinguished from each other, but some also overlap. In particular, the classroom management and interpersonal perspectives overlap. In the research reviewed in this chapter, teaching has been studied from an interpersonal perspective. The interpersonal perspective describes and analyzes teaching in terms of the relationship between teacher and students. The analysis of the teacher role in this perspective contributes to our understanding of the teacher's classroom management. Two elements are central to this perspective: the communicative systems approach and a model to describe teacher behavior. We discuss these two elements before turning to research results.

THE COMMUNICATIVE SYSTEMS APPROACH

When analyzing teachers' contributions to relationships with students, their behavior can be considered a form of communication. Three definitions of communicative behavior can be distinguished. In the first, behavior is called communication only if the sender and receiver perceive the same meaning. A second definition considers behavior communicative whenever the sender consciously and purposefully intends to influence someone else. We adopt the third and most comprehensive definition that considers as communication every behavior that someone displays in the presence of someone else. This choice is an element of the so-called systems approach (Watzlawick, Beavin, & Jackson 1967) that assumes that one cannot *not communicate* when in the presence of someone else; whatever a person's intentions are, the others will infer meaning from this behavior. For example, if teachers ignore students' questions because they do not hear them, then students, for example, might infer that the teacher is too busy, that the teacher thinks that the students are too dull to understand, or that the teacher considers the questions impertinent. The message that students take from the teacher's inattention can often be different from that which the teacher intends.

In the systems approach to communication, the focus is on the effects of someone's actions on the other. It focuses on the *pragmatic* aspects; that is, pragmatic as to the effects on the other involved. We now discuss several features of this approach that include two aspects and three levels of communication, the cyclical character of exchanges of communication, and the frequent disagreement about who is responsible for problems in communication. We conclude with an emphasis on perceptions following from this pragmatic aspect.

Content and Relationship

According to the systems approach, every form of communication has a *content* and a *relation* aspect (Watzlawick et al., 1967), also referred to as the report and the command aspects of behavior (cf. La France & Mayo, 1978). The content conveys information or description; the relational aspect carries instructions about how to interpret the content. Therefore, in a class, teacher and students often relate in ways that are outside the subject matter (content).

Message, Interaction, and Pattern

Within the systems approach to communication, three levels of communication are distinguished. The lowest level consists of one single unit of behavior, the *message* level, with a content and relation aspect. For instance, the words, "I want to help you to learn," can be combined with either a smile or a frown. In the latter case, the interpersonal aspect of this communication may be perceived as: "I think you are too stupid to learn" (Marshall & Weinstein, 1986). A series of exchanged interpersonal messages is called an *interaction*, the second communicative level. An example of an interaction occurs when the teacher asks a specific student a question, and the student ignores the teacher. The teacher then asks another student the same question, without paying any further attention to the first student. The students in the class will perhaps understand from this event that the teacher wants to avoid a confrontation with the first student. Therefore, they may expect that they can determine their own activities without a very high risk of confronting the teacher. When after a while the exchange of interpersonal messages becomes cyclic, and when action and reaction (or cause and effect) are hard to distinguish, then recurrent patterns can be identified in the exchange of messages. This is the most extended level of communication, the *pattern* level. The longer the students and the teacher interact, the more their behavior will become predictable, because their mutual expectations get confirmed and reconfirmed, and thus these will be regarded as the norm and form a stable basis for reactions.

Circularity

The notion of circularity in the systems approach to communication highlights that someone's behavior influences someone else and that the behavior of the second person on his or her in turn influences the first. Watzlawick and his colleagues (1967) described vividly how patterns in relationships may evolve and be sustained; for example, the friendly behavior of one person communicating with someone else may evoke friendly behavior from the other, thus creating a pleasant relationship. On the other hand, criticism and anger may evoke the same behavior from the other, creating an escalating relationship of mutual distrust, hostility, or aggression (see Wubbels, Créton, & Holvast, 1988; Lapointe, 2003).

Interchanges in series of messages can be either *symmetrical* or *complementary*, depending on whether they are based on equality or difference. In the case of symmetry, the behavior of the one is followed by the same kind of behavior from the other. In the complementary case, the communicating sides show opposite behavior. The teacher–student relationship, with respect to the aspect of power, is structurally a complementary relationship. The teacher is the expert, the grown-up, the elder, the one who is responsible; the student on the other hand has still to learn everything, is a child to whom little responsibility is assigned in most cases. The teacher teaches, assesses, and punishes; the student is taught, is assessed, and is punished.

In a structural complementary relationship, both types of interchanges in series of messages (symmetrical and complementary) can, and usually will, occur. For example, a teacher's respect and caring for students can evoke and intensify students' respect and caring for the teacher, a positive symmetrical interchange. Negative symmetrical escalation, in fact a form of pathology, occurs, for example, when a teacher answers student disruptive behavior with severe punishment that may provoke aggressive behavior of the student, even more harsh punishment, and so on.

In case of complementary communication, rigidity can evolve: The roles of teacher and student can intensify such that students do not take any initiative. The positions of teacher and students in the complementary relationship join with each other, leaving the possibility that complementary behaviors intensify, so that the differences become greater and greater and students start to behave more immaturely, less independently, and more irresponsibly.

Who Is to Blame?

Participants in the communication process continually exchange messages. This process may be interpreted as an uninterrupted sequence of interchanges in which cause and effect cannot be distinguished. Watzlawick et al. (1967, p. 54) argued that participants in the interaction, however, always introduce causation or order in the sequence of events. People who are communicating name messages in terms of stimulus and response; one message is considered to be the cause of the other. Teacher and students may have entirely different opinions about which behavior is cause and which is effect. They see the behavior of (the) other(s) as cause of and justification for their own behavior (e.g., the other is to blame). In most disorderly lessons, when the behavior of the teacher or students is unreasonable, unreasonable behavior may escalate. For instance, when students capitalize on every opportunity to create disturbances, or when the teacher punishes the wrong students, there may be general agreement about *if* and *how* certain events have taken place, but disagreement about *which* behavior is cause and which is result, and thus who was to blame. Both sides may feel that the other is the one who started the exchange.

If both sides show little understanding of each other's behavior, their interaction often has an escalating character. Teacher and students may find themselves in a vicious circle in which they intensify each other's behavior. The solution to this problem cannot be found by looking for who is right. The very assumption that such a sequence of messages has a "beginning" is erroneous according to Watzlawick et al. (1967). Only by changing one's own behavior can one change the behavior of the other person, and thus break the destructive spiral.

Perceptions

The pragmatic orientation of the communicative systems approach (i.e., what is the effect of communication on someone else) has evolved in our conceptualization of the interpersonal perspective as we focused on the *perceptions of students* of the behavior of their teachers. We have focused not so much on the stated intentions of the teacher, but on the students' perceptions evoked by what occurs in the classroom, what students think about their teacher, and what they learn and do. Of course, intentions are important variables; they may influence the teacher's way of teaching and thus, for example, may help explain differences in the relationships of teachers with different classes, or with different students in one class.

Teachers' intentions can be important factors for designing training or for counseling about changes in patterns in interpersonal relationships between students and teachers (see the section on improving relationships). However, intentions have limited utility in helping to understand the pragmatic effects of communication. In the remainder of this chapter, we focus on student perceptions, but also include teacher perceptions when relevant.

THE MODEL FOR INTERPERSONAL TEACHER BEHAVIOR

The perceptions of students about their interpersonal relationships with their teacher have been mapped and studied in our research with the model for interpersonal teacher behavior (MITB). This model is based on Timothy Leary's research on the interpersonal diagnosis of personality (1957) and its application to teaching (Wubbels, Créton, & Hooymayers, 1985). The Leary model has been investigated extensively in clinical psychology and psychotherapeutic settings (Strack, 1996) and has proven effective in describing human interaction (Foa, 1961; Lonner, 1980). Although not conclusive, there is evidence that the Leary model is cross-culturally generalizable (Brown, 1965; Dunkin & Biddle, 1974; Lonner, 1980; Segall, Dasen, Berry, & Poortinga, 1990). In the Leary model, two dimensions are important. Leary called them Dominance-Submission and Hostility-Affection. Although these two dimensions have occasionally been given other names (i.e., Brown [1965] used Status and Solidarity, Dunkin and Biddle [1974] used Warmth and Directivity), they have generally been accepted as universal descriptors of human interaction. The two dimensions have also been applied to education. Slater (1962) used these dimensions to describe pedagogical relationships, and Dunkin and Biddle (1974) demonstrated their importance in teachers' efforts to influence classroom events. Robertson (2002) used two similar dimensions, assertiveness and cooperation, to describe classroom management behavior.

In the Model for Interpersonal Teacher Behavior the two dimensions are *Influence* (Dominance-Submission) and *Proximity* (Opposition-Cooperation). These dimensions can be represented in an orthogonal coordinate system (See Fig. 45.1). The two dimensions, represented as two axes, underlie eight types of teacher behavior: leadership, helpful/friendliness, understanding, giving students freedom and responsibility, uncertainty, dissatisfaction, admonishing, and strictness (see Fig. 45.2)

In Fig. 45.2 the sectors are labeled DC, CD, and so on according to their position in the coordinate system (much like the directions in a compass). For example, the two sectors "leadership" and "helpful/friendliness" are both characterized by Dominance and Cooperation. In the DC sector, the Dominance aspect prevails over the Cooperation aspect covering teacher enthusiasm, motivating, and the like. The adjacent CD sector includes more cooperative and less dominant perceptions; the teacher shows helpful, friendly, and considerate behavior. Figure 45.2 provides an overview of typical teacher behaviors that relate to each of the eight sectors of the model.

MEASUREMENT OF PERCEPTIONS OF INTERPERSONAL TEACHER BEHAVIOR

For the measurement of students' perceptions of interpersonal teacher behavior, different instruments are needed for the message and interaction level and for the pattern level.

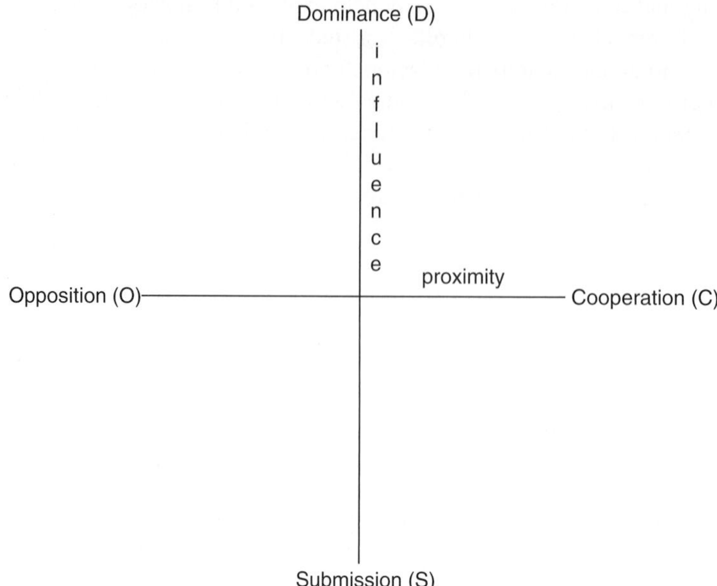

FIGURE 45.1. Two-dimensional coordinate system of the model for interpersonal teacher behavior.

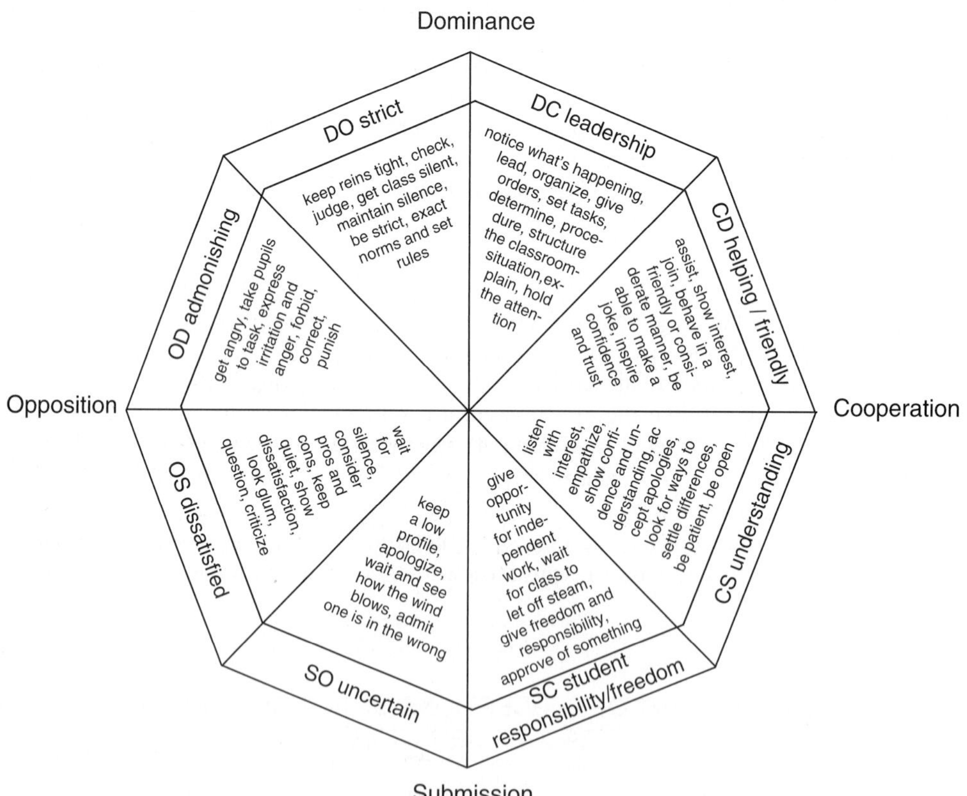

FIGURE 45.2. Model for interpersonal teacher behavior.

Dominance (D) The teacher determines the student's activities.	5–4–3–2–1	**Submission (S)** The students can determines their own activities.
Cooperation (C) The teacher shows approval of the students and their behavior.	5–4–3–2–1	**Opposition (O)** The teacher shows disapproval of the sutdents and their behavior.

FIGURE 45.3. Rating scales for observation of students' perceptions at the message and interaction level.

Message and Interaction Level

At the message level, not much research on student perceptions has been carried out. Van Tartwijk (1993) and van Tartwijk, Brekelmans, Wubbels, Fisher, and Fraser (1998) reported studies using an instrument to measure students' perceptions of interpersonal messages. These studies used two rating scales corresponding to the two dimensions of the model (see Fig. 45.3). Observers were trained to take the role of students. These observers viewed lessons that had been videotaped from the back of the classroom and gave their estimation of the students' perceptions on the two rating scales for 180 fragments of 8 seconds chosen randomly from 10 complete lessons (van Tartwijk, 1993), and 68 fragments of 1 minute showing various situations (van Tartwijk et al., 1998). In one a teacher is writing on the blackboard with his back to the classroom, and some students are listening, whereas others are talking. Another example shows the teacher speaking angrily to a student, and hitting another student with the class looking on. To establish reliability in both studies, several observers were used and acceptable interrater reliability (Kendalls' Tau between 0.69 and 0.81 and Pearson correlations between 0.71 and 0.82) were found. In a small-scale study van Tartwijk (1993) also compared the observers' ratings with the ratings of three students resulting in Pearson correlations of over 0.80. Further indications for validity were the 0.06 nonsignificant correlations between the ratings for the two dimensions.

Pattern Level

The perceptions of teachers and students at the pattern level can be measured with the Questionnaire on Teacher Interaction (QTI). To map interpersonal teacher behavior, the QTI was designed according to the two-dimensional Leary model and the eight sectors (Wubbels et al., 1985). It was originally developed in The Netherlands, and a 64-item American version was constructed in 1988 (Wubbels & Levy, 1991). The Dutch items were formulated, based on large numbers of interviews with both teachers and students (Wubbels & Levy, 1993). The original Dutch version consists of 77 items to be rated on a 5-point Likert scale ranging from Never/Not at All to Always/Very. The items are divided into eight scales corresponding with the eight behavior types. The instrument has been translated into the following languages: English, French, German, Hebrew, Russian, Slovenian, Swedish, Norwegian, Finnish, Spanish, Mandarin Chinese, Singapore Chinese, and Indonesian.[1] In Table 45.1 typical items are provided for each of the eight sectors of the QTI.

[1]The QTI was intended for use in secondary education and formed the basis of several new versions such as for primary education (e.g., Goh, & Fraser, 1996) and for higher education teachers (e.g., Soerjaningsih, Fraser, & Aldridge, 2002), for supervisors of student teachers (Kremer-Hayon & Wubbels, 1993a), and one for teachers about school managers (the Questionnaire on Principal Interaction, e.g., Kremer-Hayon & Wubbels, 1993b; Fisher & Cresswell, 1998). The instrument also formed the starting point for adaptations that are being used in postcompulsory education (Hockley & Harkin, 2000).

TABLE 45.1
Number of Items and Typical Item for Each of the Eight Scales of the Dutch and U.S. Version of the QTI

		No. of Items		
		Dutch	U.S.	Typical Item
DC	Leadership	10	7	S/He is a good leader
CD	Helpful/Friendly	10	8	S/He is someone we can depend on
CS	Understanding	10	8	If we have something to say s/he will listen
SC	Student responsibility/ Freedom	9	8	S/He gives us a lot of free time in class
SO	Uncertain	9	7	S/He seems uncertain
OS	Dissatisfied	11	9	S/He is suspicious
OD	Admonishing	9	8	S/He gets angry
DO	Strict	9	9	S/He is strict

Students can rate their current teacher on the QTI, and teachers can also record their perceptions about their own behavior (their self-perceptions). Teachers may also record their responses from the perspective of how they would like to be (i.e., their ideal perceptions). Each completed questionnaire yields a set of eight *scale scores*. Scale scores equal the sum of all item scores and are then rescaled to range between 0 and 1. When the QTI has been administered to students, scale scores of students from the same class can be aggregated to a class mean.

In some studies reviewed for this chapter, the teacher–student relationship was analyzed on the basis of *dimension scores* (i.e., the scale scores are converted linearly to dimension scores[2]). The closer the scales are to the Dominance/Submission dimension (strict, leadership, uncertainty, and student responsibility/freedom), the more they contribute to this dimension, and similarly helpful/friendliness, understanding, dissatisfied, and admonishing contribute most to the Cooperation/Opposition dimension. Graphic representations of the eight scale scores ("interpersonal profiles") can be used to report on the teacher–student relationship (see Fig. 45.11 for examples).[3]

Several studies have been conducted on the reliability and validity of the QTI. These have included, among others, Dutch (e.g., Brekelmans, Wubbels, & Créton, 1990; den Brok, 2001; Wubbels et al., 1985), American (Wubbels & Levy, 1991), and Australian (Fisher, Fraser, & Wubbels, 1992; Fisher, Henderson, & Fraser, 1995). Recently, a cross-national validity study was completed comparing students' responses to the questionnaire in Singapore, Brunei, the United States, The Netherlands, Slovakia, and Australia (den Brok, Fisher et al., 2003). In all these studies, both reliability and validity were satisfactory. The homogeneity of each of the eight groups of items expressed in internal consistencies (Cronbach's α) for student ratings at class level is generally above 0.80. The agreement between the scores of students

[2]To this end the eight scores are represented as vectors in a two-dimensional space, each dividing a section of the model of interpersonal behavior in two and with a length corresponding to the height of the scale score. We then compute the two coordinates of the resultant of these eight vectors.

[3]These graphic representations are achieved by shading in each sector of the model of interpersonal teacher behavior. The ratio of the length of the perpendicular bisector of the shaded part and the length of the perpendicular bisector of the total sector equals the ratio of the observed score and the maximum score for that sector.

in a single class usually meets the general requirements for observer agreement. The internal consistencies (Cronbach's α), when students' scores in one class are considered as repeated measures, are above 0.90 (Brekelmans et al., 1990). Internal consistencies for teacher self-perceptions and teacher ideals are usually a bit lower, but hardly ever below 0.65. The variance in students' ratings at the class level is much higher than for most other learning environments questionnaires indicating that the QTI discriminates well between classes. For the American version, the percentage of variance at the class level is between 36 and 59 (Wubbels & Levy, 1991) and in the Dutch version, between 48 and 62 (e.g., den Brok, 2001). Although most of the variance in students' ratings is at the teacher level, there is an interaction between teacher level and the class level indicating that students perceive their teachers as varying in their relationships across classes (Brekelmans, den Brok, Bergen, & Wubbels, 2004; den Brok, 2001; Levy, den Brok, Wubbels, & Brekelmans, 2003). This effect is, however, not very large. From a generalizability study (Shavelson, Webb, & Burstein, 1986) on students' ratings, it was concluded (Brekelmans, 1989), that the QTI should be administered to at least 10 students in a class for the data to be reliable. The QTI does not need to be administered more than once per year, because interpersonal style remains relatively stable. At least two classes of students should complete the questionnaire for each teacher for a reliable measure of overall style.

With respect to validity, for example, factor analyses on class means and LISREL analyses (den Brok, 2001; den Brok, Levy, Wubbels & Rodriguez, 2003; Wubbels & Levy, 1991) determined that the two-factor structure did indeed support the eight scales. For students' ratings Brekelmans et al. (1990) demonstrated that both factors explain 80% of the variance on all the scales of the Dutch QTI. Similar results were obtained for the version in the other countries (den Brok, Fisher et al., 2003). For both students' ratings and teacher self- and ideal perceptions, scales appear to be ordered in a circumplex structure, meaning that two independent factors are found, with a circular ordering of the scales (Wiggins, Philips, & Trapnell, 1989).

INTERPERSONAL PROFILES

To describe research results for interpersonal profiles, we first turn to the profiles of teacher-student relationships that have been found with the help of the Model for interpersonal teacher behavior and the QTI. A profile is the particular combination of eight scale scores resulting from the administration of the QTI. When describing patterns of interpersonal relationships in classrooms using cluster analyses of students' ratings, eight different types of profiles could be distinguished in Dutch and American classes (Brekelmans, 1989; Brekelmans, Levy, & Rodriguez, 1993)[4].

These profiles have been named Directive, Authoritative, Tolerant/Authoritative, Tolerant, Uncertain/Tolerant, Uncertain/Aggressive, Drudging, and Repressive. In Fig. 45.4, we summarize each of the eight types on the basis of the two dimension scores of the profile by means of a main point in the coordinate system. Although we characterize these profiles in terms of the teacher's style, it is important to remember that these are descriptions of a single teacher in one particular class. Classes of experienced or veteran teachers usually have the same type of interpersonal pattern, but there can be differences between classes for the same teacher (Brekelmans, Wubbels, & den Brok, 2002). For beginning teachers, the variation across classes can be considerable (Brekelmans et al., 2002; Somers, Brekelmans, & Wubbels, 1997).

[4]That eight types of patterns have been found and that the QTI has eight scales may raise misunderstandings. The 2 eights have nothing to do with each other.

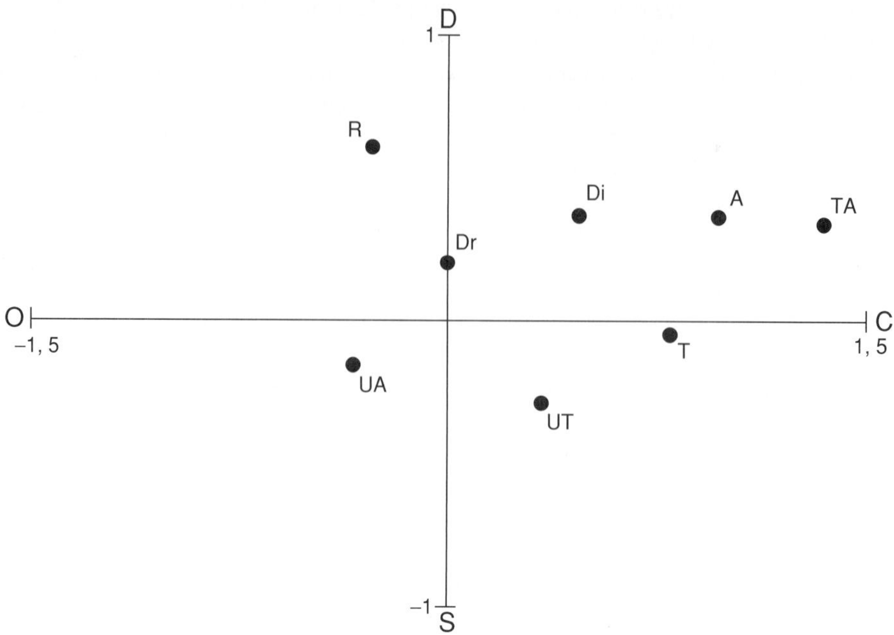

A=Authoritative, Di=Directive, Dr=Drudging, T=Tolerant, R=Repressive, TA= Tolerant/Authoritative, UA=Uncertain/Aggressive, UT=Uncertain/Tolerant

FIGURE 45.4. Main points of the eight types of patterns of interpersonal relationships.

The Authoritative, the Tolerant/Authoritative, and the Tolerant type are patterns wherein students perceive their teachers as relatively high on the Proximity dimension, with the Tolerant type lowest on the Influence dimension. Less cooperative than the three previous types are the Directive, the Uncertain/Tolerant, and the Drudging type, with the Uncertain/Tolerant type lowest on the Dominance dimension. The least cooperative patterns of interpersonal relationships have been indicated as Repressive and Uncertain/ Aggressive. In Repressive-type classes, teachers are the most dominant of all eight types.

In Table 45.2, descriptions of the classroom environment typical for each of the eight types are presented based on observation research (Créton & Wubbels, 1984; Brekelmans 1989; Wubbels & Levy, 1993).

INTERPERSONAL RELATIONS ACROSS THE TEACHING CAREER

From the outset of our research program, it appeared that many teachers were not sufficiently able to create positive learning environments. Beginning and experienced teachers encounter (different) problems in this domain. These problems can be described with the help of results of cross-sectional and longitudinal studies on the teacher–student relationship and teacher experience level. In a first longitudinal study (e.g., Brekelmans et al., 2002), data were gathered from 41 teachers (self- and ideal perceptions) and their students (actual perceptions) in the first 3 to 8 years of their careers. The number of classes participating in gathering annual data varied from one to five per year per teacher.

TABLE 45.2
Descriptions of Classroom Environments Typical for the Eight Categories in the Typology of Interpersonal Styles

Interpersonal Profile Type	*Classroom Environment*
Directive	The learning environment in a class with teachers with a Directive profile is well structured and task oriented. Directive teachers are organized efficiently and normally complete all lessons on time. They dominate class discussion, and generally hold students' interest. These teachers usually are not close to their students, though they are occasionally friendly and understanding. They have high standards and are seen as demanding. Things seem businesslike, but the teachers have to work at it. They get angry at times and have to remind the class that they are there to work. They like to call on students who misbehave and are inattentive. This normally straightens them up quickly.
Authoritative	The Authoritative atmosphere is well structured, pleasant, and task oriented. Rules and procedures are clear and students do not need to be reminded. They are attentive, and generally produce better work than their peers in the Directive teachers' class. Authoritative teachers are enthusiastic and open to students' needs. They take a personal interest in them, and this comes through in the lessons. Although their favorite method is the lecture, Authoritative teachers frequently use other techniques. The lessons are well planned and logically structured.
Tolerant and Authoritative	Tolerant and Authoritative teachers maintain a structure that supports student responsibility and freedom. They use a variety of methods, to which students respond well. They frequently organize their lessons around small-group work. Although the class environment resembles the climate in the Authoritative class, Tolerant/Authoritative teachers develop closer relationships with students. They enjoy the class and are highly involved in most lessons. Both students and teachers can be seen laughing, and there is very little need to enforce the rules. These teachers ignore minor disruptions, choosing instead to concentrate on the lesson. Students work to reach their own and the teachers' instructional goals with little or no complaining.
Tolerant	There seem to be separate Dutch and American views of Tolerant teachers. To the Dutch, the atmosphere is pleasant and supportive and students enjoy attending class. They have more freedom in this class than in those listed previously, and have some real power to influence curriculum and instruction. Students appreciate their teachers' personal involvement and their ability to match the subject matter with their learning styles. They often work at their own pace and the class atmosphere sometimes may be a little confused as a result. In the United States, however, Tolerant teachers are seen to be somewhat disorganized. Their lessons are not prepared well and they do not challenge students. These teachers often begin the lesson with an explanation and then send the students off to individually complete an assignment. Although the teachers are interested in students' personal lives, their academic expectations for them are not evident.
Uncertain/Tolerant	Uncertain/Tolerant teachers are cooperative but do not show much leadership in class. Their lessons are poorly structured, are not introduced completely, and do not have much follow-through. They generally tolerate disorder, and students are not task oriented. Uncertain/Tolerant teachers are quite concerned about the class, and are willing to explain things repeatedly to students who have not been listening. The atmosphere is so unstructured, however, that only the students in front are attentive while the others play games, do homework, and the like. Students are not provocative, however, and the teachers manage to ignore them while loudly and quickly covering the subject. Uncertain/Tolerant teachers' rules of behavior are arbitrary, and students do not know what to expect when infractions occur. The teachers' few efforts to stop the misbehavior are delivered without emphasis and have little effect on the class. Sometimes these teachers react quickly, and at other times completely ignore inattentiveness.

(*continued*)

TABLE 45.2
Continued

Interpersonal Profile Type	*Classroom Environment*
	Class performance expectations are minimal and mostly immediate rather than long range. The overall effect is of an unproductive equilibrium in which teachers and students seem to go their own way.
Uncertain/Aggressive	This class is characterized by an aggressive kind of disorder. Teachers and students regard each other as opponents and spend almost all their time in symmetrically escalating conflicts. Students seize nearly every opportunity to be disruptive, and continually provoke the teachers by jumping up, laughing, and shouting out. This generally brings a panicked overreaction from the teachers, which is met by even greater student misbehavior. An observer in this class might see the teacher and students fighting over a book that the student has been reading. The teacher grabs the book in an effort to force the student to pay attention. The student resists because he or she thinks the teacher has no right to his or her property. Because neither one backs down, the situation often escalates out of control. In the middle of the confusion Uncertain/Aggressive teachers may suddenly try to discipline a few students, but often manage to miss the real culprits. Because of the teachers' unpredictable and unbalanced behavior, the students feel that the teacher is to blame. Rules of behavior are not communicated or explained properly. These teachers spend most of their time trying to manage the class, yet seem unwilling to experiment with different instructional techniques. They prefer to think, "first, they'll have to behave." Learning is the least important aspect of the class, unfortunately.
Repressive	Students of Repressive teachers are uninvolved and extremely docile. They follow the rules and are afraid of the teachers' angry outbursts. These teachers seem to overreact to small transgressions, frequently making sarcastic remarks or giving failing grades. Repressive teachers are the epitome of complementary rigidity. These teachers' lessons are structured, but not well organized. Whereas directions and background information are provided, few questions are allowed or encouraged. Occasionally, students will work on individual assignments, for which they receive precious little help from the teachers. The atmosphere is guarded and unpleasant, and the students are apprehensive and fearful. Because the Repressive teachers' expectations are competition oriented and inflated, students worry a lot about their exams. The teachers seem to repress student initiative, preferring to lecture while the students sit still. They perceive the teachers as unhappy and impatient and their silence seems like the calm before the storm.
Drudging	The atmosphere in a Drudging teacher's class varies between the disorder with the Uncertain/Aggressive and Uncertain/Tolerant teachers and sometimes the Directive teacher's class atmosphere. One thing is constant, however: These teachers continually struggle to manage the class. They usually succeed (unlike the other two types), but not before expending a great deal of energy. Students pay attention as long as the teachers actively try to motivate them. When they do get involved, the atmosphere is oriented toward the subject matter and the teachers do not generate much warmth. They generally follow a routine in which they do most of the talking and avoid experimenting with new methods. Drudging teachers always seem to be going downhill and the class is neither enthusiastic nor supportive nor competitive. Unfortunately, because of the continual concern with class management these teachers sometimes look as though they are on the verge of burnout.

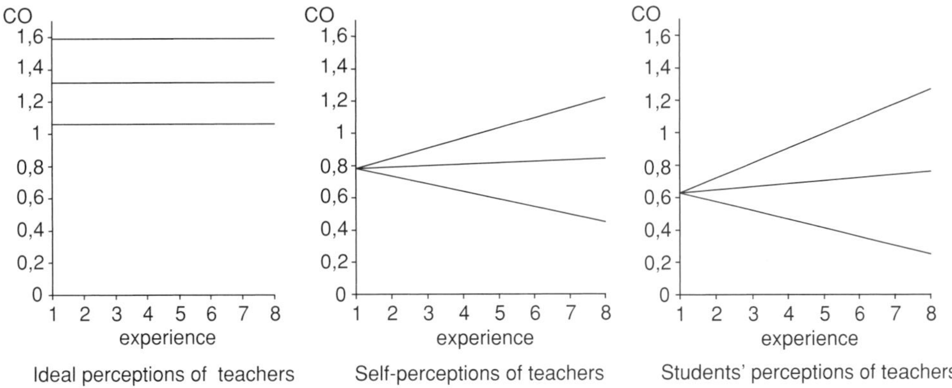

FIGURE 45.5. (Estimated) Proximity scores in the first eight years of the teaching career (longitudinal study).

A second longitudinal study (Somers et al., 1997) used data of 197 student teachers (self- and ideal perceptions) and their students (actual perceptions) to follow them during teacher education and the first 3 years of their careers.

For a cross-sectional study (e.g., Brekelmans et al., 2002), data were gathered from 573 teachers (self- and ideal perceptions) and more than 25,000 students (actual perceptions) located in about 100 different secondary schools throughout The Netherlands. Student teachers and teachers teaching all kind of subjects and from all parts of The Netherlands participated in the three studies. We first describe the development of the teacher–student relationship during the teaching career both at the level of dimension scores and at the level of the typology in Table 45.2. Then we turn to the character of the problems teachers encounter.

Proximity and Influence Dimensions

In both longitudinal studies, teachers' ideal perceptions appeared to be stable during the first decade of their careers for both dimensions, whereas teachers' self-perceptions and students' perceptions on the Proximity dimension hardly changed. It appeared that dominant behavior grew for most teachers toward their ideal every year in the first 8 years of their careers. The variation among individual teachers, however, can be large. As an example, Fig. 45.5 shows for both students' perceptions and teachers' self- and ideal perceptions, the growth rates for an "average" teacher along with two lines representing the growth rate for teachers one standard deviation above and below average. For some there is a significant upward trend and for others downward, resulting in an average of no growth.

Figures 45.6 and 45.7 plot the mean Influence (DS) and Proximity (CO) scores for students' and teachers' ideal and self-perceptions based on cross-sectional data. The mean Influence and Proximity scores of teachers' ideal perceptions did not differ significantly (5% level) across levels of seniority (grouped in six stages, see Fig. 45.6). Throughout their careers, teachers apparently agree on the amount of influence and proximity desired in the classroom. Students' and teachers' perceptions of actual behavior, however, varied noticeably for teachers across experience levels. Students' perceptions of the dominant behavior of student teachers and teachers with 1 to 5 years of experience also differed significantly from the other five groups. An increase in dominant behavior could be seen from the student teaching period through 6 to 10 years. After this point, there was little change. Teachers' self-perceptions showed the same

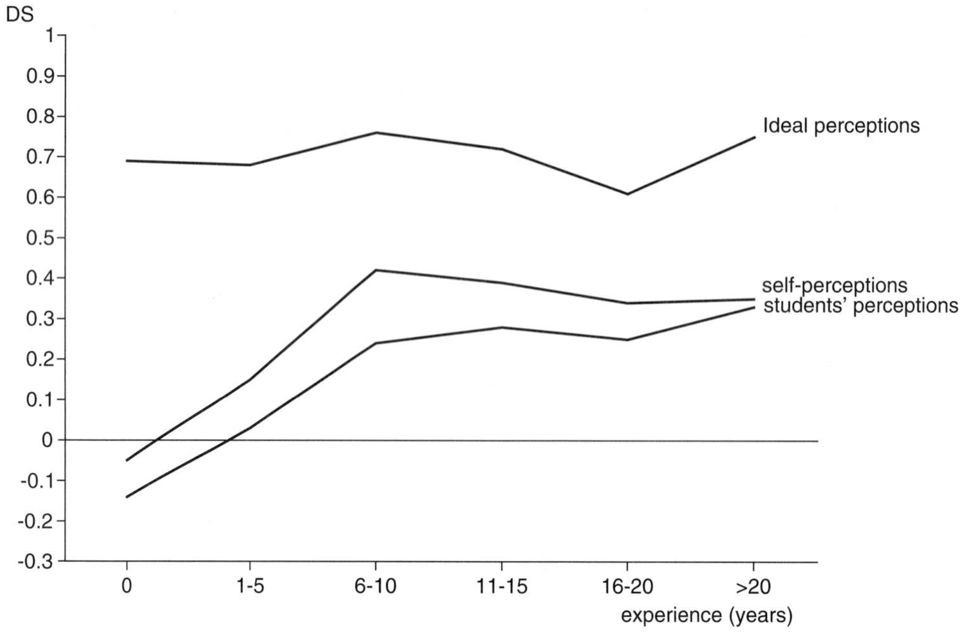

FIGURE 45.6. Mean Influence (DS) scores by experience level (cross-sectional study).

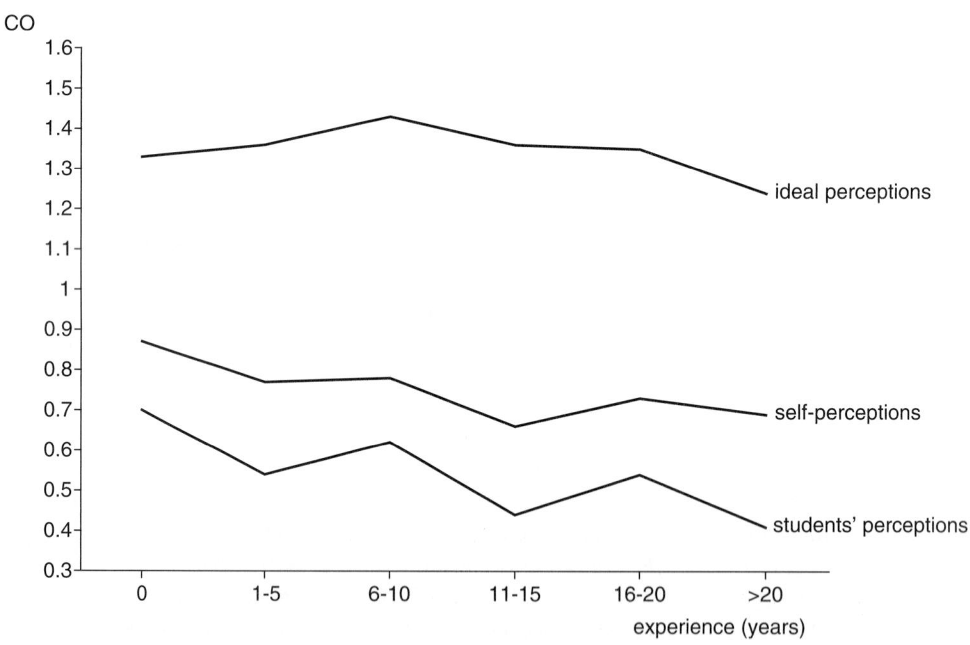

FIGURE 45.7. Mean Proximity (CO) scores by experience level (cross-sectional study).

pattern. The upward trend in students' and teachers' self-perceptions found in the longitudinal study possibly levels off after the first decade of teaching.

In the cross-sectional study, the experience-related differences in the Proximity dimension were much smaller than on the Influence dimension and only a few were significant. According to students, student teachers behaved more cooperatively than 1–5 and 11–15 year teachers. For teachers' self-perceptions, only the difference between student teachers and teachers with 11 to 15 years of experience was significant. This indicates a moderate decline in Proximity scores throughout the career. Apparently, when teachers grow older they appear to distance themselves from their students making the classroom atmosphere less personal and more businesslike

An interesting detail in the results of the second longitudinal study was a dip in the students' perceptions of dominance in the second student teaching placement. This means that the students perceive less leadership and more uncertainty. Student teachers participated in two placements: the first in a group of three students with continuous observation of a cooperating teacher and the second individually without observations. The dip can be interpreted from the reality shock perspective (e.g., Corcoran 1981; Muller Fohrbrodt et. al., 1978). In the first student teaching practicum (the triad period), the environment is relatively safe and the "mistakes" of the student teachers in management and leadership behavior do not have full (negative) consequences for the classroom atmosphere. The presence of the cooperating teacher may keep the students in order and protects the student teacher so that a positive classroom atmosphere does not deteriorate. In the student teacher's individual placement, however, without the shield of the cooperating teacher, student teachers bear the full consequences of their behavior. This results in more discipline problems, and student teachers do experience the need to show more leadership and less uncertain behavior. It is, however, much more difficult now to enforce the positive working environment than with the help of the cooperating teacher. Students perceive student teachers now lower on leadership and higher on uncertainty than before, and according to the students, apparently their student teachers are not able to be convincing leaders. It appears that they have not yet found how to do this. The higher levels in the first year show that they learn in this domain during the second placement.

Profiles

As an example of profile results, Table 45.3 presents the percentages of mean interpersonal profiles (students' perceptions) for the first and second student teaching placement and the first and second year of the professional career (Somers et al., 1997). Table 45.3 shows that the major profiles in the student teaching placement were the Tolerant and the Uncertain/Tolerant profile. A larger proportion of interpersonal profiles fitted the more structured and task-oriented Authoritative profiles in the first and second year of the career.

Brekelmans et al. (2002) found that of all ideal perceptions, three fourths (73%) were most similar to the Tolerant/Authoritative profile, whereas 25% were most similar to the Authoritative type. At all experience levels, more than 90% of the teachers preferred one of these two relatively similar interpersonal profiles.

As to the interpersonal profiles, it appears that according to their students, the most frequently found profiles in the first year of the teaching career are the Tolerant and the Uncertain/Tolerant profile. More student teachers than first-year teachers conform to the Tolerant and Uncertain/Tolerant type. The presence of these profiles decreases as teachers become more experienced. Then, according to their students, a larger proportion of interpersonal profiles of teachers fit the more structured and task-oriented Authoritative and Directive profiles. During the first decade of the teaching career, the number of Authoritative profiles increases, and after about 5 years of experience the Directive type moves to the top. Toward the end of the teaching career, the number of teachers with a Repressive profile increases (Brekelmans et al., 2002).

TABLE 45.3
Percentages of Mean Interpersonal Profiles (Students' Perceptions) for the First and Second Student Teaching Placement (STP) and the First and Second Year of the Career

Interpersonal Profile Type	*First STP (n = 197)*	*Second STP (n = 197)*	*First Year (n = 55)*	*Second Year (n = 19)*
Directive	2	4	11	5
Authoritative	10	7	15	42
Tolerant/Authoritative	11	11	11	11
Tolerant	50	47	42	32
Uncertain/Tolerant	25	28	16	11
Uncertain/Aggressive	2	1	–	
Repressive	–	–	–	–
Drudging	1	3	5	–

RELATIONAL PROBLEMS OF TEACHERS

For many beginning teachers, it appears to be difficult to create and maintain order in class (e.g., Veenman, 1984), and this can be seen from the relatively low students' perception score on leadership and high scores on uncertainty at the beginning of the career discussed in the previous section. It appears that most teachers learn to cope with these problems in the first years of their careers. The growth of the frequency of the Repressive teacher type toward the end of the career suggests that older teachers have a specific problem in their relationships with students: They become overly strict and authoritarian.

Beginning Teachers

One explanation for the observations described in the previous section may be the following. At the start of their careers, most teachers are 20 to 25 years old and have not, to any large degree, served in leadership roles. From this point of view, the professional role does not coincide very well with their stage of personal development. Beginning teachers are often confronted with the lack of a behavioral repertoire (in particular in managerial and instructional strategies) and inadequate cognitions in this area. This can result in students' perceptions of their interpersonal style as Uncertain/Tolerant and Tolerant, with a relatively low influence score. This situation urges teachers to do something about it. The need for change is reinforced by the ideal perception of beginning teachers, mainly a classroom situation with the teachers (themselves) in control. Through daily classroom practice, the young teachers may learn how to develop dominance patterns. This interpretation is consistent with Huberman's (1993) description of modal sequences in the professional engagement of teachers during their careers (survival and discovery, stabilization, experimentation/diversification). The first two phases of Huberman's sequence (survival and discovery) can be recognized from the preceding discussion.

According to the preceding interpretation, beginning teachers mainly attribute (consciously or unconsciously) problems in interacting with students to the influence area. The ability to empathize with students (recent peers) and to show cooperative behaviors is considered by them to be a less problematic area. The greater attention to Dominant behavior is probably reflected in the fact that there is more dispersion with teachers' perceptions of the Influence dimension than with students' perceptions, whereas students perceive larger differences between teachers on the Proximity dimension (e.g., Levy et al., 2003; den Brok, Levy, Rodriguez, & Wubbels, 2002).

With the greater attention to Dominant behavior, practice and experimentation on the Proximity dimension fade somewhat into the background. The previous interpretation of the differences in changes in dominant and cooperative behavior is relevant when teachers show an increase in dominant behavior (as most teachers do) and rather stable or decreasing cooperative behavior. There are teachers with an increase in cooperative behavior in the first years of their teaching careers. This may be due to an increasing behavioral repertoire or a better understanding of classroom processes.

Experienced Teachers

Considering the descriptions of the repressive teacher in Table 45.2, the growth of the number of repressive teachers, also visible in decreasing cooperative behavior toward the end of the teaching career, is problematic. We suppose that the decrease of cooperative behavior is not due to a lack of an adequate behavioral repertoire in the cooperative sectors. We think that especially some very experienced teachers tend to become stricter when they get older, becoming sometimes unreasonable in their demands. Because of the distance, both emotionally and in age, older teachers may be less connected with the students' lifestyles. Therefore, these teachers may become more and more dissatisfied with student behavior, thus becoming a problem for themselves as well as for their students. These high demands on, and low connection with, students can provoke student protest that at first can be handled easily, but can gradually become a real threat for a positive classroom atmosphere. Thus the teachers are faced with a difficult problem, and they may feel required to act in an even more demanding and admonishing manner, stimulating a negative communicative spiral: the teacher showing ever more oppositional behavior as a reaction to students' protest behavior. So the origin of the decrease in Cooperative behavior may be due to an inadequate repertoire, and inadequate cognitions about the cause of the problem. Giving responsibility to students is inherently risky, because it appears that many people when they intend to give responsibility also show uncertainty.[5] This uncertainty can provoke student disorderly behavior and shape undesirable classroom situations. Teachers need to be able to give students responsibility for their own work without showing uncertainty or demonstrating weakness. Training to give students freedom and responsibility thus may be a prominent part of inservice education for very experienced teachers. In addition, training on setting norms and standards in a clear but not provocative way may also be useful.

TEACHER POSITION IN CLASS AND NONVERBAL BEHAVIOR

This section first reports on studies on the position of the teacher in class and then about nonverbal behavior. According to the systems approach, nonverbal behavior is particularly important for the perception of the relationship aspect of communication. Differences between beginning and experienced teachers in nonverbal behavior in relation to the position in class may help explain the problems of beginning teachers.

Position

In a joint Dutch and Australian study, the relationship between the students' perceptions of their teacher's interpersonal style and judges' ratings of the interpersonal aspect of these teachers'

[5]The closeness of these two sectors in the model (implying high correlations between the two adjacent scales) is an empirical validated indication of this.

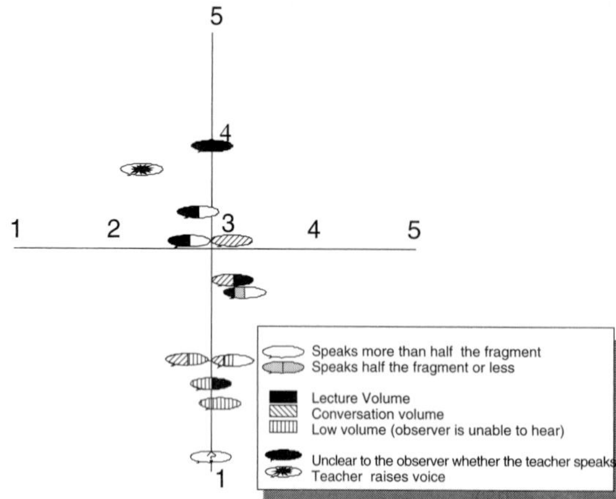

Voice

The relation between the Voice channel and the DS ratings shows that the longer teachers speak using a lecturing volume, the more they are perceived as dominant, and the longer teachers speak in such a way that they cannot be heard by the observer, the more the teachers' behavior is perceived as submissive.
For the CO ratings, whether teachers raise their voice is the most important distinctive feature.

FIGURE 45.8. Dimension scores and the use of voice.

messages was investigated (van Tartwijk et al., 1998). Strong and strong-to-medium significant correlations were established between students' perceptions and judges' ratings during whole-class teaching, whereas no significant correlations were found between students' perceptions and judges' ratings during individual seatwork. These findings suggest that teachers who present themselves as teachers with a specific interpersonal style when they have a central position in the classroom (when they are "on stage") will probably create a working climate that will last for the whole lesson and beyond. Whole-class teaching seems important for establishing the "image" the students have of their teacher. Subsequently, this image will also guide the students' communication with their teacher during seatwork (cf. Weber & Mitchell, 1995).

Nonverbal Behavior

Van Tartwijk (1993) studied the contribution of nonverbal behaviors to the perception of the relationship at the message level with the help of five channels of behavior (cf. Harper, Wiens, & Matarazzo, 1978): space (the teacher's use of classroom space), body (position and movement of the trunk, arms, and head), face (various expressions), visual behavior (duration of the teacher looking at the students), and voice (the noncontent aspects of speech). About one thousand 8-second video fragments selected from the videotaped lessons of 53 teachers at work in their classrooms were shown to raters. The raters estimated the students' perception of the teacher behavior in these fragments on rating scales corresponding to the Influence and Proximity dimensions (Fig. 45.3). Subsequently the nonverbal behavior in the fragments was scored with a specially designed observation instrument for nonverbal teacher behavior.

All channels could be used to explain variance in the Influence ratings, with voice being by far the most important. Figure 45.8 presents this relationship for voice. In this figure, nonverbal behaviors were plotted on a vertical axis according to the mean DS rating. The mean CO ratings of nonverbal behaviors were plotted on the horizontal axis. Only the Face and Voice channels were important for explaining variance in the CO ratings, with the facial expression having the strongest relationship (see Fig. 45.9).

A summarizing view across channels is presented in Fig. 45.10.[6] The figure to the left shows that behaviors such as looking at the students continuously and speaking loud and

[6]This figure is based on the results of a Homals analysis, a technique for optimal scaling. In this analysis fragments are quantified in such a way that fragments that resemble each other get a similar value on a dimension, whereas

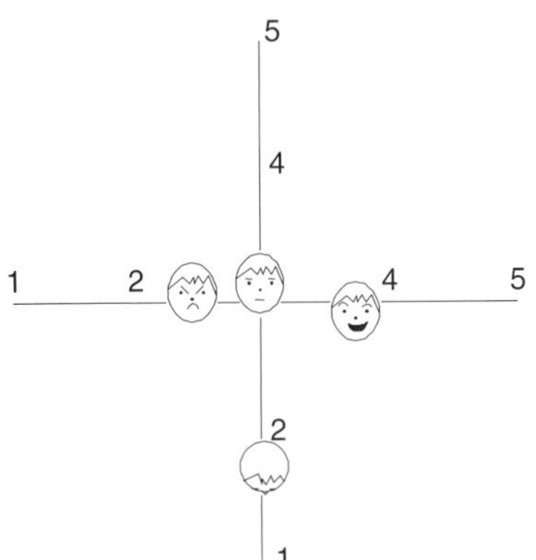

Face

For the DS ratings, the visibility of the face for the students was the most important factor. Not surprising if compared with the importance of an upright head position for a rating as relatively dominant.
The most important facial expression for the CO ratings were laughing, neutral, or angry facial expressions.

FIGURE 45.9. Dimension scores and facial expression.

FIGURE 45.10. Combinations of behavior with a relatively high (left) and low (right) influence perception. In the left position the teacher is relatively far from the student, with his or her head in upright position, scanning and talking long in a rather loud voice. In the right position the teacher is close to the students with his or her head down so that his or her facial expression cannot be seen.

emphatically were often observed together. On average, this combination of behaviors was rated as highly dominant. In the figure to the right, we see that the behaviors such as not being heard, being close to the students, and bending toward the students often go together and yield a low influence score.

Beginning Teachers' Problems

In Kounin's (1970) landmark study on discipline problems and classroom management, it was found that management success of teachers, in terms of freedom from deviancy, correlated with "withitness" (the teacher demonstrates that he or she knows what is going on) and "overlapping" (the teacher's ability to attend to two issues simultaneously). The major relationship in the study by van Tartwijk (1993) between nonverbal behaviors and interpersonal perception can be interpreted using Kounin's concepts: The more the teacher facilitates visual contact with the class, the more his or her behavior is perceived as dominant. When nonverbal behaviors such as visual contact with class and emphatic verbal presence (speaking continuously with a loud voice) are combined, the teacher's messages were rated most dominant.

fragments which do not resemble get a more different value. This analysis was used to identify the combinations of nonverbal behaviors from the various channels that occurred relatively often together.

However, there appeared a distinct difference between beginning and experienced teachers' nonverbal behavior that may be an important cause for the unsatisfying relationships of some beginning teachers with their students. Behaviors that facilitated visual contact (looking to students) and signaling withitness and overlapping were demonstrated by experienced teachers almost twice as much as by student teachers. These behaviors are typical for teachers during whole-class teaching. No differences were found between beginning and more experienced teachers for the nonverbal behaviors that are typical for a teacher interacting with individual students, such as speaking in a low volume, head and trunk bent forward, and a nonfrontal body orientation toward the majority of students in the class (see the right of Fig. 45.10). This indicates that the nonverbal behaviors of beginning and experienced teachers differ, not so much when they interact with individual students during individual seatwork, but foremost during whole-class teaching.

The previous results support the need for beginning teachers to portray the image of an experienced teacher whenever they address the class as a group. However, they probably should avoid whole-class teaching for a longer period. Staying on stage too long often increases the risk of not being able to sustain one's part.

TEACHER INTERPERSONAL BEHAVIOR AND COGNITIVE AND AFFECTIVE OUTCOMES

Classroom environment studies that have included the interpersonal perspective on teaching usually indicate a strong and positive relationship between perceptions of Influence and Proximity or their related subscales and cognitive and affective student outcomes.

Profiles

The Brekelmans (1989) study investigated the relationship between student outcomes and students' perceptions of teacher interpersonal behavior in terms of the interpersonal profiles as described in Table 45.2. In Table 45.4, estimations for the (statistical) effects of the eight different profiles of students' perceptions of interpersonal profile type on physics achievement and attitude scores are presented (after correction for the influences of other variables).[7]

The results of Table 45.4 show that, on average, the teacher with a Repressive profile has the highest achievement outcomes. Teachers with disorderly classrooms (Profiles 5, 6, 8) reflect relatively low student achievement, whereas Directive, Authoritative, and Tolerant teachers have relatively high outcomes. The Authoritative and Directive teachers have the highest student attitude scores. Students of the Drudging, Uncertain/Aggressive, and Repressive teachers have the worst attitudes toward physics.

Scales, Dimensions, and Cognitive Outcomes

In Brekelmans' (1989) study, students' perceptions of teacher influence were related to cognitive outcomes. The higher a teacher was perceived on the influence dimension, the higher the outcomes of students on a physics test. In her study, teacher influence was the most important variable at the class level. Other studies found positive correlations or regression coefficients

[7]The signs have no absolute meaning. In the analysis one of the types has to be chosen as point of reference. This is the Drudging type and the numbers and signs indicate the position relative to this type.

TABLE 45.4
Effects on Achievement and Attitudes of Students' Perceptions of the Interpersonal Profile of Their Physics Teachers

Interpersonal Profile Type	*Effect on Achievement*	*Effect on Attitude*
1 Directive	0.17	0.62
2 Authoritative	0.07	0.79
3 Authoritative/Tolerant	Missing[a]	Missing[a]
4 Tolerant	0.23	0.53
5 Uncertain/Tolerant	−0.17	0.51
6 Uncertain/Aggressive	−0.15	0.20
7 Repressive	0.40	0.38
8 Drudging[b]	0	0

[a]Too few cases to include in the analyses;
[b]reference group

for the leadership scale and cognitive student outcomes (Goh & Fraser, 2000; Henderson, 1995).

Similar relationships have also been found for the Proximity dimension and Proximity-related scales such as helpful/friendly and understanding, and to a lesser degree student responsibility/freedom (Goh & Fraser, 2000; Henderson, 1995; Evans, 1998). The more teachers were perceived as cooperative, the higher students' scores on cognitive tests. However, relationships between proximity and cognitive outcomes are not always straight forward. In some studies, it could only be proven that opposition, or dissatisfaction and admonishing behavior were related to lower performance, but not that friendliness and understanding behavior were related to higher performance (Rawnsley, 1997). In other studies, the relationship between proximity and cognitive outcomes is not linear, but curvilinear (i.e., lower perceptions of proximity go with low outcomes, but intermediate and higher values with higher performance until a certain ceiling of optimal proximity has been reached; den Brok, 2001; den Brok, Biekelmans, & Wubbels, in press). If report card grades have been used as outcome measures, relationships with interpersonal behavior are inconclusive (Levy, Wubbels, & Brekelmans, 1992; van Amelsvoort, Bergen, Lamberigts, & Setz, 1993; van Amelsvoort, 1999). No relationship between student perceptions of teacher proximity and influence and their report card grades was found in these studies. In Fig. 45.11, a graphical profile is displayed of two physics teachers (from the Brekelmans study), one with relatively high and one with relatively low student achievement.

Scales, Dimensions, and Affective Outcomes

Studies investigating associations between the teacher–student relationship and affective outcomes display a much more consistent pattern than studies investigating the relationship with cognitive outcomes. All studies find a positive relationship of both influence and proximity with affective outcome measures, usually measured in terms of subject-specific motivation. Generally, effects of proximity are somewhat stronger than effects of influence. In a study with physics teachers and their students, Brekelmans (1989) found a clear relationship between proximity and student motivation for physics. In Fig. 45.12 graphical profiles are presented from two physics teachers, one with relatively low and one with relatively high student attitudes.

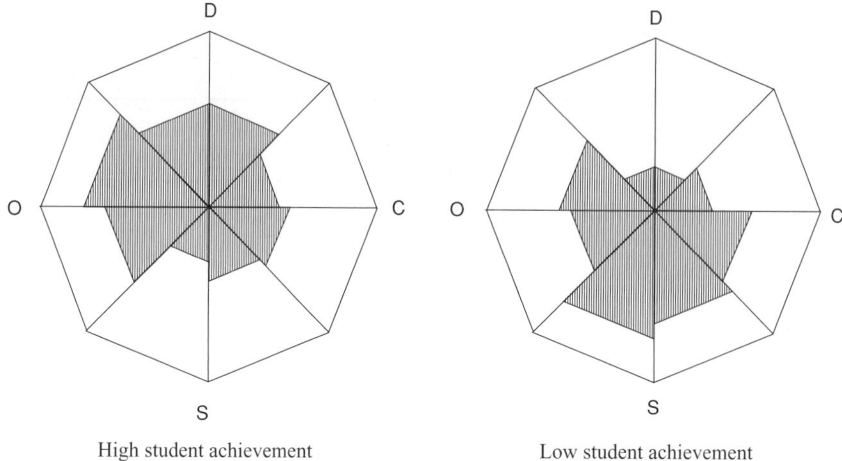

FIGURE 45.11. Interpersonal profiles of teachers with relatively high and low student outcomes.

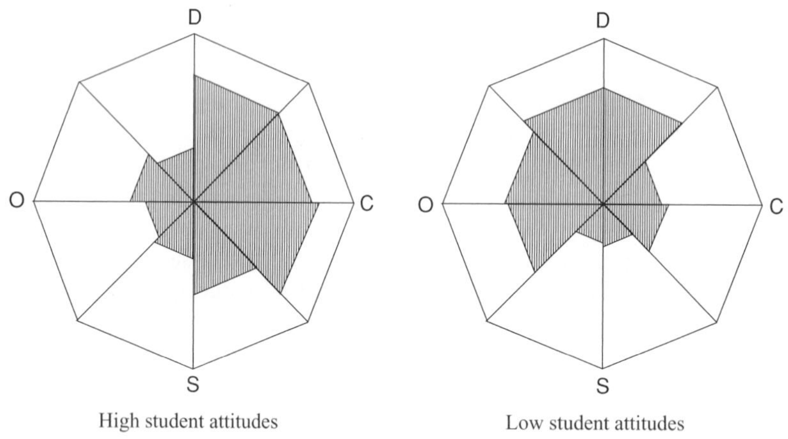

FIGURE 45.12. Interpersonal profiles of teachers with relatively high and low student attitudes.

The higher the perception of proximity, the higher the motivation of the students. With more specific measures of students' subject-specific motivation, other studies find positive relationships for helpful/friendly and understanding behavior with pleasure, confidence, effort, and relevance of students (Derksen, 1994; van Amelsvoort et al., 1993; Setz, Bergen, van Amelsvoort, & Lamberigts, 1993; van Amelsvoort, 1999). Strong and positive associations have also been demonstrated between several interpersonal scales, such as leadership and helpful/friendly, and affective outcomes, whereas negative relationships have been found with admonishing, dissatisfaction, and, in most cases, strictness (Goh & Fraser, 2000; Henderson, 1995; Rawnsley, 1997; Evans, 1998; van Amelsvoort et al., 1993; Setz, Bergen, van Amelsvoort, & Lamberigts 1993; van Amelsvoort, 1999). The weakest associations have been found between interpersonal behavior and confidence (Derksen, 1994; van Amelsvoort et al., 1993; Setz et al., 1993; van Amelsvoort, 1999). Van Amelsvoort (1999) demonstrated that the effect of interpersonal teacher behavior on students' subject-specific motivation is both direct as well as indirect via student motivation and regulation processes. In his study, a causal model was tested that linked students' perceptions on the QTI (in terms of dimension scores) to students' pleasure, confidence, and effort. He found two (statistically) significant causal paths leading from proximity to students' pleasure: One path linked the two variables directly; the other path linked proximity to student regulation of emotions, which in turn affected effort, and effort affected pleasure. Teacher proximity as perceived by students may thus affect both directly students' state of mind, but also indirectly via learning activities performed by students.

In a recent study on English as Foreign Language (EFL) teachers, den Brok (2001) found that interpersonal behavior was mainly related to the affective student outcomes, whereas other kinds of behavior were more relevant for cognitive outcomes. For all of the affective student outcome variables—pleasure, relevance, confidence, and effort—a positive and strong effect was found for teacher proximity. For some of the affective variables—pleasure, relevance, and effort—influence also had a positive effect.

Students' Learning Activities

Some of the most important mediating factors between students' perceptions of teacher behavior and student outcomes are student's learning activities (Shuell, 1996; den Brok, Bergen, & Stahl, 2002). These learning activities are, in turn, very likely to originate from students' perceptions of their teachers' regulation of learning activities and interpersonal behavior (den Brok, 2001). Brekelmans, Sleegers, and Fraser (2001) investigated relations between students' perceptions of interpersonal teacher behavior and students' perceptions of teacher elicitation and regulation of learning activities, in particular the degree to which teachers activated students to perform and initiate learning activities by themselves (teaching for active learning). Somewhat surprisingly, increasing perceptions of teacher activation seemed to be helped by stronger perceptions of influence. A similar result was found in another study on EFL teachers (den Brok, 2001). This perhaps can be understood from the earlier reported result that teaching at central moments in the lesson is crucial for the kind of relationship that develops (van Tartwijk et al., 1998). From this study it appeared that in these moments leadership will be shown quite naturally, whereas the responsibility given to students comes more to the fore during group and independent work, lesson segments that contribute less to the general perceived teacher–student relationship. To give students appropriate freedom and responsibility during group and independent work, it appeared to be important for a teacher to be a strong leader in central lesson segments. The learning environment they create in central moments lives further in individual work.

Conclusion

In general, we conclude from the studies mentioned earlier that with respect to student outcomes appropriate teacher–student relationships are characterized by a rather high degree of teacher influence and proximity toward students. Interestingly and reassuring, results of studies on students' and teachers' preferred teacher–student relationships (e.g., Créton & Wubbels, 1984) support the appropriateness of high amounts of influence and proximity.

RELATIONS BETWEEN TEACHERS' AND STUDENTS' PERCEPTIONS

Studies have shown usually considerable differences between teachers' and students' perceptions of learning environments (e.g., Fraser, 1998). We first discus the correlations between scales of the various perceptions, then we turn to the scores and differences between scores, and finally, we focus on a comparison of the teacher, student, and ideal profiles.

Scale Correlations

Wubbels, Brekelmans, and Helmans (1987) calculated correlations between the students' perceptions scale scores and teachers' self-perception scale scores. They showed that the correlations between the scales of the teachers' self-perceptions and the students' perceptions were highest for scales of the same sector in the model. So for example the teachers' self-perception on DC correlates highest with the students' perception on DC and lower with other students' perception scales. The correlations, however, even between the same scales in the model were only moderately high, ranging between 0.18 and 0.53, implying some disagreement between teachers and students. Students and their teachers agreed most about the amount of the teacher's leading and strict behavior and least about their understanding and friendly behavior.

Scale and Dimension Scores

Although a small number of studies report nonsignificant differences between students' and teachers' perceptions (Ben-Chaim & Zoller, 2001; Wubbels & Levy, 1991), most studies show rather distinct differences on the level of scale scores as well as on the level of the dimensions of influence and proximity (Brekelmans & Wubbels, 1991; Fisher, Fraser, Wubbels, & Brekelmans, 1993; Levy et al., 1992; Wubbels & Brekelmans, 1997). On average, teachers reported higher ratings of their own leadership, helpful/friendly, and understanding behavior than did their students, whereas they reported lower perceptions of their own uncertain, dissatisfied, and admonishing behavior (e.g., den Brok, Levy et al., 2002; Fisher & Rickards, 1999; Harkin & Turner, 1997; Rickards & Fisher, 2000; Wubbels et al., 1987; Wubbels, Brekelmans, & Hooymayers, 1992; Yuen, 1999). Some studies also report higher teacher than student perceptions of strictness and lower teacher than student perceptions of giving responsibility (Fisher & Rickards, 1999; Rickards & Fisher, 2000).

Behaviors for which teachers reported higher perceptions than their students—leadership, helpful/friendly, and understanding—have found to be positively related to student achievement and motivation, whereas behaviors for which lower teacher than student perceptions were reported were negatively associated with student achievement and motivation. This means that many teachers made a more favorable judgment about the learning environment than did their students.

Ideal, Self, and Student Profiles Compared

In a study by Wubbels et al. (1992) for the differences between teacher self-, ideal, and students' perceptions, the mean of the eight differences on the scales of the QTI was taken as a general difference measure for a profile. This mean difference between self- and students' perception as well as between ideal and self-perception was for 92% of the teachers far larger than the measurement errors. The differences are most distinct for the ideal and students' perceptions of the behavior. So according to the students' views, most teachers do not attain their ideal. From the difference between self-report and ideal, we see that also teachers think that they do not reach their ideal.

It appears that the more the teacher and his or her students disagree in their perceptions of teacher behavior, the more students perceive the teacher as uncertain, dissatisfied, and admonishing. These types of behavior have been shown to be counterproductive with respect to the promotion of cognitive and affective student outcomes. Studies indicate that if student perceptions of influence and proximity were higher, the difference between students' and teachers' perceptions was smaller (Brekelmans & Wubbels, 1991; Wubbels et al., 1987, 1992). In the study by Wubbels et al. (1992) it was shown that for about two thirds of the teachers the teacher's perception of his or her own behavior occupies a position between the teacher's ideal about interpersonal behavior and the students' perception. An example is shown in Fig. 45.13. These teachers see their behavior more like their ideal than their students. Thus, the difference between students' and the teacher's perceptions could be caused by wishful thinking on the part of the teacher, which may have the function to reduce cognitive dissonance (Festinger, 1957).

For another group of teachers (about one third), the self-report is lower than the students' perceptions of the actual behavior, whereas the ideal is higher than both actual behavior and self-report. An example of this pattern is found in Fig. 45.14. The teachers in this group view their behavior more negatively (in the light of their ideal) than it is. This arrangement of profiles can function to protect the teacher against potential disappointment resulting from confrontation with more negative students' perception. Evidence for the influence of such thought

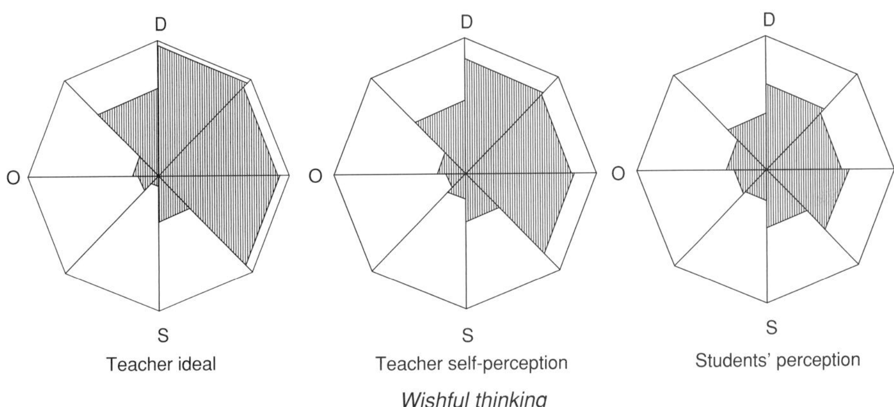

FIGURE 45.13. Teacher ideal, self-report, and students' perceptions of one teacher. The self-report occupies a position between students' perceptions and ideal.

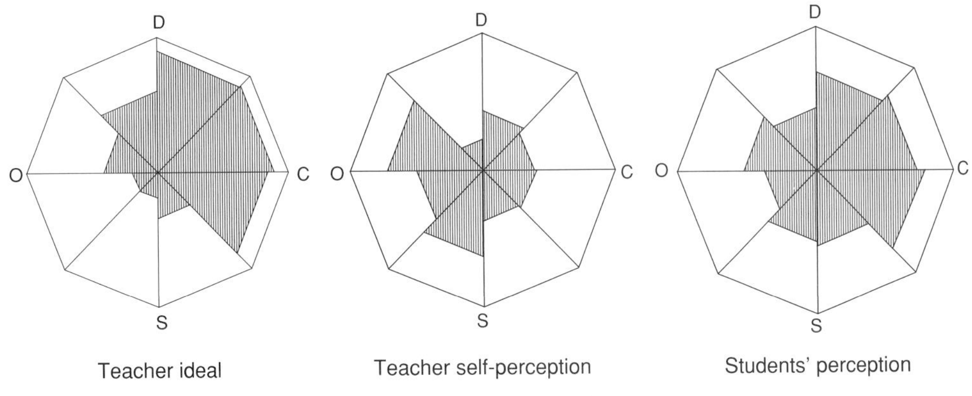

FIGURE 45.14. Teacher ideal, self-report, and students' perceptions of one teacher. The self-report is further away from the ideal than the students' perceptions.

processes was found in teachers' explanations of their own ratings (Wubbels, Brekelmans, & Hooymayers, 1993).

It remains unclear to what extent differences in perceptions may be related to teacher experience. A cross-sectional study by Brekelmans and Wubbels (1991) shows no significant relationships between teacher experience and the difference between students' and teachers' perceptions of influence and proximity. However, longitudinal studies indicate that differences with respect to proximity become larger during the teaching career, whereas they remain equal or become smaller for influence (Brekelmans et al., 2002; Brekelmans, Holvast, & van Tartwijk, 1993). Other evidence is provided by a small study involving six individual teachers and qualitative data in the form of classroom observations and teacher interviews (Fisher, Fraser, & Creswell, 1995). In the latter study, however, experience seemed to influence differences in perceptions together with (initial) interpersonal teaching style.

Differences between students' and teachers' perceptions of interpersonal behavior may also be related to ethnicity or cultural background of teachers and students. In one study, differences between Caucasian American students and their Caucasian teachers were lower than between Asian American or Hispanic American students and their (Caucasian) teachers (Levy, Wubbels, Brekelmans, & Morganfield, 1997). A study comparing U.S. and Dutch teachers showed that statistically nonsignificant differences between American students and their teachers were somewhat smaller than between Dutch students and their teachers (Wubbels & Levy, 1991). In a third study, Hispanic American teachers displayed larger divergence with all of their students (whether being Hispanic American, Asian American, Caucasian American, African American, or Native American) than did Asian American teachers (den Brok, Levy et al., 2002). However, the latter study also showed that divergence between teacher and student perceptions is not related to both participants "being of the same cultural background."

IMPROVING RELATIONSHIPS

From the research studies reviewed we have clear indications of what interpersonal relationships with students teachers should strive for and what nonverbal behaviors when having a central position in class are helpful in creating these positive relationships. It is desirable that teachers develop dominant and cooperative behavioral patterns and accompanying cognitions and attitudes. Further, the importance of accurate teacher perceptions of their relationship with students has been established. This section suggests intervention and QTI feedback strategies, and mentions results of an intervention study.

Intervention Strategies and Feedback

Training for beginning teachers in strict and leadership behavioral skills may be effective in developing both the Influence and the Proximity dimension. Adequate differentiation between "leadership" and "strict" behavior and between "freedom and responsibility" and "uncertain" behavior (the transition from the cooperative to the opposite sectors of the model of interpersonal behavior) is vital, but complex. It is our experience that a behavioral training component to improve relationships on the Influence dimension is crucial, because especially beginning teachers often lack an adequate behavioral repertoire. We think the Proximity dimension may require procedures and interventions in teacher education that are somewhat different from the behavioral emphasis on the Influence dimension. On the Proximity dimension, a cognitive component to training and staff development may be more important to help teachers to use their skills more adequately and to help them select the appropriate skills in particular situations. Giving teachers insight into the circular processes of communication and the futility of trying to solve the problem by blaming the other party may help to activate interpersonal behavior that was already part of their behavioral repertoire.

The QTI can be used as a feedback instrument for teachers. It can be useful to compare student and teacher self- and ideal perceptions, for example, in light of the two possible different positions of these three perceptions to each other. Further, it is important for teachers when they interpret their profiles to be aware of the stage they are in in their careers because of the changes that have been found in relationships during the teaching career. For a teacher, administering the questionnaire several years in a row may help monitor and influence the development of relationships during the career. For professional development purposes, comparison of the students and teacher perceptions in different classes may be helpful: Teachers might learn from the perception in what they consider as good classes for classes where relationships with students are not that well. For this purpose, we have good experiences with interviews of the teacher with their students based on the data gathered with the questionnaire. In these interviews one can try to find out what is going on in the minds of the students. The most important function of these interviews is however to engage in metacommunication. According to Watzlawick et al. (1967) this kind of communication by itself helps improve relationships.

Although we have some informal evidence, the number of intervention studies that can corroborate the ideas presented earlier about the use of the QTI as a feedback instrument unfortunately is scarce. In a program in Brunei aimed at stimulating teachers' science teaching (by reducing their teacher-centered role and their inclination to stimulate rote learning), teachers' behavior was assessed with the QTI (Scott, Fisher, & den Brok, 2003). Analyses of variance showed that project teachers were perceived as more helpful/ friendly than nonproject teachers at the same schools. However, this study used only a posttreatment measurement (no pretest).

As part of a Dutch professional development program focusing on teaching for active learning, teachers were also coached with respect to their interpersonal competencies (Derksen, 1995). This 18-week program consisted of coaching on the job, university and school-based meetings, and assessment by means of questionnaires, one being the QTI. Because interpersonal teaching competencies were regarded as important prerequisites to teaching competencies for active learning, during the first 3 to 5 weeks of the program teachers were mainly coached with respect to the teacher–student interpersonal relationship. (For a few teachers, interpersonal teacher behavior covered the whole program.) Analyses of variance on data of 15 teachers from one school (out of five) participating in the program showed some changes in interpersonal teacher behavior (Derksen, 1995). The QTI was administered three times: before and directly after the professional development program, as well as 4 months after the program (retention measurement). Directly after the training, teachers, on average, were perceived as more uncertain by their students. After 4 months, however, teachers were perceived as more friendly, as providing more student responsibility/freedom and as less dissatisfied, admonishing, and strict. Moreover, uncertainty had decreased again and was on the level as just before the program.

CONCLUDING REMARKS

It can be concluded that the systems approach to classroom communication and the model for interpersonal teacher behavior have contributed significantly to our understanding of classroom management processes. The importance of high influence and proximity perceptions at the pattern level has been related to nonverbal aspects at the message level when teachers are in a central position in class. Studies on the teaching career send clear messages to preservice and inservice teacher education.

The studies reviewed in this chapter show that the QTI is a useful research tool, but research on the QTI as a feedback instrument for teachers is insufficient to prove its usefulness. The QTI meets the standards of the American Evaluation Association (1999) for accuracy, reliability, and validity. The use of the QTI is practical in light of the time and money involved in administering the questionnaire and calculating the results and the intrusiveness of the process.

Throughout this chapter we have considered student and teacher perception data as a value in its own: The teacher and his or her students have perceptions of their relationship and both are significant for research and for professional development. At the end of this chapter, it might be useful to mention that in secondary education, students' perceptions usually have a high quality (e.g., d'Apollonia & Abrami, 1996): They bear stronger resemblance to observer data than teacher's self-perceptions do (Marsh, 1982). Nevertheless we want to emphasize that for feedback or evaluation purposes the QTI needs to be used in a respectful way and embedded in appropriate, open, and fair procedures, and it must take into account the differences in teachers careers, and differences across classes. The students' perceptions are only one of the possible inputs and certainly not the last or only word.

The research program is to be continued both in The Netherlands and in other parts of the world. Recent and ongoing studies on interpersonal relationships include teacher–student relationships in multicultural classrooms and the classroom management competence of teachers in these settings. Much needed and on its way are intervention evaluations, for example, in-teacher training programs for interpersonal teacher behavior. For input in such programs, a recently started study on the development of relationships in the first 10 lessons in a class will be significant.

ACKNOWLEDGMENTS

We wish to thank Barry Fraser, Curtin University, Australia, Carolyn Evertson, and Carol Weinstein for their comments on the draft of this chapter.

REFERENCES

Amelsvoort, J. van. (1999). *Perspective on instruction, motivation and self-regulation*. Unpublished doctoral dissertation, Nijmegen, The Netherlands: Katholieke Universiteit Nijmegen. [In Dutch]

Amelsvoort, J. van, Bergen, T., Lamberigts, R., & Setz, W. (1993). *Teacher behaviour, student motivation and school outcomes*. Nijmegen, The Netherlands: Katholieke Universiteit Nijmegen/ITS. [In Dutch]

American Evaluation Association. (1999). *The personnel evaluation standards. Summary of the standards*. Retrieved July, 21, 2005 from http://www.eval.org/Evaluation Documents/perseval.html

d'Apollonia, S., & Abrami, P. (1996, April). *Variables moderating the validity of student ratings of instruction: A meta-analysis*. Paper presented at the annual meeting of the American Educational Research Association, New York.

Ben-Chaim, D., & Zoller, U. (2001). Self-perception versus students' perception of teacher personal style in college science and mathematics courses. *Research in Science Education, 31*, 437–454.

Brekelmans, M. (1989). *Interpersonal teacher behaviour in the classroom*. Utrecht, The Netherlands: W.C.C. [In Dutch]

Brekelmans, M., Brok, P. den, Bergen, T., & Wubbels, T. (2004, April). *Exploring students' perceptions of their teachers' interpersonal communication style*. Paper presented at the annual meeting of the American Educational Research Association, San Diego, CA.

Brekelmans, M., Holvast, A., & van Tartwijk, J. (1993). Changes in teacher communication styles during the professional career. *Journal of Classroom Interaction, 27*, 13–22.

Brekelmans, M., Levy, J., & Rodriguez, R. (1993). A typology of teacher communication style. In T. Wubbels & J. Levy (Eds.), *Do you know what you look like?* (pp. 46–55). London: Falmer Press.

Brekelmans, M., Sleegers, P., & Fraser, B. (2000). Teaching for active learning. In R. J. Simons, J. van der Linden, & T. Duffy (Eds.), *New learning* (pp. 227–242). Dordrecht, The Netherlands: Kluwer Academic Publishers.

Brekelmans, M., & Wubbels, T. (1991). Student and teacher perceptions of interpersonal teacher behavior: A Dutch perspective. *The Study of Learning Environments, 5*, 19–30.

Brekelmans, M., Wubbels, T., & den Brok, P. (2002). Teacher experience and the teacher-student relationship in the classroom environment. In S. C. Goh & M. S. Khine (Eds.), *Studies in educational learning environments: An international perspective* (pp. 73–100). Singapore: World Scientific.

Brekelmans, M., Wubbels, T., & Créton, H. A. (1990). A study of student perceptions of physics teacher behavior, *Journal of Research in Science Teaching, 27*, 335–350.

Brok, P. den. (2001). *Teaching and student outcomes. A study on teachers' thoughts and actions from an interpersonal and a learning activities perspective.* Utrecht, The Netherlands: W.C.C.

Brok, P. den, Bergen, T., & Stahl, R. (2002, April). *Students' perceptions of teacher regulatory behaviors during learning activities*. Paper presented at the annual meeting of the American Educational Research Association, New Orleans, LA.

Brok, P. den, Brekelmans, M., & Wubbels, T. (in press). Interpersonal teacher behaviour and student outcomes. *School Effectiveness and School Improvement.*

Brok, P. den, Fisher, D., Brekelmans, M., Rickards, T., Wubbels, T., Levy, J., & Waldrip, B. (2003, April). *Students' perceptions of secondary teachers' interpersonal style in six countries: A study on the validity of the Questionnaire on Teacher Interaction*. Paper presented at the annual meeting of the American Educational Research Association, Chicago. (ERIC Document Reproduction Services No. ED475164)

Brok, P. den, Levy, J., Wubbels, T., & Rodriguez, M. (2003). Cultural influences on students' perceptions of videotaped lessons. *International Journal of Intercultural Relations, 27*, 355–374.

Brok, P. J., den Levy, J., Rodriguez, R., & Wubbels, T. (2002). Perceptions of Asian-American and Hispanic-American teachers and their students on interpersonal communication style. *Teaching and Teacher Education, 18*, 447–467.

Brophy, J. E., & Good, T. L. (1986). Teacher behaviour and student achievement. In M. C. Wittrock (Ed.), *Handbook of research on teaching* (3rd ed., pp. 328–375). New York: Macmillan.

Brown, R. (1965). *Social psychology*. London: Collier-McMillan.

Corcoran, E. (1981) Transition shock: The beginning teacher paradox. *Journal of Teacher Education, 32*, 19–23.

Creemers, B. P. M. (1994). *The effective classroom.* London: Cassell.

Créton, H. A. & Wubbels, T. (1984). *Discipline problems with beginning teachers.* Utrecht, The Netherlands: W.C.C. [In Dutch]

Derksen, K. (1994). *Between taking over and activating instruction* (Master's thesis). Nijmegen, The Netherlands: Vakgroep Onderwijskunde. [In Dutch]

Derksen, K. (1995, August). *Activating instruction: The effects of a teacher-training programme.* Paper presented at the 6th Conference of the European Association for Research on Learning and Instruction, Nijmegen, The Netherlands.

Doyle, W. (2006). *Classroom management in early childhood and elementary classrooms.* In C. Evertson & C. Weinstein (Eds), Handbook of Classroom Management (pp. 97–125). Mahwah, NJ: Lawrence Erlbaum Associates, Inc.

Dunkin M., & Biddle, B. (1974). *The study of teaching.* New York: Holt, Rinehart & Winston.

Evans, H. (1998). *A study on students' cultural background and teacher-student interpersonal behaviour in Secondary Science classrooms in Australia.* Unpublished doctoral dissertation. Perth Australia: Curtin University of Technology.

Festinger, L. (1957). *A theory of cognitive dissonance.* Evanston, IL: Row Peterson.

Fisher, D., & Cresswell, J. (1998). Actual and ideal principal interpersonal behaviour. *Learning Environments Research, 1*, 231–247.

Fisher, D., Fraser, B., & Cresswell. J. (1995). Using the Questionnaire on Teacher Interaction in the professional development of teachers. *Australian Journal of Teacher Education, 20*, 8–18.

Fisher, D. L., Fraser, B. J., & Wubbels, T. (1992, June). *Teacher communication style and school environment.* Paper presented at the 1992 ECER conference, Enschede, The Netherlands.

Fisher, D. L., Fraser, B. J., Wubbels, T., & Brekelmans, M. (1993). Associations between school learning environment and teacher interpersonal behavior in the classroom. *The Study of Learning Environments, 7*, 32–41.

Fisher, D. L., Henderson, D., & Fraser, B. J. (1995). Interpersonal behaviour in senior high school biology classes. *Research in Science Education, 25*, 125–133.

Fisher, D. L., & Rickards, T. (1999, June). *Teacher-student interpersonal behavior as perceived by science teachers and their students.* Paper presented at the Second International Conference on Science, Mathematics and Technology Education, Taipei, Taiwan.

Foa, U. G. (1961). Convergence in the analysis of the structure of interpersonal behavior. *Psychological Review, 68*, 341–353.

Fraser, B. J. (1998). Science learning environments: Assessment, effects and determinants. In B. J. Fraser & K. G. Tobin (Eds.), *International handbook of science education* (pp. 527–564). London: Kluwer Academic Publishers.

Goh, S., & Fraser, B. J. (2000). Teacher interpersonal teacher behaviour and elementary students' outcomes. *Journal of Research in Childhood Education, 14*, 216–231.

Goh, S. C., & Fraser, B. J. (1996). Validation of an elementary school version of the Questionnaire on Teacher Interaction. *Psychological Reports, 79*, 515–522.

Harkin, J., & Turner, G. (1997). Patterns of communication styles of teachers in English 16–19 education. *Research in Post-Compulsory Education, 2*(3), 261–280.

Harper, R. G., Wiens, A. N., & Matarazzo, J. D. (1978). *Nonverbal communication: The state of the art*. New York: John Wiley.

Henderson, D. G. (1995). *A study of the classroom and laboratory environments and student attitude and achievement in senior Secondary Biology classes*. Unpublished doctoral dissertation. Perth, Australia: Curtin University of Technology.

Hockley, M., & Harkin, J. (2000). Communicating with students with learning difficulties in further education. *Educational Action Research, 8*(2), 341–360.

Huberman, M. (1993). Steps toward a developmental model of the teaching career. In L. Kremer-Hayon, H. C. Vonk, & R. Fessler (Eds), *Teacher professional development: A multiple perspective approach* (pp. 93–118). Amsterdam, The Netherlands: Swets & Zeitlinger.

Kounin J. S. (1970). *Discipline and group management in classrooms*. New York: Holt, Rinehart & Winston.

Kremer-Hayon, L. & Wubbels, T. (1993a). Supervisors' interpersonal behavior and student teachers' satisfaction. In T. Wubbels, & J. Levy (Eds.), *Do you know what you look like?* (pp. 123–135). London: Falmer Press.

Kremer-Hayon, L., & Wubbels, T. (1993b). Principals' interpersonal behavior and teachers' satisfaction. In T. Wubbels, & J. Levy (Eds.), *Do you know what you look like?* (pp. 113–122). London: Falmer Press.

La France, M., & Mayo, C. (1978). *Moving bodies: Nonverbal communication in social relationships*. Monterey, CA: Brooks/Cole.

Lapointe, J. M. (2003). Teacher-student conflict and misbehavior: Toward a model of the extended symmetrical escalation. *Journal of Classroom Interaction, 38*(2), 11–19.

Leary, T. (1957). *An interpersonal diagnosis of personality*. New York: Ronald Press.

Lee, O. (1995). Subject matter knowledge, classroom management, and instructional practices in middle school science classrooms. *Research in Science Teaching, 32*, 423–440.

Levy, J., Brok, P. den., Wubbels, T., & Brekelmans, M. (2003). Significant variables in students' perceptions of teacher interpersonal communication styles. *Learning Environments Research, 6*, 5–36.

Levy, J., Wubbels, T., & Brekelmans, M. (1992). Student and teacher characteristics and perceptions of teacher communication style. *Journal of Classroom Interaction, 27*, 23–29.

Levy, J., Wubbels, T., Brekelmans, M., & Morganfield, B. (1997). Language and cultural factors in students' perceptions of teacher communication style. *International Journal of Intercultural Relations, 21*, 29–56.

Lonner, W. J. (1980). The search for psychological universals. In H. C. Triandis & W. W. Lambert (Eds.), *Handbook of cross cultural psychology* (Vol. 1, pp. 143–204). Boston: Allyn & Bacon.

Marsh, H. W. (1982). Validity of students' evaluations of college teaching: A multitrait- multimethod analysis. *Journal of Educational Psychology, 74*, 264–279.

Marshall, H. H., & Weinstein, R. S. (1986). Classroom context of student-perceived differential teacher treatment. *Journal of Educational Psychology, 78*(6), 707–754.

Morine-Dershimer, G. (1986). Introduction: Perspectives on a teaching episode. *Teaching and Teacher Education, 2*, 299–300.

Muller Fohrbrodt, G., Cloetta, B., & Dann, H. D. (1978). *Der Praxisschock bij Jungen Lehrern* [The reality shock with young teachers]. Stuttgart, Germany: Klett.

Rawnsley, D. G. (1997). *Associations between classroom learning environments, teacher interpersonal behaviour and student outcomes in Secondary Mathematics classrooms*. Unpublished doctoral dissertation. Perth: Curtin University of Technology.

Rickards, T., & Fisher, D. L. (2000, April). *Three perspectives on perceptions of teacher-student interaction: A seed for change in science teaching*. Paper presented at the annual meeting of the National Association for Research in Science Teaching, New Orleans, LA.

Robertson, J. (2002). The Boss, the manager and the leader: Approaches to dealing with disruption. In B. Rogers (Ed.), *Teacher leadership and behaviour management* (pp. 20–39). London: Sage.

Scott, R., Fisher, D., & Brok, P. den. (2003, August). *Specialist science teachers' classroom behaviors in 12 primary schools*. Paper presented at the annual conference of the European Science Education Research Association, Noordwijkerhout, The Netherlands.

Segall, M. H., Dasen, P. R., Berry, J. W., & Poortinga, Y. H. (Eds.). (1990). *Human behavior in global perspective: An introduction to cross-cultural psychology*. New York: Pergamon Press.

Setz, W., Bergen, T., van Amelsvoort, J., & Lamberigts, R. (1993). *Perceived and observed behaviour of teachers*. Nijmegen, The Netherlands: Katholieke Universiteit Nijmegen/ITS. [In Dutch]

Shavelson, R. J., Webb, N. W., & Burstein L. (1986). Measurement of teaching. In M. C. Wittrock (Ed.), *Handbook of research on teaching* (3rd ed., pp. 50–91). New York: Macmillan.

Shuell, T. J. (1996). Teaching and learning in a classroom context. In D. C. Berliner & R. C. Calfee (Eds.), *Handbook of educational psychology* (pp. 726–763). New York: Macmillan.

Slater, P. E. (1962). Parental behavior and the personality of the child. *Journal of Genetical Psychology, 101*, 53–68.

Soerjaningsih, W., Fraser, B. J., & Aldridge, J. M. (2002, April). *Instructor-student interpersonal behavior and student outcomes at the university level in Indonesia.* Paper presented at the annual meeting of the American Educational Research Association, New Orleans, LA.

Somers, T., Brekelmans, M., & Wubbels, T. (1997, August). *Development of student teachers on the teacher-student relationship in the classroom.* Paper presented at the 7th Conference of the European Association for Research on Learning and Instruction, Athens, GA.

Strack, S. (1996). Special series: Interpersonal theory and the interpersonal circumplex: Timothy Leary's Legacy. *Journal of Personality Assessment, 66*, 211–307.

Tartwijk, J. van. (1993). *Sketches of teacher behavior: The interpersonal meaning of nonverbal teacher behavior in the classroom.* Utrecht, The Netherlands: W.C.C. [in Dutch]

Tartwijk, J. van, Brekelmans, M., Wubbels, T., Fisher, D. L., & Fraser, B. J. (1998). Students perceptions of teacher interpersonal style: The front of the classroom as the teacher's stage. *Teaching and Teacher Education, 14*, 1–11.

Veenman, S. A. M. (1984). Perceived problems of beginning teachers. *Review of Educational Research, 54*, 143–178.

Watzlawick, P., Beavin, J. H., & Jackson, D. (1967). *The pragmatics of human communication.* New York: Norton.

Weber, S., & Mitchell, C. (1995). *'That's funny, you don't look like a teacher': Interrogating images and identity in popular culture.* London: Falmer Press.

Wiggins, J. S., Philips, N., & Trapnell, P. (1989). Circular reasoning about interpersonal behavior: Evidence concerning some untested assumptions underlying diagnostic classification. *Journal of Personality and Social Psychology, 56*, 296–305.

Wubbels, T., & Brekelmans, M. (1997). A comparison of student perceptions of Dutch physics teachers' interpersonal behavior and their educational opinions in 1984 and 1993. *Journal of Research in Science Teaching, 34*(5), 447–466.

Wubbels, T., Brekelmans, M., & Hermans, J. (1987). Teacher behavior: An important aspect of the learning environment? *The Study of Learning Environments, 3*, 10–25.

Wubbels, T., Brekelmans, M., & Hooymayers H. P. (1992). Do teacher ideals distort the self-reports of their interpersonal behavior? *Teaching and Teacher Education, 8*, 47–58.

Wubbels, T., Brekelmans, M., & Hooymayers H. P. (1993). Comparison of teachers' and students' perceptions of interpersonal behavior. In T. Wubbels, & J. Levy (Eds.), *Do you know what you look like?* (pp. 64–80). London: Falmer Press.

Wubbels, T., Créton, H., & Holvast, A. J. C. D. (1988). Undesirable classroom situations. *Interchange, 19*, 25–40.

Wubbels, T., Créton, H. A., & Hooymayers, H. P. (1985). *Discipline problems of beginning teachers, interactional teacher behavior mapped out* [Abstract]. *Resources in Education, 20*(12), 153. (ERIC Document Reproduction Services No. ED260040).

Wubbels, T., Créton, H. A, & Hooymayers, H. P. (1987). A school-based teacher induction programme. *European Journal of Teacher Education, 10*, 81–94.

Wubbels, T., & Levy, J. (1991). A comparison of interpersonal behavior of Dutch and American teachers. *International Journal of Intercultural Relations, 15*, 1–18.

Wubbels, T., & Levy, J. (1993). *Do you know what you look like?* London: Falmer Press.

Yuen, H. K. (1999). Communication styles of tertiary teachers. In J. James (Ed.), *Quality in teaching and learning in higher education* (pp. 3–8). Hong Kong: Hong Kong Polytechnic University.

46

Classroom Discipline in Australia

Ramon Lewis
La Trobe University, Victoria, Australia

INTRODUCTION

In addressing classroom management this chapter focuses primarily on what teachers do in response to student misbehavior, rather than what they do to avoid it. The term used for such behavior is classroom discipline. The discussion first establishes the significance of teachers' disciplinary behavior in classrooms. Second, the gap that exists between Australian students' and teachers' perceptions of good disciplinary practice and that which is practiced in Australian classrooms is examined. Finally, the impact of various discipline strategies on students is considered. In conducting this analysis, all patterns within the data are established before interpreting their significance and any implications for practice.

IMPORTANCE OF CLASSROOM DISCIPLINE

Classroom discipline serves a number of functions. One of the most important is to facilitate students' subject learning (Bagley, 1914; Lewis, 1997a; Wolfgang, 1995). Without adequate responses to students' inappropriate behavior, teachers will be unable to present even their best-planned lessons (Barton, Coley, & Wenglinsky, 1998; Charles, 2001).

A second recognized function of classroom discipline is to facilitate good citizenship (Anderson, Avery, Pederson, Smith, & Sullivan, 1997; Barber, 1998; Bennet, 1998; Cunat, 1996; McDonnell, 1998; Osborne, 1995; Osler & Starkey, 2001; Pearl & Knight, 1999; Print, 1996/1997).

Within Australia, there is a great deal of concern about the need for schools to provide students with a curriculum capable of preparing them for democratic citizenship and social competence (Ainley, Batten, Collins, & Withers, 1998; Civics Expert Group, 1994; Curriculum Corporation, 1998; Kennedy, 1996, 1998; Lewis, 2001; Mellor, Kennedy, & Greenwood, 2001).

In the words of Dr. Brendon Nelson, the Australian Federal Minister for Education, "Civics and citizenship education is an important national priority. Our democracy depends on informed participation. Schools play a crucial role in helping to foster such participation" (Nelson, 2002, p.1).

The significant role that schools play in developing appropriate values in their students is also recognized by teachers. For example, Mellor et al. (2001) reported that 98% of 352 Australian teachers surveyed believed that civic education matters a great deal for Australia.

In an ongoing attempt to promote appropriate values, the national Curriculum Corporation developed, and continues to promote, a package entitled "Discovering Democracy" (Curriculum Corporation, 1998). As a result of being exposed to this curriculum, students are expected to "develop personal character traits, such as respecting individual worth and human dignity, empathy, respect for the law, being informed about public issues, critical mindedness and willingness to express points of view, listen, negotiate and compromise" (Curriculum Corporation, 1994, p. 7). However, it is acknowledged that civics education programs focusing on knowledge transmission alone have limited effect. The values that are to be promoted have to be incorporated into the day-to-day experience of students if they are to be truly understood and become an integral part of their character. Experiencing democracy appears to be a good way to build civic knowledge and gain some commitment to civic processes. (Mellor et al., 2001, p. 134).

In addition to establishing order and promoting citizenship values through classroom discipline, a third function of discipline is to facilitate within students more generally the development of appropriate morals and values (Fenstermacher, 2001; Narvaez, Bentley, Gleason, & Samuels, 1998; Hansen, 2001; Lickona, 1996; Pring, 2001; Richardson & Fenstermacher, 2001), and character (Benninga & Wynne, 1998; Fisher, 1998; Glanzer, 1998; Houston, 1998; Jones & Stoodley, 1999; Rothstein, 2000; Ryan & Bonlin, 1999; Schaeffer, 1999; Siebold, 1998).

In a bid to achieve one or more of these aims some educators strongly support what Wolfgang (1995) would call interventionist strategies such as reward and punishment (Canter & Canter, 1992; Swinson & Melling, 1995). Others, in contrast, argue for strategies that provide for more student involvement in decision making, such as one-to-one discussion and class meetings (Freiberg, Stein, & Huang, 1996; Hyman & Snook, 2000; Kohn, 1996, 1998; Pearl & Knight, 1999; Schneider, 1996). This chapter investigates the effectiveness of various discipline strategies in the Australian context by considering how closely teachers' and students' conceptions of best practice is implemented in Australian classrooms. In addition, it reports on the perceived impact of teachers' disciplinary behavior on the attitudes of students toward their schoolwork, the teacher, and the misbehaving students.

ASSESSING THE IMPACT OF CLASSROOM DISCIPLINE

Before ideal and real classroom discipline can be compared, and the impact of classroom discipline assessed, teachers' disciplinary behavior must be measured. However, validly observing teachers dealing with inappropriate student behavior in classrooms is not easily accomplished. Two factors adversely influence the validity of such observations. First, once an observer (or recording device) is present, students may alter their characteristic behavior. Some may become more provocative because of the additional adult audience, whereas for others, the adult presence may lessen the likelihood of misbehavior. Second, teachers who are aware that they are being observed may alter their characteristic behavior. Some may toughen up and become more controlling, whereas others may tend to avoid confrontation by increasing their ignoring of inappropriate behavior or by responding more gently.

A further difficulty associated with assessing the impact of classroom discipline via observations relates to cost. Obtaining sufficient observations to approximate a representative sample of a teacher's disciplinary behavior is extremely expensive, involving a number of visits to a teacher's classroom to ensure a valid sample of behavior. Consequently in preparing a chapter on classroom discipline in Australia, it was not surprising to find that all relevant research had used the perceptions of students and the self-reports of teachers.

MISBEHAVIOR AND RELATED TEACHER STRESS

When addressing the issue of classroom discipline and the associated teacher stress it is common for the Australian popular press to sensationalize the problem. For example, articles entitled "Safety of Teachers Must Come First" (O'Halloran, 2003), "Critical Delay on "Bad Kid Classes" ("Critical Delay," 2002), or "Counsellors Needed for School Discipline Crisis ("Counsellors Needed," 2002) appear to suggest that school misbehavior threatens both teachers and students. However, research that reports levels of student misbehavior does not indicate the presence of a very significant problem (Fields, 1986; Hart, Wearing, & Conn, 1995; Johnson, Oswald, & Adey, 1993; Oswald, Johnson, & Whittington, 1997; Lewis, 2001) Similarly, Australian research on teacher stress and concern levels shows that they are both only moderate (Applied Psychology Research Group, 1989; Dinham 1993; Independent Education Union 1996; Lewis, 1999a, 2001; Louden 1987; Otto, 1986; Pithers & Soden, 1998; Sinclair 1992; Smith, 1996).

In the most recent research reporting on misbehavior in Australian classrooms and teachers' levels of concern over discipline issues, Lewis, Romi, Xing, and Katz (2005) presented data from 491 secondary teachers from Melbourne (as well as 98 from Israel and 159 from China). They demonstrated that approximately two thirds of the Australian sample of teachers report that they expect "hardly any" or "none" of their students to misbehave, and all but three of the remaining respondents indicate that only "some" students will misbehave. When asked "to what extent is the issue of classroom discipline and student misbehavior an issue of concern to you?" 61% report that it is no more than a minor stressor, 27% say moderate, and only 12% state that discipline is a major source of stress. In summary it can be seen that there is little support for the view that there is a crisis in classroom discipline in Australia. Nevertheless, over one third of Australian teachers appear to be experiencing at least moderate levels of stress as a result of classroom discipline and student misbehavior.

In summary, in addition to the obvious need to prevent student misbehavior from interfering with the teaching–learning process, classroom discipline remains significant because of the demand in Australia that schools provide students with a curriculum capable of preparing them for democratic citizenship and social competence (Ainley et al., 1998; Civics Expert Group, 1994; Curriculum Corporation, 1998; Kennedy, 1996, 1998; Lewis, 2001; Mellor, et al., 2001).

Having established the significance of students' misbehavior and classroom discipline in Australia it is now appropriate to address the major focus of this chapter, namely, how perceptions of teachers' classroom discipline strategies compare to perceptions of best practice.

STUDENTS' PREFERRED DISCIPLINARY STRATEGIES

In a series of studies conducted between 1980 and 1987 Lewis and Lovegrove gathered data from year 9 students (approximately 14 to 15 years old) regarding their teachers' classroom discipline. All of the studies were conducted in Victoria, Australia. Initially 34 characteristics defining good or bad teachers, and 46 disciplinary strategies used by such teachers were generated from taped group interviews of five classes of year 9 students. These then formed the focus of a number of surveys. In one study (Lovegrove & Lewis, 1982), in which 264 year

9 students were surveyed, respondents indicated which strategies their best and worst teachers used. As a result, it was possible to identify strategies most preferred by students.

In a later study (Lewis & Lovegrove, 1983), year 9 students were once again surveyed. On this occasion 364 respondents used a modified version of the earlier instrument to describe one of their current teacher's disciplinary practices. They also indicated the extent to which they liked this teacher. Consequently, in this study it was possible to make inferences regarding not only the discipline preferred by students but also teachers' current classroom practice.

A third study replicated the second with an additional 710 year 9 students. This was followed by a fourth study in which a slightly modified version of the previous questionnaire was administered to a sample of 408 year 9 students. In this investigation respondents were asked to indicate the extent to which a "good" teacher is characterized by the disciplinary items provided. In synthesizing all these data, Lewis and Lovegrove (1987a) highlighted the discipline strategies preferred by students in the following terms:

> One can infer that students appear to desire the teacher to take responsibility for the maintenance of order in the classroom and not involve either parents or other teachers. They want clear rules, designed in conjunction with students and based on a number of reasons including the needs of the students and the teacher. The use of sanctions should occur after a warning, should involve only the miscreant and should be applied in a calm manner, minimising embarrassment to the miscreant. The sanctions used should focus on isolating students who misbehave and should not include arbitrary or harsh punishments. They should be applied consistently. Finally, good teachers should recognise appropriate behavior, both by individuals and by the class. (p. 100)

In comparison to the range of discipline strategies assessed by Lewis and Lovegrove, King, Gullone, and Dadds (1990) provided only four possible teacher responses to student misbehavior for 616 Melbourne elementary and secondary students to consider. These were permissiveness (let the student get away with it), physical punishment (smack the child), discussion (talk with the child), and exclusion (put the student in another room). These alternative responses were used for three independent problems, namely a student refusing to pick up books, student aggression toward a classmate, and temper tantrums in the classroom. In each situation the students rated discussion as the most desirable teacher action, followed by exclusion, then physical punishment, and finally permissiveness. Clearly there are some similarities with the results discussed earlier. Students wish teachers to intervene, they are supportive of isolation as a form of consequence, and they prefer to receive explanations as to why the behavior is unacceptable. Their support for talking with the child was not something that students in the earlier studies had the opportunity to evaluate; however, in the teachers' preferences section that follows, it is clearly identified as a desirable technique.

TEACHERS' PREFERRED DISCIPLINARY STRATEGIES

In 1991, 427 elementary and 556 secondary school teachers were provided with a list of 61 disciplinary strategies and asked to indicate the extent to which each would characterize an "ideal" teacher (Lewis, Lovegrove, & Burman, 1991). The items listed were those provided to students in earlier studies, but were augmented by the addition of a number of items to cover areas such as discussions with and involvement of students.

The results indicate that elementary school teachers described an ideal teacher's discipline as being based on very clear rules, determined in part by the students. Students would also help identify the punishments to be applied to misbehaving students. Ideal teachers would be very much in charge, although when necessary they would involve the parents of students who misbehave. Explanations regarding the need for appropriate behavior would be primarily based on disruption to the class, and to a lesser extent, disruption to the teacher. Good behavior would be modeled and rewarded, and punishments would take the form of logical consequences and social isolation aimed only at the students who misbehave. Students would be allowed an opportunity to explain their side of the story and be assisted to see the impact their misbehavior had on others. In this way they would be expected to identify how to improve their behavior in future. At all times the ideal elementary teacher would avoid becoming angry and yelling at or embarrassing misbehaving students.

In general there is strong agreement between the secondary teachers' responses and those of the elementary teachers. The main differences lie in the areas of recognition of appropriate behavior, inclusion in decision making, and punishments. Secondary teachers provide less, yet still considerable, support for rewarding or praising students for doing what is expected. They also want less student involvement in defining both rules and sanctions for misbehavior. In addition, secondary teachers profess greater support for a range of assertive strategies. For example, they are more likely to characterize "ideal" teachers as making greater use of demands for appropriate behavior, isolation of misbehaving students inside or outside the classrooms, and detention. They are also less disapproving of yelling at misbehaving students and embarrassing them than are elementary teachers. Possible explanations for these differences are examined later in the chapter.

In summarizing preferred teacher discipline, it can be seen that the views of teachers and students are very similar. Both appear to support the concept of an interventional teacher having clear rules (with some student input into their definition). According to the data, teachers should provide warnings or explanations based on disruption to learning and to a lesser extent teaching, recognition of appropriate behavior, and punishment for misbehaving students only (primarily catch-up work, social isolation, and detention). Then they should consistently and calmly follow through, but in doing so minimize embarrassment of students. Finally, counseling is strongly supported by teachers and students (when the latter were provided an opportunity to comment).

In interpreting these findings it is useful to briefly refer to a theory of power developed by French and Raven (1959). This analysis of power in relationships continues to provide a valuable framework for those examining classroom discipline (Tauber, 1999). In dealing with the misbehavior of students, teachers may knowingly or unknowingly draw upon five kinds of power (Tauber, 1999). The first is Coercive power. It is the power a teacher has over a student that comes from the student's desire to avoid punishment associated with inappropriate classroom behavior. The second is Reward power. Teachers who provide desired recognitions and rewards for appropriate behavior have such power. The third, Legitimate power, is the power that is inherent in the role occupied by teachers. It is bestowed on them by society, coming with the position they occupy. The fourth is Referent or relationship power. This is the power that students give to teachers whose relationships they value. It stems from respect for, or liking of, the teacher. Teachers with Referent power are trusted by students, as friends are trusted. The fifth and final power, Expert power, stems from students' belief that the teacher has the ability to pass on important knowledge and skills, and they will gain something valuable if they cooperate.

According to the students' preferences for discipline strategies reported previously, they appear to attribute Legitimate power to teachers, in that they expect them to take charge of student behavior. The presence of clear, fully explained rules, which form the basis for teachers to make demands and follow through if students fail to comply, supports such an argument. Teachers should use Coercive power in the form of logical or reasonable consequences. Students also support the isolation of students who misbehave but want to minimize the likelihood of emotional discomfort. This expressed need for calm, reasonable teachers provides evidence of the relevance of Referent power. Further support for Referent power relates to the expressed desire by teachers for students to have a voice, both individually and as a class group. It is interesting to note that compared to elementary teachers, secondary teachers appear to provide less support for both Referent and Reward power while giving greater emphasis to Legitimate and Coercive power.

STUDENTS' PERCEPTIONS OF TEACHERS' DISCIPLINARY BEHAVIOR

In addition to investigating students' preferences for discipline, Lewis and Lovegrove (1988) also reported the results of two surveys of students' perceptions of their current teachers' disciplinary practices. The survey contained 39 disciplinary strategies in one study and a subset of 36 of these in the other. In general students report that teachers' disciplinary behavior is consistent with the way they would like it to be. Teachers are seen as very unlikely to ignore misbehavior and tend to deal with it themselves rather than enlisting the aid of parents or other teachers. They are likely to explain to misbehaving students that they, and to a lesser extent other students, are adversely effected by the misbehavior. Rules are clear but students are very unlikely to be allowed to work these out by themselves and they generally have no role in determining the sanctions to be applied to misbehaving students. Teachers are seen to generally target only the misbehaving students and not involve innocent bystanders. Although they will praise the class if all students are behaving well, individual students are not likely to receive recognition for behaving appropriately. Inappropriate behavior is met with explanations that focus on its disruptive nature and the threat of being moved within or outside the class, and detention. Teachers are seen as unlikely to use more arbitrary punishments such as yard duty, and very unlikely to make misbehaving students complete extra schoolwork or to write out multiple numbers of lines.

In more recent research, Lewis (2001) reported on teachers' classroom behavior by noting the perceptions of 592 year 6 (elementary) students and 2,938 (secondary) students from years 7, 9, and 11. In this study the 39 survey items describing teachers' disciplinary behavior provide measures of the extent of usage of six discipline strategies. The first strategy indicates the extent to which teachers recognized the appropriate behavior of individual students or the class (e.g., rewards individual students who behave properly). The second provides a measure of the frequency with which teachers punished students who misbehaved, increasing the level of punishment if necessary (e.g., increases the level of punishment if a misbehaving student stops when told, but then does it again). Third, respondents reported on whether the teacher talked with students to discuss the impact of their behavior on others, and negotiated with students on a one-to-one basis (e.g., gets students to change the way they behave by helping them understand how their behavior affects others). The fourth strategy focused on the extent to which the teacher involved students in classroom discipline decision-making (e.g., organizes the class to work out the rules for good behavior). The fifth strategy showed whether the teacher hinted at, and gave nondirectional descriptions of, unacceptable behavior (e.g., describes what students are doing wrong, and expects them to stop). And the final strategy comprised the use of aggressive strategies (e.g., yells angrily at students who misbehave).

Elementary students report that their teachers very frequently hint that there is a problem when students misbehave, allow students to have input into the definition of classroom rules, and praise and reward both individuals and the class when students behave appropriately. They are seen to frequently discuss with students the impact their misbehavior has on others (in a bid to have them change the way they behave), and punish students who misbehave, increasing the level of consequence if students argue or repeat the misbehavior. Rarely are elementary teachers perceived to act aggressively by humiliating students or acting unfairly.

TABLE 46.1
Aggregation Items

	Response Distributions					
Items	*Nearly Always*	*Most of the Time*	*A Lot of the Time*	*Some of the Time*	*Hardly Ever*	*Never*
Elementary Students						
Yells angrily at students who misbehave	13	13	12	31	25	7
Makes sarcastic comments to students who misbehave	5	5	8	17	18	47
Keeps the class in because some students misbehave	14	11	9	20	22	23
Puts down students who misbehave	3	5	3	8	19	63
Secondary students						
Yells angrily at students who misbehave	13	12	11	26	25	13
Makes sarcastic comments to students who misbehave	9	7	8	18	23	36
Keeps the class in because some students misbehave	12	15	8	26	22	18
Puts down students who misbehave	6	5	5	13	23	49

In contrast, secondary teachers are seen as less likely to use all strategies apart from punishment and aggression. They appear to frequently hint and punish, only sometimes recognize appropriate behavior and have discussions with students, and hardly ever involve students in decision making or act aggressively against them. Nevertheless, as reported by Lewis (2001, p. 312), "both primary and secondary teachers are seen, at least sometimes, to yell angrily at students who misbehave and to keep a class in because some students misbehave." To investigate further the extent of perceived teacher aggression, data were examined for some of the individual items composing the aggression scale. Table 46.1 reports the data for the four most commonly reported items.

Inspection of the data in Table 46.1 shows that 62% of secondary students and 68% of elementary students report that their teachers at least sometimes yell in anger at students who misbehave. In addition, 42% of secondary and 35% of elementary respondents report that their teachers at least sometimes use sarcasm, and 30% and 19%, respectively, report the use of put-downs. Finally, 45% and 60% of secondary and elementary teachers, respectively, are seen to at least sometimes keep the class in because some students misbehave. These figures are substantial and a cause for concern.

TEACHERS' PERCEPTIONS OF TEACHERS' DISCIPLINARY BEHAVIOR

Students are not the only ones to have reported on teachers' classroom disciplinary behavior. Australian teachers' perceptions of the strategies they use to discipline students in classrooms have also been extensively investigated. For example, Oswald et al. (1997) reported on the responses of a comprehensive sample of approximately 3,400 South Australian teachers asked

TABLE 46.2
Teachers' perceptions of their disciplinary behavior.

Variable	*Elementary* ($N = 141$) Ave Item Mean	*Elementary* ($N = 141$) Ave Item Std Dev	*Secondary* ($N = 354$) Ave Item Mean	*Secondary* ($N = 354$) Ave Item Std Dev	*t*	Prob	Alpha	No. of Items
Discipline								
Recognition	5.1	0.8	4.0	1.1	11.9	<.001	.83	4
Discussion	4.6	0.9	4.0	0.9	6.6	<.001	.81	4
Aggression	1.6	0.4	1.8	0.5	− 4.8	<.001	.67	6
Punishment	3.4	1.1	3.2	1.0	1.4	.160	.81	5
Involvement	3.9	1.1	2.5	1.1	12.8	<.001	.58	2
Hint	4.5	0.9	3.9	0.9	6.1	<.001	.76	6

to indicate which discipline strategies they used to deal with student misbehavior. The most commonly used strategies are reported to be reasoning with students, in and out of class, and having discussions with the class. Almost half of the teachers surveyed stated that they used these strategies often. In addition, there was a range of more interventional strategies used less frequently, yet still often enough to be common. These include verbal reprimand, sending a student out of class, setting extra work, removing privileges, giving detention, or involving the students' parents. Compared to elementary teachers, secondary teachers were noticeably less likely to reason and discuss issues with students, even though these were still their most commonly used strategies (Oswald et al., 1997).

As indicated previously, students' data from 3,430 students in 37 schools in Victoria have recently been published (Lewis, 2001). In that study, the views of approximately 500 teachers were also collected regarding discipline in 35 of these schools. These views are now considered. The number of teachers completing the survey ranged from 1 to 17 in the 19 elementary schools and from 1 to 53 in the 18 secondary schools. This was partly because some schools distributed copies of the questionnaire to all teachers whereas in others only the teacher responsible for coordinating the distribution of questionnaires to students completed a teacher survey. In total, 145 elementary and 363 secondary teachers completed questionnaires. The survey provided data on the same 39 disciplinary strategies that were given to students (refer to Lewis & Lovegrove, 1988). Each item required a response on a 6-point scale to indicate how frequently the teacher used the particular discipline technique "when trying to deal with misbehavior." The response alternatives provided—Nearly Always, Most of the Time, A Lot of the Time, Some of the Time, Hardly Ever, and Never—were coded 6 to 1, respectively. For purposes of comparability with the students' results, data for scales comprising between two and six items will be reported.

Table 46.2 reports for each scale the average of all respective item means, and where applicable, the average standard deviation of these items, Cronbach Alpha coefficient of internal consistency, and the number of scale items. In addition, for each measure, the elementary teachers' reports are compared to those of teachers in secondary schools using *t* tests for independent means. Therefore *t* and *p* values are also reported. Because with large sample sizes even small differences are statistically significant, a conservative level of statistical significance will be used ($p < .001$). As can be seen from the Cronbach alpha coefficients in Table 46.2, the reliability of each scale was acceptable although two were modest. One of these however (Involvement) contained only two items.

In general, elementary teachers' perceptions are quite similar to those of their students. They report very frequent recognition and reward of appropriate behavior, discussion with students and hinting, and frequent student involvement in decision making. They punish only a little more often than sometimes and hardly ever become aggressive. As can be seen by inspection of the t values in Table 46.2, the most noticeable differences between elementary and secondary teachers occur for student involvement, recognition and reward for good behavior, discussion with students aimed at exploring their reason for behaving inappropriately, and nondirective hints. There is also a small but significant difference in the perceived usage of aggression, which is seen as more likely to occur in secondary schools. These differences in teachers' perceptions correspond closely with those reported for elementary and secondary students. It is noticeable that although there is substantial agreement between elementary students' and teachers' perceptions of classroom disciplinary behavior, the same cannot be said for teachers and students in secondary schools. Compared to the students, secondary teachers report a more "user-friendly" style consisting of greater use of discussion and reward, and less punishment.

As can be seen in Table 46.2, the mean score for the six aggression items indicated that these strategies were reported as used less frequently than "hardly ever" by teachers. Similar to the students' responses however, inspection of individual item means shows that 36% of teachers state that they at least sometimes yell in anger at misbehaving students and 22% at least sometimes keep a class in when only some students misbehave. These proportions are substantial.

In summary, a comparison of preferred and practiced discipline appears to show that elementary teachers are generally acting consistently with the ideals of both students and teachers in the area of classroom discipline. Secondary teachers also approximate the ideal identified by teachers and students, but with three areas of contention. First, it appears that, according to students, they fail to provide sufficient recognition for appropriate behavior, particularly to individual students. This observation has been highlighted in an earlier study that examined the disciplinary behavior of teachers rated by students as the best they had experienced in their 9 years of schooling (Lewis et al., 1991): "Students indicate that good teachers should praise kids when they behave properly but in this case the best teachers are actually seen to avoid doing so" (p. 102). Second, secondary teachers should provide more of a voice for students, both individually and collectively, for example, in determining expectations for appropriate behavior in class and, to a lesser extent, choice of sanctions. Finally, to act more in accord with perceptions of best practice, teachers should reduce their use of group punishments and loss of temper when handling misbehavior in classrooms. In terms of the power analysis discussed earlier, teacher aggression can be seen to contribute toward increasing their Coercive and Legitimate power but reducing their Referent power. To act more in accord with a conception of perceived best practice, secondary teachers would need to increase their Reward and Referent power, while reducing their use of the more extreme forms of Coercive and Legitimate power.

Styles of Discipline

In attempting to identify the real and perceived ideal classroom discipline behavior of teachers it is possible to examine the results of a number of studies that have considered styles of discipline rather than discipline strategies. For example, as part of a large-scale qualitative investigation into South Australian teachers' views on classroom discipline, Johnson and Whittington (1994) identified four distinct styles of discipline. The first, the Traditional style, was teacher-in-charge. It primarily consisted of establishing clear rules and a number of escalating punishments for noncompliance. The second was called Liberal-Progressive and promoted social equality, mutual respect, shared responsibility, cooperation, and self-discipline. The third style involved a Socially Critical Orientation, and as such saw student disruption as reasonable resistance to oppression. The last style considered was Laissez-faire, which derived from the free-choice movement within schooling. After examining transcripts of interviews with teachers totaling 80,000 words, Johnson and Whittington concluded:

> The vast majority of teachers held either traditional or liberal progressive views of school discipline. For secondary teachers (Yrs 8-12), roughly 70% embraced mainly traditional views of discipline while about a quarter held liberal progressive views. The reverse was true at the elementary level (Yrs 3-7) with approximately two-thirds of teachers embracing liberal progressive views and 305 holding traditional views. At the junior elementary level (Reception, Yr1 & Yr 2), an overwhelming majority of about 90% of teachers held liberal progressive views compared with about 10% who held traditional views. (p. 271)

Research conducted by Lewis (1999a) also examined perceptions of three theoretical styles of teacher discipline. In these studies the styles of discipline were called Control, Management, and Influence, two of which align somewhat closely with those of Johnson and Whittington. The first of these three styles is Control and it corresponds to Johnson and Whittington's Traditional style, with the addition of recognition for appropriate behavior. The remaining two, Group Management and Influence, both reside within Johnson and Whittington's Liberal Progressive model.

In Group Management it is the teacher and students as a group who are responsible for the definition of norms and the securing of prosocial behavior. When applying this style, teachers organize students to make their own decisions. They choose to allow power to reside with the students and themselves as a group, where all have equal rights to contribute toward the determination of behavior standards. Consequently rules, and consequences for inappropriate behavior, are defined at classroom meetings during which the teacher is a group leader, but chooses not to use any more power to decide classroom policy than any other group member. Once policy is established, the teacher carries it out. The ultimate sanction in the group management style is to be excluded from the group until one is willing to behave appropriately.

The style of Influence is one that encourages students to become responsible for their own behavior. It is the teachers' role to influence each student so that he or she decides to behave well. They encourage students to learn their own way of behaving with minimum adult control, and negotiate with students on a one-to-one basis, acting as an advisor or consultant. They are careful however not to force their views on students. Whenever possible teachers allow students to experience the natural consequences of their behavior, so that they can choose to modify the way they behave.

In 1991, Lewis, Lovegrove, and Burman reported three studies that note teachers' levels of support for these styles of discipline, and in one of these studies, their perceptions regarding the extent to which they are implementing them. In one study 74 elementary and 171 secondary teachers indicated the suitability of each of the styles for 30 distinct classroom management issues such as damage to school property, completion of homework, physical aggression to other students, talking while the teacher is instructing the class, and so on. The data did not permit measurement of the levels of support for each style but did allow an indication of the extent to which teachers wished to include the voices of students in decision making. The results confirmed findings discussed earlier, in that "Elementary teachers wish to include their grade 4-6 students in decision-making about classroom behavior, to a greater extent than secondary teachers wish to involve year 7-9 students" (Lewis et al., 1999, p. 280). In a second investigation 427 elementary and 556 secondary teachers responded to an 18-item questionnaire designed to assess their level of support for each of the three discipline styles described earlier, namely Control, Group Management, and Influence. Although there were significant gender and year level effects reported, the general findings show that teachers see as most ideal a style of discipline that facilitates a sharing of decision making between teacher and students. They provide only a little less support for a style based on clear rules together with recognition for appropriate behavior and punishments for misbehavior. Finally, they fail to support a discipline style that encourages students to independently manage their own behavior. The final study of discipline styles by Lewis (1999a) notes not only the level of teacher support for each of the three discipline styles but also the extent of their perceived usage. Inspection of 294 secondary teachers' preferred styles shows that between 57% and 66% of respondents wish to use each of the styles at least half of the time. However there is slight preference for control in that 36% of teachers wish to implement this style at least most of the time compared to 28% and 26%, respectively, for Influence and Group Management.

When it comes to practice rather than preference, Lewis (1999a) stated: "Teachers report that they are generally using an approach to discipline based on clear rules, punishment for misbehavior, and recognition and reward for good behavior. Seventy three percent of respondents were claiming to use a style of Control at least most of the time compared to 7 percent and 10 percent for the styles of Group management and Influence respectively." (pp. 6–7)

These results appear remarkably consistent with the findings of Johnson and Whittington quoted earlier. In summary the data for preferred styles and strategies appear consistent across studies and over time. Preferences are for an interventional, assertive teacher who allows students a communal voice when it comes to rule definition and a private voice when it comes to discussing their misbehavior in a bid to have them plan for a better future. Nevertheless elementary and secondary teachers vary in their emphasis. Whereas elementary teachers stress more heavily student involvement, secondary teachers emphasize punishment. In terms of current practice, the data for styles support the analysis of strategies conducted previously in showing that teacher practice is more assertive and less inclusive of students voices than is preferred practice. Secondary teachers in particular report at most only a slight preference for Control in ideal terms, but in practice they place an overwhelming emphasis on it. In summary, the basis of the discipline implemented by teachers appears to be a combination of Referent, Reward, Legitimate, and Coercive power, with elementary teachers emphasizing the first two powers, and secondary teachers the latter two. Overall, when compared to the teachers' idea of ideal classroom discipline, secondary teachers appear to place too much stress on Legitimate and Coercive power and not enough on Reward or Referent power.

Having established what discipline strategies are preferred and what are provided, it is of value to examine research conducted in Australia to identify the impact teachers' discipline behavior has on students. The range of outcome measures considered include student interest in the subject matter being taught, distraction from learning, attitude to the teacher, and the belief that the teacher's action was justified. All of these variables have been associated with perceptions of discipline, and the results of relevant studies shed light on why some classroom discipline strategies can be argued to be preferable to others.

THE IMPACT OF CLASSROOM DISCIPLINE ON STUDENTS' ATTITUDES AND RESPONSIBILITY

After examining the results of two independent studies of students' reports of their teachers' disciplinary behavior and their attitudes to the subject taught by that teacher, Lewis and Lovegrove (1988) concluded that students may become less interested in subjects taught by teachers who display anger, mistarget and punish innocent students, and do not provide warnings before issuing punishments. This may occur even though the importance attached to the subject is not affected. These results appear very consistent with those of Fisher, Fraser, and others who, in a series of studies, demonstrated that students who perceived their teachers as admonishing and strict were those with more negative attitudes toward the subject being taught (e.g., Fisher, Henderson, & Fraser, 1997; Henderson, Fisher, & Fraser, 2000). The difficulty with correlational studies however is attributing causation. Although, as before, it is tempting to assume that teachers' unreasonable behavior causes negative student attitudes, the opposite is equally possible. Less interested students are more readily distracted and potentially distracting. Teachers dealing with such student behavior are more likely to act unreasonably. The most plausible explanation for correlations between teachers' controlling behavior and students' misbehavior and negative affect is one that involves both relationships. That is, there is a circularity to the pattern of interaction. In the words of Wubbels, Brekelmans, den Brok, and van Tatwijk, in Chapter 45 of this handbook, "The notion of circularity in the systems approach to communication highlights that someone's behavior influences someone else and that the behavior of the second person on his or her turn influences the first" (p. 1163). In this case, teachers' coercive reactions to students' negative attitudes and behavior reinforces students' negativity.

In a comprehensive report that attempts to highlight the impact of teachers' disciplinary behavior on students, Lewis and Lovegrove (1987b) examined the results of two independent studies that focussed directly on this issue. A total of 1,065 students described their teachers' disciplinary behavior and how they felt when "kids misbehave and get disciplined by the teacher." Four reactions were identified. These were students' fear of the teacher, attitude toward (liking of) the teacher, distraction from schoolwork, and sympathy for the misbehaving student. On the basis of replicated findings, Lewis and Lovegrove noted that professed students' reactions to teacher anger, mistargeting, having unclear rules, moving students without a warning, using arbitrary sanctions, and failing to recognize appropriate behavior included distraction from schoolwork, less liking of the teacher, and more sympathy for the miscreant. The use of embarrassment and teacher anger also appeared to generate fear in students. In general there was a substantial minority of students who were adversely affected by witnessing or receiving classroom discipline. For example, 35% of respondents were more than sometimes distracted from their schoolwork as a result of disciplinary strategies being implemented. Twenty percent were made anxious to the same extent, and 42% felt less positively toward the teacher and more sympathetic toward the miscreant when teachers responded to misbehaving students. These proportions are sufficiently large to indicate cause for concern.

To further investigate the relationship between discipline strategies and students' reactions to them, the data from the students' responses in an earlier study (Lewis, 2001) were augmented by the addition of those of another 2,259 secondary students, collected in a subsequent study. These data were then submitted to additional analyses. In both studies, students were asked to report how they "feel when your teacher deals with misbehavior in class." To document students' responses, a 10-item questionnaire was adapted from the one used in the study reported earlier (Lewis & Lovegrove, 1987b) and a common 4-point response format was adopted. Some of the 10 items comprising the questionnaire required students to report how often they felt distracted by their teacher's discipline strategies (e.g., not able to get on with my work properly, put off my work). Some others focussed on how often they felt the teacher's behavior was justified (e.g., the students deserved it, it was necessary), and a third group of items assessed the students' dislike of the teacher (e.g., annoyed at the teacher, sick of the teacher picking on kids). To respond, students indicated whether they Nearly Always, Most of the Time, Some of the Time, Hardly Ever, or Never felt the way described in the questionnaire item. Responses were coded from 4 to 1, respectively. In total, data were analyzed from 592 students in grade 6, 1,713 students in years 7 or 8, 1,624 in 9 or 10, and 846 students in 11 or 12.

Table 46.3 reports the number of items in each scale (n), the scales' average item means, standard deviations of the average item means, and alpha coefficients of internal consistency.

TABLE 46.3
Reaction to Discipline

Scale	*Secondary Students (N = 4183)*				*Elementary Students (N = 592)*			
	No. of Items	*Ave Item Mean*	*Ave Item Std Dev*	*Alpha*	*No. of Items*	*Ave Item Mean*	*Ave Item Std Dev*	*Alpha*
Distracted	5	2.0	0.7	.82	5	2.3	0.8	.81
Action Justified	2	2.4	0.6	.67	2	2.5	1.0	.68
Dislike Teacher	2	2.0	1.0	.76	2	2.0	0.6	.69

These reliability data show good internal consistency for the longer scale and although the internal consistency figures are low for the two item scales it is partly a function of small scale length. Despite some reservations therefore, the scales were used to examine students' reactions to the discipline provided by their teachers. In interpreting the findings it is important to note that students who observe a teacher disciplining another target student are likely to be affected by the teacher's behavior. This ripple effect was reported by Kounin (1970) over 35 years ago.

Examination of the scale means indicates that secondary students are, on average, more than "some of the time" distracted by their teachers' use of discipline strategies and often feel negatively toward the teacher when he or she deals with misbehavior. They are however more than sometimes of the belief that the teachers' intervention was necessary. Elementary students report about the same level of negative affect as do the secondary students, but more distraction, even though they are more likely to see the teacher's interventions as justified. It is of interest to recall that in the Lewis and Lovegrove (1987b) study, which examined year 9 students' reaction to discipline, the proportions of students "more than sometimes" distracted, seeing the teachers' behavior as unjustified, and feeling negative toward the teacher were 35%, 42%, and 42%, respectively. The corresponding figures for the same year level, over 15 years later, are 39%, 49%, and 32%. For elementary students the proportions are 48%, 51%, and 38%, respectively. Consequently there does not appear to be a great deal of difference in secondary students' reaction to discipline over time, although in more recent times, secondary teachers appear less likely to be thought of more negatively for implementing disciplinary strategies. In general these proportions are very substantial and indicate that many students are adversely affected by witnessing or experiencing their teacher's handling of students' misbehavior in their classrooms.

To allow examination of the magnitude of the relationship between specific discipline strategies perceived by students, and their reactions to that teacher's disciplinary style, Tables 46.4 and 46.5 below report the relevant correlations. In attempting to interpret these correlations there was concern about the extent to which the way students were treated could color not only their reactions to a teacher but also their perceptions of the strategies used by that teacher. If this "halo effect" were substantial, then there would be serious questions associated with the validity of their reports. To consider such a possibility, students' responses to two additional questions on the survey were analyzed. These questions focused on levels of student misbehavior. The first stated, "How often do you misbehave in this teacher's class?" and the second, "How many of the students in your class misbehave in this teacher's lessons?" For both questions, students responded by selecting one of four alternatives. For the former question the alternatives were Almost Never, Only a Little, Sometimes, and Often. For the latter they were

TABLE 46.4
Associations Between Discipline Strategies and Secondary Students' Reaction to Discipline

	Punishment	*Discussion*	*Recognition*	*Aggression*	*Involvement*	*Hinting*
Dislike Teacher	.19	−.24	−.26	.51	−.04	−.07
Distracted	.18	−.15	−.15	.39	.01	−.01
Teacher Action Justified	.05	.24	.23	−.17	.17	.17
No. of St's Misbehaving	.13	−.07	−.09	.29	.03	.03

TABLE 46.5
Associations Between Discipline Strategies and Elementary Students' Reaction to Discipline

	Punishment	*Discussion*	*Recognition*	*Aggression*	*Involvement*	*Hinting*
Dislike Teacher	.05	−.25	−.20	.28	−.18	−.16
Distracted	.24	−.01	−.08	.45	.01	−.14
Teacher Action Justified	.03	.22	.21	−.17	.17	.15
No. of St's Misbehaving	.04	−.00	−.07	.19	.02	.06

Hardly Any or None, Some, Many, and Nearly All. In both cases the responses were coded from 1 to 4, respectively.

To determine the extent to which a student's personal treatment influenced the treatment he or she said was received by the entire class, these two sets of answers were cross-tabulated. It was observed that the sets of responses correlated at 0.29 because of a tendency for students who were more likely to misbehave being more likely to perceive misbehavior in their classrooms. This correlation could be due to the increased likelihood that there is more misbehavior in the classes in which misbehaving students are situated, or it may be the result of a "halo effect." Nevertheless, 73% of the 2,730 students who reported misbehaving Almost Never, or at most Only a Little, still perceived Many or Nearly All students in their class as misbehaving. This indicates that the reports of the majority of students regarding teachers' discipline in classes were not related to their own treatment for misbehavior but were probably a reflection of the way they saw their misbehaving classmates treated. In summary, these data provide support for the validity of use of students' perceptions of their teachers' classroom discipline strategies.

The first three rows of data in Tables 46.4 and 46.5 record the relationships between discipline strategies and student reaction for both elementary and secondary teachers, respectively. Because the sample sizes were large, some correlations less than 0.1 were still statistically significant ($p < .001$). However, only correlations 0.15 or greater were considered sufficiently substantial to be worthy of comment. Inspection of these data indicates that teachers who use more punishment more often are seen as more distracting when they respond to misbehavior. Punishment also associates with secondary students' dislike of the teacher. For all students Aggression has a reasonably strong association with distraction and dislike of the teacher. Aggression also relates to students' belief that the teachers' disciplinary actions are unjustified. The use of recognitions and the conduct of discussions with students associates with a more positive reaction toward the teacher and a greater belief that the teacher's interventions are necessary. For secondary students only, teacher recognition and discussion are also related to less distraction.

Finally, greater use of both hinting and the involvement of students in decision-making surrounding classroom discipline relates to a stronger belief that the discipline actions taken by the teacher are warranted. For elementary students, greater use of these two strategies is also associated with a more positive attitude to the teacher. These strategies are not significantly associated with either attitude to teacher or distraction. The results for teacher aggression and recognition of appropriate behavior generally replicate the findings reported earlier.

As a consequence of the previous analysis it may be argued that application of Reward and Referent power generally results in less distraction when teachers deal with misbehavior, and more trust and liking of the teacher. Teachers who rely more on the use of Coercive power on the other hand appear to be more likely to distract their students when they handle misbehavior in classrooms and also generate more negativity toward them in secondary schools.

Having established teachers' general patterns of classroom discipline, it was of interest to examine how they discipline classes in which more children misbehave. Consequently, the bottom rows of Tables 46.4 and 46.5 record, for elementary and secondary students, respectively, the correlations between the proportions of students misbehaving in a class and the extent of usage of the various disciplinary strategies. Only two correlations exceeded 0.13. For all students, Aggression correlated significantly with the perceived misbehavior of the class. These data may indicate that teacher aggression promotes student misbehavior, teachers react aggressively when more students misbehave, or that there is circularity of interaction and both of these explanations apply.

Even though it was stated earlier that, in general, correlations less than 0.1 are statistically significant but not of importance, there are four correlations between disciplinary strategies and classroom misbehavior that defy this generalization. The magnitude of these correlations is small enough that they appear unimportant. However, that they are not large and not positive is in itself very important. As indicated before, the last rows of correlations in Tables 46.4 and 46.5 show that the number of students who misbehave in a class correlates less than 0.1 with both Discussion and Recognition in both elementary and secondary schools. Consequently it can be argued that teachers fail to provide more recognition and discussion for misbehaving students in classes where one would assume there is greater need for these powers, as there is more misbehavior occurring.

If teachers are adapting their choice of disciplinary strategies to their clientele, one might have hypothesized that with classes of students more prone to misbehavior, teachers would have found more need for generating Reward power by recognizing responsible behavior, to increase its likelihood, just as they have found more need for Coercive power comprising punishment and aggressive responses. As indicated before, however, they not only fail to provide more recognition for appropriate behavior, they also fail to generate the Referent power that can arise from having productive discussions with misbehaving students. It is acknowledged that not all discussions teachers have with misbehaving students result in better relationships, because some teachers talk at, or to them. However, those discussions that allow students' views and feelings to be heard, while still highlighting the damaging impact their misbehavior has on themselves and on other students, should increase the teacher's Referent power considerably.

DISCUSSION

From the summary of the research reviewed in this chapter, it can be argued that elementary teachers in Australia generally appear to implement their ideas of best discipline practice, in that they desire to use and are generally seen to implement a calm style of discipline characterized by the use of clear expectations for student behavior, formed in part by the students themselves. They then hint at, explain to, and discuss with students the need for appropriate behavior.

Finally, they provide recognition to those students behaving appropriately, and calmly punish misbehaving students.

To some extent, secondary teachers also act in accordance with their own best intentions, by characteristically explaining, warning, and providing punishments for misbehavior. There are however a number of noticeable exceptions. Secondary students report substantially less access to recognition of appropriate behavior, and less discussion with teachers about misbehavior than is desired. Both elementary and secondary students also note the likelihood of too many teachers getting angry with misbehaving students and yelling at them, or punishing innocent students by keeping classes in for detention.

In trying to understand these findings, it is of value to briefly contemplate four categories of students who may inhabit classrooms. The first (Category A) contains children who generally respond appropriately to the curriculum and undertake whatever work they are given by the teacher. These children usually seem to assume that the work is important enough to attempt, and easy enough to be mastered. Such students respond to hints such as a teacher pausing, moving closer, inspecting the child's work, or saying that there is a problem. The second group of students (Category B) is less interested in the work or less confident of their ability to complete it. Consequently they are occasionally distracted and sometimes distracting. The behavior of these children can often be controlled via the judicious use of rewards and punishment. The third group of students (Category C) is sufficiently difficult to warrant sending them out of the classroom. Either they resist the teacher's attempts to apply punishment, ignore the rewards, or in some other way fail to submit to the authority of the teacher. However this happens only occasionally. When it does, the teacher provides an opportunity for a "chat." It is during this discussion that the teacher helps the student become aware of the unreasonable impact his or her behavior has on the other students. Once the child acknowledges that his or her behavior is a problem, a plan or contract is developed for avoiding repetition of such unreasonable behavior in the future. Although one chat will normally not be sufficient, after a number of these chats students in Group C decide to act more appropriately. The final group of students (Category D) is those who repeatedly misbehave despite the use of all of the previous strategies.

The studies reviewed in this chapter appear to indicate that secondary teachers are very frequently using hints and assertive strategies to respond to classroom misbehavior. This is probably because such strategies meet the needs of students in Categories A and B and, because teachers on average report that only some of their students misbehave, the students in Categories A and B form the majority of students in most classrooms. Although they could use one-on-one discussions before giving out punishments such as isolation and detention, it appears that this kind of response to misbehavior may only be reserved for students who are unwilling to respond to the teacher's Legitimate power, Coercive power, or Reward power, although it needs to be noted that Reward power is not readily offered to individual students. It may be argued that it is only after the application of Legitimate and Reward power is ignored or resisted, that teachers adopt strategies based primarily on Referent power, and try to change students from the inside out rather than from the outside in.

In contrast, elementary teachers appear to rely more heavily on Referent and Reward power than Coercive, and could be argued to value more highly their relationship with students. The greater likelihood for secondary teachers to be characterized by less support for, and exercise of, Referent and Reward power has been recently noted by Hargreaves (2000). After analysis of interviews with over 50 teachers, he stated:

> Many elementary (primary) teachers secure their psychic rewards by establishing close emotional bonds or emotional understanding with their students as a foundation for teaching and learning. (p. 817)

> Secondary school teachers often feel not known by their students; and their emotional connections with them feel more distant than is true for their elementary colleagues. (p. 821)

The most likely explanation for elementary teachers' greater reliance on Referent power relates to differences in how elementary and secondary schools are organized. Teachers in elementary schools are responsible for approximately 25 to 30 children, and are with them for most of the day. In such settings teachers and students may develop strong loyalties, which facilitate the effectiveness of Referent power. In contrast, secondary teachers may teach up to 200 students in a day, seeing groups of 20 to 25 for periods of less than an hour. Consequently in each respective setting, teachers' choice of techniques may be strongly influenced by the characteristics of the students they teach and the way schooling is organized.

A second explanation, not unrelated to the first, is that teachers in secondary schools may see themselves as teachers of information and classes rather than teachers of individual children. This inference appears consistent with the outcome of an analysis of almost 200 elementary and 100 secondary schools' proposed codes of conduct for student behavior (Lewis, 1999b):

> These findings would indicate a stereotypical distinction between primary (elementary) and secondary schools. The former appear to focus on involving, supporting and educating the whole child while the latter emphasise more surveillance and punishments to secure the establishment of the order necessary to facilitate the learning of school subjects. (p. 57)

As stated earlier, one purpose of classroom discipline is to establish order to permit teachers to instruct students in the formal curriculum of the school (e.g., reading, writing, and arithmetic). A second purpose is to provide an appropriate educational experience to shape the students' values and to teach them about the rights of individuals, particularly individuals in conflict. The data reviewed in this chapter tend to suggest that secondary teachers may be providing more emphasis to the former than the latter. Such an emphasis may already be evident during teacher training according to Wilson and Cameron (1996), who argued that teachers in training move from a very caring perspective to a more managerial outlook. In their analysis of the journals of teachers in training, these authors noted that first-year student teachers are concerned with notions of relating to and understanding their students. However, by third year, they see their students less as people and more as learners.

With regard to the impact of teachers' disciplinary strategies, it is clear from the analyses presented earlier that in both elementary and secondary schools, teacher aggression and, to a lesser extent, punishment are ineffective in fostering positive student affect and behavior. In contrast Hinting, Discussions, Recognition, and Involvement may be helpful in this regard. Yet, more difficult students generally experience more of the former but no more of the latter. It is not surprising that students who are subject to, or witness, more teacher aggression, or even escalating punishment in the face of resistance, may react negatively toward the teacher, and be more distrustful of the teacher's perceived intentions, as the data in this chapter indicate. Many senior teachers who have misbehaving students sent to them will testify that often, the student's genuinely held belief is that "The teacher hates me!" However, when a teacher provides recognition and reward for appropriate behavior (particularly for that of difficult students) he or she demonstrates that it is the student's behavior that is the focus of the disciplinary interventions and not a dislike of the child. It is reasonable to expect that such teachers are more likely to be trusted when they do need to deal with misbehavior.

Similarly, a teacher who talks to misbehaving students about his or her concern over the impact their behavior has on other students directly challenges the miscreants' hypothesis that they, not the behavior, are the target of the disciplinary intervention. Consequently it is to be expected that more frequent use of discussions would result in a more positive student affect.

That being the case, it is problematic to note that teachers dealing with less responsible students are not more likely (and in some cases are less likely) to be using productive power such as Reward and Referent power manifested in strategies such as Hinting, Discussing, Recognizing, and Involving. It is equally problematic to see an increased use of Coercive power in the form of Aggression and Punishment, given that they are at best of limited usefulness, and at worst counterproductive in terms of the students' attitude to the teacher, their concentration on their work, and their evaluation of the need for teacher intervention.

If teachers are reacting to the level of responsibility displayed by students, it is possible that when more students misbehave, teachers may become overwhelmed by the level of misbehavior and consequently frustrated. Teachers with insufficient power in the classroom may feel confronted by their own lack of ability to ensure that all students are learning and are respectful of rights. According to the levels of aggression reported earlier, they may even become angry and hostile toward less responsible students. The emotionality in teachers' responses may not only be related to the number of students misbehaving but could also be influenced by the perceived severity of the misbehavior. For example, according to one of the teachers interviewed by Hargreaves (2000), commenting on a 5-year-old boy who refused demands to go to the principal, "You can't help but get angry and agitated when those kinds of things happen" (p. 819). Angry or upset teachers, as argued by Glasser (1997), may not be interested in being reasonable toward unreasonable and disrespectful students. They therefore may find it unpalatable to recognize difficult students when they act appropriately. Rewarding "Neanderthals" for being normal may not come naturally. Similarly they may find it unpleasant and unproductive to spend time letting such students tell their side of events, trying to get them to acknowledge that their behavior is unfair and needs to change.

Possibly because of teachers' nonproductive responses to these more difficult students, approximately one third of the students in Australian classrooms appear more than sometimes "distracted" when their teacher deals with misbehavior. As a result of witnessing, or being the target of, such a disciplinary response, many also see the teacher's behavior as unjustified and feel more negatively toward the teacher. The proportion of students affected is large enough to be of concern. If teachers were more aware of the negative impact their disciplinary behavior has on students' concentration on their schoolwork they might rate their concern about misbehavior and classroom discipline as higher than moderate.

There are other reasons to be concerned over teachers' relative unwillingness to use empowering strategies, such as Discussion and Involvement, with more difficult students. These generally relate to the educational purpose of classroom discipline discussed earlier. First, a number of experienced educators recommend these strategies as the only effective way of producing responsible students (Metzger, 2002; Roeser, Eccles, & Sameroff, 2000; Ryan & Patrick, 2001). As stated by Pastor (2002), when determining which discipline strategies are most desirable, we need to note that

> When we separate our approach to discipline from our principles, we influence the ethical tone of the school community. Valuing good character and seeking the development of personal responsibility determine the school's response to discipline problems. Discipline is not primarily a matter of keeping things under control by making choices for students . . . it is a matter of helping students learn to make good choices and be responsible for those choices. (p. 657)

In discussing the alternatives for discipline, Maehr and Midgeley (1991) made a similar point, highlighting the limitations of Coercive power, in comparison to Referent power: "Discipline procedures can reflect sheer force or attempts to develop critical thinking about implications of one's behavior" (p. 412).

Metzger (2002, p. 657), in supporting a recommendation for more inclusion of students' voices, focused on the relevance of discipline to the development of democratic citizens when she stated, "As we seek to prepare children to be productive citizens of a democracy, teaching them to understand and exercise their choices and voices becomes paramount."

Not only is the need to provide strategies that involve students recommended by experienced educators, so is the need to avoid aggressive disciplinary strategies. For example, the two most important pieces of advice offered by Metzger (2002) to teachers trying to ensure the likelihood that students will remain motivated to behave responsibly are first, don't escalate, deescalate! Second, let students save face. Clearly both of these processes, which would generate Referent power, are incompatible with an aggressive teacher response to misbehavior, and may also be at variance with escalating punishment in the face of resistance (especially for the more difficult children).

A second reason to ensure teachers minimize the use of aggressive responses toward students is the need to provide an appropriate model for children. For example, according to Fenstermacher (2001), the best way to create responsible or mannered students is to ensure that they are around responsible teachers: "The manner of a teacher takes on particular importance, insofar as it serves as a model for the students . . . as something the student will see and believe proper, or imitate, or accept as a standard for how things will be" (p. 644).

Consequently, in discussing the success of a character education program (Community of Caring), Jones and Stoodley (1999) noted, "Asking staff members to examine their own actions and their own role modeling is what makes the program work" (p. 45).

The final implication of this study relates to an observation by Roeser et al. (2000), commenting on how to facilitate the likelihood of teachers' increasing their use of Referent power while decreasing their Coercive power, including aggressive responses, even to the most difficult of students:

> Creating professional work environments where teachers feel supported by other professionals and school leaders in relation to their own needs for competence, autonomy, and quality relationships is essential to their decision to create these conditions for students. (p. 466)

It may well be that in order for teachers to increase their reliance on discipline strategies based on Referent power and decrease their use of those reflecting Coercive power they will need to experience more validation and better quality relationships with both colleagues and administration. The need for support for teachers attempting to improve the effectiveness of their professional practice is widely acknowledged (Hart et al., 1995; Punch, & Tuetteman, 1996; Rogers, 1992, 2002).

REFERENCES

Ainley, J., Batten, M., Collins, C., & Withers, G. (1998). *Schools and the social development of young Australians*. Melbourne: Australian Council for Educational Research.

Anderson, C., Avery, P. G., Pederson, P. V., Smith, E. S., & Sullivan, J. L. (1997). Divergent perspectives on citizenship education: A Q-method study and survey of social studies teachers. *American Educational Research Journal, 34*(2), 333–364.

Applied Psychology Research Group. (1989). *Teacher stress in Victoria: A survey of teachers' views*. Australia: University of Melbourne.

Bagley, W. C. (1914). *School discipline*. New York: Macmillan.

Barber, B. R. (1998). The apprenticeship of liberty: Schools for democracy. *School-Administrator, 55*(5), 10–12.

Barton, P. E., Coley, R. J., & Wenglinsky, H. (1998). *Order in the classroom: Violence, discipline and student achievement*. Princeton, NJ: Policy Information Center. Educational Testing Service.

Bennett, W. (1998) The place to harvest patriots. *School-Administrator, 55*(5), 38–40.

Benninga, J. S., & Wynne, E. A. (1998). Keeping in character. *Phi Delta Kappan, 79*(6), 439–445.

Canter, L., & Canter, M. (1992). Lee Canter's assertive discipline: Positive behavior management for today's classroom. Santa Monica CA: Canter & Associates.

Charles, C. (2001). *Building classroom discipline: From models to practise* (7th ed). New York: Longman.

Civics Expert Group. (1994). *Whereas the people... Civics and citizenship education.* Canberra: Australian Government Publishing Service.

Schools in Crisis: call for another 700 Counsellors (2002, July 17). *Sydney Morning Herald*, p. 2.

Critical delay on 'bad kid classes.' (2002, August 25). *Sun Hevald*, p. 3.

Cunat, M. (1996). Vision, vitality and values: Advocating the democratic classroom. In L. E. Beyer (Ed.), *Creating democratic classrooms. The struggle to integrate theory and practice* (pp. 127–149). New York: Teachers College Press.

Curriculum Corporation. (1994). *A statement on studies of society and environment for Australian schools.* Commonwealth Department of Employment Training and Youth Affairs. Canberra. ACT Australia.

Curriculum Corporation. (1998). *Discovering democracy.* Commonwealth Department of Employment Training and Youth Affairs. Canberra. ACT Australia.

Dinham, S. (1993). Teachers under stress. *Australian Educational Researcher, 20*(3), 1–16.

Fenstermacher, G. D. (2001). On the concept of manner and its visibility in teaching practice. *Journal of Curriculum Studies, 33*(6), 639–653.

Fields, B. (1986). The nature and incidence of classroom behaviour problems and their remediation through preventive management. *Behaviour Change, 3*(1), 53–57.

Fisher, D., Hehderson, D., & Fraser, B. (1997). Laboratory environments and student outcomes in senior school biology. *American Biology Teacher, 59(2)*, 14–19.

Fisher, S. (1998). Developing and implementing a K-12 character education Program. *Journal of Physical Education, Recreation and Dance, 69*(2), 21–23.

Freiberg, H. J., Stein, T. A., & Huang, S. (1995). Effects of a classroom management intervention on student achievement in inner-city elementary schools. *Educational Research and Evaluation, 1*(1), 36–66.

French, J. R. P., & Raven, B. H. (1959). The bases of social power. In I. D. Cartwright (Ed.), *Studies in social power* (pp. 150–167). Ann Arbor, MI: Institute for Social Research.

Glanzer, P. L. (1998). The character to seek justice: showing fairness to diverse visions of character education. *Phi Delta Kappan, 79*(6), 434–436, 438, 448.

Glasser, W. (1997). A new look at school failure and school success. *Phi Delta Kappan, 78*(8), 597–602.

Hart P. M., Wearing, A. J., & Conn, M. (1995). Conventional wisdom is a poor predictor of the relationship between discipline policy, student misbehavior and teacher stress. *British Journal of Educational Psychology, 65*(1), 27–48.

Hansen D. T. (2001). Reflections on the Manner in Teaching Project. *Journal of Curriculum Studies, 33*(6), 729–735.

Hargreaves, A. (2000). Mixed emotions: Teachers' perceptions of their interactions with students. *Teaching and Teacher Education, 16*, 811–826.

Henderson, D., Fisher, D., & Fraser, B. J. (2000). Interpersonal behaviour, learning environments and student outcomes in senior biology classes. *Journal of Research in Science Teaching, 37*, 26–43.

Houston, P. D. (1998). The centrality of character education. *School Administrator, 55*(5), 6–8.

Hyman, I. A., & Snook, P. A. (2000). Dangerous schools and what you can do about them. *Phi Delta Kappan*, 81(7), 489–501.

Independent Education Union. (1996). *Education and stress.* Report on the survey conducted by the Victoria and NSW IEU on workloads and perceptions of occupational stress among union members employed in Catholic schools, and Education offices and in independent schools. Melbourne, Australia.

Johnson, B., Oswald, M., & Adey, K. (1993). Discipline in South Australian primary schools. *Educational Studies, 19*(3), 289–305.

Johnson, B., & Whittington, V. (1994) Teachers' views on school discipline: A theoretical framework. *Cambridge Journal of Education, 24*(2), 261–277.

Jones, S. C., & Stoodley, J. (1999). Community of Caring: A character education program designed to integrate values into a school community. *National Association of Secondary School Principals, 83*(609), 46–51.

Kennedy, K. J. (1996). *New challenges for civics and citizenship.* Australian Capital Territory. Australia. Australian Curriculum Studies Association.

Kennedy, K. J., (1998). Preparing teachers for the new civics education. *Asia-Pacific Journal of Teacher Education and Development, 1*(2), 33–40.

King N. J., Gullone, E., & Dadds, M. R. (1990). Student perceptions of permissiveness and teacher-instigated disciplinary strategies. *British Journal of Educational Psychology, 60*, 322–329.

Kohn, A. (1996). *Beyond discipline: From compliance to community.* Alexandria, VA: Association for Supervision and Curriculum Development.

Kohn, A. (1998). Adventures in ethics versus behaviour control: A reply to my critics. *Phi Delta Kappan, 79*(6), 455–60.

Kounin, J. S. (1970). *Discipline and group management in classrooms.* New York: Holt, Rinehart & Winston.

Lewis R. (1997a). *The discipline dilemma* (2nd ed.). Melbourne: Australian Council for Educational Research.

Lewis, R. (1997b). Discipline in schools. In L. J. Saha (Ed.), *International encyclopedia of the sociology in education* (pp. 404–411). Oxford, England: Permagon Press.

Lewis, R. (1999a). Teachers coping with the stress of classroom discipline. *Social Psychology of Education. 3*, 1–17.

Lewis. R. (1999b). Preparing students for democratic citizenship: Codes of conduct in Victoria's Schools of the Future. *Educational Research and Evaluation, 5*(1), 41–61.

Lewis, R. (2001). Classroom discipline and student responsibility: The students' view. *Teaching and Teacher Education, 17*(3), 307–319.

Lewis, R., & Lovegrove, M. N. (1983). Rolling with the punches in modern classrooms. *Journal of Australian Studies, 13*, 32–39.

Lewis, R., & Lovegrove, M. N. (1987a). The teacher as a disciplinarian: How do students feel? *Australian Journal of Education, 31*(2), 173–186.

Lewis, R., & Lovegrove, M. N. (1987b). What students think of teacher's classroom control techniques: Results from four studies. In J. Hastings, J. Schwieso (Eds.), *New directions in educational psychology, Vol. 2: Behaviour and motivation* (pp. 93–113). London; Philadelphia: Falmer Press.

Lewis, R., & Lovegrove, M. N. (1988). Students' views on how teachers are disciplining classrooms. In R. Slee (Ed). *Discipline and schools: A curriculum perspective* (pp. 268–283). South Melbourne, Australia: Macmillan.

Lewis, R., Lovegrove, M. N., & Burman, E. (1991). Teachers' perceptions of ideal classroom disciplinary practices. In M. N. Lovegrove, & R. Lewis (Eds.) *Classroom discipline* (pp. 86–113). Melbourne, Australia: Longman Cheshire.

Lewis, R., Romi. S., Xing, Q., & Katz, Y. (2005). A comparison of teachers' classroom discipline in Australia, China and Israel. *Teaching and Teacher Education, 21*, 729–741.

Lickona, T. (1996) Teaching respect and responsibility. Reclaiming children and youth. *Journal of Emotional and Behavioural Problems, 5*(3), 143–151.

Louden, L. W. (1987). *Teacher stress*. Summary report of the Joint Committee of Inquiry Into Teacher Stress appointed by the minister for education and planning in W.A., Perth, W.A. Govt. Printer.

Lovegrove, M. N., & Lewis, R. (1982). Classroom-control procedures used by relationship -centred teachers. *Journal of Education for Teaching, 8*(1), 55–66.

Maehr, M. L., & Midgely, C. (1991). Enhancing Student motivation: A schoolwide Approach. *Educational Psychologist, 26*(3/4), 399–427.

McCarthy, C., Johnson, B., Oswald, M., & Lock, G. (1992). Violence in schools, *SAIT Journal, 24*(11), 16–17.

McCraith, C., (1994, November). *Violence in schools: principals' perspectives.* University of Newcastle: Paper presented at the Australian Association for Research in Education.

McDonnell, S. (1998). Ethics and freedom. *School Administrator, 55*(5), 18–20.

Mellor, S. Kennedy, K. & Greenwood, L. (2001). *Citizenship and democracy, Students' knowledge and beliefs: Australian 14 Year olds and the Civic Education study, Melbourne; Australia.* Council for Educational Research.

Metzger, M. (2002). Learning to discipline. *Phi Delta Kappa, 84*(1), 77–84.

Nelson, B. (2002). *About discovering democracy. Civics and citizenship education.* A ministerial statement Retrieved *1, 5, 12*, 2004. From http://www. curriculum.edu.au/democracy/aboutdd.htm

O'Halloran, M. (2003, April 17). Safety of teachers must come first. *Newcastle Herald*, p. 9.

Osborne, K. (1995). *In defence of history: Teaching in the past and the meaning of democratic citizenship.* Toronto, Canada: Our School-Our Selves Educational Foundation.

Osler, A., & Starkey, H. (2001). Citizenship education and natural identities in France and England: Inclusive or exclusive? *Oxford Review of Education, 27*(2), 287–305.

Oswald, U., Johnson, B., & Whittington, V. (1997, November). *Classroom discipline problems in South Australian government and independent schools.* Paper presented at Australian Association of Educational Research Conference. Retrieved November 8, 2004, from http://www.aare.edu.au/97pap/oswam463.htm

Otto, R. (1986). *Teachers under stress.* Melbourne, Australia: Hill of Content.

Pastor, P. (2002). School discipline and the character of our schools. *Phi Delta Kappan, 83*(9), 658–661.

Pearl, A., & Knight, A. (1999). *The Democratic schooling: Classroom theory, to inform Practices.* Cresskill, NJ: Hampton Press.

Pithers, R. T., & Soden, R. (1998). Scottish and Australian teacher stress and strain: A comparative study. *British Journal of Educational Psychology, 68*, 269–279.

Pring, R. (2001). Education as a moral practice. *Journal of Moral Education, 30*(2), 101–112.

Print, M. (1996/1997). Renaissance in citizenship education: An Australian perspective. *International Journal of Social Education, 11*(2), 37–52.

Punch, K. F., & Tuetteman, E. (1996). Reducing teacher stress: The effects of support in the work environment. *Research in Education, 56*, 63–72.

Richardson, V., & Fenstermacher, G. D. (2001). Manner in teaching: The study in four parts. *Journal of Curriculum Studies, 33*(6), 631–637.

Roeser, R. W., Eccles, J. S., & Sameroff, A. J. (2000). School as a context of early adolescents' academic and social-emotional development: A summary of the research findings. *The Elementary School Journal, 101*(5), 443–471.

Rogers, W. (1992). *Supporting teachers in the workplace.* Milton Queensland, Australia: Jacaranda Press.

Rogers, W. (2002). *I get by with a little help . . . Colleague support in schools.* Melbourne, Australia: Australian Council for Educational Research.

Rothstein, R. (2000). Towards a composite index of school performance. *The Elementary School Journal, 100*(5), 409–441.

Ryan, K., & Patrick, H. (2001). The classroom social environment and changes in adolescents' motivation and engagement in the middle school. *American Educational Research Journal, 38*(2), 437–460.

Ryan, K., & Bohlin, K. E. (1999). *Building character in schools: Practical ways to bring moral instruction to life.* San Francisco, Jossey-Bass.

Schaeffer, E. F. (1999). It's time for schools to implement character education. *National Association for Secondary School Principals, 83*(609), 1–8.

Schneider, E. (1996). Giving students a voice in the classroom. *Educational Leadership, 54*(1), 22–26.

Siebold, D. (1998). Making students better people. What role should schools play in shaping children's character? *Our Children, 23*(5), 6–10.

Sinclair, K. (1992). Morale, satisfaction and stress in schools. In C. Turney, N. Hatton, K. Laws, K. Sinclair, & D. Smith (Eds.), *The School Manager.* Sydney, Australia: Allen and Unwin.

Smith, P. (1996). Catering for student diversity: Strategies for reducing teacher stress, *Independent Education, 26*(4), 13–14.

Swinson, J., & Melling, R. (1995). Assertive discipline: Four wheels on this wagon: A Reply to Robinson and Maines. *Educational Psychology in Practice, 11*(3), 3–8.

Tauber, R. T. (1999). *Classroom management: Sound theory and effective practice.* PA: Westport, Conn Bergin & Garvey.

Wolfgang, C. H. (1995). *Solving discipline problems: Strategies for classroom teachers.* (3rd ed.). Boston: Allyn & Bacon.

Wilson, S., & Cameron, R. (1996). Student teacher perceptions of effective teaching. A developmental perspective. *Journal of Education for Teaching, 22*(2), 181–196.

47

Classroom Management in Postwar Japan: The Life Guidance Approach

Kanae Nishioka
Kyoto University

INTRODUCTION

This chapter explores the development of classroom management strategies in Japan, where the cultivation of children's interpersonal relations and children's groups is the main focus of attention. In the first section I offer an account of the general characteristics of classroom management in Japan. This account elucidates group-based classroom management and how students play an active role in managing their classroom. Subsequently I outline the issues to be discussed in later sections.

Schools in Japan have been commonly understood as a place not only for academic teaching but also for socializing children. Socializing efforts were promoted intially by dedicated practitioners in schools with the support and criticism of colleagues and university researchers. The initial central concept in these endeavors is often identified as *seikatsu shido, literally* translated as life guidance. It mainly addresses problems in the lives of children and the construction of their groups in the classroom.

Emphasis is placed on groups rather than individuals. In group-centered schooling, attention is given to a sense of belonging, developing close relationships and collaboration among students, and creating a peer-based system in which to discuss issues in the group. Groups here can mean small groups within a class, a whole class, an entire school, and even a local community. Teachers in Japan have endeavored to create peer groups in their class because they consider the group as providing the best way not only to socialize but also to develop individual children. Needless to say, gathering students together does not automatically result in the development of groups. Hence teachers experimented and forged various strategies to promote classroom communities.

Several strands of the life guidance approach have been launched to date. This chapter draws on the relevant materials generated by teachers who were dedicated in enhancing this approach, but not on observational data and case studies on teachers' actions in the classroom. Teachers' efforts in life guidance have attracted national attention; promoting intense debate among educators and leaving an important legacy in the field. Although this chapter does not offer a comprehensive analysis of classroom management in general, the reader will be acquainted with a highly influential strand in Japan.

CLASSROOM MANAGEMENT IN JAPAN

General Characteristics

Compulsory education is offered for 9 years, from age 6 to 15, encompassing 6 years of elementary education (age 6–12) and 3 years of lower secondary education (age 12–15; equivalent to middle school education in the United States of America). It may be followed by 3 years of upper secondary education (age 15–18; equivalent to high school education). Although upper secondary education is not compulsory, more than 90% of students remain in schools after age 15. In 1999, "secondary education schools" were introduced to implement secondary education for 6 years from age 12 to age 18; but the number of such schools is still limited (MESSC, 2000, p. 14).

When we look at classroom management, there is a significant difference between elementary schools and secondary schools. In elementary schools, a homeroom teacher normally teaches most subjects to the same class for 2 years. On the other hand, in lower and upper secondary schools, a homeroom teacher teaches normally one subject to his or her class while subject specialists teach the other subjects.

The homeroom classes are, however, very important units in both elementary and secondary schools. Because ability grouping is not very common, students spend most of their time with their classmates. The maximum number of students per class in public elementary and lower secondary schools is set at 40 by law. As of 1998, the average number of students per class is 27.4 in elementary schools and 32.7 in lower secondary schools (MESSC, 2000, p. 62).

Students perform a wide array of activities and tasks with their classmates. Table 47.1 presents a timetable in a public elementary school in the academic year 2004–2005 (a Japanese academic year starts in April and ends in March). In the table, we can find some general characteristics of students' school lives, which are common in both elementary and secondary schools. It is usual that each school day starts with a "morning class meeting" (or a whole-school assembly) and ends with an "end-of-day class meeting." Both the students and the homeroom teacher have lunch in the classroom and clean the room together. During "class activities" time, students play sports, make plans for school events, discuss how to deal with class problems, and sometimes make rules for the class. School events include an excursion, a school trip, an "athletic" day, and a "cultural festival" day. On an athletic day or a cultural festival day the classes sometimes participate as a team and compete with each other.

One of the recent changes in the timetable is the introduction of "morning activities." Since 1999 the decline in academic standards has attracted much public attention. In 2002 the minister of education implemented a new policy emphasizing student academic performance. In response to that policy many schools introduced a short period identified as "morning activities" during which students mainly practice math, reading, and writing.

It is common for students to assume roles that promote student self-management. Each class has a division-of-work chart for self-management. There are two students, one boy and one girl, who conduct class meetings held as part of "class activities." Students take a turn in performing daily duties. Called *nicchoku* (i.e., monitors for the day), a boy and a girl lead the morning class meeting and the end-of-day class meeting, and they are responsible for signaling the beginning and end of a lesson with a commanding voice. Classes are commonly divided into several small groups called *han* consisting of four to six students. One of the students in each han serves as the han leader, whose responsibility is to facilitate discussion among members. There are various *kakari* (students in charge of various activities in the class): kakari

TABLE 47.1
Week Timetable for Third-Graders (2004–2005)

	Monday	*Tuesday*	*Wednesday*	*Thursday*	*Friday*
8:15	Whole-School Assembly	Morning Class Meeting	Morning Class Meeting	Morning Class Meeting	Morning Class Meeting
8:30	Morning Activities	Morning Activities	Morning Activities	Morning Activities	Morning Activities
8:40 **Period 1**	Class Activities	Calligraphy	Japanese Language	Japanese Language	Japanese Language
9:25	Recess	Recess	Recess	Recess	Recess
9:35 **Period 2**	Japanese Language	Moral Education	Physical Education	Arithmetic	Arithmetic
10:20	Recess	Recess	Recess	Recess	Recess
10:40 **Period 3**	Music	Science	Arithmetic	Social Studies	Art and Handcraft
11:25	Recess	Recess	Recess	Recess	Recess
11:35 **Period 4**	Social Studies	Japanese Language	Science	Music	Art and Handcraft
12:20	Lunch	Lunch	Lunch	Lunch	Lunch
13:10	Cleaning	Cleaning	Cleaning	Cleaning	Cleaning
13:25	Recess	Recess	Recess	Recess	Recess
13:50 **Period 5**	Arithmetic	Period for Integrated Study	Japanese Language	Period for Integrated Study	Physical Education
14:35	End-of-day Class Meeting	Recess	End-of-day Class Meeting	End-of-day Class Meeting	End-of-day Class Meeting
14:45 **Period 6**		Period for Integrated Study			
15:30		End-of-day Class Meeting			
15:40					

for school lunch, cleaning, attending to small animals, maintaining the class garden, publishing class newsletters, and the like.

A school normally has a student council and committees. The student president, deputy presidents, and secretaries are elected by students at the school assembly. Various committees are also organized to plan school events, improve the school environment, and broadcast news during the lunch recess, among other activities.

It must be noted that "special activities," including classroom activities, student council, club activities, and school events, comprise part of the formal curriculum. The National Courses of Study allocate one school hour per week to special activities.

Thus the school is both a place for teaching academic subjects and an important social space for socializing the children. Correspondingly, classes in Japan are not mere collections of students organized for teaching but cooperative communities where children experience both of these aspects of education. Some researchers speak of such characteristics of Japanese classroom management. For example, Iwama (1989) pointed out that Japan's school management system is much more "group-oriented" than that of America and that this management characteristic reflects Japanese culture. Kataoka (1992) suggested that Japanese classroom management and "student guidance" have a positive influence on students' moral development and academic interest. Lewis (1995) pointed out that teachers in Japan aim to foster whole-child development. As Shimahara (1998) suggested, classroom management is intended to create not only order for teaching and learning, but also a community in which children learn "sensitivity to other people, [and] qualities such as empathy, thoughtfulness, and kindness" (p. 235).

Preceding Research

A number of researchers have conducted ethnographic research on routine activities in Japan's classrooms and have reported their findings. I selectively review them to provide a background for this chapter. The following passages present images of classroom activities.

Let us first focus on the children's participation in classroom management. Lewis (1995) indicated that "Japanese students assume much authority. Even first graders quiet their classmates, help solve disputes, lead class meetings, and shape class rules and activities" (p. 1). A morning class meeting of first-graders is described as follows:

> Students play and talk noisily until the two student monitors for the day [i.e., the nicchoku] come to the front of the classroom and ask their 34 classmates to be seated. Most students take their seats and quiet down quickly, but the monitors must quiet several children by calling their names. All students are seated and quiet when, a few moments later, Ms. Ishii [the teacher] enters the room. On a cue from the monitors, all students rise, bow, and chorus, "Teacher, good morning." Ms. Ishii bows and greets them in return. Students take their seats, except for the monitors, who announce, in unison, the beginning of morning meeting and the first item on the agenda: attendance. Ms. Ishii calls the roll. . . .
>
> The two monitors announce, from the board, the next item for the morning meeting: "Things to tell the class." A child raises his hand and one student monitor calls on him. "My tooth fell out last night," the boy volunteers. At that, a number of children begin shouting out how many teeth they've lost. The monitors ask children to raise their hands if they want to talk. It takes 2 minutes for the monitors to quiet the class, and Ms. Ishii sits silent during this time. Finally, the class settles down and the monitors call on several more students, who share some personal news with the class. The monitors then announce the next item: news from the teachers. [After Ms. Ishii speaks, the monitors announce the end of the meeting and the beginning of the lesson.] (Lewis, 1995, pp. 37–38)

Other researchers depict very similar scenes taking place in the classes of different age groups. Tsuneyoshi (2001) recounted a morning meeting in a fourth-grade classroom, in which the monitors for the day conducted the meeting, and the student health monitors (i.e., kakari in charge of health supervision), instead of the teacher, checked the attendance and the health condition of the students (p. 21). LeTendre (2000) also found similar activities in the lower secondary school he studied. At this level the monitors also conduct the meetings. The students' autonomy is so pronounced that the homeroom teachers are hardly present at the morning meetings in that school. The student monitors collect homework assignments, record absences, and check students' health (pp. 38–39). N. Sato (2004), who observed two fifth-sixth grade classrooms at two elementary schools with different social backgrounds, reported that the teacher at one school holds daily class meetings during lunch whereas the other teacher holds no daily meetings but only weekly class meetings. In short, students manage themselves and their activities at both schools.

Though the lack of space does not allow me to discuss this in more detail, it is common practice for students to make their own rules and to reflect at end-of-day meetings on whether they have followed those rules. Such meetings are also conducted by the monitors.

The importance of the han or small groups in classroom management is another practice that attracted the attention of those researchers. Lewis (1995) wrote, "Small groups are at the heart of elementary school life. The four or so members of a group together pursue a wide range of activities—from art to lunch to science" (p. 1). She described how han members worked together in a science experiment, preparing lunch and cleaning up. She also observed that the teacher often named the han instead of individual children in lessons to elicit students' ideas or when the children reflected on themselves at the end-of-day class meetings. LeTendre (2000), Tsuneyoshi (2001), and N. Sato (2004) also observed similar activities in the classes of different age groups.

These findings show that there are similarities in classroom management strategies between different levels of schooling. Group-based classroom management, where children actively perform their roles and organize themselves into han, is very popular. This group ethos is commonly emphasized.

Evolution of Life Guidance

Let us address two questions. First, what strategies are used to develop a classroom community? As I mentioned before, simply gathering children into a group and letting them spend time together does not automatically generate a classroom community. Most children would feel that they get more out of working on their own without having to worry about others. How can a teacher change this perception? When some children disturb others how should a teacher direct such children? And how can he or she teach the other children regarding the constructive way to handle those children? Would the teacher's methods of forming a feeling of classroom community be different in subject lessons?

Second, how defensible in ethical terms is it to create a feeling of classroom community? It appears to be a good way to maintain order in the classroom, to assist students to understand the rules of life in a society, and to help them take responsibility. But does this mean that children are really making their own rules? Or are they just following the teacher's hidden intentions? In the latter case, a classroom community would be a form of regimented system. Another problem is that everybody's responsibility can mean nobody's responsibility. The nicchoku system embodies the typical Japanese concept of leadership. All children take turns in performing the duties of the nicchoku (monitors for the day). As Lewis (1995) argued, "leadership is not a privilege accorded to the well-behaved few. It's a regular responsibility of all students" (p.105). When the group itself does something wrong, who takes responsibility for it?

When we look back at the prewar history of Japan, there was a period of military dictatorship in which fascism laid emphasis on groups. According to Amano (1993) and M. Sato (1998), when modern schools were first established in 1872, classes were mere collections of children. Group-based classroom management first appeared during the Taisho era (1912-1926). During the 1920s and the 1930s group-based classroom management gradually became widespread and popular while fascism gripped the whole nation. Multifunctional groups were organized in classrooms, and teachers encouraged students to participate in classroom management. Fascism came to an end when Japan was defeated in the Second World War, but similar methods of classroom management are still popular in schools.

In the following sections, I focus on the strategies and theoretical formulations developed by a group of educators who paid much attention to the question of ethics outlined above. This group has developed a distinct approach to seikatsu shido or life guidance stemming from the teachers' movements in prewar Japan, which tried to promote democracy among children in defiance of imperial centralism. At that time, the school curricula were controlled by the national government, and the subject called *tsuzurikata* (composition) was the only area in which teachers could construct their own curriculum. The term *seikatsu shido* was introduced in Mitsushige Minechi's[1] book, *New Teaching Methods of Culture-Centered Composition* (*Bunka Chushin Tsuzurikata Shin-Kyojuhou*) in 1922 for the first time (see Funagoshi, 2001, p. 279). The movements that proliferated from this work were clamped down on and eventually prohibited before and during the war. But postwar promoters of life guidance have made efforts to reestablish this educational legacy.

The teachers who have developed strategies for life guidance shared their ideas and practice in voluntarily organized circles of like-minded educators and often wrote books presenting the detailed descriptions of their practice. Those teachers and researchers strove to construct the methods for fostering individuals for life in a democratic community.

Debates over the life guidance approach led to the development of four trends of life guidance in the postwar period. The following sections explore these trends. Table 47.2 presents a schematic view of the evolving approaches to life guidance. Note that the period shown in the table is the time span during which the respective trend was most influential.

The movements of life guidance were briefly mentioned by Shimahara (1998). In my knowledge, however, there is no in-depth research on the theoretical formulations of life guidance written in English. A number of researchers have written papers in Japanese to provide a broad view of the life guidance movements: for example, Takeo Shishido (1985), Yukio Fujiwara (1990, 1993, 2000), and Kenji Oride (2003).

REVIVAL OF LIFE COMPOSITION

Publication of *School Echoing in the Mountains*

The first trend of life guidance was based on the revived movement of *seikatsu tsuzurikata* (life composition). Life composition means written work done at school or as homework, in which students critically construct and reflect on their encounters with the external world. Life composition also refers to the teaching approach that promotes such compositions and takes advantage of them in organizing classroom discussions.

The prewar teachers who promoted life composition emphasized the importance of enabling children to describe and reflect on the reality of their lives in their writings so that they could come to grips with the problems they experience. The revival of life composition was

[1] In Japan, a family name comes before the first name, but I put all the first names first in order to avoid confusion in this chapter.

TABLE 47.2
Four Trends of *Seikatsu Shido* or Life Guidance

Name of Trend	*Period*	*Main Advocators*	*Main Points of Emphasis*
Life Guidance, based on Life Composition (*Seikatsu Shido*, based on *Seikatsu Tsuzurikata*)	Late 1940s–1950s	Seikyo Muchaku, Kenjiro Konishi, Tetsufumi Miyasaka	– Developing the students' consciousness through writing – Organizing class discussions based on the students' compositions
Strategies to Build a Classroom Community (*Gakkyu Shudanzukuri* Approach)	1960s–1970s	Chuji Onishi, Tsunekazu Takeuchi	– Developing a formal system for discussing issues in classes – The "forming *han*, leaders and discussion" method (the "*han-kaku-togi zukuri*" method)
Strategies to Build Learning Groups (*Gakushu Shudanzukuri* Approach)	1970s–1980s	Hitoshi Yoshimoto	– Applying the "forming *han*, leaders and discussion" method in lessons – Establishing discipline for learning and organizing questions
New Strategies to Build a Classroom Community (New Approach to *Gakkyu Shudanzukuri*)	Late 1980s–2000s	Kenji Oride, Tsunekazu Takeuchi	– Organizing voluntary networks of the children with attention to troubled children – Reorganizing the lesson content from the children's points of view

occasioned by the publication in 1951 of *School Echoing in the Mountains* (*Yamabiko Gakko*) by Seikyo Muchaku, a Buddhist priest and teacher (see also Muchaku, 1995). The book was a milestone, a pioneering piece in the history of life guidance in the country. It is an anthology of life compositions written by lower secondary students, and when published it became a sensational best-seller.

Before its dazzling economic growth during the 1960s, Japan was a poor, agricultural country devastated by wartime destruction. The lower secondary school at which Muchaku taught was in an extremely poor, remote village situated in the mountains. His students and their parents were suffering from extreme poverty and distress, and they struggled to live. The school was dilapidated. In the postscript of the anthology, Muchaku wrote: "In reality, there was no single map [for geography lessons] and no equipment for science experiments. The school building had thatched roofs, the classrooms were dark, and blizzards came into the school building through the broken paper sliding doors" (Muchaku, 1951, p. 197).

Muchaku was unwavering in supporting his students to overcome their perpetual defeatism and resignation in the face of debilitating poverty. He taught students to write life compositions to understand their social conditions and to reflect on how to cope with them. He emphasized two lines of attack in his teaching. First, he taught students how to write about the realities of their lives in detail as they were lived. When he read students' diaries, he wrote questions to stimulate their reflection, such as "What did you play today?" and "Why did you feel lonely?" When a student just enumerated the things she had done, he told her to focus on a specific event, such as cooking rice or studying at night. Though Muchaku wanted his students to recognize the social problems they face in their daily lives, he did not limit the topics of discussion to such issues. But as students learned to write in detail, their compositions began to reveal the reality of their lives. Second, he collected students' compositions so that the class could share them and discuss the life problems described in them. For example, he compared two compositions that displayed contrasting perspectives. In the collection he also posed three questions: Are our family lives really peaceful? What does "peaceful" mean to you? What kinds of thinking and attitudes should we have to make our lives more peaceful and happier? (Muchaku, 1950). Students discussed their lives on the basis of the compositions they wrote.

Here is a part of the most well-known composition in the anthology written by Koichi Eguchi, a boy whose mother suffered relentless economic hardship and was critically ill. The piece was titled "My Mother's Death and After It":

> After my mother entered the dispensary she came near death. Yet she still kept saying to me in a delirium: "Did you fetch firewood?", "Have you made pickles?", "Have you washed vegetables?" and so on. When I visited her and heard such words, I couldn't comfort her although I thought "This might be my mother's last moments." I couldn't help but worry about my housework to be finished at home, and I went home without talking to her much.
>
> On the eve of my mother's death, November 12th, I was very distressed because I did not know how I could finish all the work. I thought "There is no way I can finish my work no matter how hard I work." Then my friends came to help me and said, "We decided to help you last evening at the [student] self-governing meeting of the local community." That really cheered me up. The task of fetching firewood, which seemed impossible to finish even if I worked on my own for many days, was finished within a half day.
>
> It was the following day before dawn on unforgettable November 13th that the news of my mother on the verge of death came from the village dispensary to my uncle in Rokkaku who relayed it to my home. Everybody gathered at her bedside. When I told my mother [what my friends did], who couldn't say a word any more, she just smiled. I will never forget that smile for the rest of my life.
>
> When I look back now, I don't think there was a time when my mother smiled from the bottom of her heart. She hardly smiled even when she was talking with somebody. If she smiled, I feel now that "she smiled instead of crying." But her smile just before her death seems different and is stuck to my heart. (Muchaku, 1951, pp. 4–8).

Koichi's father was already dead, and the boy took care of his grandmother and his younger brother and sister. He was torn between his fear over his mother's illness and the survival of the family that was her obsession until her death. The excerpt is a good illustration of life compositions and how students could help each other when they discussed their personal distress in the class. This composition won an award given by the minister of education.

Publication of *Classroom Revolution* and Miyasaka's Theoretical Formulation

Before the publication of *School Echoing in the Mountains*, there was a movement that tried to promote life guidance. But the influence of *School Echoing in the Mountains* on fledgling life guidance was significant and extensive. Other educators followed suit and shared their practice and innovation through publications (e.g., Kondo, 1954; Konishi, 1955; Tsuchida, 1955; Toda, 1956). Kenjiro Konishi, an elementary teacher, published *Classroom Revolution* (*Gakkyu Kakumei*) in 1955. This work received far-reaching positive feedback throughout the country and was regarded as "an example that epitomizes the development of postwar life guidance practice" (Ota, Miyasaka, & Shiromaru, 1956, p. 40).

In *Classroom Revolution*, Konishi (1955; see also Konishi, 1966) presented a detailed description and analysis of the dynamics of the power structure of his class of 5th-graders. There was a boy named Naoaki in the class. He had many attributes as a group leader: His academic performance was the best among the boys; he was good at all sports; he was good-looking; and his father was the vice principal of the school. Konishi assumed that Naoaki was a natural leader rather than the boss of his class. In January, however, late in the academic year Konishi came across a diary written by Katsuro who bitterly complained about Naoaki's bossy behavior. The boy asked the teacher to allow him to read his diary in a class meeting to disclose his feelings. When the teacher inquired if Katsuro was certain he wanted to do that, the boy withdrew his request because he became frightened of the reactions of Naoki and his peers.

After that incident, Konishi made comments in Katsuro's diary encouraging Katsuro to reject Naoaki's unreasonable demands. The boy responded that he did not have the courage to do so and subsequently stopped writing about the problem after about 2 weeks. The fifth academic year ended in March without much change in the classroom dynamics.

When the students returned as 6th-graders in April, Konishi started end-of-day class meetings of 10 to 20 minutes, in which children reflected on various events in the classroom. Konishi encouraged students not only to disapprove of each other's faults and weaknesses but also to point out the merits of other students. Students were also encouraged to reflect on their own faults before they were pointed out by peers. He told his class that the teacher could also be criticized by students.

As these meetings continued for a half year the class succeeded in creating an open atmosphere in which their feelings could be discussed frankly. Finally one day in October Katsuro pointed out Naoaki's continued bullying behavior in the meeting and demanded an apology. Other students followed suit without hesitation. Thoroughly overwhelmed, Naoaki stood up weeping and apologized: "As everybody said, I have done cunning things and selfish things against you for a long time. I won't do such things from now on, so please forgive me" (Konishi, 1955, p. 203). This was a dramatic turnaround. This meeting prompted a change of the power structure of the 6th-graders. Having lost support from his peers, Naoaki stopped bullying the class. Konishi, however, worried that Naoaki would lose his self-esteem completely and that Katsuro would become a new boss. So he encouraged Naoaki not to be docile and stood by his side when necessary. Fortunately, as a new classroom culture began to develop, the boys learned how to behave, and the students enjoyed an uninhibited atmosphere for the rest of the last year in the elementary school.

Classroom Revolution is a record of how Konishi changed the culture of the class. He presented a living history of that class illuminating how it could change by the powerful voices expressed in students' compositions and by creating a free atmosphere in the classroom. His practice encouraged other teachers and had an important impact on teaching in Japan.

Before *Classroom Revolution* the life composition approach largely focused on individual students. By contrast *Classroom Revolution*'s focus shifted from individual students to the classroom culture, and power relationships in the class, and it demonstrated that change in power relationship could be brought about by the children themselves.

The publication of innovative teacher practice stimulated nationwide discussion on life guidance. Tetsufumi Miyasaka (1956), a professor at Tokyo University, elaborated on the concept of life guidance. He argued that "in short, life guidance is teaching the way to live" (p. 13) and that a teacher needs to guide not only children's behavior but also their ways of seeing, thinking, and feeling. He conceptualized classroom management as consisting of three steps: (1) creating an emotionally receptive ethos in the classroom; (2) enabling each student to disclose the reality of his or her life; and (3) creating a classroom culture where each person's problem is viewed as everybody's problem (Miyasaka & Haruta, 1957). Miyasaka insisted that life guidance is a process that should be embedded in every domain of schooling.

Criticism of Miyasaka's Conceptualization

Miyasaka's theory, however, was criticized by a group of teachers in Kagawa prefecture headed by Chuji Onishi. Miyasaka maintained that a feeling of classroom community can be created when children express themselves freely. In contrast, Onishi and his colleagues emphasized that group discipline must be developed before the children come to feel free to express themselves. They argued, "it is not right to start by creating an emotionally receptive ethos and then to create a community; it is our final goal to enable children to express themselves freely in such a receptive ethos" (Japan Teachers' Union, 1962, p. 120).

Onishi (1964) also criticized the practice described in *Classroom Revolution.* He argued that it was wrong for Konishi (1955) to assume initially that Naoki "hardly had the characteristics of a boss but he had many traits for a good leader" (p. 173). Onishi pointed out that those characteristics of a good leader were exactly the same attributes of a boss, and that the emergence of a good leader and a bullying boss follow the same process. To prevent a leader from becoming a boss, he insisted, it was essential to develop a classroom community in which students as a group acquired the ability to criticize the leader. Onishi passed negative judgment on Konishi for waiting for 9 months without making effort to build a classroom community.

The main purpose of life composition was originally to develop students' consciousness through writing but not necessarily to change the quality of groups. Japanese Composition Association (Nihon Sakubun no Kai) (1962), which was the main network of teachers who advanced the life composition approach, addressed the relationship between life composition and life guidance. The association argued that the main purpose of student compositions should be to develop children's skills of expression. Children's descriptions of their perceptions, thoughts, and activities presented in their compositions could be used to solve problems in their daily lives; but this was not the essential part of the composition approach, they argued. Thus the later development of the composition approach put more emphasis on developing children's writing skills. Some theorists, including Miyasaka (1963) and Ogawa (1966), argued that the association had abandoned the "life composition" approach and come to focus on mere "compositions."

EMERGING STRATEGIES TO BUILD A CLASSROOM COMMUNITY

Proposal for Creating Small Groups for Discussion

The second trend of life guidance was launched based on Onishi's approach. Onishi and his colleagues emphasized strategies for "building a classroom community" (*gakkyu shudanzukuri*). Now let us take a look at the distinct features of Onishi's practice.

During the 1960s Onishi devised a method for creating han or small groups and the leader as the core for discussion (*han-kaku-togi zukuri*). Onishi's method is described in his book *A Class That Has Leaders* (*Kaku no Iru Gakkyu*) published in 1963 (see also Onishi, 1991). The literal translation of *kaku* is "core," but Onishi meant "leader" by that term. The term *leader* in Japanese does not always signify individual leadership, but it often refers to an influential individual who supports members' participation and the decision-making process. As mentioned before, Onishi criticized classroom management based on the life composition approach for not paying enough attention to power relationships among students. Let us review four features of Onishi's practice at his lower secondary school.

First, Onishi collected information about the students in various ways. Before he met his 8th grade class in the new academic year, he checked the list of enrolled students in his homeroom for potential leaders and troublemakers, basing his review on their academic performance, physique, and the comments written by the teacher of the previous year. After the academic year started, he carefully observed the students and talked with them to identify the potential leaders and troublemakers, communicated with them in writing, and sometimes contacted their parents.

Second, Onishi underlined problem solving by students by urging them to learn from their experience rather than following his direction. He even let students fail to manage their class. However, when they recognized their failure, he gave them suggestions to solve the problems. For example, he allowed students to organize a han with their favorite friends first because that was their choice. His only demand was that members of a han would do various activities cooperatively, such as cleaning and studying. A han leader's task was to direct and support the members in the han, and han could be reorganized at the student's request. Boys and girls organized themselves separately. The teacher told the students that it was going to be their responsibility to create han without fearing if those han did not function well. Within a month, girls encountered an unfair decision made by the boys, the majority in the class. They complained to the teacher about it, but he told them in response that if they had mixed boys and girls when organizing the han, the problem would not have occurred, because the boys in the same han would have supported the girls. A girl said, "We did not know that the han had such an important role" (Onishi, 1963, p. 50). Following the teacher's advice, they persuaded the class to reorganize the han.

Third, Onishi gradually changed the system of classroom management. Although the first han were created by students themselves, he organized the han for the second time. When organizing the han for the third time, students elected the han leaders who chose the members. This put pressure on the han leaders to create good han.

Fourth, Onishi established the student procedure to check and control each other's behavior. At first, the leaders in the class were just like "errand boys/girls" for the other students, but he gradually taught them what leadership entails. When students did not collaborate with the leader, he reprimanded them stating that it was their responsibility to follow the leader's direction because they elected the leader. At the same time, he reiterated that it was the han leader's responsibility to issue necessary direction. When a student did not speak up in a meeting, chatted during a lesson, or did not clean the room properly, it was the han leader's duty to demand that han members do the task properly. Onishi introduced the system of nicchoku (monitors for the day) as supervisors. If a han was not working properly, it was the monitor's charge to check and bring the problem up in the end-of-day meetings for discussion. If a monitor was unfair, the class was expected to point it out. The teacher sometimes stirred and calmed the class members so that individual students received an appropriate level of censure.

Ultimately, Onishi was interested in transferring authority to the students. The students gradually learned the strategies he used for classroom management. As the number of students who could be effective han leaders increased, some of them started giving advice to each other just as the teacher did. The students also started organizing task groups of volunteers to solve particular problems identified by the students themselves.

Strategies to Develop a Formal System for Discussion

Let us discuss how Onishi's practice led to further exploration on building a classroom community. Onishi actively shared his practice and ideas at meetings of the Japanese Society for

Life Guidance Studies (Zenkoku Seikatsu Shido Kenkyu Kyogikai), referred to as Zenseiken hereafter. Zenseiken was organized in 1959 by researchers and teachers who were taking part in the annual conferences on research on education under the auspices of the Japan Teachers' Union (JTU). According to Shimahara (1998), JTU enrolled 90% of the teachers at that time. Zenseiken is a nationwide voluntary network of union teachers and university researchers interested in life guidance. It was reported that more than 3,000 people participated in the annual conferences of Zenseiken during the 1970s. In 2001, the organization still had approximately 4,000 members. I review Zenseiken's proposals next.

The first educator to lead Zenseiken was Miyasaka to whom I referred earlier; subsequently, Tsunekazu Takeuchi became the central leader of the network. Takeuchi, a university professor, was a former student of Miyasaka. They, however, had different views of life guidance. Miyasaka maintained that life guidance must be embedded in the whole schooling process whereas Takeuchi insisted that life guidance should be promoted mainly in the domain of special activities, not in the academic area.

Takeuchi (1962) argued that school education involves two functionary processes: controlling-managing and teaching-learning. It is imperative, he suggested, to identify the specific area of activity to organize students' self-governed community, which would assume a significant level of authority. Supporting Onishi's proposal for han creation in principle, he further suggested that general student meetings of the whole school be added as part of student community building.

Thus Zenseiken formulated the method of creating student groups in part based on Onishi's practice. Zenseiken's Standing Committee (ZSC, hereafter) published *Introduction to Building a Classroom Community (Gakkyu Shudanzukuri Nyumon)* in 1963 and its second edition in 1971. Both editions, which reflected the Soviet pedagogy with emphasis on "democratic centralism," presented strategies that may be adopted in the three stages of group development in a class and a school as a whole: (1) the initial "get-together stage," (2) the "early stage," and (3) the "later stage." The second edition described the community-building process in more detail and with more refinement.

At the get-together stage the teacher leads the class. He or she organizes the han, randomly assigning students to different han; or as an alternative, students can organize han with their favorite friends. Han leaders are selected by the teacher or through election. The teacher gives two initial suggestions: Everyone must speak out if he or she is put in a disadvantaged position and everybody must obey what the whole class decides.

At the early stage, class and han leaders become gradually independent from the teacher and begin to lead the class. The process has three phases. First, han leaders are elected by the whole class, and each han leader chooses his or her members. Han activities are supervised by the monitors (nicchoku). The whole class becomes capable of making proper decisions independently. Second, those students who have built the ability to lead the class, called "cores" (kaku), support the han leaders. At this phase the kaku are separated from han leaders; they check whether the han leadership is working and provide support to the han leaders. Also at this phase, the class members come to take it for granted to appraise themselves or other members in the class. Third, when more than half the members of the class have developed the ability to act as leaders the class starts to control itself. Han are reorganized periodically and student task groups deal with the problems in the entire class to be solved.

At the later stage, a firm sense of community is established in the class. The class independently makes proper decisions, as a group, to recall a leader when necessary. Each student feels fully entitled to participate in the process of decision making. As aforementioned, formal han give way gradually to voluntary task groups addressing issues picked out by the students. Eventually, students will start thinking beyond the limits of their classroom and begin taking into account matters affecting the management of the school as a whole. As the system of these three developmental stages suggests, Zenseiken emphasized explicit direction from a teacher at the get-together stage, but students were gradually granted opportunities to control their own community.

Thus Zenseiken's proposed approach is highly structured, and the idea of the three stages was applied to various contexts in rather simplistic ways. Zenseiken's strategists believed it was practical to organize a class as a social unit, in which formal decision making as a group was strongly emphasized.

Critique of Strategies for Building a Classroom Community

The preceding Zenseiken's strategies for building a classroom community were critiqued during the 1960s and 1970s. Four main points of criticism emerged. First, Zenseiken's three-stage proposal did not pay enough attention to the developmental stages of children. Ohashi (1964) commented that the two initial suggestions by the teacher (ZSC, 1963) were applied to all children without considering their age. Ogawa (1971) agreed that there was hardly any analysis of children's developmental stages in Zenseiken's proposal and questioned whether the strategies could be applied to younger students in elementary schools as well as students in upper secondary schools.

Second, some educators questioned the practicality of giving unlimited power to student groups. Ohashi (1964) asserted that strong emphasis on competition among han could lead to a situation where students criticize each other on the basis of their moralistic judgment rather than a careful examination of the deprived backgrounds of the troublemaking students. Teachers' intervention is called for when such a situation arises. Shiromaru (1964) also argued that the excessive emphasis on the primacy of groups over individuals would produce totalitarianism. He emphasized the necessity of ethical or intellectual development of students as the basis of collective decision making of the group.

Oride (2003) recently pointed out that Zenseiken's proposal was based on "democratic centralism" practiced in the Soviet Union, which also influenced the labor movements and the organizational principles of political parties in Japan. In fact, ZSC (1971) commented as follows: "the organizational principle of a democratic group is democratic centralism, and it is a self-governing group where people act in unity, aiming at achieving one single purpose [decided by the group]" (p. 56). This activates a system in which the group guides and controls itself, and gives priority to group decision making and the implementation of the group's decisions with less regard for individual students. Oride charged that this system can be repressive and produce problems for children outside the mainstream. Interestingly, however, classroom practitioners who were adherents of the Zenseiken's initiative tended to blame themselves if the Zenseiken's strategies did not work in their schools (Oride, 2003). Thus it took some time for Zenseiken to reconsider its proposal for building a classroom community.

Third, some argued for a revival of the life composition methods to develop children's awareness of realities. For example, Ogawa (1971) wrote that if there was not enough teaching in how to recognize students' own needs and how to express their values and demands, the management methods that looked like self-management by students would actually be no more than another form of teacher control. Thus he argued that Zenseiken should have learned more from the life composition methods that related students' daily lives to schooling.

Fourth, some critics pointed out that the Zenseiken's approach did not take into account student cultural and political activities. Ogawa (1971) insinuated that the formal han proposed by Zenseiken smacked of regimented schooling. In Zenseiken's proposal (ZSC, 1971), voluntary circles and cultural activities were introduced only at the "later stage," but Ogawa contended that such spontaneous and creative networks of the students had relevance from the beginning of the process of building a classroom community.

PROPOSAL FOR BUILDING LEARNING GROUPS

Collaborative Thinking in Lessons

The third trend of life guidance was promoted by Hiroshi Yoshimoto, a member of Zenseiken. Yoshimoto, an influential professor at Hiroshima University, applied the method of building a classroom community to teaching lessons. He called his approach the methods for "building learning groups" (*gakushu shudanzukuri*).

Yoshimoto paid special attention to Miyasaka's postulate (1962): The educational process involves two interrelated aspects, teaching lessons and creating a feeling of classroom community. And life guidance is inclusive of both. As we may recall, Miyasaka's approach was contrasted with Takeuchi's, which separated the two domains in the school curriculum.

Like Miyasaka, Yoshimoto (1974) maintained that the purpose of schooling is twofold: (1) teaching and transmitting cultural values to children and (2) teaching democratic ways of life in society and working in groups. He called the first aspect "instruction" and the second "discipline." He maintained that instruction is the part of education that forms knowledge, cognition, and skills whereas discipline fosters will, emotion, social behavior, and attitudes. When those two aspects of education are addressed the development of a person as a whole is enhanced. Yoshimoto's proposal is to integrate those two aspects in the instructional process.

When he argued for building learning groups, Yoshimoto was especially interested in the concept of *shudan shiko* (see Fujiwara, 1997, 2000). *Shudan shiko* is translated by some Japanese researchers as "group-thinking," but may be best understood as "collaborative thinking." It is a collaborative process involving interaction in whole-class discussion. Kihaku Saito and Yoshio Toi were two well-known practitioners who organized lessons according to this collaborative method. Saito (1958), who was the principal of an elementary school, gained leadership in teaching as he integrated his observation of teachers into his conception of teaching. Even when a student made a mistake in a lesson, he proposed to take advantage of that mistake to create a collaborative thinking process in which the class reflected on it without embarrassing the student. He forged a creative approach to teaching.

Likewise Toi (1962) used students' misconceptions creatively to promote collaborative thinking. When such misconceptions were presented in class, he demanded that students as a group inquire into the process in which these conceptions were constructed and the reasons for that construction. When Toi found that an underachieving student presented an inaccurate interpretation of a novel in his notebook, he told the student to share his interpretation with the class. Other students immediately reacted saying his interpretation was wrong, but the teacher stood on the student's side demanding that they offer evidence that supported their interpretation. This method prompted the entire class to read the novel again carefully in order to gain a deeper understanding.

Strategies for Building Learning Groups

We shall now turn to the strategies for building learning groups proposed by Yoshimoto. To facilitate the process of effective collaborative thinking in lessons, Yoshimoto (1974) identified two crucial elements in teaching: (1) establishing discipline for learning and (2) organizing stimulating questions. The first element included a process for organizing lessons in which all children participate in discussion and for establishing order for independent and collaborative learning. The second element consisted of deepening collaborative thinking and changing and developing students' cognitive process. The first element reflects the influence of Onishi's approach with emphasis on small group discussion based on han.

Let us look closely at the first element. To ensure all children participate in discussion, Yoshimoto suggested that teachers ask han to answer questions collectively instead of calling individual children. If the teacher raised questions and named individual students, it would take 40 minutes even if each student spoke only for 1 minute. This problem could be solved by han's cooperative work. Just giving time for han to discuss, however, was not enough to generate active discussion among han members. Yoshimoto emphasized the importance of clarifying the questions when the teacher prepared for lessons. Time is also a critical factor in a lesson. Yoshimoto suggested that time allocation to han be determined not only by the teacher but also by the han which should be free to request a specific amount of time necessary to work on a task at hand. In addition, he proposed that han members assess each other's performance. For example, at the end of a lesson or in an end-of-day meeting, students would be expected to evaluate their participation and contributions as well as problems. In this way, each student's difficulties were clarified and ways to overcome them could be suggested.

To establish order for independent and collaborative learning Yoshimoto expected han leaders to promote discipline for learning. For example, they must caution han members if they lost concentration on the task at hand. Han leaders were told to maintain effective time management. Yoshimoto assumed that if the teacher needed to exert external and formal control over a group, then the group did not have a sense of order. Students with an internal and conscious sense of order, he maintained, would discipline themselves and share their expectations with others. As Yoshimoto pointed out, the teacher's direct and verbal directions are almost useless in promoting active participation of students in learning. He stressed well-defined methods to develop self-discipline among students in lessons.

Let us now discuss the second element: organizing questions to generate stimulating discussion. Without thoughtful questions presented to students there would not be any meaningful discussion in the class. From Yoshimoto's perspective, thinking about and formulating pertinent and stimulating questions to be presented in a lesson is a crucial component of effective classroom management.

Yoshimoto argued that if you ask monolithic questions that have one right answer, students would just memorize the set of questions and answers and never gain cognitive skills for further inquiry. He emphasized the relevance of interaction among students as a way to develop their cognitive skills. For example, the teacher should be expected to teach children how to relate to each other's words: "I agree with A because...," "I want to add to B's opinion...," "I disagree with C because...." Interaction is also good for training for children to listen to each other.

Yoshimoto asserted that it was crucial for teachers to formulate stimulating questions based on careful research on the materials to be taught. He categorized three types of such questions. The first type is called "restricting" questions. He argued that questions such as "What do you think about this?" or "Just say what you think or feel," are so vague that students would have difficulty responding. The teacher must be specific in formulating questions. For example, rather than asking students to "Draw your mother's face," they should ask students to "Draw your mother's face when you come home," or ask "What is your mother's face like when you come home?"

The second type is called "relationship" questions. Yoshimoto proposed two kinds of relationship questions: questions that seek comparision, and questions which relate lesson content to the children's lives. In the first case, the teacher is expected to tell students to determine what is known and what is not known and to integrate their conclusions in a coherent statement by defining the relationship between the two. In the second case, the teacher would tell students to compare their opinions with evidence, reported materials, and their own experience. Students would begin to differentiate subjectivity and objectivity and how their lives are embedded in a broader context.

The third type of question categorized by Yoshimoto may be called "denial" questions. A denial question induces a sense of conflict, contradiction, and difficulty at a higher level of cognitive operation than that at which students usually work. These conflicts or contradictions shake the student's previous ideas and lead them to construct a new interpretation. Yoshimoto cited a typical example of a denial question from a lesson conducted by Saito (1963). In the lesson, children discussed where the forest exit was located in a particular story. They thought that the exit must be at the edge of the forest. As the children did not accept the teacher's view they began to seek more knowledge about the definition of the term *exit*.

As Yoshimoto's instructional method gained popularity in Japan, he published an edited book, which included case studies of lessons contributed by the teachers who applied his ideas. These case studies illustrated how students' ideas were constructed through comparison and teachers' stimulating inquiries (Yoshimoto, 1972).

Critique of the Approach of Building Learning Groups

Other Zenseiken members became critical of Yoshimoto's approach, which was built on Miyasaka's view that schooling is an integrated process. The strongest criticism came from Masaharu Haruta, and the debate between Yoshimoto and Haruta continued for several years. As mentioned earlier, for Yoshimoto, instruction and "discipline" (training in behavior) were two interrelated aspects of subject lessons. In contrast, Haruta (1975) argued that instruction and discipline were two separate functions of education, and he contended that teachers should distinguish different purposes for lessons and special activities. His view reflected Zenseiken's position (ZSC, 1971), which maintained that during subject lessons, discipline, or training in behavior, is subordinate to instruction, whereas during special activities, instruction is subordinate to discipline. Although Haruta admitted that all educational activities involve those two functions, he insisted that greater emphasis should be placed on instruction or what he called the "organized learning of knowledge and skills." This emphasis on the distinction between subject lessons and special activities was shared by Onishi (1966) and Takeuchi (1975).

In his rebuttal Yoshimoto contended that if instruction and discipline were dichotomized, teaching in subject lessons would become a one-way transmission of knowledge, whereas special activities would be left to students' self-government and freedom. Haruta saw Yoshimoto's view as undermining the high status of instruction.

It is evident that Zenseiken members differed in terms of the definition of building a community for learning and personal development. This led to a prolonged debate on instruction and discipline. Onishi (1966) perceived a class as "a place where all the problems of children's lives flow into," but his ultimate intention was to develop alternative groups for solving problems in children's lives and finally to reestablish "a class" as a group particularly for learning subjects (pp. 10–11). Takeuchi (1975) also expected that students would develop beyond the need for formal direction by a teacher; when this happened, a teacher would become a special member of the students' society and start offering more personal guidance. On the other hand, Yoshimoto (1974) argued that the teacher's authority is not undermined even when students' self-governing skills develop. "Self-governing activities [of students] without a teacher's guidance would rapidly stagnate or fail," he wrote (p. 48).

Expounding strategies for building learning groups, Yoshimoto (1978) called attention to responsive relationships between the teacher and children and among the children. He offered the following developmental stages of such responsive relationships (1979): (1) children look at the speaker when the teacher or a child is talking to them; (2) when being asked a question or talked to, children respond by gesture (e.g., nodding, inclining their heads); (3) children become active inquirers by asking questions and making suggestions; and (4) children analyze, compare, and generalize the content of the lesson, by using words such as "To give the details . . . ," "Therefore . . . in short," "I follow, I don't agree, I agree . . . ," "That is because . . . ," and so on. In the 1980s Yoshimoto (1985) identified the attributes of good lessons by way of the metaphor of drama. For him the classroom is a theater where evolving responsive relationships unfold.

Yoshimoto's metaphor of the classroom as theater reflected changing relationships between teachers and students at all levels. Since the 1970s pressure for high school and college entrance examinations was intensifying. Society became urbanized, affluent, and diversified. Both adults and children adopted materialism as a dominant social ethos and internationalization as Japan's trade penetrated all corners of the globe. Consequently children's needs and interests became diversified, and they resisted traditional authoritarianism and uniformity in schools through creative tactics involving violence, truancy, disruption, and outright challenge to authorities. Japanese parents, children, and teachers experienced a legitimacy crisis beginning in the late 1970s. This had an immense influence on teaching and classroom management, especially the relationship between teachers and students.

NEW DEVELOPMENT OF STRATEGIES FOR BUILDING A CLASSROOM COMMUNITY

Latest Strategies for Building a Classroom Community

The fourth trend of life guidance emerged in the late 1980s and was widely discussed in the Zenseiken circle during the 1990s. As students' problems proliferated throughout the country, teachers affiliated with Zenseiken began to formulate new strategies for life guidance different from Onishi's approach.

Let us first review life guidance developed by Machiko Harada (2001) as an example. There were four violent children (the "bad kids") in the 5th grade at her elementary school. Three of them, Tomoya, Yosuke, and Yamato, were assigned to Harada's class; the last child, Rikiya—the boss among the four—was in another class in the same grade. All four children were notorious for their interruption of lessons, truancy, and bullying. The teacher previously responsible for the four children had disciplined them severely, but their disorderly classroom conduct had merely worsened.

When Harada started the new academic year, she decided to take an active interest in them instead of disciplining them. In response, the children started to display curiosity about their new teacher. Every time Harada reprimanded them, they exhibited aggressively negative reactions to her, but she was convinced that the new strategy was working.

At the same time, Harada helped create an informal network of the victims of bullying in order to give them a secure place to express their feelings. One day, Harada secretly gathered these victims and asked them why they thought the three boys continued to bully other students. The victims said that they did not know the reasons and that they had never thought about the question. She asked them to help her, saying, "There is no child who bullies without a reason. No, I don't mean that Kaori or Ayaka [the victims] were wrong. There must be reasons for what bullies do. I am going to find them out by talking with Tomoya, the other boys, and their mothers. Please think about it" (p. 119). Thus a "cheering-up society," an informal support network of children, started. The network involved a feedback system that enabled students to engage in talks about bullying, victimization and the desire for respectful relationships.

Harada gradually developed rapport with the three bullying boys. Though the boys continued to interrupt lessons, they would come up to her afterwards, telling her that they would love to talk with her. After half a month, Harada came to know that they were also threatened by the boss, Rikiya. Each of the three children was bullied by Rikiya, and the four boys were united in bullying other children. She discovered that Rikiya himself was a victim of his father's violence. As the situation became fully understood, the "cheering-up society" became a supporting group for the three boys in Harada's class. Two months later, as the three children started feeling comfortable in the class, they gained independence from Rikiya.

During this process, however, their violent behavior, truancy, and chatting in lessons continued. Other students remained scared of their violent classmates, and it was not possible for them to discuss their problems openly. Harada encouraged them to discuss the problems in class newsletters where she allowed them to present their undisguised reactions to bullying in anonymity. Even the "bad kids" had an opportunity to express their emerging thoughts to support human rights in the newsletters. As they were distributed to the class she invited other students' reactions. Thus, the class's "invisible understanding" gradually evolved.

Then, one day, the teacher held a meeting to discuss problems in lessons. She read students' anonymous statements that disparaged the three bullying boys: "I want enjoyable lessons, but somebody always laughs at us," "We cannot give our opinions because somebody would mock us," and "I cannot understand the lesson because somebody keeps chatting loudly." The bullies could not bear those condemnations and ran away, but soon they were brought back to the classroom. The teacher asked, "Why did you run away?" Yamato replied, "They are all disparaging us. It makes me feel sick!" Tomoya said, "It is sneaky. Teacher, tell me. Who wrote what?" Harada told them that it was necessary to protect the identity of the students who wrote these remarks. She told them that they would be able to give their opinions openly someday. The bullies darted angry looks at other students, but in the meantime they started writing their own remarks such as: "It is troublesome to copy what is on the blackboard to our notebooks. Meaningless!", "I don't like arithmetic lessons because only those who understand it will speak," and so on. The teacher admitted their opinions were also legitimate (pp. 125–126). Through these interactions, it gradually became possible to discuss problems openly in the class.

This informal network approach represents a shift in life guidance from the earlier paradigm for building a classroom community based on han. In the emerging approach the formal system of han does not play a role. Instead, a more informal network addressed the victims and later the bullying kids. The teacher did not prompt students to discuss openly the problems in the classroom for some time until they felt secure.

Since the late 1980s some classroom teachers have been turning away from formal systems such as han and committees in favor of student voluntary networks. For example, Jun'ichi Kurishiro (2002) reported that when his 8th-grade students held a farewell event for the graduating 9th-graders, they organized voluntary work groups across all classes that planned various activities. All students, including those often stigmatized for poor academic performance, could participate in interclass cooperative projects. These shifts in life guidance occurred because the social context of students' lives were affected by changing society and families.

Building a Community Based on Student Participation

The shift in teaching practice discussed in the preceding section led researchers to revise their theory-induced strategies. In the latest editions of *Introduction to Building a Classroom Community* (ZSC, 1990 for elementary schools; ZSC, 1991 for lower secondary schools) Zenseiken dropped the controversial three stages for building a classroom community. Whereas in the 1971 edition, the chapter on building a classroom community focused on organizing han, the later editions emphasize the organization of discussion instead of han activities. The new editions place an emphasis on creating a supportive classroom environment. Teachers are advised to pay attention to individual children's needs, desires, problems, and how they view their lives (ZSC, 1990). This advice is particularly critical because children tend to conceal their personal feelings and difficulties at school. Because it is rare for children to frankly express their complaints in their conversations with teachers, Zenseiken advises practitioners to enhance their communication with children through writing as well as dialogue (ZSC, 1991).

In 1994 Zenseiken's conference committee formulated the theme for the 36th Zenseiken conference titled "Learning, Self-Governance and the Promotion of Student Participation." The conference theme clearly reflects an emerging emphasis on student participation. At the conference greater attention was given to the imperative of communication between teachers and students to understand their personal interests and problems, and the need to develop close relationships with students to provide informed guidance and support to students.

Oride (2003) declared that "democratic centralism," which was the pivotal concept for Zenseiken in building a classroom community during the 1960s and 1970s, was now outdated. Democratic centralism pursued the goals of the group and its integrity within a formal and hierarchical system of decision making. He suggested that such a system cannot meet the needs of children at present. Students' interests and problems are now multifaceted and diverse. Oride maintained that "participatory democracy" should be promoted so as to hear students' voices and attend to their needs.

Revival of Life Guidance Through Lessons

Another line of pursuit in the Zenseiken circle is the revival of life guidance through lessons. Practitioners have returned to Miyasaka's pedagogy and begun to reexamine the purpose of lessons with particular attention to children's needs. A representative scenario can be found in Kazuko Yoshida (1997). In a lesson on "Family Law" at her upper secondary school, Yoshida asked the students, "What do you think about the problems of adultery and divorce described in the film *Champ*?" Some of the students complained that the question was crude and stupid, so Yoshida suggested that they formulate a better question that would lead to a meaningful discussion (p. 121). They did so, and were then able to examine the content in a way that was relevant to the social and cultural contexts of their own lives.

It is worth emphasizing this revival has produced another approach to "life guidance through lessons" that is different from Yoshimoto's. Whereas Yoshimoto argued for building students' groups in subject lessons, the theorists of the fourth trend emphasized the importance of reexamining the lesson content from students' perspectives. Takeuchi (1989) commented that teachers routinely organize lessons whose main purpose is to impart "'official knowledge' defined by the authority" into the mind of the student (p. 14). These lessons squash students' ideas and feelings constructed in their everyday life. It is vital, in Takeuchi's view, that teachers first of all learn from children's points of view in order to create a curriculum which challenges children's perspectives (p. 15). He (1993) advocated a curriculum in which students critically examine their social situations from the perspective of the rights of individuals and groups, start working on them, and, by doing so, develop their "knowledge, skills, attitudes and values" (p. 217). Oride (2003) supported Takeuchi's argument and pointed out the importance of enhancing global perspectives and understandings of essential concepts in students, and of students' collaborative communities for problem solving (pp. 267–270).

In summary, I have discussed the postwar development of classroom management promoted by innovative practitioners and members of Zenseiken. We paid attention to a set of proposals formulated by practitioners and theoreticians in that organization to create and re-create life guidance, which is the central concept of classroom management. Zenseiken's position shifted from democratic centralism, the socialist ideology, to a flexible view of managing students in postindustrial Japan.

It may be worth mentioning that people have started noticing that the characteristics of students' problems have been changing. Students are no longer docile and orderly in the classroom. During the 1980s, it was "delinquent kids" who actively resisted, rebelled, and asserted their needs and identities. Since the 1990s, it has often been observed that "normal kids" suddenly become furious and harm other children. Children tend to have much difficulty in expressing themselves, even though they have "stormy hearts." This seems to be why practitioners and university professors have recognized the centrality of understanding students and their values.

CONCLUSION

The first section of this chapter outlined the general characteristics of classroom management in Japan. The group-based approach we explored centered on the creation and application of han, or small groups. Subsequent sections reviewed four main trends of life guidance in postwar Japan. Practitioners and theoretically oriented university researchers developed various approaches to creating a feeling of classroom community. Practitioners of the life composition methods developed shortly after the war sought to enhance students' critical consciousness through writing. This uniquely Japanese method enabled teachers to organize class discussion based on student writings. Teachers endeavored to build a classroom community during the 1960s and 1970s to enhance discussing problems in classes. The concept of han was introduced as a central tool in life guidance. Some practitioners applied the han-focused approach to teaching lessons during the 1970s and 1980s. After the tumultuous 1980s the paradigm of building a classroom community shifted to new strategies to promote students' participation and decision making. Reexamination of the lesson content has also become a focus.

This chapter paid particular attention to Zenseiken and the efforts of its teachers to actively explore strategies for creating communities in a classroom. The final question not explored in this chapter is: To what extent have these strategies been shared with, and adopted by, grassroots teachers in the entire country? Have they been generalized as commonly accepted methods of classroom management? These questions call for further research.

Various issues have been raised throughout this chapter. Should life guidance be promoted in both lessons and special activities? Should it be restricted to special activities? Which one of the following should be emphasized over the other: the enhancement of critical consciousness or the development of certain types of student behavior? Should teachers develop a formal system to handle students' grievances and deviant behavior? Should they rather develop informal and voluntary networks of students to attack them as they develop?

Based on my examination of the four trends of classroom management, I believe that we should conduct life guidance both in special activities and in lessons, but teachers should use different strategies in the different domains of schooling. In special activities, it is necessary to create supportive networks of students as well as formal systems of discussion. Student groups in special activities are designed to teach students how to become active citizens. Teachers and children ultimately need to share power as citizens even though teachers must guide students with creative strategies. This is why creating student communities is most appropriate in special activities. On the other hand, teachers are specialists and must assert their authority in teaching lessons. The main objective of the lesson is to teach the subject content, not to create groups. Teachers, nevertheless, need to consider how subject content is being embedded in each child's real life, in order to develop a more meaningful curriculum. Learning in the content area does change students' cognitive skills and perspectives, which would also lead to changes in their attitudes and behaviors in their community.

Lastly, it is worth emphasizing the importance of the way the theories of life guidance have developed throughout the postwar era. As Stigler and Hiebert (1999) pointed out, Japanese schools have a tradition of continuously improving educational practice based on the initiatives of the teachers. It is largely the teachers who develop new ideas and put them into practice. Based on their accumulated practice and knowledge, classroom teachers and university researchers collaboratively develop educational theories. These initiatives of the teachers are indispensable for better classroom management.

ACKNOWLEDGMENTS

I wish to express my sincere gratitude to the reviewers: Tracey Gannon, Karen Leach, Catherine Lewis, Nobuo K. Shimahara, Carol Weinstein, and Theo Wubbels. This chapter owes much to their thoughtful comments. My special thanks are due to Professor Shimahara, who has kindly examined the entire manuscript and made numerous helpful suggestions. I am also very grateful to Koji Tanaka for valuable advice and encouragement.

REFERENCES

Amano, M. (1993). *Research on the history of educational evaluation and assessment: Genealogy of the evaluation and assessment theories in educational practice* [Kyoiku hyokashi kenkyu: kyoiku jissen ni okeru hyoka-ron no keifu]. Tokyo: Toshindo.

Fujiwara, Y. (1990). Several trends of the research on learning groups during the 1980s [1980 nendai ni okeru gakushu shudan kenkyu no doukou]. In the *Bulletin of College of Education, University of the Ryukyus* [Ryukyu Daigaku Kyoiku Gakubu Kiyo], No. 36, I, pp. 207–217.

Fujiwara, Y. (1993). The process of forming the theory of teaching lessons based on the idea of building learning groups (2): Development of Hitoshi Yoshimoto's theory of teaching lessons after 1971 [Gakushu shudanzukuri wo kitei toshita jugyo shido-ron no keisei katei (2): 1971 nen iko ni okeru Yoshimoto Hitoshi no jugyo shido-ron no tenkai]. In the *Bulletin of College of Education, University of the Ryukyus* [Ryukyu Daigaku Kyoiku Gakubu Kiyo], No. 42, I, pp. 161–181.

Fujiwara, Y. (1997). Examining the concept of collaborative thinking developed in lesson study in postwar Japan [Sengo Nihon no jugyo kenkyu-shi ni okeru shudan shiko gainen no kento]. In the *Bulletin of College of Education, University of the Ryukyus* [Ryukyu Daigaku Kyoiku Gakubu Kiyo], No. 51, I, pp. 21–31.

Fujiwara, Y. (2000). Significant points and remaining issues in research on learning groups in the field of lesson study in postwar Japan [Sengo jugyo kenkyu ni okeru gakushu shudan kenkyu no seika to kadai]. In the *Bulletin of College of Education, University of the Ryukyus* [Ryukyu Daigaku Kyoiku Gakubu Kiyo], No. 56, pp. 69–79.

Funagoshi, M. (2001). Guidance [Seikatsu shido]. In Y. Kubo et al. (Eds.), *Dictionary of modern education history* [Gendai Kyoiku-shi Jiten] (pp. 279–280). Tokyo: Tokyoshoseki.

Harada, M. (2001). Being with the "bad kids" ["Warugaki" tachi to tomoni]. In ZSC [Zenseiken's Standing Committee: Zenseiken Jonin Iinkai] (Ed.), *Overcoming violence: How to confront disorder in classrooms* [Boryoku wo koeru: Kyoshitsu no muchitsujo to dou mukiauka] (pp. 116–132). Tokyo: Otsuki-shoten.

Haruta, M. (1975). Examining the theories of Yoshimoto (1) [Yoshimoto riron wo kentosuru (1)]. In Zenseiken (Ed.), *Life Guidance* [Seikatsu Shido], No. 214, Tokyo, Meijitosho, pp. 67–76.

Iwama, H. (1989). Japan's group orientation in secondary schools." In J. Shields (Ed.), *Japanese schooling: Patterns of socialization, equality, and political control* (pp. 73–95). University Park: Pennsylvania State University Press.

Japan Teachers' Union [JTU: Nihon Kyoshokuin Kumiai]. (Ed.). (1962). *Education practices for the people: Theories on life guidance* [Kokumin no tameno kyoiku jissen: Seikatsu shido-ron]. Tokyo: Author.

Japanese Composition Association [JCA: Nihon Sakubun no Kai]. (1962). Let's move forward with convictions based on our meaningful tradition: Proposal of an action plan for the future [Igiaru dento no motoni kakushin wo motte zenshinshiyo: Kongo no katsudo hoshin an]. In JCA (Ed.), *Compositions and Education* [Sakubun to Kyoiku], Vol. 13, No. 9 (August), Tokyo, Yuri-shuppan, pp. 94–115.

Kataoka, T. (1992). Class management and student guidance in Japanese elementary and lower secondary schools. In R. Leestma & H. Walberg (Eds.), *Japanese educational productivity* (pp. 69–102). Ann Arbor: University of Michigan, Center for Japanese Studies.
Kondo, E. (1954). *Life guidance for children left behind* [Okureta kodomo no seikatsu shido]. Tokyo: Meijitosho.
Konishi, K. (1955). *Classroom revolution* [Gakkyu kakumei]. Tokyo: Makishoten.
Konishi, K. (1966) . Revolution of the class [Gakkyu no kakumei]. In S. Miyahara & I. Kokubu (Eds.), *A selection of records of education practices*: Vol. 3 [Kyouiku jissen kiroku senshu: Dai 3- kan] (pp. 67–95). Tokyo: Shin-Hyoron.
Kurishiro, J. (2002). Discussion drives students: Examining the practice of the "Farewell Event for Graduating 9th Graders" [Hanashiai ga yaruki wo hikidasu: "3 Nensei wo Okuru Kai" no torikumi wo megutte]. In Zenseiken (Ed.), *Life Guidance [Seikatsu Shido]*, No. 583, Tokyo, Meijitosho, pp. 57–68.
LeTendre, G. (2000). *Learning to be adolescent: Growing up in U.S. and Japanese middle schools*. New Haven, CT: Yale University Press.
Lewis, C. (1995). *Educating hearts and minds: Reflections on Japanese preschool and elementary education*. New York: Cambridge University Press.
MESSC [Ministry of Education, Science, Sports and Culture: Mombusho]. (2000). *Education in Japan 2000: A graphic presentation*. Tokyo: Gyosei.
Miyasaka, T. (1956). The essence of life guidance [Seikatsu shido no honshitsu]. In T. Miyasaka (Ed.), *Course-book school education, Vol. 11: Guidance* [Kouza gakko kyoiku, Dai 11-kan: Seikatsu shido] (pp. 11–38). Tokyo: Meijitosho.
Miyasaka, T. (1962). *Basic theories on life guidance* [Seikatsu shido no kiso riron], Tokyo: Seishin-shobo.
Miyasaka, T. (1963). *Collectivism and life composition* [Shudan-shugi to seikatsu tsuzurikata]. Tokyo: Meijitosho.
Miyasaka, T. & Haruta, M. (1957). Tenth section: Life guidance [Daiju bunkakai: Seikatsu shido]. In Japan Teachers' Union [JTU: Nihon Kyoshokuin Kumiai] (Ed.), *Education in Japan: Vol. 6* [Nihon no Kyoiku: Dai 6 shu] (pp. 345–384). Tokyo: Kokudosha.
Muchaku, S. (Ed.). (1950). *Locomotive 2* [Kikansya 2] (originally an unpublished collection of students' compositions). In Japanese Composition Association [JTU: Nihon Sakubun no Kai] (Ed.) (1994), *Class collections of compositions in prewar and postwar Japan* [Senzen-sengo Nihon no gakkyu bunko] (pp. 211–276). Tokyo: Ozorasha.
Muchaku, S. (Ed.). (1951). *School echoing in the mountains* [Yamabiko gakko]. Tokyo: Seidosha.
Muchaku, S. (Ed.). (1995). *School echoing in the mountains* [Yamabiko gakko]. Tokyo: Iwanami-shoten.
Ogawa, T. (1966). *Life composition and education* [Seikatsu tsuzurikata to kyoiku]. Tokyo: Meijitosho.
Ogawa, T. (1971). Book review: *Introduction to Building a Classroom Community (2nd Ed.)*: A summative reflection on ten years of "forming *han*, leaders and discussion" method [Shohyo: *Gakkyu Shudanzukuri Nyumon (Dai 2-han)*: "Han-Kaku-Togi zukuri" 10 nen no soukatsu]. In Zenseiken (Ed.), *Life Guidance* [Seikatsu Shido], No. 160, Tokyo: Meijitosho, pp. 80–83.
Ohashi, K. (1964). An analysis on the *Introduction to Building a Classroom Community (The Latter Part)* [Gakkyu Shudanzukuri Nyumon no bunseki (Ge)]. In Zenseiken (Ed.), *Life Guidance* [Seikatsu Shido], No. 57, Tokyo, Meijitosho, pp. 64–72.
Onishi, C. (1963). *A class that has leaders* [Kaku no iru gakkyu]. Tokyo: Meijitosho.
Onishi, C. (1964). *A class that has han* [Han no aru gakkyu]. Tokyo: Meijitosho.
Onishi, C. (1966). The Process of forming learning groups [Gakushu shudan no keisei katei]. In Zenseiken (Ed.), *Life Guidance* [Seikatsu Shido], No. 83, Tokyo, Meijitosho, pp. 9–22.
Onishi, C. (1991). *Onishi Chuji's writings on educational techniques* [Onishi Chuji kyoiku gijutsu chosakushu]. Tokyo: Meijitosho.
Oride, K. (2003). *Education in civil society: Characteristics of relationships and methods* [Shimin syakai no kyoiku: Kankei-sei to houhou]. Tokyo: Sofusha.
Ota, T., Miyasaka, T., & Shiromaru, F. (1956). Development of classroom management after *School Echoing in the Mountains* [Yamabiko Gakko igono gakkyu keiei no hatten]. In Nationwide Network for Research on the Science of Education [Kyoiku Kagaku Kenkyu Zenkoku Renraku Kyogikai] (Ed.), *Education [Kyoiku]*, No. 58 (April), pp. 37–43.
Saito, K. (1958). *Academic achievements that continue for the future* [Mirai ni tsunagaru gakuryoku]. Tokyo: Mugishobo.
Saito, K. (1963). *Lessons: That transform children* [Jugyo: Kodomo wo henkaku surumono]. Tokyo: Kokudosya.
Sato, M. (1998). Classroom management in Japan: A social history of teaching and learning. In N. Shimahara (Ed.), *Politics of classroom life: Classroom management in international perspective* (pp. 189–214). New York: Garland.
Sato, N. (2004). *Inside Japanese classrooms: The heart of education*. New York: Routledge/Falmer.
Shimahara, N. (1998). Classroom management in Japan: Building a classroom community. In N. Shimahara (Ed.), *Politics of classroom life: Classroom management in international perspective* (pp. 215–238). New York: Garland.
Shiromaru, F. (1964). Keynote report [*Kicho hokoku*]. In Zenseiken (Ed.), *Life Guidance* [Seikatsu shido], No. 63 Tokyo, Meijitosho, pp. 82–90.

Shishido, T. (1985). Theories on life guidance [Seikatsu shido-ron]. In T. Ogawa & H. Kakinuma (Eds.), *Education theories in postwar Japan, the latter volume*, [Sengo-Nihon no kyoiku riron (Ge)] (pp. 112–152). Kyoto Japan: Minerva-shobo.

Stigler, J., & Hiebert, J. (1999). *The teaching gap: Best ideas from the world's teachers for improving education in the classroom*. New York: Free Press.

Takeuchi, T. (1962). The position of students' community-building in school education [Gakko kyoiku ni okeru seito shudanzukuri no ichi]. In Zenseiken (Ed.), *Life Guidance [Seikatsu Shido]*, No. 38, Tokyo, Meijitosho, pp. 106–114.

Takeuchi, T. (1975). Examining studies on the guidance of learning groups [Gakushu shudan no shido no kenkyu wo megutte]. In Zenseiken (Ed.), *Life Guidance* [Seikatsu Shido], No. 212, Tokyo, Meijitosho, pp. 11–20.

Takeuchi, T. (1989). Introduction to lessons for teachers: Reexamination of life guidance through subjects [Kyoshi no tameno jugyo nyumon: Kyoka wo toshite no seikatsu shido saiko]. In Zenseiken (Ed.), *Life Guidance* [Seikatsu Shido], No. 393, Tokyo, Meijitosho, pp. 9–18.

Takeuchi, T. (1993). Why turn learning into a problem now? [Ima naze gakushu wo mondai ni surunoka]. In The Japan Society for the Study of Education [Nihon Kyoiku Gakkai], *The Japanese Journal of Educational Research* [Kyoikugaku Kenkyu], *60*(3), 211–218.

Toda, T. (1956). *Fellows called class* [Gakkyu toiu nakama]. Tokyo: Makishoten.

Toi, Y. (1962). *Inquiry into lessons of Japanese language* [Kokugo jugyo no tankyu]. Tokyo: Meijitosho.

Tsuchida, S. (1955). *First graders of the village* [Mura no ichinensei]. Tokyo: Shin-Hyoronsha.

Tsuneyoshi, R. (2001). *The Japanese model of schooling: Comparisons with the United States*. New York: Routledge/Falmer.

Yoshida, K. (1997). *Creation of the educational practice of feminism: Freedom to reorganize a "family"* [Feminism kyoiku jissen no sozo: "Kazoku" eno jiyu]. Tokyo: Aoki-shoten.

Yoshimoto, H. (1974). *Theories on disciplinal teaching* [Kun'ikuteki kyoju no riron]. Tokyo: Meijitosho.

Yoshimoto, H. (1978). Self-governing groups and learning groups, 7: What educational evaluative activities mean (2) [Jichiteki shudan to gakushu shudan, 7: Shidoteki hyoka katsudo towa nanika (2)]. In *Research on Special Activities* [Tokubetsu Katsudo Kenkyu], No. 130 (October), Tokyo, Meijitosho, pp. 126–131.

Yoshimoto, H. (1979). "Self-governing groups and learning groups, 12: What establishing lessons means (2) [Jichiteki shudan to gakushu shudan, 12: Jugyo no seiritsu towa nanika (2)]. In *Research on Special Activities* [Tokubetsu Katsudo Kenkyu], No. 135 (March), Tokyo, Meijitosho, pp. 126–131.

Yoshimoto, H. (1985). *Introduction to establishing lessons: Creating dramas in the classrooms!* [Jugyo seiritsu nyumon: Kyoshitsu ni dorama wo!]. Tokyo: Mijitosho.

Yoshimoto, H. (Ed.). (1972). *Introduction to building learning groups* [Gakushu shudanzukuri nyumon]. Tokyo: Meijitosho.

Zenseiken's Conference Committee [Zenseiken Kicho Teian Iinkai]. (1994). Keynote proposal: Learning, self-governance and the promotion of "student participation" [Kicho teian: "Sanka" ni Hirakareta gakushu to jichi wo]. In Zenseiken (Ed.), *Life Guidance* [Seikatsu Shido], No. 473, Tokyo, Meijitosho, pp. 118–125.

ZSC [Zenseiken's Standing Committee: Zenseiken Jonin Iinkai]. (1963). *Introduction to building a classroom community* [Gakkyu shudanzukuri nyumon]. Tokyo: Meijitosho.

ZSC. (1971). *Introduction to building a classroom community* (2nd ed.) [Gakkyu shudanzukuri nyumon (Dai 2-han)]. Tokyo: Meijitosho.

ZSC. (1990). *The new edition of introduction to building a classroom community: Elementary schools* [Shinban gakkyu shudanzukuri nyumon: Syogakko]. Tokyo: Meijitosho.

ZSC. (1991). *The New edition of introduction to building a classroom community: Lower secondary schools* [Shinban gakkyu shudanzukuri nyumon: Chugakko]. Tokyo: Meijitosho.

About the Authors

Carolyn M. Evertson is professor of education emerita, Peabody College, Vanderbilt University. She received her undergraduate degree in elementary education and her doctorate in educational psychology from The University of Texas at Austin and directed the Classroom Organization and Effective Teaching Program at The University of Texas Research and Development Center for Teacher Education. Her background in elementary education influenced a program of research at the Center that focused on classroom management. She and her colleagues conducted the first systematic studies of how teachers orchestrate activities and achieve order in classrooms from the first days of school. This work was extended to other programs of research exploring how teachers manage classrooms in different school contexts. At Vanderbilt University this research formed the basis for *COMP: Creating Conditions for Learning*, a program that has assisted over 75,000 teachers in understanding and enacting productive classroom environments. Her writings include over 100 chapters, articles, books, and monographs on classroom management, teacher education, learning in classroom settings, and research on teaching. Her books include two textbooks for beginning teachers (co-authored with Edmund Emmer and Murray Worsham), *Classroom Management for Elementary Teachers* and *Classroom Management for Middle and High School Teachers* (Allyn & Bacon) in their 7th editions. She can be contacted at carolyn.evertson@vanderbilt.edu

Carol S. Weinstein is professor emerita in the Department of Learning and Teaching at Rutgers Graduate School of Education. She received her bachelor's degree in psychology from Clark University in Worcester, Massachusetts, and her master's and doctoral degrees from Harvard Graduate School of Education. Her early research focused on the impact of classroom design on students' behavior and attitudes. She pursued this topic for many years, writing about the ways that classroom environments can be designed to facilitate teachers' goals and to foster children's learning and development. Her interest in organizing classroom space eventually expanded to include classroom organization and management in general. She is the author of *Secondary Classroom Management: Lessons From Research and Practice* (McGraw-Hill, 2003), *Elementary Classroom Management: Lessons From Research and Practice* (with Andrew J. Mignano, Jr.; McGraw-Hill, 2003), and numerous chapters and articles on classroom management and teacher education students' beliefs about caring and control. Most recently, she has focused on the need for "culturally responsive classroom management," or classroom management in the service of social justice. In 2000, Dr. Weinstein was recognized for her efforts with the "Contributing Researcher Award" from the American Federation of Teachers for "bridging the gap between theory and practice in effective classroom management." She can be contacted at csw@rci.rutgers.edu

Victor Battistich is associate professor of education at the University of Missouri, St. Louis. His interests center on how the social context of schools influences children's socioemotional and moral development. His publications have examined the effects of classroom practices and student–teacher relationships, school climate, school-based intervention programs, and comprehensive school reform efforts on the positive development of youth. He can be contacted at vicb@umsl.edu.

Miriam Ben Peretz is professor emerita on the Faculty of Education, University of Haifa, Israel. She studies the interaction between teachers and curriculum and teachers' learning from experience. Her recent publications have examined the role of the teachers' lounge in improving learning environments in schools and issues of reform policies. She can be contacted at mperetz@construct.haifa.ac.il.

Cheryl Mason Bolick is an assistant professor in the School of Education at the University of North Carolina at Chapel Hill. The focus of her research is the integration of technology into social studies education. Her most recent work addresses teaching and learning with digital history resources. She can be contacted at cbolick@unc.edu.

Hank Bohanon is an assistant professor, School of Education at Loyola University of Chicago, where he is program advisor for the special education program. He has been a research co-ordinator for the Rehabilitation Research and Training Center on Positive Behavior Support. He received his doctorate from the University of Kansas in special education. He is currently conducting research in the Chicago public schools on high school PBS. He can be reached at hbohano@luc.edu.

Amanda Rabidue Bozack, M.A. educational psychology, is a research assistant and doctoral student in educational psychology at The University of Arizona. Her research interests include motivation, comprehensive school reform, and teacher professional development.

Ellen Brantlinger is professor of special education in the curriculum and instruction department at Indiana University. She is interested in disability studies, social class and schooling issues, critical theory, and qualitative research. Her recent books include *Dividing Classes: How the Middle Class Negotiates and Rationalizes School Advantage* and *Who Benefits From Special Education: Remediating (Fixing) Other People's Children*. She can be reached at brantlin@indiana.edu.

Mieke Brekelmans is associate professor at IVLOS, Institute of Education at Utrecht University (The Netherlands). Her interest is the study of teaching from multiple perspectives, in particular the interpersonal and learning activities perspective. Her focus is on the relation between teacher thinking and action, and the development of teaching during the professional teacher career. She can be contacted at j.m.g.brekelmans@ivlos.uu.nl.

Jere Brophy is University Distinguished Professor of Teacher Education and Educational Psychology at Michigan State University. A clinical and developmental psychologist by training, he has conducted research on teachers' achievement expectations and related self-fulfilling prophecy effects, teachers' attitudes toward individual students and the dynamics of teacher–student relationships, students' personal characteristics and their effects on teachers, relationships between classroom processes and student achievement, teachers' strategies for managing classrooms and coping with problem students, and teachers' strategies for motivating students to learn. Most recently, he has focused on curricular content and instructional method issues involved in teaching social studies for understanding, appreciation, and life application. He can be contacted at jereb@msu.edu.

Kathy Carter is professor of education in the Department of Teaching and Teacher Education at The University of Arizona. Her research centers around classroom processes and instruction, classroom management, and learning to teach. Presently, her research involves narrative understandings of teaching as they are acquired through improvisational and dramatic theatre and case methods in teaching. She can be contacted at kcarter@email.arizona.edu.

Heather Casey is a doctoral candidate in literacy education at Rutgers University, Graduate School of Education. She studies effective middle school literacy teachers and practices from a sociocultural perspective. Her dissertation is titled "Making Room for the Middle: Understanding Effective Middle School Teachers and Their Work With Struggling Readers and Writers." She can be contacted at HCasey1@aol.com.

Marilyn Cochran-Smith is the John Cawthorne Chair in Teacher Education at Boston College and editor of the *Journal of Teacher Education*. She was AERA president for 2004–2005. She has written multiple award-winning articles and books on teaching and teacher education research, policy, and practice as well as on teaching and teacher education for social justice. She can be contacted at cochrans@bc.edu.

Ian Cohen, M.Ed., is a doctoral candidate in school psychology at Temple University. His research interest is the relationship between education and mental health issues. He has published and presented on topics such as classroom climate, emotional intelligence, school bullying, and posttraumatic stress disorder. Ian will be completing a school psychology internship at the Dallas Independent School District during the 2005–6 school year. He can be contacted at icohen@temple.edu.

James M. Cooper is professor emeritus in the Curry School of Education at the University of Virginia, where he served as Commonwealth Professor of Education (1984–2004) and dean of the school (1984–1994). His books and articles address the areas of teacher education, supervision of teachers, case studies in teacher education, and technology and teacher education. He was the principal investigator for a $2.8 million grant from the U.S. Department of Education for the Preparing Tomorrows Teachers to Use Technology program. He can be contacted at jimcooper@virginia.edu.

Scot Danforth is associate professor, College of Education, The Ohio State University. Scot is co-author (with Terry Jo Smith) of *Engaging Troubling Students: A Constructivist Approach* (2004, Corwin Press) and co-editor (with Steven D. Taff) of *Crucial Readings in Special Education* (2003, Prentice Hall). His latest work is a co-edited (with Susan Gabel) volume called *Vital Questions Facing Disability Studies in Education* (in press, Peter Lang).

Perry den Brok is associate professor at the IVLOS Institute of Education at Utrecht University. His research focuses on students' perceptions of teaching in a multicultural and cross-cultural context. His most recent publications have examined ethnic and cultural differences in students' perceptions of their teachers' interpersonal behavior and the association between teacher interpersonal behavior and student outcomes in various countries. He can be contacted at p.j.denbrok@ivlos.uu.nl.

Walter Doyle is professor of education at The University of Arizona. He studies classroom task and activity systems, design tasks, and curriculum processes in teaching. His most recent work has focused on narrative and curriculum in teacher education, concepts of modern teaching, and real work in schools. He can be contacted at wdoyle@u.arizona.edu.

Billie Eilam is a senior lecturer at the University of Haifa, Israel. Her research focuses on the learning sciences as related to curriculum design, contextual and cultural factors, with emphasis on cognitive skills and skills related to visual representations in particular. Many of her studies examine the application of learning theories in authentic learning situations. She can be contacted at beilam@construct.haifa.ac.il.

Maurice J. Elias is a professor of psychology at Rutgers, The State University of New Jersey, and Leadership Team vice-chair for the Collaborative for Academic, Social, and Emotional Learning (www.CASEL.org). He devotes his research and writing to the area of social–emotional intelligence in children, schools, and families and is co-author of *Building Learning Communities With Character: How to Integrate Academic and Social-Emotional Learning* (ASCD, 2002). He can be contacted at RutgersMJE@aol.com.

Edmund T. Emmer is professor and chair of the Department of Educational Psychology at The University of Texas at Austin. His research interests include the identification of effective teaching and classroom management practices, the role of emotion in teaching, and programs for management and discipline. His recent work has also examined classroom management in cooperative learning activities and the use of technology in teacher education. He can be contacted at emmer@mail.utexas.edu.

Katherine Falk is the project coordinator for the Vanderbilt Behavior Research Center. Her research interests focus on the relationship between problem behavior and academic achievement, particularly in the area of reading. She may be reached at katherine.b.falk@vanderbilt.edu.

Catherine Fallona is associate professor and chair of teacher education at the University of Southern Maine. She studies topics that shed insight on the methods, style, manner, beliefs, knowledge, learning, and development of novice and expert teachers. She is particularly interested in the moral dimensions of teaching. She can be contacted at cfallona@usm.maine.edu.

Pamela Fenning is an associate professor of school psychology at Loyola University Chicago. She studies schoolwide discipline policies and practices. Recently, she has written about the role of written discipline policies in proactive and equitable school discipline. She can be reached at pfennin@luc.edu.

H. Jerome Freiberg is John & Rebecca Moores Professor at the University of Houston in the Department of Curriculum and Instruction. He is editor of the *Journal of Classroom Interaction* and founder of the Consistency Management and Cooperative Discipline Program. He is an author or co-author of eight books and over 100 scholarly works. He has received awards in both research and teaching. He can be contacted at freiberg@mail.uh.edu.

Isaac A. Friedman is the director and senior researcher at Henrietta Szold Institute, the national institute for research in the behavioral sciences in Israel. He was formerly a professor at the

Hebrew University School of Education, Jerusalem, Israel. He studies teacher burnout and teacher professional self. He has developed a new bipolar model of teacher professional self to predict and explain teacher classroom behavior. He can be contacted at Isaac@szold.org.il or szold@szold.org.il.

Kim Fries is an assistant professor of education at the University of New Hampshire. She studies teaching, teacher education, teacher research, and pedagogical issues such as classroom management and discipline. Her most recent publications have included topics ranging from the history of teacher education, the politics of teacher education, and coteaching as a pedagogical tool. She can be contacted at kim.fries@unh.edu.

Geneva Gay is professor of education at the University of Washington, Seattle, where she teaches graduate courses in general curriculum theory and multicultural education. Her research focuses on the intersections of race, ethnicity, and culture in education, the meanings of culturally responsive teaching, and using the experiences and cultural funds of knowledge of students of color to improve their educational opportunities and outcomes. She writes about, and works with, educational agencies to help teachers improve their knowledge of and skills in multicultural education. She can be reached at ggay@u.washington.edu.

Mary Claire Gerwels is a lecturer at The University of Texas at Austin. She is an instructor in the teacher certification program for elementary teachers. Her most recent research interests have focused on the effects of technology in classrooms on teachers and students. She can be reached at maryclaire.gerwels@mail.utexas.edu.

Maribeth Gettinger is professor of school psychology in the Department of Educational Psychology, University of Wisconsin, Madison. She directs the Early Childhood Program at the Waisman Center on Mental Retardation and Human Development. Her current research reflects two lines of inquiry. The first is student learning time, specifically the relationship between learner and instructional variables and learning time. Her second line of research focuses on academic assessment and remediation. Her e-mail address is mgetting@wisc.edu

Kjell Granström is professor of education at Linköping University, Sweden. He is an authorized psychologist and reader in communication. His research interest concerns daily life in the classroom, which includes teacher–student interaction and students' internal interaction during lessons. His publications have examined communication in the classroom in relation to different classroom features; for instance class size, organizational structure, and the influence of gender and age. His e-mail address is kjegr@ibv.liu.se.

Daniel T. Hickey is an associate professor in the Learning Sciences Program at Indiana University. His research focuses on classroom assessment and its alignment with external testing. He also studies design-based research methods and their relationship with traditional research models and socio-cultural approaches to instruction and motivation. He can be contacted at dthickey@indiana.edu.

Kathleen V. Hoover-Dempsey is associate professor of psychology, human development, and education and chair of the Department of Psychology and Human Development at Vanderbilt University. Her research program focuses on understanding why parents become involved in their children's education, how their involvement activities influence student outcomes, and what achievement-related outcomes are most strongly influenced by parental involvement. She may be reached at kathleen.v.hoover-dempsey@vanderbilt.edu.

Anita Woolfolk Hoy is professor of education at The Ohio State University. She studies teachers' thinking and beliefs, particularly teachers' sense of efficacy, and the role of educational psychology in the preparation of teachers. She is editor of the journal *Theory Into Practice* and author of *Educational Psychology* (Allyn & Bacon), now in its 10th edition. Anita can be contacted at hoy.17@osu.edu.

Irwin Hyman was professor of school psychology at Temple University. Irwin published numerous books and articles on corporal punishment, posttraumatic stress disorder, student alienation, school discipline, school consultation, and student victimization. His over 50 years of service to the profession and discipline of school psychology earned him the "Legend Award" from the National Association of School Psychologists in 2003. He was a lifelong opponent of corporal punishment, appearing on hundreds of television shows and radio broadcasts.

David W. Johnson is a professor of educational psychology and codirector of the Cooperative Learning Center at the University of Minnesota. He received his doctorate from Columbia University in social psychology. He is past editor of the *American Educational Research Journal*. His theorizing and research focuses on cooperation and competition, constructive controversy, integrative negotiations, experiential learning, and group dynamics. He can be reached at johns010@umn.edu.

Roger T. Johnson is a professor of education and codirector of the Cooperative Learning Center at the University of Minnesota. He received his doctorate from the University of California at Berkeley in science education. His work focuses on inquiry learning, cooperation and competition, and constructive controversy. Together with his brother David, he is the author of over 400 research articles and book chapters and over 40 books. He can be contacted at johns009@tc.umn.edu

Vern Jones is professor and chair of the education department in the Graduate School of Education and Counseling at Lewis & Clark College. His research and practice areas are classroom management, schoolwide student behavior, and students with emotional and behavior disorders. He can be reached at jones@lclark.edu.

James M. Kauffman is professor emeritus of education at the University of Virginia. His primary areas of research are children's emotional and behavioral disorders and behavior management. He has recently published books on behavior management, characteristics of emotional and behavioral disorders, and the history of special education for children and youth with emotional and behavioral disorders. His e-mail address is jmk9t@virginia.edu.

Bryony Kay, M.Ed., is a doctoral candidate in school psychology at Temple University. She is currently a school psychologist for the Delaware County Intermediate Unit. Her research is in the area of bullying and student victimization. She can be contacted at Brvkecr@aol.com

Kristy Kohler is a doctoral student in school psychology in the Department of Educational Psychology at the University of Wisconsin-Madison. Her research and scholarly interests include early intervention and prevention, home–school collaboration, and evidence-based practice. Currently, she is working on her dissertation research, which involves an examination of parent involvement in an early intervention program targeted to serve disadvantaged children and families. She can be contacted at kmkohler@wisc.edu.

Timothy J. Landrum is an associate professor on the general faculty and senior scientist at the University of Virginia. His research and writing focus on classroom and behavior management, emotional and behavioral disorders, early literacy assessment, and the translation of research into practice. He can be reached at TimL@virginia.edu.

Kathleen Lynne Lane is an assistant professor at Peabody College of Vanderbilt University. She conducts research in how to design, implement, and evaluate school-based interventions to prevent the development of and manage existing instances of emotional or behavior disorders. For additional information on this topic, please contact Kathleen Lynne Lane at kathleen.lane@vanderbilt.edu.

Judith M. Lapointe (Université Laval, Canada) is a postdoctoral researcher at the University of Houston. Her primary area of research is teacher–student interactions and classroom discipline. She also studies student teachers' development of expertise in classroom management and critical thinking in online learning communities. She can be reached at jlap333@yahoo.ca.

John Larmer is the associate director of program development at the Buck Institute for Education. He manages teacher training programs, dissemination, and development of problem-based social studies curriculum units for high school. He has recently written units for courses in U.S. government, and was a contributing author for the Buck Institute's *Project Based Learning Handbook*. He can be contacted at johnlarmer@bie.org.

Barbara Larrivee is a professor in the Department of Learning, Literacy and Culture at California State University. Her areas of interest include classroom management, creating a learning community based on respectful dialogue and authentic communication, and conflict resolution. Her most recent book is *Authentic Classroom Management: Creating a Learning Community and Building Reflective Practice* (Allyn & Bacon, 2005). Her current research focuses on developing structures for enhancing critical reflection on classroom behavior and infusing personal beliefs and values into a professional identity. Dr. Larrivee can be reached at blarrive@csusb.edu.

Ramon Lewis is an associate professor of education at Latrobe University. He studies the gap between theory and practice in the area of classroom management. His most recent publications have examined the impact on students of various classroom disciplinary techniques. He can be contacted at r.lewis@latrobe.edu.au.

Timothy J. Lewis is professor and chair, Department of Special Education at the University of Missouri. His research focuses on social behavior problems among students with disabilities and those at risk. He conducts research across a continuum of behavioral support strategies including schoolwide preventative practices, small-group instructional strategies, and individual systems of positive behavior support guided by functional behavioral assessment. He can be contacted at LewisTJ@missouri.edu.

Rachel A. Lotan is associate professor (teaching) and director of the Stanford Teacher Education Program. Her work focuses on teaching and learning in academically and linguistically heterogeneous classrooms. Her recent articles describe strategies teachers and teacher candidates can use to create equitable classrooms. She can be reached at rlotan@stanford.edu.

Matthew Mahon, M.Ed., is pursuing his Ph.D. in school psychology at Temple University and is currently completing his internship at Elwyn Nonpublic School Program in Philadelphia.

His research has examined the traumatic effects of school victimization and bullying in several different countries. He can be contacted at matthew.mahon@temple.edu.

Thom Markham is the senior program director for the Buck Institute for Education. He directs BIE's national training program in project-based learning for secondary schools and is the author of the *Handbook for Standards-focused Project Based Learning*. He specializes in educational reform and youth development. He can be contacted at thom@bie.org.

Mary Rose McCarthy is an assistant professor at Pace University. Her research interests are educational policy and the history of desegregation in northern cities. She is co-author of *Critical Issues in Education*. Her recent research explored the politics of disciplinary policies and practices in secondary schools. She can be at contacted at mmccarthy2@pace.edu.

Mary McCaslin is a professor of educational psychology at The University of Arizona. Her research interests include classroom processes and the coregulation of student learning, motivation, and identity development. She can be contacted at mccaslin@u.arizona.edu.

John Mergendoller is the executive director of the Buck Institute for Education, a not-for-profit research, development and training organization. His research focuses on the implementation of problem- and project-based learning, and the impact of these instructional approaches on student understanding, motivation, and skill development. He can be reached at john@bie.org.

Andy Miller is special professor of educational psychology at the University of Nottingham, UK. He is responsible for the initial and postexperience training of educational (school) psychologists. He focuses on challenging behaviors in schools and his research integrates psychological theory and rigorous research methodologies with professional practice. He can be contacted at Andy. Miller@nottingham.ac.uk.

H. Richard Milner is assistant professor of education in the Language, Literacy and Culture program in the Department of Teaching and Learning at Peabody College of Vanderbilt University. His research interests focus on teacher learning and change in curriculum development, urban education, and equity, race, and racism in teaching and learning. He can be reached at rich.milner@vanderbilt.edu.

Greta Morine-Dershimer is an emeritus professor of the University of Virginia. Her research over many years has focused on classroom interaction, classroom discourse, and teacher and pupil thinking and learning in elementary and high school settings. She directed teacher preparation programs at universities in New York, California, and Virginia, served as vice president of AERA for Division K (Teaching and Teacher Education) from 1988 to 1990, and was editor of the international research journal, *Teaching and Teacher Education*, from 1998 to 2002. She can be contacted at gm4p@virginia.edu.

Lesley Mandel Morrow is Professor II at Rutgers, The State University of New Jersey. She studies issues dealing with early literacy with a focus on organization and management of the language arts program. She works in urban at-risk communities. Her recent publications focus on fluency development and pre-school teachers' continuous professional development in literacy. She can be contacted at lmorro@rci.rutgers.edu.

Lisa Napoleon M.Ed., counseling, is a doctoral student in educational psychology and an academic counselor in the C.A.T.S. Academics Program at The University of Arizona. Her research interests include African American adolescent identity development.

Lori L. Newcomer is a research assistant professor in the Department of Special Education at the University of Missouri and director of professional development at the MU Center on Positive Behavioral Interventions and Support. She is currently active in research on a continuum of behavioral support strategies including schoolwide preventative practices, classroom management, small-group instructional strategies, and individual systems of positive behavior support guided by functional behavioral assessment. She can be contacted at NewcomerL@missouri.edu.

Kanae Nishioka is associate professor of education at Kyoto University, Japan. She studies school-based curriculum development and classroom instruction and assessment. Her recent publications include books on portfolio assessment (based on collaborative research with school teachers) and a co-authored, university textbook on curriculum. She can be contacted at nishioka@educ.kyoto-u.ac.jp.

Larry Nucci is professor of educational psychology at the University of Illinois at Chicago. His research focus is on the development of children's concepts of morality, social norms, and zones of behavioral discretion and privacy. He is author of *Education in the Moral Domain* (Cambridge University Press, 2001), and editor of *Conflict, Contradiction, and Contrarian Elements in Moral Development and Education* (Lawrence Erlbaum Associates, 2005). He can be reached at lnucci@uic.edu.

Robert C. Pianta is director of the Center for Advanced Study in Teaching and Learning (CASTL) at the University of Virginia, and a professor in both the Curry School of Education, where he holds the Novartis U.S. Foundation Chair in Education, and in the Department of Psychology. A former special education teacher, he is a developmental, school, and clinical child psychologist whose work focuses on how children's experiences at home and in school affect their development. He is particularly interested in how relationships with teachers and parents, and experiences in classrooms, can help improve outcomes for at-risk children and youth. He is the author of more than 200 publications on early childhood development, transition to school, school readiness, and parent–child and teacher–child relationships. He can be reached at pianta@virginia.edu.

M. Karega Rausch is research associate at the Center for Evaluation and Education Policy at Indiana University, School of Education. His research interests include minority disproportionality in school discipline and special education. His most recent publications have examined the extent of usage and the outcomes of school disciplinary options, and explored school leaders' use of preventative alternatives to student removal. He can be contacted at marausch@indiana.edu.

Jason Ravitz is research director at the Buck Institute for Education. He is responsible for studies that advance knowledge about teaching and learning. His recent work has focused on assessing implementation and impacts of the institute's curriculum in problem-based economics and developing technology-supported strategies for supporting and studying use of problems and projects among students, teachers and schools. He can be contacted at jason@bie.org.

Johnmarshall Reeve is a professor at the University of Iowa. He studies all aspects of motivation with a special focus on the interpersonal styles teachers use to motivate their students. Recent publications use self-determination theory to understand the nature of autonomy and how teachers can provide learning environments that support students' autonomy and classroom engagement. Professor Reeve may be contacted at johnmarshall-reeve@uiowa.edu.

D. Ray Reutzel is the Emma Eccles Jones Distinguished Professor of Early Childhood and Elementary Education at Utah State University. He has studied how classroom environments can be made print rich in support of early literacy acquisition. His most recent publications focus on assessing the print richness of classroom environments and how to provide effective comprehension instruction for younger children. He can be contacted at ray.reutzel@usu.edu.

Virginia Richardson is professor of teaching and teacher education at the University of Michigan. She studies teacher change, teacher beliefs, teacher education, and the moral dimensions of classrooms. Her most recent work focuses on the assessment of teacher education programs and the ways in which "the moral" becomes a part of the teacher education curriculum. She can be reached at richardv@umich.edu.

Mary Richter is a doctoral candidate at the University of Missouri. Her research focuses on administration of special education, schoolwide systems of behavioral support for students with disabilities and those at risk, and effective behavioral management training for practitioners. She can be contacted at marymrichter@sbcglobal.net.

Sarah Ricord Griesemer is a doctoral student in school psychology at the University of Texas at Austin. She is currently studying social aggression and its correlates in elementary-aged students. She is specifically interested in the impact of a child's social goals and friendship status on their engagement in social aggression. She can be contacted at smricord@mail.utexas.edu.

Sheri Robinson is currently a consultant in private practice. She works primarily with schools to develop prosocial prevention programs to reduce disruptive, aggressive, and bullying behaviors. Her most recent publications examine predictive variables associated with overt and relational aggression. She can be contacted at sheri.robinson@mail.utexas.edu.

Nancy Jo Schafer is an instructor in early childhood education at Georgia State University. She is currently studying the use of teacher video clubs as a professional development method for improving teachers' effectiveness at creating mathematical discourse communities and improving classroom management. She can be contacted at ecenjs@langate.gsu.edu.

David Schimmel is professor of education at the University of Massachusetts, Amherst, and visiting professor at Harvard University's Graduate School of Education. He is the author of over 60 articles and co-author of five books about law and education including *Teachers and the Law, 6th ed.* (2003). His current interest is incorporating legal literacy into preservice and inservice teacher education programs and helping principals become more conscious and effective law teachers.

Yoni Schwab is a doctoral candidate in clinical psychology at Rutgers, The State University of New Jersey. His research focuses on the impact of social and emotional learning (SEL) on academic achievement. He also works on integrating SEL with progressive classroom management practices and outreach to parents. He can be reached at yschwab@eden.rutgers.edu.

Russell Skiba is professor of counseling and educational psychology at Indiana University. His research has been in the areas of school violence prevention, school suspension and expulsion, and equity in education. His most recent publications have addressed measurement issues in school safety research, and explored factors contributing to minority disproportionality in school discipline and special education. He can be contacted at skiba@indiana.edu.

Leslie Soodak is a professor of education at Pace University. Her research focuses on factors that promote quality inclusive education for children with disabilities and effective parent–professional partnerships in these settings. Her most recent research explored the politics of exclusionary discipline policies in special and general education. She can be contacted at lsoodak@pace.edu.

Laura Stough is associate professor of educational psychology at Texas A&M University. Her research attempts to address the problems of educational equity through the development of teacher knowledge and pedagogical expertise, particularly in the areas of classroom management and special education. Dr. Stough can be contacted at lstough@coe.tamu.edu.

Alexander Tabori, M.Ed., is pursuing his doctorate in school psychology at Temple University and is a school psychology intern at Wordsworth Academy. He studies student victimization in the schools by students and educators, PTSD, and bullying. He has presented at various workshops and conferences on bullying intervention and prevention programs. His recent research has examined student victimization and PTSD in 15 countries. He can be contacted at avtabori@temple.edu

Angela Thomas holds an M.A. in educational psychology (emphasis: physical education) from The University of Arizona. Her interests include physical education and the promotion of wellness of elementary and middle school students.

Robert Trussell is an instructor of special education at William Woods University. His research interests include classroom universals and teacher instructional practices that reduce problem behaviors. He is a returned Peace Corps volunteer and has worked with children with challenging behaviors for 20 years in both educational and mental health settings. He can be contacted at robert.trussell@williamwoods.edu.

Jan van Tartwijk is associate professor at the ICLON, Institute for Education, of Leiden University. After working with juvenile delinquents, he went to Utrecht University in 1989. There, he studied the interpersonal significance of nonverbal teacher behavior and communication processes between students and teachers in multicultural classrooms. He also specialized in the use of portfolios in teacher and medical education. Currently he studies teachers' cognitions about classroom communication processes and how these cognitions affect teacher behavior. He can be reached at JTartwijk@iclon.Leidenuniv.nl

Veronica B. Vasquez holds both a B.A. in secondary education and an M.A. in educational psychology from The University of Arizona. She is currently teaching middle school language arts in El Mirage, Arizona. Her research interests include learning strategies of Mexican American middle school students and the impact of emotion on knowledge acquisition.

Joan M. T. Walker is an Assistant Professor in the School of Education at Long Island University (effective January 2006). Her research focuses on how children's perceptions of parent and teacher practices influence their learning and engagement in school. She is also interested in links between teachers' beliefs about children and families and their teaching practices.

Marilyn Watson is recently retired from the Developmental Studies Center, where she was the program director of the Child Development Project (CDP), and headed the Center's work in preservice education. She is interested in the implications of attachment theory for classroom management and its the role in children's social, emotional, and moral development. Her recent book, *Learning to Trust: Transforming Difficult Elementary Classrooms Through Developmental Discipline,* documents one inner-city teacher's efforts to build a classroom community supportive of all her students' ethical and intellectual development. She can be contacted at watsonms@direcway.com.

Virginia Wayman holds a Ph.D. in music education with a minor in educational psychology from The University of Arizona. She is an assistant professor of music education at the University of Texas Pan-American. Her research interests include music education of middle school students and music teacher education.

Meredith Weber, M.Ed., is pursuing her doctorate in school psychology at Temple University where she is also an instructor in the education department. She has presented workshops on intervention and prevention programs for school bullying. Meredith will be working at the Children's Hospital of Philadelphia on a program to reduce bullying in overly aggressive elementary school girls during the 2005-6 school year. She can be contacted at meriw@temple.edu.

Joseph Wehby is an associate professor in the Department of Special Education at Peabody College of Vanderbilt University. His research interests include the assessment of teacher–student interactions and the development of classroom-based interventions for addressing the behavioral and academic needs of students with emotional and behavioral disorders. He can be reached at joseph.wehby@vanderbilt.edu.

Kathryn Wentzel is professor of human development in the College of Education, University of Maryland, College Park. Her research interests concern parents, peers, and teachers as motivators of adolescents' classroom behavior and academic accomplishments. Currently, she is examining dimensions of students' interpersonal relationships with teachers and peers that promote the adoption of group values and goals, and that promote beliefs that the classroom is a safe, responsive, helpful, and emotionally supportive place to learn. She can be contacted at wentzel@umd.edu.

Theo Wubbels is professor of education and vice dean for academic affairs of the Faculty of Social and Behavioral Sciences at Utrecht University, The Netherlands. He studies interpersonal relationships between teachers and students and between principals and teachers. Recently this work has been extended to multicultural schools. He can be contacted at Th.Wubbels@fss.uu.nl.

Estie Yankelevitch, Ph.D., is an associate teacher at the University of Haifa, Department of Israel Studies. Her field of research is in the history of education. Her recent research concerns agricultural education in the agricultural high schools in Palestine 1870–1948. She can be contacted at eyankel1@univ.haifa.ac.il.

Jizhi Zhang, M.A., educational psychology, is a research assistant and doctoral student in educational psychology at The University of Arizona. Her research interests include student motivation and emotion.

Author Index

B

C

D

E

F

G

H

I

J

K

M

O

P

S

T

U

V

X

Y

Z

Subject Index

A

C

D

E

F

G

H

I

J

K

L

M

N

O

P

Q